NEW YORK PRACTICE

Sixth Edition

David D. Siegel
Late Distinguished Professor of Law Emeritus
Albany Law School

Patrick M. Connors
Albert and Angela Farone Distinguished Professor of Law in New York Civil Practice
Albany Law School

HORNBOOK SERIES®
STUDENT EDITION

WEST
ACADEMIC
PUBLISHING

For Cecelia, Fiona, George, and Donal,
and the prior dedicatees: their moms and granny

DAVID D. SIEGEL

For my parents, Kitty and Bill, who always stressed
the importance of education

PATRICK M. CONNORS

In Memoriam

Professor David D. Siegel, the leading commentator on the CPLR since its adoption in 1963, passed away on October 9, 2014, just short of his 83rd birthday.

In rare instances, a scholar becomes such a presence in his or her field of discipline that serious consideration of a matter within that realm cannot be undertaken without reference to the author's body of work. Over five decades, Professor Siegel achieved this status in his field of concentration, New York Practice, a subject synonymous with his name. It is virtually impossible to author a meaningful piece on this fascinating subject without reference to Professor Siegel's voluminous scholarship. Thousands of judicial opinions grappling with the broad array of thorny and weighty issues that arise under the umbrella of civil procedure make the point. These decisions, and the briefs that preceded them, cite to and rely heavily upon Professor Siegel's writings. *See* Patrick M. Connors, The King of New York Practice, 72 Alb. L. Rev. 447 (2009).

Many readers had the distinct pleasure of being a student in Professor Siegel's classes and attending his CPLR Update programs, where another set of his talents was on display. His enthusiasm for the subject was contagious and, when accompanied by his unique wit and insight, made for an unforgettable learning experience. If you meet lawyers who do not find the CPLR interesting and fun, you can almost be certain that they never witnessed Professor Siegel at work.

Law schools exist today in a period of turmoil in legal education. Sadly, there is a substantial gap between what a student learns in law school, often at great monetary expense, and the essential knowledge required to effectively practice law. If law schools want to seriously address this problem, an examination of the career of Professor Siegel would be a good place to start. Unlike virtually any law professor of his time, Professor Siegel cultivated a broad audience of judges and lawyers who rely constantly on his writing, while also bridging the gap for generations of law students to enter the practice of law.

Preface to the Sixth Edition

As the late Professor Siegel frequently observed, New York Practice is a scene in motion. The subject never rests. Events are frequent, both major and minor, and there have been many developments since the publication of the fifth edition in 2011. Although the Civil Practice Law and Rules (CPLR) has governed civil practice in New York for over five decades, the landscape is constantly changing as lawyers continue to press for every sort of procedural advantage for their clients. The Legislature and Judiciary add to the mosaic by amending statutes, promulgating court rules, and issuing decisions interpreting the procedural laws of The Empire State.

Sometimes these endeavors close gaps in the procedural landscape, but on occasion they create new problems and pitfalls that require analysis. We attempt to address it all here. This edition covers most statutory, caselaw, and rule developments through the beginning of 2017, and will be supplemented twice a year, in January and July. Numerous recent cases are discussed or cited, but cases from the mid-1960s to the mid-1970s, when the main caselaw on the CPLR was developed, remain a body of prime authority and, therefore, our continued focus.

This edition includes a federal chapter (Chapter 23) that Professor Siegel devised, and I assisted with, beginning with the second edition published in 1991. The chapter summarizes the civil jurisdiction and practice of the federal courts and compares and contrasts it with New York practice in a number of particulars. It has turned out to be one of the largest chapters in the book, and one of the most rewarding to construct and refine. Federal Civil Procedure and New York Practice, when placed side by side, often present an intertwined series of comparisons and contrasts that are helpful to developing a body of knowledge on procedure. Comparing and contrasting is a sure way to avoid procedural pitfalls, and avoiding such missteps is a principal goal of the federal chapter.

The sixth edition of New York Practice includes several new sections that address significant procedural developments arising during the 21st century. They include:

§ 12A. Commercial Division of Supreme Court: addressing the requirements for litigating an action in the Commercial Division and the various rules of practice in that court.

§ 63A. Commencement of Actions by Electronic Filing ("E-Filing"): addressing the developments in commencing actions via e-filing in various counties throughout New York State's court system and the numerous statutes and rules containing e-filing procedures. Several existing sections were also revised to address issues arising in e-filed actions, including: § 202 (filing and service of papers in e-filed actions); § 246 (providing motion papers to the court in e-filed actions); § 250 (entry of orders in e-filed actions); § 533 (calculating appeal time in e-filed actions); §§ 11, 524, 536 (e-filing of records and briefs in appeals to the appellate division and the Court of Appeals).

§ 76B. Curing Technical Defects in Service: addressing the Court of Appeals decision in Ruffin v. Lion Corp. allowing CPLR 2001 to cure certain service defects.

Chapter 13, entitled "Disclosure," was substantially expanded to include additional discussion of the various issues that have arisen concerning the disclosure of electronically stored information ("ESI"), including who pays the cost of such disclosure (§§ 353, 362), the proper methods for seeking ESI from parties and nonparties (§ 362), and penalties for failure to preserve relevant ESI (§ 367).

I have always taught professional responsibility alongside New York Practice, and there are many important areas of intersection. The book now integrates a discussion of many relevant ethical issues that arise in conjunction with various procedural issues. They include: multijurisdictional practice (§ 10), expanded treatment of statute of limitations issues, including the doctrine of "continuous representation" in legal malpractice actions (§§ 35, 42), withdrawal from representation (§ 115), communications with represented parties (§ 202), Judiciary Law section 470's physical office requirement (§ 202), the lawyer's ethical duties in the disclosure process (§ 352A), compensation to fact witnesses (§ 382), and mandatory arbitration of fee disputes (§§ 456, 603).

This edition also includes hundreds of updated citations so lawyers and judges can easily find the most recent caselaw in a particular area.

Frequent references are made to our McKinney's Practice Commentaries, New York Law Journal columns, and law review articles, which provide more expanded treatments of matters necessarily set forth in a relatively abbreviated form here. These citations also allow for reference to many items that cannot be comprehensively addressed in a one-volume work. Similarly, there are frequent references to Professor Siegel's pieces in the New York State Law Digest and Siegel's Practice Review, which provide similar coverage. The form of citation to the New York State Law Digest is by issue number: "NYSLD No. 462," for example, refers to issue number 462 of the Digest. Most references are to lead notes, appearing on page 1 of an issue. Unfortunately, most of these issues are not available online, but hard copies are usually resting on the shelves of a good law library. The form of citation to Siegel's Practice Review is by issue number and page: "SPR 223:4," for example, refers to page 4 of Issue 223. Most issues of the Practice Review are available in hard copy, and all are available on WESTLAW.

We study and practice law in The Information Age. This treatise is designed to provide far more than a recitation of procedural law, although it does a fair bit of that. Very few procedural issues arise in a vacuum, and this book coordinates various topics that frequently intersect in the practice of law with cross-references to other relevant portions of the text. Judges, lawyers, and law students often benefit from the integration the book offers, which provides context and allows the reader to view the complete dimensions of a procedural problem. This was Professor Siegel's design in authoring the initial editions of the treatise, and I have done my best to continue to achieve that goal.

Another critical aspect of writing effectively on civil procedure is access to the front lines, where the rubber meets the road and statutes and rules are interpreted and applied to resolve actual controversies. Following in Professor Siegel's footsteps, I frequently provide continuing legal education programs to lawyers at law firms and bar association functions, and to judges and court attorneys at programs offered by the Office of Court Administration. Recently, I have spoken to groups of lawyers and judges in Albany, Bronx, Broome, Essex, Jefferson, Kings, Nassau, New York, Onondaga, Otsego, Oswego, Rockland, Saratoga, Suffolk, and Westchester Counties, and in Montreal, Canada for the Federation of Bar Associations of the Fourth Judicial District. The interactions at such programs with judges, lawyers, and those who work in the court system help to provide invaluable ideas and perspective, which are reflected on these pages.

Law schools exist today in a period of turmoil in legal education. Sadly, there is a substantial gap between what a student learns in law school, often at great monetary expense, and the essential knowledge required to effectively practice law. This gap will likely expand after the implementation of the Uniform Bar Exam in New York in July of 2016. See § 10. This book and the supplements that will follow remain dedicated to bridging that gap for law students to enter the practice of law, and to assist new lawyers in providing value to their clients and law firms.

This Sixth Edition is done in two forms. The Practitioner's Edition is in hard cover, with a pocket in the back for the supplements that will update it biannually. The abridged Student Edition, in soft cover, omits the chapters on federal practice and on arbitration, which have their own courses in law school, and the materials on landlord-tenant proceedings and small claims, which are often incidents of other courses, like real estate transactions and consumer rights.

The book is also available on ProView, Thomson Reuters' eReader app. This enables customers to access the publication when they are at court, travelling to court, or at their office or home, from a tablet, smartphone, laptop, or desktop. Information on obtaining the book in the ProView eBook format is provided immediately following this preface.

A treatise of this sort is in some respects only as good as its index, so we've sought over the years to make our index a thorough one. But in point of convenience and speed, the recent technology explosion displaces the traditional index altogether when the item indexed is available in electronic form, as this book is. In addition to being available in electronic form on ProView, it is also on WESTLAW, with a search engine that goes through the whole book in no time, highlighting the searched term and then, through "links," permitting the viewer, with just a "click," to call up on screen for instant access almost any item cited in the book—cases and statutes, of course, but also authorities like ours: the SPR, the McKinney's Commentaries, and other sections of this text. These electronic formats move the conventional "index" closer to the museum, but it's not there yet; so, with the anti-electronic holdouts in mind, the index is included.

For aid in reviewing the manuscript and checking citations, I am indebted to my research assistants at Albany Law School: Mara Afzali, Katie Birchenough, and Steven Cummings (ALS 2017); Anneliese Aliasso, Allison Bartlett, and Sarah Baum (ALS 2018). I have also received several valuable suggestions over the years from my first research assistant at Albany Law School, John Higgitt (ALS 2001), whose publications are frequently referenced in the text. My writing has always benefitted from the insights of Albany Law School's former research librarian, Bob Emery, who provided assistance to me in countless ways for sixteen years. My reliable and cheerful administrative assistant at Albany Law School, Theresa Colbert, has also assisted me in so many tasks necessary for the publication. Elena Renner, the publisher's Principal Attorney Editor, also helped guide me through my first edition of the book.

In 2000, after 3 years of clerking for Judge Richard D. Simons at the New York Court of Appeals and nine years of full time practice at Hancock & Estabrook in Syracuse, I decided to pursue a full time teaching position at Albany Law School. That decision was primarily inspired by the many great teachers I have had in my life. The education I received from the Marianists at Chaminade High School helped me to excel under the guidance of the Jesuits at Georgetown University. Professor Walter I. Giles, who taught so many budding lawyers at Georgetown, had a profound impact on my career and showed me how a teacher could shape the life of a student in so many ways. I then received a great legal education at St. John's University School of Law, where I had the pleasure of taking Professor David Siegel's Federal Jurisdiction class in 1986 and New York Practice class in 1987. Just as the Beatles and Rolling Stones have borrowed and stolen so much from Chuck Berry, the King of Rock and Roll, I have borrowed and stolen from Professor Siegel, the King of New York Practice. He has laid down the law on how to teach and write on procedure, and I have been very fortunate to be able to follow his path in the classroom, at lectures to the bench and bar, and in this remarkable treatise.

Finally, special thanks to my wife Margyt, our children Aron and Jessye, and our standard poodle Theo, who have all been patient and supportive through this endeavor.

PATRICK M. CONNORS

Saratoga Springs, New York
May, 2018

Summary of Contents

Page

IN MEMORIAM V

PREFACE TO THE SIXTH EDITION VII

CHAPTER 1. INTRODUCTION 1

CHAPTER 2. THE COURTS AND THEIR JURISDICTION............................**15**
A.   The Court System...15
B.   Transfers Between Courts 40
C.   Forum Non Conveniens..46
D.   Other Restrictions on Jurisdiction 53
E.   Conditions Precedent to Suit 55

CHAPTER 3. THE STATUTE OF LIMITATIONS......................................**65**
A.   Introductory...65
B.   The Applicable Periods...68
C.   Altering the Period 80
D.   Accrual 83
E.   Interposition 97
F.   Extensions and Tolls 107
G.   Foreign Claims 123

CHAPTER 4. PERSONAL JURISDICTION...**127**
A.   Introductory...127
B.   The Summons 128
C.   The Methods of Service 161
D.   Getting into the Courthouse 196
E.   The Jurisdictional Bases 211
F.   Service Outside New York 272
G.   Rem Jurisdiction...275
H.   Vacating Defaults 295

CHAPTER 5. APPEARANCE **299**

CHAPTER 6. VENUE...**313**
A.   Introductory...313
B.   Venue in Particular Actions...316
C.   Change of Venue 322

CHAPTER 7. PARTIES **327**
A.   Joinder of Claims and Actions...327
B.   Necessary Joinder of Parties 336
C.   Permissive Joinder of Parties 342
D.   Proper Parties..345

E.   Procedure for Joinder Problems 351
F.   Class Actions 354
G.   Interpleader 378
H.   Impleader 386
I.   Contribution 422
J.   Intervention 446
K.   Substitution 454
L.   Poor Persons 462
M.   Infants and Incompetents 466

CHAPTER 8. PAPERS **475**

CHAPTER 9. PLEADINGS **499**
A.   Basic Rules of Pleading 499
B.   Specific Items 514
C.   Demand for Relief 521
D.   Election of Remedies 524
E.   Splitting 530
F.   The Answer 531
G.   Counterclaims 540
H.   Cross-Claims 546
I.   The Reply 550
J.   Corrective Motions 552
K.   Service of Pleadings 554
L.   Verification 565
M.   Amendment of Pleadings 572
N.   Bill of Particulars 580

CHAPTER 10. MOTION PRACTICE **593**

CHAPTER 11. ACCELERATED JUDGMENT **639**
A.   Introductory 639
B.   Motion to Dismiss 640
C.   Summary Judgment 670
D.   Summary Judgment in Lieu of Complaint 693
E.   Default Judgment 700
F.   Voluntary Discontinuance 713
G.   Confession of Judgment 717
H.   Tenders and Offers 722
I.   Action on Submitted Facts 723

CHAPTER 12. PROVISIONAL REMEDIES **727**
A.   Introductory 727
B.   Arrest 736
C.   Attachment 736
D.   Injunction 762
E.   Receivership 776
F.   Notice of Pendency 779
G.   Seizure of Chattel 785

CHAPTER 13. DISCLOSURE **797**
A. Generally...797
B. Excluded Matters 810
C. Devices and Methods in Perspective 831
D. Protection Against Abuse..842
E. The Devices Individually 846
F. Compelling Disclosure...890

CHAPTER 14. PRETRIAL INCIDENTS **901**
A. Calendar Practice 901
B. Preferences..911
C. Pretrial Conference 917
D. Laxness Dismissals 919
E. Mode of Trial...930
F. Subpoenas and Oaths...949

CHAPTER 15. THE TRIAL.. **965**
A. Introductory 965
B. Selecting a Jury 967
C. The Trial Proper 974
D. The Verdict..987
E. Trial Motions 995

CHAPTER 16. THE JUDGMENT **1013**
A. Contents of Judgment 1013
B. Interest...1016
C. Fees, Costs, and Disbursements..1028
D. Recording the Judgment 1043
E. Recording Satisfaction 1054
F. Vacating Judgments and Orders..1058
G. Renewal of Judgment 1069
H. Declaratory Judgment..1075

CHAPTER 17. RES JUDICATA... **1089**
A. Introductory 1089
B. General Requisites 1094
C. Comparison with Other Doctrines 1100
D. Res Judicata in Particular Situations...1105
E. Collateral Estoppel 1118
F. Identity of Parties...1119
G. Identifying the Issue 1127
H. Multiparty Situations...1134
I. Different Courts...1148
J. Procedural Incidents 1159

CHAPTER 18. ENFORCEMENT OF JUDGMENTS.................................. **1163**
Introductory...1163
PART I. ENFORCEMENT OF NON-MONEY JUDGMENTS
A. Judgments Involving a Chattel or Realty...................................1165

B. Enforcement by Contempt 1168

PART II. ENFORCEMENT OF MONEY JUDGMENTS

A. In General 1181
B. Property Subject to Enforcement 1183
C. Devices in Perspective..1206
D. Property Executions 1211
E. Income Execution 1225
F. The "Supplementary Proceedings" 1238
G. Incidental Matters..1257
H. Priorities and Liens..1261
I. Protection Against Abuse..1272
J. Contempt as Back-Up Device 1275

CHAPTER 19. APPEALS **1279**
A. Introductory...1279
B. Appealability..1285
C. Reviewability 1302
D. Taking the Appeal 1313
E. Perfecting the Appeal..1328
F. Incidental Appellate Practice 1341
G. Concluding the Appeal 1344

CHAPTER 20. SPECIAL PROCEEDINGS **1351**

PART I. THE SPECIAL PROCEEDING, IN GENERAL
PART II. THE ARTICLE 78 PROCEEDING

A. Introductory...1368
B. Scope of the Proceeding..1370
C. Procedural Basics 1386
D. Mechanics...1395

TABLE OF CASES 1407

TABLE OF STATUTES AND CPLR CITATIONS...1451

TABLE OF COURT RULES..1473

INDEX...1477

Table of Contents

———

			Page

In Memoriam..V

Preface to the Sixth Edition...............................VII

CHAPTER 1. INTRODUCTION..1
- § 1.   Purpose of This Book 1
- § 2.   The CPLR 3
- § 3.   Other Procedural Tools 4
- § 4.   One Form of Action 6
- § 5.   Administration of the Courts 8
- § 6.   Liberal Construction..9
- § 7.   Forms 12

CHAPTER 2. THE COURTS AND THEIR JURISDICTION..................15
- A.   The Court System...15
  - § 8.   Kinds of Jurisdiction 15
  - § 9.   Court System; Geography 17
  - § 10.   Court of Appeals 20
  - § 11.   Appellate Division..21
  - § 12.   Supreme Court...23
  - § 12A.   Commercial Division of Supreme Court..............25
  - § 13.   Appellate Term 27
  - § 14.   County Courts 27
  - § 15.   Surrogate's Court...29
  - § 16.   Family Court 30
  - § 17.   Court of Claims 31
  - § 18.   New York City Criminal Court.............................33
  - § 19.   New York City Civil Court 33
  - § 20.   District Courts 35
  - § 21.   City Courts 36
  - § 22.   Town and Village Courts....................................37
  - § 23.   Aggregating or Reducing Claims 38
- B.   Transfers Between Courts 40
  - § 24.   Mistake in Choice of Court.................................40
  - § 25.   Transfer Up for More Relief 41
  - § 26.   Transfer Down on Consent 42
  - § 27.   Transfer Down Without Consent.........................43
- C.   Forum Non Conveniens 46
  - § 28.   Forum Non Conveniens......................................46
  - § 29.   Forum Non Conveniens and Corporations............51
- D.   Other Restrictions on Jurisdiction 53
  - § 30.   Unlicensed Plaintiff Corporation........................53
  - § 31.   Interference with Interstate Commerce.................54

E.   Conditions Precedent to Suit..55
     § 32.   Conditions Precedent to Suit; Notice of Claim; Leave to Serve Late
             Notice...55

CHAPTER 3. THE STATUTE OF LIMITATIONS................................... 65
A.   Introductory...65
     § 33.   Statute of Limitations, Generally...65
     § 34.   Theory; "Suspension of Remedy" Reckoning...............................67
B.   The Applicable Periods...68
     § 35.   The Various Time Periods...68
     § 36.   Equity Actions; Laches...75
     § 37.   Multiple Theories...77
C.   Altering the Period...80
     § 38.   Statutory Alterations...80
     § 39.   Agreements to Shorten or Lengthen the Period............................82
D.   Accrual..83
     § 40.   "Accrual" of the Claim..83
     § 41.   Accrual in Warranty Cases..86
     § 42.   Accrual in Malpractice Cases..88
     § 43.   "Discovery" Accruals...95
     § 44.   Wrongful Death Cases...96
E.   Interposition..97
     § 45.   "Interposition" of the Claim; "United in Interest"........................98
     § 46.   Provisional Remedy as Interposition...100
     § 47.   Delivery to Sheriff or Clerk..101
     § 48.   Counterclaims..101
     § 49.   Claim in Amended Pleading...103
F.   Extensions and Tolls..107
     § 50.   Extensions and Tolls, Generally..107
     § 51.   Toll Where Action Stayed...108
     § 52.   Termination of Prior Action..109
     § 53.   Defendant's Absence..116
     § 54.   Disabilities as Tolls..117
     § 55.   Tolling for Death..120
     § 56.   Estopping Defendant from Pleading Limitation...........................121
G.   Foreign Claims..123
     § 57.   Foreign Claims; the "Borrowing" Statute.....................................123

CHAPTER 4. PERSONAL JURISDICTION... 127
A.   Introductory...127
     § 58.   Personal Jurisdiction, Introduction...127
B.   The Summons...128
     § 59.   Summons Service in New York as Jurisdictional Basis.................129
     § 60.   Issuance of Summons; Accompanying Papers..............................130
     § 61.   Form of Summons Served with Complaint...................................134
     § 62.   Form of Summons Served with 305(b) Default Notice..................135
     § 63.   Commencement of Action; When and by Whom Summons Served........136
     § 63A. Commencement of Actions by Electronic Filing ("E-Filing")........150
     § 64.   Amendment of the Summons...156

§ 65. Amending Summons to Change Parties; Supplemental Summons 158
C. The Methods of Service 161
§ 66. Personal Delivery of Summons Under CPLR 308(1).............................161
§ 67. Enticement into Jurisdiction 165
§ 68. Sovereign Immunity and Immunity from Service..................................166
§ 69. Whom to Serve in Behalf of Various Defendants 168
§ 70. Service on a Corporation 174
§ 71. "Sewer Service"; the Amendment of CPLR 308....................................178
§ 72. Deliver-and-Mail Service Under CPLR 308(2) 179
§ 73. Service on Rule 318 Agent Under CPLR 308(3) 182
§ 74. Affix-and-Mail Service Under CPLR 308(4)..183
§ 75. Court-Ordered Service Under CPLR 308(5) 186
§ 76. Service in Matrimonial Actions 191
§ 76A. Personal Service by Mail..193
§ 76B. Curing Technical Defects in Service..195
D. Getting into the Courthouse 196
§ 77. General Filing Requirements; Federal Practice Compared...................196
§ 77A. The Individual Assignment System (IAS)...198
§ 77B. Getting a Judge Assigned: Request for Judicial Intervention (RJI) 200
§ 77C. Form of Request for Judicial Intervention (RJI) 202
§ 77D. The Preliminary Conference 204
§ 78. Getting an Index Number 208
§ 79. Proof of Service 208
E. The Jurisdictional Bases..211
§ 80. Basis for Jurisdiction; CPLR 301..211
§ 81. Domicile as Basis 212
§ 82. The Corporate "Presence" Doctrine 213
§ 83. Comparing Corporate "Doing Business" Tests 220
§ 84. "Longarm" Jurisdiction, Background 222
§ 85. Longarm Jurisdiction Under CPLR 302, Generally................................224
§ 86. "Transacts Any Business" Under CPLR 302(a)(1)...................................225
§ 86A. "Contracts Anywhere" Under CPLR 302(a)(1)..239
§ 87. "Tortious Act" Under CPLR 302(a)(2) 243
§ 88. Without/Injury Within New York Under CPLR 302(a)(3) 245
§ 89. Real Property Longarm Cases Under CPLR 302(a)(4)............................254
§ 90. Longarm Jurisdiction for Support and Other Relief Under
CPLR 302(b) 255
§ 91. The Restricted Appearance Under CPLR 302(c) 257
§ 92. Jurisdiction Versus the Merits 257
§ 93. Burden of Proving Jurisdiction..258
§ 94. Overlap of Longarm Bases 260
§ 95. Agency as Jurisdictional Basis 261
§ 96. Attorney as Agent Under CPLR 303 265
§ 97. The Nonresident Motorist Statute 266
§ 98. Jurisdiction by Written Agreement...269
§ 99. Continuing Jurisdiction...270
F. Service Outside New York 272
§ 100. Service Outside New York Under CPLR 313...272

G. Rem Jurisdiction 275
    § 101.   Rem Jurisdiction, Generally 275
    § 102.   Rem Jurisdiction of Marital Status 277
    § 103.   In Rem Jurisdiction Under CPLR 314(2) 279
    § 104.   Quasi in Rem Jurisdiction...281
    § 105.   The Doctrine of Seider v. Roth...287
    § 106.   Sequestration in Matrimonial Actions 292
    § 107.   Service by Publication 293
H. Vacating Defaults..295
    § 108.   Vacating Default Judgment 295

CHAPTER 5. APPEARANCE **299**
    § 109.   Appearance, Generally 299
    § 110.   How and When to Appear 300
    § 111.   Making and Preserving a Jurisdictional Objection 301
    § 112.   Informal Appearance...304
    § 113.   Appearance in "Rem" Actions; "Limited" Appearance 305
    § 114.   Adding Claims in Various Appearance Situations................307
    § 115.   Representation by Attorney 308

CHAPTER 6. VENUE.. **313**
A. Introductory...313
    § 116.   Venue, Generally 313
    § 117.   Agreement to Fix Venue..315
B. Venue in Particular Actions 316
    § 118.   Venue in Transitory Actions 317
    § 119.   Venue for Corporations and Other Private Creatures 318
    § 120.   Venue for Governmental Entities.......................................319
    § 121.   Venue in Local Actions 320
    § 122.   Special Venue Requirements in Consumer Credit Cases 321
C. Change of Venue...322
    § 123.   Change of Venue from Improper to Proper County; "Demand"
               Procedure...322
    § 124.   Discretionary Grounds for Change of Venue 324
    § 125.   Effecting the Change of Venue 326

CHAPTER 7. PARTIES **327**
A. Joinder of Claims and Actions...327
    § 126.   Joinder of Claims...327
    § 127.   Consolidation, Joint Trial, Severance, and Separate Trial, Defined......328
    § 128.   Consolidation and Joint Trial 329
    § 129.   Severance and Separate Trial..333
    § 130.   Bifurcated Trial 334
B. Necessary Joinder of Parties 336
    § 131.   Necessary Joinder of Parties, Background 336
    § 132.   Necessary Joinder of Parties, CPLR Approach...................337
    § 133.   Avoiding Dismissal for Nonjoinder.....................................338
C. Permissive Joinder of Parties 342
    § 134.   Permissive Joinder of Parties 342

§ 135.   Joinder in the Alternative..344
D.   Proper Parties..345
§ 136.   Standing to Sue..345
§ 137.   "Real Party in Interest"..349
E.   Procedure for Joinder Problems 351
§ 138.   Motion to Add or Drop Parties; Procedure........................351
F.   Class Actions...354
§ 139.   Class Actions, Background...354
§ 140.   Prerequisites to Class Action; the Old Law Reviewed 358
§ 141.   Prerequisites to Class Action; Present Law...........................359
§ 142.   Order Allowing Class Action..364
§ 143.   Notice of Class Action...367
§ 144.   Opting Out 369
§ 145.   "Fluid Recovery"...374
§ 146.   Defendant's Side as Class 374
§ 147.   Pervasive Court Discretion in Class Action; Settlement and
          Judgment..375
G.   Interpleader..378
§ 148.   Interpleader, Generally..378
§ 149.   Liberal Use; Discharge of Stakeholder..................................379
§ 150.   Mode of Trial...381
§ 151.   Discretionary Tools...381
§ 152.   The Stakeholder's Jurisdictional Dilemma...........................382
§ 153.   Rem Jurisdiction as Interpleader Basis.................................384
§ 154.   Interpleader in the Federal Courts 385
H.   Impleader..386
§ 155.   Third-Party Practice, or "Impleader," Generally..................386
§ 156.   Basic Procedure for Impleader..389
§ 157.   Indemnification as Impleader Basis; Other Bases 391
§ 158.   Effect if Impleader Complaint Negates Main Claim.............394
§ 159.   Impleader as Premature Suit 395
§ 160.   Impleader in Insurance Situations...396
§ 161.   Discretionary Powers of Dismissal, Severance, and Like Steps............396
§ 162.   Statute of Limitations on Impleader Claims 397
§ 163.   Rights of Third-Party Defendant..398
§ 164.   Additional Claims Among the Parties....................................400
§ 165.   Enforcement of Third-Party Judgment.................................401
§ 166.   Successive Impleaders...402
§ 167.   Impleader in Various Courts and Proceedings 402
§ 168.   Vouching-In...403
§ 168A. "Joint" Tort Liability Adjustment; Background 404
§ 168B. "Joint" Tort Liability Adjustment; The 50%-or-Less Tortfeasor 406
§ 168C. "Joint" Tort Liability Adjustment; Provisos and Exceptions.................408
§ 168D. "Joint" Tort Liability Adjustment; Burdens of Proof............418
§ 168E. The Comparative Negligence Rule of CPLR Article 14–A....................420
I.   Contribution..422
§ 169.   Contribution, Introductory..423
§ 170.   The Picture Before Dole v. Dow Chemical Co......................424
§ 171.   The Arrival of Dole 425

§ 172. Contribution Under CPLR Article 14...427
§ 173. Methods of Seeking Contribution 430
§ 174. The Old Contribution Rules Contrasted; Judgment Limited to Excess 431
§ 175. Some Problem Areas in Contribution...432
§ 176. Effect of Settlement with Fewer than All Tortfeasors 437
§ 177. Discretionary Tools in Handling Contribution Claims; Sequence of Trial 445
J. Intervention 446
§ 178. Intervention, Generally...446
§ 179. Intervention of Right Under Special Statutes 447
§ 180. Intervention of Right Where Representation Inadequate 448
§ 181. Intervention of Right in Property Cases 451
§ 182. Permissive Intervention 452
§ 183. Procedure for Intervention 453
K. Substitution 454
§ 184. Substitution of Parties 454
§ 185. Abatement of Claims 456
§ 186. Procedure for Substitution..457
§ 187. Public Body or Officer as Party..459
§ 188. Unknown Parties 460
§ 189. The Unincorporated Association...461
L. Poor Persons 462
§ 190. Poor Person Status 462
§ 191. Procedure to Secure Poor Person Status..463
§ 192. What Poor Person Designation Accomplishes 464
M. Infants and Incompetents..466
§ 193. Representation of Infant 466
§ 194. Representation of Incapacitated Person 467
§ 195. Representation Distinguished from Service 468
§ 196. Guardian Ad Litem Distinguished from Other Guardianships.............469
§ 197. Procedure for Appointment of Guardian Ad Litem 469
§ 198. Qualifications, Rights, and Authority of Guardian Ad Litem 471
§ 199. Risks if No Proper Representative Present 471
§ 200. Settlement of Infant's or Incapacitated Person's Claim........................472

CHAPTER 8. PAPERS...475
§ 201. Form of Papers..475
§ 202. Service of Papers; Method and Time Computation 480
§ 203. Service on All Parties 488
§ 204. Stipulations...489
§ 205. Affidavits and Affirmations 495
§ 206. Undertakings 497

CHAPTER 9. PLEADINGS 499
A. Basic Rules of Pleading...499
§ 207. Pleadings, Background..499
§ 208. The Basic Pleading Requirement 500
§ 209. Theory of the Pleadings Rule Abolished 503

§ 210.   Some Forms..505
§ 211.   Pleading in the Federal and Lower Courts Compared...........507
§ 212.   Separate Statement and Numbering 509
§ 213.   Statements Deemed Repeated; Writings 511
§ 214.   Various Techniques of Pleading...512
B.   Specific Items...514
§ 215.   Pleading Certain Specific Matters; CPLR 3015...................514
§ 216.   Particularity in Specific Actions; CPLR 3016......................517
C.   Demand for Relief...521
§ 217.   Demand for Relief; "Wherefore" Clause 521
D.   Election of Remedies 524
§ 218.   Election of Remedies; Separate Actions 525
§ 219.   Election of Remedies; Within an Action 528
E.   Splitting 530
§ 220.   Splitting...530
F.   The Answer...531
§ 221.   The Answer; Denials 531
§ 222.   Marked Pleadings...534
§ 223.   Affirmative Defenses 534
G.   Counterclaims...540
§ 224.   Counterclaims, Generally 540
§ 225.   Counterclaims; Parties with Several Capacities 543
§ 226.   Counterclaim Against Assignee-Plaintiff............................544
H.   Cross-Claims...546
§ 227.   Cross-Claims 546
§ 228.   Form of Answer..548
I.   The Reply 550
§ 229.   The Reply; Further Pleadings...550
J.   Corrective Motions 552
§ 230.   Motions to Correct Pleadings; CPLR 3024..........................552
K.   Service of Pleadings 554
§ 231.   Service of Pleadings; Responding Time...............................554
§ 231A.   Leave Time for Trouble 559
L.   Verification 565
§ 232.   Verification of Pleadings, Generally...................................566
§ 233.   Who May Verify 568
§ 234.   Form of Verification...569
§ 235.   Remedy for Defective Verification 571
M.   Amendment of Pleadings 572
§ 236.   Amendment as of Course 572
§ 237.   Amendment by Leave...574
N.   Bill of Particulars 580
§ 238.   Bill of Particulars, Generally 580
§ 239.   Procedure for Bill of Particulars 585
§ 240.   Amending and Supplementing the Bill...............................586
§ 241.   Remedies in Connection with Bill of Particulars................587
§ 242.   Variances..590

CHAPTER 10. MOTION PRACTICE **593**

§ 243.   Motion Practice, Generally 593
§ 244.   Ex Parte Motions 597
§ 245.   Where Motion Made (Venue of Motions) 600
§ 246.   The Motion Papers 603
§ 247.   Motion Notice Requirements 607
§ 248.   Order to Show Cause 612
§ 249.   Cross-Motion 616
§ 250.   Deciding the Motion; Drawing and Entering the Order 619
§ 251.   Trial of Issue of Fact Arising on Motion 627
§ 252.   Some Forms 627
§ 253.   Motion Affecting Prior Order 630
§ 254.   Motion to Reargue or Renew 632
§ 255.   Stay 637

CHAPTER 11. ACCELERATED JUDGMENT **639**
A.   Introductory 639
§ 256.   Accelerated Judgment; CPLR Article 32 639
B.   Motion to Dismiss 640
§ 257.   The Motion to Dismiss, CPLR 3211 Generally 640
§ 258.   The Dismissal Grounds: CPLR 3211(a) 642
§ 259.   Defense Based on "Documentary Evidence"; Paragraph 1 644
§ 260.   Subject Matter Jurisdiction; Paragraph 2 645
§ 261.   Lack of Capacity to Sue; Paragraph 3 645
§ 262.   Other Action Pending; Paragraph 4 646
§ 263.   Affirmative Defenses Usable on Dismissal Motion; Paragraph 5 649
§ 264.   Non-Interposable Counterclaim; Paragraph 6 651
§ 265.   Failure to State a Cause of Action; Paragraph 7 652
§ 266.   Lack of Personal Jurisdiction; Paragraph 8 655
§ 267.   Lack of Rem Jurisdiction; Paragraph 9 656
§ 268.   Dismissal for Indispensable Party; Paragraph 10 657
§ 269.   Motion to Dismiss Defense 657
§ 270.   Treating 3211 Motion as Summary Judgment 659
§ 271.   Immediate Trial of Fact Issue Under CPLR 3211 661
§ 272.   Time for 3211 Motion 662
§ 273.   Single Motion Rule 663
§ 274.   Option to Plead Instead of Move; Waiver 665
§ 275.   Leave to Replead 667
§ 276.   Res Judicata Effect of CPLR 3211 Disposition 668
§ 277.   Motion Under CPLR 3211 Extends Responding Time 669
C.   Summary Judgment 670
§ 278.   Summary Judgment, Generally 670
§ 279.   Time to Move for Summary Judgment 672
§ 280.   Actions in Which Summary Judgment Available 679
§ 281.   Proof on Summary Judgment Motion 682
§ 282.   Searching the Record 686
§ 283.   Summary Judgment Under 3212 Based on 3211 Ground 687
§ 284.   Immediate Trial of Fact Issue Under CPLR 3212 688
§ 285.   Partial Summary Judgment; Effect of Counterclaim 689

§ 286. Salvaging Something from Abortive Motion..............................691
§ 287. Res Judicata Effect of Summary Judgment Motion.............................692
D. Summary Judgment in Lieu of Complaint 693
§ 288. Summary Judgment Motion in Lieu of Complaint; CPLR 3213 693
§ 289. Money Instrument as Basis for CPLR 3213 Motion........................694
§ 290. Judgment as Basis for CPLR 3213 Motion 695
§ 291. Procedure Under CPLR 3213...697
§ 292. Effect of Denial; Conversion..698
E. Default Judgment...700
§ 293. Taking Default Judgment 700
§ 294. Time for Default Application 704
§ 295. Papers on Default Application 706
§ 296. Notice of Default Application 709
F. Voluntary Discontinuance 713
§ 297. Voluntary Discontinuance, Methods 713
§ 298. Effect of Discontinuance..716
G. Confession of Judgment...717
§ 299. Confession of Judgment, Generally..717
§ 300. Affidavit for Confession of Judgment 718
§ 301. Filing, Enforcement, and Effect of Confessed Judgment....................720
§ 302. Vacating Confessed Judgment...721
H. Tenders and Offers..722
§ 303. Tenders and Offers; CPLR 3219–3221 722
I. Action on Submitted Facts..723
§ 304. Action on Submitted Facts 723
§ 305. Disposition of Submission 724

CHAPTER 12. PROVISIONAL REMEDIES... 727
A. Introductory...727
§ 306. Provisional Remedies, Generally..727
§ 307. Provisional Remedies; Constitutional Requirements........................730
B. Arrest 736
C. Attachment 736
§ 313. Attachment, Generally...736
§ 314. Grounds for Attachment..737
§ 315. Attachment; Status of Constitutionality...................................739
§ 316. Applying for the Attachment 741
§ 317. Attachment Discretionary...745
§ 318. The Various Time Periods Concerning Attachment..........................746
§ 319. Summons Service Within 60 Days 747
§ 320. Levy of the Attachment..748
§ 321. "Perfecting" the Levy..751
§ 322. Examples of Interplay of Attachment Requirements.........................753
§ 323. What Property Attachable?..754
§ 324. Disclosure to Aid Attachment 757
§ 325. Defendant's Remedies: Vacatur; Discharge; Annulment; Action on Undertaking..758
§ 326. Disposition of Property; Disputes; Priorities 761

D.   Injunction...762
    § 327.   Preliminary Injunction, Grounds 763
    § 328.   Required Showing; Discretion................................765
    § 329.   Applying for the Injunction..................................768
    § 330.   Temporary Restraining Order 771
    § 331.   Vacating or Modifying Injunction or TRO..............775
E.   Receivership..776
    § 332.   Temporary Receivership...776
    § 333.   Applying for the Receivership 778
F.   Notice of Pendency 779
    § 334.   Notice of Pendency, Generally 779
    § 335.   Procedure for Filing...781
    § 336.   Cancellation of Notice..783
G.   Seizure of Chattel...785
    § 337.   Replevin Action, Generally 785
    § 338.   Constitutionality of Preliminary Seizure..............787
    § 339.   Applying for the Seizure.......................................788
    § 340.   The Seizure and Subsequent Proceedings 791
    § 341.   Commencing the Action 793
    § 342.   Judgment in Replevin Action................................795

CHAPTER 13. DISCLOSURE **797**
A.   Generally...797
    § 343.   Disclosure; Introduction 797
    § 344.   Disclosure Criteria; CPLR 3101(a)........................799
    § 345.   Disclosure from Parties and Nonparties 805
B.   Excluded Matters 810
    § 346.   Privileged Matter...810
    § 347.   Attorney's Work Product.......................................812
    § 348.   Materials Prepared for Litigation.........................814
    § 348A. Identification of Experts; Statement of Expected Testimony 823
    § 349.   Revelation of Names of Witnesses.........................829
C.   Devices and Methods in Perspective 831
    § 350.   The Disclosure Devices; Priority of Use 831
    § 351.   Method of Bringing on Disclosure; Stipulation or Notice 833
    § 352.   Instances Where Order Initially Required.............835
    § 352A. Requirement to Supplement Prior Responses 839
D.   Protection Against Abuse..842
    § 353.   Protective Order; CPLR 3103 842
E.   The Devices Individually 846
    § 354.   Deposition on Oral Questions: The "EBT" 847
    § 355.   Place of Deposition..848
    § 356.   Taking the Deposition 850
    § 357.   Executing the Deposition 855
    § 358.   Use of Deposition 857
    § 359.   Deposition on Written Questions...........................861
    § 360.   Commission or Letters Rogatory 863
    § 361.   Interrogatories 864
    § 362.   Discovery and Inspection 868

§ 363.   Physical and Mental Examinations.......................880
§ 364.   Notice to Admit 885
§ 365.   Demand for Address 889
F.   Compelling Disclosure...890
§ 366.   Order Compelling Disclosure; Rulings 890
§ 367.   Sanctions for Nondisclosure...............................892

CHAPTER 14. PRETRIAL INCIDENTS.............................. **901**
A.   Calendar Practice 901
§ 368.   Calendar Practice, Introductory 901
§ 369.   Note of Issue...903
§ 370.   Statement of Readiness...................................905
§ 371.   Form of Note of Issue and Statement of Readiness......908
B.   Preferences..911
§ 372.   The "General" Preference 911
§ 373.   The "Special" Preference 913
C.   Pretrial Conference 917
§ 374.   Pretrial Conferences 917
D.   Laxness Dismissals 919
§ 375.   Dismissal for Want of Prosecution; CPLR 3216.........919
§ 376.   Dismissal of Abandoned Cases; CPLR 3404 926
E.   Mode of Trial...930
§ 377.   Triability by Jury.......................................931
§ 378.   Demand and Waiver of Trial by Jury......................935
§ 379.   Triability by Referee 940
§ 380.   Triability by the Court 946
§ 381.   Advisory Jury 948
F.   Subpoenas and Oaths..949
§ 382.   Subpoenas; Issuance......................................949
§ 383.   Service of Subpoena 953
§ 384.   Motion to Quash Subpoena 956
§ 385.   Disobedience of Subpoena 957
§ 386.   Form of Subpoena 958
§ 387.   Notice to Produce 960
§ 388.   Oaths and Affirmations...................................960

CHAPTER 15. THE TRIAL.. **965**
A.   Introductory..965
§ 389.   The Trial, Introductory..................................965
B.   Selecting a Jury..967
§ 390.   Impaneling a Jury 967
§ 391.   Alternate Jurors...969
§ 392.   Challenges to Jurors.....................................970
C.   The Trial Proper 974
§ 393.   Sequence of Trial 974
§ 394.   Separate Trial of Issues; Bifurcation...................976
§ 395.   Right to Open and Close..................................977
§ 396.   Objections and Rulings...................................979
§ 397.   Summation 981

§ 398.   The Charge 983
D.   The Verdict 987
    § 399.   Kinds of Verdict 987
    § 400.   Delivery of the Verdict..990
    § 401.   Defective Verdicts; Impeachment......................................993
E.   Trial Motions 995
    § 402.   Motion for Judgment During Trial....................................995
    § 403.   Motion for Mistrial..999
    § 404.   Motion to Conform the Pleadings to the Proof................1000
    § 405.   Post-Trial Motion for Judgment 1003
    § 406.   Motion for New Trial on the "Weight of the Evidence" 1006
    § 407.   Additur and Remittitur 1007
    § 408.   Motions for "Judgment," Compared 1010

CHAPTER 16. THE JUDGMENT 1013
A.   Contents of Judgment...1013
    § 409.   Content of Judgment 1013
    § 410.   Interlocutory Judgment...1015
B.   Interest...1016
    § 411.   Allowance of Interest...1017
    § 412.   Rate of Interest 1025
C.   Fees, Costs, and Disbursements..1028
    § 413.   Fees, Costs, and Disbursements, Generally 1028
    § 414.   Costs 1029
    § 414A.   "Frivolity" Sanctions..1031
    § 415.   Disbursements 1040
    § 416.   Taxation of Costs and Disbursements..............................1041
    § 417.   Form of Judgment..1042
D.   Recording the Judgment..1043
    § 418.   Entry of Judgment..1043
    § 419.   The Judgment-Roll 1046
    § 420.   Correcting the Judgment; Nunc Pro Tunc Changes..........1046
    § 421.   Docketing the Judgment 1049
    § 422.   Transcripting Judgments Between Courts and Counties......1051
    § 423.   Changes Affecting Judgments and Dockets......................1053
E.   Recording Satisfaction 1054
    § 424.   Satisfaction-Piece..1055
    § 425.   Entry of Satisfaction..1056
F.   Vacating Judgments and Orders..1058
    § 426.   Motion to Vacate Judgment or Order, Generally 1058
    § 427.   Excusable Default...1060
    § 428.   Newly Discovered Evidence 1062
    § 429.   Fraud or Misconduct...1063
    § 430.   Lack of Jurisdiction 1064
    § 431.   Reversal of Underlying Judgment.....................................1066
    § 432.   Conditioning the Vacatur 1068
    § 433.   Restitution..1069
G.   Renewal of Judgment...1069
    § 434.   Renewal of New York Judgment 1070

§ 435. Registration of Full Faith and Credit Judgment 1072
H. Declaratory Judgment 1075
§ 436. Declaratory Judgment, Generally 1076
§ 437. Uses of Declaratory Judgment 1078
§ 438. Procedure in Declaratory Action; Limitations of Time 1082
§ 439. Trial by Jury in Declaratory Action 1084
§ 440. Judgment in Declaratory Action 1085
§ 441. Need for Follow-Up Relief 1086

CHAPTER 17. RES JUDICATA **1089**
A. Introductory 1089
§ 442. Res Judicata, Introductory 1089
§ 443. Members of the Res Judicata Family 1091
B. General Requisites 1094
§ 444. Necessity of Final Judgment 1094
§ 445. Res Judicata for Order 1096
§ 446. Necessity for Disposition on "Merits" 1096
§ 447. Preclusion for "Might Have Been Litigated" Items 1098
C. Comparison with Other Doctrines 1100
§ 448. Law of the Case 1100
§ 449. Relation to Stare Decisis 1102
§ 450. "Merger" and "Bar" 1103
D. Res Judicata in Particular Situations 1105
§ 451. Application to Default and Consent Judgments 1105
§ 452. Application to Counterclaims 1106
§ 453. Civil Use of Criminal Findings 1108
§ 454. Res Judicata in Representative and Class Situations 1109
§ 455. Res Judicata for Jurisdictional Issues 1109
§ 456. Res Judicata for Administrative and Arbitral Decisions 1112
E. Collateral Estoppel 1118
§ 457. Collateral Estoppel, Introductory 1118
F. Identity of Parties 1119
§ 458. Identity of Estopped Party 1119
§ 459. Different Capacities 1122
§ 460. Identity of Estopping Party; "Mutuality" of Estoppel 1122
§ 461. "Privity" 1123
G. Identifying the Issue 1127
§ 462. Identity of Issue Test 1127
§ 463. Law and Fact, Ultimate and Evidentiary 1129
§ 464. Underlying Facts Bind, Litigated or Not 1131
§ 465. Gratuitous Findings 1132
H. Multiparty Situations 1134
§ 466. Multiparty Situations; a Perspective 1134
§ 467. The Full and Fair Opportunity Test; Factors to Consider 1136
§ 468. Multiparty Vehicle Tort Examples 1142
I. Different Courts 1148
§ 469. Effect When Different Courts Involved 1148
§ 470. Nonjury Determinations; Court of Claims Problems 1152
§ 471. Recognition of Domestic Judgments; Full Faith and Credit 1153

§ 472.   Recognition of Foreign-Country Judgments; "Comity" 1156
J.   Procedural Incidents 1159
§ 473.   Evidentiary Sources to Establish Matters Estopped 1160
§ 474.   Estoppel Only for Given Issue 1160
§ 475.   Raising the Issue; Burden of Proof 1161

CHAPTER 18. ENFORCEMENT OF JUDGMENTS 1163
Introductory 1163
§ 476.   Enforcement of Judgments, Generally 1163

PART I. ENFORCEMENT OF NON-MONEY JUDGMENTS
A.   Judgments Involving a Chattel or Realty 1165
§ 477.   Judgment Awarding Possession of Chattel 1165
§ 478.   Judgment Awarding Possession of Realty 1166
§ 479.   Judgment Directing Sale of Realty 1167
§ 480.   Judgment Directing Conveyance of Realty 1168
B.   Enforcement by Contempt 1168
§ 481.   Enforcement by Contempt; Grounds 1168
§ 482.   Criminal and Civil Contempt Distinguished; Punishment 1172
§ 483.   Constitutionality of Contempt Procedure 1175
§ 484.   Procedure to Punish for Contempt 1177

PART II. ENFORCEMENT OF MONEY JUDGMENTS
A.   In General 1181
§ 485.   Enforcement of Money Judgments, Introductory 1181
B.   Property Subject to Enforcement 1183
§ 486.   Property Applicable to the Judgment, Introductory 1184
§ 487.   Examples of Leviable Property Rights 1185
§ 488.   Creditor Stands in Debtor's Shoes 1190
§ 489.   Contingent Intangibles 1192
§ 490.   Exemptions 1197
§ 491.   Proper Garnishee 1202
C.   Devices in Perspective 1206
§ 492.   The Enforcement Devices, Introductory 1206
§ 493.   Courts in Which Enforcement Devices Available 1207
D.   Property Executions 1211
§ 494.   The Executions, Generally 1211
§ 495.   Property Execution, Issuance, and Contents 1211
§ 496.   Levy on Personal Property 1214
§ 497.   Property "Capable of Delivery" 1218
§ 498.   Selling the Personal Property 1220
§ 499.   Levy on Real Property 1221
§ 500.   Selling the Real Property 1222
§ 501.   Sheriff's Return 1225
E.   Income Execution 1225
§ 502.   Income Execution, Contents and Service 1226
§ 503.   Income Execution; Computing the 10% 1229
§ 504.   Priorities Among Income Executions 1233
§ 505.   Employer's Obligations on Income Execution 1234
§ 506.   Sheriff's Obligation on Income Execution 1235

§ 507. Modifying the Income Execution 1236
§ 507A. Special Income Execution for Support 1236
F. The "Supplementary Proceedings" 1238
§ 508. Restraining Notice 1238
§ 509. Disclosure in Aid of Enforcement 1242
§ 510. Delivery Order or Judgment 1247
§ 511. Installment Payment Order 1252
§ 512. Receivership 1254
§ 513. Arrest 1256
G. Incidental Matters 1257
§ 514. Death of Judgment Debtor 1257
§ 515. Protecting the Garnishee 1259
§ 516. Prejudgment Enforcement 1260
H. Priorities and Liens 1261
§ 517. Priorities and Liens on Real Property 1261
§ 518. Rights in Personal Property, Introductory 1264
§ 519. Rights in Personal Property; Judgment Creditor Versus
Transferee 1265
§ 520. Rights in Personal Property; Judgment Creditors Among
Themselves 1267
§ 521. Proceeding to Determine Adverse Claims 1270
I. Protection Against Abuse 1272
§ 522. Protective Order 1272
J. Contempt as Back-Up Device 1275
§ 523. Contempt Enforcement of Certain Devices 1275

CHAPTER 19. APPEALS 1279
A. Introductory 1279
§ 524. Appeals, Introductory 1279
§ 525. "Aggrieved" Party 1283
B. Appealability 1285
§ 526. Appeals to Appellate Division 1285
§ 527. Appeals to Court of Appeals as of Right 1291
§ 528. Appeals to Court of Appeals by Permission 1298
§ 528A. Certification to Court of Appeals by Other Courts 1300
C. Reviewability 1302
§ 529. Reviewability in Particular Courts 1303
§ 530. Scope of Review from Final Judgment 1306
D. Taking the Appeal 1313
§ 531. Taking an Appeal; How 1313
§ 532. Subsequent Orders 1315
§ 533. Time to Appeal or Move for Leave 1319
§ 534. Omissions, Defects, and Time Extensions 1322
§ 535. Injunctions and Stays 1324
E. Perfecting the Appeal 1328
§ 536. "Perfecting" the Appeal, Introductory 1328
§ 537. The Transcript 1332
§ 538. The Record 1334
§ 539. The Briefs and Appendices 1337

§ 540.   Calendar Practice and the Argument.................................1340
F.   Incidental Appellate Practice 1341
§ 541.   Motions in Appellate Courts 1341
§ 542.   Dismissal of Appeal for Want of Prosecution.........................1342
G.   Concluding the Appeal...1344
§ 543.   Disposition of Appeal...1344
§ 544.   Reargument...1347
§ 545.   Remittitur..1348

CHAPTER 20. SPECIAL PROCEEDINGS 1351
§ 546.   Special Proceedings, Introductory 1351

PART I. THE SPECIAL PROCEEDING, IN GENERAL
§ 547.   The "Special Proceeding," Described 1352
§ 548.   Statute of Limitations in Special Proceedings......................1354
§ 549.   Venue in Special Proceedings 1355
§ 550.   Procedure in Special Proceedings 1357
§ 551.   Parties to Special Proceedings 1357
§ 552.   Pleadings in Special Proceedings...............................1358
§ 553.   Bringing the Proceeding..1359
§ 554.   Motions in Special Proceedings 1364
§ 555.   Disclosure in Special Proceedings 1365
§ 556.   Hearing and Disposition of Special Proceeding.....................1366

PART II. THE ARTICLE 78 PROCEEDING
A.   Introductory...1368
§ 557.   Article 78 Proceeding, Introductory 1368
B.   Scope of the Proceeding...1370
§ 558.   Mandamus...1371
§ 559.   Prohibition..1375
§ 560.   Certiorari..1378
§ 561.   Mandamus-Certiorari Borderline 1380
§ 562.   Judicial Review of Penalty or Discipline.........................1384
§ 563.   Overstepping Outer Borders of Article 78 1385
C.   Procedural Basics 1386
§ 564.   Parties in Article 78 Proceeding 1387
§ 565.   Venue of Article 78 Proceeding 1388
§ 566.   Statute of Limitations in Article 78 Proceeding 1390
D.   Mechanics 1395
§ 567.   Bringing the Proceeding..1395
§ 568.   Hearing and Determination; Transfer to Appellate Division..............1399
§ 569.   Trial of Issue of Fact in Article 78 Proceeding....................1401
§ 570.   Judgment and Enforcement in Article 78 Proceeding.................1402

TABLE OF CASES 1407

TABLE OF STATUTES AND CPLR CITATIONS..1451

TABLE OF COURT RULES...1473

INDEX..1477

NEW YORK PRACTICE
Sixth Edition

Chapter 1

INTRODUCTION

Table of Sections

§ 1.   Purpose of This Book
§ 2.   The CPLR
§ 3.   Other Procedural Tools
§ 4.   One Form of Action
§ 5.   Administration of the Courts
§ 6.   Liberal Construction
§ 7.   Forms

§ 1.   Purpose of This Book

This book has been designed as a basic text on civil practice and procedure in the New York State courts. It seeks to afford a broad perspective in each subject, setting forth the basics and stressing the problem areas that appear most often. It also endeavors to correspond as much as possible to actual practice, going heavily into things regularly met by lawyers and judges and more lightly—or not at all—into matters seldom if ever encountered, no matter what the quantity of verbiage a statute or rule may devote to them. For the practicing lawyer, it highlights pitfalls in practice, warning of their whereabouts and suggesting pathways around them. For the judge, it addresses not only matters already governed by a statute or rule or covered by caselaw but also problems likely to arise; it suggests avenues of resolution and collateral matters to be alert to in the process.

The book's awareness of the law student and newly admitted lawyer is reflected in the fact that every topic starts from scratch, building rather than assuming. By so doing, it also seeks to offer both the lawyer and the judge a quick refresher in an area they may have been away from for a while. The hope is to reduce to nil the "gap" one often hears described between what a student learns in law school and what the new lawyer actually meets afterwards in practice. There should not be such a gap.

Much effort has been made to avoid what this writer has sometimes perceived to be a fault in law books. They start off with great energy, devoting much time and attention to subjects met early in the study, but then grow weary, or concerned about space, and for that reason allow later subjects—equally and perhaps even more important—to fall by the way, inadequately covered or not covered at all. It is no accident, for example, that the chapter on the enforcement of money judgments in this book, Chapter 18, rivals both in coverage and in size the earlier chapters on personal jurisdiction, Chapter 4, and parties, Chapter 7. The rationale is hardly a subtle one: to what avail a spring of jurisdiction when one knows nothing about realizing on a judgment that comes out of it? The book also lays needed stress, in Chapter 13, on discovery and disclosure, that mass of devices whereby an attorney prepares to meet an adversary's case in court. There is much of the conceptual in the study of subjects like jurisdiction and parties, grand stuff for the give and take of a classroom. Disclosure and enforcement, on the other hand, involve less of the conceptual and much of the practical confronted in the daily life of the lawyer. The text feels an equal commitment to all of them.

There are independent chapters, towards the end of the book, on appeals and special proceedings, the latter including a separate treatment of both the Article 78 proceeding and the ubiquitous Summary Proceeding ("Landlord-Tenant") to Recover the Possession of Real Property. These are designed at least in part to supply practitioners some recourse to these important topics if they want a perspective or a review of them. The same is true of Small Claims, a subject of much moment to the average citizen and many a client; it has a short but independent chapter of its own.

There's a chapter on arbitration, Chapter 22. Arbitration continues to expand in great strides, and so, too, is the body of caselaw accompanying it. Since it's the next-to-last chapter in the book, much effort has been made to assure it a proper place in the skyline: an imposing structure next to the courthouse and not some shack off to the side.

The last chapter, Chapter 23, on federal jurisdiction and practice, is a special one devised to emphasize contrasts with New York practice and to point out special pitfalls for lawyers steeped in New York procedure, who step into the federal courts without the same familiarity with federal practice. It also performs the reverse function of cluing lawyers with primarily a federal practice experience into major points of difference with state practice.

To facilitate access to the wide range of subjects that fall under the heading of civil practice, they have been subdivided into as many separate sections as feasible. Their captions appear in the table of contents at the front of the book, and are repeated under the boldface headings used within each chapter. These headings, under which related sections are gathered, offer a quick reference point for review of a given area. Cross-references have been generously sprinkled about the text to connect one subject with another without unnecessary repetition. Very few procedural issues arise in a vacuum, and this book coordinates various topics that frequently intersect in the practice of law.

"SPR" references appear frequently. They refer to Siegel's Practice Review, a monthly newsletter authored by the late Professor Siegel that reported on developments in New York civil practice. Because the SPR treatments are of course more extensive than space allows in a single-volume work or its supplements, an effort has been made to include these SPR references whenever the subject or case under discussion has received an SPR treatment. Similarly, there are frequent references to our CPLR McKinney's Practice Commentaries (available on Westlaw) and New York Law Journal columns, which provide more expanded treatments of matters necessarily set forth in a relatively abbreviated form here. These citations also allow for reference to many items that cannot be comprehensively addressed in a one-volume work.

The SPR is available exclusively on Westlaw, with a full set of links giving it a two-way connection to this treatise. The form of an SPR citation is by Issue number and page, separated by a colon. The citation "SPR 226:4," for example, refers to page 4 of Issue 226 of Siegel's Practice Review.

§ 2.   The CPLR

The Civil Practice Law and Rules, officially citable as "CPLR,"[1] is the major tool of New York civil practice. It governs in all courts of civil jurisdiction except to the extent that an inconsistent statute governs. The purpose of this deference by the CPLR is to make it the generally applicable body of procedural law while also enabling more specific statutes to govern in special situations or in courts with particularized functions.

The CPLR became effective under Governor Nelson Rockefeller on September 1, 1963, replacing the Civil Practice Act of 1921, which superseded the Code of Civil Procedure—known as the Throop Code after Montgomery Throop—of the 1870s. That, in turn, replaced the famous Field Code—after David Dudley Field—of 1848. The Field Code was a major American step forward in the modernization of civil procedure and a national inspiration that is still felt in many other states and in the Federal Rules of Civil Procedure. At this juncture, the CPLR has governed procedure for more than five decades, longer than any other prior procedural code in New York.[2]

The CPLR is largely the product of an Advisory Committee on Practice and Procedure, appointed in 1955 to modernize practice. The committee was appointed by the Temporary Commission on the Courts, whose other major effort was the reorganization of the New York courts that became effective September 1, 1962. The committee wrote a number of reports, which are valuable references in practice and are cited from time to time in this book.

There are slots for 100 articles in the CPLR, not all of them filled. Gaps appear wherever the legislature thought it wise to keep openings for future use. The first numbered CPLR provision is 101, the last 10005. This system enables each number to identify the article in which the provision appears, as well as the provision's position within the article. Dropping the last two digits leaves the article number: § 101 is in Article 1 (drop the 01), § 10005 is in Article 100 (drop the 05), etc.

Within a given article the numbering of provisions is usually consecutive, but there are sometimes gaps. These, too, represent a legislative judgment about where room should be left for future activity. In Article 32, for example, the first numbered provision is 3201 and the next 3211, while in Article 3 the initial provisions are numbered consecutively.

The careful reader will notice that some CPLR provisions are preceded by a section designation (§) and others by the word "Rule." The former are strictly statutes and can be altered only by the legislature. Originally, those designated "Rule" could be altered by either the legislature or the Judicial Conference, the predecessor to the Office of Court Administration. So provided section 229(3) of the Judiciary Law, but it was repealed in 1978 in conjunction with the overhaul of judicial administration[3] without being

---

[1]   CPLR 101.

[2]   On September 1, 2013, the CPLR celebrated its 50th year regulating procedure in New York State's civil courts. See Patrick M. Connors, *The CPLR Turns 50! Taking Stock of Good, Bad and Ugly*, N.Y.L.J., Sept. 11, 2013, at 3, col. 1.

[3]   The subject of judicial administration is discussed in § 5. In the article referenced in the footnote above, we lament the mysterious repeal of this provision in 1978 and the subsequent compilation of supplemental procedural provisions by the courts in the Uniform Rules, the rules of a judicial district, county rules, individual court rules, preliminary conference orders, and various scheduling orders. The pre-1978 system of amending the CPLR, which was analogous to the one in place for amending the Federal Rules of

addressed in the superseding legislation. It thus appears that even the alteration of a mere "Rule" is now lodged in the legislature alone.[4]

Both the statutes and the rules in the CPLR are law as long as they don't conflict. If they do, presumably the statute controls. It isn't possible to guess which CPLR provisions are statutes and which are rules. The designations are often arbitrary. Which one a given provision is can be learned only by looking it up.

CPLR 101 authorizes the citation of CPLR provisions without indicating whether the provision cited is a statute or rule. "Blue-bookers" should take note that this manner of citation has become the common practice.

A definitions section, CPLR 105, singles out a number of commonly used words and phrases in the procedural lexicon and gives them a specific meaning for CPLR use. They will be mentioned from time to time as they become relevant.

§ 3.   Other Procedural Tools

The supreme court in New York, which is a court of primarily original, not appellate, jurisdiction, is governed directly by the CPLR.[1] It does not have an individual court act. Neither do the county courts, whose civil practice also comes directly from the CPLR. But each of the other courts of original jurisdiction in the state has a "court act."

A court act prescribes the court's jurisdiction and regulates selected procedures in varying degrees. Each court is governed first by its own court act, but as long as there is no conflict between the court act and the CPLR, civil practice in the court is governed by the CPLR as well. In some courts having their own court acts, in fact, the CPLR is relevant far more often than the court act itself because the latter addresses only a handful of selected procedures thought to need special treatment in the court.

This is especially the case in the courts governed by the so-called "uniform acts," which govern the lower courts of civil jurisdiction. These acts are largely uniform among themselves, right down to the numbering system. Four were considered necessary because of certain differences among the lower courts in jurisdiction and, to some extent, procedure as well. The four are the New York City Civil Court Act, which governs the civil court in New York City; the Uniform District Court Act, modeled on the New York City Civil Court Act and governing civil practice in the Nassau and Suffolk county district courts (those are the only two counties that presently have district courts); the Uniform City Court Act, modeled on the Uniform District Court Act and governing civil practice in all city courts (61 of them) outside New York City; and finally the Uniform Justice Court Act, modeled on the Uniform City Court Act and governing civil practice in all of the town and village courts (often collectively called "justice courts") of the state. The jurisdiction of those courts will be treated in separate sections later.

Article 2 in each of the uniform acts sets forth the subject matter jurisdiction of the courts governed by the particular act. The remainder of each act singles out certain

Civil Procedure, could be revisited and possibly adjusted to allow for the compilation of New York's procedural rules in one repository.

[4]   This applies only to a "Rule" appearing in the CPLR and should not be confused with the individual rules of particular courts or categories of courts. Those rules, including the Uniform Rules for the New York State Trial Courts, are adopted and regulated by the Chief Administrator of the Courts. See §§ 3 and 5.

[1]   See § 12.

procedures in order to simplify them, recognizing that these courts service the smaller cases.

The surrogate's court has its own court act, called the Surrogate's Court Procedure Act, or SCPA. The same is true of the family court, governed by the Family Court Act. Since those courts handle business substantially different from the ordinary run of civil litigation, their court acts are more profuse on procedure and the need to rely on the CPLR in those courts is consequently reduced. But the CPLR is still applicable when consistent.[2]

The court of claims, where the State is the only defendant, is governed by the Court of Claims Act, which sets forth the court's jurisdiction. It has only a handful of procedural provisions, with the result—intended—that the CPLR is the major procedural tool in that court.

The Real Property Actions and Proceedings Law (RPAPL) contains a number of special provisions relevant only in certain categories of actions affecting real property. These provisions are additional to the CPLR, which is still the major tool in those actions.[3] The CPLR is also the major tool in matrimonial actions, although the Domestic Relations Law contains some special procedural instruction, which will be referred to from time to time.

Some of the consolidated laws have important procedural provisions. These, too, will be cited and discussed as they arise. Among the better known are the Business Corporation Law sections that deal with process service,[4] and the non-resident motorist statute.[5]

Superimposed on all of this are the rules of court. Prior to January 6, 1986, there were numerous sets of rules, each court having its own. These were rescinded on that date and a few sets of "Uniform Rules" promulgated in their place. Each category of court has its own set of uniform rules, as follows:

Part 200:   Uniform Rules for Courts Exercising Criminal Jurisdiction

Part 202:   Uniform Civil Rules for the Supreme Court and the County Court; containing § 202.70 Rules of the Commercial Division of the Supreme Court

Part 205:   Uniform Rules for the Family Court

Part 206:   Uniform Rules for the Court of Claims

Part 207:   Uniform Rules for the Surrogate's Court

Part 208:   Uniform Civil Rules for the New York City Civil Court

Part 210:   Uniform Civil Rules for the City Courts Outside of the City of New York

---

    [2]   SCPA 102; Fam. Ct. Act § 165(a). For discussion of the application of the CPLR in the Family Court, see In re Baby Boy O., 298 A.D.2d 677, 679, 748 N.Y.S.2d 811, 813 (3d Dep't 2002); Schwartz v. Schwartz, 23 A.D.2d 204, 206–08, 259 N.Y.S.2d 751, 753–55 (1st Dep't 1965).

    [3]   Further discussion of the interplay of the RPAPL and CPLR is in § 571 (Practitioner's Edition), in the treatment of the summary proceeding.

    [4]   Bus. Corp. Law §§ 304–307; see §§ 70, 95.

    [5]   Veh. & Traf. Law § 253; see § 97.

Part 212: Uniform Civil Rules for the District Courts

Part 214: Uniform Civil Rules for the Justice Courts

There is additionally a Part 125, entitled "Uniform Rules for the Engagement of Counsel," of interest to every trial lawyer in the state. It has instructions for the resolution of "conflicting engagements," a perennial friction in practice when lawyers find their presence demanded in two or more courts at the same time.

The Uniform Rules, notably Part 202 (which governs in the supreme court), will often be cited in this book, especially when fundamental procedures (not mere incidents) are affected. Among the fundamentals that come from the uniform rules are those governing certain aspects of motion practice, and those governing the "note of issue" and "certificate of readiness," the papers whose filing puts the case on the court's trial calendar.[6]

Unfortunately, a given court governed by the CPLR and an assigned set of uniform rules may also see fit to publish individual rules. As we will see in our travels, there are also instances in which a judicial district and county has its own set of rules governing aspects of procedure. These various rules lurking in all sorts of places can present a minefield, even for the seasoned practitioner, and we will highlight them at appropriate junctures. New York's vast judiciary and diverse geography require some deviations in procedure throughout the state. Nonetheless, those responsible for these various local rules need to place a higher premium on uniformity.

The rules are also the source of the compulsory arbitration procedure for claims under a certain figure, officially called the "Alternative Method of Dispute Resolution by Arbitration."[7]

§ 4.   One Form of Action

Law and equity have long been merged in New York and the old common law forms of action have been abandoned. The distinctions between law and equity are officially abolished,[1] but in some respects linger. They are still relevant, for example, in determining the right to trial by jury. They persist also in that claims sounding in what was once equity, and which appeal to the conscience of the court, are still subject to certain equitable defenses, such as laches and unclean hands, to which law claims are not.

The CPLR governs in both actions and special proceedings. The reader who knows what a motion is can quickly learn the mechanics of a special proceeding. An action is the plenary prosecution of a right, seeking a final judgment. A motion is generally an application made within the action for some item of incidental relief, usually involving some step in the processing of the action while on its march to a final judgment. The procedures of a motion, to be met in detail in a later chapter,[2] are quick and expeditious. The movant picks a motion day—a day on which the court or the individual judge

---

[6]   These are discussed in §§ 369 and 370. A "calendar" is just a list of cases awaiting hearing or trial or other disposition. See § 368.

[7]   The governing provisions are in Part 28 of the Rules of the Chief Judge—available in the annually recompiled McKinney's N.Y. Rules of Court softcover—promulgated on the authority of CPLR 3405. See § 585B (Practitioner's Edition).

[1]   CPLR 103(a).

[2]   Chapter 10.

assigned to the case hears motions—and notifies the court and the other parties of the relief sought. The motion comes on at the appointed time for hearing, and for disposition shortly thereafter.

A special proceeding is as plenary as an action in that it seeks the vindication of a right in a final judgment,[3] but it is brought on with the procedure and speed of a motion.[4] With so expeditious a path, the special proceeding is of course preferable to an action whenever it's available, but it's available only when a statute specifically prescribes it.[5] Otherwise, the usual procedures of a plenary action must be followed.

Examples of authorized special proceedings are many. Some are contained in the CPLR itself, such as the Article 78 proceeding, whose primary mission is to facilitate judicial review of administrative decisions, and the special proceedings authorized by Article 75 to test whether a given dispute is arbitrable. Among the most highly specialized (and frequently brought) of special proceedings is the Summary Proceeding to Recover Possession of Real Property, the device used to settle landlord-tenant disputes quickly. It is governed in detail by Article 7 of the Real Property Actions and Proceedings Law. Special proceedings are treated in depth in Chapter 20.

In the CPLR, "[t]he word 'action' includes a special proceeding."[6] This enables procedures that are applicable in terms to an "action" to govern in special proceedings as well, whenever appropriate,[7] without having constantly to repeat the words "special proceeding."

Sometimes a lawyer will assume that a special proceeding lies in a given situation when in fact it does not. Sometimes it can be a close question. In older practice, the bringing of a special proceeding when an action was appropriate, or vice versa, resulted in dismissal. Dismissal is no longer permitted in that situation. Under CPLR 103(c), as long as jurisdiction over the parties has been obtained, the court today must convert the case to proper form.[8] The defect is nothing more than a "mischaracterization,"[9] and the conversion entails nothing more than a court order reciting, for example, that the pleadings in the special proceeding are to be deemed the pleadings in an action and directing that the case proceed henceforth as if it were an action in which the answer has just been served.[10]

Similarly, a party may sometimes make a mere motion for relief that technically requires a special proceeding, or take pains to commence a special proceeding when a mere motion will do. If no prejudice was demonstrated, it was held that a like conversion

---

[3]   CPLR 411.

[4]   Compare CPLR 403 (special proceeding), with CPLR 2214 (motion).

[5]   CPLR 103(b).

[6]   CPLR 105(b).

[7]   For discussion of the procedures that are unique to the special proceeding, see §§ 550 et seq.

[8]   CPLR 103(c) came into New York practice as part of the original CPLR, which went into effect on Sept. 1, 1963. It had no forebear.

[9]   Altona Citizens Committee, Inc. v. Town of Altona, 77 A.D.2d 954, 430 N.Y.S.2d 894 (3d Dep't 1980), order aff'd, 54 N.Y.2d 908, 445 N.Y.S.2d 131, 429 N.E.2d 809 (1981).

[10]   See First Nat. City Bank v. City of New York Finance Administration, 36 N.Y.2d 87, 94, 365 N.Y.S.2d 493, 498, 324 N.E.2d 861, 864 (1975); Phalen v. Theatrical Protective Union No. 1, Intern. Alliance of Theatrical and Stage Emp., AFL-CIO, 22 N.Y.2d 34, 41, 290 N.Y.S.2d 881, 887, 238 N.E.2d 295, 299 (1968); Hodges v. Beattie, 68 A.D.3d 1597, 893 N.Y.S.2d 289 (3d Dep't 2009) (supreme court properly converted "plaintiffs' order to show cause and supporting papers to a summons and complaint").

to the appropriate form may be allowed.[11] While a Court of Appeals decision[12] indicated otherwise for a while,[13] it was overruled on its specific facts by one statute[14] and overruled more completely by a 2003 amendment of CPLR 103(c). Hence CPLR 103(c) now explicitly authorizes this type of conversion in the court's discretion and lets it work both ways: motion to proceeding and proceeding to motion. It can be helpful in a variety of situations.[15]

It has also been held that a proceeding mistakenly captioned under one statute may be treated as having been brought under the proper one.[16] The court may not, however, extend the applicable statute of limitations governing the proceeding.[17]

CPLR 103(c) has even been invoked to treat a special proceeding as an appeal.[18]

§ 5.   Administration of the Courts

The authority and responsibility for administrative supervision of the courts is in the chief judge of the Court of Appeals, who shall, says the state constitution, "after consultation with the administrative board, . . . establish standards and administrative policies for general application throughout the state," and submit them to the Court of Appeals. The policies are "promulgated," however, only after "approval" by the Court.[1] Thus, the Court of Appeals has the ultimate authority over the "standards" and "policies" of judicial administration, which practically speaking amounts to a kind of veto power.

The chief judge has the initiative of administration. This is exercised through a chief administrator whom the chief judge appoints and through deputy administrators and "administrative judges" of the various courts, whom the chief administrator in turn appoints. The appointment of the chief administrator is made "with the advice and consent of the administrative board." The chief administrator serves at the "pleasure" of the chief judge, in whose behalf she carries out the day-to-day administration of the court system.[2]

The administrative board is a five-judge body consisting of the presiding justice of each of the four departments in the appellate division, and the chief judge, who acts as chair.[3] The chief judge's administrative functions are carried out in periodic

---

[11]   See generally Empire Mut. Ins. Co. v. Palladino, 54 A.D.2d 863, 388 N.Y.S.2d 601 (1st Dep't 1976).

[12]   Matter of Solkav Solartechnik, G.m.b.H. (Besicorp Group, Inc.), 91 N.Y.2d 482, 672 N.Y.S.2d 838, 695 N.E.2d 707 (1998).

[13]   See the discussion in the lead note of NYSLD No. 462.

[14]   CPLR 7502(a)(iii). This concerns the procedure for confirming an arbitration award, for which see § 591 (Practitioner's Edition).

[15]   See Albanese v. Albanese, 4 Misc. 3d 1023(A), 798 N.Y.S.2d 342 (Sup. Ct., Nassau County 2004); see also SPR 129:1 and 133:3. The failure to file the initiatory papers with the proper court can cause its own set of problems. See § 63.

[16]   See, e.g., Malatestinic v. Board of Educ. of City of New York, 132 A.D.2d 661, 518 N.Y.S.2d 34, 40 Ed. Law Rep. 956 (2d Dep't 1987), treating a proceeding brought under Article 78 of the CPLR (relating to administrative action) as one brought under Article 75 (relating to arbitration).

[17]   Watkins v. Board of Educ. of Port Jefferson Union Free School Dist., 26 A.D.3d 336, 809 N.Y.S.2d 522 (2d Dep't 2006).

[18]   See Carroll v. Gammerman, 193 A.D.2d 202, 602 N.Y.S.2d 841 (1st Dep't 1993) (SPR 19:2).

[1]   N.Y. Const. art. VI, § 28(c); Jud. Law § 211(2).

[2]   N.Y. Const. art. VI, § 28(a), (b); Jud. Law § 210(3).

[3]   N.Y. Const. art. VI, § 28(a); Jud. Law § 210(2).

"consultation" with the board. There is also a "judicial conference," representative of all of the state's courts.[4]

The Judiciary Law elaborates the functions of each of the components of this administrative hierarchy, including the functions of:

— the chief judge and the Court of Appeals, in Judiciary Law § 211;

— the chief administrator, in § 212;

— the administrative board, in § 213;

— the judicial conference, in § 214–a.

The Office of Court Administration (OCA) is the physical base of judicial administration in New York.[5] Administrative and related directives are channeled through the Office of Court Administration to the various courts, either directly or through designated local administrators and administrative judges.[6] OCA is also the statistical repository of the court system, keeping track of such controversial items as pro bono hours.[7]

Through an advisory committee on civil practice, appointed by the chief judge and consisting of lawyers, court clerks, and professors, OCA watches over the CPLR and its court rules and tries to keep them up to date with the procedural needs of litigation. OCA also conducts other procedural studies, which may be found along with judicial statistics in its published annual reports. OCA reports annually to the legislature with its recommendations for procedural changes and updating. These annual reports, which are available in law libraries and online, serve as excellent research tools and can provide insights regarding amendments to the CPLR and on the status of many matters needing reform.

The "jurisdiction" of the courts is largely, if not completely, controlled by constitution and statute. Within each court's jurisdiction, however, the distribution and management—which is what "administration" means—of the court's business is directed and overseen by the administrative judges. A simple example is the special "commercial division" set up in the supreme court in some counties to facilitate the handling of commercial cases. The extensive rules of the commercial division are contained in section 202.70 and are addressed in further detail below.[8]

§ 6.   Liberal Construction

CPLR 104: Construction

The direction contained in the CPLR about how it shall be construed is in CPLR 104:

Construction. The civil practice law and rules shall be liberally construed to secure the just, speedy and inexpensive determination of every civil judicial proceeding.

---

[4]   Jud. Law § 214.

[5]   The Office of Court Administration has its principal offices at 25 Beaver Street, New York, New York 10004 and website address at: https://www.nycourts.gov/Admin/oca.shtml.

[6]   See Joseph W. Bellacosa, *Judicial Administration—Spell It O-C-A Not O-R-C-A,* 58 N.Y. St. B.J. 6, 11 (1986).

[7]   22 N.Y.C.R.R. § 118.1.

[8]   See § 12A.

"Civil judicial proceeding" means actions and special proceedings collectively. It includes everything but a criminal action.[1]

CPLR 104 is modeled on Rule 1 of the Federal Rules of Civil Procedure, which makes federal caselaw available by analogy should a point arise that has not been addressed by a New York case. A sound approach to CPLR 104 would be this: when a provision is met and differing applications are suggested for it, its intent should be determined and its language subordinated to what is known to be its intent. In other words, find the direction in which the provision aims, and when two constructions are equally permissible, apply the one that will send it farther in its intended direction.

There are two provisions in the CPLR of such pervasive relevance to all of procedure—and to the "liberal" construction that CPLR 104 espouses—that they should be noted at the outset of any study of New York practice. They are CPLR 2001 and 2004.

CPLR 2001: Mistakes, omissions, defects and irregularities

CPLR 2001, governing mistakes and omissions in general, reads as follows (with emphasis added as appropriate):

> At any stage of an action, *including the filing of a summons with notice, summons and complaint or petition to commence an action [or special proceeding]*, the court may permit a mistake, omission, defect or irregularity, including the failure to purchase or acquire an index number or other mistake in the filing process, to be corrected, upon such terms as may be just, or, if a substantial right of a party is not prejudiced, the mistake, omission, defect or irregularity shall be disregarded, provided that any applicable fees shall be paid.

While CPLR 2001 can forgive a multitude of sins, virtually all mistakes in commencing the action were at one time deemed jurisdictional and hence beyond the corrective reach of the statute. An amendment in 2007 rejected that limitation by adding the language we've italicized above. It has worked well in a number of cases, but there are still some situations that are deemed so fundamentally "jurisdictional" that CPLR 2001 can't help. The most notable of these is the failure to file the initiatory papers with the appropriate clerk, a by-product of the infamous *Mendon Ponds* decision.[2] In Ruffin v. Lion Corp.,[3] the Court extended CPLR 2001's reach to defects in serving process.

CPLR 2001 and its instruction should be treated as part of the liberal construction edict. It puts procedure into perspective by reminding bench and bar that procedure is a means, not an end. Even if some CPLR requirement is violated, the possibility of avoiding prejudice to the other parties by a mere act of contrition, such as the correction of the mistake, permits the court to grant relief "upon such terms as may be just." And if the error prejudices no one, the court can merely direct that it be ignored, even relieving the errant party of the trouble of correcting it. This provision is of great value

---

[1] CPLR 105.

[2] Mendon Ponds Neighborhood Ass'n. v. Dehm, 98 N.Y.2d 745, 751 N.Y.S.2d 819, 781 N.E.2d 883 (2002); see Goldenberg v. Westchester County Health Care Corp., 16 N.Y.3d 323, 921 N.Y.S.2d 619, 946 N.E.2d 717 (2011) (NYSLD No. 617) (holding that the defect of failing to file the summons and complaint within the statute of limitations is of the jurisdictional variety that cannot be forgiven under CPLR 2001). Extensive treatment of the CPLR 2001 amendment and subsequent caselaw interpreting it appears in § 63, placed there because it's the section primarily concerned with commencement.

[3] Ruffin v. Lion Corp., 15 N.Y.3d 578, 915 N.Y.S.2d 204, 940 N.E.2d 909 (2010) (SPR 228:3) (NYSLD No. 612). The *Ruffin* decision is discussed in further detail in § 100.

in practice. If a given mistake can be categorized as a mere irregularity, which it should be if no party can be deemed substantially prejudiced by it, CPLR 2001 should be invited onto the scene and made at home. Caselaw decades prior to *Mendon Ponds* pointed in that direction,[4] and it's a direction CPLR 2001, especially in light of its 2007 amendment, seeks to take once again.[5]

CPLR 2004: Extensions of time generally

CPLR 2004, the provision governing extensions of time, is another fundamental statute in practice. It reads as follows:

> Except where otherwise expressly prescribed by law, the court may extend the time fixed by any statute, rule or order for doing any act, upon such terms as may be just and upon good cause shown, whether the application for extension is made before or after the expiration of the time fixed.

Considering the large number of time periods met in civil practice (and to be considered in this book), CPLR 2004 provides some assurance that occasional tardiness need not be fatal. But this early notification about the court's generosity in extending time periods is not offered as a panacea to the tardy, as good practice requires prompt responses to time-limited demands, or at minimum a stipulation with one's adversary extending the time (which would ordinarily obviate an application to the court for an extension).[6] The statute is intended more as an admonition to practitioners who would hold their opponents too rigidly to time requirements. CPLR 2004 is in the wings and can be put on stage by mere motion. As the statute recognizes, the application for an extension can even be made after the time period has expired. The Court of Appeals has noted several factors that may be considered on CPLR 2004 motions, "such as the length of the delay, whether the opposing party has been prejudiced by the delay, the reason given for the delay, whether the moving party was in default before seeking the extension, and, if so, the presence or absence of an affidavit of merit."[7]

The courts are not patient with lawyers who make too much of untimeliness when jurisdiction is not involved. Judges resent that their own time "should have been expended in a matter that properly should have been disposed of by the exercise of simple courtesy between attorneys,"[8] and they expect this mutual courtesy to encompass reasonable time extensions when requested.[9]

---

[4]   See, for example, the excellent treatment by Judge (later Chief Judge) Breitel, speaking for a unanimous court in Patrician Plastic Corp. v. Bernadel Realty Corp., 25 N.Y.2d 599, 608, 307 N.Y.S.2d 868, 875–76, 256 N.E.2d 180, 185 (1970).

[5]   This matter is elaborated elsewhere. See § 64, which discusses jurisdictional defects versus mere irregularities in conjunction with summons service. The provisional remedies, treated in Chapter 12, are the major exception to the rule of liberal construction in CPLR 104. They are considered to be drastic in nature and are given a tighter construction. See § 306.

[6]   See § 204, discussing stipulations.

[7]   Tewari v. Tsoutsouras, 75 N.Y.2d 1, 12, 550 N.Y.S.2d 572, 577, 549 N.E.2d 1143, 1148 (1989).

[8]   Bermudez v. City of New York, 22 A.D.2d 865, 254 N.Y.S.2d 420, 421 (1st Dep't 1964).

[9]   For a brief time during the early 1980s, courtesy between lawyers in the granting of extensions of time to plead disappeared almost entirely because of a short-lived caselaw rule that denied the courts discretion to consider "law office failures"—the cause of most pleading delays—as excuses. This led to a refusal of pleading and other time extensions between lawyers in the hope of obtaining an irrevocable default against the other side. A statute, CPLR 2005, was added in 1983 to overrule the case that started it all—Barasch v. Micucci, 49 N.Y.2d 594, 427 N.Y.S.2d 732, 404 N.E.2d 1275 (1980)—and restore judicial discretion to take "law office failures" into consideration along with any other explanations a tardy party might offer. In the process, it put an end to the short-lived era of "trial by ambush," as some lawyers called it. See § 231.

There are two statutory exceptions to the power of CPLR 2004 to extend time. One is the statute of limitations itself, i.e., the time in which an action has to be commenced. It is not subject to discretionary extensions.[10] The second is the time in which to take an appeal.[11] Occasionally some other time period is treated, perhaps unexpectedly, as a statute of limitations, with the result that it, too, is outside the reach of CPLR 2004,[12] but the exceptions are few and the uses of CPLR 2004 many.

In Powers v. Foley,[13] the Second Department concluded that CPLR 2004 "applies to extensions of time for the doing of acts in actions and proceedings and not for the doing of acts which are substantive in character and provided for under other statutes." In Monahan v. Hartka,[14] the Third Department ruled that CPLR 2004 "has no application 'to time limits set forth in statutes or regulations other than those contained in the CPLR.'" There is not, however, uniformity on the point.[15] In Navillus Tile, Inc. v. LC Main, LLC,[16] the Second Department concluded that a court may extend the time prescribed for the duration of a lien in section 17 of the Lien Law. The court cited to CPLR 2004 to support its conclusion but did not make reference to the above caselaw. The Court of Appeals demonstrated some interest in the issue by granting leave to appeal in *Navillus Tile*, but the appeal was withdrawn.

§ 7.   Forms

CPLR 107 authorizes the chief administrator of the courts to promulgate forms for civil practice. When she does so, the forms become official forms and they "shall," says the statute, "be sufficient . . . [to] illustrate the simplicity and brevity of statement" required by the CPLR.[17] A number of official forms were promulgated under this provision, but in what we view as an unfortunate development, the courts have rescinded them in an administrative order that became effective on July 1, 2016.[18] This development closely followed on the heels of, and was prompted by, the abrogation of Federal Rule of Civil Procedure 84 ("Forms") effective December 1, 2015.[19]

New York's official forms were certainly dated and needed revisions here and there. Nor were they comprehensive. Nonetheless, they served as a helpful blueprint when drafting pleadings and the like, especially for those new to the practice of law. Rather than simply abandoning the official forms, the courts should have sought to improve upon them to conform to current practice. This is especially the case today, with the

---

[10]   CPLR 201.

[11]   CPLR 5514(c).

[12]   This happened with the period in which to test whether an issue is arbitrable under CPLR 7503(c). See § 593 (Practitioner's Edition).

[13]   Powers v. Foley, 25 A.D.2d 525, 267 N.Y.S.2d 459 (2d Dep't 1966).

[14]   Monahan v. Hartka, 17 A.D.3d 758, 793 N.Y.S.2d 552 (3d Dep't 2005).

[15]   See, e.g., Judith S. v. Howard S., 46 A.D.3d 318, 847 N.Y.S.2d 529 (1st Dep't 2007) ("Third Department . . . ignored the clear breadth of [CPLR 2004], denying its application to time limits set forth in any statutes or regulations 'other than those contained in the CPLR' "); see generally Alexander, McKinney's Practice Commentaries, CPLR 2004 (discussing relevant caselaw); John R. Higgitt, *Requests to Extend Deadlines and the Reach of the CPLR*, N.Y.L.J., Oct. 10, 2013.

[16]   Navillus Tile, Inc. v. LC Main, LLC, 98 A.D.3d 979, 950 N.Y.S.2d 748 (2d Dep't 2012), lv. granted 20 N.Y.3d 854, 958 N.Y.S.2d 698, 982 N.E.2d 618, appeal withdrawn.

[17]   See Scholastic Inc. v. Pace Plumbing Corp., 129 A.D.3d 75, 83, 8 N.Y.S.3d 143, 149–50 (1st Dep't 2015) (official forms deemed "sufficient as a matter of law").

[18]   See AO/119/16, dated May 23, 2016, https://www.nycourts.gov/rules/comments/orders/AO119–16.pdf.

[19]   See § 620 (Practitioner's Edition).

Uniform Bar Exam in place. Many people will now be admitted to practice in New York after studying the CPLR for approximately 3 hours.[20] Furthermore, Part 523 of the Court of Appeals Rules now allows lawyers to practice in our courts "temporarily" even though they may have no knowledge of New York practice and procedure.[21] A revised set of official forms would have been a great aid to these lawyers and the courts before whom they will be appearing.

The rescinded forms are still certainly helpful and are set forth in the text at relevant junctures. There are other myriad forms available through law publishers for civil practice in general and for pleadings in particular. These forms are helpful but not official. With the increase in e-filing and the availability of court records on the internet, lawyers can also seek to obtain pleadings and papers that passed muster in another case. Often the form used by a law publisher is one that got by without objection in an actual case.

The lawyer must be careful to remember that while forms are suitable for guidance, they will often need to be tailored for the particulars of the case at hand. There is no magic in print and, indeed, some printed forms that had been used repeatedly have been suddenly rejected by the courts because of intervening changes in the law or in constitutional attitudes, among other reasons.[22] The warning, therefore, is not to use privately published forms mindlessly or simply copy a paper from another litigation. With a small injection of imagination, however, these sources can be excellent guides.

---

[20] See Patrick M. Connors, *Lowering the New York Bar: Will New Exam Prepare Attorneys for Practice?,* N.Y.L.J., Feb. 26, 2016, at 4.

[21] See Patrick M. Connors, *No License Required: Temporary Practice in New York State,* N.Y.L.J., Mar. 10, 2016, at 4.

[22] See, e.g., Long Island City Sav. and Loan Ass'n v. Suggs, 78 Misc. 2d 16, 355 N.Y.S.2d 550 (Sup. Ct., Nassau County 1974).

Chapter 2

THE COURTS AND THEIR JURISDICTION

Analysis

A. The Court System
B. Transfers Between Courts
C. Forum Non Conveniens
D. Other Restrictions on Jurisdiction
E. Conditions Precedent to Suit

A. THE COURT SYSTEM

Table of Sections

§ 8.   Kinds of Jurisdiction
§ 9.   Court System; Geography
§ 10.   Court of Appeals
§ 11.   Appellate Division
§ 12.   Supreme Court
§ 12A.   Commercial Division of Supreme Court
§ 13.   Appellate Term
§ 14.   County Courts
§ 15.   Surrogate's Court
§ 16.   Family Court
§ 17.   Court of Claims
§ 18.   New York City Criminal Court
§ 19.   New York City Civil Court
§ 20.   District Courts
§ 21.   City Courts
§ 22.   Town and Village Courts
§ 23.   Aggregating or Reducing Claims

§ 8.   Kinds of Jurisdiction

There are many ways to subdivide "jurisdiction." Initially, a distinction should be made between "subject matter" jurisdiction and "personal" jurisdiction. Personal jurisdiction has to do with the court's authority to bind a particular party to its judgment. A plaintiff submits to that authority by bringing an action in the court; the defendant is subjected to it when she is served with the court's process under circumstances that require her to defend the action—i.e., when a jurisdictional basis exists against her, a topic explored in a later chapter.[1] An objection in this category of jurisdiction is waivable,

---

[1]   Chapter 4. The discussion of bases for personal jurisdiction is in § 59 and §§ 80 et seq.

and one way a defendant waives it is by contesting on the merits without properly raising the defense of lack of personal jurisdiction.

Another category is "rem" jurisdiction, which is really a subcategory of personal jurisdiction, turned to only when the latter is lacking. Like personal jurisdiction, it is subject to waiver. With "rem" jurisdiction, the court has obtained actual or constructive custody of some property of the defendant, so that it is able, even without personal jurisdiction, to render a judgment effective at least to the extent of divesting the defendant of any interest in that property.[2]

Subject matter jurisdiction is a more rigid concept. It concerns the court's competence to entertain a given kind of case. A court gets its subject matter jurisdiction from the constitution and laws of the sovereign it serves. If the jurisdiction is not so conferred, the court lacks "subject matter" jurisdiction of the case. This defect is generally not curable by waiver, consent, estoppel, laches, or anything else.

Jurisdiction of the subject matter cannot be conferred on the court, even by stipulation of the parties. The objection may be taken at any stage of the action, even if it has not been previously raised by the parties. Furthermore, the court may, on its own motion whenever its attention is called to the issue, refuse to proceed further and dismiss the action.[3]

If a court lacks subject matter jurisdiction, its judgment is void, which generally means that the judgment is subject to collateral attack. That is, it can be resisted when the question of its validity subsequently arises in another forum.[4] Thus, for example, if a city court, which lacks matrimonial jurisdiction, purports to divorce the parties, the judgment would be of no effect in New York or elsewhere. Fortunately, problems of subject matter jurisdiction are relatively infrequent in the New York courts in contrast with the federal courts.[5]

One aspect of the contrast between the federal and New York courts highlights the difference between "general" and "limited" jurisdiction. Federal courts sitting within the states are all courts of limited jurisdiction; they can hear only such cases as Congress has authorized by statute. If the case is not within a jurisdiction-giving Act of Congress, a United States district court is incompetent to entertain it. All of the courts in the New York state system, original and appellate both, are also courts of limited jurisdiction, but with the important exception of the New York State Supreme Court, the state's sole court of "general" jurisdiction. "General" jurisdiction implies all the jurisdiction that a court of original instance can have. In fact, the supreme court is given its name because it possesses "supreme" jurisdiction. Since used in contradistinction to "limited jurisdiction," the phrase "general jurisdiction" is sometimes taken to mean "unlimited," but that goes too far. While there are some exceptions to be discussed under supreme court jurisdiction later,[6] "general" comes pretty close to meaning "unlimited." The jurisdiction of a court of general jurisdiction is presumed; that of a court of limited jurisdiction must, whenever questioned, be specifically demonstrated, i.e., it must be

---

[2]   Rem jurisdiction is discussed beginning in § 101.

[3]   Robinson v. Oceanic Steam Nav. Co., 112 N.Y. 315, 324, 19 N.E. 625, 627 (1889).

[4]   A "collateral" attack should be distinguished from a "direct" attack. See § 455, discussing res judicata effect of jurisdictional determinations. The prime examples of the direct attack are the motion to vacate the judgment, made to the court that rendered it, and the appeal.

[5]   See § 611 (Practitioner's Edition).

[6]   See § 12.

shown that the particular claim is within some law or constitutional provision conferring subject matter jurisdiction.

It is important not to confuse "limited" with "impotent." In the phraseology of subject matter jurisdiction, "limited" signifies only that the categories of cases the court may hear are restricted. Several strictures narrow the appellate path to the New York Court of Appeals, for example, but when a case has accurately negotiated them and the court's jurisdiction is properly exercised in the case, the Court's powers are potent, indeed: on all matters of New York law, the Court of Appeals is the court of last resort. In a like way, the U.S. Supreme Court, the highest court in the land, may be said to have the most limited jurisdiction of all.

Another and different use of the phrases "general" and "limited" goes back to the topic of personal jurisdiction. When jurisdiction of a nondomiciliary is predicated not on the defendant's presence in the state but on the claim's arising out of some in-state event for which the defendant is responsible, this is sometimes termed "specific jurisdiction." Conversely, "general jurisdiction" is used to describe the category in which the corporate defendant, for example, has been found to be "at home" in the state and hence subject to jurisdiction on any claim, related or not to the state.[7]

Other possible pairings of subject matter jurisdiction are self-explanatory: civil and criminal is one set; original and appellate is another. Some courts can have a bit of each. Several in New York are in that category.

Another sorting is into courts of record and courts not of record. This is relatively unimportant in the present age because all courts keep records. Today, whether a court is officially a court "of record" depends entirely on the legislature. If the court is listed in section 2 of the Judiciary Law, it is a court of record; if not, it's not. All of the state's courts are courts of record, because so listed, except the town and village courts.

§ 9.   Court System; Geography

New York is divided into four judicial departments, each of which is subdivided into judicial districts consisting of counties. The map appearing below illustrates this. The districts are relevant mainly for the election of supreme court justices and for administration, but some judicial districts also author rules governing procedure. The role of the counties in civil practice is more important. Venue in supreme court actions, for example, is based on a county nexus.

A chart of the court system, appearing after the map, illustrates a number of differences among the courts. Each court, and its jurisdiction, will be discussed in ensuing sections.

The Court of Appeals is the state's court of last resort. Below it is the main intermediate appellate court—the appellate division—which is present in each of the four judicial departments. The main court of original jurisdiction is the supreme court, whose place on the chart is larger and higher than that of the other trial-level courts to recognize that the supreme court has general jurisdiction, while all the others have limited jurisdiction. On the next level are the family court, the court of claims, the surrogate's court, and the county court. They have been put on that level because the

---

[7]   See § 82.

state constitution gives their process territorial scope equal to that of the supreme court: it may be served in any part of the state.[1]

Below those courts are six more. The three on the next level down are the New York City civil and criminal courts and the district courts. The legislature may permit their process to be served statewide.[2] The city, town, and village courts are on the last level because their process cannot be served beyond an adjoining county. The constitution has thus put them in a niche below the others.[3] The box for the city courts has been made larger than that assigned to the town and village courts to flag the fact that judges of the city courts—and of all of the other courts on the chart—must be lawyers, while the justices of the town and village courts need not be[4] and most aren't.

The supreme court box has an appellate term inserted at the bottom. The appellate term is a court that exists only if the appellate division of the particular department creates it. An appellate term can hear appeals from the county courts and from the courts on the bottom two levels.

The lines indicate appellate paths. Broken lines indicate that whether the appeal follows that path depends on either of two factors: the kind of case (capital cases, for example, would go directly to the court of appeals from the trial court) or whether the particular appellate division has created an appellate term and directed lower court appeals to it. The First and Second Departments have in certain instances, the others have not.

Direct appeal to the Court of Appeals, bypassing intermediate appellate courts, also lies in certain cases involving constitutional issues.[5] Lines so indicating have been omitted: they would run from most of the courts on the chart.

---

[1]   N.Y. Const. art. VI, § 1(c). As will be seen in the study of personal jurisdiction, process may today be served even beyond the state in many instances. See § 100.

[2]   N.Y. Const. art. VI, § 1(c).

[3]   N.Y. Const. art. VI, § 1(c).

[4]   N.Y. Const. art. VI, § 20(a).

[5]   See CPLR 5601(b)(2).

JUDICIAL DEPARTMENTS
AND
JUDICIAL DISTRICTS

See
McKINNEY'S JUDICIARY LAW
§§ 70 and 140

1st Judicial Dept. includes Judicial District 1, 12
2nd Judicial Dept. includes Judicial Districts 2, 9, 10, 11, 13
3rd Judicial Dept. includes Judicial Districts 3, 4, 6
4th Judicial Dept. includes Judicial Districts 5, 7, 8

12th – Bronx

1st – N.Y.

13th – Richmond

2nd – Kings

11th – Queens

The New York State Court System

§ 10. Court of Appeals

The highest court of the state is the New York Court of Appeals. It has jurisdiction in both criminal and civil matters, but appellate only. The Court consists of a chief judge and six associate judges who are appointed by the governor for 14-year terms from a list recommended by the Commission on Judicial Nomination. The appointments are subject to senate ratification. Five judges are needed for a quorum, four for a decision.[1] The constitution itself restricts the jurisdiction of the Court of Appeals, which may be said to be a court of very limited jurisdiction.

The Court reviews only questions of law, except in two instances in which it reviews the facts.[2] One is on an appeal from a criminal judgment imposing the death penalty; the other from an appellate division decision reversing or modifying a judgment, finding new facts, and directing that a final judgment be entered on the new facts.[3] The reason for reviewing the facts in the death case is that the appeal bypasses the appellate division,[4] and it is New York's policy to allow at least one appellate review of the facts.

---

[1]   N.Y. Const. art. VI, § 2(a).

[2]   The jurisdiction of the Court of Appeals is treated in detail in §§ 527–528.

[3]   N.Y. Const. art. VI, § 3(a); see § 529.

[4]   N.Y. Const. art. VI, § 3(b).

That rationale explains the second situation, too: the new facts found by the appellate division warranting a reversal or modification have not been subjected to any further review. Most of the appeals to the Court are from the appellate division. In certain narrow instances, in addition to the death case, direct appeal from a lower court is allowed.[5]

The Court also promulgates the rules for the admission of attorneys to practice[6] and appoints and oversees the Board of Law Examiners, which is responsible for the administration of the bar exam.[7] In July 2016, the New York State Bar Exam was essentially replaced by the Uniform Bar Exam, with applicants to the New York bar also required to pass the fifty question, open book New York Law Exam.[8] Given the scant knowledge of New York law required to pass these exams and become a member of the New York bar, it is highly probable that there will be a substantial number of newly admitted attorneys who have minimal knowledge of our state's law.

In accordance with its authority to promulgate rules regulating the admission of attorneys to practice in the state, the Court adopted Part 523 of the Rules of the Court of Appeals, which became effective on December 30, 2015, allowing lawyers not licensed in New York to practice in the state temporarily. Representing a dramatic departure for New York, the new rule tracks much of the language in Rule 5.5 of the ABA Model Rules of Professional Conduct, entitled "Multijurisdictional Practice of Law."[9]

The Court of Appeals is the only court in the state permitted to render an advisory opinion. It may do so when asked to answer a question of New York law by the U.S. Supreme Court, a federal court of appeals, or a sister state's highest court.[10]

The Court of Appeals has adopted a system requiring the submission of briefs and record material in digital format.[11]

§ 11. Appellate Division

The formal name of the court is the appellate division of the supreme court. There are four judicial departments in the appellate division. The justices are duly elected members of the supreme court whom the governor has designated to sit on the appellate division. The First and Second departments have a regular allotment of seven justices each and the Third and Fourth departments have five each, but all in fact have far more than those numbers through certification procedures that enable the governor to appoint additional justices as judicial business requires. Sadly, many appellate division seats remain unfilled for long periods of time, resulting in substantial backlogs and smaller panels to hear appeals. Whatever the total number of justices assigned to an appellate division, a panel for a given case cannot exceed five in any department. Four justices are required for a quorum and three are needed for a decision.[1]

---

[5]   N.Y. Const. art. VI, § 3(b)(2); CPLR 5601(b)(2).

[6]   Jud. Law § 53.

[7]   Jud. Law §§ 56, 461, 462.

[8]   See Patrick M. Connors, *Lowering the New York Bar: Will New Exam Prepare Attorneys for Practice?*, N.Y.L.J., Feb. 26, 2016, at 4.

[9]   The new Part 523 is discussed in Patrick M. Connors, *No License Required: Temporary Practice in New York State,* N.Y.L.J., Mar. 10, 2016, at 4.

[10]   N.Y. Const. art. VI, § 3(b)(9); see § 528A.

[11]   See § 536.

[1]   N.Y. Const. art. VI, § 4(b).

The court's jurisdiction is primarily appellate.[2] It hears appeals from the supreme and county courts,[3] the family court,[4] the surrogate's court,[5] the court of claims,[6] and appellate term of the supreme court.[7] The appellate division reviews both the law and the facts,[8] including exercises of discretion made at the trial level.

The court also has some original jurisdiction, prominent among which is the admission and supervision of attorneys.[9] Other instances include where the facts are not in dispute, in which event an action on submitted facts (which requires the decision of only questions of law) may be commenced in the appellate division;[10] where an Article 78 proceeding in the nature of mandamus or prohibition is sought against a supreme court justice[11] (which would be incongruous in any court below the appellate division); and several other special proceedings that the legislature has chosen to expedite by giving them direct access to the appellate division.[12]

It is sometimes noted that the appellate division, as a branch of the supreme court, has all of the latter's original jurisdiction;[13] at other times doubt is expressed about that.[14] But even if the assumption is that the appellate division has it all, it has been held that "as a matter of administrative convenience, it will ordinarily decline to take original jurisdiction," though it "may do so whenever it sees fit."[15] Even when original jurisdiction is expressly conferred on the appellate division by statute, the court may sometimes be seen exerting itself to resist it.[16]

Practically speaking, the only matters of which the appellate division regularly assumes original jurisdiction are the few expressly conferred.

Chapter 237 of the Laws of 2015 authorizes the use of mandatory e-filing in the appellate division at the discretion of each department. Each department is permitted to adopt mandatory e-filing rules for: (1) appeals; (2) motions for permission to appeal; (3) commencement of any proceeding over which the court has original jurisdiction; and (4) the filing and service of papers in pending actions and proceedings.[17] The law excludes from mandatory e-filing those same actions that are excluded from it in the

---

[2] The jurisdiction of the appellate divisions is treated in detail in § 526.

[3] CPLR 5701. County court appeals may be directed instead to an appellate term if a given department has established one. Const. art. VI, § 8(d).

[4] Fam. Ct. Act § 1111.

[5] SCPA 2701, CPLR 5701.

[6] Ct. of Claims Act § 24.

[7] CPLR 5703(a).

[8] CPLR 5501(c).

[9] Jud. Law § 90, CPLR 9401.

[10] CPLR 3222(b)(3); see § 304.

[11] CPLR 506(b)(1).

[12] See, e.g., Tax Law § 2016, the proceeding to review a determination of the Tax Appeals Tribunal affecting a capital gains tax on a real property transfer.

[13] See, e.g., Merritt Hill Vineyards Inc. v. Windy Heights Vineyard, Inc., 61 N.Y.2d 106, 472 N.Y.S.2d 592, 460 N.E.2d 1077 (1984).

[14] See, e.g., Waldo v. Schmidt, 200 N.Y. 199, 93 N.E. 477 (1910).

[15] In re Association of Bar of City of New York, 222 A.D. 580, 585, 227 N.Y.S. 1, 6 (1st Dep't 1928).

[16] See, e.g., In re Willmark Service System, Inc., 21 A.D.2d 478, 251 N.Y.S.2d 267 (1st Dep't 1964).

[17] See CPLR 2112.

trial courts.[18] The parties can still consent to e-filing in such actions.[19] Thankfully, the legislation recommends that "[t]o the extent practicable, rules promulgated by the appellate division in each judicial department pursuant to this section shall be uniform."[20] It is our hope that all four departments in the appellate division will find it practicable in every instance!

As of this writing, the First Department maintains a modified system of e-filing.[21] There are currently no rules for the electronic filing of records and briefs in the Second, Third, or Fourth Departments, but rules for electronic filing in the appellate division have been proposed.

§ 12. Supreme Court

The supreme court is a single court of statewide jurisdiction, with a branch in each county. Its process may be served anywhere in the state,[1] and in some instances to be studied later, beyond. Justices are elected to the court from judicial districts, for 14-year terms.[2]

There are some who contend that the title "supreme" court is a misnomer because it is not "supreme" in the same sense as the United States Supreme Court. It is actually two rungs below the state's court of last resort, which is the Court of Appeals. The supreme court is, however, supreme in the sense that it is the state's court of "general" jurisdiction. This refers to original jurisdiction and means that the court has almost all of the jurisdiction the state can confer, i.e., that it possesses supreme jurisdiction. The word "almost" is used because a qualification is necessary. Although usually juxtaposed with "limited," "general" in this context does not mean "unlimited." There are two broad categories of original jurisdiction that the supreme court lacks: cases in which exclusive jurisdiction has been conferred by Congress on the federal courts,[3] and actions against the State of New York, where jurisdiction is conferred exclusively on the court of claims.[4]

With those exceptions, perhaps expanded to include the few instances in which the appellate division exercises original jurisdiction, the supreme court has all the rest of original jurisdiction. It is the superseder of all the jurisdiction, civil and criminal, exercised by the English law courts and court of chancery. When law and equity merged under the 1846 New York Constitution, the supreme court received the equity jurisdiction, too.[5]

There are many other courts of original jurisdiction in New York, and it is the policy of the state to have these other courts handle matters of which they have jurisdiction even though the supreme court has it too. The supreme court can probate a will, for

---

[18] See § 63A.

[19] See CPLR 2111.

[20] CPLR 2112. Proposed Statewide Rules of the Appellate Division were circulated on May 25, 2017.

[21] See § 536.

[1] N.Y. Const. art. VI, § 1(a), (c).

[2] N.Y. Const. art. VI, § 6(c).

[3] The Supremacy Clause of the Federal Constitution accounts for this. U.S. Const. art. VI. Examples of exclusive federal jurisdiction are bankruptcy matters, 28 U.S.C.A. § 1334, and patent and copyright infringement suits, 28 U.S.C.A. § 1338(a), among many others.

[4] This limitation on supreme court jurisdiction results from the fact that suit against the state requires a waiver of sovereign immunity and the state, in making the waiver, has conditioned it on the court of claims having exclusive jurisdiction. See Ct. of Claims Act §§ 8, 9.

[5] In re Steinway, 159 N.Y. 250, 53 N.E. 1103 (1899).

example, even though that function is the primary business of the surrogate's court.[6] It also has jurisdiction of a summary proceeding even though it is the state's policy to have the summary proceeding (landlord-tenant business) tried in the lower courts.[7] In these instances of concurrent jurisdiction, when a case is brought in the supreme court that could have been brought in some other court, the supreme court will usually transfer it to the appropriate other court even while acknowledging that it—the supreme court— has jurisdiction of the matter.[8] It will make that acknowledgement even in the face of a statute purporting to give another court "exclusive" jurisdiction.[9] How can such a statute be disregarded? The reason is this:

The intention to secure the supreme court's general jurisdiction is in the constitution itself. It is even provided that when new classes of actions are created, the supreme court "shall have jurisdiction" over them even though another court may receive the jurisdiction as well.[10] This means that the supreme court gets the jurisdiction from the new law automatically, even if some other court is the only court named in the jurisdiction-conferring statute.[11]

It is also the state's policy to have a money action brought in the lowest court jurisdictionally competent to entertain it. To this end, there are relatively minimal costs punishments for cases brought in the supreme court when, whatever the amount sought, the judgment ends up below a stated sum.[12] But if the reason for bringing the case in the supreme instead of a lower court is that the latter's summons could not reach the defendant for want of territorial jurisdiction, or that the lower court would otherwise lack jurisdiction, the costs punishment does not apply.[13]

Appeals from the supreme court go in almost all instances to the local appellate division.[14]

The CPLR is of course the main source of procedure in the supreme court, but Part 202 of the Uniform Rules provides further procedural detail for practice in the supreme court (along with the county courts) and will be referred to at a number of places in this book.

---

[6]   Pollicina v. Misericordia Hosp. Medical Center, 82 N.Y.2d 332, 604 N.Y.S.2d 879, 624 N.E.2d 974 (1993).

[7]   See Post v. 120 East End Ave. Corp., 62 N.Y.2d 19, 475 N.Y.S.2d 821, 464 N.E.2d 125 (1984).

[8]   See 3505 Realty Corp. v. Weinberger, 41 Misc. 2d 254, 245 N.Y.S.2d 150 (Sup. Ct., Bronx County 1963).

[9]   See, e.g., People v. Davis, 27 A.D.2d 299, 278 N.Y.S.2d 750 (1st Dep't 1967).

[10]   N.Y. Const. art. VI, § 7(b).

[11]   Kagen v. Kagen, 21 N.Y.2d 532, 289 N.Y.S.2d 195, 236 N.E.2d 475 (1968). The case establishes that even grants of jurisdiction to other courts made prior to the effective date of the new judiciary article (N.Y. Const. art. VI, eff. September 1, 1962) are to be deemed within supreme court jurisdiction. See also People v. Correa, 15 N.Y.3d 213, 907 N.Y.S.2d 106, 933 N.E.2d 705 (2010).

[12]   CPLR 8102. In New York City, costs are denied to the plaintiff who brings the action in the supreme court and recovers less than $6,000. CPLR 8102(1). Outside New York City, a recovery of less than $500 in the supreme court brings about the denial of costs. CPLR 8102(2).

[13]   See, e.g., Friedman v. Great Atlantic & Pac. Tea Co., 174 Misc. 185, 20 N.Y.S.2d 392 (Sup. Ct., Schenectady County 1940), decided in 1940 when the county court lacked jurisdiction of a foreign corporation (an impediment removed in 1971 by amendments of §§ 190 and 190–a of the Judiciary Law).

[14]   CPLR 5701.

§ 12A. Commercial Division of Supreme Court

In 1995, the commercial division of the supreme court was opened in Monroe and New York County to adjudicate and expedite commercial cases in the supreme court. Over the next two decades, the commercial division has steadily expanded to several counties, including Albany, Kings, Nassau, New York, Onondaga, Queens, Suffolk, and Westchester, as well as the entire Seventh and Eighth Judicial Districts.

Monetary Thresholds

There are monetary thresholds for adjudicating an action in the commercial division, which vary from county to county. Only compensatory damages are to be considered in measuring whether the threshold has been reached. Excluded from the measurement are punitive damages, interest, costs, disbursements, and counsel fees. As of this writing, the monetary thresholds for the commercial division are:

New York County—$500,000

Nassau County—$200,000

Kings County—$150,000

Eighth Judicial District, Queens, Suffolk and Westchester Counties—$100,000

Seventh Judicial District and Albany and Onondaga Counties—$50,000

Uniform Rule 202.70(a) lists these applicable thresholds and should be checked periodically by attorneys who litigate in the commercial division.

Categories of Action and Assignment to Commercial Division

The categories of action that qualify as "commercial" are defined in subdivision (b) of Rule 202.70. These actions must meet the monetary thresholds above or seek equitable or declaratory relief. The categories include the obvious claims arising from business dealings, including breach of contract, business torts, securities transactions, partnership disputes, shareholder derivative actions, commercial real property transactions (excluding actions for the payment of rent only), "commercial class actions" (without consideration of the monetary threshold), and many others. The rules also list several actions that cannot be heard in the commercial division, even if the monetary threshold is met, including suits to collect professional fees and actions seeking a declaratory judgment as to insurance coverage for personal injury or property damage.[15]

Proceedings to stay or compel arbitration,[16] affirm or disaffirm arbitration awards,[17] and related injunctive relief pursuant to CPLR Article 75 involving the categories of commercial actions listed in Rule 202.70(b) can also be entertained in the commercial division, assuming the applicable monetary thresholds are met.[18] Where an arbitration agreement provides for the arbitration to be heard outside the United States, the monetary thresholds do not apply.

---

[15] 22 N.Y.C.R.R. § 202.70(c).

[16] See § 592 (Practitioner's Edition).

[17] See § 601 (Practitioner's Edition).

[18] 22 N.Y.C.R.R. § 202.70(b)(12).

A party seeking assignment of an action to the commercial division must act promptly. Under Rule 202.70(d), a party can seek assignment of its case to the commercial division within 90 days following service of the complaint by filing a Request for Judicial Intervention (RJI)[19] certifying that the case meets the jurisdictional requirements for commercial division assignment. Assignment to the commercial division is sought through an addendum filed with the RJI.[20] The failure to timely file the RJI and addendum may preclude the parties from seeking a commercial division assignment.[21] If the RJI is filed without the addendum seeking assignment to the commercial division, but within 90 days of the service of the complaint, any other party may seek the assignment by letter to the administrative judge within ten days from the receipt of the RJI.[22]

Rules of Practice in the Commercial Division

Given the current state of affairs in New York State courts, lawyers must unfortunately work with several different sets of rules in the commercial division. These include the CPLR, the Uniform Rules,[23] the Rules of the Commercial Division of the Supreme Court,[24] and any rules of the individual assigned judge.[25] Procedural directives may also reside in county rules or rules of a judicial district.[26] In sum, one must wade through several sets of rules before charting a procedural course.

Uniform Rule 202.70 contains the Uniform Rules of practice for the commercial division and is supplemented by the other rules in Part 202, unless the commercial division rules provide specifically to the contrary.[27] The commercial division rules are extensive, however, and address many matters including the form and length of papers;[28] preliminary and compliance conferences;[29] disclosure disputes, motions, and advance notice of motions;[30] orders to show cause and temporary restraining orders;[31] motions for summary judgment;[32] and settlement and pretrial conferences.[33] Some of these rules appear to conflict with the CPLR.[34]

---

[19]   See § 77B.

[20]   22 N.Y.C.R.R. § 202.70(d); Form UCS–840C.

[21]   See 22 N.Y.C.R.R. § 202.70(e) (allowing belated transfer of action into the commercial division under certain circumstances).

[22]   See 22 N.Y.C.R.R. § 202.70(e). Query what happens when an action is commenced by summons and notice under CPLR 305(b)?

[23]   22 N.Y.C.R.R. Part 202.

[24]   22 N.Y.C.R.R. § 202.70(g).

[25]   See, e.g., 22 N.Y.C.R.R. § 202.70(g), Com. Div. Rule 14 ("Disclosure Disputes. If the court's Part Rules address discovery disputes, those Part Rules will govern discovery disputes in a pending case.").

[26]   See, e.g., Kings County Supreme Court Uniform Civil Term Rules, Part C (6) (prescribing time periods to move for summary judgment).

[27]   22 N.Y.C.R.R. § 202.70(g).

[28]   22 N.Y.C.R.R. § 202.70(g), Com. Div. Rules 6 and 17.

[29]   22 N.Y.C.R.R. § 202.70(g), Com. Div. Rules 7 and 8.

[30]   22 N.Y.C.R.R. § 202.70(g), Com. Div. Rules 14 and 16.

[31]   22 N.Y.C.R.R. § 202.70(g), Com. Div. Rules 19 and 20.

[32]   22 N.Y.C.R.R. § 202.70(g), Com. Div. Rule 19–a.

[33]   22 N.Y.C.R.R. § 202.70(g), Com. Div. Rule 30.

[34]   Compare 22 N.Y.C.R.R. § 202.70(g), Com. Div. Rule 13(c) (requiring exchange of reports and depositions of testifying experts), with CPLR 3101(d)(1)(iii) (requiring "court order upon a showing of special circumstances" before ordering further disclosure beyond that in CPLR 3101(d)(1)(i)).

New or amended commercial division rules descend upon the practicing bar in spurts, making it somewhat difficult to keep abreast of that court's special procedures. The best way to track rule developments in the commercial division is through the New York court's website dedicated to the "Administrative Rules of the Unified Court System & Uniform Rules of the Trial Courts" and requests for public comment to proposed rules at: http://nycourts.gov/rules/comments/. This site is not limited to developments in the commercial division but also contains information on amendments to the court rules generally. As of this writing, however, this site contains more recent information than the commercial division's website, which can be found at: https://www.nycourts.gov/courts/comdiv/.

§ 13.   Appellate Term

This court exists at the pleasure of the appellate division of the particular department. At present, only the First and Second Department have created an appellate term. The court consists of three to five (usually three) supreme court justices assigned to hear appeals from certain lower courts.[1] In both the First and Second departments, the appellate term hears appeals from the New York City Civil and Criminal Court.[2] In the Second Department, an appellate term also hears appeals from the district, city, town, and village courts in all cases, and from the county courts in civil cases and in certain criminal cases.[3]

No more than three justices may sit as a panel; two make a quorum and two are also needed for a decision.[4]

Appeals from the appellate term go to the appellate division.[5]

§ 14.   County Courts

There is a county court in each of the 57 counties outside New York City. Its judges are elected for 10-year terms.[1] It has criminal jurisdiction, including over felonies, and substantial civil jurisdiction.[2]

The court does not have a separate court act for its civil practice. The CPLR applies directly, and Part 202 of the Uniform Civil Rules for the Supreme Court and County Court supplies further procedure.[3] The only need for a separate statute is to elaborate the subject matter jurisdiction of the court—the basics of which are constitutionally supplied[4]—and this is done in the Judiciary Law, primarily in sections 190 and 190–a.

Unlike the supreme court, which is a single statewide court, the county court is treated as distinct to each county. It has jurisdiction of money actions up to $25,000.[5]

---

[1]   N.Y. Const. art. VI, § 8.
[2]   22 N.Y.C.R.R. §§ 640.1; 730.1(b).
[3]   22 N.Y.C.R.R. § 730.1(d).
[4]   N.Y. Const. art. VI, § 8(c).
[5]   CPLR 5703(a).
[1]   N.Y. Const. art. VI, § 10.
[2]   N.Y. Const. art. VI, § 11(a).
[3]   22 N.Y.C.R.R. § 202.1(a).
[4]   N.Y. Const. art. VI, § 11(a).
[5]   Jud. Law § 190(3).

There is an additional jurisdictional requirement in money actions in the county courts. The defendant, or all of the defendants if there are more than one, must either reside or have a business office in the county at the time the action is commenced. If a business office is relied on instead of a residence, it must also be shown that the claim arose in the county. These are statutory requirements,[6] and since they are jurisdictional, the action is dismissed if they are not met.[7] But while the statutory requirements appear to concern subject matter jurisdiction, which would make them unwaivable objections, they are treated as going to personal jurisdiction, with the result that they can be waived if not timely interposed.[8]

Prior distinctions between foreign and domestic corporations in money actions in the county court[9] were largely abandoned in 1971 and today the county court can entertain a money claim, within the applicable monetary figure, against either kind of corporation as long as it has an office or facility in the county.[10]

The court can hear certain real property actions if the land is in the county, and here there is no monetary limitation.[11] It has replevin jurisdiction if the chattel is in the county and its value does not exceed the court's monetary jurisdiction.[12] It also has jurisdiction of incompetency proceedings affecting county residents or their real property within the county[13] and of summary proceedings to recover real property in the county.[14]

Appeals go to the appellate division,[15] except in the Second Department, where appeals (in all but felony cases) go to the appellate term.[16]

The county court itself acts as an appellate court for certain lower court decisions. In the Third and Fourth Departments, it hears appeals from city courts[17] and from town and village courts.[18]

If the summons and complaint are served together in a county court action brought for more than the court's monetary jurisdiction, the court has been held to lack even the jurisdiction needed to allow an amendment to reduce the demand to fit the money maximum.[19] But since the county court is today empowered by the constitution to transfer such a case to the court that does have the needed jurisdiction,[20] the court should by analogy have the power to permit an amendment that would retain the case.

---

[6] Jud. Law § 190(3).

[7] Bonk v. Hodgkins, 68 Misc. 2d 148, 326 N.Y.S.2d 140 (Schenectady County Court 1971).

[8] Meyers v. American Locomotive Co., 201 N.Y. 163, 94 N.E. 605 (1911).

[9] See Wachtel v. Diamond State Engineering Corporation, 215 A.D. 15, 213 N.Y.S. 77 (2d Dep't 1925).

[10] Jud. Law § 190–a as amended in 1971. A corporation having such an office or facility is the equivalent of a resident for this purpose.

[11] Jud. Law § 190(1). Among the real property actions are the typical ones of partition, mortgage foreclosure, specific performance, deed rescission, reformation, etc.

[12] Jud. Law § 190(3).

[13] Jud. Law § 190(4).

[14] RPAPL 701(1). For the distinction between a real property action and a summary proceeding, see § 571 (Practitioner's Edition).

[15] CPLR 5701.

[16] 22 N.Y.C.R.R. § 730.1(d). There are no county courts in the First Department.

[17] Uniform City Ct. Act § 1701.

[18] Uniform Just. Ct. Act § 1701.

[19] Heffron v. Jennings, 66 A.D. 443, 73 N.Y.S. 410 (4th Dep't 1901).

[20] N.Y. Const. art. VI, § 19(b).

On a money counterclaim (as opposed to main claim), the constitution specifies that the county court has jurisdiction without limit as to amount. And it authorizes the legislature to give the county court whatever equity jurisdiction it wishes.[21] The equity jurisdiction so far conferred under this power is primarily in the real property actions already mentioned.

The court's process may be served anywhere in the state[22] and in some instances beyond.[23]

The practitioner should inquire about which categories of jurisdiction the county court in a particular county customarily exercises. It may be found that in a given county the court is used primarily as the felony court, while civil matters are brought in the supreme court. These are administrative variations one meets even though the court may technically have jurisdiction over a range of cases.

It is permissible, if a statute so directs, for one judge to simultaneously perform the function of county judge, surrogate, and family court judge, or any combination of the three.[24] This wearing of several judicial robes is found in the more rural counties.

§ 15. Surrogate's Court

There is a surrogate's court in each county of the state. Each has at least one judge, called a surrogate; some have two. Election is by county. In the New York City counties, the term is 14 years; elsewhere, 10.[1]

The surrogate's court handles all matters concerning the affairs of decedents' estates. Its basic grant of jurisdiction is contained in section 12(d) of Article VI of the State Constitution and in section 201 of the Surrogate's Court Procedure Act (SCPA). The SCPA is profuse in procedural detail; thus, although the CPLR applies in the court,[2] it is less needed there than in the lower courts that try the usual civil actions. Further details of procedure for the surrogate's court are found in Part 207 of the Uniform Rules.

As long as "affairs of decedents" is the subject, the court has subject matter jurisdiction whether the claim involves law or equity.[3] This includes all the jurisdiction needed to entertain matters involving both testamentary and, as of 1980, "lifetime" inter-vivos trusts.[4] While the surrogate's court has often entertained proceedings that are in the nature of a declaratory judgment action, there is still some debate on whether it possesses subject matter jurisdiction over such claims.[5]

The court's process is servable anywhere in the state[6] and in some circumstances beyond.[7] Appeals go to the appellate division.[8]

---

[21] N.Y. Const. art. VI, § 11(b).

[22] N.Y. Const. art. VI, § 1(c).

[23] See CPLR 313, to be studied later in § 100.

[24] N.Y. Const. art. VI, § 14.

[1] N.Y. Const. art. VI, § 12(a), (c); Jud. Law § 179.

[2] SCPA 102; CPLR 101.

[3] SCPA 201(2), (3). See Practice Commentary on McKinney's SCPA 201.

[4] SCPA 209(6). See Practice Commentary on McKinney's SCPA 201.

[5] See Practice Commentary on McKinney's CPLR 3001.

[6] N.Y. Const. art. VI, § 1(c).

[7] SCPA 210, 211.

[8] SCPA 2701; CPLR 5701.

On August 31, 2015, the Governor signed Chapter 237 of the Laws of 2015, which became effective immediately. The legislation continues to authorize programs for consensual and mandatory e-filing in surrogate's court.[9]

§ 16. Family Court

There is a family court in each county of the state. There is at least one judge on each family court and as many more as statute provides.[1] The term is 10 years, elective outside New York City, appointive (by the mayor) within.[2]

The court's jurisdiction covers almost the complete range of family matters, whether they would qualify as criminal or civil in other contexts.[3] Officially, the terminology of "criminal" court is avoided. It is generally regarded as a civil court[4] but has been termed "a unique court, completely dissimilar to any other . . . [and] is primarily a social court designed to handle the complex problems of family life."[5] Its jurisdiction includes neglect, support, and paternity proceedings; adoption, guardianship and custody; juvenile delinquency and persons in need of supervision; family offenses; and conciliation proceedings. The jurisdiction is supplied by the Family Court Act (FCA). The court's procedure is supplied by the FCA and by Part 205 of the Uniform Rules. Procedure is necessarily less formal than in other courts. Process is servable statewide.[6] Appeals go to the appellate division.[7]

The item that the lay person and even the general practitioner perhaps most associate with a "family" court is the matrimonial action (divorce, annulment, separation, etc.). Ironically, the family court lacks jurisdiction of it. The matrimonial action is in the exclusive jurisdiction of the supreme court[8] although the family court may entertain certain custody and support incidentals of such actions if the supreme court refers them to the family court.[9]

Adoption proceedings[10] are in the concurrent jurisdiction of the supreme, family, and surrogate's courts.[11]

---

[9] CPLR 2111(b)(2)(B). The new law and the surrogate's courts that are currently under consensual or mandatory e-filing are discussed in more detail in § 63.

[1] Fam. Ct. Act § 131.

[2] N.Y. Const. art. VI, § 13(a).

[3] The family and criminal courts have concurrent jurisdiction over a number of acts involving family members, many of which would be strictly criminal if family were not involved. See Fam. Ct. Act § 812.

[4] In re Lang, 44 Misc. 2d 900, 255 N.Y.S.2d 987 (Fam. Ct., New York County 1965).

[5] In re Anonymous, 37 Misc. 2d 827, 831, 238 N.Y.S.2d 792, 796 (Fam. Ct., Nassau County 1962).

[6] N.Y. Const. art. VI, § 1(c). CPLR 302(b) and 313 apply in the family court and authorize service outside the state in support proceedings. See Fam. Ct. Act § 165; CPLR 101. Fam. Ct. Act § 154(b) allows extrastate service in proceedings "to establish paternity or to . . . [affect] support" when the required New York contacts are satisfied.

[7] Fam. Ct. Act § 1111.

[8] Infanto v. Infanto, 66 Misc. 2d 699, 321 N.Y.S.2d 928 (Fam. Ct., Queens County 1971).

[9] N.Y. Const. art. VI, § 13(c). If not incidental to a matrimonial action, the family court does have jurisdiction of these proceedings.

[10] Dom. Rel. Law Article 7.

[11] Fam. Ct. Act § 641; see Kaplan v. Meskin, 108 A.D.2d 787, 789, 485 N.Y.S.2d 117, 120 (2d Dep't 1985).

§ 17. Court of Claims

The court of claims has jurisdiction "to hear and determine claims against the state or by the state against the claimant."[1] Its jurisdiction is set forth in detail in the Court of Claims Act.[2] In a landmark decision in 1996,[3] the Court of Appeals expanded its jurisdiction by adopting what is described as the "constitutional tort." While characterizing its decision as providing a "narrow remedy," the Court held that the State of New York is liable in damages for violations of the equal protection and search and seizure clauses of the state constitution and that the court of claims has jurisdiction to hear those claims.[4]

While the Court of Claims Act governs procedure in the court, its provisions are few and the CPLR, which is applicable in the court pursuant to its own terms as well as under a direction from the Court of Claims Act,[5] is used there more frequently than in the surrogate's or family courts.[6] Administrative matters and details of court of claims procedure are found in Part 206 of the Uniform Rules.

Judges are appointed by the governor by and with the advice and consent of the senate; the term is nine years.[7]

The court is statewide but divided into districts for administrative purposes.[8] Appeals are to the appellate division.[9] Process is servable statewide.[10] On August 31, 2015, the Governor signed Chapter 237 of the Laws of 2015, which continues to authorize programs for consensual e-filing in the Court of Claims.[11] As of this writing, claims for personal injury or property damage being brought in the Court of Claims' New York District may now be filed electronically through the New York State Courts Electronic Filing system (NYSCEF). This district comprises the five boroughs of New York City as well as Suffolk and Nassau Counties. NYSCEF is also available for filing claims and other court papers in the Court of Claims' Albany District, which comprises Albany, Clinton, Columbia, Essex, Franklin, Greene, Rensselaer, Saratoga, Schenectady, Ulster, Warren, and Washington Counties.[12]

Multiparty occurrences involving the State pose special problems. If the State is one of several tortfeasors, for example, it can be sued only in the court of claims, while the other tortfeasors must be sued in other courts.[13] Suit against the State employees

---

[1] N.Y. Const. art. VI, § 9.

[2] Ct. of Claims Act § 9.

[3] Brown v. State, 89 N.Y.2d 172, 652 N.Y.S.2d 223, 674 N.E.2d 1129, 75 A.L.R.5th 769 (1996).

[4] The case is the subject of the lead note in NYSLD No. 444. A 3-year statute of limitations has been held to govern this category of claim. Brown v. State, 250 A.D.2d 314, 681 N.Y.S.2d 170 (3d Dep't 1998) (SPR 80:2).

[5] CPLR 101; Ct. of Claims Act § 9(9).

[6] See McNamara, *The Court of Claims: Its Development and Present Role in The Unified Court System,* 40 St. John's L. Rev. 1 (1965).

[7] N.Y. Const. art. VI, § 9.

[8] Uniform Rule 206.4.

[9] Ct. of Claims Act § 24.

[10] N.Y. Const. art. VI, § 1(c).

[11] CPLR 2111(a). See § 63.

[12] Information about e-filing in the Court of Claims is available on its website at www.nycourts.gov/courts/nyscourtofclaims/.

[13] See Cocchi v. State, 52 Misc. 3d 561, 30 N.Y.S.3d 481 (Ct. Cl. 2016) (providing helpful examples).

responsible for the tort must also be brought in the supreme or some lower court of ordinary civil jurisdiction; the employees may not be sued in the court of claims even if the State would have to indemnify them.[14] The possibility of inconsistent verdicts because of these restrictions is well recognized.[15] Moreover, the options of consolidation or joint trial of suits in the supreme court or court of claims is not available.[16]

Apportionment problems in tort cases involving the State are especially confusing,[17] and the courts struggle with these issues. This is due, in part, to the fact that a divestiture of the right to trial by jury can result if a person is compelled to first seek relief in a court of claims action (where there is no jury). A judgment as to one of the court of claims parties may bind that party elsewhere, such as in a supreme court action.[18]

The State itself, the defendant in the court of claims, cannot implead a potential indemnitor or additional tortfeasor.[19] Moreover, if the State brings suit as a plaintiff in some other court, which the State often must do, the defendant there cannot counterclaim.[20] In the court of claims itself, however, where the State is the defendant, counterclaims are allowed by the State against the claimant.[21] Furthermore, by commencing an action in the court of claims, a claimant impliedly consents to the interposition by the State of a counterclaim and may be deemed to have waived her right to a jury trial on the counterclaim.[22]

Because the State is so often involved in multiparty occurrences and transactions, it would of course be helpful to merge the court of claims into the supreme court to avoid some of these problems. That was one of the proposals of a court reorganization referendum that got a start at the 1986 legislative session, but it never made it through the following session, as required to start the referendum process. The merger continues to be the subject of discussion around water coolers in law offices facing the problem of multiparty actions involving the State, but it has not yet passed the study stage.

We have frequently repeated the dogma that the only defendant in the court of claims is the State, yet that is not always the case. The court of claims may have

---

[14]   Morell v. Balasubramanian, 70 N.Y.2d 297, 520 N.Y.S.2d 530, 514 N.E.2d 1101 (1987).

[15]   Braun v. State, 203 Misc. 563, 117 N.Y.S.2d 601 (Ct. Cl. 1952).

[16]   See *Cocchi*, 52 Misc.3d at 563, 30 N.Y.S.3d at 483. The court found limited solace for the plaintiff/claimant in this dilemma, as disclosure in the two separate actions can be coordinated and the parties can be invited to the depositions, with transcripts made available to all.

[17]   See generally Artibee v. Home Place Corp., 132 A.D.3d 96, 14 N.Y.S.3d 817 (3d Dep't 2015), aff'd as modified, 28 N.Y.3d 739, 49 N.Y.S.3d 638, 71 N.E.3d 1205 (2017), discussed in § 168C.

[18]   See Tierney v. State, 55 A.D.2d 158, 389 N.Y.S.2d 709 (4th Dep't 1976) and Valentino v. State, 44 A.D.2d 338, 355 N.Y.S.2d 212 (3d Dep't 1974). Discussion of res judicata and collateral estoppel problems involving the court of claims, including instances in which its judgment can affect a later case triable by jury, appears in § 470.

[19]   See Horoch v. State, 286 A.D. 303, 143 N.Y.S.2d 327 (3d Dep't 1955), order resettled, 286 A.D. 977, 144 N.Y.S.2d 721 (3d Dep't 1955), noting, however, that while impleader is precluded, interpleader is allowed. (For the difference between the two, see §§ 148 and 155.) If, without impleader, rights can be adjusted among those already parties, that is permissible. See General Foods Corp. v. State, 18 Misc. 2d 293, 188 N.Y.S.2d 635 (Ct. Cl. 1959).

[20]   Commissioners of State Ins. Fund v. Trio Asbestos Removal Corp., 9 A.D.3d 343, 345, 780 N.Y.S.2d 362 (2d Dep't 2004).

[21]   Ct. of Claims Act § 9(3).

[22]   *Tierney*, 55 A.D.2d at 162, 389 N.Y.S.2d at 712.

jurisdiction over certain State agencies as well as over the State itself.[23] Certain public authorities that are considered to have a distinct legal existence are sued in the court of claims, including the New York State Thruway Authority, the City University of New York, the Roswell Park Cancer Institute Corporation, the Olympic Regional Development Authority, and the Power Authority of the State of New York (for appropriations claims only).[24] The jurisdictional question depends on whether the agency is considered an arm of the State, which is often perplexing,[25] and often cited as another good reason for the court's merger into the supreme court. Practitioners faced with the issue will sometimes bring suit against the entity in both courts, just to be on the safe side.[26]

Because of the doctrine of sovereign immunity, the failure to file a claim against the State within the time prescribed by the Court of Claims Act has been held to deprive the court of subject matter jurisdiction, with consequences more serious than those met with a conventional statute of limitations dismissal.[27]

§ 18.   New York City Criminal Court

This court exists only in New York City and has only criminal jurisdiction. It is mentioned here only as part of a perspective on the court system.

It handles the misdemeanors and lesser offenses. Felonies in New York City are tried in the supreme court. Its judges are appointed by the mayor for 10-year terms.[1] Procedure in the court is governed by the New York City Criminal Court Act and by the Criminal Procedure Law. Appeals go to an appellate term.[2]

§ 19.   New York City Civil Court

This court is one of the busiest in the world. It has only civil jurisdiction and functions only in the City of New York. It has monetary jurisdiction up to $25,000, including jurisdiction of replevin actions when the value of the chattel does not exceed that amount.[1] It also has jurisdiction of real property actions, analogous to those of which the county court has jurisdiction, but the monetary limit of $25,000, inapplicable in the county court in these cases, does apply in the civil court.[2]

The civil court has jurisdiction of the summary proceeding, in which, in addition to a judgment of dispossession, judgment for rent may be rendered in any sum, unlimited by the usual $25,000 restriction that governs in the conventional civil action.[3] It has been

---

[23]   See Easley v. New York State Thruway Authority, 1 N.Y.2d 374, 153 N.Y.S.2d 28, 135 N.E.2d 572 (1956).

[24]   This information, and some additional points on procedure in the Court of Claims, can be found at its website: https://www.nycourts.gov/COURTS/nyscourtofclaims/faq.shtml#who.

[25]   See Belscher v. New York State Teachers' Retirement System, 45 A.D.2d 206, 357 N.Y.S.2d 241 (4th Dep't 1974); Ryan v. State, 35 Misc. 3d 260, 939 N.Y.S.2d 266 (Ct. Cl. 2011).

[26]   See the lead note in SPR 135:1, built around Plath v. New York State Olympic Regional Development Authority, 304 A.D.2d 885, 758 N.Y.S.2d 410 (3d Dep't 2003).

[27]   See § 35.

[1]   N.Y. Const. art. VI, § 15(a).

[2]   See 22 N.Y.C.R.R. §§ 640.1 (First Department) and 730.1(b)(2) (Second Department).

[1]   N.Y. Const. art. VI, § 15(b); New York City Civ. Ct. Act § 202.

[2]   See New York City Civ. Ct. Act § 203, which also sets forth the methods by which to gauge whether the monetary limitation is met.

[3]   New York City Civ. Ct. Act § 204.

held, however, that sums due under an acceleration clause in a lease are not "rent" for this purpose but rather just contract damages and hence do remain subject to the court's limited monetary jurisdiction.[4]

The civil court also has jurisdiction of interpleader claims within the $25,000 figure.[5] The monetary limit does not apply to counterclaims, but it has been held applicable to cross-claims.[6] The court's equity jurisdiction is generally limited by statute to the real property actions and to actions to rescind or reform contracts not involving more than $25,000,[7] but a 1972 amendment addressed to residential housing problems in New York City widely expands equity jurisdiction in housing cases.[8] Additionally, the civil court has also been deemed to possess jurisdiction of actions for unjust enrichment involving only money damages.[9]

In New York City, the so-called Small Claims "court" is part of the New York City Civil Court, entertaining money cases up to $5,000.[10] Distinct from cases brought as small claims is the procedure, authorized by CPLR 3405 and elaborated in Part 28 of the Rules of the Chief Judge, for the arbitration of claims of $10,000 or under. Arbitration in that instance is compulsory.[11]

Judges of the court are elected and serve 10-year terms.[12]

Procedure is governed by the New York City Civil Court Act, the prototype of the uniform acts governing practice in the state's lower courts, and by Part 208 of the Uniform Rules. Article 2 of the court act sets forth the court's jurisdiction; the rest of it aims to simplify certain procedures and make them less expensive. As long as it is not inconsistent with the relatively few things governed by the court act, the CPLR applies in the court.[13]

Process is servable anywhere in New York City and in certain instances beyond.[14] Appeals are to the appellate term.[15] The city marshals as well as the sheriff are the court's enforcement officers.[16]

---

[4]   172 Van Duzer Realty Corp. v. Globe Alumni Student Assistance Ass'n, Inc., 24 N.Y.3d 528, 534, 2 N.Y.S.3d 39, 42, 25 N.E.3d 952, 955 (2014); Ross Realty v. V & A Fabricators, Inc., 42 A.D.3d 246, 836 N.Y.S.2d 242 (2d Dep't 2007) (SPR 198:4). The *Ross Realty* case involved a district court, but as *172 Van Duzer Realty* demonstrates, the holding is relevant in all of the state's lower courts, whose jurisdiction is summarized in §§ 20–22. The res judicata issues in *172 Van Duzer Realty* are discussed in further detail in § 469.

[5]   New York City Civ. Ct. Act § 205.

[6]   N.Y. Const. art. VI, § 15(b); New York City Civ. Ct. Act § 208(b). See 125 Church Street Development Co. v. Grassfield, 170 Misc. 2d 31, 648 N.Y.S.2d 515 (N.Y. City Civ. Ct. 1996), noted in SPR 64:4.

[7]   See New York City Civ. Ct. Act §§ 208(c), 213.

[8]   See New York City Civ. Ct. Act § 110.

[9]   Binderman v. Kazdan, 145 Misc. 2d 628, 630, 547 N.Y.S.2d 984, 986 (N.Y. City Civ. Ct. 1989).

[10]   New York City Civ. Ct. Act Article 18. Small Claims, though often called a "court," is not one. It is merely a simplified procedure—invoked at the option of the claimant—set up in some of the lower court acts. Small Claims procedure is the subject of Chapter 21 (Practitioner's Edition).

[11]   See § 585B (Practitioner's Edition). Do not confuse this category of arbitration with the well-known consensual arbitration governed by Article 75 of the CPLR, discussed in §§ 586 et seq. (Practitioner's Edition).

[12]   N.Y. Const. art. VI, § 15(a).

[13]   CPLR 101; New York City Civ. Ct. Act § 2102.

[14]   See New York City Civ. Ct. Act Article 4.

[15]   New York City Civ. Ct. Act § 1701. See the appellate term rules in 22 N.Y.C.R.R. §§ 640.1 (First Department) and 730.1(b)(1) (Second Department).

[16]   New York City Civ. Ct. Act § 701.

On August 31, 2015, the Governor signed Chapter 237 of the Laws of 2015, which continues to authorize programs for consensual and mandatory e-filing in the New York City Civil Court, but mandatory e-filing can only be imposed in a narrow category of actions, commonly known as no-fault cases.[17]

§ 20.   District Courts

There are two district courts in the state, one covering Nassau County and the other covering the western part of Suffolk County. They are unrelated to and shouldn't be confused with the district courts of the United States. Their civil jurisdiction and practice is governed by the Uniform District Court Act (UDCA),[1] with further procedural detail supplied by Part 212 of the Uniform Rules. The district court has criminal jurisdiction of misdemeanors and lesser offenses as determined and governed by the Criminal Procedure Law.

The court's civil jurisdiction in money and replevin actions goes up to $15,000.[2] It also has jurisdiction of the summary proceeding, in which judgment for rent is not limited in amount.[3] As with the county courts and the New York City Civil Court, counterclaim jurisdiction is without monetary limitation.[4]

The district court has little equity jurisdiction[5] although it can entertain interpleader claims within the $15,000 limit[6] and claims for unjust enrichment seeking a money judgment.[7] In Nassau and western Suffolk, the Small Claims part is to be found in the district court. Small Claims jurisdiction goes up to $5,000.[8] Cases for $6,000 and under may be sent to compulsory arbitration as authorized by CPLR 3405 and implemented by Part 28 of the Rules of the Chief Judge.[9]

Process is limited to the county except in certain designated instances.[10] Appeals go to the county court unless an appellate term has been established for such appeals.[11] Judges are elected to 6-year terms.[12] District courts can be adopted elsewhere (the

---

[17]   CPLR 2111(b)(2)(C). The new law is discussed in more detail in § 63.

[1]   The Uniform District Court Act is modeled on the New York City Civil Court Act, right down to the numbering system. The differences are mainly in those areas in which the constitution or legislative preference has varied jurisdiction or practice.

[2]   N.Y. Const. art. VI, § 16(d); Uniform Dist. Ct. Act § 202.

[3]   Uniform Dist. Ct. Act § 204. Money due under an acceleration clause in a lease is not "rent" for this purpose. See § 19.

[4]   Uniform Dist. Ct. Act § 208(b); see Jeffrey M. Rosenblum, P.C. v. Casano, 45 Misc. 3d 1218(A), 7 N.Y.S.3d 242 (Dist. Ct., Nassau County 2014).

[5]   An amendment of Uniform Dist. Ct. Act § 203 expanded the courts' equity jurisdiction broadly in housing cases. See the 2005 Commentary on Uniform Dist. Ct. Act § 203 (McKinney's Book 29A, Part 3) and the lead note in SPR 167:1.

[6]   Uniform Dist. Ct. Act § 205.

[7]   See Jeffrey M. Rosenblum, P.C. v. Casano, 45 Misc. 3d 1218(A), 7 N.Y.S.3d 242 (Dist. Ct., Nassau County 2014). The district court lacks subject matter jurisdiction to entertain a declaratory judgment claim, which "is exclusively equitable in nature." *Jeffrey M. Rosenblum, P.C.*, 45 Misc. 3d at 1218(A).

[8]   Uniform Dist. Ct. Act Article 18.

[9]   See § 585B (Practitioner's Edition).

[10]   Uniform Dist. Ct. Act Article 4.

[11]   Uniform Dist. Ct. Act § 1701. An appellate term has been established. See the appellate term rules in 22 N.Y.C.R.R. § 730.1(d).

[12]   N.Y. Const. art. VI, § 16(h).

purpose would ordinarily be to supersede the justice courts), but only if approved by local referendum.[13]

The CPLR governs in the court as long as it is not inconsistent with the UDCA.[14]

§ 21.   City Courts

There is a city court in each of the 61 cities outside New York City. Most go by the formal name of "City Court," but other names are occasionally used. Whatever the names, their civil jurisdiction and practice is governed by the Uniform City Court Act (UCCA),[1] with further procedural detail supplied by Part 210 of the Uniform Rules. Monetary jurisdiction was set for a long time at a $6,000 maximum. A statute raised it to $10,000 in 1988 and to $15,000 in 1991, where it now stands.[2] The CPLR applies to the extent that it is consistent with the UCCA.[3] It usually is.

In addition to money and replevin claims, which are also subject to the applicable money limit, the city court entertains the summary proceeding. A rent judgment in a summary proceeding is not subject to a monetary limitation,[4] nor is a counterclaim in any case.[5] The court has interpleader jurisdiction within the applicable money limit.[6] The court has little equity jurisdiction.[7]

In city court money actions, certain local contacts have to be shown akin to those already met in the county court, but not identical.[8] No such requirements are imposed in the civil court or in the district courts.

Process is servable anywhere in the county where the city sits, and in some instances in an adjoining county,[9] but the constitution prevents it from going farther.[10] The city courts also have criminal jurisdiction of misdemeanors and below, as supplied and regulated by the Criminal Procedure Law.

Appeals go to the county court unless the local appellate division has set up an appellate term to hear them, as the Second Department has done.[11]

---

[13]   N.Y. Const. art. VI, § 16(b) & (c).

[14]   CPLR 101; Uniform Dist. Ct. Act § 2102.

[1]   Uniform City Ct. Act § 102. The UCCA is modeled on the UDCA much as the UDCA is modeled on the New York City Civ. Ct. Act, right down to the numbering system, making for much uniformity among the acts and helping the practitioner to step from one court's practice into another's with less difficulty.

[2]   The jurisdiction of the city courts may not exceed that of the district courts. Const. art. VI, §§ 17(a), 16(d). It does not purport to.

[3]   CPLR 101; Uniform City Ct. Act § 2102.

[4]   Uniform City Ct. Act § 204. Money due under an acceleration clause in a lease is not "rent" for this purpose. See § 19.

[5]   Uniform City Ct. Act § 208(b).

[6]   Uniform City Ct. Act § 205.

[7]   An amendment of Uniform City Ct. Act § 203 (effective January 1, 2006) expanded the courts' equity jurisdiction broadly in housing cases. See the 2005 Commentary on Uniform City Ct. Act § 203 (McKinney's Book 29A, Part 3) and the lead note in SPR 167:1.

[8]   Uniform City Ct. Act § 213. See the Commentary on McKinney's Uniform City Ct. Act § 213 (Vol. 29A, Part 3).

[9]   Uniform City Ct. Act Article 4.

[10]   N.Y. Const. art. VI, § 1(c).

[11]   Uniform City Ct. Act § 1701. See the Second Department's appellate term rules, 22 N.Y.C.R.R. § 730.1(d). There are no city courts in the First Department.

In the cities outside New York City, it is the city court that has the Small Claims part, entertaining through its informal procedures money claims not exceeding $5,000.[12] And on the authority of CPLR 3405, implemented by Part 28 of the Rules of the Chief Judge, these cases can be sent to compulsory arbitration.[13]

§ 22.   Town and Village Courts

Each county in the state outside New York City is divided into towns. Within these towns, villages are sprinkled around the state by the score. Most of these towns and villages have courts serviced respectively by town justices and village justices. The town court is also known as the "justice of the peace" and the village court as the "village police justice." Collectively they are known as the justice courts,[1] the easiest terminology to use here. There are almost 1,300 such courts in the state.

These courts have criminal jurisdiction of misdemeanors and below, as set forth and regulated in the Criminal Procedure Law.

Civil jurisdiction and practice in each town and village court is governed by the Uniform Justice Court Act (UJCA), the last of the quartet of uniform acts,[2] with further procedural detail furnished by Part 214 of the Uniform Rules. The justice courts have monetary and replevin jurisdiction up to $3,000 and, unlike the other civil courts, this limitation also applies to counterclaims.[3] The court has jurisdiction of the summary proceeding if the property is in the municipality in which the court serves, and a judgment for rent is not limited in amount.[4]

The geographical restriction is important. The rigidity of the concept of subject matter jurisdiction in the town courts is illustrated in a case in which a summary proceeding was brought in the wrong town, but a rent judgment for $35,000 was rendered anyway. Nothing happened for some dozen years after that until a creditor now docketed the judgment with a county clerk, making it a supreme court judgment,[5] whereupon the debtor sued in the supreme court to enjoin enforcement. The injunction was granted because the original town court presuming to exercise subject matter jurisdiction lacked it due to the geographical infirmity.[6]

Each town and village court has a Small Claims part, in which the ceiling of $3,000 applies,[7] even though it was raised in 2004 to $5,000 in the civil, district, and city courts. The practical effect of the increase in small claims jurisdiction is that all money claims brought in a town or village court qualify as a small claim and can be pursued as such by the plaintiff. Lawyers must also be alert to inquire whether the compulsory

---

[12]   Uniform City Ct. Act Article 18.

[13]   See § 585B (Practitioner's Edition).

[1]   See the definitions contained in § 2101 of the Uniform Justice Court Act (UJCA).

[2]   Uniform Just. Ct. Act § 2300(b)(1), (2). The UJCA is modeled on the Uniform City Court Act and thus traces back through the Uniform District Court Act to the original New York City Civil Court Act. All four acts were originally designed for maximum uniformity but have lost much of it because of piecemeal and uncoordinated amendments made since the middle of the 1960s.

[3]   Uniform Just. Ct. Act § 208. Interposition of a counterclaim for more than $3,000 waives the balance. See the Commentary on § 208 in McKinney's Uniform Just. Ct. Act (Vol. 29A, Part 2).

[4]   Uniform Just. Ct. Act § 204. Note, however, that money due under a lease's acceleration clause does not qualify as "rent" for this purpose. See § 19.

[5]   See § 422 for the procedure on docketing a lower court judgment.

[6]   Burke v. Aspland, 56 A.D.3d 1001, 867 N.Y.S.2d 759 (3d Dep't 2008) (SPR 206:4).

[7]   Uniform Just. Ct. Act Article 18. Small Claims and their procedures are the subject of Chapter 21.

arbitration procedures authorized by CPLR 3405 and implemented by Part 28 of the Rules of the Chief Judge[8] have been made applicable in a given justice court.

The justice courts have no significant equity jurisdiction. They are the only courts in the state whose judges need not be lawyers[9] and most are not. The summons, servable in the home county,[10] cannot constitutionally be permitted to go beyond an adjoining county.[11]

As with the city courts under the Uniform City Court Act, a special provision appears in the UJCA requiring local contacts to be demonstrated as an additional jurisdictional prerequisite in money actions.[12]

Appeals are to the county court[13] unless an appellate term has been set up to hear them.[14]

A three-part series of articles in The New York Times in 2006 documented several problems in the justice courts, including town and village justices who mishandled money, made racist remarks, released friends without bail, denied some defendants representation, and jailed defendants without trials.[15] Then Chief Judge, Judith S. Kaye, subsequently made several significant changes to procedures in justice courts, requiring, among other things, that a transcription be kept of proceedings.[16]

§ 23.   Aggregating or Reducing Claims

Suppose a plaintiff interposes several claims in a lower court action, or that several plaintiffs join their claims in a lower court—as they may do when the claims have common origins.[1] If each separate cause of action fits within the court's original jurisdiction when independently measured, all the claims may be joined and are deemed within the court's jurisdiction even though their total may exceed it.[2] This is

---

[8]   See § 585B (Practitioner's Edition).

[9]   N.Y. Const. art. VI, § 20(a), (c).

[10]   Uniform Just. Ct. Act § 403.

[11]   N.Y. Const. art. VI, § 1(c).

[12]   See Uniform Just. Ct. Act § 213 and its Commentary in McKinney's UJCA.

[13]   Uniform Just. Ct. Act § 1701.

[14]   See the Second Department's appellate term rule, 22 N.Y.C.R.R. § 730.1. There are no town or village courts in the First Department.

[15]   See William Glaberson, *Broken Bench: In Tiny Courts of N.Y., Abuses of Law and Power,* N.Y. Times, Sept. 25, 2006, at A1; Glaberson, *Broken Bench: Small Town Justice, With Trial and Error,* N.Y. Times, Sept. 26, 2006, at A1; Glaberson, *Broken Bench: How a Reviled Court System Has Outlasted Critics,* N.Y. Times, Sept. 27, 2006, at A1.

[16]   See William Glaberson, *Justice Courts In Small Towns To Be Upgraded,* N.Y. Times, Nov. 26, 2006; N.Y.S. Unified Court Sys., Action Plan for the Justice Courts 26 (Nov. 2006); Judith S. Kaye, Chief Judge of the State of New York, State of the Judiciary 2007 (Feb. 26, 2007).
While the Chief Judge asked the legislature for $10 million for technology upgrades for the justice courts, the Enacted SFY 2007–08 budget allocated a $5 million appropriation to the judiciary "[f]or expenses necessary to provide aid to the justice courts." See Chapter 51 of the laws of 2007. An additional $5 million was allocated in the Enacted SFY 2008–09 budget. See Chapter 51 of the laws of 2008.

[1]   See CPLR 1002(a); §§ 126, 134.

[2]   See Andrew Carothers, M.D., P.C. v. Progressive Ins. Co., 42 Misc. 3d 30, 979 N.Y.S.2d 439 (App. Term, 2d Dep't 2013), aff'd, 150 A.D.3d 192, 51 N.Y.S.3d 551 (2d Dep't 2017) (although aggregate amount in controversy was approximately $18 million, each of the causes of action were within the monetary jurisdiction of the New York City Civil Court).

accomplished by section 211 in each of the lower court acts[3] and is thus the clear rule in the civil, district, city, town, and village courts. Some cases had apparently sustained such aggregation in the county court, too,[4] but the Second Department, within which they were decided, later distinguished or overruled them and rejected aggregation in county courts.[5] The county court has no counterpart for the lower court acts' section 211, but by analogy to that section—which after all reflects a broad legislative intent about how lower court jurisdictional problems are to be handled—the aggregation ought to be allowed.

Suppose that a single cause of action is brought in one of the lower courts for a sum in excess of its jurisdiction. As will be seen shortly, the case can be transferred to a court having adequate jurisdiction.[6] But if the plaintiff is willing to reduce the demand to bring it within the subject matter jurisdiction of the lower court, may the plaintiff do that and thus have the case retained there?

Several cases, even of recent vintage, continue to hold against such a jurisdiction-preserving amendment,[7] an unfortunately technical approach that relies on the general rule that subject matter jurisdiction cannot be conferred by consent. The court is not, however, acquiring "subject matter jurisdiction" by consent in this situation. That would be the case only if the court were asked to keep the action at its original figure. All the plaintiff is consenting to is a reduction of its demand to *fit* the court's subject matter jurisdiction. Cases forbidding this are the kind that make the laity suspicious of the law, judges, and lawyers.[8]

What about the opposite: an addition to the claim, accruing after the action was commenced, that brings its total beyond the court's monetary jurisdiction? There is authority sustaining jurisdiction to entertain the increase.[9]

It has been held that in a bifurcated trial in a tort action—in which issues of liability are tried before damages[10]—the plaintiff's share of the damages under the comparative negligence rule[11] can be excluded in determining the court's monetary jurisdiction. This rule preserves jurisdiction in the lower court, even if the addition of plaintiff's share exceeds the court's monetary cap.[12]

---

[3]   The New York City Civ. Ct. Act and the Uniform Dist. Ct. Act, Uniform City Ct. Act, and Uniform Just. Ct. Acts, McKinney's Vol. 29A, Parts 2 and 3.

[4]   Baron v. Bobroy, Inc., 11 A.D.2d 766, 205 N.Y.S.2d 173 (2d Dep't 1960); Weber v. Kowalski, 85 Misc. 2d 349, 358 n.2, 376 N.Y.S.2d 996, 1007 n.2 (Sup. Ct., Dutchess County 1975).

[5]   Mandel v. Kent, 70 A.D.2d 903, 417 N.Y.S.2d 306 (2d Dep't 1979).

[6]   See § 24.

[7]   See, e.g., Providian Nat'l Bank v. Capolino, N.Y.L.J., March 2, 2000, at 35, col.2 (White Plains City Ct. 2001) (SPR 101:3), and Bloom & Krup Appliance Corp. v. A.H.C. Appliance Corp., N.Y.L.J., Dec. 9, 2003, at 20, col.3–4 (Dist. Ct., Nassau County; Asarch, J.).

[8]   See the discussion in SPR 143:2–3.

[9]   See, e.g., Board of Managers of the Mews at North Hills Condominium v. Farajzadeh, 189 Misc. 2d 38, 730 N.Y.S.2d 180 (App. Term, 2d Dep't 2001) (SPR 121:3–4), which allowed the addition with the observation that all that would happen otherwise is that the plaintiff would commence a separate action, a wasteful duplication. See also Bay Crest Ass'n v. Paar, 47 Misc. 3d 9, 4 N.Y.S.3d 812 (App. Term, 2d Dep't 2015) (multiple years of assessment fees and attorney's fees were not separate and distinct causes of action).

[10]   See § 130.

[11]   CPLR 1411; see § 168E.

[12]   Azzopardi v. St. Vincent's Medical Center of Richmond, 132 Misc. 2d 412, 503 N.Y.S.2d 700 (N.Y. City Civ. Ct. 1986).

B. TRANSFERS BETWEEN COURTS

Table of Sections

§ 24.   Mistake in Choice of Court

§ 25.   Transfer Up for More Relief

§ 26.   Transfer Down on Consent

§ 27.   Transfer Down Without Consent

§ 24.   Mistake in Choice of Court

If an action is initially brought in a court that lacks subject matter jurisdiction of it—the "wrong court," to give it a simple handle—it need not be dismissed. Rather, it should be transferred to the court that does have jurisdiction. One way to accomplish this is to ask the supreme court, by motion, to transfer the case from the wrong court to the right court, a power conferred on the supreme court by CPLR 325(a).

Another is to ask the wrong court itself to transfer the case to the right court, but this can be done only if the wrong court has been given such transfer power. The state constitution directly authorizes certain courts to transfer out of themselves, and to the proper court, actions of which they lack subject matter jurisdiction. The courts so authorized are the county courts,[1] the surrogate's court,[2] the family court,[3] and the New York City civil and criminal courts.[4] When such power exists in the wrong court, the parties have the choice of making the transfer motion in that court under the appropriate constitutional provision or in the supreme court under CPLR 325(a). So, for example, if an action is brought in the civil court for $50,000, the transfer to the supreme court may be made by motion to the supreme court under CPLR 325(a) or by motion to the civil court under the constitutional provision.

Courts still lower than those listed can be given such transfer powers by statute,[5] but until that happens, CPLR 325(a) will have to do the job. When one of those courts is involved, the transfer motion will have to be made to the supreme court.

Procedure in conjunction with a transfer motion under CPLR 325 is governed by CPLR 326, which, while not explicitly applicable to transfers made directly under the constitution, would be an appropriate guidepost there, too.

A special provision for transferring cases between lower courts, subdivision (g) of CPLR 325, applies to all district, city, town, and village courts. It governs not when there has been a mistake in choice of court but when the judges of any one of those courts are for any reason incapable of acting in the case or if a jury cannot be formed. It permits a judge of the county court in which the lower court is located, on motion, to transfer the

---

[1]   N.Y. Const. art. VI, § 19(b).

[2]   N.Y. Const. art. VI, § 19(d).

[3]   N.Y. Const. art. VI, § 19(e).

[4]   N.Y. Const. art. VI, § 19(f). Since these courts are empowered to correct jurisdictional defects by transferring a case out, by analogy they should be able to entertain such amendments as the plaintiff may request to enable the case to remain where it is. Thus, if a case initially seeks more than the court can give, but the plaintiff is willing to amend to bring the case within the court's jurisdiction, the court should itself be able to allow the amendment and keep the case. Older cases held to the contrary, however, such as Heffron v. Jennings, 66 A.D. 443, 73 N.Y.S. 410 (4th Dep't 1901), and some more recent ones still do. See § 23.

[5]   N.Y. Const. art. VI, § 19(i).

case to any other of those four categories of court in either the same county or an adjoining county, as long as the transferee court has the requisite subject matter and personal jurisdiction.

While CPLR 325(a), authorizing a transfer from the wrong to the right court, is generally thought of as applying to transfers among trial courts, it has also been held applicable to permit a transfer to the appellate division when the latter is the right court (as when the proceeding involved is within the appellate division's original jurisdiction).[6]

§ 25.   Transfer Up for More Relief

When an action is brought in a court that does have jurisdiction of it, but the plaintiff now wants more or different relief than the court can grant, the governing provision is CPLR 325(b) and the procedure is to make the transfer motion in the court to which the transfer is sought. That would be the next highest court locally available for the case. This usually happens when the plaintiff wants to raise the monetary demand in a money (usually a tort) action to a sum beyond the limits of the original court.

Distinguish this situation from that involved under CPLR 325(a), treated in the prior section. There the assumption is that the action has been brought in the wrong court to begin with, and there the statute authorizes only the supreme court to transfer the case.

An example under CPLR 325(b) would be an action commenced in the Nassau County District Court for $6,000 (which is within its jurisdiction) but in which the damages later appear to be $20,000 (which is not). The case may be transferred to the local county court, which has $25,000 jurisdiction. The motion for the transfer is made to the county court on those facts, not to the supreme court.

The motion also includes a CPLR 3025(b) request for leave to amend the ad damnum clause of the complaint to demand the greater relief.[1] Whether to allow the amendment and order the transfer is in the court's discretion.[2] It will turn on how convincingly the plaintiff justifies the greater relief and excuses the delay in obtaining the evidence that supports it.

A transfer up under CPLR 325(b) can be granted even in a case that was previously transferred down under other provisions, such as subdivision (c) or (d) of CPLR 325. It turns, again, on whether the new proof of damages is sufficiently convincing.[3]

In the event a jury trial has been waived in the lower court, the waiver becomes inoperative after it is transferred up under CPLR 325(b), thus reopening the door for a jury demand.

---

[6]   See Hopper v. Commissioner of Taxation and Finance, 224 A.D.2d 733, 637 N.Y.S.2d 494 (3d Dep't 1996) (SPR 49:4).

[1]   Francilion v. Epstein, 144 A.D.2d 633, 535 N.Y.S.2d 65 (2d Dep't 1988).

[2]   See Kornfeld v. Wagner, 12 N.Y.2d 348, 239 N.Y.S.2d 668, 190 N.E.2d 15 (1963).

[3]   See, e.g., Huston v. Rao, 74 A.D.2d 127, 427 N.Y.S.2d 36 (2d Dep't 1980); Hornung v. Mucci, 52 A.D.2d 904, 383 N.Y.S.2d 379 (2d Dep't 1976).

If the case is commenced in a lower court and a CPLR 325(b) motion to transfer up fails, the plaintiff who is compelled to settle within the lower court's jurisdictional limit may have a malpractice claim against his lawyer.[4]

§ 26. Transfer Down on Consent

CPLR 325(c) offers yet a further variation on the transfer theme. Here, as in 325(b), the action has been brought in the right court, but in this instance the plaintiff later determines that the need for damages is less than he thought and the case can therefore fit the jurisdiction of a local lower court. In this instance, the motion is made to the court in which the action is pending. It seeks leave to amend the complaint to reduce the damages demand to a figure within the lower court's jurisdiction and to transfer the case down to that court.

If the defendant has counterclaimed, his consent to the transfer is needed.

If the action could not have been brought in the proposed transferee court because of limitations on personal jurisdiction, such as where the defendant could not have been reached with the court's process because of territorial limits, the transfer is precluded.

Sometimes, a plaintiff who fails to appreciate the small worth of the case is helped to that realization by an enthusiastic judge during a pretrial conference of some kind,[1] with the defendant helping the judge help the plaintiff see the light. This is primarily a phenomenon of the personal injury case. The practice varies administratively from place to place, but it boils down to a preliminary review of the medical evidence by a judge with experience in tort cases, to see if the case can reasonably sustain a verdict in a sum sufficient to justify keeping it in the original court. This usually occurs in the supreme court, so we will use that as the example. If the judge thinks the case can earn such damages, it gets what is popularly known as a "general preference" and stays in the supreme court. Otherwise, a little gentle arm-twisting takes place to get the plaintiff to invoke CPLR 325(c) and consent to let the case go down to a lower court voluntarily.

If the plaintiff refuses, the practice under CPLR 325(c) is merely to deny the case a "general preference" in the supreme court, which means it goes to the bottom of the calendar with the privilege of remaining there indefinitely.[2] A plaintiff in that posture must either appeal the order denying the general preference or reduce the demand and let the case go down under CPLR 325(c). In the next section, we treat the nonconsensual transfer down under CPLR 325(d), which has greatly reduced dependence on the "general" preference tool used in connection with 325(c).

If there is no barrier to a transfer, as where the relief initially sought in the higher court would have been within the lower court's jurisdiction all the while, so that no reduction in damages is needed, a transfer can be made without consent and usually

---

[4]   See David v. Mallilo & Grossman, 17 Misc. 3d 1103(A), 851 N.Y.S.2d 57 (N.Y. City Civ. Ct. 2007) (noting that motion to transfer action to supreme court was denied because "[a]ll of the facts on which plaintiff relie[d] in support of the motion were known or available to plaintiff at the time the complaint was served."), aff'd 19 Misc.3d 142(A), 862 N.Y.S.2d 813 (App. Term, 1st Dep't 2008).

[1]   See 22 N.Y.C.R.R. § 202.12(c)(6) ("The matters to be considered at the preliminary conference shall include . . . removal to a lower court pursuant to CPLR 325, where appropriate."); see § 77D.

[2]   For a treatment of preferences, and the differences between a "general" and "special" preference, see §§ 372 and 373.

without complications.[3] From time to time, one even sees the supreme court making a transfer down without the plaintiff's consent in a case beyond the lower court's monetary limits—and with those limits remaining—but cases so holding[4] have been discredited.[5] One possible theory to justify such a transfer is that the supreme court has rendered a limited summary judgment in the case to the effect that as a matter of law the facts pleaded cannot justify a verdict in excess of the lower court's jurisdiction. Even for that, however, the general view is that legislative authorization is needed, and there is none.

If granted, a transfer down under CPLR 325(c) invalidates any existing jury waiver, setting the stage for a jury demand in the transferee court.

Once a case has been transferred down, the transferee court should generally not transfer it back. It would likely be deemed an attempt by the lower court to do the unseemly: review a higher court's order.[6] If the plaintiff is aggrieved, the appropriate step is to appeal the order transferring the case down.

§ 27.   Transfer Down Without Consent

The denial of a general preference, as discussed in the preceding section, was the primary remedy against a plaintiff who would not voluntarily reduce the complaint's monetary demand. The court could not transfer the case down without the reduction although occasionally a case would run against the tide and try.[1]

Onto that scene arrived an overhaul to the judiciary article of the state constitution in 1962. Part of it was a little noticed provision, subdivision k of section 19 of Article VI, which authorized the legislature to dispense with monetary limitations in transferred cases. The amendment permits the legislature to allow a transferee lower court to disregard its usual monetary limitations (even those set elsewhere in the constitution), but only in a case transferred to the lower court (not one commenced in it). The legislature accepted the invitation by enacting CPLR 325(d) in 1968, but this subdivision merely passed the buck farther, delegating to the appellate division the power to invoke this monetary dispensation by rule.[2]

The upstate departments invoked CPLR 325(d) promptly, the downstate departments somewhat later, all in separate rules. Those were abrogated on January 6, 1986, when the Uniform Rules took effect. Today, transfers under CPLR 325(d) are governed by one Rule, Uniform Rule 202.13, but not uniformly.

The supreme court can make a CPLR 325(d) transfer to the civil court in New York City.[3] In the Third and Fourth Departments, and the five counties of the 9th District (immediately north of New York City), the supreme court can make the transfer to either

---

[3]   See Frankel Associates, Inc. v. Dun & Bradstreet, Inc., 45 Misc. 2d 607, 257 N.Y.S.2d 555 (Sup. Ct., New York County 1965).

[4]   E.g., Haas v. Scholl, 68 Misc. 2d 197, 325 N.Y.S.2d 844 (Sup. Ct., Westchester County 1971).

[5]   See Frydman v. Arcure, 75 A.D.2d 863, 427 N.Y.S.2d 888 (2d Dep't 1980).

[6]   See, e.g., Unterberg v. Scarsdale Imp. Corp., 128 Misc. 2d 873, 491 N.Y.S.2d 571 (Sup. Ct., Westchester County 1985).

[1]   See notes 4 (*Haas*) and 5 (*Frydman*) in § 26.

[2]   The power presumably resides today in the chief administrator, as a constitutional matter, see § 5, not in the appellate division. But when an issue like that arises—caused by the legislature overlooking a few of the numerous statutes that required conforming amendments when the power of judicial administration was altered in a 1977 amendment of the state constitution (art. VI, § 28)—the chief administrator usually avoids the problem by eliciting the approval of the appellate division for the proposed change.

[3]   22 N.Y.C.R.R. § 202.13(a).

a county or city court.[4] In Nassau and Suffolk counties, transfer can be made from the supreme court to the county, city, or district courts.[5] Only the supreme court has this transfer power except in a handful of counties in which the county court has also been given it.[6]

The Rules should be periodically checked for any changes in the implementation of CPLR 325(d)'s transfer provision. In 1998, for example, the pretrial conference Rule authorizing a CPLR 325(d) transfer down from the supreme to the New York City Civil Court was amended to permit the transfer only if it can be administratively established that the civil court will be able to try the case within 30 days of the pretrial conference at which the transferring issue in the higher court arises.[7]

Cases whose need of supreme court monetary jurisdiction is doubtful—doubtfulness is supposed to be the criterion, anyway—can thus get transferred down without consent in many parts of the State today, the lower court getting the case, and, in the bargain, jurisdiction to award all the money originally demanded.

The lower court judges are often chagrined by these transfers.[8] It is not only the "doubtful" supreme court case that gets transferred down under CPLR 325(d): there have been instances of wrongful death cases being so transferred, and almost every such case has a potential for greater damages than any lower court can award. Civil court judges report verdicts—sustainable verdicts—in transferred cases many times in excess of the civil court's basic jurisdiction,[9] although it was not the intention of the constitution to authorize indiscriminate transfers of this kind. The provision was intended for cases near the monetary border or at least visible from it.

Indiscriminate transfers have resulted in other abuses. In Kings County, for example, plaintiffs were bringing cases in the supreme court that were unlikely to justify a recovery in excess of $10,000—the civil court's basic limit at the time—and therefore likely to be transferred down, which was apparently just what the plaintiffs desired. Their aim was to keep open the possibility of getting more money—the very fact that the transfer was predicated on CPLR 325(d) meant that the transferee court was not bound by its usual monetary limitations—while also securing an early trial. The civil court at the time was up to date with its calendars, while the supreme court was behind.[10]

It will sometimes happen, ironically, that the transferee court will not be ahead of supreme court calendars but substantially behind. It has nevertheless been held that a case's mere "languishing" in the lower court is not ground for taking it back.[11]

---

[4]   22 N.Y.C.R.R. § 202.13(b), (d), and (e).

[5]   See 22 N.Y.C.R.R. § 202.13(c), (h), and (i); Philadelphia Indem. Ins. Co. v. Goggins-Starr, 30 Misc. 3d 459, 913 N.Y.S.2d 878 (Dist. Ct., Nassau County 2010).

[6]   See 22 N.Y.C.R.R. § 202.13(f) to (i).

[7]   22 N.Y.C.R.R. § 202.26(g)(2); see the discussion in SPR 74:1.

[8]   See, e.g., Denner v. Katz, 75 Misc. 2d 51, 347 N.Y.S.2d 365 (N.Y. City Civ. Ct. 1973), aff'd as modified, 77 Misc. 2d 53, 351 N.Y.S.2d 308 (App. Term 1973).

[9]   See, e.g., Roy v. Hartogs, 85 Misc. 2d 891, 381 N.Y.S.2d 587 (App. Term, 1st Dep't 1976).

[10]   The courts answered this problem, at least for a while, by holding that cases patently below a $10,000 potential would be transferred down, as plaintiffs expected, but without dispensing with transferee limits. See, e.g., Offner v. Rothschild, 87 Misc. 2d 565, 386 N.Y.S.2d 188 (Sup. Ct., Kings County 1976). *Offner* relied on the *Haas* case, note 4 in § 26, as authority for such an involuntary transfer, but that authority has since been undermined. See § 26, note 5.

[11]   See Bess v. Fordham Road Storage Partners, N.Y.L.J., March 27, 2003, at 20, col.6 (Sup. Ct., Bronx County; Renwick, J.), discussed in SPR 139:3.

Although the money limits of a transferee court expand on a CPLR 325(d) transfer, they expand only up to the amount demanded in the plaintiff's complaint in the original court. Suppose it appears later, after a transfer down, that the damages are even greater. May the lower (the transferee) court entertain an application under subdivision (b) of CPLR 325[12] to send the case back? At least one court has said no, holding that the motion to increase and transfer back must be made to the original transferor, the supreme court.[13]

After a transfer back up to the original court under CPLR 325(b), however, the case would presumably become ripe once again for another transfer down under 325(d). In view of this, perhaps the supreme court, entertaining the 325(b) motion to increase and transfer up in a case previously transferred down under 325(d), can with just another breath grant only the increase part, and let the case stay right where it is—in the lower court.

Discussion up to now has addressed the usual money action. What about other relief? When equitable relief is demanded in a supreme court action, for example, even if a money demand is also included, it has been held that CPLR 325(d) does not permit a transfer down to a lower court, which would normally lack equity jurisdiction.[14] A difficult issue therefore arises in a CPLR 325(d) transferred-down case when the transferee court finds that it lacks jurisdiction. It has been held that the lower court still can't transfer the case back. In one case that posed the problem, it was suggested that the plaintiff move before the supreme court to "retransfer" the case.[15]

And what about personal jurisdiction? Before an action is sent down under CPLR 325(d), it must be shown that the defendants would have been within the personal jurisdiction of the lower court had the action been initially commenced there. Suppose it would not have been. Assume, for example, that the supreme court has sent down to the New York City Civil Court a case in which the summons was served in Westchester County. That would give jurisdiction of the defendant in the supreme court, whose process is statewide, but the process of the civil court does not extend beyond New York City unless the claim itself has contacts with the city.[16] Assume that it has not. In one such case,[17] the transferee lower court held itself without the power to return the case to the supreme court but also held that it nevertheless lacked jurisdiction to hear the case and could not go ahead with it. It dismissed the action, which of course poses a dilemma for the plaintiff.[18]

---

[12] See § 25.

[13] Huston v. Rao, 74 A.D.2d 127, 427 N.Y.S.2d 36 (2d Dep't 1980).

[14] Chung v. Kim, 170 A.D.2d 232, 565 N.Y.S.2d 510 (1st Dep't 1991); see Priel v. Linarello, 44 A.D.3d 835, 843 N.Y.S.2d 436 (2d Dep't 2007).

[15] See BLF Realty Holding Corp. v. Kasher, 183 Misc. 2d 953, 707 N.Y.S.2d 793 (App. Term, 1st Dep't 2000), treated along with connected problems in SPR 98:3.

[16] See § 404 of the New York City Civ. Ct. Act and the Commentary on it.

[17] Spinnell v. Doris L. Sassower, P.C., 155 Misc. 2d 147, 589 N.Y.S.2d 230 (N.Y. City Civ. Ct. 1992).

[18] See the discussion in SPR 3:4; see also Philadelphia Indem. Ins. Co. v. Goggins-Starr, 30 Misc. 3d 459, 913 N.Y.S.2d 878 (Dist. Ct., Nassau County 2010) (SPR 238:4) (defendant waived defense of lack of personal jurisdiction in lower court by not raising issue promptly after transfer).

C. FORUM NON CONVENIENS

Table of Sections

§ 28.   Forum Non Conveniens

§ 29.   Forum Non Conveniens and Corporations

§ 28.   Forum Non Conveniens

History of Doctrine

The doctrine of forum non conveniens, or inconvenient forum, has its origins in caselaw. It is a body of rules designed to keep out of the New York courts cases in which jurisdiction technically exists both of the subject matter and of the person, but in which there are no significant New York contacts to warrant entertainment of the matter. If, for example, P, a resident of Peru, commences a supreme court action against D, a resident of Denmark, for a breach of contract arising in Columbia, and D is served with process while passing through New York, the court secures jurisdiction of D. But if the case has nothing to do with New York, it should not be the burden of the New York court system and the New York taxpayer to support it.

Recognizing its status as an international commercial center with many of the world's largest law firms, New York has over the years been liberal about making its courts available for foreign actions. The rule has traditionally been that its courts will entertain jurisdiction of foreign-arising claims involving nonresidents if "special circumstances" are established for doing so.[1]

In one major case, the plaintiffs were Canadian residents (defendant of Brazil) seeking to impress a trust on assets allegedly belonging to plaintiffs and located in many parts of the world. Some of the assets were in New York and one of the alleged conduits in the transfer of the assets was a New York corporation. The court held that these circumstances warranted entertainment of the suit, that New York was as appropriate a forum as any other, and that the conveniens doctrine is relevant not only in tort cases (as had been thought) but in contract and property cases as well.[2]

Until 1972, there was a generally recognized rule that if any party to the action was a New York resident or domestic corporation, the court would have to entertain the case and that the conveniens doctrine would not apply.[3] That was changed by Silver v. Great American Insurance Co.,[4] in which the Court of Appeals held that the doctrine "should turn on considerations of justice, fairness and convenience and not solely on the residence of one of the parties." In *Silver*, the plaintiff was a physician who resided in Hawaii and alleged that the defendant (a New York corporation) had defamed him in both Hawaii and New York. On remand from the Court of Appeals, the appellate division, free now to apply its discretion even though one of the parties was a resident, dismissed for inconvenient forum,[5] finding Hawaii more appropriate.

---

[1]   Taylor v. Interstate Motor Freight System, 309 N.Y. 633, 132 N.E.2d 878 (1956).

[2]   Bata v. Bata, 304 N.Y. 51, 105 N.E.2d 623 (1952).

[3]   De La Bouillerie v. De Vienne, 300 N.Y. 60, 89 N.E.2d 15, 48 A.L.R.2d 798 (1949).

[4]   Silver v. Great Am. Ins. Co., 29 N.Y.2d 356, 361, 328 N.Y.S.2d 398, 402, 278 N.E.2d 619 (1972).

[5]   Silver v. Great Am. Ins. Co., 38 A.D.2d 932, 330 N.Y.S.2d 156 (1st Dep't 1972).

CPLR 327(a) and Discretionary Factors

The conveniens doctrine, including the *Silver* contribution, was codified in 1972. Embodied today in CPLR 327(a), it reads:

> When the court finds that in the interest of substantial justice the action should be heard in another forum, the court, on the motion of any party, may stay or dismiss the action in whole or in part on any conditions that may be just. The domicile or residence in this state of any party to the action shall not preclude the court from staying or dismissing the action.

CPLR 327(a) is only a codification, confirmatory rather than innovative.

If the plaintiff is a New York resident, a conveniens dismissal, although permissible, is less likely than when the defendant is the New York resident. The obvious reason is that the New York courts are primarily for the use of New Yorkers. But the Court of Appeals has said that a conveniens dismissal can visit even a case in which all parties are New York residents,[6] a result that should be rare, indeed, reserved solely for a case in which all of the other contacts—situs of the transaction, performance, witnesses, documents, physical evidence, etc.—are elsewhere.

The conveniens doctrine is one of judicial discretion "to be exercised by reviewing and evaluating all the pertinent competing considerations," which include, among other things, the burden on the New York courts, the hardship to the defendant that an action in New York would entail, and the availability elsewhere of a reputable forum.[7] If the "elsewhere" is a foreign country rather than a sister state, a conveniens dismissal is permissible but somewhat less likely. It depends on how much confidence we have in the jurisprudence of the foreign nation.[8] While no single factor is controlling, all relevant considerations raised by the parties must be weighed by the court. The burden rests upon the defendant challenging the forum to demonstrate that New York is not a convenient forum to conduct the litigation.[9]

While a decision to dismiss an action on forum non conveniens grounds is almost always a discretionary one, in Mashreqbank PSC v. Ahmed Hamad Al Gosaibi & Bros. Co.,[10] the Court concluded that under the facts before it, the case was "one of the relatively uncommon ones in which dismissal on forum non conveniens grounds is required as a matter of law." In *Mashreqbank*, the parties were not New York residents; no relevant conduct apart from fund transfers occurred in New York; none of the parties identified any important New York witnesses or New York documents; New York law did not apply to the dispute; there were other available forums to adjudicate the dispute;

---

[6]   Westwood Associates v. Deluxe General, Inc., 53 N.Y.2d 618, 438 N.Y.S.2d 774, 420 N.E.2d 966 (1981), aff'g 73 A.D.2d 572, 422 N.Y.S.2d 1014 (1st Dep't 1979).

[7]   Islamic Republic of Iran v. Pahlavi, 62 N.Y.2d 474, 479, 478 N.Y.S.2d 597, 600, 467 N.E.2d 245 (1984); Varkonyi v. S. A. Empresa De Viacao Airea Rio Grandense (Varig), 22 N.Y.2d 333, 337–38, 292 N.Y.S.2d 670, 673, 239 N.E.2d 542 (1968).

[8]   In the *Islamic* case, the foreign sovereign itself was the plaintiff seeking the aid of the New York courts to get at assets allegedly stolen by its former monarch. Its own courts were clearly the most appropriate for the suit, but it appeared that the world had little confidence in them and that their judgments would not be readily recognized and enforced in other nations. Holding that the plaintiff had only itself to blame for that, the Court of Appeals ordered the suit dismissed under the conveniens doctrine. *Islamic*, 62 N.Y.2d at 483, 478 N.Y.S.2d at 602.

[9]   *Islamic*, 62 N.Y.2d at 479, 478 N.Y.S.2d at 599–600.

[10]   Mashreqbank PSC v. Ahmed Hamad Al Gosaibi & Bros. Co., 23 N.Y.3d 129, 138, 989 N.Y.S.2d 458, 463, 12 N.E.3d 456, 461 (2014) (NYSLD No. 653).

no property related to the dispute was located in New York; and the Court noted that "no other circumstance support[ed] an argument that New York is an appropriate forum."[11]

CPLR 327(b) and Forum Selection Clauses

How does an "ouster" agreement figure on the forum non conveniens scene? An "ouster" agreement is a provision in a contract purporting to confer exclusive jurisdiction of a given dispute on a court in a given forum, thereby presuming to put it beyond ("oust") the jurisdiction of all other courts. Such an agreement was once regarded in New York as void on public policy grounds. Today, an agreement that purports to oust New York of jurisdiction by stipulating to exclusive jurisdiction elsewhere, while not by itself decisive, gets added to the list of factors a New York court will consider on a forum non conveniens balancing.[12]

Addressing an "ouster" agreement requiring that any action under the contract be brought in a Minnesota court, the Court of Appeals held in Boss v. American Express Financial Advisors, Inc.[13] that absent pressing reasons for maintaining a case in a New York court, New York will honor the forum selection clause. The contract contained not just a choice of forum clause but also a choice of law clause which stipulated to have Minnesota law govern the substantive issues in the case. There were objections to that clause, but the Court held that under the combination of the choice of forum and choice of law provisions in the contract, New York should dismiss the action under the conveniens doctrine and leave the substantive issues for a Minnesota court to resolve.

"In short," the Court concluded, "objections to a choice of law clause are not a warrant for failure to enforce a choice of forum clause." It is important to note that the Court did not hold the forum selection clause as a total superseder of the forum non conveniens doctrine embodied in CPLR 327. Rather, the clause is just another element on the list of things for a court to consider in a conveniens sifting.

Quite in contrast to an ouster agreement that seeks to strip New York of jurisdiction is the reverse kind: the one that seeks to confer jurisdiction on the New York courts exclusively.[14] A 1984 amendment that added subdivision (b) to CPLR 327 allows the parties to a commercial transaction to virtually guarantee that any disputes under the contract will be litigated in New York. CPLR 327(b) refers to General Obligations Law section 5–1402, which in turn refers to section 5–1401.[15] General Obligations Law section 5–1401(1) provides that if the parties to a "contract, agreement or undertaking" of at least $250,000 stipulate that New York law will govern their rights and duties, the choice of law provision will be honored "whether or not such contract, agreement or

---

[11]   *Mashreqbank*, 23 N.Y.3d at 138–39, 989 N.Y.S.2d at 463, 12 N.E.3d at 461.

[12]   Export Ins. Co. v. Mitsui S. S. Co., 26 A.D.2d 436, 274 N.Y.S.2d 977 (1st Dep't 1966).

[13]   Boss v. American Express Financial Advisors, Inc., 6 N.Y.3d 242, 811 N.Y.S.2d 620, 844 N.E.2d 1142 (2006) (NYSLD No. 554).

[14]   See also Garthon Business Inc. v. Stein, 138 A.D.3d 587, 590, 31 N.Y.S.3d 19, 23 (1st Dep't 2016) (forum selection clause in contract can bind the parties even after contract's termination).

[15]   The three statutes were supported by New York City to propitiate commercial interests. See the memorandum of the city's legislative representative on page A-689 of McKinney's 1984 Session Law News. A federal court in New York, however, would not be bound by such a contract. See item 8 on the list of choice of forum factors in § 616 (Practitioner's Edition). It has been held that these provisions, which mandate recognition of a forum selection clause in cases for $1 million or more, do not necessarily act as a bar to recognition of such a clause in smaller cases. National Union Fire Ins. Co. of Pittsburgh, Pa. v. Worley, 257 A.D.2d 228, 690 N.Y.S.2d 57 (1st Dep't 1999).

undertaking bears a reasonable relation to this state." If the parties have chosen New York law under this provision, then General Obligations Law section 5–1402(1) provides that if the agreement creates an obligation of at least $1 million, and the parties have stipulated to the jurisdiction of the New York courts, the forum non conveniens doctrine is superseded and the New York courts must entertain a dispute under the contract.

This important trio of statutes came to the forefront in IRB-Brasil Resseguros, S.A. v. Inepar Investments, S.A.,[16] where the Court of Appeals concluded that when there is an express choice of New York law in a contract pursuant to General Obligations Law section 5–1401, there is no need for a court to undertake a conflict-of-laws analysis. New York law will govern the contract, even if New York's choice of law rules would point to the substantive law of another jurisdiction. In *IRB-Brasil*, the guarantee at issue was for an amount well in excess of $250,000 ($27 million!) and contained both a New York choice of law clause and a New York forum selection clause. The Court of Appeals applied New York law to find that the guarantee was enforceable, rejecting the application of Brazilian substantive law that would have voided the guarantee. The Court noted that the General Obligations Law provisions were designed to provide certainty to contracting parties and "permit parties to select New York law to govern their contractual relationship and to avail themselves of New York courts despite lacking New York contacts . . . ."[17] A nonresident plaintiff suing under such a contract may, however, be subject to the statute of limitations of the jurisdiction where the claim arose.[18]

Some decisions predating *IRB-Brasil* have indicated, however, that even if a given case falls technically within the scenario outlined in CPLR 327(b), a dismissal or stay of the New York action in deference to an action pending elsewhere is still permissible. For example, in AIG Financial Products Corp. v. Penncara Energy, LLC,[19] the Court expressed doubts that "the Legislature intended [the statutes] to sanction preemptive and piecemeal litigation." Therefore, it upheld a trial court decision staying a New York action pursuant to CPLR 3211(a)(4) and allowed the subject dispute to continue in an action pending in Pennsylvania, which the Court found to have the predominant contacts with the transactions involved. While the contract in *AIG Financial* apparently had the clauses that seemingly made keeping the case mandatory under CPLR 327(b), the Court noted that the forum selection clause conferred "non-exclusive" jurisdiction. This suggests that if the clause had conferred the jurisdiction on the New York courts "exclusively," the Court would not have found room to require the stay it ordered in *AIG*.

A related situation is one that involves a "service of suit" provision in a contract. This requires a party, when asked by the other side, to submit to the jurisdiction of a court in a particular place. A "service of suit" clause will accomplish the submission of the dispute to the selected court's jurisdiction, but it won't guarantee that the court there will exercise the jurisdiction or that the suit will not be dismissed on other procedural grounds. The jurisdiction selected can still apply its own forum non conveniens doctrine

---

[16]   IRB-Brasil Resseguros, S.A. v. Inepar Investments, S.A., 20 N.Y.3d 310, 958 N.Y.S.2d 689, 982 N.E.2d 609 (2012) (NYSLD No. 637).

[17]   *IRB-Brasil*, 20 N.Y.3d at 315, 958 N.Y.S.2d at 692, 982 N.E.2d at 612.

[18]   2138747 Ontario, Inc. v. Samsung C & T Corp., 144 A.D.3d 122, 39 N.Y.S.3d 10 (1st Dep't 2016), lv. granted, 29 N.Y.3d 913, 2017 WL 2682196 (2017); see § 57.

[19]   AIG Financial Products Corp. v. Penncara Energy, LLC, 83 A.D.3d 495, 922 N.Y.S.2d 288 (1st Dep't 2011).

and dismiss the case if it finds that foreign contacts predominate and that there's no special reason for the court to entertain the case.[20]

Dismissal or Stay

While the New York forum non conveniens doctrine, when successfully invoked, usually brings a dismissal, a stay is sometimes used instead. CPLR 327(a) permits either. This contrasts with federal practice, where the doctrine usually does no more than transfer the case to a more appropriate federal district,[21] and where dismissal is the exception rather than the rule.

The dismissal or stay may be conditional to ensure the availability of a forum to adjudicate the dispute.[22] The court can, for example, dismiss on condition that the moving defendant stipulate to accept service in a designated forum elsewhere, thus easing the plaintiff's jurisdictional path there,[23] or require the defendant to stipulate to waive the defense of the statute of limitations when sued elsewhere.[24] Interesting issues arise when the defendant does so stipulate and then violates the stipulation.[25]

The conveniens doctrine is not restricted to personam cases; it may also be applied in actions based on rem jurisdiction.[26]

Raising a Forum Non Conveniens Objection

The forum non conveniens objection is raised by a simple motion on notice. It is expressly authorized by CPLR 327(a). Under prior law, the objection, although not the same as subject matter jurisdiction, fell into that category for the purpose of authorizing a dismissal motion under CPLR 3211(a)(2).

It takes a motion by a party to invoke the conveniens doctrine. The court cannot invoke it sua sponte. A court would occasionally raise the objection on its own, on the ground that it might otherwise be imposed on unduly merely because the lawyers on both sides wanted to use the court even for cases lacking reasonable contacts with the forum, but the Court of Appeals appears to have put an end to that. In VSL Corp. v. Dunes Hotels and Casinos, Inc.,[27] the Court held in a brief memorandum that "[u]nder CPLR 327(a) a court may stay or dismiss an action in whole or in part on forum non

---

[20] A "conveniens" dismissal in that setting was the result in Brooke Group Ltd. v. JCH Syndicate 488, 87 N.Y.2d 530, 640 N.Y.S.2d 479, 663 N.E.2d 635 (1996), a New York action against a Lloyd's insurance syndicate based in London.

[21] 28 U.S.C.A. § 1404(a); see § 618 (Practitioner's Edition).

[22] Boyle v. Starwood Hotels & Resorts Worldwide, Inc., 110 A.D.3d 938, 973 N.Y.S.2d 728 (2d Dep't 2013) (court required the defendant to stipulate, as a condition to dismissal of New York action on forum non conveniens grounds, "to waive jurisdictional and statute of limitations defenses in the United Kingdom, France, and the United Arab Emirates" and any other defenses not available in New York at the time of the commencement of the action), aff'd, 23 N.Y.3d 1012, 992 N.Y.S.2d 773, 16 N.E.3d 1252 (2014).

[23] See Boyle, 110 A.D.3d at 940, 973 N.Y.S.2d at 730; Barry v. American Home Assur. Co., 38 A.D.2d 928, 329 N.Y.S.2d 911 (1st Dep't 1972), aff'd, 31 N.Y.2d 684, 337 N.Y.S.2d 259, 289 N.E.2d 180 (1972).

[24] Boyle, 110 A.D.3d at 940, 973 N.Y.S.2d at 730; Ginsburg v. Hearst Publishing Co., 5 A.D.2d 200, 170 N.Y.S.2d 691 (1st Dep't 1958), aff'd, 5 N.Y.2d 894, 183 N.Y.S.2d 77, 156 N.E.2d 708 (1959).

[25] See Cesar v. United Technology of New York, 148 Misc. 2d 918, 562 N.Y.S.2d 903, 1990 A.M.C. 1595 (Sup. Ct., New York County 1990), aff'd, 173 A.D.2d 394, 570 N.Y.S.2d 25 (1st Dep't 1991) (NYSLD No. 380).

[26] Vaage v. Lewis, 29 A.D.2d 315, 288 N.Y.S.2d 521 (2d Dep't 1968). A special forum non conveniens provision governs in child custody cases, which can involve personam or rem jurisdiction, or a combination of both. See Dom. Rel. Law § 76–f; DeJac v. DeJac, 17 A.D.3d 1066, 794 N.Y.S.2d 208 (4th Dep't 2005), lv. denied, 20 A.D.3d 946, 797 N.Y.S.2d 789 (discussing application of statute).

[27] VSL Corp. v. Dunes Hotels and Casinos, Inc., 70 N.Y.2d 948, 949, 524 N.Y.S.2d 671, 671, 519 N.E.2d 617, 617 (1988).

conveniens grounds only upon the motion of a party; a court does not have the authority to invoke the doctrine on its own motion."

Subsequently, in Mashreqbank PSC v. Ahmed Hamad Al Gosaibi & Bros. Co.,[28] the Court concluded that even though no party formally moved to dismiss the main action based on forum non conveniens, the *VSL Corp.* holding did not bar such relief where "the issue was briefed and argued at Supreme Court." It should be noted, however, that in *Mashreqbank,* a third-party defendant moved to dismiss the third-party action on forum non conveniens grounds, which prompted the court to raise the issue of dismissing the main action on such grounds. There is no stated time limit on when the motion can be made, but a defendant bent on avoiding inconvenience should make the motion before answering. Since the conveniens ground has sometimes been treated as synonymous with subject matter jurisdiction, however—a matter elaborated in the next section—it might be thought permissible to make the motion at any time, because an objection to subject matter jurisdiction lies at any time. The assumption is unsound. If a defendant has subjected itself to the inconvenience of a trial, and lost on the merits, a court should not accept its inconvenience argument if saved until then. It should simply hold that the defendant has waived it. This does not mean that a rigid time period must be singled out to govern the conveniens motion; it merely suggests that a motion that claims inconvenience to the defendant should not be delayed until it has seriously inconvenienced the court and the plaintiff (who, because the objection was saved, has gone on to prepare for trial). This reasoning applies as well to the Business Corporation Law section 1314(b) objection in an action against a foreign corporation, discussed in the next section.

While primarily a feature of supreme court practice, the conveniens doctrine is occasionally seen in one of the lower courts. It was the subject of conflicting decisions in the New York City Civil Court in the same county (Queens). One applied the doctrine to dismiss a case that was thought more appropriate to another county,[29] while the other refused a conveniens dismissal on the facts and expressed doubt about whether the civil court could entertain such a dismissal on any facts.[30]

§ 29. Forum Non Conveniens and Corporations

Business Corporation Law ("BCL") section 1314, on the scene long before the arrival of the CPLR's general forum non conveniens statute codified in CPLR 327, applies to certain cases involving defendant foreign corporations. If the plaintiff is a New York resident or domestic corporation, BCL section 1314(a) unequivocally states that the action "may be maintained." This implies that the court must entertain the suit against the foreign corporation. It has not yet been resolved whether CPLR 327(a), which authorizes dismissal on forum non conveniens grounds if otherwise warranted, even though one of the parties is a New Yorker, will change this rigid requirement of BCL section 1314(a) and permit a dismissal in such a case. It should. CPLR 327, as the later statute, can be deemed to make a pro rata dent in section 1314(a).

---

[28] Mashreqbank PSC v. Ahmed Hamad Al Gosaibi & Bros. Co., 23 N.Y.3d 129, 133, 989 N.Y.S.2d 458, 459, 12 N.E.3d 456, 457 (2014).

[29] Neuro Rehab. Health Care v. N.Y. Central Mut. Fire Ins. Co., N.Y.L.J., Feb. 4, 1997, at 29, col.3 (N.Y. City Civ. Ct.; Weiss, J.).

[30] Suffolk Chiropractic Center v. Geico Ins. Co., 171 Misc. 2d 855, 656 N.Y.S.2d 107 (N.Y. City Civ. Ct. 1997). See the discussion of this and the *Neuro* case in SPR 54:3 and 55:3.

When the plaintiff is a nonresident or a foreign corporation suing a foreign corporation, section 1314(b) applies. It authorizes entertainment of the action only if at least one of the following five requirements is met:

(1)   The action is for damages for breach of a contract made or to be performed in New York or relates to property that was in New York when the contract was made.

(2)   The "subject matter" of the case, presumably meaning some kind of identifiable property, is in New York.

(3)   The claim arose in New York (unless it seeks to affect title to foreign real property).

(4)   The defendant would be subject to jurisdiction under CPLR 302 (the "longarm" jurisdiction statute, to be met later).[1]

(5)   The defendant is authorized to do, or is doing, business in New York.

If the only item satisfied is number 5 on the list—that the corporation is authorized to do, or is doing business in New York—caselaw imposes the additional requirement that a special circumstance be shown before the action will be entertained.[2] The reason is that so many foreign corporations have a New York presence that some leverage is needed to exclude cases having nothing to do with the corporation's New York activities and in which no other factor is present to make New York an appropriate forum.[3]

If one of the first four items on the BCL section 1314(b) list is satisfied, however, it presumably suffices by itself to require entertainment of the suit. Here, a clash with CPLR 327(a), which in general terms authorizes conveniens dismissals without getting into the kinds of specifics that section 1314(b) contains, is less likely, but still possible. Meeting one of the specific requirements of section 1314(b) would in most cases qualify as the kind of discretionary factor that would also warrant retention of the suit under CPLR 327(a).

The test for determining whether the corporation is "doing business" under section 1314(b)(5) has essentially been held to be the same as the one that determines amenability to personal jurisdiction under CPLR 301,[4] treated later.[5]

Section 1314 should be deemed a forum non conveniens statute[6] although some old cases refer to it as going to subject matter jurisdiction.[7] The conveniens doctrine is often discussed as if it were the same as subject matter jurisdiction, but it is not the same, either technically or practically. The more current thinking of the Court of Appeals is

---

[1]   See § 84.

[2]   Yesuvida v. Pennsylvania R. Co., 200 Misc. 815, 111 N.Y.S.2d 417 (Sup. Ct., Kings County 1951).

[3]   If the case falls under CPLR 327(b) however, which makes the exercise of jurisdiction mandatory in certain commercial cases, see § 28, notes 15–17 and accompanying text, the requirements of Bus. Corp. Law § 1304(b) are not applicable. Gen. Oblig. Law § 5–1402(1).

[4]   Fremay, Inc. v. Modern Plastic Machinery Corp., 15 A.D.2d 235, 240, 222 N.Y.S.2d 694, 699–700 (1st Dep't 1961).

[5]   See § 82. The famous "corporate presence" or "doing business" test has since been all but declared unconstitutional by the Supreme Court in its 2014 decision in Daimler AG v. Bauman, 571 U.S. 117, 134 S. Ct. 746, 187 L. Ed. 2d 624 (2014); see § 82.

[6]   See ABKCO Industries, Inc. v. Lennon, 85 Misc. 2d 465, 377 N.Y.S.2d 362 (Sup. Ct., New York County 1975), aff'd in part, modified in part, 52 A.D.2d 435, 384 N.Y.S.2d 781 (1st Dep't 1976).

[7]   See, e.g., Robinson v. Oceanic Steam Nav. Co., 112 N.Y. 315, 19 N.E. 625 (1889).

that "when a court, on the ground of forum non conveniens, dismisses an action which it could entertain, it is exercising a discretionary power."[8] One need only add that there is nothing discretionary about subject matter jurisdiction.

Even the rule that a court will not allow itself to become embroiled in the "internal affairs" of a foreign corporation—corporate structure, stock and bond set-ups, rights of shareholders inter se, etc.—once thought to go rigidly to subject matter jurisdiction, has more recently been placed in the more flexible category of forum non conveniens.[9]

D. OTHER RESTRICTIONS ON JURISDICTION

Table of Sections

§ 30.   Unlicensed Plaintiff Corporation
§ 31.   Interference with Interstate Commerce

§ 30. Unlicensed Plaintiff Corporation

Business Corporation Law section 1312 precludes a foreign corporation that is doing business in New York from maintaining a New York action without having duly licensed itself and paid all required fees and taxes. This is a revenue measure, designed to place foreign corporations on the same footing as domestic ones. Its purpose is therefore fulfilled when the foreign corporation complies and the state gets its money. Thus, if the plaintiff corporation is in breach of the statute when it begins an action, but duly (and retroactively) complies while the action is pending, the action is validated ab initio and may proceed unhindered.[1] But nothing less than full compliance will suffice; the mere payment of security for costs, for example, which a different statute exacts of nonresident plaintiffs, is not sufficient.[2]

Section 1312 should not be confused with section 1314 of the BCL. The latter is a statute concerned mainly with defendant foreign corporations while section 1312 is a money measure aimed at plaintiff foreign corporations.

Section 1312 is not jurisdictional, but rather affects the corporation's legal capacity to sue.[3] This means that the defendant had best make an objection under the statute affirmatively, by motion or answer[4]—or risk waiving it—despite some indications that compliance should be pleaded by plaintiff as a condition precedent to suit.[5] It should be so administered, in any case, as to preclude a plaintiff in violation of it from realizing any benefits from an action until compliance is had.

---

[8]   Bata v. Bata, 304 N.Y. 51, 55, 105 N.E.2d 623, 625 (1952).

[9]   Broida v. Bancroft, 103 A.D.2d 88, 478 N.Y.S.2d 333 (2d Dep't 1984) (shareholder derivative action); but see Raharney Capital, LLC v. Capital Stack LLC, 138 A.D.3d 83, 25 N.Y.S.3d 217, 217–18 (1st Dep't 2016) (holding that New York courts do not have subject matter jurisdiction to judicially dissolve a foreign business entity, which power "is entirely distinct from resolving a dispute over [a corporation's] internal affairs.").

[1]   Arp Films, Inc. v. Marvel Entertainment Group, Div. of Cadence Industries Corp., 645 F. Supp. 876, 879 n.3 (S.D.N.Y. 1986); Oxford Paper Co. v. S. M. Liquidation Co., 45 Misc. 2d 612, 257 N.Y.S.2d 395 (Sup. Ct., New York County 1965).

[2]   CPLR 8501(a); see Dixie Dinettes, Inc. v. Schaller's Furniture, Inc., 71 Misc. 2d 102, 335 N.Y.S.2d 632 (N.Y. City Civ. Ct. 1972).

[3]   CPLR 3211(a)(3); Digital Centre, S.L. v. Apple Industries, Inc., 94 A.D.3d 571, 942 N.Y.S.2d 488 (1st Dep't 2012).

[4]   McKenzie Banking Co. v. Billinson, 79 A.D.3d 1728, 914 N.Y.S.2d 843 (4th Dep't 2010).

[5]   *Oxford*, 45 Misc. 2d at 613, 257 N.Y.S.2d at 397–98.

The statute also applies in federal courts sitting in New York, at least when the basis of federal subject matter jurisdiction is diversity of citizenship.[6]

What constitutes "doing business" sufficient to invoke section 1312 is apparently tested by the same yardstick used to determine the former "doing business" test under CPLR 301,[7] but there are periodic statements to the effect that the tests are not the same.[8]

The statute does not apply if the commerce that the corporation is engaged in is exclusively interstate.[9]

The statute applies only to corporations suing as plaintiffs. It doesn't apply to a foreign corporation brought in as a defendant, which can, without having to carry out the statutory licensing requirements, defend the action and even interpose a counterclaim against the plaintiff if it is related to the plaintiff's claim.[10] It has even been held that a defendant not in compliance with the statute can commence a third-party action.[11]

§ 31.   Interference with Interstate Commerce

Another category of objection to the entertainment of jurisdiction, analogous to forum non conveniens but occupying a separate niche and occasioning separate inquiry because it's based on the Federal Constitution, is that the maintenance of the suit will constitute an undue burden on the defendant's interstate commerce. This is an objection that has fallen into disuse in recent years, apparently because of the rapidity of transportation today and because New York's reasonable forum non conveniens rules are apt to dispose of the case before the commerce objection is reached. An action likely to interfere unreasonably with the defendant's interstate commerce is also likely to run afoul of New York's own conveniens' rules and be shown the door by that route.

The common carrier was the primary beneficiary of this interstate commerce rule, as illustrated in Baltimore Mail S. S. Co. v. Fawcett,[1] where a steamship company was sued on a claim arising in Virginia. It was held that the action could not be entertained because the need to defend a suit far from the place of the occurrence and the main centers of its business would constitute an unreasonable burden on the defendant's transportation business.

All lawsuits are a burden. To succeed with the commerce objection, the defendant must show on the facts of the particular case that it would be an "oppressive and

---

[6]   Woods v. Interstate Realty Co., 337 U.S. 535, 69 S. Ct. 1235, 93 L. Ed. 1524 (1949); Netherlands Shipmortgage Corp., Ltd. v. Madias, 717 F.2d 731, 735, 1984 A.M.C. 141, 72 A.L.R. Fed. 562 (2d Cir. 1983); *cf.* Grand Bahama Petroleum Co., Ltd. v. Asiatic Petroleum Corp., 550 F.2d 1320, 1324 (2d Cir. 1977) ("BCL § 1312(a) may not be raised in an action to compel arbitration brought pursuant to the United States Arbitration Act with diversity as the jurisdictional basis.").

[7]   See § 82.

[8]   E.g., Von Arx, A. G. v. Breitenstein, 52 A.D.2d 1049, 384 N.Y.S.2d 895 (4th Dep't 1976), aff'd, 41 N.Y.2d 958, 394 N.Y.S.2d 876, 363 N.E.2d 582 (1977); see § 83.

[9]   International Text-Book Co. v. Tone, 220 N.Y. 313, 115 N.E. 914, 3 A.F.T.R. (P-H) P 3296 (1917).

[10]   See C.B.I. Drywall Corp. v. Anton Airfood, Inc., N.Y.L.J., Oct. 5, 2000, at 32, col.4 (Sup. Ct., Queens County; Milano, J.).

[11]   Complexions, Inc. v. Industry Outfitters, Inc., 2011 WL 13070424 (N.D.N.Y. 2011).

[1]   Baltimore Mail S. S. Co. v. Fawcett, 269 N.Y. 379, 199 N.E. 628, 104 A.L.R. 1068 (1936), cert. den. 298 U.S. 675, 56 S.Ct. 939.

unreasonable" burden,[2] a difficult showing at best in a state with sound conveniens rules. The objection does not often succeed today.[3]

It is perhaps ironic that a carrier, which would usually have the readiest facilities to transfer records pertaining to a foreign lawsuit, should have been the chief beneficiary of the commerce rule. It is clear today, however, that the rule, rare though its application be, also applies to other categories of defendant.[4]

E. CONDITIONS PRECEDENT TO SUIT

Table of Sections

§ 32.   Conditions Precedent to Suit; Notice of Claim; Leave to Serve Late Notice

§ 32.   Conditions Precedent to Suit; Notice of Claim; Leave to Serve Late Notice

Notice of Claim Provisions and Pleading Requirements

In a few instances, a condition precedent may have to be met before suit is allowed. The most common of these is the notice of claim, a requirement that the potential defendant be notified of the existence of the claim within a given period after the claim arises. This requirement may come from a contract[1]—of which the insurance policy is the prime example—or from a statute.

Various requirements with short time periods are imposed for filing claims against the state in the court of claims. These requirements are governed by section 10 of the Court of Claims Act, which contains procedures for serving a "written notice of intention to file a claim." Such written notice constitutes commencement of an action in the court of claims. This provision should be the first thing consulted by one with a claim against the state.

The most notable—or, to plaintiffs' lawyers, notorious—notice of claim provision is that of section 50–e of the General Municipal Law. It applies to tort claims against a public corporation which includes, among other things, a city, county, town, village, fire district, and school district.[2] The notice of claim must ordinarily be served on the entity within 90 days after the claim arises, i.e., the accident occurs.[3] In sum, when a plaintiff desires to pursue a claim against a public corporation, two procedural steps must be properly completed. First, the plaintiff must satisfy the notice of claim requirements.

---

[2]   International Mill. Co. v. Columbia Transp. Co., 292 U.S. 511, 520, 54 S. Ct. 797, 800, 78 L. Ed. 1396 (1934).

[3]   See, e.g., Ceravit Corp. AG v. Black Diamond S. S. Corp., 46 Misc. 2d 979, 260 N.Y.S.2d 848, 1965 A.M.C. 1751 (App. Term, 1st Dep't 1965).

[4]   Banque De France v. Supreme Court of State of New York, 287 N.Y. 483, 41 N.E.2d 65 (1942), cert. den. 316 U.S. 646, 62 S.Ct. 1279. The commerce objection did not succeed and the action in New York was sustained, the main reason being that the plaintiff would otherwise have had to bring its action in a Nazi-occupied country. That alternative made the New York suit reasonable. The case incidentally shows the similarity between the elements that go into the New York forum non conveniens doctrine and those that count under the federally inspired interference-with-commerce test.

[1]   See Cuzdey v. American Motorists Ins. Co., 45 A.D.2d 134, 357 N.Y.S.2d 143 (3d Dep't 1974), aff'd, 37 N.Y.2d 939, 380 N.Y.S.2d 648, 343 N.E.2d 287 (1975).

[2]   See Gen. Constr. Law § 66.

[3]   Gen. Mun. Law § 50–e(1)(a). In wrongful death actions, the 90 days runs from the appointment of a representative of the decedent's estate. Gen. Mun. Law § 50–e(1)(a).

Second, the plaintiff must commence the action within the one year and ninety day statute of limitations, pleading compliance with the notice of claim requirements.[4] This is due to the fact that when a notice of claim requirement is statutorily imposed, it is usually deemed an element of the substantive cause of action and as such, its satisfaction must be pleaded in the complaint. The defendant can raise the defect either as a defense in the answer or by motion to dismiss for failure to state a cause of action.

The 90-day period in section 50–e of the General Municipal Law moves fast; some lawyers, amateur relativity theorists, swear it runs faster than other 90-day periods. If the client retains the lawyer with time still left in which to get the notice of claim served, and it is not served, the lawyer is open to a malpractice charge.[5]

When the claim against a governmental entity is on a ground other than tort, a notice of claim requirement may still obtain, and yet not be found in a relatively uniform provision like the one supplied in General Municipal Law section 50–e for tort cases. The lawyer should make inquiry forthwith. For example, contract actions may be governed by separate statutes for different municipalities.[6] One way to gain information on this front is to search for prior decisions in which the entity was sued for similar claims and ascertain if any notice of claim arguments were raised. Lawyers following this path can at least be sure to avoid the mistakes of their predecessors.

In Margerum v. City of Buffalo,[7] the Court of Appeals held that "[h]uman rights [law] claims are not tort actions under [section] 50–e and are not personal injury, wrongful death, or damage to personal property claims under section 50–i." Therefore, General Municipal Law section 50–e does not require a notice of claim for such claims asserted against a city. A concurring opinion noted that the Court has "held that an employment discrimination claim brought against a *county* under the Human Rights Law is subject to County Law § 52(1)'s notice-of-claim requirement."[8] Section 52(1) of the County Law is broader than the above General Municipal Law provisions, requiring a notice of claim for various claims against a county including claims "for damage, injury or death, *or for invasion of personal or property rights, of every name and nature . . . .*"

A notice of claim is not required when the relief being sought from the municipality is equitable in nature, even if incidental money damages are sought.[9] For example, a continuing trespass extends the time for the plaintiff to sue to enjoin the trespass without worrying about a notice of claim. But if damages are also accruing and the plaintiff intends to claim them, it is not a bad idea to consider serving a timely notice of

---

    4   See Gen. Mun. Law § 50–i(1); Wally G. ex rel. Yoselin T. v. New York City Health and Hospitals Corp., 27 N.Y.2d 672, 675 n.2, 37 N.Y.S.3d 30, 31–32 n.2, 57 N.E.3d 1067, 1068–69 n.2 (2016). When a notice of claim is imposed by contract instead of by statute, the plaintiff need not plead its satisfaction, but will have to prove satisfaction if the defendant raises the issue. See CPLR 3015(a); § 215.

    5   See Glamm v. Allen, 57 N.Y.2d 87, 94 n.2, 453 N.Y.S.2d 674, 678 n.2, 439 N.E.2d 390, 393, n.2 (1982).

    6   See, e.g., CPLR 9802 (governing villages) and Town Law § 65(3). As to counties, see Meed v. Nassau County Police Dept., 70 Misc. 2d 274, 332 N.Y.S.2d 679 (Sup. Ct., Nassau County 1972).

    7   Margerum v. City of Buffalo, 24 N.Y.3d 721, 5 N.Y.S.3d 336, 28 N.E.3d 515 (2015).

    8   *Margerum*, 24 N.Y.3d at 733, 5 N.Y.S.3d at 341, 28 N.E.3d at 520 (Read, J. concurring) *citing* Mills v. Monroe County, 89 A.D.2d 776, 453 N.Y.S.2d 486 (4th Dep't 1982), aff'd, 59 N.Y.2d 307, 309, 464 N.Y.S.2d 709, 451 N.E.2d 456 (1983).

    9   Fontana v. Town of Hempstead, 18 A.D.2d 1084, 239 N.Y.S.2d 512 (2d Dep't 1963), aff'd, 13 N.Y.2d 1134, 247 N.Y.S.2d 130, 196 N.E.2d 561 (1964).

claim for the damages segment (or segments) anyway, regardless of whether such damages are "incidental" or not.[10]

As the above discussion demonstrates, a lawyer should never be self-indulgent in analyzing a given claim against a government unit. If there is any doubt whatsoever about whether a notice of claim provision is applicable, the lawyer should apply it and carry out its requirements to the letter. Suppose for example, that a municipality has withheld money or property of X even after the dismissal of a criminal action in which the property was seized. X wants it back and sues for it. This is not a typical personal injury or property damage claim of the kind usually associated with section 50–e, but notice of claim is nevertheless required, at least for any claims based on state law, and X can't avoid it by trying to cast the claim for relief in some other form.[11]

Contents and Service of Notice of Claim

The purpose of the notice of claim is to enable the public corporation to investigate claims and obtain evidence promptly.[12] Drawing and serving the notice is a simple step to carry out. It's a sworn-to writing naming the claimant and attorney; and describing the nature of the claim; the when, where, and how of its arising; and the injuries claimed insofar as they are discernible.[13] It is served on the would-be defendant by personal delivery or by registered or certified mail to one upon whom a summons could be served in the defendant's behalf, or, if the defendant has a "regularly engaged" attorney, to the attorney.[14] Confusion on this front has resulted in carnage in a legion of cases.[15]

Effective June 15, 2013, the Uniform Notice of Claim Act provides that service of the notice of claim can now be made on the Secretary of State in lieu of service on the municipal entity.[16] This alternative method of service, also set forth in General Municipal Law section 53, is similar to the method long enjoyed by plaintiffs serving corporations through the Secretary of State under the Business Corporation Law.[17] There may be some danger lurking here. If the governmental entity does not qualify as a "public corporation, as defined in subdivision one of section sixty-six of the general construction law" and has not adopted General Municipal Law section 50–e for the service of a notice of claim, service via the Secretary of State under these new provisions

---

[10] See Bulzomi v. Inc'd Village of Westbury, N.Y.L.J., Sept. 4, 2003, at 22, col.5 (Sup. Ct., Nassau County; Franco, J.) (SPR 150:4).

[11] Such as a proceeding under Article 78 of the CPLR. See § 557; Neumark v. New York City Police Property Clerk, 122 A.D.2d 210, 504 N.Y.S.2d 744 (2d Dep't 1986).

[12] State v. Waverly Central School Dist., 28 A.D.2d 628, 280 N.Y.S.2d 505 (3d Dep't 1967).

[13] Gen. Mun. Law § 50–e(2) ("Form of notice; contents"). The courts have repeatedly relied on General Municipal Law section 50–e(6), discussed below, in concluding that a lack of swearing to the notice of claim may be excused or corrected. See, e.g., Figgs v. County of Suffolk, 54 A.D.3d 671, 863 N.Y.S.2d 258 (2d Dep't 2008); Gass v. Hahn, 98 A.D.2d 741, 469 N.Y.S.2d 445 (2d Dep't 1983).

[14] Gen. Mun. Law § 50–e(3)(a) ("How served; when service by mail complete; defect in manner of service; return of notice improperly served"). An amendment that took effect on September 19, 2010, allows service of a notice of claim on New York City—and only on New York City—by electronic means. The amendment is the subject of the lead note in SPR 220:1.

[15] See, e.g., Khela v. City of New York, 91 A.D.3d 912, 937 N.Y.S.2d 311 (2d Dep't 2012) (service of notice of claim on legal department of the New York City Department of Transportation held insufficient in action against New York City).

[16] Gen. Mun. Law § 50–e(3)(f), governing "all actions and proceedings accruing on or after" June 15, 2013.

[17] See §§ 70, 95.

may not be available.[18] Furthermore, the new provision may not be used to serve process in the actual action.[19]

If the notice is served on time, but in an improper manner, the defect is waived if the defendant demands an examination of the plaintiff (to which the defendant is entitled to under General Municipal Law section 50–h).[20] Defects in the manner of service are also waived if it is shown that the defendant actually received the notice within the required time, unless the notice of claim is returned to the plaintiff within 30 days after being received with a statement specifying the alleged defect.[21] If the defendant does that, the plaintiff then has 10 days in which to serve a new notice curing the defect.[22] This obviously takes the profit out of the defendant's attempt to exploit mere defects in method of service. That, incidentally, is its purpose.

Ordinary mail is an improper method of service of the notice of claim. Nonetheless, it has been sustained if the mail is *actually received* within the 90 days, which opens the door to issues of fact connected with service. The mere posting of ordinary mail within the 90 days does not suffice, as it does when the registered or certified mail expressly prescribed by section 50–e is used.[23] Using one of the prescribed methods, which produces a post office receipt or affidavit of service, also assures the claimant better proof if the defendant denies service.

Defects in the contents of the notice not shown to prejudice the defendant, such as an omission of how the claim arose or the items of damage, have also been held curable or disregardable,[24] but the courts are not consistent about that. In Caselli v. City of New York,[25] for example, in which the accident site was misdescribed, the court voided the notice even though the defendant municipality's own police department had on record a proper site description. In a later case from the Court of Appeals, Brown v. City of New York,[26] it was held that a notice of claim suffices if it locates the accident site well enough to enable the municipality to investigate. A plaintiff careless about the site description faces the question of whether it does. In *Brown*, the court held that it did, but the cautious plaintiff may find it safer to follow the stricter standard set in *Caselli.*

In another Court of Appeals case taking a peculiarly strict view of the notice of claim,[27] there was a dispute between the city (D) and its bus companies (collectively, P) about the proper formula to be applied in figuring certain cost increases. P served timely notices of claim and then brought timely suit for overdue payments, presenting the formula dispute. While the action pended, additional payments fell due. Even though all conceded that however the formula dispute might be resolved, the resolution would be

---

[18]   Gen. Mun. Law § 50–e(3)(f).

[19]   See CPLR 311(a); § 70 (discussing service of process on municipal entities).

[20]   Gen. Mun. Law § 50–e(3)(c).

[21]   Gen. Mun. Law § 50–e(3)(c).

[22]   Gen. Mun. Law § 50–e(3)(d).

[23]   Scantlebury v. New York City Health and Hospitals Corp., 4 N.Y.3d 606, 797 N.Y.S.2d 394, 830 N.E.2d 292 (2005).

[24]   Gen. Mun. Law § 50–e(6); see, e.g., Smith v. Scott, 294 A.D.2d 11, 740 N.Y.S.2d 425 (2d Dep't 2002); Montana v. Incorporated Village of Lynbrook, 23 A.D.2d 585, 256 N.Y.S.2d 651 (2d Dep't 1965).

[25]   Caselli v. City of New York, 105 A.D.2d 251, 483 N.Y.S.2d 401 (2d Dep't 1984).

[26]   Brown v. City of New York, 95 N.Y.2d 389, 718 N.Y.S.2d 4, 740 N.E.2d 1078 (2000) (NYSLD No. 492).

[27]   Varsity Transit, Inc. v. Board of Educ. of City of New York, 5 N.Y.3d 532, 806 N.Y.S.2d 457, 840 N.E.2d 569 (2005).

binding as to all payments, the court nevertheless held that a separate notice of claim was required for each of the new payments claimed.

Application for Leave to Serve Late Notice of Claim

Defects in manner of service or in the content of the notice of claim have been a continuous source of grief for plaintiffs, but by no means the main one. That spot is still reserved for timeliness. Before September 1, 1976, the grounds on which the late service of a notice of claim might be allowed were narrow and narrowly construed. The case annotations under section 50–e in the General Municipal Law were literally a graveyard of meritorious claims barred by lateness,[28] and the court had no general discretion to allow a late service of the notice of claim. This changed with the 1976 amendment of section 50–e,[29] but if the continuing annotations are any indication, the turn-around has not proved as complete as would-be plaintiffs might wish.

A major accomplishment of the amendment is the expansion of judicial discretion to allow late service,[30] but with a cutoff: the court cannot extend the time to serve a notice of claim longer than the applicable statute of limitations and any available tolls, i.e., the time in which to start an action. Hence the court can, on application, stretch the 90-day notice of claim period of section 50–e up to the 1 year and 90 days statute of limitations in section 50–i of the General Municipal Law, plus any applicable tolls.[31]

In Williams ex rel. Fowler v. Nassau County Medical Center,[32] the Court of Appeals treats the factors that figure on an application for leave to serve a late notice of claim, including the plaintiff's infancy, the defendant's knowledge of the facts from other sources, and the issue of whether the defendant would be prejudiced by the grant of leave.[33] General Municipal Law section 50–e(5) empowers the court to take into consideration whether the defendant or its attorney or insurance carrier had actual knowledge of the facts constituting the claim within the 90-day period "or within a reasonable time thereafter." The "actual knowledge" factor "contemplates 'actual knowledge of the essential facts constituting the claim,' not knowledge of a specific legal

---

[28] To spare federal civil rights claims a similar interment, the U.S. Supreme Court has held that the 90-day notice of claim requirement does not apply in a case predicated on 42 U.S.C.A. § 1983. Felder v. Casey, 487 U.S. 131, 108 S. Ct. 2302, 101 L. Ed. 2d 123 (1988). The New York Court of Appeals had previously held to the contrary in 423 South Salina Street, Inc. v. City of Syracuse, 68 N.Y.2d 474, 510 N.Y.S.2d 507, 503 N.E.2d 63 (1986), cert. den. 481 U.S. 1008, 107 S.Ct. 1880, 95 L.Ed.2d 488 (1987).

[29] The amendment was drafted by Professor Paul S. Graziano at the behest of the New York State Judicial Conference in a study set forth in its entirety in 21st Jud. Conf. Rep. Leg. Doc. No. 90, p. 362 (1976). The study offers a devastating picture of the quagmire built over the years around the notice of claim requirement.

[30] Gen. Mun. Law § 50–e(5).

[31] If a tolling provision extends the statute of limitations, such as for the plaintiff's infancy, it will also stretch the time for the court's discretionary grant of leave to file a late notice. Cohen v. Pearl River Union Free School Dist., 51 N.Y.2d 256, 434 N.Y.S.2d 138, 414 N.E.2d 639 (1980); see § 54. The statute of limitations applicable to a public authority may, however, be construed to be a "condition precedent" to the claim rather than just an ordinary statute of limitations—rendering it immune to any tolling. See § 34 for the difference. See, e.g., Savino v. Demiglia, 128 A.D.2d 858, 513 N.Y.S.2d 776 (2d Dep't 1987), substituted opinion on reargument, 133 A.D.2d 389, 519 N.Y.S.2d 384 (2d Dep't 1987) (NYSLD No. 332).

[32] Williams ex rel. Fowler v. Nassau County Medical Center, 6 N.Y.3d 531, 814 N.Y.S.2d 580, 847 N.E.2d 1154 (2006) (NYSLD No. 558).

[33] Of the few grounds accepted under prior law to excuse a late filing, infancy was the most successful. See Murray v. City of New York, 30 N.Y.2d 113, 331 N.Y.S.2d 9, 282 N.E.2d 103 (1972); Crume v. Clarence Central School Dist. No. 1, 43 A.D.2d 492, 353 N.Y.S.2d 579 (4th Dep't 1974).

theory."[34] Nonetheless, a medical provider's possession or creation of medical records, standing alone, will not establish that it had actual knowledge of a potential injury where the records do not indicate that the provider's employees inflicted any injury on the plaintiff.[35]

In Newcomb v. Middle Country Central School District,[36] the Court focused on whether the defendant would be substantially prejudiced in defending the matter by permitting service of a late notice of claim. Examining this factor, the Court held "that it is an abuse of discretion as a matter of law when . . . a court determines, in the absence of any record evidence to support such determination, that a respondent will be substantially prejudiced in its defense by a late notice of claim."[37] While the length of delay in serving the notice of claim and the lack of actual knowledge of the facts underlying the claim are relevant to whether the late notice substantially prejudiced the public corporation, such prejudice cannot simply be inferred from these facts. Furthermore, the Court ruled that "the burden initially rests on the petitioner to show that the late notice will not substantially prejudice the public corporation" by "present[ing] some evidence or plausible argument that supports a finding of no substantial prejudice."[38] If petitioner satisfies this burden, the public corporation must then rebut that proof with "a particularized evidentiary showing that the corporation will be substantially prejudiced if the late notice is allowed."[39]

Other relevant factors on a General Municipal Law section 50–e(5) application include the would-be plaintiff's death during the 90-day period and the disabilities of mental or physical incapacity. The court may also consider whether the plaintiff withheld service of a notice of claim in "justifiable reliance" on settlement negotiations and whether there was any excusable error in identifying precisely which public corporation was liable for the particular accident.[40] Under no circumstances should an attorney rely on settlement negotiations to the extent of letting the time for serving a notice of claim expire. If negotiations are pending, the attorney can serve the notice of claim accompanied by a polite letter advising that it is only a precaution. Even if the court ultimately buys the "settlement talks" argument and extends the time to serve a notice of claim, the lawyer may have lost much sleep in the interim.

"[T]he application for the extension may be made before or after the commencement of the action but not more than 1 year and 90 days after the cause of action accrued."[41] May the complaint itself, if it is served within 1 year and 90 days and contains all the information required in the notice of claim, serve in place of a notice of claim? It cannot; it has been held that leave to serve late must be made by a distinct application because its purpose is to jog the municipality into immediate investigative activity, an aim that

---

[34]   *Williams*, 6 N.Y.3d at 537, 814 N.Y.S.2d at 582; Wally G. ex rel. Yoselin T. v. New York City Health and Hospitals Corp., 27 N.Y.3d 672, 677, 37 N.Y.S.3d 30, 32, 57 N.E.3d 1067, 1069 (2016).

[35]   *Williams*, 6 N.Y.3d at 537, 814 N.Y.S.2d at 583.

[36]   Newcomb v. Middle Country Cent. School Dist., 28 N.Y.3d 455, 45 N.Y.S.3d 895, 68 N.E.3d 714 (2016).

[37]   *Newcomb*, 28 N.Y.3d at 460, 45 N.Y.S.3d at 897, 68 N.E.3d at 716.

[38]   *Newcomb*, 28 N.Y.3d at 466, 45 N.Y.S.3d at 901, 68 N.E.3d at 720.

[39]   *Newcomb*, 28 N.Y.3d at 467, 45 N.Y.S.3d at 901, 68 N.E.3d at 720.

[40]   See, e.g., Bender v. New York City Health & Hospitals Corp., 38 N.Y.2d 662, 382 N.Y.S.2d 18, 345 N.E.2d 561 (1976).

[41]   Pierson v. City of New York, 56 N.Y.2d 950, 453 N.Y.S.2d 615, 439 N.E.2d 331 (1982). The application can also be made within any applicable tolling period.

will not necessarily be implemented merely by including among the allegations of the complaint the elements that a notice of claim requires.[42]

General Municipal Law section 50–e(7) provides, in pertinent part, "[w]here the application is for leave to serve a late notice of claim, it shall be accompanied by a copy of the proposed notice of claim." In Grasso v. Nassau County,[43] the Second Department noted that where no proposed notice of claim is submitted with an application to serve a late notice of claim, that defect constitutes "sufficient justification by itself to deny the . . . motion." Lawyers making an application for leave to serve a late notice of claim should note this rule, which constitutes another mine in a dangerous field that can destroy any action against a municipal entity.

The municipality can raise the defect of late or otherwise defective service well into the case, sometimes even after the note of issue has been served.[44] The defendant municipality is not obliged to tell plaintiff that the notice of claim requirement has not been timely satisfied, even when there's a clear opportunity to do so when the defendant is advising the plaintiff of a different defect.[45] The problem can become particularly acute when the unwitting plaintiff serves a notice of claim beyond the 90 day time frame in General Municipal Law section 50–e(1). As many courts have held, the service of a late notice of claim without leave of court is a nullity.[46] The defect is often exposed by the municipal entity only after the time to request permission to serve a late notice of claim under General Municipal Law section 50–e(5) has expired. In exceedingly rare instances, however, a court will find circumstances egregious enough to estop a municipality from asserting a notice of claim omission.[47]

An application to serve a late notice of claim or to cure some other defect is made to the supreme or county court of the appropriate county.[48] Even if the action against the municipality has been brought in a federal court, an application for leave to serve a late notice must, under the explicit instruction of General Municipal Law section 50–e(7), be made to the supreme court or a county court in the New York State system.[49]

Some New York City Civil Court decisions have held this provision unconstitutional as a denial of equal protection insofar as it empowers the county courts upstate, but not the civil court in New York City, to entertain the application to permit late service. Disregarding the restriction for that reason, they hold that the civil court can itself

---

[42] Kellogg v. Office of Chief Medical Examiner of City of New York, 24 A.D.3d 376, 806 N.Y.S.2d 528 (1st Dep't 2005).

[43] Grasso v. Nassau County, 109 A.D.3d 579, 580–81, 970 N.Y.S.2d 608, 609–10 (2d Dep't 2013).

[44] See Scantlebury v. New York City Health and Hospitals Corp., 4 N.Y.3d 606, 797 N.Y.S.2d 394, 830 N.E.2d 292 (2005) (municipal defendant successfully raised defect in service of notice of claim approximately 2 1/2 years after action was commenced).

[45] Davis v. City of New York, 250 A.D.2d 368, 673 N.Y.S.2d 79 (1st Dep't 1998); Vandermast v. New York City Transit Authority, 23 Misc. 3d 1129(A), 889 N.Y.S.2d 508 (Sup. Ct., Kings County 2009), aff'd, 71 A.D.3d 1127, 896 N.Y.S.2d 910 (2d Dep't 2010) (SPR 215:4).

[46] See, e.g., Plaza ex rel. Rodriguez v. New York Health and Hospitals Corp. (Jacobi Medical Center), 97 A.D.3d 466, 949 N.Y.S.2d 25 (1st Dep't 2012), aff'd, 21 N.Y.3d 983, 970 N.Y.S.2d 923, 993 N.E.2d 409 (2013).

[47] Brown v. City of New York, 264 A.D.2d 493, 694 N.Y.S.2d 461 (2d Dep't 1999).

[48] Gen. Mun. Law § 50–e(7).

[49] Washington v. Borough of Manhattan Community College, 2016 WL 7410717 (S.D.N.Y. 2016); Woods v. New York City Dept. of Sanitation, 1999 WL 476305 (S.D.N.Y. 1999).

entertain the application.[50] Plaintiffs purporting to rely on such caselaw must consider that until the Court of Appeals definitively rules on this point, the plaintiff risks losing all by making the extension motion in the New York City Civil Court.

What form should the application for leave to serve a late notice of claim take? The application is likely to be made when no jurisdiction has yet been obtained over the would-be defendant. If that's the case, the papers bringing on the application, even if denominated a "motion," should be served in the same manner as a summons in order to assure that jurisdiction is acquired. The best procedural course is to bring the application on as a special proceeding.[51] That would secure the guidance of Article 4 of the CPLR, which includes a provision, CPLR 403(c), requiring that the initiatory papers in a special proceeding be served in the same manner as a summons.

If, however, an action has already been commenced against the municipal entity, the plaintiff is not precluded from thereafter making the application. General Municipal Law section 50–e(5) specifically provides that "[a]n application for leave to serve a late notice shall not be denied on the ground that it was made after commencement of an action against the public corporation." Assuming jurisdiction over the municipal entity has already been obtained, the application to serve a late notice of claim can be made as a motion in the pending action or even as a cross-motion in response to a motion to dismiss for failure to serve a timely notice of claim.[52]

If time is tight on the statute of limitations against a municipal entity, it may be advisable to simply commence the action and on the same day, move by order to show cause to serve a late notice of claim. This will also require a subsequent amendment of the complaint to plead compliance with the notice of claim requirements as mandated by General Municipal Law section 50–i(1)(b). This avoids the situation in which the plaintiff is granted leave to serve a late notice of claim but then must scramble to commence the action within the statute of limitations.

Public Authorities

A party seeking leave to serve a late notice of claim will always experience uneasy moments. While the standards governing a motion to serve a late notice of claim are clearly more liberal under the present section 50–e(5) than they were before (although, as already noted, not as liberal as some hoped), this generosity is restricted to cases in which the defendant is a municipal corporation or other entity governed by section 50–e. The standards in General Municipal Law section 50–e(5) do not apply, for example, to a notice of claim requirement "with respect to the state or a state agency," such as the Port Authority, where the notice requirement is "jurisdictional."[53]

When planning to bring suit against a public authority, it is imperative to check with that authority's applicable notice of claim statute. One way to do this is to insert

---

[50] See, e.g., Sommerfield v. Office of the Comptroller, 25 Misc. 3d 1240(A), 906 N.Y.S.2d 783 (N.Y. City Civ. Ct. 2009); Arvelo ex rel. Arvelo v. City of New York, 182 Misc. 2d 101, 695 N.Y.S.2d 653 (N.Y. City Civ. Ct. 1999) (SPR 94:3–4).

[51] Lewin v. County of Suffolk, 239 A.D.2d 345, 657 N.Y.S.2d 734 (2d Dep't 1997), the court suggests that the special proceeding is the only proper vehicle to obtain jurisdiction and thus a motion would be improper. The court in *Lewin* did treat the motion as a special proceeding, however, as permitted under CPLR 103(c).

[52] See Grasso v. Nassau County, 109 A.D.3d 579, 970 N.Y.S.2d 608 (2d Dep't 2013).

[53] See Belpasso v. Port Authority of New York and New Jersey, 103 A.D.3d 562, 959 N.Y.S.2d 442 (1st Dep't 2013).

the name of the public authority into a legal research database, such as Westlaw, to see if any opinions from cases against that entity discuss notice of claim provisions. For actions against a public authority or public benefit corporation, section 2980 of the Public Authorities Law, enacted in 1990, does adopt General Municipal Law section 50–e for uniform use in wrongful death actions. In other categories of action, like personal injury, whether section 50–e applies depends on the statute governing the particular authority.[54]

Deep in the bowels of the Unconsolidated Laws, where nary a plaintiff's lawyer is known to wander, lurk notice of claim provisions governing claims against the Port Authority of New York and New Jersey.[55] In New York City Asbestos Litigation,[56] plaintiff and his wife served a "Notice of Claim for Personal Injury from Asbestos" on the Port Authority. It was undisputed that plaintiffs' initial suit against the Port Authority was premature and could be treated as a nullity because it ran afoul of section 7107 of the Unconsolidated Laws, which requires that 60 days pass between the notice of claim and the commencement of suit. After plaintiff died, his widow became the administratrix of plaintiff's estate and sought to join the Port Authority in an action asserting claims for personal injury and wrongful death. She did not, however, serve a new notice of claim. The Court of Appeals held that plaintiff's death did not require service of a new notice of claim and that the wrongful death action could go forward, essentially because the requirements of the notice of claim provisions in the Unconsolidated Laws "were sufficiently met" in the notice previously served.[57]

The applicable notice of claim provision in C.S.A. Contracting Corp. v. New York City School Const. Authority[58] was contained in the belly of the Public Authorities Law, another infamous source of confusion that has divested many plaintiffs of their claims. The provision, section 1744(2), requires that a notice of claim in contract cases (among others) be served "within three months after the accrual." "Accrual" in this instance was construed to be the time the plaintiff contractor finished the work. The 3-month period was held to run from then, even though there was not even the hint of a dispute between the parties at that time, and the service in C.S.A. was held too late.

C.S.A. is a perplexing decision. If there is no dispute, how can one even assume that the plaintiff has retained a lawyer? In situations like this, plaintiffs at the outset are usually just contractors, and it will rarely occur to them to seek out a lawyer unless and until the entity for which the work was performed has refused to pay. By that time, under the C.S.A. decision, the 3-month period would likely have already expired, causing a plaintiff to forfeit its claim before it even knew it had one. The C.S.A. case seems to

---

[54]   See Chapter 804 of the Laws of 1990, which enacts a set of uniform provisions governing public authorities in wrongful death actions, Pub. Auth. Law §§ 2980–2982, but continues to retain separate provisions for other categories. Some public authorities have adopted § 50–e, but not all have, so it remains imperative to check out each authority's applicable statute individually. This is true of the notice of claim as well as the statute of limitations itself, which is the subject of the next chapter.

[55]   See Unconsol. Laws §§ 7107, 7108.

[56]   In re New York City Asbestos Litigation, 24 N.Y.3d 275, 998 N.Y.S.2d 150, 22 N.E.3d 1018 (2014).

[57]   The *New York City Asbestos Litigation* decision will have impact in cases in which a notice of claim must be served pursuant to the General Municipal Law. See Mingone v. State, 100 A.D.2d 897, 898, 474 N.Y.S.2d 557, 560 (2d Dep't 1984) (notice of claim relating to an action to recover damages for the personal injuries sustained by the decedent, which was timely served on the county during her lifetime, was sufficient to provide notice of the wrongful death action).

[58]   C.S.A. Contracting Corp. v. New York City School Const. Authority, 5 N.Y.3d 189, 800 N.Y.S.2d 123, 833 N.E.2d 266 (2005) (NYSLD No. 550).

encourage plaintiffs' lawyers in all doubtful cases—and doubt is not hard to come by in disputes involving public authorities, especially in contract cases—to make it a standing practice to serve a notice of claim immediately upon the client's completion of the work.

Employees of Municipal Entities

An employee of the municipality may also, of course, be cast in liability for an unintentional tort that the employee committed while on municipal business. This poses the question of whether and when the municipality must indemnify the employee,[59] which poses in turn the question: when do notice of claim and like defects in an action against a municipality also bar the claim against the employee? When the indemnification obligation exists, a failure to serve a notice of claim on the municipality will ordinarily let the employee off the hook too.[60] But what if the employee is driving her own car while on the municipality's business, and has her own insurance policy, and may therefore not need indemnification from the municipality? The indication is that the case can proceed against the individual even though the municipality may now be out of the picture because it was not served with a notice of claim.[61]

Although the notice of claim is the foremost illustration of a condition precedent to suit—and has preoccupied this section and accounted for its length—there are some others. In a few rare instances, for example, such as an action against a person judicially declared to be incompetent, leave to sue the appointed guardian must be secured from the court in advance.[62] This is true also of an action against a receiver. It has been held, however, that the failure to obtain such advance permission is not jurisdictional and can therefore be cured with a nunc pro tunc order after the action has been commenced.[63]

---

[59]   See § 50–b of the General Municipal Law, for example, governing communities outside New York City. The statute requires that the employee be "saved harmless" as long as she is shown to be "acting in the discharge of his duties and within the scope of his employment."

[60]   See the note in SPR 83:3.

[61]   See Schmidt v. Board of Co-op. Educational Services of Nassau County, 253 A.D.2d 433, 676 N.Y.S.2d 623 (2d Dep't 1998) (SPR 83:3).

[62]   Depalois v. Pellegrino, 16 Misc. 3d 1133(A), 851 N.Y.S.2d 57 (N.Y. City Civ. Ct. 2007).

[63]   Copeland v. Salomon, 56 N.Y.2d 222, 451 N.Y.S.2d 682, 436 N.E.2d 1284 (1982) (receiver).

Chapter 3

THE STATUTE OF LIMITATIONS

Analysis

A.   Introductory
B.   The Applicable Periods
C.   Altering the Period
D.   Accrual
E.   Interposition
F.   Extensions and Tolls
G.   Foreign Claims

A.   INTRODUCTORY

Table of Sections

§ 33.   Statute of Limitations, Generally
§ 34.   Theory, "Suspension of Remedy" Reckoning

§ 33.   Statute of Limitations, Generally

"At common law there was no fixed time for the bringing of an action. Personal actions were merely confined to the joint lifetimes of the parties. The Statute of Limitations was enacted to afford protection to defendants against defending stale claims after a reasonable period of time had elapsed during which a person of ordinary diligence would bring an action. The statutes embody an important policy of giving repose to human affairs."[1]

The periods enacted are arbitrary; they represent what the legislature deems a sufficient period in a particular kind of case. There are explicit provisions prescribing how time periods are to be computed, but many of them are in the General Construction Law.[2]

Although the statute of limitations is generally deemed "procedural," there is little else in the law that can destroy a case so quickly, and from the defendant's point of view, so conveniently. What better gift for a defendant than a victory without even having to address the merits? The impact is in a real sense "substantive" and the plaintiff's lawyer should abandon all other pursuits when a case first comes to the office and determine, by the most conservative estimates, the latest possible day for commencing an action. A notation should then be made on that day in a long-term diary, and an additional warning notation should be made—that the last day is coming up—a week earlier, a

---

[1]   Flanagan v. Mount Eden General Hospital, 24 N.Y.2d 427, 429, 301 N.Y.S.2d 23, 25, 248 N.E.2d 871, 872 (1969).

[2]   See §§ 20, 24, 25, and 25–a of the Gen. Constr. Law. See also § 34 and more particularly § 202 on the service of papers generally.

month earlier, and several months earlier: 6 or 8 months earlier, we think, at least with respect to claims having a statute of limitations measured in years.

A recurring theme in this book is that as a general rule it is wise to commence actions, if at all possible, with at least 6 or 8 months to spare on the statute of limitations. The reason is that things can happen during the early stages of a case, often unexpectedly, with or without fault on the lawyer's part, that can lead to the dismissal of an action without reaching the merits. When one of these things does occur, like a jurisdictional objection based on something as paltry as a technical defect in the summons, it is nice to know that the time is still open for a new action. It can probably be shown by facts and figures that the lawyer who has made it a habit to leave time under the statute of limitations for a new action will enjoy full sleep cycles and also end up with a longer life expectancy on the actuarial charts.[3] We have devoted a special section, 231A, entitled "Leave Time for Trouble," demonstrating how an unanticipated contingency that brings about a mild inconvenience at worst when time for trouble has been reserved can impose capital punishment when it has not. We urge all readers, especially the infrequent litigator, to peruse that section carefully.

The reason that the statute of limitations is so uncompromising and so violent is not hard to trace. CPLR 2004 gives the courts broad discretion to extend periods of time contained in the CPLR for doing a myriad of things, "[e]xcept where otherwise expressly prescribed by law." The statute of limitations is one of those express exceptions. CPLR 201 provides that "[n]o court shall extend the time limited by law for the commencement of an action."[4] The result is that although it is subject to a variety of statutory tolls and extensions, to be met later, the statute of limitations is not subject to a discretionary judicial extension of time no matter how compelling the reason for the delay may be.

Calculating the statute of limitations should not be thought of as a single issue, but rather a determination on four separate matters. A mistake on any one can lead to disaster for the plaintiff and concomitant celebration for the defendant. The first issue is the time period that governs the particular claim.[5] The second issue is when the claim accrues for statute of limitations purposes, which is usually the moment of injury in a personal injury action, or the date of breach in a contract claim.[6] The third issue is whether the relevant time period may be subject to extensions, often referred to as tolling provisions.[7] Finally, the fourth issue is the timely interposition of the claim within the relevant limitations period.[8] That important act is accomplished through the timely filing of the initiatory papers (summons and notice, summons and complaint, or petition) under CPLR 304, followed by timely service of process. These critical matters are addressed in detail in the sections that follow.

---

[3] Attempts at commencement on the last day of the statute of limitations are probably the principal cause of high blood pressure among litigation lawyers.

[4] Another major exception is the time in which to serve and file a notice of appeal. See § 533; see also § 6.

[5] See § 35.

[6] See §§ 40 to 41.

[7] See §§ 50 to 55.

[8] See §§ 45 to 49.

§ 34.   Theory; "Suspension of Remedy" Reckoning

The theory of the statute of limitations generally followed in New York is that the passing of the applicable period does not wipe out the substantive right; it merely suspends the remedy.[9] But the application of the statute of limitations usually dismisses the action as permanently as a final judgment on the merits, at least insofar as further suit in New York is concerned. Clients told that they've lost only their remedy, not their right, have not been known to embrace their attorneys in tearful relief.

One of the practical consequences of the above theory is that it makes the statute of limitations an affirmative defense to be pleaded and proved by the defendant. The statute of limitations must be raised either by a pre-answer motion to dismiss or as a defense in the answer;[10] a defendant who does neither waives it.[11]

Most of the periods of limitation supplied by New York law, in or out of the CPLR, are of this suspend-the-remedy type. Occasionally, one meets the other kind, often referred to as a "condition precedent," in which the passing of the stipulated period abolishes the underlying right. It is seldom a happy meeting for the plaintiff, appearing more often than not when a foreign cause of action is involved, but a few survive under New York law, too.[12] Probably the most common criterion applied by the courts when they conclude that a time period is of the condition precedent kind is where a cause of action unknown to the common law is created by statute and a time period is included in the very statute that creates the claim.[13] Paradoxically, the quintessential example of that standard—the wrongful death cause of action—has a statute of limitations[14] that has been construed to be of the ordinary suspend-the-remedy kind.[15]

In the exceptional instance of the abolish-the-right kind of period, i.e., a condition precedent, the complaint must plead and the plaintiff has the burden of proving that the claim was brought on time. A condition precedent is deemed a substantive part of the plaintiff's cause of action. In the more usual case of the statute of limitations, in which the burden of raising the timeliness issue is on the defendant, the plaintiff need not even refer to the time element in the complaint.[16] The most significant consequence of the condition precedent category of time period is that it is not subject to the tolling provisions.[17] Applied to an ordinary statute of limitations, a tolling provision operates to extend the period.[18]

---

[9]   Faison v. Lewis, 25 N.Y.3d 220, 233, 10 N.Y.S.3d 185, 194, 32 N.E.3d 400, 409 (2015); Hulbert v. Clark, 128 N.Y. 295, 28 N.E. 638 (1891).

[10]   CPLR 3211(a)(5); CPLR 3018(b); see Scholastic Inc. v. Pace Plumbing Corp., 129 A.D.3d 75, 76, 78, 8 N.Y.S.3d 143, 145, 146 (1st Dep't 2015) (addressing the particularity required under CPLR 3013 when pleading a statute of limitations defense); § 208.

[11]   CPLR 3211(e).

[12]   See, e.g., Savino v. Demiglia, 128 A.D.2d 858, 513 N.Y.S.2d 776 (2d Dep't 1987), substituted opinion on reargument, 133 A.D.2d 389, 519 N.Y.S.2d 384 (2d Dep't 1987) (involving a statute of limitations against a public authority).

[13]   See, e.g., Romano v. Romano, 19 N.Y.2d 444, 280 N.Y.S.2d 570, 227 N.E.2d 389 (1967) (annulment action).

[14]   Two years under EPTL 5–4.1.

[15]   Sharrow v. Inland Lines, 214 N.Y. 101, 108 N.E. 217 (1915).

[16]   See *Romano,* 19 N.Y.2d at 447, 280 N.Y.S.2d at 572–73, 227 N.E.2d at 391.

[17]   See, e.g., McMurray v. New York State Div. of Housing and Community Renewal, 72 N.Y.2d 1022, 1024, 534 N.Y.S.2d 924, 531 N.E.2d 645, 646 (1988).

[18]   For treatment of New York's tolling provisions, see §§ 50 et seq.

When the United States brings a claim, it is subject to neither the statute of limitations nor the doctrine of laches except to the extent that it agrees to be.[19] When the State of New York sues, however, a statute provides that it is just as subject to these defenses as a private litigant.[20]

In reckoning a statute of limitations, the day of accrual is excluded and the count begins the next day.[21] With a limitation period measured in years, this makes the event's anniversary date in the last year the last day for the commencement of the action.[22] Thus, if an accident occurs on January 3, 2017, the last day on which to bring a personal injury action, which is subject to a 3-year period, is January 3, 2020.[23]

When the last day of the period falls on a Saturday, Sunday, or public holiday, the time for commencing the action is extended to "the next succeeding business day."[24] In our adversary system, the plaintiff's lawyer who plays the statute of limitations that close is asking for trouble, and the defendant's lawyer owes it to her client to take advantage of the plaintiff's tardiness.

B. THE APPLICABLE PERIODS

Table of Sections

§ 35.   The Various Time Periods
§ 36.   Equity Actions; Laches
§ 37.   Multiple Theories

§ 35.   The Various Time Periods

The various time periods are generally keyed to the kind of claim being brought. Most are in the CPLR on lists contained in CPLR 211 through CPLR 217–a; some are in other laws. It is not necessary to repeat all of the lists here, but it is worthwhile to stress certain items.

CPLR 211: 20-year period

CPLR 211 lists the claims subject to a 20-year period, the longest period supplied by the CPLR. The major one here is the action on an already rendered money judgment. Because of the language of CPLR 211(b), the passing of the 20-year period has been held to create a conclusive presumption of payment and an absolute bar to suit. This means that it is construed to be of the abolish-the-right (or "condition precedent") rather than

---

[19]   U.S. v. Summerlin, 1940–2 C.B. 435, 310 U.S. 414, 60 S. Ct. 1019, 84 L. Ed. 1283 (1940); In re Feinberg's Estate, 18 N.Y.2d 499, 277 N.Y.S.2d 249, 223 N.E.2d 780 (1966); U.S. v. Lyons, 292 A.D.2d 683, 740 N.Y.S.2d 145 (3d Dep't 2002); see 28 U.S.C.A. § 2415, and the discussion in Cracco v. Cox, 66 A.D.2d 447, 414 N.Y.S.2d 404 (4th Dep't 1979). Laches is discussed in § 36.

[20]   CPLR 201; State v. Waverly Central School Dist., 28 A.D.2d 628, 280 N.Y.S.2d 505 (3d Dep't 1967).

[21]   See Gen. Constr. Law § 20, which prescribes how time periods are counted. See also § 202 on the service of papers generally.

[22]   See Evans v. Hawker-Siddeley Aviation, Ltd., 482 F. Supp. 547 (S.D.N.Y. 1979).

[23]   See Marino v. Proch, 258 A.D.2d 628, 685 N.Y.S.2d 761 (2d Dep't 1999).

[24]   Gen. Constr. Law § 25–a. For a list of public holidays that New York recognizes, see Gen. Constr. Law § 24.

the more common suspend-the-remedy kind,[1] a situation the legislature has seen fit to preserve.[2]

CPLR 212: 10-year period

The major claim subject to the 10-year period of CPLR 212 is the one based on 10 years of possession of realty, commonly known as a claim of adverse possession.[3]

CPLR 213: 6-year period

The claims subject to a 6-year period are listed in CPLR 213. The most notable of these is the claim in contract, express or implied.[4] It includes a cause of action for indemnification, whether the obligation to indemnify arises expressly or by operation of law. Thus, where P sues D for personal injuries based on negligence (or any other theory) at the very last moment of the 3-year statute of limitations and D, after the negligence period has expired, seeks to implead X for indemnification or contribution on the ground that X's conduct is responsible to some degree for the tort, the impleader claim is timely. This is because D's claim against X sounds in indemnity, i.e. contract, rather than in negligence or whatever other theory (e.g., warranty, strict products liability, etc.) may underlie P's main claim.[5]

In installment-contract situations, the 6-year period is deemed to commence separately on each installment as it accrues.[6] The 6-year statute of limitations in a mortgage foreclosure action begins to run from the due date for each unpaid installment, but if the debt has been accelerated by a demand or commencement of an action, the entire sum becomes due and the statute of limitations begins to run on the entire mortgage.[7]

An action to enforce a distributive award in a matrimonial action is governed by a 6-year statute of limitations.[8]

Sales contracts subject to the Uniform Commercial Code, which covers the sale of nearly everything except real property and services,[9] are governed by the 4-year period in UCC section 2–725, to which the CPLR defers.[10] The breach of warranty in conjunction with the sale of a product (including a personal injury claim so predicated) is a common contract category met under the UCC and is therefore governed by this 4-year provision. The sale of real property or services continues to be subject to the CPLR 6-year period.

---

[1] See § 34.

[2] 5th Rep. Leg. Doc. No. 15, p. 50 (1961). Because of supervening federal law, it has been held that a judgment on a student loan can be collected even after 20 years. See New York State Higher Educ. Services Corp. v. Fabrizio, 73 A.D.3d 158, 900 N.Y.S.2d 159, 55 A.L.R. Fed. 2d 653 (3d Dep't 2010) (holding that federal statute removing statutes of limitation as to collection of student loans preempted CPLR 211(b)).

[3] CPLR 212(a). This is a change from the 15-year period previously applicable. Civ. Prac. Act. § 34 (repealed 1963).

[4] CPLR 213(2).

[5] Emil v. James Felt & Co., Inc., 45 A.D.2d 677, 356 N.Y.S.2d 303 (1st Dep't 1974). This matter is elaborated in § 162.

[6] See Vigilant Ins. Co. of America v. Housing Authority of City of El Paso, Tex., 87 N.Y.2d 36, 45, 637 N.Y.S.2d 342, 347, 660 N.E.2d 1121, 1126 (1995).

[7] See, e.g., Goldman Sachs Mortg. Co. v. Mares, 135 A.D.3d 1121, 23 N.Y.S.3d 444 (3d Dep't 2016).

[8] Kraus v. Kraus, 131 A.D.3d 94, 14 N.Y.S.3d 55 (2d Dep't 2015) (citing to CPLR 213(1) and (2)).

[9] N.Y. UCC §§ 2–102, 2–105.

[10] CPLR 213(2).

In some cases, it may be difficult to determine the category of action. It has been held that if services is the principal item sold and a chattel that is part of the sale is merely incidental, the 6-year period governs, as in the sale of funeral services that include a casket.[11] The breach of a warranty contained in the lease of a chattel, as opposed to its sale, has been given the 6-year rather than the 4-year period.[12]

The residual or "catch-all" period of 6 years is contained in CPLR 213(1), which applies to "an action for which no limitation is specifically prescribed by law." In Capitol Records, LLC v. Harrison Greenwich, LLC, the court ruled on what it deemed to be "an issue of first impression: the applicable statute of limitations for a New York common law copyright infringement claim."[13] The court first concluded that the CPLR governs the statute of limitations for such claims and not the federal statute governing claims under the Federal Copyright Act, which is 3 years.[14] In that the CPLR does not specifically prescribe a limitations period for common law copyright infringement, the court held that the 6-year limitations period in CPLR 213(1) applies. This provision also applies in equity actions, which are treated in the next section.

CPLR 214: 3-year period

The 3-year claims are in CPLR 214. They are in the main the unintentional torts. The personal injury claim, whether predicated on negligence or the more recent "strict tort liability" or "strict products liability" theory, is here in CPLR 214(5). This 3-year period is also the one applicable to a federal civil rights action brought in either a federal or state court in New York under the often invoked 42 U.S.C. section 1983.[15]

A 3-year period also governs a claim for an "injury to property,"[16] which covers not only property damage in a negligence case but also a wide range of other harms—

---

[11]   Joseph P. Suchy, Inc. v. Stuerzel, 82 Misc. 2d 40, 370 N.Y.S.2d 316, 17 U.C.C. Rep. Serv. 453 (App. Term, 1st Dep't 1975); see also Gibraltar Management Co., Inc. v. Grand Entrance Gates, Ltd., 46 A.D.3d 747, 848 N.Y.S.2d 684 (2d Dep't 2007) (applying the 6-year statute of limitations, finding the contract was predominantly for the performance of labor and for construction services rather than the materials involved in the construction).

[12]   Owens v. Patent Scaffolding Co., Division of Harsco Corp., 50 A.D.2d 866, 376 N.Y.S.2d 948, 18 U.C.C. Rep. Serv. 699 (2d Dep't 1975).

[13]   Capitol Records, LLC v. Harrison Greenwich, LLC, 44 Misc. 3d 428, 429, 986 N.Y.S.2d 837, 838 (Sup. Ct., New York County 2014).

[14]   See 17 U.S.C.A. § 507(b).

[15]   Wilson v. Garcia, 471 U.S. 261, 105 S. Ct. 1938, 85 L. Ed. 2d 254 (1985). Having been supplied with no time period by federal law, a § 1983 claim borrows the period applicable to the most nearly analogous state cause of action. The *Wilson* case finds the personal injury claim to be the most analogous. See Commentary C4–41 on Fed. R. Civ. P. Rule 4 in 28 U.S.C.A. The period of 1 year and 90 days applicable to tort claims against municipalities under Gen. Mun. Law § 50–i (discussed further on in this section) is superseded by this 3-year period in § 1983 cases, and the 90-day notice of claim requirement of Gen. Mun. Law § 50–e, generally applicable to tort claims against municipalities (see § 32), does not apply in a § 1983 case. See Felder v. Casey, 487 U.S. 131, 108 S. Ct. 2302, 101 L. Ed. 2d 123 (1988), in effect overruling 423 South Salina Street, Inc. v. City of Syracuse, 68 N.Y.2d 474, 510 N.Y.S.2d 507, 503 N.E.2d 63 (1986), cert. den. 481 U.S. 1008, 107 S.Ct. 1880, 95 L.Ed.2d 488 (1987), which had ruled the other way.

[16]   CPLR 214(4).

including conversion—under the broad definition of "injury to property" used in New York practice.[17] Replevin also gets a 3-year period under CPLR 214(3).[18]

Another frequently invoked 3-year period is contained in CPLR 214(2) governing "an action to recover upon a liability, penalty or forfeiture created or imposed by statute."[19] Thus, when a cause of action unknown to the common law is created by statute and a specific period is not enacted to accompany it, CPLR 214(2) governs and the period is 3 years. Judiciary Law section 487 exposes an attorney who "[i]s guilty of any deceit or collusion, or consents to any deceit or collusion, with intent to deceive the court or any party" to criminal liability and treble damages in a civil action. In Melcher v. Greenberg Traurig, LLP,[20] the Court of Appeals examined the history of the Judiciary Law provision and concluded that a cause of action for attorney deceit existed as part of New York's common law before the first New York statute governing attorney deceit was enacted in 1787. Although "[t]he 1787 statute enhanced the penalties for attorney deceit by adding an award for treble damages," the cause of action previously existed under New York's common law. In that an action to recover for attorney deceit was not "created or imposed by" Judiciary Law section 487, as is required by the language in CPLR 214(2), an action under the section is subject to the 6-year statute of limitations in CPLR 213(1) because it is "an action for which no limitation is specifically prescribed by law . . . ."[21]

A malpractice claim, which is in essence a claim of negligence against a professional, gets 3 years in nonmedical cases, such as against lawyers, accountants, and architects.[22] This provision has had an interesting history. For a while, the malpractice period against nonmedical professionals had been stretched to 6 years under a Court of Appeals decision, Santulli v. Englert, Reilly & McHugh, P.C.,[23] which held that because there is also a contractual relationship between the parties in these situations, the plaintiff has the option of relying on the 6-year period in CPLR 213(2) as an alternative. An amendment of CPLR 214(6) that took effect in 1996 overruled *Santulli* and restored the 3 years exclusively, "regardless of whether the underlying theory is based in contract or tort."[24]

---

[17]   See Sporn v. MCA Records, Inc., 58 N.Y.2d 482, 462 N.Y.S.2d 413, 448 N.E.2d 1324 (1983). Gen. Constr. Law § 25–b defines an injury to property as any "actionable act, whereby the estate of another is lessened, other than a personal injury, or the breach of a contract." Any case involving a property loss and not otherwise supplied with a time period is therefore subject to the 3-year period of CPLR 214(4).

[18]   See Solomon R. Guggenheim Foundation v. Lubell, 77 N.Y.2d 311, 567 N.Y.S.2d 623, 569 N.E.2d 426 (1991).

[19]   CPLR 214(2). This had been a 6-year period under § 48(2) of the old Civil Practice Act but was reduced to 3 with the adoption of the CPLR in order to coordinate it with the 3 years applicable to personal injury and property damage claims predicated on negligence, which often involve an additional count based on the breach of a statutory duty.

[20]   Melcher v. Greenberg Traurig, LLP, 23 N.Y.3d 10, 988 N.Y.S.2d 101, 11 N.E.3d 174 (2014) (NYSLD No. 652).

[21]   *Melcher*, 23 N.Y.3d at 15, 988 N.Y.S.2d at 104, 11 N.E.3d at 177.

[22]   CPLR 214(6).

[23]   Santulli v. Englert, Reilly & McHugh, P.C., 78 N.Y.2d 700, 579 N.Y.S.2d 324, 586 N.E.2d 1014 (1992).

[24]   See SPR 48:2. The 3-year period may sometimes be extended under a kind of "continuous representation" theory analogous to, and adopted from, the continuous treatment theory applicable in medical malpractice cases. See § 42. CPLR 214–d governs in actions against, among others, architects, engineers, and land surveyors. The statute imposes additional burdens on plaintiffs in these actions where the work was performed 10 years prior to commencement of the action. See the discussion in SPR 51:2.

In Kliment v. McKinsey & Co.,[25] the Court of Appeals ruled that the amendment applies—and makes the 3-year period of CPLR 214(6) exclusive—even when the defendant is charged with violating an explicit term in an express contract. The Court stressed, however, that the provision at issue in the architectural contract, which required that plans, drawings, and specifications comply with applicable building codes, was "not inconsistent with an architect's ordinary professional obligations."[26] Query whether the breach of a contractual term that required performance beyond that encompassed by the ordinary standard of care of a professional would be subject to a 6-year statute of limitations?

Since "malpractice" is basically only a claim of negligence against a professional, only those who qualify as "professionals" are the beneficiaries of the amendment to CPLR 241(6). Those who do not remain subject to the 6-year period in CPLR 213(2) if the claim is based on breach of contract. This result has proved painful to insurance brokers and agents, among others, whose claim to the professional status that would enable them to rely on the 3-year period of CPLR 214(6) was rejected by the Court of Appeals in Chase Scientific Research, Inc. v. NIA Group, Inc.[27] The Court in *Chase* reviewed the criteria that make an individual a "professional"—and entitled to rely on the 3-year period of CPLR 214(6)—and concluded that the licensing requirement imposed on insurance agents and brokers doesn't rise to the level of education and training exacted of professionals like lawyers, architects, accountants, engineers, etc.[28] Hence, insurance agents and brokers may not invoke CPLR 214(6) and are therefore subject to the 6-year period of CPLR 213(2) for a breach of contract claim.

On the subject of legal malpractice specifically, when the claim is based on the lawyer's failure to obtain a recovery for the client against a third-party, it has been held that the client is entitled, as damages, to only that which could have actually been recovered in an action against the third-party.[29] This requires consideration of the third-party's insurance, solvency, etc.,[30] in addition to the fact that a New York judgment has a 20-year life span under CPLR 211(b) "and that, even if the judgment is not collectible at the time of its entry, it may become collectible at any time during that life span."[31]

Negligent hiring and negligent supervision claims often accompany claims for malpractice. The statute of limitations applicable to these causes of action is 3 years.[32]

---

[25] Kliment v. McKinsey & Co., Inc., 3 N.Y.3d 538, 788 N.Y.S.2d 648, 821 N.E.2d 952 (2004) (NYSLD No. 542).

[26] *R.M. Kliment*, 3 N.Y.3d at 542, 788 N.Y.S.2d at 651, 821 N.E.2d at 955.

[27] Chase Scientific Research, Inc. v. NIA Group, Inc., 96 N.Y.2d 20, 725 N.Y.S.2d 592, 749 N.E.2d 161 (2001).

[28] See the lead note in NYSLD No. 498. In an odd twist that sometimes occurs when the "accrual" feature of the statute of limitations is integrated with the applicable period itself, a plaintiff's claim may sometimes be too late *because* it gets the 6 years in CPLR 213(2) rather than the 3 in CPLR 214(6). This is attributable to the "continuous treatment" theory applicable to malpractice claims against professionals, discussed in § 42 and more extensively in SPR 104:4.

[29] McKenna v. Forsyth & Forsyth, 280 A.D.2d 79, 720 N.Y.S.2d 654 (4th Dep't 2001) (SPR 109:2).

[30] The *McKenna* court adds that the burden is on the client to show how much of a recovery he could have had.

[31] Lindenman v. Kreitzer, 7 A.D.3d 30, 35, 775 N.Y.S.2d 4, 9 (1st Dep't 2004). *Lindenman* disagrees with *McKenna* and holds that the burden of proving noncollectibility must be borne by defendant attorney, but only after plaintiff proves the value of the lost judgment.

[32] See Calamari v. Panos, 131 A.D.3d 1088, 1090, 16 N.Y.S.3d 824, 827 (2d Dep't 2015).

CPLR 214–a: 2 years and six months period

A malpractice category unto itself is that involving medical professionals. A claim for medical, dental, or podiatric malpractice gets only 2 1/2 years,[33] while the claim against all other professionals, as noted above, gets 3. This shorter period applies only to "medical" misconduct, however. While a hospital and nurse as well as a physician enjoy the shorter period for activities qualifying as "medical" treatment, they don't for other conduct constituting mere negligence, such as failing to supply competent personnel or to establish proper emergency room rules, where the usual 3-year period in CPLR 214 applies.[34] The services of a psychologist, while of course professional, have also been held to be beyond the "medical" category, making the 3-year rather than the 2 1/2-year period applicable.[35] Similarly, the 3-year statute of limitations in CPLR 214(6) applies to claims arising from the services of a chiropractor, where the treatment is "separate and apart from any other treatment provided by a licensed physician" and is not performed at the request of a physician.[36]

When P is injured through the fault of D's examining physician during the course of disclosure in a CPLR 3121(a) examination, P's claim is for medical malpractice, rather than ordinary negligence, and is hence governed by the 2 1/2-year period in CPLR 214–a.[37]

CPLR 215: 1 year period

The 1-year claims are in CPLR 215. The most significant here are the intentional torts, like assault, defamation, and the violation of the right of privacy.[38] 1 year is also the period in which to confirm an arbitration award into a judgment.[39]

CPLR 217: 4 month period

The proceeding under CPLR Article 78, which replaces the old writs of certiorari to review and mandamus, must be brought within 4 months from the time the determination becomes "final and binding" (certiorari) or a demand to perform a duty is refused (mandamus).[40] Article 78 also replaces the writ of prohibition, but since that writ is used mainly to test whether an officer or judge has jurisdiction, there is usually no time limitation on it.[41]

The 4-month period has also been held to apply to disputes involving the constitutionality of the assessment of real property, even if the gist of the attack is on the validity of the rate schedule that grounds the assessment—the kind of constitutional

---

[33] CPLR 214–a.

[34] Bleiler v. Bodnar, 65 N.Y.2d 65, 489 N.Y.S.2d 885, 479 N.E.2d 230 (1985).

[35] Karasek v. LaJoie, 92 N.Y.2d 171, 677 N.Y.S.2d 265, 699 N.E.2d 889 (1998).

[36] Perez v. Fitzgerald, 115 A.D.3d 177, 981 N.Y.S.2d 5 (1st Dep't 2014) (SPR 266:2).

[37] Bazakos v. Lewis, 12 N.Y.3d 631, 883 N.Y.S.2d 785, 911 N.E.2d 847 (2009) (reversing ruling of appellate division that claim was for ordinary negligence governed by 3-year period in CPLR 214(5)). It's an unusual situation in which a physician sued for personal injury is relieved to know the charge against him is medical malpractice!

[38] CPLR 215(3).

[39] CPLR 215(5); see CPLR 7510, 7514(a); § 601 (Practitioner's Edition). The 1-year period runs from the "delivery" of the award.

[40] CPLR 217(1).

[41] See § 566.

issue that in other contexts might earn a longer period by being brought in the form of a declaratory judgment.[42]

Statutes of Limitations Periods Outside the CPLR

Some of the more important time periods supplied by statutes other than the CPLR are the 5-year period for divorce or separation on certain grounds[43] and the already mentioned 4-year period governing breaches of sales contracts (including the breach of warranty) under the UCC.[44] A 2-year period running from the date of death applies to a wrongful death claim.[45]

The periods applicable to claims against the State are in section 10 of the Court of Claims Act. These are shorter than the CPLR periods and, because of the doctrine of sovereign immunity, the failure to serve and file the claim within the time prescribed by the Court of Claims Act may, where the defense is properly interposed under Court of Claims Act section 11(c), deprive the court of jurisdiction.[46] In many actions, the time to serve and file a claim may be extended by the timely service of a notice of intention to file a claim. The periods can be expanded to CPLR length by the court on motion under section 10(6) of the Court of Claims Act upon consideration of six enumerated factors.[47] Similarly, a claimant who timely serves a notice of intention to file a claim but fails to timely serve or file a claim may move for permission to treat the notice of intention as a claim pursuant to section 10(8)(a) of the Court of Claims Act.

A tort action against a municipality must be brought within 1 year and 90 days under General Municipal Law section 50–i, which, as a statute of limitations, should not be confused with the 90-day notice of claim period of section 50–e, also applicable in such cases.[48] General Municipal Law section 50–i(1)(c) adopts a 2-year statute of limitations in wrongful death actions against a municipal entity, running from the date of the death. If a municipality is required to indemnify the employee responsible for the act that created the liability, as it is, for example, when the employee operates a municipal vehicle in the scope of employment,[49] the 1 year and 90 days statute of limitations also applies to an action against the employee. Furthermore, a condition precedent to the

---

[42]   See Press v. Monroe County, 50 N.Y.2d 695, 431 N.Y.S.2d 394, 409 N.E.2d 870 (1980), treated in the lead note in NYSLD No. 252. *Press* holds that the application of the shorter period is indispensable to the continuity of government, which depends on the tax collection process, but a federal court has held that if the claim is posed as a due process violation under the federal civil rights statute, 42 U.S.C.A. § 1983, a 3-year period applies and supersedes the 4-month period. Cloverleaf Realty of New York, Inc. v. Town of Wawayanda, 572 F.3d 93 (2d Cir. 2009). The problem aimed at in *Press* is not treated in the case, which is the subject of a two-part lead note in Issues 597 and 598 of the NYSLD.

[43]   See Dom. Rel. Law § 210. In Tuper v. Tuper, 98 A.D.3d 55, 946 N.Y.S.2d 719 (4th Dep't 2012) (SPR 251:4), the Fourth Department concluded that a cause of action under the new "irretrievable breakdown" ground for divorce contained in Dom. Rel. Law § 170(7), also known as the "no-fault" divorce ground, is subject to this 5-year limitations period.

[44]   N.Y. UCC § 2–725.

[45]   EPTL 5–4.1.

[46]   See Ct. of Claims Act § 10(6); Alston v. State, 97 N.Y.2d 159, 737 N.Y.S.2d 45, 762 N.E.2d 923 (2001).

[47]   Ct. of Claims Act § 10(6); see Malkan v. State, 145 A.D.3d 1601, 42 N.Y.S.3d 898 (4th Dep't 2016), leave to appeal denied, 29 N.Y.3d 907, 57 N.Y.S.3d 712, 80 N.E.3d 405 (2017) ("A determination by the Court of Claims to grant or deny a motion for permission to file a late . . . claim lies within the broad discretion of that court and should not be disturbed absent a clear abuse of that discretion"); L.F. O'Connell Associates, Inc. v. State, 176 Misc. 2d 697, 674 N.Y.S.2d 900 (Ct. Cl. 1998), noted in SPR 75:4.

[48]   For treatment of the notice of claim provisions in § 50–e, see § 32.

[49]   See Gen. Mun. Law § 50–b.

action against the municipal employee is that the 90-day notice of claim have been served on the municipality.[50]

Chapter 500 of the Laws of 2012, entitled the Uniform Notice of Claim Act, added CPLR 217–a to Article 2 in an attempt to bring some uniformity to the "patchwork" of laws governing the statute of limitations for claims against municipal entities. CPLR 217–a is helpful in that it provides notice to any plaintiff planning to sue a municipal entity that there are likely two significant obstacles that must be negotiated: (1) the notice of claim provisions in section 50–e of the General Municipal Law, and (2) the shortened statute of limitations in section 50–i of the General Municipal Law. The statute then attempts to adopt a minimum 1-year and 90 day statute of limitations for any action seeking damages for personal injuries or for injuries to real or personal property against a governmental entity to which a notice of claim provision applies. This minimum period applies "[n]otwithstanding any other provision of law to the contrary, and irrespective of whether the relevant statute is expressly amended by the uniform notice of claim act."[51] CPLR 217–a does not apply to claims for wrongful death, which are still governed by a 2-year statute of limitations,[52] and claims against the State of New York.[53]

Statute of Limitations on Derivative Claims

The statute of limitations on a derivative claim is the same time period as the statute of limitations on the main claim from which it derives.[54] The Second Department has ruled, however, that a husband's derivative claim for loss of services is subject to the 3-year statute of limitations in CPLR 214, even if the primary claim is for medical malpractice governed by the 2 1/2-year period in CPLR 214–a.[55] We are not aware of another instance in which a derivative claim is subject to a different statute of limitations than the primary claim. The derivative claim may not be entitled to the same tolling periods applicable to the main claim, such as the continuous treatment toll or infancy toll.[56]

§ 36. Equity Actions; Laches

There is no time period addressed to the "equity" action as such. It falls under the "catch-all" provision in CPLR 213(1) and gets 6 years as "an action for which no limitation is specifically prescribed by law." This 6-year period "applies in such equity actions as accounting,[1] injunction,[2] and reformation of contract.[3]

The substantive law rule that equity will not intercede unless the plaintiff has no adequate remedy at law has a limitations' counterpart, too. If the plaintiff does have an adequate legal remedy, but sues for equitable relief instead, the equitable claim, even if

---

[50]   See Fitzgerald v. Lyons, 39 A.D.2d 473, 336 N.Y.S.2d 940 (4th Dep't 1972); § 32.

[51]   CPLR 217–a.

[52]   See Gen. Mun. Law § 50–i(1)(c), discussed above.

[53]   See § 10 of the Ct. of Claims Act, discussed above.

[54]   See Maxson v. Delaware, L. & W.R. Co., 112 N.Y. 559, 563–564, 20 N.E. 544, 546 (1889).

[55]   See Chambers v. Mirkinson, 68 A.D.3d 702, 890 N.Y.S.2d 99 (2d Dep't 2009); Schrank v. Lederman, 52 A.D.3d 494, 860 N.Y.S.2d 556 (2d Dep't 2008).

[56]   See §§ 42, 54.

[1]   Schwartz v. Lois Associates, 149 A.D.2d 307, 539 N.Y.S.2d 360 (1st Dep't 1989).

[2]   Petnel v. American Tel. & Tel. Co., 280 A.D. 706, 117 N.Y.S.2d 294, 95 U.S.P.Q. 389 (3d Dep't 1952).

[3]   Hanover Fire Ins. Co. v. Morse Dry Dock & Repair Co., 270 N.Y. 86, 200 N.E. 589 (1936).

the court is disposed to entertain it under less rigid modern concepts, will be measured by the period of limitations applicable to the law claim, which is usually shorter. This made more of a difference under prior law when the residual (equity) period was 10 years.[4] When P sued for an accounting (equity), for example, in a case in which simple breach of contract (law) was found to be just as effective, the equity claim was held subject to the legal 6-year period.[5] Today, with the old residual of 10 now reduced to 6, the point in the cited example would be academic.

There is indeed a nonsequitur in this approach. Presumably, even today, equitable relief is entertainable only when no legal remedy is adequate, so that law's adequacy in a given situation would preclude the equitable claim altogether, and on that ground alone, avoid the problem of deciding which statute of limitations to apply. That the problem exists, and has been addressed in the cases, suggests that the courts today will entertain equitable relief in some cases even though there is an adequate remedy at law, while at the same time insisting that the period applicable to the law claim, at least when shorter, govern the equitable one. There is an internal contradiction in this. The lesson to the lawyer who would retain control of the time element is never to let the "law" period lapse in expectation of securing the longer "equitable" period.

If the legal alternative is inadequate, the plaintiff who sues in equity is not beholden to the law period. Suppose, for example, that P is a judgment creditor and that judgment debtor D has fraudulently transferred assets to frustrate collection of the judgment. P can disregard the transfers and just issue execution on the judgment, i.e., proceed at law. But it is recognized that such a procedure is impractical because the property sought stands in the name of others, a situation in which sheriffs will balk and further proceedings will be necessary. Thus, the plaintiff who seeks in equity to set aside the transfers is entitled to the equity period because the legal relief is inadequate.[6] But if P does seek legal relief, such as by a subsequent action for damages for fraud, the law period will apply.[7] The reason for this is that the inadequate-remedy-at-law rule has no converse: a plaintiff suing at law is not to be denied legal relief (nor is the equity period to be applied to the claim) merely because an equitable remedy happens to be available.

In those equity actions in which relief lies in the discretion of the court, such as an action for the specific performance of a contract or for an injunction, the doctrine of laches applies. It applies in addition to, but independent of, the statute of limitations.[8] The bringing of the action within the 6-year period of CPLR 213(1) is mandatory, but if the defendant can show on the facts that: (1) the plaintiff has been guilty of undue delay, and (2) the delay has been prejudicial (both showings are needed to support the defense of laches), the court can dismiss the action even though it was brought within the applicable statute of limitations.[9] Whether the delay was so unreasonable as to invoke the laches doctrine is a sui generis inquiry.[10]

---

[4]   Civ. Prac. Act. § 53 (repealed 1963).

[5]   Keys v. Leopold, 241 N.Y. 189, 149 N.E. 828 (1925).

[6]   Hearn 45 St. Corporation v. Jano, 283 N.Y. 139, 27 N.E.2d 814 (1940).

[7]   Nasaba Corporation v. Harfred Realty Corporation, 287 N.Y. 290, 39 N.E.2d 243 (1942).

[8]   Groesbeck v. Morgan, 206 N.Y. 385, 99 N.E. 1046 (1912); Richardson v. Vajiradhammapadip Temple, 24 A.D.3d 649, 807 N.Y.S.2d 392 (2d Dep't 2005).

[9]   In re Flamenbaum, 22 N.Y.3d 962, 978 N.Y.S.2d 708, 1 N.E.3d 782 (2013) (NYSLD No. 648) (defendant failed to establish affirmative defense of laches).

[10] Herrick v. Watters, 50 A.D.2d 627, 374 N.Y.S.2d 745 (3d Dep't 1975).

The foregoing shows "laches" in its traditional role, but the term is sometimes carelessly used today as shorthand to describe any situation, even within an otherwise timely action at law, in which a party is denied relief of some kind for having waited an unreasonably long time before seeking it.[11]

The doctrine of "laches may not be interposed as a defense against the State when acting in a governmental capacity to enforce a public right or protect a public interest."[12] Furthermore, the defense is not available against a claim of continuing wrong.[13]

The approach that holds an equity claim subject to the same statute of limitations that would govern an equally effectual law claim has an analogy in the declaratory judgment action. If declaratory judgment is the only effective remedy the plaintiff has, it will get the 6-year residual period of CPLR 213(1).[14] But if another adequate remedy is available, with a shorter period, the shorter period applies.[15]

§ 37. Multiple Theories

From but a single wrong a plaintiff may have many possible theories of recovery. The plaintiff should, as a rule, interpose all of them in her action. A common example today is the personal injury caused by a defective product. It may give rise to several theories of recovery, including: (1) negligence, which gets a 3-year period under the "personal injury" provision of CPLR 214(5); (2) "strict products liability,"[1] which is also a tort and is governed by the same provision—and, as with negligence, the period starts to run from the injury;[2] and (3) breach of warranty, which gets a 4-year period under UCC § 2–725. With warranty, the period starts from the sale of the defective item rather than from the time of injury.[3]

In a case in which plaintiff has multiple theories of recovery, but has suffered only one harm, she has but a single cause of action and each of the available supporting theories is merely a different count in support of the single claim.[4] In a sense, it is technically inaccurate to say that a plaintiff so situated has multiple causes of action or multiple claims. Since the plaintiff can have but one recovery for the wrong, regardless of the multiple theories available and even though each may carry a different period of limitations, the plaintiff has in the ultimate sense but a single claim.[5]

---

[11]   See SPR 203:1.

[12]   Capruso v. Village of Kings Point, 23 N.Y.3d 631, 641–42, 992 N.Y.S.2d 469, 475, 16 N.E.3d 527, 533 (2014).

[13]   *Capruso*, 23 N.Y.3d at 641–42, 992 N.Y.S.2d at 475, 16 N.E.3d at 533.

[14]   See Saratoga County Chamber of Commerce, Inc. v. Pataki, 100 N.Y.2d 801, 815, 766 N.Y.S.2d 654, 661, 798 N.E.2d 1047, 1054 (2003).

[15]   Dormer v. Suffolk County Police Benev. Ass'n, Inc., 95 A.D.3d 1166, 945 N.Y.S.2d 144 (2d Dep't 2012) (4-month period of CPLR 217 applied where Article 78 proceeding would lie for the relief sought in the declaratory action). This point is discussed in more detail in the chapter that includes the declaratory judgment. See § 438.

[1]   See Velez v. Craine & Clark Lumber Corp., 33 N.Y.2d 117, 350 N.Y.S.2d 617, 305 N.E.2d 750 (1973).

[2]   Victorson v. Bock Laundry Mach. Co., 37 N.Y.2d 395, 373 N.Y.S.2d 39, 335 N.E.2d 275 (1975).

[3]   See § 41.

[4]   The official language of the CPLR is "cause of action," CPLR 3211(a)(7), while the federal language is "claim." See Fed. R. Civ. P. 12(b)(6). While the two are sometimes said to differ, see, e.g., Garcia v. Hilton Hotels Intern., 97 F. Supp. 5 (D.P.R. 1951), the differences are not satisfactorily explained. Since both require a cognizable substantive basis for relief, there is little to pick between them. This text prefers "claim" because it is shorter but uses the word interchangeably with the phrase "cause of action."

[5]   See § 212.

The strict liability ground has in common with the warranty ground that both dispense with proof of negligence. For that reason, and because strict liability was a relative latecomer, it was thought for a while that strict liability had pushed warranty off the personal injury scene altogether.[6] That notion was dispelled by a 1975 amendment of UCC section 2–318, the warranty statute,[7] and the Court of Appeals now upholds the view that warranty is still an available alternative to strict liability.[8] Since the statute of limitations is the principal element affected—warranty offering 4 years from sale as an alternative to the 3 years from injury that applies to strict products liability—the plaintiff does no harm asserting breach of warranty as an extra count. For safety's sake, however, the plaintiff should bring the case within 3 years of the injury to assure that no inadvertent time omission will bar the negligence and strict liability grounds.[9]

It had been thought in some quarters that in a product-caused tort, the warranty and strict liability grounds were—except for the statute of limitations—substantively identical. The Court of Appeals rejected that idea in 1995 in Denny v. Ford Motor Co.,[10] finding a distinction between them and sustaining a verdict that had found a breach of warranty while rejecting a claim of strict liability. Strict liability requires a "weighing" of the product's dangers against its advantages, the Court said; marketing the product, with its dangers, might be held acceptable by the jury should it find that reasonable alternatives were not available to the manufacturer. But that won't necessarily insulate against a warranty claim, the Court concluded.[11]

The warranty versus strict products liability example manifests how one count in support of a claim can offer substantial advantages or support remedies not available on the other. The 4-year warranty period can sometimes preserve a personal injury claim sued on after the 3-year tort period—which governs both the negligence and strict liability counts—has expired. Paradoxically, the 3-year period for tort may sometimes prove longer than the warranty 4! The 3 years run from injury; the 4 years run from the sale. If the injury occurs long after the sale, a 3-year tort ground may still be alive when the 4-year warranty claim is already dead.

In one case, the plaintiff pleaded 5 counts in support of a claim for injury caused by the inhalation of dust years earlier: negligence, nuisance, breach of contract, fraud, and breach of a statutory duty. The plaintiff was seeking a longer period than the negligence 3 years, which had lapsed. The court held that the first 4 counts, however denominated, all required proof of negligence and so were in effect only negligence claims and were barred by the 3-year statute. But the fifth count, alleging violation of a statute and

---

[6]　　See Martin v. Julius Dierck Equipment Co., 43 N.Y.2d 583, 403 N.Y.S.2d 185, 374 N.E.2d 97 (1978).

[7]　　See Singer v. Federated Dept. Stores, Inc., 112 Misc. 2d 781, 447 N.Y.S.2d 582 (Sup. Ct., New York County 1981).

[8]　　Heller v. U.S. Suzuki Motor Corp., 64 N.Y.2d 407, 488 N.Y.S.2d 132, 477 N.E.2d 434, 40 U.C.C. Rep. Serv. 917 (1985).

[9]　　See § 41 and the lead note in NYSLD No. 268.

[10]　　Denny v. Ford Motor Co., 87 N.Y.2d 248, 639 N.Y.S.2d 250, 662 N.E.2d 730 (1995).

[11]　　The case is the subject of the lead note in NYSLD No. 435.

requiring no proof of negligence, was held to qualify as a statutory claim entitled to the then applicable 6-year measure[12] and was sustained.[13]

The same conduct will sometimes constitute both a breach of contract and the tort of conversion. The conversion claim has only a 3-year period;[14] adding a count in contract may secure the application of the longer contract period[15] if it should be needed. But in other contract and tort situations, the courts have been ambivalent, suspecting subterfuges conjured up by tardy plaintiffs to avoid a lapsed claim. In one case, for example, a plaintiff's contract claim, on which the time period ran from the breach, had expired. The plaintiff tried to plead a claim in fraud, whose time can start at discovery[16] and would have been alive, but the Court of Appeals held the claim barred.[17] The Court said that "in applying the Statute of Limitations we look for the reality, and the essence of the action and not its mere name."[18] If a plaintiff makes out the elements of a fraud claim, however, why shouldn't the plaintiff have the benefit of it, including its postponed-until-discovery accrual? The *Brick* case seems to reward a fraud merely because it also happens to be a breach of contract, which tends to teach a wrongdoer that sometimes two wrongs can make a right.

A later decision addresses the plaintiff's use of alternative contract and tort theories in a case against architects. In Sears, Roebuck & Co. v. Enco Associates, Inc.,[19] the defendant was an architectural firm that allegedly misdesigned ramps leading to the plaintiff's store. The plaintiff sought various items of property damage. Suit was brought more than 3, but less than 6, years after the ramp was completed. This, on a technical measure, meant that the action would be timely if the claim sounded in contract, but untimely if it had to rely on tort. The Court of Appeals, noting that the essence of the relationship between the parties was a contractual one, held that the statute of limitations is not concerned with the theory but with the remedy. It sustained the action as timely, but with the proviso that the only damages that could be recovered were those associated with contract.[20]

The *Sears* lesson, applicable in any action in which multiple theories of liability are asserted, would seem to be that if the plaintiff sues within the time applicable to all the available grounds, the plaintiff is entitled to exploit them all—tort, contract, whatever—and is entitled to the damages associated with any of them.[21]

---

[12]   Note that the statutory claim today gets only 3 years. CPLR 214(2).

[13]   Schmidt v. Merchants Despatch Transp. Co., 270 N.Y. 287, 200 N.E. 824, 104 A.L.R. 450 (1936). In another respect, dealing with when a tort claim accrues when based on exposure to a dangerous substance, the *Schmidt* case is overruled by the 1986 adoption of CPLR 214–c; see § 40.

[14]   CPLR 214(4).

[15]   CPLR 213(2); N.Y. UCC § 2–725(1).

[16]   CPLR 213(8); see § 43.

[17]   Brick v. Cohn-Hall-Marx Co., 276 N.Y. 259, 11 N.E.2d 902, 114 A.L.R. 521 (1937).

[18]   *Brick*, 276 N.Y. at 264, 11 N.E.2d at 904.

[19]   Sears, Roebuck & Co. v. Enco Associates, Inc., 43 N.Y.2d 389, 401 N.Y.S.2d 767, 372 N.E.2d 555 (1977).

[20]   As discussed below, CPLR 214(6) now requires that a malpractice suit against an architect be brought within 3 years, regardless of whether the theory is based in contract or tort. See also § 35.

[21]   The Court of Appeals has had difficulty on other fronts, however, in deciding when to permit a tort theory to emerge from a contract-based relationship. See, e.g., Board of Educ. of Hudson City School Dist. v. Sargent, Webster, Crenshaw & Folley, 71 N.Y.2d 21, 523 N.Y.S.2d 475, 517 N.E.2d 1360 (1987) (dealing with contribution among tortfeasors); NYSLD No. 340.

A later Court of Appeals case that relied on *Sears*, Video Corp. of America v. Frederick Flatto Associates, Inc.,[22] involved a defendant insurance broker's failure to obtain adequate insurance for the plaintiff. The plaintiff alleged, among other things, that the defendant failed to use due care, which is tort language. But since the wrong had its genesis in contract, the court held the claim timely even though brought after the 3 years applicable to tort.[23]

The Second Department in Baratta v. Kozlowski[24] saw the *Video* case as "portentous" for implicitly extending the rationale of *Sears*. *Sears* involved a formal written contract, the court pointed out, while *Video* extended the holding in *Sears* to less formal contract-based arrangements as well. As *Baratta* anticipated, this ultimately led to the Court of Appeals 1992 decision in Santulli v. Englert, Reilly & McHugh, P.C.,[25] holding that claims against lawyers, because also contract-based, could also rely on the 6 years of CPLR 213(2) instead of being restricted to the malpractice 3 of CPLR 214(6). While *Santulli* was, at least in part, legislatively overruled in a 1996 amendment, its rationale may apply in actions against those who do not qualify as professionals.[26]

After the 1996 overruling of *Santulli* in the amendment of CPLR 214(6), it is still necessary to determine precisely whether a given claim sounds in malpractice because, if it does, it is restricted to the 3 years of CPLR 214(6) and can't rely on the contractual 6 years of CPLR 213(2), even if it is pleaded as a breach of contract claim. In Kliment v. McKinsey & Co.,[27] the Court of Appeals held that when the claim asserted is one for breach of contract, but at its root is one for malpractice, it is subject to the 3-year malpractice period of CPLR 214(6).[28]

While there are some complications about what damages are available on what claim, and which claim gets what period, one point emerges clearly from the foregoing discussion. The plaintiff who timely commences an action as to all theories within the shortest of the applicable statutes of limitation is in the best position to get it all.

C. ALTERING THE PERIOD

Table of Sections

§ 38.   Statutory Alterations
§ 39.   Agreements to Shorten or Lengthen the Period

§ 38.   Statutory Alterations

Constitutional considerations intervene when the legislature attempts to revive an expired period or curtail an existing one.

---

[22] Video Corp. of America v. Frederick Flatto Associates, Inc., 58 N.Y.2d 1026, 462 N.Y.S.2d 439, 448 N.E.2d 1350 (1983).

[23] A "professional" whom a client sues for want of due care would be entitled to rely exclusively on the 3-year malpractice period of CPLR 214(6), but insurance brokers and agents do not qualify as "professionals" for this purpose. See § 35.

[24] Baratta v. Kozlowski, 94 A.D.2d 454, 464 N.Y.S.2d 803 (2d Dep't 1983).

[25] Santulli v. Englert, Reilly & McHugh, P.C., 78 N.Y.2d 700, 579 N.Y.S.2d 324, 586 N.E.2d 1014 (1992).

[26] The evolution and overruling of *Santulli* in CPLR 214(6) is discussed in § 35.

[27] Kliment v. McKinsey & Co., Inc., 3 N.Y.3d 538, 788 N.Y.S.2d 648, 821 N.E.2d 952 (2004).

[28] See § 35.

If the passage of the period has as a practical matter resulted in the vesting of an interest in tangible property, real or personal, the federal due process clause has been held to preclude its revival.[1] If the claim is a mere chose in action, however, such as a money action on a contract, the Federal Constitution is apparently no barrier to revival,[2] but the state constitution may be. The New York Constitution's due process clause[3] has been construed to require all revivor statutes to be demonstrably reasonable.[4] The question must be answered sui generis and it is of course the courts that have the ultimate say on reasonableness. In one leading case in which the claim had expired while its owner had disappeared in a Nazi-occupied country, a revivor statute, afterwards made a permanent part of New York law,[5] was sustained as reasonable under the circumstances.[6] Revivor legislation is considered drastic and the intent to revive must be clear.[7]

An example of significant "revival" legislation appeared in a 1986 tort reform package,[8] one part of which enacted CPLR 214–c, adopting a "discovery" rule in so-called "exposure" cases, i.e., cases involving personal injury or property damage caused by exposure to a deleterious substance.[9]

An abridgement statute—one curtailing an existing period—poses a problem only as to claims existing, but not yet interposed, when it becomes operative. It is constitutionally required that the plaintiff be allowed at least a reasonable time in which to interpose an existing claim, measured from the abridgement statute's effective date.[10] As long as the plaintiff has at least a reasonable time from then, which is initially for the legislature but ultimately for the courts to determine sui generis,[11] it makes no difference that the unexpired period of the superseded statute would have been much longer. The 1996 curtailment to 3 years of the nonmedical malpractice statute of limitations in CPLR 214(6), which had been set at 6 years by caselaw,[12] is an example of an abridgement statute that posed constitutional issues.[13]

---

[1]   Stewart v. Keyes, 295 U.S. 403, 55 S. Ct. 807, 79 L. Ed. 1507 (1935).

[2]   Campbell v. Holt, 115 U.S. 620, 6 S. Ct. 209, 29 L. Ed. 483 (1885). This distinction is difficult to defend: a substantial money claim will be a much greater threat to a defendant in a given case than a claim that asserts an interest in tangible property of less economic value.

[3]   Const. Art. I, § 6.

[4]   Robinson v. Robins Dry Dock & Repair Co., 238 N.Y. 271, 144 N.E. 579, 1924 A.M.C. 1575 (1924); see Barrett v. Wojtowicz, 66 A.D.2d 604, 613, 414 N.Y.S.2d 350, 356 (2d Dep't 1979).

[5]   CPLR 209(c).

[6]   Gallewski v. H. Hentz & Co., 301 N.Y. 164, 93 N.E.2d 620 (1950).

[7]   Hopkins v. Lincoln Trust Co., 233 N.Y. 213, 135 N.E. 267 (1922).

[8]   Chapter 682 of the Laws of 1986.

[9]   See § 40.

[10]   Brothers v. Florence, 95 N.Y.2d 290, 300–01, 716 N.Y.S.2d 367, 372, 739 N.E.2d 733, 738 (2000); see Wilson v. Iseminger, 185 U.S. 55, 22 S. Ct. 573, 46 L. Ed. 804 (1902).

[11]   See Parmenter v. State, 135 N.Y. 154, 31 N.E. 1035 (1892); Alston v. Transport Workers Union of Greater New York, 225 A.D.2d 424, 639 N.Y.S.2d 359 (1st Dep't 1996).

[12]   See §§ 35, 37.

[13]   See *Brothers*, 95 N.Y.2d at 300–01, 716 N.Y.S.2d at 371–72, 739 N.E.2d at 737–38. The issue was tracked in SPR 48:2, 53:2, 55:2, 56:2, and 58:2.

§ 39.   Agreements to Shorten or Lengthen the Period

CPLR 201 allows the parties to provide by contract for a shorter time limitation than the law supplies, but the period agreed to must be reasonable.[1] If it is found unreasonable by the courts, it is disregarded. This, too, is a sui generis inquiry. A 3-month limit in a bill of lading has been held reasonable, for example,[2] while a 2-month limit in a steamship ticket has been found unreasonable.[3] The steamship ticket was an adhesion contract and the court's scrutiny is closer there. If the period is cut back to mere days, it is likely to be held unreasonable as a matter of law, as happened in one case involving a cutback to a 15-day period.[4] The statute of limitations for sales contracts governed by the UCC may also be shortened by the original agreement, but there an arbitrary limit is imposed: the period can't be cut back to less than a year.[5]

An agreement to lengthen the statute of limitations is invalid if made before the cause of action accrues, but will be honored in certain circumstances if made afterwards.[6] The agreement must be in a signed writing and, if it is, it needs no consideration.[7] Such a postaccrual agreement will start the applicable statutory period running all over again unless the agreement itself stipulates a shorter period.

Those are the rules for contract cases. There is no statutory rule for extension agreements, commonly known as "tolling agreements," in tort and other noncontract cases.[8] If such an agreement is made in a noncontract case, however, it should be a basis on which to estop the defendant from pleading the statute of limitations.[9] Any other view would seem to tell parties, who think that with a little more time they can resolve their dispute, that when the deadline nears they can't buy more time with a mutually agreed-to extension. That would force onto the courts' calendars a lawsuit that might otherwise have been avoided, which would be at war with the state's policy of encouraging settlements.

---

[1]   Executive Plaza, LLC v. Peerless Ins. Co., 22 N.Y.3d 511, 518, 982 N.Y.S.2d 826, 828, 5 N.E.3d 989, 991 (2014).

[2]   North British & Mercantile Ins. Co. v. Central Vermont R. Co., 9 A.D. 4, 40 N.Y.S. 1113 (3d Dep't 1896), aff'd, 158 N.Y. 726, 53 N.E. 1128 (1899).

[3]   Kemelhor v. Furness, Withy & Co., 139 Misc. 64, 248 N.Y.S. 659, 1931 A.M.C. 1085 (N. Y. C. Mun. Ct. 1931).

[4]   Brown & Guenther v. North Queensview Homes, Inc., 18 A.D.2d 327, 239 N.Y.S.2d 482 (1st Dep't 1963).

[5]   N.Y. UCC § 2–725(1).

[6]   See John J. Kassner & Co., Inc. v. City of New York, 46 N.Y.2d 544, 551, 415 N.Y.S.2d 785, 789–90, 389 N.E.2d 99, 103 (1979). N.Y. UCC § 2–725(1), governing sales transactions, also precludes an extension agreement in the original contract.

[7]   Gen. Oblig. Law § 17–103(1).

[8]   See In re Stantec Consulting Group (Fonda-Fultonville Cent. School Dist.), 36 A.D.3d 1051, 1052, 827 N.Y.S.2d 762 (3d Dep't 2007) ("General Obligations Law § 17–103(1), by its express terms, applies to tolling agreements relating to actions arising out of a contract," and not to tort claims), lv. denied 9 N.Y.3d 807, 843 N.Y.S.2d 537, 875 N.E.2d 30 (2007).

[9]   Subdivision 4(b) of Gen. Oblig. Law § 17–103 provides that the statute "does not affect" the court's estoppel powers. Estoppel to plead the statute of limitations is treated in § 56.

D. ACCRUAL

Table of Sections

§ 40.   "Accrual" of the Claim
§ 41.   Accrual in Warranty Cases
§ 42.   Accrual in Malpractice Cases
§ 43.   "Discovery" Accruals
§ 44.   Wrongful Death Cases

§ 40.   "Accrual" of the Claim

After determining the applicable period governing the claim, attention must turn to when the claim "accrued." The statute of limitations starts to run when the claim "accrues,"[1] and while in most cases it is not hard to determine the moment of accrual, a few situations pose problems.

In the personal injury case predicated on negligence, the applicable 3-year period starts at the moment of injury. The majority of automobile, airplane, construction, sidewalk, etc., accidents are in that category. But this time-of-injury rule worked to the plaintiff's detriment when the cause of the injury was more subtle. Schmidt v. Merchants Despatch Transp. Co.,[2] a 1936 decision, is a classic illustration of the problem. The cause of the injury in *Schmidt* was the inhalation of dust more than 3 years before the suit. The resulting injury did not appear until many years after the inhalation, but the Court nonetheless held that the claim accrued when the dust was inhaled because the injury was suffered at that time even though it was not discerned until much later. The plaintiff, said the Court, could have sued immediately and shown such damages as "would result" from the inhalation. In other words, the plaintiff should have sued promptly upon the inhalation and then convinced a jury that a carcinoma would appear several years later. That preposterous view, which conflicts with New York's physical harm requirement,[3] prevailed for half a century. There were many efforts to overrule it. None succeeded, until 1986.

In 1986, with the enactment of CPLR 214–c, the legislature at last adopted a "discovery" rule for personal injury and property damage cases based on "exposure" to a foreign substance.[4] Under CPLR 214–c(2), the 3-year time period in such cases begins to run not from the exposure itself, as *Schmidt* held, but from the later time when the plaintiff discovers or with reasonable diligence should have discovered the injury. There is no outer time limit. As long as the claim is brought within 3 years from discovery, or the moment when with reasonable diligence plaintiff should have discovered the injury, it makes no difference when the exposure first came about. It could have been decades

---

[1]   CPLR 203(a).

[2]   Schmidt v. Merchants Despatch Transp. Co., 270 N.Y. 287, 200 N.E. 824 (1936).

[3]   See Caronia v. Philip Morris USA, Inc., 22 N.Y.3d 439, 982 N.Y.S.2d 40, 5 N.E.3d 11 (2013) (NYSLD No. 650), discussed below.

[4]   Exposure is defined by CPLR 214–c(1) to include "direct or indirect . . . absorption, contact, ingestion, inhalation, implantation or injection" of any substance harmful to the body. Actions governed by the statute are sometimes collectively referred to as the "toxic torts." "Implantation" was added in 1992 to overcome Martin v. Edwards Laboratories, Div. of American Hosp. Supply Corp., 60 N.Y.2d 417, 469 N.Y.S.2d 923, 457 N.E.2d 1150 (1983), which had held that malfunctioning devices like a prosthesis or contraceptive, "intended to have a continuing function," are governed by the usual time-of-injury rule. See Alexander, Commentary C214–c:1 on McKinney's CPLR 214–c.

earlier. In *Rothstein v. Tennessee Gas Pipeline Co.*,[5] for example, the exposure had been to a substance given the plaintiff 40 years earlier to facilitate an x-ray.[6]

The assumption, of course, is that the plaintiff knows what caused the injury. If the plaintiff does not know, but discovers the cause and can attribute it to the defendant within 5 years after discovering the injury, CPLR 214–c(4) permits the plaintiff, as an alternative, to bring suit within 1 year from the discovery of the cause. The burden on the plaintiff in this scenario is heavy, as she must allege and prove that the scientific information from which to draw conclusions about cause was not available within the 3-year period in CPLR 214–c(2), discussed above.[7] The state of technical and scientific knowledge that the statute is referencing is the general knowledge of the scientific community, not the particular plaintiff's own actual knowledge.[8]

The delayed-accrual rules of CPLR 214–c also apply to the service of a notice of claim.[9] They do not apply in medical or dental malpractice actions, however,[10] where the more limited "discovery" accrual rule of CPLR 214–a continues to govern.

CPLR 203(g), treated in more detail below,[11] purports to reduce to 2 years any longer period measured from discovery. It probably should not apply to CPLR 214–c, not only because 214–c is a later enactment silent as to the effect of 203(g), but also because, in enacting postponed accrual for toxic tort actions, CPLR 214–c(2) specifically says that it is "the three-year period" that "shall be computed from the date of discovery." But just in case the courts hold otherwise, a plaintiff is safer by suing within 2 years of the discovery of the injury.

While CPLR 214–c changed the accrual rule announced by the Court of Appeals in *Schmidt*, the Court has nonetheless adhered to the "long-held" "requirement that a plaintiff sustain physical harm before being able to recover in tort."[12] Therefore, it refused to recognize an "independent cause of action for medical monitoring" in favor of present or former smokers "absent any evidence of present physical injury or damage to property."[13]

The claim of repetitive stress injury (RSI) by a keyboard user alleging an improperly designed computer keyboard, alleged more frequently in the computer age, has been held to accrue at the onset of symptoms or upon the last use of the keyboard, whichever is earlier.[14]

---

[5]　　Rothstein v. Tennessee Gas Pipeline Co., 87 N.Y.2d 90, 637 N.Y.S.2d 674, 661 N.E.2d 146 (1995). The *Rothstein* case is treated in NYSLD No. 433.

[6]　　See NYSLD No. 321 (discussing application of CPLR 214–c in a property damage case); § 44 (application of CPLR 214–c in wrongful death action).

[7]　　In Giordano v. Market America, Inc., 15 N.Y.3d 590, 915 N.Y.S.2d 884, 941 N.E.2d 727 (2010) (NYSLD No. 448:3), the Court held that an injury occurring even mere hours after "exposure" can nevertheless be deemed "latent" and thereby be governed by CPLR 214(c)(4)'s requirements.

[8]　　See Matter of New York County DES Litigation, 89 N.Y.2d 506, 655 N.Y.S.2d 862, 678 N.E.2d 474 (1997) (NYSLD No. 448).

[9]　　See CPLR 214–c(3); see also Ct. of Claims Act § 10(7) (addressing claims against the State). The notice of claim is addressed in § 32.

[10]　　CPLR 214–c(5).

[11]　　See § 43.

[12]　　*Caronia*, 22 N.Y.3d at 446, 982 N.Y.S.2d at 43, 5 N.E.3d at 14.

[13]　　*Caronia*, 22 N.Y.3d at 452, 982 N.Y.S.2d at 47, 5 N.E.3d at 18.

[14]　　See Blanco v. American Tel. & Tel. Co., 90 N.Y.2d 757, 666 N.Y.S.2d 536, 689 N.E.2d 506 (1997) (NYSLD No. 459).

When several claims are joined in one complaint, a plaintiff must be mindful of the accrual dates being claimed for them, lest an early accrual date stated for one have a detrimental effect on another. That happened in a case in which an early accrual date was pleaded on a loss of services claim in order to maximize the period of damages. That accrual date was held to bind on the coplaintiff's personal injury claim as well, where the effect was to bar it.[15]

In certain instances a demand may be necessary before a claim accrues, as where a depositor seeks to withdraw from an ordinary bank account,[16] or where one from whom property has been taken seeks to recover it from the innocent third person who may now have possession of it.[17] In cases in which a demand would otherwise seem necessary, it ceases to be, and the period begins to run without it, if on the facts it appears that a demand would be futile.[18]

In Hahn Automotive Warehouse, Inc. v. American Zurich Insurance Co.,[19] the Court concluded that CPLR 213(2)'s 6-year statute of limitations applicable to breach of contract claims begins to run when a party possesses the legal right to demand payment from another, rather than when invoices are issued later. According to the Court, the statute of limitations in these cases, which involved monies owed by an insured to an insurer under adjustable policies, was triggered when the insurer had the right to demand payment, not when it actually made the demand.

The 1-year period applicable in defamation cases[20] begins to run from the moment that the actionable words are published. In the case of a mass-circulated publication such as a book or magazine or Sunday newspaper supplement, which often reaches the public before the day scheduled for formal distribution, the formal distribution is nonetheless the moment of accrual.[21] If the rule were otherwise, many a defamer could escape liability by letting a segment of the public see the words a year before the general public does.

This is an aspect of what is known as the "single publication" rule, which holds that the publication gives rise to a single cause of action no matter how many copies of the publication are circulated.[22] A similar rule applies to internet defamations where the statute of limitations starts when the matter is first added to the website. The claim does not start anew each time the site is accessed.[23]

---

[15] See Barlow v. Sun Chemical Co., 15 Misc. 3d 953, 838 N.Y.S.2d 387 (Sup. Ct., Westchester County 2007) (SPR 185:3).

[16] CPLR 206(a)(2). In the law of commercial paper the period of limitations on a demand instrument begins to run "upon its date or, if no date is stated, on the date of issue," i.e., immediately, and without awaiting a demand. N.Y. UCC § 3–122(1)(b). A claim against an indorser on any instrument accrues "upon demand following dishonor." N.Y. UCC § 3–122(3).

[17] Solomon R. Guggenheim Foundation v. Lubell, 77 N.Y.2d 311, 317–18, 567 N.Y.S.2d 623, 626, 569 N.E.2d 426, 429 (1991).

[18] See Tillman v. Guaranty Trust Co. of New York, 253 N.Y. 295, 171 N.E. 61 (1930).

[19] Hahn Automotive Warehouse, Inc. v. American Zurich Ins. Co., 18 N.Y.3d 765, 944 N.Y.S.2d 742, 967 N.E.2d 1187 (2012) (NYSLD No. 631).

[20] CPLR 215(3).

[21] Tomasino v. William Morrow & Co., Inc., 174 A.D.2d 734, 571 N.Y.S.2d 571 (2d Dep't 1991); Sorge v. Parade Publications, Inc., 20 A.D.2d 338, 247 N.Y.S.2d 317 (1st Dep't 1964).

[22] Hoesten v. Best, 34 A.D.3d 143, 821 N.Y.S.2d 40 (1st Dep't 2006).

[23] Firth v. State, 98 N.Y.2d 365, 747 N.Y.S.2d 69, 775 N.E.2d 463 (2002) (NYSLD No. 513).

While the desultory distribution of additional copies of books or magazines from stock after initial publication will not start the year running anew, a general republication will. In Rinaldi v. Viking Penguin, Inc.,[24] for example, several thousand copies of a text not originally bound in hardcover and another several thousand of the hardcovers that had not been sold were used in a softcover issue. This was held to be a general reissuance of the book, starting the 1-year statute of limitations afresh. Similarly, if a defendant moves defamatory material to a different Internet address, this is akin to a republication and will start the statute of limitations anew.[25]

Continuing wrongs, such as a continuous trespass, avoid the barrier of the statute of limitations altogether by being deemed to accrue constantly.[26] In Town of Oyster Bay v. Lizza Industries, Inc.,[27] the Court ruled "that injuries to property caused by a continuing nuisance involve a 'continuous wrong' and, therefore, generally give rise to successive causes of action that accrue each time a wrong is committed."[28] Nonetheless, the Court concluded that defendants' alleged tortious conduct consisted of specific acts of negligent excavation and backfilling that, of necessity, occurred before the construction was complete in the 1980s. In that an action to recover damages for injury to property must be commenced within 3 years of the date of the injury under CPLR 214(4), these tort claims commenced after the turn of the century were barred.

Special limitations issues arise in warranty, malpractice, and wrongful death cases, which get separate treatment in ensuing sections. We will note here that a claim against a nonmedical professional governed by CPLR 241(6) normally accrues at the end of the representation, or upon the conclusion of the work that gives rise to the malpractice.[29] The limitations' and accrual aspects of an indemnity claim, especially when asserted by a defendant by way of impleader, are treated in the chapter on third-party practice.[30]

§ 41. Accrual in Warranty Cases

A breach of warranty claim in connection with a product accrues upon "tender of delivery"[1]—roughly speaking, from the date of sale[2]—and not when the wrong is discovered or an injury occurs. This poses problems when a warranty has allegedly been given for a period longer than the 4 years applicable to a warranty claim under UCC

---

[24] Rinaldi v. Viking Penguin, Inc., 52 N.Y.2d 422, 438 N.Y.S.2d 496, 420 N.E.2d 377 (1981).

[25] Firth v. State of New York, 306 A.D.2d 666, 761 N.Y.S.2d 361 (3d Dep't 2003).

[26] See 509 Sixth Ave. Corp. v. New York City Transit Authority, 15 N.Y.2d 48, 255 N.Y.S.2d 89, 203 N.E.2d 486 (1964).

[27] Town of Oyster Bay v. Lizza Industries, Inc., 22 N.Y.3d 1024, 1031, 981 N.Y.S.2d 643, 648, 4 N.E.3d 944, 949 (2013) (NYSLD No. 650).

[28] See also Capruso v. Village of Kings Point, 23 N.Y.3d 631, 641, 992 N.Y.S.2d 469, 474, 16 N.E.3d 527, 532 (2014) ("[U]nder the continuing wrong doctrine, plaintiffs are able to challenge defendants' ongoing violation of the public trust doctrine at any time while the violation lasts, without being barred by the statute of limitations.").

[29] See, e.g., Town of Oyster Bay v. Lizza Industries, Inc., 22 N.Y.3d 1024, 981 N.Y.S.2d 643, 4 N.E.3d 944 (2013) (NYSLD No. 650) (in action against an architect or contractor, "the accrual date for Statute of Limitations purposes is completion of performance"); Shumsky v. Eisenstein, 96 N.Y.2d 164, 726 N.Y.S.2d 365, 750 N.E.2d 67 (2001) (action to recover damages for legal malpractice accrues when malpractice is committed, but statute can be tolled during period of continuous representation on the matter); Ackerman v. Price Waterhouse, 84 N.Y.2d 535, 620 N.Y.S.2d 318, 644 N.E.2d 1009 (1994) (in malpractice action against accountant, claim accrues on the date the accountant's work product is received by the client, and not when the IRS assesses a deficiency).

[30] See § 162.

[1] N.Y. UCC § 2–725(2).

[2] Heller v. U.S. Suzuki Motor Corp., 64 N.Y.2d 407, 488 N.Y.S.2d 132, 477 N.E.2d 434 (1985).

section 2–725. If the warranty's breach is not discovered until, say, 7 years later, i.e., the product's defect does not appear until then, this can lead to some unpalatable results. In one case, equipment allegedly under a 30-year warranty proved defective more than the then-applicable 6 years after the sale. No matter, held the court: the warranty claim still accrued at the sale and had lapsed.[3] The result is still possible today. The way to avoid it is to follow the advice contained in UCC section 2–725(2) and see to it that in the sales contract itself the warranty "explicitly extends to future performance." If that is done, "the cause of action accrues when the breach is or should have been discovered."[4]

The advantage of having express warranty commitments instead of relying on implied warranties is illustrated even in cases governed by pre-UCC law. In Bulova Watch Co., Inc. v. Celotex Corp.,[5] for example, a roofer's express promise to repair a "bonded" roof for a 20-year period after the sale of the roofing materials was held to give the plaintiff/customer a separate claim, and a fresh accrual for limitations purposes, for each breach. Hence, as long as each claim of breach of the repair obligation arising within the 20-year period was sued on within the period as measured from that particular breach, the claim is timely.

If an explicit warranty extending to future performance is not used, the 4-year UCC warranty will run from the tender of delivery by the defendant even in personal injury cases, and this has produced some bizarre law in New York. In Mendel v. Pittsburgh Plate Glass Co.,[6] D sold plate glass in 1958 to a bank. In 1965, P was hurt by the glass. Alleging breach of warranty, P sued D within 3 years after the injury. The Court of Appeals, on a 4–3 vote, held that the warranty claim accrued in 1958 and was barred by 1962—years before the plaintiff was hurt. The dissent in Mendel urged that there existed, quite apart from warranty, the theory of strict liability in tort and that the plaintiff's claim could be kept alive on that ground, which accrues 3 years from the injury.[7]

What the majority in Mendel brought about, therefore—but only for a while, as it turned out—was the substantive divestiture of a "strict liability" theory. This theory, which dispenses with proof of negligence, is something like a warranty claim with the added benefit of a tort limitations' accrual. The Mendel decision was later restricted to warranty, and the "strict liability" ground was substantively reinstated,[8] accompanied by a time-of-injury accrual. This was confirmed by the Court of Appeals in Victorson v. Bock Laundry Mach. Co.[9] It supports the conclusion that although the Mendel case still dictates the limitations' rules on a warranty claim—4 years, but with accrual at tender of delivery—their severity can usually be avoided by turning instead to the theory of strict products liability. It may offer the injured person an equivalent prospect of recovery but with the benefit of tort limitations' accrual rules.[10]

---

[3]   Citizens Utilities Co. v. American Locomotive Co., 11 N.Y.2d 409, 230 N.Y.S.2d 194, 184 N.E.2d 171 (1962).

[4]   N.Y. UCC § 2–725(2); see Wyandanch Volunteer Fire Co., Inc. v. Randon Const. Corp., 29 A.D.3d 685, 816 N.Y.S.2d 119 (2d Dep't 2006).

[5]   Bulova Watch Co., Inc. v. Celotex Corp., 46 N.Y.2d 606, 415 N.Y.S.2d 817, 389 N.E.2d 130 (1979).

[6]   Mendel v. Pittsburgh Plate Glass Co., 25 N.Y.2d 340, 305 N.Y.S.2d 490, 253 N.E.2d 207 (1969).

[7]   See § 40.

[8]   See Codling v. Paglia, 32 N.Y.2d 330, 345 N.Y.S.2d 461, 298 N.E.2d 622 (1973), and Velez v. Craine & Clark Lumber Corp., 33 N.Y.2d 117, 350 N.Y.S.2d 617, 305 N.E.2d 750 (1973).

[9]   Victorson v. Bock Laundry Mach. Co., 37 N.Y.2d 395, 373 N.Y.S.2d 39, 335 N.E.2d 275 (1975).

[10]   See § 37.

The lawyer should also remember that warranty itself may in some instances offer a limitations' advantage: when the injury occurs close in time to the sale, for example, the 4 years measured from the sale are likely to give the plaintiff a longer time than 3 years measured from the injury.

In 1985, in Heller v. U.S. Suzuki Motor Corp.,[11] the Court of Appeals resolved an important question on accrual in warranty cases that had been open for a long time. It was often thought that suit against a warranty defendant was timely as long as the plaintiff sued within 4 years after the tender of delivery of the damage-causing product from a retailer; that the time of sale by a defendant other than the retailer, such as a manufacturer or distributor, was irrelevant. Not so, held *Heller*. Each defendant along the line of manufacture and distribution is entitled to a separate accrual date based on its own sale of the product and can't be kept exposed to a warranty suit indefinitely merely because a retailer or intermediate jobber has kept a manufacturer's product on its shelves or in its stock room for an inordinate time before selling it.

Most of the discussion above pertains to warranties under the UCC, but similar accrual rules pertain to warranties in other contexts. In ACE Securities Corp. v. DB Structured Products, Inc.,[12] defendant seller made numerous representations and warranties "as of the [c]losing date" concerning the characteristics of almost 9,000 mortgages that were placed into a pool. Plaintiffs commenced this action against defendant alleging breaches of the representations and warranties and defendant's refusal to comply with a repurchase obligation in the contract. The Court ruled that plaintiffs' failure to properly commence the action within 6 years after the closing date, when the breach of warranty occurred, required its dismissal. The *ACE* Court distinguished its prior holding in *Bulova*, noting that "the remedial clause in *Bulova Watch* expressly guaranteed *future* performance of the roof and undertook a promise to repair the roof if it did not satisfy the seller's guarantee."[13] By contrast, the defendant seller in *ACE* did not guarantee the future performance of the mortgage loans. Rather, it represented and warranted certain facts about the loans' characteristics as of the closing date.

§ 42. Accrual in Malpractice Cases

Medical Malpractice

On a claim for medical malpractice (including dental and podiatric malpractice), which today has a 2 1/2-year statute of limitations under CPLR 214–a,[1] several points about accrual must be noted. The statute says that the period runs from "the act, omission or failure complained of or last treatment where there is continuous treatment for the same illness, injury or condition." The basic rule, therefore, is that the claim

---

[11]   Heller v. U.S. Suzuki Motor Corp., 64 N.Y.2d 407, 488 N.Y.S.2d 132, 477 N.E.2d 434 (1985).

[12]   ACE Securities Corp. v. DB Structured Products, Inc., 25 N.Y.3d 581, 15 N.Y.S.3d 716, 36 N.E.3d 623 (2015).

[13]   *ACE*, 25 N.Y.3d at 595, 15 N.Y.S.3d at 722, 36 N.E.3d at 629.

[1]   Note that only claims for medical, dental, and podiatric malpractice carry the 2 1/2-year period. A malpractice claim against other professionals, e.g. lawyers, architects, and accountants, is governed by CPLR 214(6) and its 3-year period. See § 35.

accrues at the time of the wrong itself, whether the plaintiff is aware of wrongdoing or not.[2]

"Continuous Treatment" Exception to Accrual

The time-of-injury rule gave rise to injustice in a number of situations under prior law and to a number of efforts to circumvent the rule.

Among the most successful of these efforts was the "continuous treatment" theory, which postpones the start of the statute of limitations until treatment in respect of the particular ailment is concluded. First adopted by caselaw,[3] the continuous treatment postponement is now codified, as the foregoing quotation from CPLR 214–a manifests. "The doctrine rests on the premise that it is in the patient's best interest that an ongoing course of treatment be continued, rather than interrupted by a lawsuit, because 'the doctor not only is in a position to identify and correct his or her malpractice, but is best placed to do so.' "[4] If the treatment has in effect been concluded, however, and a further examination is undertaken at the plaintiff's request "for the sole purpose of ascertaining . . . the patient's condition," the examination does not qualify as a continuous treatment so as to start the period anew. The same is true even if it is the doctor who initiates the new contact, as long as the prior course of treatment had been terminated.[5]

The treatment must be continuous rather than merely intermittent.[6] Termination of treatment is deemed to occur not upon the patient's last actual visit to the doctor but upon the last scheduled one if it is later.[7] In an action in which the plaintiff had a continuing relationship with the defendant doctors, the court ruled that treatment occurred on each date a prescription was received.[8] The plaintiff's "consultation with an attorney to explore one's [malpractice] options does not, of itself, defeat a showing of treatment" so as to immediately start the statute of limitations. In other words, a consultation with an attorney does not necessarily constitute a termination of "treatment" under the continuous treatment rule.[9]

The continuous treatment doctrine has been visited several times by the Court of Appeals. In its 1991 decision in Daniel J. v. New York City Health and Hospitals Corp.,[10] the court described more specifically how the continuous treatment doctrine operates. Before *Daniel J.*, it had been understood as merely postponing the moment of "accrual" until the last treatment. Looking at the matter more closely, the Court decided that instead of operating to postpone "accrual" of the claim, the doctrine functions merely as a "toll," suspending the running of the statute during the period of continuous treatment.

---

[2]   If the child is injured by medical malpractice while in the womb, its malpractice claim starts at birth. LaBello v. Albany Medical Center Hosp., 85 N.Y.2d 701, 628 N.Y.S.2d 40, 651 N.E.2d 908 (1995). See also B.F. v. Reproductive Medicine Associates of New York, LLP, 136 A.D.3d 73, 22 N.Y.S.3d 190 (1st Dep't 2015) (parents' claim for wrongful birth accrued on birth of impaired child, even though defendants' treatment concluded more than 6 months prior to that time); Ciceron v. Jamaica Hosp., 264 A.D.2d 497, 498, 694 N.Y.S.2d 459, 461 (2d Dep't 1999).

[3]   See Borgia v. City of New York, 12 N.Y.2d 151, 237 N.Y.S.2d 319, 187 N.E.2d 777 (1962).

[4]   Nykorchuck v. Henriques, 78 N.Y.2d 255, 258, 573 N.Y.S.2d 434, 436, 577 N.E.2d 1026, 1028 (1991).

[5]   See Rizk v. Cohen, 73 N.Y.2d 98, 538 N.Y.S.2d 229, 535 N.E.2d 282 (1989).

[6]   Davis v. City of New York, 38 N.Y.2d 257, 379 N.Y.S.2d 721, 342 N.E.2d 516 (1975).

[7]   Richardson v. Orentreich, 64 N.Y.2d 896, 487 N.Y.S.2d 731, 477 N.E.2d 210 (1985).

[8]   Stilloe v. Contini, 190 A.D.2d 419, 599 N.Y.S.2d 194 (3d Dep't 1993).

[9]   See Guarino v. Sharzer, 281 A.D.2d 188, 721 N.Y.S.2d 631 (1st Dep't 2001) (SPR 128:4).

[10]   Daniel J. v. New York City Health and Hospitals Corp., 77 N.Y.2d 630, 569 N.Y.S.2d 396, 571 N.E.2d 704 (1991).

Hence, the claim does "accrue" at the time of the original injury, but the running of the statute of limitations period is in effect immediately tolled until treatment is concluded. This may seem inconsequential, but it has impact on another toll, the CPLR 208 infancy toll. The latter toll is subject to a 10-year maximum in medical malpractice actions.[11] *Daniel J.* requires that the 2 tolls be calculated separately and not tacked on to each other. Therefore, the 10-year cut-off period of the infancy toll is to be measured from the actual "accrual" of the claim, and not from the later point to which the continuous-treatment doctrine in effect postpones the running of the statute of limitations.

In Nykorchuck v. Henriques,[12] a lump in the plaintiff's breast, ultimately diagnosed as cancer and requiring surgery, was first brought to the doctor's attention in 1979, when he said he'd have to "keep an eye on it." The plaintiff made subsequent visits to the doctor over the next several years, but the doctor never established a course of treatment for the condition. Therefore, "[i]n the absence of continuing efforts by a doctor to treat a particular condition," the policy behind the continuous treatment doctrine was not on the line. While the failure to diagnose and treat a condition may well be negligent, the Court held that such failure does not constitute a course of continuous treatment.

In a situation like *Nykorchuck*, the malpractice claim is essentially one for misdiagnosis and the 2 1/2-year statute of limitations runs separately from each misdiagnosis. The Court has also held that a patient unaware of a misdiagnosis gets no postponed accrual because here, too, the policy of the continuous treatment doctrine is not implicated.[13]

Because the continuous treatment doctrine is so frequently invoked in medical malpractice actions, it has appeared in a variety of scenarios.[14] In one case, for example, the doctrine was held inapplicable against a hospital when subsequent treatment was at a different hospital even though both hospitals had the same owner.[15] The Court held that where plaintiff is relying on continuous treatment provided by someone other than the allegedly negligent doctor, there must be "an agency or other relevant relationship" between the health care providers.[16]

What about treatment by different units of the same hospital? Is that the same thing? The appellate division said it was in Plummer v. New York City Health and Hospitals Corp.,[17] but the Court of Appeals, in reversing,[18] sidestepped the continuous-treatment-by-an-institution theory, which thus remains to be addressed by it.

The considerations underlying the continuous treatment theory are also inapplicable to a laboratory that misdiagnoses cancer by misreading tissue slides. Hence,

---

[11]   See § 54.

[12]   Nykorchuck v. Henriques, 78 N.Y.2d 255, 573 N.Y.S.2d 434, 577 N.E.2d 1026 (1991).

[13]   See Young v. New York City Health & Hospitals Corp., 91 N.Y.2d 291, 670 N.Y.S.2d 169, 693 N.E.2d 196 (1998).

[14]   See Introductory Statement to NY PJI 2:149 (containing a comprehensive discussion of the caselaw).

[15]   See Allende v. New York City Health and Hospitals Corp., 90 N.Y.2d 333, 660 N.Y.S.2d 695, 683 N.E.2d 317 (1997).

[16]   *Allende*, 90 N.Y.2d at 339, 660 N.Y.S.2d at 699, 683 N.E.2d at 321.

[17]   Plummer v. New York City Health and Hospitals Corp., 285 A.D.2d 374, 729 N.Y.S.2d 70 (1st Dep't 2001).

[18]   Plummer ex rel. Heron v. New York City Health and Hospitals Corp., 98 N.Y.2d 263, 746 N.Y.S.2d 647, 774 N.E.2d 712 (2002) (NYSLD No. 511).

the tolling of the statute of limitations that the theory may earn against a physician generally won't be available against a lab.[19]

"Continuous Representation" Exception to Accrual

A kind of continuous treatment theory with equivalent accrual benefits, commonly known as "continuous representation," has been applied to suits against other professionals, including lawyers,[20] accountants,[21] and architects,[22] where the applicable period is 3 years.[23] But there, too, an ongoing professional relationship with respect to the subject matter that gives rise to the malpractice claim must be shown.

In Muller v. Sturman,[24] the court held that a client who seeks to exploit the theory in a legal malpractice action must show continuous representation by the lawyer on the same matter that gives rise to the alleged malpractice and "not merely continuity of a general professional relationship." The malpractice in *Muller* was alleged to be the lawyer's failure to sue on a certain note, but the court held that there was not "an ongoing, continuous, developing and dependent relationship" on the matter "marked with trust and confidence." Rather, there had been a drifting apart and the client did not try to press for suit on the note.

The Court of Appeals discusses the "continuous representation" theory in Shumsky v. Eisenstein,[25] where it examined the facts in depth to determine the moment when it could logically be concluded that the representation had ended, which is always a key inquiry in this kind of case.[26] In a more recent Court of Appeals decision, Gotay v. Breitbart,[27] the key issue was the date the law firm terminated the attorney-client relationship. Reversing the appellate division, which found that the law firm did not clearly establish when its representation had ceased, the Court of Appeals in a brief memo found that the claim was barred by the statute of limitations and that the continuous representation doctrine did not apply.

The Court had an opportunity to apply the doctrine again in Grace v. Law,[28] where a law firm withdrew from representing the plaintiff in a medical malpractice action in federal court after discovering it had a conflict of interest. The exact date of the transfer of the representation to the successor law firm was not clear, but on December 8, 2008, an order was signed by the federal district court directing the substitution of counsel.[29] Plaintiff, who was dissatisfied with the results achieved by both firms, commenced a legal malpractice action against both of them on December 5, 2011. The law firm that withdrew from the representation in the federal court action moved for summary judgment based on the 3-year statute of limitations in CPLR 214(6), claiming that

---

[19] McDermott v. Torre, 56 N.Y.2d 399, 452 N.Y.S.2d 351, 437 N.E.2d 1108 (1982).

[20] Shumsky v. Eisenstein, 96 N.Y.2d 164, 726 N.Y.S.2d 365, 750 N.E.2d 67 (2001).

[21] Williamson ex rel. Lipper Convertibles, L.P. v. PricewaterhouseCoopers LLP, 9 N.Y.3d 1, 840 N.Y.S.2d 730, 872 N.E.2d 842 (2007) (finding toll inapplicable to facts).

[22] Regency Club at Wallkill, LLC v. Appel Design Group, P.A., 112 A.D.3d 603, 976 N.Y.S.2d 164 (2d Dep't 2013).

[23] CPLR 214(6); see § 35.

[24] Muller v. Sturman, 79 A.D.2d 482, 484, 437 N.Y.S.2d 205, 207 (4th Dep't 1981).

[25] Shumsky v. Eisenstein, 96 N.Y.2d 164, 726 N.Y.S.2d 365, 750 N.E.2d 67 (2001) (NYSLD No. 497).

[26] See Johnson v. Proskauer Rose LLP, 129 A.D.3d 59, 9 N.Y.S.3d 201 (1st Dep't 2015).

[27] Gotay v. Breitbart, 12 N.Y.3d 894, 884 N.Y.S.2d 677, 912 N.E.2d 1056 (2009).

[28] Grace v. Law, 24 N.Y.3d 203, 997 N.Y.S.2d 334, 21 N.E.3d 995 (2014).

[29] *Grace*, 24 N.Y.3d at 207, 997 N.Y.S.2d at 335, 21 N.E.3d at 996.

plaintiff should have known by September 26, 2008, that the firm was no longer able to represent him and that successor counsel would be taking over the representation. The plaintiff countered that he did not learn of the substitution of counsel until December 8, 2008, when the official order substituting counsel was signed by the federal district court. The Court affirmed the Fourth Department's denial of defendant's motion for summary judgment, agreeing that it was "unclear" when the firm's representation of plaintiff in the federal action concluded.[30]

We again stress that if a lawyer plans to withdraw from the representation of a client, she should act promptly and clearly communicate with the client in writing when the representation is concluded.[31] The First Department's decision in *Gotay*, which was reversed by the Court of Appeals, nonetheless provides sound advice in the area, especially in light of the Court's subsequent decision in *Grace*:

> The Court of Appeals has recognized it as "essential that the terms of [attorney-client] representation . . . be set down with clarity" . . . Although the need for such clarity has most often been remarked upon in connection with fee disputes, it is no less critical to have an explicit and accurate understanding of any other fundamental issue pertaining to the attorney-client relationship, including, obviously, the elemental issue of whether there is a relationship at all. There is no room for uncertainty on these matters, especially where, as here, attorneys deal with laypersons unversed in the nuances and intricacies of legal practice and expression; what may seem crystal clear to a lawyer may be utterly lost upon the client. If the attorney-client relationship has come to an end, that fact should be absolutely clear to all parties involved.[32]

The facts in the Court of Appeals decision in In re Lawrence[33] are nothing short of remarkable. The defendant law firm represented the client in estate litigation for over twenty years, which concluded with a mammoth and unexpected settlement of over $100 million. Thereafter, a dispute arose over the amount of the lawyer's contingency fee calculated under a revised retainer agreement, which totaled approximately $44 million, and several gifts that the client had made to individual lawyers during the representation ranging in amounts from $1.5 to $2 million!

The estate's claims for refund of the gifts, which were made in 1998, were subject to dismissal under the statute of limitations unless they were subject to the continuous representation doctrine. The *Lawrence* Court noted that the continuous representation doctrine can only be applied if "two prerequisites" are met: "a claim of misconduct concerning the manner in which professional services were performed, and the ongoing

---

[30]   *Grace*, 24 N.Y.3d at 212, 997 N.Y.S.2d at 338, 21 N.E.3d at 999. See also Farage v. Ehrenberg, 124 A.D.3d 159, 996 N.Y.S.2d 646 (2d Dep't 2014), *lv. denied*, 25 N.Y.3d 906, 10 N.Y.S.3d 525, 32 N.E.3d 962 (2015) ("[W]here . . . facts establish a client's discharge of counsel on a date preceding execution and filing of the Consent to Change Attorney form, the continuing representation toll of the statute of limitations for legal malpractice runs only to the date of the actual discharge and not to the date of the later Consent to Change Attorney.").

[31]   See also New York Rules of Professional Conduct, Rule 1.16(d) ("If permission for withdrawal from employment is required by the rules of a tribunal, a lawyer shall not withdraw from employment in a matter before that tribunal without its permission."); Rule 1.16(e) ("Even when withdrawal is otherwise permitted or required, upon termination of representation, a lawyer shall take steps, to the extent reasonably practicable, to avoid foreseeable prejudice to the rights of the client, including giving reasonable notice to the client, [and] allowing time for employment of other counsel . . . ."); CPLR 321(b) (providing procedures for changing an attorney on consent and motions for withdrawal from representation).

[32]   Gotay v. Breitbart, 58 A.D.3d 25, 29, 866 N.Y.S.2d 638, 641 (1st Dep't 2008), rev'd, 12 N.Y.3d 894, 884 N.Y.S.2d 677, 912 N.E.3d 1056 (2009).

[33]   In re Lawrence, 24 N.Y.3d 320, 998 N.Y.S.2d 698, 23 N.E.3d 965 (2014).

provision of professional services with respect to the contested matter or transaction."[34] The Court ultimately dismissed the claim as time-barred, concluding that the continuous treatment doctrine generally cannot be applied to a financial dispute between the professional and her client, such as a dispute over a fee or a gift.[35]

Continuous Treatment Toll for Derivative Claim

The First and Third Departments have concluded that the continuous treatment toll is personal to the patient and does not apply to a derivative claim.[36] In Miller v. Rivard,[37] the Third Department had previously held that if the continuous treatment doctrine tolled the statute of limitations on the plaintiff's primary cause of action, "the policy reasons underlying the doctrine would require its application to toll the Statute of Limitations on [a] derivative claim." The holding in *Miller* is not mentioned in the Third Department's more recent decisions that reach a contrary conclusion.[38] Relying on the Third Department's decision in *Miller*, the Second Department had ruled that the continuous treatment toll applies to a plaintiff's derivative claim even though the CPLR 208 tolls for infancy and insanity do not.[39] The Second Department also apparently reconsidered the matter and has, more recently, concluded that "the continuous treatment toll is personal to the patient and not available to extend [a] husband's loss of consortium claim."[40] The Fourth Department, citing to the Second Department's prior position, adheres to the rule that if the continuous treatment doctrine applies to toll the statute of limitations with respect to the main claim, it will similarly toll the statute of limitations on the derivative claim.[41]

While a derivative claim is often interposed as an afterthought, in certain instances it can be quite substantial and even more significant than the primary claim. Lawyers need to be cautious here, especially given the irreconcilable case law in the Second and Third Departments. If at all possible, a plaintiff with a significant derivative claim should attempt to commence the action within the statute of limitations and assume that no toll applies. Until this important conflict is resolved by the Court of Appeals, this may be the only prudent way to proceed, even if commencement of the suit might jeopardize the doctor-patient relationship.[42]

---

[34] *In re Lawrence*, 24 N.Y.3d at 341, 998 N.Y.S.2d at 712, 23 N.E.3d at 980.

[35] The Court's discussion of the continuous representation doctrine will likely be debated in future cases where the client claims that the lawyer charged an excessive fee or engaged in self-dealing. See, e.g., New York Rules of Professional Conduct, Rule 1.5(a) (outlining factors to be considered in determining if fee is excessive); Rule 1.8(a) (containing requirements for business transactions with clients).

[36] See, e.g., Baer v. Law Offices of Moran & Gottlieb, 139 A.D.3d 1232, 1233, 32 N.Y.S.3d 359, 361 (3d Dep't 2016); Devadas v. Niksarli, 120 A.D.3d 1000, 1008, 992 N.Y.S.2d 197, 204 (1st Dep't 2014) (derivative claim for loss of services).

[37] Miller v. Rivard, 180 A.D.3d 331, 339, 585 N.Y.S.2d 523, 528 (3d Dep't 1992).

[38] See *Baer*, 139 A.D.3d at 1233, 32 N.Y.S.3d at 361; Cahill v. Lat, 39 A.D.3d 1013, 1014, 834 N.Y.S.2d 363 (3d Dep't 2007).

[39] See Cappelluti v. Sckolnick, 207 A.D.2d 763, 616 N.Y.S.2d 398 (2d Dep't 1994); § 54.

[40] See Chambers v. Mirkinson, 68 A.D.3d 702, 706, 890 N.Y.S.2d 99, 103 (2d Dep't 2009).

[41] See Dolce v. Powalski, 13 A.D.3d 1200, 787 N.Y.S.2d 595 (4th Dep't 2004).

[42] See Patrick M. Connors, *For Whom the Statute Tolls,* N.Y.L.J., Mar. 29, 2017, at 4.

Foreign Object Exception to Accrual

In medical malpractice litigation, one of the most prominent injustices occurred in surgery cases in which a foreign object was left inside the plaintiff.[43] Periodically urged to adopt a "discovery" accrual in these instances, the legislature regularly refused, until the Court of Appeals took the step itself in 1969 in Flanagan v. Mount Eden General Hospital.[44] The legislature then addressed the matter in 1975 with the adoption of CPLR 214–a, which, in "foreign object" cases only, allows the action to be commenced within 1 year from the date the plaintiff discovered the wrong or facts that would reasonably lead to its discovery, "whichever is earlier." The 1-year period is an alternative, and the action is still timely if commenced within 2 1/2 years after the wrongful act, regardless of when the injury was discovered.

Some cases prior to 1975 did not insist that something be left inside the patient. They applied the discovery rule announced in the *Flanagan* decision even to injuries inflicted on internal organs during an operation, notwithstanding that nothing foreign was left behind.[45] These cases were displaced when the Court of Appeals subsequently adopted a far more restrictive view of the "foreign object" rule. It held in Rodriguez v. Manhattan Medical Group, P.C.,[46] for example, that an intrauterine device is a fixation device and not a "foreign object." Therefore, the failure to remove it does not earn a "discovery" accrual for limitations purposes. In short, the "foreign object" exception in CPLR 214–a cannot apply to what amounts to a misdiagnosis by a doctor retained to remove a device but who negligently fails to do so. A mere misdiagnosis is still subject to a time-of-wrong accrual, even if the plaintiff does not discover it until later.[47]

CPLR 214–a excludes from the "foreign object" category any "chemical compound, fixation device or prosthetic aid or device." There would thus be no discovery accrual in actions involving the failure to remove those items. A suture inserted into the wrong organ during surgery has been held a "fixation device," not a "foreign object," and hence does not get the benefit of the "foreign object" rule.[48] It has even been held that a surgeon's failure to remove a "stent" that the surgeon inserted with the very intention of removing it at a later time is also not a "foreign object" case.[49] In Walton v. Strong Memorial Hospital,[50] the Court of Appeals revisited *Flanagan* and its progeny in a comprehensive opinion and ruled that a fragment remaining from a catheter that was placed in plaintiff's heart during surgery in 1986 is a foreign object for purposes of the discovery rule of CPLR 214–a. The Court emphasized that while "every fixation device is intentionally placed for a continuing (even if temporary) treatment purpose . . . it does not follow that everything that is intentionally placed for a continuing treatment purpose is a fixation device."[51]

---

[43] See, e.g., Conklin v. Draper, 229 A.D. 227, 241 N.Y.S. 529 (1st Dep't 1930), aff'd, 254 N.Y. 620, 173 N.E. 892 (1930).

[44] Flanagan v. Mount Eden General Hospital, 24 N.Y.2d 427, 301 N.Y.S.2d 23, 248 N.E.2d 871 (1969).

[45] See, e.g., Dobbins v. Clifford, 39 A.D.2d 1, 4, 330 N.Y.S.2d 743, 747 (4th Dep't 1972).

[46] Rodriguez v. Manhattan Medical Group, P.C., 77 N.Y.2d 217, 566 N.Y.S.2d 193, 567 N.E.2d 235 (1990).

[47] Rockefeller v. Moront, 81 N.Y.2d 560, 601 N.Y.S.2d 86, 618 N.E.2d 119 (1993).

[48] See Rockefeller v. Moront, 81 N.Y.2d 560, 601 N.Y.S.2d 86, 618 N.E.2d 119 (1993).

[49] LaBarbera v. New York Eye and Ear Infirmary, 91 N.Y.2d 207, 668 N.Y.S.2d 546, 691 N.E.2d 617 (1998).

[50] Walton v. Strong Memorial Hosp., 25 N.Y.3d 554, 14 N.Y.S.3d 757, 35 N.E.3d 827 (2015).

[51] *Walton*, 25 N.Y.3d at 572, 14 N.Y.S.3d at 769, 35 N.E.3d at 839.

It might cross the reader's mind that fixation devices and other objects might qualify as harmful "substances" under CPLR 214–c, the so-called "exposure" statute,[52] and that claims relating to them might therefore earn a postponed accrual. That crossed the legislature's mind as well: CPLR 214–c(5) states explicitly that CPLR 214–c does not apply in medical or dental malpractice actions.

§ 43. "Discovery" Accruals

The general rule in New York practice is that a cause of action accrues on the date of injury regardless of when the injury is discovered. As noted in the section above, there are limited exceptions in which a claim will accrue upon discovery of the injury.[1] Aside from the "discovery" accrual applicable in foreign object cases in the medical malpractice area, there are very few other instances where a time period is started from the plaintiff's "discovery" of the wrong. We'll see some below, but we note at the outset that CPLR 203(g)[2] operates in a very limited category of actions and is a legislative intervention regarding these claims. It concludes that if the time to commence an action "is computed from the time when facts were discovered or from the time when facts could with reasonable diligence have been discovered," the maximum time the plaintiff ought to have is 2 years from that moment.[3] With most such "discovery" accruals, therefore, CPLR 203(g) superimposes itself, but also provides that the claim can still keep its stated period measured from the wrong itself if that is longer. The result is that in each of these "discovery" cases there are actually 2 measurements: (1) the stated period running from the wrong itself, and (2) the 2-year period running from the wrong's discovery. The plaintiff can use whichever is longer.

Fraud is one of the most common claims whose period, which is 6 years, has a discovery accrual.[4] The operation of CPLR 203(g) on it gave the plaintiff either 6 years from the fraud or 2 years from the discovery of the fraud, whichever is longer. In 2004, CPLR 213(8) was amended to specifically incorporate CPLR 203(g)'s discovery rule. If actual fraud underlies the claim, this discovery rule is applicable even when the plaintiff is seeking equitable relief, such as in a creditor's action to set aside a fraudulent conveyance.[5]

Expressly excepted from the operation of CPLR 203(g) is the 4-year warranty period of UCC section 2–725, which has a discovery accrual in certain instances, and the "foreign object" claim in medical malpractice cases, which is preempted by CPLR 214–a, discussed in the prior section. Apparently, the 3-year period applicable in the so-called "exposure" cases, for which a discovery rule was enacted in 1986, is also exempt from the 203(g) reduction, but the statute does not mention CPLR 214–c.[6]

---

[52] See § 40.

[1] See, e.g., CPLR 214–c, discussed in § 40.

[2] Until 1992, the designation of this provision was subdivision (f); a 1992 amendment changed it to (g). In conducting research, especially when using a tool like Westlaw, keep in mind that the many pre-1992 cases that deal with it cite it as (f).

[3] See McLaughlin, The Discovery Provisions of Article Two, 10th Jud. Conf. Rep. Leg. Doc. No. 90, p.96 (1965).

[4] CPLR 213(8).

[5] See Quadrozzi Concrete Corp. v. Mastroianni, 56 A.D.2d 353, 392 N.Y.S.2d 687 (2d Dep't 1977).

[6] See § 40.

Another period running from discovery is the breach of warranty of authority,[7] the claim a victim has against one who falsely represents his capacity to act as agent for another. This is a category of contract and has a 6-year period,[8] which would be reduced to 2 under CPLR 203(g) insofar as measured from discovery. It is not clear what the starting point of the alternative 6-years-from-wrong would be in that case. Apparently, it would be sometime after the agent makes her last representation of authority,[9] and the plaintiff would have either that period or 2 years from discovery of the misrepresentation, whichever is longer.

The Court of Appeals is asked periodically to adopt a "discovery" rule of accrual for actions against nonmedical professionals governed by CPLR 214(6), but has declined.[10] It has applied a "continuous representation" theory in these actions, however, and this often has the effect of extending the time for commencement.[11]

§ 44. Wrongful Death Cases

The wrongful death statute of limitations is supplied by EPTL 5–4.1. It is 2 years and runs from the moment of death.[1] But the statute also provides that the action lies only if the defendant "would have been liable to the decedent" for the wrong if death had not ensued. This has been construed to require that the day of death be looked at to determine if, on that day, the decedent had a timely claim against the wrongdoer for the injuries from which the death resulted. If, for example, the basis of liability is negligence, which carries a 3-year period, and on the date of death the 3 years for the negligence action had not yet expired, this condition precedent is met and the action would lie.

There are thus two statutes of limitation to be investigated in a wrongful death action. The first is the 2-year period measured from death—the claim must in any event be brought within that time—and the second is the period applicable to the decedent's underlying cause of action (3 years for negligence, 4 years for breach of warranty, 1 year for assault, etc.). On the day of death, the relevant statute of limitations for the underlying personal injury claim must still be alive.[2]

Take this example: P is injured in an accident involving D's negligent driving on June 1, 2015. P dies from his injuries on June 2, 2018, without having commenced an action. A wrongful death claim, even if brought within 2 years after death, is barred: the statute of limitations on the underlying claim had expired before P died. Had P in the example died on or before June 1, 2018, the wrongful death claim would lie. Even if P had not in fact sued for the personal injury, he could have done so timely on that day. Of course, if a timely suit had been commenced by P prior to his death and was still pending at that time, the condition precedent is met even if the statute of limitations applicable

---

[7] CPLR 206(b).

[8] CPLR 213(2).

[9] See Moore v. Maddock, 251 N.Y. 420, 167 N.E. 572 (1929). CPLR 206(b) was intended to clarify *Moore*, but confusion persists under the impact of CPLR 203(g).

[10] See, e.g., Shumsky v. Eisenstein, 96 N.Y.2d 164, 726 N.Y.S.2d 365, 750 N.E.2d 67 (2001) (NYSLD No. 497) (malpractice action against attorney); Ackerman v. Price Waterhouse, 84 N.Y.2d 535, 620 N.Y.S.2d 318, 644 N.E.2d 1009 (1994) (malpractice action against accountant); §§ 35, 40.

[11] See § 42.

[1] A wrongful death claim is often accompanied by a survival claim. See § 55.

[2] Kelliher v. New York Cent. & H.R.R. Co., 212 N.Y. 207, 105 N.E. 824 (1914).

to the underlying claim has now long since expired.[3] The timely commencement of the negligence suit and its pendency at the moment of death give the plaintiff a viable claim against the defendant at that time, which is what EPTL section 5–4.1 insists on.

The predeath settlement of the underlying claim, however, or the predeath satisfaction of a judgment recovered on it, destroys the necessary condition precedent and bars the death claim.[4] This can obviously pose a delicate problem for the plaintiff's lawyer to whom a substantial personal injury settlement is tendered by the tortfeasor while the client is in extremis. Acceptance of the settlement bars any wrongful death claim that might otherwise accrue to the client's dependents.

A point should be made about the availability of a wrongful death claim in the so-called "exposure" case in which CPLR 214–c postpones the running of the statute of limitations until the plaintiff has discovered the injury.[5] CPLR 214–c specifically refers only to personal injury and property damage cases, which has led one court to conclude that the "discovery" rule of CPLR 214–c does not apply in a wrongful death action.[6] If, however, a wrongful death action is timely commenced, the provisions in CPLR 214–c would be relevant to the issue of whether the decedent had a timely personal injury cause of action at the time of her death.[7] The incidents of CPLR 214–c about postponed accrual based on discovery of the injury and discovery of the cause would be applicable in making that determination.[8] CPLR 214–c would also appear to apply to a survival action in which the personal representative generally has at least one year from the date of death in which to commence an action.[9]

The statute of limitations in wrongful death actions against a municipal entity governed by General Municipal Law section 50–(i) is 2 years after death rather than the 1 year and 90 days period governing general tort claims.[10]

E. INTERPOSITION

Table of Sections

§ 45.   "Interposition" of the Claim; "United in Interest"
§ 46.   Provisional Remedy as Interposition
§ 47.   Delivery to Sheriff or Clerk
§ 48.   Counterclaims
§ 49.   Claim in Amended Pleading

---

[3]   The complaint could be amended to add the wrongful death claim. See Caffaro v. Trayna, 35 N.Y.2d 245, 360 N.Y.S.2d 847, 319 N.E.2d 174 (1974); §§ 49, 237.

[4]   Doe v. State, 189 A.D.2d 199, 206–07, 595 N.Y.S.2d 592, 597 (4th Dep't 1993).

[5]   See § 40.

[6]   Annunziato v. City of New York, 224 A.D.2d 31, 37, 647 N.Y.S.2d 850, 854 (2d Dep't 1996).

[7]   *Annunziato*, 224 A.D.2d at 37, 647 N.Y.S.2d at 854.

[8]   See § 40.

[9]   CPLR 210(a); see § 55.

[10]   Gen. Mun. Law § 50–i(1)(c).

§ 45. "Interposition" of the Claim; "United in Interest"

As we noted above,[1] calculating the statute of limitations requires a determination on four separate matters. The first is the time period that governs the particular claim,[2] the second is when the claim accrues for statute of limitations purposes,[3] and the third is whether the relevant time period may be subject to extensions, often referred to as tolling provisions.[4] In this section and those that follow,[5] we address the fourth issue: the timely interposition of the claim within the relevant limitations period, as required by CPLR 203(a).

A claim is deemed interposed when the action is filed[6]—the summons and complaint or summons and notice are the papers filed[7]—even though service of these papers, also known as initiatory papers, need not be made until 120 days after the filing.[8]

In New York practice, it had long been the rule that the service of the initiatory papers marked the commencement of the action and therefore constituted the moment that "interposed" the claim under CPLR 203(a),[9] in contrast with federal practice where the filing of the complaint marks interposition of the claim regardless of when the summons is ultimately served.[10] In 1992, however, the legislature changed the rule in the supreme and county courts,[11] essentially adopting the federal practice and deeming the action "commenced" and the claim interposed upon the filing of the initiatory papers with the clerk.

In the lower courts—the civil, district, city, and town and village courts—service rather than filing continued to be the measure of commencement for a while, but in 2005 they, too, were changed to "filing" courts, with the exception of the town and village courts.[12] This was done in an amendment of section 400 in each of the New York City Civil, Uniform District, and Uniform City court acts.[13]

---

[1]   See § 33.

[2]   See § 35.

[3]   See §§ 40 to 41.

[4]   See §§ 50 to 55.

[5]   See §§ 46 to 49.

[6]   CPLR 203(c).

[7]   CPLR 304(a).

[8]   CPLR 306–b. This same interposition rule applies in a special proceeding, but only a petition need be filed to interpose the claim. CPLR 304(a); see § 553. The notice of petition or order to show cause must accompany the petition when service is made on the respondent. CPLR 306–b.

[9]   There is a history behind this, and being alert to it is not a mere academic exercise: numerous cases are on the books involving the application of superseded provisions and they can crop up during research at any time.

[10]   Fed. R. Civ. P. 3; see § 621 (Practitioner's Edition). If subject matter jurisdiction in the federal action is based on diversity of citizenship, however, the moment that a claim is deemed "interposed" for statute of limitations purposes is governed by state law, not by Rule 3. See § 625 (Practitioner's Edition).

[11]   L.1992, ch. 216. The change affects the surrogates' courts, too, where claims are asserted through special proceedings, for which see the Commentary to SCPA 301 on McKinney's SCPA 301 and the note in SPR 35:4.

[12]   The town and village courts remain "service" courts. See Uniform Just. Ct. Act § 400 ("An action is commenced in this court and jurisdiction acquired by service of a summons.").

[13]   There are some significant differences from supreme court practice, however. A two-part treatment of the changeover, in SPR 164 and SPR 165, discusses the differences.

Making the mistake of assuming that service still constitutes commencement in any of these courts today—as by making service within the statute of limitations but not filing until afterwards—brings dismissal of the action.[14]

Interposing the claim by filing should rarely prove difficult, especially in an e-filed action, but if it does, and time is running out, CPLR 304(a) permits the plaintiff to seek an ex parte order from a judge directing that the filing take place within 5 days after the judge signs the order. The mere signing of such an order marks the moment of "interposition" in that instance—i.e., commencement—for a statute of limitations measure.[15]

A plaintiff who plans to mail the initiatory papers to the clerk, which is permissible, should remember that commencement doesn't occur until the clerk receives the mail, opens the papers, and files them. Furthermore, in a busy county clerk's office, these latter acts may not all occur on the same day. Filing is not deemed to occur on mere posting of the initiatory papers.[16]

Allowing a mere notice to accompany the summons instead of requiring a complaint is somewhat unique to New York practice[17] and, for various reasons, often a bad way to start things off. Using a complaint at the very outset is usually the better practice.[18] When an action is commenced with a summons and notice, the complaint comes later, after a demand is made.[19] The option of filing the summons without a complaint is not available in the lower courts where the complaint must be served with the summons pursuant to their own court acts.[20]

If there are several defendants and they are "united in interest," commencement of the action as to one will be deemed interposition of the claim as against the others[21] even though the others will of course have to be named and served before the court gets jurisdiction of them. This provision essentially permits commencement of the action against other defendants after the statute of limitations has expired, as long as there has been timely commencement as to one defendant with whom they are united in interest. To qualify as "united" under this rule, however, the defendants' interests must be without mutual hostility. Where P sought to rescind an insurance policy, for example, the beneficiary and the insured were both "united" in their wish to preserve the policy and service on the beneficiary within the applicable period therefore preserved the claim as against the insured as well.[22]

---

[14]   See. e.g., Perrone v. Jim Doyle Ford, Inc., 13 Misc. 3d 312, 818 N.Y.S.2d 907 (Dist. Ct., Nassau County 2006).

[15]   CPLR 203(c), 304(a).

[16]   See Cranesville Block Co., Inc. v. Spring Apartments, LLC, 53 A.D.3d 998, 999, 863 N.Y.S.2d 116, 117 (3d Dep't 2008), lv. denied 11 N.Y.3d 711, 872 N.Y.S.2d 73, 900 N.E.2d 556.

[17]   See CPLR 304(a), 305(b); § 60. In federal practice, the complaint must accompany the summons. See § 623 (Practitioner's Edition).

[18]   See § 60.

[19]   CPLR 305(b), 3012(b).

[20]   See § 902(a)(1) in each of the New York City Civil, Uniform District, Uniform City, and Uniform Justice court acts, and Commentary C3012:3 on McKinney's CPLR 3012. In the lower courts, the complaint itself may be a simple "indorsement" on or with the summons. A note comparing the supreme court "notice" pleading and the lower courts' "indorsement" pleading appears in SPR 90:3.

[21]   CPLR 203(c).

[22]   Prudential Ins. Co. of America v. Stone, 270 N.Y. 154, 200 N.E. 679 (1936).

It has been held that unity of interest doctrine will not apply between (e.g.) a blood center that provides blood and the hospital that administers it.[23] While a physician and the professional service corporation of which the physician is a member may be united in interest under this rule, the unity does not necessarily exist between the member physicians[24] because while the corporation is liable for the acts of Dr. A as a matter of substantive law, Dr. B individually is not. The "united in interest" doctrine, therefore, often follows the substantive law.

The test is often pragmatic. Joint tortfeasors owning or driving different cars in an accident that injures the plaintiff are not united in interest. Each is hostile to the other and would gladly lay liability at the other's door. But if the joint tortfeasors are the owner and driver of the same car, with the owner only derivatively responsible for the driver, both have been held united in interest against the plaintiff and commencement as to one preserves the claim against the other.[25] Even that conclusion can be debated, however,[26] especially in an action in which the owner claims that the driver did not have permission to drive the vehicle.[27] Therefore, it is best to assume hostility among tortfeasors of any kind and to see to it that proper commencement is effected as to each before the statute expires.[28]

§ 46.   Provisional Remedy as Interposition

There are 4 provisional remedies in New York practice, each having a CPLR article of its own. They are attachment (Article 62), injunction (63), receivership (64), and notice of pendency (65). They are studied later,[1] but are mentioned now for their ostensible bearing on the statute of limitations.

Some of the provisional remedy statutes provided for procedure when the remedy was applied for before "commencement" of the action.[2] Paragraphs 3 and 4 of CPLR 203(b) were designed to let the pre-action granting of a provisional remedy constitute "commencement" for statute of limitations purposes. These provisions had a role to play when service marked commencement but became largely irrelevant when filing displaced it because a provisional remedy cannot be obtained today prior to commencement of the action.[3]

---

[23]   Mondello v. New York Blood Center-Greater New York Blood Program, 80 N.Y.2d 219, 590 N.Y.S.2d 19, 604 N.E.2d 81 (1992).

[24]   Connell v. Hayden, 83 A.D.2d 30, 443 N.Y.S.2d 383 (2d Dep't 1981).

[25]   Rahi v. Fang, 245 A.D.2d 13, 665 N.Y.S.2d 641 (1st Dep't 1997).

[26]   See Parker v. Port Authority of New York and New Jersey, 113 A.D.2d 763, 764–65, 493 N.Y.S.2d 355, 357–58 (2d Dep't 1985); Halucha v. Jockey Club, 31 Misc. 2d 186, 220 N.Y.S.2d 567 (Sup. Ct., New York County 1961).

[27]   Poulard v. Papamihlopoulos, 254 A.D.2d 266, 678 N.Y.S.2d 383 (2d Dep't 1998) (suggesting that the owner and driver may not be united in interest if there was a claim that driver did not have owner's permission).

[28]   The *Connell* decision, note 24 above, offers a review of the relationships that satisfy the united in interest standard. 83 A.D.2d at 42–51, 443 N.Y.S.2d at 393–97.

[1]   §§ 306 et seq.

[2]   See, e.g., § 6213 (attachment) before its 1992 amendment.

[3]   See § 45.

While perhaps still applicable in the town and village courts under the Uniform Justice Court Act, provisional remedies in those courts are rare and only the remedy of seizure of a chattel is authorized.[4]

§ 47.   Delivery to Sheriff or Clerk

At one time, an important provision on the statute of limitations—and a favorite of lawyers who waited for the last minute to commence actions—was CPLR 203(b)(5). It allows a last minuter to secure an extra 60 days for service with a mere delivery of the summons to the clerk of the court in an action in New York City or to the sheriff of the county in an action outside the 5 boroughs. CPLR 203(b)(5), which only applies when an action is commenced by service of process, lost its attraction when the filing system for commencing actions was enacted in 1992 in the supreme and county courts, and in 2005 in the civil, district, and city courts.[1] The procedure apparently survives in the town and village courts, where actions are still commenced by service, but we are not likely to ever see it invoked there.

§ 48.   Counterclaims

A counterclaim is contained in the defendant's answer, but it has the advantage of being deemed interposed, for statute of limitations purposes, as of the moment the claim in the complaint was interposed.[1] This means that a counterclaim is deemed interposed when the plaintiff filed the main action,[2] and this applies whether or not the counterclaim is related to the plaintiff's claim.[3]

Suppose, for example, that in a supreme court action the statute of limitations on D's counterclaim expires on January 6, 2018. P commences the action on January 5, 2018, and the answer containing D's counterclaim is served on January 30, 2018. The counterclaim is in all respects timely.[4]

Assume now that the counterclaim is untimely even if measured by the moment of the main action's commencement. All is not necessarily lost. If D's counterclaim arises from the same transaction or occurrence as P's claim, it may be interposed regardless of timeliness, but in this situation it will suffice only to neutralize or set off P's claim. In this scenario, D will not be allowed to take an affirmative judgment against P for any balance that might be due in D's favor.[5] This is the limitations aspect of a doctrine known as "equitable recoupment." For example:

P, a physician who treated D, sues D for his fee within the 6-year contract period applicable to it.[6] D counterclaims for medical malpractice, which has a 2 1/2-year period,[7]

---

[4]   See Uniform Just. Ct. Act § 209.

[1]   See § 45. There was much to say about CPLR 203(b)(5) prior to the adoption of the filing system, and we said it in this section in the 4th edition of this book.

[1]   CPLR 203(d). Subdivision (d) was lettered (c) before a 1992 amendment gave it its present designation. Because it is frequently cited in the caselaw, lawyers must keep this relettering in mind, especially when using a research tool like Westlaw.

[2]   CPLR 304.

[3]   See Chevron Oil Co. v. Atlas Oil Co. of Utica, 28 A.D.2d 644, 280 N.Y.S.2d 731 (4th Dep't 1967).

[4]   See Proskauer Rose Goetz & Mendelsohn LLP v. Munao, 270 A.D.2d 150, 151, 704 N.Y.S.2d 590, 591 (1st Dep't 2000).

[5]   See Title Guarantee & Trust Co. v. Hicks, 283 A.D. 723, 127 N.Y.S.2d 340 (2d Dep't 1954).

[6]   CPLR 213(2); see § 35.

[7]   CPLR 214–a; see § 42.

contending that he was injured by the treatment. Assume that even as measured by the moment of the main action's commencement, the counterclaim is too late. Nevertheless, because it arises out of the transaction on which P sues, the counterclaim may still be entertained but only to the extent, and no further, of cancelling out what P may be owed.[8] Nor need the counterclaim be of the same theory as the main claim to invoke this recoupment doctrine. The malpractice counterclaim sounds in tort in the hypo above, for example, while the main claim is in contract. This is permissible.

D can't exploit the recoupment theory merely by showing some general relationship between counterclaim and main claim. The Court of Appeals has indicated that only an outright "recoupment" earns this treatment, i.e., a claim for recovery by D based on something "growing out" of P's claim. Thus, where P's claim was to recover for rent overcharges based on a wrongful computation of increases, and D, the landlord, sought by counterclaim to reform the lease, the reformation claim was held not to arise "out of" P's claim and was denied this limitations advantage.[9]

A counterclaim barred by time by all measures, but interposed as a recoupment because it arises out of the complaint's transaction, is being used, in effect, as a defense. That is permissible because CPLR 203(d) applies to defenses as well as counterclaims.

The structure of CPLR 203(d) is misleading. It has a brief first sentence and an extended second one, suggesting that the first one is the general rule and the second one its exception. In point of the number of situations affected, it's the other way around. The first sentence states that a counterclaim is deemed interposed "when a pleading containing it is served," which would mean the service of the answer. But most counterclaims are asserted in D's original answer, and these are deemed interposed, pursuant to the second sentence of CPLR 203(d), as of the time of commencement of the main action.

Then when would the first sentence apply? If D later in the case should get leave to amend the answer to include a counterclaim having no relationship to P's claim or to anything contained in D's original answer, the counterclaim would be deemed interposed only as of the service of the motion to amend the answer. That would give the first sentence of CPLR 203(d) something to operate on.[10]

Although not expressly addressed by the statute, CPLR 203(d) applies to cross-claims as well as counterclaims.[11] In one case, for example,[12] P sued D and X for personal injury. D interposed an answer containing a cross-claim against co-defendant X for contribution in respect of P's injuries and another for D's own property damage. For the contribution part, which amounts in essence to an indemnification claim, there are special limitations advantages[13] and there was thus no time problem. But there was a potential problem for the property damage cross-claim. The answer containing it was

---

[8] In this regard CPLR 203(d) apparently overrules Fish v. Conley, 221 A.D. 609, 225 N.Y.S. 27 (3d Dep't 1927). See Advisory Committee 2d Rep. Leg. Doc. No. 13, pp. 50, 494–95 (1958).

[9] SCM Corp. v. Fisher Park Lane Co., 40 N.Y.2d 788, 792, 390 N.Y.S.2d 398, 402, 358 N.E.2d 1024, 1027 (1976).

[10] Cf. Werner Spitz Const. Co. v. Vanderlinde Elec. Corp., 64 Misc. 2d 157, 314 N.Y.S.2d 567 (Monroe County Ct. 1970). Under CPLR 3025(b), the proposed amended answer would be served with the motion to amend. See § 237.

[11] Mitchell v. Olar, 138 A.D.3d 1490, 30 N.Y.S.3d 470 (4th Dep't 2016).

[12] Colichio v. Bailey, 77 A.D.2d 694, 429 N.Y.S.2d 504 (3d Dep't 1980).

[13] See §§ 35, 162.

served more than the applicable 3 years after the accident, and hence the cross-claim could be sustained as timely only if it was allowed a relation back to the original commencement of the action. It was allowed.

What about the situation in which P sues D, D impleads X, and X counterclaims against D? Does the counterclaim relate back, for a timeliness measure, to the time of commencement of P's original action against D, or only to D's filing of the third-party complaint on X? It should be the latter. In this example, X, the third-party defendant, is the one claiming the limitations advantage, and for CPLR 203(d) purposes, the relation back is to the pleading interposed against the one so claiming, i.e., the third-party complaint.[14]

§ 49.   Claim in Amended Pleading

Amendment to Add Claim Against Existing Party

Section 203(f) is the CPLR's principal "relation back" statute.[1] It provides that for limitations' purposes a claim in an amended pleading will be deemed to relate back to the time the claim in the original pleading was interposed as long as the original one gives notice of the transaction or occurrence out of which the claim in the amended pleading arises.[2]

If such notice is not given by the original pleading, the new claim will be measured for timeliness only by service of the amended pleading that contains it. If the amendment is one for which leave of court is necessary, which requires a motion,[3] it has been held that the claim can be deemed interposed as of the service of the motion papers containing the proposed amendment instead of the later time when the motion is granted.[4] This of course assumes a grant of the motion. A denial of the motion makes the matter academic.

A simple example of a relation back is where the amendment adds an assault claim arising out of the same incident as the negligence claim contained in the original complaint.[5] Since the original complaint's claim is deemed interposed as of the original filing of the action,[6] the assault claim asserted by amendment gets the advantage of relating back to the original commencement of the action if the original complaint gives notice of the elements of the assault claim. When, however, the nature of a newly asserted cause of action, such as negligent hiring, is distinct from the causes of action

---

[14]   See Goldberg v. Sitomer, Sitomer & Porges, 97 A.D.2d 114, 469 N.Y.S.2d 81 (1st Dep't 1983), aff'd, 63 N.Y.2d 831, 482 N.Y.S.2d 268, 472 N.E.2d 44 (1984).

[1]   The 1992 legislation that adopted the "filing" system for commencing actions in the supreme and county courts unfortunately relettered most of the subdivisions of CPLR 203. Subdivision (f) of the current CPLR 203 had previously been subdivision (e). Researchers must keep this change in mind.

[2]   CPLR 203(f) is the counterpart of the often invoked Rule 15(c) of the Federal Rules of Civil Procedure, which is similar to, but not the same as, CPLR 203(f). There have been disputes about which to choose in a federal action predicated on diversity of citizenship jurisdiction. See § 615 (Practitioner's Edition).

[3]   For the difference between an amendment that a party can make as of right and one that requires leave, see §§ 236 and 237.

[4]   Vastola v. Maer, 48 A.D.2d 561, 370 N.Y.S.2d 955 (2d Dep't 1975), aff'd, 39 A.D.2d 1019, 387 N.Y.S.2d 246, 355 N.E.2d 300 (1976). CPLR 3025(b) now requires that the motion include the proposed amended pleading. See § 237.

[5]   See Watso v. City of New York, 39 A.D.2d 960, 333 N.Y.S.2d 492 (2d Dep't 1972); see Pendleton v. City of New York, 44 A.D.3d 733, 737, 843 N.Y.S.2d 648, 652 (2d Dep't 2007) (amended complaint alleging Civil Rights Act cause of action related back to negligent hiring and training allegations contained in original complaint).

[6]   CPLR 203(c).

for medical malpractice and lack of informed consent asserted in the original complaint and requires different factual allegations than those contained in the original complaint, the new cause of action will not relate back to the commencement of the action.[7]

This rule is sometimes operative even if the amendment's claim technically belongs to a different plaintiff, as long as the defendant has the requisite notice. A wrongful death claim in an amended complaint, for example, which belongs to dependents of the decedent and not to the decedent himself, was held by the Court of Appeals in Caffaro v. Trayna[8] to relate back to the original complaint, which pleaded only the decedent's claim for medical malpractice from which the death later resulted.[9]

Some subsequent decisions seem inconsistent with *Caffaro*. In Laudico v. Sears, Roebuck and Co.,[10] for example, it was held that a wife's loss of services claim could not be related back to her husband's damages claim, from which it derived. But isn't it a kind of derivative claim in behalf of another, the same scenario that *Caffaro* operates on? Disagreeing with the *Laudico* case and other cases to the same effect, Anderson v. Carney[11] holds that a spouse's derivative claim, sought to be interposed through an amended pleading, does relate back to the time of the interposition of the personal injury claim from which it derives.

With a counterclaim, a triple relation back can sometimes be seen. If an amended answer adds a counterclaim arising out of an occurrence mentioned in the original answer, it relates back to the original answer;[12] the original answer then relates back to the complaint's claim;[13] and the complaint relates back to the commencement of the action.[14]

Amendment to Add New Party

CPLR 203(f) is usually invoked to add an additional claim the plaintiff has against a defendant who is already a party. What about a potential defendant whom the plaintiff wants to add as a party? Brock v. Bua[15] sets forth the rules for applying CPLR 203(f) in that situation.

P in *Brock* sued A, but did not initially join B. Then, with a supplemental summons and complaint for which leave was duly obtained,[16] P added B as a defendant. The

---

[7] Calamari v. Panos, 131 A.D.3d 1088, 1089–90, 16 N.Y.S.3d 824, 827 (2d Dep't 2015).

[8] Caffaro v. Trayna, 35 N.Y.2d 245, 360 N.Y.S.2d 847, 319 N.E.2d 174, 71 A.L.R.3d 924 (1974).

[9] *Caffaro* holds that it makes no difference that the wrongful death claim technically did not exist when the original complaint was served and only arose afterwards; that the notice purpose of current CPLR 203(f) is still fulfilled. See Commentary C3025:12 on McKinney's CPLR 3025. *Caffaro* is distinguished in Goldberg v. Camp Mikan-Recro, 42 N.Y.2d 1029, 398 N.Y.S.2d 1008, 369 N.E.2d 8 (1977), which held that there can be no relation back when the plaintiff who commences the wrongful death action has not been duly appointed as a personal representative. But a different statute, CPLR 205(a), treated in § 52, was later held to offer a statute of limitations extension for a new action in such a case. Carrick v. Central General Hospital, 51 N.Y.2d 242, 434 N.Y.S.2d 130, 414 N.E.2d 632 (1980). *Goldberg* therefore ends up as an inconvenience at worst—it requires a new action—and is even regarded in some quarters as overruled. See Snay v. Cohoes Memorial Hosp., 110 A.D.2d 1021, 487 N.Y.S.2d 899 (3d Dep't 1985).

[10] Laudico v. Sears, Roebuck and Co., 125 A.D.2d 960, 510 N.Y.S.2d 787 (4th Dep't 1986).

[11] Anderson v. Carney, 161 A.D.2d 1002, 557 N.Y.S.2d 575 (3d Dep't 1990).

[12] CPLR 203(f).

[13] CPLR 203(d).

[14] CPLR 203(c).

[15] Brock v. Bua, 83 A.D.2d 61, 443 N.Y.S.2d 407 (2d Dep't 1981).

[16] See CPLR 1003; § 65.

statute of limitations had by this time expired and the only way to preserve the claim against B was to have it deemed interposed at the time of the commencement of the action against A. That would require a relation back through use of CPLR 203(f) or a combination of 203(f) plus 203(c).[17] To earn such a relation back, *Brock* held that the plaintiff must show:

1. that the claims against both A and B arose out of the same conduct, transaction, or occurrence;

2. that there is such a unity of interest between A and B that the commencement of the action against A amounts to notice to B, thus warning B to prepare his case and negating any prejudice to B in maintaining a defense on the merits; and

3. that B knew, or should have known, that the action would have been brought against him as well as against A, but for the excusable mistake of the plaintiff in identifying the parties.

In the *Brock* case, P met the first two tests but failed the third and was denied a relation back. B in *Brock* was a corporation and A its president. The libel on which the suit was based was in a letter written by A on B's own stationery, from which P would have notice of B's involvement. P's mistake in initially omitting B was therefore not excusable, and timely suit against A thus did not save the claim against B.[18]

The *Brock* test was adopted by the Court of Appeals in Mondello v. New York Blood Center-Greater New York Blood Program,[19] where it was applied to the "united in interest" provision,[20] the provision the Court of Appeals deems relevant when P seeks to add a new party, with subdivision (f) apparently deemed applicable only when P seeks to add a new claim against a person already a party.[21] Then, in a follow-up to *Mondello*, the Court held that when the as-yet-unjoined B had notice of the claim within the applicable statute of limitations, from whatever source, this divested B of any claim of prejudice. In that situation, the Court ruled that, with regard to the third *Brock* element, plaintiff did not have to show that the mistake in failing to join B at the outset was "excusable." Rather, the plaintiff need only show that B was not joined because of a "mistake."[22]

The use of an "amendment" to assert a claim against one not already a party is, in essence, an effort to add that party. That's why the issue so often becomes bound up with the statute of limitations, but the addition of the party must also be accomplished successfully. The proper procedure to add a new party to an action is by the filing and service of a supplemental summons and amended complaint on that person.[23] Until 1996, the formal addition of the new party through use of a supplemental summons

---

[17]   CPLR 203(c) is the "united in interest" provision that enables commencement as to A to be deemed commencement as to the later-joined B as long as both are "united in interest." See § 45.

[18]   *Brock* relies, incidentally, on the test assumed to apply under the analogous Fed. R. Civ. P. 15(c), but that rule was amended in 1991, and the amendment would probably lead to a different result if applied to facts like those in the *Brock* case.

[19]   Mondello v. New York Blood Center-Greater New York Blood Program, 80 N.Y.2d 219, 590 N.Y.S.2d 19, 604 N.E.2d 81 (1992).

[20]   CPLR 203(c); see § 45.

[21]   See the discussion in SPR 17:2.

[22]   See Buran v. Coupal, 87 N.Y.2d 173, 638 N.Y.S.2d 405, 661 N.E.2d 978 (1995) (NYSLD No. 436).

[23]   CPLR 305(a), 1003; see § 65.

required court leave. A 1996 amendment of CPLR 1003 allows it by other means as well, one of which is by stipulation of all parties who have appeared in the action. Another dispenses even with a stipulation if the plaintiff acts early enough in the litigation.[24]

If a party is added to the action pursuant to CPLR 305(a) and 1003 within the statute of limitations, the *Brock* test need not be satisfied. If court leave is required and the motion is made while the statute of limitations is still alive against the party sought to be added, the lapse of time between the making of the motion and its granting has been held a tolling period, i.e., a period during which the running of the statute of limitations has been suspended.[25] In any event, the plaintiff should personally serve the party sought to be added with the motion papers and a proposed supplemental summons and amended complaint within the statute of limitations if at all possible.

Some lawyers in that situation feel more comfortable by not relying on the motion-to-add procedure at all, preferring instead to bring a separate action against the new party now, while time is still open, and then just moving to consolidate the new action with the pending one. It entails an additional filing fee, but they deem that a small price to pay for getting the new party into court immediately.

If the links that would satisfy the *Brock* standards exist, it has been held permissible to relate back to the original commencement of the action not only a claim the plaintiff seeks to add in the same action but even one sought to be added to a separate but connected action.[26]

Plaintiff Adding Direct Claim Against Third-Party Defendant

A related situation that has repeatedly arisen concerns a claim that a plaintiff wants to assert against a third-party defendant who has been impleaded. P has sued D on time, and D has impleaded X. If all D seeks of X is contribution or indemnity to cover P's main claim against D, D's claim against X is timely because of the special limitations' advantages applicable to third-party claims.[27] But what if P amends her complaint after D impleads X, as P may do as a matter of right,[28] and asserts a claim directly against X? How shall the statute of limitations be applied to that? Resolving a conflict among the cases, the Court of Appeals held in Duffy v. Horton Memorial Hosp.[29] that as long as D's commencement of the third-party action against X took place within the statute of limitations applicable to P's claim against X, P's later amendment to assert that claim directly against X is timely. The rationale is that X will be on notice of his involvement in the action at the moment he is named as a third-party defendant.

---

[24] See §§ 65, 138; SPR 43:1. It would seem that any time an amendment of a summons would be allowed to avoid the barrier of the statute of limitations, the amendment of a pleading should be allowed to as well.

[25] See Perez v. Paramount Communications, Inc., 92 N.Y.2d 749, 686 N.Y.S.2d 342, 709 N.E.2d 83 (1999) (NYSLD No. 471).

[26] See Town of Guilderland v. Texaco Refining and Marketing, Inc., 159 A.D.2d 829, 552 N.Y.S.2d 704 (3d Dep't 1990).

[27] See §§ 35, 162.

[28] See CPLR 1009.

[29] Duffy v. Horton Memorial Hosp., 66 N.Y.2d 473, 497 N.Y.S.2d 890, 488 N.E.2d 820 (1985).

Counterclaim by Third-Party Defendant Against Plaintiff

And what about an attempt by a third-party defendant to amend her answer to assert a counterclaim directly against P?[30] It has been held that even that claim can be deemed to relate back to the original action's commencement as long as the claim arose out of the same series of transactions or occurrences alleged in the complaint.[31] Although the court relied on the language of what is now CPLR 203(f) in reaching its conclusion, that provision does not appear to support the result. CPLR 203(d), which applies to the interposition of counterclaims, would seem to be the better base from which to ground such a conclusion.[32]

F.   EXTENSIONS AND TOLLS

Table of Sections

§ 50.   Extensions and Tolls, Generally
§ 51.   Toll Where Action Stayed
§ 52.   Termination of Prior Action
§ 53.   Defendant's Absence
§ 54.   Disabilities as Tolls
§ 55.   Tolling for Death
§ 56.   Estopping Defendant from Pleading Limitation

§ 50.   Extensions and Tolls, Generally

Although the court cannot in its discretion extend the statute of limitations,[1] there are a handful of statutory provisions and a few caselaw doctrines that can and do. These are generally known as tolling provisions. They can take various forms. They may suspend the running of the statute during a stated period, or start it all over again as of a given moment, or offer an alternative period. It must be remembered, however, that tolling provisions are not as a rule applicable to that relatively uncommon period of limitation known as a "condition precedent."[2]

As a general rule, in the absence of any indication to the contrary, the tolling provisions apply in both actions and special proceedings.[3]

A written and signed acknowledgment of a debt or other obligation starts the statute of limitations running anew.[4] This applies to contract claims, not torts.[5] A letter can

---

[30]   The rights of an impleaded third-party include the right to counterclaim against the main plaintiff. CPLR 1008.

[31]   T.R. America Chemicals, Inc. v. Seaboard Sur. Co., 116 Misc. 2d 874, 456 N.Y.S.2d 608 (Sup. Ct., New York County 1982).

[32]   See § 48.

[1]   CPLR 201, 2004; see § 33.

[2]   Yonkers Contracting Co., Inc. v. Port Authority Trans-Hudson Corp., 93 N.Y.2d 375, 690 N.Y.S.2d 512, 712 N.E.2d 678 (1999); see § 34.

[3]   CPLR 103(b), 105(b); see Elliot v. Green Bus Lines, Inc., 58 N.Y.2d 76, 459 N.Y.S.2d 419, 445 N.E.2d 1098 (1983).

[4]   Gen. Oblig. Law § 17–101.

[5]   Maryland Cas. Co. v. Byrne, 172 Misc. 152, 15 N.Y.S.2d 68 (N.Y. City Ct. 1939).

satisfy here.[6] Whatever form the writing takes, it must imply a promise to pay. "It should contain nothing inconsistent with an intention on the part of the debtor to pay it."[7] So if D does acknowledge the debt, but in a writing claiming that P owes D even more than D owes P, there is no implied promise to pay and the writing will not start the statute anew.[8]

Wholly apart from any written acknowledgment, an actual payment made by D under circumstances establishing that it is intended as a part payment towards a larger debt starts the period running anew on the balance.[9] The effect will be the same even if the payment is made after the period has expired; the period will start up all over again as of the part payment.[10] It does not matter how P (the creditor) applies the payment; it is entirely a matter of how the debtor intended that it be applied. So held Crow v. Gleason,[11] a leading case in which P had let horses to D over a period of time, each time making a debit on D's account. P did not bill D periodically for the total balance, however, but he did bill individual lettings. P claimed that a payment D had made was a part payment toward the whole balance, but the proof was just as consistent with D's claim that the last payment he made was for only the most recent letting and not towards the whole claimed balance. The payment was at best ambiguous and from it, therefore, no unequivocal intent to pay the balance could be drawn. On such facts, the statute of limitations could not begin anew on the claims that were untimely.

In the case of joint debtors, payment by one does not renew the period as to the other. The same is true between principal and surety.[12]

The so-called "mutual" account should be distinguished from these situations. It is one in which two parties have agreed to a course of dealings in which each periodically furnishes something to the other, each keeping a running account of credits and debits in the expectation that the party in whose favor a balance exists will send the other a bill from time to time. This kind of account is governed by CPLR 206(d), and if it is found to exist, only the last entry (on either side) need be alive under the statute of limitations in order to preserve the whole balance.[13]

§ 51.   Toll Where Action Stayed

If the commencement of an action is stayed by court order or by statute, the period of the stay is not part of the running of the applicable statute of limitations period.[1] Where, for example, a federal court enjoined P from suing D, the period of the injunction was not part of the running of the statute of limitations.[2]

---

6   Lorenzo v. Bussin, 7 A.D.2d 731, 180 N.Y.S.2d 625 (2d Dep't 1958), aff'd, 7 N.Y.2d 1039, 200 N.Y.S.2d 423, 167 N.E.2d 73 (1960).

7   Manchester v. Braender, 107 N.Y. 346, 349, 14 N.E. 405, 406 (1887).

8   Curtiss-Wright Corp. v. Intercontinent Corp., 277 A.D. 13, 97 N.Y.S.2d 678 (1st Dep't 1950).

9   See Skaneateles Sav. Bank v. Modi Associates, 239 A.D.2d 40, 668 N.Y.S.2d 819 (4th Dep't 1998); P.H. Carlyon, Inc. v. Roberts, 188 Misc. 569, 64 N.Y.S.2d 792 (Chautauqua County Ct. 1946), aff'd, 271 A.D. 1060, 70 N.Y.S.2d 133 (4th Dep't 1947).

10   Brooklyn Bank v. Barnaby, 197 N.Y. 210, 90 N.E. 834 (1910).

11   Crow v. Gleason, 141 N.Y. 489, 36 N.E. 497 (1894).

12   Peoples Trust Co. of Malone v. O'Neil, 273 N.Y. 312, 7 N.E.2d 244 (1937).

13   See Green v. Disbrow, 79 N.Y. 1, 1879 WL 10842 (1879).

1   CPLR 204(a).

2   Chance v. Guaranty Trust Co. of New York, 164 Misc. 346, 298 N.Y.S. 17 (Sup. Ct., Kings County 1937), aff'd, 251 A.D. 855, 297 N.Y.S. 293 (2d Dep't 1937).

Suit against a municipality for tort cannot be brought until 30 days have passed after a notice of claim has been served.[3] It has been held, however, that this stay does not get the benefit of the CPLR 204(a) toll for the reason that the legislature has more than compensated for it by adding 90 days to the previously applicable 1-year statute of limitations.[4]

If an application is made under General Municipal Law section 50–e(5) for leave to serve a late notice of claim, the period of the application's pendency tolls the running of the statute of limitations. So held the Court of Appeals in Giblin v. Nassau County Medical Center,[5] noting that while the relevant statutes don't "specifically proscribe the prosecution of an action," they have the same effect because an action does not properly lie until it can be shown that a notice of claim was duly served.[6]

The toll applies only to a statutory or court-ordered stay, not to one agreed to by contract, such as a tolling agreement.[7] But in such a case, the agreement would likely work an estoppel against the defendant and accomplish the same end that way.[8]

The period during which the arbitrability of a claim is being determined by the courts, measured from the initial demand for arbitration until a final judicial determination that arbitration is not required[9] (if that should be the holding) is expressly removed from the running of the statute of limitations under CPLR 204(b). The toll applies whether it turns out that the obligation to arbitrate was clear or merely arguable. The Court of Appeals has held that in either case, the time of the arbitrability test is a tolling period.[10]

When the statute of limitations expires on a claim while suit on it has been stayed because of federal bankruptcy proceedings against the debtor, federal law offers the creditor (the would-be plaintiff) a fresh period of 30 days for suit, measured from the termination of the bankruptcy stay.[11] But that's just a minimum. If state law offers the creditor more, as CPLR 204(a) does by holding the statute of limitations tolled for the whole period of the stay, it has been held that the creditor is entitled to rely on the longer state period.[12]

§ 52. Termination of Prior Action

If an action is brought within the applicable statute of limitations period and is terminated, CPLR 205(a) may give the plaintiff 6 months from that termination in which

---

[3]   Gen. Mun. Law § 50–i(1)(b).

[4]   Gen. Mun. Law § 50–i; see Joiner v. City of New York, 26 A.D.2d 840, 274 N.Y.S.2d 362 (2d Dep't 1966).

[5]   Giblin v. Nassau County Medical Center, 61 N.Y.2d 67, 74, 471 N.Y.S.2d 563, 566, 459 N.E.2d 856, 859 (1984).

[6]   See Gen. Mun. Law § 50–i(1)(b) (requiring plaintiff to plead service of the notice of claim in complaint).

[7]   See § 39.

[8]   See Robinson v. City of New York, 24 A.D.2d 260, 265 N.Y.S.2d 566 (1st Dep't 1965).

[9]   CPLR 7502, 7503.

[10]   Joseph Francese, Inc. v. Enlarged City School Dist. of Troy, 95 N.Y.2d 59, 710 N.Y.S.2d 315, 731 N.E.2d 1123 (2000) (NYSLD No. 486).

[11]   11 U.S.C.A. § 108(c).

[12]   Zuckerman v. 234–6 W. 22 Street Corp., 167 Misc. 2d 198, 645 N.Y.S.2d 967 (Sup. Ct., New York County 1996). It is of course assumed that the claim has survived the bankruptcy proceedings, which the claim in Zuckerman (mortgage foreclosure) did.

to sue anew even though the original statute of limitations has by now expired or has less than 6 months remaining.[1] If the original statute of limitations has greater than 6 months remaining, the plaintiff can enjoy what remains of that period and CPLR 205(a) does not apply to the second action.[2]

Thus, where the original action was dismissed "without prejudice" due to the plaintiff corporation's lack of capacity, the 6 months in which to sue afresh was available to the plaintiff to establish in the second action that it had subsequently acquired standing.[3]

At one time the statute said that the second suit had to be for the "same cause of action" as the first, but it was construed liberally: the second action need merely have arisen out of the same transaction as the first. A breach of warranty claim meeting that requirement in round two was held to earn the extension, for example, even though the claim dismissed in round one was for fraud.[4] Just so there would be no mistake about that, a 1978 amendment of CPLR 205(a) removed the phrase "cause of action" and substituted broader language intended to assure the 6 months to a later claim arising out of the same "transaction or occurrence or series of transactions or occurrences" as the earlier one.

A further amendment of CPLR 205(a) in 1978 added the requirement that in order for the second action to be timely, it must be shown that the claim would have been timely had it been interposed in the first action. The possibility that CPLR 205(a) might be applied to revive a claim that had already expired when the earlier action was brought is thus avoided with the statutory language requiring that the first "action is timely commenced."

The commencement ritual in a court of claims action is governed by sections 10 and 11 of the Court of Claims Act and involves both a filing and a service on the attorney general. If the action is dismissed for an omission of either act, it has not been "timely commenced" and CPLR 205(a) does not apply to offer its 6 months for a new action.[5]

CPLR 205(a) has been applied to a personal injury claim that had been dismissed because the action had been commenced after the death of the named plaintiff, which is not permissible without the appointment of a personal representative. That was in George v. Mt. Sinai Hospital,[6] where the attorney did not know that his client had died. A second action, with a proper personal representative as plaintiff, was then commenced within 6 months after the dismissal and was sustained.

The Court in *George* distinguished Goldberg v. Camp Mikan-Recro,[7] where on similar facts an attempted relation back (within the original action) under CPLR 203(f) was not allowed. The Court then undertook to reconcile both cases in Carrick v. Central

---

[1]   There are certain dismissals that are not eligible for CPLR 205(a)'s gift, which are discussed below.

[2]   Bonilla v. Tutor Perini Corp., 134 A.D.3d 869, 870, 20 N.Y.S.3d 537 (2d Dep't 2015).

[3]   Landau v. LaRossa, Mitchell & Ross, 11 N.Y.3d 8, 862 N.Y.S.2d 316, 892 N.E.2d 380 (2008); see Patrick M. Connors, *Court Was Rich With CPLR and Practice Questions,* N.Y.L.J., Sept. 2, 2008, 240 (no. 44) (Special Section: Court of Appeals the Year in Review) S2.

[4]   Titus v. Poole, 145 N.Y. 414, 40 N.E. 228 (1895).

[5]   So held a divided Court of Appeals in Dreger v. New York State Thruway Authority, 81 N.Y.2d 721, 593 N.Y.S.2d 758, 609 N.E.2d 111 (1992), treated in the lead note in NYSLD No. 397.

[6]   George v. Mt. Sinai Hospital, 47 N.Y.2d 170, 417 N.Y.S.2d 231, 390 N.E.2d 1156 (1979).

[7]   Goldberg v. Camp Mikan-Recro, 42 N.Y.2d 1029, 398 N.Y.S.2d 1008, 369 N.E.2d 8 (1977).

General Hospital,[8] where the plaintiff wife had not yet obtained letters of administration when she brought a claim for the wrongful death of her husband, and the action was therefore dismissed. Then, after obtaining proper letters, she brought a new action within 6 months after the dismissal and it was sustained under CPLR 205(a).

It is welcome news that substantive forfeiture of the claim need not be the consequence of an omission to obtain letters earlier, but the distinction that *Carrick* makes of the *Goldberg* case is unfortunate. *Goldberg* involved essentially the same defect as *Carrick* but sought to preserve the action with a relation-back amendment. It was not allowed. But *Carrick* does allow an altogether new action on the claim, with the award of the CPLR 205(a) 6 months. The bottom line is that a plaintiff who sues without first obtaining the requisite letters will at minimum be put to the burden of a new action to cure the defect. The device of a mere amendment to preserve the original action under CPLR 203(f) won't work.

The Court was presented with a somewhat related issue under CPLR 205(a) in Reliance Ins. Co. v. PolyVision Corp.[9] In *Reliance*, plaintiff parent corporation filed a second action after the original action commenced in the name of its subsidiary was dismissed because the subsidiary was not the real party in interest. Defendant moved to dismiss the later action on statute of limitations grounds, arguing that the new plaintiff, while a related corporate entity to the plaintiff in the first action, was not entitled to the benefit of CPLR 205(a). Examining the text of CPLR 205(a) and its prior caselaw, the *Reliance* Court concluded that "the benefit provided by the section is explicitly, and exclusively, bestowed on 'the plaintiff' who prosecuted the initial action." While the statute specifically allows the second action to be commenced by the plaintiff's executor or administrator if the plaintiff has died and her cause of action survives, it does not offer the 6-month gift to a different plaintiff in other circumstances. The Court of Appeals ruled that under CPLR 205(a), "the plaintiff in the new lawsuit may appear in a different capacity, such as a duly appointed administrator, but the identity of the individual on whose behalf redress is sought, [must] remain] the same."[10]

The *Reliance* issue has arisen in mortgage foreclosure actions where a second suit is sometimes commenced in the name of a different plaintiff. In Wells Fargo Bank, N.A. v. Eitani,[11] the Second Department held that a plaintiff in a mortgage foreclosure action that satisfies all of the other requirements of CPLR 205(a) is entitled to the statute's 6 month gift if it is the successor in interest to the plaintiff in the first action and is the current holder of the note and mortgage.

The Court of Appeals held in Morris Investors, Inc. v. Commissioner of Finance of City of New York[12] that CPLR 205(a) is also available when a special proceeding is dismissed even though—as pointed out in the dissent in that case—the award of 6

---

      [8]   Carrick v. Central General Hospital, 51 N.Y.2d 242, 434 N.Y.S.2d 130, 414 N.E.2d 632 (1980). *Carrick* is treated in the lead note in NYSLD No. 254.

      [9]   Reliance Ins. Co. v. PolyVision Corp., 9 N.Y.3d 52, 845 N.Y.S.2d 212, 876 N.E.2d 898 (2007).

      [10]   The *Reliance* decision is discussed in further detail in Patrick M. Connors, *Court Was Rich With CPLR and Practice Questions,* N.Y.L.J., Sept. 2, 2008, 240 (no. 44) (Special Section: Court of Appeals the Year in Review) S2.

      [11]   Wells Fargo Bank, N.A. v. Eitani, 148 A.D.3d 193, 47 N.Y.S.3d 80 (2d Dep't 2017).

      [12]   Morris Investors, Inc. v. Commissioner of Finance of City of New York, 69 N.Y.2d 933, 516 N.Y.S.2d 635, 509 N.E.2d 329 (1987).

months will prove longer than the statute of limitations applicable to the original proceeding itself.[13]

In W. T. Grant Co. v. Srogi,[14] the Court of Appeals stated the general rule that "there should be no resort to the provisions of the CPLR in instances where the Real Property Tax Law [("RPTL")] expressly covers the point in issue." The Court applied that rule in Westchester Joint Water Works v. Assessor of City of Rye,[15] to reach the conclusion that the CPLR 205(a) toll was not available to a petitioner in a tax certiorari proceeding that was dismissed for failing to comply with the notice requirements in the RPTL.[16]

Exceptions to CPLR 205(a)

CPLR 205(a) is a skyscraper on New York's procedural skyline. What has made it so prominent are not the cases already noted, which in many instances have awarded the 6 months, but rather the numerous cases that have refused to award it. These are primarily the result of a quartet of exceptions contained in the statute. If the prior action was terminated by (1) voluntary discontinuance, (2) want of personal jurisdiction over the defendant, (3) dismissal for neglect to prosecute, or (4) final judgment on the merits, CPLR 205(a)'s 6 months is not offered.

The first exception, voluntary discontinuance, is straightforward enough, with the procedures for this tool outlined in CPLR 3217.[17] The fourth exception, a final judgment on the merits, need not detain us because in that instance the second suit would usually be met by the res judicata defense in CPLR 3211(a)(5) and be subject to dismissal.[18] The troublemakers responsible for amassing so much caselaw under the statute are exceptions (2), lack of personal jurisdiction, and (3), neglect to prosecute.

(i)   Lack of Personal Jurisdiction

The dismissal for want of personal jurisdiction was added as an exception to CPLR 205(a) in 1992 in an attempt to codify the caselaw that originally established it. This exception continues to be the bearer of bad news for plaintiffs. If the earlier action was dismissed for lack of personal jurisdiction of the defendant, the 6 months do not append.[19] The Court of Appeals 1984 decision in Markoff v. South Nassau Community Hosp.[20] held that there is no CPLR 205(a) extension after a dismissal for want of personal jurisdiction regardless of the specific nature of the defect. Hence, whether the earlier jurisdictional dismissal was for want of proper service of process (despite good basis),[21] want of basis (despite good service),[22] lack of proper filing of initiatory papers,[23] or

---

[13]   For the statute of limitations that applies in a special proceeding, see §§ 35 and 548.

[14]   W. T. Grant Co. v. Srogi, 52 N.Y.2d 496, 438 N.Y.S.2d 761, 420 N.E.2d 953 (1981).

[15]   Westchester Joint Water Works v. Assessor of City of Rye, 27 N.Y.3d 566, 572, 36 N.Y.S.3d 415, 417, 56 N.E.3d 197, 199 (2016).

[16]   See RPTL 708(3).

[17]   See §§ 297, 298.

[18]   See § 263.

[19]   Wydallis v. U.S. Fidelity & Guar. Co., 63 N.Y.2d 872, 874, 482 N.Y.S.2d 472, 473, 472 N.E.2d 322, 323 (1984); Erickson v. Macy, 236 N.Y. 412, 140 N.E. 938 (1923).

[20]   Markoff v. South Nassau Community Hosp., 61 N.Y.2d 283, 473 N.Y.S.2d 766, 461 N.E.2d 1253 (1984).

[21]   See §§ 66 to 76A.

[22]   See §§ 80 to 99.

[23]   See § 63.

anything else going to personal jurisdiction, the action is as good as dead if its only hope is CPLR 205(a).

A dismissal for want of subject matter, as opposed to personal, jurisdiction does get the 6 months.[24] This is especially good news for plaintiffs who are considering suit in a federal court in New York but who are uncertain about federal jurisdiction. If the federal action is dismissed for lack of subject matter jurisdiction, such as where the plaintiff thought the claim arose under federal law, but the court disagreed, or where the plaintiff asserted diversity of citizenship and it turned out to be lacking, the 6 months will append to the dismissal and preserve a new action.[25]

Turnabout is fair play in this arena, and a plaintiff whose action is dismissed from a New York State court can likewise seek to rely on CPLR 205(a) to commence an action in a federal court.

It must also be shown that the prior action was brought in a court in New York. It has been held that the 6-month extension period will not append to an action brought in either a state or federal court outside New York.[26]

(ii) Dismissal for Neglect to Prosecute

Troublemaker number (3) on CPLR 205(a)'s exceptions list is the dismissal for neglect to prosecute, and it's just as boisterous.

The main neglect to prosecute statute is CPLR 3216.[27] A dismissal made under that provision is squarely within this exception in CPLR 205(a) and is expressly referenced toward the end of the subsection. But plaintiffs must be warned straightaway that CPLR 3216 is not the only source of dismissal that falls within the CPLR 205(a) "neglect to prosecute" exception. There is a battery of other provisions in the CPLR and Uniform Rules that can result in death due to a neglect to prosecute.[28] They include the dismissal of an action for failure to disclose,[29] the dismissal for failure to restore the case to the trial calendar within one year after it has been marked "off,"[30] the dismissal for failure to timely serve a complaint in response to a demand for one,[31] a dismissal for failure to file a certificate of merit in a medical malpractice action,[32] a dismissal for failure to file a notice of medical malpractice action,[33] and a dismissal when the plaintiff does not

---

[24]   Gaines v. City of New York, 215 N.Y. 533, 109 N.E. 594 (1915).

[25]   Dyer v. Cahan, 150 A.D.2d 172, 540 N.Y.S.2d 785 (1st Dep't 1989); see also Carver v. Nassau County Interim Finance Authority, 142 A.D.3d 1003, 38 N.Y.S.3d 197 (2d Dep't 2016), lv. denied, 28 N.Y.3d 911, 47 N.Y.S.3d 226, 69 N.E.3d 1022 (2016) (CPLR 205(a) applied after state law claims in federal action were dismissed for lack of supplemental jurisdiction).

[26]   See Guzy v. New York City, 129 A.D.3d 614, 12 N.Y.S.3d 71 (1st Dep't 2015) (dicta); Baker v. Commercial Travelers Mut. Acc. Ass'n, 3 A.D.2d 265, 161 N.Y.S.2d 332 (4th Dep't 1957).

[27]   See § 375.

[28]   See Commentary C3126:8 on McKinney's CPLR 3126 and Commentary C3216:33 on McKinney's CPLR 3216.

[29]   CPLR 3126(3); Andrea v. Arnone, Hedin, Casker, Kennedy and Drake, Architects and Landscape Architects, P.C., 5 N.Y.3d 514, 806 N.Y.S.2d 453, 840 N.E.2d 565 (2005); see § 367.

[30]   CPLR 3404; see § 376.

[31]   CPLR 3012(b); see § 231.

[32]   CPLR 3012–a; see § 231.

[33]   CPLR 3406; see § 77.

appear and proceed, or announce her readiness to proceed, at a scheduled call of a calendar or at any conference.[34]

An amendment of CPLR 205(a) that took effect in 2008 imposed an additional dimension of practice on the "neglect to prosecute" exception, potentially divesting it of its prior virulence. A plainly pro-plaintiff measure, the amendment added a very important last sentence to CPLR 205(a), which reads:

> Where a dismissal is one for neglect to prosecute the action made pursuant to rule thirty-two hundred sixteen of this chapter or otherwise, the judge shall set forth on the record the specific conduct constituting the neglect, which conduct shall demonstrate a general pattern of delay in proceeding with the litigation.

A neglect to prosecute dismissal under CPLR 3216, or any of the dismissals noted above that can qualify as a "neglect to prosecute" under CPLR 205(a), that fails to set forth on the record conduct demonstrating a "general pattern of delay" will allow the plaintiff to invoke the 6 month gift and commence a second action. The compelling reason for the amendment being made in CPLR 205(a) instead of in CPLR 3216—the CPLR's explicit neglect-to-prosecute statute—is as indicated above: there are a substantial number of other dismissals, neither predicated on nor even mentioning CPLR 3216, that can fall under the CPLR 205(a) "neglect to prosecute" caption. These others are also aimed at by the 2008 amendment, which refers to neglect to prosecute dismissals made pursuant to CPLR 3216 "or otherwise," a pair of words that seemingly draws in every dismissal if it amounts to a want of prosecution and the plaintiff afterwards attempts to bring a new action on the authority of CPLR 205(a). If the defendant should argue that the dismissal, of whatever name, is in any way viewable as a "neglect to prosecute," the plaintiff would still be entitled to the CPLR 205(a) 6 months unless the record in the dismissed case manifests—as the amendment now requires—"specific conduct" evincing "a general pattern of delay."[35] Therefore, the defendant moving to dismiss an action based on any form of neglect to prosecute must foresee that CPLR 205(a) may offer an opportunity to recommence the action after the dismissal and should request that the judge make specific findings regarding neglect in an attempt to put an end to the litigation.

An interesting 2009 case on the amendment, Stora v. City of New York,[36] holds that if the earlier dismissal, despite seeming to be for a want of prosecution or the equivalent, was not *intended* by the dismissing court to be considered such, the plaintiff does get the CPLR 205(a) 6 months, and in *Stora* the plaintiff did. The court concluded that the dismissal of the first action under CPLR 3126 based on plaintiff's failure to oppose

---

[34]   22 N.Y.C.R.R. § 202.27(b); see § 376; Marrero v. Crystal Nails, 114 A.D.3d 101, 978 N.Y.S.2d 257 (2d Dep't 2013) ("[t]he fact that the prior action was expressly dismissed pursuant to 22 N.Y.C.R.R. 202.27(b) does not preclude a determination that the prior action was, in fact, dismissed, in large measure, for neglect to prosecute"); Franchise Acquisitions Group Corp. v. Jefferson Valley Mall Ltd. Partnership, 73 A.D.3d 1123, 900 N.Y.S.2d 906 (2d Dep't 2010) (holding that record did not support conclusion that the dismissal of plaintiff's prior action pursuant to 22 N.Y.C.R.R. § 202.27(b) was "for neglect to prosecute"); Doyle v. American Home Products Corp., 583 F.3d 167 (2d Cir. 2009) (dismissal of plaintiff's prior state court action under 22 N.Y.C.R.R. § 202.27(b) for failure to attend a court ordered status conference constituted a dismissal for neglect to prosecute).

[35]   An early case illustrating a proper recital of the required delay "pattern" is Lopez ex rel. Farias v. State, 21 Misc. 3d 563, 864 N.Y.S.2d 282 (Ct. Cl. 2008); see also Patrick M. Connors, *A Second Bite at the Apple Under CPLR 205(a) Extension,* N.Y.L.J., Sept. 20, 2010, at 3.

[36]   Stora v. City of New York, 24 Misc. 3d 906, 879 N.Y.S.2d 904 (Sup. Ct., New York County 2009).

motions seeking dismissal arising out of an alleged failure to comply with disclosure orders did not preclude application of 6 month extension under CPLR 205(a). The decision, which would certainly have come out differently prior to the amendment, raises a number of questions. How, for example, does the present judge know what the earlier judge intended except through the recitations of the decision? In *Stora* that wasn't hard: the same judge was assigned to both actions.[37]

Calculating CPLR 205(a)'s Six Month Period

When an order has terminated the prior action, the 6 months for a new action under CPLR 205(a) run from the order itself,[38] and not from a later judgment entered on it,[39] or from the time that the plaintiff is served with a copy of such an order or judgment.[40] This makes for an important comparison to appellate practice. In determining when the 30-day period begins to run in which to take an appeal, CPLR 5513(a) explicitly provides that it will not start until the objectionable order or judgment is served on the loser with notice of entry.[41] CPLR 205(a) has no counterpart for that and hence offers no such postponements of the starting time for the running of the 6 months.

While the period supplied by CPLR 205(a) will be measured from an appellate determination if the earlier action went through an appellate stage, this applies only where an appeal was available and was in fact taken. In Malay v. City of Syracuse,[42] the Court ruled that where an appeal is taken as of right but is dismissed by the intermediate appellate court due to the plaintiff's failure to perfect the appeal, the prior action terminates for the purposes of CPLR 205(a) when the intermediate appellate court dismisses the appeal, not when the underlying order appealed from is entered. The Court noted that it was not reaching the unpreserved issue of whether the Second Circuit's dismissal of plaintiff's appeal constituted a "voluntary discontinuance" or a "neglect to prosecute" within the meaning of these exceptions to CPLR 205(a).

If the appeal required leave and the application was denied, the 6 months will not be measured from the denial of leave or, analogously, from a denial of a request for rehearing from an appellate court or the denial of a certiorari petition to the U.S. Supreme Court.[43] Since the statute of limitations is involved, it is important to draw that lesson sharply: if there is any doubt about whether the application for leave to appeal (or for certiorari) will be acted on in time to commence a new action should the leave be denied, and there is yet time to act, the practitioner should commence the new action as a safeguard. It can be discontinued[44] if it should prove unnecessary.

---

[37] The ramifications of *Stora* are discussed in Commentary C3126:8 on McKinney's CPLR 3126 and SPR 210:1.

[38] Ross v. Jamaica Hosp. Medical Center, 122 A.D.3d 607, 996 N.Y.S.2d 118 (2d Dep't 2014) (holding that the 6-month period runs from the entry of the order of dismissal of first action).

[39] Burns v. Pace University, 25 A.D.3d 334, 809 N.Y.S.2d 3 (1st Dep't 2006).

[40] Pi Ju Tang v. St. Francis Hosp., 37 A.D.3d 690, 830 N.Y.S.2d 311 (2d Dep't 2007).

[41] See § 533.

[42] Malay v. City of Syracuse, 25 N.Y.3d 323, 12 N.Y.S.3d 1, 33 N.E.3d 1270 (2015).

[43] Lehman Bros., Inc. v. Hughes Hubbard & Reed, L.L.P., 92 N.Y.2d 1014, 1016, 684 N.Y.S.2d 478, 479, 707 N.E.2d 433, 434 (1998); Cohoes Housing Authority v. Ippolito-Lutz, Inc., 65 A.D.2d 666, 409 N.Y.S.2d 811 (3d Dep't 1978), aff'd, 49 N.Y.2d 961, 428 N.Y.S.2d 948, 406 N.E.2d 803 (1980).

[44] See CPLR 3217; §§ 297–98.

How is the calculation made when the first action in New York is timely commenced under CPLR 202, the borrowing statute,[45] but is then dismissed? In Norex Petroleum Ltd. v. Blavatnik,[46] plaintiff's federal action was subject to the statute of limitations of Alberta, Canada because plaintiff was not a resident of New York and the claims accrued in that province.[47] Plaintiff timely commenced the action in the Southern District of New York, but it was ultimately dismissed under Federal Rule 12(b)(6) for failure to state a claim. In *Norex*, the Court of Appeals held that plaintiff's second action in New York State court was not again subject to CPLR 202 and the laws of Alberta, which had no savings provision similar to CPLR 205(a). Rather, the action was timely because it was commenced within 6 months from the dismissal of the timely federal action.[48]

Service Requirements in CPLR 205(a) Actions

An important and technical point to take note of in all CPLR 205(a) situations is that mere "commencement" of the second action within the 6-month period by filing initiatory papers[49] doesn't suffice under CPLR 205(a). The statute also requires, explicitly, that service in the new action be made within the 6 months. In Pyne v. 20 E. 35 Owners Corp.,[50] for example, where the filing occurred within the 6-month period but service came after it, the new action was held barred. The plaintiff can't, for example, just file the summons and complaint in the new action within the 6-month period, which constitutes "commencement," and then rely on CPLR 306–b for the 120 days it allows for service following filing.[51] If the new action is commenced near the 6-month deadline, the postponement of service in expectation of an extra 120 days from CPLR 306–b can prove fatal. Furthermore, if the plaintiff in the second action uses the substituted service methods in CPLR 308(2) and (4), both service steps must be carried out within the 6 month period.[52]

§ 53.   Defendant's Absence

---

[45] See § 57.

[46] Norex Petroleum Ltd. v. Blavatnik, 23 N.Y.3d 665, 992 N.Y.S.2d 503, 16 N.E.3d 561 (2014).

[47] See CPLR 202; § 57.

[48] The *Norex* decision is discussed in further detail in § 57.

[49] CPLR 304(a); see § 45.

[50] Pyne v. 20 E. 35 Owners Corp., 267 A.D.2d 168, 700 N.Y.S.2d 450 (1st Dep't 1999).

[51] On summons service and the time for it, see § 63.

[52] See §§ 72, 74.

If the defendant is outside New York when a claim accrues against her, the statute of limitations does not start until she enters, or returns to, New York. If she is in New York when it accrues, but leaves afterwards, she must remain out for at least 4 months in order for her absence to be a toll, in which event the entirety of the absence constitutes a tolling period. This absence toll is contained in CPLR 207, which goes on to state an exception, which almost swallows up the rule.

If the defendant is subject to the jurisdiction of the New York courts without being personally served in the state, the toll for absence does not apply. So, when a basis of personal jurisdiction exists, such as under CPLR 301 or 302, on which service outside New York is authorized by CPLR 313,[1] the toll of CPLR 207 does not apply,[2] and this means that CPLR 207 and its absence toll does not apply in most cases. The advent of longarm jurisdiction,[3] which is what CPLR 302 supplies, has reduced the utility of CPLR 207. Under prior law, when extrastate service was allowed only in a few narrow instances, plaintiffs had more occasion to depend on a limitations' toll based on the defendant's absence.

It has been held that as long as service beyond the state is permissible, the absence toll is inapplicable even if service is difficult and the plaintiff has to move for an order for service as a last resort.[4] If the defendant is regularly in New York, moreover, so that a diligent process server could get at him—as where the defendant was a New Jersey resident but worked in New York and was here daily—the purpose of this absence provision is not at hand and its toll does not apply.[5]

If, unknown to the plaintiff, the defendant is residing in the state under an alias, the period of such residence is also one in which the statute of limitations is suspended under CPLR 207. But with the numerous ways constitutional service can still be made under the flexible provisions of CPLR 308, even despite inability to find the defendant,[6] a plaintiff who postpones suit in reliance on this provision is today taking some risk.

§ 54.   Disabilities as Tolls

Infancy[1] and insanity are disabilities resulting in tolls under CPLR 208. Imprisonment used to be, but was dropped in 1973 and no longer tolls the statute.

Under CPLR 208, if the applicable statute of limitations is less than 3 years, the entire period of disability is a tolling period, i.e., the statute of limitations does not run during it. If the applicable period is 3 years or longer, the plaintiff will have at least 3 years for suit from the time the disability ceases, but only if needed. If the time left on

---

[1]   See § 82 et seq.

[2]   Yarusso v. Arbotowicz, 41 N.Y.2d 516, 393 N.Y.S.2d 968, 362 N.E.2d 600 (1977). In JPMorgan Chase Bank, N.A. v. Maurer, 2015 WL 4566686 (S.D.N.Y. 2015), the court ruled that the exception in CPLR 207(3) applies only when personal jurisdiction can be acquired over a defendant, and not when in rem jurisdiction exists under CPLR 314. See § 104.

[3]   See §§ 84 to 90.

[4]   New York State Higher Educ. Services Corp. v. Bandler, 168 A.D.2d 752, 753, 564 N.Y.S.2d 211, 212 (3d Dep't 1990); Goodemote v. McClain, 40 A.D.2d 22, 337 N.Y.S.2d 79 (4th Dep't 1972). The provision authorizing court-ordered service is CPLR 308(5), discussed in § 75.

[5]   Mack v. Mendels, 249 N.Y. 356, 164 N.E. 248, 61 A.L.R. 386 (1928).

[6]   CPLR 308(5) and the power it gives the court to devise a service method may prove especially helpful when the defendant can't be found. See § 75.

[1]   See CPLR 105(j) (defining infant as a person who has not yet reached the age of 18).

the original statute exceeds 3 years when the disability ends, in other words, the extension is not needed and CPLR 208 does not give it.

There are yet further qualifications in the statute, but they are self-explanatory. The statute itself is more an exercise in arithmetic than in law, but several points can be stressed.

CPLR 208 applies only when it is the plaintiff who is under the disability. The defendant can be both insane and an infant—a crazy kid—but there's no toll.

In a wrongful death case, it is the duly appointed personal representative who has title to the claim, and he of course must be of age, so there is ordinarily no toll even if some of the beneficiaries of the potential wrongful death recovery are infants.[2] But if the sole distributee of the decedent is an infant, and the decedent dies intestate, it has been held that the statute of limitations on the wrongful death claim will toll until either a guardian is appointed for the infant or the infant comes of age.[3] Should the decedent leave a will, however, and the will appoints an adult as executrix and as guardian of the infant children, the adult/executrix is the person "entitled to commence [the] action" within the meaning of CPLR 208, and the infancy of the beneficiaries in that situation will, once again, not count.[4]

In a controversial decision in 1998, the Second Department held that when the parents retain a lawyer for the infant, the infancy toll stops, reasoning that under CPLR 208, the disability must be "because" of infancy and that the retention of counsel effectively cancels the infancy as a disabling factor.[5] The decision was not only controversial, but generated conflict, and was in due course overruled by the Court of Appeals in 1999.[6] That restored the infancy toll to where the bar understood it to be: the infant is entitled to a toll for the period of infancy without regard to whether a lawyer has been properly retained for the infant or, as on the facts of the case, the parents have themselves acted on behalf of the infant by, for example, serving a timely notice of claim on a municipal defendant.

This principle has been held to apply to the insanity toll as well.[7] Furthermore, the appointment of a guardian ad litem for the plaintiff during the period of insanity does not cancel the toll.[8]

The CPLR 208 disability must exist "at the time the cause of action accrues." If it accrues afterwards, there is no toll. This is significant only when insanity is the ground. (There is as yet no reported case in New York in which a plaintiff of age when the claim accrued became an infant afterwards.)

---

[2]   Mossip v. F. H. Clement & Co., 283 N.Y. 554, 27 N.E.2d 279 (1940), aff'g 256 A.D. 469, 10 N.Y.S.2d 592 (4th Dep't 1939).

[3]   Hernandez v. New York City Health and Hospitals Corp., 78 N.Y.2d 687, 578 N.Y.S.2d 510, 585 N.E.2d 822 (1991). This toll for a wrongful death action has been held inapplicable to a decedent's survival action. See Heslin v. County of Greene, 14 N.Y.3d 67, 896 N.Y.S.2d 723, 923 N.E.2d 1111 (2010) (NYSLD No. 604); § 55.

[4]   Baez v. New York City Health and Hospitals Corp., 80 N.Y.2d 571, 592 N.Y.S.2d 640, 607 N.E.2d 787 (1992).

[5]   Henry v. City of New York, 244 A.D.2d 93, 676 N.Y.S.2d 616 (2d Dep't 1998).

[6]   Henry v. City of New York, 94 N.Y.2d 275, 702 N.Y.S.2d 580, 724 N.E.2d 372 (1999).

[7]   Costello v. North Shore University Hosp. Center for Extended Care and Rehabilitation, 273 A.D.2d 190, 709 N.Y.S.2d 108 (2d Dep't 2000).

[8]   Carrasquillo v. Holliswood Hosp., 37 A.D.3d 509, 829 N.Y.S.2d 693 (2d Dep't 2007).

Insanity resulting from the very injury involved in the action does invoke the toll even though the insanity does not appear until later.[9] The Court of Appeals has held that the toll must be "narrowly interpreted" and won't cover, for example, "the temporary effects of medications administered in the treatment of physical injuries."[10] Nor will the statute provide a toll based on an alleged post-accident "neurosis" as long as the plaintiff can still manage her affairs.[11]

The insanity need not have been formally adjudicated at the moment the claim accrued.[12] The plaintiff will be entitled to the insanity toll if she can establish that she was "unable to protect [her] legal rights because of an overall inability to function in society."[13] This circumstance should invoke the toll not only for a plaintiff under the outright incompetency status that "insanity" usually implies, but also for a plaintiff under mere "conservatorship" status, as it was once called (and still is in the CPLR),[14] which, with less stigma, is designed for an individual not necessarily insane but nevertheless unable to manage his affairs. CPLR 208 specifies only insanity, however, and the plaintiff should not assume that it will be applied to a lesser state until the point is fully settled.

CPLR references to such terms as "conservator," "conservatee," "committee," and "incompetent" are really archaic now since the 1993 adoption of Article 81 in the Mental Hygiene Law prescribing that these terms be replaced by "guardian" and "incapacitated person," and containing an instruction that the older terms be deemed replaced by, or in any event to include, the new ones.[15]

There are maximums imposed on the CPLR 208 toll. Under the insanity toll, the time within which to commence the action cannot be extended beyond 10 years from accrual of the claim. The infancy toll can allow for commencement after 10 years from the accrual of the claim, however, except in an action for medical, dental, or podiatric malpractice, where the 10-year cut-off does apply even to infants.

There can be instances in which the plaintiff is entitled to two separate tolls, such as a CPLR 208 toll for infancy and a CPLR 214–a toll for continuous treatment.[16] In Daniel J. v. New York City Health and Hospitals Corp.,[17] the Court of Appeals emphasized that the two tolls must be calculated separately and not tacked on to each other. Therefore, the 10-year cut-off period of the infancy toll is to be measured from the actual "accrual" of the claim, i.e., the time of the original injury, and not from the later point at which the continuous-treatment ended.[18]

---

[9]   Chartener v. Kice, 270 F. Supp. 432 (E.D.N.Y. 1967).

[10]   Eisenbach v. Metropolitan Transp. Authority, 62 N.Y.2d 973, 479 N.Y.S.2d 338, 468 N.E.2d 293 (1984).

[11]   McCarthy v. Volkswagen of America, Inc., 55 N.Y.2d 543, 549, 450 N.Y.S.2d 457, 460, 435 N.E.2d 1072, 1075 (1982).

[12]   Hammer v. Rosen, 7 N.Y.2d 376, 198 N.Y.S.2d 65, 165 N.E.2d 756 (1960); Lynch v. Carlozzi, 284 A.D.2d 865, 866, 727 N.Y.S.2d 504, 506 (3d Dep't 2001).

[13]   Cerami v. City of Rochester School Dist., 82 N.Y.2d 809, 812, 604 N.Y.S.2d 543, 624 N.E.2d 680 (1993) (applying "*McCarthy* rule" to Workers' Compensation Law's tolling provision for incompetency).

[14]   See, e.g., CPLR 1201.

[15]   L.1992, ch. 698. See § 194; SPR 5:4.

[16]   See § 42.

[17]   Daniel J. v. New York City Health and Hospitals Corp., 77 N.Y.2d 630, 569 N.Y.S.2d 396, 571 N.E.2d 704 (1991).

[18]   See § 42.

Neither kind of disability precludes suit from being brought in the plaintiff's behalf during the disability. Indeed, given the variety of persons who can sue in behalf of an incapacitated plaintiff,[19] relatively few claims by those under CPLR 208 disabilities are postponed so long that they have to invoke the toll.

The CPLR 208 disability toll applies only to the claim of the incapacitated person proper. A derivative claim by one who is not under a disability, such as the claim of a parent for loss of the infant's services, does not get the toll.[20]

Another disability toll is that for military service. This one comes not from the CPLR but from the Military Law[21] and differs from the CPLR 208 tolls in that: (1) it applies whether it is the plaintiff or the defendant who is in military service, and (2) the period of service is a tolling period no matter when the claim accrued, i.e., the disability of military service does not have to exist when the claim accrues, as is required of the infancy and insanity disabilities.

Other disabilities emanating from war are recognized and treated in CPLR 209.

§ 55. Tolling for Death

CPLR 210 addresses the situation in which either a potential plaintiff or a potential defendant dies. If the would-be plaintiff dies, her personal representative has at least a year from death in which to commence an action, commonly called a survival action.[1] This is an alternative period, not an extension, and is used only if needed. If at the moment of death more than a year remains on the original statute of limitations period, this provision adds nothing.[2] Any period remaining on the statute is still available; the time left is not cut back to a year.[3]

Frequently, a survival claim is accompanied by a claim for wrongful death.[4] A helpful decision demonstrating the limitations' interplay between the decedent's personal injury claim and the statutory distributees' wrongful death claim is Brandt v. Hashinsky.[5] There, the personal representative joined both the survival and wrongful death claims in one action, which was commenced a year and a half after death. At the moment of death, there were only a few months to go on the personal injury claim, which therefore needed, and got, the one-year death alternative. But the suit was not brought within the year and so the personal injury claim was barred. The wrongful death claim, however, was timely as it was brought within two years of death and the deceased's underlying claim was alive at the time of death.[6]

---

[19]   See CPLR 1201; § 193.

[20]   Lewis v. New York City Transit Authority, 100 A.D.2d 896, 474 N.Y.S.2d 555 (2d Dep't 1984); see also Baer v. Law Offices of Moran & Gottlieb, 139 A.D.3d 1232, 32 N.Y.S.3d 359 (3d Dep't 2016); Bazile v. City of New York, 94 A.D.3d 929, 943 N.Y.S.2d 131 (2d Dep't 2012); Quinones v. NYRAC, 277 A.D.2d 110, 111, 717 N.Y.S.2d 36 (1st Dep't 2000). Disagreement on whether the continuous treatment toll applies to derivative claims still lingers. See § 42.

[21]   N.Y. Mil. Law § 308.

[1]   CPLR 210(a).

[2]   Barnes v. County of Onondaga, 103 A.D.2d 624, 630, 481 N.Y.S.2d 539, 545 (4th Dep't 1984), aff'd, 65 N.Y.2d 664, 491 N.Y.S.2d 613, 481 N.E.2d 245 (1985).

[3]   Tamburello v. Mooney, 51 Misc. 2d 1093, 274 N.Y.S.2d 437 (Sup. Ct., Albany County 1966).

[4]   See § 44.

[5]   Brandt v. Hashinsky, 16 Misc. 2d 564, 177 N.Y.S.2d 648 (Sup. Ct., Kings County 1958).

[6]   See § 44.

When the would-be defendant dies before suit, there is a straight 18-month toll.[7] It is easier to remember it this way: 18 months are tacked on to whatever period remains on the statute of limitations. This is an addition and not, as where the potential plaintiff dies, a mere alternative.[8] Suit in such case must be brought against the decedent's personal representative. If none is appointed at the behest of the decedent's family, an omission on the defendant's side that may be aimed specifically at frustrating the suit, the plaintiff is herself authorized to apply to the surrogate's court for the appointment.[9]

A claim that does not accrue to P until after D's death exists not against D, but against D's estate, and gets no death extension. To this an important exception has been carved out when both parties die in a common disaster, as happened in Gibson v. Meehan,[10] in which D died immediately and P a few days later. The claim for P's wrongful death thus arose after D had died, which would ordinarily have precluded a toll for D's death, but the court rejected the technical construction in this situation and added the 18 months to the 2-year wrongful death period in which P could sue.

§ 56.   Estopping Defendant from Pleading Limitation

Under New York law, the general rule is that a claim accrues at the moment of injury, and not the later moment that plaintiff discovers it.[1] Nonetheless, "[o]ur courts have long had the power, both at law and equity, to bar the assertion of the affirmative defense of the Statute of Limitations where it is the defendant's affirmative wrongdoing . . . which produced the long delay" in bringing suit. Thus spoke the Court of Appeals in General Stencils, Inc. v. Chiappa,[2] a conversion claim against an embezzling bookkeeper, but the lawyer should not take the case as a general authority for liberal use of the estoppel doctrine. In that case, there was an inherent secrecy in the very nature of the defendant's actionable conduct.

The estoppel doctrine is in fact applied sparingly and may not be used by a naive plaintiff who lets the claim lapse on a general understanding (or hope?) that it will be settled. An actual agreement between P and D reasonably leading to postponement of suit can and should work an estoppel,[3] but anything less than that should not be depended on. It's easy enough to start the action amicably, with the plaintiff perhaps informing the defendant that suit is being commenced just as a precaution, and continue settlement talks afterwards.

The estoppel doctrine is one of caselaw, today acknowledged by statute.[4] Even so, if there is still time to sue and the defendant will not agree in writing to an extension, the plaintiff is better off assuming that the doctrine does not exist and commencing a timely lawsuit.

In the ordinary run of litigation, like damage claims in tort or breach of contract, there is rarely to be found anything like the stealth involved in embezzlement. Unlike

---

[7]   CPLR 210(b).

[8]   Schwartz v. Public Adm'r of Bronx County, 27 A.D.2d 913, 278 N.Y.S.2d 968 (1st Dep't 1967).

[9]   SCPA 1002(1).

[10]   Gibson v. Meehan, 7 N.Y.2d 93, 195 N.Y.S.2d 649, 163 N.E.2d 874 (1959).

[1]   See §§ 40 to 44.

[2]   General Stencils, Inc. v. Chiappa, 18 N.Y.2d 125, 128, 272 N.Y.S.2d 337, 340, 219 N.E.2d 169, 171 (1966).

[3]   See Robinson v. City of New York, 24 A.D.2d 260, 265 N.Y.S.2d 566 (1st Dep't 1965); see § 39.

[4]   Gen. Oblig. Law § 17–103(4)(b).

the situation in the *Chiappa* case, if the facts that give rise to the claim are open enough so that the plaintiff knows she has a cause of action, she acts at her peril by delaying suit based on what the defendant says or does afterwards. The situation that can invoke the doctrine, by whatever name—and it's always a tough sell for the plaintiff—is where the court is convinced that plaintiff was misled into withholding suit by specific representations made by the defendant (not hard to prove) and that plaintiff reasonably relied on those representations (very hard to prove). Plaintiffs must allege "an act of deception, separate from the ones for which they sue, on which an equitable estoppel could be based."[5]

The point is brought home in Calamari v. Panos[6] where plaintiffs commenced a timely medical malpractice action. When they tried to amend the complaint pursuant to CPLR 203(f) to add claims alleging negligent hiring and negligent supervision, defendants successfully interposed the statute of limitations defense as to those claims.[7] The court rejected plaintiffs' argument that defendant should be estopped from asserting the statute of limitations defense because employees of defendant misrepresented both the procedures that the doctors performed and the plaintiff's medical condition and thereby prevented plaintiffs from timely asserting their causes of action alleging negligent hiring and negligent supervision. In light of the fact that plaintiffs commenced a medical malpractice action based on the underlying facts, the court concluded that "it is clear that any such misrepresentations were no longer operative as of at least that date and, thus, did not prevent the plaintiffs from timely asserting causes of action that arose within the three-year period before that date . . . ."[8]

In rare instances, estoppel can work in something as ordinary as a negligence case. In Croop v. Odette,[9] for example, an estoppel was sustained, but it is interesting to note that the sustaining was at the pleading stage. The plaintiff had yet to prove that his reliance on the defendant's representations was justification for letting the statute of limitations pass.

If there is a fiduciary or other special relationship between the parties, estoppel may have easier sailing. In Simcuski v. Saeli,[10] for example, the defendant was the plaintiff's physician. The doctor damaged a nerve in the plaintiff's neck while performing an operation. When the plaintiff lost sensation in her right side and brought this to the doctor's attention, he assured her that it was only temporary and would correct itself in time. Relying on this advice, the plaintiff refrained from seeking other help although timely attention could have corrected or cured her condition, which became permanent. The doctor's intentional concealment of an act of malpractice and misrepresentation as to its cure had the direct effect of getting the plaintiff to forego suit and, on these facts (as pleaded), the plaintiff could reasonably rely on the representations. Thus, in a malpractice action brought after the expiration of the applicable period, enough was spelled out to work an estoppel against the doctor and prevent him from invoking the

---

[5]   See Corsello v. Verizon New York, Inc., 18 N.Y.3d 777, 944 N.Y.S.2d 732, 967 N.E.2d 1177 (2012).

[6]   Calamari v. Panos, 131 A.D.3d 1088, 16 N.Y.S.3d 824 (2d Dep't 2015).

[7]   See § 49.

[8]   *Calamari*, 131 A.D.3d at 1090–91, 16 N.Y.S.3d at 827.

[9]   Croop v. Odette, 29 Misc. 2d 606, 219 N.Y.S.2d 805 (Sup. Ct., Oneida County 1960), aff'd, 14 A.D.2d 724, 218 N.Y.S.2d 532 (4th Dep't 1961).

[10]   Simcuski v. Saeli, 44 N.Y.2d 442, 406 N.Y.S.2d 259, 377 N.E.2d 713 (1978).

time bar. While *Simcuski* has been cited in over 800 reported decisions, the plaintiff's lawyer must be forewarned that the conduct in those cases rarely justifies an estoppel.

The estoppel doctrine discussed in this section falls under the category of "equitable estoppel" and should not be confused with the "equitable tolling" doctrine one occasionally sees in the federal courts that, in special circumstances, may be invoked to excuse the late commencement of an action. The doctrine is treated in Zerilli-Edelglass v. New York City Transit Authority,[11] which denied plaintiff the tolling while observing that it can rarely be invoked successfully. The equitable tolling doctrine has no precise New York counterpart.[12]

G. FOREIGN CLAIMS

Table of Sections

§ 57.   Foreign Claims; the "Borrowing" Statute

§ 57.   Foreign Claims; the "Borrowing" Statute

In the "conflict of laws" realm, CPLR 202 is known as a "borrowing" statute. It is designed to apply when a foreign cause of action is sued upon in New York and it determines whether the foreign or our local statute of limitations applies.

CPLR 202 first provides that when the cause of action accrues outside New York to one who was at the time a New York resident, only the New York statute of limitations applies in an action commenced here. The foreign one is disregarded. Another way of looking at the issue is that those who reside in and pay New York State taxes receive the benefit of the New York statute of limitations when they commence an action here. For a time, "resident" here was construed to mean "domiciliary,"[13] but the Court of Appeals rejected that construction in Antone v. General Motors Corp.,[14] holding that it means just what it says: resident. Hence the *Antone* plaintiff, who technically had a New York domicile when he was injured in a Pennsylvania accident, but was residing in Pennsylvania at the time, could not rely solely on the New York statute of limitations.[15]

If a claim that originally accrued to a New York resident is paid by the New Yorker's foreign insurer and it's the insurer that's suing on the claim as subrogated plaintiff, the insurer stands in the insured's shoes and can rely exclusively on the New York period.[16]

As seen above, CPLR 202 does not always require a "borrowing." The "borrowing" takes place only when the foreign claim accrues to a nonresident, which includes a

---

[11] Zerilli-Edelglass v. New York City Transit Authority, 333 F.3d 74, 25 A.L.R. Fed. 2d 837 (2d Cir. 2003).

[12] Giordano v. College of Staten Island, 32 Misc. 3d 1221(A), 934 N.Y.S.2d 33 (Sup. Ct., Richmond County 2011); but see Pearl v. City of Long Beach, 296 F.3d 76, 82–3, 88 (2d Cir. 2002) (observing that the doctrine of equitable tolling, or equitable estoppel, appears to be the same in state and federal court); SPR 141:4.

[13] See, e.g., Jones v. Greyhound Bus Lines, 73 Misc. 2d 109, 341 N.Y.S.2d 159 (Sup. Ct., Orange County 1973).

[14] Antone v. General Motors Corp., Buick Motor Div., 64 N.Y.2d 20, 484 N.Y.S.2d 514, 473 N.E.2d 742 (1984).

[15] His claim was put through the borrowing process and subjected to the shorter Pennsylvania statute of limitations, which barred it.

[16] U.S. Fidelity & Guaranty Co. v. E. W. Smith Co., 46 N.Y.2d 498, 414 N.Y.S.2d 672, 387 N.E.2d 604 (1979).

foreign corporation.[17] Under the statute, the New York period is looked to on the one hand, and, on the other, the period applicable under the laws of the place "where the cause of action accrued." The two are then compared and the shorter of the two is applied. If the claim has expired under either the New York or foreign period, in other words, it's barred. Therefore, the statute really dictates a comparison, with a "borrowing" of the foreign period only if it is the shorter of the two compared.[18] The primary purpose of CPLR 202 is to prevent forum shopping by a nonresident plaintiff seeking to take advantage of a more favorable statute of limitations in New York, and the courts have tried to carry out this intent when interpreting the statute.[19]

The periods that are compared are the entire periods. That is, the New York period, with all relevant New York extensions and tolls integrated, is one prong of the comparison, and the foreign period, with the foreign tolls and extensions integrated, is the other.[20] The New York tolls are not superimposed on the foreign period or vice versa.[21]

The question of where the cause of action "accrued" can be a sticky one, especially in this age of more sophisticated choice of law principles. The doctrine of Babcock v. Jackson,[22] adopting what has become known as the "most significant contacts" test to determine which state's substantive law governs a given issue in a case with foreign elements, was thought likely to have an effect as well on "where" a cause of action accrues under CPLR 202. The Court of Appeals dispelled this notion in Global Financial Corp. v. Triarc Corp.[23] and rejected for CPLR 202 the "contacts" approach used in choosing substantive law. The Court said that having applied the more traditional test to define accrual under CPLR 202 in tort cases—that a cause of action accrues at the time and place of the injury—it would now extend the same rule to contract cases because by so doing the "guesswork" involved in the "contacts" test is avoided.

The action in *Global* was by a plaintiff seeking commissions for finding an investment company to buy shares in the defendant, a breach of contract action for exclusively economic injury. In a case like that, the Court held, the claim should be deemed to accrue where the plaintiff "sustained its alleged injury," which is the state in which the plaintiff experiences the economic loss engendered by the breach. In *Global*, where the plaintiff was a foreign corporation, that would be either its state of incorporation (Delaware) or the state of its principal place of business (Pennsylvania). Because the statute of limitations had expired under both state's laws when the plaintiff first brought the action, the Court found no need to pinpoint which one controlled. Whichever of the two states might have qualified as the place of accrual, the claim was barred.

---

[17]   American Lumbermens Mut. Cas. Co. of Illinois v. Cochrane, 309 N.Y. 1017, 133 N.E.2d 461 (1956), aff'g 284 A.D. 884, 134 N.Y.S.2d 473 (1st Dep't), aff'g 129 N.Y.S.2d 489 (Sup. Ct., New York County 1954).

[18]   See Kirsch v. Lubin, 248 N.Y. 645, 162 N.E. 559 (1928).

[19]   See *Antone*, 64 N.Y.2d at 27, 484 N.Y.S.2d at 517, 473 N.E.2d at 745.

[20]   See *Antone*, 64 N.Y.2d at 31, 484 N.Y.S.2d at 519, 473 N.E.2d at 747.

[21]   Cellura v. Cellura, 24 A.D.2d 59, 263 N.Y.S.2d 843 (4th Dep't 1965).

[22]   Babcock v. Jackson, 12 N.Y.2d 473, 240 N.Y.S.2d 743, 191 N.E.2d 279 (1963). See Neumeier v. Kuehner, 31 N.Y.2d 121, 335 N.Y.S.2d 64, 286 N.E.2d 454 (1972), for a review of the *Babcock* influence on the decade following it.

[23]   Global Financial Corp. v. Triarc Corp., 93 N.Y.2d 525, 693 N.Y.S.2d 479, 715 N.E.2d 482 (1999) (NYSLD No. 476).

It is the federal bench that has been most involved with these New York issues. In diversity cases, the federal courts are required to apply state choice of law principles,[24] and they have tried to predict how the New York Court of Appeals would want CPLR 202 construed. One Second Circuit case, Sack v. Low,[25] in which the claim might have accrued in part in each of two other states, holds that CPLR 202 should be construed to bar the claim if the laws of either of those foreign states would bar it. Securities fraud accounts for a significant segment of federal judicial business. Citing the *Sack* case, the Second Circuit has held that in securities fraud litigation "the cause of action for purposes of New York's borrowing statute . . . accrues in the state where the loss resulting from the misrepresentation was sustained. The New York courts are in accord."[26]

In a prognostication of what it thought the New York Court of Appeals would say, the Second Circuit held in 1981 that if a given defendant would not be subject to jurisdiction in a particular state, the claim could not be deemed to arise in that state under CPLR 202 and its statute of limitations would therefore not be borrowed with respect to that defendant.[27] The prediction proved wrong with the New York Court of Appeals holding to the contrary in 1997 in Insurance Co. of North America v. ABB Power Generation, Inc.[28]

The *ABB* case was a contract claim in which California, with a 4-year statute of limitations as compared to New York's 6, had almost all the contacts. In a dispute involving the breakdown of a multimillion dollar generating plant, the victim's insurer paid the loss and then, subrogated, sued *ABB*, the alleged wrongdoer, in New York. A contract between the parties called for arbitration in New York, which was how New York got involved in this essentially California dispute in the first place. Piercing through the complications, the issue boiled down to whether New York, under CPLR 202, would borrow the shorter period of a foreign state even as against a party who could not be sued in that state for want of jurisdictional contacts. New York would, the Court responded, because "the purposes underlying the borrowing statute do not require that amenability to suit be demonstrated before an action can be said to accrue in a particular jurisdiction."

The question of when the foreign claim is "interposed" (i.e., whether by filing, service, or any other procedure), as compared to what period applies, is a New York matter in all cases. CPLR 202 does not call for borrowing another state's method of commencing an action.[29]

While CPLR 202 may govern the statute of limitations for an action originally commenced in New York, if the action is dismissed and plaintiff commences a second action in reliance on CPLR 205(a)'s 6 month period,[30] will CPLR 202 be turned to again?

---

[24]   Erie R. Co. v. Tompkins, 304 U.S. 64, 58 S. Ct. 817, 82 L. Ed. 1188 (1938); Klaxon Co. v. Stentor Electric Mfg. Co., 313 U.S. 487, 61 S. Ct. 1020, 85 L. Ed. 1477 (1941). A "diversity" case is one in which federal jurisdiction is based on the fact that the parties are citizens of different states. See 28 U.S.C.A. § 1332.

[25]   Sack v. Low, 478 F.2d 360, 17 Fed. R. Serv. 2d 372 (2d Cir. 1973).

[26]   Industrial Consultants, Inc. v. H. S. Equities, Inc., 646 F.2d 746 (2d Cir. 1981).

[27]   Stafford v. International Harvester Co., 668 F.2d 142, 32 U.C.C. Rep. Serv. 1331 (2d Cir. 1981).

[28]   Insurance Co. of North America v. ABB Power Generation, Inc., 91 N.Y.2d 180, 668 N.Y.S.2d 143, 690 N.E.2d 1249 (1997) (NYSLD No. 456).

[29]   Drummy v. Oxman, 280 A.D. 800, 113 N.Y.S.2d 224 (2d Dep't 1952).

[30]   See § 52.

In Norex Petroleum Ltd. v. Blavatnik,[31] plaintiff commenced an action in the federal district court for the Southern District of New York. In that plaintiff was a nonresident of New York and its claims accrued in Alberta, Canada, CPLR 202 governed the timeliness of the federal action and the statute of limitations of Alberta was applied by the federal district court because it was shorter than the applicable New York statute of limitations. Although plaintiff's action was timely, it was ultimately dismissed under Federal Rule 12(b)(6) for failure to state a claim.

Relying on CPLR 205(a), plaintiff commenced an action in New York County Supreme Court within 6 months from the dismissal of the federal action. Defendants moved to dismiss the action on multiple grounds, including that the New York State action was untimely under CPLR 202 because Alberta did not have any similar savings statute to, in essence, borrow. The New York Court of Appeals reversed the order dismissing the action and concluded that the second action was timely because it was commenced within 6 months of the dismissal of the first action, which had been timely under CPLR 202. In sum, the court rejected the defendants' argument that CPLR 202 should again be applied to the second action. If an initial action is timely commenced in a federal or state court within New York State and overcomes any hurdles presented by CPLR 202, it can be the beneficiary of CPLR 205(a)'s 6-month gift if it is dismissed for failure to state a claim. The plaintiff need not again satisfy CPLR 202 in the second action. Rather, it merely needs to commence the second action within 6 months from dismissal of a timely initial action.

---

[31]   Norex Petroleum Ltd. v. Blavatnik, 23 N.Y.3d 665, 992 N.Y.S.2d 503, 16 N.E.3d 561 (2014).

Chapter 4

PERSONAL JURISDICTION

Analysis

A. Introductory
B. The Summons
C. The Methods of Service
D. Getting into the Courthouse
E. The Jurisdictional Bases
F. Service Outside New York
G. Rem Jurisdiction
H. Vacating Defaults

A. INTRODUCTORY

Table of Sections

§ 58.   Personal Jurisdiction, Introduction

§ 58.   Personal Jurisdiction, Introduction

In this chapter, we examine how the court gets jurisdiction to bind the parties to its determination. The plaintiff submits to the court's jurisdiction when she invokes it by suing. Other parties must be brought within it. The steps that accomplish this are the stuff of this chapter, entitled "personal jurisdiction." A subcategory of it is "rem" jurisdiction, which is usually turned to only as an alternative when personal jurisdiction is lacking. The rem materials come towards the end of the chapter.[1]

Exercising personal jurisdiction always requires homage to the due process clause, the principal constitutional restraint on potential excesses of state judicial power. The traditional requirements of that clause are (1) notice, and (2) opportunity to be heard,[2] a team so pervasively publicized that the lawyer may be prone to overlook that the team is really a trio, not a duet. There is a third member, often even louder than the other two:

Suppose a two-car accident occurs in New York between drivers N and F. N is a New Yorker, F a Floridian. A few months later N is served in New York with a Florida summons advising him of a personal injury action F has brought in Florida, and with a complaint stating a claim arising from the New York accident and advising N that he has 30 days in which to appear and answer. Has N been given due notice and an opportunity to be heard? He has been given both. But has the New York service given the Florida court jurisdiction? It has not, and the barrier is the Due Process Clause. It requires not just notice and an opportunity to be heard. It has a third requirement—

---

[1]   See §§ 101–07.
[2]   Mullane v. Central Hanover Bank & Trust Co., 339 U.S. 306, 70 S. Ct. 652, 94 L. Ed. 865 (1950).

jurisdictional basis—and that's what Florida lacked here. A state cannot subject a nondomiciliary to its jurisdiction without a thread of some kind, often referred to as a "nexus," connecting the state, the defendant, and the case. Those threads are the "bases" of personal jurisdiction.

In the example put above, New York could have subjected F to its jurisdiction if suit had been brought in New York by N and F was served in Florida. The fact that the accident occurred in New York would have given New York the jurisdictional basis that Florida lacked. The basis in this case is called "longarm" jurisdiction; it involves a claim arising out of the defendant's activity within the state.[3]

Jurisdictional basis on the one hand and the requirement of notice on the other, although both are products of due process and each is essential to jurisdiction, are best investigated separately. A failure to separate them can breed confusion. In fact, while studying this chapter, it is helpful to think of personal jurisdiction as three things, rather than one: (1) proper commencement and filing of initiatory papers,[4] (2) proper service of process,[5] and (3) a proper basis of jurisdiction over the defendant.[6] All three of these items must be separately established to obtain a judgment that can be enforced in New York, and is entitled to full faith and credit throughout the United States.

The CPLR begins its jurisdictional article, Article 3, by treating jurisdictional basis. That's what CPLR 301 and 302 are all about. Only later on, with CPLR 307 and 308 et seq., does the article get into the question of how to make service, and only with CPLR 313 are we told when and how service may be made outside New York. The provisions overlap, and treatment of one often entails a preliminary reference to another. Our treatment will stress methods of service first, concentrating at the outset on service in New York in cases in which all the defendants are in the state.

The reader would do well to read CPLR 301, 302, and 313 at the outset. It will show that everything studied about service within the state will apply with equal force to service outside the state when CPLR 313 is finally reached. The only impact, in fact, of such celebrated provisions as CPLR 302, the "longarm" statute, is that its applicability invokes CPLR 313 and permits service on the defendant, with full personam effect, anywhere in the world. CPLR 313 does little more than dissolve state lines. As far as method of service is concerned, the steps still come from CPLR 308 and the other sections concerned with the mechanics of service. When it applies, CPLR 313 just changes the words "within the state," wherever they appear in the method statutes, into "anywhere," and supplies some additional categories of people who can make service pursuant to those methods.

B. THE SUMMONS

Table of Sections

§ 59. Summons Service in New York as Jurisdictional Basis
§ 60. Issuance of Summons; Accompanying Papers
§ 61. Form of Summons Served with Complaint

---

[3] See §§ 85 to 87.

[4] See § 63.

[5] See §§ 66 to 76A.

[6] See §§ 80 to 99, 101–07.

§ 62.   Form of Summons Served with 305(b) Default Notice

§ 63.   Commencement of Action; When and by Whom Summons Served

§ 63A.   Commencement of Actions by Electronic Filing ("E-Filing")

§ 64.   Amendment of the Summons

§ 65.   Amending Summons to Change Parties; Supplemental Summons

§ 59.   Summons Service in New York as Jurisdictional Basis

If the summons, accompanied as it must be in New York practice by either a complaint or brief default notice,[1] is personally delivered to the defendant in New York, the several requirements of due process are fulfilled simultaneously as long as there has been a proper commencement by filing.[2] The reason is that local service of these initiatory papers is its own basis for jurisdiction. If service is made outside New York, no matter how perfectly, it must be separately demonstrated that there is some basis—some New York connection—justifying the extraterritorial service. Delivery of the summons to the defendant while the defendant is physically in the state is therefore the only instance in which the separate demands of due process—basis on the one hand, notice and opportunity to be heard on the other—overlap.

This is the residuum of the capias ad respondendum, the writ which at common law commanded the sheriff to bring the defendant physically before the court. That was how a law action was begun. The writ has long since given way to mere local service of the summons on the defendant[3] and for a long time service within the state was the only way to get personal jurisdiction of an unwilling defendant. So declared Pennoyer v. Neff[4] in 1877, and *Pennoyer* reigned well into the 20th century. The demands of commerce and the increasing ease of communication and movement ultimately made their mark. As a result, jurisdictional notions were generously expanded, and *Pennoyer's* restrictive attitude abandoned.

To this day, however, personal delivery of a properly filed set of initiatory papers to the individual defendant within the state, no matter how transient the defendant's presence, will still give personal jurisdiction, and in that way the old capias lingers on. This jurisdiction lies regardless of the nature of the claim—it can be wholly foreign—and regardless of the defendant's domicile or residence. The doctrine of forum non conveniens can dismiss such a case, of course,[5] but that does not change the fact that the court obtained jurisdiction for the sole reason that the defendant was served in New York. Under present concepts, this ancient idea would doubtless have demanded reconsideration a long time ago if the conveniens doctrine had not been available as a kind of insulation, casting out cases in which appropriate New York contacts were lacking even though the defendant may have been in the state at the moment of service.

While on the state side, any constitutional pressure to reexamine this transient service rule is abated by the accessibility of the conveniens doctrine, on the federal side there is no constitutional pressure at all after the U.S. Supreme Court 1990 decision in

---

[1]   See § 60. The summons and complaint, or summons and notice, are referred to in this chapter as the "initiatory papers."

[2]   See § 63.

[3]   International Shoe Co. v. State of Wash., Office of Unemployment Compensation and Placement, 326 U.S. 310, 66 S. Ct. 154, 90 L. Ed. 95, 161 A.L.R. 1057 (1945).

[4]   Pennoyer v. Neff, 95 U.S. 714, 24 L. Ed. 565, 1877 WL 18188 (1877).

[5]   See § 28.

Burnham v. Superior Court of California, County of Marin,[6] which affirmed the constitutionality of transient service on an individual as a jurisdictional basis. Service on a nonresident individual within the state, even on a claim unrelated to the State, thus continues to give full personam jurisdiction.[7]

Because service of a properly filed set of initiatory papers in New York State is its own jurisdictional basis, as well as the act that gives the defendant notice of the action and an opportunity to be heard, it is a good starting point in our treatment.

§ 60.   Issuance of Summons; Accompanying Papers

The plaintiff's attorney issues and signs the summons in New York, and under nothing more than the attorney's signature the summons is deemed official process of the court. This is in contrast to federal practice where the clerk issues the summons.[1] Sufficient copies of the summons should be issued so that a separate one can be served on each party. This is a good precaution whatever their interests may be. Even married defendants have been held entitled to individual summonses.[2]

In New York practice, the moment that commences an action is the filing of the summons and complaint or summons and notice.[3] In a special proceeding the commencement moment is the filing of the petition.[4] The filing step is important to keep in mind because it's what satisfies the statute of limitations by interposing the claim. Service of the initiatory papers on the defendant comes afterwards.[5]

This filing system for commencement is similar to federal practice—on which it's in fact based—where the first step is the filing of the complaint[6] and where service on the defendant also comes afterwards,[7] but the incidents of service differ substantially between federal and state practice and attorneys must be alert to this.[8]

In supreme and county court practice under the CPLR, the summons must be filed and served with either the complaint or a brief CPLR 305(b) notice (as described below), at plaintiff's option.[9] This is one of the differences from federal practice, in which the summons and complaint are served together.[10] In the lower courts in New York, the complaint does accompany the summons, but it often takes the form of a brief

---

[6]   Burnham v. Superior Court of California, County of Marin, 495 U.S. 604, 110 S. Ct. 2105, 109 L. Ed. 2d 631 (1990).

[7]   The few exceptions to this rule, such as under what are known as the testimonial immunity and enticement doctrines, will be noted later. See §§ 67, 68.

[1]   Fed. R. Civ. P. 4(b); see § 621 (Practitioner's Edition).

[2]   McCormack v. Gomez, 137 A.D.2d 504, 524 N.Y.S.2d 247 (2d Dep't 1988).

[3]   CPLR 304, and § 400 in each of the New York City Civ. Ct. Act, Uniform Dist. Ct. Act, and Uniform City Ct. Act. See § 45.

[4]   For details on commencement practice in special proceedings, see § 553.

[5]   The incidents and details of summons service following commencement are treated in § 63.

[6]   Fed. R. Civ. P. 3.

[7]   Fed. R. Civ. P. 4(m).

[8]   The Individual Assignment System used in New York practice, and the Request for Judicial Intervention (RJI) procedure for getting a judge assigned to a case, which are not jurisdictional, are treated later. See §§ 77A and 77B.

[9]   CPLR 304(a), 305(b), 306–b; see also Fox v. City of Utica, 133 A.D.3d 1229, 18 N.Y.S.3d 918 (4th Dep't 2015) (action dismissed where plaintiff filed "verified claim" without a summons), lv. denied 23 N.Y.3d 901.

[10]   Fed. R. Civ. P. 4(c)(1).

"indorsement" on the summons.[11] Leaving lower court practice to the prescriptions of the lower court acts, we concentrate henceforth on supreme and county court practice.

When the summons is served with the complaint, it notifies the defendant to answer the complaint within a specified time. The period is 20 or 30 days from when service is complete, depending on the place and method of service. If the service is by personal delivery to the defendant in New York, the period is 20 days; if the service is by a different means in New York, or by any method at all outside New York, the period is 30 days.[12] Although the summons in such an instance commands the defendant to answer the complaint, the defendant has the option of instead moving to dismiss the complaint or compel its amendment.[13] There was an official form for the summons, promulgated as Official Form 1 by the Office of Court Administration, but it was rescinded with the other official forms in 2016.[14] It is reprinted in the next section because it is still a useful template.

CPLR 305(b): Notice

When the summons is filed and served without a complaint,[15] it must be accompanied by a brief notice, commonly called a "default notice," as provided by CPLR 305(b). The notice must briefly state the object of the action and the relief sought, including the sum of money being sought if the claim is for money.[16]

The notice can be set forth on the summons itself or can accompany the summons as a separate paper. Former Official Form 3 contained a summons and notice. It is reprinted two sections hence.

Prior to 1979, a third option was available. A bare summons could be used to start things off, accompanied by neither a complaint nor a notice. That option was eliminated in 1979 in amendments made in CPLR 305(b) and 3012(b). The use of a bare summons is now a jurisdictional defect and results in a dismissal for want of personal jurisdiction.[17] Worse than that, should the statute of limitations now have expired, this category of dismissal does not get the six months of CPLR 205(a) for a new action.[18]

It has been held that the defendant's service of a notice of appearance and demand for the complaint will waive an objection to the plaintiff's commencement of the action

---

[11]   See § 902(a)(1) in each of the New York City Civ. Ct. Act, Uniform Dist. Ct. Act, and Uniform City Ct. Act, McKinney's Vol. 29A, Part 3; § 60.

[12]   CPLR 3012(a), (c).

[13]   CPLR 3211(e), 3024(c).

[14]   See § 7.

[15]   When this happens the complaint is served later under the demand procedure prescribed in CPLR 3012(b). See § 231.

[16]   In personal injury and wrongful death actions, no monetary sum may be stated in the complaint at the outset. See CPLR 3017(c); § 217. That should be the case with the CPLR 305(b) notice, too, but when CPLR 3017(c) was amended to impose that restriction, there was no coordinate amendment made in CPLR 305(b), which bars statement of the monetary sum only in medical malpractice cases.

[17]   Parker v. Mack, 61 N.Y.2d 114, 472 N.Y.S.2d 882, 460 N.E.2d 1316 (1984).

[18]   *Parker*, 61 N.Y.2d at 115–16, 472 N.Y.S.2d at 882, 460 N.E.2d at 1316; see § 52.

with a naked summons,[19] but using a bare summons is not authorized and the plaintiff who does so is asking for trouble.[20]

It may not even be safe to use the CPLR 305(b) notice itself. It is better, as a general rule, to file and serve a regular complaint with the summons. That's because one can never be entirely sure how much to include in a "notice" to be sure it's sufficient under CPLR 305(b). Today, with the bare summons option eliminated, an insufficient notice is likely to result in dismissal because it is the equivalent of commencing an action with only a bare summons. Add to that a statute of limitations problem, and the peril of relying on CPLR 305(b) becomes plain.

Some caselaw suggests, perhaps too reassuringly, that not much is needed to qualify as a CPLR 305(b) notice. There are indications from some cases and the former official form that statements as brief as "damages for breach of contract," "libel," "legal services," "motor vehicle negligence," "automobile negligence," and even simple "negligence," suffice,[21] but the Court of Appeals has not yet spoken to the point and the filing and service of a summons and complaint is the better precaution until it has.

The problem is highlighted in the First Department's decision in Roth v. State University of New York,[22] which teaches all comers not to use the CPLR 305(b) notice unless they know what they are doing, they are doing it very carefully, and the statute of limitations is not on the scene. The notice in *Roth* had a description far more extensive than the tiny acceptables enumerated above or in the then official form. It specified violations of a number of statutes and its demand for relief included damages of every kind, including pain and suffering, punitive damages, back pay, interest, and attorney's fees. It was still held inadequate to satisfy CPLR 305(b) and the action was dismissed for lack of personal jurisdiction. That meant that the six-month extension for a second action was beyond reach. Given that the plaintiff not only appealed to the appellate division, but also unsuccessfully sought leave to appeal to the Court of Appeals, we can safely assume that the statute of limitations had expired.

Except in instances in which the statute of limitations is a long way off, the plaintiff should make it a rule not to use CPLR 305(b). It often appears in reported decisions as the unsuccessful tool of a lazy lawyer.[23]

---

[19] Bal v. Court Employment Project, Inc., 73 A.D.2d 69, 424 N.Y.S.2d 715 (1st Dep't 1980); Aversano v. Town of Brookhaven, 77 A.D.2d 641, 430 N.Y.S.2d 133 (2d Dep't 1980). These cases, however, are of questionable authority today. See Sibley v. Lake Anne Realty Corp., 136 A.D.2d 619, 619, 523 N.Y.S.2d 865, 865–66 (2d Dep't 1988) (the Second Department, addressing its holding in *Aversano*, noted that the "Court of Appeals subsequent decision in *Parker v. Mack* . . . which stressed the mandatory nature of CPLR 305(b), casts doubt on whether such a waiver occurs"). Today, if a summons is filed without a proper CPLR 305(b) notice, it may constitute a failure to file the necessary papers, "a nonwaivable jurisdictional defect." Miller v. Waters, 51 A.D.3d 113, 116, 853 N.Y.S.2d 183, 185 (3d Dep't 2008). Let this debate be resolved in someone else's case.

[20] See LeConte v. City of New York, 129 Misc. 2d 719, 493 N.Y.S.2d 745 (Sup. Ct., Queens County 1985) (defendant's appearance in an action does not waive the right to make a timely jurisdictional objection to defective notice).

[21] See Rowell v. Gould, Inc., 124 A.D.2d 995, 508 N.Y.S.2d 794 (4th Dep't 1986); Viscosi v. Merritt, 125 A.D.2d 814, 510 N.Y.S.2d 30 (3d Dep't 1986) (NYSLD No. 330).

[22] Roth v. State University of New York, 61 A.D.3d 476, 876 N.Y.S.2d 403 (1st Dep't 2009), lv. denied, 13 N.Y.3d 711, 893 N.Y.S.2d 512, 921 N.E.2d 204.

[23] SPR 209:1 (article addressing *Roth* decision entitled "Grand Example of Why Mere CPLR 305(b) Notice Should Not Be Used to Commence Action"). Practitioners should note that while the CPLR 305(b) notice is an alternative for commencing an action with a complaint, it may not be used at all in a special proceeding. See § 553.

If the statute of limitations is so close that there is no time to draft a good complaint, perhaps the lawyer can just draft a bad one, which requires little talent or time. Ironically, a bad complaint can usually be amended as a matter of right to cure critical defects,[24] with the action preserved, while an inadequate notice can't be amended in that fashion and can therefore result in a jurisdictional dismissal.[25]

If the CPLR 305(b) notice is adequate, it is a sufficient predicate for a default judgment if the defendant fails to appear.[26] If the defendant does appear or serves a demand for the complaint, a complaint will still have to be served.[27] The back and forth procedures that then become necessary[28] cost time and money and can delay the plaintiff's action by weeks or months. Therefore, unless the plaintiff is almost certain there will be a default, and the expiration of the statute of limitations is not within sight, she should for this additional reason make it a practice to commence actions with a summons and complaint.

Defendant's Responses to a CPLR 305(b) Notice

When the complaint does not accompany the summons, instead of requiring the defendant to answer a complaint, the summons requires the defendant to appear in the action, which the defendant does by serving a notice of appearance on the plaintiff's attorney.[29] The time in which to appear is, again, either 20 or 30 days from when service is complete, depending on the place and method of service.[30] It is customary in New York practice to accompany the notice of appearance with a demand for the complaint[31] and in fact the two things are often done in the same paper. No jurisdictional objection is waived by the service of a notice of appearance.[32]

Alternatively, a defendant who is contemplating the possibility of raising jurisdictional issues in another forum, if and when an action to enforce the New York judgment is commenced there, may proceed with a demand for the complaint served without a notice of appearance. CPLR 3012(b) specifically admonishes that a demand for the complaint is not "of itself . . . an appearance in the action." Once the complaint is served pursuant to a CPLR 3012(b) demand, defendant now has an additional 20 days to actually appear in the New York action.[33] If she elects not to appear in New York, she can simply walk away from the action, default, and raise any jurisdictional objections she may have if the plaintiff institutes a proceeding to enforce the default judgment in

---

[24] See CPLR 3025(a); § 236. Note the problems plaintiffs make for themselves when they use CPLR 305(b) in tight cases, even where they ultimately prevail and service is sustained. This is well illustrated in Micro-Spy, Inc. v. Small, 9 A.D.3d 122, 778 N.Y.S.2d 86 (2d Dep't 2004) (SPR 151:3).

[25] Scaringi v. Elizabeth Broome Realty Corp., 154 Misc. 2d 786, 791, 586 N.Y.S.2d 472, 475 (Sup. Ct., New York County 1991), aff'd, 191 A.D.2d 223, 594 N.Y.S.2d 242 (1st Dep't 1993), contains another good lesson on why the better habit is to use a complaint instead of a notice. See the lead note in NYSLD No. 394.

[26] CPLR 3215(f); see § 295.

[27] CPLR 3012(b).

[28] CPLR 3012(a), (b).

[29] CPLR 320(a).

[30] CPLR 320(a).

[31] CPLR 3012(b). The complaint must be served within 20 days after the service of the notice of appearance, and the defendant then has 20 days after service of the complaint in which to answer or move. See § 231 and Commentary C3012:10 on McKinney's CPLR 3012.

[32] See § 111.

[33] CPLR 3012(b). This allows the defendant time to review the complaint and ascertain if she wants to appear in New York through a CPLR motion to dismiss, CPLR 3211(a), or by an answer.

another jurisdiction.[34] If, however, the defendant serves a notice of appearance in the New York action, she must then assert any jurisdictional defenses in that action or they are waived.[35]

Defendants' lawyers entertaining the possibility of removing a state action to a federal court if there should be some federal basis on which to do so must be aware of the time limits applicable to removal, and alert to the fact that the time for removal may run from the service of a CPLR 305(b) notice, and not necessarily from the later service of the complaint.[36]

§ 61. Form of Summons Served with Complaint

SUPREME COURT OF THE STATE OF NEW YORK
COUNTY OF NEW YORK

A.B., Plaintiff,

against   Summons

C.D., Defendant.   Index No. _____

To the above-named defendant:

You are hereby summoned and required to serve upon plaintiff's attorney an answer to the complaint in this action within twenty days after the service of this summons, exclusive of the day of service, or within thirty days after service is complete if this summons is not personally delivered to you within the State of New York. In case of your failure to answer, judgement will be taken against you by default for the relief demanded in the complaint.

The basis of the venue designated is [specify basis, as: the residence of plaintiff, which is (set forth address)].

Dated:

                                    _____[Signature]_____
                                    _____[Print name]_____
                                    Attorney for Plaintiff
                                    Address:
                                    Telephone Number:

---

[34] Generally, a defendant only has one opportunity to raise a jurisdictional objection. See § 455 (noting that a defendant is entitled to a day in court on the question of jurisdiction and that a defendant can seek that day in a second court as long as she did not appear and use it up in the first).

[35] For further discussion of service of the demand for the complaint without a notice of appearance, see Commentary C3012:14 on McKinney's CPLR 3012.

[36] See § 619 (Practitioner's Edition).

The above was Form 1 of the Official Forms, which was rescinded with the other official forms in 2016.[1] It is reprinted here with some modification because it is still a useful template. The basis of the venue is required by CPLR 305(a). As shown in the form, it is satisfied by the simple addition of a sentence. The subject of venue is met in Chapter 6.

§ 62.   Form of Summons Served with 305(b) Default Notice

SUPREME COURT OF THE STATE OF NEW YORK
COUNTY OF NEW YORK

A.B., Plaintiff,

     against

C.D., Defendant.

Summons with Notice

Index No. _____

To the above-named defendant:

You are hereby summoned to appear in this action by serving a notice of appearance on plaintiff's attorney within twenty days after the service of this summons, exclusive of the day of service, or within thirty days after service is complete if this summons is not personally delivered to you within the State of New York.

Take notice that the nature of this action and the relief sought is to recover damages for breach of contract, and that in case of your failure to appear judgment will be taken against you by default for the sum of twenty thousand dollars with interest from June 1, 2016, plus the costs and disbursements of this action.

The basis of the venue designated is [specify basis, as: the residence of plaintiff, which is (set forth address)].

Dated:

                           _____[Signature]_____
                           _____[Print name]_____
                           Attorney for Plaintiff
                           Address:
                           Telephone Number:

The above was Form 3 of the Official Forms, but with the "nature" of the action substituted for the "object" of the action that the official form contained, and some additional modification. The change reflects an amendment of CPLR 305(b) effective in 1979, an incident of several amendments whose main mission was to withdraw the

---

[1]   See § 7.

option of serving a bare summons. This form was rescinded with the other official forms in 2016.[1] It is reprinted here because it is still a useful template.[2]

We warn at several points in this book that it is not a good practice to use a CPLR 305(b) notice. The device often appears in the cases as the unsuccessful tool of a lazy lawyer.[3]

How much of a statement is necessary to satisfy as a description of the "nature" of the action? According to the form, a mere naming of the action ("damages for breach of contract"), plus a statement of the amount sought, suffices, but the plaintiff's lawyer should include more or, better still, make it a general practice not to use CPLR 305(b). The problem of including an inadequate description today is that it is the equivalent of serving a bare summons, which is no longer permissible and which brings about a jurisdictional dismissal and possibly the barrier of the statute of limitations. Until the Court of Appeals clarifies how much is necessary to satisfy the CPLR 305(b) requirement, the cautious practitioner does best by starting every action with the filing and service of a summons and complaint.

§ 63.   Commencement of Action; When and by Whom Summons Served

In the early editions of this book, the caption of this section was simply "When and by Whom Summons Served." The moment of commencement in the New York courts at that time was marked by the service of the initiatory papers, not their filing. That changed for the supreme and county courts in 1992, when filing was made the moment of commencement, and then for the civil, district, and city courts as well in 2005.[1]

Because some complications were introduced with the new system, the caption of this section changed as of the Third Edition to add "Commencement of Action." The section's reformulated obligation is significant: to cover all of the basic issues connected with "commencement" under the new filing system. Since the service of the initiatory papers is involved at one point or another in the commencement process in all courts, some preliminary general observations are in order.

General Introductory Points About Service

Service of a summons and complaint or summons and notice, otherwise known as the initiatory papers, may be made on any day except Sunday, which ideally should be a day of rest. Service on a holiday is allowed, but service of the summons on a Sunday in civil cases is permitted only when accompanied by an injunction needed to avoid irreparable injury.[2] Otherwise, Sunday service is void,[3] even if service is made outside the state in a jurisdiction that permits it on Sunday.[4] A plaintiff whose summons was served on Sunday was even allowed to recognize its invalidity himself and reject an

---

   [1]   See § 7.

   [2]   The June 1, 2016 date is the date of the breach, from which category I interest will run. See § 411.

   [3]   See, e.g., § 60.

   [1]   In the town and village courts, service continues to mark commencement. Uniform Just. Ct. Act § 400; see § 45.

   [2]   Jud. Law § 5. A writ of habeas corpus may of course be served on any day. CPLR 7005.

   [3]   Gen. Bus. Law § 11.

   [4]   Carbon Capital Management, LLC v. American Exp. Co., 88 A.D.3d 933, 936, 932 N.Y.S.2d 488 (2d Dep't 2011); see § 100 (discussing service outside New York).

answer tendered by a defendant who was apparently willing to overlook the defect.[5] If both parties disregard the defect and proceed on the merits to judgment, however, one wonders whether the statute[6] will still insist that the service is so "absolutely void" as to permit the defendant to undo the judgment at that stage.

Service on a Saturday is a misdemeanor if made "maliciously" on one who actually celebrates Saturday as the sabbath,[7] and caselaw permits the service to be invalidated on motion if that showing is made.[8]

If an action is dismissed due to a violation of the above laws, it constitutes a dismissal for lack of personal jurisdiction and the plaintiff is not entitled to CPLR 205(a)'s six month extension.[9]

The initiatory papers, and any other papers in litigation, may be served by any person 18 or over and not a party.[10] The plaintiff's attorney, or a member of the plaintiff's family, may serve them. Even the guardian ad litem of an infant plaintiff[11] or a director or officer of a corporate plaintiff, may serve them.[12] They are not parties to the action. Even if a party does serve the initiatory papers, the defect must be raised by the defendant promptly or is deemed waived.[13] It can be raised by a CPLR 3211(a) motion to dismiss or, if no such motion is made, as a defense in the answer.[14] If the defect is raised by an answer and the plaintiff wants it disposed of promptly, the plaintiff can test the defense by moving to strike it under CPLR 3211(b). Furthermore, since the objection falls into the category of improper service, the defendant herself, when she asserts the objection as a defense in the answer, is obligated, within 60 days after service of the answer, to move for judgment on the objection, or it's deemed waived.[15]

Even in federal practice today, service may be made by any person 18 or over and not a party.[16] Before 1983, the marshals were the main summons servers in federal practice, but an amendment to Rule 4 took them out of summons service almost entirely.[17]

Filing and Service of Initiatory Papers

As of 1992, the "filing" method of commencing actions took effect in the supreme and county courts in New York. In 2005, it was adopted for the civil, district, and city

---

[5]   Scott Shoe-Machinery Co. v. Dancel, 63 A.D. 172, 71 N.Y.S. 263 (1st Dep't 1901).

[6]   Gen. Bus. Law § 11.

[7]   Gen. Bus. Law § 13; see Tenenbaum v. Setton, 49 Misc. 3d 39, 18 N.Y.S.3d 498 (App. Term, 2d Dep't 2015).

[8]   Jewish Center of Baldwin v. Winer, 216 N.Y.S.2d 153 (Sup. Ct., Nassau County 1961). Muslims may not have a "sabbath" by the same criteria that other faiths apply, but Friday is generally deemed the equivalent by Muslims. It would seem to be wise, therefore—and certainly thoughtful—for any plaintiff who knows that a proposed defendant is a Muslim, and devout, to refrain from service on Friday.

[9]   *Tenenbaum*, 49 Misc.3d at 41, 18 N.Y.S.3d at 499; see § 52.

[10]   CPLR 2103(a).

[11]   Donnelly v. Donnelly, 29 Misc. 2d 469, 217 N.Y.S.2d 850 (Sup. Ct., Queens County 1961).

[12]   Outdoor Supply Co. v. Westhome Sec. Corp., 140 Misc. 48, 249 N.Y.S. 571 (App. Term, 1st Dep't 1931).

[13]   Myers v. Overton, 2 Abb. Pr. 344, 1855 WL 6165 (N.Y.C.P. 1855).

[14]   CPLR 3211(e); see § 274.

[15]   CPLR 3211(e); see § 266.

[16]   Fed. R. Civ. P. 4(c)(2).

[17]   This and a number of other changes effected by the 1983 amendments are treated in the Commentaries on Federal Rule 4 in 28 U.S.C.A. See § 624 (Practitioner's Edition).

courts as well.[18] All of the ensuing discussion concerns actions, not special proceedings, which are separately discussed elsewhere.[19]

The reader will find in the filing procedures some similarities to federal practice, but there are some significant differences, too. Lawyers familiar in any measure with federal practice can therefore be led astray by assuming that the two practices are identical.

The first step for commencing an action in a New York State court is for the plaintiff to file the summons and complaint or summons and notice, i.e., the initiatory papers, with the clerk of the court.[20] CPLR 306–b then allows 120 days after the filing in which to effect service on the defendant.[21] As long as service is made within that period, or within the period as extended by the court, the service relates back to the filing. Therefore, if the filing was within the applicable statute of limitations and service is complete within CPLR 306–b's time frame, the action is timely. Stated otherwise, if the last day of the statute of limitations is January 5th, and the filing takes place on or before that day, service made at any time within 120 days of the filing constitutes timely commencement.[22]

The filing system described above for the supreme and county courts, while now in large part applicable as well in the lower courts, is not identical.[23]

While details of the procedure for commencing a special proceeding and the time elements connected with it—they're different from those that apply in actions—are left to a later chapter,[24] we may note here that the paper whose filing marks the commencement of the special proceeding is just the petition, which is essentially the equivalent of a complaint or CPLR 305(b) notice in an action.[25] Prior to 2001, commencement of a special proceeding also required the filing of a notice of petition or an order to show cause, the close cousins of the summons in an action. That was changed in an amendment to CPLR 304(b) permitting the filing of the petition alone to suffice as "commencement."[26] While the notice of petition or order to show cause need not be filed with the petition, they must accompany the petition when it is served.[27]

---

[18] The filing system also applies in the appellate division in the infrequent situations in which an action or proceeding may be initiated there. See Spodek v. New York State Com'r of Taxation and Finance, 85 N.Y.2d 760, 628 N.Y.S.2d 256, 651 N.E.2d 1275 (1995). For practice in the surrogate's court, see SCPA 301 and the Commentaries on it in McKinney's SCPA; see also § 45.

[19] See § 553.

[20] CPLR 304(a). We will henceforth assume that "complaint" includes a notice as well if the CPLR 305(b) notice is used. See § 60 for a discussion of the use of a CPLR 305(b) notice. See also *"Who Is the 'Clerk'? The Mendon Ponds Problem,"* below.

[21] The 120-day idea came from Rule 4(m) of the Federal Rules of Civil Procedure, which has since been changed to 90 days. See § 625.

[22] If the last day is drawing near and for any reason the clerk's office is inaccessible for a filing, the plaintiff can seek an ex parte order from a judge extending the filing time for up to five days. CPLR 304(a); see § 45.

[23] See § 400(3) in the New York City Civ. Ct. Act, Uniform Dist. Ct. Act, and Uniform City Ct. Act. The differences are discussed in SPR 164:1 and SPR 165:1.

[24] See § 553.

[25] CPLR 304(a).

[26] See §§ 45, 553.

[27] CPLR 306–b; see § 553.

Extending Time for Service

If service cannot be made within the 120 days prescribed by CPLR 306–b, the plaintiff can move for an extension of time to make service. There is no arbitrary limit on how long an extension the court can grant. It can grant whatever it believes the facts call for, and can do so in a series of extensions, if need be, when genuine difficulties are being experienced in effecting service.[28]

The plaintiff should show "good cause" for the extension, but CPLR 306–b also allows the court to grant it without good cause if the court finds it warranted "in the interest of justice." Either showing will allow the court to grant an extension. This poses the anomaly of inviting a court to allow an enlargement of time in its discretion when the plaintiff can show no good cause for invoking that discretion. An equivalent peculiarity exists under Federal Rule 4(m), however, and the federal cases have grappled with it.[29] The New York courts have also had many bouts with the issue, and look to the federal court decisions under Rule 4(m) for guidance on the matter.[30]

In one early case, the court granted the extension of time because the statute of limitations would otherwise bar the claim, the delay was only 28 days, and there was no prejudice to the defendant in the delay. The court said that prejudice means the impairment of the ability to defend, not the mere loss of the technical advantage of having a statute of limitations defense.[31] In another case where the delay was 177 days, the time extension was not allowed.[32]

The issue finally reached the Court of Appeals in 2001 in the *Leader* trio of cases.[33] In two of them, the lower courts had allowed the time extension; in the third, the extension was denied. All three, however, were affirmed, demonstrating that when and whether to extend the 120-day period for summons service for "good cause" or in the "interest of justice" is a matter within the court's discretion. In none of the three cases before it was the Court prepared to say that the appellate division had abused its discretion. Given the large role discretion plays in this arena, the Court could offer no magic formula to determine how the elements in any given case would fare on a motion for an extension.[34]

---

[28]   See SPR 61:2–3.

[29]   See, e.g., Boley v. Kaymark, 123 F.3d 756, 758, 39 Fed. R. Serv. 3d 200 (3d Cir. 1997) (noting that federal Advisory Committee "plainly had in mind . . . 'authoriz[ing] the court to relieve a plaintiff of the consequences of an application of this subdivision even if there is no good cause shown' "); SPR 63:2.

[30]   See, e.g., Leader v. Maroney, Ponzini & Spencer, 97 N.Y.2d 95, 105, 736 N.Y.S.2d 291, 298, 761 N.E.2d 1018 (2001) (NYSLD No. 504 lead note).

[31]   Busler v. Corbett, 259 A.D.2d 13, 696 N.Y.S.2d 615 (4th Dep't 1999).

[32]   Estate of Jervis v. Teachers Ins. and Annuity Ass'n, 181 Misc. 2d 971, 696 N.Y.S.2d 378 (Sup. Ct., New York County 1999), aff'd, 279 A.D.2d 367, 720 N.Y.S.2d 21 (1st Dep't 2001); see SPR 103:1.

[33]   Leader v. Maroney, Ponzini & Spencer, 97 N.Y.2d 95, 736 N.Y.S.2d 291, 761 N.E.2d 1018 (2001).

[34]   Professor Vincent Alexander's article on the subject in the New York Law Journal of January 16, 2001 (pp. 3–4), draws two lists: one of factors the courts have considered "good cause" and the other of factors the courts have noted in determining whether to allow the time extension "in the interest of justice" even in the absence of good cause. Readers will find the lists helpful, and especially interesting in the overlap of some of the entries. See also Woods v. M.B.D. Community Housing Corp., 90 A.D.3d 430, 933 N.Y.S.2d 669 (1st Dep't 2011) (in determining that the "interest of justice" standard was established, the supreme court made " 'a careful judicial analysis of the factual setting of the case and a balancing of the competing interests' including the 'expiration of the [s]tatute of [l]imitations, the meritorious nature of the cause of action, the length of delay in service, the promptness of a plaintiff's request for the extension of time, and prejudice to defendant.' ").

In Slate v. Schiavone Const. Co.,[35] the Court of Appeals returned to an examination of the extension provisions in CPLR 306–b and gave them a more rigorous reading, making an extension seemingly harder to obtain afterwards.[36]

As the last sentence in CPLR 306–b contemplates, the extension can be granted even after the expiration of the 120 days. The plaintiff's request for the extension can also take the form of a cross-motion made in opposition to the defendant's motion to dismiss for lack of timely service.[37] But a plaintiff does well to seek the extension within the 120 days before any motion to dismiss. Doing so may itself serve as some indication of diligence, which can help demonstrate that "good cause" and "the interests of justice" warrant an extension.[38]

When service is being made by publication, which has to be effected in a series of publishings within a prescribed time period,[39] the availability of a time extension may prove more than helpful; it may prove indispensable.[40]

There may be a special need for a time extension when service is being made in a foreign country, especially one with primitive procedures or an indifferent bureaucracy. Federal Rule 4(m) factors this in simply by making its current 90-day time limit inapplicable when service is being made in a foreign nation. CPLR 306–b doesn't exempt foreign country service from its 120-day requirement, but the situation would be one with a special appeal to the court's discretionary extension powers.[41]

If service in any case is attempted, but fails, and a dismissal motion on that ground occurs within the 120-day period (an unlikely contingency), or if the plaintiff has developed apprehensions about whether the service is good and in an exercise of caution prefers to make a second one within the remaining time (a likelier contingency), the plaintiff can do that.[42]

If the plaintiff is getting down to the wire and can't make service because, for example, she doesn't know where the defendant resides or works and hence cannot use the substituted service provisions in CPLR 308(2) and (4), she can consider moving for an ex parte order under CPLR 308(5), under which the court can invent a method of

---

[35]   Slate v. Schiavone Const. Co., 4 N.Y.3d 816, 796 N.Y.S.2d 573, 829 N.E.2d 665 (2005).

[36]   See NYSLD No. 544; see also Nicodene v. Byblos Restaurant, Inc., 98 A.D.3d 445, 446, 949 N.Y.S.2d 684, 685 (1st Dep't 2012) ("In light of plaintiff's prima facie showing of the merit of his claim, his prompt contact with defendant's carrier, the settlement negotiations with the carrier and the absence of prejudice to defendants, an extension of time to effect service [under CPLR 306–b] is warranted."). The decisions in *Leader* and *Slate* and their construction of CPLR 306–b should apply in the lower courts as well, which have a similar 120-day period for service and a similar provision for extending it. See § 411 in the New York City Civ. Ct. Act, Uniform Dist. Ct. Act, and Uniform City Ct. Act.

[37]   See *Woods*, 90 A.D.3d at 430–31, 933 N.Y.S.2d at 670 (although plaintiff failed to satisfy his burden of establishing proper service by a preponderance of the evidence at a traverse hearing, court concluded that "plaintiff's cross-motion for an extension of time to serve the summons and complaint pursuant to CPLR 306–b should be granted in the interest of justice").

[38]   See Posada v. Pelaez, 37 A.D.3d 168, 830 N.Y.S.2d 55 (1st Dep't 2007) (extension of 120 period unwarranted where plaintiff did not move for an extension "until faced with a motion to dismiss, approximately seven months after the 120-day period had expired").

[39]   See § 107.

[40]   See SPR 63:2.

[41]   See SPR 61:2.

[42]   See SPR 62:2.

service for the plaintiff.[43] The motion should also seek an extension of time to serve under CPLR 306–b if the 120-day period is near expiration.[44]

A dismissal for failure to make service within the 120-day period may be made only on the defendant's motion. The court can't do it sua sponte.[45] This is consistent with New York's rule that a defect of personal jurisdiction is for the defendant to plead and prove, or it is waived.[46]

Altering Initiatory Papers After Filing but Before Service

Under the commencement by filing system, the filing of one set of initiatory papers takes place up front, followed by the service of another set. The papers served must be the same as those filed. It's a bad idea to make changes in the papers after their filing and before their service, lest, for statute of limitations purposes, the needed link back to the moment of filing be impaired.[47] Even if the plaintiff detects some omission in the papers after their filing, it is best not to chance an amendment until the defendant has appeared.[48] In Gamiel v. Sullivan & Liapakis, P.C.,[49] the court held that merely altering the attorney's name on the summons and complaint after filing, but before service, did not void jurisdiction. Practitioners should not let a decision like that invite too casual an attitude. Taking *Gamiel* as an invitation to start making changes in the papers between filing and service sets up a guessing game with potentially harsh consequences.

The lesson can be learned from afar by studying the decision in Johns v. Van Brunt Motors, Inc.,[50] where the plaintiffs probably experienced some sleepless nights. In *Johns*, plaintiffs commenced the action by the filing of a summons and complaint and then successfully moved under CPLR 306–b for an extension of time to make service upon defendant in France. Ultimately, plaintiffs served defendant in France with a summons and notice rather than a complaint. The Third Department, relying on the Court of Appeals decision in Ruffin v. Lion Corp.[51] and CPLR 2001, concluded that the supreme court did not abuse its discretion in choosing to disregard the "irregularities" in the service of process. The court emphasized that the summons and complaint used to commence the action were timely filed and the summons with notice was served upon defendant within the time provided by supreme court in its order under CPLR 306–b. In addition, the defendant did not claim that its ability to defend was compromised because it was served with a summons with notice, as opposed to a summons and complaint, and acknowledged ultimately receiving a copy of the summons and complaint that had been filed by plaintiffs with the county clerk after making a demand for same.

---

[43]   See § 75. Court ordered service of this kind is available today even against a corporation. See CPLR 311(b).

[44]   See Hollow v. Hollow, 193 Misc. 2d 691, 747 N.Y.S.2d 704 (Sup. Ct., Oswego County 2002) (motion under both CPLR 308(5) and 306–b).

[45]   CPLR 306–b. In federal practice, a sua sponte dismissal of this kind is explicitly authorized by Fed. R. Civ. P. 4(m).

[46]   CPLR 3211(a)(8), (e); see § 274.

[47]   See SPR 5:2, 15:3, 17:3, 19:2, 35:2, and 59:2.

[48]   See SPR 67:3–4.

[49]   Gamiel v. Sullivan & Liapakis, P.C., 259 A.D.2d 385, 687 N.Y.S.2d 129 (1st Dep't 1999).

[50]   Johns v. Van Brunt Motors, Inc., 89 A.D.3d 1188, 932 N.Y.S.2d 568 (3d Dep't 2011) (SPR 246:4).

[51]   Ruffin v. Lion Corp., 15 N.Y.3d 578, 915 N.Y.S.2d 204, 940 N.E.2d 909 (2010); see § 100.

If the mistake that needs correction is serious, and the time for a new action is still open, many a cautious attorney might even opt to commence a second action rather than chance a change in the papers before their service.

CPLR 2001 Amendment Allows for Correction of Many Filing Mistakes

In Gershel v. Porr,[52] the Court of Appeals made a strict construction of the filing system's requirements,[53] but a few months later, in Fry v. Village of Tarrytown,[54] held that the defendant can waive defects and does so by appearing and defending without raising objection. The commencement by filing requirements were essentially held to fall under the umbrella of "personal" as opposed to "subject matter" jurisdiction, which is what made them waivable.[55]

After *Gershel* and *Fry*, dismissals for unprejudicial and technical defects in commencement by filing continued. Efforts to relieve these rigidities through legislation didn't succeed until 2007, when two bills were passed to address them: Chapters 125 and 529.[56]

Chapter 529 amended only CPLR 2001, the CPLR's section on correcting "mistakes, omissions, defects and irregularities." CPLR 2001 has from the outset provided that any unprejudicial "mistake, omission, defect or irregularity" may be corrected by the court without deadly consequences to the offending party. The statute was held inapplicable, however, to mistakes made at the very commencement of the action because the courts stamped those defects "jurisdictional" and hence beyond a CPLR 2001 cure. The 2007 amendment extended CPLR 2001 to apply to mistakes in

the filing of a summons with notice, summons and complaint or petition to commence an action . . . including the failure to purchase or acquire an index number or other mistake in the filing process . . . provided that any applicable fees shall be paid.[57]

The amendment was sponsored by New York's Advisory Committee on Civil Practice, and in its report[58] it refers explicitly to the *Gershel* and *Fry* cases, evincing an intent to overrule them. That the legislature adopted that segment of the report as its own memo on Chapter 529 manifests its intent to do the same.

The most immediate catalyst of the CPLR 2001 amendment, however, was Harris v. Niagara Falls Bd. of Educ.,[59] which addressed the frequent situation in which there has been some kind of court application made before the actual commencement of the action.[60] The most common example is that of a plaintiff seeking to sue a municipality in tort, but who has not timely served the notice of claim required by section 50–e of the

---

[52]   Gershel v. Porr, 89 N.Y.2d 327, 653 N.Y.S.2d 82, 675 N.E.2d 836 (1996).

[53]   *Gershel* is discussed in the lead note in NYSLD No. 446.

[54]   Fry v. Village of Tarrytown, 89 N.Y.2d 714, 658 N.Y.S.2d 205, 680 N.E.2d 578 (1997).

[55]   See § 274 (discussing waiver of defense of personal jurisdiction under CPLR 3211(e)).

[56]   See SPR 188:1; SPR 189:1 (detailing the background of these statutes).

[57]   In the lower courts under § 400(3) of the New York City Civ. Ct. Act, Uniform Dist. Ct. Act, and Uniform City Ct. Act, the courts are instructed to be liberal in allowing omission of an index number to be cured. See SPR 164:1, SPR 165:1.

[58]   2007 Report of Advisory Committee to the Chief Administrative Judge (pages 24–26).

[59]   Harris v. Niagara Falls Bd. of Educ., 6 N.Y.3d 155, 811 N.Y.S.2d 299, 844 N.E.2d 753 (2006).

[60]   See Patrick M. Connors, *Problems at the Starting Gate*, N.Y.L.J., Jan. 12, 2006, at 3 (with T. Gleason).

General Municipal Law.[61] The plaintiff can move to extend the time to serve the notice of claim for up to 1 year and 90 days from the accrual of the claim.[62] The application is made in a special proceeding, which itself requires the payment of a filing fee and the assignment of an index number.[63]

The plaintiff in *Harris* brought that proceeding and paid the fee, and the extension of time was granted, thus enabling the plaintiff to bring the action. But now, when the plaintiff brought the action proper, he paid no new fee and simply filed the initiatory papers under the index number of the earlier proceeding. The court in *Harris* held that a new fee was required and, more significantly, that the failure to secure a separate index number with a new fee was a jurisdictional error. Instead of just allowing the fee to be paid late, since the initiatory papers were properly filed and a late payment of the fee would prejudice no one, the Court held the defect uncorrectable and dismissed the action. *Harris* typified the unfortunate dismissals resulting from the restricted construction of CPLR 2001.

An omission like that in *Harris* should no longer require dismissal in light of the amemded CPLR 2001, which can now forgive many sins committed in the commencement process. As long as the proper papers are filed with the proper clerk within the applicable statute of limitations, the plaintiff may be allowed to pay the required fee—if it's not paid with the filing—at such later point when the issue is raised. It will be the rare case in which the clerk will not insist on being paid the fee right up front, but stranger events have transpired in New York civil procedure. (In the clerk's office, collecting the fee is ecclesiastical business.) Furthermore, the objection of non-payment does not go to subject matter jurisdiction in any event, but only to personal jurisdiction, which makes it waivable by the defendant. Neither the court nor the clerk is subject to such a waiver, of course, and can insist on payment of the fee at any point at which its absence is noticed. The important thing is that New York State somehow gets its money. As long as it does—and assuming that the initiatory papers were tendered for filing before the expiration of the statute of limitations—the amendment of CPLR 2001 is aimed to forgive and forget this type of transgression.

The CPLR 2001 amendment should also apply to other occasions of a pre-action application, such as an application for pre-action disclosure under CPLR 3102(c).[64] There, too, the application generates an index number and fee. A number of cases held that when the action itself is brought later, a new fee and index number are necessary. Under the CPLR 2001 amendment, the failure to pay a new fee should be curable by a late payment, with the action preserved, as long as the initiatory papers are tendered to the proper clerk within the applicable statute of limitations.[65] It must be stressed, however, that just about all applications of CPLR 2001 are left to the court's discretion, as the language of the statute is the court "may permit a mistake . . . to be corrected."

It's helpful to note some of the other situations that can benefit from the CPLR 2001 amendment.

---

[61] See § 32.

[62] See Gen. Mun. Law § 50–e(5); § 32.

[63] See § 32.

[64] See § 352.

[65] See MacLeod v. County of Nassau, 75 A.D.3d 57, 903 N.Y.S.2d 411 (2d Dep't 2010) (SPR 223:1); Commentary C3102:6 on McKinney's CPLR 3102.

Take Soto v. Freda,[66] for example, in which the plaintiff failed to fill out a "cover sheet" to go with the initiatory papers as the particular county's local practice required. The problem arose because the messenger sent by the office to file the papers was partially blind and couldn't read it. The failure was nevertheless treated as a jurisdictional defect at first, and the case was dismissed, generating expensive follow-up proceedings before the dismissal was canceled and the filing sustained. A 2007 amendment to CPLR 2102(c), discussed below, should today bar such a rejection of the papers by the county clerk in the first place.

Another case presumably overruled by the CPLR 2001 amendment is Meiselman v. McDonalds Restaurants,[67] where the plaintiff paid the filing fee with a check that bounced. A dismissal resulted. Under the amended CPLR 2001, that should be correctable even if the plaintiff's embarrassment isn't.

In Goldenberg v. Westchester County Health Care Corp.,[68] the Court of Appeals provided some definitive guidance on just how far the amended CPLR 2001 can go to cure defects and mistakes made in the filing process. In *Goldenberg*, a medical malpractice action, the plaintiff successfully brought a special proceeding under General Municipal Law section 50–e(5) and obtained permission to serve a late notice of claim. Instead of filing the summons and complaint at that point, he simply served the initiatory papers along with the notice of claim. The Court held that the defect of failing to file the summons and complaint within the statute of limitations is of the jurisdictional variety that cannot be forgiven under CPLR 2001. Therefore, the action had to be dismissed.

If the plaintiff in *Goldenberg* had filed the summons and complaint under the index number assigned to the special proceeding, as was done in *Harris*, CPLR 2001 could likely have come to the rescue. By comparison, the failure to file the proper initiatory papers (summons and complaint, summons and notice, petition) with the proper clerk within the statute of limitations is a sin that even the amended CPLR 2001 cannot forgive. For example, applying *Goldenberg*, the Second Department dismissed an action as a "nullity" where the plaintiff had obtained an index number and made a motion by order to show cause within the action but somehow never filed a summons and complaint or summons and notice.[69]

The amended version of CPLR 2001, as interpreted by the Court of Appeals in *Goldenberg*, would not appear to save a case in which the plaintiff has filed only a bare summons, accompanied by neither a CPLR 305(b) notice nor a complaint. In Parker v. Mack,[70] the Court of Appeals ruled that to be a jurisdictional defect, and it remains so.[71]

---

[66]   Soto v. Freda, 196 Misc. 2d 623, 766 N.Y.S.2d 299 (Sup. Ct., New York County 2003).

[67]   Meiselman v. McDonalds Restaurants, 305 A.D.2d 382, 759 N.Y.S.2d 506 (2d Dep't 2003).

[68]   Goldenberg v. Westchester County Health Care Corp., 16 N.Y.3d 323, 921 N.Y.S.2d 619, 946 N.E.2d 717 (2011) (NYSLD No. 617).

[69]   O'Brien v. Contreras, 126 A.D.3d 958, 6 N.Y.S.3d 273 (2d Dep't 2015); see Wesco Ins. Co. v. Vinson, 137 A.D.3d 1114, 26 N.Y.S.3d 870 (2d Dep't 2016) (plaintiff's action dismissed as a nullity where it obtained an index number and moved by order to show cause to fix the amount of its workers' compensation lien, but did not file or serve a summons, complaint, or petition); Fox v. City of Utica, 133 A.D.3d 1229, 18 N.Y.S.3d 918 (4th Dep't 2015) (filing of a "verified claim" without summons could not be corrected under CPLR 2001).

[70]   Parker v. Mack, 61 N.Y.2d 114, 472 N.Y.S.2d 882, 460 N.E.2d 1316 (1984).

[71]   See § 60. Furthermore, the Sponsor's Memorandum and the Report of the Advisory Committee accompanying the 2007 amendment to CPLR 2001 "explicitly state that it was not the intention of the Legislature to overrule *Parker*." Miller v. Waters, 51 A.D.3d 113, 117, 853 N.Y.S.2d 183, 186 (3d Dep't 2008).

In Maddux v. Schur,[72] a variation on *Parker*, the plaintiff purchased an index number and filed a complaint, but never filed a summons. The Third Department dismissed the action as a nullity, ruling that it was beyond the reach of CPLR 2001's curative powers.

We may note, incidentally, a related misstep: that of serving the initiatory papers before filing them—the wrong sequence. That, too, is a jurisdictional defect, but the Second Department has held it to be one of only personal, not subject matter, jurisdiction, which has at least one benevolent aftermath from the plaintiff's vantage point: the defect may be waived by the defendant. If the defendant does waive it, the court may not raise and apply the objection on its own.[73] In Oyague v. Schwartz,[74] however, plaintiff's application for a default judgment was denied because he did not file his summons and complaint with the county clerk prior to serving defendant. The Third Department's decision cited to *Goldenberg* in reaching its conclusion, which indicates that it believes that this defect cannot be cured by CPLR 2001. In a decision that predates *Goldenberg*, the First Department concluded that although the petitioner erroneously served the petition and notice of petition on respondent one day prior to purchasing an index number and filing the petition with the court, CPLR 2001 afforded the court discretion to allow petitioner to correct the defect.[75]

A key problem in these cases is that the summons will not bear the index number and the date of its filing with the county clerk, which is required by CPLR 305(a). Therefore, the summons that is served may be deemed a nullity and that conclusion might possibly void service. Nonetheless, it would appear that this defect would fall under the personal jurisdiction umbrella and be waived if not raised by the defendant.[76] If the defect is raised, but the proper initiatory papers are filed with the clerk of the court within the statute of limitations, it would appear that CPLR 2001, which has also been construed to apply to defects in service of process, could still come to the rescue in this situation.[77]

The other bill enacted in 2007, Chapter 125, aimed in the same direction as the bill that amended CPLR 2001. Sponsored by the New York State Bar Association's CPLR Committee, it amended several CPLR provisions—105, 304, 306–a, and 2102—to achieve its goal, stated in the legislative memos in both the Senate and Assembly, to be a response to Mendon Ponds Neighborhood Ass'n. v. Dehm.[78] In that case, the filing fee was tendered and accepted by the "county clerk," the proper person with whom to file, and an index number was issued. As was the apparent custom in the county involved, the initiatory papers were then filed with another clerk, designated the "supreme court clerk." This wrought a tragic dismissal due to the improper filing of the initiatory papers, and at a moment too late to start over.

Whether Chapter 125 will ever overrule *Mendon Ponds*, as it clearly aimed to do, is doubtful. Chapter 529 may have hoped to do that, too, but never expressly mentioned

---

[72]   Maddux v. Schur, 139 A.D.3d 1281, 30 N.Y.S.3d 590 (3d Dep't 2016).

[73]   See Khlevner v. Khlevner, 48 A.D.3d 428, 851 N.Y.S.2d 637 (2d Dep't 2008) (SPR 194:2).

[74]   Oyague v. Schwartz, 93 A.D.3d 1044, 940 N.Y.S.2d 686 (3d Dep't 2012).

[75]   United Services Auto. Ass'n v. Kungel, 72 A.D.3d 517, 899 N.Y.S.2d 190 (1st Dep't 2010) (SPR 220:2).

[76]   CPLR 3211(e); see § 266.

[77]   Ruffin v. Lion Corp., 15 N.Y.3d 578, 915 N.Y.S.2d 204, 940 N.E.2d 909 (2010); see § 100.

[78]   Mendon Ponds Neighborhood Ass'n. v. Dehm, 98 N.Y.2d 745, 751 N.Y.S.2d 819, 781 N.E.2d 883 (2002).

the decision.[79] Because of the decisions in *Mendon Ponds* and *Goldenberg*, a central question remains: who is the clerk in the supreme and county courts? A mistake made on this front can lead to a dismissal that cannot be saved by CPLR 2001.

Who Is the "Clerk of the Court"? The *Mendon Ponds* Problem

One would think that the "supreme court clerk" would be the clerk of the supreme court for filing purposes. As many lawyers have learned the hard way, that is not the case. The "county clerk" is the clerk of the supreme and county courts, and that is the office where initiatory papers must be filed.[80] This can be confusing to the newcomer because the "county clerk" is seldom the "clerk" who processes the case and whom the practitioner takes to be the "clerk" for the myriad steps in litigation. Various other non-judicial personnel serve that function, and all are considered "clerks," yet some things have to be effected through the office of the "county clerk" alone.[81] The county clerk's office is in large measure a financial office, to which all the fees connected with litigation are paid. It is not the office through which the daily business of litigation is conducted, however. That's done through other "clerk" offices.

The confusion generated by these unfortunate titles always had the potential for damage, but it actually did little until the *Mendon Ponds* decision.[82] The fault that produced the dismissal lay in the office of the county clerk, who did not accept the initiatory papers when presented with the check that paid for an index number, but it was the plaintiff[83] who paid the price of it.

Analogous difficulties had previously arisen in urban and suburban courts in which the "clerk's" office has many subdivisions. With which clerk must the initial filing of the summons and complaint be made? Some of these issues had to be resolved by caselaw.[84] It was hoped after *Mendon Ponds* that county clerks, who would appear to have the overall responsibility for these matters, would so order or reorder their offices and personnel as to assure, by one means or another, that this kind of draconian result would not again visit a plaintiff, but that was evidently not to be, at least not everywhere.

As we discuss in the next section, commencement of actions by e-filing is slowly, but surely, becoming the norm throughout the state. That will alleviate some of the problems that exist today in those actions that must be commenced with hard copy papers, but not all. In the meantime, plaintiffs can consider pursuing the practice used in New York County, where two sets of papers are prepared, one set to file with the county clerk along with the filing fee, and the other to file with whatever clerk by whatever name functions locally to process the case. To assure that the county clerk accepts not just the fee, but

---

[79] See Miller v. Waters, 51 A.D.3d 113, 853 N.Y.S.2d 183 (3d Dep't 2008) (SPR 195:1), another wrong-clerk case. In *Miller*, the filing of the initiatory papers with the "administrative clerk" instead of the county clerk brought dismissal.

[80] See New York State Constitution, Article VI, § 6(e); County Law §§ 525(1), 909; CPLR 105(e); *Mendon Ponds*, 98 N.Y.2d at 747, 751 N.Y.S.2d at 820.

[81] Some of these others may bear names that can easily mislead practitioners—such as "supreme court clerk" or "chief clerk of [name of county] supreme and county courts"—into thinking that this is also the office of the "county clerk" since, after all, only the "county clerk" is by statute the clerk of the supreme and county courts in the county.

[82] The *Mendon Ponds* case is discussed at length in the lead note in NYSLD No. 515.

[83] It was actually the petitioner, not the plaintiff, because this was a special proceeding. We use "plaintiff" to signify both as the CPLR does in its definitions section. See CPLR 105(b).

[84] See, e.g., Federal Deposit Ins. Corp. v. Goodman, N.Y.L.J., July 13, 1994, at 25, col.5 (Sup. Ct., New York County; Schackman, J.) (SPR 21:1); see also SPR 49:3 ("Who's the Clerk").

the initiatory papers as well, the applicant should bring along a dog that growls and bares its teeth.

Rules on Filing, Rejecting Papers

CPLR 2102, which defines the "filing of papers" and did its job in about five lines, was amended in 2007 by Chapter 125 to add more than twice that, and was divided into three lettered paragraphs. The most significant addition here is in the new paragraph (c), which provides:

> [a] clerk shall not refuse to accept for filing any paper presented for that purpose except where specifically directed to do so by statute or rules promulgated by the chief administrator of the courts, or order of the court.

A Uniform Rule amendment[85] and an extensive accompanying memo implements CPLR 2102(c) with some explicit directions on where rejection of papers is mandatory and suggestions about other instances where it's not.[86]

The CPLR 2102 amendment was designed to counter what some among the bar have called "clerkitis"—the clerk's rejection of papers tendered for filing. But just like cholesterol, not all clerkitis is bad. Good clerkitis is the intrusion of the clerk, especially but not only at commencement time, that gives the filer a timely warning about a deficiency in the papers tendered.[87]

An example of this has occurred when a plaintiff attempted to use a verified complaint in place of an affidavit on an application for a default judgment. A statute indicates that that's okay,[88] but the cases say that in some situations it's not. The clerk is more likely than the plaintiff is to know this. Hence a rejection of the wrong paper by the clerk may be just the education the plaintiff needs to correct the misstep in time.[89]

Uniform Rule 202.5(d) elaborates on the clerk's duty to accept papers tendered for filing, listing five instances in which the county clerk or a chief clerk of the supreme court or county court "shall" refuse papers.[90] They include where: (i) the paper does not have an index number, (ii) the summons, complaint, petition, or judgment sought to be filed contains an "et al" or otherwise does not contain a full caption,[91] (iii) the paper is sought to be filed in the wrong court, (iv) the paper is not signed in accordance with Uniform Rule 130–1.1–a,[92] or (v) the hard copy paper is sought to be filed in an action subject to e-filing and does not fall within the exceptions recognized in the rules for electronic filing.[93] The rule also recognizes that papers can be rejected if "otherwise

---

[85] 22 N.Y.C.R.R. § 202.5(d).

[86] See SPR 217:1.

[87] See the two-part series on this theme in the lead notes in SPR 89:1 and SPR 90:1, entitled "Three Cheers for the Meddlesome Clerk."

[88] CPLR 3215(f); see § 295.

[89] See SPR 194:4. The court system itself may not be too happy with the requirement in CPLR 2102(c), which, in compelling clerks to accept virtually all papers, may impose an additional burden on judges to resolve disputes that the clerk's rejection could have avoided. See SPR 189:1–2.

[90] A memo that accompanied 22 N.Y.C.R.R. § 202.5(d) offered a "summary of the considerations" behind the new rule in general. See SPR 217:1.

[91] See CPLR 2101(c); § 201.

[92] See §§ 201, 414A.

[93] See 22 N.Y.C.R.R. § 202.5–b(d)(1).

provided by statute, Chief Administrator's rule or order of the court."[94] If the clerk rejects the paper, it must stamp it with the date and provide the reason for the refusal on the paper.[95] That will at least create a record for a party who seeks to challenge the rejection and who may need to prove that the paper would have been filed timely.

Interesting in this connection are cases on the effect of the clerk's time-and-date stamp, which of course becomes critical when the statute of limitations is involved. The stamp creates a presumption about when the papers were received in the clerk's office, but it's rebuttable. It was deemed rebutted in Resch v. Briggs,[96] where the last day of the statute of limitations was April 18, 2006. The county clerk's stamp said the papers were received on April 19, 2006, which would have made them too late under the three-year statute of limitations applicable to the case. The plaintiff's proof, which established that the initiatory papers were forwarded via a UPS express overnight envelope, was held to rebut the presumption and to show that delivery was made in time.

The more likely prospect in arguments like this is that the date stamp will prevail, as it did in Cranesville Block Co., Inc. v. Spring Apartments, LLC,[97] where the plaintiff sent the initiatory papers to the county clerk via regular mail and the tardiness cost the plaintiff a mechanic's lien. In another particularly tragic case, Reyes-Peralta v. Ngernak,[98] the plaintiff had proof that she purchased an index number and an RJI, but did not have a clerk-stamped copy of the papers. Under the facts of the case, the court was constrained to conclude that no filing of the summons and complaint actually occurred and that the nonfiling amounted to a defect in subject matter jurisdiction that could not be cured under CPLR 2001.

The lesson to be distilled from these decisions is that every lawyer representing a plaintiff in an action, or a petitioner in a special proceeding, should have a subfile containing a time stamped copy of the initiatory papers designating a filing in the county clerk's office within the statute of limitations.

In e-filed cases, arguments like these will no longer be as common because the New York State Courts Electronic Filing System (NYSCEF) will produce a notification of the receipt of e-filed documents.[99] Furthermore, the party filing the document will no longer be at the whim of the postal service, an overnight mail drop box, or the closing hours at the county clerk's office as "[d]ocuments may be transmitted at any time of the day or night to the NYSCEF site."[100] In an action still governed by paper filing, lawyers should never trust regular mail, or even overnight delivery, if the statute of limitations is approaching. Although the envelope may be received by the clerk's office in time, there is no telling when it will be opened and stamped by a human being.

---

    [94]   22 N.Y.C.R.R. § 202.5(d)(1); see, e.g., 22 N.Y.C.R.R. § 202.27–a(i) (requiring county clerk or other applicable clerk of the court to refuse to accept for filing a default judgment application that does not comply with the requirements of consumer credit rules); § 295.

    [95]   22 N.Y.C.R.R. § 202.5(d)(2).

    [96]   Resch v. Briggs, 51 A.D.3d 1194, 856 N.Y.S.2d 317 (3d Dep't 2008) (SPR 198:2–3).

    [97]   Cranesville Block Co., Inc. v. Spring Apartments, LLC, 53 A.D.3d 998, 863 N.Y.S.2d 116 (3d Dep't 2008) (SPR 203:4).

    [98]   Reyes-Peralta v. Ngernak, 30 Misc. 3d 168, 909 N.Y.S.2d 901 (Sup. Ct., Nassau County 2010) (SPR 228:3).

    [99]   22 N.Y.C.R.R. § 202.5–b(d)(3).

    [100]   22 N.Y.C.R.R. § 202.5–b(d)(3)(i).

Plaintiff's Lawyer Accountable for Process Server's Acts

All problems of service were compounded for plaintiffs' attorneys when—quite by coincidence, and not at all a product or by-product of the commencement by filing system—the Court of Appeals held in Kleeman v. Rheingold[101] that the plaintiff's attorney is responsible for the activities of the process server and cannot escape the responsibility by relying on the theory that the process server is an independent contractor. Hence, a foul-up by a process server that brings about a dismissal of the action too late for a new one under the statute of limitations will be laid at the door of the attorney who retained the process server and will render the attorney liable to the client for legal malpractice.[102] Therefore, before filing away a process server's affidavit of service, the lawyer should carefully review it to ensure that it complies with any required procedures for service in CPLR 308 and that service has been completed within the time frames prescribed by CPLR 306–b, discussed above.

Contrasting the Former CPLR 306–b

We must give at least some attention to the original, and eccentric—and now thankfully superseded—CPLR 306–b, if only because of its profuse caselaw. In the course of their research, lawyers will often meet these cases and find them difficult to account for without knowing this background, which can therefore offer the simple assurance that the case found may now be safely ignored.

The vice of the original 1992 version of CPLR 306–b was its uncompromising rigidity. Not only did service have to be made within 120 days; the plaintiff also had to secure and file proof of service within that time. The failure to file such proof within the 120 days—even if service was timely and properly made—resulted in the action's being "deemed dismissed." The dismissal occurred automatically, calling for neither a direction by a judge nor even an entry by the clerk. The court had no discretion whatever to extend the time period no matter how diligent the plaintiff's efforts at service.

This wrongheaded procedure resulted in innumerable dismissals even in cases in which the plaintiff was proceeding with diligence, but was experiencing difficulties beyond her control.

There was one favor conferred on the plaintiff under this 1992 system. If a "deemed" dismissal occurred on the 120th day, the plaintiff then had a second 120-day period in which to commence a new action—with a new fee—and the second action was then allowed to relate back to the moment that the first was commenced, so that if the first action was filed within the statute of limitations, the second action would also be deemed timely. This seemed generous enough, but it, too, was undone by its inflexibility. As generous as 240 days may seem, there were situations in which that won't suffice. The original CPLR 306–b did not provide for that; the court had no power to let the plaintiff go beyond the 240th day.

---

[101] Kleeman v. Rheingold, 81 N.Y.2d 270, 598 N.Y.S.2d 149, 614 N.E.2d 712 (1993) (NYSLD No. 402).

[102] A concern for lawyers after *Kleeman* is just how far this liability goes. If a presumably independent process server is the attorney's agent for the purpose of imposing a respondeat superior liability on the attorney, are others hired by the lawyer also to fit that mold, such as an expert witness? Is the attorney responsible for the expert's actions? Ituarte v. Kolbrener, N.Y.L.J., Dec. 9, 1993, at 27, cols. 4–5 (Sup. Ct., Nassau County; McCaffrey, J.) (SPR 12:4), says no.

Horror stories under this "deemed dismissal" procedure abounded.[103] With the court once again empowered to intervene with the flexible tool of the time extension for service offered by the 1998 revision of CPLR 306–b, these stories will hopefully be at an end.

§ 63A.   Commencement of Actions by Electronic Filing ("E-Filing")

The commencement of an action by electronic means, while accelerated in federal practice,[1] has been slow to take hold in New York. Since 1999, the legislature granted the courts permission to experiment with e-filing. The authorization was rather limited, with the Office of Court Administration (OCA) only empowered to take several baby steps along the way. In 2009, OCA was permitted to invoke mandatory e-filing, but only in selected courts and actions. With the legislative authorization for several important aspects of the e-filing system set to expire on September 1, 2015, the Governor signed Chapter 237 of the Laws of 2015 on August 31, 2015, which became effective immediately.

Previously, mandatory e-filing could only be implemented in counties by legislative action. The new law vests OCA with the authority to implement mandatory e-filing in the supreme court in any county and in almost all types of actions. This authorization is now permanent and will not sunset in the future. The legislation contains an important restriction of sorts, requiring that the local county clerk consent to the adoption of mandatory e-filing before it can become effective in that county.[2] This important stipulation is designed to ensure that mandatory e-filing is not imposed in a county that does not have the infrastructure in place to accommodate the procedure, and was probably necessary to obtain support for the measure from the county clerks.

Chapter 237 also continues to authorize programs for consensual and mandatory e-filing in Surrogate's Court,[3] and the New York City Civil Court,[4] and programs for consensual e-filing and filing by facsimile in the Court of Claims.[5] The present authorization for the use of consensual and mandatory e-filing in Family Court and certain criminal courts also continues although that authorization has not yet been exploited.

Categories of Action Excluded from Mandatory E-Filing

Several categories of action are excluded from mandatory e-filing, including matrimonial actions,[6] Election Law proceedings, CPLR Article 70 habeas corpus proceedings, CPLR Article 78 proceedings, and Mental Hygiene Law proceedings.[7] Parties in these actions presumably could consent to e-filing in an action where the Chief Administrative Judge has expressly permitted consensual e-filing.

---

[103]   These are chronicled in what became almost a regular department in Siegel's Practice Review, usually under a caption devoted to "The Filing System."

[1]   See § 636.

[2]   CPLR 2111(a).

[3]   See CPLR 2111(b)(2)(B).

[4]   See CPLR 2111(b)(2)(C).

[5]   See CPLR 2111(a).

[6]   See CPLR 105(p) (defining "matrimonial action").

[7]   See CPLR 2111(b)(2)(A).

In residential foreclosure actions involving a "home loan"[8] and consumer credit proceedings,[9] OCA can require that the initiatory papers be e-filed.[10] Any subsequent papers (i.e., interlocutory papers) served in these actions are not subject to mandatory e-filing.[11] Counties that had already adopted mandatory e-filing of all papers in these actions before the effective date of the new legislation (specifically: Erie, Essex, New York, Queens, Rockland, Suffolk, and Westchester in residential foreclosure actions; Erie, New York, Onondaga, Rockland, and Westchester in consumer credit proceedings) may, however, continue to impose mandatory e-filing of all papers until August 31, 2018.[12]

Opting Out of Mandatory E-Filing

An attorney for a party may opt out of mandatory e-filing in certain designated situations.[13] The opt-out is accomplished through the filing of a prescribed form with the county clerk in the county where the action is pending.[14] An attorney can opt out of mandatory e-filing when she "certifies in good faith" that one of the following conditions are present: (1) she lacks sufficient computer hardware, (2) she lacks a connection to the Internet, (3) she lacks a scanner or other device by which documents may be converted to an electronic format (would an "other device" include a cell phone with a camera?), or (4) "she lacks the requisite knowledge in the operation of such computers and/or scanners necessary to participate" in e-filing.[15] There is a significant exception of sorts to the "requisite knowledge" provision in item 4 above. "[T]he knowledge of any employee of an attorney, or any employee of the attorney's law firm, office or business who is subject to such attorney's direction, shall be imputed to the attorney."[16]

The last clause in CPLR 2111(b)(3)(B) also grants the court the authority, upon motion, to exempt any attorney from mandatory e-filing for any other "good cause."[17] Where a party is not represented by counsel, "the clerk shall explain such party's options for electronic filing in plain language and shall inquire whether he or she wishes to participate."[18] The unrepresented party is then free to participate in e-filing and, after participating, is free "to opt out of the program for any reason via presentation of a prescribed form to be filed with the clerk of the court where the proceeding is pending."[19]

Various Laws, Rules, and Administrative Orders Governing E-Filing

Among other things, Chapter 237 created a new Article 21–A of the CPLR, entitled "Filing of Papers in the Courts by Facsimile Transmission and by Electronic Means."

---

[8]   See RPAPL 1304(5).

[9]   See CPLR 105(f).

[10]   CPLR 2111(b)(2)(A).

[11]   CPLR 2111(b)(2)(A).

[12]   CPLR 2111(b)(2–a).

[13]   CPLR 2111(b)(3).

[14]   CPLR 2111(b)(3).

[15]   CPLR 2111(b)(3)(A), (B).

[16]   CPLR 2111(b)(3)(B).

[17]   See 22 N.Y.C.R.R. § 202.5–bb(e)(3) ("Exemption of counsel upon a showing of good cause.").

[18]   CPLR 2111(b)(3)(B).

[19]   CPLR 2111(b)(3)(B); see 22 N.Y.C.R.R. § 202.5–bb(e)(1) ("Exemption of unrepresented litigants."). Query whether a pro se party who is also an attorney can opt out of mandatory e-filing under the above provisions?

CPLR 2110 adopts the definitions of "facsimile transmission" and "electronic means" already contained in CPLR 2103(f). CPLR 2111 then addresses the commencement of actions and filing and service of papers in the trial courts by electronic means (e-filing) and by facsimile transmission. Filing by facsimile transmission is only permitted in the Court of Claims, where it has worked well for a long time.[20]

CPLR 2112 addresses the filing of papers by electronic means in the Appellate Division.[21] If a county has adopted mandatory e-filing in a particular category of action, it is important to note that the filing and service of a notice of appeal pursuant to CPLR 5515(1) is subject to the e-filing rules.[22]

One of the goals of the 2015 legislation was to relocate statutes governing e-filing from the bowels of the Unconsolidated Laws to appropriate and more accessible provisions of the consolidated laws, such as the CPLR. Negotiating the requirements of e-filing still requires one to traverse an unwieldy set of laws and rules in various places. First, one must look to the enabling legislation authorizing consensual and mandatory e-filing, and Article 21–A of the CPLR to ascertain the courts and categories of actions in which e-filing is permitted or required. Then, one must consult the provisions of the Uniform Rules governing consensual and mandatory e-filing. Rule 202.5–b governs procedures when consensual e-filing has been authorized in the court.[23] Rule 202.5–bb governs procedures in actions in which e-filing is mandatory.[24] Unless otherwise provided in the latter rule, the provisions of Rule 202.5–b that govern consensual e-filing also apply in actions in which e-filing is mandatory.[25] Both of these rules were substantially amended when Chapter 237 of the Laws of 2015 became effective on August 31, 2015.[26] Finally, one must consult the most recent administrative order to ascertain the counties and categories of action in which e-filing is required or permitted.[27] The ultimate goal should be to include all of these procedures in the CPLR or a court's governing act.

Several counties have published "Protocols" explaining how traditional courthouse and county clerk requirements for the processing of cases are applied in e-filed matters.[28] Then, of course, there is always the assigned judge's individual rules, which may require submission of hard copies (known as "working copies") even in an e-filed action.[29] While

---

[20]   CPLR 2111(a).

[21]   See § 11. On June 1, 2017, OCA circulated a "Request for Public Comment on Proposed Rules for Electronic Filing in the Appellate Division of Supreme Court." Lawyers prosecuting appeals should check the status of these proposed rules.

[22]   CPLR 2111(c); see §§ 531, 533.

[23]   22 N.Y.C.R.R. § 202.5–b.

[24]   22 N.Y.C.R.R. § 202.5–bb.

[25]   22 N.Y.C.R.R. § 202.5–bb(a)(1).

[26]   See https://iappscontent.courts.state.ny.us/NYSCEF/live/legislation.htm.

[27]   See https://iappscontent.courts.state.ny.us/NYSCEF/live/legislation.htm, supra. As we went to press, the most recent administrative order was AO/170A (August 16, 2017).

[28]   See, e.g., Protocol on Courthouse and County Clerk Procedures for Electronically Filed Cases, Supreme Court, New York County (revised March 9, 2016).

[29]   See, e.g., Protocol on Courthouse and County Clerk Procedures for Electronically Filed Cases, § B, 6(a), Supreme Court, New York County (revised March 9, 2016) ("Various Justices require that, in all NYSCEF cases assigned to them, unless otherwise directed, counsel submit working copies [, i.e., hard copies,] of e-filed documents . . . . Generally, in these Parts, documents intended for judicial review must be filed with the NYSCEF system first and the required working copy must be delivered to the court thereafter."); see also § 246 (discussing problems that can arise when moving party in e-filed action fails to submit working copies of motion to court).

e-filing certainly offers many significant advantages over paper filing, we wonder if they are fully achieved in a system that still contains a hodgepodge of local and individual court rules requiring the submission of hard copies of documents.

Counties and Actions with Mandatory and Consensual E-Filing

By Administrative Order AO/170A/17 dated August 16, 2017, the Chief Administrative Judge established or continued mandatory e-filing in certain actions in the following counties:

Supreme Court, Bronx County—all medical, dental, and podiatric malpractice actions.

Supreme Court, Dutchess County—all actions except CPLR Article 70 and 78 proceedings, Election Law proceedings, matrimonial and Mental Hygiene Law matters, consumer credit transactions as defined by CPLR 105(f), and residential foreclosure actions as defined in RPAPL 1304.

Supreme Court, Erie County—all actions except CPLR Article 70 and 78 proceedings, Election Law Proceedings, in rem tax foreclosures, matrimonial and Mental Hygiene Law matters, and proceedings under RPTL 730.

Supreme Court, Essex County—all tax certiorari (excluding proceedings under RPTL 730), eminent domain matters, and all foreclosure actions involving real property (excluding mechanics liens and in rem tax foreclosures).

Supreme Court, Kings County—all Commercial Division matters (commercial cases as defined in 22 N.Y.C.R.R. § 202.70(a), (b), and (c)), and all tort actions.

Supreme Court, Nassau County—all commercial matters (without regard to the amount in controversy), civil forfeitures, in rem tax foreclosures, and tax certiorari (including proceedings under RPTL 730).

Supreme Court, New York County—all actions except CPLR Article 70 and 78 proceedings, Election Law proceedings, matrimonial and Mental Hygiene Law matters.

Supreme Court, Niagara County—all actions except CPLR Article 70 and 78 proceedings, Election Law proceedings, matrimonial and Mental Hygiene Law matters, in rem tax foreclosures, proceedings under RPTL 730, consumer credit transactions as defined by CPLR 105(f), and residential foreclosures as defined in RPAPL 1304.

Supreme Court, Oneida County—all actions except CPLR Article 70 and 78 proceedings, Election Law proceedings, matrimonial and Mental Hygiene Law matters, residential foreclosure proceedings under RPAPL 1304, proceedings under RPTL 730, name change applications, emergency medical treatment applications, and consumer credit transactions as defined in CPLR 105(f).

Supreme Court, Onondaga County—all actions except CPLR Article 70 and 78 proceedings, Election Law proceedings, matrimonial and Mental Hygiene Law matters, foreclosure actions addressing real property and mechanics liens, proceedings under RPTL 730, name change applications, and emergency medical treatment applications.

Supreme Court, Queens County—all medical, dental, and podiatric malpractice actions, and all foreclosure actions (including commercial foreclosures) addressing real property and mechanics liens. A separate administrative order announced the launch of a pilot project for residential foreclosure actions subject to mandatory electronic filing in Supreme Court, Queens County. Effective March 23, 2015, a "Residential Foreclosure Addendum" and a "What is E-Filing?" Information Sheet shall accompany the initiating papers that must be personally served upon a party in residential foreclosure actions.[30]

Supreme Court, Rockland County—all actions except CPLR Article 70 and 78 proceedings, Election Law proceedings, matrimonial and Mental Hygiene Law matters.

Supreme Court, Suffolk County—all matters except CPLR Article 70, 75, and 78 proceedings, civil forfeiture actions, consumer credit transactions as defined in CPLR 105(f) (except initial filing of commencement papers by a represented party, which is mandatory), Election Law proceedings, emergency medical treatment applications, matrimonial and Mental Hygiene Law matters, name change applications, other special proceedings, tort actions (except medical, dental, and podiatric malpractice actions, which are mandatory).

Supreme Court, Westchester County—all actions except CPLR Article 70 and 78 proceedings, Election Law proceedings, matrimonial and Mental Hygiene Law matters, and name change applications.

Surrogate's Court in Albany, Cayuga, Chautauqua, Erie, Franklin, Jefferson, Livingston, Monroe, Montgomery, Oneida, Onondaga, Ontario, Schenectady, Seneca, Steuben, Warren, Wayne, Westchester, and Yates Counties—all probate and administration proceedings and related miscellaneous proceedings.

The administrative order also established or continued the consensual e-filing program in the following counties for various types of actions: Albany, Bronx, Broome, Chatauqua, Cortland, Dutchess, Erie, Kings, Livingston, Nassau, Niagara, Oneida, Onondaga, Ontario, Orange, Queens, Richmond, Rockland, Steuben, Suffolk, Tompkins, and Westchester.

Additionally, parties to matrimonial actions should take note of Appendix B to Administrative Order AO/170A/17. The appendix sets forth additional rules and conditions for the consensual electronic filing of matrimonial actions in supreme court. Except as otherwise required by the administrative order and appendix, the provisions of 22 N.Y.C.R.R. section 202.5–b governing consensual e-filing in supreme court still apply. See Appendix B, AO/170A/17 ("Rules Governing the Consensual Electronic Filing of Matrimonial Actions in Supreme Court").

The consensual e-filing program was also established or continued for various actions in several Surrogate's Courts, the New York City Civil Court, and the Albany and New York District of the Court of Claims.

The administrative order references the dates that mandatory and consensual e-filing became effective in the above counties. The specifics on all of the above matters, and any changes (which have been occurring with some frequency), can be checked at: https://iappscontent.courts.state.ny.us/NYSCEF/live/legislation.htm. For the practitioner unfamiliar with e-filing, inquiry must continue to be made locally, in each particular court, to determine whether e-filing applies there and, if it does, any individual peculiarities that must be noted about it.

---

[30] See AO/59/15, March 18, 2015.

One incidental issue likely to be met with e-filing is when a competition arises between judgments against the same defendant: which one takes priority as a lien on the defendant's real property? Will a judgment from a court with e-filing have an advantage in that kind of competition?[31]

Second Department Forgives Mistake of Commencing E-Filed Action on Training System!

In Grskovic v. Holmes,[32] the Second Department concluded that CPLR 2001 can be invoked "to remedy defects in the e-filing of summonses, summonses with notice, and complaints, when the defect results in a statute of limitations problem for the filing party." The plaintiff in *Grskovic* wanted to commence an action in Westchester County, a mandatory e-filing county. Plaintiff's counsel established a temporary user account with the Office of Court Administration's e-filing system to file the initiatory papers. Unfamiliar with the system, plaintiff's counsel mistakenly "filed" the initiatory papers in a practice simulation instead of the actual "live" system. Counsel argued that he was led to believe by subsequent emails from the system that the filing transaction, which occurred within the statute of limitations, was accomplished properly. Shortly after the statute of limitations expired, plaintiff's counsel learned that the filing was not achieved in the live system, i.e., within the actual courthouse. The Second Department concluded that CPLR 2001 should save the action: the court allowed the plaintiff to "correct" the improper filing nunc pro tunc to the date counsel erroneously filed the papers in the practice simulation, a correction that made the action timely.

Court Invokes CPLR 2001 to Forgive E-Filing of Incorrect Initiatory Papers That Did Not Name Defendant

In McCord v. Ghazal,[33] plaintiffs purchased an index number in conjunction with their e-filed action, but filed incorrect papers from a related case with a similar caption. The defendant was not named as a party in the papers. Relying on the Second Department's decision in *Grskovic*, discussed above, the court concluded that it was "permitted to correct a mistake caused 'in large part, by the glitches in the new e-filing system and counsel's unfamiliarity with it.'" Therefore, it denied defendant's motion to dismiss for lack of subject matter and personal jurisdiction. The court emphasized that plaintiffs' counsel timely electronically commenced a new action, properly identified defendant as a party in the e-filing system, paid the proper fee for an index number, uploaded a document identified as a "summons with notice" in the e-filing system, served defendant with the proper summons with notice the following day, properly uploaded an affidavit of service for the summons with notice with the corresponding index number purchased, and promptly uploaded the correct summons with notice upon learning of the initial filing error.

This latter act occurred after the statute of limitations expired. The court observed that "[t]he only error in commencing this action was the selection of the wrong file on plaintiffs' counsel's computer when prompted by the e-filing system to select the file to be uploaded." In that the uploading of the summons with notice was performed in a

---

[31]   SPR 231:2.

[32]   Grskovic v. Holmes, 111 A.D.3d 234, 972 N.Y.S.2d 650 (2d Dep't 2013) (NYSLD No. 646).

[33]   McCord v. Ghazal, 43 Misc. 3d 767, 984 N.Y.S.2d 572 (Sup. Ct., Kings County 2014).

mistaken manner, the court concluded that it could correct the mistake under CPLR 2001.

Supreme Court Distinguishes *Grskovic* and Refuses to Forgive Late E-Filing After County Clerk Rejected Hard-Copy Filing

As demonstrated in the *Grskovic* and *McCord* decisions discussed above, the courts have shown sympathy when a lawyer commits what might be called "a rookie mistake" in e-filing an action. We suspect that over time judges will become somewhat stingier in invoking CPLR 2001 to correct these errors, and a recent decision demonstrates that the tide may be turning. In Feld v. Ginsburg,[34] the client disputed the counsel fee charged by his lawyer and the matter proceeded to arbitration under Uniform Rule Part 137.[35] The notice of arbitration award and arbitration award were mailed to plaintiff on September 2, 2014. On October 7, 2014, plaintiff commenced this action via e-filing for de novo review pursuant to section 137.8 of Part 137, which requires a party aggrieved by a Part 137 arbitration award to commence an action "within 30 days after the arbitration award has been mailed." If no action is commenced within 30 days of the mailing of the arbitration award, the award becomes final and binding.

The *Feld* court noted that the "30-day period is absolute and the court does not have discretion to excuse the late commencement of the action for de novo review." Therefore, plaintiff client's action for de novo review, which was commenced by e-filing thirty-five days after the mailing of the notice of arbitration award, was dismissed as untimely.

Distinguishing the Second Department's decision in *Grskovic*, the court stressed that the county clerk actually rejected plaintiff's attempt to file a hard copy of the summons and complaint and notified plaintiff before the expiration of the thirty-day period that the initiatory papers had to be e-filed. Nonetheless, plaintiff failed to e-file the summons and complaint until after the expiration of the thirty-day period.

§ 64.   Amendment of the Summons

The court may at any time "allow any summons . . . to be amended, if a substantial right" of the defendant is not violated.[1] Insubstantial defects are mere irregularities and are thus subject to this kind of amendment,[2] but if there is a violation of a substantial right, the defect is jurisdictional and an amendment is precluded. The courts are not of one mind about where to draw the line, however, which suggests that the drafting of the summons—or the filling out of a printed form if one is used—is another place where lawyers must take great care to avoid errors. The omission from the summons of the court and county, for example, was held to be a jurisdictional defect in Tamburo v. P & C Food Markets, Inc.,[3] while a similar defect in Tobia v. Town of Rockland[4] was held to be a mere correctable irregularity. *Tobia* cited the fact that even before the service the parties were notified of the omission, but that distinction hardly seems enough to dictate the difference between salvation and dismissal.

---

[34]   Feld v. Ginsburg, 46 Misc. 3d 1216(A), 9 N.Y.S.3d 593 (Sup. Ct., Westchester County 2015).

[35]   See §§ 456, 603 (Practitioner's Edition).

[1]   CPLR 305(c).

[2]   See CPLR 2001; § 201.

[3]   Tamburo v. P & C Food Markets, Inc., 36 A.D.2d 1017, 321 N.Y.S.2d 487 (4th Dep't 1971).

[4]   Tobia v. Town of Rockland, 106 A.D.2d 827, 484 N.Y.S.2d 226 (3d Dep't 1984).

A mere defect in naming a defendant who has been duly served and who knows from all of the papers served that he is the intended defendant is a mere amendable irregularity that can be corrected under CPLR 305(c).[5] Where, for example, the proper defendant was served but was designated as Emma Stockton instead of the correct Mary Stockton, a name change by amendment was allowed. The action was for mortgage foreclosure; the complaint was served with the summons (always helpful because it identifies the claim for the defendant); and the defendant was not misled.[6]

The so-called idem sonans cases, in which there are only minor spelling defects, such as Rus-Kap for Russ-Kap or Schutz for Schultz, always present mere amendable irregularities as long as the right person has been served.[7]

It has been acknowledged that "[n]o rule or measure has ever been devised by which we may determine in every case, with definite certainty, whether a defect is jurisdictional or is a mere irregularity,"[8] for which reason many of the cases in this area seem irreconcilable. The rule of prejudice is as close to a rule of thumb as we have even though there continues to be some judicial disagreement on what is actually prejudicial.

What about the "d/b/a" cases, in which an entity or individual "doing business as" something or other is sued in its doing-business name instead of its technically correct name? Commenting on how little there is about that in the cases, the court in Victor Auto Parts, Inc. v. Cuva[9] sustained an action naming the "d/b/a," rather than the corporate entity, even at the post-judgment stage.[10] It is of course risky at best for a plaintiff to let things go that far; the proper name should be substituted at the plaintiff's earliest opportunity. A required showing in any event is that service was made on the proper person, whatever the name used in the papers.

A defect in naming the defendant can result in disaster when a defendant corporation is served through the secretary of state.[11] The initiatory papers in this scenario might be forwarded to the named entity, which may be an entirely separate entity from the actual defendant in the action. When serving a summons and complaint on the secretary of state, jurisdiction will only be obtained over the named party, and an amendment of the summons will not be permitted even if the papers ultimately wind up in the hands of the correct defendant.[12]

An action against a decedent must be brought against his personal representative[13] and, therefore, it is not a mere irregularity to bring it against the decedent. That defect was held jurisdictional and the action a nullity in Marte v. Graber, where the action was

---

[5]   West v. City of New York, 143 A.D.3d 810, 39 N.Y.S.3d 65, 336 Ed. Law Rep. 425 (2d Dep't 2016). This will avoid the issues encountered when seeking to add an additional defendant to an action under CPLR 1003, discussed in § 65.

[6]   Stuyvesant v. Weil, 167 N.Y. 421, 60 N.E. 738 (1901).

[7]   Russ-Kap, Inc. v. Connolly, 197 Misc. 464, 95 N.Y.S.2d 887 (Sup. Ct., Nassau County 1950).

[8]   Valz v. Sheepshead Bay Bungalow Corporation, 249 N.Y. 122, 134, 163 N.E. 124, 128 (1928).

[9]   Victor Auto Parts, Inc. v. Cuva, 148 Misc. 2d 349, 560 N.Y.S.2d 269 (Sup. Ct., Monroe County 1990).

[10]   The court retained intact an income execution and even made it operative on past as well as future payments. (This is an issue more frequently met in small claims procedure—see §§ 1813 and 1814 in the New York City Civ. Ct. Act, and in the Uniform Dist. Ct. Act and Uniform Just. Ct. Act—with which the Victor result is consistent.)

[11]   See §§ 70, 95.

[12]   See Smith v. Giuffre Hyundai, Ltd., 60 A.D.3d 1040, 1042, 876 N.Y.S.2d 450, 452 (2d Dep't 2009).

[13]   See § 55.

commenced against the defendant three months after he died.[14] Therefore, the summons could not be amended to correct the defect.

When a claim is brought in a court of limited jurisdiction in an amount beyond its monetary limit, the summons should be amendable to reduce the sum demanded to bring it under the court's ceiling, but, as noted earlier,[15] some judges still take the narrower view that bars such an amendment. In that instance, it may technically be the complaint containing the ad damnum, rather than the summons, that is being amended. The "complaint" in lower court practice quite often takes the form of just a sentence or two (called an "indorsement") written on the face of the summons.[16]

Note that while a pleading can sometimes be amended by a party as of right, without judicial permission,[17] the amendment of a summons pursuant to CPLR 305(c) requires a court order.[18]

§ 65. Amending Summons to Change Parties; Supplemental Summons

When the plaintiff draws the initial summons, she can name any defendants she wants and effect service on all of them to make them parties. Joining additional parties afterwards is more involved. Until 1996, the rule was that the plaintiff could not add parties without court leave, even if all existing parties were willing to stipulate to it.

That changed with a 1996 amendment of both CPLR 305(a) and 1003. If the plaintiff acts no later than the 20th day after the defendant's service of the answer, the plaintiff may add additional parties without leave[1] and does so by filing with the clerk a "supplemental" summons—along with the complaint that the new defendant is required to answer—and then serving both on the new party.[2] While the cited provisions don't say so, it is a good idea to serve copies of the supplemental summons on all existing parties who have appeared, to assure that all are aware of the new joinder.[3]

The amendments also allow the addition of new parties if all existing parties who have appeared so stipulate. In the absence of a stipulation, and if the time for the additional joinder as of right has expired, the plaintiff must obtain court leave for the joinder. The failure to join a defendant in accordance with the procedures in CPLR 1003

---

[14] Marte v. Graber, 58 A.D.3d 1, 867 N.Y.S.2d 71 (1st Dep't 2008) (SPR 205:2). There is a toll of the statute of limitations when a would-be defendant dies, which might make a new action against the decedent's duly designated personal representative possible at this stage. CPLR 210(b); see § 55.

[15] See § 23.

[16] See § 902(a)(1) in the New York City Civ. Ct. Act, and in the Uniform Dist. Ct. Act and Uniform Just. Ct. Act, McKinney's Vol. 29A, Parts 2 and 3; § 60.

[17] CPLR 3025(a); see § 236.

[18] Amendments that in fact or in effect seek to add or change parties are discussed in the next section. The amended summons and the "supplemental" summons—the latter being the one designed to add a party—are distinguished in § 65.

[1] CPLR 1003. If there are multiple defendants, it has been held that the 20 days for joining an additional party run from the service of the last answer to come in. Dynaire Corp. v. Germano, N.Y.L.J., Aug. 1, 1996, at 22, col.1 (Sup. Ct., New York County; Friedman, J.).

[2] CPLR 305(a).

[3] See CPLR 2103(e); § 203.

constitutes a jurisdictional defect requiring dismissal of the action against that defendant.[4]

Nonetheless, if a party is improperly added outside the time frames in CPLR 1003, she had better raise a prompt objection.[5] In Wyatt v. City of New York,[6] the court ruled that plaintiffs added MTA Bus Company as a defendant without court leave outside the time periods in CPLR 1003. The court concluded, however, that defendants waived their right to assert the issue because they failed to plead a proper objection in either their original or amended answer. For good measure, a defendant in this scenario should not only raise the affirmative defense of lack of personal jurisdiction, but also a specific objection to improper joinder.[7]

It is important to keep in mind that the amendments to CPLR 1003 do not resolve any statute of limitations problems.[8] How the statute of limitations fares in joinder cases, therefore, remains unchanged by the amendments. This gets embroiled in the so-called "relation-back" doctrine, in which, if the original statute of limitations has already expired when a new party is joined, it may still be possible to preserve the claim against the new party if the claim can be deemed to "relate back" to the time of the interposition of the original claim.

The relation back doctrine that applies in amendment cases is treated in the statute of limitations chapter.[9] Amendment of the complaint to add a new claim on the one hand, and the additional joinder of a party on the other, are really separate subjects, but they sometimes overlap, and one of the overlaps is in the delicate area of the statute of limitations. When the statute of limitations has expired as against the party whom the plaintiff now wants to add, a supplemental summons, even if allowed under CPLR 1003, is likely to be too late. The 1996 amendments may facilitate the joinder, but don't guarantee its timeliness.

Suppose, however, that the problem is just some kind of misdescription of the defendant, rather than a matter of adding an entirely new defendant. In that situation, the plaintiff may be able to convince the court to allow a mere "change of title," redesignating the defendant as named to the defendant as it should have been named. This is done by an amendment of the summons,[10] but it can only be accomplished if the court is persuaded that the error is one of mere misdescription, thus negating prejudice.

Two things must be shown for an amendment of this kind. First, it must be clear from all the papers served, including the notice or complaint accompanying the summons,[11] that the defendant now sought to be added (or "redesignated") should have

---

[4] Crook v. E.I. du Pont de Nemours Co., 181 A.D.2d 1039, 582 N.Y.S.2d 581 (4th Dep't 1992), aff'd, 81 N.Y.2d 807, 595 N.Y.S.2d 388, 611 N.E.2d 289 (1993).

[5] See He-Duan Zheng v. American Friends of Mar Thoma Syrian Church of Malabar, Inc., 67 A.D.3d 639, 640, 889 N.Y.S.2d 55 (2d Dep't 2009).

[6] Wyatt v. City of New York, 46 Misc. 3d 1210(A), 9 N.Y.S.3d 596 (Sup. Ct., New York County 2015).

[7] See Commentary C3018:14 to McKinney's CPLR 3018.

[8] Statute of limitations and other issues in conjunction with joining additional parties under the 1996 amendments are explored in the lead note in SPR 43:1.

[9] See § 49.

[10] CPLR 305(c); see § 64.

[11] Of course, the kind of information needed to place the defendant on such notice is more likely to come from a complaint than from a CPLR 305(b) notice. This demonstrates another advantage that a plaintiff gains, especially a plaintiff having difficulty ascertaining the appropriate defendants, when starting things off with a summons and complaint, instead of using the cheap alternative of a summons and mere notice. See § 60.

known that it was the intended defendant. Second, it must be shown that the summons was served on a person authorized by law to be served in behalf of the intended defendant.[12] That's what happened, for example, in a case in which the plaintiff sought to sue the Pierce Brake Service Center, Inc., but named it as Pierce Muffler Shops. The latter was in fact a different corporation, but the same personnel controlled both and service was made on X, who was an officer of both and hence servable in behalf of either.[13] Because of the nature of the claim sued on, moreover, the papers made clear which defendant was intended. An amendment was allowed.[14] The effect of an amendment of this kind is to dispense with a supplemental summons and to allow the original moment of commencement against the misnamed defendant to be deemed the moment of commencement as against the redesignated defendant, possibly sparing the plaintiff's claim from the limitations' barrier.[15]

Sometimes the problem arises when the plaintiff has named the defendant as a corporation and it turns out to be a partnership, or vice versa. The same dual test applies, and destiny will play a role in its success. If the plaintiff designates the defendant as a corporation and has the summons served on X thinking X is a corporate officer (servable in the corporation's behalf),[16] the plaintiff is in luck if, when it turns out that the defendant is a partnership, X turns out to be one of the general partners, who can be served in the partnership's behalf.[17]

That satisfies one of the requirements. The other is that the papers make clear who the intended defendant is. If both requirements are met, an amendment is allowed to redesignate the corporation as a partnership and limitations problems are avoided.[18] Conversely, where the plaintiff seeks to amend the summons to redesignate a defendant partnership as a corporation, the one presumably served as a partner had best turn out to be someone on the list of those who may be served in behalf of the corporation. If the person served is not on the list, the amendment is precluded.[19]

If no such amendment or a relation back is permissible on the facts, the interposition of the claim against the newly joined party will be deemed the key moment for a statute of limitations measure.[20]

If a motion is made to add a party, those who are already parties need only be given notice of the motion through the ordinary mail channels applicable to service of interlocutory papers within actions.[21] This applies even when the plaintiff seeks to make the new person an additional plaintiff instead of defendant. Where P commenced an action against X and Y, for example, and then sought to add A as an additional plaintiff, defendants X and Y were not entitled to be served with the supplemental summons anew via CPLR 308 service methods, notwithstanding that the new plaintiff was now adding

---

[12]   See § 64.

[13]   CPLR 311(a)(1); see § 70.

[14]   Luce v. Pierce Muffler Shops, 51 Misc. 2d 256, 272 N.Y.S.2d 845 (Sup. Ct., Onondaga County 1966), aff'd, 28 A.D.2d 826, 282 N.Y.S.2d 724 (4th Dep't 1967).

[15]   See Benware v. Schoenborn, 198 A.D.2d 710, 604 N.Y.S.2d 290 (3d Dep't 1993).

[16]   See CPLR 311(a)(1).

[17]   See CPLR 310; § 69.

[18]   De Witt v. Abraham Bros. Horse & Mule Co., 170 A.D. 610, 156 N.Y.S. 658 (1st Dep't 1915).

[19]   See Grant v. Miles Shoes, 205 Misc. 554, 127 N.Y.S.2d 743 (Sup. Ct., Schenectady County 1954).

[20]   See § 45; CPLR 305(a) (directing filing of supplemental summons).

[21]   CPLR 2103(b); see § 202.

its claim.[22] As a rule, it is only the party to be added who must be served with the supplemental summons, and even service on that party is dispensed with if he consents to jurisdiction, as the new plaintiff did in the example.

Note that most of the situations that fall under this topic involve an endeavor to effect some change on the defendant's side.

C. THE METHODS OF SERVICE

Table of Sections

§ 66.   Personal Delivery of Summons Under CPLR 308(1)

§ 67.   Enticement into Jurisdiction

§ 68.   Sovereign Immunity and Immunity from Service

§ 69.   Whom to Serve in Behalf of Various Defendants

§ 70.   Service on a Corporation

§ 71.   "Sewer Service"; the Amendment of CPLR 308

§ 72.   Deliver-and-Mail Service Under CPLR 308(2)

§ 73.   Service on Rule 318 Agent Under CPLR 308(3)

§ 74.   Affix-and-Mail Service Under CPLR 308(4)

§ 75.   Court-Ordered Service Under CPLR 308(5)

§ 76.   Service in Matrimonial Actions

§ 76A.   Personal Service by Mail

§ 76B.   Curing Technical Defects in Service

§ 66. Personal Delivery of Summons Under CPLR 308(1)

Having studied the first prerequisite for obtaining personal jurisdiction, the proper commencement and filing of the initiatory papers, we now turn to an examination of the second requirement: proper service of process.

CPLR 308 dictates the mechanics of service. It consists of five subdivisions, each of which spells out a method for service of process.[1] The first contains the age-old method of personal delivery of the initiatory papers (summons and complaint or summons and notice) to the defendant within the State. The second, commonly known as "deliver and mail," is treated later.[2] Either of these first two methods may be used at the outset. No effort need be made at personal delivery under CPLR 308(1) prior to use of the deliver-and-mail method of CPLR 308(2).[3]

We concentrate in this section on what satisfies as personal delivery under CPLR 308(1).

---

[22]   Patrician Plastic Corp. v. Bernadel Realty Corp., 25 N.Y.2d 599, 307 N.Y.S.2d 868, 256 N.E.2d 180 (1970).

[1]   CPLR 308 also dictates the methods of out-of-state service when CPLR 313 authorizes it. See § 100. CPLR 308 only refers to the service of the "summons," and we will often use that terminology in our treatment of service of process. As discussed earlier, the plaintiff must serve exactly what she files to commence the action, and this will necessitate serving the summons with the complaint or CPLR 305(b) notice to secure jurisdiction. See § 63.

[2]   See § 72.

[3]   Nor need CPLR 308 be resorted to at all in first instance. For example, personal service by mail is available as an alternative under CPLR 312–a. See § 76A.

All the process server has to do is tender the summons to the defendant. The summons need not be, and in fact should not be, in any container or envelope. Any effort to conceal the fact that it is a summons will vitiate service. In one case, for example, a husband saw his wife off on a sea trip and bid her bon voyage by having his associate give her a present for her mother and an instruction not to open it until she finished her journey. She followed his instructions and found the gift to be a summons in a divorce action. When she finally worked her way back to New York, she easily got the service and all subsequent proceedings vacated.[4]

It is even helpful to have the summons exposed to view when tendered. The tender can be in silence, although it is customary to announce that it's a summons. The normal reaction of anyone to whom a paper is tendered, except in many parts of New York City, is to extend a hand to receive it. But if the defendant does not do that, the process server need only leave the summons on a table or other item nearby, or on the sidewalk in front of the defendant, or behind him as he walks away, "provided that the defendant is made aware that this is being done."[5]

In one case, the defendant deliberately ran off to his car, locked all the windows, and sat staring straight ahead as the process server showed the summons through a window. Off drove the car with the summons stuck in the space between door and window. Service was sustained.[6]

The act of service should be unambiguous. If there is reasonable basis for the defendant to doubt that service of process was intended as such, it will be set aside. Where the defendant was an elderly woman in a nursing home, for example, and the process server, after asking her about her son's whereabouts, left the summons on a nightstand in an envelope marked with the son's name, the court held that the act of service was not unconditional and clear and the service was set aside.[7]

Once confronted, it is usually best for a defendant to accept the service. Indeed, lawyers should ordinarily advise clients expecting suit to accept service of a summons. If personal delivery is unsuccessful, other methods will be resorted to, equally valid but less likely to give notice, and the defendant may even end up paying as a disbursement whatever additional costs are incurred for such service. The only exception in which avoidance may perhaps bring tactical advantage is where the statute of limitations is at hand.

The so-called "redelivery" scenario is important. Redelivery refers to the situation in which the process server serves not the right person, but someone else who immediately or close in time, delivers the process to the right person. A number of older cases sustained this kind of service on the theory that the intermediary, retained or not by the plaintiff, in effect acted as the process server, but a more stringent requirement was imposed by the Court of Appeals in its 1968 decision in McDonald v. Ames Supply Co.[8]

---

[4] Bulkley v. Bulkley, 6 Abb. Pr. 307, 1858 WL 7234 (N.Y. Sup 1858).

[5] Carver Federal Savings Bank v. Shaker Gardens, Inc., 135 A.D.3d 1212, 23 N.Y.S.3d 685 (3d Dep't 2016).

[6] Levine v. National Transp. Co., 204 Misc. 202, 125 N.Y.S.2d 679 (Sup. Ct., Queens County 1953), aff'd, 282 A.D. 720, 122 N.Y.S.2d 901 (2d Dep't 1953).

[7] In re Bonesteel's Will, 16 A.D.2d 324, 228 N.Y.S.2d 301 (3d Dep't 1962).

[8] McDonald v. Ames Supply Co., 22 N.Y.2d 111, 291 N.Y.S.2d 328, 238 N.E.2d 726 (1968).

The defendant in *McDonald* was a corporation and the server went to the building in which the corporation had its office and gave the summons to a receptionist, who later that same day gave it to the appropriate corporate official, i.e., someone on the CPLR 311(a)(1) list of permissible servees.[9] The process server had apparently made no effort to see if he could serve a listed person, or even to determine whether the receptionist was a corporate employee (she was not). The Court felt that to sustain the service would encourage carelessness on the part of process servers. To avoid that, it pronounced the "due diligence" test: only if it is demonstrated that a diligent effort was made to find and serve the right person will service on the intermediary, with her prompt redelivery to the right person, be allowed. Subsequent cases have looked for diligence on a sui generis basis and have deemed the *McDonald* standard satisfied when they found it.[10] In *McDonald*, the person served was not an employee of the corporation. When the person was an employee, and represented that she was authorized to accept process, the service was upheld.[11]

The reader should take note of yet another point tacitly made in *McDonald* and like cases. The subject treated here is personal delivery under CPLR 308(1), and CPLR 308 is captioned "[p]ersonal service upon a natural person." Where does service on a corporation, which is governed by CPLR 311(a)(1), fit in? Or, for that matter, how do we fit in any other category of defendant covered in some provision other than CPLR 308, such as a partner governed by CPLR 310? The answer is that those other provisions are at root only lists of persons on whom the summons may be served on behalf of defendants of various categories. The method of "delivering" the summons to one of the listed persons, however, is governed as a practical matter by CPLR 308(1) and its caselaw. CPLR 311, moreover, which lists those corporate agents who can be served on behalf of the corporation, also speaks of "delivering" the summons, and for that reason involves the same principles. *McDonald* actually construed and applied CPLR 311(1), but the case is an equally influential lesson on CPLR 308(1).[12]

Members of the defendant's family who answer the door when the process server knocks are often cast in a redeliverer's role. Earlier caselaw held that when the defendant from a few feet away sees the process server (and vice versa) and hears him announce that he has a summons, delivery of the summons to the person who answered the door with subsequent redelivery by that person to the defendant is satisfactory,[13] but that if server and defendant do not see each other, it is not.[14] These cases have lost importance in view of the later adoption of CPLR 308(2), in which the delivery of the summons to the one who answered the door (assuming that person is "of suitable age and discretion") is good service on the defendant provided that it is followed by the second

---

[9]   See § 70 (discussing service on a corporation).

[10]   See Aguilera v. Pistilli Const. & Development Corp., 63 A.D.3d 765, 767, 882 N.Y.S.2d 145, 147 (2d Dep't 2009).

[11]   Fashion Page, Ltd. v. Zurich Ins. Co., 50 N.Y.2d 265, 428 N.Y.S.2d 890, 406 N.E.2d 747 (1980). The person served was the secretary of a corporate officer.

[12]   Some of the other provisions governing service, such as CPLR 309 (infants and incompetents) and 310(a) (partnerships), do not always offer an instruction as specific as "delivering" the summons; they sometimes just speak of "personally serving" it and tacitly leave to CPLR 308(1) and its caselaw all the mechanics.

[13]   Buscher v. Ehrich, 12 A.D.2d 887, 209 N.Y.S.2d 941 (4th Dep't 1961).

[14]   Ives v. Darling, 210 A.D. 521, 206 N.Y.S. 493 (3d Dep't 1924).

step of mailing provided for in that statute.[15] CPLR 308(1) becomes academic in such a case.

A major case on CPLR 308(2), in fact, Bossuk v. Steinberg,[16] should have impact on CPLR 308(1) as well. One part of 308(2)'s two-part service method is a delivery of the summons to a person of suitable age at the defendant's premises. *Bossuk* holds that when that person won't open the door to receive it, leaving the summons outside the door is an adequate delivery. That should apply under CPLR 308(1), too, when it is the defendant himself standing behind the door and refusing to open it. As long as it is established that the person is in fact the defendant, the logic of *Bossuk* should apply to CPLR 308(1) and sustain as an adequate personal delivery a service made by leaving the summons outside the door, announcing the fact, and leaving.

Bossuk has proved helpful in serving apartment house defendants. In Spector v. Berman,[17] for example, the process server went to the apartment house and rang the defendant's downstairs doorbell. The defendant answered on the intercom and he and the server identified themselves, but the defendant would not come down to meet the server or allow him into the building so as to be able to go upstairs to the apartment. So the server said he was putting the summons into the mail slot and did. The service was upheld. In *Bossuk*, the server and deliveree had been separated by only a door; in *Spector*, they were separated by two doors and a few flights of stairs. A distinction without a difference, held the *Spector* court. "The defendant did not acquire an immunity from the *Bossuk* principle simply because there were two doors and some steps involved."[18]

When it is not clear that the person served is the defendant himself, however, it is obvious that the precaution of mailing an additional copy of the summons, as CPLR 308(2) requires to satisfy that provision, can't hurt. The additional step of mailing, in other words, takes the importance out of whether the deliveree is the defendant or just some person found at his home or office. Without the mailing, paragraph 1 is relied on, and paragraph 1 is just not safe to depend on in these "redelivery" cases, even when the deliveree is, for example, the defendant's son, and even though the son promptly gives the papers to his father.[19]

In many of these cases in which service is attacked, the attack takes the form of a prompt CPLR 3211(a)(8) motion to dismiss for lack of jurisdiction.[20] The plaintiff in answering such a motion is often tempted to argue that the service must have been good or the defendant would not have had sufficient notice to be in court attacking it. That argument doesn't work. It would "negate the statutory procedure for setting aside a

---

[15]　See § 72.

[16]　Bossuk v. Steinberg, 58 N.Y.2d 916, 460 N.Y.S.2d 509, 447 N.E.2d 56 (1983); see § 72.

[17]　Spector v. Berman, 119 A.D.2d 565, 500 N.Y.S.2d 735 (2d Dep't 1986).

[18]　*Spector*, 119 A.D.2d at 566, 500 N.Y.S.2d at 736.

[19]　See Macchia v. Russo, 67 N.Y.2d 592, 505 N.Y.S.2d 591, 496 N.E.2d 680 (1986). The personal service by mail provision of CPLR 312–a, already mentioned, if successful, may make some of these points about CPLR 308 academic, but it requires a cooperative defendant. See § 76A.

[20]　See CPLR 3211(e); § 266. An alternative is to include the objection as a defense in the answer, a ploy some defendants would use regularly in the hope of postponing an adjudication of the issue until they could be sure that, should the defense be upheld at some later point, the plaintiff would by then be clearly out of time for a new action. A 1996 amendment of CPLR 3211(e) takes the profit out of that practice in most instances by requiring a defendant who pleads the objection of improper service as a defense to move for judgment on the defense within 60 days, or waive it. See § 274; SPR 50:3.

defectively served summons,"[21] which is ordinarily a prompt motion to dismiss, and would perhaps encourage defendants to suffer defaults and instead move later, after the lapse of a respectable period, to vacate the judgment based on the service defect. That postpones disposition of the jurisdictional question, however, which is often detrimental to both sides, and a burden on the system.

We can draw an important conclusion from the above, which will be helpful in our continued study of service of process. At the outset of this chapter, we discussed the traditional requirements of due process: (1) notice, and (2) opportunity to be heard.[22] Yet, when one drills down within the deep body of law governing service of process, it is apparent that the defendant's notice of the lawsuit is not controlling. There will be many instances in which the defendant is on notice of the lawsuit, but the action will be dismissed for lack of proper service because the plaintiff failed to adhere to the statutory requirements in CPLR 308. Conversely, we will see situations in which the defendant had no notice of the action, but personal jurisdiction is sustained because the plaintiff strictly complied with CPLR 308.

§ 67.   Enticement into Jurisdiction

The use of false pretenses to entice a defendant from beyond the court's territorial jurisdiction to within it, so as to serve him with process, is ground for upsetting the service.[1] But a phony representation that prompts only a short move by the defendant from one place to another within the state is not. So held Gumperz v. Hofmann,[2] where the process server just telephoned defendant's hotel room from the lobby and asked him to come down to receive a letter. Down came the defendant and was served with process instead, hardly an inconvenience worth taking judicial notice of.

The lawyer should still be wary, however, about substantially inconveniencing a defendant even if the false pretext doesn't bring about a crossing of jurisdictional lines. It is not hard to imagine the court vitiating service if the defendant is enticed from Buffalo to Brooklyn, for example—a trip of several hundred miles—just to make it easier to serve him in a supreme court action even though the service could have been made with equal effect in Buffalo. In the age of longarm jurisdiction, moreover, when CPLR 313 often permits service to be made anywhere in the world, an enticement from Hawaii (or Tibet) to New York might not, territorially speaking, make a shred of jurisdictional difference, but it is not the kind of thing the courts would want to encourage. Setting aside service in such a case may be the only lawful deterrent, lest the outraged defendant gratify himself with a little self-help.

A sincere invitation to a would-be defendant to come into the state for settlement talks will not be deemed an enticement if the talks break down and service is made at that time,[3] but cases like that are all sui generis and require difficult probing into subjective intentions. A plaintiff who would preserve his action should steer clear of any misconstruable invitations, and defendants can be notorious misconstruers.

---

21   *McDonald*, 22 N.Y.2d at 115, 291 N.Y.S.2d at 331, 238 N.E.2d at 728.

22   See § 58.

1   Garabettian v. Garabettian, 206 A.D. 502, 201 N.Y.S. 548 (1st Dep't 1923).

2   Gumperz v. Hofmann, 245 A.D. 622, 283 N.Y.S. 823 (1st Dep't 1935), aff'd 271 N.Y. 544, 2 N.E.2d 687 (1936).

3   See, e.g., Waljohn Waterstop, Inc. v. Webster, 37 Misc. 2d 96, 232 N.Y.S.2d 665 (Sup. Ct., Kings County 1962).

A classic recent example of enticement is Maydanik v. Cieri,[4] involving a Virginia accident between New Jersey and Virginia cars. P was a passenger in one of them. She wanted New York jurisdiction, but because the case had nothing to do with the State, the only way she could get it was to make service on the New Jersey defendant (D) within New York. As part of a fictional promotion, therefore, with "randomly selected" winners, D received tickets to see the Broadway show "The Producers." Into the State he came, and what appeared to be a gentleman sat next to him in the theater. But this was no gentleman; this was a process server, who tried to serve D on the way out after the show, spoiling an otherwise lovely evening at the St. James Theater. D made a motion to dismiss based on this enticement, which was granted.

§ 68.   Sovereign Immunity and Immunity from Service

Sovereign Immunity

We have briefly met the doctrine of sovereign immunity, which New York has waived to the extent of allowing itself to be sued in the court of claims only.[1] Foreign sovereigns also get immunity from New York process in their governmental functions, but not necessarily in other capacities. In tort actions, for example, the general rule is that the immunity does not apply if the occurrence causing the damage was incidental to a "proprietary," as opposed to a "governmental," function. Thus, where Missouri set up a commission to arrange for the State's participation in the World's Fair in Flushing, the purpose was primarily to amuse visitors and there was no immunity.[2] Similarly, when one of the cars involved in a New York accident was on the business of South Carolina, the State was held subject to New York jurisdiction on a tort claim arising out of the accident.[3]

Diplomatic immunity is an offspring of sovereign immunity. It protects individuals representing foreign sovereigns. But while it protects ambassadors and their staffs, even in private, nongovernmental litigation,[4] it has been held inapplicable to private suits against foreign consuls, consular officials being considered commercial rather than diplomatic representatives of their governments.[5] Doubts about diplomatic or consular status are often resolved by reference to documents secured by a party from the U.S. Department of State.[6] Even if mere consular status is shown, the New York courts may avoid decision of the immunity question today on the ground of exclusive federal jurisdiction. A federal statute provides that "all civil actions and proceedings against . . . consuls or vice-consuls" are under the exclusive jurisdiction of the U.S. district courts.[7]

---

[4]   Maydanik v. Cieri, 11 Misc. 3d 1087(A), 819 N.Y.S.2d 849 (Sup. Ct., Richmond County 2006) (SPR 175:1).

[1]   See § 17.

[2]   Tiernan v. Missouri New York World's Fair Commission, 48 Misc. 2d 376, 264 N.Y.S.2d 834 (Sup. Ct., New York County 1965). Analogously, the immunity of foreign nations is governed by federal statutes—applicable in federal and state courts alike—whose main aim is also to immunize governmental, but not commercial activity. See 28 U.S.C.A. §§ 1604–1607.

[3]   Morrison v. Budget Rent A Car Systems, Inc., 230 A.D.2d 253, 657 N.Y.S.2d 721 (2d Dep't 1997) (SPR 57:1).

[4]   See Carrera v. Carrera, 174 F.2d 496 (D.C. Cir. 1949).

[5]   Carrera v. Carrera, 174 F.2d 496 (D.C. Cir. 1949); see also State of Ohio ex rel. Popovici v. Agler, 280 U.S. 379, 50 S. Ct. 154, 74 L. Ed. 489 (1930).

[6]   See French v. Banco Nacional de Cuba, 23 N.Y.2d 46, 295 N.Y.S.2d 433, 242 N.E.2d 704 (1968).

[7]   28 U.S.C.A. § 1351.

The defense of sovereign immunity is waivable. It was held to be waived, for example, when the defendant—the instrumentality of a foreign government—answered, counterclaimed, and participated in several years of litigation maneuvering before finally seeking to assert the immunity defense.[8]

Immunity from Service

An entirely separate immunity doctrine protects nondomiciliaries of New York from civil process while they are voluntarily in the state to participate in legal proceedings of any kind, whether as mere witnesses or even as parties. To win this immunity, the participation must be voluntary; it will not apply to one here under the compulsion of a subpoena or an arrest.[9] But if D voluntarily entered the state for judicial proceedings in the first place and was then served with a subpoena or then gave bail, so that his later return might be said to be under compulsion, the fact that his original appearance was voluntary is the key factor and the immunity therefore applies to his subsequent appearance.[10]

New York has been generous with the doctrine. The original proceeding for which D voluntarily comes into the state can be civil or criminal, and in federal or state court. The doctrine applies to participation in pretrial proceedings[11] and even to mere appellate argument[12] where the client's presence is hardly necessary. It does not apply to a nonresident lawyer who is here for the proceeding, however, because the lawyer is here in pursuit of his business and not just to facilitate New York litigation.[13] But it does apply to a nonresident plaintiff here to take part in his own action.[14] In fact, New York allows the immunity not only in judicial proceedings, but in arbitral, legislative, and administrative hearings as well.[15]

The immunity applies to any civil action brought against the voluntary participant, whether or not the new action is related to the matter for which he is in the state. But if it is a related matter, there is likely to be a basis for subjecting that person to jurisdiction through service outside New York, and that may dissolve the immunity because of an important exception that has evolved.

Whenever it is shown that the action sought to be commenced against the visitor is one in which full personam jurisdiction could be obtained over him without service in New York, such as where CPLR 302 and 313 authorize service outside New York,[16] or a

---

[8]   Aboujdid v. Singapore Airlines, Ltd., 67 N.Y.2d 450, 503 N.Y.S.2d 555, 494 N.E.2d 1055 (1986).

[9]   See Glendon v. Glendon, 45 Misc. 2d 855, 258 N.Y.S.2d 20 (Sup. Ct., Kings County 1964), mod'd, 24 A.D.2d 492, 261 N.Y.S.2d 443 (2d Dep't 1965).

[10]   Thermoid Co. v. Fabel, 4 N.Y.2d 494, 176 N.Y.S.2d 331, 151 N.E.2d 883 (1958).

[11]   New England Industries v. Margiotti, 270 A.D. 488, 60 N.Y.S.2d 430 (1st Dep't 1946), aff'd, 296 N.Y. 722, 70 N.E.2d 540 (1946).

[12]   Chase Nat. Bank of City of New York v. Turner, 269 N.Y. 397, 199 N.E. 636 (1936).

[13]   Kutner v. Hodnett, 59 Misc. 21, 109 N.Y.S. 1068 (Sup. Ct., New York County 1908).

[14]   Petrova v. Roberts, 245 N.Y. 518, 157 N.E. 841 (1927). A possible way to proceed against such a plaintiff, assuming a counterclaim cannot be entertained, is to use CPLR 303 and serve his attorney so as to make him a defendant in a separate action. See § 96.

[15]   Thorp v. Adams, 11 N.Y.S. 479 (Sup. Ct., 1st Dep't 1890); Stern v. Worth, 167 Misc. 605, 4 N.Y.S.2d 392 (N.Y. City Ct. 1938).

[16]   See Brause 59 Co. v. Bridgemarket Associates, 216 A.D.2d 200, 628 N.Y.S.2d 660 (1st Dep't 1995); § 100.

designation of a state agent for service is in effect,[17] the purpose of the immunity falls and with it falls the immunity itself.[18]

To take advantage of the immunity from service, the person should show that she came to New York solely for the proceeding. A dual purpose will probably lose the immunity. The immunity covers a reasonable period before the proceeding, in order to prepare for it, and a reasonable period afterwards for return home.[19] The question of reasonableness naturally depends on the facts of each case.

This immunity, too, is waivable, and is waived like any objection to personal jurisdiction: by not raising it either in a motion to dismiss or in the answer.[20]

Another point relevant to immunity is that presence within a federal military installation in New York will not insulate the defendant from personal service and New York jurisdiction.[21]

Finally, a word should be said about whether there is any rule against serving a defendant in the courthouse. Although the courts frown on such endeavors, wary of a breach of the peace, such service has been sustained when a breach was not threatened.[22] There have apparently been a growing number of courthouse service attempts, often in connection with a proceeding trying to quash a prior attempt at service. The issue became important enough in one court to generate the consolidation of five such endeavors, producing a combined opinion. In each of the five cases, the original service was by other than personal delivery and was contested, thus necessitating a second service. In three of them the second service was "in the courtroom or its vicinity," and in another the service was made "while the respondent was actually testifying." The court criticized but sustained the service.[23]

§ 69. Whom to Serve in Behalf of Various Defendants

For various categories of defendants, there are lists of persons who may be served in the defendant's behalf. We review many of these below, with corporations treated separately in the next section.

a. Infants. An infant is anyone who has not yet reached the age of 18.[1] Suit against an infant requires no prior court leave, but service has to be made on someone listed in CPLR 309(a). Various persons are listed: a parent or guardian having legal custody (service on the parent is the most common method) or, if the infant is married and living with a spouse who is of age, on the spouse. If no such person is in the state, service may be made on anyone with whom the infant resides, or on the infant's employer. The infant herself must also be served if she is 14 or over, which means two services and two sets of process in that case. If two are necessary and only one is made,

---

[17] See Chauvin v. Dayon, 14 A.D.2d 146, 217 N.Y.S.2d 795 (3d Dep't 1961).

[18] Merigone v. Seaboard Capital Corp., 85 Misc. 2d 965, 381 N.Y.S.2d 749 (Sup. Ct., Nassau County 1976).

[19] See Application of Robinson, 18 A.D.2d 449, 240 N.Y.S.2d 82 (1st Dep't 1963).

[20] CPLR 3211(e); see §§ 266, 274.

[21] See Reybold v. Reybold, 45 A.D.2d 263, 357 N.Y.S.2d 231 (4th Dep't 1974).

[22] See Baumgartner v. Baumgartner, 273 A.D. 411, 77 N.Y.S.2d 668 (1st Dep't 1948).

[23] Department of Housing Preservation & Development of City of New York v. Koenigsberg, 133 Misc. 2d 893, 509 N.Y.S.2d 270 (N.Y. City Civ. Ct. 1986). The procedure challenged entailed the service of an order to show cause and a petition, but the holding is relevant to ordinary summons service, too.

[1] CPLR 105(j). The age of majority in New York was reduced in 1974 from 21 to 18.

the defect is jurisdictional,[2] and it will not do to show that the infant hired an attorney who appeared for her.[3] Such an appearance cannot cure the jurisdictional defect for the reason that an infant cannot hire her own attorney; someone authorized to appear for the infant must do the hiring.[4]

If a basis for extraterritorial service exists in the case, state lines disappear under CPLR 313 and either or both of the persons on whom service has to be made may be served outside New York.[5] Absent such basis, the unavailability in New York of one of the two people required to be served vitiates jurisdiction.[6]

The question of who may be served in an action against an infant should not be confused with who may appear for the infant, which is the subject of Article 12 of the CPLR and is treated later.[7] The service by mail method of CPLR 312–a[8] is not available against an infant.

b. Incompetents and Conservatees: "Incapacitated Persons." CPLR references to such terms as "conservator," "conservatee," "committee," and "incompetent," still contained in CPLR 309(b) and 309(c) and yet other CPLR provisions, are archaic. In 1993, a new Article 81 of the Mental Hygiene Law took effect. Recognizing varying kinds and degrees of dependency, it abolishes the older language and substitutes for all of it the term "incapacitated person" for the dependent person and "guardian" for the person appointed to look after the dependent person's needs. It also instructs that the older terms be deemed to include the new ones.[9] In that the CPLR continues the older terminology in several places, the terms may be used interchangeably in this text. Using the newer terminology—"incapacitated person" and "guardian"—to describe relationships that had several different descriptions prior to the enactment of Article 81 of the Mental Hygiene Law has the additional merit of offering the convenience of a single set of terms.[10]

If the defendant is an incapacitated person for whom a guardian has been appointed, CPLR 309(b) and 309(c) provide that service must be made on the guardian as well as on the incapacitated person. The court can by order dispense with service on the incapacitated person. The plaintiff would apply for such an order when, for example, the defendant is confined or dangerous. Unless a court order is secured, the plaintiff proceeds at his peril by failing to serve the incapacitated person. Incapacitated persons and infants are wards of the court and innocent procedural defects, disregardable in other contexts, can become decisive and jurisdictional when a ward is concerned. In one especially harsh case in which the guardian was served but the incapacitated person was not, and the plaintiff failed to secure an order dispensing with service on the

---

[2] K.M. ex rel. Mobley v. Mobley, 44 Misc. 3d 1225(A), 997 N.Y.S.2d 669 (Sup. Ct., Kings County 2014). If the nonresident motorist statute, Veh. & Traf. Law § 253, is used against the infant, which is permissible, it has been held that its methods apply to the exclusion of CPLR 309(a), thus dispensing with the dual service on which the latter insists. Nelson v. Fraboni, 38 A.D.2d 633, 326 N.Y.S.2d 934 (3d Dep't 1971).

[3] Randall v. Randall, 12 Misc. 2d 468, 172 N.Y.S.2d 985 (Sup. Ct., Bronx County 1958).

[4] See § 193.

[5] See Fox v. Gower, 48 Misc. 2d 1043, 266 N.Y.S.2d 658 (Sup. Ct., Monroe County 1966); § 100.

[6] See Higgins v. Blauvelt, 49 Misc. 2d 327, 267 N.Y.S.2d 461 (Sup. Ct., New York County 1966).

[7] See § 193.

[8] See § 76A.

[9] See § 194.

[10] All prior proceedings taken under the old terminology are in any event preserved until set aside or modified by a judge under the superseding law. See L.1992, c.698, § 4.

incapacitated person, the jurisdictional defect resulted in a dismissal of a mortgage foreclosure action too late for a new one, with the effect of forfeiting a mortgage loan.[11]

The motion for the order dispensing with service on the incapacitated person is presumably ex parte. If the court in a given case wants someone notified of the motion, including the incapacitated person, the court can reject the ex parte application, treat it as an order to show cause—which enables the court to prescribe the details of the motion procedure[12]—and dispose of it accordingly. As wards of the court, incapacitated persons are entitled to its extra protective powers.

Suit against an incapacitated person for whom a guardian has been appointed requires leave of court, but the courts have not treated the failure to secure advance leave as jurisdictional and have permitted the defect to be cured with a nunc pro tunc order.[13]

If the defendant has not been declared an incapacitated person, but appears to the plaintiff to be in such a condition, the plaintiff starts the action in the usual way by merely serving the defendant. Jurisdiction is thereby secured and whatever other protection is necessary for the defendant is provided by CPLR Article 12, dealing with appearances.[14] If no attorney appears for the defendant, the plaintiff can call to the court's attention any debility she perceives in the defendant and let the court decide whether it is necessary to appoint someone to protect the defendant's interests.[15]

As with an infant, the mail service provision of CPLR 312–a[16] is inapplicable to an incapacitated person.

c. **Partnerships, etc.** In New York, a partnership can be a plaintiff or a defendant in its own name without all the partners being named.[17] When the partnership is the defendant, it should be named as such. Then, to get jurisdiction of it, service need only be made on one of the general partners.[18] Those are the rules applicable to the general partnership.

Statutory provisions that were transferred to the CPLR in 1999 and are now embodied in CPLR 310–a provide for service on a limited partnership and on a limited liability partnership, creatures not to be confused with the general partnership governed by CPLR 310.

CPLR 310–a(a) enumerates various persons who may be served in behalf of a limited partnership. The limited partnership, which is an investment vehicle, consists of both general and limited partners. Service should be made on one of the general ones. Service should not be made on a limited partner, who is neither a necessary nor even a

---

[11] Sinley v. Estco, Inc., 25 Misc. 2d 172, 200 N.Y.S.2d 939 (Sup. Ct., Nassau County 1960). Ward or not, one must question the need for so rigid an approach when the service omission is so innocent.

[12] See § 248.

[13] See Depalois v. Pellegrino, 16 Misc. 3d 1133(A), 851 N.Y.S.2d 57 (N.Y. City Civ. Ct. 2007); § 194.

[14] See § 194.

[15] CPLR 1201, 1202.

[16] See § 76A.

[17] CPLR 1025.

[18] CPLR 310(a).

proper party to an action involving a limited partnership,[19] unless the action specifically involves the rights of limited partners as such.[20] As an alternative, service may be made on the limited partnership via the secretary of state.[21] If service proves impracticable by any prescribed means, the same court-ordered-service alternative that CPLR 308(5) offers for service on an individual[22] is available for service on the limited partnership.[23]

The methods set forth in subdivisions (a) and (b) of CPLR 310–a, on their face applicable to the limited partnership, should also apply to service on the limited liability partnership.[24] That conclusion is based on the language in CPLR 310–a(c), which states that "[a] limited liability partnership *may also be served* pursuant to section 121–1505 of the partnership law," allowing service on the secretary of state. This method would appear to be additional to those authorized by subdivisions (a) and (b), but ambiguities should be avoided by serving the secretary of state.[25] Still another creature to be distinguished from the others just noted is the limited liability company, for which service is prescribed by CPLR 311–a.[26] Limited Liability Company Law sections 303(a) and 304 also permit service of process on the secretary of state as an agent for a limited liability company defendant.

Novel procedural issues occasionally arise about these relatively recent organizational forms, and are likely to continue to for a while,[27] but on the subject of the general partnership some important and well established principles have evolved. These interplay, moreover, with substantive rules governing the general partnership. The practitioner does well to consider them all before drawing up any litigation papers.

Naming the partnership and serving any individual general partner enables the plaintiff to secure a judgment good against assets held by the partnership. If the plaintiff seeks a judgment good against the personal assets of an individual partner, too, he must see to it that the partner is also named in the caption and is individually served. Otherwise, the words "not summoned" are written next to the names of unsummoned partners when the judgment is docketed,[28] which means that their individual property is unavailable to satisfy the judgment. Where a client had a malpractice claim against her lawyers, for example, who were operating as a professional service corporation (P.C.), and interposed the claim only against the P.C. and not against any individual attorney, the judgment was held inoperable against the individuals.[29] While there may be ways to cure the omission with subsequent proceedings, such as a new and separate action to charge the individuals with that part of the judgment that could not be satisfied out of

---

[19]   Some older cases upheld service on a limited partner—e.g., Ballestero v. HAF Edgecombe Associates, L.P., 239 A.D.2d 308, 657 N.Y.S.2d 1002 (2d Dep't 1997); Micheli Contracting Corp. v. Fairwood Associates, 73 A.D.2d 774, 423 N.Y.S.2d 533 (3d Dep't 1979)—but they would appear to be overruled by CPLR 310–a.

[20]   See Partnership Law § 115.

[21]   See CPLR 310–a(a), which adopts Partnership Law § 121–109 for service on a limited partnership.

[22]   See § 75.

[23]   CPLR 310–a(b).

[24]   See Green v. Gross and Levin, LLP, 101 A.D.3d 1079, 1080, 958 N.Y.S.2d 399, 400 (2d Dep't 2012); Lamba v. Lasala, N.Y.L.J., Oct. 19, 2001, at 21, col.1 (Sup. Ct., New York County) (concluding that Legislature intended limited liability partnerships to be covered by CPLR 310–a(a) and (b)).

[25]   See SPR 87:2.

[26]   Extensive discussion of the 1999 amendments that address service on the limited partnership, the limited liability partnership, and the limited liability company appears in the lead note in SPR 87:1.

[27]   See, e.g., SPR 143:2.

[28]   CPLR 5018(a); see § 421.

[29]   See Somer & Wand, P.C. v. Rotondi, 219 A.D.2d 340, 642 N.Y.S.2d 937 (2d Dep't 1996).

partnership assets,[30] there are problems with that course of action.[31] These can be avoided by initially naming and securing jurisdiction over the individual partners whose property is, or merely may be, sought for application to a judgment.[32]

Unlike the situation that obtains with a corporation, each partner, or in any event each general partner, carries the partnership about for jurisdictional purposes, so that personal delivery of the summons in New York to a general partner by itself gives jurisdiction of the partnership without regard to the partnership's whereabouts or the nature of the claim.[33] Lest this notion suggest too broad an exercise of jurisdiction, the lawyer should remember the availability of the forum non conveniens doctrine,[34] which precludes the entertainment of actions having no business imposing on the New York courts notwithstanding the existence of jurisdiction.

The mechanics of serving a partnership has been the subject of some dispute. While an individual being sued and served as such is subject to the substituted service methods of paragraphs 2 and 4 of CPLR 308, there was doubt about whether those methods could be used when the individual was a partner being served in behalf of the partnership. To address the matter, and presumably to make dependence on CPLR 308 unnecessary when serving a partner in the partnership behalf, subdivisions (b) through (e) were added to CPLR 310 in 1991. These contain their own prescriptions, but the First Department, reviewing them in Bell v. Bell, Kalnick et al.,[35] said they added (and continue to add) nothing to the options that existed before the amendment and are, therefore, superfluous.[36] In *Bell*, the court sustained service under CPLR 308(2)—deliver and mail[37]—on a receptionist at the office of an individually named partner, with mail the following day to that partner in an unmarked envelope.[38]

Corporations can be partners, too. When they are, additional issues about service arise. When corporation C is a partner in partnership X, for example, which is in turn a partner in partnership Y, service on a corporate officer of C under CPLR 311(a)(1), which lists those who can be served on behalf of a corporation,[39] constitutes service on both partnerships and satisfies CPLR 310.[40]

If the plaintiff is suing both the partnership and an individual partner, and both are named in the summons, the named partner may be served in both his own and the

---

[30]   See CPLR 1502; § 421.

[31]   One problem, for example, is that the earlier judgment may not be entitled to collateral estoppel in the subsequent action, thus requiring the relitigation of the issues, with the prospect of an inconsistent result. Procedural issues like these are by-products of the common law's indecision about the nature of the partners' substantive liabilities. See Werner, *Shared Liability: An Alternative to the Confusion of Joint, Several, and Joint and Several Obligations*, 42 Alb. L. Rev. 1 (1977).

[32]   See SPR 51:4.

[33]   Rait v. Jacobs Bros., 49 Misc. 2d 903, 268 N.Y.S.2d 750 (Sup. Ct., Nassau County 1966). There, the general partner who was served resided in New York, but the result would apparently be the same if, although residing elsewhere, he was served in New York.

[34]   See § 28.

[35]   Bell v. Bell, Kalnick, Klee & Green, 246 A.D.2d 442, 668 N.Y.S.2d 177 (1st Dep't 1998).

[36]   See Foy v. 1120 Ave. of Americas Associates, 223 A.D.2d 232, 646 N.Y.S.2d 547 (2d Dep't 1996).

[37]   See § 72.

[38]   A mere receptionist suffices for service under CPLR 308(2), while only a "managing agent" would do under CPLR 310(b). See SPR 71:1.

[39]   See § 70.

[40]   885 W.E. Residents Corp. v. Coronet Properties Co., 220 A.D.2d 305, 632 N.Y.S.2d 556 (1st Dep't 1995).

partnership's behalf. It has been held that there need only be one copy of the initiatory papers served on the partner in this instance.[41] The same rule has been held to apply to a corporation being sued along with a corporate officer.[42] In an action against an infant, however, where the parent may be served for the infant, additional service must be made on the infant if the infant is 14 or over.[43] When an infant in that age range is being served pursuant to CPLR 308(2), and the parent is the person of suitable age to whom a delivery of the summons is being made in behalf of the infant under that provision, two summonses must be presented to the parent.[44] We see no logical way to distinguish these situations and would advise plaintiffs to use two sets of initiatory papers in all of them.[45] Conservationist efforts can be implemented in other endeavors.

d. Associations. The unincorporated association is amenable to jurisdiction under New York law without naming or serving all of its members, who may in some cases number in the thousands. Suit by or against the association may be brought in the name of its president or treasurer.[46] When the association is the defendant, naming and serving that official gives jurisdiction of the association. As with a partnership, such an officer is held to carry the association about with her, so that service on that officer while she is present in New York, whatever her mission and whatever the nature of the claim, gives jurisdiction of the association.[47] Were the conveniens doctrine[48] not available to insulate inappropriate cases from this loose jurisdictional concept, its use would present constitutional issues.

e. Estates and Trusts. Assuming jurisdictional basis, the question of whom to serve in an action against an estate or trust is merely a matter of identifying the real party in interest. In the case of the estate, the real party in interest is the personal representative (executor or administrator); in the case of an express trust, the trustee.[49] Such person is the proper defendant and is the one to be served. But unlike the association and partnership, these fiduciaries do not necessarily carry their estates and trusts with them. Thus, a foreign personal representative in New York on only personal business unrelated to the estate or trust is not amenable to jurisdiction in her fiduciary capacity merely because she is served in New York.[50]

f. Foreign Nations and Agencies. Service on a foreign nation or agency is governed not by New York but by federal law, applicable in federal and state courts alike. There is one set of service methods when the defendant is the foreign nation itself or one of its political subdivisions,[51] and a separate set when the defendant is an "agency or instrumentality" of the foreign nation.[52] The federal statutes address even such details

---

[41]   Brown v. Sagamore Hotel, 184 A.D.2d 47, 590 N.Y.S.2d 934 (3d Dep't 1992); see also *Green*, 101 A.D.3d at 1080, 958 N.Y.S.2d at 400 (service on limited liability partnership).

[42]   See § 70.

[43]   CPLR 309(a).

[44]   See § 72.

[45]   See SPR 11:4.

[46]   CPLR 1025. A "labor organization" can be served via service on any of its major officers. See Gen. Ass'ns Law § 13.

[47]   Gross v. Cross, 28 Misc. 2d 375, 211 N.Y.S.2d 279 (Sup. Ct., New York County 1961).

[48]   See § 28.

[49]   CPLR 1004.

[50]   Cf. Doughney v. Fauset, 9 Misc. 2d 759, 170 N.Y.S.2d 419 (Sup. Ct., New York County 1958).

[51]   28 U.S.C.A. § 1608(a).

[52]   28 U.S.C.A. § 1608(b).

as the time service is deemed made, the time in which to answer, and the requirements applicable to a default judgment.[53] Counterpart New York provisions will, of course, have to defer to these federal directions in any instance of conflict. All of this assumes that the defendant is amenable to jurisdiction, i.e., that some exception to what would otherwise be its sovereign immunity is applicable. That, too, is governed by federal law.[54]

§ 70. Service on a Corporation

Those who may be served in behalf of a corporation—domestic or foreign, no distinction is made—are listed in CPLR 311(a)(1). They are an officer, director, managing or general agent, cashier or assistant cashier, or "any other agent authorized by appointment or by law to receive service." Someone stationed at a cash register to receive money from customers does not qualify as a "cashier" or a "managing agent."[1] By cashier is meant someone at a high level who has charge of the corporation's funds. The person who gives out shoes in a bowling alley doesn't qualify.[2]

Most frequently met in the caselaw is the question of who qualifies as a "managing or general agent." Those words are liberally construed and even include someone in charge of only a corporate branch office.[3] If there are a handful of employees at a corporate office, the person who appears to be in charge qualifies as a managing agent for service, and needs no formal title indicating high position.[4] Someone holding himself out as "a person of responsibility" at the corporate office qualifies,[5] but a mere office boy, such as a stand-in for the usual freight agent at a railroad station, has been held not to qualify even though he forwards the summons promptly to the right person.[6] The test is not whether the summons was in fact forwarded, but whether the one served bears such a relationship to the corporation as to compel the inference that it will be.[7] Furthermore, in cases where there has been a redelivery of the summons to the correct person, the courts have imposed a "due diligence" test. Only if it is demonstrated that a diligent effort was made to find and serve the right person under CPLR 311(a)(1) will service on an intermediary, with her prompt redelivery to the right person, be allowed.[8]

If the officer served, X, is also being sued individually—both the corporation and individual being named in the caption—it has been held that a single service on X satisfies as commencement against both.[9] But when the service on X is made in behalf of the corporation and in behalf of A, another individual (corporate connected or not),

---

[53] 28 U.S.C.A. § 1608, subdivisions (c), (d), & (e).

[54] See 28 U.S.C.A. §§ 1605–1607.

[1] Weiss v. Glatt Pack Kosher, Inc., 138 A.D.2d 591, 526 N.Y.S.2d 174 (2d Dep't 1988).

[2] Oustecky v. Farmingdale Lanes, Inc., 41 Misc. 2d 979, 246 N.Y.S.2d 859 (Sup. Ct., Nassau County 1964).

[3] See Green v. Morningside Heights Housing Corp., 13 Misc. 2d 124, 177 N.Y.S.2d 760 (Sup. Ct., New York County 1958), aff'd, 7 A.D.2d 708, 180 N.Y.S.2d 104 (1st Dep't 1958).

[4] See Municipal Mortgage Co. v. 461 Eighth Ave. Co., 195 A.D. 370, 186 N.Y.S. 322 (1st Dep't 1921).

[5] Buckner v. D & E Motors, Inc., 53 Misc. 2d 382, 278 N.Y.S.2d 932 (Sup. Ct., Erie County 1967).

[6] Isaf v. Pennsylvania R. Co., 32 A.D.2d 578, 299 N.Y.S.2d 231 (3d Dep't 1969); see Arce v. Sybron Corp., 82 A.D.2d 308, 441 N.Y.S.2d 498 (2d Dep't 1981) ("a low level clerical employee who possessed no supervisory or administrative duties" does not qualify as a person under CPLR 311(a)(1) who can accept service on behalf of a corporation).

[7] Mastan v. Desormeau Dairy-Vend Service, Inc., 11 A.D.2d 860, 203 N.Y.S.2d 343 (3d Dep't 1960).

[8] See McDonald v. Ames Supply Co., 22 N.Y.2d 111, 115–16, 291 N.Y.S.2d 328, 332, 238 N.E.2d 726, 728–29 (1968); § 66.

[9] In re Dissolution of Stony Creek Preserve, Inc., 121 A.D.3d 1376, 995 N.Y.S.2d 346 (3d Dep't 2014).

such as where A works at the corporate office and delivery is being made to X as a person of suitable age and discretion at A's place of business under CPLR 308(2),[10] two copies of the summons must be served on X, one for each.[11]

When the defendant is a domestic corporation, or a licensed foreign one, it will have designated the secretary of state as its agent for service on any claim.[12] Service on the secretary in such an instance is always available as an alternative to service under the CPLR. The method of service in that case is governed by section 306(b) of the Business Corporation Law ("BCL"), which consists of delivering to the secretary or to his deputy or designee in Albany two copies of the summons. The secretary retains one for his files and sends the other by certified mail to the corporation at its office address as it appears in those files. The jurisdictional act is the delivery of the two copies to the secretary. The latter's failure to forward one to the corporation does not void the service.[13]

While service on a licensed corporation can be carried out pursuant to BCL 306, service on an unlicensed foreign corporation is governed by BCL 307. The methods under the two statutes differ, and using one method in a case in which the other BCL method governs may void the service.[14]

In an action against an insurance company doing business in New York, an alternative is to serve the superintendent of financial services, whom all such insurers must designate as an agent for service.[15]

CPLR 311(a), in paragraphs 2 through 8, also lists those to be served in behalf of various governmental subdivisions. Keeping the paragraph numbers just as they appear in CPLR 311(a), service is made on those entities as follows:

2. New York City: serve the corporation counsel or its filed-in-New-York-County designee;

3. any other city: the mayor, comptroller, treasurer, counsel, or clerk or, if none, whoever carries out an equivalent function;

4. a county: the chair or clerk of the board of supervisors, clerk, attorney, or treasurer;

5. a town: the supervisor or the clerk;

6. a village: the mayor, clerk, or any trustee;

7. a school district: a school officer;[16]

8. a park, sewage, or other district: the clerk, any trustee, or any member of the board.

---

[10]   See § 72.

[11]   Raschel v. Rish, 120 A.D.2d 945, 502 N.Y.S.2d 852 (4th Dep't 1986), aff'd, 69 N.Y.2d 694, 512 N.Y.S.2d 22, 504 N.E.2d 389 (1986).

[12]   Bus. Corp. Law § 304. We explore the issue of whether such designation constitutes the corporation's consent to personal jurisdiction in New York in § 95. The issue has become an important one in light of recent Supreme Court caselaw. See § 82.

[13]   Shanker v. 119 East 30th, Ltd., 63 A.D.3d 553, 881 N.Y.S.2d 98 (1st Dep't 2009); see Farrell, *Survey of New York Practice*, 28 Syracuse L. Rev. 379, 405–6 (1977).

[14]   See § 95.

[15]   Ins. Law § 1212(b); see Ins. Law § 107(a)(41).

[16]   See Educ. Law § 2(13).

It is apparently not sufficient that the plaintiff just follow these service provisions to the letter. If there happens to be some extra requirement lurking in a local law that requires someone other than a person on the above list to be served, the CPLR service may not suffice. It did not suffice, for example, in Horowitz v. Incorporated Village of Roslyn,[17] where a plaintiff suing a county effected service on the county clerk as explicitly authorized by CPLR 311(a)(4), but failed to serve the county executive or county attorney as stipulated by the Nassau County Administrative Code. Even though the clerk promptly turned the summons over to the county attorney, the action was dismissed.

In Ling Ling Yung v. County of Nassau,[18] the Court of Appeals indicated implicitly that the *Horowitz* result was wrong, but for a reason that perpetuates the problem. While the customary rule is that a special provision will govern over a general one, the Court held that the general one will prevail over the special one if the general one—the CPLR provision here—is the more recent enactment, which was the case in *Horowitz*. This rationale leaves the door open to the problem of having the CPLR directing service in certain actions, and the local law governing in others, all depending on what law was adopted first. It is unfortunate that so much should ride on this sort of uncertain test and practitioners should avoid the guesswork and make service that will comply with the CPLR and any applicable local law.

It is submitted that when two provisions offer different methods of service, a better way to reach the same result is to conclude that the two merely supply alternatives, making each of the people listed in either law a proper servee. That would entail a finding that the two laws are consistent, however, and the plaintiff in *Yung*, perhaps too obligingly, conceded that they were not. The best rule, of course, and perhaps the only one that can protect against hidden traps of this kind, is to leave plenty of time for trouble.[19] A plaintiff with a few months left over on the statute of limitations when the defendant springs that kind of objection may grumble a bit, but will keep breathing.

When serving a notice of claim on a municipal entity, these sorts of traps can be avoided by simply serving the secretary of state.[20] The service of the initiatory papers in the action, however, must be made in accordance with CPLR 311(a).

Service on the State itself is governed by CPLR 307, which is rarely used because as a rule, the State can be sued only in the court of claims and the Court of Claims Act[21] governs commencement of suit there.

Service on a court, board, or commission is governed by CPLR 312.

The "public authority" is not on the CPLR 311 list, or covered anywhere else in the CPLR. This is an indefensible omission that needlessly expends the time and energy of plaintiffs. Sometimes the plaintiff can't find even in the Public Authorities Law a statute that governs service on the particular authority she wishes to sue. In such an instance, the public authority has been likened to an ordinary business corporation and service permitted on someone listed in CPLR 311(a)(1),[22] but the lesson to a plaintiff planning

---

[17]   Horowitz v. Incorporated Village of Roslyn, 144 A.D.2d 639, 535 N.Y.S.2d 79 (2d Dep't 1988).

[18]   Ling Ling Yung v. County of Nassau, 77 N.Y.2d 568, 569 N.Y.S.2d 361, 571 N.E.2d 669 (1991).

[19]   See § 231A.

[20]   Gen. Mun. Law § 50–e(f); see § 32.

[21]   See Ct. of Claims Act § 11.

[22]   See Ware v. Manhattan and Bronx Surface Transit Operating Authority, 49 Misc. 2d 704, 268 N.Y.S.2d 519 (Sup. Ct., New York County 1965); see also Psathas v. Catskill Regional Off-Track Betting Corp.,

suit against any kind of "authority" is, once again, to leave some time for homework. If quick research doesn't resolve all questions, call the authority, ask for counsel, and put the question to counsel. Then, confirm any answer in writing. Realize, however, that this is the enemy and ask, ever so politely, for citations in support. Another source that may help is punching the authority's name and a few key words—summons, process, service, etc.—into Westlaw to see if scanning a few cases answers the question.

In each instance of service under CPLR 311(a), service should be made by CPLR 308(1) personal delivery to one of the persons listed. CPLR 311(a) specifically directs the "delivering" of the summons, and thus seems to make CPLR 311 preemptive of method of service, requiring personal delivery only and precluding use of the various substituted service methods offered by CPLR 308 when an individual is the defendant. Other provisions, such as CPLR 309 governing infants and incompetents, speak of "serving" the persons listed, which offers ground for making all of the methods of CPLR 308—whose caption is personal "service"—available for service in those instances, including the deliver-and-mail method of 308(2) and the affix-and-mail method of 308(4). Caselaw indicates that those methods are not available against corporations, however;[23] that CPLR 308 is for individuals and CPLR 311 is for corporations, and that the two don't mix.

A helpful provision in serving individual defendants is CPLR 308(5),[24] which allows the court to invent a method of service when the prescribed methods prove impracticable. A similar authorization applies for use against corporations under subdivision (b) to CPLR 311, allowing the court to invent a method upon a showing that the plaintiff can't make timely service on the corporation by the prescribed methods.[25]

Keep in mind that discussion in this section is directed only to method of service—whom to serve in the corporate behalf—not the issue of amenability to jurisdiction, also known as jurisdictional basis. To establish personal jurisdiction over the corporate defendant in New York, the plaintiff must also properly commence the action with a timely and proper filing of the initiatory papers and establish a jurisdictional basis over the corporation. If the corporation is a foreign one and does not have its principal place of business in New York, the mere fact that service is made on a corporate official in New York does not provide a basis of jurisdiction of the corporation.[26] The corporation being an entity distinct from its personnel, those personnel do not—as do those to be served for a partnership or association[27]—carry the corporation around with them. The test for establishing a jurisdictional basis over the corporation, which has undergone some radical change in recent years, is treated later.[28]

---

173 A.D.2d 1070, 1071, 570 N.Y.S.2d 407 (3d Dep't 1991) (defendant conceded that, as a public benefit corporation, it was to be served in accordance with CPLR 311(a)(1)).

[23]   Lakeside Concrete Corp. v. Pine Hollow Bldg. Corp., 104 A.D.2d 551, 479 N.Y.S.2d 256 (2d Dep't 1984), aff'd, 65 N.Y.2d 865, 493 N.Y.S.2d 309, 482 N.E.2d 1225 (1985).

[24]   See § 75.

[25]   See SPR 74:2.

[26]   See § 59 (discussing how personal service on an individual in the state simultaneously establishes a basis of jurisdiction over that individual).

[27]   See § 69.

[28]   See § 82.

§ 71. "Sewer Service"; the Amendment of CPLR 308

When a process server swears to service in an affidavit duly returned to the plaintiff, but the server did not in fact make the service, the perjury usually results in a default judgment taken against the unnotified defendant. Such a situation, commonly referred to as "sewer service," reached epidemic proportions in the 1960s, especially in the civil court in New York City. The problem led to the 1973 enactment of a provision[1] authorizing, through administrative channels, an en masse vacatur of fraudulently secured default judgments,[2] sparing each defendant victimized by the practice the burden of making an individual motion in each case. Prior to January 1, 1990, when CPLR 312–a took effect to allow personal service by simple, first-class mail,[3] the major step undertaken to discourage sewer service was an amendment of CPLR 308 in 1970 to make service easier.

As originally enacted, CPLR 308 had four subdivisions. The third was popularly known as "substituted service." It was a two-part requirement: a mailing plus either a delivery to some person or an affixing at some premises. But it was usable only if with due diligence service could not be made under CPLR 308(1), the personal delivery method. The 1970 amendment's chief purpose was to allow some kind of substituted service to be used in the first instance as an alternative to personal delivery without the condition precedent of a "diligence" requirement.[4]

The amendment divided the original "substituted service" provision into two parts, one the deliver-and-mail procedure now in CPLR 308(2) and the other the affix-and-mail procedure now in CPLR 308(4). The latter continues to be available only if the plaintiff can establish that after exercising due diligence, the other methods did not work. But the deliver-and-mail method of the recast CPLR 308(2) became, and remains, available in first instance without any prior effort having to be made at personal delivery under CPLR 308(1). The change eased service requirements and reduced instances of "sewer service," but it still appears, and occasionally flares up, as in 2009 when it prompted the intervention of the attorney general. His efforts, largely on the criminal side and largely aimed at process servers, also have disciplinary implications for attorneys and serious civil consequences for the plaintiffs in whose cases the sewer service is used.[5]

Prior to the 1973 amendment, the words "substituted service" described what was then CPLR 308(3). When that was broken down into present subdivisions two and four, "substituted service" lost some focus. The phrase can today mislead to either subdivision two or four and should be avoided in favor of the numerical CPLR citation, or the respective phrases "deliver and mail" for CPLR 308(2) and "affix and mail" for CPLR 308(4). Further confusing matters, the phrase "substituted service" is sometimes used to refer to any method of summons service other than personal delivery. The lawyer should be sensitive to inquire into precisely how the phrase is being used in a given context.

---

[1]   Originally § 217–a of the Jud. Law, now subdivision (c) of CPLR 5015.

[2]   It codifies a practice initiated earlier in the New York City Civil Court by its Administrative Judge at the time, Edward Thompson, and is sometimes called "Thompson's Law."

[3]   See § 76A.

[4]   See 16th Jud. Conf. Rep. Leg. Doc. No. 90, p. A38 (1971).

[5]   See SPR 208:1 (recalling, among other things, the possibility of a mass vacatur of offending default judgments through the administrative tool of CPLR 5015(c)).

As part of the 1970 amendment, the former CPLR 308(2), dealing with service on a CPLR 318 agent,[6] became CPLR 308(3), and the court ordered service of the former 308(4) became 308(5). The personal delivery method of CPLR 308(1) remained unchanged. Paragraph 6, added to CPLR 308 in a still later amendment, does not provide for an additional method of service and is treated later.[7]

In researching a process-service problem, the lawyer may meet pre-1970 cases using the older numbers. The 1970 reshuffling should be recalled and references in older cases adjusted accordingly.

§ 72.   Deliver-and-Mail Service Under CPLR 308(2)

This is a two-part requirement whose advantage is that it is an alternative to personal delivery under CPLR 308(1) and can be used without any prior effort to deliver the summons to the defendant personally. Nor does it require a court order.[1] It has some complications, however, and has to be negotiated carefully. Since jurisdiction turns on it, it is not a good place for mistakes, especially if the statute of limitations is closing in.

The first requirement is a delivery "to a person of suitable age and discretion" at defendant's "actual place of business, dwelling place or usual place of abode."[2] The second is a mailing either to the defendant's "last known residence" or to his actual (presently used) place of business. Both the delivery and the mailing are required for jurisdiction, and both steps must be taken within 20 days of each other.[3] Furthermore, both steps must take place within 120 days of the filing of the initiatory papers.[4]

The person of suitable age need not be an adult. A responsible teenager, for example, will do. The criterion should be whether the person can be expected to advise the defendant of the service. This requirement is modeled on Rule 4(e)(2)(B) of the Federal Rules of Civil Procedure and caselaw on that provision is some guidepost, at least as far as age is concerned.[5] But it must be noted that although modeled on the federal provision, CPLR 308(2) is not identical. Under the federal rule, for example, the deliveree must be someone who "resides" at the premises, which is not a New York requirement. An apartment house doorman has been held to qualify under CPLR 308(2), for example, at least when access to the defendant's own apartment has been refused.[6] The doorman should also qualify if, although access is allowed, no one is at home. The very purpose of the required second step of the mailing is designed as a precaution lest the deliveree, whoever that may be, not in fact deliver the papers to the defendant.

As noted above, the delivery can be made "at the actual place of business, dwelling house or usual place of abode" of the defendant. Underscore "actual"; it means that the place is presently being used by the defendant. If an outright, presently used residence

---

[6]   See § 73.

[7]   See § 72.

[1]   The exception, in which a court order is required, is the matrimonial action. See § 76.

[2]   CPLR 308(2).

[3]   CPLR 308(2).

[4]   CPLR 306–b; see § 63.

[5]   See, e.g., United States v. Zwaal, 2015 WL 9902896 (N.D.Cal. 2015), report and recommendation adopted, 2015 WL 9906943 (N.D.Cal. 2015) (a sixteen-year-old is a person qualified to receive process under FRCP 4).

[6]   Braun v. St. Vincent's Hospital & Medical Center, 57 N.Y.2d 909, 456 N.Y.S.2d 763, 442 N.E.2d 1274 (1982); F. I. duPont, Glore Forgan & Co. v. Chen, 41 N.Y.2d 794, 396 N.Y.S.2d 343, 364 N.E.2d 1115 (1977).

of the defendant is known, it satisfies for both prongs of the CPLR 308(2) requirement. But the provision does not use the word "residence." The precise meaning of the phrases used has yet to be discerned, but it is rather clear that something less than an outright "residence" can satisfy as a "dwelling house"[7] or "place of abode."[8]

An important point about the delivery aspect of CPLR 308(2) is addressed in Bossuk v. Steinberg.[9] If the "suitable age and discretion" person comes to the door but won't open it, as when the delivery is being made to the defendant's home, *Bossuk* holds that the process server's merely leaving the summons outside the door will qualify as an adequate delivering.[10]

A serious problem may arise when the plaintiff is relying on a delivery of the summons to a person of suitable age at what is assumed to be the defendant's presently used residence, and the assumption proves false. The problem comes from Feinstein v. Bergner.[11] It involves CPLR 308(4), the affix-and-mail requirement, treated later,[12] but has important bearing on CPLR 308(2) as well. (Under paragraph 4, the affixing is made at the same premises to which a delivery is made when paragraph 2 is being used.)

In *Feinstein*, the residence at which the affixing was made under paragraph 4 was the address the defendant had furnished at the scene of the accident involved in the action. He had been living with his parents at the time, but it was no longer his residence at the moment of commencement. His parents still lived there, however. The Court of Appeals upset the service, and it was now too late for the plaintiff to start over under the statute of limitations.

The *Feinstein* facts seemed to be tailor-made for an estoppel against the defendant, and an estoppel was in fact invoked on similar if not identical facts in McNeil v. Tomlin,[13] but the practitioner does well to note *Feinstein* and to take steps to avoid falling into its trap.[14]

The mailing requirement can be carried out either at a "last known residence," or at an actual, i.e., presently used, place of business. Ordinary first class mail is the method. Neither registered nor certified mail is required, and while it is probably permissible, many lawyers deliberately avoid registered and certified mail when it is not explicitly required, fearing the complications caused when postal officials can't find the defendant or other proper person to sign the required receipt. If postal evidence of a mailing is sought, a simple certificate of first-class mailing can be secured from the post office when the mail is posted.[15]

---

[7]   Karlin v. Avis, 326 F. Supp. 1325 (E.D.N.Y. 1971), sustained as a "dwelling house" a New York apartment that was one of four places where the defendant divided his time. It holds that the defendant need not be a New York "resident" in order to qualify as a dwelling house.

[8]   See Rich Products Corp. v. Diamond, 51 Misc. 2d 675, 273 N.Y.S.2d 687 (Sup. Ct., Erie County 1966).

[9]   Bossuk v. Steinberg, 58 N.Y.2d 916, 460 N.Y.S.2d 509, 447 N.E.2d 56 (1983).

[10]   The bearing the *Bossuk* case has on the common method of personal delivery to the defendant under paragraph 1 of CPLR 308 is discussed in § 66.

[11]   Feinstein v. Bergner, 48 N.Y.2d 234, 422 N.Y.S.2d 356, 397 N.E.2d 1161 (1979).

[12]   See § 74.

[13]   McNeil v. Tomlin, 82 A.D.2d 825, 439 N.Y.S.2d 430 (2d Dep't 1981). *McNeil* gives the *Feinstein* case only a "cf."

[14]   *Feinstein* is further discussed in § 74.

[15]   This certificate, signed by the postal official at the point of sending, is to be distinguished from certified mail in that it requires no signed paper, even by a postal official, at the other end.

The mail that constitutes one of the two service steps under CPLR 308(2) should be distinguished from the outright mail service allowed by CPLR 312–a, which is separately treated later.[16]

If the mailing is to the place of business, the envelope must be labeled "personal and confidential" and not bear any indication that it comes from a lawyer or relates to a lawsuit, restrictions that don't apply to a mailing made to a last known residence. Because these requirements are designed to spare the defendant embarrassment, their violation has been held to void jurisdiction and bring about a dismissal.[17]

When the defendant has an office but also carries on activities at other places, the plaintiff should not automatically deem these others a "place of business." The mere fact, for example, that a physician has a relationship with a hospital and performs operations there does not make the hospital a place of business at which a delivery of the summons may be made to a person of suitable age (etc.) in behalf of the physician under CPLR 308(2), at least not when the physician has an office elsewhere and (e.g.) bills from there.[18]

If either of the two CPLR 308(2) requirements is to be carried out outside New York State, it will be necessary to establish a basis for extraterritorial jurisdiction under CPLR 313. If the case has no contacts with New York, for example, a personal delivery to the defendant in New York under CPLR 308(1) will give jurisdiction, but a delivery to some suitable-age person in New York under CPLR 308(2) coupled with a mailing to the defendant's residence outside New York will not.[19]

In an action against an infant, the parent may be served, but if the infant is 14 or over, the infant must be separately served as well.[20] When the infant is being served pursuant to CPLR 308(2), and the father is the person of suitable age to whom a delivery is being made in behalf of the infant, two summonses must be presented to the father: one for himself and one for the infant.[21] Contrast this with corporate service where it has been held that a single summons served on a corporate officer satisfies as service on the officer individually and on the corporation as well.[22] In view of these inconsistencies, it's best to use two sets of papers in all of these instances.[23]

When CPLR 308(2) is used, the filing of proof of service is required. It must be made within 20 days after the delivery or mailing, "whichever is effected later." Service then becomes "complete" 10 days after proof of service is filed, which means only that the defendant's responding time will not start until then. The responding time is 30 days.[24] Integrating the 10-day period, the easiest way to remember this point is that when CPLR 308(2) is used, the defendant actually has 40 days in which to respond, measured from the filing of proof of service.

---

[16] See § 76A.

[17] Mastropierro v. Bennett, 233 A.D.2d 483, 650 N.Y.S.2d 287 (2d Dep't 1996).

[18] Glasser v. Keller, 149 Misc. 2d 875, 567 N.Y.S.2d 981 (Sup. Ct., Queens County 1991).

[19] See Durgom v. Durgom, 47 Misc. 2d 513, 262 N.Y.S.2d 874 (N.Y. City Civ. Ct. 1965).

[20] CPLR 309(a); see § 69.

[21] Giving the father only one was held insufficient service in Kolodzinski v. Ferreiras, 168 A.D.2d 431, 562 N.Y.S.2d 554 (2d Dep't 1990).

[22] T.E.A. Marine Automotive Corp. v. Scaduto, 181 A.D.2d 776, 581 N.Y.S.2d 370 (2d Dep't 1992); see § 70.

[23] On this point, see also the discussion of partnerships in § 69.

[24] CPLR 320(a), and 3012(a), (c).

The "completion" of service under CPLR 308(2) has nothing to do with the statute of limitations, incidentally, which is satisfied if the service acts are carried out within 120 days after the timely filing of the initiatory papers.[25] Both the delivery and the mailing must be carried out within the 120-day period for service that follows the filing of the action.[26] Delivery within the applicable period, but mailing a day later, has been held unsatisfactory.[27] If the mail is posted within the period it will satisfy, however, even though not received until after.[28] It is imprudent, to say the least, to play things that close.

CPLR 308(2) may not be used against a corporate defendant.[29] Because other alternatives are often available against a corporation,[30] the 308(2) option should not be missed.

A paragraph numbered 6 was added to CPLR 308 in 1994. It expands the meaning of the "place of business" referred to in paragraphs 2 and 4 of CPLR 308. CPLR 308(6) provides:

> [f]or purposes of this section, "actual place of business" shall include any location that the defendant, through regular solicitation or advertisement, has held out as its place of business.

This was designed to make a simple letter drop address, being used for business purposes, a proper address at which to carry out both steps of the service requirements of paragraph 2 (the deliver and mail provision) or paragraph 4 (the affix and mail provision). A number of problems arise under this statute, however, not least of which is that CPLR 308 has been held unavailable for use against corporations, which, ironically, are the entities that paragraph 6 was primarily aimed at. There are also issues about whether the claim sued on must have arisen out of business done from the mail drop address and whether the address has to be shown to be an active one at the time of service.[31] Because of this, careful lawyers have been hesitant to trust this provision, especially where there's a potential statute of limitations problem in the case.

§ 73.   Service on Rule 318 Agent Under CPLR 308(3)

CPLR 318 authorizes a person or entity to designate a person to act as agent for service of process. It is done in an acknowledged writing on which the agent endorses consent. The writing is then filed with the county clerk of the county in which the designor "resides or has its principal office." It's effective for three years. If such an agent exists, CPLR 308(3) allows service of process to be made on the agent in behalf of that principal.

CPLR 308(3) and its CPLR 318 companion count for little in New York practice. Theoretically, the designation makes it easier for a plaintiff to effect service, but the

---

[25]   See § 63. Proof of service is treated in more detail later. See § 79.

[26]   See CPLR 306–b; § 63.

[27]   Furey v. Milgrom, 44 A.D.2d 91, 353 N.Y.S.2d 508 (2d Dep't 1974). *Furey* concerned CPLR 308(4) in an era where service marked commencement, but its conclusions govern CPLR 308(2) as well, and would likely apply under CPLR 306–b. The posting was made a day after the statute of limitations expired.

[28]   Weill v. Erickson, 49 A.D.2d 895, 373 N.Y.S.2d 370 (2d Dep't 1975), aff'd, 37 N.Y.2d 851, 378 N.Y.S.2d 39, 340 N.E.2d 473 (1975).

[29]   See § 70.

[30]   See § 70 and § 95.

[31]   See the extended treatment of CPLR 308(6) in the lead notes in SPR 26:1 and 27:1.

easing of the plaintiff's path is never the defendant's purpose. The practical accomplishment of the designation is to prevent the statute of limitations from tolling if the defendant should leave the state or be absent.[1] That was also its effect under prior law,[2] but it was more important there because there were few other things that could prevent a tolling for the defendant's absence. Under the CPLR, on the other hand, the mere fact that there exists an in personam basis for jurisdiction authorizing extraterritorial service, such as under CPLR 302 and 313,[3] denies the plaintiff a limitations' toll for the defendant's absence[4] and vastly reduces the significance of CPLR 318 and its agency. Hence its rare use.

No attempt need be made to discover a CPLR 318 agency as a condition for using some other service provision. CPLR 308(4), for example, the affix-and-mail method, requires a prior effort to use paragraphs 1 and 2, but not paragraph 3, of CPLR 308. The reason is that a plaintiff can't be sure where such an agency may be on file. Suppose the defendant has several residences, for example. Or suppose the defendant has several offices. Which is the "principal" one, at which the filing of the designation is required? Realizing that a wrong guess, and a search of the clerk's records in the wrong county, can have jurisdictional consequences, the legislature has isolated CPLR 308(3). It is sometimes suggested that these agencies be centralized in a state office, such as the secretary of state's. That would help, but it is not likely to divest CPLR 308(3) and 318 of their wide reputation for unimportance.

§ 74.   Affix-and-Mail Service Under CPLR 308(4)

Like paragraph 2 of CPLR 308, service under paragraph 4 is a two-step process. There are really only two major differences between the two. The first is that under paragraph 4, an affixing to the premises replaces the delivery requirement of paragraph 2. The second is that paragraph 4 may not be used unless service under paragraphs 1 and 2 "cannot be made with due diligence."[1]

Because of this due diligence requirement, service under paragraph 4 requires a more detailed affidavit of service. The affidavit must set forth the particular steps taken in attempting service under the other provisions.[2] This enables the court to determine whether due diligence was used. Form affidavits in this kind of case are usually inadequate and have been rejected.[3]

As to what constitutes "due diligence," it is a sui generis test. The courts don't like to count service attempts,[4] but a single visit to the premises, when no one is at home,

---

[1]   See CPLR 207(1).

[2]   Civ. Prac. Act §§ 19, 227 (repealed 1963).

[3]   See §§ 84, 100.

[4]   CPLR 207(3); see § 53.

[1]   As noted in § 73, an attempt at service on an agent under paragraph 3 of CPLR 308 is not a condition precedent to service under paragraph 4.

[2]   See CPLR 306(c).

[3]   See, e.g., Blatz v. Benschine, 53 Misc. 2d 352, 278 N.Y.S.2d 533 (Sup. Ct., Queens County 1967).

[4]   See Huntington Utilities Fuel Corp. v. McLoughlin, 45 Misc. 2d 79, 255 N.Y.S.2d 679 (Sup. Ct., Suffolk County 1965).

will not suffice. A few visits on different occasions and at different times to both residence and place of business, if known, will.[5]

A mere showing of many visits will not automatically do. If the server deposes that for five straight business days he went to the defendant's residence at 10 a.m. and found no one home, he is more likely to be credited with obtuseness than with diligence. He should vary the time of his visits. At least for purposes of satisfying the diligence requirement of CPLR 308(4), it should be shown that the process server made genuine inquiries about the defendant's whereabouts and places of employment.[6]

If it is known that the place is no longer used by the defendant, such as where it was the defendant's residence but no longer is, an attempt to execute the two requirements of CPLR 308(4) at that place will fail.[7]

While a "last known residence" suffices for the mailing requirement, it does not suffice for the affixing requirement, as the plaintiff learned to her chagrin in Feinstein v. Bergner,[8] a case with an important lesson for all plaintiffs using either paragraph 2 or 4 of CPLR 308.

Feinstein involved an automobile accident in which P was injured and her husband killed. D at the accident scene revealed his proper address—D then lived with his parents—but when P got around to service several years later, D no longer resided there although his parents still did. After two unsuccessful attempts to deliver the summons at that address under paragraph 2 of CPLR 308, the process server turned to paragraph 4 for an affixing.[9]

As to the mailing to D at the parental address, that was okay because it qualified as a "last known" residence, but the affixing part of the statute requires a presently used premises (business or residential) and since the parental address no longer qualified as that, the affixing was unacceptable and resulted in a jurisdictional dismissal of the action—too late to start a new one.

As expanded in the dissenting opinion in *Feinstein*, the facts indicate that D left no forwarding address with the post office. The result was that the post office delivered the mailed summons to his parents' address, and D's father, receiving it at that address, mailed it on to D. But if the address was one still thought by the post office to be D's present residence, shouldn't P be entitled to make the same assumption for a CPLR 308(4) affixing?

It does not appear whether D notified his insurance carrier or the motor vehicle bureau of his change of address, as it is incumbent on him to do under the Court of Appeals decision in Dobkin v. Chapman,[10] or whether P checked with those sources.

---

[5]   O'Connor v. O'Connor, 52 Misc. 2d 950, 277 N.Y.S.2d 424 (Sup. Ct., Suffolk County 1967); see also CPLR 306(c) (stating requirements for proof of service under CPLR 308(4)).

[6]   Smith v. Wilson, 130 A.D.2d 821, 515 N.Y.S.2d 146 (3d Dep't 1987).

[7]   Polansky v. Paugh, 23 A.D.2d 643, 256 N.Y.S.2d 961 (1st Dep't 1965).

[8]   Feinstein v. Bergner, 48 N.Y.2d 234, 422 N.Y.S.2d 356, 397 N.E.2d 1161 (1979). The case is the subject of the lead note in NYSLD No. 239.

[9]   An incidental but important point, and one helpful to plaintiffs, is that the two visits under paragraph 2 were found by the lower courts to satisfy the "due diligence" requirement, which must be met before service can be made under paragraph 4. On this point, the Court of Appeals was "unprepared to say that the finding was erroneous as a matter of law."

[10]   Dobkin v. Chapman, 21 N.Y.2d 490, 289 N.Y.S.2d 161, 236 N.E.2d 451 (1968). *Dobkin* is treated at length in § 75. It concerns court ordered service under paragraph 5 of CPLR 308, but what it says about a

Hence the *Feinstein* decision should not be deemed to annul the obligation of a person involved in a vehicle tort to supply prompt and accurate address changes to his insurer and to the motor vehicle bureau, if not to the injured person directly (which *Dobkin* also allows as an alternative).

The *Dobkin* case does not suggest that the defendant leave a forwarding address with the post office, but since that seems the most obvious step for any person to take to keep everyone apprised of an address change, the omission of such a suggestion was probably a mere inadvertence in *Dobkin*. In the *Feinstein* case, in any event, the very fact that the mailing went through to the parental address, which was the one originally furnished by D to P, is an element that should support an estoppel against D and sustain jurisdiction. The classic lines of an estoppel would seem to be spelled out in that D represented at the accident scene that the parental address was his; he ratified that representation by failing to leave a forwarding address with the post office; P relied on that as D's continuing address; and P would be seriously damaged if D should be allowed to prevail.

A practical lesson for the plaintiff's lawyer is to make full inquiry of both the motor vehicle bureau and D's insurer. The failure to apprise the bureau of an address change worked an estoppel against D in McNeil v. Tomlin,[11] for example, where substituted service was made at what was still the address of record in bureau files. The *Feinstein* case got only a "cf."

After *Feinstein*, plaintiffs in a similar situation must apparently be prepared to turn to CPLR 308(5), i.e., to make an ex parte motion to have the court direct service. Perhaps it would be appropriate for P to do so not only when P knows that D's previously furnished address is no longer used, but also when P does not know whether it is or not. P would seem to be able to set a proper foundation for a CPLR 308(5) application by making inquiries about D's present address of the vehicle bureau, D's insurer, the post office, and perhaps D's family at the original address (with an ordinary letter). The job is not all that big; it entails several pieces of correspondence and a waiting period for responses. Of course, the plaintiff who has waited to the last minute for suit obviously can't spare the time. The luxury of an opportunity to make those inquiries is reserved only to plaintiffs who leave ample time for trouble.[12]

Should the responses all indicate that there has been no change of address, although in fact there has been, it is quite possible that the court on a CPLR 308(5) application would take the position that it should offer no aid because service is available under CPLR 308(4). But that poses an interesting question. If the court does take that position, and P turns of necessity to paragraph 4, P is likely to be met with the same dismissal motion that D made in *Feinstein*, and on the same grounds. An estoppel against D in that instance would seem inevitable.

---

defendant's obligations in regard to changes of address should apply regardless of the provision the defendant is being served under.

[11]   McNeil v. Tomlin, 82 A.D.2d 825, 439 N.Y.S.2d 430 (2d Dep't 1981).

[12]   See § 231A.

These details about the mailing aspect of CPLR 308(4) should apply as well to the mailing part of the deliver-and-mail statute, CPLR 308(2). Conversely, cases on mailing under the latter should apply here under CPLR 308(4), too.[13]

Getting back to the "affixing" part of CPLR 308(4), how should it be carried out? It must be done in such a way as to avoid damage. A railroad spike is too much. A tack should do nicely. So should a reasonably secure taping. Wrapping the summons around the doorknob with a rubber band has also been sustained.[14] A method should be used that ensures "a genuine adherence"; wedging the summons between door and door jamb has been held insufficient.[15] When the defendant lives in an apartment to which the server can't gain access, there is some suggestion that the affixing may be to the main lobby door of the apartment house.[16]

Filing of proof, and "completion" of, service and the defendant's responding time are the same under this provision as under CPLR 308(2).[17]

A contrast should be made between CPLR 308(4) and section 735 of the Real Property Actions and Proceedings Law. The latter governs in the summary proceeding to recover possession of real property (the so-called "landlord-tenant" case),[18] and requires, in addition to a mailing, an affixing to a "conspicuous" part of the premises.[19] It has been held that if only that provision is satisfied, a default by the tenant will justify only an eviction judgment, but that if the service also satisfies the "due diligence" requirements of CPLR 308(4), the landlord will also be entitled to a money judgment for rent arrears.[20]

§ 75.   Court-Ordered Service Under CPLR 308(5)

This provision was born in the CPLR. It may be invoked whenever service proves "impracticable" under the earlier paragraphs of CPLR 308.[1] Under paragraph 5, all the plaintiff has to do is make an ex parte motion—a motion without notice to any other potential party—requesting the court to devise a method of service. The court can by order direct any kind of service it wishes, restricted only by the basic demands of due process, the facts of the particular case, and the judge's imagination.

---

[13]   Paragraph 2 is treated in § 72, which should also be consulted for the relevance of CPLR 308(6), which among other things defines the "actual place of business"—as that phrase is used in both paragraphs 2 and 4 in CPLR 308—to include a mail drop address. Difficulties about using CPLR 308(6), also discussed in § 72, have made some lawyers hesitant to rely on it.

[14]   Merchandise Nat. Bank of Chicago v. Lister, 5 A.D.2d 653, 174 N.Y.S.2d 102 (1st Dep't 1958).

[15]   PacAmOr Bearings, Inc. v. Foley, 92 A.D.2d 959, 460 N.Y.S.2d 662 (3d Dep't 1983).

[16]   See Mittelman v. Mittelman, 45 Misc. 2d 445, 257 N.Y.S.2d 86 (Sup. Ct., Queens County 1965).

[17]   See § 72. Proof of service is more fully treated in § 79.

[18]   The summary proceeding is treated in §§ 571 et seq. (Practitioner's Edition).

[19]   Because the word "conspicuous" appears in the affixing requirement of RPAPL 735, the phrase "conspicuous service" is often used in connection with summary proceedings. Because the consequences differ, as the text shows, the phrase should not be used to describe service under CPLR 308(4).

[20]   See Avgush v. Berrahu, 17 Misc. 3d 85, 847 N.Y.S.2d 343 (App. Term, 2nd Dep't 2007); 1405 Realty Corp. v. Napier, 68 Misc. 2d 793, 328 N.Y.S.2d 44 (N.Y. City Civ. Ct. 1971). Since the money judgment sought in the summary proceeding is for rent for use of the very premises at which service is made, it is difficult to countenance this kind of distinction between what suffices for eviction and what suffices for a rent judgment. Service good for one would seem to be adequate for both. The matter remains in controversy. See SPR 139:4.

[1]   CPLR 308(3), providing for service on a Rule 318 agent, is excepted; no effort to use it need precede an application under paragraph 5. See § 73.

One early case involved a defendant domiciled in Spain, but subject to New York longarm jurisdiction under CPLR 302(a)(1). The court on a CPLR 308(5) motion, assisted by the plaintiff's showing of the defendant's relationship with people in New York, made an order directing that the summons be delivered in the defendant's behalf to the defendant's New York literary agent, even though the agent was not involved in the transaction sued on. That was done, and the service was sustained.[2]

When is service under the earlier paragraphs sufficiently "impracticable" to invoke paragraph 5? It is clear that service need not prove "impossible" under those paragraphs. The same due diligence required under paragraphs 1 and 2 as a prelude to the use of the affix-and-mail method of paragraph 4 can also set the stage for the use of paragraph 5, necessitating only the additional showing that paragraph 4 will not work either. If, for example, the plaintiff has diligently tried to find the defendant's New York place of business or dwelling house or place of abode, and failed, the paragraph 5 stage should be set, but such showing should not be necessary. CPLR 308(5) does not require "due diligence," but rather a showing of "impracticability," i.e., that the methods of service under CPLR 308(1), (2) and (4) will simply not work.[3]

If it is simply want of a proper effort on the plaintiff's part that creates the service problem, even in situations in which there are numerous defendants, the plaintiff will not be allowed help from CPLR 308(5).[4]

Some caselaw suggests, even if only implicitly, that the plaintiff need not attempt service in a foreign country as a condition precedent to the use of paragraph 5, i.e., that inability to effect service within New York suffices for a paragraph 5 application,[5] but that's an undependable assumption. If the defendant resides at a known address in the foreign country, for example, and nothing is indicated to show that service there would be impracticable or unduly expensive, an application for court-ordered service under CPLR 308(5) should be denied.[6]

If service under one of the earlier paragraphs would be unjustifiably expensive, the expense has been held to be a factor tending to make the service sufficiently "impracticable" to invoke paragraph 5.[7] But if without undue trouble or expense service can be arranged for outside the state, or, in the case of paragraphs 2 or 4, can be made by executing one of the two requirements within the state and the other outside, the plaintiff should take those steps. The court may of course deny a paragraph 5 motion if a prescribed method appears feasible, remitting the plaintiff to try that method without prejudice to a further paragraph 5 application if the method does prove futile.

The leading New York authority on methods that can suffice under paragraph 5 and the factors to be considered by the court in devising the method is known as the *Dobkin* trilogy. The Court of Appeals decided three cases together—Dobkin v. Chapman, Sellars

---

[2]   Totero v. World Telegram Corp., 41 Misc. 2d 594, 245 N.Y.S.2d 870 (Sup. Ct., New York County 1963).

[3]   Markoff v. South Nassau Community Hosp., 91 A.D.2d 1064, 458 N.Y.S.2d 672 (2d Dep't 1983), aff'd, 61 N.Y.2d 283, 473 N.Y.S.2d 766, 461 N.E.2d 1253 (1984). In *Markoff*, the plaintiff didn't make that showing.

[4]   See Horner v. Waste Management of New York, Inc., Sup. Ct., Oneida County, Dec. 13, 1995 (Index No. 94–12613; Tenney, J.), discussed in SPR 39:3.

[5]   This point seems implicit in the *Totero* case, note 2, above.

[6]   See SPR 84:2 (discussing Corbo v. Stephens, 177 Misc. 2d 338, 677 N.Y.S.2d 211 (App. Term, 2d Dep't 1998), aff'd, 272 A.D.2d 502, 709 N.Y.S.2d 99 (2d Dep't 2000)).

[7]   See Dolgow v. Anderson, 43 F.R.D. 21 (E.D.N.Y. 1967). The cost would have been $120 to make service in Missouri—but that was in 1967 dollars and that was half a century ago.

v. Raye, and Keller v. Rappoport—delivering a consolidated opinion and setting forth guidelines for the use of CPLR 308(5).[8] In each of the three cases there had been an accident in New York, thus invoking longarm jurisdiction under CPLR 302(a)(2) and allowing service outside the state, if necessary, under CPLR 313. There was, in other words, no problem of jurisdictional basis. It was strictly a question of proper service of process, the second requirement for establishing personal jurisdiction.[9] The problem in each case was how to make service.

In *Dobkin*, D at the scene of the accident had furnished P a Pennsylvania address. Ordinary mail to that address was not returned, but registered mail was. In *Sellars* and in *Keller*, D gave P his apparently correct New York address, but afterwards moved. Registered mail in *Sellars* was returned "Moved—Left No Address."[10] In *Keller*, inquiries of D's former neighbors, of the New York Motor Vehicle Bureau, and of D's former employer did not reveal D's present whereabouts.

In each of the three cases, an order was made under paragraph 5, as follows:

a.   in *Dobkin*, an order was made directing service on D by ordinary mail at the address D had given P;

b.   in *Sellars*, there were two orders, one directing service pursuant to V&TL § 253, which requires service on the secretary of state[11] along with a mailing, plus a second directing service by publication when the mail was returned;

c.   in *Keller*, the order directed two steps, a mailing to D at the address D furnished, plus a delivery of the summons to D's insurance carrier.

In all three cases, the Court of Appeals sustained the methods used, even though it was far from certain that the methods would assure notice to the defendants. Due process does not guarantee notice, the court pointed out; it requires only that the plaintiff do under the circumstances what is reasonably calculated to give the defendant notice. The Court stressed that if the defendant failed to get notice, it would have been his own fault, observing that in accident cases, the plaintiff's needs must also be taken into account. And the Court laid down the rule that it is the defendant's duty in such cases to make information about his whereabouts available, either by keeping his address current with state licensing authorities, or with his insurance carrier, or with the injured person by direct communication. Although the Court doesn't specify it, perhaps equally

---

[8]   Dobkin v. Chapman, 21 N.Y.2d 490, 289 N.Y.S.2d 161, 236 N.E.2d 451 (1968).

[9]   See § 58.

[10]   In § 97 is discussion of the nonresident motorist statute, Veh. & Traf. Law § 253, which prescribes its own method of service and is available as an alternative in automobile tort cases. The unsuccess of registered or certified mail under § 253 has been held to vitiate the service. This rigidity in treating the mail aspect of § 253 should perhaps be reconsidered and abated under the reasoning of the *Dobkin* case. A mailing constitutional under one statute, CPLR 308(5), should not, on the same facts, be unconstitutional under another, Veh. & Traf. Law § 253. The fact that under the former the mailing results from a court order while under the latter it is directly required by statute should not make a constitutional difference. But see National Equipment Rental, Limited v. Szukhent, 375 U.S. 311, 84 S. Ct. 411, 11 L. Ed. 2d 354, 7 Fed. R. Serv. 2d 23 (1964), and its distinguishing of Wuchter v. Pizzutti, 276 U.S. 13, 48 S. Ct. 259, 72 L. Ed. 446, 57 A.L.R. 1230 (1928). Under a 1978 amendment of § 253, a procedure is set up for using ordinary mail if the registered or certified mail is returned "unclaimed." It is not clear just how far this will go to overrule earlier cases involving the "moved, left no address" situation. The plaintiff's lawyer might do better to seek an order of service under CPLR 308(5) than to rely on § 253 in a doubtful situation.

[11]   See § 97.

acceptable would be for the defendant to leave an accurate and active forwarding address with the post office.

The Court was influenced by the fact that the three cases in *Dobkin* were tort cases involving plaintiffs with personal injuries and that in some of the cases, the defendant's insurer was known. It also stressed that in the event of a default—because the defendant might really not get notice—New York's default-vacating provisions are available and are generously applied.[12]

There was some early authority that with a nunc pro tunc order the court could validate under CPLR 308(5) a method of service undertaken by the plaintiff without prior court leave,[13] but such a procedure is perilous and should be avoided. It's just an attempt to legitimize an unauthorized service retroactively and the practice has since been disapproved.[14]

In tort cases in which the plaintiff knows who the defendant's insurer is, service on the insurer in behalf of the insured is a common prescription under CPLR 308(5).[15] It is sometimes suggested that a liability insurer that does not itself know the insured's whereabouts will disclaim liability and thus deny the plaintiff a solvent source of recovery. But that point did not detain the court in the *Keller* case and, indeed, a disclaimer merely because the insured has not kept in touch with the insurer is not easily upheld in New York where the injured person's interest in the insurance policy is also recognized.[16]

Methods under paragraph 5 should always be trimmed to fit the case. In one instance in which demonstrators had taken over a building and blocked its entry, the posting of a temporary restraining order in the vicinity of the building and the announcement of its injunctive edict through a bullhorn were sustained by analogy to CPLR 308(5).[17] In a federal action also involving a court's broad discretionary powers, service in a hostile foreign nation was ordered by telex, with the airspace and electronic communication functioning as the process server.[18]

That medium has played an even more prominent role in serving process under CPLR 308(5) in the 21st Century. Email has been held a permissible method of service when the circumstances are appropriate, as they were found to be in Hollow v. Hollow,[19] a divorce action in which the defendant insulated himself from service in his employer's compound while in Saudi Arabia. The *Hollow* decision also recognizes that an application for service under CPLR 308(5) may be joined with a request for an extension of time to effect the service under CPLR 306–b. The courts have also permitted service via

---

[12]   CPLR 317, 5015(a)(1); see § 108.

[13]   See Rodgers v. Rodgers, 32 A.D.2d 558, 300 N.Y.S.2d 275 (2d Dep't 1969).

[14]   DeCarvalhosa v. Adler, 298 A.D.2d 293, 748 N.Y.S.2d 755 (1st Dep't 2002) (SPR 133:2).

[15]   See, e.g., Lerman v. Church, 54 Misc. 2d 402, 282 N.Y.S.2d 622 (Sup. Ct., New York County 1967).

[16]   See Thrasher v. U.S. Liability Ins. Co., 19 N.Y.2d 159, 278 N.Y.S.2d 793, 225 N.E.2d 503 (1967).

[17]   Cornell University v. Livingston, 69 Misc. 2d 965, 332 N.Y.S.2d 843 (Sup. Ct., Tompkins County 1972).

[18]   New England Merchants Nat. Bank v. Iran Power Generation and Transmission Co., 495 F. Supp. 73, 29 Fed. R. Serv. 2d 1212 (S.D.N.Y. 1980).

[19]   Hollow v. Hollow, 193 Misc. 2d 691, 747 N.Y.S.2d 704 (Sup. Ct., Oswego County 2002) (SPR 130:1).

Facebook, which may actually be more reasonably calculated to provide notice to millennials, who rarely enter a post office or read a newspaper.[20]

There are also decisions from the appellate level that have approved of service via email. In Safadjou v. Mohammadi,[21] the plaintiff commenced a matrimonial action and submitted evidence that defendant left the United States with the parties' child and declared her intention to remain in Iran with her family. The supreme court initially ordered service of process under CPLR 308(5) by three methods: (1) personal service upon defendant's parents in Iran; (2) mail service upon defendant at her parents' address in Iran; and (3) service upon defendant by plaintiff's Iranian attorneys in accordance with Iranian law. When plaintiff was unable to complete personal service upon defendant's parents in Iran, the court relieved him of that obligation and instead permitted service "via email at each of defendant's known email addresses."

The Fourth Department affirmed supreme court's order, concluding that CPLR 308(5)'s "impracticability" standard was met on the facts of the case and that plaintiff satisfied the demands of due process by making the requisite showing that service by email was " 'reasonably calculated to apprise defendant of the pending lawsuit.' "[22] It is important to note that the *Safadjou* court did not approve a CPLR 308(5) court order that provided solely for email service. Email was one of three methods of court ordered service, all of which had been attempted. Even though the *Hollow* court granted an application under CPLR 308(5) that incorporated only email service, it may be prudent to couple a request for service via email with other alternative methods of service to ensure due process is satisfied. As we note below, when there is an appellate reversal of an order granting an application for court ordered service, it may be too late to correct the problem.

The plaintiff's affidavits on the ex parte motion, in addition to showing the prescribed methods to be impracticable, should set forth all facts that can aid the court in deciding on a potential method of service. Indeed, the plaintiff's lawyer should be prepared to recommend a few feasible methods.

The subject of court-ordered service under paragraph 5 in matrimonial actions is also separately treated.[23]

An appellate court should be hesitant to overturn a lower court order directing service under CPLR 308(5) unless the plaintiff can be shown to be at fault in some way in the evidence laid before the court. If the plaintiff sets forth all of the facts accurately, and suggests several methods of service, and the nisi prius judge selects a method he deems satisfactory to due process and directs its use, the overturning of that method on

---

[20]   See Baidoo v. Blood-Dzraku, 48 Misc. 3d 309, 5 N.Y.S.3d 709 (Sup. Ct., New York County 2015) (permitting plaintiff in matrimonial action to serve defendant via private message through Facebook pursuant to the court ordered service provisions in CPLR 308(5), with follow-up phone calls and texts to alert defendant of Facebook service); Matter of Noel B. v. Maria A., F-00787-13/14B, N.Y.L.J. 1202670317766, at *1 (Fam. Ct., Richmond County Sept. 12, 2014) (granting motion for court ordered service by permitting petitioner to send a digital copy of process to the respondent via her Facebook account, and to follow up with a mailing of those documents to respondent's last known street address).

[21]   Safadjou v. Mohammadi, 105 A.D.3d 1423, 964 N.Y.S.2d 801 (4th Dep't 2013).

[22]   *Safadjou*, 105 A.D.3d at 1425, 964 N.Y.S.2d at 804; see also Alfred E. Mann Living Trust v. ETIRC Aviation S.a.r.l., 78 A.D.3d 137, 141, 910 N.Y.S.2d 418, 422 (1st Dep't 2010) (where defendant consented to service of process via email in contract, court noted that service of process by email "is not prohibited under either state or federal law, or the Hague Convention"); John R. Higgitt, *The Emergence of "E-Service" Under CPLR 308(5)*, 85 N.Y. St. B. J. 28 (2013).

[23]   See § 76.

appeal can mean the end of the plaintiff's case, as where the statute of limitations has expired and a new action would now be barred. It would be an unusual example of a party being made to pay the price of a judge's error. An appellate court should therefore give all possible deference to the discretion exercised below, saving a reversal for only that case in which the court sees no alternative as a matter of law.[24]

While service under paragraph 5 of CPLR 308 may not be directed against a corporation,[25] a separate statute allows the equivalent in corporate cases.[26]

§ 76. Service in Matrimonial Actions

The matrimonial actions, including divorce, annulment, and separation, have special provisions governing commencement and an interesting history leading up to them. The key provision is section 232 of the Domestic Relations Law. The developments about to be noted evolved when service rather than filing marked commencement of a matrimonial action in the supreme court, which has exclusive jurisdiction of matrimonial actions.

Prior to 1974, section 232 provided for service by the usual personal delivery method, but if that proved unfeasible, the only other method allowed was service by publication. Paragraphs 2, 3, and 4 of CPLR 308 contained clauses expressly precluding their use in matrimonial actions and, because section 232 was deemed preemptive, resort to court-ordered service under CPLR 308(5) was also held by some courts to be precluded.

Then came Boddie v. Connecticut,[1] in which the U.S. Supreme Court held that due process prevents a state from denying a divorce plaintiff access to its courts solely because of inability to pay costs and fees. Based on the fact that service by publication was required by New York as the only alternative to personal delivery, and was expensive (in addition to being nearly useless as a way of giving notice), ensuing caselaw in New York held that if the government required such service, then the government would have to pay for it for indigent matrimonial plaintiffs. A conflict then arose among departments as to whether local government or the State would have to foot the bill. The Court of Appeals resolved the conflict in Deason v. Deason[2] by holding it to be a local burden: in New York City, a city charge, and elsewhere a county charge. The court in *Deason* also hinted that court-ordered service under CPLR 308(5) might be available in matrimonial actions, and on remand the trial court took the hint and so held.[3]

Section 232 was then amended in 1974 to permit service by any of the methods of CPLR 308, with concomitant amendments of paragraphs 2, 3, and 4 of CPLR 308 to recognize the change, which they do with a simple cross-reference to DRL section 232. An important qualification, however, is that only the personal delivery method of CPLR

---

[24] At worst the appellate court should try to keep the action alive with a remand to have a more appropriate method chosen. See Wishni v. Taylor, 75 A.D.3d 747, 749, 903 N.Y.S.2d 813 (3d Dep't 2010) (rejecting plaintiff's argument that supreme court properly granted CPLR 308(5) service, but extending plaintiff's time to serve the amended summons and complaint upon defendant for an additional 30 days); Standifer v. Goord, 285 A.D.2d 912, 727 N.Y.S.2d 823 (3d Dep't 2001) (SPR 128:4) (involving order to show cause in special proceeding); see § 553.

[25] CPLR 311 governs corporations and does not admit of a CPLR 308(5) application. See LTD Trading Enterprises v. Vignatelli, 176 A.D.2d 571, 574 N.Y.S.2d 745 (1st Dep't 1991).

[26] See CPLR 311(b) and the discussion in § 70.

[1] Boddie v. Connecticut, 401 U.S. 371, 91 S. Ct. 780, 28 L. Ed. 2d 113 (1971).

[2] Deason v. Deason, 32 N.Y.2d 93, 343 N.Y.S.2d 321, 296 N.E.2d 229 (1973).

[3] Deason v. Deason, 73 Misc. 2d 964, 343 N.Y.S.2d 276 (Sup. Ct., Albany County 1973).

308(1) may be used without court leave in a matrimonial action. The other CPLR 308 methods are available, but all require an order of court in the matrimonial action whereas only service under CPLR 308(5) requires one in other actions.[4]

Service by publication is still available in the matrimonial action as a court-ordered alternative[5] but should be used only as a last resort.[6]

The matrimonial action is in the jurisdiction of the supreme court exclusively so, like all other supreme court actions, it is commenced today by the filing of the initiatory papers.[7] The same time restrictions that then come into play for service, notably the 120-day period and the requirements applicable to it,[8] apply equally to matrimonial actions.[9]

Pinpointing the moment of commencement is important for several reasons, one of them being that it marks the "interposition" of the claim for statute of limitations purposes. In relatively few instances, however, is there a statute of limitations issue in a matrimonial context.

In an ordinary civil action in the supreme court, the summons is accompanied by either a complaint or by the brief notice prescribed by CPLR 305(b).[10] Section 232 has its own instructions for matrimonial actions, however, providing that if the complaint does not accompany the summons, the summons itself must contain a notice that the action is for matrimonial relief, specifying its nature—e.g., "Action for a divorce," "Action for a separation," etc. Here a mistake in labeling can have jurisdictional consequences. A "separation" label will not be allowed to support a divorce judgment, for example, especially if there has been a default.[11]

Also required, if the complaint does not accompany the summons, is that the summons include a demand for any ancillary relief sought (support, custody of children, etc.). The omission of the request for ancillary relief is not jurisdictional, however; it just bars the ancillary relief if the defendant should default.[12]

The requirements of labeling the summons to recite that it's for matrimonial relief and of having it specify any ancillary relief sought do not apply if the complaint accompanies the summons at the outset.

For custody matters in matrimonial actions, Article 5–A of the Domestic Relations Law is an adoption of the Uniform Child Custody Jurisdiction Act, which includes an extensive set of jurisdictional bases on which custody jurisdiction can be predicated. It exploits a mixture of jurisdiction conceptually akin to the "longarm" jurisdiction

---

[4] See Baidoo v. Blood-Dzraku, 48 Misc. 3d 309, 5 N.Y.S.3d 709 (Sup. Ct., New York County 2015) (permitting plaintiff in matrimonial action to serve defendant via a private message through Facebook pursuant to the court ordered service provisions in CPLR 308(5)); § 75.

[5] See CPLR 314(1), discussed in § 102, and CPLR 315.

[6] See *Baidoo*, 48 Misc.3d at 316, 5 N.Y.S.3d at 715 (court ordered service via Facebook under CPLR 308(5), but refused to order additional service by any other method, such as publication under CPLR 315, noting that "publication service is . . . almost guaranteed not to provide a defendant with notice of the action for divorce").

[7] Dom. Rel. Law § 211, CPLR 304.

[8] See § 63.

[9] For detailed treatment of the commencement of matrimonial actions, see the Commentaries by Justice Alan D. Scheinkman on McKinney's Dom. Rel. Law §§ 211 and 232.

[10] See § 60.

[11] See Fishman v. Fishman, 42 N.Y.2d 856, 397 N.Y.S.2d 774, 366 N.E.2d 862 (1977).

[12] See Rosen v. Rosen, 161 Misc. 2d 795, 614 N.Y.S.2d 1018 (Sup. Ct., Queens County 1994) (SPR 33:3).

underlying CPLR 302,[13] as well as to the rem jurisdiction found in CPLR 314.[14] It often becomes necessary in custody proceedings to give notice to a person outside the State. A 2006 amendment of DRL section 75–g aims to facilitate such notice by expanding alternatives for it.

§ 76A.　Personal Service by Mail

CPLR 312–a, providing for service of the summons by ordinary mail and dispensing with the use of a process server, was enacted in 1989.[1] As will be seen shortly, the procedure requires the defendant's cooperation, and some attorneys have reported that cooperation is so infrequent that some of them don't even bother with CPLR 312–a. Service by mail undertaken timely and used carefully, however, can avoid some of the problems associated with the more traditional methods of service. The idea of trying it should not be rejected out of hand, at least where the end of the statute of limitations is nowhere in sight.

Mail service is available as an immediate initial option. No effort need be made to make service by any other means before using the mail method of CPLR 312–a. And anyone at all, even the plaintiff herself, can be the mailer. The method is available against all categories of defendants—individuals, corporations and other entities, partnerships, governmental agencies, the State itself, etc.—with the exception of infants and incapacitated persons.[2] The method used is ordinary, first-class mail.

The summons is accompanied by the notice or complaint (whichever the plaintiff is opting for),[3] by two copies of a "statement of service by mail and acknowledgment of receipt," and by a postpaid envelope addressed to the sender.[4] The form of this statement and acknowledgment is explicitly prescribed in the statute.[5] The defendant's obligation is to subscribe and "affirm"[6] the acknowledgment[7] and return one copy of it in the envelope supplied. If it is not returned, the plaintiff will have to issue the summons to a process server in the usual way and have it served by some other method.

The penalty to the defendant for not acknowledging, thus making service by another method necessary, is that the court may assess against the defendant the "reasonable

---

[13]　See §§ 84 et seq.

[14]　See § 102.

[1]　CPLR 312–a was modeled on the federal rule, Rule 4(c)(2)(C)(ii) of the Federal Rules of Civil Procedure, as it was at the time of the enactment of CPLR 312–a. Ironically, the federal procedure of service by mail was abrogated shortly afterwards under an amendment of Rule 4 that went into effect on December 1, 1993. Adopted in place of service by mail under the 1993 federal amendment is a formal procedure whereby the plaintiff can seek from the defendant a waiver of service. See Fed. R. Civ. P. 4(d) and Commentaries C4–15 to C4–18 on Rule 4 in 28 U.S.C.A., and § 623 (Practitioner's Edition). No comparable waiver procedure exists in New York practice.

[2]　CPLR 309, which governs service on such persons, is not included in the listing of statutes in CPLR 312–a(a) for which service by mail can be used as an alternative. For discussion of who an "incapacitated person" is, see caption b. in § 69.

[3]　See § 60.

[4]　CPLR 312–a(a).

[5]　CPLR 312–a(d).

[6]　This is apparently intended to adopt the form of affirmation that attorneys and other professionals are permitted to make in lieu of an affidavit. See CPLR 2106; § 205.

[7]　CPLR 312–a(c). The returned acknowledgment is proof of service, the equivalent of the affidavit of service used when service is made by other means.

expense" of the other service.[8] The statement and acknowledgment include a notice to that effect.

Service by another method after abortive mail service must indicate that an attempt was made to serve by mail under this provision.[9] Perhaps just an additional clause can be included in the summons to satisfy this requirement or an additional paper served with the summons.

The defendant has 30 days in which to return the acknowledgment.[10] If the complaint is served with the summons, an answer has to be served within 20 days after the defendant returns the acknowledgment. If a notice instead of a complaint is served with the summons, the statute is less clear. Presumably the acknowledgment acts as the equivalent of a demand for the complaint and starts the plaintiff's 20-day period for serving the complaint.[11]

If the defendant is a corporation or other entity, or in any instance in which someone other than the named defendant signs the acknowledgment, the signer must indicate her authority or her relationship to the defendant.

Because only the "reasonable expense" of the other service is assessed when service by some other means is made necessary because of the defendant's failure to acknowledge, the sum may be so inconsequential that defendants feel no qualms at all about refusing to acknowledge, especially if there is any chance of putting the plaintiff out of time altogether with a little delay. The prospect of also having to pay an attorney's fee for the extra time that may be entailed when the plaintiff's attorney has to arrange for other service would give the defendant more incentive to acknowledge voluntarily, but such a fee is apparently not to be included in the assessment.

Putting the plaintiff out of time always refers to the statute of limitations, and on that front, plaintiffs who use mail service must be extremely wary for these additional reasons:

The plaintiff has 120 days in which to make service.[12] The time for making the service, the time for the defendant to ponder whether to acknowledge it (the defendant has at least 30 days for that), and the time for the return of the acknowledgment even if the defendant does decide to return it, all comes out of the 120-day period. When the plaintiff using mail service finally determines that the defendant is not going to return the acknowledgment, there may be precious little of the 120 days left in which to make service by some other means. It is for reasons like this that many plaintiffs, or in any event those at the tail end of the statute of limitations, stay away from mail service altogether.

The statute explicitly authorizes mail service in a special proceeding as well as in an action, but it is probably an altogether bad idea to try it in a special proceeding.[13] The special proceeding, like a motion, requires the setting of a specific return day for a hearing, which can be as close as a few weeks after commencement of the proceeding.[14]

---

[8]   CPLR 312–a(f).

[9]   CPLR 312–a(e).

[10] CPLR 312–a(b).

[11] See § 231.

[12] See § 63.

[13] For a discussion of special proceedings, see § 547.

[14] See § 550.

How can a petitioner who serves the initiatory papers on (e.g.) July 1st confidently make them returnable on July 15th when the validity of the service depends on the respondent's voluntary acceptance of the service and the respondent need not even decide whether to accept it until July 31st or later? And if a short statute of limitations applies to the special proceeding—like the four-month period of CPLR 217 that applies to the common Article 78 proceeding[15]—reliance on CPLR 312–a is even more hazardous. For the time being, plaintiffs would do best to restrict their use of CPLR 312–a to plenary actions, and, even there, to actions in which the statute of limitations has a long time to go.

§ 76B. Curing Technical Defects in Service

In Ruffin v. Lion Corp.,[1] the Court concluded that the plaintiff's failure to fulfill the service requirements of CPLR 313 because the process server's residence rendered him unauthorized to serve process constituted a defect that may be disregarded under CPLR 2001. The *Ruffin* decision is monumental in that it grants courts the power to invoke CPLR 2001 to disregard any number of defects that can arise when plaintiff attempts to make service under CPLR 308, sections 306 and 307 of the Business Corporation Law, section 253 of the Vehicle and Traffic Law, and various other provisions. Defects that have arisen in this realm are explored in sections 63, 66 through 76A, 95, and 97. The holdings in many cases discussed therein, which resulted in dismissal of an action for lack of proper service, must be reconsidered in light of the Court's holding in *Ruffin*.

The *Ruffin* Court cautioned, however, that CPLR 2001 may be used to cure only a "technical infirmity." Furthermore, the Court instructed that "[i]n deciding whether a defect in service is merely technical, courts must be guided by the principle of notice to the defendant . . . ."[2] In providing guidance to future cases involving the use of CPLR 2001 to cure a defect in service, the Court stated:

> Defendant's actual receipt of the summons and complaint is not dispositive of the efficacy of service. For example, simply mailing the documents to defendant or emailing them to defendant's Web address would present more than a technical infirmity, even if defendant actually receives the documents, inasmuch as these methods in general introduce greater possibility of failed delivery. Likewise, delivery of a summons and complaint to the wrong person . . . is a substantial defect. On the other hand, delivery of a summons and complaint by a process server who is unauthorized to serve simply because of his place of residence will not affect the likelihood that the summons and complaint will reach defendant and inform him that he is being sued.[3]

Just how far does CPLR 2001 go to permit courts to forgive defects that arise in serving process? Debates on the subject will surely arise in future cases because the stakes are so high where, as in *Ruffin*, the plaintiff faces the prospect of dismissal of an action outside the statute of limitations.

---

[15]   See §§ 557 et seq.

[1]   Ruffin v. Lion Corp., 15 N.Y.3d 578, 915 N.Y.S.2d 204, 940 N.E.2d 909 (2010) (SPR 228:3) (NYSLD No. 612).

[2]   *Ruffin*, 15 N.Y.3d at 582, 915 N.Y.S.2d at 206, 940 N.E.2d at 911.

[3]   *Ruffin*, 15 N.Y.3d at 583, 915 N.Y.S.2d at 207, 940 N.E.2d at 912.

An early entrant on the scene indicating that courts might not be so generous in allowing CPLR 2001 to cure service defects is the decision in George Doulaveris & Son, Inc. v. P.J. 37 Food Corp.[4] In *George Doulaveris*, deliver-and-mail service was made pursuant to section 735(1) of the Real Property Actions and Proceedings Law ("RPAPL"), which governs in a summary proceeding to recover possession of real property (the so-called "landlord-tenant" case).[5] The statute contains requirements similar to those imposed by CPLR 308(2), but they are not identical. Nonetheless, the court's decision is instructive for those making service under the deliver-and-mail provisions in either statute as it addresses the scope of CPLR 2001's curative powers.

The petitioner in *George Doulaveris* complied with the "delivery" requirements in RPAPL section 735(1), but failed to properly satisfy the provision's "mailing" requirements. Instead of mailing the notice of petition and petition to the respondent tenant, the papers were addressed to an entity named "CTOWN." The New York City Civil Court concluded that this constituted an insignificant defect within the meaning of CPLR 2001 and was, therefore, not fatal. The appellate term reversed and granted the respondent tenant's motion to dismiss the petition. The court concluded that the petitioner landlord did not satisfy the mailing prong of the substituted service requirements in RPAPL section 735(1), which requires that the notice of petition and petition be mailed "to the respondent." Citing *Ruffin*, the court disagreed with the civil court's determination that the error in addressing the papers was de minimis. Rather, the appellate term categorized the defect as "substantial," placing it beyond the reach of CPLR 2001's healing powers. Quoting from the *Ruffin* decision, the court stressed that "[a] tenant's 'actual receipt of the petition and notice of petition is not dispositive of the efficacy of service.' "

D. GETTING INTO THE COURTHOUSE

Table of Sections

§ 77.   General Filing Requirements; Federal Practice Compared
§ 77A.   The Individual Assignment System (IAS)
§ 77B.   Getting a Judge Assigned: Request for Judicial Intervention (RJI)
§ 77C.   Form of Request for Judicial Intervention (RJI)
§ 77D.   The Preliminary Conference
§ 78.   Getting an Index Number
§ 79.   Proof of Service

§ 77. General Filing Requirements; Federal Practice Compared

Before we conclude this discussion about how an action is commenced, note should be taken of the procedure for opening a file of the case in the clerk's office, and several connected matters. To the student or young lawyer trying to keep everything in perspective, the intervention of these and the several ensuing sections—about opening a case, getting an index number, filing papers, the individual assignment system (IAS), the request for judicial intervention (RJI), the preliminary conference, and proof of service—may seem to burst out of nowhere. We've put them here under the caption

---

[4]   George Doulaveris & Son, Inc. v. P.J. 37 Food Corp., 39 Misc. 3d 1, 961 N.Y.S.2d 722 (App. Term, 2nd Dep't 2013).

[5]   See § 575 (Practitioner's Edition).

"Getting into the Courthouse" because there is no obvious, single juncture in litigation at which to address them. They can become relevant at any number of points.

The step that initiates an action is the filing of the summons and complaint;[1] hence the filing takes place right at the outset, with the case getting an index number right off and having its place identified in the clerk's files. This is akin to federal practice where the filing of the complaint commences the action.[2]

While an initial filing of the summons and complaint now takes place at the outset, which opens a file of the case and secures an index number straightaway, the full mandatory filing system as used in federal practice has not been adopted in New York. In federal practice, there is a general requirement that any paper served on any party be filed with the court either before service or "within a reasonable time after service."[3] This is sometimes called the mandatory filing system. It has no counterpart in civil practice in New York, although e-filed actions come close.[4] The New York requirement is to file the initial summons and complaint. While additional filings of one sort or another may be required for a few specific things in litigation practice—such as for motion papers[5] and for the note of issue[6]—there is nothing like the across-the-board federal practice of requiring the filing of everything that is served between the parties. In New York practice, this frees many papers from any filing requirement, including answers, replies, amended and supplemental pleadings, notices in disclosure proceedings, demands for bills of particulars, etc.

Under the filing system, whatever postcommencement filing of a paper takes place will have an existing file to refer to. The existence of the file is no assurance, however, that a judge will have yet been assigned to the case. As a general rule, no judge is assigned until a paper known as a Request for Judicial Intervention (RJI) is filed,[7] and that usually doesn't take place until some procedure is started that requires the attention of a judge, such as a motion. Local practice might profitably be checked into in this regard, however; the practice of assigning of a judge as soon as a case is filed might be in effect as a matter of local option.

There are some situations in which a file is started even before commencement of an action. One is where a would-be plaintiff is applying for leave to file a late notice of claim or for preaction discovery as an aid to bringing the action. Those steps require an index number and the payment of the fee for it—virtually every application to the court requires an index number—even though the action may not yet have been formally commenced. Commencement may be necessary after the preaction application is disposed of and, if it is, there is likely to be the requirement of a new index number, or in any event a new fee.[8]

Effective August 30, 2013, newly enacted CPLR 3012–b requires the filing of a "certificate of merit" with the complaint in any residential foreclosure action involving a

---

[1]   See § 45.

[2]   Fed. R. Civ. P. 3. The summons need not be filed with the complaint in federal practice but often is. See Commentary C4:12 on Federal Rule 4 in 28 U.S.C.A.

[3]   Fed. R. Civ. P. 5(d)(1).

[4]   See § 63A.

[5]   CPLR 2214(c); see § 246.

[6]   CPLR 3402(a); see § 369.

[7]   See § 77B.

[8]   See § 63.

home loan in which the defendant is a resident of the property subject to the foreclosure.[9] The requirement is similar to the one imposed under CPLR 3012–a, which requires that a special certificate of merit accompany the complaint in medical, dental, and podiatric malpractice actions.[10]

In medical (including dental and podiatric) malpractice actions a further filing requirement has been imposed. CPLR 3406 requires that in any such action the plaintiff file a notice describing the action within 60 days,[11] but the point that starts the 60 days is not the commencement of the action; it's the joinder of issue (the moment when the defendant serves an answer).[12] The notice is designed to trigger the scheduling of a pretrial conference that will expedite the action. The plaintiff's omission to serve a timely notice under CPLR 3406(a) may be punished with money sanctions, but not a dismissal. Dismissal can ensue, however, for a failure to carry out the requirements of an order emanating from the pretrial conference.[13] The notice is relatively easy to complete. A plaintiff unable to serve it timely should seek a time extension under CPLR 2004 as promptly as possible.[14]

CPLR 3409 was enacted in 2011 to require the court to hold a "mandatory settlement conference" in medical, dental, and podiatric malpractice actions. This occurs at a later stage of the action, within 45 days after the filing of the note of issue in the action.

Another statute germane to note here is CPLR 3408, enacted in 2008 and amended and expanded several times since. It's part of a package of amendments designed to ease the foreclosures of residential mortgages that threaten to dispossess the mortgagor. The design is to get the parties and court together, hopefully generating some kind of agreement about payments that will keep the mortgagor in residence.[15] Effective with actions commenced on or after August 30, 2013, CPLR 3408(a) was amended to require that every plaintiff in a residential foreclosure action "file proof of service within twenty days of such service, however service is made . . . ." This filing will trigger the scheduling of the mandatory settlement conference required by CPLR 3408.[16]

§ 77A. The Individual Assignment System (IAS)

Prior to January 6, 1986, an action in a New York court was not assigned to a given judge and might eventually occupy the time of many judges. If a motion had to be made, for example, it would come before whatever judge happened to be assigned to the court's motion part at the time. Several motions often meant that several different judges had to become familiar with the background of the case, only to have yet another judge preside at the trial. This system, known as the "master calendar" system, was felt in many quarters to be duplicative and wasteful. Under an "individual" calendar system,

---

[9]   See Commentaries on McKinney's CPLR 3012–b.

[10]   See Commentaries on McKinney's CPLR 3012–a.

[11]   See 22 N.Y.C.R.R. § 202.56, a detailed implementation of CPLR 3406.

[12]   A form for the notice is prescribed in 22 N.Y.C.R.R. § 202.56. Further procedures are elaborated there.

[13]   See Tewari v. Tsoutsouras, 75 N.Y.2d 1, 550 N.Y.S.2d 572, 549 N.E.2d 1143 (1989). It may be questionable today whether *Tewari* is an absolute bar to dismissal, even if there is no order. See Gordon v. Sea Crest Health Care Center, LLC, 73 A.D.3d 1125, 900 N.Y.S.2d 905 (2d Dep't 2010) (SPR 223:3).

[14]   See § 6.

[15]   The original CPLR 3408 is discussed in SPR 201:3; the 2009 amendment in SPR 217:3.

[16]   See § 77D.

as long used in the local federal courts, a case gets assigned to but a single judge, to whom it then belongs from cradle to grave: all motions and applications go to that judge, who presides at the trial as well.

Effective January 6, 1986, that kind of system, or something close to it, officially denominated the "Individual Assignment System," or IAS, took effect in New York as part of the Uniform Rules that also became effective on that day. The IAS is implemented by these provisions:

For	Uniform Rule
Supreme and County courts	202.3
Family Court	205.3
Court of Claims	206.3
City courts outside New York City	210.3

For the time being, the IAS is not being used in the New York City Civil Court or in the Nassau or Suffolk district courts.[1] And the system is apparently deemed unnecessary in the surrogates' courts—most of which have only one surrogate—and in the town and village courts.

While most cases fall into the system and end up in the hands of a single judge, there are some exceptions. Under the IAS rules applicable in the supreme court, which we will henceforth use for illustration, special "parts" can be set up for particular categories of cases, such as matrimonial actions, condemnation cases, tax assessment reviews, cases against a municipality, commercial cases, etc.[2]

If such parts are established, judges will be specially assigned to them, perhaps being exempted from regular caseloads in the process. The rule also says that if several judges are assigned to any such part, the assignment of cases to those judges "shall be at random" within the part.

Some judges can be kept in "reserve" to try cases in "exceptional" circumstances. Other judges may be directed to hear matters when the assigned judge is not available. And in a provision that may hold the cure for periodic ailments that can from time to time appear in any individual assignment system, a transfer can be ordered, administratively, "of any action or proceeding ... from one judge to another in accordance with the needs of the court."[3] What these exceptions consist of, and where they can be found, are matters of local regulation—despite the "uniform" in the Uniform Rules—and must therefore be checked out on a local basis.

The chief administrator is empowered to permit a given court, or a court in a given district or county, to inaugurate what is called a "dual track system of assignment." This is really a modified individual assignment system. Under the dual track system, a case gets assigned to one judge for all pretrial proceedings, but to a different judge for the trial itself.[4] A similar system—if it's not, indeed, the same one under a different name— is the "trial assignment part" or "TAP" system, under which trial-ready cases get transferred to a "calendar" judge who first tries to settle the case and then transfers it

---

[1]   See 22 N.Y.C.R.R. §§ 208.3, 212.3.

[2]   See, e.g., 22 N.Y.C.R.R. § 202.3(c)(2).

[3]   22 N.Y.C.R.R. § 202.3(c)(5).

[4]   22 N.Y.C.R.R. § 202.3(c)(6).

to a standby judge for trial if it doesn't settle. Whether the dual track or TAP procedure is applicable locally must also be ascertained by local inquiry.

One of the options considered before the IAS system was adopted was to use the federal system of having a judge assigned to the case as soon as the action is commenced. That option was rejected. Instead, a judge is assigned only upon the first step taken in the action that requires one—which the mere commencement of the action ordinarily does not. Hence, no judge is automatically assigned at the outset, but only at that later point when one is needed. When and how a case is assigned to a judge involves a paper known as a Request for Judicial Intervention, or "RJI," discussed in a separate section.[5] Practice in a special proceeding, which does require the assignment of a judge at the very outset, is also the subject of a separate section.[6]

Critics of the IAS among the bar have argued that the IAS works well only when the assigned judge is a good one. The system's proponents counter that if any judges aren't doing their job, the IAS will be more prone to expose them. In any event, they conclude, there are tools within the system—some of them already noted—for meeting problems as they arise. There is also the factor that most intermediate (non-final) orders are appealable of right in New York practice,[7] in contrast with the federal system where precious few are.[8] The immediate appealability of just about any order serves as a safeguard against abuses by a judge under the IAS[9] or, for that matter, under any system.

§ 77B. Getting a Judge Assigned: Request for Judicial Intervention (RJI)

Implementing the Individual Assignment System entails the early assignment of the case to a judge. How early? If a case is to be assigned to a single judge, one might expect a procedure whereby a judge is assigned to the case at its very commencement, as in the federal courts.[1]

Adoption of such a procedure for the New York courts was considered and rejected. The way a case gets assigned to a judge under the IAS is through the filing of a paper known as a Request for Judicial Intervention, or RJI. In the supreme court, to which discussion will be confined here, the governing provision is Uniform Rule 202.6. To the rule is appended an official form of RJI, which is reprinted below in section 77C.

The filing of the RJI activates the IAS machinery and gets the case assigned to a judge, who is designated the "assigned judge"[2] and who then has the case until the end, subject to some exceptions built into the IAS.[3] But when is an RJI filed?

---

[5]   § 77B.

[6]   § 550.

[7]   See CPLR 5701(a)(2), discussed in § 526.

[8]   See § 642 (Practitioner's Edition).

[9]   See, e.g., Goldheart Intern. Ltd. v. Vulcan Const. Corp., 124 A.D.2d 507, 508 N.Y.S.2d 182 (1st Dep't 1986) (precluding judges from requiring a party to obtain permission before making a motion).

[1]   See the discussion in § 77A.

[2]   22 N.Y.C.R.R. § 202.3(b).

[3]   The "dual track" system may have been put into operation locally, for example, entailing an assignment to one judge for pretrial purposes, but to another for the trial. Or special parts may have been set up in the court to hear particular categories of cases. See § 77A.

The first need of judicial attention is the occasion for the filing of an RJI. Hence Uniform Rule 202.6 requires that if a judge has not already been assigned to the case, an RJI, in duplicate, must accompany any of the following:

— a notice of motion

— an order to show cause

— an application for an ex parte order

— a notice of petition

— a note of issue

— a notice of medical, dental, or podiatric malpractice action[4]

— a statement of net worth in matrimonial actions[5] or

— a request for a preliminary conference.

The "preliminary conference," treated in more detail below in section 77D, is a procedure prescribed by Uniform Rule 202.12.[6]

Note that if judicial attention is not yet needed, there is no authorization for filing an RJI.

The assignment of an index number to a case occurs upon the filing of the first paper in the action (at which time the filing fee is paid),[7] but not even in the supreme and county courts, where the filing of the summons and complaint constitutes the commencement of the action, does the filing necessarily trigger the assignment of a judge. The paper filed will occasion such an assignment only if it is one of those listed above, i.e., a paper that an RJI must accompany. If the paper filed is merely proof of service, for example, an RJI does not go along with it unless other papers that accompany the proof of service—such as papers moving for a default judgment against the defendant—fall into one of the categories on the above list and call for an RJI.

Certain circumstances may prevent the filing of the summons and complaint in supreme and county court practice, and time may be short under the statute of limitations. The plaintiff in that situation may apply to a judge for an order directing filing within five days, which amounts to commencement of the action.[8] This is a variety of ex parte order, which is one of the events that technically requires the filing of an RJI. Presumably, therefore, an application for such an order should be accompanied by an RJI. This seems a paltry event to occasion the permanent assignment of a judge. It has other peculiarities.[9]

If and when a judge is assigned, notice of the assignment will presumably be given to all parties by the clerk. If not, whichever party is notified of the assignment would do well to identify the assigned judge to the other parties. Here again, inquiry into local

---

[4]   A special mandatory filing requirement applies in these cases. See CPLR 3406 and 22 N.Y.C.R.R. § 202.56.

[5]   See 22 N.Y.C.R.R. § 202.16, implementing the requirement imposed by Dom. Rel. Law § 236.

[6]   The "preliminary" conference should not be confused with the "pretrial" conference of 22 N.Y.C.R.R. § 202.26, treated in § 374.

[7]   Getting an index number is the subject of § 78.

[8]   CPLR 304(a); see § 45.

[9]   See captions 9 and 12 in the lead note in NYSLD No. 391.

practice should be made. Try as any "uniform" compilation may, distinct local variations inevitably evolve, like regional accents on the Queen's English.

§ 77C. Form of Request for Judicial Intervention (RJI)

The following is the official form of RJI used in the supreme court, as drafted and promulgated by the Office of Court Administration and as reprinted from the annually recompiled "McKinney's New York Rules of Court."

REQUEST FOR JUDICIAL INTERVENTION
UCS-840 (7/2012)

	For Court Clerk Use Only:
	IAS Entry Date
	Judge Assigned
	RJI Date

_____COURT, COUNTY OF_____

Index No: _____   Date Index Issued:_____/_____/_____

CAPTION: Enter the complete case caption. Do not use et al or et ano. If more space is required, attach a caption rider sheet.

Plaintiff(s)/Petitioner(s)

-against-

Defendant(s)/Respondent(s)

NATURE OF ACTION OR PROCEEDING: Check ONE box only and specify where indicated.

MATRIMONIAL
- ☐ Contested
  NOTE: For all Matrimonial actions where the parties have children under the age of 18, complete and attach the **MATRIMONIAL RJI Addendum.**
  For Uncontested Matrimonial actions, use RJI form UD-13.

TORTS
- ☐ Asbestos
- ☐ Breast Implant
- ☐ Environmental: _____
  (specify)
- ☐ Medical, Dental, or Podiatric Malpractice
- ☐ Motor Vehicle
- ☐ Products Liability:_____
  (specify)
- ☐ Other Negligence:_____
  (specify)
- ☐ Other Professional Malpractice:_____
  (specify)
- ☐ Other Tort:_____
  (specify)

OTHER MATTERS
- ☐ Certificate of Incorporation/Dissolution   [see **NOTE** under Commercial]
- ☐ Emergency Medical Treatment
- ☐ Habeas Corpus
- ☐ Local Court Appeal
- ☐ Mechanic's Lien
- ☐ Name Change
- ☐ Pistol Permit Revocation Hearing
- ☐ Sale or Finance of Religious/Not-for-Profit Property
- ☐ Other:_____
  (specify)

COMMERCIAL
- ☐ Business Entity (including corporations, partnerships, LLCs, etc.)
- ☐ Contract
- ☐ Insurance (where insurer is a party, except arbitration)
- ☐ UCC (including sales, negotiable instruments)
- ☐ Other Commercial:_____
  (specify)

  NOTE: For Commercial Division assignment requests [22 NYCRR § 202.70(c)], complete and attach the **COMMERCIAL DIV RJI Addendum.**

REAL PROPERTY: How many properties does the application include?____
- ☐ Condemnation
- ☐ Mortgage Foreclosure (specify):   ☐ Residential   ☐ Commercial
  Property Address:_____
  NOTE: For Mortgage Foreclosure actions involving a one- to four-family, owner-occupied, residential property, or an owner-occupied condominium, complete and attach the **FORECLOSURE RJI Addendum.**
- ☐ Tax Certiorari - Section: _____ Block: _____ Lot: _____
- ☐ Tax Foreclosure
- ☐ Other Real Property:_____
  (specify)

SPECIAL PROCEEDINGS
- ☐ CPLR Article 75 (Arbitration)   [see **NOTE** under Commercial]
- ☐ CPLR Article 78 (Body or Officer)
- ☐ Election Law
- ☐ MHL Article 9.60 (Kendra's Law)
- ☐ MHL Article 10 (Sex Offender Confinement-Initial)
- ☐ MHL Article 10 (Sex Offender Confinement-Review)
- ☐ MHL Article 81 (Guardianship)
- ☐ Other Mental Hygiene:_____
  (specify)
- ☐ Other Special Proceeding:_____

STATUS OF ACTION OR PROCEEDING: Answer YES or NO for EVERY question AND enter additional information where indicated.

	YES	NO	
Has a summons and complaint or summons w/notice been filed?	☐	☐	If yes, date filed: _____/_____/_____
Has a summons and complaint or summons w/notice been served?	☐	☐	If yes, date served: _____/_____/_____
Is this action/proceeding being filed post-judgment?	☐	☐	If yes, judgment date: _____/_____/_____

NATURE OF JUDICIAL INTERVENTION: Check ONE box only AND enter additional information where indicated.

☐ Infant's Compromise
☐ Note of Issue and/or Certificate of Readiness
☐ Notice of Medical, Dental, or Podiatric Malpractice   Date Issue Joined: _____/_____/_____
☐ Notice of Motion   Relief Sought: _____   Return Date: _____/_____/_____
☐ Notice of Petition   Relief Sought: _____   Return Date: _____/_____/_____
☐ Order to Show Cause   Relief Sought: _____   Return Date: _____/_____/_____
☐ Other Ex Parte Application   Relief Sought: _____
☐ Poor Person Application
☐ Request for Preliminary Conference
☐ Residential Mortgage Foreclosure Settlement Conference
☐ Writ of Habeas Corpus
☐ Other (specify): _____

RELATED CASES: List any related actions. For Matrimonial actions, include any related criminal and/or Family Court cases.
                        If additional space is required, complete and attach the **RJI Addendum**. If none, leave blank.

Case Title	Index/Case No.	Court	Judge (if assigned)	Relationship to Instant Case

PARTIES: For parties without an attorney, check "Un-Rep" box AND enter party address, phone number and e-mail address in space provided.
               If additional space is required, complete and attach the **RJI Addendum**.

Un-Rep	Parties: List parties in caption order and indicate party role(s) (e.g. defendant; 3rd-party plaintiff).	Attorneys and/or Unrepresented Litigants: Provide attorney name, firm name, business address, phone number and e-mail address of all attorneys that have appeared in the case. For unrepresented litigants, provide address, phone number and e-mail address.	Issue Joined (Y/N):	Insurance Carrier(s):
☐	Name: Role(s):		☐ YES ☐ NO	
☐	Name: Role(s):		☐ YES ☐ NO	
☐	Name: Role(s):		☐ YES ☐ NO	
☐	Name: Role(s):		☐ YES ☐ NO	
☐	Name: Role(s):		☐ YES ☐ NO	

I AFFIRM UNDER THE PENALTY OF PERJURY THAT, TO MY KNOWLEDGE, OTHER THAN AS NOTED ABOVE, THERE ARE AND HAVE BEEN NO RELATED ACTIONS OR PROCEEDINGS, NOR HAS A REQUEST FOR JUDICIAL INTERVENTION PREVIOUSLY BEEN FILED IN THIS ACTION OR PROCEEDING.

Dated: _____/_____/_____   _____
                                                  SIGNATURE

_____   _____
ATTORNEY REGISTRATION NUMBER   PRINT OR TYPE NAME

§ 77D. The Preliminary Conference

With the adoption of the Uniform Rules in 1986, the practice of a "preliminary conference" was introduced, governed by section 202.12 of the Uniform Rules. It was at first mandatory in all but a few cases, but was found to be unnecessary or unwanted in many cases and was therefore made optional, to take place at a party's request.[1]

The Uniform Rules in fact provide for two conferences. The "preliminary conference" that we treat here is a discussion among judge and parties that takes place early, ordinarily before the filing of the note of issue (which puts the case on the trial calendar).[2] The other is the "pretrial conference,"[3] which occurs after a note of issue is filed. The function of a "pretrial" conference is to administer the finishing touches to an already prepared case before it goes to trial. The "preliminary" conference that we take up here, if it doesn't bring about a settlement of the case, is designed to get the case ready in the first place by lining it up for the customary preparatory procedures, mainly the use of the disclosure devices of Article 31 of the CPLR.[4]

Officially, the preliminary conference is an early meeting between the lawyers and judge designed to (1) simplify the issues, (2) establish a timetable for using and completing the disclosure devices, including any electronic discovery,[5] (3) add other parties, if necessary, and (4) discuss settlement and other issues the court deems appropriate.[6]

Uniform Rule 202.12(b) now requires that in litigation "reasonably likely to include electronic discovery . . . [c]ounsel shall, prior to the preliminary conference, confer with regard to any anticipated electronic discovery issues." Furthermore, the rule requires that "[w]here a case is reasonably likely to include electronic discovery . . . [c]ounsel for all parties who appear at the preliminary conference must be sufficiently versed in matters relating to their clients' technological systems to discuss competently all issues relating to electronic discovery." To satisfy this obligation, counsel may bring a client representative or outside expert to assist in e-discovery discussions. The rule contains "a non-exhaustive list of considerations for determining whether a case is reasonably likely to include electronic discovery," thereby triggering the dual requirements of conferring with opposing counsel prior to the preliminary conference and acquiring sufficient knowledge regarding the client's technological systems. The list includes such considerations as whether "potentially relevant electronically stored information ('ESI') exist[s]"; whether "any of the parties intend to seek or rely upon ESI"; whether there are "less costly or less burdensome alternatives to secure the necessary information without recourse to discovery of ESI"; whether "the cost and burden of preserving and producing ESI [is] proportionate to the amount in controversy"; and "the likelihood that discovery of ESI will aid in the resolution of the dispute."[7] Uniform Rule 202.12(c)(3) contains a

---

[1]   The preliminary conference as used in the supreme and county courts is the subject here. Other courts may have preliminary conference rules, but they are likely to be cast in general terms, with less detail. See, e.g., 22 N.Y.C.R.R. § 206.10 (court of claims) and 22 N.Y.C.R.R. § 210.10 (city courts).

[2]   The note of issue is the subject of § 369.

[3]   The pretrial conference, prescribed and governed by 22 N.Y.C.R.R. § 202.26, is discussed in § 374.

[4]   The disclosure devices are studied in §§ 343 et seq.

[5]   Electronic discovery could always be considered at the conference, but an amendment in 2009 included an express reference to it, as if by way of reminder that it's a subject worth talking about. See SPR 207:2. Electronic filing (more widely known today as e-filing), i.e., the commencement of actions through electronic means, should not be confused with electronic disclosure. See § 63A (discussing e-filing).

[6]   22 N.Y.C.R.R. § 202.12(c).

[7]   22 N.Y.C.R.R. § 202.12(b)(1).

list of "non-exhaustive" factors that can be considered in establishing the method and scope of any electronic discovery.[8]

In an attempt to avoid the time and expense of attending a preliminary conference, the parties can stipulate to a timetable governing disclosure using the form stipulation and order prescribed by OCA.[9] If the court "so orders" the stipulation, the conference is as a rule cancelled.[10] In any event, where the litigation is "reasonably likely to include electronic discovery," the parties should reduce the scope of their conference to writing so they can establish compliance with the new requirement.

Despite the uniformity at which the conference rule aims, however, what the conference turns out to be depends in large measure on the individual judge. It thus behooves each lawyer, whatever she may cull from the specific instruction of the applicable rule, to determine the practice and propensities of the assigned judge.

A request for a preliminary conference may be made by any party at any time after service of process.[11] The conference ordinarily precedes use of the disclosure devices. If nothing has occurred earlier to occasion the assignment of a judge to the case with an RJI,[12] an RJI must accompany the request for the conference.

The contents of the request are prescribed in the rule. If the request procedure is properly followed, the court orders the conference, fixes its date and time—which as a rule must be within 45 days from the time the RJI is filed[13]—and notifies the parties.

The rule adds the time-worn requirement, previously articulated only in some local provisions, that all attorneys attending the conference be "thoroughly familiar with the action and authorized to act" on the client's behalf.[14]

The making of motions after the conference is scheduled, but before it has been conducted, is discouraged. The motion "may be denied unless there is shown good cause" why relief is needed before the conference can take place.[15] The date of the preliminary conference can be advanced upon application of a party showing "special circumstances," and the court can, in its discretion, hold additional conferences.[16]

In matrimonial actions, medical malpractice actions, and, in New York City, tax certiorari proceedings, the preliminary conference is permitted only to the extent consistent with other rules that govern those things in more detail.[17]

At the conclusion of the conference, the judge is required to make a written order embodying any directions she has made at the conference.[18] If the case is not settled, and

---

[8]   For further discussion of the amendments to the Uniform Rules regarding electronic disclosure, and examination of electronic disclosure in general, see § 362; Commentary C3120:2A to McKinney's CPLR 3120.

[9]   See 22 N.Y.C.R.R. § 202.12(b).

[10]   22 N.Y.C.R.R. § 202.12(b) ("If all parties sign the form and return it to the court before the scheduled preliminary conference, such form shall be 'so ordered' by the court, and, unless the court orders otherwise, the scheduled preliminary conference shall be cancelled.").

[11]   22 N.Y.C.R.R. § 202.12(a).

[12]   This stands for Request for Judicial Intervention. See § 77B.

[13]   22 N.Y.C.R.R. § 202.12(b).

[14]   22 N.Y.C.R.R. § 202.12(b).

[15]   22 N.Y.C.R.R. § 202.12(h).

[16]   22 N.Y.C.R.R. § 202.12(g), (j).

[17]   See 22 N.Y.C.R.R. § 202.12(k).

[18]   22 N.Y.C.R.R. § 202.12(d).

disclosure directions are included in the order, the order must establish a timetable directing that disclosure proceedings be completed within 12 months "unless otherwise shortened or extended by the court."[19] The "unless" clause is needed to acknowledge unusual circumstances that may in a given case require more than the usual allotment of time.

Instead of an order, the judge's directions can be taken down by a reporter and transcribed, the parties to share the cost and the transcript to be filed by the plaintiff.[20] When a note of issue is later filed, one of the things its accompanying certificate of readiness[21] must attest to is compliance with the preliminary conference's order or transcript.[22]

A special preliminary conference, required by the addition of CPLR 3408 in 2008 and 2009[23] and implemented in Uniform Rule 202.12–a, applies in residential mortgage foreclosure actions. Born of the transactions undertaken in the troubled 2003–2008 period of subprime lending, it requires the court to conference the case within 60 days after the filing of proof of service with the clerk. The design is to get the parties and court together, hopefully generating some kind of agreement about payments that will keep the mortgagor in residence and the lender satisfied. Effective with actions commenced on or after August 30, 2013, CPLR 3408(a) was amended to require that every plaintiff in a residential foreclosure action "file proof of service within twenty days of such service, however service is made . . . ." This filing will trigger the scheduling of the CPLR 3408 mandatory settlement conference.[24]

There have been some rigorous applications of this new requirement. In one case, IndyMac Bank F.S.B. v. Yano-Horoski,[25] in which the plaintiff obstinately refused to cooperate at the CPLR 3408 conference, the court invoked its equitable powers and canceled both the mortgage and note of the plaintiff for "duplicity" and "opprobrious demeanor."[26] The judgment in *IndyMac* was reversed by the Second Department, which reinstated the judgment of foreclosure and sale along with the note and mortgage.[27] The court concluded that the "severe sanction" of cancelling the mortgage and note was not authorized by any statute or court rule.

---

[19]   22 N.Y.C.R.R. § 202.12(b). This is for "standard" cases, a word used to distinguish them from "complex" cases, which have a 15-month outer time limit. Whether a case is "complex" is determined administratively.

[20]   22 N.Y.C.R.R. § 202.12(d).

[21]   See § 370 for certificate of readiness practice.

[22]   22 N.Y.C.R.R. § 202.12(e).

[23]   CPLR 3408 is the prime CPLR involvement in this important realm, but developments in the area have been numerous, with a number of other statutes involved that can affect procedure. Some of these developments are tracked in SPR 201:3, 216:1, 217:2, 219:4, 221:1, 222:3, 227:2 and 4, 228:2, and 229:4. See Commentary on McKinney's CPLR 3408.

[24]   Hon. Mark C. Dillon, *The Newly Enacted CPLR 3408 for Easing the Mortgage Foreclosure Crisis: Very Good Steps, but not Legislatively Perfect*, 30 Pace L. Rev. 855 (2010); see § 77.

[25]   IndyMac Bank, F.S.B. v. Yano-Horoski, 26 Misc. 3d 717, 890 N.Y.S.2d 313 (Sup. Ct., Suffolk County 2009) (SPR 216:1).

[26]   A similar application was made by the same court—and judge—in Emigrant Mortg. Co. Inc. v. Corcione, 28 Misc. 3d 161, 900 N.Y.S.2d 608 (Sup. Ct., Suffolk County 2010) (SPR 221:1). The court subsequently granted a motion for reargument and renewal and vacated its prior order. Emigrant Mortgage Co. Inc. v. Corcione, 2010 WL 7014850 (Sup. Ct., Suffolk County 2010).

[27]   IndyMac Bank, F.S.B. v. Yano-Horoski, 78 A.D.3d 895, 912 N.Y.S.2d 239 (2d Dep't 2010) (SPR 227:2); see NYSLD No. 612.

§ 78.   Getting an Index Number

The filing of the initiatory papers, which commences the action,[1] also occasions the payment of the filing fee[2] and the assignment of an index number.[3]

As noted earlier, there are occasions when judicial relief is required before the action is formally commenced, such as with an application for preaction discovery,[4] or for leave to file a late notice of claim.[5] In those instances, the preaction application will usually be sought in a special proceeding that will require its own file and index number before commencement.[6] If the occasion then arises to commence the action proper—as where an application for leave to file a late notice of claim has been granted—the payment of a new fee for a new index number will be required.[7] At one time, the failure to take those steps qualified as jurisdictional and required dismissal of the action, but an amendment of CPLR 2001 converted that into a mere correctable irregularity, permitting the late payment of any fee due, as long as the proper initiatory papers are filed on time.[8]

Whoever does the initial filing, and whatever the occasion that generates it, the index number once assigned adheres to the case permanently. The party who obtains the number, almost always the plaintiff, must communicate it in writing to all other parties.[9]

If the defendant has had to pay the filing fee, as where the defendant wants to move to dismiss in a would-be action in which the plaintiff has failed to secure an index number, a statute enables the defendant to get reimbursed by the plaintiff through an application to the clerk, and even authorizes the clerk to order a dismissal of the action if the plaintiff fails to pay.[10]

§ 79.   Proof of Service

CPLR 306 governs proof of service. With service by mail under CPLR 312–a, proof of service consists of the defendant's signed acknowledgment of receipt and requires nothing more than that.[1] With other methods, proof takes the form of a certificate if service is made by a sheriff or other enforcement officer of the court. If made by some other person—as by a process server, the most common instance—that person's affidavit is proof of service.[2] The person served can admit service in writing,[3] which would then dispense with other kinds of proof, but admissions of that kind, more common for

---

[1]   See § 45. For commencement procedure in special proceedings, see §§ 550 and 553.

[2]   For the fees applicable in the supreme and county courts, see CPLR 8018(a).

[3]   In the town and village courts, service marks commencement. See § 400 in the Uniform Justice Court Act; § 45.

[4]   CPLR 3102(c); see § 352.

[5]   See § 32.

[6]   See §§ 32, 35, and 63, under the subcaption "CPLR 2001 Amendment . . . ."

[7]   See, e.g., Goldenberg v. Westchester County Health Care Corp., 16 N.Y.3d 323, 921 N.Y.S.2d 619, 946 N.E.2d 717 (2011) (NYSLD No. 617); see § 63.

[8]   See § 63.

[9]   See, e.g., 22 N.Y.C.R.R. § 202.5(a).

[10]   CPLR 306–a(b). This appears to confer on the clerk what seems a judicial power. There are several problems with this statute. See its treatment in Caption 4 of the lead note in NYSLD No. 390.

[1]   CPLR 312–a(b), 306(d).

[2]   CPLR 306(d).

[3]   CPLR 306(e).

interlocutory papers served back and forth between attorneys after the action is begun, are not common for summons service.

The certificate or affidavit specifies the papers served, the person on whom service was made, the when and how of the service,[4] and facts showing that the process server was a proper person, i.e., a hominid 18 or over and not a party.[5] It must also include a description of the person to whom the summons was delivered—including sex, color of skin and hair, approximate age, weight, and height, and other identifying features.[6] These requirements were enacted to help discourage sewer service,[7] but they can prove impracticable for even the most upright process server, who often has only the briefest glance at the person served. The defendant doesn't often invite the process server in for a cup of tea and then pose for him under a bright light. Fortunately, the courts have approached these requirements pragmatically, holding them satisfied as long as the person served proves to be the person intended. In that event, defects in proof of service are played down.[8] Other evidence can also be included in the server's affidavit to establish the identity of the person served, such as correspondence addressed to that person and seen by the process server.[9]

This approach evinces judicial sensitivity to the process server's problems. It makes defects in these regards significant only when there is doubt about the identity of the person to whom process was delivered, or, indeed, when sewer service is suspected.

When service is made under paragraph 4 of CPLR 308—the affix-and-mail provision, which requires a showing that service under paragraphs (1) and (2) could not be performed with "due diligence"—the affidavit of service must detail the "dates, addresses and the times of attempted service" under those earlier paragraphs.[10]

There is no general requirement that proof of service be filed in all cases. For a while after the 1992 adoption of the filing system for commencing actions in the supreme and county courts, there was, but it was short lived.[11] Although there's no general requirement for the filing, some of the methods of service do impose one, like paragraph 2 (the deliver-and-mail method) and paragraph 4 (the affix-and-mail method) of CPLR 308,[12] but the failure to file proof of service under those provisions is a mere correctable irregularity.[13] It may require court leave, but if the plaintiff files late without court leave and the defendant doesn't take issue with it, the filing should stand.

---

[4]   CPLR 306(a).

[5]   CPLR 2103(a); 306(a).

[6]   CPLR 306(b). In matrimonial actions, there is the additional requirement, when the defendant spouse is served directly, that the process server set forth how he knew that the person served was the defendant. Dom. Rel. Law § 232(b).

[7]   See § 71.

[8]   See Mrwik v. Mrwik, 49 A.D.2d 750, 372 N.Y.S.2d 693 (2d Dep't 1975).

[9]   Coutain v. Coutain, 76 Misc. 2d 982, 353 N.Y.S.2d 294 (Sup. Ct., Kings County 1974).

[10]   CPLR 306(c).

[11]   Under the original CPLR 306–b in the 1992 legislation, the filing of proof of service became for a while not only a jurisdictional requirement, but a rigid and malevolent one, mandating the filing of proof of service within 120 days after the filing of the summons and complaint and visiting a mandatory dismissal on the case if the deadline was missed. This got the filing of proof of service enmeshed in the commencement of the action and the follow-up of service of process. It was cured in a 1998 amendment, as noted in § 63.

[12]   See §§ 72 and 74.

[13]   Lopez v. Quickset Printers, Inc., 70 Misc. 2d 732, 334 N.Y.S.2d 808 (Sup. Ct., Nassau County 1972).

The main consequence of a late filing under these provisions is that it extends the defendant's responding time.[14] Service under paragraphs 2 or 4 of CPLR 308 is not "complete" until 10 days after the filing of proof of service, and that means that the defendant's responding time doesn't start until the expiration of that period.

There is no express requirement for the filing of proof of service when service is made by court order under paragraph 5 of CPLR 308, but the court can of course include directions on that matter in the order.

Proof of service loses its importance under these provisions if the defendant makes a timely appearance and defends without contesting jurisdiction. But it is a key item if the defendant defaults; it then becomes an indispensable part of the papers that must be filed for a default judgment.[15] It also becomes important if the defendant disputes jurisdiction. If, for example, the defendant moves to dismiss based on nonservice, the affidavit of service will be the plaintiff's chief item in opposition.

If a testimonial hearing is ordered on the issue of service, which occurs when the court is unable to resolve the issue on papers alone, there is some dispute as to whether the process server's affidavit may be taken in evidence. Some courts say that it may not; that if the dispute goes to viva voce hearing, the process server himself must be called as a witness.[16] Other courts hold that the affidavit, while not decisive, may at least be received in evidence.[17] Although in the context of a testimonial hearing an affidavit is usually unacceptable hearsay, perhaps an exception is warranted for the process server's affidavit when service is contested, at least when the server is unavailable to give testimony. A rigid rule excluding the affidavit in testimonial hearings could result in a jurisdictional dismissal whenever the defendant merely says he was not served—simply because the one who served him is not there in person to say otherwise. The problem is recognized in Denning v. Lettenty[18] where the process server died before the hearing. The court held that the affidavit makes out a prima facie case of service and that the defendant then has the burden of refuting it, which he does not do merely by saying that he did not see or find the summons.

A federal statute,[19] applicable in state as well as federal courts, requires that when the defendant defaults and the plaintiff applies for a default judgment, the plaintiff must include in the application an affidavit that the defendant, or the person of whom the defendant is a dependent, is not in military service. This is commonly known as the "military affidavit." An extensive treatment of it appears in Citibank, N.A. v. McGarvey,[20] pointing out that investigation at the time of service does not suffice; the affidavit must attest to the nonmilitary status at the time a default judgment is applied for. The court also holds, however, that the defendant who would vacate the judgment on the ground of a defective affidavit must come forward with proof that the individual involved was in fact on active duty because if he or she was not, the judgment will be

---

[14]   William Iser, Inc. v. Garnett, 46 Misc. 2d 450, 259 N.Y.S.2d 996 (Sup. Ct., Nassau County 1965).

[15]   See CPLR 3215(f), discussed in § 295.

[16]   Prudential Property and Cas. Ins. Co. v. Holtzman, 135 A.D.2d 696, 522 N.Y.S.2d 595 (2d Dep't 1987).

[17]   See, e.g., Otto v. Royal Palm Bar, 86 N.Y.S.2d 307 (App. Term, 1st Dep't 1949).

[18]   Denning v. Lettenty, 48 Misc. 2d 185, 264 N.Y.S.2d 619 (Sup. Ct., New York County 1965).

[19]   50 U.S.C.A. § 3931.

[20]   Citibank, N.A. v. McGarvey, 196 Misc. 2d 292, 765 N.Y.S.2d 163 (N.Y. City Civ. Ct. 2003).

allowed to stand. An absent or defective nonmilitary affidavit makes the judgment voidable, in other words, not void.[21]

E. THE JURISDICTIONAL BASES

Table of Sections

§ 80.   Basis for Jurisdiction; CPLR 301

§ 81.   Domicile as Basis

§ 82.   The Corporate "Presence" Doctrine

§ 83.   Comparing Corporate "Doing Business" Tests

§ 84.   "Longarm" Jurisdiction, Background

§ 85.   Longarm Jurisdiction Under CPLR 302, Generally

§ 86.   "Transacts any Business" Under CPLR 302(a)(1)

§ 86A.   "Contracts Anywhere" Under CPLR 302(a)(1)

§ 87.   "Tortious Act" Under CPLR 302(a)(2)

§ 88.   Without/Injury Within New York Under CPLR 302(a)(3)

§ 89.   Real Property Longarm Cases Under CPLR 302(a)(4)

§ 90.   Longarm Jurisdiction for Support and Other Relief Under CPLR 302(b)

§ 91.   The Restricted Appearance Under CPLR 302(c)

§ 92.   Jurisdiction Versus the Merits

§ 93.   Burden of Proving Jurisdiction

§ 94.   Overlap of Longarm Bases

§ 95.   Agency as Jurisdictional Basis

§ 96.   Attorney as Agent Under CPLR 303

§ 97.   The Nonresident Motorist Statute

§ 98.   Jurisdiction by Written Agreement

§ 99.   Continuing Jurisdiction

§ 80.   Basis for Jurisdiction; CPLR 301

Having completed treatment of the service of the summons—the "notice" aspect of due process—we can turn to the "basis" part of it.

Whenever the summons is served on the defendant outside the state, or even within the state by some substituted method (since as a general rule it is only personal delivery within the state that simultaneously serves as its own jurisdictional basis),[1] due process requires that the court have some foundation for jurisdiction. Any of several things can satisfy as a "jurisdictional basis," including the defendant's New York domicile,[2] or, in the case of a corporate defendant, its "at home" presence in New York.[3] The designation

---

[21]   See SPR 143:3; Memorandum from Fern A. Fisher, Deputy Chief Administrative Judge, New York City Courts, Civil Court of the City of New York on Non-Military Affidavits (May 27, 2010) (on file with nycourts.gov).

[1]   See § 59.

[2]   See § 81.

[3]   See § 82.

by the defendant of an agent for New York service, either express or implied, can also be a basis;[4] or the defendant's agreement to submit to New York jurisdiction in a contract.[5]

To one degree or another, all of these things were recognized as jurisdictional bases prior to the adoption of the CPLR on September 1, 1963. It is the terse but potent mission of CPLR 301 to carry forth for use under the CPLR all of those prior law bases. It says that the courts "may exercise such jurisdiction over persons, property, or status as might have been exercised heretofore." The "property" and "status" references are to rem jurisdictional bases and are met later.[6] The "persons" part accomplishes the carry-over of anything that previously supported in personam jurisdiction.

CPLR 301 having brought forward everything prior law offered as a jurisdictional basis, CPLR 302, the so-called "longarm" statute, then goes on to establish additional bases for extraterritorial jurisdiction of nondomiciliaries, not exploited under prior law. It does this so successfully that today longarm jurisdiction, in which the claim arises from an activity conducted by the defendant within the state, accounts for a substantial part of the courts' civil calendars.

A coordinate note is that whenever either CPLR 301 or 302 supplies a jurisdictional predicate, CPLR 313 immediately becomes applicable to permit summons service to be made outside New York as well as within.

All of these matters are the subject of the ensuing sections.

§ 81.   Domicile as Basis

A defendant who is a New York domiciliary is amenable to the jurisdiction of the New York courts no matter where served with process. This is a basis constitutionally recognized by the U.S. Supreme Court[1] and exploited by statute in New York. CPLR 313 subjects a New York domiciliary to service of process even outside New York on any cause of action. Of course, the fact of New York domicile will usually mean that the defendant is physically available for service within the state, but since domicile is not synonymous with residence, this is not always so. "Domicile" implies physical presence coupled with an intention to remain indefinitely, i.e., to make the state one's "home," while residence entails mere physical presence not necessarily accompanied by that intention.[2]

If the defendant is merely en route to a new domicile but has not yet reached it, the rule is that she has failed to achieve the new domicile and therefore retains the old one.[3] The key time to look to in this instance is the commencement of the action, for it's at that moment that the defendant must be shown to be a domiciliary in order for the plaintiff to exploit this basis. The question arises whether the defendant's residence in New York, without domicile, would also constitute a jurisdictional basis. The Court of Appeals said in Dobkin v. Chapman that "[r]esidence itself may provide a foundation for the exercise

---

[4]   See § 95.

[5]   See § 98.

[6]   See §§ 101 et seq. Quasi in rem jurisdiction, one of the rem categories exploited by New York extensively prior to the CPLR and for a long time after it, was vastly reduced by the U.S. Supreme Court in 1977 and thus, despite CPLR 301, is not available to the extent it was under prior law. See § 104.

[1]   Milliken v. Meyer, 311 U.S. 457, 61 S. Ct. 339, 85 L. Ed. 278, 132 A.L.R. 1357 (1940); Restatement (Second) Conflict of Laws § 29.

[2]   See Rawstorne v. Maguire, 265 N.Y. 204, 192 N.E. 294 (1934).

[3]   See Zimmerman v. Mingo, 171 A.D.2d 662, 567 N.Y.S.2d 142 (2d Dep't 1991).

of personal jurisdiction over an absent defendant by means of substituted service,"[4] but did not elaborate. If the defendant, although technically domiciled elsewhere, maintains a regular New York residence, it would not be unreasonable to conclude that he thereby establishes a relationship with New York and that the State may exploit it jurisdictionally. Perhaps that is what the *Dobkin* dictum implies. The fact is, however, that all three cases disposed of in *Dobkin* involved New York accidents and therefore had longarm bases for jurisdiction, which made dependence on other bases unnecessary.[5]

The Restatement takes the position that residence is a good jurisdictional basis "unless the individual's relationship to the state is so attenuated as to make the exercise of such jurisdiction unreasonable."[6]

§ 82.   The Corporate "Presence" Doctrine

We have seen that the oldest and easiest way to get personal jurisdiction of a natural person defendant is to deliver the summons to him personally while he is physically present in New York.[1] With the natural person, "presence" is spelled out by determining where the legs and feet are planted.

No such facile determination can be made of a corporation's presence because it is an intangible entity distinct from the humans who run it. One who happens to be a corporate director or officer or like person does not necessarily carry the corporation about with her for jurisdictional purposes. If, for example, such officer is in New York on private rather than corporate business when properly served,[2] jurisdiction of the corporation does not necessarily result. The question is not whether a corporate officer is in New York, or was properly served, but whether the corporation is present here for jurisdictional purposes.

For the purpose of comparing the corporation to the individual so as to determine whether the corporation is physically "present" in the state, decisional law invented the "doing business" test. The corporation carries on its business through its employees and agents and the "doing business" test looked at the aggregate of the activities conducted in the state on that business. If those activities were found to be conducted on a regular day-to-day basis, the corporation was deemed "present" in the state and, by analogy to the natural person, found here physically. That finding rendered the corporation amenable to the jurisdiction of the New York courts on any claim at all, whether or not related to the state.

The finding of such corporate presence in New York was one of the bases of jurisdiction carried over by CPLR 301, which meant that it invoked CPLR 313, which in turn allowed service to be made on the corporation outside the state if need be.[3] The

---

[4]   Dobkin v. Chapman, 21 N.Y.2d 490, 506, 289 N.Y.S.2d 161, 174, 236 N.E.2d 451, 460 (1968), citing Fishman v. Sanders, 15 N.Y.2d 298, 258 N.Y.S.2d 380, 206 N.E.2d 326 (1965).

[5]   The *Dobkin* trilogy of cases and the service methods used in each are treated in § 75.

[6]   Restatement (Second) Conflict of Laws § 30.

[1]   See § 66.

[2]   See § 70.

[3]   Whatever the basis of jurisdiction may be against the corporation, service on it is made in the usual way, i.e., by serving one of the individuals listed in CPLR 311(a)(1). See § 70. If the corporation is an unlicensed foreign one subject to jurisdiction in New York, Bus. Corp. Law § 307 authorizes service on the secretary of state as an alternative. In that instance the secretary is an implied-in-law agent, in contrast to his actual designation as agent for the domestic and licensed foreign corporation. See § 95.

basis here was not the nature of the claim or its New York contacts; it was the physical presence of the corporation in New York.

This basis of jurisdiction had long been recognized by the U.S. Supreme Court,[4] but its most popular and often quoted articulation was that of Judge Cardozo, writing for the New York Court of Appeals in Tauza v. Susquehanna Coal Co.:[5] "if the corporation is here, not occasionally or casually, but with a fair measure of permanence and continuity, then, whether its business is interstate or local, it is within the jurisdiction of our courts."[6] Despite its pedigree, the long line of cases applying this standard, and the fact that *Tauza* itself was cited by the United States Supreme Court several times, the doctrine has essentially been overruled and declared unconstitutional in the Supreme Court's 2014 decision in Daimler AG v. Bauman.[7] In *Daimler*, twenty-two Argentinian residents commenced an action in federal court in California against defendant, an automobile manufacturer headquartered in Germany. The complaint sought damages arising from criminal actions committed by defendant's Argentinian subsidiary outside the United States. Plaintiffs claimed general jurisdiction over defendant in California predicated on the acts of another one of its other subsidiaries, which was a major distributor of defendant's cars in California and various other states. Even though defendant's subsidiary was present in California with a fair degree of permanence and continuity, the Supreme Court held that the "Due Process Clause of the Fourteenth Amendment precludes the [California] Court from exercising jurisdiction over [defendant] in this case, given the absence of any California connection to the atrocities, perpetrators, or victims described in the complaint."[8]

There were questions in *Daimler* regarding the particulars of the parent-subsidiary relationship, but the landmark holding did not rest on them. The Court ruled that even if it were to assume that the activities of defendant's California subsidiary "are imputable to [defendant], there would still be no basis to subject [defendant] to general jurisdiction in California, for [defendant's] slim contacts with the State hardly render it at home there."[9] Relying on its 2011 decision in Goodyear Dunlop Tires Operations, S.A. v. Brown,[10] where it held that a court may assert general "all-purpose" jurisdiction over a foreign corporation to hear any claim against it only when the corporation's connections with the forum state are of such a quality "as to render [it] essentially at home in the forum State."[11]

Applying constitutional principles of due process, the *Daimler* Court stressed that "only a limited set of affiliations with a forum will render a defendant amenable to all-purpose jurisdiction there."[12] Noting that an individual is subject to general jurisdiction

---

[4]   See, e.g., International Harvester Co. of America v. Commonwealth of Kentucky, 234 U.S. 579, 34 S. Ct. 944, 58 L. Ed. 1479, 3 A.F.T.R. (P-H) P 2902 (1914). Shaffer v. Heitner, 433 U.S. 186, 97 S. Ct. 2569, 53 L. Ed. 2d 683 (1977), which banned the use of the "quasi in rem" category of jurisdiction in all but a few instances (see § 104), includes a footnote that seems designed to preserve the corporate presence doctrine as a basis of personal jurisdiction. See footnote 19 in *Shaffer*.

[5]   Tauza v. Susquehanna Coal Co., 220 N.Y. 259, 267, 115 N.E. 915, 917, 3 A.F.T.R. (P-H) P 3297 (1917).

[6]   See, e.g., Bryant v. Finnish Nat. Airline, 15 N.Y.2d 426, 260 N.Y.S.2d 625, 208 N.E.2d 439 (1965).

[7]   Daimler AG v. Bauman, 571 U.S. 117, 134 S. Ct. 746, 187 L. Ed. 2d 624 (2014) (SPR 265:1).

[8]   *Daimler*, 134 S. Ct. at 751.

[9]   *Daimler*, 134 S. Ct. at 760.

[10]   Goodyear Dunlop Tires Operations, S.A. v. Brown, 564 U.S. 915, 131 S. Ct. 2846, 180 L. Ed. 2d 796 (2011); see § 88.

[11]   *Goodyear*, 564 U.S. at 919, 131 S. Ct. at 2851.

[12]   *Daimler*, 134 S. Ct. at 760.

where she is domiciled,[13] the Court reasoned that the appropriate equivalent for a corporation is its "place of incorporation and principal place of business."[14] The Court conceded that it was not holding that these are the "*only*" two places where a corporation can be subject to general jurisdiction, but gave the *Tauza* decision the constitutional cold shoulder by concluding that a corporation is not subject to general jurisdiction "in every State in which a corporation 'engages in a substantial, continuous, and systematic course of business.' "[15] Applying this reasoning, the *Daimler* Court concluded that defendant was not "at home" in California because its subsidiary distributor was incorporated in Delaware and had its principal place of business in New Jersey.[16] The fact that defendant's subsidiary was the largest supplier of luxury vehicles to the California market, with several billions of dollars in annual sales there, could not render it subject to general jurisdiction in the Golden State. While it did not entirely rule out "the possibility that in an exceptional case . . . a corporation's operations in a forum other than its formal place of incorporation or principal place of business may be so substantial and of such a nature as to render the corporation at home in that State," defendant's "activities in California plainly d[id] not approach that level."[17] The Court's holding, which constitutes a major boon to the corporate world, essentially overrules a legion of cases on the books in New York that find general jurisdiction under the "doing business" test.

In short, the holding in *Daimler* permits a state to exercise general jurisdiction over a corporation in three instances: (1) when the corporation is incorporated in the state, (2) when the corporation has its principal place of business in the state, or (3) "in an exceptional case" where the corporation's activities in the state are "so substantial and of such a nature as to render the corporation at home in that State." There will likely be considerable litigation on whether a corporation's activities fall within the "exceptional case" category, but the facts in *Daimler* do not augur that this level of activity will often be found. The defendant's subsidiary had "multiple California-based facilities," including a regional office and car preparation center in the state and it was the largest supplier of luxury vehicles to the California market with several billions of dollars in annual sales there.[18] Despite this, it was still not "at home" in the forum state.

An "exceptional case" argument arose in Aybar v. Aybar,[19] where plaintiffs sought to obtain general jurisdiction over defendant *Goodyear* in New York. Defendant Goodyear, an Ohio corporation with its principal place of business in that state, moved to dismiss the action for lack of personal jurisdiction based on the Supreme Court's decision in *Daimler*.[20] The court denied the motion, relying on plaintiffs' unrefuted allegations that *Goodyear* had operated numerous stores in New York since approximately 1924 and employed thousands of workers who engaged in daily activities

---

[13] See § 81.

[14] *Daimler*, 134 S. Ct. at 760.

[15] *Daimler*, 134 S. Ct. at 761.

[16] *Daimler*, 134 S. Ct. at 761–62.

[17] *Daimler*, 134 S. Ct. at 761 n.19.

[18] *Daimler*, 134 S. Ct. at 752.

[19] Aybar v. Aybar, 2016 WL 3389889, *1 (Sup. Ct., Queens County 2016).

[20] The court initially ruled that CPLR 302, New York's longarm statute, could not provide a basis of personal jurisdiction over *Goodyear* because it manufactured and sold the subject tire out of state and the plaintiffs' injuries were sustained in Virginia. Aybar v. Aybar, 2016 WL 3389889, *2 (Sup. Ct., Queens County 2016).

in those stores. Based on this conduct, the *Aybar* court held that *Goodyear's* activities within New York were "so continuous and systematic that the company is essentially at home here" and therefore subject to general jurisdiction.[21] *Aybar* is the first reported decision in New York to find such an "exceptional case" and deem a foreign corporation, whose principal place of business was not in New York State, to nonetheless be "at home" here.[22] The *Aybar* court issued a separate decision denying co-defendant Ford's motion to dismiss for lack of personal jurisdiction, which was based on the same reasoning.[23]

Given the large number of corporations formed in Delaware, that state will likely see an increase in the number of actions commenced there in the wake of *Daimler*. What about the company that is incorporated in Delaware, but then obtains a license to do business in New York? In *Daimler*, there was no mention of whether the defendant or its subsidiary was licensed to do business in California, nor whether that would have affected the outcome. That issue is explored in further detail below.[24]

The plaintiffs in *Daimler* were all Argentinian residents and their claims arose from events that occurred not only outside California, but entirely outside the United States. Yet, the Court's holding will likely have a significant impact on New York residents who sue at home for claims arising in other states. For example, take a New York resident plaintiff who is injured after falling on defendant hotel's property in Florida, where the hotel chain has its principal place of business. Now assume the hotel chain also operates ten properties in New York and is incorporated in Delaware. Unless a New York court concludes that this is "in an exceptional case" where the corporation's activities in the state are "so substantial and of such a nature as to render the corporation at home" here, a motion to dismiss for lack of personal jurisdiction will likely succeed.[25]

If the above prediction proves to be correct, it constitutes a radical departure from notions of personal jurisdiction over a corporation as they existed for almost 100 years prior to *Daimler*, and there are likely many pending actions in New York state courts where jurisdiction is based on a similar set of facts.[26] There can be no question that the defendant hotel corporation in the above hypothetical is engaged in a substantial, continuous, and systematic course of business in New York, yet that is not enough to establish general jurisdiction over the corporation in the wake of *Daimler*. Moreover, the plaintiff's residence or domicile in New York, standing alone, has little or no bearing in determining whether a corporation is subject to general jurisdiction in New York.[27] CPLR 302, New York's longarm statute, might provide a basis of specific jurisdiction if, for example, plaintiff can establish that the claim arose out of a transaction of business within the state.[28] That would be doubtful in most cases, and likely impossible in a situation in which plaintiff was merely visiting a guest at defendant's hotel in Florida.

---

[21] Aybar v. Aybar, 2016 WL 3389889, *3 (Sup. Ct., Queens County 2016).

[22] The court also found an additional basis for personal jurisdiction over *Goodyear*, deeming it to have consented to general jurisdiction in New York by obtaining a license to do business here and designating the secretary of state as its agent for service of process. *Aybar*, at *3; see also § 95.

[23] Aybar v. Aybar, 2016 WL 3389890, *4 (Sup. Ct., Queens County 2016).

[24] See § 95.

[25] *Daimler*, 134 S. Ct. at 761 n.19.

[26] See §§ 111, 266 (discussing defendant's avenues for raising the issue).

[27] See Walden v. Fiore, 134 S. Ct. 1115, 1122, 188 L. Ed. 2d 12 (2014) ("Put simply, however significant the plaintiff's contacts with the forum may be, those contacts cannot be 'decisive in determining whether the defendant's due process rights are violated.' ").

[28] See CPLR 302(a)(1); §§ 84 to 86.

What remains for the plaintiff in this scenario? She can take the long trip back to Florida to institute the action or possibly a shorter trip to Delaware on Amtrak to commence the suit where the hotel is incorporated. As noted above, if the hotel has obtained a license to do business in New York, that may provide another possibility for securing general jurisdiction in New York, but there is no certainty on that front.

The *Daimler* court observed that "specific jurisdiction [a.k.a. longarm jurisdiction] has become the centerpiece of modern jurisdiction theory, while general jurisdiction [has played] a reduced role."[29] There can be no question that general jurisdiction will play an even more decreased role in litigation against corporations after this momentous decision.[30]

A further dimension to determining if a corporation is "at home" in New York State is added when it is alleged that Corporation X, while acting for Corporation D in New York, is doing so as an independent agent. As noted above, this issue was essentially avoided in *Daimler* because the Court reached its conclusions about general jurisdiction while assuming that all of the activities of defendant's California subsidiary were imputable to the defendant for purposes of the inquiry.[31] If truly independent—a money making entity in its own right even though the money comes from acting as an agent for other corporations—D would not be subject to New York jurisdiction based on X's activities.

But if it can be shown that X is acting not as an independent entity, but in effect as a mere employee or department of D, D can be held within jurisdiction based on X's presence in the state. Assume that X Corporation, for example, is concededly incorporated in New York or has its principal place of business here. It is alleged that X is acting for D, and that under the law of agency X's New York presence on behalf of D constitutes D being present in the state. This is indeed a possibility. Some major New York cases involve that situation, further complicated (or facilitated?) by interlocking ownership or directorship.

The rules that govern these inquiries are essentially rules of agency. One corporation can be acting as another's agent so pervasively as to constitute the principal "present" in New York even though ownership and directorship of the two corporations is entirely separate. As a result of the Court of Appeals decisions in Taca Intern. Airlines, S. A. v. Rolls-Royce of England, Limited,[32] and Frummer v. Hilton Hotels Intern., Inc.,[33] however, the fact of interlocking ownership has taken on an influential role.

In *Taca*, the corporation that the plaintiff wanted to get at was E, the parent Rolls-Royce corporation, an English company. E owned all the stock of C, the Canadian Rolls Royce corporation, which in turn owned all the stock of N, a Delaware corporation licensed to do business and concededly present in New York. It was alleged that E was doing regular business in New York through N. It was shown that there were some

---

[29] *Daimler*, 134 S. Ct. at 755.

[30] For further discussion of *Daimler*, see Patrick M. Connors, *Impact of Supreme Court Decisions on New York Practice [Part I]*, N.Y.L.J., June 18, 2014, at 116 and Patrick M. Connors, *Impact of Recent U.S. Supreme Court Decisions on New York Practice [Part II]*, N.Y.L.J., July 21, 2014, at 13.

[31] *Daimler*, 134 S. Ct. at 760.

[32] Taca Intern. Airlines, S. A. v. Rolls-Royce of England, Limited, 15 N.Y.2d 97, 256 N.Y.S.2d 129, 204 N.E.2d 329 (1965).

[33] Frummer v. Hilton Hotels Intern., Inc., 19 N.Y.2d 533, 281 N.Y.S.2d 41, 227 N.E.2d 851 (1967), cert. denied 389 U.S. 923, 88 S. Ct. 241 (1967).

directors in common; that the business of N was solely to sell E's products; that the employees of N got their training from E in England; that it was E's warranties that accompanied N's sales of E's cars but that N performed on E's engines the requirements of those warranties; that key employees were exchanged both ways between N and E; and that all of N's income went to C and appeared on C's balance sheet and ultimately on E's. These and yet other factors suggested agency. The question was whether N was an independent entity or a mere department of E. The court held that N, for all the facade of separateness, was at root a mere department, and that E was therefore present in New York through N's activities in the state.

In *Frummer*, which involved the Hilton Hotel chain, the corporations seem to have maintained an even more punctilious separateness, but the interlocking ownership was apparent, and complex. The defendant was L, the London Hilton, an English corporation. Clearly present in New York was R, the Hilton Reservation Service. A different foreign corporation in the Hilton setup owned L and, together with still another one, owned R. R took and confirmed reservations in New York for L and other hotels in and out of the Hilton chain. Jurisdiction was sustained on a 4–3 vote, the majority finding that R was doing all the business in New York that L "could do were it here by its own officials."[34] The dissent took issue, finding that the majority was sustaining jurisdiction "over a foreign corporation simply because of its relationship with subsidiary or affiliated corporations."[35]

Perhaps the meat of the *Frummer* decision is in the general aura created by the fact of interlocking ownership. The question of the New York presence of the parent through the local activities of its subsidiary will turn on rules of agency, suggests the majority, "and the fact that the two are commonly owned is significant only because it gives rise to a valid inference as to the broad scope of the agency."[36] In other words, New York adheres to principles of agency, but once agency is indicated by the facts, the additional fact of the parent-subsidiary relationship can intervene to stretch the agency into an outright parental "presence." It is instructive to distinguish yet another case in which a local entity took reservations for hotels outside New York. In Miller v. Surf Properties, Inc.,[37] the local service in New York took reservations for Florida hotels, but that did not result in the hotels' corporate presence in New York. A major distinction is that the reservation service in *Miller* was an independently owned profit-making organization, which enabled the court to regard it as an independent contractor. In *Frummer* the reservation service was not independently owned and was not a profit-maker; the majority concluded that it was run just for the benefit of the Hilton chain.

We can apply these principles instructively to two other major international corporations, the German Volkswagen Corporation and the Japanese Toyota Corporation. Volkswagen escaped New York "presence" jurisdiction in Delagi v.

---

[34] *Frummer*, 19 N.Y.2d at 537, 281 N.Y.S.2d at 44, 227 N.E.2d at 854. This statement in *Frummer* had impact on the later case of Gelfand v. Tanner Motor Tours, Limited, 385 F.2d 116 (2d Cir. 1967), cert. denied 390 U.S. 996, 88 S. Ct. 1198 (1968), in which the corporation was held to be doing business in New York through an entirely independent representative because it would otherwise have had to go to New York to perform the service for itself. The service was the taking of reservations for the defendant's sightseeing bus business and the court stressed the large number of bookings that originated in New York and the high percentage of the defendant's overall tour business generated in New York.

[35] *Frummer*, 19 N.Y.2d at 540, 281 N.Y.S.2d at 46, 227 N.E.2d at 855 (Breitel, J., dissenting).

[36] *Frummer*, 19 N.Y.2d at 538, 281 N.Y.S.2d at 45, 227 N.E.2d at 854.

[37] Miller v. Surf Properties, Inc., 4 N.Y.2d 475, 176 N.Y.S.2d 318, 151 N.E.2d 874 (1958).

Volkswagenwerk A.G. of Wolfsburg, Germany.[38] It owned all the stock of the New Jersey corporation that imported Volkswagens into this country, but the cars got into New York through a franchisee owned by American investors independent of the German and New Jersey companies. The franchisee picked the cars up at various delivery points, none of them in New York. Various devices by which the German corporation exercised ultimate control over the activities of the New York franchisee were shown, but these did not confer jurisdiction. The Court of Appeals said that it "has never held a foreign corporation present on the basis of control, unless there was in existence at least a parent-subsidiary relationship."[39]

That statement appears to confirm what the dissent contended in *Frummer*: that the interlocking aspect of ownership was being given a decisive role jurisdictionally. Indeed, it was the failure of the Japanese Toyota Corporation to mind these Ps and Qs that resulted in their being held to a New York presence in Sunrise Toyota, Ltd. v. Toyota Motor Co.:[40] the California corporation doing business in New York was wholly owned by the Japanese parents.

Prior to the Supreme Court's decision in *Daimler*, it may have come as a surprise to learn that a company like the German Volkswagen Corporation, despite its thousands of cars on the New York highways, is not "present" in the state. But the "mere sales of a manufacturer's product in New York," said the court in *Volkswagen*, "however substantial, have never made the foreign corporation manufacturer amenable to suit in this jurisdiction."[41] In the wake of *Daimler*, the plaintiff will not only need to establish a sufficient agency relationship under the above caselaw but also that the corporate agent in New York is "at home" here so that it is subject to general jurisdiction. That essentially means that the plaintiff must establish that the agent is incorporated in New York or has its principal place of business here. Although, as discussed above, the *Daimler* Court assumed that all of the activities of defendant's California subsidiary were imputable to the defendant for purposes of its jurisdictional inquiry, it did issue some dicta that is sure to draw attention in future cases. The Court observed that the "subsidiary . . . might be its parent's agent for claims arising in the place where the subsidiary operates, yet not its agent regarding claims arising elsewhere."[42] That would indicate that the test for establishing that the parent is subject to general jurisdiction in New York based on the acts of its subsidiary requires significantly more than simply establishing a parent-subsidiary relationship. The above discussion, and the upheaval that *Daimler* brought to an already unpredictable area of the law, render it very difficult for the lawyer to provide advice to plaintiffs and defendants alike. There are, however, a few points of relative certainty.

First, a need to measure whether a corporation is "at home" "in New York is confronted only when the cause of action itself has no New York roots. If it does have such a connection, the case gets longarm jurisdiction under CPLR 302 and does not need any corporate "presence" help from CPLR 301.[43] In *Taca*, for example, the suit was for

---

[38]   Delagi v. Volkswagenwerk A.G. of Wolfsburg, Germany, 29 N.Y.2d 426, 328 N.Y.S.2d 653, 278 N.E.2d 895 (1972).

[39]   *Delagi*, 29 N.Y.2d at 432, 328 N.Y.S.2d at 657, 278 N.E.2d at 897; see Birnbaum, *1972 Survey of New York Law, Civil Practice*, 24 Syracuse L. Rev. 447, 457–58 (1973).

[40]   Sunrise Toyota, Ltd. v. Toyota Motor Co., 55 F.R.D. 519, 16 Fed. R. Serv. 2d 539 (S.D.N.Y. 1972).

[41]   *Delagi*, 29 N.Y.2d at 433, 328 N.Y.S.2d at 657, 278 N.E.2d at 898.

[42]   *Daimler*, 134 S. Ct. at 759.

[43]   See §§ 84 to 90.

Nicaraguan property damage; in *Frummer*, for an injury in London; in *Delagi*, for an accident in Germany. Had those occurrences taken place in New York, CPLR 302 would likely have given jurisdiction and made a *Daimler* "at home" inquiry unnecessary.

Second, even if the claim has no CPLR 302 contacts and something else is needed as a basis for personal jurisdiction of a corporate defendant, that basis automatically appears if the corporation is incorporated in New York State or has its principal place of business here.[44] Whether a foreign corporation incorporated in Delaware, for example, that obtains a license to do business in New York is "at home" in New York is a hotly debated issue after *Daimler*. Prior to *Daimler*, there was a general understanding that this application, which requires the corporation to designate the secretary of state as its agent for service of process,[45] was enough to support jurisdiction no matter where the claim arose. The act of obtaining the license to do business in New York amounted to a consent to general jurisdiction in New York and service could be made in that instance on the secretary of state[46] or, as an alternative, on any of the corporate agents listed in CPLR 311(a)(1).[47]

The need to use what was formerly known as the "presence" doctrine, and is now properly labelled the "at home" doctrine after *Daimler*, arises only when (1) the defendant is not incorporated in New York and does not have its principal place of business here, and (2) the cause of action does not arise out of an activity conducted in New York.

While designed historically to determine the amenability of a corporation to general jurisdiction in New York, it had been held that the "doing business" test extended also to a nondomiciliary individual working in New York, permitting extrastate service on the individual although the claim does not arise out of New York activities.[48] The doing business test was also extended to nondomiciliary individuals in language to suggest that it can also be used against foreign partnerships and associations.[49] When so applied, it enabled any claim to be asserted against the defendant, whether or not the claim arose out of the business conducted in New York. The extent to which this assertion of general jurisdiction survives after the Supreme Court's holding in *Daimler* has yet to be determined. In any event, the test is an alternative; jurisdiction can still rest, instead, on local service on an individual, such as a partner or on the association's president or treasurer, who carry around the partnership or association for purposes of obtaining jurisdictional basis.[50]

§ 83. Comparing Corporate "Doing Business" Tests

The former "doing business" test examined in the prior section was used to determine whether a corporation was amenable to New York jurisdiction. As discussed

---

[44]   *Daimler*, 134 S. Ct. at 760.

[45]   Bus. Corp. Law § 304.

[46]   Bus. Corp. Law § 306(b).

[47]   See § 70.

[48]   See FCNB Spiegel Inc. v. Dimmick, 163 Misc. 2d 152, 619 N.Y.S.2d 935 (N.Y. City Civ. Ct. 1994), citing ABKCO Industries, Inc. v. Lennon, 52 A.D.2d 435, 384 N.Y.S.2d 781 (1st Dep't 1976), treated in § 83.

[49]   See ABKCO Industries, Inc. v. Lennon, 52 A.D.2d 435, 384 N.Y.S.2d 781 (1st Dep't 1976).

[50]   See § 69.

above, the test was declared unconstitutional by the Supreme Court in its 2014 decision in Daimler AG v. Bauman.[1]

We have also met two other corporate "doing business" tests, and they likely survive the carnage caused by *Daimler*. One arises under section 1314(b)(5) of the Business Corporation Law, a provision that requires a showing in certain cases that a defendant corporation is doing business in New York before the court is authorized to entertain the case. We can call this one the BCL 1314 test.[2]

The third arises under section 1312 of the Business Corporation Law, which precludes a plaintiff foreign corporation from maintaining a New York action if it is doing business in New York without having duly licensed itself to do so.[3] We will refer to this one as the BCL 1312 test.

Are these tests the same? As a practical matter they ought to be. One should be able to take all of the cases just reviewed under the former doing business test and apply them under the other provisions as well. It seems idle to go through this exercise afresh for the other provisions, using different tests, especially because there is no convincing evidence that the policies underlying the three tests substantially diverge. But while the former doing business and BCL 1314 tests were said by caselaw to be the same,[4] the doing business and BCL 1312 tests were said by caselaw to differ.[5] The extent of the difference is not clear, but more appears to be demanded for the BCL 1312 test because of its penal effect in precluding suit by a foreign corporation.

Section 1301(b) of the Business Corporation Law lists certain corporate activities and provides that these by themselves shall not constitute "doing business" for BCL purposes, and this applies to both the 1312 and 1314 tests. The activities listed include bringing or defending a proceeding, holding directors' or shareholders' meetings, maintaining bank accounts, or maintaining offices or agencies for securities activities. Doing only those things does not establish a corporate presence.

By listing activities that may not alone be taken to satisfy the 1312 or 1314 doing business tests, however, BCL 1301 evinces an intention that whatever tests do apply to those provisions should be the same. If that is so—and caselaw has yet to meet this matter full face—then the BCL 1314 test has the unique distinction of being the same as two other tests that differ. This suggests that the three tests are all the same or that someone has had too much wine.

---

[1]   Daimler AG v. Bauman, 571 U.S. 117, 134 S. Ct. 746, 187 L. Ed. 2d 624 (2014) (SPR 265:1).

[2]   See § 29.

[3]   See § 30.

[4]   Fremay, Inc. v. Modern Plastic Machinery Corp., 15 A.D.2d 235, 222 N.Y.S.2d 694 (1st Dep't 1961); see also Simonson v. International Bank, 16 A.D.2d 55, 225 N.Y.S.2d 392 (1st Dep't 1962), aff'd with opinion, 14 N.Y.2d 281, 251 N.Y.S.2d 433, 200 N.E.2d 427 (1964).

[5]   Beja v. Jahangiri, 453 F.2d 959 (2d Cir. 1972); William L. Bonnell Co. v. Katz, 23 Misc. 2d 1028, 196 N.Y.S.2d 763 (Sup. Ct., New York County 1960). The difference is rooted in fears for the constitutionality of Bus. Corp. Law § 1312's predecessors and has to do with possible interference with interstate commerce, at least as that prospect was perceived in an earlier era. See International Text-Book Co. v. Tone, 220 N.Y. 313, 115 N.E. 914, 3 A.F.T.R. (P-H) P 3296 (1917).

§ 84.   "Longarm" Jurisdiction, Background

In 1945, in the landmark case of International Shoe Co. v. Washington,[1] the U.S. Supreme Court said that if the claims sued on "arise out of or are connected with . . . activities within the state," the State can exercise personal jurisdiction of the defendant in respect of those claims no matter where the defendant is served with process. This came to be known as "longarm" jurisdiction. It allows the State to exercise extraterritorial jurisdiction of a nondomiciliary defendant based on contacts the defendant had with the state if—and this is the key "longarm" factor—the claim arises out of those contacts. Operations within the state, if the claim is a product of those very operations, "make it reasonable and just according to our traditional conception of fair play and substantial justice" to subject the one conducting those operations to extraterritorial jurisdiction.[2]

Even cases prior to *International Shoe* had begun to escape the strictures of the celebrated Pennoyer v. Neff of 1877,[3] which regarded personal jurisdiction as permissible only when the defendant is personally served within the state. The nonresident motorist statutes, for example, under which an implied designation of a state official as an agent for service automatically results if a claim arises from in-state driving,[4] were sustained as constitutional.[5] But those and like statutes still paid lip service to *Pennoyer* by regarding the within-the-state service on the state official as the jurisdiction-getting act. In 1940, however, outright extrastate service, with personam effect, was sustained in Milliken v. Meyer[6] on the basis that the defendant was a domiciliary of the forum.

The facts of *International Shoe* show that the State in that case was still looking for a local "agent" on which to effect service, but as a matter of historical perspective, it is nonetheless the *International Shoe* case that takes the credit for renouncing *Pennoyer* and allowing the states to extend their summons beyond their borders, as long as it is limited to instances in which the claim arises from those "minimum contacts" a defendant must have with the forum in order to satisfy due process.

It is the Due Process Clause of the 14th Amendment that oversees exercises of State jurisdiction, and it is the U.S. Supreme Court that oversees the clause, thus accounting for that court's key role in the area of longarm jurisdiction. The court in *International Shoe* indicates that whether there is longarm jurisdiction in any given case is a sui generis inquiry:

> Whether due process is satisfied must depend rather upon the quality and nature of the activity in relation to the fair and orderly administration of the laws which it was the purpose of the due process clause to insure.[7]

---

[1]   International Shoe Co. v. State of Wash., Office of Unemployment Compensation and Placement, 326 U.S. 310, 66 S. Ct. 154, 90 L. Ed. 95, 161 A.L.R. 1057 (1945).

[2]   *International Shoe*, 326 U.S. at 320, 66 S. Ct. at 160. The *International Shoe* facts suggest that the activities of the defendant corporation in the state might have been regular enough to constitute a corporate "presence" under the former doing-business test, which would have allowed jurisdiction against it on any claim (see § 82), but the court took it as the occasion to pronounce the elements of the "longarm" category of jurisdiction, and it is that category for which *International Shoe* stands as the major historical precedent.

[3]   Pennoyer v. Neff, 95 U.S. 714, 24 L. Ed. 565, 1877 WL 18188 (1877).

[4]   Veh. & Traf. Law § 253. See § 97.

[5]   Hess v. Pawloski, 274 U.S. 352, 47 S. Ct. 632, 71 L. Ed. 1091 (1927).

[6]   Milliken v. Meyer, 311 U.S. 457, 61 S. Ct. 339, 85 L. Ed. 278, 132 A.L.R. 1357 (1940).

[7]   *International Shoe Co.*, 326 U.S. at 319, 66 S.Ct. at 160.

For a while there wasn't much guidance from the Supreme Court, especially in tort cases. *International Shoe* of 1945 involved the collection of state taxes. The next U.S. Supreme Court address to longarm jurisdiction was in 1957 in McGee v. International Life Ins. Co.,[8] an action on an insurance policy. And a year later, in 1958, came Hanson v. Denckla,[9] a complicated wills-trust case.[10] Those three cases were all the Supreme Court had to say about longarm jurisdiction until 1980—a 35-year period as measured from *International Shoe's* 1945 beginning—and not one was a tort case. For all the hundreds and perhaps thousands of longarm tort cases in the interim, from both state and federal courts, it was not until 1980, in World-Wide Volkswagen Corp. v. Woodson,[11] that the tort case was addressed, and with more restrictive notions about how far a state may go than had been assumed under some state statutes, including New York's.[12]

It is by statute or rule that longarm jurisdiction is exploited. Some states responded to *International Shoe's* invitation more quickly than others, and some limited their longarm statutes to specific activities while others went all the way by enacting a general statute authorizing jurisdiction whenever it would be compatible with due process.[13] Illinois was one of the quicker responders but chose to restrict its longarm jurisdiction to claims arising out of designated activities.[14] New York didn't get around to general longarm jurisdiction until September 1, 1963, when the CPLR took effect. It contained New York's first general longarm statute, CPLR 302, which was originally modeled on the Illinois statute.[15]

CPLR 302 does not go as far as due process permits. It delineates only certain categories. But although these don't go all the way,[16] they go far, as will be seen.

"Longarm" and like categories, in which jurisdiction is predicated not on the defendant's regular presence in the state but on the claim's arising out of some in-state event for which the defendant is responsible, is sometimes called "specific jurisdiction," with the term "general jurisdiction" used to describe the "presence" category, which supports jurisdiction of all claims against the defendant, related or not to the state.[17]

---

[8]   McGee v. International Life Ins. Co., 355 U.S. 220, 78 S. Ct. 199, 2 L. Ed. 2d 223 (1957).

[9]   Hanson v. Denckla, 357 U.S. 235, 78 S. Ct. 1228, 2 L. Ed. 2d 1283 (1958).

[10]   In *Hanson*, Florida tried to exercise personal jurisdiction over Delaware trustees and over property in Delaware on the basis that if the transactions which sent the property to Delaware were stricken down the property would revert to a Florida estate. Jurisdiction was rejected. The court noted the liberal trend set by the *McGee* case of the prior year but added that "it is a mistake to assume that this trend heralds the eventual demise of all restrictions on the personal jurisdiction of state courts."

[11]   World-Wide Volkswagen Corp. v. Woodson, 444 U.S. 286, 100 S. Ct. 559, 62 L. Ed. 2d 490 (1980).

[12]   This matter is elaborated in § 88, in treating one of New York's longarm tort provisions.

[13]   E.g., Cal. Code Civ. Proc. § 410.10: "A court of this state may exercise jurisdiction on any basis not inconsistent with the Constitution of this state or of the United States."

[14]   Ill. Ann. Stat., ch. 735, § 5/2–209.

[15]   See 2d Rep. Leg. Doc. No. 13, p. 39 (1958).

[16]   New York does have one of those all-the-way longarm statutes, but it's applicable only in the surrogate's court. See SCPA 210.

[17]   See Daimler AG v. Bauman, 571 U.S. 117, 134 S. Ct. 746, 754–58, 187 L. Ed. 2d 624 (2014); Burger King Corp. v. Rudzewicz, 471 U.S. 462, 105 S. Ct. 2174, 85 L. Ed. 2d 528 (1985). The "general jurisdiction" phrase juxtaposed here with "specific jurisdiction" operates in the area of personal jurisdiction and should not be confused with that other realm in which "general jurisdiction" is paired with "limited jurisdiction" in categorizing the subject matter jurisdiction of the courts. On the latter, see § 8.

§ 85.   Longarm Jurisdiction Under CPLR 302, Generally

CPLR 302(a) opens with the language that "[a]s to a cause of action arising from any of the acts enumerated in this section, a court may exercise personal jurisdiction over any nondomiciliary, or his executor or administrator, who in person or through an agent" does any of the things listed. Before turning to seriatim treatment of the listed activities, several general observations should be made about the statute.

CPLR 302(a) is applicable to all categories of defendants. It speaks of a "nondomiciliary," but that includes a corporation, association, partnership, trustee of a trust—any entity or creature capable of being made a defendant in a lawsuit—as well as a natural person. And it applies whether the listed activities were carried on by the defendant in person or through an agent.

If the would-be CPLR 302 defendant dies before the action is commenced, it may be commenced against his personal representative, who is just as amenable to jurisdiction in a longarm case as the decedent himself would have been.[1] And if a duly served CPLR 302 defendant dies during the lawsuit, his foreign personal representative need only be substituted in his place. This requires no new action; it entails only that the representative be served with the papers that bring on the motion to substitute,[2] and those papers are servable outside New York with personam effect under CPLR 302(a) and 313.[3]

Longarm jurisdiction under CPLR 302 is available in the federal courts in New York; state extraterritorial bases of personal jurisdiction have been adopted by the Federal Rules of Civil Procedure without regard to the basis on which federal subject matter jurisdiction may rest (diversity of citizenship, federal question, etc.).[4] Some of the state's lower courts have their own longarm statutes and these, when applicable, permit service outside the area serviced by the particular court just as CPLR 302 and 313 dispense with state lines in the supreme court.[5]

Longarm jurisdiction is usable against any person sought to be made a party to an action in any procedural mode. It can be used in third-party practice, for example,[6] such as by D when impleading X for contribution or indemnification in respect of the claim on which P is suing D, as long as local contacts are demonstrated in respect of the third-party claim itself. The court does not get extraterritorial jurisdiction of the alleged indemnitor (X in the example) merely because it has jurisdiction of the party claiming indemnification (D in the example).[7]

---

[1]   Such a rule had earlier been applied and constitutionally sustained under the nonresident motorist statute, (now) Veh. & Traf. Law § 253, in Leighton v. Roper, 300 N.Y. 434, 91 N.E.2d 876, 18 A.L.R.2d 537 (1950).

[2]   CPLR 1015 authorizes the substitution in case of death and CPLR 1021 supplies the procedure, which is a mere motion.

[3]   See Rosenfeld v. Hotel Corp. of America, 20 N.Y.2d 25, 281 N.Y.S.2d 308, 228 N.E.2d 374 (1967), which also sustains the constitutionality of CPLR 302 and 313 in this respect.

[4]   Fed. R. Civ. P. 4(k)(1)(A). See § 626 (Practitioner's Edition).

[5]   See § 404 in the New York City Civ. Ct. Act, and in the Uniform Dist. Ct. Act and Uniform City Ct. Act, McKinney's Vol. 29A, Part 3.

[6]   Moss v. Frost Hempstead Corp., 43 Misc. 2d 357, 251 N.Y.S.2d 194 (Sup. Ct., Nassau County 1964). Third-party practice is treated in §§ 155 et seq.

[7]   See Asahi Metal Industry Co., Ltd. v. Superior Court of California, Solano County, 480 U.S. 102, 107 S. Ct. 1026, 94 L. Ed. 2d 92 (1987); Media Corp. of America v. Motif Mfg. Co., Inc., 524 F. Supp. 86 (S.D.N.Y.

The statute is also available against one who was a domiciliary at the time of the alleged CPLR 302 acts. In several cases it appeared that the defendant had moved from New York after the acts but before suit. He then ingeniously alleged that he could not be amenable to jurisdiction under CPLR 302(a) because it applies only to nondomiciliaries; and that he could not be subjected to extrastate service as a domiciliary because that requires domicile at the time of suit and by that time he had left the state. A few lower court judges bought the argument but the Court of Appeals finally held that there is no such "gap" in jurisdiction and that CPLR 302(a) may also be applied to defendants domiciled here at the time of the acts.[8]

While a nondomiciliary or nonresident plaintiff may use CPLR 302—it is not restricted to the use of New York plaintiffs—the doctrine of forum non conveniens[9] can of course intervene to dismiss the case if, notwithstanding jurisdiction, New York involvement is too tenuous to impose the case on the New York courts.

Note that CPLR 302(a) does not require that the cause of action arise in New York. It requires only that it arise "from" the acts listed in the section. The claim can therefore arise elsewhere and still give New York jurisdiction as long as there are adequate New York acts "from" which it arises, as will be seen in ensuing sections.

§ 86. "Transacts Any Business" Under CPLR 302(a)(1)

If the defendant transacts business in New York and the claim arises from it, jurisdiction is conferred by the first clause of CPLR 302(a)(1), "transacts any business within the state,"[1] and the defendant is subject to service outside New York under CPLR 313. Stated otherwise, a plaintiff relying on longarm jurisdiction under the first clause in CPLR 302(a)(1) must establish two elements: (1) the defendant transacted business within the state, and (2) the cause of action arose from that transaction of business.[2] If either element is not met, jurisdiction cannot be conferred under CPLR 302(a)(1).

This provision is invoked regularly; the question is invariably whether what the defendant did in New York constitutes a sufficient "transaction" to satisfy the statute. The inquiry is sui generis, the annotations on CPLR 302(a)(1) numerous; the lawyer bent on securing longarm jurisdiction should consult them straightaway. The cases are so plentiful that despite extensive factual variations, the lawyer will often find a case fairly close to her own. Our mission is to set forth illustrative cases, especially from the appellate courts, to establish the general principles and to illustrate a few of the more common situations.

The leading cases, as might be expected, are for the most part the early ones. Among the first from the New York Court of Appeals was Longines-Wittnauer Watch Co. v.

1981). The latter case is discussed in the lead note in NYSLD No. 269, including how the indemnitee might try to protect itself.

[8]   State v. Davies, 24 A.D.2d 240, 265 N.Y.S.2d 358 (3d Dep't 1965), appeal granted order amended, 25 A.D.2d 690, 268 N.Y.S.2d 927 (3d Dep't 1966) and aff'd, 18 N.Y.2d 950, 277 N.Y.S.2d 146, 223 N.E.2d 570 (1966). The same rule applies to a foreign corporation that was "present" at the time of the acts but left the state afterwards. Sharp Export Limited v. Mulco Products, Inc., 50 Misc. 2d 611, 270 N.Y.S.2d 787 (Sup. Ct., Nassau County 1966).

[9]   See §§ 28 and 29.

[1]   The "contracts anywhere" clause, the second segment of CPLR 302(a)(1), is separately treated in § 86A.

[2]   See, e.g., Johnson v. Ward, 4 N.Y.3d 516, 519, 797 N.Y.S.2d 33, 34, 829 N.E.2d 1201, 1202 (2005) (SPR 154:3).

Barnes & Reinecke, Inc.,[3] in which D was a foreign corporation with its principal place of business in Illinois. P was a New York corporation that bought $118,000 worth of complicated machinery from D, which D shipped f.o.b. Chicago. Some preliminary negotiations had taken place in New York but the original contract was executed in Chicago. Most significantly, D sent several of its employees, including two engineers, into New York for several months to help install the machinery. When P later sued D for breach of warranty, jurisdiction under CPLR 302(a)(1) was sustained. The court would not determine whether any particular one of the New York contacts sufficed; it indicated that the test is not quantitative but qualitative and that the inquiry should determine whether "defendant has engaged in some purposeful activity in this State in connection with the matter in suit."[4] In *Longines*, defendant did engage in such purposeful activity and was subject to longarm jurisdiction. The case also clarifies that for a contract action to be sustainable under CPLR 302(a)(1), the contract need not necessarily have been made in New York.

A case in which longarm jurisdiction was shortly afterwards rejected is Kramer v. Vogl.[5] There D was an Austrian leather manufacturer which, by an agreement made in Europe, made P its exclusive American distributor. All of D's contacts with P in New York were by mail. P bought the leather from D outright and it was shipped f.o.b. European ports.[6] P sued D for fraud, alleging that D gave distribution rights to others in violation of the agreement. The court held that D had not transacted any business in New York. Selling and sending goods into New York pursuant to orders sent from New York does not by itself give longarm jurisdiction.

Longines and *Kramer* sometimes act as poles between which yet other cases are set to see which one the new case will gravitate towards. McKee Elec. Co. v. Rauland-Borg Corp.[7] was such a case. D manufactured sound equipment in Illinois and shipped it f.o.b. Chicago to P in New York. P was one of D's distributors and the distribution contract was made in New York. The goods proved defective and P sustained losses for which it now sued D in breach of contract and conspiracy. The case thus far seems much like *Kramer*. But when difficulties arose, D sent one of its employees, a trouble-shooter, into New York to confer with P. He did so for about a day. Although that tended to push the case closer to *Longines*, a majority of the Court held that it did not push hard enough and that this contact was "so infinitesimal" as to make no difference. *Kramer* governed, and jurisdiction was turned down.

One reconciliation is that the crew sent into New York in *Longines* was indispensable to the agreement; if there were not a commitment to send them, no agreement would have been made. The sending of the trouble-shooter in *McKee*, on the

---

[3]   Longines-Wittnauer Watch Co. v. Barnes & Reinecke, Inc., 15 N.Y.2d 443, 261 N.Y.S.2d 8, 209 N.E.2d 68 (1965).

[4]   The court relied on the U.S. Supreme Court's requirement, in Hanson v. Denckla, 357 U.S. 235, 253, 78 S. Ct. 1228, 1240, 2 L. Ed. 2d 1283 (1958), that the defendant be shown to have "purposefully avail[ed] itself of the privilege of conducting activities" within the state and thereby "invok[ed] the benefits and protections of its laws."

[5]   Kramer v. Vogl, 17 N.Y.2d 27, 267 N.Y.S.2d 900, 215 N.E.2d 159 (1966).

[6]   The f.o.b. feature frequently appears in these cases. Its influence, when the defendant is the seller of goods, apparently consists in the fact that an f.o.b. shipment cuts off the seller's obligations, and therefore its contacts, at the f.o.b. point. The f.o.b. aspect was played down in Galgay v. Bulletin Co., Inc., 504 F.2d 1062 (2d Cir. 1974), where the plaintiff was the seller. For an explanation of "f.o.b.," see N.Y. UCC § 2–319.

[7]   McKee Elec. Co. v. Rauland-Borg Corp., 20 N.Y.2d 377, 283 N.Y.S.2d 34, 229 N.E.2d 604 (1967) (4–3 decision).

other hand, can be contrasted as a mere gesture to P rather than as an understood part of the bargain. A minority of three in *McKee* would not draw that contrast and would have sustained jurisdiction.

In Singer v. Walker,[8] a case decided in a consolidated opinion with *Longines*, jurisdiction was sustained under CPLR 302(a)(1) for the tort of personal injury, establishing that this paragraph about transacting business is not limited to contract or other commercial actions but can apply to torts as well if they arise from the transaction. In *Singer*, neither the negligent act nor the resulting injury occurred in New York, but jurisdiction was still sustained. D was a foreign manufacturer and made, among other things, what it labeled "unbreakable" geological hammers. These were shipped in substantial quantities into New York and P's aunt bought one in New York from a dealer and gave it to P, an infant, who was injured while using it on a Connecticut trip. Jurisdiction was upheld as arising out of D's transaction of business in New York under CPLR 302(a)(1).

Singer is somewhat of a maverick. It apparently holds, or at least the *Kramer* court thought so, that if a foreign seller, otherwise beyond 302(a)(1) jurisdiction, "solicits business in this State by means of catalogue, advertisements, or other promotional material circulated here"[9] (D did those things in *Singer*), it can be subjected to jurisdiction for causes of action connected with local purchase of its products. Those promotional activities in *Singer* would then appear to be the jurisdiction-giving factor that distinguishes the jurisdiction-rejecting *Kramer* case. It may also be significant that *Singer* involved personal injury and *Kramer* only a property right, but the courts do not say outright that that makes a jurisdictional difference.

CPLR 302(a) has two paragraphs devoted to torts, paragraphs 2 and 3, but they both exclude defamation.[10] Perhaps ironically, paragraph 1 has been held available for a defamation claim if it can be shown to arise out of the defendant's transaction of business in New York. That this is so makes longarm jurisdiction a New York possibility in defamation cases, and makes relevant in turn two major U.S. Supreme Court cases on the subject, involving national publications: Calder v. Jones[11] (involving the National Enquirer) and Keeton v. Hustler Magazine, Inc.,[12] both decided in 1984. Not only the publication itself but also the individuals writing and editing it were found to be within the jurisdiction of the forum, which in each case was one of many states in which the publications were sold and circulated, but not one in which any of the writing or editing was done. The generous reach allowed the longarm statutes (California's and New Hampshire's) involved in these libel cases suggest that the Supreme Court views differently, and more expansively, longarm efforts aimed at intentional as against unintentional torts.[13]

---

8   Longines-Wittnauer Watch Co. v. Barnes & Reinecke, Inc., 15 N.Y.2d 443, 261 N.Y.S.2d 8, 209 N.E.2d 68 (1965), cert.denied sub nom. Estwing Mfg. Co. v. Singer, 382 U.S. 905, 86 S.Ct. 241 (1965).

9   *Kramer*, 17 N.Y.2d at 31, 267 N.Y.S.2d at 903, 217 N.E.2d at 161.

10   See § 87.

11   Calder v. Jones, 465 U.S. 783, 104 S. Ct. 1482, 79 L. Ed. 2d 804, 10 Media L. Rep. (BNA) 1401 (1984).

12   Keeton v. Hustler Magazine, Inc., 465 U.S. 770, 104 S. Ct. 1473, 79 L. Ed. 2d 790, 10 Media L. Rep. (BNA) 1405 (1984).

13   The cases are discussed in the lead note in NYSLD No. 297.

The Second Circuit in Best Van Lines, Inc. v. Walker[14] rejected longarm Internet jurisdiction in a defamation case. An Iowa defendant in *Walker* put a business-damaging statement on his website: a blacklist of moving companies with P's name on it. Applying CPLR 302(a)(1), the court found D lacking the minimal New York contacts required for jurisdiction. The *Walker* court observed that New York courts construe CPLR 302(a)(1)'s "transacts any business within the state" clause "more narrowly in defamation cases than they do in the context of other sorts of litigation."[15]

In SPCA of Upstate New York, Inc. v. American Working Collie Ass'n,[16] the New York Court of Appeals agreed with the *Walker* court's assessment in yet another action involving the assertion of longarm jurisdiction over nondomiciliary defendants who allegedly defamed a plaintiff on the Web. In *SPCA*, numerous mistreated collies were rescued and placed in plaintiff's facility in Queensbury, New York. The defendants were an Ohio-based club devoted to promoting the welfare and protection of collies and its president, a resident of Vermont. The club, which had no office or employees in New York, provided leashes, collars, care, and monetary support for the collies at plaintiff's facility. After the president visited plaintiff's facility on two occasions, she returned to her residence in Vermont and authored and posted a number of writings on her club's website addressing the condition of the dogs and the treatment being provided by plaintiff. Plaintiff commenced this action alleging that certain statements in the posted writings were defamatory.

The *SPCA* Court, in affirming the dismissal of the action, concluded that defendants' activities in New York—two short visits totaling less than three hours, three phone calls from Vermont, and the donation of cash and leashes—"were quite limited." Although the alleged defamatory statements were posted on the Web, the Court emphasized that they "were not written in or directed to New York" and "were equally accessible in any other jurisdiction." In addition, there was "no substantial relationship between the allegedly defamatory statements and defendants' New York activities," which were limited to providing financial and medical assistance to the dogs in plaintiff's facility. The Court noted in dicta that if defendant placed the dogs with plaintiff in New York or complained about the treatment its volunteers received from plaintiff, that may have given rise to a "sufficiently substantial relationship between the allegedly defamatory statements and defendants' New York activities as to warrant a finding of long-arm jurisdiction."[17]

When the defendant is a corporation, it is necessary to distinguish between "general jurisdiction,"[18] rendering the corporation subject to jurisdiction on any claim regardless of where it arises, and the "specific jurisdiction" provided by the "transacts any business" standard applicable under CPLR 302(a)(1). Under the standards set forth by the Supreme Court in Daimler AG v. Bauman,[19] the defendant corporation will only be subject to general jurisdiction, i.e., "at home" in New York, if it is incorporated in New York or has its principal place of business here. If the defendant corporation is not "at

---

[14]   Best Van Lines, Inc. v. Walker, 490 F.3d 239 (2d Cir. 2007).

[15]   *Best Van Lines*, 490 F.3d at 248.

[16]   SPCA of Upstate New York, Inc. v. American Working Collie Ass'n, 18 N.Y.3d 400, 940 N.Y.S.2d 525, 963 N.E.2d 1226 (2012) (NYSLD No. 628).

[17]   *SPCA*, 18 N.Y.3d at 405, 940 N.Y.S.2d at 529, 963 N.E.2d at 1230.

[18]   See § 82.

[19]   Daimler AG v. Bauman, 571 U.S. 117, 134 S. Ct. 746, 187 L. Ed. 2d 624 (2014); see § 82.

home" in New York, but it is shown that the claim arises out of whatever the local activity was, the activity can qualify as a "transaction of business" within the intendment of CPLR 302(a)(1) and support personal jurisdiction in New York for a claim arising from the transaction of business. This is now commonly referred to as "specific" jurisdiction.[20]

Under neither category is jurisdiction present against a foreign hotel or like entity which does no more than maintain a listing in a New York telephone directory, even if a toll-free number is furnished. A number of hotels do this, and the courts have apparently decided that this activity, without more, will not confer jurisdiction either under CPLR 301 or 302(a)(1).[21] Similarly, the fact that a foreign corporation conducts an interactive website that is accessible to New Yorkers is not sufficient, standing alone, to confer general or specific jurisdiction over the defendant.[22]

Two classic buy-and-sell situations should be highlighted, for in each of them longarm jurisdiction has been refused under the "transacts" clause of CPLR 302 (although it might be accepted under the "contracts" clause treated in the next section). One, already seen in *Kramer*, is where P is a New York buyer who orders goods from D, a foreign seller. The mere shipment of goods to New York on an order sent by P from New York does not give longarm jurisdiction against the foreign seller, such as for breach of warranty. Conversely, if P is a New York seller and D the foreign buyer who simply sends an order to P in New York, by telephone or otherwise, pursuant to which P ships the goods f.o.b. New York, there is no longarm jurisdiction against the foreign buyer, such as for the price of the goods.[23] Additional contacts might mean jurisdiction, but those bare facts alone do not. If, for example, the foreign buyer came to New York in addition to conducting negotiations by telephone and mail, longarm jurisdiction for the purchase price of the goods could result,[24] but it won't if the trip to New York was on an unrelated transaction.[25]

In Galgay v. Bulletin Co., Inc.,[26] D was a Pennsylvania publisher that ordered more than a million dollars in special machinery from P, a manufacturer located in New York. The goods were made pursuant to the contract and shipped f.o.b. New York, an agent of D coming to New York to pick up the equipment. The contract also stipulated to the application of New York substantive law. The Second Circuit analogized the case, a contract claim by P against D for the balance due, to the simple situation in which a foreign buyer orders goods from a New York seller, and rejected jurisdiction. The analogy might be appropriate if the goods ordered were stock items, whatever the quantity ordered, but it is submitted that when the order is for the manufacture of special, expensive, and sophisticated machinery, especially when combined with the several other contacts manifest on the *Galgay* facts, longarm jurisdiction should exist. When a nondomiciliary arranges for a company to manufacture in New York a substantial

---

[20]   See *Daimler*, 134 S. Ct. at 751–58 (noting "distinction between general or all-purpose jurisdiction, and specific or conduct-linked jurisdiction"), and the discussion at the very end of § 84.

[21]   See, e.g., Ziperman v. Frontier Hotel of Las Vegas, 50 A.D.2d 581, 374 N.Y.S.2d 697 (2d Dep't 1975).

[22]   See Bossey ex rel. Bossey v. Camelback Ski Corp., 21 Misc. 3d 1116(A), 873 N.Y.S.2d 509 (Sup. Ct., Suffolk County 2008).

[23]   M. Katz & Son Billiard Products, Inc. v. G. Correale & Sons, Inc., 20 N.Y.2d 903, 285 N.Y.S.2d 871, 232 N.E.2d 864 (1967), aff'g 26 A.D.2d 52, 270 N.Y.S.2d 672 (1st Dep't 1966).

[24]   See Harry Winston, Inc. v. Waldfogel, 292 F. Supp. 473, 5 U.C.C. Rep. Serv. 1241 (S.D.N.Y. 1968).

[25]   Pacamor Bearings, Inc. v. Molon Motors & Coil, Inc., 102 A.D.2d 355, 477 N.Y.S.2d 856, 39 U.C.C. Rep. Serv. 410 (3d Dep't 1984).

[26]   Galgay v. Bulletin Co., Inc., 504 F.2d 1062 (2d Cir. 1974).

quantity of made-to-order equipment, the mission of longarm jurisdiction would seem to be at hand. Subsequent cases have nevertheless placed *Galgay* in the simple category of a sale "by telephone or mail from a New York plaintiff" and insulated the buyer from New York jurisdiction.[27]

The fact that a contract has been made in New York does not by itself guarantee jurisdiction if other contacts are lacking,[28] although it is always a factor to be considered.[29] But if the contract contemplates an ongoing relationship between a New Yorker and the nondomiciliary, rather than a random or single transaction, the contract's negotiation and execution in New York will likely tip the scales in favor of jurisdiction, as it did in George Reiner & Co., Inc. v. Schwartz.[30]

The defendant in *George Reiner* was a Massachusetts resident who responded to an ad placed by the plaintiff, a New York corporation, in the Boston Globe. The defendant then came to New York at plaintiff's expense and after a day's discussions and negotiations[31] made a contract to be the plaintiff's New England salesman. For four years the relationship continued, the defendant working out of his Massachusetts home. The plaintiff then sued for the excess of defendant's drawings over earned commissions and longarm jurisdiction in New York was sustained under CPLR 302(a)(1). Quoting and stressing the language of the U.S. Supreme Court in Hanson v. Denckla,[32] that jurisdiction is authorized when "the defendant purposefully avails itself of the privilege of conducting activities within the forum State, thus invoking the benefits and protection of its laws," the Court of Appeals held that the defendant's physical presence in New York when he made the contract, coupled with its contemplation of an ongoing relationship between the parties, constituted such conduct and satisfied as a CPLR 302(a)(1) "transaction." The casual New York visit of the trouble-shooter in *McKee*, discussed earlier in this section, was distinguished; it was not at all the source, as the *George Reiner* visit was, of the parties' contract and continuing arrangement.

The court did note, however, that the panel in *McKee* did not weigh the possible New York execution of the original distributorship contract, hinting that perhaps jurisdiction would have been sustained if it had; that the *McKee* court chose instead to rely on the aggregate of activities, as *Longines* had, and found the aggregate inadequate, however sufficient it may have been in *Longines*.

Some of the *George Reiner* language might be read to suggest that the mere making of the contract in New York is by itself sufficient to support CPLR 302(a)(1) longarm jurisdiction. But the Court of Appeals said in Presidential Realty Corp. v. Michael Square West, Ltd.,[33] shortly after the *George Reiner* decision, that if the formal execution

---

[27] See, e.g., Concrete Pipe & Products Corp. v. Modern Bldg. Materials, Inc., 213 A.D.2d 1023, 624 N.Y.S.2d 496 (4th Dep't 1995), holding that the principle applies to a nondomiciliary who leases as well as to one who buys.

[28] McNellis v. American Box Bd. Co., 53 Misc. 2d 479, 278 N.Y.S.2d 771 (Sup. Ct., Onondaga County 1967).

[29] See the review of "transaction" cases in Standard Wine & Liquor Co. v. Bombay Spirits Co., 20 N.Y.2d 13, 281 N.Y.S.2d 299, 228 N.E.2d 367 (1967).

[30] George Reiner & Co., Inc. v. Schwartz, 41 N.Y.2d 648, 394 N.Y.S.2d 844, 363 N.E.2d 551 (1977).

[31] For treatment of how negotiations conducted in New York figure in determining "transacts" jurisdiction, especially when the contract itself is technically executed outside the state, see Moser v. Boatman, 392 F. Supp. 270 (E.D.N.Y. 1975).

[32] Hanson v. Denckla, 357 U.S. 235, 78 S. Ct. 1228, 2 L. Ed. 2d 1283 (1958).

[33] Presidential Realty Corp. v. Michael Square West, Ltd., 44 N.Y.2d 672, 405 N.Y.S.2d 37, 376 N.E.2d 198 (1978).

of the contract takes place in New York only because the parties happen to be physically in the state at the moment of execution, longarm jurisdiction will not attach under CPLR 302(a)(1). That was the situation in *Presidential*, where the agreement had been negotiated in three southern cities and it was only because the plaintiff wanted further talks, which took place at its New York office, that the formal execution of the contract took place in the state.

Note the converse proposition in the *Longines* case: that the making of the contract outside New York will not preclude "transaction" jurisdiction in New York if other contacts are present.

The case of Parke-Bernet Galleries, Inc. v. Franklyn[34] is an important one. It involves the agency aspect of CPLR 302(a). P was an auction gallery and D a Californian who wanted to participate in P's New York auction without coming to New York. P let one of its employees hold an open telephone line to D in California during the auction. Through this employee, D put in his bids, won a few, and then refused to pay. Longarm jurisdiction was sustained on the ground that the employee, although on P's payroll, had actually been made an agent by D, a kind of borrowed servant.

An intriguing line of cases involves a New York plaintiff who has in one way or another been retained to act in New York for the foreign defendant, and where the plaintiff himself brings suit against the defendant for something connected with their arrangement. To get longarm jurisdiction in that situation, the plaintiff tries to impute his own New York acts to the defendant, as, for example, when P is a New York lawyer hired to act for D in New York and who now sues D for his fee. The Court of Appeals in Haar v. Armendoris Corporation[35] held that there is no longarm jurisdiction in such a case; that New York acts performed by P for D cannot be jurisdictionally imputed to D in a suit by P.

It is helpful to contrast the decision in *Haar* with the Court of Appeals more recent decision in Fischbarg v. Doucet.[36] In *Fischbarg*, the California defendants retained P to perform legal services for them, which P did in New York. Defendants established an "ongoing" and "continuing" attorney-client relationship with P by "repeatedly projecting themselves into New York—via telephone, mail, email and facsimile." The Court based its finding of longarm jurisdiction under CPLR 302(a)(1) not on the acts P performed for D in New York, but rather on D's communications with P as a result of projecting itself into New York to establish an attorney-client relationship with P.

There are some instances in which P's overall New York activities can be imputed to D.[37] If, for example, P's New York activities are solely in behalf of D—P performs services for no one else—they may bolster such an imputation and support jurisdiction.[38] It seems equally clear, however, that if P acts for D and others, such as where P is an

---

[34]   Parke-Bernet Galleries, Inc. v. Franklyn, 26 N.Y.2d 13, 308 N.Y.S.2d 337, 256 N.E.2d 506 (1970).

[35]   Haar v. Armendoris Corporation (State Report Title: Haar v. Armendaris), 31 N.Y.2d 1040, 342 N.Y.S.2d 70, 294 N.E.2d 855 (1973), reversing on the dissenting opinion in 40 A.D.2d 769, 337 N.Y.S.2d 285 (1st Dep't 1972).

[36]   Fischbarg v. Doucet, 9 N.Y.3d 375, 849 N.Y.S.2d 501, 880 N.E.2d 22 (2007) (NYSLD No. 577).

[37]   See the caselaw review in Amins v. Life Support Medical Equipment Corp., 373 F. Supp. 654 (E.D.N.Y. 1974).

[38]   See A. Millner Co. v. Noudar, Lda., 24 A.D.2d 326, 266 N.Y.S.2d 289 (1st Dep't 1966).

independent broker, his New York activities will not be ascribed to D and therefore will not support longarm jurisdiction of his suit against D.[39]

These agent-against-own-principal situations in which jurisdiction is refused must of course not be confused with the case in which a third person is suing the principal after having dealt with the principal through the agent. In that instance there may indeed be an imputation of the agent's acts to the principal under CPLR 302(a).[40]

The refusal to impute the agent's activities to the principal when the agent himself is the plaintiff is also the rationale used to protect the New York courts from what might otherwise be a deluge of litigation emanating from ordinary stock transactions. Assume that P is a national brokerage house. D visits an office of P outside New York with a sell order, which P processes through its own channels back to New York, where the order is executed on a national exchange. D now refuses to turn over the stock, which P has to replace. In an action by P for the replacement cost, is there longarm jurisdiction in New York? Caselaw has said no. This is at root just another illustration of suit by agent against principal where the agent is trying to bring off a jurisdictional imputation of its own acts to the principal.[41] Whatever the rationale, a different rule would in effect lend New York longarm jurisdiction to any transaction that ultimately results in a purchase or sale on one of New York's national exchanges.

The defendant is apparently protected in these stock transactions only when he engages in them on his own turf, however. If, for example, the defendant is a customer who deals directly with the broker's New York office by phone or mail in a number of transactions instead of dealing with the broker at the broker's local office outside New York, longarm jurisdiction may indeed be upheld.[42]

In the *Fischbarg* decision noted earlier, a California client's "ongoing" and "continuing" attorney-client relationship with plaintiff lawyer in New York through repeated communications with the lawyer via telephone, mail, email, and facsimile was held to support New York longarm jurisdiction in a fee action. What about the converse—an out-of-state lawyer acting for a New York plaintiff? Out-of-state lawyers don't automatically confront New York longarm jurisdiction if the New Yorker is unhappy with their services. California lawyers acting for a New York plaintiff, but acting only in California without coming into New York, escaped longarm jurisdiction in a malpractice action brought in federal court in New York in Mayes v. Leipziger.[43] It is important to stress that the defendant lawyers' services had been solicited in California.

In one category of typical textile industry transactions, an important segment of New York commerce, longarm jurisdiction was rejected in Dero Enterprises, Inc. v. Georgia Girl Fashions, Inc.[44] W was a New York clothing wholesaler and R a Georgia retailer that occasionally used A, a New York company, as a purchasing agent. When W approached A looking for buyers, A produced R, telling R about W's line. R bought, but the clothes were alleged to be defective and R wouldn't pay. W sued. The court said there

---

[39]   Glassman v. Hyder, 23 N.Y.2d 354, 296 N.Y.S.2d 783, 244 N.E.2d 259 (1968).

[40]   Orient Mid-East Lines, Inc. v. Albert E. Bowen, Inc., 297 F. Supp. 1149 (S.D.N.Y. 1969).

[41]   Hertz, Newmark and Warner v. Fischman, 53 Misc. 2d 418, 279 N.Y.S.2d 97 (N.Y. City Civ. Ct. 1967).

[42]   See Deutsche Bank Securities, Inc. v. Montana Bd. of Investments, 7 N.Y.3d 65, 818 N.Y.S.2d 164, 850 N.E.2d 1140 (2006) (NYSLD No. 559) (discussed below); Rothschild v. Thompson, 78 A.D.2d 795, 433 N.Y.S.2d 6 (1st Dep't 1980).

[43]   Mayes v. Leipziger, 674 F.2d 178 (2d Cir. 1982).

[44]   Dero Enterprises, Inc. v. Georgia Girl Fashions, Inc., 598 F. Supp. 318 (S.D.N.Y. 1984).

was no New York jurisdiction, stressing that it was W, the New York party, that had initiated the contact with R. There might have been jurisdiction if R had been the initiator.

Another conclusion, important in the realm of commercial paper, that has spared the New York courts what might otherwise be an undue category of longarm cases: that making the paper payable in New York does not by itself constitute a "transaction" sufficient to confer jurisdiction of an action brought on the paper, such as a promissory note.[45]

Just as CPLR 302(a)(1) may be used on a tort claim, so may it be used for a contract of a non-commercial nature. It has been held that the statute may be applied to the obligations arising under a separation agreement made in New York.[46] This "transaction" jurisdiction under CPLR 302(a)(1) should not be confused with anything offered by CPLR 302(b), which applies only in the context of an outright matrimonial action—a separation agreement can be the subject of a simple contract action—or family court proceeding.

When longarm jurisdiction is asserted against a corporate officer or employee as well as against the corporation, can the individual avoid jurisdiction by alleging that he was acting only in behalf of the corporation and that he is therefore insulated from individual jurisdiction, just as he is insulated from personal liability as a matter of substantive law? This is the "fiduciary shield" doctrine, and the Court of Appeals appeared to reject it in 1988 in Kreutter v. McFadden Oil Corp.[47]

New Yorker P gave $70,000 to a Texas company present in New York to invest in an oil-related venture. He got back not even an acknowledgment. He sued, naming several corporate defendants and X, a power behind some of the corporations and a nondomiciliary of New York. X tried to invoke the shield doctrine, but the court found the "transacts any business" clause satisfied as against X on sustainable allegations that those who conducted New York activities in this matter did so, in part, as X's agent. X contended that he was acting only in the corporations' behalf and that he could not be personally bound unless there was a piercing of the corporate veil. But that, answered the court, relates to substantive liability, and what the substantive liability may come to is not relevant at the jurisdictional stage. "Liability may be considered only after it is decided . . . that the defendant is subject to . . . jurisdiction . . . ."[48]

This conclusion about irrelevancy may become a troublesome point in a case based solely on breach of contract, which *Kreutter*, however, was not. The claims asserted in *Kreutter* included tort claims (fraud and conversion) along with contract claims, and as long as tort is part of the package, it is reasonably clear that there is no shield for an individual to hide behind.[49] Perhaps, from the point of view of a plaintiff seeking jurisdiction of the individual as well as the corporation, it would be a good idea to see whether there isn't some tort theory that can be added to the complaint. The fact that

---

[45] American Recreation Group, Inc. v. Woznicki, 87 A.D.2d 600, 448 N.Y.S.2d 51 (2d Dep't 1982); Hubbard, Westervelt & Mottelay, Inc. v. Harsh Bldg. Co., 28 A.D.2d 295, 284 N.Y.S.2d 879 (1st Dep't 1967).

[46] Kochenthal v. Kochenthal, 28 A.D.2d 117, 282 N.Y.S.2d 36 (2d Dep't 1967). Whitaker v. Whitaker, 32 A.D.2d 595, 299 N.Y.S.2d 482 (3d Dep't 1969), appears to take a contrary position, but it actually viewed itself only as a matrimonial action, not a contract action on a separation agreement.

[47] Kreutter v. McFadden Oil Corp., 71 N.Y.2d 460, 527 N.Y.S.2d 195, 522 N.E.2d 40 (1988).

[48] *Kreutter*, 71 N.Y.2d at 470, 527 N.Y.S.2d at 200, 522 N.E.2d at 45.

[49] See the discussion of the *CPC* case in § 87.

there were tort claims present in *Kreutter* seemed to lead to a sustaining of longarm jurisdiction that a complaint couched only in contract might not have achieved. If this kind of maneuver can bring a plaintiff jurisdiction, while a straight contract claim would not, we must note that it doesn't take much for an imaginative plaintiff's lawyer to add a tort claim to what would otherwise be a strictly commercial lawsuit.

Transacting business through electronic communication, such as instant messaging and Internet activities, got the attention of the New York Court of Appeals in Deutsche Bank Securities, Inc. v. Montana Bd. of Investments,[50] in which the defendant agreed to sell bonds from its base in Montana to a New York buyer and was held subject to New York jurisdiction on a claim related to the transaction. The agreement to sell, which was transmitted through an instant messaging service, was found to be a transaction of business in New York under CPLR 302(a)(1). Defendants "using electronic and telephonic means to project themselves into New York to conduct business transactions" can be subject to longarm jurisdiction here for claims arising from the transaction.[51]

What role do Internet activities play in longarm jurisdiction? A substantial one, and growing more substantial by the day. The subject got one of its earliest extensive treatments from a federal district court in Citigroup Inc. v. City Holding Co.,[52] in which the court said that if the website is used only "passively," such as just by making data available, it's just the same as an advertisement in a national magazine and won't give the benefit of longarm jurisdiction to those answering the ad. But the jurisdiction does loom into prospect if the site's activities take a more active form, as where the site "repeatedly transmits computer files to customers." In the middle is the "interactive" site that allows for an exchange of data; there, whether longarm jurisdiction exists depends "on the level and nature of the exchange."[53]

In Paterno v. Laser Spine Institute,[54] the Court of Appeals weighed in on the subject in a case in which plaintiff clicked on an Internet advertisement for Laser Spine Institute ("LSI"), a facility specializing in spinal surgery with its principal place of business in Florida. After numerous telephone and electronic communications with LSI to ascertain if surgical procedures might alleviate his pain, he ultimately travelled from his home in New York to LSI's Florida facility for evaluation and surgery. Plaintiff made two separate trips to Florida and underwent three surgeries in two months at LSI, but experienced severe pain following each procedure. For approximately three months following the third surgery, plaintiff alleged that he communicated daily with LSI surgeons and staff via text messages, emails, and telephone calls to resolve the pain. An LSI surgeon spoke by telephone with plaintiff's New York-based doctors concerning his condition and ordered an MRI, which was performed in New York. LSI invited plaintiff to travel back to Florida at LSI's expense for a fourth procedure, but plaintiff declined

---

[50] Deutsche Bank Securities, Inc. v. Montana Bd. of Investments, 7 N.Y.3d 65, 818 N.Y.S.2d 164, 850 N.E.2d 1140 (2006) (NYSLD No. 559).

[51] *Deutsche Bank*, 7 N.Y.3d at 71, 818 N.Y.S.2d at 167.

[52] Citigroup Inc. v. City Holding Co., 97 F. Supp. 2d 549 (S.D.N.Y. 2000) (SPR 99:2).

[53] In *Citigroup*, jurisdiction did result against D, who did more than merely post data about mortgage loans: it allowed customers to seek the loans on line and to "chat." That was held sufficient under all of the first three paragraphs of CPLR 302(a) to give jurisdiction over D in a trademark action by P suing D for palming off P's product as D's.

The appellate division elaborates on the "passive" issue in Grimaldi v. Guinn, 72 A.D.3d 37, 895 N.Y.S.2d 156 (2d Dep't 2010) (SPR 218), showing that what starts off as "passive" can readily lead to involvements that go beyond "passive" and into longarm jurisdiction, as occurred in the case.

[54] Paterno v. Laser Spine Institute, 24 N.Y.3d 370, 998 N.Y.S.2d 720, 23 N.E.3d 988 (2014).

and elected to have surgery in New York with another doctor. Plaintiff commenced a medical malpractice action in New York against LSI and several LSI surgeons relying on longarm jurisdiction under CPLR 302(a)(1) and (3).

The Court of Appeals unanimously affirmed the dismissal of the action. The Court acknowledged that "[t]he lack of an in-state physical presence is not dispositive of the question whether a nondomiciliary is transacting business in New York," citing to its prior decisions in *Fischbarg* and *Deutsche Bank*.[55] In those prior decisions, the Court concluded that CPLR 302(a)(1) longarm jurisdiction could exist over commercial actors who project themselves into New York electronically to conduct business transactions via email, text messaging, and the somewhat ancient art of telephone communication. In *Paterno*, however, the Court concluded that the defendants' contacts with New York, when viewed on the whole, did not rise to the level of conducting a transaction of business in New York under CPLR 302(a)(1).

The Court deemed LSI's website to be a "passive website . . . which merely impart[s] information without permitting a business transaction, [and is] . . . generally insufficient to establish personal jurisdiction."[56] Nonetheless, plaintiff recounted that he had several telephone calls and email communications with LSI representatives over several months, sent MRIs and blood work to LSI, and that LSI sent prescriptions to his New York-based pharmacies. The Court rejected the notion that these numerous contacts could establish jurisdiction because "it is not the quantity but the quality of the contacts that matters under our long-arm jurisdiction analysis."[57] On that front, the Court classified LSI's contacts with plaintiff as "responsive in nature" and not of the type that demonstrate the purposeful availment necessary to confer personal jurisdiction over nondomiciliary defendants.

The careful observer could reasonably view the *Paterno* decision as an indication that the Court of Appeals is tightening the reins on the application of CPLR 302(a)(1), which has been rather broadly construed in some recent decisions.[58] Plaintiffs must take note of this possible trend, along with recent United States Supreme Court decisions that significantly curtail general jurisdiction under CPLR 301 and longarm jurisdiction under CPLR 302(a).[59] If plaintiff commences an action in New York and the existence of general or longarm jurisdiction is not crystal clear, the plaintiff must carefully calendar the statute of limitations in the jurisdiction where the defendant is incorporated or has its principal place of business, or the place where the claimed wrong occurred.[60] This will at least keep the door open to a holding action if jurisdictional prospects in New York are bleak.[61]

The difficulties of establishing jurisdiction in today's world, where a hotel can sport a familiar name on the Internet, but be actually owned by a separate corporate entity, are vividly demonstrated in Stern v. Four Points.[62] In *Stern*, plaintiff alleged that she

---

[55]   *Paterno*, 24 N.Y.3d at 376, 998 N.Y.S.2d at 725, 23 N.E.3d at 993.

[56]   *Paterno*, 24 N.Y.3d at 377, 998 N.Y.S.2d at 726, 23 N.E.3d at 994.

[57]   *Paterno*, 24 N.Y.3d at 378, 998 N.Y.S.2d at 726, 23 N.E.3d at 994.

[58]   See, e.g., Licci v. Lebanese Canadian Bank, 20 N.Y.3d 327, 960 N.Y.S.2d 695, 984 N.E.2d 893 (2012), discussed below.

[59]   See §§ 82, 88.

[60]   See § 231A.

[61]   See § 262.

[62]   Stern v. Four Points, 133 A.D.3d 514, 19 N.Y.S.3d 289 (1st Dep't 2015).

made a reservation from a computer terminal in New York for a room in a Sheraton hotel in Michigan using an interactive website maintained by Starwood Hotels and Resorts Worldwide, Inc. and used by Sheraton hotels. While at the Michigan hotel, plaintiff tripped over a walkway in the lobby and fractured her knee. The hotel was owned by defendant ZLC, a Michigan corporation, which moved to dismiss for lack of jurisdiction. In support of its motion, ZLC submitted proof that, at the time of the accident, it used the trademark name "Sheraton" pursuant to a license agreement, but had no other hotels and no bank accounts, real estate, or other contacts with New York.

The First Department acknowledged that ZLC's participation in the interactive website for Sheraton hotels may have demonstrated that it transacted business in New York under CPLR 302(a)(1), but plaintiff failed to establish the second element of a longarm claim as described in the first paragraph of this section: that the claim arose from the transaction of business. Rather, plaintiff's injuries arose from the allegedly defective condition of the Michigan hotel. As is often the case when a claim is based on Internet activity, any nexus between the transaction of business on the website and plaintiff's injuries were deemed "too remote to support the exercise of long-arm or specific jurisdiction under CPLR 302(a)(1)."[63]

What about something like a humble eBay transaction on the Internet? Sayeedi v. Walser,[64] a New York City Civil Court action, involved a common scenario: a New York plaintiff's purchase through eBay of a relatively modest item (in Sayeedi, an engine) from an out-of-stater (in Sayeedi, a Missourian). The court addressed a question many New Yorkers have confronted after their eBay purchases have come up short on the merits. Claiming the engine, represented as new, was defective, P in Sayeedi sued for damages. The question was whether the seller, a Missouri resident, was subject to New York longarm jurisdiction under the "transaction of business" standards of the applicable longarm statute.[65] If the eBay transaction can be deemed a transaction of business in New York—which under the Civil Court Act means New York City rather than the State at large—P would succeed on the issue of jurisdiction and be able to maintain the suit at home without having to pursue D in Missouri. But he did not succeed in Sayeedi. In an extended treatment of the subject, the court formulated the main issue as whether a nonresident defendant is subject to New York jurisdiction on the basis of a single on-line auction for goods placed on an international website.

The court answered no and added that "[t]he few courts that have found personal jurisdiction over purely on-line auction sales have focused primarily on the sophistication of the seller." It found that this defendant didn't fit the description. If the seller advertised that she was a "Top Rated Seller" on eBay, would that change the jurisdictional result? Furthermore, does an eBay seller ever intend to "transact" business within New York State, or is the agreement to simply sell to the highest bidder in any State? Should it matter that the highest bidder is actually in New York and that the transaction, in effect, takes place here through electronic means?

---

[63] *Stern*, 133 A.D.3d at 514, 19 N.Y.S.3d at 290; see *SPCA*, 18 N.Y.3d at 404–05, 940 N.Y.S.2d at 528, 963 N.E.2d at 1229; Snegur v. Grupo Iberostar, 2016 WL 74414 (E.D.N.Y. 2016) ("Courts have consistently held that the in-state activity of booking a hotel room is too remote from negligence alleged to have taken place at a foreign hotel to satisfy [CPLR 302(a)(1)].").

[64] Sayeedi v. Walser, 15 Misc. 3d 621, 835 N.Y.S.2d 840, 62 U.C.C. Rep. Serv. 2d 352 (N.Y. City Civ. Ct. 2007) (SPR 186:3).

[65] In the civil court, the longarm statute is § 404(a)(1) of the New York City Civ. Ct. Act, which is modeled on CPLR 302(a)(1) and thus able to resort to the caselaw on the latter.

Longarm inquiries under CPLR 302(a)(1) range far and wide, from eBay transactions to the funding of terrorist organizations through international monetary transactions using correspondent bank accounts in New York, the subject of the Court of Appeals decision in Licci v. Lebanese Canadian Bank.[66] In *Licci*, which highlights the dimensions of long-arm jurisdiction under CPLR 302 in our increasingly global world, plaintiffs included citizens of the United States, Canada, and Israel, who resided in Israel and were injured there in rocket attacks claimed to have been launched by the terrorist organization Hizballah. While the defendants were not members of that organization, they were banks that allegedly assisted Hizballah in committing the terrorist attacks by "facilitating international monetary transactions" with it.

Plaintiffs brought various claims against the Lebanese Canadian Bank ("LCB") in New York State court and asserted personal jurisdiction under CPLR 302(a)(1). "LCB did not operate any branches or offices, or maintain any employees in the United States, much less New York." Rather, its only point of contact with the United States was a correspondent banking account with co-defendant American Express Bank in New York. Plaintiffs alleged that LCB used this correspondent account to transfer millions of dollars to agents of Hizballah, who it knew was a terrorist organization, and that these transactions through "wire transfers 'caused, enabled and facilitated the terrorist rocket attacks' that injured them and their families."[67]

The action was removed to federal district court, but returned to our state system in the form of two certified questions forwarded to the New York Court of Appeals by the Second Circuit. The certified questions pertained to the two inquiries commonly at issue under the first clause in CPLR 302(a)(1): (1) whether the defendant "transacts any business" in New York and, if so, (2) whether the cause of action asserted "aris[es] from" such a business transaction.[68]

Examining its prior caselaw in this arena, the Court agreed with the Second Circuit's conclusion that the first prong of the long-arm jurisdiction inquiry under CPLR 302(a)(1) can be "satisfied by [a] defendant's use of a correspondent bank account in New York, even if no other contacts between the defendant and New York can be established, *if* the defendant's use of that account was purposeful."[69] The Court acknowledged that this analysis "may be complicated by the nature of inter-bank activity, especially given the widespread use of correspondent accounts nominally in New York to facilitate the flow of money worldwide, often for transactions that otherwise have no other connection to New York, or indeed the United States."[70] Nevertheless, the Court held that a complaint alleging a foreign bank's repeated use of a correspondent account in New York

---

[66]   Licci v. Lebanese Canadian Bank, 20 N.Y.3d 327, 960 N.Y.S.2d 695, 984 N.E.2d 893 (2012) (NYSLD No. 636).

[67]   *Licci*, 20 N.Y.3d at 332, 960 N.Y.S.2d at 697, 984 N.E.2d at 895.

[68]   See Johnson v. Ward, 4 N.Y.3d 516, 519, 797 N.Y.S.2d 33, 34, 829 N.E.2d 1201, 1202 (2005) (SPR 154:3).

[69]   Licci ex rel. Licci v. Lebanese Canadian Bank, SAL, 673 F.3d 50, 66 (2d Cir. 2012), certified question accepted, 18 N.Y.3d 952, 944 N.Y.S.2d 472, 967 N.E.2d 697 (2012) and certified question answered, 20 N.Y.3d 327, 960 N.Y.S.2d 695, 984 N.E.2d 893 (2012).

[70]   *Licci*, 20 N.Y.3d at 338, 960 N.Y.S.2d at 702, 984 N.E.2d at 900.

on behalf of a client could support a claim that defendant transacted business in the state under CPLR 302(a)(1).[71]

As for the second inquiry under CPLR 302(a)(1), and the second question certified by the Second Circuit, the New York Court of Appeals held that plaintiffs' claims under the Anti-Terrorism Act, the Alien Tort Statute, and for negligence or breach of statutory duty in violation of Israeli law, arose from LCB's transaction of business in New York within the meaning of CPLR 302(a)(1). The Court emphasized that this portion of the longarm inquiry "is relatively permissive" and requires, "at a minimum, a relatedness between the transaction and the legal claim such that the latter is not completely unmoored from the former."[72] CPLR 302(a)(1) does not, however, require that every element of a pleaded claim arise from a transaction of business in New York. The Court noted that "where at least one element of the claim arises from defendant's New York contacts, "the relationship between the business transaction and the claim asserted supports specific jurisdiction under the statute."[73]

Longarm inquiries go on and on. The foregoing treatment, long as it is, sets forth only a few essentials about what constitutes a "transaction of business" under CPLR 302(a)(1). The matter is of great moment in any case in which it is even arguably applicable because the very issue of jurisdiction depends on it. The plaintiff who makes out a "transaction" in New York gets New York jurisdiction and need not sue elsewhere. That can be a very significant matter in this global economy that is somehow connected by electronic communication.[74] But important as these sui generis longarm investigations may be, the candid negotiator with CPLR 302(a)(1) will confess that they are tedious—and sometimes even the cause of low blood pressure among judges. One federal judge opened an opinion with the cheerless lament that his case requires yet "another decision in the interminable line of cases applying the New York long-arm statute, CPLR § 302."[75]

Interminable or not, CPLR 302 atones in importance for what it generates in boredom. It is no small gift for a plaintiff and her New York lawyer to be able to choose the forum, and CPLR 302 is a key factor in the choice.

2008 Adoption of CPLR 302(d): Foreign Defamation Judgment

On that note, we take temporary leave of paragraph 1 of CPLR 302(a). The next section returns to it with a treatment of its "contracts anywhere" clause and subsequent sections treat other CPLR 302(a) paragraphs, but there's one more piece of business to take up here, concerning subdivision (d) of CPLR 302, added in 2008. We treat it here because it's really related to the transaction of business category of subdivision (a)(1). It concerns what has come to be known as "libel terrorism."

The new subdivision is designed to meet the unique problem posed by Ehrenfeld v. Bin Mahfouz,[76] involving an alleged libel by a New York writer against a wealthy Saudi.

---

[71]　See also Zottola v. AGI Group, Inc., 63 A.D.3d 1052, 882 N.Y.S.2d 445 (2d Dep't 2009) (SPR 211:1) (citing as a significant element in finding jurisdiction over defendant seller under CPLR 302(a)(1) that contract called for plaintiff buyer to deposit payment into the seller's New York bank account).

[72]　*Licci*, 20 N.Y.3d at 339, 960 N.Y.S.2d at 702, 984 N.E.2d at 900.

[73]　*Licci*, 20 N.Y.3d at 341, 960 N.Y.S.2d at 703, 984 N.E.2d at 901.

[74]　See Patrick M. Connors, *The Golden Age of Personal Jurisdiction,* N.Y.L.J., May 19, 2008, at 3.

[75]　Orient Mid-East Lines, Inc. v. Albert E. Bowen, Inc., 297 F. Supp. 1149, 1150 (S.D.N.Y. 1969).

[76]　Ehrenfeld v. Bin Mahfouz, 9 N.Y.3d 501, 851 N.Y.S.2d 381, 881 N.E.2d 830 (2007).

The writing appeared in a book written by New Yorker P and sold in Great Britain. The book accused D, a Saudi businessman, of giving financial aid to terrorism. D said it was libelous and sued P in London, serving her in New York. She didn't defend and D took a default judgment for a large sum of money. P did not possess any assets against which to enforce the judgment in Britain, and the judgment probably wouldn't have been enforceable in New York anyway, where she did have assets, because the United Kingdom's defamation law is fundamentally different from our own laws that strongly support free speech under the First Amendment.[77] In any event, it did not appear that D was interested in collecting the judgment. Rather, he sought to deter writers like P, and, even more significantly, publishers in New York, from publishing writings like P's.

The English judgment was a cloud over P's head and she sought to remove it in a New York action seeking a declaration that the British judgment would not be recognized here. For that she sought longarm jurisdiction under CPLR 302(a)(1), but the court in *Ehrenfeld* held that there was none; that D was not transacting business in New York, the necessary jurisdictional predicate under that statute.

The resulting clamor quickly produced Chapter 66 of the Laws of 2008, purporting to overrule the case and to allow longarm jurisdiction in it and in like cases, with amendments adding subdivision (d) to CPLR 302 and a paragraph 8 to CPLR 5304(b).[78] The new law faces serious constitutional obstacles, among other problems, and will likely be the subject of future litigation when it is invoked. It has generated very little reported caselaw since it was adopted almost a decade ago.

§ 86A. "Contracts Anywhere" Under CPLR 302(a)(1)

A 1979 amendment of paragraph 1 of CPLR 302(a) expanded longarm jurisdiction to reach a defendant who "contracts anywhere to supply goods or services in the state," a jurisdictional category distinct from the "transacts any business" of the first clause, and a study in itself. Hence this separate section.

In commercial transactions, which are what the "contracts anywhere" clause principally aims at, the U.S. Supreme Court has taken a generous view of longarm jurisdiction. *Burger King Corp. v. Rudzewicz*[1] is the major indicator. Burger King, the fast food giant, had its base in Florida. Under a Florida longarm statute purporting to assert jurisdiction of anyone who "[b]reach[es] a contract in this state by failing to perform acts required by the contract to be performed in this state," *Burger King* was allowed to obtain Florida jurisdiction over a Michigan franchisee who never set foot in Florida. Among the obligations the franchisee undertook in Michigan, however, where it had its operation, was to send periodic payments under the franchise agreement to Florida. The court held this a major ingredient in satisfying due process.[2]

Relying on *Burger King*, the Second Circuit sustained New York jurisdiction over two California individuals in another franchise case,[3] holding that with contacts even greater than those that sufficed in *Burger King*, they "reached into New York to obtain

---

[77]   See CPLR 5304(b)(4) (noting that a foreign country judgment need not be recognized if "the cause of action on which the judgment is based is repugnant to the public policy of this state").

[78]   These are discussed in SPR 196:4 and 197:2. The background of the controversy appears in Siegel, *"Perspective"*, N.Y.L.J., March 12, 2008.

[1]   Burger King Corp. v. Rudzewicz, 471 U.S. 462, 105 S. Ct. 2174, 85 L. Ed. 2d 528 (1985).

[2]   The case is the subject of a lead note in NYSLD No. 308.

[3]   Retail Software Services, Inc. v. Lashlee, 854 F.2d 18 (2d Cir. 1988).

the benefits of selling seven franchises [computer software stores] to be operated in the state." Misrepresentations and omissions on behalf of the now bankrupt corporation for which the defendants purportedly acted were claimed. The main negotiations had apparently been made at a California meeting and in telephone calls to New York, but the statements were also allegedly contained in franchise registrations and ads in New York.

This generous view of longarm jurisdiction in cases of intentional conduct, like *Burger King* (a commercial case) and the *Calder* and *Keeton* cases (involving intentional torts),[4] may be contrasted with the more restrictive view taken when accidents are involved.[5]

The utility of the "contracts anywhere" clause is plain in the vast realm of Internet orders and in mail solicitations. Every time a New Yorker orders something online or by mail and the seller at the other end sends it on, he has apparently contracted "to supply goods" in the state and on the face of CPLR 302(a)(1) that would mean jurisdiction. But the lawyer has to be circumspect about using the "contracts anywhere" clause of CPLR 302(a)(1) in small cases.

Suppose, for example, that a New Yorker orders a $1,500 computer from a Chicago retailer. It is sent but does not work right. Will the statute require the retailer to defend an action for breach of warranty in New York? Same example, but with a $150 radio from a department store in St. Louis, or a $35 speaker ordered on eBay from a small shop in Tucson, Arizona? Does the exercise of longarm jurisdiction in such small cases satisfy the constitution?[6]

On the constitutional front, there have been cases in New York, involving relatively modest transactions, in which the New York courts have refused recognition to a sister-state judgment because it was found to be predicated on a jurisdictional foundation that violated due process because the rendering state had insufficient contacts with the defendant (a New Yorker), when the very same contacts, in converse circumstances, would have satisfied the "contracts anywhere" clause of CPLR 302(a)(1) to the letter.[7]

And even if a given exercise of the "contracts anywhere" clause would satisfy constitutional standards, the time and trouble of invoking the statute in a small case must be weighed against the stakes involved. The growth of Internet transactions has, however, given rise to more tests of jurisdiction in smaller cases. In this connection there are several points to make about the lower courts.

They also have longarm statutes. Section 404 in the New York City Civil Court Act and in each of the Uniform District and Uniform City court acts[8] is modeled on CPLR 302 so as to reach defendants outside the lower court's territory when the transaction or event has local contacts. Only the Civil Court Act was amended to add the "contracts anywhere" clause, however,[9] but requiring that the contacts be with New York City

---

[4]   See § 86.

[5]   See § 88.

[6]   Note the "bigness" point mentioned in § 88.

[7]   See, e.g., Pinna v. Davis, 67 A.D.2d 967, 413 N.Y.S.2d 460 (2d Dep't 1979).

[8]   McKinney's Vol. 29A, Part 3.

[9]   The amendment was made in 1983, four years after the 1979 amendment that added the "contracts anywhere" clause to CPLR 302.

rather than with the state in general. The district and city court acts were not so amended, and remain without this potentially far-reaching clause.

This means that within New York City small cases that depend on the contracts-anywhere language can be brought in the civil court, but that outside New York City they have to be brought in the supreme court. In this respect, however, note that the costs statute that would otherwise punish the bringing of such cases in the supreme court, CPLR 8102, does not apply to cases that depend for jurisdiction on the "contracts anywhere" clause. CPLR 8102 visits its costs sanction only on a case in which jurisdiction could have been obtained over the defendant in a lower court. In this category of cases—those brought in the supreme court outside New York City—jurisdiction can't be obtained over the defendant in the lower court because its longarm statute doesn't contain the contracts-anywhere clause. Thus, even the smallest cases falling under the new language of CPLR 302(a)(1) can apparently be brought in the supreme court outside New York City without facing the CPLR 8102 costs deterrent.

The plaintiff shouldn't bother with the "contracts anywhere" clause in small cases, however, unless convinced that the defendant will voluntarily pay a judgment or has assets in New York against which the judgment can be easily enforced. Otherwise the judgment will have to be taken to the defendant's jurisdiction and made the subject of an action there to convert it into a judgment of that place. Only then could plaintiff proceed to make use of enforcement devices likely to reach the defendant's assets. The cost of these steps may make their attempted use uneconomical in small cases. The point should in any event be discussed with the client, lest the client get a satisfaction of judgment accompanied by a bill from her own attorney for a fee that exceeds it.

Sending an employee into the state to repair a piece of machinery has been held to be the furnishing of services in New York and thus to support jurisdiction of a claim connected with the service. In Island Wholesale Wood Supplies, Inc. v. Blanchard Industries, Inc.,[10] the court examined the language of the 1979 amendment, held that the legislature intended it "to extend jurisdiction to the limits of due process" and concluded that it must therefore be given "a broad construction."

Does the new clause alter the significance of the "f.o.b." shipment that often insulated the seller from jurisdiction under the "transacts any business" clause?[11] The court in Blanchard described this as a "difficult question," but found it unnecessary to decide it. Perhaps the court decided it implicitly anyway. The "broad construction," the court finds the statute calling for is certainly not consistent with the idea that a seller can insulate itself merely by shipping goods f.o.b. its own jurisdiction.

Practitioners should be aware that some of the cases in which jurisdiction was rejected under the original "transacts any business" clause of CPLR 302(a)(1), including several cited in the report of the Law Revision Commission that drafted and recommended the "contracts anywhere" language,[12] involve fact patterns that would today fall under the new contracts-anywhere language. If research produces old "transacts any business" cases that reject jurisdiction, they should be reviewed to see if they fit under the "contracts anywhere" description. Two cases that might be successfully

---

[10]   Island Wholesale Wood Supplies, Inc. v. Blanchard Industries, Inc., 101 A.D.2d 878, 476 N.Y.S.2d 192 (2d Dep't 1984).

[11]   See § 86.

[12]   The commission's 1979 report is reprinted at page A-57 of McKinney's 1979 New York Session Law News.

refitted in that way are the *Kramer* and *McKee* cases previously reviewed under the "transacts" clause.[13]

In treating that clause in section 86, two "classic buy-and-sell situations" (as we labeled them) are discussed, in each of which jurisdiction was rejected. One of these, involving a New York plaintiff's purchase from a nondomiciliary seller, would seem to fall under the new contracts-anywhere phrase. The *Kramer* case, involving a continuing sales arrangement, is a prime example, but the new language, literally applied, would also reach one-shot sales and transactions involving small and even paltry sums. (The *Kramer* sales were substantial.)

What of stock exchange transactions? D, the owner of a few nationally traded shares, lives in Oregon. He goes to the local office of a national broker to sell, and the order goes through the broker's channels to its New York office, where the sale is made on one of the New York exchanges. D does not turn over the shares. He says he has good reason. Will suit in New York obtain jurisdiction of D? Are the shares "goods" so that D can be said to have contracted "to supply goods" in New York? It could mean quite an additional burden for the New York courts were they deemed jurisdictionally competent to reach all the sellers of any stock traded on one of New York's national exchanges. Even if the shares are "goods," moreover, in the example given the defendant could be deemed to have contracted to furnish the shares not in New York, but in Oregon, the defendant's home, so that it is the plaintiff broker, not the defendant seller, who is responsible for the trip the shares make to New York.

In a similar situation, in which the out-of-state defendant (D) was the buyer instead of the seller and ordered the shares merely by telephoning the New York broker (P) on a single transaction, D was held not subject to longarm jurisdiction in an action by P on the agreement for the reason that D did not conduct "sufficient purposeful activity" for jurisdiction.[14]

Ironically, some situations in which jurisdiction seems quite fair to exercise remain beyond the language of the "contracts anywhere" clause in CPLR 302(a)(1). One example is in Galgay v. Bulletin Co., Inc., also discussed in the prior section.[15] The Pennsylvania publisher in *Galgay* ordered more than a million dollars in special machinery from the New York plaintiff, which the plaintiff made and shipped. Jurisdiction of a claim for a balance due was nevertheless rejected. Unless the money that the publisher contracted to pay can qualify as "goods" under the contracts-anywhere clause, an unlikely

---

[13] See § 86.

[14] L.F. Rothschild, Unterberg, Towbin v. McTamney, 59 N.Y.2d 651, 463 N.Y.S.2d 197, 449 N.E.2d 1275 (1983), affirming on the appellate division opinion in 89 A.D.2d 540, 452 N.Y.S.2d 630 (1st Dep't 1982). The *L.F. Rothschild* decision was distinguished in Deutsche Bank Securities, Inc. v. Montana Bd. of Investments, 7 N.Y.3d 65, 71–2, 818 N.Y.S.2d 164, 167, 850 N.E.2d 1140 (2006) (NYSLD No. 559), where defendant was "a sophisticated institutional trader that entered New York [via instant messaging] to transact business here by knowingly initiating and pursuing a negotiation with [plaintiff's] employee in New York that culminated in the sale of $15 million in bonds." See § 86.

[15] Galgay v. Bulletin Co., Inc., 504 F.2d 1062 (2d Cir. 1974).

conclusion,[16] the publisher has not contracted to furnish either "goods" or "services" in New York and so remains beyond jurisdiction.[17]

What about making a promissory note calling for payment in New York? Such doing is analogous in that it implicitly poses the question of whether agreeing to pay money in New York may be considered an agreement to furnish goods in New York within the intendment of the contracts-anywhere clause. The question arose in American Recreation Group, Inc. v. Woznicki,[18] where the court held that making a promissory note payable in New York cannot by itself subject the maker to longarm jurisdiction if all the rest of the defendant's contacts with the case are outside New York.

A similar issue that has periodically arisen under CPLR 302(a)(1)'s "contracts anywhere" clause is whether it extends to a person who, from outside the state, guarantees the performance of a contract to be carried out within the state. In a scholarly treatment of the subject in Summit Const. Services Group, Inc. v. Act Abatement, LLC,[19] the court held that a person who, from outside the state, signs a guaranty of the performance of a New York project is subject to New York jurisdiction on the guaranty.

The furnishing of a drug outside the state, by a Massachusetts physician to whom the New York plaintiff went for treatment, even if the intent was that the plaintiff take the drug home, does not support jurisdiction under the "contracts anywhere" clause.[20] The court said that in enacting this provision the legislature "was not concerned with limited provision of supplies incident to medical treatment."

Cases on similarly worded sister-state statutes can also offer guidance on the scope and application of the "contracts anywhere" clause of CPLR 302(a)(1).[21]

§ 87. "Tortious Act" Under CPLR 302(a)(2)

CPLR 302(a)(2) is likely the most frequently cited subdivision in the longarm statute and applies to any tort, intentional or unintentional, in which the actionable conduct takes place in New York. It does not apply when the tortious conduct takes place outside New York, even though it causes injury within New York. That's the construction of the statute in Feathers v. McLucas,[1] decided in 1965. In that case, K was a Kansas

---

[16] But compare in this respect the language of the Florida statute in the *Burger King* case, above, which was held to embrace mere payments of money required to be sent to the state.

[17] It is not certain, however, that the New York Court of Appeals would agree with the *Galgay* court's release of the defendant from the "transacts any business" clause were a similar fact pattern to arise today. See § 86.

[18] American Recreation Group, Inc. v. Woznicki, 87 A.D.2d 600, 448 N.Y.S.2d 51 (2d Dep't 1982).

[19] Summit Const. Services Group, Inc. v. Act Abatement, LLC, 34 Misc. 3d 823, 935 N.Y.S.2d 499 (Sup. Ct., Westchester County 2011) (SPR 241:2).

[20] Etra v. Matta, 61 N.Y.2d 455, 474 N.Y.S.2d 687, 463 N.E.2d 3 (1984).

[21] Several are cited by the report of the Law Revision Commission (note 12 above), the amendment's sponsor. Massachusetts, for example, has a "contracting to supply services or things" provision, Massachusetts Annotated Laws, C.223A, § 3(b), which got a broad construction in Sarno v. Florida East Coast Ry. Co., 327 F. Supp. 506 (D. Mass. 1971), a services case. The uniform act, Unif. Interstate and Int'l Proced. Act § 1.03(a)(2), 13 U.L.A. 361 (1986), settles on a similar provision. Other statutes the reader can consult are those that go all the way with longarm jurisdiction, i.e., that assume jurisdiction whenever due process permits it. California has such a statute, for example. See § 84.

[1] Longines-Wittnauer Watch Co. v. Barnes & Reinecke, Inc., 15 N.Y.2d 443, 261 N.Y.S.2d 8, 209 N.E.2d 68 (1965), cert. den. sub nom. Estwing Mfg. Co., v. Singer, 382 U.S. 905, 86 S.Ct. 241 (1965). *Feathers* is the third of three cases the Court of Appeals consolidated into a single opinion that played a key role in the development of longarm jurisdiction early in the life of the CPLR. The other two are the *Longines* and *Singer* cases, treated in § 86, which sustained jurisdiction under CPLR 302(a)(1).

corporation that manufactured tanks in Kansas. It sold one of these to M, a Missouri corporation. M mounted it on a wheelbase and sold it to C, a Pennsylvania corporation and an interstate carrier. After the tank was filled with propane gas and sent on its way to Vermont, it exploded while passing through New York and injured P. P sued K in New York and served process in Kansas. The court dismissed the case for lack of jurisdiction.

Jurisdiction was rejected by the court because CPLR 302(a)(2) requires that the tortious "act" take place in New York. The occurrence of only the injury in New York does not satisfy. In *Feathers*, whatever "tortious act" K was guilty of in its manufacturing process had occurred outside New York.

Feathers came as a surprise. Since CPLR 302 was modeled on the Illinois statute, and a major Illinois case[2] had sustained jurisdiction on similar facts, it was widely assumed that it would also be sustained in New York. But it was not. The net result of *Feathers* was the prompt amendment of CPLR 302(a) to add what is now paragraph 3, the subject of the next section. *Feathers* remains the lord of paragraph 2, however, which continues to require that the "tortious act" take place in New York. Thus, where P purchased pills in Germany and brought them back to New York, and the pills resulted in deformities to later born children, paragraph 2 did not give jurisdiction because the pills were manufactured outside New York.[3]

The statute has also been held inapplicable to a paternity claim when the act involved is consensual rather than tortious.[4] No matter. While subdivision (a)(2) of CPLR 302 may exclude certain paternity suits, the plaintiff can turn to subdivision (b), added and altered afterwards, for longarm jurisdiction on a paternity claim today.[5]

Defamation is expressly excepted from the "tort" parts of CPLR 302(a)—paragraphs 2 and 3—because it was feared that national and international libels and slanders could too easily find their way into New York and impose unduly on its courts. But jurisdiction of a defamation arising out of the defendant's transaction of New York business has been sustained under paragraph 1, which does not have a defamation exclusion.[6]

In many of the instances in which CPLR 302(a)(2) confers jurisdiction, it will be found that some other statute also confers it. If, for example, negligent driving in New York results in an accident, the injured party can invoke either CPLR 302(a)(2) or the nonresident motorist statute,[7] or both.

What about longarm jurisdiction over an individual who was on a corporate mission at the time of the tort? When an individual is acting solely in behalf of a corporation on a strictly commercial matter, like the negotiation of a contract, the individual has no personal liability for it as a substantive matter under the "fiduciary shield" doctrine, and this would presumably also insulate the individual from longarm jurisdiction as a

---

[2]   Gray v. American Radiator & Standard Sanitary Corp., 22 Ill. 2d 432, 176 N.E.2d 761 (1961). See 2d Rep. Leg. Doc. No. 13, p. 39 (1958).

[3]   Harvey v. Chemie Grunenthal, G.m.b.H., 354 F.2d 428 (2d Cir. 1965), cert. denied 384 U.S. 1001, 86 S.Ct. 1923 (1966).

[4]   Anonymous v. Anonymous, 49 Misc. 2d 675, 268 N.Y.S.2d 710 (Fam. Ct., Queens County 1966). Longarm statutes elsewhere, albeit different in terminology, have been stretched to offer jurisdiction in similar instances. See, e.g., Neill v. Ridner, 153 Ind. App. 149, 286 N.E.2d 427 (1972).

[5]   See § 90.

[6]   The New York courts have, however, construed CPLR 302(a)(1) more narrowly in defamation actions than they do in the context of other sorts of litigation. See § 86.

[7]   Veh. & Traf. Law § 253, treated in § 97.

procedural matter. There is doubt about whether the doctrine applies in the commercial realm today, but in the tort sphere, it is clear that it does not apply at all.[8] The corporate employee is individually liable for any tort he commits, whether or not the corporation is derivatively liable as well, and when subjected to longarm jurisdiction under one of the tort provisions, the individual cannot erect the "fiduciary shield"—i.e., plead that he was only acting in behalf of the corporation—as a defense to jurisdiction. After some conflict on the point among lower courts, the Court of Appeals held in CPC Intern. Inc. v. McKesson Corp.,[9] that in a tort case under CPLR 302(a)(2), the "fiduciary shield" doctrine does not apply and the individual is therefore subject to longarm jurisdiction for the tort.

Perhaps jurisdiction in this regard is just following the substantive law, the individual being subject to jurisdiction for the corporate act only when he is substantively liable for the corporate act.[10] With tort, unlike contract, an individual purporting to act for another does not escape personal liability under some kind of innocent agency theory.

Because of the *Feathers* strictures and the statute's language, CPLR 302(a)(2) is used only in the relatively clear-cut situation of a tort actually committed in New York. It generates less caselaw than the situations in which conduct outside New York results in injury within the State, a jurisdictional niche filled by CPLR 302(a)(3), treated in the next section.

§ 88.   Without/Injury Within New York Under CPLR 302(a)(3)

Paragraph 3 of CPLR 302(a) was added in 1966 in response to the restrictive interpretation the Court of Appeals made of CPLR 302(a)(2) in the *Feathers* case.[1] It was the product of a study conducted by the Judicial Conference.[2] Like paragraph 2, paragraph 3 applies in personal injury as well as property damage cases and even in commercial tort cases that:

General Elements in CPLR 302(a)(3)

In all instances under paragraph 3, it must be shown that: (1) the defendant committed a tortious act outside New York, (2) the cause of action arose from that act, and (3) the act caused injury within New York. Those three requirements must be met in all cases, but the plaintiff must also satisfy either of the two subparagraphs of paragraph 3. One additional showing is necessary if subparagraph (i) is used, which makes a total of four showings needed for 302(a)(3)(i) jurisdiction; two additional showings are necessary if subparagraph (ii) is relied on, for a total of five.

The two subparagraphs of paragraph 3 are the principal sources of dispute, but there has also been activity on the introductory clause in paragraph 3 containing the omnibus requirements of a tortious act outside New York and injury within, which are

---

[8]   See the discussion of the *Kreutter* case in § 86.

[9]   CPC Intern. Inc. v. McKesson Corp., 70 N.Y.2d 268, 519 N.Y.S.2d 804, 514 N.E.2d 116 (1987). Subsequently, in *Kreutter*, the Court held that the fiduciary shield doctrine does not apply to any other provisions of the long-arm statute.

[10]   It is submitted that this ought to be the rule, but it is not at all clear that it is. See the discussion of this point and of the *CPC* case generally in the lead note in NYSLD No. 336.

[1]   See § 87.

[2]   The study is published in 11th Jud. Conf. Rep. 132 (1966).

applicable to both subparagraphs. When co-conspirators are involved, for example, there have been some apparently conflicting decisions on whether the tortious activity of one can be imputed to the other as a "tortious act" for longarm jurisdiction.[3]

Recent Supreme Court Caselaw

Before delving into the New York caselaw interpreting the requirements in CPLR 302(a)(3)(i) and (ii), several United States Supreme Court decisions must be examined, including its 2014 decision in Walden v. Fiore.[4] *Walden* involved the assertion of longarm jurisdiction by a federal court in Nevada over a Drug Enforcement Agency (DEA) agent, who improperly seized $97,000 of plaintiffs' cash while they were at a stopover in an airport in Georgia en route to their Nevada residence. The Nevada longarm statute relied upon by plaintiffs to assert jurisdiction over the Georgia DEA agent was a general one, permitting its courts to exercise jurisdiction over persons "on any basis not inconsistent with . . . the Constitution of the United States."

In a unanimous opinion, the Supreme Court concluded that the Nevada district court lacked personal jurisdiction over the defendant. The Court focused on the "minimum contacts" necessary between the defendant and the forum state and found those insuffcient to create longarm jurisdiction in the action. The Court stressed that the central jurisdictional inquiry is the contacts that "defendant himself" creates with the forum state, and not plaintiff's connection with same.[5] Furthermore, the Court observed that " 'minimum contacts' analysis looks to the defendant's contacts with the forum State itself, not the defendant's contacts with persons who reside there."[6] While the Court acknowledged that "physical presence in the forum is not a prerequisite to jurisdiction . . . physical entry into the State—either by the defendant in person or through an agent, goods, mail, or some other means—is certainly a relevant contact."[7]

Applying these principles, the Court noted that defendant "approached, questioned, and searched respondents, and seized the cash at issue, in the Atlanta airport," and "never traveled to, conducted activities within, contacted anyone in, or sent anything or anyone to Nevada."[8] In language that is pertinent to the application of CPLR 302(a)(3), the Supreme Court criticized the Ninth Circuit's opinion to the extent it "shift[ed] the analytical focus from [defendant's] contacts with the forum to his contacts with [plaintiffs . . . and his] knowledge of [plaintiffs'] strong forum connections."[9] Defendant's conduct toward plaintiffs, whom he knew had Nevada connections, and the fact that it was foreseeable that plaintiffs would suffer harm in Nevada were insuffcient to establish minimum contacts with the forum state. The key jurisdictional inquiry "is not where the plaintiff experienced a particular injury or effect but whether the defendant's conduct connects him to the forum in a meaningful way."[10] When examined from this perspective, it was undisputed that no part of defendant's conduct occurred in Nevada.

---

[3]   See Lehigh Valley Industries, Inc. v. Birenbaum, 389 F. Supp. 798 (S.D.N.Y. 1975), aff'd, 527 F.2d 87 (2d Cir.), distinguished in Hargrave v. Oki Nursery, Inc., 636 F.2d 897 (2d Cir. 1980).

[4]   Walden v. Fiore, 134 S. Ct. 1115, 1122, 188 L. Ed. 2d 12 (2014).

[5]   *Walden*, 134 S. Ct. at 1122.

[6]   *Walden*, 134 S. Ct. at 1122.

[7]   *Walden*, 134 S. Ct. at 1122.

[8]   *Walden*, 134 S. Ct. at 1124.

[9]   *Walden*, 134 S. Ct. at 1124.

[10]   *Walden*, 134 S. Ct. at 1125. For further discussion of *Walden*, see Patrick M. Connors, *Impact of Supreme Court Decisions on New York Practice [Part I]*, N.Y.L.J., June 18, 2014, at 116 and Patrick M.

Just three years prior to the decision in *Walden*, the Supreme Court foreshadowed the tightening of the reins on the application of longarm jurisdiction under CPLR 302(a)(3) in two decisions. In Goodyear Dunlop Tires Operations, S.A. v. Brown,[11] a unanimous Court held that a tire made by a U.S. company's foreign affiliate, causing the death of two North Carolina minors in Paris, doesn't give the decedents' home state jurisdiction over the affiliate. An important aspect of the case is its definitive rejection of the so-called "stream of commerce" argument that plaintiffs hoped to get the Court to adopt against manufacturers, which had been frequently invoked in lower court decisions. The argument posits that if the defendant company manufactures an item outside the forum state and: (1) puts the item into the "stream of commerce" internationally, (2) the item is in some way defective, and (3) the defect causes injury in the forum, the injured person should be able to secure in his home courts full in personam jurisdiction of the foreign manufacturer. Hints in prior cases that it might adopt the doctrine were proved idle and laid to rest in *Goodyear*, with the Court stressing that the plaintiffs' claims were unrelated to any activity of the affiliate in the forum state.

In the second decision, J. McIntyre Machinery, Ltd. v. Nicastro,[12] the Court rejected longarm jurisdiction in New Jersey for a person injured by a machine there, reasoning that the British manufacturer didn't specifically target New Jersey for its products. Here the Court was fragmented. A three-justice dissent said that the manufacturer did not have to aim its product at New Jersey specifically; that under the Court's precedents it was enough that the manufacturer aimed to cover the whole country with its products. A four judge plurality rejected this notion, commenting that the application of the "stream of commerce" metaphor would result in assertions of longarm jurisdiction that did not comport with due process.

The Application of CPLR 302(a)(3) in the 21st Century

With the backdrop of this recent Supreme Court caselaw, we can now turn to a detailed examination of what is required to establish longarm jurisdiction under CPLR 302(a)(3) today. In addition to the three items always necessary under CPLR 302(a)(3), the plaintiff seeking to satisfy subparagraph (i) is required to show that the defendant:

> regularly does or solicits business, or engages in any other persistent course of conduct, or derives substantial revenue from goods used or consumed or services rendered, in the state.

This subparagraph requires at root a showing that the defendant has some overall contact with New York, or derives some substantial commercial benefit from New York. The cause of action sued on, however, need not necessarily be related to those New York activities. Requiring those activities is designed to assure only that the defendant's overall contact with New York is substantial enough to make it reasonable to subject the defendant to jurisdiction here.

If the defendant is a corporation "at home" in New York, it is of course subject to "general" jurisdiction under CPLR 301 and no help is needed from CPLR 302. In this

---

Connors, *Impact of Recent U.S. Supreme Court Decisions on New York Practice [Part II]*, N.Y.L.J., July 21, 2014, at 13.

[11] Goodyear Dunlop Tires Operations, S.A. v. Brown, 564 U.S. 915, 131 S. Ct. 2846, 180 L. Ed. 2d 796 (2011).

[12] J. McIntyre Machinery, Ltd. v. Nicastro, 564 U.S. 873, 131 S. Ct. 2780, 180 L. Ed. 2d 765 (2011) (SPR 235:3).

connection, note that the "does business" requirement of CPLR 302(a)(3)(i) was not intended to require as much activity as the former "doing business" test required.[13] In the words of the statute, any "persistent course of conduct" should do.

Of the several items listed in subparagraph (i), the one most often relied on is the defendant's derivation of "substantial revenue from goods used or consumed" in New York. A uniformly dependable yardstick for what is or is not "substantial" has not yet been devised, but a proportion test is one measure, comparing the defendant's overall income with its New York portion. While such a test has been used,[14] there is no rigid rule about what percentage suffices.

A quantity test can be used in the alternative. The amount of revenue the defendant derives from New York may be great, for example, and yet constitute only a small percentage of the defendant's overall business. That was the situation in Allen v. Canadian General Electric Co.[15] In *Allen*, the $9 million of New York income was only 1% of the defendant's overall business. The defendant contended that the small percentage meant that the $9 million was not "substantial revenue." The contention was rejected and jurisdiction sustained, but the defendant got an award for keeping a straight face throughout the proceedings.

Gross and net income are looked at,[16] but whether the sums involved are "substantial" requires a factual inquiry in each case.

If the plaintiff is depending on subparagraph (ii), the requirements differ. Here the plaintiff must show that the defendant:

> expects or should reasonably expect the act to have consequences in the state
> and derives substantial revenue[17] from interstate or international commerce.

As far as the statute is concerned, the commerce need not take in the State of New York. It can be interstate commerce on the West Coast only, for example. This aspect of subparagraph (ii) can be called the "bigness" requirement. It's imposed not to guarantee an overall contact with New York, as subparagraph (i) is designed to do, but to assure that the defendant is economically big enough to be able to defend a New York lawsuit without undue hardship. It is the expectation aspect of subparagraph (ii) that is supposed to tie the case to New York and satisfy due process.

The expectation requirement is a general one. The defendant need not foresee the specific injury-producing event in New York. In the case of a product, for example, it has been held that it is sufficient if the defendant knew that it was likely to end up in New York and (if defective) do injury.[18]

That the commerce showing under subparagraph (ii) need not take in New York State, and that the expectation aspect suffices to give New York the requisite due process

---

[13]   12th Jud. Conf. Rep. 343 (1967). Today's "at home" standard for establishing general jurisdiction, and the former "doing business" test, are discussed in § 82.

[14]   See Gillmore v. J. S. Inskip, Inc., 54 Misc. 2d 218, 282 N.Y.S.2d 127 (Sup. Ct., Nassau County 1967).

[15]   Allen v. Canadian General Elec. Co. Ltd., 65 A.D.2d 39, 410 N.Y.S.2d 707 (3d Dep't 1978), aff'd, 50 N.Y.2d 935, 431 N.Y.S.2d 526, 409 N.E.2d 998 (1980).

[16]   See Allen v. Auto Specialties Mfg. Co., 45 A.D.2d 331, 357 N.Y.S.2d 547 (3d Dep't 1974).

[17]   The test for what constitutes "substantial" revenue should be similar to that used under subparagraph (i).

[18]   Gonzales v. Harris Calorific Co., 64 Misc. 2d 287, 315 N.Y.S.2d 51 (Sup. Ct., Queens County 1970), aff'd, 35 A.D.2d 720, 315 N.Y.S.2d 815 (2d Dep't).

nexus, are the assumptions underlying subparagraph (ii), but they are too rosy a set of conclusions today, especially after the Supreme Court's decision in *Walden*. The same may be said of subparagraph (i)'s contentment with a simple showing that the defendant "derives substantial revenue from goods used or consumed" in New York. In a major pronouncement on longarm jurisdiction in 1980, years after the 1966 enactment of CPLR 302(a)(3), the U.S. Supreme Court took a considerably more restrictive view about longarm jurisdiction in World-Wide Volkswagen Corp. v. Woodson,[19] its first address to longarm jurisdiction in a tort case. The due process standard under *World-Wide* is more restrictive of state options in accident cases than had been assumed under many of the state statutes—including CPLR 302(a)(3)—and it is likely that many jurisdiction-sustaining decisions under them, reexamined in the light of *World-Wide* and *Walden*, would not pass the jurisdictional test today.

The plaintiffs in *World-Wide* were New Yorkers when they bought an Audi automobile from a retailer (R) in an upstate New York village. The regional distributor of the car (W, for wholesaler) operated in New York, New Jersey, and Connecticut. Both R and W were New York corporations. The plaintiffs were on their way to Arizona in the car when it was involved in an accident in Oklahoma, the state whose jurisdictional statute was involved—and found unconstitutional in its application—in *World-Wide*. Alleging personal injuries caused by the defective design of the car, the plaintiffs sued four defendants. In addition to R and W, they joined M and N in the Oklahoma action; M was the foreign manufacturer and N the importer and national distributor of Audi cars.

The Oklahoma statute on which jurisdiction was predicated was akin to subparagraph (i) of New York CPLR 302(a)(3), the subparagraph that seeks to exercise jurisdiction whenever a tortious act outside the state causes injury within the state if (among other things) the particular defendant "derives substantial revenue from goods used or consumed . . . in this state."

In respect of the New York defendants R and W, the U.S. Supreme Court found "a total absence of those affiliating circumstances that are a necessary predicate to any exercise of state-court jurisdiction." Those defendants "carry on no activity . . . close no sales . . . perform no services . . . avail themselves of none of the privileges and benefits of Oklahoma law . . . [and] solicit no business there." Hence, in respect of R and W, the due process clause barred Oklahoma from assuming jurisdiction.

R's activities were centered around its upstate New York village and W's activities, although they crossed state lines, did so only to enter the two adjoining states of New Jersey and Connecticut, not Oklahoma. But W's activities were nevertheless interstate, if not national, and in this regard the *World-Wide* case can be viewed as a restriction not only on subparagraph (i) of CPLR 302(a)(3), but also on subparagraph (ii). One of the latter's jurisdictional predicates is that the defendant derives substantial revenue from interstate commerce even if New York is not included in that commerce, but the fact that W in the *World-Wide* case was involved in interstate commerce didn't ensure jurisdiction in the forum state.

While the *World-Wide* decision seems on its face to have bad jurisdictional news for tort plaintiffs—including a refusal by the Supreme Court to accord an automobile any unique jurisdictional status on a "dangerous instrumentality" theory, as had often been

---

[19]   World-Wide Volkswagen Corp. v. Woodson, 444 U.S. 286, 100 S. Ct. 559, 62 L. Ed. 2d 490 (1980).

relied on in prior cases—a bit of probing beneath the surface may reveal a more optimistic message for tort plaintiffs. Both M, the manufacturer, and N, the national distributor, remained parties to the litigation, not having brought any jurisdictional objection before the Supreme Court. Even if they had, there is language in the Court's opinion suggesting that as to them, the jurisdictional objections would not have succeeded and Oklahoma jurisdiction would have been sustained. That would give the plaintiffs jurisdiction over the two final links in the chain of purchase, and solvent sources for any sum awarded as damages, so that in many cases it would be unimportant that the immediate seller and the regional distributor are jurisdictionally unavailable. Indeed, Justice Blackmun in a dissenting opinion in *World-Wide* expresses puzzlement at why the plaintiffs should be so insistent on jurisdiction over the retailer and wholesaler when the obviously solvent manufacturer and national distributor did not challenge Oklahoma jurisdiction.

Seven years later, in Asahi Metal Industry Co., Ltd. v. Superior Court of California, Solano County,[20] the Court came close to rejecting the "stream of commerce" test that was seemingly relied upon in *World-Wide*. In that case, a motorcycle accident in California was allegedly caused by a defective tire tube and its valve. While jurisdiction over the tube manufacturer, a Taiwanese company selling its product by the thousands in California, was present there, jurisdiction over the Japanese valve manufacturer, from which the Taiwanese company bought the valve assemblies and which it tried to implead, was rejected. As noted above, the definitive rejection of the "stream of commerce" theory would occur in the Court's 2011 decision in *Goodyear*.

Jurisdiction with respect to only an indemnification claim between the two companies was at issue in *Asahi*, and a majority of the Court stresses that point. Would a different view prevail if the injured plaintiff were the one seeking jurisdiction of the valve manufacturer? The possibility is not foreclosed, but is severely diminished today in light of the decisions in *Goodyear* and *Walden*.

It may of course happen in a given case that fault is traceable to something that the retailer or regional distributor did—something that does not implicate the national distributor or manufacturer. In a case like *World-Wide*, that would mean no jurisdiction in the other state. But a case of that nature would seem the exception rather than the rule. Defective design or manufacture is more often likely to be the liability predicate, and with warranty and/or strict products liability available as liability theories against the manufacturer and national distributor, who are available jurisdictionally throughout the country, the regional distributor may not be missed.

The expectation element, a key one under the jurisdictional requirements of subparagraph (ii) of CPLR 302(a)(3), gets much attention in the *World-Wide* case, but is given less effect than the New York statute envisioned. In its 2014 decision in *Walden*, the Supreme Court made clear that defendant's expectation that a plaintiff might suffer harm in the forum state, standing alone, is not a sufficient basis on which to ground jurisdiction.

The decisions in *Walden* and *World-Wide* have impact on longarm jurisdiction generally so that their jurisdictional precepts will be guideposts regardless of the particular statute being used. It is sometimes possible, for example, to fit under CPLR

---

[20]　Asahi Metal Industry Co., Ltd. v. Superior Court of California, Solano County, 480 U.S. 102, 107 S. Ct. 1026, 94 L. Ed. 2d 92 (1987).

302(a)(1), as a "transaction of business," a fact pattern that may also fit the statutory language of paragraphs 2 or 3 of CPLR 302(a), the tortious-act provisions. An attempted jurisdictional exercise that runs afoul of constitutional restrictions, however, as occurred in *Walden* and *World-Wide*, would fail whether predicated on the particular language of the statute the court has before it—in *World-Wide*, the Oklahoma statute akin to New York's CPLR 302(a)(3)(i)—or even a general longarm provision, as in *Walden*.

Now for a look at some cases decided before *Walden* or even *World-Wide* to see whether their fact patterns can survive a reexamination. Would the case that occasioned the adoption of CPLR 302(a)(3), for example, the *Feathers* decision,[21] itself be a casualty of the tightened standards?[22] To whom do we analogize the Kansas tank manufacturer involved in the *Feathers* case? If to the car manufacturer in *World-Wide*, jurisdiction would likely be upheld. Did the tank manufacturer in *Feathers* intend to blanket the country with its tanks as the Volkswagen Company intended to blanket the country with its cars in *World-Wide*? That would be a key inquiry. Each prior case requires a similar scrutiny under the principles of the *World-Wide*, *Goodyear*, and *Walden* decisions.

Furthermore, in *Feathers* it was contended that all of defendant manufacturer's business was carried on from its plant and offices in Kansas City, Kansas, that defendant never had any agents, representatives, offices, or other facilities in New York, and there was no claim that it ever transacted or solicited any business here.[23] In the aftermath of *Walden* and *World-Wide*, it is highly unlikely that minimum contacts could be established against a similarly situated manufacturer today merely because, under CPLR 302(a)(3)(ii), it "expects or should reasonably expect the act [of negligent manufacturing] to have consequences in the [New York] state."

Another illustration of subparagraph (ii) in operation in an earlier decision is Brown v. Erie-Lackawanna R. Co.[24] There the defendant was a foreign railroad engaged in interstate commerce. It leased a car to X, which used it in New York where it came loose, went wild, and killed the plaintiff's intestate. All the CPLR (a)(3)(ii) elements were met and jurisdiction was sustained: (1) act outside New York (negligent maintenance), (2) injury within New York, (3) cause of action arising from the act, (4) expectation that the car would be used in New York and could do damage here, and (5) derivation of substantial revenue from interstate commerce. But would the case pass muster under *Walden* and *World-Wide*?

The facts of each such earlier decision have to be reinvestigated along lines that would meet current due process requirements, and often there may not be sufficient facts visible on the face of the opinion to support a reappraisal.

It is required in all CPLR 302 cases that the claim arise out of the activities complained of; it's part of the statute's introductory language and hence implicit in all exercises of jurisdiction under it. For good measure, the Court of Appeals emphasizes it

---

[21]   See § 87.

[22]   As far as the statutory overruling of the *Feathers* case is concerned (which occurred long before the *World-Wide* case came down from the U.S. Supreme Court), CPLR 302(a)(3)(ii) did its job well. The *Feathers* litigation, dismissed under paragraph 2 of CPLR 302(a), see § 87, was promptly recommenced after paragraph 3 was added a year or so later. Defendant's counsel reported that jurisdiction was then conceded and the case settled.

[23]   Longines-Wittnauer Watch Co. v. Barnes & Reinecke, Inc., 15 N.Y.2d 443, 459, 261 N.Y.S.2d 8, 20, 209 N.E.2d 68, 76 (1965).

[24]   Brown v. Erie-Lackawanna R. Co., 54 Misc. 2d 225, 282 N.Y.S.2d 335 (Sup. Ct., Oneida County 1967).

as a formal fifth requirement in the CPLR 302(a)(3)(ii). This the Court does in its 2000 LaMarca v. Pak-Mor Manufacturing Co. decision.[25]

In *LaMarca*, which is a quintessential Court of Appeals model of CPLR 302(a)(3)(ii) jurisdiction, the Court sustained jurisdiction over D, a Texas company. The company manufactured a loading device at its Virginia factory where it was installed on a sanitation truck that D's New York distributor picked up in Virginia and delivered to the Town of Niagara in New York. The town was the employer of P, who was injured a few months later when he fell off the back of the truck while standing on the loader's riding platform. The five enumerated CPLR 302(a)(3)(ii) requirements as recited in *LaMarca* are—verbatim—that the plaintiff show that:

— the defendant committed a tortious act outside the state;

— the cause of action arises from that act;

— the act caused injury to person or property within the State;

— defendant expected or should reasonably have expected the act to have consequences in the State; and

— the defendant derived substantial revenue from interstate or international commerce.

In *LaMarca*, the first three elements were concededly present. The fourth and fifth, while disputed, were resolved in the plaintiff's favor. It also appears that the holding in *LaMarca* would survive analysis under the Supreme Court's 2014 decision in *Walden*. The defendant in *LaMarca* did establish several contacts with New York, including a New York distributor and "district representative," to increase sales of its products in New York. The defendant also advertised in nationally published trade magazines using the logo "Sanitation for the Nation," thereby projecting itself into the New York market. Those facts provided a meaningful connection between defendant and the New York forum, which was a key element missing in *Walden*.

Miscellaneous Issues Arising Under CPLR 302(a)(3)

There are several other general things worth stressing under the statute. Under CPLR 302(a)(3), the original injury must occur in New York. If the injury occurs outside New York and just becomes manifest in New York, or has its greatest consequences in New York, or results in loss of earnings in New York, the statute is not satisfied and jurisdiction does not obtain.[26] In Paterno v. Laser Spine Institute,[27] for example, the Court rejected plaintiff's argument that longarm jurisdiction existed under CPLR 302(a)(3) against a group of defendants that had surgically treated plaintiff's spine at their facility in Florida. In that "the situs of the injury in medical malpractice cases is the location of the original event which caused the injury, and not where a party experiences the consequences of such injury," plaintiff could not establish an injury in New York.[28]

---

[25] LaMarca v. Pak-Mor Mfg. Co., 95 N.Y.2d 210, 713 N.Y.S.2d 304, 735 N.E.2d 883 (2000) (NYSLD No. 487).

[26] Black v. Oberle Rentals, Inc., 55 Misc. 2d 398, 285 N.Y.S.2d 226 (Sup. Ct., Onondaga County 1967).

[27] Paterno v. Laser Spine Institute, 24 N.Y.3d 370, 998 N.Y.S.2d 720, 23 N.E.3d 988 (2014).

[28] *Paterno*, 24 N.Y.3d at 381, 998 N.Y.S.2d at 728, 23 N.E.3d at 996. The *Paterno* decision, which also raised issues of longarm jurisdiction under CPLR 302(a)(1), is discussed in further detail in § 86.

The Court also held in a commercial setting that injuries do not have a New York situs merely because the plaintiff has a New York domicile. In Fantis Foods, Inc. v. Standard Importing Co., Inc.,[29] P and D were competitors in wholesaling imported cheese. D was a New York corporation. D impleaded X, a nondomiciliary importer, alleging conversion, but it was shown that the goods at issue were shipped f.o.b. Greece and were addressed to Chicago. Apparently all D could show in support of its longarm claim in the third-party action was consequential damage to itself in New York. This did not suffice for jurisdiction of X because the original injury must occur in New York, and in *Fantis*, it was not established that it did.

Longarm jurisdiction was tried, unsuccessfully, against a physician practicing in his own state, Vermont, to whom a New York physician sent a New York patient who lived near the Vermont border. The patient later died of cancers the defendant allegedly failed to notice. On these facts, a divided Court of Appeals held that the physician was not involved in "interstate commerce" under CPLR 302(a)(3)(ii) because his practice was confined to Vermont.[30]

That CPLR 302(a)(3) applies to commercial as well as personal torts is best illustrated by the influential decision in Sybron Corp. v. Wetzel,[31] where the Court of Appeals applied it to sustain longarm jurisdiction for injunctive relief against a New Jersey defendant, D. D was about to retain the services of X, one of P's former employees in possession of P's trade secrets. D had no New York office or employees and could therefore be reached only through longarm jurisdiction, if at all. The Court held that he was subject to longarm jurisdiction.

Other important points in *Sybron* are that no tort had as yet been committed, and the action was for an injunction, not damages. The Court held that the longarm statute is available for injunctive relief and for mere "anticipatory" relief at that—as long as the requisite longarm elements are demonstrated. The elements of subparagraph (ii) of CPLR 302(a)(3) were held satisfied in *Sybron*, with stress on the fact that P would suffer great injury in New York through loss of customers if its trade secrets were to get out.

Nor does CPLR 302(a)(3) confine itself to claims sounding directly in tort. It may be used for any claim merely "arising" from a tortious act.[32] It applies to warranty claims, for example.[33]

There have been cases on how far the statute will reach to take jurisdiction of nondomiciliary defendants who have carried on activity through the Internet. In Bensusan Restaurant Corp. v. King,[34] for example, in which a New York jazz club tried to sue a club in a moderate sized Missouri town for using the plaintiff's name on its website and violating its trademark, the Second Circuit held—prognosticating—that the New York Court of Appeals would not uphold jurisdiction of the Missouri defendant.[35]

---

[29]   Fantis Foods, Inc. v. Standard Importing Co., Inc., 49 N.Y.2d 317, 425 N.Y.S.2d 783, 402 N.E.2d 122 (1980).

[30]   Ingraham v. Carroll, 90 N.Y.2d 592, 665 N.Y.S.2d 10, 687 N.E.2d 1293 (1997) (NYSLD No. 455).

[31]   Sybron Corp. v. Wetzel, 46 N.Y.2d 197, 413 N.Y.S.2d 127, 385 N.E.2d 1055 (1978).

[32]   See Garbellotto v. Montelindo Compagnie Navegacion, S. A., 294 F. Supp. 487, 1969 A.M.C. 101 (S.D.N.Y. 1969).

[33]   Naples v. City of New York, 34 A.D.2d 577, 309 N.Y.S.2d 663 (2d Dep't 1970).

[34]   Bensusan Restaurant Corp. v. King, 126 F.3d 25, 44 U.S.P.Q.2d 1051 (2d Cir. 1997).

[35]   The subject of Internet jurisdiction also arises under the "transacts any business" clause of CPLR 302(a)(1), for which see § 86.

If the defendant is a bigger enterprise with operations through the Internet that reach well beyond its own bailiwick, other courts have sustained longarm jurisdiction.[36] In an extensive review in Hearst Corp. v. Goldberger,[37] however, a federal magistrate in New York's Southern District declined to follow cases upholding what it described as "Internet Personal Jurisdiction."

The Court of Appeals discusses longarm jurisdiction through Internet activities in Penguin Group (USA) Inc. v. American Buddha.[38] Applying CPLR 302(a)(3)(ii), the Court held that uploading a New York publisher's books onto the Internet, even outside the State, gives copyright infringement jurisdiction to the New York courts. The Court held that the situs of injury in such actions for purposes of determining long-arm jurisdiction under CPLR 302(a)(3)(ii) is the residence or location of the principal place of business of the copyright holder.

CPLR 302(a)(3) is obviously not perfect.[39] In view of recent U.S. Supreme Court cases, especially the decision in *Walden*, its application is not even entirely constitutional in certain instances. But it still poses numerous jurisdictional opportunities if constitutional strictures are kept in mind. If there is doubt in a given case, it may be worth a try to get jurisdiction in the New York courts, as long as the lawyer keeps a careful eye on statute of limitations requirements applicable in the state or states to which the plaintiff would have to turn for suit should jurisdiction in New York be rejected.[40]

§ 89.   Real Property Longarm Cases Under CPLR 302(a)(4)

This paragraph has generated few cases. It subjects the defendant to longarm jurisdiction on a claim arising out of the ownership, use, or possession of New York real property. It has been applied to a claim to compel D to convey the realty to P or pay damages in the alternative.[1] That kind of case arises from D's ownership of the property. An early one that arose from the possession of the property was a suit by a landlord against a dentist who leased premises and then reneged on the lease and moved to Maine. Jurisdiction was upheld for unpaid rent, reletting charges, incidental charges, and attorney's fees.[2]

When B is not a domiciliary or resident of New York and never enters the state, but contracts to buy New York land by negotiating for it from outside the state and then fails to make the required payments and complete the transaction, it was held in Black River

---

[36]   See, e.g., Inset Systems, Inc. v. Instruction Set, Inc., 937 F. Supp. 161, 155 A.L.R. Fed. 745 (D. Conn. 1996).

[37]   Hearst Corp. v. Goldberger, 1997 WL 97097 (S.D.N.Y. 1997).

[38]   Penguin Group (USA) Inc. v. American Buddha, 16 N.Y.3d 295, 921 N.Y.S.2d 171, 946 N.E.2d 159 (2011) (NYSLD No. 617, p.3).

[39]   Drawing a specific and yet perfect statute is impossible because of the numerous potential factual variations. The 11th Jud. Conf. Rep. 132 (1966), cited in note 2, above, concedes this and leaves it implicitly to caselaw, armed with the Due Process Clause, to guard the outer borders of these longarm exercises.

[40]   See § 231A, item 5.

[1]   Tebedo v. Nye, 45 Misc. 2d 222, 256 N.Y.S.2d 235 (Sup. Ct., Onondaga County 1965).

[2]   Hempstead Medical Arts Co. v. Willie, N.Y.L.J., Dec. 9, 1963, at 18, col.6 (Sup. Ct., Nassau County; Farley, J.).

Associates v. Newman[3] that B is subject to the personal jurisdiction of the New York courts in a specific performance suit by the seller.[4]

Suppose now that a loan is transacted outside New York between nonresidents and a mortgage on New York real property is given to secure it, with the mortgage, in form satisfactory to New York law, being sent to New York for recording, but without any of the parties entering the state. There would be no difficulty about later getting New York jurisdiction to foreclose the mortgage, because mere rem jurisdiction would suffice for that, but suppose a deficiency arises, the land not bringing in enough to pay the debt. Under the reasoning of the *Black River* case, CPLR 302(a)(4) should supply jurisdiction to support a deficiency judgment, even though the deficiency arises on the loan, and even though the loan itself, when viewed apart from the mortgage, did not have New York contacts. Since the mortgage, which did have the requisite New York contacts, was given as security for the loan, the foreclosure action should fall under New York jurisdiction in all its incidents.

It is permissible for the cause of action to accrue after the land has been disposed of. If the claim arises from the ownership, use, or possession of the land and can be traced to just that, it should make no difference that at the moment of its arising the defendant no longer has an interest in the land.[5]

§ 90.   Longarm Jurisdiction for Support and Other Relief Under CPLR 302(b)

CPLR 302(b) gives the court longarm personal jurisdiction in certain family actions. It applies in the matrimonial action[1] in the supreme court and in any family court proceeding in which support is claimed. At first it offered longarm jurisdiction only for "support or alimony." With subsequent amendments, however, designed to recognize all of the property categories applicable after the 1980 adoption of the equitable distribution system in matrimonial actions,[2] it offers longarm jurisdiction for "support, alimony, maintenance, distributive awards or special relief in matrimonial actions."

CPLR 302(b) applies to either spouse. While it is usually the husband or father against whom money is sought and who is liable for it in family matters, the wife or mother may also face this liability today.[3] Whenever the particular defendant (respondent in a family court proceeding) is substantively liable for the money or property demanded, CPLR 302(b) offers longarm jurisdiction to assist in getting it.

The statute has several requirements. The party against whom the demand is made need not be a domiciliary or resident of New York, but the party making the demand must be a resident when the demand is made—which is ordinarily when the suit is brought. It must also be shown that:

---

[3]   Black River Associates v. Newman, 218 A.D.2d 273, 637 N.Y.S.2d 880 (4th Dep't 1996).

[4]   The *Black River* case is the subject of the lead note in SPR 41.

[5]   See Karrat v. Merhib, 62 Misc. 2d 72, 307 N.Y.S.2d 915 (Sup. Ct., Oneida County 1970).

[1]   The matrimonial action is defined by CPLR 105 to include divorce, separation, annulment, and several actions declaring on the validity of the marriage or a purported foreign divorce.

[2]   Dom. Rel. Law § 236. See Scheinkman, Introductory Commentary on McKinney's Dom. Rel. Law § 236.

[3]   See Dom. Rel. Law §§ 236 and 240.

(1) New York was the matrimonial domicile of the parties before their estrangement; or

(2) "the defendant abandoned the plaintiff" in New York; or

(3) the claim for the relief "accrued under the laws" of New York or "under an agreement executed" in New York.

The first requirement, about matrimonial domicile, was construed by the Second Department in Lieb v. Lieb[4] to require that the matrimonial domicile be shown to have existed immediately prior to the estrangement, not at some more distant time in the past. But in Paparella v. Paparella,[5] in which the parties' departure from the state was recent, the state had been their matrimonial domicile for many years, and the plaintiff had resumed a New York residence at action time, the Fourth Department held the statute satisfied. *Paparella* distinguishes the *Lieb* case as involving "attenuated" New York contacts.

Disagreeing with *Lieb* as "unnecessarily restrictive" and taking note of the other departments' views, the Third Department sustained the use of CPLR 302(b) in a case in which New York had been the matrimonial domicile of the parties years earlier but had long since ceased to be when they separated.[6]

An attempt to use CPLR 302(b) as a predicate for support jurisdiction in a paternity suit was rejected in 1981 in Nilsa B. B. v. Clyde Blackwell H.[7] At the time, the language of requirement number 3 on the above list was that "the obligation to pay" must have accrued under New York law. The court held that no such obligation "accrues" until a filiation order is entered, i.e., that the "obligation" means one already embodied in a judicial direction. The legislature responded with an amendment of CPLR 302(b) in 1982, striking out the "obligation to pay" and substituting the "claim for" language set forth above. The statute should therefore be available for support jurisdiction in a paternity suit today on a showing that the child was born in New York or perhaps merely conceived in New York, though born elsewhere.[8] Given the benevolent purpose of this provision, the claim should be deemed to "accrue" under New York law under either showing.

When the statute applies, it invokes CPLR 313 and permits service without regard to state lines.

CPLR 302(b) may not be used to support matrimonial relief as such, i.e., a divorce, separation, etc. But if the plaintiff spouse is a New York domiciliary, the marriage itself is deemed to have a New York presence and qualifies as a res supporting rem jurisdiction for matrimonial relief under CPLR 314(1). Nor does CPLR 302(b) supply jurisdiction to award custody of a child. Section 76 et seq. of the Domestic Relations Law supplies the jurisdictional bases for custody awards. Both matrimonial and custody jurisdiction are discussed elsewhere.[9]

---

[4]　Lieb v. Lieb, 86 Misc. 2d 75, 381 N.Y.S.2d 757 (Sup. Ct., Queens County 1976), aff'd, 53 A.D.2d 67, 385 N.Y.S.2d 569 (2d Dep't 1976).

[5]　Paparella v. Paparella, 74 A.D.2d 106, 426 N.Y.S.2d 610 (4th Dep't 1980).

[6]　See Levy v. Levy, 185 A.D.2d 15, 592 N.Y.S.2d 480 (3d Dep't 1993), noted in SPR 1:3.

[7]　Nilsa B. B. v. Clyde Blackwell H., 84 A.D.2d 295, 445 N.Y.S.2d 579 (2d Dep't 1981).

[8]　See Shirley D. v. Carl D., 224 A.D.2d 60, 648 N.Y.S.2d 650 (2d Dep't 1996) (applying Fam. Ct. Act § 154).

[9]　See § 102.

Note, however, that a single action can involve three different jurisdictional statutes and satisfy all of them: CPLR 302(b) for support, CPLR 314(1) for matrimonial relief, and Domestic Relations Law § 75–d for custody.

Under the Uniform Interstate Family Support Act,[10] applications for support can be made by the family against an out-of-state support obligee. These applications are made in the family court.[11]

§ 91.   The Restricted Appearance Under CPLR 302(c)

The state's policy is to encourage longarm defendants to submit to New York jurisdiction without contesting it. As an incentive, CPLR 302(c) guarantees defendants that if they do appear in the action, the appearance may not be exploited by the plaintiff to add non-longarm claims against them. If, for example, the plaintiff in a case predicated on longarm jurisdiction should seek to amend the complaint to add an additional claim, that claim would also have to fall within the longarm standards of CPLR 302. If the new claim does not, it may not be interposed in the action through amendment or otherwise.

This has come to be known as the "no piling on" rule, or more formally as the "restricted appearance,"[1] to distinguish it from other kinds of appearances met later.[2] It is applicable only when jurisdiction is based "solely" on CPLR 302. If any other jurisdictional basis is used, CPLR 302(c) does not apply although some other statute may apply and offer analogous protection.[3]

§ 92.   Jurisdiction Versus the Merits

Suppose P sues nondomiciliary D for an assault allegedly committed in New York, serving D outside the state. P bases jurisdiction on CPLR 302(a)(2), defendant's commission of a "tortious act" in New York. D moves to dismiss for lack of jurisdiction, contending that he did not commit any tortious act. The court denies the motion and sustains jurisdiction. To do this, the court has to find that D committed the "tortious act," which is the jurisdictional prerequisite of CPLR 302(a)(2). But if the court does, isn't it also finding for the plaintiff on the merits, since the tort is precisely what P is suing for? Is P entitled at that moment to have liability determined in his favor and the case set down merely for an assessment of damages?

The question looks challenging because of this curious overlap of jurisdictional and merits requirements, but the courts have come up with practical solutions and the challenge is theoretical only. Distilling a single conclusion from a number of cases in the area, we may say this: the jurisdictional and merits questions, no matter how similar, are separate. A holding for jurisdictional purposes does not dictate how the case must be decided on the merits.

---

[10]   Article 5–B of the Fam. Ct. Act.

[11]   As of December 31, 1997, the UIFSA superseded and broadened the Uniform Support of Dependents Law, which had a similar mission. See the Introductory Commentary of Merril Sobie on Article 5–B in McKinney's Family Court Act in Fam. Ct. Act § 580–101.

[1]   See Homburger and Laufer, *Appearance and Jurisdictional Motions in New York*, 14 Buff. L. Rev. 374, 388 (1964).

[2]   See §§ 109 and 112.

[3]   See §§ 113 and 114, which discuss the limited and qualified appearances.

Conversely, a merits determination will not go back and undo a jurisdictional finding. In the example given, suppose that jurisdiction is sustained, the case goes through the usual pretrial preparation, and that at the main trial on the merits the jury finds that D did not commit a tort. Will the dismissal of P's case at that stage be on the merits, or merely for lack of jurisdiction (because a jurisdictional fact has now been found wanting)?

It will be on the merits. The jurisdictional line having long since been crossed, the case will not retreat to it no matter how inconsistent the two determinations may seem. This is a simple fact of life when jurisdiction depends in some measure on the merits, as longarm jurisdiction often does. The practical and theoretical justifications for these conclusions are ample, however, so they aren't really so contradictory after all.

To sustain longarm jurisdiction, P has to show facts that, assuming they are actionable, would give rise to longarm jurisdiction under CPLR 302. P's conclusion that the acts are "tortious" is generally accepted at the jurisdictional stage. If the defendant was the performer of acts and the complaint "adequately frames a cause of action in tort arising from those acts," the jurisdictional requirement is met.[1]

Another situation can be placed under the caption of this section: that in which a successor corporation, while found to be substantively liable for the acts of its predecessor corporation, is not subject to longarm personal jurisdiction in the state even though the predecessor corporation would have been. That appears to be the law on the subject, as recognized and applied, for example, by the appellate division in Semenetz v. Sherling & Walden, Inc.,[2] but the Court of Appeals in that case affirmed on other grounds,[3] sidestepping the jurisdictional question.

There is an irony in this. How can a state with so adequate a connection with the case as to bind it to its substantive law—and a potentially vast liability—be found, nevertheless, without the jurisdiction to hear the case in its courts in the first place?[4]

§ 93. Burden of Proving Jurisdiction

A jurisdictional question can arise in any case, but it is more challenging in the longarm case, and therefore, plaintiff's burden on the matter is best treated in that context.

It is often said that the plaintiff has the burden of proving jurisdiction whenever the issue is raised,[1] but it would seem that conclusion is either taken a bit lightly in longarm cases, or else amounts to a bout with semantics. If, for example, D moves to dismiss and a factual dispute arises between P and D as to whether D performed longarm acts, a judge with some doubts might be inclined to sustain jurisdiction and let the case go to trial on the merits. Technically, however, if each side makes out an equally convincing case, the party with the burden of proof is supposed to lose, and a longarm

---

[1]   Evans v. Planned Parenthood of Broome County, Inc., 43 A.D.2d 996, 997, 352 N.Y.S.2d 257, 259 (3d Dep't 1974). This approach also avoids the issue of divestiture of the right to trial by jury if the court's finding of jurisdiction were allowed to be dispositive of the merits as well.

[2]   Semenetz v. Sherling & Walden, Inc., 21 A.D.3d 1138, 801 N.Y.S.2d 78 (3d Dep't 2005), aff'd, 7 N.Y.3d 194, 818 N.Y.S.2d 819, 851 N.E.2d 1170 (2006).

[3]   Semenetz v. Sherling & Walden, Inc., 7 N.Y.3d 194, 818 N.Y.S.2d 819, 851 N.E.2d 1170 (2006) (NYSLD No. 559).

[4]   See the note in SPR 166:3.

[1]   See, e.g., Coast to Coast Energy, Inc. v. Gasarch, 149 A.D.3d 485, 53 N.Y.S.3d 16 (1st Dep't 2017).

plaintiff seldom loses on a close jurisdictional point. A judge can avoid the issue, and sustain jurisdiction, just by finding that the two sides are not "equally" convincing; that the plaintiff's showing is a mite stronger—just strong enough to discharge this "burden" of proof on the jurisdictional question. What is actually happening, however, is that the plaintiff is being given the benefit of the doubt on the jurisdictional point, a result theoretically at war with the notion that the burden of proof of jurisdiction is on the plaintiff.

Whoever may have this "burden," the degree of proof needed to sustain jurisdiction is certainly not as heavy as that needed to sustain a recovery on the merits.[2] In other words, the plaintiff may have the "burden," but it's a burden that discharges more easily than other burdens.

In Peterson v. Spartan Industries, Inc.,[3] a dispute arose over facts on which longarm jurisdiction depended. P needed to use the disclosure devices against D to help develop the jurisdictional facts. The court held that P is entitled to compel D to submit to disclosure in such an instance without first making out even a "prima facie showing of jurisdiction"; that P makes a "sufficient start" just by showing that his position is not "frivolous." Apparently, the mere fact that the defendant has moved to dismiss sets up a sufficient nexus for the court to take the limited step, not of sustaining jurisdiction, but of making the defendant submit to an examination on the facts on which jurisdiction depends. How else would the court get the limited jurisdiction it needs to let P even examine D on the jurisdictional question? In one case in which the defendant failed to deny that it was served, insisting that it was the plaintiff's burden to prove every detail about service including a description of the defendant, the defendant's silence was held to concede jurisdiction.[4]

When the federal courts meet the question of whether they have enough jurisdiction to decide issues on which that very jurisdiction depends, they have developed the theory of "jurisdiction to determine jurisdiction."[5] At least where the parties are before the court, even if only to pose a jurisdictional question, the court gets at least as much jurisdiction as it needs to determine the jurisdictional issue. The doings noted above under the New York longarm statute are analogous and fall conceptually—if not explicitly—under the doctrine of "jurisdiction to determine jurisdiction."

If the jurisdictional facts are so in dispute that they can't be resolved from affidavits and other submissions on the dismissal motion, a hearing may be required. A fast resolution of a jurisdictional question is usually preferred. The court does have the option to refrain from deciding the objection and directing the defendant to use it instead as a defense in the answer,[6] the idea in that case being to postpone its resolution until the main trial, but the alternative is unattractive because if the later decision is against jurisdiction, all the intervening effort preparing for trial will have been wasted. And for plaintiffs, postponement of the issue can be more than just a waste of time; because of statute of limitations considerations, it can destroy the case.

---

[2]   Buckley v. Redi-Bolt, Inc., 49 Misc. 2d 864, 268 N.Y.S.2d 653 (Sup. Ct., Rensselaer County 1966).

[3]   Peterson v. Spartan Industries, Inc., 33 N.Y.2d 463, 354 N.Y.S.2d 905, 310 N.E.2d 513 (1974).

[4]   See Kulpa v. Jackson, 3 Misc. 3d 227, 773 N.Y.S.2d 235 (Sup. Ct., Oneida County 2004), noted in SPR 152:4. Service in *Kulpa* was made outside the country pursuant to the Hague Convention, which the court treats at length in the opinion.

[5]   See U.S. v. United Mine Workers of America, 330 U.S. 258, 67 S. Ct. 677, 91 L. Ed. 884 (1947).

[6]   CPLR 3211(d).

When one hears, therefore, that courts do not favor viva voce hearings for only a jurisdictional question, with the calling of witnesses and the usual testimonial proof, it is usually a federal source that's doing the talking.[7] In New York practice, such hearings are frequent, especially if the statute of limitations would now be dead on a new action should the present one be dismissed. The dismissal would be for want of personal jurisdiction, a category of dismissal that does not get the six months that CPLR 205(a) would otherwise offer for a new action.[8] In practical terms, therefore, the prospect is that the disposition of this mere "jurisdictional" question can mean the death of the case substantively. This prompts the court to dispose of the question immediately for the obvious reason that if the decision is against jurisdiction, it will save the time and trouble of a lengthy trial on the merits.

A jurisdictional objection by a defendant and an immediate trial of an issue of fact connected with it has been frequent enough in New York to earn a special word of description: in common usage it's called a "traverse." In the world at large, the word has many colorful meanings, but in New York practice has come to be applied almost exclusively to the trial of an issue of fact arising on a motion to dismiss for want of personal jurisdiction—most often for some defect in the manner of service, but sometimes just to determine whether there are sufficient longarm contacts to support extraterritorial jurisdiction.

If such a trial seems necessary, and the situation is one in which jurisdictional and merits requirements overlap,[9] the parties might stipulate that the result of the jurisdictional trial be deemed binding on the merits as well. That would expedite the case, but that phenomenon, too, is seen more often in federal than New York State practice.[10]

§ 94. Overlap of Longarm Bases

It will sometimes happen that several different provisions offer a predicate for jurisdiction. They may be different statutes altogether or different subdivisions of the same statute. Two and sometimes even three of CPLR 302(a)'s paragraphs can apply in the same case, for example, as where D is a nondomiciliary in the business of owning and operating New York City apartment houses. If D's negligence in the maintenance of a common hallway injures P, P may base jurisdiction against D on paragraph 1 of CPLR 302(a) (transacting business), paragraph 2 (tortious act), or paragraph 4 (claim arising out of the ownership of realty).

There are other statutes on the books that will overlap CPLR 302 from time to time. A notable example is the nonresident motorist statute,[1] separately treated later.[2] If it applies, service may be made on the secretary of state as the implied-in-law agent of the nondomiciliary defendant. Through this "agency," jurisdiction is secured on service technically made in New York, but at root it's a kind of longarm jurisdiction since it gives

---

[7] See, e.g., Unicon Management Corp. v. Koppers Co., 38 F.R.D. 474, 9 Fed. R. Serv. 2d 12B.22, Case 7 (S.D.N.Y. 1965).

[8] CPLR 205(a); see § 52.

[9] See § 92.

[10] See, e.g., U.S. v. Montreal Trust Co., 35 F.R.D. 216, 64–1 U.S. Tax Cas. (CCH) P 9477 (S.D.N.Y. 1964).

[1] Veh. & Traf. Law § 253.

[2] See § 97.

jurisdiction of a nondomiciliary notified outside the state. When there's this kind of overlap, the plaintiff can predicate jurisdiction on either statute and use the service of process provisions of the one chosen.

Other statutes that use the "agency" theory in one form or another, requiring that a person or corporation actually designate a local agent for service, or merely deeming such agent to be appointed automatically, also have a longarm mission that can overlap CPLR 302. These are discussed under the separate category of "agency as jurisdictional basis."[3] They, too, are alternatives to CPLR 302 when an overlap exists.

§ 95.   Agency as Jurisdictional Basis

The court can get personal jurisdiction of the defendant by service on someone whom the defendant has designated as agent for service, either in connection with the particular claim or with claims, generally. The agency can be express or implied.

One express agency already met is under CPLR 318, which allows a defendant to designate any person of choice as an agent for service.[1] That one is voluntary. Other kinds may be mandatory, like the designation of the secretary of state by licensed corporations and the superintendent of financial services by insurance companies.[2] These designees may be used for any claim against the defendant. Still another is the designation of the surrogate's court clerk that an estate fiduciary is required to make before letters are granted.[3]

An express designation voluntarily made by a would-be defendant can be as broad or as narrow as the parties stipulate. It can be limited to only certain claims. An example of a limited one would be a contract that designates an agent for service as to claims arising under the contract. (The designation of an agent for service as authorized by CPLR 318 is not an exclusive method, and therefore does not preclude contractual designations of a less formal kind.)

There are several implied agencies on the books. An implied agency is a designation, usually of a state official, which results not from an actual designation by the would-be defendant, but as the automatic consequence of some act the defendant commits or is responsible for in New York. A classic illustration is the nonresident motorist statute,[4] and such statutes exist today for boats[5] and planes[6] as well as ground vehicles.

A broad implied agency, the superintendent of financial services now being the agent,[7] exists against unauthorized insurers under section 1213 of the Insurance Law on a variety of insurance contacts so extensive that it has been said to go to the "very perimeters" of due process.[8] This separate and comprehensive treatment of what

---

[3]   See § 95.

[1]   See § 73; CPLR 308(3).

[2]   Bus. Corp. Law § 304; Ins. Law § 1212, treated in § 70. The condominium declaration is another example of a required secretary of state designation for service. See Real Prop. Law § 339–n(7).

[3]   SCPA 708.

[4]   Veh. & Traf. Law § 253, treated in § 97.

[5]   Nav. Law § 74.

[6]   Gen. Bus. Law § 250.

[7]   The Department of Insurance has merged into the Department of Financial Services and now the appropriate "superintendent" to serve is "the superintendent of financial services of this state." Ins. Law § 107(a)(41).

[8]   Ford v. Unity Hospital, 32 N.Y.2d 464, 470–71, 346 N.Y.S.2d 238, 242, 299 N.E.2d 659, 663 (1973).

amounts to longarm jurisdiction in insurance matters, incidentally, is the reason why CPLR 302(a), the state's general longarm statute, has no separate insurance category although its Illinois model had.[9]

These and like statutes will often be found to overlap some part of CPLR 302. When that happens, the plaintiff can base jurisdiction on CPLR 302 and make service under the usual CPLR provisions, or rely instead on the special statute and make service as that statute provides.[10]

When the corporation is a domestic or licensed foreign corporation, the designation of the secretary of state as agent for service is express and the governing provision on service is Business Corporation Law (BCL) section 306, treated earlier.[11] In this connection, note yet another provision: BCL 307, which contains an implied designation of the secretary of state as agent of any *unlicensed* foreign corporation that is subject to jurisdiction under any part of Article 3 of the CPLR. Since a corporation subject to CPLR jurisdiction is also subject to CPLR service, BCL 307 simply offers the alternative of serving the secretary of state in these instances, just as BCL 306 does for licensed corporations. But while both BCL 306 and BCL 307 involve designations of the secretary of state as agent for service, the methods of service differ and the difference can have jurisdictional consequences.

Under BCL 306, the designation is an actual one and the secretary of state has a listing of the corporation's address on her records, while under BCL 307, the designation is an implied one, spelled out only from the corporation's activity in New York, and the secretary has no such record. That's what generates a difference in the methods of service. Under BCL 306, two copies of the summons are delivered to the secretary of state, with the secretary mailing one to the corporation. By contrast, under BCL 307 the secretary is served with only one copy and it is the plaintiff who must personally serve, or forward by registered mail, another copy to the corporation.[12] The Court of Appeals held in Flick v. Stewart-Warner Corp.[13] that when BCL 306 instead of BCL 307 is mistakenly used for service on an unlicensed corporation, jurisdiction will not obtain even if the secretary, gratuitously, manages to mail a copy of the summons to the corporation and the corporation gets it.

The Court adhered to this rigid construction of BCL 307 a few years later in Stewart v. Volkswagen of America, Inc.[14] The statute has a progression of options in which each becomes available only if the preceding one can't be satisfied. The court called it a "menu" and held that a plaintiff can't choose from it at random, but must go in sequence.

Consent to Personal Jurisdiction Based on Designation of Agent in New York

The mere fact that service of process is made on a corporate official in New York does not create a basis of jurisdiction over the corporation itself,[15] in the way that

---

[9] Ill. Ann. Stat., ch. 735, § 5/2–209.

[10] See § 94.

[11] See § 70.

[12] Bus. Corp. Law § 307(b).

[13] Flick v. Stewart-Warner Corp., 76 N.Y.2d 50, 556 N.Y.S.2d 510, 555 N.E.2d 907 (1990).

[14] Stewart v. Volkswagen of America, Inc., 81 N.Y.2d 203, 597 N.Y.S.2d 612, 613 N.E.2d 518 (1993). The case is the subject of the lead note in NYSLD No. 406.

[15] See § 70.

personal service on an individual in the state simultaneously establishes a basis of jurisdiction over that individual.[16] The plaintiff must independently establish that there is a basis of jurisdiction over the corporate defendant. The standard used for decades to measure whether a corporate defendant is subject to general jurisdiction in New York, the famous "corporate presence" or "doing business" test, has been declared unconstitutional by the Supreme Court in its 2014 decision in Daimler AG v. Bauman.[17]

Even if a corporate defendant's activities in New York do not render it "at home" and subject to general jurisdiction in the state in light of the holding in *Daimler*, could the corporation be deemed to have consented to personal jurisdiction in New York if it obtains a license to do business in the state?[18] This issue will take on greater significance after the *Daimler* Court's evisceration of the "doing business" test.

As noted above, when the defendant is a licensed foreign corporation, it will have designated the secretary of state as its agent for service of process on any claim.[19] The courts have held that this designation constitutes consent to personal jurisdiction in New York.[20] There has, however, been some disagreement on the subject.[21] In 2016, the Second Circuit examined "the applicable Connecticut law" and ruled "that by registering to transact business and appointing an agent under the Connecticut statutes—which do not speak clearly on this point—[the defendant] did not consent to the state courts' exercise of general jurisdiction over it."[22] The court also observed in dicta that New York's BCL section 304 "has been definitively construed" to vest the New York courts with general jurisdiction over a corporation that designates the New York Secretary of State as its agent for service of process.[23]

In Aybar v. Aybar,[24] plaintiffs alleged that they were injured in an auto accident in Virginia while passengers in a car manufactured by defendant Ford and equipped with defendant Goodyear's defective tire. In addition to finding that both companies were "essentially at home" in New York and, therefore, were subject to general jurisdiction,[25] the *Aybar* court also found an additional basis for personal jurisdiction over Goodyear and Ford. The court deemed that both companies consented to general jurisdiction in New York by obtaining licenses to do business here and designating the secretary of

---

[16]   See § 59.

[17]   Daimler AG v. Bauman, 571 U.S. 117, 134 S. Ct. 746, 187 L. Ed. 2d 624 (2014) (SPR 265:1); see § 82.

[18]   Cf., § 98 ("Jurisdiction by Written Agreement").

[19]   Bus. Corp. Law § 304 ("Statutory designation of secretary of state as agent for service of process").

[20]   See, e.g., Flame S.A. v. Worldlink Intern. (Holding) Ltd., 107 A.D.3d 436, 437, 967 N.Y.S.2d 328, 330 (1st Dep't 2013) ("New York courts have personal jurisdiction over [defendant] because, at the time this action was commenced, [defendant] was registered to do business in New York."), lv. denied, 22 N.Y.3d 855, 979 N.Y.S.2d 561, 2 N.E.3d 929; Augsbury Corp. v. Petrokey Corp., 97 A.D.2d 173, 175–76, 470 N.Y.S.2d 787, 789 (3d Dep't 1983); STX Panocean (UK) Co., Ltd. v. Glory Wealth Shipping Pte Ltd., 560 F.3d 127, 131, 2009 A.M.C. 748 (2d Cir. 2009) ("It is well-settled under New York law that registration [by foreign corporations to do business in New York] under § 1304 [of the Business Corporation Law] subjects [them] to personal jurisdiction in New York.").

[21]   See, e.g., Bellepointe, Inc. v. Kohl's Dept. Stores, Inc., 975 F. Supp. 562, 564 (S.D.N.Y. 1997) (recognizing disagreement on the matter, but following what it deemed to be "the rule set forth by the Second Circuit that a license to do business is not dispositive on the issue of personal jurisdiction"). There is a helpful discussion of the subject in Professor Alexander's McKinney's Practice Commentaries to CPLR 301.

[22]   Brown v. Lockheed Martin Corp., 814 F.3d 619, 623 (2d Cir. 2016).

[23]   *Brown*, 814 F.3d at 640.

[24]   Aybar v. Aybar, 2016 WL 3389889, *1 (Sup. Ct., Queens County 2016); see § 82 for a further discussion of the case.

[25]   See § 82.

state as an agent for service of process under BCL section 304. Citing to the Court of Appeals ruling in Bagdon v Philadelphia & Reading Coal & Iron Co.,[26] the *Aybar* court observed that "foreign corporations have been on notice since 1916 that registration to conduct business in this state amounts to consent to general jurisdiction here, and they can always cancel their registration if their business interests lead them to do so."[27]

What about the unlicensed foreign corporation in the aftermath of *Daimler*? As noted above, BCL section 307 contains an implied designation of the secretary of state as agent of any unlicensed foreign corporation that is subject to jurisdiction under any part of Article 3 of the CPLR. Therefore, after *Daimler*, unless the unlicensed foreign corporation has its principal place of business in New York or the corporation's activities in the state are "so substantial and of such a nature as to render the corporation at home in that State," both unlikely prospects, it will not be subject to general jurisdiction in the state.[28] That will require reliance on the longarm statute, CPLR 302, to authorize service on the unlicensed foreign corporation through the secretary of state.

Similar issues arise when an international bank opens a branch in New York State and is required as part of its license application to appoint the Superintendent of the Department of Financial Services as its agent to accept process.[29] In B & M Kingstone, LLC v. Mega Intern. Commercial Bank Co., Ltd.,[30] Mega was a bank with its principal place of business in Taiwan, but it maintained a New York branch. The First Department held that Mega could be compelled to fully respond to an information subpoena served upon it to enforce a money judgment. The *B&M* court concluded that under *Daimler*, New York did not have general jurisdiction over Mega's worldwide operations.[31] Mega's New York branch was, however, subject to jurisdiction requiring it to comply with the information subpoenas because it consented to the necessary regulatory oversight in return for permission to operate as a bank in New York. Emphasizing this quid pro quo arrangement, the First Department quoted extensively from Vera v. Republic of Cuba,[32] which explained that "[i]n order to benefit from the advantages of transacting business in [New York], a foreign bank must register with and obtain a license from the Superintendent of the Department of Financial Services ('DFS'), and file a written instrument 'appointing the superintendent' " as its agent for service of process "in any action or proceeding against it on a cause of action arising out of a transaction with its New York agency or agencies or branch or branches." In sum, the *B&M* court held that "Mega's New York branch is subject to jurisdiction requiring it to comply with the appropriate information subpoenas, because it consented to the necessary regulatory oversight in return for permission to operate in New York."[33]

---

[26]   Bagdon v. Philadelphia & Reading Coal & Iron Co., 217 N.Y. 432, 111 N.E. 1075 (1916).

[27]   *Aybar*, 2016 WL 3389889 at *3.

[28]   *Daimler*, 134 S. Ct. at 762 n.19; see § 82.

[29]   See Banking Law § 200(a).

[30]   B & M Kingstone, LLC v. Mega Intern. Commercial Bank Co., Ltd., 131 A.D.3d 259, 15 N.Y.S.3d 318 (1st Dep't 2015).

[31]   See Gucci America, Inc. v. Weixing Li, 768 F.3d 122, 112 U.S.P.Q.2d 1445 (2d Cir. 2014) (applying *Daimler*, the Second Circuit ruled that district court did not have general jurisdiction over Bank of China to enforce a prejudgment asset freeze injunction).

[32]   Vera v. Republic of Cuba, 91 F. Supp. 3d 561, 570 (S.D.N.Y. 2015), rev'd on other grounds, 867 F.3d 310 (2d Cir. 2017) (quoting New York Banking Law § 200(a)).

[33]   *B & M Kingstone*, 131 A.D.3d at 260, 15 N.Y.S.3d at 319–20.

§ 96.   Attorney as Agent Under CPLR 303

If nondomiciliary P sues D in the supreme court, D can interpose any claim as a counterclaim because the supreme court has general jurisdiction. But if P sues D in some other court, whose subject matter jurisdiction of counterclaims is limited and does not embrace D's claim, D will have to sue on her claim separately in a court that has the requisite jurisdiction. When D tries to effect service on P in that separate action, however, she may find that P himself is outside the state, or in New York in connection with the P v. D suit and therefore immune from summons service for that reason.[1]

The answer to D's dilemma in that situation is to effect service of the summons on the attorney who is representing P in the P v. D action. CPLR 303 authorizes this. (The clerk becomes the person to serve if P is appearing pro se.) This automatic designation is available only on behalf of D in the P v. D action. A stranger can't exploit it.

In Deutsche Bank AG v. Vik,[2] a nondomiciliary corporation had commenced an action against a bank in New York County Supreme Court (Action #1). The bank subsequently commenced an action (Action #2), also in New York County Supreme Court, against several defendants, including the nondomiciliary corporation and its sole shareholder. In Action #2, plaintiffs relied on CPLR 303 and served process on the attorneys who appeared on behalf of the corporation when it commenced Action #1. As the *Deutsche Bank* court noted, CPLR 303 contains a limitation on this method of service and requires that the claims stated in Action #2 be of such a nature that they could have been prosecuted as counterclaims in Action #1 "had the action been brought in the supreme court."

In Action #2, the defendant corporation argued that the plaintiff bank's claims against it and its sole shareholder, who was not a party to Action #1, could not have been asserted as counterclaims therein and, therefore, the latter action should be dismissed for lack of proper service. CPLR 3019(a), entitled "Subject of counterclaims," states that "[a] counterclaim may be any cause of action in favor of one or more defendants . . . against one or more plaintiffs . . . or a plaintiff and other persons alleged to be liable." In sum, the provision allows a defendant to assert a counterclaim against the plaintiff and a third party, X, who can be joined by defendant in the action.[3] Although the bank's claims in Action #2 were asserted against both the nondomiciliary corporation and its sole shareholder, the court concluded that it would have been proper for the bank to have added the shareholder as a counterclaim defendant in Action #1. Therefore, the *Deutsche Bank* court ruled that service upon the corporation's attorney pursuant to CPLR 303 in Action #2 was proper and denied the motion to dismiss.

While the point was not addressed in *Deutsche Bank*, we wonder if the method of service offered by CPLR 303 is available in Action #2 if Action #1 was brought in supreme court. The language of the statute appears to contemplate a situation in which Action #1 has not been commenced in the supreme court.[4] The automatic designation under CPLR

---

[1]   See § 68.

[2]   Deutsche Bank AG v. Vik, 2015 WL 458284 (Sup. Ct., New York County 2015), aff'd, 142 A.D.3d 829, 40 N.Y.S.3d 23 (1st Dep't 2016).

[3]   See § 224; Commentary C3019:6 on McKinney's CPLR 3019.

[4]   CPLR 303 (permitting service on an attorney in Action #2 "if such separate action would have been permitted as a counterclaim had [Action #1] been brought in the supreme court") (emphasis added).

303 is good only during the pendency of P's action; it terminates with final judgment.[5] It has also been held that it applies only when P commences a court action or proceeding; that commencement of a New York arbitration, for example, will not invoke CPLR 303.[6]

It may seem a bit odd to immunize P from service while allowing service on his attorney. It would be more palatable simply to deprive nondomiciliaries of immunity from service when they themselves use the New York courts. But why tempt fate? CPLR 303 works in this situation and should be used.

Since CPLR 303 applies only to a suit in New York "by a person not subject to personal jurisdiction," it should not apply when, in whatever suit D wants to bring against P, P would be amenable to extraterritorial service. So, for example, if D's claim has a longarm jurisdictional basis against P under CPLR 302, D may not use CPLR 303 to make service on P's attorney, and of course doesn't need to.

§ 97.   The Nonresident Motorist Statute

Section 253 of the Vehicle and Traffic Law ("VTL") is the best known of the provisions that imply the designation of a state official for service, and there is enough caselaw on it to merit separate treatment.

Section 253 is sometimes confused with section 388 of the VTL, but its mission is quite different. Section 253 is just a jurisdiction giver. Section 388 is a substantive liability creator, imputing to the owner of a vehicle the conduct of one driving with the owner's permission, so as to make the owner, and her insurance policy, available to pay the damages of an injured third person.

Under section 253, a nonresident driving in New York or owning a vehicle being driven in New York with permission is "deemed equivalent" to the appointment of the secretary of state for service of process with respect to any claim emanating from an accident or collision growing out of the "use or operation" of the vehicle in New York. The statute then supplies in detail the method of service, which requires the mailing of a copy of the summons to the secretary in Albany (or a personal delivery of a copy to one of its branch offices) plus a mailing of summons, complaint, and notice to the defendant by registered or certified mail, return receipt requested, with a provision for ordinary mail if the registered mail should be refused.

The implied designation exploited in the nonresident motorist statute is really an ingenious way around the strictures of Pennoyer v. Neff.[1] The statute is at root just a "longarm" statute whose underlying theory is the same as CPLR 302. But *Pennoyer* precluded extrastate service, regardless of local contacts, thus forcing state legislatures to resort to some substitute. The substitute here was the "deemed" designation of a local state official who could then be served within the state in the defendant's behalf with personam effect. The "jurisdictional" service is the one made in New York on the secretary of state; the mailing of a copy to the defendant outside New York gives defendant the notice that due process also requires, but is not the "jurisdictional" act and hence does not have to occur in New York. Section 253, on the books for years before

---

[5]   Banco Do Brasil v. Madison S. S. Corp., 61 Misc. 2d 1028, 307 N.Y.S.2d 341 (Sup. Ct., New York County 1970).

[6]   Gillespie & Co. of New York v. Coleport Fabrics, Inc., 48 Misc. 2d 333, 264 N.Y.S.2d 653 (Sup. Ct., New York County 1965).

[1]   Pennoyer v. Neff, 95 U.S. 714, 24 L. Ed. 565, 1877 WL 18188 (1877).

outright extraterritorial service was allowed under "longarm" jurisdiction,[2] was a lip server to the restrictive demands of the now-abandoned *Pennoyer* decision.

The section details the follow-up procedures, including the filing of the mailing receipt along with the other papers after the receipt comes back. Service is complete upon the filing.[3] An alternative to the mailing is personal delivery to the defendant outside New York.

There will often be an overlap between VTL section 253 and CPLR 302(a)(2), which supplies longarm jurisdiction for a tortious act committed in New York. When both provisions apply, the plaintiff can choose either, using the ordinary service methods of the CPLR if CPLR 302 is chosen. If both statutes were always certain to apply to the same situations, the plaintiff's choice would be based only on which one's service provisions would be easier on the facts of the case. But that's the question: are the two statutes so similar that one always applies when the other does? Probably not. CPLR 302(a)(2) bases its jurisdiction on the defendant's alleged "tortious act" in New York. All section 253 requires is that the claim emanate from an accident arising out of the "use or operation" of the vehicle in New York. Although section 253 does not predicate jurisdiction on a showing of a "tort," it is tort that the plaintiff invariably claims when suing under section 253, thus tending to make the two provisions parallel in that respect.

The lawyer in any event does well to note some of the situations to which section 253 has been extended. For example, under section 253(1), the nondomiciliary owner of a vehicle is subject to jurisdiction whenever the vehicle was driven in New York with her permission, regardless of whether the driver was an "agent" of the owner, as would be required under CPLR 302(a)(2). Where the vehicle was left unattended, with motor idling, and it rolled forward and tipped over a stove, resulting in the burning of P's property, P's suit for property damage was held to arise out of the "operation" of the vehicle.[4] And where D negligently allowed a slippery condition to exist on the floor of a truck while it was being unloaded, this was held a "use" of the truck and gave jurisdiction when P fell.[5] Similarly, where P slipped on an oil accumulation on a boat, the oil coming from a defective hose leading to the boat from D's truck, the accident was held to arise from the truck's "use."[6]

In another case D took his mother's car without permission and then let his friend drive it while D sat in the passenger seat. An accident occurred. D, although neither the owner nor the driver of the car, was held to be "using" the vehicle and was subject to jurisdiction under section 253.[7]

---

[2]   See § 84.

[3]   See § 72 for the significance of when service is "complete."

[4]   Raspante v. Trans. Supply & Management, Inc., 214 N.Y.S.2d 583 (Sup. Ct., Oneida County 1960), aff'd, 11 A.D.2d 1090, 207 N.Y.S.2d 447 (4th Dep't).

[5]   Aranzullo v. Collins Packing Company, 14 N.Y.2d 578, 248 N.Y.S.2d 874, 198 N.E.2d 255 (1964), aff'g 18 A.D.2d 1068, 239 N.Y.S.2d 398 (1st Dep't 1963). The appellate division opinion points out that the addition of the word "use" was intended to give jurisdiction even with respect to accidents occurring when the vehicle is not moving.

[6]   Landolphi v. Wilhelmsen, 39 Misc. 2d 950, 241 N.Y.S.2d 942 (Sup. Ct., Kings County 1963).

[7]   Wahler v. Thompson, 36 Misc. 2d 847, 234 N.Y.S.2d 105 (Sup. Ct., Onondaga County 1962), rev'd on other grounds, 26 A.D.2d 895, 274 N.Y.S.2d 862 (4th Dep't 1966).

Would each of the above situations also satisfy CPLR 302(a)(2) as involving a "tortious act" by D? It's nice to know the inquiry may not be necessary as long as VTL section 253 stands on the books as an alternative.

Turning back to the service part of section 253, we should stress that present caselaw is prone to void the service entirely in some situations (and frustrate use of section 253 altogether) if the mailing does not work out right. If D voluntarily gives P an incorrect address, D may be estopped from pleading noncompliance and jurisdiction can result,[8] but if the address given by D was correct and he merely moves, with the result that the certified mail is returned "moved, left no address," the follow-up ordinary mail has been disallowed, service held invalid, and jurisdiction denied.[9]

In Cayo v. Saggar,[10] P claimed that the post office furnished a California forwarding address for D. The details aren't clear, but just one day before the statute of limitations was due to expire, P served D through the secretary of state pursuant to sections 253 and 254 of the VTL. P seemed to have made much effort to locate D, but these efforts did not satisfy the court, faulting P for failing to check with the Department of Motor Vehicles to determine the address it currently had listed with it. "Under controlling law," says the court, "the plaintiff's failure to search the records of the DMV renders the service void, no matter how extraordinary other attempts were . . . to find the defendant."[11] Cayo's lesson is that "the starting point for verifying an address is the DMV, not the USPS," and that service of process should never be made at the eleventh hour.[12]

Under a different statute—CPLR 308(5) on court-invented service—the Court of Appeals has held that the order can direct mail to an address D furnished even though D later moved and left no forwarding address. Jurisdiction will be upheld in such an instance on the ground that a would-be defendant involved in an accident is under a duty to see to it that persons hurt in the accident have continuing access to data about the defendant's whereabouts.[13] Such a rule should logically apply to like situations under section 253 and would mean the overruling of cases that void the section 253 service even though it was D's own failure to leave a forwarding address that accounted for his not getting notice. The analogy is tempting, but whether the courts will buy it remains to be seen. Indeed, the Court of Appeals itself, in a case on paragraph 4 of CPLR 308 (the affix-and-mail method of service), later cast doubt on whether the defendant is under a duty to keep advice current about his whereabouts.[14]

The best the practitioner can do is be aware of these things and use whatever scheme has proved tried-and-truest on the particular facts.

What about a return marked "unclaimed"? Caselaw had held that it voids the service,[15] but a 1978 amendment of section 253 overruled these decisions to allow a

---

[8]   Greenwood v. White, 25 A.D.2d 73, 266 N.Y.S.2d 1012 (3d Dep't 1966).

[9]   Bauman v. Fisher, 12 A.D.2d 32, 208 N.Y.S.2d 317 (3d Dep't 1960).

[10]   Cayo v. Saggar, 31 Misc. 3d 1209(A), 929 N.Y.S.2d 198 (Sup. Ct., Queens County 2011).

[11]   Cayo, 2011 WL 1364471 at *1; see McCaslin v. Peterson, 13 Misc. 3d 1206(A), 824 N.Y.S.2d 755 (Sup. Ct., Chautauqua County 2005), aff'd, 23 A.D.3d 1028, 803 N.Y.S.2d 456 (4th Dep't).

[12]   Cayo, 2011 WL 1364471 at *1; see § 231A.

[13]   See § 75. The Dobkin trilogy, treated in the cited section, holds such mail service to be constitutional when the defendant moves without advising of the move.

[14]   See the discussion of the Feinstein case in § 74.

[15]   Grandison v. College Truck Renting Corp., 26 A.D.2d 260, 273 N.Y.S.2d 567 (1st Dep't 1966).

follow-up procedure by ordinary mail when the registered or certified mail is returned unclaimed. The amendment does not address the "moved, left no address" situation, however, and there is therefore some peril in treating that as an "unclaimed" delivery. Here, too, therefore, the lawyer should investigate whether CPLR 302(a) offers an alternative jurisdictional basis. If it does, and there's any doubt about the procedures to be followed under section 253, the lawyer can avoid section 253 and instead apply under paragraph 5 of CPLR 308 for a court order inventing a method of service.

The practitioner who uses VTL section 253 should note all of its procedural incidents, including filing of proof of service and the time when service is deemed complete.

Lawyers will find the working out of these problems comfortable only if they have left plenty of time for trouble should the statute of limitations be anywhere around. If the statute is closing in, an oversight can prove fatal.[16]

§ 98. Jurisdiction by Written Agreement

A court can get jurisdiction from the parties' written contract, in which they simply stipulate that the New York courts will have jurisdiction to hear any dispute, or a given dispute, arising under the agreement. The constitutionality of this basis was sustained in National Equipment Rental, Limited v. Szukhent,[1] and the basis is exploited by the New York courts. Sometimes, as in *Szukhent* itself, the contract also contains the designation of an agent for service, in which event the "agency" may be deemed the jurisdictional basis. But other cases involve agreements containing the jurisdictional submission without an agency designation,[2] and these illustrate how the contractual submission itself can serve as the basis.

If the agreement provides for jurisdiction, but says nothing about service, service would be made as usual under the CPLR. And since caselaw made use of this jurisdictional basis prior to the adoption of the CPLR,[3] CPLR 301 should be deemed to carry it forth for present use, thus invoking CPLR 313. This in turn means that when consent jurisdiction of this kind is involved, service may be made within or without the state.

The agreement providing for New York jurisdiction may also provide for a non-CPLR method of service. If the agreed method is reasonable, it will be allowed to supersede CPLR methods. Where, for example, the contract provided for certified mail, service by that means was upheld.[4]

No particular form of language is necessary. It can be as "refreshingly simple and brief" as a letter, and merely say that as to any (or a given) dispute arising under the

---

[16] See § 231A.

[1] National Equipment Rental, Limited v. Szukhent, 375 U.S. 311, 84 S. Ct. 411, 11 L. Ed. 2d 354, 7 Fed. R. Serv. 2d 23 (1964).

[2] See, e.g., National Equipment Rental, Limited v. Dec-Wood Corp., 51 Misc. 2d 999, 274 N.Y.S.2d 280 (App. Term, 2d Dep't 1966).

[3] See, e.g., National Equipment Rental, Limited v. Graphic Art Designers Inc., 36 Misc. 2d 442, 234 N.Y.S.2d 61 (Sup. Ct., Nassau County 1962).

[4] *Dec-Wood*, 51 Misc. 2d at 1000, 274 N.Y.S.2d at 280.

arrangement the parties "consent to the jurisdiction of any court within the State of New York."[5]

The agreement involved in the *Szukhent* case came close to being upset as an adhesion contract. There were four dissenters in the U.S. Supreme Court and the adhesion factor played a role. A later lower court case in New York refused a submission under circumstances it found "unconscionable."[6] But perhaps this apprehension is unwarranted. If the dispute has New York contacts, it will likely have a longarm basis for jurisdiction under CPLR 302 and the contractual submission in such an event would be superfluous. If, on the other hand, the controversy lacks significant New York contacts, the forum non conveniens doctrine[7] may intercede to dismiss it. The contract may supply jurisdiction to the court, but if the case lacks reasonable New York contacts, the contract can't ordinarily compel the court to exercise the jurisdiction.

A contractual agreement is very commonly the source of an arbitrator's jurisdiction.[8] When there's an agreement to arbitrate, the courts' involvement is limited. The courts decide, if asked, only whether the dispute is arbitrable and whether the arbitration was timely sought.[9] If it's found arbitrable and goes to arbitration, the courts' only further involvement is later, in determining whether the arbitrators' award should be confirmed into a judgment, modified, or vacated.[10] But even for that limited involvement, the courts must have some source of their own jurisdiction over the parties. The same agreement that authorized the arbitration in New York may be deemed to authorize the New York courts to entertain whatever personal jurisdiction they need to carry out the narrow judicial involvement in the arbitral process. Indeed, even the means of service needed to commence the connected judicial proceedings may be drawn from or through the agreement to arbitrate. Where, for example, the parties agreed to arbitrate according to a certain body of rules, and among those rules is one authorizing service on a party's attorney in any connected court proceeding, the court's jurisdiction and the facilitated service were both sustained.[11]

§ 99.   Continuing Jurisdiction

In a matrimonial action in which alimony is awarded or in a family court proceeding in which support is ordered,[1] the judgment or order may provide for payments to be made in periodic installments. It may become necessary later on to enter an arrears judgment on accrued installments or to move the court to modify the amounts up or down based on changed circumstances. Suppose, however, that the defendant or respondent, clearly within the in personam jurisdiction of the court at the outset, has since left the state. Is

---

[5]   Albert Levine Associates, Inc. v. Hudson, 43 F.R.D. 392, 393 (S.D.N.Y. 1967).

[6]   Paragon Homes, Inc. v. Carter, 56 Misc. 2d 463, 288 N.Y.S.2d 817, 4 U.C.C. Rep. Serv. 1144 (Sup. Ct., Nassau County 1968), aff'd, 30 A.D.2d 1052, 295 N.Y.S.2d 606, 5 U.C.C. Rep. Serv. 991 (2d Dep't). The plaintiff was a New York assignee of a contract entirely between nonresidents and a simple forum non conveniens dismissal was at that time precluded because of the plaintiff's New York residence.

[7]   See § 28.

[8]   See CPLR 7501.

[9]   CPLR 7502, 7503. See § 589 (Practitioner's Edition).

[10]   CPLR 7510, 7511, 7514. See §§ 601, 602 (Practitioner's Edition).

[11]   Board of Ed. of Half Hollow Hills Central School Dist. of Huntington and Babylon v. Half Hollow Hills Teachers Ass'n, Inc., 79 Misc. 2d 223, 358 N.Y.S.2d 285, 87 L.R.R.M. (BNA) 2281 (Sup. Ct., Suffolk County 1974). These matters are more fully explored in Chapter 22 (Practitioner's Edition).

[1]   Dom. Rel. Law § 236; Fam. Ct. Act §§ 442, 443.

he still subject to the personal jurisdiction of the court on an application to affect the judgment in some way even if served with the motion papers outside New York?

If the judgment to be affected is that of the supreme court in a matrimonial action in which the defendant was originally within the court's personam jurisdiction, continuing jurisdiction of that kind exists.[2] If it arose in a family court proceeding, there is some debate even though there was personam jurisdiction at the outset. An appellate division case holds that continuing jurisdiction in the family court applies only to subject matter, not personal, jurisdiction.[3] A later family court case in the same department, apparently unaware of the appellate division decision of a few months earlier, holds that there is a continuation of personal jurisdiction as well,[4] which would seem to be the more appropriate conclusion.

The constitutionality of continuing jurisdiction has been upheld where the personal representative of an estate subsequently left the state of appointment. The personal representative was held subject to continuing personal jurisdiction in a proceeding (for example) to remove him and require him to account.[5] New York exploits this constitutional permission indirectly by having the personal representative designate the clerk of the surrogate's court as agent for service.[6]

Continuing jurisdiction has been applied in New York after judgment was rendered in favor of a plaintiff against tortfeasors A and B, with full jurisdiction, so as to enable A to get a contribution judgment against B even though B afterwards moved from the state.[7] By analogy, once judgment has been rendered against a defendant with jurisdiction, that jurisdiction ought to continue, at least as against the defendant himself, for all steps necessary to enforce the judgment. Exploitation of the continuing jurisdiction doctrine would allow the extrastate service of papers in connection with appropriate enforcement devices,[8] but New York has not yet taken that broad a position. One of the devices most helpful in the enforcement of a New York judgment, for example, is a subpoena used to make the defendant reveal data about his assets. Such a subpoena is authorized by CPLR 5224 and should be servable, with personam effect, even on a defendant who moved from the state after judgment. But other provisions have been construed—unfortunately, it is submitted—to preclude extraterritorial subpoena service,[9] thereby depriving the enforcement realm of the helpful and reasonable device of continuing jurisdiction when a subpoena is the needed weapon. The courts are not of one mind on the matter. Some appear to be taking a more liberal view.[10]

---

[2] See Schneidman v. Schneidman, 188 Misc. 765, 65 N.Y.S.2d 876 (Sup. Ct., Kings County 1946).

[3] Wasserman v. Wasserman, 43 A.D.2d 951, 352 N.Y.S.2d 207 (2d Dep't 1974).

[4] Iannone v. Iannone, 78 Misc. 2d 294, 355 N.Y.S.2d 992 (Fam. Ct., Suffolk County 1974).

[5] Michigan Trust Co. v. Ferry, 228 U.S. 346, 33 S. Ct. 550, 57 L. Ed. 867 (1913).

[6] SCPA 708(1).

[7] Ohlquist v. Nordstrom, 143 Misc. 502, 257 N.Y.S. 711 (Sup. Ct., Chautauqua County 1932), aff'd, 238 A.D. 766, 261 N.Y.S. 1039 (4th Dep't 1933), aff'd, 262 N.Y. 696, 188 N.E. 125.

[8] CPLR Article 52 supplies these devices, some of which are mere motion procedures, such as the installment payment order of CPLR 5226 (see § 511), which would be easier to implement if extrastate service of notice is permitted.

[9] See DuPont v. Bronston, 46 A.D.2d 369, 362 N.Y.S.2d 471 (1st Dep't 1974). It may be that *DuPont* is no longer followed. See AABCO Sheet Metal Co., Inc. v. Lincoln Center for Performing Arts, Inc., 249 A.D.2d 39, 670 N.Y.S.2d 494 (1st Dep't 1998), but see also DeLeonardis v. Subway Sandwich Shops, Inc., N.Y.L.J. March 20, 1998, at 28, col.3 (Sup. Ct., New York County; Tompkins, J.).

[10] See Coutts Bank (Switzerland) Ltd. v. Anatian, 275 A.D.2d 609, 713 N.Y.S.2d 45 (1st Dep't 2000), and the discussion of it in SPR 104:1.

The Restatement regards jurisdiction as continuing "throughout all subsequent proceedings which arise out of the original cause of action," as long as there was jurisdiction to begin with and notice of subsequent steps is given.[11]

F. SERVICE OUTSIDE NEW YORK

Table of Sections

§ 100.   Service Outside New York Under CPLR 313

§ 100. Service Outside New York Under CPLR 313

As has been noted many times already, CPLR 313 permits service outside the state whenever the defendant is a New York domiciliary or there exists a basis for jurisdiction against the defendant under either CPLR 301 or 302.

The 301 bases that authorize this extrastate service include corporate presence in New York under the "at home" test.[1] The fact that the corporation is incorporated in New York or has its principal place of business in New York—the new standards for asserting general jurisdiction over a corporation[2]—will usually assure that an appropriate corporate agent is available for service in New York.[3] But whether one is or not, extrastate service on the corporation under CPLR 313 is permissible.[4]

Another CPLR 301 basis on which extrastate service may be predicated is where the defendant has agreed by contract to submit to New York jurisdiction.[5]

CPLR 313 does not supply any of the mechanical methods of service, other than to somewhat expand the list of people who can serve process outside the state. The statute adopts the methods for service of process from other provisions in Article 3, mainly CPLR 308. Thus, as soon as CPLR 313 is activated in a case in which an individual is the defendant, the lawyer must then turn back to CPLR 308 for the methods, the practical impact of CPLR 313 merely being to translate the words "within the state," wherever found in CPLR 308, into "within or without the state." The net result of a successful invocation of CPLR 313, therefore, is simply to remove state lines as an impediment to process.

All of the paragraphs of CPLR 308 are available for service outside the state, and with the same conditions.[6] The Court of Appeals confirms this in a review of the subject in Morgenthau v. Avion Resources Ltd.[7]

---

[11]   Restatement (Second) Conflict of Laws § 26.

[1]   See § 82.

[2]   See § 82.

[3]   CPLR 311(a). See § 70. Service through the secretary of state will also likely be available in these circumstances. See § 95.

[4]   Decisionware, Inc. v. Systems Equipment Lessors, Inc., 45 A.D.2d 971, 359 N.Y.S.2d 586 (2d Dep't 1974).

[5]   See § 98.

[6]   Service on a Rule 318 agent under CPLR 308(3) would probably be an exception, since that agent, designated in papers filed with New York clerks, would usually not be amenable to service outside the state. But if he were, even CPLR 308(3) could be used for extrastate service.

[7]   Morgenthau v. Avion Resources Ltd., 11 N.Y.3d 383, 869 N.Y.S.2d 886, 898 N.E.2d 929 (2008) (NYSLD No. 589).

Thus, for example, service outside New York could be initially made under paragraphs 1 or 2 of CPLR 308, but before paragraphs 4 or 5 could be used, their conditions precedent would have to be satisfied, as with a showing of prior attempts to make service under paragraphs 1 and 2 to permit service under paragraph 4.

If CPLR 313 applies, it is even permissible under two-step service requirements such as the deliver-and-mail method of paragraph 2 and the affix-and-mail method of paragraph 4, to execute one step within the state and the other outside. CPLR 313 being applicable, state lines lose significance. But, one of the bases of jurisdiction on which CPLR 313 relies would have to be present. Without such a basis, service may not be "split" in this fashion and would have to take place entirely within the state because there would be no authority for carrying out either step outside the state.[8]

If service is made outside the country, the plaintiff must be alert to the Hague Convention on the Service Abroad of Judicial and Extrajudicial Documents, a treaty to which the United States subscribes.[9] It requires that any conditions imposed on service by the nation in which the service takes place must be fulfilled, such as that service shall not be made by mail, or that a translation accompany the papers served, etc.[10] But as long as there's no treaty that requires deference to the law of the foreign nation as to method of service, the New York provisions have an unfettered run. The *Morgenthau* case,[11] where service of process on several defendants was carried out in Brazil, illustrates this.

An important point clarified by the U.S. Supreme Court is that the convention and its demands apply only when the defendant has to be served in the foreign country. If the defendant, as is often the case, is amenable to service anywhere in the United States, the convention does not apply.[12]

Who may make the extrastate service?

Any New York resident 18 and over who is not a party to the action may make it,[13] but so may anyone authorized to make service under the laws of the place of service, even though such person could not make service under New York law. Any person "duly qualified [as an] attorney, solicitor, barrister, or equivalent" in the place of service is also authorized by CPLR 313 to act as a process server. It turns out, therefore, that those who may serve New York process outside New York sometimes make up a longer list than those authorized to serve it within.

There is an unfortunate pitfall in the first category of process servers listed in CPLR 313, and lawyers must be careful to avoid it. While a person 18 and over and not a party may make the out-of-state service, that person must be a New York resident. This is counterintuitive, especially considering that CPLR 313 authorizes service outside New York! In Ruffin v. Lion Corp.,[14] a lawyer who had served process in Pennsylvania was

---

[8]   See Durgom v. Durgom, 47 Misc. 2d 513, 262 N.Y.S.2d 874 (N.Y. City Civ. Ct. 1965).

[9]   The convention is reprinted following Rule 4 in 28 U.S.C.A.

[10]   See Chase, *Serving Summons Abroad*, N.Y.L.J., June 28, 1983, at 1, col.1.

[11]   *Morgenthau*, 11 N.Y.3d at 391, 869 N.Y.S.2d at 891–92, 898 N.E.2d at 934–35.

[12]   Volkswagenwerk Aktiengesellschaft v. Schlunk, 486 U.S. 694, 108 S. Ct. 2104, 100 L. Ed. 2d 722, 11 Fed. R. Serv. 3d 417 (1988). See § 624 (Practitioner's Edition).

[13]   See CPLR 2103(a); § 63.

[14]   Ruffin v. Lion Corp., 15 N.Y.3d 578, 915 N.Y.S.2d 204, 940 N.E.2d 909 (2010) (SPR 228:3) (NYSLD No. 612).

confronted with the problem when a defendant moved to vacate a $450,000 default judgment.[15] The plaintiff acknowledged that the process server was not authorized to make service under CPLR 313. Although he was at least 18 and not a party to the action, he was not a New York resident. Nor was he a sheriff authorized to make service under Pennsylvania law or a lawyer admitted in that state. After the appellate division granted the motion to vacate the default judgment, the plaintiff begged for mercy before the Court of Appeals and received it when that court held that this particular "technical infirmity" could be disregarded under CPLR 2001.[16]

The New York rule against serving process on Sunday[17] applies to extrastate service, and it makes no difference that the place where service is made allows Sunday service.[18]

CPLR 313 permits service to be made on the defendant's personal representative if the would-be defendant dies before suit, which raises an old issue about what happens when the defendant dies during the action instead of before it. The appropriate step is, of course, to substitute the personal representative in place of the defendant, but the question arises whether the representative is subject to extrastate service of the papers that bring on the substitution.

It is clear today that if the original jurisdiction against the decedent was based on longarm contacts or on some other basis authorizing out-of-state service, the representative is also subject to out-of-state service for the purpose of substitution.[19] But if the only predicate of jurisdiction over the decedent was that he was personally served in New York, older caselaw, not explicitly overruled, holds that the court has no jurisdiction whereby to substitute his nondomiciliary representative,[20] i.e., there is no authority for service of the substitution papers on the representative outside New York.

It would seem, however, through a combination of CPLR 301 and 313, that this old caselaw is overruled and that substitution, through extrastate service on the personal representative, would today be permitted in either situation. CPLR 313 says that if the "person," apparently meaning the original defendant, was subject to jurisdiction under CPLR 301, then so is his personal representative. Since personal delivery within New York to D himself is the oldest of jurisdictional bases and is carried over by CPLR 301, one may conclude that CPLR 313 covers it. It should make no difference that the representative is being substituted rather than initially sued, or that in one instance initial jurisdiction was through local service (a recognized CPLR 301 basis), while in another it was founded on longarm jurisdiction (a CPLR 302 basis). Both bases are specified in CPLR 313.

---

[15]   See CPLR 5015(a)(4); § 430.

[16]   The *Ruffin* decision is monumental in that it grants courts the power to invoke CPLR 2001 to disregard any number of defects that can arise when plaintiff attempts to make service under CPLR 308, sections 306 and 307 of the Bus. Corp. Law, section 253 of the Veh. & Traf. Law, and various other provisions. Defects that have arisen in this realm are explored in §§ 63, 66 through 76A, 95, and 97. The holdings in many cases discussed therein, which resulted in dismissal of an action for lack of proper service, must be reconsidered in light of the Court's holding in *Ruffin*.

[17]   See § 63.

[18]   Eisenberg v. Citation-Langley Corp., 99 A.D.2d 700, 471 N.Y.S.2d 595 (1st Dep't 1984).

[19]   Rosenfeld v. Hotel Corp. of America, 20 N.Y.2d 25, 281 N.Y.S.2d 308, 228 N.E.2d 374 (1967). See § 85.

[20]   McMaster v. Gould, 240 N.Y. 379, 148 N.E. 556, 40 A.L.R. 792 (1925); Helme v. Buckelew, 229 N.Y. 363, 128 N.E. 216 (1920).

Territorial service in New York as an automatic jurisdictional predicate, while subject to legitimate criticism, was recently reaffirmed by the U.S. Supreme Court.[21] As long as it exists, there seems scant reason to say that a defendant served here during his lifetime, and thus brought within New York jurisdiction that way, can frustrate the jurisdiction just by dying.

G. REM JURISDICTION

Table of Sections

§ 101.   Rem Jurisdiction, Generally
§ 102.   Rem Jurisdiction of Marital Status
§ 103.   In Rem Jurisdiction Under CPLR 314(2)
§ 104.   Quasi in Rem Jurisdiction
§ 105.   The Doctrine of Seider v. Roth
§ 106.   Sequestration in Matrimonial Actions
§ 107.   Service by Publication

§ 101. Rem Jurisdiction, Generally

Rem jurisdiction turns on the presence within the state of a res—a thing—of some kind. It is generally turned to only when personam jurisdiction of D is unavailable. It enables the court to give P a judgment against D good to the extent of D's interest in the res.

Rem jurisdiction can be subdivided into several categories, which it helps to do for analysis. For convenience of reference, we can break it down into three parts and call them:

1. strictly in rem;

2. in rem; and

3. quasi in rem.

Categories 1 and 2 have this in common: they both involve an action in which P is after the particular thing. Rather than seeking a general money judgment, P wants possession of the particular item of property, wants to establish his ownership or other interest in it, or to exclude D from an interest in it.

The difference between 1 and 2 is that with "strictly in rem" jurisdiction, the action is brought against the thing, but binds everyone in the world, whether named in the action or notified of it. The action in rem against a ship under admiralty jurisdiction is the most common example of this today, but that category of action is not seen in the New York courts because it is exclusively federal.[1] There is at least one item of "strictly in rem" jurisdiction of which the New York courts do have jurisdiction, however: the proceeding to register land title under Article 12 of the Real Property Law.[2] It is rarely

---

[21]   See § 59.

[1]   28 U.S.C.A. § 1333(1). Admiralty and maritime actions that may be brought in state courts under the "saving to suitors" clause contained in § 1333(1) do not include the strictly in rem action against the vessel. Such an action was not known to the common law, and only items of relief recognized at common law, such as maritime suits seeking only money (as most do), may at the plaintiff's option go into state court through the saving to suitors clause in § 1333.

[2]   See Real Prop. Law § 391.

seen today, however, and should not be confused with any other action affecting an interest in land. Practically speaking, therefore, "strictly in rem" jurisdiction is not a significant part of New York practice.

The second item on the list, "in rem" jurisdiction, does still play a role in 21st Century procedure, at least theoretically. While also brought to affect an interest in a particular and identifiable property of some kind, an action in this "in rem" category of action produces a judgment binding only on those who have been named as parties and duly notified—the usual understanding of what due process requires. In this category are many actions familiar to the lawyer, including foreclosure of a mortgage or other lien on real or personal property in the state, replevin, ejectment, an action to quiet title, etc. There is no need to draw out the list. As long as the property is in the state and P is seeking only to affect interests in it, this category of jurisdiction does the job.[3]

The third category, which we have labeled "quasi in rem" jurisdiction, differs from the first two in that it does not seek to affect interests in any particular property. Here, all P wants is money. P wants to bring an ordinary money action against D, but can't get personal jurisdiction of D. Through the use of appropriate judicial process, quasi in rem jurisdiction purports to let P actually or constructively seize any property D may have in the state, thus assuring P that any money judgment P may get in the action will be enforceable at least to the extent of the property seized. In New York, the device used for this purpose in the ordinary money action is called "attachment."[4] As will be seen three sections hence, this "quasi in rem" category of rem jurisdiction has been severely circumscribed by the U.S. Supreme Court.

The reader should take careful note that the three rem subdivisions used above are for reference purposes only. In fact, the Restatement uses the words "in rem" to describe item 1 on the list, the strictly in rem jurisdiction, and applies "quasi in rem" to categories 2 and 3 together.[5] Characterization is of secondary importance, however. The three-part division used above, although perhaps not as accurate historically, is more helpful for study and reference.

When all three categories are to be referred to collectively, we can simply call them "rem" jurisdiction, without a qualifying word.

Rem jurisdiction can also support a matrimonial action, ingeniously theorizing that the "marital res" is present in the state if the plaintiff spouse is domiciled there even though the defendant spouse is not. This makes rem jurisdiction over the marital status sufficient to support matrimonial relief (divorce, separation, etc.) against an absent spouse.[6]

---

[3] The concept has been advanced that in rem jurisdiction over property located outside the state may be exercised by a court if it can be shown that the other state or nation, where the property is located, is cooperating in the venture. See U.S. v. All Funds on Deposit in any Accounts Maintained in Names of Meza or De Castro, 63 F.3d 148 (2d Cir. 1995), noted in SPR 40:4.

[4] See §§ 313 to 326.

[5] See Introductory Note on Topic 2 of Chapter 3, Restatement (Second) Conflict of Laws. Noting this categorization, the U.S. Supreme Court, in circumscribing quasi in rem jurisdiction in Shaffer v. Heitner, 433 U.S. 186, 97 S. Ct. 2569, 53 L. Ed. 2d 683 (1977), was at pains to state that in the Restatement's terminology it was only the second type of "quasi in rem" jurisdiction that was being restricted—the category 3 "quasi in rem" jurisdiction that we describe above as we refer to it in this book. See § 104.

[6] See § 102.

CPLR 314 exploits all of the available rem bases of jurisdiction. Its several parts are studied in the ensuing sections. Whenever CPLR 314 applies, the introductory sentence to the statute recognizes that service may be made on the defendant inside or outside New York. But unless there happens to be some personam basis coincidentally applicable, only rem jurisdiction results.

§ 102. Rem Jurisdiction of Marital Status

CPLR 314(1) authorizes the use of rem jurisdiction in a matrimonial action. The marriage, sometimes termed the "marital res" or "matrimonial res" or "marital status," is deemed present within the state as long as one of the spouses is a domiciliary (not a mere resident) of the state. (It's usually the plaintiff spouse who is the domiciliary when this category of jurisdiction is relied on.) The presence of the marital res allows the court, along rem jurisdictional lines, to affect the marriage, such as by divorce or separation.[1] The action is brought in the usual way, and the defendant may be served anywhere. If he or she defaults, the resulting judgment of (e.g.) divorce is valid and must be recognized by all other American jurisdictions under the Full Faith and Credit Clause.[2]

In some instances, New York, as a matter of its own internal law, requires that the plaintiff show not just that he or she is a domiciliary at the time of commencement of the action, but has been so for a year, or in some cases two years, prior to suit.[3] This requirement is not, however, jurisdictional.[4]

If there is personam jurisdiction of the defendant spouse, this rem category of jurisdiction of course becomes academic. It is needed and hence used only when personam jurisdiction of the defendant is lacking.

Distinguish CPLR 302(b), which offers personam jurisdiction for monetary relief in marital and family disputes in certain circumstances. CPLR 302(b) applies only to monetary relief, however, not to the matrimonial remedy itself. In a given case, of course, the court may have rem jurisdiction to affect the marriage under CPLR 314(1) as well as personam jurisdiction sufficient to affect the parties' monetary rights under CPLR 302(b), but the matrimonial relief (divorce, separation, etc.) does not get longarm personam jurisdiction under CPLR 302 and must rely on rem jurisdiction under CPLR 314(1) if some other personam basis is lacking.

Nor does the presence of rem matrimonial jurisdiction afford a basis to affect the custody of a child. For custody, the rule was that the court needed personam jurisdiction of the parent whose custody right was to be affected, or else personam jurisdiction of the child. In the latter instance, a kind of rem jurisdiction was working: having the child before it, the court could affect the absent parent's right to the custody of the child.[5] The

---

[1]   Geary v. Geary, 272 N.Y. 390, 6 N.E.2d 67, 108 A.L.R. 1293 (1936).

[2]   Williams v. State of North Carolina, 317 U.S. 287, 63 S. Ct. 207, 87 L. Ed. 279, 143 A.L.R. 1273 (1942). A footnote in the U.S. Supreme Court's opinion in Shaffer v. Heitner, treated in § 104, seems designed to assure that this "status" category of rem jurisdiction is not undone by the strictures *Shaffer* places on quasi in rem jurisdiction. See note 30 at Shaffer v. Heitner, 433 U.S. 186, 208, 97 S. Ct. 2569, 2582, 53 L. Ed. 2d 683 (1977).

[3]   Dom. Rel. Law § 230. The statute, which imposes certain durational residency requirements, speaks in terms of "residence," but has been construed to mean "domicile." Black v. Black, 108 A.D.3d 842, 968 N.Y.S.2d 722 (3d Dep't 2013).

[4]   See § 430.

[5]   See Levitt v. Kinori, 80 Misc. 2d 557, 363 N.Y.S.2d 707 (Sup. Ct., Suffolk County 1974), aff'd 47 A.D.2d 598, 365 N.Y.S.2d 785 (2d Dep't 1975).

adoption of Article 5–A of the Domestic Relations Law, which took effect in 1978, made some changes in custody matters. The article is an adoption of the Uniform Child Custody Jurisdiction and Enforcement Act.[6] It has an extensive set of jurisdictional bases on which custody jurisdiction can be predicated,[7] exploiting a mixture of both personam and rem jurisdiction conceptually akin to the "longarm" jurisdiction underlying CPLR 302 as well as the rem jurisdiction found in CPLR 314. Under this act, the physical presence of the child is a jurisdictional predicate unless certain other factors are met.[8]

Rem jurisdiction in the matrimonial context is really in a class by itself. If it had to be fitted into one of the three categories we devised in the preceding section, it would come somewhere between the first two. A judgment in a matrimonial action comes close to binding the whole world, so it is not in category 2, which is the "in rem" jurisdiction binding only on notified persons. On the other hand, the judgment may be attackable by some nonparties,[9] which keeps it out of the "strictly in rem" category of number 1 on the list.

The "matrimonial action" in which the rem jurisdiction is authorized by CPLR 314 is defined in CPLR 105. It includes not just divorce, annulment, and separation, but also actions that seek a declaratory judgment affecting the marriage or a purported divorce of it.[10]

If P brings a declaratory action seeking to affect only P's own marriage with D, P can sometimes use this rem category of jurisdiction even though the judgment may affect the marriage of a nonparty, as occurred, for example, in Sacks v. Sacks.[11] W-1 sued H to declare invalid a Mexican divorce H purportedly obtained from W-1. W-1's New York domicile was held to give jurisdiction of the declaratory action even though a judgment for W-1, invalidating the Mexican divorce, could indirectly undo H's marriage with W-2. W-2 was held bound by the rem judgment as long as duly notified (i.e., named as a party and served, even if only outside the state).

In the *Sacks* case, New York had substantial contacts with the parties to be affected by the judgment. Later developments indicate that such New York contacts may be indispensable to justify even this in rem exercise of jurisdiction. The Court of Appeals held in Carr v. Carr[12] that where H had no New York marital domicile with either W-1 or W-2 at any time, W-2 had no New York contacts of any kind, and W-1 did not attempt to bring a New York action until after H had died, New York had no jurisdiction to entertain the action. (After H died, W-1 in Carr had moved to New York and brought a declaratory judgment action to undo a divorce H had obtained from W-1 in a foreign country.) The Court dismissed the action, saying that this rem theory, which uses the plaintiff's local domicile as its jurisdictional touchstone, "however useful and appropriate it may be during the joint lives of the husband and wife, ceases to have any vitality or legal substance after the death of either."

---

[6]   It consists of §§ 75–a through 75–*l* of the Dom. Rel. Law.

[7]   These are listed in Dom. Rel. Law §§ 76 et seq.

[8]   See Dom. Rel. Law § 76.

[9]   See Johnson v. Muelberger, 340 U.S. 581, 71 S. Ct. 474, 95 L. Ed. 552 (1951).

[10]   Chittenden v. Chittenden, 46 Misc. 2d 347, 259 N.Y.S.2d 738 (Sup. Ct., Monroe County 1965).

[11]   Sacks v. Sacks, 47 Misc. 2d 1050, 263 N.Y.S.2d 891 (Sup. Ct., New York County 1965).

[12]   Carr v. Carr, 46 N.Y.2d 270, 413 N.Y.S.2d 305, 385 N.E.2d 1234 (1978).

Even if H were still alive when W-1 brought the declaratory action in New York, the impression one draws from *Carr* is that since a voiding of the divorce, which is what W-1 sought in the action, would have incidentally destroyed W-2's marriage with H, such a doing could not be tolerated at a place lacking contacts with either W-2 or the first marriage.

§ 103. In Rem Jurisdiction Under CPLR 314(2)

CPLR 314(2) exploits for the New York courts the whole range of in rem actions brought to affect interests in specific and identifiable property found in New York. Whether real or personal, if the property is in New York and all P wants to do is affect D's interest in it—no matter what the merits of the action may require by way of proof to sustain the relief sought—the fact that the property is in the state gives the court all the jurisdiction it needs.

The courts have sometimes overlooked this simple fact of life with in rem jurisdiction, erroneously mixing jurisdiction and the merits together. In one case, for example, Morgenstern v. Freudenberg,[1] in which P was seeking an interest in an item of property concededly in the state—which is the only requirement for in rem jurisdiction—the court said that it needed personam jurisdiction of D because P could have no right to the property until a P-D agreement was first rescinded. That proposition is questionable.[2] As long as the resulting judgment is limited to affecting interests in property in New York, the court can, on an in rem foundation, do anything at all with regard to the merits. Not only can it rescind a contract; it can declare D a witch or a vagabond, as long as the resulting judgment does no more than exclude D from an interest in the New York property.

Dependence on this in rem category of jurisdiction has been much reduced under the CPLR for the reason that longarm jurisdiction almost always applies today under CPLR 302 to give personam jurisdiction in cases that in the past had to depend on in rem jurisdiction. Some major New York in rem cases of yesteryear can illustrate this.

In a case involving a contract to sell New York real property, it was always possible for buyer B to get in rem jurisdiction sufficient to compel the nondomiciliary seller S to convey the property, as in a specific performance action. Since all B wanted from S was the property, its New York situs made in rem jurisdiction effectual.[3] But when S was seeking specific performance from B, a nondomiciliary buyer, in rem jurisdiction did not suffice because what S wanted from B was money, and that needed personam jurisdiction. It still does, but today CPLR 302(a)(4) is likely to supply it. When a nondomiciliary buyer contracts to buy New York land, he may be said to be making a "use" of the land under the cited provision. Alternatively, such a contract may qualify as a transaction of New York business and thereby be subject to longarm jurisdiction under CPLR 302(a)(1).

In another old New York case, mortgagor R, a nondomiciliary, gave mortgagee E a mortgage on some New York real property that R owned. E later had to foreclose the mortgage in New York and did so, but the sale of the parcel did not fetch enough to pay

---

[1]   Morgenstern v. Freudenberg, 7 Misc. 2d 273, 165 N.Y.S.2d 934 (Sup. Ct., New York County 1957).

[2]   The *Morgenstern* case finds dubious support in what is at best an unfortunate dictum in Jackson v. Jackson, 290 N.Y. 512, 517, 49 N.E.2d 988, 990–91, 147 A.L.R. 668 (1943).

[3]   Garfein v. McInnis, 248 N.Y. 261, 162 N.E. 73 (1928). If S is ordered to make a deed to B and refuses, the sheriff may be directed to make it in S's behalf. CPLR 5107. The effect is the same.

the debt and a deficiency judgment resulted. Treating that deficiency just as if it were a personam judgment, E then tried to levy execution on the judgment against a different parcel R happened to own in New York. E could not do that, held the court:[4] the foreclosure was good against only the mortgaged property, and the action, lacking personam jurisdiction, could not support any other relief. Today, of course, personam jurisdiction could arise in such a foreclosure action. As with the prior specific performance example, the mortgage transaction could be seen as a New York transaction of business under CPLR 302(a)(1) or as arising out of the ownership, use, or possession of New York real property under CPLR 302(a)(4), either of which would support personam jurisdiction. That would validate a deficiency judgment and permit a levy of execution on it against any other property of R found in New York.

The lesson to the lawyer, if the issue arises today, is to look carefully at in rem cases decided before 1963, the year of the CPLR. See if the fact pattern can invoke one of today's longarm jurisdictional bases. If it can—and it apparently can so often today that this ordinary category of in rem jurisdiction is now rarely used—personam jurisdiction is at hand and the availability of in rem jurisdiction is academic.

One interesting recent example of the utility of in rem jurisdiction is in a domestic dispute involving equitable distribution. The Court of Appeals ruled that if the property that is the subject of the dispute between spouses or former spouses is in New York, in rem jurisdiction can be invoked to support the action even if neither of the parties is a New Yorker. In personam jurisdiction, in other words, is not indispensable for an equitable distribution of marital property.[5]

When "in rem" jurisdiction is used, i.e., when the action seeks to affect interests in specific property, there is no rule—as there is with attachment in quasi in rem actions to be discussed in the next section—that judicial process of some kind must issue in advance of the action so as to bring the property into the court's actual or constructive possession before jurisdiction is exercised. The fact that the property is in New York usually suffices without such a step. A statutory exception is the replevin action. When an action to recover a chattel (replevin) rests on an in rem foundation, and personam jurisdiction of the defendant is lacking, the chattel must be seized before service of process can be made.[6]

Notice is not dispensed with merely because an action rests on rem rather than personam jurisdiction,[7] as was sometimes supposed in the past. New York requires that the intended defendants be named and served in the action in the usual way. The only advantage is that CPLR 314 allows the service to be made outside New York.

The methods of service are for the most part the same as when CPLR 313 applies to allow extrastate service in a personam action, i.e., CPLR 308 and the other provisions on service govern, but with the words "within the state" now read as "within or without

---

[4]   Schwinger v. Hickok, 53 N.Y. 280, 1873 WL 10369 (1873).

[5]   See McCasland v. McCasland, 68 N.Y.2d 748, 506 N.Y.S.2d 329, 497 N.E.2d 696 (1986), reversing 110 A.D.2d 318, 494 N.Y.S.2d 534 (3d Dep't 1985) in which a divided panel had held personam jurisdiction necessary.

[6]   This requirement is imposed by CPLR 314(3). The seizure is effected by the sheriff pursuant to a court order secured under CPLR Article 71.

[7]   See Griffin v. Griffin, 327 U.S. 220, 66 S. Ct. 556, 90 L. Ed. 635 (1946).

the state." Another possible method of service in the rem categories of action is publication, to be discussed later.[8]

The category of rem jurisdiction we have been discussing, in which the property involved is the very subject of the claim in suit, is not affected by the U.S. Supreme Court's decision in Shaffer v. Heitner.[9] The restrictions pronounced by that case affect only quasi in rem jurisdiction, treated in the following section.

§ 104. Quasi in Rem Jurisdiction

If P seeks a mere money judgment against D but can't get personam jurisdiction of D, the doctrine of quasi in rem jurisdiction allows P to attach any property D happens to have in New York and use it as a jurisdictional basis. Even if D is then served outside New York and defaults, the doctrine assures P that a resulting judgment will be good at least to the extent of the seized property. Very active in New York until 1977, this doctrine was greatly restricted by the U.S. Supreme Court in Shaffer v. Heitner[1] during that year. There are a few situations in which the *Shaffer* case still permits quasi in rem jurisdiction, but these are narrowly confined. We will return to them later.

The objection of the *Shaffer* case was that in this category of jurisdiction, the coincidental local presence of a nondomiciliary's property was being used to force the nondomiciliary to submit to the court's jurisdiction to litigate a claim having no relationship to the forum, contrary to the demands of due process. While perhaps justified during an earlier era, when strictures on personal jurisdiction prompted the exploitation of rem concepts in order to move jurisdiction forward, the doctrine could no longer be tolerated in the current era in which personam jurisdiction is free from its earlier confinement. The major case accounting for that freedom is of course International Shoe Co. v. Washington,[2] the founding father of longarm jurisdiction and the subject of study earlier.[3] In *International Shoe*, the U.S. Supreme Court held that a forum can entertain personal jurisdiction over a nondomiciliary served outside the state as long as she has had such minimal contacts with the forum, in respect of the claim, that the forum's entertainment of the suit would not offend the basic concepts of fairness underlying due process. In *Shaffer*, the Court extends the same or in any event a similar minimal contacts test to quasi in rem jurisdiction, the category in which, among the three listed in section 101 earlier, the property attached is unrelated to the claim sued on. The Court holds that "the relationship among the defendant, the forum, and the litigation" must be the center of the inquiry.[4]

On *Shaffer*'s facts, the relationship was not demonstrated and jurisdiction failed. The suit was a corporate derivative action brought in Delaware. Jurisdiction over certain directors and officers was based on the seizure of stock they held in the corporation.[5] Neither the individuals nor the claim had any relationship to Delaware.

---

[8]   See § 107.

[9]   Shaffer v. Heitner, 433 U.S. 186, 97 S. Ct. 2569, 53 L. Ed. 2d 683 (1977).

[1]   Shaffer v. Heitner, 433 U.S. 186, 97 S. Ct. 2569, 53 L. Ed. 2d 683 (1977).

[2]   International Shoe Co. v. State of Wash., Office of Unemployment Compensation and Placement, 326 U.S. 310, 66 S. Ct. 154, 90 L. Ed. 95, 161 A.L.R. 1057 (1945).

[3]   See § 84.

[4]   *Shaffer*, 433 U.S. at 204, 97 S.Ct. at 2580.

[5]   Under Delaware law, the situs of shares in a Delaware corporation is always in Delaware, apparently without regard to where the certificates representing the shares may be. Note that Delaware might have been

The highest point to which the U.S. Supreme Court had ever carried quasi in rem jurisdiction was in Harris v. Balk.[6] It came down in 1905, during the restrictive reign of Pennoyer v. Neff,[7] which declared that personal jurisdiction can result only if D is served within the state. *Harris* was an endeavor, enlightened for its age, to circumvent *Pennoyer*'s personam restrictions by expanding rem jurisdiction. *Harris* allowed a court that lacked personam jurisdiction of D to attach a debt owed to D by G by the service on G of an attachment order while G was in the state.

P in *Harris* lived in Maryland and had a money claim against D, who lived in North Carolina and of whom personam jurisdiction was unavailable in Maryland. G was also a North Carolinian concededly in debt to D. G happened through Maryland one day and P had G served with a Maryland attachment purporting to seize the G-to-D debt. G paid the debt to the Maryland sheriff and it was credited to the P v. D claim. When D later tried to sue G on the debt in North Carolina, G's payment on the Maryland attachment was allowed as a complete defense.[8]

The *Shaffer* case overrules *Harris* and like decisions[9] that purport to rest jurisdiction of a money claim on the coincidental local presence of some property belonging to the defendant. Perhaps it would be better, in view of *Harris*'s thoughtful endeavor to move forward without wounding *Pennoyer*'s pride, to say that the *Shaffer* case gives *Harris* honorable retirement after yeoman service. It's kinder than the brush-off that a mere overruling implies. And the retirement of *Harris* is only a partial one at that:

It must be stressed that *Shaffer* addresses and affects only the quasi in rem jurisdictional use to which the *Harris* case put the attached property. In other respects, *Harris* is probably still good law. Its manner of theorizing the situs of a debt, for example—finding it present in the forum when the debtor is present in the forum—does not appear to be undone by *Shaffer*. If an attaching creditor seeks seizure of the debt not for jurisdictional, but for mere security purposes—personam jurisdiction being present—*Harris* should still be available to theorize the situs of the debt through the presence of the debtor. The same should be true when the debt is sought to satisfy a valid in personam judgment already rendered against the person to whom the debt is owed.[10]

The question outstanding, then, is the extent to which quasi in rem jurisdiction survives at all after *Shaffer*. When may a defendant's local property be attached, not merely as security when jurisdiction in personam exists, but to *supply* a limited

---

allowed to exercise personam longarm jurisdiction on the facts of *Shaffer*, predicated on Delaware's interest in the directorial and managerial activities of its corporations, but Delaware chose to lay jurisdiction entirely on the quasi in rem basis and *Shaffer* disposed of the constitutional issues on that basis alone.

[6] Harris v. Balk, 198 U.S. 215, 25 S. Ct. 625, 49 L. Ed. 1023 (1905).

[7] Pennoyer v. Neff, 95 U.S. 714, 24 L. Ed. 565, 1877 WL 18188 (1877).

[8] The fact that G in *Harris* conceded his debt to D simplified matters. Had G disputed that he owed the debt, and had a Maryland court assumed to adjudicate whether he did or not, personam jurisdiction of D would have been required before an adjudication that G did not owe D the debt could be jurisdictionally upheld. See and compare New York Life Ins. Co. v. Dunlevy, 241 U.S. 518, 36 S. Ct. 613, 60 L. Ed. 1140 (1916).

[9] See, e.g., Pennington v. Fourth Nat. Bank of Cincinnati, Ohio, 243 U.S. 269, 37 S. Ct. 282, 61 L. Ed. 713 (1917).

[10] See Koehler v. Bank of Bermuda Ltd., 12 N.Y.3d 533, 883 N.Y.S.2d 763, 911 N.E.2d 825 (2009); see §§ 491, 510. Fixing the situs of an intangible, towards which *Harris* makes a substantial and probably still viable contribution, is reserved for general treatment in the enforcement of judgments chapter. See §§ 489, 491. *Harris* should also remain good law for the purpose of protecting the garnishee—the debtor's debtor—who has paid a debt over to a sheriff pursuant to a valid attachment or execution. See § 326.

jurisdiction to adjudicate a claim when personam jurisdiction is lacking and when the property has no relationship to the claim?[11] *Shaffer* appears to permit this in several situations:

1.   *Minimal Contacts.*

Shaffer authorizes quasi in rem jurisdiction when the forum has the requisite minimal contacts in the *International Shoe* sense. An initial reaction to this would be that the presence of such contacts would authorize outright personam ("longarm") jurisdiction under CPLR 302, making quasi in rem jurisdiction superfluous. But that's not necessarily so. As indicated during the earlier discussion of longarm jurisdiction, CPLR 302 does not go the constitutional limit.[12] Should a case arise in which the defendant's contacts with the forum in respect of the subject claim are sufficient to permit New York jurisdiction under due process but technically beyond the contacts statutorily required by CPLR 302, a "gap" exists. If the defendant in a case falling within that gap should happen to have property in New York, *Shaffer* would seem to authorize quasi in rem jurisdiction. In this instance, the action would be restricted to quasi in rem jurisdiction not because of constitutional strictures, but because of the failure of New York law to go as far on the personam track as due process permits.

And even in situations in which New York would choose to go the limit, there is obviously a gap within the Due Process Clause itself—as *Shaffer* reads it—between what is needed for outright personam jurisdiction and what will satisfy for the less demanding purposes of quasi in rem jurisdiction. Some cases have appeared manifesting what the courts have considered contacts sufficient for the rem measure, but just short on the personam scale. For example:

An early case following *Shaffer* is the Second Circuit decision in Intermeat, Inc. v. American Poultry, Inc.[13] P was a New York corporation that sold meat to D, an Ohio corporation without a New York office and presumably without the New York activities that would mean either "presence" jurisdiction of D under CPLR 301 or longarm jurisdiction of D under CPLR 302. D sold much of its own product to New York buyers, however, and one of these, the A&P supermarket, owed D money. That debt is what P attached in New York. Analyzing how D bought the meat from P, including paper work and deliveries, and how and to whom D sold the meat, the court found some $7 million annually (about 30%) of D's business to involve New York. It sustained the quasi in rem jurisdiction, holding that the contacts test for that is "narrower" for than for personam jurisdiction.

Another case is Banco Ambrosiano, S.P.A. v. Artoc Bank & Trust Ltd.,[14] involving a loan between foreign banks. The loan had no connection with New York except that it called for initial deposit and subsequent repayment in New York banks, which were the correspondent banks of the two foreign banks concerned. D's sole contact with the state was the account it maintained with the New York bank, but since that was "the very account through which [D] effectuated the transaction at issue," the account was held

---

[11]   The *Shaffer* case makes plain that the strictly in rem and in rem classes of jurisdiction, categories 1 and 2 on the list formulated in § 101, remain valid, or are at least unaffected by *Shaffer*.

[12]   See §§ 84 et seq.

[13]   Intermeat, Inc. v. American Poultry Inc., 575 F.2d 1017, 23 U.C.C. Rep. Serv. 925 (2d Cir. 1978).

[14]   Banco Ambrosiano, S.P.A. v. Artoc Bank & Trust Ltd., 62 N.Y.2d 65, 476 N.Y.S.2d 64, 464 N.E.2d 432 (1984).

attachable and gave quasi in rem jurisdiction in the action even though there wasn't enough for personam jurisdiction.[15]

Majique Fashions, Ltd. v. Warwick & Co., Ltd.[16] is still another example. D was to inspect goods for P in Asia. Alleging a failure to inspect and/or negligent inspection, P brought a New York action against D, but D had no New York office. It did have several New York accounts, however, in one of which P was to make the deposit required by the P-D contract. Noting additionally that D could foresee that its behavior could result in harm to P in New York, i.e., introducing a foreseeability element by a kind of tacit analogy to CPLR 302(a)(3)(ii), the court held the *Shaffer* trio of elements satisfied.

Dependence on analogizing the foreseeability element to CPLR 302(a)(3)(ii) may be risky today because of the rejection of foreseeability as a definitive longarm factor by the U.S. Supreme Court in World-Wide Volkswagen Corp. v. Woodson, decided in 1980, after the *Majique* case was decided.[17] But a distinction from *World-Wide*, an unintentional tort case,[18] can be made in that in *Majique* and like cases the contact that the defendant had with New York, whatever it consisted of, was intentional. The U.S. Supreme Court appears to be allowing longarm jurisdiction greater scope in cases involving deliberate as opposed to accidental conduct,[19] and in this respect foreseeability may still count as an influential factor if the defendant's conduct was intentional, as it invariably is in contract cases.

Yet a further application of quasi in rem jurisdiction occurred in a situation in which longarm personal jurisdiction is usually rejected. This has to do with agency. In the earlier discussion of longarm jurisdiction,[20] it is shown that in an agency situation in which P claims that its own acts in New York should be imputed to D for jurisdictional purposes because they were performed as agent of D, New York will not ordinarily make the imputation. It has been held that such an imputation can be made, however, in a case involving mere quasi in rem jurisdiction.[21] This would be another illustration of where activities insufficient to support personal jurisdiction may nonetheless satisfy the less demanding standards of quasi in rem jurisdiction. Some lower courts tend in that direction, in any event.

Stipulations in a contract for the arbitration of a controversy in New York, or for the application of New York commercial law to govern the transaction substantively, have also been cited as significant New York contacts in cases sustaining quasi in rem jurisdiction under *Shaffer*.[22]

The above are mere illustrations. There are others. One commentator has suggested from a sampling of these post-*Shaffer* cases that the courts are disinclined "to take

---

[15]   The subject is treated in the lead note in NYSLD No. 295.

[16]   Majique Fashions, Ltd. v. Warwick & Co., Ltd., 67 A.D.2d 321, 414 N.Y.S.2d 916 (1st Dep't 1979).

[17]   World-Wide Volkswagen Corp. v. Woodson, 444 U.S. 286, 100 S. Ct. 559, 62 L. Ed. 490 (1980); see also Asahi Metal Industry Co., Ltd. v. Superior Court of California, Solano County, 480 U.S. 102, 107 S. Ct. 1026, 94 L. Ed. 2d 92 (1987). Note that CPLR 302(a)(3)(ii) does not use foreseeability as its standard, but rather that defendant "expects or should reasonably expect . . . ."

[18]   The case is treated at length in § 88.

[19]   See §§ 86, 86A, and 88.

[20]   See § 86 on the "transacts any business" provision of CPLR 302(a)(1).

[21]   Drexel Burnham Lambert, Inc. v. D'Angelo, 453 F. Supp. 1294 (S.D.N.Y. 1978).

[22]   See, e.g., ACLI Intern. Inc. v. E. D. & F. Man (Coffee) Ltd., 76 A.D.2d 635, 430 N.Y.S.2d 858 (2d Dep't 1980).

[*Shaffer*] seriously," seeing *Shaffer* as being treated lightly if not, indeed, being "brushed aside" altogether.[23]

2. *All Property in New York.*

Suppose the defendant has moved all of his property to New York. The *Shaffer* case holds that even in that situation, the State may not adjudicate a claim against the defendant if the claim and the defendant have no nexus with the State. But the case does say that an attachment of the property may be allowed in that situation as security for a judgment being sought on the claim in an appropriate forum.[24] This suggests that if New York is the property state, it can allow an attachment before the foreign action has gone to judgment. There is at present no statutory authority in New York for an attachment in that situation, however. The closest New York comes is the allowance of an attachment after the foreign action has gone to judgment, in conjunction with a New York action now being brought on that judgment.[25]

3. *No Other Forum.*

Shaffer leaves the door open to quasi in rem jurisdiction in an unrelated forum if it should be shown that there is no other and presumably more appropriate forum in which to litigate the claim.[26] That would not be a common situation, except perhaps in wartime or a state of severely strained relations between the domestic and the would-be foreign forum. If the defendant should happen to have property in the domestic forum in that situation, but not be amenable to its personal jurisdiction, the quasi in rem seizure of the property as a jurisdictional base on which to proceed to an adjudication of the claim's merits could evidently be allowed. This also supposes that it would not otherwise be unfair to proceed against the absent defendant. It would be, for example, if the defendant were interned on enemy soil.

Procedure in Quasi in Rem Cases

Since quasi in rem jurisdiction, although curtailed, still exists in the foregoing situations and has proved itself tenacious in the years since *Shaffer* came down, its procedural requisites should be reviewed.

CPLR 314(3) is the statute that exploits this category of jurisdiction in New York, ordinarily using the order of attachment as the expedient for the seizure of the property. In deference to the lingering requirement of Pennoyer v. Neff, it requires that the attachment be secured and levied before service of process.[27]

---

[23]   See Barker, *New York Practice*, N.Y.L.J., Dec. 28, 1987, at 1, col.1.

[24]   *Shaffer*, 433 U.S. at 210, 97 S.Ct. at 2583.

[25]   CPLR 6201, paragraph 5. Paragraph 3 of CPLR 6201, which authorizes an attachment when the defendant disposes of or secretes property with the intent to defraud creditors, contemplates a New York action, not a foreign one, on the underlying claim. See § 314. If the New York courts were to permit an anticipatory action, i.e., one brought here in anticipation of a judgment yet to be obtained elsewhere, the provisions of CPLR 6201(3) might be stretched to support an attachment if New York were the state to which, rather than from which—as is usually contemplated—the defendant has transferred property.

[26]   See note 37 at *Shaffer*, 433 U.S. at 211, 97 S.Ct. at 2584.

[27]   Pennoyer v. Neff, 95 U.S. 714, 24 L. Ed. 565, 1877 WL 18188 (1877). The requirement that for quasi in rem jurisdiction the constructive seizure must precede service may be the most significant part of *Pennoyer* that still remains in force in New York. And it does so not under constitutional compulsion, but as an internal New York preference.

The procedure is simple. Subject to detailed study later,[28] we can note briefly that P gets the order of attachment from the court, usually by ex parte application,[29] and delivers it to the sheriff. The sheriff must levy on it before the summons is served. In the case of real property, the sheriff levies by filing a notice of attachment with the clerk of the real property's county.[30] To levy against personal property, the sheriff merely serves a copy of the order of attachment on the garnishee.[31] As soon as the sheriff files the order of attachment (in the case of real property) or serves it upon the garnishee (in the case of personal property), there has been a "levy" sufficient to permit service of the summons.[32] CPLR 314(3) insists that this levy precede summons service. If it does not precede, the property will not be deemed attached and jurisdiction will not obtain.[33] The filing of the action must precede the levy under the filing system for commencing actions—as long as service follows it.[34]

Service in this quasi in rem category may be made outside New York on the express authority of CPLR 314. If D should default, and P's claim is not completely satisfied out of the previously attached property, P has a subsisting claim against D for the balance and can sue on it without facing any charge of having "split" the claim. The judgment will not be binding on any issue in the subsequent action, however, for the obvious reason that the court's jurisdiction existed only as to the property attached and could not affect D's personal rights beyond that.[35]

This category of jurisdiction works not only on tangible property of D found in New York, but on any intangible property for which a New York situs can be fixed. If, for example, D maintains an account at a New York bank, the account can be attached for quasi in rem purposes. The sheriff merely serves a copy of the order of attachment on the bank, which in this instance is the garnishee.

Fixing the situs of an intangible can sometimes be a problem, so the CPLR tries to establish a situs for some of the more significant intangibles. A negotiable instrument, for example, has its situs wherever the instrument is, as does a certificate of stock representing interests in a corporation, and in each instance, the person holding the instrument or certificate is the proper garnishee on whom to serve a copy of the

---

[28]   See §§ 316 et seq.

[29]   CPLR 6201, 6211, 6212; see § 316.

[30]   CPLR 6216.

[31]   CPLR 6214(a). Remember that a garnishee in New York practice is any person who has possession of property belonging to D or who owes a debt to D. CPLR 105.

[32]   As will be seen later in the study of attachment, § 319, the summons must be served within 60 days after the order of attachment is granted or it loses its validity under CPLR 6213. Thus, the levy must precede the service and both must occur within 60 days from the order of attachment. This sequence is mandatory, however, only where, as here, attachment is being used for its quasi in rem jurisdictional function. When used for mere security, i.e., when there is personam jurisdiction in the action, the levy need not necessarily precede the service of the summons.

[33]   Nemetsky v. Banque De Developpement De La Republique Du Niger, 48 N.Y.2d 962, 425 N.Y.S.2d 277, 401 N.E.2d 388 (1979); Dimmerling v. Andrews, 236 N.Y. 43, 139 N.E. 774 (1923).

[34]   CPLR 306–b ordinarily allows 120 days for service after filing. A plaintiff securing an attachment for quasi in rem use, however, must make service within 60 days after the granting of the order of attachment. CPLR 314(3), 6213; see § 319. Thus, in a supreme or county court action, service within the 120 days, but after the 60 day period, may preserve the action, but will forfeit the attachment. If the action is based on quasi in rem jurisdiction, however, the entire action is subject to dismissal.

[35]   Benadon v. Antonio, 10 A.D.2d 40, 197 N.Y.S.2d 1 (1st Dep't 1960).

attachment.[36] If P wants to levy against an interest D has in an estate, the personal representative of the estate is the appropriate garnishee.[37]

Before Harris v. Balk[38] was for the most part retired by *Shaffer*, New York made a remarkable exploitation of what the Court of Appeals perceived as *Harris*'s quasi in rem jurisdictional opportunities. This it did with the doctrine of Seider v. Roth,[39] an intriguing entry in American jurisprudence born in 1966 in Albany and interred at the tender age of 14 in Washington, D.C. *Seider* needs the privacy of a separate section. It follows.

§ 105.   The Doctrine of Seider v. Roth

P was a New Yorker injured in a Vermont collision with D, a Canadian. D's car was covered by a liability policy issued in Canada by G, a Connecticut insurer. P clearly had no personam basis on which to sue D in New York, nor did D have in New York any tangible or even intangible property of a traditionally recognizable kind, such as a bank account. But it was shown that G, the Connecticut insurer, was doing business in New York and hence had a New York presence. In effect exploiting the *Harris v. Balk* doctrine, discussed in the prior section, P claimed that G owed to D the obligations to defend and indemnify any claim that might be brought against D within the policy; that these obligations constituted attachable "property" under New York law; and that they had a New York situs because G, the "ower" of the obligations, was doing business in New York. On a 4–3 vote, the New York Court of Appeals accepted that rationale in Seider v. Roth[1] and sustained a quasi in rem attachment of these peculiar obligations.

The doctrine threw open the doors of the New York courts to all New Yorkers injured anywhere in the country—or the world—as long as it could be shown that the alleged tortfeasor's insurer happened to maintain an office in New York. The doctrine was exploited heavily for 14 years, until 1980, when the U.S. Supreme Court overruled it in Rush v. Savchuk.[2] Actually involved in *Rush* was Minnesota's short-lived adoption of the doctrine. For the 14 years of *Seider*'s New York life, the U.S. Supreme Court never accepted a New York *Seider*-based case for review. But upon Minnesota's adoption of the doctrine almost a decade and a half later, the court reviewed and overturned it promptly, finding it a deprivation of the insurer's property without due process by subjecting it to jurisdiction in a state with which neither its insurance policy nor its insured had sufficient contact.

The overruling took place on January 21, 1980. Under due process, held the Supreme Court, a *Seider*-based case lacks the requisite contacts even for quasi in rem jurisdiction. Thus ended a bizarre jurisdictional saga.

Since the *Seider* basis for jurisdiction can no longer be used, almost all discussion of it is of historical interest only. *Seider* was widely relied on, however, and was cited so often at many different procedural stages of numerous actions in both the state and federal courts that it still crops up in the course of researching procedural issues. When

---

[36]   See CPLR 6202, 5201(c)(4).

[37]   CPLR 5201(c)(2). See § 491 for further discussion of who the proper garnishee is in diverse situations.

[38]   Note 6 above.

[39]   Seider v. Roth, 17 N.Y.2d 111, 269 N.Y.S.2d 99, 216 N.E.2d 312 (1966).

[1]   Seider v. Roth, 17 N.Y.2d 111, 269 N.Y.S.2d 99, 216 N.E.2d 312 (1966).

[2]   Rush v. Savchuk, 444 U.S. 320, 100 S. Ct. 571, 62 L. Ed. 2d 516 (1980).

it does, it sometimes adds a difficult twist to the issue or poses some special peculiarity understandable only if one is familiar with *Seider*. We therefore include here a synopsis of the doctrine and its doings from its pronouncement in the mid-1960s through its demise in 1980.

Immediately upon its pronouncement, *Seider* posed both theoretical and practical problems. While P had previously been allowed to attach insurance proceeds to which D was entitled, the insurance in those instances was burglary or fire or casualty, or insurance of some similar kind, in which D had a direct interest and which existed as an attachable property independently of the main action, for which it was to be used as a jurisdictional crutch.[3] The G-to-D debt in such cases had an economic viability of its own and could be used for quasi in rem jurisdictional support by one of D's creditors (P).[4]

In *Seider*, the "obligations" attached were a liability insurer's obligation to defend and indemnify a tortfeasor, and it was argued that neither of these obligations could even be said to exist until an action has been brought by P against D with jurisdiction. How could two obligations that don't exist until there is jurisdiction, supply that jurisdiction? It was like trying to pull oneself up by the bootstraps,[5] and this posed theoretical difficulties. When the property of D that P is pursuing is an intangible "debt" of some kind, CPLR 5201(a) allows its seizure only if the debt is either past due or certain to become due. The "debts" involved in *Seider* were neither. CPLR 5201(a) sought to avoid the kinds of problems *Seider* presented, but the statute was nevertheless construed to allow the attachment and *Seider* was on its way.

On the practical side, there were equivalent difficulties. If the defendant, D, duly notified, defaulted, for example, and a default judgment is entered, and enforcement undertaken against the attached property, the CPLR requirement is that the property be sold at public auction.[6] Who bids at a sheriff's auction on an insurer's obligation to defend or indemnify? That and a number of other problems were never addressed by the courts. Some were avoided, others ignored.

The history of *Seider* is fascinating. Its highlights are these:

1.   The cases, both state and federal,[7] in which *Seider*'s theory was exploited for jurisdiction began to proliferate. One of them, Simpson v. Loehmann,[8] brought to the New York Court of Appeals the question of *Seider*'s federal constitutionality, an issue, curiously, that the *Seider* case itself had not raised. It was contended that *Seider* went beyond the permissible limits of due process. The New York Court of Appeals in *Simpson* rejected the argument and sustained *Seider*'s constitutionality, but in a set of opinions that manifested that if the Court of Appeals had the case to decide all over again—this

---

[3]   See, e.g., Baumgold Bros. v. Schwarzschild Bros., 276 A.D. 158, 93 N.Y.S.2d 658 (1st Dep't 1949), aff'd, 302 N.Y. 628, 97 N.E.2d 357 (1951).

[4]   See the concurring opinion of Breitel, J., in Simpson v. Loehmann, 21 N.Y.2d 305, 314, 287 N.Y.S.2d 633, 640, 234 N.E.2d 669, 674 (1967). G, who is the insurer in the text's examples, stands for garnishee.

[5]   Seider v. Roth, 17 N.Y.2d 111, 115, 269 N.Y.S.2d 99, 103, 216 N.E.2d 312, 315 (1966) (dissenting opinion).

[6]   Such are the directions of CPLR 5230(a), 5232 and 5233, for enforcement of a judgment in an action predicated on attachment.

[7]   The federal courts make use of the forum state's quasi in rem attachment procedures and essentially follow the state rules governing them. Fed. R. Civ. P. 4(n)(2). See § 627 (Practitioner's Edition).

[8]   Simpson v. Loehmann, 21 N.Y.2d 305, 287 N.Y.S.2d 633, 234 N.E.2d 669 (1967).

in 1967, just a year after *Seider* came down—it would reject *Seider* as a matter of New York law without even reaching the constitutional issue.[9]

2.   Lower court judges in New York would of course deem themselves bound by the New York Court of Appeals view of *Seider*'s constitutionality, but federal judges were not so deferential. At the time, CPLR 320(c) insisted that an attachment defendant submit to personam jurisdiction if she wanted to defend the action, or else default and forfeit whatever of her property was attached. Citing this obviously unfair "leverage" aspect of the attachment, a federal court in Podolsky v. Devinney[10] declared *Seider* unconstitutional, the New York Court of Appeals' view to the contrary notwithstanding. Such coercive use of rem jurisdiction to exact a personam appearance seemed to be an unanswerable constitutional point. In the *Seider* context, it would mean that a defendant driving his own car in his own state would have to submit to the personam jurisdiction of a New York court—and the reputed generosity of a New York jury—which would mean in turn that if liability were assessed at a sum beyond his insurance coverage, unlikely though such a prospect might be if the defendant were sued at home or where the accident occurred, he would have to pay the difference out of pocket.

3.   There now followed a kind of miracle. A motion had been made in the New York Court of Appeals to reargue the *Simpson* case. The Court of Appeals took that occasion, not to do battle with *Podolsky*'s reasoning, but to reconstrue CPLR 320(c) to divest it of its coercive effect in *Seider*-based cases. After setting forth certain conclusions, the Court said that "[t]his, it is hardly necessary to add, means that there may not be any recovery against the defendant . . . in an amount greater than the face value" of the insurance policy. In other words, the Court was, by construction, divesting CPLR 320(c) of its "leverage" use and inviting the defendant to appear and defend without facing a personam judgment.[11] It was good that the Court added the clarification, "hardly necessary" though the Court thought it was, because few would have perceived it otherwise.

That was only part of the miracle. The Court further concluded, again without setting forth its reasoning, that the things attached in *Seider* were not the obligations to defend or indemnify, but the face amount of the insurance policy.[12] The *Simpson* reargument opinion was an unsigned per curiam with the distinction of being unanimous. The Court had manifested in earlier opinions that it could not reach consensus on the *Seider* components and apparently decided that it would be best to reach as many unanimous conclusions as need be to offer guidance to the lower courts and preserve *Seider*'s validity, but the less said about reasons the better. Perhaps it is

---

[9]   One of the judges in the *Seider* majority of four had in the interim retired and Judge Charles D. Breitel, no friend of the *Seider* doctrine, was appointed to the vacancy. As a matter of New York internal law, Judge Breitel voted to support *Seider* only because he did not think that the mere coincidence of a change in judicial personnel on the Court of Appeals should undo a recent and important statutory interpretation. *Simpson*, 21 N.Y.2d at 314, 287 N.Y.S.2d at 640, 234 N.E.2d at 674.

[10]   Podolsky v. Devinney, 281 F. Supp. 488 (S.D.N.Y. 1968).

[11]   Simpson v. Loehmann, 21 N.Y.2d 990, 991, 290 N.Y.S.2d 914, 916, 238 N.E.2d 319, 320 (1968), opinion denying reargument. CPLR 320(c) was later amended to add paragraph (1), codifying this result and authorizing a limited appearance in all instances (not just *Seider* cases) in which attachment is the sole predicate of jurisdiction. That stands as the law today. See § 113.

[12]   The *Simpson* reargument opinion purports to quote the "court's opinion" with respect to the main argument, which was not the court's opinion at all in the original *Simpson* decision but only that of Chief Judge Fuld with one other judge concurring, 21 N.Y.2d 305, 307, 287 N.Y.S.2d 633, 634, 234 N.E.2d 669, 671. The unanimous per curiam opinion on reargument in effect adopts whatever parts of Judge Fuld's earlier opinion it quotes.

commendable that the judges made so concerted an effort at consensus, albeit in the humbling forum of a per curiam denial of a motion to reargue. But *Seider* compensated in impact for what it lacked in grace.

4. The *Simpson* reargument opinion, compelled in essence by the *Podolsky* case, took what was then deemed to be the major constitutional objection out of *Seider*: the coercive use of an attachment to squeeze an in personam submission out of a nondomiciliary defendant who had no contacts with New York. With that, the *Seider* doctrine was sustained as constitutional by a divided Second Circuit in Minichiello v. Rosenberg, and certiorari was denied.[13]

5. When the plaintiffs were nonresidents, the use of *Seider* was foreclosed on forum non conveniens grounds,[14] but in a discretionary disposition that left the door open to keeping jurisdiction in such cases in special circumstances. The door was then closed and locked by the Court of Appeals in Donawitz v. Danek,[15] a medical malpractice action based on a foreign injury, but with at least some medical treatment in New York. Although special circumstances were apparently present in *Donawitz* because several of the defendants were New Yorkers and within personam jurisdiction, the action was nonetheless dismissed as against a New Jersey physician on the ground that the duty to defend and indemnify "is not of sufficient substance to support quasi in rem jurisdiction where the plaintiff is a nonresident."[16]

6. *Seider* involved a liability insurance policy applicable to a vehicle, but it was cited as authority for attaching other liability policies, including a homeowner's policy[17] and a medical malpractice policy (which the *Donawitz* case involved).

7. Courts in other states, asked to adopt *Seider*'s approach, almost uniformly refused.[18] Only one or two went along.[19] One of these, New Hampshire, made a kind of retaliatory adoption of *Seider*, stressing that a New Hampshire seizure of an insurance policy in connection with a foreign accident is, because of *Seider*, peculiarly appropriate when the defendant is a New Yorker.[20]

8. Numerous problems arose as Seider wended its way through jurisprudence. Questions appeared about whether there was jurisdiction to impose disclosure obligations on a mere "quasi in rem defendant," on the res judicata and collateral estoppel impact of a quasi in rem judgment in subsequent actions, on disclaimers of

---

[13] Minichiello v. Rosenberg, 410 F.2d 106 (1968), upheld en banc at page 117 (1969), cert.denied 396 U.S. 844, 90 S.Ct. 69 (1969). The court took the unusual step of suggesting that the New York Court of Appeals reexamine the *Seider* doctrine, reissuing the invitation several years later in Beja v. Jahangiri, 453 F.2d 959 (2d Cir. 1972). The invitations were not accepted.

[14] Vaage v. Lewis, 29 A.D.2d 315, 288 N.Y.S.2d 521 (2d Dep't 1968).

[15] Donawitz v. Danek, 42 N.Y.2d 138, 397 N.Y.S.2d 592, 366 N.E.2d 253 (1977).

[16] *Donawitz*, 42 N.Y.2d at 142, 397 N.Y.S.2d at 595, 366 N.E.2d at 256. It is difficult to understand how the presence in New York of the insurer's obligations can be made to depend on where the plaintiff lives, a point made in both the concurring and dissenting opinions in *Donawitz*.

[17] See Flemming v. Williams, 30 A.D.2d 834, 293 N.Y.S.2d 45 (2d Dep't 1968) (Connecticut homeowner's policy on Connecticut accident).

[18] See, e.g., Javorek v. Superior Court, 17 Cal. 3d 629, 131 Cal. Rptr. 768, 552 P.2d 728 (1976); Howard v. Allen, 254 S.C. 455, 176 S.E.2d 127 (1970); Ricker v. Lajoie, 314 F. Supp. 401 (D. Vt. 1970); De Rentiis v. Lewis, 106 R.I. 240, 258 A.2d 464 (1969).

[19] See, e.g., Rintala v. Shoemaker, 362 F. Supp. 1044 (D. Minn. 1973).

[20] Forbes v. Boynton, 113 N.H. 617, 313 A.2d 129 (1973). Chief Judge Friendly, writing for the en banc majority in *Minichiello*, had warned that *Seider* might be taken up "defensively" in this way. 410 F.2d at 119.

coverage by the insurer, on federal jurisdiction, on choice of law, on statute of limitations, on preferences, and on many other matters of which treatment proliferated.[21]

9.   *Seider* went onto the books as a kind of indirect direct action against a liability insurer.[22] At root, it regards the insurer as the real party in interest and circumvents New York's rule against direct actions. With the "limited appearance" read into *Seider* by the *Simpson* reargument opinion, *Seider* had the major merit of giving a New York plaintiff a New York forum, which was of course the purpose of the *Seider* doctrine, but without the unpalatable attempt to subject the nondomiciliary insured to personal liability.

Seider's demerit was not its result, which made an insurer come to a plaintiff rather than making the plaintiff hunt out the insurer, but its lawlessness. CPLR 5201(a) said that inchoate rights not sure to ripen into reality were not leviable; *Seider*, by ignoring the statute, held that they were. CPLR 320(c) said there was to be no limited appearance, but *Seider*, assisted by its offspring (the *Simpson* reargument opinion), said that there was. Insurance Law § 167(7)[23] said there was to be no direct action against a liability insurer; *Seider* said in effect that there was.

10.   The Court of Appeals wearied of *Seider*, but felt constrained to stand by it as a precedent. Neuman v. Dunham[24] is one indication. The plaintiff was a New York resident injured in a Pennsylvania accident. When the New York *Seider*-based action was brought, the Pennsylvania two-year statute of limitations had expired, but the New York three-year period was alive. CPLR 202 provides that when a foreign claim accrues to a New Yorker, only the New York period governs. The defendant pointed out, however, that, but for *Seider*, the action could not have been brought in New York at all; that insult should not be added to injury by subjecting the defendant to the longer New York period after subjecting him to such flimsy New York jurisdiction. Evincing a mixture of institutional loyalty and professional impatience, the Court applied CPLR 202 and sustained the action "on the ground of *stare decisis* alone." A year later, acknowledging *Seider*'s bad press, a majority of the Court voted to retain *Seider* based on "considerations of institutional stability and the mandates of *stare decisis*" and because "it would be scandalous for us to abandon it at this time."[25]

11.   There were yet other statutes destined to be "deconstrued," had *Seider* not been overturned. CPLR 6214(b), for example, "freezes" attached property, requiring that it be

---

[21]   See, e.g., Stein, *Jurisdiction by Attachment of Liability Insurance*, 43 N.Y.U. L. Rev. 1075 (1968), and the sources cited in the panel and en banc opinions in *Minichiello*, 140 F.2d at 106.

[22]   New York generally does not allow a direct action, requiring that the insured first be sued. See § 437. Only after securing judgment against the insured can the policy be looked to. The Judicial Conference, based upon a study by Professor Maurice Rosenberg, recommended that a direct action be allowed (in conjunction with which *Seider* would be legislatively overturned), see 16th Jud. Conf. Rep. 289 (proposed statute) and 264 (study) (1971), but it was never adopted. It was hoped, by supporters of the *Seider* rule, that the fact that the insurer in a *Seider* case is the real party in interest and that the *Seider* attachment is available only at the behest of a New York plaintiff, would save *Seider* by giving the case a New York nexus sufficient to meet the requirements of Shaffer v. Heitner. (*Shaffer* requires a relationship between the defendant, the claim, and the forum. See § 104.) If the insurer could be regarded as the defendant, and if its doing business in the forum could be deemed to invoke that forum's interest in protecting its residents from injuries inflicted by tortfeasors insured with that insurer no matter where the conduct occurs, *Seider* could sneak under the *Shaffer* fence. As things turned out, of course, it didn't work.

[23]   Now Ins. Law § 3420; see § 437 (discussing a limited exception to the rule).

[24]   Neuman v. Dunham, 39 N.Y.2d 999, 387 N.Y.S.2d 240, 355 N.E.2d 294 (1976), aff'g Neuman v. Dunham, 49 A.D.2d 733, 374 N.Y.S.2d 296 (1st Dep't 1975).

[25]   *Donawitz*, 42 N.Y.2d at 142, 397 N.Y.S.2d at 595, 366 N.E.2d at 255.

held to the credit of the attaching plaintiff. CPLR 5234(b) gives the plaintiff an outright lien on the attached property. With that in mind, look at this situation:

There are 10 persons injured in a State X accident. Two are New Yorkers who return to New York and attach the policy under *Seider* in a New York action. The other eight sue in State X, their domicile, and get judgments against the insured, seeking now to satisfy their judgments out of the insurance policy, as they are surely entitled to do, but the insurer refuses to pay the judgments, pleading that the policy has been attached in New York and can be used only for the claims of the two New York plaintiffs. That is precisely what CPLR 6214(b) and 5234(b) say, but their literal application in such an instance would have been patently unconstitutional, a deprivation of the property rights of the eight State X plaintiffs. Had *Seider* not been overturned when it was—by the U.S. Supreme Court *Rush* case in 1980—those two statutes, too, would have eventually joined CPLR 5201(a), old CPLR 320(c), and former Insurance Law section 167(7), in that special purgatory *Seider* reserved for statutes that got in its way.

§ 106. Sequestration in Matrimonial Actions

If the defendant/spouse in a matrimonial action is not subject to the court's personam jurisdiction, his or her property may be sequestered and used for the support of the family.[1] Just as with attachment, which is not available in matrimonial actions[2] for the reason that sequestration has been made available instead, any property interest that the defendant has in the state can be sequestered. The procedure is by motion. If the motion is granted the court appoints a sequestrator—this can be the plaintiff spouse—to seize the defendant's property and dispose of it pursuant to court direction. The motion can initially be ex parte and the seizure can be made before the defendant has notice. But notice must be given at some time before the property is actually used.[3]

Caselaw authorizes the use of this sequestration device for quasi in rem jurisdiction, i.e., to secure property of the support debtor out of which monetary awards can be satisfied even though he or she is beyond personam jurisdiction.[4] In this respect, one must of course ask today whether this kind of jurisdiction can continue in matrimonial actions in view of the general ban on quasi in rem jurisdiction pronounced by the U.S. Supreme Court in Shaffer v. Heitner.[5]

Shaffer requires a showing that the defendant and the case have some relationship to the forum. It should be possible to satisfy the court of that relationship in most matrimonial actions. Even if the defendant support debtor is not a New York domiciliary, the fact that his or her family is domiciled in New York—a general condition precedent to the exercise of any kind of matrimonial jurisdiction under section 230 of the Domestic Relations Law—combined with the fact that the defendant has property in New York should, in respect of a support obligation, afford the kind of nexus *Shaffer* contemplates.

---

[1]   Dom. Rel. Law § 233. We are here concerned with sequestration only for quasi in rem jurisdictional use. Its other use, governed by Dom. Rel. Law § 243, is as an enforcement (rather than jurisdictional) device to implement support and alimony orders and judgments already rendered. Property sequestered for jurisdictional use under § 233 may afterwards be applied for enforcement under § 243.

[2]   CPLR 6201.

[3]   Matthews v. Matthews, 240 N.Y. 28, 147 N.E. 237, 38 A.L.R. 1079 (1925).

[4]   Geary v. Geary, 272 N.Y. 390, 6 N.E.2d 67, 108 A.L.R. 1293 (1936).

[5]   Shaffer v. Heitner, 433 U.S. 186, 97 S. Ct. 2569, 53 L. Ed. 2d 683 (1977). The *Shaffer* case is discussed more fully in § 104.

These conclusions should obtain even in view of the U.S. Supreme Court decision in Kulko v. Superior Court of California,[6] which holds that a mere showing of a child's presence in a state is not by itself an adequate jurisdictional basis for a support award in favor of the child against its nonresident father. But *Kulko* involved personam jurisdiction and in this section we are addressing only quasi in rem jurisdiction. An additional showing that the defendant/parent has property in New York should supply nexus enough for quasi in rem jurisdiction under the criteria of the *Shaffer* case. The additional "contact" that the presence of the property constitutes, although inadequate to satisfy personam jurisdiction, should suffice to support the more limited quasi in rem jurisdiction.[7]

Unlike attachment, which by statute must precede the service of process in an action when the attachment is used for quasi in rem jurisdiction,[8] sequestration need not precede service. It can come after and can be sought at any time up to judgment. If personam jurisdiction of the defendant is not obtained during the action, the monetary award in the judgment will of course be enforceable only out of sequestered property.

Pennoyer v. Neff,[9] whence clearly comes the requirement that quasi in rem seizure must precede judgment, is a bit ambiguous as to whether it even has to precede the service of process in the action. New York in effect reads *Pennoyer* both ways. When used for jurisdictional purposes, an order of attachment in an ordinary money action must precede service,[10] while an order of sequestration in a matrimonial action has been allowed to follow it.[11] Following it is not mandatory, however. The sequestration can precede the service of process. But if it does, service must be made within a reasonable time afterwards.[12]

The need for sequestration as a quasi in rem jurisdictional substitute for personam jurisdiction in matrimonial actions was much reduced by the addition of CPLR 302(b) in 1974. CPLR 302(b) offers personam jurisdiction for money claims in matrimonial actions and in family court matters based on certain prescribed longarm contacts that the case has with the state.[13]

For equitable distribution, too, quasi in rem jurisdiction can be invoked if the property affected is in New York.[14]

§ 107. Service by Publication

We've saved this method of service for last because as a matter of due process, it is "the method of notice least calculated to bring to a potential defendant's attention the pendency of judicial proceedings."[1] Service by publication amounts only to a gesture and

---

[6] Kulko v. Superior Court of California In and For City and County of San Francisco, 436 U.S. 84, 98 S. Ct. 1690, 56 L. Ed. 2d 132 (1978).

[7] The *Kulko* case is the subject of the lead note in NYSLD No. 223.

[8] CPLR 314(3).

[9] Pennoyer v. Neff, 95 U.S. 714, 24 L. Ed. 565, 1877 WL 18188 (1877).

[10] CPLR 314(3), 6213; see § 104.

[11] Matthews v. Matthews, 247 N.Y. 32, 159 N.E. 713 (1928).

[12] *Matthews*, 247 N.Y. at 34, 159 N.E. at 714. Note that there is no arbitrary period for service in this situation, such as there is for attachment (60 days after order of attachment under CPLR 6213); see § 319.

[13] See § 90.

[14] McCasland v. McCasland, 68 N.Y.2d 748, 506 N.Y.S.2d 329, 497 N.E.2d 696 (1986).

[1] Boddie v. Connecticut, 401 U.S. 371, 382, 91 S. Ct. 780, 788, 28 L. Ed. 2d 113 (1971).

"when notice is a person's due, process which is a mere gesture is not due process."[2] In a case with many defendants, all of whom have a common interest, such as a proceeding to settle a trust fund with many beneficiaries, a reasonable effort to give personal notice to each may justify a general service by publication if some can't be personally notified after reasonable effort. The mass reached can be expected to protect the interest of the few not reached.[3] But because of supervening due process demands, the use of service by publication in an ordinary one-on-one personam action is risky at best and should be avoided.

In one case in which New York City had condemnation rights to upstate waterways, the city notified certain riparian owners by two methods: by publication and by posting notice on nearby trees—a boon to the tree-reading public. This was all done pursuant to a then-applicable statute and the service was sustained by the New York courts. The U.S. Supreme Court summarily and unanimously reversed, held the methods unconstitutional, and suggested that all the plaintiff had to do to satisfy due process was send each of the riparian owners a letter.[4]

The scheme of the CPLR in regard to service by publication satisfies due process requirements. CPLR 315 is the governing statute. First of all, it permits service by publication only in the rem categories of action, i.e., those listed in CPLR 314. Then it provides that even in those cases, publication can be ordered only "if service cannot be made by another prescribed method with due diligence," which methods include among other things any and all of the usual service methods contained in CPLR 308. Where, for example, the plaintiff/wife in a matrimonial action[5] knew a military address for the defendant/husband, a retired soldier living in Germany, but made no effort to contact him or to learn of his whereabouts through that address, a divorce predicated on service by publication was vacated.[6] Service by publication, said the court, "should be utilized only as a last resort where all other methods are unavailable." The unavailability of other methods had not been established.

With CPLR 308(5) on the books as the ultimate alternative—authorizing the court to invent a method of service if nothing else works—the need for publication even in the rem case should be reduced to near the vanishing point.

Technically, service by publication can still be found even in the personam case despite its being restricted by CPLR 315 to rem cases. A court may order service by publication on a CPLR 308(5) application in a personam action, for example, but it is obviously a last resort there, too.[7] If it is done, some other method should also be ordered, as a due process precaution.

---

[2]   Mullane v. Central Hanover Bank & Trust Co., 339 U.S. 306, 315, 70 S. Ct. 652, 657, 94 L. Ed. 865 (1950).

[3]   *Mullane*, 339 U.S. at 319, 70 S. Ct. at 659.

[4]   Schroeder v. City of New York, 371 U.S. 208, 83 S. Ct. 279, 9 L. Ed. 2d 255, 89 A.L.R.2d 1398 (1962). As a matter of fact, it would probably be a lot faster and cheaper for the plaintiff to use the newspapers and the trees. The extensive search of county records needed to identify all riparian interests along a waterway costs time and poses pitfalls, but due process mandates the effort.

[5]   The matrimonial action is a category in which in rem jurisdiction of the "marital res" can support jurisdiction (see § 102) and in which service by publication under CPLR 315 may be available.

[6]   Caban v. Caban, 116 A.D.2d 783, 497 N.Y.S.2d 175 (3d Dep't 1986).

[7]   See Fidelity Nat. Title Ins. Co. v. Smith, 2015 WL 9851735, *1 (Sup. Ct., New York County 2015) (ordering service of process by publication in accordance with CPLR 316, while also extending time to make service under CPLR 306–b).

The mechanics of publication, in the relatively rare instances when it is ordered—and publication can come about only by court order—are contained in CPLR 316. The publication is to be in two newspapers, designated by the judge, and is to run at least once in each of four consecutive weeks. For the matrimonial action, where service by publication is permissible, but less likely today,[8] publication need be in only one newspaper once in each of three consecutive weeks.[9] The statute also requires—but only in the matrimonial action—that the summons be mailed to the defendant.[10]

First publication of the summons must be made within 30 days after the order for service by publication is granted. This is strict. It has been held that even a short delay will void the service.[11] Service is complete on the 21st day after first publication in a matrimonial action, on the 28th day in all other actions.

When an order of attachment has been obtained in what starts out to be a quasi in rem action,[12] the summons is served on the defendant only after the attachment has been levied. If it is served by publication and it turns out that the defendant is a New Yorker, does the service by publication give personam jurisdiction? For a long time under the old Civil Practice Act (CPA) the question remained unanswered. After the CPA became history, Fishman v. Sanders[13] answered the question and said yes, personam jurisdiction results, but specified that the question was being answered only under the CPA, not under the CPLR. A definitive answer under the CPLR will apparently have to wait until it is superseded sometime in the 21st Century by something else.[14]

H. VACATING DEFAULTS

Table of Sections

§ 108.   Vacating Default Judgment

§ 108. Vacating Default Judgment

A duly served defendant who does not appear and against whom a default judgment is taken may move to vacate the judgment within a year. Two CPLR provisions authorize this: CPLR 317 and CPLR 5015(a)(1).[1] CPLR 317 applies when service was made by a method other than personal delivery to the defendant under CPLR 308(1) or to the defendant's CPLR 318 agent under CPLR 308(3). CPLR 5015(a)(1) is broader, giving the court discretion to vacate a judgment for "excusable default" regardless of the method of

---

[8]   See § 76.

[9]   CPLR 316(a).

[10]   CPLR 316(b).

[11]   Caton v. Caton, 72 Misc. 2d 544, 339 N.Y.S.2d 92 (Sup. Ct., Monroe County 1972).

[12]   This category of jurisdiction is discussed in § 104.

[13]   Fishman v. Sanders, 15 N.Y.2d 298, 258 N.Y.S.2d 380, 206 N.E.2d 326 (1965).

[14]   Service by publication is not likely to be ordered on such a defendant under the CPLR. Given the broad discretion of the court under CPLR 308(5), limited only by judicial imagination, the occasion to order service by publication should be rare indeed today. And given a basis for extraterritorial jurisdiction, as there was in *Fishman* (the defendant was a tortfeasor involved in a New York accident as well as a domiciliary), the procedure today would indeed be to get a service order under CPLR 308(5), such as an order directing mail to the defendant's last known address, which can give personam jurisdiction even if D no longer lives there. See § 75, treating CPLR 308(5).

[1]   CPLR 5015 is studied in more detail later, in the chapter on judgments. See §§ 426 et seq.

service. Hence, a defendant to whom CPLR 317 is unavailable because she was personally served may move to vacate under CPLR 5015(a).[2]

We are assuming here that the court has jurisdiction, both of the subject matter and of the defendant's person, and that all the defendant wants to do is have the default opened and be allowed to defend on the merits. The situation is not to be confused with the one in which jurisdiction is also contested, such as where the defendant contends that service was never properly made.[3] In a lack-of-jurisdiction case, the defendant wants the default judgment vacated and the action dismissed. In the present discussion, jurisdiction is assumed and all the defendant is asking is a vacatur of the default coupled with a reopening of the action so that the defendant can defend it on the merits.

If the defendant believes jurisdiction is lacking, but is apprehensive that the court will not agree, which happens often enough, the defendant's step is to request relief in the alternative: move to vacate the default judgment and either dismiss the action or, if jurisdiction is sustained, open the default and allow a defense on the merits.

Each of the two provisions purports to require that the motion to vacate the default be made within a year, but each starts the year at a different time. CPLR 317 starts the year from the time the defendant "obtains knowledge of entry of the judgment," apparently without regard to the source through which the knowledge came. CPLR 5015(a)(1) starts its year from the time the defendant is formally served with "written notice" of the entry of the judgment, apparently without regard to whether she knew about it before then or not. If that formal service is never made, the one year never starts.[4]

CPLR 317 has a five-year cut-off, which means that the motion under it does not lie if more than five years have elapsed since the entry of judgment. No such limitation inhibits CPLR 5015(a)(1).

The differences between the two provisions might appear to require the drawing of a sharp line between them in situations in which either may be invoked—which would be whenever service is made by a method other than personal delivery to the defendant or her agent—so as to clarify just which one governs what. That might be helpful, but it isn't indispensable for the reason that the one-year period is not a statute of limitations[5] and is therefore not rigid. The court has inherent discretionary power to vacate a default in the interests of justice and retains this power even though the allotted year has expired.[6] This is true of CPLR 317[7] as well as CPLR 5015(a)(1).[8] But then, to what avail the one-year requirement? It is not clear, but if the year has expired, the excuse for the default had best be all the more compelling.

The foregoing should evince how liberal the New York courts are about vacating defaults. It's in the broad discretion of the court. Given a reasonable excuse for the default and a meritorious defense, the court is likely to grant the vacatur. There are even

---

[2]   See Commentary on McKinney's CPLR 5015.

[3]   See CPLR 5015(a)(4); § 430.

[4]   Redfield v. Critchley, 277 N.Y. 336, 14 N.E.2d 377 (1938).

[5]   Ladd v. Stevenson, 112 N.Y. 325, 19 N.E. 842 (1889).

[6]   Machnick Builders, Ltd. v. Grand Union Co., 52 A.D.2d 655, 381 N.Y.S.2d 551 (3d Dep't 1976).

[7]   2d Rep. Leg. Doc. No. 13, p. 169 (1958).

[8]   3d Rep. Leg. Doc. No. 17, p. 204 (1959).

instances of deliberate defaults being vacated, usually with a stiff costs penalty,[9] but a defendant had best have analyzed things quite closely before suffering a default intentionally. The more usual vacatur basis is a showing that as a practical matter circumstances disabled the defendant from protecting her interests.[10]

As alluded to above, the New York rule of thumb is that a motion to vacate a default requires two showings: (1) an excuse for the default and (2) an "affidavit of merits," as it is commonly called, in which the defendant is required to satisfy the court that she has a meritorious defense.[11] This offers assurance that vacating the default will not be a wasted effort; that the defendant does have a reasonable position on the merits and is not just delaying the inevitable. (If the defendant has no defense on the merits, the rule's theory is that a default judgment is just as good as any other to close out the case.)

The affidavit of merits should be made by the defendant herself, or by someone else with first-hand knowledge of the facts. An affidavit of merits made by one without such knowledge will be ignored as having no probative force, which means that the motion papers will be deficient and that the motion to vacate will likely be denied. Quite often in the reported cases the affidavit of merits submitted is that of the defendant's lawyer. Unless the lawyer happens to have been involved in the transactions between the parties, however, which occasionally happens in a commercial or real property case, but virtually never in a tort action, the lawyer's affidavit of merits is essentially worthless. Even if the lawyer did have an involvement and consequently possesses personal knowledge of the facts, it is still better to have the client furnish the affidavit of merits. An attorney's affidavit of merits is prone to rouse the court's suspicion.

Caselaw construing the predecessor of CPLR 317 held that a motion to vacate a default needs the usual affidavit of merits, in common with the caselaw construing CPLR 5015(a)(1), but that it does not need an excuse for the default, as CPLR 5015(a)(1) requires.[12] The present structure of CPLR 317, requiring the defendant to show that he did not get notice "in time to defend," suggests that an excuse for the default is just as necessary on a CPLR 317 as on a 5015(a)(1) motion.[13] Caselaw continues to hold, however, that the CPLR 317 applicant does not have to excuse the default; that she just has to show that she didn't receive notice in time to defend, even if the reason for not receiving notice was her own fault.[14]

Many of the reported cases on default-opening motions involve a corporate defendant served through the secretary of state's office.[15] A common scenario is that the defendant failed to get notice because it failed to keep its address current on the secretary's books, as it is required to do by law, and that the secretary therefore mailed the summons to an old address and the corporation never got it. The omission ought to be laid at the defendant's door, generating at least a money sanction as a condition for a vacatur, but some courts nevertheless continue to forgive the omission and grant

---

[9]   See, e.g., Hensey Properties, Inc. v. Lamagna, 23 A.D.2d 742, 258 N.Y.S.2d 495 (1st Dep't 1965).

[10]   Benadon v. Antonio, 10 A.D.2d 40, 197 N.Y.S.2d 1 (1st Dep't 1960).

[11]   *Benadon*, 10 A.D.2d at 42, 197 N.Y.S.2d at 4.

[12]   Carpenter v. Weatherwax, 277 A.D. 264, 98 N.Y.S.2d 673 (3d Dep't 1950).

[13]   If the reason the defendant defaulted is that he did not get notice in time to defend because of the method of service, that itself may be a good excuse and satisfy as such.

[14]   See Wharton v. 241 Corp., 99 A.D.2d 979, 473 N.Y.S.2d 17 (1st Dep't 1984), citing and relying on Taieb v. Hilton Hotels Corp., 60 N.Y.2d 725, 469 N.Y.S.2d 74, 456 N.E.2d 1197 (1983).

[15]   Bus. Corp. Law § 306. See § 70.

vacaturs by such corporate applicants almost as a matter of course. The defendant does best to cite CPLR 317 on its default-vacating motion, however. CPLR 5015(a)(1), since it requires a decent excuse for the default, doesn't work in this situation.[16] It has been held, however, that if the defendant makes the default vacatur application under CPLR 5015, it can be treated in appropriate circumstances as having been made under the more advantageous 317.[17]

This generous attitude towards corporations may have prompted some of them to take too much for granted, even when there has been no address change, such as by letting certified mail sent to a present address remain unclaimed. It has been held that if the corporation does know about the mail—and it is of course Post Office policy to see that it does—leaving the mail unclaimed can produce a default judgment that will not be vacated under CPLR 317 or anything else.[18] It has also been held that if the corporation, having had a default vacated on wrong-address grounds, still doesn't get its address corrected, the next default will stick.[19]

In the early 1980s, there was a great to-do about defaults predicated on what are known as "law office failures"—omissions on the part of the attorney or someone connected with the attorney's office. It started in 1980 with the Court of Appeals decision in Barasch v. Micucci,[20] which held categorically that "law office failures" may not be accepted as excuses for the plaintiff's late service or nonservice of a complaint under CPLR 3012(b). Then, in Eaton v. Equitable Life Assur. Soc. of U.S., Inc.[21] in 1982, the holding was extended to defendants' defaults in answering, the more typical category of default and the one addressed in the present section. Thenceforth referred to as the *Barasch/Eaton* rule to denote its application to defaults in pleading on either side, it had the parties lying in ambush for each other, hoping for a default and jumping in for it as soon as things were ripe.

Barasch/Eaton was overruled by the legislature in 1983 with the addition of CPLR 2005 and the addition of subdivision (d) to CPLR 3012. Discretion to consider law office failures along with other excuses then reverted to approximately where it was before the *Barasch/Eaton* era. It must be stressed, however, that the legislation merely restores judicial discretion; it does not assure a defaulter that all will be forgiven.

Costs sanctions, including hefty attorney's fees, are a frequent condition now for the excusing of a default.[22]

---

[16]   The lead note in NYSLD No. 290 addresses this subject.

[17]   Eugene Di Lorenzo, Inc. v. A.C. Dutton Lumber Co., Inc., 67 N.Y.2d 138, 501 N.Y.S.2d 8, 492 N.E.2d 116 (1986).

[18]   See Rifenburg v. Liffiton Homes, Inc., 107 A.D.2d 1015, 486 N.Y.S.2d 529 (4th Dep't 1985). The court in *Rifenburg* remanded the case to determine whether the corporation had notice of the certified mail, the vacatur to be denied if it had.

[19]   Paul Conte Cadillac, Inc. v. C.A.R.S. Purchasing Service, Inc., 126 A.D.2d 621, 511 N.Y.S.2d 58 (2d Dep't 1987).

[20]   Barasch v. Micucci, 49 N.Y.2d 594, 427 N.Y.S.2d 732, 404 N.E.2d 1275 (1980).

[21]   Eaton v. Equitable Life Assur. Soc. of U.S., Inc., 56 N.Y.2d 900, 453 N.Y.S.2d 404, 438 N.E.2d 1119 (1982).

[22]   The 1983 amendments and more on the *Barasch/Eaton* background are discussed in § 231. The hectic few years before the overruling of *Barasch/Eaton* are chronicled in lead notes in NYSLD No. 271, after *Eaton* came down, and NYSLD No. 282, when the overruling legislation took effect.

Chapter 5

APPEARANCE

Table of Sections

§ 109.   Appearance, Generally
§ 110.   How and When to Appear
§ 111.   Making and Preserving a Jurisdictional Objection
§ 112.   Informal Appearance
§ 113.   Appearance in "Rem" Actions; "Limited" Appearance
§ 114.   Adding Claims in Various Appearance Situations
§ 115.   Representation by Attorney

§ 109. Appearance, Generally

An appearance is a participation of some kind in an action. It comes in several varieties and lawyers should spare themselves the idle pursuit of trying to give it a precise definition. It is at root a way of submitting to the court's jurisdiction either for a particular purpose or for all purposes.

Under prior law, there existed a "special" appearance, which was used by the defendant for the sole purpose of objecting to the court's jurisdiction of his person, and prior law was strict about it. The only way the jurisdictional objection could be raised was by motion with the "special appearance" label, and jurisdiction had to be the only objection stated. If accompanied by any merits objection, the jurisdictional objection was ipso facto waived.[1]

The CPLR abolished the "special" appearance, and since the "general" appearance was used only to differentiate it from the special one, both categories have disappeared under the CPLR. The main provision in point is CPLR 320(a), and it speaks only of an "appearance." Under the CPLR, lawyers have to know (1) what constitutes an "appearance" and (2) how to make and preserve a jurisdictional objection, and they should absorb the two topics independently before negotiating the interplay between them. The two are no longer wedded as they were under prior law.

Some unique categories of appearance do exist under present law, such as the so-called "restricted" and "limited" and perhaps even "qualified" appearances; these will be treated shortly.[2] There also remains an "informal" appearance.[3] But the "special" and "general" appearances are gone.

---

[1]   Civ. Prac. Act § 237–a (repealed 1963). The statute and the background of New York appearances under prior law are treated in Frumer & Graziano, *Jurisdictional Dilemma of the Nonresident Defendant in New York—A Proposed Solution*, 19 Ford. L. Rev. 125 (1950).

[2]   See §§ 113–14.

[3]   See § 112.

§ 110. How and When to Appear

A plaintiff appears in an action merely by bringing it. A defendant can appear in any of the three ways listed in CPLR 320(a):

1. by serving a notice of appearance; or

2. by serving an answer; or

3. by making a motion which has the "effect" of extending the answering time.

Two motions have the automatic "effect" of extending the answering time: the motion to correct a pleading of CPLR 3024,[1] seen infrequently, and the dismissal motion of CPLR 3211,[2] seen all the time. The making of either kind of motion is therefore an appearance in the action.

If the summons is served with the notice that CPLR 305(b) allows[3] instead of with a complaint, the defendant can respond by serving a notice of appearance[4] and a demand for the complaint.[5] These are usually incorporated into one paper, which can read as simply as: "Take notice that the defendant, through the undersigned as attorney, hereby appears in the action and demands a copy of the complaint."

By serving such a paper the defendant formally "appears" in the action, but the appearance does not constitute a waiver of any jurisdictional objection; the objection can be made later.[6]

The time in which to take this responsive step to the summons depends on the place and method of its service. If the summons is served by personal delivery to the defendant in New York, the responding period is 20 days; if it is served by any other means in New York, or by any means at all (including personal delivery) outside New York, the responding period is 30 days after service is complete.[7] If service by publication is used and the defendant appears during the period of publication, the defendant's appearance itself completes the service[8] and dispenses with further publications.[9]

---

[1]   See CPLR 3024(c).

[2]   See CPLR 3211(f).

[3]   See § 60.

[4]   CPLR 320(a).

[5]   CPLR 3012(b). Procedure when the complaint is served with the summons is treated in § 231.

[6]   Although the notice of appearance is an appearance under CPLR 320(a), the demand for the complaint under CPLR 3012(b) by itself is not. See § 60. Even though the demand, when accompanied by a notice of appearance, constitutes an "appearance" under CPLR 320(a), it does not waive jurisdictional objections. See § 111.

[7]   CPLR 320(a).

[8]   CPLR 320(d).

[9]   For the significance of when service is "complete," see § 72.

§ 111. Making and Preserving a Jurisdictional Objection

An objection to jurisdiction of the subject matter may be taken at any time and in just about any form,[1] but the rules about the objection to personal jurisdiction—including rem jurisdiction—are more demanding[2] and run as follows:

Before the 1963 adoption of the CPLR, an objection to personal jurisdiction could be taken only by a motion made in conjunction with a special appearance.[3] The CPLR abolished the special appearance—an appearance made for the sole purpose of objecting to jurisdiction—and permits the objection to be taken in either of two ways, at the defendant's option: by a motion to dismiss under CPLR 3211[4] or as a defense in the answer.[5] The fact that the defendant may have appeared earlier does not necessarily mean that the jurisdictional objection is waived. Where, for example, the summons is served with only a CPLR 305(b) notice and the defendant responds by serving a notice of appearance and demand for the complaint, the response is an appearance in the action, but since the defendant's answering time is still open, and in fact will not even begin to run until the plaintiff responds to the demand by serving the complaint, whatever jurisdictional objection the defendant may have is preserved.

When the complaint is finally served in that situation, the defendant may now assert the jurisdictional objection either by moving or answering. If the defendant chooses the motion route, which is usually preferable—because it disposes of the objection early, and, if it succeeds, gets rid of the case fast—the defendant may join in the motion any other grounds for dismissal listed in CPLR 3211(a).[6] (Under prior law and its special appearance, the addition of other grounds brought an immediate waiver of the jurisdictional objection.)

Technical defects in carrying out the various requirements of the filing system have also been held waived if the defendant or respondent proceeds with the merits without raising the objection either by motion or answer; the court may not raise the objection on its own motion.[7]

If the jurisdictional objection is one that comes into being only after the time for making a CPLR 3211 motion or serving an answer has expired, the waiver rule does not apply and the objection may be asserted when it does arise. Where, for example, the defect is a failure to perfect an initially valid order of attachment in a case based on quasi in rem jurisdiction—a failure that voids the levy and the quasi in rem jurisdiction along with it[8]—the objection may be asserted in a motion for summary judgment.[9]

---

[1]   CPLR 3211(a)(2), (e); see Commentary C3211:11 on McKinney's CPLR 3211.

[2]   See Homburger & Laufer, *Appearance and Jurisdictional Motions in New York*, 14 Buffalo L. Rev. 374 (1965).

[3]   Civ. Prac. Act § 237–a (repealed 1963).

[4]   CPLR 3211(a)(8) (personam objection) or (9) (rem objection).

[5]   CPLR 3211(e), 320(b), 320(c)(2).

[6]   See CPLR 3211(e).

[7]   Fry v. Village of Tarrytown, 89 N.Y.2d 714, 658 N.Y.S.2d 205, 680 N.E.2d 578 (1997); see Goldenberg v. Westchester County Health Care Corp., 16 N.Y.3d 323, 327, 921 N.Y.S.2d 619, 620–21, 946 N.E.2d 717, 719 (2011) (NYSLD No. 617) (ruling that defendant did not waive defense of filing error). In this sense, the defects fall under the category of personal, not subject matter, jurisdiction. See the discussion of the *Fry* case in § 63 and in the lead note in NYSLD No. 448.

[8]   See § 104 and § 321.

[9]   See Rich v. Rich, 103 Misc. 2d 723, 426 N.Y.S.2d 936 (Sup. Ct., New York County 1980).

If the defendant has defaulted and a judgment has been entered in a case in which the defendant believes jurisdiction was lacking, the jurisdictional objection may be taken by a motion to vacate the default judgment.[10] Furthermore, if the defendant has any other objections such as would have been joinable on a CPLR 3211 motion had there been no default, these, too, may be joined on the motion to vacate the judgment.[11] They may be joined in the alternative: the defendant can seek vacatur of the judgment plus either (1) dismissal of the action for want of jurisdiction or, should jurisdiction be sustained, (2) an opening of the default with leave to defend on the merits.[12] The court would ordinarily pass first on the jurisdictional objection. Only if it finds jurisdiction present would it then go on to rule on the request to open the default. That's the obvious order in which to dispose of the alternative objections, but a court sometimes overlooks this and reverses the sequence.[13]

Although most of the objections on the CPLR 3211(a) list may be taken either by motion or by answer, at the defendant's option, the objections to personal jurisdiction under paragraph 8 and to rem jurisdiction under paragraph 9 are subject to a special requirement. If no CPLR 3211 motion is made at all, those objections may be included as defenses in the answer. But if the defendant does make a CPLR 3211 motion, on any ground at all, and omits from it a personal or rem jurisdictional objection, those objections are waived and may not be included in any later answer.[14] This is to discourage the making of a CPLR 3211 motion unless it includes those fundamental jurisdictional objections, objections so basic that the court should have a chance to dispose of them before being burdened with having to address anything else.

If the objection is taken as a defense in the answer instead of by motion, it evinces the defendant's preference to defer determination of the objection until later, perhaps until the trial itself. The plaintiff, however, may bring the issue to prompt adjudication by moving to dismiss the defense under CPLR 3211(b). Indeed, if there is a potential statute of limitations problem in the case, the plaintiff will be glad to have that option. (Always relevant to the plaintiff, when the defendant has interposed a jurisdictional objection, is the timing of its adjudication.)[15]

One of the objections to personal jurisdiction, and perhaps the most common one at that—the objection of improper service—invokes another special rule: if the defendant asserts the objection in the answer, the defendant must then move for judgment on it within 60 days thereafter or the objection is waived.[16] If the defense is instead based on a lack of jurisdictional basis, the 60-day limitation does not apply and it can be raised on a motion for summary judgment made within the deadlines set in CPLR 3212(a).[17]

Since the CPLR allows the defendant to take the jurisdictional objection by motion or answer, it has been held that when the answer method is used, the pleading of a

---

[10]   CPLR 5015(a)(4); see § 430.

[11]   Mutual Home Dealers Corp. v. Alves, 23 A.D.2d 791, 258 N.Y.S.2d 786, 2 U.C.C. Rep. Serv. 726 (2d Dep't 1965).

[12]   CPLR 5015(a)(1); see § 427.

[13]   *Mutual Home Dealers Corp.*, 23 A.D.2d at 792, 258 N.Y.S.2d at 788.

[14]   CPLR 3211(e); Dominion of Canada General Ins. Co. v. Pierson, 27 A.D.2d 484, 280 N.Y.S.2d 296 (3d Dep't 1967).

[15]   The urgency of this timing when the statute of limitations is approaching the scene is explored in a three-part series of lead notes in NYSLD Nos. 274–76.

[16]   CPLR 3211(e); see § 266; SPR 50:3.

[17]   See § 279.

counterclaim—which is also contained in the answer—does not waive the jurisdictional objection if the counterclaim is related to the plaintiff's claim.[18] To hold otherwise would nullify the CPLR permission to plead rather than move on a jurisdictional objection. But it has been held that the pleading of an unrelated counterclaim does waive an objection to jurisdiction.[19]

To determine relatedness in this situation, the Court of Appeals has adopted a collateral estoppel test. If there are common issues between the main claim and the counterclaim, such that the resolution of any common issue in the course of adjudicating the main claim would also be dispositive of the issue if it should arise on the counterclaim, "relatedness" is established and the risk of waiving the objection to jurisdiction merely by pleading the counterclaim is avoided.[20]

While these rules presumably apply as well to a cross-claim,[21] D's impleader of a third-party defendant is not necessarily inconsistent with D's preservation of a jurisdictional objection and therefore does not waive it.[22]

The spectacle has arisen of a defendant serving an answer and objecting to jurisdiction in an action in which he has not even been served with process. In one case, although not served, D was named as a defendant along with others. The fact that D is named, held the court, gives D a sufficient nexus with the case to support his application to dismiss for want of jurisdiction. Until a court rules on jurisdiction, D's position is insecure—perhaps service was attempted, but D was unaware of it, for example. As a named party, served or not, D may, if he fancies himself entitled to a jurisdictional dismissal, interpose the objection and ask for it.[23]

If the defendant moves to dismiss for want of personal jurisdiction in an ordinary in personam action, she had best stay on and defend on the merits if the motion is denied. If the defendant leaves the action after the denial, a default judgment will result and it will be binding in personam under the full faith and credit doctrine.[24] The defendant therefore derives no advantage at all by attempting to withdraw after losing a jurisdictional objection in a personam action, although withdrawal may offer a benefit in certain rem cases.[25]

Under New York law, an immediate appeal may be taken from an order denying a motion to dismiss for lack of jurisdiction,[26] even though it is of course not final, i.e., does not terminate the case. But the defendant has the alternative, little used with jurisdictional objections, of foregoing an immediate appeal and instead seeking appellate review of the order as part of a later appeal from the final judgment on the merits, should

---

[18]   Goodman v. Solow, 27 A.D.2d 920, 279 N.Y.S.2d 377 (1st Dep't 1967).

[19]   Liebling v. Yankwitt, 109 A.D.2d 780, 486 N.Y.S.2d 292 (2d Dep't 1985).

[20]   Textile Technology Exchange, Inc. v. Davis, 81 N.Y.2d 56, 595 N.Y.S.2d 729, 611 N.E.2d 768 (1993). The various tactical considerations confronted by the defendant in this situation are discussed in a lead note on the *Textile* case in SPR 4:1.

[21]   See Commentary C3211:60 on McKinney's CPLR 3211. Counterclaims and cross-claims may be interposed in New York practice even though unrelated to any other claim in the case, CPLR 3019(a) and (b) (see §§ 224 and 227), in contrast with federal practice (for which see § 632 (Practitioner's Edition)).

[22]   Italian Colony Restaurant v. Wershals, 45 A.D.2d 841, 358 N.Y.S.2d 448 (2d Dep't 1974).

[23]   Colbert v. International Sec. Bureau Inc., 79 A.D.2d 448, 437 N.Y.S.2d 360 (2d Dep't 1981).

[24]   See § 471.

[25]   See § 113.

[26]   CPLR 5701(a)(2)(v); see § 526.

that judgment be adverse.[27] At whatever stage the jurisdictional point is appealed, an appellate determination that jurisdiction was lacking will result in a dismissal, incidentally cancelling out a trial on the merits if one has already taken place.

The rule in American jurisprudence is that each defendant is entitled to one day in court on a jurisdictional question. If the defendant asserts the objection by motion or answer in the original action, she uses up that day in court at that time and is bound by the court's holding on the issue. In fact, if she appears in the action and defends on the merits, even without raising a jurisdictional objection, the rule is that by appearing (1) she had the opportunity to raise it, (2) her silence about it forfeited it, and (3) that's the equivalent of a day in court on the issue and precludes any other American court, under the Full Faith and Credit Clause, from later questioning the first court's jurisdiction.[28] Even if the defendant did not appear in the first court at the outset, but made her jurisdictional objection there by a motion to vacate a default judgment after one was entered against her, that post-judgment motion constitutes the day in court under this rule so that an adverse decision on the motion to vacate, sustaining jurisdiction, seals it and precludes collateral attack on it later in any other court.[29]

§ 112. Informal Appearance

In addition to the formal appearances listed in CPLR 320(a),[1] the law continues to recognize the so-called "informal" appearance. It comes about when the defendant, although not having taken any of the steps that would officially constitute an appearance under CPLR 320(a), nevertheless participates in the case in some way relating to the merits. Thus, where the defendant's lawyer showed up at the trial and questioned witnesses on the merits, the defendant was held to have appeared in the action and thereby submitted himself to jurisdiction.[2]

Participation at the pretrial stage of proceedings can also bring about an informal appearance, such as where the defendant submits to the taking of his deposition or seeks to take the plaintiff's deposition on any matter touching the merits of the case.[3]

The occasion for this kind of appearance, an infrequent thing, may be a case in which there are multiple defendants, some of whom have appeared and are defending. This affords a context in which another defendant, duly named in the summons but perhaps not served, hears about the action from the other defendants. Taking no step that would constitute a formal appearance, he nevertheless participates and addresses the merits in some way as in the above examples.

An informal appearance can also occur if the defendant participates in the trial of a damages issue after a judgment by default has been rendered establishing liability.[4]

---

[27] CPLR 5501(a)(1). Compare Application of Dorfman, 187 Misc. 1048, 66 N.Y.S.2d 591 (Broome County Ct. 1946), which was decided in the now expired era of the special appearance but whose conclusions, allowing deferral of appellate review of jurisdictional objections until later appeal on the merits, would still obtain under CPLR 5501. See § 530.

[28] Sherrer v. Sherrer, 334 U.S. 343, 68 S. Ct. 1087, 92 L. Ed. 1429, 1 A.L.R.2d 1355 (1948).

[29] Vander v. Casperson, 12 N.Y.2d 56, 236 N.Y.S.2d 33, 187 N.E.2d 109 (1962).

[1] See § 110.

[2] Henderson v. Henderson, 247 N.Y. 428, 160 N.E. 775 (1928).

[3] McGowan v. Bellanger, 32 A.D.2d 293, 301 N.Y.S.2d 712 (3d Dep't 1969).

[4] The default concedes liability, but not damages. See § 293.

A defendant who desires to preserve any kind of jurisdictional objection had best not appear informally. The consequence of the informal appearance is that while it is a full submission to jurisdiction, and in fact perfects jurisdiction otherwise lacking, it is also a waiver of any jurisdictional objection the defendant might otherwise have had.[5] A jurisdictional objection, as has been seen,[6] must be interposed only by motion or answer, and if no motion was made and the time to answer has expired, as where the defendant was served and let the time pass without a responsive step, an informal appearance at a later point forfeits the only opportunity the defendant had for assertion of a jurisdictional objection.

§ 113. Appearance in "Rem" Actions; "Limited" Appearance

A few special points have to be made about appearances and the making of jurisdictional objections in the rem categories of actions, rare as they are today. The method of taking the objection is the same as in the personam action, i.e., by motion to dismiss or as a defense in the answer, but the appearance itself can have different consequences in certain actions or at certain stages. The following discussion assumes that there is no personam jurisdiction in the action and that only rem jurisdiction is claimed.

If the sole basis of jurisdiction is the attachment of the defendant's local property,[1] New York allows the defendant what has become known as a "limited" appearance. In this kind of action, and only in this one, the defendant is permitted to appear and defend without facing any personam consequences. Whether he defaults, or defends and loses, the resulting judgment is effective only to the extent of—and execution on the judgment can be levied only against—the property previously attached. This is the gift of CPLR 320(c)(1),[2] a provision added in a 1969 amendment. The amendment codifies the result of the reargument opinion in Simpson v. Loehmann,[3] which interpolated a limited appearance into the pre-amendment version of CPLR 320(c). The *Simpson* case did that in a *Seider* situation, i.e., where the property attached was the defendant's liability insurance policy,[4] but the amendment allows the limited appearance in any case in which attachment is the sole basis for jurisdiction.

If the defendant exploits the limited appearance and defends on the merits, the action follows the usual procedures. The only consequence is that a judgment for the plaintiff will have limited effect. In the realization that even a victory may afford the plaintiff only partial satisfaction of the claim, i.e., satisfaction only to the extent of the attached property, thus necessitating yet another action later to collect the balance, the plaintiff sometimes seeks a special preference for the attachment-based action so as to get it tried early. The courts are not ordinarily receptive to this. They reason that the

---

[5] An informal appearance can also impinge on other matters, including the right to dismissal of an action under CPLR 3215(c) where the plaintiff has failed to timely apply for a default judgment. See § 294.

[6] See § 111.

[1] This is the quasi in rem jurisdiction treated in § 104. As discussed in that section, this category of jurisdiction was much curtailed by the U.S. Supreme Court in Shaffer v. Heitner, 433 U.S. 186, 97 S. Ct. 2569, 53 L. Ed. 2d 683 (1977), but subsists in several situations.

[2] See also CPLR 5230(a).

[3] Simpson v. Loehmann, 21 N.Y.2d 990, 290 N.Y.S.2d 914, 238 N.E.2d 319 (1968).

[4] See § 105.

plaintiff could have sued for everything at once in a court with personam jurisdiction and spared everyone the extra action.[5]

If the defendant contends that even quasi in rem jurisdiction is lacking for some reason—insufficient service, defective attachment, etc.—she can move to dismiss for want of rem jurisdiction under CPLR 3211(a)(9). If that motion is not successful, the defendant loses nothing by staying in and defending on the merits. Doing so does not result in personam jurisdiction. The limited appearance still insures that the judgment will be valid only as against the attached property.

That is not so, however, with any other category of rem jurisdiction, such as the usual "in rem" category described in section 103. These others are governed by CPLR 320(c)(2), and here, an appearance does confer personal jurisdiction even though there was no personal jurisdiction to start with. If the defendant maintains that even the rem jurisdiction was lacking at the outset, he may make the dismissal motion under CPLR 3211(a)(9). If the defendant wins on that motion, all is dismissed and he can go home. But if the motion is denied, and the rem jurisdiction sustained, the defendant now faces a choice: he must either withdraw from the litigation, thus allowing a default judgment to be entered against him—which forfeits without contest whatever interest he has in the property involved in the case—or he may remain in the action and defend on the merits. By remaining, however, he submits himself to personam jurisdiction and a judgment in the action is not confined to the defendant's interest in the property.

It is to be seen, therefore, that except in the attachment case, where the defendant is allowed a limited appearance, in all other rem actions in New York, an appearance subjects the defendant to a kind of leverage in which the defendant must either submit to personam jurisdiction (by appearing and defending) or forfeit his interest in the property (by defaulting). In some cases, this can pose the same kind of constitutional objection that resulted in the caselaw adoption of the limited appearance in the *Seider* situation discussed earlier.[6] But given the expanded modern bases for personam jurisdiction, today's diminished reliance on rem jurisdiction[7] makes the issue largely academic.

Suppose the defendant does not know precisely what kind of jurisdiction the plaintiff is asserting—personam or rem or quasi in rem—and that she has some jurisdictional objections. Even the plaintiff may be unsure of what kind of jurisdiction exists.[8] The objection to personal jurisdiction is made under paragraph 8 of CPLR 3211(a), the rem objection under paragraph 9. The unsure defendant should base the dismissal motion on both paragraphs and in the moving papers request that the court specify, in the order deciding the motion, what kind of jurisdiction, if any, exists. Since different consequences append to later steps in the case, depending on the kind of jurisdiction sustained, a judicial determination sustaining any kind should clarify what kind it is.

As with the objection to personam jurisdiction, an order denying a motion to dismiss for want of rem jurisdiction may be appealed immediately or deferred for appellate

---

[5]   See Tjepkema v. Kenney, 59 Misc. 2d 670, 299 N.Y.S.2d 943 (Sup. Ct., New York County 1969), an action based on the since-overruled *Seider* doctrine. See § 105.

[6]   See the paragraphs numbered 2 and 3 in the discussion of *Seider* in § 105.

[7]   See § 103.

[8]   See Kelly v. Stanmar, Inc., 51 Misc. 2d 378, 273 N.Y.S.2d 276 (Sup. Ct., Albany County 1966).

review until later appeal of an adverse judgment on the merits.[9] In either instance, the appellate court will be the final judge of jurisdiction. Under CPLR 320(c)(2), if the defendant has stayed in the action and defended after her jurisdictional motion was denied, thus submitting to personam jurisdiction, a later appellate finding that the court lacked rem jurisdiction—and that the jurisdictional motion should have been granted—will result in a dismissal, incidentally cancelling the trial, if already had, and with it the personam "submission" that had been in essence coerced from the defendant.

§ 114. Adding Claims in Various Appearance Situations

Assume that a nondomiciliary defendant is temporarily in the state and is served with a summons and CPLR 305(b) notice, the latter setting forth a contract claim. Assume no longarm or other basis for extraterritorial service exists. The defendant serves a notice of appearance and a demand for the complaint. Is the complaint that the plaintiff now serves confined to the contract claim of which the CPLR 305(b) notice advised the defendant, or may the complaint put in additional claims not referred to in the notice? The New York Court of Appeals held in Everitt v. Everitt,[1] that the complaint is not confined to the claim described in the notice, which was a contract claim for $46,900 in *Everitt,* and may as a matter of right plead any other claim the plaintiff has. The *Everitt* plaintiff added a tort claim for $350,000.

The justification for this result is that when the defendant is personally served in New York, the service is a good jurisdictional predicate for any claim.

By way of dictum, the court added in *Everitt* that had the action been commenced by service of the summons and complaint together, "[i]t may well be that . . . the complaint cannot be amended by adding new causes of action after the defendant has left the State."[2] That presumably means that the defendant has "left the State" without further participation in the action, i.e., without even putting in an appearance, because when the defendant does appear in that kind of case, the plaintiff has been held entitled to add, in an amended complaint, even claims of which the original complaint gave no notice. The appellate division held in Mendoza v. Mendoza[3] that in an amendment as of course—an amendment a party is entitled to make without court leave[4]—the plaintiff can as a matter of right add whatever she wishes in the amended complaint whether the original complaint gave notice of the matter or not. *Mendoza* allowed an amendment to add a fraud claim to an original complaint that had pleaded only a cause of action to annul a marriage.

If the defendant has appeared and the amendment is sought by court leave,[5] which is necessary when the of-right amendment is used up or the time for it has expired, whether to allow new or additional claims is in the court's discretion.[6]

---

[9]   See § 111.

[1]   Everitt v. Everitt, 4 N.Y.2d 13, 171 N.Y.S.2d 836, 148 N.E.2d 891 (1958).

[2]   *Everitt,* 4 N.Y.2d at 16, 171 N.Y.S.2d at 838, 148 N.E.2d at 893.

[3]   Mendoza v. Mendoza, 4 Misc. 2d 1060, 77 N.Y.S.2d 169 (Sup. Ct., New York County 1947), aff'd, 273 A.D. 877, 77 N.Y.S.2d 264 (1st Dep't 1948).

[4]   CPLR 3025(a); see § 236.

[5]   CPLR 3025(b).

[6]   Alkalaj v. Alkalaj, 190 Misc. 326, 73 N.Y.S.2d 678 (Sup. Ct., New York County 1947).

The Court of Appeals in Einstoss' Estate[7] introduced the possibility of what might be called a "qualified" appearance when it refused to recognize an Alaskan judgment that had failed to honor a condition the defendant had stipulated to when he appeared. P had sued D in an Alaska court to foreclose a mortgage. In that action, D was served outside Alaska and the court got no personam jurisdiction.[8] The State of Alaska was a co-defendant. D agreed to appear in the action, thereby facilitating P's proceedings, but only on the understanding that P would not seek a personam judgment against D. The co-defendant State of Alaska ignored that P-D understanding, however, interposed a cross-claim jurisdictionally dependent on D's appearance and took a default judgment against D. There were further complications that contributed to the Court of Appeals refusal to recognize the judgment on the cross-claim, but the main ground was that since the judgment had depended jurisdictionally on the appearance, it could not at the same time violate the condition that had legitimately qualified the appearance.

Whether such a "qualified" appearance will be permissible in internal New York practice has yet to be elaborated, but if the defendant would attempt it, he had best do no more than D did in *Einstoss*: put in the appearance; duly qualified; and then participate no further. But in that case, why appear at all? One advantage is that the defendant who appears but does not defend is entitled to notice of subsequent proceedings[9] whereas the outright defaulter is not.

The still nebulous "qualified" appearance should not be confused with the already discussed "restricted" and "limited" appearances. The "restricted" one is authorized by CPLR 302(c) and applies to preclude a plaintiff from adding against a CPLR 302 ("longarm") defendant any additional claims not also having an extraterritorial jurisdictional basis under CPLR 302.[10] The "limited" appearance is permitted by CPLR 320(c)(1) in the case in which jurisdiction rests solely on the local attachment of the defendant's assets.[11] Even if the defendant appears in the attachment case, incidentally, the amendment of the complaint to add claims should not matter because, whatever is added, a judgment in the action will still be enforceable only against the attached property.

With these restricted and limited appearances, the defendant is actually defending the case on the merits. Hence, except for the special advantage built into the particular kind of appearance, such a defendant is subject to the usual procedural rules. He is, for example, subject to a deposition and other pretrial proceedings.[12]

§ 115. Representation by Attorney

Adult natural persons may prosecute or defend an action in person, but a corporation and association may do so only through an attorney.[1] It has been held,

---

[7]   In re Einstoss' Estate, 26 N.Y.2d 181, 309 N.Y.S.2d 184, 257 N.E.2d 637 (1970).

[8]   There is no indication in the report that Alaska had a longarm or like statute for extraterritorial jurisdiction. It would seem that if it had, the Alaskan judgment would have been entitled to full faith and credit because of the personal jurisdiction that would have resulted based on the apparent contacts Alaska had with the claim.

[9]   See CPLR 3215(g)(1); § 296.

[10]   See § 91.

[11]   See § 113.

[12]   See Gazerwitz v. Adrian, 28 A.D.2d 556, 280 N.Y.S.2d 233 (2d Dep't 1967).

[1]   CPLR 321(a).

however, that the assignee of a corporation may sue in person.[2] Infants and incapacitated persons—incompetents, conservatees, etc.[3]—can neither appear for themselves nor hire lawyers. Appearance in their behalf must be made by persons authorized by CPLR 1201. The common practice is for the appropriate CPLR 1201 person to retain an attorney to act in behalf of the ward.

Exceptions apply in the small claims parts of the lower courts. A corporation can appear without a lawyer in the "commercial" small claims part of the New York City Civil Court and of the district and city courts[4] and in the usual small claims part of those courts and of the town and village courts. In the usual (non-"commercial") part, the corporation is allowed only to defend (not prosecute) a small claim.[5]

An appearance by an attorney in purported behalf of a nondomiciliary, but without the latter's authority, confers no jurisdiction and any judgment based on it will be vacated on motion.[6] An unauthorized appearance in behalf of a New Yorker was upheld by the old case of Denton v. Noyes,[7] but the holding was roundly criticized[8] and appears to have been abandoned.[9] An unauthorized appearance, even for a New York resident, would thus seem to be void.

CPLR 321(b) authorizes a change of attorney by merely filing with the clerk a consent signed by the retiring attorney and signed and acknowledged by the party. Notice of the change must then be given to all other parties. Absent the client's consent, an attorney seeking to withdraw from representing a party in an action must make a motion to withdraw.[10] If the motion route is necessary, the attorney will need to establish grounds under Rule 1.16 of the New York Rules of Professional Conduct.[11]

Regardless of the method or grounds for withdrawal, the outgoing lawyer should clearly communicate with the client at every step along the way, preferably in writing. The Court of Appeals decision in Grace v. Law[12] highlights the point. In *Grace*, the Court affirmed the denial of defendant law firm's motion for summary judgment to dismiss a

---

2   Kamp v. In Sportswear Inc., 39 A.D.2d 869, 332 N.Y.S.2d 983 (1st Dep't 1972), rev'g on dissenting opinion below, 70 Misc. 2d 898, 335 N.Y.S.2d 306 (App. Term, 1st Dep't 1972).

3   The terminology of "incapacitated person" is generally used today in place of incompetent and conservatee, and "guardian" in place of committee and conservator. See § 69, paragraph (b).

4   See Article 18–A in the New York City Civ. Ct. Act and in the Uniform Dist. Ct. Act and Uniform City Ct. Act, and the Commentaries on them in McKinney's Vol. 29A, Part 3.

5   See § 1809(2) in the three acts cited above and in the Uniform Justice Court Act (McKinney's Vol. 29A, Part 2). A 1987 amendment adding § 501 to the Uniform Justice Court Act appears to permit a corporation to appear in town and village courts without a lawyer in any category of action, not just a small claim. See the Commentary on McKinney's UJCA § 501.

6   Vilas v. Plattsburgh & M.R. Co., 123 N.Y. 440, 25 N.E. 941 (1890).

7   Denton v. Noyes, 6 Johns. 296, 1810 WL 1155 (N.Y. Sup. 1810).

8   See, e.g., Note, *Unauthorized Appearance*, 25 St. John's L. Rev. 325 (1951).

9   The Third Department held in Wickham v. Liberty Mut. Ins. Co., 73 A.D.2d 742, 423 N.Y.S.2d 273 (3d Dep't 1979), that *Denton* and like cases "have no present-day validity." The Second Department agreed in Skyline Agency, Inc. v. Ambrose Coppotelli, Inc., 117 A.D.2d 135, 502 N.Y.S.2d 479 (2d Dep't 1986).

10   CPLR 321(b)(2). The motion is made by order to show cause, with appropriate notice to the client and all other parties.

11   22 N.Y.C.R.R. Part 1200. New York Rules of Professional Conduct, Rule 1.16(b) contains four grounds for mandatory withdrawal; Rule 1.16(c) contains thirteen grounds for permissive withdrawal. See, e.g., Ferdico v. Zweig, 82 A.D.3d 1151, 919 N.Y.S.2d 521 (2d Dep't 2011); Jessamy v. Doran Group, 36 Misc. 3d 1220(A), 959 N.Y.S.2d 89 (Sup. Ct., Westchester County 2012). An attorney seeking to withdraw from representing a client by either consent under CPLR 321(b) or on motion should review Rule 1.16 in its entirety, along with the accompanying comments, which outline the many duties of a lawyer in that circumstance.

12   Grace v. Law, 24 N.Y.3d 203, 997 N.Y.S.2d 334, 21 N.E.3d 995 (2014); see § 42.

legal malpractice action based on the statute of limitations because it was "unclear" when the firm's representation of the plaintiff in a federal action concluded.

If, because of death, illness, disbarment, suspension, or any other disabling reason, a party's attorney becomes unable to act before judgment, leave of court is needed before any further step may be taken against that party unless she is given at least 30 days notice to appoint a new attorney.[13]

In Countryman v. Watertown Housing Authority,[14] the court listed three of the most commonly recognized grounds for a withdrawal motion:

(1)   the client's failure to keep in touch with counsel;[15]

(2)   the "deterioration" of the relationship;[16] and

(3)   the non-payment of fees.[17]

The *Countryman* court held that the attorney did not establish valid grounds for withdrawal and "the fact that a lawsuit is of questionable liability, limited damages, and a likely unfavorable trial result is not the type of impairment of the attorney-client relationship that permits withdrawal of counsel."

What happens when a party purports to discharge his lawyer without following the authorized procedure, such as with a mere letter, and then by himself negotiates a settlement with the opposing party, who has a lawyer? The Second Department in Moustakas v. Bouloukos[18] allowed the party so doing to rescind the settlement. The Third Department, however, disagreed and held that a party is bound by what he does on his own after deliberately discharging his lawyer and electing to proceed pro se.[19]

An interesting problem concerning representation sometimes arises in a case involving liability insurance. In Chemprene, Inc. v. X-Tyal Intern. Corp.,[20] for example, P, through an attorney, sued D. D interposed a counterclaim against P. P carried insurance on the liability asserted in the counterclaim and was entitled to have the insurer defend it. Must P choose but a single lawyer both to prosecute P's main claim and defend P on the counterclaim? Not necessarily, ruled the Court of Appeals, especially when there is a "possibility of diverse interests and a need for two attorneys." The matter is for the trial court to determine on the facts of the particular case in its discretion. In

---

[13]   CPLR 321(c); see Moray v. Koven & Krause, Esqs., 15 N.Y.3d 384, 912 N.Y.S.2d 547, 938 N.E.2d 980 (2010) (NYSLD No. 613) ("action was automatically stayed by operation of CPLR 321(c) on the date when plaintiff's attorney was suspended from the practice of law," necessitating vacatur of order dismissing action); compare RDLF Financial Services, LLC v. Bernstein, 93 A.D.3d 421, 938 N.Y.S.2d 891 (1st Dep't 2012) (defendant, representing himself and his law firm, not entitled to stay under CPLR 321(c) because his removal from the bar was the product of his own wrongdoing).

[14]   Countryman v. Watertown Housing Authority, 13 Misc. 3d 632, 820 N.Y.S.2d 757 (Sup. Ct., Jefferson County 2006).

[15]   See New York Rules of Professional Conduct, Rule 1.16(c)(7).

[16]   See New York Rules of Professional Conduct, Rule 1.16(c)(7).

[17]   See New York Rules of Professional Conduct, Rule 1.16(c)(5).

[18]   Moustakas v. Bouloukos, 112 A.D.2d 981, 492 N.Y.S.2d 793 (2d Dep't 1985).

[19]   Imor v. Imor, 119 A.D.2d 913, 501 N.Y.S.2d 195 (3d Dep't 1986). Justice Levine's dissent in *Imor* cogently observed that "[i]n dealing directly with defendant without at least obtaining informal, direct confirmation from defendant's attorney-of-record that he was no longer in the case, plaintiff's counsel came perilously close to a violation of the canons of ethics." *Imor*, 119 A.D.2d at 915, 501 N.Y.S.2d at 198 (Levine, J. dissenting); see New York Rules of Professional Conduct, Rule 4.2, cmt. 3 (noting that "no contact" rule "applies even though the represented party initiates or consents to the communication").

[20]   Chemprene, Inc. v. X-Tyal Intern. Corp., 55 N.Y.2d 900, 449 N.Y.S.2d 23, 433 N.E.2d 1271 (1982).

Chemprene, the trial court did not require the plaintiff to choose and the Court of Appeals upheld the trial court.

When an attorney is discharged, or a substitution is made, an issue often arises about whether, and on what, the attorney may have a lien. A distinction must be made between a "retaining" lien, which attaches to any papers or property of the client in the lawyer's possession, and a "charging" lien under Judiciary Law section 475, which applies to the proceeds of a given action.[21]

---

[21] See Justice Leon Lazer's instructive discourse in Kaplan v. Reuss, 113 A.D.2d 184, 495 N.Y.S.2d 404 (2d Dep't 1985), aff'd, 68 N.Y.2d 693, 506 N.Y.S.2d 304, 497 N.E.2d 671 (1986), the subject of the lead note in NYSLD No. 318.

Chapter 6

VENUE

Analysis

A. Introductory
B. Venue in Particular Actions
C. Change of Venue

A. INTRODUCTORY

Table of Sections

§ 116.   Venue, Generally
§ 117.   Agreement to Fix Venue

§ 116. Venue, Generally

Venue means the geographical subdivision in which an action may be brought. The supreme court, for example, has statewide jurisdiction, but the suit can't be maintained anywhere merely at the plaintiff's whim. If the defendant insists, the action must be prosecuted in a proper "venue," for purposes of which the supreme court is subdivided into counties. The venue rules of Article 5 of the CPLR determine which of the counties is proper for the particular supreme court action.

There is little occasion to apply Article 5 of the CPLR, and especially CPLR 503, the main venue-choosing provision of the CPLR, in any other court but the supreme court. Venue rules are needed only for courts with territorial subdivisions. The county courts, for example, have none. Each is an independent entity in the particular county and whether or not to sue in a county court is a question of jurisdiction, not venue. The venue-fixing provisions of Article 5 therefore do not apply in the county courts. Nor do they apply in the lower courts. Like the county court, each of the city, town, and village courts is independent in its municipality and therefore needs no "venue" provisions as such.[1] The New York City Civil Court and the district courts in Nassau and Suffolk counties, on the other hand, do have subdivisions—the civil court consists of the five New York City counties and the district courts consist of districts into which the county is divided—but they have their own venue provisions[2] and are thus not governed by the venue-laying provisions of the CPLR.[3]

---

[1]   A provision analogous to a venue provision applies in the city courts (Uniform City Ct. Act § 213) and in the town and village courts (Uniform Just. Ct. Act § 213). It keeps out of those courts cases that don't belong there for want of municipal contacts. See the Commentaries on those provisions in McKinney's Vol.29A, Parts 2 and 3.

[2]   Article 3 in both the New York City Civ. Ct. Act and Uniform Dist. Ct. Act supplies the venue rules in those courts. See McKinney's Vol. 29A, Part 3.

[3]   The family court, established in each county of the state, also comes in for occasional treatment as a "statewide" court so as to permit the transfer of a case from one county to another. See Prospero v. Prospero, 39 A.D.2d 634, 331 N.Y.S.2d 318 (4th Dep't 1972).

Venue presupposes that the court already has both subject matter and personal jurisdiction because an absence of either would produce a jurisdictional dismissal and make a venue question academic. Venue even assumes that there is no forum non conveniens objection in the case because that, too, would be a dismissal ground. A mere defect of venue, on the other hand, is not a dismissal ground in New York practice.[4]

This is in contrast with federal practice. If suit in a U.S. district court is brought in the wrong district, a federal statute permits dismissal, although transfer is the more common remedy.[5] If suit in the New York supreme court is brought in the wrong county, the New York statute precludes dismissal; the court is required to entertain the case unless the venue is changed to a proper county on motion.[6] Curiously, just the reverse occurs between the two court systems on a forum non conveniens objection. Successful application of the conveniens doctrine in New York dismisses the action,[7] while in the federal courts it usually results in a mere transfer to the more convenient district.[8]

A judgment is valid even though rendered by the supreme court in an improper county of venue. Hence, the worst that can happen to an improperly venued supreme court action is a change of venue to a proper county.[9]

It is also true of supreme court practice that as long as the case can get by jurisdictional and conveniens objections, there will always be some proper county of venue.[10]

When specific real or personal property is involved in the action, venue can, and sometimes must, be based on the situs of the property. If it is, the action is called a "local" one for venue purposes.[11] All other actions qualify as "transitory" (the popular but unofficial term), and these, which include the ordinary money actions, are by far the more numerous. In the transitory action, venue is keyed to residence.[12] If there are multiple parties and claims, or even an ordinary P v. D suit with several claims, venue proper as to any one of the claims satisfies for the whole action, including the claims that would have demanded different venue if sued on alone.[13]

Venue is measured by the plaintiff's claim; it is not ordinarily affected by a counterclaim.[14] The defendant who interposes a counterclaim therefore submits it to the venue the plaintiff has selected.

---

[4] An exception may be deemed to come from CPLR 513, applicable in a consumer credit transaction (as defined in CPLR 105). It requires the clerk to refuse to file the summons if it appears on its face that the venue is improper.

[5] 28 U.S.C.A. § 1406(a) (permitting the federal court to "dismiss, or if it be in the interest of justice, transfer" an action to a proper district); see § 617 (Practitioner's Edition).

[6] CPLR 509.

[7] See § 28.

[8] 28 U.S.C.A. § 1404(a). See § 618 (Practitioner's Edition).

[9] Benson v. Eastern Bldg. & Loan Ass'n, 174 N.Y. 83, 66 N.E. 627 (1903).

[10] CPLR 503(a), 502.

[11] CPLR 507, 508, treated in § 121.

[12] CPLR 503, treated in § 118.

[13] CPLR 502.

[14] Taconic Inn Corp. v. Holsapple, 188 Misc. 322, 65 N.Y.S.2d 262 (Sup. Ct., New York County 1946).

A change of venue requires a motion. That the change cannot be made by the court sua sponte is an old rule[15] generally still followed.[16] One might think that under more modern administrative standards that notion would have to give way, lest a given county, by simple agreement among opposing lawyers, becomes unduly burdened with cases not locally germane. That's about what happened in one case when an amendment of the special venue statute applicable in proceedings affecting arbitration[17] was ignored by hundreds of insurers bringing special proceedings to stay certain arbitrations. They brought the proceedings in Nassau—the county of their offices but no longer a proper venue under the statute—instead of in the insureds' counties, which were the only proper venue. The lower court, on its own motion, dismissed the proceedings,[18] but its action was rejected by the appellate division. Not only was dismissal not an option, held the latter, but even a change of venue could not be granted without a motion by a party.[19]

The court does have the power to change venue, even when not specifically requested to do so, in conjunction with a motion to consolidate under CPLR 602,[20] or a motion under CPLR 3211(a)(4) to dismiss an action because of a duplicative action already pending elsewhere.[21]

§ 117. Agreement to Fix Venue

CPLR 501 permits the parties to fix venue by contract. They can even choose a county that would not otherwise be proper under CPLR Article 5. It is said that it is "mandatory" to uphold the contract choice,[1] but there is questionable older authority that the agreement need not be upheld if "public policy" is violated, as where the county selected is the residence of neither party nor otherwise connected with the subject of the suit.[2] Another court held that the contract choice can't be said to violate public policy because statute expressly authorizes it, but the parties in that case chose a county without a heavy calendar.[3] If the parties opt for an unrelated county that does have a substantial backlog, the public policy argument may yet offer a distinction. The problem is whether the distinction can make a difference in the face of a statute as unambiguous as CPLR 501.

The trend today in New York State courts is to honor contractual venue agreements as demonstrated in the Second Department's decision in Puleo v. Shore View Center for Rehabilitation and Health Care.[4] In *Puleo*, plaintiff's decedent was a resident of a health

---

[15]   CPLR 509; see Phillips v. Tietjen, 108 A.D. 9, 95 N.Y.S. 469 (2d Dep't 1905).

[16]   See Brooks v. Dalsheim, 103 A.D.2d 986, 479 N.Y.S.2d 817, 819 (3d Dep't 1984).

[17]   CPLR 7502(a). See § 565.

[18]   Allstate Ins. Co. v. Gonzalez, Index #18449/00, Feb. 21, 2001 (Adams, J.). For further background on this special situation, see the lead note in SPR 107.

[19]   Travelers Indem. Co. of Illinois v. Nnamani, 286 A.D.2d 769, 730 N.Y.S.2d 522 (2d Dep't 2001) (SPR 113:3–4).

[20]   Smith v. Witteman Co., 10 A.D.2d 793, 197 N.Y.S.2d 877 (4th Dep't 1960); see §§ 127–28.

[21]   See § 262.

[1]   Harvey v. Colonial Home Imp. Co., 57 Misc. 2d 196, 291 N.Y.S.2d 755 (Sup. Ct., Oneida County 1965).

[2]   See Syracuse Plaster Co. v. Agostini Bros. Bldg. Corp., 169 Misc. 564, 7 N.Y.S.2d 897 (Sup. Ct., Onondaga County 1938). The case is of questionable authority, however, after the holding in the arbitration-connected cases discussed in § 116.

[3]   Callanan Industries, Inc. v. Sovereign Const. Co., Ltd., 44 A.D.2d 292, 354 N.Y.S.2d 486 (3d Dep't 1974).

[4]   Puleo v. Shore View Center for Rehabilitation and Health Care, 132 A.D.3d 651, 17 N.Y.S.3d 501 (2d Dep't 2015).

care facility located in Brooklyn. Upon the decedent's admission to the facility, her daughter signed an "Admission Agreement" containing a forum selection clause stating that "[e]ach of the parties to this Agreement irrevocably (a) submits to the exclusive jurisdiction of the courts of the State of New York in the County of Suffolk . . . for purposes of any judicial proceeding that may be instituted in connection with any matter arising under or relating to this Agreement." The agreement also provided that "[i]n addition to the parties signing this Agreement, the Agreement shall be binding on the heirs, executors, administrators, distributors, successors, and assigns of the parties."[5]

After the decedent died, the plaintiff, as the administrator of the decedent's estate, commenced a medical malpractice action against the operator of the facility in Supreme Court, Kings County. The defendant successfully convinced the Second Department to change venue from Kings County to Suffolk County based on the agreement's forum selection clause. Furthermore, the Second Department ruled that the defendant was not required to serve the plaintiff with a written demand to change venue or make a motion to change venue within the tight time constraints in CPLR 511(a) and (b)[6] because it was relying on CPLR 501 and the contractual venue clause. According to the last sentence in CPLR 511(a), the motion to change venue based on a contractual designation need only "be made within a reasonable time after commencement of the action," and defendant satisfied that criteria. Relying on its prior decisions,[7] the court ruled that "the plaintiff failed to show that enforcement of the forum selection clause would be unreasonable, unjust, or in contravention of public policy, or that the inclusion of the forum selection clause in the agreement was the result of fraud or overreaching."[8]

The only ground expressly recognized by CPLR 501 for rejecting a contract-selected venue is a finding that an impartial trial can't be had in the selected county. When the ground is merely that the convenience of witnesses will be better served elsewhere, there is a dispute about whether the agreement can be overridden.[9]

As with any case of improper venue, the remedy when an action is brought in other than the county agreed on is a change of venue to the stipulated county, not a dismissal.[10]

B. VENUE IN PARTICULAR ACTIONS

Table of Sections

§ 118.   Venue in Transitory Actions

§ 119.   Venue for Corporations and Other Private Creatures

§ 120.   Venue for Governmental Entities

---

[5]   *Puleo*, 132 A.D.3d at 652, 17 N.Y.S.3d at 502.

[6]   See § 123.

[7]   See, e.g., Molino v. Sagamore, 105 A.D.3d 922, 963 N.Y.S.2d 355 (2d Dep't 2013); see also Karlsberg v. Hunter Mountain Ski Bowl, Inc., 131 A.D.3d 1121, 16 N.Y.S.3d 746 (2d Dep't 2015); Bhonlay v. Raquette Lake Camps, Inc., 120 A.D.3d 1015, 991 N.Y.S.2d 765 (1st Dep't 2014).

[8]   *Puleo*, 132 A.D.3d at 652, 17 N.Y.S.3d at 502.

[9]   Gardner & North Roofing & Siding Corp. v. Demko, 82 Misc. 2d 922, 370 N.Y.S.2d 294 (Sup. Ct., Oneida County 1974), holds that it can't be. Kenron Awning & Window Corp. of Eastern New York v. Abbott, 43 Misc. 2d 552, 251 N.Y.S.2d 593 (Sup. Ct., Onondaga County 1964), holds that it can. The "convenience" ground is one of the discretionary ones treated in § 124.

[10]   See Graziano v. Indemnity Ins. Co. of North America, 1 N.Y.2d 817, 153 N.Y.S.2d 74, 135 N.E.2d 604 (1956).

§ 121.   Venue in Local Actions

§ 122.   Special Venue Requirements in Consumer Credit Cases

§ 118. Venue in Transitory Actions

Section 503 is the main venue-setting provision of the CPLR. It is captioned "venue based on residence." The word "transitory" is popularly used to describe an action in which venue is based on residence. The majority of actions, including money actions, are in this "transitory" category.

The general New York rule is that the plaintiff may bring the action in any county in which any one of the parties, on the plaintiff's or on the defendant's side, resides. A party may have multiple residences for venue purposes.[1] The choice of venue is the plaintiff's, at least initially. The plaintiff makes the choice based on a number of considerations, including calendar congestion, convenience of witnesses, convenience to the plaintiff and his attorney, and, alas, inconvenience to the defendant. The plaintiff more often than not chooses to sue at home.

In recent decades, Bronx County has become such a favored venue of plaintiffs with personal injury claims that some plaintiffs' attorneys have had their clients move to the Bronx—or purport to—in situations in which the Bronx had nothing to do with the case and would otherwise not qualify as proper venue. In several reported cases, the ploy didn't work.[2]

If no party is a resident—which assumes that the case has managed to get by a forum non conveniens objection—the plaintiff may bring the action in any county she wishes. It is this aspect of CPLR 503(a), that establishes that no action in the supreme court will ever want for proper venue.

In determining where "residence" is, the moment of commencement of the action is looked to under CPLR 503(a), which also acknowledges that a party can have more than one residence. If the party has several, any of them is proper venue, thus expanding the plaintiff's choices.

While multiple residences are permissible, a party can as a rule have only one "domicile." Domicile is the place a person calls home, however many residences she may maintain. "Residence" as used in the venue provisions means just that, not domicile.[3] This is in contrast to the statutes governing matrimonial actions where "residence" is usually construed to mean domicile.[4]

Although residence does not require the continuity that domicile does, it still requires "more stability than occasional stopovers at a hotel." Even when P maintained a year-round room at the hotel, a showing that his presence there was sporadic and only business-connected prevented it from qualifying as a residence for venue purposes.[5] But

---

[1]   CPLR 503(a); Echevarria v. Sadker, 106 A.D.3d 567, 967 N.Y.S.2d 12 (1st Dep't 2013).

[2]   See Koschak v. Gates Const. Corp., 225 A.D.2d 315, 639 N.Y.S.2d 10 (1st Dep't 1996); Brown v. Doxsee Sea Clam Co., (Sup. Ct., Bronx County 1997) (Index No. 18388/92, Salman, J.). See the "Ode to the Bronx" in SPR 47:4 and its reprise in SPR 67:4.

[3]   For treatment of the differences between domicile and residence, see In re Newcomb's Estate, 192 N.Y. 238, 84 N.E. 950 (1908).

[4]   See, e.g., Usher v. Usher, 41 A.D.2d 368, 343 N.Y.S.2d 212 (3d Dep't 1973).

[5]   Hammerman v. Louis Watch Co., 7 A.D.2d 817, 818, 181 N.Y.S.2d 65, 67 (3d Dep't 1958). If that county were the party's principal business office, it would today qualify as proper venue. See § 119.

if the party, while residing most of the year in County X, regularly maintains a residence in County Y even if only for vacation purposes, there is indication that County Y can also serve as proper venue.[6]

A trailer to which the party regularly returns, blocked up on a rented site, is a residence.[7] So is the place of a party's prolonged hospitalization, at least when the party evinces an intention to remain at the hospital.[8]

The assignee of a claim may not sue in his own county unless it is also the assignor's or some other party's.[9] This prevents an assignment from securing venue advantages. Assignees for the benefit of creditors and the holders of negotiable instruments are exempted from this limitation and can sue at home.[10]

Fiduciaries who sue and are sued in their own name are deemed residents of the county of their appointment as well as of the county where they actually reside, thus expanding venue choices in cases involving them.[11] These fiduciaries include an executor, administrator, trustee, committee, conservator, guardian,[12] and receiver. The theory of this provision is that the fiduciary, rather than the estate or person represented, is the proper party to the litigation.

§ 119. Venue for Corporations and Other Private Creatures

The domestic and licensed foreign corporation is deemed a resident for venue purposes. Its residence is the county in which its certificate, as filed with the Secretary of State, officially lists its office: that county has been held to be the "principal office" of the corporation under CPLR 503(c) regardless of where the actual "principal" office may be.[1] An unlicensed foreign corporation is not a resident, with the result that suit by or against it must be brought in some other party's county. A derivative action may be brought in the residence county of one of the shareholder plaintiffs[2] even though the action is brought in the right of the corporation. A special proceeding for a judicial dissolution is venued in the judicial district in which the office of the corporation, as designated in the certificate of incorporation, is located.[3]

In addition to the usual venue choices, suit by or against a common carrier, such as a railroad, may be brought alternatively in the county where the claim arose.[4]

---

[6]　See Fromkin v. Loehmann's Hewlett, Inc., 16 Misc. 2d 117, 184 N.Y.S.2d 63 (Sup. Ct., Queens County 1959).

[7]　Vrooman v. Vrooman, 183 Misc. 233, 50 N.Y.S.2d 694 (Sup. Ct., Otsego County 1944).

[8]　Bradley v. Plaisted, 277 A.D. 620, 102 N.Y.S.2d 295 (3d Dep't 1951).

[9]　CPLR 503(e).

[10]　CPLR 503(e).

[11]　CPLR 503(b).

[12]　The guardian meant here is a general or testamentary guardian. Not included is the mere guardian ad litem, who is appointed solely for the purpose of a particular litigation (see § 196) and whose residence county is irrelevant.

[1]　Carlton Group, Ltd. v. Property Markets Group, Inc., 134 A.D.3d 1018, 1019, 21 N.Y.S.3d 704, 705 (2d Dep't 2015).

[2]　Tashenberg v. Breslin, 89 A.D.2d 812, 453 N.Y.S.2d 538 (4th Dep't 1982).

[3]　*Tashenberg*, 89 A.D.2d at 812, 453 N.Y.S.2d at 539.

[4]　CPLR 503(c).

If the corporation is of a kind not required to designate an office in filed papers, such as a foreign insurance company, it may be deemed a resident of the county in which it actually maintains an office.[5]

It has been seen that the unincorporated association may sue or be sued through its president or treasurer.[6] The residence of that person—whichever one is suing or being sued in the particular case—is a proper venue, but the suit may be brought alternatively in the county of the association's principal office.[7]

A partnership's principal office is a proper residence for venue. So is the actual residence of the partner "suing or being sued"—language of CPLR 503(d) that has been construed to permit venue in the partner's residence county "only where that partner is himself a plaintiff or defendant."[8] So, if a given partner's own county is to be made the venue, he should be named as a party in the summons along with the partnership in its own name and should be individually served with process.[9]

CPLR 503(d) also treats an "individually-owned business" as a partnership for this purpose. The effect is to add as a permissible venue the county of the individual's principal office, but only as to claims arising out of the business.[10] Professionals like physicians and lawyers are deemed an individually owned business under this provision because when they offer services to the public, they are "engaged in a business."[11]

In virtually all of the above situations, the "principal office" county is just an alternative. The cases are essentially transitory ones in which venue may of course be based on the residence of any of the natural-person parties.

§ 120. Venue for Governmental Entities

Given that the legislature is laying down the law, governmental defendants usually get the favor of being suable only in their own counties. An action against a county must be brought in that county,[1] for example, and one against a city, town, village, school district, or district corporation must be brought in the county of the defendant's location.[2] An action against the City of New York is brought in the county where the claim arose or in New York County if the claim did not arise in New York City.[3] These venue requirements supersede anything to the contrary contained in the particular unit's charter, thus assuring the practitioner proper venue by reference to the CPLR alone, but they apply only when the unit is a defendant. When the unit is the plaintiff, the usual

---

[5] See State Farm Ins. Co. v. Brother Transp., Inc., 15 Misc. 3d 1110(A), 839 N.Y.S.2d 437 (Sup. Ct., Nassau County 2007).

[6] See § 69, paragraph d.

[7] If the particular unincorporated creature has filed a certificate with a state office, which an association may do, see Gen. Ass'ns Law § 18, the office listed in that paper should, by analogy to the *Carlton* case on corporations (note 1, above), be deemed its residence. Otherwise, the office that qualifies as the "principal" one will have to be decided as an issue of fact.

[8] Bensaull v. Fanwood Estates, 128 Misc. 2d 110, 488 N.Y.S.2d 944 (Sup. Ct., New York County 1984).

[9] See § 69, paragraph c.

[10] Friedman v. Law, 60 A.D.2d 832, 400 N.Y.S.2d 562 (2d Dep't 1978).

[11] Harrington v. Cramer, 129 Misc. 2d 489, 493 N.Y.S.2d 390 (Sup. Ct., New York County 1985).

[1] CPLR 504(1).

[2] CPLR 504(2). This also applies to actions against the "officers, boards or departments" of these governmental units.

[3] CPLR 504(3). The New York City Transit Authority is treated the same way for venue purposes. CPLR 505(b).

venue rules apply and the case may be brought in the defendant's or in the plaintiff's county. If one of these units sues another, such as city against city, CPLR 504 should apply and limit suit to the defendant's county.

CPLR 505(a) provides that venue in an action involving a public authority is where its principal office is "or where it has facilities involved in the action." This is the governing rule whether the authority is a plaintiff or defendant.[4] But a special statute, Unconsolidated Law section 7106, governs the venue of actions against the Port Authority, and it provides that venue shall be laid in any county "situated wholly or partially within the port of New York district." In Velez v. Port Authority of New York and New Jersey,[5] the court noted that CPLR 505(a) only applies to public authorities constituted under the laws of the State of New York and that provision does not apply to the Port Authority, which was created by New York and New Jersey. Moreover, where a specific statute like section 7106 is in conflict with a general act covering the same subject matter, such as CPLR 505(a), the specific statute controls. As the Bronx is within the Port of New York district, an action may be brought in the Bronx despite the fact that the Port Authority's principal office is not situated there and regardless of whether the accident giving rise to the action occurred there. Hooray for the plaintiffs' bar!

All of these rules apply to plenary actions involving these governmental entities and should not be confused with a special proceeding, such as the Article 78 proceeding that may be brought against a governmental agency or unit. The special proceeding has a special venue provision.[6]

It has been held that a municipality may be impleaded into an action pending in a county other than the one in which an original suit against the municipality would have to be brought; that the best the municipality can do in a case like that is seek a change of venue back to its own county and whether it is entitled to that in a given case is in the court's discretion.[7]

§ 121. Venue in Local Actions

While most actions are of the "transitory" kind in which venue is based on residence, the action that "would affect the title to, or the possession, use or enjoyment of, real property" qualifies as a local action and must be brought in the county where the real property is situated.[1] It is not sufficient that the action merely involves realty; it must be shown to "affect" it in some way before coming under this venue provision. It has been held, for example, that an action to recover commissions on the sale of realty does not "affect" it, however much it may involve it, and is not a local action.[2] The courts have not been consistent here. A mere trespass action, for example, which may involve the realty but does not really "affect" it, has been held, albeit reluctantly, a local one.[3]

---

[4]   CPLR 505(a).

[5]   Velez v. Port Authority of New York and New Jersey, 111 A.D.3d 449, 974 N.Y.S.2d 417 (1st Dep't 2013).

[6]   CPLR 506(b), treatment of which is deferred to § 565, in the chapter on special proceedings.

[7]   Holmes v. Greenlife Landscaping, Inc., 171 A.D.2d 916, 567 N.Y.S.2d 193 (3d Dep't 1991).

[1]   CPLR 507.

[2]   McNamara Realty, Inc. v. Hutchinson, 54 Misc. 2d 810, 283 N.Y.S.2d 422 (Sup. Ct., Albany County 1967).

[3]   Geidel v. Niagara Mohawk Power Corp., 46 Misc. 2d 990, 261 N.Y.S.2d 379 (Sup. Ct., Nassau County 1965).

An action to rescind a land sale contract is a local one, whether the contract is executory or already executed.[4] Some old caselaw had distinguished the two situations by holding only the case of the executed contract to be a local one.[5]

While there is as yet no definitive appellate ruling on venue in cases involving a cooperative apartment, there is caselaw at the trial level analyzing the purpose of having a realty action deemed local—the purpose is the centralization and certainty of realty records—and concluding that an action for the specific performance of a contract to sell cooperative shares is not a local action and need not be brought in the cooperative's county.[6] In contrast is the condominium, each unit of which "shall for all purposes constitute real property."[7]

The action to recover a chattel may be treated as either local, and brought where the chattel is, or as transitory, with venue based on residence.[8] (The real property action is not allowed the option of being treated as transitory).

§ 122. Special Venue Requirements in Consumer Credit Cases

To remedy certain abuses in a "consumer credit transaction," CPLR 503(f) requires that the action be brought in the defendant's (the consumer's) county or in the county where the transaction occurred. The net result of this is to preclude the plaintiff from suing in its own county unless it also happens to satisfy as the defendant's or the transaction's county. If the defendant is a nonresident and the transaction occurred outside New York, the usual residence options of CPLR 503(a) apply.

The "consumer credit transaction" (CCT) is defined by CPLR 105 as one "wherein credit is extended to an individual and the money, property or service which is the subject of the transaction is primarily for personal, family or household purposes." Whether the transaction qualifies as a CCT in a given case is obviously a question of fact. The plaintiff who would avoid trouble had best give the defendant the benefit of the doubt, treat the transaction as a CCT, and sue where the defendant resides or the transaction took place.

The summons must state the basis of venue in all New York actions and must identify the case as a CCT if it is one.[1] In a CCT, the clerk is required to reject (refuse to file) a summons which "upon its face" shows that venue has been laid in the wrong county.[2] A clerk rejecting the summons must so indicate on it and name the counties that would be proper.[3] The plaintiff must then file the summons in a proper county along with proof of its service on the defendant and further proof that the defendant has been served additionally—in this instance by registered or certified mail—with a notice telling the defendant what occurred and about her extended answering time. In this situation,

---

[4]   Merrill Realty Co., Inc. v. Harris, 44 A.D.2d 629, 353 N.Y.S.2d 570 (3d Dep't 1974).

[5]   See Birmingham v. Squires, 139 A.D. 129, 123 N.Y.S. 906 (1st Dep't 1910).

[6]   Suddin v. Lynbrook Gardens Co., 127 Misc. 2d 406, 486 N.Y.S.2d 155 (Sup. Ct., New York County 1985).

[7]   Real Prop. Law § 339–g.

[8]   CPLR 508.

[1]   CPLR 305(a).

[2]   CPLR 513(a).

[3]   CPLR 513(b).

the defendant's answering time does not begin to run until 10 days after the summons is filed in the proper county.[4]

C. CHANGE OF VENUE

Table of Sections

§ 123.   Change of Venue from Improper to Proper County; "Demand" Procedure
§ 124.   Discretionary Grounds for Change of Venue
§ 125.   Effecting the Change of Venue

§ 123. Change of Venue from Improper to Proper County; "Demand" Procedure

When D contends that P has laid venue in an improper county and D seeks to change it to a proper county as a matter of right, D must follow the special "demand" procedure of CPLR 511(b).

With or before the answer,[1] D must serve on P a written demand that venue be changed to the county D specifies as proper.[2] Within five days after service of the demand, P must do one of two things:

1. serve on D a written consent agreeing to the change; or

2. serve on D an affidavit showing either that the county chosen by P is proper or that the one to which D seeks transfer is not.

If P takes step 1, the consent is filed pursuant to CPLR 511(d) and the change D wants is effected. If P takes step 2, it is now incumbent on D to move to change the venue, and the court to decide whether the change is in order. If P takes neither step within the 5 days, D is allowed to make the motion in the county to which she seeks transfer.[3] This can be a tactical advantage. But it is the only advantage conferred by P's failure to respond within the 5 days. P's failure does not automatically entitle D to the venue change; it merely gives D a broader option on where to move for it. Nor does P, by omitting to respond, forfeit the right to resist the motion. Wherever D moves, P may still oppose the motion and show that his chosen county is proper or that D's is not.[4]

P's affidavit (responding to the demand) must at least purport to justify P's choice or to negate D's. An affidavit that purports to do neither has been deemed no affidavit at all, thus permitting D to move in the proposed transferee county.[5] In HVT, Inc. v.

---

[4]   CPLR 513(c). Here, there is indication that the statute was drafted for the lower courts rather than supreme court practice. It speaks of the time within which an answer is to be "filed," there being no such requirement in supreme court practice (where the requirement is that the answer merely be served on the plaintiff's lawyer). The drafters apparently had in mind § 902(a)(2) of (e.g.) the New York City Civil Court Act, in which the defendant answers to the clerk rather than to the plaintiff's lawyer directly.

[1]   CPLR 511(a).

[2]   D may apply under CPLR 2004 to extend the time to make the demand. Levkovich v. Vivian Hotel Corp., 27 A.D.2d 754, 279 N.Y.S.2d 1018 (2d Dep't 1967).

[3]   This means that D may make the motion either in the county in which P has laid venue or in the proposed transferee county, and it may even include a variety of other venue options under CPLR 2212(a), depending on local rules adopted under CPLR 2212(d). See § 245.

[4]   McDermott v. McDermott, 267 A.D. 171, 45 N.Y.S.2d 321 (1st Dep't 1943).

[5]   Payne v. Civil Service Emp. Ass'n, 15 A.D.2d 265, 222 N.Y.S.2d 725 (3d Dep't 1961).

Safeco Ins. Co. of America,[6] D made the requisite demand to change venue and it was then P's obligation to show either that P's chosen venue was correct or that the one advocated by D was wrong. For this, the court stressed, P's affidavit responding to the demand must aver facts showing one of these two things. P's affidavit in *HVT* was deemed inadequate because it did not contain the needed factual showing. The consequence under CPLR 511(b), therefore, is that while D must still move for a change of venue, D may make the motion in the county to which D seeks the transfer.

If P has several choices (such as counties X and Y) available, but lays venue in an improper county (Z), P's right of first choice will be forfeited to D. Thus if P, opposing D's motion, urges that the change be to X, while D wants Y, Y will be the county to which the venue is ordered changed.[7] The point is that P may lose first choice to D by laying initial venue in an altogether improper county.

If D has followed the demand procedure and P has served an appropriate affidavit within the allotted 5 days, D must move for the venue change within 15 days from the time she served the demand.[8] Since 5 of those days have already expired awaiting P's response, D must move promptly for the change. If the motion is made within the 15 days, and it establishes that P's county is improper while the one D wants is proper, D generally gets the change as a matter of right—unless the court directs that the action be retained where it is or transferred to yet another county on one of the discretionary change of venue grounds, such as the convenience of witnesses,[9] discussed in the next section.

If D does not so move within the 15 days, she is no longer entitled to a change of venue as of right. The change does lie in the court's discretion, however, so D may still make the motion at any time before trial, but because of its tardiness, D in that situation is not entitled to the change as a matter of right. If there is strong reason to prefer the proper county, such as where real property records are involved in what qualifies as a local action, the court's discretion is likely to favor the change, tardy as the motion may be.[10]

It has been held that the demand procedure for a change of venue from an improper to the proper county may also be invoked by a third-party defendant, who should serve the demand for the change with its answer.[11]

A defendant relying on a contractual venue clause[12] to obtain a change of venue is not required to serve the plaintiff with a written demand to change venue or make a motion to change venue within the tight time constraints in CPLR 511(a) and (b). According to the last sentence in CPLR 511(a), the motion to change venue based on a

---

[6]   HVT, Inc. v. Safeco Ins. Co. of America, 77 A.D.3d 255, 908 N.Y.S.2d 222 (2d Dep't 2010) (NYSLD No. 610).

[7]   Kelson v. Nedicks Stores, Inc., 104 A.D.2d 315, 478 N.Y.S.2d 648 (1st Dep't 1984).

[8]   The Court of Appeals held in Simon v. Usher, 17 N.Y.3d 625, 934 N.Y.S.2d 362, 958 N.E.2d 540 (2011) (NYSLD No. 624), that the 5-day extension in CPLR 2103(b)(2) is afforded to such a motion. See § 202.

[9]   Windhurst v. Town of Thompson, 78 A.D.2d 930, 433 N.Y.S.2d 516 (3d Dep't 1980).

[10]   Reichenbach v. Corn Exchange Bank Trust Co., 249 A.D. 539, 292 N.Y.S. 732 (1st Dep't 1937).

[11]   See Kearns v. Johnson, 238 A.D.2d 121, 655 N.Y.S.2d 498 (1st Dep't 1997) (SPR 57:3).

[12]   See CPLR 501.

contractual designation need only "be made within a reasonable time after commencement of the action."[13]

§ 124. Discretionary Grounds for Change of Venue

In addition to authorizing a change of venue from an improper to a proper county,[1] CPLR 510 offers two other grounds for a change of venue: (1) that there is reason to believe that an impartial trial can't be had in a proper county,[2] or (2) that the convenience of material witnesses and the ends of justice will be promoted by a change.[3]

These discretionary grounds can be applied even though the venue selected by the plaintiff is proper and can even bring about a change to a county that would not be a proper one under the initial venue-fixing rules.

The demand procedure set up by CPLR 511(b) for the change from an improper to a proper county has no application to a change of venue sought on these discretionary grounds.[4] Here, the change must be sought by direct motion made "within a reasonable time after commencement."[5] What's "reasonable" is of course sui generis. 5 months has been held reasonable when no prejudice traceable to the delay could be shown.[6]

Since change on a discretionary ground does not follow the demand procedure, the motion for such a change may not be made in the proposed transferee county. Nor will the court in that county, if the motion to change venue is made there on the improper-to-proper ground in CPLR 510(1), entertain any of the discretionary grounds should the movant try to throw them in for good measure.[7]

The defendant is not the only one permitted to move for a venue change on these discretionary grounds. The plaintiff can,[8] and so can a third-party defendant.[9]

The impartial trial ground does not appear often. An example of it was an action by a Kings County judge who in his own court sued a doctor for malpractice. The case was transferred to another county to avoid the "unconscious bias" of his colleagues.[10] In a similar case, in which the surrogate of a county brought a private lawsuit in the supreme court of that county, the defendant's motion to change venue was denied because the court found nothing to suggest that there could not be an impartial trial.[11] A change of venue is probably advisable in all such cases even from the point of view of the party— the judge, in these examples—who is presumably the beneficiary of "unconscious bias"; he can find himself the victim, instead, when his colleagues bend over backward to avoid even the appearance of prejudice.

---

[13]   See Puleo v. Shore View Center for Rehabilitation and Health Care, 132 A.D.3d 651, 17 N.Y.S.3d 501 (2d Dep't 2015); Medina ex rel. Valentin v. Gold Crest Care Center, Inc., 117 A.D.3d 633, 988 N.Y.S.2d 578 (1st Dep't 2014); § 117.

[1]   CPLR 510(1).

[2]   CPLR 510(2).

[3]   CPLR 510(3).

[4]   Baker v. Julius Pollak & Sons, 277 A.D. 11, 97 N.Y.S.2d 694 (1st Dep't 1950).

[5]   CPLR 511(a).

[6]   Ryan v. Great Atlantic & Pac. Tea Co., 30 A.D.2d 549, 290 N.Y.S.2d 849 (2d Dep't 1968).

[7]   See Nevelson v. Piesner, 272 A.D. 555, 74 N.Y.S.2d 105 (4th Dep't 1947).

[8]   Kenford Co. v. Erie County, 38 A.D.2d 781, 328 N.Y.S.2d 69 (4th Dep't 1972).

[9]   Champlain Creameries v. Hovey, Stanter & Co., 141 N.Y.S.2d 271 (Sup. Ct., New York County 1955).

[10]   Arkwright v. Steinbugler, 283 A.D. 397, 128 N.Y.S.2d 823 (2d Dep't 1954).

[11]   Midonick v. Peppertree Hill Development Corp., 49 A.D.2d 721, 373 N.Y.S.2d 2 (1st Dep't 1975).

Juror prejudice can give rise to a motion under CPLR 510(2), but there are ways to monitor that problem short of changing venue. When a power company brought suit locally to recover some $62,000,000 of alleged overcharges from a fuel company—costs that are of course passed along to the consumer—the action was transferred out of the county whose consumers were directly affected.[12] The Third Department's decision in Blaine v. International Business Machines Corp.[13] examined a similar problem, but stopped short of changing venue. The proper venue in *Blaine* was Broome County where defendant IBM began its operations in the Village of Endicott in 1924 and employed as many as 16,000 people in the 1980s. Hundreds of plaintiffs commenced nine similar actions alleging that defendant released toxic chemicals from its manufacturing facility into the environment, thereby contaminating the air and groundwater and causing the plaintiffs to, among other things, suffer medical problems and real estate devaluation. In the first action scheduled to proceed to trial—which only addressed the claims of a limited number of plaintiffs—IBM moved to change venue under CPLR 510(2) to one of three neighboring counties. It alleged that an impartial trial could not be held in Broome County because the jury pool contained a large number of plaintiffs' relatives as well as IBM's former employees and their families. Supreme court denied the motion without prejudice to renew at the close of voir dire.

The Third Department affirmed, concluding that the supreme court did not abuse its discretion. The court emphasized that under CPLR 4110(b), any relative within the sixth degree of consanguinity or affinity to a party is automatically disqualified from jury service. Furthermore, in response to defendant's statistical analysis of potential jurors in Broome County, the court noted "that juries are not randomly selected" and that "[j]ury questionnaires and the voir dire process should filter out relatives and decrease the chances of empaneling such a person." Although defendant alleged that 24,000 of its former employees were still living in Broome County, the Third Department emphasized that "only persons 'in the employ of a party' are specifically listed in the statute [(CPLR 4110(a))] as subject to a challenge to the favor from serving as [a] juror . . . ." While former employees of a party may be biased for various reasons, the court concluded that these biases could "be addressed through a comprehensive juror questionnaire sent to prospective jurors before jury selection and through the jury selection process itself."[14]

Perhaps the most frequent ground for a discretionary change of venue is the convenience of witnesses. The witnesses whose convenience counts here are the "material" ones: those who can testify to the facts of the occurrence or transaction involved in the case. And the convenience of witnesses testifying on issues of liability is "entitled to greater weight" than that of witnesses testifying only on damages.[15]

Expert witnesses will not ordinarily be considered, but this applies only to those who are to be called solely for opinion. If they can testify to material facts, their convenience is a factor.[16]

---

[12] Long Island Lighting Co. v. New England Petroleum Corp., 80 Misc. 2d 183, 362 N.Y.S.2d 350 (Sup. Ct., Queens County 1974).

[13] Blaine v. International Business Machines Corp., 91 A.D.3d 1175, 937 N.Y.S.2d 405 (3d Dep't 2012).

[14] *Blaine*, 91 A.D.3d at 1177, 937 N.Y.S.2d at 407; see § 392 (discussing challenges to jurors).

[15] Katz v. Goodyear Tire and Rubber Co., 116 A.D.2d 506, 497 N.Y.S.2d 376 (1st Dep't 1986).

[16] See Delair v. T. Southworth Tractor & Mach. Co., 142 N.Y.S.2d 449 (Sup. Ct., Franklin County 1955).

A witness who is employed by a party or otherwise under the party's control carries little weight on a change of venue scale.[17] Indeed, the general rule is that the convenience of the parties and their employees is not to be considered on the motion.[18]

P's choice of forum will not be disturbed unless there is a clear balance in favor of D's witnesses.[19] It has also been held that where, on a change of venue motion, the convenience of witnesses is fairly evenly balanced between sides, a "transitory action should be tried in the county where the cause of action arose."[20]

The motion for a change of venue based on the convenience of witnesses requires a detailed affidavit from the moving party setting forth "what he expects to prove by the alleged witnesses and that he cannot safely proceed to trial without the testimony of such witnesses as he is advised by his counsel."[21] Even more ideal, although not essential, are affidavits secured from the potential witnesses themselves.

§ 125. Effecting the Change of Venue

If a change of venue is ordered, or if P has served on D a written consent to the change under the demand procedure, CPLR 511(d) directs that the order be entered, or the consent filed, with the clerk in the original county. That clerk is then required to deliver all papers in the action, including certified copies of any minutes that may already have been taken, to the clerk of the transferee court. That clerk must now make them part of her records as if the case had originally been brought there. Subsequent proceedings then follow on the same assumption unless otherwise directed by the court. To avoid confusion as to where an appeal may be taken from the order granting the change, it is specifically provided that it be in the department in which the motion for the change was made and decided.

If a stay of proceedings has been applied for in conjunction with the motion to change venue, the court is precluded from granting the stay "unless it appears from the papers that the change is sought with due diligence."[1] The lesson to a defendant who wants the proceedings suspended while the change is sought is to seek it promptly.

---

[17]   Hoffman v. Boston & Maine R.R., 259 A.D. 958, 20 N.Y.S.2d 460 (3d Dep't 1940).

[18]   *Katz*, 116 A.D.2d at 507, 497 N.Y.S.2d at 377.

[19]   Cf. Marzello v. Kiamesha Concord, Inc., 26 A.D.2d 986, 274 N.Y.S.2d 1002 (3d Dep't 1966).

[20]   *Katz*, 116 A.D.2d at 507, 497 N.Y.S.2d at 377; Strosberg v. Kiamesha Concord, Inc., 26 A.D.2d 723, 271 N.Y.S.2d 767, 769 (3d Dep't 1966).

[21]   Dairymen's League Co-op. Ass'n v. Brundo, 131 Misc. 548, 549, 227 N.Y.S. 203, 206 (Sup. Ct., Oneida County 1927).

[1]   CPLR 511(c).

Chapter 7

PARTIES

Analysis

A.   Joinder of Claims and Actions
B.   Necessary Joinder of Parties
D.   Proper Parties
E.   Procedure for Joinder Problems
F.   Class Actions
G.   Interpleader
H.   Impleader
I.   Contribution
J.   Intervention
K.   Substitution
L.   Poor Persons
M.   Infants and Incompetents

A.   JOINDER OF CLAIMS AND ACTIONS

Table of Sections

§ 126.   Joinder of Claims
§ 127.   Consolidation, Joint Trial, Severance, and Separate Trial, Defined
§ 128.   Consolidation and Joint Trial
§ 129.   Severance and Separate Trial
§ 130.   Bifurcated Trial

§ 126.   Joinder of Claims

A plaintiff may join in a single action as many claims as the plaintiff has against the defendant whether the claims are related or not.[1] The idea is to get everything over with at once. If the claims are totally unrelated and would confuse a jury, or unduly influence it in some way, the remedy is a severance.[2] Even that can be avoided. The court can, in its discretion, have each claim tried to the same jury, consecutively but separately, thus enabling the claims to remain in one action and sparing the court's calendar an additional case, which is what a severance produces.[3]

This liberal permission to interpose any claims at all includes a defendant putting in counterclaims or cross-claims, as long as all those initially made parties have been made so in satisfaction of the joinder-of-parties rules. The generosity of CPLR 601(a),

---

[1]   CPLR 601(a).

[2]   See *Sporn v. Hudson Transit Lines*, 265 A.D. 360, 38 N.Y.S.2d 512 (1st Dep't 1942). Severance is treated in § 129.

[3]   See § 129 on severance and separate trial.

allowing the interposition of any claims at all "when there are multiple parties," assumes that those parties are in the suit on the authority of one of the provisions of Article 10 of the CPLR, the article on parties. If, for example, A and B are both injured in the same accident, they may join as plaintiffs in a single action against D for their respective injuries. CPLR 1002(a), the statute on permissive joinder of parties, allows this.[4] A and B, as legitimate coparties under that provision, may now exploit the join-any-claim permission of CPLR 601(a). That would permit A, for example, to add against D yet another claim not arising out of the accident and not having any link at all with B.

§ 127. Consolidation, Joint Trial, Severance, and Separate Trial, Defined

These four items make up a kind of set determining when actions may be merged or separated. They need some definition before being treated individually.

Consolidation and severance are diametrical opposites. Consolidation takes two or more actions and fuses them into one; severance takes one action and separates it into two or more.

Joint trial and consolidation are much the same in accomplishment, but differ in mechanics. Joint trial, like consolidation, puts two or more actions together, but with joint trial, the actions maintain their separate identities. With consolidation, there is a total fusion of the actions. They take on one caption and culminate in one judgment—which pronounces on the rights of all the parties involved—and result in but a single bill of costs. With joint trial, the actions keep their separate captions and go to separate verdicts—although perhaps delivered by the jury at the same time—and to separate judgments and bills of costs. Consolidation fuses them organically, while joint trial, available on the same criteria as consolidation under CPLR 602, offers the same advantages without the additional paper work that consolidation entails.[1]

If one party would find herself on both sides of the versus sign if the cases were merged, then joint trial is probably preferable to consolidation just to avoid confusing the jury.[2] It should be preferable for other reasons as well. Since joint trial usually secures the same advantages as consolidation without the latter's papers-altering inconvenience, the thoughtful attorney ought to prefer it more often than the older caselaw indicates. The reason that consolidation has been sought more often than mere joint trial may be the bar's unawareness of the differences.[3]

Whether the one or the other prevails in a given case, the pair is favored by the courts, rising even to the level of "public policy." This can be seen when a contract presumes to bar consolidation or joint trial of designated claims. While there is no absolute prohibition against such a contract provision, it will be scanned closely to see if it treads unduly on the court's prerogative and will be disregarded if it does. Disregarding it in a lease case, the court stressed that the devices may even be invoked by the court sua sponte.[4]

---

[4]   Permissive joinder is treated in § 134.

[1]   See Vidal v. Sheffield Farms Co., 208 Misc. 438, 141 N.Y.S.2d 82 (Sup. Ct., Bronx County 1955).

[2]   See Padilla v. Greyhound Lines, Inc., 29 A.D.2d 495, 288 N.Y.S.2d 641 (1st Dep't 1968).

[3]   *Padilla*, 29 A.D.2d at 497–98, 288 N.Y.S.2d at 643–44.

[4]   Ultrashmere House, Ltd. v. 38 Town Associates, 123 Misc. 2d 102, 473 N.Y.S.2d 120 (Sup. Ct., New York County 1984).

The relationship between severance and separate trials is analogous to that between consolidation and joint trials. While the severance cleaves the action in two and sends each claim off as a distinct case for all purposes (separate judgments, etc.), the separate trial can often accomplish the same thing without the cleavage. Two unrelated claims in a single action, for example, need not be severed to avoid jury confusion. The court can merely have one tried first, right through to a verdict, before the second is touched. This is all in the court's discretion. Severance is not a favored device today because of the additional burden it imposes on judicial calendars. (One action becomes two.) The separate trial is usually a satisfactory alternative.

Consolidation and joint trial are authorized by CPLR 602; severance and separate trials, by CPLR 603. Individual treatment of them follows.

§ 128. Consolidation and Joint Trial

When two or more actions are pending before a court and they involve "a common question of law or fact," CPLR 602(a) permits the court, on motion, to consolidate them or order them jointly tried. If they are pending in different divisions of the court, such as where they are both in the supreme court but in different counties, the order would also have to include a change of venue for one or several of them. If they are pending in different courts altogether, it would also entail a removal from one court to another. If so, the removal is from the lower to the higher court, not vice versa.

While any court can consolidate or jointly try cases pending before itself, only two courts in the state have the power to remove cases from other courts in conjunction with these devices. The county court has the power, but only over district, city, town, and village courts in the same county. The supreme court has the power over all courts. It is the only court that can reach within or beyond its county and bring to itself for consolidation or joint trial an action pending in any other court of original jurisdiction.[1] In order for the supreme court or the county court to effect a removal and consolidation,[2] at least one of the actions to be affected has to be pending in the removing court. Where, for example, two actions are pending in two different lower courts and no related case is in the supreme court, the supreme court may not reach down to put the two together.[3]

The courts are often reluctant to transfer an action from the small claims part for consolidation or joint trial with an action in a higher court. In Moise v. Brown,[4] for example, the court emphasized that the small claims part is designed to enable a claim to proceed without the formality required in a supreme court or New York City Civil Court action and, therefore, denied the motion to consolidate an action in a small claims part with a supreme court action. The plaintiff in the small claims part should not be deprived of the benefits of that simpler forum.[5]

---

[1] CPLR 602(b). Excepted, of course, is the court of claims action, which is not removable to the supreme court. Conversely, the court of claims cannot remove actions pending in supreme court. These matters were addressed in Cocchi v. State, 52 Misc. 3d 561, 30 N.Y.S.3d 481 (Ct. Cl. 2016), which is discussed in further detail in § 17.

[2] Since the standards for consolidation and joint trial are the same, and what differences exist between them have been covered in the prior section, everything said henceforth about consolidation will, unless otherwise indicated, also apply to the joint trial.

[3] Curriere v. Roeill, 55 Misc. 2d 1049, 287 N.Y.S.2d 747 (Sup. Ct., Nassau County 1967).

[4] Moise v. Brown, 26 Misc. 3d 1224(A), 907 N.Y.S.2d 438 (Sup. Ct., Kings County 2010).

[5] See § 582.

Unless a New York State court action is duly removed to a U.S. district court,[6] where it can then be consolidated with other federal actions under federal procedure,[7] neither a federal nor a state court can consolidate one of its own actions with one pending in the other's system. But the parties to separate federal and state actions can, if they wish, stipulate to consolidate their disclosure proceedings and other pretrial steps.[8]

Consolidation and joint trial are today preferred remedies because they reduce calendar congestion and economize legal and judicial effort. When consolidation is proposed, the burden today is on the resisting party to show that it would prejudice him,[9] and the mere fact that his case may be somewhat delayed by the consolidation will not suffice to bar it.

While consolidation can't be made of a court of claims case with a case pending in some other court, if the State is a proper party to the other-court action, as where it brought an action in supreme court or intervened in it voluntarily, consolidation with other claims is permissible.[10]

There is no stated time limit on a motion to consolidate, but it can't as a rule be made before issue has been joined—the pleadings are all in—in the several actions affected because not until then can the court know whether the actions present common issues. Since the motion lies in the court's discretion, the applicant should move promptly. Substantial delay causing prejudice, determined on a sui generis basis, can be an enemy.

Consolidation is even more liberal than the permissive joinder of parties is today and that is liberal indeed. For the initial joinder of different parties in one action, CPLR 1002 requires not only that the several claims have a question of law or fact in common, but also that they be shown to emanate from the same transaction or occurrence or series of them.[11] The latter showing is not required for consolidation, which requires only the common question of law or fact.

The court's discretion guards against fusing separate actions that technically meet this requirement, but which on balance should not be put together. Because of the greater requirement for permissive joinder under CPLR 1002, a showing that the parties in two separate actions could have sued, or been sued, in but a single action a fortiori satisfies the requirement for consolidation.[12] This applies only to the standard governing the joinder of parties, however, and not necessarily to the standard that governs the joinder of claims by the same party. Where, for example, P has two separate but unrelated claims against D and joins them in one action, as he may do under CPLR 601,

---

[6]   28 U.S.C.A. §§ 1441, 1446, 1447. See § 619 (Practitioner's Edition).

[7]   See Fed. R. Civ. P. 42(a).

[8]   See General Aniline & Film Corp. v. Photo-Marker Corp., 28 A.D.2d 990, 284 N.Y.S.2d 106 (1st Dep't 1967). A special procedure exists for consolidating actions for pretrial purposes only, a matter noted at the end of this section.

[9]   Vigo S. S. Corp. v. Marship Corp. of Monrovia, 26 N.Y.2d 157, 309 N.Y.S.2d 165, 257 N.E.2d 624 (1970).

[10]   Fox v. Tioga Const. Co., Inc., 1 Misc. 3d 909(A), 781 N.Y.S.2d 624 (Sup. Ct., Oneida and Albany Counties 2004).

[11]   See § 134.

[12]   See Tanbro Fabrics Corp. v. Beaunit Mills, Inc., 4 A.D.2d 519, 167 N.Y.S.2d 387 (1st Dep't 1957).

his bringing them as separate actions does not authorize their consolidation if they have no common question of law or fact.[13]

Two actions can be consolidated despite the fact that one is a law claim (triable by jury) and the other an equitable one (triable by the court), but the consolidation does not divest the right to the jury on the law claim.[14] The point is not unique to consolidation. It can arise in a single action in which the plaintiff has joined the two different categories of claims, or in which the defendant meets the plaintiff's law claim with an equitable counterclaim, or vice versa. Issues of who tries what in that situation are recognized and resolved by CPLR 4102(c).[15]

It is also permissible today to consolidate an action with a special proceeding,[16] and even with a summary proceeding to recover the possession of real property, the so-called landlord-tenant case.[17] But in the latter situation, it should require some very special circumstance indeed before the summary proceeding is divested of its "summary" nature and subjected to the delay common to an action.[18]

The differences between consolidation and joint trial, noted in an earlier section,[19] are more cosmetic than consequential, but a consequential difference does sometimes appear, suggesting that a lawyer seeking to put two cases together should first ponder the differences between the two devices. Hope v. Fortunato[20] can aid those deliberations.

In *Hope*, while actions 1 and 2 were separate, the time period for a summary judgment motion in action 1 expired, and the time period of the other action, action 2, which might have been open for the motion had the case retained its own distinct identity under a "joint trial" order, lost that identity with the consolidation—moved for by the action 2 plaintiff—and subjected action 2 to the time elements of action 1. (This was how the judge construed things, anyway.) The effect was to bar, as too late, a summary judgment motion in action 2.

Since consolidation is a favored step in the court system, it would seem that the party seeking the consolidation in *Hope* was made to pay a penalty for doing so. What the court might better have done is find the circumstances unique enough to allow the summary judgment motion belatedly based on "good cause."[21]

So popular is the consolidation/joint-trial pair today that attorneys often make little effort to resist it when it's moved for, trying instead just to secure certain incidental rights. The major of these is the right to open and close to the jury.[22] The plaintiff ordinarily has this right, which gives her the first statement to the jury as the case starts and the last word before the jury retires. The latter especially is a grand advantage.

---

[13] Gibbons v. Groat, 22 A.D.2d 996, 254 N.Y.S.2d 843 (3d Dep't 1964).

[14] Philip Shlansky & Bro. v. Grossman, 273 A.D. 544, 78 N.Y.S.2d 127 (1st Dep't 1948).

[15] See § 378.

[16] In re Elias, 29 A.D.2d 118, 286 N.Y.S.2d 371 (2d Dep't 1967).

[17] Notarius v. Hess Oil & Chemical Corp., 30 A.D.2d 663, 292 N.Y.S.2d 1 (2d Dep't 1968).

[18] See Hotel New Yorker Pharmacy, Inc. v. New Yorker Hotel Corp., 40 A.D.2d 967, 968, 338 N.Y.S.2d 697, 699 (1st Dep't 1972) (dissenting opinion).

[19] See § 127.

[20] Hope v. Fortunato, 20 Misc. 3d 1117(A), 867 N.Y.S.2d 17 (Sup. Ct., Kings County 2008) (SPR 199:1).

[21] CPLR 3212(a); see § 279.

[22] CPLR 4016.

What wouldn't Brutus give in retrospect for the last word, especially with Marlon Brando playing Anthony?

When separate actions are consolidated and involve different plaintiffs, both want the right to open and close. The rule is that, other things being equal, the right belongs to the plaintiff whose action was commenced first. And it makes no difference that the earlier action may have been in a lower court. This race is generally to the swift regardless of which court the swift sued in.[23] If three actions are consolidated, the plaintiff in the earliest one will open first and sum up last, the plaintiff in the second-commenced action will open second and sum up next-to-last, etc. It is customary for the judge who orders consolidation to determine, in the order, who has this open-and-close right, but when joint trial is ordered it is more the custom to leave the matter to the trial judge.[24]

When the actions to be consolidated are supreme court actions in different counties, the parties now vie to secure the most favorable venue for the consolidated action. The same rule applies: other things being equal, the county that gets the consolidated action is the one where the earliest of the actions was venued.[25]

One phenomenon that can undo the "other things being equal" assumption (and venue the merged action elsewhere) is a showing that one of the counties involved has a light calendar while the other's is backlogged. The fact that one can offer a speedier trial is a factor,[26] although not necessarily a decisive one. There is also some preference to have a consolidated action tried where the claim arose,[27] a standard justified by the fact that it is the place most likely to serve the witnesses' convenience, another matter the court considers.

If the several actions are pending in the supreme court in different counties, the consolidation motion may be made in any one of them[28] and should be made on notice to all parties to all of the actions affected.[29]

Under the Individual Assignment System,[30] a consolidation order can of course entail removing a case not merely from another court, but specifically from another judge of coordinate jurisdiction. Indeed, it may even entail sending the consolidated cases *to* another judge, as where the latter sits in the venue chosen for the consolidated action.

---

[23] Brink's Exp. Co. v. Burns, 230 A.D. 559, 245 N.Y.S. 649 (4th Dep't 1930). The case also says that the party otherwise entitled to the opening and closing right in the consolidated action waives it if he is the one who moves for the consolidation, but that notion has long since been abandoned in New York.

[24] Rockaway Boulevard Wrecking & Lumber Co. v. Raylite Elec. Corp., 25 A.D.2d 842, 270 N.Y.S.2d 1 (1st Dep't 1966).

[25] Rae v. Hotel Governor Clinton, Inc., 23 A.D.2d 564, 256 N.Y.S.2d 741 (2d Dep't 1965).

[26] See Poly Const. Corp. v. Oxford Hall Contracting Corp., 24 A.D.2d 637, 262 N.Y.S.2d 206 (2d Dep't 1965).

[27] Braff v. Par-Du Leasing, Inc., 25 A.D.2d 897, 269 N.Y.S.2d 222 (3d Dep't 1966).

[28] Velasquez v. Pine Grove Resort Ranch, Inc., 77 Misc. 2d 329, 354 N.Y.S.2d 65 (Sup. Ct., Ulster County 1974).

[29] Barch v. Avco Corp., 30 A.D.2d 241, 291 N.Y.S.2d 422 (4th Dep't 1968), indicated that if actions are pending in counties X and Y and a consolidation motion is made in X, the parties to the Y action need not respond to the X motion. This overlooks that CPLR 602 is itself authority for the making of the motion in any of the counties involved, i.e., that the venue of the motion is not in this instance dictated exclusively by CPLR 2212(a), which otherwise governs the venue of a motion. See § 245. Commentary C3211:17 on McKinney's CPLR 3211 suggests alternatives for the parties if *Barch* remains law. See also Kent Development Co., Inc. v. Liccione, 37 N.Y.2d 899, 378 N.Y.S.2d 377, 340 N.E.2d 740 (1975); § 262.

[30] See § 77A.

It is therefore a good idea for the judge entertaining the consolidation motion to consult with the other judges concerned. Friction may otherwise result and require administrative resolution.

All of this discussion has concerned the full consolidation (or joint trial) of actions, which generates their merger for all purposes, right through to trial and judgment. Following the federal example of 28 U.S.C. § 1407, the statute that allows in federal practice the transfer of actions among districts in order to consolidate at least discovery proceedings, a New York "Litigation Coordinating Panel" was set up in 2003 to permit the "quasi" consolidation of pretrial proceedings in related actions pending before New York courts in different counties. The procedure was set up by rule.[31]

If two actions do not have a common question of law or fact as is required for consolidation or joint trial under CPLR 602(a), the court can transfer an action to the same part where a related action is pending "solely for 'purposes of disposition.' "[32] So held the Second Department in Bermejo v. New York City Health and Hospitals Corp., which emphasized "that both actions were related to the same underlying incident . . . ."[33]

The court's power to impose conditions when making a consolidation order can resolve sometimes thorny problems. It may be, for example, that the configuration of the different actions or their issues will pose an evidentiary problem: the admissibility of proof as against one party that would not be admissible against another. The court can meet these issues by ordering the impanelment and use of two separate juries, the one to be temporarily excused while testimony is offered that is proper for only the other to hear.[34]

§ 129. Severance and Separate Trial

The severance is the ubiquitous device for lopping off claims and making separate actions of them. Because there are no stated statutory criteria for a severance, it is available from its main niche in CPLR 603 in any instance in which a sound exercise of judicial discretion suggests it. There are other listings for it in the CPLR, probably unnecessary because of CPLR 603, but these are overlaps at worst. One is CPLR 3212(e) in conjunction with partial summary judgment; another is CPLR 3215(a) on default judgments; and yet another is CPLR 5012 in connection with judgments generally.

The occasions for the use of a severance are many and will be treated in this book as their contexts arise. One common application is where the liberal joinder rule of CPLR 601 has resulted in the interposing of claims so unrelated that the jury would be confused by them.[1] Another is where a party's retention in a particular context would unduly prejudice it, as where a disclaiming liability insurer has been impleaded by its insured

---

[31]   See 22 N.Y.C.R.R. § 202.69, noted in SPR 124:1 and treated in Herrmann and Ritts, *New York Adopts Procedures for Statewide Coordination of Complex Litigation*, 75 N.Y. St. B.J. 20 (2003).

[32]   Bermejo v. New York City Health and Hospitals Corp., 133 A.D.3d 808, 809, 20 N.Y.S.3d 401, 402 (2d Dep't 2015).

[33]   *Bermejo*, 133 A.D.3d at 809, 20 N.Y.S.3d at 402.

[34]   See *Fox*, 1 Misc. 3d 909(A), 781 N.Y.S.2d 624.

[1]   See, e.g., Pierce v. International Harvester Co., 65 A.D.2d 254, 411 N.Y.S.2d 456 (4th Dep't 1978).

in an ordinary negligence action. The Court of Appeals requires a severance of the impleader claim as a matter of law in that instance.[2]

Despite the court's broad powers of severance under CPLR 603, severance cannot be ordered once consolidation of those very claims has previously been ordered by another judge.[3] In that situation, the severance is barred by the doctrine of the law of the case.[4]

No time limit is placed on the motion to sever or separately try. As with the consolidation motion, it should not be made before issue is joined because not until then can the issues be seen.[5] Substantial delay causing prejudice may also be considered.

The power to order separate trials co-exists with the severance power in CPLR 603. Often, if not always, a direction for separate trials can be used instead of a severance. Where, for example, unrelated claims have been joined and their trial together would confuse the jury, they can be tried in succession. One can be disposed of in its entirety before the other is even touched, and without the need of a severance. This really concerns the sequence of trial, in this regard overlapping CPLR 4011, which allows the court broad discretion in determining "the sequence in which the issues shall be tried." Perhaps one difference between the two provisions is that under CPLR 4011, the trial judge controls the sequence, whereas CPLR 603 apparently contemplates a pretrial order directing the separate trial of certain claims or issues.[6]

A CPLR 603 motion can be denied without prejudice to a later application at the trial for similar relief. In view of this power to order separate trials and avoid jury confusion that way, perhaps the principal justification today for an outright pretrial severance of multiple claims is where they should not be kept together even for the pretrial remedies, such as depositions and other disclosure devices, although those items, too, can be separately managed within the framework of the same case.

If claims are related, they should ordinarily be tried together. Separate trials in such an instance would require some special reason.[7]

§ 130. Bifurcated Trial

The ordinary definition of bifurcate is to divide into two parts. In New York practice, bifurcation has come to mean the trial of the liability issue in a personal injury or wrongful death case separately from, and prior to, trial of the damages issues.[1] The advantage of doing this is that if the liability issue is determined in the defendant's favor, there is no need to try damages, which can involve expensive expert witnesses and other proof. The plaintiff often resists an attempt to bifurcate, especially when the liability

---

[2] Kelly v. Yannotti, 4 N.Y.2d 603, 176 N.Y.S.2d 637, 152 N.E.2d 69 (1958). The common method to test the validity of the disclaimer, so as to determine whether the insurer is obliged to defend a pending suit against the insured, is a separate declaratory judgment action. See § 437.

[3] Dain & Dill, Inc. v. Betterton, 39 A.D.2d 939, 333 N.Y.S.2d 237 (2d Dep't 1972).

[4] This is an intra-action res judicata doctrine. See § 448.

[5] See Hamm v. Richards, 12 A.D.2d 953, 210 N.Y.S.2d 871 (2d Dep't 1961).

[6] This point would be academic in courts with the Individual Assignment System (IAS), in which a case goes to one judge at the outset and stays with that judge throughout, but it's significant in courts that still use the so-called "Master Calendar" system instead of the IAS. See § 77A.

[7] See Greenberg v. City of Yonkers, 45 A.D.2d 314, 358 N.Y.S.2d 453 (2d Dep't 1974), aff'd, 37 N.Y.2d 907, 378 N.Y.S.2d 382, 340 N.E.2d 744 (1975).

[1] See NY PJI 1:2A ("Split Trial—Liability").

issue is a close one, because he understandably wants to exploit the sympathy factor and have the jurors aware of the injuries and damages when they deliberate liability. The defendant, for the opposite reason, usually prefers bifurcation.

The Uniform Rules state that judges are "encouraged" to order a bifurcated trial in personal injury cases, not directing when it should be ordered, but merely prescribing some procedure when it is.[2] Even under the rules, therefore, bifurcation is in the court's discretion.

Whether to bifurcate depends on whether the two issues are wholly distinct and whether there is a substantial saving that can result. Bifurcation was seldom used under prior law.[3] It came into vogue in the mid-1960s and has achieved wide judicial acceptance as the "authorized and accepted practice."[4] An incisive treatment of the subject is in Carpenter v. County of Essex,[5] where the court reviewed some of the factors that can result in the denial of bifurcation.

In Mercado v. City of New York,[6] the court ordered a retrial of only a damages question in a case in which the damages were deemed excessive, but liability was clearly established. Where the nature of the plaintiff's injuries has a direct bearing on the question of liability, as when there is a serious question of whether the defendant's conduct was the proximate cause of the particular injury, the jury should consider the two items simultaneously and bifurcation is not appropriate.[7]

If bifurcation is ordered and the liability trial produces a verdict for the plaintiff, the damages trial goes forward. Its precise time is fixed by the court. The judge may direct that the damages trial proceed forthwith and before the same jury, which the rules prefer to be the course because the main advantage of the split trial would otherwise be lost.[8] But if the parties have to go through further preparation for the damages trial, such as the calling of busy expert witnesses, it may be tried before the same jury after a brief adjournment or before a new jury if the delay is prolonged. The rules allow for that, too, provided the judge states "in the record" why it's necessary.[9]

The delay between trials may even be occasioned by the defendant's appeal of the liability judgment and his securing of a stay of further proceedings in conjunction with it.[10] There is a general policy, however, against allowing an appeal from a liability finding before damages are tried. It has been held that such an appeal lies only when an

---

[2] In the supreme court and in the county courts, the applicable rule is 22 N.Y.C.R.R. § 202.42. Other courts may have similar rules. See, for example, 22 N.Y.C.R.R. § 208.35, applicable in the civil court, and 22 N.Y.C.R.R. § 206.19, applicable in the court of claims.

[3] See Hacker v. City of New York, 25 A.D.2d 35, 266 N.Y.S.2d 194 (1st Dep't 1966).

[4] Williams v. City of New York, 36 A.D.2d 620, 318 N.Y.S.2d 536, 537 (2d Dep't 1971).

[5] Carpenter v. County of Essex, 67 A.D.3d 1106, 888 N.Y.S.2d 278 (3d Dep't 2009) (SPR 219:1).

[6] Mercado v. City of New York, 25 A.D.2d 75, 265 N.Y.S.2d 834 (1st Dep't 1966).

[7] Schwartz v. Binder, 91 A.D.2d 660, 457 N.Y.S.2d 109 (2d Dep't 1982); see Matthew H. v. County of Nassau, 131 A.D.3d 135, 14 N.Y.S.3d 38 (2d Dep't 2015) (unified trial required where severity of the infant plaintiff's injuries had an important bearing upon the question of defendants' constructive knowledge of the vicious propensities of dogs).

[8] See Trimboli v. Scarpaci Funeral Home, Inc., 37 A.D.2d 386, 326 N.Y.S.2d 227 (2d Dep't 1971), aff'd, 30 N.Y.2d 687, 332 N.Y.S.2d 637, 283 N.E.2d 614 (1972).

[9] See the rules cited in note 2, above.

[10] The *Trimboli* case discussed above shows the additional interest the defendant may have to pay if the defendant is responsible for this further delay in the damages trial. See § 411.

interlocutory judgment has been permitted by the court on the liability finding.[11] Whether to permit one is in the court's discretion.[12]

While the economizing aims of bifurcation are generally realized by having liability tried before damages, and the rules prescribe that as the norm,[13] it will occasionally happen that economy is better served by reversing the order and trying damages first, as when an issue of wilful misconduct, which goes to liability, does not become relevant unless damages are shown to exceed a certain figure.[14] The rules cover that, too.[15]

Bifurcation can give way to what might be called trifurcation in certain cases, such as the multi-defendant tort case involving the apportionment of culpability under the doctrine of Dole v. Dow Chemical Co.[16] and its codifying statutes.[17] The three separable issues would be (1) whether there is any liability at all, and if so, (2) what are the parties' respective shares of it, and (3) what are the plaintiff's damages. As a rule, little is gained by keeping (1) and (2) separate. The responsibilities of defendants to the plaintiff, as well as to themselves, are best determined by the jury at one time. Indeed, the Court of Appeals frowns on "trifurcation" if it subdivides the liability phase.[18] It should be even less justifiable under the comparative negligence rule adopted in New York in 1975[19] since that rule entails an allotting of actual fault among all the parties, including the plaintiff, and it would be awkward to apportion percentages, supposed to total 100%, in segments that each total less.

B. NECESSARY JOINDER OF PARTIES

Table of Sections

§ 131.   Necessary Joinder of Parties, Background
§ 132.   Necessary Joinder of Parties, CPLR Approach
§ 133.   Avoiding Dismissal for Nonjoinder

§ 131. Necessary Joinder of Parties, Background

A plaintiff ordinarily has little trouble determining the parties to sue. She knows who the defendants should be and simply names them, serves them, and gets an action going. One does not often find a "necessary joinder" problem in practice.

In many situations, P has a claim not only against X, but against X and Y jointly, or jointly and severally. She may own the claim absolutely or contingently. She may own it herself, or share it with A, or with A and B, and the sharing may be outright, or on some condition. Perhaps the liability P asserts against several defendants is not "joint"

---

[11]   See Jack Parker Const. Corp. v. Williams, 35 A.D.2d 839, 317 N.Y.S.2d 911 (2d Dep't 1970).

[12]   A treatment of this question appears in Bank of New York v. Ansonia Associates, 172 Misc. 2d 70, 656 N.Y.S.2d 813 (Sup 1997) (SPR 69:3). See § 526.

[13]   See note 2, above.

[14]   See Harari-Raful v. Trans World Airlines, Inc., 41 A.D.2d 753, 341 N.Y.S.2d 655 (2d Dep't 1973), involving the Warsaw Convention.

[15]   22 N.Y.C.R.R. § 202.42, for example, while prescribing liability and then damages as the sequence, permits the court to order "otherwise."

[16]   Dole v. Dow Chemical Co., 30 N.Y.2d 143, 331 N.Y.S.2d 382, 282 N.E.2d 288 (1972). See § 171.

[17]   See Articles 14 and 14–A of the CPLR.

[18]   See Greenberg v. City of Yonkers, 37 N.Y.2d 907, 378 N.Y.S.2d 382, 340 N.E.2d 744 (1975).

[19]   CPLR 1411. See § 168E.

in the substantive law sense, but the relief P wants is such that X, or X and A, or X and Y, or Y and A, or any of a myriad of others, can in some way be affected. Must these others be made parties to the action? If so, which of them? And shall they be plaintiffs or defendants? May they sometimes be joined and at other times be omitted? These questions are the crux of the subject known as "necessary joinder."

Prior law endeavored to formulate criteria whereby some persons in some situations were to be deemed "indispensable" parties without whom the action could not continue and whose lack of joinder would force a dismissal. Others were to be only "conditionally necessary," and their joinder was desirable, but the action could nonetheless continue without them if they were beyond jurisdiction.[1] This approach proved futile. The Advisory Committee candidly noted that the subject of necessary joinder "defies definitive statement" and must rest in each instance in the sound discretion of the court.[2]

Acknowledging that in a given case a particular person could prove "indispensable" in the sense that it would not be effectual to proceed in her absence, the committee decided that the matter "should be determined in the light of all the factors and interests involved including those of the court." Stressing that "there is no single certain criterion" that would prove airtight by itself,[3] the committee therefore adopted an approach of maximum flexibility, leaving the matter to be determined by the court on a case by case basis and with an abundance of discretion. This approach is embodied in CPLR 1001, treated in the next section.

§ 132. Necessary Joinder of Parties, CPLR Approach

CPLR 1001(a) provides:

Persons who ought to be parties if complete relief is to be accorded between the persons who are parties to the action or who might be inequitably affected by a judgment in the action shall be made plaintiffs or defendants.

The phrase "persons who ought to be parties" is used with the aim of escaping from the rigorous caselaw built up around the word "indispensable" that prior law used. CPLR 1001 omits it. The joinder of an ought-to-be-party person is directed whenever either of the following is indicated:

1. his joinder would make the relief between those already parties more complete; or

2. the judgment may in some way inequitably affect him.

The second item does not necessarily require a showing that the judgment would be entitled to res judicata or collateral estoppel effect against such person; indeed, if he has not been joined, it probably couldn't be.[1] The possibility that a judgment rendered without him could have an adverse practical effect on him is enough to indicate joinder.[2]

---

[1]   See Civ. Prac. Act § 193 (repealed 1963).

[2]   1st Rep. Leg. Doc. No. 6(b), p.29 (1957).

[3]   1st Rep. Leg. Doc. No. 6(b), p.30 (1957).

[1]   See § 458.

[2]   An illustration of this practical approach appears in City of New York v. Long Island Airports Limousine Service Corp., 48 N.Y.2d 469, 423 N.Y.S.2d 651, 399 N.E.2d 538 (1979). See and compare Fed. R. Civ. P. 19(a).

The problem is usually avoided if the plaintiff (P) merely resolves doubts in favor of joinder. If the person has an interest in any way adverse to P, she should be made a defendant. If she has some share in P's claim and ought to be a co-plaintiff, P should consult her, for she might consent to join with P in bringing the action. If she resists, P can make her a defendant,[3] as the main aim is to get her into the case. The court will render judgment as need be regardless of who is on what side of the "versus" sign.[4]

A serious problem arises, therefore, in but a single situation: when the person who "ought to be joined" is not subject to the personal jurisdiction of the court and will not submit to it voluntarily. If X ought to be joined and is subject to jurisdiction, CPLR 1001(a) directs that she be named and joined now. Hence the underlying premise of the joinder statute is that there is no occasion to determine if X is "indispensable" as long as jurisdiction of X can be obtained. X simply gets joined and the problem is done with. The point sometimes seems to be overlooked by the courts, but as long as the statute of limitations is still alive for an action that joins the needed party, the harm is minimal.[5] Of course, if the plaintiff has had ample opportunity to join the needed parties and fails to, dismissal may result.[6]

It's when jurisdiction is not obtainable that the problem reaches its peak. The next section treats that.

§ 133. Avoiding Dismissal for Nonjoinder

The Advisory Committee's resolution of the necessary joinder problem is in CPLR 1001(b). The assumption throughout the ensuing treatment is that the ought-to-be-joined person is not subject to personal jurisdiction.

Dismissal of the action for nonjoinder of a given person is a possibility under the CPLR,[7] but it is only a last resort. Before reaching that point, the court should stretch its judicial imagination to see if it can devise some way of allowing the action to proceed without that person's joinder. CPLR 1001(b) gives the court plenary power to keep the action alive without that person "when justice requires." To aid the court in making that determination the statute lists five things the court "shall" consider:

1. whether the plaintiff has another effective remedy in case the action is dismissed on account of the nonjoinder;

2. the prejudice that may accrue from the nonjoinder to the defendant or to the person not joined;

3. whether and by whom prejudice might have been avoided or may in the future be avoided;

4. the feasibility of a protective provision by order or in the judgment; and

---

[3]   CPLR 1001(a) specifically provides for this.

[4]   Adding someone as a party plaintiff is of course easier when he consents, see Abschagen v. Goldfarb, 8 A.D.2d 750, 185 N.Y.S.2d 339 (3d Dep't 1959), but if he should be a plaintiff and will not consent he can be made a defendant. The federal description allows him to be made an "involuntary plaintiff," Fed. R. Civ. P. 19(a), a distinction perhaps important for federal jurisdictional purposes (measuring whether there is diversity of citizenship between the parties, for example) but carrying little difference in New York practice.

[5]   See, e.g., Storrs v. Holcomb, 245 A.D.2d 943, 666 N.Y.S.2d 835 (3d Dep't 1997).

[6]   See Llana v. Town of Pittstown, 245 A.D.2d 968, 667 N.Y.S.2d 112 (3d Dep't 1997).

[7]   CPLR 1003, 3211(a)(10).

5.   whether an effective judgment can be rendered in the absence of the person who is not joined.

The list is not exhaustive, but it covers most of the possibilities that come to mind. It makes no distinction between law and equity actions. It is a challenge to the court as well as to the lawyers, and it requires both imagination and energy. It implicitly instructs that a determination of "indispensability" is to be reached only after the list has been thoughtfully negotiated and found to offer no alternative. A few examples will illustrate.

a.   P and X were joint lessors of Chicago real property leased to D. P sued D in New York for money due under the lease. X, an Illinoisan, would not join in the action and was not subject to New York jurisdiction. The Court held that P could maintain the action without X, but P would of course have to account to X for his share of the proceeds.[8] The same result can be reached today under CPLR 1001(b), especially paragraph 4 (authorizing a protective provision in the judgment requiring P to account to X). Ironically, however, even a dismissal may be appropriate in that kind of case today. Perhaps P sued in New York because he could not get jurisdiction over D in the sister state where the real property was. If it were shown that jurisdiction could be had in that state today under a longarm statute akin to CPLR 302(a)(4), then CPLR 1001(b)(1) might be applied to dismiss the action without prejudice to suit in Illinois where personal jurisdiction would be available against both X and D. Forum non conveniens[9] is another basis on which such a dismissal might rest.

b.   Husband H and Wife W are joint buyers of real property. D is the seller. H sued D to recover the down payment, but without joining W, from whom H had separated. The court dismissed the action for nonjoinder of W, apparently finding nothing in CPLR 1001(b) that could preserve the action.[10] But if New York real property were involved, CPLR 302(a)(4), the longarm statute, might have offered jurisdiction over W, wherever she might have to be served. If so, W should simply have been ordered joined. It does not appear that counsel raised the possibility. If the real property were elsewhere, and the other jurisdiction had an equivalent longarm statute, this could have been called to the court's attention and the action dismissed on that basis under CPLR 1001(b)(1), remitting the parties to suit in the real property state.

If those possibilities did not exist, however, dismissal may have been the only fair thing from D's point of view. Suppose, for example, that W had wanted specific performance as a remedy instead of the damages that H sued for? If a situation like that should arise, one course that might be followed today is for the court to dismiss the New York action on condition that D submit to jurisdiction wherever W would be subject to it, thus assuring H a forum in which he could sue with jurisdiction over everyone.

c.   The Federal Rules of Civil Procedure have grappled with this problem, producing some caselaw pertinent to CPLR 1001(b). Consider the following example

---

[8]   Keene v. Chambers, 271 N.Y. 326, 3 N.E.2d 443 (1936). The *Keene* case should cast some doubt on cases that automatically conclude that a co-obligee is indispensable to the litigation, such as Natter v. Isaac H. Blanchard Co., 153 A.D. 814, 138 N.Y.S. 969 (1st Dep't 1912), especially in view of present CPLR 1001(b).

[9]   See § 28.

[10]   Mechta v. Scaretta, 52 Misc. 2d 696, 276 N.Y.S.2d 652 (Sup. Ct., Queens County 1967).

involving a shareholders' derivative action on behalf of a corporation (New York having at one time held the corporation indispensable in this kind of case).[11]

Shareholder P brought an action to compel the declaration of a dividend. P could not get jurisdiction over all or even a majority of the corporation's directors and was able to serve only three out of twelve. The court held that the absent directors were not necessary parties.[12] It noted that it had jurisdiction of the corporation and that it had all of the tools that any court of equity needs to effectuate a judgment. If the declaration of a dividend were directed by the court, rare though that may be substantively, the court could see to it that the corporation paid it, levying against local property of the corporation if necessary. Under CPLR 1001(b)(5), the New York courts would have equal power in a similar situation, assuming that the case could survive an application of the forum non conveniens doctrine.

d. The nonjoinder problem has appeared in the insurance context. P insured X's life and afterwards sued the beneficiaries to rescind the policy. One of them moved to dismiss for P's failure to join the estate of X, who had since died. The court denied the motion and held that the insured, in this case the estate of X, was not an indispensable party.[13] It held that if P could gain rescission against those whom P did join (the beneficiaries), P would have a meaningful judgment even though it might not bind X's estate. Should X's estate later sue the insurer, and the insurer be required to relitigate the case between itself and the estate, that would be no skin off the beneficiaries' necks. They will have their day in court now and can't avoid it merely because subsequent relitigation between insurer and insured is possible later. If anyone were to be inconvenienced by that relitigation prospect, it would be P, and P was not complaining.

Now suppose that suit is brought by beneficiary B against Insurer to collect on the policy. Insurer moves to dismiss for the nonjoinder of X, the insured, who is beyond jurisdiction. Is the situation the same? It differs significantly. If B collects from Insurer, and Insurer is afterwards sued by X in a separate action, the prior judgment may not bind X, who can therefore collect all over again from Insurer—as where the factfinders in the second suit disagree with those in the first. In that situation, dismissal for nonjoinder may be justified but, again, it should be so conditioned as to maneuver the parties into some other court that has or would get (through a protective provision in the New York disposition) jurisdiction over everyone.

In circumstances like these, the insurer can of course turn to its interpleader remedies,[14] but even the need of interpleader as a cure has diminished in this age of expanded extraterritorial jurisdiction. Cases in which an ought-to-be-joined person is not amenable to jurisdiction have become increasingly rare.

A prime possibility when such a case does crop up, already alluded to several times, is for the court to see whether any sister state or reasonably accessible (and trusted) foreign court would have jurisdiction over all of the interested persons if New York does not. P's action could then be dismissed on condition that within a stated period D

---

[11] See the pre-CPLR case of Carruthers v. Jack Waite Mining Co., 306 N.Y. 136, 116 N.E.2d 286 (1953).

[12] Kroese v. General Steel Castings Corp., 179 F.2d 760, 15 A.L.R.2d 1117 (3d Cir. 1950).

[13] New England Mut. Life Ins. Co. v. Brandenburg, 8 F.R.D. 151 (S.D.N.Y. 1948).

[14] Interpleader (see §§ 148 et seq.) is the device whereby a stakeholder—one who owes money or has property that several are making conflicting claims to—can avoid double liability by bringing the conflicting claimants to court, thereby subjecting them to a judgment that protects the stakeholder from later suit by any of them.

stipulate to submit to jurisdiction in the other court, where the absent X would be subject to suit. Such a disposition would be a combined exercise under paragraphs 1 and 4 of CPLR 1001(b). It's in effect a leverage use of whatever jurisdiction the court has: if D wants the action dismissed for nonjoinder of a third person, D may have the dismissal only by consenting to jurisdiction in a court in which the third person can be joined as a party.[15]

A classic illustration of what the CPLR drafters had in mind in devising CPLR 1001(b) is the First Department's *SafeNet* decision.[16] N was not joined in the action because N was not subject to the court's personal jurisdiction. Had N been truly indispensable to the litigation, a dismissal of the action might have been possible for N's nonjoinder. But the whole thrust of CPLR 1001(b) is to avoid that and keep the action going without the joinder if at all possible. Going down the whole CPLR 1001(b) list of factors in the *SafeNet* case, the court suggests what might be done to avoid the dismissal, and avoids it.

With extraterritorial jurisdiction so broadly available today, the problem of joining a "necessary" party seldom appears, and more seldom still does it reach the Court of Appeals. Two cases with the problem did get to that Court in recent years, one of them occasioning a reminder of how far a court has to go before dismissing for nonjoinder.

In the *Red Hook* case,[17] the Court held that even if the claim against the unjoined party appears to be time-barred, the statutory factors enumerated in CPLR 1001(b) must still be considered before the court can dismiss for nonjoinder. A dissent in the case pointed to the futility of joining a party only to produce a prompt statute of limitations dismissal of the claim against it. In the later *Windy Ridge* decision,[18] the Court distinguished its prior holding in *Red Hook*, where the parties assumed that jurisdiction over the necessary party could only have been obtained by his consent or appearance. As in *Red Hook*, the statute of limitations on the claim against the necessary parties in *Windy* had expired, but the Court concluded that this time bar, standing alone, did not mean that the parties were not "subject to the jurisdiction of the court" under CPLR 1001(b). Therefore, the necessary parties were properly joined and, in turn, successfully obtained dismissal of the action on statute of limitations grounds. This required dismissal of the case against the remaining party due to the failure to join the necessary parties.

In Swezey v. Merrill Lynch, Pierce, Fenner & Smith, Inc.,[19] the Court again reviewed the five factors in CPLR 1001(b) in an action in which the Republic of the Philippines invoked sovereign immunity and could not be joined as a party. In its analysis of the factors, the Court applied "the general rule that an assertion of immunity

---

[15]   A brief memorandum in Cushing-Murray v. Adams, 49 A.D.2d 874, 373 N.Y.S.2d 191 (2d Dep't 1975), states that the dismissal may not be conditioned on the defendant's stipulating to submit to jurisdiction elsewhere. This is a needlessly broad restriction. One of the court's options is "a protective provision by order of the court," under CPLR 1001(b)(4). An order conditioning dismissal on a submission to jurisdiction in a more appropriate forum seems well within the possibilities contemplated.

[16]   L-3 Communications Corp. v. SafeNet, Inc., 45 A.D.3d 1, 841 N.Y.S.2d 82 (1st Dep't 2007) (SPR 193:3).

[17]   Red Hook/Gowanus Chamber of Commerce v. New York City Bd. of Standards and Appeals, 5 N.Y.3d 452, 805 N.Y.S.2d 525, 839 N.E.2d 878 (2005) (NYSLD No. 553).

[18]   Windy Ridge Farm v. Assessor of Town of Shandaken, 11 N.Y.3d 725, 864 N.Y.S.2d 794, 894 N.E.2d 1183 (2008) (NYSLD No. 585).

[19]   Swezey v. Merrill Lynch, Pierce, Fenner & Smith, Inc., 19 N.Y.3d 543, 950 N.Y.S.2d 293, 973 N.E.2d 703 (2012) (NYSLD No. 634, p. 3).

by a sovereign entity requires dismissal of an action in which it is a necessary party if the entity's claims are not frivolous and there is a potential for injury to its interests."[20]

Rule 19 of the Federal Rules of Civil Procedure was recast in 1966 to meet the same kind of problem that CPLR 1001(b) addresses. This enables us to take note of the U.S. Supreme Court's first major decision on the revised rule. It notes that "a court does not know whether a particular person is 'indispensable' until it has examined the situation to determine whether it can proceed without him,"[21] the very premise on which CPLR 1001 is bottomed.

This subject sometimes overlaps the less serious "misnomer" cases discussed earlier, in which a proper party was served, but under a technically incorrect name in the summons.[22]

C. PERMISSIVE JOINDER OF PARTIES

Table of Sections

§ 134.   Permissive Joinder of Parties
§ 135.   Joinder in the Alternative

§ 134. Permissive Joinder of Parties

The CPLR is generous about the joinder of multiple parties. Parties with separate and distinct claims may join—and those against whom the claims exist may be joined—in a single action if the several claims (1) arise out of "the same transaction[s], occurrence[s], or series of transactions or occurrences," and (2) have in common any "question of law or fact."[1] These standards apply to the voluntary joinder of claims by multiple plaintiffs as well as to the joinder of multiple defendants by one or more plaintiffs.

A simple example of plaintiffs' joinder is where several plaintiffs injured in the same accident join their separate claims for personal injuries or property damage (or both) in a single action. As long as a common thread ties all of the claims together, enabling the court to say that they all arise out of a common series of transactions or occurrences, the first criterion is met. In Akely v. Kinnicutt,[2] for example, where D circulated a fraudulent prospectus in connection with a stock floater and 193 different persons relied on it, all were permitted to join their fraud claims in a single action even though the claim of each was distinct and in no way dependent on any other's. The second requirement, that there be a common question of law or fact, was also met. The question of whether or not the prospectus was false was one such common question.

Note that the existence of separate questions, distinct to each plaintiff, does not defeat the joinder as long as there is some common question, too. In *Akely*, there were several questions unique to each plaintiff, among them the issues of whether that particular plaintiff relied on the prospectus and what his damages were, but that didn't

---

[20]   *Swezey*, 19 N.Y.3d at 553, 950 N.Y.S.2d at 300, 973 N.E.2d at 710.

[21]   Provident Tradesmens Bank & Trust Co. v. Patterson, 390 U.S. 102, 119, 88 S. Ct. 733, 743, 19 L. Ed. 2d 936 (1968).

[22]   See § 64.

[1]   CPLR 1002(a) (for plaintiffs) and (b) (for defendants).

[2]   Akely v. Kinnicutt, 238 N.Y. 466, 144 N.E. 682 (1924).

bar joinder. *Akely* also establishes that neither does the fact that the diverse claims arise at different times bar the joinder; the transactions can still constitute a "series." The defendant's argument that she should be allowed a separate jury on each claim is given short shrift by the court.

The word "transaction" in CPLR 1002 connotes a consensual dealing. "Occurrence" includes nonconsensual happenings, such as tort claims. It was added to expand the scope of permissive joinder.[3]

The statute works the same way on the defendant's side. Where P was insured with two companies, for example, each insuring a separate part of the same loss—thus giving rise to separate and independent claims against the two when a burglary loss occurred—the insured was permitted to join both companies in a single action.[4] The common questions were the fact of the burglary and the value of the insured merchandise.

CPLR 1002(c) provides that "[i]t shall not be necessary that each plaintiff be interested in obtaining, or each defendant . . . in defending against, all the relief demanded or as to every claim included in an action." As long as the threads of "series of transactions" and "common question of law or fact" run through the several claims, the absence of an interest by each litigant in the claims asserted by or against the others offers no barrier to joinder.

Of course, despite their valid joinder, the distinctness of the claims may in some instances make it impractical or infeasible to hear all of them together, but for that CPLR 1002(c) has a flexible remedy. It provides that the court "may order separate trials or make other orders to prevent prejudice," among which would be an order severing some of the claims and sending them off as separate actions.[5] The remedy of a severance would be particularly appropriate where, because of the broadness of joinder, a person finds herself involved in a case with an "adverse" party with whom she has no argument.

In short, the CPLR sets broad boundaries for permissive joinder and simply invites the court to curtail them if the exigencies of a given case indicate.

While joinder by different plaintiffs against one defendant ordinarily requires, under CPLR 1002(a), that the claims arise out of a single transaction or series of transactions, an exception is carved out for consumer credit transactions[6] by CPLR 601(b),[7] which provides that five separate consumer credit transactions may now be joined in a single action provided that all are against the same defendant and all the plaintiffs are represented by the same attorney.

In the lower courts, which have monetary limitations on their jurisdiction, the CPLR provisions on permissive joinder are equally applicable. As long as each of the claims falls within the court's monetary jurisdiction when independently measured, the court may entertain them all in one action. There is even permission for a single

---

[3]   15th Jud. Council Rep. 211, 216 (1949).

[4]   Bossak v. National Surety Co. of New York, 205 A.D. 707, 200 N.Y.S. 148 (1st Dep't 1923).

[5]   See CPLR 603, 1003.

[6]   See the definition in CPLR 105.

[7]   Subdivision (b) was added to CPLR 601 in a 1996 amendment. The amendment is treated in SPR 52:2–3.

judgment to be rendered for more than the court's monetary jurisdiction, as long as none of the claims exceeds the jurisdiction individually.[8]

§ 135. Joinder in the Alternative

Particularly helpful to plaintiffs is the permission of CPLR 1002(b) to join defendants "in the alternative," so that when P has a claim but does not know who, as between X and Y, is liable on it, P can sue them both. A typical situation is where goods left P's possession, went through the hands of several others (carrier, dyer, cutter, packer, warehouseman, return carrier, etc.), and then came back into P's possession with some of the goods missing or damaged, but with all of the handlers denying it was their fault. P may sue them all, establishing the condition of the goods when they left P, the condition in which they were returned, and the fact that each of the defendants handled the goods somewhere in between. This is enough to throw onto the defendants the burden of coming forward with proof of their due care, thus helping to fix liability as among themselves.[1] P's showing satisfies as a prima facie case in this kind of situation, and a defendant's silence in the face of such proof can therefore be taken by the factfinder as an admission of liability. What generally occurs is that each defendant tries, if he can, to pin liability on some other, with the plaintiff ending up the beneficiary rather than the victim.

The final judgment can be based on any proof in the record regardless of who introduced it. A statute explicitly so providing under prior law[2] was omitted from the CPLR (probably inadvertently), but no matter; the same conclusion has been reached under the CPLR[3] and no other would be appropriate. Thus, if the evidence that implicates defendant X is introduced by defendant Y, P has full use of it.

Joinder in the alternative is available on even more remote contingencies. In one case P's agent, A, was supposed to have brought timely suit in P's behalf against D. It was questionable whether he did. P sued A and D in the alternative, asserting primary liability against D but pleading for judgment against A in the event that the statute of limitations now barred P's claim against D. The suit was allowed in that form.[4] The "common question" was whether the statute of limitations had expired on P's claim against D.

A concomitant of joinder in the alternative is pleading in the alternative, which is also invited by the CPLR.[5]

Suit in the alternative generally involves alternative defendants, but it can apply to plaintiffs. A situation can arise, for example, in which two or more persons do not know who, as between them, should sue as plaintiff. In that situation today, suit by the plaintiffs in the alternative should be allowed. It was allowed in the past,[6] but not when

---

[8] See § 23.

[1] S. & C. Clothing Co. v. United States Trucking Corporation, 216 A.D. 482, 215 N.Y.S. 349 (1st Dep't 1926).

[2] Civ. Prac. Act § 212(1) (repealed 1963).

[3] Shaw v. Lewis, 55 Misc. 2d 664, 286 N.Y.S.2d 758 (N.Y. City Civ. Ct. 1968), aff'd, 58 Misc. 2d 1072, 299 N.Y.S.2d 615 (App. Term, 1st Dep't).

[4] Great Northern Tel. Co. v. Yokohama Specie Bank, 297 N.Y. 135, 76 N.E.2d 117 (1947).

[5] CPLR 3014. See Tanbro Fabrics Corp. v. Beaunit Mills, Inc., 4 A.D.2d 519, 167 N.Y.S.2d 387 (1st Dep't 1957) (discussing the interplay between the joinder and pleading provisions).

[6] See, e.g., Roecklein v. American Sugar Refining Co., 222 A.D. 540, 226 N.Y.S. 375 (2d Dep't 1928).

the claim of each was clearly exclusive. Where, for example, both maker and payee sued a bank on a check, the court held the two misjoined as plaintiffs because the claim of each destroyed the other's.[7] CPLR 1002(a) should permit joinder even in that kind of case today.

D. PROPER PARTIES

Table of Sections

§ 136.   Standing to Sue
§ 137.   "Real Party in Interest"

§ 136. Standing to Sue

Questions of proper parties generally focus on who must be made defendants. Less frequent is the question of who should be the plaintiff. One category that occasionally raises the issue is known as "standing to sue."

It is the law's policy to allow only an aggrieved person to bring a lawsuit. One not affected by anything a would-be defendant has done or threatens to do ordinarily has no business suing, and a suit of that kind can be dismissed at the threshold for want of jurisdiction without reaching the merits. When one without the requisite grievance does bring suit, and it's dismissed, the plaintiff is described as lacking "standing to sue" and the dismissal as one for lack of subject matter jurisdiction. A want of "standing to sue," in other words, is just another way of saying that this particular plaintiff is not involved in a genuine controversy, and a simple syllogism takes us from there to a "jurisdictional" dismissal: (1) the courts have jurisdiction only over controversies; (2) a plaintiff found to lack "standing" is not involved in a controversy; and (3) the courts therefore have no jurisdiction of the case when such a plaintiff purports to bring it.

A "standing" issue is sometimes found in a case involving administrative action. A good example is Dairylea Cooperative, Inc. v. Walkley,[1] in which the Commissioner of Agriculture and Markets granted L, a milk dealer, a license to distribute milk in an area already serviced by P. P sought to annul the determination,[2] which had been made without a hearing, and the question was whether P, as a mere competitor, had standing to bring the suit. The Court concluded that P had the requisite standing because P was able to show: (1) that the administrative action would harm P, and (2) that P's interest was "arguably" within the "zone of interest" to be protected by the statute involved. (In the *Dairylea* case, it was a licensing statute.) The Court said that "[o]nly where there is a clear legislative intent negating review . . . or lack of injury in fact will standing be denied."[3] The test today is a liberal one, according to *Dairylea*, and the right to challenge administrative action, articulated under the "standing" caption, is an expanding one.

While the public interest was involved in *Dairylea*, the crux of the case was a private argument between commercial competitors. This facilitated a finding of direct aggrievement at least sufficient to conclude that one competitor had the capacity to

---

[7]   See Olsen v. Bankers' Trust Co., 205 A.D. 669, 199 N.Y.S. 700 (1st Dep't 1923).

[1]   Dairylea Cooperative, Inc. v. Walkley, 38 N.Y.2d 6, 377 N.Y.S.2d 451, 339 N.E.2d 865 (1975).

[2]   P brought an Article 78 proceeding (see §§ 557 et seq.), the New York procedure for contesting administrative action.

[3]   *Dairylea*, 38 N.Y.2d at 11, 377 N.Y.S.2d at 455, 339 N.E.2d at 868.

contest official activity that benefitted the other. In awarding standing to sue, the Court was hardly deciding a matter of urgent public policy.

Economic interest in the outcome of a case will not assure a plaintiff standing to sue if the plaintiff's claim is based on a statute that seeks to implement non-economic interests, as was the case in Society of Plastics Industry, Inc. v. County of Suffolk,[4] where the Court barred a plastics maker from attacking a county's "plastics law" under the State Environmental Quality Review Act. The Court found that the attackers were motivated by economic interests while standing under that statute is available only to those with non-economic (environmental, aesthetic, etc.) interests. Elaborating on that in Save the Pine Bush, Inc. v. Common Council of City of Albany,[5] to be returned to below, which involved a protected area in Albany known as the Pine Bush, the Court of Appeals ruled that those who use the area "more than most other members of the public" have the requisite standing to contest activities that affect its wildlife. The Court said that nothing in *Plastics* suggests that residence nearby is an indispensable element.

The *Plastics* Court held that when challenging government action in land use matters, "the plaintiff, for standing purposes, must show that it would suffer direct harm, injury that is in some way different from that of the public at large."[6] In Sierra Club v. Village of Painted Post,[7] the Court took the opportunity to further explain this "special injury" requirement of standing. Petitioners in *Sierra Club* brought an Article 78 proceeding challenging respondents' water sale agreement and lease of land to construct a "water transloading facility" where water would be withdrawn, loaded, and transported via rail line. One of the petitioners resided in respondent village and lived within a block and a half of the rail line and transloading facility. The Fourth Department ruled that he lacked standing and dismissed the petition.

The Court of Appeals reversed, noting that while more than one resident was directly impacted by the noise created by the increased train traffic, "[t]he number of people who are affected by the challenged action is not dispositive of standing."[8] Therefore, the Fourth Department erred in requiring petitioner to show harm different from other village residents who also lived along the train line and suffered similar noise impacts. Quoting from its opinion in *Society of Plastics*, the *Sierra Club* Court stressed that the harm "alleged must be specific to the individuals who allege it, and must be 'different in kind or degree from the public at large,' but it need not be unique."[9] Petitioner was not alleging a generalized indirect effect from the increased train noise, "but rather a particularized harm that may also be inflicted upon others in the community who live near the tracks."[10]

A singular involvement of the standing doctrine in the economics sphere has been in the so-called "taxpayer" suit, an action brought by a citizen-taxpayer, with a minimal personal stake, to test the constitutionality of an expenditure of state money. New York

---

[4]   Society of Plastics Industry, Inc. v. County of Suffolk, 77 N.Y.2d 761, 570 N.Y.S.2d 778, 573 N.E.2d 1034 (1991) (NYSLD No. 379). The decision is often referred to by just one word: "Plastics."

[5]   Save the Pine Bush, Inc. v. Common Council of City of Albany, 13 N.Y.3d 297, 301, 890 N.Y.S.2d 405, 406, 918 N.E.2d 917, 918 (2009) (NYSLD No. 601; SPR 601:1).

[6]   *Soc'y of Plastics*, 77 N.Y.2d at 774, 570 N.Y.S.2d at 785–86, 573 N.E.2d at 1041–42.

[7]   Sierra Club v. Village of Painted Post, 26 N.Y.3d 301, 22 N.Y.S.3d 388, 43 N.E.3d 745 (2015).

[8]   *Sierra Club*, 26 N.Y.3d at 311, 22 N.Y.S.3d at 392, 43 N.E.3d at 749.

[9]   *Sierra Club*, 26 N.Y.3d at 311, 22 N.Y.S.3d at 392, 43 N.E.3d at 749.

[10]   *Sierra Club*, 26 N.Y.3d at 311, 22 N.Y.S.3d at 392, 43 N.E.3d at 749.

was among the few states to preclude such an action; it found the plaintiff's interest either lacking, or so infinitesimal as to be in effect lacking, and thus adjudged the plaintiff to be without "standing."[11]

What was involved was really a policy determination that the validity of legislative expenditures should not be broadly supervised by the courts. This was a fundamental decision about the separation of powers, and one of great moment, and yet the closing of the judicial door was attributed, with a strained effort, to a lack of "standing." There has since been, incidentally, a total change of heart in New York on the taxpayer suit, which is now allowed to challenge state expenditures just as it has for years been allowed to challenge municipal expenditures.[12] The Court of Appeals made the change in Boryszewski v. Brydges,[13] noting the expanding attitude towards "standing." The legislature made the same change almost simultaneously with the enactment of Article 7–A of the State Finance Law,[14] elaborating procedure and imposing certain conditions.

In Aurora Loan Services, LLC v. Taylor,[15] the Court of Appeals addressed the issue of standing in mortgage foreclosure actions. The Court emphasized that "the note, and not the mortgage, is the dispositive instrument that conveys standing to foreclose under New York law."[16] Furthermore, the holder of the note is generally deemed the owner of the underlying mortgage because "the mortgage passes as an incident to the note." Therefore, the physical delivery of the note to the plaintiff from its owner prior to commencement of a foreclosure action may, in certain circumstances, be sufficient to transfer the mortgage obligation and create standing to foreclose. The *Aurora* Court ruled that the affidavit of the plaintiff's "legal liaison," which stated that she examined the original note herself, coupled with the adjustable rate note attachments submitted with the plaintiff's summary judgment papers, demonstrated the note's chain of ownership and that it was in the plaintiff's possession prior to commencement of the foreclosure action. This was sufficient to confer standing and, absent a CPLR 3120(1)(i) document demand, the plaintiff was not required to produce the original mortgage note.

While these developments suggest that neither the legislature nor the Court of Appeals is about to allow the "standing to sue" category to become the controversial battleground in New York practice that it has become in the federal courts, a New York decision occasionally appears that is hard to fit in. In New York State Ass'n of Nurse Anesthetists v. Novello,[17] for example, a group of nurse anesthetists sought to attack a health department "guideline" requiring that at all in-office surgeries involving anesthesia there be present at all times either a duly qualified anesthesiologist or the surgeon himself. The presence-throughout of only a nurse anesthetist thereupon became unacceptable, of course reducing their employment prospects. An association of nurse anesthetists directly impacted by the guideline was nevertheless held without standing to contest it. The case is either a momentary aberration, or else a harbinger of a more

11   See St. Clair v. Yonkers Raceway, Inc., 13 N.Y.2d 72, 242 N.Y.S.2d 43, 192 N.E.2d 15 (1963).

12   See Gen. Mun. Law § 51.

13   Boryszewski v. Brydges, 37 N.Y.2d 361, 372 N.Y.S.2d 623, 334 N.E.2d 579 (1975).

14   State Fin. Law §§ 123 to 123(j).

15   Aurora Loan Services, LLC v. Taylor, 25 N.Y.3d 355, 12 N.Y.S.3d 612, 34 N.E.3d 363 (2015).

16   *Aurora*, 25 N.Y.3d at 361, 12 N.Y.S.3d at 615, 34 N.E.3d at 366.

17   New York State Ass'n of Nurse Anesthetists v. Novello, 2 N.Y.3d 207, 778 N.Y.S.2d 123, 810 N.E.2d 405 (2004).

restrictive attitude about which further input must be awaited from the Court of Appeals.[18]

In the federal courts, in addition to serving as the door-closer for taxpayer suits seeking to test federal spending measures,[19] the standing doctrine has also come to mirror the prevalent views of the U.S. Supreme Court on the scope and reach of federal judicial jurisdiction. When a majority of the Supreme Court was of an expansive mind, "standing" was generously accorded taxpayers to test legislative enactments and administrative action.[20] In one case, the Court seemed almost to be interring the "standing" barrier and laying out a red carpet for a variety of suits previously thought insulated by restrictive notions of "standing."[21] When through personnel changes the Supreme Court then retrenched to a more restrained view of the federal judicial function, it was the "standing" doctrine that got trotted out once again to rebuild the wall.[22]

In federal practice, one also finds under the "standing" caption, or related to it, a number of other headings under which a court may refuse to entertain a case: justiciability, advisory opinion, political question, ripeness, mootness, etc.[23] Their significance in New York State practice is discussed by the New York Court of Appeals in New York State Inspection, Sec. and Law Enforcement Employees v. Cuomo,[24] an unsuccessful attempt by correction personnel to stop the closing of a correctional facility. The issues involved were found "political" (i.e., of a kind that must be left to the other branches of government) instead of "justiciable" (of a kind that the courts can entertain). As for the "advisory opinion," the New York courts can't grant one. An actual controversy is required, with one notable exception. A 1985 constitutional amendment[25] empowered the New York Court of Appeals, and only that Court, to entertain requests for advisory opinions on New York law submitted by the U.S. Supreme Court, a federal court of appeals, or a sister state's highest court.[26]

While the expanded use, or in any event theoretical availability, of the class action in New York[27] may increase the occasions for determining standing and like questions touching also on matters of policy, we can still conclude, and with some relief, that "standing" is not now and is not likely to become the arena it constitutes in federal

---

[18]   The difficulty of reconciling the *Anesthetists* case with the general caselaw on standing appears in the dissenting opinion of Judge Robert Smith. See the discussion of the case in the lead note in NYSLD No. 533.

[19]   Commonwealth of Massachusetts v. Mellon, 262 U.S. 447, 43 S. Ct. 597, 67 L. Ed. 1078 (1923).

[20]   See, e.g., Flast v. Cohen, 392 U.S. 83, 88 S. Ct. 1942, 20 L. Ed. 2d 947 (1968); U.S. v. Students Challenging Regulatory Agency Procedures (SCRAP), 412 U.S. 669, 93 S. Ct. 2405, 37 L. Ed. 2d 254 (1973).

[21]   See Association of Data Processing Service Organizations, Inc. v. Camp, 397 U.S. 150, 151, 90 S. Ct. 827, 829, 25 L. Ed. 2d 184 (1970), reciting that "[g]eneralizations about standing to sue are largely worthless as such."

[22]   See U.S. v. Richardson, 418 U.S. 166, 94 S. Ct. 2940, 41 L. Ed. 2d 678 (1974).

[23]   See § 612 (Practitioner's Edition).

[24]   New York State Inspection, Sec. and Law Enforcement Employees, Dist. Council 82, AFSCME, AFL-CIO v. Cuomo, 64 N.Y.2d 233, 485 N.Y.S.2d 719, 475 N.E.2d 90 (1984) (NYSLD No. 305).

[25]   The amendment added paragraph 9 to section 3(b) of Article VI of the State Constitution.

[26]   A Court of Appeals rule, 22 N.Y.C.R.R. § 500.27, entitled "Discretionary proceedings to review certified questions from federal courts and other courts of last resort," implements the new procedure, whose first invoking—there have been many since—appears to have occurred in Kidney by Kidney v. Kolmar Laboratories, Inc., 68 N.Y.2d 343, 509 N.Y.S.2d 491, 502 N.E.2d 168 (1986) (NYSLD No. 329). The certification procedure implemented by the rule has been the source of many recent decisions from the Court of Appeals. See § 528A.

[27]   See §§ 139 et seq.

practice. With the taxpayer suit having been expressly adopted in New York, and with the Court of Appeals having acknowledged that in general "standing" is to be measured generously, the occasion for closing the court's doors to a plaintiff by finding that his interest is not even sufficient to let him address the merits, which is what a "standing" dismissal means, should be infrequent. Ordinarily, only the most officious interloper should be ousted for want of standing.

An example of this more generous attitude is seen in *Save the Pine Bush*,[28] already mentioned above, involving local citizens seeking to protect a park area from development. The Court held that those who used the Pine Bush area "more than most other members of the public" did have the requisite standing.[29]

It's hard to draw a sharp line between the plaintiff's lack of "capacity" to sue, which is governed by CPLR 3211(a)(3) and is a waivable affirmative defense under CPLR 3211(e), and the issue of "standing" to sue, which can get lumped under the category of "subject matter jurisdiction" and thereby become an unwaivable defense, i.e., be interposable at any time.

The point is illustrated in the close division among the justices of the appellate division in Security Pacific Nat. Bank v. Evans,[30] in which a defunct corporation (since absorbed into another) brought a foreclosure action. The defendant did not raise any issue about this until a holdover proceeding was brought four years later, now arguing— in resisting the contention that it waived objection to the matter—that this was a question of "standing," went to subject matter jurisdiction, and hence could not be waived. A majority of the court disagreed, finding the "standing" objection, at least in this context, to be the mere alter ego of "capacity" and hence subject to waiver.

In Landau v. LaRossa, Mitchell & Ross,[31] the Court of Appeals itself treated lack of "capacity" and lack of "standing" as twins, holding that a dismissal on either ground will not invoke the res judicata doctrine to block a new action.

§ 137. "Real Party in Interest"

Under section 210 of the old Civil Practice Act every action was required to be prosecuted "in the name of the real party in interest," except in certain enumerated circumstances. The successor provision, CPLR 1004, omits that statement as obvious on the one hand (who else would bring the action?), misleading on the other (does it require in a trust case, for example, that the beneficiaries rather than the trustee bring suit?), and "an inept statement of . . . substantive law" in any event.[1] Low praise, indeed.

We thus have an acknowledgment that the questions of who may bring suit and against whom it may be brought are really questions of substantive rather than procedural law and must be answered as such. Who owns the cause of action? Whose right has been interfered with? Who interfered with it?

---

[28]   *Save the Pine Bush*, 13 N.Y.3d at 301, 890 N.Y.S.2d at 406, 918 N.E.2d at 918.

[29]   The case is treated in the lead note in NYSLD No. 601.

[30]   Security Pacific Nat. Bank v. Evans, 31 A.D.3d 278, 820 N.Y.S.2d 2 (1st Dep't 2006).

[31]   Landau v. LaRossa, Mitchell & Ross, 11 N.Y.3d 8, 862 N.Y.S.2d 316, 892 N.E.2d 380 (2008) (NYSLD No. 584); see § 52.

[1]   1st Rep. Leg. Doc. No. 6b, p.33 (1957).

CPLR 1004 confines its specific references to a few basic legal relationships, mostly of a fiduciary character, by providing that suit may be brought by or against these representatives instead of the person represented:

1. an executor or administrator of a decedent's estate;

2. a guardian of an infant's property;

3. a committee of a declared incompetent;

4. a conservator of a conservatee;

5. a trustee of an express trust;

6. an insured to whom the insurer has become subrogated; and

7. the intermediary in a third-party beneficiary situation.

Number 2 on the list does not include the mere guardian ad litem, whose brief tenure in the infant's life is only to act as a representative in a particular litigation. Nor does it include the parent of the infant, even though the parent may be served in the infant's behalf under CPLR 309(a). CPLR 309(a) requires, among other things, that the infant be served as well as the parent when the infant is 14 or over, a requirement that can't be circumvented by naming only the parent as the party. It is apparently only the formally appointed "guardian of the property" of an infant,[2] a person not met very often, who may be designated the party in place of the infant.[3]

With respect to numbers 3 and 4 on the list, note the archaic terminology. The committee/incompetent and conservator/conservatee descriptions have both been officially replaced by guardian/incapacitated person.[4]

For number 5, it should be noted that in an ordinary action between the trust and a stranger, the trustee is of course the proper party and the beneficiaries do not belong in the case. But the beneficiaries should be joined if the action or proceeding affects the validity of the trust itself,[5] or if there is a dispute between trustee and beneficiaries.

Number 6 on the list concerns the situation in which the insurer has paid the loss to its insured and stepped into the shoes of the insured for the purpose of making a claim against, and suing if need be, the third person who caused the loss. The action may still be maintained in the insured's name. The insured may have given the insurer a "subrogation receipt," but CPLR 1004 makes clear that the right of subrogation does not depend on the title of the document that confers the right. It can be any "agreement" evincing a purpose to give over to the insurer all or part of the insured's claim. The aim is to prevent the jury from knowing that the claim was covered by insurance,[6] and in all but name the action is prosecuted and paid for by the insurer. If the insurer has paid the insured only part of the claim, this device enables the action to be maintained in the insured's name for the entirety of the claim, but with the portion already paid now being paid back to the insurer out of the proceeds.

---

[2] See § 196 for the distinctions among "guardians."

[3] See Cramer v. Henderson, 123 Misc. 2d 159, 473 N.Y.S.2d 672 (Sup. Ct., Yates County 1984).

[4] See § 69, paragraph (b).

[5] McKnight v. Bank of New York & Trust Co., 254 N.Y. 417, 173 N.E. 568 (1930).

[6] Leone v. Lohmaier, 205 Misc. 467, 128 N.Y.S.2d 618 (Sup. Ct., Monroe County 1954).

Number 7 on the list, while presumably governing in the third-party beneficiary situations encountered in contract law, is most often met in agency cases, particularly when the persons involved, although acting as agents, have acted throughout in their own names.[7]

CPLR 1004 is phrased permissively ("may") so that, under categories 6 and 7 anyway, the insurer (rather than the insured) and the third-party beneficiary (rather than the benefactor) should have the option of bringing the action in its own name.

The opening language of CPLR 1004, "[e]xcept where otherwise prescribed by order of the court," enables the court to intercede in any of the listed situations so as to require the joinder of the various behind-the-scenes persons who would not otherwise have to be joined.

E. PROCEDURE FOR JOINDER PROBLEMS

Table of Sections

§ 138.   Motion to Add or Drop Parties; Procedure

§ 138. Motion to Add or Drop Parties; Procedure

CPLR 1003 supplies the procedure for defects of joinder. It provides that parties may be added or dropped by the court, on motion of any party or on its own initiative, at any stage of the action and upon such terms as may be just.

The court may thus act on its own without waiting for a motion and will do so whenever need appears. Where, for example, an argument ensued between parents as to how money was being expended for the children, the children's guardian ad litem was ordered joined by the court so as to assure a representation unfettered by the emotions that hampered the parents.[1]

The court may take this sua sponte action at any time and may make its orders conditional.

A formal motion to add or drop parties, whether made by P or D, must be made on notice to all who are already parties, but notice need not be given to the person sought to be added. If that person does not come into the action voluntarily, he must be served with a "supplemental summons,"[2] which must specify the pleading he is required to answer. The court can adjust the procedure in the order directing joinder, but in the absence of a court direction the new party should have a 20- or 30-day answering time, just as any original defendant would, depending on the time and manner of service.[3]

Under CPLR 1003, the "[m]isjoinder of parties is not a ground for dismissal of an action." The remedy to cure a misjoinder is simply to drop the improperly joined party. If an action has been tried with an improper party present and judgment has been

---

[7]   See Watts v. Phillips-Jones Corporation, 211 A.D. 523, 207 N.Y.S. 493 (2d Dep't 1925), aff'd, 242 N.Y. 557, 152 N.E. 425 (1926).

[1]   See Rosenblatt v. Birnbaum, 20 A.D.2d 556, 245 N.Y.S.2d 72 (2d Dep't 1963), aff'd, 16 N.Y.2d 212, 264 N.Y.S.2d 521, 212 N.E.2d 37 (1965).

[2]   CPLR 305(a).

[3]   CPLR 320(a), 3012(c).

rendered as to all parties, the improper party can be dropped at that point and the judgment preserved as to the others.[4]

Substantial delay causing prejudice will be considered by the court. If the litigation has proceeded to the point where X, a defendant, has appeared and answered, P has no absolute right to drop X and X may resist the attempt, especially if P could sue X all over again later. P's endeavor to "drop" X in that situation is just a "discontinuance" in disguise and will be treated as such.[5] This means that the court need not permit it if P has any ulterior motive, e.g., if P doesn't like the way the case has been going and simply wants to start over.[6]

As previously discussed,[7] the ultimate remedy for nonjoinder of a necessary party is a dismissal, but dismissal is only a last resort. If the needed person is subject to jurisdiction, the court merely orders her joined; if she is not subject to jurisdiction, the court must negotiate the CPLR 1001(b) list to find some possible alternative because only the complete absence of alternatives justifies considering whether the absent person is indispensable (so as to dismiss the action if she is). Prior law had a futile "dual motion" procedure, in which on D's first motion the court would order P to try to serve X even if it was clear that X could not be served or otherwise brought within jurisdiction. Only after some time passed during which P was supposed to make that attempt could D then move for dismissal for X's nonjoinder. This requirement of two motions has been abandoned.[8] Dismissal can be ordered straight-away upon D's initial motion if X proves to be indispensable and if the CPLR 1001(b) list offers no alternative. The rub is that with a bit of imagination an alternative is likely to be found and a dismissal—at least an unconditional one—therefore avoided in just about all cases.

When S is in the position of a stakeholder with two claimants, C-1 and C-2, making conflicting claims against him, he can, as will be seen, interplead them.[9] If C-1 sues S, S can defensively interplead C-2.[10] If S can't get jurisdiction of C-2 in the latter situation, he would of course like to have the action dismissed for the nonjoinder of C-2. Pre-CPLR caselaw suggested that there can be no dismissal for nonjoinder in such a case.[11] Today, however, the devices of CPLR 1001(b) should be available to help the stakeholder so that he is not faced with the prospect of double liability if there is anything the court can do to avoid it, such as dismiss the action on the condition that C-1 submit to jurisdiction in a place where jurisdiction is available over C-2.[12] Occasionally, the courts have treated a situation that smacks of the interpleader problem as only a joinder question,[13] a flexibility that CPLR 1001(b) should encourage.

---

[4]   Kosiba v. City of Syracuse, 287 N.Y. 283, 39 N.E.2d 240 (1942).

[5]   In re Cowles' Will, 22 A.D.2d 365, 255 N.Y.S.2d 160 (1st Dep't 1965), aff'd, 17 N.Y.2d 567, 268 N.Y.S.2d 327, 215 N.E.2d 509 (1966); see CPLR 3217, § 297.

[6]   See Commentary C3217:12 on McKinney's CPLR 3217. Voluntary discontinuance is the subject of §§ 297 and 298.

[7]   See § 133.

[8]   See Blumenthal v. Allen, 46 Misc. 2d 688, 260 N.Y.S.2d 363 (Sup. Ct., New York County 1965).

[9]   CPLR 1006(a). See § 148.

[10]   CPLR 1006(b).

[11]   See Petrogradsky Mejdunarodny Kommerchesky Bank v. National City Bank of New York, 253 N.Y. 23, 170 N.E. 479 (1930).

[12]   See the examples in § 133.

[13]   See and compare Cohen v. Douglas L. Elliman & Co., 279 A.D. 161, 108 N.Y.S.2d 386 (1st Dep't 1951).

Before 1996, the plaintiff could not, after the action was commenced, alter the line-up of defendants without court leave. After the initial papers set the roster of defendants, the addition of a new defendant required permission of the court. A 1996 amendment of CPLR 1003 changed that. While a court order is still a permissible way to add a party, the joinder is also allowed by stipulation of all parties who have appeared in the action. If the plaintiff acts early in the case, moreover, not even a stipulation is required. Drawing on CPLR 3025(a), the statute that allows each party one amendment of its pleading as a matter of course (i.e., without leave or stipulation),[14] CPLR 1003 allows the plaintiff one opportunity to join an additional party as a matter of right as long as the plaintiff acts within any of three time periods:

— within 20 days after service of the original summons;

— at any time before the time for responding to the summons expires; or

— within 20 days after the service of a pleading responding to the summons.

If a party is improperly added outside the time frames in CPLR 1003, she had better raise a prompt objection, as the defect can be waived.[15]

Some questions can arise under this statute, especially when a party other than the plaintiff seeks to add parties, as on a counterclaim or cross-claim, or when several defendants named in the original summons were served at different times. The plaintiff is best off assuming that the time periods are measured from the earliest service, responding time, etc.,[16] but it has been held, to the plaintiff's advantage, that in multiple defendant cases the 20 days run from the service of the answer of the last defendant to serve one.[17]

A supplemental summons is used to join the new party.[18]

The time between the making of a motion to add X as a party and the entry of an order granting the motion is a period during which the statute of limitations is tolled,[19] but incidental questions arise here that should make the lawyer watchful.[20] Some lawyers prefer not to rely on the statute of limitations suspension applicable to the time during which a motion to add a party is pending, preferring instead to bring a separate action against the proposed new defendant and then just move to consolidate it with the pending one.[21] When the statute of limitations is on the scene, one can never label that a bad policy, whatever the extra dollars it may cost in filing and motion fees.

The motion should in any event include a proposed supplemental summons and amended complaint.

---

[14]   See § 236.

[15]   See § 65.

[16]   See the extended discussion in SPR 43:1.

[17]   Dynaire Corp. v. Germano, N.Y.L.J., Aug. 1, 1996, at 22, col.1 (Sup. Ct., New York County; Friedman, J.).

[18]   CPLR 305(a). The supplemental summons should be filed and then served on the new party. It has been held that no additional fee is required when a new party is added. Kheyfets v. El Amari, Inc., 231 A.D.2d 684, 647 N.Y.S.2d 982 (2d Dep't 1996) (SPR 50:4).

[19]   Perez v. Paramount Communications, Inc., 92 N.Y.2d 749, 686 N.Y.S.2d 342, 709 N.E.2d 83 (1999) (NYSLD No. 471).

[20]   See the discussion in SPR 77:2.

[21]   See § 49.

F. CLASS ACTIONS

Table of Sections

§ 139.   Class Actions, Background
§ 140.   Prerequisites to Class Action; the Old Law Reviewed
§ 141.   Prerequisites to Class Action; Present Law
§ 142.   Order Allowing Class Action
§ 143.   Notice of Class Action
§ 144.   Opting Out
§ 145.   "Fluid Recovery"
§ 146.   Defendant's Side as Class
§ 147.   Pervasive Court Discretion in Class Action; Settlement and Judgment

§ 139. Class Actions, Background

A unique remedy afforded by procedural law is the "class action," a device whereby a few persons get together and bring an action in behalf of themselves and an entire category or "class" of persons. The class is described as such but its other members, who may be numerous indeed, are not joined. The few who take the initiative and bring the action are called the representatives. The device can also operate on the defendant's side—this is less common—the plaintiff naming and joining only a few of the members of the class, but designating the whole class as a defendant.[1]

The class action is a major exception to the general rule of law that only those individually brought within the jurisdiction of the court can be bound by its judgment. When the class action is properly used, it operates as res judicata for or against all members of the class,[2] although the extent of this binding effect is "not precisely defined by judicial opinion."[3] The res judicata aspect accounts for much, but by no means all, of the judicial ambivalence manifested towards the class action over the years. The energetic antagonism of the would-be opponents of the class, often powerful corporate interests, contributes. One must also cite the fact that a class action involves the courts in a much more active managerial role than they are accustomed to in our adversary system, and some judges aren't very much turned on by that.

When it works, the class action permits into litigation the related claims of numerous persons, each with a stake too small to be worth litigating by itself, with the prospect, therefore, that without a device like the class action, they would refrain from suit and literally make the wrongdoer the beneficiary of the very massiveness of its own wrong. The class action is a spur to the vindication of rights that simple economics would otherwise deter.[4]

There are two key years in the development of the class action in New York. The first is 1849, a year after the original Field Code. By an 1849 amendment of that code,

---

[1]   See § 146.

[2]   Supreme Tribe of Ben Hur v. Cauble, 255 U.S. 356, 41 S. Ct. 338, 65 L. Ed. 673 (1921); Graham v. Board of Sup'rs, 25 A.D.2d 250, 269 N.Y.S.2d 477 (4th Dep't 1966). For the res judicata effect of federal class judgments, see Berry Petroleum Co. v. Adams and Peck, 518 F.2d 402, 411–13 (2d Cir. 1975).

[3]   Hansberry v. Lee, 311 U.S. 32, 41, 61 S. Ct. 115, 118, 85 L. Ed. 22, 132 A.L.R. 741 (1940).

[4]   See Weinstein, *Revision of Procedure: Some Problems in Class Actions*, 9 Buff. L. Rev. 433, 435 (1960).

the class action took the form it was to have for well over a century.[5] It kept that form, even becoming a national model, right through the CPLR of 1963, where it was carried forth as CPLR 1005. Subdivisions (b) and (c) of CPLR 1005 were traceable to then-recent Judicial Council recommendations;[6] subdivision (a) was merely a restatement of prior law,[7] and prior law meant the Field Code provision.[8]

The second historic year for the class action in New York was 1975, when the ferment of the previous decade, whose prime agent was Rule 23 of the Federal Rules of Civil Procedure and the great activity spawned around it, finally distilled some new spirits in New York. In 1975, CPLR 1005 was repealed and a new Article 9 enacted, consisting of CPLR 901–909. The new article, explored in ensuing sections, is an enlightened and powerful one, in some respects more ambitious than Federal Rule 23, on which it was largely but not entirely based. Article 9 will be easier to negotiate if at least its immediate background is looked at first.

The amended Federal Rule 23, giving the class action the active role it afterwards achieved in the federal courts, took effect in 1966. It quickly became the enthusiastic expedient for bringing into court some of the major substantive issues of the age,[9] involving, to cite just a few examples, the rights of African Americans,[10] migratory workers,[11] prisoners,[12] demonstrators,[13] and soldiers.[14] It also became an activist model for class action reform in other states. In those states, and in others in which no new statute was enacted, but the state's old one was more expansively construed, consumer rights found a new friend. California, for example, applied its old statute to sustain some imaginative consumer actions.[15]

But while these other states, either with new statutes or with a reconstruction of older ones, were forging new ground with the class action device, New York was marking time. Not yet replaced by Article 9, CPLR 1005 continued to be narrowly construed. The Court of Appeals would from time to time prod the legislature to replace the statute with a more modern one,[16] but the Court would not undertake through the construction route to break new ground itself. In Hall v. Coburn Corp.,[17] for example, a consumer action, the Court rejected use of the class action in an opinion that left no doubt that it regards

---

[5] The code provision was itself devised from preexisting chancery practice. See 1st Rep. Leg. Doc. No. 6(b), p.35 (1957).

[6] See 18th Jud. Council Rep. 217 (1952). The cited report is a major study of the class action by Professor Adolf Homburger.

[7] Civ. Prac. Act § 195 (repealed 1963).

[8] A different subdivision (a) proposed by the CPLR's draftsmen, containing the substance of the 1952 Judicial Council recommendation, see 1st Rep. Leg. Doc. No. 6b, p.34 (1957), was rejected and the Field Code provision restored in 1962 and carried forward. See 6th Rep. Leg. Doc. No. 8, p.153 (1962).

[9] See Meyer, *Social Utility of Class Action,* 42 Brook. L. Rev. 189 (1976).

[10] E.g., Cypress v. Newport News General and Nonsectarian Hospital Ass'n, 375 F.2d 648 (4th Cir. 1967) (en banc).

[11] E.g., Petersen v. Talisman Sugar Corp., 478 F.2d 73, 84 L.R.R.M. (BNA) 2061 (5th Cir. 1973).

[12] E.g., Wallace v. McDonald, 369 F. Supp. 180 (E.D.N.Y. 1973).

[13] E.g., Sullivan v. Murphy, 478 F.2d 938 (D.C. Cir. 1973).

[14] E.g., Committee for G. I. Rights v. Callaway, 370 F. Supp. 934 (D.D.C. 1974), rev'd on other grounds, 518 F.2d 466 (D.C. Cir. 1975).

[15] See, e.g., Daar v. Yellow Cab Co., 67 Cal. 2d 695, 63 Cal. Rptr. 724, 433 P.2d 732 (1967); Vasquez v. Superior Court, 4 Cal. 3d 800, 94 Cal. Rptr. 796, 484 P.2d 964 (1971); but see City of San Jose v. Superior Court, 12 Cal. 3d 447, 115 Cal. Rptr. 797, 525 P.2d 701 (1974).

[16] See Moore v. Metropolitan Life Ins. Co., 33 N.Y.2d 304, 352 N.Y.S.2d 433, 307 N.E.2d 554 (1973).

[17] Hall v. Coburn Corp. of America, 26 N.Y.2d 396, 311 N.Y.S.2d 281, 259 N.E.2d 720 (1970).

suits like this as an indirect procedural way of altering substantive rights, a legislative function the Court said it would not usurp.

The Court afterwards drew back at least a bit from that view. In Ray v. Marine Midland Grace Trust Co.,[18] it said that "there has been a continuing development and definition of the appropriate sphere of class actions," and indicated that it would be inappropriate to regard CPLR 1005 as intending to keep the class action static. This was as encouraging a suggestion of upcoming judicial relief in this area as had ever been tendered in New York, but it served more as a legislative spur than as a herald of future Court of Appeals action.

In 1975, just a year after the *Ray* case, Article 9 was enacted and CPLR 1005 laid to rest. It is just as well that the legislature acted. Had the Court of Appeals tried to extend the "continuing development" it spoke of in the *Ray* case, it would have been hard pressed to collate and reconcile the massive and conflicting caselaw handed down on the New York class action over the years, cases that Professor Adolf Homburger, long a champion of the class action, said "defy logical analysis" and lose sight of the purpose of the class action.[19]

The drive for an expanded New York class action accelerated when the U.S. Supreme Court curtailed the jurisdictional scope of the federal class action, thereby creating a gap which, were it to be filled at all, could be filled only by a generous state class action provision, which New York did not have. The federal curtailment had several causes.

The main one is that while Federal Rule 23's procedural authorization for a class action is generous, it may be used only when there is some basis for federal subject matter jurisdiction. Rule 23 regulates procedure only; it can't expand the subject matter jurisdiction of the federal courts,[20] authorization for which must be found in some federal statute. When a case invokes a statute conferring federal jurisdiction based on the cause of action arising under federal law—the popularly described "federal question jurisdiction"—there is no minimal monetary requirement[21] and the federal class action confronts no jurisdictional barrier on that account. But when the cause of action does not arise under federal law and the sole basis on which federal jurisdiction rests is the diversity of citizenship of the parties, there is a problem.

The diversity statute is 28 U.S.C. § 1332. It requires complete diversity: the citizenship of each plaintiff must differ from that of each defendant.[22] On the citizenship aspect, the Supreme Court has treated the class action generously: for diversity purposes, only the representatives' citizenship need differ from those of the other side; the citizenships of unjoined class members need not be considered.[23]

But § 1332 also has a monetary requirement; a case based on diversity must (at the present time) involve more than $75,000. On that aspect, the court has been less

---

[18]   Ray v. Marine Midland Grace Trust Co., 35 N.Y.2d 147, 151, 359 N.Y.S.2d 28, 31, 316 N.E.2d 320, 322 (1974).

[19]   18th Jud. Council Rep. 223–224 (1952).

[20]   See Fed. R. Civ. P. 82.

[21]   See 28 U.S.C.A. § 1331. It's more accurate to describe this as the "arising under" jurisdiction since there are many contexts in which a federal issue arises but in which the claim itself is not a federal one. See § 611.

[22]   Strawbridge v. Curtiss, 7 U.S. 267, 2 L. Ed. 435, 1806 WL 1213 (1806).

[23]   Supreme Tribe of Ben Hur v. Cauble, 255 U.S. 356, 41 S. Ct. 338, 65 L. Ed. 673 (1921).

generous. It held that the claim of each of the representatives must meet the monetary minimum independently; that the interests of the representatives can't be aggregated to reach it.[24]

Advocates of the class action then argued that if at least one or a few of the representatives can meet the monetary requirement individually, the claims of the others (including those of the members of the class) ought to be sustained under recognized federal doctrines of "pendent" or "ancillary" jurisdiction so as to permit the federal court to entertain the whole class suit. In Zahn v. International Paper Co.,[25] the Supreme Court rejected that alternative, too, thus severely limiting the federal class action in diversity cases—or at least those in which the class consists of numerous persons with relatively small individual money claims. People in that category, however, are supposed to be the class action's major beneficiaries.[26]

With the federal arena practically closed to the huge diversity of citizenship category for a substantial number of years, the class action would have to look to state hospitality. In New York, it did so in vain—until 1975. The New York problem before 1975 was that the class action was well received only when the relief sought was something like an injunction or a declaratory judgment. There, with one judgment, the court could satisfy the whole class and be done with the case. But when more was at stake, like the separate monetary interests of all of the members of the class, judicial hackles were up and the class action was out. Professor Homburger documents this in his 1971 study of the class action, a study done almost two decades after his earlier one[27] and from which emerges the new Article 9. He concludes that:

> in the absence of a limited fund or a substantive relationship of some sort among the members of the class, the New York courts [would] not countenance class actions for separate and distinct relief of individual members of the class even if the basic issues of law or fact around which the controversy [revolved were] common to all.[28]

The new Article 9 not only countenanced such class actions; it offered them a red carpet, or so its sponsors intended. The carpet did not prove as posh as planned, however. The judicial reception was mixed, as will be seen.

---

[24]   Snyder v. Harris, 394 U.S. 332, 89 S. Ct. 1053, 22 L. Ed. 2d 319 (1969).

[25]   Zahn v. International Paper Co., 414 U.S. 291, 94 S. Ct. 505, 38 L. Ed. 2d 511 (1973).

[26]   There was an on-going a dispute about whether the 1990 adoption of 28 U.S.C.A. § 1367, the statute on "supplemental" jurisdiction that codifies the federal caselaw doctrines of "pendent" and "ancillary" jurisdiction, was intended to overrule the *Zahn* case. The Supreme Court resolved the conflict in Exxon Mobil Corp. v. Allapattah Services, Inc., 545 U.S. 546, 125 S. Ct. 2611, 162 L. Ed. 2d 502 (2005) (when one party party satisfies the $75,000 jurisdictional threshold, it secures supplemental jurisdiction for additional plaintiffs). The Class Action Fairness Act of 2005 made many changes to the requirements for diversity jurisdiction in class actions and eased some of the difficult burdens placed on plaintiffs by Supreme Court caselaw. The Act is discussed in section 630 (Practitioner's Edition).

[27]   The earlier one is the 1952 study for the Judicial Council, cited in note 19 above.

[28]   Homburger, *State Class Actions and the Federal Rule,* 17th Jud. Conf. Rep. 242, 250 (1972). The study is republished in that report with the permission of the Columbia Law Review, where it first appeared in 71 Col. L. Rev. 609, 619 (1971). See also Weinstein, *Revision of Procedure: Some Problems in Class Actions,* 9 Buff. L. Rev. 433 (1960). The Homburger and Weinstein articles are good bibliographical starting points for the student who would read more deeply on the class action. So is the advisory committee note on Fed. R. Civ. P. 23 (which may be found in the 28 U.S.C.A. volume covering that rule). Another series of general lessons on the class action and some of its difficulties may be found in the majority and dissenting opinions in Eisen v. Carlisle and Jacquelin, 417 U.S. 156, 94 S. Ct. 2140, 40 L. Ed. 2d 732 (1974).

§ 140.   Prerequisites to Class Action; the Old Law Reviewed

The old New York criterion for the class action, the one embodied in subdivision (a) of the repealed CPLR 1005 (which had been carried over with little change from the Field Code amendment of 1849), read as follows:

> Where the question is one of a common or general interest of many persons or where the persons who might be made parties are very numerous and it may be impracticable to bring them all before the court, one or more may sue or defend for the benefit of all.

The number that would satisfy as "many persons" or as "very numerous" was decided on a case-by-case basis.[1] Most of the attention of the cases was directed at what would satisfy as "a common or general interest." The straitjacket that the class action found itself in was woven of the courts' insistence that the interests of the class members be so uniform that each could be said to desire the same relief, or in any event a substantial part of it. In Brenner v. Title Guarantee & Trust Co.,[2] for example, D sold shares in a bond secured by a mortgage. Many bought. Alleging that the sales were induced by fraudulent representations, three buyers sued in behalf of all to recover the purchase prices. The Court would not allow it in class form, but did allow it as an ordinary action.[3] Although there were common issues, the Court found that they were not common interests. The fact that each of the buyers had a separate and distinct cause of action was not by itself the deterrent because that's often the case with class actions. The major rejecting factor in *Brenner* was that it could not be said that each of the buyers wanted the same relief. Some might want back the purchase price, others might prefer a formal rescission in equity, still others a tort action for fraud damages. There might even be a group not deeming themselves defrauded at all, and who, aware of the facts, would have wished to preserve the transaction. Under the criteria applicable under CPLR Article 9 today, a case like *Brenner* ought to pass the class action test without difficulty.

Brenner is prototypical of where class status would be denied under prior law: the case in which the court would have to award money judgments in different sums to a large number of people. While that wasn't an absolute deterrent,[4] it was almost so. If the money claims could be satisfied only out of a limited fund, class action status was more generously awarded, such as where the plaintiffs were looking to the bond of a surety company to make good on losses caused by a defalcation.[5] On close examination, one might even find cases in which class form was permitted for money claims not limited to a fund,[6] but in context, these could almost be called accidents. With the exception of the "fund" cases, the judicial restriction of class form to where only injunctive or declaratory relief was sought was carried virtually to the point of exclusiveness, and that was no gift at all to the "class action" concept. There was little more for the court to do in that kind

---

[1]   See pp. 226–229 of the Homburger study in the 18th Jud. Council Rep. (1952).

[2]   Brenner v. Title Guarantee & Trust Co., 276 N.Y. 230, 11 N.E.2d 890, 114 A.L.R. 1010 (1937).

[3]   Actual joinder is permitted in a case like this because the claims arise out of a related series of transactions and involve common questions. CPLR 1002(a). Akely v. Kinnicutt, 238 N.Y. 466, 144 N.E. 682 (1924), is an example. See § 134. Actual joinder should not be confused with class form, in which the injured persons are represented rather than joined.

[4]   See, e.g., Lichtyger v. Franchard Corp., 18 N.Y.2d 528, 277 N.Y.S.2d 377, 223 N.E.2d 869 (1966).

[5]   See Guffanti v. National Surety Co., 196 N.Y. 452, 90 N.E. 174 (1909).

[6]   See, e.g., Case v. Indian Motocycle Co., 300 N.Y. 513, 89 N.E.2d 246 (1949).

of case than in an ordinary action. The presence of the "class" was reduced to a mere esthetic formality. The final judgment would just enjoin or declare, and as far as time and trouble were concerned, it was the same to the court whether the injunction or declaration was at the behest of a single plaintiff or a mob.

Kovarsky v. Brooklyn Union Gas Co.[7] is a good illustration. There the Court allowed the class action for a declaration that a certain service charge by a public utility was unlawful, and an injunction restraining its collection in the future, but the Court would not order an accounting, which would have led to a huge number of individual money judgments, in nominal sums, returning prior charges. Whether the new class action provision will invite new remedies in a situation like that, such as by using what has become known as the "fluid recovery,"[8] still lacks definitive judicial determination.

This almost total barrier to the use of class actions for money was legislatively removed with the adoption of CPLR Article 9 in 1975. A few of the old anti-money cases will be reexamined below to see how they should fare today under the new article.

§ 141. Prerequisites to Class Action; Present Law

Subdivision (a) of CPLR 901 sets forth the basic conditions for a class action. It says that "[o]ne or more members of a class may sue or be sued as representative parties on behalf of all if:

1. the class is so numerous that joinder of all members, whether otherwise required or permitted, is impracticable;

2. there are questions of law or fact common to the class which predominate over any questions affecting only individual members;

3. the claims or defenses of the representative parties are typical of the claims or defenses of the class;

4. the representative parties will fairly and adequately protect the interests of the class; and

5. a class action is superior to other available methods for the fair and efficient adjudication of the controversy."

The drafters believe this formulation to be more uniform than the federal rule, which they found "overlapping and more complex."[1] The first four items have counterparts in subdivision (a) of Federal Rule 23. The requirements of paragraph 2, about common questions predominating, and paragraph 5, about the class action being superior to other available methods, have counterparts in Federal Rule 23(b)(3), but while they are stated only as alternative requirements in the federal provision, they are made uniform prerequisites for all class actions under CPLR 901(a).

Since CPLR 901(a) is intentionally phrased "in pragmatic and functional terms avoiding any reference to the abstract nature of the substantive rights involved,"[2] it contains no limitation based on the kind of substantive claim asserted. It has no stated preference for one kind of claim against another, presumably making itself available to

7   Kovarsky v. Brooklyn Union Gas Co., 279 N.Y. 304, 18 N.E.2d 287 (1938).

8   See § 145.

1   20th Jud. Conf. Rep. 206–207 (1975).

2   20th Jud. Conf. Rep. 206–207 (1975).

any as long as the CPLR 901(a) requirements are met. Nor is the 901(a) list exclusive. As will be seen in a later section discussing CPLR 902 and the procedure whereby the court by order determines whether the action may proceed in class form,[3] there are a number of other matters that must also be considered by the court before determining whether to allow a class action.

All of these requirements—the basics from CPLR 901(a) and the several additional from CPLR 902—must be examined individually in each case to see if the case passes muster in class form. Each case is sui generis,[4] but with the obvious support that Article 9 gives the class action, the courts' examination of the prerequisites in each individual case should at least be divested of its pre-1975 hostility. The New York caselaw on Article 9 continues to develop, and the lawyer also has the innumerable cases on Federal Rule 23 to turn to for ideas and guidance,[5] but given the highly individual nature of each case requesting class form, the emanations of the cases offer only general aid.

While it is more usual for a handful of representatives to get together for the suit, even one alone can bring it. So provides CPLR 901(a), in common with its federal counterpart in Rule 23(a). The caselaw condones a single representative if the representative is a good one. The court is not concerned so much with the number of representatives as with the quality of their lawyers.[6] Because of the high degree of judicial management required in a class action, and the great numbers affected by the result, the court is especially sensitive to assure quality representation. If one person brings the action, but with a lawyer of repute and ability, the court will be more content than if several sue with a staff of lawyers about whom the court has doubts. These doubts are seldom expressed, to be sure, but they result in more intense judicial scrutiny of the proceedings.

When several attorneys are on the scene to represent the class, and come from different firms, there may occasionally arise some dispute as to who will control the litigation on the class's side (subject, of course, to judicial oversight). This can be resolved by the court on motion or sua sponte; the court can assign control of the case to lawyer X, but with instruction that she consult with lawyers Y and Z before taking designated steps. Application to the court can be made if agreement on a given point can't be achieved.

There is no set quantity that will make the membership so "numerous" under CPLR 901(a)(1) as to make actual joinder "impracticable." As under prior law, the number will vary from case to case. Even for such initial requisites, the court's discretion controls. The requirement must be weighed in context.

The class action is especially appropriate when a fraud, such as that contained in a stock prospectus, has harmed many.[7] It is also fitting in the kind of situation met in

---

[3] See § 142.

[4] Borden v. 400 East 55th Street Associates, L.P., 24 N.Y.3d 382, 998 N.Y.S.2d 729, 23 N.E.3d 997 (2014) (reviewing standards for class certification in CPLR 901(a) and concluding that the appellate division did not abuse its discretion by affirming the supreme court's grant of class certification).

[5] See, e.g., Huebner v. Caldwell & Cook, Inc., 139 Misc. 2d 288, 526 N.Y.S.2d 356 (Sup. Ct., Monroe County 1988).

[6] See, e.g., Hohmann v. Packard Instrument Co., 399 F.2d 711, 12 Fed. R. Serv. 2d 383 (7th Cir. 1968).

[7] See and compare Brenner v. Title Guarantee & Trust Co., 276 N.Y. 230, 11 N.E.2d 890, 114 A.L.R. 1010 (1937).

Kovarsky v. Brooklyn Union Gas Co.,[8] in which all the utility users in a large municipality were unlawfully charged for a certain service. In that case, the class device was sustained for injunctive and declaratory relief, but not for the return of the improperly collected money. Under CPLR 901(a), it should be sustainable for the money, too, whatever the logistics of getting the money back into proper hands.

No longer should one hear the frequent insistence of old caselaw that the class action is usable for money recoveries only when a limited fund is involved. Under CPLR 901(a), most of the non-"fund" cases in which prior law rejected the class action[9] should be overruled and the class action allowed. CPLR 901(a) should also, of course, continue to permit a class action in cases in which old CPLR 1005 did, and that means continued utility of the class weapon when an injunction or declaration is the principal aim, a conclusion buttressed by CPLR 904(a).[10]

The class need not have a common interest in all of the issues. CPLR 901(a)(2) makes this clear when it requires that common issues "predominate" rather than preempt. If it appears that there are several common issues, but one predominates for one part of the class and another for a different part, the class can be divided into "subclasses and each subclass treated as a class."[11] So, for example, if a defendant, in furtherance of a commercial scheme, issues two fraudulent documents (e.g., prospectuses), large numbers relying on each to their detriment, a class action need not be disallowed merely because two issues (the fraud with respect to each document) predominate. The court can order a severance, making separate class actions of the two groups, or merely keep the case, but with "subclass" treatment within it.

It is not of great moment that damages differ individually among the various members of the class, numerous though they be. In Vickers v. Home Federal Sav. and Loan Ass'n of East Rochester,[12] for example, allowing a class action under federal truth-in-lending provisions, the court held that the fact that the representatives seek damages in different amounts than the class members, or even a different category of remedy altogether, does not bar a class action or necessarily impair the representatives' capacity to act fairly for all. The court can allow class status for the purpose of trying the common issue and then, through various discretionary alternatives, set up a mechanism whereby each class member can individually prove his damages.[13] Indeed, there is explicit authority for a class action brought to try only a particular issue rather than all issues.[14]

So, for example, a class action can be brought to establish only the fraudulence of a document relied on by many. If the fraud is established, the many may then bring separate actions to test the individual elements of reliance and damages. In those later actions, the fraud issue will then get collateral estoppel effect and the class action will have served its purpose admirably.

---

[8]   Kovarsky v. Brooklyn Union Gas Co., 279 N.Y. 304, 18 N.E.2d 287 (1938), discussed in § 140.

[9]   E.g., Society Milion Athena v. National Bank of Greece, 281 N.Y. 282, 22 N.E.2d 374 (1939).

[10]   CPLR 904(a), discussed in § 143, dispenses with initial notice to the class when injunctive or declaratory relief is the main object of the action.

[11]   CPLR 906(2).

[12]   Vickers v. Home Federal Sav. and Loan Ass'n of East Rochester, 56 A.D.2d 62, 390 N.Y.S.2d 747 (4th Dep't 1977).

[13]   See, e.g., Nix v. Grand Lodge of Intern. Ass'n of Machinists and Aerospace Workers, 479 F.2d 382, 83 L.R.R.M. (BNA) 2486 (5th Cir. 1973).

[14]   CPLR 906(1).

Disputes about whether common issues predominate over individual issues often engender disagreement among the judges. Rosenfeld v. A. H. Robins Co., Inc.[15] illustrates. The action was brought in behalf of all women injured by an allegedly defective intrauterine device. Despite the numerousness of the class and the majority's concession that there were at least several issues in the case that would lend themselves to class treatment, the court rejected class form. Not only would damages be individual to each class member's case, stressed the majority, but causality and reliance (on the manufacturer's representations) would be individual as well. The dissent accented, instead, the common issues and notably the common opportunity to obtain disclosure, which in *Rosenfeld*, by the defendant's own concession, would involve some 100,000 documents—obviously beyond the economic ability of each class member to pursue on her own.

The *Rosenfeld* case illustrates how much of the class action's future depends on the attitude of the judges. The factors that must be considered before determining whether to permit an action in class form are so flexible that equally reasonable minds can flex them either way.

Another factor is whether the court finds the class action "superior" to other kinds of action, an element listed in CPLR 901(a)(5). The New York courts apparently don't find the class action superior when its main purpose is just to establish a legal principle of importance to many. They find adequate in that situation the doctrine of stare decisis: whether the plaintiffs are few or many, the courts postulate that the precedent set by the case on a general issue of law will be available statewide. The want of enthusiasm for the class action on this point is especially apparent when governmental obligations are involved, such as in an action to determine entitlement to public assistance.[16]

This coin has a flip side, however. Governmental obligations were involved in Beekman v. City of New York,[17] for example, where the court nevertheless sustained a class action in behalf of all New York City firemen denied terminal leave and vacation prior to a certain day. Although each member of the class was seeking individual damages—the factor that often turned the courts off, rather than on to a class action— separate suits by all of them were deemed virtually certain to follow if class form were denied. The court indicated that although the class was large, it was nevertheless "defined and limited," and hence, the action was more manageable than one in behalf of "indefinite numbers."

Perhaps a lesson for advocates of class form is that they will help their cause if they can convince the court that far from being an encumbrance, the class action will spare the court numerous separate actions; that the interest of each class member is sufficient to spur a separate action by each if the court refuses to allow them to proceed as a class.

When a case involves more than just a legal principle, in other words, manifesting as well that there are throngs out there who are up in arms about the wrong and will sue on their own if not allowed their day in court within the framework of the class action, the courts are less likely to reject the action by pointing to the stare decisis doctrine.

---

[15]   Rosenfeld v. A. H. Robins Co., Inc., 63 A.D.2d 11, 407 N.Y.S.2d 196 (2d Dep't 1978).

[16]   See, e.g., Gaillard v. Lavine, 51 A.D.2d 181, 380 N.Y.S.2d 7 (1st Dep't 1976).

[17]   Beekman v. City of New York, 65 A.D.2d 317, 411 N.Y.S.2d 620 (1st Dep't 1979).

In this connection, consider again the *Brenner* case discussed above and in the prior section. Under the old New York statute, *Brenner* refused class status to an action brought to recover the purchase price of shares in a mortgage-secured bond. Shouldn't class status now be allowed in a case like that under CPLR 901(a)? The action was based on fraud and the class device, since it would enable the fraud issue to be adjudicated in one instead of numerous actions, ought to be deemed "superior" to other methods to protect the class.[18] Any device that would allow one action to do a job that would otherwise have to be done by many should by definition be considered "superior."

Another factor is that were all the potential class members to bring separate actions, the common issue would permit consolidation of all of them[19] and the courts would be almost certain to grant such a consolidation. This is not to suggest that class status is permissible whenever consolidation could ensue if each class member were to bring separate suit. It is only to stress that as far as CPLR 901(a)(5) is concerned, New York does deem a single action a "superior" way to adjudicate multiple claims. To that extent, the analogy is compelling.

A probing self-examination into the old and to some degree continuing judicial resistance to the class action appears in the Second Department case of Friar v. Vanguard Holding Corp.[20] *Friar* sustained in class form an action in behalf of all persons who sold real property to buyers for whom defendant D was acting as mortgage lender. D allegedly forced the sellers to pay a certain tax at the closings, in violation of law. *Friar* is a convincing decision, and yet not unanimous. A First Department case subscribing to *Friar*'s more generous attitude toward the class action is Brandon v. Chefetz,[21] which allowed class status to numerous minority shareholders against two of the major ones for obtaining special breaks for themselves in a corporate take-over situation.[22]

The use of the class action in multiparty personal injury cases is discussed in the next section.[23]

An action to recover a statutory penalty is expressly barred from class form unless the statute imposing the penalty specifically says otherwise.[24] But this CPLR ban may not apply if the action is brought in federal court.[25] In Borden v. 400 East 55th Street Associates,[26] the Court of Appeals stressed that under the language of CPLR 901(b),

---

[18]   See, e.g., Dolgow v. Anderson, 43 F.R.D. 472, 11 Fed. R. Serv. 2d 565 (E.D.N.Y. 1968), rev'd on other grounds, 438 F.2d 825 (2d Cir. 1970).

[19]   CPLR 602(a).

[20]   Friar v. Vanguard Holding Corp., 78 A.D.2d 83, 434 N.Y.S.2d 698 (2d Dep't 1980). The case is the subject of a more extended treatment in NYSLD No. 255.

[21]   Brandon v. Chefetz, 106 A.D.2d 162, 485 N.Y.S.2d 55 (1st Dep't 1985).

[22]   The court sustained class status only in respect of New York shareholders, however. The power to exercise jurisdiction over nonresident class members was unclear at the time, but was shortly afterwards recognized by the U.S. Supreme Court. See the *Phillips* case discussed in § 144.

[23]   See § 142.

[24]   CPLR 901(b). This exception was added by the legislature; it was not part of the Judicial Conference draft. See 20th Jud. Conf. Rep. 206–207 (1975). Penalty provisions under federal truth-in-lending statutes were held to authorize a class action in terms satisfactory to CPLR 901(b), and such a class action was sustained in Vickers v. Home Federal Sav. and Loan Ass'n of East Rochester, 56 A.D.2d 62, 390 N.Y.S.2d 747 (4th Dep't 1977). The sustaining may have avoided some constitutional issues under the Supremacy Clause. See Homburger, *The 1975 New York Judicial Conference Package: Class Actions and Comparative Negligence,* 25 Buff. L. Rev. 415, 423–24 (1976).

[25]   See Shady Grove Orthopedic Associates, P.A. v. Allstate Ins. Co., 559 U.S. 393, 130 S. Ct. 1431, 176 L. Ed. 2d 311 (2010); § 630 (Practitioner's Edition).

[26]   *Borden,* 24 N.Y.3d at 393, 998 N.Y.S.2d at 733, 23 N.E.3d at 1001.

which imposes this restriction, "it is not dispositive that a statute imposes a penalty so long as the [class] action brought pursuant to that statute does not seek to recover the penalty." Therefore, the *Borden* Court held that a class action is permissible to seek recovery of actual damages sustained as a result of rent overcharges despite the fact that the Rent Stabilization Law imposes treble damages on the finding of a willful violation of its provisions. In other words, "if a statute imposes a nonmandatory penalty, the plaintiffs may waive the penalty to bring the claim as a class action."

§ 142. Order Allowing Class Action

No court permission is needed in advance of a class action. The representatives simply bring it. But CPLR 902 requires that the plaintiffs, shortly after the action is begun, move for an order permitting maintenance of the class action, thus promptly affording the court in each class action an opportunity to determine whether the requirements of class form have been met. The time within which the plaintiff must make this motion is 60 days after the defendant's answering time has expired. This policy of requiring early court attention to class-action appropriateness is borrowed from the federal class action rule, but while the federal rule requires only that the adjudication be made "at an early practicable time,"[1] the New York provision imposes a stated time limit and thus offers greater assurance of prompt disposition of the matter.[2]

In addition to determining whether the stated requirements of CPLR 901 are met, the court on the motion must also consider the factors listed in CPLR 902. Five are listed:

1. the interest of members of the class in individually controlling the prosecution or defense of separate actions;

2. the impracticability or inefficiency of prosecuting or defending separate actions;

3. the extent and nature of any litigation concerning the controversy already commenced by or against members of the class;

4. the desirability or undesirability of concentrating the litigation of the claim in the particular forum;[3] and

5. the difficulties likely to be encountered in the management of a class action.[4]

The list is illustrative, not exhaustive. Any other factors the court deems relevant may also be considered. The apparent merits of the class claim may be looked at, for example.[5]

The listed factors are to be considered in all class actions, and not, as under the federal rule, in only some of them.[6] The second listed item, about the impracticability of

---

[1] Fed. R. Civ. P. 23(c)(1).

[2] The period may, however, be extended for good cause. See Argento v. Wal-Mart Stores, Inc., 66 A.D.3d 930, 888 N.Y.S.2d 117 (2d Dep't 2009).

[3] See Bloom v. Cunard Line, Ltd., 76 A.D.2d 237, 430 N.Y.S.2d 607 (1st Dep't 1980). This is just a kind of forum non conveniens rule specifically acknowledged for the class action.

[4] See Homburger, *State Class Actions and the Federal Rule*, 71 Colum. L. Rev. 609, 652 (1971).

[5] See 20th Jud. Conf. Rep. 607–608 (1975).

[6] Compare paragraph (3) of Fed. R. Civ. P. 23(b), which is an alternative to the Rule's paragraphs (1) and (2).

separate actions,[7] has no counterpart in the federal rule (although it is of course a matter the federal judge can and often does consider); the other four items on the list do have federal counterparts.[8]

If the court, after considering all of the required CPLR 902 factors, finds favorably on them, and finds all of the CPLR 901 prerequisites satisfied as well, it will make an order permitting the class action. If it does, the order must describe the class.[9] The order can be conditional, and it may be amended, either on motion of a party or on the court's own motion, at any time before the case is decided on the merits.[10]

And so it appears that CPLR 902 is every bit as much of a key section as CPLR 901.

The matters to be considered by the court in deciding whether class form is warranted, which are essentially discretionary, can be used to implement or frustrate the broad purposes of the legislature, depending entirely on the attitude of the judges. A given factor in a case can be viewed in a negative light and that illumination can easily be allowed to obscure positive beams emanating from other factors, thus defeating the class action at the threshold.

Until the various factors are put into some sequence of stress and dominance, individual cases may be uncomfortably dependent on the predilections of individual judges. Lawyers considering or involved in class actions should therefore keep a running check on caselaw, even on a departmental basis. While the ultimate destiny of the class action in New York under the current Article 9 would seem to depend on the Court of Appeals, the facts of the daily life of the class action indicate that the Court of Appeals may have little occasion to address the subject. As a practical matter, therefore, the appellate divisions thus end up as the custodians of the class action for the following reasons:

The Court of Appeals is a law court. It doesn't review exercises of discretion unless they rise to the level of an "abuse," which not many do. Since "[c]lass action certification is a question vested in the sound discretion of the court,"[11] and for exercises of discretion, the appellate division is in effect the court of last resort, it may be the fate of the class action to run hot and cold depending on the temperature in the local appellate division.[12] The Court of Appeals may be called on from time to time to answer a question of law connected with the class action, but the big question in almost every attempted class action is whether the particular action qualifies for class status. Since the Court of Appeals ends up with little role on that point, it turns out to have little role in the class action in New York. When it has before it a case in which class status was acted on below—one way or the other—and there was basis for going either way, the Court of Appeals sees little option but to affirm.

---

[7]   This is an important factor in small claimants' consumer actions. See Homburger, *State Class Actions and the Federal Rule*, 71 Colum. L. Rev. at 637.

[8]   See subparagraphs A to D in Fed. R. Civ. P. 23(b)(3), and compare (b)(1).

[9]   CPLR 903.

[10]   CPLR 902.

[11]   Askey v. Occidental Chemical Corp., 102 A.D.2d 130, 137, 477 N.Y.S.2d 242, 247 (4th Dep't 1984).

[12]   See Weinberg v. Hertz Corp., 116 A.D.2d 1, 499 N.Y.S.2d 693 (1st Dep't 1986), aff'd, 69 N.Y.2d 979, 516 N.Y.S.2d 652, 509 N.E.2d 347 (1987), and the year-end review of the class action by Thomas A. Dickerson in the New York Law Journal of December 30, 1987.

A good example is Small v. Lorillard Tobacco Co., Inc.,[13] a composite of five attempted class actions, one against each of the major tobacco companies. The trial court eliminated some issues and then certified the class. The appellate division then reviewed all the Article 9 factors, disagreed with the trial court, and decertified. On further appeal, the Court of Appeals reviewed each discretionary item considered below. On none did the Court suggest what it would have done if the discretion to be exercised was its own; it merely noted how the appellate division had exercised its discretion on each issue, found that there was room on the record to support each such exercise, and affirmed.

Another example is Harris v. Shearson Hayden Stone, Inc.,[14] a case seemingly tailor-made for class relief, but rejected for it by a closely divided (3–2) appellate division. Here was an intriguing battle between the class action of Article 9 on one side and the Article 75 requirement of arbitration on the other. A major brokerage house "floated" remittances to commodities customers, i.e., drew checks on distant banks to prolong collection (a practice also known as "kiting"), which in this case prolonged the broker's retention of the high interest the money was earning in the meantime. Aggrieved customers brought a class action against the practice. Class status was rejected because all of the customers had signed contracts containing arbitration agreements. Having consented to arbitration, they were held to have waived the right to sue in court and with it the right to use the class action.[15]

A definitive answer is still awaited to the question of whether the class action will be allowed in multiparty accident cases, at least for the liability issue: will it be allowed in the massive plane or train tragedy in which numerous persons are injured or killed? The Federal Advisory Committee, thorough and even committed though they may have been in other regards, hedged on this one. They said that the "mass accident . . . is ordinarily not appropriate for a class action," citing the prospect of varying defenses "affecting the individuals in different ways."[16] But such a delicate approach to the "mass accident," at least on the ground cited, may be unwarranted. What part, after all, do "defenses" play when 100 people on a plane or 200 on a train were reading magazines or sleeping or conversing when they were suddenly subjected to injury or death? Can comparative negligence be expected to play any realistic role at all in these occurrences?

Two important factors suggest that the question of using the class action in mass accident cases may have been tabled, indefinitely if not permanently. Expanded application of the collateral estoppel (issue preclusion) doctrine[17] is one contributing factor. The New York Court of Appeals held in 1984, almost a decade after the 1975

---

[13] Small v. Lorillard Tobacco Co., Inc., 94 N.Y.2d 43, 698 N.Y.S.2d 615, 720 N.E.2d 892 (1999) (NYSLD No. 479).

[14] Harris v. Shearson Hayden Stone, Inc., 82 A.D.2d 87, 441 N.Y.S.2d 70 (1st Dep't 1981), aff'd, 56 N.Y.2d 627, 450 N.Y.S.2d 482, 435 N.E.2d 1097 (1982).

[15] This arbitration-versus-class-action issue often arises where the contract with the arbitration clause also purports to waive the use of the class action. In AT&T Mobility LLC v. Concepcion, 563 U.S. 333, 336, 131 S. Ct. 1740, 1744, 179 L. Ed. 2d 742 (2011), the contract provided for arbitration of all disputes between cell phone customers and the carrier, but required that claims be brought in the parties' "individual capacity, and not as a plaintiff or class member in any purported class or representative proceeding." The lower courts found the class arbitration waivers in consumer contracts unconscionable under California law and refused to order arbitration. The Supreme Court reversed and ordered arbitration, holding that the Federal Arbitration Act (FAA) preempted California law. Concepcion, 563 U.S. at 351, 131 S.Ct. at 1752. In sum, the FAA, when it applies to the contract at issue, prohibits states from conditioning the enforceability of certain arbitration agreements on the availability of class-wide arbitration procedures. See §§ 587, 607.

[16] See Advisory Committee notes to amended (1966) Fed. R. Civ. P. 23 in 28 U.S.C.A.

[17] The doctrine is treated in §§ 457 et seq.

enactment of Article 9, that once one victim has successfully sued a tortfeasor, other victims of the same tort may be allowed, in their individual lawsuits, a free estoppel ride on the liability finding.[18] That accomplishes in many instances what the class action might otherwise have to be depended on for. It enables a nonparty to make use of the doctrine against one who was a party to the first action and thus fully heard on the issue. The doctrine does not work *against* the nonparty, however,[19] so that a victory by the tortfeasor against the plaintiff in one action could not be invoked against a different plaintiff in another. This means that the estoppel doctrine is only a partial resolution.

The second factor, and perhaps a fuller answer to the question of using the class action in the mass tort case, is the opting-out procedure, treated below.[20] The first factor listed for consideration in CPLR 902 is "the interest of members of the class in individually controlling the prosecution . . . of separate actions." In personal injury actions, plaintiffs usually prefer to retain their own lawyers, choose their own venues (those reputed to offer the highest verdicts), and make their own settlements. The potential recovery in most personal injury suits makes such an independent prosecution economically worthwhile. Hence an attempt to use a class action for victims of a mass tort would probably result in many if not most of them invoking the "opting out" procedure, frustrating the class suit by that route.

Perhaps the class action would have better sailing, therefore, in a mass accident case in which individual damages to most victims are relatively modest. It may then be economical for them to have the liability issue presented in one trial, damages then to be resolved individually, either as follow-ups in the same (the class) action or in separate actions. The point is that at least in some mass accident cases, the class action can be of value. The door should be left open to it.

The venue rules as they apply in class actions are reviewed in Kidd v. Delta Funding Corp.,[21] which holds that venue in a class action must be based on the residence of an actual party—i.e., one of the representatives, not a mere class member. If a motion affecting venue is timely brought, it should be determined before an application is made to certify the class.[22]

§ 143. Notice of Class Action

There was no requirement under prior law that the members of the class be notified of an action brought in their behalf. There still is none in a class action "brought primarily for injunctive or declaratory relief," although the court may in its discretion require notice if it's deemed necessary to protect the class and the cost of the notice will not be too burdensome.[1] But in any other kind of class action today, including the one that seeks money, "reasonable notice of the commencement of a class action shall be given to the class in such manner as the court directs."[2] The giving of notice is thus

---

[18] See Koch v. Consolidated Edison Co. of New York, Inc., 62 N.Y.2d 548, 479 N.Y.S.2d 163, 468 N.E.2d 1 (1984), discussed in § 467, and the lead note in NYSLD No. 309.

[19] See § 458.

[20] See § 144.

[21] Kidd v. Delta Funding Corp., 270 A.D.2d 81, 704 N.Y.S.2d 66 (1st Dep't 2000).

[22] See Mazzocki v. State Farm Fire & Cas. Co., 170 Misc. 2d 70, 649 N.Y.S.2d 656 (Sup. Ct., New York County 1996).

[1] CPLR 904(a).

[2] CPLR 904(b).

mandatory in other than injunctive and declaratory cases, but its method has been left to the discretion of the court. There is therefore room to allow in a given case notice by publication or by some other collective method,[3] thus saving the great expense that can attend individual notification, but the method chosen will of course have to be tailored to the facts. The court can authorize publication, for example, while also ordering actual notice, by mail or otherwise, to designated class members or groups of them, or to a certain number of class members selected at random or as the court directs. In determining the method of notice, CPLR 904(c) requires the court to consider:

1. the cost of giving notice by the various possible methods;[4]

2. the resources of the parties; and

3. the stake of each class member and the likelihood that significant numbers of them might wish to be excluded from the class, and thus not be bound by the judgment.[5]

The court can assist itself in determining this likelihood (under the third item) by having notice sent to a random sampling of the class.[6]

The content of the notice must be approved by the court,[7] and this is so whether the requirement of notice is a discretionary matter, as in an injunction or declaratory judgment action, or mandatory, as in a money action.[8] The plaintiff can seek the court's directions and approval by motion, which should be on notice to adverse parties. If need be, the motion can be brought on by order to show cause in which the court can determine what notice the adverse parties shall be given. It will be recalled that under CPLR 902, the plaintiff must move for an order allowing the action in class form. Perhaps that requirement can be combined with the CPLR 904 requirements in regard to notifying the class and having the court approve the notice's content. It would seem permissible for the plaintiff, by a single motion, to seek (1) court leave to prosecute the action in class form as required by 902, (2) (if leave is granted) court determination of the method by which the class is to be notified of the action's pendency, and (3) court approval of the contents of the notice.

The CPLR is specific about the expense of notification and who must bear it, thus avoiding the dispute that arose in this regard under the federal rule.[9] Unless the court says otherwise, the plaintiff must bear the expense of notifying the class. That can be costly and sometimes prohibitively costly if individual notice is required, as opposed to

---

[3] Cf. Fed. R. Civ. P. 23(c)(2) and Eisen v. Carlisle and Jacquelin, 417 U.S. 156, 94 S. Ct. 2140, 40 L. Ed. 2d 732 (1974).

[4] In this connection the Judicial Conference called attention to the situation in which the class consists of corporate shareholders and the corporation is also a party, where the notification can be as competent and inexpensive as merely ordering the corporation to enclose the notice in its next mailing to shareholders. See 20th Jud. Conf. Rep. 209 (1975), citing Dolgow v. Anderson, 43 F.R.D. 472, 500, 11 Fed. Serv. 2d 565 (E.D.N.Y. 1968), rev'd on other grounds, 438 F.2d 825 (2d Cir. 1970).

[5] This list is the formulation of the legislature. The Judicial Conference proposal was more general, but did mention several of these considerations in its notes. See 20th Jud. Conf. Rep. 208–209 (1975).

[6] CPLR 904(c)(III).

[7] CPLR 904(c).

[8] An example of a notice approved by the court in a class action seeking money damages appears as an appendix to Vickers v. Home Federal Sav. and Loan Ass'n of East Rochester, 56 A.D.2d 62, 390 N.Y.S.2d 747 (4th Dep't 1977).

[9] See *Eisen*, 417 U.S. at 172, 94 S. Ct. at 2150. *Eisen* interprets only Fed. R. Civ. P. 23, however, not the Constitution, thus leaving it open to the states to fashion their own procedures.

the collective notice offered by something like publication. But the court is empowered, "if justice requires," to make the defendant pay all or part of the notice expense. The court can investigate the potential merits of the case to help its determination. The court may even conduct a preliminary hearing to determine how notice costs should be apportioned.[10]

The flexibility built into these steps under Article 9 are a contrast with the strictures pronounced by the U.S. Supreme Court for the federal class action in its 1974 *Eisen* case,[11] where it construed Federal Rule 23 to require individual notice to each member of the class and to require the plaintiff's (the class's) side to bear the expense of it without the defendant's being made to chip in. The contrasting New York pliancy is illustrated in Eugenia J. Fiala v. Metropolitan Life Insurance,[12] where the court came up with a CPLR prescription that allowed collective notice, ordered the defendant to share the cost of the notice, and required inclusion of the notice in mass mailings sent out by the defendant.

A hearing on any of the ingredients that go into a class action certification, including a preliminary look at the merits, is sometimes called a "mini-hearing."[13]

§ 144. Opting Out

CPLR 903 provides in part that "[w]hen appropriate the court may limit the class to those members who do not request exclusion from the class within a specified time after notice." This contemplates that the notice served on the class members, advising them of the pendency of the action and its purpose, will also offer each member an opportunity to notify the court that he or she does not wish to be part of the class or subject to the judgment. This procedure is popularly known as "opting out." When and how it's used is left to the discretion of the court under CPLR 903.[1] Under the federal counterpart, on which it's modeled, the opting out offering is mandatory in certain cases.[2] As contemplated by the Judicial Conference, the opting out procedure under the New York statute would be used:

    i.   when representation of the entire class is not needed for a just disposition of the controversy;

    ii.   when the class members have a significant practical interest in individually controlling the litigation; and

    iii.   when individual notice is feasible without imposing a prohibitive economic or administrative burden on the parties.[3]

---

[10]   CPLR 904(d).

[11]   *Eisen*, 417 U.S. at 172, 94 S.Ct. at 2150.

[12]   Eugenia J. Fiala v. Metropolitan Life Insurance, 2006 WL 4682149 (N.Y. Sup 2006), aff'd as modified, 52 A.D.3d 251, 859 N.Y.S.2d 426 (1st Dep't 2008).

[13]   See Chimenti v. American Express Co., 97 A.D.2d 351, 467 N.Y.S.2d 357 (1st Dep't 1983).

[1]   The opting-out procedure was ordered in Vickers v. Home Federal Sav. and Loan Ass'n of East Rochester, 56 A.D.2d 62, 390 N.Y.S.2d 747 (4th Dep't 1977), and a copy of the notice implementing it, called an "Exclusion Request," is appended to the opinion.

[2]   See Fed. R. Civ. P. 23(c)(3).

[3]   20th Jud. Conf. Rep. 208 (1975). A special and more specific opting-out provision, contained in Gen. Bus. Law § 342–b, applies to governmental entities being represented as a "class" by the attorney general suing for damages caused by monopolistic practices (see Gen. Bus. Law § 340) or violations of the federal antitrust laws.

With the opting out procedure available, the New York courts can be less hesitant about allowing a class action in personal injury cases. As mentioned two sections earlier, a factor that can be cited against the use of class form in personal injury cases is that the plaintiffs, for tactical reasons, often want individual control of their own cases.[4] Those who do can opt out; class form can still be retained for the rest and still result in a substantial benefit to the class (and to the court's calendars).

Item (iii) on the list concerns notice of the action's pendency. Since notice is not required when the relief sought is injunctive or declaratory (although it remains a court option in those cases),[5] the fact that the opting out procedure is initiated in the notice means that its primary use would be in other categories of class action, categories in which notice is mandatory.[6] Even when notice is mandatory, however, the method of notice is still left to judicial discretion. Since the opting out procedure confers an important right, it would be inappropriate to offer it in a collective form of notice, such as by publication or by posting in public places. It's therefore contemplated that the court will order opting out steps mainly when it has also decided to require individual notice and that the court will order individual notice only when the "economic or administrative burden" of giving such notice is not "prohibitive."[7] Whether it is depends in large measure on the numbers involved. If the class has many thousands, the burdens are real. In one case, for example, in which the class was estimated at 10 million, the court formulated an opting out notice that allowed collective notification, ordered the defendant to share the cost of it, and required the notice-giving paper to be included in mass mailings sent out by the defendant.[8]

In actions in which the class members would have different remedies to choose from—as opposed to those in which each class member would clearly be seeking money and nothing else—and in which the circumstances indicate that there might be conflict among them as to the remedy pursued, the effectiveness of the opting out procedure may be decisive of whether the court will allow a class action at all. Whether opting out is workable may also depend on the feasibility of identifying the class members. Gaynor v. Rockefeller,[9] for example, was an action under the old class action statute by African Americans alleged to have been denied admission to certain unions. They sued for declaratory and injunctive relief. Pointing out that some of the class members might prefer a complaint to the Human Rights Commission or an action for money damages, and that the claim of each class member would turn on its own particular facts, the Court disallowed class form. It said:

> a class action may not be maintained where the wrongs asserted are individual to the different persons involved and each of the persons aggrieved "may

---

[4]   This is one of the factors to be considered in determining whether to allow a class action. CPLR 902(1); see § 142.

[5]   CPLR 904(a).

[6]   CPLR 904(b).

[7]   20th Jud. Conf. Rep. 208 (1975).

[8]   See Eugenia J. Fiala v. Metropolitan Life Insurance., 2006 WL 4682149 (N.Y. Sup 2006), aff'd as modified, 52 A.D.3d 251, 859 N.Y.S.2d 426 (1st Dep't 2008).

[9]   Gaynor v. Rockefeller, 15 N.Y.2d 120, 256 N.Y.S.2d 584, 204 N.E.2d 627 (1965).

determine for himself the remedy which he will seek" and may be subject to "a defense not available against others."[10]

Rejection of class form for actions meeting that description is no longer a categorical mandate but is still a prospect on a case-by-case basis after the court's analysis of all the required factors that go into a class certification. Using the *Gaynor* facts, for example, one question would be whether the individual class members are identifiable. If they are, an opting out notice can be sent to each of them and each can determine whether he wants the collective remedy proposed (in which case he can stay in) or some other remedy (in which case he can opt out and follow his own course). The appropriateness of different remedies, the relevance of different options, and the existence of individual defenses, are of course factors that must be initially considered before class form is sustained under the basic requirements of CPLR 901, but the availability of the opting out procedure is germane to the court's thinking when it negotiates those factors.

If a given member does opt out, she is excluded from the class and a judgment unfavorable to the class does not bind her. But what if the judgment is in favor of the class? There is some dispute about whether one who opted out may make collateral estoppel use of the judgment in an individual action later.[11] Because a class action carries res judicata consequences only when the several requirements applicable to it have been faithfully met, it has even been urged that a class member who has not opted out (although offered the opportunity) may still seek to be relieved of the effects of the judgment by showing that the prerequisites of a class action were not met.[12]

There should also be room within the structure of Article 9 to use a kind of "opting in" procedure. When the class is very numerous, for example, and all or most of its members can't be identified and there is a likelihood of diversity in their choice of remedies even if they could be, the court should be able to order a collective notice, such as by publication in an appropriate periodical, in which the proposed class relief is stated and the members of the class are offered the right to opt in. Under such a procedure, only those specifically responding would be included in the class and permitted to share its fruits. That would not preclude separate actions by those not responding, but it could substantially curtail the total number of actions by enabling the class action to dispose of many, if not all, of the potential claims.

When the remedy sought is one that redounds to the whole class automatically, opting out will seldom, if ever, be appropriate. Here again the injunctive and declaratory actions are the examples—the same ones that found welcome even under prior law. *Greer v. Smith*[13] is typical. The defendant operated a fat-rendering plant in the city of Rye. Refuse from it was emptied into a pond, which in turn polluted a local brook, spreading obnoxious odors through the neighborhood. A few local residents brought a class suit for an injunction and it was allowed. The court noted that "the tortious act [nuisance] in its entirety operates on all."[14] And all that was before the court was the

---

[10] *Gaynor*, 15 N.Y.2d at 129, 256 N.Y.S.2d at 590, 204 N.E.2d at 631. The court was quoting from its own prior decision in Society Milion Athena v. National Bank of Greece, 281 N.Y. 282, 292, 22 N.E.2d 374, 377 (1939).

[11] See Homburger, *State Class Actions and the Federal Rule*, 71 Colum. L. Rev. 609, 647, republished in 17th Jud. Conf. Rep. 242, 270 (1972).

[12] Homburger, *State Class Actions and the Federal Rule*, 71 Colum. L. Rev. at 646, 17th Jud. Conf. Rep. 269–270.

[13] Greer v. Smith, 155 A.D. 420, 140 N.Y.S. 43 (2d Dep't 1913).

[14] *Greer*, 155 A.D. at 423, 140 N.Y.S. at 45.

request for an injunction, which meant that in one thrust the wish of all could be satisfied. Also noted by the court was the fact that each member of the class could, in his own right, have brought the action for the same relief without doing so in class form or otherwise involving any other class member. Each had, in other words, a private right to the same relief individually, which is true of most class actions.

Dissent among the class as to the remedies to be pursued is seldom in prospect when it is an injunction or mere declaration that's sought, but, as the *Gaynor* case shows, it may be. Whether potential dissent about relief should preclude class form altogether, or allow class form only after use of the opting out procedure, has to be approached practically. Class status should not be denied and the opting out procedure should not be invoked if choice of a different remedy is just a fanciful or remote possibility; both alternatives should be reserved for cases in which it is reasonable and perhaps even likely that a substantial number of class members would not go along with the relief asked for by the representatives who brought the suit. In such instances, the formation of subclasses may be a way out of the dilemma.

If the courts were to take an approach any more rigid than that, the class action could not exist. When the class is large, it can perhaps always be demonstrated that at least one or two among the class do not want the relief sought. Suppose, for example, that several of the Rye residents in the *Greer* case found the odors innocuous, or even pleasant; or, indeed, that they were employed at the offending plant. Should they be allowed to bar the suit in class form? The larger the group, the greater the prospect that it will include a few mavericks or iconoclasts of unique taste and preference. What must govern here is not the remote possibility that one or a handful of the members of a large class might personally prefer to resist the suit. The courts must look to cultural realities—to a prevailing norm of human behavior. If by that standard it can be said that all but a few loners are going along with the relief, the potential dissent of the reclusive few should not be a barrier. The facts of Onofrio v. Playboy Club of New York, Inc.[15] can serve as an example:

Five out of 50,000 members of the class (club members) sought in behalf of the class damages of over $1 million for the club's failure to fulfill its agreement to operate and maintain a private club. An individual money judgment (or series of judgments) was sought returning the membership fee of $25 to each member of the class. Class form was denied in this old law case and one of the bases for the denial was that the remedy desired by some class members might differ from the monetary one sought. In a case like *Onofrio* today, class form should be sustainable under Article 9, but would possible preferences for different remedies prompt utilization of the opting out procedure? What other remedies might class members seek? An injunction requiring maintenance of the club? Will equity undertake that, entailing as it does the management of an involved project and a running check on the good faith of its operators? A declaratory judgment that the club should be opened? Is that not even less effectual than an injunction? Is there a real and reasonable prospect that individual class members could show money damages in excess of the $25 they paid for membership? Factors like these must all be considered, but if alternative choices of remedy prove in context to be unfeasible or unreasonable, then perhaps not even the opting out step should be required.

---

[15] Onofrio v. Playboy Club of New York, Inc., 15 N.Y.2d 740, 257 N.Y.S.2d 171, 205 N.E.2d 308 (1965), reversing on dissenting opinion below, 20 A.D.2d 3, 6, 244 N.Y.S.2d 485, 488 (1st Dep't 1963).

The availability of the opting out procedure accounted for the affirmative answer to a long-outstanding question. May a court entertain jurisdiction over nonresident members of the class? The issue was finally resolved by the U.S. Supreme Court in Phillips Petroleum Co. v. Shutts,[16] involving the plaintiffs' side as the class (the usual scenario) under a state's class action statute.

Rarely has a court any occasion to address how it gets jurisdiction of a plaintiff. It's jurisdiction over the defendant that produces battle, and acres of caselaw. But the class action is an exception. If the members of the plaintiff class come from many places, by what right does a court in a state other than a given class member's domicile presume to entertain jurisdiction of her? Shall we apply to a plaintiff something like the "minimum contacts" test that we apply to measure extraterritorial jurisdiction of a defendant?[17] The U.S. Supreme Court in Phillips said no, sustaining Kansas jurisdiction over a huge class of plaintiffs even though only a fraction of them had Kansas contacts. It was the opting out device, which Kansas law had and the court properly used in Phillips, that was held to satisfy the demands of due process. The members were notified of the suit and if they didn't want to be bound by the Kansas proceedings, they had only to say so in response to the opting out notice. Many did.[18] Those who didn't would be bound by the judgment.

Addressing the jurisdiction-over-nonresidents issue in Matter of Colt Indus. Shareholder Litigation,[19] the New York Court of Appeals held that while the opting-out procedure would be mandatory when it's damages that the nonresident would be seeking, it does not apply to a class action's demand for equitable or collective relief, such as an injunction or a declaratory judgment. The issues raised in Jiannaras v. Alfant,[20] mirrored those in Matter of Colt as the class action complaint sought predominately equitable relief, but the proposed settlement would also release any monetary damage claims of out-of-state class members. The Jiannaras Court noted that under Matter of Colt and the Supreme Court's decision in Phillips, the ability of those out-of-state class members to pursue monetary damages constituted constitutionally protected property rights. Therefore, the Court affirmed the order of the Second Department that refused to approve the settlement of the class action because it did not include an opt-out provision for out-of-state class members.

The Jiannaras decision also contains a helpful discussion highlighting some distinctions between federal class actions and those brought in New York State court. The Court stresses a point made in the first paragraph of this section: while Federal Rule 23(c)(2) requires notice and opt-out rights for only one type of class action, Article 9 of the CPLR permits the court to exercise its discretion and require notice and an opt-out provision in any class action.[21]

---

16   Phillips Petroleum Co. v. Shutts, 472 U.S. 797, 105 S. Ct. 2965, 86 L. Ed. 2d 628 (1985).

17   See § 84.

18   The case is discussed in the lead note in NYSLD No. 311.

19   Colt Industries Shareholder Litigation v. Colt Industries Inc., 77 N.Y.2d 185, 565 N.Y.S.2d 755, 566 N.E.2d 1160 (1991) (NYSLD No. 375).

20   Jiannaras v. Alfant, 27 N.Y.3d 349, 33 N.Y.S.3d 140, 52 N.E.3d 1166 (2016).

21   Jiannaras, 27 N.Y.3d at 354, 33 N.Y.S.3d at 143, 52 N.E.3d at 1169; see CPLR 903, 904.

§ 145. "Fluid Recovery"

In Onofrio v. Playboy Club of New York, Inc.,[1] discussed in the prior section, the possibility of different choices of remedy among the class members was cited as a major reason for refusing class form. But the real explanation lay in the prospect that at one point or another, the court might have to render 50,000 individual money judgments, or one massive judgment awarding $25 plus incidental sums to each of 50,000 different persons, each of whom would have to be identified and ultimately named. That kind of prospect was a sotto voce, but influential deterrent in many old law cases. Without expanding the topic unduly, we should mention what has become known nationally as the "fluid recovery," which may supply a compromise solution in cases like Onofrio.

The fluid recovery contemplates a judgment against the defendant in a sum sufficient to divest it of all the fruits of its wrong, but the beneficiaries are the class to which the past victims belong, rather than the specific victims themselves.[2] Fluid recovery can be accomplished, for example, by requiring the seller of a product or service regulated by law to reduce its price not just to the maximum, but below it, and to continue selling it at the reduced price until sufficient losses have been sustained to repay the general body of users of the product or service who had been previously overcharged.[3] That promises a remedy if the monetary wrong is so massive that it's impracticable, if not impossible, to reimburse the actual victims, and almost any remedy is better than simply letting the wrongdoer get off scot-free.

The part of the fluid recovery concept that divests the wrongdoer of illicit gains has already gained judicial support, even when there was nothing to do with an unclaimed part of the recovery but turn it over to the State. In a later phase of Friar v. Vanguard Holding Corp., the facts of which were noted earlier,[4] the wrongdoer was required to disgorge its wrongful charges, but not all of the overcharged victims could be found. Some $14,000 was left over and the defendant sought to get it back. Nothing doing, held the court: "permitting reversion of the unclaimed funds to this defendant would be equivalent to awarding it the benefit of its own wrongdoing, a result which should not be sanctioned."[5] The court directed the money to be turned over to the state as abandoned property. That, too, is a "fluid recovery."

§ 146. Defendant's Side as Class

A suit against a defendant class is permitted by CPLR 901, but is seen far less frequently than one on plaintiffs' side, and is approached even more cautiously by the courts. The sensitive nerve here is an attempt by the plaintiffs, who initially designate those who are to be the defendant/class's representatives, to pick out weak ones. The

---

[1]   Onofrio v. Playboy Club of New York, Inc., 15 N.Y.2d 740, 257 N.Y.S.2d 171, 205 N.E.2d 308 (1965), reversing on dissenting opinion below, 20 A.D.2d 3, 6, 244 N.Y.S.2d 485, 488 (1st Dep't 1963).

[2]   See Homburger, *Private Suits in the Public Interest in the United States of America*, 23 Buff. L. Rev. 343, 371–73 (1973); Malina, *Fluid Class Recovery as a Consumer Remedy in Anti-Trust Cases*, 47 N.Y.U. L. Rev. 477 (1972); Comment, *Due Process and Fluid Class Recovery*, 53 Or. L. Rev. 225 (1975). The New York statutes neither invite nor prohibit a fluid recovery, leaving the matter to the courts on a case-by-case basis. See Homburger, *The 1975 New York Judicial Conference Package: Class Actions and Comparative Negligence*, 25 Buff. L. Rev. 415, 429–30 (1976).

[3]   See Comment, *Manageability of Notice and Damage Calculation in Consumer Class Actions*, 70 Mich. L. Rev. 338, 363–73 (1971).

[4]   Friar v. Vanguard Holding Corp., 78 A.D.2d 83, 434 N.Y.S.2d 698 (2d Dep't 1980); see § 141.

[5]   *Friar*, 125 A.D.2d at 446, 509 N.Y.S.2d at 376.

court can check into that and will doubtless be diligent in doing so. If the action otherwise satisfies class form, but the court is uncomfortable about those who have been designated the representatives of the defendant class, the court can designate others, additionally or alternatively. An example of a defendant-as-class action which passed muster even under prior law is Northwestern Telegraph Co. v. Western Union Telegraph Co.,[1] in which the defendants were the shareholders of the plaintiff corporation in a dispute involving whether certain moneys paid by a third person should go to the shareholders directly or to the corporation itself.

A situation like that should not be confused with the well known derivative action in which shareholders sue in the right of the corporation. The derivative action, a species of class action (in which the class is usually on the plaintiffs' side), is subject to more detailed statutory regulation.[2]

Dudley v. Kerwick[3] is an unusual example of class status being conferred on both sides. Some 88% of the landowners of a town got themselves ordained as "ministers" of the "Universal Life Church" through a simple mail application procedure that apparently did not involve the rigors of seminary training. So ordained, they then got tax exemptions on religious grounds. The unordained 12% that thereupon inherited the town's entire tax bill, if not the earth, ungratefully renounced the inheritance and brought suit to lift the exemptions.[4] It was allowed in class form on both sides.

§ 147. Pervasive Court Discretion in Class Action; Settlement and Judgment

Recognizing how the class action eludes precise statutory direction, the CPLR gives the court broad discretion in the management of the class action and the protection of the class. Old CPLR 1005(b) did this in general terms by allowing the court to "impose . . . terms" to protect the class at any stage of the action. CPLR 907 offers at least as much discretion to the court "in the conduct of class actions," but contains a more detailed list illustrating the kinds of protective steps the court can take. CPLR 907 allows the court to make an order:

1. determining the course of proceedings or prescribing measures to prevent undue repetition or complication in the presentation of evidence or argument;

2. requiring, for the protection of the members of the class, or otherwise for the fair conduct of the action, that notice be given in such manner as the court may direct to some or all of the members of any step in the action, or of the proposed extent of the judgment, or of the opportunity of members to signify whether they consider the representation fair and adequate, or to appear and present claims or defenses, or otherwise to come into the action;

3. imposing conditions on the representative parties or on intervenors;

---

[1]   Northwestern Telegraph Co. v. Western Union Telegraph Co., 197 Misc. 1075, 99 N.Y.S.2d 331 (Sup. Ct., New York County 1950).

[2]   See Bus. Corp. Law § 626.

[3]   Dudley v. Kerwick, 84 A.D.2d 884, 444 N.Y.S.2d 965 (3d Dep't 1981).

[4]   The case is discussed in the lead note in NYSLD No. 261.

4. requiring that the pleadings be amended to eliminate therefrom allegations as to representation of absent persons;

5. directing that a money judgment favorable to the class be paid either in one sum, whether forthwith or within such period as the court may fix, or in such installments as the court may specify; and/or

6. dealing with similar procedural matters.

The last item, number 6 on the list, manifests that the list is illustrative, rather than exclusive. The first four items have counterparts in Rule 23(d) of the Federal Rules of Civil Procedure. The fifth, which addresses the terms of payment of a money judgment rendered in behalf of the class, lacks a federal analog; it's an indulgence felt by the Judicial Conference to be due the defendant "so as to avoid harsh economic and social consequences."[1] Under its general power over "similar procedural matters" (the sixth item), there should still be room for the court in an appropriate case to direct the "fluid recovery" discussed earlier.[2]

Protection of the opponent of the class is just as much an aim of CPLR 907 as protection of the class itself. The gubernatorial message approving Article 9 stressed the presence of powers whereby the court can "prevent abuse of the class action device" and thus assure respect for "the rights of the class as well as those of its opponent."[3]

Under item 2, the court can permit class members to appear and participate without a formal motion to intervene.[4] The motion of course remains an alternative available to any class member who wants in.[5]

CPLR 907 explicitly states that orders for the conduct of class actions "may be altered or amended as may be desirable from time to time." All of these CPLR 907 orders, original or amending, may be sought by motion of a party, or made by the court sua sponte.

CPLR 908 provides that a class action may not be dismissed, discontinued, or compromised without the court's approval, and even provides that if any such step is proposed, notice of it "shall be given to all members of the class in such manner as the court directs." The notice is mandatory, but again, its method lies in the court's discretion.[6] By requiring court leave for a compromise or settlement, CPLR 908 makes it harder for the defendants to buy the plaintiffs off with a settlement advantageous to the representatives, but not necessarily to the class itself. That was the famous "strike suit" phenomenon, most visible in the corporate derivative actions of yesteryear, which was easier to bring off before the reins of the class action were taken from the parties and turned over to the court. By placing control in the court, CPLR 908 seeks not only to bar the plaintiffs from being bought, but also to prevent the defendants from getting off

---

[1] See 20th Jud. Conf. Rep. 210 (1975).

[2] See § 145.

[3] See 1975 N.Y. Sess. Laws 1748 (McKinney).

[4] See 20th Jud. Conf. Rep. 210 (1975).

[5] CPLR 1012(a)(2), 1013.

[6] Notice of settlement was optional with the court under the prior law counterpart, the old CPLR 1005(b)(1).

too cheaply in the bargain. For the above reasons, among others, professional ethics are an especially sensitive matter in the class action.[7]

CPLR 908's notice requirement applies even when the settlement is sought before class status has been certified.[8] It would otherwise be possible, by foreclosing the members of the class from a hearing on the subject, for the representatives to make a private settlement beneficial to themselves, a possibility the notice requirements are designed to foreclose.

While notice of a settlement, or of a dismissal or discontinuance, must be given to the class under the terms of CPLR 908, notice of judgment on the merits is not mandatory, but left to judicial discretion under CPLR 907.

The merits judgment in a class action, whether for or against the class, must "include and describe those whom the court finds to be members of the class."[9] It means that a mere description of the class suffices.[10] The naming of the individual members of the class is not a general requirement, although the court must of course have discretion to require naming in given instances, especially if the opting out procedure has been used (where the judgment may have to recite that it's not binding on certain persons).

According to the Judicial Conference, the issue of the res judicata or collateral estoppel effect of the judgment on one who is a member of the class, but who neither appeared nor opted out, can be determined only in a subsequent action in which that member is a party.[11]

The class action is one of the rare exceptions to the American rule that attorney's fees may not be awarded to the winner against the loser. CPLR 909 expressly provides that if the class prevails, the court has discretion to award a fee to the representatives' attorneys based on the "reasonable value" of the legal services rendered, and to impose this sum on the class's opponent. This controversial provision was not recommended by the Judicial Conference because it was felt that it would have rough going in the legislature. It was, therefore, omitted from the Conference's 1975 proposals, although contained in the CPLR Committee's original 1972 recommendations.[12] Paradoxically, legislative hands reinserted the provision and included it in the initial enactment of Article 9. Attorney's fees were not expressly authorized by statute under prior law, but caselaw allowed them.[13]

In Flemming v. Barnwell Nursing Home and Health Facilities, Inc.,[14] the Court of Appeals held that under CPLR 909 attorney's fees may be awarded out of a successful class action recovery only to "the representatives of the class." In that case, however, the fees were sought not by the class representatives, but by a member of the class who objected to the fees that the court proposed to award to the class representatives.

---

[7]   See Homburger, *Private Suits in the Public Interest in the United States of America*, 23 Buff. L. Rev. 343, 373–75 (1973).

[8]   Avena v. Ford Motor Co., 85 A.D.2d 149, 447 N.Y.S.2d 278 (1st Dep't 1982).

[9]   CPLR 905.

[10]   See and compare Fed. R. Civ. P. 23(c)(3), which uses "describe" in its paragraph (A) but "specify" in its paragraph (B), generating different options for the court depending on the kind of class action involved.

[11]   See 20th Jud. Conf. Rep. 209 (1975).

[12]   See 18th Jud. Conf. Rep. A27, A41 (1973).

[13]   Cf. Runcie v. Bankers Trust Co., 16 N.Y.S.2d 917 (Sup. Ct., Nassau County 1939).

[14]   Flemming v. Barnwell Nursing Home and Health Facilities, Inc., 15 N.Y.3d 375, 912 N.Y.S.2d 504, 938 N.E.2d 937 (2010).

Flemming held that the statute would not support that. In 2011, the legislature amended CPLR 909 so that it now does support such a recovery, authorizing the award not only to the class representatives, but also "to any other person that the court finds has acted to benefit the class." It's a direct overruling of the *Flemming* case.

The memo in support of the bill points out that an objection to the fees being awarded to the class representatives would, if successful, be a step that would benefit the class and is hence consistent with the purpose of CPLR 909. The memo recites that "[i]n many class action cases, objecting parties successfully argue that the proposed settlement is inadequate, that the class should be expanded or, as in *Flemming*, that the fees proposed for the class representatives are too high. The court should also have the discretion to compensate counsel for those efforts."

Friar v. Vanguard Holding Corp., cited several times already for other matters,[15] treats the method of computing attorney's fees in class actions, including use of the so-called "lodestar" fee.

G. INTERPLEADER

Table of Sections

§ 148. Interpleader, Generally
§ 149. Liberal Use; Discharge of Stakeholder
§ 150. Mode of Trial
§ 151. Discretionary Tools
§ 152. The Stakeholder's Jurisdictional Dilemma
§ 153. Rem Jurisdiction as Interpleader Basis
§ 154. Interpleader in the Federal Courts

§ 148. Interpleader, Generally

Interpleader is the situation in which someone faces a possible multiple liability at the hands of conflicting claimants. It allows that person, who in interpleader context is known as a "stakeholder," to bring all the claimants into court to fight it out, producing a judgment binding on all the claimants and, under the doctrine of res judicata, forever protecting the stakeholder, S, from further suit on the matter at the behest of any of them.

S can take the initiative and simply bring an action of interpleader, making all of the claimants defendants.[1] Or, if one of the claimants (C-1) brings an action against S, S can interplead the other claimants (C-2 etc.) from her position as defendant. The latter procedure is called "defensive" interpleader.[2]

S commences an action of interpleader as he would any other, describing the situation in the complaint and pleading that the defendants be made to put in their claims. In defensive interpleader, in addition to serving a summons and interpleader complaint on the other claimants (the ones to be added), S must serve copies of all prior

---

[15] Friar v. Vanguard Holding Corp., 78 A.D.2d 83, 434 N.Y.S.2d 698 (2d Dep't 1980); see §§ 141 and 145.

[1] CPLR 1006(a).

[2] CPLR 1006(b).

pleadings already served in the action.[3] Failure to serve the other pleadings is not a jurisdictional defect, however, so that the omission does not impair jurisdiction and a default judgment can follow if the person interpleaded fails to respond.[4]

A liability insurer can presumably pay off judgments rendered against the insured in the sequence in which the judgments are presented to the insurer, but the interpleader device is also available to the insurer. One insurer that used it was commended by the court for doing so,[5] apparently based on the justice of having all claims prorated rather than encouraging a race.[6]

No court order is necessary for either an action of interpleader or defensive interpleader. Whether as plaintiff or defendant, S simply commences the interpleader action. Most of the old requirements that once severely circumscribed the interpleader remedy are no longer applicable. CPLR 1006(d) addresses the point by stating that:

> It is not ground for objection to interpleader that the claims of the several claimants or the titles on which their claims depend do not have a common origin or are not identical but are adverse to and independent of one another
> . . . .

It was once otherwise.[7] Today the only real criterion is whether S "is or may be" subject to conflicting claims. C-1 may be claiming the proceeds of an insurance policy as its named beneficiary, C-2 the same proceeds under an alleged contract with the insured, C-3 the same through the insured's estate, etc. It makes no difference. As long as it appears that the claims are or simply "may be" mutually exclusive, i.e., that only one of the claimants should prevail, the interpleader device is available. S can use it unless the alleged conflicting claim "is so patently without substance that [S] can reject it without risk that . . . an independent action . . . may be able to establish a right" to the fund or property.[8]

Interpleader is also available in the lower courts of civil jurisdiction, as long as the money or property involved is within the court's subject matter jurisdiction.[9]

§ 149. Liberal Use; Discharge of Stakeholder

CPLR 1006(f) sets up a procedure whereby the stakeholder can move to be discharged. This can be done only when it is established that the stakeholder is no more than that, and that the sole battle is between the claimants. If a discharge is allowed,

---

[3]   CPLR 1006(b). The interpleader summons and complaint must be filed with the court, for defensive as well as original interpleader, and a filing fee paid in either instance. See SPR 22:1.

[4]   Donas v. European American Bank and Trust Co., 106 Misc. 2d 437, 431 N.Y.S.2d 873 (Sup. Ct., New York County 1980).

[5]   See Boris v. Flaherty, 242 A.D.2d 9, 672 N.Y.S.2d 177 (4th Dep't 1998).

[6]   See the discussion in the lead note in SPR 75:1. In a similar situation in which one insured tried to intervene in the other's personal injury action to avoid the latter preempting the insurance proceeds, intervention was denied. See David v. Bauman, 24 Misc. 2d 67, 71, 196 N.Y.S.2d 746, 750 (Sup. Ct., Nassau County 1960), § 181.

[7]   See Frumer, *On Revising the New York Interpleader Statutes*, 25 N.Y.U. L. Rev. 737 (1950). The main revision was in 1954, amending the old Civil Practice Act (see Civ. Prac. Act §§ 285 et seq.) at the instigation of the Judicial Council. See 20th Jud. Council Rep. 271, 319 (1954).

[8]   Boden v. Arnstein, 293 N.Y. 99, 103, 56 N.E.2d 65, 67 (1944).

[9]   See § 205 in each of the New York City Civ. Ct. Act, Uniform Dist. Ct. Act, and Uniform City Ct. Act. There is no § 205 in the Uniform Just. Ct. Act; the town and village courts lack interpleader jurisdiction.

the stakeholder leaves the action fully protected: the claimants will be left behind to fight things out and will be bound by the judgment afterwards reached on the merits.

The procedure for the discharge is a motion, on affidavits or any other proof, and it can be made at any time after the pleading time of all the parties has expired. If a discharge is granted, the court can order the money or property paid into court, delivered to a designated person, or retained by the stakeholder pending further order of the court. The order of discharge makes appropriate provision for "expenses, costs and disbursements" and these "may be charged against the subject matter of the action,"[1] i.e., are payable out of the money or property interpleaded. Interpleader is also one of the few instances in which an attorney's fee may be allowed out of the stake.[2] The courts will typically award attorney's fees to a neutral stakeholder with no interest in the disputed matter who was forced to participate in a dispute between the two claimants.[3]

The stakeholder does not have an automatic right to be discharged. The law is liberal about the use of the interpleader device to get into court any dispute in which conflicting liability is merely possible, but discharging the stakeholder before a trial on the merits is another matter entirely. It is clear today, for example, that S may use interpleader even if his position is that he is not liable at all to any of the claimants.[4] In making interpleader available when S "is or may be" liable to two or more claimants, CPLR 1006(a) recognizes its utility even if the merits ultimately show that S is liable to no one, or liable to all the claimants individually, or to some but not all. It's the existence of the last possibility that makes interpleader available procedurally, and the resulting judgment is valid whatever the merits turn out to be.

Suppose, for example, that C-1 sues S, who defensively interpleads C-2, and that the court sustains the interpleader, but the merits then resolve that S is independently liable to both C-1 and C-2. Each will take judgment against S.[5] The interpleader device, which enabled S to bring C-2 into the C-1 action and get both sides of his liability resolved, has in that instance filled a gap that would otherwise have needed other devices, such as consolidation[6] or impleader,[7] but it is not a guarantee to S that she will end up with but a single liability.

To be discharged, so as not to have to stay on for the trial, S has to convince the court, as a matter of law, that she is liable to only one or a designated number, but not to all the claimants, i.e., that this is a fight among the claimants in which S is really just a bystander.

---

[1] Under CPLR 1006(f), the interest rate applicable to a party asserting a claim, absent agreement to the contrary, is that set by the Federal Reserve Bank of New York for member banks.

[2] See CPLR 1006(f); Sun Life Ins. and Annuity Co. of New York v. Braslow, 38 A.D.3d 529, 831 N.Y.S.2d 497 (2d Dep't 2007).

[3] See Mahon, Mahon, Kerins & O'Brien, LLC v. Moskoff, 85 A.D.3d 738, 926 N.Y.S.2d 540 (2d Dep't 2011).

[4] CPLR 1006(d).

[5] An example of where S would incur such a multiple liability is where S is a seller of realty who has given, inadvertently or otherwise, an exclusive sales right to several brokers if they produce a buyer on given terms, and several produce.

[6] CPLR 602. Consolidation would come into play, for example, when C-1 and C-2 sue S separately. See § 128.

[7] Given the broader approach to impleader today, S could probably even implead C-2 into a C-1 action under CPLR 1007. See § 157.

The proof offered by S to support a discharge should be as weighty on the single-liability issue as the proof needed to support a summary judgment motion under CPLR 3212. The effect of an order of discharge is essentially the same as the grant of summary judgment: it is the equivalent of a trial. If the court has any doubt about whether S is just a stakeholder, or for any good reason feels that S should remain in the action as a party, it will deny S's motion to be discharged.[8]

If S does get the discharge, the resulting judgment between the claimants protects S from further suit by any of them—winners or losers.

§ 150. Mode of Trial

If the case is one of genuine interpleader, one in which two or more claimants are battling for the same money or property and the stakeholder is indifferent as between them, or, indeed, has made a deposit into court and been discharged, the case sounds in equity, through which interpleader evolved, and is presumably not triable by jury.[1] But if the nature of the dispute is such that it would have been jury triable had it not made its appearance in an interpleader context, the right to a jury remains.

An example is Geddes v. Rosen,[2] in which C-1 sued S to recover an escrow fund and S defensively interpleaded C-2. It appeared that if a certain sale were not consummated, C-1 would have a claim directly against C-2 rather than against S. The parties were held entitled to jury trial. Apparently, the way to test this sometimes difficult issue[3] is to inquire whether, without the interpleader remedy, there would be an adequate remedy at law to litigate the underlying dispute. If there would be, the right to jury trial remains despite the fact that the issue has come into court in an interpleader vehicle.

§ 151. Discretionary Tools

A wide range of discretionary tools is available to handle problems in interpleader cases. CPLR 1006(c) sees to this by empowering the court to make such "order as may be just."

One situation contemplated by CPLR 1006(c) is where S as defendant wants to interplead C-2, but another action is pending between them on the same dispute. If the other action is in a New York court, it can be consolidated or ordered to joint trial with the suit in which S is a defendant.[1] Or one can be dismissed or stayed in deference to the other.[2]

The consolidation (or joint trial) remedy is the most cohesive of the several supplied by the CPLR because it enables the several actions to be united, with a broad range of advantages. Only a single common question of law or fact is needed for consolidation or joint trial,[3] and either device can avoid expense and embarrassment. Where, for example, C-1 has two possible grounds of recovery, only one of them involving other potentially

---

8   See Nelson v. Cross & Brown Co., 9 A.D.2d 140, 192 N.Y.S.2d 335 (1st Dep't 1959).

1   Clark v. Mosher, 107 N.Y. 118, 14 N.E. 96 (1887).

2   Geddes v. Rosen, 22 A.D.2d 394, 255 N.Y.S.2d 585 (1st Dep't 1965), aff'd, 16 N.Y.2d 816, 263 N.Y.S.2d 10, 210 N.E.2d 362 (1965).

3   See the dissenting opinion of Breitel, J., in Geddes, 22 A.D.2d at 400, 255 N.Y.S.2d at 591.

1   As to which court can effect the consolidation or joint trial, see § 128.

2   CPLR 3211(a)(4). See § 262.

3   CPLR 602.

conflicting claimants, it's advantageous to C-1 to be able to litigate both grounds in one action even though only one involves an interpleadable controversy.[4] Were they pending in separate actions, consolidation could fuse them.

Within the action, whether the action is the product of consolidation, interpleader, or initial joinder, the court has available the severance and separate trial devices,[5] and general control of the sequence of trial,[6] to aid its hearing and disposition of the issues.

§ 152. The Stakeholder's Jurisdictional Dilemma

If S, either by an action of interpleader or by defensive interpleader, can bring all conflicting claimants under the roof of but a single court, she will get her protection from double liability because the judgment of that court will bind all claimants. But when, for lack of jurisdiction over all claimants, S cannot maneuver all of them before a single court, she meets her most serious problem. The New York legislature has tried to remedy the problem in two ways, neither very effective. One is the attempted use of rem jurisdiction for a mere money claim, the subject of the next section. The other is the procedure now found in CPLR 216.

The CPLR 216 procedure applies where C-1 has brought an action against S in New York in which S cannot interplead C-2 because C-2 is a nondomiciliary and not otherwise subject to extraterritorial service. Under CPLR 216, S gets an order from the court authorizing S to serve on C-2, by registered mail at C-2's last known address, a notice of the pending action accompanied by a summons and complaint and a copy of the order.[1] S then shows the court that he has made such service, whereupon the court stays the pending C-1 v. S action for one year.[2] The hope is that during the year C-2 will either intervene in C-1's action voluntarily or else commence a separate action in New York,[3] which could then be consolidated with C-1's.

If C-2 takes neither step within the year, the only effect of all this CPLR 216 business is that an action by C-2 against S will be met by the bar of the statute of limitations (which is why the stuff of CPLR 216 appears in Article 2 of the CPLR). The whole impact of this provision is to abbreviate to 1 year the period of limitation otherwise applicable to C-2's claim.[4] This is all quite effective against any endeavor by C-2 to sue S in New York after the allotted year. The trouble is that it does not prevent C-2 from catching and suing S in some other state, or country, which need not recognize or apply

---

[4]   See American Motorists Ins. Co. v. Oakley, 172 Misc. 319, 14 N.Y.S.2d 883 (Sup. Ct., Broome County 1939), discussed in 20th Jud. Council Rep. 271, 276 (1954).

[5]   CPLR 603.

[6]   CPLR 4011.

[1]   CPLR 216(a)(2). The procedure applies where the money is payable under a contract and involves more than $50.

[2]   CPLR 216(a)(3).

[3]   See Solicitor for Affairs of His Majesty's Treasury v. Bankers Trust Co., 304 N.Y. 282, 107 N.E.2d 448 (1952).

[4]   CPLR 216(a)(1). When the year passes and the case resumes, S may defend on the merits against C-1. The use of the CPLR 216 procedure does not waive S's rights. See *Solicitor*, 304 N.Y. at 282, 107 N.E.2d at 448.

the New York statute of limitations.[5] S thus remains subject to double liability, and the CPLR 216 procedure proves well intentioned but ineffective.[6]

An obvious question is this: if S cannot get C-2 before the same court, why doesn't she just move to dismiss C-1's action for failure to join a necessary party?[7] The trouble on that score is some old caselaw indicating that a stakeholder's inability to interplead the other claimant is not a defense to C-1's suit. The main decision in point is Petrogradsky Mejdunarodny Kommerchesky Bank v. National City Bank of New York,[8] but perhaps the case should not be read as absolutely precluding such a defense today. First, *Petrogradsky* involved the unique problem of Russian assets in the United States before our recognition of the then Soviet Union. Second, procedural developments since then offer the court significant and perhaps even decisive alternatives. One is CPLR 1001(b). Recast in the CPLR (from what it had been in the old Civil Practice Act), it now permits the court a broad range of discretion in shaping relief when someone who ought to be a party has not been joined.[9] If, for example, there is any other forum before which C-2 can reasonably be brought, the New York court might just dismiss C-1's action without prejudice to an action in such other forum, even exacting from S a stipulation to submit to that other forum's jurisdiction. Such a step would avoid the problem at which the ineffective CPLR 216 aims, and with less strain.

Due process might even be found today to mandate the pursuit of other available courses. Due process is offended when a court compels a litigant to relinquish property without the assurance that he will not confront liability again in another forum.[10] A court risks offending the constitution in that way if, with alternatives available, it disregards them and insists on continuing with C-1's case in C-2's absence, thus exposing S to a double liability unnecessarily.

Another barrier to dismissal of a C-1 v. S action under prior law was where either party was a New York resident. The residency would have precluded a forum non conveniens dismissal. Today, however, if "in the interest of substantial justice the action should be heard in another forum . . . [t]he domicile or residence in this state of any party . . . shall not preclude the court from staying or dismissing the action."[11]

Also relevant is the advent of longarm jurisdiction under CPLR 302 and like statutes. CPLR 302 authorizes personam jurisdiction against nondomiciliaries when the case has New York contacts—which many such interpleader cases have—making CPLR 216 superfluous for that reason, too. Indeed, the national omnipresence of longarm jurisdiction may have resolved just about all of the stakeholder's jurisdictional problems. If the subject matter of the interpleader dispute has roots anywhere in the United States, it is almost certain that the state involved will have a longarm statute ready to reach out and assume personal jurisdiction of all claimants. And, of course, there is the statute

---

    [5]   Warner v. Buffalo Drydock Co., 67 F.2d 540, 1933 A.M.C. 1610 (C.C.A. 2d Cir. 1933).

    [6]   The procedure also applies when the conflict is as to specific property within the state instead of mere money, CPLR 216(b), but the need for it in that situation is questionable because rem jurisdiction under CPLR 314 will usually afford the stakeholder all the jurisdiction required. See § 153.

    [7]   The motion lies under CPLR 3211(a)(10); see §§ 131–33.

    [8]   Petrogradsky Mejdunarodny Kommerchesky Bank v. National City Bank of New York, 253 N.Y. 23, 170 N.E. 479 (1930).

    [9]   See § 133.

    [10]   See W. U. Tel. Co. v. Com. of Pa., by Gottlieb, 368 U.S. 71, 82 S. Ct. 199, 7 L. Ed. 2d 139 (1961).

    [11]   CPLR 327. See Silver v. Great Am. Ins. Co., 29 N.Y.2d 356, 328 N.Y.S.2d 398, 278 N.E.2d 619 (1972); § 28.

that seeks to "reify" a sum of money so as to bind claimants under a rem jurisdictional theory, the next topic.

§ 153. Rem Jurisdiction as Interpleader Basis

If the dispute concerns specific property instead of money, and the property is located in New York, rem jurisdiction will usually suffice even in an interpleader situation to secure for S a judgment binding even on claimants served outside New York and not amenable to the State's personal jurisdiction.[1] That will be so whenever S wants only to affect the claimants' right in the subject property. But will rem jurisdiction avail when the subject obligation involves no specific property, nor even a trust or other limited fund, but a mere monetary obligation?

A naked attempt to convert mere money into "property" so as to exploit rem jurisdiction, as CPLR 1006(g) purports to allow, has been held unconstitutional both by the New York Court of Appeals[2] and the U.S. Supreme Court,[3] a combination that would normally discourage the most tenacious advocate. But CPLR 1006(g) is not easily dissuaded. It still authorizes the court, upon S's motion, to permit a sum of money to be paid into court[4] and thereby deemed a "res" so as to invoke the rem jurisdiction offered by CPLR 314(2). This would presumably enable service on the claimants to be made outside the state and bind them to the judgment to the extent of their "interest" in the money—that is, if it works.

It should work despite the older caselaw, for the reason that CPLR 1006(g) does not authorize this procedure as to any money at all. It allows it only when the money is "payable in the state pursuant to a contract or claimed as damages for unlawful retention of specific real or personal property in the state." So limited—and this factor seems to have been overlooked by the courts[5]—CPLR 1006(g) can be treated as a kind of longarm statute, analogous to CPLR 302. If the particular interpleader situation involves substantial New York contacts—which it should often do when the requirements of CPLR 1006(g) are met—the case satisfies federal constitutional criteria evolved after the earlier restrictive cases[6] and should be jurisdictionally sustainable on an outright personam basis.

If that's so, then CPLR 1006(g), far from going too far, doesn't even go as far as it can. CPLR 1006(g) is not a blunderbuss effort to convert money into a res. It's just a kind of longarm statute requiring the usual contacts analysis called for in that category of jurisdiction.[7]

---

[1] CPLR 314(2).

[2] Hanna v. Stedman, 230 N.Y. 326, 130 N.E. 566 (1921).

[3] New York Life Ins. Co. v. Dunlevy, 241 U.S. 518, 36 S. Ct. 613, 60 L. Ed. 1140 (1916).

[4] Alternatively, the court can order the money paid to a designated person or retained by the stakeholder to the credit of the action.

[5] See, e.g., Cordner v. Metropolitan Life Ins. Co., 234 F. Supp. 765 (S.D.N.Y. 1964).

[6] The potentate of general longarm jurisdiction is International Shoe Co. v. State of Wash., Office of Unemployment Compensation and Placement, 326 U.S. 310, 66 S. Ct. 154, 90 L. Ed. 95 (1945), decided in 1945, long after the U.S. Supreme Court's *Dunlevy* case of 1916, in note 3, above, and the New York Court of Appeals' *Hanna* case of 1921, in note 2, above. See also Shaffer v. Heitner, 433 U.S. 186, 97 S. Ct. 2569, 53 L. Ed. 2d 683 (1977), discussed in § 104.

[7] See § 84, discussing longarm jurisdiction in general. A contacts analysis of this kind occurred in Atkinson v. Superior Court In and For Los Angeles County, 49 Cal. 2d 338, 316 P.2d 960 (1957) (Traynor, J.), where the court went as far as it thought it could based on local contacts, while rejecting any arbitrary conclusions about whether money could be converted into a res.

§ 154. Interpleader in the Federal Courts

Perhaps the most meaningful resolution of the stakeholder's jurisdictional problem before the arrival of general longarm jurisdiction was the procedure Congress authorized in the federal courts, commonly known as federal statutory interpleader.[1] It was designed for cases in which federal jurisdiction is based on diversity of citizenship. Still exploited when the need arises, it offers four distinct advantages:

First, it measures subject matter jurisdiction by the citizenship of the claimants, disregarding the citizenship of the stakeholder and sustaining jurisdiction as long as any two of the claimants are of diverse citizenship.[2] Thus, if there are a dozen adverse claimants, all of them citizens of State X except one, who is a citizen of State Y, the diversity requirement is met. This is known as "minimal" diversity and its constitutionality has been sustained.[3]

Second, while the usual diversity case requires that the amount in controversy exceed $75,000, the minimum is set at only $500 in statutory interpleader cases.[4]

Third, while the general rule in federal actions is that in the absence of special statutory authority service of process may not cross state lines, i.e., that the district court's personal jurisdiction is limited to those reachable by process within the state in which the particular federal court sits,[5] process service in statutory interpleader is allowed nationwide.[6]

Fourth, the venue requirements are relaxed; the stakeholder may bring the action in any district in which any claimant resides.[7]

This generous federal quartet will often serve the stakeholder at least as well, if not better, than the New York remedies. But if the stakeholder can't satisfy even the relaxed jurisdictional requirements of federal statutory interpleader—as where there is no diversity of citizenship at all or the amount in controversy is less than $500—she must turn to the state remedies, such as they are. Worth noting again is that with the general longarm jurisdiction available under statutes like CPLR 302, the state interpleader remedies treated in the prior two sections, as well as the federal statutory remedy treated in this one, are needed much less frequently today.

---

[1]   There is also "rule" interpleader in the federal courts. Fed. R. Civ. P. 22 authorizes interpleader, but does not give it the special advantages of subject matter jurisdiction, personal jurisdiction, and venue accorded to "statutory" interpleader, to be noted shortly.

[2]   28 U.S.C.A. § 1335(a)(1).

[3]   State Farm Fire & Cas. Co. v. Tashire, 386 U.S. 523, 87 S. Ct. 1199, 18 L. Ed. 2d 270 (1967). The general diversity of citizenship statute, 28 U.S.C.A. § 1332, in contrast to § 1335, requires complete diversity, Strawbridge v. Curtiss, 7 U.S. 267, 2 L. Ed. 435, 1806 WL 1213 (1806), which means that the citizenship of each plaintiff must differ from that of each defendant. For who qualifies as a "citizen" of a state in diversity parlance, see § 611 (Practitioner's Edition).

[4]   28 U.S.C.A. § 1335(a).

[5]   Fed. R. Civ. P. 4(k). See § 626 (Practitioner's Edition) and Commentaries C4:29 et seq. on Rule 4 in 28 U.S.C.A.

[6]   See 28 U.S.C.A. § 2361, which also authorizes the interpleader court to enjoin the claimants from maintaining conflicting suits in state or other federal courts.

[7]   28 U.S.C.A. § 1397. The general venue requirements in a diversity case, found in 28 U.S.C.A. § 1391(a), are not quite as generous. See § 617 (Practitioner's Edition).

H. IMPLEADER

Table of Sections

§ 155. Third-Party Practice, or "Impleader," Generally

§ 156. Basic Procedure for Impleader

§ 157. Indemnification as Impleader Basis; Other Bases

§ 158. Effect if Impleader Complaint Negates Main Claim

§ 159. Impleader as Premature Suit

§ 160. Impleader in Insurance Situations

§ 161. Discretionary Powers of Dismissal, Severance, and Like Steps

§ 162. Statute of Limitations on Impleader Claims

§ 163. Rights of Third-Party Defendant

§ 164. Additional Claims Among the Parties

§ 165. Enforcement of Third-Party Judgment

§ 166. Successive Impleaders

§ 167. Impleader in Various Courts and Proceedings

§ 168. Vouching-In

§ 168A. "Joint" Tort Liability Adjustment; Background

§ 168B. "Joint" Tort Liability Adjustment; The 50%-or-Less Tortfeasor

§ 168C. "Joint" Tort Liability Adjustment; Provisos and Exceptions

§ 168D. "Joint" Tort Liability Adjustment; Burdens of Proof

§ 168E. The Comparative Negligence Rule of CPLR Article 14-A

§ 155. Third-Party Practice, or "Impleader," Generally

Officially it's called "third-party practice;"[1] popularly it's known as "impleader," the name this text will most often use. When P sues D, and D claims that X will be, or merely may be, liable to D for all or part of that which P may recover of D, impleader enables D to bring X into the P v. D action and have the D v. X dispute resolved at the same time. In this procedure, D is denominated the "third-party plaintiff" and X the "third-party defendant." For ease of reference in our examples, D will remain D and X will represent the impleaded third-party defendant.

The advantages of impleader are many. It avoids multiplicity of suits since without impleader, D would have to bring a separate later action against X. (D may still do that. Impleader is not compulsory.) It saves time, money, and effort, and it reduces the prospect of inconsistent verdicts. If a separate action were used, the court or jury in that action could ignore the result of the P v. D action—assume it was determined in favor of P against D—and determine that D should not have been held liable to P, leaving X with no liability to D despite the P v. D victory (which could not bind nonparty X).[2]

The third-party claim is also known as a "claim over," especially when D is seeking straight indemnity from X to cover D's liability to P.

---

[1] CPLR 1007.

[2] For the background and historical development of impleader, see 11th Jud. Council Rep. 370, 375 (1945).

When an issue arises concerning impleader, it more often than not touches on the basic question of whether impleader lies rather than in some detail of the procedure for its use. Whether it lies depends on the substantive law applicable to D's claim against X. If X as a matter of substantive law, as applied to the facts that D pleads against X, would be required to reimburse D for all or part of P's recovery against D, impleader lies. The source of X's obligation is secondary. It may come from an express contract or it may be implied in law. Here are a few common examples:

(a) O owns some property and hires K, a contractor, to repair the sidewalk. K repairs it negligently and P trips and is injured. P sues O, who (assume) bears liability for the defect. O can implead K.[3]

(b) A and B are joint venturers involved in a commercial project. They agree to split expenses and liabilities 50–50. P sues A on one of the enterprise's projects. A may implead B to make B share the liability.[4]

(c) P sues G, a general contractor, for breach of an agreement to build a house. The defect is in the plumbing done by S, a plumbing subcontractor hired by G. G may implead S.[5]

(d) P sues O, the owner of a car, for injuries P suffered when the car, driven by X, struck P. Since the fault is X's driving, O may implead X.[6]

(e) P is injured in a two-car accident. The drivers are D-1 and D-2. If P sues only one driver, the one sued may implead the other.[7]

(f) P is injured by tortfeasor D. X is a hospital or a physician or like person who then negligently treats P, aggravating the injury. P sues D for all the damages P suffered in the accident, because under tort law D is substantively liable for the original as well as the aggravated damages. D may implead X, however, who must indemnify D for such part of the damages as X caused.[8]

(g) P is an employee injured on a construction job and sues D, the owner or general contractor, who bears liability for the injury. Maintaining that the fault belongs in whole or in part to P's employer, X, against whom P cannot bring a direct action because of the exclusivity of the workers' compensation remedy, D may implead employer X for indemnity or contribution, but in this instance with an important qualification, discussed below.

---

[3]   See Koerner, *Modern Third-Party Practice—Substantive or Procedural?*, 3 N.Y. L. Forum 159, 166–68 (1957).

[4]   McCabe v. Queensboro Farm Products, Inc., 22 N.Y.2d 204, 292 N.Y.S.2d 400, 239 N.E.2d 340 (1968).

[5]   See Comment, *Third-Party Practice in New York*, 37 Cornell L.Q. 721, 744–45 (1952).

[6]   See Traub v. Dinzler, 309 N.Y. 395, 131 N.E.2d 564 (1955). Be careful to distinguish O's personal rights in this situation from those of O's insurer. If X, the driver, is an additional insured under O's liability policy, as X usually is, O's insurer, who is conducting O's defense, may not implead X. But if the amount demanded by P from O exceeds the policy, O may implead X to make good the excess. See Beck v. Renahan, 46 Misc. 2d 252, 259 N.Y.S.2d 768 (Sup. Ct., Nassau County 1965), aff'd, 26 A.D.2d 990, 275 N.Y.S.2d 1010 (2d Dep't 1966).

[7]   This involves contribution among tortfeasors, for which see §§ 169 et seq. The impleader device is used to implement contribution just as it is outright indemnification.

[8]   See Musco v. Conte, 22 A.D.2d 121, 254 N.Y.S.2d 589 (2d Dep't 1964).

Third-Party Action Against Plaintiff's Employer

Under the 1996 enactment of the Omnibus Workers' Compensation Reform Act,[9] D may implead P's employer only if: (1) it can be shown that P suffered a "grave" injury in the accident, as defined by statute, or (2) if there is a "written contract entered into prior to the accident or occurrence by which the employer had expressly agreed to contribution to or indemnification of [D]."[10]

Under Workers' Compensation Law section 11, the categories of "grave injury" are:

death, permanent and total loss of use or amputation of an arm, leg, hand or foot, loss of multiple fingers, loss of multiple toes, paraplegia or quadriplegia, total and permanent blindness, total and permanent deafness, loss of nose, loss of ear, permanent and severe facial disfigurement, loss of an index finger or an acquired injury to the brain caused by an external physical force resulting in permanent total disability.[11]

The Court of Appeals has given the statutory list a strict construction. As for the "loss of multiple fingers," the Court held in Castro v. United Container Machinery Group, Inc.,[12] that the loss of multiple fingertips does not qualify and therefore does not support the impleader of the employer. Although the loss of the index finger and the loss of use of a hand is on the list, the loss of the thumb is not. An appellate division said that the loss of the thumb amounts to the loss of the use of the hand and therefore qualifies as a "grave injury," but adhering to a strict construction, the Court of Appeals reversed and said no.[13] Tell that to Charles Darwin!

The Court of Appeals has found some of the items on the "grave injury" list, such as the loss of multiple fingers, to be "objectively ascertainable,"[14] but others less so, like the "permanent and severe facial disfigurement" category that it found was not established in Fleming v. Graham.[15] The *Fleming* Court held that this category implies "a highly limited class of disfiguring injuries beyond minor scarring or lacerations" and that both "permanency" and "severity" are conditions precedent to a finding of "facial disfigurement."[16]

Regarding the "written contract" ground for impleader of P's employer, in Flores v. Lower East Side Service Center, Inc.,[17] the Court concluded that the contract entered into can give rise to a third-party action against the employer, even if it is not signed, provided there is objective evidence establishing that the parties intended to be bound. Subsequently, in Rodrigues v. N & S Building Contractors, Inc.,[18] the Court rejected the

---

[9]   Work. Comp. Law § 11.

[10]   Work. Comp. Law § 11.

[11]   See Patrick M. Connors, *Court of Appeals Revisits "Grave Injury,"* N.Y.L.J., Jan. 21, 2005, at 1 (with Tom Gleason).

[12]   Castro v. United Container Machinery Group, Inc., 96 N.Y.2d 398, 736 N.Y.S.2d 287, 761 N.E.2d 1014 (2001) (NYSLD No. 501).

[13]   Meis v. ELO Organization, LLC., 97 N.Y.2d 714, 740 N.Y.S.2d 689, 767 N.E.2d 146 (2002).

[14]   *Castro*, 96 N.Y.2d at 401, 736 N.Y.S.2d at 288–89, 761 N.E.2d at 1015–16.

[15]   Fleming v. Graham, 10 N.Y.3d 296, 857 N.Y.S.2d 8, 886 N.E.2d 769 (2008) (NYSLD No. 583).

[16]   *Fleming*, 10 N.Y.3d at 300–01, 857 N.Y.S.2d at 12, 886 N.E.2d at 773.

[17]   Flores v. Lower East Side Service Center, Inc., 4 N.Y.3d 363, 795 N.Y.S.2d 491, 828 N.E.2d 593 (2005) (NYSLD No. 544).

[18]   Rodrigues v. N & S Building Contractors, Inc., 5 N.Y.3d 427, 805 N.Y.S.2d 299, 839 N.E.2d 357 (2005) (NYSLD No. 552).

argument that the indemnification provision must specify the sites, persons, and the types of losses covered. The Court concluded that "[s]o long as a written indemnification provision encompasses an agreement to indemnify the person asserting the indemnification claim for the type of loss suffered, it meets the requirements of the statute."[19]

In New York Hosp. Medical Center of Queens v. Microtech Contracting Corp.,[20] the Court dismissed a hospital's action for common law and contractual indemnification and contribution commenced against an employer who hired two undocumented aliens to conduct demolition work at the hospital. The hospital argued that the employment contracts between the employer and the injured employees were illegal under federal law and unenforceable. Therefore, the hospital maintained that the employer could not invoke the protections of Workers' Compensation Law section 11 to defeat the claims for indemnification and contribution. The Court noted that it "essentially rejected the hospital's argument" in its 2006 decision, Balbuena v. IDR Realty LLC,[21] where it permitted an undocumented alien to seek recovery of lost wages in a personal injury action against a landowner based on violations of the Labor Law. Viewing this matter as "the other side of the coin," the Court observed that if the illegality of the employment contract did not defeat the employees' rights to recover under the Labor Law "in Balbuena, it should not defeat the employer's statutory rights" under Workers' Compensation Law section 11.

The need to determine impleadability is what involves the law of procedure in these essentially substantive issues, along with sticky problems about burden of proof. There have been disagreements about who has the burden on the "grave injury" issue.[22] The situation is unique in that it casts D into the position of wanting to show that P's injury is "grave" just so as to be able to implead P's employer as a standby indemnitor. (Where else in the law does one see the accused tortfeasor trying to show that the plaintiff's injuries are "grave?") While P himself would seem technically to be just a bystander in this D v. X dispute, which usually appears on X's motion to dismiss D's attempted impleader of X, P is also permitted to weigh in on the motion with proof of the graveness of his injury.[23]

§ 156. Basic Procedure for Impleader

Impleader requires no court leave under the CPLR. D merely files a summons and third-party complaint and serves those papers on X along with copies of all prior pleadings in the action.[1] The methods of service are the same as those that apply to the initial commencement of an action, i.e., they're governed by Article 3 of the CPLR. X

---

[19] *Rodrigues*, 5 N.Y.3d at 433, 805 N.Y.S.2d at 302, 839 N.E.2d at 360.

[20] New York Hosp. Medical Center of Queens v. Microtech Contracting Corp., 22 N.Y.3d 501, 982 N.Y.S.2d 830, 5 N.E.3d 993 (2014).

[21] Balbuena v. IDR Realty LLC, 6 N.Y.3d 338, 812 N.Y.S.2d 416, 845 N.E.2d 1246 (2006) (NYSLD No. 556).

[22] See the lead note in SPR 122:1.

[23] See Way v. George Grantling Chemung Contracting Corp., 289 A.D.2d 790, 736 N.Y.S.2d 424 (3d Dep't 2001) (SPR 122).

[1] CPLR 1007. A separate filing fee must be paid for this, but no separate index number is assigned (the index number of the main action remains applicable, usually with an "x" appended to it). The omission to serve the prior pleadings is sometimes held a jurisdictional defect, but the better view is that it is at worst a correctible irregularity. See Wings & Wheels Exp. Inc. v. Sisak, 73 Misc. 2d 846, 342 N.Y.S.2d 891 (Sup. Ct., Queens County 1973).

must answer the third-party complaint.[2] The answering time is determined by the place and method of service, just as if X were a defendant initially sued.[3]

D is also required to serve a copy of the third-party complaint on P's attorney, which must be done "simultaneously" with the "issuance for service" of the third-party complaint.[4] This enables P to keep abreast of any impleader introduced into the action.

The same bases for extraterritorial jurisdiction available against an original defendant are available against a third-party defendant. Thus, whenever the requirements of CPLR 313 are met as to the third-party claim, service of process may be made on the third-party defendant without regard to state lines. It has been held, however, that local contacts must be demonstrated in respect of the third-party claim itself; that a forum does not get extraterritorial jurisdiction of X, an alleged indemnitor, merely because D, the alleged indemnitee, purports to implead X into the action in which D has been sued by P—with jurisdiction—on the underlying obligation.[5]

The only CPLR statement about the time for impleader is that D must not undertake it until D has served an answer to the main complaint.[6] It's permissible any time afterwards, but D must be wary of substantial delay causing prejudice. If D has unduly delayed the impleader and a resisting party can establish prejudice, the court can in its discretion dismiss or sever it,[7] thus remitting D to a separate later action against X. Whether there has been such undue delay as to warrant a dismissal or severance is of course a sui generis inquiry. The courts recognize that since D would still have the right to bring a separate action against X, an impleader claim should not ordinarily be dismissed for tardiness unless the delay has been palpably prejudicial,[8] as where D waits until after P has been granted summary judgment against D before impleading X.[9]

A prime example of such prejudice is Pierce v. International Harvester Co.[10] The case had gone to trial and went to both judgment and appeal without any attempt to implead. Only after the appellate court had reversed (on a point not touching the impleader issues) and remanded the case for a new trial was an impleader finally undertaken by D. Too late, held the court; the delay was in years and P's case was sharpened and ready for the retrial. It would not be fair to P to subject the case to the delays that so belated an impleader would entail.

While D can later sue X, the would-be third-party defendant, after paying out on such judgment as P might obtain, and without statute of limitations problems,[11] this is

---

[2]   CPLR 1008.

[3]   See CPLR 3012; § 110.

[4]   CPLR 1007.

[5]   Media Corp. of America v. Motif Mfg. Co., Inc., 524 F. Supp. 86 (S.D.N.Y. 1981). The case is discussed, and suggestions made about how the indemnitee might try to protect itself, in the lead note in NYSLD No. 269. See Asahi Metal Industry Co., Ltd. v. Superior Court of California, Solano County, 480 U.S. 102, 107 S. Ct. 1026, 94 L. Ed. 2d 92 (1987); § 88.

[6]   CPLR 1007.

[7]   CPLR 1010.

[8]   See Manganaro v. Estwing Mfg. Co., 27 A.D.2d 711, 276 N.Y.S.2d 891 (1st Dep't 1967).

[9]   Nickerson v. City of New York, 309 A.D.2d 588, 765 N.Y.S.2d 510 (1st Dep't 2003). X is not bound by the P v. D judgment; it's the same as if D tried to bring a separate indemnity action against X after losing to P, in which it is of course open to X to refute P's claim against D. See SPR 144:1.

[10]   Pierce v. International Harvester Co., 65 A.D.2d 254, 411 N.Y.S.2d 456 (4th Dep't 1978).

[11]   See § 162.

not an ideal alternative for D. Lost to D would be the advantage of having the same jury that found D liable to P also determine whether D is to be made whole by X. More significant still is that X would not be bound by the P v. D judgment and could relitigate the merits of P's claim and any damages awarded.[12]

D should make it a rule to implead X as early as possible for the additional reason that it avoids duplication of effort. Much of the preparation will be the same as that required for the main claim, including use of the disclosure devices. The best rule of thumb for D is to implead X right after the service of the answer to the main complaint.

When X, the impleaded person, is a municipality or other governmental entity against which initial suit would not ordinarily lie unless it has first been served with a notice of claim, the notice of claim requirement is dispensed with. The notice of claim requirement applies only when the governmental entity is an original defendant, not a third-party defendant.[13]

If P has already joined D and X as co-defendants in the original action, there will of course be no need for D to implead X in order to assert a claim over. In that situation, D may assert the claim as a mere cross-claim in D's answer, which need not be accompanied by a summons and which can be served by mere mail.[14] A difference between the devices of cross-claim and impleader is that a cross-claim may be asserted by one defendant against another for any cause of action at all,[15] whether or not related to the main claim. An indemnity claim is only one of the things a cross-claim can include, while impleader under the CPLR is usually found to embrace only the indemnity/contribution type claim, although its use has been expanded in recent years, as the next section discusses.

§ 157. Indemnification as Impleader Basis; Other Bases

It's tempting to think of impleader as being used only when D has an out-and-out "indemnification" claim against X. That's its primary function, and if we include contribution, which is a variety of indemnification, it accounts for the great majority of third-party claims. If D's claim is solely for "indemnification" or "contribution," it means that X is liable to D only if D is liable to P, and that if D can get off P's hook, X avoids liability to D automatically.

Although it accounts for most impleaders, a formal, substantive "indemnity" or "indemnification" or "contribution" claim is not indispensable to the use of impleader today. An older case in point is B.M.C. Mfg. Corp. v. Tarshis,[1] in which P contracted to buy steel from D, and D turned around and made a contract to buy the steel from X. The contracts were independent and a breach of the D-X contract would have permitted suit by D against X without regard to whether D would be liable to P. Thus, D's claim against X was not for "indemnification," but when P sued D, D was nevertheless allowed to implead X. It was held sufficient that X, by breaching the contract with D, had "exposed" D to all or part of the liability P was asserting.

---

[12]   *Nickerson*, 309 A.D.2d at 588, 765 N.Y.S.2d at 510.

[13]   Valstrey Service Corp. v. Board of Elections, Nassau County, 2 N.Y.2d 413, 161 N.Y.S.2d 52, 141 N.E.2d 565 (1957).

[14]   See § 202.

[15]   CPLR 3019(b).

[1]   B.M.C. Mfg. Corp. v. Tarshis, 278 A.D. 266, 104 N.Y.S.2d 254 (3d Dep't 1951).

Under a liberal approach, impleader should lie whenever the link between the P-D and D-X claims is such as to suggest the practical soundness of having them heard together. There is no requirement under the CPLR that the two claims be related by a common question of law or fact, although in most cases they are. That point was made in Norman Co. v. County of Nassau,[2] which stated that the true test today "is simply whether the third-party defendant may be liable to defendant/third-party plaintiff, for whatever reason, for the damages for which the latter may be liable to plaintiff."[3] *Norman* was a liberal reading of the impleader statutes, and yet it still looked for an indemnity link of some kind.

While usually present, and always a strong glue for impleader, the indemnity link was largely abandoned as an impleader requirement in George Cohen Agency, Inc. v. Donald S. Perlman Agency, Inc.,[4] a major pronouncement on the impleader device. The Court held that impleader is no longer to be limited solely to claims of indemnity or contribution. "[I]t has grown beyond its early limitations," said the Court, "and should now be seen primarily as a tool for economical resolution of inter-related lawsuits."

P in the *George Cohen* case sold an insurance portfolio to D and took back notes in payment. When D defaulted and P sued, D claimed that he was fraudulently induced to buy the portfolio by both P and X. He sought to implead X, who maintained that the impleader would not lie because it was not exclusively to indemnify D for what P was claiming. The Court upheld D in his contention that impleader should lie for any claims related to P's main claim, including any that D might have against P and X jointly. The argument that D should just bring separate actions and then move to consolidate them with P's action pursuant to CPLR 602 was rejected by the Court as "a needless procedural dance."

If any claims impleaded under the generous *George Cohen* view would unduly impede the litigation in any way, the court has plenty of room for a cure with the severance and separate trial tools of CPLR 603.

George Cohen is a commercial case, but its expansive view of impleader helps in the tort area as well. Suppose, for example, that A and B in their separate cars collide and injure P, who sues only A. A impleads B. Both before and after the *George Cohen* case, A could assert against the impleaded B an indemnification or contribution claim in respect of P's main claim. But before the case, A could not add against B—or it was in any event debatable—a claim for A's own personal injuries or property damage suffered in the accident. It is now clear that A can add such claims.

A concomitant of this key decision is that no longer is a defendant's money demand against the impleaded third-party defendant limited to the sum the original plaintiff has demanded in the main action.

The *George Cohen* case should be deemed to overrule older cases that barred impleader in a variety of situations in which factual links were present to make

---

[2]   Norman Co. v. Nassau County, 63 Misc. 2d 965, 314 N.Y.S.2d 44 (Sup. Ct., Nassau County 1970).

[3]   *Norman*, 63 Misc.2d at 969, 314 N.Y.S.2d at 50. Quoting the *Norman* case, the appellate division adopted this expansive view of impleader in Holloway v. Brooklyn Union Gas Co., 50 A.D.2d 603, 375 N.Y.S.2d 396 (2d Dep't 1975).

[4]   George Cohen Agency, Inc. v. Donald S. Perlman Agency, Inc., 51 N.Y.2d 358, 434 N.Y.S.2d 189, 414 N.E.2d 689 (1980) (NYSLD No. 253).

impleader useful, but an outright indemnity claim was missing. Take Horn v. Ketchum,[5] for example, in which P sued D for realty commissions. D impleaded X, to whom D had apparently paid the commissions in error. Noting that D could bring an action against X to recover the commissions regardless of P's claim against D, the court disallowed the impleader. Today it would be allowed.

A relevant consideration under the *George Cohen* approach is that in a case like *Horn*, the common questions would have enabled the two disputes, had they been brought as separate actions, to be consolidated or jointly tried.[6] The court has broad discretion in the handling of an impleader claim,[7] and can simply treat the claim as a separate action and merely order it consolidated or jointly tried with the main claim,[8] thus enabling the two to be heard together by that route.[9] When it is shown that the consolidation or joint trial route would be available were D's claim brought separately, the *George Cohen* case indicates that D should be allowed to get the claim in with the impleader device.

Courts still occasionally speak of the need for "some minimal jural relationship, aside from possible common questions of fact or law [which is all consolidation requires], between the liability of the defendant asserted in the main action and the liability-over claim in the third-party complaint,"[10] suggesting that an impleader without that link would be error. If so, it is submitted that the error is harmless as long as a common question of fact or law exists. In this circumstance, the court should ask whether it would order consolidation or joint trial if the claim were brought separately and consolidation or joint trial were sought. If the court answers the question yes, it should sustain the impleader with nothing more than a citation of CPLR 2001, the statute permitting the court to ignore unprejudicial errors. If, under that test, it appears that a consolidation would not be ordered, the court can simply sever the impleaded claim and send it off as a separate action.

When the impleader claim is based on a contract, the contract's terms will of course govern the claim. If it is a straight indemnity agreement, the claim over may seek judgment for all of the main claim. If it's an agreement only to share the loss, the impleader can be used to secure whatever portion the contract provides for.[11]

Another major source of indemnification is an obligation to indemnify implied by law. A leading example here is the tort case in which tortfeasor X, derivatively liable for the tort of Y, seeks to implead Y. At one time, X in this situation would be denominated the "passive" tortfeasor and Y the "active" one.[12] Also during an earlier era, an indemnity contract would not be deemed to cover the indemnitee's "active" negligence unless it did

---

[5]   Horn v. Ketchum, 27 A.D.2d 759, 277 N.Y.S.2d 177 (3d Dep't 1967); see Cleveland v. Farber, 46 A.D.2d 733, 361 N.Y.S.2d 99 (4th Dep't 1974) (holding that where wrong committed by third-party defendants was "separate, distinct and not related in any way to the wrong committed by third-party plaintiff," the third-party complaint was properly dismissed).

[6]   CPLR 602; see § 128.

[7]   CPLR 1010.

[8]   Ellenberg v. Sydharv Realty Corp., 41 Misc. 2d 1078, 247 N.Y.S.2d 226 (Sup. Ct., Kings County 1964).

[9]   See § 161.

[10]   Zurich Ins. Co. v. White, 129 A.D.2d 388, 518 N.Y.S.2d 469 (3d Dep't 1987).

[11]   See McCabe v. Queensboro Farm Products, Inc., 22 N.Y.2d 204, 292 N.Y.S.2d 400, 239 N.E.2d 340 (1968).

[12]   See § 170. Related to this is "contribution," a separate topic, for which the impleader device also supplies the procedure. See the treatment of contribution in §§ 169 et seq.

so expressly,[13] but today such an obligation can arise by implication if the particular contract lends itself to it,[14] constituting a kind of mixed express-implied indemnification agreement.

The impleader claim, especially after the liberalizing edict of the *George Cohen* case, need not rest on the same underlying ground or theory as the main claim, which was yet another notion of an earlier time. The main claim, for example, may be in tort and the claim over in contract, or vice versa.[15] The main claim may be based on warranty and the claim over on negligence.[16] The test is simply whether what X has done has exposed D in any measure to the liability P is asserting. Indeed, as has already been stressed, impleader may even be used today when the claim over is independent of the main claim and only common questions of law or fact offer a nexus for it.

What about attorney's fees? If D is entitled to have X cover D for D's liability to P, does X also have to pay D's attorney's fees? The matter was considered in Chapel v. Mitchell,[17] in which the Court of Appeals held that when D's common law indemnification claim against X prevails, X must pay D's attorney's fees for defending P's suit, but is not liable for D's attorney's fees in prosecuting the impleader claim. Issues necessarily arise under this rule about how to apportion the efforts of D's attorneys between the defense of P's claim and the pursuit of the impleader claim, and apportionment may be even more contentious when the indemnification sought by the impleader claim is for only part of the main claim, such as in the contribution instead of outright indemnification situation.[18]

§ 158. Effect if Impleader Complaint Negates Main Claim

If D's impleader complaint against X pleads a state of facts that would, if proved, relieve D of all liability to P, it has been held that impleader does not lie and that the impleader complaint must be dismissed. Thus, where P sued D for injuries caused by D's manufacture of defective goods, and D pleaded that X's alterations of the goods were the cause of P's injuries, the impleader was barred. The court said that "a claim over for indemnity is insufficient where its allegations would, if established, preclude liability on the part of the one asserting it."[1]

Cases of that kind usually involve tort claims and the old active-passive dichotomy that at one time determined impleader rights.[2] With the arrival of the *Dole* case,[3]

---

[13] Thompson-Starrett Co. v. Otis Elevator Co., 271 N.Y. 36, 2 N.E.2d 35 (1936).

[14] See Levine v. Shell Oil Co., 28 N.Y.2d 205, 321 N.Y.S.2d 81, 269 N.E.2d 799 (1971).

[15] See Sommer v. Federal Signal Corp., 79 N.Y.2d 540, 583 N.Y.S.2d 957, 593 N.E.2d 1365 (1992); Sol Lenzner Corp. v. Aetna Cas. & Sur. Co., 20 A.D.2d 305, 246 N.Y.S.2d 950 (4th Dep't 1964).

[16] In tort cases today, especially the action for personal injuries caused by a product, many theories are used: negligence, breach of warranty, strict liability in tort, and sometimes even the breach of a statutory duty. Their allotment between main claim and impleader claim—if each claim does not list all possible theories, as they can usually be trusted to do—is not decisive of the question of allowing impleader as long as each wrong listed is a possible factor in the plaintiff's injury.

[17] Chapel v. Mitchell, 84 N.Y.2d 345, 618 N.Y.S.2d 626, 642 N.E.2d 1082 (1994).

[18] See the discussion of the *Chapel* case in the lead note in NYSLD No. 420. The court in *Chapel* addressed only the common law indemnity claim, i.e., the one arising by implication of law instead of by express contract, distinguishing the contractual situation.

[1] Beckerman v. Walter J. Munro, Inc., 25 A.D.2d 448, 449, 266 N.Y.S.2d 996, 998 (2d Dep't 1966).

[2] See, e.g., LaRosa v. Edward J. Furhmann & Co., 34 A.D.2d 881, 311 N.Y.S.2d 948 (4th Dep't 1970), and the discussion of the active/passive rule in § 170.

[3] Dole v. Dow Chemical Co., 30 N.Y.2d 143, 331 N.Y.S.2d 382, 282 N.E.2d 288 (1972). See § 171.

however, and its subsequent codification in Article 14 of the CPLR, allowing the sued tortfeasor to implead other alleged participants in the tort, impleader by D should be sustainable today even if there is a possibility that the fault will be found to belong entirely to X and relieve D of liability altogether.

The logical relationship of the claims should determine, and the capacity of one claim to negate the other is itself a factor establishing such a relationship. The Court of Appeals decision in the 1980 George Cohen Agency, Inc. v. Donald S. Perlman Agency, Inc. case[4] is relevant on this point with its approval of the appellate division statement that "it is the logical relationship of the claims which should determine whether third-party practice is appropriate, not the mechanistic approach of the past."[5]

§ 159. Impleader as Premature Suit

Impleader is one of the rare instances in which the law permits what amounts to a premature action. That is so, in any event, when the impleader is used for straight indemnity because should P lose on the claim against D, there will be nothing for which X has to indemnify D. In fact, the statute of limitations on D's cause of action for indemnity does not even begin to run until D has paid P's judgment.[1] Yet impleader permits the D v. X dispute to be set in motion even before P has had judgment entered against D. Impleader "does not vitiate the requirement of a showing of actual loss before there may be recovery, but does permit an indemnitee to obtain a conditional judgment fixing the potential liability without the need for payment until it is shown that the judgment in the principal action has been satisfied in whole or part."[2]

Ordinarily, however, the D v. X suit does not mature to the point of being litigable until P has at least sued D. Thus, if P has merely made a claim against D without actually putting it into litigation, it has been held that the D v. X suit for indemnity does not yet lie.[3] But as long as the underlying P v. D action is pending, even if pending outside New York, a separate D v. X suit for what amounts to indemnity has been permitted. It was allowed in W.T. Grant Co. v. Uneeda Doll Co.,[4] for example, an early case on pleading under the CPLR.[5] Since the impleader of X into the P v. D action is almost always preferable to a separate indemnity action by D against X afterwards, it would seem that one of the few instances in which D would be justified in bringing a separate action would be where personal jurisdiction of X is not available in the state where the P v. D action is pending, which may have been the problem in *Grant*.

---

[4]   George Cohen Agency, Inc. v. Donald S. Perlman Agency, Inc., 51 N.Y.2d 358, 434 N.Y.S.2d 189, 414 N.E.2d 689 (1980); section § 157.

[5]   George Cohen Agency, Inc. v. Donald S. Perlman Agency, Inc., 69 A.D.2d 725, 734, 419 N.Y.S.2d 584, 589 (2d Dep't 1979), aff'd, 51 N.Y.2d 358, 434 N.Y.S.2d 189, 414 N.E.2d 689 (1980).

[1]   See § 162.

[2]   McCabe v. Queensboro Farm Products, Inc., 22 N.Y.2d 204, 208, 292 N.Y.S.2d 400, 403, 239 N.E.2d 340, 342 (1968). *McCabe* actually involved a separate D v. X action (because it had been severed from the P v. D. action), but even as a separate action it was allowed to go forward. For enforcement of judgment problems, see § 165.

[3]   Lasker-Goldman Corp. v. Delma Engineering Corp., 32 A.D.2d 513, 298 N.Y.S.2d 747 (1st Dep't 1969).

[4]   W. T. Grant Co. v. Uneeda Doll Co., 19 A.D.2d 361, 243 N.Y.S.2d 428 (1st Dep't 1963), aff'd, 15 N.Y.2d 571, 254 N.Y.S.2d 834, 203 N.E.2d 299 (1964).

[5]   See the discussion in Commentary C3014:8 on McKinney's CPLR 3014.

§ 160.   Impleader in Insurance Situations

When an insurer is so positioned as to be liable to D for all or part of what P is claiming of D, the insurer as a general rule is just as subject to impleader as any other person or entity. But there is a notable exception made for liability insurance.

The usual liability policy provides that when the insured (D) is sued for a covered tort, the insurer will supply the attorney, handle the defense, and pay any resulting judgment. There is therefore no need to implead an insurer if it fulfills those obligations. If the insurer should disclaim coverage, however, and D does implead it, the impleader will likely be a waste of time when the insurance involved is liability insurance because the insurer is entitled to a severance of the third-party claim on demand, as held by the Court of Appeals in Kelly v. Yannotti.[1] The purpose is to avoid prejudice to the insurer at the hands of a jury because a jury in New York—a land of compulsory automobile liability insurance!—is assumed not to know that D is insured. If a jury has by chance been waived, however, the severance may be refused and the insurer kept in.[2]

If D is the owner of a car driven by X, and D but not X is sued, the insurer may not ordinarily implead X if X is an additional insured under the policy, as X usually is.[3]

When an insurer is the named defendant on a cause of action brought by the plaintiff insured, whatever the kind of insurance involved, the insurer ordinarily may implead a third person who is responsible for the insured loss even though the insurer's right of equitable subrogation does not technically accrue until it has paid its insured under the policy.[4] But there is another exception here, this one applicable when automobile collision coverage is the insurance involved.[5] Third-party practice by the insurer is barred there to spare the plaintiff/insured the delay in its presumably modest property damage suit.[6]

§ 161.   Discretionary Powers of Dismissal, Severance, and Like Steps

CPLR 1010 expressly authorizes the dismissal or separate trial of the impleader claim. Its further permission for the court to make "such other order as may be just" covers several other discretionary possibilities, such as severance, consolidation, joint trial, etc. The rule requires the court to consider "whether the controversy between the third-party plaintiff and the third-party defendant will unduly delay the determination of the main action or prejudice the substantial rights of any party." When prejudice does appear, it is usually because of delay, although other possibilities exist.[1]

Since one of the major advantages of impleader is having the same jury that passes on D's liability to P then determine X's liability to D, an impleader claim with an

---

[1]   Kelly v. Yannotti, 4 N.Y.2d 603, 176 N.Y.S.2d 637, 152 N.E.2d 69 (1958).

[2]   See Koolery v. Lindemann, 91 N.Y.S.2d 505 (Sup. Ct., Kings County 1949).

[3]   See § 155.

[4]   Krause v. American Guarantee & Liability Ins. Co., 22 N.Y.2d 147, 292 N.Y.S.2d 67, 239 N.E.2d 175 (1968).

[5]   Ross v. Pawtucket Mut. Ins. Co., 13 N.Y.2d 233, 246 N.Y.S.2d 213, 195 N.E.2d 892 (1963); see *Policy Held to Limit Insurer's Right to Implead Tortfeasor*, 38 St. John's L. Rev. 406, 421 (1964).

[6]   See the distinction offered in *Krause*, 22 N.Y.2d at 156, 292 N.Y.S.2d at 73–4, 239 N.E.2d at 180.

[1]   One example is the prejudice that may result to a liability insurer if retained in the same action in which its insured is being sued. See § 160.

arguable basis should rarely be dismissed, at least not if it has been timely interposed. If D's claim against X is a genuine indemnity one, every effort should be made to have it tried to the same jury. (There may be more justification for dismissal or severance when the impleader claim is not for outright indemnity).[2] If the problem is that the simultaneous trial of the impleader claim will create undue complications for the jury, the appropriate remedy is a separate trial. This enables the main claim to be tried to a verdict, with the impleader claim to be tried immediately afterwards to the same jury.

If the impleader claim has a question of law or fact in common with the main claim, but impleader does not appear to be appropriate, a remedy is to treat the impleader claim as if brought separately and order it, or just deem it, consolidated or jointly tried with the main claim.[3]

§ 162. Statute of Limitations on Impleader Claims

When the claim over is a formal indemnity cause of action, whether based on an express agreement or implied in law, it gets two important benefits for purposes of the statute of limitations. The first is that the period that applies to it is the 6 years applicable to contract;[1] the second is that the period does not start running until the underlying claim is paid.[2] This is so even if the basis of the indemnity claim is tort, such as where one tortfeasor seeks partial indemnification from another. So held Musco v. Conte[3] in 1964, during the age of restricted contribution among tortfeasors. The restrictions were lifted in 1972 in Dole v. Dow Chemical Co.,[4] and since contribution is just a form of indemnification, the Court of Appeals then held in Bay Ridge Air Rights, Inc. v. State of New York[5] that the same statute of limitations rules govern contribution. *Bay Ridge* concerned the time requirements applicable to a tortfeasor's contribution suit against the State (a co-tortfeasor) in the court of claims, the tortfeasor having been previously sued in another court.

The postponed accrual rule relieves the tortfeasor of any pressure to bring a contribution suit until at least after the underlying action has given rise to a judgment and the judgment has been paid. It is especially helpful when barriers of subject matter jurisdiction preclude impleader—impleader is usually the best course if it's available— such as when a tortfeasor is sued in the supreme court and wants to implead the State as a co-tortfeasor, but can't because the State can be sued only in the court of claims. A separate action in the court of claims is necessary in that situation, and it's nice to know it doesn't face time problems.

There had been some difficulty under prior law when warranty was the basis underlying the impleader claim. Assume that P sued D for personal injuries and that D impleaded X for indemnity or contribution. If the underlying basis of D's impleader claim was X's negligence, the law treated the claim as a formal indemnity cause of action and

---

2   See Norman Co. v. Nassau County, 63 Misc. 2d 965, 314 N.Y.S.2d 44 (Sup. Ct., Nassau County 1970).

3   CPLR 602; see Ellenberg v. Sydharv Realty Corp., 41 Misc. 2d 1078, 247 N.Y.S.2d 226 (Sup. Ct., Kings County 1964); § 157.

1   CPLR 213(2); see § 35.

2   Bunker v. Bunker, 80 A.D.2d 817, 437 N.Y.S.2d 326 (1st Dep't 1981).

3   Musco v. Conte, 22 A.D.2d 121, 254 N.Y.S.2d 589 (2d Dep't 1964).

4   Dole v. Dow Chemical Co., 30 N.Y.2d 143, 331 N.Y.S.2d 382, 282 N.E.2d 288 (1972); see §§ 169–171.

5   Bay Ridge Air Rights, Inc. v. State, 44 N.Y.2d 49, 404 N.Y.S.2d 73, 375 N.E.2d 29 (1978).

gave it the limitations' benefits. If its basis was warranty, however, some cases[6] continued to treat it as a formal "warranty" cause of action even in third-party context, and denied it the limitations' advantages. They held in that situation that even though D sought only indemnification from X for whatever D might have to pay P, the D v. X claim would not get the indemnity 6-year statute of limitations, but rather only the warranty 4,[7] and that the period would run not from a payment by D to P, but from the sale of the warranted item by X to D. The different treatment when the impleader claim was rooted in warranty was an unjustifiable enigma in New York[8] and was abandoned with the Court of Appeals decision in 1980 in McDermott v. City of New York,[9] overruling the earlier caselaw. Today, it should make no difference in a tort case whether the claim over sounds in negligence, strict liability, warranty, or something else. Whatever its underlying theory of wrong, if the claim over seeks only indemnity from X to cover D for what P may recover of D, it gets the special set of statute of limitations advantages described in this section.

§ 163. Rights of Third-Party Defendant

The third-party defendant, X, may of course assert any defenses she has to the third-party claim, but X is also given "the rights of a party adverse to the other parties in the action, including the right to counter-claim, cross-claim and appeal."[1] There is some doubt as to whether this broad right allows X to interpose unrelated claims that X may happen to have. CPLR 1008 might be read to admit unrelated claims, but an easy remedy in any event, if things get too complicated, would be for the court merely to sever the unrelated ones pursuant to CPLR 603 and let them pend as separate actions, or to order separate trials.

Perhaps most importantly, CPLR 1008 also permits X to assert any defenses D may have against P's main claim. This recognizes that X's liability is usually contingent upon D's and that whatever can defeat P's claim against D will ipso facto destroy D's claim over against X. It also acknowledges that if X is solvent and D is reasonably sure of getting an indemnity judgment over, D's kinship or friendship with P might prompt D to be lax in his own defense on the theory that X will have to make everything good to D anyway. CPLR 1008 in effect permits X to prosecute D's case against P if D should prove remiss, and caselaw warns D that if D gets lazy about his own rights, he may end up with a liability to P unindemnified by X. Upon interposing a defense omitted by D, in other words, X may be let off the hook while D stays on. For example:

P neglected prosecution of his claim against D, and D could have moved to dismiss it on that ground.[2] D did not so move, but X did in D's behalf. The court dismissed the main action, but only insofar as X was concerned, leaving D to face liability to P with no further prospect of indemnity from X.[3] We may formally denominate this a disappointment to D, and if D was remiss out of some relationship with P—family and

---

[6] E.g., C.K.S., Inc. v. Helen Borgenicht Sportswear, Inc., 22 A.D.2d 650, 253 N.Y.S.2d 56 (1st Dep't 1964).

[7] N.Y. UCC § 2–725.

[8] See Siegel, *Procedure Catches Up—and Makes Trouble*, 45 St. John's L. Rev. 63, 69–70 (1970).

[9] McDermott v. City of New York, 50 N.Y.2d 211, 428 N.Y.S.2d 643, 406 N.E.2d 460 (1980).

[1] CPLR 1008.

[2] For neglect to prosecute dismissals today, see CPLR 3216, treated later in § 375.

[3] Lewis v. Borg-Warner Corp., 64 Misc. 2d 454, 315 N.Y.S.2d 56 (Sup. Ct., Orange County 1968), modified 37 A.D.2d 609, 325 N.Y.S.2d 314 (2d Dep't 1971).

friend relationships are not uncommon between P and D in tort actions, for example—D may wish he had another chance.

Such a D-against-P defense may be used by X even if the defense has since become barred to D because of some omission on his part. Thus, where it appeared that D had been so lax that he would not even be able to assert his defense against P in an amended pleading, the diligent X was still permitted to use the defense, and with the same unhappy consequences for D.[4]

CPLR 1008 had been applied even to the defense of lack of personal jurisdiction, such as for improper service.[5] In 2011, the legislature amended CPLR 1008 to make an exception for that defense, precluding X from raising it if D didn't.[6] The amendment purports in one breath to except only the defense of lack of proper service, but later sweeps in any defect in personal jurisdiction. Therefore, any of the three categories of jurisdictional objection not asserted, and therefore waived by D, may not be interposed by the third-party defendant, X.[7]

In light of CPLR 1008, a prudent defendant who has impleaded a third-party defendant may wish to forget subtleties and just interpose against the plaintiff any and all available defenses, including those that won't bar fresh suit, lest the third-party defendant (X) assert them later in the litigation in D's behalf under CPLR 1008, but at that point by no means in D's best interest.

The rule permitting X to interpose one of D's defenses against P does not necessarily permit X to use a defense he might himself have against P if P were to try to sue X directly. Thus, where X is P's employer and direct suit by P against X would be barred by the exclusivity of workers' compensation relief, X is not permitted to use that defense when, after P has sued D, X is impleaded by D.[8]

The right of X to use defenses available to D can have some impact on appeal, too. Suppose, for example, that P has won against D and D has won a judgment over against X. X appeals, but D does not. If X shows on the appeal that P should not have had judgment against D, the appellate court can reverse and dismiss D's judgment against X while leaving the P v. D judgment intact for D's failure to appeal.[9] Some older cases had held that the appellate court does have discretion to reverse the main P v. D judgment "in the interest of justice" in that situation,[10] but the Court of Appeals afterwards said no.[11] Not appealing in such an instance is a perilous course for D in any

---

[4]   See Marrone v. John A. Johnson & Sons, Inc., 283 A.D. 1114, 131 N.Y.S.2d 853 (2d Dep't 1954) (involving defense of statute of limitations).

[5]   See, e.g., Charles v. Long Island College Hosp., 47 A.D.3d 665, 850 N.Y.S.2d 173 (2d Dep't 2008).

[6]   See SPR 236:1.

[7]   See § 58 (discussing three categories of personal jurisdiction objection).

[8]   Bellefeuille v. City and County Sav. Bank, 43 A.D.2d 335, 351 N.Y.S.2d 738 (3d Dep't 1974).

[9]   Frankel v. Berman, 10 A.D.2d 838, 199 N.Y.S.2d 261 (1st Dep't 1960).

[10]   See, e.g., Rome Cable Corp. v. Tanney, 21 A.D.2d 342, 250 N.Y.S.2d 304 (4th Dep't 1964).

[11]   See Hecht v. City of New York, 60 N.Y.2d 57, 467 N.Y.S.2d 187, 454 N.E.2d 527 (1983) (NYSLD No. 285). It's not clear whether the result would be the same today. In Sharrow v. Dick Corp., 86 N.Y.2d 54, 629 N.Y.S.2d 980, 653 N.E.2d 1150 (1995), for example, a nonappealing defendant was allowed the advantage of an appellate victory won by a third-party defendant. As manifest from the discussion further on, in the appeals chapter, the cases are in conflict on this issue and have yet to be reconciled. See § 543.

event. D should cover all contingencies by taking his own appeal, at least when his indemnitor, X, has appealed.[12]

X's right to stand in D's shoes applies even to steps at the trial itself. Where, for example, it had been stipulated that the claim over would be tried to the court, although P's main claim against D was tried to a jury, X had to be given a chance to sum up to the jury on the main claim.[13]

§ 164. Additional Claims Among the Parties

The main plaintiff, P, may assert directly against the third-party defendant, X, any claim P may have against X,[1] doing so merely by amending the complaint to add the claim. P has 20 days in which to do this, measured from the service on P of X's answer to the third-party complaint. While CPLR 1008 requires X to serve the answer to the third-party complaint only on the main defendant, D, CPLR 2103(e) requires that any paper served on any party must be served on every other party.[2] Hence, X must serve a copy of the answer on P as well. P's time to amend so as to assert a direct claim against X will not start to run until P is so served.

If P makes the amendment within the required 20 days, P needs no court leave; after the 20 days, P does. In both instances, however, P's claim may also be subject to a statute of limitations defense.[3] When the amended complaint is served on X, no summons need accompany it because X is already a party.[4]

There is still some doubt about whether D, the main defendant who impleaded X, can assert against X claims unrelated to P's claim. Unrelated claims were not allowed under prior law.[5] While the Court of Appeals has more recently held that impleader is no longer to be restricted to indemnity and contribution claims, and that D may use the device to assert any claims D may have against X that bear any relationship to P's main claim against D, including D's own claim for damages against X,[6] there is still some doubt about whether a claim wholly unrelated to anything in the transaction or event underlying P's main claim would be permissible.

Several things point to permitting it. CPLR 601 as a general matter allows broad joinder of claims "when there are multiple parties," and there is specific authority in CPLR 1008 for the interposition of claims among impleaded parties.[7]

On all of these questions, the soundest conclusion would be to allow the free interposition of claims between and among all parties legitimately joined at the outset

---

[12]   See § 543.

[13]   Phillips v. Chevrolet Tonawanda Division of General Motors Corp., 43 A.D.2d 891, 352 N.Y.S.2d 73 (4th Dep't 1974).

[1]   CPLR 1009. The kinship that P's several claims must have under CPLR 1002(b) for the initial joinder of a defendant does not apply to P's claims against X under CPLR 1009. See § 134 (discussing joinder of parties).

[2]   See § 203.

[3]   See § 49.

[4]   See Harlem River Consumers Co-op., Inc. v. Manufacturers Hanover Trust Co., 68 Misc. 2d 608, 327 N.Y.S.2d 903 (N.Y. City Civ. Ct. 1972).

[5]   See, e.g., Otto v. Wegner, 11 Misc. 2d 499, 172 N.Y.S.2d 115 (App. Term, 1st Dep't 1958).

[6]   George Cohen Agency, Inc. v. Donald S. Perlman Agency, Inc., 51 N.Y.2d 358, 434 N.Y.S.2d 189, 414 N.E.2d 689 (1980); see § 157.

[7]   CPLR 1008 authorizes third-party defendants to counterclaim and cross-claim. See Bellefeuille v. City and County Sav. Bank, 43 A.D.2d 335, 351 N.Y.S.2d 738 (3d Dep't 1974).

or subsequently impleaded, leaving judicial discretion to keep order with an ad hoc application of such remedies as an order for a separate trial or severance or even a discretionary dismissal, all of which are available to the court.[8]

Assuming that a claim by D against X is relevant enough to remain, the *George Cohen* case holds that D's demand against X can exceed the sum P is seeking of D on the main claim.[9] (When impleader was strictly limited to indemnity claims, a corollary was that the impleader claim could not exceed the sum demanded on the main claim).

§ 165. Enforcement of Third-Party Judgment

Since an impleader judgment is in most cases one to make X indemnify D for all or part of what P recovers of D, it cannot be allowed to go to actual enforcement until D has paid something to P. It may go to judgment before payment of the underlying obligation, and the judgment may even be formally entered, but it will necessarily be only "a conditional judgment fixing the potential liability" until there is some proof of "payment of the main judgment."[1] If D should seek to enforce its judgment against X before paying any part of P's judgment, X may move the court to cancel the enforcement step.[2]

If the main defendant, D, is unable for any reason to pay P on the main judgment, this circumstance will ordinarily redound to the benefit of any person against whom D has an impleader judgment, but against whom P has not been awarded a direct judgment. If X is the impleaded party, D cannot compel X to pay P directly, nor can P collect from X directly. This arises in contribution more often than in the indemnity context and is elaborated later, with some discussion of a possible way for P to circumvent the barrier.[3]

The court can work out any needed details in arranging for enforcement. It may even require that D's judgment over be articulated in conditional terms, with leave to D to apply to strike the condition and make the judgment enforceable upon proof of a designated kind (such as an affidavit) presented to the court or the clerk, attesting to the datum that D has paid P on the main judgment.

If there was a default by X on the third-party claim, D at one time faced an apparent dilemma because of the 1-year time limit that CPLR 3215(c) imposes on the taking of default judgments.[4] D couldn't have judgment against X unless and until something was adjudicated in favor of P against D, and the contested P v. D suit might be a long way from trial. The dilemma doesn't exist today. Caselaw has held that the requirement that a default judgment be entered within a year after the default occurs does not apply to

---

[8]   CPLR 603, 1010. See § 161. If a party would have a statute of limitations problem if a new action would now have to be brought on a dismissed claim, severance instead of dismissal would be the more appropriate step.

[9]   *George Cohen*, 51 N.Y.2d at 366, 434 N.Y.S.2d at 194, 414 N.E.2d at 693.

[1]   McCabe v. Queensboro Farm Products, Inc., 22 N.Y.2d 204, 208, 292 N.Y.S.2d 400, 403, 239 N.E.2d 340, 342 (1968).

[2]   See CPLR 5240. Enforcement occurs under Article 52 of the CPLR, met and treated in Chapter 18, below.

[3]   See § 175.

[4]   See § 294.

third-party defaults. The year in that instance commences only upon entry of judgment in favor of P against D on the main claim, whenever that may be.[5]

§ 166. Successive Impleaders

The third-party defendant—X in our examples—may also do some impleading. X may bring in any person who "is or may be liable to him for all or part of the third-party claim."[1] And that person may do the same against yet another. The parties to such later impleaders are sometimes called fourth-party plaintiffs and defendants, fifth-party ones, etc.[2]

When a counterclaim is asserted against the plaintiff, the plaintiff has the same impleader rights vis-a-vis the counterclaim as an original defendant has on the main claim.[3]

The usual discretionary tools—dismissal, severance, separate trial—remain available to prevent things from getting out of hand.

§ 167. Impleader in Various Courts and Proceedings

Impleader is applicable to all New York courts of original civil jurisdiction except the court of claims.[1] It has limited use in courts of special jurisdiction, such as the surrogates' and family courts, but it's important in the lower courts of civil jurisdiction. It's of course limited to the subject matter jurisdiction of the particular court.

In regard to personal jurisdiction, some lower court provisions are designed to assist impleader by allowing service of process on a third-party defendant beyond the area to which the court's summons is ordinarily restricted.[2]

While impleader requires no permission in an action, it is permissible in a special proceeding only by leave of court.[3] The summary proceeding to recover the possession of real property under Article 7 of the Real Property Actions and Proceedings Law is one kind of special proceeding. Because of its summary nature,[4] the use of impleader is perhaps even less appropriate there than in any other kind of special proceeding. It is nevertheless tried from time to time and there are at present conflicting decisions on whether it's permissible. One occasional context of its appearance has been a proceeding brought by the landlord against the tenant for the non-payment of rent, with the tenant seeking to implead the local welfare official allegedly responsible for the rent payment.[5]

---

[5] Multari v. Glalin Arms Corp., 28 A.D.2d 122, 282 N.Y.S.2d 782 (2d Dep't 1967). See § 294; Commentary C3215:13 on McKinney's CPLR 3215.

[1] CPLR 1011.

[2] See Sheftman v. Balfour Housing Corp., 37 Misc. 2d 468, 234 N.Y.S.2d 791 (Sup. Ct., Queens County 1962).

[3] CPLR 1011.

[1] See Patti v. State, 47 Misc. 2d 622, 263 N.Y.S.2d 158 (Ct. Cl. 1965).

[2] See New York City Civ. Ct. Act § 408, removing city lines for purposes of process service; Uniform Dist. Ct. Act § 408, removing county lines; and Uniform City Ct. Act § 408, allowing service in adjoining counties. All three acts are in McKinney's Vol. 29A, Part 3.

[3] CPLR 401.

[4] See § 571 (Practitioner's Edition), discussing in general the function of the summary proceeding.

[5] See § 577 (Practitioner's Edition).

§ 168. Vouching-In

The device known as "vouching-in" is the "common-law counterpart and antecedent of statutory impleader,"[1] and while with the growth of impleader it has fallen into disuse, it's still permitted under caselaw and still puts in an occasional appearance.

Where X bears an indemnification relationship to D, who has been sued by P, D can "vouch in" X by merely giving X notice of the pending action and offering X control of the defense.[2] The notice need not be formal; it has even been held that it can be oral.[3] D would be wise to make the notice as formal as possible, of course; such expedient as a certified mailing would make proof of the notice, if needed, easier later on. The notice does not make X a party, but X may seek to intervene as such.

If P does get judgment against D, the judgment does not operate directly against X. Whether or not X has participated, it will still be necessary for D to bring a separate action against X for indemnification. The vouching-in notice will have accomplished this much, however: in the later action, X will not be permitted to relitigate the issues resolved between P and D in the prior suit. D's burden in the indemnity action against X will therefore be to prove only the indemnification relationship, the fact of the prior judgment, and that a vouching-in notice was duly given to X. Were X not vouched in, X would be allowed in the indemnity suit to relitigate the P v. D dispute as well, perhaps convincing the fact trier, to the obvious detriment of D, that P should not have prevailed, or at least prevailed to the extent she did. In short, the vouching-in device gives the P v. D judgment collateral estoppel effect as against X.

Because outright impleader is more effectual in that it makes X a party to the P v. D action, and, if P wins, enables D to get a simultaneous indemnity judgment against X, it's of course preferable to the more cumbersome vouching-in device. But if for one reason or another D can't implead X, the vouching-in notice may offer some help. It would seem, however, that whenever vouching-in would lie, so would outright impleader. We do know that for D to implead X, D needs a basis for jurisdiction.[4] If X is outside the state and there is no basis for extraterritorial jurisdiction of X, impleader will be unavailable. It is sometimes urged that vouching-in will serve in such a case, but the notion supposes that a vouching-in notice has a jurisdictional reach beyond that of impleader. Indeed, the Uniform Commercial Code seems to assume just that, without comment.[5] Since the vouching-in device has the effect of binding X to the result of the P v. D action, however, its jurisdictional support should be no less than that which supports outright impleader. Hence, if impleader is jurisdictionally barred, vouching-in would appear to be barred as well.[6]

---

[1] Glens Falls Ins. Co. v. Wood, 8 N.Y.2d 409, 412, 208 N.Y.S.2d 978, 980, 171 N.E.2d 321, 322 (1960).

[2] Hartford Accident & Indemnity Co. v. First Nat. Bank & Trust Co. of Hudson, 281 N.Y. 162, 22 N.E.2d 324, 123 A.L.R. 1149 (1939).

[3] Bouleris v. Cherry-Burrell Corp., 45 Misc. 2d 318, 256 N.Y.S.2d 537 (Sup. Ct., Albany County 1964).

[4] See, e.g., Ferrante Equipment Co. v. Lasker-Goldman Corp., 26 N.Y.2d 280, 309 N.Y.S.2d 913, 258 N.E.2d 202 (1970); see § 156.

[5] See N.Y. UCC § 3–803.

[6] See and compare *Glens Falls Ins. Co.*, 8 N.Y.2d at 412, 208 N.Y.S.2d at 980, 171 N.E.2d at 322, and Comment, *Constitutional Limitations on Vouching*, 118 U. Pa. L. Rev. 237 (1969). For D's right to recover from X the cost of defending P's suit in a vouching-in context, see Clarke v. Fidelity & Cas. Co. of New York, 55 Misc. 2d 327, 285 N.Y.S.2d 503 (Sup. Ct., New York County 1967).

In Castignoli v. Van Guard,[7] after an impleader claim against X was dismissed for want of personal jurisdiction, D served a vouching-in notice on X, which the trial court refused to vacate. On appeal the decision was reversed, but only on the ground that the notice was served late, which seemed to preserve the lower court decision as some authority giving vouching-in a broader jurisdictional scope than impleader itself has.[8]

It would be of obvious benefit to X, as soon as X is purportedly vouched in, to be able to use something like a motion to strike the notice so as to test the validity of the device in the particular action, i.e., secure a determination of whether X bears an indemnification relationship to D and is therefore required to assume the defense. It has been held that the court in the P v. D action has no general authority to strike the notice, even on X's motion,[9] but the conclusion is questionable. It's premised on the distinction between outright impleader and a mere vouching-in notice, as if the latter has no significant impact. But it has: use of vouching-in can make the underlying issues in the main action subject to collateral estoppel use against the person vouched-in, which is impact enough. Although the issue of X's obligation to indemnify would be open in D's later suit against X if not earlier determined, X should not be compelled to wait until then to have the issue decided. It would mean having to pick up the burden of D's defense just as a precaution, and that would seem an unreasonable burden to impose on X if X can summarily establish the absence of any possible indemnification relationship to D.

Vacatur of the vouching-in notice on the basis of its untimely service is apparently permissible,[10] and it would be useful to permit a vacatur motion on the substantive validity ground as well. If X is impleaded outright, X may move to dismiss.[11] When X is instead vouched in, a motion to strike the vouching-in notice is nothing more than the equivalent of the motion to dismiss the impleader claim.

§ 168A. "Joint" Tort Liability Adjustment; Background

At this point, impleader having been completed and contribution to follow, we inject Article 16 of the CPLR, enacted in 1986. It makes adjustments in the liability of tortfeasors. This section is background.

The rule of "joint and several" liability has long been the rule in tort cases, meaning that each tortfeasor is responsible not only for the share of plaintiff P's damages that she herself caused ("several" liability), but also for the shares attributable to the other culpable tortfeasors ("joint" liability). The practical impact of this rule is that as long as any one of the tortfeasors—call her S—is solvent, able to pay the whole judgment though in point of fault accountable for just a small part of it, P can collect all from S. S can then turn around and seek recompense from the other tortfeasors based on their shares. That's what "contribution" is all about under Article 14 of the CPLR.[1] But if the others can't pay, S ends up with the whole bill.

---

[7]   Castignoli v. Van Guard, Sup. Ct., Nassau County (Index No. 34415/94, Jan. 30, 1996; Collins, J.), rev'd 242 A.D.2d 357, 661 N.Y.S.2d 280 (2d Dep't 1997).

[8]   See the discussion in the lead note in SPR 70:1.

[9]   *Bouleris*, 45 Misc.2d at 319–20, 256 N.Y.S.2d at 538–39; Urbach v. City of New York, 46 Misc. 2d 503, 259 N.Y.S.2d 975 (Sup. Ct., Kings County 1965).

[10]   See Cole v. Long Island Lighting Co., 14 A.D.2d 922, 222 N.Y.S.2d 293 (2d Dep't 1961).

[11]   CPLR 1010.

[1]   The treatment of contribution begins in §§ 169 et seq.

The rule of "joint and several" liability thus assures that if there is to be a loser in the pack, it won't be P, the injured person. Rather, it will be the solvent tortfeasor, whom the argot often calls the "deep pocket."

Until 1986, apportionments among tortfeasors affected only an adjustment of their rights among themselves after P had been paid by any liquid source among them. The injustice of the traditional rule of joint and several liability is that a tortfeasor guilty of only the smallest share of wrongdoing will sometimes end up having to pay all or most of P's damages, at best receiving in return a contribution judgment against the other tortfeasors, who may be insolvent. What good is a juicy judgment against a juiceless debtor?

The paying tortfeasor, S, always complained when that happened, but for a variety of reasons no cure was offered. Probably the chief reason was that the plaint was really that of S's insurer, and as long as the cycle of increasing premiums made sure that the insurer would ultimately recoup from somewhere, the pressure just never rose to the point of legislative reaction. It finally reached that point in 1986, with the enactment of Article 16 of the CPLR (sections 1600 to 1603). Among the major forces advocating the enactment were the state's municipalities, the classic "deep pocket."

A municipality is often the "deep pocket" in a multiparty tort case, exposed to liability for something like a pothole, an unmarked intersection, a defective traffic light, an overhanging tree limb, etc. In many of these circumstances, the facts suggested that this type of defect played only a small role in causing the accident, a few percentage points at most. Meanwhile, the real culprit, at fault even in a jury's eyes for perhaps 90% or 95% of the tragedy, was, for example, a driver filled with alcohol, drugs, or simply rage. The culprit's insurer might have to pay the injured person its whole policy, but that might be only the minimum sum called for by the state's compulsory insurance rule, which always falls short of the damages sustained in a serious personal injury case. Hence, the responsibility for paying a $1 million judgment, for which the municipality was at most only a few thousand dollars responsible, might wind up entirely in the municipality's lap. That municipality might, in turn, only have contribution rights against a wholly uninsured motorist.

Municipal officials complained that their insurance premiums had been burgeoning to the point that insurance was sometimes unavailable. So did many others, but the municipal voices were apparently the strongest, loudest, and most audible. (A municipality will usually have the ear of a legislator.) Although the municipalities were the medium, many other tortfeasors ended up as beneficiaries.

Albeit with a myriad of exceptions and conditions, the legislative response to the "joint" liability issue was the undistinguished piece of statutory prose known as Article 16, enacted as part of Chapter 682 of the Laws of 1986.[2]

Article 16 makes an adjustment in "joint" liability, but only in part, and with many exceptions. First, the adjustment affects only "non-economic" damages.[3] There is no change in the rule of joint and several liability in respect to economic damages such as

---

[2] Chapter 682 is a concession to defendants, but not without a quid pro quo for plaintiffs: Chapter 682 is also the chapter that enacted CPLR 214–c, the provision that at last adopted a "discovery" rule for the statute of limitations in "exposure" cases. See § 40.

[3] CPLR 1600.

loss of earnings, hospital, and medical expenses. Pain and suffering, mental anguish, and loss of consortium are the major "non-economic" elements that the rule operates on.[4]

Second, only a "personal injury" claim is affected.[5] Tortfeasor liability on property damage and wrongful death claims remains joint and several in respect of all damages. This is consistent: damages on those claims are economic in nature and are therefore unaffected by the "non-economic" target of Article 16. If property damage and wrongful death claims are joined with a personal injury claim in the action, as they often are, the old rules apply to them and there will be the need to adjust figures and judgments accordingly with the assistance of a special verdict.[6] Article 16 operates only on the personal injury claim and only on its non-economic damages segment.

As we proceed through the subject of CPLR Article 16 and its inner workings, it is helpful to keep the broad picture in mind. The general rule in New York tort law is still that of joint and several liability. Defendants will try to establish their entitlement to Article 16's protections from this cruel doctrine by demonstrating that they are 50% or less at fault. Plaintiffs, in turn, will try and establish that there is an exception to Article 16 that governs,[7] placing the entire matter right back in the wonderful world of joint and several liability, regardless of the defendant's percentage of fault. That is typically the back and forth that occurs in personal injury actions, and it can have significant consequences.

We treat CPLR Article 16 here because it is a subject that should be covered before getting into the "contribution" topic. Contribution adjusts rights among tortfeasors, but does not affect their exposure to the plaintiff. Article 16 does affect their exposure to the plaintiff, and when it does it may simultaneously diminish the need for contribution. As we will discuss, rights of indemnity and contribution remain intact under Article 16.[8]

§ 168B. "Joint" Tort Liability Adjustment; The 50%-or-Less Tortfeasor

To earn the benefit of Article 16 and be rid of "joint" tort liability—securing what we might call "several-only" status—a tortfeasor must be found to have "fifty percent or less of the total liability assigned to all persons liable."[1] If found more than 50% at fault, the tortfeasor's liability remains joint. Example:

P brings a personal injury claim against T1 and T2 and gets a verdict of which $100,000 represents non-economic damages.[2] T1 is found 60% culpable, T2 40%. T2, as a beneficiary of CPLR Article 16, is responsible to P for only $40,000. T1 remains responsible to P for the full $100,000 because he is more than 50% responsible. If T1 pays that to P, T1 can then seek contribution of $40,000 from T2. But if T2 can't pay, T1 is the loser. If T2 pays P T2's own $40,000 share, on the other hand, T2 would obviously not get contribution from T1 because T2 has paid P only what T2 is individually

---

[4]   CPLR 1600.

[5]   CPLR 1601.

[6]   See § 399.

[7]   See CPLR 1602; § 168C.

[8]   See §§ 168B and 168C.

[1]   CPLR 1601(1).

[2]   Remember that in this and all of the following examples, unless otherwise noted, damage sums refer to only the non-economic segment of the verdict, which is the only segment that Article 16 operates on. See § 168A.

responsible for. P in that situation can of course collect the balance of $60,000 from T1, or try to.

If in the above example the whole verdict were $150,000, the additional $50,000 being for economic damages (e.g., loss of earnings and medical costs), T2 would be severally liable for her own $40,000 segment of the $100,000, the non-economic portion, but both jointly and severally liable, along with T1, for the whole of the $50,000, the economic portion.

If T1 is only derivatively liable for the tort of T2, as in an employer-employee context, and T2 is 100% responsible for the accident, T1 may have 0% culpability but retains 100% liability. CPLR 1602(2)(iv) makes this clear by providing that liabilities arising under the "respondeat superior" doctrine are not altered by Article 16. T1 is of course entitled to indemnification from T2 if T1 pays P all in this situation.

If employee T2 is 40% at fault and a separate tortfeasor, T3, is 60% at fault, employer T1 is responsible for T2's 40%, but T1 and T2 are both relieved of joint liability for T3's 60% share; they are beneficiaries of the 50%-or-less test. T3, on the other hand, fails that test and is jointly liable to P for the whole verdict, including the T1/T2 40% share.[3]

Is the plaintiff's share of fault factored in?

The comparative negligence rule of Article 14–A of the CPLR enables a plaintiff responsible in some measure for her own damages to recover from the defendants nevertheless, but with her damages—both economic and non-economic (there's no distinction made when figuring how much to deduct for the plaintiff's own share)—diminished by the percentage of culpability the jury has ascribed to the plaintiff. That remains intact under Article 16.[4] But how will the plaintiff's percentage of fault figure in determining the Article 16 liabilities of the defendants?

Take a sidewalk-fall case in which P's non-economic damages are found to be $100,000, with P found to have comparative fault of 40% while T1 (who supposedly fixed the sidewalk) is found 40% at fault and T2 (the property owner) 20% at fault. If P's 40% share counts in calculating whether either T1 or T2 is entitled to a several-only judgment, then both are entitled to it; neither has joint liability for the other's share because each is less than 50% at fault. But if P is factored out, and the 40% and 20% shares of the defendants are extrapolated to 100%, then T1 becomes 66 2/3% responsible and T2 33 1/3% responsible. That still means the benefit of Article 16 for T2, but not for T1, who now goes on the hook for T2's share. If T2 is insolvent, then the factoring out of P's comparative fault means that T1 pays T2's $20,000 share, while if P is factored in, P is the loser to the extent of the $20,000.

Which shall it be? Article 16 does not address the point, a fundamental one. CPLR 1601 speaks in one breath of the "total liability assigned to all persons liable" and in another of "the relative culpability of each person causing or contributing to the total liability for non-economic loss." The word "culpability" is comparative negligence language as used in Article 14–A and suggests that P's share is considered. The word

---

[3]   Rights of contribution and indemnification under these and other circumstances are, as already noted, discussed §§ 169 et seq.

[4]   CPLR 1602(2)(iii).

"liability," on the other hand, suggests to most ears the shares of those who will have to pay a judgment, which would mean defendants only.

There are arguable points on both sides. Probably more consistent with the overall structure of Article 16 is that P's share should not be considered. The extensive narrowing-down of the rule in CPLR 1601 through the numerous exceptions contained in CPLR 1602 favors the view that had the legislature considered the point, it would have excluded P's own share of fault from the joint versus joint-and-several tabulation. When P turns to the defendants, moreover, it is only for the sum left over after P's share of the damages has come off the top, which is the way the comparative negligence rule operates. With respect to that left-over sum—$60,000 in the above example (after subtracting P's share of $40,000 from the $100,000 total)—the shares of T1 and T2 are indeed the extrapolated 66 2/3% and 33 1/3%.

If we assume that T2 can't pay, however, a curious mockery can appear if such an extrapolation is used (i.e., if P's share is excluded from consideration). In the above example, where P is 40% at fault, P collects $60,000, T1 picking up T2's share. But if the percentages are instead assessed at P 20% and T1 and T2 40% each, P recovers only $40,000, because, even with extrapolation, T1 and T2 end up with 50% shares and a 50% share for T1 means that T1 does not face joint liability and does not have to pick up the insolvent T2's $40,000 share. The rule of "extrapolation" in these examples, in other words, gives more money to the less deserving plaintiff: $60,000 to the 40%-at-fault plaintiff and only $40,000 to the 20%-at-fault plaintiff. Defendants opposing an "extrapolation" construction have quite an argument on that point.

There is some caselaw addressing the issue, and a law review article devoted exclusively to the subject of extrapolation by an appellate division justice.[5] In Robinson v. June,[6] for example, drunk rowdies X and Y assaulted P outside T's tavern. The jury found X and Y together responsible for 45% of P's injuries and the tavern 50% responsible under the Dram Shop Act. The other 5% was P's share. Because X and Y were guilty of intentional conduct, they retain joint liability under an exception to the rule met later.[7] The tavern, which with 50% fault would presumably get the benefit of "several" liability, ended up with joint liability when the extrapolation step—after eliminating P's 5% share from the calculus—brought its 50% share to 52.63%.[8] The Court of Appeals also appears to have adopted the extrapolation rule applied in Robinson, although in a somewhat indirect way, in its decision in Frank v. Meadowlakes Development Corp.[9]

§ 168C. "Joint" Tort Liability Adjustment; Provisos and Exceptions

There are a number of qualifications and exceptions in Article 16, all of them apparently pro-plaintiff, the result of intense legislative trading that required a lot of

---

[5]   See Dillon, *The Extrapolation of Defendants' Liabilities Under CPLR Article 16 Where the Plaintiff Is Contributorily Negligent: An Update Toward Resolving a Perceived Ambiguity of CPLR 1601*, 73 Alb. L. Rev. 79 (2009).

[6]   Robinson v. June, 167 Misc. 2d 483, 637 N.Y.S.2d 1018 (Sup. Ct., Tompkins County 1996).

[7]   CPLR 1602(5); see § 168C.

[8]   The case is discussed in SPR 40:1.

[9]   Frank v. Meadowlakes Development Corp., 6 N.Y.3d 687, 816 N.Y.S.2d 715, 849 N.E.2d 938 (2006) (NYSLD No. 556). The extrapolation issue is discussed in SPR 174:1.

small steps back after the agreement had been made in the back rooms to take the main pro-defendant step forward.[1]

When Share of Nonparty Tortfeasor Not Considered

It must be noted that the general rule is that a nonparty's share of fault can be considered by the jury in apportioning damages under Article 16. That's good news for a named defendant, who will be trying to point fingers elsewhere and bring her proportionate share to 50% or less. However, CPLR 1601(1) provides an exception to this general rule and states that in determining shares of fault, "the culpable conduct of any person not a party to the action shall not be considered . . . if the claimant proves that with due diligence he or she was unable to obtain jurisdiction over such person." The idea is that if plaintiff (P) can get jurisdiction over one tortfeasor (T1), but not another (T2), that's T1's bad luck: T1 must carry T2's share. Nonetheless, T1, the tortfeasor joined in the action, should not simply accept the composition of the parties as chosen by P, but should scan the terrain to be sure that all other tortfeasors over whom jurisdiction can be asserted are there with T1. Generally, the only time T1 can accept the absence of another tortfeasor who is subject to jurisdiction is where T1 knows that T2 has settled the case and is insulated from suit by the settlement statute.[2] But absence because of settlement is not what CPLR 1601 means; the absence that Article 16 is concerned with is where T2 is not subject to "jurisdiction."

The use of the term "jurisdiction" in CPLR 1601(1) means both personal and subject matter jurisdiction.[3] If either is lacking over T2, that tortfeasor's proportionate share of fault will not be considered by the jury. Personal "jurisdiction" may be lacking, for example, because T2 is not a domiciliary of New York and no basis for longarm jurisdiction is available.[4] Problems of process service, as long as there is some basis for service outside the state, should not normally be a barrier to jurisdiction or an excuse for P's failure to join T2. If worse comes to worst, P should seek court-ordered service upon T2.[5] If P fails to do so, that may provide grounds for T1 to convince the court that P failed to exercise due diligence in securing jurisdiction over T2, opening the door to allow T1 to introduce T2's share of fault to the jury.

As noted above, T1 should not simply wait for P to join T2 and then, if P is not successful, rely on an argument that P failed to exercise due diligence. P may, for a variety of reasons, drag his heels. T1 should make every effort to implead T2. If impleader is made, it alone will establish that T2 is amenable to jurisdiction and assure the injection of T2's share into the case, increasing T1's chance of getting down to a proportionate share of 50% or less.

There is a paradox in this provision about not considering the share of fault of a tortfeasor beyond the court's jurisdiction. T2 will be beyond jurisdiction mainly when the claim accrued outside New York. It is in that kind of claim that longarm jurisdiction might not be available to secure jurisdiction of other tortfeasors in the action. But if the

---

[1]   Much of the text here is excerpted from this writer's lead notes in editions 322–24 of the NYSLD. The notes are more extensive. Parts will merely be footnoted as they become relevant.

[2]   The settlement statute is § 15–108 of the General Obligations Law, for which see § 176. T1 will usually obtain a reduction of the verdict under the statute for T2's settlement.

[3]   Artibee v. Home Place Corp., 28 N.Y.3d 739, 747–48, 49 N.Y.S.3d 638, 643–44, 71 N.E.3d 1205, 1210–11 (2017).

[4]   See §§ 84–89.

[5]   CPLR 308(5), 311(b); see § 75.

claim accrued in another place, the statute may be going too far in its assumption that New York law and its peculiar Article 16 workings can even be applied to the case.[6]

What about a case in which P can't get jurisdiction of an intentional tortfeasor because he can't be identified, like an assailant who made off? It has been held that the unintentional tortfeasor alleged to be responsible in some measure for the tort, and within the court's jurisdiction, may not diminish its own share based on the unidentified assailant's. The latter, in other words, is deemed beyond jurisdiction.[7] This assumes that P has made diligent efforts to identify the assailant to obtain jurisdiction, something the unintentional tortfeasor will want to carefully probe in disclosure.

Article 16 and the Court of Claims

CPLR 1601(1) also applies when the State is one of the tortfeasors or the court of claims is one of the courts involved. When the injured person sues the State in the court of claims and the State wants to show the fault of the other tortfeasors—the others of course beyond court of claims jurisdiction, but at least shown to be subject to the personal jurisdiction of some other New York court—CPLR 1601(1) expressly allows the State to have the court of claims consider the fault of these absent tortfeasors to the end of possibly reducing the State's share to 50% or below.

The converse situation, where a defendant is sued in supreme court and wants to introduce the share of fault of the nonparty State, is not expressly provided for in the statute In Artibee v. Home Place,[8] plaintiffs sued defendant landowner for injuries sustained while driving on a state highway when a branch from defendant's tree fell and struck plaintiff's car. Plaintiff also sued the State in the court of claims. The appeal in *Artibee* pertained only to the supreme court action.

The Third Department ruled that defendant was entitled to an apportionment of the State's fault to permit it to establish that its share of fault was 50% or less. The Court of Appeals reversed, concluding that the factfinder in supreme court cannot apportion fault to the State under CPLR 1601(1). The Court noted that apportionment of fault against a nonparty tortfeasor is generally available under CPLR 1601(1), unless "the claimant proves that with due diligence he or she was unable to obtain jurisdiction over" the nonparty tortfeasor "in said action (or in a claim against the state, in a court of this state)." As noted above, the statutory language permits the State in a court of claims action to seek apportionment against a private tortfeasor who is subject to jurisdiction in any court in the state. "The statute does not, however, contain similar, express enabling language to allow apportionment against the State in a Supreme Court action."[9] Furthermore, in such action, the plaintiff can easily establish that she is unable to obtain jurisdiction over the State, regardless of the degree of diligence employed.[10] In this respect, the *Artibee* Court ruled that the term "jurisdiction" in CPLR 1601(1) means both personal and subject matter jurisdiction.[11] The Court stressed that "if a defendant

---

[6]   See NYSLD No. 322.

[7]   Kennedy v. City of Yonkers, 264 A.D.2d 507, 694 N.Y.S.2d 715 (2d Dep't 1999).

[8]   *Artibee*, 28 N.Y.3d at 742, 49 N.Y.S.3d at 639–40, 71 N.E.3d at 1206–07. The Court of Appeals decision in *Artibee* was handed down just before going to press with the sixth edition. The Third Department's decision and various other aspects of CPLR Article 16 are discussed in further detail in Patrick M. Connors, *Striving to Understand Article 16, The Rubik's Cube of the CPLR*, N.Y.L.J., Sept. 23, 2015, at 3.

[9]   *Artibee*, 28 N.Y.3d at 745, 49 N.Y.S.3d at 641, 71 N.E.3d at 1208.

[10] See § 17.

[11] *Artibee*, 28 N.Y.3d at 747–48, 49 N.Y.S.3d at 643–44, 71 N.E.3d at 1210–11.

believes that it has been held liable in Supreme Court for what is actually the State's negligent conduct, the defendant can sue the State for contribution in the Court of Claims." It must be noted, however, that the State will not be bound by the amount of the judgment or the apportionment of fault in the supreme court action.[12]

Article 16 and Bankruptcy

Prior to the Court's decision in *Artibee*, for the purposes of applying CPLR 1601(1), a tortfeasor absent from the proceedings because of bankruptcy was not considered beyond the court's "jurisdiction." Therefore, a bankrupt entity's share of fault—or the share of many bankrupt entities in the realm of asbestos litigation—was included in apportioning fault for purposes of CPLR Article 16.[13] That was good news for solvent defendants. Given *Artibee's* conclusion that the term "jurisdiction" in CPLR 1601(1) means both personal and subject matter jurisdiction,[14] this area of the law needs to be reexamined.

Effect of Settlement Under General Obligations Law § 15–108

The legislature made no detailed analysis of the effect that a settlement between, for example, P and T1, but not T2, might have on CPLR Article 16. But just to be sure that the settlement statute, section 15–108 of the General Obligations Law,[15] is not in any way undermined by Article 16, CPLR 1601(2) provides that "[n]othing in this section shall be construed to affect or impair any right of a tortfeasor under section 15–108." The section appears to be compatible with Article 16 in most situations.[16]

Contribution and Indemnification Rules Intact

CPLR 1602(1) retains contribution and indemnification rights intact. Does CPLR Article 16 apply as between the third-party plaintiff and the third-party defendant? In other words, what should the rule be when an owner of premises is vicariously liable for all of an injured worker's damages and brings a third-party action seeking indemnity from the employer, who is less than 50% at fault. Is the owner entitled to complete indemnity from that party, or indemnity only for that party's pro rata share of fault (as long as that share is 50% or less of the total)? The latter, holds the Court of Appeals in Frank v. Meadowlakes Development Corp.[17] The same rule would presumably apply when the faultless, but vicariously liable, party is a contractor, or anyone else with a claim over against an at-fault party.

One wonders, however, if CPLR Article 16 should even apply to claims for indemnity or contribution. Those claims are essentially contractual in nature, and therefore do not involve the non-economic damages that Article 16 operates on, such as "pain and

---

[12] See § 470.

[13] See Kharmah v. Metropolitan Chiropractic Center, 288 A.D.2d 94, 733 N.Y.S.2d 165 (1st Dep't 2001); In re New York City Asbestos Litigation, 194 Misc. 2d 214, 750 N.Y.S.2d 469 (Sup. Ct., New York County 2002), aff'd, 6 A.D.3d 352, 775 N.Y.S.2d 520 (1st Dep't 2004) (SPR 130:4). The Second Circuit held to the contrary on this point in In re Brooklyn Navy Yard Asbestos Litigation, 971 F.2d 831 (2d Cir. 1992).

[14] *Artibee*, 28 N.Y.3d at 747–48, 49 N.Y.S.3d at 643–44, 71 N.E.3d at 1210–11.

[15] See § 176.

[16] See NYSLD No. 323 and the examples cited there.

[17] Frank v. Meadowlakes Development Corp., 6 N.Y.3d 687, 816 N.Y.S.2d 715, 849 N.E.3d 938 (2006) (NYSLD No. 556).

suffering, mental anguish, [or] loss of consortium."[18] The *Frank* Court did not address this issue.

"Non-Delegable" Duty Exception

CPLR 1602(2)(iv) provides that the limited liability permitted by Article 16 "shall not be construed to impair, alter, limit, modify, enlarge, abrogate or restrict . . . any liability arising by reason of a non-delegable duty."

Non-delegable duties are often at the heart of construction site accident cases under Article 10 of the Labor Law, which includes the popular Labor Law sections 240 and 241, and the strict liabilities they impose on owners and contractors at construction sites. A tortfeasor running afoul of such a provision, even though found only 30% responsible for the accident, for example, remains 100% accountable to the plaintiff for all damages if that 30% is predicated on one of the cited Labor Law statutes, which impose non-delegable duties. A separate provision in CPLR Article 16 also supplies this Labor Law exception, however: CPLR 1602(8).

Not necessarily needed in actions involving Labor Law sections 240 and 241, therefore, the "non-delegable duty" language in CPLR 1602(2)(iv) would have to find other terrain to travel on. It did, and quite a ride it was.

In what came as an unpleasant surprise to the state's municipalities, who championed Article 16 and are generally regarded as having spurred its adoption, a municipality was denied the benefits of Article 16 under the "non-delegable duty" provision in Rubinfeld v. City of New York,[19] where the court found nondelegable a city's duty to maintain traffic signals. The possible impact of the "non-delegable duty" language, which was apparently inserted towards the end of the frantic behind-the-scenes maneuverings in Albany that produced Article 16, may not have been appreciated at the time. Total liability for something like the non-delegable duty to maintain a traffic light failure, when a jury ascribes only a small percentage of fault to it, was the very kind of thing from which Article 16 was designed to insulate municipalities.

Under this interpretation of the non-delegable duty provision in CPLR 1602(2)(iv), whenever a municipal duty was breached and it was also found to fall in this broad "non-delegable" category, the municipality was deprived of the possibility of an Article 16 reduction for the percentage of fault attributable to others. This left the "deep pocket" municipality with a 100% exposure to the plaintiff, even though the percentage in which its wrong contributed to the accident was only a small one. In sum, it left municipalities largely without standing to enjoy the insulation of Article 16 when, in fact, the municipalities were supposed to be the article's primary beneficiaries.

It took some intricate steps, but the broad construction given the "non-delegable duty" provision by cases like *Rubinfeld* was ultimately rejected by the Court of Appeals in Rangolan v. County of Nassau.[20] In *Rangolan*, a county was sued for putting the plaintiff prisoner into the same cell with another prisoner on whom he had informed. The inevitable result, of course, was an assault, the subject of the *Rangolan* lawsuit. While the duty to protect the prisoner would indeed be a "non-delegable duty," the Court

---

[18]   CPLR 1600.

[19]   Rubinfeld v. City of New York, 170 Misc. 2d 868, 652 N.Y.S.2d 688 (Sup. Ct., Kings County 1996) (SPR 59:3).

[20]   Rangolan v. County of Nassau, 96 N.Y.2d 42, 725 N.Y.S.2d 611, 749 N.E.2d 178 (2001) (NYSLD No. 496).

in *Rangolan* was faced with the meaning of the phrase as used in CPLR 1602(2)(iv). The statute's design, held the Court in *Rangolan*, was not to create an exception, but merely to assure that tortfeasors with a nondelegable duty be saddled with the share of fault of the entity to whom they delegated the duty. The Court reasoned that "CPLR 1602(2)(iv) is not an exception to limited liability but a savings provision that preserves vicarious liability."[21] Therefore, if a municipality delegates a nondelegable duty, such as the maintenance of its roads, to an independent contractor, the municipality remains vicariously liable for the contractor's share of fault and cannot rely on CPLR 1601(1) to apportion liability between itself and the contractor.[22]

An example of the application of CPLR 1602(2)(iv)'s savings provision after *Rangolan* will help. Assume that plaintiff is injured in an automobile accident due to a defective road designed by a municipality, but maintained by an independent contractor. Plaintiff sues the driver of the car that struck him, the municipality, and the independent contractor. The jury apportions fault in equal shares, finding each defendant to be 1/3 at fault and renders a verdict of $100,000 for pain and suffering. The municipality will be liable for the full $100,000. Although the municipality's own share of fault is less than 50%, because it delegated the nondelegable duty to maintain its roads to an independent contractor, it is saddled with the percentage of fault of the contractor in addition to its own share and is therefore approximately 67% responsible for Article 16 purposes.

Now assume the same accident, lawsuit, and verdict, with the jury apportioning fault as follows: driver 60%; municipality 20%; independent contractor 20%. In this example, the municipality is entitled to the protections of CPLR Article 16. Although it delegated a nondelegable duty to an independent contractor, when it assumes the contractor's share of fault, it is only 40% responsible for Article 16 purposes. With its share of fault below 50% and the verdict comprised of non-economic damages, it is only liable for $40,000. Prior to the Court's holding in *Rangolan*, the municipality would not be entitled to Article 16 protection because it breached a non-delegable duty.

Special Rule When Plaintiff's Employer Is at Fault

An odd situation results from subdivision 4 of CPLR 1602. The subdivision concerns the well known scenario in which employee E is injured on the job in part by the fault of employer R, but can't sue R because of the exclusivity of the remedy of workers' compensation in that situation. E can sue any other person, however, such as T, responsible in part for E's injury, and T is then permitted, in certain circumstances, to implead R for contribution in this anomalous but frequent New York scenario.

If grave injury to E is not shown, section 11 of the Workers' Compensation Law would bar impleader of R altogether.[23] That scenario is addressed by CPLR 1601(1), which provides "that the culpable conduct of any person shall not be considered in determining any equitable share herein to the extent that action against such person is

---

[21]   *Rangolan*, 96 N.Y.2d at 45, 725 N.Y.S.2d 614, 749 N.E.2d at 181. While the plaintiff in *Rangolan* lost the battle regarding CPLR 1602(2)(iv) in the Court of Appeals, it ultimately won the war by establishing that the county was 63.5% at fault, putting it beyond the possibility of protection under CPLR Article 16.

[22]   See Faragiano ex rel. Faragiano v. Town of Concord, 96 N.Y.2d 776, 725 N.Y.S.2d 609, 749 N.E.2d 184 (2001).

[23]   See § 155.

barred because the claimant has not sustained a 'grave injury' as defined in section eleven of the workers' compensation law."

If E has sustained a grave injury as defined by section 11 of the Workers' Compensation Law, then T is permitted to maintain a third-party action against R for indemnity or contribution.[24] Even in this situation, however, CPLR 1602(4) will not permit an apportionment of R's fault for Article 16 purposes. That means if T and R are the only parties in E's action, T will be subject to joint and several liability for the entirety of any verdict that E obtains, even if T is only 25% responsible for the accident. The only bright spot here for T is that he will at least have a claim for contribution against R for any amount that T pays E over his 25% share.[25] That's a small consolation if R is insolvent.

As discussed in section 155 above, a "grave injury" suffered by E is not the sole condition permitting T to implead R. An additional ground for impleader of R exists if there is a "written contract entered into prior to the accident or occurrence by which the employer [R] had expressly agreed to contribution to or indemnification of . . . [T]."[26] If such a contract exists, CPLR 1602(1)(a) provides that the limitations to joint and several liability in Article 16 will not apply to a claim for indemnification arising thereunder.

Intentional Conduct and "Reckless Disregard" Cases Excepted

At two junctures, the point is made that a tortfeasor found guilty of intentional conduct gets no Article 16 benefit, whatever the percentage of fault allotted to him. He remains subject to joint and several liablity. Subdivisions 5 and 11 of CPLR 1602 so provide, the latter requiring a showing that the defendant acted "in concert" with another.

The specific language of subdivision 5 is that it removes the benefits of CPLR Article 16 from any action "requiring proof of intent." Defendants guilty of torts like assault and fraud, which have intent elements, remain wholly in the joint and several class of liability.

What about a case involving both categories of tortfeasor, one intentional (like an assailant), and the other unintentional (like the landlord whose failed maintenance of front door security was a contributing factor to letting the assailant in)? Is the unintentional one entitled to request that the jury apportion the fault of the intentional one, so as to possibly bring itself to the 50% mark, or below? The Court of Appeals answered yes to that question in Chianese v. Meier.[27]

One would expect that the jury in such a case would assign the lion's share of fault to the intentional tortfeasor. That's the likelihood, but not the certainty. A jury is free to find the act of the unintentional tortfeasor, however lacking in any specific design to damage the plaintiff, so flagrant in context—vis-à-vis the act of the intentional tortfeasor—that the jury will assign less fault to the latter and more to the unintentional tortfeasor.

That's what happened in the *Rangolan* case, discussed above, after remand. In *Rangolan*, a county put an informer back into the cell with the prisoner he informed on,

---

[24] See § 155.

[25] See § 172.

[26] Work. Comp. Law § 11.

[27] Chianese v. Meier, 98 N.Y.2d 270, 746 N.Y.S.2d 657, 774 N.E.2d 722 (2002) (NYSLD No. 511).

and the informer was predictably attacked and seriously injured.[28] The plaintiff lost the battle in the Court of Appeals, which found that the nondelegable duty provision in CPLR 1602(2)(iv) is not an exception to limited liability, but a savings provision that preserves vicarious liability. Yet, it turned out that the plaintiff was not in need of the exception after all as the county (the unintentional tortfeasor) got assessed 63.5% of fault and the assailant (the intentional one) only 36.5%.[29] That apportionment finding placed the county above the 50% cap, disqualifying it from seeking the protections of Article 16 in any event.

Subdivision 7 of CPLR 1602 adds that a tortfeasor acting "with reckless disregard for the safety of others" is also to be denied several-only status. This of course induces the plaintiff to inject the "reckless disregard" issue into as many cases as possible.

One might at first assume that a tortfeasor found guilty of "reckless disregard" conduct is not likely to be found 50% or less at fault by a jury. But the unexpected can happen as it did with the intentional/unintentional tortfeasors in the *Rangolan* case. If there are several causes of P's injury, for example, and T1's act is 70% responsible while T2's is only 30% responsible, a finding, nevertheless, that T2's conduct was the result of T2's "reckless disregard for the safety of others" would make T2 liable to P for 100%. If T1 were unable to pay the judgment, the "reckless disregard" finding against T2 would assure P's collection of the whole judgment against T2, a party less than 50% at fault.

The Motor Vehicle Exception

Reading through Article 16 from the beginning and seeking to summon up examples of its prescriptions, the uninitiated are apt to use as an example perhaps the most common source of all personal injuries: the motor vehicle accident. This makes the exception contained in subdivision 6 of CPLR 1602 all the more influential, and interesting. It says that the several-only advantage conferred by Article 16 does

not apply to any person held liable by reason of his use, operation, or ownership of a motor vehicle or motorcycle, as those terms are defined respectively in [sections 311 and 125] of the vehicle and traffic law.

Example. P sues T1 and T2, drivers of two cars who injured pedestrian P. P's non-economic damages are $100,000, with T1 found 60% at fault and T2 40%. Each is liable to P for the full $100,000: T2, although less than 50% at fault, gets no several-only status. He was a driver and drivers are not beneficiaries of Article 16. That would also be true if T2 were sued as owner of the car. But it would not be true, and T2 would be allowed the several-only status, if T2 were the manufacturer of the car, or its designer, or some other tortfeasor involved with the car in a capacity other than "use, operation, or ownership."

And there are exceptions to this exception. The definitions referred to in the statute exclude police and fire vehicles from the "vehicle" exclusion, for example, so that drivers and owners of those vehicles, most notably municipalities, do get the benefits of Article 16's several-only exposure. This is consistent with one of the prime motives known to underlie Article 16, as noted earlier: the protection of municipal entities, the usual owners and operators of fire and police vehicles. But it is not a consistent consistency because other municipal vehicles are not excepted and do retain the joint liability for the

---

[28]   *Rangolan*, 96 N.Y.2d at 45, 725 N.Y.S.2d 614, 749 N.E.2d at 181.

[29]   See SPR 131:3.

municipality. Garbage trucks would be an example. Shall we describe them as exceptions to the exception of the exception that CPLR 1602(6) constitutes?

Take an example. Four vehicles collide, injuring pedestrian P, who sues six defendants: O1, the owner of car 1 (for the negligence of the driver for whom O1 is derivatively liable under New York law); G1, a garage that negligently repaired the brakes of car 1; D2, the driver of car 2; M2, the manufacturer of car 2 (for negligent clutch design); V3, the village that owns vehicle 3, a police car on duty at the time; and C4, a city that owns vehicle 4, a garbage truck that was in the village at the time to dump some trash under a city-village contract.

The jury finds P's non-economic damages to be $100,000 and finds all defendants in some degree at fault: 20% for O1 for the ownership of the negligently driven vehicle, 20% for G1 for negligent brake repair, 30% for D2 for negligent driving, 10% for M2 for negligent car design, 15% for V3 for negligent driving, and 5% for C4 for negligent driving. Integrating just how each defendant qualifies under the interlocking exceptions noted, P would be entitled to judgment against:

O1   for $100,000; the private car owner falls under the exception and so loses the several-only status, even though his vehicle had only a 20% share of fault;

G1   for $20,000; a garage is not under the exception, so it gets the status;

D2   for $100,000; although only 30% at fault, a private car driver falls under the exception and so loses the status;

M2   for $10,000; a manufacturer is not under the exception, so it gets the status;

V3   for $15,000; a police car owner falls under the exception to the exception and so gets the status;

C4   for $100,000; a garbage truck owned by a city falls beyond the exception to the exception, so the city loses the status, although its vehicle was only 5% at fault.

It's not hard, just involved.

Medical Malpractice and "Successive Tortfeasor" Cases

We've said nothing up to now about how Article 16 figures in medical malpractice actions, or when tortfeasors are not "concurrent" and "joint," but "independent" and "successive."

Article 16 applies in medical malpractice actions, of course, to the extent it can find a situation in which tortfeasors would be "jointly" liable there. If, for example, two doctors worked on P concurrently, and the jury assigns MD1 60% responsibility and MD2 40% responsibility, MD2 would have several-only standing while MD1 would retain joint responsibility for MD2's share.

More typical, though, and clearly more challenging under Article 16, is the accident-plus-malpractice situation, which brings us into the "successive tortfeasors" arena.

The operation of Article 16 should be carefully analyzed in a situation in which a successive rather than concurrent liability is involved. The classic example is where P is hurt at the hands of tortfeasor T (a driver, contractor, sidewalk owner, etc.) and is then treated for her injury by MD, whose malpractice aggravates the injury. Under existing tort law, before even considering Article 16, T has joint and several liability and is responsible for both his own and MD's share, but MD's liability is several only: MD is responsible to P for only MD's own share, not T's. With respect to MD, therefore, Article 16 offers no gift because MD already has several-only status.

Suppose the jury finds that only 20% of P's damages were caused by the conduct of T in bringing about the accident and that MD's negligent medical treatment accounts for the other 80%. MD is still accountable for only his own 80%, not T's 20%. MD has several-only status from prior law, independent of Article 16, and keeps it without having to depend on Article 16's 50% threshold.

But what of T? Does T's 20% invoke Article 16 and relieve him of MD's 80% share? It would appear that T retains 100% exposure to P, including MD's share, for several reasons. One is that CPLR 1601(1) operates only when there are two or more tortfeasors "jointly liable." T and MD in this frequent context are not "jointly liable"; they are successive, not concurrent, tortfeasors. While T is liable for MD's share, MD is not liable for T's.

Another reason is the policy ground behind the original rule refusing to declare T and MD "joint" tortfeasors. Its theory is that T was the evil one whose conduct brought about P's injury while MD was the benevolent one who at least tried to put things right. Hence the law differentiates between the initial group, the tortfeasor or tortfeasors accountable in varying measures for the infliction of P's original injury, and the subsequent or "successive" group, the medical profession that gets involved only as a consequence.

While there is obvious evidence in Article 16 of a wish to adjust liabilities among the first group so as to relieve of "joint" liability those among them with light involvement, and while we can also find an intention to retain an initial tortfeasor's liability for all of the ensuing medical malpractice, things become murky, and a good deal more interesting, when there are several members of the original tortfeasor group and the question is whether responsibility should be placed on all of them for all of the subsequent medical malpractice, without regard to their percentages of fault for the original tort. Example:

Passenger P is hurt in a car designed by M and driven by D over a road maintained by Town T. P is taken for treatment to MD, whose treatment aggravates P's injury. P sues all four. The jury sets P's non-economic damages at $100,000. It finds that the original accident caused 40% of P's damages, the other 60% being caused by MD. For the original accident that caused 40% of P's damages, the assigned responsibility is M 10%, D 70%, and T 20%. How do we resolve that case under Article 16?

For the $40,000 segment of P's pain and suffering damages caused by the original accident, M and T, each with less than a 50% share, should be severally liable for only their own shares, which would be $4,000 for M and $8,000 for T. D, whose 70% passes the Article 16 threshold, should be accountable to P for the whole $40,000, and is also subject to the exception in CPLR 1602(6) as the driver of a car.

But what about the responsibility of M, D, and T for MD's $60,000 share? Is each of them responsible for the whole $60,000 regardless of the shares assessed against them for the initial $40,000? An argument can be made to that effect. Since each contributed in some measure to the original accident that occasioned the medical treatment, they could each be made jointly accountable for the whole of MD's share. That would make their total exposure to P: M $64,000, T $68,000, and D $100,000.

MD's exposure to P continues, as under prior law, to be for only his own $60,000 share of P's damages.

In this example, M and T, with only 10% and 20% culpability for the accident, which is itself accountable for only 40% of P's damages, are made to bear full responsibility to P for MD's 60% share of those damages.

Perhaps, in a "successive" tort situation, it would be more consistent with Article 16 (and its wish to insulate the less-than-50% tortfeasors from joint liability) to hold each of the original tortfeasors responsible for the MD-caused damages only in the percentages in which they are found accountable for the initial damages. Of the $60,000 assigned to MD, that would make M jointly liable for $6,000 and T jointly liable for $12,000. D, on the other hand, having failed Article 16's 50% threshold test initially, would continue to bear joint liability for the whole of the $60,000.

These situations involving a physician should not be frequent. They would arise only when the damages involved in phase two, the medical treatment, are not paid, and they imply an ability to pay on the part of the original tortfeasors greater than the "successive" group's ability to pay. But there can be "successive" tort situations in which the second-round injury is not caused by medical treatment, but by (e.g.) a second collision. Inability of the second-round tortfeasor to pay in that situation may be more frequent, and the above illustrations consequently less academic.

§ 168D. "Joint" Tort Liability Adjustment; Burdens of Proof

A tortfeasor seeking to obtain several-only status under Article 16 has the burden of proving it was 50% or less at fault. So provides CPLR 1603. It essentially amounts to a defense that should be pleaded as such in the answer, but there is some dispute on the subject that is discussed below. It can be pleaded hypothetically: "If I am liable at all, I am 50% or less so and entitled to the protections of CPLR Article 16." This burden is consistent with the defendant's wish to lay as much fault as possible at the door of co-tortfeasors so as to maximize his own contribution rights against them under Article 14 of the CPLR.[1]

When an Article 16 issue is present, the question has arose as to whether it is an affirmative defense and it generated a conflict among the departments about whether the defendant is obliged to furnish a bill of particulars to the plaintiff. The Fourth Department held in Ryan v. Beavers[2] that Article 16 is an affirmative defense and that the defendant must particularize it on demand. A divided Second Department afterwards held otherwise in Marsala v. Weinraub, concluding that Article 16 need not be pleaded as an affirmative defense because the statute automatically applies whenever a defendant's share of the liability is 50% or less.[3] The conflict is noted and the elements that figure in it are discussed in Maria E. v. 599 West Associates,[4] in which the court takes the position that Article 16 need not be pleaded unless it falls under the definition

---

[1]   See §§ 169 et seq.

[2]   Ryan v. Beavers, 170 A.D.2d 1045, 566 N.Y.S.2d 112 (4th Dep't 1991).

[3]   Marsala v. Weinraub, 208 A.D.2d 689, 690, 617 N.Y.S.2d 809, 810 (2d Dep't 1994).

[4]   Maria E. v. 599 West Associates, 188 Misc. 2d 119, 726 N.Y.S.2d 237 (Sup. Ct., Bronx County 2001) (SPR 115:3).

of a defense as set forth in CPLR 3018(b). Defendants' attorneys who want to be on the safe side should follow the suggestions in Justice Ritter's concurrence in *Marsala*: plead Article 16 as a defense and be prepared to particularize it.[5] That's sound advice until the Court of Appeals determines the issue and resolves the conflict. Unless and until the Court of Appeals rules to the contrary, defense attorneys would seem to do best in all departments by pleading, whenever relevant, the exception to joint and several liability under Article 16. Let this issue ultimately be decided in someone else's case. If the Court concludes that CPLR Article 16 is an affirmative defense, even defendants in the Second Department will want to be sure they have preserved it in their answer.

Although the question of whether CPLR Article 16 must be pleaded as an affirmative defense is still unresolved, the Court of Appeals has held that a plaintiff who fails to plead an exception to Article 16 waives it.[6] That can result in a substantial forfeiture to the plaintiff, who may be denied access to the wonderful world of joint and several liability against a defendant based on a mere pleading defect. Where would the plaintiff plead this? It may be premature before the answer is served, but some plaintiffs plead exceptions to CPLR Article 16 right out of the gate in the complaint. Although a reply is not permitted as of right to a CPLR Article 16 defense, assuming the defendant pleads it, the plaintiff may ask the court for permission to serve a reply including an exception to CPLR Article 16.[7] The plaintiff can also seek to amend the complaint as of right to include any relevant exceptions after receiving an answer that includes an Article 16 defense.[8]

Whatever the defendant may do in this pleading realm, it behooves the plaintiff in the course of bill of particulars or pretrial disclosure practice to inquire into whether the defendant seeks to hold anyone else accountable for the plaintiff's claim. It has been held that the defendant is under no duty to volunteer names of persons it may hold accountable under Article 16, so that a plaintiff failing to specifically inquire into the subject in pretrial practice can't complain if the defendant at the trial unexpectedly places some blame on a third person not identified earlier.[9]

A defendant seeking to preserve her Article 16 rights should be alert against any step that might later prevent her from pointing fingers at a co-defendant. In one case, for example, in which P sued A and B, and in which A successfully moved for summary judgment against P, B did not oppose the motion. The court held that B forfeited the right to implicate A at the trial, thus diminishing B's own chances of avoiding joint liability by having A's liability remain an issue in the case.[10]

As discussed above, under CPLR 1603 it is D's burden to prove it was 50% or less at fault. Quite distinct is D's right to prove P's own "comparative" fault, which D must inject as an affirmative defense. That's governed by a separate statute, CPLR 1412. D's confusion of the two articles resulted in D's waiver of the comparative negligence defense in Jones v. Kalache,[11] where D pleaded Article 16, erroneously assuming it would cover

---

[5] See the discussion in the lead notes in SPR 29–30.

[6] Morales v. County of Nassau, 94 N.Y.2d 218, 703 N.Y.S.2d 61, 724 N.E.2d 756 (1999).

[7] CPLR 3011; see § 229.

[8] See CPLR 3025(a); see § 236.

[9] See Rodi v. Landau, 170 Misc. 2d 180, 650 N.Y.S.2d 514 (Sup. Ct., Rockland County 1996).

[10] See Drooker v. South Nassau Communities Hosp., 175 Misc. 2d 181, 669 N.Y.S.2d 169 (Sup. Ct., Nassau County 1998) (SPR 72:3); see also SPR 77:3.

[11] Jones v. Kalache, 30 Misc. 3d 998, 915 N.Y.S.2d 479 (Sup. Ct., Westchester County 2011).

the comparative negligence defense as well. It didn't, resulting in a serious forfeiture by D.[12]

§ 168E. The Comparative Negligence Rule of CPLR Article 14–A

This is an appropriate point to introduce New York's comparative negligence rule, lest confusion between it and the contributory negligence rule (which it replaced) add unnecessary complications to the discussion of contribution that begins in the next section.

Prior to 1975, New York applied a rule of "contributory negligence" in tort cases. Under it, a plaintiff (P) guilty of contributing in any measure at all to her own injuries would recover nothing. Technically applied, this meant (for example) that a defendant 95% at fault in causing an accident would get off the hook completely. The 5% culpability that P had would bar any recovery at all. The rule often disposed juries to disregard contributory fault altogether in order to preserve a recovery for a seriously hurt plaintiff. Many lawyers urged adoption of a "comparative" negligence rule, under which a plaintiff guilty of culpable conduct does recover, but with her damages diminished by the percentage of her own culpability. "To keep the jury honest," they argued that a new rule should be adopted.

Article 14–A of the CPLR, consisting of sections 1411 to 1413, adopts such a rule. It was enacted in 1975 and made applicable to all causes of action accruing on or after September 1, 1975.[1]

The rule is one of "pure" comparative negligence, which enables a plaintiff to recover even if responsible for more than 50% of her own damages, the damages just being reduced by whatever percentage the fact finder, usually a jury, finds to be the plaintiff's own fault.

The rule bases the reduction not on allotments of culpability contributing to the accident or occurrence—this is an important point—but to the plaintiff's damages,[2] which is broader. In an automobile accident case, for example, it permits a comparative fault deduction based on the extent to which the plaintiff's damages were caused by her failure to wear a seat belt, an omission that may have played no role at all in causing the accident.[3]

The burden of pleading and proving the plaintiff's comparative culpability is on the defendant. It has been made an affirmative defense,[4] and a defendant should make sure to plead it as such in the answer.[5] A waiver by D of the right to show P's comparative fault in a tort action resulted when D confused Article 14–A of the CPLR with Articles 14 and 16. That happened in Jones v. Kalache,[6] a medical malpractice action in which D

---

[12]   See § 168E.

[1]   CPLR 1413.

[2]   CPLR 1411.

[3]   See 1A NY PJI3d 2:87 ("Motor Vehicle Accidents—Comparative Negligence of a Passenger") (discussing comparative negligence of passenger and failure to wear an available seat belt). In some situations, it can of course play a role even on the issue of causation. See Curry v. Moser, 89 A.D.2d 1, 454 N.Y.S.2d 311 (2d Dep't 1982).

[4]   CPLR 1412.

[5]   See § 223.

[6]   Jones v. Kalache, 30 Misc. 3d 998, 915 N.Y.S.2d 479 (Sup. Ct., Westchester County 2011) (NYSLD No. 615).

pleaded an Article 16 defense when he meant to plead an Article 14–A comparative fault defense. At a charge conference, when he asked the court to include a charge to the jury on the plaintiff's share of fault, the court refused it on the ground that the right was waived with the defendant's pleading omission. The defendant unsuccessfully argued that the pleading of the Article 16 defense in effect covered the Article 14–A defense as well.

Tort lawyers in defense work, and notably those who defend tort actions only from time to time, should sit down with all three CPLR articles in front of them—Article 14 (contribution),[7] Article 14–A (comparative fault), and Article 16 (limitations on joint and several liability)[8]—and see how they differ in their recitation of defendants' responsibilities.[9] It's a relatively light task, and it can readily avoid the kind of substantive forfeiture the defendant sustained, almost casually, in the *Jones* case. Like the contribution and apportionment rules of the *Dole* case and its CPLR Article 14 codification, which concern adjustments of liability among the tortfeasors and are taken up beginning in the next section, the comparative negligence rule of Article 14–A is essentially a rule of substantive law. But it, too, is a CPLR product and is often bound up with matters of procedure.

We introduce it here, between two batches of sections concerned with the defendants' rights and obligations, for several reasons. One is that in charging the jury about where the defendants stand under the law, the judge has to fit in at the same time what the plaintiff's rights and duties are and how they affect the defendants' liabilities. Another reason is that what the plaintiff gets from the defendants may be very much affected by the adjustment in joint and several liability made by Article 16 of the CPLR, treated in the preceding sections. By contrast, what the defendants' liabilities may be among themselves, as taken up in the ensuing sections under the "contribution" caption, are very much affected by both the Article 16 adjustment and the comparative culpability adjustment treated here.

The interplay of culpabilities, responsibilities, obligations, faults, rights, duties, etc., under these various provisions, including those on contribution yet to be negotiated, can be challenging, sometimes creating both conceptual problems substantively and practical problems procedurally. An example is Caiazzo v. Volkswagenwerk, A.G.,[10] treated later.[11]

A derivative claim, like one for loss of consortium, is diminished under the comparative negligence rule by the same percentage that diminishes the claim of the injured person from whom the claim derives. Thus, if a woman is found responsible for 30% of her own injuries, her husband's loss of services claim is also diminished by 30%.[12]

The role the assumption of risk doctrine plays within the framework of the comparative negligence rule has occasioned some difficulty. Assumption of the risk

---

[7]   See §§ 169–177.

[8]   See §§ 168A–168D.

[9]   See Patrick Connors, *Back to Basics: Careful Pleading Under CPLR Article 30*, N.Y.L.J., May 18, 2015, at 3.

[10]   Caiazzo v. Volkswagenwerk A.G., 647 F.2d 241 (2d Cir. 1981), rev'g 468 F.Supp. 593 (E.D.N.Y. 1979).

[11]   See § 175.

[12]   Maidman v. Stagg, 82 A.D.2d 299, 441 N.Y.S.2d 711 (2d Dep't 1981); see Florsz v. Ogruk, 184 A.D.2d 546, 585 N.Y.S.2d 220 (2d Dep't 1992).

under CPLR 1411 is an affirmative defense that the defendant must plead and prove.[13] The doctrine must be distinguished from comparative negligence because in an appropriate case it can lead to outright dismissal of the claim,[14] as opposed to the diminished recovery that comparative negligence allows the plaintiff. In Custodi v. Town of Amherst,[15] for example, plaintiff fell and sustained serious injuries when one of her rollerblade skates allegedly struck a two-inch height differential at the edge of defendants' driveway. Defendants moved for summary judgment dismissing the complaint based, in part, on the argument that plaintiff assumed the risk of such an injury by voluntarily engaging in recreational rollerblading.

The Court of Appeals noted that while the legislature abolished contributory negligence and assumption of risk as complete defenses when it adopted CPLR 1411, a "limited vestige of the assumption of the risk doctrine—referred to as 'primary' assumption of the risk—survived the enactment of CPLR 1411 as a defense to tort recovery in cases involving certain types of athletic or recreational activities."[16] Reviewing its extensive jurisprudence in this area, the Court concluded that, "[a]s a general rule" the doctrine of assumption of the risk should only be invoked to bar the assertion of a claim in "cases appropriate for absolution of duty, such as personal injury claims arising from sporting events, sponsored athletic and recreative activities, or athletic and recreational pursuits that take place at designated venues."[17]

In language that is sure to be cited by a legion of plaintiff's lawyers in future cases, the *Custodi* Court warned that the doctrine of primary assumption of the risk "would swallow the general rule of comparative fault [in CPLR 1411] if sidewalk defects or dangerous premises conditions were deemed 'inherent' risks assumed by non-pedestrians who sustain injuries, whether they be joggers, runners, bicyclists or rollerbladers." Therefore, the Court concluded that the assumption of the risk doctrine did not apply to bar plaintiff's action.

We sum up in this area with some cautionary advice. Unless and until the Court of Appeals rules to the contrary, defendants' attorneys would seem to do best in all departments by pleading, whenever relevant: (1) comparative fault under CPLR Article 14–A, (2) the exception to joint and several liability under Article 16, and (3) assumption of the risk under CPLR 1411, as affirmative defenses, and being ready to serve bills of particulars on them.

I. CONTRIBUTION

Table of Sections

§ 169.   Contribution, Introductory

§ 170.   The Picture Before Dole v. Dow Chemical Co.

---

[13]   See Micallef v. Miehle Co., Division of Miehle-Goss Dexter, Inc., 39 N.Y.2d 376, 382, 384 N.Y.S.2d 115, 118–19, 348 N.E.2d 571 (1976) (assumption of risk is waived if not specifically pleaded).

[14]   See Morgan v. State, 90 N.Y.2d 471, 662 N.Y.S.2d 421, 685 N.E.2d 202 (1997) (NYSLD No. 454) (quartet of cases in which three were barred by the doctrine of assumption of the risk on motions for summary judgment at the very threshold of the action, and a fourth in which the doctrine was found insufficient by itself to bar a trial in the action).

[15]   Custodi v. Town of Amherst, 20 N.Y.3d 83, 957 N.Y.S.2d 268, 980 N.E.2d 933 (2012) (NYSLD No. 637, p. 2).

[16]   *Custodi*, 20 N.Y.3d at 87, 957 N.Y.S.2d at 270, 980 N.E.2d at 935.

[17]   *Custodi*, 20 N.Y.3d at 89, 957 N.Y.S.2d at 271, 980 N.E.2d at 936.

§ 171. The Arrival of Dole
§ 172. Contribution Under CPLR Article
§ 173. Methods of Seeking Contribution
§ 174. The Old Contribution Rules Contrasted; Judgment Limited to Excess
§ 175. Some Problem Areas in Contribution
§ 176. Effect of Settlement with Fewer than All Tortfeasors
§ 177. Discretionary Tools in Handling Contribution Claims; Sequence of Trial

§ 169. Contribution, Introductory

Contribution is the right of a wrongdoer who has paid the injured person's damages to make other wrongdoers contribute to what has been paid. It has always been a phenomenon primarily of the tort realm, arising automatically when certain factors are present and not requiring any kind of agreement between or among the wrongdoers. After the 1987 Court of Appeals decision in Board of Educ. of Hudson City School Dist. v. Sargent, Webster, Crenshaw & Folley,[1] it will apparently have to be regarded as exclusively a tort phenomenon. The *Hudson* case holds that contribution under CPLR 1401 does not apply when the one from whom it is sought is liable only in contract.[2]

"Contribution" differs from "indemnity" in that it "is not founded on nor does it arise from contract and only ratable or proportional reimbursement is sought," while indemnity "springs from a contract, express or implied, and full, not partial, reimbursement is sought."[3]

Actually, the matter of terminology is more historical than accurate. When A seeks to make B "contribute" to tort damages paid by A to the plaintiff, A may also be said to be seeking to make B "indemnify" A for that portion of the hurt that was B's fault. In practical effect, contribution can be described as partial indemnity and indemnity can be described as total contribution. It is nonetheless convenient to separate the two items along the lines suggested above, using "indemnity" to describe a situation in which B should reimburse everything A has paid and "contribution" to describe B's obligation to contribute to what A has paid the plaintiff.

With the 1974 enactment of Article 14 of the CPLR, in essence codifying the Court of Appeals decision in Dole v. Dow Chemical Co.,[4] a tortfeasor sued alone in a situation in which multiple parties are at fault is allowed to bring in the other tortfeasors and make them share—"contribute" to—the damages paid to the injured person. It had previously been A's fate, if made the sole defendant, to bear all the damages alone with no right to bring in or otherwise pursue the other tortfeasors to make them share the load.

---

[1] Board of Educ. of Hudson City School Dist. v. Sargent, Webster, Crenshaw & Folley, 71 N.Y.2d 21, 523 N.Y.S.2d 475, 517 N.E.2d 1360 (1987).

[2] The case and its problems are discussed in Barker, *The Badly Performed Contract*, N.Y.L.J., Nov. 28, 1988, at 3, and in the lead note in NYSLD No. 340.

[3] McFall v. Compagnie Maritime Belge S.A., 304 N.Y. 314, 327–8, 107 N.E.2d 463, 470–1, 1952 A.M.C. 1860 (1952).

[4] Dole v. Dow Chemical Co., 30 N.Y.2d 143, 331 N.Y.S.2d 382, 282 N.E.2d 288 (1972).

§ 170. The Picture Before Dole v. Dow Chemical Co.

The Dole v. Dow Chemical Co. decision[1] burst onto the scene suddenly. It's helpful to set that scene.

At common law, the injured person, P, could pick from among the tortfeasors, singling out any one or any combination of them to pay P's damages. P could, for example, sue only tortfeasor A, and if P did, A had no recourse against any other tortfeasor. In these cases involving multiple tortfeasors, B and C and all of the others were off the hook at P's whim. The common law had various reasons for this. One was that the law should not lend its hand to adjust rights among wrongdoers.[2] Another was that the rule would discourage torts by warning each tortfeasor that there is no safety in numbers; that if P should sue A alone, A would have no recourse against the other tortfeasors so that P could therefore single A out and make A pay all of P's damages alone.[3]

Those motivations may have been relevant as applied to the intentional tort, but the restrictive rule they created was imported without critical analysis to govern in the era of the unintentional tort as well where the rule's application was irrational. Before *Dole*, only a few developments took place to abate the rigors of the rule, and the abatement was only partial.

One was the creation of a statutory right of contribution. This was itself limited. It still depended on P's voluntarily joining more than one tortfeasor, and so it still left A to face liability alone when P chose to sue A without B. It was a step towards a rule of contribution, but a grudging one.[4]

Another development was the caselaw creation of the so-called "passive-active" dichotomy. If A, the named tortfeasor, could show that it was merely "passive" in conduct while the real culprit was B, whose conduct was "active," A would be allowed to implead B. It was usually a case of all or nothing, however. If A was merely "passive" and B "active," B would be required not merely to contribute to what A paid the injured person, but to indemnify A for all of it. It was in effect a "contribution" label sewn into what was really an "indemnity" garment.

The passive-active standard was easy enough to apply in cases of straight derivative or automatic liability. If, for example, P sued O, the owner of a building, for injuries sustained in P's fall on a defective sidewalk, O could implead G, the general contractor whose negligent repair actually caused the defective condition. In a situation like that, O was rather clearly "passive" in conduct and G "active." Similarly with a master, M, sued for the tortious wrong of a servant, S. M was only derivatively liable, which qualified as passive, and M could therefore implead S. And a car owner, O, sued for injuries caused by the driving of D, could implead D.[5]

---

[1]   Dole v. Dow Chemical Co., 30 N.Y.2d 143, 331 N.Y.S.2d 382, 282 N.E.2d 288 (1972).

[2]   *Dole*, 30 N.Y.2d at 147, 331 N.Y.S.2d at 386, 282 N.E.2d at 291.

[3]   See *Developments in New York Practice,* Dole v. Dow Chemical Co.: *A Revolution in New York Law*, 47 St. John's L. Rev. 185 (1972).

[4]   See § 174, comparing the old CPLR 1401 with the new Article 14.

[5]   See Farrell and Wilner, Dole v. Dow Chemical Co.: *A Leading Decision—But Where?*, 39 Brook. L. Rev. 330 (1972).

The endeavor to apply the passive-active criterion in other situations, however, was hard and sometimes theoretically unacceptable. In many cases, the same conduct on the part of a tortfeasor could be phrased by an able lawyer in either passive or active terms. If P pleaded against A "actively," A was ipso facto barred from impleading B. Illustrative cases were numerous. The problem was well illustrated and discussed by Justice (later Chief Judge) Charles Breitel in Bush Terminal Bldgs. Co. v. Luckenbach S.S. Co.[6] The *Bush* case demonstrated how allegations of commission versus omission could be used in an attempt to parallel active versus passive conduct and how erratic that attempt could be, and how P's choice of words would nonetheless be allowed to control so substantial a right as whether A could secure contribution from B. Cases involving the so-called "nondelegable" duty were notorious examples of unfairness; the person with the statutory "nondelegable" duty was deemed guilty of "active" negligence and thereby automatically precluded, no matter how innocent, from impleading any other person, no matter how guilty.[7] Throughout this era, the language in P's complaint controlled the defendant's impleader right. The impleader was allowed if P alleged "passive" conduct by D, but was precluded if P pleaded "active" behavior.[8] This was the case even though these matters concerned only the rights of the tortfeasors inter se, a matter on which P was at best indifferent. These misfortunes are largely swept away by the *Dole* decision.

As sound as the *Bush* analysis was—more than a decade before *Dole* it pressed for the adoption of an approach that would determine primary and secondary grades of culpability rather than the artificially denominated "active" and "passive" classes—the decision was reversed by the Court of Appeals[9] along the old lines. Its lessons came in due course, however, to prevail in the Court of Appeals with the 1972 *Dole* decision, and in the legislature with the 1974 adoption of CPLR Article 14, codifying *Dole*.

§ 171.　The Arrival of Dole

The active-passive lines on the caselaw front, coupled with the old CPLR 1401 and its limited right of contribution on the statutory front, continued to stand until March 22, 1972, when the Court of Appeals handed down Dole v. Dow Chemical Co.[1] The decision in *Dole* abruptly abandoned the active-passive restriction and granted the named tortfeasors the right to interpose a contribution claim against any other tortfeasor alleged to have participated in the tort, joining the others as parties if necessary. The relative percentages of the several tortfeasors' culpabilities were henceforth to be gauged by the jury and their relative liabilities apportioned accordingly.

The rights of P, the injured person, remained the same, however. After 1975, with the adoption of the comparative negligence rule in Article 14–A of the CPLR,[2] there would of course be a reduction of P's damages for P's own percentage of culpable conduct, but even under *Dole*, P would still take judgment for the balance against each of the

---

[6]　Bush Terminal Bldgs. Co. v. Luckenbach S.S. Co., 11 A.D.2d 220, 202 N.Y.S.2d 172 (1st Dep't 1960), rev'd, 9 N.Y.2d 426, 214 N.Y.S.2d 428, 174 N.E.2d 516 (1961).

[7]　See, e.g., Milne v. Chandler and Hatlee, 45 Misc. 2d 593, 257 N.Y.S.2d 476 (Sup 1964), aff'd, 23 A.D.2d 711, 257 N.Y.S.2d 460 (3d Dep't 1965).

[8]　Kennedy v. Bethlehem Steel Co., 282 A.D. 1001, 125 N.Y.S.2d 552 (4th Dep't 1953), aff'd, 307 N.Y. 875, 122 N.E.2d 753 (1954).

[9]　Bush Terminal Bldgs. Co. v. Luckenbach S.S. Co., 9 N.Y.2d 426, 214 N.Y.S.2d 428, 174 N.E.2d 516 (1961), with Chief Judge Desmond and Judge (later Chief Judge) Fuld dissenting.

[1]　Dole v. Dow Chemical Co., 30 N.Y.2d 143, 331 N.Y.S.2d 382, 282 N.E.2d 288 (1972).

[2]　See § 168E.

defendant tortfeasors, jointly and severally.[3] If P joined A and B as defendants and P's damages were assessed at $20,000 and P's own fault at 25%, the $20,000 would be reduced to $15,000, but P would take a full $15,000 judgment against A and B and could collect it all from either one. Under *Dole*, whatever proportions of fault were found in A and B governed only contribution between them. If P sued only A, who impleaded B, P's judgment would run only against A, but A would get a judgment over against B for whatever the jury found B's share to be.[4]

The apportionment rule of *Dole* applies in all unintentional tort situations,[5] and is not limited to specific contexts, such as vehicle accident cases. *Dole* in fact involved no cars at all. P was sent by his employer, R, to clean out an enclosure that had been sprayed with D's product, but the enclosure had not yet been adequately defumigated. P inhaled poisonous fumes and died. His widow sued D. D impleaded R. Before *Dole*, the impleader would have been precluded because D was accused of acts—improperly labeling and circulating a poison product—which would have qualified as "active" negligence. *Dole*, as noted in section 170 just above, abandoned that standard and allowed the impleader.

The involvement in *Dole* of the employee/employer relationship requires a word of explanation here. The widow in *Dole* could not sue R, the employer, directly because as against R workers' compensation was (and remains) the exclusive remedy.[6] But when suit by or in behalf of the employee is brought against some other person liable for the tort, the latter may turn around and implead the employer. The theory is that such a third-party claim is one for indemnity or contribution, which are contractual in nature, and are therefore not precluded by the exclusivity of the workers' compensation remedy. *Dole* is a typical illustration of this phenomenon in New York, which subjects the employer indirectly (via having to make good as a third-party defendant) to the common law tort liability for which suit by the employee may not be brought against the employer directly. It also accounts for the monumental effort some lawyers make, when a tort case involving an employee marches into the office, to uncover some person other than the employer on whom liability might be pinned. That opens the door to common law tort damages, without which the more modest workers' compensation sums, which do not permit recovery for pain and suffering, would be all the employee could get.

Before *Dole*, the defendant could implead a third-party (employer or otherwise) only for indemnification, i.e., full coverage for the defendant's exposure to the plaintiff. The passive-active dichotomy governed and impleader was available only for indemnity, not mere contribution. *Dole* allowed the impleader device of CPLR 1007 to be used to bring in tortfeasors merely for contribution purposes.

---

[3] Kelly v. Long Island Lighting Co., 31 N.Y.2d 25, 334 N.Y.S.2d 851, 286 N.E.2d 241 (1972).

[4] Until 1986, when Article 16 was adopted adjusting the "joint and several liability" rule in tort cases (see §§ 168A through 168D), the courts of course had to assume that insofar as defendants were "joint" tortfeasors—as opposed to "successive" or "independent" tortfeasors, for example—each defendant was accountable to P for all of P's damages regardless of the defendant's own allotted proportion, which counted only in determining contribution rights among the defendants. Under Article 16, and subject to its many exceptions treated in § 168C, a tortfeasor whose culpability is assessed at 50% or less is no longer responsible to the plaintiff for the shares of non-economic damages apportioned to other tortfeasors.

[5] It should be noted that CPLR 1411, embodying the comparative negligence rule enacted after *Dole* was decided, does not purport to restrict itself to unintentional conduct.

[6] Work. Comp. Law § 11.

We may remark that the *Dole* decision (and the statutory package of Article 14 that codifies it)[7] pronounces in essence a rule of substantive law. *Dole* creates a right of contribution where none existed before, as substantive a doing as the law can manage. The CPLR was chosen as the site of its codification because the ruling affects procedure in so many ways. *Dole* can be viewed as a kind of comparative negligence rule applicable only among tortfeasors, and the case must be given credit for accelerating New York's 1975 adoption of a full comparative negligence rule,[8] which applies to the plaintiff in replacement of the contributory negligence rule that was in effect when *Dole* came down in 1972.

On the subject of the employee/employer relationship and its status in the indemnity/contribution realm, notice should be taken of the enactment of the Omnibus Workers' Compensation Reform Act of 1996,[9] which permits a defendant sued by an employee to implead the employer only when it is shown that the employee has suffered a "grave injury," as defined by statute.[10] In sum, the *Dole* decision is still good law when a third-party action is commenced against the plaintiff's employer, but only when the defendant-third-party plaintiff can establish that plaintiff sustained a grave injury.

§ 172. Contribution Under CPLR Article 14

Article 14 of the CPLR, enacted in 1974, codifies the basics of the *Dole* decision. It creates a right of contribution for a named tortfeasor regardless of whether the other tortfeasors have also been named by P, the injured person.[1] If P joins them initially, the contribution can be sought within the action via cross-claims. If P doesn't, the named tortfeasor can implead those P has omitted.[2]

The amount of contribution to which a tortfeasor is entitled is the "excess" she pays beyond her own "equitable share" of the injured person's judgment. But the one from whom the contribution is sought need not pay more than his own share; he can't be made to recompense the paying tortfeasor for yet another tortfeasor's share. (This means that tortfeasor A, from whom P has collected all, can get only B's share from B, but can't make B contribute part of the share of insolvent tortfeasor C, which A then has to absorb alone. This is an established injustice that Article 14 perpetuates.)

The "equitable share" of each tortfeasor is the "relative culpability" of that tortfeasor as found by the jury or other fact trier.[3] When Article 14 was first enacted, a plaintiff suing two or more tortfeasors and winning against all would take judgment against all of them in the full amount of the verdict. Today, with CPLR Articles 14–A and 16 on the books, P takes judgment in the full sum—less the plaintiff's own share of comparative fault, if any has been found—only against tortfeasors found responsible for more than 50% of the liability; those with 50% or less are on P's hook for only their own percentage

---

[7]   Article 14 is discussed in § 172.

[8]   CPLR 1411. See § 168E.

[9]   L.1996, ch. 635.

[10]   See Work. Comp. Law § 11; § 155. The Omnibus Act and its effect on the liability of employers is discussed at length in SPR 48:1 and 49:1 and in Connors and Gleason, *Court of Appeals Revisits "Grave Injury" Issue,* N.Y.L.J., Jan. 21, 2005, at 3.

[1]   CPLR 1401. Article 14 was adopted on the recommendation of the Judicial Conference and was based on a study by Professor M.E. Occhialino which appears in 19th Jud. Conf. Rep. 217 (1974).

[2]   CPLR 1403.

[3]   CPLR 1402.

of non-economic damages, assuming no exceptions to Article 16 apply.[4] If a given tortfeasor is in the more-than-50% category (whom we can designate M), M is jointly and severally liable for the entire judgment. If M pays out more than its proportionate share, M has a contribution claim against any other tortfeasor who has not paid P its proportionate share of the judgment. A tortfeasor who has not paid more than its proportionate share, possibly because of the protections in Article 16, will not have a contribution claim against other tortfeasors.

If it appears that the relationship between any tortfeasors is such that one is entitled to outright indemnification from the other, the right remains unimpaired.[5] Suppose, for example, that P sues E (employee) and R (employer) for E's negligent tort, for which R bears only derivative liability. While of course liable to P for the whole of P's damages, R is entitled to full indemnification from E rather than mere contribution.

If two causes concur to cause the tort, both contribution and indemnification can be sought in the same action.[6] For example:

P alights from a bus and has one foot on a defective part of the sidewalk. At that moment the bus takes off and P is injured. Both the premature takeoff and the defective sidewalk combine to produce the injury. P sues B, the bus company, O, the owner of the land, and K, the contractor who had purportedly fixed the sidewalk (and who would be responsible to O if the sidewalk was not properly fixed). The jury finds for P against all, and awards only non-economic damages, further finding that the driving was 60% responsible and the sidewalk condition 40% responsible for P's damages. P obtains judgment for all of P's damages against B (because it is more than 50% at fault, B retains joint and several liability under CPLR Article 16), but for only 40% of P's damages from O and K (who are relieved of joint and several liability under Article 16). Assume that B pays the whole judgment. B is entitled to 40% contribution from O and/or K. Should O pay any part of that, however, O would be entitled to recover back from K whatever O pays because between them there is an indemnification relationship.[7]

Liability for the same personal injury, injury to property, or wrongful death is the factor that allows contribution under CPLR 1401. It applies not only to joint tortfeasors, but also to concurrent, successive, independent, alternative, and even intentional tortfeasors.

The statute has had some interesting applications. In one case A, an attorney representing client P, failed to sue in time, relying on D's false settlement promises. P then sued D for fraud. D impleaded A for having also contributed to the lapse of P's claim. The court sustained the impleader.[8] Both A and D contributed to P's loss, notwithstanding the distinct sources of their liability—fraud by D, negligence by A.

---

[4]   See §§ 168A–168D. Article 16 applies only to P's "non-economic" damages, primarily the pain and suffering element of an award; in respect of economic damages, such as loss of earnings and medical costs, Article 16 makes no change. See § 168A.

[5]   CPLR 1404(b); CPLR 1602(2)(ii); see Logan v. Esterly, 34 N.Y.2d 648, 355 N.Y.S.2d 381, 311 N.E.2d 512 (1974). CPLR 1404(b) also preserves subrogation rights, such as the right of A's insurer, after paying the judgment P got against A, to seek contribution from the other tortfeasor, B.

[6]   If an express contract of indemnification is involved, it will govern; neither *Dole* nor the new Article 14 changes that. CPLR 1404(b). See Williams v. D. A. H. Const. Corp., 42 A.D.2d 877, 346 N.Y.S.2d 862 (2d Dep't 1973).

[7]   See and compare Bundy v. City of New York, 23 A.D.2d 392, 261 N.Y.S.2d 221 (1st Dep't 1965), decided under CPLR 1401 prior to the 1974 amendment.

[8]   Taft v. Shaffer Trucking, Inc., 52 A.D.2d 255, 383 N.Y.S.2d 744 (4th Dep't 1976).

In another case on contribution between attorneys, the wife's first attorney was apparently responsible for her losing out on alimony because after she had obtained a default judgment for it against her husband, the judgment was vacated based on mistakes made by her attorney. She sued the attorney for malpractice. He then impleaded the wife's second attorney, who, he said, was also responsible in some measure for the lost alimony because he failed to take such steps, after being retained, that would have at least reduced the amount of the loss. Since both attorneys might be shown to have a role in the alimony loss for which the wife had sued the first attorney, the links needed for contribution were present and the first attorney was allowed to seek it with an impleader of the second even though the wife's second attorney did not owe a duty to the first.[9]

Each party's responsibility will be apportioned according to the party's "equitable share" and "relative culpability"[10] regardless of theory, the mixture of theories, or the consistency of theories either among the apportionment claims or between them and the main claim. The contribution claim can thus be based on negligence, breach of warranty, breach of statutory duty, strict products liability, or any other theory, as long as it contributed to the damages suffered by the person to whom the party seeking contribution has been found liable.[11]

Another bus accident case, Zuckerman v. City of New York,[12] can illustrate. P in *Zuckerman* fell when about to enter a bus. She alleged that the sole cause of her injury was a defective sidewalk, for which C (the city) and T (the transit authority) were both responsible. She sued both, and C, seeking contribution from T, added as a ground T's negligent operation of the bus. The added theory was held permissible even though it was not asserted by plaintiff in her complaint. The case manifests that tortfeasors seeking contribution among themselves are not bound by the theories introduced by the plaintiff.

This would appear to be a natural corollary of the *Dole* rule itself, which is designed to take out of the plaintiff's hands the power—by suing fewer than all tortfeasors—to deny the ones sued any recourse against others not named in the action. Since *Dole* enables the sued tortfeasor to implead the others for contribution, it should follow that the impleading tortfeasor should not be bound by the theories on which the plaintiff relies. Just as a tortfeasor sued alone may implead another for contribution, so may he add against the other a ground of liability at least arguably supportable on the facts, whether or not depended on by the plaintiff on the main claim.[13]

"Dram Shop" cases often involve the right of contribution. The New York Dram Shop Act[14] creates a cause of action against one who sells liquor to an intoxicated person, in

---

9　　Schauer v. Joyce, 54 N.Y.2d 1, 444 N.Y.S.2d 564, 429 N.E.2d 83 (1981).

10　　CPLR 1402; see 1B NY PJI3d 2:275 ("Comparative Fault—Apportionment of Fault Between Defendants").

11　　Doundoulakis v. Town of Hempstead, 51 A.D.2d 302, 381 N.Y.S.2d 287 (2d Dep't 1976), rev'd on other grounds, 42 N.Y.2d 440, 398 N.Y.S.2d 401, 368 N.E.2d 24 (1977).

12　　Zuckerman v. City of New York, 66 A.D.2d 248, 413 N.Y.S.2d 657 (1st Dep't 1979), rev'd, 49 N.Y.2d 557, 427 N.Y.S.2d 595, 404 N.E.2d 718 (1980). The case was reversed by the Court of Appeals on a different point.

13　　As noted in the footnote above, the Court of Appeals reversed *Zuckerman*, but on a ground that apparently leaves these principles intact. *Zuckerman*, 49 N.Y.2d at 557, 427 N.Y.S.2d, 404 N.E.2d at 718 at 595. The reversal ground was that the new theory was introduced into the case in an unacceptable form.

14　　Gen. Oblig. Law § 11–101.

behalf of any person injured by reason of that drunkenness. When such a liability is asserted against the seller, it has been held that the seller can seek contribution from the intoxicated person.[15]

Defendants need to be careful to treat contribution rights under CPLR Article 14 separate from the comparative fault defense in CPLR Article 14–A and the CPLR Article 16 defense. In Jones v. Kalache,[16] a medical malpractice action in which D pleaded an Article 16 defense when he meant to plead an Article 14–A defense asserting plaintiff's comparative fault, the result was a forfeiture by D of the right to a jury charge on comparative fault.[17] A similar forfeiture arose in Ilyayeve v. City of New York,[18] where the defendant hospital's answer contained six separately captioned affirmative defenses, including a CPLR Article 16 defense and a demand for apportionment, but no cross-claim for contribution against the co-defendants. The court rejected the argument that the hospital's demand for an apportionment of any liability constituted a cross-claim, stressing that the apportionment request "can simply be relevant to its Article 16 affirmative defense, i.e., that if its fault is 50% or less, it be liable to [plaintiff] only for its apportioned share of liability as to non-economic loss."[19]

§ 173. Methods of Seeking Contribution

If P has initially joined tortfeasors A and B, each can seek contribution from the other with a mere cross-claim. If only A is joined, A can implead B for contribution. If the contribution is sought from a plaintiff, a counterclaim may be used.[1]

A separate action is still permitted, in lieu of impleader, at the tortfeasor's option. Therefore, A, without attempting to implead B, can simply pay P's judgment and then sue B for contribution, but this is a decidedly poor alternative. If impleader is possible, it should be used to avoid inconsistent verdicts and duplication of proof.[2]

An important point is that notice of claim requirements, such as might be applicable in a suit against a municipality by the injured person,[3] do not apply to contribution claims, whether asserted by a pleading within the original action, or by impleader, or in a separate action later.[4]

If the tortfeasors are in the action initially, each should assert its contribution claim as an affirmative cause of action, usually a cross-claim. If that is done, and it can be

---

[15]   Zona v. Oatka Restaurant and Lounge, Inc., 68 N.Y.2d 824, 507 N.Y.S.2d 615, 499 N.E.2d 869 (1986). For further discussion of contribution rights in dram shop cases, see Weinheimer v. Hoffman, 97 A.D.2d 314, 470 N.Y.S.2d 804 (3d Dep't 1983).

[16]   Jones v. Kalache, 30 Misc. 3d 998, 915 N.Y.S.2d 479 (Sup. Ct., Westchester County 2011).

[17]   The *Jones* decision is discussed in further detail in § 168E. That treatment is designed to warn defendants about confusing their obligations under these three articles.

[18]   Ilyayeve v. The City of New York, 2016 WL 4490623 (Sup. Ct., New York County 2016).

[19]   See §§ 168B, 168C.

[1]   CPLR 1403. An example of a counterclaim asserting contribution would be where A, driving with her son S as passenger, collides with B. If A sues B in behalf of herself and S, B's contribution claim against A, in respect of S's claim, may be interposed as a counterclaim.

[2]   See § 155.

[3]   See § 32.

[4]   See Quinn v. Spitale, 203 A.D.2d 674, 610 N.Y.S.2d 370, 90 Ed. Law Rep. 747 (3d Dep't 1994) (claim for contribution may be maintained against defendant absent compliance with notice of claim requirement in Education Law § 3813); Zillman v. Meadowbrook Hospital Co., Inc., 45 A.D.2d 267, 358 N.Y.S.2d 466 (2d Dep't 1974).

deemed mandatory under CPLR 1403[5]—there should be no need to ask or answer whether there is any other way that contribution rights can be injected into the case, or whether the judge can inject them sua sponte. If there is no undue prejudice to the other side, a pleader omitting a cross-claim for contribution from its original pleading may be permitted to assert it in an amended one.[6] If all parties omit contribution claims, they may be found to have waived them, although it is difficult to reach that conclusion in view of the fact that even a separate action is a permissible way of seeking contribution.[7]

§ 174. The Old Contribution Rules Contrasted; Judgment Limited to Excess

The lawyer conducting research into the contribution area will periodically meet pre-*Dole* cases built around the old contribution law. To adjust those cases to the present CPLR Article 14, it's helpful to contrast prior law.

Four things had to concur under the pre-1974 version of CPLR 1401 before the right of contribution among tortfeasors arose. The first three requirements have been abandoned. Only the fourth remains: it limits the paying tortfeasor to a contribution judgment for only the excess he actually pays beyond his own share. These are the four requirements of prior law, with the result under present law juxtaposed:

First. The injured person (P) had to name two or more tortfeasors in her initial summons and complaint. Article 14 doesn't require that now. It permits tortfeasor A, if sued alone, to implead B and any other tortfeasors. Contribution rights are no longer contingent on P's election to join several tortfeasors as original defendants.

Second. P had to secure jurisdiction over two or more of the tortfeasors. If she got jurisdiction over A, but not over B—because B was not served or for any other reason—A's contribution right against B died right there. The new law makes those considerations irrelevant by enabling A to implead B.[1]

Third. P had to obtain a joint judgment against A and B. If the jury found against A but in favor of B, A's right of contribution would not arise. If A paid the judgment, A could not even prosecute an appeal against B, either in its own or in P's right. Under the new law no joint judgment is needed. If A or B are joined but the verdict goes only against A, A can today take an appeal in an endeavor to obtain a reversal and hold B in for contribution. If P sues only A, A can implead B or bring a separate action later against B.

Fourth. Under prior law, A could have a contribution judgment against B only if A paid P's judgment and only for the excess paid beyond A's own share. And the contribution judgment could not exceed B's share. As noted above, this part of prior law continues. The paying A is still restricted to recovering only the excess A pays beyond her own share. Furthermore, A cannot recover from B more than B's proportionate share. These lingering rules can produce some unfair results. For example:

---

[5]   See Ilyayeve v. The City of New York, 2016 WL 4490623 (Sup. Ct., New York County 2016), where defendant who failed to assert cross-claim could not assert contribution rights. The decision is discussed in further detail in § 172.

[6]   CPLR 3025(b), discussed in § 237, permits liberal amendment of pleadings.

[7]   CPLR 1403.

[1]   CPLR 1403. A must still, however, establish jurisdiction over B in the third-party action. See § 156.

Assume that in an accident involving the driving of three private cars,[2] one of the passengers, P, is injured. Judgment for P has been rendered for $60,000 with the tortfeasors' shares found to be $30,000 for A, $20,000 for B, and $10,000 for C. A pays the whole judgment. A may not collect more than $20,000 from B. This means that if C should be insolvent and have no available insurance coverage, A, the paying tortfeasor, ends up assuming responsibility for C's whole share of the judgment.[3] This is an apparent inequity of both the old and the new law.

When the right of contribution did arise under prior law, its proportions were based on the number of concurring causes and not the "relative culpability" now provided by CPLR 1402. If, for example, P had sued two drivers, A and B, the ultimate contribution between them under this equal shares formula would have been 50%–50%; if three drivers, 33 1/3% each. Those percentages were arbitrary and automatic and were applied by the court; the jury did not pass on them. Today the jury decides actual percentages of fault, with contribution rights adjusted accordingly.

§ 175. Some Problem Areas in Contribution

A few situations in practice pose unique questions in the contribution area.

a. *Non-Supervision of Child.*

Assume a two-car collision involving drivers A and B. A's child, C, is a passenger and is injured. A, on behalf of C, sues B. B may counterclaim against A for contribution in respect of C's injuries. The case presents no unique difficulty. But now assume that instead of a two-car collision, C runs out into the street while playing and is hit by B's car. Parent A, on behalf of child C, sues B. B asserts a counterclaim against A for contribution, this time on the ground that it was A's nonsupervision of C that contributed to the accident. After much litigation and a number of lower court decisions and opinions, the Court of Appeals held in Holodook v. Spencer[1] that the counterclaim in the second situation does not lie as a matter of substantive law; that the infant has no direct tort claim against the parent for nonsupervision; and that since a nonsupervision claim does not exist directly against a parent in favor of the infant, it cannot be asserted against the parent by a third person seeking contribution, i.e., the third person's right is in a sense derivative of the infant's.[2]

This rationale enabled the courts to avoid imposing personal liability on the parent for what is usually an uninsured liability. In the first example, in which A is charged with A's own negligent driving, A's liability is covered by insurance, which is compulsory in New York at least to certain levels.[3] In the second instance, it is unlikely that parent A will carry insurance coverage for a "non-supervision" claim with the result that A would have to pay any contribution judgment out of A's own pocket. It is appealing at first blush to conclude that if A's nonsupervision, as found by the jury, accounts for such-

---

[2] There is no adjustment of liability under Article 16 of the CPLR in this situation, so the liability of each tortfeasor to the plaintiff remains joint and several. See CPLR 1602(6); § 168C.

[3] See CPLR 1402. An analogous problem occurs when P, who has a judgment against D, cannot collect from D. Even if D should have a judgment-over against X, and X is solvent, it may not avail P. D's inability to pay can become a shield for X. See paragraph (d) in § 175.

[1] Holodook v. Spencer, 36 N.Y.2d 35, 364 N.Y.S.2d 859, 324 N.E.2d 338 (1974).

[2] When a person other than a parent, such as a grandparent or uncle, undertakes to control, care for, or supervise an infant, a cause of action for negligent supervision may be brought against such person. See Adolph E. by Susan E. v. Lori M., 166 A.D.2d 906, 560 N.Y.S.2d 567 (4th Dep't 1990).

[3] See Veh. & Traf. Law §§ 311, 312.

and-such a percent of the accident, it is only fair that A pay that percent. But countervailing considerations are that if A knows he will have to make good out of his own pocket for a part of his child's recovery,[4] he will be less diligent in prosecuting the claim (if he prosecutes it at all), and that if a contribution judgment should bankrupt A or otherwise press him too hard, C himself will suffer as an infant member of the family.[5]

Although insurance seems to be a decisive factor between the lines, it is rarely recited by the courts to differentiate the cases. The judiciary has preferred to bar the nonsupervision claim as a simple matter of substantive law. The difficulty is that this approach is only a partial answer. In the first situation discussed above, in which parent A was a driver, he does face a contribution counterclaim by B. Yet A's insurance policy can be as low as the current insurance minimum prescribed by law. If B's contribution claim is sustained for more than that, the excess will have to come out of A's pocket, posing the same problems just noted, but without a "non-supervision" door to close on them.

An interesting and important distinction was made of the *Holodook* case in Nolechek v. Gesuale.[6] A partially blind infant was allowed by his parent to use a motorcycle. Doing so, he rode onto the defendant's land, did not see a cable that closed off a road, and was killed. In a wrongful death case brought by the parent, the defendant counterclaimed for contribution. The Court of Appeals allowed the counterclaim, but not on the "non-supervision" ground, which *Holodook* had now foreclosed. Rather, the court found that the parent had entrusted a "dangerous instrument" (the motorcycle) to the infant, in whose hands it damaged the defendant economically.[7] The departure that this theory makes from the conventional "dangerous instrument" cases is that here the damages sought by the contribution-claiming defendant were not for a personal injury, but rather for monetary exposure "resulting from potential liability" in a lawsuit.

Reasonable minds may obviously differ about this rationale. *Holodook* purported to bar such claims altogether, as falling under the "non-supervision" category. The *Nolechek* Court was in fact divided, but only one judge dissented (on the ground that the decision undermines the *Holodook* barrier).

The same rules that the *Holodook* case applies to nonsupervision by a parent apply as well to nonsupervision by unemancipated minor siblings. Sister S (10 years old) took her younger brother B (4 years old) next door to D's place, where D's dog bit B. B sued D, and D sought to implead S on the ground that S did not properly supervise B. The impleader claim was not allowed.[8]

---

[4]   The child's recovery is ordinarily unavailable to the use of the parent. See CPLR 1206, 1210.

[5]   It has been observed that allowing such a cause of action would adversely affect family unity by creating a direct conflict between parent and child. Lastowski v. Norge Coin-O-Matic, Inc., 44 A.D.2d 127, 133, 355 N.Y.S.2d 432, 439 (2d Dep't 1974). The case of Gelbman v. Gelbman, 23 N.Y.2d 434, 297 N.Y.S.2d 529, 245 N.E.2d 192 (1969), which removed the immunity barrier that had previously blocked a tort suit between parent and child, is distinguished on the ground that it exposed preexisting tort liabilities but did not create any new ones and that the nonsupervision claim was not a preexisting one. See *Holodook*, 36 N.Y.2d at 49–51, 364 N.Y.S.2d at 871–72, 324 N.E.2d at 345–46.

[6]   Nolechek v. Gesuale, 46 N.Y.2d 332, 413 N.Y.S.2d 340, 385 N.E.2d 1268 (1978).

[7]   See 1B NY PJI3d 2:260 ("Liability for the Conduct of Another—Family Relationship—Liability of Parent for Tort of Child—Negligence in Permitting Use of Instrumentality").

[8]   Smith v. Sapienza, 52 N.Y.2d 82, 436 N.Y.S.2d 236, 417 N.E.2d 530 (1981).

b.   *Applicability of Insurance to Impleaded Spouse.*

Section 3420(g) of the Insurance Law provides that no liability insurance policy shall be deemed to cover damages suffered by the insured's spouse unless it covers them expressly. (It usually doesn't cover them expressly.) Thus, when the insured, H, is driving and his wife, W, is injured, the insurance policy does not cover an action by W against H and the insurer need not defend nor indemnify H.

But now assume that H, with W a passenger, is driving his car when it collides with a car driven by X. W sues X, who impleads H with a contribution claim based on H's negligent driving. Does H's insurance policy cover him in that third-party context? The Court of Appeals had held in State Farm Mut. Auto. Ins. Co. v. Westlake[9] that it does not. The Court reasoned that even if the prospect of collusion, which it was the statute's purpose to avoid, is not present in the impleader situation—where both H and W would want to impose liability only on X rather than on their own insurer—the statute explicitly bars the spousal exposure and can be changed only by the legislature. The legislature accepted the invitation in 1976, overruling *State Farm* and amending the statute to provide that coverage is excluded "only where the injured spouse, to be entitled to recover, must prove the culpable conduct of the insured spouse." Since W, when suing X, levies all of her proof against X and none against H, and it is only X who is trying to implicate the impleaded H, the insurance policy in this contribution situation does cover H, who is therefore entitled under the statutory amendment to both defense and indemnity from his insurer.

c.   *Imputation of Control to Owner Present in Car.*

Suppose that the owner of car one, O-1, is a passenger in it while D-1 is driving, and there is a collision with D-2's car. O-1 sues D-2 for O-1's damages. The old case of Gochee v. Wagner[10] held that in such a situation O-1 could not recover if D-1 was also guilty of negligence; that if O-1 was present in the car, he was presumed to have control of D-1; and that the driver's negligence was therefore to be imputed to the owner.[11]

Recognizing that it was incongruous to retain so arbitrary a fault-imputing rule in light of the *Dole* case, the Court of Appeals in Kalechman v. Drew Auto Rental, Inc.,[12] overruled *Gochee.* The result is that an owner, or any other person with control of the car, such as a borrower who lets yet another person drive it, can today be held accountable, when suing for her own damages, only for her own demonstrable culpability, if any. The driver's negligence will not be imputed to her automatically.

The lawyer should not confuse this situation, in which the owner is a plaintiff, with that in which the owner is a defendant being sued by an injured third person. In that case the driver's negligence does indeed get imputed to the owner.[13]

---

[9]   State Farm Mut. Auto. Ins. Co. v. Westlake, 35 N.Y.2d 587, 364 N.Y.S.2d 482, 324 N.E.2d 137 (1974).

[10]   Gochee v. Wagner, 257 N.Y. 344, 178 N.E. 553 (1931).

[11]   New York at this time had a rule of contributory negligence, which barred a plaintiff from all recovery if plaintiff was to blame at all, a result afterwards changed with the adoption of the comparative negligence rule. See § 168E.

[12]   Kalechman v. Drew Auto Rental, Inc., 33 N.Y.2d 397, 353 N.Y.S.2d 414, 308 N.E.2d 886 (1973).

[13]   Veh. & Traf. Law § 388.

d.   P's Attempt to Bypass D and Collect Directly from X.

P can seek satisfaction of her judgment only against those whom she has joined and kept as defendants, or against those she has pleaded against after their impleader.[14] If P cannot collect her judgment from those parties, she will not be able to collect from a person against whom only an impleader (third-party) judgment stands. Example:

P sues D, and D impleads R, P's employer (whom P could not sue directly because of the exclusivity of workers' compensation).[15] P gets a $50,000 judgment against D and D gets a contribution judgment of $30,000 against R. If D is insolvent and cannot pay P's judgment, P still cannot "jump over" D and collect anything directly from R. R in that situation escapes payment.

This is the result of the Court of Appeals ruling in Klinger v. Dudley,[16] which involved an even more unpalatable loss to P. P in *Klinger* had sued A and B, among others, but a summary judgment of dismissal had been awarded to B based on an order of preclusion that B had secured against P for P's failure to serve a bill of particulars.[17] B did remain in the action but only with respect to A's contribution cross-claim against him.

In due course, P had judgment against A, and A had judgment over against B. A was unable to pay a good part of P's judgment. The question was whether B could be made to pay P any part of B's own proportionate share before A, the only party with a judgment against B, had paid P more than his own pro rata share. The Court held that B had no such obligation; that B's duty was to contribute only upon A's payment beyond his proportionate share, not upon A's mere exposure to liability.

There was lively colloquy for a while among bench and bar about whether there would be any way around this *Klinger* barrier, i.e., any way whereby P, with a judgment against an insolvent D, could collect directly or indirectly from a solvent third-party defendant, X, against whom D had a contribution judgment.[18] In due course, a lending scheme to accomplish just such a circumvention was sustained by the Court of Appeals in Feldman v. New York City Health & Hospitals Corporation.[19]

P in *Feldman* was injured in D's car and was treated at H hospital. P sued D and did not join H, but D impleaded H. P obtained judgment for $835,000, but of course it did not run against H, which was nevertheless found to have 54% responsibility for the damages and against which D had the usual inchoate judgment-over for contribution. D was able to pay only $25,000 (D's insurance coverage). The rest of the decision discusses an elaborate agreement among P, D, and one L, whereby L lent D the money to pay P, thus setting the stage for D to pay more than its proportionate share and collect from H on the judgment over. The money was carefully escrowed so that L would not lose control

---

[14]   CPLR 1009; see § 164.

[15]   See § 171.

[16]   Klinger v. Dudley, 41 N.Y.2d 362, 393 N.Y.S.2d 323, 361 N.E.2d 974 (1977).

[17]   See CPLR 3042(d); § 241 for discussion of preclusion orders.

[18]   Commentary C5230:4 on McKinney's CPLR 5230 goes into some of the suggestions that were advanced as possibilities for P.

[19]   Feldman v. New York City Health & Hospitals Corporation, 56 N.Y.2d 1011, 453 N.Y.S.2d 683, 439 N.E.2d 398 (1982), adopting the nisi prius opinion of Justice Aronin, Skagen v. New York City Emp. Retirement System, 108 Misc. 2d 448, 437 N.Y.S.2d 497 (Sup. Ct., Kings County 1981).

of it while a court test pended to test the arrangement's validity. The arrangement gave L 25% of the recovery, and was upheld.

The fact that in *Feldman* an outside lender came off with 25% of the recovery (and presumably 25% of the lawyer's contingency fee?) for a no-risk loan suggests that the *Klinger* case, which makes these circumventions necessary, deserves some additional scrutiny.[20]

The third-party defendant in the *Feldman* case was not the plaintiff's employer, and could have been joined in the original suit. To give some effect to the policies of the Workers' Compensation Law that insulates an employer from common law liability to its employee, the Court of Appeals later held in Reich v. Manhattan Boiler & Equipment Corp.[21] that a *Feldman*-type loan will not be permitted when the third-party defendant is the employer of the plaintiff.[22]

> e. *Difficulties in Dividing Fault.*

As noted earlier,[23] the interplay of the plaintiff's duty to himself (implicating the comparative negligence rule of CPLR Article 14–A), the defendants' rights and duties vis-a-vis the plaintiff (implicating the joint and several liability rules of CPLR Article 16), and the defendants' rights and duties among themselves (implicating the contribution rules of Article 14), can sometimes create both conceptual problems substantively and practical problems procedurally. An example arising even before Article 16 was on the scene is the 1979 decision in Caiazzo v. Volkswagenwerk, A.G.[24]

The case involved a multiparty problem. P was injured when he was thrown from his car as a result of D's negligence in driving his car into P's, which was not moving. P did nothing to cause the accident. It was caused solely by D. But P added to his own injuries by failing to wear a seat belt. P's damages would, therefore, have to be diminished by the proportion in which P's seatbelt omission might be found by the jury to have contributed to P's injuries. An added complication, however, was that P's being thrown from the car was allegedly contributed to by yet another cause: the negligent design or manufacture of the car door, implicating manufacturer M. D was responsible for all of P's damages, save those caused by the seat-belt omission, which was a defense for D to prove.[25] This meant that D would also be accountable for M's proportionate share, for which D was responsible for having caused the accident. M was not liable for D's share, however, because M was implicated only in the door design, which contributed to P's injuries, but not to the causation of the accident.

The court met the issues by stressing burdens of proof, in essence leaving the apportionment of damages dilemma to the jury and apparently prepared to accept the jury's verdict as long as its allotments appeared rational. The *Caiazzo* decision was an early entry on a field presenting many such skirmishes, including an aggravating

---

[20] The *Feldman* case and its lending scheme are treated in the lead note in NYSLD No. 273.

[21] Reich v. Manhattan Boiler & Equipment Corp., 91 N.Y.2d 772, 676 N.Y.S.2d 110, 698 N.E.2d 939 (1998).

[22] See the discussion of the *Reich* case in the lead note in NYSLD No. 464.

[23] See § 168E.

[24] Caiazzo v. Volkswagenwerk A.G., 647 F.2d 241 (2d Cir. 1981), rev'g 468 F.Supp. 593 (E.D.N.Y.).

[25] See § 223, discussing need to plead as a separate defense the plaintiff's failure to wear a seat belt.

dimension generated by the later addition of Article 16, which modified the rules of joint and several liability applicable to tortfeasors.[26]

§ 176. Effect of Settlement with Fewer than All Tortfeasors

A settlement with one tortfeasor does not bar the injured person's suit against any other tortfeasor, but special rules govern the effect that the settlement will have. Throughout the ensuing discussion, P will stand for the injured person, S for the settling tortfeasor, and N for the nonsettling tortfeasor. The applicable rules come from section 15–108 of the General Obligations Law.

If S settles in good faith with P, and is released by P, P may still sue N. If P does, N will be allowed to inject the issue of S's culpability into the case even though S is not a party. In that action, the jury will make findings of the relative shares of fault of parties P and N as well as nonparty S.[1] If the jury brings in a verdict against N, and also finds S at fault, the court will reduce the verdict against N by whichever of the following three figures is the highest:

1.   the amount stipulated in the release;

2.   the consideration paid for the release;[2] or

3.   the settling tortfeasor's equitable share of the damages as found by the jury (or other fact-trier).

The reduction is made by the court in the absence of the jury,[3] and the judgment that P takes against N is only for the reduced amount.

The impact of this is that if S's share of the verdict is found in the P v. N action to be more than S settled for, the difference is P's loss, while if S's share is found to be less than the settlement—not a frequent occurrence—the difference is S's loss. Take these examples.

P and S settle an automobile accident case for $10,000. The jury in P's action against N finds P's damages to be $100,000 with N and S each responsible for half. S's equitable share is $50,000; that amount is subtracted from the verdict—because it is higher than the $10,000 settled for—leaving P with a $50,000 judgment against N. With a $50,000 judgment against N and the $10,000 settlement with S, P ends up with $60,000. The difference between that and the $100,000 that the jury found to be P's damages is $40,000. That $40,000 is P's loss.

Again assume that P and S settle for $10,000, but now the jury in P's action against N brings in a verdict of $12,000 for P, with S found 40% responsible and N 60%. S's equitable share comes to $4800, which is less than his settlement figure of $10,000. Since the $10,000 is the higher, the $10,000 is the figure deducted from P's verdict. This leaves N to pay a $2,000 judgment, although N's equitable 60% share of P's $12,000 damages would otherwise have come to $7200. The $5200 difference between N's equitable share and the judgment that P actually takes against N is windfall for N and S's loss.

---

[26]   See §§ 168A–168D.

[1]   See NY PJI 2:275A–2:275C (containing jury instructions for apportionment of fault of settling tortfeasors).

[2]   This figure is usually the same as that stipulated in the release so that items 1 and 2 are generally the same and will be assumed to be the same in the examples used in this section.

[3]   CPLR 4533–b.

A possibility like that might appear to discourage settlement by S, but a settlement that turns out to be greater than what a jury actually determines the settler's share to be was apparently deemed too uncommon to warrant a different approach. And it will still be true that the big gift to S when S settles is that S will no longer be subject to the predilections of a jury while the nonsettling N is still taking his chances.

Under section 15–108, a tortfeasor who has settled a matter obtains a state of peace on the contribution front. Subsection (b) generally relieves the settling tortfeasor from liability to any other person for contribution, while subsection (c) prohibits the settlor from seeking contribution from any other person. Therefore, having settled with P, S cannot afterwards seek contribution in respect of P's injuries from any other tortfeasor.[4] But by the same token, the settlement immunizes S from any contribution claim *by* any other tortfeasor in respect of P's injuries.[5] When P settles with S and then sues N, N can't implead S for contribution.[6]

Suppose the nonsettling tortfeasor, N, defaults in P's action. It has been held that N thereupon forfeits the right to have the settlement sum to which S—the settling tortfeasor—agreed applied in reduction of the damages thereafter found. The right to the reduction comes from General Obligations Law section 15–108, held Dixon v. Globe Realty Of New York, Inc.,[7] which requires the right to be pleaded as an affirmative defense, and a defaulting defendant hasn't pleaded one.[8]

If the settlement does not occur until after P, having sued both S and N, has had judgment against S on the main claim and S has had a contribution judgment against N, S's contribution claim against N is not wiped out by a settlement. So held the Court of Appeals in Rock v. Reed-Prentice Division of Package Machinery Co.[9] At this post-judgment stage, a settlement by S with P in a sum less than the judgment is clearly advantageous to N because it reduces the contribution judgment S has against N (N's proportionate share now being applied to the settlement figure instead of to the judgment figure). A post-judgment settlement like that is therefore compatible with the purpose of section 15–108, held the court, which is to foster settlements.

The rule of the *Rock* case, allowing post-judgment settlements without the parties' forfeiting the advantages of section 15–108, is especially helpful when the State is one of the tortfeasors and the restrictions on court of claims jurisdiction enter the picture. It has been held that if the State is cast in judgment in a court of claims action, in which the cotortfeasor could of course not be joined because of jurisdictional restrictions,[10] and

---

[4]   Gen. Oblig. Law § 15–108(c).

[5]   Gen. Oblig. Law § 15–108(b).

[6]   A 2007 amendment of § 15–108 added a subdivision (d) to the statute. Everything noted so far is retained by the amendment, but with the proviso that the consideration paid for the release given by P to S be for more than one dollar. If it's for one dollar or less, the arithmetic described above is canceled and if S is let out by P in such a settlement, N is allowed to implead S if N wishes to do so later. See the example in Calise v. Heartland Medical Services, P.C., 18 Misc. 3d 332, 852 N.Y.S.2d 643 (Sup. Ct., Richmond County 2007). The amendment is discussed in SPR 193:4. Those who want this condition built into their settlement have the shorthand way of securing it: they need only see to it that the settlement recites a consideration of one dollar or less.

[7]   Dixon v. Globe Realty Of New York, Inc., 13 Misc. 3d 1202(A), 824 N.Y.S.2d 753 (Sup. Ct., Kings County 2006) (SPR 182:4).

[8]   See § 223.

[9]   Rock v. Reed-Prentice Division of Package Machinery Co., 39 N.Y.2d 34, 382 N.Y.S.2d 720, 346 N.E.2d 520 (1976).

[10]   See § 17.

the State settles with the claimant after the judgment has been rendered, the settlement at that post-judgment point does not bar the State from bringing a contribution claim in the supreme court against the other tortfeasor, based on the settlement figure.[11]

But while a post-judgment settlement may preserve contribution rights, a pretrial settlement won't, even if the settlement in terms tries to. Lettiere v. Martin Elevator Co., Inc.[12] illustrates. P sued S, who impleaded R (P's employer, who was immune from direct suit by P because of the exclusivity of workers' compensation). S was willing to settle, but wanted a jury to decide R's share so as to support a judgment for S against R for contribution. S settled with P before the trial for $250,000, with the stipulation that the trial proceed to determine R's proportionate share (which percentage S wanted applied to the settlement figure, so that S could have a contribution judgment against R accordingly). The scheme didn't work and S ended up with no contribution at all. The *Rock* case was distinguished for the point within the litigation at which the settlement occurred, and perhaps even more importantly because in *Rock*, it was the judgment that determined P's damages while in *Lettiere*, the settlement did, thereby invoking section 15–108 in *Lettiere* and barring the contribution claim.

In a later case in the Court of Appeals, Gonzales v. Armac Industries, Ltd.,[13] the settlement was made in a percentage figure instead of in dollars, but brought about the same result. It was a typical P v. D case in which D impleaded R, P's employer. The P-D settlement provided for an admission by D of 2% fault, the 2% to be applied to anything the jury might award. This is just *Lettiere* in disguise, held the Court, trying to do with percentages what *Lettiere* tried unsuccessfully to do with a dollar amount, but both are the same in that they are pretrial settlements that invoke the settlement statute and let the impleaded third person (in this case the employer) out entirely.

An unusual situation in which a pretrial settlement did immunize the settling tortfeasor from contribution even though the settlement depended in some measure on the verdict appears in Reynolds v. Morka Enterprises, Inc.[14] The only matter between the settling parties that depended on the outcome of the action was an additional $50,000 in damages. S paid P $100,000 and agreed to pay up to $50,000 more unless P recovered at least that much from N. The purpose was to assure P at least $150,000 in all. In making the computations called for by section 15–108, N would have the benefit of having the settlement figure of $150,000 applied in reduction of the verdict (N to be liable to P only if the verdict exceeded $150,000). For this reason, the settlement condition was found to contain no prejudice to N, and S was therefore permitted the benefits of section 15–108: immunity from a contribution claim by N.

What about a conventional bifurcated trial situation—with none of the unusual *Reynolds* elements to contend with—in which the settlement occurs right in the middle of things: after a liability finding, but before damages are determined? It was held in

---

[11]   State of New York v. County of Sullivan, 43 N.Y.2d 815, 402 N.Y.S.2d 397, 373 N.E.2d 291 (1977), rev'g on the dissenting opinion of Presiding Justice Koreman in State v. Sullivan County, 54 A.D.2d 29, 33, 386 N.Y.S.2d 253, 256 (3d Dep't 1976).

[12]   Lettiere v. Martin Elevator Co., Inc., 62 A.D.2d 810, 406 N.Y.S.2d 510 (2d Dep't 1978), aff'd, 48 N.Y.2d 662, 421 N.Y.S.2d 879, 397 N.E.2d 390 (1979).

[13]   Gonzales v. Armac Industries, Ltd., 81 N.Y.2d 1, 595 N.Y.S.2d 360, 611 N.E.2d 261 (1993) (NYSLD No. 401).

[14]   Reynolds v. Morka Enterprises, Inc., 82 A.D.2d 199, 442 N.Y.S.2d 664 (3d Dep't 1981). The case, a complicated one with a number of parties, is summarized in NYSLD No. 262.

Makeun v. State[15] that section 15–108 does apply and bars contribution by S against N. The *Rock* case is distinguished because in *Rock* the judgment determined the damages and the settlement came after, while in *Makeun* the settlement determined the damages.

As is evident from the numerous decisions discussed in this section, General Obligations Law section 15–108 contains many intricacies and must be carefully negotiated by parties entering into a settlement. This point is vividly made in Carlin v. Patel,[16] where a settling defendant forfeited contribution rights against two other parties based on the timing of the settlement. In *Carlin*, plaintiffs sued three defendant doctors for medical malpractice, but subsequently discontinued the action against two of them. The remaining defendant still had cross-claims for contribution against these two defendants, which were subsequently converted into a third-party action. The parties to the third-party action agreed to sever that action from the main action and to conduct a trial at a later date to resolve the contribution claims.

In plaintiffs' main action, the jury returned a verdict finding defendant liable and awarding $2.4 million in damages. Following the verdict, but before entry of the judgment, defendant settled with plaintiffs. Thereafter, the two third-party defendants moved for summary judgment dismissing the third-party action on the ground that General Obligations Law section 15–108(c) now barred any claim seeking contribution from them. The Fourth Department agreed. The *Carlin* court noted that while a tortfeasor who settles with an injured party generally cannot seek contribution from any other alleged tortfeasor, the statute does not apply to post-judgment settlements. This is the rule enunciated by the Court of Appeals in its *Rock* decision, and the one the settling defendant was seeking to avail itself of in *Carlin*.[17]

In 2007, the legislature added a new subsection (d) to General Obligations Law section 15–108, which defines the releases and covenants within the scope of the statute.[18] This amendment provides, among other things, that "[a] release . . . between a plaintiff or claimant and a person who is liable or claimed to be liable in tort shall be deemed a release . . . for the purposes of this section only if . . . such release . . . is provided *prior to entry of judgment.*"[19] The Fourth Department noted, therefore, that the new provision retains the rule enunciated in *Rock* that "a tortfeasor who settles with an injured party after the entry of a judgment retains the right to seek contribution from other tortfeasors."[20] In *Carlin*, the defendant doctor settled with plaintiffs after the $2.4 million verdict, but prior to the entry of the judgment. This sequence, the Fourth Department holds, results in defendant third-party plaintiff's forfeiture of his right to seek contribution from the two third-party defendants "under the plain language in General Obligations Law section 15–108."

Since a settlement by S under section 15–108 does not prevent N from injecting S's fault into a P v. N action even though S is not a party, the question arises whether N is entitled to have the jury know of the settlement, as reflecting, for example, on S's motivation, interest, and credibility. An interesting "gang-up" case, Meleo v. Rochester

---

[15]   Makeun v. State, 98 A.D.2d 583, 471 N.Y.S.2d 293 (2d Dep't 1984).

[16]   Carlin v. Patel, 99 A.D.3d 1220, 951 N.Y.S.2d 807 (4th Dep't 2012) (SPR 251:1).

[17]   *Rock*, 39 N.Y.2d at 40–41, 382 N.Y.S.2d at 723, 346 N.E.2d at 523–24.

[18]   The amendment is discussed in a footnote above.

[19]   Gen. Oblig. Law § 15–108(d) (emphasis added).

[20]   *Carlin*, 99 A.D.3d at 1221, 951 N.Y.S.2d at 808.

Gas and Elec. Corp.,[21] holds that at least in some circumstances a jury's being kept in ignorance of the settlement may so prejudice the nonsettling N as to require the overturning of a verdict against him.[22]

Meleo was a gas explosion case. All defendants except N settled, but the settling ones were allowed—rightly or wrongly—to remain in the case for apportionment purposes. They turned all their guns on N, and with P's sights similarly oriented, it was no surprise that N was found exclusively at fault. Allowing the settling tortfeasors to remain in the action while at the same time preventing the jury from knowing about the settlement stacked the deck, held the court. It granted a new trial.

Often in a tort case two claims are interposed, one for the personal injury suffered by the decedent and one for the wrongful death in which it culminated. The claims belong to different persons—the first to the decedent's estate, the second to statutory designees—and must therefore be kept distinct. If S settles both claims with P (the decedent's personal representative who is prosecuting both of them), but in one sum, who determines how that sum shall be divided and allocated for the purpose of applying section 15–108 in an action by P against N? It has been held that the allocation is to be decided by the fact trier in the P v. N action; that allocations purportedly made by P and S can't bind N.[23]

Didner v. Keene Corp.[24] held that a formal release is not necessary to establish that there has been a settlement, as long as the circumstances of the settlement make clear that it's a binding one.

Didner also resolved the issue of how settlement credits are to be allotted in multiparty cases in which some tortfeasors settle and some don't. Sometimes, there are a number of settlors, and the verdict in the action against the nonsettlors, which assesses the shares of responsibility of both the settling and nonsettling defendants, indicates that for some of the settlors the settlement figure is higher than their pro rata share of the verdict, and for others the opposite. Should the court consider each settlor separately and reduce the verdict by the higher of the two figures for each, or should it aggregate all of the settlors' pro rata shares on one side, and all their settlements on the other, and reduce the verdict by the higher of the two aggregated figures?

Didner adopts the "aggregate" rule, rejecting the alternative, which it describes as the "pick-and-choose" method. The Court acknowledges that section 15–108(a) does not supply a direct answer to the question, but holds that the "aggregate" rule more closely comports with the overall purpose of the settlement statute, which is to encourage settlements. Doing the opposite—allowing a reduction for the higher of the settlement versus the apportioned share of each settlor separately—would give the holdout defendant the best of both worlds with respect to every settling tortfeasor, which would not serve to encourage settlements.

---

[21] Meleo v. Rochester Gas and Elec. Corp., 72 A.D.2d 83, 423 N.Y.S.2d 343 (4th Dep't 1979) (NYSLD No. 244).

[22] In more recent years, the nonsettling party's right to know of any settlement in the case has grown more secure. See, e.g., Osowski v. AMEC Const. Management, Inc., 69 A.D.3d 99, 887 N.Y.S.2d 11 (1st Dep't 2009) (SPR 214:1). The disclosure of settlement agreements is discussed in § 348.

[23] Casey v. State, 119 A.D.2d 363, 507 N.Y.S.2d 159 (2d Dep't 1986). The facts of the case and the practical reasons for its conclusion are summarized in NYSLD No. 327.

[24] Didner v. Keene Corp., 82 N.Y.2d 342, 604 N.Y.S.2d 884, 624 N.E.2d 979 (1993) (NYSLD No. 408).

Suppose that after a settlement has been reached with some tortfeasors, the others, who remain in the action, fail to inject into the trial the issue of the shares of the settling ones, with the result that there are no jury-apportioned figures applicable to the settlors to juxtapose with the settlement figures. The problem arose and is resolved in Williams v. Niske,[25] another and more complicated Court of Appeals decision on section 15–108.

In the *Williams* case, the fault of some of the settling tortfeasors was not injected into the trial. That may have been inadvertent. A better test of the effect of such an omission occurred in the later Court of Appeals decision in Whalen v. Kawasaki Motors Corp.,[26] in which N deliberately refrained from injecting S's fault into the trial and in which an added factor was the comparative fault of P. S settled for $1.6 million. The verdict at trial was $2,415,000, with N 8% at fault and P's comparative fault at 92%. P argued that N was entitled to no deduction at all for S's settlement because N did not introduce S's fault into the trial. That would have given P a $193,000 judgment against N (the verdict reduced by P's own 92%). N argued that its $193,000 share should be reduced to nothing by crediting S's settlement against it. The Court rejected both arguments, holding that the settlement does count even without an apportionment of fault for S against which to juxtapose it, but it is applied, first, to reduce the verdict, in this case down to $815,000, and then P's 92% share is applied to reduce that. The result was a judgment for P against N for $65,000.[27]

The effect of the bankruptcy of some but not all tortfeasors is addressed in New York City Asbestos Litigation: Brooklyn Naval Shipyard Cases.[28] Shall some appropriate ratio be found whereby to allot a portion of the bankrupts' shares to the settlors and a portion to the nonsettlors? The Court in the *Asbestos* case says no, holding that all must be allocated to the nonsettlors. General Obligations Law section 15–108 contemplates adjusting what a plaintiff recovers from a nonsettlor by deducting something for what a settlor paid. Tortfeasors—here the bankrupts—who have paid the plaintiff nothing can't qualify as settlors under the statute, and the nonsettlors can't expect any diminution of the verdict to reflect the shares of the non-payers, which would violate the usual tort rule of joint and several liability.[29]

Suppose tortfeasor D is found at fault for 10% of P's damages, with P's own share assessed at 90%, but that also in the picture is general contractor G, who, under a Labor Law statute, bears absolute liability to P for all of P's damages. If G settles with P, is G entitled to indemnity from D for everything, or only D's 10% share? Everything holds the First Department in Risko v. Alliance Builders Corp.[30] because, vis-à-vis G, D is not entitled to factor in P's own 90% share.

Presumably it's open to D to show that the settlement was not reasonable. But if it's found to be, a 10% fish apparently ends up on a 100% hook.

---

[25] Williams by Williams v. Niske by Niske, 81 N.Y.2d 437, 599 N.Y.S.2d 519, 615 N.E.2d 1003 (1993) (NYSLD No. 405).

[26] Whalen v. Kawasaki Motors Corp., 92 N.Y.2d 288, 680 N.Y.S.2d 435, 703 N.E.2d 246 (1998).

[27] See the treatment of the *Whalen* case in the lead note in NYSLD No. 466.

[28] New York City Asbestos Litigation: Brooklyn Naval Shipyard Cases, 82 N.Y.2d 821, 605 N.Y.S.2d 3, 625 N.E.2d 588 (1993), affirming "for reasons stated in the opinion by Justice Israel Rubin at the Appellate Division," In re New York City Asbestos Litigation, 188 A.D.2d 214, 593 N.Y.S.2d 43 (1st Dep't 1993).

[29] Apparently these cases were not governed by the 1986 enactment of Article 16 of the CPLR— attenuating the joint and several liability rule—which would likely require adjustment in light of it. See §§ 168A–168D.

[30] Risko v. Alliance Builders Corp., 40 A.D.3d 345, 835 N.Y.S.2d 551 (1st Dep't 2007) (SPR 198:4).

The *Riviello* Problem: "Indemnification" Versus "Contribution"

A line of cases culminating in the Court of Appeals decision in Riviello v. Waldron[31] holds section 15–108 of the General Obligations Law inapplicable to indemnification situations. Hence, when S, the settling tortfeasor, is solely at fault, and N, the non-settling tortfeasor against whom an action is brought, bears a liability entirely derivative of S's, the arithmetic of section 15–108 does not apply. P will be allowed judgment against N undiminished by the proportion of responsibility found by the jury to belong to S (in *Riviello* it was 100%), and S can be impleaded into the action and made to indemnify N in full.

S in *Riviello* was a tavern employee who injured P while tossing a knife. S settled with P and now P sued N, the employer/tavern. The Court held that the relationship between S and N involved total indemnification, not contribution, and was therefore not governed by General Obligations Law section 15–108, which applies exclusively to the contribution situation. Hence, N is not entitled to a credit for the pro rata share of the fault that a jury might impute to S—it would be likely to impute 100%—because that's a mandate of the settlement statute and the statute doesn't apply. Nor is S insulated from impleader by N to make good on whatever N has to pay out to P, because that insulation, too, is a product of the statute. This means in turn that the law prior to the adoption of section 15–108 applies, which credits N with only the actual amount of the settlement and subjects S to impleader and full exposure after all—in the process discouraging settlements in the future in all cases in which indemnification instead of contribution might prove to be the relationship involved.

It takes all incentive away from a primary wrongdoer, like S in *Riviello*, to settle a claim unless P is also willing to release all who derive liability from S. *Riviello* therefore has the unfortunate effect of subverting the intent of the settlement statute, which the Court of Appeals, as evidenced by a number of cases already noted in this section, has otherwise been sensitive to avoid. The ultimate contradiction of *Riviello* is that the person from whom the law should be most enthusiastic about extracting a settlement in multiparty cases—the culprit solely at fault in the accident—is the one deterred from settling.

There were interesting follow-ups on *Riviello*. In McDermott v. City of New York,[32] the facts were the converse of *Riviello* in that S was apparently the party with only the derivative liability and N presumably the true culprit. P was an employee of S, the City of New York, and sued S for an injury caused by a sanitation truck malfunction. S impleaded the truck's manufacturer, N. Now came the settlement by S with P, and N maintained that this invoked section 15–108 and required dismissal of the impleader claim seeking contribution. The Court said no; that what S was seeking here was indemnification, not contribution, and that section 15–108 therefore did not apply.

If the fact trier in a case like *McDermott* should find that N, the manufacturer, is not exclusively at fault, however, and that S, the employer, bears some culpability, be it ever so little, the case would be magically transmuted into a "contribution" claim, which would invoke section 15–108 and require the dismissal of S's impleader claim against N, which shows once again the unsoundness of the *Riviello* construction. It generates litigation that section 15–108 sought to avoid, sometimes forcing a judicial hearing or

---

[31]   Riviello v. Waldron, 47 N.Y.2d 297, 418 N.Y.S.2d 300, 391 N.E.2d 1278 (1979).

[32]   McDermott v. City of New York, 50 N.Y.2d 211, 428 N.Y.S.2d 643, 406 N.E.2d 460 (1980).

even a jury trial just to determine whether the situation involves contribution, which would invoke the protections of section 15–108, or indemnification, which would not.[33]

A more graphic illustration of *Riviello*'s workings is the hold-harmless agreement treated at the appellate division stage of D'Ambrosio v. City of New York.[34] P was hurt by something sticking up out of a sidewalk and sued the City (N) which impleaded the abutting owner (S). At this point, P settled with S for $22,500, and in an interesting wrinkle gave S an indemnity agreement to the effect that should S ever have to pay out more on P's claim, P would make it good to S. The jury found for P for $100,000 and found fault against both N and S, apportioning it at 65% for N and 35% for S. The appellate division, deeming the case one in indemnity rather than contribution under the *Riviello* rule, held N to have only a derivative liability, S being solely at fault.[35] On this matter-of-law "indemnity" premise the appellate division held section 15–108 inapplicable, thus sustaining N's impleader of S and requiring S to recompense N for anything that N might have to pay P.

But now look at the impact of the voluntary hold-harmless agreement that P gave S when the case was settled. Whatever S pays N, S gets back from P. This results in a round robin in which P collects from N, N from S, and S back from P, the "obvious effect" of which, notes the appellate division dissent, is that P ends up with only the amount of the original settlement S agreed to anyway.[36] One lesson is that if S wants to settle, but is apprehensive about losing the advantages of section 15–108 because of the *Riviello* holding, S will derive at least some benefit if S can get a hold-harmless agreement from P in the settlement.

The motive in *D'Ambrosio* was to counter the effects of the *Riviello* case. The same motive, but a different tactic, appears in Williams v. New York City Health and Hospitals Corp.,[37] where the settlement between P and S provided that P would not assert any claim against N that could support an "indemnity" claim by N against S.

P in this *Williams* case—don't confuse it with another *Williams* case done earlier in this section—had a claim against hospital H and radiologist R. P settled with R and that barred H from seeking contribution from R. But because of *Riviello*, it did not bar H from asserting an indemnification claim against R. Hence, as part of the settlement, P stipulated that he would not assert against H any claim on which H might be vicariously liable for R as through the doctrine of respondeat superior. The court upheld the agreement and barred P from asserting any such claims, thereby assuring that H would have no basis for impleading R. H's attempted impleader of R was therefore dismissed.

Another variation on the dissonant themes forced into the settlement realm by *Riviello* is what to do when there are tortfeasor "units," with a "contribution" obligation

---

[33]   For an example of the "harsh consequences" that can attend a characterizing of a case as "indemnification" instead of "contribution," and vice versa, see Flood v. Re Lou Location Engr., 487 F. Supp. 364 (E.D.N.Y. 1980), aff'd, 636 F.2d 1201 (2d Cir. 1980) and aff'd, 636 F.2d 1202 (2d Cir. 1980).

[34]   D'Ambrosio v. City of New York, 79 A.D.2d 965, 438 N.Y.S.2d 224 (1st Dep't 1981), afterwards reversed by the Court of Appeals on a different point in D'Ambrosio v. City of New York, 55 N.Y.2d 454, 450 N.Y.S.2d 149, 435 N.E.2d 366 (1982).

[35]   It was in this respect that the Court of Appeals reversed, holding that henceforth in these "special benefit" sidewalk situations, an apportionment of fault will be required between municipality and abutting owner instead of a full recovery over. See the summary of the *McDermott* case in NYSLD No. 245.

[36]   See the summary of the appellate division *D'Ambrosio* opinion in NYSLD No. 256.

[37]   Williams v. New York City Health and Hospitals Corp., 262 A.D.2d 231, 694 N.Y.S.2d 355 (1st Dep't 1999) (SPR 95:3).

existing between the units (each unit responsible for a distinct part of the tort) and an "indemnification" obligation existing among the members of one of the units (as where one member's liability is entirely derivative of another member's conduct). A leading case in point is Mead v. Bloom.[38]

The accident was allegedly caused by the bad driving of D (of a car owned by O and being driven on the business of R), bad brake repair by B, and bad car design by GM. R, a member of the "unit" responsible for the bad driving and who had an "indemnification" relationship with D, settled. It was held that B was entitled to the benefits of the section 15–108 arithmetic for R's settlement, i.e., that R's "indemnification" relationship with a member of his own unit would not invoke *Riviello* (and cancel out the statutory benefits of section 15–108) as between R and a member of a different unit, there clearly being a "contribution" relationship between units.[39]

Nonsettling tortfeasors, otherwise immune from a contribution claim by tortfeasor S after he settles, can waive that immunity and were held to have done so in Mitchell v. New York Hospital.[40] A whole bunch of alleged tortfeasors stipulated in writing that one of their number, S, could pay P all, with S thereafter entitled to proceed against the others to have his contribution rights against them determined. S paid all and proceeded against the others, who promptly tried to violate their stipulation by moving to dismiss S's contribution claim. Their motion was denied, and they were sent to bed without dinner.

The policies underlying the federal civil rights legislation may sometimes deny a nonsettling tortfeasor a reduction for a settlement made by another tortfeasor as where the effect would be to let the civil rights offender avoid all punishment for his conduct.[41]

Article 16 of the CPLR, adopted in 1986, which alleviates the "joint" liability of certain tortfeasors,[42] specifically provides that it is not to be construed to impair settlements under General Obligations Law section 15–108.[43]

§ 177. Discretionary Tools in Handling Contribution Claims; Sequence of Trial

Ordinarily, it will pose no undue difficulty for either the court or jury to have the contribution claims tried right along with the other liability issues. But the court can vary the steps as need be. It can have P's claim against tortfeasors A and B tried first to a verdict, and then, if the verdict is for P against both, have A and B try their contribution claims to the same jury. That will usually be unnecessary. In most cases, it would be an outright waste. A preferable step, if any at all should be needed, is to try all of the issues together, but feed them to the jury in spurts. That is, the court can charge the jury to

---

[38]   Mead v. Bloom, 62 N.Y.2d 788, 477 N.Y.S.2d 326, 465 N.E.2d 1262 (1984), affirming on Justice Boomer's opinion in the appellate division, Mead v. Bloom, 94 A.D.2d 423, 464 N.Y.S.2d 904 (4th Dep't 1983).

[39]   These points are elaborated in the lead note in NYSLD No. 293.

[40]   Mitchell v. New York Hosp., 61 N.Y.2d 208, 473 N.Y.S.2d 148, 461 N.E.2d 285 (1984).

[41]   See Banks v. Yokemick, N.Y.L.J., Dec. 14, 2001, at 28, col.4 (S.D.N.Y.; Marrero, J.) (SPR 123:3).

[42]   See §§ 168A–168D.

[43]   CPLR 1601(2). Some examples of the interplay of Article 16 problems and settlement problems appear in the lead note in NYSLD No. 323.

pass only on P's rights against A and B, and then, if the verdict comes in against both, charge the jury to go out again and this time find their relative culpabilities.[1]

It is usually best to have all issues of liability tried together, especially now, with CPLR Article 16 on the books. Article 16 adjusts the rules about joint and several liability as they bear on the tortfeasors' exposure to the plaintiff,[2] an exposure which would in any event have to be part of the initial liability hearing, so there is even more reason now than before to have contribution rights among the tortfeasors heard and determined simultaneously. All these things concern percentages of culpability of all of the parties: of the tortfeasors to P on the one hand (involving Article 16 and adjusted tort liability), among the tortfeasors inter se on the other hand (involving Article 14 and contribution rights among tortfeasors), and, if we may be allowed a third hand (which this subject can surely use), of course P's own comparative fault under Article 14–A. Except in unusual circumstances, all three things should be heard and determined together.

The use of a special verdict will clarify the jury's conclusions.[3]

Enforcement questions, such as the form a contribution judgment should take and the moment when the judgment becomes enforceable, can be guided by the rules applicable to impleader judgments.[4]

J. INTERVENTION

Table of Sections

§ 178.   Intervention, Generally
§ 179.   Intervention of Right Under Special Statutes
§ 180.   Intervention of Right Where Representation Inadequate
§ 181.   Intervention of Right in Property Cases
§ 182.   Permissive Intervention
§ 183.   Procedure for Intervention

§ 178. Intervention, Generally

Intervention is a procedure whereby an outsider can become a party to a pending action on her own initiative. It is sometimes available as of right,[5] sometimes only in the court's discretion,[6] but it must be sought by motion in all instances.[7] The courts are liberal in its allowance today—a relatively recent development[8]—and distinctions between intervention of right and discretionary intervention are not sharply drawn.[9]

---

[1]   See 1B NY PJI3d 2:275 ("Comparative Fault—Apportionment of Fault Between Defendants").

[2]   See §§ 168A et seq.

[3]   A general verdict merely announces the jury's conclusion without revealing any particular ground or answering any particular question. The special verdict, a list of questions that the jury answers specifically, is more revealing of jury deliberations and is the preferred tool today. See § 399.

[4]   See § 165.

[5]   CPLR 1012, discussed in §§ 179 and 181.

[6]   CPLR 1013, discussed in § 182.

[7]   The procedure for intervention is in § 183.

[8]   For a brief history of intervention as a procedural device, see 1st Rep. Leg. Doc. No. 6b, p.46 (1957), and 11th Jud. Council Rep. 396 (1945).

[9]   See Raymond v. Honeywell, 58 Misc. 2d 903, 297 N.Y.S.2d 66 (Sup. Ct., Dutchess County 1968).

The applicant can seek to intervene on either side of the case, plaintiff's or defendant's. Once let in, the intervenor becomes a party for all purposes.[10]

Intervention is available in a special proceeding, but requires court leave there too.[11] Sometimes a special provision authorizing intervention harmlessly overlaps the more general provisions of CPLR 1012 and 1013.[12]

§ 179. Intervention of Right Under Special Statutes

The first basis recognized for intervention as of right under CPLR 1012(a) is when a statute confers "an absolute right to intervene."[1] This is of course superfluous in that if some special statute confers the right, it doesn't need additional permission from the CPLR. The provision can be taken as a simple reminder of the existence of such statutes.

Several of these others are in CPLR 1012 itself, in subdivisions (b) and (c).

Subdivision (b) applies when the constitutionality of a state or local statute or regulation is involved. Paragraph 1 of the subdivision requires that notice be given to the attorney-general when it's a state provision that's challenged and the State is not a party. Paragraph 2 does the same with respect to local laws and regulations: if the city, county, town, or village whose provision is involved is not a party, it must be notified of the constitutional challenge. In each instance, the State or municipality, if so disposed, has an absolute right to intervene "in support" of the provision's validity.

The party making the constitutional attack would ordinarily be the one to give the required notice. Whoever wants to keep the constitutional challenge alive had better see to it that the notice is given. The court is precluded from entertaining the attack "unless proof of service of the notice . . . is filed" with the court.[2]

A special provision has a similar requirement for actions that merely "involve" the retirement benefits of public employees and without requiring that an issue of constitutionality be involved. Here the State Comptroller is the one who has to be notified, and in this instance, the obligation to notify is placed on the court itself.[3]

Statutes authorizing intervention of right are found elsewhere in the state's consolidated laws. One well known example gives the co-respondent in an adultery-based divorce action the right to intervene and defend.[4]

---

[10]   See Incorporated Village of Island Park v. Island Park-Long Beach, Inc., 81 N.Y.S.2d 407 (Sup. Ct., Nassau County 1948), aff'd, 274 A.D. 930, 83 N.Y.S.2d 542 (2d Dep't).

[11]   CPLR 401.

[12]   See, e.g., CPLR 7802(d), authorizing intervention in an Article 78 proceeding. When a specific provision like that exists for a given special proceeding, it preempts the general provision. CPLR 103(b).

[1]   CPLR 1012(a)(1).

[2]   CPLR 1012(b)(3).

[3]   CPLR 1012(c). Before an amendment of CPLR 1012 that took effect in 2005 (L.2003, ch. 296), the court also had the notification obligation in actions involving a constitutional attack on a state or local provision. The amendment relieved the court of that obligation and shifted it over to the parties. Some of the procedural questions that can arise under the amendment are discussed in SPR 140:2.

[4]   Dom. Rel. Law § 172(1).

§ 180. Intervention of Right Where Representation Inadequate

CPLR 1012(a)(2) permits a nonparty to intervene in an action as a matter of right

[w]hen the representation of the person's interest by the parties is or may be inadequate and the person is or may be bound by the judgment . . . .

The most notable example of this is the class action, one of the few instances in our law in which nonparties may be directly bound by the result of a litigation.[1] Another example is where the proposed intervenors seek to protect their rights even though they are supposedly represented by a governmental entity already a party.[2] There have even been cases in which the activities of one governmental agency or municipality are taken in behalf of, or have a direct effect on, another. When that happens, the latter may intervene as of right, too.[3]

The showing required under CPLR 1012(a)(2) is that the representation "may" be inadequate and that the proposed intervenor "may" be bound by the judgment. It is the possibility, rather than the certainty, that governs. Well-reasoned caselaw holds that the movant should be given the benefit of the doubt.[4] The potentially binding nature of the judgment on the proposed intervenor is the factor that invokes this provision, even if the law that purports to do the binding is foreign rather than New York law.[5]

Whether the movant will be "bound" by the judgment has reference to the res judicata family of doctrines.[6] "The stare decisis effect of the judgment is not enough,"[7] although it may be relevant for permissive intervention, which can be sought under CPLR 1013 when the intervenor's claim or defense has a question of law in common with the pending action.[8]

It has been held that even with regard to the of-right provisions, the courts have some discretion.[9] This appears to contradict the seemingly mandatory nature of CPLR 1012, but the statute does say that the intervention must be "timely." Timeliness itself is a factor that varies from case to case and the court of course has some discretion in measuring it.

CPLR 1012 may be analogized to Rule 24(a) of the Federal Rules of Civil Procedure, especially since the pre-1966 version of the federal provision was the model for CPLR 1012 and its predecessors.[10] Rule 24(a) was amended in 1966 to broaden intervention of

---

[1] See § 139.

[2] See Village of Spring Valley v. Village of Spring Valley Housing Authority, 33 A.D.2d 1037, 308 N.Y.S.2d 736 (2d Dep't 1970).

[3] Teleprompter Manhattan CATV Corp. v. State Bd. of Equalization and Assessment, 34 A.D.2d 1033, 311 N.Y.S.2d 46 (3d Dep't 1970). The court suggests that whenever the party to the suit is not "the real party in interest," the real one may intervene. That can happen in representative cases, see CPLR 1004, although a better remedy, if the representative's representation is inadequate, is to take appropriate steps to oust that one and substitute a better one.

[4] See Unitarian Universalist Church of Central Nassau v. Shorten, 64 Misc. 2d 851, 315 N.Y.S.2d 506 (Sup. Ct., Nassau County 1970), vacated on other grounds, 64 Misc. 2d 1027, 316 N.Y.S.2d 837.

[5] See Nardone v. Morris A. Fierberg Co., 40 A.D.2d 60, 337 N.Y.S.2d 884 (3d Dep't 1972).

[6] See § 443.

[7] *Unitarian Universalist Church*, 64 Misc.2d at 854, 315 N.Y.S.2d at 511. The distinction between the res judicata and stare decisis doctrines is discussed in § 449.

[8] See § 182.

[9] E.g., Reurs v. Carlson, 66 Misc. 2d 968, 323 N.Y.S.2d 370 (Sup. Ct., Westchester County 1971).

[10] See 1st Rep. Leg. Doc. No. 6b, p.46 (1967).

right in the federal courts. The Rule requires the movant in federal court to show that he has an interest in the subject matter of the action and that the pending action "may as a practical matter impair or impede his ability to protect" that interest.[11] The New York statute does not go as far, but with CPLR 1013 standing in the wings—offering discretionary intervention in almost every situation in which the applicant falls technically short of CPLR 1012's of-right intervention—the accomplishments of the current Federal Rule 24(a) can pretty well be extracted from the present CPLR 1012.

The subject of intervention lacked sparkle until late in the 1990s, when a controversy erupted concerning the efforts of health insurers to intervene as plaintiffs in their insureds' personal injury actions. It also involved the so-called "collateral source" rule of CPLR 4545, which allows a defendant tortfeasor to show that items of damages claimed by the plaintiff are duplicated by payments the plaintiff has received or will receive from outside ("collateral") sources, like health insurance. It allows the court to reduce the recovery by the sums so collected, a boon to liability insurers.

Health insurers, belatedly deciding that they should be getting their payments back out of any recovery, realized by its insured against the tortfeasor, instead of the tortfeasor getting credit for the items under the collateral source rule, began to include in the insurance contracts subrogation clauses and clauses making the insurance payments a lien on any recovery the insured might get against the tortfeasor.

The health insurers also came to distrust the way their insureds—the plaintiffs in the tort actions—were prosecuting their claims. Indifferent to the insured items for the very reason that insurance covered them, the plaintiffs were accused of orienting their proof of damages away from the items covered by insurance and emphasizing the items, like loss of earnings and pain and suffering, that the insurance did not cover. To give the insured items a fair shake in the proof, the insurers began to make motions to intervene as plaintiffs so as to handle that aspect of the proof themselves.

All four departments addressed the intervention issue, and all decided that a health insurer could not be allowed to intervene in this situation: Independent Health Ass'n, Inc. v. Grabenstatter (4th Dep't);[12] Humbach v. Goldstein (2d Dep't);[13] Berry v. St. Peter's Hosp. of City of Albany (3d Dep't);[14] and Halloran v. Don's 47 West 44th Street Restaurant Corp. (1st Dep't).[15] The *Humbach* case stressed the tortfeasor/defendant's collateral source rights under CPLR 4545, holding that the health insurer stands in P's shoes so that if P is subject to a collateral source reduction in favor of D, then so is P's health insurer.

The Fourth Department in a later case allowed the intervention by the health insurer, now creating a conflict among departments. The Court of Appeals, noting and discussing the matter in Fasso v. Doerr,[16] does not resolve the conflict because there was no need to in that case, where the parties had allowed the intervention by stipulation.

---

[11]   See Town of Chester, N.Y. v. Laroe Estates, Inc., 137 S. Ct. 1645, 198 L. Ed. 2d 64, 97 Fed. R. Serv. 3d 1671 (2017) ("an intervenor of right must have Article III standing in order to pursue relief that is different from that which is sought by a party with standing").

[12]   Independent Health Ass'n, Inc. v. Grabenstatter, 254 A.D.2d 722, 678 N.Y.S.2d 220 (4th Dep't 1998).

[13]   Humbach v. Goldstein, 229 A.D.2d 64, 653 N.Y.S.2d 950 (2d Dep't 1997).

[14]   Berry v. St. Peter's Hosp. of City of Albany, 250 A.D.2d 63, 678 N.Y.S.2d 674 (3d Dep't 1998).

[15]   Halloran v. Don's 47 West 44th Street Restaurant Corp., 255 A.D.2d 206, 680 N.Y.S.2d 227 (1st Dep't 1998).

[16]   Fasso v. Doerr, 12 N.Y.3d 80, 875 N.Y.S.2d 846, 903 N.E.2d 1167 (2009) (NYSLD No. 591).

The Court did, however, address in general the issue of the health insurer's subrogation rights vis-a-vis the insured, holding that the health insurer cannot seek reimbursement out of the recovery the insured (P) gets from the tortfeasor unless the recovery fully compensates P for all losses. If it doesn't, held the Court, the health insurer, "who has been paid by the insured to assume the risk of loss—has no right to share in the proceeds of the insured's recovery from the tortfeasor." In other words, the insurer may seek subrogation against only those funds and assets that remain after P has been "made whole" as to all damages. In *Fasso*, P was made whole by accepting a settlement from the tortfeasor to add to what P got from the health insurer, but that still left more than $1 million in liability insurance available and it was out of that sum that the health insurer sought to satisfy its subrogation right. In that scenario, it was apparently entitled to.

What about a settlement? Is the health insurer entitled to a piece of any settlement? The Court of Appeals decision in Teichman by Teichman v. Community Hosp. of Western Suffolk[17] figures here. In *Teichman*, an infant's claim was settled for a large sum, but without any indication of the components of the settlement. An insurer that had made medical payments to the infant sought reimbursement for those payments out of the settlement. Because the settlement's components were not revealed, the Court in *Teichman* noted the possibility that the settlement included some medical expenses and held that the insurer should be allowed to litigate the matter.

A 2009 amendment overturned that. The amendment[18] provides that except for explicit statutory liens, a settlement with a tortfeasor will not be deemed to include items covered by health insurance (and hence there's nothing a health insurer can expect from it). While that answers the issue of the health insurer's intervention—negatively—in settlement cases, it leaves the matter open, with all its connected issues, when there has been no settlement.[19]

With a subrogation right, can't the health insurer bring a separate action against the tortfeasor/defendant for the sums it has expended so far and then just move to consolidate that action with the insured's own tort action? The basic ingredients for consolidation under CPLR 602 are present, but wouldn't such a consolidation be a back door to the same position the health insurers have been denied on the intervention front?[20]

The seeming conflict between the plaintiff's health insurer on one side, with its subrogation and lien weapons, and the defendant and its liability insurer on the other, with its "collateral source" right under CPLR 4545, appears to have been resolved in favor of the latter, but the last word has yet to be heard about that. Emotions don't run high here, except among procedural junkies, probably for the very reason that it's essentially a contest between insurers.

---

[17]   Teichman by Teichman v. Community Hosp. of Western Suffolk, 87 N.Y.2d 514, 640 N.Y.S.2d 472, 663 N.E.2d 628 (1996).

[18]   L.2009, ch. 494, § 8, Part F, enacting § 5–335 of the Gen. Oblig. Law.

[19]   See Patrick Connors, *New Laws After Fasso Leave Health Insurer Out in the Cold*, 243 (no. 18) N.Y.L.J. (January 28, 2010); SPR 216:1.

[20]   At least one case has held, on grounds of prematurity, that such a separate suit by the health insurer does not even lie. See the notes in SPR 89:3 and SPR 96:3.

To the plaintiff, who has been paid by the health insurer for the sums in dispute, it makes little difference whether the defendant gets a deduction for them or the health insurer gets them back.

We have treated this issue here, under intervention of right instead of intervention by permission,[21] because it seems to fall so perfectly under CPLR 1012(a)(2), which invites intervention when representation by the existing parties "is or may be inadequate and the [proposed intervenor] is or may be bound by the judgment." The plaintiff's purported representation of the health insurer's interest in this context is wholly inadequate, unless one postulates that while the health insurer may have an interest, it has—because of the collateral source rule of CPLR 4545—no right. That seems to be where the courts stand, but as noted, we await the final word on that.

In jury cases, whatever collateral source deductions are needed are made by the court after the verdict is in.[22]

§ 181. Intervention of Right in Property Cases

Paragraph 3 of CPLR 1012(a) confers the right to intervene

[W]hen the action involves the disposition or distribution of, or the title or a claim for damages for injury to, property and the person may be affected adversely by the judgment.

The paragraph is primarily concerned with the case in which some tangible property, real or personal, or identifiable intangibles, such as stocks or bonds, or even a limited money fund, is the subject of the action. It seeks to assure the right to intervene to anyone with an interest in the subject property. Unlike paragraph 2, it does not require a showing that the intervenor may be bound by the judgment; only that he "may be affected adversely" by it. For example:

L (landlord) leases land to T (tenant). P claims title to the land and sues to evict T. L, who also claims title, may intervene as of right even though L would not be bound by a P v. T judgment rendered in L's absence.

The courts are especially prone to authorize intervention when it appears needed to assure an adversary proceeding. In Mann v. Compania Petrolera Trans-Cuba S.A.,[1] for example, X was a shareholder in a nationalized Cuban corporation and brought an action in New York to preserve the corporation's local assets. The Cuban government appointed S to appear in behalf of the corporation but O, the corporation's president and an opponent of the Cuban government, also asserted that right. After hearing argument on the point, the court found for O and authorized O's lawyer to represent the corporation. Now S moved to intervene, not necessarily as the corporation's factotum but as the person whom the Cuban government recognized as its spokesman. The difficulty was that the same issues posed on that intervention application were previously disposed of, adversely to S, on the hearing to determine who should represent the corporation. The court held that the earlier determination did not control, and allowed S to intervene. An

---

[21]   Permissive intervention is treated in § 182.

[22]   The various points before, within, or after the trial at which proof of collateral source payments may be sought or offered are noted in the Second Department's *Firmes* decision, cited in § 399 and treated in SPR 194:1.

[1]   Mann v. Compania Petrolera Trans-Cuba S.A., 17 A.D.2d 193, 234 N.Y.S.2d 1001 (1st Dep't 1962).

influential factor was that O and X seemed to be allied on the merits, leaving no one to plead the other side.

In New York at present, the notion prevails that when plaintiffs injured in a single accident bring separate suits against the tortfeasor in separate courts, the race to the coverage offered by the tortfeasor's liability insurance policy is to the swift. Whoever gets judgment first is entitled to first crack at the insurance proceeds even if the judgment would exhaust the proceeds and leave nothing for the other injured persons whose suits are still pending. One set of plaintiffs in such a position sought in one case to intervene in the other set's lawsuit when it appeared that judgment in the latter was imminent. They were denied leave to intervene. The main objection was untimeliness, the court said, citing its obligation under CPLR 1013 (permissive intervention) to consider whether the parties to the pending action would be prejudiced by the application.[2]

It is submitted that in a case like that the insurance proceeds should be deemed "property" under CPLR 1012(a)(3) and intervention authorized as of right. Timeliness would still be a factor, of course, but not decisive.

Another possibility is for the insurer to interplead the insurance proceeds, giving all claimants a pro rata bite of the apple. An insurer that brought that kind of interpleader action was commended by the court for doing so.[3]

§ 182. Permissive Intervention

When the proposed intervenor's claim or defense has any question in common with a claim or defense involved in the action, intervention is permitted under CPLR 1013 "in the discretion of the court." It is so easy to establish such a common question that the courts have had to be circumspect about exercising this discretion.[1]

When the common question relied on is one of law, the endeavor to intervene is analogous to an application to an appellate court for leave to file a brief amicus curiae, and the disposition is governed by similar factors. Are both sides of the legal issue already well represented in the action? If they are, adding parties may merely make the case more cumbersome. If they are not, the intervention motion of course enables the court to strengthen the existing representation.

The court has to be wary of numbers. If, for example, the legality of rent control or some phase of it were involved in a case, literally tens of thousands of tenants and landlords would have sufficient interests in the outcome to apply to intervene. The discretion of the court is the dike against this potential flood. An appropriate step would be to admit one or a few groups or associations shown to be strongly representative of their side. If the interests pressing for intervention are concentrated among a manageable few, the numbers difficulty does not appear and the few can be allowed to intervene.

---

[2] David v. Bauman, 24 Misc. 2d 67, 71, 196 N.Y.S.2d 746, 750 (Sup. Ct., Nassau County 1960). The motion by the plaintiff in the second action was made only after the plaintiff in the first action had won summary judgment on liability. This made timeliness a factor, and perhaps the decisive one.

[3] See Boris v. Flaherty, 242 A.D.2d 9, 672 N.Y.S.2d 177 (4th Dep't 1998) (SPR 75:1); § 148.

[1] CPLR 1013 is modeled on Fed. R. Civ. P. 24(b). See 1st Rep. Leg. Doc. No. 6b, p.46 (1957).

Since intervention under CPLR 1013 is permissive, the court can of course impose conditions on its allowance.[2]

One appropriate place to grant a discretionary application under CPLR 1013 would be where there's a question in the case about whether intervention exists as of right under CPLR 1012, and the question is a close one.[3]

Intervention by permission under CPLR 1013 can be compared with consolidation under CPLR 602, which is allowed whenever two or more actions involve a common question of law or fact. Consolidation is a favored remedy today[4] because it fuses separate actions into one and relieves judicial calendars accordingly.

On a CPLR 1013 application, the court must consider whether the intervention (1) "will unduly delay the determination of the action" or (2) "prejudice the substantial rights of any party." The two factors listed are not exclusive, however. Another that the court can consider is whether, if intervention is refused, the applicant is likely to bring a separate action and then move for consolidation, and how that motion would likely be decided. If consolidation is perceived as inevitable, the court may as well permit intervention.

§ 183. Procedure for Intervention

The procedure for intervention, whether of right under CPLR 1012 or in the court's discretion under CPLR 1013, is a mere motion, which should be on notice to all parties to the pending action. A copy of a proposed pleading setting forth the claim or defense on which the movant bases the intervention request must accompany the motion.[1] It has been held that omission of the pleading is jurisdictional; that in its absence the court has "no power" to entertain the motion.[2] That may be unnecessarily rigid, but it's a warning to aspiring intervenors to see that the pleading is included.[3] The court should have "power" at least to hold the motion in abeyance while it allows the movant to supply the missing pleading.

The intervenor gets no rights as a party unless and until the motion to intervene is granted,[4] at which time she gets them all, including the right to counterclaim, cross-claim, implead, appeal, etc.

Whether made under CPLR 1012 or 1013, the application must be "timely." That question is always sui generis. The movant should of course apply as early as possible, but intervention has been allowed in appropriate circumstances even at the appellate stage, for the purpose of permitting the intervenor to take the appeal.[5] Indeed, it has been granted to enable the intervenor to move to vacate a default judgment taken

---

[2]   See City of Buffalo v. State Bd. of Equalization and Assessment, 44 Misc. 2d 716, 254 N.Y.S.2d 699 (Sup. Ct., Albany County 1964).

[3]   Cf. United Services Auto. Ass'n v. Graham, 21 A.D.2d 657, 249 N.Y.S.2d 788 (1st Dep't 1964).

[4]   See § 128.

[1]   CPLR 1014.

[2]   Carriage Hill, Inc. v. Lane, 20 A.D.2d 914, 249 N.Y.S.2d 455 (2d Dep't 1964).

[3]   See Ryder v. Travelers Ins. Co., 37 A.D.2d 797, 324 N.Y.S.2d 804 (4th Dep't 1971).

[4]   See Brown v. Waryas, 45 Misc. 2d 77, 255 N.Y.S.2d 724 (Sup. Ct., Dutchess County 1965), holding that the moment at which the intervenor becomes a party is the entry of the order granting intervention.

[5]   See, e.g., Unitarian Universalist Church of Central Nassau v. Shorten, 64 Misc. 2d 851, 315 N.Y.S.2d 506 (Sup. Ct., Nassau County 1970), vacated on other grounds, 64 Misc. 2d 1027, 316 N.Y.S.2d 837.

against the original defendant.[6] But intervention at that stage will not be allowed merely to permit the intervenor to accomplish now what it could have done as of right, but deliberately omitted to do earlier. So, for example, where a liability insurer, relying on an untested disclaimer, refused to defend its insured in a tort case and the unrepresented defendant defaulted, the insurer was now denied leave to intervene—so as to move to vacate the default judgment—and the judgment stood.[7]

K. SUBSTITUTION

Table of Sections

§ 184.   Substitution of Parties

§ 185.   Abatement of Claims

§ 186.   Procedure for Substitution

§ 187.   Public Body or Officer as Party

§ 188.   Unknown Parties

§ 189.   The Unincorporated Association

§ 184. Substitution of Parties

Whenever an occurrence during an action logically indicates that an interest in the case has passed from one of the parties to an outsider, the outsider may as a rule be substituted for the party. There are a number of provisions on the subject, covering CPLR 1015 through 1022, but the foregoing general statement summarizes the lot of them. Some of the specifics are the following:

Death of a party during an action is the most common cause of substitution. If the claim does not abate upon death—and in New York most claims do not[1]—the action will nonetheless be suspended, at least as to the decedent, until substitution is made.[2] The same is true on appeal; all is suspended until proper substitution is made.[3] The CPLR says that upon the death of a party, the court "shall" order substitution.[4] The substitute in the case of a decedent is of course the decedent's personal representative.

In the ordinary action, the death of a party in effect divests the court of jurisdiction to continue until proper substitution has been made,[5] so that any step taken without the substitution may be deemed void, including even an appellate decision.[6]

---

[6]   Gonzalez v. Industrial Bank (of Cuba), 13 A.D.2d 770, 215 N.Y.S.2d 632 (1st Dep't 1961).

[7]   See Krenitsky v. Ludlow Motor Co., 276 A.D. 511, 96 N.Y.S.2d 102 (3d Dep't 1950). This kind of case appears less frequently today because of the expanded use of the declaratory judgment action to test the validity of insurance disclaimers. See § 437. The declaratory action should be brought while the main tort action pends and before any default is taken. A stay can be sought in the tort action until the declaratory action is concluded.

[1]   See § 185.

[2]   In re Einstoss' Estate, 26 N.Y.2d 181, 309 N.Y.S.2d 184, 257 N.E.2d 637 (1970). For death before judgment, but after verdict or decision, see CPLR 5016(d).

[3]   Price v. Booth, 21 A.D.2d 680, 249 N.Y.S.2d 1007 (2d Dep't 1964).

[4]   CPLR 1015(a).

[5]   Moore v. Washington, 34 A.D.2d 903, 311 N.Y.S.2d 310 (1st Dep't 1970).

[6]   Thompson v. Raymond Kramer, Inc., 23 A.D.2d 746, 258 N.Y.S.2d 671 (1st Dep't 1965).

If it is the plaintiff who dies, those interested in the plaintiff's estate had best have a personal representative appointed and substituted or the action will just lie dormant.[7]

If the defendant dies, and the defendant's estate is insubstantial, the plaintiff may find the defendant's family singularly unenthusiastic about having a personal representative appointed and substituted—they have little motive to expedite the plaintiff's suit—and yet the action can't proceed until that's done. The plaintiff in that situation can make the application to have a representative appointed and substituted for the deceased defendant.[8] It may even happen that a defendant will have to seek the appointment of a representative in behalf of a deceased plaintiff if the defendant wants to take some further step in the case.[9]

In multiparty cases, there may be no need for substitution when one of the parties dies. Where, for example, the plaintiff is suing several tortfeasors, the death of one doesn't preclude the action from continuing against the others. In that instance, the court need merely note the death on the record.[10] Of course, if the plaintiff wants a judgment in the action to bind the decedent's estate, the plaintiff does have to assure that a proper substitution is made for the decedent.

Other events that permit substitution under explicit statutes are an adjudication of a party's incompetency (the committee is substituted) or conservatorship (the conservator is substituted),[11] and the appointment of a receiver for a party (the receiver is substituted).[12]

Any "transfer of interest" during the action, such as by assignment of the claim by the plaintiff, is also a permissible ground for substitution of the transferee, but in this instance, the court has discretion to permit the action to proceed with the original parties.[13]

The above list is not exhaustive of events permitting substitution.[14] Common sense appears to be the major criterion.

It is logical that a practitioner with a general problem about amending a summons or complaint to add or change parties would look here, under "substitution," for answers. The topic can pose more delicate issues, however, often bound up with the statute of

----

[7] The appointment is sought from and made by the appropriate surrogate's court. The supreme court has jurisdiction to make the appointment, but will exercise it only in pressing circumstances. See Castrovinci v. Edwards, 59 Misc. 2d 696, 299 N.Y.S.2d 1017 (Sup. Ct., Westchester County 1969).

[8] See SCPA 1002.

[9] See De Rijdt v. Robert Straile Co., 58 Misc. 2d 543, 296 N.Y.S.2d 601 (Sup. Ct., Queens County 1968).

[10] CPLR 1015(b).

[11] CPLR 1016. Although the terms incompetent/committee and conservatee/conservator continue to be used in the CPLR and other statutes, the terms incapacitated person/guardian are the preferred references today and the other terms should be deemed changed accordingly. See § 54.

[12] CPLR 1017.

[13] CPLR 1018.

[14] See, for example, Lazar v. Merchants' Nat. Properties, Inc., 22 A.D.2d 253, 254 N.Y.S.2d 712 (1st Dep't 1964), allowing an initially balky corporation in a derivative action to change its mind and be substituted as plaintiff, i.e., switched from the defendant's side to replace the shareholder plaintiff on whose initiative the action was first brought.

limitations, and is treated in the sections on the so-called "relation back" doctrine,[15] the amendment of the summons,[16] and the amendment of pleadings.[17]

§ 185. Abatement of Claims

Whether a claim abates upon the death of a party, or survives it, is a matter of substance, not procedure, but a brief discussion of abatement is helpful in conjunction with the substitution of parties. Most claims survive the death of either or both parties. Abatement of a claim upon the death of a person is rare today.

A rule of nonabatement had long been applied in contract and property cases, precluding abatement on the death of either the plaintiff or defendant (or both), and thus permitting an action to be commenced by or against (or between) their personal representatives. But abatement continued in personal injury cases. It took legislation, enacted in 1935, to preserve the personal injury claim for postdeath suit.[1] Earlier, the macabre notion had lingered that if one could but direct the course of his negligence it might be economically preferable to kill rather than merely injure a person.

Today it is clear that neither a personal injury claim nor a property damage claim[2] abates upon the death of either the injured or the injuring person.[3]

The major category in which abatement still occurs upon death is the matrimonial suit.[4] Since the action is entirely personal, the death of either party before its conclusion by judgment abates the claim—substantively dissolves it. This applies even in mere separation actions.[5] In some situations, however, a statute evinces an intent to preserve even a matrimonial cause of action. Section 140(e) of the Domestic Relations Law, for example, allows an annulment action predicated on fraud to be maintained by the parent or guardian of the innocent spouse. This was held to confer the cause of action substantively on that person, with the result that when the innocent spouse sued, but died before final judgment, the claim was held to survive and substitution of the parent or guardian was held permissible.[6] Section 140(c) of the same law similarly evinces an

---

[15] See § 49.

[16] See § 65.

[17] See § 237.

[1] See the 1935 Report of the New York Law Revision Commission, Leg. Doc. No. 60, pp. 157–225, and the historical discussion contained in Holmes v. City of New York, 269 A.D. 95, 54 N.Y.S.2d 289 (2d Dep't 1945), aff'd, 295 N.Y. 615, 64 N.E.2d 449.

[2] Section 37–a of the General Construction Law defines "personal injury" to include "libel, slander and malicious prosecution; also an assault, battery, false imprisonment, or other actionable injury to the person either of the plaintiff, or of another." Injury to property is also broadly defined in the General Construction Law. See § 35, note 17.

[3] EPTL 11–3.2.

[4] See In re Crandall's Estate, 196 N.Y. 127, 89 N.E. 578 (1909). The interlocutory three-month period following initial judgment, during which the matrimonial decree was not final and so not yet effective, was involved in *Crandall* but, as noted shortly in the text, has since been abolished (L.1968, ch. 645). Today, a matrimonial decree becomes final immediately upon entry.

[5] Hoff v. Dugan, 266 A.D. 790, 41 N.Y.S.2d 691 (2d Dep't 1943).

[6] In re Estate of Haney, 14 A.D.2d 121, 1961 WL 18207 (4th Dep't 1961). A non-abatement rule applies when it is the innocent spouse who dies. This enables the litigation to continue, dissolving the marriage and preventing the wrongdoing spouse from sharing in the innocent one's estate. Abatement does occur, however, when it is the wrongdoing spouse who dies, see Sampson v. Lancaster, 39 Misc. 2d 467, 240 N.Y.S.2d 659 (Sup. Ct., New York County 1963), thus preserving the marriage and enabling the innocent spouse to share in the wrongdoer's estate. Determining guilt or innocence in matrimonial context is a tougher thing to do today, after the 1960s liberalization of the divorce and separation laws. Those, too, are matters of substantive law, which we touch here only on a tangent and only as incidental to the subject of the substitution of parties.

intent to preclude abatement in certain annulment actions based on mental retardation or illness.

Often in the reported cases, the spouse's death occurred during the three-month period after the rendition of "interlocutory" judgment, but before the entry of "final" judgment (a procedure no longer used). In Cornell v. Cornell,[7] an interlocutory divorce was granted, but plaintiff P didn't have final judgment entered on it. She nevertheless remarried. Eight years later, her first husband, the presumably divorced one, died. Years after that, her second husband died and P sought to elect against the second husband's estate. Her election was resisted on the ground that she was still married to the first husband and that the second marriage was therefore void. The Court granted a nunc pro tunc order permitting entry of a final judgment on the years-old interlocutory divorce, holding that P's failure to enter a timely final judgment was a mere ministerial omission, correctable retroactively. With that, clarifying that P's marriage had been dissolved, P had a wife's standing with respect to her second husband's estate.

Problems of this kind are largely swept away by the abolition of the interlocutory period following a matrimonial judgment.[8] Applying the rule of the *Cornell* case today should enable a nunc pro tunc order to effect retroactive entry of a matrimonial judgment in any instance in which the case has been decided on its merits and only the ministerial act of entering the judgment is needed.[9] CPLR 5016(d) appears to support this view by providing that as long as the case has been decided, whether by jury verdict or court decision, the subsequent death of a party before the formal entry of judgment does not require a substitution of parties. Entry can be made in the name of the original parties. This evidences an intent to prevent substantive consequences from appending to a delayed entry of judgment after the merits of a case have been fully, and clearly, decided. With the abolition of the interlocutory period in matrimonial actions, this general aim of CPLR 5016(d) should also be given effect in those actions.

Few categories other than the matrimonial action involve an abatement. It has been held that a claim for the invasion of the right of privacy abates upon the death of the one whose right was purportedly invaded[10] and that a claim for a penalty will abate upon the death of the one entitled to it.[11]

The abatement of claims discussed here fits under the legal caption of "survival" of claims; it is generally viewed, as already noted, as a question of substantive law. The "revival" of a claim, on the other hand, such as by legislative enactments affecting the statute of limitations, is a separate, but sometimes overlapping, topic[12] that as a general rule falls into the "procedural" category.[13]

§ 186. Procedure for Substitution

Whatever the event mandating or suggesting substitution, the procedure for it comes from CPLR 1021. The procedure is a motion, which should be on notice to all

---

[7] Cornell v. Cornell, 7 N.Y.2d 164, 196 N.Y.S.2d 98, 164 N.E.2d 395 (1959).

[8] See *Crandall*, 196 N.Y. at 131–32, 8 N.E. at 580.

[9] See and compare Figueroa v. Figueroa, 53 Misc. 2d 1028, 281 N.Y.S.2d 392 (Sup. Ct., Kings County 1967).

[10] See Rome Sentinel Co. v. Boustedt, 43 Misc. 2d 598, 252 N.Y.S.2d 10 (Sup. Ct., Oneida County 1964).

[11] Brackett v. Griswold, 103 N.Y. 425, 9 N.E. 438 (1886).

[12] See § 38.

[13] Cf. Baltimore & O.R. Co. v. Joy, 173 U.S. 226, 19 S. Ct. 387, 43 L. Ed. 677 (1899).

parties. If the event requiring substitution is a party's death and the motion is made by other than the decedent's side, notice of it can't be served on the decedent's attorney because the attorney's authority dissolves when the client dies.[1] In that case, the notice should be served on the would-be representative, and since he is not already a party, there is some indication that the motion papers should be served in the same manner as a summons.[2] If guidance is needed about whom to serve, the motion can be brought on by order to show cause.[3] The motion may be made by any party or by the successor of the deceased party. If the one who should be substituted doesn't appear voluntarily, she may be made a defendant.

If the substitution-requiring event occurs before judgment, substitution should be made "within a reasonable time" or the action may be dismissed as to the party for whom substitution is needed. But what a "reasonable" time is will always depend on the facts of the particular case.[4] There may even have to be a substitution before determining whether the delay was unreasonable since without substitution, that side can't be heard on the issue.[5]

If the substitution-requiring event occurs after judgment, the motion should be made within 4 months. If an appeal has been or could be taken, the substitution motion may be made to the original or appellate court,[6] but unless the substitution is made within the 4-month period, only the appellate court holds the remedy, and one of the things it can do is dismiss the appeal, outright or conditionally.

When death is the substitution-requiring event, those interested in the decedent's estate must be given an opportunity "to show cause why the action or appeal should not be dismissed."[7] This requirement contemplates the case in which the decedent was the plaintiff, or the appellant on appeal, i.e., the one who would want the action continued or the appeal prosecuted.

Many of the decisions address the situation in which it is the plaintiff who has died and the defendant seeks a dismissal. The defendant can't have the dismissal unless he has given notice to the plaintiff's side to get a substitution made and waited a reasonable time for that to happen. Equally important to keep in mind is the consequence when the defendant does fulfill those requirements, but the plaintiff's side does not take the steps needed to effect the substitution. There a dismissal can indeed result.

Suppose it does. What happens when the lawyer purporting to appear for the plaintiff's side—still without proper substitution—then tries to appeal the dismissal? The appeal is likely to be dismissed because the death of the plaintiff freezes the status quo and cancels the lawyer's authority to proceed at any level until proper substitution is made.[8]

---

[1]   See Friedlander v. Roxy Theatre, Inc., 204 Misc. 740, 127 N.Y.S.2d 765 (Sup. Ct., Bronx County 1953), aff'd, 283 A.D. 860, 129 N.Y.S.2d 896 (1st Dep't 1954).

[2]   See Lewis v. Lewis, 43 Misc. 2d 349, 250 N.Y.S.2d 984 (Sup. Ct., Nassau County 1964).

[3]   See § 248.

[4]   It has been held that the period of 2 years, for example, is not an unreasonable period as a matter of law. Rosenfeld v. Hotel Corp. of America, 20 N.Y.2d 25, 281 N.Y.S.2d 308, 228 N.E.2d 374 (1967).

[5]   De Rijdt v. Robert Straile Co., 58 Misc. 2d 543, 296 N.Y.S.2d 601 (Sup. Ct., Queens County 1968).

[6]   If the case is on its way from one appellate court to another, the motion can be made in either one or in the trial court. CPLR 1021.

[7]   This is the actual language used by CPLR 1021.

[8]   See Hyman v. Booth Memorial Hosp., 306 A.D.2d 438, 761 N.Y.S.2d 306 (2d Dep't 2003) (SPR 148:3).

The appellate division in Gonzalez v. Ford Motor Co.[9] discusses who should be served with the notice to effect substitution. The plaintiff in *Gonzalez* was a father suing for damages for the death of his son. During the action, the father died. Persons interested in the son's estate included his wife and child, living in Spain. The notice should have been served on them, held the court, and since they were not already parties, it should have been served on them in the same manner as a summons. The family, interested in preserving the action, would then presumably take the proper steps to have a personal representative appointed to prosecute it. A judgment of dismissal made by the lower court was vacated because those steps were not taken.[10]

If it's the defendant who has died, his family may not show much interest in getting a personal representative appointed, especially when the estate is modest. Why make it easier for the plaintiff to continue the action? There's a remedy for the plaintiff in that situation. If no one on the defendant's side applies to get a personal representative appointed, the plaintiff can himself petition for an order appointing a representative for the decedent.[11] The petition should ordinarily be made to the surrogate's court.[12]

In practical terms, the requirement is designed to assure a hearing to the decedent's side, whichever side that may be, before permitting any step detrimental to that side.

If the time within which to take any procedural step in the case is running when the substitution-requiring event occurs, the time "is extended as to all parties until fifteen days after substitution is made."[13] This can amount to quite an extension, and in this instance, it applies explicitly even to the rarely extendable period in which to appeal.[14]

§ 187. Public Body or Officer as Party

Whenever suit is brought by or against "a public officer, body, board, commission or other public agency" in its official capacity, only the title of the office or agency need be used in the action. The name of the office's incumbent doesn't have to be added unless the court requires it.[1] The office or agency is the real party, and the incumbent's name is not needed.[2]

A plaintiff may save some bother later by designating the office rather than the incumbent now. If there should be a change in office, as by election or appointment, there would then be no need to amend the papers in the action: a statute dispenses with substitution when the office, and not its occupant, has been named while indicating that substitution is necessary if the individual's name has been added.[3] In practice, substitution even in the latter instance is often ignored (harmlessly, it would seem). If

---

[9]   Gonzalez v. Ford Motor Co., 295 A.D.2d 474, 744 N.Y.S.2d 468 (2d Dep't 2002).

[10]   *Gonzalez* is further discussed in SPR 132:3.

[11]   SCPA 1002(1). See the note in SPR 44:4.

[12]   Jones v. Vetter, 188 Misc. 2d 475, 727 N.Y.S.2d 875 (Sup. Ct., Nassau County 2001). The supreme court can also make the appointment, but ordinarily won't make it without some special reason. See Harding v. Noble Taxi Corp., 155 A.D.2d 265, 547 N.Y.S.2d 29 (1st Dep't 1989) (SPR 129:3).

[13]   CPLR 1022.

[14]   See CPLR 5514(c).

[1]   CPLR 1023.

[2]   See Heslin v. Schechter, 3 Misc. 2d 42, 148 N.Y.S.2d 625 (Sup. Ct., New York County 1956).

[3]   CPLR 1019.

substitution is sought, it is by motion on notice to both the successor and predecessor. The court can dispense with service on the latter.

A special statute, CPLR 1026, governs the question of proper parties in suits involving judicial administration. It applies to determinations of the Court of Appeals, and to those of the Chief Judge and the Administrative Board of the Courts, made in their administrative (rather than judicial) capacities, i.e., determinations made pursuant to Article 7–A of the Judiciary Law, the article that governs judicial administration. To avoid even the facial impression that the Chief Judge or the Court of Appeals or any other judge is being sued as such, CPLR 1026 requires that all actions and proceedings brought to review such determinations name only "the chief administrator of the courts, in his representative capacity" as the adverse party.

§ 188. Unknown Parties

CPLR 1024 provides that when suit is brought against someone whose "name or identity" is unknown, the plaintiff may bring the action against that person "by designating so much of his name and identity as is known." The use of a fictitious name, with a description added, is not required. Indeed, its use can be misleading. If it is used, it should be of the clearly fictitious variety: Mary Doe, Richard Roe, etc.

The description is the important thing in this situation. It should be complete enough to identify the defendant so as to afford notice to the person answering to the description and an opportunity to defend. As long as it does that, it satisfies due process and "the form of description . . . is immaterial."[1]

A diligent effort to learn the party's name is a condition precedent to the use of CPLR 1024,[2] which should therefore be turned to only as a last resort. Even if it suffices for jurisdiction, use of a description, with or without a fictitious name, is likely to create trouble at the enforcement of judgment stage, if not before.[3] The correct name should be ascertained and inserted before then.

An extensive address to the unknown party issue appears in Bumpus v. New York City Transit Authority,[4] in which the court reviews difficulties in identifying and serving parties unknown at action time and suggests remedies to which the plaintiff can resort in seeking to identify them.[5]

As soon as the person's name becomes known, all later proceedings must be taken under the correct name "and all prior proceedings shall be deemed amended accordingly."[6] The plaintiff does not need court leave to amend the papers to insert the name of the party sued fictitiously once the name is determined.[7] If there's any confusion in fixing the point at which prior papers in the action are to be "deemed" amended to

---

[1]   City of Mount Vernon v. Best Development Co., 268 N.Y. 327, 330, 197 N.E. 299, 300 (1935).

[2]   See Porter v. Kingsbrook OB/GYN Associates, P.C., 209 A.D.2d 497, 618 N.Y.S.2d 837 (2d Dep't 1994).

[3]   See Kiamesha Concord, Inc. v. Pullman, 52 Misc. 2d 210, 274 N.Y.S.2d 431 (Sup. Ct., New York County 1966). If execution on the judgment is sought through the sheriff's office, the sheriff can be expected to insist on insertion of the party's proper name before levying.

[4]   Bumpus v. New York City Transit Authority, 66 A.D.3d 26, 883 N.Y.S.2d 99 (2d Dep't 2009).

[5]   The case is the subject of a note in SPR 211:3.

[6]   CPLR 1024.

[7]   Woodburn Court Associates I v. Wingate Management Co., Inc., 243 A.D.2d 1043, 663 N.Y.S.2d 445 (3d Dep't 1997).

reflect the defendant's true name, a court order can be obtained containing a formal recitation.

To use this designation-by-description, the plaintiff must have a cause of action. It can't be used just to enable the plaintiff to conduct a fishing expedition, perhaps with the idea of later amending the papers to specify the defendant on a cause of action thereby uncovered.[8] But if the plaintiff does have a cause of action, and the defendant is merely being evasive about furnishing its proper name, which the plaintiff through reasonable efforts can't determine precisely, the plaintiff may find CPLR 1024 helpful indeed—especially if the statute of limitations is closing in. The plaintiff in that case should commence the action with an appropriate description, effect timely service—using substituted means if needed, as they're likely to be—and thus secure jurisdiction of the misnamed or unnamed defendant, then use the disclosure devices[9] to seek to determine the defendant's right name promptly,[10] and, finally, move to amend the caption to insert it. The statute of limitations of course adds tension in these situations.

It has been held that the plaintiff can file papers with a fictitious designation of the defendant, but must then learn the name of the party within the 120-day period allowed for service by CPLR 306–b so as to be able to effect service with papers that properly name the defendant.[11] But it may of course happen that the plaintiff will not be able to determine the defendant's right name in time for service. That will not be fatal as long as the proper person has been served, albeit under a fictitious name. And if for want of the defendant's right name the plaintiff is unable to make service by a prescribed method, service might be sought under CPLR 308(5), under which the court can invent a service method for the plaintiff.[12]

All discussion so far has addressed only the situation in which the defendant is the party being named fictitiously. What about the plaintiff's using a fictitious name for herself? It has been held that in a proper case—one in which there's a good reason for a plaintiff to seek public anonymity—the plaintiff may use a fictitious name in court papers even for herself as long as she properly identifies herself to the other side.[13]

§ 189. The Unincorporated Association

Procedure can take the substantive law only as it finds it. With the unincorporated association, it finds it unclear. The question of when the entire membership is liable for the act of the association is for the substantive law to answer.[1] We will assume here for

---

[8]　See Matthews v. Schusheim, 42 Misc. 2d 176, 247 N.Y.S.2d 285 (Sup. Ct., Nassau County 1964).

[9]　These are in Article 31 and are studied in Chapter 13. The plaintiff should wait for the defendant's answer before turning to disclosure since the defendant may appear through an attorney who may be willing to volunteer the client's right name.

[10]　Statute of limitations problems may otherwise confront the plaintiff. See Piccinich v. Forest City Tech Place Associates, 234 A.D.2d 528, 651 N.Y.S.2d 203 (2d Dep't 1996), and the note in SPR 72:4 on the procedure for suing unknown parties and avoiding statute of limitations problems.

[11]　See Luckern v. Lyonsdale Energy Ltd. Partnership, 229 A.D.2d 249, 654 N.Y.S.2d 543 (4th Dep't 1997).

[12]　Section 75. See Harkness v. Doe, 261 A.D.2d 846, 689 N.Y.S.2d 586 (4th Dep't 1999).

[13]　See E.K. v. New York Hospital-Cornell Medical Center, 158 Misc. 2d 334, 600 N.Y.S.2d 993 (Sup. Ct., Orange County 1992), noted in SPR 19:4, in which the plaintiff did not want it revealed that she had been under care for mental illness. The action was in fact against a hospital and its employee for wrongfully disclosing the datum.

[1]　The caselaw is not consistent. See *Developments in the Law—Judicial Control of Actions of Private Associations*, 76 Harv. L. Rev. 983 (1963). Substantively, it would seem that the association and all of its membership should be subjected to liability for any act (tortious, contractual, or otherwise) performed or

our procedural purpose that the liability being asserted is one for which the entire membership must ultimately answer.

Procedurally, an action may be brought by or against an unincorporated association in New York merely by naming its president or treasurer,[2] and, when the association is the defendant, by serving the one named.[3] This obviates naming and serving all of the members, a requirement that would as a practical matter impede if not prohibit suit whenever the association has a large membership, as it often has.

If suit against the association goes to judgment, it is enforceable only against association property, i.e., property owned jointly by all of the members.[4] If, however, an execution on the judgment is returned in any part unsatisfied, suit may be brought against the members "or, in a proper case . . . any of them."[5]

The plaintiff does have the option to forego suit against the association collectively and bring it instead against the members directly,[6] but rarely pursues that alternative for obvious practical reasons.

Suit by or against the members of an association may be maintained in the form of a class action if requirements applicable to that category of action[7] are otherwise met.[8]

L. POOR PERSONS

Table of Sections

§ 190.   Poor Person Status
§ 191.   Procedure to Secure Poor Person Status
§ 192.   What Poor Person Designation Accomplishes

§ 190.   Poor Person Status

A person "unable to pay the costs, fees and expenses necessary to prosecute or defend" an action or appeal may apply for poor person status.[1] The status can be sought by any party at any stage of the action on affidavit proof of such inability. The seeker

---

committed in its behalf or in the course of its business under simple principles of agency. The courts may be moving in that direction, see Madden v. Atkins, 4 N.Y.2d 283, 174 N.Y.S.2d 633, 151 N.E.2d 73 (1958), but the issue remains unresolved, as will be manifest when one reads in the *Madden* case the distinction sought to be made of Martin v. Curran, 303 N.Y. 276, 101 N.E.2d 683 (1951), probably the genesis of the problem. The subject remains blurry, as shown more recently in Salemeh v. Toussaint ex rel. Local 100 Transp. Workers Union, 25 A.D.3d 411, 810 N.Y.S.2d 1 (1st Dep't 2006). A dissenting opinion in *Salemeh* refers to *Martin* as of "dubious validity when decided and . . . even less deserving of recognition today," but the majority adheres to what *Martin* itself said in 1951: that any change in this rule of liability must be made by the legislature. The point remains unaddressed, although the United States has had over a dozen different presidents since then.

    [2]   CPLR 1025; Gen. Ass'ns Law § 13.

    [3]   See § 69, d.

    [4]   Gen. Ass'ns Law § 15. The judgment is not good against the individual assets of the president or treasurer through whom the association litigated.

    [5]   Gen. Ass'ns Law § 16. The quoted language, "in a proper case," is an acknowledgement that the legislature, too, is uncertain about when substantive liability exists against the entire membership.

    [6]   Gen. Ass'ns Law § 17. See Mandell v. Moses, 209 A.D. 531, 205 N.Y.S. 254 (3d Dep't 1924), aff'd, 239 N.Y. 555, 147 N.E. 192.

    [7]   See §§ 141–142.

    [8]   House v. Schwartz, 18 Misc. 2d 21, 37–8, 188 N.Y.S.2d 308, 324–25 (Sup. Ct., New York County 1959).

    [1]   CPLR 1101(a).

need no longer show, as was once required, that he or she is not worth $300 in cash or available property; the Advisory Committee rejected that standard as too rigid.[2]

The applicant is required to set forth in the affidavit the amount and sources of her income and a list of her property and its value. This broad look into resources is the necessary basis for the court's determination of whether to grant the application, which lies in the court's discretion. It has been held that eligibility for public assistance or legal aid under other statutes and standards, while germane, does not conclusively entitle the litigant to poor person status under Article 11 of the CPLR.[3]

The applicant's motives may also be investigated, because if leave is granted it is the public that pays the way.[4]

In addition to stating inability to pay and listing income and assets, the affidavit must set forth the nature of the action and include a statement of facts sufficient to enable the court to determine whether there is any merit to the applicant's claim or defense. Finally, it must assert whether any other person is interested in the recovery sought and whether such other person is able to pay for the litigation. This was designed primarily to enable the court to determine whether a plaintiff applicant has an attorney working on a contingent fee basis, in which event poor person status will not be granted.[5]

§ 191. Procedure to Secure Poor Person Status

The usual procedure for securing poor person status is by motion to the court of original instance. When the status is sought for purposes of an appeal, however, the motion may be made to the original or appellate court.[1] It had been held preferable even in that instance to make it to the original court: the appellate court would often deny the application without prejudice to renewal below,[2] or perhaps just transfer the application to let the lower court handle it, but a 1987 amendment requires the appellate court itself to entertain the application if made before it.[3]

If an action has already been commenced, notice of the motion must be given to all parties. Notice is also required to be given to the corporation counsel if the action is in New York City and to the county attorney in actions outside the city because it is the municipality that has to pay for transcripts later on.[4] This notice is apparently required whether the application is made before or after commencement of the action.

The court may require the movant to append to her application an attorney's certificate stating that the attorney has examined the action and finds merit in the applicant's contentions.[5]

The plaintiff seeking poor person status can file the summons and complaint along with an affidavit of inability to pay costs and fees,[6] and upon doing so will be assigned

---

2   2d Rep. Leg. Doc. No. 13, p. 389 (1958).

3   Lancer v. Lancer, 70 Misc. 2d 1045, 335 N.Y.S.2d 138 (Sup. Ct., Nassau County 1972).

4   2d Rep. Leg. Doc. No. 13 at 388 (1958).

5   2d Rep. Leg. Doc. No. 13 at 390 (1958).

1   CPLR 1101(a).

2   See, e.g., Jenks v. Murphy, 21 A.D.2d 346, 250 N.Y.S.2d 848 (4th Dep't 1964).

3   L.1987, ch. 312, amending CPLR 1101(a).

4   CPLR 1101(c).

5   CPLR 1101(b).

6   CPLR 1101(a).

an index number or a filing number, whatever's appropriate to the court involved, without paying a fee. The application will then be referred to a judge. If the judge approves the application, the plaintiff will be notified by a written order that fees are waived. If the application is disapproved, the written order will instruct the plaintiff that the action will be dismissed if the fee is not paid within 120 days, measured from "the date of the order."[7] This presumably means the time of the order's service on the plaintiff, but it might be construed more rigidly to mean that the time runs from the date on the order, whatever the delay in its service on the plaintiff, so the plaintiff intent on pursuing the claim should pay the fee expeditiously if the application is denied.

Meanwhile, nothing is said in CPLR 1101(d) about giving the plaintiff any different time—than that provided in CPLR 306–b (which is a 120-day period)—for effecting service of the summons after the filing, whatever the status may be of the plaintiff's poor-person application to the court. The plaintiff has gotten the index number promptly under this provision, so it is expected that the plaintiff will proceed to service promptly, bound by the 120-day provisions of CPLR 306–b. If it turns out that the plaintiff's application for poor person status is denied, the plaintiff will have to pay the filing fee within 120 days of the order so advising, whether service has already been effected or not.

Poor person applicants should not confuse the 120 days for service (which is governed by CPLR 306–b and starts from the initial filing) with the 120 days for paying the fee (which is governed by CPLR 1101(d) and starts from the date of the court order denying the poor person application). But since each of these 120-day periods is presumably subject to extension in the discretion of the court,[8] short delays caused by their confused interplay should be readily curable.

If the plaintiff is represented by a "legal aid society or . . . other nonprofit organization . . . furnishing . . . legal services to indigent persons," or by a lawyer working for such a group, and the group or lawyer certifies that the plaintiff meets the poor person standards, the fee is waived without application to the court.[9]

A special provision governs poor person applications by prison inmates.[10]

§ 192. What Poor Person Designation Accomplishes

The privileges conferred on one who qualifies as a poor person are listed in CPLR 1102. A major one is that the court may assign an attorney.[1] There is no absolute right to assigned counsel in civil litigation, however. The Court of Appeals held in In re Smiley[2] that whether to make the assignment in a given case is in the discretion of the court.

The applicant may already have an attorney, and often appears in court through a lawyer previously assigned by one of the governmental, quasi-governmental, or even private organizations (including law firms acting pro bono) that offer legal assistance

---

[7] CPLR 1101(d).

[8] See CPLR 306–b; § 63.

[9] CPLR 1101(e).

[10] CPLR 1101(f).

[1] CPLR 1102(a).

[2] In re Smiley, 36 N.Y.2d 433, 369 N.Y.S.2d 87, 330 N.E.2d 53 (1975). For the position of the U.S. Supreme Court on the requirement to assign counsel under the due process clause, and for the difference between criminal and civil actions in this respect, see Lassiter v. Department of Social Services of Durham County, N. C., 452 U.S. 18, 101 S. Ct. 2153, 68 L. Ed. 2d 640 (1981).

generally or in special situations. It may even be the attorney who is bringing the poor person application.

If the court does appoint a lawyer, is the lawyer entitled to compensation? There had been some dispute about whether the lawyer is entitled to be paid out of public funds. The *Smiley* case then held that the lawyer is not; that it is for the legislature and not the courts to appropriate money for this purpose. There is a general expectation among judges that lawyers will accept unpaid assignments for indigent litigants, from time to time, as a professional obligation.[3] While not abating that traditional responsibility,[4] *Smiley* acknowledges that the lawyer's own constitutional rights may be infringed by judicial resort to the involuntary assignment too often.[5]

Once the status is granted, the poor person is not liable for any costs or fees in the action. But if the poor person recovers a judgment, some or all of those items as well as a reasonable sum for the assigned attorney may be ordered paid out of the recovery, as may anything the municipality has paid for a transcript.[6] CPLR 1102(b) entitles the poor person to two free copies of the transcript (one copy is filed with the court). These are a municipal charge. But it has been held that the free copy covers only the main trial or hearing and not necessarily pretrial depositions,[7] even though these can be expensive and play an important and sometimes even decisive role in litigation.

This statutory allowance of a transcript and suspension of court costs and fees has avoided a clash with the Federal Constitution, whose supervening requirements have been felt on related fronts. Out-of-court expenses, for example, are not necessarily dispensed with when poor person status is allowed under the terms of CPLR Article 11. Notorious among these expenses had been the cost of service by publication in matrimonial actions. The U.S. Supreme Court then held this to be a governmental expense if government, as was the case in New York, insists on imposing a method of service that incurs a substantial expense.[8] New York responded to the problem in Deason v. Deason,[9] making the cost of service by publication a government expense, but imposing it on the municipality rather than the State. Confirmatory legislation followed.[10]

If an appeal is involved, a party who has been granted poor person status need submit only typed briefs and appendices to the appellate court, "furnishing one legible copy for each appellate justice."[11] Besides a motion for poor-person status, an appellant can instead move the appellate court for a more limited privilege: leave to appeal on a typed transcript and typed briefs in a minimum number of copies, which accomplishes the more limited but still substantial benefit of eliminating the need to print, offset, or otherwise machine-reproduce those papers. That kind of motion accomplishes only what

---

[3] See Jacox v. Jacox, 43 A.D.2d 716, 350 N.Y.S.2d 435 (2d Dep't 1973); New York Rules of Professional Conduct, Rule 6.1 ("Voluntary Pro Bono Service").

[4] See Yearwood v. Yearwood, 54 A.D.2d 626, 387 N.Y.S.2d 433 (1st Dep't 1976).

[5] See also Menin v. Menin, 79 Misc. 2d 285, 359 N.Y.S.2d 721 (Sup. Ct., Westchester County 1974), aff'd 48 A.D.2d 904, 372 N.Y.S.2d 985 (2d Dep't 1975).

[6] CPLR 1102(d).

[7] Lester v. Lester, 69 Misc. 2d 528, 330 N.Y.S.2d 190 (Sup. Ct., Sullivan County 1972).

[8] Boddie v. Connecticut, 401 U.S. 371, 91 S. Ct. 780, 28 L. Ed. 2d 113 (1971).

[9] Deason v. Deason, 32 N.Y.2d 93, 343 N.Y.S.2d 321, 296 N.E.2d 229 (1973).

[10] The matter is discussed in the section on service in matrimonial actions. See § 76.

[11] CPLR 1102(c). For further details on matters like this, the lawyer should consult the individual rules of the appellate court.

the appellate court prescribes, however. An order granting such leave, for example, does not automatically entitle the applicant to go back to the lower court and insist on a free transcript,[12] while an order granting full poor-person status does.

M. INFANTS AND INCOMPETENTS

Table of Sections

§ 193.   Representation of Infant
§ 194.   Representation of Incapacitated Person
§ 195.   Representation Distinguished from Service
§ 196.   Guardian Ad Litem Distinguished from Other Guardianships
§ 197.   Procedure for Appointment of Guardian Ad Litem
§ 198.   Qualifications, Rights, and Authority of Guardian Ad Litem
§ 199.   Risks if No Proper Representative Present
§ 200.   Settlement of Infant's or Incapacitated Person's Claim

§ 193. Representation of Infant

An infant, who is any person not yet 18 years old,[1] can't appear in its own behalf or by an attorney of its own hiring. An infant must appear through one of the persons listed in CPLR 1201, and if it is to appear by attorney, the attorney must be retained by the appropriate person on the list.

The first person on the list is a formally (judicially) designated guardian of the property—not to be confused with a mere guardian ad litem[2]—if the infant should have one, which it rarely does. Absent such guardian, the infant may be represented by the parent having legal custody. Statistically, it is most often the parent who does the representing. If no parent has custody of the infant, an appearance may be made in behalf of the infant "by another person or agency having legal custody." This has been held to mean custody determined by judicial decree; a long-standing but informal custody will not by itself suffice.[3] Finally, if the infant is married to and resides with an adult spouse, the spouse may appear for the infant.

There is no requirement that an infant appear by a guardian ad litem, i.e., a guardian appointed solely for the purpose of representing the infant in a particular litigation. Such a guardian may of course be appointed by the court if no one on the CPLR 1201 list is available or willing to represent the infant. And even if there is such a person, the court may still appoint a guardian, as upon a finding of conflict of interest or any other cause.[4] Because the infant is a ward of the court, it takes little "other cause" to prompt appointment of a guardian ad litem. In a suit by a father, for example, to make the mother account for money paid to her for the child's support under a separation agreement, with each parent claiming to represent the child's best interests, the court

---

[12]   Moriarity v. Butler Bin Co., 21 A.D.2d 865, 251 N.Y.S.2d 44 (1st Dep't 1964), aff'd, 15 N.Y.2d 901, 258 N.Y.S.2d 429, 206 N.E.2d 361 (1965).

[1]   CPLR 105.

[2]   See § 196.

[3]   Villafane v. Banner, 87 Misc. 2d 1037, 387 N.Y.S.2d 183 (Sup. Ct., New York County 1976).

[4]   CPLR 1201.

held that it would be best for a guardian ad litem to be appointed,[5] for the reason that the parents could not prevent their own interests from becoming confused with the child's.

§ 194.　Representation of Incapacitated Person

CPLR 1201 and other parts of the CPLR and other laws still use the terminology of "incompetent," for whom a "committee" has been appointed, and "conservatee," for whom a "conservator" has been appointed but all four phrases have been officially replaced by two: "incapacitated person," for whom a "guardian" has been appointed. The replacement terminology comes from Article 81 of the Mental Hygiene Law. A brief instruction in section 4 of the enacting bill[1] directs that "[w]herever a statute uses the terms conservators or committees, such statute shall be construed to include the term guardian notwithstanding the provisions of this article unless the context otherwise requires."[2]

The appointment of a "conservator" was a lighter step than the appointment of a committee. The situation was one in which a person was subject to an infirmity that disabled the person from caring for property or discharging obligations to dependents, but did not call for the more drastic, and stigmatic, "incompetency" determination. CPLR 1201 requires that an adjudicated incompetent appear in litigation through its committee and that a person adjudicated a conservatee appear through its conservator. To parallel CPLR 1201, we will use its terminology when it's necessary to distinguish between the two categories of disability; otherwise we will use the new terms. As with infants, so with incapacitated persons: if there is any conflict of interest or if for "other cause" the court deems it best, it may appoint a guardian ad litem.[3]

If the person has not been adjudicated an incapacitated person, but nevertheless appears to be "incapable of adequately prosecuting or defending his rights," a guardian ad litem may be appointed.[4]

It is not a good idea for one party to proceed against another knowing the other to be incapable of looking after his rights, despite the absence of a formal adjudication to that effect. Thus, where P knew that D had been institutionalized but nonetheless sued and took a default judgment against D, the court, analogizing the situation to where an improperly represented infant has been proceeded against, held the judgment jurisdictionally void, vacated it, and opened the default.[5] So, when D's ability to look after his interests is doubtful, it may even be politic for P to make sure that D is properly represented. The thing for P to do in D's behalf, if no one else steps in to do it first, is move to have a guardian ad litem appointed for D. Without such a guardian, a judgment against D may be in jeopardy even if D purported to appear by an attorney of her own

---

　　[5]　Rosenblatt v. Birnbaum, 20 A.D.2d 556, 245 N.Y.S.2d 72 (2d Dep't 1963), aff'd, 16 N.Y.2d 212, 264 N.Y.S.2d 521, 212 N.E.2d 37 (1965).

　　[1]　L.1992, ch. 698.

　　[2]　All prior proceedings taken under the old terminology are of course preserved until set aside or modified by a judge under the new article. See SPR 5:4.

　　[3]　CPLR 1201. See Matter of Berman, 24 A.D.2d 432, 260 N.Y.S.2d 736 (1st Dep't 1965).

　　[4]　Attorneys representing clients incapable of adequately prosecuting or defending their rights must be aware of their obligations under New York Rules of Professional Conduct, Rule 1.14, entitled "Client With Diminished Capacity."

　　[5]　Oneida Nat. Bank & Trust Co. of Central New York v. Unczur, 37 A.D.2d 480, 326 N.Y.S.2d 458 (4th Dep't 1971).

choosing,[6] apparently on the theory that D lacked even the competence to choose a lawyer.

Suit against an incompetent for whom a committee has been appointed requires leave of court,[7] a rule that can be viewed as applicable to suit against a conservator, too. The matter is not of great moment as long as a failure to secure advance leave is not treated as jurisdictional, and caselaw indicates it's not.[8]

§ 195. Representation Distinguished from Service

When the infant or incapacitated person is the defendant, a distinction must be drawn between service of process, which is made pursuant to CPLR 309, and appearance, which is governed by CPLR 1201.

Service on an incapacitated person is made by serving both him and the guardian, unless service on the incapacitated person is dispensed with.[1]

For service on an infant, CPLR 309(a) governs and contains a list of people who may be served in the infant's behalf,[2] but the lawyer should not confuse the CPLR 309(a) list of servees with the CPLR 1201 list of appearers. They are similar but not the same. The CPLR 1201 list sets up rigid priorities concerning who may appear; the CPLR 309(a) roster of servees is more an offering of alternatives.

The plaintiff about to sue an infant or incapacitated person need not concern herself initially with CPLR 1201. She should merely effect service pursuant to CPLR 309. Doing so secures jurisdiction.[3] Ordinarily it is only then that CPLR 1201 becomes relevant, now alighting to determine who may appear for the defendant. Presumably, someone on the defendant's side will see to it that a proper person appears and defends. Only if that does not happen need the plaintiff take the initiative to assure that an appropriate guardian is appointed for the defendant.[4]

If an infant has a "guardian of the property," whichever of the guardianships that may be deemed to refer to,[5] CPLR 1004 permits the guardian instead of the infant to be named as the party.[6] It is better not to rely on that authorization and to see to it that the infant is named, too. The authorization applies, in any event, only when a formally appointed "guardian of the property" is present; it does not apply to some other person, such as a parent, through whom the infant usually appears. Nor can the requirement of CPLR 309(a), that the parent and infant both be served to start the action, be circumvented by theorizing that the parent qualifies as a "guardian" in the CPLR 1004 sense so as to dispense with both the naming and serving of the infant.[7]

---

[6]   See Rand v. Lockwood, 65 Misc. 2d 182, 316 N.Y.S.2d 950 (Sup. Ct., Nassau County 1970).

[7]   Sinley v. Estco, Inc., 25 Misc. 2d 172, 200 N.Y.S.2d 939 (Sup. Ct., Nassau County 1960).

[8]   Van Vooren v. Cook, 191 Misc. 794, 77 N.Y.S.2d 173 (Sup. Ct., Ontario County 1948), aff'd, 274 A.D. 966, 85 N.Y.S.2d 526 (4th Dep't).

[1]   CPLR 309(b), (c). See § 69.

[2]   See § 69.

[3]   If the defendant is an incapacitated person, leave to sue should be secured in advance. See § 194, note 7.

[4]   See § 197.

[5]   See § 196 for the distinction between a guardian ad litem and other guardianships.

[6]   See § 137.

[7]   See Cramer v. Henderson, 123 Misc. 2d 159, 473 N.Y.S.2d 672 (Sup. Ct., Yates County 1984).

§ 196. Guardian Ad Litem Distinguished from Other Guardianships

A guardian ad litem is appointed only to represent someone in litigation, which is what "ad litem" means. The phrase "special guardian" is no longer used in civil practice.[1]

The guardian ad litem should not be confused with more permanent guardianships for infants. CPLR 1210 supplies one of them, just called a "guardian," who is as a rule appointed when the child's parents are dead or disabled or when there is friction between them. It is sometimes used to resolve custody disputes.[2] Those disputes are more likely to arise in matrimonial litigation, however, where the court can make directions as to custody, which is in effect guardianship, through regular orders and judgments. These often include money directions (maintenance, support, etc.) as well.[3] Habeas corpus, and alternatively a mere petition and order to show cause, are also recognized as ways to secure custody of a child.[4] Those devices are plenary in themselves; they need not be connected to a matrimonial action. They secure guardianship (without calling it that) as effectively as would a direct application for it. They doubtless contribute to the disuse into which the CPLR 1210 guardianship has fallen.

The surrogate's court can appoint a guardian of the infant's person and/or property even if both parents are alive.[5] The county court has some analogous jurisdiction of infants,[6] the family court shares that authority with both courts,[7] and of course the supreme court has it concurrently with all of them.[8] A surviving parent can appoint a guardian for the person or property, or both, of the children, by inter-vivos instrument or by will.[9] If by will, the appointee is known as a "testamentary" guardian.

Any of these guardians should ordinarily qualify as the "property" guardian authorized by CPLR 1201 to appear for an infant in litigation, and all should be distinguished from the mere guardian ad litem. The latter is appointed only for an action or special proceeding, and the appointment will ordinarily be made only when the infant does not have one of the other formally decreed or recognized guardians or custodians or when its parents and other potential CPLR 1201 appearers are dead, disabled, or in conflict of interest.

§ 197. Procedure for Appointment of Guardian Ad Litem

CPLR 1202 supplies the procedure for the appointment of a guardian ad litem. It's a motion made in the court in which the action has been or is about to be brought. The motion may be made at any time and may be made by a party or by the court sua sponte. It's ordinarily made by someone on the side of the infant or incapacitated person, such as "a relative, friend or a guardian, committee of the property, or conservator."[1] In the

---

[1] See In re Becan, 26 A.D.2d 44, 270 N.Y.S.2d 923 (1st Dep't 1966).

[2] See and compare Application of Brown, 17 N.Y.S.2d 188 (Sup. Ct., Nassau County 1939).

[3] See Dom. Rel. Law §§ 236, 240.

[4] Dom. Rel. Law § 240.

[5] SCPA 1701. See also SCPA 1750 et seq., authorizing guardianships for mentally retarded persons.

[6] Jud. Law § 190(4).

[7] Fam. Ct. Act § 661.

[8] N.Y. Const. art. VI, § 7(b); Kagen v. Kagen, 21 N.Y.2d 532, 289 N.Y.S.2d 195, 236 N.E.2d 475 (1968).

[9] Dom. Rel. Law § 81.

[1] CPLR 1202(a)(2).

case of an infant over 14, the infant itself can make the application.[2] Since the infant and incapacitated person are wards of the court, the question of who calls to the court's attention the need for a guardian ad litem is not important.

If the defendant is the ward, the plaintiff should be sensitive that the person who shows up to represent the defendant is one duly authorized by CPLR 1201. A defect here can jeopardize any judgment the plaintiff may recover. If the plaintiff has serious doubts about the qualifications of the person purporting to represent the defendant and no one on the defendant's side moves for the appointment of a guardian ad litem within 10 days after service of the summons is complete, the plaintiff may make the motion herself.[3]

If the ward has a duly appointed guardian, notice of the motion to appoint a guardian ad litem must be served on that person. If the ward has not, notice is served on the one with whom the ward resides. If the ward is over 14, the ward must also be served with notice of the motion, but an adjudicated incapacitated person need not be.[4] If the court does appoint a guardian ad litem, the designation will not take effect until the appointee submits to the court a written consent accompanied by proof of financial ability to answer for any potential negligence or misconduct.[5]

In an action against an infant, as has been indicated, the plaintiff merely effects service pursuant to CPLR 309 without any preliminary court order or application. There is no authority for the court to appoint a guardian ad litem for the defendant in advance of commencement of the action so as to enable summons service itself to be made on the guardian. In an ordinary action, in fact, the court is without power to appoint a guardian ad litem for the defendant until jurisdiction is secured, and it is service under CPLR 309 that secures jurisdiction.[6] A special proceeding, however, may be commenced either by service in the usual way, i.e., pursuant to CPLR 309 in the case of an infant or incapacitated person,[7] or by an order to show cause.[8]

If the order to show cause is used, the court can determine the method of service in the order itself. Early in the life of the CPLR, some caselaw held that this would also authorize the court, in advance of service, to both appoint a guardian ad litem for the prospective respondents and direct service on the appointee in their behalf,[9] but that procedure did not catch on and does not appear to be used today.[10] The alternative is in any event unavailable in an ordinary action because the order to show cause procedure itself is not available as an alternative to start an action.

---

[2]   CPLR 1202(a)(1).

[3]   CPLR 1202(a)(3).

[4]   CPLR 1202(b).

[5]   CPLR 1202(c).

[6]   Soto v. Soto, 30 A.D.2d 651, 291 N.Y.S.2d 37 (1st Dep't 1968).

[7]   CPLR 403(c).

[8]   CPLR 403(d). See § 553.

[9]   In re Beyer, 21 A.D.2d 152, 249 N.Y.S.2d 320 (1st Dep't 1964).

[10]   See Application of Pugach, 29 A.D.2d 518, 285 N.Y.S.2d 258 (1st Dep't 1967), aff'd, 23 N.Y.2d 901, 298 N.Y.S.2d 306, 246 N.E.2d 160 (1969). The holding of the *Beyer* case, *Beyer*, 21 A.D.2d at 152, 249 N.Y.S.2d at 320, the main decision that authorized precommencement appointment of a guardian ad litem for a respondent in a special proceeding, was in any event restricted to cases in which the ordinary procedure "would constitute a danger to the infant's interest," In re Legget's Trust, 25 A.D.2d 727, 268 N.Y.S.2d 911 (1st Dep't 1966), at best a remote contingency.

§ 198. Qualifications, Rights, and Authority of Guardian Ad Litem

Any adult person who is capable of protecting the interests of the ward and has no conflict of interest may be appointed guardian ad litem.[1] The person need not be a lawyer.[2]

The court is authorized to permit the guardian ad litem "a reasonable compensation" for her services, which may be ordered paid by an adverse party, from the ward's recovery (if any), or from other of the ward's property.[3] It has been noted that such guardians are often required "to accept most moderate compensation for their services." The compensation will of course depend on the nature of the services rendered.[4] The value of a nonlegal service performed by a guardian who happens to be a lawyer is not "enhanced just because an attorney does it."[5]

The authority of a guardian ad litem for an infant terminates when the infant reaches majority[6] if it has not been terminated by the court before. If the attorney appearing for the ward before majority is to continue representation after it, it must now be with the ward's consent, not just the guardian's. If an infant has been appearing all the while without acceptable representation, such as where she instead of her parent or guardian retained the attorney, the infant's continued appearance after reaching majority has been held to validate all of the prior proceedings nunc pro tunc.[7]

§ 199. Risks if No Proper Representative Present

Prior to the 1963 adoption of the CPLR, an infant could appear only by a guardian ad litem. A by-product was that the absence of the guardian could carry severe consequences, not necessarily for the ward but for the adverse party. Indeed, even where a guardian ad litem had been duly appointed, evidence of improper representation could result in the setting aside of any proceedings taken against the ward,[1] while there was a concomitant tendency, if the proceedings went the ward's way, to uphold them regardless of defects in the representation.[2]

Although there is no requirement that a guardian ad litem do the representing today, the infant and incapacitated person are still wards of the court. Evidence of improper representation, no matter by whom, can still imperil whatever an adverse party may otherwise accomplish in the case. Prior caselaw will therefore continue to have much to say. The counseling point for the adverse party, whether as plaintiff or defendant, is to take no joy from evidence of weak representation of the ward's interest.

---

[1]   Specific direction to this effect in prior law was omitted from the CPLR as "self-evident." See 2d Rep. Leg. Doc. No.13, p.372 (1958). In the surrogate's court, a guardian ad litem must be a New York attorney. SCPA 404.

[2]   Bolsinger v. Bolsinger, 144 A.D.2d 320, 533 N.Y.S.2d 934 (2d Dep't 1988).

[3]   CPLR 1204.

[4]   See In re Becan, 26 A.D.2d 44, 270 N.Y.S.2d 923 (1st Dep't 1966).

[5]   *Bolsinger*, 144 A.D.2d at 321, 533 N.Y.S.2d at 935.

[6]   In re Fassig's Estate, 58 Misc. 2d 252, 295 N.Y.S.2d 146 (Sur. Ct., Nassau County 1968).

[7]   See Petker v. Rudolph, 168 Misc. 909, 6 N.Y.S.2d 296 (Sup. Ct., Bronx County 1938), aff'd, 258 A.D. 1040, 17 N.Y.S.2d 1020 (1st Dep't 1940).

[1]   See and compare Glogowski v. Rapson, 20 Misc. 2d 96, 198 N.Y.S.2d 87 (Sup. Ct., Monroe County 1959).

[2]   See, e.g., Rima v. Rossie Iron-Works, 120 N.Y. 433, 24 N.E. 940 (1890).

A victory in such an instance may be short-lived.[3] The adverse party in such a situation would therefore do well to assume the initiative of getting a guardian ad litem appointed for the ward.[4]

The ward status retained by infants and incompetents accounts for the provision precluding default judgments against them until proper representation has been secured.[5]

The status also accounts for the requirement of a court order before a controversy involving a ward can be submitted to out-of-court arbitration.[6] Presumably the ward's guardian can move for such an order. A curious case in this respect is In re Doe,[7] which holds that the court has no jurisdiction to appoint a guardian to represent an incapacitated person in arbitration. The person's psychiatrist in *Doe* testified that Doe can't participate "in any legal process or in any meaningful productive activity, but is capable of managing his affairs and does not need a guardian within the meaning of the Mental Hygiene Law."

The court accepted the psychiatrist's conclusions as if they were binding, but the conclusions to be reached based on a psychiatrist's—or any expert's—testimony are for the court to draw, not for the expert to dictate.[8] Dictatorial experts could otherwise end up running the court system.

§ 200. Settlement of Infant's or Incapacitated Person's Claim

The settlement of the claim of an infant or incapacitated person requires court approval, which is applied for with a motion or special proceeding. If an action has been brought, there is a pending litigation that furnishes a context and a motion is the procedure. If no action has been brought, context is lacking and a special proceeding is used, brought in the court in which, based on the amount of the settlement, an action for that sum would have been brought. Whether the motion or special proceeding is the appropriate device, it should be brought on by order to show cause.[1] If the motion procedure is used, an approval of the settlement results in an order and the order has the effect of a judgment.

CPLR 1208 prescribes the papers to be submitted and the incidental procedure to be followed. The rules elaborate.[2] These requirements should be carried out to the letter. On the hearing of the settlement application, the applicant, the ward, and the ward's

---

[3] See Oneida Nat. Bank & Trust Co. of Central New York v. Unczur, 37 A.D.2d 480, 326 N.Y.S.2d 458 (4th Dep't 1971); Anderson v. Anderson, 164 A.D. 812, 150 N.Y.S. 359 (1st Dep't 1914).

[4] CPLR 1202(a)(3).

[5] CPLR 1203. A default taken in violation of this requirement will be vacated. State Bank of Albany v. Murray, 27 A.D.2d 627, 275 N.Y.S.2d 985 (3d Dep't 1966). CPLR 1203 was not amended in 1981 to add the conservatee when the surrounding provisions in Article 12 were (L.1981, ch. 115), but it is best read as applying to a conservatee as well. The court's general power to vacate default judgments would in any event cover the situation.

[6] CPLR 1209. The statute makes an exception for uninsured and underinsured motorist cases where court permission for arbitration of the infant's claim is not required.

[7] In re Doe, 184 Misc. 2d 519, 709 N.Y.S.2d 372 (Sup. Ct., Queens County 2000).

[8] See the discussion of the case in SPR 100:2–3.

[1] CPLR 1207, by providing that "[n]otice of the motion or petition shall be given as directed by the court," means to require use of the show cause procedure. See § 248.

[2] 22 N.Y.C.R.R. § 202.67, applicable in the supreme and county courts, supplies detailed procedure for the settlement application. Uniform Rules of other courts then adopt that rule by reference, e.g., 22 N.Y.C.R.R. §§ 208.36 (New York City Civil Court), 212.36 (district courts), and 210.36 (city courts).

attorney must attend before the court "unless attendance is excused for good cause."[3] The ward and representative must be consulted about the settlement—often referred to in practice as a "compromise"—and it can't ordinarily be effected by their attorney without consultation.[4] But even though consultation is necessary, the court can approve the settlement over the ward's objection[5] and even over the objection of the representative,[6] unlikely though that may be.[7]

Sometimes the ward's representative, deeming a settlement at a given figure a fair one and of a mind to encourage the defendant to pay it quickly, may try to push the settlement by purporting to give the defendant an agreement indemnifying the defendant for anything that a court may later award beyond the settlement sum. To discourage this, such agreements have been declared invalid.[8] They of course don't bind the ward, but neither may they be enforced against the representative. The voiding of such agreements has been deemed necessary to prevent the representative, perhaps motivated by selfish interest, from relaxing diligence in behalf of the ward.

The disposition of the proceeds of an infant's claim is prescribed by statute[9] as is the procedure for applying an infant's property towards the infant's support and maintenance.[10]

The court's approval of an infant's settlement does not necessarily bar an action for legal malpractice against the lawyer who negotiated the settlement for the infant. While the settlement acts like a judgment and (absent fraud or the like) forever protects the opposing party from the claim, it has been held that it offers no such insulation to the infant's lawyer, against whom malpractice may be established on the basis of simple professional negligence or incompetence in negotiating the settlement.[11]

---

[3]   CPLR 1208(d). Bittner v. Motor Vehicle Acc. Indemnification Corp., 45 Misc. 2d 584, 257 N.Y.S.2d 521 (Sup. Ct., New York County 1965), demonstrates the strictness of the court's approach to CPLR 1208.

[4]   See Fasano v. City of New York, 22 A.D.2d 799, 254 N.Y.S.2d 133 (2d Dep't 1964).

[5]   Armour v. Broadman, 283 A.D. 351, 128 N.Y.S.2d 281 (1st Dep't 1954), aff'd, 307 N.Y. 896, 123 N.E.2d 90.

[6]   Glogowski v. Rapson, 20 Misc. 2d 96, 198 N.Y.S.2d 87 (Sup. Ct., Monroe County 1959).

[7]   See Lee v. Gucker, 27 A.D.2d 722, 279 N.Y.S.2d 697 (1st Dep't 1967).

[8]   Valdimer v. Mount Vernon Hebrew Camps, Inc., 9 N.Y.2d 21, 210 N.Y.S.2d 520, 172 N.E.2d 283 (1961).

[9]   CPLR 1206.

[10]   CPLR 1211.

[11]   See Fletcher v. Hatch, 197 A.D.2d 775, 602 N.Y.S.2d 718 (3d Dep't 1993).

Chapter 8

PAPERS

Table of Sections

§ 201.   Form of Papers
§ 202.   Service of Papers; Method and Time Computation
§ 203.   Service on All Parties
§ 204.   Stipulations
§ 205.   Affidavits and Affirmations
§ 206.   Undertakings

§ 201. Form of Papers

Size of Papers & Print Size

CPLR 2101 governs the form of papers in New York practice, with further elaboration in the rules.[1] All papers are to be of letter size, 11 × 8 1/2 inches,[2] with the exception of summonses, subpoenas, notices of appearance, notes of issue, and exhibits.[3] Exhibits can be of any size. These excepted papers are usually printed forms that have traditionally been short and which continue to be acceptable in reduced size. Use of the short paper even in those few instances is optional; when the needs of the case require it, the usual letter size may be used. Where, for example, the action involves so many parties that the usual short-form summons can't contain them, a regular letter-size paper can be used. And it can be typed. There is no mystique in print and the CPLR does not require printing. It requires only that "[t]he writing shall be legible and in black ink."[4] Printed forms are acceptable whenever they do the job. The mere fact that they are in print guarantees nothing, of course, else anyone with a little printing press could claim the earth.

Except for the summons, print size must be at least 10–point type. For the summons, the minimum is 12-point type.[5] While it has been held that using smaller than

---

[1]   22 N.Y.C.R.R. § 202.5 of the Uniform Rules, governing papers filed in the supreme and county courts, contains several instructions on form, in effect codifying a number of practices, like requiring the cover and the first page of each paper to state the action's venue and provide a brief description of the paper. There are equivalent uniform rules for the filing of papers in other courts: 22 N.Y.C.R.R. §§ 205.7 (family court); 206.5 (court of claims); 207.4 (surrogate's court); 208.4 (N.Y.C. Civil Court); 212.4 (district courts); and 210.4 (city courts).

[2]   The old legal size (14 × 8 1/2) was abandoned by amendment of CPLR 2101 in 1973, effective in 1974. The appellate courts apparently didn't deem themselves bound by the new letter size and some continued to use the longer legal size. By early 1988, the Court of Appeals and three of the four appellate division departments had gone over to letter size voluntarily, the Second Department holding out for a while, but finally going along as well. These being the events that tried men's souls in the late 20th century, they're chronicled in NYSLD Nos. 339 and 347.

[3]   CPLR 2101(a). Orders of protection and temporary orders of protection are also exempt from the size limitations.

[4]   CPLR 2101(a).

[5]   CPLR 2101(a).

12-point is not jurisdictional,[6] the lawyer should not take chances with as key a document as a summons.[7] Litigation backs, oversize sheets into which documents are folded and stapled by some lawyers—voluntarily, because such backs are not required—may continue to use smaller type.[8] They're sometimes called "blue-backs," but they vary in color, depending on the aesthetic preference of the particular firm. Although not required, they are available through legal stationers and have a number of handy printed forms on them, such as verifications (for use with pleadings), affidavits of service, notices of entry or settlement, admissions of service, and the like, to use in conjunction with the particular paper enclosed within the back. Firms with heavy litigation practices sometimes order stocks of these forms with the firm name, address, and telephone number printed on them. Unless there's a need to use one of the form boxes included on the back, in which event the back may spare the use of a separate paper for the needed form (like a notary's affidavit, notice of entry, etc.), it may be idle as well as environmentally unfriendly to use a back.

Captions

Each paper used in the case should have a caption. This consists of the name of the court and the venue of the action, its title, and, to the right of the title, what the paper is—complaint, answer, notice of motion, demand for change of venue, etc. The case's index number should also appear to the right of the title,[9] and in courts using the Individual Assignment System (IAS),[10] such as the supreme court, the name of the judge should also be set forth if one has been assigned.[11]

The only three papers required to name all parties are the summons, complaint, and judgment. All others need only name the first party on each side, with an "et al." or the like to indicate that there are more.[12]

Name, Address, and Telephone Number of Lawyer or Party and Signature Rule

Each paper served or filed must bear the name, address, and telephone number of the lawyer for the party serving or filing it, or of the party herself if she is appearing pro se.[13] It was for a long time sufficient if the attorney's name was typed or printed; an

---

[6]   See United States Fid. & Guar. Co. v. King Van, Sup. Ct., Nassau County, Dec. 12, 1995 (Index No. 8196/95; Ain, J.), noted in SPR 40:3.

[7]   See the discussion in SPR 28:1.

[8]   See SPR 27:2, which discusses a memorandum circulated to the clerks by the Office of Court Administration so providing, noting that the various notices, verifications, certifications, and the like that appear on litigation backs are just "secondary or ancillary material . . . peripheral to the case resolution process."

[9]   CPLR 2101(c); 22 N.Y.C.R.R. § 202.5(a).

[10]   See § 77A.

[11]   See 22 N.Y.C.R.R. § 202.5(a).

[12]   CPLR 2101(c).

[13]   CPLR 2101(d). Under CPLR 2103–a, enacted in 2004, the court can permit a party to conceal an address or telephone number "in any civil proceeding." The court in Ahamed v. Cabs Nursing Home, Index No. 8512/08 (Sup. Ct., Nassau County; Dec. 16, 2009; Winslow, J.) (SPR 216:3), added the social security number to that list, advising that the court "will not entertain or otherwise execute any document that contains a social security number . . . [if it] would have the inevitable effect of making private information available to the public." A new rule requiring attorneys to redact certain confidential information from papers filed in court is addressed at the end of this section.

actual subscription was not required.[14] That was changed as of March 1, 1998, when an amendment of the sanctions rule, Rule 130–1 of the Rules of the Chief Administrator, took effect. It requires the actual subscription, by an attorney, on all papers "served on another party or filed or submitted to the court,"[15] and that includes pleadings, motions, and any other paper that has traditionally born the printed or typed name of the lawyer.

The signature automatically constitutes the attorney's certification—without any formal attestation or certification language being required—of the integrity of the paper to the best of the attorney's knowledge after conducting "an inquiry reasonable under the circumstances."[16] The bar had many questions about the signing requirement and its implications,[17] including how far the lawyer has to go in checking into the facts supplied by the client before certifying the paper with a signature. Early caselaw addressed to some procedural incidentals held that in the absence of prejudice to the other side, the inadvertent omission of a signature is curable by supplying it late[18] and that this applies even to the summons.[19]

Lawyers must note that a significant violation of the signature requirement, as by signing a paper the lawyer knows or should know contains false or misleading data, amounts to a frivolous litigation practice and can result in heavy sanctions.[20]

A typing or printing of the name must appear beneath the signature to assure that it can be read.[21]

The attorney should sign himself, not have others do it. In at least one unreported case, an attorney's allowing others to affix his signature to a summons and complaint brought a dismissal "with prejudice,"[22] a draconian result but a good warning to the bar nevertheless. Depending on the nature of the paper and the attorney's actual involvement with the facts underlying it, false statements in such a paper can be found the responsibility of the lawyer, leading to imposition of the sanctions provided in Part 130 just as if the lawyer had signed it himself.

In a pair of Second Department cases in 2008, In re Shapiro[23] and In re Moroff,[24] an attorney's regular practice of having others sign his name brought a six-month suspension. The practice affected thousands of court filings. (In one district court alone,

---

[14]   See In re Edward Shapiro, P.C., 9 Misc. 3d 369, 374, 801 N.Y.S.2d 694, 698 (N.Y. City Civ. Ct. 2005); 2d Rep. Leg. Doc. No.13, p.174 (1958).

[15]   22 N.Y.C.R.R. § 130–1.1–a.

[16]   22 N.Y.C.R.R. § 130–1.1–a(b). The language of the rule is that merely "[b]y signing a paper, an attorney . . . certifies."

[17]   The signature rule and sanctions that can be imposed for frivolous pleading are discussed in further detail in § 414A. See the three-part treatment in SPR 66:1–68:1.

[18]   Di Russo v. Hendrick, Sup. Ct., Westchester County, March 9, 1998 (Index No. 2033/97, Lefkowitz, J.), treated in SPR 69:2.

[19]   See SPR 70:1.

[20]   Sanctions are treated in § 414A.

[21]   CPLR 2101(a).

[22]   See SPR 144:3.

[23]   In re Shapiro, 55 A.D.3d 291, 863 N.Y.S.2d 784 (2d Dep't 2008), reinstatement granted, 63 A.D.3d 951, 880 N.Y.S.2d 534 (2d Dep't 2009).

[24]   In re Moroff, 55 A.D.3d 200, 863 N.Y.S.2d 800 (2d Dep't 2008), reinstatement granted, 63 A.D.3d 944, 880 N.Y.S.2d 537 (2d Dep't 2009).

some 4600 matters needed refiling). The punishment would have been greater but for the lawyer's candid confession of fault.[25]

In e-filed actions, the relevant rules provide that "[a]n electronically filed document shall be considered to have been signed by, and shall be binding upon, the person identified as a signatory" if, among other things: "(i) it bears the physical signature" of the attorney "and is scanned into an electronic format that reproduces" the signature; (ii) the attorney "has electronically affixed the digital image of his or her signature to the document"; or (iii) it is e-filed under the attorney's user identification and password.[26] This constitutes compliance with the signature requirement in Part 130.[27] Therefore, while an attorney can permit another, such as a secretary or paralegal, to e-file documents with the attorney's user identification and password, the attorney will be responsible for the content of those papers.[28]

Originals vs. Copies

The CPLR is generally content to have copies rather than originals used, whether for service or filing.[29] CPLR 2101(e) expressly provides that unless "otherwise specifically prescribed, copies, rather than originals, of all papers, including orders, affidavits and exhibits may be served or filed." It is common practice to save the "original" for the court, serving mere copies on parties. (In this technological age, it may be hard in many cases to distinguish between them). In Gehring v. Goodman,[30] in which a clerk had refused to accept a mere copy of the affidavit required under CPLR 3218(b) in conjunction with a confession of judgment, the aggrieved lawyer brought an Article 78 proceeding against the clerk, who was then directed to accept the copy. Similarly, in Rechler Equity B-1, LLC v. AKR Corp.,[31] the Second Department concluded that the supreme court should not have denied the plaintiff's motion for summary judgment on the ground that the affidavits submitted in support thereof were not "originally" signed. Citing to CPLR 2101(e), the *Rechler Equity* court ruled that the photocopies of the plaintiff's affidavits submitted in support of the motion for summary judgment should have been considered. Unless for some good reason the original is not available, it's obviously wiser to furnish the original than have to go to the kind of trouble, time, and expense involved in *Gehring* and *Rechler Equity*.[32]

CPLR 2101(g) requires that any paper served or filed electronically, such as in an e-filed action, be capable of reproduction by the recipient into such form as will satisfy the requirements noted in this section about the form of papers generally.[33] The use of a means of transmission that sends an actual copy of the paper, rather than just the recitation of its contents, will apparently do the job.

---

[25]   See the discussion of the cases in SPR 203:2.

[26]   22 N.Y.C.R.R. § 202.5–b(e)(1). While this rule is contained in the rules for the consensual e-filing program, it also applies in cases governed by mandatory e-filing. See 22 N.Y.C.R.R. § 202.5–bb(a)(1).

[27]   22 N.Y.C.R.R. § 202.5–b(e)(2).

[28]   The status of e-filing in New York State courts is discussed in § 63A.

[29]   CPLR 2101(e).

[30]   Gehring v. Goodman, 25 Misc. 3d 802, 884 N.Y.S.2d 646 (Sup. Ct., New York County 2009) (SPR 213:3).

[31]   Rechler Equity B-1, LLC v. AKR Corp., 98 A.D.3d 496, 949 N.Y.S.2d 457 (2d Dep't 2012) (SPR 249:2).

[32]   A rule has now been implemented which specifically lists the papers that a clerk is authorized to reject. See 22 N.Y.C.R.R. § 202.5(d)(1). See § 63.

[33]   See 22 N.Y.C.R.R. § 202.5–b(a)(2)(i) (defining "electronic means" in e-filed actions).

If a copy of some paper is required to be formally "certified"—distinguish this from the automatic certification that accompanies a lawyer's signature—the certification need not be made by the clerk with whom the paper is on file; it can be made by the attorney.[34]

Defects in Form

CPLR 2101(f) provides that if no one is prejudiced by it, a defect in mere form shall be disregarded or at worst corrected. This provision overlaps CPLR 2001, the CPLR's general statute about forgiving or amending harmless mistakes,[35] but it's even less tolerant of nit-picking. When the defect is one of mere form, the one served with the paper must, in order to preserve the objection, return the paper within fifteen days with "a statement of particular objections." If the defect is truly one of mere form, the complaining party will even then be disappointed because the best he can expect is an amendment to correct the form.

Acknowledgments

At several points inside and outside the CPLR, an "acknowledgment" is called for.[36] An "acknowledgment" is a statement or accompanying paper whereby the signer of an instrument attests, before a notary or person of like authority, that he, she, or it is the signer of the instrument.

For acknowledgments made within New York, section 309–a of the Real Property Law prescribes the form for in-state acknowledgments, section 309–b for acknowledgments made outside New York. The acknowledgment forms were included in the Real Property Law because deeds to real property are perhaps the best known instruments calling for an acknowledgment. But a number of other provisions having nothing to do with real property, including some in the CPLR itself,[37] also call for an acknowledgment. What form should be used for these others?

For both categories—those that adopt outright the acknowledgment form used for deeds and those that merely call for an acknowledgment without the reference—use of the form prescribed in the Real Property Law, appropriately tailored, is advisable. For the one category, it satisfies explicitly and for the other, it furnishes the best model.[38]

Redaction of Personal Confidential Information

The Administrative Board of the Courts recently promulgated Uniform Rule 202.5(e), which requires the redaction of certain confidential personal information ("CPI") from court filings. Compliance with the rule—effective January 1, 2015—was voluntary through February 28, 2015, but is now mandatory. The new rule covers actions

---

[34]   CPLR 2105. The thing certified is that the paper has been compared with the original and "found to be a true and complete copy." That's all a certification is. At one time it was necessary for the certifier to compare the original and the copy line by line and word by word—visions of the clerk on a high stool in a Dickens setting—but today xerography does the job.

[35]   See §§ 6, 63.

[36]   See, e.g., CPLR 321(b) (on substitution of attorneys); CPLR 2502(d) (on undertakings); CPLR 3121(a) (on furnishing medical authorizations); Gen. Oblig. Law § 5–1501B(1) (on powers of attorney); etc.

[37]   See note 36 above.

[38]   See Midfirst Bank v. Agho, 121 A.D.3d 343, 350, 991 N.Y.S.2d 623, 629 (2d Dep't 2014); SPR 91:2; McKinney's Practice Commentaries to CPLR 2309; see also § 388.

that are using the New York State Courts Electronic Filing System ("NYSCEF")[39] as well as those proceeding with actual hard copy papers.

Under the rule, CPI includes "(i) the taxpayer identification number of an individual or an entity, including a social security number, an employer identification number, and an individual taxpayer identification number, except the last four digits thereof; (ii) the date of an individual's birth, except the year thereof; (iii) the full name of an individual known to be a minor, except the minor's initials; and (iv) a financial account number, including a credit and/or debit card number, a bank account number, an investment account number, and/or an insurance account number, except the last four digits or letters thereof."[40] Parties filing a paper with CPI, whether in redacted or unredacted form, should secure a "Redaction Cover Page" from the clerk's office and fill out the appropriate information. NYSCEF has been modified to allow parties filing papers electronically to check a box to indicate whether the paper is redacted.

Any document containing unredacted CPI should only be filed under the terms of a court order.[41] The responsibility to comply with the rule lies primarily with the parties and the county clerks have not been vested with authority to reject a document presented for filing that contains CPI.[42] While some county clerks have implemented procedures to address the filing of papers containing social security numbers in compliance with General Business Law section 399–dd and Public Officers Law section 96–a, the new court rule requires broader redaction than that required under those statutes.

§ 202. Service of Papers; Method and Time Computation

Initiatory Papers vs. Interlocutory Papers

The only kind of service studied so far is service of the initiatory papers, which is governed by CPLR 308.[1] CPLR 308 allows various methods, but nothing as simple as mere mailing.[2] For the service of almost all the rest of the mass of papers that fly back and forth in litigation after jurisdiction has been secured, ordinary first-class mailing has been the common method of service.

CPLR 308 and its punctilious demands apply to the service of jurisdiction-getting papers. The summons is the main one, securing jurisdiction of the defendant in an action. Another is the notice of petition, or order to show cause, securing jurisdiction of a respondent in a special proceeding.[3] The subpoena is also considered a jurisdiction-getting paper, in this instance securing jurisdiction of a witness.[4] Those papers must therefore be served in the same manner as a summons,[5] and so it falls to CPLR 308 to govern them.

---

[39] See § 63A.

[40] 22 N.Y.C.R.R. § 202.5(e)(1).

[41] See 22 N.Y.C.R.R. § 202.5(e)(2), (3).

[42] See 22 N.Y.C.R.R. § 202.5(d)(1) (listing papers that court clerks are authorized to reject).

[1] See §§ 66–76A.

[2] CPLR 312–a permits personal service of initiatory papers by mail, but requires the cooperation of the recipient. See § 76A.

[3] See § 553.

[4] See § 382.

[5] CPLR 403(c) (special proceedings); CPLR 2303 (subpoenas). CPLR 308 would also govern in any other instance in which service is directed to be made in the same manner as a summons. Such service is required, for example, by CPLR 5231(d) and (e) for an income execution.

But for almost all other papers served and filed in litigation after jurisdiction has been secured—papers sometimes called "interlocutory" or "intermediary" papers—CPLR 2103 governs. Its subdivision (a) is the source of the permission for any nonparty 18 and over to serve papers in New York practice.[6] In Neroni v. Follender,[7] the court ruled that service of motion papers by a party in "violation of this provision 'is a mere irregularity which does not vitiate service' where . . . no resulting prejudice is shown." Subdivision (b) then supplies the rules about how interlocutory papers are to be served, which makes it one of the busier provisions of the CPLR.

Computing Time Periods for Service

It's appropriate to note preliminarily how time periods are computed in New York practice[8] since many papers in litigation have to be served on or before a particular day. The day from which a time period runs is excluded in the computation.[9] If a plaintiff has 20 days to reply to a counterclaim,[10] for example, and the answer containing the counterclaim is served on April 1, the last day for serving the answer is April 21. The count starts on April 2 and counting 20 days with April 2 as the first day makes the last day the 21st. If the last day falls on a Saturday, Sunday, or legal holiday,[11] the time is extended until "the next succeeding business day."[12] The time extensions applicable when a paper is served by mail or by an overnight service, to be discussed below, must be factored in accordingly.

Service upon Attorney

Perhaps the most significant aspect of CPLR 2103(b) is its requirement that interlocutory papers be served on the attorney rather than the party. Only if the party is appearing without an attorney, or if the attorney "cannot be served," may the service be made on the party directly.[13] Hence, as soon as it's perceived that a party is appearing by an attorney, all further contacts with that party by the opposing attorney, including the service of papers, must be made through the attorney.[14] For example, the plaintiff appears in an action by an attorney as soon as a summons bearing the lawyer's name is served on the defendant. Therefore, all future communications with the plaintiff, including the service of papers, must be made through the plaintiff's attorney. CPLR 2103(b)'s rule requiring service upon an attorney covers the whole of the litigation, and

---

[6]   This also applies to summons service. There is no CPLR rule that summons servers be licensed, but there may be a local requirement to that effect as there is in New York City for those serving more than a certain number of summonses a year. See N.Y.C. Admin. Code §§ 20–403–20–410.

[7]   Neroni v. Follender, 137 A.D.3d 1336, 1337, 26 N.Y.S.3d 621, 623 (3d Dep't 2016).

[8]   Passing mention was made of the applicable General Construction Law statutes in §§ 33 and 34 while discussing the statute of limitations where inaccurate time reckoning can of course have its most serious consequences.

[9]   See, e.g., Gen. Constr. Law § 20.

[10]   See CPLR 3012(a).

[11]   The list of legal holidays is in Gen. Constr. Law § 24.

[12]   See Gen. Constr. Law §§ 25 (for periods set by contract) and 25–a (for periods set by statute), which also contain instructions for when a particular hour is specified. If no hour is specified, and it rarely is, service may be made at any time on the last day.

[13]   CPLR 2103(c). Attorneys should make all possible efforts to avoid serving a represented party directly, as doing so can run afoul of Rule 4.2(a) of the New York Rules of Professional Conduct. If neither the party nor his attorney is servable, the paper can simply be filed with the clerk. CPLR 2103(d).

[14]   See New York City Bar Association Ethics Opinion 2009–1 (2009) (lawyer generally prohibited from sending papers directly to a represented person and simultaneously to her counsel).

can even go beyond. A notice of appeal, for example, must still be served on the other side's attorney.

The first clause in CPLR 2103(b) authorizes the court to determine whom to serve in doubtful situations. A judge's aid can be obtained by resorting to an order to show cause.[15]

Methods of Service and Completion of Service

The attorney may of course be served by personal delivery,[16] but that method is generally used only when there is some special hurry or when lawyers' offices are in close proximity. The most common method is ordinary first-class mail to the lawyer's office address[17] as set forth on the last paper served by that lawyer in the action. The paper must be enclosed in a properly stamped envelope,[18] and it is deemed served—i.e., service is deemed complete—when it is merely dropped into the letter box or mail chute or other official post office gadget, or delivered into a postal official's hand.[19] Until 2016, the receptacle or office had to be in New York State, but the legislature has amended CPLR 2103(f)(1) to define "[m]ailing" as depositing the interlocutory paper with the "United States Postal Service within the United States."[20]

Delivery through an overnight delivery service, like Federal Express, United Parcel Service, or the U.S. Post Office's own "Express Mail," is also permitted and deemed complete when the paper is delivered into the custody of the particular service prior to the latest time the service requires in order to assure overnight delivery.[21]

Service by facsimile ("fax") is also permitted for interlocutory papers. When fax service is used, it is also necessary to mail a copy of the paper to the fax recipient, which makes this already antiquated method of service needlessly cumbersome.[22] Fax service also requires the consent of the recipient. Including a fax number in the address block on a paper served in the action signifies such consent, but it has been held that its inclusion only on an office letterhead does not.[23] The point is somewhat mooted by the rule that permission to use fax, even if granted, can be withdrawn at any time merely by serving a notice on the other parties in the action.[24] Fax service is complete "upon the

---

[15]	Orders to show cause are treated in § 248.

[16]	CPLR 2103(b)(1).

[17]	CPLR 2103(b)(2). Paragraph 3 of CPLR 2103(b) allows service on the attorney by delivering it to the person in charge of the attorney's office or inserting it into the office letter drop. Paragraph 4 allows service at the lawyer's residence, but only if service can't be made at the office.

[18]	If the postage is insufficient but the adverse party pays the difference and accepts the paper, all is in order and the recipient can't later reject or return it. In re Hart's Estate, 53 Misc. 2d 555, 558, 279 N.Y.S.2d 119, 122 (Sur. Ct. 1967), aff'd, 30 A.D.2d 781, 292 N.Y.S.2d 1017 (2d Dep't 1968) ("[F]ailure to properly prepay postage does not per se invalidate service, and delivery to the addressee or receipt by the addressee and retention waives any defect in insufficiency in postage.").

[19]	CPLR 2103(f)(1).

[20]	For further discussion of the amendment, see Patrick M. Connors, *Turn and Face the Changes: E-filing Among 2015 Amendments to CPLR*, N.Y.L.J., Jan. 19, 2016, at 3.

[21]	CPLR 2103(b)(6).

[22]	CPLR 2103(b)(5). The fax statute speaks of "mailing" an additional copy of the faxed paper, but this would apparently include the alternative of the overnight delivery service provided for in CPLR 2103(b)(6).

[23]	See Levin v. Levin, 160 Misc. 2d 388, 609 N.Y.S.2d 547 (Sup. Ct., Nassau County 1994). The case involved an order to show cause, which can be deemed a category of process. The court can prescribe that service of an order to show cause be made via facsimile even without the recipient's consent. See CPLR 403(d), CPLR 2214(d).

[24]	CPLR 2103(b)(5).

receipt by the sender of a signal from the equipment of the attorney served indicating that the transmission was received, and the mailing of a copy of the paper to that attorney."

Although service by ordinary mail is deemed complete upon the mere posting, a showing that the paper was never received will usually prompt the court to undo any default predicated on the absence of a response. A mere denial of receipt, however, especially when set forth in unconvincing affidavits or in a case in which the party denying receipt has a prior history of delay, will not suffice to raise an issue of proper service.[25] Simple courtesy among members of the bar usually prompts the serving attorney to inquire into the reason for an adversary's lack of response. When that comity is extended, these problems are usually resolved.

Affidavits of Service

A lost argument about the mailing or receipt of a mailed paper can sometimes have serious consequences, such as the forfeiture of the right to appeal.[26] It is to the credit of the bar that there are so few disputes—at least relatively few—about whether or not a mailed paper was received, and to the credit of the bench that so few of these few get as far as the "contest" stage. Occasionally, the contest comes on, however, and has telling effect. It did in Engel v. Lichterman,[27] for example, and went all the way to the Court of Appeals. It was a dispute about whether a conditional order, which allowed P a new period in which to serve a bill of particulars,[28] was received by P. D said he mailed the order and had a properly executed affidavit of service to prove it. D won the argument when P could only protest that he didn't receive it. The Court apparently did not believe P, and D ended up with summary judgment dismissing the medical malpractice action. P had been lax in earlier phases of the case, whose lesson is the negative effect dilatory conduct can have on a procrastinator's credibility,[29] even on so seemingly picayune a point as whether a mailed paper was received.[30]

The one who actually deposits the paper at the post office or at an official depository, usually a secretary or someone else in the lawyer's employ, should fill out the affidavit of mail service. This may be done on the litigation back encasing the original or on a separate sheet. Whichever is used, it's retained as proof of service for ultimate filing in court.

Attorneys have often recited in an affidavit or affirmation of service that they have "caused" papers to be served rather than having actually "served" the particular papers. The appellate division has held that an affirmation of service containing this language is defective, vacating a default judgment for that reason.[31]

---

[25]   See Engel v. Lichterman, 95 A.D.2d 536, 541–42, 467 N.Y.S.2d 642, 645–46 (2d Dep't 1983), aff'd, 62 N.Y.2d 943, 479 N.Y.S.2d 188, 468 N.E.2d 26 (1984).

[26]   Lichtman v. Mount Judah Cemetery, 269 A.D.2d 319, 705 N.Y.S.2d 23 (1st Dep't 2000).

[27]   Engel by Engel v. Lichterman, 62 N.Y.2d 943, 479 N.Y.S.2d 188, 468 N.E.2d 26 (1984).

[28]   Bill of particulars practice is taken up in §§ 238 et seq.

[29]   See § 231A.

[30]   The *Engel* case is treated in a lead note in NYSLD No. 300.

[31]   See Peter-MacIntyre v. Lynch Intern., Inc., 52 A.D.3d 424, 862 N.Y.S.2d 351 (1st Dep't 2008), more fully discussed in § 205.

To secure a piece of more objective evidence that a paper was mailed, lawyers sometimes use certified or even registered mail. While permissible,[32] it is not necessary,[33] and it will sometimes bring on delays as when the post office does not deliver the envelope because it cannot obtain a signature on a receipt. The lawyer who wants some post office evidence of a mailing can simply obtain from the post office clerk a "Certificate of Mailing,"[34] not to be confused with either "certified" or "registered" mail. Its cost is nominal. It recites that a piece of first-class mail was presented to the post office for mailing and requires no signature from the adversary.

Add-Ons for Recipient of Paper

We meet at this point the provisions about the additional days the recipient gets for responding to a paper when it is served by mail or by an overnight delivery service. The additional times are 5 or 6 days when the paper is served by mail, but only 1 day if served through an overnight delivery service. CPLR 2103(b)(2) provides that whenever a period of time is measured from the service of a paper, and that paper is served by mail, the party required to take the responsive step gets 5 additional days if the paper was mailed from New York State and 6 additional days if mailed from outside New York.[35] This recognizes that the service of the paper was deemed complete upon posting and it compensates for the delay in mail delivery.

These add-ons have ubiquitous applications and in fact have to be superimposed on a number of time periods we have already met. Where, for example, D serves on P a demand for a change of venue, P has 5 days in which to respond to it.[36] If the demand was served by mail in New York, however, which is usually the procedure, the 5 days become 10.[37] The additional days are added to the stated period whenever the time to perform a procedural act runs from the service of a paper and the paper is served via mail. The CPLR has a big array of these periods.

Lawyers need to be careful here because the add-ons will only be available where: (1) the time to perform an act runs from the service of a paper; and (2) the paper is served by regular mail. Therefore, they will not apply when a particular statute specifically provides that the *receipt* of the paper starts the time for responding as occurs, for example, with the 90-day demand procedure that must precede a motion to dismiss for neglect to prosecute.[38] Similarly, if a time period runs from the filing of a paper, as with the time to move for summary judgment under CPLR 3212(a), the add-ons are inapplicable.[39] Furthermore, the add-ons will ordinarily not apply in an e-filed action

---

[32]　See Cohen v. Shure, 153 A.D.2d 35, 548 N.Y.S.2d 696 (2d Dep't 1989).

[33]　Registered mail is especially gratuitous because it's more expensive, designed as it is primarily for the shipment of valuables.

[34]　Postal Service PS Form 3817.

[35]　The paper must still be mailed via the United States Postal Service within the United States. Before 1983, the add-on was 3 days. Older cases involving the issue will often refer to the 3-day period.

[36]　CPLR 511(b). See § 123.

[37]　Similarly, the 15 days within which to make a motion to change venue under CPLR 511(b) becomes 20 if the demand to change venue is served via regular mail. See § 123.

[38]　CPLR 3216(b)(3); see Public Service Mut. Ins. Co. v. Zucker, 225 A.D.2d 308, 309, 639 N.Y.S.2d 5, 7 (1st Dep't 1996) (concurring opinion). The dismissal for neglect to prosecute is treated in § 375.

[39]　See Group IX, Inc. v. Next Printing & Design Inc., 77 A.D.3d 530, 909 N.Y.S.2d 434 (1st Dep't 2010); Dexter v. 16th Street Holdings, L.L.C., 2012 WL 116102 (Sup. Ct., New York County 2012) (denying motion made three days late as untimely where defendant could not show "good cause" for late filing). The timing of summary judgment motions is discussed in further detail in section 279.

because service of the interlocutory paper is made simultaneously with the filing of the document rather than by mail.[40]

When an overnight delivery service is used, the 5-day addition is reduced to a mere 1-day addition regardless of where the papers are deposited.[41] No additional time for responding is prescribed when fax service is used, but since fax service is not complete until the mailing of the faxed paper, it can be argued that the time addition applicable to mailing will be available to the recipient. Otherwise, because a fax transmission is immediate, there would presumably be no time extension, a situation an attorney can avoid for the present by withholding from adversaries permission for fax service.

If any confusion should arise in a given situation about just how long a responding period is, whether because of the additional day or days or otherwise, the one expecting the response should not be too hasty to treat the other side as in default. Attorneys must bear in mind the court's broad power under CPLR 2004 to extend time periods and to do so even after the applicable period has expired.[42] That power is likely to be invoked swiftly to preclude confrontations over minor time omissions traceable to the impact of the applicable add-ons, or to disagreements about what kind of time extension attends what kind of service, at least in situations when the time provision involved does not have jurisdictional impact.

What happens, for example, when the paper calling for a response is sent by overnight delivery on a Friday—which postulates that it would be received by Saturday—but the paper doesn't arrive until Monday, for whatever reason (the office was closed on Saturday, the service doesn't deliver on Saturday, the sender failed to request Saturday delivery, etc.)? What period of extension applies in that scenario? Still just the one day? Or does it now become equivalent to an ordinary mailing and get the five-day addition that applies to a mailed paper? The courts have not definitively answered the question.

With most papers, missing the mark by a day or two would not be fatal because of the courts' general power to extend time periods under CPLR 2004. But that would not be so when the time to appeal is involved, which is rigidly applied and not subject to discretionary extensions under CPLR 2004.[43]

The additional time is added to responding periods not only when it is a statute or rule that sets the responding time, but also when a court order does,[44] as illustrated in the *Engel* case discussed above.

It must always be kept in mind that the add-ons apply only to papers served within an already commenced and pending litigation. They do not apply to papers served in an administrative proceeding[45] or other out-of-court proceedings, such as an arbitration.[46] This is so even if the particular paper is the final step in the proceeding and its service

---

[40]   22 N.Y.C.R.R. § 202.5–b(f)(2)(ii).

[41]   CPLR 2103(b)(6), added in 1989. Before that, the 5-day addition for responding was held to apply even when express mail, with a guaranteed next-day delivery, was used. See Rolm Corp. v. F. Garofalo Elec. Co., Inc., 127 Misc. 2d 662, 487 N.Y.S.2d 309 (Sup. Ct., Queens County 1985).

[42]   See § 6, in which CPLR 2004 is discussed.

[43]   § 6; see § 534 and the note on the sent-on-Friday problem in SPR 99:3.

[44]   Corradetti v. Dales Used Cars, 102 A.D.2d 272, 477 N.Y.S.2d 779 (3d Dep't 1984).

[45]   See De Milt v. Tax Appeals Tribunal of State of N.Y., 232 A.D.2d 824, 649 N.Y.S.2d 66 (3d Dep't 1996) (SPR 70:3).

[46]   See § 593 (Practitioner's Edition).

starts the running of the statute of limitations on the court action that may be brought to review the determination.[47] Indeed, it is especially in that situation that a party must avoid thinking that there's extra time. Some cases below Court of Appeals level hold or assume that the extensions do apply in those situations.[48] Lawyers who put all their eggs into that extension basket are likely to lose the eggs.[49]

Filing of Papers and E-Filing

The filing of all papers with the court, as opposed to their service on other parties, is not a general requirement of New York law, as has already been noted.[50] Filing is required in some instances,[51] however, and permissible in just about all. Whether required or volunteered, the filing takes place with the clerk of the court in which the action has been brought.[52]

Discussion has so far centered mainly on the service of a paper. Every now and again, there's a dispute about the *filing* of a paper. When a paper has to be filed in court by a particular date, the clerk's date/time stamp affixed to a copy of the paper and returned to the server is a comforting reassurance of the paper's timely filing. Dare a party ever contest the clerk, and claim filing at an earlier time than the date/time stamp indicates? It has worked in a few cases,[53] but it's always risky—and almost always seen only when a party has waited until the last minute to file something, thereby necessitating the contest.

When an action is subject to mandatory e-filing, or parties to an action have consented to e-filing, filing and service occurs simultaneously. In e-filed actions, "a party causes service of an interlocutory document to be made upon another party participating in e-filing by filing the document electronically."[54] The NYSCEF system immediately transmits an e-mail message to all of the attorneys participating in e-filing containing a link to the document. The add-ons discussed above will not apply in an e-filed action because service of papers is generally not made via regular or overnight mail.[55] Therefore, if the time to perform a procedural act runs from the service of a document, the period will run from the moment the document is e-filed. When the day arrives where most New York State actions are subject to e-filing, many of the disputes that are the subject of this section will be nonexistent or significantly diminished.

---

[47]   Fiedelman v. New York State Dept. of Health, 58 N.Y.2d 80, 459 N.Y.S.2d 420, 445 N.E.2d 1099 (1983); see Lester v. New York State Office of Parks, Recreation & Historic Preservation, 60 A.D.3d 680, 874 N.Y.S.2d 568 (2d Dep't 2009).

[48]   See, e.g., Miller v. General Elec. Co., 102 A.D.2d 966, 477 N.Y.S.2d 834 (3d Dep't 1984).

[49]   See *Lester*, 60 A.D.3d at 681, 874 N.Y.S.2d at 568.

[50]   See § 77.

[51]   A prime example is the note of issue, CPLR 3402(a), without whose filing the case doesn't get on the calendar. It's discussed in § 369. Another example is the filing of proof of service made under CPLR 308(2) (deliver and mail service) or CPLR 308(4) (affix and mail service). See §§ 72, 74.

[52]   CPLR 2102.

[53]   See § 63.

[54]   22 N.Y.C.R.R. § 202.5–b(f)(2)(ii) ("Service of interlocutory documents in an e-filed action."). While this rule is contained in the rules for the consensual e-filing program, it also applies in cases governed by mandatory e-filing. See 22 N.Y.C.R.R. § 202.5–bb(a)(1).

[55]   But see Global Custom Integrations, Inc. v. JDP Wholesale Enterprises, Inc., 40 Misc. 3d 909, 968 N.Y.S.2d 852 (Sup. Ct., Westchester Co. 2013) (holding that when service is made by first-class mail, rather than solely by e-filing, see 22 N.Y.C.R.R. § 202.5–b(f)(2)(ii), the 5-day extension to respond in CPLR 2103(b)(2) applied).

Specific Statutory Instruction on Service

In several cases, a party who had a clear and statutory formula for the service of a paper readily at hand nonetheless ignored it and made service by another means instead. A defendant in one case, for example, served a CPLR 3216 demand—a device used in conjunction with the neglect to prosecute procedure[56]—by federal express despite the statute's calling for the more economical means of registered or certified mail. It was nevertheless held okay in Secreto v. IBM Corp.[57] We suggested that such an assurance not be relied on in other contexts, especially when process is involved, i.e., a paper securing jurisdiction or commencing a proceeding of some kind.[58] When the same sort of deviation was later tried in New York Central Mutual Fire Ins. Co. v. Czumaj,[59] for example, the court was not nearly as permissive. *Czumaj* involved a demand for arbitration under CPLR 7503(c), which calls for the demand's service by CPLR 308's methods or registered or certified mail, return receipt requested.[60] When the demand was served by federal express instead, it was held invalid for that reason and the arbitration was permanently stayed.

A similar warning that unauthorized substitution is bad business is Newman v. State,[61] where "priority mail" was used instead of the "certified mail" called for by section 11(a) of the Court of Claims Act. The service was held invalid, resulting in the dismissal of the action for untimeliness.

Judiciary Law § 470's Physical Office Requirement

As noted above, CPLR 2103(b) generally requires that interlocutory papers be served on the party's attorney rather than the party. This subdivision also lists several methods of service, including personal delivery, regular mail, and overnight delivery to the attorney's law office. Judiciary Law section 470 works in tandem with CPLR 2103(b) by requiring nonresident attorneys to maintain an "office for the transaction of law business" in New York State.

In this "virtual" age, where almost every activity known to man and woman can be accomplished electronically or in a "cloud," Judiciary Law section 470 has come under some intense scrutiny. It is especially a problem for those who want to conduct their practice in a "virtual law office," where attorneys have an online presence, but no bricks and mortar facility to meet with clients or accept service.[62]

In Schoenefeld v. State,[63] the Court of Appeals, on a certified question from the Second Circuit, interpreted Judiciary Law section 470 to require nonresident attorneys

---

[56]   This is discussed in § 375.

[57]   Secreto v. International Business Machines Corp., 194 Misc. 2d 512, 755 N.Y.S.2d 566 (Sup. Ct., Dutchess County 2003).

[58]   SPR 134:3.

[59]   New York Cent. Mut. Fire Ins. Co. v. Czumaj, 9 A.D.3d 833, 780 N.Y.S.2d 254 (4th Dep't 2004) (SPR 157:2).

[60]   See § 593 (Practitioner's Edition).

[61]   Newman v. State, 5 Misc. 3d 640, 783 N.Y.S.2d 796 (Ct. Cl. 2004) (SPR 159:4).

[62]   See, e.g., New York State Bar Association Opinion 1025 (2014), 2014 WL 5369076 (opining that an attorney may operate ethically via a purely virtual law office, provided the attorney complies with all applicable laws and rules, including the minimum requirements as set forth in Jud. Law § 470); Association of the Bar of the City of New York Committee on Professional Ethics, Formal Opinion 2014–2 (discussing requirements for lawyers who plan to practice via a virtual law office).

[63]   Schoenefeld v. State, 25 N.Y.3d 22, 6 N.Y.S.3d 221, 29 N.E.3d 230 (2015).

to maintain a physical law office within the state. After return of the certified question, the Second Circuit held that section 470 "does not violate the Privileges and Immunities Clause because it was not enacted for the protectionist purpose of favoring New York residents in their ability to practice law."[64] Given the decisions of the Court of Appeals and Second Circuit, attorneys must note that the First Department has concluded that an attorney's failure to maintain a New York office as required by Judiciary Law section 470 requires the dismissal of an action commenced by such attorney, without prejudice to commencing a new action.[65] The Second Department has taken a far more lenient approach.[66]

§ 203.　Service on All Parties

Lawyers sometimes wonder whether they are required to serve a given set of papers on all parties, or only on adverse parties, or those affected by the particular papers. CPLR 2103(e) does not leave them guessing. It requires that each paper be served "on every other party who has appeared." Thus, attorneys must make it their practice to draw papers in sufficient copies to enable one to be served on each of the other parties to the action, no matter whose side they are on, and without regard to any notions about who is or isn't interested in the particular paper. All the parties will make that judgment for themselves.

Parties who have not appeared ordinarily need not be served. If the particular party's time to appear has not yet expired, the one seeking to serve some paper on that party should wait for expiration of that party's appearance time before assuming the party is in default. When it expires without an appearance, the party is in default and need not be served with further papers. If a new or additional claim is being asserted against a party who has not appeared, however, even if that party is long in default, it must not only be served on her but must also be served in the same manner as a summons.[1] This is to prevent a default from being taken against the nonappearing party on some claim of which she did not have due notice. It therefore applies whether or not the original responding time has expired.[2]

If the party—ordinarily a defendant—who wants to serve some paper does not know who has or has not appeared, so as to assess her duties under CPLR 2103(e) and CPLR 3012(a), she may demand a list of the appearers from the plaintiff's attorney, who knows

---

[64]　Schoenefeld v. Schneiderman, 821 F.3d 273, 276 (2d Cir. 2016), cert. denied, 137 S. Ct. 1580, 197 L. Ed. 2d 705 (2017). The case is discussed in further detail in Patrick M. Connors, *Judiciary Law § 470 Meets Temporary Practice Under Part 523*, N.Y.L.J., May 24, 2016, at 3.

[65]　See, e.g., Webb v. Greater New York Auto. Dealers Ass'n, Inc., 93 A.D.3d 561, 940 N.Y.S.2d 608 (1st Dep't 2012); Kinder Morgan Energy Partners, LP v. Ace American Ins. Co., 51 A.D.3d 580, 859 N.Y.S.2d 135 (1st Dep't 2008).

[66]　See, e.g., Sovereign Bank v. Calderone, 84 A.D.3d 778, 921 N.Y.S.2d 878 (2d Dep't 2011) ("even had the defendant demonstrated that the plaintiff's counsel was in violation of Jud. Law § 470, such violation would 'not provide a basis for the defendant to have the complaint against him dismissed.' "). The Third Department has imposed discipline on lawyers who fail to comply with Jud. Law § 470. See Matter of Marin, 250 A.D.2d 997, 673 N.Y.S.2d 247 (3d Dep't 1998) lv. den., 92 N.Y.2d 818, 685 N.Y.S.2d 420, 708 N.E.2d 177 (1999).

[1]　CPLR 3012(a) ("[a] subsequent pleading asserting new or additional claims for relief shall be served upon a party who has not appeared in the manner provided for service of a summons"); see Caronia v. Peluso, 2016 WL 799364 (Sup. Ct., Suffolk County 2016) (defendant's application for default judgments on its cross-claims against owner and operator of auto was denied for lack of proper service).

[2]　First Nat. City Bank v. Elsky, 62 Misc. 2d 880, 312 N.Y.S.2d 325 (N.Y. City Civ. Ct. 1970); see Mazie v. Mazie, 77 A.D.2d 878, 430 N.Y.S.2d 672 (2d Dep't 1980); Citibank N. A., In Interest of Dale Olds Inc. v. Hamilton, 114 Misc. 2d 1082, 1085–86, 453 N.Y.S.2d 295, 298 (N.Y. City Civ. Ct. 1982).

who they are because they appear by serving their papers on him.[3] The plaintiff must furnish the list and must include in it the names and addresses of the parties' attorneys. A defendant who wants to assert cross-claims against co-defendants via regular mail, for example, may have to depend on a list furnished by the plaintiff under this provision.

The aim of CPLR 2103(e) is to keep all parties posted of all steps taken in the action. Those who fail to appear are deemed to waive that right. One who does appear, but then defaults at some later stage of the proceedings, is not held to this waiver and therefore retains the right to be served with all papers. This can be an important right indeed. A party may wish, for example, to concede liability but contest at the damages trial,[4] or to keep track of foreclosure proceedings against her so as to assure that the sale of her property fulfills applicable requirements,[5] or, in a multiparty case, to see what co-defendants are doing so as to ascertain whether she might be the beneficiary of some defense they put in.

Even the service of a tardy notice of appearance or answer should suffice to require that all further papers be served on the one interposing the appearance or answer since both qualify as an "appearance" under CPLR 320(a), whether timely or not.[6]

§ 204. Stipulations

The parties can stipulate to almost anything in an action. The litigation is theirs and they can pretty much dispose of their rights any way they want to. But if they contemplate the need of any judicial aid in carrying out their stipulation, they must conform to the dictates in CPLR 2104. The statute requires that stipulations be: (1) in writing and subscribed by the party to be bound, or the party's attorney; (2) reduced to the form of an order and entered, often referred to as the "so-ordered" stipulation; or (3) made between counsel in open court.[1] Any agreement between parties or their attorneys relating to the action that falls into one of these three categories can be enforced by the court.

Unless "reduced to the form of an order and entered," says CPLR 2104, the stipulation must be "subscribed" by the party to be bound by it. Because the statute requires a signed writing, it has been held that an e-mail that does not contain an

---

[3] CPLR 2103(e); see § 110 for what constitutes an appearance.

[4] A defendant who appears, but later defaults, automatically gets the right to be notified of when the damages trial is to take place. A nonappearing defendant can assure himself this notice merely by serving the plaintiff with a demand pursuant to CPLR 3215(g)(2). See § 296.

[5] Even an appearance made after the entry of judgment entitles the appearer to notice of all subsequent steps. See and compare Jamaica Savings Bank v. Spiro, 206 Misc. 897, 135 N.Y.S.2d 728 (Nassau County Court 1954); see also Home Sav. Bank v. Chiola, 203 A.D.2d 525, 526, 611 N.Y.S.2d 235, 236 (2d Dep't 1994) ("Even though a defendant defaults in pleading, his appearance entitles him to service of all papers and notice of all proceedings through and subsequent to judgment."); Bank of New York Mellon v. Piercey, 40 Misc. 3d 1219(A), 975 N.Y.S.2d 707 (Sup. Ct., Suffolk County 2013) ("[S]ervice of the notice of appearance by counsel for defendant . . . after a default in answering has occurred merely entitles the defendant to notice of all subsequent proceedings in the action.").

[6] The court in the *Jamaica* case suggests that a late answer is by itself an insufficient appearance to require notice of further steps, a doubtful conclusion when made, and even more doubtful today. Involved in the case was a foreclosure sale that would have been undone had the court held otherwise. But see Jaworower v. Rovere, 98 Misc. 377, 380, 162 N.Y.S. 1075 (Sup. Ct., Kings County 1917), aff'd, 177 A.D. 740, 164 N.Y.S. 515 (2d Dep't 1917) (service of answer, rejected as untimely, does not constitute appearance in action).

[1] It has been held that an arbitration panel qualifies as the equivalent of a court for this purpose. Central New York Regional Market Authority v. John B. Pike, Inc., 120 A.D.2d 958, 503 N.Y.S.2d 462 (4th Dep't 1986).

electronic signature won't do for a stipulation, at least not a stipulation of settlement.[2] The Second Department appeared to have second thoughts on the matter and, in *Forcelli v. Gelco Corp.*,[3] concluded that an email could satisfy CPLR 2104 even without a signature. In *Forcelli*, a claims adjuster with the insurer of one of the defendants offered $230,000 to settle an automobile accident case, and the plaintiffs' counsel orally accepted. Later that day, the adjuster sent an email message to plaintiffs' counsel confirming the terms of the settlement. The Second Department concluded that when an email contains all of the "material terms of a settlement and a manifestation of mutual accord, and the party to be charged, or his or her agent, types his or her name under circumstances manifesting an intent that the name be treated as a signature, such an email message may be deemed [to satisfy] . . . CPLR 2104."[4]

If made in open court, the stipulation should be taken down by the stenographer.[5] The purpose, of course, is to assure irrefutable proof of the agreement. It has been held that not even the "personal notes" of a judge qualify as an "open court" stipulation.[6]

Oral stipulations would be absolutely taboo if CPLR 2104 were applied rigidly, but they are nevertheless used by lawyers, especially for incidental matters like an extension of time for responding to some paper. To the bar's credit, an oral stipulation is not often disavowed. Even when it is, the courts have from time to time accepted it anyway as when "there is no dispute" that the parties entered into it.[7] It has been said that "a party is precluded from invoking CPLR 2104 to avoid an oral stipulation if it appears that the stipulation was made."[8] But if one side chooses to deny it, how can the other always be confident of proving it? It's risky to rely on oral stipulations, and especially risky to make it a habit. In some of the more generous cases upholding oral stipulations, it will be found that reliance on the stipulation led to some kind of default and that the court could simply have invoked its broad default-vacating powers[9] to undo the default without even addressing the stipulation.[10]

It is also worth noting that whether to vacate a default is a matter of discretion, and that in matters of discretion the appellate division is, in effect, the court of last resort.

---

[2] DeVita v. Macy's East, Inc., 36 A.D.3d 751, 828 N.Y.S.2d 531 (2d Dep't 2007) (SPR 183:2); see also Rubin v. Deckelbaum, 2014 WL 3924611 (Sup. Ct., Kings County 2014) (concluding that parties' email exchange did not constitute enforceable stipulation under CPLR 2104).

[3] Forcelli v. Gelco Corp., 109 A.D.3d 244, 972 N.Y.S.2d 570 (2d Dep't 2013).

[4] *Forcelli*, 109 A.D.3d at 244, 972 N.Y.S.2d at 570; see also Stefaniw v. Cerrone, 130 A.D.2d 483, 515 N.Y.S.2d 66 (2d Dep't 1987) (holding that party who prepared stipulation is bound by it without an actual subscription).

[5] Gonyea v. Avis Rent A Car System, Inc., 82 A.D.2d 1011, 442 N.Y.S.2d 177 (3d Dep't 1981). If the stipulation constitutes a settlement, the lawyer may also want to ensure that the stenographer transcribes the communication of the settlement to the client and the client's decision regarding the settlement. See New York Rules of Professional Conduct, Rule 1.2(a) ("A lawyer shall abide by a client's decision whether to settle a matter."); Rule 1.4(a)(1)(iii) (requiring lawyer to communicate all settlement offers to client).

[6] In re Estate of Janis, 210 A.D.2d 101, 620 N.Y.S.2d 342 (1st Dep't 1994) (SPR 34:3). There is some indication in In re Dolgin Eldert Corp., 31 N.Y.2d 1, 334 N.Y.S.2d 833, 286 N.E.2d 228 (1972), that a stipulation in the judge's chambers would not satisfy as one made in "open court," but an important factor is that the substance of the alleged stipulation in *Dolgin* was disputed. The test should be whether the stipulation, if not otherwise in writing, was taken down by a stenographer.

[7] Rhulen Agency, Inc. v. Gramercy Brokerage, Inc., 106 A.D.2d 725, 484 N.Y.S.2d 156 (3d Dep't 1984).

[8] La Marque v. North Shore University Hosp., 120 A.D.2d 572, 573, 502 N.Y.S.2d 219, 220 (2d Dep't 1986).

[9] See § 426.

[10] See the discussion in *La Marque*, 120 A.D.2d at 573, 502 N.Y.S.2d at 220–21.

Moreover, discretion can take different turns in different courts and even among different panels of the same court. All in all, it's bad business to rely on oral stipulations.

The stipulation must be clear and all matters claimed to be covered by it must be set out. The court "cannot be asked to divine what was in counsel's mind or to seek the intent from other evidence."[11]

The party who consents to stipulate away some right, however minor, may of course condition it. D ordinarily has the option, for example, of using the answering time to either answer or move to dismiss.[12] But if P stipulates to extend D's time, P can limit the extension to allow late service of the defendant's answer, but refuse to extend it for the making of a motion.[13] A stipulation extending the answering time without that qualification would be deemed to extend the moving time as well.[14] It must be remembered that a stipulation extending the answering time with certain qualifications must normally be signed be both parties as both parties are offering to be bound by it.

In practice, the answering time is one of the most common periods extended, and the stipulation extending it is often oral. But even this frequent and pro forma extension must technically be in writing. It is sound practice for one of the parties to draw up the stipulation promptly and forward it to the other side already signed (as where the one allowing the time extension graciously prepares the stipulation) or for signing and return (as where the one seeking the extension prepares it). Some offices, when they seek the stipulation, draw it and send it to the other side's attorney with a stamped, self-addressed envelope for convenience.

It has become a common practice for a plaintiff who is asked for an extension of time to answer to ask the defendant for the quid pro quo of a waiver of jurisdictional defenses. This is a good idea, especially when the statute of limitations is closing in. If the defendant resists, the plaintiff can gauge his tactics accordingly. (The very refusal of the defendant to waive jurisdictional objections should rouse the plaintiff's suspicion that the defendant may be maneuvering for a time extension in order to assert a jurisdictional objection later when it may now be too late for a new action if the objection succeeds).

It is common courtesy for lawyers to grant each other reasonable time extensions in litigation and Rule 1.2(e) of the New York Rules of Professional Conduct provides that "[a] lawyer may exercise professional judgment to . . . accede to reasonable requests of opposing counsel, when doing so does not prejudice the rights of the client." In fact, the lawyer can agree to reasonable extensions of deadlines without the client's consent as long as the client's rights are not prejudiced. The question arises whether, in light of the lawyer's discretion, the plaintiff acts improperly when exacting a jurisdictional waiver

---

[11] Columbia Broadcasting System, Inc. v. Roskin Distributors, Inc., 31 A.D.2d 22, 24, 294 N.Y.S.2d 804, 806 (1st Dep't 1968), aff'd, 28 N.Y.2d 559, 319 N.Y.S.2d 449, 268 N.E.2d 128 (1971); see Sterling Fifth Associates v. Carpentille Corp., Inc., 10 A.D.3d 282, 781 N.Y.S.2d 72 (1st Dep't 2004).

[12] CPLR 320(a); 3211(e); see § 110.

[13] North County Communications Corp. v. Verizon New York, Inc., 196 Misc. 2d 149, 152, 762 N.Y.S.2d 238, 240 (Sup. Ct., Albany County 2003) (citing Venizelos v. Venizelos, 30 A.D.2d 856, 293 N.Y.S.2d 20 (2d Dep't 1968)).

[14] See CPLR 3211(e); Rich v. Lefkovits, 56 N.Y.2d 276, 279–80, 452 N.Y.S.2d 1, 3, 437 N.E.2d 260, 262 (1982).

from the defendant as a condition for the grant of an extension of time to appear. We think not, especially if the prospect of a jurisdictional dismissal is substantial.[15]

The court can of course enforce the terms of any valid stipulation and will usually do so on motion.[16] The court also has the power to permit a stipulation to be withdrawn, but will exercise it only for good cause, such as where its purpose has been frustrated or where a condition that it contemplated has not materialized.[17] For example, a mutual misassumption about the amount of insurance applicable in a tort case was held to be a sufficient ground to vacate a settlement in Madar v. 1333 Realty LLC.[18] The parties thought the coverage was $25,000, but it was actually $250,000. The insurer was in liquidation and the Liquidation Bureau mistakenly advised plaintiff P that the coverage was $25,000. The settlement for that sum followed, and only afterwards did the bureau advise P that coverage was 10 times that, prompting a motion by P to vacate the settlement, and a grant of the motion.

Depression, stress, and general pressure applied by a party's attorney when entering into a stipulation of settlement will generally not be sufficient to disrupt it.[19] Fraud, collusion, mistake, accident, and the like may be grounds for setting aside the stipulation, especially if the status quo is restorable.[20] The remedy is a motion to vacate the stipulation, made to the court in which the action is pending, or to the court in which the stipulation was entered if there is no action pending.[21] If the stipulation had the effect of discontinuing or dismissing the action, however—such often happens with a stipulation of settlement—some older cases hold that a plenary action is necessary to undo the stipulation,[22] or even to enforce it.[23] The Court of Appeals cast doubt on those cases, however, when it more recently held that even in that situation a mere motion can do the job, captioned in the presumably settled action.[24] This is a sound result and a motion ought to suffice, just as it suffices to vacate a judgment on a myriad of grounds.[25]

---

[15] The New York State Standards of Civility provide that "[i]n the absence of a court order, a lawyer should agree to reasonable requests for extensions of time or for waiver of procedural formalities when the legitimate interests of the client will not be adversely affected." III, A. These standards are treated in SPR 66, and see the lead note in SPR 163:2.

[16] See Baumis v. General Motors Corp., 102 A.D.2d 961, 477 N.Y.S.2d 827 (3d Dep't 1984).

[17] See Rebell v. Trask, 220 A.D.2d 594, 597–98, 632 N.Y.S.2d 624, 627 (2d Dep't 1995); Central Valley Concrete Corp. v. Montgomery Ward & Co., 34 A.D.2d 860, 310 N.Y.S.2d 925 (3d Dep't 1970); Ware v. Grossman, 177 Misc. 2d 320, 676 N.Y.S.2d 844 (Dist. Ct., Nassau County 1998).

[18] Madar v. 1333 Realty LLC, N.Y.L.J., Dec. 31, 2009 (decision date December 8), at 27, col.3 (Sup. Ct., Kings County; Ruchelsman, J.) (SPR 219:3).

[19] Ng v. Chalasani, 51 Misc. 3d 134(A), 36 N.Y.S.3d 408, 2016 WL 1532590, *1 (App. Term, 2d Dep't 2016).

[20] In re Frutiger's Estate, 29 N.Y.2d 143, 324 N.Y.S.2d 36, 272 N.E.2d 543 (1971); see Childs v. Levitt, 151 A.D.2d 318, 319, 543 N.Y.S.2d 51, 53 (1st Dep't 1989).

[21] Matter of Horton's Estate, 51 A.D.2d 856, 379 N.Y.S.2d 569 (4th Dep't 1976); see e.g., In re New York Skyline, Inc., 432 B.R. 66, 83, 53 Bankr. Ct. Dec. (CRR) 85 (Bankr. S.D.N.Y. 2010) ("a party may not seek relief from a stipulation in a court other than where it was originally entered."); LaVigna v. Capital Cities/ABC, Inc., 245 A.D.2d 75, 76, 665 N.Y.S.2d 410, 411 (1st Dep't 1997) ("[A] stipulation 'so ordered' by the [Federal] District Court . . . . which was never vacated or appealed, cannot be collaterally attacked in State court.").

[22] E.g., Schweber v. Berger, 27 A.D.2d 840, 277 N.Y.S.2d 855 (2d Dep't 1967).

[23] Yonkers Fur Dressing Co. v. Royal Ins. Co., 247 N.Y. 435, 160 N.E. 778 (1928).

[24] Teitelbaum Holdings, Ltd. v. Gold, 48 N.Y.2d 51, 421 N.Y.S.2d 556, 396 N.E.2d 1029 (1979).

[25] See §§ 426 et seq., treating CPLR 5015.

Stipulations of Settlement

CPLR 2104 applies to stipulations of settlement, as well as to stipulations affecting the management and incidentals of the case.[26] Attorneys purporting to represent their clients at settlement talks are assumed to be acting with authority. The Court of Appeals has even invoked the doctrine of apparent authority to prevent a party from reneging on a settlement by claiming that his attorney acted without his permission.[27]

A controversial 2003 amendment to CPLR 2104 added the last sentence to the statute, which states that "[w]ith respect to stipulations of settlement and notwithstanding the form of the stipulation of settlement, the terms of such stipulation shall be filed by the defendant with the county clerk." The primary purpose of this addition mandating the filing of all settlements was to generate a fee ($35)[28] upon the filing, as the amendment was part of a budget measure.[29]

The curious requirement that the "terms" of the settlement be filed became a point of controversy. Does it mean that the detailed background of the settlement, including the consideration given for it by each side to the other, must be filed and thus exposed to public view? There is nothing whatsoever in the background of the amendment to suggest that it was designed to accomplish that end; no indication that it sought to implement a policy of public disclosure, such as to publicize a defect in a widely used product. The legislature wanted the state treasury to collect an extra $35. That was all. Until a definitive judicial ruling on the matter, or a legislative clarification, it remains controversial, especially because at least one party to a stipulation of settlement usually insists on confidentiality.[30]

Disclosure of "Hi/Lo" and Settlement Agreements

Disputes arising over stipulations often concern stipulations of settlement of one kind or another, such as a so-called "hi/lo" agreement made before a verdict comes in a damages trial. In a "hi/lo" agreement, D guarantees P will get no less than a specified sum, and P agrees that D will not have to pay more than a specified sum, regardless of the verdict. In one such case that came before the Court of Appeals, In re Eighth Judicial Dist. Asbestos Litigation (Reynolds),[31] the Court ruled that if P and D-1 make such an agreement, D-2 must be made aware of it. The stipulation in *Reynolds* was that D-1 would assure P's getting at least $155,000, and P agreed that D-1 would not be required to pay more than $185,000. It proved a good deal for D-1, but a short-lived one. The trial

---

[26]   In re Dolgin Eldert Corp., 31 N.Y.2d 1, 334 N.Y.S.2d 833, 286 N.E.2d 228 (1972); see Armonk Snack Mart, Inc. v. Robert Porpora Realty Corp., 42 Misc. 3d 1208(A), 984 N.Y.S.2d 630 (Sup. Ct., Westchester County 2014).

[27]   Hallock v. State, 64 N.Y.2d 224, 231, 485 N.Y.S.2d 510, 513, 474 N.E.2d 1178, 1181 (1984). A loss of consortium claim has been held to be an adjunct of the injured spouse's personal injury claim for settlement purposes so that the settlement of the injured party's claim, whether it mentions the consortium claim or not, automatically releases it. Buckley v. National Freight, Inc., 90 N.Y.2d 210, 659 N.Y.S.2d 841, 681 N.E.2d 1287 (1997).

[28]   See CPLR 8020(d).

[29]   L.2003, ch. 62, Part J, § 28.

[30]   The controversial issue of whether settlement agreements with a party or nonparty are subject to disclosure is explored at greater length in § 348 and in the McKinney's Practice Commentaries to CPLR 3101, C3101:18A ("Disclosure of Settlements"). The various paths lawyers have been considering in order to keep the details of their settlements confidential are tracked in Siegel's Practice Review. See SPR 137:2–4, 139:1, 140:1, which cover early stages of the controversy.

[31]   In re Eighth Judicial Dist. Asbestos Litigation, 8 N.Y.3d 717, 840 N.Y.S.2d 546, 872 N.E.2d 232 (2007) (NYSLD No. 573).

proceeded against both defendants and produced a damages verdict of $3,750,000, with D-1 confronted with no greater exposure than the $185,000 stipulated. Bad luck got D-1: the concealment of the agreement was held unfair to D-2, who had the right to know about it for many, including tactical, reasons. A new trial was ordered by the Court on both liability and damages.

Consistent with the *Reynolds* decision, the First Department held in Mahoney v. Turner Const. Co.,[32] that where settling defendants plan to participate in the trial as it continues against the nonsettlor, the latter is entitled to know the terms of the settlement. In *Mahoney*, the settlement recited that it was to be confidential, requiring the court to balance that factor against the nonsettlor's right to know those parts of the settlement that affect him. The appellate division remanded the case for an in camera examination of the settlement to consider a protective order for preserving the claim of confidentiality to the extent consistent with the rights of the nonsettlor.

Delays in Signing Settlement Agreements

Suppose that settlement terms have been reached, but the plaintiff's lawyer delays signing—for various tactical reasons. That happened in Bonnette v. Long Island College Hosp.,[33] a medical malpractice action in which things didn't pan out for the plaintiff. Plaintiff died before the settlement was signed. The death of a plaintiff reduces potential damages greatly, and did so in *Bonnette* to what all assumed would be substantially less than the agreed settlement offer. It's the decedent's family's bad luck, held *Bonnette*. Since the settlement was not reduced to writing, the defendant, while having agreed to it, was not bound by it, and was permitted to withdraw from it. Perhaps the real bad luck on this scene is that of the plaintiff's lawyer, who might well be subject to an action for legal malpractice if the delay in getting the stipulation signed is found unjustifiable.

Stipulation Signed by Nonparty

What happens when a stipulation within an action is subscribed to by a nonparty, as happened in White House Manor, Ltd. v. Benjamin?[34] The stipulation there was to settle an unjust enrichment claim. A church, never formally a party to the action, "agreed to be a party to the . . . Stipulation," but the lower court held the church in breach of terms of other contracts between those who were already parties, but which were beyond the subject of the stipulation. This, held the Court of Appeals, was the equivalent of granting summary judgment against the church, and the stipulation was found to offer no foundation for that.

The rule that emerges from *Benjamin* is that a nonparty agreeing to be a party to a stipulation becomes a party only for the relief addressed in the stipulation itself. With that case now on the books as a lesson, the nonparty should see to it that the point is made clear in the stipulation itself.

Res Judicata Effect of Settlement

If a stipulation of settlement is properly made in an action, is it subject to the same res judicata rules that apply to a judgment? The appellate division in 34 Funding

---

[32] Mahoney v. Turner Const. Co., 61 A.D.3d 101, 872 N.Y.S.2d 433 (1st Dep't 2009) (SPR 205:2).

[33] Bonnette v. Long Island College Hosp., 3 N.Y.3d 281, 785 N.Y.S.2d 738, 819 N.E.2d 206 (2004) (NYSLD No. 540).

[34] White House Manor, Ltd. v. Benjamin, 11 N.Y.3d 393, 870 N.Y.S.2d 835, 899 N.E.2d 941 (2008) (NYSLD No. 590).

Associates, Inc. v. Pollak[35] said yes. The stipulation, made in a mortgage foreclosure case, was signed by the mortgagor. Now, the mortgagor wanted to assert additional claims for money the receiver and mortgagee allegedly retained improperly. Those claims "arose out of the same transaction," held the court, and "could have been part of the stipulation." Hence, "res judicata bars [the mortgagor] from litigating" them now.[36]

§ 205. Affidavits and Affirmations

Affidavits

An affidavit is a sworn written statement. Its utility at the trial itself, where live testimony from cross-examinable witnesses is the primary source of proof, is limited if not altogether nullified. But it's the foremost source of proof on motions.

The affidavit ordinarily begins with its venue (the state, county, and city in which it is made), contains an opening statement such as, "Mary Jones, being duly sworn, says," and then marches into a recitation of whatever Mary Jones wants to swear to. At the end is her signature, subscribed and sworn to before a person authorized to administer oaths, usually a notary public, who then attests with his own signature that the affidavit was "Sworn to before me this 16th day of March 2016." This is followed by the notary's stamp, including her number, or by the number written in.

It has been held that an affidavit properly signed and in other respects proper is sufficient even if it omits the statement that the affiant was duly sworn, but this is not an arena within which one should take chances.[1] A defective affidavit can be deemed the equivalent of no proof at all, resulting in harsh consequences, such as an award of summary judgment dismissing an action. CPLR 105(u) states that a " 'verified pleading' may be utilized as an affidavit whenever the latter is required." In Sanchez v. National R.R. Passenger Corp.,[2] the Court of Appeals ruled that this provision permitted a verified complaint and verified bill of particulars to be considered as affidavits in opposition to a motion for summary judgment.

Affirmations

Certain professionals have been authorized by CPLR 2106 to make written statements by mere affirmation, including words to the effect that their averments are "true under the penalties of perjury."[3] Such statements are the equivalent of affidavits without the need of a swearing ceremony or a notary's signature. The professionals allowed merely to affirm in this way constitute an odd and unholy quadrumvirate: attorneys, doctors, osteopaths, and dentists who are licensed to practice in New York State. One using this provision must actually subscribe the affirmation.[4]

---

[35]   34 Funding Associates, Inc. v. Pollak, 26 A.D.3d 182, 811 N.Y.S.2d 352 (1st Dep't 2006).

[36]   See § 444, addressing res judicata effects of settlements.

[1]   Collins v. AA Trucking Renting Corp., 209 A.D.2d 363, 618 N.Y.S.2d 801 (1st Dep't 1994). It has also been held that a notary's failure to sign the jurat is not a jurisdictional defect. See SPR 26:2.

[2]   Sanchez v. National R.R. Passenger Corp., 21 N.Y.3d 890, 965 N.Y.S.2d 775, 988 N.E.2d 511 (2013). The decision is discussed in further detail in § 246.

[3]   False swearing in either an affidavit or CPLR 2106 affirmation constitutes perjury under Chapter 210 of the Penal Law.

[4]   Dowling v. Mosey, 32 A.D.3d 1190, 821 N.Y.S.2d 326 (4th Dep't 2006) (affirmation defective where orthopedist's signature was affixed by rubber stamp); see the discussion below regarding electronic signatures.

If one of these professionals is a party to the action, she cannot affirm under CPLR 2106 and must submit an affidavit.[5] The court's decision in Tomeo v. Beccia,[6] highlights another one of the pitfalls of the statute. In *Tomeo*, the plaintiff submitted an affirmation from its expert doctor in response to defendant hospital's motion for summary judgment. The Second Department ruled that the affirmation "did not constitute competent evidence, because [the doctor] was not authorized by law to practice medicine in New York State." Therefore, the court dismissed plaintiff's action against the defendant hospital due to plaintiff's failure to raise a triable issue of fact in opposition to defendant's prima facie showing on its motion for summary judgment.

Effective January 1, 2015, CPLR 2106 was amended to add a new subsection (b) to permit the use of an affirmation by any person who subscribes and affirms the statement while located outside the geographic boundaries of the United States and its territories. The predecessor statute remains unchanged and is housed in a new subdivision (a). The amendment expressly notes that such affirmation "may be used in an action in lieu of and with the same force and effect as an affidavit." The new provision also contains a form, which states that the affirmation is made "under the penalties of perjury under the laws of New York," and notes that any such affirmation shall substantially conform to the form.

This amendment was designed, in part, to alleviate the burden imposed by CPLR 2309(c) on parties who submit statements from people residing in foreign countries, which is a common occurrence in major commercial litigation. The problem has also surfaced in personal injury litigation.[7] It is important to note that the requirements of CPLR 2309(c) are still imposed when the oath or affirmation is made outside New York State, but within the United States and its territories.[8] In sum, a bartender in Montreal can affirm under penalties of perjury under CPLR 2106(b), but a lawyer or doctor licensed in New Jersey must submit an affidavit that complies with CPLR 2309(c).

One of the most common affidavits or affirmations seen in litigation is the affidavit or affirmation of the service of a paper. Ideally, this document should be made by the person—lawyer or not—who actually serves the paper, including the person who merely posts the paper if it's being served by mail.[9]

Electronic Signatures

As noted above, one who affirms under CPLR 2106 must actually subscribe the affirmation. Will an electronic signature suffice? Section 304(2) of the State Technology Law states that "unless specifically provided otherwise by law, an electronic signature may be used by a person in lieu of a signature affixed by hand [and that] [t]he use of an electronic signature shall have the same validity and effect as the use of a signature affixed by hand." Relying on this provision in Martin v. Portexit Corp.,[10] the First

---

[5]   Harris v. Krauss, 87 A.D.3d 469, 928 N.Y.S.2d 295 (1st Dep't 2011); Kalir v. Ottinger, 2011 WL 6968334 (Sup. Ct., New York County 2011) (SPR 243:3). Whether this defect can be cured with an affidavit of the party submitted on a motion for renewal is addressed in § 254.

[6]   Tomeo v. Beccia, 127 A.D.3d 1071, 7 N.Y.S.3d 472 (2d Dep't 2015).

[7]   See Green v. Fairway Operating Corp., 72 A.D.3d 613, 898 N.Y.S.2d 848 (1st Dep't 2010) ("The affidavit of plaintiff's witness, purportedly sworn to in the Dominican Republic, lacks the certificate of conformity . . . required by CPLR 2309(c), and therefore is not properly before the Court.").

[8]   See § 388.

[9]   See § 202.

[10]   Martin v. Portexit Corp., 98 A.D.3d 63, 948 N.Y.S.2d 21 (1st Dep't 2012) (SPR 246:2).

Department concluded that a physician's affirmation containing an electronic signature complied with CPLR 2106 and was admissible on a motion for summary judgment.

The First Department found the Second Department's decision on the matter in Vista Surgical Supplies, Inc. v. Travelers Insurance Co.,[11] to be "unpersuasive" and declined to follow it. In *Vista*, the Second Department ruled that medical reports were "inadmissible since they contained computerized, affixed, or stamped facsimiles of the physician's signature." The court concluded that the reports failed to comply with CPLR 2106 "since they were not subscribed and affirmed, but merely contained facsimiles of the physician's signature without any indication as to who placed them on the reports . . . ."

Note that *Martin* applied the State Technology Law to an affirmation, not an affidavit. Given the need for a swearing ceremony attendant with an affidavit, there may be issues—as yet unexplored in the caselaw—regarding the use of e-signatures on affidavits.

The Notary Public

A notary who continues to notarize documents after his commission has expired may be subject to both civil and criminal liability, but parties to lawsuits in which the documents so notarized are used apparently need not worry. The documents' validity is preserved by a statute[12] intended to allow the public to continue relying on "the presumption of validity" attending a notarized document.[13]

Two recent cases illustrate the liabilities of notaries who fail to properly administer an oath or who are otherwise guilty of misconduct in connection with the notarial process. One is Plemmenou v. Arvanitakis,[14] involving a false notarization. The other is Edwards v. Rockaway Storage Inc.,[15] involving the notary's failure to administer the oath.[16]

§ 206. Undertakings

Various provisions in the CPLR impose the requirement that an undertaking— often referred to simply as a bond—be furnished in conjunction with a particular procedure. These are common with the provisional remedies, for example, where undertakings may be required by law,[1] or by the court in its discretion.[2] In some

---

[11] Vista Surgical Supplies, Inc. v. Travelers Ins. Co., 50 A.D.3d 778, 860 N.Y.S.2d 532 (2d Dep't 2008) (SPR 246:2).

[12] Exec. Law § 142–a.

[13] Parks v. Leahey & Johnson, P.C., 81 N.Y.2d 161, 164, 597 N.Y.S.2d 278, 280, 613 N.E.2d 153, 155 (1993).

[14] Plemmenou v. Arvanitakis, 39 A.D.3d 612, 833 N.Y.S.2d 596 (2d Dep't 2007), overruled only in respect of a procedural point in Butler v. Catinella, 58 A.D.3d 145, 868 N.Y.S.2d 101 (2d Dep't 2008).

[15] Edwards v. Rockaway Storage, Inc., 30 Misc. 3d 1215(A), 924 N.Y.S.2d 308 (Sup. Ct., Queens County 2008).

[16] See the discussion of these cases in SPR 199:4 and SPR 202:4.

[1] E.g., in conjunction with an attachment, CPLR 6212(b); see § 316, preliminary injunction, CPLR 6312(b); see § 329, or receivership, CPLR 6403; see § 332.

[2] E.g., in conjunction with a temporary restraining order, CPLR 6313(c); see § 330, or notice of pendency ("lis pendens"), CPLR 6515; see § 336.

instances, the furnishing of an undertaking may be optional, such as where it's given to stay the execution of a judgment pending an appeal.[3]

Wherever in the CPLR an undertaking may be statutorily or judicially mandated, or voluntarily furnished by the party, the detailed rules governing it will be found centralized in Article 25 of the CPLR.

While the lawyer usually understands an undertaking to be an obligation assumed by a surety to pay a sum of money on a stated contingency, and that's of course one recognized definition of the term,[4] the CPLR permits the one who is required to furnish an undertaking in a stated sum to deposit, instead, cash or United States or New York bonds in that sum.[5]

A "surety" is someone, corporate or individual, who issues the bond or otherwise undertakes to back the bonded person's promise. The other side, for whose protection the bond is issued, can object to the surety as inadequate ("except" to the surety) or require the surety to show that it has assets sufficient to cover its undertaking (make the surety "justify"). Acknowledging the paucity of caselaw on Article 25, the court in City of New York v. Britestarr Homes, Inc.[6] treats how excepting to sureties under CPLR 2506 and justifying sureties under CPLR 2507 interplay—and how a motion under CPLR 2508 for a new or additional undertaking, which is permissible at any time, can cover an omission to make prompt use of the other provisions.

More will be said about undertakings in particular situations as those situations are met.[7]

---

[3] See CPLR 5519(a)(2); see § 535.

[4] CPLR 2501(1).

[5] CPLR 2501(2).

[6] City of New York v. Britestarr Homes, Inc., 150 Misc. 2d 820, 570 N.Y.S.2d 882 (Sup. Ct., Bronx County 1991).

[7] See, e.g., § 325.

Chapter 9

PLEADINGS

Analysis

A. Basic Rules of Pleading
B. Specific Items
C. Demand for Relief
D. Election of Remedies
E. Splitting
F. The Answer
G. Counterclaims
H. Cross-Claims
I. The Reply
J. Corrective Motions
K. Service of Pleadings
L. Verification
M. Amendment of Pleadings
N. Bill of Particulars

A. BASIC RULES OF PLEADING

Table of Sections

§ 207. Pleadings, Background
§ 208. The Basic Pleading Requirement
§ 209. Theory of the Pleadings Rule Abolished
§ 210. Some Forms
§ 211. Pleading in the Federal and Lower Courts Compared
§ 212. Separate Statement and Numbering
§ 213. Statements Deemed Repeated; Writings
§ 214. Various Techniques of Pleading

§ 207. Pleadings, Background

The liberalization of pleadings is one of the major accomplishments of the CPLR. The common law hoped that by requiring the parties to trade pleadings back and forth, the whole controversy could shortly be reduced to but a single succinct issue or just a few clearly defined ones. The hope was forlorn, its offshoot was the exaltation of form over substance, its heritage was a set of forms of action into which all civil claims of whatever variety had to be squeezed, and the squeezing gave rise to the extended use of fictions.

The Advisory Committee tackled the pleadings problem in its first report where it offers both a background study[1] and a helpful bibliography.[2]

Under the old Civil Practice Act, the pleader had to set forth the "facts" relied on "but not the evidence" by which they would be proved.[3] The requirement to plead "facts" precluded the pleading of a conclusion of law. In the construction process, the cases carried this so far that it became taboo to plead "negligence" in a negligence case because it was too conclusory.[4] But to furnish too much detail, on the other hand, made the pleading too evidentiary. The pleader thus walked a tightrope with an abyss on either side—one ready to consume him if the pleading was so summary that it amounted to a conclusion of law and the other just as hungry if it tilted towards too much evidence. This rigidity was found to be too demanding without being productive and was abandoned.

The major culprit, around which the caselaw had built these rigid requirements, was the word "facts." The Advisory Committee therefore abandoned the word and with it fell the cases. If a pleading today otherwise satisfies the new pleading requirements—to be taken up shortly—its inclusion of a legal theory is permissible.[5] Nor is there any specific barrier in the CPLR against the inclusion of "evidence." It doesn't belong in the pleading, and including it is a burden assumed by the pleader gratuitously, but the inclusion does not by itself invalidate the pleading.

The decline in the importance of pleadings has its counterpart in the ascent of the disclosure devices.[6] Today those devices enable the parties to probe their adversaries' positions more incisively than pleadings ever could, and the free availability of the disclosure devices more than fills any gap left by the relaxation of the old pleadings requirements.

§ 208. The Basic Pleading Requirement

CPLR 3013 provides:

Statements in a pleading shall be sufficiently particular to give the court and parties notice of the transactions, occurrences, or series of transactions or occurrences, intended to be proved and the material elements of each cause of action or defense.

Those few words are the theme of pleadings under the CPLR. The word "statements" instead of "facts" is used mainly to eliminate the caselaw previously built around "facts." Averments in pleadings are still, of course, primarily factual.[1]

The main mission of an affirmative pleading—as opposed to the defensive pleading taken up beginning in section 221 below—whether it is the main claim in the complaint, or a counterclaim or cross-claim in the answer, etc., is to give "notice" of the event out of which the grievance arises. If the pleading can be said to give that notice, the first pleading requirement is satisfied. If the allegations also cover the substantive material

---

[1]   1st Rep. Leg. Doc. No. 6(b), p. 261 (1957).

[2]   1st Rep. Leg. Doc. at 266.

[3]   Civ. Prac. Act § 241 (repealed 1963).

[4]   See Newell v. Woodward, 241 A.D. 786, 270 N.Y.S. 258 (3d Dep't 1934).

[5]   1st Rep. Leg. Doc. at 63.

[6]   Article 31 of the CPLR supplies the disclosure devices. They're studied in Chapter 13.

[1]   See Commentary C3013:4 on McKinney's CPLR 3013.

elements that make up the particular cause of action relied on, the second requirement is met and the pleading satisfies the CPLR.

The major challenge to an affirmative pleading is a motion under CPLR 3211(a)(7) to dismiss it for failure to state a cause of action; a pleading that meets the two stated requirements defeats that motion.[2]

All pleadings must be liberally construed. Draftsmanship is secondary. Under the CPLR, if a cause of action can be spelled out from the four corners of the pleading, a cause of action is stated and no successful motion lies under CPLR 3211(a)(7) based on a failure to plead one. The pleading can be pathetically drawn; it can reek of miserable draftsmanship. That is not the inquiry. We want only to know whether it states a cause of action—any cause of action. If it does, it's an acceptable CPLR pleading.[3]

The CPLR intention to make pleadings less rigid and to measure their validity solely by whether they state a cause of action was given a decisive judicial boost when, only half a year after the CPLR took effect, the First Department handed down Foley v. D'Agostino.[4] It sustained as adequately pleaded several derivative causes of action and in the course of doing so sent the word out that the CPLR drafters' intention to relieve pleadings of their formalism was going to get not mere lip service, but full judicial cooperation, a view afterwards consistently approved by the Court of Appeals.[5]

It's not necessary that the claim pleaded be given any particular name. It can even be named wrong.[6] It's sufficient if the pleading alleges any cause of action that the law recognizes and on which it offers relief.[7] Its substance prevails over its articulateness.[8] Giving notice is the key. It has sometimes even been held under the CPLR that if the other party has gotten the requisite notice from some other source in the case, such as statements written on the summons itself, the notice requirement may be deemed satisfied.[9]

The several elements that make up the substantive claim must of course be covered by the allegations, but even in that fundamental regard, an omission that appears to be remediable by a mere amendment will be remedied by just that and not a dismissal. One of the substantive elements that make up a fraud claim, for example, is a showing that P relied on D's misrepresentation.[10] When reliance is not alleged, the complaint violates

---

[2]   See Siegel, A Perspective on Pleading Under the CPLR: A Motion Yardstick, 38 St. John's L. Rev. 190, 198 (1963).

[3]   This is not to encourage sloppy pleading. If the pleading, although it states a cause of action and satisfies CPLR 3013, is so jumbled or disorderly that it can't be answered, the defendant can move to compel a more definite statement. That motion lies under CPLR 3024(a), studied in § 230, but that's a matter distinct from whether the pleading states a cause of action and whether the pleading states a cause of action is the inquiry on a motion under CPLR 3211(a)(7).

[4]   Foley v. D'Agostino, 21 A.D.2d 60, 248 N.Y.S.2d 121 (1st Dep't 1964).

[5]   See, e.g., Guggenheimer v. Ginzburg, 43 N.Y.2d 268, 401 N.Y.S.2d 182, 372 N.E.2d 17 (1977).

[6]   Barrick v. Barrick, 24 A.D.2d 895, 264 N.Y.S.2d 888 (2d Dep't 1965).

[7]   CPLR 3017(a) governs the relief clause. See § 217.

[8]   Dulberg v. Mock, 1 N.Y.2d 54, 150 N.Y.S.2d 180, 133 N.E.2d 695 (1956), so held even under prior law.

[9]   See Lederman v. McLean Trucking Co., 41 A.D.2d 5, 342 N.Y.S.2d 570 (2d Dep't 1973). This is not to encourage the pleading to omit giving notice in reliance on its being given elsewhere. It just helps set the tenor for the liberalization of pleadings.

[10]   See § 216, item (b).

CPLR 3013, but it has been held that a simple amendment can add the allegation and cure the defect.[11]

So successful was the *Foley* case in setting the tone for liberal pleadings that some practitioners may have gone a bit too far. The same court, the First Department, had to remind the bar a few months later in another case that "it is still essential . . . that the pleading enable the defendant to determine the nature of the plaintiff's grievances and the relief he seeks in consequence of the alleged wrongs."[12] Missing in that case were some material elements, a clear violation of CPLR 3013, but the plaintiff was still allowed to replead.[13]

It is only a want of notice or the absence of a material element that violates CPLR 3013. The lack of either prejudices the defendant because she can't prepare her case. Thus, a defendant who can show that CPLR 3013 has been violated can show prejudice— the indispensable condition precedent to any application to the court for a remedy against an allegedly defective pleading.

CPLR 3026 says that pleadings shall be liberally construed. Even more significantly, it adds that "[d]efects shall be ignored if a substantial right of a party is not prejudiced." As will be seen, there are other pleading requirements besides those in CPLR 3013, applicable generally or in particular situations, but when CPLR 3013 has been fulfilled, the likelihood is much reduced that some other defect will breed the prejudice needed to justify judicial intervention. Taking note of some of these other provisions, such as CPLR 3015 and 3016,[14] which impose special pleading requirements in designated situations, the court in *Foley* said that these, too, must be subordinated to CPLR 3013,[15] i.e., that a pleading satisfying CPLR 3013 is not likely to prejudice the other side even if some other provision is technically violated. When one of these others is violated in such a way as to prejudice the other party, moreover, the breach is likely to offend CPLR 3013 as well. The theme, in other words, is set by CPLR 3013, and everything else among the pleadings' requirements must be in harmony with it.

A major address to the CPLR's pleading rules is contained in Scholastic Inc. v. Pace Plumbing Corp.,[16] where the defendant pleaded sixteen affirmative defenses "within a boilerplate, catchall paragraph" that also asserted "any other matter constituting an avoidance or an affirmative defense which further investigation of this matter may prove applicable herein." Following disclosure, defendant moved for summary judgment dismissing the complaint based on, among other grounds, the statute of limitations. In response to defendant's motion, plaintiff argued that defendant failed to adequately plead the statute of limitations pursuant to CPLR 3013 and, therefore, waived the defense. The First Department reversed the supreme court's order dismissing the action and reinstated the complaint with a set of extensive writings, including a signed majority opinion and a two-judge concurrence, dedicated primarily to the pleading issues raised by the plaintiff.

---

[11] Brickner v. Linden City Realty, Inc., 23 A.D.2d 560, 256 N.Y.S.2d 533 (2d Dep't 1965).

[12] Shapolsky v. Shapolsky, 22 A.D.2d 91, 253 N.Y.S.2d 816, 817 (1st Dep't 1964).

[13] Repleading is discussed in § 275.

[14] CPLR 3015 is discussed in § 215; CPLR 3016, in § 216.

[15] *Foley*, 21 A.D.2d at 63–4, 248 N.Y.S.2d at 125–6.

[16] Scholastic Inc. v. Pace Plumbing Corp., 129 A.D.3d 75, 76, 78, 8 N.Y.S.3d 143, 145 (1st Dep't 2015).

The entire First Department ruled that this method of pleading "the defense within a laundry list of predominantly inapplicable defenses did not provide plaintiff with the requisite notice" required under CPLR 3013.[17] Furthermore, the court ruled that the defense was inadequately pleaded because of the failure to separately state and number it with the others[18] and that these defects prejudiced the plaintiff under the standard outlined in *Foley*.[19] Nonetheless, "because it concluded that the prejudice could be cured by permitting discovery on the statute of limitations issue," the court remanded the matter to supreme court to allow defendant to correct its defective pleading and for plaintiff to obtain necessary discovery.[20]

Throughout this chapter, we will return to many of the points made in *Foley* and *Scholastic* and look at some forms of pleadings to give color and body to the discussion in this section, which at this stage may still be the sterile product of introductory discourse.

§ 209. Theory of the Pleadings Rule Abolished

At various stages of prior law, a rule was applied to the effect that plaintiffs had to prove and recover on the very theory on which they pleaded. Where, for example, P pleaded in tort, but was able to prove only a contract claim, P was denied a judgment.[1] This was known as the "theory of the pleadings" rule. The CPLR has abandoned it.[2] It is today permissible, although of course not advisable, to prove a theory different from that pleaded, as long as the pleading gives notice of the transaction out of which the proved claim arises and covers its material elements. If no prejudice is shown, CPLR 3017(a) allows the court to grant "any type of relief . . . appropriate to the proof whether or not demanded," and CPLR 3025(c) permits an amendment to conform the pleadings to the proof. As long as the pleading embraces the elements of the proved claim, the fact that the pleading theorized it as something else is immaterial.[3]

Even before the CPLR, the Court of Appeals indicated that a plaintiff would not be bound by the theory pleaded if the theory proved was adequately embraced in the transactions of which the pleading gave notice and if no prejudice was generated by the variance. In the well known case of Diemer v. Diemer,[4] the plaintiff husband sued for separation because his wife would not submit to sexual relations with him. His theory was that this was cruel and inhuman treatment. The Court of Appeals held that it was not, but proceeded to sustain the separation on the unpleaded and unargued theory of abandonment: it held that the wife's conduct amounted to an abandonment, if not to cruel treatment, and that either was a permissible ground for separation. Whatever criticism may be directed at such a conclusion—the parties were not even offered an

---

[17] *Scholastic*, 129 A.D.3d at 79, 8 N.Y.S.3d at 146.

[18] See CPLR 3014 ("Separate causes of action or defenses shall be separately stated and numbered."); § 212.

[19] *Scholastic*, 129 A.D.3d at 80–81, 8 N.Y.S.3d at 147–48.

[20] *Scholastic*, 129 A.D.3d at 76, 8 N.Y.S.3d at 145. For further discussion of the *Scholastic* decision, see Commentary to McKinney's CPLR 3013, 3014, 3018, 3024, 3026 and Patrick Connors, *Back to Basics: Careful Pleading Under CPLR Article 30*, N.Y.L.J., May 18, 2015, at 4.

[1] Barnes v. Quigley, 59 N.Y. 265, 1874 WL 11386 (1874).

[2] Lane v. Mercury Record Corp., 21 A.D.2d 602, 252 N.Y.S.2d 1011 (1st Dep't 1964), aff'd, 18 N.Y.2d 889, 276 N.Y.S.2d 626, 223 N.E.2d 35 (1966).

[3] See McGinnis v. Bankers Life Co., Des Moines, Iowa, 39 A.D.2d 393, 334 N.Y.S.2d 270 (2d Dep't 1972).

[4] Diemer v. Diemer, 8 N.Y.2d 206, 203 N.Y.S.2d 829, 168 N.E.2d 654 (1960).

opportunity to brief and argue the point—it surely inters all lingering notions about the existence of a theory-of-the-pleadings rule.

With the demise of that rule, and the substitution of a rule based on notice and prejudice, the only remaining problem concerns trial by jury. If, for example, P pleads an equitable claim, which does not get tried by jury,[5] but ends up proving a legal one, which does, an award of judgment would incidentally divest D of her right to trial by jury.

The converse is of course no problem and apparently never was. When P sues at law, and a jury is present, but ends up proving an equity theory, judgment on the equity ground is permissible.[6] The judge, presiding at the trial all the while, can decide the facts and the jury's presence can be treated as superfluous. But when the case is pleaded in equity, and no jury is present to try it, the establishment of a mere law claim may not ground judgment if the defendant objects.[7]

The courts remain sensitive to preserving the right to trial by jury. Even when the case is denominated one in equity, the courts will allow its trial by jury if they believe it to be in essence a law case.[8] As a practical matter, the claim's sufficiency for pleading purposes is not relevant to whether relief flowing from it is legal or equitable;[9] the only problem to be resolved in these situations is how to preserve the right to trial by jury.

The problem is addressed by CPLR 4103. Although the plaintiff waives the right to trial by jury by pleading a claim in equity and proceeding at law, the defendant doesn't waive the right to demand trial by jury on it. The defendant must therefore be given an opportunity to demand a jury. If the defendant does demand it, a new trial will be required, which will nullify the one just had before the judge. It's a high price to pay, but in the legislature's view a reasonable price in order to protect the right of trial by jury.

A similar problem arises when the plaintiff pleads both equitable and legal claims. When both kinds are pleaded in respect of the same transaction, the plaintiff waives jury trial on the legal claim, but, again, the defendant doesn't.[10] The defendant must specifically demand jury trial on the legal claim, however, or he, too, will be held to waive it.[11]

In Cioffi v. S.M. Foods, Inc.,[12] plaintiff commenced an action for personal injuries and also attempted to pierce a defendant's corporate veil to hold its principals individually liable. The court noted that the request to pierce the corporate veil does not constitute an independent cause of action against the corporation. While the piercing of a corporate veil is equitable in nature, the court concluded that plaintiffs' personal injury action sought only legal relief in the form of money damages. "The fact that they relied

---

[5] As to what claims are triable by jury in New York, see § 377.

[6] Emery v. Pease, 20 N.Y. 62, 1859 WL 8319 (1859).

[7] Jackson v. Strong, 222 N.Y. 149, 118 N.E. 512 (1917).

[8] See, e.g., City of Syracuse v. Hogan, 234 N.Y. 457, 138 N.E. 406 (1923), in which an action asking for the equitable relief of injunction to remove an encroachment and to reform a deed was found to be at root an ejectment claim to test title (a law action) and thus was required to be tried by jury.

[9] See Advance Music Corp. v. American Tobacco Co., 296 N.Y. 79, 70 N.E.2d 401 (1946).

[10] CPLR 4102(c). If the claims arise out of separate transactions, the plaintiff does not waive jury trial of the law claim by joining the two. Di Menna v. Cooper & Evans Co., note 14, below.

[11] I. H. P. Corp. v. 210 Central Park South Corp., 12 N.Y.2d 329, 239 N.Y.S.2d 547, 189 N.E.2d 812 (1963).

[12] Cioffi v. S.M. Foods, Inc., 129 A.D.3d 888, 10 N.Y.S.3d 620 (2d Dep't 2015).

upon the equitable theory of piercing the corporate veil did not amount to a waiver of the right to a jury trial."[13]

Yet another situation in which this problem of jury trial arises is where P sues in equity, but D counterclaims with a legal cause of action. That happened in DiMenna v. Cooper & Evans Co.,[14] where P sued to foreclose a mechanic's lien (equity and no jury) and D counterclaimed for damages (law and jury trial) regarding the same transaction. The problem in a case like this is that the judge (the fact-finder on the equity claim) and the jury (the fact-finder on the law claim) can disagree on who breached the contract—or on some other fact on which both claims depend—in such a way as to create an irreconcilable conflict. That prospect was avoided in *DiMenna*, in which the jury's verdict was held to bind all parties on all claims, because D had apparently not insisted in time that the judge determine the facts on P's equity claim. But even if D had, the court could avoid the problem, and still can today, by treating the jury, impaneled as of right to hear the law claim, as a merely "advisory" jury[15] to hear the equitable claim. Although the court can reject a merely advisory verdict, it ought to treat such a unique case as one triable of right by jury. When the U.S. Supreme Court, in an analogous situation, had before it several related maritime claims, some jury triable and some not, it held that the presence of one that was jury triable required all of the claims to be submitted to the jury and the verdict to be treated as binding on all of them.[16]

§ 210. Some Forms

There were a few handfuls of official forms of pleadings.[1] These were designed to offer the practitioner samples of "the simplicity and brevity of statement" contemplated by the CPLR.[2] In what we view as an unfortunate development, the courts rescinded the Appendix of Official Forms for the CPLR in 2016.[3] Nonetheless, the former official forms still provide helpful templates for practitioners drafting complaints and we will review some samples below.

Former Official Form 6, to illustrate, is a complaint in an action for goods sold and accepted. Its body, exclusive of the "wherefore" (the relief) clause, has only a few lines, reading:

Defendant owes plaintiff $20,000 for goods sold to, and accepted by, defendant between June 1, 1966 and December 1, 1966.

It fully satisfies CPLR 3013. The money lent complaint, Former Official Form 9, is even shorter:

---

[13]   *Cioffi*, 129 A.D.3d at 894, 10 N.Y.S.3d at 627.

[14]   Di Menna v. Cooper & Evans Co., 220 N.Y. 391, 115 N.E. 993 (1917). Today, too, the interposition of a legal counterclaim where the plaintiff has brought an equitable claim does not waive jury trial of the counterclaim, CPLR 4102(c), but a specific demand for jury trial is still required and without it a waiver does result. CPLR 4102(a). These matters are elaborated in § 378.

[15]   In any case in which the court is to be the fact finder, the judge has the power to give the question to an advisory jury, CPLR 4212, but in that case the verdict does not bind and the judge can disregard it and find the facts contra. See § 381.

[16]   Fitzgerald v. U.S. Lines Co., 374 U.S. 16, 83 S. Ct. 1646, 10 L. Ed. 2d 720 (1963).

[1]   They were promulgated in the 1960s by the Judicial Conference. Today, the power to promulgate forms is in the Chief Administrator of the Courts. CPLR 107. See §§ 5, 7.

[2]   The language is that of CPLR 107, which confers the power to promulgate forms. See § 7.

[3]   See § 7.

Defendant owes plaintiff $20,000 for money lent by plaintiff to defendant on June 1, 1965.

Even the presumably involved tort case had an official illustration. Former Official Form 12 is a complaint in the so-called "pedestrian knockdown" case and has only three paragraphs:

> 1.   On June 1, 1966, in a public highway called Broadway in New York City, defendant C.D. negligently drove a motor vehicle against plaintiff who was then crossing the highway.

> 2.   That motor vehicle was then owned by defendant E.F. and driven by defendant C.D. with defendant E.F.'s permission.

> 3.   Solely as a result of defendant C.D.'s negligence, plaintiff was personally injured, lost earnings and incurred expenses for [e.g., care and treatment, etc.].

In several regards the form is archaic, and yet it still shows the simplicity aimed at. The last paragraph reflects the contributory negligence rule, applicable when the form was drafted. (The form was never amended and updated.) Claims accruing on or after September 1, 1975, are governed by the comparative negligence rule,[4] which makes any culpable conduct of the plaintiff an affirmative defense for the defendant to plead,[5] which in turn makes it unnecessary for the plaintiff to plead that the defendant was "solely" to account for the occurrence.[6] There should also be added to the form an allegation that the plaintiff sustained a "serious injury" or "economic loss greater than basic economic loss" and that the matter is, therefore, proper for a court action, another requirement adopted after the form was promulgated.[7]

In each instance, a "wherefore" clause concludes the complaint, setting forth the demand for relief.

These are simple cases. More involved ones will naturally entail more extended pleading, but the brevity the forms are designed to illustrate comes across. Former Official Form 15, for example, a specific performance claim to convey land, has only five brief paragraphs.

All of these forms, which at one time bore the imprimatur of the court system itself, are generally far terser than those in the commercial form books. The lawyer should not hesitate to adjust any form she consults to the needs of the case.

The simplicity and brevity of New York's pleading requirements are further demonstrated in the Third Department's decision in 12 Baker Hill Road, Inc. v. Miranti,[8] a breach of contract action. In *12 Baker Hill Road*, the court rejected defendant's argument that plaintiff's amended complaint was defective because it did not specify the provision of the contract that was allegedly breached. The court stressed that "the primary function of a pleading is to apprise an adverse party of the pleader's claim."[9] To accomplish this goal, a complaint must be sufficiently detailed to meet CPLR 3013's

---

[4]   CPLR 1413; see § 168E.

[5]   CPLR 1412.

[6]   See § 168E.

[7]   CPLR 3016(g); see § 216.

[8]   12 Baker Hill Road, Inc. v. Miranti, 130 A.D.3d 1425, 14 N.Y.S.3d 787 (3d Dep't 2015).

[9]   *12 Baker Hill Road*, 130 A.D.3d at 1426, 14 N.Y.S.3d at 789.

instruction "to give the court and parties notice of the transactions, occurrences, or series of transactions or occurrences, intended to be proved and the material elements of each cause of action or defense." Furthermore, the Third Department stressed that "[w]hen examining the facial sufficiency of the complaint, it must be construed liberally, and any technical defects may be ignored in the absence of prejudice to the opposing party."[10]

In *12 Baker Hill Road*, the amended complaint's fourth cause of action alleging breach of contract identified the parties and the property that was the subject of the contract, alleged that defendant agreed to purchase the property for $75,000, and claimed that defendant breached the contract, resulting in damages. That was sufficient to satisfy CPLR 3013, and the plaintiff "was not required to attach a copy of the contract or plead its terms."[11]

With the rescinding of the official forms, decisions such as *12 Baker Hill Road* will take on more prominence in providing guidance on what it takes to satisfy New York's pleading rules, which now stand in stark contrast to the more demanding pleading requirements in federal courts.[12]

The lawyer who fears pleading error most often chooses to err on the side of too much rather than too little. It's interesting, therefore, to note that there may sometimes be just as much danger in pleading too much. In one case, for example, the complaint on a promissory note had thirty paragraphs. The court compared it with former Official Form 5, which has only three. It held the complaint "inordinate" and unacceptable.[13]

§ 211. Pleading in the Federal and Lower Courts Compared

The federal pleading requirement comes from Rule 8 of the Federal Rules of Civil Procedure, which requires "a short and plain statement of the claim showing that the pleader is entitled to relief." The federal "claim" is for all practical purposes the same as the New York "cause of action,"[1] and the measure of whether the pleading passes muster was at one time essentially the same under both Federal Rule 8 and CPLR 3013.

In the well known federal case of Dioguardi v. Durning,[2] for example, decided early in the life of the Federal Rules, a plaintiff conversant with neither the law nor the English language appeared and pleaded pro se. He babbled on—even his spelling illustrated his accent—but the Court of Appeals for the Second Circuit sustained his complaint as stating not one but two claims. The lesson is not to encourage poor pleading, but to deter technical attacks on sufficient pleading. Pleading requirements in federal courts became far more demanding than those in New York State courts after a pair of recent United States Supreme Court decisions.[3] Therefore, the current state of the law

---

[10]   *12 Baker Hill Road*, 130 A.D.3d at 1426, 14 N.Y.S.3d at 789; see § 208.

[11]   *12 Baker Hill Road*, 130 A.D.3d at 1426, 14 N.Y.S.2d at 789 (quoting Griffin Bros., Inc. v. Yatto, 68 A.D.2d 1009, 415 N.Y.S.2d 114 (3d Dep't 1979)).

[12]   See § 631 (Practitioner's Edition).

[13]   Domestic Finance Corp. v. Milner, 59 Misc. 2d 867, 868, 300 N.Y.S.2d 636, 637 (Sup. Ct., Onondaga County 1969).

[1]   Occasionally, a case tries to distinguish the two terms, e.g., Garcia v. Hilton Hotels Intern., 97 F. Supp. 5 (D. Puerto Rico 1951), but without much success.

[2]   Dioguardi v. Durning, 139 F.2d 774 (2d Cir. 1944).

[3]   See Bell Atlantic Corp. v. Twombly, 550 U.S. 544, 127 S. Ct. 1955, 167 L. Ed. 2d 929 (2007); Ashcroft v. Iqbal, 556 U.S. 662, 129 S. Ct. 1937, 173 L. Ed. 2d 868 (2009); § 631 (Practitioners Edition).

on the federal side under Rule 8 of the Federal Rules of Civil Procedure is no longer a very helpful guide for a lawyer trying to comply with CPLR 3013.

As liberal as pleadings are under the CPLR, they are even more so in the lower courts in New York under the uniform court acts. In the New York City Civil Court and in the district, city, town, and village courts, pleading by mere "indorsement" is permitted in money actions. An indorsement is a brief statement of "the nature and substance of the cause of action."[4] It can be appended to the summons or merely written or typed on it. In some lower courts, an "indorsement" pleading may even be checked boxes on a form furnished by the clerk.[5]

In other than money actions, a formal pleading is generally required even in the lower courts, and there may be provisions in the rules of a particular court requiring formal pleadings even in particular categories of money action,[6] or, to the contrary, dispensing with formal pleading altogether in all actions under stated circumstances, such as where the plaintiff appears pro se.[7]

An indorsement pleading need not satisfy even the modest requirements of the CPLR,[8] which probably means that an indorsement can be little more than a short name or description of the cause of action.[9] If a formal complaint is required in one of the lower courts in a given case, whether by statute or rule, and an indorsement is used instead, the defect should be an amendable irregularity and a formal complaint should be permitted nunc pro tunc.[10] If only a bare summons is served, however, with neither a formal complaint nor an indorsement accompanying it, the defect has been held jurisdictional, resulting in a dismissal.[11] (As a result of CPLR amendments effective in 1979, the service of a bare summons was eliminated as an option even in supreme and county court practice and with the same result for a violation: dismissal of the action.)[12]

In the supreme and county courts, the summons may be accompanied by a mere notice under CPLR 305(b) instead of a complaint, the complaint to follow later under a

---

[4]   See § 902(a) in the New York City Civ. Ct. Act and in the Uniform Dist., City, and Just. Ct. Acts, McKinney's Vol. 29A, Parts 2 and 3.

[5]   See Holloway v. New York City Transit Authority, 182 Misc. 2d 749, 699 N.Y.S.2d 261 (N.Y. City Civ. Ct. 1999) (SPR 90:3) (differentiating pleading requirements in the higher and lower courts and comparing "notice" and "indorsement" pleading).

[6]   See, e.g., 22 N.Y.C.R.R. § 212.7, applicable in the district courts.

[7]   See, e.g., 22 N.Y.C.R.R. § 208.7, applicable in the New York City Civ. Ct. Act.

[8]   See § 903 in the New York City Civ. Ct. Act and in the Uniform Dist., City, and Just. Ct. Acts, McKinney's Vol. 29A, Parts 2 and 3.

[9]   See the Commentary on § 903 in the New York City Civ. Ct. Act. Since indorsement pleading is permissive rather than mandatory in the lower courts, lawyers there often elect the more formal pleading, but under the CPLR today, the "formal" pleading itself is hardly a burdensome task.

[10]   Creative Woodworking Co. v. Bohn, 44 Misc. 2d 369, 253 N.Y.S.2d 711 (N.Y. City Civ. Ct. 1964). Compare Knauer v. Long Island Airports Limousine Service Corp., 53 Misc. 2d 1017, 280 N.Y.S.2d 343 (App. Term, 1st Dep't 1967). It has been held that if the rules authorize the court with an ex parte order to permit an indorsement complaint, the order can be granted nunc pro tunc. Onorati v. National Automatic Laundry & Cleaning Council, Inc., 85 Misc. 2d 236, 379 N.Y.S.2d 295 (N.Y. City Civ. Ct. 1976).

[11]   See Young v. Franklyn, 93 Misc. 2d 508, 402 N.Y.S.2d 966 (N.Y. City Civ. Ct. 1978); see also Parker v. Mack, 61 N.Y.2d 114, 472 N.Y.S.2d 882, 460 N.E.2d 1316 (1984) (supreme court action).

[12]   See § 60.

demand procedure.[13] It has been held that what satisfies as a CPLR 305(b) notice in a supreme court action also satisfies as an "indorsement" pleading in the lower courts.[14]

§ 212. Separate Statement and Numbering

If CPLR 3013 can be considered the commanding general of pleadings, then CPLR 3014 should be deemed its chief of staff. CPLR 3014 contains, among other things, the instructions about numbering and stating allegations. Its preference is that every pleading "consist of plain and concise statements in consecutively numbered paragraphs"—already illustrated in former Official Form 12 as set forth two sections back—and that each paragraph "contain, as far as practicable, a single allegation."

As a general rule, the assignment of a separately numbered paragraph to each factual allegation aids clarity and facilitates responsive pleading. Admissions and denials in the answer thereby secure clearer reference points. But this numbering requirement is governed by the "practicable" standard. If presentation is facilitated by including a few facts in a single paragraph, it is permissible. Paragraph two of former Official Form 12, for example, reads that the "motor vehicle was then owned by defendant E.F. and driven by defendant C.D. with defendant E.F.'s permission." There are three factual averments in that paragraph—ownership, operation, and permission— and yet it is not only good pleading, but also was official pleading. Breaking the statement down into three separately numbered paragraphs is of course permissible, but would be awkward and verbose.

An adverse party who feels prejudiced by the pleader's failure to separately state and number can make a motion to compel it.[1] An adverse party is not required to make such a motion if the disputed pleading does not necessitate a response, and a failure to move in these circumstances cannot be deemed a waiver of the CPLR 3014 defect.[2]

Since factual averments within a single cause of action must be separately numbered, of course separate causes of action must also be separately stated and numbered. This sometimes necessitates the unrewarding search for a definition of a "cause of action"—a phrase of "shifting meanings" which "may mean one thing for one purpose and something different for another."[3] It is one of the most "theory-ridden of legal concepts" and cannot be defined except in its particular context.[4] The ultimate test of whether the plaintiff has one or several causes of action is usually resolved by applying the double recovery test: ask whether, if the plaintiff were to get a satisfied judgment on theory A, she could then turn around and seek more in a suit on theory B. It is usually easier to put and answer that question than to define a "cause of action," and yet the answer often supplies the needed definition. If the second recovery is permissible, the pleader has in fact two separate causes of action; if it is not, the pleader has but one cause of action, perhaps sustainable on several theories or grounds or counts.

---

[13]   See § 60.

[14]   Martinez v. College Gardens Co-op, Inc. N.Y.L.J., Jan. 24, 2000, at 31, col.2 (N.Y. City Civ. Ct.; Brigantti-Hughes, J.).

[1]   See CPLR 3024; § 230.

[2]   Scholastic Inc. v. Pace Plumbing Corp., 129 A.D.3d 75, 79, 8 N.Y.S.3d 143, 147 (1st Dep't 2015).

[3]   U.S. v. Memphis Cotton Oil Co., 1933–1 C.B. 307, 288 U.S. 62, 67–68, 53 S. Ct. 278, 280, 77 L. Ed. 619 (1933).

[4]   U.S. v. Dickinson, 331 U.S. 745, 748, 67 S. Ct. 1382, 1385, 91 L. Ed. 1789 (1947).

Where, for example, the plaintiff sustains one injury but it is actionable under the common law as well as under a statute, a frequent occurrence today, the plaintiff has but one cause of action.[5] Perhaps the most frequently met of this species today is the personal injury caused by a product. It often supports three theories—negligence, breach of warranty, and strict liability—but it is only one cause of action.

The plaintiff who has separate grounds to support a single cause of action is entitled to the damages offered by the most generous of them. Not all of the counts or grounds will necessarily offer the same quantum of damages. A medical injury, for example, may support both a malpractice and a breach of contract claim. The contract claim does not support an award for pain and suffering, however,[6] while the malpractice claim does. The plaintiff who joins and prevails on both grounds of course recovers for pain and suffering even though it pertains to but one ground. And of course the damages element available to both counts, such as for medical treatment, can't be duplicated. No matter how many counts support it, the plaintiff can recover for it only once.

How does this translate into our present purpose, which is to determine separate numbering requirements? Technically, if there's but one cause of action, its various possible theories or counts need not be separately stated and numbered as such. The facts needed to cover them all can be consecutively numbered, but introduced as only one claim: "Cause of action number one" or (favorite terminology among the more ancient members of the bar) "As and for a first cause of action." Quite often separate theories in support of but a single claim are separately numbered, harmlessly enough, as if they were distinct causes of action. The plaintiff who has only one claim—one ultimate "cause of action"—will still be entitled to be recompensed for each item of damages only once. The availability of separate theories does not occasion a windfall for the plaintiff.

Errors of mere verbalization either way—stating separate claims as one or dividing one into two or more—should at worst be correctible by amendment and if unprejudicial should be ignored.[7]

As a general rule, all items of damage emanating from but a single occurrence, event, or transaction and due at the time of suit are deemed parts of but a single cause of action and should all be joined. Omitting an item of damages risks waiver under the "splitting" rule.[8] But in regard to a tort New York takes the position that its property damage and personal injury aspects are separate causes of action and may be sued on as such;[9] or, if they are sued on together (the more appropriate and more frequent step), they should be separately numbered. Today, moreover, unless the property damage part of the tort claim is small enough to go into the small claims part of one of the lower courts,[10] an action on it and a separate action on the personal injury claim may result in consolidation of both on motion of the defendant.

CPLR 3014 also requires that "[s]eparate . . . defenses shall be separately stated and numbered," yet lawyers sometimes ignore these dictates. For example, in Scholastic Inc. v. Pace Plumbing Corp., defendant pleaded sixteen affirmative defenses "within a

---

[5]   Payne v. New York, S. & W.R. Co., 201 N.Y. 436, 95 N.E. 19 (1911).

[6]   Robins v. Finestone, 308 N.Y. 543, 127 N.E.2d 330 (1955).

[7]   CPLR 3026.

[8]   See § 220.

[9]   Reilly v. Sicilian Asphalt Paving Co., 170 N.Y. 40, 62 N.E. 772 (1902).

[10]   See § 582 (Practitioner's Edition).

boilerplate, catchall paragraph" that also asserted "any other matter constituting an avoidance or an affirmative defense which further investigation of this matter may prove applicable herein."[11] It is the rare decision in which a defect under CPLR 3014 for failing to separately state and number allegations or affirmative defenses is found to be prejudicial, but the entire *Scholastic* court agreed that defendant's one-sentence paragraph, containing virtually every affirmative defense known to man, failed to provide plaintiff with adequate notice of the specific defense of the statute of limitations, on which a motion to dismiss was granted. The court ruled that the defense "was inadequately pleaded because of its failure to separately state and number the defense and that plaintiff was prejudiced by the defective pleading."[12] Nonetheless, concluding that "the prejudice was curable by permitting discovery on the statute of limitations issue," the court remanded the matter to the motion court to allow defendant to correct its defective pleading and for plaintiff to obtain necessary discovery.[13]

§ 213. Statements Deemed Repeated; Writings

The prior section, on the separate numbering requirement, treated the case in which a pleading sets forth several distinct causes of action or several different counts or theories in support of the same cause of action. In such cases, it is often necessary, at a later point in the pleading, to rely again on something alleged earlier in the same pleading. CPLR 3014 provides that prior statements are "deemed repeated or adopted subsequently in the same pleading," thus dispensing with repetition or even further reference and automatically summoning forth the earlier allegations to support the later claim or count.

If needed for a "clear presentation," however, CPLR 3014 does encourage repetition of the earlier statements, but even there it allows the repetition to be made merely by referring to the numbers of the earlier paragraphs, dispensing with the duplication of their substance. When, for example, a second count or claim is pleaded in a complaint, introduced by language like "Second cause of action [count, claim, ground, theory, etc.]," and most of its elements are the same as those of the first claim and have already been pleaded, the next numbered paragraph can simply say "Plaintiff repeats the allegations of paragraphs two, four, and five." Further paragraphs can then add the new allegations distinct to the second claim or count.

The allegations are cumulative for all purposes. Even those of a defense stated in an answer, for example, are deemed repeated for purposes of a counterclaim to follow in that answer.[1] Allegations in a pleading in a prior litigation, however, are not deemed repeated and may not be incorporated by reference; they have to be set forth independently.[2]

The pleader who wishes to make a writing a part of the pleading need merely attach a copy of it. CPLR 3014 then makes it part of the pleading "for all purposes." It is usual

---

[11]   *Scholastic*, 129 A.D.3d at 76, 78, 8 N.Y.S.3d at 145, 146.

[12]   *Scholastic*, 129 A.D.3d at 76, 8 N.Y.S.3d at 145; see CPLR 3013; § 208.

[13]   *Scholastic*, 129 A.D.3d at 76, 8 N.Y.S.3d at 145. For further discussion of the *Scholastic* decision, which addresses a multitude of pleading issues, see § 208.

[1]   Nussenblatt v. Nussenblatt, 62 Misc. 2d 792, 309 N.Y.S.2d 397 (Sup. Ct., Queens County 1970).

[2]   Card v. Budini, 29 A.D.2d 35, 285 N.Y.S.2d 734 (3d Dep't 1967).

to make some reference to the writing in the body of the pleading. If a conflict arises between the writing itself and allegations made in the pleading, the writing prevails.[3]

§ 214. Various Techniques of Pleading

CPLR 3014 recognizes and approves several special techniques of pleading.

Inconsistency is allowed, either among claims or among defenses. This is done to recognize the unpredictability of litigation. A plaintiff can in one cause of action ask for rescission of a contract and in a second ask for its specific performance, all in the same complaint. A defendant can plead in one defense that she never made the contract and in a second that the contract is illegal. A party can't predict what the fact finding will be and is entitled at the pleading stage to introduce into the case everything she's got. Hence a cause of action is not subject to dismissal merely because it "contradicts the underlying theory" of one already pleaded.[1] The defense of workers' compensation coverage, for example, is not precluded by an earlier defense denying that the plaintiff was even an employee.[2]

While allowed to plead inconsistent claims, a party can't ordinarily be allowed an inconsistent recovery, i.e., judgment. The doctrine of election of remedies, treated later,[3] sees to that. If the claims or theories are consistent, then a judgment can of course embody both or all of them. In a personal injury action, for example, the doctrine of res ipsa loquitur, at one time deemed inconsistent with proof of specific acts of negligence, is no longer considered so;[4] both grounds can go to the jury (and to judgment) together.

Alternative pleading is also recognized and invited by CPLR 3014. This is the pleading counterpart of CPLR 1002, which allows the joinder of parties in the alternative. The example given earlier in the book, of joinder in the alternative[5]—in which P, unable to determine who as among various handlers of his goods was responsible for damage, sues them in the alternative—is also an example of a complaint that pleads in the alternative: the plaintiff pleads facts indicating that at least one of the defendants must be responsible and thereby establishes a sufficient prima facie case to require each of the defendants to come forward with proof in self-exoneration. The proof offered by any defendant may be used against any other;[6] the jury will decide who (if anyone) is responsible.

A common example of pleading in the alternative is an injured pedestrian's complaint in a negligence case involving two cars. He alleges formally that both cars were responsible, a sufficient pleading basis on which the jury can find either responsible. Former Official Form 13 is a complaint in a pedestrian injury case in which the plaintiff does not know which of two cars hit him.[7] It is a further example of alternative pleading.

---

[3]   805 Third Ave. Co. v. M.W. Realty Associates, 58 N.Y.2d 447, 461 N.Y.S.2d 778, 448 N.E.2d 445 (1983).

[1]   Cohn v. Lionel Corp., 21 N.Y.2d 559, 563, 289 N.Y.S.2d 404, 408, 236 N.E.2d 634, 637 (1968).

[2]   George v. Sparwood Realty Corp., 34 A.D.2d 768, 311 N.Y.S.2d 422 (1st Dep't 1970).

[3]   See § 219.

[4]   Abbott v. Page Airways, Inc., 23 N.Y.2d 502, 297 N.Y.S.2d 713, 245 N.E.2d 388 (1969).

[5]   See § 135.

[6]   Shaw v. Lewis, 55 Misc. 2d 664, 286 N.Y.S.2d 758 (N.Y. City Civ. Ct. 1968), aff'd, 58 Misc. 2d 1072, 299 N.Y.S.2d 615 (App. Term, 1st Dep't).

[7]   See § 210.

Hypothetical pleading is another technique authorized by CPLR 3014. Whenever a hypothesis, with or without an "if" or "when" or similar clause, would aid presentation of a pleader's case, the pleader can use it. P pleads, for example, for the specific performance of a contract, but pleads also that if the court in its discretion refuses the relief of specific performance—which as an equitable remedy lies in the discretion of the court—then P wants damages for breach of contract. (Damages are a law claim in which judicial discretion plays no role.) In an assault case, for another example, D pleads that he never touched P (defense of mistaken identity), but that if D did, then P had it coming (defense of justification). These hypothetical techniques, among their other possible functions, are one way of interjecting inconsistent claims or defenses.

A few months before Foley v. D'Agostino[8] offered the First Department the full opportunity it had been seeking to implement the CPLR's purpose of divesting pleadings of their rigidity,[9] the court used the case of W. T. Grant Co. v. Uneeda Doll Co.[10] as a kind of herald and in the bargain gave expansive approval to the use of hypotheses. Retailer R in Uneeda bought dolls from manufacturer M and sold one of these to customer C. C was injured by the product and sued R in Connecticut. Before the suit went to judgment, R sued M in New York for indemnification, for whatever C might recover of R, on the ground that it was all M's responsibility. M moved to dismiss on the ground that R's claim was premature, but the court sustained R's claim as a hypothetical pleading: "if" C recovers of R "then" R is entitled to recover from M.

In a situation of that kind, stays, continuances, and like remedies can be used in the New York action to await the result of C's Connecticut suit, on which any judgment in the New York indemnification action would of course depend. Whether there was some barrier in the *Uneeda* case to R's impleading M into the Connecticut action—which would have been the ideal step for R to take—does not appear. Perhaps it was a jurisdictional problem.[11] When jurisdiction is not a problem, as where the underlying action is pending in a New York court and impleader of M is clearly available, a separate indemnification action before the thing to be indemnified has been adjudicated will likely be disallowed.[12] A third-party action by R against M would, however, be permissible before C has obtained a judgment against R.[13]

In Scholastic Inc. v. Pace Plumbing Corp.,[14] discussed at length above in section 208, defendant pleaded sixteen affirmative defenses within a single catchall paragraph that also asserted "any other matter constituting an avoidance or an affirmative defense which further investigation of this matter may prove applicable herein." This gave the First Department an occasion to address certain limitations to hypothetical pleading. The *Scholastic* court acknowledged that while defendant was permitted to plead its affirmative defenses hypothetically, "which it apparently attempted to do by 'reserving' those defenses unto itself," it could only do so "insofar as those defenses were concise,

---

[8]   Foley v. D'Agostino, 21 A.D.2d 60, 248 N.Y.S.2d 121 (1st Dep't 1964).

[9]   See § 208.

[10]   W. T. Grant Co. v. Uneeda Doll Co., 19 A.D.2d 361, 243 N.Y.S.2d 428 (1st Dep't 1963).

[11]   See Commentary C3014:8 on McKinney's CPLR 3014.

[12]   See Morey v. Sealright Co., 41 Misc. 2d 1068, 247 N.Y.S.2d 306 (Sup.Ct., Onondaga County 1964).

[13]   See § 159.

[14]   Scholastic Inc. v. Pace Plumbing Corp., 129 A.D.3d 75, 76, 78, 8 N.Y.S.3d 143, 145 (1st Dep't 2015).

separately numbered, and sufficiently stated."[15] In one of the more informative treatments of hypothetical pleading under CPLR 3014, the court held:

A permissive hypothetical pleading does not extend so far as to authorize a defendant to plead each and every affirmative defense that might exist without regard to its relevance to the cause(s) of action presented by the complaint. Permitting such conduct here would effectively sanction deception on the part of defendant, whether intentional or not, thereby avoiding the CPLR's notice requirement. In other words, defendant's formulation of its laundry list of defenses in hypothetical terms does not exempt it from the other requirements of CPLR 3014.[16]

B. SPECIFIC ITEMS

Table of Sections

§ 215.   Pleading Certain Specific Matters; CPLR 3015
§ 216.   Particularity in Specific Actions; CPLR 3016

§ 215. Pleading Certain Specific Matters; CPLR 3015

For certain items, CPLR 3015 requires particularity in pleading. Before its several subdivisions are treated, a few related points should be made.

There is no requirement in New York practice that jurisdiction be pleaded. Even with the lower courts, whose subject matter jurisdiction is limited, there is no statutory requirement, as there is in federal practice,[1] that subject matter jurisdiction be pleaded. Whether there is subject matter jurisdiction is technically an affirmative defense for the defendant to raise by motion or answer,[2] and the plaintiff is allowed, when the defense is raised, to establish the court's subject matter jurisdiction whether the complaint has mentioned it or not. The same is true of personal jurisdiction: the complaint need not say anything about it. If personal jurisdiction is lacking, the defendant must raise the objection by motion or answer,[3] and the plaintiff can, in response, adduce whatever is needed to show that personal jurisdiction exists.

Some cases nevertheless held for a time, at least in lower court actions in which process had been served beyond the lines of the municipality serviced by the court, that the complaint had to allege the basis for personal jurisdiction.[4] It was even held that in the absence of the jurisdictional allegation, not even enough jurisdiction is obtained to support an amendment of the complaint to add it.[5] Carried to its logical end, this kind of

---

[15] *Scholastic*, 129 A.D.3d at 79–80, 8 N.Y.S.3d at 147 (citing CPLR 3013, 3014); see also Kowalczyk v. Village of Monticello, 107 A.D.3d 1365, 1366, 969 N.Y.S.2d 566, 568 (3d Dep't 2013) ("[A] party cannot employ a catch-all provision in an attempt to preserve any and all potential defenses/objections for future use without affording notice to the opposing party . . . .").

[16] *Scholastic*, 129 A.D.3d at 80, 8 N.Y.S.3d at 147. For further discussion of this type of "catchall" pleading of affirmative defenses, which is a very troublesome practice, see Commentary C3018:16A to McKinney's CPLR 3018.

[1] Fed. R. Civ. P. 8(a); see §§ 611, 631 (Practitioner's Edition).

[2] CPLR 3211(a)(2), (e).

[3] CPLR 3211(a)(8), (e).

[4] E.g., All-State Credit Corp. v. Riess, 61 Misc. 2d 677, 306 N.Y.S.2d 596 (App. Term, 2d Dep't 1970), criticized but followed in Henry Sash & Door Co. v. Medi-Complex Limited, 69 Misc. 2d 269, 329 N.Y.S.2d 892 (Dist. Ct., Suffolk County 1972).

[5] *All-State Credit Corp.*, 61 Misc. 2d at 679, 306 N.Y.S.2d at 598.

reasoning would mean that the court would lack even the jurisdiction to declare jurisdiction absent, which in turn should void its decision as a precedent—for want of jurisdiction! The appellate division afterwards righted things in Fishman v. Pocono Ski Rental Inc.,[6] overruling that line of cases. "There is no requirement . . . that the complaint allege the basis for personal jurisdiction," said the court; "lack of personal jurisdiction is an affirmative defense" for the defendant to raise.

It should be unnecessary to plead in the complaint any item that needs an affirmative defense to inject it into the case. Allegations of when a claim accrued, for example, are not an integral part of the claim itself and should therefore need no statement in the complaint: the statute of limitations, to which such allegations pertain, is an affirmative defense for the defendant to plead and prove.[7] An exception to this rule applies in the rare instance where the relevant time period is a condition precedent. In these instances, the complaint must plead, and the plaintiff has the burden of proving, that the claim was brought on time.[8]

The same conclusions apply to the statute of frauds, also an affirmative defense:[9] caselaw has held that the complaint should plead whether the contract was oral or written.[10] Some former official forms are to the same effect,[11] again suggesting by implication that it is a good thing to do. Although a bill of particulars seems the more appropriate place for such things,[12] it is certainly no burden to include the allegations in the pleading itself, even if they are not part of the substantive claim. Their omission, however, should never be deemed to invalidate the claim or ground a dismissal.

When a given matter, though not ordinarily deemed an integral part of a substantive cause of action, is considered integral on a given one, it must of course be pleaded. Special damages, for example, is not required to give substance to most claims, but it is for some. When it is, as it is for tort claims not having a common law origin, it must of course be pleaded.[13]

The various subdivisions of CPLR 3015 add particularity requirements for several things, but only a few. Subdivision (a) makes it unnecessary for a plaintiff to plead satisfaction of a contractual condition precedent. The pleading burden here is on the defendant to specifically raise the issue of the plaintiff's nonperformance of the condition. If the defendant does plead it, the plaintiff then has the burden of proving that she satisfied the condition.

It has been held that if the plaintiff voluntarily pleads on the issue, although not required to by CPLR 3015(a), the plaintiff injects the issue into the case and thereby relieves the defendant of having to raise it in the answer.[14]

---

[6]   Fishman v. Pocono Ski Rental Inc., 82 A.D.2d 906, 907, 440 N.Y.S.2d 700, 701 (2d Dep't 1981).

[7]   CPLR 3018(b), 3211(a)(5), (e).

[8]   See § 34.

[9]   CPLR 3018(b), CPLR 3211(a)(5), (e).

[10]   Hanson v. Hanson, 203 Misc. 396, 119 N.Y.S.2d 11 (Sup. Ct., New York County 1953).

[11]   E.g., former Official Form 15, ¶ 1.

[12]   The bill of particulars is treated later. See §§ 238 et seq.

[13]   Zausner v. Fotochrome, Inc., 18 A.D.2d 649, 235 N.Y.S.2d 698 (1st Dep't 1962).

[14]   Allis-Chalmers Mfg. Co. v. Malan Const. Corp., 30 N.Y.2d 225, 331 N.Y.S.2d 636, 282 N.E.2d 600 (1972).

While relieved of pleading her own performance under a contract, the plaintiff must still, of course, plead the facts constituting the defendant's alleged breach.[15] It should also be noted that CPLR 3015(a) applies only to a condition precedent imposed by a contract. When it's imposed by a statute, like section 50–e of General Municipal Law (the notice of claim requirement in tort cases),[16] the plaintiff retains the burden both of pleading and of proving the condition's fulfillment.

A tendering back of benefits received from a transaction is no longer a condition precedent to an action to void the transaction; the court can adjust the equities in the judgment.[17] Since there is no omnibus requirement of such a tender as a substantive condition to relief, there is of course no requirement to plead it.

If any party to the action is known to be a corporation, that fact must be alleged, along with a specification of the place of incorporation.[18] There is no analogous requirement in regard to noncorporate parties, although a plaintiff who picks his own county of residence as the venue of a supreme court action must specify his residence address on the summons.[19] Having corporate status pleaded is helpful for several purposes, such as a motion to dismiss an action when it appears that it has been brought by a corporate plaintiff doing business in New York without authority.[20] This requirement to plead corporate status has nothing of the importance it can have in federal practice, however, where it may reflect on subject matter jurisdiction in a case based on the diversity of citizenship of the parties.[21]

With the growth in recent years of other forms of carrying on business, like the professional corporation (PC), the limited liability company (LLC), the limited liability partnership (LLP) (to be distinguished from the mere "limited partnership"), etc., it is a good idea to identify the nature of the entity or creature in the pleading when it is involved as a party in litigation, whether technically required or not.[22]

Whenever it is appropriate in a pleading to refer to a previously rendered judgment or decision of any court or board or other tribunal, it may be referred to without pleading facts showing the rendering tribunal's jurisdiction.[23]

A signature on a negotiable instrument is admitted unless the opponent's pleading specifically denies it.[24] The same is true of signatures on commercial paper in general under Articles 3[25] and investment securities under Article 8[26] of the Uniform Commercial Code. If the signature is specifically denied, the burden of proving the instrument's validity shifts back to the party claiming under it.

---

[15] Baby Show Exhibition Co. v. Crowell Pub. Co., 174 A.D. 368, 161 N.Y.S. 205 (1st Dep't 1916).

[16] See § 32.

[17] CPLR 3004.

[18] CPLR 3015(b).

[19] CPLR 305(a).

[20] Bus. Corp. Law § 1312. See § 30.

[21] 28 U.S.C.A. § 1332(c), Fed. R. Civ. P. 8(a). See § 611 (Practitioner's Edition).

[22] Treatment of how to effect service on some of these creatures appears in a lead note in SPR 87:1; see § 69.

[23] CPLR 3015(c). See Commentary C3015:4 on McKinney's CPLR 3015.

[24] CPLR 3015(d).

[25] N.Y. UCC § 3–307(1), overruling Hoffstaedter v. Lichtenstein, 203 A.D. 494, 196 N.Y.S. 577 (1st Dep't 1922).

[26] N.Y. UCC § 8–114(1).

CPLR 3012–b, which requires the filing and service of a "certificate of merit" with the initiatory papers in certain residential foreclosure actions, contains a provision that creates an exception to CPLR 3015(d). Pursuant to CPLR 3012–b(d), the provisions in CPLR 3015(d) are "not . . . applicable to a defendant who is not represented by an attorney." Therefore, a pro se litigant is apparently free to enter a general denial and later maintain that any signature appearing on a negotiable instrument is not hers. The exception to CPLR 3015(d) contained in CPLR 3012–b(d) was likely intended to apply only in residential foreclosure actions, but it is not so limited. Based on the literal language of the statute, it would apply to actions on a simple promissory note if the defendant is not represented by an attorney. We also wonder if the exception to CPLR 3015(d) would operate in a case where the actual pro se defendant is a lawyer.[27]

A special provision, CPLR 3015(e), governs business plaintiffs who are required to be licensed by the consumer affairs departments of New York City and certain other downstate suburban counties.[28] When they sue a consumer on a business claim, they have to plead the license. In 2012, the statute was amended to require the plaintiff to plead that she was duly licensed at the time the services were rendered, rather than at the time the litigation was commenced.[29] The new law also recognizes that a business plaintiff can seek to amend the complaint with the name and number of the license held at the time the work was performed. The amendment was designed to permit an unlicensed contractor who has retired, or who has had to close their business, to still pursue relief as long as a license was in effect at the time the work was performed. In 2013, the language in CPLR 3015(e) regarding "an after-acquired license," which caused some confusion,[30] was removed by the legislature.

In Marraccini v. Ryan,[31] the Court of Appeals ruled that "a licensed home improvement contractor who enters into a contract using a name other than the one on his license is not barred from enforcing the contract unless the other party is deceived or otherwise prejudiced by the misnomer." Because CPLR 3015(e) is a consumer protection measure, it has been held that it does not apply to an unlicensed contractor who furnishes materials not to a "consumer," but to a company. There, suit is maintainable against the company free of the CPLR 3015(e) barrier.[32]

These minutiae of pleadings under CPLR 3015 are easy to forget, making it necessary to negotiate the statute whenever drawing a complaint. Keeping at hand a small reprint of the statute for quick consultation when drawing a complaint can prove helpful. Covering it with a laminating sheet or keeping it under the glass top of a desk in a litigation office can prove convenient at pleading-drafting time. Any paralegal assisting with the drafting process should also be provided a copy of the statute.

§ 216. Particularity in Specific Actions; CPLR 3016

For most causes of action, there are no special pleading requirements. CPLR 3013 and 3014 do the job alone. But for a handful of actions, CPLR 3016 introduces some

---

[27] See Commentary to McKinney's CPLR 3012–b and Commentary C3015:5 to McKinney's CPLR 3015.

[28] The counties presently on the list are Nassau, Suffolk, Westchester, Rockland, and Putnam.

[29] See SPR 250:1.

[30] See B & F Bldg. Corp. v. Liebig, 76 N.Y.2d 689, 563 N.Y.S.2d 40, 564 N.E.2d 650 (1990) (requiring license to be in effect at time work is performed).

[31] Marraccini v. Ryan, 17 N.Y.3d 83, 85, 926 N.Y.S.2d 399, 950 N.E.2d 135 (2011).

[32] Bayonne Block Co., Inc. v. Porco, 171 Misc. 2d 684, 654 N.Y.S.2d 961 (N.Y. City Civ. Ct. 1996).

specific requirements. Before these are negotiated, we should again note the admonition contained in Foley v. D'Agostino:[1] that the theme is still set by CPLR 3013 and that CPLR 3016 is merely the exaction of additional detail in a few selected instances. Omission of such detail, moreover, should be curable by mere amendment or, if a bill of particulars is a likely place for it, the detail can be left to the bill.[2] Treatment (not verbatim statement) of the subdivisions of CPLR 3016 follows:

(a) Defamation. In a libel or slander case, the defamatory words must be quoted verbatim. This is strictly enforced and any paraphrasing or use of qualifying words makes the complaint defective.[3] The words' applicability to the plaintiff, however, may be stated generally. If extrinsic facts are relied on to give defamatory import to the words, or if the persons to whom the words were uttered had special knowledge that gave the words their defamatory impact, those facts should be pleaded.[4] The plaintiff must also plead with specificity the identity of third persons to whom the allegedly defamatory statements were made or read.[5] A bill of particulars is available if the defendant needs more detail.[6]

(b) Fraud, etc. Detail of the wrong is required in actions based on misrepresentation, fraud, mistake, wilful default, breach of trust, or undue influence. This is the subdivision that the *Foley* case specifically subordinated to CPLR 3013, noting that satisfaction of CPLR 3013, which imposes the fundamental requirement that notice of the transaction be given and the material elements of the claim be set forth, will usually satisfy CPLR 3016(b) as well. The consequence of a violation of CPLR 3016(b) is in any event a mere amendment[7] as long as the facts that the statute calls for exist and merely need pleading. If the case is dismissed outright, the explanation will usually lie not in the failure to plead detail, but in the court's being convinced from everything pleaded that there simply was no fraud or similar misconduct.

The Court of Appeals said in 1977 in Lanzi v. Brooks[8] that CPLR 3016(b):

> requires only that the misconduct complained of be set forth in sufficient detail to clearly inform defendant with respect to the incidents complained of and is not to be interpreted so strictly as to prevent an otherwise valid cause of action in situations where it may be "impossible to state in detail the circumstances constituting a fraud."

The Court stressed that the failure to allege "a necessary element of the cause of action" is not to be confused with what it plainly views as the less serious defect of omitting some detail. Should the detail be unavailable at the pleading stage, but the

---

[1]   Foley v. D'Agostino, 21 A.D.2d 60, 248 N.Y.S.2d 121 (1st Dep't 1964).

[2]   See Pernet v. Peabody Engineering Corp., 20 A.D.2d 781, 248 N.Y.S.2d 132 (1st Dep't 1964).

[3]   Gardner v. Alexander Rent-A-Car, Inc., 28 A.D.2d 667, 280 N.Y.S.2d 595 (1st Dep't 1967). An amendment, however, may allow the verbatim words to be inserted.

[4]   Danko v. F. W. Woolworth Co., 29 A.D.2d 855, 288 N.Y.S.2d 509 (1st Dep't 1968).

[5]   Raymond v. Marchand, 125 A.D.3d 835, 4 N.Y.S.3d 107 (2d Dep't 2015).

[6]   Pappalardo v. Westchester Rockland Newspapers, 101 A.D.2d 830, 475 N.Y.S.2d 487 (2d Dep't 1984), aff'd, 64 N.Y.2d 862, 487 N.Y.S.2d 325, 476 N.E.2d 651 (1985).

[7]   See Marcucilli v. Alicon Corp., 41 A.D.2d 932, 343 N.Y.S.2d 367 (2d Dep't 1973).

[8]   Lanzi v. Brooks, 43 N.Y.2d 778, 780, 402 N.Y.S.2d 384, 385, 373 N.E.2d 278, 279 (1977) (quoting Jered Contracting Corp. v. New York City Transit Authority, 22 N.Y.2d 187, 292 N.Y.S.2d 98, 239 N.E.2d 197 (1968)); see Eurycleia Partners, LP v. Seward & Kissel, LLP, 12 N.Y.3d 553, 559, 883 N.Y.S.2d 147, 150, 910 N.E.2d 976 (2009) ("CPLR 3016(b) is satisfied when the facts suffice to permit a reasonable inference of the alleged misconduct.").

complaint, notwithstanding an absence of detail, satisfactorily states a basic claim in fraud, the complaint can be sustained and the needed detail left to abide pretrial disclosure or, if need be, the trial itself. The court recognized that it's difficult for the plaintiff to cite detail since the wrong is often "peculiarly" in the defendant's knowledge.[9]

CPLR 3016(b) wouldn't be on the New York books at all but for the fact that it's in the Federal Rules,[10] which New York's Advisory Committee followed in this respect.[11] It has more justification in federal civil practice, which lacks a bill of particulars to furnish detail unrevealed by a complaint, while New York practice retains the bill for the kind of detail CPLR 3016(b) calls for.[12]

(c) Separation or divorce. In a separation or divorce action, the time, place, and circumstances of each act the defendant is accused of must be specified. This provision has been rigidly applied. Even the bill of particulars has been held to be an inappropriate alternative source.[13] The need for this kind of provision—a product of pre-CPLR thinking—derived from the unavailability of free disclosure in matrimonial actions whereby to enable the defendant to secure the needed detail. Disclosure is still relatively restricted in those actions under the CPLR.[14] The "irretrievable breakdown" ground for divorce adopted by the legislature in 2010[15] does not require a showing of any "misconduct" by either party and, therefore, the requirements of CPLR 3016(c) are inapplicable to it.[16]

(d) Judgment. In a suit on a judgment, the complaint must state the extent to which the judgment has been satisfied. This is to guard against a possible double recovery. It contemplates, among other things, the situation in which the earlier judgment was predicated on quasi in rem jurisdiction and the instant one is for the balance still due on the claim because the property seized in the first action did not suffice to satisfy the judgment. If the earlier quasi in rem judgment came from a New York court, it would recite on its face that it is enforceable only to the extent of duly attached property,[17] and the fear underlying CPLR 3016(d) would be unwarranted in this context.[18]

(e) Foreign law. Federal and sister-state law must be given judicial notice without even being requested by a party,[19] but foreign law does not get the notice automatically. CPLR 3016(e) requires that each party relying on foreign-country law set forth the substance of that law in her pleading. Doing so will probably produce the fringe benefit, incidentally, of making judicial notice mandatory pursuant to CPLR 4511(b). CPLR 4511(b) says that if the party relying on foreign law (1) requests judicial notice for it, (2) shows the court what the foreign law is, and (3) notifies other parties of reliance on the

---

9   *Lanzi*, 43 N.Y.2d at 780, 402 N.Y.S.2d at 385, 373 N.E.2d at 279.

10   Fed. R. Civ. P. 9(b).

11   See 1st Rep. Leg. Doc. No. 6(b), pp. 67–8 (1957).

12   See § 238.

13   Pustilnik v. Pustilnik, 24 A.D.2d 868, 264 N.Y.S.2d 400 (2d Dep't 1965).

14   See § 344; Commentary C3101:15 on McKinney's CPLR 3101.

15   See Dom. Rel. Law § 170(7).

16   Tuper v. Tuper, 98 A.D.3d 55, 946 N.Y.S.2d 719 (4th Dep't 2012) (SPR 251:4).

17   Benadon v. Antonio, 10 A.D.2d 40, 197 N.Y.S.2d 1 (1st Dep't 1960).

18   These matters are elaborated in Commentaries C3016:6 and 7 on McKinney's CPLR 3016. For discussion of the present (and much diminished) status of quasi in rem jurisdiction, see § 104.

19   CPLR 4511(a).

foreign law, the court "shall" take judicial notice. Including the substance of the foreign law in the pleading comes close, by itself, to fulfilling all three of those requirements. The failure to plead foreign law can be excused and need prove no more fatal, or serious, than any other omission under CPLR 3015 or 3016. In Edwards v. Erie Coach Lines Co.,[20] the Court of Appeals stressed that "the fact that the court can on its own volunteer to give the foreign law judicial notice under CPLR 4511(b) should further divest CPLR 3016(e) of any undue rigidity."

(f)   Schedule of goods or services. Whenever the plaintiff's claim involves the furnishing of goods, materials, or services in a significant quantity, the plaintiff can make use of CPLR 3016(f) and include in the complaint a schedule of the various items with agreed price, date of sale or performance, etc. Using such a detailed schedule has the effect of requiring the defendant to address in the answer and deny specifically whatever item in the schedule the defendant disputes. A general denial in this instance is inadequate to contest any individual item.[21] But if the defendant's position is that it had no dealings with the plaintiff at all—e.g., that the sales were to a different person— or if the defendant assumes any other posture going to the entirety of the claim and not just disputing individual components, the specific denials stipulated by CPLR 3016(f) are not required.[22]

When the CPLR 3016(f) schedule is used, the complaint must be verified, which in turn requires verification of the answer.

(g)   No-fault requirement. Because the no-fault law, which took effect in 1974, precludes ordinary tort suit in personal injury vehicle cases in New York unless certain criteria are met, CPLR 3016(g) commands that the complaint in every such action allege that the requirement has been satisfied. Either "serious injury"[23] or "economic loss greater than basic economic loss"[24] can be shown. Satisfaction of the requirement need merely be "stated" in the pleading. The detail needed to satisfy the no-fault requirement is the province of the bill of particulars.

(h)   Not-for-profit entities. CPLR 3016(h) is the concomitant of section 720–a of the Not-For-Profit Corporation Law, which is designed to expand the immunities of uncompensated officials of not-for-profit organizations by excluding suit against them except for acts of gross negligence or for conduct intended to cause harm.[25] Subdivision (h) requires the complaint in such an action to be verified and to allege whether it is based on such conduct.[26]

The point made at the end of section 215, above, about keeping at hand a small reprint of CPLR 3015 for quick consultation when drawing a complaint, applies to CPLR 3016, too. Its minutiae are hard to remember and a handy check list is helpful. Keeping

---

[20]   Edwards v. Erie Coach Lines Co., 17 N.Y.3d 306, 328, 929 N.Y.S.2d 41, 50, 952 N.E.2d 1033, 1042 (2011).

[21]   Duban v. Platt, 23 A.D.2d 660, 257 N.Y.S.2d 109 (2d Dep't 1965), aff'd, 17 N.Y.2d 526, 267 N.Y.S.2d 907, 215 N.E.2d 164 (1966).

[22]   Edwin F. Guth Co. v. Gurland, 246 A.D. 67, 284 N.Y.S. 333 (1st Dep't 1935).

[23]   This is defined in Ins. Law § 5102(d). A comprehensive discussion of the categories of serious injury under the no-fault law and the pattern charges for each category are contained in New York Pattern Jury Instructions—Civil, Introductory Statement preceding 2:75 and in sections 2:88A through 2:88G.

[24]   This is defined in Ins. Law § 5102(a).

[25]   See Commentary C3016:11 on McKinney's CPLR 3016.

[26]   See Kamchi v. Weissman, 125 A.D.3d 142, 160–62, 1 N.Y.S.3d 169, 183–84 (2d Dep't 2014) (discussing interplay between CPLR 3016(h) and motion to dismiss under CPLR 3211(a)(11)).

the list in a side drawer or under the glass top of a desk can make it a convenient tool at pleading-drafting time. And putting a laminating sheet over it can lend the list an elegance that can make a deep impression on a client, especially a naive one.

C. DEMAND FOR RELIEF

Table of Sections

§ 217.   Demand for Relief; "Wherefore" Clause

§ 217. Demand for Relief; "Wherefore" Clause

Subdivision (a) of CPLR 3017 provides for the relief clause in pleadings. It requires that every pleading containing a cause of action, which of course includes the complaint, "shall contain a demand for the relief to which the pleader deems himself entitled."[1] In money actions, demand for a specific sum is commonly included,[2] except in personal injury and wrongful death actions, which are governed by a special provision in subdivision (c) to be discussed later. If the plaintiff expects to take a default judgment against the defendant in an action other than personal injury or wrongful death, a statement of the amount demanded is of course indispensable.[3]

The relief clause, often called the "wherefore" clause, appears at the end of the pleading. In a money action it's popularly called the "ad damnum."

The relief clause does not count in determining whether a cause of action is stated[4] except perhaps in those cases in which a showing of damage is a substantive element of the claim. Even a prayer for the wrong relief does not vitiate the pleading as long as the pleading otherwise states a cause of action recognized by the law. Relief of different kinds may be requested, a natural corollary of the permission that CPLR 3014 offers to plead inconsistent claims. Relief may also be asked for in the alternative, another parallel to CPLR 3014.

Subdivision (a) of CPLR 3017 authorizes the court to grant "any type of relief within its jurisdiction appropriate to the proof whether or not demanded, imposing such terms as may be just." The only stated exception is where the defendant defaults. There, the only relief that can be had against the defendant in a default judgment is that of which she had due notice prior to the default.[5]

This authorization to grant even undemanded relief if the proof supports it is generous. It can be cited to justify legal relief where equitable relief was asked for, and vice-versa—even relief of a different kind or category than that originally demanded— as long as the pleading gave notice of the underlying transaction and covered the elements of the cause of action (thus precluding the adverse party from claiming

---

[1]   CPLR 3017(a).

[2]   It's not indispensable in all situations. See Silvestris v. Silvestris, 24 A.D.2d 247, 265 N.Y.S.2d 173 (1st Dep't 1965); Commentary C3017:1 on McKinney's CPLR 3017.

[3]   CPLR 3215(b).

[4]   Lehmann v. Kingston Plaza, Inc., 44 Misc. 2d 63, 252 N.Y.S.2d 964 (Sup. Ct., Ulster County 1964).

[5]   CPLR 3215(b).

prejudice).[6] When both legal and equitable relief are demanded and the plaintiff on the facts can't have both, the ultimate choice of which it's to be is with the court.[7]

For a while it was held that a verdict in a money action could not exceed the amount demanded in the complaint.[8] In one well known case, Naujokas v. H. Frank Carey High School,[9] the jury, apparently unaware that the complaint demanded only $50,000,[10] brought in a verdict for $250,000. The appellate division would not permit judgment for more than the $50,000.[11]

Naujokas and similar cases were overruled by the New York Court of Appeals in Loomis v. Civetta Corinno Const. Corp.,[12] where the court held that the plaintiff may be allowed to keep a verdict that exceeds the amount demanded in the complaint as long as there is no prejudice to the defendant.[13] An example of prejudice would be the case in which the original demand in a tort case is within the defendant's insurance coverage, but the verdict exceeds it. In this situation, the defendant would have lost her chance to appear through a lawyer of her own choosing to protect her personal liability.[14]

The lesson under *Naujokas* and similar cases was that the tort race was to the greedy; that an endeavor to assess a tort claim realistically could hurt the client, while the addition of nothing—one small zero—in the demand clause would supply a figure that, however voracious, would cover all possible contingencies. Indeed, because of cases like *Naujokas*, inflated demands were as much the product of caution as of greed. Though it should not abate caution, the *Loomis* case should at least remove the fear that sent monetary demands in tort cases into outer space.

An amendment to raise the sum demanded in advance of the trial, and even at the trial itself but in advance of the verdict, while not granted for the mere asking, is less controversial. As long as prejudice is absent, the amendment is permissible,[15] and prejudice at this stage is less likely than at the post-verdict stage.

CPLR 3017(a) can't be used to force on a pleader relief the pleader doesn't want. In Ross v. Ross,[16] for example, W sued H for a separation and found herself awarded a

---

[6]　See Commentaries C3017:4–6 on McKinney's CPLR 3017.

[7]　Ungewitter v. Toch, 31 A.D.2d 583, 294 N.Y.S.2d 1013 (3d Dep't 1968), aff'd, 26 N.Y.2d 687, 308 N.Y.S.2d 858, 257 N.E.2d 40 (1970).

[8]　Since the complaint itself can't state a specific sum today, reference in the discussion that follows may be taken to be to the amount revealed in the plaintiff's demand pursuant to the defendant's request for a figure under the special procedure now set up in CPLR 3017(c).

[9]　Naujokas v. H. Frank Carey High School, 33 A.D.2d 703, 306 N.Y.S.2d 195 (2d Dep't 1969).

[10]　There was at the time no uniform rule in New York about whether a jury could be told the amount demanded in the complaint. See Williams v. Long Island R. R., 41 A.D.2d 940, 343 N.Y.S.2d 700 (2d Dep't 1973); Commentary C3017:1 on McKinney's CPLR 3017. The Court of Appeals afterwards held in Tate by McMahon v. Colabello, 58 N.Y.2d 84, 459 N.Y.S.2d 422, 445 N.E.2d 1101 (1983), that amounts could be suggested to the jury during summation.

[11]　The same conclusion, but involving smaller figures, was reached in Wyman v. Morone, 33 A.D.2d 168, 306 N.Y.S.2d 115 (3d Dep't 1969). Support for the result was found in the Advisory Committee's notes, 1st Rep. Leg. Doc. No.6(b), p.68 (1957), but it flew in the face of the plain language of CPLR 3017(a).

[12]　Loomis v. Civetta Corinno Const. Corp., 54 N.Y.2d 18, 444 N.Y.S.2d 571, 429 N.E.2d 90 (1981).

[13]　See the lead note in NYSLD No. 265. A motion to amend to conform the pleadings to the proof under CPLR 3025(c)—in this case to conform to both the proof and the verdict—would be the procedural step for the plaintiff to take in this situation.

[14]　See Commentary C3017:7 on McKinney's CPLR 3017.

[15]　See § 237.

[16]　Ross v. Ross, 84 A.D.2d 569, 443 N.Y.S.2d 419 (2d Dep't 1981), aff'd, 55 N.Y.2d 999, 449 N.Y.S.2d 481, 434 N.E.2d 717 (1982).

divorce she didn't ask for. Her proof would have supported a divorce, but it was H who asked for it. H wanted to remarry, but abandonment was the ground and H was the abandoner, so he wasn't entitled to a divorce. Only W was, but she didn't want it. Reversing, the appellate division vacated the divorce that W earned but did not want, and H wanted but did not earn.[17] The case supports the theory that when a movable object is displaced by a resistible force, the plaintiff appeals.

Actions for personal injury and/or wrongful death are subject to the special requirements of subdivision (c) of CPLR 3017. CPLR 3017(c) prohibits the plaintiff from pleading a specific amount of monetary damages in those categories of action, but provides a procedure whereby the defendant can request that plaintiff set forth the amount sought in a "supplemental demand." If the supplemental demand is not served within fifteen days, "the court, on motion, may order that it be served."

If the action is in the supreme court, the plaintiff must state that the amount sought exceeds the jurisdiction of all lower courts that might otherwise have had jurisdiction.[18]

As noted in the federal chapter at the end of the book,[19] the supplemental demand procedure is often invoked to ascertain if the amount in controversy exceeds $75,000 and will support removal of the action to federal court. In Ardelean v. Affuso,[20] where removal of the action did not appear to be an option, defendant nonetheless requested a supplemental demand from the plaintiff. Plaintiff responded that "[a] jury will decide the total damages to which the [p]laintiff is entitled to at the time of trial . . . ." The court ruled that this response was insufficient to comply with the statute and ordered plaintiff to provide a specific sum.

In addition to being able to ascertain if the action qualifies for removal, there are good reasons for a defendant to ascertain as early as possible how much the plaintiff is seeking. If there is "excess" insurance in the picture, for example, it may be necessary to determine whether the amount sought surpasses the figure at which the excess insurance kicks in. Another example may be to enable the defendant or its insurer to assess a proper "reserve" to earmark for the case. The defendant may also want to lure plaintiff into serving an exorbitant demand, which can then be communicated to the jury in an attempt to demonstrate plaintiff's greed. That may explain the vague nature of plaintiff's original response in *Ardelean*.

Some cases addressing the prior restrictions on pleading damages, which were limited to medical and dental malpractice actions and actions against a municipal corporation, held that a violation of the CPLR 3017(c) pleading restriction can be cured with a mere amendment striking the reference to the demand,[21] but the imposition of a money sanction in an appropriate sum might better implement this aspect of CPLR 3017(c). Whether CPLR 3017(c)'s restriction on including a specific sum in the complaint should also be applied to bar the mention of a specific sum in the parties' opening or

---

[17]   This is somewhat akin to the brief life enjoyed by the "reverse summary judgment" in matrimonial actions, for which see § 278.

[18]   CPLR 3017(c). The purpose is to implement the state's policy of having a money claim brought in the lowest court that can entertain it. See § 12.

[19]   See § 619 (Practitioner's Edition).

[20]   Ardelean v. Affuso, 35 Misc. 3d 476, 939 N.Y.S.2d 689 (Sup. Ct., Queens County 2012) (SPR 244:1).

[21]   See, e.g., Twitchell v. MacKay, 78 A.D.2d 125, 434 N.Y.S.2d 516 (4th Dep't 1980).

closing to a jury was the subject of some dispute, and conflict,[22] but was finally resolved by a 2004 amendment of CPLR 4016(b) allowing the mention in the closing statement but barring it in the opening.[23]

The issue has even arisen as to whether a failure to include the demand in a CPLR 305(b) notice—when the notice is used at the outset instead of a complaint—makes the notice defective. The purpose of the CPLR 305(b) device is to set the stage for a default judgment without putting the plaintiff to the burden of drawing a complaint, so it's a contradiction to suggest that the notice can ever omit the monetary demand. CPLR 305(b) still bars it in medical malpractice actions, however, for which two sources can be credited: (1) it's the category that first inspired the restriction, and (2) the legislature failed to coordinate CPLR 3017(c), governing the complaint, with CPLR 305(b), governing the notice. It has been held in any event that the omission is not jurisdictional and can be cured by amendment.[24] Given the rigidity surrounding the CPLR 305(b) notice, these cases should not be relied upon until the Court of Appeals addresses the issue.[25]

A special reference to the role that CPLR 3017(c) plays in court of claims practice is necessary here. The Court of Claims Act has its own instruction in point, in section 11(b). It requires that "the total sum claimed" be set forth. It had no exception such as CPLR 3017(c) makes for the personal injury and wrongful death claims, so practitioners versed in the CPLR, but not at home in court of claims practice, quite often brought their CPLR experience with them and omitted a monetary demand in court of claims actions. Asserting that the CPLR must defer to the Court of Claims Act when there's a conflict, the Court of Appeals in Kolnacki v. State[26] held that the omission of the monetary demand was a jurisdictional defect, uncurable by amendment. For that technical pleading omission alone, the whole claim was lost in *Kolnacki*, earning the case a bad press and a prompt overruling by the legislature, which amended section 11(b) to except specifically from its demand requirement all wrongful death and personal injury actions. In all but those two actions, however, the "total sum claimed" must still be pleaded in the court of claims. Attorneys must remember that; *Kolnacki* remains on standby to condemn omissions of the sum in any other than the two excluded categories.[27]

D. ELECTION OF REMEDIES

Table of Sections

§ 218.   Election of Remedies; Separate Actions

§ 219.   Election of Remedies; Within an Action

---

[22]   Bechard v. Eisinger, 105 A.D.2d 939, 481 N.Y.S.2d 906 (3d Dep't 1984), said it would be and barred the mention. Braun v. Ahmed, 127 A.D.2d 418, 515 N.Y.S.2d 473 (2d Dep't 1987), went the other way.

[23]   See NY PJI 2:277A ("Damages—Comment by Counsel During Closing Remarks").

[24]   Day v. Davis, 47 A.D.3d 750, 850 N.Y.S.2d 189 (2d Dep't 2008); Sherk v. Sherk, 37 A.D.3d 1062, 829 N.Y.S.2d 774 (4th Dep't 2007); Premo v. Cornell, 71 A.D.2d 223, 423 N.Y.S.2d 64 (3d Dep't 1979).

[25]   See § 60.

[26]   Kolnacki v. State, 8 N.Y.3d 277, 832 N.Y.S.2d 481, 864 N.E.2d 611 (2007) (NYSLD No. 568).

[27]   See Commentary C3013:15A on McKinney's CPLR 3013; (SPR 188:3).

§ 218. Election of Remedies; Separate Actions

The doctrine of the election of remedies is related to res judicata but more by affinity than by blood. Res judicata requires a final judgment on the merits.[1] The election of remedies doesn't. The doctrine becomes relevant, although today not necessarily operative, when a plaintiff with two or more remedies to choose from in respect of the same wrong sues on only one. The remedy sued on is deemed the one elected, and technically speaking, the election of the one bars later suit on the others. When the doctrine was rigidly applied, the election was deemed made as soon as the complaint was served. But there is little occasion today to treat the doctrine technically. It is "a harsh and arbitrary principle designed only to prevent vexatious litigation,"[2] and the courts have held that it should not be extended.[3]

If a plaintiff with theories A and B available to support a claim sues only on theory A, and the case is disposed of on its merits, it is the doctrine of res judicata that bars later suit on theory B. This is because res judicata—in this regard now known as "claim preclusion"—is conclusive "not only as to any matters actually litigated . . . but also as to any that might have been . . . litigated."[4] Since theory B could also have been litigated in the first action, final judgment on the merits in that action, albeit only with regard to theory A, invokes res judicata to preclude later suit on theory B. But res judicata is not on the scene when no final judgment has been rendered on the merits, and that's where the election of remedies doctrine may become relevant.

The general rule is that not just any final judgment invokes res judicata, only a final judgment on the merits. This led to some election of remedies cases difficult to square with res judicata, mainly because of the occasional difficulty one meets in determining precisely what a "merits" result is. Judge Cardozo wrote that

> An election of remedies presupposes a right to elect . . . . If in truth there is but one remedy, and not a choice between two, a fruitless recourse to a remedy withheld does not bar recourse thereafter to the remedy allowed.[5]

That would presumably mean that if the plaintiff didn't really have theory A available, even though she thought she did, a dismissal on ground A would not, under the election doctrine, preclude later suit on ground B. But shouldn't the res judicata doctrine do the precluding in that case? That was the conflict. Fitzgerald v. Title Guarantee & Trust Co.[6] and Smith v. Kirkpatrick[7] illustrate.

In *Fitzgerald*, P's first suit had been in contract and was held barred by the statute of limitations. So P turned around and brought a second action for the same relief, but grounded it on fraud, a fraud claim being alive under the accrual-at-discovery rule.[8] The court sustained the claim, holding that it couldn't be barred by the election of remedies

---

[1]   See § 443.

[2]   Strong v. Reeves, 280 A.D. 301, 305, 114 N.Y.S.2d 97, 101 (3d Dep't 1952), aff'd, 306 N.Y. 666, 116 N.E.2d 497 (1953).

[3]   Smith v. Kirkpatrick, 305 N.Y. 66, 111 N.E.2d 209 (1953).

[4]   Schuylkill Fuel Corp. v. B. & C. Nieberg Realty Corp., 250 N.Y. 304, 306–7, 165 N.E. 456, 457 (1929). See § 447.

[5]   Schenck v. State Line Telephone Co., 238 N.Y. 308, 311, 144 N.E. 592, 593 (1924).

[6]   Fitzgerald v. Title Guarantee & Trust Co., 290 N.Y. 376, 49 N.E.2d 489 (1943).

[7]   *Smith*, 305 N.Y. at 69–71, 111 N.E.2d at 211–12.

[8]   CPLR 213(8), 203(g); see § 43.

doctrine because since P had no live contract claim when he first sued, he couldn't have "elected" the nonexistent remedy.

Similarly, in *Kirkpatrick*, where P's first action in contract was dismissed because the contract was oral and was barred by the statute of frauds, a second suit in quantum meruit was allowed. The Court held that all the former action determined was that a contract could not be proved, not that no services were rendered or goods delivered. The *Kirkpatrick* case does endeavor to square the result with the doctrine of res judicata by finding the "causes of action" different, but in the ultimate sense, P in *Kirkpatrick* had but one cause of action for services rendered, whether based on contract or quantum meruit.

The Court of Appeals had second thoughts about cases like *Fitzgerald* and *Kirkpatrick* and overruled them, closing this gap between the election and res judicata doctrines in a pair of cases handed down on the same day: O'Brien v. City of Syracuse[9] and Smith v. Russell Sage College.[10]

In *O'Brien*, P had brought an action involving a public taking of property, but lost it when he couldn't establish the taking. P then brought the second action in trespass. The Court held that any claim based on a trespass arising out of the acts involved in the earlier action would be barred under the doctrine of res judicata.

Russell Sage involved a statute of limitations point analogous to that in *Fitzgerald*. But in *Russell Sage*, P did have, during the first action, knowledge of the facts on which he sought to predicate the second action. What P should have done, said the *Russell Sage* court, was move to amend the complaint during the first action to add the additional claim there.

One lesson from these two cases is that if there is yet time to amend in action number one, as when knowledge of the additional facts comes to the plaintiff during the pretrial stage, the plaintiff should seek the amendment forthwith and will forfeit the claim if she doesn't. A corollary, however, is that if knowledge of the additional facts does not reach the plaintiff in time, a second action on the new count should be permissible.[11]

The main lesson to the lawyer is that the omission of a count or ground or theory today, whether or not amounting to a forfeiture under an "election of remedies" label, may amount to a forfeiture under the res judicata banner and hurts just as much. In every suit on an oral contract (the *Kirkpatrick* situation), for example, the plaintiff should therefore consider joining a quantum meruit count if goods have been delivered or services rendered, whatever the chance the quantum meruit claim has of success under the language of the particular statute of frauds involved.

And in any action on any claim, the plaintiff should sift all possible bases and—unless she has some well considered tactical reason in mind—join them all to be sure that a statute of limitations advantage available on any one of them (the *Fitzgerald* situation) is not omitted.

The *Kirkpatrick* and *Fitzgerald* cases applied the election doctrine too generously, doing so in apparent fidelity to the legislature's wish to avoid the harshness of the

---

[9]   O'Brien v. City of Syracuse, 54 N.Y.2d 353, 445 N.Y.S.2d 687, 429 N.E.2d 1158 (1981).

[10]   Smith v. Russell Sage College, 54 N.Y.2d 185, 445 N.Y.S.2d 68, 429 N.E.2d 746 (1981).

[11]   The *O'Brien* and *Russell Sage* cases are further treated in § 447. They are also the subject of a lead note in NYSLD No. 267.

doctrine, a harshness manifest in a number of old cases. The legislature overruled those old cases one by one over the years. Each involved a special situation and the aggregate of the statutes doing the overruling are now gathered up in CPLR 3002,[12] which is simply a list of a few prime instances of legislative relief. Treating CPLR 3002 in more detail and footnoting the cases overruled, its subdivisions run this way:

(a) Action against several persons. If P has a claim against both X and Y jointly and severally, suit and even rendition of judgment against X does not bar later suit against Y.[13] Satisfaction of the X judgment will bar the Y suit, of course, because the law does not allow duplicate recoveries. The initial joinder of both X and Y, which is of course permissible,[14] would avoid such issues.

(b) Agent and undisclosed principal. This involves the agency area and assumes that substantively both the agent and the undisclosed (but later revealed) principal are liable to P. P's suit and unsatisfied judgment against one will not bar later suit against the other.[15] Again, satisfaction of the first judgment does bar the second suit.

(c) Conversion and contract. Theft from P gives P a conversion claim against the thief, but in that situation New York law also allows P in effect to "ratify" the conversion and sue instead in contract on the theory of an implied obligation to repay or return the thing taken.[16] This can supply a statute of limitations advantage because while the conversion ground is an injury to property and gets only three years,[17] the contract ground gets six.[18] When P's claim exists against several persons, CPLR 3002(c) becomes operative. It provides that if P sues one of the liable persons and recovers judgment on either ground, and the judgment is not satisfied, later suit against any of the others is still permissible on either or both grounds.[19] Again, satisfaction of a judgment, meaning that P has been recompensed for his damages, bars further suit by P against anyone. If the first judgment is unsatisfied, however, note that CPLR 3002(c) applies to permit the second suit only against the previously unsued persons. It does not authorize a second suit against X on the conversion ground after rendition of judgment against him on the contract ground, or vice-versa. Sound initial practice would avoid all of these questions: the attorney should make it a general rule to join all liable persons and all possible theories in one action.[20]

(d) On contract and to reform. If P sues D on a written contract and does not recover, he may afterwards sue to reform that contract and then sue on it as reformed.[21] Without this provision, several doctrines might bar the later reformation action, including the election of remedies and res judicata doctrines. If P sues on a contract and does recover, he may not ordinarily sue later for a reformation.

---

[12]   See the discussion in the *Kirkpatrick* case, 305 N.Y. at 74, 111 N.E.2d at 214.

[13]   CPLR 3002(a), overruling Fowler v. Bowery Sav. Bank, 113 N.Y. 450, 21 N.E. 172 (1889).

[14]   CPLR 1002(b).

[15]   CPLR 3002(b), overruling Georgi v. Texas Co., 225 N.Y. 410, 122 N.E. 238 (1919).

[16]   Dentists' Supply Co. of N.Y. v. Cornelius, 281 A.D. 306, 119 N.Y.S.2d 570 (1st Dep't 1953), aff'd, 306 N.Y. 624, 116 N.E.2d 238.

[17]   CPLR 214(4).

[18]   CPLR 213(2).

[19]   CPLR 3002(c), overruling Terry v. Munger, 121 N.Y. 161, 24 N.E. 272 (1890).

[20]   Compare Hahl v. Sugo, 169 N.Y. 109, 62 N.E. 135 (1901).

[21]   CPLR 3002(d), overruling Steinbach v. Relief Fire Ins. Co., 77 N.Y. 498, 1879 WL 10734 (1879).

(e) *Damages plus rescission.* The old case of Weigel v. Cook[22] held that in an action to rescind an agreement, the plaintiff could not also seek damages. It overlooked that rescission alone might not be enough because of D's conduct; that damages might also be necessary to restore P to status quo; and that a refusal to allow damages plus rescission could be a windfall to the wrongdoer. The legislature recognized this and with CPLR 3002(e) and its predecessor overruled the *Weigel* case. Thus, where D's fraud induced the contract, entitling P to rescind it but also causing P monetary injury, which rescission alone would not requite, P may seek (and get) both in one action. They are not to be deemed inconsistent remedies.

(f) *Vendee's lien.* The lien a buyer gets when she buys real property was at one time deemed forfeit if the contract of sale was rescinded. CPLR 3002(f) provides that the buyer's suit to rescind or otherwise disaffirm the agreement does not automatically forfeit the lien. Old caselaw[23] had made the lien wholly contingent on the contract, and disaffirmance of the contract was held to carry with it destruction of the lien. CPLR 3002(f) overrules that.

We can conclude this discussion with the lesson taught by Hahl v. Sugo,[24] in which P brought and won an ejectment action based on the encroachment of D's wall on P's land. An ejectment judgment is enforceable by an execution delivered to the sheriff,[25] but the sheriff in *Hahl* returned it unsatisfied because he found it "impracticable" to enforce. P then brought a new action seeking equitable relief, which, had it succeeded, would have earned P a judgment directing D to remove the encroachment himself under penalty of contempt. The equitable action was held barred, however, because of P's earlier election of the ejectment count.

The lesson is that it's easy enough to ask for the equitable relief to begin with. If D tries to defeat the equitable relief by pleading the adequacy of the legal (the ejectment) remedy, P should cite the *Hahl* case. The warning, once again, is to make it a rule to join in the very first action brought all counts, grounds, and theories that support one's claim,[26] but the plaintiff must also be aware that joining the legal and equitable demands will result in the waiver of trial by jury on the legal one.[27]

It will be noted that all of the discussion in this section has concerned the situation in which the plaintiff did not bring suit on all possible grounds or against all of the arguably liable persons. When the plaintiff does join all claims and defendants in one action, a different and much easier election of remedies problem arises, if it arises at all. It's discussed in the next section.

§ 219. Election of Remedies; Within an Action

The majority of the prior section discussed the more serious election of remedies situation: that in which not everything was interposed in the first action, thereby

---

[22] Weigel v. Cook, 237 N.Y. 136, 142 N.E. 444 (1923).

[23] Davis v. William Rosenzweig Realty Operating Co., 192 N.Y. 128, 84 N.E. 943 (1908).

[24] *Hahl*, 169 N.Y. at 116–18, 62 N.E. at 137–38.

[25] CPLR 5102.

[26] Another illustration of why all possible grounds should be joined at the outset appears in Application of Galich, 59 Misc. 2d 836, 300 N.Y.S.2d 670 (Monroe County Ct. 1969), where omission of a fraud count in exclusive reliance on a contract claim apparently resulted in a later forfeiture of the judgment when the defendant went bankrupt. See § 219.

[27] See § 378.

generating a second one. Here we deal with the case in which everything has been joined—all claims, grounds, theories, counts, and persons potentially liable.

If in this situation the several counts asserted are consistent, no election of remedies problem should arise at all. If, for example, P sues D for injuries sustained in an accident, and P can show that D was negligent, breached a warranty, and violated a statutory duty, P can interpose all of those bases of liability. At no time will she have to elect among them; the remedies are consistent.

The sensitive situation, therefore, is one in which the several theories or demands for relief are inconsistent. There is explicit CPLR authority for an inconsistent pleading[1] but not for an inconsistent judgment. If the remedies sought are mutually exclusive, the plaintiff will have to elect from among them at some point in the case. If the plaintiff does not voluntarily elect, the trial judge will determine what that point is.[2] Probably the only safe conclusion one can reach is that the election will have to be made before judgment. The judgment should not ordinarily embody inconsistent items of relief although one occasionally does encounter such a judgment.[3] But the election can be reasonably postponed right up to the point of judgment.

Suppose, for example, that P is suing D to rescind a contract for fraud or for specific performance in the alternative in the event that the fraud claim is not sustained. Rescission and specific performance are about as inconsistent as demands can be. Yet the trial judge can postpone the election until after the trial. The trial, in fact, may manifest that the plaintiff has no election after all. It may find, for example, that the defendant is not guilty of fraud, which would mean that rescission is barred, leaving only the plaintiff's alternative demand for specific performance. The fact-finding process, in other words, can be allowed to precede the election whenever there is any doubt about what the plaintiff has to elect from. And if the facts found do sustain both items of relief, the election can be compelled after trial but before judgment. The election of remedies within an action is left almost entirely to judicial discretion.

A plaintiff who makes it a practice to join all available theories and grounds may realize a fringe benefit and become the beneficiary of an unanticipated advantage. Conversely, the plaintiff may become the victim of an unsuspected detriment when some grounds are omitted. Application of Galich[4] can illustrate. P sued in contract for goods delivered and won, getting a money judgment against D. But because it was based only on contract, it was afterwards discharged in D's bankruptcy. Had it been based on fraud, it would have survived the discharge. The omission of the fraud ground, which may have been meritorious, therefore resulted in the demise of a judgment that might otherwise have remained enforceable.

---

[1]   CPLR 3014. See § 214.

[2]   Baratta v. Kozlowski, 94 A.D.2d 454, 464 N.Y.S.2d 803 (2d Dep't 1983).

[3]   A replevin judgment, for example, recites the money value of the chattel so that the sheriff can enforce it like a money judgment if the chattel can't be found, CPLR 7108(a), 5102, although of course a recovery of the chattel itself is inconsistent with a money award for its value.

[4]   Application of Galich, 59 Misc. 2d 836, 300 N.Y.S.2d 670 (Monroe County Ct. 1969).

E. SPLITTING

Table of Sections

§ 220.   Splitting

§ 220. Splitting

The splitting doctrine is related to the election of remedies. While the election doctrine generally deals with a claim having different theories or counts, the splitting doctrine is usually concerned with a money claim sued on in spurts instead of at one time.[1] If P has a money claim against D and sues for only part of what is presently due, P forfeits the rest under the splitting rule. A simple example is where a landlord sues a monthly tenant for rent for only one month although several months rent is due at the time. An action like that splits the claim and forfeits the part due but not joined at the time of suit.[2] This is the law's approach to all installment contracts: suit must join all installments due at the moment of commencement. Amounts not due at commencement but accruing later, albeit under the same agreement, of course cannot be joined at that time and so are not deemed split off; they can ground a later action.[3] If additional installments fall due while the action is pending, it is usually a good idea to move to amend the complaint to include them.

The main question to ask in order to resolve a splitting problem is the old one about whether the plaintiff has but one cause of action or several. If several—and P is sure of it!—P may safely sue on them separately or in any event omit from suit on one the amounts due on the other. Thus, where P's two claims against D arise out of two entirely separate contracts, P's suit on one is not a splitting and therefore not a waiver of the other.[4] Of course, a wrong guess about whether P has one or several causes of action can result in a splitting, which suggests that P make it a practice to resolve all doubt in favor of joining all sums due from D even if they probably emanate from separate transactions and constitute separate causes of action. Even if separate and distinct, the joinder is permissible[5] and obviously preferable to the inadvertent forfeiture that the splitting rule threatens.

If P sues D on a quasi in rem jurisdictional foundation, attaching D's property but getting no personam jurisdiction, P's judgment will be effective only to the extent of the property attached.[6] If the property does not suffice to pay P's whole claim, P may bring later suit for the balance. In this situation, the earlier judgment is not deemed a splitting or given any other kind of res judicata treatment in the second action.[7]

Since the splitting doctrine was designed to prevent unreasonable harassment, it will not be applied when good reason is shown for omitting part of the claim from an

---

[1]   The distinction is a handy one, but not sharp. The Restatement, for example, also describes as a "splitting" an attempted use, in a second action, of "grounds or theories" omitted from the first. See Restatement (Second) of Judgments § 25 (1982).

[2]   See Maloney v. McMillan Book Co., 52 Misc. 2d 1006, 277 N.Y.S.2d 499 (Syracuse City Ct. 1967).

[3]   See Industrial Development Foundation of Auburn, N. Y., Inc. v. U.S. Hoffman Machinery Corp., 16 A.D.2d 600, 229 N.Y.S.2d 857 (4th Dep't 1962).

[4]   Secor v. Sturgis, 16 N.Y. 548, 1858 WL 7351 (1858).

[5]   CPLR 601; see § 126.

[6]   See §§ 104 and 113.

[7]   Benadon v. Antonio, 10 A.D.2d 40, 197 N.Y.S.2d 1 (1st Dep't 1960).

earlier action. Where, for example, a judgment was duly obtained and paid in an action to enforce shareholders' liability against A and B based on their ownership of a certain number of shares, and it was later learned that A and B in fact owned more shares, a second suit, based on ownership of the additional shares, was allowed. Tracing the ownership had been made difficult by A and B themselves because of complicated assignments and bookkeeping entries. Finding that if the defendants were vexed by the second suit it was not in this instance an unreasonable vexing, the Court held that the reason for the splitting rule, and hence the rule itself, was inapplicable.[8]

The splitting rule will also be set aside when a duality of actions can be explained by the presence of different parties in interest, even though it might apply were there but a single party in interest. Where, for example, an insured is paid for part of a loss by an insurer, and then sues the person who caused the loss for the uninsured part, a later suit by the insurer to recover the part that it paid will not be deemed a splitting, even if prosecuted nominally in the name of the insured.[9]

The benefit of the splitting doctrine is subject to waiver. An illustration is where D objects to the court's hearing a certain part of P's claim for the reason that that part is the subject of a separate action: D waives the doctrine and can't assert it in the other action.[10] A waiver has also been held to result when the defendant acquiesces in multiple suits. Since the purpose of the rule is "to protect defendants from being vexed by multiple suits, it stands to reason that acquiescence by the defendant will work a waiver," as it did in a case in which P brought two actions against D arising out of the same transaction and D went along with this, making no motion to consolidate the two or to dismiss one based on the pendency of the other.[11]

F. THE ANSWER

Table of Sections

§ 221.   The Answer; Denials
§ 222.   Marked Pleadings
§ 223.   Affirmative Defenses

§ 221. The Answer; Denials

The answer is the defendant's pleading. It has several chores to perform.[1] The first is found in CPLR 3018(a), which requires the defendant to respond to the complaint with denials or admissions.

---

[8]   White v. Adler, 289 N.Y. 34, 43 N.E.2d 798, 142 A.L.R. 898 (1942).

[9]   See Clarcq v. Chamberlain Mobile Home Transport, Inc., 58 Misc. 2d 227, 294 N.Y.S.2d 550 (Sup. Ct., Monroe County 1968).

[10]   Stoner v. Culligan, Inc., 32 A.D.2d 170, 300 N.Y.S.2d 966 (3d Dep't 1969).

[11]   Brown v. Lockwood, 76 A.D.2d 721, 740, 432 N.Y.S.2d 186, 199 (2d Dep't 1980).

[1]   The rules to be discussed in this section apply not only to the defendant's answer to the complaint, but to all responsive pleadings, like a plaintiff's reply to a counterclaim, a co-defendant's answer to a cross-claim when an answer is demanded, etc. For purposes of this treatment, all responsive pleading steps are discussed in terms of the defendant answering the complaint.

There are three kinds of denials:

1.   If the defendant knows at first hand that the allegation is false, the denial is outright, without any qualifying language: "Defendant denies the allegations of paragraphs 2 and 3 of the complaint."

2.   If the defendant does not know at first hand, but has information (and believes it) suggesting the falsity of an allegation, the denial is on information and belief: "Upon information and belief, defendant denies the allegations of paragraphs 5 and 6 of the complaint."

3.   If the defendant has no knowledge one way or the other and can't say whether the allegation is true or false, the denial is of knowledge or information sufficient to form a belief: "Defendant denies knowledge or information sufficient to form a belief of the allegations of paragraphs 7 and 8 of the complaint."

Silence in a responsive pleading is an admission. In the above example, paragraphs 1 and 4 of the 8 paragraph complaint, not having been addressed by the answer, are deemed admitted.

Whichever form of denial is used, the plaintiff has the burden of proving the matter denied. And under a denial, whatever its form, the defendant is entitled at the trial to disprove any fact the plaintiff is required to prove.

Denials must be made in good faith. A denial of knowledge or information sufficient to form a belief of something the defendant must know one way or the other can lead to trouble for the defendant although the consequences are not clear. If the denials lend an aura of sham to the whole of the defendant's posture in the litigation, they may be deemed to go to the crux of his case and lead to summary judgment. That's what happened in effect in Dahlstrom v. Gemunder[2] where P sued an agent whose defense was that his principal had paid P. In a reply, P denied knowledge or information about the payment. The Court held that P may not just "close his eyes and ears for the purpose of avoiding knowledge and information,"[3] and P in *Dahlstrom* paid the ultimate price for doing so by being barred from any recovery. If P is genuinely in the dark, as where she is an executrix who had no personal part in the transaction involving her decedent, her denials of knowledge would not suggest bad faith and would not invoke consequences.

If the subject of a given allegation of a complaint is only presumptively in D's knowledge, the denial-of-knowledge form is permissible to meet the allegation. If some of the denials in that situation are good while some are bad and some borderline, there is not likely to be enough to support a summary judgment against the responsive pleader.[4] And there is no motion available under the CPLR to strike denials.[5] One risk the bad faith denier runs, however, is that the matter purportedly denied may be deemed admitted. It is not a common result, nor something the other side can assume will happen unless and until the court so holds, but even a denial made upon information and belief, type 2 on the list, may be deemed ineffective and the matter addressed

---

[2]   Dahlstrom v. Gemunder, 198 N.Y. 449, 92 N.E. 106 (1910). The *Dahlstrom* case involved a judgment on the pleadings, a remedy superseded under the CPLR by summary judgment under CPLR 3212.

[3]   *Dahlstrom*, 198 N.Y. at 454, 92 N.E. at 108.

[4]   See Kirschbaum v. Eschmann, 205 N.Y. 127, 98 N.E. 328 (1912).

[5]   Abrahao v. Perrault, 147 A.D.2d 824, 824–25, 537 N.Y.S.2d 913, 914 (3d Dep't 1989); see Commentary C3018:4 on McKinney's CPLR 3018 (suggesting possible remedies).

deemed admitted if the court is convinced that the denier had to know the fact first hand one way or the other.[6]

Certain other denial techniques are frowned on and can get the denier in trouble. One of these is the inconsistent-version denial. Here, the responsive pleader does not deny a fact directly, but sets forth a different version in the expectation that the reader will imply or infer a denial. This technique should not be used; it has been held inadequate to deny the fact[7] and may therefore result in its admission.

Another unacceptable ploy, related to the inconsistent-version denial, is the so-called "negative pregnant"—a negation pregnant with an admission. "The defect known as negative pregnant usually arises where the answer denies immaterial allegations of the complaint, which relate to time and place merely."[8] P pleads, for example, that at 9:51 p.m. on January 31, 2017, D drove a car against P at the corner of Holland and Delaware Avenues in Albany, New York, and D in response says that "D denies that at 9:51 p.m. on January 31, 2017, D drove a car against P at the corner of Holland and Delaware Avenues in Albany, New York." This is a negative pregnant. Perhaps the accident occurred at 9:30 p.m., or on February 1, 2017, or not at the very corner, etc. D is hiding behind an incident, hoping to evade the crux of the allegation because some inconsequential phase of it is not entirely accurate.

A "general denial," as it is popularly known, is usually a terse but total denial of everything contained in the complaint: "Defendant denies all the allegations of the complaint." If intended in good faith, it's acceptable, and if the complaint is terse, it may be appropriate. But the more precise and detailed the complaint is, the less appropriate the general denial becomes. If used against a complaint containing extended allegations, it may create the same aura of frivolity or sham that the wrong kind of specific denial, as previously discussed, can amount to. The courts frown on general denials in such instances, but unless the judge is convinced that it is patently phony, there is not likely to be any serious consequence appended to it,[9] except perhaps an award of costs.[10] Every now and again a judge who condemns a flippant general denial that doesn't intend to deny everything discourses on the limited remedies available against it.[11] If the context suggests that the general denial is totally frivolous, it can result in a money sanction.[12]

A good faith general denial, like any legitimate denial, enables the defendant to adduce evidence in respect of any matter of which the plaintiff has the burden of proof.[13]

In some instances, a general denial is explicitly forbidden. If a schedule of goods or services is used under CPLR 3016(f), for example,[14] the defendant must address

---

[6]   See City of Rochester v. Diksu Corp., 47 Misc. 2d 407, 262 N.Y.S.2d 690 (Sup. Ct., Monroe County 1965).

[7]   Smith v. Coe, 170 N.Y. 162, 63 N.E. 57 (1902).

[8]   Kellogg v. Freeland, 195 N.Y.S. 912, 913 (Sup. Ct., Erie County 1922).

[9]   See Doyle v. Buturlinsky, 26 A.D.2d 717, 271 N.Y.S.2d 349 (3d Dep't 1966).

[10]   See Rouse v. Champion Home Builders Co., 47 A.D.2d 584, 363 N.Y.S.2d 167 (4th Dep't 1975).

[11]   See Safa Turistik Esya Hali v. Dreier, N.Y.L.J., Jan. 15, 2003, at 19, col.5 (N.Y. City Civ. Ct.; Billings, J.) (SPR 133:1).

[12]   See § 414A.

[13]   Hoffstaedter v. Lichtenstein, 203 A.D. 494, 196 N.Y.S. 577 (1st Dep't 1922).

[14]   See § 216.

specifically any enumerated item that she wants to refute. Contractual conditions precedent and signatures on negotiable instruments must also be specifically denied.[15]

Although silence in response to a given allegation is an admission, admissions may also be made expressly: "D admits the allegation of paragraph 11 of the complaint." Silence is probably better. As a general rule, the only time a responsive pleader should make an admission expressly is when the allegation addressed also contains some matter that has to be denied. D should in that instance deny the allegations of the subject paragraph "except that D admits thus-and-so." In other words, single out the fact to be admitted and deny the rest. Don't do the reverse, singling out the matter to be denied and admitting the rest. That only increases the chance of an inadvertent admission.[16]

When a pleading requires no response, such as a reply, or an answer containing no affirmative claims, all of it, including any affirmative defenses it may contain, is deemed denied.[17]

If convenient and clear, a single numbered paragraph can contain D's responses to several paragraphs of the complaint. This does not violate the separate numbering requirement of CPLR 3014.[18]

§ 222. Marked Pleadings

A marked pleading is one that states an affirmative cause of action and whose numbered allegations each bear, usually in the left margin, some indication of what the adverse party's response is. Using the complaint and answer as the illustration, each paragraph of the complaint would have a "D" pencilled in if the allegation is denied outright; "I&B" or "DI&B" if it's denied on information and belief; "DKI" if it's something of which knowledge or information is denied; and "A" if admitted. If a paragraph has several allegations, some of which are denied in one form, some in another, some admitted, etc., any set of markings clearly showing the response to each allegation would satisfy.

Marked pleadings must be submitted to the trial judge. CPLR 4012 requires that they be furnished by the party who files the note of issue in the case (either party can file it under CPLR 3402). The court's rules may require marked pleadings on other occasions in connection with motions, pretrial conferences, etc., and of course a court can require marked pleadings in any given case.

§ 223. Affirmative Defenses

Under a denial, a defendant can disprove anything the plaintiff is required to prove.[1] But a number of matters are not the plaintiff's burden to prove as part of the cause of action and are thus the defendant's burden to broach in the answer and sustain

---

[15]   CPLR 3015(a), (d); see § 215.

[16]   See Commentary C3018:8 on McKinney's CPLR 3018.

[17]   CPLR 3018(a).

[18]   See paragraph one of former Official Form 17, which includes all of D's responses on fewer than half a dozen lines.

[1]   The text uses the example of a defendant answering a complaint, but the obligation to plead affirmative defenses applies to any party required to respond to an affirmative claim, such as a plaintiff replying to a counterclaim, a co-defendant answering a cross-claim, a third-party defendant answering an impleader claim, etc.

at the trial, i.e., to plead and to prove. These are the "affirmative defenses." They're defined, and the main ones listed, in CPLR 3018(b).

Most of the affirmative defenses are well known and the attorney does not have to stop to figure out what they are. The well known ones are the several explicitly listed in CPLR 3018(b):

arbitration and award

collateral estoppel

culpable conduct of the plaintiff under the comparative negligence rule

discharge in bankruptcy

illegality

fraud

infancy or other disability of the defendant

payment

release

res judicata

statute of frauds

statute of limitations

The list is not exhaustive. Other things may qualify as affirmative defenses and will if they meet either of the following two descriptions contained in CPLR 3018(b): (1) the matter is one that would be likely to surprise the plaintiff; or (2) the matter raises issues of fact not appearing on the face of the complaint. The "surprise" standard is not very helpful for determining whether a given item must be raised by way of defense. Few things in the parties' dealings are likely to "surprise" the plaintiff. Should P be surprised to learn that he sued too late, or that his contract is oral, or that his claim was previously adjudicated? More meaningful is the second standard: that the matter raises factual issues not introduced by the complaint.

Other matters than those listed have also been held to be affirmative defenses, such as truth in a defamation action,[2] adverse possession,[3] qualified privilege,[4] and standing to sue,[5] to name but a few.[6] The claim that a prior settlement among some of the parties to an action was not reasonable should be pleaded as an affirmative defense.[7] Another affirmative defense comes from Article 16 of the CPLR, the article added in 1986 to relieve of "joint" liability certain tort defendants with culpability of 50% or less. Defendants in that category bear "several-only" liability, meaning that they are responsible to the plaintiff for only their own shares of the plaintiff's non-economic

---

[2]   Fregoe v. Fregoe, 33 A.D.3d 1182, 826 N.Y.S.2d 755 (3d Dep't 2006).

[3]   Falco v. Pollitts, 298 A.D.2d 838, 747 N.Y.S.2d 874 (4th Dep't 2002).

[4]   Lerwick v. Kelsey, 24 A.D.3d 918, 806 N.Y.S.2d 732 (3d Dep't 2005).

[5]   Fossella v. Dinkins, 66 N.Y.2d 162, 495 N.Y.S.2d 352, 485 N.E.2d 1017 (1985).

[6]   To provide a checklist for lawyers drafting answers, a discussion of affirmative defenses not listed in CPLR 3018(b) is contained in Commentary C3018:14 on McKinney's CPLR 3018.

[7]   See Thome v. Benchmark Main Transit Associates, LLC, 125 A.D.3d 1283, 3 N.Y.S.3d 475 (4th Dep't 2015) (granting third-party defendant's motion to amend the answer to include this affirmative defense); Commentary C3018:15 to McKinney's CPLR 3018.

damages.[8] The burden of proof on this score is on the defendant.[9] It amounts to an affirmative defense and should be pleaded as such, but there is some appellate division conflict on the matter.[10] The defendant's attorney should consider it an additional item on the list contained in CPLR 3018(b).

Some matters may be affirmative defenses needing injection by the defendant depending on the particular situation. In Bello v. Transit Authority of New York City,[11] for example, "emergency" as a justification for a defendant's conduct was held to be an affirmative defense only if the plaintiff was not aware of the emergency. In *Bello* itself, however, the plaintiff was. There was a bomb scare on a bus and some passengers yelled "stop," which the driver did. The plaintiff was injured while exiting the bus. Because the plaintiff was just as aware of the circumstances as the driver, the "emergency" did not qualify as an affirmative defense in plaintiff's tort action and hence could be entertained without the defendant's having pleaded it.

A few points should be made about the culpable conduct defense embodied in the comparative negligence rule. There have been several decisions in automobile tort cases on the need to plead as a separate defense the plaintiff's failure to wear a seat belt. At least one case has held that the seat belt defense must be separately pleaded; that it would not be deemed embraced even by a general defense alleging the plaintiff's negligence.[12] Others hold that the general defense of the plaintiff's culpable conduct covers the seat belt defense as well.[13] A later statutory change appears to mandate the pleading of the seat belt defense distinctly.[14]

The cautious lawyer will conclude that it does no harm to articulate the seat belt defense as a separately numbered one, and that's probably the best course as long as the answer does not appear to put all its eggs in that basket. The defendant should keep in mind that being too specific with defenses in a pleading can sometimes have a restricting effect at the trial.[15] If the seat belt omission is not the only culpable conduct the defendant plans to show against the plaintiff, words should be chosen to make that clear in the answer.

The defendant's rule of thumb should be to treat as an affirmative defense— pleading it and being prepared to prove it—anything she is not sure of being able to introduce pursuant to her denials.[16] The defendant may thereby be assuming a "burden" of pleading and perhaps even of proof that she might otherwise not have had, but that's more a theoretical than practical element.[17] Assuming a doubtful burden more than offsets the alternative prospect: that of forfeiting a defense for not having realized that

---

[8]   See § 168A.

[9]   CPLR 1603.

[10]   See § 168D.

[11]   Bello v. Transit Authority of New York City, 12 A.D.3d 58, 783 N.Y.S.2d 648 (2d Dep't 2004) (SPR 156:1).

[12]   Brodvin v. Hertz Corp., 487 F. Supp. 1336, 29 Fed. R. Serv. 2d 982 (S.D.N.Y. 1980).

[13]   Fernandez v. Vukosa, 108 Misc. 2d 48, 436 N.Y.S.2d 919 (N.Y. City Civ. Ct. 1980).

[14]   See Veh. & Traf. Law § 1229–c(8) and Costanza v. City of New York, 147 Misc. 2d 94, 553 N.Y.S.2d 616 (N.Y. City Civ. Ct. 1990).

[15]   See the *Linton* case discussed below.

[16]   See Northway Engineering, Inc. v. Felix Industries, Inc., 77 N.Y.2d 332, 567 N.Y.S.2d 634, 569 N.E.2d 437 (1991), where the defendant pleaded as a defense, gratuitously, something it could have preserved through a mere denial. See the discussion in NYSLD No. 378.

[17]   See Commentary C3018:16 on McKinney's CPLR 3018.

it was one. It has been held, moreover, that the defendant does not even assume the burden in such an instance; that the burden remains the plaintiff's despite the defendant's gratuitous assertion of the matter as a "defense."[18]

While we encourage defendants to plead any relevant defense to avoid a waiver, sometimes a defendant will go too far. For example, in Scholastic Inc. v. Pace Plumbing Corp.,[19] defendant pleaded sixteen affirmative defenses "within a boilerplate, catchall paragraph" that also asserted "any other matter constituting an avoidance or an affirmative defense which further investigation of this matter may prove applicable herein." The First Department condemned the all too common practice of "boilerplate" pleading, observing:

> "[A] party cannot employ a catch-all provision in an attempt to preserve any and all potential defenses/objections for future use without affording notice to the opposing party." Moreover, neither plaintiff nor the court ought to be required to sift through a boilerplate list of defenses, or "be compelled to wade through a mass of verbiage and superfluous matter," to divine which defenses might apply to the case.[20]

In Scholastic, the First Department ruled that defendant failed to properly plead the statute of limitations, essentially "because its inclusion of the defense within a laundry list of predominantly inapplicable defenses did not provide plaintiff with the requisite notice" required under CPLR 3013.[21] The Scholastic decision is a reminder that the defendant should take care to plead only those affirmative defenses that have a basis in law and fact. For example, the defendant should not plead plaintiff's failure to wear an available seat belt in a contract action. (It's happened!) We wonder, however, whether the remedy imposed by the court in Scholastic—the remittal of the matter to supreme court to allow amendment of the answer in conformance with CPLR 3013 and CPLR 3014—will be sufficient to deter defendants from the "kitchen sink" approach to pleading.[22]

In tort actions involving multiple tortfeasors, it is almost always advisable for each defendant to include in its answer an allegation placing at least some blame on the others, whether the others are named in the main action or not. By so doing, the defendant preserves its rights under at least two statutes that may prove germane later even if the defendant is not thinking about them now.[23] One is Article 16 of the CPLR and the insulation it offers defendants from joint and several liability in certain circumstances.[24] The other is General Obligations Law section 15–108, which reduces a

---

[18] Beece v. Guardian Life Ins. Co. of America, 110 A.D.2d 865, 488 N.Y.S.2d 422 (2d Dep't 1985); see Commentary C3018:16 on McKinney's CPLR 3018.

[19] Scholastic Inc. v. Pace Plumbing Corp., 129 A.D.3d 75, 76, 78, 8 N.Y.S.3d 143, 145 (1st Dep't 2015).

[20] Scholastic, 129 A.D.3d at 79–80, 8 N.Y.S.3d at 147 (citing CPLR 3013, 3014); see also Kowalczyk v. Village of Monticello, 107 A.D.3d 1365, 1366, 969 N.Y.S.2d 566, 568 (3d Dep't 2013) ("[A] party cannot employ a catch-all provision in an attempt to preserve any and all potential defenses/objections for future use without affording notice to the opposing party . . . .").

[21] Scholastic, 129 A.D.3d at 79, 8 N.Y.S.3d at 146.

[22] See Kowalczyk, 107 A.D.3d at 1366, 969 N.Y.S.2d at 567–68 (respondent who failed to specifically plead statute of limitations defense, but instead "purported 'to reserve[ ] [respondent's] right to assert [such] further affirmative defenses as [may be] appropriate as investigation and discovery continue,' " deemed to have waived statute of limitations defense.) (alterations in original). For further discussion of the Scholastic decision, see § 208.

[23] See Ward v. City of Schenectady, 204 A.D.2d 779, 611 N.Y.S.2d 932 (3d Dep't 1994) (SPR 30:1).

[24] See §§ 168A through 168D.

nonsettling defendant's exposure based on settlements the injured person has reached with other tortfeasors.[25]

Defendants need to be careful, however, to treat contribution rights under CPLR Article 14 separate from the comparative fault defense in CPLR Article 14–A and the CPLR Article 16 defense. In Jones v. Kalache,[26] a medical malpractice action, defendant was requesting a comparative fault charge at a closing charge conference. In his answer, defendant asserted an affirmative defense of CPLR Article 16, which provides an exception to joint and several liability, but did not assert the defense of comparative fault or a claim for contribution against plaintiff.

CPLR 1412 specifically requires that a defendant plead and prove comparative fault. The court concluded that defendant's pleading of the Article 16 defense did not provide plaintiff with notice that defendant was asserting a comparative negligence defense and held that "in the absence of pleading a comparative negligence affirmative defense or specific facts alleging such an affirmative defense, defendant is not entitled to a charge of comparative negligence."[27]

If the plaintiff introduces in the complaint a matter that would ordinarily be an affirmative defense for the defendant to plead, the defendant's omission to plead it should not be held a forfeiture. So holds Green Bus Lines, Inc. v. Consolidated Mut. Ins. Co.,[28] where the issue was whether certain insurance coverage was excluded, a matter for the defendant to plead and prove. But while the defendant was relieved of the burden of pleading on the issue—because the plaintiff had assumed it—it was nevertheless held to retain the burden of proof of it at the trial.

Laches is an affirmative defense for the defendant to plead. The doctrine of laches may have several meanings, and recent Second Department cases illustrate two of them. The first, in Blinds To Go (U.S.), Inc. v. Times Plaza Development, L.P.,[29] holds the defense unavailable in a mere damages action because damages is an action at law and laches is a defense available only against an equitable action. That's the classic application of the laches doctrine, whose postulate is that even though the statute of limitations is still alive on the claim, the plaintiff waited too long to sue on it and the defendant has been demonstrably prejudiced by the delay, barring equitable relief.[30]

The second, in Rosenstrauss v. Women's Imaging Center of Orange County,[31] illustrates another common use that has lazily evolved for "laches" today: a shorthand statement that any step a party has sought in a case was sought inexcusably too late and must be denied for that reason. In *Rosenstrauss*, the action had been dismissed under CPLR 3404 and the plaintiff didn't move to get the case restored until 11 years

---

[25]   See § 176.

[26]   Jones v. Kalache, 30 Misc. 3d 998, 915 N.Y.S.2d 479 (Sup. Ct., Westchester County 2011) (SPR 230:1) (NYSLD No. 615).

[27]   See § 168E, where the *Kalache* decision is discussed at length in a treatment designed to warn defendants about confusing their obligations under CPLR Articles 14, 14–A, and 16.

[28]   Green Bus Lines, Inc. v. Consolidated Mut. Ins. Co., 74 A.D.2d 136, 426 N.Y.S.2d 981 (2d Dep't 1980).

[29]   Blinds To Go (U.S.), Inc. v. Times Plaza Development, L.P., 45 A.D.3d 714, 846 N.Y.S.2d 296 (2d Dep't 2007).

[30]   See In re Flamenbaum, 22 N.Y.3d 962, 978 N.Y.S.2d 708, 1 N.E.3d 782 (2013) (NYSLD No. 648) (concluding that the defense's two part showing of undue delay and resulting prejudice was not established); see § 36.

[31]   Rosenstrauss v. Women's Imaging Center of Orange County, 56 A.D.3d 454, 866 N.Y.S.2d 759 (2d Dep't 2008).

later! "Laches," said the court of the plaintiff's delay, and refused to vacate the dismissal.[32]

Defenses can be complete or partial. They are subject to the usual pleading rules and get the usual pleading advantages. Under CPLR 3014, they can be inconsistent and may be pleaded in the alternative or hypothetically.

As the former official forms illustrate,[33] brevity is not only permissible but encouraged. The Court of Appeals held in Immediate v. St. John's Queens Hospital[34] that the phrase "statute of limitations" is a sufficient pleading of that defense. In a brief memorandum opinion, the Court concluded that "[i]t was sufficient under CPLR 3013 that respondent pleaded the 'statute of limitations' as a defense; it was not required to identify the statutory section relied on or to specify the applicable period of limitations."[35] In *Scholastic*, a First Department panel disagreed on the particularity required under CPLR 3013 when pleading a statute of limitations defense. The majority reasoned that the brief notation of "statute of limitations" as a defense in an answer, as it appeared in *Scholastic*, might not be adequate in all cases to satisfy CPLR 3013 and recommended that the Court of Appeals revisit the issue addressed in *Immediate*.[36] The majority, relying on former Official Form 17, contended that the affirmative defense of "statute of limitations" needs to include the specific time period relied upon, at least in certain cases.[37]

Where does that leave things now in the First Department? A defendant interposing a statute of limitations defense should err on the side of caution and follow the format in former Official Form 17, specifically stating the time period relied upon. This may not be necessary in cases where there is one defendant, one theory of recovery, one possible accrual date, and only a single applicable statute of limitations. But why tempt fate? Until the matter is resolved by the Court of Appeals or the legislature, it is best to plead the affirmative defense of the statute of limitations by including any applicable time period.[38]

Sometimes, terseness in pleading may be the safer course. In Linton v. Unexcelled Fire-Works Co.,[39] for example, P sued D for wrongful discharge. D set up the defense of justification, setting forth many specific instances. Then at the trial D tried to prove even further instances. He was precluded from doing so on the ground that P was entitled to rely on the list of instances D had volunteered in the answer. The Court hinted that if D had pleaded justification in general terms, he might have been able to prove any specific instances of it because the plaintiff would not then have been misled.[40]

Another example, a century later, of what we might call "over pleading" appears in Hatch v. Tran,[41] in which a defendant who pleaded that the complaint wasn't "properly served" (which concerns the method of service) was precluded from afterwards

---

[32]   See SPR 203:1 (discussing these distinct applications of the "laches" doctrine).

[33]   See § 228, showing former Official Form 17.

[34]   Immediate v. St. John's Queens Hospital, 48 N.Y.2d 671, 421 N.Y.S.2d 875, 397 N.E.2d 385 (1979).

[35]   *Immediate*, 48 N.Y.2d at 673, 421 N.Y.S.2d at 876, 397 N.E.2d at 386.

[36]   *Scholastic*, 129 A.D.3d at 82, 8 N.Y.S.3d at 149.

[37]   *Scholastic*, 129 A.D.3d at 89 n.1, 8 N.Y.S.3d at 154 n.1.

[38]   See Commentary C3018:19 to McKinney's CPLR 3018.

[39]   Linton v. Unexcelled Fire-Works Co., 124 N.Y. 533, 27 N.E. 406 (1891).

[40]   Linton v. Unexcelled Fire-Works Co., 124 N.Y. 533, 537, 27 N.E. 406, 407 (1891).

[41]   Hatch v. Tran, 170 A.D.2d 649, 567 N.Y.S.2d 72 (2d Dep't 1991).

contending that there was no jurisdictional basis. Both objections, in addition to a defective filing,[42] are embraced within the category of want of personal jurisdiction set forth in CPLR 3211(a)(8), however, and the defendant would probably have preserved all just by asserting the general defense of want of personal jurisdiction.[43]

Many of the affirmative defenses may at the defendant's option be raised by a motion to dismiss instead of being pleaded in the answer. It depends on whether the particular defense is among the motion grounds listed in CPLR 3211(a). A comparison of that provision and CPLR 3018(b) made later in the book[44] shows which of the defenses are available for use on a dismissal motion.

An affirmative defense should be included in the defendant's initial answer, but it has been held that if it is not, it's generally permissible for the defendant to include it in an amended answer made as of course.[45] That amendment is made pursuant to CPLR 3025(a). If the time for making the of-course amendment has expired,[46] the defendant must seek leave of court under CPLR 3025(b) before amending to add the defense. Whether to grant leave lies in the discretion of the court and usually turns on whether the other side would be unreasonably prejudiced by the amendment.[47]

In a given case, a defense may be preserved through conduct even though not included in the answer. It has been held, for example, that D's omission of a defense from the answer becomes unprejudicial and can even be made the basis of a summary judgment or dismissal motion when the subject matter of the defense is explored through the disclosure devices and the element of surprise is thereby removed from the case.[48] That won't often happen. It's always best that the defendant plead the defense and not take chances.

G. COUNTERCLAIMS

Table of Sections

§ 224.   Counterclaims, Generally
§ 225.   Counterclaims; Parties with Several Capacities
§ 226.   Counterclaim Against Assignee-Plaintiff

§ 224. Counterclaims, Generally

A counterclaim is a claim the defendant (D) interposes against the plaintiff (P). It is contained in the answer, following the denials and defenses.[1] The CPLR permits D to

---

[42]   See § 58.

[43]   This is in contrast with federal practice, which, in Fed. R. Civ. P. 12(b), lists these defects separately and requires the defendant to specify the one relied on. See § 635 (Practitioner's Edition).

[44]   See § 263.

[45]   Iacovangelo v. Shepherd, 5 N.Y.3d 184, 800 N.Y.S.2d 116, 833 N.E.2d 259 (2005) (NYSLD No. 548); see § 237. If a defendant makes a pre-answer motion to dismiss under CPLR 3211(a) and neglects to include the defense of lack of personal jurisdiction, that defense is waived and cannot be included in the answer. CPLR 3211(e); see § 274.

[46]   The time for an amendment as of course is limited to the early stages of the action. See § 236.

[47]   See § 237.

[48]   See Rogoff v. San Juan Racing Ass'n, Inc., 77 A.D.2d 831, 431 N.Y.S.2d 16 (1st Dep't 1980), aff'd, 54 N.Y.2d 883, 444 N.Y.S.2d 911, 429 N.E.2d 418 (1981).

[1]   See the form answer in § 228.

use as a counterclaim any claim D has against P, related or not to P's action.[2] If it's unrelated and would unduly confuse the jury, it can be severed or ordered separately tried;[3] but it can't be dismissed, as at one time it could,[4] merely because it is inconvenient or unrelated. The usual pleading rules applicable to a plaintiff's statement of a claim in the complaint apply to counterclaims as well.[5]

When P invokes the court's jurisdiction by bringing suit, P also subjects herself to the court's jurisdiction in respect of the defendant's counterclaims. Hence, no process service need be made on P for counterclaim jurisdiction. It has also been held that once P serves a summons and notice on D, P can't avoid the court's counterclaim jurisdiction by trying to abandon the action without serving a complaint.[6]

All counterclaims are permissive in New York, but this classification can be misleading. In general terms, D can use his claim as a counterclaim or save it and sue on it separately. D may save it for separate suit even when it is a related counterclaim, i.e., when it arises out of the same transaction or occurrence as P's claim. The decision in Batavia Kill Watershed Dist. in County of Greene v. Charles O. Desch, Inc.[7] illustrates the rule and its somewhat misleading handle.

In *Batavia*, Owner O retained contractor G on a project. G sued O for breach of their agreement. O had a damages claim against G arising out of the transaction, but did not interpose it as a counterclaim, successfully defending and defeating G's suit and only afterwards bringing an action against G for O's own damages. The trial court held that O waived the right to bring the separate action against G. Its reason was that O had told the jury in G's action that O had suffered damage at G's hands, but made no affirmative claim against G for relief, thus possibly misleading the jury into thinking that O was absorbing its damages and thereby making the jury all the more sympathetic to O. The appellate division nevertheless reversed and not only allowed O to bring the separate action, but on the merits applied the collateral estoppel (issue preclusion) doctrine in favor of O against G.[8]

Things worked out well for O in the *Batavia* case and furnished a classic example of the permissive nature of New York's counterclaim rule even as applied to related counterclaims. But the notion that a defendant with a related claim can safely withhold it and sue on it later can be misleading and perilous. The reason is that any fact adjudicated or legal conclusion reached in the P v. D action will be conclusive and binding if it should become germane—as it became in *Batavia*—in D's later action against P,[9] and not always with such happy results for D. Had O, who was the defendant in the *Batavia* setting, lost in the first action, for example, it being established that O and not G was the breacher of the contract, the estoppel would have gone against O and brought

---

[2]   CPLR 3019(a).

[3]   See § 129.

[4]   See Civ. Prac. Act § 262 (repealed 1963).

[5]   CPLR 3019(d); see § 208.

[6]   See Edelman v. Edelman, 88 Misc. 2d 156, 386 N.Y.S.2d 331 (Sup. Ct., Nassau County 1976).

[7]   Batavia Kill Watershed Dist. in County of Greene v. Charles O. Desch, Inc., 57 N.Y.2d 796, 455 N.Y.S.2d 597, 441 N.E.2d 1115 (1982), affirming on the appellate division opinion reported in 83 A.D.2d 97, 444 N.Y.S.2d 958 (3d Dep't 1981).

[8]   See §§ 457 et seq. The *Batavia* case is the subject of a lead note in NYSLD No. 258. The reversing appellate division case is summarized in Digest No. 267 and the Court of Appeals affirmance in Digest No. 276.

[9]   See Pace v. Perk, 81 A.D.2d 444, 440 N.Y.S.2d 710 (2d Dep't 1981).

about a dismissal of the second action.[10] This suggests that unless a defendant with a related counterclaim has some special tactical reason for saving it (and taking a chance on losing it through the estoppel route), he should use it as a counterclaim in the plaintiff's original action and not depend on the notion that all counterclaims are "permissive." O swam against the tide in *Batavia* and had a victory that a similarly situated defendant might not enjoy the next time around.

D will likely want to use his claim at least as a defense to P's action, if not as an outright counterclaim, but in one case in which D did so he was held to have waived the right to sue on the same subject matter afterwards. In Musco v. Lupi,[11] P sued D for money due under a contract. D defended and won on the ground that P, and not D, had breached the contract. D's later suit against P for damages for breach of that same contract was held barred, a holding not at all at home with the ostensibly "permissive" counterclaim rule. *Batavia* could be read as overruling *Musco*, but the appellate division in *Batavia* purports merely to distinguish it on the ground that in *Musco* the court in the first action had specifically invited D to amend and assert a counterclaim and D didn't accept it. That seems a tenuous distinction; D had the right to assert a counterclaim and the judicial invitation, however cordial, was hardly relevant. The trial court in *Batavia* cited an even better reason, already noted, for holding D to a waiver—D had led the jury to think that D was generously absorbing the loss caused it by P—but the appellate division still reversed and said there was no waiver.

In federal practice related claims such as those in *Batavia* and *Musco* would be denominated "compulsory"[12] and the failure to use them as counterclaims would waive them.[13] Only unrelated counterclaims in the federal courts fall under the permissive category.[14] But what if a defendant in a federal action withholds a counterclaim that arises out of the same transaction or occurrence as plaintiff's claim and then turns to a New York State court and commences an action to assert that claim under our permissive counterclaim rule? In Paramount Pictures Corp. v. Allianz Risk Transfer AG,[15] the First Department ruled that "the later assertion in a state court action of a contention that constituted a compulsory counterclaim (FRCP rule 13[a]) in a prior federal action between the same parties is barred under the doctrine of res judicata." This principle of law required dismissal of the complaint in the state court action.[16]

If P's claim is brought in a lower court, and D prefers the supreme court for D's claim (or must turn to the supreme court because the lower court lacks subject matter jurisdiction of D's claim), an alternative open to D is to commence a prompt separate suit on his claim in the supreme court and then make a motion to remove and consolidate P's action.[17]

---

[10] The doctrine of collateral estoppel is studied in Chapter 17. See §§ 457 et seq.

[11] Musco v. Lupi, 6 Misc. 2d 930, 164 N.Y.S.2d 84 (Sup. Ct., Orange County 1957).

[12] Fed. R. Civ. P. 13(a).

[13] See Cummings v. Dresher, 18 N.Y.2d 105, 108, 271 N.Y.S.2d 976, 978, 218 N.E.2d 688, 690 (1966) (Fuld, J., concurring).

[14] Fed. R. Civ. P. 13(b).

[15] Paramount Pictures Corp. v. Allianz Risk Transfer AG, 141 A.D.3d 464, 468, 36 N.Y.S.3d 11, 15 (1st Dep't 2016), leave to appeal granted, 28 N.Y.3d 909, 47 N.Y.S.3d 224, 69 N.E.3d 1020 (2016).

[16] The *Paramount* decision is discussed in further detail in §§ 452, 632 (Practitioner's Edition).

[17] CPLR 602(b). If P's claim is in a small claims part, the motion to consolidate will likely be denied. See § 582 (Practitioner's Edition).

A counterclaim needs a reply.[18] If D pleads something that is in effect a counterclaim, but not formally denominated one, P need not reply to it[19] although from P's point of view it may be wiser to.[20] The reply must be served within 20 days of the answer.[21]

If D has a claim against P and some other person, X, who is not a party, the CPLR allows D to interpose the claim against P while simultaneously joining X as an adverse party on the claim. D just serves the answer containing the counterclaim on both P and X, but with the service on X accompanied by a summons and made by the usual methods of summons service.[22] To take advantage of this permission to add X, the counterclaim should exist at least in part against P. A common example is where the plaintiff bringing suit against D is an assignee of the claim, rather than the person to whom the claim originally accrued, and where D counterclaims on something due from the assignor and adds the assignor as a party.[23]

A few points should be noted about counterclaims in some of the lower courts. The subject matter jurisdiction of the New York City Civil Court and of the district, city, town, and village courts in respect of a counterclaim is always at least as broad as that governing the main claim, but in some instances, counterclaim jurisdiction is broader. Jurisdiction of money counterclaims, for example, although subject in the town and village courts to the same monetary limitation that governs the main claim,[24] is unlimited in the New York City Civil Court and in the district and city courts.[25] Those courts also have jurisdiction of a counterclaim to rescind or reform the transaction out of which the main claim arises.[26]

§ 225. Counterclaims; Parties with Several Capacities

If a party has several capacities, a counterclaim involving that party may be used only in respect of the capacity in which she appears in the action.[1] Where T is a trustee, for example, and brings an action in behalf of the trust, the defendant can interpose as a counterclaim any claim existing against T in T's trustee capacity, or against the whole body of beneficiaries of the trust, but can't interpose a claim existing against T personally and having no relationship to the trust.[2] The same rule applies when the plaintiff is a trustee in effect even though not in name.[3]

---

[18] CPLR 3011.

[19] Fromm v. Glueck, 161 Misc. 502, 293 N.Y.S. 530 (Sup. Ct., Greene County 1937).

[20] See Commentary C3011:9 on McKinney's CPLR 3011.

[21] CPLR 3012(a).

[22] A preliminary filing and fee paying must be made for this joinder of X as an additional party. See CPLR 3019(d) and the discussion in SPR 22:2–3.

[23] See § 226.

[24] Uniform Just. Ct. Act § 208, McKinney's Vol. 29A, Part 2.

[25] See § 208 in the New York City Civ., Uniform Dist., and Uniform City Ct. Acts, McKinney's Vol. 29A, Part 3. The county court also has unlimited monetary jurisdiction over counterclaims. See § 14.

[26] See § 208 in the New York City Civ., Uniform Dist., and Uniform City Ct. Acts, McKinney's Vol. 29A, Part 3. The Civil Court also has jurisdiction to order a partnership accounting by way of counterclaim in certain instances. New York City Civ. Ct. Act § 208(c)(2).

[1] Corcoran v. National Union Fire Ins. Co. of Pittsburgh, Pa., 143 A.D.2d 309, 532 N.Y.S.2d 376 (1st Dep't 1988).

[2] CPLR 3019(c). See Commentary C3019:16 on McKinney's CPLR 3019.

[3] See, e.g., Helman v. Dixon, 71 Misc. 2d 1057, 338 N.Y.S.2d 139 (N.Y. City Civ. Ct. 1972).

If P sues a partnership (consisting of X, Y, and Z) on a partnership liability, the partnership may of course interpose any claim it has against P even though not all of the partners were served.[4] If the partnership were to interpose against P a claim owned personally by partner X, however, it would have to be with X's permission because it amounts to an assignment by X to the partnership of an asset owned individually by X.

When the partnership is the plaintiff, only a claim existing against the partnership collectively, or against the partners together, may be used as a counterclaim. If the claim exists against partner X personally, but not against the partnership or partners Y and Z, the defendant may not use it.[5]

CPLR 3019(a) is rather broadly phrased in regard to representative situations and might even be read as permitting D, sued by P for (e.g.) assault, to counterclaim for money due to D from a decedent for whom P just happens to be the executor. It must therefore be stressed that CPLR 3019(a) was "not intended to alter the well-settled rule requiring a counterclaim to be a claim against the plaintiff in the capacity in which [the plaintiff] sues."[6]

An exception is where there is a complete merger of a party's several capacities. If P sues as administrator of an estate of which he is the sole heir, for example, D may in some instances use as a counterclaim a claim existing against P personally.[7] Similarly, where the merger of capacities is on D's side—where D is sued individually, for example, but happens to be the sole shareholder of a corporation which has a claim against P—D can use that claim as a counterclaim.[8]

The remedy against a counterclaim interposed in violation of this "capacities" rule is a motion under CPLR 3211(a)(6) to dismiss the counterclaim.[9]

§ 226. Counterclaim Against Assignee-Plaintiff

When P is the assignee of a cause of action and sues D on it, D may of course interpose against P any claim D has directly against P. But to what extent, if at all, may D interpose against P a claim that D has only against R, the assignor who originally owned the assigned claim now owned by P? Different rules apply, depending on whether the would-be counterclaim has a relationship to the assigned claim.

When the counterclaim arises out of the same transaction or occurrence as that out of which the assigned claim arises, i.e., when it is a related counterclaim, it may be used as an offset by D. That is, it may be interposed as a counterclaim against P but only to the extent of neutralizing P's claim.[1] Should a balance be due in D's favor, D may not have affirmative judgment against P for it.

This is an example of the doctrine of equitable recoupment, and it applies even if the counterclaim was not yet in existence or owned by D when R assigned the main claim to P. Where P sued for the balance due for fans sold by R to D, for example, and D

---

[4] Fox Chase Knitting Mills v. Handal, 232 A.D. 498, 250 N.Y.S. 416 (1st Dep't 1931).

[5] Ruzicka v. Rager, 305 N.Y. 191, 111 N.E.2d 878 (1953).

[6] 1st Rep. Leg. Doc. No. 6(b), p. 71 (1957).

[7] Anderson v. Carlson, 201 A.D. 260, 194 N.Y.S. 112 (2d Dep't 1922).

[8] Conant v. Schnall, 33 A.D.2d 326, 307 N.Y.S.2d 902 (3d Dep't 1970).

[9] See § 264.

[1] See Peerless Ins. Co. v. Michael Beshara, Inc., 75 A.D.3d 733, 736, 903 N.Y.S.2d 833, 835–36 (3d Dep't 2010).

counterclaimed against P for commissions earned on the sale of those fans and for certain freight charges on them, the counterclaims were held good for offset purposes even though they may have technically accrued after the assignment and presumably even after D was notified of the assignment.[2]

When the counterclaim that D would interpose against P is unrelated to the assigned claim, the time that D is notified of the assignment becomes a key moment. The law's policy is to preserve such claims as D may legitimately have against R and to preclude R, through the simple expedient of an assignment, from divesting D of use of those claims as counterclaims. Thus, any claim D already has against R when D learns of the assignment is usable against P, the assignee—again, only to the extent of an offset—even if it has no relationship to the assigned claim.[3] But any claim against R that comes into D's ownership afterwards is not usable against P. This is to prevent D, after getting such notice, from deliberately acquiring someone else's claim against R, perhaps at a discount—R may be having solvency problems—so as to use it against P. A lesson to P in this situation is to give prompt notice to D of any claim assigned to P by R.

In any circumstances in which D is allowed to interpose against P the claim D has against R, whether it is a related counterclaim (and interposable regardless of when D got it) or an unrelated one (but already in D's hands when notified of the assignment), D can join R as an additional party on the counterclaim,[4] which would enable D to get an affirmative judgment against R for anything that might be left over after the claim has been used as an offset against P.

If P is not merely the assignee of a cause of action, but the complete successor of R and of R's liabilities, as in a merger of two corporations, these qualifications become irrelevant and P faces the counterclaim in full.

With some exceptions, the law recognizes an agreement whereby D consents with R not to use against the assignee, P, a claim D has against R, but the agreement had best be drawn carefully because it has been severely circumscribed by statute[5] and is distrusted by the courts. In an adhesion contract, its likelihood of success is remote.[6]

Throughout this discussion we have assumed that the thing assigned by R to P is a mature cause of action. If it is something close, but really something else, these rules may be irrelevant and D's claim may be altogether unusable as a counterclaim. Suppose, for example, that R sells a building to P, after which, while P is owner, rent falls due from a tenant, D. When sued by P for rent, D may not counterclaim P for something due from R. It was P, now the owner, who furnished the consideration for which P now sues, and D's claim against R doesn't belong in the action at all.[7]

---

[2] James Talcott, Inc. v. Winco Sales Corp., 14 N.Y.2d 227, 250 N.Y.S.2d 416, 199 N.E.2d 499 (1964).

[3] Gen. Oblig. Law § 13–105; N.Y. UCC §§ 3–306, 9–318(1)(b).

[4] CPLR 3019(d); D.P.C. Corp. v. Jobson, 15 A.D.2d 861, 224 N.Y.S.2d 772 (4th Dep't 1962).

[5] Section 302(9) of the Personal Property Law bars from any "retail installment contract" any provision by which the buyer agrees not to assert defenses against the seller's assignee. Coordinately, Pers. Prop. Law § 403(4) subjects the assignee to all such defenses. Both statutes limit these defenses to offset use, however, insulating the assignee from any affirmative judgment for a balance that the buyer may claim.

[6] See B. W. Acceptance Corp. v. Richmond, 46 Misc. 2d 447, 259 N.Y.S.2d 965 (Sup. Ct., New York County 1965).

[7] See Stafford Sec. Co. v. Kremer, 258 N.Y. 1, 179 N.E. 32 (1931).

H. CROSS-CLAIMS

Table of Sections

§ 227.   Cross-Claims
§ 228.   Form of Answer

§ 227. Cross-Claims

A cross-claim is a claim by one defendant against another; in New York, it can be for any claim at all, whether or not related to the plaintiff's claim.[1] This is in contrast to federal practice where a cross-claim is interposable only if related to some other claim in the case.[2] If, for reasons of relevancy or otherwise, a cross-claim should prove unnecessarily burdensome in a given case, it can be severed or ordered separately tried.[3]

One of the popular uses of a cross-claim by defendant A is for indemnification or contribution from co-defendant B in respect of a tort claim for which the injured person, P, is suing both of them. This is only one of the uses of a cross-claim, however. A cross-claim can be a claim by A against B for A's own injuries suffered in the accident, or a claim on a promissory note, or, theoretically, a claim for divorce if A and B happen to be married. Here we can distinguish the cross-claim from the impleader (third-party claim) of CPLR 1007. A third-party claim is designed primarily for an indemnity or indemnity-like claim, including a contribution claim,[4] whereas a cross-claim can interpose those or any other claims. Another distinction is that a third-party claim entails summons service because it joins someone not yet a party, while a cross-claim, addressing someone already in the action, does not.

The cross-claim is a popular expedient for interposing apportionment claims in tort cases under CPLR 1401 and 1403.[5] Such claims are virtually pro forma in multi-defendant tort actions. The last sentence to CPLR 3019(b) allows a cross-claim to assert that another party "may be liable to the cross-claimant for all or part of a claim asserted in the action against the cross-claimant." In Ilyayeve v. The City of New York,[6] plaintiff sued New York City, its fire department, and a hospital whose ambulance personnel attended to plaintiff's decedent. The hospital's answer contained six separately captioned affirmative defenses, including a CPLR Article 16 defense. The answer also demanded "that the liability, if any, be apportioned" but contained no cross-claim against the city, the fire department, or any other named co-defendants. The court rejected the argument that the hospital's demand for an apportionment of any liability constituted a cross-claim, stressing that the apportionment request was only relevant to its Article 16 affirmative defense that its fault was 50% or less. The hospital's answer did not even mention contribution or assert that anyone might be liable to it for all or part of the plaintiff's claims against the hospital. Furthermore, the answer failed to refer to any co-defendant or contain a separately captioned cross-claim against any co-defendant.

---

[1]   CPLR 3019(b).

[2]   Fed. R. Civ. P. 13(g); see § 632 (Practitioner's Edition).

[3]   See CPLR 603; § 129.

[4]   CPLR 1007. Its use was expanded by the Court of Appeals in 1980. See § 157.

[5]   See § 173.

[6]   Ilyayeve v. The City of New York, 2016 WL 4490623, *1 (Sup. Ct., New York County 2016).

Defendants often encounter problems in multiparty actions when failing to separately address the interrelated concepts of comparative fault, apportionment of fault among defendants, and CPLR Article 16.[7] These concepts, which usually appear as affirmative defenses in the answer, need to be treated separately from Article 14 of the CPLR, which provides the procedural vehicles for one defendant to make another contribute to what the injured plaintiff is seeking, either within the same action or through a separate action.[8]

The cross-claim is pleaded in the defendant's answer[9] and is subject to the usual rules for pleading a cause of action. As with a counterclaim, it is also interposable against a nonparty as well as the co-defendant. The nonparty is joined by filing a copy of the answer containing the cross-claim along with a summons, paying a filing fee, and then serving the answer and summons on the nonparty being joined.[10] Suppose, for example, that P, injured in an accident involving tortfeasors A, B, and C, sues only A and B. A in his answer can cross-claim both B and C for contribution, but, since C is not a party, C would have to be served with a summons accompanying the answer containing the cross-claim, while B would be served with only the answer and the service would be by mere mail to his attorney.[11]

A cross-claim requires an answer only if the pleading containing the cross-claim demands one. In the absence of a demand, the allegations of the cross-claim are deemed denied.[12] While this applies to all cross-claims, it was designed primarily to dispense with answers to contribution cross-claims, which are interposed almost automatically between joint tortfeasors in personal injury and wrongful death cases. Answers in that situation are straight denials and recriminations and were found to add nothing to the case but paper. A better remedy might have been to dispense with answers only to contribution cross-claims, but the legislature made it the burden of the cross-claimant in all cases to demand an answer if he wants one.

In the situation mentioned above, in which a nonparty is being joined as an additional adverse party on a cross-claim, it would be preferable for the new party to answer the cross-claim whether or not an answer is demanded, so that the new party's posture in the case can be discerned. Under the terms of CPLR 3011, however, apparently even such a new party need answer only when an answer is demanded. The court can in any event require an answer in its discretion. If an answer is to be made by a party, it should be served within 20 days after service of the pleading containing the cross-claim.[13] When the cross-claim is being served on a nonparty, such as C in the example used above, the answering time would be a 20- or 30-day period under the usual rules governing summons service.[14]

As noted above, the defendant's answer is the place for the cross-claim, but the co-defendant against whom the cross-claim is to be used may not yet have been served in

---

[7] See §§ 168D, 168E.

[8] See §§ 169 to 177.

[9] CPLR 3011.

[10] CPLR 3019(b), (d).

[11] CPLR 2103(b)(2). See § 202. Of course an alternative and far more common way for A to join C is by impleader under CPLR 1007.

[12] This is the result of a 1977 amendment of CPLR 3011. Previously, all cross-claims required answers.

[13] CPLR 3012(a).

[14] CPLR 3012(c). See § 231.

the main action and thus subjected to the jurisdiction of the court. The courts, recognizing such problems, are not strict about the time for cross-claiming if no prejudice is shown.[15] Furthermore, there is always the ubiquitous CPLR 2004 to authorize an extension of time or forgive short lapses of time if need be.

If defendant A would cross-claim co-defendants but does not know whether they have yet appeared—if they have, service could be made by mere mail to their attorneys[16]—A can demand a list of the appearers from the plaintiff.[17]

§ 228. Form of Answer

The following is Form 17 of the recently rescinded Official Forms, but it is still a helpful model for drafting an answer.[1] It illustrates denials (¶ 1), affirmative defenses (¶¶ 2–5), and the proper positions of counterclaims and cross-claims. The first paragraph of the counterclaim would be numbered 6, picking up after the last allegation made under the affirmative defenses. Note that the wherefore clause first requests dismissal of the complaint—which is the relief sought by the defendant based on the denials and defenses—and then affirmative relief on the counterclaim and cross-claim.

---

[15] See Manganaro v. Estwing Mfg. Co., 27 A.D.2d 711, 276 N.Y.S.2d 891 (1st Dep't 1967).

[16] CPLR 2103(b)(2).

[17] CPLR 2103(e). For discussion of service on a nonappearing co-defendant, see Commentary C3012:7 on McKinney's CPLR 3012.

[1] See § 7.

SUPREME COURT OF THE STATE OF NEW YORK
COUNTY OF NEW YORK

A.B., Plaintiff,

      against

C.D. and E.F., Defendants.

Answer

Index No. _____

1. Defendant C.D. admits the allegations in paragraphs 1 and 4 of the complaint; states that he lacks knowledge or information sufficient to form a belief as to the truth of the allegations in paragraph 2 of the complaint; and denies each and every other allegation in the complaint.

First Affirmative Defense

2. The cause of action set forth in the complaint did not accrue within six years next before the commencement of this action.

Second Affirmative Defense

3. Defendant C.D. entered into the contract annexed to the complaint as Exhibit A in reliance upon the truth of the oral statements made by plaintiff to defendant C.D. on or about July 1, 2016, that [specify alleged misrepresentation].

4. Plaintiff made those statements in order to induce defendant C.D. to enter into the contract and with the intention that defendant C.D. rely upon plaintiff's statements.

5. In fact and to the knowledge of plaintiff at the time he made those statements they were false in that [state facts].

Counterclaim

[Here set forth any cause of action as a counterclaim in the manner in which a claim is pleaded in a complaint].

Cross-Claim Against Defendant E.F.

[Here set forth any cause of action as a cross-claim against defendant E.F. in the manner in which a claim is pleaded in a complaint].

Wherefore defendant C.D. demands judgment (1) against plaintiff dismissing the complaint, (2) against plaintiff on the counterclaim in the sum of _____ dollars, plus interest, (3) against defendant E.F. on the cross-claim in the sum of _____ dollars, plus interest, and (4) against plaintiff and defendant E.F. for costs and disbursements.

                      ___[Signature]_____

                      ___[Print name]_____

                      Attorney for Defendant C.D.

                      Address:

                      Telephone Number:

I. THE REPLY

Table of Sections

§ 229.   The Reply; Further Pleading

§ 229. The Reply; Further Pleadings

CPLR 3011 lists the few pleadings used in New York practice. The plaintiff's initial pleading is the complaint and the defendant's is the answer. The only other one listed is the plaintiff's reply.

A main purpose of CPLR 3011 is to state the instances in which a responsive pleading is required. The defendant's answer to the complaint is of course mandatory. But a reply by the plaintiff, as will be elaborated shortly, is required only when the answer contains a counterclaim. A third-party (impleader) complaint requires an answer; so does an interpleader complaint. Prior to a 1977 amendment of CPLR 3011, every cross-claim also required an answer, but this was found to be generating too much superfluous paper in tort cases, as described in a prior section.[1] Under the amendment, a cross-claim requires an answer only when the cross-claimant demands one, which she can do with appropriate language in the answer containing the cross-claim, perhaps in an additional paragraph. While motivated by the tort case, however, the amendment is not limited to the tort case; it requires a demand before any cross-claim need be answered. In the absence of a demand, the allegations of the cross-claim are deemed denied.

An auxiliary function of CPLR 3011 is to give all claims and pleadings a label, but any CPLR provision authorizing the assertion of a claim in any context should be given effect without regard to whether CPLR 3011 has an apt label for it. "The rights of parties are not ultimately determined by the names given their pleadings."[2] If that approach is not taken, labels take over and substance becomes lost in the shuffle.

A reply is the plaintiff's response to an answer. It is required when the answer contains a counterclaim[3] and, indeed, the failure to reply in that situation amounts to a default on the counterclaim.

Sometimes the same matter will lend itself to use either as a defense or a counterclaim. If the defendant has used it as a counterclaim, the plaintiff who withholds a reply on the assumption that it is only a defense risks a default. Usury, for example, can be treated as a mere defense, negating the plaintiff's claim, or as an outright counterclaim seeking affirmative relief, such as rescission of the usurious contract. A plaintiff who failed to reply to a usury allegation when it was denominated a counterclaim was held to be in default.[4] A plaintiff in doubt does best to serve a reply. If the plaintiff, in doing so, has guessed wrong, and the defendant moves to dismiss the

---

[1]   See § 227.

[2]   Axelrod & Co. v. Telsey, 77 Misc. 2d 1035, 1038, 353 N.Y.S.2d 596, 599 (Sup. Ct., New York County 1973).

[3]   CPLR 3011. As to whether a reply, required because the answer contains a counterclaim, may also respond to defenses, see Commentary C3011:10 on McKinney's CPLR 3011.

[4]   Loew v. McInerney, 159 A.D. 513, 144 N.Y.S. 546 (2d Dep't 1913). Defaults are vacatable, however, and vacatur of a default in this situation would likely be granted for the mere asking if sought expeditiously. See § 108.

reply, it amounts to a concession that the defendant is seeking no affirmative relief. The plaintiff can live with that.

If there is no counterclaim in the answer, not only need the plaintiff not reply; he may not even do so voluntarily. Absent a counterclaim, a reply is permissible only by court order.[5] Either party can move for the order. Affirmative defenses contained in an answer having no counterclaim (and therefore requiring no reply) are deemed denied.[6]

Whether to order a reply to a non-counterclaiming answer is in the court's discretion. A reply will not be ordered unless the court is convinced that it will serve some useful purpose.[7] It is sometimes ordered when the answer has something like a statute of frauds defense, so as to compel the plaintiff by reply to say whether the contract was oral; or a statute of limitations defense, to compel the plaintiff to set forth relevant dates.[8] An alternative might be to require the plaintiff to state such facts in the complaint,[9] but since they are matters of defense, the complaint should not have to reflect on them at all. The courts are not disposed to make any pleading do that kind of extra bidding today; the bill of particulars and the disclosure devices are more likely to get that assignment.

A reply should not be used by the plaintiff to amend the complaint or to set forth new matter.[10] Nor should a reply ordinarily state an affirmative cause of action. The plaintiff who wants to add another claim at that stage should amend the complaint, obtaining leave to do so if necessary.[11] If the reply does state a claim, however, and in the context of the particular case it seems an appropriate thing to do, it has been held permissible. Thus, if there are two defendants, and defendant A counterclaims plaintiff P for damage to A's car, and P maintains that defendant B is the one responsible for that damage, P may, in the same reply that responds to the counterclaim, include a "cross-claim" against defendant B for contribution or indemnification in respect of the counterclaim.[12] This is sound. The pressing of recriminations and apportionment claims back and forth among parties to a tort suit is frequent; in a context like the one supposed the reply is not merely an appropriate, but even an obvious place for such claims.

In a case decided before the enactment of CPLR Article 14 codifying the right to contribution,[13] defendant X interposed a counterclaim against P for which P maintained that defendant Y was required to indemnify P. Had Y not been a party, P could have impleaded Y for the indemnification.[14] But Y was a party, so P simply included the indemnity claim against Y (calling it a "cross-complaint") in the same reply that responded to the counterclaim, a seemingly sound procedural step. The court disallowed it,[15] apparently remitting P to implead Y into an action in which Y was already a party,

---

5   CPLR 3011.
6   CPLR 3018(a).
7   See Olsen & Chapman Const. Co. v. Village of Cazenovia, 30 A.D.2d 738, 291 N.Y.S.2d 388 (3d Dep't 1968).
8   See, e.g., Barker v. O'Grady, 98 Misc. 42, 162 N.Y.S. 262 (Sup. Ct., Monroe County 1916).
9   See § 215.
10 Eidlitz v. Rothschild, 33 N.Y.S. 1047 (Gen. Term., 1st Dep't 1895).
11 CPLR 3025(a), (b); Habiby v. Habiby, 23 A.D.2d 558, 256 N.Y.S.2d 634 (1st Dep't 1965).
12 De Mato v. Suffolk County, 79 Misc. 2d 484, 360 N.Y.S.2d 570 (Sup. Ct., Suffolk County 1974).
13 See §§ 170 and 171.
14 CPLR 1011.
15 Chambland v. Brewer, 51 Misc. 2d 231, 272 N.Y.S.2d 903 (Sup. Ct., Queens County 1966).

an idle and wasteful formality. The "cross-complaint," under that or any other label, should have been allowed. In the face of a clear legislative intent to allow the indemnity claim, the label appended to the pleading interposing it should have been subordinate.[16]

The reply is ordinarily the final pleading because "[t]here shall be no other pleading unless the court orders otherwise."[17] Suppose, however, that P's reply to a counterclaim contains the defense of the statute of limitations. The court can order D to cross-reply to that defense with the relevant dates. Under old law it sometimes did.[18] But such a step is largely wasteful in view of the availability, as already noted, of the bill of particulars and the disclosure devices to do the job.

J.   CORRECTIVE MOTIONS

Table of Sections

§ 230.   Motions to Correct Pleadings; CPLR 3024

§ 230.   Motions to Correct Pleadings; CPLR 3024

There are two statutorily recognized corrective motions—motions that seek to compel an amendment of a pleading rather than to dismiss it. Both are in CPLR 3024.

Subdivision (a) of CPLR 3024 is the motion for a more definite statement. It's available only to a party required to respond to the objectionable pleading. It may be used by the defendant against the complaint and by the plaintiff against a counterclaim, for example, but it's not available to the plaintiff if the answer contains no counterclaim because in that case the plaintiff doesn't have to respond to the answer.

The movant's burden is to show that the pleading, whether it states a claim or not, is so jumbled or disorderly that she "cannot reasonably be required to frame a response." If the pleading is answerable and what the movant is really seeking is an amplification of it, the motion for a more definite statement will be denied and the movant remitted to seek a bill of particulars.[1]

Subdivision (b) of CPLR 3024 contains the only motion the CPLR recognizes for striking objectionable matter from a pleading.[2] It permits a motion to strike out "scandalous or prejudicial matter unnecessarily inserted in a pleading." Mere repetitiveness is not a ground for a motion to strike.[3] Nor is a mere showing that irrelevant matter has been included.[4] (Corrective motions had been allowed on those grounds under prior law.)[5] Nor does an allegation of scandalousness by itself suffice. An allegation of mayhem in an assault claim is scandalous, for example, but belongs in the pleading, as does a charge of adultery in a divorce case. "Prejudice" by itself has little

---

[16]   Axelrod & Co. v. Telsey, 77 Misc. 2d 1035, 353 N.Y.S.2d 596 (Sup. Ct., New York County 1973).

[17]   CPLR 3011.

[18]   See, e.g., Rosner v. Globe Valve Corp., 276 A.D. 462, 95 N.Y.S.2d 531 (1st Dep't 1950).

[1]   State v. New York Movers Tariff Bureau, Inc., 48 Misc. 2d 225, 254, 264 N.Y.S.2d 931, 963 (Sup. Ct., New York County 1965).

[2]   Koos v. Ludwig, 22 A.D.2d 666, 253 N.Y.S.2d 380 (1st Dep't 1964).

[3]   See Cassissi v. Yee, 46 Misc. 3d 552, 557, 995 N.Y.S.2d 443, 447–48 (Sup. Ct., Westchester County 2014).

[4]   In re Emberger's Estate, 24 A.D.2d 864, 264 N.Y.S.2d 277 (2d Dep't 1965).

[5]   See *Cassissi*, 46 Misc.3d at 557, 995 N.Y.S.2d at 448. Rule 103 of the old (pre-1963) Rules of Civil Procedure.

meaning here because most of what a party pleads is intended to prejudice the other side. The key words are "unnecessarily inserted," which makes relevancy the measuring rod.

Matter directly relevant to the claim stays in. If something is prejudicial or scandalous, while only indirectly relevant at best, it has been held that it may be stricken out even if it can later be made to appear sufficiently relevant at the trial to be admitted into evidence.[6] In Guiliana v. Chiropractic Institute of N. Y.,[7] for example, where P sued a chiropractic facility for letting an inexperienced student treat P, allegations that D allowed other unready students to work on other unwary patients were stricken out— "though possibly pertinent as proof" at the trial—because not a necessary part of P's claim. The *Guiliana* case is best treated as one in which the objectionable matter was only indirectly relevant. It should not be read as authority to strike out anything not needed for the statement of the claim. Reading it so would needlessly encourage corrective motions of this kind in a vast range of cases for the reason that so little is needed today to state a cause of action that the inclusion of anything beyond the barest bones can lead disputatious adversaries to cry "prolix" and run to court. Hence, despite cases like *Guiliana*, relevancy is still the best key to whether matter is "unnecessarily" pleaded, and the best key to relevancy is whether it would be admissible in evidence at the trial.

In addition to the explicit corrective motions of subdivisions (a) and (b) of CPLR 3024, there is also the motion to separately state and number, which arises by implication from CPLR 3014.[8] This is akin to the motion for a more definite statement in that the need of it is usually felt only by a party required to respond to the objectionable pleading. The motion would be appropriate, for example, if a more accurate numbering of allegations would better enable one of several defendants to determine which of the allegations are meant for him.[9] In Scholastic Inc. v. Pace Plumbing Corp.,[10] plaintiff pleaded the statute of limitations "within a boilerplate, catchall paragraph" that also asserted fifteen other affirmative defenses, including "any other matter constituting an avoidance or an affirmative defense which further investigation of this matter may prove applicable herein."

The court noted that while plaintiff could have moved to compel separate numbering, "it was not required to make such a motion because defendant's answer did not necessitate a responsive pleading."[11] Therefore, plaintiff did not waive its contention that it was prejudiced by this kitchen-sink approach to pleading and could not "be forced to accept the defective answer simply because it declined to make a motion to compel separate numbering."[12]

There is some dispute between departments as to whether an order on a separate numbering motion is appealable only by permission, like an order on either of the

---

[6]   See Schachter v. Massachusetts Protective Ass'n, 30 A.D.2d 540, 291 N.Y.S.2d 128 (2d Dep't 1968).

[7]   Guiliana v. Chiropractic Institute of N. Y., 45 Misc. 2d 429, 430, 256 N.Y.S.2d 967, 968 (Sup. Ct., Kings County 1965).

[8]   See Weicker v. Weicker, 26 A.D.2d 39, 40, 270 N.Y.S.2d 640, 641 (1st Dep't 1966).

[9]   See Shapolsky v. Shapolsky, 22 A.D.2d 91, 253 N.Y.S.2d 816 (1st Dep't 1964).

[10]   Scholastic Inc. v. Pace Plumbing Corp., 129 A.D.3d 75, 76, 78, 8 N.Y.S.3d 143, 145 (1st Dep't 2015).

[11]   *Scholastic*, 129 A.D.3d at 79, 8 N.Y.S.3d at 147.

[12]   *Scholastic*, 129 A.D.3d at 79, 8 N.Y.S.3d at 147. For further discussion of the *Scholastic* decision, see § 208.

expressly listed corrective motions of CPLR 3024,[13] or as of right,[14] because not set forth expressly in CPLR 3024. The Second Department has held that it is appealable as of right;[15] the First, that permission is needed.[16]

The time to make a corrective motion is within 20 days after the objectionable pleading is served.[17] This is so even though there may be a 30-day period applicable to the answering time.[18] The time limit applicable to the expressly listed motions of CPLR 3024 should apply as well to the separate numbering motion.

The service of an answer waives the right to move for a more definite statement or for separate numbering,[19] since answering establishes answerability, which both motions are designed to assist. But it does not necessarily waive the motion to strike objectionable matter. If the matter is scandalous and irrelevant, for example, it is just as much so before as after answering. This has prompted the courts to be less rigid with the time requirements for the motion to strike.[20]

The mere making of a corrective motion extends D's answering time. If the motion is denied, D may serve the answer within 10 days after being served with notice of entry of the order denying the motion. If the motion is granted, P is required to serve an amended complaint curing the defects within 10 days after notice of entry of the order granting the motion.[21] D then has 20 days to answer the amended complaint.[22]

This discussion of the corrective motions has assumed the defendant to be the moving party and an objectionable complaint to be the pleading moved against. Any party against whom a pleading is interposed may of course make equivalent use of the corrective motions.

K. SERVICE OF PLEADINGS

Table of Sections

§ 231.   Service of Pleadings; Responding Time
§ 231A.   Leave Time for Trouble

§ 231. Service of Pleadings; Responding Time

Response to the summons is made within either a 20- or 30-day period, depending on the place and method of service. If the summons is served by personal delivery in New York, the responding period is 20 days; if served by any other means, or by any means at all outside New York, the period is 30 days. CPLR 320(a) so provides when the complaint does not accompany the summons; CPLR 3012(c) so provides when it does.

---

[13] See CPLR 5701(b)(2), (3).

[14] See CPLR 5701(a)(2)(v), discussed in § 526 in the appeals chapter.

[15] Weicker v. Weicker, 26 A.D.2d 39, 270 N.Y.S.2d 640 (1st Dep't 1966).

[16] Consolidated Airborne Systems, Inc. v. Silverman, 23 A.D.2d 695, 257 N.Y.S.2d 827 (2d Dep't 1965).

[17] CPLR 3024(c).

[18] CPLR 3012(c).

[19] Albemarle Theatre, Inc. v. Bayberry Realty Corp., 27 A.D.2d 172, 277 N.Y.S.2d 505 (1st Dep't 1967).

[20] See Szolosi v. Long Island R. Co., 52 Misc. 2d 1081, 277 N.Y.S.2d 587 (Sup. Ct., Suffolk County 1967).

[21] CPLR 3024(c).

[22] CPLR 3012(a).

If P should serve D by two methods, each having a different answering time, such as where a corporate defendant is served via the secretary of state, which affords a 30-day period, as well as by personal delivery to an officer, which offers 20 days, D may take advantage of the longer period and is not in default when the shorter one expires.[1]

The defendant's responsive step when the summons is served without a complaint is to appear and demand a copy of the complaint or simply demand a copy of the complaint.[2] The defendant's responsive step when the summons and complaint are served together is to serve an answer or make a motion.[3]

CPLR 320(a), governing the time to appear when the complaint is not served with the summons, and CPLR 3012(b), allowing the defendant to demand a copy of the complaint, should be read together. Since the demand is a step taken in response to the summons, it should be made within the period for appearing as offered by CPLR 320(a). Before CPLR 3012(b) was amended in 1978, some old caselaw suggested that when a complaint was not served with the summons, the defendant could stymie the plaintiff altogether by just doing nothing; that the plaintiff could not then serve a complaint voluntarily.[4] Some later caselaw disagreed.[5] The amended CPLR 3012(b) not only permits, but requires the plaintiff to serve a complaint if the defendant appears in the action, even if the defendant does not serve a demand.

If the defendant does not respond at all after being served with a summons, whether the summons has with it a complaint or mere CPLR 305(b) notice, the plaintiff can apply for a default judgment under CPLR 3215.[6] If the defendant needs or just wants additional answering time, he should get a written stipulation from the plaintiff, or a court order, extending the time.[7]

If the summons was served "bare," accompanied by neither a complaint nor a notice, the defendant can move to dismiss the action on the ground that the defect is jurisdictional.[8] That would be an appropriate tactic for the defendant if the statute of limitations would now bar a new action by the plaintiff. But if the statute is still alive, and a dismissal would just result in a new and timely service by the plaintiff, with proper papers, the defendant should consider whether a motion to dismiss is worth the bother.[9]

It has been held in lower court practice, too, that if no complaint of any kind accompanies the summons, the defect is jurisdictional and the action can be dismissed on the defendant's motion.[10] In the lower courts, too, the summons and complaint are

---

[1]   Olson v. Jordan, 181 Misc. 942, 43 N.Y.S.2d 348 (Sup. Ct., New York County 1943).

[2]   CPLR 320(a), 3012(b); see § 60.

[3]   CPLR 3011, 3211(e); see § 110.

[4]   See Gluckselig v. H. Michaelyan, Inc., 132 Misc. 783, 230 N.Y.S. 593 (Sup. Ct., New York County 1928), aff'd, 225 A.D. 666, 231 N.Y.S. 757 (1st Dep't).

[5]   E.g., Keyes v. McLaughlin, 49 A.D.2d 974, 373 N.Y.S.2d 891 (3d Dep't 1975).

[6]   See § 295.

[7]   See § 204.

[8]   See § 60.

[9]   Some of the unsuspected implications of the 1978 change that bars the service of a naked summons appear in the 1978 Commentary C3012:1 on McKinney's CPLR 3012.

[10]   See Paskus, Gordon and Hyman v. Peck, 41 Misc. 2d 1004, 246 N.Y.S.2d 874 (N.Y. City Civ. Ct. 1964).

served together, but the complaint can be a mere "indorsement" on the face of the summons.[11]

The common procedure when only a CPLR 305(b) notice is served with the summons is for the defendant to serve on the plaintiff a single paper embodying both a notice of appearance and a demand for the complaint. CPLR 3012(b) states explicitly that the demand by itself is not an appearance, and this is the tool that can be used by a defendant who may wish to default in the New York action and assert jurisdictional objections in another forum when plaintiff seeks to enforce the default judgment there.[12] After the summons has been served, as noted earlier,[13] other papers in the action—and this includes all later pleadings as well—become "interlocutory" or "intermediate" papers and may be served by mail on the party's attorney. When the complaint accompanies the summons, the methods of service applicable to the summons of course govern. When it does not, but is served later pursuant to the defendant's demand, the complaint qualifies as an interlocutory paper and may be served on the defendant's attorney by ordinary mail.

In medical malpractice actions, including those for dental and podiatric malpractice, a special certificate of merit must accompany the complaint,[14] whenever it may be served. Effective August 30, 2013, the statute now has a companion, CPLR 3012–b, which requires the filing of a "certificate of merit" in any residential foreclosure action involving a home loan in which the defendant is a resident of the property subject to the foreclosure.[15]

It is common practice, and deemed common courtesy among attorneys, to allow one another reasonable extensions of time to plead. While often oral, these are in every sense stipulations and, routine though the stipulation to extend the time to plead may be, it should be in writing.[16] The Court of Appeals spoke to this in a case in which a plaintiff, asked by the defendant for an extension of time to answer, wanted to qualify the extension to exact of the defendant a waiver of jurisdictional defenses as a quid pro quo. The Court held that in that case the plaintiff must also have the defendant sign the stipulation, or the qualification won't bind and the defendant's jurisdictional objection will be preserved.[17]

The party who needs an extension of time to appear or plead, but can't get it from the other side, can move the court for it pursuant to CPLR 3012(d). If the other side threatens to take a default before the motion can come on for a hearing, the motion can be accelerated by the procedure of an order to show cause.[18] While CPLR 2004 applies to

---

[11] See § 902 in the New York City Civ. Ct. Act and in the Uniform District, City, and Justice Court Acts, McKinney's Vol. 29A, Parts 2 and 3. The indorsement is somewhat akin to the CPLR 305(b) notice applicable in supreme and county court practice. See § 211.

[12] See § 60.

[13] See § 202.

[14] CPLR 3012–a requires that in medical, dental, and podiatric malpractice actions, the complaint, whenever served, must have with it the certificate of the plaintiff's lawyer attesting that she consulted with an appropriate expert and believes, based on the consultation, that there is a "reasonable basis" for the action. For the sanction applied for a violation of this requirement, see the McKinney's Commentaries on CPLR 3012–a.

[15] See Commentaries to McKinney's CPLR 3012–b.

[16] CPLR 2104. See § 204.

[17] See Klein v. Mount Sinai Hosp., 61 N.Y.2d 865, 474 N.Y.S.2d 462, 462 N.E.2d 1180 (1984).

[18] See § 248.

extensions of all sorts of time periods arising during litigation, CPLR 3012(d) specifically addresses an "[e]xtension of time to appear or plead." The latter provision permits the court to extend "the time to appear or plead, or compel the acceptance of a pleading untimely served, upon such terms as may be just and upon a showing of reasonable excuse for delay or default." While the statute does not expressly require it, the Second Department has repeatedly held that a defendant must not only provide a reasonable excuse for the delay in appearing but must also "demonstrate a potentially meritorious defense to the action."[19] By contrast, the First Department does not require a defendant to demonstrate the existence of a meritorious defense on an application under CPLR 3012(d).[20] The Third Department appears to be of two minds on the subject.[21] The Fourth Department has required a reasonable excuse for the delay and an affidavit of merit for applications under CPLR 3012(d).[22]

If, however, a default judgment has already been entered, a party moving under CPLR 5015(a)(1) to vacate a default at that stage must demonstrate both a reasonable excuse for the delay in appearing and a meritorious defense to the action.[23] Note too that in the category of default where the plaintiff tries to avoid dismissal for failure to timely serve a complaint after a demand for the complaint has been made pursuant to CPLR 3012(b), the plaintiff must demonstrate both a reasonable excuse for the delay in serving the complaint and a meritorious cause of action.[24]

Neither party, when under the gun with an obligation to plead, should be casual about time limits, perhaps a bit too serene in the assumption—usually sound enough—that the court will be generous about vacating a default judgment even if the other side should obtain one. Omissions of a few days and perhaps even a few weeks have been forgiven, but attorneys have been notoriously remiss in this matter with little heed of the consequences. Delays of months and years have been seen in the cases,[25] mainly delays by plaintiffs in not serving a complaint pursuant to a demand as prescribed by CPLR 3012(b), which rules the roost when only a summons and notice are used in initial service. These most often produce dismissals, and every such dismissal can qualify as a neglect to prosecute within the meaning of CPLR 205(a),[26] which means in turn that no additional time for a new action may be available if the original statute of limitations has expired (as it usually has).

---

[19]   Deutsche Bank Nat. Trust Co. v. Kuldip, 136 A.D.3d 969, 25 N.Y.S.3d 653 (2d Dep't 2016); see also KI 12, LLC v. Joseph, 137 A.D.3d 750, 26 N.Y.S.3d 573 (2d Dep't 2016).

[20]   See Hirsch v. New York City Dept. of Educ., 105 A.D.3d 522, 961 N.Y.S.2d 923 (1st Dep't 2013); Vazquez v. Beharry, 82 A.D.3d 649, 919 N.Y.S.2d 336 (1st Dep't 2011).

[21]   See Bank of New York Mellon v. Jinks, 127 A.D.3d 1367, 7 N.Y.S.3d 634 (3d Dep't 2015) (affirming grant of extension based on reasonable excuse); but see Anthony DeMarco & Sons Nursery, LLC v. Maxim Const. Service Corp., 126 A.D.3d 1105, 4 N.Y.S.3d 732 (3d Dep't 2015).

[22]   Gribbins v. Rushford Lake Recreation Dist., 96 A.D.3d 1369, 946 N.Y.S.2d 324 (4th Dep't 2012).

[23]   See, e.g., Eugene Di Lorenzo, Inc. v. A.C. Dutton Lumber Co., Inc., 67 N.Y.2d 138, 141, 501 N.Y.S.2d 8, 10, 492 N.E.2d 116, 118 (1986); John Wiley & Sons, Inc. v. Grossman, 132 A.D.3d 559, 18 N.Y.S.3d 610 (1st Dep't 2015); see § 427.

[24]   See Gear Up, Inc. v. City of New York, 140 A.D.3d 515, 34 N.Y.S.3d 17 (1st Dep't 2016); Lobel v. Hilltop Village Cooperative, No. 4, 138 A.D.3d 938, 28 N.Y.S.3d 633 (2d Dep't 2016); Roberts v. Northington, 128 A.D.3d 1487, 8 N.Y.S.3d 814 (4th Dep't 2015). These issues are explored in further detail in the Commentaries to McKinney's CPLR 3012.

[25]   See, e.g., Kahn v. Samson Management Corp., 44 A.D.2d 571, 353 N.Y.S.2d 227 (2d Dep't 1974).

[26]   Wright v. Farlin, 42 A.D.2d 141, 346 N.Y.S.2d 11 (3d Dep't 1973); see § 52.

The problem of defaults like this—defaults by plaintiffs—became an epidemic for a while after the Court of Appeals handed down Barasch v. Micucci[27] in 1980, dealing with pleading defaults based on "law office failures." The epidemic subsided under 1983 legislation, but it left behind some scars. It also left behind some good lessons, and to preserve them, we've made the brief but painful history of *Barasch* an independent subtopic, following.

The Era of Barasch and "Law Office Failure": March 25, 1980 to June 21, 1983

Barasch came down with an audible thud on March 25, 1980. From that day until June 21, 1983, when amendments overruling the case took effect—principally the amendments adding CPLR 2005 and subdivision (d) of CPLR 3012—New York practice was a chaotic arena. Each side would pounce on the other with a default application for just about any delay at all in the service of a pleading.

Barasch held—as a matter of law, and unanimously—that law office failure is not an acceptable excuse for the late service or nonservice of a pleading. "Law office failure" is a caption that embraces most of the reasons tendered over the years to excuse defaults: the attorney confused folder numbers in the office, misplaced the file, misplaced a secretary, became ill, was on trial in Elmira, was on Elba deposing a retired general, was indisposed for personal reasons, relied on an inexperienced associate, moved offices, changed partners, went to the races, ad infinitum. With apologies to the adage about the candle and the darkness, it is better to serve a timely complaint than to define a law office failure.

Applied in *Barasch* to a plaintiff's delay in serving a complaint, the holding was afterwards extended to a defendant's default in serving an answer, but this time by a closely divided (4–3) Court of Appeals in Eaton v. Equitable Life Assur. Soc. of U.S., Inc.,[28] handed down on June 15, 1982. At one point or another during *Barasch's* more than three-year reign, moreover, the summary rejection of law office failure as an excuse was extended to delays affecting bills of particulars, failures to prosecute within the action (after the pleading stage), failures to show up at a calendar call, etc.

While the question of whether to allow the late service of a pleading or bill of particulars or to excuse a calendar failure had been traditionally regarded as a matter of judicial discretion to be exercised on a case-by-case basis, the effect of *Barasch* was to withdraw all discretion and virtually mandate a default judgment for the omission. Said the court in *Barasch*:

> [T]hose excuses which may be roughly categorized under the heading of "law office failures" cannot properly serve as a basis for defeating a motion to dismiss under CPLR 3012 (subd b) . . . .

Barasch described itself as a "rare" instance in which a dismissal was required as a matter of law. But it was by no means a rare case. It was therefore easy to predict that *Barasch* would have the impact that it in fact ended up with. The impact was great. The

---

[27]   Barasch v. Micucci, 49 N.Y.2d 594, 427 N.Y.S.2d 732, 404 N.E.2d 1275 (1980). The *Barasch* case is the subject of the lead note in NYSLD No. 247.

[28]   Eaton v. Equitable Life Assur. Soc. of U.S., Inc., 56 N.Y.2d 900, 453 N.Y.S.2d 404, 438 N.E.2d 1119 (1982). The *Eaton* case is the subject of the lead note in NYSLD No. 271.

cases were often described by the lawyers concerned as horror stories (meritorious claims lost, meritorious defenses barred, all for relatively innocent omissions).[29]

The overruling of *Barasch* was effected by the enactment of both CPLR 2005, explicitly permitting the court to consider "law office failure" as an excuse for a pleading delay, and CPLR 3012(d), permitting the court, in excusing a pleading default, to impose "such terms as may be just."

The lawyer must remember that the overruling of *Barasch* and its progeny is not a guarantee that all pleading defaults will be forgiven upon the presentation of any excuse at all, law-office connected or not. All the overruling does is restore discretion to the court to consider law office failure alongside any other excuses in determining whether to forgive the late service of a pleading or some other default. If the delay has been long, or the reasons are particularly weak, or for any other combination of factors judicial discretion is not impressed with the showing, the court can reject the party's request to be relieved of the default and just let it stand. In more than a few cases after the *Barasch* overruling, the courts did just that.[30]

The preference of some judges, with *Barasch* no longer pressuring them, is to excuse defaults upon the condition that the defaulter pay the other side costs (including attorney's fees) in a sum the judge deems appropriate to the delay and to the excuse offered.[31] There is ample authority for that under the "such terms as may be just" provision of CPLR 3012(d).

The accused defaulter must be sure to include among his motion papers, along with his excuses, an affidavit of merits. In a case involving a plaintiff's lateness in serving a complaint, the Court of Appeals held—even after *Barasch*—that the absence of the affidavit from the plaintiff's opposing papers still mandates an unconditional dismissal "as a matter of law."[32]

The affidavit of merits had best be that of the party; rarely will the lawyer's affidavit or affirmation do the job because rarely will the lawyer have first-hand knowledge of the claim. And the affidavit should be included in the original papers. The Court of Appeals has held that it is no abuse of discretion for a court to reject the late filing of a party's affidavit after the prior (and useless) submission by the lawyer of his own.[33]

§ 231A. Leave Time for Trouble

A default caused by a failure to take a step within a prescribed time, or by a defect in the procedure for the taking, can occur in a variety of contexts in litigation and at every stage of it. A treatment designed to warn about the consequences of leaving insufficient time to remedy a mistake or omission, and the unsuspecting ways in which it can destroy a claim or defense, has no obvious chronological niche in a practice text. It is nevertheless helpful to centralize a set of warnings under one heading, which requires a more or less arbitrary choice of place. The place we choose for this treatment is a

---

[29] These cases may be found in the various installments of the New York State Law Digest, enumerated in the lead note in Digest 282 (June 1983).

[30] See, e.g., Bernard by Bernard v. City School Dist. of Albany, 96 A.D.2d 995, 465 N.Y.S.2d 793 (3d Dep't 1983).

[31] See Commentary C3012:19 on McKinney's CPLR 3012. The commentary also treats defects other than pleading omissions that can turn delays into fatal defaults.

[32] Kel Management Corp. v. Rogers & Wells, 64 N.Y.2d 904, 488 N.Y.S.2d 156, 477 N.E.2d 458 (1985).

[33] Foitl v. G.A.F. Corp., 64 N.Y.2d 911, 488 N.Y.S.2d 377, 477 N.E.2d 618 (1985).

separate section right here, following the *Barasch* era of pleading defaults. It could as well appear at the very beginning of the chapter on the statute of limitations, nearly 100 sections back,[1] or following the study of the dismissal for neglect to prosecute, more than 100 sections further on,[2] or at any assortment of other places.

Choice of place is secondary. What is important is that every student of practice in the courts, novice and veteran alike, make at least some effort to coordinate and review the subject in one sitting and try to settle deep in mind the often unappreciated advantage of doing all things, whenever possible, with time to spare.

That an action has to be started within the applicable statute of limitations, or that a pleading has to be served by a stated date to avoid a default, may be obvious enough. But there are a number of less obvious steps in litigation whose misdoing can carry dire consequences only because of the time element. Things like that crop up insidiously in the course of daily litigation practice, in both the New York and federal courts, and quite often the only thing prominent about them is the consequence: a dismissal or default of some kind too late to allow for a redoing, and with the consequent forfeiture of a claim or defense, and, not unlikely, a malpractice claim against the lawyer.

An inadequate notice served with a summons under CPLR 305(b), for example, might be assumed to be amendable. It is not, however,[3] and when the plaintiff who doesn't know that finds it out, it will be only the time element that dictates the consequence. If there is time for a new action, the defect is minor; if there is not, the defect is fatal. The inadequacy of the notice may be the apparent offender here, but the real culprit is time: the bringing of the action so near the expiration of the statute of limitations that when the defect arises—even one that arises as early within a case as this one does—there is no time left for a new action.

Simply put, the plaintiff in these situations has failed to leave time for trouble, and the statute of limitations was waiting in the wings. It waits like that with a mass of things whose misdoing may seem innocent enough on the surface. If time was left for trouble, the case stays on the surface and the litigant can correct the defect. But if a time margin has not been left, the case can sink dead away. This has happened time and again, at many junctures of litigation. The mission of this section is to set forth at least an illustrative list of them.

1. The Statute of Limitations.

We begin with the obvious. Starting cases too late under the statute of limitations is a good way to lose both cases and clients. If litigation is inevitable—and lawyers should not develop the habit of judging inevitability solely by the approach of the statute of limitations—it is wise as a rule of thumb, if there is any choice in the matter, to start the action with six or eight months to spare under the applicable period. The case should be diaried with conservative rather than rosy assumptions.[4] Unexpected threshold problems can arise and bring dismissal. These are illustrated in the separately captioned paragraphs below.

---

[1]   The statute of limitations treatment begins with § 33.

[2]   The neglect to prosecute dismissal is the subject of § 375.

[3]   See § 60, and the discussion of the *Parker* case in § 52.

[4]   See § 33.

2. *Inadequate Notice Under CPLR 305(b).*

This is the example referred to above. As was shown earlier in this book, in the treatment of the CPLR 305(b) notice, there is no safe formula for determining how much suffices to satisfy as a proper "notice." If the notice is found improper, by only a word or phrase, the result is a dismissal, the dismissal is jurisdictional, and there is no time extension offered by CPLR 205(a) for a new action.[5] Had the action been brought with several months to go, any objection to the adequacy of the CPLR 305(b) notice would have had to be raised by the defendant by way of motion or answer, which would have called the defect to the plaintiff's attention and permitted the bringing of a new action before the statute of limitations expired.

3. *Defect in Summons Service.*

Among lawyers representing defendants in litigation, most notably in tort litigation—the personal injury, wrongful death, and medical malpractice actions—there has been almost a tradition of raising an objection to service of process. The reward of a dismissal on so facile a ground is such a temptation that few can resist it even if the prospect of a dismissal is only a remote one. Some attorneys include the defense in the answer without even having ascertained the facts from the client. If the statute of limitations is closing in, the sustaining of the defense will work a dismissal when it is too late to start over. CPLR 205(a) does not offer its six months for a new action when the earlier action was dismissed for want of proper service.[6]

One of the best examples of this kind of lastminutism conduct is Feinstein v. Bergner,[7] involving service under paragraph 4 of CPLR 308. Paragraph 4 is the affix-and-mail provision.[8] The affixing must be made to a premises presently used by the defendant or the defendant's actual place of business. In *Feinstein*, the place at which the affixing was made under paragraph 4 had been the defendant's residence earlier, but was no longer so when the action was commenced. His parents still lived there, though, and the mailing, the second required step, did get through to the defendant. No matter, held the Court of Appeals. Service was no good, and it was now too late for the plaintiff to start again.[9]

Almost any plaintiff can make a mistake like that, but the only plaintiff who gets no second chance is the one who has left no time for trouble. Suing with enough time for a new action, should a jurisdictional defect about service be raised, may even be a way for the plaintiff to find out about the defendant's present whereabouts within the action itself, when the defendant spills the beans on a motion to dismiss. What a delight for the plaintiff when an education accompanies the dismissal, and there's still time to do things right!

Service under the recently enacted CPLR 312–a is by ordinary mail and requires a signed acknowledgment.[10] Suppose the acknowledgment is forged, or, simply, that it is

---

[5]   See § 60. Serving no notice or complaint at all with the summons is also, of course, a jurisdictional defect. See also § 52.

[6]   See the treatment of the *Markoff* case in § 52.

[7]   Feinstein v. Bergner, 48 N.Y.2d 234, 422 N.Y.S.2d 356, 397 N.E.2d 1161 (1979).

[8]   See § 74.

[9]   The case has equal bearing on service under paragraph 2 of CPLR 308, the deliver-and-mail requirement. See § 72.

[10]   See § 76A.

made by one without authority to act for the defendant. That and similar issues can arise under CPLR 312–a, and should the action be dismissed for want of jurisdiction, it will be reassuring to the plaintiff to know that there is still time to make the service afresh.

Not even court-ordered service under CPLR 308(5) can be considered airtight. An appellate court can disagree and hold the method approved by the lower court invalid.[11] Again, the only thing that can save the plaintiff is that there is still a bit of time to start a new action.

Soto v. Freda[12] adds a new dimension to the absurdity of last minute casualness. On the last day of the statute of limitations, and in late afternoon to boot, the plaintiff's attorney sent an office messenger to file the required commencement papers. It was in New York County, where the local procedure requires that a cover sheet be filled out and also filed. The messenger would have been glad to fill out the sheet, but his vision was impaired and he couldn't read it. Nor would personnel in the clerk's office help him. The papers were thus refused. Ludicrously prolonged steps followed—including an Article 78 proceeding[13] and an appeal—before the matter finally came back into the supreme court's hands where the court validated the filing with a nunc pro tunc order.[14]

The problem of filing involved in the *Soto* case may be abated today by virtue of an amendment of CPLR 2001, the mistakes-correcting provision, which was extended in 2007 to apply even to some mistakes made at filing time, mistakes which before that had been deemed "jurisdictional" and required dismissal.[15]

Finding an adjective to describe the absurdity of waiting until the last part of the last day and then imposing on a messenger with impaired vision to take the required step would challenge a lexicographer.

4.   *Serving the Wrong Person.*

The plaintiff need not be guilty of such nonsensical conduct to meet the misfortunes of leaving too little time for trouble. Even a comparatively innocent plaintiff who thought he started things in time can confront a jurisdictional quirk of some kind, such as where the person served appears to be the right one to serve under one statute, but where another unsuspected statute crops up with a different instruction. This point is illustrated in Horowitz v. Incorporated Village of Roslyn,[16] treated earlier.[17] The suit was against a county and the plaintiff served the county clerk as authorized by CPLR 311(4). But unknown to the plaintiff, there was also a service provision in the Nassau County Administrative Code, requiring service on the county executive or county attorney. The clerk turned the summons over to the county attorney, but the action was dismissed just the same.

Unless the plaintiff is virtually clairvoyant, the only way to protect against a hidden trap like this is to sue with plenty of time for a new action. Defects of this kind arise

---

[11]   See § 75.

[12]   Soto v. Freda, 196 Misc. 2d 623, 766 N.Y.S.2d 299 (Sup. Ct., New York County 2003).

[13]   The Article 78 proceeding is treated in §§ 557 et seq.

[14]   The court held that a failure to include something like a cover sheet, while within a given court's local prerogative to require, may not be treated as a jurisdictional defect. See § 63.

[15]   Treatment of CPLR 2001 and its 2007 amendment appears in several prior sections. See §§ 6, 63, 70, and 201.

[16]   Horowitz v. Incorporated Village of Roslyn, 144 A.D.2d 639, 535 N.Y.S.2d 79 (2d Dep't 1988).

[17]   See § 70.

early in the litigation, or can in any event be flushed out of the defendant by an alert plaintiff early in the litigation, so that the plaintiff can take remedial steps as needed and on time. A motion by the defendant will raise a jurisdictional objection promptly and enable the plaintiff to start a new action just as promptly, if one is necessary. If the defendant raises the objection by way of defense in the answer instead of by motion, which is the defendant's option,[18] the plaintiff can test the defense quickly with a motion to strike it under CPLR 3211(b).[19]

If the defendant's first step is to ask the plaintiff for an extension of time to plead, a frequent first step, the plaintiff should exact from the defendant in return either a stipulation waiving jurisdictional defenses or at least a conversation about whether the defendant has any. If the defendant hesitates, the plaintiff should refuse the extension and insist on a timely answer, which will show whether or not the objection exists.[20]

Analogous to serving the wrong person is naming the wrong person in the first place. The Court of Appeals has held that when the designated defendant is "a nonexistent entity"; the person served is not a proper person to serve in behalf of the intended entity; and the intended entity eventually gets notice of the action but only after the expiration of the statute of limitations; the plaintiff has lost it all.[21] Just allowing some extra time up front could have enabled the plaintiff to fix things up.[22]

5.   *Other Jurisdictional Defects.*

A dismissal for a defect of personal jurisdiction based not on flawed service but on want of a jurisdictional basis, such as where longarm jurisdiction is lacking,[23] is even more serious because here a proper service will not cure the defect. A new action will have to be brought in some other place, and the statute of limitations of that place will be the one applicable. It is wise to have checked that out before commencing the New York action, so that time enough is left for a new action in the other place, under *its* statute of limitations, should the New York action fail. This involves a lot of research and a lot of timing, but the reward will be the ability to start afresh for having left time for trouble.[24]

Plaintiffs must take note of a possible trend in New York State law limiting the scope of longarm jurisdiction[25] and the recent United States Supreme Court's decisions in Daimler AG v. Bauman[26] and Walden v. Fiore,[27] which significantly curtail presence jurisdiction under CPLR 301 and longarm jurisdiction under CPLR 302(a)(3)(ii).[28] If plaintiff commences an action in New York and the existence of presence or longarm jurisdiction is not crystal clear, the plaintiff must carefully calendar the statute of limitations in the jurisdiction where the defendant is incorporated or has its principal

---

[18]   See § 111.

[19]   See § 269.

[20]   See the series of lead notes in NYSLD Nos. 274–76 on the timing of jurisdictional objections.

[21]   Maldonado v. Maryland Rail Commuter Service Admin., 91 N.Y.2d 467, 672 N.Y.S.2d 831, 695 N.E.2d 700 (1998).

[22]   See the discussion of the *Maldonado* case in NYSLD No. 461.

[23]   See § 80.

[24]   See the trio of New York State Law Digest lead notes cited in note 20 above.

[25]   See Paterno v. Laser Spine Institute, 24 N.Y.3d 370, 998 N.Y.S.2d 720, 23 N.E.3d 988 (2014); § 86.

[26]   Daimler AG v. Bauman, 571 U.S. 117, 134 S. Ct. 746, 187 L. Ed. 2d 624 (2014).

[27]   Walden v. Fiore, 134 S. Ct. 1115, 188 L. Ed. 2d 12 (2014).

[28]   See §§ 82, 88.

place of business, or the place where the claimed wrong occurred. Furthermore, any defenses to personal jurisdiction lurking in the answer must be promptly addressed before the statute of limitations expires in these venues.[29] If this is not possible, a holding action should be commenced in defendant's home state or the place where the claimed wrong occurred, assuming the latter place can be clearly determined.[30] Following this procedure will ensure plaintiff that even if he loses the jurisdictional battle in New York, the ultimate war on the merits can still be won in another forum.

6. Dispensing with Reliance on Relation-Back Doctrine.

All of the tension connected with the so-called "relation-back" doctrine, embodied in CPLR 203(f)[31] for New York practice and in Rule 15(c) of the Federal Rules of Civil Procedure for federal practice,[32] is tension created by the time element. The plaintiff who has omitted a claim and wants to add it now can do so only if the statute of limitations on it is still alive. If it is not alive at amendment time, the plaintiff's hope is that it can be "related back" to the time of the original commencement of the action, which requires a showing that the new claim arises out of the same transaction that the original one does. If it can't be related back, the claim is lost. A showing that the original statute of limitations is still alive will make it unnecessary to depend entirely on the relation back provision, but the statute will be alive only for plaintiffs who have left time for trouble.

7. Need to Add New Parties.

Something in the early stages of litigation, usually something coming out of one of the disclosure devices,[33] may suggest that the plaintiff needs to join someone as an additional party, which requires the service of a supplemental summons;[34] or, indeed, that the plaintiff has joined the wrong party to begin with and must now go out and get the right one. If the original statute is still alive, that should be no problem. If it is dead, it is a problem that may have no solution.

8. Procrastinator's Credibility Affected.

It was also noted earlier that the lawyer who procrastinates at one point in litigation may find his credibility impaired at a later point[35] and that it may cost the client the case. That appears to be what happened in Engel by Engel v. Lichterman,[36] a dispute about whether a conditional order allowing P a new period in which to serve a bill of particulars was received by P. D said he mailed the order. P protested that he didn't receive it, but the Court did not believe P, who had been lax in earlier phases of the action. D ended up with summary judgment. The case teaches what a negative effect dilatory conduct can have on an attorney's credibility, even on so seemingly picayune a point as whether a mailed paper was received.

A more impressive lesson still is that the timely commencement of an action, and with jurisdiction perfected, is no guarantee against meeting up with the statute of limitations later. Failing to do things timely within the action can bring on a dismissal,

---

[29] See § 269; CPLR 3211(b) (allowing plaintiff to move to dismiss any defenses in defendant's answer).

[30] See § 262.

[31] See § 49.

[32] See § 615 (Practitioner's Edition).

[33] These are studied beginning with § 343.

[34] See § 65.

[35] See § 202.

[36] Engel by Engel v. Lichterman, 62 N.Y.2d 943, 479 N.Y.S.2d 188, 468 N.E.2d 26 (1984).

such as for neglect to prosecute the case diligently,[37] and a new action after a dismissal at this later stage is all the more likely to meet the statute of limitations barrier. One might guess that since a dismissal of this kind is not for want of jurisdiction, it will get the six months of CPLR 205(a) for a new action. It will not. Lack of prosecution is another item on the list of things to which CPLR 205(a) will not accord a six-month statute of limitations extension.[38]

The courts have often warned that procrastination even after the proper commencement of an action can invoke the policies of repose underlying the statute of limitations.[39]

9.　Timely Filing but Late Service.

Service of process, which under CPLR 306–b has to be made within 120 days after the action is filed (and within an even shorter time in a special proceeding),[40] has some flexibility built in, especially in contrast with the filing step. The court can extend the 120-day service period for "good cause or in the interest of justice." That by itself suggests how much more relaxed the service requirement is when juxtaposed with the filing requirement. But service, too, took on a tension in 2005 when the Court of Appeals in Slate v. Schiavone Const. Co.[41] gave the 120-day service requirement a rigorous reading, making an extension harder to get afterwards.[42] So now there, too, a leave-time-for-trouble lesson is in order: don't be lax about the 120 days. If because of the *Slate* decision an extension is not granted, and the statute of limitations has by now expired, a dismissal for want of timely service will—even though the action was filed on time—mean the end of the case.

10.　Similar Problems on the Federal Side.

Similar problems can arise in the federal courts, which have in addition a prize problem not often met in the New York courts: it is often difficult in a federal action predicated on a federal question (as opposed to diversity of citizenship) to determine what statute of limitations applies to the case in the first place.[43]

* * *

In all practices, there is a bonus for the litigant who leaves time for trouble.

L.　VERIFICATION

Table of Sections

§ 232.　Verification of Pleadings, Generally

§ 233.　Who May Verify

§ 234.　Form of Verification

§ 235.　Remedy for Defective Verification

---

[37]　See § 375.

[38]　See § 52.

[39]　See Sortino v. Fisher, 20 A.D.2d 25, 245 N.Y.S.2d 186 (1st Dep't 1963), treated in § 375.

[40]　See § 553.

[41]　Slate v. Schiavone Const. Co., 4 N.Y.3d 816, 796 N.Y.S.2d 573, 829 N.E.2d 665 (2005).

[42]　See the lead note on the *Slate* case in NYSLD No. 544.

[43]　See § 615 (Practitioner's Edition).

§ 232. Verification of Pleadings, Generally

A verification is an affidavit swearing to the truth of a pleading.[1] Verification is largely optional under the CPLR and would, for the most part, have been abandoned if the Advisory Committee had had its way. The committee recognized that the pleading, although technically the statement of the party, is really the product of the lawyer. It proposed to have the lawyer certify instead of having the party verify.[2] The legislature rejected the proposal and restored verification in pretty much the same form it had under prior law.

The requirement of verification is supposed to encourage honesty in pleading. A false verification is technically a perjury,[3] but district attorneys seldom become involved, excusing themselves on the ground of more pressing problems. Earlier in our legal history, the requirement of swearing may have been underwritten by a genuine fear of hell, but hell has had little impact on New York practice. Quite the contrary. Verification, in a word, has nothing more to recommend it than the legislature.

With a legislative imprimatur, but with almost all of its teeth gone, verification still smiles grotesquely from the pages of the CPLR, which requires us to give it at least a few pages of homage.

In only a few instances is verification mandatory. All pleadings must be verified in a matrimonial action, except the part of a responsive pleading that responds to a charge of adultery (because—not to upset the reader unduly—adultery is a crime and pleading with respect to it invokes privilege).[4] In a summary proceeding to recover the possession of real property (the usual landlord-tenant vehicle), the petition must be verified.[5] Among the CPLR instances of mandatory verification of a complaint are where it contains or has appended the schedule of goods and services available for optional use under CPLR 3016(f),[6] or where it seeks to charge an obligor with an amount still unsatisfied after prior suit by the obligee against a co-obligor.[7] The pleadings in an Article 78 proceeding also require verification.[8]

To continue this stimulating saga, we note that in a few instances an answer must be verified even if the complaint is not. If the complaint charges the defendant with fraud, a statute requires the answer to be verified.[9] Such conduct is likely to amount to a criminal charge, however, which would invoke the privilege against self-incrimination and dispense with verification altogether,[10] but these are mere constitutional requirements and must not be allowed to impede the jolly meanderings of the law of verification. Another instance of required verification of the answer is that of a corporate defendant being sued on a promissory note,[11] a requirement so trivial that it lacks the

---

[1] CPLR 3020(a).

[2] See 1st Rep. Leg. Doc. No. 6(b), pp. 73 to 74 (1957).

[3] See, e.g., Penal Law §§ 210.10, 210.15.

[4] Dom. Rel. Law § 211. Penal Law § 255.17 still makes adultery a criminal act.

[5] RPAPL 741.

[6] See § 216.

[7] CPLR 1502.

[8] CPLR 7804(d).

[9] CPLR 3020(b)(1).

[10] Kellogg v. Match Supply Co., 165 A.D. 885, 151 N.Y.S. 361 (3d Dep't 1915), recognized this problem two practice acts ago. See Commentary C3020:5 on McKinney's CPLR 3020.

[11] CPLR 3020(b)(2).

minuscule electric charge needed to adhere it to some portion of the brain.[12] There is also a requirement in the CPLR that a defense be verified if it "does not involve the merits."[13] This would embrace such defenses as lack of jurisdiction, lack of capacity, other action pending, failure to join a party, and a number of others. Court files are filled, however, with unverified answers embracing such defenses, and there is mounting evidence that no one cares. The fact that no one cares speaks well of bench and bar.

With the few exceptions above and a few others in which verification is mandatory, verification is optional. When opted for, it requires that all subsequent pleadings (including those of adverse parties) also be verified.[14] Note too that if a pleading is verified, any bill of particulars in respect of it must also be verified and, furthermore, any bill of particulars in a negligence action must be verified regardless of whether the pleading is verified.[15] If any matter in a responsive pleading would be privileged under any of the rules of evidence, the pleader need not verify as to the privileged portion of the responsive pleading (although she must verify as to the rest).[16] If the privilege is that against self-incrimination, every doubt is resolved in favor of the responsive pleader, who will be excused from verifying if the matter can have any incriminatory tendency whatever.[17]

The answer of an infant need not be verified, whether the complaint is or not.[18] It is one of the unsuspected advantages of youth. "Ah, to be sixteen again, and not have to verify my answer!"

Subsequent claims, such as counterclaims or cross-claims or third-party claims, may be verified even if the complaint is not.[19] Pleadings responding to those claims would then need verification.

It is the lawyer who manages the entire pleading phase of the action. The meaningful deterrent to false pleading is not verification, but the threat of disciplinary proceedings against the lawyer who, knowing the facts, falsifies them. That threat presumably obtains whether the pleading is verified or not. Today, moreover, there hangs over all deliberately false pleading the threat that it will be denominated a frivolous practice and will invoke a money sanction against lawyer or client or both.[20] That, too, applies whether the pleading is verified or not.

CPLR 105(u) states that a " 'verified pleading' may be utilized as an affidavit whenever the latter is required." In Sanchez v. National R.R. Passenger Corp.,[21] the Court of Appeals ruled that this provision permitted a verified complaint and verified

---

[12] The provision is archaic. If the suit is based on a promissory note, it would probably not be brought as an ordinary action at all; it would likely be brought under CPLR 3213, which dispenses with pleadings altogether. See §§ 288 et seq.; Commentary C3020:5 on McKinney's CPLR 3020.

[13] CPLR 3020(c).

[14] CPLR 3020(a). A pleading mandatorily verified will also, of course, require verification of subsequent pleadings.

[15] CPLR 3044.

[16] CPLR 3020(a). Knight v. Maybee, 44 Misc. 2d 152, 253 N.Y.S.2d 59 (Sup. Ct., Erie County 1964).

[17] Travelers' Ins. Co. v. Mulligan, 231 A.D. 222, 247 N.Y.S. 85 (1st Dep't 1931).

[18] CPLR 3020(a).

[19] CPLR 3020(a).

[20] See § 414A.

[21] Sanchez v. National R.R. Passenger Corp., 21 N.Y.3d 890, 965 N.Y.S.2d 775, 988 N.E.2d 511 (2013); see § 246.

bill of particulars to be considered as affidavits in opposition to a motion for summary judgment.[22]

We can't leave this subject without warning readers about practice in the court of claims, where the claim itself, and the notice of intention to file a claim—if that device is used to start things off instead (the claim itself to come later)—must be verified.[23]

§ 233. Who May Verify

The general rule is that the party and not the lawyer makes the verification.[1] The practitioner does well to leave verification to the client. Seldom does the lawyer know the facts at first hand and it takes little effort to have the client make the affidavit of verification.

If there are multiple parties "united in interest," one who has knowledge of the facts may verify for all.[2] Here joint tortfeasors have been held united in interest.[3] An infant has been held competent to verify.[4] Any officer can verify on behalf of a domestic corporation,[5] and anyone acquainted with the facts can verify on behalf of a governmental unit or agency.[6]

CPLR 3020(d)(3), which is likely to be the provision most often involved when cases on verification appear, reads as follows:

> [I]f the party is a foreign corporation, or is not in the county where the attorney has his office, or if there are two or more parties united in interest and pleading together and none of them acquainted with the facts is within that county, or if the action or defense is founded upon a written instrument for the payment of money only which is in the possession of an agent or the attorney, or if all the material allegations of the pleading are within the personal knowledge of an agent or the attorney, the verification may be made by such agent or attorney.

It is this paragraph that permits an agent or attorney to verify in place of the party.[7] An attorney or agent who has "personal knowledge" of the facts can apparently verify on behalf of a party of any kind (individual, corporate, etc.). But the attorney who lacks such knowledge, and has to verify on second-hand information, must satisfy one of the other grounds listed in the excerpt quoted above. Perhaps the most frequently invoked ground

---

[22] The use of verified pleadings as affidavits on motions is explored in further detail in Commentary C3020:1 to McKinney's CPLR 3020.

[23] Ct. of Claims Act § 11(b).

[1] CPLR 3020(d).

[2] CPLR 3020(d).

[3] Finn Hannevig & Co. v. Frankel, 207 A.D. 180, 201 N.Y.S. 762 (1st Dep't 1923). This is somewhat in contrast with what "united in interest" means under CPLR 203(b), where its purpose is to determine when an action is deemed commenced under the statute of limitations. There, joint tortfeasors have been held not to be united in interest. See § 45.

[4] Serani v. Rowe, 43 Misc. 2d 307, 250 N.Y.S.2d 918 (Sup. Ct., Suffolk County 1964). Serani involved a 19-year-old. Today infancy stops at 18, de jure if not de facto. CPLR 105.

[5] CPLR 3020(d)(1).

[6] CPLR 3020(d)(2).

[7] When the verification is the attorney's, it may of course be made by mere affirmation, CPLR 2106, instead of by formal affidavit. See § 205.

is where the client "is not in the county where the attorney has his office."[8] In metropolitan centers, it is this provision that enables the lawyer to verify when the client lives in one of the suburban counties. In New York City, it accounts for the quantity of attorney verifications coming out of Manhattan (New York County). The attorney permitted to verify is not only the attorney of record, but any associated with that attorney,[9] which would of course embrace partners.

§ 234. Form of Verification

The form of verification is governed by CPLR 3021. There were some official forms to illustrate. Although the official forms were rescinded in 2016, they are still illustrative of the requirements in the CPLR. The following is former Official Form 20, the verification by a party; the "Jurat" at the lower left is a notary's statement to the effect, "Sworn to before me this __ day of _____, ____," followed by the notary's signature and, usually on a rubber stamp, the notary's identifying number and other data.

STATE OF NEW YORK
CITY OF BUFFALO
COUNTY OF ERIE

    A.B., being duly sworn, states that he is the plaintiff in this action and that the foregoing complaint is true to his own knowledge, except as to matters therein stated to be alleged on information and belief and as to those matters he believes it to be true.

_____
[Signature]
_____
[Print name]

[Jurat]

The form set forth just above follows the letter of the first sentence of CPLR 3021, which allows the party to state summarily his belief in those matters alleged "on information and belief," i.e., those allegations of which he lacks direct knowledge. With neither category of allegation need it be stated how the information was come by. This is in contrast with the verification made by someone other than the party, as illustrated by former Official Form 21, the verification by the party's attorney:

---

[8]   At one time it had to be shown, before an attorney would be allowed to verify, that the client was not in the attorney's residence county, not mere office county, see Treen Motors Corporation v. Van Pelt, 106 Misc. 357, 174 N.Y.S. 500 (Sup. Ct., Kings County 1919), but the office county is now the relevant one under CPLR 3020(d)(3).

[9]   Teichman v. Ker, 60 Misc. 2d 789, 303 N.Y.S.2d 985 (Sup. Ct., Nassau County 1969).

STATE OF NEW YORK
CITY OF NEW YORK
COUNTY OF NEW YORK

J.K., being duly sworn, states that he is the attorney for plaintiff in this action and that the foregoing complaint is true to his own knowledge, except as to matters therein stated on information and belief and as to those matters he believes it to be true; that the grounds of his belief as to all matters not stated upon his knowledge are correspondence and other writings furnished to him by plaintiff and interviews with officers and employees of plaintiff; and that the reason why the verification is not made by plaintiff is that [e.g., plaintiff is a foreign corporation].

_____ [Signature] _____

_____ [Print name] _____

[Jurat]

There are two major differences between the above and the prior (the party's) form. First, as to matters alleged in the pleading only upon information and belief, the nonparty verifier must state the grounds of her belief. The party verifier doesn't have to. As the attorney form shows, however, brief references to such things as correspondence, writings, and interviews are deemed sufficient. Second, there must appear a statement of why the party is not doing the verifying.[1] Anything contained in CPLR 3020(d) that authorizes the verification to be made by other than the party need merely be referred to in the verification itself to satisfy this requirement.

If a nonparty verifier fails to specify the grounds for information-and-belief allegations, the verification is defective. If the defect is in the purported verification of a complaint, the answer then need not be verified.[2]

Forms of verification, both individual and corporate (including an affirmation for use by an attorney), are usually contained on the litigation backs available at legal stationers[3] and need merely be filled in and executed to meet verification requirements.

The practitioner should note a peculiarity about verification. Usually, when papers in litigation are being prepared and served, originals are saved for the court's file and copies are served on parties and retained by the server. The copies seldom have signatures executed. Though there are no rigid rules about this, execution usually takes place on the original only—to the extent that an original can be distinguished from a copy in this technical age[4]—with the copies merely conformed. Some caselaw has held, however, that adverse parties are entitled to fully executed copies of verifications, i.e., the notary's signature must appear on the copy served on the opposing party; that service of anything less entitles the recipient to treat the pleading as unverified.[5] More recent

---

[1] CPLR 3021.

[2] Bowery Sav. Bank v. Ward, 188 A.D. 593, 177 N.Y.S. 219 (1st Dep't 1919).

[3] See § 201.

[4] See § 201.

[5] See Crimmins v. Polhemus, 189 Misc. 183, 68 N.Y.S.2d 819 (Syracuse Mun. Ct. 1947).

cases reject that position, holding that service of a mere conformed copy suffices.[6] Perhaps the cautious lawyer does best to have the notary subscribe the original, destined for the court's file, as well as each copy to be served on another party.

§ 235. Remedy for Defective Verification

If P voluntarily verifies the complaint but the verification is defective, D may treat it as unverified[1] and just serve an unverified answer to it. If P refuses the answer, insisting that it be verified, D can move to compel P's acceptance of it.[2] In Mamoon v. Dot Net Inc.,[3] defendants argued in support of their CPLR 3211 motion to dismiss that the complaint was improperly verified by the plaintiff's attorney. The First Department classified the argument as "a red herring" because the complaint was not required to be verified.

The remedy for defects when verification is mandatory, whether because mandated by statute or because the pleading responds to a verified pleading, is more involved. The recipient of an unverified or defectively verified pleading may, if he is entitled to a verified one, "treat it as a nullity" provided he gives the serving attorney notice "with due diligence" that he is so treating it and the specific nature of the defect.[4] The Court of Appeals has never "employed a specific time period to measure due diligence."[5] While some courts have construed "due diligence" in CPLR 3022 to mean "within twenty-four hours," the issue is obviously one where the judge has discretion.[6] The admonition to the nit-picker is to pick quickly. The notice must also specify the particular reasons for deeming the verification defective, such as that the verification was made by a nonparty without first-hand knowledge.[7] If the particulars are not specified, the notice is inadequate.[8] In Treen Motors Corporation v. Van Pelt,[9] P returned D's answer because of a defective verification, but failed to specify what the defect consisted of. The result was held to be the same as if P had accepted the answer and the default judgment P hoped for didn't materialize. If P, entitled to a verified answer, had returned it to D with a proper statement of reasons, P could then have applied for a default judgment.[10] For good measure, the *Treen* case added that "pleaders insisting upon strict compliance with

---

[6]   Scaringe v. Kinley, 154 A.D.2d 836, 546 N.Y.S.2d 702 (3d Dep't 1989).

[1]   CPLR 3022.

[2]   See Commentary C3022:1 on McKinney's CPLR 3022.

[3]   Mamoon v. Dot Net Inc., 135 A.D.3d 656, 25 N.Y.S.3d 85 (1st Dep't 2016).

[4]   CPLR 3022.

[5]   Miller v. Board of Assessors, 91 N.Y.2d 82, 86 n.3, 666 N.Y.S.2d 1012, 1014 n.3, 689 N.E.2d 906, 908 n.3 (1997).

[6]   E.g., Lentlie v. Egan, 94 A.D.2d 839, 463 N.Y.S.2d 542 (3d Dep't 1983), aff'd, 61 N.Y.2d 874, 474 N.Y.S.2d 467, 462 N.E.2d 1185 (1984); see also Rozz v. Law Offices of Saul Kobrick, P.C., 134 A.D.3d 920, 22 N.Y.S.3d 113 (2d Dep't 2015) ("due diligence" not established where plaintiff waited fifteen days after receiving an unverified answer before raising an objection). The "due diligence" requirement is treated in further detail in Commentary C3022:2 to McKinney's CPLR 3022.

[7]   See, e.g., Lefrak v. Robinson, 115 Misc. 2d 256, 454 N.Y.S.2d 571 (Mount Vernon City Court 1982), voiding a petition in a summary proceeding governed by § 741 of the RPAPL (which adopts the relevant CPLR verification provisions) but preserving the proceeding so as to permit new service.

[8]   See Gaffey v. Shah, 131 A.D.3d 1006, 17 N.Y.S.3d 46 (2d Dep't 2015) ("the plaintiffs' rejection of the defendant's answer was ineffective, as it failed to specify the reasons or objections with sufficient specificity" as required by CPLR 3022; therefore, the alleged "defect was properly ignored by the Supreme Court").

[9]   Treen Motors Corporation v. Van Pelt, 106 Misc. 357, 174 N.Y.S. 500 (Sup. Ct., Kings County 1919).

[10]   See State v. McMahon, 78 Misc. 2d 388, 356 N.Y.S.2d 933 (Sup. Ct., Albany County 1974).

the rules of practice must follow the same themselves."[11] The *Treen* case is of 1919 vintage, showing an early—and healthy—judicial impatience with the carping and captious devotee of insignificant detail.

CPLR 3026, the provision that mandates disregarding all pleading defects if no substantial right is prejudiced, has been given a role in verification. The verification provisions are part of the pleadings article and are therefore subject to CPLR 3026. There is so scant an advantage emanating from verification that the party who deems herself entitled to a verified pleading can be deemed unprejudiced if she doesn't get it. These considerations have prompted at least one court, citing CPLR 3026, to hold that even where a complaint is required to be verified, no prejudice can result if it is not.[12]

In court of claims practice, where the claim and the notice of intention to file a claim must be verified,[13] some draconian caselaw applied the verification requirement rigidly, dismissing a claim for want of verification even though the earlier filed notice of intention was properly verified.[14] The Court of Appeals afterwards went out of its way to reject that rigidity, volunteering in a dictum that the same flexibility in the application of the verification rules that apply in the supreme court—and the cures for their violation (noted above)—must also be applied in the court of claims.[15]

M. AMENDMENT OF PLEADINGS

Table of Sections

§ 236.   Amendment as of Course
§ 237.   Amendment by Leave

§ 236. Amendment as of Course

The CPLR allows each party to amend its pleading once without leave of court.[1] This is commonly known as an amendment as of course. Since it must be made early in the case, it is at root just a final version of the original pleading. The pleader may make the amendment as of course within any of three time periods:

1. within 20 days after the pleading itself has been served; or

2. within the period that the adverse party has for responding to it (so that when the defendant has a 30-day answering period, for example, the plaintiff may amend the complaint within that period); or

3. within 20 days after a responsive pleading is served.[2]

---

[11]   *Treen*, 106 Misc. at 361, 174 N.Y.S. at 503.

[12]   Capital Newspapers Division-Hearst Corp. v. Vanderbilt, 44 Misc. 2d 542, 254 N.Y.S.2d 309 (Sup. Ct., Albany County 1964). There were special considerations in the *Capital* case, which was a labor dispute in need of prompt resolution on the merits. That may deprive the case of status as a general anti-verification precedent. For further discussion of remedies for defects when verification is required, see Commentary C3022:2 on McKinney's CPLR 3022.

[13]   Ct. of Claims Act § 11(b).

[14]   Martin v. State, 185 Misc. 2d 799, 713 N.Y.S.2d 831 (Ct. Cl. 2000).

[15]   Lepkowski v. State, 1 N.Y.3d 201, 770 N.Y.S.2d 696, 802 N.E.2d 1094 (2003) (NYSLD No. 529).

[1]   CPLR 3025(a).

[2]   CPLR 3025(a).

The last period is probably the most meaningful since it also enables a plaintiff to remedy some defect in the complaint to which attention has been called in the answer. Any other party pleading a cause of action, such as a defendant with a cross-claim or counterclaim, should also keep that in mind. Upon realizing, before a responsive pleading is in, that there's some defect in the complaint (counterclaim, etc.), the pleader should consider waiting until the response is served before using up her one as-of-course amendment. If saved until then, it can cure the error or omission initially realized as well as any pointed out by the responsive pleading.

The second and third alternative time periods listed are available only when the pleading to be amended requires a response. If it doesn't require one, like an answer containing no counterclaim, the only period for the of-course amendment of the answer is the first one listed: within 20 days after its own service.

If the pleading to be amended does require a response—take the complaint as an example—and the defendant, instead of answering, moves to dismiss the complaint under CPLR 3211 or to correct it under CPLR 3024, the making of either kind of motion automatically extends the defendant's responding time[3] and by so doing extends as well the time in which the plaintiff may amend the complaint as of course. This enables the plaintiff, even before the motion is heard, to amend the complaint and perhaps even correct the defect to which the defendant's motion calls attention.[4]

The amendment as of course can include anything that could have been included in the original pleading. It can add separate and distinct causes of action or substitute a different one for the original.[5] Similarly, when a summons is served with only a CPLR 305(b) notice at the outset and the defendant demands the complaint in due course, the complaint can also include matter not referred to in the 305(b) notice.[6] This naturally assumes, however, that no other impediment is present. Where, for example, jurisdiction of the claim is based on CPLR 302's longarm contacts, a special statute provides that no non-CPLR 302 claims may be added after the defendant has appeared in the action.[7]

When the pleading being amended is a responsive one, the responder can sometimes end up with two as of course amendments. Suppose, for example, that D amends the answer. That's D's first of-course amendment. P then amends the complaint and D answers the amended complaint, as D must.[8] D may then amend that answer as of course, and that's D's second one.[9] The reason for this is that P's service of an amended complaint restarted the cycle.

As will be seen, the many important objections listed in CPLR 3211(a) may be taken either by motion to dismiss under CPLR 3211(a) or by way of defense in the answer,[10]

---

[3]   CPLR 3211(f), 3024(c).

[4]   As to whether an amendment that purports to cure the moved-against defect abates the motion, see § 273.

[5]   Mendoza v. Mendoza, 4 Misc. 2d 1060, 77 N.Y.S.2d 169 (Sup. Ct., New York County 1947), aff'd, 273 A.D. 877, 77 N.Y.S.2d 264 (1st Dep't 1948).

[6]   Everitt v. Everitt, 4 N.Y.2d 13, 171 N.Y.S.2d 836, 148 N.E.2d 891 (1958). See Commentary C3025:3 on McKinney's CPLR 3025.

[7]   CPLR 302(c). See § 91.

[8]   CPLR 3025(d).

[9]   Brooks Bros. v. Tiffany, 117 A.D. 470, 102 N.Y.S. 626 (1st Dep't 1907).

[10]   See § 274.

but they are waived if taken by neither.[11] If one of those objections is not taken by motion and is also omitted from the original answer, the waiver might still be avoided by including the objection in an amended answer made as of course.[12] The Court of Appeals confirms this in Iacovangelo v. Shepherd,[13] wherein defendant answered in the first instance and was permitted to raise the objection of lack of personal jurisdiction in an amendment of right. It must be remembered, however, that if D makes a CPLR 3211(a) motion to dismiss and does not include that ground, a special provision in CPLR 3211(e) holds it waived altogether.[14]

An amendment without leave of court is sometimes authorized by some other provision. Where, for example, X has been impleaded into the P v. D action, P is given 20 days, measured from the service on P of X's answer to the third-party complaint, in which to amend the main complaint to add a claim directly against X.[15] CPLR 1003 authorizes the addition of parties to the action and must be carefully negotiated.[16]

If the pleading being amended required a responsive pleading, so does the amended one. Where P amends the complaint, D must serve an answer to it even though D has already troubled to answer the original complaint. The period within which to serve the responsive pleading is 20 days after service of the amended one.[17] If the amendment as of course has been used up, or the period for making it has expired, the pleader who would now amend must either obtain the other parties' stipulation or get a court order under CPLR 3025(b).[18] The latter is the amendment by leave, treated in the next section.

§ 237. Amendment by Leave

Motion to Amend Pleading

CPLR 3025(b) provides that:

A party may amend his pleading, or supplement it by setting forth additional or subsequent transactions or occurrences, at any time by leave of court or by stipulation of all parties. Leave shall be freely given upon such terms as may be just including the granting of costs and continuances.

This is among the most important and often used provisions in practice. It assures flexibility throughout the action and adjusts the pleadings to the substantive rights involved whenever it can be done without prejudice. If there is no prejudice to the other side, leave to amend must be freely given. The courts stress this time and again.[1]

A 2012 amendment to CPLR 3025(b) provides that "[a]ny motion to amend or supplement pleadings shall be accompanied by the proposed amended or supplemental pleading clearly showing the changes or additions to be made to the pleading." The statute has no prescription for precisely how the pleading changes are to be indicated. It

---

[11] CPLR 3211(e).

[12] Solarino v. Noble, 55 Misc. 2d 429, 286 N.Y.S.2d 71 (Sup. Ct., New York County 1967).

[13] Iacovangelo v. Shepherd, 5 N.Y.3d 184, 800 N.Y.S.2d 116, 833 N.E.2d 259 (2005) (NYSLD No. 548).

[14] See § 274.

[15] CPLR 1009; see §§ 49, 164.

[16] See § 65.

[17] CPLR 3025(d).

[18] Orlik v. National Carbon Co., 176 A.D. 600, 163 N.Y.S. 768 (1st Dep't 1917).

[1] See McCaskey, Davies and Associates, Inc. v. New York City Health & Hospitals Corp., 59 N.Y.2d 755, 757, 463 N.Y.S.2d 434, 434, 450 N.E.2d 240 (1983).

would seem that any method that makes the changes clear to the other side will do, as the idea is to call the changes to the attention of the recipient as clearly and succinctly as possible. This amendment has already made its mark in caselaw. In Drice v. Queens County Dist. Attorney,[2] for example, the Second Department cited several of its prior cases in affirming an order denying a motion to serve an amended complaint because, among other things, the movant failed to provide a copy of the proposed amended complaint.[3]

There is no stated time limit for the amendment by leave under subdivision (b), as there is for the amendment of course under CPLR 3025(a). Nor is there a stated limit on the number of by-leave amendments a party may have.

The CPLR 3025(b) amendment lies in the discretion of the court and may be denied on such discretionary grounds as prejudice, delay, undue advantage, etc.[4]

Motion to Supplement Pleading

CPLR 3025(b) governs both the amendment and the supplement of a pleading. By grouping them together, it downplays the difference between the two, but differences do remain.[5] Technically, a "supplement" to a pleading adds something that has only come into existence since the earlier pleading, such as an additional installment falling due in a contract action or an additional claim becoming actionable in the interim. An "amendment" is any change at all in a pleading, without regard to whether the relevant facts existed at the time of the initial pleading. By combining the amendment and the supplement and directing that leave be "freely given" for both, CPLR 3025(b) rejects the old practice, applicable in law cases, restricting the action to facts in existence when it was first brought, and instead adopts for all actions the equity practice of allowing the case to take cognizance of facts arising right up to the time of the trial.[6] It must be remembered, however, that while sometimes an amendment can be made without leave of court under CPLR 3025(a), a supplement requires either leave of court or a stipulation under CPLR 3025(b).[7]

What Constitutes Prejudice?

Causes of action can be added or subtracted by amendment, whether they involve changes of fact or changes of theory. If the theory alone is changed, but the facts remain as originally pleaded, a problem should not often be met because there is little the other

---

[2]   Drice v. Queens County Dist. Attorney, 136 A.D.3d 665, 665, 23 N.Y.S.3d 896, 897 (2d Dep't 2016).

[3]   See Fermas v. Ampco System Parking, 2016 WL 743777 (Sup. Ct., Queens County 2016) (supreme court denied motion to amend because defendants failed to submit proposed amended answer that actually highlighted the difference between the original answer and the proposed amended answer); Supplementary Practice Commentaries to McKinney's CPLR 3025.

[4]   See Kimso Apartments, LLC v. Gandhi, 24 N.Y.3d 403, 411, 998 N.Y.S.2d 740, 745, 23 N.E.3d 1008, 1013 (2014) (reversing appellate division and granting defendant's motion to amend answer to assert a counterclaim due to lack of any prejudice); Leutloff v. Leutloff, 47 Misc. 2d 458, 262 N.Y.S.2d 736 (Sup. Ct., Onondaga County 1965).

[5]   Town Bd. of Town of Fallsburgh v. National Sur. Corp., 53 Misc. 2d 23, 277 N.Y.S.2d 872 (Sup. Ct., Sullivan County 1967), aff'd, 29 A.D.2d 726, 286 N.Y.S.2d 122 (3d Dep't 1968).

[6]   See Renwick v. Town of Allegany, 18 A.D.2d 877, 879, 236 N.Y.S.2d 902, 905 (4th Dep't 1963) (concurring opinion).

[7]   Hernandez v. City of New York, 2016 WL 1449413, *2 n.5 (Sup. Ct., Kings County 2016) (supplementing of complaint as of right not permitted, but defendants found to have waived any procedural defect).

party would now have to do by way of new preparation.[8] Conceptual rather than factual changes are always easier because the opponent will at least be on notice of the facts. Inadvertent omissions are also curable with the of-leave amendment, as where a denial[9] or even a defense[10] has been left out of an answer through oversight. Objections listed in CPLR 3211(a)—most CPLR 3211(a) objections must be taken either by motion or answer[11]—may generally be added in an amended answer if omitted from the original one.[12] While this has been held to be automatically permissible for an amendment as of course under CPLR 3025(a),[13] it will be allowed in an amendment by leave under 3025(b) only if there is no prejudice to the plaintiff.[14] It is up to the plaintiff to show prejudice in that situation.[15]

What does constitute prejudice sufficient to defeat an amendment? It must obviously be a showing of prejudice traceable not simply to the new matter sought to be added, but also to the fact that it is being added at a relatively late stage in the proceedings.[16] Almost everything parties seek to add to their pleadings is designed to prejudice the other side. That's what litigation is all about. So, the showing of prejudice that will defeat the amendment must be traced right back to the omission from the original pleading of whatever is sought to be added in the proposed amendment. Some special right must be lost in the interim, or some change of position, or some significant trouble or expense must be encountered, which could have been avoided had the original pleading contained what the amendment proposes to add.[17]

For example, D answered a personal injury action with only a general denial and a year later wanted to amend the answer to add the defense that P was an employee of D and that workers' compensation was therefore the exclusive remedy. The time in which to seek such compensation had meanwhile expired. The court denied the motion to amend: had the amendment been allowed, it would have meant the substantive loss of all of plaintiff's claims.[18] In a similar case in which the time to apply for compensation was still alive, however, the late defense was allowed.[19] If P had notice from other sources of D's intention to rely on the defense, prejudice can be deemed avoided by that route,

---

[8]   Rife v. Union College, 30 A.D.2d 504, 294 N.Y.S.2d 460 (3d Dep't 1968).

[9]   LaBate v. Meyerbank Elec. Co., 23 A.D.2d 503, 256 N.Y.S.2d 420 (2d Dep't 1965).

[10]   Ciunci v. Wella Corp., 23 A.D.2d 754, 258 N.Y.S.2d 994 (1st Dep't 1965).

[11]   CPLR 3211(e); see § 274.

[12]   If a defendant makes a pre-answer motion to dismiss under CPLR 3211(a) and neglects to include the defense of lack of personal jurisdiction, that defense is waived and cannot be included in the answer. CPLR 3211(e); see § 274.

[13]   See Solarino v. Noble, 55 Misc. 2d 429, 286 N.Y.S.2d 71 (Sup. Ct., New York County 1967), and the discussion in § 236.

[14]   See Commentary C3025:7 on McKinney's CPLR 3025.

[15]   See M. Kramer & Sons, Inc. v. Facilities Development Corp., 135 A.D.2d 942, 522 N.Y.S.2d 351 (3d Dep't 1987) (granting defendant's motion to amend its answer to assert as additional affirmative defenses that the action was untimely pursuant to CPLR 213 and the parties' contractual agreement shortening the applicable statute of limitations); Lermit Plastics Co., Inc. v. C. W. Lauman & Co., Inc., 40 A.D.2d 680, 336 N.Y.S.2d 187 (2d Dep't 1972).

[16]   Edenwald Contracting Co., Inc. v. City of New York, 60 N.Y.2d 957, 471 N.Y.S.2d 55, 459 N.E.2d 164 (1983); St. Paul Fire & Marine Ins. Co. v. Town of Hempstead, 291 A.D.2d 488, 738 N.Y.S.2d 226 (2d Dep't 2002).

[17]   See Fulford v. Baker Perkins, Inc., 100 A.D.2d 861, 474 N.Y.S.2d 114 (2d Dep't 1984); A.J. Pegno Const. Corp. v. City of New York, 95 A.D.2d 655, 463 N.Y.S.2d 214 (1st Dep't 1983).

[18]   Ciccone v. Glenwood Holding Corp., 44 Misc. 2d 273, 253 N.Y.S.2d 576 (N.Y. City Civ. Ct. 1964).

[19]   Murray v. City of New York, 43 N.Y.2d 400, 401 N.Y.S.2d 773, 372 N.E.2d 560 (1977).

and an amendment allowed, perhaps with a money sanction against the dilatory defendant.[20]

Another example: D answered with denials only, and P prepared his whole case accordingly. On the eve of trial, D wanted to add defenses that could readily have been pleaded earlier. The amendment to add them was denied.[21] Here, the prejudice was the loss of the time and effort expended in preparing a case against a pleading from which significant material had been needlessly withheld. The emerging tactical lesson is that if the plaintiff, half expecting the answer to contain a defense like lack of jurisdiction, statute of limitations, or the like, sees the answer come in without the defense and with the time to amend as of course now expired, the plaintiff should promptly take preparatory steps: draw and serve a bill of particulars if one has been demanded, immediately initiate use of the disclosure devices, respond promptly to any disclosure demands the defendant has made,[22] etc. In other words, get busy. The plaintiff is then prepared to cite those steps—taken on the strength of an answer barren of defenses—if the defendant seeks leave to add a defense later.

Yet another example of prejudice would be where the allowance of a late defense by the present defendant would deprive the plaintiff of recourse against some other person because of the lapse of time.[23]

Although leave to amend under CPLR 3025(b) should be "freely given," the courts are more hesitant to grant such motions when the facts on which they're based were known to the movant from the beginning and could have been pleaded without trouble earlier.[24] As a rule, mere lateness is not a barrier to the amendment, but lateness coupled with significant prejudice is. Those are the classic elements of the laches doctrine, the major obstacle to a CPLR 3025(b) amendment. Where, for example, D wanted to amend its answer to add a counterclaim but waited a year after the joinder of issue and only after P had moved for a trial preference, the amendment was rejected. The court pointed to all the pretrial procedures that would now have to attend the belated counterclaim, such as dismissal motions, bill of particulars procedures, disclosure devices, and even appeals from those steps, and held it prejudicial to hinder the plaintiff with those new things at this late stage.[25] Furthermore, "[w]here the application for leave to amend is made long after the action has been certified for trial, 'judicial discretion in allowing such amendments should be discrete, circumspect, prudent, and cautious.' "[26]

Conditional Order Granting Amendment

The amendment may be allowed conditionally, and the conditions can pertain to time and money, among other things. If the amendment is sought close in time to the trial, for example, but the court is disposed to grant it, the court can adjourn the trial to enable the adverse party to prepare to meet the new matter. It may also impose costs as a condition to granting the motion. There are indications that tardy amendments, which

---

[20] See, e.g., Godell v. Greyhound Rent A Car, Inc., 24 A.D.2d 568, 262 N.Y.S.2d 318 (2d Dep't 1965).

[21] See James-Smith v. Rottenberg, 32 A.D.2d 792, 302 N.Y.S.2d 355 (2d Dep't 1969).

[22] Disclosure is the subject of Chapter 13, §§ 343 et seq.

[23] See Pace v. Perk, 81 A.D.2d 444, 440 N.Y.S.2d 710 (2d Dep't 1981).

[24] See, e.g., Dawley v. McCumber, 45 A.D.3d 1399, 1400, 845 N.Y.S.2d 888, 889 (4th Dep't 2007); L. B. Foster Co. v. Terry Contracting, Inc., 25 A.D.2d 721, 268 N.Y.S.2d 618 (1st Dep't 1966).

[25] O'Hara v. Tidewater Oil Co., 23 A.D.2d 870, 259 N.Y.S.2d 263 (2d Dep't 1965).

[26] Alrose Oceanside, LLC v. Mueller, 81 A.D.3d 574, 915 N.Y.S.2d 643 (2d Dep't 2011).

in the past might have been refused outright, may be allowed today with a costs assessment imposed instead.[27] In a case involving an inexcusable lateness in seeking an amendment to add defenses, for example, the court allowed the amendment, but only on the condition that D pay P a stated sum, including attorney's fees, to cover the cost of preparing to meet the new defense.[28]

While not a usual part of a costs award in New York, attorney's fees can be awarded as part of a disposition whenever a court, in granting relief, is permitted to grant it conditionally.[29] It's a shorter and kinder step than the outright denial of the relief, in this case the denial of an amendment that the court might otherwise be disposed to grant. Other examples of this will be seen in practice on the bill of particulars[30] and disclosure.[31]

Consideration of Merits on Motion to Amend

On a motion to amend, the court will not ordinarily consider the merits of the proposed new matter unless it is so obviously lacking in merit as to have no chance of success whatever, in which case the motion may be denied on that ground.[32] Some courts have even said that a grant of the motion without looking at the merits may needlessly generate a later motion to test the merits. Labeling that procedure wasteful, they hold that at least the prima facie merit of the new matter should be considered on the amendment motion.[33]

The Second Department took issue with courts conducting an early examination of the merits of a proposed amendment in Lucido v. Mancuso,[34] a decision that extensively reviews the history of the amendment by leave of court. The court's perception was that the liberality of CPLR 3025(b) has eroded over the years, that the courts too often delve into the merits of the proposed amendment on the motion to amend, that the history of the provision does not countenance this, and that the practice should therefore stop. Hence, in its view, the proof needed for the amendment should be relaxed, and if there's a sustainable merits attack that can be made against the proposed new claim, it should be raised by the defendant afterwards, as on a motion for summary judgment. The *Lucido* court expressly overruled the line of cases holding that a motion seeking leave to amend a personal injury complaint to assert a cause of action for wrongful death must be supported by competent medical proof of the causal connection between the alleged negligence and the death of the original plaintiff.[35]

---

[27]   See Armstrong v. Peat, Marwick, Mitchell & Co., 150 A.D.2d 189, 540 N.Y.S.2d 799 (1st Dep't 1989).

[28]   Mirabella v. Banco Indus. de la Republica Argentina, 34 A.D.2d 630, 309 N.Y.S.2d 400 (1st Dep't 1970).

[29]   See Whiteman Osterman & Hanna, LLP v. Albany-Troy Neurosurgical Associates, P.C., 50 A.D.3d 1305, 854 N.Y.S.2d 678 (3d Dep't 2008) (while noting that "[g]ranting a party permission to amend a pleading may be subject to certain conditions, including costs and reasonable counsel fees," the court exercised its discretion to reverse so much of the supreme court's order that awarded counsel fees).

[30]   See § 241.

[31]   See § 367.

[32]   Heller v. Louis Provenzano, Inc., 303 A.D.2d 20, 25, 756 N.Y.S.2d 26, 30 (1st Dep't 2003); Blueberry Investors Co. v. Ilana Realty Inc., 184 A.D.2d 906, 907, 585 N.Y.S.2d 564, 565 (3d Dep't 1992). A totally groundless motion of that kind may also risk a sanction as a frivolous practice. See § 414A.

[33]   See, e.g., East Asiatic Co. v. Corash, 34 A.D.2d 432, 312 N.Y.S.2d 311 (1st Dep't 1970).

[34]   Lucido v. Mancuso, 49 A.D.3d 220, 851 N.Y.S.2d 238 (2d Dep't 2008) (SPR 194:3).

[35]   *Lucido*, 49 A.D.3d at 232, 851 N.Y.S.2d at 246.

Amendment of Ad Damnum

A common motion to amend under CPLR 3025(b) was one to raise the demand in the wherefore clause (the so-called "ad damnum") in a money action. The courts had mixed emotions about this.[36] Under current law, however, CPLR 3017(c) prohibits a party from stating a specific amount of monetary damages in a pleading alleging personal injury or wrongful death causes of action.[37] Therefore, motions to amend the ad damnum are not encountered often today. If such a motion is necessary, the Court's pronouncement in Loomis v. Civetta Corinno Const. Corp.[38] should govern. Therein, the Court held that "in the absence of prejudice to the defendant, a motion to amend the ad damnum clause, whether made before or after the trial, should generally be granted."[39] This standard should also apply to a motion to amend a supplemental demand served pursuant to CPLR 3017(c) in personal injury and wrongful death actions. If this sounds a bit familiar, it may be because a related round on this subject appearing earlier[40] met this problem in its more difficult phase: the motion to increase the ad damnum after a verdict has come in for more than the sum demanded in the complaint. That post-verdict motion is made under CPLR 3025(c), the motion to conform the pleadings to the proof,[41] while the instant motion, which is made before the trial, is made under CPLR 3025(b).

Statute of Limitations Issues

For purposes of the statute of limitations, matter in an amended pleading is deemed to relate back to the earlier one as long as the earlier one gave notice of the transaction or occurrence out of which the new matter arises.[42] This has been generously applied by the Court of Appeals. For a while there had been some debate, for example, as to whether a wrongful death claim sought to be added by amendment could be allowed to relate back to the original complaint, which pleaded only the claims for personal injury, from which the death ensued.[43] An argument was made that such a relation back was conceptually untenable because the wrongful death claim did not exist at the earlier time and because it does not belong to the same owner.[44] Those arguments were rejected and the relation back allowed in Caffaro v. Trayna,[45] a Court of Appeals decision inviting a pragmatic rather than technical approach to the relation-back provision.

Insofar as an amendment seeks to add, drop, or change a party, discussion will often center on alterations the plaintiff seeks to effect in the roster of defendants. Much of the reasoning in the cases applies to attempts to alter not just the complaint, but the summons as well.[46] Note, however, that *Caffaro* was at root an endeavor to add or change

---

[36] See Commentary C3025:14 on McKinney's CPLR 3025.

[37] See section 217.

[38] Loomis v. Civetta Corinno Const. Corp., 54 N.Y.2d 18, 23, 444 N.Y.S.2d 571, 573, 429 N.E.2d 90 (1981).

[39] *Loomis*, 54 N.Y.2d at 23, 444 N.Y.S.2d at 573.

[40] See § 217.

[41] That motion is treated in § 404.

[42] CPLR 203(f). The relation-back doctrine of CPLR 203(f) is more fully discussed in § 49.

[43] See Commentary C3025:12 on McKinney's CPLR 3025.

[44] The personal injury claim belongs to the injured person and goes to that person's estate upon death, while the wrongful death claim itself belongs to the deceased's dependents, EPTL 5–4.4, not the estate.

[45] Caffaro v. Trayna, 35 N.Y.2d 245, 360 N.Y.S.2d 847, 319 N.E.2d 174, 71 A.L.R.3d 924 (1974).

[46] See CPLR 1003; § 65.

plaintiffs. That change, too, is permissible by mere amendment, with prejudice once again the key. And it must of course be the kind of prejudice that entails

some change of position or hindrance in the preparation of a case or significant trouble or expense that could have been avoided if the original pleading had contained what the amended one seeks to add.[47]

It was noted in Bellini v. Garsalle Realty Corp.[48] that this simple amendment solution may be allowed even when a statute of limitations problem is involved as where it is urged that the amendment is an attempt to assert a new cause of action. Even there, said the court,

[i]t is well settled that amendment of a pleading to assert a new cause of action, even one which technically belongs to different persons, or to substitute new parties, related to the original parties, is not precluded [merely] because an independent de novo action would be time barred. The amendment may relate back to the earlier pleading so long as the earlier pleading gave the adverse party sufficient notice of the transaction out of which the new claim arises.

Sometimes the change in plaintiffs is verbalized in terms of "standing" and without much attention to the relationship between the originally named plaintiff and the one sought to be substituted.[49]

Service of Amended Pleading and Responsive Pleadings

If the amendment is allowed, the amended pleading must be served on the other parties. The court usually prescribes the time for service of the amended pleading in the order granting leave to amend. If the amended pleading requires a responsive pleading— as it will if the original pleading did—the response must be served within 20 days.[50] An amended complaint will require a fresh answer by all defendants even if the amendment pertains to the acts of only one.[51]

N. BILL OF PARTICULARS

Table of Sections

§ 238. Bill of Particulars, Generally

§ 239. Procedure for Bill of Particulars

§ 240. Amending and Supplementing the Bill

§ 241. Remedies in Connection with Bill of Particulars

§ 242. Variances

§ 238. Bill of Particulars, Generally

A "bill of particulars" in civil practice is an amplification of a pleading. It supplies more detail than required in a pleading and, therefore, affords the adverse party a more

---

[47] Frankart Furniture Staten Island, Inc. v. Forest Mall Associates, 159 A.D.2d 322, 552 N.Y.S.2d 599 (1st Dep't 1990).

[48] Bellini v. Gersalle Realty Corp., 120 A.D.2d 345, 501 N.Y.S.2d 674 (1st Dep't 1986).

[49] See, e.g., JCD Farms, Inc. v. Juul-Nielsen, 300 A.D.2d 446, 751 N.Y.S.2d 421 (2d Dep't 2002).

[50] CPLR 3025(d).

[51] Wells Fargo Bank, NA v. Gerasimou, 2016 WL 909522 (Sup. Ct., Queens County 2016).

thorough picture of the claim or defense being particularized. It's designed to limit the proof and prevent surprise at the trial.[1]

Party with Burden of Proof Must Supply Bill

The bill of particulars is tied to the burden of proof. Parties are required to particularize only that of which they have the burden of proof,[2] and a bill of particulars is as a rule served only when demanded.[3] Plaintiffs must particularize their claims and defendants their defenses, counterclaims, cross-claims, and third-party claims. But the defendant need not particularize denials contained in the answer because the matters involved are the plaintiff's burden to prove, not the defendant's.[4] This is in contrast with the disclosure devices of CPLR Article 31 where burden of proof is irrelevant.[5]

Bill of Particulars as Disclosure Device?

It is the general rule that a bill of particulars is not usable to obtain evidence.[6] The supplying of evidentiary material is not its office.[7] The bill is supposed to offer a more expansive statement of the pleader's contentions rather than the evidentiary basis on which they rest. Thus, where P sued D for breach of a contract for P to do a musical score for D, which P said he did, D was not entitled to a copy of the score as part of a bill of particulars.[8]

D would be able to get it, however, by using the disclosure device of CPLR 3120(1)(ii).[9] The disclosure devices are probably the most important in litigation, but they can be expensive. They are worth the expense in substantial cases, but they can quickly prove too costly—even though needed just as much—in smaller cases.

Some thoughtful decisions have suggested that the bill of particulars be allowed a disclosure function in actions with relatively small stakes,[10] and the First Department sided with that view in Twiddy v. Standard Marine Transport Services, Inc.,[11] holding that while it is not the mission of the bill of particulars to secure materials more appropriately left to the disclosure devices of Article 31 of the CPLR, "the rule is not an inflexible one." If the party on whom the demand is served makes no showing of prejudice, the demand for the bill can be allowed to serve as a disclosure notice as well and was allowed to in *Twiddy*. "A rigid adherence to the purpose behind a bill of

---

[1]   Northway Engineering, Inc. v. Felix Industries, Inc., 77 N.Y.2d 332, 335, 567 N.Y.S.2d 634, 636, 569 N.E.2d 437 (1991); State v. Horsemen's Benev. & Protective Ass'n (New York Division), 34 A.D.2d 769, 311 N.Y.S.2d 511 (1st Dep't 1970).

[2]   *Northway Engineering, Inc.*, 77 N.Y.2d at 336, 567 N.Y.S.2d at 637; Hydromatics, Inc. v. County Nat. Bank, 23 A.D.2d 576, 256 N.Y.S.2d 438 (2d Dep't 1965).

[3]   CPLR 3041, the basic statute on the bill of particulars, provides that a party "may require" the other to serve a bill.

[4]   L. F. Dommerich & Co. v. Diener & Dorskind, Inc., 31 A.D.2d 516, 294 N.Y.S.2d 613 (1st Dep't 1968); see § 221.

[5]   CPLR 3101(a); see § 344.

[6]   Arroyo v. Fourteen Estusia Corp., 194 A.D.2d 309, 309, 598 N.Y.S.2d 471, 472 (1st Dep't 1993); Yardarm Club Hotel, Inc. v. Morgan, 22 A.D.2d 700, 253 N.Y.S.2d 920 (2d Dep't 1964).

[7]   *Horsemen's Benevolent*, 34 A.D.2d at 770, 311 N.Y.S.2d at 512.

[8]   Elman v. Ziegfeld, 200 A.D. 494, 193 N.Y.S. 133 (1st Dep't 1922).

[9]   See § 362.

[10]   See, e.g., Block v. Fairbairn, 68 Misc. 2d 931, 328 N.Y.S.2d 497 (Sup. Ct., Ulster County 1972).

[11]   Twiddy v. Standard Marine Transport Services, Inc., 162 A.D.2d 264, 556 N.Y.S.2d 622 (1st Dep't 1990).

particulars in this case," the court said, "would only result in additional meaningless time-consuming motion practice."

The Advisory Committee had planned to abolish the bill of particulars altogether (it has been abolished in federal civil practice), but the legislature restored it in substantially the same form it had under prior law.[12] The committee's idea was to have the disclosure devices fill the gap. With that history, it would not be amiss to give the bill a reasonable disclosure function in smaller cases if doing so would save the parties substantial expense.

Bill of Particulars Supplements Pleading

Technically a bill of particulars is not a pleading, but just an expansion of one. The extent to which it can be treated as a pleading has met some judicial ambivalence. If a pleading is attacked because it lacks certain detail, for example, the courts are likely to sustain the pleading and just remit the complainer to a bill of particulars, the disclosure devices, or both.[13] This suggests that if in a given case some item that arguably belongs in the pleading can instead be gotten through the bill, the bill can for that purpose be treated as the pleading itself. Some courts had held that a pleading omission could not be remedied by the bill,[14] but the Court of Appeals later said that in considering the sufficiency of a pleaded cause of action, the bill may be looked to as well.[15]

Things appear to end up this way: if the bill is being used in the case, or the court on some motion can direct a bill, the bill can be made to carry out some of the pleading's function.[16] Since the adverse party now has the information in both items, it should make no difference.

What Can Be Demanded in the Bill?

What a party may demand in a bill—and the demand, as long as it is reasonable, determines the bill's contents—is necessarily personal to the particular case. Whatever the pleading pleads, the bill must particularize. With the exception of the personal injury action, where the items that may be demanded have been codified into a list,[17] the things that may be demanded and thus must be particularized are a sui generis inquiry. An eminent New York surrogate learned this when he had occasion to research the matter. Surrogate Wingate came out of the books aghast at the mass of cases—literally hundreds—each establishing only what had to be particularized in the given case. These cases, he noted in 1935, had no general utility, "no application to cases presenting divergent states of fact."[18] The decades since then have added more cases but not more utility.

"In furnishing the particulars requested, a bill should follow the designation of the items set forth in the demand and each item of the demand must be answered separately

---

[12]　See Commentary C3041:1 on McKinney's CPLR 3041.

[13]　See, e.g., Serio v. Rhulen, 24 A.D.3d 1092, 1094, 806 N.Y.S.2d 283, 285 (3d Dep't 2005); Pernet v. Peabody Engineering Corp., 20 A.D.2d 781, 248 N.Y.S.2d 132 (1st Dep't 1964).

[14]　E.g., Melino v. Tougher Heating & Plumbing Co., 23 A.D.2d 616, 256 N.Y.S.2d 885 (3d Dep't 1965).

[15]　Nader v. General Motors Corp., 25 N.Y.2d 560, 565, 307 N.Y.S.2d 647, 650, 255 N.E.2d 765, 767 (1970).

[16]　MacDonald v.Howard, 91 A.D.2d 1119, 1120, 458 N.Y.S.2d 331, 332 (3d Dep't 1983).

[17]　CPLR 3043(a), set out later on in this section.

[18]　In re Herle's Estate, 157 Misc. 352, 356, 283 N.Y.S. 588, 592 (Sur. Ct., Kings County 1935).

and categorically under its own number and subdivision."[19] The laws relied on as well as the facts alleged have to be particularized,[20] especially when the laws concerned are foreign.[21] General damages are "the natural and probable consequence of the breach . . . while special damages are extraordinary in that they do not so directly flow from the breach."[22] While special damages are the proper subject of a bill,[23] general damages need not be particularized.[24]

In a personal injury action, the items to be particularized are enumerated in a statutory list. This is designed to reduce arguments and the need for unwanted court applications in this most numerous category of litigation. The list is in CPLR 3043(a). In addition to supplying the personal injury items specifically, the statute gives some idea of how a bill of particulars demand functions generally. CPLR 3043(a) provides that in actions for personal injuries the following particulars may be required:

(1)   The date and approximate time of day of the occurrence;

(2)   Its approximate location;

(3)   General statement of the acts or omissions constituting the negligence claimed;

(4)   Where notice of condition is a prerequisite, whether actual or constructive notice is claimed;

(5)   If actual notice is claimed, a statement of when and to whom it was given;

(6)   Statement of the injuries and description of those claimed to be permanent, and in an action designated in [Insurance Law section 5104(a)] for personal injuries arising out of negligence in the use or operation of a motor vehicle in this state, in what respect plaintiff has sustained a serious injury, as defined in [Insurance Law section 5102(d)], or economic loss greater than basic economic loss, as defined in [Insurance Law section 5102(a)];

(7)   Length of time confined to bed and to house;

(8)   Length of time incapacitated from employment; and

(9)   Total amounts claimed as special damages for physicians' services and medical supplies; loss of earnings, with name and address of the employer; hospital expenses; nurses' services.

The court can add to or subtract from the above list in a given case.[25] For example, a demand for a bill of particulars is an appropriate vehicle for obtaining information on

---

[19]   Coonradt v. Walco, 55 Misc. 2d 557, 560, 285 N.Y.S.2d 421, 425 (Sup. Ct., Rensselaer County 1967).

[20]   Sacks v. Town of Thompson, 33 A.D.2d 627, 304 N.Y.S.2d 729 (3d Dep't 1969); see Castellano v. Norwegian Christian Home and Health Center, Inc., 24 A.D.3d 490, 808 N.Y.S.2d 289 (2d Dep't 2005) (responses in bill of particulars were proper since they enumerated the specific statutes, codes, rules, and regulations alleged in the complaint to have been violated by the defendants).

[21]   Haines v. Cook Elec. Co., 20 A.D.2d 517, 244 N.Y.S.2d 483 (1st Dep't 1963); see CPLR 3016(e); § 216.

[22]   American List Corp. v. U.S. News and World Report, Inc., 75 N.Y.2d 38, 43, 550 N.Y.S.2d 590, 593, 549 N.E.2d 1161 (1989).

[23]   Penn-Ohio Steel Corp. v. Allis-Chalmers Mfg. Co., 9 A.D.2d 620, 191 N.Y.S.2d 65 (1st Dep't 1959).

[24]   Arett Sales Corp. v. Island Garden Center Queens, Inc., 25 A.D.2d 546, 267 N.Y.S.2d 623 (2d Dep't 1966).

[25]   CPLR 3043(c).

collateral sources, such as insurance.[26] The list is, nonetheless, the standard for personal injury litigation and the court seldom has occasion to stray far from it.

Note that item 6 involves the no-fault law, requiring elaboration of the facts on which the plaintiff relies to take the case out of the no-fault realm and permit it to be brought as an ordinary fault action. CPLR 3016(g) requires the pleading of those facts, but while the pleading need merely allege them in conclusory form, the bill must elaborate them. Attorneys with automobile personal injury practices recognize these requirements and fulfill them almost automatically.[27] A comprehensive discussion of the categories of serious injury under the no-fault law and the pattern charges for each category are contained in New York Pattern Jury Instructions—Civil.[28] These pattern charges, and the accompanying comments, can provide immeasurable assistance to a lawyer preparing a bill of particulars.

"A plaintiff does not have to set forth in a bill of particulars the specific acts of negligence committed by the defendant where he relies on the doctrine of Res ipsa loquitur."[29] At one time, it was thought inconsistent in a negligence case for the plaintiff to rely both on the doctrine of res ipsa loquitur as well as on specific acts of negligence. Upon reexamination, the Court of Appeals determined that the two things are not necessarily inconsistent and held that both may be relied on in a given case.[30] When they're both relied on, the specific acts of negligence claimed must be particularized, as item 3 on the CPLR 3043(a) list manifests.[31]

If an account is pleaded, the adverse party is entitled to demand a copy of the items of the account. CPLR 3041 in fact defines "bill of particulars" to include "items of an account" when an account is involved. If a pleader has used CPLR 3016(f) and included a schedule of goods and services,[32] the pleading should contain sufficient detail as to make unnecessary the account contemplated by CPLR 3041. But if the account has been pleaded without the itemization of CPLR 3016(f), the pleader can be required to furnish an itemization through a demand under CPLR 3041.

Verification and Limitations on Use of Bill

If a pleading is verified, any bill of particulars in respect of it or copy of the items of an account alleged in it must also be verified.[33] But in a negligence case, the bill of

---

[26] McKenzie v. St. Elizabeth Hospital, 81 A.D.2d 1003, 1004, 440 N.Y.S.2d 109, 110 (4th Dep't 1981); Lewis v. MTA Bus Co., 51 Misc. 3d 1204(A), 36 N.Y.S.3d 408 (Sup. Ct., New York County 2016); see § 180 (discussing collateral source offsets).

[27] One of the showings that will take the case out of the no-fault realm is that the plaintiff sustained a "serious injury" as defined by statute. The kinds of injury that qualify as "serious" are reviewed by the Court of Appeals in Oberly v. Bangs Ambulance Inc., 96 N.Y.2d 295, 727 N.Y.S.2d 378, 751 N.E.2d 457 (2001) (NYSLD No. 497), and the kinds of proof needed to sustain the "serious" showing are reviewed in Toure v. Avis Rent A Car Systems, Inc., 98 N.Y.2d 345, 746 N.Y.S.2d 865, 774 N.E.2d 1197 (2002) (NYSLD No. 512).

Issues sometimes arise about whether the granting of summary judgment to the plaintiff on liability in a vehicle accident case (damages to abide a trial), or the defendant's default in the action (which establishes liability, but then requires a hearing on the damages issue), is also deemed to establish "serious injury" and sustain the case as a tort action. See SPR 133:2.

[28] See NY PJI Introductory Statement preceding §§ 2:75 and 2:88A–2:88G.

[29] Horan v. Syosset Hospital, 35 A.D.2d 729, 315 N.Y.S.2d 396 (2d Dep't 1970).

[30] Abbott v. Page Airways, Inc., 23 N.Y.2d 502, 297 N.Y.S.2d 713, 245 N.E.2d 388 (1969); see § 214.

[31] See Horan, 35 A.D.2d at 729, 315 N.Y.S.2d at 397; Fizette v. Riverview Plaza, Inc., 40 Misc. 2d 1, 242 N.Y.S.2d 594 (Sup. Ct., Seneca County 1963).

[32] See § 216.

[33] CPLR 3044.

particulars must be verified whether or not the pleading is.[34] The reason for this is known to few living organisms, but might be explained by the penchant for exaggeration among the plaintiff's bar.

Because the bill of particulars tends to duplicate the function of the interrogatory, CPLR 3130(1) provides that one cannot use both devices against the same party, except in a matrimonial action.[35]

§ 239. Procedure for Bill of Particulars

The procedure governing the bill of particulars is in CPLR 3042, which was overhauled in 1994, effective January 1, 1995. The procedures applicable before then will be noted only when a contrast seems especially helpful.[1]

A mere demand starts things off. The party seeking the bill of particulars serves a "written demand" on the other side stating the items with respect to which particulars are desired. In this treatment, the party who serves the demand will be S (for seeker), and the party on whom the demand is served will be R (for recipient).

There is no stated time for when the demand may be served, but ordinarily it should not be served before joinder of issue. The common practice for the defendant is to serve the demand with or after the answer. If the plaintiff wants a bill regarding affirmative defenses in the answer, the plaintiff can demand it any time after the answer is served; if the answer contains a counterclaim, a demand for a bill of particulars pertaining to the counterclaim may be served with or after the reply.

Under the CPLR, the service of a bill is not a condition precedent to the opening of disclosure proceedings, but the court can make it so if it finds reason to in a given case.[2]

R has 30 days in which to respond to the demand. R must review the demand promptly and decide which particulars she is willing to furnish and which particulars she objects to. R must answer the unobjectionable ones and in the same response include a statement of reasons for not responding to the others.[3] Each objection must be stated "with reasonable particularity."[4] R's response within the 30 days must cover everything. Objecting to one or more items is not ground for withholding or even delaying a response to the unobjectionable items, nor is there any delay or extension of time allowed.[5]

If S has any objections to the bill that R furnishes or, indeed, where R has altogether failed to serve a bill, S's remedy is a motion to compel compliance, which is governed by CPLR 3042(c) and (d). If R's failure is deemed "willful," the motion can include a request

---

[34]   CPLR 3044.

[35]   See § 361.

[1]   An extensive treatment comparing and contrasting the new and old procedures appears in a three-part series of notes in SPR 23:1 through SPR 25:1.

[2]   See, e.g., Rochester Radio Supply Co., Inc. v. State, 43 A.D.2d 897, 351 N.Y.S.2d 234 (4th Dep't 1974).

[3]   CPLR 3042(a).

[4]   CPLR 3042(a).

[5]   Note the similarity of this change to the one made a year earlier, effective January 1, 1994, with respect to the disclosure devices of the interrogatory, the discovery notice, and the notice of physical and mental examination. See §§ 361–62.

for penalties under CPLR 3042(d).[6] For irresponsible behavior on S's side, such as the service of improper or unduly burdensome demands, CPLR 3042(e) provides penalties.[7]

§ 240. Amending and Supplementing the Bill

CPLR 3042(b) allows the particularizer one amendment of the bill as of right, provided it is made prior to the filing of the note of issue.[1] This amendment can make any change in the bill enabling the party to include in it whatever could have been included in the original bill, just as an amendment as of course can make any change in a pleading under CPLR 3025(a).[2] But the latter is restricted in time to the outset of the action, while CPLR 3042(b) keeps the bill's amendment time open during the whole pre-note of issue period.

If the of right amendment of the bill introduces a substantial change, the other side may still resort to the disclosure devices to prepare to meet it. That's one of the purposes of making the cut-off time the filing of the note of issue.[3]

What does the recipient do who has received a valid demand, but who does not yet know all of the details needed to draw the bill of particulars? The recipient should draw the bill as completely as then able to and candidly note the present inability to go any further, setting forth an explanation under oath.[4] This can occur, for example, when the recipient needs to conduct a deposition of the demander in order to secure the necessary data.[5] A more common situation along this line is the personal injury action in which the likely duration of the injuries and damages is not yet known when the demand is served.[6] That used to be a dilemma, but isn't any longer. The plaintiff can obviously use the of-right amendment to update damages, but if the amendment has been used up, or the note of issue has already been filed thereby cutting off the right to amend without court leave, the personal injury plaintiff can turn to yet another device enacted to meet this updating problem: the supplemental bill.

CPLR 3043(b) allows the plaintiff in a personal injury case to serve a supplemental bill of particulars, also as a matter of right, but only "with respect to claims of continuing special damages and disabilities." The supplemental bill permits the plaintiff to expand on the extent of the injuries and damages[7]—an especially helpful opportunity in the personal injury case in which the extent of the injuries was not known earlier in the action—and it may be served even after the note of issue is filed, as long as it is served at least 30 days before the trial.[8] It can't be used, however, to add a new cause of action or assert a new injury. While the statutory language in CPLR 3043(b) does not prohibit

---

[6] CPLR 3042(c); see § 241.

[7] See § 241.

[1] For note of issue practice, see § 369.

[2] See Geller v. Port Jefferson Obstetrics and Gynecology, P.C., 294 A.D.2d 537, 742 N.Y.S.2d 872 (2d Dep't 2002); § 236.

[3] Disclosure proceedings must ordinarily be concluded before the note of issue is filed, the note of issue having to be accompanied by a certificate of readiness attesting to the completion of disclosure proceedings, among other things. See §§ 352, 369 and 370.

[4] Waldman v. Allen, 87 A.D.2d 817, 448 N.Y.S.2d 770 (2d Dep't 1982).

[5] Waldman, 87 A.D.2d 817, 448 N.Y.S.2d at 770.

[6] See, e.g., Marshall v. Zimmerly's Exp., 30 A.D.2d 929, 294 N.Y.S.2d 85 (2d Dep't 1968).

[7] Tate by McMahon v. Colabello, 58 N.Y.2d 84, 459 N.Y.S.2d 422, 445 N.E.2d 1101 (1983).

[8] An extensive discussion of this "supplement" provision, including its interplay with the "amendment" provision discussed above, is in Commentary C3043:2 on McKinney's CPLR 3043.

a party from adding a new "theory" in support of an existing cause of action, the courts have consistently prohibited a party from serving a supplemental bill of particulars that includes one.[9]

If the note of issue has been filed, cutting off an amendment as of right, or if the amendment has already been used up even though the note of issue has not yet been filed, or if the time for the of-right supplement of the damages claims in a personal injury case has expired, court leave will be required for any change in the bill.[10] If the note of issue has already been filed and there is any doubt as to whether the proposed additions to the bill of particulars constitute an "amendment," as opposed to a "supplement," a motion to amend is the only prudent course of action. If a party serves what is actually an amended bill of particulars after the filing of the note of issue, but labels it a "supplemental" bill, the courts will place substance over form and treat the bill as a nullity.[11]

The standard used by the courts in considering whether to allow the amendment is generally that applicable to the pleading itself under CPLR 3025(b).[12] In the absence of prejudice, the motion should be freely granted.[13] In fact, the absence of prejudice, such as where the party had knowledge all the while of just what it is that her adversary wants to add to the bill, may make it an abuse of discretion to refuse the amendment.[14] After the filing of the certificate of readiness, however, which is designed to assure that the case is ready for trial before being added to the calendar,[15] motions of this kind will be entertained only when unanticipated circumstances are shown, particularly if the motion is made on the eve of trial.[16]

§ 241. Remedies in Connection with Bill of Particulars

If the party receiving the demand for a bill of particulars (R) serves a bill that the seeker (S) deems inadequate, S may not return it, as that's not the remedy.[1] Under subdivision (c) of CPLR 3042, S's remedy for that, as well as for R's failure to serve a bill at all, is to:

> move to compel compliance or, if such failure is willful, for the imposition of penalties pursuant to subdivision (d) of this rule.

This is intended to replace the prior procedure under which S could do nothing more than make a motion to preclude, which was almost invariably granted conditionally, giving R a second chance to supply the bill as a matter of right. The old procedure did

---

[9]   See, e.g., Jurkowski ex rel. Cosgrove v. Sheehan Memorial Hosp., 85 A.D.3d 1672, 926 N.Y.S.2d 781 (4th Dep't 2011); Barrera v. City of New York, 265 A.D.2d 516, 697 N.Y.S.2d 132 (2d Dep't 1999); see also Commentary C3043:2 on McKinney's CPLR 3043.

[10]   Stipulation in lieu of motion can of course accomplish these things, and the courts are usually delighted with the substitute. The lawyer should always try to adjust these items with the other side before running to the judge with a motion.

[11]   See, e.g., Jurkowski, 85 A.D.3d at 1674, 926 N.Y.S.2d at 783.

[12]   Cardy v. Frey, 86 A.D.2d 968, 969, 448 N.Y.S.2d 291, 292 (4th Dep't 1982); Maloney v. Union Free School Dist. No. 7, 46 A.D.2d 789, 360 N.Y.S.2d 699 (2d Dep't 1974).

[13]   Kerlin v. Green, 36 A.D.2d 892, 320 N.Y.S.2d 200 (4th Dep't 1971).

[14]   Ackerman v. City of New York, 22 A.D.2d 790, 253 N.Y.S.2d 775 (2d Dep't 1964).

[15]   See § 370.

[16]   Cardy, 86 A.D.2d at 969, 448 N.Y.S.2d at 292–93; Hernandez v. Ezrow, 24 A.D.2d 730, 263 N.Y.S.2d 372 (4th Dep't 1965).

[1]   See Lutza v. Bollacker, 36 A.D.2d 789, 319 N.Y.S.2d 371 (3d Dep't 1971).

not contemplate penalties right away. Only if R disobeyed the court order could S seek penalties, which of course entailed a second trip to court. Under CPLR 3042(c), the court is not limited to a simple conditional preclusion order. If R's behavior is found "willful," sanctions can be applied on the initial motion to compel compliance.

If R does not respond in any way at all within the 30-day period, a start may already have been made towards a finding of willfulness. If R needs more time, R should contact S and seek an extension of time by stipulation. If the stipulation is refused, R may move the court for a time extension.[2]

S will be wasting S's own time, as well as R's, by making a compliance motion without first trying to work things out with R and at least offering one extension of time. Any and all motions affecting the bill of particulars, whether made by S or R, must include a detailed affirmation by the moving party's lawyer "that counsel has conferred with counsel for the opposing party in a good faith effort to resolve the issues raised by the motion."[3] Furthermore, unless there is something on the scene to show that R's omission was willful, so that the result of S's motion will be not merely a compliance order but a sanction to go with it, S may end up with a court order carrying no meat that just sets the stage for yet a further court application should this order now be disobeyed.

Prior to the 1995 amendment that overhauled bill of particulars practice, the courts were not quick to find conduct willful and impose sanctions. They should not be as hesitant under the present statute. Manifestly indifferent conduct by R should qualify as willful. The purpose of the amendment, in the words of the committee that drafted it, is to:

> curtail pronounced and widespread abuses which have arisen under present law . . . [where] [i]nitial requests for bills of particulars routinely are ignored. Some attorneys routinely serve demands that are . . . prolix and burdensome[,] demands [that] . . . harass opponents . . . [and] [s]till other attorneys routinely serve patently defective bills.[4]

The penalties sword of course cuts two ways, slashing at whichever side is at fault: R, covered by subdivision (d) of CPLR 3042, and S, covered by subdivision (e).

Subdivision (d) says that if R, the recipient of the demand for the bill:

> willfully fails to provide particulars which the court finds ought to have been provided . . ., the court may make such final or conditional order with regard to the failure or refusal as is just, including such relief as is set forth in [CPLR 3126].

CPLR 3126 is the statute that provides the penalties for a failure to make disclosure under Article 31.[5] Its penalties move in degrees, from an order establishing the relevant facts against the recalcitrant party, to a preclusion order, to the ultimate civil penalty of finding the party in default. The listed penalties are not exclusive, however. Under CPLR

---

[2]   See CPLR 2004.

[3]   22 N.Y.C.R.R. § 202.7(a), (c); see Kovacs v. Castle Restoration and Const., Inc., 262 A.D.2d 165, 692 N.Y.S.2d 63 (1st Dep't 1999) (order of preclusion held to be improper where plaintiff failed to submit affirmation establishing that a good faith attempt was made to resolve the bill of particulars dispute with defense counsel before moving to preclude).

[4]   See the memorandum of the Office of Court Administration at p.3304 of McKinney's 1994 Session Laws.

[5]   See § 367.

3126, the court can make any orders that it finds "just," and a popular one is an order giving the wrongdoer another chance, but only on condition that it pay a stated sum to cover the other side's costs and attorney's fees associated with the misconduct.[6]

The reference to CPLR 3126 makes all of these remedies available as well for R's bill of particulars omissions, including the money assessment. Just as the remedies that CPLR 3126 contains are not exhaustive of the court's options there, the entirety of the CPLR 3126 package is not exhaustive of the court's options here, with the bill of particulars. The court can dip into the CPLR 3126 pot if it finds it appropriate, but doesn't have to. It can, independently of CPLR 3126, make its own "just" order under CPLR 3042(d).

The phrase "final or conditional" in subdivision (d) enables the court to include, with whatever penalty it chooses, a qualification, such as suspending the penalty "unless" compliance is forthcoming within a set time. "Unless" dispositions have been common in bill of particulars practice,[7] but the word "final" in subdivision (d) would seem to make it permissible for the court to visit the ultimate sanction of a default on the wrongdoing party.

If the remedy selected by the court is a conditional preclusion order, and the condition has been violated, what's the next step? The ultimate remedy is summary judgment against R on the simple (and obvious) premise that since R is precluded from putting in a case, there is no reason for prolonging the agony of the litigation. Although delays even beyond the time offered by a conditional preclusion order can be forgiven, and for good cause will be,[8] summary judgment is exactly what awaits the recalcitrant party who presses his luck too far and who has no good reason for the delay.[9] When a plaintiff does that, the court may even specify that the judgment is "on the merits," or "with prejudice,"[10] clarifying that any attempted new action will be met by the defense of res judicata. The continued disregard of court orders in bill of particulars practice has been held to justify the appending of such a fatal qualification to the dismissal.[11]

Penalties Against S, the Demanding Party

Subdivision (e) is the tool that R, the recipient of the demand, may be able to use against S, the party who is seeking the particulars, but it may be invoked only if the court finds that S's demand is "improper or unduly burdensome." Demanding things not relevant to the case would be "improper," for example; demanding things that may be technically relevant but of a nature or quantity disproportionate in context would invoke the "unduly burdensome" standard.

---

[6]   See § 367.

[7]   See Whitfield v. State, 28 A.D.3d 541, 542, 814 N.Y.S.2d 185, 187 (2d Dep't 2006).

[8]   See, e.g., Abramowitz v. Berger, 20 A.D.2d 903, 248 N.Y.S.2d 936 (2d Dep't 1964).

[9]   See, e.g., Gibbs v. St. Barnabas Hosp., 16 N.Y.3d 74, 917 N.Y.S.2d 68, 942 N.E.2d 277 (2010); Kwiatek v. Buffalo Truck Sales & Service, 178 A.D.2d 948, 948, 579 N.Y.S.2d 252, 252 (4th Dep't 1991). Cases in the First Department suggesting that summary judgment is not an appropriate remedy were decided when summary judgment was available only in certain actions, and are not authority today, when summary judgment is no longer so restricted. See § 280.

[10]   See Palmer v. Fox, 28 A.D.2d 968, 283 N.Y.S.2d 216 (4th Dep't 1967), aff'd, 22 N.Y.2d 667, 291 N.Y.S.2d 361, 238 N.E.2d 751 (1968).

[11]   See Mitchell v. Kiamesha Concord, Inc., 94 A.D.2d 914, 463 N.Y.S.2d 626 (3d Dep't 1983).

If S's demand for a bill of particulars is unduly burdensome, the courts will not ordinarily prune the demand, but will rather strike it in its entirety.[12] The court may also impose a sanction in addition to vacating or modifying the demand. Presumably the sanction would be monetary, but one can conjure up a situation in which it could be worse. Under subdivision (e), there is no explicit invitation to apply CPLR 3126, as there is in subdivision (d) in dealing with remedies against R, but there is general language of subdivision (e) that permits "such order as is just." In that may be found a route to CPLR 3126, and its various sanctions, should the court choose to use it.[13]

Under subdivision (e), the only conduct on the part of S, the demanding party, that can invoke a sanction is the service of an improper or excessive demand. Other conduct by S that would seem appropriate for a sanction, but which does not come down to an improper or excessive demand, is not subject to a penalty under subdivision (e). If S's conduct rises to the level of "frivolous," however, it can be made the subject of a sanction under Rule 130–1.[14] That happened in Bank of Rochester v. Volpe,[15] for example, where the demanding party moved to preclude before the bill of particulars was even due.

In both subdivisions (d) and (e), the court's remedial powers are summed up in the phrase permitting the court to make such order "as is just," thus leaving the matter almost entirely within the court's hands and broad discretion.[16]

§ 242. Variances

Variances between the bill of particulars and the pleading together on one side, and the proof at trial on the other, are usually resolved today by giving the proof the upper hand and allowing the pleading and the bill to be amended to conform to the actual evidence, at least when no prejudice is shown.[1] And if the proof is within the purview of the pleading, but not in conformity with the bill, or vice versa, the variance may be held inconsequential.[2] It is therefore difficult today to say just what the consequence of a variance will be. If the other side can't convince the court that it was misled by the variance, the court is not likely to penalize it. The bill of particulars, in other words, appears to have lost some of its purpose in narrowing the issues.[3] It's an amplification and therefore an adjunct of the pleading and as such enjoys the same liberal rules of construction that prevent pleadings from being handled too rigidly.

Practically speaking, the other side will not be heard to complain unless (1) the bill of particulars has actually misled it, and (2) it is prejudiced as a result. This is not common today, but when it occurs, pain is usually inflicted. The lawyer would do well to

---

[12]   See, e.g., Erbesh v. Schwartz, 21 A.D.3d 532, 799 N.Y.S.2d 905 (2d Dep't 2005).

[13]   See SPR 25:1–2.

[14]   Rule 130–1, the sanctions rule applicable in civil actions, is treated in § 414A.

[15]   First Nat. Bank of Rochester v. Volpe, 219 A.D.2d 867, 632 N.Y.S.2d 732 (4th Dep't 1995).

[16]   A similar deference to the court's judgment appears in several other procedural provisions that may provide additional guidance by analogy. See SPR 25:2.

[1]   CPLR 3025(c) (see § 404); Kimso Apartments, LLC v. Gandhi, 24 N.Y.3d 403, 998 N.Y.S.2d 740, 23 N.E.3d 1008 (2014); Sharkey v. Locust Valley Marine, Inc., 96 A.D.2d 1093, 467 N.Y.S.2d 61 (2d Dep't 1983).

[2]   See, e.g., Pogor v. Cue Taxi Service, Inc., 43 Misc. 2d 487, 251 N.Y.S.2d 635 (N.Y. City Civ. Ct. 1964), aff'd, 45 Misc. 2d 933, 258 N.Y.S.2d 60 (App. Term, 1st Dep't 1965).

[3]   See Commentary C3042:10 on McKinney's CPLR 3042. The advent of liberal disclosure under Article 31 of the CPLR, see Chapter 13, below, probably accounts for this.

absorb the lesson of Mammarella v. Consolidated Edison Co. of New York, Inc.,[4] for example. It was a wrongful death action and D demanded of P particulars as to the deceased's employment and loss of earnings, among other things. P responded to that portion of the demand with a pithy "not applicable," indicating that no damages were being claimed for those things. D therefore didn't prepare to address them. P was nevertheless allowed at the trial to prove such losses and when a verdict of $55,000 came in for P, it was discernible that $35,000 of the total was imputable to the very things P had so casually denominated "not applicable." The appellate division, holding D to have been unfairly misled, reduced the verdict from $55,000 to $20,000 and ordered P to take that or a whole new trial—together with the risk that a new jury might find liability lacking and that P would end up with nothing. That's the kind of consequence that awaits a party who takes too much for granted in bill of particulars practice.[5]

---

[4] Mammarella v. Consolidated Edison Co. of New York, Inc., 44 A.D.2d 571, 353 N.Y.S.2d 38 (2d Dep't 1974).

[5] See Kenney v. Zimmerman, 185 A.D.2d 690, 586 N.Y.S.2d 80 (4th Dep't 1992).

Chapter 10

MOTION PRACTICE

Table of Sections

§ 243.   Motion Practice, Generally

§ 244.   Ex Parte Motions

§ 245.   Where Motion Made (Venue of Motions)

§ 246.   The Motion Papers

§ 247.   Motion Notice Requirements

§ 248.   Order to Show Cause

§ 249.   Cross-Motion

§ 250.   Deciding the Motion; Drawing and Entering the Order

§ 251.   Trial of Issue of Fact Arising on Motion

§ 252.   Some Forms

§ 253.   Motion Affecting Prior Order

§ 254.   Motion to Reargue or Renew

§ 255.   Stay

§ 243. Motion Practice, Generally

A motion is an application for an order.[1] It is usually made within the framework of an existing action or proceeding and is ordinarily made on notice, but some motions may be made without notice. A motion made without notice is called an ex parte motion.

Orders are the devices whereby the courts manage litigation and resolve various intra-action disputes between the parties. Motions are the expedients for securing the orders. Most motions concern only incidents, i.e., they seek orders processing some housekeeping phase of the case, such as the pleadings, or they seek via motion disclosure; others seek relief that is actually or in effect final, such as motions to dismiss or for summary judgment.

As for who may move for what, there is one grand rule of thumb: any order the court can make, an interested party may seek via motion. Some orders may be granted by the court on its own motion, otherwise known as a sua sponte motion, but the great majority of orders result from motions made at the initiative of a party.

When Is a Motion Made?

A motion on notice is deemed made when the motion papers are served.[2] When they are served by mail, which is perhaps the most usual method, the moment of service occurs when the stamped and properly addressed envelope containing the papers is dropped in the letter box.[3] Thus, when the envelope leaves the fingers and drops into the

---

[1]   CPLR 2211.

[2]   CPLR 2211.

[3]   CPLR 2103(b)(2).

box, the movant has "made" the motion even though the motion is not returnable in court until a number of days later and even though it will be several days before the motion papers are received by the court or the other parties. In an e-filed action, a motion is made when the motion papers are filed.[4]

It is necessary to pinpoint the moment of service because many motions have to be made within a specified time.[5] The mere posting within that time usually satisfies the requirement. A motion by the defendant for a more definite statement, for example,[6] must be made within 20 days after the complaint is served.[7] Posting the motion papers on or before the 20th day or filing them in an e-filed action fulfills that requirement.

An ex parte motion, when such motion is permitted,[8] is "made" when the motion papers and proposed order are submitted to the court.[9]

Written Motions Versus Oral Motions

Most motions are made on written papers. The ensuing sections will discuss the various steps in making, scheduling, and disposing of motions. At the trial itself, oral motions are common, especially for the purpose of resolving evidentiary disputes. The courts are, however, hesitant to entertain an oral motion to dismiss or an oral motion for summary judgment at that juncture.[10] The court has sometimes entertained an oral motion—i.e., one not made by a formal written notice of motion—in other contexts when the parties were before it and when it appeared that no prejudice would result from the informal procedure. Thus, where P brought a special proceeding against D and both were before the court on the return day of the proceeding, D's oral motion to dismiss for lack of jurisdiction (based on defective service of the initiatory papers) was entertained. Prejudice to P was avoided in that the court held its decision off until P could submit opposing affidavits, which the court reviewed when it got them. The procedure was upheld.[11]

The fact that the court may occasionally entertain an oral motion in a context that ordinarily calls for the conventional written one is not something a lawyer should depend on. It should on no account be taken as an invitation to withhold papers in the hope that an oral request during a court hearing will do the job.

Uniform Rules, Individual Court Rules, Protocols, and the RJI

The subject of motion practice is much affected by the adoption of the Individual Assignment System (IAS) that went into effect on January 6, 1986,[12] as part of the Uniform Rules. Two important uniform rules supplement the CPLR and must be

---

[4]   22 N.Y.C.R.R. § 202.5–b(f)(2)(ii). While this rule is contained in the rules for the consensual e-filing program, it also applies in cases governed by mandatory e-filing. See 22 N.Y.C.R.R. § 202.5–bb(a)(1).

[5]   See, e.g., CPLR 3212(a) (prescribing time periods for summary judgment motions), discussed in § 279.

[6]   CPLR 3024(a); see § 230.

[7]   CPLR 3024(c).

[8]   See § 244.

[9]   2d Rep. Leg. Doc. No. 13, p. 181 (1958).

[10]   See Martinez v. Premium Laundry Corp., 137 A.D.3d 419, 420, 25 N.Y.S.3d 867, 867 (1st Dep't 2016); Commentary C2214:23A to McKinney's CPLR 2214.

[11]   Shanty Hollow Corp. v. Poladian, 23 A.D.2d 132, 259 N.Y.S.2d 541 (3d Dep't 1965), aff'd, 17 N.Y.2d 536, 267 N.Y.S.2d 912, 215 N.E.2d 168 (1966).

[12]   See § 77A.

consulted by any party making a motion in a supreme court action: section 202.7, entitled "Calendaring of motions; uniform notice of motion form; affirmation of good faith"; and section 202.8, entitled "Motion procedure." Furthermore, almost everything said about motion practice today—and this has to be kept in mind in consulting the ensuing sections that review the CPLR's diverse requirements on motion practice—has to be qualified to caution that if the case is in the hands of a single judge, that judge's preferences have to be negotiated with respect to many of the details of motion procedure. Some judges have drawn and published their own individual rules, sometimes called "information sheets," instructing on diverse procedures, such as the day and time the judge hears motions, whether an appearance is required, whether oral argument is allowed, deadlines for the filing of motion papers or requests for adjournment, etc. In e-filed actions, these individual rules are contained in "protocols," and lawyers must be careful to take note of them.[13]

Despite the uniformity at which the Uniform Rules aim, when it comes to motions, the IAS unfortunately brings about less, rather than more, uniformity. The lawyer with any question at all about a motion after consulting the CPLR, the Uniform Rules, and of course the particular judge's rules if there are any, would seem to have no alternative but to call the judge's chambers and find out specifically how the judge wants things done. Guidance may also be found on a court's website.

For motion practice in supreme and county courts, the Uniform Rules have two rules noted above, 202.7, which contains a helpful notice of motion form, and 202.8, which contains other procedural guidelines for motions.[14] Other Uniform Rule provisions govern motion practice in other courts, including the Court of Claims,[15] the New York City Civil Court,[16] the District Courts,[17] and the City Courts.[18]

When a party desires to make the first motion in an action and no judge is yet assigned, the rules require that the motion "be made returnable before the court" and that "a copy of the moving papers, together with a request for judicial intervention [RJI], shall be filed with the court."[19] But even there, it doesn't hurt for the lawyer in doubt to ask about local trimmings in a call to the clerk in the county where the action is venued.[20]

Requiring Court Permission to Make Motion

Some judges early in the life of the IAS, following the controversial practice of some federal judges, required that their permission be obtained before a motion could be made in one of their assigned cases. The appellate division has rejected that restriction on

---

[13]   See, e.g., Protocol on Courthouse and County Clerk Procedures for Electronically Filed Cases, § B, 6(a), Supreme Court, New York County (revised March 9, 2016) ("Various Justices require that, in all NYSCEF cases assigned to them, unless otherwise directed, counsel submit working copies [, i.e., hard copies,] of e-filed documents . . . .").

[14]   These are reviewed in the lead note in NYSLD No. 313.

[15]   22 N.Y.C.R.R. §§ 206.8, 206.9.

[16]   22 N.Y.C.R.R. §§ 208.10, 208.11.

[17]   22 N.Y.C.R.R. §§ 212.10, 212.11.

[18]   22 N.Y.C.R.R. §§ 210.8, 210.9.

[19]   22 N.Y.C.R.R. § 202.8(b); see § 77B (describing how a case gets assigned to a judge through the filing of a Request for Judicial Intervention (RJI)).

[20]   Motion venue, too, is affected by the IAS. See § 245.

numerous occasions, holding in Goldheart Int'l Ltd. v. Vulcan Constr. Corp.,[21] for example, that a judge can't refuse to entertain a properly made motion. Other judges and court rules have required a kind of "conference" before a formal motion is made, hoping to resolve the dispute that might otherwise entail a motion. If this is seen as just a back door to requiring pre-motion permission in all instances, it may also meet appellate division disapproval. But if it doesn't substantially add to the burdens of the lawyers and is seen as a device for resolving in a telephone call or in a brief visit to chambers that which might otherwise require the time, effort, and expense of a formal motion, the practice might be upheld.

Because some judges continued the practice of requiring prior leave for motions, the First Department returned to the matter with an even more direct reproach in Hochberg v. Davis.[22] In an Article 78 proceeding brought against a judge by an aggrieved party, the court set aside a judge's rule exacting such permission and this time added the admonition that the "information sheets" used by some judges as the equivalent of rules are not valid unless filed with the Chief Administrator. In so doing, the court therefore made another point the bar wanted clarified: that a preliminary leave requirement for motions can't be tolerated for "information sheets" any more than for outright "rules." To the extent that a permission requirement is felt to be a way of avoiding frivolous motions, the court pointed out that the answer to a frivolous motion is a frivolity sanction.[23]

The rules of the commercial division of the supreme court currently require that parties planning to make motions first submit letters and then participate in court conferences.[24] If a moving party fails to comply with the rules, it "may result in [the] motion being held in abeyance until the court has an opportunity to conference the matter."[25] In Briarpatch Ltd., L.P. v. Briarpatch Film Corp.,[26] neither side requested a pre-motion conference prior to filing a motion and cross-motion and the court marked both motions off the calendar with leave to renew after compliance with the rules. Instead of marking the motions off the calendar, the First Department ruled that supreme court "should have scheduled a conference and then decided the motions if the conference did not resolve the parties' disputes."[27] Marking a motion off the calendar in this fashion can wreak havoc on a party who is under a deadline for making a motion, especially when the time period has now passed.

New York allows an appeal from non-final orders on motions.[28] That, plus the further availability of a mandamus-type proceeding against a judge to compel the

---

[21]   Goldheart Int'l Ltd. v. Vulcan Constr. Corp., 124 A.D.2d 507, 508 N.Y.S.2d 182 (1st Dep't 1986). The Second Circuit also curtailed the get-permission-first rule used by some federal district judges. See Richardson Greenshields Sec., Inc. v. Lau, 825 F.2d 647 (2d Cir. 1987).

[22]   Hochberg v. Davis, 171 A.D.2d 192, 575 N.Y.S.2d 311 (1st Dep't 1991).

[23]   See 22 N.Y.C.R.R. § 130–1, treated in § 414A.

[24]   See, e.g., 22 N.Y.C.R.R. § 202.70, Com. Div. Rule 14 (stating preference to resolve disclosure disputes via court conference rather than motion); Com. Div. Rule 24 (requiring party contemplating a motion to submit a "motion notice letter" and participate in a conference before making the motion).

[25]   22 N.Y.C.R.R. § 202.70, Com. Div. Rule 14.

[26]   Briarpatch Ltd., L.P. v. Briarpatch Film Corp., 68 A.D.3d 520, 891 N.Y.S.2d 352 (1st Dep't 2009).

[27]   *Briarpatch Ltd., L.P.,* 68 A.D.3d at 520, 891 N.Y.S.2d at 353; see Costigan & Co., P.C. v. Costigan, 304 A.D.2d 464, 758 N.Y.S.2d 312, 313 (1st Dep't 2003) ("Since . . . [the commercial division] rule [at issue] effectively conditions the making of a motion on prior judicial approval, it violates a party's statutory right to make a motion and is void.").

[28]   See § 526.

exercise of mandatory duties,[29] serve as checks on possible IAS abuses. In a proceeding brought against one supreme court justice, for example, it was held that upon the request of an aggrieved party, a judge must sign an order reflecting a motion's outcome or otherwise make a written record on which an appeal can be predicated.[30]

Filing of Motions and Fees

Until 2003, no fee was charged for the making of a motion. In what came as a surprise to bench and bar alike—it was part of the state budget[31]—a fee was imposed for the first time for the making of a motion, taking effect July 14, 2003. The fee, exacted in the supreme and county courts, but not in the lower courts, is $45.[32] It must be paid in conjunction with a variety of motions.

The problems associated with fee collection are almost all logistical, but are virtually nonexistent in an e-filed action where any applicable fees must generally be payed upon the e-filing of a paper.[33] In actions not subject to e-filing, how and when is the fee to be paid with different categories of motions? As ensuing sections will explore, there are a variety of these: the usual pretrial motions; pre-action motions; post-judgment motions; cross-motions; ex-parte motions; motions to renew, reargue, or resettle; orders to show cause; motions that commence actions;[34] motions during trial; oral motions; sua sponte motions; etc.[35]

There appears to be a consensus that only formal written motions generate the required fee. The assumption appears to be that oral motions don't, because it's the filing of the papers that begets the fee, and the oral motion is not ordinarily a paper begetter. If a given oral motion should end up on paper and be filed, however, it too will require a fee.

§ 244. Ex Parte Motions

Although New York statutory law is not explicit on the point, the general rule from the cases is that motions must be made on notice. Practically speaking, the only time a party should attempt to move ex parte is when a statute or rule explicitly authorizes it.[1] Only a few statutes do this. One is the motion for an order devising a method of summons service.[2] Another is the motion for an order in the supreme or county courts extending the plaintiff's time to file an action, pursuant to which the court can grant an extension of up to five days. In this instance, the mere signing of the order marks the commencement of the claim for limitations purposes.[3] This motion is usually made when interim relief, such as a temporary restraining order, is sought on a weekend or holiday

---

[29] CPLR 7803(1); see § 558.

[30] Grisi v. Shainswit, 119 A.D.2d 418, 507 N.Y.S.2d 155 (1st Dep't 1986). There is of course a general requirement that orders be in writing. See CPLR 2219(a), discussed in § 250.

[31] L.2003, ch. 62, Part J.

[32] CPLR 8020(a).

[33] 22 N.Y.C.R.R. § 202.5–b(d)(2).

[34] CPLR 3213 is an example. See § 291.

[35] Many of the issues raised by the fee requirement are addressed in a two-part treatment in SPR Issues 136:1 and 137:2.

[1] See Essex v. Newman, 220 A.D.2d 639, 632 N.Y.S.2d 636 (2d Dep't 1995) (deleting provision in order fixing rental payments ex parte and directing future applications to fix rental payments to be made by motion on notice).

[2] CPLR 308(5), 311(b). See § 75.

[3] See CPLR 304(a). See § 45.

before an action can be commenced in the matter by filing in the county clerk's office. Other instances in which a motion can be made ex parte are found among the provisional remedies.[4]

Some caselaw holds that a motion may be made ex parte even without statutory authority if the other side would not be "prejudiced or affected in the least" by the relief sought.[5] This is a difficult notion to accept because the very issue of whether a party is affected by a motion is an issue on which that party is entitled to be heard.[6] Cases upholding ex parte applications made without statutory invitation are happily infrequent, and there is a widespread and healthy judicial distaste for such attempts.[7] Lawyers should make it their business to make all motions on notice unless there is an unambiguous statute or rule at hand authorizing the particular motion to be made ex parte.

There is an important rule the lawyer should remember on all ex parte motions. All of them. There is a strong policy against having one judge overrule another of coordinate jurisdiction, or putting a judge into the embarrassing position of doing so inadvertently, or even confronting a judge with the possibility of overruling herself because she has forgotten some earlier ruling she made in the case. Recognizing that on an ex parte motion there is no adverse party to offset the movant's one-sided presentation, it is required that the moving papers on every ex parte application include an affidavit attesting to whether this or any similar relief has been moved for previously and, if so, what new facts justify this new application.[8] The affidavit should describe precisely what occurred on the earlier application.

In addition, Rule 3.3(d) of the New York Rules of Professional Conduct reinforces CPLR 2217(b). It provides that, "[i]n an ex parte proceeding, a lawyer shall inform the tribunal of all material facts known to the lawyer that will enable the tribunal to make an informed decision, whether or not the facts are adverse."[9] This provision imposes an independent obligation on a lawyer making an ex parte motion to disclose the result of any prior motion for similar relief.

The Individual Assignment System (IAS),[10] under which a case goes to a single judge and stays there throughout, might be thought to reduce the need for this attestation of prior activity because the prior activity in the case would presumably have been before the same judge. But that notion gives too much credit to judicial memory, especially when the judge may have hundreds of cases to track. There are, in any event, exceptions from place to place under the IAS in which the system is not operative and in which the case does get exposed to different judges.

---

[4]   See, e.g., CPLR 6211(a), 6313(a).

[5]   See, e.g., In re Salmon, 34 Misc. 251, 253, 69 N.Y.S. 215, 216 (Sup. Ct., Monroe County 1901).

[6]   See Fosmire v. Nicoleau, 144 A.D.2d 8, 536 N.Y.S.2d 492 (2d Dep't 1989), aff'd, 75 N.Y.2d 218, 551 N.Y.S.2d 876, 551 N.E.2d 77 (1990).

[7]   See *Essex*, 220 A.D.2d at 640, 632 N.Y.S.2d at 637; Cooke v. Wozen Equities, Inc., 143 Misc. 2d 578, 540 N.Y.S.2d 629 (Sup. Ct., New York County 1988).

[8]   CPLR 2217(b).

[9]   See New York Rules of Professional Conduct, Rule 3.3, cmt. 14 ("The lawyer for the represented party has the . . . duty to make disclosures of material facts known to the lawyer that the lawyer reasonably believes are necessary to an informed decision.").

[10]   See § 77A.

An order on an ex parte application is not appealable.[11] If an adverse party wants the order vacated, she should move for the vacatur on notice. The order granting or denying the vacatur will then be appealable. He may alternatively seek vacatur of the order by an ex parte application made to the judge who granted it,[12] but if that application is denied, the order of denial will not be appealable. The party has yet another alternative: to move, ex parte, to have the appellate court or one of its judges vacate or modify the order. CPLR 5704(a) expressly authorizes this, and even authorizes a movant whose ex parte motion below has been denied to seek its grant from the appellate court.[13] CPLR 5704 contemplates a simple, ex parte motion procedure before the appellate court, not a full-blown appeal procedure with its attendant time, trouble, and expense. The First Department declared in 1964 that it would only entertain such applications "in unusual circumstances,"[14] remitting the movant to repeating the motion before the lower court, this time on notice—so that the resulting order would be appealable. This hostility to CPLR 5704 did not spread to all of the other departments[15] and, indeed, the indications are that it is no longer present even in the First Department.

Under the IAS, all motions, including the ex parte motion, must as a rule be made to the assigned judge.[16] If an ex parte motion is made in a case in which a judge has not yet been assigned, the papers must be accompanied by a Request for Judicial Intervention.[17] It is this "RJI" that occasions the assigning.[18] If there is time pressure that can't await the usual local assignment machinery, an inquiry about any special procedure should be made promptly of the clerk. There may be a judge on "standby" for such an exigency. In populous counties, there may even be a regularly assigned "standby" judge, the equivalent of the judge presiding at what used to be widely known as "Special Term, Part II" in some counties to handle such emergency applications. The fact that the order to show cause, the prime servant of an emergency, can also fall into the "ex parte" category gives this subject extra importance.[19]

A standby judge may be available under local procedure even for emergency applications in cases in which a judicial assignment is already in effect as where the assigned judge is indisposed or off on circuit to a distant part of the judicial district. Uniformity on these matters is illusive, and a call to the clerk reassuring.

As will be seen more fully in the treatment of the venue of motions,[20] each supreme court justice carries the ex parte powers of the court around wherever he or she may be and can be approached for ex parte relief in any part of the state,[21] presumably without regard to where the action is venued or who the assigned judge is. But the Uniform Rules

---

[11]   See CPLR 5701(a)(2).

[12]   CPLR 2221(a)(2).

[13]   The appellate division has these ex parte powers only in respect of the lower courts of which it has appellate jurisdiction. CPLR 5704(a). In the First and Second Departments, the appellate term and its justices have like powers for their lower courts, which include the New York City Civil Court, the district courts, etc. CPLR 5704(b).

[14]   See In re Willmark Service System, Inc., 21 A.D.2d 478, 251 N.Y.S.2d 267 (1st Dep't 1964).

[15]   People v. Conway, 62 A.D.2d 1107, 404 N.Y.S.2d 170 (3d Dep't 1978) (finding *Willmark*'s "unusual circumstances" standard satisfied, court entertained CPLR 5704 application).

[16]   22 N.Y.C.R.R. § 202.8(a).

[17]   22 N.Y.C.R.R. § 202.8(b).

[18]   See § 77B.

[19]   The order to show cause is the subject of § 248.

[20]   Section 245.

[21]   CPLR 2212(b).

qualify this to require the judge approached to refer the ex parte application to the appropriate county or judge "unless . . . the urgency of the motion requires immediate determination."[22]

As noted in section 243 above, a fee must be paid upon the filing of motion papers in the supreme and county courts. The ex parte motion is not excepted from this requirement. The logistics of paying the fee can be tricky with ex parte motions, however, which may go directly to a judge without initial processing through the clerk's office. It should be okay to defer the fee paying until the papers are later filed with the county clerk,[23] but, once again, an inquiry into local preferences can't hurt. A strong argument can be made that the fee should be imposed even if the court denies the motion as the motion has nonetheless been made.

§ 245. Where Motion Made (Venue of Motions)

The question of where a motion may be made, i.e., what counties are proper venue for the motion, arises rarely today. Uniform Rule section 202.8(a) states that "[a]ll motions shall be returnable before the assigned judge."

Since the supreme court is a court of statewide jurisdiction with local subdivisions, proper venue for supreme court motions may need pinpointing. The county court, on the other hand, is independent in each county that has one, and all counties except those in New York City have one. Therefore, all motions in county court actions are made returnable in that county except under special circumstances.[1]

A motion on notice in a supreme court action has a broad choice of venues under CPLR 2212(a). Due to the Individual Assignment System (IAS), however, under which a case goes to a single judge and remains with that judge for all purposes,[2] the "choice" is usually illusory today. As noted above, under the IAS, all motions must be returnable before the assigned judge.[3] An effort was made to reconcile the statutes on motion practice, embodied for the most part in Article 22 of the CPLR, with the IAS-implementing Uniform Rules, but unfortunately the "reconciliation" did not rework the statutes to coordinate with the rules. Rather, it merely added language at key points subordinating the statutes to such rules as the chief administrator may adopt.[4] The rules adopted pursuant to those authorizations can be uniform, as where something in the Uniform Rules addresses the matter, or just local. Given practices, whether by adoption in a rule or by direction through administrative order or otherwise, may be prescribed for application only in a given district or county or court.

The lesson to the lawyer is to check things out on a local basis—indeed, with the individual assigned judge if there is one—if there is any doubt whatever about procedures followed locally.

---

[22]   22 N.Y.C.R.R. § 202.7(e); see Commentary C2212:8 on McKinney's CPLR 2212.

[23]   See the discussion in SPR 136:4.

[1]   See CPLR 2213. As to the venue of motions in the lower courts, see Commentary C2212:6 on McKinney's CPLR 2212.

[2]   See § 77A.

[3]   22 N.Y.C.R.R. § 202.8(a).

[4]   See CPLR 2212(d), 2213(c), 2217(d), 2221(b).

CPLR 2212(a) is in dire need of radical revision or repeal, but procedural reforms are not high on the legislature's "to do" list.[5] Regardless of whether it's applicability has been reduced, CPLR 2212(a) remains on the books, and therefore, we offer the following treatment of it, but with the admonition that much of it is likely academic.

CPLR 2212 offers a choice of counties, or shall we say *purports* to offer a choice of counties, in which to make a motion in a supreme court action. The motion may be noticed to be heard, i.e., made returnable, in the county in which the action is pending (the most common choice), or in any other county in the same judicial district, or in any county physically adjoining the pendency county even if not in the same district.[6] The original and legitimate purpose of this surprisingly broad choice was to recognize the frequent unavailability of motion terms and permanently assigned justices in the more rural counties, a problem not met in the urban counties (where alternatives to the pendency county were therefore less frequently used for motions). Whatever the motivations, the provision, at least until the advent of the IAS, continued to make for a lot of judge shopping.

The generous venue alternatives of CPLR 2212(a) can't comfortably co-exist with a system that insists that all motions in a case go to but a single judge. Subdivision (d) of CPLR 2212 therefore confers on the chief administrator the power to withdraw the 2212(a) alternatives. The power is supposed to be exercised "by rule," but whether an administrative "rule" or "order" or perhaps just a local practice is in effect in a given area must, once again, be inquired into locally. In a case in which a judge has already been assigned, motions will presumably be following the judge thenceforth wherever the judge may be at a given time.

Following the judge about can of course be a problem in upstate districts covering large areas because the judge may be on assignment to a distant county. At least for emergency applications, such as ex parte applications that can't wait, there will presumably be some more expeditious alternative set up in the county in which the action was commenced and in which the assigned judge is ordinarily resident.[7]

Assuming that once a judge has been assigned, the CPLR 2212(a) venue options dissolve and the motion must be made to the assigned judge, that still leaves the situation in which a motion is made prior to a judge being assigned to the case. There, at least, it would seem that the movant can exercise his CPLR 2212(a) options and make the motion in a county other than the main action's venue. Rule 202.8(b) of the Uniform Rules addresses the point, however, and appears to discourage the exercising of these 2212(a) choices. It sets up a procedure for getting a judge assigned—whichever county has initially been made the motion venue—and to allow the party to re-notice the motion in accordance with the assigned judge's calendar, of course notifying the parties when all this is done.[8]

The IAS does seem to sound the death knell of that favorite old use of the CPLR 2212(a) motion options, already noted: judge shopping. And if it's not the death knell, then it's at least some early tolling. An attempt to invoke the CPLR 2212(a) venue

---

[5]   See Sullivan & Donovan, L.L.P. v. Bond, 175 Misc.2d 386, 387, 669 N.Y.S.2d 131, 132 (Sup. Ct., Bronx County 1997) (noting that it "may be a suitable time for the Legislature to consider abrogating [CPLR 2212(a),] especially in view of the adoption of the Individual Assignment System.").

[6]   CPLR 2212(a).

[7]   See § 244.

[8]   See Commentary C2212:1A on McKinney's CPLR 2212.

alternatives by making a motion in the Bronx in an action pending in Westchester was rejected in Sullivan & Donovan, LLP v. Bond,[9] for example, where the court denied the motion without prejudice to its renewal in Westchester. The court held, in effect, that the statute does not apply when the alternative venue imposes on an urban county.[10] Even before the IAS came in, the use of the venue options had been excluded from some counties by caselaw.[11]

Although a county may have no resident supreme court justice, each county outside New York City usually has a sitting county court judge. Recognizing this, the CPLR allows the rules to permit supreme court motions to be made to the county judge in certain circumstances.[12] The lawyer should find out if such a rule is applicable in the particular county, at least in the Second, Third, and Fourth departments. There are no county courts in the First Department.[13]

If a supreme court motion is made returnable in an altogether wrong county, the result should be nothing more serious than a change of venue back to a proper county as happens when the action itself has been improperly venued.[14] It has even been observed that the parties can stipulate to a venue for their motion,[15] which of course implies that motion venue is not jurisdictional. Some caselaw has indicated that it is,[16] but on closer reflection certain courts so indicating have come round to the view that it is not.[17] Even the consequence of holding the matter jurisdictional should not often be serious; however, instead of a transfer, it merely results in a denial of the motion, or perhaps in its mere "dismissal," without prejudice to its being made anew in a proper county. Pressed too far, the treatment of a venue defect as jurisdictional can do unnecessary damage.

If the supreme court on a wrongly venued motion (to which no one objects) passes on its merits, the order on the motion should be deemed valid.[18]

The subject up to now has been the usual motion on notice. What about the ex parte motion?

CPLR 2212(b) provides that an ex parte supreme court motion may be made at a motion term duly prescribed for such motions or—take note—to any justice of the court anywhere in the state, but here, too, the rules can take away what the statute presumes to give. One of the Uniform Rules does a little of this taking away. It provides that an ex

---

[9] Sullivan & Donovan, L.L.P., 175 Misc.2d at 388, 669 N.Y.S.2d at 132.

[10] See the discussion in SPR 63:4.

[11] In Cordero v. Grant, 95 Misc. 2d 153, 407 N.Y.S.2d 383 (Sup. Ct., New York County 1978), for example, New York County, which has one of the heaviest calendars in the state, was held to be unavailable as a motion venue for actions pending in other counties. The case is discussed in Commentary C2212:1 on McKinney's CPLR 2212. CPLR 2212(d), incidentally, in permitting administrative withdrawal of the 2212(a) venue options, requires that "the practice in counties within the city of New York shall be uniform."

[12] CPLR 2212(c).

[13] See § 14.

[14] See CPLR 509–511; § 123.

[15] See 2d Rep. Leg. Doc. No. 13, p. 183 (1958).

[16] United Jewish Appeal-Federation of Jewish Philanthropies of New York, Inc. v. Young Men's and Young Women's Hebrew Ass'n, Inc., 30 A.D.3d 504, 817 N.Y.S.2d 352 (2d Dep't 2006).

[17] Compare Newell v. Huston, 35 A.D.2d 908, 317 N.Y.S.2d 66 (4th Dep't 1970), with Cwick v. City of Rochester, 54 A.D.2d 1078, 388 N.Y.S.2d 753 (4th Dep't 1976). The latter warns, however, that counsel's contriving a wrong motion venue for its own convenience will not be countenanced. See Commentary C2212:7 on McKinney's CPLR 2212.

[18] See Commentary C2212:7 on McKinney's CPLR 2212.

parte motion made to a judge outside the action's venue county "shall be referred to the appropriate court in the county of venue," but it also leaves an important power intact by adding the qualification "unless the judge [to whom the ex parte application is presented] determines that the urgency of the motion requires immediate determination."[19] Hence, the rules do preserve each judge's power to act ex parte when an emergency is at hand even in a case not assigned to the judge.

Where does a judge get the power to issue orders on a beach or golf course? The answer is that each justice of the supreme court carries the ex parte powers of the court around with her. The judge can be approached at any time or place (in or out of court) with an ex parte motion. If the motion is made far from the action-pending county, and to a wholly inappropriate justice (one not even in the same judicial district), the reason had best be good. The consequence, otherwise, is that the motion may be denied without even reaching its merits, leaving the movant to repeat it before the assigned judge or at least in a more appropriate place. This statewide authority in connection with ex parte motions is designed to help the litigants and their lawyers in emergencies. Therefore, if there is no emergency or special reason for the far-from-home motion, the justice approached need merely refuse the requested order.[20] Indeed, under the Uniform Rules, the judge is required to refuse it unless there's "urgency."[21] While the application for an ex parte order can be made to a supreme court justice "out of court," it must be made in a "county in the state."[22] The limitations in this regard are traceable to the New York State Constitution, which provides that a "justice of the supreme court may perform the duties of office or hold court in any county."[23]

Perhaps the prime beneficiary of this statewide authority is the order to show cause, the litigant's best friend in a tight situation. The show cause order starts off ex parte. It is no small advantage to be able to present it to any available justice if there's an emergency at hand.[24]

The requirement that a fee be paid for the making of a motion, imposed for the first time in 2003,[25] can in point of logistics be relevant to the place of making a motion.[26]

§ 246. The Motion Papers

Contents of Motion Papers

The moving papers generally consist of three items: (1) a notice of motion or order to show cause; (2) affidavits and affirmations with exhibits; and (3) a memorandum of law. The notice of motion specifies the time and place of the hearing as well as the relief requested[1] while the affidavits, affirmations, and memorandum of law state the grounds for the relief. A motion can seek relief "in the alternative or of several different types."[2]

---

[19]   22 N.Y.C.R.R. § 202.7(e).

[20]   See Commentary C2212:9 on McKinney's CPLR 2212.

[21]   22 N.Y.C.R.R. § 202.7(e).

[22]   CPLR 2212(b).

[23]   N.Y. Const. art. VI, § 26(a); see Commentary C2212:8 on McKinney's CPLR 2212.

[24]   See § 248 for discussion of the order to show cause.

[25]   See CPLR 8020(a); § 243.

[26]   The fee is required in the supreme and county courts, but not in the lower courts. The subject of motion fees is addressed in § 243.

[1]   See § 247 for the applicable time requirements.

[2]   CPLR 2214(a).

Whatever motion remedies one party fancies herself entitled to against another at any given time, in other words, may all be joined in one motion if the movant is so disposed.

The main supporting papers on a motion are affidavits and affirmations,[3] but any relevant exhibits, documents, depositions, etc., are also included. The supporting papers should be referred to in the notice of motion as illustrated in the form contained in section 252. Opposing papers are also made up principally of affidavits and affirmations with supporting documents and a memorandum of law. Reply papers consist of affidavits, affirmations, and sometimes a reply memorandum of law.

CPLR 2214(a) requires that a notice of motion list "the relief demanded and the grounds therefor." On occasion, a movant will attempt to seek relief in reply papers that is additional to, or different from, that sought in the moving papers. The practice is generally a sloppy one, and courts will often deny the relief even when the moving papers contain a general prayer for "such other and further relief" as the court deems just and proper.[4] In Eujoy Realty Corp. v. Van Wagner Communications, LLC,[5] defendant contended that plaintiff's theory of recovery under the lease in question was not pleaded in its complaint. The Court of Appeals rejected this argument, but also went on to note that "even if [plaintiff] had, in fact, presented a new legal argument about the lease to Supreme Court in a reply brief, neither that court nor the Appellate Division would have been prohibited from considering it."[6] The Court distinguished those cases in which "sloppy and potentially prejudicial motion practice" leads to a situation where "facts [are] presented for the first time in a reply *affidavit* 'to which the [non-moving party] had no right to reply without court permission.' "[7]

The decision in *Eujoy Realty Corp.* prompts several observations. The Court of Appeals confirmed that courts have discretion to consider legal arguments made or legal relief sought for the first time in reply papers.[8] Yet, the trial court also has broad discretion not to consider them, and should follow this course if the non-movant can establish prejudice.[9] The *Eujoy Realty Corp.* decision distinguishes the situation in which new facts are submitted for the first time in a reply affidavit. The Court of Appeals appears to take a dimmer view of this practice, while not expressly prohibiting it.[10]

CPLR 105(u) states that a " 'verified pleading' may be utilized as an affidavit whenever the latter is required." In Sanchez v. National R.R. Passenger Corp.,[11] the Court of Appeals ruled that this provision permitted a verified complaint and verified bill of particulars to be considered as affidavits in opposition to a motion for summary

---

[3]   See § 205.

[4]   Willette v. Willette, 53 A.D.3d 753, 754–55, 861 N.Y.S.2d 204, 205 (3d Dep't 2008); see Madden v. Town of Greene, 95 A.D.3d 1426, 1427, 942 N.Y.S.2d 911, 911–12 (3d Dep't 2012); Commentary C2214:5 on McKinney's CPLR 2214.

[5]   Eujoy Realty Corp. v. Van Wagner Communications, LLC, 22 N.Y.3d 413, 981 N.Y.S.2d 326, 4 N.E.3d 336 (2013).

[6]   *Eujoy Realty Corp.,* 22 N.Y.3d at 422, 981 N.Y.S.2d at 332, 4 N.E.3d at 342.

[7]   *Eujoy Realty Corp.,* 22 N.Y.3d at 422, 981 N.Y.S.2d at 332, 4 N.E.3d at 342.

[8]   See Blumenstyk v. Singer, 2014 WL 3870616 (Sup. Ct., New York County 2014).

[9]   See, e.g., *Willette,* 53 A.D.3d at 754–55, 861 N.Y.S.2d at 205 (denying relief requested for first time in reply affidavit); Lumbermens Mut. Cas. Co. v. Morse Shoe Co., 218 A.D.2d 624, 626, 630 N.Y.S.2d 1003, 1005 (1st Dep't 1995) ("Arguments advanced for the first time in reply papers are entitled to no consideration by a court entertaining a summary judgment motion. This Court has and will require consistent application of the rule.").

[10]   See Commentary C2214:10 on McKinney's CPLR 2214.

[11]   Sanchez v. National R.R. Passenger Corp., 21 N.Y.3d 890, 965 N.Y.S.2d 775, 988 N.E.2d 511 (2013).

judgment. These documents were relied upon by the Court in reversing the order of the Appellate Division dismissing the action and in finding that a question of fact existed regarding the date of plaintiff's injury. It is difficult to reconcile the Court's decision in *Sanchez* with its prior precedent on the subject.[12] Until the point is clarified, lawyers submitting proof on a motion for summary judgment should submit affidavits from those with personal knowledge, rather than simply relying on verified pleadings or bills of particulars.

Service of Motion Papers

The moving papers should not be served until they're ready. In one case where the lawyer served deficient moving papers accompanied by a statement that later "a further more detailed affirmation will be furnished"—a kind of "stay tuned to this station" announcement—the court denied the motion with $100 costs and a $500 sanction.[13] It said that it is "unheard of" that a party should deliberately make a motion with inadequate supporting papers in the mere expectation of supplementing them at some future time. When read together, CPLR 2211, CPLR 2214(a), and Uniform Rule 202.8(c) require that all papers supporting the motion be served simultaneously.

In the absence of an agreement between the parties, or if the motion has already been submitted, leave is required before motion papers already served can be supplemented. Supplemental affirmations should be used sparingly to clarify limited issues and should not be relied upon as a matter of course to correct deficiencies in a party's motion papers.[14]

If the motion concerns either the bill of particulars or disclosure, an affirmation must also be included in the moving papers to the effect that the movant's lawyer has consulted with the other side in a good faith effort to resolve the dispute, but without success.[15] The contents of the affirmation are prescribed by the Uniform Rules.[16]

Providing Motion Papers to the Court

Each party furnishes the court with all papers that it has served.[17] In addition, the moving party must supply the court with "all other papers not already in the possession of the court necessary to the consideration of the questions involved."[18] This requirement has come under some increased scrutiny in the electronic age. In Biscone v. JetBlue Airways Corp.,[19] plaintiff commenced a putative class action, which was ultimately converted to an e-filed action. Plaintiff thereafter made a motion for leave to renew or reargue a motion for class certification that had been denied. Rather than supplying a complete set of the papers submitted in support of the original motion, plaintiff merely referenced the previously e-filed documents by citing electronic docket entry numbers.

---

[12] See § 232.

[13] Rosenman Colin Freund Lewis & Cohen v. Edelman, 165 A.D.2d 533, 568 N.Y.S.2d 590 (1st Dep't 1991).

[14] Ostrov v. Rozbruch, 91 A.D.3d 147, 936 N.Y.S.2d 31 (1st Dep't 2012) (SPR 241:2); see Commentary C2214:23 on McKinney's CPLR 2214; Patrick M. Connors, *'Just One More Thing': Supplemental Submissions on Summary Judgment,* 54 N.Y.L.J., Sept. 17, 2012, at 248.

[15] 22 N.Y.C.R.R. § 202.7(a).

[16] 22 N.Y.C.R.R. § 202.7(c).

[17] CPLR 2214(c).

[18] CPLR 2214(c).

[19] Biscone v. JetBlue Airways Corp., 103 A.D.3d 158, 957 N.Y.S.2d 361 (2d Dep't 2012) (SPR 253:3).

The Second Department affirmed the denial of the motion on the ground that the moving papers were insufficient because plaintiff failed to furnish a complete copy of the papers as required by CPLR 2214(c). In reaching its conclusion, the court relied upon the rationale of several trial court decisions that have concluded that when a party moving for reargument or renewal fails to submit the papers relied upon in connection with the initial motion, it renders the motion for leave to renew and/or reargue defective. In sum, courts should not be required to search court records—even those maintained electronically—to decide a motion.[20]

The *Biscone* decision prompted an amendment to CPLR 2214(c), adding a new sentence stating:

> Except when the rules of the court provide otherwise, in an e-filed action, a party that files papers in connection with a motion need not include copies of papers that were filed previously electronically with the court, but may make reference to them, giving the docket numbers on the e-filing system.

Assuming the supreme court judge that decided *Biscone* had no individual rule or protocol governing motions for reargument or renewal that required including all papers that were submitted with the underlying motion, this amendment would have saved the day for the movant. That is, however, a big assumption.

Many supreme court judges require that in all e-filed cases assigned to them, counsel submit hard copies, also known as "working copies," of e-filed documents that are intended for the court's review.[21] Any party submitting papers on a motion in an e-filed action must be certain what specific papers a judge may want provided as "working copies." Simply relying on the amended statute and referencing papers that were previously electronically filed in the matter may result in a denial of the motion if it is deemed that the individual "rules of the court provide otherwise." In actions that are not subject to e-filing, the amendment to CPLR 2214(c) provides no relief and parties must be sure to provide the court with hard copies of all papers "necessary to the consideration of the questions involved" on the motion.[22]

Problems under CPLR 2214(c) commonly arise on motions for reargument or renewal under CPLR 2221 and motions to dismiss under CPLR 3211. Those statutes do not expressly state the papers that must be submitted on motions thereunder.[23] The statute governing motions for summary judgment, CPLR 3212, does specify that "[a] motion for summary judgment shall be supported by affidavit, by a copy of the pleadings

---

[20] There are decisions in the First Department that are difficult to square with the Second Department's decision in *Biscone*. See, e.g., Studio A Showroom, LLC v. Yoon, 99 A.D.3d 632, 952 N.Y.S.2d 879 (1st Dep't 2012) (trial court "properly overlooked" defendant's failure to include the pleadings with its motion for summary judgment where "the pleadings were filed electronically and thus were available to the parties and the court."); Commentary C2214:23 on McKinney's CPLR 2214.

[21] See, e.g., Protocol on Courthouse and County Clerk Procedures for Electronically Filed Cases, § B, 6(a), Supreme Court, New York County (revised March 9, 2016). ("Various Justices require that, in all NYSCEF cases assigned to them, unless otherwise directed, counsel submit working copies of e-filed documents . . . . Generally, in these Parts, documents intended for judicial review must be filed with the NYSCEF system first and the required working copy must be delivered to the court thereafter.").

[22] See Commentary C2214:23 on McKinney's CPLR 2214.

[23] See § 254, discussing deficient submissions on motions to reargue or renew; § 265, discussing deficient submissions on motions to dismiss for failure to state a cause of action. See 1501 Corp. v. Leilenok Realty Corp., 2015 WL 2344489 (Sup. Ct., Queens County 2015) (denying CPLR 3211(a)(7) motion to dismiss because moving party failed to annex copy of amended complaint it sought to dismiss).

and by other available proof, such as depositions and written admissions."[24] Despite this express direction, there are many cases in which a motion for summary judgment is denied because the moving party has failed to attach the pleadings.[25]

CPLR 2214(c) states that if a needed paper is in the possession of an adverse party, the moving party can, in the notice of motion, require that it be produced at the hearing. Only papers duly served on all parties and furnished to the court in accordance with CPLR 2214 should be considered on a motion unless for good cause the court otherwise directs.[26]

Memorandum of Law

Before the adoption of the Uniform Rules, there was no omnibus requirement about serving on the other side a memorandum or brief used on a motion. The Uniform Rules today require the movant to include in her moving papers any brief she intends to use on the motion, and the opposing party to include any responding brief in the answering papers.[27] Rule or not, common courtesy insists that no lawyer spring a memorandum or brief on an adversary without giving her some chance to peruse it before the return day and to draw her own in rebuttal.[28] Furthermore, common sense dictates that a party will want to get all the moving papers into the court's hands sufficiently in advance of the return date to enable the court to consider the arguments.

§ 247. Motion Notice Requirements

Picking a Return Date and Negotiating Various Rules

The moving party determines when a motion on notice shall be heard, but she has to consult the court's or judge's calendar practice first. The movant picks out a "return day" sufficiently far off to assure that the notice requirements of CPLR 2214(b) can be met and to assure as well that the day picked is a day on which the assigned judge hears motions.

Under the practice used before adoption of the Individual Assignment System (IAS), the motion was made returnable to the court rather than the judge. There was usually a motion term in session on every business day in urban and most suburban counties, but in a rural county, there might be only one every few weeks or even months. In the larger counties, the movant would also have to determine the "part" before which the motion was to be returnable, with local rules prescribing these things. Most contested motions were returnable before a single part, usually called "Special Term, Part I" in metropolitan counties, while certain motions might be of a kind directed to a special part (matrimonial, condemnation, tax assessment, etc.).

Under the IAS, "[a]ll motions shall be returnable before the assigned judge."[1] Therefore, it is the practice of the individual assigned judge that has to be noted in all

---

[24]   CPLR 3212(b).

[25]   See § 281.

[26]   CPLR 2214(c); see Mosheyeva v. Distefano, 288 A.D.2d 448, 733 N.Y.S.2d 499 (2d Dep't 2001) (holding that the supreme court improvidently exercised its discretion in accepting and considering the plaintiffs' untimely answering papers); Commentary C2214:14 on McKinney's CPLR 2214.

[27]   22 N.Y.C.R.R. § 202.8(c). The rule also reminds us that affidavits are for the facts and briefs for the law. In clean and crisp practice, the two missions are kept distinct.

[28]   See Commentary C2214:20 on McKinney's CPLR 2214.

[1]   22 N.Y.C.R.R. § 202.8(a).

respects: the day or days on which the judge hears motions; the place of the hearing; the time of day; whether oral argument is allowed; etc. The Uniform Rules have many details, requiring that all motion papers be filed on or before the return date[2] and addressing also the setting up of oral argument,[3] adjournments of the return date,[4] and the holding of the preliminary conference in conjunction with a motion affecting disclosure or a bill of particulars.[5] As the time elements in the CPLR for the making of motions are discussed in this section, the reader should keep in mind the need to also consult the Uniform Rules, the rules of the judicial district, the county rules, as well as the particular judge's own rules (sometimes known as "information sheets"). In e-filed actions, individual rules are often contained in "protocols," and lawyers must be careful to take note of them.[6] If a clear path can still not be discerned, the judge's chambers should be consulted.

"While guidance on procedure may sometimes need to be sought from the judge's chambers, the judge's advance permission is not required to make a motion.[7]

Notice Requirements

CPLR 2214(b), designed as it is to assure reasonable notice periods for moving and answering papers, remains applicable under the Uniform Rules and the IAS. It requires that the movant give all other parties at least 8 days notice of the motion, which becomes 13 if the motion papers are served by mail, as is often the case.[8] When that minimum notice period is used, however, the adverse party can mail her answering papers to the movant as late as 2 days before the motion is to be heard, which usually means that the movant will not receive them in time to respond properly at the hearing.[9] Furthermore, the moving party is not entitled to a reply.

To assure receipt of the answering papers earlier than that, and to secure the "last word" on the motion, the movant can use the 16–7–1 notice option offered by CPLR 2214(b). If the movant gives at least 16 days notice of the motion, or 21 days if the motion is served via mail,[10] she can require the adverse party to serve answering papers and any cross-motion[11] no later than 7 days before the return day. Even if those papers are mailed on the 7th day prior to the return day, the movant will still get them several days before and will be able to prepare to meet them. When this option is used, a common

---

[2]   22 N.Y.C.R.R. § 202.8(a); see § 246.

[3]   22 N.Y.C.R.R. § 202.8(d).

[4]   22 N.Y.C.R.R. § 202.8(e).

[5]   22 N.Y.C.R.R. § 202.8(f); see the discussion in SPR 3:3.

[6]   See, e.g., Protocol on Courthouse and County Clerk Procedures for Electronically Filed Cases, Supreme Court, New York County (revised March 9, 2016).

[7]   See Costigan & Co., P.C. v. Costigan, 304 A.D.2d 464, 758 N.Y.S.2d 312, 313 (1st Dep't 2003). The judge can, however, require that the dispute be "conferenced" before being made the subject of a motion. See § 243.

[8]   CPLR 2103(b)(2). If motion papers are served via mail outside New York State, the movant must provide 14 days notice. CPLR 2103(b)(2). If motion papers are served via overnight delivery, the movant must provide 9 days notice. CPLR 2103(b)(6); see § 202.

[9]   The additional days afforded to a party responding to a document served by mail pursuant to CPLR 2103(b)(2) do not apply to the service of answering or reply papers. See Ryan v. Town of Cortlandt, 134 A.D.2d 420, 521 N.Y.S.2d 43 (2d Dep't 1987); see Commentary C2214:8 on McKinney's CPLR 2214.

[10]   If motion papers are served via mail outside New York State, the movant must provide 22 days notice. See CPLR 2103(b)(2). If motion papers are served via overnight delivery, the movant must provide 17 days notice. CPLR 2103(b)(6); see, e.g., § 202.

[11]   See § 249.

practice, a specific statement should be included in the notice of motion requiring that answering papers be served at least 7 days prior to the return day.[12]

In an e-filed action, the motion will be deemed served when filed and there will be no need to add any additional days to the notice periods in CPLR 2214(b).[13]

When picking out a motion day satisfactory to the notice requirements in CPLR 2214(b), the movant should recognize that various delays may occur before the moving papers can actually be served and that the notice requirement is measured not from the day the papers are prepared or dated, but from the moment of service. Therefore, it is sound practice to hold off preparing the notice of motion until all required affidavits and other proof have been gathered up and legal memoranda drawn. This enables a return day to be picked out with more precision because the movant knows that the motion papers are all at hand and ready for posting.

It is also good practice to make motions returnable at least three weeks away from the planned date of mailing and to always include a demand in the motion that the other side serve answering papers at least 7 days before the return day. This enables the motion to be served by mail, gives sufficient notice to support the 7-day demand, and leaves a few days for a delayed mailing if some snag prevents posting on the day planned.

If speed is needed, the shorter 8 day notice period can be used, forfeiting the right to 7-day answering papers and a reply. If even 8 days notice is too much under the circumstances, the order to show cause is the remedy.[14]

The reply papers in this 16–7–1 situation need only be served one day before the return day.[15] If delayed until that time, however, it will arrive in the opposing side's hands too late—probably after the return day has come and gone and will not likely be provided to the court on time.[16] The CPLR does not resolve that problem, although the Uniform Rules require that "all" papers be filed with the court no later than the return day[17] and that includes reply papers.

The problem usually arises only between lawyers denying one another professional courtesies. Judges usually resolve late service disputes with some pragmatic response, such as offering the parties more time, requiring the trading of as-yet-unreceived papers in the courthouse corridor, adjourning the argument of the motion, etc. Judges do not like arguments about these things—or the lawyers who make them necessary. These problems can be avoided altogether if lawyers voluntarily take the extra step, after serving the reply via mail in accordance with CPLR 2103(b)(2) (or any other paper close to the return date), of promptly forwarding the paper via facsimile, email, or personal delivery to assure its receipt, if at all possible, a reasonable time prior to the hearing on the return day.[18] As long as the original service of the reply was proper, this additional "courtesy service" need not comply with the rules regarding service of interlocutory

---

12   CPLR 2214(b). See the last paragraph in the form of notice of motion contained in § 252.

13   22 N.Y.C.R.R. § 202.5–b(f)(2)(ii). While this rule is contained in the rules for the consensual e-filing program, it also applies in cases governed by mandatory e-filing. See 22 N.Y.C.R.R. § 202.5–bb(a)(1).

14   CPLR 2214(d); see § 248.

15   Hemingway v. Pelham Country Club, 14 A.D.3d 536, 789 N.Y.S.2d 178 (2d Dep't 2005).

16   See § 246.

17   22 N.Y.C.R.R. § 202.8(a).

18   See Commentary C2214:9–11 on McKinney's CPLR 2214.

papers. These sorts of problems will be ameliorated in e-filed cases where filing and service of papers occur simultaneously.

While CPLR 2214(b) provides for *minimum* notice time on motions, it sets no arbitrary outer limit. Theoretically, therefore, a moving party can make a motion returnable way off into the future. The absence of an outer time limit has a reason: the infrequency of motion terms in some parts of the state.[19] Since many motions have to be "made" within a specified period,[20] making them timely in certain rural counties can be difficult if there is no available return date to include on the papers.[21]

This absence of an outer time limit can lead to abuse. An example of this is where a movant may want the automatic stay of disclosure that can result upon the making of certain motions under CPLR 3211, 3212, or 3213.[22] If a movant under a court order to make disclosure seeks to avoid the direction by making a CPLR 3211(a)(7) motion with a far out return day, the court, upon being advised of this, is likely to foil the plot.[23] If the conduct really strikes the court as frivolous,[24] moreover, the court can even apply a money sanction against the abuser.

Inadequate Notice

Opinion is divided on the effect of giving inadequate notice, that is, making the motion returnable too early. Some courts have held it jurisdictional, at least when there has been no appearance by the other side,[25] and deny the motion without prejudice or "dismiss" it (which is the same thing).[26] Others hold that inadequate notice is not jurisdictional "unless there is substantial prejudice" and that there is no prejudice when the opposing party prepared a response on the merits and in fact submitted it to the court.[27] In these circumstances, the court has discretion to give the adverse party more time, even adjourning the motion for that purpose. If the motion has been the subject of voluntary adjournment by the parties and the adjournments have added enough time to compensate for the short notice, the initial defect should be disregarded.[28]

An irony in all of this is that the opposing party who does more—shows up rather than defaults—may get less. The motion may be entertained, while that against the defaulter usually gets denied. If the parties cannot mutually agree to resolve a dispute about inadequate notice, it is always advisable for the adverse party to seek judicial intervention as soon as possible rather than assume that the court will simply deny the motion.[29] The failure to give any notice at all, in an instance where notice is required and where the unnotified party is not before the court, should invalidate the motion

---

[19] See 2d Rep. Leg. Doc. No. 13, p. 181 (1958).

[20] See § 243.

[21] See Commentary C2214:11 on McKinney's CPLR 2214.

[22] See CPLR 3214(b); §§ 277, 279.

[23] See Town of Southampton v. Salten, 186 A.D.2d 796, 589 N.Y.S.2d 355 (2d Dep't 1992); Commentary C2214:11 on McKinney's CPLR 2214, and SPR 13:4.

[24] See § 414A.

[25] See, e.g., Bianco v. Ligreci, 298 A.D.2d 482, 748 N.Y.S.2d 503 (2d Dep't 2002).

[26] See Commentary C2214:13 on McKinney's CPLR 2214.

[27] National Microtech, Inc. v. Satellite Video Services, Inc., 107 A.D.2d 860, 484 N.Y.S.2d 303 (3d Dep't 1985); see Piquette v. City of New York, 4 A.D.3d 402, 771 N.Y.S.2d 365 (2d Dep't 2004), lv. denied 3 N.Y.3d 605, 785 N.Y.S.2d 21, 81 N.E.2d 663.

[28] See Hudson v. Eck, 70 A.D.3d 1261, 896 N.Y.S.2d 218 (3d Dep't 2010); Coonradt v. Walco, 55 Misc. 2d 557, 285 N.Y.S.2d 421 (Sup. Ct., Rensselaer County 1967).

[29] See Commentary on C2214:12 on McKinney's CPLR 2214.

altogether.[30] It would be equivalent to making the motion ex parte, which is permissible only when explicitly authorized by statute or rule.[31]

Filing and Service of Motion Papers

The original motion papers are usually filed with the court (they used to be called the "ribbon copy" before the word processor replaced the typewriter and the duplicating machine replaced carbon paper). Copies are served on all other parties regardless of whether a party is on the same side or an opposing side or whether the movant fancies a party to be interested in the motion or not.[32] The time by which the moving papers have to be filed with the court is a matter usually regulated by rule.[33] Upon receiving the papers, the clerk or judge's assistant will usually add the motion to the motion calendar for the return day specified in the notice of motion. Again, individual judges' rules have to be consulted on this.

Keep in mind that in the supreme and county courts a fee must be paid when filing a motion.[34] The fee is due upon the filing of the papers with the county clerk, which suggests that the fee need not necessarily be paid at earlier junctions along the motion road, including service of the motion. Given the geographic and administrative differences among the state's counties, however, there must always be a local inquiry about when and how the fee is to be paid.[35]

If the motion is the first step in the action that requires judicial attention, no judge having yet been assigned to the case, the motion papers must include a Request for Judicial Intervention (RJI),[36] which brings about the assignment of a judge to rule on the motion. A special rule prescribes procedure in that situation.[37]

The motion papers filed with the court should be accompanied by an affidavit attesting to the service of copies on each of the parties. While the CPLR and Uniform Rules generally do not require that an affidavit of service be filed with the motion papers, many local rules do contain such a requirement.[38] The affidavit of service is required to ensure that the notice requirements in CPLR 2214(b) have been satisfied. The affidavit should be completed by the person who actually served the papers.[39]

Adjournment and Withdrawal of Motions

Uniform Rule section 202.8(e) addresses adjournments. It requires that stipulations of adjournment of the return date shall be in writing and shall be submitted to the

---

[30]   Zaidi v. New York Bldg. Contractors, Ltd., 61 A.D.3d 747, 877 N.Y.S.2d 381 (2d Dep't 2009); Burstin v. Public Service Mut. Ins. Co., 98 A.D.2d 928, 471 N.Y.S.2d 33 (3d Dep't 1983); see Commentary C2211:7 on McKinney's CPLR 2211.

[31]   See § 244.

[32]   CPLR 2103(e).

[33]   See 22 N.Y.C.R.R. § 202.8(a) (discussed above) and any applicable local rules or orders. If they don't offer the answer, call the judge's chambers or the clerk.

[34]   See CPLR 8020(a); § 243.

[35]   For further discussion of fee matters, see § 243, and the two-part treatment in SPR 136:1 and 137:1.

[36]   See § 77B.

[37]   22 N.Y.C.R.R. § 202.8(b); see § 243; Commentary C2214:18 on McKinney's CPLR 2214.

[38]   See, e.g., Supreme Court, Civil Branch, New York County, *Motions and Special Proceedings by Notice of Motion/Petition,* ("The original notice of motion/petition, proof of service, and affirmation of good faith in a hard-copy case shall be presented to the General Clerk's Office no later than five business days before the original return date, but no earlier than 30 days prior to that date.").

[39]   See § 202.

assigned judge.[40] The rule provides that a "stipulation shall be effective unless the court otherwise directs," but places a limitation on adjournments submitted without court permission.[41] If the parties cannot stipulate to an adjournment, the rule requires that a request for an adjournment "be submitted in writing, upon notice to the other party, to the assigned judge on or before the return date."[42] Individual judges frequently have rules regarding adjournments of motions and it is imperative that a lawyer carefully review them well in advance of the return date of the motion. Ordinarily, a motion may be withdrawn by its maker at any time before it is submitted,[43] but the judge or clerk and the other parties should be at least notified[44] if not, indeed, consulted. After submission, the motion may not ordinarily be withdrawn, even if the judge has not yet decided it, except upon the judge's order or upon stipulation of all the parties, to which the judge is not likely to object.[45] The "submission" ordinarily occurs when the oral argument of the motion is concluded or, if it is to be submitted on papers alone without argument, on the return day.[46]

Oral Argument

Whether oral argument of the motion is required, or even permissible, is a matter within the discretion of the assigned judge.[47] If oral argument is desired, the movant asks for it in the notice of motion or order to show cause while another party must request it on the top page of their answering papers.[48] "Where all parties to a motion request oral argument, oral argument shall be granted unless the court shall determine it to be unnecessary."[49]

§ 248. Order to Show Cause

An order to show cause is basically only a substitute for a notice of motion.[1] Instead of serving a notice of motion in accordance with the instructions in CPLR 2214(a) and (b), the applicant in the first instance presents a proposed order to show cause and the accompanying motion papers to a justice of the court. This initial step is usually done ex parte. If the judge reviewing the order to show cause decides to grant it, the judge signs it and returns it to the applicant. At this point, it becomes the equivalent of a regular notice of motion, and the applicant serves it on the other side with the other motion papers.

---

[40]   See CPLR 2104 (setting forth requirements for stipulations); § 204.

[41]   22 N.Y.C.R.R. § 202.8(e)(1) ("No more than three stipulated adjournments for an aggregate period of 60 days shall be submitted without prior permission of the court.").

[42]   22 N.Y.C.R.R. § 202.8(e)(2).

[43]   Caplash v. Rochester Oral & Maxillofacial Surgery Associates, LLC, 48 A.D.3d 1139, 851 N.Y.S.2d 769 (4th Dep't 2008); Oshrin v. Celanese Corp. of America, 37 N.Y.S.2d 548 (Sup. Ct., New York County 1942), aff'd, 265 A.D. 923, 39 N.Y.S.2d 984 (1st Dep't), aff'd, 291 N.Y. 170, 51 N.E.2d 694 (1943).

[44]   See Commentary C2211:9 on McKinney's CPLR 2211.

[45]   Deutsche Bank Nat. Trust Co. v. Young, 2012 WL 6019543 (Sup. Ct., Suffolk County 2012) ("a motion may not be withdrawn after the return date without the consent of all parties or without leave of Court"); Wallace v. Ford, 44 Misc. 2d 313, 314, 253 N.Y.S.2d 608, 610 (Sup. Ct., Erie County 1964).

[46]   See Santoli v. 475 Ninth Ave. Associates, LLC, 2007 WL 2815374 (Sup. Ct., New York County 2007); *Wallace*, 44 Misc.2d at 314, 253 N.Y.S.2d at 610.

[47]   22 N.Y.C.R.R. § 202.8(d).

[48]   22 N.Y.C.R.R. § 202.8(d).

[49]   22 N.Y.C.R.R. § 202.8(d).

[1]   See CPLR 2211.

The order to show cause has several features, among them that it can shorten the notice time.[2] An ordinary notice of motion can't be brought on for hearing earlier than the eighth day after the motion papers are served.[3] With an order to show cause, the hearing can be brought on at any time the court directs, which can be fewer than eight days or as close as the very day on which it is signed. If the court is convinced there is a real emergency, it can schedule the hearing for a few hours later or, in the direst case, "forthwith" the service of the order to show cause.

An ordinary notice of motion merely notifies the recipient that a motion is being made for specified relief. The burden of proof is on the movant. Although in most cases it is just as innocent as an ordinary notice of motion, the order to show cause gets its name by directing the recipient to "show cause" why the particular relief being asked for should not be granted. It sounds as if the burden of proof is being shifted to the recipient. It isn't. It specifies the time and place of the hearing on the application, but when the hearing comes on, the burden of proof is where it always is on a motion: on the movant.

If the order to "show cause" is served on the lawyer, it usually holds no terror; the lawyer knows it for what it is. But if it is directed to a lay person, as it often is, it sounds to the recipient as if some monster with sharp fangs is pointing a crooked and threatening finger. It's all bluster—no more or less malevolent than an ordinary notice of motion.

The order to show cause is presented to the court ex parte. It will prescribe at least three things and may also include temporary relief as follows:

(1) The court determines the return date and time, as already mentioned, and the place as well. The court may provide that oral argument is required on the return date.[4]

(2) The court determines whom to serve with the order to show cause. Usually, of course, this is the other side's attorney. If any difficulty should arise about who the attorney is, or if there is doubt about whether the attorney's authority subsists,[5] the procedure of order to show cause may resolve this dilemma by having the court decide the matter.

(3) The court determines the method by which the order to show cause is to be served and will usually direct a method consistent with the time element. If it is not returnable too soon, mail may be sufficient, but this would be the rare case. If the order to show cause is to come on for hearing fast, the court will direct personal delivery, email, fax, or any other quick and effective method consistent with the needs of the case. An order to show cause directing "personal service" has been held to invoke CPLR 308, thereby authorizing deliver-and-mail service under 308(2), for example, rather than only personal delivery under 308(1).[6]

---

[2]   CPLR 2214(d).

[3]   CPLR 2214(b); see § 247.

[4]   22 N.Y.C.R.R. § 202.8(a).

[5]   When a motion is made long after a judgment has been rendered, for example, such as one to vacate the judgment pursuant to CPLR 5015, there may be doubt as to whether the former attorney still represents the client.

[6]   Weill v. Erickson, 49 A.D.2d 895, 373 N.Y.S.2d 370 (2d Dep't 1975), aff'd, appeal dismissed, 37 N.Y.2d 851, 378 N.Y.S.2d 39, 340 N.E.2d 473 (1975); see Rothkopf v. Rothkopf, 191 A.D.2d 685, 686, 595 N.Y.S.2d 506, 506 (2d Dep't 1993) ("since the order to show cause stated that it was to be served by 'personal service', we

(4) The court may include a provision staying designated proceedings or enjoining specified out-of-court conduct in the order, thus retaining the status quo until a hearing is had. Although the order to show cause can contain any kind of stay that the court has the power to grant,[7] the most important one is the temporary restraining order. The temporary restraining order, popularly called a "TRO" by the bar is the device that holds the status quo pending a hearing for a preliminary injunction.[8] The order to show cause is its traditional vehicle.

All four of the above items are illustrated in the form of order to show cause contained in section 252.

The CPLR says nothing more about an order to show cause than that it may be used "in a proper case,"[9] which leaves it entirely to the judge's discretion to determine what a proper case is.[10] Any fact suggesting a problem as to any of the four items listed above would be sufficient to invoke judicial discretion and justify the show cause procedure, which is in fact liberally used.

A judge cannot be compelled to sign an order to show cause, such as through a proceeding under Article 78 of the CPLR.[11] Because the order to show cause is in first instance a species of ex parte order, if the judge refuses to sign it, an application for it can be made to the appellate court under CPLR 5704.[12]

It is the time of the service of the order, not the date the court signs it, that counts as the "making" of the motion.[13] The point becomes a key one whenever there is a time limit on the motion involved, as illustrated in Property Clerk v. Chevers,[14] where the validity of a counterclaim depended on a showing that it had been duly preceded by the timely service of a notice of claim.[15] No notice was served and time was running out even on the period in which the defendant could move to extend the notice of claim period.[16] On the last day to move, the defendant applied for and got an order to show cause, but did not serve it on that day. The motion was held too late.

Since the order to show cause is initially sought ex parte, it is always necessary on an order to show cause application to include an affidavit attesting to whether this or

---

conclude that any of the four methods of personal service enumerated in CPLR 308 would be sufficient to confer jurisdiction over the plaintiffs").

[7]   See the discussion of stays in § 255.

[8]   CPLR 6301, 6313; see § 330.

[9]   That's the first sentence of CPLR 2214(d), a general and pervasively important provision in civil practice. We might call it the feast, just to contrast it to the second sentence, which adds this crumb: an order to show cause bringing on a motion against a state body must also be served on an assistant attorney general. See Commentary C2214:30 on McKinney's CPLR 2214.

[10]   City of New York v. West Winds Convertibles Int'l, Inc., 16 Misc. 3d 646, 837 N.Y.S.2d 555 (Sup. Ct., Kings County 2007).

[11]   Rosenthal v. Agate, 29 A.D.3d 809, 813 N.Y.S.2d 916 (2d Dep't 2006). The Article 78 proceeding is taken up in §§ 557 et seq.

[12]   Greenhaus v. Milano, 242 A.D.2d 383, 661 N.Y.S.2d 664 (2d Dep't 1997); see § 244.

[13]   CPLR 2211.

[14]   Property Clerk v. Chevers, Sup. Ct., New York County, March 1, 1991 (Index No. 41097/90; Cahn, J.).

[15]   See Gen. Mun. Law § 50–e, treated in § 32.

[16]   Gen. Mun. Law § 50–e(5).

similar relief has previously been applied for and what new facts, if any, have appeared to justify the new motion, etc.[17]

If a show cause application is the first step taken in an action requiring a judge's attention, it must be accompanied by a Request for Judicial Intervention.[18] Under the Individual Assignment System (IAS), an order to show cause has to be made to the assigned judge.[19] If made to some other judge, or outside the county of the action's venue, as CPLR 2212(b) allows,[20] the rules require that it be referred back to the proper county—and under the IAS that means back to the assigned judge if there is one— "unless . . . the urgency of the motion requires immediate determination."[21] The "unless" clause covers the emergency situation, about which other applicable procedures should be consulted locally. If the assigned judge is unavailable, for example, there may be some other judges on "standby" in the county of the action's venue.[22]

In some instances, the show cause procedure to bring on a motion has been made mandatory.[23] And whenever a given statute requires a motion to be brought on in such manner as the court may direct, or requires that the motion papers be served on such persons as the court may designate, or by such notice as the court may determine, it contemplates that the procedure of order to show cause will be used.[24] If the show cause procedure is required in a given instance and an ordinary notice of motion is used instead, the defect has sometimes been held jurisdictional, precluding the court from passing on the motion's merits even though notice resulted.[25] The better view, however, is that the defect should be ignored as harmless and the merits treated.[26] The movant should avoid issues like that by using the show cause procedure whenever it seems to be required.

Since an order to show cause is a species of motion, a fee must be paid for it in supreme and county court actions. Because the fee is required to be paid upon the filing of the papers with the county clerk, the order to show cause can be processed in full before payment of any fee, as long as the payment is made before the papers are filed with the county clerk. Since an order to show cause is often presented to a judge out of court, moreover, it would be awkward to tender the fee with the order. (It would be

---

[17] CPLR 2217(b); see § 244.

[18] 22 N.Y.C.R.R. §§ 202.6(a), 202.8(b); see § 77B.

[19] 22 N.Y.C.R.R. § 202.8(a).

[20] As a species of ex parte application, the order to show cause falls under CPLR 2212(b) and 22 N.Y.C.R.R. § 202.7(e), applicable in the supreme court, and may be presented to any judge of the court anywhere in the state.

[21] 22 N.Y.C.R.R. § 202.7(e). Under CPLR 2212(d), the rules are allowed to supersede the statutory venue requirements of the other parts of CPLR 2212. See § 245.

[22] See § 244.

[23] Prior to 1977, the procedure for punishing a civil contempt was required to be by order to show cause under Jud. Law § 757 as it then was. Amendments in 1977 made an ordinary notice of motion acceptable, Jud. Law § 756, Dom. Rel. Law § 245, the show cause procedure thereupon becoming only an alternative as it is with motions in general. See § 484.

[24] See, e.g., CPLR 5015(a) ("on motion . . . with such notice as the court may direct").

[25] See, e.g., Papadakos v. Papadakos, N.Y.L.J., January 29, 1968, at 20, col. 5 (Sup. Ct., Suffolk County 1968).

[26] Hornok v. Hornok, 121 A.D.2d 937, 504 N.Y.S.2d 660 (1st Dep't 1986).

tantamount to requiring the judge to perform cashier functions). In any event, the logistics of the fee payment must be inquired into locally.[27]

§ 249. Cross-Motion

What Is a Cross-Motion? Notice of Cross-Motion

After the motion has been made and served on all parties pursuant to CPLR 2103(e),[1] some other party, whether on the same or the opposing side, may also want some motion relief. That party can of course make an independent motion, setting up a different return day. But if the relief sought is against the moving party, she can instead make what is known as a "cross-motion." A cross-motion is a motion made against the moving party returnable at the same time and place as the pending motion. Like any motion, a cross-motion is deemed made when the notice of cross-motion is served, not when the original motion is made.[2]

Under CPLR 2215, the cross-moving party must serve "an explicit "notice of cross-motion,"[3] a requirement added by a 1980 amendment designed to overcome the problem—complained about by moving parties and judges—of a demand for cross-relief encountered only in the middle of the opposing papers instead of in a formal notice appearing at the very top of them. The proper practice under the amendment, when the opposing party wants both to oppose the main motion as well as obtain affirmative relief of her own, is to include a notice of cross-motion as the lead-off paper, right on the top of the batch, with accompanying affidavits in support. The affidavits can offer proof against the main motion as well as in support of the cross-motion, but they should not be the housing for the demand for cross-relief.[4] Before the amendment, even an opposing affidavit asking for cross-relief was held acceptable.[5] It is not acceptable today, however,[6] and it is surely "not enough to request such relief orally on the return date of the movant's motion."[7] The notice of cross-motion should conform essentially to an original notice of motion, except that it sets no different time for a return date.

Relief on a Cross-Motion

Any kind of relief can be demanded on a cross-motion, just as on any motion, and it need not be responsive or even related to the relief demanded on the main motion.[8] Supporting affidavits and other papers may of course be used on a cross-motion, but they are optional. If all the proof relied on by the cross-movant is already before the court in the papers used on the main motion, for example, they may be exploited by the cross-motion, which requires only a notice.

---

[27] A general discussion of the fee requirement appears in § 243, and in a two-part treatment in SPR 136:1 and SPR 137:1.

[1] See § 247.

[2] McCabe v. The Inc. Village of Flower Hill, 2012 WL 9496352 (Sup. Ct., Nassau County 2012); Dugas v. Bernstein, 5 Misc. 3d 818, 786 N.Y.S.2d 708 (Sup. Ct., New York County 2004).

[3] Estate of Briger, 95 A.D.2d 887, 464 N.Y.S.2d 31 (3d Dep't 1983); see Dossous v. Corporate Owners Bayridge Nissan, Inc., 101 A.D.3d 937, 956 N.Y.S.2d 174 (2d Dep't 2012).

[4] See Commentary C2215:1D on McKinney's CPLR 2215.

[5] Plateis v. Flax, 54 A.D.2d 813, 388 N.Y.S.2d 245 (3d Dep't 1976).

[6] Free In Christ Pentecostal Church v. Julian, 64 A.D.3d 1153, 881 N.Y.S.2d 773 (4th Dep't 2009).

[7] Guggenheim v. Guggenheim, 109 A.D.2d 1012, 486 N.Y.S.2d 489 (3d Dep't 1985).

[8] CPLR 2215.

Notice Periods and Add-Ons

The advantage of the cross-motion is that it requires less notice time: the notice demanding cross-relief may be personally served or filed in an e-filed action as late as the third day before the return day set by the original motion. Recognizing how unreasonable it is to expect that papers dropped in a letter box three days before the return day of the motion will reach the other side in time for any kind of meaningful response, the legislature amended CPLR 2215 in 2007. CPLR 2215 now has its own add-ons if the cross-motion is served via mail or overnight delivery, superseding those in CPLR 2103(b)(2) and (6).[9] If the cross-motion is served via regular mail pursuant to CPLR 2103(b)(2), the movant must serve the papers 6 days prior to the return date of the original motion.[10] If the cross-motion is served via overnight delivery, it must be served 4 days before the return date of the original motion.[11]

CPLR 2214(b) was also amended in 2007 to add a far more civilized method for making a cross-motion on 7 days notice. To ensure that another party cannot make a cross-motion on 3 days notice, the party making the original motion must allow for 16 days notice of the original motion and include a 7-day demand in the notice of motion requiring that any cross-motion and the answering papers be served 7 days prior to the return date.[12] In this situation, the add-ons contained in CPLR 2215, discussed above, will require that a cross-motion be served via regular mail at least 10 days prior to the return date, while a cross-motion that is served via overnight delivery must be served 8 days prior to the return date. If, however, the cross-motion is personally served or made in an e-filed action, the add-ons are inapplicable. Moreover, if the party making the original motion does so on 8 days notice (13 days if the motion is served via mail), or neglects to include the 7 day demand, any other party can make a cross-motion on 3 days notice, with any applicable add-ons. That will not provide the moving party with much chance to review the papers, especially if the return date is on a Monday and the cross-motion papers are personally served late Friday afternoon.

It is important to remember that while a cross-motion can be made by any party, and not just a party moved against on the main motion, it must be made against the party that made the original motion.[13] The courts have held that "[a] cross motion is an improper vehicle for seeking relief from a nonmoving party."[14] Therefore, if a party is making a motion against anyone other than the party that made the original motion, even if seeking the same relief, the motion must conform to the longer notice periods in CPLR 2214(b). In instances where a cross-motion is improperly made against a non-moving party who was prejudiced by a lack of opportunity to be sufficiently heard on the issues raised on the cross-motion, the courts will normally deny it without prejudice to renewal in compliance with the time periods in CPLR 2214(b).[15]

---

[9]   See § 202.

[10]   CPLR 2215(a).

[11]   CPLR 2215(b).

[12]   See § 247.

[13]   CPLR 2215.

[14]   See *Dugas*, 5 Misc. 3d at 824 n.2, 786 N.Y.S.2d at 713 n.2.

[15]   See Mango v. Long Island Jewish-Hillside Medical Center, 123 A.D.2d 843, 507 N.Y.S.2d 456 (2d Dep't 1986); see also Terio v. Spodek, 25 A.D.3d 781, 785, 809 N.Y.S.2d 145, 149 (2d Dep't 2006).

Service of Cross-Motion with Answering Papers

Assume a party makes a motion returnable on 16 days notice and includes a proper 7 day demand for answering papers and any cross-motion. If another party makes a cross-motion via regular mail, that party will be required to serve the cross-motion 10 days prior to the return date. That party's answering papers on the main motion, however, need only be served 7 days prior to the return date, even if regular mail is used.[16] If the cross-motion and answering papers are served together via regular mail 7 days prior to the return date of the original motion, the cross-motion will not be made on sufficient notice, even though the answering papers will be timely. This could result in an outright denial of the cross-motion if the party who made the original motion can show prejudice due to a lack of opportunity to be sufficiently heard on the issues raised on the cross-motion. Therefore, if the answering papers and cross-motion are served together, they must be served in conformance with the more demanding time periods governing the cross-motion.

Any party serving a cross-motion should also ensure that such papers are promptly filed with the court. While Uniform Rule section 202.8(a) merely requires that the papers be filed with the court on or before the return date, the party's best interests are served if the court has had as much time as possible to review the papers comprising the cross-motion. The requirement that a fee be paid for the making of a motion in supreme and county court actions also applies explicitly to cross-motions.[17]

Answering Papers on a Cross-Motion

One of the larger black holes in the CPLR was the failure to provide any mechanism for serving answering papers to a cross-motion. That issue was left hanging for almost a half-century due to the absence of a specific instruction from CPLR 2214(b) and 2215. While CPLR 2215 still remains silent, CPLR 2214(b) now ever so subtly permits a party to serve answering papers in response to a cross-motion. CPLR 2214(b) states that where answering papers and a cross-motion are required to be served 7 days in advance of the return day, "any reply or *responding affidavits* shall be served at least one day before such time."[18] The "responding affidavits" should be deemed those responding to a cross-motion, but the statutory language is not a model of clarity. Furthermore, a good argument can be made that under this interpretation of CPLR 2214(b), a party who makes a motion on 8 days notice, or fails to include a 7 day demand, is not entitled to submit a response to any cross-motion.[19]

If a cross-motion is properly served on 3 days notice, it is usually best for the parties to reach an agreement on adjourning the motions and provide for the service of answering papers to the cross-motion (and perhaps reply papers on both motions).[20] This will offer benefits to both sides and make for a better presentation of the arguments on the return date. If judges are required to resolve timeliness issues on cross-motions, they do so on a case-by-case basis, usually with some pragmatic response, such as by offering

---

[16]   CPLR 2214(b); see § 247.

[17]   CPLR 8020(a). Discussion of payment of the fee in a cross-motion context appears in SPR 136:3.

[18]   CPLR 2214(b) (emphasis added).

[19]   See Commentary C2215:1E on McKinney's CPLR 2215.

[20]   See Commentary C2214:19 on McKinney's CPLR 2214.

the parties more time, requiring the trading of as-yet-unreceived papers in the courthouse corridor, adjourning the motion, etc.

As we suggest in section 247, above, many problems can be avoided altogether if after serving papers on a cross-motion in accordance with CPLR 2214 and 2215, lawyers voluntarily take the extra step of promptly forwarding the papers via facsimile, email, or personal delivery to assure their receipt, and if at all possible, within a reasonable time prior to the hearing on the return day. As long as the original service of the cross-motion papers was proper under the CPLR, this additional "courtesy service" need not comply with the rules regarding service of interlocutory papers. These sorts of problems will be ameliorated in e-filed cases where filing and service of papers occur simultaneously.

§ 250. Deciding the Motion; Drawing and Entering the Order

Time to Decide Motion; Reducing Decision to Written Order

The court has 60 days from the submission of the motion (20 days in the case of a motion relating to a provisional remedy)[1] in which to decide it.[2] The period is precatory rather than jurisdictional; however, a decision made after the required time is valid and a party who tries to attack a late decision only after he learns that it has gone against him will meet an estoppel.[3] An Article 78 proceeding[4] is available to compel a judge to render an overdue decision,[5] but is rarely used for that purpose. Attorneys are apprehensive that it will not merely get them a decision, but also enable them to predict what the decision will be.

A motion culminates in an order,[6] which must be reduced to a writing, and the written order must conform strictly to the decision. In the event of conflict, the decision controls.[7] It is the common practice for the winner on the motion to draw the order and see to its entry unless the court or clerk does it as happens with some boiler-plate orders. For example, if it is a standard kind of motion giving rise to a simple and standard order, it may be the practice in some courts for the clerk to draw the order—which usually entails nothing more than the filling out of a printed form—and entering it, notifying the parties of so doing. This kind of order is sometimes known as a "short-form" order, an informal rather than official terminology.

A court rule now provides that "[u]nless the circumstances require settlement of an order, a judge shall incorporate into the decision an order effecting the relief specified in the decision."[8] This is designed to save the parties the need to draft and submit an order, making the decision itself serve also as the order whenever possible.

---

[1]   The provisional remedies are listed in CPLR 6001 and are separately provided for in CPLR Articles 62–65. They are treated in Chapter 12, beginning with § 306.

[2]   CPLR 2219(a).

[3]   Slavuter v. Slavuter, 304 A.D.2d 820, 757 N.Y.S.2d 874 (2d Dep't 2003).

[4]   See CPLR 7802(a), 7803(1).

[5]   See, e.g., Weinstein v. Haft, 60 N.Y.2d 625, 467 N.Y.S.2d 350, 454 N.E.2d 933 (1983) ("Mandamus will lie to compel the determination of a motion"); Liang v. Hart, 132 A.D.3d 765, 17 N.Y.S.3d 771 (2d Dep't 2015).

[6]   CPLR 2211.

[7]   Scheuering v. Scheuering, 27 A.D.3d 446, 811 N.Y.S.2d 100 (2d Dep't 2006); Di Prospero v. Ford Motor Co., 105 A.D.2d 479, 480 N.Y.S.2d 784 (3d Dep't 1984).

[8]   See 22 N.Y.C.R.R. § 202.8(g), applicable in the supreme and county courts.

The requirement that the order be in writing is explicit in CPLR 2219(a). Practitioners nevertheless report instances in which oral directions are issued by judges, such as in the course of conferences or proceedings in chambers, or even by telephone, which amount to orders but are not reduced to a writing or otherwise recorded (as when no stenographer is present). This practice impedes appellate review, should an aggrieved party seek it. A 1996 amendment of CPLR 2219(a) responded to the situation by requiring that any such "order or ruling" made by a judge "be reduced to writing or otherwise recorded" if any party requests it.

The amendment does not apply to the trial itself. Rulings made in the course of a trial, such as in response to objections, are not the equivalent of orders and are merely noted in the record, with appellate review of the rulings to abide the final judgment that concludes the trial.[9]

If the order as drawn is deemed incorrect by the other side, i.e., not a proper reflection of the court's decision, the way to correct things is by a motion to resettle the order.[10] This is usually done by application to the motion judge, but a correction of this kind has even been made on an appeal.[11] "Resettlement," which connotes the revising of the order to make it reflect the decision more accurately, "is a procedure designed solely to correct errors or omissions as to form, or for clarification. It may not be used to effect a substantive change in or to amplify the prior decision of the court."[12]

Entry, Filing, and Service of the Order

As the form for a court order in section 252 illustrates, the order is to be dated and is to bear the judge's signature or initials. It should recite, in addition to the decision, the papers on which it was based.[13] This recitation will be important in compiling the record on appeal and lawyers should take pains to see that it is accurate.[14] CPLR 2220(a) states that "[a]n order determining a motion shall be entered and filed" with the clerk of the court where the action is pending. The statute has transposed the terms, as the order is first filed with the clerk, who then enters it. No distinction is made under the CPLR between a court order and a judge's order made out of court.[15] The stated requirement of entry and filing applies to both.[16] If the motion has been brought and decided in some other county, as it sometimes may be in supreme court practice,[17] the winner of the motion should also see to its entry and filing in the action-pending county.[18]

---

[9]   See § 526; SPR 43:2.

[10]   See Foley v. Roche, 68 A.D.2d 558, 566, 418 N.Y.S.2d 588, 593 (1st Dep't 1979); see Commentary C2220:4A on McKinney's CPLR 2220.

[11]   See Rowlee v. Dietrich, 88 A.D.2d 751, 451 N.Y.S.2d 467 (4th Dep't 1982).

[12]   Foley v. Roche, 68 A.D.2d 558, 566, 418 N.Y.S.2d 588, 593 (1st Dep't 1979); see Simon v. Mehryari, 16 A.D.3d 664, 792 N.Y.S.2d 543 (2d Dep't 2005).

[13]   CPLR 2219(a).

[14]   See CPLR 5526 (record on appeal shall include, among other things, "the papers and other exhibits upon which the judgment or order was founded"); § 538.

[15]   See CPLR 2219(a).

[16]   CPLR 2220.

[17]   See CPLR 2212(a); § 245.

[18]   See Commentary C2220:2 on McKinney's CPLR 2220.

If the order directs the payment of money, CPLR 2222 permits it to be docketed like a judgment[19] and enforced in the same manner.[20] The rarely cited CPLR 2222 is a sleeper provision that, when coupled with the 9% interest offered by CPLR 5004, can have a dramatic impact on a money award. The First Department's decision in Han Soo Lee v. Riverhead Bay Motors,[21] demonstrates the point. In *Han Soo Lee*, the supreme court issued an order awarding former counsel in the matter $50,000 as his proportionate share of the contingency fee in the underlying personal injury action. The First Department ruled that because CPLR 2222 directs that, upon request, "the clerk shall docket as a judgment an order directing the payment of money," supreme court correctly concluded that the clerk erred by refusing to enter the order as a judgment when requested to do so. Therefore, the court ruled that statutory interest at 9% should be calculated from the date the order was presented to the clerk pursuant to CPLR 5003. The former counsel also sought stage 2 interest to run from the award to the judgment,[22] but the court concluded that the award was not a "verdict, report or decision" under CPLR 5002. Therefore, former counsel was limited to interest from the date the order should have been entered and docketed as a judgment under CPLR 2222.

The winning party should see to it that the order is filed and entered, along with the papers submitted (which likely have already been filed with the court) and any written decision, and that the order is then served on the losing party with notice of entry.[23] The point should be stressed right up front that, generally speaking, an order is not enforceable, or even appealable,[24] until it has been entered and served on the loser with notice of entry.[25] A First Department case[26] in which a pharmacist had been penalized with an administrative exclusion from Medicaid participation zeroes in on this point:

On the pharmacist's petition, the trial court overturned the agency decision. The appellate division then reversed the trial court and upheld the agency in a decision published in the New York Law Journal on February 28, 1991, but no notice in writing was given the petitioner until a letter dated March 12, 1991. The court held that the Law Journal publication was not the moment at which the order took effect; the written notice to the petitioner or his lawyer was the moment. There was approximately a two-week hiatus between the two events, and during that time, held the court, the lower court decision held sway and the petitioner remained a Medicaid participant and was entitled to reimbursements for that period. The court acknowledges that while there is no statutory requirement that an order be served before it is effective, caselaw so holds,[27]

---

[19]   CPLR 2222, 5018.

[20]   The devices for enforcing money judgments are in Article 52 of the CPLR. See §§ 485 et seq.; see also § 285, addressing partial summary judgment directing entry of money judgment.

[21]   Han Soo Lee v. Riverhead Bay Motors, 134 A.D.3d 656, 656, 21 N.Y.S.3d 624 (1st Dep't 2015).

[22]   See § 411.

[23]   CPLR 2220(b); see 22 N.Y.C.R.R. § 202.5–b(h)(3) (in an e-filed action, "[a] party shall serve notice of entry of an order or judgment on another party by serving a copy of the order or judgment and written notice of its entry"). While this rule is contained in the rules for the consensual e-filing program, it also applies in cases governed by mandatory e-filing. See 22 N.Y.C.R.R. § 202.5–bb(a)(1).

[24]   Matter of Ryan v. Nolan, 134 A.D.3d 1259, 1261 n.1, 21 N.Y.S.3d 469, 471, n.1 (3d Dep't 2015).

[25]   Fried v. Carlucci & Legum, Cascione, Chechanover & Purcigliotti, P.C., 309 A.D.3d 829, 766 N.Y.S.2d 83 (2d Dep't 2003).

[26]   Raes Pharmacy, Inc. v. Perales, 181 A.D.2d 58, 586 N.Y.S.2d 579 (1st Dep't 1992).

[27]   See, e.g., Wells Fargo Bank, N.A. v. Frierson, 150 A.D.3d 1045, 55 N.Y.S.3d 332 (2d Dep't 2017).

and if the party has an attorney, service on the attorney is an "all but universally codified" requirement.

Ordinarily, an order is "filed" and "entered" at the same time, a practice so common that some lawyers think of the two steps as contemporaneous and consider both of them embraced under "entry." In e-filed actions, the county clerk "or his or her designee shall file orders and judgments of the court electronically, which shall constitute entry of the order or judgment."[28] In actions not subject to e-filing, complications still arise. The judge's mere act of signing the order in such actions does not constitute filing or entry. Occasions will arise when the order is signed, but for one reason or another is not promptly filed and entered with the clerk. There have also been occasions where an order is signed and filed, but not entered.[29] If the record before the appellate court does not reflect that a written order was filed and entered, an appeal from the order can be dismissed,[30] and an argument can be made that the order has no effect. Therefore, lawyers need to take pains to insure not only that orders and judgments are timely submitted for signature, but also that they are ultimately filed, entered, and served on all parties with notice of entry.

Practices will differ on these procedural details. In some places, the judges may themselves see to the filing and entry of their orders; in others, it may be the convention for the judges to leave the securing of the entry to the winning party. At least one case has held that in this age of the photocopy machine, the clerk's stamp "Filed" on a copy of the order will itself connote entry.[31] As long as it is not plainly offensive to the rules, the practice of a court may depend on the kind of order, the judicial department, the size of the court, the geographical distribution of the judges, the predilection of the particular judge, simply local habit, or other factors. Whatever it is, significant consequences can attend violations of these otherwise incidental "details."

"Order Filed," "Submit Order," "Settle Order"

What does "settle" mean? What does "submit" mean? The lawyer should be familiar with these terms, so often met in motion practice.[32] If the decision on the motion concludes with "order filed," or words to that effect, this usually signifies that the judge or clerk has drawn and filed the order and that it is already entered. The winning party in that instance should obtain the order and serve it on all other parties with notice of entry, which is merely a notice that the order was entered on such-and-such date and place.

If the decision ends with "submit order" or similar words, this signifies that the winning party is to draw the order and submit it to the clerk for entry, with proof of service on all parties. A "submit order" direction usually means that the adverse party need not be consulted in advance. If the order does not conform to the decision (the clerk

---

[28]   22 N.Y.C.R.R. § 202.5–b(h)(1).

[29]   See *Matter of Ryan*, 134 A.D.3d at 1261 n.1, 21 N.Y.S.3d at 471, n.1.

[30]   See, e.g., People v. Goodwin, 131 A.D.3d 1284, 15 N.Y.S.3d 896 (3d Dep't 2015); People v. Kemp, 130 A.D.3d 1132, 12 N.Y.S.3d 394 (3d Dep't 2015).

[31]   Resource Funding Co. v. McNamara, 150 Misc. 2d 1041, 570 N.Y.S.2d 762 (Sup. Ct., New York County 1990).

[32]   See Commentary C2220:4 on McKinney's CPLR 2220 (discussing meaning of terms "submit," "settle," etc.).

can usually be relied upon to see that it does), the adverse party can make a motion to resettle the order, as discussed above, after it is served on him following entry.

If the decision says "settle order," an alternative used for more complicated relief, the court is signifying that it wants the winning party to draft the order and work out the proposed draft with the adverse party so that the latter can determine whether it also fits her understanding of the motion's decision. If the parties can agree, the order can be entered without trouble. If they can't, a motion to settle must be made and the court determines the form and content of the order. Procedure for the motion to settle, including the time periods applicable to it, is governed in the supreme and county courts by Uniform Rule section 202.48(c). The losing party may tender his own suggested form of order, known as a proposed counter order.[33]

If the phrase used in the decision does not clearly connote the procedure the judge wants followed with respect to the drawing and entry of the order, or, indeed, if the decision contains no direction at all, a clarification should be obtained from the clerk or the judge's chambers.[34]

Time for Drawing and Submitting Proposed Orders and Judgments

As noted above, Uniform Rule section 202.8(g) was designed to encourage judges to include sufficient instruction in a decision so that the decision itself can serve as the dispositive order—with the decision reciting as much—thereby making a separate order unnecessary.[35] What if the court has not signed an order to accompany the decision? Just how much time does the winner have to draft a proposed order and submit it to the court for signature? Before 1986, there was no uniform time limit at all. A case would occasionally come along to invoke the laches doctrine against a long-delayed attempt at entry,[36] but that was rare. The law relied on the winner's incentive to start the loser's appeal time running as soon as possible, as entry and service of the order are the acts that start the time to appeal in New York practice.[37]

Uniform Rule section 202.48(a) closed that procedural gap in supreme and county courts.[38] It requires that the order be settled or submitted for signature "within 60 days after the signing and filing of the decision."[39] The rule applies to the submission of a judgment as well as of an order, and failure to submit on time "shall be deemed an

---

[33]   22 N.Y.C.R.R. § 202.48(c)(2) ("[a]ny proposed counter-order or judgment shall be submitted with a copy clearly marked to delineate each proposed change to the order or judgment to which objection is made.").

[34]   See the note on "Muddling the Distinction Between 'Submit Judgment' and 'Settle Judgment' and Abandoning a Victory as a Result," in SPR 52:3. The differences between the "submit" and "settle" instructions are discussed by the Court of Appeals in Funk v. Barry, 89 N.Y.2d 364, 653 N.Y.S.2d 247, 675 N.E.2d 1199 (1996).

[35]   See the lead note in SPR 5:1.

[36]   See, e.g., Vickery v. Village of Saugerties, 106 A.D.2d 721, 483 N.Y.S.2d 765 (3d Dep't 1984), aff'd, 64 N.Y.2d 1161, 490 N.Y.S.2d 735, 480 N.E.2d 349 (1985), involving a judgment in an Article 78 proceeding. Orders and judgments are generally treated alike for time-for-entry purposes.

[37]   See CPLR 5513; see § 533.

[38]   It behooves lawyers to check into the Uniform Rules applicable to each category of court they practice in to see if there is any similar rule there. See Commentary C2220:3 on McKinney's CPLR 2220.

[39]   22 N.Y.C.R.R. § 202.48 applies in the supreme and county courts. Similar rules address similar matters in other courts, including the surrogate's court (22 N.Y.C.R.R. § 207.37), the N.Y.C. Civil Court (22 N.Y.C.R.R. § 208.33), the district courts (22 N.Y.C.R.R. § 212.33), and the city courts (22 N.Y.C.R.R. § 210.33).

abandonment of the motion or action."[40] With this limit on the victor's time to translate the victory into an order and submit it for signing, the winner can no longer dally. In e-filed actions, "[u]nless the court directs otherwise, any document that requires a judge's signature shall be transmitted electronically and in hard copy to the court."[41] Therefore, unless the court directs otherwise, the lawyer who has prevailed on a motion that requires settlement or submission of an order (a point discussed in further detail below) will want to take both steps, and maintain proof that the hard copy of the proposed order was submitted within 60 days of the filing of the decision. Similarly, in actions still prosecuted with paper, the lawyer will want some proof from the court, e.g., a stamped copy of the proposed order, to establish compliance with Uniform Rule section 202.48(a).

The lawyer should not confuse the 60-day period the court has for deciding a motion, which comes from CPLR 2219(a) and is anything but rigid, with the 60-day period the winner of the motion has for submitting the proposed order, which is governed by Uniform Rule section 202.48. Such confusion can lead to tragedy.

For a while, some courts held that the 60-day time period for getting an order entered after a motion, or a judgment entered after a decision in a court-tried case, applied also to the entry of a judgment following a jury verdict. The Court of Appeals rejected that idea in Funk v. Barry,[42] adopting in effect the position taken by the First Department in Helfant v. Sobkowski:[43] the 60-day rule applies only to orders and judgments that have to be submitted to the court for signature, which is not the procedure on a verdict. Hence, the 60-day rule does not apply when reducing verdicts to judgments.

Funk, the leading decision on the 60-day entry rule, also held that the time limit does not apply at all unless the court's decision explicitly calls for the submission or settlement of an order or judgment. Hence, a decision that contains no instructions about the drawing of the dispositive order will not produce "abandonment" consequences for the prevailing party. In that situation, the main spur to the winning party's securing entry of the order and serving a copy of it on the other side with notice of entry is the continuing rule that the order will have no effect and the losing party's time to appeal will not start to run until that is done.[44]

The courts do have the power to excuse a delay in honoring the 60-day rule "for good cause shown,"[45] permitting late submission of the order, but they have indicated that the delay will not be excused just for the asking. In what was probably the first case on the 60-day limit, a defendant who got a complaint dismissed found it reinstated, and the plaintiff's action preserved, by letting some five months elapse after the dismissal decision without reducing the victory to an order and getting it entered.[46] The defendant's excuse was "the heavy press of work, the great volume of motions and the

---

[40] 22 N.Y.C.R.R. § 202.48(b).

[41] 22 N.Y.C.R.R. § 202.5–b(d)(5).

[42] *Funk*, 89 N.Y.2d at 368, 653 N.Y.S.2d at 250, 675 N.E.2d at 1202.

[43] Helfant v. Sobkowski, 174 A.D.2d 340, 570 N.Y.S.2d 552 (1st Dep't 1991).

[44] *Funk* is treated at length in the lead note in NYSLD No. 445.

[45] 22 N.Y.C.R.R. § 202.48(b); see Commentary C2220:3F on McKinney's CPLR 2220 (discussing caselaw applying the "good cause" standard).

[46] Urena v. N.Y.C. Health and Hospitals Corp., Sup. Ct., New York County, April 24, 1987 (Index No. 6549/86: Sklar, J.).

limitations of the staff in the Office of the Corporation Counsel."[47] All of that together, held the court, is not "good cause" under Uniform Rule section 202.48(b) sufficient to be relieved of the abandonment.

If good cause is not shown, and the worst does happen—the motion victory is deemed abandoned—the impact of the abandonment can pose a dilemma.[48] In Feldman v. New York City Transit Authority,[49] for example, the defendant won on its motion for summary judgment, but then abandoned the victory by failing to secure entry. Remarking that to allow the defendant to keep its victory, perhaps with only a monetary slap on the wrists for the delay, was not sufficient, the First Department held that the abandonment stuck. In effect, the *Feldman* court treated the failure to comply with Uniform Rule section 202.48(a) as the equivalent of a denial of the motion on the merits and allowed the case to proceed. Should such a case now be tried even though it has been judicially determined that there is nothing to try? Does the abandonment mean to turn things around 180 degrees so as to declare summary judgment for the opposing side, the one that lost on the motion?[50]

The peculiarity of the situation prompted the Second Department to take a different view of the matter in a similar summary judgment situation in Russo v. City of New York.[51] Holding that a court should not be burdened with a "demonstrably meritless action," the court imposed motion costs but let the defendant keep the summary judgment. In an analogous situation, the Second Department let a defendant keep its judgment with a nunc pro tunc order. The trial court had directed judgment for D after P's proof was in and directed D to settle the judgment. D failed to settle the judgment, and did not have good cause for its failure, so the trial court deemed D's victory abandoned and restored the case to the calendar. Reversing, the appellate division said that a nunc pro tunc order should have been used; that the trial court's disposition would not bring the "repose" to judicial proceedings that the rule contemplates.[52]

An unusually draconian application of the 60-day rule was made by the appellate division in Farkas v. Farkas,[53] resulting in the forfeiture of a $750,000 judgment by the plaintiff wife in a bitter matrimonial dispute in which it appeared that the defendant was a card-carrying scoundrel who would not have been at all prejudiced by the court's allowance of a late entry of the judgment. In *Farkas*, the First Department reversed a trial court's apparent finding of "good cause" to allow a late submission of a $750,000 judgment and ordered "the claim underlying the judgment dismissed as abandoned pursuant to 22 N.Y.C.R.R. 202.48(b)." The hearts of the plaintiff's lawyers raced at high speeds for several months until the Court of Appeals issued its decision in the matter.[54] The majority in *Farkas* ruled that the $750,000 judgment was not subject to the 60-day

---

[47]   Urena v. N.Y.C. Health and Hospitals Corp., Sup. Ct., New York County, April 24, 1987 (Index No. 6549/86: Sklar, J.).

[48]   See Commentary C2220:3G on McKinney's CPLR 2220 (discussing possible penalties for failure to comply with 60-day rule).

[49]   Feldman v. New York City Transit Authority, 171 A.D.2d 473, 567 N.Y.S.2d 228 (1st Dep't 1991).

[50]   See the discussion in the lead note in NYSLD No. 382; Commentary C2220:3G on McKinney's CPLR 2220.

[51]   Russo v. City of New York, 206 A.D.2d 355, 614 N.Y.S.2d 55 (2d Dep't 1994).

[52]   Meany v. Supermarkets Gen. Corp., 239 A.D.2d 393, 658 N.Y.S.2d 338 (2d Dep't 1997), and the discussion in SPR 79:4.

[53]   Farkas v. Farkas, 40 A.D.3d 207, 835 N.Y.S.2d 118 (1st Dep't 2007).

[54]   Farkas v. Farkas, 11 N.Y.3d 300, 869 N.Y.S.2d 380, 898 N.E.2d 563 (2008) (5–2 decision). The case is discussed in NYSLD No. 587.

rule in Uniform Rule section 202.48, in part because these amounts were already awarded in prior judgments.[55]

If the 60-day entry issue is not raised, and an order is entered on the decision more than 60 days later, the order is fully valid.[56]

The consequence of "abandonment" is obviously aimed at a movant who has won on the motion. In the reverse situation, just as common, in which the motion has been denied, making the one moved against the winner, it has been held that the 60-day period does not apply.[57] Perhaps the rule is intentionally aimed only at the winning movant and does not intend to prescribe so dire a result as "abandonment" when the other side prevails and the motion is denied. That party, too, however, should not dally in getting the order entered. Digging into the facts of some involved cases, like Aetna Cas. & Sur. Co. v. F & F Maintenance, Inc.,[58] may reveal that the 60-day abandonment rule was indeed applied even against the victorious opponent of the motion.

What lesson should be distilled from all this? Simple: if you're a winner in any context (movant or opponent), forget all technical rules and get your victory promptly reduced to a proposed order; submit it to the judge; and have it signed, filed, and entered. It really isn't safe to make optimistic assumptions about the 60-day rule, even in the face of what would seem to be a unanimous set of appellate division views. The Court of Appeals has yet to address many issues pertaining to the rule, and it has been known to come up with an occasional procedural surprise.

How do the parties learn of the filing of the decision directing that the order be settled or submitted, which triggers the 60-day rule in Uniform Rule section 202.48(a)? Obviously, the prevailing party can't undertake the chore of drawing the order, securing its entry, serving it on the other side with notice of entry, etc., without being aware that the decision has been filed. It therefore behooves the lawyer to find out about the decision promptly. The method whereby a party may learn of the decision varies from place to place. In actions that are subject to e-filing, "all signed decisions...shall be converted into electronic form and transmitted to the NYSCEF site by the appropriate clerk."[59] This will put all parties on notice of the decision.[60] In the New York City metropolitan area, the New York Law Journal announces certain decisions. Elsewhere, local law newspapers may do so, or the clerk may advise the parties by mail or perhaps even by phone, or the parties may simply be expected to keep in touch with the clerk's office. In some places, a party wanting notice of the court's decision, or a copy of it, may be asked to furnish the judge or clerk a stamped and self-addressed envelope. Again, an inquiry

---

[55] The dissent in *Farkas* contains an insightful discussion of the thorny issue of "abandonment" and the appropriate penalties to be imposed for a violation of 22 N.Y.C.R.R. § 202.48. See Commentary C2220:3G on McKinney's CPLR 2220.

[56] See Alexander v. C.P. Craska, Inc., Sup. Ct., Bronx County, Feb. 3, 1992 (Index No. 13273/90; Friedman, J.), in which the order directed an attorney to turn over a file. It was disobeyed and the disobedience was punished as a contempt.

[57] See Matter of Estate of Germain, 138 A.D.2d 918, 526 N.Y.S.2d 662 (3d Dep't 1988), treated in the lead note in NYSLD No. 326; Matter of Kerrigan, 169 A.D.2d 833, 565 N.Y.S.2d 203 (2d Dep't 1991); Rotella v. Wegmans Food Mkts., Inc., 289 A.D.2d 1014, 735 N.Y.S.2d 447 (4th Dep't 2001); Bell v. New York Higher Educ. Assistance Corp., 166 A.D.2d 228, 560 N.Y.S.2d 439 (1st Dep't 1990).

[58] Aetna Cas. & Sur. Co. v. F & F Maintenance, Inc., 168 A.D.2d 876, 564 N.Y.S.2d 550 (3d Dep't 1990).

[59] 22 N.Y.C.R.R. § 202.5–b(d)(5).

[60] 22 N.Y.C.R.R. § 202.5–b(h)(3).

into local practice is needed for the uninitiated, especially the visiting lawyer whose county base is elsewhere.

What happens when the loss of a party's claim is attributable to a court's delayed decision, an issue that arose in Matter of Goffredo v. City of New York.[61] The party was nevertheless held the loser, but two justices vociferously (and justifiably) dissented.[62]

There's a provision in the motion article for the enforcement of mandates,[63] but that subject is deferred until the chapter on the enforcement of judgments.[64]

For an even more comprehensive discussion of the requirements of Uniform Rule section 202.48, the reader should consult the McKinney's Practice Commentaries to CPLR 2220.

§ 251. Trial of Issue of Fact Arising on Motion

CPLR 2218 authorizes a separate trial of an issue of fact arising on a motion. It applies to all motions except the motion for summary judgment under CPLR 3212, which has its own, and very restrictive, provision on the subject.[1] The main motion on which a fact issue is likely to warrant a separate preliminary trial is the motion to dismiss under CPLR 3211. The rule governing CPLR 3211 motions also has its own provision authorizing such a trial, however, so CPLR 2218, even if also applicable there, is essentially not needed.[2]

As a general principle, no issue of fact arising on any motion should be ordered to immediate trial unless there is some compelling reason for it—such as where jurisdiction depends on it or where it is a succinct issue whose resolution might avoid a trial by bringing about a dismissal or stay of the action.[3] If the hearing needed to resolve the issue is likely to be a lengthy one, that factor militates against ordering the separate trial.[4] Further investigation of this matter is reserved for the treatment of CPLR 3211.[5]

§ 252. Some Forms

It will be helpful to illustrate a few papers connected with motion practice. For some things, there are official forms, but unfortunately most of the official forms were rescinded in 2016.[1] Official or not, the forms below present a helpful template for lawyers, which can be adjusted based on the needs of the case.

(a) Form of notice of motion. Uniform Rule section 202.7(b) contains a sample notice of motion, applicable in the supreme and county courts. It has been adjusted slightly here to incorporate the 7-day demand for cross-motions:

---

[61]   Goffredo v. City of New York, 33 A.D.3d 346, 830 N.Y.S.2d 11 (1st Dep't 2006).

[62]   See the lead note in SPR 178:1.

[63]   CPLR 2223.

[64]   Chapter 18 (§§ 476 et seq.).

[1]   See § 284.

[2]   CPLR 3211(c).

[3]   See Brown v. Micheletti, 97 A.D.2d 529, 530, 468 N.Y.S.2d 160, 162 (2d Dep't 1983).

[4]   Korn v. Korn, 56 A.D.2d 837, 392 N.Y.S.2d 73 (2d Dep't 1977); Stowell v. Berstyn, 26 A.D.2d 828, 274 N.Y.S.2d 120 (2d Dep't 1966).

[5]   See § 271.

[1]   See § 7.

.... COURT OF THE STATE OF NEW YORK

COUNTY OF ....

....x

A.B.,   Notice of Motion

                Plaintiff,   Index No.

        -against-   ....

C.D.,   Name of Assigned Judge

                Defendant.   ....

                                       Oral argument is requested □

                                       (check box if applicable)

....x

Upon the affidavit of ...., sworn to on ...., 20..., and upon (list supporting papers if any), the .... will move this court (in Room ....) at the ...., ... Courthouse, ..., New York, on the ..... day of ......, 20..., at ..... (a.m.) (p.m.) for an order (briefly indicate relief requested).

The above-entitled action is for (briefly state nature of action, *e.g.*, personal injury, medical malpractice, divorce, etc.).

This is a motion for or related to interim maintenance or child support. □ (check box if applicable)

An affirmation in compliance with Uniform Rule section 202.7 (a) and (c) that a good faith effort has been made to resolve the issues raised in this motion is annexed hereto. (required only where the motion relates to disclosure or to a bill of particulars)

Pursuant to CPLR 2214(b), any answering affidavits, and any notice of cross-motion and accompanying papers, are required to be served upon the undersigned at least seven days before the return date of this motion. See CPLR 2215. □ (check box if applicable)

Dated:

                                             ....[Signature]..................................

                                             ....[Print name]..................................

                                             Attorney[1] (or attorney in charge of

                                             case if law firm) for moving party.

                                             Address:

                                             Telephone number:

TO: ....[Print name]..................................

             Attorney[1] for (other party)

             Address:

             Telephone number:

             ....[Print name]..................................

             Attorney[1] for (other party)

             Address:

             Telephone number:

[1] If any party is appearing pro se, the name, address, and telephone number of the party shall be stated.

(b) Form of order to show cause. The following is a form (not an official form) of order to show cause to vacate an execution and default judgment, which includes a temporary restraining order:

SUPREME COURT OF THE STATE OF NEW YORK
COUNTY OF NEW YORK

A.B., Plaintiff, against C.D. and E.F., Defendants.	Order to Show Cause Index No. _____

Upon the affidavits of C.D. and his attorney, J.R., sworn to on March 10, 2018, and upon the default judgment entered in the office of the clerk of this court on February 8, 2018, and upon a copy of an execution issued to the Sheriff of the City of New York in this action and bearing receipt date of March 1, 2018, and upon all prior papers and proceedings in this cause, it is hereby

ORDERED, that the plaintiff show cause before this court, at IAS Part 27, to be held at the Courthouse at 60 Centre Street in the City and County of New York, at 9:30 a.m. on March 16, 2018, why an order should not be entered in this action vacating the execution and the judgment in this action in its entirety for lack of jurisdiction and for total lack of service of process of any kind, or granting such other and further relief as may seem just and proper to the court; and it is further

ORDERED, that until further order of this court and pending the hearing and determination of this application, the plaintiff and his attorney and all purporting to act in his behalf, and the Sheriff of the City of New York, are hereby stayed from taking any further step to levy the execution or otherwise enforce the judgment.

LET SERVICE of a copy of this order and of the papers on which it is based, by personal delivery to the plaintiff's attorney, or to a person of suitable age and discretion at his office, and to the Sheriff of the City of New York, or to a deputy Sheriff in the County of New York, on or before March 12, 2018, be deemed sufficient service thereof.

This order has been signed by me this 11th day of March, 2018, and shall upon presentation be entered in the office of the clerk.

                             _____
                                  [Signature]
                                  Ira Gammerman
                                  Justice, Supreme Court
                                  New York County

(c) Form of court order. CPLR 2219(a) provides that there is to be no difference between a court order and a judge's order made out of court (such as on an ex parte motion). The following is essentially what was previously known as Official Form 27, an order on a motion, made on notice, to dismiss the complaint:

SUPREME COURT OF THE STATE OF NEW YORK
COUNTY OF NEW YORK

A.B., Plaintiff,	Order
against	Index No. _____
C.D. and E.F., Defendants.	Name of Assigned Judge: _____

Upon defendant's notice of motion dated December 1, 2017, for a dismissal of the complaint and for dismissal of the first, second and third causes of action therein, and upon the complaint, the affidavit of C.D. sworn to December 1, 2017, and the affidavit of A.B. sworn to December 8, 2017, and [plaintiff having appeared in opposition] [or] [there being no appearance in opposition], it is ordered that:

1. The first cause of action is dismissed. The plaintiff may upon application to the court, within _____ days from service of a copy of this order with notice of entry thereof, submit evidence to the court to justify the granting of leave to plead again.

2. The motion to dismiss the second cause of action is denied, with leave to assert the statute of limitations as a defense in defendant's answer.

3. All further proceedings on the third cause of action are stayed, except upon leave of this court, until the final determination of the action entitled <u>A.B., Plaintiff v. X.Y.Z., Inc., Defendant</u>, presently pending in the Superior Court of New Jersey (Index No. _____), on condition that defendant file a stipulation, within _____ days from service of a copy of this order with notice of entry thereof, that all discovery proceedings in the action in the Superior Court of New Jersey shall be usable in this action with the same force and effect as though originally taken herein.

4. In all other respects the motion of the defendant is denied.

New York, New York, December 20, 2017

[Signature] _____
[Print name to be signed or initialed]
Justice, Supreme Court
New York County

§ 253. Motion Affecting Prior Order

CPLR 2221, and to a lesser extent CPLR 2217, address the situation in which one judge may be asked to do something in an action that another judge refused to do, or to undo something the other judge did. The situation is far less frequent under the

Individual Assignment System (IAS),[1] in which one judge is assigned to the action and "[a]ll motions [are] returnable before the assigned judge,"[2] but it can still happen.

This may occur, for example, when the assigned judge is unavailable, for any variety of reasons. It can arise in those areas of the state following the so-called "dual track" system, in which the assigned judge leaves the case as of the filing of the note of issue and another takes over for the trial. The trial judge may be asked to take a step inconsistent with the previous judge's order. It can also arise in special categories of cases that have been exempted from IAS treatment and which are handled in special "parts."[3] Finally, it can arise in courts in which the IAS is not in effect at all.

Whenever the situation is at hand, the concerns of CPLR 2221, and to some degree CPLR 2217, are at hand. Both were amended in 1986 to empower the chief administrator by rule to exclude the application of either provision from any given department, district, or county.[4] This means that local practice may vary and that a local inquiry will sometimes be necessary. If no such implementing rule is found, the cited CPLR provisions govern.

CPLR 2221, the main provision in point, provides that any motion affecting a prior order shall be made only to the judge who made that order unless she is unable to hear it. Excepted from such a requirement is the order rendered by default. Since nothing was judicially passed on in that instance, the later motion can be made to any judge of the court, but must be made on notice. If the earlier order was granted ex parte, the later motion affecting it may be made ex parte to the same judge or on notice to any other judge.

Again, the reminder that these instructions give way when the IAS is strictly applicable. There, everything must go to the assigned judge.

Under CPLR 2221, a motion made to the wrong judge must be transferred to the right one. The design of the rule is to prevent a second judge of the same court from sitting in effect as an appellate court over a colleague—a procedure the appellate courts have long frowned on.[5] It has even been held that when the prior order was made by a judge sitting only temporarily in the court by administrative assignment, the transfer of the second motion may be made to that judge even after the assignment has expired and the judge is back on his own court. In sum, the judge's jurisdiction of the matter is deemed to continue.[6]

To fall under CPLR 2221, the second motion must "affect" the earlier order. If it does not affect it at all, but is merely another motion in the same action, that's where CPLR 2217(a) comes in, making it permissible (but not mandatory) to refer the motion to the judge who heard the earlier motion.[7] The aim here is to conserve judicial energy.

---

[1]   See Rosenshein v. Rosenshein, 158 A.D.2d 268, 550 N.Y.S.2d 670 (1st Dep't 1990).

[2]   22 N.Y.C.R.R. § 202.8(a); see also Clearwater Realty Co. v. Hernandez, 256 A.D.2d 100, 102, 681 N.Y.S.2d 270, 272 (1st Dep't 1998) ("a subsequent action in the course of the same litigation should be referred to the judge that entertained the earlier proceedings").

[3]   See § 77A for discussion of these points about the Individual Assignment System and its exceptions.

[4]   Chapter 355 of the Laws of 1986.

[5]   See, e.g., Sloan v. Beard, 125 A.D. 625, 110 N.Y.S. 1 (2d Dep't 1908).

[6]   Prudential Lines, Inc. v. Firemen's Ins. Co. of Newark, N. J., 109 Misc. 2d 281, 440 N.Y.S.2d 155 (Sup. Ct., New York County 1981); see Guaman v. Tran, 52 A.D.3d 656, 860 N.Y.S.2d 197 (2d Dep't 2008) (directing that the motion to reargue be submitted to the referee who decided the original motion to dismiss).

[7]   CPLR 2217(a).

The aim of CPLR 2221, on the other hand, is to avoid judicial conflict. It is not necessary, however, in order to invoke CPLR 2221 and *require* the application to be made to the same judge, that the second motion be an outright attempt to have the second judge undo what the first judge did. It is sufficient if the second motion merely touches on or influences the first. Where a respondent, for example, in a proceeding to review a tax assessment, had secured an extension of time from Judge X and then a second from Judge Y, the appellate division criticized the procedure and said it would have been more appropriate to seek the second extension from Judge X.[8] Doubt about whether the second motion affects the first should be resolved by assuming that it does and by moving before the same judge that heard the first motion. The inability of that judge to hear it should, as a rule, be the sole ground for moving before a different judge.

Many kinds of motions qualify as motions "affecting" a prior order. Specifically assigned by CPLR 2221(a) to this category are motions to renew or reargue the prior motion; or to stay, vacate, or modify the order entered on it; or to secure leave to appeal the order. Other motions may fall into the CPLR 2221 category even though not explicitly listed, like a motion to resettle the order.[9]

A motion may be transferred to a different judge even if it has no effect whatever on a prior order if the judge to whom the motion is made is "for any reason unable to hear it."[10]

§ 254. Motion to Reargue or Renew

Motion to Reargue Versus Motion to Renew

A motion to reargue is based on no new proof; it seeks to convince the court that it overlooked or misapprehended something on the first go around and ought to change its mind. The motion to renew (or rehear)[1] is based on new or additional proof not used the first time around or a change in the law. Both should be distinguished from the motion to resettle, which just corrects the order to reflect what is in the decision or in some other way affects only the form of the order.[2]

An extensive body of guiding caselaw evolved to govern the motions to reargue or renew. Most of it is codified in subdivision (d) of CPLR 2221, on the motion to reargue, and subdivision (e), on the motion to renew.[3] The codification occurred in 1999. While the intention was to make it a mere codification, i.e., to clarify without changing, a few changes may have been made, most likely inadvertently. These will be noted.

The first change concerns the proof needed on the motion to renew. Ideally, it should be shown that the proof being offered on the motion has been only recently discovered and that the movant is acting with reasonable dispatch in bringing it before the court. Nonetheless, while a renewal motion may be based on "new facts not offered on the prior

---

8   Lansingburgh Realties, Inc. v. Commissioner of Assessments and Taxation of City of Troy, 42 A.D.2d 646, 345 N.Y.S.2d 152 (3d Dep't 1973).

9   See § 250.

10   CPLR 2217(c).

1   The motion to renew is sometimes called a motion to "rehear." No consequence appends to the distinction. "Renew" is the almost universally used term. See Commentary C2221:9 on McKinney's CPLR 2221.

2   See § 250.

3   The codification is discussed at length in SPR 86:1.

motion,"[4] there is no express requirement in the statute that the facts be "newly discovered" as some of the decisions indicate. This is consistent with some pre-amendment caselaw indicating that the new proof need not necessarily be newly discovered.[5] CPLR 2221(e)(3) does, however, explicitly require a "reasonable justification for the failure to present such facts on the prior motion." In In re Defendini,[6] the Second Department framed a helpful interpretation of the statute, observing that "[t]he requirement that a motion for renewal be based on new facts is a flexible one, and it is within the court's discretion to grant renewal upon facts known to the moving party at the time of the original motion if the movant offers a reasonable excuse for the failure to present those facts on the prior motion."

Time to Make Motion to Reargue or Renew

Under the 1999 codification, CPLR 2221(d)(3) provides that the motion to reargue "shall be made within thirty days after service of a copy of the order determining the prior motion and written notice of its entry."

That language is summary and somewhat arbitrary. Under the law that existed prior to the statute, when an appeal had been duly taken from the original order, and was pending, the motion to reargue could be made during the pendency of the appeal and any time up to the appeal's submission. The jurisdiction of the original court to entertain the reargument motion was not deemed terminated by the mere taking of the appeal. That was a good rule. It gave the lower court an opportunity to obviate the appeal by altering the decision to correct the determination that generated the appeal in the first place. The new rule, with its arbitrary 30-day time limit on the motion to reargue, can be construed to divest the original court of that jurisdiction, which would in turn force through an appeal that might not be necessary.

There are thus good policy reasons for retaining the old rule. Some lower court cases nevertheless held that it was displaced by the adoption of CPLR 2221(d)(3) and that a motion to reargue is now strictly limited to 30 days from the time of the service of the objectionable order notwithstanding the pendency of an appeal from it. The First Department rejected that construction, however, and held in favor of the older rule in Leist v. Goldstein,[7] and the Second Department did likewise in Itzkowitz v. King Kullen Grocery Co., Inc.[8] Under these appellate decisions, the pendency of an appeal from the order continues to be a time period available for a motion to reargue, which is indeed the preferable construction.

A connected issue arises, obfuscated rather than helped by the amendment of CPLR 2221(d)(3). This is where the aggrieved person himself serves the order on the winner, the reverse of the usual procedure in which the winner serves it.[9] When the winner serves the order by mail, the loser clearly gets the additional five days allowed by CPLR

4　　CPLR 2221(e)(2).

5　　See, e.g., Webb & Knapp v. United Cigar-Whelan Stores Corp., 276 A.D. 583, 96 N.Y.S.2d 359 (1st Dep't 1950).

6　　In re Defendini, 142 A.D.3d 500, 502, 35 N.Y.S.3d 495, 497 (2d Dep't 2016); see Commentary C2221:9 on McKinney's CPLR 2221.

7　　Leist v. Goldstein, 305 A.D.2d 468, 760 N.Y.S.2d 191 (1st Dep't 2003); see Garcia v. Jesuits of Fordham, Inc., 6 A.D.3d 163, 774 N.Y.S.2d 503 (1st Dep't 2004).

8　　Itzkowitz v. King Kullen Grocery Co., Inc., 22 A.D.3d 636, 804 N.Y.S.2d 350 (2d Dep't 2005).

9　　See § 250.

2103(b)(2), extending the 30 days in which to appeal[10] or move to reargue[11] to 35 days. But does the loser get the additional five days when it is he himself who serves the order and serves it by mail? Caselaw had said yes, and the yes apparently applied to both the appeal step of CPLR 5513 as well as the reargument step of CPLR 2221.

Here, another 1999 amendment needs integration. It added a subdivision (d) to CPLR 5513 explicitly allowing the loser to add the extra five days to the 30-day appeal period even when it is the loser who has served the order. But that's just for the taking of an appeal. No similar amendment was made for the motion to reargue, and the opportunity to just borrow the appeal steps for application to the reargument motion—which is what happened before the amendment—may be lost because of the independent codification of the reargument motion in CPLR 2221(d)(3). The warning to the loser who elects to serve the order herself, and to serve it by mail,[12] is that while she may be extending by five days her time to appeal, she may not be extending her time to move to reargue.

CPLR 2221(e) does not prescribe a specific time period for making a motion to renew. There are, however, several time limitations recognized in the caselaw that a party moving for renewal must consider. The case must still be "sub judice" to allow for a motion for renewal. A change in the law occurring after the case has gone to final judgment, with the appeal time having expired, cannot as a general rule be made the basis to change the result of the case.[13] While CPLR 2221(e)(3) requires a party seeking renewal based on new facts to provide a reasonable justification for failing to present the facts on the prior motion, it does not require a similar justification when moving for renewal based on a change in the law. Nonetheless, a party seeking renewal based on a change in the law that would change the earlier determination should act expeditiously.[14]

After a final judgment has been entered, a party can still resort to CPLR 5015(a)(2) and move for relief from the judgment based on "newly discovered evidence."[15]

Papers on a Motion to Reargue or Renew

In Biscone v. JetBlue Airways Corp.,[16] the Second Department concluded that the moving papers on a motion for reargument/renewal were insufficient because plaintiff failed to furnish a complete set of the papers relied upon in making the original motion as required by CPLR 2214(c). The decision is explored in greater detail above,[17] but we note it here because the problem seems to arise most frequently in motions for reargument or renewal under CPLR 2221, which does not clearly specify the papers that

---

10   CPLR 5513(a).

11   CPLR 2221(d)(3).

12   See SPR 86:2–3.

13   See Dinallo v. DAL Elec., 60 A.D.3d 620, 874 N.Y.S.2d 246 (2d Dep't 2009).

14   Bray v. Gluck, 235 A.D.2d 72, 663 N.Y.S.2d 725 (3d Dep't 1997); see Commentary C2221:9A on McKinney's CPLR 2221; see also Glicksman v. Board of Education/Central School Bd. of Comsewogue Union Free School Dist., 278 A.D.2d 364, 717 N.Y.S.2d 373 (2d Dep't 2000) (where motion for renewal was made after judgment was entered and the time to appeal had expired, it should have been denied as untimely).

15   Maddux v. Schur, 53 A.D.3d 738, 861 N.Y.S.2d 814 (3d Dep't 2008); see § 428.

16   Biscone v. JetBlue Airways Corp., 103 A.D.3d 158, 957 N.Y.S.2d 361 (2d Dep't 2012) (SPR 253:3).

17   See § 246.

need to be submitted.[18] A party moving for reargument or renewal should be sure to include three things on the motion: (1) the motion for renewal and/or reargument; (2) the papers submitted on the underlying motion; and (3) the underlying order. The papers submitted on the underlying motion are particularly important on a motion for reargument because the movant will want to point to the things on the original motion that the court "overlooked or misapprehended."[19]

Using a Motion to Renew to Cure a Procedural Defect on a Motion

Recently, we have seen a number of occasions in which a party makes a procedural error on a motion, such as submitting an affirmation when an affidavit is required,[20] and attempts to cure the error on a motion to renew, which includes the proper papers. The Second Department took a somewhat rigid position on such renewal motions, denying them regardless of the lack of prejudice if the party failed to provide a reasonable justification for the defects in the documents originally submitted.[21] By contrast, the First Department appears to allow the trial court the discretion to grant motions to renew in the absence of prejudice even where the original failure was due to a party's procedural mistake.[22] The Third Department apparently agrees with the First Department on the matter.[23]

Even the Second Department took a more lenient approach on such motions in Defina v. Daniel,[24] where the court ruled that the lawyer's mistake of including an affirmation instead of a notarized affidavit constituted law office failure and provided "a reasonable justification for the plaintiff's failure to provide the affidavit to the court in opposing the original motion." Upon granting renewal, the Second Department considered the affidavit and concluded that it created a question of fact, necessitating a reversal of the order of summary judgment in defendant's favor.

The decision in Defina, and the generosity it bestowed on a moving party who failed to include the proper documents with its motion papers, should not be embraced by the practicing bar. The decisions in this realm are not always forgiving and are difficult to reconcile.[25] Furthermore, the Court of Appeals has not weighed in on the matter. Who would want to be before that Court, or any other, on a motion to renew arguing that the "reasonable justification for the failure to present [proper papers] on the prior motion"[26] was because of a lack of procedural knowledge?

---

[18] Compare CPLR 3212(b) (specifying which papers must be submitted on motion for summary judgment).

[19] CPLR 2221(d)(2).

[20] See § 205.

[21] See, e.g., Austin v. McPherson, 111 A.D.3d 610, 974 N.Y.S.2d 281 (2d Dep't 2013); Singh v. Mohamed, 54 A.D.3d 933, 864 N.Y.S.2d 498 (2d Dep't 2008).

[22] See, e.g., B.B.Y. Diamonds Corp. v. Five Star Designs, Inc., 6 A.D.3d 263, 775 N.Y.S.2d 34 (1st Dep't 2004); Kalir v. Ottinger, 2011 WL 6968334 (Sup. Ct., New York County 2011) (applying the First Department's rule, the court granted the motion for renewal, despite the fact that defendants submitted defective documents on two prior occasions); see also SPR 243:3.

[23] Wilcox v. Winter, 282 A.D.2d 862, 722 N.Y.S.2d 836 (3d Dep't 2001).

[24] Defina v. Daniel, 140 A.D.3d 825, 33 N.Y.S.3d 421 (2d Dep't 2016).

[25] See Commentary C2221:9 on McKinney's CPLR 2221.

[26] CPLR 2221(e)(3).

Appealability of Orders on Motions to Reargue or Renew

Appealability of orders on reargument and renewal motions should be carefully noted. An order on a motion to renew is appealable whether it grants or denies the motion. An order on a motion to reargue is appealable only if it grants the motion. An order denying a motion to reargue is not appealable; it would amount to an extension of time in which to appeal the original order.

An order granting a motion to reargue is appealable even if, after the granting, the prior decision is adhered to.[27] It has also been held that an order granting reargument supersedes the original order.[28] Therefore, an appeal must be taken from the latter order granting reargument.[29]

Challenging issues—and pitfalls—arise when an order is in fact on appeal and a party makes a motion to the lower court to reargue or renew it during the appeal's pendency. If a new order somehow eventuates, and the party aggrieved by it appeals it, what effect has that on the original appeal? The subject has been troublesome enough to earn some special statutory attention. It's reviewed in the later chapter on appeals.[30]

There's an ongoing question about whether a non-appealing defendant may be allowed to exploit a co-defendant's appellate victory if the issues disposed of in the appealed case would also benefit the non-appealer. A motion to renew after the co-defendant's appellate victory was used to achieve that result—successfully—in Koscinski v. St. Joseph's Medical Center.[31]

Mislabeling of Motion

If a motion is based on new proof, but is erroneously termed a "reargument" motion, the mislabel will be ignored and the motion will be treated as one to renew.[32] And vice-versa.[33] This is of course important on the question of appealability.[34]

The motion to reargue and the motion to renew are listed in CPLR 2221(a) and must therefore be made to the judge who made the original order. That instruction, a product of the now largely superseded Master Calendar System, is self-evident under its replacement, the Individual Assignment System (IAS). It remains relevant in a number of situations even in the IAS era.[35]

Motions to reargue, reconsider, renew, etc., are not exempt from the fee-for-each-motion requirement that applies in the supreme and county courts.[36]

---

[27] See CPLR 2221(f) (noting that if a motion to reargue or renew is granted, "the court may adhere to the determination on the original motion").

[28] See Dennis v. Stout, 24 A.D.2d 461, 260 N.Y.S.2d 325 (2d Dep't 1965).

[29] Bliss v. Jaffin, 176 A.D.2d 106, 573 N.Y.S.2d 687 (1st Dep't 1991).

[30] See § 532.

[31] Koscinski v. St. Joseph's Medical Center, 47 A.D.3d 685, 850 N.Y.S.2d 162 (2d Dep't 2008); see § 543.

[32] Board of Ed. of Scotia-Glenville Central School Dist. v. Shapiro, 85 A.D.2d 763, 445 N.Y.S.2d 270 (3d Dep't 1981).

[33] Weiss v. Deloitte & Touche, LLP, 63 A.D.3d 1045, 1047, 882 N.Y.S.2d 229, 232 (2d Dep't 2009).

[34] See § 532.

[35] See § 253.

[36] See SPR 137:1.

§ 255. Stay

A stay is a suspension of the case or some designated step in it. It is a kind of injunction with which a court freezes proceedings at a particular point. It can be used to stop the prosecution of the action altogether, or to hold up only some phase of it. The stay can be granted during the action's pendency, or even afterwards during an appellate or enforcement stage by staying an execution about to be levied on a judgment.[1]

The word "stay" in New York practice usually connotes a court's suspension of its own proceedings, not those of another court. Although the terminology of "stay" is sometimes applied to the enjoining by one court of an action being brought in another, the latter is more accurately considered an "injunction." That relief partakes of all of the principles of equity applicable to injunctions and may be sought only from a court with equitable powers adequate to entertain injunctive relief. In New York, the main tribunal with equity jurisdiction is of course the supreme court where a plenary action would ordinarily be needed to enjoin the prosecution of an action in another forum.[2] Very rarely, if ever, can a state court injunction stop a federal action.[3]

Pursuant to CPLR 2201, any court in New York can stay its own proceedings "in a proper case, upon such terms as may be just." The stay is sought with a mere motion, but it must have good ground to support it. It is left to the court to determine what a "proper case" is as a matter of discretion, which must be exercised with circumspection.[4] It may be prudent, for example, to stay an action for a brief time if the point of law involved is about to be definitively decided by an appellate court whose decision would bind, but such a decision had best be imminent;[5] the mere pendency of such a case on appeal is not by itself ground on which to stay an action.[6]

One of the most common examples of a stay is one that is granted to suspend one action because of the pendency of another action in some other court between the same parties on the same claim. That stay rests more on CPLR 3211(a)(4), which even authorizes a dismissal in such an instance, than on CPLR 2201.[7] Most of the stays one sees in civil practice, in fact, are not the product of CPLR 2201, the general stay statute, but of some specific stay-authorizing statute applicable to a particular situation. There are a number of these. Among the more prominent are the stay of a judgment's enforcement during an appeal[8] and the stay of an action brought in violation of an agreement to arbitrate.[9]

---

[1]   See § 252, form of order to show cause.

[2]   See Indestructible Metal Products Co. v. Summergrade, 197 A.D. 199, 188 N.Y.S. 642 (1st Dep't 1921); see also Shaid v. Consolidated Edison Co. of New York, Inc., 95 A.D.2d 610, 622, 467 N.Y.S.2d 843, 851 (2d Dep't 1983).

[3]   See Commentary C2201:6 on McKinney's CPLR 2201.

[4]   See Commentary C2201:7 on McKinney's CPLR 2201.

[5]   Assenzio v. A.O. Smith Water Products, 2015 WL 5283301 (Sup. Ct., New York County 2015); Miller v. Miller, 109 Misc. 2d 982, 441 N.Y.S.2d 339 (Sup. Ct., Suffolk County 1981).

[6]   Compare In re Weinbaum's Estate, 51 Misc. 2d 538, 273 N.Y.S.2d 461 (Sur. Ct., Nassau County 1966).

[7]   See § 262.

[8]   CPLR 5519; see § 535.

[9]   CPLR 7503(a); see § 592 (Practitioner's Edition).

If one of the parties is in military service and therefore lacks the freedom of movement that civilians have, a federal statute, also applicable in state courts,[10] requires a stay of the action on the application of the military person unless the court finds that the military service does not impair preparation of the case.[11] Where, for example, it appeared that the defendant was in service but intended to put his case in through a third-party witness, the court found that "the defendant's ability to defend . . . [was] not materially affected by his military service" and denied the stay.[12]

The willful violation of a stay is a contempt of court and may be punished as such.[13] If the reason for the stay is no longer valid, it may be vacated. The party seeking the vacatur need merely move for it.

---

[10]   50 U.S.C.A. § 3931(d); see also Mil. Law § 304 (analogous state statute); Commentary C2201:11A on McKinney's CPLR 2201.

[11]   Mirisoloff v. Monroe, 16 A.D.3d 1161, 791 N.Y.S.2d 255 (4th Dep't 2005).

[12]   Deacon v. Witham, 131 Misc. 2d 217, 499 N.Y.S.2d 317 (Hudson City Ct. 1985). *Deacon* was a small claims case, to which the statute applies just as it does to any other.

[13]   Young v. Young, 130 Misc. 2d 527, 496 N.Y.S.2d 317 (Sup. Ct., New York County 1985); see Commentary C2201:16 on McKinney's CPLR 2201; see also § 481, treating the contempt remedy in the enforcement chapter.

Chapter 11

ACCELERATED JUDGMENT

Analysis

A. Introductory
B. Motion to Dismiss
C. Summary Judgment
D. Summary Judgment in Lieu of Complaint
E. Default Judgment
F. Voluntary Discontinuance
G. Confession of Judgment
H. Tenders and Offers
I. Action on Submitted Facts

A. INTRODUCTORY

Table of Sections

§ 256.   Accelerated Judgment; CPLR Article

§ 256. Accelerated Judgment; CPLR Article 32

Article 32 of the CPLR, entitled "Accelerated Judgment," contains the motion to dismiss,[1] the summary judgment motions,[2] and, among a few other things, the provisions governing the default judgment,[3] the dismissal for want of prosecution,[4] the voluntary discontinuance,[5] the confession of judgment,[6] and the action on submitted facts.[7] All of these devices have one unifying thread: they all contemplate the possibility of disposing of the case, or some significant part of it, without having to try the merits.

In attempting to follow some kind of logical sequence for these devices—recognizing that no sequence is perfect because variations from case to case are too unpredictable—Article 32 is reasonably accurate in its grouping. Because of an amendment to the want of prosecution rule, CPLR 3216, however, which ties it to the note of issue, CPLR 3216 will be treated later, in calendar practice, where the note of issue is a key item.[8] With that exception, the contents of Article 32 will be treated in this chapter.

---

[1]   CPLR 3211.
[2]   CPLR 3212 and 3213.
[3]   CPLR 3215.
[4]   CPLR 3216.
[5]   CPLR 3217.
[6]   CPLR 3218.
[7]   CPLR 3222.
[8]   See §§ 369 and 370. The want of prosecution motion is treated in § 375.

B. MOTION TO DISMISS

Table of Sections

§ 257.   The Motion to Dismiss, CPLR 3211 Generally
§ 258.   The Dismissal Grounds: CPLR 3211(a)
§ 259.   Defense Based on "Documentary Evidence"; Paragraph 1
§ 260.   Subject Matter Jurisdiction; Paragraph 2
§ 261.   Lack of Capacity to Sue; Paragraph 3
§ 262.   Other Action Pending; Paragraph 4
§ 263.   Affirmative Defenses Usable on Dismissal Motion; Paragraph 5
§ 264.   Non-Interposable Counterclaim; Paragraph 6
§ 265.   Failure to State a Cause of Action; Paragraph 7
§ 266.   Lack of Personal Jurisdiction; Paragraph 8
§ 267.   Lack of Rem Jurisdiction; Paragraph 9
§ 268.   Dismissal for Indispensable Party; Paragraph
§ 269.   Motion to Dismiss Defense
§ 270.   Treating 3211 Motion as Summary Judgment
§ 271.   Immediate Trial of Fact Issue Under CPLR 3211
§ 272.   Time for 3211 Motion
§ 273.   Single Motion Rule
§ 274.   Option to Plead Instead of Move; Waiver
§ 275.   Leave to Replead
§ 276.   Res Judicata Effect of CPLR 3211 Disposition
§ 277.   Motion Under CPLR 3211 Extends Responding Time

§ 257. The Motion to Dismiss, CPLR 3211 Generally

CPLR 3211 is the main dismissal motion in New York civil practice. It contains in subdivision (a) the diverse grounds for the dismissal of a cause of action and in subdivision (b) the motion to dismiss a defense. CPLR 3211 is the mechanical expedient that can convert a substantive conclusion into a dispositional reality—a legal theory into an order or judgment.

It does this in many important realms of procedural law. Earlier chapters in this book, for example, that studied topics like subject matter jurisdiction, statute of limitations, and personal jurisdiction—all extensive studies in themselves—each had a singular purpose. One sought to determine whether the court had the power to entertain a given kind of action, another to determine if the action was timely brought, still another to determine if the particular defendant could be subjected to the court's jurisdiction. For these and for many other procedural realms already met, and some yet to come, the whole inquiry is converted into an actual result through the singular expedient of the motion to dismiss supplied by CPLR 3211. It's the bridge that leads the inquiry to its conclusion, one way or the other. Or, to choose another metaphor, it's the waistline of the hour glass that converts the conclusions housed in the top sphere into the order or judgment that inhabits the bottom.

CPLR 3211(a) and its dismissal grounds are available for use by any party against whom a cause of action is asserted. It is of course most commonly used by the defendant against the plaintiff, and that situation will supply the context of the examples we will be using. But it's equally available for use by a plaintiff against a defendant's counterclaim, a defendant against a co-defendant's cross-claim, a third-party defendant against the third-party plaintiff's complaint, etc.

The same is true of the CPLR 3211(b) motion to strike a defense. Although most often seen as the plaintiff's motion to strike one of the defendant's defenses, it is equally the tool of a defendant who wants to move against a defense used by a plaintiff in replying to a counterclaim, of a cross-claiming defendant against a defense interposed to the cross-claim, of a third-party plaintiff against the third-party defendant's defenses, etc.

It may be noted in general that CPLR 3211 does not countenance, or even recognize, any differences among its various grounds as far as evidence is concerned. Pleadings, affidavits, depositions, documentary proof, admissions, letters, and any other papers or proof having an evidentiary impact in the particular situation may generally be considered on any CPLR 3211 motion[1] regardless of its ground.[2] This is so whether the motion contends that the pleading, though adequate on its face, lacks merit or requires dismissal on some other basis, which obviously does require extrinsic proof. If the contention is that the pleading is facially defective as a matter of law and the movant is even willing to concede the truth of the factual allegations of the attacked pleading, extrinsic proof is of course unnecessary. The point is that even in that situation, the proof may be permissible.

An increasing number of motions to dismiss under CPLR 3211 have been denied because the movant neglected to include a copy of the pleadings with the motion. The statute governing motions for summary judgment, CPLR 3212, specifies that "[a] motion for summary judgment shall be supported by affidavit, by a copy of the pleadings and by other available proof, such as depositions and written admissions."[3] Unfortunately, CPLR 3211 contains no similar direction. Yet, many courts have reasonably concluded that the pleadings are "necessary to the consideration of the questions involved" on a CPLR 3211 motion and require that they be included with the motion.[4]

If the one whose claim or defense is being attacked by a CPLR 3211 motion contends that facts adequate to defeat the motion do exist but can't then be stated, that party should explain this to the court in the opposing affidavits. CPLR 3211(d) permits the court in a situation like that to deny the motion without passing on its merits and allow the movant to assert the objection in its responsive pleading. By that means the objection is put off until a later moment in the litigation, by which time the needed evidence will presumably be available. Alternatively, CPLR 3211(d) lets the court retain the motion but adjourn its determination until further affidavits are secured or depositions taken or opportunity otherwise afforded for such other steps as the court may deem appropriate. This provision is applicable even when the additional evidence pertains to a mere jurisdictional objection.

---

[1]   See CPLR 3211(c), adopting for 3211 the evidentiary rule of CPLR 3212(b), governing summary judgment.

[2]   An exception is CPLR 3211(a)(1), treated in § 259.

[3]   CPLR 3212(b).

[4]   See CPLR 2214(c); § 246.

In Peterson v. Spartan Industries, Inc.,[5] for example, P claimed jurisdiction under CPLR 302(a)(1), the "transaction of business" longarm statute,[6] and D moved to dismiss under CPLR 3211(a)(8) on the ground that jurisdiction was lacking because D did not transact business in New York. It was contended that until jurisdiction was established by P, there was not even enough basis to allow P to seek disclosure from D related to jurisdiction. Rejecting that contention, the Court of Appeals sustained the use of CPLR 3211(d) even there and permitted P to use the discovery device,[7] one of the disclosure tools, to aid in garnering evidence to oppose D's CPLR 3211 motion. Not even a prima facie showing of jurisdiction is necessary to sustain such use of CPLR 3211(d), the Court said; the mere making of the CPLR 3211 motion is basis enough to require the defendant to reveal facts relevant to it.[8]

§ 258. The Dismissal Grounds: CPLR 3211(a)

A motion to dismiss a cause of action may not be made on just any ground. It must find authority somewhere. CPLR 3211(a) is the principal somewhere, listing the various grounds on which a dismissal motion may be predicated. Its list is almost exclusive, but not quite. There are a handful of other provisions on which a dismissal motion may be based. The more prominent of these are:

(1) CPLR 327, dismissal for forum non conveniens;

(2) CPLR 3012(b), dismissal of the action for failure to serve a duly demanded complaint;

(3) CPLR 3126, dismissal for failure to comply with disclosure obligations; and

(4) CPLR 3216, dismissal for neglect to prosecute.

With the above exceptions, and perhaps a few others, CPLR 3211(a) and its list of dismissal grounds is just about it.

The grounds listed in CPLR 3211(a) may be raised by motion, but the motion is optional. They may instead be used as defenses in the answer.[1] As will be seen later, most of them may even be divided up, some raised by motion and, if the motion fails, the rest raised by answer.[2]

It is permissible to use CPLR 3211(a) against all claims pleaded, or against one, or a selected few. Indeed, the rule may even be used to dismiss but part of a single cause of action if the part is severable without macerating the whole pleading.[3] Therefore, the CPLR 3211(a) motion is available as to any severable part of a single claim, whether it relates only to the relief clause or to some part of the theory or theories sued on. An example is where P sues D for both compensatory and punitive damages in respect of

---

[5]   Peterson v. Spartan Industries, Inc., 33 N.Y.2d 463, 354 N.Y.S.2d 905, 310 N.E.2d 513 (1974).

[6]   See §§ 84 to 86.

[7]   This device, which comes from CPLR 3120, is one of the most popular of Article 31's disclosure weapons. See § 362.

[8]   *Peterson,* 33 N.Y.2d at 467, 354 N.Y.S.2d at 908, 310 N.E.2d at 515.

[1]   CPLR 3211(e).

[2]   See § 274.

[3]   See Aronov v. Regency Gardens Apartments Corp., 34 A.D.3d 404, 823 N.Y.S.2d 542 (2d Dep't 2006).

the same wrong. The claim for punitive damages is not a separate cause of action.[4] If D can convince the court on a motion under CPLR 3211(a), most likely paragraph 7 for failure to state a cause of action, that the malice needed to sustain the punitive damages award is plainly wanting, the court can dismiss the punitive damages demand while retaining the rest of the case for trial in respect of compensatory damages. Note that in such a situation the court does not technically "dismiss" a claim or part of it, as CPLR 3211(a) formally articulates. It merely strikes out the part of the complaint containing the rejected matter, in this instance the allegations that reflect only on punitive damages as well as the punitive damages demand in the relief clause. This is all permissible procedure under CPLR 3211.

If D is in doubt as to which of the several CPLR 3211(a) grounds might apply in a given case, such as where they seem to overlap, D's rule of thumb is to join all of them. It may happen, for example, that P is purporting to sue in behalf of an estate that he has not been duly appointed to represent. That defect would support an objection under paragraph 3 that P lacks capacity to maintain the action, as well as under paragraph 7 that P is not stating a cause of action belonging to him. Either or both paragraphs can ground the motion.

If the wrong ground is designated on the motion, but some other CPLR 3211(a) ground does apply, the court can treat the motion as having specified the right ground, as long as no prejudice can be claimed. In one case where D based his motion on paragraphs 1, 2, and 8, for example, the court granted it on grounds 3 and 7 instead. The court based its decision on the general relief clause contained in the notice of motion—which all well-drawn motions include[5]—and on the absence of prejudice to P.[6] If P did not have notice of the undesignated grounds from any appropriate source, or if the court is convinced that P's opposing proof would have differed if the intended grounds had been properly designated, the court can of course deny the motion, stay it for further affidavits, etc.

Some of the 11 numbered paragraphs of CPLR 3211(a) are self-explanatory and can be treated succinctly. Others require more extensive comment. With the exception of paragraph 11, which has a narrow mission,[7] the CPLR 3211(a) list is important enough in civil practice to warrant a separate treatment for each entry. The ensuing sections offer that seriatim treatment.

---

[4] Rocanova v. Equitable Life Assur. Soc. of U.S., 83 N.Y.2d 603, 616–17, 612 N.Y.S.2d 339, 344, 634 N.E.2d 940, 945–46 (1994).

[5] See Tirado v. Miller, 75 A.D.3d 153, 901 N.Y.S.2d 358 (2d Dep't 2010); Commentary C2214:5 on McKinney's CPLR 2214. A general relief clause favored by lawyers for its reassuring prolixity is to ask, after reciting the specific relief sought on the motion, for "such other, further, and/or different relief as to the court may seem just and proper." The last clause, too, has the sort of archaic word order and patronizing pomposity that many moving lawyers find moving. Limiting the adjectives and conforming the word order to Modern English Usage are acceptable alternatives, but only in well established law firms.

[6] Nehmadi v. Davis, 95 A.D.3d 1181, 1184, 945 N.Y.S.2d 122, 125 (2d Dep't 2012).

[7] Paragraph 11 was added in 1986, designed to cover only one situation: that in which an uncompensated official of a not-for-profit organization is the defendant and seeks a dismissal of the action based on the absence of gross negligence or harmful intent. Coordinate legislation immunizes such officials from suit unless one or the other of the two elements is present. All this comes from L.1986, ch. 220, and is discussed in Commentary C3211:33 on McKinney's CPLR 3211.

§ 259. Defense Based on "Documentary Evidence"; Paragraph 1

Rather than single out a particular category of objection, as most of the other paragraphs of CPLR 3211(a) do, paragraph 1 permits the dismissal motion whenever the defense is founded on "documentary evidence." This was not a basis for dismissal under pre-CPLR law and there is not much in the legislative history to tell us what qualifies as "documentary" under this paragraph.

When a mortgage and note unambiguously made the property itself the plaintiffs' sole recourse, thereby barring a personal action, the documents were held to suffice under paragraph 1 to support a dismissal of the personal action.[1] A judgment has also been held to be an acceptable document for paragraph 1 purposes.[2] Mortgages, deeds, contracts, and the like would also seem to qualify for use under CPLR 3211(a)(1).[3] Some courts have, however, been stingy in construing what is acceptable under the statute. A paper will only qualify as "documentary evidence" if it satisfies the following criteria: (1) it is unambiguous; (2) it is of undeniable authenticity; and (3) its contents are essentially undeniable.[4] As the caselaw demonstrates, it is difficult to meet this standard. For example, the Second Department has concluded that affidavits, letters, and emails "were not the types of documents contemplated by the Legislature when it enacted" CPLR 3211(a)(1).[5] The First Department has concluded to the contrary, ruling that emails can qualify as "documentary evidence" under the statute if they meet the "essentially undeniable" test.[6] In light of the fact that many courts permit any evidence in admissible form to be submitted in support of a CPLR 3211(a)(7) motion to demonstrate that the plaintiff does not have a cause of action, a defendant relying on an email should consider invoking both subdivisions (a)(1) and (a)(7) in a CPLR 3211 motion.[7]

Even if the "documentary evidence" standard is satisfied, the proof must "utterly refute[ ] plaintiff's factual allegations, conclusively establishing a defense as a matter of law."[8] In Sbarra Real Estate, Inc. v. Lavelle-Tomko,[9] for example, the Third Department

---

[1] Bronxville Knolls, Inc. v. Webster Town Center Partnership, 221 A.D.2d 248, 634 N.Y.S.2d 62 (1st Dep't 1995).

[2] Heaney v. Purdy, 29 N.Y.2d 157, 324 N.Y.S.2d 47, 272 N.E.2d 550 (1971) (proof of judgment in another forum); see Dynamic Medical Imaging P.C. v. State Farm Fire and Cas. Co., 27 Misc. 3d 357, 894 N.Y.S.2d 847 (Dist.Ct., Nassau County 2010).

[3] Anderson v. Armentano, 139 A.D.3d 769, 771, 33 N.Y.S.3d 294, 296 (2d Dep't 2016). Subdivision (d) of CPLR 3212 had a provision about the use of documentary evidence in connection with summary judgment in a matrimonial action. The subdivision was repealed in 1978, but those things that qualified as documents under it should still qualify as documentary evidence under CPLR 3211(a)(1). See Brill v. Brill, 10 N.Y.2d 308, 222 N.Y.S.2d 321, 178 N.E.2d 720 (1961).

[4] See Fontanetta v. Doe, 73 A.D.3d 78, 86, 898 N.Y.S.2d 569, 575 (2d Dep't 2010).

[5] Anderson, 139 A.D.3d at 771, 33 N.Y.S.3d at 296; see JBGR, LLC v. Chicago Title Ins. Co., 128 A.D.3d 900, 11 N.Y.S.3d 83 (2d Dep't 2015).

[6] See Kolchins v. Evolution Markets, Inc., 128 A.D.3d 47, 58–59, 8 N.Y.S.3d 1, 8–9 (1st Dep't 2015); Amsterdam Hospitality Group, LLC v. Marshall-Alan Associates, Inc., 120 A.D.3d 431, 992 N.Y.S.2d 2 (1st Dep't 2014).

[7] See, e.g., Liberty Affordable Housing, Inc. v. Maple Court Apartments, 125 A.D.3d 85, 92, 998 N.Y.S.2d 543, 548 (4th Dep't 2015); Clarke v. Laidlaw Transit, Inc., 125 A.D.3d 920, 923, 5 N.Y.S.3d 138, 142 (2d Dep't 2015); see also Higgitt, McKinney's CPLR Practice Commentaries, CPLR 3211, C3211:27.

[8] Goshen v. Mutual Life Ins. Co. of New York, 98 N.Y.2d 314, 326, 746 N.Y.S.2d 858, 865, 774 N.E.2d 1190, 1197 (2002); see J.P. Morgan Securities Inc. v. Vigilant Ins. Co., 21 N.Y.3d 324, 334, 970 N.Y.S.2d 733, 738, 992 N.E.2d 1076, 1081 (2013).

[9] Sbarra Real Estate, Inc. v. Lavelle-Tomko, 84 A.D.3d 1570, 921 N.Y.S.2d 919 (3d Dep't 2011); see Vaughns v. Kirkland, 85 A.D.3d 770, 924 N.Y.S.2d 845 (2d Dep't 2011) ("[D]etermination of whether the [out-

concluded that the parties' conflicting interpretations of the settlement agreement at issue raised issues of fact requiring further development and denied the CPLR 3211(a)(1) motion to dismiss. The *Sbarra Real Estate* decision demonstrates the relative ease with which a plaintiff can derail a CPLR 3211(a)(1) motion to dismiss.

An additional difficulty is encountered on motions under CPLR 3211(a)(1) because the statute contemplates that the defense will be established by the "documentary evidence" alone. Therefore, affidavits, which are the most common source of proof on most motions and which are available for use on CPLR 3211(a) motions grounded on any other paragraph, can't be made the basis for a paragraph 1 motion. Nor can depositions, apparently. If it turns out that documentary evidence is available, but that affidavit or deposition support is also necessary and that no other CPLR 3211(a) ground appears to be applicable, an alternative for the defendant is to forget about CPLR 3211, serve an answer, and then promptly move for summary judgment under CPLR 3212, where the other papers may be included without difficulty.[10]

The Advisory Committee noted that most of the grounds supported by documentary evidence are in paragraph 5, including estoppel, arbitration and award, and discharge in bankruptcy, and that paragraph 1 was added only to cover something like a defense based on the terms of a written contract.[11] All in all, CPLR 3211(a)(1) has not been very helpful and can't be deemed very important in practice.

§ 260. Subject Matter Jurisdiction; Paragraph 2

Chapter 2 of this book is occupied at length with the courts and their jurisdiction. Whenever a court lacks jurisdiction of the subject matter of a case, the way to raise the objection is by motion to dismiss under CPLR 3211(a)(2). As is true of all the objections listed in CPLR 3211(a), so with this one: it may be taken as a defense in the answer instead of by motion, but the motion is usually the more expeditious route.

There is no time limit for moving to dismiss on the ground of lack of subject matter jurisdiction. The defect is deemed to go to the root of the court's power and, therefore, is never waived and can be raised at any time.[1]

Until 1972, CPLR 3211(a)(2), while phrased in terms of "subject matter" jurisdiction, was also used to raise the objection of forum non conveniens, an objection that also gives rise to a dismissal. Nonetheless, the two categories of objection are not the same.[2] Today, a motion to dismiss on the ground of forum non conveniens is based instead on CPLR 327(a).[3]

§ 261. Lack of Capacity to Sue; Paragraph 3

" 'Capacity[ ]' . . . concerns a litigant's power to appear and bring its grievance before the court."[1] If the party asserting the claim lacks capacity to sue, a motion to dismiss lies

---

of-court prelitigation] settlement agreement was binding on the plaintiff would have been premature at this early stage, and inappropriate in the context of a CPLR 3211 motion.").

10   See CPLR 3212(b); § 281.

11   1st Rep. Leg. Doc. No. 6(b), p. 85 (1957).

1   CPLR 3211(e); see §§ 272, 274.

2   See §§ 28 to 29.

3   The forum non conveniens doctrine is treated in §§ 28–29.

1   Community Bd. 7 of Borough of Manhattan v. Schaffer, 84 N.Y.2d 148, 155, 615 N.Y.S.2d 644, 647, 639 N.E.2d 1, 2 (1994).

under CPLR 3211(a)(3). If an infant, for example, purports to sue pro se or even to retain an attorney—only someone listed in CPLR 1201 can do that for the infant[2]—the infant would lack capacity to sue and this ground of objection could be invoked.

The paragraph 3 objection can sometimes overlap paragraph 7. A trust situation can illustrate this. Where, for example, a plaintiff without even an arguable title or right as a trustee presumes to sue in behalf of the trust, the plaintiff lacks capacity to sue and is subject to the paragraph 3 dismissal. But it would also be true that the complaint, interposed by so irrelevant a person, would fail to state a cause of action, thus invoking the paragraph 7 objection as well. As suggested earlier,[3] the defendant in a situation like that should invoke both grounds in the dismissal motion.

If the plaintiff's capacity to sue depends on status, and the status is disputed, an action brought to clarify the status can't be defeated with the capacity objection. Where, for example, P sued for a declaration that a certain voting trust agreement was valid and that P was its proper trustee, a motion to dismiss on the ground that P lacked capacity to sue as trustee was denied; it was the very matter in issue.[4]

It is sometimes difficult to distinguish between lack of capacity to sue and the conceptually distinct issue of "standing to sue," treated as a separate topic in section 136.[5] The courts have permitted a defendant to challenge a plaintiff's standing by moving under CPLR 3211(a)(3).[6]

§ 262. Other Action Pending; Paragraph 4

Paragraph 4 of CPLR 3211(a) is designed to avoid duplicative litigation. It's one of the more active paragraphs of CPLR 3211(a) and has generated substantial caselaw. It implements its purpose by permitting the court to dismiss the action whenever it is shown that another action between the same parties on the same cause is pending elsewhere. The elsewhere need not be a New York court, moreover; it can be a federal court anywhere in the country or a court in a sister state.

The general rule is that for the instant action to be dismissed because of the other's pendency, the other must have been commenced first[1]—i.e., the race here is usually to the swift—but the rule is not rigid. If the other action was technically commenced first because the summons and notice was filed earlier, for example, but the latter action was commenced with the filing of a summons and complaint and came to issue earlier, it should be permissible to dismiss the other action pursuant to CPLR 3211(a)(4) in deference to the latter one.[2]

Most of the cases under this subdivision were decided before 1992, when service of the initiatory papers marked commencement of the action, but as of 1992 it's the filing

---

[2]   See § 193.

[3]   See § 258.

[4]   Kittinger v. Churchill Evangelistic Ass'n, 239 A.D. 253, 267 N.Y.S. 719 (4th Dep't 1933).

[5]   See and note also the Court of Appeals 2008 decision in Landau v. LaRossa, Mitchell & Ross, 11 N.Y.3d 8, 862 N.Y.S.2d 316, 892 N.E.2d 380 (2008) (NYSLD No. 584).

[6]   Wells Fargo Bank Minnesota, Nat. Ass'n v. Mastropaolo, 42 A.D.3d 239, 243, 837 N.Y.S.2d 247, 250 (2d Dep't 2007) ("[S]tanding and capacity to sue are sufficiently related that they should be afforded identical treatment.").

[1]   Izquierdo v. Cities Service Oil Co. (Pa.), 47 Misc. 2d 1087, 264 N.Y.S.2d 58, 1966 A.M.C. 381 (Sup. Ct., Kings County 1965); see Montalvo v. Air Dock Systems, 37 A.D.3d 567, 830 N.Y.S.2d 255 (2d Dep't 2007).

[2]   Wharton v. Wharton, 244 A.D.2d 404, 664 N.Y.S.2d 73 (2d Dep't 1997).

of those papers that marks commencement, so that the action filed first would today be the action commenced first.[3]

To invoke CPLR 3211(a)(4), it should be shown that the two causes are essentially the same. If they aren't, there is no duplication and the purpose of the provision falls. If the only difference between the two actions is that the relief demand differs, but it appears that the relief demanded in either action could by amendment be demanded in the other, the motion to dismiss should be granted.[4] If the action moved upon involves more than the other one does, however, and the other can't be made to do as much, the dismissal should be denied.[5] When the earlier action is quasi in rem, for example, and its judgment will be good only to the extent of attached property, the subsequent in personam suit, which is not subject to such a limitation, will not be dismissed.[6]

If in the earlier action by P against D, D interposes a counterclaim and then commences a separate action (D v. P) on that claim, D's action is dismissible under this provision: the claim in the earlier context can be a counterclaim instead of a main claim if the requirements of paragraph 4 are otherwise met.[7]

Dismissal on this ground does not ordinarily lie before at least the complaint is served in the present action, and the pleadings relevant to the inquiry should also have been served in the other action because only then can the court determine the identity of the cause. An action in which only a summons and notice are initially served is therefore not likely to be treated as a prior pending action for CPLR 3211(a)(4) purposes until the complaint has been served.[8] Hence, if no complaint has yet been served in the other action, a paragraph 4 motion in the instant action proposing to defer to the other is at best premature.[9]

There should also be a substantial identity of parties.[10] If the present parties are also parties to the prior suit, this requirement would be met, but if there are additional parties in the instant action and it appears that it will thus afford broader relief than the other, the court may take this into consideration. If the parties are not the same, even though the two lawsuits have pretty much the same purpose, the court may be disinclined to apply paragraph 4 and dismiss because it may in effect leave the parties in the dismissed action to depend on whatever representation the other parties have secured in the other action. Where stockholder X brought a derivative action in the corporate behalf against certain directors, for example, and stockholder Y brought a

---

[3]   For discussion of the effect of the filing system on determining which of two competing actions is to be accorded priority on an application under CPLR 3211(a)(4), see Kevorkian v. Harrington, 158 Misc. 2d 464, 601 N.Y.S.2d 522 (Sup. Ct., New York County 1993) (SPR 9:3), and D'Gani v. Dagani, N.Y.L.J., May 22, 1995, at 27, col.4 (Sup. Ct., New York County; Silbermann, J.) (SPR 39:3).

[4]   See Falzerano v. DeLuca, 154 A.D.2d 431, 545 N.Y.S.2d 930 (2d Dep't 1989); Stanley Elec. Service, Inc. v. City of New York, 26 A.D.2d 951, 275 N.Y.S.2d 222 (2d Dep't 1966).

[5]   See Safier v. Cohl, 95 A.D.2d 933, 463 N.Y.S.2d 937 (3d Dep't 1983).

[6]   See Tjepkema v. Kenney, 59 Misc. 2d 670, 299 N.Y.S.2d 943 (Sup. Ct., New York County 1969); see § 104.

[7]   Frank Pompea, Inc. v. Essayan, 36 A.D.2d 745, 320 N.Y.S.2d 441 (2d Dep't 1971); Donenfeld v. Brilliant Technologies Corp., 20 Misc. 3d 1139(A), 872 N.Y.S.2d 690 (Sup. Ct., New York County 2008).

[8]   *Wharton*, 244 A.D.2d at 405, 664 N.Y.S.2d at 73; John J. Campagna, Jr., Inc. v. Dune Alpin Farm Associates, 81 A.D.2d 633, 438 N.Y.S.2d 132 (2d Dep't 1981).

[9]   See United Enterprises, Ltd. v. Hill, 185 A.D.2d 206, 587 N.Y.S.2d 160 (1st Dep't 1992); Louis R. Shapiro, Inc. v. Milspemes Corp., 20 A.D.2d 857, 248 N.Y.S.2d 85 (1st Dep't 1964).

[10]   Barringer v. Zgoda, 91 A.D.2d 811, 458 N.Y.S.2d 42 (3d Dep't 1982).

similar derivative action, the second action was not dismissed but instead consolidated with the first.[11]

Consolidation is possible instead of dismissal because the court has a broad range of discretion, and as a result a whole bag of other tools, in disposing of a motion under paragraph 4. The paragraph says that "the court need not dismiss . . . but may make such order as justice requires." If both actions are pending in New York courts, for example, consolidation or joint trial is permissible and in many instances preferable to dismissal.[12] Consolidation and joint trial ordinarily require a motion by one of the parties, but as an alternative to dismissal on a paragraph 4 motion, the court can order it sua sponte.[13] Neither consolidation nor joint trial should be ordered, however, unless all parties to all actions affected have been notified.[14]

A stay instead of a dismissal is another permissible alternative under the discretion afforded by paragraph 4. A stay can be especially appropriate when the action to which the instant one is asked to defer is pending outside the state, whether in another state's court or in a federal court. While permissible under paragraph 4, an outright dismissal would surrender, or in any event impede, the New York court's ability to lend its aid if some unforeseen difficulty should later arise in connection with the other action. Therefore, a stay may be preferable in these circumstances. When a stay is used, later difficulties in the action pending in another forum can permit the New York action to proceed to provide whatever aid may be appropriate, through the simple expedient of a motion to vacate the stay.

CPLR 2201 is the CPLR's general authorization for the issuance of stays,[15] supplying the courts this power in a brief but sweeping statement. It may therefore be viewed as the authority for a stay even under CPLR 3211(a)(4), but in paragraph 4 cases it isn't needed because the provision's "such order as justice requires" language would independently support a stay in many contexts. One in which it would not, however, is where the other action is pending in a court of a foreign country, a situation to which paragraph 4 doesn't apply. CPLR 2201 can be turned to as authority in that instance, staying the instant action in deference to the foreign one.[16] That would be done, of course, only when the foreign forum appears by just about all standards to be the more appropriate one. If it is, a stay of the present action would be the most that could be granted in these circumstances. Absent an outright forum non conveniens objection to the New York action, there would be no authority to dismiss it merely because of the pendency of a similar one in a foreign nation.

If both actions are pending in New York courts, yet another alternative is available to a court pursuant to its powers to "make such order as justice requires": an order directing the discontinuance of one of them. In one case, it was the first action that was

---

[11]   Dresdner v. Goldman Sachs Trading Corp., 240 A.D. 242, 269 N.Y.S. 360 (2d Dep't 1934). Statements in the *Dresdner* case about dismissal being precluded if the other action is in a federal court or a court in another state no longer apply under CPLR 3211(a)(4).

[12]   See, e.g., Reckson Associates Realty Corp. v. Blasland, Bouck & Lee, Inc., 230 A.D.2d 723, 645 N.Y.S.2d 873 (2d Dep't 1996). For the distinctions between consolidation and joint trial, see §§ 127–28.

[13]   *John J. Campagna, Jr.,* 81 A.D.2d at 634, 438 N.Y.S.2d at 133; Marcus v. Antell, 2013 WL 6179284 (Sup. Ct., New York County 2013).

[14]   Kent Development Co., Inc. v. Liccione, 37 N.Y.2d 899, 378 N.Y.S.2d 377, 340 N.E.2d 740 (1975).

[15]   See § 255.

[16]   See Commentary C2201:10 on McKinney's CPLR 2201.

ordered discontinued and the second allowed to stand, both having been brought in the same court.[17] Dispositions under CPLR 3211(a)(4) can also be conditional.

If the defendant tries to play games with this provision, he may find the court wanting in team spirit. Suppose, for example, that after D moves to dismiss the first action for lack of jurisdiction over D, P commences a precautionary second action while the motion is pending. Then suppose that D moves to dismiss the second action on the ground of the pendency of the first. The motion will be denied,[18] in effect working an estoppel against D, and a sanction may even be imposed on D for what the courts deem duplicitous conduct.[19] Alternatively, the court can stay the present action to see what happens with the jurisdictional motion in the first. If the first is dismissed, the second can then be continued. If the motion to dismiss the first is denied, the second can then be dismissed.

Suppose that the New York action has been brought just as a precautionary back-up to an action elsewhere, lest the statute of limitations or a problem of jurisdiction be held to bar the action in that other place. Will New York allow itself to be used as a kind of holding action in that situation? The Court of Appeals indicated yes in Flintkote Co. v. American Mut. Liab. Ins. Co.,[20] discussing the use of a stay to keep the New York action alive lest some "unforeseen difficulty should arise in connection with the other [foreign] action." Further indications appeared to similar effect.[21] An extensive address to the issue appears in Rye Psychiatric Hospital Center, Inc. v. State of New York.[22]

Federal practice has no statute precisely the same as paragraph 4 of CPLR 3211(a). Guidance for what a federal court would do when the equivalent of a CPLR 3211(a)(4) motion is made before it—to dismiss or stay the federal action in deference to a state court action, for example—is found principally in caselaw.[23]

§ 263. Affirmative Defenses Usable on Dismissal Motion; Paragraph 5

Most of the objections listed in paragraph 5 are those officially denominated as affirmative defenses by CPLR 3018(b). At the defendant's option, they may be raised on a CPLR 3211(a)(5) dismissal motion instead of being pleaded as defenses in the answer. The defenses for which the option is offered are:

---

[17] Dunn v. Dunn, 86 A.D.2d 772, 448 N.Y.S.2d 277 (4th Dep't 1982); Cogen Properties, Ltd. v. Griffin, 78 Misc. 2d 936, 358 N.Y.S.2d 929 (Sup. Ct., Sullivan County 1974).

[18] Clark v. Bilt-Rite Land Corp., 82 Misc. 2d 1026, 372 N.Y.S.2d 466 (Sup. Ct., Orange County 1975).

[19] See Scheichet & Davis v. Sukoff, Sup. Ct., New York County, Aug. 12, 1991 (Index No. 8056/90, per Cohen, J.) (SPR 149:3), finding the defendant's conduct frivolous and imposing a money sanction of $500 pursuant to Rule 130–1. For treatment on Rule 130–1, see § 414A.

[20] Flintkote Co. v. American Mut. Liability Ins. Co., 67 N.Y.2d 857, 501 N.Y.S.2d 662, 492 N.E.2d 790 (1986), affirming on the appellate division opinion in Flintkote Co. v. American Mut. Liability Ins. Co., 103 A.D.2d 501, 480 N.Y.S.2d 742 (2d Dep't 1984).

[21] See Houston v. Trans Union Credit Information Co., 154 A.D.2d 312, 546 N.Y.S.2d 600 (1st Dep't 1989); Hollendonner v. Kiem, 138 A.D.2d 230, 525 N.Y.S.2d 43 (1st Dep't 1988); and the lead note in NYSLD No. 364.

[22] Rye Psychiatric Hospital Center, Inc. v. State of New York, N.Y. Ct. Cl., Motion No. M-42081, July 3, 1990 (Margolis, J.).

[23] See, e.g., Moses H. Cone Memorial Hosp. v. Mercury Constr. Corp., 460 U.S. 1, 103 S. Ct. 927, 74 L. Ed. 2d 765 (1983), and Wilton v. Seven Falls Co., 515 U.S. 277, 115, 115 S. Ct. 2137, 132 L. Ed. 2d 214 (1995), major addresses to the issue. The *Mercury* case and the situation in general is the subject of the lead note in NYSLD No. 281.

arbitration and award

collateral estoppel

discharge in bankruptcy

infancy or other disability of the moving party

payment

release

res judicata

statute of limitations

statute of frauds

Only three of the CPLR 3018(b) defenses are not adopted by CPLR 3211(a)(5): comparative negligence (that the plaintiff was guilty of culpable conduct), illegality, and fraud. The illegality defense can nonetheless be squeezed under CPLR 3211(a)(7) because if the claim is illegal, a motion would lie to dismiss it for failure to state a cause of action. That leaves the culpable conduct and fraud defenses as the only two on the CPLR 3018(b) list that are not imported for alternative motion use by CPLR 3211(a)(5). The reason for the omission is that the two almost invariably involve issues of fact that make them inappropriate for the matter-of-law treatment that CPLR 3211(a) contemplates. Furthermore, a plaintiff's comparative fault does not require dismissal of the action, as it did under the reign of contributory negligence.

That issues of fact on a fraud claim are too subjective for cursory motion disposition does not prevent fraud from sneaking back for CPLR 3211 treatment in other guises, however,[1] but even when it does it is not likely suitable to the cursory disposition that CPLR 3211 has in mind. The issues are likely to generate a denial of the motion and be saved for resolution at the trial later.

Other affirmative defenses—besides those listed in CPLR 3018(b), whose list is not exhaustive[2]—may not be used on a dismissal motion under CPLR 3211 unless one of the objections listed in 3211(a) can somehow be made to cover it. That's sometimes possible. The affirmative defense of the election of remedies, for example, essentially a member of the "res judicata" family, can be fitted under that objection.[3]

---

[1] Allowing fraud to become the dispositive issue through any CPLR 3211 channel is of course inconsistent with the reason for not including the defense of fraud in paragraph 5 in the first place, but other channels do exist. If the defendant raises the defense of fraud in the answer, for example, the plaintiff can move to strike the defense under CPLR 3211(b). Fraud can also become the key issue in conjunction with some other objection raised under CPLR 3211(a). D may claim release under paragraph 5, for example, and P, in response, may contend that the release was procured by fraud. See Barker v. Conley, 267 N.Y. 43, 195 N.E. 677 (1935); see e.g., Farber v. Breslin, 47 A.D.3d 873, 877, 850 N.Y.S.2d 604, 608 (2d Dep't 2008) ("a motion to dismiss should be denied where fraud or duress in the procurement of the release is alleged.").

[2] See § 223.

[3] See Merrick v. Merrick, 163 Misc. 2d 929, 934, 622 N.Y.S.2d 852, 855 (Sup. Ct., New York County 1995), aff'd, 225 A.D.2d 491, 639 N.Y.S.2d 818 (1st Dep't 1996); cf. Incorporated Village of Laurel Hollow v. Laverne, Inc., 43 Misc. 2d 248, 250 N.Y.S.2d 951 (Sup. Ct., Nassau County 1964), modified, 24 A.D.2d 615, 262 N.Y.S.2d 622 (2d Dep't 1965).

The "arbitration and award" that constitutes the first item on the paragraph 5 list requires a showing that arbitration has already been had and gone to award.[4] Only then is a dismissal of the action, presumably brought in disregard of the award, the proper remedy.[5] If a defendant, sued in court on a claim that the defendant maintains is arbitrable, wants to compel its arbitration, the remedy is not a dismissal motion under CPLR 3211(a)(5), but a motion to stay the action and compel arbitration under CPLR 7503(a).[6]

The "infancy or other disability" listed in paragraph 5 refers to the defendant's disability; paragraph 3, dealing with "incapacity to sue," is concerned with the plaintiff's disability.

The courts have frequently observed that on a CPLR 3211(a)(5) motion to dismiss a claim on statute of limitations grounds, the moving party "must establish, prima facie, that the time in which to commence the action has expired. The burden then shifts to the [opponent] to raise an issue of fact as to whether the statute of limitations is tolled or is otherwise inapplicable."[7] For example, in Ross v. Jamaica Hosp. Medical Center,[8] the defendants established, prima facie, that the two and one half year statute of limitations for medical malpractice in CPLR 214–a had elapsed. In opposition, the plaintiff failed to raise a triable issue of fact as to whether the statute of limitations was tolled pursuant to CPLR 205(a) and the action was dismissed.[9]

§ 264. Non-Interposable Counterclaim; Paragraph 6

The various grounds listed in CPLR 3211(a) may be used against any affirmatively pleaded cause of action, with the exception of paragraph 6, which is concerned with only a counterclaim. Paragraph 6 is the ground invoked when a counterclaim has been interposed in violation of the "capacity" rule. A counterclaim may be interposed by or against a party only in the capacity in which that party is present in the case. If the plaintiff is a partnership, for example, the defendant may interpose only a counterclaim that lies against the partnership. A claim existing against only one of the partners, personally, would not be usable.[1] Should the defendant attempt to use it, the plaintiff's remedy would be a motion to dismiss the counterclaim under CPLR 3211(a)(6).

Although a counterclaim that violates the capacities rule may be dismissed under paragraph 6, and any counterclaim in the case is subject to dismissal on any of the other grounds listed in CPLR 3211(a), there is no authority under the CPLR to dismiss an otherwise valid counterclaim merely because it is not convenient to have it present in

---

[4]   Marracino v. Alexander, 73 A.D.3d 22, 23, 897 N.Y.S.2d 555, 556 (4th Dep't 2010) (noting that an arbitration award may not serve as the foundation of the defense of "arbitration and award" unless the award is subject to confirmation pursuant to CPLR article 75).

[5]   *Marracino,* 73 A.D.3d at 23, 897 N.Y.S.2d at 556; Langemyr v. Campbell, 23 A.D.2d 371, 261 N.Y.S.2d 500 (2d Dep't 1965).

[6]   See § 592 (Practitioner's Edition).

[7]   Baptiste v. Harding-Marin, 88 A.D.3d 752, 930 N.Y.S.2d 670 (2d Dep't 2011).

[8]   Ross v. Jamaica Hosp. Medical Center, 122 A.D.3d 607, 996 N.Y.S.2d 118 (2d Dep't 2014).

[9]   See also Farage v. Ehrenberg, 124 A.D.3d 159, 996 N.Y.S.2d 646 (2d Dep't 2014), lv. denied, 25 N.Y.3d 906, 10 N.Y.S.3d 525, 32 N.E.3d 962 (2015) (applying similar burdens of proof in legal malpractice action in which continuous representation toll was unsuccessfully asserted).

[1]   See § 225.

the case. Such authority did exist under prior law,[2] but the worst that can befall such a counterclaim under the CPLR is a severance, sending it off as a separate action.

§ 265. Failure to State a Cause of Action; Paragraph 7

One of the most important and frequently used dismissal grounds is the failure to state a cause of action of paragraph 7. The motion of course lies if the pleading is defective on its face, and in that respect it's the equivalent of the old common law demurrer (presumably long since abandoned in New York), which conceded the truth of everything pleaded but contended that, even so, the pleading stated nothing actionable under the law.

More important under the CPLR is that the paragraph 7 motion may be made even against a claim perfectly pleaded.[1] At least the way the CPLR's drafters envisioned it, the motion may—upon affidavits and the same kind of other proof that might be used on any CPLR 3211 motion—go behind the pleading and prove that the claim, although artfully stated, lacks merit. Since pleadings have been so successfully informalized by the CPLR,[2] so that it does not take much to successfully "state" a cause of action, the paragraph 7 motion is used more often today to attack the merits of the claim than to attack its articulation. Of course, in order to succeed on the motion, the defendant must convince the court that nothing the plaintiff can reasonably be expected to prove would help; that the plaintiff just doesn't have a claim. The criterion for determining such a motion is akin to that used to decide a motion for summary judgment.[3] Therefore, the court may under CPLR 3211(c) treat the motion as such if the court is so disposed and the proof warrants it.[4]

What if the court elects not to treat a CPLR 3211(a)(7) motion as one for summary judgment under CPLR 3211(c)? Is there any way to get behind the well-dressed pleading and expose the weakness in the proof? The Court of Appeals decision in Rovello v. Orofino Realty Co., Inc.[5] held that as long as the complaint states a claim on its face, the plaintiff need not—in response to the defendant's paragraph 7 objection—come forward with affidavits or other proof unless the court does in fact elect to treat the motion as one for summary judgment under CPLR 3211(c).

The *Rovello* rule has resulted in many decisions holding that the court cannot even *consider* the defendant's affidavits on a CPLR 3211(a)(7) motion unless and until it has elected to exercise its treat-as-summary-judgment power.[6] Yet, New York appellate courts reviewing orders emanating from pre-answer motions to dismiss under CPLR 3211(a)(7) have also recognized that it may be appropriate, in limited circumstances, to

---

[2]   Civ. Prac. Act § 262 (repealed 1963). See Jayell Films v. A.F.E. Corp., 67 N.Y.S.2d 77 (Sup. Ct., New York County 1946).

[1]   Tender Loving Care Agency, Inc. v. Hladun, 111 A.D.2d 162, 488 N.Y.S.2d 790 (2d Dep't 1985).

[2]   Foley v. D'Agostino, 21 A.D.2d 60, 248 N.Y.S.2d 121 (1st Dep't 1964); see Camarda v. Vanderbilt, 100 A.D.2d 836, 473 N.Y.S.2d 831 (2d Dep't 1984); § 208.

[3]   In some respects, the CPLR 3211(a)(7) motion not aimed at only the face of the pleading is like a short-cut to summary judgment, the motion that CPLR 3212 supplies only after the joinder of issue. A CPLR 3211 motion doesn't have to wait for that. See § 272.

[4]   See CPLR 3211(c); § 270.

[5]   Rovello v. Orofino Realty Co., Inc., 40 N.Y.2d 633, 389 N.Y.S.2d 314, 357 N.E.2d 970 (1976).

[6]   See, e.g., Henbest & Morrisey Inc. v. W.H. Ins. Agency Inc., 259 A.D.2d 829, 686 N.Y.S.2d 207 (3d Dep't 1999), which, citing *Rovello*, holds that on the CPLR 3211(a)(7) motion the complaint must be judged exclusively on its face; the court can't even consider affidavits.

consider a defendant's affidavits even if the court does not elect to treat the motion as one for summary judgment under CPLR 3211(c).[7] This line of cases can be traced to language in the *Rovello* decision, which states that "affidavits submitted by the defendant will *seldom* if ever warrant the relief he seeks *unless too the affidavits establish conclusively that plaintiff has no cause of action*."[8]

Almost four decades later, the Court reaffirmed the *Rovello* rule in Miglino v. Bally Total Fitness of Greater New York, Inc.,[9] where it stated that it was limited "to an examination of the pleadings to determine whether they state a cause of action" on a motion under CPLR 3211(a)(7). Citing *Rovello*, the *Miglino* Court concluded that where the defendant does not move for summary judgment, a "plaintiff may not be penalized for failure to make an evidentiary showing in support of a complaint that states a claim on its face."[10] Unfortunately, the *Miglino* Court did not expressly address or distinguish the caselaw that has permitted consideration of defendant's evidentiary affidavits on a pure CPLR 3211(a)(7) motion to dismiss for failure to state a cause of action, including its own decision in Guggenheimer v. Ginzburg.[11] The question of whether this line of caselaw has been impliedly overruled by *Miglino* has been raised in recent appeals before the appellate division, but the decisions are not of one mind on the subject.[12]

This discussion might lead defendants to assume that they should not even bother submitting affidavits on a CPLR 3211(a)(7) motion, but they should make no such assumption unless, of course, it is their intention to test only the face of the complaint.[13] A suggestion to the defendant who wants to go beyond the face of the pleadings, attack the plaintiff's claim on the merits, and flush out a merits response from the plaintiff without facing the peculiarities of the *Rovello* rule is to serve an answer and then move outright for summary judgment under CPLR 3212, where affidavits may of course be included and must be considered by the court in this context.

For purposes of a paragraph 7 motion, especially when it attacks the pleading on its face, the allegations of the pleading are deemed to be true. More than that, the pleading will be deemed to allege whatever may be implied from its statements by reasonable intendment.[14] In sum, the pleader is entitled to every favorable inference that might be drawn.[15]

While the general rule about the CPLR 3211(a) objections is that any of them can at the defendant's option be used as a defense in the answer instead of being taken by

---

[7]   See John R. Higgitt, *CPLR 3211(a)(7): Demurrer or Merits-Testing Device?*, 73 Alb. L. Rev. 99 (2009); SPR 97:4.

[8]   *Rovello,* 40 N.Y.2d at 636 (emphasis added); see also Guggenheimer v. Ginzburg, 43 N.Y.2d 268, 275, 401 N.Y.S.2d 182, 185, 372 N.E.2d 17, 20 (1977) ("When evidentiary material is considered [on a CPLR 3211(a)(7) pre-answer motion to dismiss], the criterion is whether the proponent of the pleading has a cause of action, not whether he has stated one . . . .").

[9]   Miglino v. Bally Total Fitness of Greater New York, Inc., 20 N.Y.3d 342, 961 N.Y.S.2d 364, 985 N.E.2d 128 (2013).

[10]   *Miglino,* 20 N.Y.3d at 351, 961 N.Y.S.2d at 370, 985 N.E.2d at 134.

[11]   Guggenheimer v. Ginzburg, 43 N.Y.2d 268, 401 N.Y.S.2d 182, 372 N.E.2d 17 (1977).

[12]   See Patrick M. Connors, *Courts Reconsider Rule Permitting Use of Affidavits on CPLR 3211(a)(7) Motion,* 253 (no. 12) N.Y.L.J. (Jan. 20, 2015).

[13]   See the discussion in §§ 270 and 275, and in the lead note in NYSLD No. 353.

[14]   *Camarda,* 100 A.D.2d at 836, 473 N.Y.S.2d at 832.

[15]   Underpinning & Foundation Constructors, Inc. v. Chase Manhattan Bank, N.A., 46 N.Y.2d 459, 462, 414 N.Y.S.2d 298, 299, 386 N.E.2d 1319, 1320 (1979); Natixis Real Estate Capital Trust 2007-HE2 v. Natixis Real Estate Holdings, LLC, 149 A.D.3d 127, 50 N.Y.S.3d 13 (1st Dep't 2017).

motion under CPLR 3211,[16] there was some doubt about whether this was true of the paragraph 7 objection of failure to state a cause of action. That objection is implicit in the very fact that there's a lawsuit, a tune imbedded in the vocal chords of just about every defendant. The Second Department had held that the objection cannot be stated in the answer and that the plaintiff may therefore move to strike such a defense under CPLR 3211(b).[17] The court reversed itself in Butler v. Catinella,[18] however, and adopted the First Department position, which is that the inclusion of the defense in the answer is surplusage at worst and that no motion by the plaintiff lies under CPLR 3211(b) to strike the defense.[19] Such a motion would, in effect, "amount[ ] to an endeavor by the plaintiff to test the sufficiency of his or her own claim."[20] Furthermore, the objection is so fundamental that the defendant can raise it at any time during the action, whether pleaded as a defense in the answer or not.[21]

The relief clause is of no great consequence on a CPLR 3211(a)(7) motion. As long as the complaint as a whole manifests a cause of action recognizable under the law, it is of no moment that the wrong relief is sought.[22]

It has also been held that if there are several claims alleged, and any one of them is sufficient, a paragraph 7 motion aimed at the whole pleading will be denied in its entirety.[23] The lesson to be derived from these cases is that when making a CPLR 3211(a)(7) motion, the movant should single out the allegedly defective claims and aim the motion at each one. It is always best to treat each cause of action separately in the affidavits, affirmations, and memorandum of law submitted in support of the motion. In this regard, the First Department has held that "[w]here a motion to dismiss for failure to state a cause of action particularizes each of the claims in the complaint, even though it is nominally addressed to the complaint as a whole, the court should treat that motion as applying to each individual cause of action alleged" and not simply deny the motion in its entirety if one claim is sufficient.[24]

As we discuss above, CPLR 2214(c) requires that the moving party furnish all of the papers to the court necessary for the consideration of the motion.[25] Courts will often rely upon CPLR 2214(c) to deny a CPLR 3211(a)(7) motion when the moving party fails to annex a copy of the pleading it seeks to dismiss.[26] What if the opponent on the motion

---

[16]   See § 258.

[17]   See, e.g., Bentivegna v. Meenan Oil Co., Inc., 126 A.D.2d 506, 510 N.Y.S.2d 626 (2d Dep't 1987).

[18]   Butler v. Catinella, 58 A.D.3d 145, 868 N.Y.S.2d 101 (2d Dep't 2008) (SPR 204:2).

[19]   Riland v. Frederick S. Todman & Co., 56 A.D.2d 350, 393 N.Y.S.2d 4 (1st Dep't 1977).

[20]   *Butler,* 58 A.D.3d at 150, 868 N.Y.S.2d at 105.

[21]   See CPLR 3211(e); §§ 269, 272. The subject is treated in the lead note in NYSLD No. 333.

[22]   Planned Consumer Marketing, Inc. v. Coats & Clark, Inc., 127 A.D.2d 355, 371, 513 N.Y.S.2d 417, 427 (1st Dep't 1987), aff'd, 71 N.Y.2d 442, 527 N.Y.S.2d 185, 522 N.E.2d 30 (1988); State v. Ole Olsen, Limited, 65 Misc. 2d 366, 317 N.Y.S.2d 538 (Sup. Ct., Westchester County 1971), aff'd, 38 A.D.2d 967, 331 N.Y.S.2d 761 (2d Dep't 1972).

[23]   See, e.g., Long Island Diagnostic Imaging, P.C. v. Stony Brook Diagnostic Associates, 215 A.D.2d 450, 626 N.Y.S.2d 828 (2d Dep't 1995); Great Northern Associates, Inc. v. Continental Cas. Co., 192 A.D.2d 976, 978, 596 N.Y.S.2d 938, 940 (3d Dep't 1993).

[24]   Gamiel v. Curtis & Riess-Curtis, P.C., 16 A.D.3d 140, 791 N.Y.S.2d 78 (1st Dep't 2005); see Recovery Racing, LLC v. Sunrise Motors, LLC, 10 Misc. 3d 1053(A), 809 N.Y.S.2d 483 (Sup. Ct., Nassau County 2005) ("Where the motion addresses each of the claims, the court will treat that motion 'as applying to each individual cause of action alleged.' ").

[25]   See § 246.

[26]   See 1501 Corp. v. Leilenok Realty Corp., 2015 WL 2344489 (Sup. Ct., Queens County 2015); Gibbs v. Kings Auto Show Inc., 47 Misc. 3d 1203(A), 15 N.Y.S.3d 711 (Sup. Ct., Kings County 2015).

submits the pleading that is being attacked? In Thompson v. Iannucci,[27] the court ruled that the mere fact that the opposition attached the pleading being attacked did not satisfy the burden of the moving party under CPLR 2214(c) and denied defendants' CPLR 3211(a)(7) motion to dismiss as "procedurally deficient." While CPLR 3211 does not expressly state the papers that need to be submitted on a motion to dismiss, the moving party must be sure to include any pleading that is being attacked.[28]

For the lawyer who finds federal comparisons helpful, CPLR 3211(a)(7) is the counterpart of Rule 12(b)(6) of the Federal Rules of Civil Procedure. That rule uses the terminology "failure to state a claim upon which relief can be granted"; the CPLR language is "fails to state a cause of action." Pleading requirements in federal courts became far more demanding than those in New York State courts after a pair of recent United States Supreme Court decisions.[29]

§ 266. Lack of Personal Jurisdiction; Paragraph 8

Whenever it's contended that the court lacks personal jurisdiction of the defendant, a dismissal motion lies under CPLR 3211(a)(8). If the lack of jurisdiction affects the whole complaint, as where the defendant maintains that he was never served with process, the motion seeks dismissal of the entire action. If it affects only a given claim, as where the defendant was served outside New York and one claim has a basis for extraterritorial service under CPLR 302 and 313, but another has not, the motion seeks to strike only the latter.

The motion lies whatever the nature of the defect, as long as the defect goes to personal jurisdiction. It lies if the claim has a basis for extraterritorial jurisdiction, but service was improper, or where service was proper, but made beyond the state without an extraterritorial basis. It applies where the initiatory papers are sufficient, but were not properly filed[1] or properly served,[2] or where the service is good, but the papers are defective.[3] It applies even when the initiatory papers are well drawn and served by a proper means within the state, but the enticement or immunity doctrine applies to bar personal jurisdiction.[4]

If the initiatory papers consist of a summons and CPLR 305(b) notice[5] and the notice or its method of service is defective, the paragraph 8 motion lies before a complaint is served. But if the complaint must be seen in order to determine a jurisdictional defect, such as where the plaintiff bases jurisdiction on a longarm statute and an investigation

---

[27] Thompson v. Iannucci, 50 Misc. 3d 1226(A), 36 N.Y.S.3d 50 (Sup. Ct., Ulster County 2015).

[28] Compare CPLR 3212(b) (specifying that "[a] motion for summary judgment shall be supported by affidavit, by a copy of the pleadings and by other available proof, such as depositions and written admissions."); see § 281.

[29] See Bell Atlantic Corp. v. Twombly, 550 U.S. 544, 127 S. Ct. 1955, 167 L. Ed. 2d 929 (2007); Ashcroft v. Iqbal, 556 U.S. 662, 129 S. Ct. 1937, 173 L. Ed. 2d 868 (2009); § 631 (Practitioners Edition).

[1] See § 63.

[2] See §§ 66 to 76A.

[3] In this regard, CPLR 3211(a)(8) is more comprehensive than its federal counterpart. Rule 12(b) of the Federal Rules of Civil Procedure lists as separate grounds lack of jurisdiction over the person, insufficiency of process, and insufficiency of service of process, all of which fall under the simple "jurisdiction of the person" category of CPLR 3211(a)(8). See § 628 (Practitioner's Edition).

[4] See §§ 67 and 68.

[5] See § 60.

of the claim is required in order to determine its New York contacts, the motion does not lie until after the complaint has been served.[6]

For tactical reasons, a defendant sometimes prefers to include an objection to personal jurisdiction as a defense in the answer instead of taking it by motion under CPLR 3211(a). If the action was timely commenced, but just barely, postponing the adjudication of the objection can, if it prevails, bring on a dismissal of the action too late for the plaintiff to start over. The plaintiff had best be alert to this.[7]

When the specific objection on the CPLR 3211(8) motion is improper service, a special rule in CPLR 3211(e) governs. If the defendant takes the objection as a defense in the answer, the defendant must move for judgment on it within 60 days from service of the answer or the objection is waived.[8] The court may grant a discretionary extension of this 60-day period, but only upon a showing of "undue hardship," a strict standard that has been held more demanding than the "good cause" showing that can earn time extensions in other contexts.[9]

Note that the 60-day rule applies only to the objection of improper service, which is just one of several specific objections that fall under the category of "jurisdiction of the person." In the aftermath of the Supreme Court's 2014 decision in Daimler AG v. Bauman,[10] which severely circumscribes the availability of general jurisdiction over a corporation, we suspect that many corporate defendants will make motions to dismiss based on a lack of jurisdictional basis over them in New York. In that this aspect of personal jurisdiction is not subject to the 60-day rule in CPLR 3211(e), it can be raised on a motion for summary judgment made within the deadlines set in CPLR 3212(a) as long as the affirmative defense is pleaded in the answer.[11] Similarly, if the defense of lack of personal jurisdiction is based on an improper filing of the initiatory papers,[12] the 60-day rule does not apply.

§ 267. Lack of Rem Jurisdiction; Paragraph 9

CPLR 3211(a)(9) refers to an objection to jurisdiction in a case in which service was made under CPLR 314 or 315. The reference means rem jurisdiction, which is governed by those provisions. Whenever rem jurisdiction of any kind is what the pleader is relying on, and the defendant maintains that even that jurisdiction is lacking for some reason (location of the res, failure of an attachment, defect in the summons, lack of summons service, etc.), the motion to dismiss is grounded on paragraph 9 of CPLR 3211(a).

Paragraph 9 can be safely made the sole ground of the motion only when the movant, D, is sure that personal jurisdiction is not even arguably present and that rem jurisdiction is the sole kind claimed. If there is any doubt whatever about the kind of jurisdiction the plaintiff is asserting, the defendant is wise to base the dismissal motion

---

[6]   Fraley v. Desilu Productions, Inc., 23 A.D.2d 79, 258 N.Y.S.2d 294 (1st Dep't 1965); Meng v. Allen, 31 Misc. 3d 1211(A), 927 N.Y.S.2d 817 (Sup. Ct., New York County 2011).

[7]   See § 269. A three-part series of lead notes on the urgency of timing the adjudication of jurisdictional objections appears in NYSLD Nos. 274–76.

[8]   See Warsowe Acquisition Corp. v. DeNoble, 116 A.D.3d 949, 983 N.Y.S.2d 859 (2d Dep't 2014); see also § 274 and SPR 50:3.

[9]   See Abitol v. Schiff, 180 Misc. 2d 949, 691 N.Y.S.2d 753 (Sup. Ct., Queens County 1999), aff'd as modified, 276 A.D.2d 571, 714 N.Y.S.2d 880 (2d Dep't 2000) (SPR 84:2).

[10]   Daimler AG v. Bauman, 571 U.S. 117, 134 S. Ct. 746, 187 L. Ed. 2d 624 (2014) (SPR 265:1); see § 82.

[11]   See § 279; Commentary C3211:55 on McKinney's CPLR 3211; SPR 50:3.

[12]   See § 63.

on paragraphs 8 (personal jurisdiction) and 9 together. Even the plaintiff may be uncertain about her bases for jurisdiction in a given case, which has prompted the courts to be forgiving if the defendant, also mistaking it, asserts the wrong ground.[1] The invoking of both grounds is a precaution that should avoid the problem. D should even include in the motion papers a request that, if any jurisdiction is found present, the court specify in its order precisely what kind it is sustaining—in rem, quasi in rem, or in personam. Different consequences, involving the law of appearances, append to different conduct of a defendant following disposition of a jurisdictional motion,[2] and since these consequences are tied in with the kind of jurisdiction that exists in the case, the disposition should be clear.

§ 268. Dismissal for Indispensable Party; Paragraph 10

We have already discussed the question of whether a dismissal lies for the plaintiff's failure to join as a party someone who is necessary to the case.[1] It was pointed out that the conclusion of whether a party's presence is necessary is reached only as a last resort today if it is reached at all. Considering the numerous alternatives available to the court,[2] it is a rare case in which such a dismissal is warranted, and so the mission of CPLR 3211(a)(10) is a curtailed one.[3] But if the issue does arise, as it does from time to time,[4] the defendant can raise the issue by a motion to dismiss under CPLR 3211(a)(10).

Since it is clear from CPLR 1001(b) that conditions may be imposed on a motion to dismiss based on the absence of a party,[5] the dispositive order on such a motion may contain conditions even though the motion is formally made pursuant to CPLR 3211(a)(10), which does not expressly authorize the imposition of conditions.

§ 269. Motion to Dismiss Defense

CPLR 3211(b) provides that a party may move to dismiss one or more defenses on the ground that a defense "is not stated or has no merit." As subdivision (a)(7) does with the motion to dismiss a cause of action, so subdivision (b) does with a defense. This subdivision allows the attack to challenge the defense as deficient on its face—i.e., argue that it fails even to verbalize a defense—or go behind a perfectly pleaded defense to test its merit. Unlike subdivision (a), which enumerates grounds on which a cause of action may be dismissed, there are no listed grounds on which a defense may be attacked. Any defense may be attacked on any ground, and there is no requirement that the court elect to treat the CPLR 3211(b) motion as one for summary judgment under CPLR 3211(c) before the court can consider affidavits. CPLR 3211(b) expressly permits the motion to dismiss "on the ground that a defense . . . has no merit."

The test and the rules of construction in disposing of the motion on its merits are also akin to those applied to the (a)(7) motion to dismiss a complaint for failure to state

---

[1]   See Kelly v. Stanmar, Inc., 51 Misc. 2d 378, 273 N.Y.S.2d 276 (Sup. Ct., Albany County 1966).

[2]   See §§ 111 and 113.

[1]   See § 133.

[2]   CPLR 1001(b).

[3]   See L-3 Communications Corp. v. SafeNet, Inc., 45 A.D.3d 1, 10–11, 841 N.Y.S.2d 82, 90 (1st Dep't 2007) (discussing factors to be applied on CPLR 3211(a)(10) motion).

[4]   See, e.g., Windy Ridge Farm v. Assessor of Town of Shandaken, 11 N.Y.3d 725, 864 N.Y.S.2d 794, 894 N.E.2d 1183 (2008) (NYSLD No. 585); Storrs v. Holcomb, 245 A.D.2d 943, 666 N.Y.S.2d 835 (3d Dep't 1997).

[5]   See CPLR 1001(b)(1), (4).

a cause of action. So, when the defense is attacked on its face, the truth of its allegations will be assumed; when the attack goes beyond, and with affidavits and other extrinsic proof aims at the defense's merit, all reasonable inferences are drawn in favor of the defense.

There was for a while a disagreement among the courts about whether the defense of failure to state a cause of action, the ground listed in CPLR 3211(a)(7), may be included in the answer instead of taken by motion. The Second Department had held that it may not be and that the plaintiff may therefore move to strike such a defense from the answer under CPLR 3211(b). The court reversed itself in Butler v. Catinella,[1] however, and adopted the First Department position, which is that the inclusion of the defense in the answer is surplusage at worst and that no motion by the plaintiff lies under CPLR 3211(b) to strike the defense.[2]

The motion to dismiss a defense is an especially important tool for the nervous plaintiff, who is always concerned with the prospect that an affirmative defense lurking in the answer might ultimately result in a dismissal of the action. Suppose, for example, that the defendant has an objection to personal jurisdiction. The defendant contends he was never served with process and got notice of the action only by coincidence, or that the service was made by an improper method, or that it was made outside the state without an extraterritorial jurisdictional basis. The defendant opts, as she may,[3] to assert the jurisdictional objection as a defense in the answer and to let it linger rather than by a prompt motion to dismiss under CPLR 3211(a)(8). If the adjudication of the defense is postponed until after the statute of limitations on the claim expires, which will likely be defendant's intention, a sustaining of the defense at that later point will result in a jurisdictional dismissal too late to enable the plaintiff to start over.[4]

By allowing the nervous plaintiff to move early in the case, CPLR 3211(b) enables the plaintiff to test the validity of an explosive defense in time to permit a new and timely action if the defense is sustained. If the plaintiff fails to make the CPLR 3211(b) motion, and the defendant obtains a jurisdictional dismissal later, after the applicable statute of limitations has expired, the attitude of the courts is that the plaintiff has only himself to blame.[5] Both sides, in fact, should take note of the tactics in and about the assertion and adjudication of a jurisdictional objection—the plaintiff in order to avoid a dismissal too late to start over in New York or another forum where jurisdiction can be secured, and the defendant in order to see whether she can't maneuver the plaintiff into just that position.[6]

The CPLR 3211(b) motion can also be an effective tool for the plaintiff against a defendant who has taken a "kitchen sink" approach to pleading affirmative defenses, asserting every defense known to man.[7] The plaintiff may not be successful in dismissing

---

[1] Butler v. Catinella, 58 A.D.3d 145, 868 N.Y.S.2d 101 (2d Dep't 2008); SPR 204:2.

[2] See § 265.

[3] CPLR 320(a), 3211(e).

[4] CPLR 205(a) does not offer its six months for a new action when the prior action was dismissed for a want of personal jurisdiction. See § 52.

[5] Dickinson v. Houston, 97 A.D.2d 665, 469 N.Y.S.2d 207 (3d Dep't 1983).

[6] There is a three-part treatment of this subject, with a variety of illustrations, under the caption, "The urgency of timing the adjudication of jurisdictional objections," in the lead notes in Nos. 274–76 of the New York State Law Digest.

[7] See, e.g., Scholastic Inc. v. Pace Plumbing Corp., 129 A.D.3d 75, 76, 78, 8 N.Y.S.3d 143, 145, 146 (1st Dep't 2015) (defendant pleaded sixteen affirmative defenses "within a boilerplate, catchall paragraph" that

all of the affirmative defenses in such circumstances, but a CPLR 3211(b) motion in the hands of the right judge will often help to narrow the issues in the litigation moving forward.[8]

A 1997 amendment of CPLR 3211(e) reduces the scope of this problem for the plaintiff when the specific basis of the objection to personal jurisdiction is improper service. It requires a defendant who takes the objection by answer to move for judgment on the defense within 60 days after its service.[9] There is no such restriction when some other ground is the foundation for the jurisdictional defense, however, like a defective summons, a want of jurisdictional basis for extraterritorial service, or an improper filing of the initiatory papers.[10] In those instances, the plaintiff's timing problem persists and the jurisdictional defense is not subject to CPLR 3211(e)'s 60-day rule.

A CPLR 3211(b) motion does what is called "searching the record." This means that the court looks not only at the answer, whose defense the plaintiff is attacking, but also at the pleading to which the answer responds, i.e., the complaint. If the complaint is defective, it and not the defense gets dismissed, without the defendant's even cross-moving for it.[11] This phenomenon is better known in connection with the summary judgment motion and is discussed more fully there.[12]

§ 270. Treating 3211 Motion as Summary Judgment

Under CPLR 3211(c), the court is empowered to treat any 3211 motion as a summary judgment motion. The effect of doing this will ordinarily mean that the resulting judgment is to be deemed a judgment on the merits, invoking the doctrine of res judicata. As will be seen later,[1] the res judicata effect of a CPLR 3211 motion not so treated is more circumscribed.

The summary judgment motion itself, governed by CPLR 3212, does not lie until after issue has been joined.[2] Since that is so, one might assume that a CPLR 3211 motion could not be given summary judgment treatment until after joinder of issue. While CPLR 3211 motions are almost always made—indeed, most of them have to be made—before the joinder of issue,[3] CPLR 3211(c) expressly permits the court to treat a CPLR 3211 motion as one for summary judgment.

Because of its res judicata impact, treating a CPLR 3211 motion as one for summary judgment is drastic. Before it can be done, therefore, the court must clearly notify the

---

also asserted "any other matter constituting an avoidance or an affirmative defense which further investigation of this matter may prove applicable herein.").

[8]   See One West Bank v. Chapilliquen, 2016 WL 1380855 (Sup. Ct., Queens County 2016) (court dismissed five of the ten affirmative defenses asserted); see also Commentary C3018:16A on McKinney's CPLR 3018.

[9]   Thompson v. Cuadrado, 277 A.D.2d 151, 717 N.Y.S.2d 109 (1st Dep't 2000) (motion to dismiss for lack of proper service made 61 days after service of the answer denied as untimely).

[10]   See § 266.

[11]   See Rand v. Hearst Corp., 31 A.D.2d 406, 408, 298 N.Y.S.2d 405, 409 (1st Dep't 1969), aff'd, 26 N.Y.2d 806, 309 N.Y.S.2d 348, 257 N.E.2d 895 (1970); see Hyman v. Hillelson, 79 A.D.2d 725, 727, 434 N.Y.S.2d 742, 745 (3d Dep't 1980), aff'd, 55 N.Y.2d 624, 446 N.Y.S.2d 251, 430 N.E.2d 1304 (1981); Rubiano v. Kelly, 136 A.D.3d 780, 782, 26 N.Y.S.3d 106, 108 (2d Dep't 2016).

[12]   See § 282.

[1]   See § 276.

[2]   CPLR 3212(a).

[3]   See § 272.

parties of its intention to make the treatment so as to enable them to submit whatever additional proof they may have to buttress their positions.[4] The nature of the ground on which the CPLR 3211 motion was made may not necessarily have elicited all the evidence that might be expected on an outright summary judgment application. This notice requirement therefore offers the parties an opportunity to submit everything they've got.[5] To implement it, the court notifies the parties that it is considering CPLR 3211(c)'s treat-as-summary-judgment option, that they have until X date in which to submit further proof, and that a determination of the motion will be held in abeyance until then.[6]

There had been some disagreement among departments about whether the notice to treat a CPLR 3211 motion as one for summary judgment under CPLR 3212 must be given by the court, or can come from some other source, such as the moving party.[7] The Court of Appeals resolved the conflict in Mihlovan v. Grozavu:[8] it must come from the court.

No matter what ground the CPLR 3211 motion was made on, any aggregate of proof before the court that arouses the court's suspicion that this is a one-sided situation on the merits with no genuine issue of fact is sufficient to invoke this treatment. Realistically speaking, the grounds most likely to produce a record thorough enough to give the court that kind of insight into the case are CPLR 3211(a)(7), the motion to dismiss a claim for insufficiency,[9] and CPLR 3211(b), the motion to dismiss a defense.[10] Technically, however, the court has the power to make the summary judgment treatment regardless of the specific ground on which the CPLR 3211 motion was originally based.

Defendants planning to make a motion to dismiss under CPLR 3211(a)(7) might assume, because of Rovello v. Orofino Realty Co., Inc.[11] and its progeny, that they should not submit any affidavits at all on the motion unless and until the court invokes its powers under subdivision (c) and elects to treat the motion as one for summary judgment.[12] That might be an unfortunate assumption. If the court does make the summary judgment treatment under CPLR 3211(c), it will usually be because something in defendant's submissions aroused its suspicion that the plaintiff may have no case at all. The chief suspicion-arousers are likely to be the defendant's moving affidavits. Caselaw holding that the court may not *consider* the defendant's affidavits on a CPLR

---

[4]   See Pine Street Homeowners Ass'n v. 20 Pine Street LLC, 109 A.D.3d 733, 971 N.Y.S.2d 289 (1st Dep't 2013); Mareno v. Kibbe, 32 A.D.2d 825, 302 N.Y.S.2d 324 (2d Dep't 1969).

[5]   State Bd. of Equalization and Assessment v. Kerwick, 72 A.D.2d 292, 425 N.Y.S.2d 640 (3d Dep't 1980), aff'd, 52 N.Y.2d 557, 439 N.Y.S.2d 311, 421 N.E.2d 803 (1981).

[6]   See, e.g., Estate of Robert Wallis, 239 N.Y.L.J. 68, 2008 N.Y. Misc. LEXIS 2243, at *1 (Sur. Ct., New York County 2008); Lustig v. Congregation B'Nai Israel of Midwood, 62 Misc. 2d 216, 308 N.Y.S.2d 480 (Sup. Ct., Kings County 1970).

[7]   See and compare Reed v. Shoratlantic Development Co., Inc., 121 A.D.2d 525, 503 N.Y.S.2d 840 (2d Dep't 1986), and Four Seasons Hotels Ltd. v. Vinnik, 127 A.D.2d 310, 320, 515 N.Y.S.2d 1, 8 (1st Dep't 1987).

[8]   Mihlovan v. Grozavu, 72 N.Y.2d 506, 534 N.Y.S.2d 656, 531 N.E.2d 288 (1988).

[9]   See Martin v. State Liquor Auth., 43 Misc. 2d 682, 252 N.Y.S.2d 365 (Sup. Ct., Albany County 1964), aff'd, 15 N.Y.2d 707, 256 N.Y.S.2d 336, 204 N.E.2d 496 (1965); Scattergood v. Jamaica Water Securities Corp., 234 A.D.2d 688, 650 N.Y.S.2d 854 (3d Dep't 1996).

[10]   See Blatz v. Benschine, 53 Misc. 2d 352, 278 N.Y.S.2d 533 (Sup. Ct., Queens County 1967).

[11]   Rovello v. Orofino Realty Co., Inc., 40 N.Y.2d 633, 389 N.Y.S.2d 314, 357 N.E.2d 970 (1976).

[12]   See § 265 and § 275 for fuller treatment of the *Rovello* case.

3211(a)(7) motion[13] does not suggest that the court cannot *read* them, and the court's reading them is the defendant's best hope of getting the court to treat the motion as one for summary judgment.[14]

If the CPLR 3211(c) treatment is invoked and the motion is disposed of as a summary judgment motion, the order should so state, especially because of the res judicata impact of the treatment.

§ 271.   Immediate Trial of Fact Issue Under CPLR 3211

CPLR 3211(c) allows the court, "when appropriate for the expeditious disposition of the controversy," to order an immediate trial of an issue of fact arising on a CPLR 3211 motion. CPLR 2218 contains such an authorization for motions generally,[1] but CPLR 3211(c) contains its own, superfluous as it may be.

The power is broad, but is exercised only when the immediate trial has some potential for ending the litigation. It's appropriate, for example, on a CPLR 3211(a)(8) motion to dismiss for lack of personal jurisdiction if a genuine issue exists about whether service of process was made or as to any other fact going to jurisdiction.[2] The rationale underpinning the rule is that it is wasteful to preserve a case and put it through pretrial processing only to dismiss it for want of jurisdiction later.

The trial of an issue of fact on a jurisdictional motion, notably one raising an issue about whether or not the defendant was properly served with process—perhaps the most prolific example of this genre—is commonly called a "traverse hearing" in New York practice, some parts of the state virtually monopolizing the word for that use. The traverse hearing is ordered, however, only when there is a genuine dispute about service, one side swearing unequivocally to one version and the other, just as unequivocally, to an inconsistent version of the facts. A hedgy or coy affidavit by the defendant, for example, perhaps saying only that he doesn't "remember" being served, won't do to dispute service,[3] which will simply be upheld.

An immediate trial would be even more appropriate to order on a CPLR 3211(b) motion to strike a defense if the motion has the potential for ending the case on the merits. Where, for example, D interposed the defense of release and P moved to dismiss it on the ground that the release was procured by fraud, it was held suitable to try the fraud issue immediately because, should D prevail on it and the release be upheld, P's action would be at an end.[4] It is this case-ending prospect, though of course not its certainty, that governs judicial discretion as to whether to order an immediate trial on a CPLR 3211 motion.

---

[13]   E.g., Miglino v. Bally Total Fitness of Greater New York, Inc., 20 N.Y.3d 342, 351, 961 N.Y.S.2d 364, 370, 985 N.E.2d 128, 134 (2013); FYM Clinical Laboratory, Inc. v. Perales, 147 A.D.2d 840, 537 N.Y.S.2d 998 (3d Dep't 1989), aff'd, 74 N.Y.2d 539, 549 N.Y.S.2d 933, 549 N.E.2d 124; see § 275.

[14]   A defendant who would sidestep the problem altogether can ignore CPLR 3211, draft and serve an answer, and then move directly for summary judgment under CPLR 3212 with the accompanying affidavits, which the court must consider in this context. See § 265. Drafting an answer may be a major undertaking in a given case, however, and therefore one the defendant would prefer to avoid.

[1]   See § 251.

[2]   See Usher v. Usher, 41 A.D.2d 368, 343 N.Y.S.2d 212 (3d Dep't 1973); see, e.g., Vandermark v. Jotomo Corp., 42 A.D.3d 931, 933, 839 N.Y.S.2d 670, 672 (4th Dep't 2007).

[3]   See LeFevre v. Cole, 83 A.D.2d 992, 443 N.Y.S.2d 533 (4th Dep't 1981).

[4]   Barker v. Conley, 267 N.Y. 43, 195 N.E. 677 (1935); see Starr v. Johnsen, 143 A.D.2d 130, 132, 531 N.Y.S.2d 589, 591–92 (2d Dep't 1988).

The word "immediate" in CPLR 3211(c) is a relative term, merely indicating that the trial should be given a preference. When the trial actually takes place turns on a number of administrative factors—under the Individual Assignment System, it turns mainly on the judge's calendar—but it touches also on whether the trial is to be by jury. Is it to be by jury?

If the claim itself would have been triable by jury and the grant of the motion would effectively put an end to the case on the merits, the disputed issue must be tried by jury if either party requests it. Thus, where P sued in contract, D moved to dismiss on the statute of frauds, and P then adduced a memo which he said satisfied the statute, an issue of fact as to whether the memo was signed by an agent of D had to be tried by jury.[5]

But if a grant of the motion would not preclude a new action for the same relief, the fact issue would not be jury triable even though the main claim itself, were its merits reached, would be. An example here would be the usual "traverse hearing." Assume a simple damages action, ordinarily jury triable, in which D moves under CPLR 3211(a)(8) to dismiss for want of proper service. A CPLR 3211(c) trial of whether service was made would not ordinarily require a jury because even if the motion were granted, and the action dismissed, P could turn right around and sue again.[6]

Taking things a step further, however, suppose that the statute of limitations has meanwhile expired, so that a new action would now be barred if the motion to dismiss for lack of jurisdiction should succeed. Will that make it necessary to try the jurisdictional issue by jury if a party insists? Controversy on this point is apparent in Cerrato v. Thurcon Constr. Corp.,[7] where the First Department held 3–2 that trial by jury is required in such circumstances.[8]

§ 272. Time for 3211 Motion

CPLR 3211(e) provides that the defendant's motion against a claim under CPLR 3211(a) must be made within the responding time. If D has 20 days to answer the complaint, and chooses to move under CPLR 3211(a) in lieu of answering, she must make the motion within the 20 days; if the responding time is 30 days,[1] or 40 days, or even more,[2] D has that time. If D is bent on moving, it is best for D to make the motion instead of answering. While CPLR 3211(e) technically permits the motion before the answer "is required," so that, for example, D's motion on the 15th day after service of process would seem permissible even though D answered on the 12th day, it has been held that the service of an answer waives the right to make the motion.[3] Even if a postanswer motion is denominated as a motion to dismiss under CPLR 3211, the court can treat it as one for summary judgment under CPLR 3212 if the papers submitted demonstrate that the

---

[5]   Herzog v. Brown, 217 A.D. 402, 216 N.Y.S. 134 (1st Dep't 1926), aff'd, 243 N.Y. 599, 154 N.E. 622.

[6]   See Commentary C3211:45 on McKinney's CPLR 3211.

[7]   Cerrato v. Thurcon Const. Corp., 92 A.D.2d 89, 459 N.Y.S.2d 765 (1st Dep't 1983).

[8]   The Second Department appears to agree with the First Department's reasoning in Cerrato. See Sosnowski v. Kolovas, 127 A.D.2d 756, 757, 512 N.Y.S.2d 148, 150 (2d Dep't 1987). The subject is treated in the Commentary C2218:3 on McKinney's CPLR 2218 and the lead note in NYSLD No. 283.

[1]   CPLR 320(a), 3012(c).

[2]   Under the substituted service methods of CPLR 308(2) and (4), where completion of service depends on filing proof of service, the responding period can be 40 days or longer. See §§ 72, 74.

[3]   Hanover Ins. Co. v. Finnerty, 225 A.D.2d 1054, 639 N.Y.S. 433 (4th Dep't 1996); Incorporated Village of Laurel Hollow v. Laverne, Inc., 43 Misc. 2d 248, 250 N.Y.S.2d 951 (Sup. Ct., Nassau County 1964), modified, 24 A.D.2d 615, 262 N.Y.S.2d 622 (2d Dep't 1965).

parties are laying bare their proof and deliberately charting a summary judgment course.[4]

These time limits apply to all of the subdivision (a) grounds except those of paragraphs 2 (subject matter jurisdiction), 7 (failure to state a cause of action), and 10 (nonjoinder of necessary party). For any of that trio, the motion to dismiss may be made at any time, although it is usually a good idea even with those objections to make the motion before answering.

With those three exceptions, the time to move is keyed to the answering time and because of that a stipulation extending the answering time will also extend the time to make the CPLR 3211(a) motion.[5] But if the stipulation specifies that the extension is offered only for pleading, not for moving under CPLR 3211(a), it has been held that it does not extend the moving time.[6] The court of course has discretion to extend the time to take either step,[7] but it may be more prone to grant the extension for the purpose of answering than for moving.[8]

CPLR 3211(a)(6), the motion to dismiss a counterclaim because it's not properly interposed in the particular action,[9] is also technically subject to the responding-time limit of CPLR 3211(e) but does not lend itself to it readily. If, for example, the counterclaim does not belong in the case because it has been interposed against the plaintiff in a capacity other than that in which the plaintiff is bringing the action,[10] the motion under paragraph 6 to strike it is akin to a paragraph 7 motion for insufficiency and perhaps ought to be allowed, as the paragraph 7 motion is, at any time. An alternative, available throughout the action, is a motion to sever the counterclaim, which is governed by CPLR 603 and has no arbitrary time limit.[11]

There is no time limit on a motion under CPLR 3211(b) to dismiss a defense.[12]

§ 273. Single Motion Rule

CPLR 3211(e) allows only one subdivision (a) pre-answer motion per case, but the movant can join in the one motion whatever grounds she possesses. This is designed to avoid duplication and repeated postponement of the service of the answer. It has been held, however, that a second motion is permissible if based on paragraph 7 (insufficiency

---

[4] See, e.g., Nowacki v. Becker, 71 A.D.3d 1496, 1497, 897 N.Y.S.2d 560 (4th Dep't 2010); see CPLR 3211(c); § 270.

[5] See Rich v. Lefkovits, 56 N.Y.2d 276, 280, 452 N.Y.S.2d 1, 3, 437 N.E.2d 260, 262 (1982).

[6] See Tatar v. Port Authority of New York and New Jersey, 291 A.D.2d 554, 737 N.Y.S.2d 874 (2d Dep't 2002) ("The motion was timely since a stipulation which extends the time in which to answer a complaint also extends the time in which to move pursuant to CPLR 3211(c), unless a contrary intent is clearly stated.").

[7] See CPLR 2004.

[8] See Smith v. Pach, 30 A.D.2d 707, 292 N.Y.S.2d 333 (2d Dep't 1968); see Apicella v. Valley Forge Military Academy and Jr. College, 97 A.D.2d 392, 467 N.Y.S.2d 211, 212 (2d Dep't 1983).

[9] See § 264.

[10] See § 225.

[11] Compare Jayell Films v. A.F.E. Corp., 67 N.Y.S.2d 77 (Sup. Ct., New York County 1946), which was decided when a counterclaim, legitimately interposed or not, could be dismissed for mere inconvenience. That power does not exist under the CPLR, which prefers the remedy of a severance.

[12] Zarnoch v. Luckina, 148 A.D.3d 1615, 50 N.Y.S.3d 709 (4th Dep't 2017) (noting that CPLR 3211(b) motion is not subject to the time limit for summary judgment motions contained in CPLR 3212(a)), lv. denied, 29 N.Y.3d 915, 63 N.Y.S.3d 5.

of the claim),[1] but the Court of Appeals seemed to assume otherwise in McLearn v. Cowen & Co.[2] Omitting the insufficiency objection from an initial CPLR 3211 motion will not waive it in any event. It is just a matter of determining what mechanical device to use for interposing the paragraph 7 objection after the defendant's CPLR 3211 motion has been used up. If CPLR 3211 is unavailable, the defendant can raise the objection just as well with a summary judgment motion under CPLR 3212 based on the grounds in CPLR 3211(a)(7).[3] It is usually best, however, for the defendant to join the insufficiency ground on any CPLR 3211 motion the defendant chooses to make on any ground, even though it's not obligatory.

Since paragraphs 2, 7, and 10 are treated uniformly for time purposes, the foregoing discussion about the insufficiency objection of paragraph 7 should apply equally to the objection of subject matter jurisdiction under paragraph 2 and the objection of failure to join a party under paragraph 10. Certainly a second motion would have to be entertained on the paragraph 2 ground of lack of subject matter jurisdiction—whatever the motion that asserts it may be called—and with paragraphs 2, 7, and 10 treated as a package by CPLR 3211(e), it would be awkward to reach any other conclusion for the other objections.

A second motion may be permitted on any of the subdivision (a) grounds if the first motion was premature and it was only because of the prematurity that the motion was not considered on its merits.[4] Where, for example, a paragraph 8 motion (lack of personal jurisdiction) was made before a complaint had been served, and it was necessary to consider the complaint because jurisdiction was based on CPLR 302 and the claim's New York contacts had to be examined, the court denied the motion without prejudice to renewal after service of the complaint.[5]

It is also permissible for a party to make a second CPLR 3211 motion if each aims at a different pleading. In one case, for example, where D moved to dismiss P's claim and then moved to dismiss a co-defendant's cross-claim, both motions were allowed.[6]

As noted above, if the CPLR 3211 motion is used up, motion relief is not yet lost. As long as the subdivision (a) objection has been preserved by being included as a defense in the answer, it can be made the subject of a summary judgment motion under CPLR 3212 after the answer has been served.[7] If it is, and the second motion is labeled a 3211 motion, the court may just treat it as if it were properly labeled a summary judgment motion and dispose of it on its merits.[8]

---

[1]   Higby Enterprises, Inc. v. City of Utica, 54 Misc. 2d 405, 282 N.Y.S.2d 583 (Sup. Ct., Oneida County 1967), aff'd, 30 A.D.2d 1052, 295 N.Y.S.2d 428 (4th Dep't 1968).

[2]   McLearn v. Cowen & Co., 60 N.Y.2d 686, 468 N.Y.S.2d 461, 455 N.E.2d 1256 (1983).

[3]   *McLearn*, 60 N.Y.2d at 689, 468 N.Y.S.2d at 462, 455 N.E.2d at 1257; see Oakley v. County of Nassau, 127 A.D.3d 946, 6 N.Y.S.3d 646 (2d Dep't 2015).

[4]   See CPLR 3211(d); § 257.

[5]   Fraley v. Desilu Productions, Inc., 23 A.D.2d 79, 258 N.Y.S.2d 294 (1st Dep't 1965); Meng v. Allen, 31 Misc. 3d 1211(A), 927 N.Y.S.2d 817 (Sup. Ct., New York County 2011).

[6]   Nassau Roofing & Sheet Metal Co., Inc. v. Celotex Corp., 74 A.D.2d 679, 424 N.Y.S.2d 786 (3d Dep't 1980); see Wallace v. Merrill Lynch Capital Services, Inc., 12 Misc. 3d 1153(A), *7, 819 N.Y.S.2d 214 (Sup. Ct., New York County 2006).

[7]   See § 283. Summary judgment motions based on CPLR 3211(a)(2), (7), and (10) can be made even if these defenses are not included in the answer.

[8]   Hertz Corp. v. Luken, 126 A.D.2d 446, 510 N.Y.S.2d 590 (1st Dep't 1987); cf. Miglino v. Bally Total Fitness of Greater New York, Inc., 20 N.Y.3d 342, 351, 961 N.Y.S.2d 364, 370, 985 N.E.2d 128, 134 (2013)

Suppose that while D's CPLR 3211(a) motion against the complaint is pending, P amends the complaint as of right.[9] When the plaintiff exercises this option, the amended complaint supersedes the original complaint and will become "the only complaint in the case."[10] Will the amendment automatically abate the motion? It should not. Even if the motion attacks the complaint under CPLR 3211(a)(7) for insufficiency on its face, for example, and the complaint as amended arguably remedies the deficiency, whether the motion formally "abates" is something that must still be determined by the court if the parties can't work it out voluntarily. The First Department has concluded that when P amends the complaint while D's dismissal motion is pending, D "has the option to decide whether its motion should be applied to the new pleadings."[11] In this regard, there is the possibility that the amended pleading does not address the defects raised in the motion.[12] Thus, unless the defendant withdraws the motion, the plaintiff should respond to it on the return day and let the court decide the abatement issue.[13] Many CPLR 3211(a) objections, moreover, are not curable by mere amendment of the complaint.

If the defendant wants to proceed with the motion, it is advisable for the parties to explore the need for supplemental submissions, as the arguments made in the original motion will often need to be adjusted to address the amended pleading. The court must also be alerted to the amendment, whether the defendant will press on with the motion, and to the possibility of supplemental submissions.[14]

§ 274. Option to Plead Instead of Move; Waiver

If D has available a number of the objections listed in subdivision (a) of CPLR 3211, subdivision (e) allows D to raise them all by a dismissal motion or, instead, plead all of them as defenses in the answer. Or, D may divide them up and take some by motion and—if the motion does not succeed—plead the rest by answer.[1] It is of course preferable as a rule to take them all by motion since an answer will not be needed at all if the motion is granted. With the exception of the trio of objections in paragraphs 2, 7, and 10 of subdivision (a), which may be taken at any time, any subdivision (a) objection is waived if it is not taken either by a CPLR 3211 motion or as a defense in the answer.[2]

There is an important caveat to the above rule for the objections of personal or rem jurisdiction, the grounds listed in paragraphs 8 and 9 of subdivision (a). These objections are deemed so fundamental that wasting the court's time on a CPLR 3211(a) motion

---

(court did not elect to treat post answer CPLR 3211 motion as a CPLR 3212 motion for summary judgment); § 265.

[9] CPLR 3025(a).

[10] D'Amico v. Correctional Medical Care, Inc., 120 A.D.3d 956, 957, 991 N.Y.S.2d 687, 690 (4th Dep't 2014).

[11] Sage Realty Corp. v. Proskauer Rose LLP, 251 A.D.2d 35, 675 N.Y.S.2d 14 (1st Dep't 1998) (SPR 74:2); see Sholom & Zuckerbrot Realty Corp. v. Coldwell Banker Commercial Group, Inc., 138 Misc. 2d 799, 801, 525 N.Y.S.2d 541, 542 (Sup. Ct., Queens County 1988) (the "better rule" is that the movant has "the option of withdrawing its motion or pressing it with regard to the amended pleading.").

[12] See Sim v. Farley Equipment Co. LLC, 138 A.D.3d 1228, n.1, 30 N.Y.S.3d 736, 738 n.1 (3d Dep't 2016).

[13] See Commentary C3211:61 on McKinney's CPLR 3211.

[14] Cf. 22 N.Y.C.R.R. § 202.8(e)(1) ("Stipulations of adjournment of the return date made by the parties shall be in writing and shall be submitted to the assigned judge.").

[1] Hertz Corp. v. Luken, 126 A.D.2d 446, 449, 510 N.Y.S.2d 590, 593 (1st Dep't 1987).

[2] CPLR 3211(e); see Raoul v. Olde Village Hall, Inc., 76 A.D.2d 319, 333, 430 N.Y.S.2d 214, 223 (2d Dep't 1980).

based on any other grounds without including the jurisdictional ones waives them.[3] If, for example, D moves to dismiss the complaint based on one of the affirmative defenses listed in CPLR 3211(a)(5) and the motion is denied, the answer that D now serves may not plead the defenses of lack of personal or rem jurisdiction, which are waived. D may, however, plead as defenses any of the other subdivision (a) objections D may have, which, although not raised on the motion, are not deemed waived.[4]

The Court of Appeals has construed this strictly, holding in Addesso v. Shemtob[5] that even in the situation in which P amends the complaint as of right while D's CPLR 3211(a) motion is pending, an answer that D afterwards serves to the amended complaint may not include the jurisdictional objection that D omitted from the motion.

If the defendant does not make a pre-answer motion to dismiss under CPLR 3211(a) and the original answer omits the jurisdictional objection, an amendment of the answer made as of course under CPLR 3025(a) can include it.[6] Assuming the affirmative defense has not been waived by the making of a pre-answer motion to dismiss under CPLR 3211(a), whether an amendment by leave of court under CPLR 3025(b) will be allowed to raise a CPLR 3211(a) objection for the first time should depend on whether the delay in asserting the objection can be shown to have prejudiced the plaintiff.[7]

CPLR 3211(e) singles out the objection of improper service of process and imposes a special additional time limit on asserting it. If the objection is taken by answer instead of by motion, as it may be, the party so asserting it must move for summary judgment under CPLR 3212 based on the objection within 60 days after serving the answer, or the objection is waived. While the objection to improper service is embraced within the category of "jurisdiction of the person" under CPLR 3211(a)(8), the other objections that go to personal jurisdiction under that paragraph, such as want of extraterritorial basis for service, improper filing, defective summons, etc., are not—when taken by answer—subject to this 60-days-to-move-for-judgment requirement.[8]

Caselaw holds that a defendant does not waive a jurisdictional objection by interposing a counterclaim related to the plaintiff's claim or by impleading a third-party defendant,[9] either step being deemed a necessary precaution should the jurisdictional objection fail. But it has been held that the defendant does waive the objection by interposing a counterclaim unrelated to the plaintiff's claim. It makes the defendant the equivalent of a plaintiff who initially invokes the court's jurisdiction.[10]

The key to determining relatedness for this purpose is the collateral estoppel (issue preclusion) doctrine. When there are issues in common between the counterclaim and the plaintiff's main claim, such that an adjudication of an issue in the course of trying the main claim would necessarily be dispositive of the same issue when it afterwards becomes relevant on the trial of the counterclaim, then the counterclaim is to be deemed a related one and, practically speaking, the defendant really has no choice but to

---

[3]   CPLR 3211(e); Competello v. Giordano, 51 N.Y.2d 904, 434 N.Y.S.2d 976, 415 N.E.2d 965 (1980).

[4]   See Montcalm Pub. Corp. v. Pustorino, 125 A.D.2d 188, 508 N.Y.S.2d 455 (1st Dep't 1986).

[5]   Addesso v. Shemtob, 70 N.Y.2d 689, 518 N.Y.S.2d 793, 512 N.E.2d 314 (1987).

[6]   Iacovangelo v. Shepherd, 5 N.Y.3d 184, 800 N.Y.S.2d 116, 833 N.E.2d 259 (2005) (NYSLD No. 548); see § 236.

[7]   See § 237; Commentary C3211:58 on McKinney's CPLR 3211.

[8]   See § 266; SPR 50:3.

[9]   See Commentaries C3211:56 on McKinney's CPLR 3211.

[10]   Liebling v. Yankwitt, 109 A.D.2d 780, 486 N.Y.S.2d 292 (2d Dep't 1985).

interpose it. Doing so, therefore, does not waive a jurisdictional defense that the defendant may also have.[11]

§ 275. Leave to Replead

On a motion to dismiss a claim for insufficiency under CPLR 3211(a)(7), or to dismiss a defense for insufficiency under CPLR 3211(b), the party whose claim or defense is attacked may want a chance to plead over if the motion is granted. If the time period to amend the pleading as of right has not expired, and the party has not used their one of-right amendment, amending the pleading to cure the alleged defects will likely be the safest course of action.[1] The court can, however, grant leave to replead when the issue of sufficiency arises on these motions.

Prior to 2006, CPLR 3211(e) allowed a party desiring leave to replead in these circumstances to expressly request that relief in the opposing papers and demonstrate that she had "good ground" to support the claims she wished to replead. The court was permitted to require the party seeking leave to replead to submit evidence to demonstrate the merit of the claims in the new pleading. A 2006 amendment to CPLR 3211(e) removed any reference to repleading in the body of the subdivision, but the title still refers to a "motion to plead over."[2]

The Second Department held in Janssen v. Incorporated Village of Rockville Centre[3] that the legislature did not intend to eliminate a motion for leave to replead when it amended CPLR 3211(e), so the device is still used in New York practice.

The party moved against should specifically ask for leave to replead in the event the motion to dismiss is granted. The party makes this request in the opposing papers and, based on the law that existed prior to 2006, is encouraged to include in them whatever evidence she has to convince the court that a claim or defense exists. The court could require further evidence, but it was held that the evidentiary requirement for leave to replead was not as stringent on a CPLR 3211 motion as on a motion for summary judgment under CPLR 3212.[4] In *Janssen*, the Second Department held that under the 2006 amendment, a less burdensome standard should govern on a motion for leave to replead pursuant to CPLR 3211(e), i.e., "the standard governing motions for leave to amend pursuant to CPLR 3025."[5] Therefore, motions for leave to replead "should be freely granted absent prejudice or surprise to the opposing party, unless the proposed amendment is devoid of merit or palpably insufficient."[6]

Is there any time limit on a motion for leave to replead? If the action has been dismissed based on a CPLR 3211(a)(7) motion, that's that; the opportunity for mere repleading is gone. But suppose the action is for one reason or another ongoing, such as where several, but not all, of plaintiff's claims were dismissed. In analyzing the 2006

---

[11]   Textile Technology Exchange, Inc. v. Davis, 81 N.Y.2d 56, 595 N.Y.S.2d 729, 611 N.E.2d 768 (1993); see the discussion in SPR 4:1.

[1]   See § 236.

[2]   A detailed treatment of the amendment and its background appears in the lead note in SPR 170:1.

[3]   Janssen v. Incorporated Village of Rockville Centre, 59 A.D.3d 15, 869 N.Y.S.2d 572 (2d Dep't 2008).

[4]   Four Seasons Hotels Ltd. v. Vinnik, 127 A.D.2d 310, 319, 515 N.Y.S.2d 1, 7 (1st Dep't 1987); Cushman & Wakefield, Inc. v. John David, Inc., 25 A.D.2d 133, 267 N.Y.S.2d 714 (1st Dep't 1966).

[5]   *Janssen,* 59 A.D.3d at 27, 869 N.Y.S.2d at 581.

[6]   *Janssen,* 59 A.D.3d at 27, 869 N.Y.S.2d at 581; see § 236.

amendment to CPLR 3211(e), the Second Department has held that in that situation there's no time limit on moving to replead.[7]

§ 276. Res Judicata Effect of CPLR 3211 Disposition

A judgment resulting from the grant of a CPLR 3211 motion is not res judicata of the entire merits of the case unless the motion was treated as one for summary judgment under CPLR 3211(c). But it is res judicata, or law of the case, of whatever it determined, and that can sometimes have the same effect. Where, for example, the first action is dismissed as barred by the statute of limitations, a second New York action that attempts to duplicate the claim will be dismissed: it is law of the case that the claim is time barred.[1]

If the first-round dismissal was under subdivision (a)(7) for a mere pleading deficiency in the cause of action, a new action with a complaint identical to the first will be barred by res judicata,[2] but a new action with a complaint that remedies the deficiency will be sustained.[3] Investigation must therefore be made to determine precisely what the ground was for the granting of the CPLR 3211 dismissal.

Until recently, caselaw sometimes invoked the election of remedies doctrine to preserve a claim that should have been barred under res judicata. In one older case, for example, in which the first action was dismissed because the contract on which it was based was oral and unprovable under the statute of frauds, a second action, pleading in quantum meruit instead of contract, was sustained. The court held that the first action did not decide that no services were rendered or goods delivered, only that no contract for those things could be proved.[4] It then added that since the quantum meruit remedy does not depend on contract, an "election" had not been made against it when the plaintiff sued in contract earlier. Taking a broader view under the res judicata doctrine, which deems concluded not only that which was litigated in the earlier action but also that which could have been litigated if it springs from the same event or transaction, the Court of Appeals overruled that old line of cases, which had allowed the election of remedies doctrine to serve as a detour around the res judicata barrier.[5]

Whenever it gives rise to a final judgment, the grant of a CPLR 3211 motion invokes the "res judicata" doctrine outright, whatever its scope may be in the particular case. The reduction of the case to a final judgment is one of the major prerequisites of the res judicata doctrine.[6] But a denial of the motion, or a grant that does not give rise to a final judgment, such as where it strikes one cause of action or defense but leaves others intact for trial, does not end in a judgment. It ends in an order denying the motion, or granting it only in part. The effect of the order in those situations is also res judicata but under a

---

   [7]   *Janssen*, 59 A.D.3d at 28–29, 869 N.Y.S.2d at 581–82 (permitting motion to replead six months after order dismissing claims was served).

   [1]   Spindell v. Brooklyn Jewish Hospital, 35 A.D.2d 962, 317 N.Y.S.2d 963 (2d Dep't 1970), aff'd, 29 N.Y.2d 888, 328 N.Y.S.2d 678, 278 N.E.2d 912 (1972).

   [2]   Flynn v. Sinclair Oil Corp., 20 A.D.2d 636, 246 N.Y.S.2d 360 (1st Dep't 1964), aff'd, 14 N.Y.2d 853, 251 N.Y.S.2d 967, 200 N.E.2d 633 (1964); Papa v. Burrows, 186 A.D.2d 375, 588 N.Y.S.2d 171 (1st Dep't 1992).

   [3]   DeRonda v. Greater Amsterdam School Dist., 91 A.D.2d 1088, 458 N.Y.S.2d 310 (3d Dep't 1983).

   [4]   Smith v. Kirkpatrick, 305 N.Y. 66, 72, 111 N.E.2d 209, 213 (1953).

   [5]   See § 218.

   [6]   See § 444.

different name. The order invokes a doctrine known as the "law of the case," which is in essence a doctrine of intra-action res judicata.[7]

The law of the case doctrine is fundamental, and powerful, in practice. It holds that once an issue is decided, it cannot again be litigated at trial level,[8] although it may of course be reviewed by an appellate court either by immediate appeal from an interlocutory order, or as part of a later appeal from a final judgment in the action.[9] Where, for example, D moves to dismiss P's complaint on one of the objections listed in CPLR 3211(a)(5) and the motion is denied, the denial is a holding that the objection lacks merit and cannot afterwards be raised as a defense in the answer.[10] The ruling can, however, be challenged on appeal.

The court may sometimes deny the CPLR 3211(a) motion without prejudice and refrain from passing on the merits, thereby allowing the defendant to plead the objection as a defense in the answer instead.[11] No law of the case doctrine would apply in that situation because a determination of the merits of the objection is being deliberately postponed.

§ 277. Motion Under CPLR 3211 Extends Responding Time

A defendant moving to dismiss a complaint under CPLR 3211 need not be apprehensive about being in default for failing to answer. Nor need she get an order extending the answering time. As long as the CPLR 3211(a) motion is itself timely,[1] the mere making of the motion automatically extends the answering time should the motion be denied. In that instance, P must serve on D a copy of the order denying the motion with notice of entry.[2] D has 10 days after that in which to answer.[3] So the mere making of the motion not only extends the answering time, but extends it substantially. Depending on when the motion comes on for hearing and how long the judge takes to decide it, the extension can run into months.

If several claims are asserted, but only one is moved against, the motion extends the answering time as to the entire complaint, including the claims not moved against.[4]

The making of a CPLR 3211 motion also suspends all pending disclosure proceedings until the motion is determined "unless the court orders otherwise."[5] Courts frequently "order otherwise" in local rules or preliminary conference orders, so lawyers need to ascertain the practice of the court and the judge.[6] An exception to the stay rule is where the motion is based solely on improper service, where no automatic stay of

---

[7] See § 448.

[8] State of N.Y. Higher Educ. Services Corp. v. Starr, 158 A.D.2d 771, 551 N.Y.S.2d 363 (3d Dep't 1990).

[9] CPLR 5701(a)(1), (2), 5501(a).

[10] Masterson v. Valley Nat. Bank of Long Island, 70 Misc. 2d 623, 334 N.Y.S.2d 356 (Sup. Ct., Nassau County 1972).

[11] See CPLR 3211(d).

[1] See § 272.

[2] See CPLR 2220(b); § 250.

[3] See CPLR 3211(f), analogous in this respect to CPLR 3024(c) and its answer-extending effect on corrective motions. CPLR 3211 is a dispositive, as opposed to merely corrective, motion.

[4] United Equity Services, Inc. v. First Am. Title Ins. Co. of New York, 75 Misc. 2d 254, 347 N.Y.S.2d 377 (Sup. Ct., Nassau County 1973); cf. Roff v. Green Hills of Glenham Condominium Ass'n, Inc., 97 A.D.3d 830, 949 N.Y.S.2d 156 (2d Dep't 2012) (Article 78 proceeding).

[5] CPLR 3214(b).

[6] See, e.g., 22 N.Y.C.R.R. § 202.70, Rule 11 (d).

disclosure results "unless the court orders otherwise."[7] The defendant who seeks the stay in that situation can bring the motion on by order to show cause.

C. SUMMARY JUDGMENT

Table of Sections

§ 278.   Summary Judgment, Generally
§ 279.   Time to Move for Summary Judgment
§ 280.   Actions in Which Summary Judgment Available
§ 281.   Proof on Summary Judgment Motion
§ 282.   Searching the Record
§ 283.   Summary Judgment Under 3212 Based on 3211 Ground
§ 284.   Immediate Trial of Fact Issue Under CPLR 3212
§ 285.   Partial Summary Judgment; Effect of Counterclaim
§ 286.   Salvaging Something from Abortive Motion
§ 287.   Res Judicata Effect of Summary Judgment Motion

§ 278. Summary Judgment, Generally

CPLR 3212, one of the busiest provisions in New York civil practice, allows the court on motion to grant summary judgment for a party. The grant means that the court, after going through the papers pro and con on the motion, has found that there is no substantial issue of fact in the case and therefore nothing to try. Summary judgment is often termed a drastic remedy and will not be granted if there is any doubt as to the existence of a triable issue.[1] As summary judgment is the procedural equivalent of a trial,[2] it is granted somewhat sparingly.[3] When saved for a proper case, it is a perfectly constitutional weapon and does not deny the parties a trial. It merely ascertains that there is nothing to try. Rather than resolve issues, it decides whether issues exist and, as is often said of the motion, issue finding rather than issue determination is its function.[4]

If the court on the motion finds genuinely controverted any fact on which liability depends, it cannot grant the motion,[5] but note that this applies only to liability. If liability is summarily established and only damages remain to be proved, the court can grant partial summary judgment, with the damages issues ordered to immediate trial.[6] In a few rare instances, to be discussed later,[7] immediate trial may be had even on certain issues on which liability depends, but as a general rule, the appearance of issues of fact in connection with liability results in the denial of the motion.

---

[7]   CPLR 3214(b).

[1]   Vega v. Restani Const. Corp., 18 N.Y.3d 499, 503, 942 N.Y.S.2d 13, 15, 965 N.E.2d 240, 242 (2012).

[2]   Mendoza v. Highpoint Associates, IX, LLC, 83 A.D.3d 1, 8, 919 N.Y.S.2d 129, 134 (1st Dep't 2011).

[3]   Ronder & Ronder, P.C. v. Nationwide Abstract Corp., 99 A.D.2d 608, 471 N.Y.S.2d 716 (3d Dep't 1984).

[4]   *Vega*, 18 N.Y.3d at 505, 942 N.Y.S.2d at 16, 965 N.E.2d at 243.

[5]   CPLR 3212(b).

[6]   Plank v. Watson Bowman Acme Corp., 46 A.D.3d 1338, 849 N.Y.S.2d 148 (4th Dep't 2007).

[7]   See § 284.

If an issue is arguable, a trial is needed and the case may not be disposed of summarily.[8] "Where the court entertains any doubt as to whether a triable issue of fact exists, summary judgment should be denied."[9] The same is true when a key issue turns on the credibility of opposing affiants. Only rarely can a credibility issue be resolved as a matter of law.[10]

CPLR 3212(b) draws an analogy between the motion for summary judgment and the motion for a directed verdict made at the trial.[11] The analogy is valid in that in both instances the court is taking the case away from the fact trier by determining that there is nothing to try, but the job on summary judgment is harder because the judge is asked to take this step on papers alone while the trial judge, on a motion for a directed verdict, has had the advantage of hearing the testimony and seeing the evidence in the flesh.

Whether to grant summary judgment in a given case is another of those inquiries that must always be sui generis. One can go through the reports and find literally hundreds of appellate cases reversing lower court grants of summary judgment. The review will show how judges can disagree on the relative strength of the same paper proof.[12] The first lesson to the lawyer is a comforting one: most of this mass of caselaw is largely useless (and therefore largely ignorable) as far as general principles are concerned. Each decision is a judicial reaction to the particular papers in a particular situation and has little precedential significance. The second lesson confirms that if the papers are such that reasonable minds may disagree on what they lead to, the court's recourse is to deny the motion and remit the parties to the trier of fact. If material facts are in dispute, or if different inferences may reasonably be drawn from facts themselves undisputed, the case must go to trial and summary judgment must be denied.[13]

If a main element in the case is a highly subjective one, such as fraud and the inherent investigation into intent that it entails, the case is likely to be unsuitable for summary judgment.[14] Nonetheless, as will be seen a few sections hence, there is no arbitrary restriction on the categories of action in which summary judgment may be sought.[15]

There have been innumerable articulations of standards by which summary judgment should be measured, but when all is said and done, the perception of whether or not the papers raise an issue of fact sufficient to ground the judgment is not the product of book-learned verbalizations of criteria, but of the judge's total experience on the bench and, before that, at the bar. Many judges will admit that they can't explain a

---

[8]   Steinberg v. Goodman, 27 N.Y.2d 304, 308, 317 N.Y.S.2d 342, 344, 265 N.E.2d 758, 760 (1970); Barrett v. Jacobs, 255 N.Y. 520, 175 N.E. 275 (1931); see *Vega,* 18 N.Y.3d at 505, 942 N.Y.S.2d at 16, 965 N.E.2d at 243.

[9]   Daliendo v. Johnson, 147 A.D.2d 312, 317, 543 N.Y.S.2d 987, 990 (2d Dep't 1989).

[10]   Rickert v. Travelers Ins. Co., 159 A.D.2d 758, 551 N.Y.S.2d 985 (3d Dep't 1990).

[11]   The motion for a directed verdict, although still called that in practice, is officially known today as a motion for judgment during trial. See CPLR 4401, treated in § 402.

[12]   See, e.g., Millerton Agway Co-op., Inc. v. Briarcliff Farms, Inc., 17 N.Y.2d 57, 268 N.Y.S.2d 18, 215 N.E.2d 341 (1966).

[13]   Shea v. Johnson, 101 A.D.2d 1018, 476 N.Y.S.2d 706 (4th Dep't 1984).

[14]   See, e.g., Falk v. Goodman, 7 N.Y.2d 87, 195 N.Y.S.2d 645, 163 N.E.2d 871 (1959); Foreign Cars of New Paltz, Inc. v. Hennessy, 124 A.D.2d 415, 507 N.Y.S.2d 512 (3d Dep't 1986).

[15]   See § 280.

summary judgment situation by a uniform standard but, as Justice Stewart noted about pornography,[16] they know it when they see it.

The mere making of a summary judgment motion under CPLR 3212 automatically suspends all pending disclosure proceedings until the motion is determined, "unless the court orders otherwise."[17] Courts frequently "order otherwise" in local rules or preliminary conference orders, so lawyers need to ascertain the practice of the court and the judge.[18] An exception to the stay rule is where the summary judgment motion is based solely on improper service where no automatic stay of disclosure results "unless the court orders otherwise."[19] The defendant who seeks the stay in that situation can bring the motion on by order to show cause.

§ 279. Time to Move for Summary Judgment

The earliest a motion for summary judgment may be made is after the joinder of issue,[1] which occurs when the answer is served in respect of the main claim and when a reply is served in respect of a counterclaim. The summary judgment motion under CPLR 3212 may not be made before the joinder of issue,[2] but a dismissal motion under CPLR 3211, which is usually made prior to joinder, can be treated as one for summary judgment.[3] Therefore, a pre-joinder summary judgment can come about that way.

This time restriction has been part of CPLR 3212(a) from the outset. There were no outer time limits under CPLR 3212(a), but they were added in 1996 in an attempt to prevent eleventh hour motions for summary judgment on the eve of trial.[4] The statute permits the court to set an outer time limit in a given case, as long as the court allows a party to move for summary judgment until at least the 30th day following the filing of the note of issue.[5] If the court sets no time limit, the statutory limit is imposed and the motion must be made by the 120th day following the filing of the note of issue. Upon a showing of "good cause," however, the court can allow a late motion in either instance.

CPLR 2103(b)(2) provides that "where a period of time prescribed by law is measured from the service of a paper and service is by mail, five days shall be added to the prescribed period."[6] The summary judgment deadlines in CPLR 3212(a) run from "the filing of the note of issue," not from its service. Although some prior appellate division caselaw had ruled to the contrary, in Group IX, Inc. v. Next Printing & Design Inc.,[7] the court noted that the 5-day add-on in CPLR 2103(b)(2) "is inapplicable to the

---

    [16]   Jacobellis v. State of Ohio, 378 U.S. 184, 197, 84 S. Ct. 1676, 1683, 12 L. Ed. 2d 793 (1964) (concurring opinion).

    [17]   CPLR 3214(b). Sometimes a special rule of court may reverse that or at least attempt to. See SPR 121:1, 130:2.

    [18]   See, e.g., 22 N.Y.C.R.R. § 202.70, Rule 11(d).

    [19]   CPLR 3214(b).

    [1]   CPLR 3212(a).

    [2]   City of Rochester v. Chiarella, 65 N.Y.2d 92, 101, 490 N.Y.S.2d 174, 179, 479 N.E.2d 810, 815 (1985).

    [3]   CPLR 3211(c). For a discussion of whether a pre-joinder 3212 motion can be treated as a 3211 motion, which pursuant to 3211(c) can then be retreated as a summary judgment motion—a series of doings which might sustain an otherwise premature CPLR 3212 motion—see Commentary C3212:12 on McKinney's CPLR 3212.

    [4]   See SPR 51:1.

    [5]   CPLR 3212(a). For note of issue practice, see §§ 368 to 369.

    [6]   See § 202.

    [7]   Group IX, Inc. v. Next Printing & Design Inc., 77 A.D.3d 530, 909 N.Y.S.2d 434 (1st Dep't 2010); SPR 227:2.

making of a summary judgment motion." In that defendant could not demonstrate "good cause" for the delayed motion, the First Department reversed the grant of partial summary judgment in its favor and dismissed the motion as untimely.[8] Defeat was thereby snatched from the jaws of victory.

In Organek v. Harris,[9] an action for wrongful death and conscious pain and suffering, plaintiff moved simultaneously for leave to amend the complaint and for partial summary judgment on liability. The supreme court granted the plaintiff's motion and, following an inquest on damages, awarded plaintiff $748,000. The Fourth Department concluded that it was premature to grant plaintiff summary judgment, while at the same time allowing him to amend his complaint, "[inasmuch as] defendant had not yet had an opportunity to serve an answer to the amended complaint and, thus, issue had not been joined." The Fourth Department reversed the award for partial summary judgment on liability, vacated the award of damages, and granted defendant twenty days to serve an answer.

While there is authority for the Fourth Department's reasoning, does this approach needlessly delay disposition of the motion for summary judgment? Issue had already been joined on the original pleadings and, unless the amended complaint significantly changed the allegations in the action and required additional disclosure,[10] we wonder if the summary judgment procedure was needlessly forestalled.

A lower court held in Santana v. City of New York[11] that CPLR 3212(a)'s deadline for moving for summary judgment doesn't apply to a pure motion to dismiss under CPLR 3211(a)(7) for failure to state a cause of action made after the filing of the note of issue.[12] If the CPLR 3211(a)(7) motion includes affidavits and challenges the proof in any way, however, it should be treated as a summary judgment subject to CPLR 3212(a)'s time restrictions.[13] A party intent on moving for summary judgment should do it within the strictly applied CPLR 3212(a) time prescription and not try to hide behind a CPLR 3211(a)(7) alternative.

In a similar vein, in Martinez v. Premium Laundry Corp.,[14] the court ruled that defendant's "oral application was not a motion to dismiss pursuant to CPLR 3211(a)(5) on the ground of release, but was, in effect, an untimely motion for summary judgment." The appellate division ruled that "[t]he court should not have entertained the oral application, since it was not supported by any motion papers, no formal motion was made on notice to plaintiff, and the application was made after jury selection had been completed." Even if the motion had been made on papers with sufficient notice, it would likely have been denied. The court stressed that the oral application was made more than seven months after the 120-day time period in CPLR 3212(a) had expired and defendant failed to make any showing of "good cause" for the delay.

---

[8]   See also Dexter v. 16th Street Holdings, L.L.C., 2012 WL 116102 (Sup. Ct., New York County 2012) (denying motion made three days late as untimely where defendant could not show "good cause" for late filing).

[9]   Organek v. Harris, 90 A.D.3d 1512, 935 N.Y.S.2d 240 (4th Dep't 2011).

[10]   See CPLR 3212(f); § 281.

[11]   Santana v. City of New York, 6 Misc. 3d 642, 787 N.Y.S.2d 651 (N.Y. City Civ. Ct. 2004); see also, Neil v. New York City Housing Authority, 15 Misc. 3d 1115(A), 839 N.Y.S.2d 434 (Sup. Ct., Kings County 2007), aff'd, 48 A.D.3d 767, 853 N.Y.S.2d 567 (2d Dep't 2008).

[12]   Recall that a CPLR 3211(a)(7) motion can be made at any time. See CPLR 3211(e); § 272.

[13]   See the discussion in SPR 166:1.

[14]   Martinez v. Premium Laundry Corp., 137 A.D.3d 419, 25 N.Y.S.3d 867 (1st Dep't 2016).

Some individual judges prohibit more than one summary judgment motion by a party in a case, but there is no stated restriction in CPLR 3212. "Multiple summary judgment motions in the same action [are] discouraged in the absence of a showing of newly discovered evidence or other sufficient cause."[15] One situation in which the courts allow a second motion for summary judgment is where "a new, as yet untested defense is permitted to be added by amendment."[16]

"Good Cause" to Entertain Late Motion

What will constitute "good cause" permitting a late motion to be considered? A number of lower court decisions had held that a strong showing of the merits of the motion would suffice. The rationale supporting this conclusion was that if the motion, however late, demonstrated that there was no issue of fact and that summary judgment was warranted, it would be idle to force the case to trial. They questioned, irrespective of a late motion, whether a case should have to go to trial when there was nothing to try.[17]

The Court of Appeals in Brill v. City of New York[18] unambiguously rejected this argument and held that CPLR 3212(a) "requires a showing of good cause for the delay in making the motion—a satisfactory explanation for the untimeliness—rather than simply permitting meritorious, nonprejudicial filings, however tardy." Hence it held that even if the merits of the motion are manifest, the delay in its making must be excused by "good cause" and that the consequence of failing to excuse the lateness is that the case will now just have to stay on the calendar until the trial, with the aspiring summary judgment party left to the devices available there.[19]

One popular assertion of "good cause" by parties moving for summary judgment outside the time periods in the statute is outstanding disclosure. In Greenpoint Properties, Inc. v. Carter,[20] the Second Department recognized that "[s]ignificant outstanding discovery may, in certain circumstances, constitute good cause for the delay in making a motion for summary judgment." Nonetheless, the court concluded that "good cause" was not present because the discovery outstanding at the time the note of issue was filed was not essential to defendant's motion. Therefore, the Second Department reversed the trial court's order granting defendant's late motion for summary judgment dismissing plaintiff's complaint.

As the *Greenpoint Properties* decision starkly demonstrates, the required linkage between the delayed disclosure and the grounds for the summary judgment motion presents needless trouble for the dilatory movant. Even if the movant believes that delayed disclosure will strengthen the motion, there is a significant chance that it will prove fruitless or that a court will disagree as to its importance. If so, the movant may

---

[15] LaFreniere v. Capital Dist. Transp. Authority, 105 A.D.2d 517, 518, 481 N.Y.S.2d 467, 468 (3d Dep't 1984); see Maggio v. 24 West 57 APF, LLC, 134 A.D.3d 621, 625, 24 N.Y.S.3d 1 (1st Dep't 2015); Jones ex rel. Cline v. 636 Holding Corp., 73 A.D.3d 409, 899 N.Y.S.2d 605 (1st Dep't 2010).

[16] See Armstrong v. Peat, Marwick, Mitchell & Co., 150 A.D.2d 189, 191, 540 N.Y.S.2d 799, 801 (1st Dep't 1989).

[17] See the discussion in SPR 79:2.

[18] Brill v. City of New York, 2 N.Y.3d 648, 781 N.Y.S.2d 261, 814 N.E.2d 431 (2004) (6–1 decision).

[19] *Brill*, 2 N.Y.3d at 653, 781 N.Y.S.2d at 265. See the discussion of the *Brill* case in the lead note in NYSLD No. 534. The whole subject of the CPLR 3212(a) time limit and its application—and prolific caselaw—is extensively reviewed in Connors, *CPLR 3212(a)'s Timing Requirement for Summary Judgment Motions*, 71 Brook. L. Rev. 1529 (Summer 2006).

[20] Greenpoint Properties, Inc. v. Carter, 82 A.D.3d 1157, 919 N.Y.S.2d 370 (2d Dep't 2011).

ultimately be unable to establish "good cause" to allow for consideration of a late motion. The prudent lawyer will frequently prefer to make a timely motion and simply rely on the proof already obtained.[21]

There are instances in which a party is not joined in the action until after the time period in CPLR 3212(a) has expired. Can that late joinder, standing alone, constitute "good cause" for a late motion for summary judgment? In Callegari v. Davis & Partners, LLC,[22] the court entertained a motion by the third-party defendant made far beyond the CPLR 3212(a) deadline. The note of issue in P's main action against D was filed on August 21, 2007, but the third-party defendant, X, wasn't joined until July 17, 2008, and did not move for summary judgment until over two years later, on July 20, 2010. The court held in rather broad language that "the fact that movant was not even a party to the action when the 120 deadline expired constitutes good cause to allow this late motion for summary judgment."[23]

An analysis of X's diligence after its joinder may be appropriate to consider in these situations. Did X have ample opportunity, through the bill of particulars and disclosure devices, to ready itself for a summary judgment application? Did the time chosen by X to make the motion show reasonable diligence under the circumstances? A similar problem can arise where two actions are consolidated and the CPLR 3212(a) deadline has already expired in the action in which the merger has occurred.[24] It is advisable in all of these situations for the party joining the action to immediately ascertain the CPLR 3212(a) deadline and, if necessary, move to strike the note of issue or request that the court permit additional time for the making of a summary judgment motion.

If there is any nonfrivolous argument that a motion for summary judgment is untimely, the movant should attempt to establish "good cause" for any possible delay in the moving papers and not wait to address the issue in a reply. This approach may display a chink in one's armor, but is far better than being precluded from making the motion. The point is made in Goldin v. New York and Presbyterian Hosp.,[25] where the supreme court granted the defendant's motion for summary judgment, which was made 67 days after the note of issue was filed. In his original moving papers, the defendant failed to demonstrate "good cause" for not making the motion before the expiration of the 60-day deadline set forth in Kings County Supreme Court Uniform Civil Term Rule Part C (6). On appeal, the Second Department denied the motion as untimely and reinstated the medical malpractice action against the defendant ruling that "[i]t was an improvident exercise of the Supreme Court's discretion to entertain the summary judgment motion and to consider the good cause arguments raised for the first time in [defendant's] reply papers." Similarly, in Bissell v. New York State Dept. of Transp.,[26] defendant made its motion more than 10 months after the expiration of CPLR 3212(a)'s 120 day deadline and failed to demonstrate "good cause" for the delay in its moving papers. Relying on *Goldin*, the Fourth Department held that supreme court "improperly considered the 'good cause' proffered by defendant for the first time in its reply papers" and reversed the order dismissing plaintiff's claim.

---

[21] See Supplementary Practice Commentary C3116:1 on McKinney's CPLR 3116.

[22] Callegari v. Davis & Partners, LLC, 2011 WL 1114421 (Sup. Ct., New York County 2011).

[23] *Callegari*, 2011 WL at 1114421.

[24] See Hope v. Fortunato, 20 Misc. 3d 1117(A), 867 N.Y.S.2d 17 (Sup. Ct., Kings County 2008); § 128.

[25] Goldin v. New York and Presbyterian Hosp., 112 A.D.3d 578, 975 N.Y.S.2d 892 (2d Dep't 2013).

[26] Bissell v. New York State Dept. of Transp., 122 A.D.3d 1434, 995 N.Y.S.2d 530 (4th Dep't 2014).

Time to Make Cross-Motion for Summary Judgment

What about CPLR 3212(a)'s time limit as applied to an application for summary judgment made by way of cross-motion? Assume X makes a timely motion for summary judgment and Y then makes a cross-motion for similar relief, affording proper notice under CPLR 2215, the cross-motion statute,[27] but just beyond the time limit of CPLR 3212(a).[28] May the cross-motion be entertained? The First Department answered yes in Filannino v. Triborough Bridge and Tunnel Authority,[29] as long as the relief sought in the cross-motion is "nearly identical" to that sought on the main motion, but then concluded that the standard was not satisfied.

D's motion for summary judgment in *Filannino* was to dismiss P's claims under Labor Law sections 200 and 241(6). P's cross-motion was for summary judgment on P's claim under Labor Law section 240(1). The court found the latter ground to be distinct from the grounds moved upon in D's main motion—albeit all are part of the Labor Law article addressing safety at construction sites—and also held that there was no "good cause" to entertain the untimely cross-motion.

Subsequently, in Maggio v. 24 West 57 APF, LLC,[30] the First Department noted that in reviewing a summary judgment motion, it may search the record and grant summary judgment to any non-moving party without the necessity of a cross-motion.[31] Therefore, it reasoned, a court "may even disregard the tardiness of a cross-motion and grant the cross movant summary judgment, on the theory that the cross-motion was not necessary in the first place."[32] The issue on which the non-movant, or late cross-movant, is awarded summary judgment must, however, be "nearly identical" to that on which the movant sought relief.[33] Is this another way of saying there is "good cause" to entertain a late motion for summary judgment if it seeks relief nearly identical to the relief sought on a timely motion for summary judgment?

Court Rules Imposing Summary Judgment Deadlines

As discussed above, CPLR 3212(a) permits the court to set its own outer time limit for making summary judgment motions, as long as that date is no earlier than 30 days after the filing of the note of issue. Courts can prescribe these short time frames in all sorts of places, including preliminary conference orders, scheduling orders, individual court rules, county rules,[34] and rules of a judicial district. In McDowell & Walker, Inc. v. Micha,[35] the Third Department applied the local rules of the Sixth Judicial District, which require that "[s]ummary judgment motions must be *filed* no later than (60) days

---

[27] See § 249.

[28] A cross-motion is "made" when it is served. See § 249.

[29] Filannino v. Triborough Bridge and Tunnel Authority, 34 A.D.3d 280, 824 N.Y.S.2d 244 (1st Dep't 2006).

[30] Maggio v. 24 West 57 APF, LLC, 134 A.D.3d 621, 24 N.Y.S.3d 1 (1st Dep't 2015).

[31] See § 282.

[32] *Maggio*, 134 A.D.3d at 628, 24 N.Y.S.3d at 8.

[33] *Maggio*, 134 A.D.3d at 628, 24 N.Y.S.3d at 8.

[34] See Kings County Supreme Court Uniform Civil Term Rule Part C (6); Lyebyedyev v. Hoffman, 84 A.D.3d 751, 921 N.Y.S.2d 866 (2d Dep't 2011) (denying motion made approximately 90 days after filing of note of issue as untimely); Drumgold v. AVA Service Corp., 37 Misc. 3d 1212(A), 964 N.Y.S.2d 58 (Sup. Ct., Kings County 2012) (denying motion made 67 days after filing of note of issue as untimely).

[35] McDowell & Walker, Inc. v. Micha, 113 A.D.3d 979, 979 N.Y.S.2d 420 (3d Dep't 2014) (emphasis added).

after the date when the Trial Note of Issue is filed," unless permission is obtained for good cause shown.

Compliance with this sort of local rule can be tricky. CPLR 3212(a) speaks in terms of when a summary judgment motion may be "made" and, pursuant to CPLR 2211, a motion is "made" when the motion or order to show cause is "served," not when it is "filed."[36] Lawyers making motions for summary judgment in the Sixth Judicial District must take pains to not only make, i.e., serve, their motions for summary judgment within 60 days from the filing of the note of issue, but also to file them within that time frame.

These sorts of local rules that require the "filing" of a motion for summary judgment within a specific time frame, rather than its mere service, are not solely an upstate phenomenon. The First Department's decision in Connolly v. 129 E. 69th Street Corp.[37] presents another stark example of the importance of ascertaining and calendaring summary judgment time frames. In *Connolly*, a New York County supreme court's individual part rules required that motions for summary judgment be "filed" within 60 days of the filing of the note of issue. Since plaintiffs filed the note of issue on July 10, 2013, the motions for summary judgment were required to be filed by September 9, 2013. While defendant "made" the motion for summary judgment on September 4, 2013, by serving it, it did not file the motion until September 10, 2013, one day after the 60-day time period expired. Therefore, the First Department found defendants' motions to be untimely and reversed the supreme court's order granting defendants' summary judgment dismissing the complaint. Try explaining that to the clients!

The Third Department held in Harrington v. Palmer Mobile Homes, Inc.[38] that a court can, with a "scheduling order," require a summary judgment motion to be made by a specified time "without reference" to the note of issue activities around which CPLR 3212(a) revolves. The scheduling order in *Harrington* required that summary judgment motions be made returnable by a date certain, and the movant did not establish good cause for missing the deadline. Therefore, the court affirmed the denial of the motion as untimely. A court ordered deadline like the one in *Harrington* can create mischief if it essentially cuts short the minimum 30-day period in CPLR 3212(a), but that apparently was not the case therein as the action was commenced in 2003 and the scheduling order didn't even issue until 2008.

In Crawford v. Liz Claiborne, Inc.,[39] there was an interplay between a preliminary conference order directing that dispositive motions be made "per local rule," the local rule itself, and the judge's individual part rules that addressed the time period to move for summary judgment. To make matters more complicated, the local rule and the judge's individual part rules were amended after the preliminary conference order was issued, but before the filing of the note of issue. The Court of Appeals reversed the First Department and ruled that the summary judgment motion was timely, but it was a very bumpy ride for the defendant who faced the prospect of going to trial on a matter in which it had been awarded summary judgment by supreme court.

---

[36] See § 243.

[37] Connolly v. 129 East 69th Street Corp., 127 A.D.3d 617, 7 N.Y.S.3d 889 (1st Dep't 2015).

[38] Harrington v. Palmer Mobile Homes, Inc., 71 A.D.3d 1274, 900 N.Y.S.2d 152 (3d Dep't 2010) (SPR 232:3).

[39] Crawford v. Liz Claiborne, Inc., 11 N.Y.3d 810, 869 N.Y.S.2d 378, 898 N.E.2d 561 (2008).

While the court clearly has the power under CPLR 3212(a) to set a date after which no summary judgment motion may be made (as long as the parties are given until at least the 30th day after the filing of the note of issue), it has been held that the court has "no authority" to require that the filing of the note of issue actually precede the motion. The statute allows the motion after issue has been joined—in the usual case that means after the answer has been served—which makes this the conferral of a right.[40] The statute's use of the note of issue's filing as a basis for measuring the outside time limit for a summary judgment motion is not an authorization for a court to direct that the filing precede the motion.

It is doubtful that this myriad of individual court rules imposing time limits on moving for summary judgment, which cause pain and heartache in so many cases, do anything to advance justice. Nonetheless, the lesson to be distilled from the above caselaw is that the lawyer must always ascertain the applicable time period to move for summary judgment in every matter in the office. The period then needs to be checked carefully and coordinated with the filing of the note of issue to ensure that the option for moving for summary judgment is not forfeited due to untimeliness. Further, in the event of a conflict between local rules and the judge's individual part rules, always follow the earlier deadline to avoid the "*Crawford* predicament."

Stipulations Extending Time to Move for Summary Judgment

In Bennett v. St. John's Home,[41] the parties entered into a written stipulation permitting a late motion for summary judgment and supreme court granted defendants' motion dismissing the complaint. Plaintiff appealed, now contending that that the motion should have been denied as untimely under CPLR 3212(a) because it was made more than 120 days after the filing of the note of issue and defendant did not make the required statutory showing of "good cause" for the delay. The Fourth Department majority concluded that plaintiff waived that contention by entering into the written stipulation before the motion was made. A dissenting justice, outlining the purpose behind the statutory time frame for moving for summary judgment contained in CPLR 3212(a), maintained that the court was not permitted to simply accept the stipulation of the parties to extend the 120-day deadline. In that the motion was made more than ten months beyond the statutory deadline, the dissent argued that it could not be considered unless the court found "good cause" for the delay. Furthermore, the dissent observed, the parties' stipulation was insufficient to excuse the delay because, under the statute, the court has the exclusive authority to extend the statutory deadline and may only do so if it finds "good cause."[42]

The Fourth Department granted leave to the Court of Appeals. Unfortunately, however, because the issue of the motion's timeliness under CPLR 3212(a) was not preserved in the supreme court, the Court of Appeals lacked power to review the matter.[43]

The ultimate answer to the question of whether a stipulation to extend the time to move for summary judgment can trump the statutory requirement of "good cause" for a delayed motion will await another day. Meanwhile, parties need to be careful in this

40   See Vasquez v. Soto, 61 A.D.3d 968, 877 N.Y.S.2d 467 (2d Dep't 2009); SPR 209:2.

41   Bennett v. St. John's Home, 128 A.D.3d 1428, 8 N.Y.S.3d 774 (4th Dep't 2015).

42   See Coty v. County of Clinton, 42 A.D.3d 612, 839 N.Y.S.2d 825 (3d Dep't 2007).

43   Bennett v. St. John's Home, 26 N.Y.3d 1033, 22 N.Y.S.3d 162, 43 N.E.3d 372 (2015).

context. Even if the court so orders a stipulation to extend the time to move for summary judgment, it may not be honored on appeal absent an independent finding of "good cause" under CPLR 3212(a). Until the Court of Appeals weighs in on this issue, the prudent course is to make the motion for summary judgment in a timely fashion and without any extension of the applicable period.

If a stipulation between the parties calls for the "filing" of a summary judgment motion within 60 days after the note of issue is filed, an actual filing must occur within that time. Merely serving the motion papers on the other side before the deadline won't do.[44] This result is consistent with the caselaw addressed under the heading above in which a court's own rule requires filing of the motion for summary judgment within a specific time frame rather than making the motion by service within such time.

§ 280. Actions in Which Summary Judgment Available

Before 1959, there was a limited list of actions in which summary judgment could be sought. If a given category of action was not on the list, the motion could not be used in it. The list was contained in Rule 113 of the old Rules of Civil Practice. In 1959, the rule was amended to abolish the list and extend the summary judgment tool to all actions except the matrimonial action.[1] In 1978, after the liberalization of New York's divorce laws, even the matrimonial exception was eliminated and today the summary judgment motion has no restrictions at all with respect to category of action.

The main accomplishment of the 1959 amendment was to permit summary judgment in negligence and other personal injury actions, a numerous category of litigation from which summary judgment had previously been excluded. The plaintiff's bar welcomed this event with fervor; they hoped it would pave the way to early grants of partial summary judgment motions in many cases on the issue of liability, obviating a trial on that issue. They awaited court tests eagerly. In a couple of key negligence cases, summary judgment was granted for the plaintiff, but on fact patterns—as it turned out—that were to offer little encouragement for the long-range use of summary judgment motions by plaintiffs in the conventional tort action.

In what was probably the first major test case, Di Sabato v. Soffes,[2] the plaintiffs were counter girls working at a corner drugstore in New York City when the defendant's car came careening into the store, dislodging coffee urns and injuring them. After the dust settled, it became apparent that nobody was at the helm of the 1957 Chrysler that was now mounted in the wall of the drugstore. The driver had double-parked across the intersection and tried to let someone out on the passenger side, but the door stuck. So he went back around and had the passenger sidle along the seat past the driver's side. During the sidling the car took off and caused the accident. On these facts, the First Department granted summary judgment for the plaintiffs on the issue of the defendant's negligence. But the vote was 3–2, and the dissenting opinion by Justice (later Chief Judge) Breitel pointed to a number of fact questions that had to be tried no matter how tempting it might be to guess that the jury would find them in the plaintiff's favor. The defendant swore, for example, that he set the brake and put the car in neutral. The dissent was of the view that if that were so, negligence as a matter of law was not

---

[44]   Corchado v. City of New York, 64 A.D.3d 429, 883 N.Y.S.2d 33 (1st Dep't 2009) (SPR 212:2).

[1]   This was based on legislative policy against the so-called "consent" divorce (the fear that the movant's proof on a summary judgment motion might by agreement be left unrefuted).

[2]   Di Sabato v. Soffes, 9 A.D.2d 297, 193 N.Y.S.2d 184 (1st Dep't 1959).

established.[3] Because of this dissent and despite the majority's grant of judgment, *Di Sabato* over the years became an influence against, not for, summary judgment in a negligence case.

If the facts are not disputed, and the only issue is one of law, summary judgment will of course be granted even in a negligence case, such as one involving a rear-end collision with a stopped vehicle.[4] If, however, the issue is at root one of negligence, it's a question of fact for the jury and summary judgment is barred. Granting summary judgment in a negligence case may take something as unusual as the defendant almost deliberately inculpating herself in her own deposition, as happened in Gerard v. Inglese,[5] an early Second Department test of the use of summary judgment in the negligence area. The defendant driver deposed that at the time of the accident, while driving at about 45 m.p.h., she took her eyes off the road to light a cigarette and hit the curb. At this point in the deposition, the plaintiffs' lawyer probably pinched himself. The plaintiffs, her passengers in the personal injury action, were awarded summary judgment.

A self-inculpating deposition accomplished the same result some years later in the Court of Appeals case of Andre v. Pomeroy.[6] The defendant driver said that the accident occurred just after she looked down to get her compact; she hit the slowed or stopped car in front of her. The plaintiff was the defendant's daughter, and the plaintiff's lawyer was a happy man. A divided Court of Appeals gave the plaintiff summary judgment.

That was a so-called rear-end collision case, which is usually a consistent candidate for summary judgment.[7] But even that case will elude summary judgment if the defendant by affidavit or deposition offers strong opposition to the motion, as where he attests that there was an oil slick on the road causing skidding, or that the brakes went suddenly and without warning, or that the defendant took suddenly ill at the wheel.[8] As the Court of Appeals has acknowledged, "[n]egligence cases by their very nature do not usually lend themselves to summary judgment."[9]

Cases like the pair noted above, in which the defendant literally gives the case away in a deposition, are a dilemma for the insurer, who usually provides and compensates the defendant's lawyer. It is often a case in which the defendant insured is being scrupulously honest or deliberately dishonest. If the latter, the reason is usually the collusion of the defendant to assure a recovery from the insurance policy to the injured plaintiffs, who are family or friends. One may wonder how enthusiastic the defendant's self-inculpating deposings would be if the sum sought by the plaintiff exceeded the defendant's insurance coverage—a sure way to test friendship or to see just how thick blood is.

---

[3]   *Di Sabato*, 9 A.D.2d at 306–7, 193 N.Y.S.2d at 195 (Breitel, J., dissenting).

[4]   See, e.g., Farkas v. Cedarhurst Natural Food Shoppe Inc., 51 A.D.2d 793, 380 N.Y.S.2d 287 (2d Dep't 1976), aff'd, 41 N.Y.2d 1041, 396 N.Y.S.2d 165, 364 N.E.2d 829 (1977); Pampris v. Egnasher, 20 A.D.3d 746, 799 N.Y.S.2d 309 (3d Dep't 2005).

[5]   Gerard v. Inglese, 11 A.D.2d 381, 206 N.Y.S.2d 879 (2d Dep't 1960).

[6]   Andre v. Pomeroy, 35 N.Y.2d 361, 362 N.Y.S.2d 131, 320 N.E.2d 853 (1974).

[7]   See Shulga v. Ashcroft, 11 A.D.3d 893, 784 N.Y.S.2d 744 (4th Dep't 2004) (granting plaintiff partial summary judgment on liability in rear end collision accident in which defendant was holding a cellular phone); 1 NY PJI 2:82 (Motor Vehicle Accidents—Rear End Collisions—Negligence).

[8]   See Normoyle v. New York City Transit Authority, 181 A.D.2d 498, 581 N.Y.S.2d 28 (1st Dep't 1992) (recognizing proposition, but holding that defendant's mere proffering of "brake failure" as an excuse for the accident was insufficient to raise triable issue of fact).

[9]   Ugarriza v. Schmieder, 46 N.Y.2d 471, 474, 414 N.Y.S.2d 304, 305, 386 N.E.2d 1324, 1325 (1979).

Although summary judgment can be awarded to the plaintiff in a negligence action, what if the plaintiff may be guilty of some culpable conduct in the matter? Should that obstruct plaintiff's path to summary judgment? This issue was the subject of conflict between the departments, but the First, in Calcano v. Rodriguez,[10] came around to the Second's way of thinking, acknowledging that the law on the subject is that "a plaintiff moving for summary judgment on the issue of liability . . . must eliminate any material issue, not only as to the defendant's negligence, but also as to whether the plaintiff's own comparative negligence contributed to the incident." *Calcano*, and subsequent First Department decisions, conclude that placing the burden on the plaintiff to disprove any comparative fault is more faithful to the Court of Appeals view of the subject, expressed in its 1993 decision in Thoma v. Ronai.[11] These latter decisions from the First Department include significant dissents and concurrences expressing disagreement on the point.[12]

In an opinion that does not cite any of the decisions above, the Fourth Department permitted a plaintiff to obtain partial summary judgment on the issue of defendant's negligence even though there was a question of fact regarding the plaintiff's comparative fault.[13] This alternative position can be supported by the argument that summary judgment on D's liability is permissible, even when there are questions of fact regarding P's comparative fault, because that course still requires a trial of damages and the trial is the proper place to try issues of, and apportion, P's fault. The rule that currently holds sway in the First and Second Departments is peculiar in that it apparently imposes on the P the burden of establishing her freedom from comparative fault even though by statute that's a burden of both pleading and proof borne by the defendant under the specific terms of CPLR 1412.[14]

Examining the problem from a different perspective, even if a plaintiff is entirely free from any comparative fault, that does not mean she will be entitled to summary judgment on liability. In Oluwatayo v. Dulinayan,[15] the First Department ruled that a plaintiff, who was an "innocent driver" and did not in any way contribute to the happening of the accident, was not merely "by virtue of such status, per se, entitled to summary judgment on liability against any or all defendant drivers." In *Oluwatayo*, plaintiff failed to demonstrate that he was entitled to summary judgment on liability against either defendant driver because of the conflicting and unresolved versions of which vehicle was responsible for the accident. The court did, however, rule that plaintiff was entitled to an order denoting his lack of culpable conduct on the issue of liability pursuant to CPLR 3212(g) in his action against the drivers of two other cars.[16]

---

[10] Calcano v. Rodriguez, 91 A.D.3d 468, 469, 936 N.Y.S.2d 185, 186–87 (1st Dep't 2012) (SPR 242:1).

[11] Thoma v. Ronai, 82 N.Y.2d 736, 602 N.Y.S.2d 323, 621 N.E.2d 690 (1993).

[12] See Rodriguez v. City of New York, 142 A.D.3d 778, 37 N.Y.S.3d 93 (1st Dep't 2016); Capuano v. Tishman Const. Corp., 98 A.D.3d 848, 950 N.Y.S.2d 517 (1st Dep't 2012); Maniscalco v. New York City Transit Authority, 95 A.D.3d 510, 943 N.Y.S.2d 486 (1st Dep't 2012). The issue is explored in further detail in Patrick M. Connors, *Can Comparative Fault Stop the Train Known as Summary Judgment?*, N.Y.L.J., Jan. 16, 2013, at 249 (no. 11).

[13] Simoneit v. Mark Cerrone, Inc., 122 A.D.3d 1246, 996 N.Y.S.2d 810 (4th Dep't 2014), amended on reargument, 126 A.D.3d 1428, 6 N.Y.S.3d 918 (4th Dep't 2015).

[14] See § 168E.

[15] Oluwatayo v. Dulinayan, 142 A.D.3d 113, 35 N.Y.S.3d 84 (1st Dep't 2016).

[16] See § 286; see also Huerta-Saucedo v. City Bronx Leasing Inc., 147 A.D.3d 695, 48 N.Y.S.3d 132 (1st Dep't 2017) (triable issues of fact precluded summary judgment on the issue of defendants' liability, but plaintiffs were entitled to an order under CPLR 3212(g) finding that they were free from comparative fault).

Is this all that significant an issue? There are significant benefits that can be derived from the award of partial summary judgment on liability. In a personal injury action, for example, interest under CPLR 5002 will begin to run from the liability determination even though damages have not yet been awarded.[17] That right, coupled with the fact that a trial on damages will now be necessary, will often tip the scales in favor of a settlement. A summary judgment is sometimes entertained on the basis of a defense not formally pleaded, but it is exceedingly rare and can be permitted only when other sources within the action have given the other side adequate notice and an opportunity to prepare.[18] This result is appropriate only when, for example, "reliance upon that defense neither surprises nor prejudices the plaintiff," as when the plaintiff knows the score from other sources in the case, such as motion papers.[19]

§ 281. Proof on Summary Judgment Motion

Any form of evidence, documentary or otherwise, may be considered on a motion for summary judgment.[1] Affidavits from those having personal knowledge of the facts are a primary source of proof.[2] Written admissions are specifically mentioned in CPLR 3212(b). The fruits of any other of the disclosure devices[3] would also be usable. As has already been seen, depositions—also listed in the statute—are excellent sources of proof.[4]

Affidavits on any motion should be made only by those with knowledge of the recited facts, and nowhere is this rule more faithfully applied than on the motion for summary judgment. The attorney's affidavit, unless the attorney happens to have first-hand knowledge of the facts, which is the exception rather than the rule, has no probative force.[5] The movant for summary judgment may be expected to include in her papers just about everything she has, but the opposing party must not overlook his own burden if the motion is to be defeated. He must avoid mere conclusory allegations and come forward to lay bare his proof.[6] The consequence of failing to do so will lead the court to infer that there is no genuine fact issue to be tried.[7] Failing to respond to a fact attested to in the moving papers, for example, will be deemed to admit it.[8] Nor will pleading ignorance of the fact be a sufficient response, unless it is shown that the ignorance is

---

[17]   Eisenberg v. Rockland County, 19 A.D.3d 536, 796 N.Y.S.2d 532 (2d Dep't 2005); see § 411.

[18]   See Dampskibsselskabet Torm A/S v. P. L. Thomas Paper Co., 26 A.D.2d 347, 352, 274 N.Y.S.2d 601, 606–07 (1st Dep't 1966).

[19]   Olean Urban Renewal Agency v. Herman, 101 A.D.2d 712, 713, 475 N.Y.S.2d 955, 957 (4th Dep't 1984).

[1]   CPLR 3212(b); Wilkinson v. Skinner, 34 N.Y.2d 53, 356 N.Y.S.2d 15, 312 N.E.2d 158 (1974).

[2]   See Viviane Etienne Medical Care, P.C. v. Country-Wide Ins. Co., 25 N.Y.3d 498, 508, 14 N.Y.S.3d 283, 291, 35 N.E.2d 451, 459 (2015).

[3]   The disclosure devices are in Article 31 of the CPLR, studied in §§ 343 et seq.

[4]   See, e.g., Andre v. Pomeroy and Gerard v. Inglese, 35 N.Y.2d 361, 362 N.Y.S.2d 131, 320 N.E.2d 853 (1974); § 280.

[5]   Zuckerman v. City of New York, 49 N.Y.2d 557, 563, 427 N.Y.S.2d 595, 598, 404 N.E.2d 718, 720 (1980); Estate of Ligaya Rodriguez, 2012 N.Y.L.J. LEXIS 3606, *5–6 (Sur. Ct., Kings County 2012).

[6]   In re Dissolution of Rencor Controls Inc., 263 A.D.2d 845, 693 N.Y.S.2d 717 (3d Dep't 1999) (special proceeding for judicial dissolution).

[7]   Banasik v. Reed Prentice Division of Package Machinery Co., 34 A.D.2d 746, 310 N.Y.S.2d 127 (1st Dep't 1970), aff'd, 28 N.Y.2d 770, 321 N.Y.S.2d 376, 269 N.E.2d 918 (1971); Monex Financial Services Ltd. v. Dynamic Currency Conversion, Inc., 2009 WL 1269482 (Sup. Ct., Nassau County 2009), aff'd, 76 A.D.3d 515, 904 N.Y.S.2d 919 (2d Dep't 2010).

[8]   Kuehne & Nagel, Inc. v. Baiden, 36 N.Y.2d 539, 369 N.Y.S.2d 667, 330 N.E.2d 624 (1975); Madeline D'Anthony Enterprises, Inc. v. Sokolowsky, 101 A.D.3d 606, 609, 957 N.Y.S.2d 88, 92 (1st Dep't 2012).

unavoidable and that with diligent effort the fact could not be ascertained in time for the motion.[9]

The evidence will be construed in a light most favorable to the one moved against,[10] but this normal rule of summary judgment practice will not be applied if the opposition is evasive, indirect, or coy. Offering only part of one's opposing proof on the assumption that it will suffice to defeat the motion, and for tactical purposes holding back the rest for trial use, can backfire. It can be done safely only when the opposer is sure that what he uses will suffice to beat back the motion. A wrong guess will find the opposer on the wrong side of a summary judgment. Although the courts sometimes grant a motion for summary judgment with leave to move to vacate it,[11] it is rare and should not be anticipated.

Drawing the line between what the moving party has to show to earn a summary judgment and what the opposing party has to show to defeat the summary judgment is a perennial battle in the courts, both federal and state. And it is a case-by-case battle, manifesting the relatively limited value of general language about who has what burden.

In New York State courts, the party moving for summary judgment has the burden to establish "a prima facie showing of entitlement to judgment as a matter of law, tendering sufficient evidence to demonstrate the absence of any material issues of fact."[12] If the moving party fails to meet that initial burden, summary judgment should be denied *regardless of the sufficiency of the opposing papers.*"[13] In these circumstances, the burden does not shift to the party opposing summary judgment to persuade the court against granting it.[14] Stated otherwise, a defendant should not be awarded summary judgment dismissing the action by simply pointing to weaknesses in the plaintiff's case.[15]

The New York rule governing burdens of proof on a summary judgment motion should be contrasted with the federal rule established in Celotex Corp. v. Catrett.[16] Therein, the Supreme Court held that "the burden on the moving party may be discharged by . . . pointing out to the district court . . . that there is an absence of evidence to support the nonmoving party's case."[17] Such an approach will not satisfy the movant's burden in a New York State court, and parties moving for summary judgment must be alert to this distinction.[18]

The failure of the opposing party to respond to a summary judgment motion does not mandate a grant of the motion. The movant must still make the usual showing

---

[9]   Kenworthy v. Town of Oyster Bay, 116 A.D.2d 628, 497 N.Y.S.2d 712 (2d Dep't 1986); Overseas Reliance Tours & Travel Service, Inc. v. Sarne Co., 17 A.D.2d 578, 237 N.Y.S.2d 416 (1st Dep't 1963); see CPLR 3212(f) (discussed later in this section).

[10]   Asabor v. Archdiocese of New York, 102 A.D.3d 524, 527, 961 N.Y.S.2d 17, 20 (1st Dep't 2013).

[11]   See Frutos v. Shapiro, 11 A.D.2d 1005, 206 N.Y.S.2d 18 (1st Dep't 1960).

[12]   Voss v. Netherlands Ins. Co., 22 N.Y.3d 728, 734, 985 N.Y.S.2d 448, 452, 8 N.E.3d 823, 828 (2014).

[13]   Vega v. Restani Const. Corp., 18 N.Y.3d 499, 503, 942 N.Y.S.2d 13, 965 N.E.2d 240 (2012).

[14]   *Voss,* 22 N.Y.3d at 734, 985 N.Y.S.2d at 452, 8 N.E.3d at 828; see Higgitt, Commentaries C3212:1 on McKinney's CPLR 3212.

[15]   See, e.g., River Ridge Living Center, LLC v. ADL Data Systems, Inc., 98 A.D.3d 724, 950 N.Y.S.2d 179 (2d Dep't 2012).

[16]   Celotex Corp. v. Catrett, 477 U.S. 317, 106 S. Ct. 2548, 91 L. Ed. 2d 265 (1986).

[17]   *Celotex Corp.,* 477 U.S. at 325, 106 S.Ct. at 2554.

[18]   Yun Tung Chow v. Reckitt & Colman, Inc., 17 N.Y.3d 29, 36, 926 N.Y.S.2d 377, 382, 950 N.E.2d 113 (2011) (Smith, J., concurring).

needed for summary judgment, which is that there is no issue of fact and that the movant is entitled to judgment as a matter of law.[19]

If a key fact in issue is within the exclusive knowledge of the moving party, the motion for summary judgment will usually be denied.[20] This situation can easily occur, for example, when the opposer is an executor or administrator of a decedent and had no actual part in the transaction or event at issue. Denial of the motion will also result when the fact is one the opposing party cannot know, as where it turns on the scope of the movant's knowledge of his own agent's act.[21]

If a key fact turns on an item of evidence whose admissibility at the trial is arguable, summary judgment must be denied.[22] Because of the drastic nature of the remedy, a rule has even arisen that occasionally permits the court to consider incompetent evidence on a motion for summary judgment, i.e., evidence that would be inadmissible at a trial, but only if it tends to defeat the motion. It cannot be considered in support of the motion. Therefore, a party opposing a summary judgment motion may be permitted to demonstrate an acceptable excuse for the failure to tender evidence in admissible form.[23] This rule has been applied, for example, when the so-called dead-person statute, CPLR 4519, was involved. Thus, where P's only opposing evidence was a communication that the statute would exclude at a trial, the evidence was nevertheless entertained and D's summary judgment motion denied on the basis of it. The court did seem to be at some pains, however, to point out that P might have some other way to make out a prima facie case,[24] thus appearing to leave the door open to a different result, and to the exclusion of the incompetent evidence, in a case in which such an alternative clearly does not exist.

Just as the proponent of a piece of evidence at trial can lay a foundation and cure a hearsay problem, the movant on summary judgment can attempt to clear the path for consideration of proof on the motion.[25] In Viviane Etienne Medical Care, P.C. v. Country-Wide Ins. Co.,[26] the Court observed that "[c]ertain affidavits and documents submitted in support of a motion for summary judgment may be deemed admissible where those documents meet the requirements of the business records exception to the rule against hearsay under CPLR 4518." In *Viviane Etienne*, plaintiff medical provider commenced an action to recover no-fault insurance benefits to reimburse it for medical services provided to defendants' insureds. In support of its motion for summary judgment, plaintiff submitted eight verification of treatment forms and an affidavit of the president

---

[19] See Liberty Taxi Management, Inc. v. Gincherman, 32 A.D.3d 276, 820 N.Y.S.2d 49 (1st Dep't 2006).

[20] Krupp v. Aetna Life & Cas. Co., 103 A.D.2d 252, 262, 479 N.Y.S.2d 992, 999 (2d Dep't 1984). The movant in such a case should be put to her proof so that the opposing party can be afforded an opportunity for cross-examination.

[21] See Esposito v. Metropolitan Transp. Authority, 264 A.D.2d 370, 371, 695 N.Y.S.2d 28, 30 (1st Dep't 1999).

[22] Gallo Painting, Inc. v. Aetna Ins. Co., 49 A.D.2d 746, 372 N.Y.S.2d 699 (2d Dep't 1975); see Supreme Automotive Mfg. Corp. v. Continental Cas. Co., 97 A.D.2d 700, 468 N.Y.S.2d 125 (1st Dep't 1983).

[23] Friends of Animals, Inc. v. Associated Fur Mfrs., Inc., 46 N.Y.2d 1065, 1068, 416 N.Y.S.2d 790, 792, 390 N.E.2d 298, 299 (1979).

[24] Phillips v. Joseph Kantor & Co., 31 N.Y.2d 307, 314–15, 338 N.Y.S.2d 882, 887–88, 291 N.E.2d 129 (1972). See also Raybin v. Raybin, 15 A.D.2d 679, 224 N.Y.S.2d 165 (2d Dep't 1962), and compare Falk v. Goodman, 7 N.Y.2d 87, 195 N.Y.S.2d 645, 163 N.E.2d 871 (1959). Another point stressed in *Phillips* is that CPLR 4519 excludes the communication with a decedent only when an interested witness offers it "upon the trial" and that the objection may therefore not be asserted or waived until then.

[25] See John R. Higgitt, *Summary Judgment Do's and Don'ts*, 85 N.Y. St. B.J. 26 (Mar./Apr. 2013).

[26] Viviane Etienne Medical Care, P.C. v. Country-Wide Ins. Co., 25 N.Y.3d 498, 508, 14 N.Y.S.3d 283, 291, 35 N.E.3d 451, 459 (2015).

of a third-party billing company it hired to create and submit the forms to insurers. The Court concluded that these documents met the business records exception to the hearsay rule contained in CPLR 4518(a) and awarded plaintiff summary judgment. Presumably, certified business records produced pursuant to CPLR 3122–a can also supply the supporting proof necessary for an award of summary judgment.[27]

If the opposing party needs further opportunity to secure affidavits or conduct disclosure or otherwise summon forth evidentiary aid in opposing the motion, the court can make any order it deems appropriate, as long as the party attests in an affidavit that such opposing facts may exist and the disclosure devices to be invoked to obtain them.[28] The court can stay the motion and give the party the needed chance to get the additional data or seek the requisite disclosure, or it can deny the motion outright with similar purpose without prejudice to renewal later.[29]

If the motion for summary judgment is made at a late point in the action, however—albeit within the time limits imposed by CPLR 3212(a)[30]—and the court finds that the opposing party has already had all the opportunity for disclosure that it now claims the need of, the disclosure may be denied and the opponent left to face the consequences of the summary judgment motion without it.[31]

One of the moving affidavits should include a statement attesting to the validity of the movant's claim or defense or to the invalidity of the other party's. This is expressly required by CPLR 3212(b). It's a pro forma part of summary judgment motion papers.

A copy of the pleadings must also be part of the moving papers on a motion for summary judgment. While their omission could presumably be remediable under CPLR 2001, some courts have held that omitting the pleadings mandates a denial or dismissal of the motion for that reason alone.[32] Summary judgment movants should take special note of this, even if it's not clear that other courts would go the same way. The motion for summary judgment is strictly time limited by CPLR 3212(a), and the time limit is strictly enforced by the courts.[33] Doing anything that results in the denial of an otherwise timely motion for summary judgment, necessitating a second one (which assumes a second one is otherwise permissible), can run into the CPLR 3212(a) time barrier, which might have been avoided with proper papers at the outset.

For a period of several years, the First and Second Departments frequently refused to consider the affidavits of experts submitted on a motion for summary judgment when the offering party failed to provide "timely" disclosure of the expert under CPLR 3101(d)(1)(i). This often resulted in the dismissal of a party's claims.[34] To address the problem, the Governor signed a bill amending CPLR 3212(b) by adding a new third sentence that states that "[w]here an expert affidavit is submitted in support of, or

[27]   See Commentary C3122–a:3 on McKinney's CPLR 3122–a.

[28]   See CPLR 3212(f), the counterpart of CPLR 3211(d). See the treatment of CPLR 3212(f) in Higgitt, *Opposing Summary Judgment Motions Under CPLR 3212(f)*, N.Y.L.J., Oct. 17, 2005, at 17.

[29]   Cassevah v. Mack, 51 A.D.3d 1132, 857 N.Y.S.2d 343 (3d Dep't 2008).

[30]   See § 279.

[31]   Dennis v. City of New York, 304 A.D.2d 611, 758 N.Y.S.2d 661 (2d Dep't 2003).

[32]   See, e.g., Notaro v. Bison Const. Corp., 32 A.D.3d 1218, 821 N.Y.S.2d 715 (4th Dep't 2006). Citing CPLR 3212(b), *Notaro* says denial must be the result regardless of the merits of the motion.

[33]   See § 279.

[34]   See, e.g., Scott v. Westmore Fuel Co., Inc., 96 A.D.3d 520, 947 N.Y.S.2d 15 (1st Dep't 2012); Construction by Singletree, Inc. v. Lowe, 55 A.D.3d 861, 866 N.Y.S.2d 702 (2d Dep't 2008); SPR 205:3.

opposition to, a motion for summary judgment, the court shall not decline to consider the affidavit because an expert exchange pursuant to subparagraph (i) of paragraph (1) of subdivision (d) of section 3101 was not furnished prior to the submission of the affidavit."[35]

§ 282. Searching the Record

CPLR 3212(b) provides that "[i]f it shall appear that any party other than the moving party is entitled to a summary judgment, the court may grant such judgment without the necessity of a cross-motion." If P moves for summary judgment against D, for example, D can end up getting summary judgment against P without even asking for it. Popularly known to bench and bar as "searching the record," this device is more likely to be remembered as the doctrine of extreme disappointment. It occurs most often when the pleading being attacked by the summary judgment motion is a responsive one, as in the example above where P's motion is actually an attack on the answer. A motion in that category requires the court to go behind the answer to examine the sufficiency of the complaint. If the complaint is defective, it and not the answer is dismissed and the plaintiff, although the movant, becomes the victim. The theory is that a bad answer is good enough for a bad complaint.

The court need not provide the movant with notice that it intends to search the record,[1] but doing so is permissible only with respect to the claim on which summary judgment is sought. The Court of Appeals has cautioned that the issue with respect to which the court proposes to search the record and grant summary judgment to the non-moving party must be an issue that is properly before the court on the motion.[2] If the particular issue is not, it can't support summary judgment for any party because the court cannot inject the issue on its own. Thus, if P has several distinct claims and moves for summary judgment only on claim X, it is only with respect to claim X that the court can sua sponte search the record.[3] There is some indication, even though the language of CPLR 3212(b) is permissive, that a searching of the record on a summary judgment motion may be mandatory.[4] It has even been known to take place on appeal.[5] And it can occur on a motion under CPLR 3211 as well as under CPLR 3212. When P moves under 3211(b) to dismiss a defense, for example, and the cause of action in the complaint turns out to be inadequate, the complaint gets dismissed instead of the defense.[6]

While the court can grant summary judgment for the non-movant by searching the record, there is no general authorization for a court to grant summary judgment sua sponte. A motion is necessary, on papers, so that all sides have an opportunity to muster their proof.[7]

---

[35] See § 348A.

[1] Kenneths Fine Repairs, LLC v. State, 133 A.D.3d 1181, 21 N.Y.S.3d 412 (3d Dep't 2015).

[2] Dunham v. Hilco Const. Co., Inc., 89 N.Y.2d 425, 654 N.Y.S.2d 335, 676 N.E.2d 1178 (1996); see NYSLD No. 446.

[3] See Costello v. Hapco Realty, Inc., 305 A.D.2d 445, 761 N.Y.S.2d 79 (2d Dep't 2003), noted in SPR 148:3.

[4] See Wilkinson v. Skinner, 34 N.Y.2d 53, 356 N.Y.S.2d 15, 312 N.E.2d 158 (1974); Manganello v. Park Slope Advanced Medical PLLC, 42 Misc. 3d 1222(A), 984 N.Y.S.2d 632 (Sup. Ct., Suffolk County 2014).

[5] See, e.g., Curry v. Davis, 241 A.D.2d 924, 661 N.Y.S.2d 359 (4th Dep't 1997).

[6] See § 269.

[7] Barrett v. Watkins, 52 A.D.3d 1000, 860 N.Y.S.2d 246 (3d Dep't 2008).

Following the prescription of human nature, the one who moves for summary judgment is the party who wants it for herself. But in matrimonial actions for a while, for tactical reasons unique to that realm, the defendant spouse was moving to have summary judgment granted for the plaintiff spouse, and it was the plaintiff who was resisting.[8] Earning for itself the name "reverse summary judgment"—a kind of party-initiated cousin of the court-initiated search-the-record phenomenon—the procedure was upheld by the Court of Appeals on the theory that a party who seeks a judgment can't be heard to complain when it's awarded to her summarily.[9] But there were legitimate complaints about this bizarre procedure. The legislature overturned it in 1984 with an amendment of CPLR 3212(e).[10]

The amendment bars reverse summary judgment only in matrimonial actions, however, where it had found some use; it is still available in other actions where it really has none. Hence, if a defendant in a million dollar commercial or tort action wants the plaintiff to have summary judgment, the court will not stand in his way, and the plaintiff can probably be prevailed upon to fully cooperate.

§ 283. Summary Judgment Under 3212 Based on 3211 Ground

The usual summary judgment motion is based on the overall merits of the case rather than on an individual defense like the statute of limitations, lack of jurisdiction, other action pending, etc. But it is permissible to base it on one of those grounds or any of the other grounds listed in CPLR 3211(a).[1] It will be recalled that the long list of CPLR 3211(a) objections may, under CPLR 3211(e), be taken either by a motion to dismiss or as defenses in the answer.[2] When the latter alternative is used, the objection, duly preserved by inclusion in the answer, may then be made the basis of a CPLR 3212(a) summary judgment motion.[3]

When making a post answer motion to dismiss based on the grounds in CPLR 3211(a)(7), the importance of labeling the motion as one for summary judgment under CPLR 3212 is highlighted in Miglino v. Bally Total Fitness of Greater New York, Inc.[4] In *Miglino*, the CPLR 3211(a)(7) motion to dismiss for failure to state a cause of action was made after the answer, but was not labeled a summary judgment motion. Therefore, the Court ruled it was improper to consider the affidavits and denied the motion.[5]

If an affirmative defense was not included in the original answer, but the defendant seeks to include it in an amended answer, the requests to amend to include the defense and for summary judgment based on it may be included in one motion.[6]

---

[8]   Explanations for this are that the defendant/husband wanted to remarry quickly, or hoped that the court would drag its heels on the equitable distribution (i.e., the money) aspects of the case if the matrimonial relief were out of the way, etc.

[9]   Leeds v. Leeds, 60 N.Y.2d 641, 467 N.Y.S.2d 568, 454 N.E.2d 1311 (1983).

[10]   L.1984, ch. 827. See Commentary C3212:29 on McKinney's CPLR 3212.

[1]   Houston v. Trans Union Credit Information Co., 154 A.D.2d 312, 546 N.Y.S.2d 600 (1st Dep't 1989).

[2]   See § 274.

[3]   See Commentary C3212:20 on McKinney's CPLR 3212.

[4]   Miglino v. Bally Total Fitness of Greater New York, Inc., 20 N.Y.3d 342, 961 N.Y.S.2d 364, 985 N.E.2d 128 (2013). See § 265.

[5]   See § 265.

[6]   See Armstrong v. Peat, Marwick, Mitchell & Co., 150 A.D.2d 189, 540 N.Y.S.2d 799 (1st Dep't 1989).

This applies not only to a defense that can constitute an effective disposition on the merits, such as the defense of payment or release,[7] but also to a defense that brings on a mere temporary abatement, i.e., dismisses without precluding a new action, such as lack of jurisdiction,[8] or the curable incapacity of the plaintiff.[9]

The grant of summary judgment based on one of these "abatement" defenses will not import the full res judicata effect carried by the usual summary judgment aimed at the merits of the case generally.[10] The lesson to the parties is to see to it that the dispositive order clarifies the particular ground on which the summary judgment is based. If it is based only on the defense of lack of jurisdiction of the defendant, for example, the order should say so. That will clarify that the merits of the claim were not disposed of in this round and that a new action lies if jurisdiction can now be obtained.

§ 284. Immediate Trial of Fact Issue Under CPLR 3212

If liability is summarily established and only damages remain in dispute, CPLR 3212(c) authorizes summary judgment and the case is set down for "an immediate trial" of the damages question. But an issue of fact going to liability requires denial of the motion; that issue may not be immediately tried.[1] This makes the summary judgment motion the sole exception to the court's general power, under CPLR 2218, to order the immediate trial of any issue of fact arising on a motion.

Before 1973, this restriction applied to any issue at all not related to damages, and this posed an anomaly. On a dismissal motion under CPLR 3211, the immediate trial of an issue of fact is permissible[2] and, as discussed in the prior section, if the CPLR 3211(a) objection is taken by answer instead of by motion, it can be made the basis of a summary judgment motion under CPLR 3212. If it is, however, and CPLR 3212 were to prohibit the immediate trial of an issue of fact arising on it, the anomaly would result that the same issue of fact that could be ordered to immediate trial if raised by a 3211 motion made on Tuesday could not be ordered immediately tried if raised on a 3212 motion accompanying an answer served on Wednesday. To avoid the anomaly, CPLR 3212(c) was amended in 1973 to allow the immediate trial even of a liability-related fact issue as long as it is shown to arise on a 3212 motion that is grounded on a 3211(a) objection pleaded as a defense or on a motion to dismiss a defense under CPLR 3211(b).

The court must of course be as circumspect in ordering the immediate trial under CPLR 3212 as it would be under CPLR 3211. The immediate trial of a liability-affecting issue of fact should be ordered only when it has some prospect of putting an end to the case.[3] If liability is established and only the damages issue needs trial, the trial should as a rule go forward immediately.[4]

---

7   CPLR 3211(a)(5).

8   CPLR 3211(a)(2), (8), (9).

9   CPLR 3211(a)(3).

10   Res judicata as applied to summary judgments is treated in § 287.

1   Stowell v. Berstyn, 26 A.D.2d 828, 274 N.Y.S.2d 120 (2d Dep't 1966); see Berman v. Town of Liberty, 91 A.D.2d 758, 458 N.Y.S.2d 20 (3d Dep't 1982).

2   CPLR 3211(c); see § 271.

3   See Commentary C3212:22 on McKinney's CPLR 3212, and § 271.

4   Before the 1973 amendment, the rule said that the court "shall" order the immediate trial of damages if liability is established. The 1973 amendment was intended only to authorize the immediate trial of liability-related fact issues arising on 3211(a) grounds, not to remove the mandatory requirement of an immediate trial of damages issues when liability is established.

The mode of trial of the damages issue, notably whether it's to be by jury, depends on the nature of the case itself. If the case would have been triable by jury had there been no summary judgment, and either party insists on a jury trial on damages, a jury is required.[5] Under the 1973 amendment authorizing the immediate trial of some liability-related fact issues, the question of whether a jury is required should depend further on whether the ground involved disposes of the case permanently. If it does not, such as where D seeks summary judgment dismissing P's action for the affirmative defense of lack of personal jurisdiction and the statute of limitations has not expired, a trial by jury should not ordinarily be necessary.[6]

§ 285. Partial Summary Judgment; Effect of Counterclaim

CPLR 3212(e) authorizes partial summary judgment. It applies to part of a single cause of action as well as to separate causes of action: summary judgment can be granted as to claim #1, but denied as to claim #2; or it can be granted as to part of claim #1, but denied as to another part as long as the part on which summary judgment is granted can be logically separated. Where P pleads two theories in respect of the same wrong, for example, one being summarily attackable (e.g., for untimeliness), but the other not, the court can, with a partial summary judgment, dismiss the one theory while retaining the other even though P has in essence only one cause of action.

Partial summary judgment may be granted "on such terms as may be just."[1] This makes available for the court's incidental use the usual broad range of procedural tools: severance, stay, separate trial, the imposing of conditions, etc.

Although the provision speaks in terms of partial summary judgment as to one or more "causes of action," it can operate on defenses in the answer as well. Where, for example, one defense is shown to be bad but the other good, the court can grant summary judgment dismissing the bad one. A motion under CPLR 3211(b) to dismiss that defense would be an alternative route to the same end.

There is a substantial body of law treating the situation in which P's claim is summarily established, but where D has interposed a counterclaim that requires trial. Or vice-versa. What effect does the counterclaim have, if any, on a grant of summary judgment for P? Despite a quantum of caselaw, it all boils down to a simple conclusion: the court can work out whatever seems fair in the particular case.

A defendant will sometimes interpose a counterclaim merely to frustrate plaintiff's entitlement to a swift recovery on a meritorious cause of action. It is clear, however, that the mere assertion of the counterclaim does not bar an otherwise warranted summary judgment on the main claim.[2] One alternative is that P be given summary judgment for all of the main claim with the entry of it stayed until the counterclaim is tried to see

---

[5]   See Cogen v. Robin Klinger Children's Entertainment, 17 A.D.3d 619, 793 N.Y.S.2d 508 (2d Dep't 2005) (defendants waived right to jury trial of damages issue before referee by not requesting it); Livingston v. Blumenthal, 248 A.D. 138, 289 N.Y.S. 5 (1st Dep't 1936). As to trial by referee, see § 379.

[6]   See § 271, which also points up the relative nature of the word "immediate" in the phrase "immediate trial"; Commentary C2218:3 on McKinney's CPLR 2218.

[1]   CPLR 3212(e).

[2]   M & S Mercury Air Conditioning Corp. v. Rodolitz, 24 A.D.2d 873, 264 N.Y.S.2d 454 (2d Dep't 1965), aff'd, 17 N.Y.2d 909, 272 N.Y.S.2d 132, 218 N.E.2d 898 (1966); Marinelli v. Shifrin, 260 A.D.2d 227, 688 N.Y.S.2d 72 (1st Dep't 1999).

what effect the counterclaim may have in diminishing P's claim in whole or in part.[3] If the main claim exceeds the counterclaim, P may be given summary judgment for the balance with the right to seek immediate enforcement of it, the rest being held in abeyance for possible offset by whatever D proves on the counterclaim.[4] If the counterclaim in that situation does not then succeed, P can be given summary judgment for the rest of the main claim at that time along with the right to proceed to enforcement. Still another example of a conditional order is requiring D to post a bond in order to stay the enforcement of P's summary judgment, the bond conditioned on D's making good whatever P is still entitled to after D's counterclaim is adjudicated.[5]

If D's counterclaim exceeds P's claim and P is given summary judgment on the main claim, the staying of entry or enforcement of the judgment until the counterclaim is adjudicated will protect D. But if there is no prospect of P's insolvency, so that D is assured of adequate enforcement of any judgment that may be warranted on the counterclaim, the stay would not even be required. P could go to immediate entry and enforcement of the summary judgment.[6]

The solvency of P is probably the main inquiry needed in this situation. It would be unfair, if P were unable to pay D's later judgment on a counterclaim, to let P get and enforce a judgment on the main claim. It would be far more palatable in that situation to hold P's claim in abeyance to be offset by whatever the counterclaim may establish. But if P is plainly solvent, and the court is convinced that the solvency will not be lost while a counterclaim pends, it can allow the main claim to go to judgment and enforcement both—and it will, especially when the counterclaim, though permissibly interposed in the action, has no relationship to the main claim.[7]

A court must be especially circumspect in imposing conditions with respect to one claim when the other has no relationship to it. The court has "wide discretion in imposing conditions upon the grant of partial summary judgment so as to avoid possible prejudice to the party against whom that judgment is granted," but the discretion "is not unlimited, and is to be exercised only if there exists some articulable reason for concluding that the failure to impose conditions might result in some prejudice, financial or otherwise . . . should that party subsequently prevail on the unsettled claims." So wrote the Court of Appeals in Robert Stigwood Organisation, Inc. v. Devon Co.,[8] adding that this is especially the case "where . . . counterclaims with respect to which partial summary judgment [is] granted are . . . independent of the plaintiff's claim[.]"

Conversely, if there is so intimate a relationship between the main claim and the counterclaim that the latter falls substantively if the main claim prevails, then the counterclaim, despite its apparent validity, must abide the trial and can't go to summary

---

[3]   CPLR 3212(e)(2); Casten v. Tannenbaum, 42 Misc. 2d 118, 246 N.Y.S.2d 954 (Sup. Ct., Queens County 1964).

[4]   Atlas Arm Co. v. Smith, 25 A.D.2d 669, 268 N.Y.S.2d 385 (2d Dep't 1966).

[5]   See Dalminter, Inc. v. Dalmine, S. p. A., 29 A.D.2d 852, 288 N.Y.S.2d 110 (1st Dep't 1968), aff'd 23 N.Y.2d 653, 295 N.Y.S.2d 337, 242 N.E.2d 488.

[6]   Pease & Elliman, Inc. v. 926 Park Ave. Corp., 23 A.D.2d 361, 260 N.Y.S.2d 693 (1st Dep't 1965), aff'd, 17 N.Y.2d 890, 271 N.Y.S.2d 992, 218 N.E.2d 700 (1966); The Bank Bldg. v. Mehling, 2016 WL 5944457, at *3 (Sup. Ct., New York County 2016).

[7]   *Pease & Elliman, Inc.,* 23 A.D.2d at 362–3, 260 N.Y.S.2d at 695–6; *The Bank Bldg.,* 2016 WL 5944457 at *3.

[8]   Robert Stigwood Organisation, Inc. v. Devon Co., 44 N.Y.2d 922, 923, 408 N.Y.S.2d 5, 6, 379 N.E.2d 1136, 1137 (1978).

judgment before then. The Court of Appeals so held in Created Gemstones, Inc. v. Union Carbide Corp.,[9] in which P was a distributor for D and concededly owed money to D under the contract. But P alleged that D failed to fulfill its obligations under the contract and sued D for damages. D thereupon interposed as a counterclaim a demand for the sum owed by P. It was found that the debt by P to D could be substantively cancelled were P to establish D's breach. Summary judgment for D was therefore held barred on the counterclaim.

When it does seem appropriate to hold back one side's claim, or part of it, to await possible offset use by the other side's claim, the holding back can be effected with either a stay of entry of the judgment or, while allowing entry, a stay of the enforcement of the judgment. In a given case, the question of which step is stayed—entry or enforcement— can make a big difference, as it did in Interstate Equipment. Corp. v. Bell.[10]

The court in *Bell* allowed P to enter judgment for only $24,000 of its $42,000 claim, the difference of $18,000—the amount of D's counterclaim—to abide the counterclaim's later trial. P docketed the $24,000 judgment with the county clerk, which made it a lien on D's real property. Then came D's bankruptcy proceeding, in which the trustee, apparently on the basis of the lien, paid the $24,000 judgment but discharged the unliened $18,000 balance that had been held in abeyance. The appellate division observed that had the trial judge opted to give P judgment for the whole amount and merely stayed execution on the potential offset part, P would have had a lien for the whole judgment and all of it would have been collected in the bankruptcy proceeding. "Significantly," stressed the court, the trial judge "did not elect the alternative of granting a judgment for the entire amount while staying execution," but the court does not discuss the factors to be applied in determining which step to take.[11]

CPLR 3212(e) permits summary judgment to be granted on "one or more causes of action, or part thereof" and provides that the court may direct "that the cause of action as to which summary judgment is granted shall be severed from any remaining cause of action[.]" CPLR 5012, in turn, provides that "[t]he court, having ordered a severance, may direct judgment upon a part of a cause of action or upon one or more causes of action as to one or more parties." A party moving for partial summary judgment (or full summary judgment for that matter) should consider specifically requesting that the court grant a severance and direct entry of judgment on any amount awarded. Without such direction, the clerk may not enter an interlocutory judgment on the order.[12]

§ 286. Salvaging Something from Abortive Motion

CPLR 3212(g) provides that if a summary judgment motion is denied or granted only in part, the court may nonetheless determine whether any of the facts involved are established. It is a discretionary tool, and the court may even interrogate counsel to see

---

[9]   Created Gemstones, Inc. v. Union Carbide Corp., 47 N.Y.2d 250, 417 N.Y.S.2d 905, 391 N.E.2d 987 (1979).

[10]   Interstate Equipment Corp. v. Bell, 288 A.D.2d 809, 733 N.Y.S.2d 763 (3d Dep't 2001).

[11]   See the discussion in SPR 120:3.

[12]   See Barrier Systems, Inc. v. A.F.C. Enterprises, Inc., 279 A.D.2d 543, 544, 719 N.Y.S.2d 597, 598 (2d Dep't 2001) ("In the absence of a court order directing the entry of judgment and severing the remaining causes of action, the clerk was without authority to issue the challenged judgment, and it therefore must be reversed."); Orix Credit Alliance, Inc. v. Grace Industries, Inc., 231 A.D.2d 502, 647 N.Y.S.2d 522 (2d Dep't 1996); see also CPLR 5016(c) ("Judgment upon the decision of a court . . . shall be entered by the clerk as directed therein."); CPLR 2222 (docketing "as a judgment an order directing the payment of money"); § 250.

what facts, if any, are uncontroverted. If the court, with or without such an interrogation, finds any facts to be beyond issue, it need only list those facts in the order denying or partially granting the motion. The facts so listed are then deemed established for all purposes in the case, relieving all parties from preparing proof on them for a trial.

The CPLR abolished the old motion to strike denials,[1] but an order under CPLR 3212(g) can sometimes carry out the same function by determining some of the denied facts to be established.[2]

Perhaps if calendars were less congested and judges had more time for each case, an order under CPLR 3212(g) establishing given facts would be more common. As things stand, however, CPLR 3212(g) appears to be little used. This is unfortunate because it can be versatile too. If a defense is formally pleaded as such, for example, a plaintiff who wants to test it can of course move to dismiss it with a motion under CPLR 3211(b). If the defense is not pleaded, but is injected into the parties' papers on a summary judgment application, the defense can be disposed of with a kind of minuscule declaratory judgment under CPLR 3212(g). That happened in E.B. Metal & Rubber Industries, Inc. v. Washington County,[3] for example, the court "declaring" that the defense of sovereign immunity was not available to the defendant in a certain property damage suit. "Such a declaration is appropriate . . . and salvages something of value from an otherwise aborted CPLR 3212 motion[,]" said the court.

More recently, CPLR 3212(g)'s utility was also demonstrated in Oluwatayo v. Dulinayan,[4] where the First Department ruled that a plaintiff who was an "innocent driver," and did not in any way contribute to the happening of the accident, was entitled to an order denoting his lack of culpable conduct on the issue of liability pursuant to CPLR 3212(g) in his action against the drivers of two other cars. The innocent plaintiff driver wanted more, arguing that he was entitled to partial summary judgment on liability against both defendant drivers. The court rejected this contention because he "failed to meet his burden to eliminate triable issues of fact as to how the accident happened and which defendant driver was responsible for the rear end collision."[5] While an award of partial summary judgment on liability against either driver was not appropriate, an order specifying "plaintiff's lack of fault or culpability is a much narrower finding[ ]" that merely establishes for all purposes in the action that plaintiff is free from any negligence and, presumably, comparative fault. The court noted that the same analysis would be applied to an action commenced by an "innocent passenger."

§ 287. Res Judicata Effect of Summary Judgment Motion

A summary judgment motion presents a snapshot of the proof at a moment in time. Therefore, the denial of the motion establishes nothing except that summary judgment

---

[1] See Chicago Dressed Beef Co. v. Gold Medal Packing Corp., 22 A.D.2d 1010, 254 N.Y.S.2d 717 (4th Dep't 1964).

[2] See Commentary C3212:36 on McKinney's CPLR 3212.

[3] E.B. Metal & Rubber Industries, Inc. v. Washington County, 102 A.D.2d 599, 479 N.Y.S.2d 794 (3d Dep't 1984). The case and the application of CPLR 3212(g) in general is the subject of a lead note in NYSLD No. 298.

[4] Oluwatayo v. Dulinayan, 142 A.D.3d 113, 120, 35 N.Y.S.3d 84, 90 (1st Dep't 2016).

[5] Oluwatayo, 142 A.D.3d at 115, 35 N.Y.S.3d at 86; see also Huerta-Saucedo v. City Bronx Leasing Inc., 147 A.D.3d 695, 48 N.Y.S.3d 132 (1st Dep't 2017) (triable issues of fact precluded summary judgment on the issue of defendants' liability, but plaintiffs were entitled to an order under CPLR 3212(g) finding that they were free from comparative fault); § 280.

is not warranted at this time.[1] So if it appears at the trial that judgment is warranted as a matter of law for one side or the other, the trial judge, despite the pretrial denial of a motion for summary judgment, may direct a verdict or grant judgment notwithstanding the verdict.[2]

The grant of summary judgment, on the other hand, does operate as an adjudication on the merits and is entitled to res judicata treatment.[3] The grant is usually based on a review of the overall merits of the case and so it is of course appropriate to give it such treatment. But it must also be recalled that the grant may be more narrowly based. It may be grounded, for example, on one of the objections listed in CPLR 3211(a).[4] When so based, the summary judgment is res judicata only of the point decided. Where, for example, D pleads as a defense lack of personal jurisdiction, and a summary judgment for the defendant is granted on that ground, a later action in which personal jurisdiction is established will not be subject to dismissal on res judicata grounds.[5]

D. SUMMARY JUDGMENT IN LIEU OF COMPLAINT

Table of Sections

§ 288.   Summary Judgment Motion in Lieu of Complaint; CPLR 3213

§ 289.   Money Instrument as Basis for CPLR 3213 Motion

§ 290.   Judgment as Basis for CPLR 3213 Motion

§ 291.   Procedure Under CPLR 3213

§ 292.   Effect of Denial; Conversion

§ 288. Summary Judgment Motion in Lieu of Complaint; CPLR 3213

CPLR 3213 recognizes that some claims have greater presumptive merit than others and should have easier access to the courts than an ordinary plenary action gets. It singles out these claims and permits them to be brought on by a summary judgment motion at the outset. Instead of a complaint accompanying the summons, a set of summary judgment motion papers does. Instead of merely having the defendant answer the complaint at any time within a stated period following service, the motion papers pick out a specific return day and require the defendant to appear and argue the case on that day.[1] The hope of the plaintiff is to have a judgment awarded on the return date.

---

[1]   Puro v. Puro, 79 A.D.2d 925, 434 N.Y.S.2d 424 (1st Dep't 1981); see Delgado v. City of New York, 144 A.D.3d 46, 50, 38 N.Y.S.3d 129 (1st Dep't 2016) (citing proposition).

[2]   S.L. Benfica Transp., Inc. v. Rainbow Media, Inc., 13 A.D.3d 348, 786 N.Y.S.2d 98 (2d Dep't 2004).

[3]   Eidelberg v. Zellermayer, 5 A.D.2d 658, 174 N.Y.S.2d 300 (1st Dep't 1958), aff'd, 6 N.Y.2d 815, 188 N.Y.S.2d 204, 159 N.E.2d 691 (1959); QFI, Inc. v. Shirley, 60 A.D.3d 656, 874 N.Y.S.2d 238 (2d Dep't 2009).

[4]   See § 283.

[5]   Of course the plaintiff must be wary of the statute of limitations in a situation like this. While a dismissal for want of personal jurisdiction does not lead to res judicata consequences, it can easily lead to a statute of limitations dismissal of a new action if the original statute has expired. There is no time extension under CPLR 205(a) for a dismissal based on lack of personal jurisdiction. See § 52.

[1]   On setting the return day of motions, see § 247. CPLR 3213 is very much like a special proceeding, see § 547, and in fact could have accomplished its result in fewer words merely by authorizing the use of a special proceeding instead of spelling out a procedure of its own.

The claims to which this expeditious treatment is afforded are those based on "an instrument for the payment of money only" or on a judgment of any kind. No other category of claim is entitled to use this "motion-action" of CPLR 3213.

Because this procedure is more expeditious than the usual action, many a resourceful plaintiff has tried to use it for items that fall rather short of what CPLR 3213 contemplates. This is so, in any event, on the "instrument" side of CPLR 3213. The "instrument" and "judgment" categories are separately treated in the next two sections.

§ 289. Money Instrument as Basis for CPLR 3213 Motion

Of the two categories of action in which CPLR 3213 allows its special treatment, the instrument for the payment of money has created by far the bigger body of caselaw. The plaintiff waves a paper at the court and insists it's "an instrument for the payment of money only," but it often falls short of the mark. In several cases, for example, a separation agreement was used, the plaintiff claiming that its money clauses satisfied as the equivalent of a money-only instrument. The courts have rejected that contention,[1] principally because the various other rights and obligations under separation agreements interplay with the monetary provisions and prevent the agreement from qualifying as a money-only obligation.

The negotiable instrument for the payment of money of course qualifies for CPLR 3213 use. So does a nonnegotiable instrument if it's for money only.[2]

One helpful standard for what qualifies as a proper CPLR 3213 "instrument" case is that offered by Seaman-Andwall Corp. v. Wright Mach. Corp.,[3] which says that a case is made out for CPLR 3213 use if two things are shown: (1) the instrument itself plus (2) proof of non-payment. The instrument doesn't qualify "if outside proof is needed." So stating in Weissman v. Sinorm Deli, Inc.,[4] the Court of Appeals rejected for CPLR 3213 treatment an indemnification commitment included in a stock agreement. The *Seaman-Andwall* standard was somewhat expanded in Cooperatieve Centrale Raiffeisen-Boerenleenbank, B.A. v. Navarro[5] where the Court held that the plaintiff must prove three things on a CPLR 3213 motion based on an unconditional guaranty: "the existence of the guaranty, the underlying debt and the guarantor's failure to perform under the guaranty." If the plaintiff is successful, "the burden shifts to the defendant to establish, by admissible evidence, the existence of a triable issue with respect to a bona fide defense."[6] Presumably any paper requiring the payment of money only and qualifying as a piece of "commercial paper" under the Uniform Commercial Code[7] would satisfy for CPLR 3213 use. Furthermore, if a given paper, although not formally a money

---

[1]   See Interman Indus. Products, Ltd. v. R.S.M. Electron Power, Inc., 37 N.Y.2d 151, 155, 371 N.Y.S.2d 675, 679, 332 N.E.2d 859, 862 (1975) (describing cases); Wagner v. Cornblum, 36 A.D.2d 427, 321 N.Y.S.2d 156 (4th Dep't 1971).

[2]   Louis Sherry Ice Cream Co. v. Kroggel, 42 Misc. 2d 21, 245 N.Y.S.2d 755 (Sup. Ct., New York County 1963); Stern v. Chemical Bank, 83 Misc. 2d 508, 511, 372 N.Y.S.2d 913, 916 (N.Y. City Civ. Ct. 1975) (listing examples of "instruments for the payment of money only").

[3]   Seaman-Andwall Corp. v. Wright Mach. Corp., 31 A.D.2d 136, 295 N.Y.S.2d 752 (1st Dep't 1968), aff'd, 29 N.Y.2d 617, 324 N.Y.S.2d 410, 273 N.E.2d 138 (1971).

[4]   Weissman v. Sinorm Deli, Inc., 88 N.Y.2d 437, 646 N.Y.S.2d 308, 669 N.E.2d 242 (1996) (NYSLD No. 438).

[5]   Cooperatieve Centrale Raiffeisen-Boerenleenbank, B.A. v. Navarro, 25 N.Y.3d 485, 15 N.Y.S.3d 277, 36 N.E.3d 80 (2015).

[6]   *Cooperatieve Centrale*, 25 N.Y.3d at 492, 15 N.Y.S.3d at 281, 36 N.E.3d at 84.

[7]   See UCC § 3–104 (defining "negotiable instrument").

"instrument," contains the requisite (and limited) terms, it will be accepted, as a mere letter was in one case.[8]

An "absolute and unconditional" guarantee is an instrument for the payment of money only,[9] even when it requires, dehors the instrument, a determination of costs, expenses, and attorney's fees.[10] Going that far afield from the instrument itself does not appear to comport with the simple standards set forth in the *Seaman* and *Weissman* cases.

If the instrument calls for something in addition to the payment of money, it doesn't qualify.[11] Numerous cases have embroiled bench and bar in the question of whether or not a given piece of paper fits the CPLR 3213 requirement.[12] Each such case takes the attention of all away from the merits and concentrates it instead on whether or not the device of CPLR 3213 is fit to pose the merits. This suggests that the plaintiff should not use CPLR 3213 without a paper that unequivocally qualifies. If the plaintiff instead brings an ordinary action and simply waits until the answer is in, she can then make a conventional summary judgment motion under CPLR 3212. It costs a little more time, but not much,[13] and the reward will be that the court will not be sidetracked and the substantive issues smoke-screened by a procedural inquiry about whether or not CPLR 3213 has been properly invoked.

Transactional lawyers involved in drafting commercial agreements and guaranties might take a look at the contractual language in the CPLR 3213 decisions above for guidance and brief their clients about the effects of entering into such agreements.

§ 290. Judgment as Basis for CPLR 3213 Motion

It is usually easy enough to apply CPLR 3213 when a judgment is the basis of the action because, in contrast with an "instrument" that must be for money only, there is no requirement that the judgment be of a particular kind. Any judgment qualifies to invoke CPLR 3213 and allow the action to be commenced with the motion procedure it supplies, but that is of course no guarantee that the court will grant the motion. That depends entirely on whether the judgment qualifies for recognition and adoption.

Sister-state judgments and those of the federal and territorial courts and the District of Columbia, since all are entitled to full faith and credit as long as rendered with jurisdiction of subject matter and parties,[1] are of course entitled to recognition and

---

[8]   See Baker v. Gundermann, 52 Misc. 2d 639, 276 N.Y.S.2d 495 (Sup. Ct., Nassau County 1966); *Stern,* 83 Misc. 2d at 511, 372 N.Y.S.2d at 916 (listing examples).

[9]   Cooperatieve Centrale, 25 N.Y.3d at 492, 15 N.Y.S.3d at 282, 36 N.E.3d at 85; European American Bank & Trust Co. v. Schirripa, 108 A.D.2d 684, 485 N.Y.S.2d 763 (1st Dep't 1985).

[10]   See Chase Manhattan Bank, N.A. v. Marcovitz, 56 A.D.2d 763, 392 N.Y.S.2d 435 (1st Dep't 1977); HCG Mezzanine Development Fund, L.P. v. Jreck Holdings, LLC, 37 Misc. 3d 1217(A), 964 N.Y.S.2d 59 (Sup. Ct., New York County 2012).

[11]   Maglich v. Saxe, Bacon & Bolan, P.C., 97 A.D.2d 19, 22, 468 N.Y.S.2d 618, 620 (1st Dep't 1983); Dann v. Bernstein, 73 A.D.2d 782, 423 N.Y.S.2d 524 (3d Dep't 1979).

[12]   See the cases collated in Interman Indus. Products, Ltd. v. R.S.M. Electron Power, Inc., 37 N.Y.2d 151, 371 N.Y.S.2d 675, 332 N.E.2d 859 (1975). Interman rejects for CPLR 3213 use a claim based on an implied account stated.

[13]   See Commentary C3213:4 on McKinney's CPLR 3213.

[1]   U.S. Const. art. IV, § 1; 28 U.S.C.A. § 1738; see V.L. v. E.L., 136 S. Ct. 1017, 194 L. Ed. 2d 92 (2016) (Georgia decree allowing plaintiff to adopt her lesbian partner's biological children was entitled to full faith and credit in Alabama).

readily qualify for a CPLR 3213 motion.[2] But, ironically, they don't need CPLR 3213: New York gives those judgments the even more expeditious device of Article 54 of the CPLR, which allows a judgment to be converted into the equivalent of a New York judgment through a mere registration procedure.[3] The only full-faith-and-credit judgments denied summary registration under Article 54 are those taken in the earlier forum either by default for nonappearance or by confession.[4] Only those, therefore, normally need to invoke CPLR 3213. Quick as it is, CPLR 3213 still sets up an adversary proceeding before converting the judgment into a New York one, in contrast to the summary registration procedure offered by Article 54.

CPLR 3213 is not restricted to money judgments. It has been held that the statute may be used to convert even a sister-state matrimonial decree into a New York judgment, thus enabling it to be enforced here.[5] But there is still some debate about how far New York will go in "adopting" a sister-state decree, replete with its periodic payment awards.[6]

CPLR 3213 should also be available to renew a judgment originally rendered by a New York court. Although not frequent—why, ordinarily, would a person who already has a New York judgment need to renew it?—there are, indeed, occasions when renewal is useful and sometimes even indispensable.[7]

It is really the foreign country judgment that can best exploit CPLR 3213—the judgment that is not entitled to full faith and credit under federal law and which therefore depends on New York's willingness to recognize it, an acquiescence loosely known as "comity." Here Article 53 of the CPLR is relevant, having much to say about which foreign country judgments must be recognized and which need not be.[8] Article 53 applies only to money judgments, however.[9] Other kinds are governed by caselaw, but as it happens, New York decisional law is quite generous in recognizing foreign judgments. This is also a res judicata topic, reserved for more extensive treatment in a later chapter.[10] Suffice it to note here that when the lawyer is seeking to convert a foreign country's judgment into its New York equivalent, so as to make it enforceable in New York, the best tool is CPLR 3213 whether the judgment is for money or something else and whether it is governed by Article 53 or by common law.

---

[2] More extensive discussion of when the Full Faith and Credit Clause applies to mandate recognition is reserved for the chapter on res judicata, since the full faith and credit doctrine is essentially just one of compulsory interstate res judicata. See § 471.

[3] See § 435 on Article 54, which is New York's adoption of the Uniform Enforcement of Foreign Judgments Act.

[4] CPLR 5401.

[5] Carbone v. Alverio, 89 A.D.2d 553, 452 N.Y.S.2d 121 (2d Dep't 1982); Mittenthal v. Mittenthal, 99 Misc. 2d 778, 417 N.Y.S.2d 175 (Sup. Ct., New York County 1979).

[6] See Blackburn v. Blackburn, 113 Misc. 2d 619, 449 N.Y.S.2d 827 (Sup. Ct., Delaware County 1982) (adopting a Georgia divorce judgment). The subject of adopting sister-state marital decrees is treated in the lead note in NYSLD No. 237. For a general discussion of the conversion of a sister-state divorce decree in a family court proceeding, see Pearson v. Pearson, 108 A.D.2d 402, 489 N.Y.S.2d 332 (2d Dep't 1985) (majority and dissenting opinions), aff'd 69 N.Y.2d 919, 516 N.Y.S.2d 629, 509 N.E.2d 324 (1987).

[7] See § 434.

[8] See Sea Trade Maritime Corp. v. Coutsodontis, 111 A.D.3d 483, 978 N.Y.S.2d 115 (1st Dep't 2013) (demonstrating issues that can arise when the basis of a CPLR 3213 proceeding is a foreign country judgment); see Commentary C3213:2 on McKinney's CPLR 3213.

[9] CPLR 5301(b).

[10] See § 472.

§ 291. Procedure Under CPLR 3213

The plaintiff using CPLR 3213 must pick out a return day just as she would on a motion for summary judgment made within an action, but the time and paper requirements vary. While an ordinary motion within an action can be brought on with notice of as few as eight days,[1] the minimal notice period when CPLR 3213 is used— since the motion papers accompany a summons and commence an action—is 20 or 30 days, depending on the place and method of service. It is based, in other words, on the time the defendant would have in which to appear under CPLR 320(a) when an ordinary action is brought.[2] If service is to be made by personal delivery in New York, for example, the earliest return day of the motion would be the 20th day after service and the motion papers should pick out a day accordingly.

The plaintiff is also permitted to add up to 10 days to the notice period. The advantage of doing this is that the plaintiff may require the defendant to serve answering papers as many days in advance of the motion day as the plaintiff has added. If P sets the return day on the 27th day after D is personally served in New York, for example, P may require D to serve answering papers seven days before the return day.[3]

The defendant's failure to serve answering papers within the required time does not authorize an immediate default, however. The plaintiff who wants a default judgment must ask for it on the return day, and the default may of course be excused by the court for good cause shown.[4] Furthermore, the failure to give the defendants the statutorily mandated time to appear and answer a CPLR 3213 motion can result in a vacatur of a default judgment and dismissal of the action.[5]

Methods of summons service are the same as in a plenary action prosecuted in the usual form, i.e., they come from CPLR 308 for individuals, CPLR 311(a)(1) for corporations, etc. But one must be wary of using substituted service methods to bring on CPLR 3213 applications. Since a specific hearing date is set under CPLR 3213 rather than an open-ended requirement to answer within X days as in an ordinary action, it may be difficult to work out the additional requirements of paragraphs 2 or 4 of CPLR 308 if the substituted service methods of those provisions are used.[6] They require the filing of proof of service and delay the start of the answering time until 10 days after that filing.[7] This suggests that it is wise to use personal delivery under CPLR 308(1) in CPLR 3213 cases. If the other methods must be resorted to, however, it would be reasonable for the court to adjust or even disregard their requirements about filing proof of service and postponing completion of service. Otherwise, it may prove difficult to satisfy both CPLR 3213 and the substituted service provisions of CPLR 308 simultaneously.[8]

---

[1]   CPLR 2214(b).

[2]   See § 110.

[3]   See Commentaries C3213:5, C3213:6 on McKinney's CPLR 3213.

[4]   CPLR 3213; CPLR 2004; see Commentary C3213:14 on McKinney's CPLR 3213.

[5]   Segway of New York, Inc. v. Udit Group, Inc., 120 A.D.3d 789, 992 N.Y.S.2d 524 (2d Dep't 2014).

[6]   See *Segway of New York, Inc.*, 120 A.D.3d 789, 992 N.Y.S.2d at 524 (service of papers on CPLR 3213 motion under leave and mail provision in CPLR 308(2) did not provide proper notice to defendant; defect could not be corrected under CPLR 2001).

[7]   See §§ 72, 74.

[8]   An analogous problem existed at one time with subpoena service under CPLR 2303. The courts made do with a common sense application of the statute and the legislature finally corrected the problem with an amendment in 1982. See Commentary C2303:2, C2303:3, on McKinney's CPLR 2303.

When there are several defendants, and difficulties arise in meeting the notice requirements because summons service on one of them fails, or because one of them contests service, or because of like problems, the court can set an adjourned date or otherwise defer the motion until the jurisdictional problem is resolved. It can order a trial of an issue of fact as to whether X was served,[9] for example, while a merits disposition is held in abeyance as to Y and Z. A new hearing date can be set as to all parties if jurisdiction against X is sustained.[10]

There are obvious similarities between the motion/action of CPLR 3213 and the special proceeding, for which Article 4 of the CPLR supplies the regulatory detail,[11] but they are not identical and the differences should be noted. Both the special proceeding and the CPLR 3213 action come on to be heard like a motion, for example, and that's a similarity. But the special proceeding, like an ordinary motion, can be brought on by an order to show cause,[12] while the CPLR 3213 application can't be,[13] which is a significant difference.

The filing system for commencement[14] applies to both actions and special proceedings, but no specific attention was given to how it applies to the CPLR 3213 procedure. Under the rules for commencement by filing, the initiatory papers must be served within 120 days after they're filed, but only a 15-day period for service running from the expiration of the statute of limitations applies in a special proceeding.[15] It is doubtful that this issue will ever be resolved as the plaintiff in a CPLR 3213 action will usually serve the summons and summary judgment papers promptly after they are filed.

As a motion, the CPLR 3213 application must also include a Request for Judicial Intervention (RJI),[16] and some adjustments will need to be made at the outset to assure that the return day set in the papers is satisfactory to the judge assigned. Because a judge is not ordinarily assigned until after the initial papers are filed, this can complicate the initial filing steps on a CPLR 3213 application, as it sometimes does with a special proceeding.[17] If a CPLR 3213 plaintiff gets all the papers ready, files them with an RJI, obtains an index number, makes sure that the assigned judge hears motions on the return date, and then serves the papers expeditiously, things should work out at least well enough. If there are any rough edges, the court should consider the plaintiff's dilemma and smooth things over as well as may be.

§ 292. Effect of Denial; Conversion

Even if CPLR 3213 is used in the proper circumstances (e.g., the instrument sued on is a proper one), it obviously doesn't guarantee the plaintiff success on the merits.

---

[9] See CPLR 2218.

[10] See Lemme v. TME Fashion Exchange, Inc., N.Y.L.J., Oct. 13, 1981, at 14, col. 5 (Sup. Ct., New York County; Stecher, J.).

[11] Special proceedings are discussed in §§ 546 et seq. The would-be CPLR 3213 plaintiff may find it helpful to consult that section.

[12] See CPLR 2214(d) (motion), CPLR 403(d) (special proceeding).

[13] Arena Bagels, Inc. v. Brooklyn Bagels, Inc., 51 Misc. 3d 1211(A), 37 N.Y.S.3d 206 (Sup. Ct., Kings County 2016); Bullard v. Bullard Orchards, Inc., 153 Misc. 2d 136, 580 N.Y.S.2d 131 (Sup. Ct., Saratoga County 1992).

[14] See § 63.

[15] CPLR 306–b; see § 63; § 553.

[16] See § 77B.

[17] See § 553.

One might say that a claim under CPLR 3213 is presumptively meritorious, but even that may be technically incorrect because nothing in CPLR 3213 alters the burden of proof otherwise belonging to the plaintiff in an action. The defendant may refute the claim and, if she does, summary judgment may be granted for the defendant instead of the plaintiff. If the refutation is not total, but establishes that genuine issues of fact exist that require trial, the court will deny the motion. In doing so, however, it will not dismiss the action. Under CPLR 3213, the court will merely convert it into an ordinary one, with the moving papers becoming the equivalent of a complaint and the answering papers an answer.[1] The case is now the equal of an action brought in conventional form in which a summary judgment motion has just been denied. Whether the issues of fact that resulted in the denial are to be preferred for trial would be governed by the same rules that govern summary judgment motions in general.[2]

When a CPLR 3213 motion is denied without reaching the merits, its conversion to an ordinary action is the usual remedy, but not the inevitable one. The language of the statute is that the court can order "otherwise." This lays the matter in the court's discretion. An interesting illustrative case is Schulz v. Barrows,[3] in which the Court of Appeals upheld an exercise of discretion to dismiss rather than convert a CPLR 3213 motion seeking to enforce a Texas judgment. The Court found that the Texas tribunal had no basis for exercising personal jurisdiction over the defendant and found no equities on the plaintiff's side to warrant a favorable exercise of discretion to retain the action. Quite the contrary. With tenuous jurisdiction at best, the plaintiff had apparently tried to get the case before a Texas court so as to expose it to an application of Texas substantive law and secure an award of punitive damages that New York—the state with all of the significant contacts in the underlying transactions—would almost certainly have denied. With the matter of conversion lying in the court's discretion, and the plaintiff through his conduct having forfeited all appeal to that discretion, plaintiff found himself out of court on his judgment-based claim and too late now even to bring an action on the underlying claim.[4]

Even if the plaintiff has mistaken his remedy altogether, and CPLR 3213 is not available because the plaintiff's claim does not even arguably present an instrument or judgment to which the statute is restricted, the action typically should not be dismissed but can simply be converted to ordinary form.[5] If, however, the plaintiff's claim "plainly fails on the merits, the court can grant summary judgment for defendant, denying the motion and dismissing the action."[6] Furthermore, if the case is unsuitable for CPLR 3213 treatment, but the defendant does not point this out, she may be held to waive objection to the use of CPLR 3213, with the court proceeding right to the merits.[7]

---

[1]   Fine v. Di Stanti, 79 A.D.2d 673, 433 N.Y.S.2d 873 (2d Dep't 1980); see Schulz v. Barrows, 263 A.D.2d 565, 572–73, 693 N.Y.S.2d 658, 665 (3d Dep't 1999), aff'd, 94 N.Y.2d 624, 709 N.Y.S.2d 148, 730 N.E.2d 946 (2000).

[2]   See § 284.

[3]   Schulz v. Barrows, 94 N.Y.2d 624, 709 N.Y.S.2d 148, 730 N.E.2d 946 (2000).

[4]   The case is the subject of extended treatments in the lead notes in SPR 93:1 (appellate division decision) and NYSLD No. 485 (Court of Appeals decision).

[5]   See CPLR 103(c); Weissman v. Sinorm Deli, Inc., 88 N.Y.2d 437, 445, 646 N.Y.S.2d 308, 312, 669 N.E.2d 242, 246 (1996).

[6]   *Weissman,* 88 N.Y.2d at 445, 646 N.Y.S.2d at 312, 669 N.E.2d at 246.

[7]   See Smith v. IG Second Generation Partners, L.P., 27 A.D.3d 265, 809 N.Y.S.2d 910 (1st Dep't 2006); P. Ballantine and Sons v. Boston Celtics Basketball Club, 36 A.D.2d 914, 320 N.Y.S.2d 876 (1st Dep't 1971).

The question of whether a counterclaim should be entertained in a CPLR 3213 action, in view of the statute's intention to get the main claim through to judgment summarily, is an interesting one. The courts are generally reticent about allowing a counterclaim to impede a legitimate CPLR 3213 claim, and while a better case can be made for entertaining a counterclaim if it is related to the plaintiff's claim than if it is not,[8] it has been held that even if a counterclaim arises out of the "same general transaction" as the main claim does, its interposition should not be allowed to impede P's ride to summary judgment on the main claim unless the counterclaim also amounts to a "defense" to the main claim.[9]

Other equities must also be considered, such as whether the plaintiff will be able to pay a counterclaim if it is disallowed here but successfully prosecuted to judgment in a separate action.[10] The simple remedy for an unrelated counterclaim, which really should not be allowed to impede a CPLR 3213 claim at all, is a severance.[11]

E. DEFAULT JUDGMENT

Table of Sections

§ 293.　　Taking Default Judgment
§ 294.　　Time for Default Application
§ 295.　　Papers on Default Application
§ 296.　　Notice of Default Application

§ 293. Taking Default Judgment

In several situations, the defendant's conduct, or complete failure to appear, amounts to a default and entitles the plaintiff to take a default judgment. The most common situation is where the defendant does not respond to the summons within the requisite time. This amounts to what CPLR 3215, the default statute, calls a failure to appear.

Nonappearance is the most frequent default basis, but not the only one. A defendant who has duly appeared can be guilty of a default at a later stage of the action, such as by failing to show up at the trial at the scheduled time. Failure to plead is also a default basis and can be distinct from a failure to appear. Where P serves only a summons and CPLR 305(b) notice at the outset, for example, D's step is to demand a copy of the complaint.[1] If P then serves the complaint and D fails to answer it, the failure to plead is a default.

---

[8]　*Fine*, 79 A.D.2d at 673, 433 N.Y.S.2d at 874.

[9]　See Harris v. Miller, 136 A.D.2d 603, 523 N.Y.S.2d 586 (2d Dep't 1988), where the main claim got summary judgment and the counterclaims were severed for pleading in a formal answer and for litigation in due course. The main claim in *Harris* was on a note executed by D to P. The counterclaims were for legal services.

[10]　See § 285; Commentaries C3213:17, C3213:18 on McKinney's CPLR 3213.

[11]　Wildeb Rest., Inc. v. Jolin Restaurant, Inc., 69 Misc. 2d 1012, 331 N.Y.S.2d 575 (Dist. Ct., Suffolk County 1972); see McMann v. Ballantyne Marine, Inc., 182 A.D.2d 1131, 586 N.Y.S.2d 225 (4th Dep't 1992).

[1]　See § 60.

The above default bases are listed in CPLR 3215(a), which also acknowledges as grounds for a default judgment any other category of dismissal ordered by the court for a "neglect to proceed."[2]

While a "default" is usually associated with an omission by the defendant, the plaintiff can also be guilty of conduct that constitutes a default. The plaintiff defaults, for example, by not showing up at the trial,[3] by refusing to submit to pretrial disclosure, or failing to reply to a counterclaim.[4] Whichever side defaults, the other is entitled to apply for a default judgment. Examples to be used in our discussion will assume it is the defendant who has defaulted, the most common situation.

The application for the default may be made to the court or to the clerk, depending on the claim involved. Application to the clerk is generally the preferable procedure because it gives the plaintiff a final judgment on papers alone, a ministerial procedure with nothing to try. Application to the court, on the other hand, usually needs more and may even require a testimonial hearing.[5] But application may be made to the clerk only when the plaintiff's claim is for "a sum certain or for a sum which can by computation be made certain[.]"[6] That would apply to liquidated contract claims, such as a claim for the delivery of X number of items at the agreed price of Y dollars each and to a claim on a money instrument. It also applies to an action on a previously rendered money judgment,[7] even if the claim underlying it was not liquidated.

All of the claims involved in the case must satisfy this "sum certain" criterion in order for the clerk to handle the default entry. If any claim does not, the default application has to be made to the court.[8] As long as all qualify, the fact that there are multiple defendants and not all of them have defaulted is not necessarily a barrier. The clerk is authorized to enter the judgment against the defaulter and at the same time enter an order severing, and thus continuing, the claim against the others.[9] The clerk's failure to enter such an order can be corrected nunc pro tunc, and it has been held that the nunc pro tunc order may even be sought ex parte.[10]

Anything that prevents mere arithmetic from reducing the claim to a sum certain requires that the application be made to the court. The Court of Appeals has indicated that only the most liquidated and undisputed of claims can be processed by the clerk.[11] This of course means that in that most numerous category, the personal injury action, and for that matter almost all tort actions, the application must go to the court rather

---

[2]   A defendant's refusal to submit to pretrial disclosure, for example, can result in a default judgment. CPLR 3126(3).

[3]   CPLR 3215(a).

[4]   CPLR 3126 and its penalties for nondisclosure, see § 367, also apply to the plaintiff. On defaults by a plaintiff, see Commentary C3215:5 on McKinney's CPLR 3215.

[5]   CPLR 3215(b).

[6]   CPLR 3215(a).

[7]   See Reynolds Securities, Inc. v. Underwriters Bank & Trust Co., 44 N.Y.2d 568, 406 N.Y.S.2d 743, 378 N.E.2d 106 (1978).

[8]   Stephan B. Gleich & Associates v. Gritsipis, 87 A.D.3d 216, 224, 927 N.Y.S.2d 349, 355–56 (2d Dep't 2011) (NYSLD No. 624).

[9]   CPLR 3215(a). Plaintiff must apply for the default judgment within one year from the default. See § 294.

[10]   Citibank Eastern, N. A. v. Minbiole, 50 A.D.2d 1052, 377 N.Y.S.2d 727 (3d Dep't 1975).

[11]   Rokina Optical Co., Inc. v. Camera King, Inc., 63 N.Y.2d 728, 480 N.Y.S.2d 197, 469 N.E.2d 518 (1984); Reynolds Securities, Inc. v. Underwriters Bank & Trust Co., 44 N.Y.2d 568, 406 N.Y.S.2d 743, 378 N.E.2d 106 (1978).

than to the clerk. The difference in procedure is that on the application to the court, damages have to be inquired into. The court is authorized to conduct that inquiry with an assessment, commonly known as an "inquest," with or without a jury, or through the appointment of a referee.[12] If the damages, although unliquidated, can be established by paper alone, and do not require oral testimony—one may draw an analogy here to the standards used on a summary judgment motion[13]—the court can make the assessment without an oral hearing.[14]

A defendant who defaults in appearing concedes only liability. New York holds that a default in a money action does not concede the amount of the plaintiff's damages.[15] The defaulting defendant is therefore permitted to appear and give proof at any damages trial or hearing.[16] The Uniform Rules have something to say about this, however. They provide that if the defendant doesn't show up for the damages hearing, the plaintiff may put in affidavits to prove damages.[17] If the defendant does show up, the rules appear to allow plaintiff to use "written statements of the witnesses, in narrative or question and answer form, signed and sworn to."[18] This appears to be a watering down of the defendant's confrontation and cross-examination rights at a damages trial, and some courts have not interpreted the rules to allow the plaintiff to submit only affidavits to prove damages where the defendant appears at the inquest.[19] Caselaw prior to the Uniform Rules had held the right to contest at a damages trial to include, even for a defaulting defendant, the pretrial tools of a bill of particulars and the disclosure devices.[20]

Perhaps the practical lesson to a defendant who wants to contest only on damages is not to default at all. The defendant might just serve an answer silent as to the liability allegations of the complaint, thereby admitting them,[21] or admitting liability explicitly, but only on the condition that full adversary rights are reserved to the defendant in regard to preparing for a damages trial.

When an inquest is necessary, whether and under what circumstances a jury is required is unclear. There appears to be broad discretion to direct a reference instead. If the claim is such that it would in due course have been tried by jury had there been no default, one may reasonably conclude that a defaulting defendant has waived it. But one cannot as simply conclude that the defendant's default can deprive the plaintiff of a jury to hear the damages question if it is the plaintiff who otherwise wants it.[22]

---

[12]   CPLR 3215(b).

[13]   See § 278.

[14]   See 22 N.Y.C.R.R. § 202.46(a) (permitting "properly executed affidavits as proof of damages[ ]" at inquest).

[15]   *Rokina*, 63 N.Y.2d at 730, 480 N.Y.S.2d at 198–99, 469 N.E.2d at 519–20; Christian v. Hashmet Management Corp., 189 A.D.2d 597, 592 N.Y.S.2d 306 (1st Dep't 1993).

[16]   Cf. James v. Powell, 19 N.Y.2d 249, 279 N.Y.S.2d 10, 225 N.E.2d 741 (1967).

[17]   22 N.Y.C.R.R. § 202.46(a).

[18]   22 N.Y.C.R.R. § 202.46(b), applicable in the supreme and county courts.

[19]   See, e.g., Suleiman v. Miamor Transp. Corp., 13 Misc. 3d 1230(A), 831 N.Y.S.2d 356 (Sup. Ct., Bronx County 2006) (stating that, with the exception of damages sought for a sum certain, "which can be determined by computation," a defaulting defendant must be given the "full opportunity" to "offer proof in mitigation of damages" including a full and fair opportunity to cross-examine plaintiff's witnesses).

[20]   See, e.g., Ayala v. Boss, 120 Misc. 2d 430, 466 N.Y.S.2d 128 (Sup. Ct., Bronx County 1983).

[21]   CPLR 3018(a); see § 221.

[22]   See Commentary C3215:7 on McKinney's CPLR 3215.

The default judgment can't exceed in amount or differ in kind of relief from that demanded in the complaint or notice served with the summons. A judgment directing the return of a chattel, for example, can't be entered if the complaint asked only damages for its retention.[23] Unlike the situation in which the defendant has appeared, where the plaintiff is usually able to amend the complaint to seek more or different relief than originally asked, the defendant who does not appear can be subjected to a judgment only for that of which she was originally notified.

The theory underlying the above rule is that the defaulting defendant is entitled to assume that nothing more will be taken through a default than was demanded in the papers served.[24] The application of this rule is problematic in a personal injury or wrongful death action because CPLR 3017(c) now prohibits a party seeking relief in such actions from stating the amount of damages sought in the "complaint, counterclaim, cross-claim, interpleader complaint, and third-party complaint . . . ."[25] If there is a default in such an action, what is the maximum sum that can be awarded to the party asserting the claim, whose pleading must remain silent as to the specific amount sought? The party asserting the personal injury or wrongful death claim should be permitted to seek whatever sum is reasonable under the circumstances to provide adequate compensation for the specific allegations in the pleading. If the defaulting party appears at the inquest in such a matter, CPLR 3017(c)'s supplemental demand procedure can be invoked to ascertain the amount of damages sought.

As indicated earlier in the book, New York is very liberal about vacating default judgments. The showing usually needed is (1) an excuse for the default and (2) an affidavit assuring the court of the merits of the defaulter's case.[26]

A default judgment is entitled to res judicata (claim preclusion) treatment.[27]

It is also to be remembered that a judgment by default is not appealable. The required procedure is to move on notice to vacate the default judgment and, if the motion is denied, to appeal the order of denial.

If a settlement is reached in a pending action, it can provide for the entry of judgment in accord with its terms and the clerk can then enter the judgment as if there had been a default.[28]

Special problems arise in motor vehicle personal injury actions when owner O appears and defends, but driver D defaults. If there's an issue about whether D had permission to drive the vehicle, that might relieve O of liability for the otherwise imputed conduct of D.[29] In one such case, the court severed the claim against D and allowed a

---

[23] Lape v. Lape, 23 A.D.2d 539, 255 N.Y.S.2d 953 (1st Dep't 1965).

[24] See Everitt v. Everitt, 4 N.Y.2d 13, 171 N.Y.S.2d 836, 148 N.E.2d 891 (1958); § 114.

[25] See § 217.

[26] See § 108 on the vacatur of default judgments. Note also, and distinguish, the procedure authorized today for the en masse vacatur of tainted default judgments through administrative channels, as in the case of an extensive consumer fraud. The procedure, now codified in CPLR 5015(c), is known as "Thompson's Law," for Edward Thompson, the then Administrative Judge of the New York City Civil Court who first used it. See Commentary C5015:13 to McKinney's CPLR 5015.

[27] The default judgment even gets collateral estoppel ("issue preclusion") effect in New York. See § 451.

[28] CPLR 3215(i); see Commentaries C3215:21, C3215:22, on McKinney's CPLR 3215.

[29] See Veh. & Traf. Law § 388.

default judgment to be entered against D with a damages assessment to follow.[30] In another, a default judgment was entered against D and then held to establish liability against O as well, thus barring O from litigating liability and leaving only the issue of damages to be adjudicated.[31]

§ 294. Time for Default Application

A plaintiff entitled to take a default judgment against a defendant, whatever the nature of the defendant's default, must "take proceedings for the entry of judgment within one year after the default."[1] Failure to take action within the year results not only in forfeiture of the default judgment against the defendant, but can also bring about the dismissal of the plaintiff's own complaint "as abandoned."[2] CPLR 3215(c) empowers the court to dismiss the complaint on its own motion, moreover, without even waiting for the defendant's request. The statute also gives the court discretion, for "sufficient cause," to excuse the default within the default, allow the action to proceed, and enter judgment after the year has expired.[3]

The ultimate entry of a default judgment can be a difficult task for the plaintiff in mortgage foreclosure actions—where defaults are common—due to all of the procedural hurdles that must be negotiated along the way.[4] In Citimortgage, Inc. v. Espinal,[5] the supreme court directed the dismissal of the mortgage foreclosure complaint, sua sponte, pursuant to CPLR 3215(c). The Second Department reversed, noting that the plaintiff took the preliminary step to obtaining a default judgment of foreclosure and sale by moving for an order of reference to compute the amount due to the plaintiff.[6] That act constituted the initiation of proceedings for the entry of a default judgment within one year of the defendant's default.[7] As the Second Department confirmed in a subsequent decision, "[i]t is not necessary for a plaintiff to actually obtain a default judgment within one year of the default."[8] Rather, the institution of proceedings to obtain a default judgment should be enough to avoid the clutches of CPLR 3215(c).[9]

The defendant can waive the plaintiff's "default within the default," and has been held to do so by appearing in the action by serving a belated answer, along with discovery

---

[30] Betances v. Ford Motor Credit Co., N.Y.L.J., Aug. 7, 2000, at 28, col.4 (N.Y. City Civ. Ct.; Brigantti-hughes, J.).

[31] Ha v. T.W. Smith Corp., 185 Misc. 2d 895, 714 N.Y.S.2d 873 (Sup. Ct., Kings County 2000); but see Balanta v. Stanlaine Taxi Corp., 307 A.D.2d 1017, 763 N.Y.S.2d 840 (2d Dep't 2003) ("The granting of a default judgment against [defendant driver] does not preclude [defendant owner] from contesting the issue of [defendant driver's] negligence."). This was a kind of application of the collateral estoppel doctrine, if not res judicata itself. See SPR 98:3, 104:2, and 105:3.

[1] CPLR 3215(c).

[2] CPLR 3215(c); see Morton v. Morton, 136 A.D.2d 902, 524 N.Y.S.2d 928 (4th Dep't 1988).

[3] Charles F. Winson Gems, Inc. v. D. Gumbiner, Inc., 85 A.D.2d 69, 448 N.Y.S.2d 471 (1st Dep't 1982), aff'd, 57 N.Y.2d 813, 455 N.Y.S.2d 600, 441 N.E.2d 1118; HSBC Bank USA v. Clayton, 146 A.D.3d 942, 944, 45 N.Y.S.3d 543, 545 (2d Dep't 2017), lv. denied, 29 N.Y.3d 1073, 2017 WL 2467939.

[4] See §§ 77, 77D (discussing adoption of CPLR 3012–b Certificate of Merit Rule and CPLR 3408 requiring settlement conferences in residential mortgage foreclosure actions); see Commentary on CPLR 3012–b to McKinney's CPLR 3012–b.

[5] Citimortgage, Inc. v. Espinal, 136 A.D.3d 857, 26 N.Y.S.3d 541 (2d Dep't 2016).

[6] See RPAPL 1321(1).

[7] See Wells Fargo Bank, N.A. v. Daskal, 142 A.D.3d 1071, 37 N.Y.S.3d 353 (2d Dep't 2016).

[8] State of New York Mortg. Agency v. Linkenberg, 150 A.D.3d 1035, 55 N.Y.S.3d 126 (2d Dep't 2017).

[9] See US Bank Nat. Ass'n v. Konstantinovic, 147 A.D.3d 1002, 48 N.Y.S.3d 182 (2d Dep't 2017).

demands.[10] Similarly, in Torres v. Jones,[11] the Court of Appeals concluded that supreme court erroneously dismissed plaintiff's claims against a defendant on the ground that she failed to timely request a default judgment pursuant to CPLR 3215(c). At the start of the defendant's deposition, counsel for the co-defendant city stated that he represented the defendant in the action and waived all jurisdictional defenses on the defendant's behalf. This conduct constituted an informal appearance on behalf of the defendant which, "unequivocally waived any right to dismissal that he might have had, including his right to dismissal upon plaintiff's failure to timely seek a default judgment under CPLR 3215(c)."[12]

While CPLR 3215(c) speaks only in terms of the plaintiff's claim, and the defendant's defaulting on it, it applies as well to a plaintiff's default on a counterclaim.[13] A strict application of the one-year time limit of CPLR 3215(c) led to dismissal of the counterclaim of a defendant who cut things too close in Giglio v. NTIMP, Inc.[14] The defendant in *Giglio* didn't apply for the default until more than the year of CPLR 3215(c) had passed from plaintiff's failure to serve a reply. The miss was by only a few days, and the court had power under CPLR 3215(c) to excuse the lateness if the defendant could show "sufficient cause." But that required the usual two-pronged requirement of an excuse for the lateness and a showing of a meritorious position on the merits, and defendant showed neither.

If the complaint is dismissed under CPLR 3215(c) and the statute of limitations has now passed, the dismissal is likely to be the end of things for the plaintiff. The dismissal qualifies as a neglect to prosecute, with the result that CPLR 205(a) may not authorize a new six-month period for a fresh action.[15] The defendant moving under CPLR 3215(c) will want to ensure that the order of dismissal sets forth specific conduct constituting plaintiff's neglect, which demonstrates "a general pattern of delay in proceeding with the litigation."[16] Otherwise, the plaintiff will be able to invoke the six month gift in CPLR 205(a).[17]

Suppose there are multiple defendants and not all of them default. Under the terms of CPLR 3215(c), the plaintiff must seek a default judgment against the defaulters within a year, and yet it may take more than a year to try the case against the defendants who have appeared. In that situation, the court, on ex parte application, can order that the inquest—the trial of the damages issues—against the defaulters take place at the same time as, or even after, the trial against the appearing defendants, without regard to the one-year limit of CPLR 3215(c).[18] The plaintiff must apply for such an order within one-year from the default.[19]

---

[10] See Myers v. Slutsky, 139 A.D.2d 709, 527 N.Y.S.2d 464 (2d Dep't 1988).

[11] Torres v. Jones, 26 N.Y.3d 742, 27 N.Y.S.3d 468, 47 N.E.3d 747 (2016).

[12] *Torres*, 26 N.Y.3d at 772, 27 N.Y.S.3d at 490; see § 112, addressing the informal appearance.

[13] Kohn v. Tri-State Hardwoods, Ltd., 92 A.D.3d 642, 937 N.Y.S.2d 865 (2d Dep't 2012).

[14] Giglio v. NTIMP, Inc., 86 A.D.3d 301, 926 N.Y.S.2d 546 (2d Dep't 2011).

[15] Shepard v. St. Agnes Hospital, 86 A.D.2d 628, 446 N.Y.S.2d 350 (2d Dep't 1982) (decided prior to 2008 amendment to CPLR 205(a)); see § 52.

[16] CPLR 205(a).

[17] See Wells Fargo Bank, N.A. v. Eitani, 148 A.D.3d 193, 47 N.Y.S.3d 80 (2d Dep't 2017) (permitting second action to be commenced under CPLR 205(a) after first action was dismissed pursuant to CPLR 3215(c)); § 52.

[18] CPLR 3215(d).

[19] CPLR 3215(d).

The one-year requirement posed a dilemma for a while in third-party actions. If defendant D impleads third-party X, it is usually for indemnification or contribution of some kind, and D's entitlement to it depends on what, if anything, P recovers from D in the main action. D is thus unable to take judgment against X until P has had judgment against D. If X should default on the third-party claim, a requirement that D take a default judgment against X within a year presupposes that the P v. D action will go to judgment within that time, which will almost never be the case. For this reason, it has been held that the one-year period in which D must apply for a default judgment against X does not start to run until the entry of a P v. D judgment in the main action.[20] By analogy to CPLR 3215(d), it might be prudent for the defendant in this scenario to apply for an ex parte order of default against X within a year from the default, with a direction that the assessment of damages await the entry of the P v. D judgment.

If the plaintiff has defaulted by failing to proceed to trial when the case is called, a one-year requirement also applies to the defendant's application for a default judgment.[21]

§ 295. Papers on Default Application

The proof needed on an application for a default judgment is governed by CPLR 3215(f), whose requirements are three:

1.   proof of summons service including a complaint or CPLR 305(b) notice;

2.   proof of the claim, including the amount due if it is a money claim; and

3.   proof of the default.

Note with respect to the first requirement that if the affidavit of service does not reveal that either the complaint or notice went with the summons, the clerk will not accept it for filing and neither court nor clerk will entertain a default application.[1] Proof of service usually takes the form of an affidavit by the process server.[2] Its contents are dictated by CPLR 306, which today purports to require even a physical description of the person served.[3]

The second requirement, proof of the claim itself, is usually made by the plaintiff's own affidavit, buttressed, if need be, by additional affidavits of others having first-hand knowledge. The affidavit of the plaintiff's lawyer, unless the lawyer happens to have that first-hand knowledge, should not be used to fulfill this requirement. While it has been held that the use of the lawyer's, rather than the client's, affidavit as proof of merit on a default application does not necessarily make the default judgment void—the defect can

---

[20]   Slovik v. Wang, 110 A.D.2d 630, 487 N.Y.S.2d 119 (2d Dep't 1985); Multari v. Glalin Arms Corp., 28 A.D.2d 122, 282 N.Y.S.2d 782 (2d Dep't 1967).

[21]   CPLR 3215(a).

[1]   If service by publication was used, the affidavit should instead show that the published notice satisfies the requirements of CPLR 316(a). In the lower courts, where an "indorsement" pleading may be used, the indorsement is the equal of a complaint for the purpose of a default application under CPLR 3215(e). See §§ 902 and 1402 in each of the New York City Civil, Uniform District, Uniform City, and Uniform Justice court acts, McKinney's Vol. 29A, Parts 2 and 3.

[2]   When service is made by mail under CPLR 312–a, the acknowledgment returned by the defendant counts as proof of service. See § 76A.

[3]   See § 79.

be waived by the other side[4]—it is a bad practice that can make trouble.[5] A verified complaint, for example, if it accompanied the summons, may serve as an affidavit of the claim,[6] but not if the verification was made by the attorney.[7]

Does the failure to include an affidavit of merits make a default judgment nevertheless entered on the papers void or merely voidable? In Manhattan Telecommunications Corp. v. H & A Locksmith, Inc.,[8] the Court of Appeals resolved a conflict in the appellate division, concluding that the failure to include an affidavit containing the facts constituting the claim in an application for a default judgment is not a jurisdictional defect that renders a default judgment a nullity that may be vacated at any time. The Court noted that "not every defect in a default judgment requires or permits a court to set it aside."[9] While "[a] failure to submit the proof required by CPLR 3215(f) should lead a court to deny an application for a default judgment," the Court held that the failure to do so is a mere error that is not "jurisdictional" in nature. This type of error can be addressed by a motion under CPLR 5015(a) for relief from the judgment but "does not justify treating the judgment as a nullity."[10]

At one time there was a special rule in matrimonial actions: mere paper proof of the claim did not suffice. The plaintiff, despite the defendant's default, would have to take the stand and testify to the facts of the claim. The requirement wasted time and effort, was unpopular with judges who resented having to preside mindlessly at what was known in some parts of the state as the "uncontested matrimonial part," and was eliminated with an amendment of the applicable statute[11] in 1978. Default judgments in matrimonial actions, as in any other kind, may now be based on paper proof of the claim. Live courtroom testimony is not required. The point is mentioned just to reassure lawyers whose research brings up the pre-1978 cases.[12]

The proof needed of the claim itself under CPLR 3215(f) is extensively reviewed by the Court of Appeals in Woodson v. Mendon Leasing Corp.,[13] in which the plaintiff was a mother standing with her 4-year-old son on a sidewalk when he was struck by a car that collided with and was sent careening by a truck. In behalf of her son, she sued the driver of the car and the driver and owner of the truck. The truck driver defaulted, the

---

[4]   Freccia v. Carullo, 93 A.D.2d 281, 462 N.Y.S.2d 38 (2d Dep't 1983); but see Woodward v. Eighmie Moving & Storage, Inc., 151 A.D.2d 892, 543 N.Y.S.2d 187 (3d Dep't 1989) (even though defect was not raised by defendant before supreme court, appellate division considered it and vacated default judgment).

[5]   See § 108.

[6]   CPLR 3215(f).

[7]   Joosten v. Gale, 129 A.D.2d 531, 514 N.Y.S.2d 729 (1st Dep't 1987).

[8]   Manhattan Telecommunications Corp. v. H & A Locksmith, Inc., 21 N.Y.3d 200, 969 N.Y.S.2d 424, 991 N.E.2d 198 (2013).

[9]   *Manhattan Telecommunications Corp.,* 21 N.Y.3d at 203, 969 N.Y.S.2d at 425, 991 N.E.2d at 199.

[10]   See §§ 108 and 427 (discussing two-part showing required for vacating a default judgment under CPLR 5015(a)(1)). For additional discussion of the Court's decision in *Manhattan Telecommunications* and the problems that can be encountered in this realm, see Patrick M. Connors, *Notable Opinions Include Application of CPLR in Contract Disputes,* N.Y.L.J., Aug. 26, 2013, at 250 (no. 40); John R. Higgitt, *A Nullity or Not?—The Status of a Default Judgment Entered Absent Compliance with CPLR 3215(f),* 73 Alb. L. Rev. 807 (2010).

[11]   Dom. Rel. Law § 211.

[12]   On this score the reader should also keep in mind the general relettering of subdivisions that was made in CPLR 3215 in 1992 to make way for a new subdivision (d). Subdivisions (a) through (c) retained their original lettering, but original subdivisions (d) through (h) were relettered (e) through (i). Practitioners should be alert to the relettering, especially when doing something like a Westlaw search.

[13]   Woodson v. Mendon Leasing Corp., 100 N.Y.2d 62, 760 N.Y.S.2d 727, 790 N.E.2d 1156 (2003); NYSLD No. 522.

insurer inexplicably defending for the owner but not the driver. In the papers submitted on the application for a default judgment, the plaintiff submitted an affidavit averring that the truck driver had driven negligently, but during later enforcement proceedings, she said in a deposition that she was not certain of a truck being involved in the accident. Pointing to this purported conflict in the plaintiff's averments, the insurer maintained that this showed that her proof on the default application was inadequate. It sought to overturn everything.

Finding the plaintiff's proof adequate in the circumstances, the Court preserved the default judgment and rejected the insurer's argument, observing that "[a]t the early stages of litigation in cases of this type it would be unreasonable to expect a plaintiff to sort out meticulously the negligent acts assignable to each defendant."[14]

The third requirement on the application is proof of the default. Here the affidavit of the plaintiff's lawyer is not just acceptable, but ideal. A literal reading of CPLR 3215(f) suggests that the affidavit of the plaintiff's attorney may be used to establish the defendant's default only when a verified complaint has been served. In fact, it is almost always the attorney's affidavit that proves the defendant's default, whether a verified complaint is used or not. It's upon the plaintiff's attorney that the defendant's notice of appearance, answer, or motion must be served.[15] The failure to serve plaintiff's attorney with these papers is what constitutes the default and is therefore known first hand by the plaintiff's lawyer, rather than by the plaintiff proper—to whom, indeed, it would be mere hearsay.[16]

Hence a trio of affidavits is the ideal composition of a default application: the server's affidavit of service, the plaintiff's affidavit of merits, and the lawyer's affidavit of the default.

The trio may become a quartet when an additional notice is required, as it is in a number of situations covered by CPLR 3215(g). Those are addressed in the next section.

There is yet another item of proof needed on the default application, this one emanating from federal law. The plaintiff must include in the application an affidavit that the defendant, or the person of whom the defendant is a dependent, is not in military service. This is commonly known as the "military affidavit" and should be made "contemporaneous" to the entry of judgment and after the default of the defendant.[17]

If personam jurisdiction is lacking, and the sole basis of jurisdiction is quasi in rem based on the attachment of the defendant's property, the application should also include an affidavit so stating and describing the property levied on and its value.[18] The judgment in that instance is enforceable only against the attached assets and the judgment itself should reflect that fact.[19]

---

[14] *Woodson,* 100 N.Y.2d at 71, 760 N.Y.S.2d at 733, 790 N.E.2d at 1162.

[15] CPLR 2103(b); see § 202.

[16] See Commentary C3215:16 on McKinney's CPLR 3215.

[17] An extensive treatment of the military affidavit appears in Citibank, N.A. v. McGarvey, noted in § 79.

[18] CPLR 3215(f).

[19] Benadon v. Antonio, 10 A.D.2d 40, 197 N.Y.S.2d 1 (1st Dep't 1960); cf., Hidalgo v. 4–34–68, Inc., 117 A.D.3d 798, 988 N.Y.S.2d 64 (2d Dep't 2014), lv. denied, 24 N.Y.3d 916, 4 N.Y.S.3d 602, 28 N.E.3d 38 (2015) ("In order to avoid confusion, 'a judgment should express its true legal effect and the precise relief awarded.' ").

Even at an inquest on damages conducted after the defendant has conceded liability by failing to appear, the plaintiff may put in paper proof of damages; live testimony is not indispensable.[20] But it has been held that this applies only if a defaulting defendant does not contest damages at the inquest.[21] If the defendant does appear at the inquest, as is his right, he is entitled to cross-examine the plaintiff's witnesses and, in that situation, the plaintiff can't rely on mere paper proof of damages, but must call live witnesses. In a personal injury action, such as an automobile accident case, this would require the plaintiff to call physicians that she is relying on to prove a "serious injury," as well as any other witnesses that will testify as to damages.[22]

Court Rules Governing Default Judgment Applications in Consumer Credit Transactions

The Uniform Rules applicable to the Supreme and County Courts, the New York City Civil Court, City Courts outside of New York City, and the District Courts have been modified to impose specific requirements on plaintiffs seeking default judgments in "consumer credit" matters.[23] When a plaintiff in a consumer credit matter, which is defined in the new Uniform Rules, applies for a default judgment through the clerk's office,[24] the plaintiff must submit the proof required under CPLR 3215(f) and additional papers mandated by the new Uniform Rules. The additional proof required by the rules includes, among other things, an "Affirmation of Non-Expiration of Statute of Limitations" executed by plaintiff's counsel and an "Additional Notice of Consumer Credit Action." This latter notice is in addition to any notice required under CPLR 3215(g) and the default judgment cannot be entered until 20 days after the notice is mailed to the defendant.

Section 202.27–a(i) requires the county clerk or other applicable clerk of the court to refuse to accept for filing a default judgment application that does not comply with the requirements of the new Rules.[25] The new rules apparently do not apply to applications made before the court under CPLR 3215(b).[26] That may be the preferable route in these matters, even when the claim is for a sum certain.

§ 296. Notice of Default Application

CPLR 3215(g), as noted in the prior section, requires that in certain instances an additional notice of the default judgment application be served on the defendant; that is additional to the notice that service of the initiatory papers under CPLR 308 provides. Proof of mailing of the notice must be filed with the application.[1] CPLR 3215(g) is a somewhat unwieldy provision. For ease of reference, the additional notice requirements

---

[20] See 22 N.Y.C.R.R. § 202.46, applicable in the supreme and county courts. A similar rule may apply in other courts. See, e.g., 22 N.Y.C.R.R. § 208.32, applicable in the New York City Civ. Ct. See also § 293.

[21] Suleiman v. Miamor Transp. Corp., 13 Misc. 3d 1230(A), 831 N.Y.S.2d 356 (Sup. Ct., Bronx County 2006). The decision is an application of 22 N.Y.C.R.R. § 202.46.

[22] *Suleiman*, 13 Misc. 3d at 1230(A), 831 N.Y.S.2d at 356.

[23] See 22 N.Y.C.R.R. §§ 202.27–a, 202.27–b; AO-185–2014, September 15, 2014; http://www.nycourts. gov/rules/ccr/ ("New Consumer Credit Rules and Resources").

[24] See CPLR 3215(a).

[25] See 22 N.Y.C.R.R. § 202.5(d)(1) (authorizing various clerks to refuse to accept papers for filing when authorized by Chief Administrator's rule).

[26] See 22 N.Y.C.R.R. § 202.27–a(j).

[1] CPLR 3215(f).

will be presented in the order in which they appear in CPLR 3215(g), with various headings to organize the discussion.

CPLR 3215(g)(1) & (2): Five-Day Notice Requirements

Default After Appearance

CPLR 3215(g)(1) requires that "whenever application [for a default judgment] is made to the court or to the clerk, any defendant who has appeared is entitled to at least five days' notice of the time and place of the application[.]" In this scenario, the default consists of something occurring after the defendant has appeared in the action, such as a failure to answer after appearing by a notice of appearance.[2] A mere demand for a copy of the complaint, not combined with a notice of appearance, does not qualify as an appearance under CPLR 3215(g)(1) that requires notice of subsequent proceedings.[3]

When the default consists of the defendant's failure to show up when the case is called for trial, CPLR 3215(g)(1) authorizes the court to dispense with this notice. This is designed to enable the court, if it wishes, to go forward with an assessment of damages immediately.

Taking Proceedings to Enter Default One Year After Default

Furthermore, if the year for taking proceedings to enter the default as prescribed in CPLR 3215(c) has expired, any defendant, whether having appeared or not, is entitled to the five-day notice.[4] This makes it plain that the plaintiff who applies for the default after the allotted year has expired is additionally penalized by having to give the defendant notice of it, violating the adage about letting sleeping dogs lie. If steps are taken to apply for the default judgment within the year, notice is dispensed with, even if the assessment itself does not take place within the year.[5] The plaintiff can't control the court's calendars and hence should not be held responsible for judicial delays in getting around to the assessment.

Defaulting Defendant Who Has Demanded Notice

Even a defendant in default for failure to appear—as noted, the most common category of default—may nonetheless want to keep apprised of later proceedings. Pursuant to CPLR 3215(g)(2), at any time before the damages hearing, the defendant may simply serve on the plaintiff a demand that notice of the hearing be served on her. A plaintiff so served must give the defendant five days notice of any reference or jury trial of the damages question.[6] This is a meaningful right for the defendant, who is allowed at the assessment to put in certain proof in mitigation of damages notwithstanding the default, which concedes only liability.[7]

Failure to Provide Notice Under CPLR 3215(g)(1)

What happens if plaintiff fails to provide the requisite proof of the additional notice required under CPLR 3215(g)(1), but the default judgment is entered nonetheless? In

---

[2]   See § 60.

[3]   Simmons v. Mercer, 146 A.D.2d 833, 536 N.Y.S.2d 862 (3d Dep't 1989).

[4]   CPLR 3215(g)(1).

[5]   Q.P.I. Restaurants Ltd. v. Slevin, 93 A.D.2d 767, 461 N.Y.S.2d 334 (1st Dep't 1983).

[6]   CPLR 3215(g)(2). This provision applies only to default applications that have to be made to the court; notice is not necessary when the claim is for a sum certain and goes before the clerk under CPLR 3215(a).

[7]   See § 293 and Commentary C3215:19 on McKinney's CPLR 3215.

Paulus v. Christopher Vacirca, Inc.,[8] the defendant appeared in the action but subsequently defaulted. The Second Department held, in an issue of "first impression" in that court, that plaintiff's failure to provide the required notice to the defendant under CPLR 3215(g)(1) before moving for leave to enter a default judgment deprived the supreme court of jurisdiction to entertain the plaintiffs' motion for leave to enter a default judgment. Therefore, the Second Department ruled that the default judgment must be vacated pursuant to CPLR 5015(a)(4) because of the failure to comply with the notice requirements of CPLR 3215(g)(1)

The First, Third, and Fourth Departments have addressed the issue of vacating a default judgment for an appearing party who received no notice of the motion for leave to enter a default judgment, but have reached different results.[9] Lawyers need to be very careful here. Not only do courts reach different conclusions when interpreting the same additional notice provision, but the failure to provide notice under CPLR 3215(g)(1) may be treated differently than the failure to provide notice required under the other provisions in CPLR 3215(g), discussed below. It's also difficult to square the holding in *Paulus*, concluding that plaintiff's failure to provide additional notice essentially rendered the default judgment void, with the Court of Appeals holding in Manhattan Telecommunications Corp. v. H & A Locksmith, Inc.[10] Therein, the Court ruled that even a defect in the proof required for an application for a default judgment is not of a jurisdictional nature such as to render a default judgment a nullity that may be vacated at any time.[11]

CPLR 3215(g)(3): Twenty-Day Notice Requirement

Default Against Natural Person in Breach of Contract Action

CPLR 3215(g)(3) requires an additional notice of a default judgment application when the defendant is a natural person who has not appeared and the action is one for money due under a contractual obligation of any kind, not just a formal or express contract.[12] In this category of action, the statute requires that a notice be mailed to the defendant, and it supplies detailed instructions for it, including when the "mailing is returned as undeliverable."[13] The mailing must be made at least 20 days before the entry of the default judgment, but may be made simultaneous with the service of the

---

[8]   Paulus v. Christopher Vacirca, Inc., 128 A.D.3d 116, 6 N.Y.S.3d 572 (2d Dep't 2015).

[9]   See Walker v. Foreman, 104 A.D.3d 460, 963 N.Y.S.2d 625 (1st Dep't 2013) (vacating judgment, court noted that the failure to give proper notice under CPLR 3215(g)(1) requires a new inquest, on proper notice); Dime Savings Bank of New York, FSB v. Higner, 281 A.D.2d 895, 722 N.Y.S.2d 651 (4th Dep't 2001) (granting motion to vacate default judgment and foreclosure sale based upon failure to provide notice to defendant homeowner who appeared informally by sending a letter to the bank's attorney denying the validity of the bank's claim); Fleet Finance Inc. v. Nielsen, 234 A.D.2d 728, 650 N.Y.S.2d 904 (3d Dep't 1996) (concluding that failure to provide notice in accordance with CPLR 3215(g)(1) and (3) does not, standing alone, warrant vacatur of a default judgment).

[10]   Manhattan Telecommunications Corp. v. H & A Locksmith, Inc., 21 N.Y.3d 200, 969 N.Y.S.2d 424, 991 N.E.2d 198 (2013).

[11]   See § 295.

[12]   Vanderveer v. Magedson, 148 Misc. 2d 185, 560 N.Y.S.2d 265 (Sup. Ct., Franklin County 1990).

[13]   CPLR 3215(g)(3)(i).

summons.[14] An affidavit attesting to the mailing must also be included on the default application.[15]

A special provision in this portion of the statute, CPLR 3215(g)(3)(iii), governs in small claims parts, summary proceedings to recover possession of real property such as those involving landlords and tenants, and actions "affecting title to real property." In those actions, CPLR 3215(g)(3)(iii) dispenses with the additional notice otherwise required by the statute. Whatever the legislative motivation for these exceptions, a supervening motive then caused an exception to be made to one of those exceptions: the action affecting title to real property. Excepting all such actions from the additional notice requirement was deemed too broad in instances of foreclosure on residential properties of not more than three units, where the presumably unsophisticated mortgagor doesn't realize from other required notice,[16] clear as it may be, that a default can bring foreclosure of the mortgage and the loss of his home. Hence an amendment— convoluted but important—carved out an exception to the exception, making the additional notice requirement applicable to residential mortgage foreclosure actions.[17]

The extra mailing requirement in CPLR 3215(g)(3) is apparently not a jurisdictional one. It has been held that a failure to carry it out will therefore not qualify by itself as a ground for vacating a default judgment.[18] The defendant who has not been served with the additional notice must establish grounds under either CPLR 317 or CPLR 5015(a) to vacate the default judgment,[19] meaning that if the judgment is proper in all other respects, the defendant won't be allowed to vacate it solely because the additional notice in CPLR 3215(g)(3) wasn't provided.

Default Against Corporation Served Pursuant to BCL § 306

As discussed in an earlier chapter, a domestic or licensed foreign corporation can be served through the secretary of state's office pursuant to section 306(b) of the Business Corporation Law.[20] If a corporation has been served via this method and defaults by not appearing, CPLR 3215(g)(4) requires that the plaintiff forward an additional copy of the summons to the corporation by first class mail "at its last known address at least twenty days before the entry of judgment." The additional service must be accompanied by a notice to the corporation that service is being made through section 306(b) of the Business Corporation Law.[21] An affidavit attesting to the mailing must be made by the person who performs the mailing and it must be included on the default application.[22] CPLR 3215(g)(4)(iii) dispenses with the additional service requirement in small claims or commercial claims parts, summary proceedings to recover possession of real property

---

[14]   CPLR 3215(g)(3)(ii). Before 1986, when an amendment moved this provision from CPLR 308 to its present niche in CPLR 3215, it had been the understanding in some places that the notice had to be given at some later time.

[15]   CPLR 3215(g)(3)(ii); CPLR 3215(f).

[16]   See RPAPL 1304 ("Required prior notices" in residential mortgage foreclosure actions); 1320 ("Special summons requirement in private residence cases").

[17]   CPLR 3215(g)(3)(iii); see SPR 189:2.

[18]   Rothschild v. Finkelstein, 248 A.D.2d 701, 670 N.Y.S.2d 331 (2d Dep't 1998); Kirkman/3HREE, Inc. v. Priority AMC/Jeep, Inc., 94 A.D.2d 870, 463 N.Y.S.2d 579 (3d Dep't 1983).

[19]   See § 108.

[20]   See §§ 70, 95.

[21]   CPLR 3215(g)(4)(ii).

[22]   CPLR 3215(g)(4)(i); CPLR 3215(f).

such as those involving landlords and tenants, and actions "affecting title to real property."

Limited Liability Company Law section 303(a) also permits service of process on the secretary of state as an agent for a limited liability company defendant.[23] The additional notice requirement in CPLR 3215(g)(4) does not, however, apply when seeking a default judgment against a limited liability company.[24]

Miscellaneous Matters

When the additional notice has to be given to a defaulting defendant in a situation in which there are other defendants who have not defaulted, it has been held that a copy of the notice need not be served on the others.[25] But at least one case has said that it does have to be served on the others if it appears that they may bear an indemnification relationship to the defaulting defendant and thus are entitled to defend in his behalf.[26] If there is any doubt on that score, requiring the notice to be served on all parties appears to be the soundest course.

The CPLR rules about default judgments are generally applicable in the lower civil courts as well as in the supreme court.[27] The additional notice of a consumer credit action required by rules passed by the Office of Court Administration in 2014 is in addition to any notice required under CPLR 3215(g).[28] It may be that additional notice of a default judgment is required by one provision, but not the other.

F. VOLUNTARY DISCONTINUANCE

Table of Sections

§ 297.   Voluntary Discontinuance, Methods
§ 298.   Effect of Discontinuance

§ 297. Voluntary Discontinuance, Methods

Any party asserting a claim may be allowed to discontinue it. That includes not only the plaintiff, but also the defendant with a counterclaim, cross-claim, or third-party claim. Our examples below will assume that the plaintiff seeks to discontinue.

There are three ways in which voluntary discontinuance can be accomplished: (1) notice; (2) stipulation; or (3) order.

(1) Discontinuance by notice. At one time a party could discontinue a claim at any moment during the litigation without any permission from court or adversary.[1] A party still has that power, but only at the very outset of the action. Under CPLR 3217(a)(1),

---

[23] See § 69.

[24] Gershman v. Ahmad, 131 A.D.3d 1104, 16 N.Y.S.3d 836 (2d Dep't 2015); see also Confidential Lending, LLC v. Nurse, 120 A.D.3d 739, 992 N.Y.S.2d 77 (2d Dep't 2014) (additional notice requirements in CPLR 3215(g) do not apply when seeking default judgment against the New York City Environmental Control Board because it "is neither a 'natural person' (CPLR 3215(g)(3)(i)), nor 'a domestic or authorized foreign corporation' that had been served with process pursuant to Business Corporation Law § 306(b).").

[25] Card v. Polito, 55 A.D.2d 123, 389 N.Y.S.2d 696 (4th Dep't 1976).

[26] Rivera v. Laporte, 120 Misc. 2d 733, 466 N.Y.S.2d 606 (Sup. Ct., New York County 1983).

[27] See § 1402 in the New York City Civil, Uniform District, Uniform City, and Uniform Justice court acts, McKinney's Volume 29A, Parts 2 and 3.

[28] See § 295.

[1] See 19th Jud. Council Rep. 197, 207 (1953).

the plaintiff can discontinue the claim merely by serving a notice of discontinuance on all parties and filing the notice, with proof of service, with the clerk. She must do so, however, within 20 days after serving the complaint or before the defendant has served a responsive pleading, whichever occurs earlier. Thus, the service of an answer or a CPLR 3211(a) pre-answer motion to dismiss[2] cuts off the plaintiff's right to discontinue by mere notice even if the 20-day period from complaint service is still open.[3] The purpose of this restriction is to prevent the plaintiff from discontinuing at whim after the defendant has troubled to respond and to require either the defendant's permission (discontinuance by stipulation) or leave of court (discontinuance by order). For that reason, too, a plaintiff whose original complaint has been answered should not be allowed, merely by amending the complaint, to get a new chance to discontinue by notice.

A discontinuance is often based on a settlement of the case. A 2003 amendment of CPLR 2104, the general statute requiring that certain stipulations be in writing, made the filing of all stipulations of settlement mandatory, and required that the "terms" of the settlement be included. This proved controversial among attorneys, who often want the "terms" of the settlement kept confidential. The issue is discussed elsewhere in this book.[4]

The voluntary discontinuance by notice can play a unique role in matrimonial actions where the commencement of the action ends the period during which income of either spouse is considered marital property subject to equitable distribution. Whatever comes in after commencement is deemed the spouse's individual property. This made a voluntary discontinuance effected by mere notice under CPLR 3217(a)(1) an extraordinary tool in McMahon v. McMahon.[5]

W commenced her divorce action against H without a complaint, as she is permitted to do, and, although the action proceeded apace, H never demanded a complaint. During this time H came into a $30 million bonanza when his brokerage firm went public. W understandably wanted that money included in equitable distribution. Because the right to discontinue by mere notice is measured by the service of pleadings, and none had yet been served in the action, W just served H with a notice of discontinuance, hoping to erase the action and revive the equitable distribution period to cover H's windfall.

It worked. The court held that W had an absolute right under the statute to discontinue in this way, whatever the impact it might have on the parties' marital rights.

(2) Discontinuance by stipulation. Discontinuance is permitted on stipulation by all parties. Under the CPLR itself,[6] the stipulation can be filed with the court at any time before the case has been submitted to the fact-trier, but under the more stringent demands of the Uniform Rules, which implement the Individual Assignment System (IAS), the requirement is that the stipulation be filed within 20 days of its execution and that the court be notified "promptly."[7]

---

[2]   Jericho Group, Ltd. v. Mid-Town Development Ltd. Partnership, 129 A.D.3d 561, 12 N.Y.S.3d 45 (1st Dep't 2015); BDO USA, LLP v. Phoenix Four, Inc., 113 A.D.3d 507, 979 N.Y.S.2d 45 (1st Dep't 2014).

[3]   Discontinuance by notice when there are several adverse parties is discussed in Commentary C3217:5 on McKinney's CPLR 3217.

[4]   See § 204.

[5]   McMahon v. McMahon, 279 A.D.2d 346, 718 N.Y.S.2d 353 (1st Dep't 2001) (SPR 105:1).

[6]   CPLR 3217(a)(2).

[7]   See 22 N.Y.C.R.R. § 202.28, applicable in the supreme and county courts. A similar rule, 22 N.Y.C.R.R. § 210.16, applies in city courts outside New York City. In courts in which the Individual

If any party is an infant or incapacitated person (incompetent or conservatee), the stipulation method is not available; a court order is needed. Nor may a class action be discontinued by mere stipulation.[8]

Old caselaw held that once an action was discontinued by stipulation, a later endeavor to vacate the stipulation and revive the case would require a plenary action. That was the holding in Yonkers Fur Dressing Co. v. Royal Ins. Co.,[9] where the discontinuance was part of a stipulation of settlement. *Yonkers* was criticized for requiring a new action when a mere motion could do the job with so much less trouble,[10] and in Teitelbaum Holdings, Ltd. v. Gold,[11] the Court of Appeals joined the criticism of its own prior holding and allowed a mere motion to enforce a settlement stipulation, which in that case called for money payments by D to P and authorized the offset of a certain debt owed by P to D. The court cited the criticism of *Yonkers*, the expeditiousness of the motion procedure, and, by analogy, the availability of mere motions to undo action-terminating judgments in other contexts. All of this suggests that *Gold* overrules *Yonkers*.

(3) Discontinuance by order. If the plaintiff's time to vacate by notice has expired and the defendant will not stipulate to discontinue, the plaintiff must turn to the third and last method: a court order. The court can allow discontinuance by order any time before submission of the case to the fact trier. After that submission, the only method of discontinuance recognized by the CPLR is a combination of stipulation and order.[12]

The courts are reasonably liberal about ordering a discontinuance. It has been held that the plaintiff should be allowed to discontinue the action at any time "unless substantial rights have accrued or his adversary's rights would be prejudiced thereby."[13] If the court detects any illegitimate motive in the plaintiff's wish to discontinue, however, it will deny the motion. Where, for example, the plaintiff realized at the trial that things were going badly and that a loss was imminent, his discontinuance motion was properly regarded by the court as merely an effort "to make another try" and was denied.[14]

If the plaintiff has tactically mistaken his forum, however, a discontinuance has been allowed. A leading case is Schimansky v. Nelson,[15] where P brought a wrongful death action in a state court in a rural county. After the case had reached an advanced stage of preparation, P realized that federal jurisdiction was available in a New York City federal court, where damages are reputedly awarded in greater sums. Conditioning its order on P's payment to D of costs and expenses to date, the court allowed P to discontinue so as to start afresh in federal court.

Assignment System (IAS) is not in operation, the notifications are made to the "clerk of the court." See 22 N.Y.C.R.R. § 208.16 (N.Y.C. Civil Court) and 22 N.Y.C.R.R. § 212.16 (district courts).

  [8] CPLR 908 (requiring court approval for discontinuance of a class action); see § 147.

  [9] Yonkers Fur Dressing Co. v. Royal Ins. Co., 247 N.Y. 435, 160 N.E. 778 (1928).

  [10] See, e.g., Commentary C3217:10 on McKinney's CPLR 3217.

  [11] Teitelbaum Holdings, Ltd. v. Gold, 48 N.Y.2d 51, 421 N.Y.S.2d 556, 396 N.E.2d 1029 (1979).

  [12] CPLR 3217(b).

  [13] Louis R. Shapiro, Inc. v. Milspemes Corp., 20 A.D.2d 857, 248 N.Y.S.2d 85, 86 (1st Dep't 1964); see GK v. JK, 55 Misc. 3d 690, 47 N.Y.S.3d 652 (Fam. Ct., New York County 2017).

  [14] Getz v. Harry Silverstein, Inc., 205 Misc. 431, 432, 128 N.Y.S.2d 436, 438 (N.Y. City Ct. 1954); see Bergassi, LLC v. Ikon Solutions, Inc., 21 Misc. 3d 1133(A), 875 N.Y.S.2d 818 (Sup. Ct., Westchester County 2008).

  [15] Schimansky v. Nelson, 50 A.D.2d 634, 374 N.Y.S.2d 771 (3d Dep't 1975).

Conditioning the order and imposing such terms as it deems just are explicitly authorized by CPLR 3217(b). A money sanction beyond just costs and expenses can be imposed, for example,[16] or the discontinuance can be granted on the condition that a given party be permitted to use, in a different action, the record accumulated in the discontinued one.[17]

§ 298. Effect of Discontinuance

CPLR 3217(c) governs the res judicata effect of a discontinuance. The general rule is that unless the discontinuance itself states otherwise, whether in the notice, stipulation, or order, it is not res judicata so as to bar a new action.

An order of discontinuance can dictate what its res judicata effect is to be. The court can specify, for example, that no later action may be brought on the claim,[1] a result that invokes res judicata. So does the shorthand phrase "with prejudice." Whatever phrase is used should make clear the court's intent.

If any action on the same claim was previously discontinued, by any method, in any federal or state court including a New York court, the discontinuance of the second action by the notice method does operate as res judicata and bars relitigation.[2] Discontinuance of the second action by the stipulation or order method, however, is not such an automatic bar. The matter in that instance is left to the terms of the stipulation or order.

Giving res judicata effect to a discontinuance-by-notice of a second action is designed to avoid harassment of the defendant. It has therefore been held that when the purpose of the second discontinuance, albeit by notice, involves no harassment, the res judicata rule will not operate and another action will be allowed. Where, for example, P discontinued the second action by notice (after discontinuance of a prior action) because D had moved to dismiss the second action for lack of jurisdiction, P's discontinuance in that instance was simply a concession of D's jurisdictional point and a third action was held permissible.[3]

Keep in mind that all of these conclusions about a later action being permissible concern only the doctrine of res judicata, not the statute of limitations. They assume that the original statute of limitations is still alive so that a later action will not meet a time barrier. Here we must refer yet again to the potent CPLR 205(a), which gives a plaintiff six months, from a prior nonmerits termination of an action, in which to sue anew notwithstanding the interim expiration of the original statute of limitations.[4] The lawyer about to discontinue must always remember that a voluntary discontinuance, by any method at all, is an exception to CPLR 205(a) and does not get the six months. A discontinuing plaintiff planning to start over must therefore always make sure either that the original statute of limitations is still alive or that the plaintiff has in hand an agreement by the defendant not to interpose the statute of limitations defense in the new action.

---

[16]   Brockman v. Turin, 130 A.D.2d 616, 515 N.Y.S.2d 545 (2d Dep't 1987).

[17]   See 1st Rep. Leg. Doc. No. 6b, p. 104 (1957).

[1]   1st Rep. Leg. Doc. No. 6b, p. 104 (1957).

[2]   CPLR 3217(c).

[3]   Headley v. Noto, 45 Misc. 2d 284, 256 N.Y.S.2d 750 (Sup. Ct., Kings County 1965), aff'd, 24 A.D.2d 493, 261 N.Y.S.2d 846 (2d Dep't); ATM One, LLC. v. Escobar, 193 Misc. 2d 157, 159–60, 747 N.Y.S.2d 286, 287–88 (Dist. Ct., Nassau County 2002).

[4]   See § 52.

The federal counterpart to CPLR 3217 is the voluntary "dismissal" found in Rule 41(a) of the Federal Rules of Civil Procedure. In Kyriacou v. Village of Airmont,[5] the original proceeding was commenced in state court but was removed by the respondents to federal court where it was then voluntarily dismissed under Federal Rule 41(a). The second proceeding, although brought in the New York court within six months of the dismissal of the federal action, was time-barred because the earlier termination was voluntary and the original statute of limitations had expired.

G. CONFESSION OF JUDGMENT

Table of Sections

§ 299.   Confession of Judgment, Generally
§ 300.   Affidavit for Confession of Judgment
§ 301.   Filing, Enforcement, and Effect of Confessed Judgment
§ 302.   Vacating Confessed Judgment

§ 299. Confession of Judgment, Generally

A confession of judgment dispenses with an adversary proceeding and gives the creditor the fruits of a successful one by permitting the creditor merely to file a judgment voluntarily confessed by the debtor. It serves as a security device by enabling the creditor to obtain judgment without an action even before a debt is due, although it may not be enforced until due. If the debt is already due, the confession of judgment is a concession of liability and still has the advantage of avoiding an action.

A confessed judgment is closely scrutinized and will be valid only if it conforms to the strict requirements of CPLR 3218.[1] It's a device virtually limited to money claims.

Confession of judgment is available for "money due or to become due," or "to secure the plaintiff against a contingent liability in behalf of the defendant."[2] The latter phrase enables it to be used in a situation where it is not certain that the defendant will ever owe the plaintiff any money. A simple example is where P agrees to act as surety or guarantor for a debt incurred by D to some third person. If D pays the debt, P will never have to. P is nonetheless allowed to enter a confessed judgment against D to cover P's potential liability in the interim, with enforcement suspended until P is actually called on to pay all or part of the debt to the third person.

The confession device is used primarily, if not exclusively, in contract situations. It is not precluded in tort cases,[3] but has little to offer there: a confession is usually sought by the creditor before payment of the debt is due and torts are not known to be negotiated in advance. Its readiest use is in a loan or other credit transaction, but here the attorney must take note of CPLR 3201, which may preclude the use of a confessed judgment in transactions of $1,500 or less involving installment purchases of personal, as opposed to

---

    [5]   Kyriacou v. Village of Airmont, 33 Misc. 3d 1221(A), 939 N.Y.S.2d 741 (Sup. Ct., Rockland County 2011).

    [1]   See Rae v. Kestenberg, 23 A.D.2d 565, 256 N.Y.S.2d 737 (2d Dep't 1965), aff'd, 16 N.Y.2d 1023, 265 N.Y.S.2d 904, 213 N.E.2d 315; Irons v. Roberts, 206 A.D.2d 683, 614 N.Y.S.2d 792 (3d Dep't 1994).

    [2]   CPLR 3218(a).

    [3]   See Luboch v. Sidey's Inc., 35 Misc. 2d 410, 411, 230 N.Y.S.2d 860, 862 (Sup. Ct., Chautauqua County 1962) (discussing a supreme court decision affirmed by the Fourth Department which had "held that a confession of a judgment for a tort is not authorized.").

business, goods. As will be seen,[4] the affidavit of the debtor is a key paper in the confession procedure, and in installment purchases for $1,500 or less, the affidavit is unacceptable if executed prior to default. This is contrary to the rule in most confession situations where a pre-default affidavit is permissible.

When joint debtors are involved, not all need confess judgment. Any of them can. The creditor may take confessed judgment against the one who does, retaining the right to bring an ordinary action against those who don't.[5]

§ 300. Affidavit for Confession of Judgment

A confessed judgment may be entered only if accompanied by an affidavit executed by the defendant—the confessor—in conformity with the requirements of CPLR 3218(a). The affidavit must state the sum in which entry is to be permitted and the defendant's residence county where the entry takes place. If the defendant is a nonresident, the affidavit should specify a county in which entry is authorized.[1]

The most important mission of the affidavit is to state the facts of the transaction on which the confession is based. If it is for a contingent liability, as in the surety or guarantee example given in the prior section, the affidavit must state the facts constituting the potential liability and manifest that the confessed judgment does not exceed it.[2]

In the more common situation, where the confessed judgment is for money, whether now due or to become due, the affidavit must concisely state "the facts out of which the debt arose" and must show that the debt is a just one.[3] It is here that the careless creditor most often has trouble. The caselaw requires a more exhaustive factual picture than the "concise" statement the statute seems to call for. Even the Advisory Committee contemplated that if the facts stated in the affidavit sufficed to state a cause of action in a pleading, they would satisfy this confession requirement,[4] but the committee had in mind older cases, decided when pleadings were more detailed. It did not anticipate how successful the CPLR would be in freeing pleadings from that detail.

So little does it take to satisfy the pleading requirements today that the creditor who merely applies the pleading standard to the confession affidavit is likely to miss the mark. County National Bank v. Vogt,[5] in which the court itself apparently overlooked the irony, illustrates. The confession in *Vogt* was for a debt, and the affidavit's statement of the transaction was in perfect conformity not only with the general pleading requirement, but also with former Official Form 9.[6] The court nonetheless held the affidavit inadequate.

---

[4]   See § 300.

[5]   CPLR 3218(d).

[1]   CPLR 3218(a)(1).

[2]   CPLR 3218(a)(3).

[3]   CPLR 3218(a)(2).

[4]   See 1st Rep. Leg. Doc. No. 6b, p. 108 (1957).

[5]   County Nat. Bank v. Vogt, 28 A.D.2d 793, 280 N.Y.S.2d 1016 (3d Dep't 1967), aff'd, 21 N.Y.2d 800, 288 N.Y.S.2d 631, 235 N.E.2d 772 (1968).

[6]   Former Official Form 9 authorizes as a pleading in a case for money lent the simple statement that "[d]efendant owes plaintiff twenty thousand dollars for money lent by plaintiff to defendant on June 1, 1965." The affidavit in *Vogt* stated that it was "for a debt justly due to the plaintiff arising from the following facts: Money loaned by Plaintiff to Defendant and not repaid" and was found inadequate (and not because the date

The lesson is clear: the confession affidavit should contain genuine detail, enough to put the confessing debtor in peril of perjury if the statement is false.[7] An affidavit saying only that liability was for "legal services rendered" was held inadequate under that standard, and a law firm's judgment against its client therefore vacated at the behest of a competing creditor.[8] The simple conclusory standards that govern pleadings must not be relied on.

The purpose of the affidavit is to protect third persons, not the judgment debtor.[9] An inadequate affidavit therefore can't be availed of by the debtor herself. The affidavit's major aim is to enable other and presumably junior creditors to investigate the claim and determine its validity[10] because if the claim is not legitimate, and junior can defeat it, junior becomes senior. The statement of facts in the affidavit should be drawn with that in mind.

The affidavit may be amended in the discretion of the court.[11] Discretion apparently turns on the nature of the affidavit's deficiency. Innocent and merely technical omissions are correctible nunc pro tunc,[12] but basic defects in the statement of underlying facts, especially when the rights of other creditors have become involved, are not likely to be correctible by amendment.[13]

The New York confession procedure must be distinguished from the old "cognovit" practice, which no longer obtains in New York but does elsewhere. A cognovit instrument at its worst purports to allow a creditor to designate any attorney to act as the debtor's attorney so as to confess judgment in the debtor's behalf and allows the judgment to be entered without notice anywhere the creditor chooses. The New York Court of Appeals held in Atlas Credit Corp. v. Ezrine[14] that such an instrument is so offensive to due process that even a judgment predicated on it in a sister state lacks jurisdiction and is therefore not entitled to full faith and credit. The U.S. Supreme Court later held in D.H. Overmyer Co. v. Frick Co.[15] that a cognovit instrument is not per se unconstitutional; that the right to notice and hearing guaranteed by due process is waivable; and that if a debtor, with knowledge and appreciation of the consequences, signs such an instrument, he waives his rights and will be bound by any judgment rendered on the instrument.

The court in *Overmyer* stressed that the debtor before it, a corporation, was represented by counsel and sophisticated in the preservation of its rights and hence could

---

was missing). *County National Bank,* 28 A.D.2d at 793, 280 N.Y.S.2d at 1018. The official forms have since been abrogated. See § 7.

[7]   Princeton Bank & Trust Co. v. Berley, 57 A.D.2d 348, 394 N.Y.S.2d 714 (2d Dep't 1977); see Allied Intern. Fund, Inc. v. Gladtke, 2016 WL 4140824, n.4 (Sup. Ct., New York County 2016).

[8]   Baehre v. Rochester Dental Prosthetics, Inc., 112 Misc. 2d 270, 446 N.Y.S.2d 901 (Sup. Ct., Erie County 1982).

[9]   Giryluk v. Giryluk, 30 A.D.2d 22, 289 N.Y.S.2d 458 (1st Dep't 1968), aff'd, 23 N.Y.2d 894, 298 N.Y.S.2d 91, 245 N.E.2d 818 (1969); Regency Club at Wallkill, LLC v. Bienish, 95 A.D.3d 879, 942 N.Y.S.2d 894 (2d Dep't 2012).

[10]   See ILMS Realty Ass'n v. Madden, 174 A.D.2d 603, 571 N.Y.S.2d 310 (2d Dep't 1991); *Baehre,* 112 Misc.2d at 272, 446 N.Y.S.2d at 902.

[11]   *County National Bank,* 28 A.D.2d at 794, 280 N.Y.S.2d at 1019; see Cole-Hatchard v. Nicholson, 73 A.D.3d 834, 901 N.Y.S.2d 660 (2d Dep't 2010).

[12]   *Princeton Bank,* 57 A.D.2d at 354, 394 N.Y.S.2d at 718.

[13]   See *Cole-Hatchard,* 73 A.D.3d at 836, 901 N.Y.S.2d at 662; Baehre, 112 Misc.2d at 276, 446 N.Y.S.2d at 905; Commentary C3218:10 on McKinney's CPLR 3218.

[14]   Atlas Credit Corp. v. Ezrine, 25 N.Y.2d 219, 303 N.Y.S.2d 382, 250 N.E.2d 474 (1969).

[15]   D. H. Overmyer Co. Inc., of Ohio v. Frick Co., 405 U.S. 174, 92 S. Ct. 775, 31 L. Ed. 2d 124 (1972).

be bound by its cognovit commitment. It left the door open to a contrary result, invalidating the cognovit procedure if the debtor should be shown to have unequal bargaining power or if the contract should be one of adhesion. After *Overmyer*, a New York court bent on refusing recognition to a cognovit-based judgment of a sister state would have to find such a factor present.

Acknowledging this in its later decision in Fiore v. Oakwood Plaza Shopping Ctr., Inc.,[16] the Court of Appeals reviewed its *Atlas* holding in light of the *Overmyer* case, found the defendants before it to have had a sufficiently strong position to intelligently waive notice and hearing, and, so finding, upheld the waiver, at least partly overruling *Atlas* and directing recognition of a cognovit-based sister-state judgment. *Fiore* was no adhesion contract and involved a $1 million project for the sale of land for a shopping mall and debtors represented by counsel.

The cognovit practice, although a precursor of confession of judgment, must be distinguished from it.[17] New York's confession rules, both in regard to the affidavit, which must be made by the debtor proper rather than by some fictional agent, and in regard to the place of entry, which is restricted, are tight and should satisfy constitutional demands. But even here the door must be left open to the invalidation of a confession contained in a particularly one-sided (in bargaining power) contract or one that runs afoul of the Uniform Commercial Code's "unconscionability" standard.[18] Turning back to a point made in the previous section, all confessions of judgment in New York, whatever their source, "are always closely scrutinized . . . and in judging them a liberal attitude should be assumed in favor of the judgment debtor."[19]

§ 301. Filing, Enforcement, and Effect of Confessed Judgment

The time within which the affidavit may be filed and the confessed judgment entered is three years from the execution of the affidavit.[1] The filing and entry take place in the county of the defendant's residence or, when the defendant is a nonresident, in the county specified in the affidavit. The filing of a confession of judgement will require an index number and the payment of the fee for same.[2] The clerk enters judgment in the supreme court[3] and it may then be enforced as if duly rendered by that court.[4]

The 3-year period is a statute of limitations. The confession procedure will therefore not work if only the affidavit of confessed judgment is filed within three years of its execution; the judgment itself must also be.[5]

---

[16] Fiore v. Oakwood Plaza Shopping Center, Inc., 78 N.Y.2d 572, 578 N.Y.S.2d 115, 585 N.E.2d 364 (1991).

[17] The history of cognovit instruments and the evolution of the more moderate New York confession procedure is traced in the *Atlas* case, 25 N.Y.2d at 225–27, 303 N.Y.S.2d at 387–88, 250 N.E.2d at 478–79.

[18] See N.Y. UCC § 2–302.

[19] Rae v. Kestenberg, 23 A.D.2d 565, 566, 256 N.Y.S.2d 737, 739 (2d Dep't 1965), aff'd, 16 N.Y.2d 1023, 265 N.Y.S.2d 904, 213 N.E.2d 315; Jaliman v. JMJ Films, Inc., 42 Misc. 3d 1233(A), 986 N.Y.S.2d 866 (Sup. Ct., Putnam County 2014).

[1] CPLR 3218(b).

[2] See § 78.

[3] If the amount sought is within the monetary jurisdiction of a lower court, the confessed judgment may be entered there if the affidavit so provides. See § 1403 in each of the New York City Civil, Uniform District, Uniform City, and Uniform Justice court acts, McKinney's Vol.29A, Parts 2 and 3.

[4] CPLR 3218(b).

[5] Moldavsky v. Nevins, 184 Misc. 2d 968, 712 N.Y.S.2d 822 (Sup. Ct., Westchester County 2000).

There may be no enforcement until something is due. Although the confessed judgment may be filed before a default occurs, no execution or other enforcement step may be taken until that time. Executions may periodically issue for such sums as fall due, but each must specify the amount now due so that the sheriff will not levy for more.[6] Should execution be sought for too much, the levy can be vacated on motion.[7]

Since the clerk must docket the judgment when she enters it,[8] the judgment becomes a lien on the defendant's real property in the county as of that time even though enforcement is not yet permissible.[9]

A confessed judgment in New York is given both res judicata and collateral estoppel effect.[10]

§ 302. Vacating Confessed Judgment

If the judgment has been entered in violation of the terms of the affidavit, it may be vacated. But as far as attacking the affidavit itself is concerned, especially in its statement of the underlying transaction, it must be remembered that the affidavit is for the protection of third persons, not the debtor.[1] While a defect in the terms of the affidavit may therefore be exploited by another creditor—even though the underlying transaction is valid—it may not be exploited by the debtor. If the transaction is proper, the affidavit is irrelevant as far as the debtor is concerned. But the debtor may of course attack the confessed judgment if the underlying transaction is bad, as where it was induced by fraud.

Whenever made by the right person on the right ground, the attack takes the form of an application to vacate the judgment. Whether this requires a plenary action or can be brought on by mere motion also turns on who is seeking the vacatur and the ground for it. If the vacatur is sought by another creditor of the debtor, a mere motion will do.[2] But if the debtor seeks it, she can use the simple motion procedure only if the judgment has been entered in violation of the affidavit's terms, such as where it states a time that has not arrived or a contingency that has not occurred. If the entry is valid on its face and the debtor's objection is based on some extrinsic factor, like fraud or misrepresentation, it has been held that a plenary action is required to do the vacating; that a mere motion won't do.[3]

---

[6]   CPLR 3218(c).

[7]   CPLR 5230, 5240.

[8]   For the difference between entry and docketing, see §§ 418 and 421.

[9]   CPLR 5203. This result was apparently intended, see 1st Rep. Leg. Doc. No. 6(b) p. 107 (1957), but see Commentary C3218:15 on McKinney's CPLR 3218. The judgment becomes a real property lien only when the judgment is entered and docketed in the supreme or county court. For the procedure on making a judgment of a lower court, including a confessed judgment, a lien on real property, see §§ 421 to 422.

[10]   See § 451.

[1]   Regency Club at Wallkill, LLC v. Bienish, 95 A.D.3d 879, 942 N.Y.S.2d 894 (2d Dep't 2012).

[2]   County Nat. Bank v. Vogt, 28 A.D.2d 793, 280 N.Y.S.2d 1016 (3d Dep't 1967), aff'd, 21 N.Y.2d 800, 288 N.Y.S.2d 631, 235 N.E.2d 772 (1968); Estate of Zelman v. Scibelli, 157 A.D.2d 705, 549 N.Y.S.2d 805 (2d Dep't 1990).

[3]   See Scheckter v. Ryan, 161 A.D.2d 344, 555 N.Y.S.2d 99 (1st Dep't 1990). It can be argued that a mere motion should be adequate even in that situation. See CPLR 5015(a)(3), and § 429.

H. TENDERS AND OFFERS

Table of Sections

§ 303.   Tenders and Offers; CPLR 3219–3221

§ 303.   Tenders and Offers; CPLR 3219–3221

The devices of tender and offer, never to be confused with the tender offers that preoccupy corporate practice and sometimes the federal penitentiaries, make up the trio of CPLR 3219, 3220, and 3221. They have in common that each is an exceedingly weak tool that enables a defendant (or any party against whom a claim is asserted) to make some kind of gesture to the plaintiff in advance of trial that concedes something in the hope of securing some incidental advantage in return. The plaintiff can accept or refuse. A refusal is at the risk of some relatively paltry penalty if the thing tendered is ultimately adjudged to have been adequate.

CPLR 3219, entitled "Tender," enables a defendant against whom a contract claim is asserted to deposit in court a sum the defendant deems sufficient to satisfy the claim, thereby requiring the plaintiff to accept the sum in full settlement, or else. The or else is that if the plaintiff rejects the tender and gets no higher sum at the trial, the plaintiff forfeits interest and costs as of the time of the tender. Here the defendant concedes liability, but disputes damages.

Under CPLR 3220, entitled "Offer to liquidate damages conditionally," it is mainly liability that the defendant disputes, although she may dispute damages as well. This offer, like the tender of CPLR 3219, is available only in contract cases, but here the defendant offers to pay a specified sum only if the plaintiff establishes liability at the trial. If the plaintiff accepts, and then wins on the liability issue at trial, the amount offered is the amount he gets. If the plaintiff rejects the offer, and then at the trial gets no greater damages than the defendant offered, the plaintiff must pay the expenses incurred by the defendant in trying damages.

The last member of this weak triumvirate, CPLR 3221, is not limited to contract cases. It is usable in all but matrimonial actions. It's entitled "Offer to compromise" and enables a defendant to offer the plaintiff judgment for a specific sum or for specified property. The plaintiff's acceptance results in judgment and closes the case. If the plaintiff rejects the offer and then does no better at the trial, the plaintiff loses costs from the time of the offer and must pay the defendant's costs as of that time.

None of the tenders or offers of CPLR 3219, 3220, or 3221 may be made known to the jury if the case goes to trial, and each of the cited provisions prescribes in detail the procedures to be followed, including time requirements. A chart comparing and contrasting the three provisions was prepared for the McKinney's Commentaries and may be found there.[1]

---

[1]   The chart, prepared by Professor Paul S. Graziano, appears with Commentary C3221:3 on McKinney's CPLR 3221.

I. ACTION ON SUBMITTED FACTS

Table of Sections

§ 304.   Action on Submitted Facts

§ 305.   Disposition of Submission

§ 304. Action on Submitted Facts

One of the most useful but unfortunately underused devices in practice today is the action on submitted facts supplied by CPLR 3222. Here the adversaries agree on the facts and disagree only on their legal implication. They draw up a paper called a "submission of controversy" in which they fully state all the facts relevant to their dispute, acknowledge it before a notary just as they would a deed, and file it with the court. The court applies the law to the submitted facts and renders judgment accordingly. There is no summons, pleading, bill of particulars, disclosure, or delay. Whenever an attorney believes there is agreement with the other side on the facts, she should contact her opposite number and try to work up a submission. Since it will result in a substantial saving for both sides, even the opposing lawyer, usually the prospective defendant's lawyer, owes it to the client to consider the use of this device.

It can be used in any kind of dispute except a matrimonial action, from which it has been excluded as a possible back door to a consent divorce. All that is needed is agreement on the facts and a mutual willingness to put them into a submission.

The whole controversy must be submitted. It has been held that the court will not take just a piece of it, such as a defense that is part of a pending conventional action.[1]

The CPLR 3222 submission is sometimes confused with the declaratory judgment. It should not be. While the declaratory judgment action can also be used as the litigation vehicle for a variety of disputes, it is prosecuted in conventional adversary form—with summons, pleadings, disclosure, trial, etc.—and can pose issues of fact just like any other action. Its main distinction from other actions is that it seeks declaratory rather than coercive relief. If the parties can agree on the facts, declaratory relief can of course be sought on a CPLR 3222 submission and often is. Declaratory judgment is treated in a subsequent chapter.[2]

The submission should be a direct statement of facts. It should simply narrate the facts rather than recite that X would testify to this and Y would testify to that.[3] It must contain a statement to the effect that "the controversy is real and . . . the submission is made in good faith."[4] It may not, in other words, be used to get an advisory opinion or otherwise involve the court in anything short of an actual controversy. Nor will it be entertained if someone not a party to the submission has an apparent interest in the outcome.[5]

---

[1]   See Braun v. C. E. P. C. Distributors, Inc., 80 A.D.2d 505, 435 N.Y.S.2d 289 (1st Dep't 1981).

[2]   See §§ 436 et seq.

[3]   Ciunci v. Wella Corp., 26 A.D.2d 109, 271 N.Y.S.2d 317 (1st Dep't 1966).

[4]   CPLR 3222(a).

[5]   See Boehm v. Dillon, 195 A.D.2d 1080, 600 N.Y.S.2d 543 (4th Dep't 1993); Justino v. Fassi, 15 A.D.2d 676, 224 N.Y.S.2d 173 (2d Dep't 1962).

The submission is filed with the clerk of the court specified in the agreement, which of course must be a court having jurisdiction of the subject matter. If it is the supreme court, the submission must also specify the county. A special advantage here is that if it is a supreme court submission, which it usually is, the parties may stipulate to have it heard by the appellate division in first instance.[6] If they do, the submission eliminates one step in the litigation process, for which reason CPLR 3222 submissions more often than not do specify the appellate division. If the case is initially submitted to the appellate division, the submission should be filed there and with the clerk of some trial-level court.[7] While CPLR 3222 is not clear on this point, filing at the supreme court will allow for easier enforcement of any judgment rendered by the appellate division.

The provisional remedies of attachment and injunction are unavailable in an action on submitted facts,[8] as are the disclosure devices and other pretrial procedures.[9]

§ 305. Disposition of Submission

The controversy in an action on submitted facts must be determined on the submission.[10] There is to be no live testimony nor even affidavits or other argumentative proof. It is permissible, however, to append a legal instrument (a contract, deed, will, mortgage etc.) if its terms are not disputed and only its legal implications are at issue.

At one time, the factual statement had to be so complete that the court was not even required to draw an inference from the facts stated. In one case, for example, a safebox user found money on the floor of a booth at a bank. The controversy concerned whether the finder or the bank was entitled to the money. The court dismissed the submission as inadequate because the submission did not state whether the place was a public place or whether a customer or a stranger dropped the money.[11] A fact trier in an ordinary action, the court noted, could draw inferences to answer such questions, but the court on a submission could not. The result was unfortunate, and no longer obtains. The court is now explicitly authorized to "find facts by inference from the facts stipulated[.]"[12]

The submission should state what judgment each party is looking for. The disposition will take the form of a judgment, just as if the case had been tried to a conclusion in due course. If the submission is before the appellate division, the court can if need be order that the judgment be entered in the supreme court of a designated county, which would enable the judgment to enjoy the usual rules about lien value and enforcement.[13]

If the submission is found by the court to be inadequate to support a judgment, the court can dismiss it or call for an additional statement.[14]

---

[6]   CPLR 3222(b)(3). As an alternative, the stipulation can choose a specific judge or referee, subject to that person's consent.

[7]   See Commentary C3222:8 on McKinney's CPLR 3222.

[8]   CPLR 3222(b)(1); see Commentary C3222:6 on McKinney's CPLR 3222.

[9]   See Commentary C3222:7 on McKinney's CPLR 3222.

[10]   CPLR 3222(b)(2).

[11]   Cohen v. Manufacturers Safe Deposit Co., 297 N.Y. 266, 78 N.E.2d 604 (1948).

[12]   CPLR 3222(b)(4).

[13]   See Commentary C3222:10 on McKinney's CPLR 3222. As noted in the prior section, that is why it is advisable for the submission to be filed with the clerk of the supreme court even when a determination is sought from the appellate division.

[14]   CPLR 3222(b)(5).

If additional facts are needed and the parties can't agree on them, an additional submission will of course not help and an ordinary plenary action will be needed to resolve the controversy.

Chapter 12

PROVISIONAL REMEDIES

Analysis

A. Introductory
B. Arrest
C. Attachment
D. Injunction
E. Receivership
F. Notice of Pendency
G. Seizure of Chattel

A. INTRODUCTORY

Table of Sections

§ 306.   Provisional Remedies, Generally
§ 307.   Provisional Remedies; Constitutional Requirements

§ 306. Provisional Remedies, Generally

CPLR 6001 lists the four official provisional remedies,[1] each of which is then given its own article for the law applicable to it. The four are attachment (Article 62), injunction (Article 63), receivership (Article 64), and notice of pendency (Article 65). The notice of pendency is more commonly known as "lis pendens." To these four may be added a few others which, while not actually "provisional," are provisional-like and are traditionally treated as part of the family. They are the order to seize a chattel in a replevin action, procedure for which is in Article 71 of the CPLR, and the order of sequestration in a matrimonial action, supplied by sections 233 and 243 of the Domestic Relations Law.

The four provisional remedies are "provisional" in the sense that they afford the plaintiff some kind of security or protection while the action is pending, but they operate only as interim devices which, at least theoretically, do not effect any permanent divestiture against the defendant. They may come close, however, and in any event they do inflict deprivations even if only "provisional." This engendered a series of constitutional determinations that reduced the freedom with which the remedies used to be granted. The constitutional limitations are discussed as an independent topic in the next section and are the subject of brief reminders as they become relevant.

---

[1] There were five when the CPLR started out in 1963. The fifth was the order of civil arrest, which was inherited from prior law and which occupied Article 61. It was rarely used and was abolished in 1979 when Article 61 was repealed. The five sections devoted to the civil arrest in the first edition of this book, §§ 308 through 312, are omitted from later editions—just left blank.

Broadly viewed, and subject to elaboration and detail as each of the remedies is separately treated in ensuing sections, the provisional remedies operate this way:

Attachment seizes the defendant's property and prevents the defendant from using it during the pendency of a money action unless the defendant discharges the attachment with a bond, whereupon the bond substitutes for the attached property and the plaintiff gets just as much security that way.

Injunction operates to require the defendant to maintain a specified status quo during the pendency of the action, usually with an instruction not to do a given act (a negative rather than positive direction).

A receiver takes possession of designated property of the defendant and protects it during the pendency of the action, preventing the defendant from selling it, squandering it, or abusing it.

The lis pendens, which is merely a paper the plaintiff files in a county clerk's office, puts the world on notice that the plaintiff has a claim to a described parcel of real property and that anyone who buys it or lends money on the strength of it or otherwise relies on the defendant's unfettered ownership of it does so subject to whatever the pending action decides to be the plaintiff's right.

The order to seize a chattel, a provisional-like remedy, is available only in a replevin action. It is not officially "provisional" because it can result in the plaintiff actually getting the chattel before the action goes to judgment. We mention it here—it is be taken up more fully in later sections[2]—only to show why the seizure order does not officially qualify as "provisional."

The same may be said of sequestration, a device used to seize property of a spouse or parent in a matrimonial action, thus enabling support and other money obligations to be paid out of the sequestered assets. Since the property seized may actually be expended—sold and reduced to money and the money used to support the family during the action—the sequestration device, too, falls beyond the merely "provisional" frame.[3]

Each of the remedies is available only in certain categories of actions or under designated conditions. For each of the four provisional remedies, the opening section of its CPLR article states those categories and conditions.

All the remedies require a court order, except the lis pendens, which the plaintiff merely files. The reader should note whether the motion for the order must be on notice or may be ex parte. Some are available ex parte. For those the constitution is on close watch.

The order to seize a chattel is added to the four provisional remedies to make a total of five. While not technically a "provisional remedy," CPLR 6001 includes it with the other four by requiring the plaintiff to state on every motion for a provisional remedy or for an order to seize a chattel whether any of the other remedies has been sought or secured in the same action against the same defendant. The court may then require the

---

[2]   See §§ 337 to 342.

[3]   Sequestration is discussed in § 106. It also performs a jurisdictional function, enabling the local assets of the spouse or parent to be seized to make good on support awards even without personal jurisdiction. It is this jurisdictional use that is stressed in § 106. But sequestration is available even when personal jurisdiction exists. Under § 243 of the Domestic Relations Law, for example, it can be used to satisfy a support order in a pending matrimonial action. The procedure is the same whether jurisdictional or enforcement use is being made of sequestration. That, too, is discussed in § 106.

plaintiff to elect from among the remedies in the event the action should qualify for more than one of them.[4] To enable the court to determine whether to require an election, the plaintiff must state, on every motion for a provisional remedy or for an order to seize a chattel, whether any of the other remedies has been sought or secured in the same action.[5] Ordinarily, only ex parte motions have to attest to such facts;[6] with the provisional remedies even motions on notice must.

The provisional remedies are usually sought by the plaintiff against the defendant, but CPLR 6001 also makes them available to a defendant for use against the plaintiff on a counterclaim or against a co-defendant on a cross-claim.

On some of the provisional remedies, the plaintiff must furnish a bond whose sureties undertake to pay any damages the defendant suffers if the remedy should prove unwarranted. These will be met in the study of the remedies individually. It should be noted at the outset, however, that even if a given remedy has no bonding requirement, the plaintiff may face a personal liability to the defendant if he misuses the remedy. It has been held, for example, that the misuse of a lis pendens can give rise to an abuse of process claim.[7]

Because the provisional remedies are drastic—suspending or reducing the defendant's property rights before a final adjudication of the merits—they are subject to rules of strict construction[8] and are therefore an exception to the CPLR's general rule of liberal construction.[9]

All four of the provisional remedies have a security function. Attachment can have a jurisdictional function as well: it is the device used in New York to secure quasi in rem jurisdiction against the defendant in a money action in the few instances in which that's permissible today.[10] Sequestration can serve a similar function in a matrimonial action.[11] The seizure of a chattel affords a rem basis on which to adjudicate a replevin claim even without personal jurisdiction of the defendant. Therefore, those three devices—attachment, sequestration, and seizure of chattel—should also be remembered for their jurisdictional utility.

All of the provisional remedies, along with the seizure of a chattel, are available in the supreme and county courts. The chattel seizure is available in all of the lower courts, too—the New York City Civil Court and the district, city, town, and village courts.

---

[4] See, e.g., LaCarrubba v. Naclerio, 1 A.D.3d 571, 767 N.Y.S.2d 633 (2d Dep't 2003); Todd-Buick v. Smith, 118 Misc. 102, 192 N.Y.S. 459 (Sup. Ct., Essex County 1922), aff'd, 202 A.D. 774, 194 N.Y.S. 985 (3d Dep't).

[5] CPLR 6001.

[6] CPLR 2217(b); see § 244.

[7] See, e.g., Parr Meadows Racing Ass'n, Inc. v. White, 76 A.D.2d 858, 428 N.Y.S.2d 509 (2d Dep't 1980). See § 336.

[8] See, e.g., Penoyar v. Kelsey, 150 N.Y. 77, 80, 44 N.E. 788, 789 (1896); Northern Blvd. & 80th St. Corp. v. Siegel, 16 A.D.2d 523, 229 N.Y.S.2d 827 (1st Dep't 1962). Both cases deal with attachment, but the discretionary nature of all the provisional remedies that require a court order—all do except the lis pendens— bring all of them under the same strict construction banner. See Sartwell v. Field, 68 N.Y. 341, 1877 WL 11865 (1877).

[9] CPLR 104; see § 6.

[10] See § 104.

[11] See § 106.

Attachment and lis pendens are available in appropriate actions in the civil, district, and city courts, but use of the injunction and receivership is restricted.[12]

§ 307. Provisional Remedies; Constitutional Requirements

The fact that some of the provisional remedies were (and to some degree still are) available by ex parte order before the defendant has been given any hearing whatsoever subjected them to extensive constitutional (due process) attack. Until 1971, in fact, the seizure of a chattel provided for by Article 71 of New York's CPLR did not even require a court order. The plaintiff's lawyer just drew and delivered to the sheriff a "requisition" along with a bond and affidavit, and the sheriff, without any court direction, would thereupon seize the designated chattel from the defendant even breaking down a door if necessary to get at it.[1] A constitutional tightening up from the U.S. Supreme Court was not unexpected. It began at the tail end of the 1960s and produced some rudimentary criteria regulating the provisional remedies.

The case that started the constitutional ball rolling was Sniadach v. Family Finance Corp. of Bay View.[2] As is common with cases that break new ground, the facts were one-sided and the statute involved in the case particularly obnoxious. It was a Wisconsin law that allowed a creditor, before suit, to garnish 50% of the debtor's wages, to be put aside to the credit of a potential judgment, the debtor being thus divested of half her income without a hearing. The Supreme Court held that a prejudgment garnishment of that kind "may as a practical matter drive a wage-earning family to the wall"[3] and struck the statute down. It is no answer, held the Court, that the wages will be returned to the debtor if she prevails on the merits: due process requires the hearing before, not after, the seizure. Perhaps such a summary procedure might be deemed to meet the requirements of due process in "extraordinary situations," the Court suggested, but none were present in *Sniadach*.

New York's counterpart law on wage seizure is called an "income execution." Found in CPLR 5231, it could probably have passed muster under *Sniadach* for two reasons. The first is that it operates on only 10%, not 50%, of the debtor's wages, a gap in degree that might be great enough to make a constitutional difference. The second and probably more important reason is that it is available only after judgment, which means that the debtor has already had a hearing on the merits and lost. Before the CPLR, New York law did allow the 10% post-judgment execution to be used for prejudgment attachment as well,[4] and there is statutory authority that could be read as continuing the practice,[5] but in fact it is no longer so used.[6]

Sniadach therefore had little impact on New York law. The same cannot be said of Fuentes v. Shevin,[7] however, which the U.S. Supreme Court handed down in 1972.

---

12 See § 209 in each of the cited lower court acts (McKinney's Vol.29A, Parts 2 and 3).

1 CPLR 7102 and 7110 prior to the 1971 amendments.

2 Sniadach v. Family Finance Corp. of Bay View, 395 U.S. 337, 89 S. Ct. 1820, 23 L. Ed. 2d 349 (1969).

3 *Sniadach*, 395 U.S. at 341–42, 89 S. Ct. at 1822–23.

4 Morris Plan Industrial Bank of New York v. Gunning, 295 N.Y. 324, 67 N.E.2d 510 (1946).

5 See CPLR 6202.

6 The New York Court of Appeals sidestepped the question in Glassman v. Hyder, 23 N.Y.2d 354, 296 N.Y.S.2d 783, 244 N.E.2d 259 (1968). See § 323. Given that the New York Court of Appeals today finds more protective force in the state constitution's due process clause than the federal clause has been given, the allowance of a prejudgment wage attachment would not likely be approved today.

7 Fuentes v. Shevin, 407 U.S. 67, 92 S. Ct. 1983, 32 L. Ed. 2d 556 (1972).

Fuentes upset the summary replevin writs authorized by the law of two other states. It would have done the same to the New York procedure, which at the time allowed a mere "requisition" by the plaintiff's lawyer to activate the sheriff's seizure, but New York had anticipated as much and had already amended its statute to eliminate the objectionable procedure.[8] New York did this in response to an earlier (1970) decision by a three-judge federal district court which had expressly overturned the New York replevin procedure.[9] The New York answer was a cautious one. Recognizing that specific constitutional limitations on replevin procedures were only in the process of being formulated, and might remain unclear for a while, New York abandoned the requisition procedure entirely and substituted in its place a motion-and-order procedure to be carried out "to conform to . . . due process."[10]

The major requirement of *Fuentes* is that a hearing precede any seizure of the defendant's property. The case involved statutes of Pennsylvania and Florida that authorized seizure without a preliminary hearing. Household goods were involved, but the court declared that the kind of property involved doesn't matter. It said that the constitution does not distinguish, and that it is not satisfied unless the defendant has an opportunity to be heard in advance of the seizure. A duly notified defendant may forfeit the opportunity merely by failing to appear at the hearing, but giving the defendant an opportunity to be heard only after the seizure does not satisfy due process except in special instances under narrowly drawn statutes (of which the *Fuentes* pair were not examples).

One of the exceptions recognized by the Court in a footnote[11] is where the seizure of property is needed to serve as a jurisdictional basis.[12] That exception proved important with attachment, the device New York uses to secure quasi in rem jurisdiction of a nondomiciliary through seizure of his local assets.[13] The other exception *Fuentes* acknowledges as permitting ex parte seizure is where a "public interest" is involved.[14]

A creditor's or seller's hope of exacting a waiver of these due process rights was dashed in *Fuentes* when the Court indicated that a waiver in an adhesion contract, where it would most likely be found, would not be effective.

The Court acknowledged that its *Fuentes* holding was going to create inconvenience and increase the expense of chattel seizure (and like procedures), but that due process is a higher consideration to which these other factors would just have to give way.

---

[8]   The statutes amended were CPLR 7102, 7103, 7104, and 7110. The year of the amendments was 1971.

[9]   Laprease v. Raymours Furniture Co., 315 F. Supp. 716 (N.D.N.Y. 1970).

[10]   CPLR 7102(d)(1), (c)(5). Further and more specific amendment of Article 71 of the CPLR was made in 1978. The current constitutional status of New York's law of chattel seizure is discussed in § 338.

[11]   *Fuentes*, 407 U.S. at 91 n.23, 92 S. Ct. at 1999 n.23, 32 L. Ed. 2d at 576 n.23.

[12]   The court cited for this proposition Ownbey v. Morgan, 256 U.S. 94, 41 S. Ct. 433, 65 L. Ed. 837 (1921), which sustained a state's rather one-sided attachment statute. We may infer that the court was now not especially enthusiastic about *Ownbey*, but that it wanted to leave the door open to ex parte seizures for at least some jurisdictional uses. It had second thoughts about that in 1977 in the *Shaffer* case, for which see § 104.

[13]   For discussion of the general constitutionality of New York's attachment remedy, using the present treatment as background, see § 315.

[14]   Cited for this proposition is Coffin Bros. & Co. v. Bennett, 277 U.S. 29, 48 S. Ct. 422, 72 L. Ed. 768 (1928), which involved a bank failure. According to footnote 23 in *Fuentes*, it is only "a most basic and important public interest" that justifies the ex parte use of a seizure device.

Fuentes was a catalyst as well as a landmark. In New York, it got the legislature to further review and update the provisional remedy statutes. It also occasioned the New York Court of Appeals' interpretation of the state constitution's due process clause, which was then found to go even farther than its federal counterpart. It is helpful to chart these two post-*Fuentes* paths separately, New York's first and the federal—to some degree academic in New York because of New York's own doings—afterwards.

New York Developments

In 1973, on the basis of the *Fuentes* decision, the New York Court of Appeals in Blye v. Globe-Wernicke Realty Co.[15] voided certain procedures under the then-applicable New York statute giving an innkeeper a lien on a guest's property.[16] The statute allowed the innkeeper by a mere notice to sell the guest's property to cover an unpaid bill. This was held to constitute state action because it amounted to the enforcement of a lien, a traditional state function.

Then in 1978, in reliance on *Blye*, the Court declared unconstitutional the enforcement procedures of the garage owner's lien,[17] again for the reason that they did not offer an advance hearing. This the Court did in Sharrock v. Dell Buick-Cadillac, Inc.[18]

By this time, the Court of Appeals, in applying the state constitution's due process clause, had gone ahead of the restrictions the U.S. Supreme Court had laid down in interpreting the federal clause. At issue in *Sharrock* was the constitutionality of provisions in the New York Lien Law authorizing the ex parte sale of a chattel to implement a lien—in the *Sharrock* case, a garage owner's lien. While concluding that the lien itself was valid, the majority held that an opportunity to be heard must be afforded the car owner before the car is sold to make good on the unpaid bill. The requirement comes not from the Federal Constitution, noted the Court of Appeals in *Sharrock*, because the U.S. Supreme Court had found no such requirement in the Federal Due Process Clause in an analogous situation,[19] but from the state constitution where the absence from the due process clause of language explicitly requiring state action facilitates a more "flexible" approach to what will or will not constitute "state action" sufficient to invoke due process protections.

Using this more flexible standard, the *Sharrock* panel found the Lien Law's relevant provisions, sections 200, 201, 202, and 204, to constitute state action and held them unconstitutional insofar as they purported to authorize a sale of the chattel without affording the owner a preliminary hearing. A number of liens other than the garage owner's lien are also governed by the cited provisions. Hence, these others were also affected by the decision, among them the liens of the artisan, jeweler, veterinarian, and trucker.

The legislature in 1980 produced a package of amendments[20] to meet the *Sharrock* objections. The heart of the package was the addition of Lien Law section 201–a, which

---

[15]   Blye v. Globe-Wernicke Realty Co., 33 N.Y.2d 15, 347 N.Y.S.2d 170, 300 N.E.2d 710 (1973).

[16]   Former Lien Law § 181.

[17]   Lien Law §§ 200, 201, 202, 204.

[18]   Sharrock v. Dell Buick-Cadillac, Inc., 45 N.Y.2d 152, 408 N.Y.S.2d 39, 379 N.E.2d 1169 (1978). The case is the subject of the lead note in NYSLD No. 225.

[19]   See the discussion of the *Flagg Bros.* case below.

[20]   L.1980, ch. 715.

authorizes the owner of the goods to commence a special proceeding against the party claiming the lien within 10 days after being served with a notice of sale. Although it requires the owner of the goods to take the initiative of bringing the proceeding, it does set up a presale hearing and it imposes on the lienor the burden of notifying the owner about the right to bring the proceeding. The proceeding may be brought in any court of appropriate monetary jurisdiction.[21]

The innkeeper's lien voided by the Court of Appeals in the *Blye* case was cited by the majority in *Sharrock*, but the dissent rejected the analogy, noting that the property seized by an innkeeper for application to an unpaid hotel bill has no direct relationship to the bill, while in the case of the garage owner, the lien is asserted against the very property bettered by the repair being sued for. The dissent also noted that the innkeeper's lien involves a seizure of the property, while with the garage the property is already in its possession.

There appears at the end of the majority opinion in *Sharrock* a footnote[22] in which the Court of Appeals implicitly invites the lawyer for such a garage owner/lienor to arrange things so that the ex parte sale can go forward, just as the Lien Law contemplates it. The lienor can do this by "securing the owner's knowing waiver of his opportunity for a hearing when possession is initially transferred." This probably means that something like a big, bold-faced or red-lettered waiver—prominent on the face of the repair authorization and perhaps additionally called to the customer's attention orally or by an obvious notice posted on the repair shop wall—will permit an ex parte sale to go forward under the Lien Law provisions without a court hearing if the bill is not paid.

The sale procedures called for to implement the garage owner's and like liens, especially as they existed before the 1980 Lien Law amendments, should be contrasted with the steps used with a mechanic's lien. With the latter, all that is contemplated ex parte is the filing of a paper to note of public record the claim of the mechanic; subsequent steps are necessary—and these on notice—to realize on the lien out of the liened property. This was found to be a distinction with a constitutional difference, and it accounts for the sustaining of New York's mechanic's lien procedures in Carl A. Morse, Inc. (Diesel Const., Division) v. Rentar Indus. Development Corp.[23]

Rentar held that although the filing of the lien diminishes the economic value of the real property, it does not bar its sale or encumbrance and therefore does not deprive the defendant of any constitutionally protected property interest. The court said that the requirement of a hearing in advance of the filing of the lien would destroy its utility for those who have expended labor or material on the premises.

---

[21] This means that the lower courts can do the job, and it would seem to make it clear that nothing of the formal nature of a "foreclosure" proceeding is needed. (The word "foreclosure" was used at a few points in the *Sharrock* opinion, but not in context to suggest the need of the formal judicial steps of a foreclosure action.) The amendments and the procedures they contemplate are treated in the lead note in NYSLD No. 251.

[22] *Sharrock*, 45 N.Y.2d at 167 n.7, 408 N.Y.S.2d at 48 n.7.

[23] Carl A. Morse, Inc. (Diesel Const., Division) v. Rentar Indus. Development Corp., 56 A.D.2d 30, 391 N.Y.S.2d 425 (2d Dep't 1977). The case was affirmed by the New York Court of Appeals on the appellate division opinion. Carl A. Morse, Inc. v. Rentar Indus. Development Corp., 43 N.Y.2d 952, 404 N.Y.S.2d 343, 375 N.E.2d 409 (1978). An appeal to the U.S. Supreme Court, sub nom. Rentar Industrial Development Corp. v. Carl A. Morse, Inc, 439 U.S. 804, 99 S. Ct. 59, 58 L. Ed. 2d 96 (1978), was then dismissed for want of a substantial federal question.

This stresses the distinction between provisional and provisional-like remedies that involve the mere filing of a paper, and those that involve the seizure of property. The only one of the New York provisional remedies effectuated through a mere filing of a paper is the notice of pendency ("lis pendens") of CPLR Article 65.[24] It puts the world on notice of the plaintiff's potential rights in designated real property of the defendant. It doesn't bar a sale or encumbrance of the property, but it of course makes those things more difficult. The *Rentar* opinion draws an analogy between the mechanic's lien and a lis pendens, thereby suggesting that the lis pendens provisions of Article 65 of the CPLR are constitutionally safe. In a direct treatment of the lis pendens, the Second Circuit in Diaz v. Paterson[25] reaches the same conclusion: because the lis pendens, unlike such provisional remedies as attachment and replevin, doesn't completely deprive the defendant of the use of the real property, its filing without preliminary input from a court does not violate due process.

Contrasting the self-help provisions of the Uniform Commercial Code—provisions that permit a lienor to sell the liened goods without court leave—shows the more expansive view of due process taken by the New York Court of Appeals than by the U.S. Supreme Court. The self-help provisions applicable to the Code's warehouser's lien,[26] for example, were sustained by the Supreme Court in Flagg Bros., Inc. v. Brooks,[27] the Court holding that they did not amount to state action and therefore did not offend the Federal Constitution. But the New York Court of Appeals went the other way in Svendsen v. Smith's Moving & Trucking Co.,[28] holding that they do offend the state constitution. *Sharrock* governed, held the Court, and while the curative 1980 Lien Law amendments treated above preserved the procedures prescribed for the garage owner's lien, they were not applicable to the UCC's warehouser's lien, which therefore remained vulnerable to constitutional attack. This led to amendments of the New York UCC.[29]

That's about where things stand today on the constitutional front, at least in New York. Since it is generally permissible for a state to impose higher standards under its due process clause than the U.S. Supreme Court does under the Federal Due Process Clause, the broader range given the New York provision may make academic in New York some of the Supreme Court cases subsequent to *Fuentes*, the catalyst that really started New York's attack along the broad front of the provisional and provisional-like remedies. But just to round out the picture, a bird's eye view of the U.S. Supreme Court's major entries subsequent to *Fuentes*, most of them the product of the 1970s—the era of the revision of the provisional remedies—is pertinent.

Federal Developments

The first of the major post-*Fuentes* cases was Mitchell v. W. T. Grant Co.,[30] in 1974. To the dissent of four justices and to the outright chagrin of one of them (Justice Stewart), a bare majority in *Mitchell* sustained the Louisiana ex parte replevin statute. *Sniadach* was distinguished because it involved only a money claim underlain by no

---

[24]   The lis pendens is taken up in §§ 334–36.

[25]   Diaz v. Paterson, 547 F.3d 88 (2d Cir. 2008); (SPR 204:4).

[26]   UCC § 7–210.

[27]   Flagg Bros., Inc. v. Brooks, 436 U.S. 149, 98 S. Ct. 1729, 56 L. Ed. 2d 185 (1978).

[28]   Svendsen v. Smith's Moving & Trucking Co., 54 N.Y.2d 865, 444 N.Y.S.2d 904, 429 N.E.2d 411 (1981).

[29]   UCC § 7–210 was amended in 1982 to provide notice requirements and § 7–211 was added to supply a special proceeding to test the lien.

[30]   Mitchell v. W. T. Grant Co., 416 U.S. 600, 94 S. Ct. 1895, 40 L. Ed. 2d 406 (1974).

specific lien on any particular property, whereas in *Mitchell* the plaintiff was after goods on which the plaintiff had a lien. That was one distinction. *Fuentes* was differentiated because the statutes involved there did not require the court to issue the process, while in *Mitchell* the court had to do the issuing—although it was allowed to do so without notice, resulting in the seizure before a hearing. The initial participation of a judge was therefore distinction number two. A third was that the statute in *Mitchell* provided for a prompt hearing after seizure, albeit on the defendant's application. Justice Stewart, who authored the *Fuentes* opinion, could not in his dissent abide these distinctions and insisted that the Court was disregarding stare decisis and overruling *Fuentes*.[31] Justice Powell, concurring with the majority, was also of the view that *Fuentes* had been overruled.[32] The others in the majority purported only to distinguish it.

So things stood until about half a year later when the Supreme Court decided North Georgia Finishing, Inc. v. Di-Chem, Inc.[33] With that case, the pendulum seemed to swing back to the debtor, this time to the relief of Justice Stewart, who was moved in concurrence to paraphrase Mark Twain and observe that the rumors (from *Mitchell*) of *Fuentes*'s death had been greatly exaggerated.[34]

North Georgia involved, and upset, another garnishment statute, this time used against the bank account of a substantial corporate debtor instead of a poor one, which is the more frequent case. The Court again declared that the kind of property involved is not a key consideration. It then cited the following factors as distinguishing *Mitchell*, and, in the eyes of some, reviving *Fuentes*:

1. the affidavit in *North Georgia* (which supported the application) did not have to be made on knowledge; in *Mitchell* it did;

2. the *North Georgia* affidavit could depose in conclusory terms; in *Mitchell* it had to set out underlying facts;

3. the *North Georgia* writ was made by the clerk, no judge participating; in *Mitchell* a judge made the order;

4. in *North Georgia* there was no provision for an early hearing and only a bond from the defendant could release the property, the bond being held insufficient recourse to substitute for a pre-seizure hearing; in *Mitchell* there was a requirement for a prompt hearing, albeit post-seizure and albeit on defendant's own motion.[35]

Presumably, if a given provisional remedy is found to satisfy each of the four *Mitchell* items listed above (which the *North Georgia* statute did not), it would get by.

* * *

Constitutional issues in the provisional remedy context are briefly reviewed later, in the treatment of the order of attachment[36] and the order to seize a chattel.[37]

---

[31] *Mitchell*, 416 U.S. at 634–35, 94 S. Ct. at 1913–14, 40 L. Ed. 2d at 429–30 (Stewart, J., dissenting).

[32] *Mitchell*, 416 U.S. at 623, 94 S. Ct. at 1908, 40 L. Ed. 2d at 423 (Powell, J., concurring).

[33] North Georgia Finishing, Inc. v. Di-Chem, Inc., 419 U.S. 601, 95 S. Ct. 719, 42 L. Ed. 2d 751 (1975).

[34] *North Georgia*, 419 U.S. at 608, 95 S. Ct. at 723, 42 L. Ed. 2d at 758.

[35] *North Georgia*, 419 U.S. at 607, 95 S. Ct. at 722–23, 42 L. Ed. 2d at 757–58.

[36] See § 315.

[37] See § 338.

B. ARREST

Table of Sections

§§ 308. to 312. [DELETED]

[NOTE: There are no sections 308 through 312. They concerned the provisional remedy of the order of civil arrest, which was abolished in 1979 with the repeal of Article 61 of the CPLR.]

C. ATTACHMENT

Table of Sections

§ 313.   Attachment, Generally

§ 314.   Grounds for Attachment

§ 315.   Attachment; Status of Constitutionality

§ 316.   Applying for the Attachment

§ 317.   Attachment Discretionary

§ 318.   The Various Time Periods Concerning Attachment

§ 319.   Summons Service Within 60 Days

§ 320.   Levy of the Attachment

§ 321.   "Perfecting" the Levy

§ 322.   Examples of Interplay of Attachment Requirements

§ 323.   What Property Attachable?

§ 324.   Disclosure to Aid Attachment

§ 325.   Defendant's Remedies: Vacatur; Discharge; Annulment; Action on Undertaking

§ 326.   Disposition of Property; Disputes; Priorities

§ 313. Attachment, Generally

An order of attachment is a device whereby a plaintiff effects a seizure of a defendant's property, the sheriff taking constructive and sometimes actual hold of it under the terms of the order. The device in New York practice is supplied by Article 62 of the CPLR. It operates on only the property of the defendant, not on his person.

The order of attachment always serves a security purpose since the property attached is held by the sheriff, actually or constructively, to apply to the plaintiff's judgment in the action if the plaintiff should win. But it can also serve a jurisdictional purpose. It is the device New York uses to implement the "quasi in rem" category of jurisdiction. Today, of course, that category of jurisdiction is much curtailed, the result of the U.S. Supreme Court decision in Shaffer v. Heitner.[1] The subject is discussed in the chapter on jurisdiction, which lists the surviving instances in which quasi in rem jurisdiction may still be allowed.[2] If one of those cases is at hand, so that quasi in rem jurisdiction is operative, the attachment is the tool used for its exploitation. If the defendant is not amenable to personal jurisdiction, but has property of any kind in New York, the plaintiff can with an order of attachment confiscate the property, thereby

---

[1]   Shaffer v. Heitner, 433 U.S. 186, 97 S. Ct. 2569, 53 L. Ed. 2d 683 (1977).

[2]   See § 104.

guaranteeing that a judgment in the action will be good at least to the extent of the property attached.

As will be seen, the seizure under an attachment is more often constructive than actual, but just as real in either case because it executes its main mission—that of depriving the defendant of the free use of the property, including the ability to sell or encumber it. It also constitutes a kind of lien on the property, giving the plaintiff first crack at it for his judgment if he wins on the merits.

The "garnishee" plays a major role in the attachment process, so it is well to introduce the garnishee at the outset. A garnishee is any person (which includes a corporation) who owes a debt to the defendant or who has in its possession or custody any property in which the defendant has an interest.[3] It is good to keep in mind this broad definition of "garnishment," a term often thought by the laity and even members of the bar to refer exclusively to a levy being made against a percentage of the defendant's income. That is indeed "garnishment," with the employer the "garnishee," but it's only one form of it. In its official definition, "garnishment" describes any situation in which a debtor's property—property of any kind—is being reached through a third person.

The garnishee is a key figure when personal rather than real property is being attached, which is most often the case, because a levy against personal property is carried out by service of the order of attachment on the garnishee while a levy against real property is effected by a mere filing.[4]

§ 314. Grounds for Attachment

There are two requirements to make out a case for an order of attachment. Both are stated in CPLR 6201. First, the plaintiff must be seeking a money judgment from the defendant. Second, the plaintiff must satisfy one of the five numbered paragraphs of CPLR 6201.

The plaintiff need not be seeking only a money judgment. Under prior law, that was the case, but today other claims, seeking something besides money or otherwise posing an inadequate basis for attachment, may be joined as long as the plaintiff seeks a money judgment among other things and satisfies one of the five enumerated requirements.[1] The matrimonial action is excepted; attachment is not available there, but isn't missed because the sequestration remedy[2] does an equivalent job in the matrimonial category.[3]

The list of five items in CPLR 6201 is for the most part self-explanatory. In addition to the money demand, the plaintiff must show that:

1. the defendant is a nondomiciliary residing without the state, or is a foreign corporation not qualified to do business in the state; or

2. the defendant resides or is domiciled in the state but cannot be personally served despite diligent efforts to do so; or

---

3   CPLR 105, 6202.

4   CPLR 6214–6216. The mechanics of the levy are detailed in § 320.

1   See Bradford v. Eden, 47 Misc. 2d 482, 262 N.Y.S.2d 788 (App. Term, 1st Dep't 1965).

2   For discussion of sequestration, see § 106.

3   See Dom. Rel. Law §§ 233, 243.

3.   the defendant, with intent to defraud creditors or frustrate the enforcement of a judgment that might be rendered in the plaintiff's favor, has assigned, disposed of, encumbered, or secreted property, or removed it from the state, or is about to do any of those acts; or

4.   the action is by a crime victim suing the perpetrator for damages caused by the crime; or

5.   the cause of action is based on a judgment, decree or order of a court of the United States or of any other court which is entitled to full faith and credit in this state, or on a judgment which qualifies for recognition under the provisions of article 53.

The easiest ground to satisfy, and statistically the most often resorted to in the past, is paragraph 1. If the defendant is an individual, the needed showing under paragraph 1 is that she is neither a domiciliary nor a resident of the state. The defendant's having either a domicile or a residence in New York, even though she may have one elsewhere, makes paragraph 1 inapplicable.[4] The theory is that either domicile or residence in New York assures a way to get personal jurisdiction of the defendant and obviates resort to the substitute of quasi in rem jurisdiction, for which paragraph 1 of CPLR 6201 was primarily designed.[5]

When the defendant is a domestic corporation, or a foreign corporation duly qualified to do business in New York, paragraph 1 does not apply. Personal jurisdiction is likely available in these instances and quasi in rem jurisdiction is not needed. But it does apply to authorize attachment against an unqualified foreign corporation. There is presently a conflict about whether such a corporation, by getting itself qualified after the attachment has been granted and levied, is entitled to have it vacated. The Second Circuit says it is.[6] The First Department disagrees and holds that it is not; that the attachment should be retained in that situation to serve its security function.[7]

With the ground listed in paragraph 3 of CPLR 6201, it is the security rather than the jurisdictional aspect of the attachment device that is being exploited. With paragraph 3, which authorizes attachment if it can be shown that the defendant is finagling with his property with intent to defraud creditors, allegations raising a mere "suspicion" of fraudulent intent have been held insufficient. "It must appear that such fraudulent intent really existed in the defendant's mind. A mere showing of removal or assignment or other disposition of property is not by itself grounds for attachment."[8]

With paragraph 5, which allows the attachment to aid in the course of converting into a New York judgment a judgment already rendered elsewhere, it is apparently both functions of an attachment—jurisdiction and security—that are served. If the judgment

---

    [4]   See Zenatello v. Pons, 235 A.D. 221, 256 N.Y.S. 763 (1st Dep't 1932).

    [5]   With quasi in rem jurisdiction its main mission, paragraph 1 has a reduced function today as a result of the U.S. Supreme Court's curtailment of this category of jurisdiction in Shaffer v. Heitner, 433 U.S. 186, 97 S. Ct. 2569, 53 L. Ed. 2d 683 (1977). See § 104 for treatment of the *Shaffer* case.

    [6]   Brastex Corp. v. Allen Intern., Inc., 702 F.2d 326 (2d Cir. 1983).

    [7]   Elton Leather Corp. v. First General Resources Co., 138 A.D.2d 132, 529 N.Y.S.2d 769 (1st Dep't 1988).

    [8]   Computer Strategies, Inc. v. Commodore Business Machines, Inc., 105 A.D.2d 167, 483 N.Y.S.2d 716 (2d Dep't 1984). "The difficulties of establishing fraud such as will support an order of attachment" are treated under that caption in SPR 212:1, discussing National Audubon Soc., Inc. v. Sonopia Corp., 2009 WL 636952 (S.D.N.Y. 2009).

debtor has moved all of his assets to New York, for example, but remains beyond New York's personal jurisdiction, there would be at hand a situation in which the *Shaffer* case apparently continues to permit the exercise of quasi in rem jurisdiction.[9]

The lawyer should note that before 1977, there were eight grounds listed in CPLR 6201 for attachment, among them showings that the defendant was about to leave the state to defraud creditors,[10] was guilty of fraud in incurring a contractual liability,[11] or converted public funds (peculation),[12] or that the action was for conversion or fraud.[13] Those four categories were abolished by the 1977 legislation[14] that produced the present CPLR 6201. These superseded provisions are mentioned only because older cases, bound to crop up during research, may refer to them and it is helpful to be aware that they're no longer on the books.

§ 315. Attachment; Status of Constitutionality

Since the attachment procedure usually begins with an ex parte motion, as will be seen in detail, it has gone through some constitutional testing. In 1974, a three-judge federal district court[1] in Sugar v. Curtis Circulation Co. held certain parts of the New York attachment statutes, as they existed prior to 1977, unconstitutional,[2] but its judgment was vacated by the U.S. Supreme Court under the name Carey v. Sugar and the case was remanded to await a definitive construction of the relevant statutes by the New York courts.[3] These matters were briefly alluded to earlier in the discussion of the constitutionality of the provisional remedies in general,[4] but it will help here to be more specific about attachment.

During this period of constitutional testing, the Judicial Conference's CPLR Committee assigned the attachment article for study.[5] From this came legislation in 1977,[6] responding to virtually all of the constitutional objections raised by the three-judge district court in *Sugar*. The constitutional objections having been thus addressed by statute, a judicial test of the original provisions was avoided. The main accomplishments of the 1977 legislation can be highlighted here. The rest of them, and each procedure summarized now, will be elaborated in later sections.

The 1977 amendments reduced the attachment grounds of CPLR 6201 from eight to four (later raised to five) paragraphs—those that were found consistent with both the

---

[9] See § 104. Paragraph 3 of CPLR 6201 might also lend itself to quasi in rem jurisdictional use. See notes 24–25 and accompanying text in § 104.

[10] Former paragraph 3 of CPLR 6201.

[11] Former paragraph 5 of CPLR 6201.

[12] Former paragraph 6 of CPLR 6201.

[13] Former paragraph 8 of CPLR 6201.

[14] L.1977, ch. 860. For further background of the 1977 legislation, see the 1977 Judicial Conference Report to the Legislature, p. 13, and the background study by Professor Donnelly in 21st Jud. Conf. Rep. 452 et seq. (1976).

[1] For a description of this court, see § 483.

[2] Sugar v. Curtis Circulation Co., 383 F. Supp. 643 (S.D.N.Y. 1974).

[3] Carey v. Sugar, 425 U.S. 73, 96 S. Ct. 1208, 47 L. Ed. 2d 587 (1976).

[4] See § 307. The reader might find it helpful to review those general constitutional considerations at this point as background.

[5] See 21st Jud. Conf. Rep. 452 et seq. (1976), containing the study by Professor Samuel J.M. Donnelly of the Syracuse University College of Law.

[6] See the 1977 Judicial Conference Report to the Legislature, p.13.

purposes of an attachment on the one hand and the requirements of the constitution on the other.

Subdivision (b) was added to CPLR 6211. It provides that when the attachment order is initially issued ex parte, as it usually is, the plaintiff must, within a specified number of days after the attachment is levied, make a motion on notice to "confirm" the attachment. The motion is usually brought on by order to show cause so as to enable the court to determine how the motion papers should be served. The procedure affords the defendant a prompt opportunity to refute the plaintiff's showing and vacate the attachment, thus protecting her property interest. Before 1977, a "confirmation" was not required as a follow-up to an ex parte attachment.

The 1977 amendments also added CPLR 6210. It seeks to encourage the plaintiff to apply for the attachment order by a motion on notice in the first instance instead of using the ex parte application and follow-up confirmation motion. It does this by authorizing the issuance of a temporary restraining order prohibiting the garnishee's transfer of assets pending further proceedings. If the CPLR 6210 restraint is sought, it is sought by order to show cause or the equivalent, with the restraining order rather than a seizure of the property being the only relief granted ex parte.

In addition, CPLR 6212(a) was amended to require the plaintiff to show not only that he has a cause of action against the defendant, but also "that it is probable that the plaintiff will succeed on the merits," a showing that was often exacted of the plaintiff as a matter of common practice even before the amendment.

As far as constitutionality is concerned, the attainment-in-chief of the 1977 legislation was the addition of subdivision (b) to CPLR 6223, unequivocally imposing on the plaintiff at any hearing to vacate, modify, or confirm the attachment "the burden of establishing the grounds for the attachment, the need for continuing the levy and the probability that he will succeed on the merits."[7] The absence of such a requirement was the major objection of the three-judge district court in the *Sugar* case. It was not clear that the burden of proof would lie with the defendant under New York caselaw,[8] but the 1977 legislation makes the point academic: it places the burden of proof squarely on the plaintiff.

A further constitutional safeguard is included in CPLR 6211(b). It permits the court, on granting an attachment ex parte, to prohibit the sheriff from taking actual (physical) custody of the property without further court direction. This was not a major accomplishment; as will be seen, the attachment usually involves only a constructive rather than an actual seizure anyway.[9]

Another stated objection of the three-judge district court was that the only ground New York would entertain on a motion by the defendant to vacate the attachment was a showing that the attachment was not needed for the plaintiff's security. This was an incorrect assumption. While that was the only ground expressly listed in CPLR 6223(a), it was by no means a negation of other possible vacatur grounds: it was included in terms in CPLR 6223 only because it had not been a vacatur ground under prior law.[10] The

---

[7]   CPLR 6211(b), the confirmation provision, adopts the burden of proof provision of CPLR 6223(b).

[8]   See, e.g., Regnell v. Page, 82 Misc. 2d 506, 369 N.Y.S.2d 936 (Sup. Ct., New York County 1975), rev'd on other grounds, 54 A.D.2d 540, 387 N.Y.S.2d 253 (1st Dep't 1976).

[9]   See § 320.

[10]   See 3d Rep. Leg. Doc. No. 17, pp. 357–58 (1959).

addition of subdivision (b) to CPLR 6223 moots that point, too; it provides explicitly that the plaintiff's failure at the hearing (to establish an attachment ground) to justify a continuing need for the attachment, or to show a probability of success on the merits, is ground to vacate the attachment.

§ 316. Applying for the Attachment

An order of attachment can be applied for by motion ex parte or on notice, at the plaintiff's option. Since giving notice at the outset may enable the defendant to remove the property, the ex parte procedure is preferred by plaintiffs.

If the ex parte procedure is used, the plaintiff can obtain the order and have it levied before the defendant is heard, but then the plaintiff must, within a specified number of days after the levy,[1] repeat the motion, this time on notice. This is known as a motion to confirm. The period within which the plaintiff must move to confirm is 5 days after the levy, except when the attachment is based on paragraph 1 of CPLR 6201—the defendant's foreign status—which is the ground usually relied on when the attachment is being used for its quasi in rem jurisdictional function. A 10-day period applies in that case.

The plaintiff's obligations become tight when the attachment has a jurisdictional function, as will be seen later,[2] and procedure is adjusted a bit to recognize this. The main adjustment is the stretching from 5 to 10 days for the post-levy confirmation motion. The court is also empowered to extend it by an additional 10 days.[3] These adjustments are designed to coordinate with the mandate of CPLR 6219, which requires the garnishee through whom the attachment is levied to serve on the sheriff a list of any assets of the defendant that the garnishee holds or any debts the garnishee owes the defendant. The garnishee ordinarily has 10 days from the levy in which to serve that statement,[4] but the information about the defendant's property is needed extra fast when the attachment is being used for its jurisdictional purpose. Hence, when the attachment is based on paragraph 1 of CPLR 6201, the garnishee has only 5 instead of 10 days in which to serve the statement, a copy of which must be served on the plaintiff as well as on the sheriff.[5]

If the attachment has been granted ex parte, which invokes the confirmation requirement—whatever time period applies to it—the motion to confirm should be made within the required time even if the garnishee, through whom the levy is sought, doesn't have any leviable property of the defendant. The rationale is that to permit the attachment to remain outstanding, without confirmation, while the plaintiff flits from garnishee to garnishee in search of property, would be inconsistent with the defendant's rights.[6]

The confirmation procedure affords the defendant the constitutionally required opportunity to be heard promptly.[7] If the motion on notice procedure is initially used, the plaintiff can obtain, ex parte, a temporary restraining order to be served on the

---

[1]   What the levy consists of is discussed in § 320.

[2]   See §§ 319 et seq.

[3]   CPLR 6211(b).

[4]   CPLR 6219.

[5]   CPLR 6211(b).

[6]   See Eisenberg v. Citation-Langley Corp., 92 A.D.2d 795, 459 N.Y.S.2d 788 (1st Dep't 1983).

[7]   CPLR 6211(b) supplies the confirmation procedure, to which the text returns later.

garnishee pending return of the motion, enjoining any transfer of the property by the garnishee in the interim. Although a temporary restraining order is ordinarily contained in an order to show cause,[8] in this instance, it apparently need not be. A show cause order is an alternative way of bringing on a notice of motion, and in this instance the motion—for the order of attachment—is being made against the defendant, not against the garnishee. The governing statute, CPLR 6210, apparently contemplates service of the temporary restraining order on the garnishee sufficiently in advance of the defendant's actual receipt of the motion papers so as to enable the plaintiff to effect the restraint's service on the garnishee before the defendant even knows about the attachment and tries to get the property back from the garnishee.

If the court grants a temporary restraining order, it may in its discretion require the plaintiff to give an undertaking.[9]

Application for the attachment can be made before or after service of the summons and at any time before final judgment.[10] In rare instances involving a judgment against a foreign sovereign, an attachment can even be granted after a judgment has been awarded.[11]

If sought after summons service, the attachment is presumably being used solely for its security purpose. When used for quasi in rem jurisdiction, the order of attachment must be sought and granted before the summons is served. Indeed, in that instance it is necessary not only that attachment be issued before the summons is served but that the levy of the order of attachment also be made before the summons is served, a requirement imposed by CPLR 314(3).

The plaintiff must furnish an undertaking. It is mandatory on an attachment motion. The court fixes the amount of the undertaking, but it can't be less than $500.[12] The undertaking is governed by Article 25 of the CPLR, which determines such matters as who may act as surety on it.[13] The condition of the undertaking in this instance is that the plaintiff will pay the defendant all costs and damages, including reasonable attorney's fees,[14] that may be sustained if the defendant should win on the merits or if it is otherwise ultimately determined that the plaintiff was not entitled to the attachment.

The main part of the plaintiff's moving papers, on a motion for an attachment as well as on a post-levy motion to confirm it, is the proof on which the plaintiff bases the motion. This always includes at least one affidavit, but it may include as many as the plaintiff can muster along with any other written proof available. The proof must

---

[8]   See § 330.

[9]   See CPLR 6313(c), which is part of Article 63 of the CPLR (which supplies the provisional remedy of preliminary injunction). And if a temporary restraining order is granted and then vacated, as where the plaintiff fails to show a likelihood of success on the merits, it has been held that the measuring of the defendant's damages will also be governed by Article 63—see CPLR 6313(c) and 6312(b)—rather than the undertakings provisions of Article 62 itself, the attachment statute. See Shu Yiu Louie v. David & Chiu Place Restaurant, Inc., 261 A.D.2d 150, 689 N.Y.S.2d 476 (1st Dep't 1999).

[10]   CPLR 6211(a). Although CPLR 6211's caption suggests that it applies only to the attachment sought "without notice," its options about when the attachment may be sought should be deemed to apply to the motion on notice as well.

[11]   CPLR 6205; see SPR 231:1–2.

[12]   CPLR 6212(b).

[13]   CPLR 2502; see § 206.

[14]   See § 325.

establish to the court's satisfaction that the plaintiff has a money cause of action, that it is "probable" that the plaintiff will succeed on the merits, and that at least one of the attachment grounds listed in CPLR 6201 has been satisfied. The plaintiff's affidavit must also attest that the amount the plaintiff is demanding from the defendant exceeds all counterclaims "known" to the plaintiff, an express requirement of the statute,[15] but one that the plaintiff can usually satisfy just by listing only those counterclaims he concedes.

The plaintiff has the burden of proof on these issues, not a very difficult burden when the application is ex parte—there is no one to deny anything—but one that becomes quite important on the post-levy motion to confirm or on any motion the defendant may make to vacate or modify the attachment.[16]

If the ex parte procedure is used, the plaintiff's affidavit must also depose as to whether this or a like application has previously been made and, if so, to whom, when, where, what happened, what new facts have come to light, etc.[17]

Each affidavit should be made by a person with first-hand knowledge of the facts sworn to. Affidavits by those whose knowledge is at best indirect will surely weaken the appeal to the court's discretion, to which the attachment is addressed. If an affidavit by one with only second-hand knowledge is necessary, it should at least include an explanation of why it is not being made by one with direct knowledge.[18]

The affidavit(s) should convince the court of the merits of the plaintiff's claim. When CPLR 6212(a) requires the plaintiff to show that it is "probable" that the action will succeed on the merits, it means that there must be something in the proof stronger than the mere prima facie case that could satisfy as a pleading. The 1977 amendment that added the "probability" language in effect codified the caselaw to that effect. "What is sufficient for a pleading may be insufficient for attachment," said Judge Cardozo in Zenith Bathing Pavilion v. Fair Oaks S.S. Corporation,[19] which well illustrates the point that for an attachment, there must be evidentiary detail stronger than the summary and conclusory allegations that suffice today in a pleading.

In *Zenith*, the plaintiff was suing for trespass for part of a vessel left on his land. He sued four defendants in the alternative, not being sure which of them was responsible. As a matter of pleading, he made out a prima facie case readily enough against all of them, as a kind of suit in the alternative if nothing else, but only against one of the defendants was there the kind of evidentiary showing sufficient to sustain the drastic remedy of attachment. Thus, only against that one was an attachment permissible and that was so even though it might develop at the trial that another, against whom attachment was initially refused for lack of evidentiary detail, was the real culprit after all.

---

[15]   CPLR 6212(a).

[16]   CPLR 6223(b). The burden of proof should also belong to the plaintiff on an initial motion on notice if that's the procedure the plaintiff chooses for the attachment, although the statutes in point, CPLR 6210, 6223(b), don't say so expressly. A statute does say so expressly in respect of a confirmation motion, used when the initial attachment application is ex parte. See CPLR 6211(b), adopting CPLR 6223(b) in this respect.

[17]   CPLR 2217(b); see § 244.

[18]   See Rubin v. Lesser, 35 Misc. 2d 172, 228 N.Y.S.2d 798 (Sup. Ct., New York County 1962).

[19]   Zenith Bathing Pavilion v. Fair Oaks S.S. Corporation, 240 N.Y. 307, 312, 148 N.E. 532, 534 (1925).

There is no requirement that the plaintiff submit a copy of the complaint as part of the moving papers.[20] But it is permissible, of course, and if the complaint is verified by the plaintiff, it can serve as an additional affidavit.[21] The moving papers should include a copy of the proposed order of attachment, but that common sense practice is not required by the statute either.

CPLR 6212(a) does not require, as a precondition to an attachment, a showing that the defendant has property in New York, much less its value.[22] Usually, the plaintiff will not bother with an attachment, however, unless she knows of, or at least suspects, that the defendant has local property, but the showing is nevertheless not required on the attachment motion. If the plaintiff ends up with an attachment that can't be levied because the sheriff can't find any property of the defendant, so much the worse for the plaintiff. The attachment order becomes a souvenir. Since the motion is addressed to the court's discretion, however,[23] a showing that the defendant has significant local property can become a contributory element in invoking that discretion.

If the attachment motion is granted, CPLR 6211(a) requires the order to specify the amount that the attachment is being allowed for, including interest, costs, and sheriff's fees and expenses. The court determines the bottom line figure. It can of course specify a lower figure than the plaintiff demands when, on the proof submitted, the plaintiff's demand appears to be inflated.

The order, which also includes the name and address of the plaintiff's lawyer, is directed to the sheriff of any county or of New York City and directs the sheriff to levy on any of the defendant's property found within his jurisdiction, up to the amount specified in the order.[24] Quite often, the sheriff must gauge the value of the property levied on so as to stop the levy when the amount specified in the order is reached.

Several additional points should be made about the confirmation motion that the plaintiff is required to make when initially obtaining the order ex parte.[25] The confirmation procedure is in CPLR 6211(b) and usually comes about as follows:

The ex parte order is delivered to the appropriate sheriff and levied. It will usually take a considerable amount of time before the sheriff effects the levy. Only when the sheriff finally levies, however,[26] does the time begin to run in which the plaintiff must make the motion to confirm.[27] The motion must be made "on such notice as the court shall direct to the defendant, the garnishee, if any, and the sheriff,"[28] which means that

---

[20]   CPLR 6212(c) requires that the summons and complaint be filed with any order of attachment that issues, but those initiatory papers will likely be filed when the action is commenced. See § 45.

[21]   See the definition of "verified pleading" in CPLR 105(u); § 205.

[22]   See ABKCO Industries, Inc. v. Apple Films, Inc., 39 N.Y.2d 670, 385 N.Y.S.2d 511, 350 N.E.2d 899 (1976).

[23]   See § 317.

[24]   CPLR 6211(a).

[25]   The confirmation requirement is a codification of the directive of Edward Thompson, who as Administrative Judge of the New York City Civil Court devised it to answer constitutional objections to the ex parte procedure as it then was.

[26]   The act of the sheriff that constitutes the "levy" is discussed in § 320.

[27]   See CPLR 6211(b).

[28]   CPLR 6211(b).

it is to be made by the procedure of an order to show cause or its equivalent—that being the common means whereby the court is able to prescribe the method of service.[29]

All the plaintiff has to do is "move" to confirm within the applicable period, i.e., serve the motion papers as directed by the court. The return day of the motion need not—and likely will not—be scheduled within the period. But if the plaintiff fails to at least "make" the motion within the period, the order and levy become void and both may be vacated on motion.

If the 5-day period for confirmation is applicable, as it is when a ground other than that of paragraph 1 of CPLR 6201 is relied on for the attachment, the 5 days are not a set period, but a maximum. CPLR 6211(b) directs the court to set the period and provides only that it is "not to exceed [5] days after levy." When attachment is based on paragraph 1 of CPLR 6201 and the 10-day confirmation period applies, the period does appear to be a set one: the court is not invited, as it is with the 5-day period, to shorten it.

CPLR 6211(b) also provides that an order of attachment granted ex parte may preclude the sheriff from taking "actual custody" of levied property without further leave of court. This is not terribly important in the average case. Provision is made in Article 62 for levy by actual seizure of the property,[30] but the far more common method of effecting an attachment levy is by the sheriff's mere service, on the garnishee, of a copy of the order of attachment,[31] resulting in a constructive rather than physical seizure.

§ 317. Attachment Discretionary

Even if the plaintiff makes out a case for attachment under CPLR 6201, its granting is still discretionary with the court. The plaintiff cannot demand it as a matter of right.[1] The Advisory Committee that produced the CPLR acknowledged its discretionary nature,[2] and if the judge should perceive from the papers that the plaintiff does not need an attachment, either for jurisdiction or security, discretion is appropriately exercised against it even though a CPLR 6201 showing has been made. As a practical matter, however, the courts are somewhat more generous in granting orders of attachment than they are with other provisional remedies, like injunction and receivership.

As indicated in the introductory section on the provisional remedies,[3] the usual rule of liberal construction applicable to the CPLR at large[4] does not apply to these remedies. It has been noted with attachment, for example, that the remedy is harsh, is in derogation of the common law, and must be construed "strictly in favor of those against whom it may be employed."[5] The lesson to the plaintiff is that an attachment will not be assured merely by eking out a prima facie showing under CPLR 6201. The affidavits should be ample and should add whatever else is both relevant and likely to influence judicial discretion.

---

[29]   See § 248, discussing order to show cause procedures.

[30]   CPLR 6215.

[31]   CPLR 6214(a). See § 320. Even the "perfection" of the levy, the follow-up steps that must be taken after the delivery of the order of attachment to the garnishee, does not require that the sheriff take actual custody of the attached property; there are alternatives. See § 321.

[1]   Sartwell v. Field, 68 N.Y. 341, 1877 WL 11865 (1877).

[2]   See 3d Rep. Leg. Doc. No. 17, p. 144 (1959).

[3]   Section 306.

[4]   CPLR 104.

[5]   Penoyar v. Kelsey, 150 N.Y. 77, 80, 44 N.E. 788, 789 (1896).

Requiring affidavits of that strength should also satisfy constitutional requirements, which, remember, are always on standby when an attachment is sought, especially when it is sought ex parte. In Connecticut v. Doehr,[6] for example, the U.S. Supreme Court struck down a state attachment statute on due process grounds where the plaintiff's claim was just a general money claim in tort, asserted no pre-existing interest in the property attached, and was accompanied by no showing of exigent circumstances such as to justify postponing the defendant's hearing until after levy of the attachment.

§ 318. The Various Time Periods Concerning Attachment

Article 62 of the CPLR sprinkles time periods about abundantly. Some of these carry sudden and stark jurisdictional consequences if overlooked, such as the time under CPLR 6211(b), already discussed, in which to move to confirm an order of attachment initially granted ex parte. At least four other time periods affect the plaintiff's obligations and should be noted in perspective at the outset:

1. A 1-day period. After the levy has been made, a procedure to be met shortly,[1] the defendant may serve a written demand on the plaintiff requiring service on the defendant of the papers on which the attachment is based. Within one day after that demand, the plaintiff must make that service.[2] The consequence of a failure here is not clear, but if the demand is served by mail it should be deemed to add five days to stretch the responding period to six, and the plaintiff should then be able to satisfy the obligation by merely posting the papers within the six-day period.[3]

2. A 10-day period. If the order of attachment is granted, the plaintiff must within 10 days thereafter file it and its underlying papers with the clerk of the court.[4] The 10-day period may be extended, but if it isn't, the omission to file within the period invalidates the order.[5] Both this and the 1-day requirement of the prior paragraph are easy to carry out and it will be assumed through all further discussion of attachment, and of various examples to be used in the course of it, that both have been met.

The attachment may be sought not just in a litigation, but also in conjunction with an arbitration.[6] If it's granted, among the papers that must be filed within the required 10 days are those with which the arbitration was commenced.[7]

3. A 60-day period. This applies only when the order of attachment is granted before service of the summons, which means that it always applies when the attachment is being used for its jurisdictional purpose (where, as will be seen, the levy of the attachment must precede service).[8] The requirement is that the summons be served

---

[6]   Connecticut v. Doehr, 501 U.S. 1, 111 S. Ct. 2105, 115 L. Ed. 2d 1 (1991).

[1]   See § 320.

[2]   CPLR 6212(d).

[3]   CPLR 2103(b)(2); see § 202.

[4]   CPLR 6212(c); CPLR 2102.

[5]   CPLR 6212(c).

[6]   See § 599 (Practitioner's Edition).

[7]   Mulder v. A.S. Goldman & Co., Inc., 183 Misc. 2d 505, 703 N.Y.S.2d 678 (Sup. Ct., New York County 1999). The court says the 10-day period can be extended before or after its expiration. Relying on that is not a good idea, however, given the strict construction that usually attends the provisional remedies. In *Mulder*, the proceedings were complicated, but the seeker of the attachment was diligent under the circumstances, so all was sustained.

[8]   CPLR 314(3). See §§ 319 and 320.

within 60 days after the granting of the order; if it is not, the order becomes invalid.[9] This is a fundamental part of the procedure when the attachment is being used for quasi in rem jurisdiction.[10] It should be kept in mind that this 60-day period and the 10-day period mentioned in the prior paragraph run from the granting of the order.

   4.   *A 90-day period.* This period is relevant when personal rather than real property is being levied on, which is most often the situation. Like the period of CPLR 6211(b) in which to confirm the attachment—the confirmation period can be either 5 or 10 days depending on the CPLR 6201 ground on which the attachment is predicated[11]—it runs from the moment of levy, which is the moment the sheriff serves a copy of the order of attachment on the garnishee.[12] Within the 90 days the plaintiff must see to it that the levy is "perfected." What perfection consists of is also a distinct subject later.[13] Note now, though, that the failure to perfect within 90 days can destroy the plaintiff's entire case. Examples will demonstrate how.[14]

   The interplay of the 60-day and 90-day provisions will become clear as we treat them in detail. A brief listing has been set forth here for reference purposes. Attachment is one remedy in which time periods often have jurisdictional consequences, which is reason enough to stress them and their interplay. (The workings of the confirmation procedure of CPLR 6211[b], which has its own comparatively rigid time periods, were treated in an earlier section.)[15]

§ 319. Summons Service Within 60 Days

   If the order of attachment is granted before service of the summons, the summons must be served within 60 days after the granting of the order or the order becomes invalid. If service by publication is being used, as it may be in this instance, only the first publication need be made within the 60 days as long as the rest of the publications are completed in due course.[1] Should the defendant die within the 60 days, the plaintiff has 60 days from whenever a personal representative is duly appointed. Finally, it's permissible for the court to extend the period, but for not more than an additional 60 days, and the motion to extend must be made before the expiration of the original 60 days.[2]

   As far as Article 62 is concerned, the levy of the attachment, which in the case of personal property consists only of the sheriff's delivering to the garnishee a copy of the order of attachment,[3] need not be made within any particular time. But when jurisdictional as opposed to mere security use is being made of the attachment, the interplay of Articles 3 and 62 of the CPLR puts a time limit on when the levy must be made. CPLR 314(3) requires, for quasi in rem jurisdiction, that the levy of the attachment precede the service of the summons while CPLR 6213 requires that the

---

[9]   CPLR 6213.
[10] See § 104.
[11] See § 316.
[12] CPLR 6214(a), (b), (e).
[13] See § 321.
[14] See § 322.
[15] See § 316.
[1]   CPLR 315, 314(3). For the number of publications needed, see CPLR 316.
[2]   CPLR 6213. The application for such an extension should be permissible ex parte.
[3]   CPLR 6214(a).

summons be served within 60 days after the attachment order is granted. Putting the two together therefore requires not only that the levy be made within the 60 days, but early enough so that summons service can follow the levy and still be within the 60 days. This is New York's statutory homage to the old notions of Pennoyer v. Neff,[4] which indicated that to secure quasi in rem jurisdiction, the absent defendant's property has to be constructively seized before service of process. If the summons is served before the levy is made, quasi in rem jurisdiction is not obtained. For example:

P gets an order of attachment against D on February 17, 2016. The summons is served on D (against whom no personam jurisdictional basis exists) in Vermont on March 29, 2016. The sheriff levies the attachment by serving it on G, a New York garnishee (who has property of D), on April 8, 2016. A motion made by D on May 13, 2016, or at any other time after the expiration of 60 days from February 17, 2016, to dismiss the action for lack of jurisdiction, will be granted. Although both summons service and levy of the attachment were made within the 60-day period, the levy did not precede the summons service as CPLR 314(3) requires.

The summons service within the 60-day period is made in the usual way, i.e., pursuant to CPLR 308 for individual defendants, CPLR 311 for corporate defendants, etc. Service by an unauthorized method will not do and can vitiate the proceedings. Thus, where the garnishee just happened to turn over to the defendant copies of the papers the sheriff delivered to the garnishee (which in this instance included the summons and complaint), that did not constitute due service and the attachment was vacated.[5]

Note, therefore, that the plaintiff who seeks an attachment has two time provisions to satisfy in making service. The service of the summons must occur within 60 days after the granting of the order of attachment, so as to satisfy CPLR 6213, and must also occur within 120 days after the filing of the action itself, to satisfy CPLR 306–b. If the plaintiff commences the action and then delays the application for an order of attachment for more than two months, for example, the plaintiff may have to effect service within a shorter period than CPLR 6213 would allow in order to satisfy the 120-day period of CPLR 306–b. Conversely, if the plaintiff secures the order of attachment shortly after filing the action, the requirement to make service within 60 days after the granting of the order will curtail the 120 days that CPLR 306–b would otherwise have allowed for service. The plaintiff must coordinate these periods. Prompt steps on all fronts should make that easy enough.

If proper proceedings are had in a case in which the defendant is not subject to personal jurisdiction, and the attachment results in the acquisition of quasi in rem jurisdiction, a judgment rendered in the action will be effective only against the attached property. This is so even if the defendant, served outside New York, appears and defends the action. This is a consequence of the "limited" appearance that New York allows to an attachment defendant.[6]

§ 320. Levy of the Attachment

The plaintiff should deliver the order of attachment to the sheriff of the county in which the property to be levied on is located. In New York City, the sheriff's office is city-

---

[4] Pennoyer v. Neff, 95 U.S. 714, 24 L. Ed. 565, 1877 WL 18188 (1877).

[5] Kieley v. Central Complete Combustion Mfg. Co., 147 N.Y. 620, 42 N.E. 260 (1895).

[6] CPLR 320(c)(1), discussed in § 113.

wide, but the delivery should be made to the branch office in the county where the property is located. The method whereby the sheriff levies the attachment depends on whether the property levied is real or personal.

A real property levy is simple. The sheriff just files a notice of attachment with the county clerk of the real property county. The notice contains the name and address of the plaintiff's attorney, names the parties to the action, states the amount specified in the order, and describes the real property. The clerk records and indexes the notice like a lis pendens, and it serves a like function: it puts the world on notice of the plaintiff's potential rights so that any later encumbrancer or buyer takes subject to the plaintiff's rights should the plaintiff win in the attachment action.[1] No follow-up step is necessary when realty is levied. The notice of attachment stands of record and warns off potential buyers and lienors. When attachment is being used jurisdictionally, and real property is being levied, this filing of the notice of attachment is all that is needed to satisfy CPLR 314(3) and enable service of the summons to be made.

Levying personal property is more involved and requires follow-up steps not satisfied by the mere filing of a paper. There are two ways in which the sheriff can levy against personal property: (1) by seizing it, or (2) by serving the order of attachment on the garnishee.

Levy by seizure is uncommon. It is permissible only when the property is tangible and hence capable of delivery, but even in that instance, the sheriff is not required to make a "seizure" unless the plaintiff so directs and—the main discouragement to this method—furnishes the sheriff indemnity, satisfactory to the sheriff or fixed by the court, against such liability as the sheriff may sustain if the proceedings taken in the plaintiff's behalf should prove unwarranted.[2]

By far the most common method of levying against personal property is the second one listed above, supplied by CPLR 6214. Here, the sheriff levies merely by serving a copy of the order of attachment on the garnishee—the one who has possession of property belonging to the defendant or who owes a debt to the defendant.[3] The service is the "levy." When the attachment is being used for jurisdiction, the service therefore satisfies CPLR 314(3), supporting quasi in rem jurisdiction and permitting summons service to go forward. The summons service must, under CPLR 6213, occur within the 60-day period after the granting of the order of attachment. There is no time stated in Article 62 within which a levy must be made, but since CPLR 314(3) requires that the levy precede the service of the summons when the attachment is being exploited for jurisdiction, CPLR 314(3) and 6213 read together require that summons service follow the levy and that both occur within 60 days after the granting of the order.

The effect of this levy by service is injunctive: it precludes the garnishee from disposing of the defendant's property to anyone but the levying sheriff unless and until the court says otherwise. This is provided by CPLR 6214(b), which offers detailed guidance as to the garnishee's obligations. The levy applies not only to property of the

---

[1] See CPLR 6216, in effect adopting CPLR 6501, the lis pendens provision treated in § 334.

[2] See CPLR 6215.

[3] CPLR 6214(a). This statute allows the levy to be made by serving the order of attachment on the defendant himself if the property is in the defendant's possession, but, as the reader can guess, the plaintiff's course is easier when there is a separate garnishee to deal with. Since the garnishee is personally liable to the plaintiff for whatever property it permits to slip through the injunctive effect of the levy, the garnishee is far more likely to cooperate in the procedure than the defendant is.

defendant then in the garnishee's possession, for example, but also to any property of which the garnishee obtains possession thereafter; not only to debts then due and owing by the garnishee to the defendant, but also debts that come due later.

As noted above, when this mode of levy is used—this levy by service—the mere service on the garnishee accomplishes the "levy" enough to assure quasi in rem jurisdiction and permit service of process in the action. However, unlike the levy by seizure, it requires some follow-up step within 90 days after the levy. Failure to take that step—which is commonly known as "perfecting" the levy—voids everything ab initio. Perfection of the levy is treated in the next section.

If the situation is such that the garnishee may not know that the property belongs to the defendant, such as where it stands of record in the garnishee's possession under some other name, or some alias of the defendant, or for any other reason, CPLR 6214(b) permits the plaintiff to include with the order a notice, which the sheriff is to serve along with the order, identifying the property specifically. Doing so subjects it to the levy. This is a helpful option for the plaintiff, but it must of course be exercised with caution. If the plaintiff is mistaken, he is liable to the true owner of the property for any interference with the ownership that the attachment may cause. The provisional remedies are not toys.

The sheriff's duties after the levy are governed by CPLR 6218, which manifests the difference between an attachment levy and a levy of execution on a judgment. In the latter instance, all of the procedures are devised to enable the sheriff to seize and sell the property, convert it to money, and pay the judgment.[4] With attachment, the sheriff's only duty if and when he gets possession of the property, whether by seizure or by the garnishee's handing it over voluntarily after a levy by service, is to "hold and safely keep" the property to answer a possible future judgment.[5] Attachment's maximum power is to keep the defendant away from the property or its free use; it does not give the property to the plaintiff.

Within 10 days after service of the order of attachment on the garnishee or such shorter time as the court directs, the garnishee must serve on the sheriff a detailed statement of debts it owes the defendant and of any property in the garnishee's possession in which the defendant has an interest.[6] When the attachment is based on paragraph 1 of CPLR 6201—the foreign status of the defendant—the garnishee has only 5 days in which to serve this statement and must also serve a copy of it on the plaintiff.[7] If the plaintiff loses out because of the garnishee's default under this provision, as where the statement the garnishee serves is false, the garnishee is liable to the plaintiff for whatever damage plaintiff suffers.[8]

---

[4]   See CPLR 5232, 5233, 5236. See §§ 496 et seq.

[5]   CPLR 6218(a). If "urgency" dictates, such as where the property attached consists of perishables, the court can direct sale of the property and its conversion into money, the money to be held in place of the property. Any money coming into the sheriff's possession under a levy must be deposited in an interest-bearing account as directed by CPLR 6218(a). Property other than money must be inventoried as provided in CPLR 6218(b).

[6]   CPLR 6219.

[7]   CPLR 6211(b). See § 316.

[8]   See Leber-Krebs, Inc. v. Capitol Records, 779 F.2d 895 (2d Cir. 1985).

§ 321. "Perfecting" the Levy

When a levy is made against real property, there is nothing further to be done; the filing with the county clerk does the whole job under CPLR 6216. The same is true of a levy against personal property when the levy is made by seizure under CPLR 6215. But when a levy is made against personal property by service of the order of attachment on a garnishee under CPLR 6214, the most common situation, some step must be taken within 90 days afterwards or the levy becomes void.[1] It is therefore only the levy by service procedure with which we are concerned in this section, for it is only there that the 90-day period for a follow-up step, popularly called "perfection" of the levy, applies.

Any one of three things will constitute "perfection" and satisfy this 90-day requirement:

(1) The garnishee need only deliver the attached property to the sheriff. The sheriff will then hold it to apply to whatever judgment the plaintiff may get in the action. This contemplates that the garnishee will deliver the property voluntarily. That would settle everything. But if the garnishee doesn't, there is also a provision for the sheriff to seize the property. CPLR 6214(c) contemplates the possibility of seizure as a follow-up step after levy by service—not to be confused with seizure under CPLR 6215 as an initial method of levy. But the explicit requirement under CPLR 6215 that the plaintiff indemnify the sheriff as a condition to initial levy by seizure has been found by implication to apply also to the seizure used only as a "perfection" step after a levy by service,[2] thus discouraging the seizure procedure in both instances. If the garnishee delivers to the sheriff all property then in its possession belonging to the defendant, later property of the defendant coming into the garnishee's custody or possession is not subject to the levy.[3]

If the property is too big to deliver, or is an intangible, such as a debt not yet due, physical delivery by the garnishee may be impracticable, but the same result is accomplished by the garnishee's serving a paper on the sheriff, agreeing to hold the property as the equivalent of the sheriff's agent. In one case,[4] in which the garnishee just set aside merchandise in response to the levy and so advised the defendant, this was held tantamount to an assignment to the sheriff and hence satisfactory. A simple letter from the garnishee to the sheriff has also been held to do the job.[5]

(2) An alternative step that would constitute a "perfection" of the levy and satisfy the 90-day requirement is for the plaintiff to begin a special proceeding against the garnishee, also giving notice of the proceeding to the parties to the action and to the sheriff.[6] The mere filing of the petition accomplishes "commencement" of the proceeding[7] for this purpose. Service of the petition along with a notice of petition or order to show

---

[1]   CPLR 6214(e).

[2]   See Lacharite v. Ducatte, 4 A.D.2d 130, 164 N.Y.S.2d 361 (3d Dep't 1957), aff'd, 4 N.Y.2d 945, 175 N.Y.S.2d 820, 151 N.E.2d 617 (1958). The Advisory Committee, in addressing this subject, did not cite the *Lacharite* case (see 3d Rep. Leg. Doc. No. 17, p. 350 (1959)), which therefore presumably still governs.

[3]   CPLR 6214(b).

[4]   Fantasy Records, Inc. v. Travelers Indem. Co., 54 Misc. 2d 799, 283 N.Y.S.2d 473 (N.Y. City Civ. Ct. 1967).

[5]   See Kalman v. Neuman, 80 A.D.2d 116, 438 N.Y.S.2d 109 (2d Dep't 1981).

[6]   CPLR 6214(e).

[7]   CPLR 304, 403; see §§ 45, 548, 553.

must of course follow the petition's filing,[8] but as long as service is made properly afterwards, the mere filing of the petition accomplishes the requisite "commencement" for the attachment purpose regardless of when the special proceeding is terminated.

The proceeding is designed to make the garnishee turn the money or property over to the sheriff. The garnishee may of course defend the proceeding with anything he might have used against the defendant had the defendant brought suit concerning the subject property. (The garnishee is not divested of his defenses merely because a creditor of the defendant, instead of the defendant herself, is seeking the property.) Although the statute authorizing the proceeding[9] states that the plaintiff may bring it against the garnishee, caselaw holds that it may be brought against the defendant if the property sought is in the defendant's possession.[10]

(3) The third and, paradoxically, the easiest alternative whereby to "perfect" the levy, at least so as to remove the onus of the 90-day period and its threat to void the levy, is to have the period extended. The court is empowered to extend the 90 days, and it takes no more than a motion by the plaintiff, on notice to the defendant to obtain the extension. The extension motion should be made within the original 90-day period because the statute says that the levy shall be "void" if the period expires without extension.[11] It has been held, however, that the period can be extended even by application made after the period has expired.[12] While tardy applications to extend the time to perfect the levy may be permissible, it is unwise for the plaintiff to proceed on that assumption. The plaintiff should get the extension while the 90-day period is still in effect until the Court of Appeals has blessed the practice.

Another bonus of the timely motion is that the extension is not limited to another 90-day period. The court can extend the original 90-day period almost indefinitely. A common disposition is for the court to extend it until 10 days after the entry of such judgment as may be rendered in the main action, which means after trial on the merits. That may be many months, and perhaps even years away. In one instance, the appellate division even extended the time until 30 days after disposition of an appeal to the Court of Appeals.[13]

With so easy a set of options—any one of the three listed items is sufficient to fulfill the 90-day requirement and remove it as a potential destroyer of jurisdiction or security—there is no excuse for the lawyer to let the 90 days lapse, thereby voiding the levy, which is precisely what happens. Where, for example, all initial steps were properly taken, but the 90-day period went by without a perfection step, all was voided: the levy, the order of attachment, and the jurisdiction obtained in the action itself, which, when quasi in rem jurisdiction is relied on, depends on an effectual levy.[14]

---

[8]   See § 553.

[9]   CPLR 6214(d).

[10]   Hom-De-Lite Realty Corp. v. Trimboli, 28 A.D.2d 1127, 284 N.Y.S.2d 141 (2d Dep't 1967).

[11]   CPLR 6214(e).

[12]   Kitson & Kitson v. City of Yonkers, 10 A.D.3d 21, 26, 778 N.Y.S.2d 503, 507 (2d Dep't 2004) (holding that "[a] motion for an extension of a levy may be made after the levy has expired, since there is no provision in the CPLR prohibiting an extension after the levy has expired"); but see Worldwide Carriers Limited v. Aris S. S. Co., 312 F. Supp. 172, 175 n.5 (S.D.N.Y. 1970).

[13]   Stines v. Hertz Corp., 22 A.D.2d 1018, 256 N.Y.S.2d 321 (2d Dep't 1964), aff'd 16 N.Y.2d 605, 261 N.Y.S.2d 59, 209 N.E.2d 105 (1965).

[14]   See Rich v. Rich, 103 Misc. 2d 723, 725, 426 N.Y.S.2d 936, 937 (Sup. Ct., New York County 1980); Sturcke v. Link, 176 Misc. 93, 26 N.Y.S.2d 748 (Sup. Ct., New York County 1941).

It has been held that if the 90 days expire, but the order of attachment remains valid, which is the case when the attachment is not being used for jurisdiction, the sheriff can relevy it and start a new 90 days running[15] as long as no other creditor sneaks in and steals priority in the interim. The New York Court of Appeals has not yet spoken to the point, however, and until it does, the plaintiff should try to avoid such a time gap. Anything done, including that easiest step of all—the obtaining of a time extension—should be done within the original 90 days.

These New York attachment procedures are also applicable, by adoption, in the federal courts in New York where they are just as rigid, and plaintiffs in federal actions should therefore be just as wary of them.[16]

§ 322. Examples of Interplay of Attachment Requirements

Illustrations can help in understanding the interplay of some of the attachment procedures. We assume here a jurisdictional use of the attachment because when the attachment is used for jurisdiction, its procedures are at their most rigid and the illustrations their most instructive. Assume a case in the supreme court in which no personam jurisdiction is available to New Yorker P. P is suing D, a domiciliary of Vermont with no residence in New York,[17] for a claim arising in Vermont. Assume the following year 2016 occurrences on the stated dates:

Feb. 19	Summons and complaint filed and order of attachment granted ex parte by the supreme court.
Feb. 26	Levy by service of the order of attachment by the sheriff on garnishee G (a New York bank where D has an account).
March 1	Motion made by P by order to show cause to confirm the attachment.
March 15	Court confirms the attachment in an order.
April 19	Summons service is made on D in Vermont.
May 20	Special proceeding is begun by P against G.
June 16	Motion is made by D to vacate everything.

The motion would be denied because all is in order. The levy preceded the service of the summons; a motion to confirm was made within the required time (within 10 days after the levy, and was granted); the summons was served within 60 days after the order was granted (satisfying CPLR 6213), and within 120 days after the filing of the action (satisfying CPLR 306–b); and, within 90 days after the levy, the levy was perfected with the commencement of the special proceeding.

Now take all the facts to be the same, but omit the May 20 special proceeding and assume that no perfection step of any kind is taken within 90 days following February 26. Under older law,[18] the June 16 motion would be granted, voiding everything. The

---

[15] Fireman's Fund Ins. Co. v. D'Ambra, 766 F.2d 95 (2d Cir. 1985).

[16] Fed. R. Civ. P. 64. See Worldwide Carriers Limited v. Aris S. S. Co., 312 F. Supp. 172 (S.D.N.Y. 1970). For treatment of the provisional remedies in federal actions, see § 640 (Practitioner's Edition).

[17] See CPLR 6201(1).

[18] See Sturcke v. Link, 176 Misc. 93, 26 N.Y.S.2d 748 (Sup. Ct., New York County 1941).

levy is void under CPLR 6214(e) for lack of perfection within 90 days; the action is dismissed for lack of quasi in rem jurisdiction, which depended on the levy; and the order of attachment is vacated because of the action's dismissal. More recent law suggests that the 90 days can be extended even by motion made after the period has expired,[19] and if that becomes the prevailing view, then P, upon excusing the delay, should be able to have the 90-day period extended by late motion which, if granted, would preserve everything. P is better off by not assuming that this generosity about allowing an extension on motion made after the passing of the 90 days will be upheld by the Court of Appeals. P should make the motion within the initial 90 days.

Take all the facts to be the same as listed, but reverse the levy and summons service: the summons is served on February 26; and the levy is made on April 19. Even assuming the granting of a proper and timely confirmation motion, a defect would subsist in that the levy did not precede service as it must under CPLR 314(3), which means that quasi in rem jurisdiction was not secured, requiring dismissal of the action. (If personam jurisdiction exists—the attachment being used for mere security rather than for quasi in rem jurisdiction—the proceedings would be valid and no dismissal would be required.)

Take all the facts to be the same as listed, but omit the perfection step of May 20 and have the summons service of April 19 made on D, not in Vermont, but in New York while D is visiting. The June 16 motion, insofar as it seeks vacatur of the levy, would be granted (unless the court allows a late application to extend the 90 days). The 90-day perfection step is required no matter what kind of jurisdiction may exist in the action, i.e., whether the attachment is being used for jurisdiction or for mere security. But insofar as the June 16 motion seeks dismissal of the action, it would have to be denied: the April 19 service in New York conferred personam jurisdiction over D and made all further questions of rem jurisdiction academic. The failure of the levy, needed for rem but not for personam jurisdiction, would become irrelevant for jurisdiction.

Take all the facts to be the same as listed, except that summons service is made on D in Vermont on May 5 instead of April 19. Here, the defect would be that the summons was not served within 60 days after the granting of the order, which makes the order void under CPLR 6213. This in turn voids the levy and that in turn defeats the quasi in rem jurisdiction that P was relying on. So here again is a scenario in which the whole edifice crumbles.

§ 323. What Property Attachable?

Article 62 does not specify what property may be attached. CPLR 6202 provides simply that whatever property can be applied to enforce a judgment under CPLR 5201 can be attached before judgment under Article 62. CPLR 5201 is the standard for both, and for this purpose the "judgment debtor" of CPLR 5201 is to be treated as the mere "defendant" that he is at attachment time.

CPLR 5201 defines property broadly. It makes no endeavor to list the innumerable categories of property interests a defendant can have. Such a list would always be incomplete, and thus restrictive despite its best endeavors. With the narrow exception of property explicitly exempted by statute from application to a judgment,[1] CPLR 5201(b)

---

[19] See § 321.

[1] CPLR 5205 and 5206 contain the main (but not the exclusive) lists of property exempted from application to a judgment and hence from an attachment as well. See § 490.

subjects to the judgment (and hence to attachment) any property interest of the defendant that is assignable or transferable. Whatever the interest is, and whether tangible or intangible, it is leviable as long as the defendant can assign or transfer it, which means that almost any property interest of the defendant is reachable. Further discussion of this matter is reserved for the chapter on the enforcement of judgments,[2] but it is especially useful when discussing attachment to refer to subdivision (a) of CPLR 5201, which is purportedly an exception to the broad property criterion of subdivision (b).

Subdivision (a) provides that when the property consists of a "debt" owing to the defendant (D) by the garnishee (G), it can be subjected to levy only if it is presently due or certain to become due in the future either upon some inevitable contingency, such as the mere passage of time, or upon demand of D. The purpose of this restriction was to preclude a levy against contingent obligations not certain to ripen into something economically real. This was found too inflexible, however, and was much reduced in scope—and the contingent intangible made much more accessible—by the Court of Appeals in its 1976 decision in ABKCO Industries, Inc. v. Apple Films, Inc.[3] The decision is discussed at length in the enforcement chapter, but since the prejudgment attachment can find itself in pursuit of an intangible just as often as a post-judgment execution can— ABKCO in fact involved an attachment—the ABKCO decision is a key one for an attaching plaintiff, too.[4]

When considering what property of the defendant may be levied on, a helpful rule of thumb is what may be called the "step into the shoes" doctrine.[5] The plaintiff generally has no greater standing than the defendant herself has in some item of the defendant's property. But the plaintiff can reach at least the interest that the defendant does have, i.e., stand in the defendant's shoes, and that is what the plaintiff tries to accomplish with the levy. This, too, will be seen in more depth in the enforcement of judgments chapter, but with this difference noted once again: when a levy of execution is made on a judgment, the sheriff's obligation is to convert the property into money (if it is not money itself) and pay the plaintiff's judgment. With attachment, the sheriff just takes possession or custody of the property, actually or constructively, and holds it, thereby keeping it away from the defendant's use but without letting the plaintiff have it either. If the plaintiff wins on the merits, what is contemplated is that the plaintiff will then issue an execution on the judgment to the same sheriff, who will then take the further enforcement steps needed to liquidate the property, convert it into money, and satisfy the plaintiff's judgment.

The fact that on an attachment there is no pressure to get and sell the property makes it simpler than the levy of execution on a judgment. If, for example, some property or debt is duly attached while in the hands of a garnishee, whether it is a tangible or a debt, and the plaintiff gets the 90-day period of CPLR 6214 extended until after judgment,[6] that simple step suspends everything until that later time when, with a judgment now on the scene, it becomes the burden of Article 52 and its enforcement of judgments devices to convert the property into money. The garnishee fulfills his

---

[2]   See §§ 486 et seq.

[3]   ABKCO Industries, Inc. v. Apple Films, Inc., 39 N.Y.2d 670, 385 N.Y.S.2d 511, 350 N.E.2d 899 (1976).

[4]   See § 489.

[5]   See § 488.

[6]   See CPLR 6214(e) and its discussion in § 321.

obligation by keeping the property interest away from the defendant in the meantime, but no one is pressing to have the interest sold or even, perhaps, measured. All of this abides final judgment and a levy of execution on it.

A problem that attachment and execution have in common is that of identifying the proper garnishee. In most situations, it is not hard; the garnishee is the person who has physical possession of some piece of the defendant's property or who owes a debt to the defendant.[7] In some instances, especially those involving intangible property interests, such as shares in a corporation or an interest in a decedent's estate, a statute assists by specifically identifying the garnishee.[8]

The plaintiff must see to it that the sheriff directs his efforts to an appropriate garnishee since address to a wrong one will frustrate the proceedings. Suppose, for example, that D is one of several persons having some beneficial interest in a trust and that the trust owns certain tangible assets. In a suit against D, D's interest in the trust, to whatever extent that interest is subject to levy, is the thing to go after, and the proper garnishee is the trustee. But no particular assets belonging to the trust may be levied on in that situation because those are the property of the trust and not the property of any one of its beneficiaries.[9] A person, other than the trustee, who happens to have possession or custody of such a trust asset would therefore not be a proper garnishee.

An analogous question concerns the attachment of partnership property, which arose often enough under prior law to earn special mention from the CPLR's drafters.[10] The only time specific property of a partnership can be attached is when the claim is against the partnership as such.[11] A given partner's individual interest in the partnership is his share of the profits and surplus,[12] and one with a claim against an individual partner must attach that rather than specific property owned by the partnership. The creditor does this either with a levy or with what is known as a charging order.[13] The latter requires a motion; the levy does not, and is therefore the preferable method when priorities among creditors are at stake.[14]

One of the major devices for the enforcement of a judgment is the income execution of CPLR 5231, which enables a judgment creditor to reach 10% of the judgment debtor's income and apply it to the judgment. Under prior law, the case of Morris Plan Industrial Bank of New York v. Gunning[15] held that this post-judgment income levy could be exploited for prejudgment attachment as well, i.e., that it would operate as a continuing levy, requiring—all pursuant to the single attachment—that the employer (the garnishee) deduct 10% every payday and send that amount to the sheriff until the plaintiff's demand was met.[16] *Morris Plan* is not followed today; whether the income

---

[7]   See the definition of garnishee in CPLR 105.

[8]   See CPLR 5201(c).

[9]   See William A. White & Sons v. Scott, 14 A.D.2d 307, 220 N.Y.S.2d 342 (1st Dep't 1961).

[10]   See 3d Rep. Leg. Doc. No. 17, p. 140 (1959).

[11]   Partnership Law § 51(2)(c).

[12]   Partnership Law § 52.

[13]   See Partnership Law § 54.

[14]   See § 520.

[15]   Morris Plan Industrial Bank of New York v. Gunning, 295 N.Y. 324, 67 N.E.2d 510 (1946).

[16]   The case allowed a New York attachment of a Pennsylvania defendant's wages, earned in Pennsylvania, despite the fact that Pennsylvania itself exempted such wages. New York theorized that the wages had a New York situs because D's employer, G, happened to be a corporation with a New York office. The Court assumed that the obligation underlying the judgment was a Pennsylvania one. New York's attempt

execution authorized by CPLR 5231 to enforce a judgment may be exploited for the prejudgment attachment is, as noted earlier,[17] a question expressly reserved by the Court of Appeals in Glassman v. Hyder.[18]

It is tempting to delve further into this property topic, but it would be duplicative of the effort required later in the enforcement of judgments,[19] in deference to which we stop here.

§ 324. Disclosure to Aid Attachment

If help is needed to determine the location or extent of the defendant's assets or even whether such assets exist, CPLR 6220 enables the plaintiff to apply for a court order directing disclosure. This makes available any disclosure device contained in Article 31, the CPLR's disclosure article,[1] if the court finds the device appropriate or helpful to reveal the nature or whereabouts of the defendant's property. Depositions on oral questions,[2] for example, and the discovery and inspection of documents,[3] may be directed.

A significant distinction is that disclosure directly under Article 31 is usually available by mere notices served between parties, while disclosure in aid of attachment under CPLR 6220 requires a court order. Since the motion for the order is required to be on "such notice as the court may direct," it should be brought on by order to show cause.[4] This enables the court to determine the method of notice and whether other parties and nonparties should be notified, including the one from whom disclosure is sought. It is helpful to have the court direct as to these items because the juncture at which this kind of disclosure is sought—after the granting of the attachment order but before the levy and often before the summons has been served—muddies the rules about the notice of motion.

Any person with data reflecting on the defendant's property may be required to make disclosure under this provision, including the defendant and the garnishee as well as one who is neither, such as a friend or relative of the defendant who does not have the defendant's property, but knows something about it.[5]

---

to subject to a New York levy wages earned (and exempted from levy) in Pennsylvania puts *Morris Plan* under a constitutional cloud. It is a question of choice of law and *Morris Plan* may have given it the wrong answer. Compare Home Ins. Co. v. Dick, 281 U.S. 397, 50 S. Ct. 338, 74 L. Ed. 926 (1930). Another relevant factor is that the plaintiff in *Morris Plan* was a New York corporation, a factor which at the time precluded a forum non conveniens dismissal. A conveniens dismissal would be permissible in a like situation today. See §§ 28 and 29.

[17] See § 307.

[18] Glassman v. Hyder, 23 N.Y.2d 354, 296 N.Y.S.2d 783, 244 N.E.2d 259 (1968).

[19] See §§ 486 et seq.

[1] See §§ 343 et seq.

[2] CPLR 3107; see §§ 354 et seq.

[3] CPLR 3120; see § 362.

[4] CPLR 2214(d); see § 248.

[5] See Heller Financial, Inc. v. Wall Street Imports, Ltd., 140 Misc. 2d 205, 529 N.Y.S.2d 969 (Sup. Ct., New York County 1988); Michelsen v. Brush, 233 F. Supp. 868 (E.D.N.Y. 1964).

§ 325. Defendant's Remedies: Vacatur; Discharge; Annulment; Action on Undertaking

The CPLR offers the attachment defendant a number of options, which can be considered seriatim.

1. Vacating or modifying the attachment. The defendant can move at any time during the action to vacate or modify the attachment order. CPLR 6223(a) supplies this right,[1] and any ground that affects the validity of the attachment is a vacatur ground. Before 1977, the motion to vacate was the principal context for the presentation of the defendant's side of the case: the order of attachment was almost always granted ex parte and there was no requirement that the plaintiff afterwards make a motion—on notice— to confirm the attachment. With the 1977 amendment adding CPLR 6211(b), which mandates such a follow-up confirmation motion in all instances in which an attachment is granted ex parte, it will likely be on the motion to confirm that the defendant's objections are raised. And since CPLR 6211(b) contemplates that the confirmation motion will be made after the levy, the motion will enable the defendant to put objections not only to the validity of the order of attachment, but also to the validity of the levy. Motions to vacate are therefore less frequent under present practice. Indeed, any issue decided on the contested confirmation motion should be deemed binding on any later motion by the defendant to vacate, under the doctrine of the law of the case.[2] Motions to vacate or modify should therefore be based on new facts arising after the disposition of the confirmation motion.

The motion to vacate may have more scope in a situation in which the plaintiff has elected to apply for the attachment by motion on notice in the first place. Since the levy would not yet have taken place in that instance, defects connected with the levy would not be raised on the motion as they might be on a post-levy motion to confirm following an ex parte attachment.

One of the vacatur grounds listed in CPLR 6223(a) is that "the attachment is unnecessary to the security of the plaintiff." The ground was not explicitly set forth under pre-CPLR law and that's the sole reason for its inclusion,[3] a point overlooked by the lower court in Carey v. Sugar, necessitating its reversal by the U.S. Supreme Court[4] as previously discussed.[5] The lower court had erroneously assumed that the expression of one vacatur ground negated all others, while it was clear under New York law that anything on which the attachment depended—any showing that the plaintiff had to make to obtain the attachment ex parte in the first place—could be negated by the defendant on a motion to vacate.

On a motion to vacate or modify the attachment, the plaintiff has the burden of establishing the grounds for the attachment—including a sustaining of the particular paragraph of CPLR 6201 depended on as well as a showing of a "probability" of success on the merits—and of convincing the court of the need for continuing the levy.[6] If these

---

[1] The garnishee and any other interested person are also authorized by CPLR 6223(a) to make this motion.

[2] See § 448.

[3] See 3d Rep. Leg. Doc. No. 17, pp. 357–58 (1959).

[4] Carey v. Sugar, 425 U.S. 73, 96 S. Ct. 1208, 47 L. Ed. 2d 587 (1976).

[5] See § 315.

[6] CPLR 6223(b).

issues should arise on a motion to confirm, as they are more likely to do today, the plaintiff retains the burden of proof on them there as well.[7]

The motion to vacate or modify is made on notice to all parties and to the sheriff.[8] The resulting order is appealable.[9]

Modification of the order is a permissible alternative to vacatur. An example of a modification would be where the court on the motion finds that the amount stated in the original order—which is the amount to be secured by the levy—has proved to be inflated and should be reduced.

On the defendant's motion to vacate the attachment, the court may give the plaintiff "a reasonable opportunity to correct any defect."[10] This clearly evinces that not every defect is a jurisdictional one requiring vacatur of the attachment. If the defect consists of a paper omission or error that can be corrected by mere amendment, amendment rather than vacatur is the remedy. Part of the plaintiff's showing is that there is a sufficient cause of action for money, for example, which tends to make the rules about the sufficiency of a pleading relevant to some extent to the plaintiff's affidavits in support of attachment. A primary purpose of this permission to allow defects to be corrected is to prevent the strict and technical old rules about pleadings—no longer applicable to pleadings themselves today—to be used to defeat the attachment.[11]

2. Discharging the attachment. A "discharge" of the attachment involves the substitution, in place of the attached property, of the defendant's undertaking, committing the defendant to pay whatever judgment the plaintiff may recover in the action, limited by the value of the property from which the defendant wants to lift the attachment. The discharge is sought by motion under CPLR 6222. If granted, it releases the property and returns it to the defendant's use. The defendant who has no basis for contesting the jurisdictional validity of the attachment, and so can't get it vacated, can turn to the discharge motion, albeit at the expense of whatever the undertaking costs.

Neither a vacatur motion under CPLR 6223 nor a discharge motion under CPLR 6222 constitutes an appearance in the action. This is to assure that a defendant making either kind of motion will not inadvertently submit to an otherwise lacking jurisdiction, a fear that is probably unwarranted under the CPLR since objections to jurisdiction are no longer wedded to the concept of a "special appearance" as they were under prior law.[12]

3. Annulling the attachment. Yet another word, to be distinguished from both the vacatur of the attachment under CPLR 6223 and its discharge under CPLR 6222, is its "annulment" under CPLR 6224. Annulment of the attachment requires no motion; it occurs automatically. If the defendant wins on the merits, for example, the attachment is automatically annulled—although the defendant may have to remind garnishees and sheriffs about it. (If the sheriff should resist, for example, and refuse return of the defendant's property, the defendant's remedy is a motion to compel the return under

---

[7]   CPLR 6211(b), adopting CPLR 6223(b).

[8]   CPLR 6223(a).

[9]   CPLR 5701(a)(2)(i); see § 526.

[10]   CPLR 6223(a).

[11]   See 3d Rep. Leg. Doc. No. 17, p. 358 (1959). Of course, as noted earlier, the other side of this coin is that what suffices for a pleading may be insufficient for an attachment where strong evidentiary detail of the merits is needed in support. See § 316.

[12]   See § 109 above. Take note also of the limited appearance permitted in attachment cases by CPLR 320(c)(1). See § 113.

CPLR 6225.) If the plaintiff wins on the merits, the annulment does not occur until the plaintiff's judgment is fully satisfied. If the action for any reason abates before judgment on the merits, such as by a dismissal under CPLR 3211 on a non-merits ground,[13] or by a voluntary discontinuance,[14] that also annuls the attachment.

4. *Action on plaintiff's undertaking.* The undertaking that the plaintiff must furnish for an attachment requires the plaintiff and the sureties on the bond to stand good to the defendant for "all costs and damages, including reasonable attorney's fees, which may be sustained by reason of the attachment if the defendant recovers judgment or if it is finally decided that the plaintiff was not entitled to an attachment."[15] Note, therefore, that all that need occur in order to invoke the condition of the plaintiff's undertaking is for the defendant to win on the merits. And even a merits victory by the plaintiff does not prevent the defendant's suit on the undertaking as where the attachment depended on a ground involving an extrinsic fact, such as a showing under CPLR 6201(1) that the defendant was neither a domiciliary nor resident of the state, and it turns out that the defendant was indeed a New Yorker.

The undertaking that the defendant (D) must furnish in order to discharge the attachment, the second remedy discussed above, guarantees collection of the plaintiff's judgment while the undertaking under discussion here, which the plaintiff (P) must supply, covers only damages sustained by D "by reason of the attachment."

Usually, the main question in connection with P's undertaking, when its condition is invoked, is whether the defendant's attorney's fees were incurred solely because of the attachment. Suppose, for example, that D wins on the merits. If D is a nondomiciliary served outside New York and the sole basis for jurisdiction is the attachment of D's New York property (i.e., jurisdiction is quasi in rem only), any defect in the attachment process that would lend itself to a vacatur motion would require that such a motion be made, or that the defendant at least point the defect out by way of opposing the plaintiff's motion to confirm. Defending on the merits—and even winning—without raising the defect means that the defendant went further than he had to. The undertaking would therefore not cover attorney's fees incurred in defending the action.

But if the attachment is in all technical regards valid, so that the only way for the defendant to protect his property is to defend on the merits, and he does so and wins, the fee of his attorney in defending the action is covered by the undertaking.[16] There the defense on the merits—remember that there was no personam jurisdiction in the case—was necessitated solely by the attachment. But where the defendant is within the court's personam jurisdiction, divesting the attachment of any jurisdictional function, it is the personam jurisdiction, and not the attachment, that requires that the action be defended. The defendant's expense of an attorney in that instance is not traceable to the attachment and is therefore not ordinarily covered by the undertaking.[17]

---

[13] E.g., paragraph 3 of CPLR 3211(a), lack of capacity to sue, or paragraph 4, the pendency of a duplicative action.

[14] CPLR 3217.

[15] CPLR 6212(b).

[16] Thropp v. Erb, 255 N.Y. 75, 174 N.E. 67 (1930). The case was codified in 1977 by an amendment of CPLR 6212(b) and the addition of 6212(e).

[17] Dinnerstein v. Max's Gas Station, 172 Misc. 27, 13 N.Y.S.2d 1014 (App. Term, 2d Dep't 1939).

Even a defendant who was within the court's personam jurisdiction may be allowed to recover attorney's fees for steps shown to have been induced by the attachment as where the defendant's commercial viability depended on lifting the attachment.[18]

While the amount of the undertaking necessarily limits the liability of the sureties, it does not limit the liability of the plaintiff himself.[19]

§ 326. Disposition of Property; Disputes; Priorities

The plaintiff's hope is that the garnishee, after the attachment levy, will turn over to the sheriff whatever money the garnishee (G) owes the defendant (D) or whatever property of D that G may be holding. Doing so offers the garnishee complete protection. Should D afterwards sue G for the debt or property, G has as a complete defense its payment to the New York sheriff at the behest of one claiming as D's creditor.[1]

If G does not voluntarily hand the property over, the plaintiff, P, can, as we have seen, bring a special proceeding to compel him to.[2] If it has been handed over to the sheriff and the attachment or its levy is then wholly or partly vacated, the court can, on the motion of any interested person—most likely the defendant—direct the sheriff to return the property. This is authorized by CPLR 6225, which gives the court, through the simple expedient of a motion, the power to undo whatever parts of the attachment process require undoing.

Now assume that some outsider, X, is claiming the property that has up to now been assumed to belong to D. Any such adverse claimant to the property may bring a special proceeding against the plaintiff to determine ownership or other interests in the property. Notice of that proceeding must be given to the sheriff and to each of the parties to the main action. And although the statute in point[3] does not say so, it would also be appropriate to join the garnishee and any outsiders who are making claim to the property. If issues of fact arise in the proceeding, the court is authorized to try them, thus obviating a new plenary action.

A few basic priority problems are addressed by Article 62. Priorities in real property of the defendant are usually easy to measure because they invariably come about by a filing of papers in the county clerk's office—levy of attachment is made by such a filing[4]— and it is just a matter of determining who filed first. Personal property is more involved.

The general way to secure a priority in the defendant's personal property, i.e., to secure a kind of lien superior to later ones of other persons, is to deliver the order of

---

[18]   See A. C. Israel Commodity Co. v. Banco Do Brasil, S.A., 50 Misc. 2d 362, 270 N.Y.S.2d 283 (Sup. Ct., New York County 1966).

[19]   See CPLR 6212(e), codifying Siegel v. Northern Boulevard & 80th St. Corp., 31 A.D.2d 182, 295 N.Y.S.2d 804 (1st Dep't 1968).

[1]   CPLR 6204. The constitutionality of CPLR 6204 was upheld by the U.S. Supreme Court in Harris v. Balk, 198 U.S. 215, 25 S. Ct. 625, 49 L. Ed. 1023 (1905), but insofar as the *Harris* case authorizes quasi in rem jurisdiction through the seizure of a debt owed to the debtor, it is largely overruled by Shaffer v. Heitner, 433 U.S. 186, 97 S. Ct. 2569, 53 L. Ed. 2d 683 (1977). See § 104. But *Harris* probably remains good law for its fixing of a debt's situs for the purpose of levying execution against it on a judgment and even for its seizure on an attachment being used for mere security rather than for jurisdictional purposes. It should also remain good law for the purpose for which it is cited here: the protection of a garnishee who has paid the debt over to the sheriff pursuant to a valid levy whether on a prejudgment attachment or on a post-judgment levy of execution.

[2]   CPLR 6214(d).

[3]   CPLR 6221.

[4]   CPLR 6216; see § 320.

attachment to "a sheriff."[5] This mere delivery, before any levy has been made, will at least give P a right higher than that of someone to whom D afterwards gratuitously transfers the property, but only if the transferee has knowledge of the order of attachment. But if D's pre-levy transfer is made to one who pays fair consideration for the property, that transferee prevails over the attaching plaintiff regardless of the transferee's knowledge.[6]

After a levy is made, it behooves the plaintiff to try to get the property into the hands of the sheriff, for many reasons. One of them is that if the sheriff has not taken possession of the property, then even if a levy has been made (as by his serving a copy of the order of attachment on G), a person who pays fair consideration for the property without knowing of the levy prevails over the plaintiff.[7] If the property is in the possession of a garnishee, the situation is less likely to occur because a garnishee who after levy prematurely returns possession of the property to D or his designee faces a personal liability to P. But if D himself has possession, D fears little in the way of additional liability, and P's efforts to get the property out of D's hands and into the sheriff's custody should therefore be all the more diligent.

Utopia for the attaching plaintiff is to have the garnishee either hold the property away from D or put it into the sheriff's hands, to have the action go forward to judgment for P against D, to issue an execution on the judgment to the same sheriff who levied the attachment, and to have that sheriff levy now on the execution, which means selling the previously attached property[8] and paying the proceeds of the sale over to P to satisfy the judgment. CPLR 6226 contemplates the situation, but it also contemplates further priority fights if there are multiple attachment creditors or other judgment creditors.

If there are several attachment creditors dealing through different sheriffs, the one whose attachment gets levied first gets priority; if they have delivered their attachment orders to the same sheriff, priority is in the order of delivery.[9]

D. INJUNCTION

Table of Sections

§ 327.   Preliminary Injunction, Grounds
§ 328.   Required Showing; Discretion
§ 329.   Applying for the Injunction
§ 330.   Temporary Restraining Order
§ 331.   Vacating or Modifying Injunction or TRO

---

[5]   CPLR 6203. The enforcement officers of the various lower courts of civil jurisdiction of the state, such as the city marshals in the case of the New York City Civil Court, are to be deemed the same as a "sheriff" for these enforcement purposes. See § 701 in each of the New York City Civil, Uniform District, Uniform City, and Uniform Justice Court Acts, McKinney's Vol. 29A, Parts 2 and 3. While the city marshals can aid in the enforcement of money judgments under CPLR Article 52 in supreme court actions, see CPLR 105(s–1), they cannot serve an order of attachment in such action.

[6]   CPLR 6203(1).

[7]   CPLR 6203(2).

[8]   CPLR 5232, 5233.

[9]   CPLR 6226. The section evinces an intent that it be read alongside CPLR 5234, to which it refers. When the contest is between attaching creditors on the one side and execution and other judgment creditors on the other, CPLR 5234 is the priority resolver. See § 520.

§ 327. Preliminary Injunction, Grounds

Article 63 of the CPLR supplies the provisional remedies of the preliminary injunction, which keeps the status quo while an action is pending, and the temporary restraining order (TRO), which keeps the status quo while a motion is brought on for a preliminary injunction. There are, however, special injunction statutes applicable in particular situations,[1] and when applicable these supersede the general CPLR provisions of Article 63,[2] which is the central and most frequently invoked authority for a preliminary injunction.

CPLR 6301 authorizes a preliminary injunction in either of two situations:[3]

1. where it appears that the defendant threatens or is about to do, or is doing or procuring or suffering to be done, an act in violation of the plaintiff's rights respecting the subject of the action, and tending to render the judgment ineffectual; or

2. in any action where the plaintiff has demanded and would be entitled to a judgment restraining the defendant from the commission or continuance of an act, which, if committed or continued during the pendency of the action, would produce injury to the plaintiff.

In the first situation, the action[4] is not necessarily brought for a permanent injunction. The plaintiff is seeking some kind of relief with respect to a particular "subject matter," and it is in respect of that very subject matter that the plaintiff needs an injunction lest the defendant do something to make a potential judgment "ineffectual." Where, for example, P sued D to rescind a contract to transport goods for P, and it was shown that D's negotiation of the bill of lading could render a rescission judgment ineffectual, P was allowed a preliminary injunction enjoining D from either negotiating or demanding payment on the bill.[5]

Since the first part of CPLR 6301 requires a specific "subject matter," an action for money only does not qualify, and of course a money action does not qualify under the second part of the statute, in which the object of the action itself is a permanent injunction. The provisional remedy of injunction is therefore unavailable in that most numerous of all actions, the money action. This was confirmed by the Court of Appeals in Credit Agricole Indosuez v. Rossiyskiy Kredit Bank,[6] and is the rule as well in federal practice.[7] The courts suggest that a plaintiff seeking to prevent the defendant from transferring assets during the pendency of a money action and unable to secure the help

---

[1]   In labor disputes, for example, there is detailed special instruction about injunctions, whether permanent or preliminary. See Lab. Law §§ 807, 808.

[2]   CPLR 101.

[3]   CPLR 6301 has no numbered subparagraphs. Its content is divided in two here to aid reference.

[4]   A preliminary injunction may also be sought in a special proceeding if it otherwise satisfies the requirements of CPLR 6301. See City Commission on Human Rights v. Regal Gardens, Inc., 53 Misc. 2d 318, 278 N.Y.S.2d 739 (Sup. Ct., Queens County 1967).

[5]   Gross v. State Cooperage Export Crating & Shipping Co., 32 A.D.2d 540, 299 N.Y.S.2d 773 (2d Dep't 1969).

[6]   Credit Agricole Indosuez v. Rossiyskiy Kredit Bank, 94 N.Y.2d 541, 708 N.Y.S.2d 26, 729 N.E.2d 683 (2000).

[7]   See Grupo Mexicano de Desarrollo S.A. v. Alliance Bond Fund, Inc., 527 U.S. 308, 119 S. Ct. 1961, 144 L. Ed. 2d 319 (1999) (applying Fed. R. Civ. P. 65, the federal counterpart of CPLR 6301).

of a preliminary injunction might look to the remedy of attachment instead, but neither case elaborates.[8]

P's apprehension in these circumstances is often that D will secrete property during the action's pendency and thus make a money judgment uncollectable. If P can corroborate that foreboding with some palpable indication of D's intent to frustrate the enforcement of a judgment—a mere suspicion will not do—the particular remedy for P would be an order of attachment under CPLR 6201(3).[9]

Although the inclusion of a money demand will not necessarily preclude an injunction if other relief satisfying the first provision of CPLR 6301 is also sought, the court will refuse the injunction if convinced that a money judgment is the true object of the action and that all else is incidental.

Equity actions are not the only ones that can qualify for an injunction under this first segment of CPLR 6301. While the money action, the major specimen of an action at law, is not an acceptable context for an injunction, other law actions may qualify if they involve a specific subject matter, such as an ejectment or replevin action. If the chattel in a replevin action is unique, there is even separate authority for the granting of an injunction,[10] but even with a chattel that is not unique, the injunction might be granted under the first part of CPLR 6301.[11]

The second part of CPLR 6301 is invoked more frequently than the first. Under the second part, P is bringing an injunction *action* against D, the well known equity action seeking a final judgment of permanent injunction. Even if the action is prima facie sustainable, it will still be a while before a trial on the merits can determine P's right to a permanent injunction. Unless enjoined in the meantime, D may do the very thing P has sued to enjoin. This latter provision of CPLR 6301 authorizes a preliminary injunction to enjoin during the action that which P seeks to enjoin permanently with a final judgment.

One riffling through the annotations on CPLR 6301 will find numerous cases on the preliminary injunction. The standards for the issuance of these injunctions are so well known that most judges don't even bother to cite the source—CPLR 6301—so that even written opinions accompanying grants of a preliminary injunction often omit citations.

The plethora of cases on the preliminary injunction should not detain the practitioner long: as far as specific principles are concerned, most of the cases play no role at all. They merely illustrate whether, on the facts of a particular case, the injunction is warranted,[12] offering little guidance for other cases (a loss?), but relieving the practitioner from having to read all the annotations (a delight!).

---

[8] Elaboration appears in a two-part series in SPR 94:1 and 95:1, showing that while an order of attachment is not available for the mere asking, it can, when granted, prove just as effective as an injunction, and in some instances can be even more effective.

[9] See § 314.

[10] CPLR 7109(a). See the discussion of restraints in replevin actions in § 339.

[11] See, e.g., Carter v. Phillips, 127 Misc. 903, 217 N.Y.S. 621 (Sup. Ct., Lewis County 1926). If the chattel lacks uniqueness, however, the element of urgency traditionally insisted on for an injunction of any kind would seem to be lacking.

[12] The same has already been noted with the bill of particulars, see § 238, and the summary judgment motion, see § 278. Cases in all three areas are for the most part sui generis dispositions offering little in the way of specific guidance.

Because the substantive equity action of injunction is the context for the seeking of a preliminary injunction when the second part of CPLR 6301 is the ground invoked, one can easily convert an inquiry about a preliminary injunction into a full-fledged equity course on injunction actions. That temptation will be resisted here, but the factors to be considered in our inquiry—adequacy of legal remedy, irreparable injury, judicial discretion, etc.—derive from that majestic body of law that falls under the caption of "equity" and necessarily figures even when the preliminary injunction being considered is to be only a transient one. One advantage to be drawn from the fact that our standards for preliminary injunctions derive from the rules of equity applicable to permanent injunctions is apparent: whenever it appears that a permanent injunction would not be granted even if the plaintiff establishes at trial the facts alleged in the complaint, it of course follows that a preliminary injunction should also be denied.[13]

While acknowledging the relationship, we should not let it obscure the fact that Article 63 is concerned not with making or remaking the substantive law of equitable injunctions, but with taking that law as it is and asking, additionally, whether enough has been shown to warrant even a preliminary restraint. The legislature itself sometimes overlooks that Article 63 was set up to govern only the provisional remedy.[14]

The preliminary injunction of Article 63 should be distinguished from a "stay" of proceedings as authorized by CPLR 2201. Technically, a "stay" refers to a court's temporary suspension of its own proceedings, while an endeavor to stop a proceeding in some other court usually involves an outright "injunction" and all of the relevant requirements of equity. If a temporary injunction is sought, it also involves Article 63. The terms of "stay" and "injunction" are sometimes used interchangeably, however, even in statutes.[15]

§ 328. Required Showing; Discretion

The plaintiff's showing on an application for a preliminary injunction must be convincing.[1] The plaintiff must show that the claim falls under either of the two categories listed in CPLR 6301 and outlined in the prior section, i.e., that it is either (1) a cause of action having a specific and identifiable subject matter, or (2) a cause of action for a permanent injunction. The plaintiff must also show that the statutorily required peril is in prospect: a potentially ineffectual judgment if the defendant does something during the action that could render the final judgment essentially moot.

---

[13]　See, e.g., Arpels v. Arpels, 8 N.Y.2d 339, 207 N.Y.S.2d 663, 170 N.E.2d 670 (1960). The Court's entire dissertation in *Arpels* is on equity's traditional reluctance to enjoin a party to a New York action from prosecuting an action elsewhere, and yet the discourse was generated by an appeal from an order disposing of an application for only a preliminary injunction.

[14]　In 1971, for example, it added to the article CPLR 6330, which determines the availability of permanent injunctive relief in obscenity cases. The section is of course designed to recognize the delicacy of prior restraints on first amendment free speech activities, see Gaetano v. Erwin, 46 A.D.2d 735, 360 N.Y.S.2d 741 (4th Dep't 1974), but it has no logical place in Article 63. It would be more appropriately housed in something like the Civil Rights Law. It's concerned only with permanent injunctions—the substantive stuff of equity—and does not even address itself to the temporary injunction, the bailiwick of Article 63. Corroborating that CPLR 6330 does not address the preliminary injunction, the only subject that justifies its appearance in Article 63, is that it took caselaw to establish that an injunction under CPLR 6301 is permissible in a CPLR 6330 case. See Vergari v. Pierre Productions, Inc., 43 A.D.2d 950, 352 N.Y.S.2d 34 (2d Dep't 1974).

[15]　See, e.g., CPLR 6312(b) and Commentaries C2201:1 to C2201:4 on McKinney's CPLR 2201.

[1]　Hui v. New Clients, Inc., 126 A.D.3d 759, 760, 5 N.Y.S.3d 279, 281 (2d Dep't 2015); Etter v. Littwitz, 47 Misc. 2d 473, 262 N.Y.S.2d 924 (Sup. Ct., Monroe County 1965).

It will not suffice for the plaintiff merely to make out a prima facie possibility of success on the merits of the claim. Standards sufficient for a pleading will not automatically do for a preliminary injunction, a point previously made with the attachment remedy,[2] but just as true here with preliminary injunctions. The plaintiff has the burden of proof and must demonstrate a likelihood of success on the merits,[3] which means a strong showing in affidavits and other proof supplying evidentiary detail. The plaintiff should then show "that he would be irreparably damaged if an injunction were not granted before trial,"[4] and should demonstrate this factually and convincingly. Mere apprehensions do not suffice; the preliminary injunction will issue only upon a showing that the defendant's wrongful acts are occurring or are threatened and reasonably likely to occur.[5] If the defendant, opposing the application, offers substantial proof of defenses tending to negate the plaintiff's claim on the merits, such as laches and unclean hands, the preliminary injunction is likely to be denied.[6]

Of course, the defendant's merely serving opposing papers disputing some of the facts on which the plaintiff's application is premised can't by itself be allowed to defeat the injunction. Because it doesn't take much to create an issue of fact, that rule would put too many aces into the defendant's hand. Some cases had been perceived as adopting such a position, however. Citing two of these,[7] the Advisory Committee on Civil Practice recommended that CPLR 6312 be amended. The legislature responded with an amendment in 1996 that adds a subdivision (c) to CPLR 6312, providing that as long as the plaintiff's papers supply the elements needed for the injunction,

the presentation by the defendant of evidence sufficient to raise an issue of fact as to any of such elements shall not in itself be grounds for denial of the motion. In such event, the court shall make a determination by hearing or otherwise whether each of the elements required for issuance of a preliminary injunction exists.

It remains, in other words, a matter of the court's balancing all the proof, including consideration—but not undue consideration—of issues of fact raised by the defendant. An evidentiary hearing is permissible, but not mandatory. The court may, as it usually does in these situations, determine the application on the papers alone.[8]

As a general rule—again borrowing from the substantive realm of equity—the injunction will not be granted if the plaintiff has an adequate remedy at law. An overly rigid adherence to this old principle, however, would undo some of the benefits wrought by the merger of law and equity. So, practically speaking, the standard has been reworked to require the injunction's denial only when the legal remedy is plain, adequate, and complete, and from a pragmatic viewpoint as efficacious as an injunction.

---

[2]   See § 316.

[3]   Metz v. People, 73 Misc. 2d 219, 341 N.Y.S.2d 940 (Sup. Ct., Nassau County 1973).

[4]   De Candido v. Young Stars, Inc., 10 A.D.2d 922, 200 N.Y.S.2d 695, 696 (1st Dep't 1960).

[5]   Eldre Components, Inc. v. Kliman, 47 Misc. 2d 463, 262 N.Y.S.2d 732 (Sup. Ct., Monroe County 1965).

[6]   *De Candido*, 10 A.D.2d at 922, 200 N.Y.S.2d at 696.

[7]   Price Paper and Twine Co. v. Miller, 182 A.D.2d 748, 582 N.Y.S.2d 746 (2d Dep't 1992); Hart Island Committee v. Koch, 137 Misc. 2d 521, 520 N.Y.S.2d 977 (Sup. Ct., New York County 1987), aff'd in part, modified in part, 150 A.D.2d 269, 541 N.Y.S.2d 790 (1st Dep't 1989).

[8]   See the discussion in SPR 43:2. The amendment was applied and even given retroactive effect in Independent Health Ass'n, Inc. v. Murray, 233 A.D.2d 883, 649 N.Y.S.2d 616 (4th Dep't 1996).

Where the doing of the act could not be readily compensated by money damages, to use a frequent example, the legal remedy is not adequate and an injunction may be allowed.[9]

Perhaps the most instructive point about the preliminary injunction is that its granting is discretionary with the court.[10] This is so even though the plaintiff has made out the minimum showing under CPLR 6301.[11] This discretion can be abused, and the appellate division may and does deny injunctions granted below, and vice-versa. But discretion is still the keynote and there is therefore little need for rigidity when resorting to the broad catalog of equitable principles governing injunctions. Under a judicious application of discretion, all manner of factors, whether pointing to or away from the injunction, can be given appropriate weight. Discretion will figure prominently, for example, in calculating the efficacy of an alternative legal remedy: if the alternative is suggested, but there is significant doubt as to how completely it would do the job, discretion can be exercised to allow the injunction so as not to remit the plaintiff to an alternative that could prove impotent. Conversely, discretion can be relied on to deny the injunction if it would be futile, as where it seeks to enjoin an act that has already been done and can't be undone, or where the issue has become academic, as where P wants to enjoin an activity that D has long since clearly discontinued.

Perhaps the highest role discretion plays is in determining whether the plaintiff would be "irreparably" injured if the injunction were withheld. The adverb is often seen in opinions treating injunctions, and yet if it were literally applied, few injunctions would issue. Whether the plaintiff's harm would be "irreparable" turns on many things, all of which can be weighed and balanced by an astute judicial exercise of discretion. If all past cases granting provisional injunctions were collated and analyzed, many if not most would not pass a rigid "irreparable injury" test. The test must be applied common sensically to give appropriate consideration to all factors. With a banner of discretion waving over the field of injunctions, pragmatism is the theme. This tends to prevent any single factor, no matter what its individual dictate might be, from rejecting the injunction out of hand in the face of countervailing considerations. Take this example:

P is the H.J. Heinz Co. It has made a contract with farmer D to get all of the tomatoes grown on D's 25–acre tract. D then threatens to sell the crop to someone else. P sues to enjoin that sale and seeks a preliminary injunction. Should P get it? The literal, to say nothing of the rigid, application of the several traditional requirements applicable to the provisional injunction would preclude its issuance. P has a remedy at law, which is to buy 25 acres of tomatoes somewhere else and sue D for the difference in price. And it would border on the incredible to conclude that the H.J. Heinz Co. could be "irreparably" injured, even if it were to lose the 25 acres of tomatoes altogether. The court nonetheless granted the injunction,[12] and rightly so. It took note that no harm would come to the defendant by granting the injunction because (1) it required him to do only that which he said he was going to do anyway (he admitted the 25–acre contract

---

[9]   See, e.g., Republic Aviation Corp. v. Republic Lodge No. 1987, Intern. Ass'n of Machinists, 10 Misc. 2d 783, 169 N.Y.S.2d 651 (Sup. Ct., Queens County 1957).

[10]   Sartwell v. Field, 68 N.Y. 341, 1877 WL 11865 (1877).

[11]   See Walsh v. New York State Liquor Authority, 45 Misc. 2d 827, 1965 WL 19789 (Sup. Ct., Suffolk County 1965), modified on other grounds 23 A.D.2d 876, 259 N.Y.S.2d 491 (2d Dep't), aff'd 16 N.Y.2d 781, 262 N.Y.S.2d 502, 209 N.E.2d 821.

[12]   H.J. Heinz Co. v. Currie, 83 N.Y.S.2d 705 (Sup. Ct., Niagara County 1948).

and said he was not violating it), and (2) a bond exacted of the plaintiff would indemnify the defendant for any resulting damages.

The plaintiff Heinz Company had an adequate remedy at law and that, considered alone under a rigid construction, would have precluded the injunction. Nor would the company have been irreparably injured, no matter what the defendant did with the 25 acres of tomatoes, and that, considered alone, would also have precluded the injunction. But these factors were not considered alone. They were part of a whole picture in which the competition of other factors, less generic in the texts and more individual to the case, prompted discretion to allow the injunction. The lesson is not that the inadequacy-of-legal-remedy and irreparable-injury factors are to be ignored; it is that both must be balanced in context. Everything is relative, even in the law of preliminary injunctions.

The courts generally prefer to couch preliminary injunctions in negative terms, especially if there is any chance that by giving P a mandatory preliminary injunction, P will get everything she wants in advance and thus lose incentive to prosecute the claim on the merits. Where, for example, P was suing to be restored to membership in an association, the Court of Appeals said that the preliminary injunction could adequately maintain the status quo by enjoining D from denying P the benefits of membership (negative injunction), but that it should not go so far as to require full reinstatement (mandatory injunction) because that might prompt P, having gotten all he wants on the preliminary injunction, to let the action lapse.[13]

There is no absolute bar to mandatory relief in a preliminary injunction if the facts warrant it, however.[14] In fact, in many instances, the line between a mandatory and negative injunction is semantic, and whenever that is so the distinction will likely be academic. What difference is there between requiring the defendant to sell his tomato crop to the plaintiff exclusively (mandatory injunction) and enjoining him from selling it to anyone but the plaintiff (negative injunction), as long as the defendant is bent on sale?

Since a preliminary injunction seeks only to retain status quo until the merits can be duly tried and adjudicated, neither its granting nor its refusal binds the trial court when the main trial comes on. There, the issues will be tried as if no preliminary injunction was ever sought.[15] The granting of a preliminary injunction, in other words, does not invoke the doctrine of law of the case.[16]

§ 329. Applying for the Injunction

The procedure for getting a preliminary injunction is a motion, which must be made on notice.[1] If the case involves urgency, a faster return date and an interim restraint can be secured with a temporary restraining order in an order to show cause, the subject of the next section. The notice of motion for the preliminary injunction may be served with or after the summons or at any time before final judgment.[2] A preliminary injunction is available only in a pending action or proceeding.

---

[13]   Bachman v. Harrington, 184 N.Y. 458, 77 N.E. 657 (1906).

[14]   See, e.g., Graham v. Board of Sup'rs, Erie County, 49 Misc. 2d 459, 267 N.Y.S.2d 383 (Sup. Ct., Erie County 1966), modified, 25 A.D.2d 250, 269 N.Y.S.2d 477 (4th Dep't).

[15]   Walker Memorial Baptist Church v. Saunders, 285 N.Y. 462, 35 N.E.2d 42 (1941).

[16]   Law of the case is a doctrine of intra-action res judicata. See § 448.

[1]   CPLR 6311(1).

[2]   CPLR 6311(1).

The proof on the motion consists of affidavits and any other evidence the plaintiff possesses. It must show satisfaction of either of the two grounds stated in CPLR 6301.[3] Bearing in mind the discretionary nature of the remedy, the fact that the plaintiff has the burden of proof, and the many equitable considerations discussed in the prior section, such as a showing of irreparable injury, the proof should be clear and convincing.

It should not be necessary to submit the complaint as part of the moving papers because the requisite facts, including those that show a cause of action, can be proved by affidavit.[4] Nonetheless, it is always advisable to include the complaint and when the application for the preliminary injunction is based on the nature of the action, i.e., where the action seeks a final judgment of injunction under the second part of CPLR 6301, it is required.[5] If the complaint fails to make out a claim satisfactory to CPLR 6301, it will result in a denial of the injunction.[6] If a verified complaint is submitted, it can be treated as an affidavit.[7]

Before getting a preliminary injunction, the plaintiff will have to submit an undertaking (bond)—this is mandatory—in an amount to be fixed by the court, conditioned that "if it is finally determined that he was not entitled to an injunction," the plaintiff will pay the defendant "all damages and costs which may be sustained by reason of the injunction."[8]

CPLR 6315 provides that the court may ascertain these damages by motion brought on by order to show cause. This is designed to facilitate things by enabling D, with a mere motion procedure, to have the amount of her damages ascertained within the framework of P's action before bringing a separate action on the undertaking to recover judgment for those damages.[9] This procedure is optional; the damages can be ascertained in the separate action.[10] It has also been held that if the damages are ascertained by motion in P's action, a judgment for them can be awarded without even requiring a separate action.[11]

Assuming that the condition of the bond has been met—and it can be met by so simple a development as D's winning the case on the merits[12]—what are the damages that may be recovered on the bond? Expenses, including attorney's fees, may be recovered, but ordinarily only for proceedings to vacate the preliminary injunction and for proceedings to assess D's damages. D is not entitled to recover an attorney's fee for the trial of P's action on the merits if it is shown, as it often can, that the trial would

---

3   See CPLR 6312(a); see § 327.

4   Somerset R. R. Corp. v. Graham, 89 A.D.2d 819, 453 N.Y.S.2d 527 (4th Dep't 1982).

5   See, e.g., Seplow v. Century Operating Co., 56 A.D.2d 515, 391 N.Y.S.2d 124 (1st Dep't 1977).

6   Rodgers v. Rodgers, 30 A.D.2d 548, 290 N.Y.S.2d 608 (2d Dep't 1968).

7   CPLR 105(u); see §§ 232, 246.

8   CPLR 6312(b). Special added conditions are imposed by paragraphs 1 and 2 of the statute for undertakings given for injunctions to stop a party from prosecuting other actions. If P wants to enjoin D's enforcement of a money judgment that D has against P, paragraph 3 of CPLR 6312(b) requires that P's undertaking be to the effect that it will make good the judgment.

9   Gross v. Shields, 130 Misc. 2d 641, 496 N.Y.S.2d 894 (Sup. Ct., New York County 1985).

10   See 4th Rep. Leg. Doc. No. 20, p. 233 (1960).

11   See, e.g., Carroll v. Kenin, 25 A.D.2d 743, 269 N.Y.S.2d 226 (1st Dep't 1966).

12   Dismissal of P's complaint carries with it an implicit finding that the injunction was unwarranted and supports a damages claim on the bond. Sweets' Estate v. Behrens, 118 Misc. 2d 1062, 462 N.Y.S.2d 398 (Sup. Ct., Schenectady County 1983).

have gone forward whether P had obtained a preliminary injunction or not.[13] By implication, the same should be true of pretrial activities in general, notably disclosure proceedings. Attorney's fees for them should be recoverable only if incurred as a result of the injunction.[14]

As long as the condition of the undertaking has been satisfied, damages are recoverable even if it is shown that P did not act in bad faith.[15] But the damages are ordinarily limited to the amount of the undertaking.[16] It has been held that there is no common law liability for an improperly issued injunction and that CPLR 6315 does not create a statutory cause of action so that the undertaking is the very basis for the damages claim.[17]

The effect on the bond of an interim appellate determination of the propriety of the injunction has been addressed by the Court of Appeals. The Court held that an interim determination that the injunction is proper does not entitle P to a discharge of the bond; that things can still go against P on the merits, which would entitle D to look to the bond despite the earlier indications that sustained the injunction.[18] But in the converse situation, in which the interim appellate determination is that the preliminary injunction is not proper, D has an immediate right to damages on the bond; the bond covers damages for wrongful *preliminary* injunction no matter how things may later turn out on the merits.[19]

The difference between the bond required for a preliminary injunction under Article 63 and the bond required for an attachment under Article 62 is highlighted in A & M Exports, Ltd. v. Meridien Intern. Bank, Ltd.[20] When the condition of the bond is invoked, the applicable statute on an Article 63 bond is CPLR 6315, requiring that the court ascertain the defendant's damages (it can't just award as damages the face amount of the bond) and that the amount of the bond constitutes the outer limit on any permissible award made. Under Article 62, on the other hand, the bond defines the surety's liability, but the plaintiff can be subjected to damages in excess of the bond's amount.

The *Meridien* case holds that even the limited temporary restraining order authorized in conjunction with an attachment under CPLR 6210 is to be considered an Article 63 injunction for the purpose of ascertaining damages, making the governing provision CPLR 6315.

---

[13] See Cross Properties, Inc. v. Brook Realty Co., Inc., 76 A.D.2d 445, 430 N.Y.S.2d 820 (2d Dep't 1980).

[14] See *Carroll*, 25 A.D.2d at 743, 269 N.Y.S.2d at 227. For a general discussion of the damages the defendant is entitled to if he prevails on the merits, including attorney's fees for defending, see Bausch & Lomb Inc. v. Hydron Pacific, Ltd., 82 Misc. 2d 576, 371 N.Y.S.2d 292 (Sup. Ct., Monroe County 1975).

[15] *Sweets' Estate*, 118 Misc. 2d at 1064, 462 N.Y.S.2d at 400.

[16] Doran & Associates, Inc. v. Envirogas, Inc., 112 A.D.2d 766, 492 N.Y.S.2d 504 (4th Dep't 1985).

[17] Honeywell, Inc. v. Technical Bldg. Services, Inc., 103 A.D.2d 433, 480 N.Y.S.2d 627 (3d Dep't 1984).

[18] J.A. Preston Corp. v. Fabrication Enterprises, Inc., 68 N.Y.2d 397, 509 N.Y.S.2d 520, 502 N.E.2d 197 (1986).

[19] Margolies v. Encounter, Inc., 42 N.Y.2d 475, 398 N.Y.S.2d 877, 368 N.E.2d 1243 (1977). On that basis, the *J.A. Preston* decision distinguishes *Margolies*. *J.A. Preston Corp.*, 68 N.Y.2d at 407–08, 509 N.Y.S.2d at 525–26, 502 N.E.2d at 202–03.

[20] A & M Exports, Ltd. v. Meridien Intern. Bank, Ltd., 222 A.D.2d 378, 636 N.Y.S.2d 35 (1st Dep't 1995).

Counsel fees are includible in the damages sustained by reason of a preliminary injuction or temporary restraining order once it is determined that injunctive relief should not have issued.[21]

Since the application for the injunction is a motion, it requires the payment of a fee, the logistics of which are discussed in the chapter on motion practice.[22]

§ 330. Temporary Restraining Order

A preliminary injunction, the official name for the device under Article 63 of the CPLR that we have been discussing, goes by other popular names. It may variously be referred to as a "temporary" injunction, or an injunction "pendente lite," or even as an "interlocutory" injunction. Whatever the alias, the device is used to enjoin the defendant from doing something while the action is pending and must be distinguished from the "temporary restraining order," whose mission is shorter lived, but more urgent. Since a motion for a preliminary injunction may be made only on notice under CPLR 6311, there is a risk that between the time the motion papers are served and the day set for the hearing, the return day, the defendant will consummate the act the plaintiff wants restrained and make all further proceedings futile. The sole mission of the temporary restraining order (TRO) is to effect a restraint against the defendant during that brief interim and keep the status quo until the judge can hear both sides.

CPLR 6301 allows the TRO only if the plaintiff shows that "immediate and irreparable injury, loss or damage will result unless the defendant is restrained before the hearing [on the preliminary injunction] can be had."[1] A plaintiff who wants a TRO does not use the ordinary motion on notice procedure to bring on the application for a preliminary injunction, but rather an order to show cause, and it's the order to show cause that includes the TRO. CPLR 6313(a), the TRO statute, requires that the time for the preliminary injunction be set by the court, and by so doing makes it clear that the show cause procedure is to be used.[2]

The plaintiff who wants a TRO frequently applies for it ex parte by presenting an order to show cause to the court. Since an order to show cause is, in this instance, a species of ex parte application, the plaintiff must inform the court in an affidavit whether this or like relief was previously applied for and what the result was of any such prior application, and must establish the requirements in Uniform Rule 202.7(f), discussed below.[3] If the judge signs the order to show cause, the judge will determine in the order itself (1) the time and place of the hearing for the preliminary injunction, (2) who shall be served with the order, (3) how and when the service shall be made, and (4) the terms of the TRO.[4] After signing by the judge, the order to show cause is returned to the plaintiff's attorney, who then effects service of it on the defendant pursuant to its terms.

---

[21] Citizens for St. Patrick's v. City of Watervliet Zoning Board of Appeals, 130 A.D.3d 1338, 15 N.Y.S.3d 492 (3d Dep't 2015).

[22] See § 243.

[1] See also CPLR 6313(a).

[2] Setting a return time different from the one required by the motion on notice statute, CPLR 2214(b), is one of the functions of an order to show cause.

[3] CPLR 2217(b); see § 244.

[4] See § 248.

Several rules apply here. If the court grants a TRO, it must set the hearing for the preliminary injunction for "the earliest possible time,"[5] which merely recognizes that an ex parte restraint against a defendant should be as brief as possible.[6] If an order to show cause containing a TRO does not contain directions as to the method of service, then service is to be made in the same manner as a summons.[7] The papers served must include the papers on which the TRO is based.[8]

If the summons has not yet been served, the summons should accompany the order to show cause and be served on the defendant at the same time. Since the order to show cause serves as the notice of application for the preliminary injunction, this procedure will satisfy the requirement of CPLR 6311(1) that notice of the application be served with or after the summons.

The usual practice is for the plaintiff to file the summons and complaint when applying for the TRO so that an action will immediately be pending and give its context to the application. It will also enable the plaintiff to secure an index number and include it on the summons and complaint, as well as on the order to show cause. The plaintiff will also need to obtain an RJI so that a judge is assigned to hear the motion.[9]

The courts should recognize, however, that the TRO is an emergency device, and if the emergency is such that the filing of the initiatory papers and securing of an index number in advance of the presentation of the order to show cause is not practicable, it should be permissible to obtain the index number later. That procedure is authorized by CPLR 304(a), which provides that "[w]here a court finds that circumstances prevent immediate filing [of the initiatory papers], the signing of an order requiring the subsequent filing at a specific time and date not later than five days thereafter shall commence the action." That procedure will provide sufficient context within which to entertain the order to show cause and TRO application.[10]

An undertaking, mandatory if a preliminary injunction is granted, is merely discretionary with the court when it grants a TRO.[11] This acknowledges that time may be so tight and the situation so urgent that opportunity may not exist even to secure an undertaking. If the court does require an undertaking, its terms are the same as the one required for the preliminary injunction.[12] If there appears to be any difficulty about getting the parties into court for a hearing, so that it looks as if the "earliest possible time" required for the hearing by CPLR 6313(a) is not going to be so early after all, the court should recognize that while it may be granting a TRO in form, it is granting a preliminary injunction in effect, and should therefore require an undertaking.[13]

Whatever showing of urgency is needed to sustain a preliminary injunction, presumably that much more is needed to justify a TRO. That's the conclusion one would

---

[5]   CPLR 6313(a).

[6]   No TRO may issue under CPLR 6313 in a labor dispute, in which injunctions are governed by Lab. Law § 807.

[7]   CPLR 6313(b).

[8]   CPLR 6313(b).

[9]   22 N.Y.C.R.R. § 202.6(a); see § 77B.

[10]   The emergency TRO, and its interplay with CPLR 304(a), is discussed in further detail in the McKinney's Practice Commentaries to CPLR 2212, C2212:8 ("Venue of Ex Parte Supreme Court Motion").

[11]   CPLR 6313(c).

[12]   These terms come from CPLR 6312(b), discussed in § 329.

[13]   Honeywell, Inc. v. Technical Bldg. Services, Inc., 103 A.D.2d 433, 480 N.Y.S.2d 627 (3d Dep't 1984).

ordinarily draw from a reading of CPLR 6301 and 6313(a), both of which reserve for the TRO the most demanding standard articulated by the injunction article—more demanding, in any event, than the requirements verbalized for the preliminary injunction itself. A little logic applied to the situation, however, can lead one to reverse these roles and require less for a TRO than for a preliminary injunction. The preliminary injunction, after all, will cover the whole period of litigation, which can be a long one, while the TRO will live for only the few days, and sometimes only the few hours, needed to bring on a hearing for the preliminary injunction. Since the preliminary injunction can ensue only after an adversary hearing, the court can weigh, in at least some leisure, the opposing views of the parties. Therefore, assuming that a TRO has issued in advance of the hearing on the preliminary injunction, the air of emergency in determining whether to issue a preliminary injunction is not as tense as that surrounding the prior TRO application. On the TRO, by contrast, the court has before it an excited if not frantic applicant pleading for an instant enjoinment lest the defendant do something even before a hearing can be had. Greater though the stated requirement may be for the issuance of a TRO than for a preliminary injunction, these realities often mean that, in practice, a judge may be more disposed to issue a TRO than a preliminary injunction.

It has up to now been assumed that the TRO can be granted ex parte without offering the defendant a hearing, the defendant to have that right only when the court hears the preliminary injunction application that the order to show cause brings on. But there are different conclusions to be reached about that under a rule adopted by the Office of Court Administration in 2006. The rule much increases the prospect that the defendant will indeed be heard on the TRO application itself. This has an interesting history, germane indeed to TRO practice today.

The requirement of CPLR 6313 that a plaintiff seeking a temporary restraining order show the threat of "immediate and irreparable injury" would always have seemed to require the showing of a threat so imminent that the judge is able to conclude that there really isn't time to allow D a hearing on the TRO. Over the years, however, many New York judges have been lax about this, too ready to accept P's statement without any input from D and routinely signing orders to show cause containing TROs. Anecdotal experience, as reported to the Advisory Committee on Civil Practice by a number of lawyers, notably lawyers in federal practice, showed that in many such cases giving notice to D would pose no significant risk of D's doing the act sought to be enjoined (so as to make any further injunction attempts futile). Convinced of this, the Office of Court Administration based its 2006 rule, Uniform Rule 202.7(f), on the federal practice. It took effect Oct. 1, 2006.

Requiring notice to D of a TRO application, except in cases of clear exigency, had become a common practice among federal judges. The New York legislature was asked annually for over 30 years to prescribe the same practice for the New York courts, too, but showed no interest. In the face of this lethargy, the Office of Court Administration picked up the initiative and adopted Uniform Rule 202.7(f), which provides among other things that an application for an order to show cause containing a TRO shall itself contain

> an affirmation demonstrating there will be significant prejudice to the [seeking] party . . . by the giving of notice. In the absence of [that] showing . . . the affirmation must demonstrate that a good faith effort has been made to notify the party against whom the temporary restraining order is sought of the

time, date and place, that the application will be made in a manner sufficient to permit the party an opportunity to appear in response to the application.

P's plea of immediate injury, in other words, often accepted pro forma on these applications in the past, now has to be accompanied by a cogent showing of what that prejudice would consist of if the TRO is made to go through a notice process. To establish the "significant prejudice" required for this private audience with the judge, the applicant should be sure to present affidavits from those with personal knowledge of the facts. That will usually require an affidavit from the client. Sanctions have been imposed against a party who secured a TRO in violation of the rule.[14]

Rule 202.7(f) excepts summary proceedings—the landlord/tenant disputes—in which orders to show cause to stay evictions have evolved a life of their own.

Part 202 of the Uniform Rules, which applies only in supreme and county courts, doesn't apply in the lower courts, including the New York City Civil Court and the state's district, city, town, and village courts. This is apparently no accident: those courts have little equity jurisdiction and hence little occasion to entertain preliminary injunctions.

As one of the introductory sections of this chapter stressed, the provisional remedies, because of their ex parte nature, are under constitutional scrutiny and some have been severely circumscribed. The preliminary injunction appears to be on safe ground because it requires notice of motion and thus offers the defendant a hearing in advance. Under Uniform Rule 202.7(f), the defendant may even be granted a hearing on the TRO, but even if that's refused in a given case, the TRO practice may be secure because: (1) it's in the court's control; (2) it requires the court to set an "earliest possible time" hearing for the preliminary injunction;[15] and (3) the TRO may be granted only if the plaintiff shows that irreparable injury will result if any delay at all is allowed. This trio suggests, in the aggregate, that the TRO in New York rests on a sturdy constitutional foundation.[16]

Statute prohibits the issuance of a temporary restraining order "against a public officer, board or municipal corporation of the state to restrain the performance of statutory duties,"[17] a provision sometimes circumvented by theorizing that it does not apply if the plaintiff can make it appear—and the plaintiff is usually hell bent to make it appear—that the body is acting unlawfully and hence not within its "statutory duties."[18] In any event, this is a restriction only on the TRO, not on the preliminary injunction. If the restriction applies, an order to show cause, although it can't in this instance include a TRO, may still be used to expedite a hearing on the preliminary injunction, which will reduce to a bare minimum the period in which the public officer

---

[14] Dixon v. Roy, 21 Misc. 3d 1117(A), 2008 WL 4635548, at *3 (Sup. Ct., Kings County 2008).

[15] CPLR 6313(a).

[16] See the discussion of the constitutional requirements in § 307. In free speech cases, the U.S. Supreme Court has forbidden a TRO unless it is shown that there is no possibility whatever of giving reasonable notice. See Carroll v. President and Com'rs of Princess Anne, 393 U.S. 175, 89 S. Ct. 347, 21 L. Ed. 2d 325 (1968). New York afterwards adopted CPLR 6330, a statute on obscenity, which acknowledges the policy against prior restraints in such cases by supplying special preferences for their trial.

[17] CPLR 6313(a).

[18] See, e.g., Komyathy v. Board of Ed. of Wappinger Central School Dist. No. 1, 75 Misc. 2d 859, 348 N.Y.S.2d 28 (Sup. Ct., Dutchess County 1973).

or body is unrestrained.[19] This can have a positive ecological impact by helping to control a potential infestation of unrestrained public officers.

Since the order to show cause is a species of motion, it requires the payment of a fee, the logistics of which are discussed in the chapter on motion practice.[20]

We can sum up this section by pointing up the neat trio of protections that Article 63 offers plaintiffs with the right stuff. Assuming the plaintiff prevails at all stages,

1. the TRO puts the defendant under a restraint while a motion for a preliminary injunction is brought on;

2. the preliminary injunction takes over from the TRO and continues the restraint during the entire pendency of the action until final judgment; and

3. the judgment of permanent injunction takes over at that point, covering the future and closing the case.

Telephone Service, Available 24/7, for Facilitating TROs

The movant facing urgent circumstances,[21] such as an assigned judge who is for some reason unavailable, or who will not be available in time to meet the needs of the particular application, should check into any local procedures that may be applicable to authorize a judge other than the assigned one to entertain ex parte applications. On this front, the Office of Court Administration issued a directive to the supreme court's administrative judges in 2008 entitled "Protocol for Emergency Applications." It is "designed to facilitate applications for [temporary restraining orders] during the evening and on weekends and holidays when the courthouse is closed." While aimed chiefly at the temporary restraining order, the protocol covers all "emergency civil applications" and invites a phone call to a central toll free number (800-430-8457) or an email to emergency@nycourts.gov, which works for the supreme court throughout the state. The number puts the caller through to administrative staff, who are instructed to take the caller's number and refer the matter to the appropriate administrative judge, who then determines if there's a "real need" to hear the case outside regular court hours. If so, the administrative judge sets up the needed procedure and provides that information to the applicant.[22] The Protocol supplements the procedures available for making motions under the CPLR and Uniform Rules rather than replacing them.

§ 331. Vacating or Modifying Injunction or TRO

The defendant may move at any time to vacate or modify the preliminary injunction or temporary restraining order. Since the preliminary injunction is granted only on notice, the motion to vacate it must also be made on notice.[1] Conversely, if the TRO was

---

[19]　CPLR 6311 also has some special requirements for preliminary injunctions against public officers and bodies, restricting the venue of motions seeking such injunctions, CPLR 6311(1), and requiring that notice of the motion be served on the attorney general as well as on the particular defendants, CPLR 6311(2).

[20]　See §§ 243, 248.

[21]　See 22 N.Y.C.R.R. § 202.7(e).

[22]　See SPR 208:4; Commentary C2212:8A to McKinney's CPLR 2212; George Bundy Smith and Thomas J. Hall, *TRO Applications When the Courthouse Is Closed,* N.Y.L.J., Oct. 30, 2008, at 3. Some federal courts have a similar rule in place, such as Rule 3 of the Southern District's Rules for the Division of Business Among District Judges.

[1]　CPLR 6314.

granted without notice, the motion to vacate or modify it may be made without notice, but only if made to the judge who granted it.[2] Only in the absence or disability of the granting judge may it be made without notice to another one. CPLR 6314 does not distinguish between TRO's granted on notice or without notice. The presumption in CPLR 6314 appears to be that the TRO was granted without notice. In those rare instances in which a party seeks to vacate a TRO granted on notice, the motion should be made on notice to the judge who granted it.

The party seeking to vacate or modify an ex parte order has yet another alternative: to move, ex parte, to have the appellate court or one of its judges vacate or modify the order. CPLR 5704(a) expressly authorizes this procedure and even authorizes a movant whose ex parte motion below has been denied to seek its grant from the appellate court.[3] CPLR 5704 contemplates a simple, ex parte motion procedure before the appellate court, not a full-blown appeal procedure with its attendant time, trouble, and expense.[4]

An ex parte order vacating or modifying a TRO, and the papers underlying the order, must be filed with the clerk and served on the plaintiff. The order is not effective unless they are. An order vacating or modifying either an injunction or TRO can be conditioned on the defendant's furnishing an undertaking, in an amount fixed by the court, that the defendant will reimburse the plaintiff for any loss occasioned by the order of vacatur or modification.[5]

The violation of either a preliminary injunction or a temporary restraining order is of course a contempt of court and may be punished as such. The procedure for the contempt punishment (which is also the enforcement device for several classes of final judgment), including distinctions between criminal and civil contempt and their applicable sanctions, is treated in the chapter on the enforcement of judgments.[6]

E. RECEIVERSHIP

Table of Sections

§ 332.   Temporary Receivership
§ 333.   Applying for the Receivership

§ 332. Temporary Receivership

Article 64 of the CPLR supplies the provisional remedy of receivership. The Article 64 receiver is a person appointed by the court to take control of designated property and see to its care and preservation during litigation. This is only a temporary receivership, functioning to preserve the property during the litigation,[1] and should therefore be distinguished from a permanent receiver, such as one appointed in conjunction with the

---

[2]   CPLR 6314.

[3]   The appellate division has these ex parte powers only in respect of the lower courts of which it has appellate jurisdiction. CPLR 5704(a). In the First and Second departments, the appellate term and its justices have like powers for their lower courts, which include the New York City Civil Court, the district courts, etc. CPLR 5704(b).

[4]   See § 244.

[5]   CPLR 6314. If the defendant is a public body or officer, it may not be subjected to this condition, an exception which to some extent overlaps the more general one in CPLR 2512.

[6]   See §§ 481 et seq.

[1]   Decker v. Gardner, 124 N.Y. 334, 26 N.E. 814 (1891).

dissolution of a corporation.[2] It should also be distinguished from two other CPLR receivers, those of CPLR 5106 and 5228.

The Article 64 receiver takes control of property during the action. If the plaintiff wins on the merits, a CPLR 5106 receiver may then be appointed to dispose of the property under the judgment. The CPLR 5106 receiver can be considered the post-judgment counterpart of the Article 64 receiver. The same person appointed under Article 64 can later be appointed under CPLR 5106, but the two provisions are independent and the use of one does not require the use of the other.

The CPLR 5228 receiver is one appointed to help enforce a money judgment. Our concentration here will be on only the temporary, or "provisional," receiver of Article 64.

This category of receivership may be sought only in an action having some specific and identifiable "property" as the "subject of the action."[3] The plaintiff must be asserting some right in that specific property, for which reason this kind of receivership is not available in an action for money only.[4] It has been held available, however, if it seeks the money proceeds of specific assets in the context of a fiduciary relationship. It is therefore available in an accounting action in equity, for example,[5] even though money is the ultimate object of the plaintiff's quest in an accounting action.

The temporary receiver is historically an aspect of equity practice. Hence, it is more often than not an equity action that qualifies for one.

Receivership is one of the rarer of the provisional remedies. Probably its best known context is the action to foreclose a mortgage on a rental or other income-producing property where a receiver may be appointed to collect the rents and profits and in effect manage the property while the foreclosure steps proceed.

The reason for the relative infrequency of this provisional remedy is that a showing that the action involves specific property is not enough. The plaintiff must also demonstrate that "there is danger that the property will be removed from the state, or lost, materially injured or destroyed."[6] This showing is indispensable, and many actions having specific property as their subject fail to satisfy it. Receivership, in common with the other provisional remedies, is considered a drastic remedy and ordinarily lies in the discretion of the court. This discretion will be exercised to deny the receivership unless the court deems it necessary to preserve the property until the action makes clear who has the right to it.[7]

The powers of a temporary receiver, which are more circumscribed than those of a permanent one, are set forth in CPLR 6401(b). The receiver is authorized to take and hold personal or real property and to sue for, collect, and sell debts or claims "upon such conditions and for such purposes as the court shall direct." The lesson is that the receiver

---

[2] See Bus. Corp. Law Art. 12; Application of Sheridan Const. Corp., 22 A.D.2d 390, 256 N.Y.S.2d 210 (4th Dep't 1965), aff'd, 16 N.Y.2d 680, 261 N.Y.S.2d 300, 209 N.E.2d 290.

[3] CPLR 6401(a). The Article 64 receivership is available in the supreme court or a county court under the terms of CPLR 6401(a), but may also be used in certain actions in the New York City Civil Court under § 209(c) of its court act (McKinney's Vol. 29A, Part 3).

[4] See Mack v. Stanley, 74 A.D. 145, 77 N.Y.S. 574 (1st Dep't 1902), in which P's action for fraud, a mere money claim, was held to preclude a receivership regardless of the nature of the underlying transaction.

[5] See Meurer v. Meurer, 21 A.D.2d 778, 250 N.Y.S.2d 817 (1st Dep't 1964).

[6] CPLR 6401(a).

[7] See E.H.A. Successor Corp. v. Vogel, 21 A.D.2d 176, 249 N.Y.S.2d 568 (1st Dep't 1964).

should see to it that whatever he does has basis in the appointing order or some subsequent one. No sale of any asset received, for example, should be made without court authorization, else the receiver may end up paying for it out of pocket, i.e., being surcharged.[8] Nor can the receiver retain counsel without explicit court approval,[9] and the approval should be obtained in advance of the retainer. There is some authority, however, for the court to ratify an appointment of counsel previously retained "under exigent circumstances."[10]

Any person capable of performing a receiver's duties can be appointed as one. Ideally, the appointee should be a disinterested person,[11] but a party is sometimes appointed.[12]

Occasionally, the appointee turns out to be disinterested in everything but his fee, and the receivership has been known to be a patronage plum. A receiver's compensation is on a commission basis, set by the court that appoints him. The commission can't exceed 5% of sums received and disbursed, but a fee of up to $100 may be allowed if the 5% computation comes to less.[13]

Upon appointment, receivers are required to take an oath[14] and give an undertaking to perform their duties faithfully. The amount is fixed by the appointing court.[15] They are also required by statute to keep accurate accounts[16] and, as officers of the court, they may be removed by the court at any time on the motion of a party or sua sponte.[17]

§ 333. Applying for the Receivership

A temporary receiver is appointed on motion, which may be made by any person having "an apparent interest" in the property to be received. The primary supporting papers are, as usual, affidavits making out a cause of action that has specific "property" as its subject matter and setting forth facts showing the danger that the property will be removed from New York or otherwise lost, injured, or destroyed, i.e., that the case comes within the requirements of CPLR 6401(a). Usually, the motion is made by the plaintiff who has brought an action, but it can be made in a pending action even by one not a party to it, as where the nonparty movant has an interest in the property involved in the action and fears that it will be removed or destroyed if left in a party's hands. Such a motion by a nonparty makes her a party, i.e., constitutes an appearance in the action.[1] There is also provision for extending the receivership to another action involving the

---

[8] A good illustration of how the court determines and supervises the receiver's powers is Security Nat. Bank v. Village Mall at Hillcrest, Inc., 79 Misc. 2d 1060, 361 N.Y.S.2d 977 (Sup. Ct., Queens County 1974).

[9] CPLR 6401(b).

[10] See Emigrant Sav. Bank v. Elan Management Corp., 114 Misc. 2d 472, 453 N.Y.S.2d 977 (Sup. Ct., Queens County 1982).

[11] Hahn v. Wylie, 54 A.D.2d 622, 387 N.Y.S.2d 255 (1st Dep't 1976).

[12] See, e.g., Broder v. Broudarge, 38 N.Y.S.2d 282 (Sup. Ct., Kings County 1942).

[13] CPLR 8004(a). The party who moved for the appointment may be required to pay the fees of the receiver and her lawyer (assuming a lawyer has been allowed) if there are no funds in the hands of the receiver out of which fees can be paid. CPLR 8004(b).

[14] CPLR 6402.

[15] CPLR 6403.

[16] CPLR 6404.

[17] CPLR 6405.

[1] CPLR 6401(a).

same property,[2] which would then require the receiver to account to the parties in both actions.

The motion for the appointment of a receiver is made on notice, but an ex parte appointment is permissible if a contract between the parties calls for it. Mortgages often contain stipulations for ex parte receiverships in the event of foreclosure, statute expressly approves of it,[3] and the constitutionality of such no-notice appointments has, at least for the time being, been upheld.[4]

The appointment may be made before or after the service of the summons.[5]

The court can permit the receivership to extend beyond judgment[6] where it would serve primarily to preserve the property during an appeal.[7] If it is sought to continue the receivership beyond judgment to aid in enforcing the judgment, the more appropriate authorizing provision would be CPLR 5106, under which, as already noted, the 6401 receiver can be continued for the enforcement purpose.

As an officer of the court, a receiver should not be sued except by leave of court, but the absence of prior leave is not a jurisdictional defect and can be cured with a nunc pro tunc order. An action brought in violation of this requirement may thereby be preserved.[8]

F. NOTICE OF PENDENCY

Table of Sections

§ 334.   Notice of Pendency, Generally
§ 335.   Procedure for Filing
§ 336.   Cancellation of Notice

§ 334. Notice of Pendency, Generally

A notice of pendency (or "lis pendens" as it is commonly called) is a paper that may be used in a real property action. The plaintiff files it with the county clerk of the real property county, putting the world on notice of the plaintiff's potential rights in the action and thereby warning all comers that if they then buy the property or lend on the strength of it or otherwise rely on the defendant's right, they do so subject to whatever the action may establish to be the plaintiff's right. The device takes advantage of the immobility of realty and the ease with which the mere filing of a paper can affect interests in it. Where mortgagee E had a lis pendens on file, for example, E prevailed

---

[2]   CPLR 6401(b).

[3]   Real Prop. Law § 254(10).

[4]   Security Nat. Bank v. Village Mall at Hillcrest, Inc., 79 Misc. 2d 1060, 361 N.Y.S.2d 977 (Sup. Ct., Queens County 1974). The constitutionality of the receivership provisions, especially when invoked ex parte, was under review for a while. See the Judicial Conference's Report to the 1977 Legislature, p. 80, and Professor Donnelly's study of the temporary receivership in 21st Jud. Conf. Rep. 483 (1976).

[5]   CPLR 6401(a).

[6]   CPLR 6401(c).

[7]   The appointment for appeal purposes is expressly authorized by CPLR 6401(a), and in this regard subdivisions (a) and (c) of CPLR 6401 overlap.

[8]   Copeland v. Salomon, 56 N.Y.2d 222, 451 N.Y.S.2d 682, 436 N.E.2d 1284 (1982).

over B even though B bought the land from mortgagor R only after being shown a satisfaction-piece signed by E. The lis pendens still stood of record at the title closing.[1]

It has been held that if the person who files the lis pendens knows of another person's prior interest, the prior interest will prevail even though it is unrecorded.[2]

CPLR 6501 allows the lis pendens to be used only in an action that can "affect the title to, or the possession, use or enjoyment of, real property."[3] The well known real property actions, such as mortgage foreclosure, specific performance, partition, etc., easily fall within the category, but despite the seemingly generous language of the statute (including the phrase "use or enjoyment"), it has been held that the lis pendens can't be used where the plaintiff claims no "right, title, or interest" in the property itself. It was therefore held unavailable in an action in which P sought to prevent D from using D's land in such a way as to create a nuisance. Although P sought an injunction, his grievance was found to be in essence just a tort claim.[4] This is perhaps unduly severe since it would be useful to a potential buyer to have notice that use of the property may be restricted—the use the buyer sees D making of the land and which the buyer may wish to make himself.

There was a dispute for a while about whether a lis pendens could be used in a summary (landlord/tenant) proceeding.[5] An amendment of CPLR 6501 explicitly bars the lis pendens from those proceedings.

The Court of Appeals has said that a lis pendens cannot be used if the real property is owned by a corporation or partnership and the plaintiff's contractual right is not to buy the land directly, but only to buy shares in the entity that owns the property. It so held in 1984 in 5303 Realty Corp. v. O & Y Equity Corp.,[6] a case that may impair some of the purpose of a lis pendens, which is to protect a plaintiff in real property transactions. The defendant/owner, unencumbered by the deterrent that the lis pendens would be to a buyer, can sell unimpeded to one who might not go near the transaction if made aware of—and were subject to—the plaintiff's claim. The Court said in the *5303* case that the plaintiff can fall back on an attachment or an injunction for protection, but this overlooks that if a conveyance is what a plaintiff wants, an attachment will not do because it is available only in a money action,[7] and an injunction, while a better prospect, depends on the defendant's fear of contempt proceedings and does not put other potential buyers on notice.

Mere money actions of course do not qualify for a lis pendens. Nor may a lis pendens be used if the plaintiff merely *could* state a real property claim, as where he might assert a lien against the premises for goods affixed to them or services rendered or money spent on them. If the complaint asserts in essence only a money claim, the plaintiff forfeits the use of the lis pendens.[8]

---

[1] Goldstein v. Gold, 106 A.D.2d 100, 483 N.Y.S.2d 375 (2d Dep't 1984), aff'd, 66 N.Y.2d 624, 495 N.Y.S.2d 32, 485 N.E.2d 239 (1985). E was seeking to have the satisfaction-piece canceled based on fraud.

[2] Gerenstein v. Williams, 282 A.D.2d 813, 723 N.Y.S.2d 257 (3d Dep't 2001).

[3] CPLR 6501.

[4] Braunston v. Anchorage Woods, Inc., 10 N.Y.2d 302, 222 N.Y.S.2d 316, 178 N.E.2d 717 (1961).

[5] See Nadeau v. Tuley, 160 A.D.2d 1130, 553 N.Y.S.2d 912 (3d Dep't 1990).

[6] 5303 Realty Corp. v. O & Y Equity Corp., 64 N.Y.2d 313, 486 N.Y.S.2d 877, 476 N.E.2d 276 (1984).

[7] CPLR 6201. See § 314.

[8] Gokey v. Massey, 278 A.D. 630, 102 N.Y.S.2d 581 (4th Dep't 1951).

The real property action can be pending in a New York court or in a federal court in New York. The lis pendens can be used in connection with either.[9]

The lis pendens must state the names of the parties to the action, state the object of the action, and describe the real property affected. The plaintiff should be as explicit as possible, but as long as the lis pendens contains such data as will at least put potential buyers and encumbrancers on inquiry, they can't claim to be misled and the lis pendens suffices.[10]

The lis pendens is effective for a period of three years measured from the date of its filing. It can be extended for like periods, but each extension must be applied for within the prior three-year period so that any extension order can be filed and indexed before the existing notice expires.[11] This avoids a gap in the constructive notice afforded by the lis pendens and prevents some third person from slipping in and taking priority. The Court of Appeals held in Matter of Sakow[12] that if the three-year period passes without extension, the extension is no longer available, so it ill behooves a plaintiff to be lax about commencement of the renewal process.[13]

Generally speaking, the filing of a lis pendens is optional with the plaintiff. In an action to foreclose a mortgage or other lien, however, like a mechanic's lien, statutes— RPAPL section 1331 and Lien Law section 43—make it mandatory.[14] In those cases, the application of *Sakow* to bar the extension would destroy the foreclosure claim substantively, for which reason it has been held that when a lis pendens is mandatory, *Sakow* does not apply and a new lis pendens is allowed even after the lapse of an earlier one.[15] A 2005 amendment adding CPLR 6516 codifies that conclusion. It applies to mortgage foreclosure actions directly, and to other actions that use RPAPL section 1331 by adoption.[16]

The constitutionality of the lis pendens was alluded to earlier.[17] Reviewing the issue in Diaz v. Paterson,[18] the Second Circuit again upheld the validity of CPLR Article 65's lis pendens procedures. The rationale is that the filing of a lis pendens does not amount to a taking in the due process sense.[19]

§ 335. Procedure for Filing

---

[9]   CPLR 6501.

[10]   Mechanics Exchange Sav. Bank v. Chesterfield, 34 A.D.2d 111, 309 N.Y.S.2d 548 (3d Dep't 1970).

[11]   CPLR 6513.

[12]   In re Sakow, 97 N.Y.2d 436, 741 N.Y.S.2d 175, 767 N.E.2d 666 (2002). The case is the subject of the lead note in NYSLD No. 508.

[13]   Some earlier caselaw had held that as long as the plaintiff at least started the extension machinery within the three-year period, as with an order to show cause to bring on the motion to extend, and even filed the order, P was allowed a nunc pro tunc order to retain the continuity of the lis pendens. Thelma Sanders & Associates, Inc. v. Hague Development Corp., 131 A.D.2d 462, 516 N.Y.S.2d 93 (2d Dep't 1987). *Sakow* calls such cases into question.

[14]   Lien Law § 43 just adopts RPAPL 1331, as shown in MCK Building Assocs. v. St. Lawrence Univ., 95 Misc. 2d 430, 759 N.Y.S.2d 309 (Sup. Ct., Lawrence County 2003).

[15]   See Campbell v. Smith, 309 A.D.2d 581, 768 N.Y.S.2d 182 (1st Dep't 2003), overruling the earlier decision to the contrary in 297 A.D.2d 502, 747 N.Y.S.2d 18 (2002), developments treated in SPR 128:1 and 140:3.

[16]   The amendment is discussed in SPR 164:4.

[17]   See § 307.

[18]   Diaz v. Paterson, 547 F.3d 88 (2d Cir. 2008).

[19]   U.S. v. Rivieccio, 661 F. Supp. 281 (E.D.N.Y. 1987).

The lis pendens is the only one of the provisional remedies that does not require a court order. The plaintiff just makes it out and files it with the clerk of the real property county.

If the lis pendens is filed before the summons has been served, the summons must be served within 30 days after the filing. If the summons has already been served, the lis pendens may be filed at any time up to final judgment. If the complaint has not already been filed, it should be filed with the lis pendens.[1] In an action in the supreme or county courts, both of which have plenary jurisdiction of the real property actions,[2] the soundest procedure for the plaintiff is to start the action itself with the filing of a summons and complaint and at the same time present the lis pendens for filing.[3] The plaintiff must then be sure to effect service of the summons within 30 days afterwards, or the lis pendens will become void. That's the condition imposed by CPLR 6512, whose impact is to deny the plaintiff the full 120-day period that CPLR 306–b would otherwise have allowed for summons service.[4]

If there are several defendants, service on one within the 30-day period satisfies CPLR 6512.[5] And if service is made under either CPLR 308(2) ("deliver and mail") or 308(4) ("affix and mail"), each of which involves two steps and contains provisions about when service is "complete," it is sufficient if the two steps are taken within the 30 days even though the service does not become "complete" until afterwards.[6]

If the clerk maintains what is known as a "block index," which is common in urban counties, the lis pendens must contain the number of the block containing the land affected.[7] A clerk who maintains such an index records the lis pendens against the block. Searchers find it there easily. If a block index is not in effect in the county, the clerk records the lis pendens against the names of all defendants named in the action,[8] in whatever alphabetized books the clerk maintains for this purpose.

If the lis pendens is properly filed, but the clerk fails to index it, and a purchaser or encumbrancer is damaged because a search fails to uncover it, liability for the omission lies with the State and damages may be sought in a court of claims action.[9]

---

[1] CPLR 6511(a).

[2] Some use of a lis pendens may be allowed in the New York City Civil Court, which has some limited real property jurisdiction. See §§ 203 and 209(d) of the New York City Civil Court Act (McKinney's Vol. 29A, Part 3).

[3] When no lis pendens is filed until after the summons has been served, CPLR 6512 would seem to require another service of the summons, this one to be made within 30 days after the filing of the lis pendens. This language is the product of a 1994 amendment of the statute that had a different mission. It was not the drafters' intention to require an additional process service. See the discussion in SPR 22:3.

[4] Letting the 30 days pass without service of the summons will not require dismissal of the action—as a passing of the 120–period would, see § 63—but it will undo the lis pendens.

[5] Micheli Contracting Corp. v. Fairwood Associates, 73 A.D.2d 774, 423 N.Y.S.2d 533 (3d Dep't 1979). The plaintiff should serve the others as promptly as possible since a failure to do so can qualify as a want of prosecution and justify a discretionary cancellation of the lis pendens under CPLR 6514(b).

[6] See William Iser, Inc. v. Garnett, 46 Misc. 2d 450, 259 N.Y.S.2d 996 (Sup. Ct., Nassau County 1965), holding that the word "completed" in CPLR 6514(a), which authorizes a cancellation of the lis pendens, refers only to service by publication. When that method is used, only the first publication need be made within the 30-day period, CPLR 6512, provided that the remaining publications are carried out in due course.

[7] CPLR 6511(b).

[8] CPLR 6511(b), (c). In a partition action, it is also recorded against the plaintiff's names if there is no block index.

[9] Ashland Equities Co. v. Clerk of New York County, 110 A.D.2d 60, 493 N.Y.S.2d 133 (1st Dep't 1985). The Court of Appeals has held that in the filing and indexing of judgments, the county clerk is a state agent

If the lis pendens has become void, it has been held that even a person who accepts title with knowledge of the lis pendens takes free of the plaintiff's claim,[10] but the buyer's or mortgagee's lawyer would do better to insist on a court order cancelling the lis pendens rather than merely assuming its nullity from facts as yet unadjudicated.[11]

The lis pendens may be amended by court leave if no prejudice would result.[12]

§ 336. Cancellation of Notice

There are several ways to cancel a lis pendens. One is for the plaintiff's attorney to file an affidavit attesting that all the defendants' time to appear has expired and none has appeared, but that of course applies only where all the defendants are in default.[1] If any defendants have appeared, a stipulation of the appearing ones (agreeing to the cancellation) must accompany the affidavit.[2] The plaintiff would of course take this step only when the defendants' default has removed all opposition, giving the claim clear sailing to judgment and enforcement (and the removal of record of the defendants' interest in the property).

The lis pendens can of course be cancelled by court order. On the motion of any aggrieved person, which is ordinarily brought on by order to show cause, the court is required to cancel the lis pendens in any of several situations. The first, already met, is where the summons has not been served within the 30 days allowed by CPLR 6512. Another is where the action has been settled, discontinued, or abated. Yet another is where the plaintiff loses on the merits and the appeal time has expired or where, having taken an appeal, the plaintiff does not get a stay of enforcement of the judgment during the appeal's pendency. Each of those things is expressly listed in CPLR 6514(a) and mandates cancellation. Not listed, but just as clearly a ground for mandatory cancellation, is a showing that the plaintiff's action doesn't qualify for a lis pendens under CPLR 6501 in the first place.

The lis pendens is in a sense a privilege that can be lost if abused. In Israelson v. Bradley,[3] for example, P filed a lis pendens in a county court realty action. The lis pendens was later cancelled for want of summons service. P then brought the same action in the supreme court and again filed a lis pendens. The lis pendens was cancelled; the court held that having abused the privilege in the first action, the plaintiff was not entitled to it in the second.[4] Note that a second action in such circumstances is not barred by res judicata (the first action not having been disposed of on the merits); it is only the privilege of the lis pendens that the plaintiff forfeits.

---

whose negligence supports a court of claims action. See National Westminster Bank, USA v. State, 76 N.Y.2d 507, 561 N.Y.S.2d 541, 562 N.E.2d 866 (1990), and the discussion in the lead note of NYSLD No. 372.

[10]   Skoler v. Rimberg, 20 A.D.2d 580, 246 N.Y.S.2d 147 (2d Dep't 1963).

[11]   See CPLR 6514; § 336.

[12]   See Lake Louise Marie Community Ass'n v. Lake Louise Marie Corp., 25 A.D.2d 475, 266 N.Y.S.2d 156 (3d Dep't 1966), which allowed an amendment to describe the property more accurately. The case did not involve any of the jurisdictional difficulties tied in with the 30-day service-of-summons requirement of CPLR 6512.

[1]   CPLR 6514(e).

[2]   CPLR 6514(d).

[3]   Israelson v. Bradley, 308 N.Y. 511, 127 N.E.2d 313 (1955).

[4]   Resort to another provisional remedy, however, such as an injunction, would not necessarily be barred in these circumstances. Vincent v. Seaman, 152 A.D.2d 841, 544 N.Y.S.2d 225 (3d Dep't 1989).

In actions to foreclose mortgages and other liens, however, where the filing of a lis pendens is mandatory, not optional, the cancellation of one lis pendens does not preclude the filing of a second one. The same is true, as noted earlier,[5] when the lis pendens lapses because of the expiration of its three-year period without renewal. While a new lis pendens would then be barred in most actions,[6] it isn't barred in the lien foreclosure actions. This has led the courts to conclude that in mortgage and lien foreclosures, the lis pendens is a right rather than just a privilege.[7]

Then there is the cancellation directed by the court as a matter of discretion. Under CPLR 6514(b), the court can order cancellation of a lis pendens as a discretionary matter, and will if it finds that the plaintiff has not prosecuted the action diligently. This is to recognize that the defendant's rights are suspended for as long as the action pends. Again, the motion to cancel is brought on by order to show cause.

Upon making any order under CPLR 6514 cancelling a lis pendens, the court may direct the plaintiff to pay the defendant such costs and expenses as the filing of the lis pendens may have occasioned.[8] Such expenses are imposed on the plaintiff, and they are not necessarily backed by an undertaking.

Undertakings are not mandatory in lis pendens practice, but they do figure in the cancellation requirements of CPLR 6515, which run as follows. Any person aggrieved by the filing of the lis pendens (presumably the defendant) may volunteer an undertaking for the plaintiff's protection in an amount to be fixed by the court. If the court finds that the undertaking is adequate for the plaintiff's protection, it will order cancellation of the lis pendens.[9] If money alone would not be adequate protection, as where the interest the plaintiff asserts is unique—this is not just an action to foreclose a lien, for example, in which the plaintiff is usually after money and nothing more—cancellation would not be ordered under this provision.

Cancellation might be ordered under another provision, however, a bit baroque in design. Even if an undertaking would not be adequate to protect the plaintiff, the court can still cancel the lis pendens if the defendant offers an undertaking and the plaintiff does not respond with the plaintiff's own undertaking to protect the defendant.[10] It's a kind of lever the defendant can pull to try to make the plaintiff furnish an undertaking in return. If the plaintiff does furnish it, its condition is that the plaintiff will indemnify the defendant for damages traceable to the lis pendens as where the defendant wins on the merits.[11] In an action for the specific performance of a realty contract, a "double bonding," requiring each side to post an undertaking to indemnify the other, has been held to be the "preferred" course.[12]

---

[5] See § 334.

[6] See the *Sakow* case discussed in § 334.

[7] See, e.g., Robbins v. Goldstein, 36 A.D.2d 730, 320 N.Y.S.2d 553 (2d Dep't 1971).

[8] CPLR 6514(c).

[9] CPLR 6515(1).

[10] CPLR 6515(2).

[11] Excepted from these undertaking trade-offs of CPLR 6515 are the actions for foreclosure of a mortgage, for partition, and for dower. In none of these will the defendant's furnishing of an undertaking authorize cancellation of the lis pendens. For the elements to be considered in fixing the amounts of the CPLR 6515 undertakings, see Ronga v. Alpern, 45 Misc. 2d 1029, 258 N.Y.S.2d 731 (Sup. Ct., Bronx County 1964).

[12] Andesco, Inc. v. Page, 137 A.D.2d 349, 530 N.Y.S.2d 111 (1st Dep't 1988).

It might be fairer, and it surely would be simpler, if the legislature were to make an undertaking by P mandatory with the lis pendens as it has with the order of attachment[13] and the preliminary injunction.[14]

The absence of an undertaking is by no means an insulation from liability for the plaintiff in a lis pendens situation. The plaintiff faces serious penalties for abusing the lis pendens device, and this is so even if there is no undertaking in the picture at all. The Second Department held in Parr Meadows Racing Ass'n, Inc. v. White[15] that the defendant has an abuse of process claim against the wrongdoing plaintiff for misuse of a lis pendens, remanding the case to have damages determined. The result on remand is a lesson to all would-be abusers of the lis pendens:

O in the *Parr* case had been about to get a favorable mortgage loan on some land when L, a lawyer, sued O on a money claim having nothing to do with the land, but in that action nevertheless filed a lis pendens. In order to lift the lis pendens and free the land for the loan, O settled the suit on unfavorable terms. When all was clear, O turned about and brought an abuse of process suit against L and proved his case. Among the remedies awarded O against L was cancellation of the settlement of L's action, a return of O's payment and a note given under the settlement, the legal fees it cost O to clear the title report, and a $5,000 attorney's fee for having to bring the abuse of process suit.[16]

G. SEIZURE OF CHATTEL

Table of Sections

§ 337.   Replevin Action, Generally
§ 338.   Constitutionality of Preliminary Seizure
§ 339.   Applying for the Seizure
§ 340.   The Seizure and Subsequent Proceedings
§ 341.   Commencing the Action
§ 342.   Judgment in Replevin Action

§ 337. Replevin Action, Generally

"Replevin" today describes an action to recover a chattel. Technically, at least in New York, "replevin" meant the device whereby the sheriff seizes the chattel before judgment,[1] a provisional-like remedy that was, and is, available as an incident of an action to recover a chattel, just as attachment is an incident of a money action. The phrase "order of seizure" is best used to describe this provisional-like remedy today, with "replevin" reserved for the substantive action itself.[2]

CPLR 7101 provides that an action may be brought under Article 71 "to try the right to possession of a chattel," and one would think from such an introduction that the whole article is designed to supply the substantive law governing the action. It is not. Common

---

[13] CPLR 6212(b).

[14] CPLR 6312(b).

[15] Parr Meadows Racing Ass'n, Inc. v. White, 76 A.D.2d 858, 428 N.Y.S.2d 509 (2d Dep't 1980).

[16] N.Y.L.J., Aug. 26, 1983, at 15, col.1 (Sup. Ct., Suffolk County, DeLuca, J.). The case is the subject of the lead note in NYSLD No. 288.

[1] See 4th Rep. Leg. Doc. No. 20, p. 249 (1960).

[2] So widespread is its use for this purpose that it is the principal definition of "replevin" found in Black's Law Dictionary (10th ed.).

law, as expanded or contracted by statute, governs who has the substantive right to the chattel. Article 71 is concerned with procedural incidents of the action, notably the provisional-like order of seizure by which the chattel can be taken before or during the action. Concentration in all but the present section will be on the seizure remedy and the other procedural aspects of the replevin action.

The reason for this overlapping of substantive and procedural functions is historical. Predecessor acts had carried forward some of replevin's substantive elements, such as rules about when D could defeat P just by showing that some third person had a higher right than either of them. That defense, known as the jus tertii, was good when it was alleged that the chattel had been wrongfully detained although properly taken at first. But when the charge was that the chattel was wrongfully taken in the first place, the defense could be used by D only if he could connect himself with the third person.[3] These and like distinctions did not have much to commend them and were abandoned by the CPLR's drafters. Today, the action lies, substantively speaking, to test "the relative possessory rights of the parties," whatever their source.[4]

Also casualties of the modern CPLR approach are the old rules about whether the action lies only if the defendant has possession of the goods now, or even if he has not, and about whether the goods were taken from the defendant by legal process or parted with voluntarily.[5] The CPLR attitude is to allow the action in all these instances and let the final judgment on the merits adjust whatever substantive rights emerge.[6]

Another question often met in the action to recover a chattel is whether the plaintiff must make a demand for its return before suing. This is not a procedural question but, in certain circumstances, at least historically, a condition precedent to the very existence of the substantive right, as where the defendant secured possession lawfully in first instance. The absence of a demand in a case like that resulted in dismissal under prior law, albeit without prejudice to a new action after a demand had been duly made.[7] Of course, if the facts showed that a demand would be futile, it was dispensed with as where the defendant was fully aware of the plaintiff's hostile claim to the chattel.[8] The futility rule is a healthy one, and continues, but there is indication that dismissal still threatens a case that shows neither a demand nor facts indicating its futility.[9]

It is unusual and perverse for P to sue D for something D would return upon P's mere demand. If P brings an action in a situation like that, and D posits that upon mere demand he would have returned the chattel or paid its value, D can be afforded that opportunity now: the court can dismiss the action on the condition that D return the chattel or pay its value. If P had no excuse for suing without making the demand, D can be awarded costs. The action in those circumstances can even be labeled "frivolous" so as to invoke the more substantial monetary penalties of the sanctions rule.[10] A dismissal

---

[3]   Civ. Prac. Act § 1093 (repealed 1963).

[4]   See 4th Rep. Leg. Doc. No. 20, pp. 253–54 (1960); Bulman v. Bulman, 57 Misc. 2d 320, 292 N.Y.S.2d 572 (Sup. Ct., Rensselaer County 1968).

[5]   See, e.g., Sinnott v. Feiock, 165 N.Y. 444, 59 N.E. 265 (1901).

[6]   See 4th Rep. Leg. Doc. No. 20 at p. 250 (1960).

[7]   See, e.g., Cohen v. M. Keizer, Inc., 246 A.D. 277, 285 N.Y.S. 488 (1st Dep't 1936).

[8]   Employers' Fire Ins. Co. v. Cotten, 245 N.Y. 102, 156 N.E. 629 (1927).

[9]   See, e.g., Agawam Trading Corp. v. Mayer Malbin Co., 37 A.D.2d 946, 325 N.Y.S.2d 757 (1st Dep't 1971).

[10]   See § 414A.

without prejudice, contemplating that P will now make the demand but face the burden of bringing yet another action if the demand is not met, is an idle relic of an earlier time, breeds suspicion and disrespect for the law, and presumably has been abandoned.

A further substantive point to make before turning to procedure, which is the main mission of Article 71, is that the action to recover a chattel, a law action, is not necessarily the plaintiff's exclusive remedy to get the chattel back. In certain commercial situations, notably under the Uniform Commercial Code, the plaintiff is permitted to use self-help.[11]

If the chattel is unique, moreover, the plaintiff can seek equitable relief. Thus, for example, where P and D had a contract whereby D agreed to return a specific item to P, a showing that the item was unique and thus irreplaceable by money[12] enabled P to sue in equity for specific performance,[13] which is backed by the contempt remedy.[14] That would still be the case, but the same thing can be accomplished within the law action itself today. An explicit CPLR provision says that if the chattel is unique, the judgment can direct its return under the threat of contempt,[15] which is of course what plaintiffs are relying on when they sue in equity.

§ 338. Constitutionality of Preliminary Seizure

The earlier section that discusses constitutional issues concerning the provisional remedies in general includes treatment of the prejudgment seizure of a chattel in a replevin action,[1] but a brief review may help.

Prior to 1971 in New York, a chattel would be seized by the sheriff on the say-so of the plaintiff's attorney, with no initial court involvement at all. The attorney merely made out and delivered to the sheriff, along with certain other papers, a "requisition," on the basis of which the sheriff was required to seize the chattel forthwith.[2] Because that procedure was declared unconstitutional by a federal court,[3] the legislature in 1971 amended several of Article 71's provisions to replace the requisition with a court order and to impose other requirements designed to satisfy constitutional requirements. Not quite sure what those requirements were at the time, the legislature left the details to the courts with the simple instruction that procedure conform to "due process of law."[4] Then, in 1978, the constitutional demands having become clearer through caselaw, the legislature further amended Article 71, more specifically CPLR 7102, 7104, 7108, and 7112, to fulfill constitutional demands with a new set of instructions.[5]

---

[11]   See the discussion of the *Jefferds* case in § 338.

[12]   The ordinary judgment in an action to recover a chattel calls for the return of its possession or for a levy on other property of the defendant to obtain the chattel's money value instead. See § 342.

[13]   Chabert v. Robert & Co., 273 A.D. 237, 76 N.Y.S.2d 400 (1st Dep't 1948).

[14]   See § 481.

[15]   See CPLR 7109(b), discussed in § 342.

[1]   See § 307.

[2]   See the pre-1971 CPLR 7102.

[3]   Laprease v. Raymours Furniture Co., 315 F. Supp. 716 (N.D.N.Y. 1970).

[4]   See the 1971 amendment of CPLR 7102(d)(1), L.1971, ch. 1051, § 1.

[5]   These are treated in §§ 339 and 340.

The gist of the constitutional exaction is that notice and an opportunity to be heard precede the issuance of a seizure order. The exception is where an important governmental interest or a need for very prompt action appears.[6]

One situation in which the seizure can be authorized by an ex parte order is where the replevin action is based on rem rather than on personam jurisdiction. If the chattel is in New York, it affords the New York courts an in rem basis on which to adjudicate rights in it even as against an absent nondomiciliary defendant of whom personal jurisdiction is lacking.[7] It is required, however, that the chattel's seizure precede service of process.[8] By analogy to attachment, where ex parte procedure has been found permissible when attachment is being used for its jurisdictional purpose,[9] a seizure of the chattel by ex parte order should also be allowable in this replevin situation.

In some instances, almost always involving a contract, statutes that permit a plaintiff to seize a chattel with no court order required at all, and without even the intervention of a public official (like a sheriff), have been sustained. The self-help provisions of the Uniform Commercial Code, for example, which allow a secured party to take peaceable possession of the collateral that secures an obligation,[10] have been upheld by the appellate division.[11] If the self-help procedure is otherwise applicable, in fact, it has been held that it can be resorted to even after an order of seizure under Article 71 has been obtained, instead of going ahead with enforcement of the order.[12]

§ 339. Applying for the Seizure

The procedure to obtain an order of seizure is a motion. The general rule, or at least the underlying assumption in the structure of CPLR 7102, the main provision in point, is that the motion will be on notice, but the order can be granted without notice (ex parte) if

> in addition to the other prerequisites . . . the court finds that . . . it is probable the chattel will become unavailable for seizure by reason of being transferred, concealed, disposed of, or removed from the state, or will become substantially impaired in value.[1]

It sounds as if the motion on notice would be the common method and the ex parte motion the exception, but if statistics were charted, the reverse might prove to be the case. Ex parte applications are not uncommon. They are just more demanding of procedural guidance. Much of CPLR 7102 is designed to furnish it.

The plaintiff's main paper on an application for a seizure order is, as with the provisional remedies generally, an affidavit, whose contents are enumerated in CPLR 7102(c). The affidavit must identify the chattel and show that the plaintiff is entitled to

---

[6]   Cedar Rapids Engineering Co. v. Haenelt, 39 A.D.2d 275, 277, 333 N.Y.S.2d 953, 955–56 (3d Dep't 1972) (holding that "facts and circumstances of the instant case do not present such a situation").

[7]   See § 103.

[8]   CPLR 314(3); see § 103.

[9]   See § 315.

[10]   See UCC § 9–609.

[11]   See Jefferds v. Ellis, 132 A.D.2d 321, 522 N.Y.S.2d 398 (4th Dep't 1987) (applying predecessor provisions of UCC § 9–609).

[12]   See General Motors Acceptance Corp. v. Ayanru, 126 Misc. 2d 607, 483 N.Y.S.2d 593 (N.Y. City Civ. Ct. 1984) (involving a car under a standard financing agreement).

[1]   CPLR 7102(d)(3).

it and that the defendant is wrongfully withholding it. It must also state whether the action has yet been commenced and, if so, its status. And it must set forth the chattel's value.

All of the substantive elements of the replevin claim should be deposed to in the affidavit. If, for example, this is one of those cases in which a demand is a condition precedent,[2] facts showing the demand (or the futility of making one) should be stated. The plaintiff must also aver that she knows of no defense to the claim.[3]

Accompanying the affidavit must be an undertaking, in not less than twice the chattel's value, to the effect that the chattel will be given to whoever is awarded possession by the final judgment and that the surety will pay any sum of money the judgment may award against the person furnishing the undertaking.[4] This undertaking may not be withdrawn until the right to possession is resolved.[5]

If the order of seizure is granted, the plaintiff delivers it to the sheriff along with the undertaking, the papers on which the order was based, and the summons and complaint, which must bear the index number of the case.[6] This of course means that the summons and complaint must be filed before the seizure; the filing being the act that commences the action and secures the index number.[7]

As long as the proceedings in respect of the chattel, including its initial seizure, are completed before the service of the summons, the risk that the defendant will be forewarned of the seizure so as to abscond with the chattel are diminished.

Whether on notice or ex parte, the motion for the order of seizure is ordinarily best made when the action is first filed and an index number assigned. If the plaintiff does make the motion before summons service, the sheriff can serve the summons and complaint on the defendant at or about the time he seizes the chattel. Also, in this motion-first-summons-later situation, the rules about the service of motion papers, so clear during the pendency of an action when all parties have appeared through their attorneys, are more difficult, and the plaintiff planning to apply for the seizure order with a motion on notice had best bring the motion on by order to show cause. That will enable the court to determine how and upon whom the motion papers should be served. It also enables the court to set an earlier return day than an ordinary motion requires and, if the plaintiff so requests, the court can include in the order to show cause a temporary restraining order (TRO) forbidding the defendant from removing or secreting the chattel until further court direction.

The TRO device, supplied by CPLR 7102(d)(2) for use in replevin context, is designed to encourage the plaintiff to tender the defendant a hearing before the seizure. It has the effect of preserving the chattel for subsequent seizure even if the defendant gets preliminary notice of the plaintiff's intent to seize it. When this procedure is used— an order to show cause including a TRO—it is contemplated that a seizure will not occur

---

[2]   See § 337.

[3]   CPLR 7102(c)(6).

[4]   CPLR 7102(e).

[5]   Monte Pub. Co. v. Cohen, 39 A.D.2d 661, 331 N.Y.S.2d 918 (1st Dep't 1972). For a discussion of the undertaking and its surety requirements, see Consolidated Edison Co. of New York, Inc. v. Alston, 110 Misc. 2d 188, 441 N.Y.S.2d 802 (N.Y. City Civ. Ct. 1981).

[6]   CPLR 7102(a).

[7]   See the discussion of the 1994 amendment of CPLR 7102(a), which accounts for these requirements, in SPR 22:3–4.

until a hearing has been afforded the defendant on the return of the order to show cause because the TRO in this situation is presumably the plaintiff's security.[8]

When the ex parte procedure is used without a TRO, the seizure precedes the hearing, but the plaintiff is then obliged to make a follow-up motion "confirming" the order of seizure.[9] Assuming that the plaintiff has satisfied the requirement of a pre-hearing seizure as noted above, the order of seizure is—recapitulating now—signed by the judge, given to the plaintiff, delivered by the plaintiff to the sheriff with the other required papers, and executed by the sheriff with a seizure of the subject chattel. Now, after the seizure, the plaintiff must move to confirm the seizure order—in essence make the motion all over again, but this time on notice. It is this confirmation motion that sets up the hearing that the defendant is constitutionally entitled to when the seizure starts off ex parte. It's a requirement of CPLR 7102(d)(4), analogous in this respect to the post-levy confirmation motion required in attachment cases when the attachment is granted ex parte.[10]

The motion to confirm must be made no more than five days after the seizure. The failure to make the motion results in a voiding of all prior proceedings and a return of the chattel to the defendant. It has been held, moreover, that merely presenting a blank order to show cause to the clerk on the last day for making a motion to confirm does not satisfy the five-day confirmation requirement.[11]

In all cases, whether on a pre-seizure motion made ex parte or on a confirmation motion, the burden of establishing the merits of the case is on the plaintiff, and it is not met by a simple showing of a prima facie case. The plaintiff must show that it is "probable" that she will succeed on the merits.[12]

The court can permit the sheriff to break down a door to get the chattel,[13] but the plaintiff who wants such an authorization must include in the affidavit facts justifying it.[14]

As far as identifying the chattel is concerned, the description need only be sufficient to enable the sheriff to single it out and seize it. The chattel need not have any intrinsic monetary value. A package of letters and personal and professional papers in identifiable condition has been held sufficient against a claim that it lacked monetary significance.[15]

---

[8] See also Morning Glory Media, Inc. v. Enright, 100 Misc. 2d 872, 420 N.Y.S.2d 176 (Sup. Ct., Monroe County 1979) (pending final outcome of action, plaintiff was entitled to a TRO "that the chattel shall not be removed from its location, transferred, sold, pledged, assigned or otherwise disposed of, or permitted to become subject to a security interest or lien until further order of this Court").

[9] CPLR 7102(d)(4).

[10] See § 316.

[11] See Quality Ford of Mt. Vernon, Inc. v. Metro Auto Leasing, Inc., 172 Misc. 2d 635, 660 N.Y.S.2d 341 (Sup. Ct., Westchester County 1997) (SPR 65:3). The court said that a plaintiff who is having trouble getting the order to show cause signed within the required time should notify the clerk, who is then charged with making an effort to accommodate the plaintiff. See § 330 (discussing "Protocol for Emergency Applications").

[12] See CPLR 7102(d)(1) and (4), which place on the plaintiff the burden of establishing all the grounds for the order.

[13] CPLR 7102(d)(1), 7110.

[14] See CPLR 7102(c)(5). See also Laprease v. Raymours Furniture Co., 315 F. Supp. 716 (N.D.N.Y. 1970), which discusses this breaking-in permission in light of the search and seizure clause of the Fourth Amendment.

[15] Hipsley v. Hipsley, 186 Misc. 458, 60 N.Y.S.2d 10 (App. Term, 1st Dep't 1946).

The hearing, whether brought on by initial motion on notice or by a confirmation motion following an ex parte seizure, is not the occasion for finally determining the merits of the replevin claim; it is designed only to determine whether a preliminary seizure is proper. The court can ordinarily decide that issue on the papers submitted pro and con and on the oral argument heard on the motion. Live testimony and the calling of witnesses, although sometimes permitted by the court, are not required.[16]

The order of seizure directs the sheriff of any county where the chattel may be found to seize it "without delay." Copies of the order, the affidavit and other papers on which the order is based, and the undertaking, all of which, as noted, are delivered to the sheriff of the appropriate county, must be served by the sheriff "upon the person from whose possession the chattel is seized." Copies of those papers must also be served on the defendant—along with the summons and complaint if not already served—and this service must be made in the same manner as a summons. If perchance the defendant has already appeared in the action, the service can be by the usual mail method or other methods for serving interlocutory papers.[17]

A frequent use of the order to seize a chattel is by a public utility seeking to replevy its meter after non-payment of its bill. A number of abuses in connection with one utility's procedures in such cases were enumerated in Consolidated Edison Co. of New York, Inc. v. Church of St. Cecilia,[18] extruding a statement of what should be done through a detailed list of what should not.

If at any time the plaintiff needs assistance in locating the chattel, she may seek leave to compel any person with light to shed on the subject to give a deposition on its whereabouts. The plaintiff may move "upon such notice as the court may direct,"[19] i.e., by order to show cause, to have the court order the deposition, or, in fact, any of the disclosure devices of Article 31 of the CPLR that can offer aid for this purpose.[20]

§ 340. The Seizure and Subsequent Proceedings

On receipt of the order, affidavit, and undertaking, the sheriff is required to seize the chattel[1] and then serve copies of those papers on the one from whom possession is taken. Copies are also to be served by the sheriff on each defendant so that if the defendant herself is not in possession, extra copies of the papers should be delivered to the sheriff to enable a set to be served on the possessor as well as on each defendant. Service on the defendants must be in the same manner as a summons.[2] This assumes that the service of the seizure papers is being made before the service of the summons and complaint in the action, as is most often the case, but if that service has already

---

[16]   Long Island Trust Co. v. Porta Aluminum Corp., 44 A.D.2d 118, 354 N.Y.S.2d 134 (2d Dep't 1974).

[17]   CPLR 7102(b). For service of interlocutory papers, see § 202.

[18]   Consolidated Edison Co. of New York, Inc. v. Church of St. Cecilia, 125 Misc. 2d 744, 480 N.Y.S.2d 284 (N.Y. City Civ. Ct. 1984).

[19]   CPLR 7112.

[20]   See CPLR 3101(a), 3102(c); G. A. C. Commercial Corp. v. La Pardo Bros. Excavating Contractors, Inc., 33 A.D.2d 777, 307 N.Y.S.2d 186 (2d Dep't 1969).

[1]   CPLR 7102(a).

[2]   CPLR 7102(b). The service is directed to follow CPLR 314, which means that the service methods of CPLR 308 et seq. may be used, within or without the State.

been made and the defendants have appeared, the other papers may be served by mailing them to their attorneys.[3]

After seizing the chattel, the sheriff's obligations depend in some measure on how the seizure order came on. If it was ex parte, the sheriff holds the chattel until served with an order of confirmation. That of course presupposes that the seizure will be confirmed, which may not happen. What is apparently meant is that when the seizure has been made ex parte, the sheriff should hold the chattel until he receives further directions from the court (or perhaps from the replevying plaintiff), whether the directions are embodied in an order of confirmation or any other kind of order. If the plaintiff does not make a confirmation motion within the required time, the order loses effect (and can be vacated on motion if need be) and the chattel must be returned "forthwith" to the defendant.[4]

If the order of seizure was granted on notice, the sheriff must hold the chattel for 10 days. This assumes that the sheriff will know whether the granting of the order was ex parte or on notice. The order should say. If for some reason it doesn't, and the sheriff doesn't know which it was, the sheriff does best either to retain the chattel until the facts on which he may safely act have been presented to him or apply to the court for a clarifying direction (especially when the chattel is of substantial value and the consequences of improper procedure are therefore all the greater).

These waiting periods—the 10 days when the seizure was on notice and the until-served-with-a-confirmation-order when the seizure was ex parte—are designed to give the defendant a chance to do any of three things: (1) except to the sureties on the plaintiff's undertaking; (2) move to impound the chattel or have it returned; or (3) reclaim the chattel.[5] If the defendant does none of those things within the waiting period, the sheriff turns the chattel over to the plaintiff.[6]

It is this last possibility that takes the seizure order out of the mere "provisional" category. The fact that the plaintiff can end up with the chattel before the case is adjudicated on the merits makes the seizure order a good deal more than a provisional remedy.

Any person claiming the right to possession of the chattel, including of course the defendant, may reclaim it after its initial seizure. The reclaimer procedure, which is governed by CPLR 7103(a) and is carried out during the waiting period, entails the service of a reclaimer notice, an affidavit showing the reclaimant to be entitled to possession, and an undertaking similar to the one the plaintiff has to furnish on the initial seizure motion.[7] Upon receipt of such reclaimer papers, the sheriff must now hold the chattel for an additional 10-day period. During this time, the plaintiff cannot again effect a seizure—that would amount to an endless Alphonse-and-Gaston routine—but he can except to the sureties on the reclaimant's undertaking or move to impound the chattel. If the plaintiff does nothing within that period, the chattel goes to the

---

[3] CPLR 2103(b)(2). See § 202.

[4] CPLR 7102(d)(4).

[5] If the seizure was on notice, the likelihood of the defendant's now being able to have the chattel summarily returned is remote. Presumably, the defendant was heard on the point and didn't prevail. The other remedies, though, the excepting, impounding, or reclaiming, would ordinarily still be open.

[6] CPLR 7102(f).

[7] A mere lienholder can't reclaim, CPLR 7103(a); the theory is that money alone will satisfy her claim and that the plaintiff's undertaking therefore gives the lienholder what protection she needs.

reclaimant, ordinarily the defendant. If more than one person purports to reclaim the chattel, the sheriff may move to have the court determine who gets it.

An impounding order keeps the chattel out of the possession of either party.[8]

If one not already a party to the action takes any of the steps authorized by CPLR 7103, such as by moving to impound or return the chattel or by serving a notice of reclaimer or exception to sureties, that person thereby becomes a party[9] and is bound by any judgment rendered in the action.

The sheriff is entitled to fees and expenses from the party to whom possession is delivered.[10] Within 20 days after the delivery, the sheriff must file a return with the clerk stating what action he's taken.[11]

Any perishables among the chattels seized may be ordered sold and the proceeds of the sale deposited in their place.[12]

The plaintiff is personally liable to the defendant if the seizure turns out to be wrongful.[13] The defendant can of course pursue the sureties on the undertaking, but is not restricted to that remedy. If the order is granted ex parte, moreover, the failure to secure its post-seizure confirmation makes the plaintiff liable for "all costs and damages, including reasonable attorney's fees, which may be sustained by reason of the granting of the order of seizure without notice," unless the court orders otherwise on good cause shown.[14] The plaintiff's personal liability is not limited, as the sureties' liability is, to the amount of the undertaking.[15]

§ 341. Commencing the Action

It will be recalled that the summons and complaint must also be delivered to the sheriff with the initial seizure papers.[1] CPLR 7102(b) contemplates that the summons and complaint will be among the papers that the sheriff serves after seizing the chattel. No time limit is set as to when that service must be made, but it is contemplated that it will be done soon after the seizure. The law's standby time period, a reasonable time, should be implied. Predecessor statutes were construed as not mandating service of process at all, which enabled a plaintiff to get the chattel through the seizure papers and to forego suit altogether.[2] Such a result is unacceptable today. CPLR 7102(a) now requires that a summons and complaint in a replevin action be filed before a chattel can be seized. Between subdivisions (a) and (b) of CPLR 7102, it is clear that the seizure of

---

8   See CPLR 7103(b). If the chattel is in the category of a necessity, there is a special and additional procedure whereby the defendant can secure its return before final judgment. See CPLR 7103(c); Morning Glory Media, Inc. v. Enright, 100 Misc. 2d 872, 420 N.Y.S.2d 176 (Sup. Ct., Monroe County 1979).

9   CPLR 7103(d).

10   CPLR 7106(a).

11   CPLR 7107.

12   CPLR 7105.

13   CPLR 7108(a).

14   CPLR 7108(a); see Armored Motor Service of America, Inc. v. Gribbon, 176 A.D.2d 1202, 576 N.Y.S.2d 700 (4th Dep't 1991) ("Because plaintiff proceeded improperly in obtaining an order of seizure ex parte, there is no 'good cause' for denying an award of damages").

15   CPLR 7108(a).

1   CPLR 7102(a). See § 339.

2   See, e.g., Kurzweil v. Story & Clark Piano Co., 95 Misc. 484, 159 N.Y.S. 231 (N.Y. City Ct. 1916).

the chattel must be followed by service of the summons and complaint on each defendant, at least in instances when the summons and complaint have not already been served.[3]

If the action has already been filed, the context would exist for the replevin proceedings, but if the summons and complaint are not served within 120 days thereafter[4] and the action is dismissed for that reason, the context would be lost. That should result in the vacatur of the seizure order and a direction that the chattel, if already taken, be returned.[5]

As discussed in the prior section, the defendant can take some step during the waiting period following the initial seizure.[6] Any such step automatically makes the defendant a party.[7] One may therefore be inclined to assume that if the defendant does nothing within the waiting period and the sheriff at the end of it turns the chattel over to the plaintiff, the defendant is conceding the plaintiff's right on the merits and that it is therefore idle to force the plaintiff to continue prosecuting the action. The assumption may be unwarranted, however. Even if the defendant would like to reclaim the chattel, which is one of the things the defendant can do during the waiting period, he may not be able to afford the undertaking indispensable to a reclaimer. The steps of the waiting period are optional with the defendant, who can take one of them, or none of them and insist that the plaintiff prosecute the action promptly and prove a right on the merits.

Although the defendant's inaction may result in the plaintiff's getting the chattel after the waiting period, that does not amount to an adjudication that it is rightfully the plaintiff's. That "adjudication" would not bind the defendant unless she has defaulted in the action proper after being duly served with the summons and complaint. Technically, therefore, the plaintiff who abandons all further proceedings upon getting the chattel at the end of the waiting period risks having to return it. As a matter of common experience, however, plaintiffs who get the chattel after the waiting period frequently let matters lapse. The case is often one in which the defendant does not have a defense and would only lose to the plaintiff if he contested. With so bleak a chance on the merits, and as a matter of economics, the defendant is deterred from taking steps to void the proceedings and get back the chattel, with the result that the plaintiff keeps the chattel—and the case, for all practical purposes, is closed.

Still, the plaintiff who would wrap the case up in an airtight legal package after getting possession of the chattel through the seizure device had best let the default consist of the defendant's failure to answer after due service of the summons and complaint, rather than the defendant's mere failure to act during the waiting period.

After the defendant has been duly served, the plaintiff should see to the diligent prosecution of the action. A discontinuance or a dismissal, which would include a

---

[3]   That was the purpose of requiring the summons and complaint to be delivered to the sheriff, CPLR 7102(a), and of requiring the sheriff to serve the defendants, CPLR 7102(b), when seizure precedes service of process. See 4th Rep. Leg. Doc. No. 20, p. 257 (1960).

[4]   See CPLR 306–b.

[5]   Cf. Sears Roebuck & Co. v. Austin, 60 Misc. 2d 908, 304 N.Y.S.2d 131 (N.Y. City Civ. Ct. 1969), which dismissed the action and voided the seizure, but did not direct return of the chattel.

[6]   CPLR 7102(f). The waiting period is 10 days following the seizure if the seizure order was granted by motion on notice. If it was granted ex parte, the waiting period is however long it takes for the plaintiff to obtain and serve on the sheriff an order confirming the seizure.

[7]   CPLR 7103(d).

dismissal for want of prosecution, requires that the chattel be returned to the one from whom it was initially taken.[8]

§ 342. Judgment in Replevin Action

The judgment in an ordinary replevin action awards possession to the winner. If the winner does not already have possession, the judgment also fixes the chattel's value,[1] measured as of the time of the trial.[2] Enforcement of an ordinary replevin judgment is through an execution delivered to the sheriff, who seizes the chattel (if he hasn't already obtained possession of it) and turns it over to the party to whom judgment was awarded. If the chattel can't be found, the sheriff levies as if on a money judgment,[3] which is the reason why the judgment fixes the chattel's value. Since the judgment can also award damages for the wrongful taking or detention of the chattel,[4] the plaintiff would do well to include a claim for such damages in the complaint. If the plaintiff is entitled to both the chattel and damages, the sheriff levies the chattel part by turning the chattel over to the plaintiff and the money part as he would any money judgment.

The remedy of money in place of the chattel is an unacceptable alternative when the chattel is unique and irreplaceable. So, if the chattel is unique, the judgment can additionally direct that the possessor deliver the chattel to the winner. The advantage of such a direction is that disobedience is enforceable as a contempt of court.[5] The general standard for determining whether or not a chattel is unique is whether it can be replaced. An item with sentimental value, a painting, a family heirloom, a pet, a patent; these and like items all qualify as unique.[6]

As noted earlier,[7] the uniqueness of the chattel can in some cases justify the plaintiff's bringing an equitable action instead of a replevin action (which is a law claim), but the availability of contempt as an enforcement remedy in a replevin judgment itself under CPLR 7109(b) will often make the equitable alternative superfluous.

---

[8]   CPLR 7108(a).

[1]   CPLR 7108(a). In certain circumstances, set forth in CPLR 7108(b), the chattel's value is not fixed in the judgment.

[2]   Colonial Funding Corp. v. Bon Jour Intern. Ltd., 148 A.D.2d 654, 539 N.Y.S.2d 405 (2d Dep't 1989).

[3]   See CPLR 5102.

[4]   CPLR 7108(a).

[5]   CPLR 7109(b).

[6]   See Morse v. Penzimer, 58 Misc. 2d 156, 295 N.Y.S.2d 125 (Sup. Ct., Oneida County 1968).

[7]   See § 337.

Chapter 13

DISCLOSURE

Analysis

A. Generally
B. Excluded Matters
C. Devices and Methods in Perspective
D. Protection Against Abuse
E. The Devices Individually
F. Compelling Disclosure

A. GENERALLY

Table of Sections

§ 343.   Disclosure; Introduction
§ 344.   Disclosure Criteria; CPLR 3101(a)
§ 345.   Disclosure from Parties and Nonparties

§ 343. Disclosure; Introduction

One of the most important articles in the CPLR is Article 31, entitled "Disclosure." It contains the aggregate of devices, including among others the deposition, discovery, and interrogatory, by which the trial lawyer, well in advance of the trial and in order to be completely prepared for it, probes into the other side's case and into whatever data or material nonparties may have reflecting on the issues. It is the trial lawyer's major preparation tool. Article 31's aim is to prevent litigation from becoming a game by requiring parties and witnesses to shed their light before the trial so as to prevent surprise at it. Its design is "to advance the function of the trial to ascertain truth and to accelerate the disposition of suits."[1]

Article 31 starts off with the criteria for disclosure. CPLR 3101(a) supplies those criteria and sets the tone for the whole article. The rest of the article supplies the various mechanical devices by which disclosure may be sought and the incidents of their use. The devices will be studied individually. There are fewer than a dozen of them, with some more useful and hence more used than others.

It should be remembered at all times that whatever the device used, the question of whether or not the datum or item sought is a disclosable one is governed by CPLR 3101(a), the article's opening section and the herald to which all inquires about disclosure must turn. It should also be remembered that there is no priority of use among the devices. There is in general no sequence in which they must be used, nor any arbitrary limitation on how many may be used or how many times any one of them may

---

[1]   Rios v. Donovan, 21 A.D.2d 409, 411, 250 N.Y.S.2d 818, 820 (1st Dep't 1964).

be used.[2] As long as the disclosure devices are legitimately sought for data or material open to disclosure under CPLR 3101(a), the lawyer will find Article 31 and its offering of devices to be largely free of any built-in limitations.

Rather than encumber each device with individual restrictions that may be appropriate in individual cases, Article 31 centralizes in one place, CPLR 3103, a broad judicial power to make what is known as a "protective order."[3] This the court does upon application, or even sua sponte, in the particular case. The protective order enables the court on an individual basis to take any needful step to prevent abuse of the easily abused disclosure devices. With the power to shield a party or nonparty from disclosure abuses centrally contained and invokable at any time, the rest of the article is free to concentrate on supplying a broad range of disclosure devices and incidents.

The word one most often hears to describe the equivalent devices in federal practice is "discovery," the title of the counterpart article in the Federal Rules of Civil Procedure being "Disclosures and Discovery."[4] New York has settled on the word "disclosure." The difference is not significant.[5] The federal rules have influenced New York disclosure, notably in the efforts of the CPLR's drafters and in the generous reception and interpretation given to the CPLR's disclosure article by the New York judiciary. The influence continues today, with the New York State courts relying on the federal rules and caselaw when determining a party's rights to disclosure of electronically stored information (ESI) and penalties that can be imposed for destruction of the information.[6]

A revision of pretrial disclosure rules that took effect on January 1, 1994, effected a number of changes in Article 31[7] that had been advocated by New York's Advisory Committee on Civil Practice for more than a decade. There was some pressure for full adoption of federal discovery practice, but a middle ground prevailed: there was no wholesale changeover to the federal rules, but several things were borrowed from them. An irony is that this partial turn to some federal practices took effect exactly one month after some significant changes in federal discovery took effect. So, just as New York took a few strides towards the federal practice, federal practice vacated its position and strode forward into a new one. The resulting gap may be even bigger than the one New York thought it was closing in on.[8]

---

    [2]   See JMJ Contract Management, Inc. v. Ingersoll-Rand Co., 100 A.D.2d 291, 475 N.Y.S.2d 528 (3d Dep't 1984). For further discussion of this priority topic, see § 350.

    [3]   See § 353.

    [4]   See Fed. R. Civ. P. 26 through 37.

    [5]   "Disclosure" was chosen because it is more comprehensive than the federal title was at that time. See 1st Rep. Leg. Doc. No. 6(b), p. 114 (1957).

    [6]   See §§ 362, 367.

    [7]   L.1993, ch. 98. These changes, integrated in this text in the sections to which they pertain, are treated in narrative form in a five-part series of articles in SPR Issues 7–11.

    [8]   The federal changes are briefly noted in § 636 (Practitioner's Edition). A similar development arose in 2015 when the New York Court of Appeals, relying heavily on federal caselaw, outlined penalties for the failure to preserve electronically stored information shortly after Rule 37(e)(2) was significantly amended to prohibit the imposition of some of those penalties. See § 367.

Article 31 applies in all New York courts of civil jurisdiction. It has a few minor modifications in some of the lower courts,[9] but it applies as is in the surrogates' courts,[10] as it of course does in the supreme and county courts.

A final introductory point is that full and free pretrial disclosure is primarily a development of the mid-20th century, accomplished in grudging steps away from the common law, where a profusion of traded pleadings were supposed to sharpen the issues, but seldom did. The emergence and growth of pretrial disclosure has been in roughly inverse proportion to the decline in the importance, and certainly in the rigidity, of pleadings. Under the old pleadings rules, the game was for lawyers to keep their cards close to their vests until the trial where they hoped to surprise their adversaries with a datum too late to meet or counter. The game works less often today, and if Article 31's devices are vigorously employed and its caselaw is faithfully applied, it will not likely work at all.

Unfortunately, the very freedom of use that has been accorded the disclosure devices sometimes generates a game of its own, with one side possessing abundant resources over-using them to the disadvantage of the other and less affluent side. Similarly, and perhaps the biggest game of all, two well-heeled parties may go at each other with the words flying, the papers piling high, and the lawyers' billable hours piling higher. The abuse is worse in the federal than in the New York courts. The cure in both, insofar as the law has evolved, is the shield of a CPLR 3103 protective order.

§ 344. Disclosure Criteria; CPLR 3101(a)

Subdivision (a) of CPLR 3101 sets up the standard for disclosure in New York practice, sounding a generous note and then leaving it to subdivisions (b), (c), and (d) to carve out a few exceptions, to be met later. The opening language of subdivision (a) contains the standard: "There shall be full disclosure of all matter material and necessary in the prosecution or defense of an action . . . ."

Seemingly, the key words in that statement are "material and necessary," the phrase used in the predecessor provision of the Civil Practice Act.[1] The CPLR's drafters felt that the phrase was too restrictive and sought to abandon it, recommending instead the equivalent of the federal standard. They proposed to require disclosure not just of relevant evidence, but also of all information "reasonably calculated to lead to the discovery of relevant evidence,"[2] criteria clearly broader than the "material and necessary" standard. But the legislature rejected the proposal and reverted to the old language, which stands to this day as the verbal formula of CPLR 3101(a).

If the courts had construed "material and necessary" under the CPLR as they did under its predecessor, however, which they had every legislative warrant to do since the

---

[9]   See, for example, Article 11 in the New York City Civ. Ct. Act, Uniform Dist. Ct. Act, Uniform City Ct. Act, and Uniform Just. Ct. Act, McKinney's Vol. 29A, Parts 2 and 3. It will be found that as a practical matter the lower the court, the less use is made of the disclosure devices. This recognizes that the devices can sometimes be expensive to use and that, as a matter of simple economics, the justification for their use diminishes as the stakes involved in the case decline.

[10]   The business of the surrogates' courts is carried on in a series of special proceedings, but CPLR 408, which governs in special proceedings and requires a court order for disclosure, expressly excludes the surrogates' courts and provides that Article 31 will govern in them directly.

[1]   Civ. Prac. Act § 288 (repealed 1963).

[2]   First Rep. Leg. Doc. No. 6(b), p. 117 (1957). See and compare the federal criteria of Fed. R. Civ. P. 26(b)(1), discussed in § 637 (Practitioner's Edition).

same language was carried forward, disclosure would not be as generous today as it has in fact become. Determining whether a given datum or item was "material and necessary" under prior law involved inquiry, and hence effort, much beyond what bench and bar are accustomed to today.[3]

The reason we are spared the effort is the gift of the Court of Appeals in Allen v. Crowell-Collier Pub. Co.,[4] which fused the dual requirements of "material and necessary" into the single word "relevant." A determination of whether a datum or item is "relevant" to the case is a lot easier than determining whether it is "material" or "necessary," or both. All disputes of basic disclosability can therefore be resolved under the CPLR merely by asking whether the thing sought is "relevant." The statutory phrase "material and necessary," said the Court of Appeals, must be "interpreted liberally to require disclosure upon request, of any facts bearing on the controversy which will assist preparation for trial by sharpening the issues and reducing delay and prolixity. The test is one of usefulness and reason."[5]

And so it appears that what the drafters could not accomplish in new statutory language, they accomplished through the Court of Appeals' construction of the old language. Under the *Allen* decision, whatever is "relevant" to the case is for that reason alone "material and necessary" to it. The Court of Appeals has continually applied this broad standard for almost half a century.[6]

Another potential problem that the original CPLR 3101(a) posed was that it spoke of "evidence" that is material and necessary, which might have been construed to permit disclosure to elicit only that which would itself qualify as "evidence" admissible at trial. It was, however, construed more broadly than that. Well-considered caselaw specifically rejected this "evidence in chief" doctrine, stating that disclosure extends as well "to all relevant information calculated to lead to relevant evidence,"[7] a standard similar to that applicable in federal court. With an amendment that took effect on January 1, 1994, changing "evidence" to "matter" in CPLR 3101(a), these generous interpretations of the statute were in effect approved by the legislature.

The concept that disclosure under the CPLR embraces information that merely leads to evidence is also apparent in the rule requiring that a party reveal the name of a witness to a fact in issue.[8] While a witness's name may not itself be "evidence," knowledge of the witness's name surely leads to evidence, and a rule that compels the revelation of a witness's name could hardly be at home in a practice that limits disclosure to "evidence" alone.

The burden of proof is immaterial to a party's right to disclosure. CPLR 3101(a) requires disclosure "regardless of the burden of proof," the purpose being to require the parties to show where they stand on each issue no matter who may have the burden of

---

[3]   See First Rep. Leg. Doc. No. 6(b), p. 117, 440 to 448 (1957). A detailed study of pre-CPLR disclosure, of which the cited pages are part, begins at page 429 of the First Report.

[4]   Allen v. Crowell-Collier Pub. Co., 21 N.Y.2d 403, 288 N.Y.S.2d 449, 235 N.E.2d 430 (1968).

[5]   *Allen*, 21 N.Y.2d at 406, 288 N.Y.S.2d at 452, 235 N.E.2d at 432.

[6]   See, e.g., Kapon v. Koch, 23 N.Y.3d 32, 988 N.Y.S.2d 559, 564, 11 N.E.3d 709, 714 (2014), discussed in § 345.

[7]   See Johnson v. New York City Health & Hospitals Corp., 49 A.D.2d 234, 374 N.Y.S.2d 343 (2d Dep't 1975); West v. Aetna Cas. & Sur. Co., 49 Misc. 2d 28, 29, 266 N.Y.S.2d 600, 602 (Sup. Ct., Onondaga County 1965), modified, 28 A.D.2d 745, 280 N.Y.S.2d 795 (3d Dep't 1967).

[8]   See § 349.

that issue at trial. The plaintiff, for example, who has the burden of proof of every substantive element of the claim, is entitled to full disclosure from the defendant of everything relevant to it, and the same right belongs to the defendant seeking disclosure from the plaintiff about an affirmative defense, on which the burden of proof at trial is on the defendant. Each party is entitled to know the other's position on every element.

This rule of disclosure should not be confused with the rule governing the bill of particulars, where the burden of proof plays a central role. A bill of particulars can only be demanded from a party on an issue on which that party has the burden of proof.[9]

The relevancy standard in CPLR 3101(a) has evolved in several contexts. For a dozen years under the CPLR, and during the reigns of all of its forebears, the defendant's liability insurance policy in a personal injury or other tort action was deemed irrelevant, and hence not subject to disclosure. It was periodically pointed out that the plaintiff's knowledge of the amount and scope of the policy during the action could accelerate a settlement, among other things, but the courts still rejected the disclosure,[10] holding that it would be up to the legislature to effect a change. The legislature, following the federal example,[11] made the change in 1975 by adding subdivision (f) to CPLR 3101. It requires disclosure of both the "existence and contents" of the policy at any time during the action if it "may" be used "to satisfy part or all of a judgment which may be entered in the action."[12] The insurance policy does not thereby become admissible at the trial or otherwise disclosable to the jury, however. Therefore, CPLR 3101(f) stands as another example of how CPLR 3101(a) will compel the disclosure of relevant information even if the information does not constitute admissible evidence at trial.

As far as CPLR 3101(a) indicates, its generous disclosure standard is applicable to all actions without qualification. Given the continuous availability of the protective order,[13] by which abuses can be remedied on a case by case basis, there would seem to be no warrant for judicial interpolation of categorical restrictions. There have nevertheless been some restrictions, notably during the early days of the CPLR when the influence of prior law limiting disclosure still held sway. A reference to the few categories of actions in which disclosure was supposed to be restricted appears in Nomako v. Ashton,[14] decided in 1964. The categories in which disclosure was supposedly restricted, all carryovers from the period before the CPLR was adopted, were the matrimonial action, the shareholders' derivative and other representative actions, and the accounting action.[15] In none of them was disclosure altogether precluded; the difference was instead embodied in such caselaw-imposed requirements that a stronger prima facie case, or a need for disclosure beyond simple relevance, be shown. All such categorical restrictions are suspect today, with the exception of the matrimonial action, whose restrictions are discussed below.

---

[9]   See § 238.

[10]   See, e.g., Mosca v. Pensky, 42 A.D.2d 708, 345 N.Y.S.2d 606 (2d Dep't 1973), aff'd, 35 N.Y.2d 764, 362 N.Y.S.2d 148, 320 N.E.2d 864 (1974), rev'g 73 Misc. 2d 144, 341 N.Y.S.2d 219 (Sup. Ct., Westchester County 1973).

[11]   See what is now Fed. R. Civ. P. 26(a)(1)(A)(iv).

[12]   See Freidman v. Fayenson, 41 Misc. 3d 1236(A), 983 N.Y.S.2d 203 (Sup. Ct., New York County 2013), aff'd, 138 A.D.3d 554, 30 N.Y.S.3d 58 (1st Dep't 2016).

[13]   See CPLR 3103; § 353.

[14]   Nomako v. Ashton, 20 A.D.2d 331, 247 N.Y.S.2d 230 (1st Dep't 1964).

[15]   See Commentary C3101:14 on McKinney's CPLR 3101.

The reason for restricted disclosure in the matrimonial action under prior law was the fear of exacerbating the tensions in the relationship and thus diminishing the prospect of reconciliation. Legislation in 1967, however, set up a procedure to require attempts at reconciliation before the action could go forward, thus clarifying that a matrimonial action already under way was one in which reconciliation had been found futile.[16] Even that preliminary reconciliation attempt proved ineffectual and it, too, was afterwards abandoned,[17] thus leaving the matrimonial action without a statutory reconciliation procedure either before or after judgment and thereby removing much of the old justification for limiting the use of disclosure. Later cases thus indicated, as earlier cases had begun to do,[18] that restrictions on disclosure in a matrimonial action should be left to individual protective orders rather than embodied in a categorical prohibition.[19] In 2010, however, the Court of Appeals in Howard S. v. Lillian S.,[20] opted to keep the blanket prohibition on "liberal discovery on issues of marital fault," leaving protective orders on a case-by-case basis to provide otherwise should the court find "egregious conduct" on the part of the offending party.[21]

All of this concerns only the issue of the ground for the divorce, and *Howard S.* does not appear to alter the rule allowing liberal disclosure of the finances of the parties in a divorce action. On the subject of the parties' finances, one of the most frequent disclosure topics in a matrimonial action, full disclosure is mandated, and without any requirement that special circumstances be shown.[22] A detailed provision in the rules also governs "financial disclosure in actions and proceedings involving alimony, maintenance, child support and equitable distribution."[23]

The defamation action, also one in which prior law had some general reservations about disclosure, is apparently free of them today.[24]

In proceedings for condemnation, appropriation, or review of tax assessments, appraisals would virtually always qualify as material prepared in anticipation of litigation and thereby secure an immunity from disclosure under CPLR 3101(d)(2). To avoid that, and to implement a special policy in such proceedings, CPLR 3140 was added in 1967 permitting the appellate division to adopt disclosure rules in such cases.[25]

While today relevance is the touchstone of pretrial disclosure, the court may sometimes have difficulty deciding what's relevant, especially when the issue involved

---

[16]   See Commentary C3101:15 on McKinney's CPLR 3101.

[17]   L.1973, ch. 1034.

[18]   E.g., Hochberg v. Hochberg, 63 Misc. 2d 77, 310 N.Y.S.2d 737 (Sup. Ct., Nassau County 1970); Lachoff v. Lachoff, 69 Misc. 2d 512, 330 N.Y.S.2d 227 (Sup. Ct., Nassau County 1972).

[19]   Lemke v. Lemke, 100 A.D.2d 735, 473 N.Y.S.2d 646 (4th Dep't 1984); see also Schaeffer v. Schaeffer, 70 Misc. 2d 1033, 335 N.Y.S.2d 510 (Sup. Ct., Nassau County 1972).

[20]   Howard S. v. Lillian S., 14 N.Y.3d 431, 902 N.Y.S.2d 17, 928 N.E.2d 399 (2010).

[21]   The *Howard* case is the subject of a note in NYSLD No. 605.

[22]   See Dom. Rel. Law § 236; Scheinkman, Practice Commentaries on McKinney's Dom. Rel. Law § 236.

[23]   22 N.Y.C.R.R. § 202.16 (applicable in the supreme court, which has exclusive jurisdiction of matrimonial actions, in all actions in which statements of net worth are required by Dom. Rel. Law § 236). Annexed to the Uniform Rules as Appendix A—it follows Part 220 in the annually recompiled McKinney's New York Rules of Court softcover—is an extensive form of "Statement of Net Worth."

[24]   See Nomako v. Ashton, 20 A.D.2d 331, 247 N.Y.S.2d 230 (1st Dep't 1964).

[25]   There are several such rules. See Commentary C3140:1 & 2 on McKinney's CPLR 3140; 22 N.Y.C.R.R. §§ 202.59 (tax assessment reviews outside New York City), 202.60 (tax assessment reviews in New York City), and 202.61 (eminent domain proceedings). The court of claims has its own rule on appraisals in appropriation cases. 22 N.Y.C.R.R. § 206.21.

is a sensitive one. A good example is the attempt in lead-paint personal injury cases to depose an infant's parents on the subject of their IQ. Among the injuries alleged by the plaintiff may be that the infant has developed a learning disability because of the lead exposure, with the defendant countering that an IQ test of the parents may reveal deficiencies in the parents themselves that can account for the infant's disability genetically, in whole or in part negating the ingestion of lead paint as the cause. On a close issue of relevance, such a deposition was refused in Andon ex rel. Andon v. 302–304 Mott Street Associates.[26] As the Court of Appeals saw things, this was a discretionary call on the record, and there was room here for the appellate division's decision to deny the deposition.

It was pointed out that the defendants' main item of proof was the affidavit of a pediatrician stating that "cognitive deficiencies are not unique to lead exposure, but may be attributed to other factors, including a child's genetic history."[27] The Court faulted the pediatrician's affidavit because while he said he was "familiar with scientific literature" on the subject, "he failed to identify those studies or attach them to his affidavit." With a more thorough attachment of authority in a future case, the relevance standard, barely missed in Andon, might be readily satisfied.

Disclosure of Information on Social Media Sites

In our computer age, electronically stored information, commonly known as ESI, will also be subject to disclosure when relevant.[28] An example of ESI would be social networking sites where people recount so many events in their lives. These sites can often contain a treasure trove of relevant information ripe for disclosure, especially when what is posted is at odds with a party's claims and deposition testimony.[29]

In Romano v. Steelcase Inc., a groundbreaking decision in this area, defendant moved for an order under CPLR 3124 granting it access to plaintiff's current and historical Facebook and MySpace pages and accounts, including all deleted pages and related information.[30] Defendant claimed that the information was relevant because plaintiff placed certain material on the public portion of her social networking sites that was inconsistent with her claims concerning the extent and nature of her injuries, especially her claims for loss of enjoyment of life.[31] The court concluded that the information sought was both material and necessary to the defense of the action and issued an order granting defendant, among other things, access to plaintiff's current and historical Facebook and MySpace pages and accounts, including all deleted pages and related information.

---

[26] Andon ex rel. Andon v. 302–304 Mott Street Associates, 94 N.Y.2d 740, 709 N.Y.S.2d 873, 731 N.E.2d 589 (2000).

[27] *Andon,* 94 N.Y.2d at 746, 709 N.Y.S. 2d at 877, 731 N.E.2d at 593.

[28] See § 362.

[29] See Patrick M. Connors, *Disclosure of Information on Social Networking Websites,* 246 N.Y.L.J., Sept. 20, 2011, at 3.

[30] Romano v. Steelcase Inc., 30 Misc. 3d 426, 907 N.Y.S.2d 650 (Sup. Ct., Suffolk County 2010) (SPR 225:1).

[31] See also Flowers v. City of New York, 151 A.D.3d 590, 55 N.Y.S.3d 51 (1st Dep't 2017) (by submitting evidence of public portions of plaintiff's social media site, defendant made a threshold showing that examination of private social media accounts will result in the disclosure of relevant information).

Not all attempts to obtain information on social networking sites have been successful. For example, in McCann v. Harleysville Insurance Co. of New York,[32] plaintiff sought supplementary uninsured/underinsured motorist coverage. Defendant insurance company appealed from two orders denying its motions to compel disclosure of photographs and seeking an authorization for access to plaintiff's Facebook account. Defendant argued that the information sought was relevant with respect to whether plaintiff sustained a serious injury in the accident. The Fourth Department affirmed, concluding that defendant failed to establish a factual predicate with respect to the relevancy of the evidence and characterized the request as "a fishing expedition."[33]

In Abrams v. Pecile,[34] the First Department cited *McCann* and denied defendant's request for access to plaintiff's social networking accounts because no showing was made that the information sought was relevant. Subsequently, in Patterson v. Turner Construction Co.,[35] the First Department displayed a seemingly more liberal attitude toward disclosure of information on social networking sites. *Patterson* was a personal injury action in which plaintiff claimed damages for physical and psychological injuries, including the inability to work, anxiety, post-traumatic stress disorder, and the loss of enjoyment of life. The supreme court granted defendants' motion "to compel an authorization for all of plaintiff's Facebook records compiled after the incident alleged in the complaint, including any records previously deleted or archived."[36] On appeal, the First Department noted that it was possible that not all of plaintiff's Facebook communications were related to the events that gave rise to plaintiff's cause of action. Therefore, the court reversed and remanded the action "for a more specific identification of plaintiff's Facebook information that is relevant, in that it contradicts or conflicts with plaintiff's alleged restrictions, disabilities, and losses, and other claims."[37] Citing to *Romano*, the court further noted that "[t]he postings on plaintiff's online Facebook account, if relevant, are not shielded from discovery merely because plaintiff used the service's privacy settings to restrict access . . ., just as relevant matter from a personal diary is discoverable."[38]

In Forman v. Henkin,[39] the First Department's majority opinion appeared to return to the more restrictive attitude reflected in its *Abrams* decision. The plaintiff in *Forman* sued for injuries sustained in a fall from defendant's horse and defendant moved to compel plaintiff to provide authorizations to obtain records of her private Facebook postings. The First Department concluded that defendant failed to make a threshold showing of relevance sufficient to require disclosure of either plaintiff's private Facebook

---

[32]　McCann v. Harleysville Ins. Co. of New York, 78 A.D.3d 1524, 910 N.Y.S.2d 614 (4th Dep't 2010).

[33]　*McCann*, 78 A.D. 3d at 1525, 910 N.Y.S.2d at 615; see also Kregg v. Maldonado, 98 A.D.3d 1289, 951 N.Y.S.2d 301 (4th Dep't 2012) (denying defendants' motion to compel the disclosure of entire contents of the plaintiff's social media accounts because there was no specific contention that the information posted on the accounts contradicted plaintiff's claims for loss of enjoyment of life).

[34]　Abrams v. Pecile, 83 A.D.3d 527, 922 N.Y.S.2d 16 (1st Dep't 2011).

[35]　Patterson v. Turner Const. Co., 88 A.D.3d 617, 931 N.Y.S.2d 311 (1st Dep't 2011).

[36]　*Patterson*, 88 A.D.3d at 617, 931 N.Y.S.2d at 311.

[37]　*Patterson*, 88 A.D.3d at 617, 931 N.Y.S.2d at 312. For a discussion of whether a party should be afforded an in camera review of postings on a social media site to ascertain what should be produced, see Melissa "G" v. North Babylon Union Free School Dist., 48 Misc. 3d 389, 6 N.Y.S.3d 445, 316 Ed. Law Rep. 1001 (Sup. Ct., Suffolk County 2015).

[38]　See *Patterson*, 88 A.D.3d at 618, 931 N.Y.S.2d at 312.

[39]　Forman v. Henkin, 134 A.D.3d 529, 22 N.Y.S.3d 178 (1st Dep't 2015), lv. granted A.D.3d (1st Dep't 2016).

photographs or information about plaintiff's private Facebook messages. The court did, however, order plaintiff to provide defendant with all photographs of herself posted on Facebook, either before or after the accident, that she intended to use at trial. A two-judge dissent suggested that the First Department reexamine its caselaw addressing the disclosure of social media postings.[40]

To the extent defendants were seeking photographs or videos on plaintiffs' social networking sites, it is hard to square the holdings in *Forman*, *McCann* and *Abrams* with CPLR 3101(i), which provides that "[i]n addition to any other matter which may be subject to disclosure, there shall be full disclosure of any films, photographs, video tapes or audio tapes, including transcripts or memoranda thereof, involving a [party to the action]." This provision generally requires production of any films, photos and videos of the plaintiff, regardless of whether the material is relevant.[41] Therefore, the approach adopted in *Romano*, at least as applied to the production of any photos, film, or audio tapes of a party on a social networking site, appears to more closely comport with the statutory and decisional law in this arena.

§ 345. Disclosure from Parties and Nonparties

CPLR 3101(a) addresses disclosure from both parties and nonparties. Under CPLR 3101(a)(1), the word "party" includes an "officer, director, member, agent or employee of a party." CPLR 3101(a)(2), (3) and (4) provide for disclosure from various nonparties. The central requirement imposed by CPLR 3101(a) on disclosure from parties and nonparties is that the information or item be relevant.[1]

Disclosure from Parties

Today, there is full disclosure among all parties, regardless of the position they hold in the case vis-a-vis one another.[2] The plaintiff gets full disclosure from the defendant, and vice versa, and the defendant from a third-party defendant, and vice versa, but these are self-evident conclusions born of the obvious adversary status of those parties. Parties not necessarily in adversary status, or at least not directly so, are also required to make full disclosure to each other, such as co-defendants, and the plaintiff and third-party defendant. The Court of Appeals has concluded that, "in preparing for the trial, each defendant now has full discovery against his co-defendant whether or not there is a claim between them."[3] There is also statutory authorization for disclosure by a third-party defendant, who "shall have the rights of a party adverse to the other parties in the action."[4] Disclosure may even be sought between plaintiffs.[5] To the extent that disclosure between any two parties in a given case appears to be wholly unnecessary, or is shown

---

[40]   *Forman,* 134 A.D.3d at 534, 22 N.Y.S.3d at 183 (Saxe, J. dissenting); see Commentary C3101:50 on McKinney's CPLR 3101.

[41]   See Tran v. New Rochelle Hosp. Medical Center, 99 N.Y.2d 383, 756 N.Y.S.2d 509, 786 N.E.2d 444 (2003) (SPR 122:3) (NYSLD No. 519) (noting that CPLR 3101(i) does not contain any limitation as to relevancy or subject matter).

[1]   See § 343.

[2]   See Hawkins v. Genesee Hospital, 86 A.D.2d 971, 86 A.D.2d 972, 448 N.Y.S.2d 288 (4th Dep't 1982); Lombardo v. Pecora, 23 A.D.2d 460, 262 N.Y.S.2d 201 (2d Dep't 1965).

[3]   Schwartz v. Public Adm'r of Bronx County, 24 N.Y.2d 65, 71–72, 298 N.Y.S.2d 955, 960, 246 N.E.2d 725 (1969).

[4]   CPLR 1008; see § 163.

[5]   See Rosado v. Valvo, 58 Misc. 2d 944, 297 N.Y.S.2d 230 (Sup. Ct., Kings County 1969).

to be sought for harassment, it can be controlled by an individual protective order under CPLR 3103.[6]

It is also permissible for a party to obtain disclosure from herself, such as by causing her own deposition to be taken. This is done, for example, when the party wants to perpetuate her own testimony for use at the trial if she is apprehensive about surviving it.[7]

Disclosure from Nonparties

When it comes to seeking disclosure from a nonparty as provided by CPLR 3101(a)(2), (3) and (4), such as a witness or a person who has possession of something related to the case, the requirement of relevancy imposed by CPLR 3101(a) is the key. If any person previously possessed a claim or defense asserted in the action, such as an assignor, CPLR 3101(a)(2) provides for disclosure of relevant information from such person. 3101(a)(3) provides for disclosure from various people in six categories that are self-explanatory. The categories of nonparties in CPLR 3101(a)(2) and (3) do not serve an important role because a party unable to establish that the nonparty from whom disclosure is sought falls within them can turn to CPLR 3101(a)(4). That subdivision permits a party to obtain disclosure from a nonparty by merely serving a subpoena on the nonparty providing notice of "the circumstances or reasons such disclosure is sought or required."

Prior to 2014, the categories of nonparties in 3101(a)(2) and (3) held greater importance because a party relying on disclosure under CPLR 3101(a)(4) had to show "special circumstances" in the Second and Third Departments, or at least something more than mere relevance.[8] In Kapon v. Koch,[9] the Court of Appeals finally addressed the issue and concluded that CPLR 3101(a)(4) "imposes no requirement that the subpoenaing party demonstrate that it cannot obtain the requested disclosure from any other source [and] so long as the disclosure sought is relevant to the prosecution or defense of an action, it must be provided by the nonparty."

The Court held that CPLR 3101(a)(4) requires a party serving a subpoena, which is necessary to compel disclosure from a nonparty,[10] to "sufficiently state the 'circumstances or reasons' underlying the subpoena (either on the face of the subpoena itself or in a notice accompanying it) . . . ."[11] The Court reasoned that "[b]ecause a nonparty is likely to be less cognizant of the issues in pending litigation than a party, section 3101(a)(4)'s notice provision mandates that the nonparty is apprised of the 'circumstances or reasons' as to why the party seeks or requires the disclosure."[12] The subpoenaing party's notice obligation under CPLR 3101(a)(4) was described as a

---

[6]　See § 353.

[7]　See Lapensky v. Gordon, 41 Misc. 2d 958, 246 N.Y.S.2d 442 (Sup. Ct., Kings County 1964); § 358.

[8]　See, e.g., Troy Sand & Gravel Co., Inc. v. Town of Nassau, 80 A.D.3d 199, 912 N.Y.S.2d 798 (3d Dep't 2010); Kooper v. Kooper, 74 A.D.3d 6, 901 N.Y.S.2d 312 (2d Dep't 2010); Commentary C3101:22 on McKinney's CPLR 3101.

[9]　Kapon v. Koch, 23 N.Y.3d 32, 38, 988 N.Y.S.2d 559, 564, 11 N.E.3d 709, 714 (2014).

[10]　CPLR 3106(b); see § 351.

[11]　Kapon, 23 N.Y.3d at 34, 988 N.Y.S.2d at 562, 11 N.E.3d at 711.

[12]　Kapon, 23 N.Y.3d at 36, 988 N.Y.S.2d at 563, 11 N.E.3d at 713.

"minimal" one that was intended "to apprise a stranger to the litigation the 'circumstances or reasons' why the requested disclosure was sought or required."[13]

The federal counterpart of CPLR 3101, Rule 26 of the Federal Rules of Civil Procedure, contains no added requirements for disclosure by a nonparty. This was often cited as a factor by a plaintiff opting for a federal rather than a New York court when a choice was available and when the testimony of a nonparty was a key element.[14] With *Kapon's* abolition of the "special circumstance" requirement from CPLR 3101(a)(4), the obtaining of disclosure from nonparties should be more in line with the discovery rules applicable in federal court.

When medical testimony is required, as is so often the case in tort actions, both CPLR 3101(a)(3) and (4) become relevant. CPLR 3101(a)(3) permits a party to obtain disclosure as a matter of right from the party's own treating physician and from any physician he has duly retained as an expert witness.[15] While P can depose P's own treating physician under this part of paragraph 3, D cannot. But D may depose P's treating physician under some other part of paragraph 3, as where the physician resides more than 100 miles from the courthouse.[16] When convinced in a given situation of the need for pretrial interrogation, the courts have also required a treating physician (as opposed to an expert) to depose under CPLR 3101(a)(4).[17]

While neither CPLR 3101(a)(3) or (4) permits one side to depose the other side's experts, some other provisions may authorize it, such as CPLR 3101(d)(1)(ii), discussed later.[18] In addition, Rule 13(c) in the Commercial Division provides for expert disclosure in commercial cases similar to that available in federal actions, including depositions, unless otherwise ordered by the court or stipulated by the parties.[19] Parties to lawsuits that are not in the Commercial Division can stipulate to disclosure from experts that is broader than that permitted by the CPLR.

When a person is a party to a lawsuit in a representative rather than personal capacity, some old caselaw holds that such person can be examined as a party only as to data come by in the representative status. With respect to anything the party has to say or give in his personal capacity, he must be treated as a nonparty witness and the requirements of either paragraph 3 or 4 of CPLR 3101(a) must be met.[20] Such an approach is of doubtful validity today, especially under the broad view taken of CPLR 3101(a)(4) in the *Kapon* decision.

Disclosure can be obtained from an infant, and under oath, with the proviso, if the matter is contested, that the court conduct "a preliminary examination to determine the competency of the infant."[21]

---

[13]   *Kapon*, 23 N.Y.3d at 39, 988 N.Y.S.2d at 565, 11 N.E.3d at 715. For a further discussion of the *Kapon* decision, see the Practice Commentary to CPLR 3101, C3101:22 ("The 'Circumstances' Rule of 3101(a)(4)"). For a discussion of the corresponding burdens of proof on a motion to quash a subpoena under CPLR 2304, see § 384.

[14]   See item 15 on the list of choice of forum factors in § 616 (Practitioner's Edition).

[15]   A 1993 amendment clarifies that dentists and podiatrists also fall under this provision.

[16]   See Roeck v. Columbia-Greene Medical Center, 248 A.D.2d 921, 670 N.Y.S.2d 269 (3d Dep't 1998).

[17]   See Bianchi v. Galster Management Corp., 131 A.D.3d 558, 15 N.Y.S.3d 189 (2d Dep't 2015).

[18]   See §§ 348 and 363.

[19]   22 N.Y.C.R.R. § 202.70(g), Commercial Div. Rule 13(c).

[20]   See, for example, Pardee v. Mutual Ben. Life Ins. Co., 238 A.D. 294, 265 N.Y.S. 837 (4th Dep't 1933).

[21]   Muscoreil By Vigneri v. Pool Mart, Inc., 107 A.D.2d 1025, 486 N.Y.S.2d 518 (4th Dep't 1985).

Disclosure from a Corporation

If a party is a corporation, each of its officers, directors, members, agents, and employees is also deemed a "party" for disclosure purposes.[22] A party who needs relevant data or material from a nonparty corporation can seek it through CPLR 3101(a)(2), (3) or (4), under which the corporate entity is treated as a "person."[23] These subdivisions should also apply to any entity, corporate or otherwise, from whom disclosure is sought through its agents.[24] A corporate employee who has the requisite knowledge and information may respond to a disclosure request on behalf of the corporation.[25] A party who can't single out the particular person in the corporation's employ to whom a disclosure request should be properly directed can direct it to the corporation as such and leave it to the corporation to designate the appropriate person to respond.

Whenever disclosure is sought from a corporation through a deposition, whether as a party or as a nonparty witness, the choice in the first instance of who will be produced in the corporate behalf is with the corporation rather than the examining party.[26] That was the general rule and it would seem to remain so despite the addition of a subdivision (d) to CPLR 3106 in 1984 presuming to change it. The change is illusory. It allows the seeking party to name the "particular officer, director, member or employee" who is to do the deposing, "unless" a notice is served by the corporation's side, at least 10 days before the scheduled deposition, identifying another person that will be produced instead.[27]

If the corporation should submit an employee who does not have the requisite knowledge, it can be compelled afterwards, with a protective order, to produce a designated employee who has.[28] The party seeking additional disclosure has the burden of demonstrating that: (1) the representatives already deposed had insufficient knowledge, or were otherwise inadequate; and (2) there is a substantial likelihood that the person sought for an additional deposition possess information that is relevant.[29]

A person who is an officer, director, member, or employee of a party at the time the deposition is taken qualifies as a "party," rather than as a mere "witness" under CPLR 3106(b).[30] Hence, deponents in these categories need not be served with a subpoena and an out-of-state employee may be required, subject to the procedures in CPLR 3106(d) outlined above, to appear for a deposition merely by serving notice on the corporate entity if it is a party in the action. The point arose in Sammy v. First American Title Ins.

---

[22]   CPLR 3101(a)(1).

[23]   See BAII Banking Corp. v. Northville Industries Corp., 204 A.D.2d 223, 612 N.Y.S.2d 141, 142 (1st Dep't 1994).

[24]   See Smith v. Robilotto, 27 A.D.2d 684, 276 N.Y.S.2d 323 (3d Dep't 1967) (for disclosure purposes, an unincorporated association should be treated the same as a corporation).

[25]   Delta Diagnostic Radiology, P.C. v. Travelers Property Cas. Co. of America, 35 Misc. 3d 147(A), 954 N.Y.S.2d 758 (App. Term, 2d Dep't 2012).

[26]   See Rector, Church Wardens and Vestrymen of St. Bartholomew's Church in City of New York v. Committee to Preserve St. Bartholomew's Church, Inc., 84 A.D.2d 516, 443 N.Y.S.2d 233 (1st Dep't 1981); Necchi S.p.A. v. Nelco Sewing Mach. Co., 23 A.D.2d 543, 256 N.Y.S.2d 347 (1st Dep't 1965).

[27]   See Commentary C3106:7 on McKinney's CPLR 3106.

[28]   JMJ Contract Management, Inc. v. Ingersoll-Rand Co., 100 A.D.2d 291, 475 N.Y.S.2d 528 (3d Dep't 1984).

[29]   Gomez v. State, 106 A.D.3d 870, 965 N.Y.S.2d 542 (2d Dep't 2013).

[30]   See Commentary C3106:3 on McKinney's CPLR 3106.

Co. of New York[31] where the chief executive officer of defendant corporation was served with a subpoena and sought to have it quashed. The court noted that the plaintiff could have sought the deposition of this witness with a CPLR 3106(d) notice served on the defendant even though the witness worked and resided in California. By contrast, a New York subpoena could not be served on the witness in California.[32]

International Disclosure

The generous scope of disclosure in New York State actions is generally far broader than that embraced by the law of most foreign lands. In Richbell Information Services, Inc. v. Jupiter Partners L.P.,[33] the court issued an extensive opinion addressing the standards to be applied in a New York State action involving international disclosure. The First Department listed several factors that should be considered in all cases involving international disclosure, i.e., when the information sought is outside the United States. The factors are borrowed from section 442 of the Restatement (Third) of Foreign Relations Law and include, among others, the importance of the requested information to the litigation, the degree of specificity of the request, the availability of alternative means for securing the information, and whether compliance with the request would undermine important interests of the state where the information is located. Conflicting foreign statutes must also be considered. Moreover, parties are only entitled to information that is relevant pursuant to CPLR 3101(a), regardless of any conflicting foreign law.[34]

Lawyers seeking disclosure from foreign nationals should be aware of the Hague Evidence Convention.[35] The convention's disclosure procedures were described in Wilson v. Lufthansa German Airlines[36] as "quite costly and cumbersome even in situations where the foreign government has agreed to cooperate." Certainly, they are more trouble than the procedures of the New York CPLR or the Federal Rules of Civil Procedure. The party seeking the disclosure would like to sidestep the convention whenever possible, and it is apparently possible whenever the foreign national is within the jurisdiction of the court, at least when the claim arose locally, as in the *Wilson* case.[37] In that situation the case holds the convention's use optional, not mandatory.

In addition, any party seeking international disclosure must also review the provisions for obtaining letters rogatory in CPLR 3108, particularly when the disclosure is sought from a nonparty.[38]

---

[31] Sammy v. First American Title Ins. Co. of New York, 2015 WL 4597115 (Sup. Ct., Queens County 2015).

[32] See § 383.

[33] Richbell Information Services, Inc. v. Jupiter Partners L.P., 32 A.D.3d 150, 816 N.Y.S.2d 470 (1st Dep't 2006).

[34] See Commentary C3101:11A in McKinney's CPLR 3101 (discussing standards for international disclosure).

[35] Its formal name is the Hague Convention on the Taking of Evidence Abroad in Civil or Commercial Matters. It can be found as an appendix to 28 U.S.C.A. § 1781. It was ratified by the United States in 1972.

[36] Wilson v. Lufthansa German Airlines, 108 A.D.2d 393, 489 N.Y.S.2d 575 (2d Dep't 1985).

[37] See 23/23 Communications Corp., d/b/a Communications Diversified v. General Motors Corporation, 172 Misc. 2d 821, 823–824, 660 N.Y.S.2d 296, 297 (Sup. Ct., New York County 1997) (court has the power to compel a corporate employer to produce at trial an employee who is located out-of-state as a witness).

[38] See § 360.

Disclosure from Arbitrators and Mediators

Arbitrators, like judges, are as a rule not subject to disclosure,[39] but a troublesome issue is whether a mediator is.

In Hauzinger v. Hauzinger,[40] the parties participated in mediation that concluded with the signing of a separation agreement. In the subsequent action for divorce, the nonparty mediator was served with a subpoena by the defendant wife seeking his deposition and any records he possessed relating to the mediation process. The supreme court denied the mediator's motion to quash the subpoena and the Fourth Department affirmed.[41] The court also refused to apply the confidentiality provisions in the Uniform Mediation Act as a matter of public policy, noting that New York has not adopted the Act.[42] The Court of Appeals affirmed *Hauzinger* in a brief memorandum[43] stressing that both sides "waived mediation confidentiality," thus keeping the issue of confidentiality—and insulation from disclosure—open in future cases.

B. EXCLUDED MATTERS

Table of Sections

§ 346.   Privileged Matter
§ 347.   Attorney's Work Product
§ 348.   Materials Prepared for Litigation
§ 348A. Identification of Experts; Statement of Expected Testimony
§ 349.   Revelation of Names of Witnesses

§ 346. Privileged Matter

Subdivision (b) of CPLR 3101 accords to "privileged matter" an immunity from disclosure. A determination of whether information is privileged is governed by the rules of evidence, which apply as they would at a trial. Whatever is privileged at the trial is privileged as well on pretrial disclosure. All privileges are included, whether they come from the constitution directly, such as that against self-incrimination;[1] from evidence statutes like those governing communications between spouses,[2] attorney and client,[3] physician and patient,[4] clergy and penitent,[5] and the like; from the law of criminal procedure, such as that governing the secrecy of grand jury proceedings;[6] or, indeed, from

---

[39] Hoeft v. MVL Group, Inc., 343 F.3d 57, 66 (2d Cir. 2003) (noting "the well-established rule that arbitrators may not be deposed absent 'clear evidence of impropriety' ").

[40] Hauzinger v. Hauzinger, 43 A.D.3d 1289, 842 N.Y.S.2d 646 (4th Dep't 2007), aff'd, 10 N.Y.3d 923, 862 N.Y.S.2d 456, 892 N.E.2d 849 (2008).

[41] See also City of Newburgh v. Hauser, 126 A.D.3d 926, 3 N.Y.S.3d 616 (2d Dep't 2015) (affirming order compelling production of documents submitted to private mediator deemed material and relevant to the defense of action).

[42] Commentary C3101:25B on McKinney's CPLR 3101.

[43] Hauzinger v. Hauzinger, 10 N.Y.3d 923, 862 N.Y.S.2d 456, 892 N.E.2d 849 (2008).

[1] U.S. Const. amends. V, XIV; see also CPLR 4501.

[2] CPLR 4502.

[3] CPLR 4503.

[4] CPLR 4504.

[5] CPLR 4505.

[6] See Melendez v. City of New York, 109 A.D.2d 13, 489 N.Y.S.2d 741 (1st Dep't 1985), discussing the circumstances under which grand jury testimony may be disclosed in a civil action.

caselaw, such as the murky "public interest" privilege, which protects certain communications made in the course of governmental activities.[7]

As long as the objection is properly asserted, all privileged matter is excluded. The original version of CPLR 3101(b) recognized this in explicit language when the objection was made by a party, but in practice anyone entitled to assert the privilege was entitled to interpose the objection, even a nonparty witness. By eliminating the word "party" and permitting the objection to be made by any "person entitled to assert the privilege," a 1993 amendment of CPLR 3101(b) confirms that a nonparty may also invoke privilege.

The Court of Appeals has instructed that the proponent of the attorney-client privilege bears the burden of establishing that the communication was: (1) between an attorney and a client, (2) made "for the purpose of facilitating the rendition of legal advice or services," (3) made in the course of a professional relationship, (4) predominantly of a legal character, (5) confidential, and (6) that the privilege was not waived.[8] Regarding waiver, New York courts have recognized the common interest doctrine of the attorney-client privilege, which generally allows two or more clients who have retained separate counsel to represent them "to shield from disclosure certain attorney-client communications that are revealed to one another for the purpose of furthering a common legal interest."[9] In Ambac Assurance Corp. v. Countrywide Home Loans, Inc., the Court held that this doctrine, which is an exception to the waiver rule, applies only in situations where the sharing of attorney-client communications took place while the clients faced "pending or reasonably anticipated litigation," and not simply where the clients shared "any common legal interest," such as a merger.[10]

If it appears that not everything involved in an examination will be privileged, the examination can be scheduled as usual, but with the deponent's right to decline privileged answers preserved.[11] This applies even to a party's attorney when, because of involvement in the transaction at issue, the attorney has been directed to submit to a deposition.[12] If it appears that all questions would fall into a privileged sphere, however, the examination can be denied in toto.[13]

The Court of Appeals has held that a report by outside counsel giving legal advice to a client doesn't lose its immunity just because it may refer to unprivileged matter, like communications with third persons.[14] The communication must, however, be "primarily or predominantly of a legal character."[15] There need not be any showing that a report

---

[7]   See, e.g., In re World Trade Center Bombing Litigation, 93 N.Y.2d 1, 686 N.Y.S.2d 743, 709 N.E.2d 452 (1999); Cirale v. 80 Pine St. Corp., 35 N.Y.2d 113, 359 N.Y.S.2d 1, 316 N.E.2d 301 (1974); see also Commentary C3101:25A on McKinney's CPLR 3101. The Freedom of Information Law (FOIL) enacted in 1974 and recast in 1977, Pub. Off. Law §§ 84–90, is relevant here. The law and its interplay with CPLR disclosure is discussed in § 348.

[8]   Ambac Assur. Corp. v. Countrywide Home Loans, Inc., 27 N.Y.3d 616, 624, 36 N.Y.S.3d 838, 842–43, 57 N.E.3d 30, 34–35 (2016).

[9]   Ambac Assur. Corp, 27 N.Y.3d at 625, 36 N.Y.S.3d at 843, 57 N.E.3d at 35.

[10]   Ambac Assur. Corp, 27 N.Y.3d at 632, 36 N.Y.S.3d at 848, 57 N.E.3d at 40.

[11]   Flanigen v. Mullen & Gunn, Inc., 45 Misc. 2d 944, 258 N.Y.S.2d 609 (Sup. Ct., Erie County 1965).

[12]   McNulty v. McNulty, 81 A.D.2d 581, 437 N.Y.S.2d 438 (2d Dep't 1981); Planned Indus. Centers, Inc. v. Eric Builders, Inc., 51 A.D.2d 586, 378 N.Y.S.2d 760 (2d Dep't 1976).

[13]   Osserman v. Osserman, 92 A.D.2d 932, 460 N.Y.S.2d 355 (2d Dep't 1983).

[14]   Spectrum Systems Intern. Corp. v. Chemical Bank, 78 N.Y.2d 371, 575 N.Y.S.2d 809, 581 N.E.2d 1055 (1991) (NYSLD No. 386).

[15]   Rossi v. Blue Cross and Blue Shield of Greater New York, 73 N.Y.2d 588, 594, 542 N.Y.S.2d 508, 511, 540 N.E.2d 703, 706 (1989).

was prepared for litigation before it can earn an attorney/client privilege under subdivision (b) of CPLR 3101. The proximity of litigation, basic in determining immunity for material prepared for litigation under CPLR 3101(d)(2),[16] is not a major factor in determining privilege under CPLR 3101(b).[17] Furthermore, the attorney/client privilege is not restricted solely to the litigation scene. If it were, a myriad of relationships that don't involve litigation would suddenly be stripped of any attorney/client privilege protections.

If a paper contains a privileged communication, it may be withheld for that reason.[18] If an issue arises as to whether the privilege obtains and it appears necessary for the court to examine the material in order to resolve the issue, the court can examine it in camera before it directs the item to be turned over to the adverse party.[19] When feasible, the privilege may be upheld by the court's just redacting the privileged portions of the paper.

Since the scope of the privilege is a matter of the law of evidence and its resolutions are adopted from that realm, it need not detain us further here.[20] The same may not be said, however, for the exclusions contained in subdivisions (c) and (d) of CPLR 3101, which Article 31 creates and which it is therefore obliged to regulate. The immunity for privileged matter conferred by subdivision (b) is absolute, in common with that conferred on an attorney's work product by subdivision (c). "[I]f a privilege applies, the [information] simply need not be produced."[21] Both of these exceptions to disclosure are to be contrasted shortly with the exemption for material prepared for litigation, created by subdivision (d)(2), which is just a conditional exemption.

§ 347. Attorney's Work Product

Subdivision (c) of CPLR 3101 makes unobtainable the "work product of an attorney"—an ill-defined category whose potential for mischief has been avoided only because the judiciary has accorded it a very narrow scope. It is a category wholly distinct from the "materials ... prepared in anticipation of litigation" of subdivision (d)(2), treated in the next section. The fact that immunity is absolute under CPLR 3101(c), while that of CPLR 3101(d)(2) is only conditional, is the factor that requires as sharp a line as possible between the two categories.

The drafters of the CPLR did not intend the two to be separate. They proposed a single subdivision covering both and as to both of them the immunity was to be only conditional, i.e., dissolvable so as to necessitate disclosure upon stated contingencies.[1] That would have codified for New York the federal approach enunciated in Hickman v. Taylor.[2] The *Hickman* case might have occasionally offered some insights into the resolution of problems arising under these New York provisions, but the value of the

---

[16] See § 348.

[17] *Spectrum Systems,* 78 N.Y.2d at 380, 575 N.Y.S.2d at 815, 581 N.E.2d at 1061.

[18] See CPLR 3122(b); *Spectrum Systems,* 78 N.Y.2d at 377, 575 N.Y.S.2d at 813, 581 N.E.2d at 1059; *Rossi,* 73 N.Y.2d at 594, 542 N.Y.S.2d at 511, 540 N.E.2d at 706; § 362.

[19] *Cirale,* 35 N.Y.2d at 119, 359 N.Y.S.2d at 5, 316 N.E.2d at 304.

[20] For a detailed discussion of the attorney-client privilege, see Barker and Alexander, Evidence in New York State and Federal Courts, §§ 5:3–5:17 (2nd ed. 2011); Farrell, Prince, Richardson on Evidence, §§ 5–101–5–214 (11th ed. 1995).

[21] *World Trade Center Litigation,* 93 N.Y.2d at 12, 686 N.Y.S.2d at 749.

[1] See 1st Rep. Leg. Doc. No. 6(b), p. 119 (1957).

[2] Hickman v. Taylor, 329 U.S. 495, 67 S. Ct. 385, 91 L. Ed. 451, 1947 A.M.C. 1 (1947).

case on the New York scene is undermined by this subdividing, with one category absolutely and the other only conditionally immune.[3]

Although it spoke of the "work product of an attorney," *Hickman* gave it no absolute immunity. The phrase was used in *Hickman* to describe such phenomena as "interviews, statements, memoranda, correspondence, briefs, mental impressions, personal beliefs, and countless other tangible and intangible" things.[4] Whatever those things might amount to in a given case, there would be no absolutes connected with them that would tie the courts' hands and bar case-by-case solutions.

In giving the "work product" of subdivision (c) an absolute immunity, the New York legislative hands that wrought the change probably assumed that without it there'd be some risk that the privileged lawyer-client communication would be invaded. But protection against that result is what subdivision CPLR 3101(b) accomplishes by immunizing—absolutely—"privileged" matter, and for that, it needs no help from subdivision (c). In one case, for example, the court noted that "reports of an attorney to his client as to the progress of pending litigation or advice and opinions rendered to a client who is on the brink of litigation should clearly be considered 'work product of an attorney' and thus within the protection of subdivision (c)."[5] But wouldn't the attorney-client privilege itself, independently applicable under subdivision (b), insulate those items just as securely? As enacted by the legislature, in other words, and as they remain on the books today, subdivisions (d)(2) (materials prepared for litigation) and (b) (privileged matter) between them essentially accomplish what the legislature stuffed into the "attorney's work product" category of subdivision (c).

The question then is: where does that leave subdivision (c)? What is it that can be categorized as an attorney's work product distinct from both privileged matter on the one side and materials prepared for litigation on the other? The more obvious the items that come to mind, the more absurd it is to think that the legislature wants them absolutely immunized from disclosure. What could be more the "work product" of an attorney than a deed, will, contract, mortgage, bond, or the like? Certainly these, if relevant to the litigation, can't be concealed from an adversary's view. *Hickman*, the U.S. Supreme Court case from which both categories emerged, offers no support for the idea that items like these are to be excluded (absolutely!) from cases in which, indeed, they may be dispositive of all the substantive rights and obligations asserted.[6]

The judiciary, in large measure tacitly, has recognized this. It has cast precious little under the "work product" category of subdivision (c), preferring instead to fit doubtful items under the "materials . . . prepared in anticipation of litigation" banner of CPLR 3101(d)(2), where the conditional immunity can be overcome and the matters ordered disclosed when stated conditions are met. Information protected under CPLR 3101(c) "is generally limited to materials prepared by an attorney, while acting as an attorney,

---

[3]   This bifurcation was the work of legislative staff after the drafters had handed over their recommendations. See 5th Rep. Leg. Doc. No. 15, p. 444 (1961).

[4]   *Hickman,* 329 U.S. at 511, 67 S.Ct. at 393.

[5]   Wickham v. Socony Mobil Oil Co., 45 Misc. 2d 311, 312, 256 N.Y.S.2d 342, 344 (Sup. Ct., Albany County 1965); but see Great American Ins. Co. of New York v. Castleton Commodities Intern. LLC, 2015 WL 6437397 (S.D.N.Y. 2015), on reconsideration, 2015 WL 6955176 (S.D.N.Y. 2015) (declining to apply a broadened "attorney work product" privilege under CPLR 3101(c) to plaintiffs' communications "given the narrowness of the provision's scope").

[6]   See Siegel, *Disclosure under the CPLR: Taking Stock After Two Years*, 11th Jud. Conf. Rep. 148 at 151–158 (1966).

which contain his or her legal analysis, conclusions, theory, or strategy."[7] It has been held that an item will not even begin to qualify as "work product" merely upon a showing that a lawyer drew it or did it; it must be shown to be something that only a lawyer could draw or do.[8] The fact that a lawyer has taken a statement from a witness, for example, does not transmute the statement into a "work product": a lay person could have taken it.[9] The general rule is that data received by the attorney from others while investigating in behalf of the client is neither privileged under CPLR 3101(b) nor necessarily "work product" under subdivision (c). This is so even though the material itself, such as a statement or report, may qualify as material "prepared in anticipation of litigation" and thus be conditionally immunized by subdivision (d)(2).

In construing the parameters of CPLR 3101(c)'s immunity, the courts have concluded that relevant information subject to disclosure under CPLR 3101(a) cannot be shielded "merely because the client has obtained his knowledge through his lawyer's investigative efforts."[10]

The dormant state in which the "work product" of subdivision (c) finds itself earns it less of a place in our study. It may have already been given more treatment than it deserves, and it's gotten that much only because in *Hickman*, it was the Siamese twin of what is now subdivision (d)(2)'s "materials . . . prepared in anticipation of litigation." The surgery that separated them in New York was a botched job; all of the vital organs went to (d), which is as active in New York practice as (c) is quiescent. Perhaps (c)'s only claim to attention, in fact, is the history it shares with (d).

§ 348. Materials Prepared for Litigation

The most exercised exclusionary category in CPLR 3101 is "materials . . . prepared in anticipation of litigation," governed by subdivision (d)(2). It gives a conditional immunity to materials otherwise discoverable under the broad criteria of subdivision (a) if it is shown that they were "prepared in anticipation of litigation."[1]

The condition that removes the immunity and makes the materials discoverable is a finding by the court "that the party seeking discovery has substantial need of the materials in the preparation of the case and is unable without undue hardship to obtain the substantial equivalent of the materials by other means."[2]

---

[7] Geffner v. Mercy Medical Center, 125 A.D.3d 802, 4 N.Y.S.3d 283 (2d Dep't 2015) (rejecting claim of protection under CPLR 3101(c) and ordering plaintiff to provide defendants with copies of an audio recording of an interview lawyer conducted with the defendant).

[8] Brunswick Corp. v. Aetna Cas. & Sur. Co., 49 Misc. 2d 1018, 269 N.Y.S.2d 30 (Sup. Ct., Erie County 1966), mod'd, 27 A.D.2d 182, 278 N.Y.S.2d 459 (4th Dep't 1967).

[9] People v. Kozlowski, 11 N.Y.3d 223, 245, 869 N.Y.S.2d 848, 862, 898 N.E.2d 891, 905 (2008).

[10] Kenford Co., Inc. v. Erie County, 55 A.D.2d 466, 470, 390 N.Y.S.2d 715, 718 (4th Dep't 1977); see Spectrum Systems Intern. Corp. v. Chemical Bank, 157 A.D.2d 444, 449, 558 N.Y.S.2d 486, 488–89 (1st Dep't 1990), aff'd as modified, 78 N.Y.2d 371, 575 N.Y.S.2d 809, 581 N.E.2d 1055 (1991).

[1] Before 1985, when subdivision (d) was amended, the counterpart category consisted of "any writing or anything created by or for a party or his agent in preparation for litigation." It generated much caselaw. The new language borrows extensively from the terminology of the counterpart provisions of Rule 26 of the Federal Rules of Civil Procedure, but in so doing makes more of a change—from prior New York law—in language than in substance. Most of the standing legion of caselaw on the old subdivision (d)—especially cases that end up allowing discovery—remain intact under the new language. The more important of those cases will be treated in this section. A treatment of the CPLR 3101(d) amendment appears in Commentary C3101:29 on McKinney's CPLR 3101.

[2] CPLR 3101(d)(2). The pre-1985 language was that "the court finds that the material can no longer be duplicated because of a change in conditions and that withholding it will result in injustice or undue

The party resisting disclosure on the ground that the item falls under subdivision (d)(2) has the burden of establishing, with specificity, that the item was prepared "exclusively in anticipation of litigation."[3] If the papers before the court don't suffice for resolution of the issue, the court can require that the item be produced for inspection in camera before the item is turned over to the other party.[4] If the court is satisfied that the particular item, report, or statement was drawn up only after consultation with counsel and upon counsel's advice, it will ordinarily get the subdivision (d)(2) immunity as material prepared for litigation.[5]

Expert Reports

The report of an expert is one example of an item prepared for litigation that is subject to the provisions of paragraph 2 of CPLR 3101(d)—not to be confused with expert disclosure, which is governed by paragraph 1 and is separately treated later.[6] The expert's report, embodying his opinion, is often a subject of dispute. The medical expert in the personal injury case is probably the first example to spring to mind because of the proliferation of tort cases in New York, but the provision embraces any expert report in any context.[7] Where an engineer at D's behest examines a washing machine alleged to have injured P, for example, the engineer's report qualifies as "material prepared in anticipation of litigation" and is governed by this provision.[8]

Court rules about the trading of medical reports in ordinary tort cases narrow the operation of subdivision (d) substantially,[9] and in one instance another statute, CPLR 3121(b), does the same thing by directing the exchange of reports of examining physicians in certain instances.[10] The reports of appraisers are also the subject of a separate provision, CPLR 3140, which allows the rules to supersede the provisions of CPLR 3101(d) in condemnation and tax review proceedings.[11] Unless such a rule exists, however, or the court makes a disposition under its expanded powers under paragraph 1 of CPLR 3101(d),[12] paragraph 2 governs the reports of experts.

A divided First Department held in a condemnation case that the condemnor's earlier appraisal report, in a sum more than the same appraiser's later one, constituted material prepared in anticipation of litigation under CPLR 3101(d)(2) and that the special showing needed to lift the immunity had not been made.[13]

---

hardship," which amounts to essentially the same thing and also preserves the great body of caselaw on the predecessor provision.

    [3]   See, e.g., Ligoure v. City of New York, 128 A.D.3d 1027, 1028, 9 N.Y.S.3d 678, 679 (2d Dep't 2015).

    [4]   Haire v. Long Is. R.R. Co., 29 A.D.2d 553, 285 N.Y.S.2d 717 (2d Dep't 1967).

    [5]   Albano v. Schwab Bros. Trucking, Inc., 27 A.D.2d 901, 278 N.Y.S.2d 780 (4th Dep't 1967).

    [6]   See § 348A.

    [7]   The exchange of medical reports of examining physicians is addressed in CPLR 3121(b): see § 363.

    [8]   Silberberg v. Hotpoint Division of General Elec. Co., 23 A.D.2d 754, 259 N.Y.S.2d 60 (1st Dep't 1965).

    [9]   See, e.g., 22 N.Y.C.R.R. § 202.17, the rule applicable in the supreme and county courts. The rule was amended effective April 17, 1998, to make it unnecessary for a party to secure a narrative report from the physician and to make acceptable the briefer notations found in such as insurance and workers' compensation forms. See Bauman, *Letter to the Editor*, N.Y.L.J., June 1, 1998, at 2. Similar changes were made in the parallel rules of other courts. See Commentary C3121:4 on McKinney's CPLR 3121; SPR 73:1–2.

    [10]   See § 363.

    [11]   See 22 N.Y.C.R.R. §§ 202.59–202.61, applicable in the supreme and county courts; Commentary C3140:1 & 2 on McKinney's CPLR 3140.

    [12]   See § 348A.

    [13]   CMRC Corp., Ltd. v. State, 270 A.D.2d 27, 704 N.Y.S.2d 219 (1st Dep't 2000) (SPR 94:2–3). Should the appraiser take the stand, however, the unused appraisal may be relevant for cross-examination and can

Statements of Witnesses and Parties

Most often seen under CPLR 3101(d)(2) are papers of one sort or another, statements and reports of diverse kinds. Whether or not a given item qualifies for the paragraph 2 immunity as litigation material is usually a sui generis inquiry, often resolved on the basis of the pro and con papers submitted on a motion for a protective order.[14] Probably the most common example of an item sought by one side, but claimed by the other to be litigation material, is a statement given by a witness. These statements ordinarily do qualify for the subdivision (d)(2) immunity and are hence undisclosable unless the stated conditions are satisfied.

To be distinguished from the statement of a witness is the statement of a party made to someone on the other side. Such a statement may have been given, for example, when a person injured in an accident is approached by the potential defendant's insurance adjuster before the injured person has retained counsel.[15] Parties are entitled as a matter of right to obtain copies of their own statements pursuant to the explicit authority of CPLR 3101(e); subdivision (d) does not govern it.[16] The rule applies to corporate parties as well as individuals.[17] Moreover, CPLR 3101(e) has been broadly interpreted to include photographs.[18] Items such as photographs and videotapes are now independently subject to disclosure under CPLR 3101(i), discussed below.

Films, Photographs, Video, and Audio Tapes of a Party

Surveillance tapes had become so commonly embroiled in tort cases (although not limited to them) that a subdivision (i) was added to CPLR 3101 in 1993 to regulate them. This subdivision allows for full disclosure of all "films, photographs, video tapes or audio tapes, including transcripts or memoranda thereof, involving a [party or agent of a party]." As if this was not broad enough, the provision goes on to require disclosure "of all portions of such material, including out-takes, rather than only those portions a party intends to use." CPLR 3101(i)'s directive, therefore, apparently overrides any protection afforded to the items as work product under CPLR 3101(d)(2).

Some background is helpful here. When defendants suspect a personal injury plaintiff is feigning or exaggerating an injury, they may try to make a surveillance videotape hoping to catch the plaintiff in robust activities to prove that the injuries are not as claimed. In 1992, the Court of Appeals, resolved a departmental dispute on the issue of disclosure of such tapes in DiMichel v. South Buffalo Ry. Co.,[19] holding that the plaintiff is entitled to their production, but must first submit to a deposition and narrate his injuries, the premise being that a malingerer can be exposed by that means.

---

be turned over to the condemnee at that point, with an adjournment offered the condemnee, if needed, to peruse the appraisal to prepare for the cross-examination. See Niagara Mohawk Power Corp. v. Town of Moreau Assessor, 8 A.D.3d 935, 779 N.Y.S.2d 608 (3d Dep't 2004).

[14]   See, e.g., Corona Courts, Inc. v. Frank G. Shattuck Co., 50 Misc. 2d 1066, 272 N.Y.S.2d 217 (Sup. Ct., Monroe County 1966).

[15]   See generally McHugh ex rel. Kurtz v. Fitzgerald, 280 A.D.2d 771, 719 N.Y.S.2d 785 (3d Dep't 2001).

[16]   Free Park Associates v. Cepeda, 55 Misc. 3d 460, 44 N.Y.S.3d 895 (Dist. Ct. Nassau County 2017); see Commentary C3101:46 on McKinney's CPLR 3101.

[17]   See, e.g., Briggs v. Spencerport Road Plaza, Inc., 19 A.D.2d 943, 244 N.Y.S.2d 17 (4th Dep't 1963) (applying provision to enable corporate party to obtain from adverse party copy of statement furnished by corporation's employee).

[18]   Saccente v. Toterhi, 35 A.D.2d 692, 314 N.Y.S.2d 593 (1st Dep't 1970).

[19]   DiMichel v. South Buffalo Ry. Co., 80 N.Y.2d 184, 590 N.Y.S.2d 1, 604 N.E.2d 63 (1992).

When CPLR 3101(i) was enacted to require that surveillance tapes be made available even if not planned for use at the trial, there was no provision for a deposition. The Court of Appeals therefore held in Tran v. New Rochelle Hosp. Medical Center[20] that the statute no longer required the presurrender deposition.[21] In response to the *Tran* decision, many defendants in personal injury cases now postpone their surveillance activities until after deposing the plaintiff, and making doubly sure at the deposition to probe the damages issues thoroughly.

In Zegarelli v. Hughes,[22] the Court held that videotapes are subsumed under the phrase "documents and things" and are, therefore, obtainable by using a CPLR 3120(1)(i) notice for discovery and inspection.[23] The Court observed that CPLR 3120 requests are customarily satisfied by the party's lawyer, who makes copies of the items sought, such as a videotape, and forwards them to the party serving the notice. "Where that is done, it is understood that the originals must be available for inspection on request."[24]

While CPLR 3101(i) was enacted with the defendant's surreptitious tapes of the plaintiff in mind, its language is broad enough to embrace any films, photographs, and audio or video tapes of a party, even those made by the party from whom disclosure is sought. In one case, for example, D was allowed a discovery of tapes P had made of her wedding, which took place about a year and a half after her alleged injury on D's train platform. The tape was held discoverable because it could depict P "in activity which contrasts with her claims that she is no longer able to exercise regularly."[25]

More recently, surveillance videotaping has become somewhat obsolete as people have taken to filming a substantial portion of their own lives and then posting the material on social media websites such as Facebook. Any picture, film or audiotape of a party posted on a social media website should be subject to disclosure under CPLR 3101(i),[26] but the courts have struggled with the issue and have not relied on CPLR 3101(i) when requiring production of such information.[27]

In the situation where the defendant procures the surveillance tapes, the unexpected may happen. Instead of refuting P's injuries, the tapes may corroborate them. In one case where that occurred, D of course did not introduce the tapes, but for the same reason P wanted to. Holding that D "was hoisted by its own petard in videotaping plaintiff," the court allowed the tapes into evidence at P's request.[28]

---

[20]   Tran v. New Rochelle Hosp. Medical Center, 99 N.Y.2d 383, 756 N.Y.S.2d 509, 786 N.E.2d 444 (2003).

[21]   See the discussion of *Tran* in NYSLD No. 519.

[22]   Zegarelli v. Hughes, 3 N.Y.3d 64, 781 N.Y.S.2d 488, 814 N.E.2d 795 (2004).

[23]   CPLR 3120(1)(i) requires a party "to produce and permit the party seeking discovery. . .to inspect, copy, test or photograph" the items produced. See § 362.

[24]   *Zegarelli*, 3 N.Y.3d at 69, 781 N.Y.S.2d at 491, 814 N.E2d at 798.

[25]   Srok v. Long Is. R.R., Sup. Ct., New York County, Aug. 18, 1993 (Index No. 1671/92; Cohen, J.). Such a tape would probably have been discoverable under the general relevancy standard of subdivision (a) of CPLR 3101 even had no subdivision (i) been enacted.

[26]   See *Tran,* 99 N.Y.2d at 388, n.2, 756 N.Y.S.2d at 512, n.2, 786 N.E.2d at 447, n.2 (noting that CPLR 3101(i) does not contain any limitation as to relevancy or subject matter).

[27]   See § 344; Commentary C3101:50 on McKinney's CPLR 3101.

[28]   Hairston v. Metro-North Commuter R.R., 6 Misc. 3d 399, 786 N.Y.S.2d 890 (Sup. Ct., New York County 2004). The details of the decision, and the routines it has generated, are discussed in Commentary C3101:50 on McKinney's CPLR 3101.

Materials in the Liability Insurer's File

Although a subdivision (d)(2) inquiry is largely a case-by-case one, there is at least one class of cases that has been carved out for wholesale treatment under the statute, and it's a big one. In the tort case in which the defendant is represented and defended by an attorney retained by the defendant's liability insurer, the insurer's whole file of the case qualifies as litigation material and is conditionally immune. This is popularly known as the *Kandel-Finegold* rule, after the principal cases that pronounced it.[29] Its theory is that this category of insurance is a kind of institutionalized attorney. Other kinds of insurance earn no such treatment,[30] and whether, in cases involving these others, a given item merits the subdivision (d)(2) immunity involves an individualized inquiry.[31] The usual items in the liability insurer's file that get the litigation-material immunity are the statements of witnesses and the reports of employees and other personnel.

The *Kandel-Finegold* rule applies only to an action in which the insurer hires a lawyer to represent the insured, not in an action against the insurer.[32] Where, for example, the insured is suing the insurer to recover for an "excess" verdict rendered against the insured and alleged to have been caused by the insurer's unreasonable failure to negotiate and settle the earlier action in good faith, the *Kandel-Finegold* rule does not apply and neither, therefore, does the subdivision (d) immunity.[33] The file is open. The insurer's file that gets the insulation, in other words, is the insurer's file accumulated in the present suit against its insured, not the file accumulated in a prior and distinct one.[34]

Accident Reports

Reports and statements made in the ordinary course of operating a business get no immunity and must therefore be distinguished from those prepared for litigation, a sometimes difficult chore when the item's existence is traceable to mixed motives and litigation is one of them. A common example is an accident report made by an employee in a restaurant, hotel, conveyance, etc. If someone is injured and sues, the proprietor's lawyer would like to make it appear that the accident report was prepared for litigation so that it won't have to be disclosed. One lawyer for a big hotel had his client route such reports directly to him in an effort to make them smack of being prepared in anticipation of litigation, and nothing else. He didn't succeed. The court noted that the reports also served internal business purposes and thus earned no protection from CPLR 3101(d)(2).[35] The decision may incidentally be credited with establishing a proposition now commonly recognized: that in order to qualify as material "prepared in anticipation

---

[29] Kandel v. Tocher, 22 A.D.2d 513, 256 N.Y.S.2d 898 (1st Dep't 1965); Finegold v. Lewis, 22 A.D.2d 447, 256 N.Y.S.2d 358 (2d Dep't 1965).

[30] See Rodolitz v. Greater New York Mut. Ins. Co., 82 Misc. 2d 1024, 371 N.Y.S.2d 89 (Sup. Ct., Nassau County 1975).

[31] See Commentary C3101:32 on McKinney's CPLR 3101.

[32] See Collins v. Jamestown Mut. Ins. Co., 56 Misc. 2d 964, 290 N.Y.S.2d 791 (Sup. Ct., Schoharie County 1968), mod'd on other grounds, 32 A.D.2d 725, 300 N.Y.S.2d 391 (3d Dep't 1969).

[33] Colbert v. Home Indem. Co., 45 Misc. 2d 1093, 259 N.Y.S.2d 36 (Sup. Ct., Monroe County 1965), aff'd, 24 A.D.2d 1080, 265 N.Y.S.2d 893 (4th Dep't).

[34] Bennett v. Troy Record Co., 25 A.D.2d 799, 269 N.Y.S.2d 213 (3d Dep't 1966).

[35] Weisgold v. Kiamesha Concord, Inc., 51 Misc. 2d 456, 273 N.Y.S.2d 279 (Sup. Ct., Sullivan County 1966).

of litigation," the item must have been prepared exclusively for litigation.[36] Incidental potential use in litigation, the courts have observed, may also be a function of such reports, but they have at least an equal if not greater mission "to prevent future accidents, discipline careless employees, or, generally, to increase the economy and efficiency of the operation."[37] Such multimotive reports, therefore, do not warrant the immunity if litigation is only one of the motives.[38]

Subdivision (g) of CPLR 3101, enacted in 1980, is addressed to "accident reports" specifically. It requires disclosure of "any written report of an accident prepared in the regular course of business operations."[39] There is no condition imposed as to whether it was prepared for litigation, but since the sole exception that it recognizes is a report prepared by a peace officer in connection with a criminal investigation, one is prone to conclude that its apparent purpose is to make a regular course-of-business accident report fully disclosable even if it was prepared exclusively for litigation and would otherwise secure the immunity of subdivision (d). That's the construction given the provision in Pataki v. Kiseda,[40] holding the accident report to be disclosable even if it was prepared "exclusively" for litigation. But the contrary has also been suggested: that subdivision (g) is just a codification of prior law,[41] and therefore effects no change.

There appears to be a consensus at least to the effect that the *Kandel-Finegold* rule, which insulates an accident report made by insured to insurer, remains intact under subdivision (g). The Third Department had held to the contrary on the point,[42] but appears to have withdrawn that position and joined the consensus.[43]

Overcoming the Conditional Immunity in CPLR 3101(d)(2)

Even if an item falls within CPLR 3101(d)(2) and gets the immunity, it must always be recalled that the immunity given is not absolute, as are the immunities for the privileged matter of subdivision (b)[44] and attorney's work product of subdivision (c).[45] The (d)(2) immunity is conditional only, and the conditions that will remove it, thereby exposing the materials to full disclosure, are that the party: (1) has "substantial need" of the materials; and (2) "is unable without undue hardship to obtain the substantial equivalent of the materials by other means."

If the materials are relevant under CPLR 3101(a),[46] they are likely to be needed, satisfying the first condition for that reason alone and making the second condition, inability to get their equivalent elsewhere, the key inquiry. A good example is a

---

[36]   See, e.g., Geffner v. Mercy Medical Center, 125 A.D.3d 802, 4 N.Y.S.3d 283 (2d Dep't 2015).

[37]   Kandel v. Tocher, 22 A.D.2d 513, 516, 256 N.Y.S.2d 898, 900 (1st Dep't 1965).

[38]   See Commentary C3101:35 on McKinney's CPLR 3101; see also Spectrum Systems Intern. Corp. v. Chemical Bank, 157 A.D.2d 444, 448, 558 N.Y.S.2d 486, 488 (1st Dep't 1990) ("In order to qualify as 'litigation' material under CPLR 3101(d), the document must have been prepared primarily if not solely for litigation"), aff'd as mod'd, 78 N.Y.2d 371, 575 N.Y.S.2d 809, 581 N.E.2d 1055 (1991).

[39]   See Commentary C3101:48 on McKinney's CPLR 3101.

[40]   Pataki v. Kiseda, 80 A.D.2d 100, 437 N.Y.S.2d 692 (2d Dep't 1981).

[41]   See Harris v. Processed Wood, Inc. (P.W.I., Inc.), 89 A.D.2d 220, 455 N.Y.S.2d 411 (4th Dep't 1982).

[42]   See Vandenburgh v. Columbia Memorial Hosp., 91 A.D.2d 710, 457 N.Y.S.2d 591 (3d Dep't 1982), and Commentary C3101:33 on McKinney's CPLR 3101. Subdivision (g) is the subject of a lead note in NYSLD No. 279, reviewing the activity of all four departments on this front.

[43]   See Gavigan v. Otis Elevator Co., 117 A.D.2d 941, 499 N.Y.S.2d 253 (3d Dep't 1986).

[44]   See § 346.

[45]   See § 347.

[46]   See § 344.

photograph taken at an accident scene at or shortly after the event. It is rarely possible to duplicate the scene and the subdivision (d)(2) conditions are easily met, requiring disclosure of the photo.[47] Another example is an item that can no longer be found and on which tests have to be conducted. In Sherman v. M. Lowenstein & Sons, Inc.,[48] for example, a garment had burned and P bought a duplicate to conduct a test on. Because of the lapse of time, D could not later find a duplicate even though D was the manufacturer, and P was required to surrender for D's testing the duplicate P bought.

But note that in the *Sherman* case, P did not have to furnish a copy of the report made by the expert. The report itself was material "prepared in anticipation of litigation" under subdivision (d)(2) and the immunity-lifting conditions of that provision had not been met because D could, upon getting the garment, have his own report made. If P could not furnish the garment, however, the court held that P would then have to furnish the report. The absence of the garment would make it impossible for D to duplicate the test and the circumstances of P's report would then satisfy the conditions in CPLR 3101(d)(2).

That appears to be the general rule. If the thing to be examined is available for examination by an expert in a party's behalf, the courts are reluctant to order disclosure of a report made by an adversary's expert, especially where no showing has been made of any difficulty in obtaining other expert testimony.[49] This conclusion applies, however, only when the matter is controlled by CPLR 3101(d)(2). When some other and more specific provision governs, and authorizes the disclosure, such as CPLR 3121(b) does with medical reports[50] and as the rules adopted under CPLR 3140 do with appraisal reports,[51] they preempt.

Freedom of Information Law

The Freedom of Information Law,[52] commonly known as FOIL, has had an impact on pretrial disclosure generally under the CPLR, and on material "prepared in anticipation of litigation" in particular. The purpose of the FOIL is to open to public scrutiny a broad range of governmental records. A key question for litigants concerns the situation in which the criteria in CPLR 3101(a) would not allow disclosure in a given instance, but the FOIL provisions would. Can the litigant invoke the FOIL in that instance, thus in effect circumventing the CPLR even though the materials are sought for use in the litigation?

The Court of Appeals, surprising bench and bar by overturning the prevalent notion on the matter, answered with an unequivocal yes in M. Farbman & Sons, Inc. v. New York City Health and Hospitals Corp.[53] The Court stated:

we refuse to read into the FOIL the restriction that, once litigation commences, a party forfeits the rights available to all other members of the public and is

---

[47]   See Flowers for Robinson v. Lyell Metal Co., Inc., 244 A.D.2d 948, 665 N.Y.S.2d 482 (4th Dep't 1997); Hayward v. Willard Mountain, Inc., 48 Misc. 2d 1032, 266 N.Y.S.2d 453 (Sup. Ct., Rensselaer County 1966).

[48]   Sherman v. M. Lowenstein & Sons, Inc., 42 Misc. 2d 770, 248 N.Y.S.2d 1000 (Sup. Ct., Queens County 1964), and on reargument, 42 Misc. 2d 771, 1964 WL 19337 (Sup. Ct., Queens County).

[49]   Gugliano v. Levi, 24 A.D.2d 591, 262 N.Y.S.2d 372 (2d Dep't 1965).

[50]   See § 363.

[51]   See § 344.

[52]   Pub. Off. Law §§ 84–90.

[53]   M. Farbman & Sons, Inc. v. New York City Health and Hospitals Corp., 62 N.Y.2d 75, 476 N.Y.S.2d 69, 464 N.E.2d 437 (1984).

confined to discovery in accordance with article 31. If the Legislature had intended to exempt agencies involved in litigation from FOIL, it certainly could have so provided.

When a public agency is one of the litigants, this means that it has the distinct disadvantage of having to offer its adversary two routes into its records, while limited to one path in the other direction.[54] In effect, the Court of Appeals responds, that's the price of open government.

The FOIL excludes from its reach, among other things, any information "specifically exempted from disclosure by state or federal statute,"[55] presenting the issue whether CPLR 3101(d)(2) and the protection it supplies to material prepared in anticipation of litigation is a "specific" exemption within the meaning of that provision. The *M. Farbman* case addressed only the general disclosure standards of the two competitors, the CPLR and FOIL, not their exemption categories. Hence the Court of Appeals saved for another day the question of whether the disclosure would be required if, while it falls within the basic criteria of the FOIL, it also falls under one of the exemption categories of CPLR 3101.[56] In Burke v. Yudelson,[57] it was held that the CPLR 3101 exclusions of subdivisions (b), (c), and (d) are all general in scope and hence not of the "specific" kind to which the FOIL defers and that something purportedly exempt by one of the CPLR provisions therefore does face disclosure if embraced as part of public records under the FOIL.

There is also the question of what procedure to use to obtain the disclosure. The CPLR and the FOIL have their own procedures. The FOIL's procedures are more elaborate and usually more time consuming. Application must be made by turns to an access officer, an appeals officer, the supreme court in an Article 78 proceeding, an appellate court, etc.[58] CPLR disclosure is more expeditious. Can CPLR procedures be used to obtain only FOIL-authorized disclosure? It has been held that they cannot.[59]

In Data Tree, LLC v. Romaine,[60] addressing the FOIL in general, the Court of Appeals makes an important incidental point about the form in which the agency maintains the records that a FOIL application seeks. The seeker in *Data Tree* wanted the records in electronic form, which of course facilitates their acquisition and review, but the court held that there is nothing in the law that requires the agency to furnish records in electronic form if the agency doesn't already keep them in that form.

---

[54]   Mosey v. County of Erie, 148 A.D.3d 1572, 50 N.Y.S.3d 641 (4th Dep't 2017).

[55]   Pub. Off. Law § 87(2)(a).

[56]   The *M. Farbman* case and the general subject of FOIL versus CPLR disclosure is treated in the lead note in NYSLD No. 296. See also Commentary C3101:23A on McKinney's CPLR 3101.

[57]   Burke v. Yudelson, 81 Misc. 2d 870, 368 N.Y.S.2d 779 (Sup. Ct., Monroe County 1975), aff'd, 51 A.D.2d 673, 378 N.Y.S.2d 165 (4th Dep't 1976).

[58]   See Pub. Off. Law § 89. The liability an agency faces when a FOIL request is found legitimate and the agency is found to have unreasonably denied it, including the payment of counsel fees, is discussed in New York Civil Liberties Union v. City of Saratoga Springs, 87 A.D.3d 336, 926 N.Y.S.2d 732 (3d Dep't 2011), and New York State Defenders Ass'n v. New York State Police, 87 A.D.3d 193, 927 N.Y.S.2d 423 (3d Dep't 2011). See SPR 235:3–4.

[59]   Moussa v. State, 91 A.D.2d 863, 458 N.Y.S.2d 377 (4th Dep't 1982). This to-each-its-own-procedure rule is also addressed in the *M. Farbman* decision.

[60]   Data Tree, LLC v. Romaine, 9 N.Y.3d 454, 849 N.Y.S.2d 489, 880 N.E.2d 10, 36 Media L. Rep. (BNA) 1394 (2007) (NYSLD No. 579).

Disclosure of Settlements

What about the disclosure of data connected with settlements? We interject the issue again here,[61] after discussion of all of the possible immunities from disclosure. It is important to note that the determination of whether to order disclosure of a settlement agreement that is relevant to a nonsettling party will usually not be governed by any of the three exceptions to disclosure in CPLR 3101. CPLR 3101(b) grants an absolute immunity from disclosure to information that is "privileged,"[62] while CPLR 3101(c) grants an absolute immunity to a limited category of information classified as "attorney work product."[63] The subject of this section, CPLR 3101(d)(2), provides a qualified immunity to material "prepared in anticipation of litigation or for trial." A settlement agreement does not fall comfortably under any of these categories of immunity, but disputes regarding the disclosure of such information have occupied the courts and the law is surprisingly unsettled in this area.[64]

In re Eighth Judicial Dist. Asbestos Litigation,[65] the plaintiff and one of two co-defendants entered into a high-low agreement, which has some of the trappings of a settlement.[66] The Court of Appeals held that "whenever a plaintiff and a defendant enter into a high-low agreement in a multi-defendant action which requires the agreeing defendant to remain a party to the litigation, the parties must disclose the existence of that agreement and its terms to the court and the nonagreeing defendant(s)."[67] Previously, it had been held that defendants are not entitled to discovery of an agreement made among the plaintiffs about maintaining unity in settling with the defendants. The court saw nothing in such an agreement relevant to the triable issues in the case.[68] Another decision held that defendants are not even entitled to data about the plaintiffs' settlements with co-defendants, despite the relevancy of settlements in computing a post-verdict judgment.[69] The court said that the matter does not become germane until after the verdict and may therefore not be the subject of pretrial disclosure.[70] There is caselaw permitting pretrial disclosure in respect of "collateral source" payments, however, which are in some ways analogous to settlement payments.[71]

---

[61] See also § 204.

[62] See § 346.

[63] See § 347.

[64] The issue is explored at length, with a discussion of some additional cases, in Commentary C3101:18A to McKinney's CPLR 3101.

[65] In re Eighth Judicial Dist. Asbestos Litigation, 8 N.Y.3d 717, 840 N.Y.S.2d 546, 872 N.E.2d 232 (2007).

[66] See § 411.

[67] *In re Eighth Judicial District Asbestos Litigation,* 8 N.Y.3d at 722–23, 840 N.Y.S.2d at 550, 872 N.E.2d at 236.

[68] See Allegretti-Freeman v. Baltis, 205 A.D.2d 859, 613 N.Y.S.2d 449 (3d Dep't 1994), noted in SPR 27:4.

[69] See § 176.

[70] In re New York County Data Entry Worker Product Liability Litigation, 162 Misc. 2d 263, 616 N.Y.S.2d 424 (Sup. Ct., New York County 1994), aff'd, 222 A.D.2d 381, 635 N.Y.S.2d 641 (1st Dep't 1995).

[71] Firmes v. Chase Manhattan Automotive Finance Corp., 50 A.D.3d 18, 35, 852 N.Y.S.2d 148, 161–62 (2d Dep't 2008). See the discussion of the *Hulse* case in SPR 29:4, and in the N.Y.L.J. of March 6, 1995 (p.1, cols.2–3). A demand for a bill of particulars would also be an appropriate vehicle for obtaining information on collateral sources. McKenzie v. St. Elizabeth Hospital, 81 A.D.2d 1003, 440 N.Y.S.2d 109 (4th Dep't 1981).

In Mahoney v. Turner Const. Co.,[72] the plaintiff entered into a stipulation of discontinuance against two co-defendants. The remaining defendants moved to compel production of a copy of the settlement agreement or a sworn statement setting out its terms, but the supreme court denied the motion. The First Department reversed, noting that "[t]he touchstone for determining whether information is discoverable in an action is whether [it] is 'material and necessary.' "[73] The court unanimously concluded that "disclosure of the terms of a settlement agreement by a settling party to a nonsettling party may be appropriate, despite the presence of a confidentiality clause in the agreement, where the terms of the agreement are 'material and necessary' to the nonsettling party's case."[74] Acknowledging that there may be instances in which a settlement agreement has no bearing on the issues remaining in the case, the court cited to its prior caselaw which observed that any doubt as to the relevance of a settlement agreement may be resolved by an in camera inspection of the document.[75]

A party seeking to prevent or limit disclosure of a settlement agreement should seek relief under CPLR 3103(a).[76] This provision grants the court far more discretion in reaching a determination on the issue than the comparatively narrow immunities from disclosure in CPLR 3101(b), (c), and (d)(2). On a motion for a protective order, the court may direct the disclosure of those portions of the agreement that it finds are "material and necessary," while shielding from disclosure those portions of it that are not and "limiting the disclosure of the settlement agreement to [the nonsettling defendants] and [their] counsel or by such other manner as Supreme Court directs."[77]

CPLR 4547, added to the evidence article of the CPLR in 1998, bars from evidence any indication that something of value was tendered or accepted during compromise negotiations and "any conduct or statement made" during them, whether offered to reflect on liability or on damages. The statute extends the exclusion beyond just the offers made during the bartering, which have traditionally been excluded, to also embrace statements made by any of the parties.[78]

§ 348A. Identification of Experts; Statement of Expected Testimony

CPLR 3101(d)(1), an entirely new provision added by a 1985 amendment, is entitled "Experts." It consists of three subparagraphs, (i), (ii), and (iii).

Subparagraph (i) is an innovation in New York. It provides that "upon request" by a party, any other party is required to identify "each person whom the party expects to call as an expert witness at the trial" and to disclose "in reasonable detail the subject matter on which each expert is expected to testify, the substance of the facts and opinions on which each expert is expected to testify, the qualifications of each expert witness and a summary of the grounds for each expert's opinion."

---

[72] Mahoney v. Turner Const. Co., 61 A.D.3d 101, 104, 872 N.Y.S.2d 433, 435 (1st Dep't 2009).

[73] *Mahoney*, 61 A.D.3d at 104, 872 N.Y.S.2d at 435.

[74] *Mahoney*, 61 A.D.3d at 104, 872 N.Y.S.2d at 436.

[75] See Masterwear Corp. v. Bernard, 298 A.D.2d 249, 250, 750 N.Y.S.2d 5, 6 (1st Dep't 2002).

[76] See § 353.

[77] *Masterwear Corp.*, 298 A.D.2d at 250–51, 750 N.Y.S.2d at 6.

[78] The statute, modeled on Rule 408 of the Federal Rules of Evidence, has some exceptions. See the Advisory Committee note on Rule 408 in 28 U.S.C.A.

It starts off with this rather big bang, but then tones down considerably. The provision is unique in CPLR Article 31 as it sets forth neither a particular time for the making of the disclosure request nor a particular time limit for responding to it. Furthermore, CPLR 3101(d)(1)(i) emphasizes that the recipient shall not be precluded from using the expert at trial "solely" because the party failed to comply with the request if the party can demonstrate "good cause" for "retain[ing] an expert an insufficient period of time before the commencement of trial to give appropriate notice thereof . . . ." But if the court can't preclude for noncompliance, then what can it do? Says the statute: "the court may make whatever order may be just." Not exactly a beacon of uniformity or predictability.

Adding to the confusion and uncertainty that seems to always accompany the application of CPLR 3101(d)(1)(i), several courts have reached the debatable conclusion that expert disclosure is not required for a treating doctor, even if that doctor will provide expert testimony.[1] This rule led to a perverse result in Andrew v. Hurh,[2] when plaintiff's own treating physician, to almost everyone's surprise, was permitted to provide expert testimony for the defendant without any disclosure under CPLR 3101(d)(1)(i). The Third Department appears to be alone in holding that "CPLR 3101(d)(1)(i) requires disclosure of any medical professional, even a treating physician or nurse, who is expected to give expert testimony."[3]

The request for expert disclosure should be made during the normal period for pretrial disclosure, prior to the filing of the certificate of readiness and note of issue.[4] If the expert has not yet been decided on when the request is made, caselaw holds that the request must be considered "to be of a continuing nature" so that the recipient is under a legal duty to respond upon the expert's retention.[5] This is consistent with the current scheme in Article 31, which requires a disclosure response to be promptly amended or supplemented when a prior response is known to be incorrect or incomplete.[6]

And what form shall the request take? Any kind of a paper appropriately captioned and clearly stating the request should do. Some courts have held that the request can be embodied as an additional paragraph in a demand for a bill of particulars.[7] Others say no, because that would confuse bill of particulars remedies with disclosure remedies.[8] The argument can be avoided by putting the request on a separate paper and appending it to and serving it with the bill of particulars demand, if one is used.

---

[1]　See, e.g., Hamer v. City of New York, 106 A.D.3d 504, 965 N.Y.S.2d 99, 292 Ed. Law Rep. 1009 (1st Dep't 2013); Jing Xue Jiang v. Dollar Rent a Car, Inc., 91 A.D.3d 603, 938 N.Y.S.2d 90 (2d Dep't 2012); Rook v. 60 Key Centre, Inc., 239 A.D.2d 926, 660 N.Y.S.2d 238 (4th Dep't 1997).

[2]　Andrew v. Hurh, 34 A.D.3d 1331, 824 N.Y.S.2d 546 (4th Dep't 2006), lv. den. 8 N.Y.3d 808, 834 N.Y.S.2d 89, 865 N.E.2d 1256 (2007).

[3]　Norton v. Nguyen, 49 A.D.3d 927, 853 N.Y.S.2d 671 (3d Dep't 2008).

[4]　See § 352; Aversa v. Taubes, 194 A.D.2d 580, 598 N.Y.S.2d 801 (2d Dep't 1993) (plaintiffs' CPLR 3101(d)(1)(i) request was deemed untimely when served one year after the filing of the note of issue and two months after the case appeared on the trial calendar).

[5]　Dunn v. Medina Memorial Hosp., 131 Misc. 2d 971, 502 N.Y.S.2d 633 (Sup. Ct., Erie County 1986). The case notes that there is no requirement that the expert be retained before depositions are taken, but such a sequence can be imposed by a judge in a given case, if deemed appropriate on the facts, through invocation of general protective order powers under CPLR 3103(a) or in a scheduling order. See 22 N.Y.C.R.R. § 202.12(c)(2); § 77D.

[6]　CPLR 3101(h); see § 352A.

[7]　E.g., Bellen v. Baghei-Rad, 148 A.D.2d 827, 538 N.Y.S.2d 663 (3d Dep't 1989).

[8]　E.g., Coleman by Coleman v. Richards, 138 A.D.2d 556, 526 N.Y.S.2d 138 (2d Dep't 1988).

The party seeking expert disclosure is only entitled to a statement of the "substance" of the facts and opinions the expert will testify to. The statute does not require that the disclosure set forth the specific facts and opinions upon which the expert will testify and can usually be satisfied in a few paragraphs.[9]

Failing to respond to a proper demand for expert disclosure can result in a party being altogether precluded from using the expert at the trial.[10] The absence of any statutory time limit on when the expert data has to be furnished has made it difficult to determine what remedy, if any, to apply in situations where the expert disclosure has not been served before the action reaches the trial stage. It has been held that when the case is still "at an early stage," the court need not set a deadline for expert disclosure,[11] but that waiting until the eve of trial to provide disclosure can result in preclusion, with obviously serious consequences if the case requires the use of an expert. Where expert testimony was essential to the plaintiff's case, for example, the plaintiff's unexcused failure to supply the expert data resulted in summary judgment for the defendant.[12]

Another problem frequently arising under CPLR 3101(d)(1)(i) occurs when a party provides expert disclosure, but it is deficient. In Rivera v. Montefiore Medical Center,[13] the Court held that supreme court did not "abuse[ ] its discretion as a matter of law in denying as untimely plaintiff's motion to preclude the testimony of defendant's expert on the grounds that the CPLR 3101(d) disclosure statement was deficient." The Court emphasized that trial courts possess broad discretion in their supervision of expert disclosure under CPLR 3101(d)(1)(i) and that the deficiency complained of in Rivera was "readily apparent" and "could have been raised—and potentially cured—before trial."[14] The Court's decision in Rivera demonstrates that where a party plans to object to the adequacy of an expert disclosure response, it should do so well in advance of trial.[15] By contrast, where a party's expert disclosure is misleading or the expert's trial testimony is inconsistent with it, the opposing party should not be precluded from raising the issue at trial.[16]

Many courts have been hesitant to preclude a party from offering expert testimony at trial and have liberally dispensed forgiveness for a failure to comply with CPLR 3101(d)(1)(i), accompanied by relatively minimal sanctions. Despite the fact that the disclosure obligation is limited to experts that a party plans to call "at trial," and is contained in a subdivision captioned "Trial preparation," several appellate division decisions nonetheless imposed relatively draconian sanctions for a failure to comply with a CPLR 3101(d)(1)(i) demand in the context of a motion for summary judgment made well in advance of the trial. The hub of activity on this front had been in the Second Department, which repeatedly, but not consistently, refused to consider the affidavits of

---

[9]   See Tate-Mitros v. MTA New York City Transit, 144 A.D.3d 454, 41 N.Y.S.3d 214 (1st Dep't 2016); Conway v. Elite Towing & Flatbedding Corp., 135 A.D.3d 893, 894, 22 N.Y.S.3d 911 (2d Dep't 2016).

[10]   E.g., Tienken v. Benedictine Hosp., 110 A.D.3d 1389, 974 N.Y.S.2d 166 (3d Dep't 2013) (SPR 18:4).

[11]   DiPiano v. Truchly, 221 A.D.2d 182, 633 N.Y.S.2d 156 (1st Dep't 1995).

[12]   In Grassel v. Albany Medical Center Hosp., 223 A.D.2d 803, 636 N.Y.S.2d 154 (3d Dep't 1996).

[13]   Rivera v. Montefiore Medical Center, 28 N.Y.3d 999, 1000, 41 N.Y.S.3d 454, 64 N.E.3d 274 (2016).

[14]   Rivera, 28 N.Y.3d at 1002, 41 N.Y.S.3d at 456, 64 N.E.3d at 276.

[15]   We have stressed this point on many occasions. See Commentary CPLR 3101:29A on McKinney's CPLR 3101 ("D) Failure To Comply With CPLR 3101(d)(1)(i) Demand, 3) Deficient CPLR 3101(d)(1)(i) Response"); see, e.g., Qian v. Dugan, 256 A.D.2d 782, 783, 681 N.Y.S.2d 408, 409 (3d Dep't 1998).

[16]   See Rivera, 28 N.Y.3d at 1002, 41 N.Y.S.3d at 456, 64 N.E.3d at 276 (noting that deficiency of expert disclosure response was "not analogous to a situation in which a party's disclosure was misleading or the trial testimony was inconsistent with the disclosure.").

experts submitted on a motion for summary judgment when the offering party failed to provide "timely" disclosure of the expert under CPLR 3101(d)(1)(i).[17] This often resulted in the dismissal of a party's claims.[18]

To address the problem in the summary judgment realm, a new third sentence was added to CPLR 3212(b) in 2015, which addresses, among other things, the supporting proof that can be submitted on a motion for summary judgment. It states:

> Where an expert affidavit is submitted in support of, or opposition to, a motion for summary judgment, the court shall not decline to consider the affidavit because an expert exchange pursuant to subparagraph (i) of paragraph (1) of subdivision (d) of section 3101 was not furnished prior to the submission of the affidavit.

The courts have been ambivalent about how to punish delayed expert disclosure, misleading attorneys into case-forfeiting conduct.[19] The ambivalence continues with no guidance yet provided by the Court of Appeals. Some courts, and even one judicial district, weary of the absence of any statutory or regulatory guidance on these issues, adopted local rules to fill the gap, requiring a response with or before the filing of the note of issue.[20] The judicial district's rule got little attention from an appellate division decision in an action that involved it,[21] with the court allowing D to use an expert who was not disclosed until six weeks before the trial. The court said the expert was of a category that P could "expect" D to call. Don't most parties "expect" the other side to use an expert whenever relevant to the issues?

Some attorneys have noted that they have even seen a total omission to respond to an expert demand forgiven at the trial itself, and the recalcitrant party permitted to produce the expert nonetheless. No lawyer should depend on such generosity. More likely is that the party who does not respond to the expert demand before the trial will be barred from expert disclosure altogether, with whatever consequence that portends. Indeed, preclusion may go even farther. In one case in which the plaintiff's expert was barred from testifying because he had not been properly identified, resulting in a hung jury, the plaintiff hoped to remedy the omission—and identify the expert—before the retrial. Nothing doing, held the court, as the barring of the expert at the first trial was now the law of the case.[22]

---

[17]   Rivers v. Birnbaum, 102 A.D.3d 26, 953 N.Y.S.2d 232 (2d Dep't 2012).

[18]   See, e.g., Kopeloff v. Arctic Cat, Inc., 84 A.D.3d 890, 923 N.Y.S.2d 168 (2d Dep't 2011); Construction by Singletree, Inc. v. Lowe, 55 A.D.3d 861, 866 N.Y.S.2d 702 (2d Dep't 2008).

[19]   See Commentary CPLR 3101:29A on McKinney's CPLR 3101; SPR 42:1. Different attitudes among the departments are cited and discussed in Marks v. Solomon, 174 Misc. 2d 752, 667 N.Y.S.2d 194 (Sup. Ct., Westchester County 1997).

[20]   See SPR 80:2–3. Lawyers practicing before courts in the Third Judicial District must be aware of the local rule, and the fact that it is housed in a relatively obscure place. See http://www.nycourts.gov/courts/3jd/JudgesRules/3JD-judges%20rules.shtml.

[21]   Gushlaw v. Roll, 290 A.D.2d 667, 735 N.Y.S.2d 667 (3d Dep't 2002) (addressing Third Judicial District's Expert Disclosure Rule); see also Frankel v. Vernon & Ginsburg, LLP, 118 A.D.3d 479, 988 N.Y.S.2d 28 (1st Dep't 2014) (denying motion to preclude plaintiff's expert from testifying at trial because "defendants have not established that they were prejudiced by receipt of the expert disclosures four days after the 30-day minimum set by local rule, or that the delay was willful or intentional.").

[22]   Noble v. Cole, 267 A.D.2d 702, 699 N.Y.S.2d 527 (3d Dep't 1999). This point is controversial. Distinguishing cases like *Noble,* Hothan v. Met. Suburban Bus Auth., N.Y.L.J., Nov. 21, 2002, at 24, col.3 (Sup. Ct., Nassau County; Winslow, J.) reached a different conclusion, allowing a defendant on a retrial to use the expert barred from use by that defendant on the earlier one. Whatever the rule, if any, ultimately settled on

Some courts express the view that, consistent with Uniform Rule 202.7(a),[23] the party objecting to nondisclosure or belated or deficient disclosure of expert data should not be permitted to raise the objection unless he tried to secure some kind of remedy for the delay during the pretrial period.[24] The First Department leaned in that direction in St. Hilaire v. White[25] where it allowed testimony by D's neurologist at the trial because:

1.   D's conduct was found "unintentional,"

2.   D alerted P that a neurologist would be called,

3.   the court offered an adjournment to enable P to bone up for cross-examination, and

4.   D was required to pay the cost of a rebuttal witness P might require.

This is just one example of a case, and from the appellate division to boot, that forgives a party's omission to respond to an expert demand and refuses any kind of significant sanction at the trial proper. There is no solid glue to hold these decisions together. Almost every decision interpreting the statute, including a healthy number of opinions from the appellate division, cannot be reconciled with some other opinion applying CPLR 3101(d)(1)(i) to a similar set of facts.[26] This substantial body of caselaw, interpreting one of CPLR Article 31's most important provisions, suffers from "Corpus Juris Secundum" (CJS) Syndrome. There is a case to support virtually every position imaginable. This can be explained, at least in part, by the fact that the New York Court of Appeals has not issued a substantial opinion interpreting the expert disclosure statute.

The statute cries out for substantial amendment to, among other things, impose a time period for expert disclosure, but none is in prospect. This state of affairs is due mainly to the strong resistance of the plaintiffs' bar in personal injury cases. This powerful lobby often tries to put off retaining an expert—and its concomitant expense—in the hope that a settlement can be reached that will obviate the retention and spare the expense.

"Further Disclosure" Permitted on Showing of "Special Circumstances"

Does the fact that the substance of the facts and opinions of the expert must be furnished under CPLR 3101(d)(1)(i) authorize the production of a written report or deposition of the expert? By itself, no.[27] But "upon a showing of special circumstances," subparagraph (iii) of CPLR 3101(d)(1) permits the court to order such further disclosure as it deems warranted, and that would presumably include the production of an expert report or a deposition, especially where the party has delayed so long in retaining the

---

this issue, it should make no difference whether the remiss party is the plaintiff, as in *Noble*, or the defendant, as in *Hothan*.

   23   See § 353.

   24   See, e.g., Neel v. Mount Sinai Hospital, N.Y.L.J., Oct. 22, 2001, at 25, col.2 (N.Y. City Civ. Ct. 2001), aff'd 196 Misc. 2d 343, 762 N.Y.S.2d 224 (App. Term, 1st Dep't 2003).

   25   St. Hilaire v. White, 305 A.D.2d 209, 759 N.Y.S.2d 74 (1st Dep't 2003).

   26   A treatment of the legion of caselaw interpreting CPLR 3101(d)(1)(i) appears in Commentary C3101:29A on McKinney's CPLR 3101. See also SPR 114:3, 116:4, 122:2, 126:2, 127:4, 135:4, and 144:2.

   27   This is in contrast with federal practice, where a "party may depose any person who has been identified as an expert whose opinions may be presented at trial." Fed. R. Civ. P. 26(b)(4)(A); see also Fed. R. Civ. P. 26(a)(2)(B) (requiring certain experts to provide a written report).

expert that the extra disclosure is deemed necessary to compensate for the delay and facilitate the requester's preparation for trial. A determination of that kind could be supported under either the "special circumstances" language of subparagraph (iii) or the "whatever order may be just" power conferred by subparagraph (i).

Another special circumstance warranting the deposing of the expert is the present unavailability of the physical evidence on which the expert's opinion is based.[28] It must be noted, however, that a finding of "special circumstances" under CPLR 3101(d)(1)(iii) justifying further disclosure is a rare event in reported decisions. By contrast, through its own rules, the commercial division of the supreme court has apparently deemed all of its cases worthy of a "special circumstances" finding regardless of the facts. This has been accomplished through the adoption of Rule 13(c) of the Rules of the Commercial Division, which provides for expert disclosure in commercial cases similar to that available in federal actions, including the exchange of reports and depositions of testifying experts unless otherwise ordered by the court or stipulated by the parties.[29]

Expert Disclosure in Medical Malpractice Actions

Note the special provision that applies to expert disclosure in medical, dental, and podiatric malpractice actions, which we'll collectively refer to as the "medical" categories. Everything CPLR 3101(d)(1)(i) requires, as quoted from the statute at the outset of this section, must be forthcoming in the medical malpractice actions, too—including a statement of the expert's qualifications—but with the notable exception that the name of the expert can be withheld. This was designed to avoid peer pressure, sometimes applied to discourage the expert from testifying against a fellow professional in the medical categories.

A problem that has generated many cases is what to do when revelation of the expert's qualifications would tend to reveal the expert's identity as well. The consensus for a time was that in the medical malpractice categories the judge should hear the arguments of the parties, examine in camera the expert's qualifications, redact such parts of them as would make identification possible, and give only the redacted version to the requester.[30] An extensive treatment of the conflict that ultimately developed on the point, and an almost full turn in the opposite direction, appears in the Second Department's decision in Thomas v. Alleyne.[31] *Thomas* concludes that the qualifications of the expert must be revealed even if the revelation would today enable the other side to identify the expert through the use of search engine technologies.[32] However, shortly before *Thomas*, the Fourth Department cited to the Second Department's prior caselaw and permitted plaintiff to disclose only that his expert was a board-certified urologist,

---

[28]   See Brooklyn Floor Maintenance Co. v. Providence Washington Ins. Co., 296 A.D.2d 520, 745 N.Y.S.2d 208 (2d Dep't 2002); Rosario v. General Motors Corp., 148 A.D.2d 108, 543 N.Y.S.2d 974 (1st Dep't 1989).

[29]   22 N.Y.C.R.R. § 202.70(g), Com. Div. Rule 13(c).

[30]   See, e.g., Jones v. Putnam Hosp. Center, 133 A.D.2d 447, 519 N.Y.S.2d 665 (2d Dep't 1987); McGoldrick v. Whitney M. Young, Jr. Health Center, Inc., 135 Misc. 2d 200, 514 N.Y.S.2d 872 (Sup. Ct., Albany County 1987). The subject is treated in the lead note in NYSLD No. 332. Redaction of identifying features can sometimes apply even to the plaintiff's examining physician if the plaintiff plans to call the physician as an expert. See Ryan v. Michelsen, 241 A.D.2d 434, 660 N.Y.S.2d 435 (1st Dep't 1997).

[31]   Thomas v. Alleyne, 302 A.D.2d 36, 752 N.Y.S.2d 362 (2d Dep't 2002) (SPR 131:1).

[32]   The computer's complicity in this plot is the subject of Gleason and Connors, *Search Engine Technology "Over-rules" Expert Witness Laws*, N.Y.L.J., Nov. 21, 2005, at 3. The article contrasts the New York rule with federal practice, which has no such restriction, noting the pros and cons on each side.

the state in which he was licensed to practice, and the state in which he taught.[33] The issue continues to be controversial.

Unless a time period has been set and violated, it has been held permissible for the party who has not yet furnished the expert data in one of the medical categories to include the affidavit of the expert, with the name redacted, in papers opposing a motion for summary judgment.[34] To guard against the use of summary judgment motions just to flush out the otherwise concealable name of an adversary's expert, the court can inspect the affidavit in camera and direct redactions accordingly.[35] But redaction is not permissible when the affidavit is being used to support, rather than oppose, the summary judgment motion.[36] It can't be used, in other words, as a sword.[37] Requiring a movant to reveal an expert's identity in these circumstances "allow[s] a nonmovant to meaningfully pursue information such as whether that expert has ever espoused a contradictory opinion, whether the individual is actually a recognized expert and whether that individual has been discredited in the relevant field prior to any possible resolution of the case on the motion."[38]

Subparagraph (ii) of CPLR 3101(d)(1), applicable only in the medical categories, offers a kind of trade-off for a party willing to name and submit to deposition the medical expert that subparagraph (i) would otherwise permit that party to withhold. If the other side is amenable, the offering party gets the same in return.

§ 349. Revelation of Names of Witnesses

Article 31 does not expressly require a party to furnish a list of witnesses,[1] but the caselaw interpreting the CPLR has confirmed that parties must reveal the name of anyone they know of who witnessed the event at issue.[2] This does not mean that upon demand each party must serve on the other a list of all the witnesses she intends to use at the trial. It doesn't cover, for example, character or expert witnesses, whatever the effect other provisions may have on compelling the disclosure of such witnesses.[3] Its concern is with those ordinary witnesses who can shed light on what happened.[4] If liability occurred all at once, such as in an accident, the witnesses included are not only those who beheld the occurrence but also those who can reflect on any fact that can help

---

[33]   Thompson v. Swiantek, 291 A.D.2d 884, 736 N.Y.S.2d 819 (4th Dep't 2002).

[34]   See, e.g., Kozlowski v. Alcan Aluminum Corp., 209 A.D.2d 930, 621 N.Y.S.2d 240 (4th Dep't 1994) (SPR 38:4); McCarty v. Community Hosp. of Glen Cove, 203 A.D.2d 432, 433, 610 N.Y.S.2d 588, 589 (2d Dep't 1994).

[35]   See, e.g., Vega v. Mount Sinai-NYU Medical Center and Health System, 13 A.D.3d 62, 786 N.Y.S.2d 23 (1st Dep't 2004); Napierski v. Finn, 229 A.D.2d 869, 646 N.Y.S.2d 415 (3d Dep't 1996) (SPR 61:4).

[36]   Rivera v. Albany Medical Center Hosp., 119 A.D.3d 1135, 1136–37, 990 N.Y.S.2d 310, 312 (3d Dep't 2014).

[37]   Marano v. Mercy Hosp., 241 A.D.2d 48, 670 N.Y.S.2d 570 (2d Dep't 1998).

[38]   *Rivera,* 119 A.D.3d at 1137, 990 N.Y.S.2d at 312.

[1]   Compare Fed. R. Civ. P. 26(a)(1)(A)(i) (requiring a party, "without awaiting a discovery request, [to] provide to the other parties [ ]the name and, if known, the address and telephone number of each individual likely to have discoverable information—along with the subjects of that information—that the disclosing party may use to support its claims or defenses, unless the use would be solely for impeachment.").

[2]   See, e.g., Rios v. Donovan, 21 A.D.2d 409, 250 N.Y.S.2d 818 (1st Dep't 1964), an early appellate address to the issue, and Wolodkowicz v. Seewell Corp., 61 A.D.3d 676, 876 N.Y.S.2d 487 (2d Dep't 2009).

[3]   See § 348A.

[4]   See, e.g., Zellman v. Metropolitan Transp. Authority, 40 A.D.2d 248, 250, 339 N.Y.S.2d 255, 257 (2d Dep't 1973); Sanfilipo v. Baptist Temple, Inc., 52 Misc. 2d 767, 276 N.Y.S.2d 936 (Sup. Ct., Monroe County 1967).

account for the accident. It embraces, for example, not just a bystander who saw the crash, but anyone who can reflect on the condition of a traffic light alleged to have played a role, or who can show whether the driver or pedestrian was drunk or sober, such as a bartender or companion, or who can testify about the speed of the vehicle, such as an old man sitting on a bench two blocks away who saw the car careening out of control around the corner, or a mechanic who warned the defendant a day earlier that his brakes were defective, and so on.

There is no satisfactory ground for distinguishing between a witness to the accident itself and one who can reflect on some cause of it.[5] All are within this rule and the names of all, if known by a party, must be revealed if requested.

It had previously been held that the only witnesses a party had to reveal were those learned of at the scene of the accident itself, as opposed to those learned of later by investigation. These latter witnesses were deemed to fall under the umbrella of CPLR 3101(d)(2) as material prepared "in anticipation of litigation" and therefore were immunized.[6] Earlier still it had been held that the only revealable witnesses were those who participated in the event in some way, as opposed to those who merely saw it.[7] Both these older approaches have been discarded as unworkable and unduly restrictive.[8]

Conflict on the point lingered into the early 1980s, with the Third Department continuing to exempt from the disclosure requirement the name of a witness through whom a tort defendant allegedly had notice of a dangerous condition that caused an accident, i.e., a "notice" witness,[9] but the court withdrew the distinction in Bombard v. Albany County in 1983.[10] The withdrawal, as the court recognized, harmonized the views of all departments on the issue.

There are instances in which the disclosure of the name and address of a patient who was a witness to negligence or medical malpractice at a medical facility may violate that patient's privilege of confidentiality of treatment.[11] The courts have concluded that where it is not possible to comply with a demand for the name and address of a witness-patient without disclosing privileged information concerning their diagnosis and treatment, discovery is prohibited.[12]

Distasteful as it is to lawyers to reveal the names of witnesses harvested through their investigative efforts, the names must be divulged. The lawyer who has gone to any expense learning of them can, on a protective order motion, ask the court to make the seeking party share the bill.

---

[5] Rivera v. Glen Oaks Village Owners, Inc., 41 A.D.3d 817, 819, 839 N.Y.S.2d 183, 187 (2d Dep't 2007).

[6] See Varner v. Winfield, 33 A.D.2d 807, 307 N.Y.S.2d 3 (2d Dep't 1969).

[7] See, e.g., Coleman v. Kirkey, 53 Misc. 2d 947, 279 N.Y.S.2d 803 (Sup. Ct., Monroe County 1967).

[8] Hartley v. Ring, 58 Misc. 2d 618, 296 N.Y.S.2d 394 (Sup. Ct., Queens County 1969), rejected the "participant" distinction such as *Coleman*, 53 Misc.2d at 947, 279 N.Y.S.2d at 803, used, but adopted the learned-of-later distinction, which *Varner*, above, later approved of. *Varner* and *Hartley* were then overruled in Zellman v. Metropolitan Transp. Authority, 40 A.D.2d 248, 339 N.Y.S.2d 255 (2d Dep't 1973), which adopts the current rule.

[9] See the lead note in NYSLD No. 243.

[10] Bombard v. Albany County, 94 A.D.2d 910, 463 N.Y.S.2d 633 (3d Dep't 1983).

[11] Gunn v. Sound Shore Medical Center of Westchester, 5 A.D.3d 435, 772 N.Y.S.2d 714 (2d Dep't 2004).

[12] See In re Grand Jury Investigation in New York County, 98 N.Y.S.2d 525, 530, 749 N.Y.S.2d 462, 779 N.E.2d 173 (2002); Kneisel v. QPH, Inc., 124 A.D.3d 729, 2 N.Y.S.3d 195 (2d Dep't 2015).

The inquiry into the names of witnesses often occurs at a deposition where in the course of the questioning the party is asked to provide the names of any witnesses. The deponent's lawyer, who would at one time interpose himself promptly and direct the client not to answer the question, must now grin and bear it or, in any event, bear it. If the question is not answered, the questioning party can take the matter to court and will likely be granted an order to compel the answer.[13] Moreover, the court may order a new trial if an undisclosed witness testifies.[14]

A CPLR 3120 discovery notice is another device that can be used to compel the revelation of witnesses, but the deposition is usually more effectual.[15]

Distinguish between the witness's name and a statement the witness may have given. The name is not immunized litigation material under CPLR 3101(d)(2), but the statement may be.[16]

C. DEVICES AND METHODS IN PERSPECTIVE

Table of Sections

§ 350.   The Disclosure Devices; Priority of Use
§ 351.   Method of Bringing on Disclosure; Stipulation or Notice
§ 352.   Instances Where Order Initially Required
§ 352A.   Requirement to Supplement Prior Responses

§ 350. The Disclosure Devices; Priority of Use

CPLR 3102(a) lists the disclosure tools, but each is later allotted a separate provision in Article 31 supplying details on the use of the tool. Following that lead, we will list each device here and briefly describe how it works, leaving later sections to elaborate on the devices individually.

1.   Deposition on oral questions.[1] This is one of the most useful and hence frequently used of the devices. It's a session around a table, usually in an attorney's office,[2] with all parties represented by their lawyers. The party or witness being deposed is questioned in depth by all the lawyers in turn while a stenographer, or sometimes tape or video recorder, takes everything down verbatim and afterwards reduces it to a transcript. It all takes place in front of an officer, usually just a notary public; just as usually the stenographer has qualified as a notary and carries out both roles.

2.   Deposition on written questions.[3] This is also a session around a table, but much rarer than the oral deposition and nowhere near as effectual. The deposition on written questions is wooden. It's used mainly for depositions outside the state. Each party furnishes written questions to the officer who is to conduct the deposition, who then goes to where the witness is and puts the written questions verbatim (no variations!), taking

---

13   See CPLR 3124; see § 366.
14   *Wolodkowicz,* 61 A.D.3d at 677, 876 N.Y.S.2d at 489.
15   See *Rios,* 21 A.D.2d at 413–14, 250 N.Y.S.2d at 822.
16   See § 348.
1   For elaboration, see § 354.
2   For the place of taking the deposition, see § 355.
3   For elaboration, see § 359.

down the answers and afterwards reducing all to a transcript. The attorneys are usually not present at the session.

3. *Interrogatories.*[4] These are questions drawn up by the attorney and sent to an opposing attorney, who usually drafts verified answers to them for the client to verify. These responses are then sent back to the first lawyer. Interrogatories differ from the deposition on written questions in that the deposition is a session around a table while interrogatories and their answers flow back and forth, usually through the mails. For reasons to be seen later, the interrogatory in New York practice has less utility than it has in federal practice and is therefore met less frequently.

4. *Commission or letters rogatory.*[5] These are used to take testimony outside the state and are usually resorted to only when an ordinary deposition will not do the job. The only apparent difference between a "commission" and a deposition on written questions (or perhaps even oral questions if that's what the parties want) is that the "commissioner" carries the court's seal while the officer settled on by the parties does not. The letter rogatory is a different animal. It is a communication addressed by a local judge to a foreign tribunal asking for its aid in the securing of disclosure in the foreign place. The letter is usually carried by some person designated by the requesting court. That person can also be designated a "commissioner."

5. *Demand for address.*[6] Each party is entitled to know the address of any other party, or of its officers and assignors.

6. *Discovery and inspection.*[7] This ranks with the oral deposition in the frequency of its use and its importance in litigation. With the discovery device, the seeker is after a thing rather than testimony. The thing is usually a paper or document of some kind, but it can be any item relevant to the case, such as electronically stored information (ESI). Through this device, a party can also be required to permit entry onto real property that the party owns or controls for inspections of various kinds.

7. *Physical and mental examinations.*[8] If the physical or mental condition of any party is in controversy, that party can be compelled with this device to submit to an examination by appropriate professionals, whose testimony and reports are important and in some cases indispensable. In personal injury cases, for example, the physical examination is as important a device as the deposition or discovery. In incompetency proceedings, the key device is the mental examination. In a commercial case, or any other in which a physical or mental condition is not ordinarily implicated, the device plays no role at all.

8. *Request for admission.*[9] With this device, a party can require another to admit or deny stated facts or the genuineness of appended documents or photographs, all under oath. It sounds much more useful than it has actually proved in practice, mainly because

---

[4]   For elaboration, see § 361.

[5]   The commission and letters rogatory are not specified on the CPLR 3102(a) list, but appear later in CPLR 3108. They are important devices, especially when disclosure from a foreign source is required. They are elaborated in § 360. For a good review of the disclosure devices in general and those used to obtain disclosure from outside the state in particular, see Wiseman v. American Motors Sales Corp., 103 A.D.2d 230, 479 N.Y.S.2d 528 (2d Dep't 1984).

[6]   See § 365.

[7]   For elaboration, see § 362.

[8]   For elaboration, see § 363.

[9]   For elaboration, see § 364.

the sanctions for inadequate responses are unfortunately paltry or unpredictable, and often grudgingly applied by the courts.

Those are the devices, briefly listed. Note that the bill of particulars is not a disclosure device, but rather an incident of pleadings,[10] although it always does tend to disclose something (as, indeed, the pleading itself does). It has been suggested that expanded use of the bill of particulars should be allowed, at least in smaller cases, to perform the task that the more expensive disclosure devices carry out in bigger ones.[11] The suggestion has merit,[12] but it has not achieved great currency. Therefore, the lawyer should not consider the bill of particulars a disclosure device until the CPLR or the courts do. Nor is there any requirement under the CPLR that a demand for a bill of particulars be served before resort is made to a disclosure device, although the court can impose that chronology through a protective order in a given case.

There is no priority in the use of the devices. They need not be sought in any particular sequence. The party resorts to whichever device will best do the job needed and in whatever order the job needs doing. Nor is there any arbitrary limit on the number of devices that may be used or, indeed, on the number of times any single device may be used. Abuses in this regard are handled by the courts on a case by case basis, usually on a motion for a protective order under CPLR 3103.[13] With a protective order, the court can prescribe whatever priority or sequence it deems appropriate to the facts (deposition first, discovery next, etc.).[14] If one disclosure device proves inadequate, the party can turn to another.[15]

The usual time for disclosure is the pretrial period after the action has been commenced, but before the trial. Certificate of readiness rules restrict the period further, requiring that disclosure be concluded before the case is even placed on the trial calendar.[16] This means that as a practical matter disclosure is conducted within the several months after the action has been commenced and the pleadings are served. The general attitude of the CPLR, embodied in its statute authorizing a motion to dismiss for neglect to prosecute, CPLR 3216, is that the plaintiff who lets an action go more than a year without seeing to the completion of the necessary disclosure devices begins to face the threat of a dismissal for lack of prosecution.[17]

Disclosure sought at times other than the pretrial period—e.g., before commencement, after calendaring, at the trial, etc.—requires leave of court.[18]

§ 351. Method of Bringing on Disclosure; Stipulation or Notice

CPLR 3102(b) provides that stipulation or notice shall be the ordinary means for bringing on disclosure, whatever the device used. Only in certain instances is a court order initially required. These are discussed in the next section. "Stipulation" means

---

[10] The bill of particulars is the subject of §§ 238 et seq.

[11] See Block v. Fairbairn, 68 Misc. 2d 931, 328 N.Y.S.2d 497 (Sup. Ct., Ulster County 1972).

[12] See Commentary C3041:11 on McKinney's CPLR 3041.

[13] See § 353.

[14] See Rios v. Donovan, 21 A.D.2d 409, 250 N.Y.S.2d 818 (1st Dep't 1964).

[15] Law Offices Binder & Binder, P.C. v. O'Shea, 44 A.D.3d 626, 848 N.Y.S.2d 178 (2d Dep't 2007); Katz v. Posner, 23 A.D.2d 774, 258 N.Y.S.2d 508 (2d Dep't 1965).

[16] This aspect of the readiness rules is discussed in § 370.

[17] See CPLR 3216 and its discussion in § 375.

[18] See § 352.

agreement among the attorneys for all the parties, usually initiated by telephone after each attorney has checked with the client. It is primarily the deposition that requires this checking, even after a deposition notice is served. Since the deposition requires a session at an appointed day, time, and place, the convenience of the parties and their lawyers must be consulted. Technically, the stipulation setting up the deposition, like any other stipulation, should be in writing and subscribed,[1] but quite often it's done orally or merely confirmed by one lawyer to another in a letter. Alternatively, the lawyer seeking the deposition may first ascertain from his adversary the availability of the proposed deponent, choose a time accordingly, and then serve notices on attorneys for all parties advising of, or merely confirming, the time and place selected.

It is technically permissible for the seeking attorney just to pick out a day, time, and place[2] for an adverse party's deposition and simply serve notices on all parties advising of it,[3] but that's inviting trouble if it's not followed up by some confirmatory communications. If the deponent is legitimately engaged at the time set and does not show up, the court is likely to require nothing more than a rescheduling, without any sanction at all. The court will not countenance deliberate discourtesies among attorneys. A refusal to work out the time and place of a deposition is a high form of discourtesy.

Although the deposition is usually the most demanding of the disclosure devices in regard to scheduling, others may need some programming too. A CPLR 3120 discovery notice, for example, which requires the producing of a paper or thing, or the inspection of a designated item or premises, may also have to be scheduled for a particular time and place, especially when it involves something of which a mere copy can't be made and furnished to the seeker by mail, fax, email attachment, etc. This will be the case when what is sought for production and inspection concerns something cumbersome, like three file cabinets, or a roomful of rare blues records, or a swimming pool, or a fire escape or gymnasium contraption, etc. The CPLR 3121(a) physical and mental examination is in the same category, as it requires the party to appear in person and thus needs the setting of a day, time, and place for the appearance. Devices that contemplate the mere sending of papers back and forth, such as interrogatories served pursuant to CPLR 3132 and requests to admit under CPLR 3123, need no designated session and thus impose fewer logistical demands.

If a stipulation is used to secure disclosure, it should ideally be the stipulation of all parties, and it is prudent for the seeking party to confirm the stipulation, if it is not already in the form of a subscribed writing, by notices served on all. If notice is used without stipulation, the notice must be served on the attorney for each party, not merely on the attorney for the party from whom disclosure is sought.[4] This point is an important one because, for example, a deposition may not be used against a person not notified of its taking.[5] There is an exception to the notice rule if the party is in default for failure to appear in the action; nothing need be served on that party.[6] The time requirements

---

[1]   CPLR 2104; see § 204.

[2]   The place of the deposition is discussed in § 355.

[3]   This is often done at the outset of an action to secure priority in taking the deposition. See CPLR 3106(a); § 354.

[4]   See CPLR 2103(e); § 203.

[5]   CPLR 3117(a)(3); see § 358.

[6]   CPLR 3105.

connected with the giving of notice are discussed in the later treatments of the devices individually since they are not uniform for all.

For the deposing of a party, notices and stipulations do the job. But if the deponent is a nonparty witness, the deponent must be served with a subpoena.[7] This recognizes that the usual sanctions available against a party who violates a notice or stipulation— such as a preclusion order or even a default judgment[8]—hold no terror for a nonparty. The use of the subpoena subjects the nonparty to the court's jurisdiction and makes available the sanction of contempt for disobedience.[9]

The party seeking disclosure from a nonparty proceeds in the first instance without an order by effecting subpoena service on the witness.[10] If objection is made that the requirements for disclosure from a nonparty in CPLR 3101(a)(3) and (4) are not met, motions to quash the subpoena and for a protective order can be sought by the nonparty witness or any party to cancel or suppress the examination.[11] If a notice, subpoena, or stipulation setting up disclosure is ignored or otherwise violated, the aggrieved party can seek a court order compelling the disclosure[12] or, if the disobedience is willful, a penalty against an offending party or person.[13]

§ 352. Instances Where Order Initially Required

In instances in which a mere notice is used to bring on disclosure, disobedience may ensue and a court order compelling disclosure may be needed. The CPLR provides for such an order,[1] but there the order is sought only as a follow-up. In some instances, the notice method is not available at all and a court order must be sought in the first instance. These situations are the following:

1. Before action commenced. If disclosure is sought before an action has been duly commenced, a court order is required. Disclosure at this stage may be obtained "to aid in bringing an action, to preserve information or to aid in arbitration."[2] The last, designed to secure the aid of a court to compel disclosure in connection with an out-of-court arbitration, is frowned on by the courts,[3] although every now and again the courts can be prevailed on to lend a hand when the disclosure is needed to present "a proper case" to the arbitrator.[4] Free use of the disclosure devices is inconsistent with the

---

[7]   CPLR 3106(b) An "officer, director, member or employee of a party" equals the party itself for this purpose and need not be served with a subpoena. CPLR 3106(b). The notice served on the party is deemed adequate to compel that person's deposition. See Sammy v. First American Title Ins. Co. of New York, 2015 WL 4597115 (Sup. Ct., Queens County 2015); § 345.

[8]   CPLR 3126; see § 367.

[9]   See § 385.

[10]   The Court of Appeals addressed the contents required in such a subpoena in Kapon v. Koch, 23 N.Y.3d 32, 988 N.Y.S.2d 559, 11 N.E.3d 709 (2014), which is discussed in detail in § 345. See also Commentary C3101:22 on McKinney's CPLR 3101.

[11]   See, e.g., *Kapon,* 23 N.Y.3d at 34, 988 N.Y.S.2d at 562, 11 N.E.3d at 712. For a discussion of the corresponding burdens of proof on a motion to quash a subpoena under CPLR 2304, see § 384.

[12]   CPLR 3124; see § 366.

[13]   For penalties against a party, see CPLR 3126; § 367. For penalties against a nonparty, see CPLR 2308(a); § 385.

[1]   CPLR 3124; see § 366.

[2]   CPLR 3102(c).

[3]   See De Sapio v. Kohlmeyer, 35 N.Y.2d 402, 406, 362 N.Y.S.2d 843, 847, 321 N.E.2d 770, 773 (1974); AXA Equitable Life Ins. Co. v. Kalina, 101 A.D.3d 1655, 956 N.Y.S.2d 743 (4th Dep't 2012); § 597 (Practitioner's Edition).

[4]   See Hendler & Murray, P.C. v. Lambert, 127 A.D.2d 820, 511 N.Y.S.2d 941 (2d Dep't 1987).

purposes of arbitration, among which are ease, expedition, and economy. Therefore, court-ordered disclosure in aid of arbitration is justified only where "extraordinary circumstances" demonstrate that "relief is 'absolutely necessary for the protection of the rights of a party' to the arbitration."[5] The parties are usually better off seeking disclosure authorizations from the arbitrators.[6]

The preservation of information—or perpetuation of testimony, as it is better known—was one of the earliest functions of disclosure. It abides,[7] but is not frequently seen. It may be used, for example, when a key witness is in extremis or about to depart the state and there is not even time to commence an action and seek disclosure within it.

Disclosure to aid in "bringing" an action is seen a bit more often.[8] It may not be used to determine whether the plaintiff has a cause of action,[9] but as long as the plaintiff can satisfy the court that there is one, the disclosure can be sought to help determine who the defendants should be[10] or the form that the action should take.[11] A set of strong affidavits demonstrating that there is a prima facie cause of action is an indispensable part of an application for preaction disclosure.[12] If, however, a would-be defendant is under a duty to allow a would-be plaintiff to inspect records, as a hospital is when a patient seeks the inspection, and the defendant violates that obligation, the right to preaction disclosure is at hand and the plaintiff's application for the disclosure does not require an affidavit of merits.[13]

If the disclosure is needed merely to help in the drafting of the complaint, an alternative procedure is to commence the action with only a CPLR 305(b) notice[14] and then seek the disclosure within the action itself. If the complaint can be drawn without the datum that the disclosure seeks, the disclosure will not be allowed at all for this purpose. Where, for example, the plaintiff seeks disclosure for the purpose of pleading the amount of damages in a case in which a damages estimate in the complaint suffices, disclosure will be refused.[15]

---

[5] Travelers Indem. Co. v. United Diagnostic Imaging, P.C., 73 A.D.3d 791, 899 N.Y.S.2d 641 (2d Dep't 2010).

[6] Geico General Ins. Co. v. Weislee, 35 Misc. 3d 1221(A), 953 N.Y.S.2d 549 (Sup. Ct., Kings County 2012); see § 597 (Practitioner's Edition).

[7] See Matter of Davis, 178 Misc. 2d 65, 677 N.Y.S.2d 889 (Ct. Cl. 1998).

[8] See Commentary C3102:4 on McKinney's CPLR 3102.

[9] Holzman v. Manhattan and Bronx Surface Tr. Operating Authority, 271 A.D.2d 346, 707 N.Y.S.2d 159 (1st Dep't 2000).

[10] Leff v. Our Lady of Mercy Academy, 150 A.D.3d 1239, 55 N.Y.S.3d 392 (2d Dep't 2017).

[11] See Konig v. WordPress.com, 112 A.D.3d 936, 978 N.Y.S.2d 92 (2d Dep't 2013) (petition dismissed for failure to allege facts indicating that a cause of action existed); Application of Pelley, 43 Misc. 2d 1082, 252 N.Y.S.2d 944 (Nassau County Ct. 1964).

[12] See Toal v. Staten Island University Hosp., 300 A.D.2d 592, 752 N.Y.S.2d 372 (2d Dep't 2002).

[13] Application of Taylor, 143 Misc. 2d 259, 540 N.Y.S.2d 162 (Sup. Ct., Kings County 1989).

[14] See § 60.

[15] L-Tron Corp. v. Davco Systems, Inc., 60 A.D.2d 25, 400 N.Y.S.2d 243 (4th Dep't 1977); Zakarias v. Radio Patents Corp., 20 A.D.2d 795, 248 N.Y.S.2d 75 (2d Dep't 1964). CPLR 3017(c) now prohibits a party from pleading the specific amount of damages sought in a complaint for personal injuries or wrongful death. See § 217.

A petition seeking preaction disclosure should demonstrate that the court in which the special proceeding is commenced has subject matter jurisdiction to hear the potential action for which the disclosure is sought.[16]

2.   *During or after trial.* If disclosure is sought after the trial has begun, it needs a court order.[17] Disclosure at this stage is rare, since disclosure must as a rule be concluded before the case can even be put on the calendar to await trial and its purpose is to aid preparation *for* the trial.[18] But it can arise, for example, where some new element is permitted to be introduced at the trial, and the pleadings or other pretrial procedures did not give notice of it.

Disclosure to aid in the enforcement of a judgment, which becomes relevant only after judgment has been rendered, is subject to a special set of provisions[19] and is not governed by CPLR 3102(d).

3.   *Disclosure to aid foreign action.* CPLR 328(b) provides that serving a paper on someone in New York in connection with a foreign proceeding requires no court order. The aid of a New York court is available pursuant to CPLR 328(a) if it proves necessary. If the paper served requires compliance of some kind, however, the assistance of a New York court is more likely to be needed and the need is felt most when disclosure is sought in New York to aid in the foreign proceeding. CPLR 3102(e) was enacted to fill that need.

CPLR 3102(e) is an adaptation of the Uniform Foreign Depositions Act. It offers the machinery of the New York court system to compel a witness found in New York to give testimony for use in a proceeding pending elsewhere. The one seeking the disclosure, usually acting through a New York attorney retained for the purpose, can apply to the supreme court or to a county court for aid, the court making whatever order is appropriate in the circumstances.

The methods and processes to be used are the same as for disclosure sought for local actions. While the specific language of CPLR 3102(e) is somewhat limiting, authorizing the New York court to compel a witness "to appear and testify," several cases have implicitly recognized that the provision may be used to obtain documents in the absence of a deposition.[20] The seeker here can be a commissioner carrying the seal of the foreign court, or the bearer of a foreign letter rogatory,[21] or just an attorney or other person authorized by the foreign law or by the parties in the foreign action as permitted by the foreign law. If an objection of any kind is raised, such as by the person to be examined as a witness, the court will seek only to ascertain that the examination is relevant to the issues in the foreign action and that the witness's rights are protected. No showing of special circumstances is required to invoke CPLR 3102(e).[22]

There appears to be a conflict about whether an application under CPLR 3102(e) has to be on notice. The appellate division has indicated that the seeking attorney may

---

[16]   Estate of Matter of Wallace, 239 A.D.2d 14, 667 N.Y.S.2d 768 (3d Dep't 1998).

[17]   CPLR 3102(d).

[18]   See §§ 369 to 370.

[19]   CPLR 5223, 5224, 5229; see § 509.

[20]   See, e.g., Application of Wolf Popper Ross Wolf & Jones, 179 A.D.2d 389, 578 N.Y.S.2d 159 (1st Dep't 1992) (ordering production of documents sought pursuant to CPLR 3102(e)); see also Commentary C3102:9 on McKinney's CPLR 3102.

[21]   See, e.g., Application of Levine, 116 Misc. 2d 922, 456 N.Y.S.2d 936 (Sup. Ct., New York County 1982).

[22]   Brandes v. Harris, 78 A.D.2d 638, 432 N.Y.S.2d 116 (2d Dep't 1980).

just use a subpoena in that situation without first seeking a prior order allowing it.[23] It would presumably be a New York attorney issuing the subpoena out of a New York court under the caption of a CPLR 3102(e) application. It has been held that a subpoena issued by an attorney in the foreign jurisdiction will not do the job.[24]

CPLR 3119 contains New York's adoption of the Uniform Interstate Depositions and Discovery Act. The Act, applicable to courts whose proceedings are entitled to recognition under the Full Faith and Credit Clause (which excludes the courts of foreign nations), prescribes an easier procedure in certain instances for seeking the aid of the New York courts to assist outside litigation. The procedure is implemented by subpoenas, dispensing with a court order, at least at the outset. The first sentence in CPLR 3102(e) exempts procedures governed by CPLR 3119 from what might otherwise be the stricter prerequisites of CPLR 3102(e).[25]

If the law of a foreign place, including a sister state, has a provision akin to CPLR 3102(e) or has adopted the Uniform Foreign Depositions Act or Uniform Interstate Depositions and Discovery Act, it will assist in the converse situation: the securing of disclosure there to aid in a New York action.[26]

4. Disclosure by the State. As a rule, the State can be sued only in the Court of Claims.[27] The State can, however, sue in any court as a plaintiff, or voluntarily intervene even as a defendant, so it is seen in other courts and in different postures. Disclosure against the State, whatever its posture and whatever the court, was at one time available only by court order. A 1984 amendment of CPLR 3102(f) eliminated that requirement and made the disclosure devices available against the State through the same procedures applicable to any other party.[28]

It has been clarified that the State is also subject to disclosure as a nonparty witness. For that reason, state officials or employees in command of data relevant to a pending action, and not otherwise privileged, can't resist disclosure by pleading either their state employment or the fact that the State is not a party.[29]

5. Prisoners. Disclosure from a prisoner requires a court order.[30] Prison doors do not open, even temporarily, for a mere notice or stipulation.

6. Discovery against nonparty witness. The discovery device of CPLR 3120, which seeks to compel the production of a paper or thing and which has always proceeded by mere notice as against a party, at one time required a court order when the item was sought from a nonparty witness.[31] This was designed to recognize the possible inconvenience that the item's production might cause the witness and to enable the court to assess the need for the discovery and the cost to the witness, perhaps providing reimbursement or even the advance payment of those costs. That was changed in a 2003

---

[23] See Application of Ayliffe and Companies, 166 A.D.2d 223, 564 N.Y.S.2d 297 (1st Dep't 1990).

[24] See Matter of Deloitte, Haskins, and Sells, 146 Misc. 2d 884, 552 N.Y.S.2d 1003 (Sup. Ct., New York County 1990).

[25] See McKinney's Practice Commentaries to CPLR 3119.

[26] See §§ 359–60.

[27] See § 17.

[28] See Commentary C3102:10 in McKinney's CPLR 3102.

[29] Kaplan v. Kaplan, 31 N.Y.2d 63, 334 N.Y.S.2d 879, 286 N.E.2d 260 (1972).

[30] CPLR 3106(c).

[31] CPLR 3120(b) so provided before its 2003 amendment.

amendment of CPLR 3120 dispensing with the preliminary court order and allowing the discovery to proceed even against a nonparty through the mere service of a subpoena duces tecum.[32]

7. *Disclosure after case on calendar.* After the case has been placed on the calendar with the filing of a note of issue accompanied by a certification of readiness,[33] as required under the rules, disclosure is available only upon a showing of "unusual or unanticipated circumstances."[34] It thus requires a motion satisfying the court that the circumstances have been met. These motions are infrequently granted.[35]

8. *Special proceedings.* In a special proceeding (as opposed to an ordinary action), all disclosure except the request to admit device must be sought by court order.[36] This does not apply in the surrogates' courts, however, which conduct their business in a series of "proceedings," but where the same methods of disclosure are used as those in the supreme court—notice, stipulation, etc.[37]

Whenever disclosure is sought without the context of an action or proceeding, as where it is sought pursuant to CPLR 3102(c) by application before the action has been commenced, there may be some confusion about the procedures for the application. How is it made? Who must be served? Unfortunately, CPLR 3102(c) is devoid of any of the necessary mechanics for seeking preaction disclosure. The courts have filled the gap, recommending that the application should be made via a special proceeding.[38] It may be helpful to bring the proceeding by order to show cause to permit the court to give direction on such things as service of process.[39] As noted above, the petition should demonstrate that the court in which the application is commenced has subject matter jurisdiction to hear the potential action for which the disclosure is sought.[40] If a party has made a motion for preaction disclosure and desires to convert it to a special proceeding, it can seek such relief from the court.[41]

§ 352A. Requirement to Supplement Prior Responses

CPLR 3101(h) contains what is known as the supplementation requirement. It requires a party to update prior disclosure responses whenever the party obtains information indicating that a prior response was "incorrect or incomplete when made, or . . . though correct and complete when made, no longer is correct and complete, and the circumstances are such that a failure to amend or supplement the response would be materially misleading."

The provision was added to the CPLR in 1993, modeled on Rule 26(e) of the Federal Rules of Civil Procedure, but the New York statute is not identical. Coincidentally, Rule

---

[32] See § 362; SPR 138:1.

[33] CPLR 3402. This is a matter of calendar practice, treated in §§ 369 to 370.

[34] See, e.g., 22 N.Y.C.R.R. § 202.21, the rule applicable in the supreme and county courts.

[35] See § 370.

[36] CPLR 408. The request to admit is governed by CPLR 3123, treated in § 364.

[37] See the Commentary on SCPA 102 in McKinney's Surrogate's Court Procedure Act.

[38] See Bumpus v. New York City Transit Authority, 66 A.D.3d 26, 33, 883 N.Y.S.2d 99, 106 (2d Dep't 2009); see Commentary C3102:6 on McKinney's CPLR 3102.

[39] Using a special proceeding secures the helpful procedural guidance of Article 4 of the CPLR. See § 550.

[40] *Matter of Wallace,* 239 A.D.2d at 16, 667 N.Y.S.2d at 770.

[41] See CPLR 103(c); § 4; SPR 129:1.

26(e) was also amended in 1993. The New York provision drew on the federal rule as it was before the federal revision, as well as on the revision itself, notably in borrowing the "incomplete or incorrect" phrase, which was floating around in drafts of what was then merely a proposed federal change.

The purpose of the federal revision is summarized in the Federal Advisory Committee Notes,[1] which state that one of its purposes is to clarify that the supplementation requirement "applies to interrogatories, requests for production, and requests for admissions, but not ordinarily to deposition testimony." The New York provision makes no exception for a deposition; it applies "to all disclosure devices."[2] Hence, a response in a deposition, if it falls under the criteria quoted above, is also subject to the supplementation requirement.

If a party was asked to identify its fact witnesses, there was a standing requirement under the prior version of the federal rule[3] to advise the other side of any new fact witnesses the party subsequently learned about. The New York provision does not adopt that requirement in terms, but if a party to a New York action was specifically asked to identify fact witnesses and gave a complete list at the time, the later uncovering of another witness would fall under the general supplementation language used in CPLR 3101(h).

Subdivision (h) makes no reference to the disclosure of expert witnesses, which the federal rule does.[4] There can be little doubt, however, that any expert disclosure provided under CPLR 3101(d)(1) is subject to the supplementation requirement in CPLR 3101(h).[5]

Supplementing is to be made "promptly" upon the party's obtaining the new information.

The language of subdivision (h) indicates some hesitation about whether a failure to supplement should result in preclusion against the party withholding the information. The legislature left the matter to the court, providing the general instruction that the court may make "whatever order may be just." Preclusion is, of course, a possibility, but the court can turn to other remedies. A failure to supplement is also backed by the penalties of CPLR 3126,[6] and it would also seem possible to subject a violator to the money sanctions of Rule 130–1 if the conduct can be found to rise to the level of "frivolous."[7]

If a dispute arises about whether a given disclosure response should have been supplemented, it is not unlikely that it will arise at the trial itself. A finding at that point that the supplementing should have been made may result in the court's precluding the use of the unrevealed information altogether.[8]

---

[1]   See the 1993 Advisory Committee Notes following Fed. R. Civ. P. 26 in the Federal Rules segment of 28 U.S.C.A.

[2]   See the 1993 Report of the Advisory Committee on Civil Practice to the Chief Administrator of the Courts (Dec. 1992), p.19.

[3]   See subparagraph (A) of paragraph (1) of the pre-1993 Federal Rule 26(e).

[4]   The subject was part of Fed. R. Civ. P. 26(e)(1) and is now covered in Fed. R. Civ. P. 26(e)(2).

[5]   See Salander v. Central General Hosp., 130 Misc. 2d 311, 316, 496 N.Y.S.2d 638 (Sup. Ct., Nassau County 1985).

[6]   See Commentary C3126:1 on McKinney's CPLR 3126.

[7]   For discussion of the frivolity sanctions, see § 414A.

[8]   See Ward v. Mehar, 264 A.D.2d 515, 694 N.Y.S.2d 726 (2d Dep't 1999); Commentary C3101:49 on McKinney's CPLR 3101; SPR 8:1.

Since the supplementation requirement is intended to apply to all of the disclosure devices—depositions, discoveries, interrogatories, etc.—it should apply no matter what the tool is that brought on the original disclosure, e.g., notice, stipulation, or court order. But what form shall the supplementation take?

The form should follow as closely as possible the form in which the original disclosure response was provided. If the information to be updated first came out in a deposition by party P, for example, P can merely send a statement to the other parties advising that the answer she gave in response to the question asked at the top of folio 49 of the deposition now appears to be incorrect and that based on subsequent information coming to the deponent's attention the answer should be changed to thus-and-so. The statement should be sworn to, just as the original deposition and any changes in form or substance to it were.[9] The other parties are entitled to this so that they can make the same use of the supplementary data at the trial as they could have made of the deposition itself. The same considerations apply to the supplementing of interrogatories, which must be answered in writing under oath.[10]

If a CPLR 3120 discovery demand is involved, and the document or thing requested was not available earlier but can be furnished by the party now, it should be furnished now, with an accompanying explanation in a letter, notice, statement, etc. Here, the supplementing is somewhat less formal. Unless some verification is required in connection with the identification of the document or thing, a swearing or affirmation in this instance would not ordinarily be necessary.

The first sentence of CPLR 3101(h) places the burden of amending or supplementing a prior response squarely on the party who has served the response.[11] While the statute anticipates automatic supplementation by each party, it has been held that a motion is permissible "to force an amendment or supplementary response."[12]

The supplementation requirement of CPLR 3101(h) only applies to a "party." Therefore, a nonparty who produces records pursuant to a CPLR 3120(1)(i) demand has no obligation to supplement the production at a later date. If additional documents might be available after an original production, a second CPLR 3120(1)(i) subpoena may be necessary.[13]

Lawyer's Duties Under Rules of Professional Conduct

If the lawyer discovers that a prior response to a disclosure request needs supplementing under CPLR 3101(h), the lawyer will normally consult with the client and there will be an agreement to amend the prior response. In rare situations, the client might object to any amendment or supplement and, for various reasons, desire to go to trial relying on the inaccurate disclosure responses. The lawyer in this scenario may be personally subject to sanctions for allowing the misrepresentation to linger and thereby engaging in frivolous conduct.[14] Short of seeking to withdraw from the representation

---

[9]   See CPLR 3116(a); § 357.

[10]   CPLR 3133(b); see § 361.

[11]   See Dehaney v. New York City Transit Authority, 180 Misc. 2d 695, 694 N.Y.S.2d 831 (N.Y. City Civ. Ct. 1997).

[12]   See Green by Cage v. Staten Island University Hosp., 161 Misc. 2d 976, 615 N.Y.S.2d 856 (Sup. Ct., Richmond County 1994), aff'd, 221 A.D.2d 416, 634 N.Y.S.2d 386 (2d Dep't 1995), noted in SPR 37:3.

[13]   See Commentary C3120:3 to McKinney's CPLR 3120.

[14]   See § 414A. By signing a disclosure response, the attorney certifies that, "to the best of [her] knowledge, information and belief, formed after an inquiry reasonable under the circumstances," the contents

pursuant to Rule 1.16 of the New York Rules of Professional Conduct, does the lawyer have any independent recourse under these difficult circumstances? Searching for a resolution to this dilemma places us at the crossroads of attorney ethics and civil procedure once again, with several provisions from different sets of laws outlining the lawyer's duties.

Rule 1.6(b)(3) allows a lawyer "to withdraw a written or oral opinion or representation previously given by the lawyer and reasonably believed by the lawyer still to be relied upon by a third person, where the lawyer has discovered that the opinion or representation was based on materially inaccurate information or is being used to further a crime or fraud." This language would allow a lawyer who has certified a prior response to disclosure under Part 130, or who has relied on a response in an affidavit, to withdraw the response or affidavit if the lawyer subsequently learns that it was, for example, "incorrect or incomplete when made."[15] The lawyer can elect this course of action even if the withdrawal of the prior response or affidavit will implicitly reveal that it is inaccurate, and the lawyer learned that the prior response was inaccurate in a confidential communication with the client.[16] It should be emphasized, however, that Rule 1.6(b)(3) does not permit the lawyer to expressly reveal that the prior disclosure response is "inaccurate" or the information supporting such contention absent the client's permission. It merely permits the withdrawal of a prior response in certain specified circumstances.

Rule 3.3(a)(3), which may also be applicable in this scenario, can require the lawyer to expressly reveal that information. The Rule states that "[i]f a lawyer, the lawyer's client, or a witness called by the lawyer has offered material evidence and the lawyer comes to know of its falsity, the lawyer shall take reasonable remedial measures, including, if necessary, disclosure to the tribunal."[17] The rule applies to information provided during pretrial disclosure[18] and may require the lawyer to reveal the client's confidential information to the court.[19]

D. PROTECTION AGAINST ABUSE

Table of Sections

§ 353.   Protective Order; CPLR 3103

§ 353. Protective Order; CPLR 3103

The protective order is the law's perpetual guard, shielding parties and nonparties alike against disclosure abuses. Addressed always to the particular situation at hand

---

of the paper are not frivolous. 22 N.Y.C.R.R. § 130–1.1–a(b). If initial responses to disclosure are inaccurate, or are rendered inaccurate through the events of time, sanctions may be imposed on a party or a party's attorney. 22 N.Y.C.R.R. §§ 130–1.1(b), (c)(3).

[15]   CPLR 3101(h).

[16]   See N.Y. St. B. Ass'n Formal Ops. 781 (2004) and 797 (2006).

[17]   See also New York Rules of Professional Conduct, Rule 3.3(b).

[18]   See New York Rules of Professional Conduct, Rule 3.3, cmt. 1 ("[The Rule] also applies when the lawyer is representing a client in an ancillary proceeding conducted pursuant to the tribunal's adjudicative authority, such as a deposition. Thus, for example, paragraph (a)(3) requires a lawyer to take reasonable remedial measures if the lawyer comes to know that a client has offered false evidence in a deposition.").

[19]   See New York Rules of Professional Conduct, Rule 3.3(c). This thorny problem is discussed in further detail in Commentary C3001:49 on McKinney's CPLR 3101.

and available on motion or sua sponte when needed, it relieves the rest of the disclosure article from having to stop at key junctures to anticipate and arm against harassment. It is helpful to quote CPLR 3103(a):

> The court may at any time on its own initiative, or on motion of any party or of any person from whom or about whom discovery is sought, make a protective order denying, limiting, conditioning or regulating the use of any disclosure device. Such order shall be designed to prevent unreasonable annoyance, expense, embarrassment, disadvantage, or other prejudice to any person or the courts.

The statute recognizes how readily the disclosure devices can be abused and wisely abandons all attempts to enumerate specific examples. The cure is an ad hoc protective order. If advantage is being taken of a given party's attorney, low on either talent, experience, or financial wherewithal; or if the party has no attorney; or if for any other reason the court detects an abuse before a party or witness has actually complained of it by motion, the court may make the order on its own motion. With a protective order, the court can limit the number of disclosure devices that may be used, but this is a rare event.[1] CPLR 3103(a) is also available, for good cause shown, to change the venue of a deposition as prescribed by CPLR 3110.[2]

When a party seeks the CPLR 3103(a) protective order by motion, which is the more common situation, the mere making of the motion suspends the scheduled disclosure until the court, disposing of the motion, decides what's to follow.[3] If the disclosure involves a nonparty witness, the moving party must notify the witness that the disclosure is suspended.[4] CPLR 3103(a) permits the witness to seek the protective order, but by contacting an opposing party, the witness may be able to get that party to make the motion in the witness's behalf. This all falls under the caption: "The Enemy of My Enemy Is My Friend."

The phrase "any person from whom discovery is sought" includes, among others, a nonparty from whom a deposition is sought and the custodian of a paper or thing from whom discovery is sought.[5] CPLR 3103(a) was amended in 2013 to allow "any person . . . *about whom* discovery is sought" to move for a protective order to address problems that arose where a nonparty's information was sought from some other third party that possessed the information, such as a bank, accountant, or utility.[6] According to the legislative history, the purpose of the amendment is not to change existing caselaw as to whether a nonparty has a protectable interest in certain records. Rather, the new language is designed to clarify that a nonparty whose information is contained in the records of another has standing to challenge a subpoena served to obtain those records.

---

[1] See, e.g., Estates Roofing Co., Inc. v. Savo, 85 Misc. 2d 1028, 381 N.Y.S.2d 198 (Dist. Ct., Suffolk County 1976).

[2] See § 355.

[3] CPLR 3103(b).

[4] CPLR 3106(b).

[5] An amendment of CPLR 3103(a), effective January 1, 1994, changed the word "witness" to the phrase "person from whom discovery is sought" to clarify that the mere custodian of a relevant paper or thing is also included. This change was an adoption of the language of Fed. R. Civ. P. 26(c).

[6] See Norkin v. Hoey, 181 A.D.2d 248, 586 N.Y.S.2d 926 (1st Dep't 1992) (noting that "the overwhelming weight of authority in this State holds that a bank customer is without standing to challenge a third-party subpoena" of her bank records).

As a general rule, the time is always open to move for a protective order. The best time to move is obviously before the disclosure has been had because, as noted above, the motion's mere making stays the disclosure until the court decides whether it is to proceed. But if the disclosure has already gone forward and the testimony or item has already been provided, a protective order may still prove useful. Any information "improperly or irregularly obtained" may be ordered suppressed under CPLR 3103(c), i.e., barred from any use at the trial.[7] In addition, if a case involves "heinous" and "egregious" conduct by the plaintiff and her lawyer, the Court of Appeals has determined that dismissal of an action is also an appropriate remedy under CPLR 3103(c).[8]

The protective order is available no matter what disclosure device is implicated. Early conflict about whether the protective order can be used to test the validity of a request to admit under CPLR 3123 has been resolved. It can be.[9] A bill of particulars is not, technically, a disclosure device[10] and is therefore not a proper subject of a CPLR 3103 protective order.[11] CPLR 3042(e) would seem to play a similar role in that context, permitting the court to, among other things, issue an order vacating a demand for a bill of particulars that is improper or unduly burdensome.[12] In the lower courts, the protective order is available against a bill of particulars if the bill is being used for harassment.[13]

The Advisory Committee, whose draft of CPLR 3103(a) got through the legislature unscathed, set forth in its report a number of matters that the court can regulate on a motion for a protective order:

1. the time, order, and place of taking depositions;

2. the number and names of persons to be questioned;

3. the time within which the information must be obtained;

4. the number, kinds of questions, or specific questions that may be asked;

5. the disclosure device or combination of devices that may be used; and

6. the matters that may or may not be inquired into.[14]

The enumerated matters are illustrative, not exclusive. There follows in the Advisory Committee's notes a list of other examples of protective orders. A perusal of the list will confirm to the lawyer the numerous possibilities and corroborate the drafters'

---

[7]   CPLR 3103(c); see Juskowitz v. Hahn, 56 Misc. 2d 647, 289 N.Y.S.2d 870 (Sup. Ct., Nassau County 1968); see also McHugh ex rel. Kurtz v. Fitzgerald, 280 A.D.2d 771, 772–73, 719 N.Y.S.2d 785, 786–87 (3d Dep't 2001) (suppression not required on CPLR 3103(a) motion because communication with unrepresented party was not in violation of "no contact" rule, currently embodied in New York Rules of Professional Conduct, Rule 4.2(a)).

[8]   Lipin v. Bender, 84 N.Y.2d 562, 620 N.Y.S.2d 744, 644 N.E.2d 1300 (1994) (NYSLD No. 419); see § 367; Commentary C3103:7 on McKinney's CPLR 3101.

[9]   Wolin v. St. Vincent's Hosp. and Medical Center of New York, 304 A.D.2d 348, 757 N.Y.S.2d 33 (1st Dep't 2003); Epstein v. Consolidated Edison Co. of New York, 31 A.D.2d 746, 297 N.Y.S.2d 260 (2d Dep't 1969).

[10]   See § 238.

[11]   See Forte v. Perry, 108 A.D.2d 895, 485 N.Y.S.2d 777 (2d Dep't 1985).

[12]   See § 241.

[13]   See § 1101 in the New York City Civil, Uniform District, Uniform City, and Uniform Justice court acts, McKinney's Vol. 29A, Parts 2 and 3, and the Commentaries on it.

[14]   First Rep. Leg. Doc. No. 6(b), p. 124 (1957).

judgment to leave disclosure rectifications to the courts on a case by case basis.[15] Provision is made to protect against the unnecessary revelation of trade secrets, for example.[16]

The CPLR does not have explicit instructions for who pays for disclosure—the seeking party or the responding party. The general attitude has been that each party pays its own way. The protective order can step in to balance the situation in which a disparity in the economic resources of the parties is disabling one from participating in the disclosure process, or empowering another to take undue advantage of it. The court can order one party to defray initially the costs of another's participation in disclosure,[17] but this is not a favored step. The later winner on the merits can recover these expenses, or at least a segment of them, from the loser as post-judgment disbursements.[18]

Pressed by the great expense that the retrieval of electronically stored information (ESI) can entail—that greedy monster of the computer age—the courts have turned to the subject in earnest. A major treatment on allotting disclosure costs appears in the First Department decision in U.S. Bank National Ass'n v. GreenPoint Mortgage Funding, Inc.,[19] where the court held that the producing party is "to bear the initial cost of searching for, retrieving and producing discovery," but that the court, in the exercise of its protective order powers, is permitted to shift the costs between the parties, as the circumstances may warrant.[20]

In ruling on motions for a protective order, the courts have consistently denied public access to pretrial proceedings, including depositions.[21] A party, however, has the right to be present at a deposition in her action and the right is placed on par with a party's constitutional right to be present at trial.[22]

The court can assign a given judge or referee to supervise all or part of the disclosure proceedings in a particular case,[23] including a judicial hearing officer.[24] It has been held that this power should be exercised sparingly, however,[25] and it is. The question is one of congestion and personnel. An example of a case warranting the appointment of a referee is where a party has a "long history of . . . intransigence" in resisting disclosure

---

[15] The list is from 1st Rep. Leg. Doc. No. 6(b), p. 125 (1957), and is printed verbatim following McKinney's CPLR 3103.

[16] See Mann ex rel. Akst v. Cooper Tire Co., 33 A.D.3d 24, 816 N.Y.S.2d 45 (1st Dep't 2006) (discussing procedure to be followed for obtaining a protective order for information constituting a trade secret).

[17] Buffone v. Aronson, 45 Misc. 2d 454, 257 N.Y.S.2d 47 (Sup. Ct., Westchester County 1965).

[18] See Fairchild Camera & Instrument Corp. v. Barletta, 21 A.D.2d 768, 250 N.Y.S.2d 679 (1st Dep't 1964); Connors, *Which Party Pays the Costs of Document Disclosure,* 29 Pace L. Rev. 441 (Spring 2009).

[19] U.S. Bank Nat. Ass'n v. GreenPoint Mortgage Funding, Inc., 94 A.D.3d 58, 63–64, 939 N.Y.S.2d 395, 399 (1st Dep't 2012).

[20] See § 362.

[21] See Scollo v. Good Samaritan Hosp., 175 A.D.2d 278, 572 N.Y.S.2d 730 (2d Dep't 1991); Lisa C.-R. v. William R., 166 Misc. 2d 817, 635 N.Y.S.2d 449 (Sup. Ct., New York County 1995) (involving a matrimonial dispute).

[22] Perez v. Time Moving & Storage, 28 A.D.3d 326, 813 N.Y.S.2d 411 (1st Dep't 2006); see Commentary C3113:7A to McKinney's CPLR 3113.

[23] CPLR 3104(a).

[24] CPLR 3104(b). A judicial hearing officer is a retired judge designated as such pursuant to § 850(1) et seq. of the Judiciary Law.

[25] DiGiovanni v. Pepsico, Inc., 120 A.D.2d 413, 502 N.Y.S.2d 23 (1st Dep't 1986).

and a "constantly available supervisor" is needed.[26] A middle step, which doesn't require the appointee to sit in on the disclosure proceedings proper, is for the court to direct that all disclosure applications in a given case be made to a designated judge or referee.[27]

The parties can stipulate to name an attorney to act as a referee.[28] The powers of the referee, including a judicial hearing officer and a lawyer appointed by the parties, are set forth in the statute.[29] Review of a referee's determination must be sought before the appointing court; it does not go directly to an appellate court even if the referee is a judicial hearing officer.[30]

"Good Faith" Affirmation Requirement on Disclosure Motions

Every motion relating to disclosure must be accompanied by the moving lawyer's affirmation that a good faith effort was first made to resolve the disclosure dispute with the other side.[31] The motion for a protective order is one of the many motions requiring this affirmation. The affirmation should not be a mere boiler-plate recitation. It has been held that "[s]ignificant, intelligent and expansive contact and negotiations must be held between counsel to resolve any dispute and such efforts must be adequately detailed in [the] affirmation [and mere] computer generated form letters or cursory telephone conversations [are not acceptable]."[32] Uniform Rule 202.7(c) prescribes the details that need to be included in the affirmation to satisfy the court that a good faith effort has been made to resolve the dispute.[33]

E. THE DEVICES INDIVIDUALLY

Table of Sections

§ 354. Deposition on Oral Questions: The "EBT"

§ 355. Place of Deposition

§ 356. Taking the Deposition

§ 357. Executing the Deposition

§ 358. Use of Deposition

§ 359. Deposition on Written Questions

§ 360. Commission or Letters Rogatory

§ 361. Interrogatories

§ 362. Discovery and Inspection

§ 363. Physical and Mental Examinations

---

[26] Baker v. General Mills Fun Group, Inc., 101 Misc. 2d 193, 420 N.Y.S.2d 820 (Sup. Ct., New York County 1979).

[27] See In re Dietrich's Will, 65 Misc. 2d 811, 318 N.Y.S.2d 72 (Sup. Ct., Erie County 1970), aff'd, 36 A.D.2d 1027, 321 N.Y.S.2d 449 (4th Dep't 1971).

[28] CPLR 3104(b); see Ploski v. Riverwood Owners Corp., 255 A.D.2d 24, 688 N.Y.S.2d 627 (1st Dep't 1999) (court can only appoint a private attorney as a referee under CPLR 3104(b) when parties stipulate).

[29] CPLR 3104(c); see also § 379 ("Triability by Referee").

[30] East End Laboratories, Inc. v. Altaire Pharmaceuticals, Inc., 100 A.D.3d 824, 825, 955 N.Y.S.2d 348 (2d Dep't 2012); see Nasir v. Tait, 128 A.D.3d 1033, 9 N.Y.S.3d 660 (2d Dep't 2015); Commentary C3104:1 on McKinney's CPLR 3104.

[31] See, e.g., 22 N.Y.C.R.R. § 202.7, the rule applicable in the supreme and county courts.

[32] See Eaton v. Chahal, 146 Misc. 2d 977, 553 N.Y.S.2d 642 (Sup. Ct., Rensselaer County 1990), a consolidated decision in six cases before the court in which the court rejected as inadequate the affirmations tendered in five of them.

[33] 22 N.Y.C.R.R. § 202.7(c).

§ 364.   Notice to Admit

§ 365.   Demand for Address

§ 354. Deposition on Oral Questions: The "EBT"

The oral deposition is one of the most probing and most important disclosure devices. There are several aspects of it to be negotiated, as the CPLR builds from the priority in taking depositions established in CPLR 3106(a) right through the ultimate use of the deposition at trial as prescribed in CPLR 3117. This section will treat the deposition's initial scheduling. Succeeding sections will discuss where and how the deposition is taken and executed and the use that can be made of the deposition at the trial or on a motion for summary judgment.

At the outset we have a question of terminology. In practice, a popular name for the oral deposition is "EBT," standing for examination before trial. The three-letter recitation is deeply ensconced in New York practice and generally accurate, but not technically so. The usual time for the deposition is after commencement of the action and before the trial, giving currency to the "EBT" description, but depositions can also be scheduled by court order before the action is begun,[1] after the trial is under way,[2] and even after it is over.[3] By avoiding time references and embracing all oral examinations, "deposition" is more accurate. "EBT" by definition embraces the most usual deposition, but is sometimes used casually to describe all of them.

CPLR 3107 contains the basic requirements for scheduling a deposition. Ideally, the deposition is set up by agreement among all parties after the deposition notice has been served, and the dates and times in the notice are usually altered by the parties agreement. Absent an agreement among the parties, the deposition notice must schedule the deposition for not earlier than 20 days after the notice is served, and not earlier than 25 days if mail is used.[4] As previously indicated, the party noticing the deposition will ordinarily want to confirm that the deponent will be able to attend the deposition at the appointed place and time. Without that consultation, usually with the deponent's attorney, the court is less likely to visit any penalty for a nonappearance.

The notice must be in writing, state when and where the deposition is to take place, and indicate who is to be deposed. It need not enumerate the matters on which the person is to be examined, as it is understood that the examination can delve into anything relevant to the case and any phraseology so indicating will suffice. The deponent's lawyer may serve a notice to depose the party who noticed the deposition, and any other party, for the same date and place, to immediately follow the deponent's deposition. The advantage here is that only 10 days notice is needed for that deposition, as compared to the 20 days required if the examination is scheduled independently.

Ordinarily, the defendant is entitled to examine the plaintiff before the plaintiff gets a turn at the defendant. The theory is that the defendant is blameless until the plaintiff

---

[1]   CPLR 3102(c); see § 352.

[2]   CPLR 3102(d); see § 352.

[3]   CPLR 5229; see § 516.

[4]   CPLR 2103(b)(2). If the deposition notice is served via mail outside New York State, a 2016 amendment to CPLR 2103(b)(2) will now require that the deposition be set not earlier than 26 days after the notice is served. See § 202.

proves otherwise.[5] The CPLR spells out this pro-defendant priority backhandedly. It provides that if a notice of deposition is served by the plaintiff before the defendant's answering time has expired, it requires leave of court, while the defendant's notice served on the plaintiff during that time does not.[6] Even this who-goes-first direction can be varied by the court in a protective order.[7] The courts are impatient with priority battles, reasonably believing that counsel can work these things out without court aid and condemning "the consummate waste of time occasioned by attorneys' picayune and pettifogging contentiousness," especially when it necessitates judicial intervention.[8] The requirement of the Uniform Rules, that every motion related to disclosure be accompanied by an affirmation of a good faith effort to resolve the dispute without resort to the court,[9] is a by-product of that kind of contentiousness.

A nonparty deponent must be served with a subpoena, which, like the notice when a party is to be examined, must be served at least 20 days before the deposition.[10] All parties are entitled to notice of a nonparty's deposition as well as a party's. Common practice is to serve notices on the parties, advising of the witness's deposition, at about the same time the witness is served with the subpoena. One difference is that the notices served on the parties are interlocutory papers which go by mail to the parties' lawyers,[11] while the subpoena must be served on the witness in the same manner as a summons.[12]

Errors and irregularities in the notice of deposition, such as an improper venue,[13] are waived unless a written objection is served on the noticing party at least three days before the scheduled deposition.[14] Other phases of the deposition cycle may come in for substantial objections, but the initial step of noticing it usually does not.

The expenses of scheduling and taking a deposition are on the party seeking it, unless the court otherwise directs, such as on a motion for a protective order.[15]

A simple form of notice to take a deposition can read as follows:

Please take notice that, pursuant to CPLR Article 31, the deposition on oral examination of the plaintiff ____, whose address is ____, will be taken on the ____ day of __, at ____ o'clock at the office of the attorney for the defendant at ____.[16]

§ 355. Place of Deposition

The venue of a deposition to be taken in the state is set by CPLR 3110, which lists the proper counties. If the person to be examined "is a party or an officer, director,

---

[5]   Klevens Const. Co., Inc. v. State, 87 Misc. 2d 108, 109, 383 N.Y.S.2d 844 (Ct. Cl. 1976).

[6]   CPLR 3106(a). After expiration of the answering time, the one who serves the notice first generally gets to take the deposition first.

[7]   See CPLR 3103(a); see § 353.

[8]   Goldberg v. Freedman, 33 A.D.2d 754, 305 N.Y.S.2d 996 (1st Dep't 1969).

[9]   See, e.g., 22 N.Y.C.R.R. § 202.7(a) & (c), applicable in the supreme and county courts; § 353.

[10]   CPLR 3106(b). The Court of Appeals addressed the contents required in such a subpoena in Kapon v. Koch, 23 N.Y.3d 32, 988 N.Y.S.2d 559, 11 N.E.3d 709 (2014), which is discussed in detail in § 345.

[11]   CPLR 2103(b)(2).

[12]   CPLR 2303; see § 383.

[13]   See CPLR 3110; § 355.

[14]   CPLR 3112.

[15]   CPLR 3116(d).

[16]   This notice is modeled on 2PT2 West's McKinney's Forms, CPLR § 6:106, which also contains caption, signature, and an additional clause used when the deponent is also to be required to produce papers or other things designated for use in conjunction with the examination. See CPLR 3111, discussed in § 362.

member or employee of a party," the deposition may be scheduled in a county in which (1) the party resides, or (2) the party "has an office for the regular transaction of business in person," or (3) the action is pending.[1] If the person to be examined is a nonparty resident, the alternative of the action-pending county is unavailable and the venue is limited to a county in which the witness resides or "is regularly employed or has an office for the regular transaction of business in person."[2] If the nonparty deponent is not a resident, then the proper venue for the deposition is the county in which she "is regularly employed or has an office for the regular transaction of business in person" or, simply, the county in which she is served.[3] If the witness can't be served here and has no contacts with the state, her testimony will have to be taken outside the state by devices to be met later.[4]

While a CPLR 3103(a) protective order can adjust the venue rules in CPLR 3110,[5] it usually will require a showing of undue hardship by the party being deposed.[6] In Weinstein v. Gindi,[7] for example, plaintiff commenced an action in Supreme Court, New York County and was ordered to appear for a deposition in Manhattan. The First Department noted that depositions of parties to an action are generally held in the county where the action is pending[8] but that "if a party demonstrates that conducting his deposition in that county would cause undue hardship, the Supreme Court in its exercise of discretion can order the deposition to be held elsewhere." The hardship alleged in *Weinstein* was somewhat novel: a warrant for plaintiff's arrest had been issued in New York upon his contempt in an unrelated action. That "self-imposed" problem, holds the court, does not constitute "undue hardship" that would excuse a plaintiff from failing to attend a court ordered deposition in the county where he commenced the action. Therefore, the First Department concluded that supreme court providently exercised its discretion in striking plaintiff's pleading and dismissing his claims.[9]

If a party resides outside New York, the convenience of that party will be considered by the court, especially when the party must travel from a foreign country. While the stated requirements of CPLR 3110 are as applicable to foreign as to domestic parties, a protective order under CPLR 3103(a) can adjust venue where the parties reside abroad, and even provide for a deposition by remote electronic means.[10] A protective order can also cancel a duly scheduled deposition of the foreign party, even if that party is the plaintiff, on condition, for example, that the party submit to local examination at a later time a stated number of days in advance of the trial.[11] That will enable the party to make but one trip to the state, deferring pretrial disclosure to that occasion when the party

---

[1]　CPLR 3110(1).

[2]　CPLR 3110(2).

[3]　CPLR 3110(2). The nonparty is served with a subpoena. CPLR 3106(b); see § 354.

[4]　See §§ 359 and 360.

[5]　See § 353.

[6]　See Yu Hui Chen v. Chen Li Zhi, 81 A.D.3d 818, 916 N.Y.S.2d 525 (2d Dep't 2011); Wygocki v. Milford Plaza Hotel, 38 A.D.3d 237, 831 N.Y.S.2d 381 (1st Dep't 2007); Commentary C3110:7 on McKinney's CPLR 3110.

[7]　Weinstein v. Gindi, 92 A.D.3d 526, 938 N.Y.S.2d 538 (1st Dep't 2012) (SPR 243:2).

[8]　See CPLR 3110(1).

[9]　See CPLR 3126(3) (authorizing a court to strike pleadings and dismiss an action based on a party's failure to comply with an order compelling disclosure); § 367.

[10]　See Feng Wang v. A & W Travel, Inc., 130 A.D.3d 974, 14 N.Y.S.3d 459 (2d Dep't 2015).

[11]　See Nama Air Cargo Co., Ltd. v. Unitrans Consol. Inc., 208 A.D.2d 604, 617 N.Y.S.2d 367 (2d Dep't 1994).

would shortly have had to come to New York for the trial anyway. This is sometimes called the "eve of trial" rule, but it's not applied just for the asking.[12]

CPLR 3110 merely prescribes the county of the deposition; it doesn't say where, within the county, the deposition may be held. The most common practice is for the noticing lawyer to schedule the deposition at her office, if the office is in a proper county. Any appropriate place within the county where a table and chairs are available in an atmosphere of decorum should do. In some counties, the courthouse has facilities for the taking of depositions as do county law libraries. This must be inquired into locally. When available, a deposition set for the courthouse is of course permissible, but not mandatory. It has been held, however, that if an opposing party objects to having a deposition at the noticing attorney's office, the court should, on application, direct that it be held elsewhere. The courthouse would seem the most appropriate place when relations between counsel have so deteriorated.[13]

When the party to be examined is a public corporation, which includes all of the municipalities (cities, counties, towns, and villages), among other entities,[14] or any of its officers, agents, or employees, the action-pending county is the only venue choice and the deposition must be set at the office of the public corporation's attorney or of its officers, agents, or employees.[15] The parties can stipulate otherwise, and the court can vary this requirement with a protective order.

For purposes of disclosure, New York City is deemed one county so that if any of its five counties answers to a requirement of CPLR 3110, the deposition can apparently be scheduled in that county, or in any of the four other counties. The protective order stands by here, too, as a remedy for abuse.

Although CPLR 3110, in setting venue, addresses itself only to the deposition, it should be taken as the guide for any disclosure device that requires a face-to-face session. It is not of moment with something like the request to admit or the interrogatory because those devices ordinarily move by mail or electronic means between lawyers' offices. But it may be relevant for the discovery device of CPLR 3120, especially in a situation in which the person must show up with the item at a stated time and place and can't merely send it on. Absent any contrary direction in a rule, it may be relevant as well to the physical or mental examination allowed by CPLR 3121.[16] Whenever, for any device, a place of in-state disclosure must be singled out and instructions are not found elsewhere, CPLR 3110 is the appropriate guidepost.[17]

§ 356. Taking the Deposition

The deposition is taken before a person authorized to administer oaths, typically a notary public.[1] Often the stenographer hired to record the questions and answers is qualified as a notary and carries out both functions. The party setting up a deposition

---

[12]   See Platman v. Pham Thu Duc, 191 A.D.2d 620, 595 N.Y.S.2d 111 (2d Dep't 1993); Rakowski v. Irmisch, 46 A.D.2d 826, 361 N.Y.S.2d 68 (3d Dep't 1974).

[13]   See Ambrose v. Wurlitzer Co., 27 A.D.2d 732, 277 N.Y.S.2d 160 (2d Dep't 1967).

[14]   See the definitions contained in Gen. Constr. Law § 66.

[15]   CPLR 3110(3).

[16]   The rule governing medical examinations in the supreme and county courts is 22 N.Y.C.R.R. § 202.17, which leaves it to the court to adjust venue if the parties can't agree to it.

[17]   See Cattat v. Alfa Romeo, Inc., 81 Misc. 2d 119, 364 N.Y.S.2d 772 (Sup. Ct., Oneida County 1975).

[1]   CPLR 3113(a).

must see to it that the officer and stenographer attend at the session, and it's always a good idea to confirm the deposition the day before it is scheduled. Stenography is still the predominant method for transcribing the testimony, but the use of videotape is permitted.[2] A rule prescribes the procedures when videotape is used.[3]

Disqualified from taking a deposition, i.e., from serving as the officer before whom it is taken, are the attorney for a party, the attorney's employees, and anyone who would be disqualified by interest, blood, or affinity from serving as a juror in the case.[4] But an employee of the attorney can operate the tape equipment when tape is used.[5]

Separate provisions list the persons authorized to conduct a deposition elsewhere in the United States and in foreign countries.[6] Objection to the person designated to take the deposition must be made before it is taken or as soon afterwards as the disqualification becomes known.[7] It is also permissible, of course, for a judge or referee to conduct the deposition,[8] or an attorney if the parties stipulate.[9]

When the session finally gets under way, with the deponents and the lawyers for all parties present along with the officer and stenographer or tape operator, the officer puts the deponent under oath and the noticing attorney starts the questioning.[10] The other attorneys will have their chance to participate in due course through cross-examination.[11] The inquiry may be into anything relevant to the case. It is no longer a defense to simply cry "fishing expedition." In the parlance of the CPLR, where relevance is the standard under CPLR 3101(a) and the *Allen* case construing it,[12] anything relevant is fair game. The once handy epithet, "fishing expedition," won't defeat the inquiry. Realistically, the questioner is indeed fishing—into every posture the deposing party takes on every fact relevant to the case. As will be seen below, the party defending the deposition can only assert a direction not to answer "when the question is plainly improper and would, if answered, cause significant prejudice to any person."[13]

The testimony, question-and-answer, colloquy, and any disputes are recorded verbatim. All objections and directions not to answer, whatever their nature, are to be noted by the officer and "the deposition shall proceed subject to the right of a person to apply for a protective order."[14] The deposition shall proceed, moreover, "without

---

[2]   CPLR 3113(b) permits the deposition to be recorded by "stenographic or other means."

[3]   See 22 N.Y.C.R.R. § 202.15, applicable in the supreme and county courts. Subdivision (j) of the rule applies when only an audio taping is sought. Counterpart rules adopting section 202.15 govern in the New York City Civil Court (22 N.Y.C.R.R. § 208.12), the district courts (22 N.Y.C.R.R. § 212.12), and the city courts (22 N.Y.C.R.R. § 210.12). The Court of Claims has its own rule on the subject (22 N.Y.C.R.R. § 206.11).

[4]   CPLR 3113(a). For an enumeration of those so disqualified, see CPLR 4110.

[5]   22 N.Y.C.R.R. § 202.15(c).

[6]   CPLR 3113(a)(2), (3). See Commentary C3113:1 on McKinney's CPLR 3113.

[7]   CPLR 3115(c).

[8]   CPLR 3102(c), 3104(a).

[9]   CPLR 3104(b). The attorney selected is not likely to be the attorney for either side, but to keep from running afoul of CPLR 3113(a), the court should make sure it isn't.

[10]   The First Department has ruled that a party has a right to be present at a deposition in her action. See Perez v. Time Moving & Storage, 28 A.D.3d 326, 813 N.Y.S.2d 411 (1st Dep't 2006); Commentary C3113:7A on McKinney's CPLR 3113.

[11]   CPLR 3113(c).

[12]   See § 344.

[13]   22 N.Y.C.R.R. § 221.2(c).

[14]   CPLR 3113(b); see 22 N.Y.C.R.R. § 221.2(c) ("If the deponent does not answer a question the examining party shall have the right to complete the remainder of the deposition.").

unreasonable adjournments."[15] The statutory intent is to prevent any objection from cancelling the whole examination if that can possibly be avoided. If the parties disagree on a question and the deponent, on counsel's advice, refuses to answer it, the examination should continue in accordance with CPLR 3113(b). Other matters can be explored until the questioner has exhausted all relevant areas of inquiry. Any unanswered questions to which the lawyer thinks answers are required may be made the subject of a later motion for a disclosure order.[16] It is also possible, if the deposition is being conducted in the courthouse or close by, to have the judge rule—during the course of the deposition—on the legitimacy of questions and the requirement of answers.[17] In sum, the court's powers under CPLR 3103(a), 3124 and 3126 remain available, but all attempts should be made to avoid resorting to this type of relief until the deposition is concluded.

In an important set of rules that went into effect on October 1, 2006, the Office of Court Administration took aim at disruptive conduct frequently met at depositions—disruptive conduct that many lawyers have perhaps come to deem their divinely conferred right—and sought, in more specific terms, to divest it of its divinity. This was done in three rules, all part of a new Part 221 of the Uniform Rules for the New York State Trial Courts, entitled "Uniform Rules for the Conduct of Depositions." A separate caption bearing that title appearing towards the end of this section goes into these rules at length.

CPLR 3113(b) authorizes any party to submit written questions to the officer, to be propounded at the session, without that party's attorney attending. This is not a sound practice, however, unless done by all parties. It leaves the deponent at the mercy of those lawyers who do attend and hampers such permissible questions and objections as might be interposed spontaneously in the client's behalf if the attorney were present.

Examination and cross-examination proceed as at a trial in open court,[18] with a few notable exceptions. If the deposition is noticed by the adverse party, which is most often the case, the deponent may then be cross-examined by her own lawyer. Cross-examination, by whomever conducted, is not limited to the subject matter of the main examination, as it ordinarily is at the trial. It can explore new ground.[19] Any party against whom the deposition may later be used[20] is also entitled to cross-examine the deponent.[21]

An interesting and controversial issue arose concerning whether a lawyer for a nonparty was entitled to participate and assert objections at the deposition. The Fourth Department said no in Thompson v. Mather,[22] relying on CPLR 3113(c). The court concluded that because a nonparty's lawyer could not object to a question posed to the

---

[15] CPLR 3113(b).

[16] See CPLR 3124.

[17] This is discussed in § 366, treating CPLR 3124.

[18] CPLR 3113(c); see Lieblich v. Saint Peter's Hosp. of City of Albany, 112 A.D.3d 1202, 977 N.Y.S.2d 780 (3d Dep't 2013).

[19] CPLR 3113(c).

[20] The uses of the deposition are treated in § 358.

[21] Beatty v. Donley, 31 Misc. 2d 164, 220 N.Y.S.2d 218 (Sup. Ct., Nassau County 1961).

[22] Thompson v. Mather, 70 A.D.3d 1436, 894 N.Y.S.2d 671 (4th Dep't 2010).

nonparty witness at trial, such objection could not be interposed at a deposition.[23] The *Thompson* decision and its progeny were legislatively overruled by a 2014 amendment to CPLR 3113(c) that expressly provides "that a non-party deponent's counsel may participate in [a] deposition and make objections on behalf of his or her client in the same manner as counsel for a party."[24]

To encourage every party to be relaxed and open at the deposition, insofar as any law can bring that off, it is provided that no objection is waived by not being made at the session. Later, if and when the particular question is read at the trial, any lawyer can object to it, and the objection at that time will be disposed of under the rules of evidence even though the question was answered without objection at the deposition. If the applicable rule bars the answer, it will be kept from the jury regardless of the fact that the answer stands forth in full flower on the folios of the deposition transcript.[25]

An exception to this rule concerns an objection to the form of the question. Here, the theory is that the prompt assertion of the objection will enable the questioner to cure it with a simple rephrasing. Mere form objections must, therefore, be noted at the deposition, or are waived.[26]

The trial lawyer is still cautious at the deposition. The fact that substantial objections need not be made does not mean that lawyers do not try to make them. The right to raise most objections is now strictly limited by Part 221 of the Uniform Rules, discussed below.[27] If they are made, disputes about them are usually resolved on a later motion to compel disclosure[28] by reference to the rules of evidence just as they would be at the trial. The courts are especially impatient with petty objections at this stage, however, and Part 221 of the Uniform Rules reflects this sentiment.[29]

When stenography is the recording method, the device used most often is that noiseless little contraption that makes the recording process very quiet and the stenographer very prosperous. The use of longhand has been held an imposition and is precluded if a party objects.[30] As already indicated, tape recording is permissible. For a time it was used only experimentally, with a stenographer present and working as a back-up.[31] While an extensive rule prescribes procedure when a deposition is taken by videotape, the issue of when the tape method may be used is not resolved in either the CPLR or the rules. It has been held, however, that a party willing to pay for the

---

[23]   See also Sciara v. Surgical Associates of Western New York, P.C., 104 A.D.3d 1256, 961 N.Y.S.2d 640 (4th Dep't 2013).

[24]   The amendment is far more sweeping than the rule announced in Women in City Government United v. City of New York, 112 F.R.D. 29, 32 (S.D.N.Y. 1986); see Commentary C3113:7 to McKinney's CPLR 3113.

[25]   CPLR 3115(d); see Johnson v. New York City Health & Hospitals Corp., 49 A.D.2d 234, 374 N.Y.S.2d 343 (2d Dep't 1975).

[26]   CPLR 3115(b), (d).

[27]   See 22 N.Y.C.R.R. § 221.1(a).

[28]   See CPLR 3124.

[29]   See 22 N.Y.C.R.R. § 221.1(a), 221.2(c); O'Neill v. Ho, 28 A.D.3d 626, 814 N.Y.S.2d 202 (2d Dep't 2006) (imposing sanctions for costs incurred in conjunction with aborted deposition session).

[30]   See Gammarata v. Bill's Garage, Inc., 40 Misc. 2d 1081, 244 N.Y.S.2d 832 (Dist.Ct., Nassau County 1963).

[31]   See, e.g., Rubino v. G. D. Searle & Co., 73 Misc. 2d 447, 340 N.Y.S.2d 574 (Sup. Ct., Nassau County 1973); see also Alava v. Peninsula General Hospital, 68 A.D.2d 875, 414 N.Y.S.2d 43 (2d Dep't 1979).

videotaping may use it without the other side's consent.[32] Logistics can be worked out by the court if the parties can't agree.[33]

Admissibility of the tape at the trial is governed basically by the same rules that apply to stenographic transcripts.[34]

Everything is done in English. If the deponent does not speak the language, the noticing party must supply and pay for a complete translation of questions and answers, subject to the court's protective order powers.[35]

What about a deposition by telephone? The Federal Rules of Civil Procedure provide that "[t]he parties may stipulate in writing or the court may upon motion order that a deposition be taken by telephone or other remote electronic means."[36] In 2005, CPLR 3113(d) was added to authorize a deposition "by telephonic or other remote electronic means" when all parties stipulate. This provision does not address whether the court can order this form of remote deposition over the objection of one of the parties. As the caselaw demonstrates, however, this authority can still be found in the protective order provisions of CPLR 3103(a).[37]

Uniform Rules for the Conduct of Depositions

Three rules are part of Part 221 of the Uniform Rules for the New York State Trial Courts, mentioned several times above. Part 221 took effect in 2006. While addressing the "conduct" of depositions, it was really designed to deter misconduct at depositions. The trio of rules are:

Rule 221.1   Objections at depositions

Rule 221.2   Refusal to answer when objection is made

Rule 221.3   Communication with the deponent

Improper and petty disputes at depositions have been condemned in many cases.[38] The new rules prohibit improper and disruptive conduct in broader terms and in more detail. Most significantly, Part 221 removes certain discretion previously reserved to lawyers under the CPLR. The CPLR allows the lawyer to interpose all objections at the deposition, but does not require it.[39] Section 221.1(a) now prevents a lawyer from asserting an objection at a deposition unless it would be waived at trial under CPLR

---

[32]   See Roche v. Udell, 155 Misc. 2d 329, 588 N.Y.S.2d 76 (Sup. Ct., Nassau County 1992) (SPR 3:4); see also Miller v. Saha, 50 Misc. 3d 1218(A), 31 N.Y.S.3d 922 (Sup. Ct., Clinton County 2016), aff'd, 151 A.D.3d 1316, 56 N.Y.S.3d 655 (3d Dep't 2017) (court acknowledged that "videotaped depositions are a superior means of presenting testimony of absent witnesses," such as doctors).

[33]   See, e.g., Fajardo v. St. Joseph's Medical Center, 192 Misc. 2d 369, 746 N.Y.S.2d 779 (Sup. Ct., Bronx County 2002).

[34]   22 N.Y.C.R.R. § 202.15(i); Bichler v. Eli Lilly & Co., 50 A.D.2d 90, 376 N.Y.S.2d 144 (1st Dep't 1975). These requirements are treated in § 358.

[35]   CPLR 3114; see Born to Build LLC v. Saleh, 43 Misc. 3d 1213(A), 990 N.Y.S.2d 436 (Sup. Ct., Nassau County 2014) (court shifted the burden for paying the costs of the interpreter from the plaintiff to the defendant under its CPLR 3103(a) protective order powers).

[36]   See Fed. R. Civ. P. 30(b)(4).

[37]   Kirama v. New York Hosp., 13 Misc. 3d 1246(A), 831 N.Y.S.2d 360 (Sup. Ct., New York County 2006); see Commentary C3113:8 on McKinney's CPLR 3113.

[38]   See, e.g., O'Neill v. Ho, 28 A.D.3d 626, 814 N.Y.S.2d 202 (2d Dep't 2006); Mora v. Saint Vincent's Catholic Medical Center of New York, 8 Misc. 3d 868, 800 N.Y.S.2d 298 (Sup. Ct., New York County 2005).

[39]   CPLR 3113(b), 3115(a).

3115(b), (c), or (d). In sum, this subsection limits the type of objections that can be raised at a deposition to those pertaining to form.[40]

Part 221 also aims at such things as "speaking objections,"[41] objections described by the Advisory Committee as those "accompanied by, or made in the form of, speeches which exceed what is necessary to preserve an objection to form." These types of objections are made to suggest an answer to a question or to convey that the deponent should not answer. But what about an attorney's explicit instruction directing a deponent not to answer a given question? That's another frequent happening that is addressed in Rule 221.2, which forbids such a direction except in three specific instances.

The first is where the answer would violate "a privilege or "right of confidentiality."[42] The second is where the court has already made an order—as at a pretrial conference or at an earlier stage of the trial—imposing a specific limitation on testimony.[43] The third is where the question is "plainly improper" and also "would, if answered, cause significant prejudice to any person."[44]

One early example of the new rule in operation is a case in which the court found it necessary to appoint a referee to supervise disclosure after P's lawyer, defending a deposition, directed P not to answer some questions and made condescending gender remarks about D's lawyer. He said at one point that he was "unaware of any rule or law which requires civility between counsel." The court made him aware—and in the process gave him a dash of immortality by quoting his obnoxious remark in the opinion.[45]

Violation of the rule can of course lead to a money sanction as well, as it did in another early case. Citing the conduct of P's lawyer in making ungrounded objections and directing the deponent not to answer questions, D moved the court for a ruling, saying the judge was a friend. That prompted P's lawyer to seek the judge's recusal, which backfired. Asserting that the relationship was professional only and dismissing the "good friends" notion out of hand, the judge broke through the digression, noted that P's lawyer's conduct clearly violated Rule 221, imposed a sanction of $2500,[46] and probably unfriended D from his social media account.

§ 357. Executing the Deposition

When stenography, still the predominant method, is used for the recording of the deposition, the stenographer in due course types up a transcript of the deposition and makes as many copies as the parties order. The expense as a rule belongs to the noticing

---

[40] See Commentary C3115:1 on McKinney's CPLR 3115, where Part 221 is discussed in detail.

[41] 22 N.Y.C.R.R. § 221.1(b).

[42] 22 N.Y.C.R.R. § 221.2(a).

[43] 22 N.Y.C.R.R. § 221.2(b).

[44] 22 N.Y.C.R.R. § 221.2(c). There are several places the lawyer can consult for background on these rules, and for caselaw interpreting them. See Commentary C3115:1 on McKinney's CPLR 3115; January 2006 Report of the Advisory Committee on Civil Practice, pp. 50–54; SPR 177:1; Connors/Gleason, *Uniform Rules for Conduct of Depositions*, N.Y.L.J., Sept. 18, 2006, at 3.

[45] See Laddcap Value Partners, LP v. Lowenstein Sandler P.C., 18 Misc. 3d 1130(A), 859 N.Y.S.2d 895 (Sup. Ct., New York County 2007) (SPR 192:2); see also Freidman v. Fayenson, 41 Misc. 3d 1236(A), 983 N.Y.S.2d 203 (Sup. Ct., New York County 2013), aff'd, 138 A.D.3d 554, 30 N.Y.S.3d 58 (1st Dep't 2016) (imposing sanctions on lawyer who violated Part 221 and engaged in frivolous conduct at deposition).

[46] Simmons v. Minerley, N.Y.L.J., Sept. 25, 2007 at 29, col. 1 (Sup. Ct., Dutchess County; Pagones, J.) (SPR 192:2).

party,[1] but agreement on this subject is usually reached with other parties if they want their own copies. Absent agreement to the contrary, the noticing party must file the deposition with the clerk unless a copy of the deposition is furnished to each party.[2]

The deposition transcript is first submitted to the deponent for perusal, usually by merely being sent to the deponent's attorney for forwarding. The deponent may correct it, and must then sign it under oath, so that deponents usually go through two swearing processes: one at the deposition itself and one on signing the transcript later. Corrections must be made at the end of the deposition,[3] where the appropriate procedure is to refer to the particular question, set forth a corrected answer, and state why the answer as initially recorded is not right. Under no circumstances should the original answer be obliterated.[4] The changes and the reasons for them should be set forth individually. Omnibus reasons set forth in general rather than specific terms will not do.[5] The deposition transcript is then signed by the deponent before an officer authorized to administer an oath, usually a notary public, and returned to the party that noticed the deposition.[6]

The general rule is that the deposition must be reviewed, corrected, and returned by the deponent within 60 days after it is submitted to her. If the deponent does not sign and return the transcript within 60 days, the unsigned transcript may be used "as fully as though signed."[7] Corrections attempted after the 60-day period has run may be ordered stricken by the court, as the intention of the rule is to allow the party taking the deposition to rely on the transcript as final at that point.[8] They have been allowed afterwards, sometimes as late as the eve of trial,[9] but allowance at that late date runs the risk of prejudicing parties who have prepared for trial based on the original answer. It therefore requires special reasons.

There is no arbitrary limit on the number of corrections that may be made by a deponent before signing the deposition, but changes must be accompanied by an adequate explanation.[10] A good one was not offered in Garcia v. Stickel,[11] where what the court describes as P's "errata sheets" were therefore rejected on D's motion because P "failed to timely submit a statement of the reasons for the numerous changes." The striking resulted in summary judgment for D. Even if an adequate explanation is provided, a large number of substantive changes in a deposition transcript can warrant a further deposition of the witness.[12] The failure to timely make changes to the

---

[1]   CPLR 3116(d).

[2]   CPLR 3116(b). The design of the statute is to ensure that parties lacking copies will always have access to the filed deposition.

[3]   CPLR 3116(a).

[4]   See 11th Jud. Conf. Rep. 148, 206–207 (1966).

[5]   See Horn v. 197 5th Ave. Corp., 123 A.D.3d 768, 999 N.Y.S.2d 111 (2d Dep't 2014); Marine Trust Co. of Western New York v. Collins, 19 A.D.2d 857, 243 N.Y.S.2d 993 (4th Dep't 1963).

[6]   CPLR 3116(a).

[7]   CPLR 3116(a).

[8]   Zamir v. Hilton Hotels Corp., 304 A.D.2d 493, 758 N.Y.S.2d 645 (1st Dep't 2003) ("courts should be circumspect about extending the 60-day period" pursuant to CPLR 2004); see 1996 Report of the Advisory Committee to the Chief Administrative Judge, 70 (Dec. 1995).

[9]   See, e.g., Keenan v. Munday, 79 A.D.3d 1415, 912 N.Y.S.2d 778 (3d Dep't 2010).

[10]   Torres v. Board of Educ. of City of New York, 137 A.D.3d 1256, 29 N.Y.S.3d 396, 329 Ed. Law Rep. 1026 (2d Dep't 2016).

[11]   Garcia v. Stickel, 37 A.D.3d 368, 831 N.Y.S.2d 380 (1st Dep't 2007).

[12]   Lieblich v. Saint Peter's Hosp. of City of Albany, 112 A.D.3d 1202, 977 N.Y.S.2d 780 (3d Dep't 2013).

deposition transcript does not bar the deponent from rebutting the statements at the trial,[13] but so testifying will of course expose the deponent to the impeachment use of the deposition.[14]

The procedure of having the officer sign on behalf of the deponent is still used in some circumstances as where the deponent dies before executing the transcript.[15]

Some lawyers have reported situations in which the side taking the deposition tries to use it on a motion before giving the deponent an opportunity to review and sign it, or in which the side required to execute the deposition itself tries to use it on a motion before signing. These are improper practices and can result in the court's rejection of the unexecuted transcript.[16]

The procedure for correcting, editing, certifying, and filing videotaped depositions is in the Uniform Rules.[17] Parties who want a stenographic transcription made of a taped deposition must make their own arrangements for it. The court in its discretion may require it.[18]

Documentary evidence and exhibits used during the deposition are annexed to and returned with the deposition transcript, absent agreement among the parties to the contrary. There usually is such an agreement. The producing party may request that the exhibits be returned, in which event each party is given an opportunity to copy or inspect them first.[19]

§ 358. Use of Deposition

With some of the disclosure devices, there's not much to know about what use can be made of the product. With the discovery device of CPLR 3120, for example, a paper or thing is produced and the party who sought it studies it or tests it, etc., and may then use it according to the usual rules of evidence.[1] With the deposition, however, there is a general policy against unfettered use at the trial. The preference is to have the deponent appear and respond to questioning in person, if reasonably possible, so that the fact-trier can observe the witness's demeanor, an important aid in appraising credibility. The deposition will have served to acquaint the parties with each others' contentions in advance of the trial—itself a most important "use" of the deposition and perhaps ultimately its major use—but an actual reading from the deposition at the trial must satisfy both the strictures of CPLR 3117(a) and "the rules of evidence."[2]

---

[13]   CPLR 3116(d); see § 358.

[14]   See CPLR 3117(a)(1); § 358; SPR 46:1.

[15]   See Chisholm v. Mahoney, 302 A.D.2d 792, 756 N.Y.S.2d 314 (3d Dep't 2003) (SPR 139:2).

[16]   See, e.g., Pina v. Flik Intern. Corp., 25 A.D.3d 772, 808 N.Y.S.2d 752 (2d Dep't 2006); Palumbo v. Innovative Communications Concepts, Inc., 175 Misc. 2d 156, 668 N.Y.S.2d 433 (Sup. Ct., New York County 1997), aff'd, 251 A.D.2d 246, 675 N.Y.S.2d 37 (1st Dep't 1998), noted in SPR 69:3–4.

[17]   See 22 N.Y.C.R.R. § 202.15(f), (g).

[18]   See 22 N.Y.C.R.R. § 202.15(g)(2).

[19]   CPLR 3116(c).

[1]   See, e.g., Viviane Etienne Medical Care, P.C. v. Country-Wide Ins. Co., 25 N.Y.3d 498, 508, 14 N.Y.S.3d 283, 291, 35 N.E.3d 451, 459 (2015) ("[c]ertain affidavits and documents submitted in support of a motion for summary judgment may be deemed admissible where those documents meet the requirements of the business records exception to the rule against hearsay under CPLR 4518."); § 281.

[2]   CPLR 3117(a).

CPLR 3117(a)(1): Use of Deposition for Impeachment of Deponent

The deposition of any deponent—party or nonparty—may be used by any party "for the purpose of contradicting or impeaching" the deponent.[3] This assumes that the deponent has taken the stand at the trial and testified to something contrary to what she previously said in the deposition: the deposition is being cited to show the contradiction. In this instance, the theory is that the deposition is not being used as "evidence in chief" of the data deposed to, but only to make the deponent out a liar, or at least untrustworthy. The hope is that the jury, thinking the deponent dishonest, will disbelieve what the deponent is now saying on the stand. As a practical matter, of course, this will cause the jury to believe the contrary. The contrary is usually what the deponent said in the deposition, however, and the deposition thus ends up getting believed through a kind of back door. To many trial lawyers this is sometimes just as forceful as "evidence in chief." It therefore matters little to them that it does not officially fall under that caption.

Although the rule provides that "any deposition" may be so used "by any party," it has been held that a party may not so use her own deposition, i.e., may not impeach herself with it. Infrequent though this may be, it does happen.[4]

CPLR 3117(a)(2): Use of Deposition of Party

CPLR 3117(a)(2) allows one party's deposition to be used "for any purpose" by any adverse party. Hence the deposition of a party or of any person who was a party at the time the testimony was given, as opposed to that of a nonparty witness, may be used as evidence in chief as well as for impeachment, by any adverse party. This means that without any special foundation being laid, the plaintiff can be allowed to read from the defendant's deposition, and vice-versa, as competent evidence of the facts deposed to. For this purpose, "party" includes "any person who at the time the testimony was given was an officer, director, member, employee or managing or authorized agent of a party."[5] The Court of Appeals held in Feldsberg v. Nitschke[6] that the phrase "for any purpose" in CPLR 3117(a)(2) does not divest the trial court of its usual discretion to determine the points during the trial at which the deposition may be used. At issue in *Feldsberg* was the location of D's vehicle at a certain moment. D's deposition addressed the matter. P called D as a witness but did not use the deposition during D's testimony. D was to return to the stand later on a different matter, however, and when D did P then sought to probe into the location issue with the deposition. The court upheld a ruling by the trial court that P had waived this use of the deposition by failing to use it earlier. A convincing three-judge dissent in *Feldsberg* views the case as one in which the trial judge did not exercise discretion in the matter, but rather deemed himself bound as a matter of law— incorrectly—to hold P to a waiver.[7]

---

[3]   CPLR 3117(a)(1).

[4]   See Mravlja v. Hoke, 22 A.D.2d 848, 254 N.Y.S.2d 162 (3d Dep't 1964) (clarification in dissenting opinion), aff'd 17 N.Y.2d 822, 271 N.Y.S.2d 271, 218 N.E.2d 314 (1966).

[5]   CPLR 3117(a)(2).

[6]   Feldsberg v. Nitschke, 49 N.Y.2d 636, 427 N.Y.S.2d 751, 404 N.E.2d 1293 (1980).

[7]   For a discussion of decisions applying *Feldsberg*, see Commentary C3117:3 on McKinney's CPLR 3117.

CPLR 3117(a)(3): Use of Deposition of "Any Person"

Subject to the above exceptions, the general rule is that before the deposition of any "person"—party or witness—may be used as evidence in chief, the requirements of CPLR 3117(a)(3) must be met. Satisfying this provision is sometimes popularly called "laying a foundation" for the use of the deposition. The statute's introductory language makes clear that in all instances under CPLR 3117(a)(3), the deposition may be used only against a party "who was present or represented at the taking of the deposition" or duly notified of the taking of the deposition, whether electing to attend it or not.[8] It is this requirement that makes it so important that all parties be notified of deposition takings through the service of the deposition notice.[9] Indeed, if in advance of a deposition session the court is made aware that not all parties have been duly notified, it can cancel the session altogether[10] or postpone it until all parties have been given the requisite notice.

Assuming proper notice has been given to the party against whom the deposition is now sought to be read, the reading may proceed only if there is some special reason for allowing it. The five subparagraphs of CPLR 3117(a)(3) are in effect a list of these special reasons. Verbatim, they allow the reading if the court finds:

(i)   that the witness is dead; or

(ii)   that the witness is at a greater distance than one hundred miles from the place of trial or is out of the state, unless it appears that the absence of the witness was procured by the party offering the deposition; or

(iii)   that the witness is unable to attend or testify because of age, sickness, infirmity, or imprisonment; or

(iv)   that the party offering the deposition has been unable to procure the attendance of the witness by diligent efforts; or

(v)   upon motion or notice, that such exceptional circumstances exist as to make its use desirable, in the interest of justice and with due regard to the importance of presenting the testimony of witnesses orally in open court.

The last item on the list is seldom met, and with the others there is necessarily a pragmatic interpretation given by the judges. Under subparagraph (iv), for example, a cursory visit to the witness's home without finding him there doesn't satisfy as a "diligent" effort and, without more, does not support use of the witness's deposition.[11] Similarly, where the plaintiff disappears after giving her deposition and can't be located even by her own lawyer, that lawyer may not put in the plaintiff's case with the deposition unless some satisfactory explanation is made to the court. The disappearance would otherwise be of the plaintiff's own doing,[12] and the plaintiff will not be allowed so casually to flout the law's preference for oral testimony in open court.

---

[8]   See Bigelow v. Acands, Inc., 196 A.D.2d 436, 601 N.Y.S.2d 478 (1st Dep't 1993).

[9]   See § 354.

[10]   See, e.g., Lake Minnewaska Mountain Houses, Inc. v. Smiley, 62 Misc. 2d 311, 307 N.Y.S.2d 739 (Sup. Ct., Ulster County 1970).

[11]   See McNerney v. New York Polyclinic Hospital, 18 A.D.2d 210, 238 N.Y.S.2d 729 (1st Dep't 1963).

[12]   See United Bank Ltd. v. Cambridge Sporting Goods Corp., 41 N.Y.2d 254, 265, 392 N.Y.S.2d 265, 274, 360 N.E.2d 943, 952, 20 U.C.C. Rep. Serv. 980 (1976); Jobse v. Connolly, 60 Misc. 2d 69, 302 N.Y.S.2d 35 (N.Y. City Civ. Ct. 1969).

If the requirements of CPLR 3117(a)(3) have been met, the party may use the deposition of any "person," which embraces a party as well as a nonparty witness. This, in effect, may allow a party to use her own deposition. When a party dies between the deposition and the trial, for example, and his personal representative is duly substituted, it is this provision that admits the decedent's deposition in behalf of the decedent's own case.

CPLR 3117(a)(4): Use of Deposition of Physician

Recognizing policy considerations as well as logistical difficulties often met in trying to coordinate the courtroom attendance of physicians, CPLR 3117(a)(4) permits any party to use a physician's deposition for all purposes, evidence in chief included, without any special justification.[13]

Use of Deposition of Former Party to Action

Suppose that P has sued both A and B and that P wants to use A's deposition against B even though A may no longer be a party at the time of the trial. If adversity existed between A and B at the time one of them was deposed, but the deponent thereafter dropped out due to a settlement, voluntary discontinuance, or summary judgment, the deposition may still be used in full by any remaining party. The rationale for use of the transcript is that both P and B were adverse to A at the time of the deposition and thus had a motive and opportunity to question A at that time.

A 1996 amendment to CPLR 3117(a)(2) was designed to address the situation and expressly provides that the deposition of a party "may be used for any purpose by any party who was adversely interested when the deposition testimony was given or who is adversely interested when the deposition testimony is offered in evidence."[14] This unfortunate language can lead to problematic results. It purports to allow P, for example, to use A's deposition against B because P and A were "adversely interested when the deposition testimony was given," even though B was not adverse to A at that time and had no motive to examine A at the deposition. The general rule, however, is that a deposition is not admissible as evidence in chief against a party unless that party had a motive and opportunity to cross-examine the deponent.[15] The important introductory language in CPLR 3117(a) will, nonetheless, likely preclude use of the deposition in this circumstance because it provides that such use is allowed under the statute only "so far as admissible under the rules of evidence."[16]

CPLR 3117(b):   Use of Part of Deposition

Subdivision (b) of CPLR 3117 seeks to assure perspective. Recognizing that a party will always try to read in only those passages of a deposition favorable to itself, it allows the court to permit any other party to read in any other passages "which ought in fairness to be considered in connection with the part read." The court should ordinarily require the other party to await the putting in of her own case before allowing a cross-reading from the deposition, rather than permit it on the heels of the initial reading during her

---

[13]   See Commentary C3117:8 on McKinney's CPLR 3117.

[14]   See SPR 46:2.

[15]   See Owens v. Sokol, 65 A.D.2d 569, 409 N.Y.S.2d 25 (2d Dep't 1978).

[16]   CPLR 3117(a); see Rivera v. New York City Transit Authority, 54 A.D.3d 545, 863 N.Y.S.2d 201 (1st Dep't 2008).

opponent's case.[17] This is so, however, only when the deposition is being used as evidence in chief. It doesn't apply when the deposition is being used for impeachment, which occurs when the witness is on the stand. For all of these matters, the trial judge must be conceded a fair measure of discretion to introduce variations when the peculiar circumstances of the case warrant them.

CPLR 3117(d):   Effect of Using Deposition

The effect of using the deposition is governed by CPLR 3117(d), whose chief assurance is that a party does not make a deponent his own witness merely by taking the deposition. As far as using the deposition is concerned, the only time a party need concern herself about adopting a deponent as her witness is when the deposition is being used as evidence in chief after a foundation for it has been laid under paragraph 3 of CPLR 3117(a). Using the deposition merely for contradiction or impeachment under paragraph 1, or a party's use of an adverse party's deposition under paragraph 2, does not adopt the deponent.

The last sentence of CPLR 3117(d) says that any party at the trial "may rebut any relevant evidence contained in a deposition, whether introduced by him or by any other party." As applied to a party's deposition, however, the lawyer should not invert that instruction: subdivision (d) allows a party by testimony at the trial to rebut what she said in a deposition, but it does not permit her to use a deposition to rebut what she says at the trial. This is not to recommend the former step either, of course, lest the other side be permitted to now impeach the party's trial testimony with the deposition testimony[18] and have a picnic with the contradiction during summation.

A party to an action that has been consolidated with another action and who does not want to be bound by depositions already taken in the other action should take some prompt initiative, reviewing the depositions and perhaps seeking to depose the same persons himself.[19]

For the use in later actions of depositions taken in earlier actions involving the same parties, there is an explicit provision.[20]

The deposition should be used only after it has been properly executed, or after the time for its review and execution have expired. Otherwise, the attempt to use it is likely to be rejected.[21]

§ 359. Deposition on Written Questions

CPLR 3108 provides that a deposition may be taken on written questions "when the examining party and the deponent so stipulate or when the testimony is to be taken without the state." With the stipulation, it can be taken anywhere; without it, it can presumably be taken only outside the state. It is elsewhere provided, however, that when an oral deposition has been duly scheduled, any party may, instead of participating in it, transmit written questions to the officer, who must then propound them to the witness

---

[17]   See Villa v. Vetuskey, 50 A.D.2d 1093, 376 N.Y.S.2d 359 (4th Dep't 1975).

[18]   See CPLR 3117(a)(1).

[19]   See Bianchi v. Federal Ins. Co., 142 Misc. 2d 82, 535 N.Y.S.2d 952 (Sup. Ct., New York County 1988).

[20]   CPLR 3117(c).

[21]   See § 357 and the discussion in SPR 69:3–4.

and take down the answers.[1] This, as already pointed out,[2] should not ordinarily be done by one party unless the others do the same because it provides the lawyers who do attend a distinct advantage over the party whose lawyer is absent.

Compared with the usual oral deposition, the deposition on written questions is a rare one. If all counsel appear, moreover, an examination that starts out on written questions can be readily converted into an ordinary oral one.[3]

In situations in which the deponent consents, there is no rule against taking oral depositions outside the state, but the additional expense for the travel and accommodation of the lawyers are practical impediments in many cases. With the deposition on written questions, which the lawyers do not ordinarily attend, expense would ordinarily be incurred only for the officer who takes the deposition.

If the testimony is to be taken of a nonparty witness, it may have to take place outside the state if the witness is not amenable to New York process and can't be persuaded to enter the state voluntarily. If the testimony is that of a party, as where a nonresident plaintiff or defendant is to be deposed, the court of course has leverage to make the party come to the state for an ordinary oral examination,[4] but even in that case it may try to reach a middle point accommodating the convenience of all if the nonresident can demonstrate undue hardship. It may, for the time being, require the deposition to proceed outside the state on written questions, for example, but require the nonresident party, within X days before the trial, to appear in the state and submit to an oral examination,[5] thereby cutting down on the number of trips the party has to make to New York.

The procedure for the formulation of the written questions, which must of course be devised in advance and delivered to the officer who is to take the deposition, is in CPLR 3109(a). It contemplates a serving of questions back and forth among the parties until the whole set is worked out. The party seeking the examination starts things off with a notice served on all other parties, setting forth the name of the person to be examined, identifying the officer who will do the examining, and containing the proposed questions. Within 15 days after the notice is served, the other parties must serve the questions they propose, called cross-questions. The initiating party then has seven days in which to serve "redirect" questions; the other parties then have five days for "recross" questions. There is some indication that objections to written questions should be raised within the time for otherwise responding to them,[6] but the stated time periods are not rigid and a protective order would in any event be available to resolve disputes that an agreement can't smooth out.

When at last formulated, the questions are delivered by the noticing party to the officer, who must proceed "promptly" to take the deposition.[7] If the deposition is to take place outside New York, the officer must be guided by any rules applicable at that place. If the witness there does not voluntarily submit to being deposed, the officer may have

---

1   CPLR 3113(b).

2   See § 356.

3   See Walborsky v. Wolf, 28 A.D.2d 1120, 285 N.Y.S.2d 176 (1st Dep't 1967).

4   See CPLR 3110(1); § 355.

5   See Zilken v. Leader, 23 A.D.2d 644, 257 N.Y.S.2d 185 (1st Dep't 1965).

6   See CPLR 3115(e), which applies, however, only to objections of form.

7   CPLR 3109(b).

to seek the aid of the courts or other tribunals of that jurisdiction, which may have a statute, akin to CPLR 3102(e),[8] designed to lend local judicial aid to the securing of depositions for use elsewhere. In the many jurisdictions that have adopted the Uniform Interstate Depositions and Discovery Act,[9] a party seeking disclosure in another United States jurisdiction for use in a New York action can call upon the Act for assistance. This course of action can be used in lieu of, or in addition to, CPLR 3108.

These problems must of course be anticipated and researched in advance. The parties' lawyers may attend the foreign deposition session to assure that all requirements have been complied with,[10] but this does not mean that one side's lawyer, without permission from the others, can simply appear and propound his questions and comments orally.[11] If a given party prefers the oral deposition, and can afford it, the court can with a protective order still bar the oral questions, or allow them only on the condition that that the monied party pay the way of the other lawyers whose clients can't afford the trip.[12]

The deposition on written questions may be used at the trial in the same manner as an oral one.

§ 360. Commission or Letters Rogatory

The second sentence of CPLR 3108 provides that "a commission or letters rogatory may be issued where necessary or convenient for the taking of a deposition outside of the state." These devices are more often resorted to when the disclosure is sought in a foreign country than in a sister state. As noted in the prior section, many sister states have adopted the Uniform Interstate Depositions and Discovery Act and a party seeking disclosure in another United States jurisdiction for use in a New York action can call upon the Act for assistance, rather than resorting to the more burdensome devices of a commission or letters rogatory.

The only apparent difference under the CPLR between an officer designated by the parties to take testimony elsewhere and a commissioner appointed to do so is that the latter, although perhaps the nominee of the parties, bears the court's imprimatur. This can make a difference if and when the officer must apply to a foreign court for disclosure aid. It all depends on the law of the place where the deposition is sought.

The deposition to be taken can be on oral or written questions, as the parties may agree or as the court directs. If on oral questions, it is commonly called an "open" commission;[1] if written, the terminology is that it's a "sealed" one. It can be used to elicit the testimony of either parties or nonparty witnesses if they reside elsewhere. It has been used to take the testimony of a plaintiff residing in a foreign country who did not plan to come to this country even for the trial,[2] although the court can require in person testimony for the trial if circumstances otherwise require it and resources permit it.

---

[8]   See the discussion of CPLR 3102(e) in § 352, paragraph numbered 3.

[9]   See CPLR 3119 (New York's adoption of the Act); Commentary C3108:5 on McKinney's CPLR 3108.

[10]   See VanDyke v. Jefferson Anesthesiology, P.C., 2001 WL 1154973 (Sup. Ct., Jefferson County 2001); Gorie v. Gorie, 48 Misc. 2d 411, 265 N.Y.S.2d 19 (Sup. Ct., New York County 1965).

[11]   See Commentary C3109:1 on McKinney's CPLR 3109.

[12]   See item 5 on the list contained in 1st Rep. Leg. Doc. No. 6(b), p.125 (1957).

[1]   Wiseman v. American Motors Sales Corp., 103 A.D.2d 230, 479 N.Y.S.2d 528 (2d Dep't 1984); see Meckert v. Sears Roebuck & Co., 275 A.D.2d 308, 712 N.Y.S.2d 56 (2d Dep't 2000).

[2]   See Bosurgi v. Chemical Bank New York Trust Co., 30 A.D.2d 950, 294 N.Y.S.2d 45 (1st Dep't 1968).

The letter rogatory, or as the Federal Rules of Civil Procedure now call it, the letter of request,[3] is a further aid to the taking of foreign testimony. A commissioner who bears the seal of the appointing court has good standing to seek the aid of a foreign tribunal if she should need it, but the bearer of a letter rogatory has even stronger call. The letter is merely a writing addressed by the New York court or its clerk to the foreign tribunal, describing the facts and showing the need for aid in taking the testimony of a local person, asking that the foreign machinery be made available for that purpose, and usually ending with the amenity that the New York courts will be happy to return the favor. Sometimes the letter is secured and carried by a "commissioner," i.e., the one appointed to take the testimony, so that these devices for extrastate disclosure often overlap and even merge. Whether one or two or more, or any combination of them, are needed is for the court to determine if the parties can't agree. There is no prescribed form for a letter rogatory.[4] It is sought by an ordinary motion.

It has been held that the letter rogatory should be resorted to last, only after a showing that other devices won't work in the particular case. The reason cited is that the letter rogatory anticipates the use of the foreign tribunal's rules and devices to aid the disclosure, and these are not as certain as our own devices are to implement our domestic values of confrontation and cross-examination of witnesses.[5] Thus, a party seeking a commission or letters rogatory must make a "strong showing of necessity" and demonstrate that the information is unavailable from other sources.[6]

Standards of disclosure are significantly broader in the United States than in most other countries. Therefore, in entertaining motions for a commission or letters rogatory to obtain disclosure in another country, the courts have imposed a more stringent test than the relatively broad relevance standard contained in CPLR 3101(a). In Punwaney v. Punwaney,[7] the court quoted from the First Department's opinion in Richbell Information Services, Inc. v. Jupiter Partners L.P.,[8] in ruling that "[t]his higher standard is whether the information sought is crucial 'to the resolution of a key issue in the litigation.'" The *Punwaney* court found the standard satisfied because the testimony sought was "crucial to proving or disproving issues in this litigation" and, therefore, granted the issuance of an open commission.

§ 361. Interrogatories

Interrogatories are written questions drawn by one party and served on another, answered by the latter under oath, and sent back. They may be served in the same manner as any other interlocutory paper,[1] and therein lies a major distinction from the deposition. The deposition requires a session at a designated time and place while

---

[3]   See Fed. R. Civ. P. 28(b).

[4]   For sample forms see 2PT2 McKinney's Forms, 6:121 (notice of motion for issuance of open commission); 6:119 (letters rogatory form).

[5]   See Matter of Siiderof, N.Y.L.J., Feb.18, 1982, at 6, col.6 (Sur. Ct., New York County; Lambert, S.). The court in *Siiderof* denied the request for letters rogatory without prejudice to a renewal of the application later, upon a showing that nothing else would do the job.

[6]   See MBIA Ins. Corp. v. Credit Suisse Securities (USA) LLC, 103 A.D.3d 486, 960 N.Y.S.2d 25 (1st Dep't 2013); Commentary C3108:5 on McKinney's CPLR 3108.

[7]   Punwaney v. Punwaney, 2016 WL 3455937 (Sup. Ct., New York County 2016).

[8]   Richbell Information Services, Inc. v. Jupiter Partners L.P., 32 A.D.3d 150, 816 N.Y.S.2d 470 (1st Dep't 2006); see § 345.

[1]   See CPLR 2103(b); § 202.

interrogatories require no meeting. In this sense, they are analogous to a take home exam where the lawyer assists the client in preparing answers to the questions posed.

Interrogatories are used to elicit answers from parties, not nonparties.[2] When available, the scope of the disclosure that may be sought with interrogatories is governed, like all the disclosure devices, by the relevance standard in CPLR 3101(a).[3] The interrogatory is not a method to secure a formal judicial admission, such as may be sought under CPLR 3123.[4] Furthermore, interrogatories cannot be used to obtain opinions or conclusions of law.[5]

Subdivision two of CPLR 3130 is much narrower in aim than subdivision one. It allows and regulates financial disclosure from nonparties in matrimonial actions. Financial disclosure in matrimonial actions is also extensively regulated by a rule.[6]

Restrictions on Use of Interrogatories

The interrogatory is a frequently used device in federal practice,[7] but it has found less use in New York practice because of certain built-in restrictions and apparently because of simple tradition as well. Interrogatories came in with the CPLR and the drafters planned to make them available in all actions, as they are in federal practice.[8] A suspicious legislature, fearful that wealthy litigants with a battery of lawyers could bury their poorer adversaries in a blizzard of paper, restricted their use in certain tort actions. The restrictions themselves then went through a metamorphosis.[9]

The legislature has relaxed the restrictions somewhat, or perhaps just changed their nature. In a line of amendments, the applicable provision became what is presently CPLR 3130(1), with the result that the device is now available in all actions, but with some qualifications. The personal injury, injury to property, and wrongful death claims still make up a trio in the statute, but now for a different purpose: when negligence is the ground of liability in any of those three, the interrogatory is no longer excluded absolutely, but a party may not use both the interrogatory and a deposition without leave of court. The party will need to therefore choose between the two, but the choice most often made is for the deposition. When something other than negligence, or in addition to negligence, is the ground, both devices are available as to all grounds and no choice is necessary.[10]

In Buxton v. Ruden,[11] the Second Department held that the plaintiff's claim "for pecuniary losses arising from the former attorney's alleged negligence" is not one for

---

[2]   Martinez v. State, 111 A.D.3d 1445, 974 N.Y.S.2d 880 (4th Dep't 2013).

[3]   CPLR 3131; see § 344.

[4]   See § 364.

[5]   See Deer Park Associates v. Town of Babylon, 121 A.D.3d 738, 993 N.Y.S.2d 761 (2d Dep't 2014).

[6]   See 22 N.Y.C.R.R. § 202.16.

[7]   See Fed. R. Civ. P. 33.

[8]   See 1st Rep. Leg. Doc. No. 6(b), p. 148 (1957).

[9]   See Commentary C3130:2 on McKinney's CPLR 3130 (discussing history of interrogatory device in New York).

[10]   See LaJoy v. State, 48 A.D.3d 1022, 852 N.Y.S.2d 461 (3d Dep't 2008) (claimant could utilize both interrogatories and depositions for the same party on both the negligence and nuisance theories asserted in the action).

[11]   Buxton v. Ruden, 12 A.D.3d 475, 477, 784 N.Y.S.2d 619, 621 (2d Dep't 2004); see also Friedler v. Palyompis, 24 A.D.3d 501, 502, 808 N.Y.S.2d 242, 243 (2d Dep't 2005) (action for broker malpractice does not fall within the limitations of CPLR 3130(1)).

"personal injury, injury to property or wrongful death" and, therefore, is not subject to the "limited scope" of the restrictions contained in CPLR 3130(1). Even if a restriction in CPLR 3130(1) applies, it can be lifted with both devices permitted against the same party if the court so directs in its discretion.[12]

Because the interrogatory tends to duplicate the function of the bill of particulars, another basic restriction in CPLR 3130(1) is that a party can't use both devices against the same party. If D has demanded a bill of particulars of P, in other words, which many defendants' lawyers do automatically upon serving an answer, he may not afterwards serve interrogatories on P. The practitioner should consider carefully whether the bill of particulars or the interrogatory would better serve his case, lest a forfeiture of the choice result from the knee-jerk service of the bill of particulars demand. Both the interrogatory and the bill of particulars are available in the matrimonial actions,[13] however, where they have evolved distinct uses. The bill of particulars is used to probe the grounds for the matrimonial relief and the interrogatory to aid financial disclosure.

Both of the "you-have-to-choose" mandates contained in CPLR 3130(1)—the interrogatory versus the bill of particulars in litigation generally, and the interrogatory versus the deposition in a negligence-based tort action—refer only to the use of both devices against the same party. It is apparently permissible for party A to use one device against party B and the other device against party C.[14] If several parties seeking the disclosure are represented by the same attorney, however, it has been held that they qualify as only one party and must elect.[15]

Use of Interrogatories

According to CPLR 3131, the answers to interrogatories "may be used to the same extent as the depositions of a party," but that may be misleading. It was held in Matter of New York City Asbestos Litigation,[16] for example, that the answer to an interrogatory may be used against the answering party as an admission, but otherwise it's just hearsay. The facts of the case were that P sued D-1 and D-2. D-1, the party that answered the interrogatory, settled out, and at the trial D-2 wanted to use the answer to show more fault by D-1, and hence less by D-2, to enable D-2 to limit its liability pursuant to the application of General Obligations Law § 15–108.[17] The court would not let D-2 use the answer.[18]

By making the admissibility of depositions the standard for admitting interrogatory answers as well, CPLR 3131 invokes CPLR 3117 and its various conditions. The latter prevents a party from introducing his own answers, for example, unless a proper foundation is laid,[19] while ordinarily allowing a party to use his adversary's answers

---

[12]   CPLR 3130(1); see Farca v. Semah, 181 A.D.2d 757, 581 N.Y.S.2d 100 (2d Dep't 1992).

[13]   CPLR 3130(1).

[14]   See Commentary C3130:3 on McKinney's CPLR 3130.

[15]   Liemer v. Kings Highway Hosp. Center, Inc., 140 Misc. 2d 94, 529 N.Y.S.2d 967 (Sup. Ct., Kings County 1988).

[16]   Matter of New York City Asbestos Litigation, 173 Misc. 2d 121, 660 N.Y.S.2d 803 (Sup. Ct., New York County 1997).

[17]   See § 176.

[18]   The court stressed the absence of the opportunity to cross-examine. See United Bank Ltd. v. Cambridge Sporting Goods Corp., 41 N.Y.2d 254, 264, 392 N.Y.S.2d 265, 360 N.E.2d 943 (1976).

[19]   CPLR 3117(a)(3). A party's attempt to use his own answers in evidence is also likely to violate the hearsay rule. See *United Bank Ltd.,* 41 N.Y.2d at 264, 392 N.Y.S.2d at 273–74, 360 N.E.2d at 951.

without such a foundation.[20] Interrogatories may also require the furnishing of copies of papers and documents relevant to the answers,[21] but a party intent on securing such items will usually find the discovery device of CPLR 3120 more effective for that purpose.[22] While CPLR 3117 is not well suited to address the use of interrogatories,[23] the important introductory language in subsection (a) of the statute will preclude use of interrogatories when doing so does not comport with "the rules of evidence."

It is interesting to ask lawyers the sequence in which they prefer to exploit the disclosure devices. In the federal courts, where the interrogatory is widely used without artificial restrictions, practitioners sometimes report that they prefer to serve interrogatories first because the answers they furnish help identify papers and other items relevant to the case. The discovery device is then often served second because it requires production of those items. Then the deposition is taken because the give-and-take of its questioning is more meaningful when relevant documents and books have been secured and perused in advance. In smaller cases, the expense involved in disclosure may color these priorities and mandate a coupling of the devices, but "[i]n complex commercial cases and when dealing with corporations, the initial use of proper interrogatories is preferred in order to save time and money."[24]

Service of Interrogatories, Answers, and Objections

The procedure for the service and answer of interrogatories is in CPLR 3132 and 3133. Interrogatories may be served by one party on another any time after commencement of the action[25] and, as previously noted, they are usually served by mail.[26] Priority in the serving of interrogatories parallels that applicable to depositions. A defendant can serve interrogatories on the plaintiff immediately after being served with the complaint while the plaintiff must wait until the defendant's answering time has expired before being allowed to serve interrogatories on the defendant.[27]

The recipient must respond within 20 days, answering unobjectionable interrogatories and stating "with reasonable particularity" the reasons for not responding to the other questions.[28] While the requirement that the recipient respond to the unobjectionable interrogatories is clearly the legislature's preference, it is not absolute. It has been held that when the demand is itself "outrageous" in its excessiveness and in the irrelevance of many of its items, the recipient may still, instead of responding to the demand at all, seek to strike it altogether with a motion for a protective order.[29] If, however, a party fails to submit answers or objections to interrogatories under CPLR 3133(a) and fails to move promptly for a protective order

---

[20]   CPLR 3117(a)(2).

[21]   CPLR 3131.

[22]   See § 362.

[23]   See *Matter of New York City Asbestos Litig.*, 173 Misc.2d at 126, 660 N.Y.S.2d at 806 (noting that implied cross reference to CPLR 3117 in CPLR 3131 "creates problems," court recommended that legislature consider amending CPLR 3131 to deal specifically with the use of interrogatories).

[24]   Barouh Eaton Allen Corp. v. International Business Machines Corp., 76 A.D.2d 873, 429 N.Y.S.2d 33 (2d Dep't 1980).

[25]   CPLR 3132.

[26]   CPLR 2103(b)(2).

[27]   CPLR 3132.

[28]   CPLR 3133(a).

[29]   See Hanover Ins. Co. v. Lama, 164 Misc. 2d 843, 629 N.Y.S.2d 945 (App. Term, 2d Dep't 1995) (SPR 33:3).

under CPLR 3103(a), it may waive the right to contest the validity of the substantive content of the demand.[30] Copies of interrogatories and of answers, no matter by which party initiated or to whom directed, must be served on all parties.[31]

Answers must be under oath. If the party is a business entity of some kind, the answers must be furnished by an employee or agent having the requisite knowledge or data. The answer should follow each question rather than be contained in a separate list.[32] With parties that are computer-equipped and literate, electronic documents can be employed which would enable the recipient to use as much space as necessary for each answer right after the question and to coordinate everything into a neat response.[33]

Once an answer has been made to an interrogatory, an amendment of it requires court leave,[34] except in the situation in which a duty to supplement arises under the general terms of CPLR 3101(h).[35] Because each answer to an interrogatory is carefully formulated under the guidance of counsel before being sent to the adverse party, an amendment is seldom needed, in contrast with the more frequent need of a deponent to correct her deposition.[36] If an amendment is sought, the motion should be made promptly.[37]

The remedy for a party's failure to respond to interrogatories is a motion under CPLR 3124 to compel a response, and the motion for a protective order under CPLR 3103 is of course on standby to cure abuses. If the court finds in a given case that the interrogatories are "burdensome, oppressive and improper," it will vacate them in toto rather than prune them.[38] As judges will attest, when they are "burdensome, oppressive and improper," they are just as much so to the court as to the adverse party.

Recipients of interrogatories often charge that there are too many. While efforts to amend the CPLR and place an arbitrary limit on their number have not been successful, the Commercial Division of the Supreme Court has adopted a rule both limiting the number of interrogatories that a party may serve to twenty-five and restricting their scope.[39]

§ 362. Discovery and Inspection

CPLR 3120 supplies the device for requiring a person to produce "any designated documents or any things" for inspection, testing, photographing, or copying. The caption of the rule begins "discovery and production," but the more popular name in practice is "discovery and inspection." Small matter. The device accomplishes both. It is available

---

[30] See Fields ex rel. Peterson v. Wendy's Old Fashioned Hamburgers of New York, Inc., 2002 WL 977163 (App. Term, 2d Dep't 2002).

[31] CPLR 3132; CPLR 3133(a).

[32] CPLR 3133(b).

[33] See Vincent v. Seaman, 142 Misc. 2d 196, 536 N.Y.S.2d 677 (Greene County Ct., 1989).

[34] CPLR 3133(c).

[35] See § 352A.

[36] See § 357.

[37] See Wilkinson v. British Airways, 304 A.D.2d 505, 758 N.Y.S.2d 642 (1st Dep't 2003) (motion to amend interrogatories made nineteen months after filing note of issue denied in absence of explanation).

[38] EIFS, Inc. v. Morie Co., Inc., 298 A.D.2d 548, 549, 749 N.Y.S.2d 43 (2d Dep't 2002); Barouh Eaton Allen Corp. v. International Business Machines Corp., 76 A.D.2d 873, 429 N.Y.S.2d 33 (2d Dep't 1980).

[39] 22 N.Y.C.R.R. § 202.70(g), Com. Div. Rule 11–a. Parties may consent to the waiver of these limitations, or the court may permit deviation from the limitations upon a showing of good cause.

against a party by mere notice and against a nonparty through a subpoena duces tecum with a copy of it served on each of the parties.[1]

Here, as with any of the other devices, the criterion for whether or not an item is subject to disclosure comes from CPLR 3101(a). CPLR 3120 merely supplies the mechanical device to get the item. Many of the cases determining whether an item in a given case is discoverable have been annotated by the publishers under CPLR 3120 instead of CPLR 3101, where they truly belong. Lawyers should be aware of that in their searches.

The papers and things that may be the subject of discovery under CPLR 3120 are as variable as litigation itself. One hesitates to offer even a few examples for fear that they may be taken as exhaustive rather than merely illustrative. CPLR 3120 permits a party to get at any tangible thing relevant—the CPLR 3101 criterion—to the case, whether composed of paper, cloth, metal, gold, silver dust, electronically stored information (ESI), or anything else. More often than not, the thing sought is a document, such as a witness's statement,[2] or tax return[3] or business record.[4] Papers of any other kind, including photographs, are equally fair game[5] as long as they are relevant. If a photograph, film, video tape, or audio tape involves a party as defined by CPLR 3101(a)(1), it is deemed relevant by statute and is subject to a CPLR 3120 demand.[6] Any object involved in the event or transaction out of which the case arises can also be the subject of a CPLR 3120 request, such as, in a tort action, the bolt whose breaking caused the fire escape to fall, the cowboy hat that caught fire, the tin can that contained the infected mushrooms, the soda bottle that exploded, etc. They can be had for examination, or for testing, or for copying, or for whatever else it seems appropriate to do to advance the litigation.

Disclosure of Electronically Stored Information

Physical things, such as many of the above items, can't be stored electronically, at least not yet. But documents and papers can be, and this electronically stored information poses some unique benefits and problems. New York courts have interpreted the language in CPLR 3120, requiring the production of "any designated documents or any things," to include any relevant electronically stored information, commonly referred to as ESI.[7] An early and major treatment appears in Lipco Elec. Corp. v. ASG Consulting

---

[1]   CPLR 3120(1); CPLR 2303. Prior to 2003, discovery from a nonparty required a motion on notice under CPLR 3120(b). A 2003 amendment repealed the subdivision and abolished the motion requirement, a point researchers should keep in mind when they come upon pre-2003 cases.

[2]   Rios v. Donovan, 21 A.D.2d 409, 250 N.Y.S.2d 818 (1st Dep't 1964).

[3]   See Altman v. City of New York, 46 Misc. 2d 133, 258 N.Y.S.2d 977 (Sup. Ct., New York County 1965), demonstrating also a substitute procedure for obtaining the tax return when the party doesn't have a copy of it. Parties claiming loss of earnings as an item of damages, as plaintiffs so often do in personal injury actions, waive any right to confidentiality of their income tax returns and must disclose them upon demand. Singh v. Singh, 51 A.D.3d 770, 857 N.Y.S.2d 707 (2d Dep't 2008). In an action for punitive damages, wealth is a legitimate topic on which the defendant may be required to make disclosure and that would also include the furnishing of copies of tax returns, but it becomes relevant on punitive damages issues only after malice has been established as part of a preliminary finding of liability. See Rupert v. Sellers, 48 A.D.2d 265, 368 N.Y.S.2d 904 (4th Dep't 1975).

[4]   See CPLR 3101(g) (disclosure of accident reports); § 348.

[5]   See Flowers for Robinson v. Lyell Metal Co., Inc., 244 A.D.2d 948, 665 N.Y.S.2d 482 (4th Dep't 1997).

[6]   See CPLR 3101(i); Zegarelli v. Hughes, 3 N.Y.3d 64, 781 N.Y.S.2d 488, 814 N.E.2d 795 (2004).

[7]   See, e.g., Tener v. Cremer, 89 A.D.3d 75, 78, 931 N.Y.S.2d 552, 554 (1st Dep't 2011); Etzion v. Etzion, 7 Misc. 3d 940, 943, 796 N.Y.S.2d 844, 846 (Sup. Ct., Nassau County 2005) ("Courts have held that the contents

Corp.,[8] which reviews problems of retrieving stored data, shows how technology can dig out supposedly erased data, and discusses who pays the costs of the dig.[9] It is worth noting that in the electronic age, documents are not always permanently deleted from a data system. In the past, paper documents could be burned, thereby permanently expunging the information contained in them for all time. Today, however, when an electronic document is deleted, the information may still linger in the bowels of a data system and can still be accessed with sufficient technology and the funds necessary to procure it.

In Tener v. Cremer,[10] the First Department delivered its maiden address on the obligation of a nonparty to produce electronically stored information deleted through normal business operations. In *Tener*, plaintiff alleged she was defamed on a website and contended that the allegedly defamatory post originated from a computer in the custody and control of a nonparty university. Approximately one year after the alleged defamation, plaintiff served a nonparty subpoena[11] on the university seeking the identity of all persons who accessed the Internet on a specific date via the IP address plaintiff identified. With the subpoena, plaintiff also served a preservation letter advising the university that the identity of the person who posted the remarks was at issue in litigation and that it should halt any normal business practices that would destroy that information.

The university did not produce the information and plaintiff moved for contempt sanctions against it.[12] In opposition, the university contended that the information sought was "automatically written over every 30 days" and that it did not have the technological capability or software to retrieve the data at issue. Plaintiff responded with an affidavit from a forensic computer expert opining that the university could still access the information using software designed to retrieve deleted information.

The First Department reversed the supreme court's order denying the motion for contempt sanctions, concluding that plaintiff's expert affidavit sufficiently outlined the steps the nonparty university could take to obtain the data. The court noted that while the CPLR does not specifically address the disclosure of ESI, several other pertinent authorities address the subject in some detail. The *Tener* opinion presents a helpful compilation of rules and guidelines in this arena for judges and practitioners, listing the Uniform Rules of the Trial Courts, the Uniform Rules of the Commercial Division, the "Guidelines for Discovery of Electronically Stored Information" for the Commercial

---

of a computer are analogous to the contents of a filing cabinet."); see also Commentary C3120:2A on McKinney's CPLR 3120.

[8] Lipco Elec. Corp. v. ASG Consulting Corp., 4 Misc. 3d 1019(A), 798 N.Y.S.2d 345 (Sup. Ct., Nassau County 2004).

[9] See SPR 153:1. An early and groundbreaking treatment of electronic discovery on the federal side is in Zubulake v. UBS Warburg LLC, 217 F.R.D. 309, 91 Fair Empl. Prac. Cas. (BNA) 1574 (S.D.N.Y. 2003). Judge Scheindlin, the author of *Zubulake*, also reviewed the proposed amendments to the Federal Rules of Civil Procedure pertaining to "electronically stored information" that were ultimately adopted in December 2006. See Shira A. Scheindlin, *Electronic Discovery Takes Center Stage*, N.Y.L.J., Sept. 13, 2004, at 4. See generally E-Discovery Committee of the Commercial and Federal Litigation Section of the New York State Bar Association, "Best Practices in E-Discovery in New York State and Federal Courts," available at www.nysba.org/ComFedReports (containing a "Glossary" of over 250 words and phrases that have evolved from e-discovery in litigation).

[10] *Tener*, 89 A.D.3d 75, 931 N.Y.S.2d 552.

[11] See CPLR 3120(1).

[12] See CPLR 2308(a) (listing contempt as possible punishment for disobedience of judicial subpoena); § 385; Practice Commentary CPLR 2308, C2308:2 ("Contempt Punishment").

Division in Nassau County, and the Conference of Chief Justices' report entitled "Guidelines for State Trial Courts Regarding Discovery of Electronically Stored Information."[13]

In the end, the court relied heavily on the "practical approach" taken by the Nassau County Guidelines and observed that "exempt[ing] inaccessible data presumptively from discovery might encourage quick deletion as a matter of corporate policy, well before the spectre of litigation is on the horizon and the duty to preserve it attaches."[14] Furthermore, the court held that plaintiff demonstrated "good cause" requiring a "cost/benefit analysis to determine whether the needs of the case warrant retrieval of the data."[15] Recognizing that the record was not sufficient for it to conduct a cost/benefit analysis, the First Department remanded the case to the supreme court for a hearing to determine:

>   (1)   whether the identifying information was written over, [ ]or whether it is somewhere else, such as in unallocated space as a text file;

>   (2)   whether the retrieval software plaintiff suggested [could] actually obtain the data;

>   (3)   whether the data will identify actual persons who used the Internet on [the date in question] via the IP address plaintiff identified;

>   (4)   which of those persons accessed [the site on which plaintiff was allegedly defamed;] and

>   (5)   a budget for the cost of the data retrieval, including line item(s) correlating the cost to [the nonparty] for the disruption.[16]

While these factors should also be relevant when disclosure is sought from a party, the First Department emphasized that when disclosure was sought from a nonparty, that should also figure into the equation.[17] Therefore, it is reasonable to conclude that if the relevant information sought from the nonparty is not readily accessible, the cost/benefit analysis will be applied more rigorously than it would if the information was sought from a party.[18]

The issue of who, between the parties, pays the costs of production dominates many actions in which electronic disclosure is sought.[19] In *Tener*, where the data was sought from a nonparty, CPLR 3122(d) requires the requesting party to defray the "reasonable

---

[13]   *Tener*, 89 A.D.3d at 78–81, 931 N.Y.S.2d at 554–56: see, e.g., 22 N.Y.C.R.R. § 202.12(c)(3)(vi) (directing that the preliminary conference should include discussion of the "anticipated cost of data recovery and [the] proposed initial allocation of such cost" in appropriate cases). The court also examined various provisions in the Federal Rules of Civil Procedure and federal caselaw addressing the disclosure of ESI that is not readily accessible. See, e.g., Fed. R. Civ. P. 45(d)(1)(D) (discussing duties of nonparty who has been directed to produce "inaccessible" ESI); Zubulake v. UBS Warburg LLC, 217 F.R.D. 309, 91 Fair Empl. Prac. Cas. (BNA) 1574 (S.D.N.Y. 2003).

[14]   *Tener*, 89 A.D.3d at 81, 931 N.Y.S.2d at 556.

[15]   *Tener*, 89 A.D.3d at 81, 931 N.Y.S.2d at 556.

[16]   *Tener*, 89 A.D.3d at 82, 931 N.Y.S.2d at 556–57.

[17]   *Tener*, 89 A.D.3d at 82, 931 N.Y.S.2d at 557; see Whitlow v. Martin, 263 F.R.D. 507, 512 (C.D. Ill. 2009).

[18]   See Commentary C3120:2A on McKinney's CPLR 3120; Patrick M. Connors, *Disclosure of Electronically Stored Information From a Non-Party*, N.Y.L.J., Jan. 23, 2012, at 247 (no. 14), where the *Tener* decision is discussed in further detail.

[19]   See Patrick M. Connors, *Which Party Pays the Costs of Document Disclosure?*, 29 Pace L. Rev. 441 (2009); § 353.

production expenses" of a nonparty. Relying on this subdivision, the First Department instructed that if the trial court finds after the hearing that the nonparty has the ability to produce the data, "the court should allocate the costs of this production to plaintiff and should consider whether to include in that allocation the cost of disruption to [the nonparty's] normal business operations."[20] Furthermore, with respect to this latter consideration, the supreme court was instructed to "also take into account that plaintiff waited one year before sending the subpoena and preservation letter."[21]

The operation of electronic instruments while driving has become increasingly implicated in automobile accident litigation[22] and discovery of a driver's cell phone records for the period surrounding the occurrence is commonly sought. Perhaps typical of such discovery cases is Detraglia v. Grant,[23] in which it was established that several such instruments were in the car when it collided with another. The court found an adequate case made out for the discovery for a one-hour time frame within which the accident occurred. It remanded the case to the lower court, however, to examine the records in camera with a view to redacting data that might unreasonably compromise privacy before ordering discovery of the rest.[24]

Entry upon and Inspection of Land

If land is involved in the case, a discovery demand under CPLR 3120 can require a party or nonparty to permit entry onto land owned or controlled by that party for "inspecting, measuring, surveying, sampling, testing, photographing or recording by motion pictures or otherwise the property or any specifically designated object or operation thereon."[25] In one case, for example, the permission sought was to take borings, tests, and measurements on the land.[26] In another, a party was allowed to get at poles and wires on another party's land,[27] the discovery device immunizing the seeker from what might otherwise be a trespass charge.

Contents and Timing of Discovery Notice or Subpoena

Against a party, CPLR 3120 discovery requires only a notice. As noted above, when discovery is sought against a nonparty, a subpoena is required. Both documents must specify the time, place, and manner of making the discovery or entry.[28] The only stated time requirement concerning a notice of discovery is that it await commencement of the

---

[20]   *Tener*, 89 A.D.3d at 82, 931 N.Y.S.2d at 557.

[21]   *Tener*, 89 A.D.3d at 82, 931 N.Y.S.2d at 557.

[22]   See generally Clark v. New York State Dept. of Motor Vehicles, 151 A.D.3d 1410, 54 N.Y.S.3d 338 (3d Dep't 2017) (confirming that petitioner was guilty of operating a motor vehicle while using a portable electronic device, court held that "Appeals Board's interpretation of Vehicle and Traffic Law § 1225–d(2)(a) as encompassing a hand-held GPS device was rational").

[23]   Detraglia v. Grant, 68 A.D.3d 1307, 890 N.Y.S.2d 696 (3d Dep't 2009) (SPR 219:3).

[24]   See also Neuman v. Frank, 82 A.D.3d 1642, 919 N.Y.S.2d 644 (4th Dep't 2011) (remitting matter to supreme court to conduct in camera review prior to ordering disclosure of any relevant cellular telephone records).

[25]   CPLR 3120(1)(ii).

[26]   See 1417 Bedford Realty Co. v. Sun Oil Co., 21 A.D.2d 684, 250 N.Y.S.2d 455 (2d Dep't 1964).

[27]   Parker v. New York Tel. Co., 47 Misc. 2d 342, 262 N.Y.S.2d 700 (Sup. Ct., Albany County 1965), aff'd, 24 A.D.2d 1067, 265 N.Y.S.2d 740 (3d Dep't).

[28]   CPLR 3120(2).

action[29] and that it give the recipient at least 20 days to respond.[30] If a specific place must be chosen for the discovery, as where the examination must take place when all sides are represented (because the item involved can't be surrendered, or because each side must observe the other lest chicanery occur, etc.), the venue rules of CPLR 3110 governing the deposition should be applied.[31] Ideal, as usual, is for the parties to come to terms on the point after the service of the notice or subpoena.

All of the scheduling mechanics should ultimately be coordinated in advance among the parties and nonparties concerned so that the mutual convenience of all is considered, as is usually done when scheduling depositions. A party should not arbitrarily insist on discovery under CPLR 3120 without consultation with the other parties and any nonparty unless perhaps the discovery will entail only the sending of a paper or document through the mails. The consultation can occur after the notice or subpoena is served with a preliminary date that satisfies the notice periods in CPLR 3120(2).

While much of the above discussion of CPLR 3120 has concerned disclosure from a party, disclosure from a nonparty is essentially the same in scope under CPLR 3101(a), permitting a party to obtain relevant materials.[32] The procedure for disclosure from a nonparty, which was overhauled in 2003, is the service of a subpoena duces tecum instead of a mere notice, with a copy of the subpoena to be served on each of the other parties.[33] The subpoena duces tecum must be served on the nonparty in the same manner as a summons.[34] The copies of it however, may presumably be served on the other parties, or at least those who have appeared in the action, like any interlocutory paper, i.e., by mere mail promptly after service on the witness.[35] Within five days after the nonparty complies by submitting the requested materials, the party receiving them must notify all the other parties of the submission and make the materials available for inspection and copying.[36]

CPLR 3122–a requires that business records produced pursuant to a CPLR 3120 subpoena duces tecum be accompanied by a certification.[37] CPLR 3122–a(a) sets forth the form and contents of the certification, essentially requiring a statement of four items necessary for admitting business records under CPLR 4518(a).[38] The aim of the statute is to ease the admissibility of the certified records and thereby reduce the need to call

---

[29] CPLR 3120(1). Since mere filing of the initiatory papers now constitutes commencement, CPLR 3120(1) would appear to give the plaintiff an advantage because the defendant is not likely to be aware of the "commencement" until service is made, which can be as long as 120 days after the filing. See CPLR 306–b; § 63; Commentary C3120:3 on McKinney's CPLR 3120; SPR 28:2 and 36:3.

[30] CPLR 3120(2). If a CPLR 3120 notice is served via regular mail, the notice period becomes 25 days. See CPLR 2103(b)(2); § 202.

[31] See § 355; Commentary C3110:2 on McKinney's CPLR 3110 and compare Cattat v. Alfa Romeo, Inc., 81 Misc. 2d 119, 364 N.Y.S.2d 772 (Sup. Ct., Oneida County 1975).

[32] See Kapon v. Koch, 23 N.Y.3d 32, 988 N.Y.S.2d 559, 11 N.E.3d 709 (2014); § 345 above. The State qualifies as a "person" from whom discovery can be sought for purposes of CPLR 3120(1). Kaplan v. Kaplan, 31 N.Y.2d 63, 334 N.Y.S.2d 879, 286 N.E.2d 260 (1972).

[33] See Velez v. Hunts Point Multi-Service Center, Inc., 29 A.D.3d 104, 811 N.Y.S.2d 5 (1st Dep't 2006).

[34] CPLR 2303(a); see § 383.

[35] See CPLR 2103(b)(2); § 202. For further details on the procedure and some incidental issues, see Commentary C3120:12 on McKinney's CPLR 3120 and the lead note in SPR 138:1.

[36] CPLR 3120(3).

[37] See Practice Commentaries to McKinney's CPLR 3122–a. Pursuant to a 2014 amendment, CPLR 3122–a's certification procedure can be used for "business records produced by non-parties whether or not pursuant to a subpoena." CPLR 3122–a(d).

[38] See CPLR 3122–a(a)(1–4).

foundation witnesses, whose role is usually perfunctory.[39] Certified business records produced pursuant to CPLR 3122–a can also supply the supporting proof necessary for an award of summary judgment.[40]

During the initial decades of the CPLR, the discovery notice had to identify the paper(s) or item(s) sought very specifically; asking for "any and all" documents of a general description was usually unacceptable. If additional information was needed before the item could be adequately identified, a landmark case, Rios v. Donovan,[41] held that a deposition should first be used to elicit the identifying data. If the data was at hand, the discovery could proceed without a preliminary deposition,[42] and the "any and all" language could be disregarded as mere surplusage as long as the notice could otherwise be seen as directed at "limited and specific subject matter."[43] One might say that when a demand for discovery used words like "all," "all other," or "any and all," a kind of suspicion arose in New York practice that the specificity required by CPLR 3120(2) was lacking even though there was no absolute barrier to the use of such words. This was in contrast with federal practice, a distinction noted by the First Department in Mendelowitz v. Xerox Corp.[44]

The specificity requirement was somewhat relaxed in 1994 in an amendment of CPLR 3120(2) that adopted the federal practice of allowing discovery by "category." The word "specifically" and the phrase "specified with reasonable particularity in the notice" were dropped, and the word "category" was added. When "an inspection, copying, testing or photographing" of an item or items is sought, CPLR 3120(2) now requires that the seeking party set them forth "by individual item or by category, and . . . describe each item and category with reasonable particularity."[45] Even under this new permission to demand by category, however, a demand may still be vacated in its entirety if it is found "unduly burdensome."[46] Therefore, blunderbuss demands for documents using broad and general descriptions, especially when they require the production of massive quantities of papers or other items, are still generally not enforced by the courts.[47]

If the seeking party doesn't know who has the paper or thing sought, but an adverse party does, the latter must reveal that person's name.[48] When entry onto land is what is desired, and an inspection of some object or operation on the land is sought, the requirement that the object or operation be "specifically designated" remains.[49]

---

[39]   See Campos v. Payne, 2 Misc. 3d 921, 766 N.Y.S.2d 535 (N.Y. City Civ. Ct. 2003).

[40]   See generally Viviane Etienne Medical Care, P.C. v. Country-Wide Ins. Co., 25 N.Y.3d 498, 508, 14 N.Y.S.3d 283, 291, 35 N.E.3d 451, 459 (2015); see § 282.

[41]   Rios v. Donovan, 21 A.D.2d 409, 250 N.Y.S.2d 818 (1st Dep't 1964).

[42]   See Taylor v. John Doe, 167 A.D.2d 984, 562 N.Y.S.2d 6 (4th Dep't 1990); Brady by Brady v. Wyeth Laboratories, Inc., 106 A.D.2d 795, 484 N.Y.S.2d 191 (3d Dep't 1984).

[43]   See Seattle Pacific Industries, Inc. v. Golden Valley Realty Associates, 54 A.D.3d 930, 864 N.Y.S.2d 500 (2d Dep't 2008).

[44]   Mendelowitz v. Xerox Corp., 169 A.D.2d 300, 573 N.Y.S.2d 548 (1st Dep't 1991).

[45]   This change in CPLR 3120 is discussed at length in Commentary C3120:4 on McKinney's CPLR 3120 and in SPR 9:2.

[46]   See Konrad v. 136 East 64th Street Corp., 209 A.D.2d 228, 618 N.Y.S.2d 632 (1st Dep't 1994).

[47]   Hochheiser v. Alin, 2015 WL 4620757 (Sup. Ct., Suffolk County 2015).

[48]   Food Fair, Inc. v. Board of Assessment Review of Town of Niskayuna, 78 A.D.2d 335, 338, 435 N.Y.S.2d 378, 380–81 (3d Dep't 1981).

[49]   CPLR 3120(1)(ii).

CPLR 3111 Demand

CPLR 3120 should not be confused with CPLR 3111, which provides for a limited kind of discovery that is sought in conjunction with a deposition. It provides that the notice or subpoena bringing on the deposition may require the production of papers and things in the custody of the deponent for use at the examination. CPLR 3120, on the other hand, supplies a discovery wholly independent of a deposition. If the particular item or items can be identified in the initial notice scheduling the deposition, the notice can require their production and, hopefully, kill two birds with one stone. If not, a preliminary deposition can be set up to identify the items, and the discovery device of CPLR 3120 then used to get them. If needed, yet another deposition can be taken, to permit further questions based on the newly revealed materials.[50]

Unless the case is one in which the use of interrogatories is restricted,[51] an interrogatory can initially inquire into the nature and whereabouts of the item, too, obviating a deposition at that stage. The CPLR 3120 discovery device can then be used to get the item, and the deposition can then be turned to afterwards, when the item will be at hand to assist with the examination. In fact, an interrogatory can be used as a kind of limited discovery device itself, requiring the production of papers that are relevant to the answers required.[52]

The line between CPLR 3111 on the one hand, and 3120 on the other, is not sharply defined and probably doesn't need to be, given the court's power by protective order to do what has to be done without overnice attention to the scope of any one device. CPLR 3111 generally requires that the item sought be in the possession or control of the deponent proper since the discovery here is in conjunction with a deposition.[53] It has also been held that "a notice pursuant to CPLR 3111 to produce materials at an examination before trial need not contain the specificity required for the discovery and inspection of materials sought pursuant to CPLR 3120."[54]

Because CPLR 3111 is an adjunct of a deposition, and notice of the deposition must of course be provided to all parties, all are also entitled to notice of whatever is being sought of the deponent through CPLR 3111. As noted above, a nonparty witness who will not submit to a deposition voluntarily must be served with a subpoena.[55] The subpoena can also contain a duces tecum clause, or be accompanied by a distinct subpoena duces tecum, to implement CPLR 3111 and require the witness to produce documents and things at the deposition. It is improper to keep notice of any of these steps from an adverse party. In one highly publicized case, Matter of Beiny,[56] a party set up a deposition of a nonparty witness and served a subpoena duces tecum on the witness to elicit key materials under CPLR 3111. Then the party cancelled the deposition, but without advising the other side, collected up the materials the subpoena had produced, armed itself with a thorough ex parte review of the materials, and used them tellingly

---

[50] See Mayer v. Albany Medical Center Hospital, 56 Misc. 2d 239, 288 N.Y.S.2d 771 (Sup. Ct., Albany County 1968), aff'd as modified, 37 A.D.2d 1011, 325 N.Y.S.2d 517 (3d Dep't 1971).

[51] See § 361.

[52] See CPLR 3131.

[53] See Western Elevating Ass'n v. Chapman, 238 A.D. 14, 263 N.Y.S. 62 (4th Dep't 1933).

[54] Early v. Nassau County, 98 A.D.2d 789, 469 N.Y.S.2d 809 (2d Dep't 1983).

[55] CPLR 3106(b); see § 354.

[56] Matter of Beiny, 129 A.D.2d 126, 517 N.Y.S.2d 474 (1st Dep't 1987), reargument denied with further opinion 132 A.D.2d 190, 522 N.Y.S.2d 511 (1st Dep't 1987).

in deposing—and surprising—the other side. An irate appellate division suppressed all of the materials, disqualified the offending law firm, and remitted the matter to the local disciplinary committee for investigation.[57]

The 2003 amendments to CPLR 3120 and 3122 were "intended to bring to an end [this] unauthorized but longstanding practice."[58] What appears to be contemplated by CPLR 3111, and to have been violated in the *Beiny* case, is that the materials produced will be produced *at* the deposition, or in any event at such time and place as will give access to all parties equally, and simultaneously. The discovery now allowed under CPLR 3120 has the same aim, as is manifest in the requirement that the party receiving the subpoenaed materials notify the other parties and make the materials available to them for inspection and copying.[59]

If an item in the possession of a nonparty is needed in conjunction with a different person's deposition (party or nonparty), it would seem permissible to either (1) secure the item in advance with a subpoena duces tecum under CPLR 3120 and schedule the deposition only after obtaining it; or (2) to schedule a discovery under CPLR 3120 by the nonparty for the same time and place as the deposition, by agreement among the parties if possible or by order of the court if not.

Implementing a Litigation Hold and Preservation Letters

The preservation of documents and various items pertinent to potential or pending litigation has always been an important issue, but it has become increasingly so in the age of ESI. In VOOM HD Holdings LLC v. EchoStar Satellite L.L.C.,[60] the First Department, relying primarily on federal caselaw, declared that it is "well settled" that once litigation is reasonably anticipated, a party must preserve relevant emails as part of a litigation hold, even if it requires suspension of a computer system's automatic-deletion function. In *VOOM*, defendant's failure to adequately preserve the electronic information constituted "gross negligence at the very least," and warranted an adverse inference charge.[61] Subsequently, in Pegasus Aviation I, Inc. v. Varig Logistica S.A.,[62] the Court of Appeals observed that a party's failure to institute a litigation hold is a relevant factor that a trial court can consider in making a determination as to the penalties to be imposed for a party's failure to preserve relevant information.

We return to the subject of penalties for nondisclosure later,[63] but note the litigation hold obligation at this juncture because parties need to be aware of it at the outset of litigation, and even before commencement of the action if litigation is reasonably anticipated. A party, or potential party, who desires to ensure preservation of relevant information may send out a letter to potential parties alerting them to the obligation to

---

[57] *Matter of Beiny,* 132 A.D.2d at 191, 522 N.Y.S.2d at 512.

[58] Velez v. Hunts Point Multi-Service Center, Inc., 29 A.D.3d 104, 110, 811 N.Y.S.2d 5, 9 (1st Dep't 2006); see CPLR 3120(3) and 2303(a); Commentary C3120:12 on McKinney's CPLR 3120.

[59] CPLR 3120(3).

[60] VOOM HD Holdings LLC v. EchoStar Satellite L.L.C., 93 A.D.3d 33, 939 N.Y.S.2d 321 (1st Dep't 2012).

[61] See Commentary C3126:8A on McKinney's CPLR 3126.

[62] Pegasus Aviation I, Inc. v. Varig Logistica S.A., 26 N.Y.3d 543, 553, 26 N.Y.S.3d 218, 46 N.E.3d 601 (2015). While the entire Court appeared to agree that the failure to impose a litigation hold is a factor that can be considered in the determination of whether discovery sanctions should issue, the decision does not address the circumstances under which the duty to impose a litigation hold arises.

[63] See § 367.

preserve the information. That may ease the path to the subsequent disclosure of the information with a CPLR 3120(1)(i) notice, or at least help to establish that there was a duty to preserve the information at that earlier moment in time. A preservation letter may also be sent to a nonparty with, or in advance of, a subpoena to alert the nonparty to preserve the information and halt any normal business practices that would destroy it.[64] The timing of the preservation letter can be a relevant factor in considering the costs to be imposed on the party who ultimately seeks the information.[65]

Responding to CPLR 3120 Demand & Objections

The proper methods for responding to a CPLR 3120 notice or subpoena are addressed in CPLR 3122(c) and (d).[66] In 1998, CPLR 3122(c) was added, requiring that the person responding to an order or notice for document discovery produce the documents "as they are kept in the regular course of business or"—note it's an "or," not an "and"—"shall organize and label them to correspond to the categories in the request." Thus, the option of choosing the method of production lies with the responding party regardless of whether the production is sought by individual item or category.[67] The responding party is likely to favor producing the documents "as they are kept in the regular course of business," which may perpetuate the kind of overbroad response CPLR 3122(c) was designed to discourage.[68] The parties should attempt to reach agreement on the method of production, possibly at the preliminary conference.[69]

Until the early 1990s, a party objecting to a discovery notice was required by CPLR 3122 to state its objections in a motion for a protective order and to make the motion within 10 days after service of the discovery notice.[70] That procedure, which imposed a very tight timeframe on the recipient, was changed in an amendment of CPLR 3122(a) that took effect in 1994, addressed to the physical and mental exam of CPLR 3121 as well as the discovery device of CPLR 3120. We discuss it here in its CPLR 3120 context, but the discussion will also apply, to the extent relevant, to its use with the CPLR 3121 devices, met later.[71]

If R (the recipient of the notice) has no objections to the notice, R should comply within the period specified in the notice, or at least work something out with S (the server of the notice) to assure that compliance will be forthcoming. What is the procedure if R does have objections? Under CPLR 3122(a), R is to serve, within the 20-day period allowed, a "response" on S, which "shall state with reasonable particularity the reasons for each objection. If objection is made to part of an item or category, the part shall be specified."

If R withholds documents that appear to be among those demanded by S, CPLR 3122(b) requires R to supply a notice, commonly referred to as a privilege log, explaining

---

[64]　See *Tener*, 89 A.D.3d at 77, 931 N.Y.S.2d at 553.

[65]　*Tener*, 89 A.D.3d at 82, 931 N.Y.S.2d at 557.

[66]　See Commentary C3122:4 on McKinney's CPLR 3122.

[67]　See CPLR 3120(2), discussed above.

[68]　See SPR 75:2.

[69]　See 22 N.Y.C.R.R. § 202.12(c); § 77D.

[70]　CPLR 3122 (before its 1994 amendment).

[71]　See § 363.

why and requires the explanation to include the following information with respect to each withheld document:[72]

> (1) the type of document;
>
> (2) the general subject matter of the document;
>
> (3) the date of the document; and
>
> (4) such other information as is sufficient to identify the document for a subpoena duces tecum.[73]

This information will provide the seeking party with at least a fighting chance to mount an argument that the information should be produced. If the inclusion of any of the enumerated information would cause disclosure of some "allegedly privileged information," R may exclude the information, but must state in the notice that it is being withheld on that ground. The reference to "privileged information" in CPLR 3122(b) is probably intended as a reference to all of the categories excluded from disclosure by CPLR 3101.[74]

If a document within the embrace of a discovery demand is not available when the demand is served, but becomes available later, it will fall under the supplementation requirement of CPLR 3101(h). This means that a copy of the document or thing will have to be furnished to the other side promptly after it is obtained or uncovered, without awaiting a new demand. Failing to furnish it may bar its use at the trial.[75]

When a party takes a deposition in a foreign language, CPLR 3114 requires the examining party to furnish a translation of it.[76] In contrast, a party surrendering a foreign-language document pursuant to a discovery demand is not required to supply a translation with it. It's the seeking party, not the producing party, who must get it translated.[77]

Motion to Compel Discovery

If S is dissatisfied with R's response, and feels entitled to more than R is willing to give voluntarily, CPLR 3122(a) suggests that S "may move for an order under rule 3124 or section 2308 with respect to any objection to, or other failure to respond to or permit inspection as requested by, the notice or subpoena."[78] The hope of the statute is to have

---

[72] CPLR 3122 is addressed in general to any CPLR 3120 discovery and any CPLR 3121 physical or mental examination, but subdivision (b) of CPLR 3122 addresses only "documents." If the discovery that S seeks is of things other than documents, and R is disposed to furnish only some of the discovery, it would be appropriate for R to follow the procedures of subdivision (b) there, too. R should produce the unobjectionable things and state in a notice the grounds of objection to the things withheld.

[73] The reference to the subpoena duces tecum here is just a handy way of assuring that the identification offered would, if included in a subpoena, be sufficient to invoke the contempt penalty if the subpoena were to be disobeyed (assuming, of course, that the document is otherwise legitimately discoverable).

[74] See CPLR 3101(c) (attorney's work product); CPLR 3101(d)(2) (material prepared in anticipation of litigation). There is nothing in the background of the 1994 change in CPLR 3122 to suggest an intention to remove those exclusions.

[75] See § 352A.

[76] CPLR 3114; see § 356.

[77] See Rosado v. Mercedes-Benz of North America, Inc., 103 A.D.2d 395, 480 N.Y.S.2d 124 (2d Dep't 1984).

[78] The references to a subpoena, and to CPLR 2308, which governs the penalty for disobedience of a subpoena, were added in 2003 to recognize that the procedure of a mere subpoena duces tecum was now being allowed for discovery from a nonparty, displacing the motion that had previously been required.

the parties iron out the objections among themselves. The court is to be imposed with a motion only if the parties can't resolve their dispute privately after a good faith effort.[79]

Because the invitation to S, the moving party, is to make the motion "under rule 3124," which provides for a motion that seeks only to have the court direct compliance, there is some doubt about whether S may, as an alternative, base the motion on CPLR 3126, the sanctions provision. That tact would allow S to skip CPLR 3124 as an intermediate step and jump right into CPLR 3126 in the hope of getting at least a conditional order directing disclosure backed by a sanction if the order is disobeyed. That was permissible before the amendment.[80] Some caselaw indicates that a CPLR 3124 stopover is still unnecessary.[81]

Costs of Disclosure Under CPLR 3120

As noted in the discussion of the *Tener* decision above, when discovery of papers or other "things" are sought from a nonparty, the party seeking the items must defray the nonparty's expenses.[82] There is no requirement that these be paid in advance, but the party who subpoenas the materials might do well to ascertain those expenses and tender them to the nonparty. If the expenses are substantial, and not offered up front, and a contempt proceeding now becomes necessary, the seeking party may find the court hesitant to hold the nonparty in contempt.

Surprisingly, the issue of which party pays the costs of discovery between them is not clearly spelled out in the CPLR. During the first four decades of the CPLR's reign, most parties to litigation were apparently able to amicably resolve disputes concerning who was to shoulder the costs of document disclosure.[83] Typically, each party paid their respective costs associated with production and rarely sought judicial intervention to resolve the occasional dispute. As noted above, a CPLR 3103(a) protective order can be issued to balance the situation in which a disparity in the economic resources of the parties is disabling one from participating in the disclosure process, or empowering another to take undue advantage of it.[84]

In the 21st Century, the issue of who, between the parties, pays the costs of production dominates many actions in which electronic disclosure is sought.[85] Several New York State court decisions have concluded that, under the CPLR, the party seeking disclosure should incur the costs associated with the production of discovery material, but the basis and soundness of such a rule is questionable.[86] In U.S. Bank Nat. Ass'n v. GreenPoint Mortgage Funding, Inc.,[87] the First Department refused to apply a blanket rule requiring the requesting party to pay all costs associated with electronic disclosure.

---

[79] See 22 N.Y.C.R.R. § 202.7(a), (c); § 353; Commentaries C3102:2 on McKinney's CPLR 3102; C3103:3A on McKinney's CPLR 3103; and C3124:1 on McKinney's CPLR 3124 (discussing application of 22 N.Y.C.R.R. § 202.7 in various contexts).

[80] See SPR 10:1.

[81] See Estate of Henry M. Riebesehl, 1998 N.Y.L.J. 7457 (Sur. Ct., Westchester County Mar. 31, 1998); Matter of T./P. Children, 165 Misc. 2d 333, 629 N.Y.S.2d 677 (Fam. Ct., Albany County 1995), noted in SPR 37:2; Commentaries C3126:6 on McKinney's CPLR 3126.

[82] CPLR 3111, 3122(d).

[83] See § 353.

[84] See § 353.

[85] See Connors, *Which Party Pays the Costs of Document Disclosure?*, 29 Pace L. Rev. 441 (2009).

[86] Connors, *Which Party Pays the Costs of Document Disclosure?*, 29 Pace L. Rev. 441 (2009).

[87] U.S. Bank Nat. Ass'n v. GreenPoint Mortgage Funding, Inc., 94 A.D.3d 58, 939 N.Y.S.2d 395 (1st Dep't 2012).

Rather, it applied the rule governing in federal court,[88] which requires the producing party to bear the cost of production unless the trial court, in the exercise of its discretion on a proper motion by the producing party, concludes that the costs should be allocated differently. Therefore, the *GreenPoint* court ruled that defendant's motion for a protective order conditioning production of discovery on compliance with a proposed discovery protocol that provided, among other things, that each party would pay for its own discovery requests, was premature.[89]

§ 363. Physical and Mental Examinations

Who May Be Subject to a CPLR 3121(a) Examination?

CPLR 3121(a) requires that a party whose physical or mental condition, or blood relationship to someone, is "in controversy," must, at the behest of another party, submit to an examination by "a designated physician." Agents, employees, and others under the party's control confront this examination, too, if their condition is in controversy. It is mainly the party proper, notably the plaintiff in the ubiquitous personal injury case, who makes the caselaw on this device.

Plaintiffs bringing personal injury actions place their physical condition in controversy and must submit to examination, incidentally waiving the doctor-patient privilege regarding the injuries asserted.[1] Although most often it is the plaintiff's condition that's in controversy, the defendant may also be required to submit to examination if his own condition is genuinely in controversy, as where impairment of the defendant's vision has become a substantial point of dispute.[2] The party's condition need not actually be "in issue," however; it need only be "in controversy," which the courts regard as a less demanding standard[3] and therefore an easier one on which to require an examination. But, the condition must be rationally in dispute. One party's pique at another's posture on the facts will not suffice. A tort defendant's simple statement that he didn't see the plaintiff at an intersection, for example, does not entitle the plaintiff to an eye examination of the defendant.[4] Similarly, the failure to recall the events surrounding an accident does not place one's physical or mental condition in controversy.[5]

Although the defendant's condition can be injected into the case by the plaintiff, injection by the plaintiff will not cause a waiver of the defendant's doctor-patient privilege. Mere denials by the defendant will not deprive her of the physician-patient privilege no matter how thoroughly the plaintiff has injected the issue.[6] If the defendant himself levies the issue, however, it does result in a waiver, as where he injects it with a counterclaim or affirmative defense.[7] When dispute arises as to whether a party's

---

[88] Zubulake v. UBS Warburg LLC, 220 F.R.D. 212, 92 Fair Empl. Prac. Cas. (BNA) 1539 (S.D.N.Y. 2003). This again demonstrates that our state courts, when addressing the disclosure of ESI, are often persuaded by the authorities emanating from the federal side.

[89] *U.S. Bank National Ass'n*, 94 A.D.3d at 65, 939 N.Y.S.2d at 400. The issue of who pays the costs of electronic disclosure is further explored in the Commentary C3120:2A on McKinney's CPLR 3120.

[1] See Arons v. Jutkowitz, 9 N.Y.3d 393, 409, 850 N.Y.S.2d 345, 351, 880 N.E.2d 831, 837 (2007).

[2] See Constantine v. Diello, 24 A.D.2d 821, 264 N.Y.S.2d 153 (4th Dep't 1965).

[3] See Fisher v. Fossett, 45 Misc. 2d 757, 257 N.Y.S.2d 821 (Sup. Ct., Erie County 1965).

[4] Courtney v. Olsen, 45 Misc. 2d 283, 256 N.Y.S.2d 748 (Sup. Ct., Westchester County 1965).

[5] Gaglia v. Wells, 112 A.D.2d 138, 139, 490 N.Y.S.2d 829 (2d Dep't 1985).

[6] Dillenbeck v. Hess, 73 N.Y.2d 278, 539 N.Y.S.2d 707, 536 N.E.2d 1126 (1989).

[7] Koump v. Smith, 25 N.Y.2d 287, 303 N.Y.S.2d 858, 250 N.E.2d 857 (1969).

condition is in controversy, the burden of showing that it is on the party seeking the examination.[8] The tendency of the courts is to allow an examination—physical, mental, or blood—if it can be shown to have some practical value in the case.[9] If the examination "presents the possibility of danger to [the] life or health" of the party, it can be dispensed with.[10]

While the personal injury action in the realm of the unintentional tort is the one that dominates when a medical examination is the topic, the examination may become relevant in a variety of other actions. An intentional tort, too, such as assault, will warrant a physical examination if injuries are claimed. Blood relationship and hence blood examination is invariably involved in a paternity suit, as is mental capacity and hence mental examination in incompetency proceedings. Physical or mental examinations, or a combination of them, can become relevant in such unsuspected places as a contract, trust, succession, insurance, custody, or matrimonial case in which undue influence, overreaching, duress, capacity, ability, or other general or specific condition is injected. Where the plaintiff sued for fraud and breach of a contract concerning a stock transaction and the defendant pleaded that he did not remember receiving or signing the plaintiff's checks, defendant's physical and mental condition was found to be sufficiently in controversy to support an examination.[11] Recognition of these diverse possibilities is the reason CPLR 3121(a) does not attempt to restrict examinations to any particular category of action.

Authorizations for Hospital Records

In any instance in which hospital records are relevant to the party's condition, CPLR 3121(a) requires that party, upon demand, to execute and acknowledge written authorizations allowing the other parties to the action to obtain and make copies of those records. The authorization must accompany any subpoena duces tecum served on a medical provider. Without it, the provider need not respond or object to the subpoena.[12] A party who obtains copies of hospital records as a result of a party's authorization is required by CPLR 3121(a) to serve a duplicate copy of the records on the party who furnished the authorization. This requirement only applies when the examining party actually makes a copy of the record.[13]

Court Rules Governing Examinations and Exchange of Reports

Some of the cases construing and applying CPLR 3121 seem to have become a bit academic today because the Uniform Rules have been promulgated to cover much of the subject and do so in great detail. On the subject of physical examinations especially,

---

[8]   *Koump*, 25 N.Y.2d at 294, 303 N.Y.S.2d at 862, 250 N.E.2d at 864.

[9]   See Carpinelli v. Manhattan Bottling Corp., 21 A.D.2d 792, 250 N.Y.S.2d 756 (2d Dep't 1964), allowing a psychogalvanic skin reaction test.

[10]   Lefkowitz v. Nassau County Medical Center, 94 A.D.2d 18, 462 N.Y.S.2d 903 (2d Dep't 1983).

[11]   Estabrook & Co. v. Masiello, 75 Misc. 2d 784, 348 N.Y.S.2d 879 (Sup. Ct., Westchester County 1973).

[12]   CPLR 3122(a)(2). While the situating of this requirement in Article 31 of the CPLR would indicate that it was intended only for the subpoena duces tecum used in pretrial disclosure, it was held applicable to the trial subpoena as well. See Campos v. Payne, 2 Misc. 3d 921, 766 N.Y.S.2d 535 (N.Y. City Civ. Ct. 2003). The result in *Campos* was legislatively overruled with 2011 amendments to both CPLR 3122(a)(2) and CPLR 2302(b) clarifying that if the court directs production of medical records for use at trial, an authorization by the plaintiff is not required. See Commentary C3122:2 on McKinney's CPLR 3122.

[13]   See Tower v. Chemical Bank, 140 A.D.2d 514, 528 N.Y.S.2d 413 (2d Dep't 1988).

practitioners should first consult the rules, which supplement CPLR 3121 with many particulars. It must be stressed that a rule violation can result in a substantial forfeiture.[14]

In actions involving personal injury and wrongful death, a lengthy rule entitled "Exchange of medical reports in personal injury and wrongful death actions" governs examinations and medical reports.[15] In Hamilton v. Miller,[16] the Court of Appeals held that Uniform Rule 202.17 does not require a party "to hire a medical provider to examine them and create a report solely for purposes of the litigation." Relying on the language in Rule 202.17(b)(1), the Court concluded that parties "need only produce reports from medical providers who have 'previously treated or examined' them."[17]

Practitioners may sometimes be surprised to find that a procedure prescribed in a rule may seem in some respects at odds with CPLR 3121.[18] Unless the matter is important enough to challenge, which it rarely is, it is politic just to follow the rule. There have been instances, however, when a court on a closer look has been prevailed on to set aside even one of its own rules as inconsistent with the statutory prescription.[19]

Notice of Examination Under CPLR 3121(a) and Objections Under CPLR 3122(a)(1)

Under CPLR 3121(a), a mere notice brings on the examination. It is served by the examining party on the examinee and the other parties, setting forth the time, the place, the conditions, and the scope of the examination. As discussed above, if an authorization to secure hospital records is sought, a demand for it may be included in the notice. The general rule is that the examinee's attorney, or a same-sex stand-in, may be present during the examination,[20] but it has been held that a videotaping of the examination may not be allowed except in "special and unusual circumstances."[21]

As far as time is concerned, CPLR 3121(a) requires that at least 20 days notice of the examination be given. Uniform Rule 202.17(a), which applies in personal injury and wrongful death actions, requires more notice than that.

Notwithstanding elaboration of the "notice" procedure, or any other procedure in either the statutes or the rules, the prevalent notion about disclosure proceedings has

---

[14] A rule involved in Delgado v. Fogle, 32 A.D.2d 85, 299 N.Y.S.2d 898 (2d Dep't 1969), for example, enabled a party to set up his own physical examination, that is, to notify other parties of his availability for examination at a stated time. The other side then had to show up with its examining physician at the appointed time, which it failed to do. The case was one of first impression, so the court forgave the default, but put the bar on notice that in the future, the rule would be strictly enforced. See Bowen v. Fiore, 42 A.D.2d 960, 347 N.Y.S.2d 749 (2d Dep't 1973).

[15] 22 N.Y.C.R.R. § 202.17, applicable in the supreme and county courts. Similar rules apply in the N.Y.C. Civil Court (22 N.Y.C.R.R. § 208.13), the district courts (22 N.Y.C.R.R. § 212.13), and the city courts (22 N.Y.C.R.R. § 210.13).

[16] Hamilton v. Miller, 23 N.Y.3d 592, 601, 992 N.Y.S.2d 190, 194, 15 N.E.3d 1199, 1203 (2014).

[17] *Hamilton*, 23 N.Y.3d at 601, 992 N.Y.S.2d at 194, 15 N.E.3d at 1203; see Commentary C3121:4 to McKinney's CPLR 3121.

[18] If all the rule offers is additional instruction, it passes muster. See Commentaries C3121:4, C3121:5 on McKinney's CPLR 3121.

[19] See, e.g., Calhoun v. Pickett, 77 A.D.2d 776, 431 N.Y.S.2d 212 (3d Dep't 1980), aff'd, 52 N.Y.2d 605, 439 N.Y.S.2d 831, 422 N.E.2d 491 (1981).

[20] See Parsons v. Hytech Tool & Die, Inc., 241 A.D.2d 936, 661 N.Y.S.2d 362 (4th Dep't 1997) (placing limitations on lawyer's location at examination).

[21] See Vargas v. City of New York, 146 A.D.3d 917, 45 N.Y.S.3d 525 (2d Dep't 2017); Lamendola v. Slocum, 148 A.D.2d 781, 538 N.Y.S.2d 116 (3d Dep't 1989).

stronger application with the physical examination than perhaps anywhere else: work things out with the other side and don't just send off notices with ultimatums in them. With other disclosure devices, the time of the parties and their lawyers is on the line; with CPLR 3121(a), the time of physicians is on the line as well. There should be consultation among the parties in advance to set up a time and place convenient to parties, to counsel, and to the examining physician. The lawyer should not, relying only on the letter of CPLR 3121(a) or even on a detailed rule in point, just serve a notice arbitrarily setting up the examination.

If the party served with the notice has objections to it, she should serve a response within 20 days, stating the objections "with reasonable particularity." That's the requirement of CPLR 3122(a)(1), which then provides that the party serving the notice may make a motion under CPLR 3124 to test the objections and/or compel compliance.[22]

The reference in CPLR 3121(a) is to examinations by a "physician." The Court of Appeals has held that while this may bar examinations by other professionals under CPLR 3121, nonphysician professionals can conduct examinations under the general and broader terms of CPLR 3101(a) whenever relevant.[23]

Defendants in personal injury actions may sometimes seek the physical examination of the plaintiff through an organization retained to conduct what has become known as an "independent medical evaluation" (IME). The courts have had occasion to question the organization's independence, as in Chapman v. Mayo,[24] where, in assigning a physician to conduct the examination, defendant made no pretense of seeking an objective report: it instructed the physician to reflect on causation, for example, "only if in negative."[25]

Defendant's Ex Parte Interview with Plaintiff's Treating Physician

The Federal Health Insurance Portability and Accountability Act (HIPAA) plays a significant role in disclosure in personal injury actions.[26] There was once a conflict among the lower courts about whether HIPAA prevented the defendant from conducting an ex-parte interview with the plaintiff's treating physician in such actions. The Court of Appeals resolved the conflict in Arons v. Jutkowitz,[27] holding that under New York's doctrine of "informal discovery," the defendant has the right to request an ex-parte interview with the plaintiff's treating physician. In holding that "an attorney may [seek to] interview an adverse party's treating physician privately when the adverse party has affirmatively placed his or her medical condition in controversy," the *Arons* decision

---

[22] For additional treatment of CPLR 3122, see § 362 and Commentary C3122:1 to McKinney's CPLR 3122.

[23] See Kavanagh v. Ogden Allied Maintenance Corp., 92 N.Y.2d 952, 683 N.Y.S.2d 156, 705 N.E.2d 1197 (1998), allowing examination by a vocational rehabilitation expert. Other cases have allowed exams by other professionals. See the lead note in NYSLD No. 469.

[24] Chapman v. Mayo, Sup. Ct., Putnam County, July 24, 2003 (Index 1694/00; Hickman, J.).

[25] The plaintiff's medical expenses alone in the case were $65,000, but the defendant at no time offered in settlement more than the $50,000 limit of the insurance policy. The court faulted the defendant and its hireling for its conduct and upheld a verdict of $1,315,000.

[26] For some background on HIPAA, see Patrick M. Connors, New York Practice, *Appellate Division is Confronted with HIPAA*, N.Y.L.J., Jan. 17, 2007, at 3, col. 1; SPR 143:4.

[27] Arons v. Jutkowitz, 9 N.Y.3d 393, 850 N.Y.S.2d 345, 880 N.E.2d 831 (2007). The case, one of three decided together, is the subject of the lead note in NYSLD No. 576. See Commentary C3121:7 on McKinney's CPLR 3121.

expressly noted that court orders allowing the interview should no longer be necessary because there is no basis for the plaintiff in such cases to refuse to furnish an authorization permitting it.[28] The Court outlined several guidelines for conducting the interview, cautioning that the defense attorney must steer clear of privileged information that has not been waived by the plaintiff in the litigation.[29] The decision instructed that "an attorney who approaches a nonparty treating physician (or other health care professional) must simply reveal the client's identity and interest, and make clear that any discussion with counsel is entirely voluntary and limited in scope to the particular medical condition at issue in the litigation."[30] HIPAA, the Court concluded, is satisfied by the preliminary securing from the plaintiff of a valid authorization for the interview.[31]

An *Arons* authorization,[32] to be distinguished from the CPLR 3121(a) hospital records authorization,[33] must be obtained from the plaintiff before the defendant may contact the treating physician. In one case, an ex parte interview with P's treating physicians by D's attorney without P's authorization voided a verdict for D.[34] The permissible topics of conversation for the physician agreeing to the ex parte interview are negotiated between the lawyers on both sides and listed in the authorization.[35]

There have been instances where the plaintiff duly furnishes the authorization to the defendant but also sends a letter to the treating physician emphasizing that the interview is voluntary and, while not demanding it, requests to be present during any interview. The court held such a request permissible in Miller v. Kingston Diagnostic Center,[36] concluding that the letter was not threatening or intimidating. The *Miller* court emphasized that the letter was copied to defendants' counsel and, distinguishing other decisions finding such letters inappropriate,[37] ruled that the letter did not interfere with defense counsel's right to ask for an ex parte interview with plaintiff's treating physician as recognized under the *Arons* decision.

The Practice Commentaries to McKinney's CPLR 3121 contain an extensive review of the procedure for obtaining and conducting an ex parte interview of an adverse party's treating physician, including the issue of communications similar to those contained in

---

[28]　*Arons*, 9 N.Y.3d at 401–02, 850 N.Y.S.2d at 346, 880 N.E.2d at 832.

[29]　See Commentary C3121:7 to McKinney's CPLR 3121.

[30]　*Arons*, 9 N.Y.3d at 410, 850 N.Y.S.2d at 352, 880 N.E.2d at 839.

[31]　In Kleeschulte v. Blair, 20 Misc. 3d 1114(A), 867 N.Y.S.2d 375 (Sup. Ct., Ulster County 2008) (SPR 199:3), it was held that P's counsel has no right to participate in D's interview with P's treating physician.

[32]　See Official Form UCS-575, discussed in Commentary C3121:7 to McKinney's CPLR 3121; SPR 195:2–3.

[33]　See Official Form UCS-960, discussed in Commentary C3121:7 to McKinney's CPLR 3121; Akalski v. Counsell, 2010 WL 4412335 (Sup. Ct., Westchester County 2010) (SPR 230:3) ("[s]ince the HIPAA and *Arons* authorizations seek different discovery and contain different notices, [defendant's] contention that the authorizations may be combined is without merit").

[34]　Straub v. Yalamanchili, 58 A.D.3d 1050, 871 N.Y.S.2d 773 (3d Dep't 2009) (SPR 208:3–4).

[35]　See Official Form UCS-575, discussed in Commentary C3121:7 to McKinney's CPLR 3121.

[36]　Miller v. Kingston Diagnostic Center, 33 Misc. 3d 496, 929 N.Y.S.2d 668 (Sup. Ct., Ulster County 2011) (SPR 240:4).

[37]　See Prindle v. Prindle, Sup. Ct., Schenectady County, July 17, 2008 (Index No. 2005–0690) (SPR 200:3) (letters to several treating physicians stating, among other things, that "your patient . . . prefers that you do not engage in such private discussions with anyone except us concerning any aspect of her medical condition, treatment or prognosis" deemed improper).

Miller. Subsequent entries in these Commentaries track many relevant developments since that time.

Exchange of Reports Under CPLR 3121(b) and Uniform Rules

A party who has conducted a CPLR 3121(a) physical or mental examination will ordinarily have the examining physician draw up a report. Any other party who wants a copy of that report can obtain it by exchanging a medical report of a CPLR 3121(a) examination that it has had conducted of the same person's condition. No consent is required to invoke this procedure, which is contained in CPLR 3121(b). It has been held that when a physician bases his report solely on hospital records and not on a personal examination of the party, the report is not subject to the exchange directed by CPLR 3121(b).[38]

The scope of this statute was addressed by the Court of Appeals in Hoenig v. Westphal,[39] which held that while CPLR 3121(b) is addressed to the exchange of medical reports in general, it applies only to the report of a nontreating physician, i.e., one whose report is made after an examination conducted pursuant to CPLR 3121(a), or otherwise made solely for litigation. The Court said that the report of a treating physician is not in that category and may therefore be discovered under the basic relevance standard in CPLR 3101(a). It is not material prepared exclusively for litigation under CPLR 3101(d)(2), in other words, and thus faces no discovery impediment from that statute. Nor may it be deemed the product of an examination conducted pursuant to CPLR 3121(a) and, therefore, is not subject to the exchange requirement of CPLR 3121(b).

As discussed above, in a given category of case a Uniform Rule may require the trading of the reports of all examining physicians, without distinction between treaters and nontreaters and without requiring the exchange contemplated by CPLR 3121(b).[40] In an action for medical, dental, or podiatric malpractice, if the person conducting the examination is to serve as an expert in the case, the policies of CPLR 3101(d)(1)(i) may be implicated, allowing the redaction of the expert's name from the report he furnishes.[41]

§ 364. Notice to Admit

Scope of Notice to Admit

CPLR 3123 supplies a disclosure device known as a "notice to admit," whereby one party can require another to admit stated facts, or the genuineness of a paper or document, or the correctness of photographs. Copies of any paper or documents involved accompany the notice unless they have already been furnished.[1] The device may be used only when the seeking party "reasonably believes there can be no substantial dispute"

---

[38]   Edelman v. Holmes Private Ambulances, Inc., 32 A.D.2d 563, 300 N.Y.S.2d 372 (2d Dep't 1969); see Kelly v. Tarnowski, 213 A.D.2d 1054, 624 N.Y.S.2d 504 (4th Dep't 1995).

[39]   Hoenig v. Westphal, 52 N.Y.2d 605, 439 N.Y.S.2d 831, 422 N.E.2d 491 (1981).

[40]   See 22 N.Y.C.R.R. § 202.17(b)(1). At one time, the rule required that the reports contain a narrative, rather than the briefer notations found in insurance and workers' compensation forms. The rule was amended in 1998 to allow the use of these forms. See Commentary C3121:7 on McKinney's CPLR 3121; SPR 73:1.

[41]   See Ryan v. Michelsen, 241 A.D.2d 434, 660 N.Y.S.2d 435 (1st Dep't 1997); see also Galdon v. Ring, 261 A.D.2d 928, 690 N.Y.S.2d 794 (4th Dep't 1999) (plaintiff permitted to redact the identity of plaintiff's treating physician on medical records and reports exchanged where physician also served as her expert witness in medical malpractice action).

[1]   CPLR 3123(a).

about the matter at the trial and when it is within the knowledge of the other party or ascertainable by him "upon reasonable inquiry."[2] The notice does not work, and even if ignored will not invoke a sanction, if the matters as to which admissions are sought are not "attuned to any reasonable belief that they [are] free from substantial dispute."[3]

The purpose of the device is to save a party the trouble and expense of proving a readily admittable fact. It will usually work well enough to compel an admission that the adverse party owned a car of a given description, for example, or was driving it on a stated occasion, or that he was or was not in the vehicle at a stated time, or that the signature that appears on the appended contract is his, or that this is the last deed signed by the party, or that this photograph accurately represents the intersection at which a collision occurred, and numerous other matters of like tenor. But it is not to be used to compel the defendant to admit that she was driving negligently, or that it was she who breached the contract or defrauded, defamed, assaulted, or embezzled from the plaintiff. It may not be used, in other words, "to cover ultimate conclusions, which can only be made after a full and complete trial."[4] Nor may it be used for technical or scientific information such as is ordinarily elicited from an expert.[5]

Nor may it be used to make one party admit what some other party knows. Demands that party X admit that party Y owned certain premises continuously for a stated period, or that Y admit that certain matters were known to party Z, were held improper in Taylor v. Blair.[6] In delineating the scope of a CPLR 3123(a) notice to admit, the First Department held that "[t]he sole function of such a notice is to expedite the trial by eliminating from contention that which is public knowledge or easily provable and which the party reasonably believes is not in dispute."[7]

What may have happened in *Taylor* is that the plaintiff drew up all the admission subjects he had listed for any of several defendants and included them in but one notice served on all of them. Even in respect of proper subjects, a separate notice to admit should be drawn for each party so as not to elicit from one something suitable for admission only by another.

Because of its inherent limitations, the notice to admit is under-used. It is also true that the matters to which it lends itself are often admitted by opposing parties in the course of the pleadings or depositions or other disclosure devices, or preliminary conferences, or are so easily and inexpensively proved that a party feels no need to avoid the proof by securing the admission.

The admission is usable in the pending action only. It has been held analogous to a pleading,[8] and therefore binds only to the same degree. While much discussion in this section is focused on the situation in which admissions are not forthcoming, when they are made the recipient has various ways to make use of them.[9]

---

[2]   CPLR 3123(a).

[3]   Marguess v. City of New York, 30 A.D.2d 782, 782, 291 N.Y.S.2d 956, 957 (1st Dep't 1968), aff'd, 28 N.Y.2d 527, 319 N.Y.S.2d 71, 267 N.E.2d 884 (1971).

[4]   DeSilva by DeSilva v. Rosenberg, 236 A.D.2d 508, 654 N.Y.S.2d 30 (2d Dep't 1997).

[5]   Berg v. Flower Fifth Ave. Hospital, 102 A.D.2d 760, 476 N.Y.S.2d 895, 42 A.L.R.4th 485 (1st Dep't 1984); Johantgen v. Hobart Mfg. Co., 64 A.D.2d 858, 407 N.Y.S.2d 355 (4th Dep't 1978).

[6]   Taylor v. Blair, 116 A.D.2d 204, 500 N.Y.S.2d 133 (1st Dep't 1986).

[7]   *Taylor*, 116 A.D.2d at 207–08, 500 N.Y.S.2d at 135.

[8]   Seidenberg v. Rosen, 114 N.Y.S.2d 279 (Sup. Ct., New York County 1952).

[9]   See Commentary C3123:4 on McKinney's CPLR 3123; SPR 100:3–4.

Relevant Time Periods and Responding to CPLR 3123 Notice

The usual time for serving the notice to admit is after the joinder of issue, but before the filing of the note of issue, which is also the usual time frame for pretrial disclosure.[10] CPLR 3123(a) also permits the device to be used 20 days after the service of the summons and any time up to 20 days before the trial. This poses at least a facial conflict with the certificate of readiness rule, which requires certification that pretrial proceedings, and most notably disclosure, are complete before the certificate, which accompanies the note of issue, may be filed.[11] Disclosure after the filing requires a showing of "unusual or unanticipated circumstances."[12] The First Department held in Hodes v. City of New York[13] that service of a notice to admit up to 20 days before the trial is okay notwithstanding the prior filing of the certificate of readiness, for the reason that the notice is not truly a disclosure device, but just a procedure designed to "crystallize issues."[14]

The recipient of a notice to admit has 20 days to respond. A recipient who wishes to admit the matter need do nothing, as silence constitutes an admission under the statute. If the party wishes to deny the matter, she must do so in a sworn writing, to be served within the 20-day period. The writing may include qualifications or explanations. Under the statute, privileged matters and trade secrets can be labeled such, for example, and admission refused on those grounds.[15]

Although it may happen that a given notice to admit will be found so unreasonable that a party ignoring it entirely will face no sanction,[16] ignoring it under ordinary circumstances is perilous. If the recipient would deny the matter, the denial should be made. If the recipient deems the notice unreasonable, she should promptly move for a protective order determining the issue one way or the other. It is clear today that the protective order of CPLR 3103 is available to test the validity of a notice to admit under CPLR 3123;[17] earlier doubts about that in the Second Department were dispelled and the availability of the protective order for this purpose acknowledged.[18] A recipient of a notice to admit who neither denies the matters nor moves to test the validity of the notice is courting trouble. If the party guesses wrong, she will be held to the usual rule that silence is an admission.[19] Indeed, the fact admitted may even prove dispositive of the claim. In one case, for example, the impact of an admission-by-silence was to concede

---

[10] See § 352.

[11] See § 371 (containing forms for note of issue and certificate of readiness).

[12] See § 370.

[13] Hodes v. City of New York, 165 A.D.2d 168, 566 N.Y.S.2d 611 (1st Dep't 1991).

[14] The notice used in *Hodes*, however, consisting of some 50 pages, was found to be a mere subterfuge to obtain more disclosure by trying to circumvent the readiness requirement with a notice to admit, and was disallowed.

[15] CPLR 3123(a).

[16] See *Marguess*, 30 A.D.2d at 782, 291 N.Y.S.2d at 957.

[17] See Wolin v. St. Vincent's Hosp. and Medical Center of New York, 304 A.D.2d 348, 757 N.Y.S.2d 33 (1st Dep't 2003).

[18] Epstein v. Consolidated Edison Co. of New York, 31 A.D.2d 746, 297 N.Y.S.2d 260 (2d Dep't 1969).

[19] See Kowalski v. Knox, 293 A.D.2d 892, 741 N.Y.S.2d 291 (3d Dep't 2002).

that the party learned of a fraud early enough to subject the claim to the bar of the statute of limitations.[20]

If the recipient of the notice wishes to deny the matter, the denial should be outright. The techniques applicable to denials in a pleading[21] have been held inappropriate to address to a notice to admit. Hence a denial "upon information and belief," or of "knowledge or information sufficient to form a belief," are not countenanced,[22] at least not when the denier has ready access to sources that will enable her either to admit or deny outright.

It has been held that, except in special situations, it must be the party, not the party's attorney, who makes the sworn statement that responds to a CPLR 3123 notice to admit.[23] While there is some dispute about that,[24] the sounder practice is of course to have the client do it.

With leave of court, an admission can be amended or withdrawn "on such terms as may be just."[25] It is rare for a court to permit a party to withdraw an express admission, but it occurred in Altman v. Kelly[26] where a defendant employer admitted that, at the time of the collision in issue, defendant employee was "acting in the scope of his employment." The plaintiff moved for summary judgment on the issue of liability against the employer, which cross moved for leave to withdraw its admissions. The Second Department reversed the award of summary judgment and granted the employer's cross-motion to withdraw its admissions under CPLR 3123(b), essentially finding that the notice to admit improperly sought admissions on the core legal and factual issues in the case.[27]

Penalties Under CPLR 3123(c)

The notice to admit device of CPLR 3123 is the only one that has its own built-in penalty for a violation and to which the usual sanctions, to be met shortly in the treatment of CPLR 3126,[28] therefore do not apply. If the party on whom the notice to admit is served duly responds with a denial, the seeking party will have to prepare to prove the matters denied, amassing witnesses and evidence for the purpose. If the seeking party does, and if the matter is proved at the trial, the sole remedy is to move for an order compelling the denying party to pay the costs of the proof. This is one of those rare instances, however, when a reasonable attorney's fee may be included. The costs award may be made even though the prover has lost the case on the merits.

CPLR 3123(c) authorizes the court to award the costs of proving the matter unless it finds "that there were good reasons for the denial . . . or that the admissions sought were of no substantial importance." Attorneys distrust provisos like that, however, and

---

[20]   Psaroudis v. Psaroudis, 30 A.D.2d 841, 293 N.Y.S.2d 24 (2d Dep't 1968), aff'd, 27 N.Y.2d 527, 312 N.Y.S.2d 998, 261 N.E.2d 108 (1970).

[21]   See § 221.

[22]   Barnes v. Shul Private Car Service, Inc., 59 Misc. 2d 967, 301 N.Y.S.2d 907 (Sup. Ct., Kings County 1969).

[23]   HSBC Bank USA, N.A. v. Carchi, 2013 WL 1281019 (Sup. Ct., Queens County 2013).

[24]   See Barnes, 59 Misc.2d at 968–69, 301 N.Y.S.2d at 908.

[25]   CPLR 3123(b); see Webb v. Tire and Brake Distributor, Inc., 13 A.D.3d 835, 786 N.Y.S.2d 636 (3d Dep't 2004).

[26]   Altman v. Kelly, 128 A.D.3d 741, 9 N.Y.S.3d 359 (2d Dep't 2015).

[27]   See Commentary C3123:1 on McKinney's CPLR 3123.

[28]   See § 367.

if they are going to keep special tabs on the costs of witnesses and evidence in regard to a certain matter, as well as special track of their own time, they want the effort to pay off with a costs award that is more certain than what CPLR 3123 offers. The "unless" clause in CPLR 3123(c) is, unfortunately, a refuge for judges unenthusiastic about the statute's costs sanctions. That appears in any event to be a widespread feeling among the bar. It's probably another reason for the relative disuse of CPLR 3123.

The motion for the costs sanction must be made "at or immediately following the trial" since it is only then that the court can determine whether the fact denied has in fact been proved. The motion should be made promptly, perhaps even before the court has adjourned, which means that the lawyer contemplating the motion should have the required proof ready—affidavits and bills and the like—on what is expected to be the trial's final day. A CPLR 3123 costs motion delayed until four days after the trial, for example, was held too late.[29]

§ 365. Demand for Address

There are several situations in which a party may need to know another party's address. This usually arises at the outset of the action, such as where it may be relevant to determine the propriety of the venue, which is most often based on residence,[1] or when service may have to be made at the residence.[2]

CPLR 3118 provides that upon demand by any party, any other must serve a verified statement of its post office address and residence and also that of any "officer or member" of the party or of any assignor to whom a claim or defense in the action once belonged. The response time is ten days. This is of course a minor disclosure device, but it has its uses. Since it operates only to require that the party reveal its own or an agent's or assignor's address, it is not the device used when the address of a nonparty witness, otherwise disclosable, is sought. There the seeker can use other devices, however, such as interrogatories or the ordinary deposition.[3]

In 2004, CPLR 2103–a was adopted, which provides for the confidentiality of a party's address and telephone number in civil proceedings. The court, upon its own motion or the motion of a party, can authorize confidentiality of the information where it "makes specific findings on the record supporting a conclusion that disclosure of such addresses or telephone numbers would pose an unreasonable risk to the health or safety of a party."[4] If these findings are made, CPLR 3118 is trumped by the confidentiality provisions in CPLR 2103–a, which apply "[n]otwithstanding any other provision of law."[5]

By analogy to CPLR 3118, which operates during the action, it has been held that a judgment debtor's attorney, upon being served with a post-judgment disclosure

---

[29]   Halligan v. Glazebrook, 59 Misc. 2d 712, 299 N.Y.S.2d 951 (Sup. Ct., Suffolk County 1969); see Commentary C3123:9 on McKinney's CPLR 3123.

[1]   See CPLR 305(a), 503; § 118.

[2]   CPLR 2103(b)(4), (c).

[3]   For disclosure of witnesses' names, which would also include their addresses, see § 349.

[4]   CPLR 2103–a(a).

[5]   CPLR 2103–a(a).

subpoena,[6] must reveal the judgment debtor's address. As a general rule, the address does not constitute privileged information.[7]

F. COMPELLING DISCLOSURE

Table of Sections

§ 366.   Order Compelling Disclosure; Rulings

§ 367.   Sanctions for Nondisclosure

§ 366. Order Compelling Disclosure; Rulings

Most of the disclosure devices are brought on by mere notices served by parties to the action. Only in a few instances, treated earlier, is a preliminary court order needed.[1] If the notice is ignored in whole or in part or if a demanded datum or thing is withheld, or if a party refuses to submit to a deposition, CPLR 3124 authorizes an application to the court for an order compelling virtually all disclosure, whatever the device that was used to seek it. CPLR 3123's notice to admit device has its own noncompliance remedies built in and is excepted from the statute.[2]

CPLR 3124, which was amended in 1993 as part of an overhaul of the disclosure article, contemplates a disclosure order without a penalty. If a sanction of some kind is sought for the disobedience of either a notice or an order, the application is made under CPLR 3126. Caselaw under the original statute held that a CPLR 3126 sanction motion need not necessarily be preceded by a disclosure order under CPLR 3124,[3] which of course made the motion under CPLR 3126 the preferred one. The design was to avoid the two-motion procedure generated by making a party go to CPLR 3124 first and allowing access to CPLR 3126 only as a follow-up. Under the 1993 amendments, however, there are at least two instances in which it appears that a bypass of CPLR 3124 in favor of a direct motion under CPLR 3126 may be precluded. When the devices involved are the discovery of CPLR 3120 or the physical or mental examination of CPLR 3121, the coordinate amendment to CPLR 3122(a) appears to require that a preliminary CPLR 3124 application be made for a court order directing disclosure without a sanction before a sanction can be invoked with a CPLR 3126 motion.[4] The courts have yet to offer a definitive resolution to that question.[5] The party seeking disclosure would of course prefer the direct route to CPLR 3126. Why seek to compel disclosure under CPLR 3124 when it can be compelled just as well with a motion under CPLR 3126, where the direction can be accompanied with a sanction or at least a threatened sanction?

When the disclosure device being used requires a session, as the ordinary deposition does, and answers to certain questions are refused on various evidentiary grounds, the hope of CPLR 3124 is that the deposition will turn to other things until everything

---

6   See CPLR 5224.

7   See Chemical Bank v. Sinoto, N.Y.L.J., December 1, 1981 (Sup. Ct., New York County; Stecher, J.).

1   See § 352.

2   See § 364.

3   Wolfson v. Nassau County Medical Center, 141 A.D.2d 815, 530 N.Y.S.2d 27 (2d Dep't 1988).

4   See §§ 362, 363; SPR 10:1.

5   At least one court has held that such preliminary resort to CPLR 3124 is not necessary. Matter of T./P. Children, 165 Misc. 2d 333, 629 N.Y.S.2d 677 (Fam. Ct., Albany County 1995) (party was not required to move pursuant to CPLR 3124 in first instance to compel disclosure under CPLR 3120; CPLR 3126 was also an option); see § 362 and SPR 37:2.

susceptible of resolution between the parties is covered.[6] The statute's preference is that all unanswered questions be gathered up afterwards in one batch and made the subject of a single, formal, written motion for a disclosure order in which the court can all at once pass on the validity of, and hence on the need to respond to, each question.[7]

There is yet another way of securing court instruction on the validity of individual questions posed at a deposition, informally known as the "let's get a ruling" system.[8] This procedure is sometimes used when the deposition is taking place in the courthouse or near enough to the courthouse to get a judge to issue an informal but nonetheless binding "ruling," usually oral, on whether a given question need be answered. This system, in which the attorneys leave the deposition table and march resolutely to the courthouse, or across the courthouse lobby, or to its staircase or elevators, to find a judge,[9] is, even where available, only an alternative to the use of the single, formal motion made after the session is concluded.[10] Whether or not CPLR 3124 intended to preserve the "let's get a ruling" alternative, it was held—almost immediately after the CPLR took effect—that the system survived.[11] The court's or a given judge's calendars may even be helped by it: it may be more economical to dispose of a key objection with an informal ruling on the propriety of a question than to encourage formal, postsession motions that constitute a disproportionate burden on motion calendars. In those areas where the IAS[12] system is in operation, it must presumably be the assigned judge who makes rulings on deposition issues. Under the old master calendar system, the ruling could be sought in some counties from the judge assigned to one of the motion parts for the day, even though the judge otherwise had nothing to do with the case. If it must today be the IAS judge, and the judge is unavailable, the formal, postsession motion may be the only remedy the examining party has.

Since any motion in the case would have to be made to the IAS judge in any case in which there is one,[13] a formal motion should be returnable before that judge, wherever she may be, or in accord with her directions. If IAS doesn't apply in the court or if for any other reason the motion needs a venue, the motion to compel disclosure under CPLR 3124 may be made in any county otherwise permissible for a contested motion in the action, which is usually the county where the action is pending. But for this purpose, the county in which the disclosure session has been set under the venue rules of CPLR 3110

---

[6] See also CPLR 3113(b) ("[a]ll objections made at the time of the examination . . . to the conduct of any person, and any other objection to the proceedings, shall be noted by the officer upon the deposition and the deposition shall proceed subject to the right of a person to apply for a protective order"); 22 N.Y.C.R.R. § 221.1(a) (after an objection is noted on the record, "the answer shall be given and the deposition shall proceed subject to the objections and to the right of a person to apply for appropriate relief pursuant to Article 31 of the CPLR"); § 356.

[7] See Commentary C3124:3 on McKinney's CPLR 3124; Freidman v. Fayenson, 41 Misc. 3d 1236(A), 983 N.Y.S.2d 203 (Sup. Ct., New York County 2013), aff'd, 138 A.D.3d 554, 30 N.Y.S.3d 58 (1st Dep't 2016) (party brought motion under CPLR 3024 to compel responses to nine questions posed at deposition).

[8] See Commentary C3124:4 on McKinney's CPLR 3124.

[9] Some judges may even entertain such a request by phone during the deposition.

[10] See Cohen v. Heine & Co., 39 A.D.2d 563, 331 N.Y.S.2d 751 (2d Dep't 1972). Since the only appealable items in New York practice are a judgment or an order, the question arises as to whether a mere "ruling," not reduced to an order, may be appealed. See § 526, and Commentary C3124:5 on McKinney's CPLR 3124.

[11] Bustard v. Kedala, Inc., N.Y.L.J., Sept. 23, 1963, at 14, col. 1 (Sup. Ct., Kings County; Brown, J.).

[12] This stands for "Individual Assignment System." See § 77A.

[13] 22 N.Y.C.R.R. § 202.8(a); see § 245.

may be treated as the county in which the action is pending unless, of course, the rules have removed this option, as they are authorized to do.[14]

A motion to compel disclosure under CPLR 3124, as is true of any kind of motion relating to disclosure, must be accompanied by the moving attorney's affirmation that there has been a good faith consultation with the other side's lawyer in an effort to resolve the dispute.[15]

§ 367. Sanctions for Nondisclosure

Given the significance of CPLR 3126 as the enforcement arm of the disclosure article, and the frequency of its citation and application in the caselaw, the sanctions that it prescribes for nondisclosure are quoted here verbatim:

> If any party, or a person who at the time a deposition is taken or an examination or inspection is made, is an officer, director, member, employee or agent of a party or otherwise under a party's control, refuses to obey an order for disclosure or wilfully fails to disclose information which the court finds ought to have been disclosed pursuant to this article, the court may make such orders with regard to the failure or refusal as are just, among them:
>
> 1. an order that the issues to which the information is relevant shall be deemed resolved for purposes of the action in accordance with the claims of the party obtaining the order; or
>
> 2. an order prohibiting the disobedient party from supporting or opposing designated claims or defenses, from producing in evidence designated things or items of testimony, or from introducing any evidence of the physical, mental or blood condition sought to be determined, or from using certain witnesses; or
>
> 3. an order striking out pleadings or parts thereof, or staying further proceedings until the order is obeyed, or dismissing the action or any part thereof, or rendering a judgment by default against the disobedient party.

CPLR 3126 Applies to Party and Persons Under Party's Control

CPLR 3126's sanctions apply to nondisclosure by a party, not by a nonparty. "Party" for this purpose includes anyone under a party's control at the time disclosure is sought, with the theory being that the control enables the party to compel the disclosure and that it is therefore fair to penalize the party if the disclosure is not forthcoming. It is not fair, on the other hand, to invoke a sanction against a party for the recalcitrance of a nonparty beyond her control. It is for this reason that the CPLR requires the use of a subpoena to compel disclosure from a nonparty.[1] The disobedience of the subpoena is a contempt of court[2] and the contempt punishment therefore serves as the enforcement remedy.[3]

---

[14] See CPLR 3125.

[15] See, e.g., 22 N.Y.C.R.R. § 202.7(a), (c); see § 353.

[1] CPLR 3106(b), 3120; see §§ 345, 351.

[2] CPLR 2308, 5104; see § 385; Commentary C3126:3 to McKinney's CPLR 3126.

[3] The procedures for invoking the contempt punishment are in the enforcement chapter. See §§ 481 et seq. In Ortega v. City of New York, 9 N.Y.3d 69, 845 N.Y.S.2d 773, 876 N.E.2d 1189 (2007) (NYSLD No. 575),

As against a party, however, the meaningful civil sanctions of CPLR 3126 obviate resort to the contempt remedy. Some doubt has been expressed, therefore, about whether contempt is even available against a party for nondisclosure.[4] The door should not be entirely closed to the use of contempt against a party. Take the situation in which a party may be willing to suffer a default rather than make a required disclosure, with serious repercussions for another party. The contempt remedy should be kept available for use even against a recalcitrant party in that context.

The situation arose in Quintanilla v. Harchack,[5] in which P sued a drunk driver and a dram shop. P needed the driver's testimony to reflect on the shop's acts, but the driver—who had indicated that the shop had given him liquor while he was obviously drunk—ignored five court orders to depose. Instead of granting the shop's request to bar the driver from testifying at the trial, the court allowed P to seek the pressures of a contempt proceeding against the driver, so as to compel disclosure under the threat of jailing.[6]

Disobedience of Order or Disclosure Notice

The CPLR 3126 sanctions are available not only when an order for disclosure has been disobeyed, but also when there is wilful disobedience of a mere notice. A court order, such as one under CPLR 3124 directing disclosure, is not a condition precedent to the invocation of CPLR 3126.[7] The statute so provides explicitly in that it applies when the party either disobeys an order, "or" wilfilly fails to disclose information which the court finds ought to have been disclosed" under CPLR Article 31.[8] This may account, at least in part, for some diminished use of CPLR 3124 today, which prescribes an order directing disclosure without a sanction.

Another reason some courts will not require resort to a CPLR 3124 order before entertaining a motion under CPLR 3126 is that an order under CPLR 3126 can be made conditionally, with the court directing the disclosure accompanied by a sanction if the direction should be disobeyed. This is a very popular step among judges today.

If a CPLR 3126 sanction motion is addressed to a mere notice to disclose, as opposed to an order, it must be shown that the disobedience was "wilful."[9] One might guess that the cases would be filled with discussion of what is and what is not "wilful" in this sense, but the law is not altogether clear in this realm. In any event, the courts usually prefer to determine whether the disclosure is required and, if it is, to issue a conditional order

where evidence was inadvertently scrapped by a nonparty, the Court held that New York does not recognize "the tort of third-party negligent spoliation of evidence."

4   See Commentary C3126:4 on McKinney's CPLR 3126.

5   Quintanilla v. Harchack, 259 A.D.2d 681, 686 N.Y.S.2d 854 (2d Dep't 1999).

6   See also Mermelstein v. Kalker, 294 A.D.2d 413, 741 N.Y.S.2d 904 (2d Dep't 2002) (holding that parties, including co-defendant employer, were free to use contempt proceedings or warrant of commitment and arrest to secure defendant former employee's deposition or trial testimony).

7   See Wolfson v. Nassau County Medical Center, 141 A.D.2d 815, 530 N.Y.S.2d 27 (2d Dep't 1988). With the devices of the discovery of CPLR 3120 and the physical or mental examination of CPLR 3121, CPLR 3122(a)(1) appears to require that a preliminary application be made under CPLR 3124 before the stage is properly set for a sanction under CPLR 3126 (see the discussion in SPR 10:1), but some caselaw has held that such a preliminary step is not necessary. See §§ 362, 366 and SPR 37:2.

8   CPLR 3126 was so construed even before a 1978 amendment clarified the matter. See Coffey v. Orbachs, Inc., 22 A.D.2d 317, 254 N.Y.S.2d 596 (1st Dep't 1964); Goldner v. Lendor Structures, Inc., 29 A.D.2d 978, 289 N.Y.S.2d 687 (2d Dep't 1968).

9   See Commentary C3126:7 to McKinney's CPLR 3126.

directing the party to make the disclosure whether the prior refusal was wilful or not. The order will normally impose a sanction "unless" the disclosure is made within a stated time. With this conditioning, the court relieves itself of the unrewarding inquiry into whether a party's resistance was wilful.

The court usually reserves the "wilful" finding for cases where it is convinced not only that the party refused disclosure in the past, but apparently will not, without judicial prodding, make it in the future either. In one case, the court considered a party's failure to comply with disclosure in related actions outside New York State as part of a "programmed response to discovery."[10] Any unnecessary trouble the seeking party has been caused in this process is usually remedied, as will be seen, by a conditional order requiring the resisting party to make the disclosure now and pay the seeking party an attorney's fee.

The recalcitrant party is best warned, however, that there is no assurance that the CPLR 3126 sanction imposed by the court will be conditional. It may indeed be imposed outright.[11]

Although the conditional order is perhaps most often used when a notice for disclosure has been disregarded, it can be used as well for the disobedience of a prior order. In other words, the invocation of CPLR 3126 for the violation of a court order rather than of a mere notice does not mean that a sanction must be applied outright. The fact that a court order has already been disobeyed will, however, influence the court's discretion in the choice of a sanction, and a CPLR 3126 penalty applied unconditionally is of course a higher possibility in that situation.

All of the disclosure devices are backed by the sanctions of CPLR 3126, with the exception of the request to admit, which carries its own set of consequences.[12] The sanctions of CPLR 3126 can also become relevant for any phase of a given device. Sanctions can be invoked, for example, not just for the failure to attend a deposition, but for the failure to answer proper questions propounded during it.[13]

A rule requires that either motion—under CPLR 3124 or 3126—must, as a motion affecting disclosure, be accompanied by the moving attorney's affirmation that a good faith effort was made with opposing counsel to resolve the dispute, but that it didn't succeed.[14] In the scenario in which a CPLR 3124 motion precedes the CPLR 3126 motion, two separate good faith efforts to resolve the matter will be required. The effort required before the CPLR 3126 motion, however, should be relatively minimal. If matters have reached this point, it is doubtful that the recalcitrant party will suddenly experience a change of heart.

---

[10]   See Mann ex rel. Akst v. Cooper Tire Co., 33 A.D.3d 24, 816 N.Y.S.2d 45 (1st Dep't 2006) (apparently involving a motion to compel under CPLR 3124, not a motion for sanctions under CPLR 3126).

[11]   Fish & Richardson, P.C. v. Schindler, 75 A.D.3d 219, 901 N.Y.S.2d 598 (1st Dep't 2010) (given the defendant's "pattern of disobeying court orders and failing to provide discovery," an unconditional order of preclusion was an appropriate penalty).

[12]   CPLR 3123(c); see § 364.

[13]   See Adamo v. Kirsch Beverages, Inc., 80 Misc. 2d 369, 363 N.Y.S.2d 58 (Dist.Ct., Suffolk County 1974).

[14]   See 22 N.Y.C.R.R. § 202.7(a), (c), applicable in the supreme and county courts; Amherst Synagogue v. Schuele Paint Co., Inc., 30 A.D.3d 1055, 1057, 816 N.Y.S.2d 782, 783 (4th Dep't 2006) (reversing supreme court's grant of CPLR 3126 order because defendants "failed to demonstrate that they made a diligent effort to resolve this discovery dispute."); § 353.

The sanctions of CPLR 3126 are also available for matters beyond the disobedience of an order or the disregard of a notice. A party who has wilfully failed to provide a bill of particulars can be met with sanctions under CPLR 3126.[15] Under subdivision (h) of CPLR 3101, a party is required to supplement prior responses in certain circumstances, and to do so voluntarily, i.e., without the other side having to serve a new notice, demand, request, interrogatory, or anything else.[16] The CPLR 3126 sanctions are available for a failure to honor the CPLR 3101(h) supplementation requirement even though no order or notice has specifically requested supplementation.[17]

Possible Sanctions Under CPLR 3126

As quoted from CPLR 3126 above, the court has several options to choose from in remedying disclosure misconduct.

The first of the illustrative sanctions is what we might call the "resolving" order, which can be used when the refusal to disclose relates to an isolatable matter. It results in an order deeming the matter to be established as the seeking party claims it to be.[18] The second is also available in that kind of situation. It involves a preclusion order akin to that which punishes a failure to furnish a bill of particulars[19] and precludes the resisting party from supporting or opposing a given claim, defense, or contention, or from giving evidence on a designated issue, or from using a particular witness.[20] Where, for example, a defendant refused to produce books reflecting on the value of certain stock, he was precluded from contending that the stock was worth less than X dollars.[21]

A resolving or preclusion order may also be used when the court finds, even if only by negative inference from the party's reaction to disclosure efforts, that the party destroyed evidence reflecting on a specific issue.[22] Suppose that an object in one side's control was lost after it was tested and made the subject of an expert's report, for example, and is therefore unavailable to the other side for testing now. It will not necessarily be precluded from evidence if there is a reasonable way to set things right. In one case in which the expert was made available for deposition and in which unredacted copies of the expert's report were made available to the other side—which took advantage of both—a preclusion order was refused.[23]

Deliberate destruction or concealment of evidence, or even negligent destruction of relevant evidence, qualifies as what is known as "spoliation" and can bring about a resolving or preclusion order under the first two subdivisions of CPLR 3126 or, indeed, a dismissal under subdivision 3. In litigation today, parties commonly seek to impose penalties on an adversary based on the failure to preserve "electronically stored

---

[15]   CPLR 3042(d); see § 241.

[16]   See § 352A.

[17]   See Commentary C3126:6 to McKinney's CPLR 3126.

[18]   CPLR 3126(1); see Osterhoudt v. Wal-Mart Stores Inc., 273 A.D.2d 673, 709 N.Y.S.2d 685 (3d Dep't 2000).

[19]   See CPLR 3042(d); § 241.

[20]   CPLR 3126(2).

[21]   Feingold v. Walworth Bros., 238 N.Y. 446, 144 N.E. 675 (1924).

[22]   See Rizzuti v. Laucella, 57 A.D.3d 755, 871 N.Y.S.2d 202 (2d Dep't 2008).

[23]   See Ashline v. Kestner Engineers, P.C., 219 A.D.2d 788, 631 N.Y.S.2d 783 (3d Dep't 1995), where there was no proof that the object was deliberately hidden or destroyed, which could of course make a difference, as it did in Hallock v. Bogart, 206 A.D.2d 735, 614 N.Y.S.2d 651 (3d Dep't 1994), noted in SPR 33:3.

information" or "ESI." In Pegasus Aviation I, Inc. v. Varig Logistica S.A.,[24] the Court of Appeals made only a passing reference to CPLR 3126 and instead relied heavily on federal law when it outlined the penalties to be imposed on a party who fails to satisfy its preservation obligations in a New York State action.[25] The *Pegasus* Court ruled that a party seeking sanctions for spoliation of evidence must show: (1) that the party having control over the evidence possessed an obligation to preserve it at the time of its destruction; (2) that the evidence was destroyed with a "culpable state of mind," which would include negligence; and (3) that the destroyed evidence was relevant to, or would have supported, the seeking party's claim or defense.

Furthermore, the *Pegasus* Court held that in resolving the second issue above, if the evidence is determined to have been "intentionally or wilfully destroyed," the relevancy of that evidence to the seeking party's claim is presumed under the third prong of the inquiry.[26] If, however, the evidence is determined to have been "negligently destroyed," the party seeking spoliation sanctions must establish that the destroyed materials were relevant to its claim or defense.[27]

It is not always a simple task to apply the above standards to a set of facts.[28] The procedural history in *Pegasus,* which includes two reversals and a dissent at both the appellate division and the Court of Appeals, makes this point. The Court ruled that the failure to institute a litigation hold to preserve relevant information did not, standing alone, constitute gross negligence[29] but "rather was one factor to consider in determining the alleged spoliator's culpable state of mind."

The Court also addressed the adverse inference jury charge contained in PJI 1:77, entitled "General Instruction—Evidence—Failure to Produce Documents or Other Physical Evidence." This charge permits, but does not require, the jury to draw negative inferences from missing documents. Therefore, the Court rejected the appellate division's conclusion that delivering this charge amounted to an award of summary judgment to the plaintiff.[30] The Court also stressed that the charge was appropriate for cases in which the information has been negligently destroyed, even if intentional conduct or gross negligence was not on the scene.

It is interesting to note that *Pegasus* was handed down exactly two weeks after an important amendment to the Federal Rules of Civil Procedure relating to spoliation went into effect. A new Rule 37(e), entitled "Failure to Preserve Electronically Stored

---

[24]   Pegasus Aviation I, Inc. v. Varig Logistica S.A., 26 N.Y.3d 543, 26 N.Y.S.3d 218, 46 N.E.3d 601 (2015).

[25]   The *Pegasus* decision essentially adopted the standards set forth by the First Department in VOOM HD Holdings LLC v. EchoStar Satellite L.L.C., 93 A.D.3d 33, 939 N.Y.S.2d 321 (1st Dep't 2012), which relied extensively on the federal law staked out in Zubulake v. UBS Warburg LLC, 220 F.R.D. 212, 92 Fair Empl. Prac. Cas. (BNA) 1539 (S.D.N.Y. 2003).

[26]   *Pegasus*, 26 N.Y.3d at 547, 26 N.Y.S.3d at 219, 46 N.E.3d at 602. The decision is discussed in further detail in Commentary C3126:8A on McKinney's CPLR 3126.

[27]   Pegasus, 26 N.Y.3d at 547–48, 26 N.Y.S.3d at 219, 46 N.E.3d at 602.

[28]   For a discussion of decisions applying the standards outlined in *Pegasus*, see Commentary C3126:8A on McKinney's CPLR 3126.

[29]   In VOOM HD Holdings LLC v. EchoStar Satellite L.L.C., 93 A.D.3d 33, 939 N.Y.S.2d 321 (1st Dep't 2012) (SPR 249:3), relied upon heavily in *Pegasus*, the court concluded that where evidence has been destroyed through gross negligence, that finding is sufficient to presume that the information was relevant and warrants an adverse inference charge.

[30]   See also Mendoza v. Highpoint Associates, IX, LLC, 83 A.D.3d 1, 919 N.Y.S.2d 129 (1st Dep't 2011) (SPR 233:1) (CPLR 3126(2) preclusion order issued against defendant does not relieve the plaintiff of the burden of proving its case).

Information," became effective on December 1, 2015. The amendment was designed to address the somewhat draconian spoliation sanctions that developed in the decisional law in several federal circuits, which required litigants to expend excessive effort and money to preserve ESI to avoid the risk of severe penalties. Rule 37(e)(2) does not permit the court to use an adverse inference charge based merely on a finding of negligence, as the Court of Appeals authorized in *Pegasus*. Under the current version of Rule 37(e), the court can only impose penalties on a spoliator, including an adverse inference instruction, upon a "finding that the party acted with the intent to deprive another party of the information's use in the litigation."[31]

Resolving and preclusion orders under CPLR 3126(1) and (2) are usually feasible only when the refusal to disclose touches on just part of the case. In that instance, they can effectively shape the sanction to the failure—to make the punishment fit the crime—which is what CPLR 3126 desires. But when a party's resistance is total, or involves a matter that goes to the core of the whole case, the sanction has to go just as far and that, as noted, invokes paragraph 3 of CPLR 3126. A default against the offending party is the ultimate punishment of paragraph 3, but it provides for steps short of that.

CPLR 3126(3) permits the court to strike out parts of a party's pleading or to stay further proceedings by that party until a disclosure order is obeyed. The ultimate penalty for nondisclosure is not favored by the courts. They save it for cases of aggravated resistance where "[l]ess drastic action would only serve to encourage dilatory conduct and reward an obstructionist approach to discovery proceedings."[32]

If the resisting party is the plaintiff, a default can consist of a dismissal of the action.[33] The matter is left to the sound discretion of the court, and because the imposition of sanctions under CPLR 3126 is in almost all instances a matter or discretion, the Court of Appeals has given notice that it is unlikely to upset the exercise of discretion in the lower courts should the matter manage to climb before it.[34] It warned in Kihl v. Pfeffer,[35] for example, that it has little patience with recalcitrance in disclosure proceedings, especially common with plaintiffs, and showed that if the appellate division has seen fit in a given case to apply the ultimate sanction of dismissal under CPLR 3126(3), the dismissal is very likely to be upheld.[36]

What remedy when it is the defendant who is doing the unreasonable resisting and the misconduct has risen to the level of warranting the ultimate penalty? The court merely holds liability established through default and, if the case is one for money, sets the case down for an assessment of the plaintiff's damages.[37]

---

[31]   Fed. R. Civ. P. 37(e)(2)(B). The amendment to Rule 37(e) is discussed in further detail in § 638.

[32]   Sawh v. Bridges, 120 A.D.2d 74, 507 N.Y.S.2d 632 (2d Dep't 1986).

[33]   See Zletz v. Wetanson, 67 N.Y.2d 711, 499 N.Y.S.2d 933, 490 N.E.2d 852 (1986).

[34]   See, e.g., Arts4All, Ltd. v. Hancock, 54 A.D.3d 286, 863 N.Y.S.2d 193, 194 (1st Dep't 2008) ("[S]ubstantial deference should be accorded to the trial court's considerable discretion to compel compliance with discovery orders, and, absent clear abuse, a penalty imposed in accordance with CPLR 3126 should not readily be disturbed."), aff'd 12 N.Y.3d 846, 881 N.Y.S.2d 390, 909 N.E.2d 83 (2009).

[35]   Kihl v. Pfeffer, 94 N.Y.2d 118, 700 N.Y.S.2d 87, 722 N.E.2d 55 (1999) (NYSLD No. 480).

[36]   But see Merrill Lynch, Pierce, Fenner & Smith, Inc. v. Global Strat Inc., 22 N.Y.3d 877, 976 N.Y.S.2d 678, 999 N.E.2d 156 (2013) (Court found a clear abuse of discretion and vacated a $99 million default judgment because the penalty "was not commensurate with the alleged disobedience").

[37]   See James v. Powell, 26 A.D.2d 525, 270 N.Y.S.2d 789 (1st Dep't 1966), rev'd on other grounds 19 N.Y.2d 249, 279 N.Y.S.2d 10, 225 N.E.2d 741 (1967).

The penalties imposed under the *Pegasus* decision for failure to preserve ESI, discussed above, are akin to a resolving order under CPLR 3126(1). The *Pegasus* decision only made passing reference to CPLR 3126, but the statute would seem to authorize harsher penalties for the destruction of ESI in an appropriate case. The First Department's decision in *VOOM*, which was heavily relied upon in *Pegasus*, suggests that the sanction imposed on the defendant therein could have been a default under CPLR 3126(3), civil litigation's equivalent of the death penalty.[38] Similarly, the Court of Appeals has recognized on previous occasions that dismissal of an action may be an appropriate sanction under CPLR 3126 if evidence is spoliated.[39]

When the refusal to disclose is based on privilege, such as that against self-incrimination, the availability of a sanction may depend on who is invoking the privilege. If the defendant does, and legitimately, no sanction may be invoked because the privilege is a shield and that's the way the defendant is using it. But when the plaintiff invokes it—the very person who brought the case to court—the invocation amounts to an attempt to use the privilege as a sword. Although the plaintiff can't be precluded from using the privilege, he will face a civil sanction under CPLR 3126 if he does[40] up to and including the ultimate sanction of a dismissal or default.

CPLR 3126 is the remedy turned to when a party has not offered enough. Suppose the reverse: that a party has gotten too much. CPLR 3103, the protective order statute, will offer a cure in that situation. When a plaintiff obtained a defendant's confidential files on the sly, for example, as in Lipin v. Bender,[41] and attempted to exploit them with her attorney, CPLR 3103(c) was also deemed to authorize the ultimate sanction of a default against the plaintiff: a dismissal of the action.[42]

Since CPLR 3126 prescribes "such orders . . . as are just," the court is not restricted to the illustrative sanctions contained in the three numbered paragraphs. As already illustrated several times, the favored device today is the conditional order in which a designated sanction is invoked "unless" the party makes the requisite disclosure within a stated time. The order often contains the added condition that the resister pay to the seeking party costs to date plus an attorney's fee in a designated sum to cover the extra time and expense engendered by the unwarranted resistance. This conditional order together with the added sanction of an attorney's fee was alighted on early as an alternative to the listed sanctions of CPLR 3126,[43] which many judges find too harsh. The authority for a money sanction under CPLR 3126 exists independently of the general

---

[38]   *VOOM HD Holdings LLC*, 93 A.D.3d at 47, 939 N.Y.S.2d at 332.

[39]   MetLife Auto & Home v. Joe Basil Chevrolet, Inc., 1 N.Y.3d 478, 482–83, 775 N.Y.S.2d 754, 756, 807 N.E.2d 865, 867 (2004); *Ortega*, 9 N.Y.3d at 76, 845 N.Y.S.2d at 776, 876 N.E.2d at 1192 (noting that if a court finds that a party destroyed evidence that "ought to have been disclosed," the court has discretion to impose any of the three penalties in CPLR 3126).

[40]   See Levine v. Bornstein, 13 Misc. 2d 161, 174 N.Y.S.2d 574 (Sup. Ct., Kings County 1959), aff'd, 7 A.D.2d 995, 183 N.Y.S.2d 868 (2d Dep't), aff'd, 6 N.Y.2d 892, 190 N.Y.S.2d 702, 160 N.E.2d 921.

[41]   Lipin v. Bender, 84 N.Y.2d 562, 620 N.Y.S.2d 744, 644 N.E.2d 1300 (1994) (NYSLD No. 419).

[42]   See § 353.

[43]   See Nomako v. Ashton, 22 A.D.2d 683, 253 N.Y.S.2d 309 (1st Dep't 1964); Di Bartolo v. American & Foreign Ins. Co., 48 Misc. 2d 843, 265 N.Y.S.2d 981 (Sup. Ct., Suffolk County 1966), aff'd, 26 A.D.2d 992, 275 N.Y.S.2d 805 (2d Dep't); Commentary C3126:11 to McKinney's CPLR 3126.

sanctions provision applicable to frivolous conduct,[44] which means that the disclosure misconduct need not rise to level of "frivolous" to support a sanction under CPLR 3126.[45]

The amount of the money sanction is also, of course, in the court's discretion,[46] and if the court finds that the resistance is the fault of the attorney, it may order the attorney—including one representing a governmental unit, like a member of the attorney general's staff[47]—to pay the sum out of pocket,[48] without reimbursement at any time from the client. The court can of course impose other conditions as well. It can require, for example, that the resister file a bond to secure the seeking party in some phase of the litigation or even to make good the potential recovery on the merits.[49]

In CDR Créances S.A.S. v. Cohen,[50] the Court affirmed an order striking pleadings and imposing a default judgment as prescribed in CPLR 3126(3). This severe sanction was imposed on a finding, "by clear and convincing evidence," that defendants had engaged in conduct that constituted a fraud on the court. The Court of Appeals noted that in addition to the sanctions under CPLR 3126, "a court has inherent power to address actions which are meant to undermine the truth-seeking function of the judicial system and place in question the integrity of the courts and our system of justice."[51] While the *CDR Créances S.A.S.* Court cites to CPLR 3126 and contains a brief discussion of the statute, the relief afforded appears to lie under the distinct inherent power of the courts to impose appropriate sanctions in actions involving a fraud on the court. Therefore, we suspect that the decision will have little impact on the more common issues arising under CPLR 3126, where a party has failed to obey an order requiring disclosure.[52]

A matter of current dispute is how a conditional order that a court makes in punishing disclosure resistance, such as a dismissal of the action "unless" the recalcitrant plaintiff acts by a stated time, is to be applied. Does the penalty take effect the instant the condition is violated or must the resister first be given a chance to excuse violating the condition? The courts are not consistent about that. In Wilson v. Galicia Contracting & Restoration Corp.,[53] the Court held that a conditional order was "self-executing" and therefore, defendant's failure to produce the requested items by the date in the order rendered it "absolute." The *Wilson* decision is a stern lesson on ignoring the condition stated in a conditional order. More often than one might suspect, however, a conditional order has been issued, and the condition not carried out, only to see the court entertaining the defaulter's argument that it had an excuse for missing the condition.[54]

---

[44] 22 N.Y.C.R.R. Part 130; see § 414A.

[45] See Mazarakis v. Bronxville Glen I Ass'n, 229 A.D.2d 661, 644 N.Y.S.2d 793 (3d Dep't 1996).

[46] It was $500, for example, in Warner v. Bumgarner, 49 Misc. 2d 488, 267 N.Y.S.2d 825 (Sup. Ct., Monroe County 1966), a heavy sanction for those times.

[47] See Kulers v. State, 141 Misc. 2d 1079, 535 N.Y.S.2d 931 (Ct. Cl. 1988).

[48] See, e.g., Rabinowitz v. Bernstein, 37 A.D.2d 963, 327 N.Y.S.2d 570 (2d Dep't 1971); Cotteral v. City of New Rochelle, 33 A.D.2d 791, 307 N.Y.S.2d 568 (2d Dep't 1969).

[49] Bredin v. Buchman, 32 A.D.2d 518, 298 N.Y.S.2d 748 (1st Dep't 1969).

[50] CDR Creances S.A.S. v. Cohen, 23 N.Y.3d 307, 991 N.Y.S.2d 519, 15 N.E.3d 274 (2014).

[51] *CDR Créances S.A.S.*, 23 N.Y.3d at 318, 991 N.Y.S.2d at 527, 15 N.E.3d at 282.

[52] See Commentary C3126:12 to McKinney's CPLR 3126.

[53] Wilson v. Galicia Contracting & Restoration Corp., 10 N.Y.3d 827, 860 N.Y.S.2d 417, 890 N.E.2d 179 (2008) (NYSLD No. 585).

[54] An example is the Fourth Department decision in Lauer v. City Of Buffalo, 53 A.D.3d 213, 862 N.Y.S.2d 675 (4th Dep't 2008) (SPR 199:2).

Judicial hesitancy to deem conditional orders self-executing is manifest in Gibbs v. St. Barnabas Hospital,[55] where the Court of Appeals concluded in a 4–3 decision that the trial court erred as a matter of law in excusing the plaintiff's failure to serve a supplemental bill of particulars before the deadline set by a conditional order of preclusion "without requiring plaintiff to establish both a reasonable excuse for his noncompliance and a meritorious cause of action."[56]

In the typical case facing dismissal under CPLR 3126, a party has: (1) failed to comply with the initial disclosure demand; (2) failed to comply with the movant's good faith effort to resolve the discovery dispute;[57] (3) failed to comply with a court's order under CPLR 3124 to provide the disclosure; and (4) failed to comply with a 30-day conditional order. Should the recalcitrant party now be given another opportunity to excuse the failure to comply with the conditional order?[58]

Statute of Limitations Issues

A word should be said about the statute of limitations when CPLR 3126(3)'s death penalty is imposed on a plaintiff and the action is dismissed for resistance to disclosure. At this point, the original statute of limitations has usually expired. The dismissal is likely to qualify as one for "neglect to prosecute" under CPLR 205(a),[59] which would deny the plaintiff the additional six months that the provision might otherwise allow for a new action. If a party is moving under CPLR 3126(3) for an order dismissing the complaint based on a failure to comply with disclosure, she should also remind the judge that in addition to seeking an order of dismissal, she is requesting that the judge outline: (1) "the specific conduct constituting the neglect"; and (2) plaintiff's "general pattern of delay in proceeding with the litigation." This detail will satisfy the requirements imposed by the 2008 amendment to CPLR 205(a).[60]

---

[55]   Gibbs v. St. Barnabas Hosp., 16 N.Y.3d 74, 917 N.Y.S.2d 68, 942 N.E.2d 277 (2010).

[56]   *Gibbs*, 16 N.Y.3d at 77, 917 N.Y.S.2d at 69. 942 N.E.2d at 278. The history of *Gibbs* and the numerous problems surrounding the enforcement of conditional orders is explored in detail in Connors, *CPLR 3126 Conditional Orders Requiring Disclosure 'Can't Get No Respect'*, 73 Alb. L. Rev. 853 (2010) and in Commentary C3126:10 to McKinney's CPLR 3126.

[57]   See 22 N.Y.C.R.R. § 202.7(a), (c); § 353.

[58]   See Connors, *CPLR 3126 Conditional Orders Requiring Disclosure 'Can't Get No Respect'*, 73 Alb. L. Rev. at 874.

[59]   Andrea v. Arnone, Hedin, Casker, Kennedy and Drake, Architects and Landscape Architects, P.C., 5 N.Y.3d 514, 806 N.Y.S.2d 453, 840 N.E.2d 565 (2005).

[60]   See § 52. It is difficult to conceive of an action properly dismissed pursuant to CPLR 3126(3) that will not also provide a basis for the court to outline the new requirements in CPLR 205(a).

Chapter 14

PRETRIAL INCIDENTS

Analysis

A. **Calendar Practice**
B. **Preferences**
C. **Pretrial Conference**
D. **Laxness Dismissals**
E. **Mode of Trial**
F. **Subpoenas and Oaths**

A. CALENDAR PRACTICE

Table of Sections

§ 368.   Calendar Practice, Introductory
§ 369.   Note of Issue
§ 370.   Statement of Readiness
§ 371.   Form of Note of Issue and Statement of Readiness

§ 368. Calendar Practice, Introductory

A "calendar" is a list of cases awaiting treatment of some kind, usually a trial. There are also motion and conference calendars, for example.[1] The phrase "calendar practice" is almost always used to refer to trial calendars and it connotes to lawyers the various rules for putting a case on one of the court's trial calendars and keeping it there until its turn for trial is finally reached. The case stands in line based on its calendar position. Whatever the prevalent delay with the particular judge or court may be, it is usually measured not from the time the action is commenced, but from the moment it is placed on the calendar. There will usually be several and sometimes many different calendars used in a given court or area or by a given judge. It's entirely a matter of administration, either with each individual judge, as in the supreme and other courts that the Individual Assignment System (IAS) operates in, or centrally, as in courts that don't have the IAS.[2]

The kinds of calendars that can be maintained, and how a case can attain them, is provided for by the rules, to which the CPLR defers. CPLR 3401 in fact mandates that these matters be managed by rule. It provides that "the chief administrator of the courts shall adopt rules regulating the hearing of causes, which may include the filing of notes of issue, the preparation and publication of calendars and the calendar practice for the

---

[1]   See 22 N.Y.C.R.R. § 202.22(a) (listing various calendars).

[2]   See 22 N.Y.C.R.R. § 202.22(a), applicable in the supreme and county courts. There are uniform calendar practice rules in the Court of Claims (22 N.Y.C.R.R. §§ 206.13 et seq.), the New York City Civil Court (22 N.Y.C.R.R. §§ 208.14, 208.17 et seq.), the district courts (22 N.Y.C.R.R. §§ 212.14, 212.17 et seq.), and the city courts (22 N.Y.C.R.R. §§ 210.14, 210.17 et seq.).

courts."[3] In the rule-drafting process, the courts involved are consulted and frequently their judicial and non-judicial staffs draft or assist in the drafting in concert with the administrative judge of the district or court. Ultimate promulgation of the rules regulating the hearing of cases, however, is a matter for the chief administrator.

Illustrative calendars in the supreme court are listed in the rules, from which the court or judge may choose. They include a general calendar, onto which a case goes when all pretrial procedures (pleading, disclosure, etc.) are completed and then various follow-up calendars—reserve, ready, military,[4] etc.—each briefly defined in the rule.[5]

The heavier the caseload, the more varied the calendars. Lawyers accustom themselves quickly to the calendar divisions applicable in the courts in which they practice.

The step that puts the case on the trial calendar in a supreme court action is the filing of a paper known as a "note of issue," as will be treated in the next section. Interlocked with the note of issue is the question of the right to trial by jury because if a jury is appropriate to the particular case and the parties want it, it is either in the filing of the note of issue, or in response to its filing, that a jury is demanded.[6] Treatment of calendaring therefore makes triability by jury a topic, which in turn necessitates treatment of the other modes of trial—court or referee. Those subjects, also part of this chapter, overlap the topic of the trial itself, but only to the extent of determining who the fact-trier shall be. Proceedings at the trial proper, from the picking of the jury right through the verdict and including all the trial motions, are treated in the next chapter.

The constant companion of the note of issue is a paper known as a "certificate of readiness."[7] This is entirely a creature of court rule, and the CPLR does not expressly acknowledge its existence. The statement of readiness, indispensable in any study directed to calendar practice, is another matter taken up in this chapter.[8]

In courts in which the IAS is fully operative, a case goes to but one judge at the outset and stays with that judge throughout, including the trial.[9] In what is called a "dual track" system, however, introduced in an amendment of the applicable rule[10] in 1988, a modification was made. With "dual track," the case stays with one judge from the outset until the filing of the note of issue, at which time it can then be assigned to a different judge for the trial. Whether dual track applies in a given court or area is of course a matter of local practice as prescribed by the chief administrator and must be checked out on a local basis.

---

[3]   It requires that the calendar rules in New York City be uniform "[i]nsofar as practicable."

[4]   A "military" calendar is for cases in which one of the parties or even a witness is in military service and the action can't go forward on mere deposition evidence. The courts try to manage things to accommodate the person in service. See, e.g., Goot v. Board of Ed. of Waterford Halfmoon High School, Saratoga County, 82 A.D.2d 985, 440 N.Y.S.2d 403 (3d Dep't 1981); see also Jusino v. New York City Housing Authority, 255 A.D.2d 41, 46, 691 N.Y.S.2d 12, 17 (1st Dep't 1999) (discussing military stay under CPLR 304).

[5]   22 N.Y.C.R.R. § 202.22(a). Also listed are some pretrial calendars, including one for preliminary conferences and another for motions. 22 N.Y.C.R.R. § 202.22(a)(1), (2).

[6]   The procedure for demanding a jury trial is treated in § 378.

[7]   22 N.Y.C.R.R. § 202.21.

[8]   See § 370.

[9]   See § 77A.

[10]   22 N.Y.C.R.R. § 202.3.

§ 369. Note of Issue

A case is placed on the calendar by the filing of a "note of issue," a paper that contains basic data about the case.[1] Ultimately, these notes of issue become a primary source of the statistics published annually about the court system by the Office of Court Administration. CPLR 3402 governs note of issue practice.

The case is entered on the calendar "as of the date of the filing of the note of issue."[2] Its turn for trial is measured by that filing and not, as sometimes assumed, by the date of the action's commencement.

As far as the CPLR is concerned, the note of issue may be filed any time after issue has been joined, or after 40 days have elapsed following the completion of summons service. But it is rarely, if ever, filed that early. Court rules, which impose many additional demands before a note of issue may be filed, virtually own the note of issue today. As part and parcel of "calendar practice," control of which is delegated to the chief administrator of the courts,[3] CPLR 3402 and its time requirements defer almost entirely to the rules.

The item in the rules that postpones the filing of the note of issue to a later stage— a much later stage than CPLR 3402(a) recites—is the "certificate of readiness," often referred to as the "statement of readiness," treated in the next section. The certificate must ordinarily accompany the note of issue.

The note of issue and the certificate of readiness are prescribed, with forms, in the rules.[4] A "notice of trial," instead of a note of issue, is used in the lower courts, as provided by their court acts,[5] but the implementing rules prescribe a certificate of readiness to accompany the notice of trial.[6] A special rule governs calendar practice in medical, dental, and podiatric malpractice actions and regulates the special notice that CPLR 3406 requires at the outset of those actions.[7]

The filing of the note of issue designating that disclosure is complete adds the case at the bottom of what is usually called the "general" calendar.[8] From there, the case's travels depend largely on what calendars the particular court or judge uses, which depends in turn on the kinds and quantity of cases the court or judge has. If nothing happens to cause a case's transfer to some other calendar, it will rise in due course to the top of the general calendar. From there it will usually be transferred to yet another list (every calendar is just a list) still closer to trial, but perhaps not quite there. Each transfer is ordinarily from the top of one calendar to the bottom of the next. The closer the particular calendar is to the actual trial calendar, sometimes called the "ready

---

[1]   See the form of note of issue contained in § 371.

[2]   CPLR 3402(a).

[3]   CPLR 3401.

[4]   See 22 N.Y.C.R.R. § 202.21(b). The rule requires that a note of issue be used in special proceedings as well as in actions. See 22 N.Y.C.R.R. § 202.21(a). Its appearance in a special proceeding is rare, however, contemplated only when the proceeding poses an issue of fact that needs a plenary trial, not a frequent occurrence. See § 556. Note of issue practice in the Court of Claims is governed by 22 N.Y.C.R.R. § 206.12.

[5]   See § 1301 in the New York City Civ. Ct. Act and in the Uniform District and City Court Acts (McKinney's Vol. 29A, Part 3).

[6]   The applicable rules are 22 N.Y.C.R.R. §§ 208.17 in the New York City Civil Court, 212.17 in the district courts, and 210.17 in the city courts.

[7]   See 22 N.Y.C.R.R. § 202.56; see § 77.

[8]   See 22 N.Y.C.R.R. § 202.22(3), applicable in the supreme and county courts.

calendar,"[9] the readier must the attorneys and their witnesses be, including expert witnesses, whose time is expensive.

In courts that don't use the Individual Assignment System (IAS), there may be a "calendar part," under that or some other name, whose assigned judge has the job of parceling cases out to "trial parts" and who has to keep cases moving to assure that no judge will be idle for lack of ready cases. It's a frequent source of friction between bench and trial bar. Busy trial lawyers with commitments in many courts ("previous engagement," as the jargon has it), each of which has its own calendar obligations and may require readiness for trial on short notice, find themselves in choppy straits when two courts are suddenly ready for their cases at the same time and neither court is too enthusiastic about deferring to the other. Occasionally a judge, idled for a day by the failure of counsel to appear for a trial, will invoke a money sanction against the offender, payable to the other side or perhaps even to the clerk for payment into the public treasury.[10]

In IAS courts, including of course the supreme court, the friction may be greater still as pressure for priority in the lawyers' time comes from individual judges. A special rule was enacted, as part of the uniform rules, addressed to "Engagement of Counsel." It prescribes which cases shall have priority of a given lawyer's time, when adjournments will be granted, and when, without adjournment, substitute counsel will be required.[11]

CPLR 3402(a) allows any party to file the note of issue. Two copies must be filed with proof of service, and the filing must take place within 10 days after the note of issue is served on the other parties. As may be guessed, it is usually the plaintiff who serves and files the note of issue. The plaintiff, after all, is the one who wants the case to go forward. But the defendant may do it in the alternative.

The filing requires payment of a fee,[12] but the fee qualifies as a disbursement which the merits winner, if she paid it, may recover from the loser.[13]

If the case is triable by jury and the party filing the note of issue wants a jury, it is demanded in the note of issue. If any other party wants the jury and the note of issue does not ask for one, that party must serve and file a demand for a trial by jury within 15 days after service of the note of issue.[14]

Preferences are a topic treated later,[15] but we should note here that if a preference is sought by the party filing the note of issue, that party must ordinarily make a motion

---

[9]   22 N.Y.C.R.R. § 202.22(6).

[10]   The occasion for doing this is usually a motion to restore after the case has been stricken from the calendar for the nonappearance of counsel. See Hood v. City of New York, 4 Misc. 3d 627, 632, 781 N.Y.S.2d 431, 435 (Sup. Ct., Bronx County 2004); Campbell v. Regency Towers, Inc., 76 Misc. 2d 33, 349 N.Y.S.2d 928 (Sup. Ct., New York County 1973).

[11]   22 N.Y.C.R.R. § 125.1. See, e.g. Warner v. Orange County Regional Medical Center, 126 A.D.3d 887, 888, 6 N.Y.S.3d 83, 85 (2d Dep't 2015) ("court's dismissal of the complaint pursuant to 22 NYCRR 125.1(f) also was an improvident exercise of discretion"); Garcia v. Riverbay Corp., 112 A.D.3d 542, 543, 976 N.Y.S.2d 877 (1st Dep't 2013) (denying motion to vacate default where "counsel made only conclusory assertions of having been engaged in another trial, without any support and without naming the time and dates of such engagement, the court, the judge or any other details").

[12]   CPLR 8020.

[13]   CPLR 8301(a).

[14]   CPLR 4102(a). Jury demands are elaborated in § 378.

[15]   See §§ 372 and 373.

for it and serve it with the note of issue.[16] If some other party desires a preference, she must move for it within 10 days after service of the note of issue.[17] In an IAS court, the motion is made to the IAS judge, or, if the court or district uses the "dual track" feature of the IAS,[18] to whichever judge or part the rules direct. If the court doesn't use the IAS, the motion for a preference may have to be directed to a special part of the court, again as the rules may prescribe.[19]

The filing of the note of issue must of course be made in the county in which venue is laid. A filing in any other county is a nullity,[20] which means that the case will not secure a calendar position. The same will probably be the case if, under the IAS, the note of issue is filed with the name of someone other than the assigned judge, who is not likely to accord it an enthusiastic welcome.

If a new party should be added after a note of issue has been filed, the party bringing in the new party must serve the new one with a copy of the note of issue within five days and must file with the clerk a statement advising of the addition of the new party and any change made to the caption, accompanied by an affidavit of service of the note of issue on the new party, and the statement on all parties who have appeared.[21] Because under the rules a note of issue is ordinarily not ripe for filing until the case is ready for trial, joinder of an additional party after the filing of the note is relatively rare. But it is possible and, if it takes place, overlooking this note of issue requirement can have repercussions.[22]

§ 370. Statement of Readiness

The "certificate of readiness," sometimes called the "statement of readiness," is a creature of the Uniform Rules rather than of the CPLR. It's the almost constant companion of the note of issue today. It attests that the case is essentially ready for trial because pretrial procedures have been completed, or that opportunity for them has come and gone, and there has been compliance with any preliminary conference order that may have been issued in the case.[1]

Since the rules are the home of the certificate of readiness, a number of rules and rule subdivisions will be cited in the footnotes in this section. The reader is advised, however, that rule changes can come down suddenly. In making changes, rulemakers are prone to renumber rules and especially subdivisions within rules freely, undermining whatever foothold the prior numbers or letters may have attained in the attention of the profession and even in reported cases that are a permanent part of the library. They don't see this as a moral issue, as authors and dedicated followers of New York practice do! The reader should bear this in mind, always double-checking to make sure a rule or subdivision's number has not been altered, along with a dozen others, to make way for

---

[16] CPLR 3403(b).

[17] CPLR 3403(b).

[18] See § 368.

[19] See Vinal v. New York Cent. R. Co., 48 Misc. 2d 362, 264 N.Y.S.2d 824 (Sup. Ct., Albany County 1965).

[20] Holihan v. Regina Corp., 54 Misc. 2d 264, 282 N.Y.S.2d 404 (Sup. Ct., Onondaga County 1967).

[21] CPLR 3402(b).

[22] See Kaufman v. Clearview Gardens Federal Credit Union, 71 Misc. 2d 945, 337 N.Y.S.2d 323 (N.Y. City Civ. Ct. 1972), involving the "notice of trial," the lower courts' equivalent of the note of issue.

[1] The preliminary conference is discussed in § 77D.

some small item stuck in between. It's no way to run a railroad, but it's often a fact of life for those who practice law.

The general rule is that the certificate must be served with the note of issue,[2] but there are some exceptions. When a pretrial proceeding can't be completed because of forces beyond the party's control, for example, the party can move the court for leave to file the note of issue without the certificate of readiness, with the court to make provision for its filing later.[3] As noted above, medical, dental, and podiatric malpractice actions have a special governing rule.[4] While the certificate of readiness, just like the note of issue, must be filed in special proceedings as well as in actions, neither is required for an application to settle the claim of an infant, incompetent, or conservatee.[5]

An official form for the certificate of readiness, manifesting the certificate's diverse requirements in a checklist of items, is included in the rule.[6] We concentrate here on the application of the certificate of readiness rule in the supreme and county courts. Other courts have their own rules.[7]

Occasional attacks were made on the certificate of readiness rule, contending that— because it requires total preparation before the note of issue can be filed—it nullifies the permission of CPLR 3402(a) to file the note of issue any time after issue is joined. These attacks were rejected, citing the express authorization that CPLR 3401 gives the chief administrator (previously it was the appellate division) to make calendar rules.[8]

The major item the courts want concluded and at rest when the case goes on the calendar is pretrial disclosure. The experience before the certificate of readiness was first adopted in the 1950s was that too much attention and effort was spent on motions for disclosure made after the case was on the calendar, engendering numerous adjournments and unnecessary delay as judicial time was spent on actions that were not ready for trial. No matter how needful the disclosure, the courts' general attitude today is that it should be complete before the case is allowed to go on the calendar under the pretext that the case is ready. All parties are held to represent that the case is ready when the certificate is filed without challenge.[9]

The disparity in the application of the rules governing the timing of disclosure, which are central to the orderly resolution of litigation, presents a nightmare for lawyers. Unfortunately, some judges have a reputation for requiring that the note of issue and certificate of readiness be filed by a date certain regardless of whether disclosure is complete. This practice wreaks havoc by distorting the procedural rules that are built around a system in which several key events are triggered by the filing of the note of issue, including the deadline for moving for summary judgment.[10] Appellate courts and

---

    [2]   See 22 N.Y.C.R.R. § 202.21(a).

    [3]   22 N.Y.C.R.R. § 202.21(d).

    [4]   22 N.Y.C.R.R. § 202.56.

    [5]   22 N.Y.C.R.R. § 202.21(a).

    [6]   22 N.Y.C.R.R. § 202.21(b). The form is set forth in § 371.

    [7]   In the Court of Claims, 22 N.Y.C.R.R. § 206.12 applies. The applicable rules in the lower courts are 22 N.Y.C.R.R. § 208.17 in the New York City Civil Court, 22 N.Y.C.R.R. § 212.17 in the district courts, and 22 N.Y.C.R.R. § 210.17 in the city courts.

    [8]   See, e.g., Bedingfield v. Dairymaid Farms, Inc., 46 Misc. 2d 146, 259 N.Y.S.2d 292 (Sup. Ct., Suffolk County 1965).

    [9]   See Jacobs v. Peress, 23 A.D.2d 483, 255 N.Y.S.2d 492 (1st Dep't 1965).

    [10]   CPLR 3212(a); see § 279.

court administrators should quickly put a halt to the practice if it is brought to their attention.

When the position of some other party is that the certificate of readiness has been prematurely filed, whether for lack of opportunity to complete disclosure proceedings or for any other reason, the remedy of that party is to move to vacate the note of issue. The party has 20 days in which to do that, measured from the service of the note of issue and certificate of readiness.[11] If, on a timely motion to vacate, the movant can show that disclosure proceedings have not yet had their fair run, the motion will be granted.[12] In addition, the court "may vacate the note of issue if it appears that a material fact in the certificate of readiness is incorrect" or if the certificate otherwise fails to comply with the requirements of the rule.[13]

If the note of issue has been vacated and the case stricken from the calendar, it can be reinstated on motion, with affidavit proof that the action is meritorious and all is now ready.[14]

In the absence of a motion to vacate, further disclosure will be deemed waived unless the party can demonstrate that "unusual or unanticipated circumstances" have developed subsequent to the filing of the note of issue and that "substantial prejudice" will result if disclosure is not permitted.[15] This has to be shown by a motion supported by affidavit. If, without such a court application, a party serves a mere disclosure notice after the note and certificate have been filed, the other side's remedy is to move to vacate the disclosure notice.[16]

The courts are not generous about finding these special requirements met, lest an attitude of judicial laxness undermine the purpose of the certificate of readiness rule.[17] The Court of Appeals has observed that "it bears emphasizing that the filing of a note of issue denotes the completion of discovery, not the occasion to launch another phase of it."[18] Post-filing disclosure thus requires something unusual or unanticipated, coupled with substantial prejudice if the disclosure is not permitted. Where the plaintiff, for example, content in a relatively small case to await the trial to develop his proof, files the note of issue and is afterwards met with the defendant's summary judgment motion, a showing that the plaintiff needs disclosure from the defendant in order to respond to the motion has been held to be a circumstance justifying post-filing disclosure.[19] A plaintiff filing the note of issue should not, however, rely on such generosity and must

---

[11]   22 N.Y.C.R.R. § 202.21(e).

[12]   See Jacobs v. Johnston, 97 A.D.3d 538, 948 N.Y.S.2d 321, 322 (2d Dep't 2012); Falk v. Kalt, 44 Misc. 2d 172, 253 N.Y.S.2d 188 (Sup. Ct., Suffolk County 1964).

[13]   22 N.Y.C.R.R. § 202.21(e); see Greco v. Wellington Leasing Ltd. Partnership, 144 A.D.3d 981, 43 N.Y.S.3d 64 (2d Dep't 2016); Commentary C3102:3 on McKinney's CPLR 3102 (discussing several Appellate Division decisions applying 22 N.Y.C.R.R. § 202.21(e) to strike the note of issue).

[14]   22 N.Y.C.R.R. § 202.21(f); see Tejeda v. Dyal, 125 A.D.3d 578, 1 N.Y.S.3d 818 (1st Dep't 2015).

[15]   22 N.Y.C.R.R. § 202.21(e); see § 352 (Item 7); Tirado v. Miller, 75 A.D.3d 153, 901 N.Y.S.2d 358 (2d Dep't 2010).

[16]   Audiovox Corp. v. Benyamini, 265 A.D.2d 135, 136, 707 N.Y.S.2d 137, 138 (2d Dep't 2000) (motion under CPLR 3103); Price v. Brody, 7 A.D.2d 204, 181 N.Y.S.2d 661 (1st Dep't 1959).

[17]   See Sapichino v. City of New York, 20 Misc. 3d 1142(A), 875 N.Y.S.2d 823 (Sup. Ct., Kings County 2008) (court noted it was unaware of any "Brooklyn rule" exception to the general time frames governing disclosure, and concluded that plaintiff waived right to disclosure after it filed note of issue and certificate of readiness).

[18]   Arons v. Jutkowitz, 9 N.Y.3d 393, 411, 850 N.Y.S.2d 345, 353, 880 N.E.2d 831 (2007).

[19]   Connell v. City of New York, 102 Misc. 2d 585, 424 N.Y.S.2d 81 (N.Y. City Civ. Ct. 1979).

assume that the filing of the note of issue and certificate of readiness waives any further pretrial proceedings.[20]

Unexpected complications after the filing of the note of issue can also do the job, such as where cases have been consolidated and it appears that disclosure has not been completed in all the actions.[21] While that can happen, it is not always the case, and some courts will deny the disclosure in similar circumstances.[22] The practitioner's attention is better directed, in all such contexts, to a prompt motion to vacate a note of issue alleged to be premature. It is more likely to preserve the right to further disclosure than a post-certificate effort to obtain it, which will more likely than not be rejected.

A plaintiff filing the certificate of readiness must fulfill its terms, including that disclosure proceedings in the case are complete. In Sapichino v. City of New York,[23] P included in the certificate what the court described as a "self designed" form in which P said that still outstanding was D's obligation to make a "discovery and inspection response." The court held that this attempt to preserve post note of issue disclosure was impermissible.

The case offers a judicial reaction to a rumor occasionally heard from lawyers in some counties: there's local practice that allows the filing of the note of issue with disclosure permitted to follow afterwards, despite the completion of disclosure that should be attested to in the accompanying certificate of readiness. P in the *Sapichino* case, apparently with that in mind, cited what the court described as "some unspecified Brooklyn rule . . . [i]n effect stating, this is how we do it in Brooklyn." The judge said he was "unaware of any 'Brooklyn' exception to the Uniform Court Rules."[24]

An attempt to get on the calendar speedily by attesting in a certificate of readiness that disclosure proceedings were either completed or not desired, and then trying to resort to the Freedom of Information Law (FOIL) to obtain further disclosure, was held impermissible in John T. Brady & Co. v. City of New York.[25]

§ 371. Form of Note of Issue and Statement of Readiness

Rule 202.21 of the Uniform Rules, applicable in the supreme and county courts, has official forms for both the note of issue and the certificate of readiness. These are set forth below, but lawyers should check to ascertain if these forms have been revised.

---

[20]   Capri Beachwear, Inc. v. AAA Stretch, Inc., 49 A.D.2d 831, 374 N.Y.S.2d 2 (1st Dep't 1975).

[21]   See Wahrhaftig v. Space Design Group, Inc., 33 A.D.2d 953, 306 N.Y.S.2d 863 (3d Dep't 1970).

[22]   See Hope v. Fortunato, 20 Misc. 3d 1117(A), 867 N.Y.S.2d 17 (Sup. Ct., Kings County 2008) ("a note of issue is effective against a new party that is brought in the case"); § 128.

[23]   *Sapichino*, 20 Misc. 3d at 1142(A), 875 N.Y.S.2d at 823.

[24]   See Gomez v. New York City Transit Authority, 19 A.D.3d 366, 795 N.Y.S.2d 909 (2d Dep't 2005).

[25]   John T. Brady & Co. v. City of New York, 84 A.D.2d 113, 445 N.Y.S.2d 724 (1st Dep't 1982). Anything the *Brady* case suggests about the FOIL not being available to litigants as an alternative to CPLR disclosure is overruled by the *M. Farbman* case discussed in § 348, but *Brady's* point about a party not being entitled to file a certificate of readiness if FOIL disclosure is in fact being pursued for litigation purposes is not necessarily overturned by *Farbman*.

(a)   Form of note of issue.

NOTE OF ISSUE

Calendar No. (if any) . . . .   For use of clerk
Index No. . . . .
. . . . Court, ... County
Name of assigned judge . . . .

Notice for trial

           Trial by jury demanded . . . .
            . . . of all issues
            . . . of issues specified below
            . . . or attached hereto
       Trial without jury . . .
       Filed by attorney for . . . .
       Date summons served . . . .
       Date service completed . . . .
       Date issue joined . . . .
         Nature of action or
         special proceeding
       Tort:
         Motor vehicle negligence . . . . . .
         Medical malpractice   . . . . . .
         Other tort   . . . . . .
       Contract   . . . . . .
       Contested matrimonial   . . . . . .
       Uncontested matrimonial . . . . . .

Special preference   Tax certiorari   . . . . . .
claimed under . . . . Condemnation   . . . . . .
. . . . Other (not itemized
on the ground that . . . . above)   . . . . . .
. . . .   (specify) . . . .

Attorney(s) for Plaintiff(s)   Indicate if this action is   . . . . . .
Office and P.O. Address: brought as a class action
Phone No.

Attorney(s) for Defendant(s)
Office and P.O. Address:
Phone No.

       Amount demanded $ . . . .
        Other relief . . . .
       Insurance carrier(s), if known:
    NOTE: The clerk will not accept this note of issue unless
        accompanied by a certificate of readiness.

The above is the body of the note of issue; the usual caption and other trappings are omitted. Observe that the note of issue is required to recite, among other things, whether a preference is claimed for the case. Preferences are the subject of the following sections.

(b) Form of certificate readiness.

CERTIFICATE OF READINESS FOR TRIAL (Items 1-7 must be checked)

		Complete	Waived	Not Required
1.	All pleadings served	. . . .	. . . .	. . . .
2.	Bill of particulars served	. . . .	. . . .	. . . .
3.	Physical examinations completed	. . . .	. . . .	. . . .
4.	Medical reports exchanged	. . . .	. . . .	. . . .
5.	Appraisal reports exchanged	. . . .	. . . .	. . . .
6.	Compliance with section 202.16 of the Rules of the Chief Administrator (22 N.Y.C.R.R. § 202.16) in matrimonial actions	. . . .	. . . .	. . . .
7.	Discovery proceedings now known to be necessary completed	. . . .	. . . .	. . . .
8.	There are no outstanding requests for discovery			
9.	There has been a reasonable opportunity to complete the foregoing proceedings			
10.	There has been compliance with any order issued pursuant to section 202.12 of the Rules of the Chief Administrator (22 N.Y.C.R.R. § 202.12)			
11.	If a medical malpractice action, there has been compliance with any order issued pursuant to section 202.56 of the Rules of the Chief Administrator (22 N.Y.C.R.R. § 202.56)			
12.	The case is ready for trial			

Dated: _____

(Signature) _____

Attorney(s) for: _____

Office and P.O. address: _____

_____

B. PREFERENCES

Table of Sections

§ 372.   The "General" Preference

§ 373.   The "Special" Preference

§ 372. The "General" Preference

A preference, as the name implies, is an order giving a case a "preferred" position on the calendar. One must be careful in New York practice to distinguish between two kinds of preferences, however. One is commonly known as a "general" preference, entirely a product of court rules. The other, which the bar has come to call a "special" preference, is supplied by CPLR 3403 and is a real preference in every sense.

The general preference is not a preference to the case that gets it, but more of a punishment to the case that doesn't. In proper sequence, the general preference should be treated first because a case required to qualify for a general preference and failing to is not likely to be allowed a special preference.[1] The special preference will be treated in the next section.

The general preference is a device for administering the calendars of the supreme court. It aims primarily at the unintentional torts, such as the ubiquitous personal injury and wrongful death actions,[2] which are so substantial a part of judicial calendars today. The function of the general preference is to keep out of the supreme court cases in which the injuries and damages are not permanent or protracted and which, in the court's view, should therefore have been brought for a smaller sum and in a lower court. If the complaint in such a case asks a sum beyond the monetary jurisdiction of the lower court, the plaintiff thereby insisting on remaining in the supreme court, the case will be denied a "general" preference.[3] The impact of the denial is that the case will go onto the calendar at the bottom and stay there; it will not, as will cases that do get the general preference, move up and get tried in due course. Attorneys sometimes facetiously call this the "oblivion" calendar.

In New York City, where the civil court is the one to which a case goes if transferred down by the supreme court, the $25,000 monetary jurisdiction maximum is the one the supreme court is presumably looking at when it determines whether to grant the case a general preference. The court or judge makes this determination in some pretrial context, perhaps a preliminary conference.[4] It's based on the pleadings and bill of particulars and on the medical information accumulated in the case, such as reports of physical examinations and hospital records. It's not the occasion for trying the case. The judge's obligation is only to ascertain whether the aggregate of the written medical

---

[1] See Rab v. Colon, 37 A.D.2d 813, 324 N.Y.S.2d 809 (1st Dep't 1971).

[2] See, e.g., Di Gilio v. William J. Burns Intern. Detective Agency, 46 A.D.2d 650, 359 N.Y.S.2d 688 (2d Dep't 1974).

[3] For an extensive discussion of the general preference rules and their purpose, see Weber v. Kowalski, 85 Misc. 2d 349, 376 N.Y.S.2d 996 (Sup. Ct., Dutchess County 1975). The *Weber* case was overruled in Mandel v. Kent, 70 A.D.2d 903, 417 N.Y.S.2d 306 (2d Dep't 1979), but not in respect of preferences, on which subject it remains an instructive discourse. The rules involved have now been superseded by the Uniform Rules.

[4] See 22 N.Y.C.R.R. § 202.12.

evidence could, if presented to a jury in testimonial form, support a verdict for more than $25,000. A mere prima facie showing of such a possibility warrants the preference.[5]

The monetary aspect is the crux of general preference practice, but it's recognized that sometimes even cases falling short of the money threshold may for other good reason justify supreme court jurisdiction and hence a general preference. If, for example, territorial restrictions applicable to the lower court, but not to the supreme court, would have made the defendant unreachable with the lower court's summons, the case is right for the supreme court and gets the preference even though the damages sought are less than $25,000.[6] Acknowledging that these rules are designed to promote judicial economy, it has been held that in a multi-plaintiff case the preference should ordinarily be awarded the whole case if any plaintiff qualifies for it individually.[7]

A denial of a general preference can as a practical matter keep a supreme court case in limbo indefinitely, if not forever. This prompted a constitutional attack, but it failed: the general preference was held to be a reasonable calendar measure and the principle to be one of "ancient and undisputed law that courts have an inherent power over the control of their calendars, and the disposition of business before them, including the order in which disposition will be made of that business."[8] The remedy for a plaintiff aggrieved by the denial of a general preference is either to appeal the order of denial or else consent to reduce the monetary demand to bring it within the lower court's jurisdiction and permit the case to be transferred down. This topic was treated earlier when CPLR 325(c) was discussed.[9]

It is CPLR 325(c) that authorizes a plaintiff to reduce the demand and consent to have the case transferred to a lower court. The judge who feels that a case's potential monetary worth doesn't require the jurisdiction of the supreme court, and who threatens to deny it a general preference for that reason, is actually doing a little arm-twisting to get the plaintiff to reduce the demand and consent to have the case transferred down under CPLR 325(c). That provision is therefore largely regarded as an adjunct of the general preference device. The 1968 enactment of subdivision (d), however, and the rules adopted pursuant to it, have dramatically reduced dependence on subdivision (c) and, indeed, on the whole system of "general" preferences.

Under the rules that implement CPLR 325(d), a transfer down does not have to be accompanied by a reduced demand to meet the lower court's jurisdiction. As discussed earlier,[10] the usual monetary limits of the lower court disappear in a case transferred down under CPLR 325(d).[11] This enables the plaintiff to retain and have determined in the transferee lower court whatever sum the complaint originally demanded. A CPLR 325(d) transfer down therefore requires no consent from the plaintiff. The problem for which the general preference was devised as a cure—to devote supreme court trial energies to those cases that have only the supreme court to call on—is now usually met

---

[5]   Freedman v. Black, 23 A.D.2d 770, 258 N.Y.S.2d 563 (2d Dep't 1965).

[6]   See Chiques v. Sanso, 72 Misc. 2d 376, 339 N.Y.S.2d 394 (Sup. Ct., Westchester County 1972).

[7]   Martin v. Suarez, 30 A.D.2d 947, 293 N.Y.S.2d 950 (1st Dep't 1968).

[8]   Plachte v. Bancroft Inc., 3 A.D.2d 437, 438, 161 N.Y.S.2d 892, 893 (1st Dep't 1957). The case traces in depth the origin of the general preference rule.

[9]   See § 26.

[10] See § 27.

[11] CPLR 325(d) is an invoking of N.Y. Const. art. VI, § 19, subd. (k)—the ultimate authority for dispensing with the ordinary monetary limitation of a lower court.

with an obligatory CPLR 325(d) transfer down instead of the denial of a general preference.

If CPLR 325(d) or its implementing rules should be repealed with respect to any particular district or county, general preference practice of the kind we have been discoursing on in this section can again become, in that locale, the only way to discourage the bringing of unworthy cases in the supreme court.

While the general preference is a serious, but not fatal, casualty of the era of CPLR 325(d) and its implementing rules, the special preference remains alive and vigorous. It's the next subject.

§ 373. The "Special" Preference

The "general" preference treated in the prior section is just a filter to keep small cases out of the supreme court. The preference set forth in CPLR 3403(a) is the real preference. Its purpose is to single out cases that for some pressing reason deserve to be tried earlier than their calendar position would ordinarily allow. It is popularly called a "special" or "statutory" preference, although CPLR 3403(a) doesn't call it by either name. The bar adopted the general/special dichotomy as a shorthand way of distinguishing between the two kinds. The general preference is presently in a state of eclipse, but the eclipse is not necessarily total and permanent, as we point out in the prior section. To the extent that it still hangs around, homeless as far as the rules are concerned, but capable of materializing out of the shadows in some places, it has to be acknowledged. Also requiring acknowledgment, then, is the proposition, announced when both preferences were an active part of the scene,[1] that a case not qualifying for a general preference is ordinarily in no position to ask for a special one.[2]

The CPLR 3403(a) preference is addressed and expanded on in the Uniform Rules, which continue to refer to it as a "special" preference.[3]

CPLR 3403(a) provides that "civil cases shall be tried in the order in which notes of issue have been filed, but the following shall be entitled to a preference:

1. an action brought by or against the state, or a political subdivision of the state, or an officer or board of officers of the state or a political subdivision of the state, in his or its official capacity, on the application of the state, the political subdivision, or the officer or board of officers;

2. an action where a preference is provided for by statute;

3. an action in which the interests or justice will be served by an early trial;

4. in any action upon the application of a party who has reached the age of seventy years;

---

[1]   For example, the rule that implements CPLR 325(d) by allowing the mandatory transfer down—22 N.Y.C.R.R. § 202.13—for a time excluded the 9th District, which consists of Westchester, Putnam, Dutchess, Rockland, and Orange counties. When that was so, the denial of a general preference was the only method of pressuring plaintiffs with inadequate cases in those counties to transfer them down to a lower court.

[2]   See Rab v. Colon, 37 A.D.2d 813, 324 N.Y.S.2d 809 (1st Dep't 1971).

[3]   See 22 N.Y.C.R.R. §§ 202.24 and 202.25, applicable in the supreme and county courts. There are uniform rules on the special preference in the New York City Civil Court (22 N.Y.C.R.R. §§ 208.20, 208.21), the district courts (22 N.Y.C.R.R. §§ 212.20, 212.21), and the city courts (22 N.Y.C.R.R. §§ 210.20, 210.21).

5. an action to recover damages for medical, dental or podiatric malpractice; [and]

6. an action to recover damages for personal injuries where the plaintiff is terminally ill and alleges that such terminal illness is a result of the conduct, culpability or negligence of the defendant."

Several of these paragraphs require some individual observations.

The preference in CPLR 3403(a)(1) must be sought by the state, the political subdivision, or the officer or board of officers of such entity. It is not available to just any party merely because a governmental creature is a party to the action.

One example of a statutorily preferred action under paragraph 2 is perhaps the most preferred action of all: the election dispute,[4] in which the whole electorate has an interest. Even the Court of Appeals arranges special and expedited calendars for election cases during the pre-voting season, usually in late summer and in autumn. An election law proceeding can be commenced in supreme court and proceed through review by the appellate division and the Court of Appeals all in the month of August.

Local practice, with or without impetus from a rule, may also develop preferences— in effect special ones—in certain situations, as for a case back for a new trial after an appeal.[5]

The preferences authorized by paragraphs 4, 5, and 6 of CPLR 3403(a) were added after the CPLR's original enactment. Paragraph 4 presently recognizes age 70 as an age at which any party should be entitled to a preference. The applicant is usually the plaintiff reaching that age, of course, but a defendant attaining it may also, under the provision's language, move for the preference. The preference is available only at the request of the party attaining that age, not some other party. Hence a plaintiff under 70 was not allowed a preference based on the defendant's having passed that age.[6]

When a party with only a derivative cause of action reaches 70, however, such as a husband with a loss of consortium claim based on his wife's injury, it has been held that a preference can be granted to the whole case even though the main claimant, in this example the wife on the personal injury claim, is under 70.[7] The preference would still need to be sought by the party who reached 70.

The paragraph 5 preference for the medical malpractice case, expanded to include dentistry and podiatry, was part of a package of 1975 legislation, affecting many statutes, designed to avert a strike by doctors stung by their burgeoning malpractice insurance premiums.[8]

The preference for terminal illness under paragraph 6 applies only when it is the plaintiff who is suffering the illness, and only when the illness is alleged to be a by-

---

[4]   See Elec. Law § 16–116, which gives the election proceeding "preference over all other causes in all courts." 22 N.Y.C.R.R. § 202.64 follows through on this with the same instruction.

[5]   See Bierzynsky v. New York Cent. R. Co., 59 Misc. 2d 315, 298 N.Y.S.2d 584 (Sup. Ct., Erie County 1969).

[6]   Libow v. Brill, 127 Misc. 2d 661, 486 N.Y.S.2d 648 (Sup. Ct., Nassau County 1985); see also Egon J. Salmon, Inc. v. Tamarin, 14 Misc. 3d 338, 340, 829 N.Y.S.2d 832, 834 (N.Y. City Civ. Ct. 2006).

[7]   Bobowski v. Toomey, 108 Misc. 2d 1061, 439 N.Y.S.2d 239 (Sup. Ct., Albany County 1981).

[8]   See L.1975, ch. 109, § 8, and the governor's accompanying message. McKinney's N.Y. Session Laws p.1739 (1975). An insurance law provision that was part of the same package contains a definition of medical malpractice that may prove helpful under paragraph 5. See Ins. Law § 5501(b).

product of the wrong for which the suit is being brought. CPLR 3403(a)(6) is silent on who can seek this preference and arguably it is not limited to the terminally ill plaintiff.

It has been held that preferences may not be "stacked." When the plaintiff qualified for two preferences, for example, the one for medical malpractice actions under paragraph 5 and the other for a plaintiff who has reached 70 under paragraph 4, the award of the first was held to preclude the second. The court said that orderly calendaring would be "virtually impossible if multiple preferences were permitted."[9]

Unique situations can arise in this realm that justify the award of a preference. It is paragraph 3 that enables the court to take them into consideration. Paragraph 3 authorizes a preference when the "interests of justice" will be served by it. This enables a variety of situations to be recognized as deserving a special preference. A plaintiff's terminal illness not arising out of the conduct sued on, for example, which is governed by CPLR 3403(a)(6), can be taken into consideration on a sui generis application under paragraph 3.

Although the paragraph 3 preference may be sought in any kind of case, it is again the personal injury action that supplies much of the caselaw. It has been held that the preference should not be granted in personal injury cases unless there is a persuasive showing of destitution or probability of death before trial[10] When the subject is the special preference, however, one can't confidently appropriate the holdings of one court or department for automatic use in another. Despite the fact that CPLR 3403(a)(3) purportedly governs uniformly across the state, there is room, in determining what will satisfy the "interests of justice," for each department to take cognizance of its own calendar conditions, and they do. Rules and practices in one department or part of it may be unwarranted in another department or part of it. The courts candidly acknowledge this.[11] Much discretion is involved, and discretionary matters because they primarily constitute issues of fact rather than of law—unless an "abuse" of discretion is involved—are not reviewed by the Court of Appeals.[12] As a practical matter, then, this leaves each department as the ultimate judge of what will be recognized locally as sufficient for a special preference. In one place, for example, the fact that the plaintiff is destitute enough to be receiving public assistance may earn an automatic preference,[13] while elsewhere it may not be decisive at all.[14]

Destitution is always an important factor, of course, and there need be no showing that the wrong sued on caused the indigency,[15] although causation is a factor that the court may consider.[16] If local calendar conditions are tight and the attitude towards special preferences consequently sparing, some courts have even been known to take into consideration in support of denying the preference the defendant's willingness to pay the plaintiff's past and continuing medical and living expenses while the action is pending.

---

[9]   Green v. Vogel, 144 A.D.2d 66, 537 N.Y.S.2d 180 (2d Dep't 1989).

[10]   See Rothschild v. Carolina Coach Co., 23 A.D.2d 729, 258 N.Y.S.2d 49 (1st Dep't 1965).

[11]   See, e.g., Smith v. Schnabel, 34 A.D.2d 603, 308 N.Y.S.2d 502 (3d Dep't 1970).

[12]   CPLR 5501(b).

[13]   See, e.g., Harvin v. Chiusano, 52 Misc. 2d 836, 276 N.Y.S.2d 701 (Sup. Ct., Kings County 1967).

[14]   See, e.g., Smith v. Schnabel, 34 A.D.2d 603, 308 N.Y.S.2d 502 (3d Dep't 1970).

[15]   Matheson v. Joy-Kar Taxi, Inc., 32 A.D.2d 544, 299 N.Y.S.2d 660 (2d Dep't 1969).

[16]   Beltran v. Borstein, 32 A.D.2d 954, 303 N.Y.S.2d 9 (2d Dep't 1969).

The First Department considered those factors in Martinkovic v. Chrysler Leasing Corp.[17]

The traditional attitude about the special preference was stated in Dodumoff v. Lyons,[18] which held that a special preference "emphatically . . . is never to be lightly granted, for the granting of a preference represents a favoring of one case over the many other cases awaiting trial on a calendar heavy with accident injury cases." As a general rule, that statement could have validity statewide, but the rigor of its application depends on local conditions. The perennial difficulty when the calendars are heavy is that whatever standards are set for the sui generis inquiry necessitated by CPLR 3403(a)(3), there are invariably a large number of cases that can meet them.

A sensitive treatment of the factors that the court would consider in an ideal legal world is in Tintner v. Marangi,[19] where an elderly couple avoided imposing on public assistance by sharing a small bedroom with their grandchildren in their son's home. The court stressed the deprivations the couple faced, psychological as well as physical, and held that if the tort recovery they were seeking would restore the plaintiffs to living circumstances of dignity, independence, and self-respect, they merited the special preference. The opinion noted that the courts should not "be required to indulge in a near-morbid exercise of anticipating whether litigant or calendar will first expire" and that the struggles of an old person to avoid public assistance should be rewarded with a grant of the preference rather than cited as a reason for its denial. It would be comforting to report a universal adoption of that approach, but it is not yet to be discerned in the cases. The circumstances of each case can appeal heavily to the judge, but the overall caseload has unfortunately required the drawing of careful lines.

Assuming a case is made out for the grant of a preference, what the nature of it will be will also depend on geography, calendar conditions, and the exigency of the factors accounting for the preference. The case can be set down for a day certain or just accelerated to an advanced calendar. The rules say that if a preference is granted, "the case shall be placed ahead of all non-preferred cases pending as of that date, unless the court otherwise orders."[20]

The special preference is ordinarily sought by motion. The motion papers are served with the note of issue if sought by the party filing the note of issue, or within 10 days after that service if sought by some other party.[21] When the ground is that the applicant has attained age 70, or is terminally ill, the motion may be made when the applicant reaches that age, or any time after the terminal nature of the illness becomes known, even though the note of issue has already been filed.[22] In personal injury and wrongful death actions, the rules impose more detailed requirements for the preference motion under the "interests of justice" provision in CPLR 3403(a)(3), including a showing that the venue of the action is proper.[23]

---

[17]   Martinkovic v. Chrysler Leasing Corp., 29 A.D.2d 636, 286 N.Y.S.2d 195 (1st Dep't 1968).

[18]   Dodumoff v. Lyons, 4 A.D.2d 626, 627, 168 N.Y.S.2d 183, 185 (1st Dep't 1957).

[19]   Tintner v. Marangi, 57 Misc. 2d 318, 292 N.Y.S.2d 779 (Sup. Ct., Rockland County 1968).

[20]   22 N.Y.C.R.R. § 202.24(d).

[21]   CPLR 3403(b).

[22]   CPLR 3403(b).

[23]   See 22 N.Y.C.R.R. § 202.24(b).

There are also rules prescribing the steps for opposing a preference application,[24] requiring the court to make sure the preference is justified even if there's no opposition to it,[25] and permitting the court, on its own motion, to withdraw a preference already granted.[26]

We have been discussing preferences in the trial of an action, the subject of CPLR 3403(a). Occasionally a preference is called for on the hearing of a motion, the best known of which is the motion for a preliminary injunction in an instance in which a temporary restraining order has been granted and is outstanding.[27] Preferences on appeal are discussed in the appeals chapter.[28]

C. PRETRIAL CONFERENCE

Table of Sections

§ 374.   Pretrial Conferences

§ 374. Pretrial Conferences

Another creature of the rules rather than the CPLR is the pretrial conference, the second of the conferences provided for by the rules. The first is the preliminary conference outlined in Uniform Rule 202.12, treated earlier.[1] The preliminary conference, a pre-note of issue session that comes early in the action if it comes at all, was mandatory when the Uniform Rules first took effect, on January 6, 1986, but was made optional as of April 1, 1988. The pretrial conference that we address here[2] has been optional from the outset. It's a device designed to get the parties and the judge together on the eve of trial for a variety of purposes, notably to evaluate the case and discuss possible settlement or, failing settlement, to resolve potential evidentiary disputes and narrow the issues by securing admissions of fact or agreements about documents.[3]

The pretrial conference occurs after the filing of the note of issue. While the rule in point, Uniform Rule 202.26, says that the judge "shall" order a pretrial conference, it adds in the same clause that the judge can dispense with it. This presumably recognizes that under the Individual Assignment System the judge has been on top of the case from the outset, perhaps including an initial review of it in a preliminary conference earlier, so that the judge knows one way or the other whether there would be any utility in going through a "pretrial" conference.

---

[24]   22 N.Y.C.R.R. § 202.25(a). The time periods in the rule are different than those governing motions under CPLR 2214. See § 247.

[25]   22 N.Y.C.R.R. § 202.25(c).

[26]   22 N.Y.C.R.R. § 202.25(b).

[27]   See CPLR 6313(a); see § 330.

[28]   See § 540.

[1]   See § 77D.

[2]   Treatment here is of Uniform Rule 202.26, applicable in the supreme and county courts. The establishment of pretrial conferences in the lower courts is also left to the chief administrator to determine by separate rule, presently 22 N.Y.C.R.R. § 208.22 in the N.Y.C. Civil Court and 22 N.Y.C.R.R. § 212.22 in the district courts. In the city courts, conferences are left to each judge to set up "as required by the needs of the court." See 22 N.Y.C.R.R. § 210.22.

[3]   The evolution of the pretrial conference is briefly discussed and some statistics on its effectiveness appeared in the Judicial Conference's Second Annual Report at page 66 et seq. (1957).

If the pretrial conference is to take place, the rule says that to the extent "practicable" it should be held between 15 and 45 days in advance of the anticipated day of trial.

The attorneys who appear at the conference must be "fully familiar with the action and authorized to make binding stipulations."[4] This is designed to discourage the firms involved from sending down junior lawyers without any authority to take meaningful steps in the case.

The court is also empowered to direct representatives of an insurer to attend at a conference—a meaningful step in personal injury and wrongful death cases—presumably subjecting the insurer to sanctions for willful failure to attend.[5] Unfortunately, the penalty prescribed in the rule for a failure to comply is inadequate, noting only that it may be deemed a default under CPLR 3404. That's the provision that would allow the striking of the case from the trial calendar, something that neither plaintiff nor defendant should suffer if an insurer fails to attend a pretrial conference.[6]

Modeled in some measure on a counterpart federal provision,[7] Uniform Rule 202.26(c) says that the conference can consider:

1. simplification of the issues;

2. securing admissions and documents "to avoid unnecessary proof";

3. "disposition" of the action (a euphemism for settlement talks) and its scheduling for trial (if there is no settlement);

4. amendment of pleadings and bill of particulars;

5. limiting the number of expert witnesses;

6. insurance coverage, if relevant; and

7. anything else deemed relevant.

Even as late as the pretrial conference, a supreme court justice retains the power to transfer the case down to a lower court under CPLR 325 if, with the benefit of all pretrial proceedings, including disclosure, now having been completed and the view of the case therefore having been brought into better focus, the justice finds that it fits within the monetary jurisdiction of a lower court and doesn't belong in the supreme court.[8] The transfer down can be based on either CPLR 325(c)[9] or CPLR 325(d).[10]

Whatever the stated reasons for a "conference"—any kind of conference—the practical experience of the bar is that with some judges, at least in tort cases, it can turn into an arm-twisting session in which the judge tries hard to get the case settled. While

---

[4]   22 N.Y.C.R.R. § 202.26(e). The rule can also be satisfied if the attorneys are "accompanied by a person empowered to act on behalf of the party represented." 22 N.Y.C.R.R. § 202.26(e).

[5]   A 2006 amendment of 22 N.Y.C.R.R. § 202.26(e) added this power.

[6]   CPLR 3404 is discussed in § 376.

[7]   Fed. R. Civ. P. 16; see § 636 (Practitioner's Edition).

[8]   See 22 N.Y.C.R.R. § 202.26(g)(1).

[9]   See § 26.

[10]   See § 27. A 1998 amendment of the applicable rule imposes a restriction on transfers down from the supreme to the New York City Civil Court under CPLR 325(d). See 22 N.Y.C.R.R. § 202.26(g)(2). It provides that if the case will not be tried faster in the civil than in the supreme court, there shall be no transfer unless it can be established that the civil court will try the case within 30 days after the conference. See the discussion in SPR 74:1. This restriction seems to have gotten short shrift in some quarters. See § 27 and SPR 139:3.

judges may encourage settlements, employing "pressure tactics" to coerce them is not permissible.[11] Some judges, self-conscious about their "track record," have developed special touches to increase their settlement credits, sending the plaintiff out while the defendant is bargained up, and then reversing the audience to bargain the plaintiff down. It's a procedure criticized publicly, but applauded privately, especially by court administrators concerned about sagging calendars and overtaxed facilities.[12] Judges have even been known to attempt—improperly—retributive measures against recalcitrant parties who don't settle on terms the judge deems fair, like the granting of a preference in the case to punish a balky defendant.[13]

D. LAXNESS DISMISSALS

Table of Sections

§ 375.   Dismissal for Want of Prosecution; CPLR 3216
§ 376.   Dismissal of Abandoned Cases; CPLR 3404

§ 375. Dismissal for Want of Prosecution; CPLR 3216

In Chapter 11, on the accelerated judgment, we discussed all of the sections in Article 32 of the CPLR except CPLR 3216,[1] which authorizes a dismissal for the plaintiff's want of diligence in the prosecution of the action. This category of dismissal was not addressed until now because developments in the 1960s tied it to the note of issue, which therefore had to be treated first.

CPLR 3216 permits a want of prosecution dismissal only after the court or a defendant has served on the plaintiff what is known as a 90-day notice (or "demand," as it is popularly referred to), giving the plaintiff a chance to serve and file the note of issue during the 90-day period following the demand. A plaintiff who serves and files the note within that time automatically avoids the dismissal regardless of how much past delay the plaintiff has been guilty of, and no matter how inexcusable the delay may have been. This pro-plaintiff provision, which in essence wipes the slate clean of past laxness and gives the plaintiff a new start, is the product of an extraordinary lobbying effort, all in reaction to the 1963 decision of Sortino v. Fisher,[2] in which the First Department abruptly overturned decades of judicial leniency and sharpened the teeth of the original CPLR 3216.

The CPLR 3216 enacted with the adoption of the CPLR merely reproduced in substance its prior-law counterpart,[3] which in terse and general terms authorized a dismissal upon a showing that the plaintiff neglected to proceed in the action. While there would occasionally be dismissals under that provision, over the years the courts, recognizing the dire consequences attending a dismissal for want of prosecution, showed themselves receptive to almost any excuse the plaintiff offered in resisting the motion.

---

[11]   See Schunk v. Schunk, 84 A.D.2d 904, 905, 446 N.Y.S.2d 672 (4th Dep't 1981).

[12]   See 22 N.Y.C.R.R. § 100.3(B)(6)(d) (provision in Rules of Judicial Conduct permitting a "judge, with the consent of the parties, [to] confer separately with the parties and their lawyers on agreed-upon matters").

[13]   See, e.g., Wolff v. Laverne Inc., 17 A.D.2d 213, 233 N.Y.S.2d 555 (1st Dep't 1962) (trial court abused discretion by ordering preference after defendant refused to offer additional money to settle action).

[1]   Although CPLR 3216 is a "rule" rather than a "statute," it is the product of the 1967 legislature. There is, in any event, little practical distinction between the two captions today. See § 2.

[2]   Sortino v. Fisher, 20 A.D.2d 25, 245 N.Y.S.2d 186 (1st Dep't 1963).

[3]   Civ. Prac. Act § 181 (repealed 1963).

It was that list of excuses, grown long with time, that the *Sortino* case reviewed in depth and rejected almost in toto. It dismissed for want of prosecution in a comprehensive opinion a number of cases the court had consolidated for appeal. The plaintiffs' bar found it devastating.

The source of the devastation should be noted right off. Although the court can specify that a CPLR 3216 dismissal is on the merits,[4] which the court would ordinarily do only if the pro and con papers delve into the merits and the court is convinced that the case has none,[5] the papers seldom go that deep. Therefore, the court rarely designates that a CPLR 3216 dismissal is "on the merits," or "with prejudice," which is generally used to connote the same thing. The fear that in a future action the defense of res judicata will be interposed is therefore not a significant factor.

The critical problem is the statute of limitations. The neglect to prosecute dismissal is one of the exceptions listed in CPLR 205(a), which means that there may not be a six-month period, from the dismissal, in which to sue again. This will certainly be the case where the order dismissing the action for neglect to prosecute "set[s] forth on the record the specific conduct constituting the neglect, which conduct shall demonstrate a general pattern of delay in proceeding with the litigation."[6] Defendants moving to dismiss under CPLR 3216 must be sure to request that the dismissal order contain such detail and should provide suggested language to the court. If the 90-day demand is served by the court, a 2015 amendment to CPLR 3216(b)(3) discussed below now requires that such detail be embodied in the demand and will make it readily accessible for inclusion in the order of dismissal. A dismissal based merely on a neglect to prosecute, without any supporting detail in the record demonstrating neglect and a pattern of delay, will likely permit the plaintiff to use CPLR 205(a)'s lifesaver for a subsequent action.

If the original statute of limitations is still open, the action can be commenced anew without time barriers, but defendants are well aware of that and will rarely make the motion until the statute has expired. The consternation of a CPLR 3216 dismissal, therefore, is the statute of limitations, and recognition of this dire prospect is what prompted the courts, before *Sortino*, to be generous in the acceptance of a plaintiff's excuses.

Handed down in December of 1963 when the CPLR was just a few months old, *Sortino* thrust at the heart of the so-called "negligence" bar: the lawyers representing plaintiffs in the omnipresent personal injury and wrongful death tort cases. The decision in *Sortino* struck a receptive chord in other courts throughout the State, and quickly became a statewide authority without Court of Appeals involvement for the reason that the elements that go into the dismissal are discretionary, rendering most determinations under the statute beyond the scope of the Court's review. The court in *Sortino* actually drew a numbered list of the various excuses tendered by plaintiffs over the years, treated them seriatim, and rejected virtually all of them. The listed excuses, and the factors relevant to their consideration, are these:

---

[4]   CPLR 3216(a).

[5]   The court has discretion, however, to make the dismissal "on the merits" without actually considering the merits. See Jones v. Maphey, 50 N.Y.2d 971, 431 N.Y.S.2d 466, 409 N.E.2d 939 (1980). It's an extraordinary thing to do. Fairer sanctions are at hand, as will be discussed.

[6]   See § 52 (discussing 2008 amendment to CPLR 205(a)).

1. Extent of delay. The court noted that no particular period is required. Mere months may qualify.

2. Law office failures. The court rejected explanations based on the mistakes of the lawyers or their employees, a common source of excuse (overlooked calendars, misread papers, misplaced files, replaced secretaries, displaced associates, and the like). From its vantage point in *Sortino*, "law office failure" became the famous catch-phrase of the later Barasch v. Micucci era and the subject of an important codification in CPLR 2005.[7]

3. Settlement negotiations. That these are continuing ceases to be an excuse shortly after the last communication between the parties.

4. Other continuing pretrial activity, such as disclosure, which will only justify a short delay.

5. Statute of limitations. That the statute has run is no excuse for denying the motion, because the purpose underlying the statute of limitations (preserving evidence and witnesses and memories) can be defeated just as much by delay after commencement as by postponing commencement itself.

6. Defendant's duty. Attempts to blame the defendant for delay are unacceptable because the plaintiff, having brought the suit, is the one obliged to press it.

7. Plaintiff's belated activity. A spurt of activity by the plaintiff only on the eve of the dismissal motion may not be recognized.

8. Disabling circumstances. These may excuse delay (personal catastrophes or the need for foreign disclosure are cited as examples), but none such were adduced in the cases before the court in *Sortino*.

9. Parallel litigation. The need, for practical reasons, to await the outcome of other litigation might be an excuse. No such need in these cases.

10. Affidavit of merits. Since a neglect to prosecute is a kind of default, the court insisted that the plaintiff's papers in response to the motion attest in strong affidavits to the merits of the case, a showing commonly required of anyone who seeks to undo a default. The court held that a delayed case is suspect on the merits, and the longer the delay the greater the suspicion.

Around the state at the time of *Sortino* were literally hundreds of cases qualifying as neglected under *Sortino*'s new guidelines, and at the prompt initiative of defendants, these cases began to get dismissed by the dozens. Cases were being lost, in effect by default, and lawyers were being left to face the possible personal consequences of a malpractice action, to which a CPLR 3216 dismissal can of course give rise if the delay is the lawyer's fault,[8] as it usually is. Possible disciplinary proceedings are also in prospect in that situation, which can mean censure,[9] or suspension,[10] or even disbarment.

---

[7] The *Barasch* case concerns the consequences of pleading defaults. See § 231.

[8] See Gladden v. Logan, 28 A.D.2d 1116, 284 N.Y.S.2d 920 (1st Dep't 1967).

[9] See In re Ribolow, 26 A.D.2d 579, 271 N.Y.S.2d 45 (2d Dep't 1966).

[10] See In re Higgins, 27 A.D.2d 340, 279 N.Y.S.2d 197 (1st Dep't 1967).

The plaintiffs' bar took great pains to seek substantial amendments to CPLR 3216 to restrict its use, and the statute in effect today reflects the fruit of those efforts.[11] Under the present version of CPLR 3216, which was substantially amended in 2015,[12] several conditions must be satisfied before an action can be dismissed for neglect to prosecute. First, the dismissal motion can't be made earlier than a year after the joinder of issue, or six months after a preliminary conference order, whichever period is later.[13] Second, the dismissal motion under CPLR 3216 must be preceded by the service on the plaintiff, by registered or certified mail, of a demand requiring resumption of prosecution and the filing and service of a note of issue by the plaintiff within 90 days following receipt of the notice.[14] The notice must warn the plaintiff that a failure to comply can serve as the basis for a motion to dismiss for lack of prosecution.[15] Third, if the written demand is served by the court, CPLR 3216(b)(3) now requires that it "set forth the specific conduct constituting the neglect, which conduct shall demonstrate a general pattern of delay in proceeding with the litigation."[16] This latter requirement that was added in the 2015 amendment does not pertain to a party, who can serve the written demand described in CPLR 3216(b)(3) based solely on the passage of time, without regard to whether the opponent engaged in a course of conduct demonstrating a general pattern of delay. Fourth, CPLR 3216(a) was also amended in 2015 to require that the dismissal be "with notice to the parties" regardless of whether it is prompted by the motion of a party or the court's own doing. Therefore, it appears that when a party is served with a 90-day demand by the court, it must also receive a separate notice that the judge intends to dismiss the action, thereby allowing the party to be heard on the matter. This amendment will bring the procedure governing CPLR 3216 dismissals sought by a court more in line with the practice governing motions by a party.

The new language in CPLR 3216(b)(3) was borrowed in substantial part from the 2008 amendment to CPLR 205(a).[17] CPLR 205(a) now requires a judge who dismisses an action for neglect to prosecute under CPLR 3216, or any other relevant statute, "to set forth on the record the specific conduct constituting the neglect, which conduct shall

---

[11]   The developments are traced in Commentary C3216:3 on McKinney's CPLR 3216.

[12]   The amendments were recommended in response to the Court of Appeals 4–3 decision in Cadichon v. Facelle, 18 N.Y.3d 230, 938 N.Y.S.2d 232, 961 N.E.2d 623 (2011) (NYSLD No. 625), a multiparty medical malpractice action that was dismissed by supreme court on its own initiative pursuant to CPLR 3216 without notice to the parties.

[13]   CPLR 3216(b)(2); see § 77D, discussing preliminary conference orders. 22 N.Y.C.R.R. § 202.12 sets out the details for a preliminary conference. It is important to note that the parties will often agree to a timetable for disclosure in a preliminary conference stipulation and order in the form prescribed by the Chief Administrator of the Courts. See 22 N.Y.C.R.R. § 202.12(b). The rule states that if the parties do sign such a stipulation, they shall agree "to a timetable which shall provide for completion of disclosure within 12 months of the filing of the request for judicial intervention for a standard case, or within 15 months of such filing for a complex case." 22 N.Y.C.R.R. § 202.12(b). If this route is followed, a motion to dismiss under CPLR 3216 should not be permitted until the time period for disclosure in the preliminary conference order has elapsed. Therefore, we wonder if this amendment to CPLR 3216(b)(2) will have any meaningful impact.

[14]   CPLR 3216(b)(3). The Court of Appeals has held that the use of ordinary mail instead of the required registered or certified mail is not a jurisdictional defect, as long as the plaintiff actually receives it. Balancio v. American Optical Corp., 66 N.Y.2d 750, 497 N.Y.S.2d 360, 488 N.E.2d 106 (1985). Federal express has also been held a permissible method, Secreto v. IBM Corp., N.Y.L.J., Jan. 27, 2003, at 24, col.1 (Sup. Ct., Dutchess County; Dillon, J.), but when a statute prescribes a specific method of service it is unwise to use any other. See SPR 134:3. The service requirements in CPLR 3216(b)(3) will also be deemed satisfied if the plaintiff has received the court's notice at, for example, a certification conference. Felix v. County of Nassau, 52 A.D.3d 653, 860 N.Y.S.2d 196 (2d Dep't 2008).

[15]   CPLR 3216(b)(3).

[16]   CPLR 3216(b)(3).

[17]   See § 52.

demonstrate a general pattern of delay in proceeding with the litigation." A court contemplating service of a CPLR 3216(b)(3) 90-day demand might check the recent caselaw construing the amendment to CPLR 205(a) to ascertain if the heightened standard of delay is met. If the court fails to include the specific conduct constituting neglect in its 90-day demand, would that render a subsequent dismissal under CPLR 3216 void?

The interplay of the above four requirements means that the defendant can't serve the demand on the plaintiff until at least nine months have elapsed since the joinder of issue. Serving the demand at that time and then waiting 90 days if the plaintiff does not comply enables the defendant to make the motion at just about the time the year in CPLR 3216(b) expires, as measured from the joinder of issue. As a practical matter, CPLR 3216 is saying that a plaintiff has at least nine months from joinder in which to get the case ready before even being reminded about the obligation to prosecute diligently. A defendant prone to move under CPLR 3216 as promptly as possible had best take careful note of this. A premature motion may not even be entertained by the court.

If the plaintiff serves and files the note of issue within the 90 days following receipt of the CPLR 3216(b)(3) demand, the court is not permitted to consider delay preceding the demand, whether measured in months or years.[18] Compliance with the demand is deemed "diligent prosecution of the action" and no motion to dismiss can be made.[19] In some decisions, the Second Department suggested that the doctrine of laches could provide a basis to dismiss an action after a lengthy delay in prosecuting it, even though a note of issue has not been filed, there has been no order pursuant to Uniform Rule 202.27,[20] and there has been no 90-day demand served pursuant to CPLR 3216(b)(3). In Arroyo v. Board of Educ. of City of New York,[21] the Second Department expressly states that those decisions should not be followed and rejects defendant's laches argument in a case that was commenced in 1992 and marked off the calendar in 1996! More than 12 years later, in October 2008, the plaintiffs moved to restore the action to the "active pre-note of issue calendar" and to schedule a preliminary conference. The supreme court denied defendant's cross-motion to dismiss the action based on laches because it did not have the power to dismiss the complaint in these circumstances, and the Second Department affirmed.

A plaintiff who lets the 90-day period pass without serving and filing the note of issue, or without at least making a manifestly good-faith attempt to get the case moving, becomes subject to the CPLR 3216 motion.[22] Not infrequently, even a good faith attempt to serve and file the note of issue within the 90 days may be frustrated by the certificate of readiness rule, which requires completion of disclosure and other pretrial proceedings before a note of issue can be filed.[23] In many instances, the plaintiff should not be penalized if the readiness rule gets in the way, as long as the she can satisfy the court that she pressed forward as diligently as possible after being served with the 90-day

---

[18]   CPLR 3216(c), (d).

[19]   CPLR 3216(c).

[20]   This rule is noted in the footnotes below and is discussed in further detail in § 376.

[21]   Arroyo v. Board of Educ. of City of New York, 110 A.D.3d 17, 970 N.Y.S.2d 229 (2d Dep't 2013) (SPR 260:3).

[22]   CPLR 3216(e).

[23]   See § 370.

demand.[24] That issue will almost certainly be raised on the motion to dismiss for neglect to prosecute, but it will be the opponent's burden to establish a "justifiable excuse for the delay and a good and meritorious cause of action."[25]

The best idea for the plaintiff who is trying to get the note of issue filed within the 90 days but finds that more time than that is needed is to ask the defendant for a stipulation extending the time, or, if the defendant won't stipulate, to make a motion for a time extension under CPLR 2004.[26] In Grant v. City of New York,[27] the court held that a timely motion seeking an extension of the 90-day period under CPLR 2004 "constitutes a sufficient, timely response to a [CPLR 3216(b)(3)] notice." Where such motion is made, the plaintiff is "not required by CPLR 3216(e) to demonstrate a reasonable excuse or meritorious cause of action in order to avoid dismissal," but rather must satisfy the less burdensome "good cause" standard in CPLR 2004.[28]

A plaintiff near the border of the 90-day period and planning to mail the note of issue to the clerk should keep in mind Stein v. Wainwright's Travel Service, Inc.[29] The case holds that when mail is used, a "filing" with the clerk—which is a requirement, along with service of the note of issue, that the plaintiff must meet within the 90 days— is not deemed to occur upon the mere mailing of the document. Rather, the later moment when the filing actually takes place is the key date for measuring compliance with the 90-day demand, which occurred on the 93rd day in Stein. The consequence to the plaintiff was a dismissal for want of prosecution. Mailing the note of issue to the county clerk on the 90th day, even if witnessed by a high priest, is therefore asking for trouble.

Nor is the plaintiff who files the note of issue after the 90 days rescued by the mere fact that the filing occurs before the defendant makes the CPLR 3216 dismissal motion. The motion still lies and the case is subject to dismissal under CPLR 3216(e).[30]

The defendant erroneously offering fewer than the required 90 days does not invalidate the notice as long as the plaintiff ends up actually being accorded the required 90 days.[31] Similarly, if a court's demand erroneously directs the note of issue to be filed within 30 days, but the court extends the filing deadline well beyond the 90-day period, the defect may be overlooked.[32]

The defendant waives no rights by serving a CPLR 3216 demand, such as the right to conduct disclosure proceedings during the 90-day period that the plaintiff has now been given to get the case ready,[33] but a waiver has been held to result, and by all parties, when the plaintiff calls the defendant's bluff and complies with the demand by serving

---

[24]   See Commentaries C3216:20, C3216:21, C3216:22 on McKinney's CPLR 3216.

[25]   CPLR 3216(e).

[26]   See Nappi v. St. John's Cemetery, 73 A.D.2d 687, 423 N.Y.S.2d 240 (2d Dep't 1979).

[27]   Grant v. City of New York, 17 A.D.3d 215, 793 N.Y.S.2d 35 (1st Dep't 2005).

[28]   Grant, 17 A.D.3d at 215, 793 N.Y.S.2d at 35; see § 6, which discusses CPLR 2004.

[29]   Stein v. Wainwright's Travel Service, Inc., 92 A.D.2d 961, 460 N.Y.S.2d 659 (3d Dep't 1983).

[30]   Scott v. Columbia Memorial Hosp., 134 A.D.2d 792, 522 N.Y.S.2d 257 (3d Dep't 1987).

[31]   Smith v. City of Troy, 77 A.D.2d 691, 429 N.Y.S.2d 796 (3d Dep't 1980), aff'd, 54 N.Y.2d 890, 444 N.Y.S.2d 918, 429 N.E.2d 425 (1981); see Lyons v. Butler, 134 A.D.2d 576, 521 N.Y.S.2d 477, 479 (2d Dep't 1987) (court lacked jurisdiction to entertain CPLR 3126 motion that was served before expiration of the requisite 90-day period).

[32]   Athanasiou v. Esposito, 212 A.D.2d 878, 622 N.Y.S.2d 148 (3d Dep't 1995).

[33]   Baxt v. Cohen, 96 A.D.2d 661, 466 N.Y.S.2d 737 (3d Dep't 1983); see EDP Hosp. Computer Systems, Inc. v. Bronx-Lebanon Hosp. Center, 13 A.D.3d 476, 478, 789 N.Y.S.2d 50, 52 (2d Dep't 2004).

the note of issue within the required time.[34] The note of issue, it must again be remembered, has to be accompanied by a certificate of readiness, which constitutes a representation by all that the case is ready.[35] A defendant who has served a 90-day demand under CPLR 3216(b)(3) should not be permitted to then move to vacate the note of issue under Uniform Rule 202.21(e) because the case is not ready for trial!

If and when the motion to dismiss for want of prosecution lies, and is made, its disposition on its merits under CPLR 3216(e) will still be largely dictated by an application of the factors outlined in the *Sortino* decision or any of the numerous subsequent decisions that approve and follow *Sortino*. Thus, while the legislative activity on CPLR 3216 has much reduced the number of cases susceptible to the motion, the cases that do face it face *Sortino* as well.

One would think, with the tense lessons of the 1960s and the ample rope that CPLR 3216 gives to plaintiffs, that the motion to dismiss for want of prosecution would virtually disappear from the practice. Hardly. Cases continue to appear all over the state in which the plaintiff bungles the absolution from all delay that CPLR 3216(c) offers, sometimes not even trying to file the note of issue after receiving the 90-day notice. Although scaled down, dismissals still appear with inexcusable frequency.[36]

Delay prior to the filing of the note of issue—delay that has put off the filing—has been the subject up to now. Until around 2001, laxness after the filing of the note of issue, while more likely to be punished by striking the case from the calendar under CPLR 3404,[37] could also bring a dismissal under CPLR 3216, "irrespective of any compliance (or non-compliance) with a 90-day notice."[38] This overlap between CPLR 3216 and CPLR 3404 often confused the bench and bar. It was addressed and presumably resolved in Lopez v. Imperial Delivery Service, Inc.[39]

In an extensive treatment, *Lopez* lined up the two statutes, traced their histories, described their scope and purpose, and drew a sharp line between them designed to avoid the mutual invasions that had been characterizing their application. CPLR 3404, the court held, assumes that the case has been fully readied for trial and appears on the trial calendar for that reason, having reached it only after the filing of the note of issue and certificate of readiness. It does not apply to strikings from other calendars, like motion or pretrial calendars or any other pre-note of issue calendar. Only if a call of the trial calendar is missed, therefore, can the one-year restoration provision of CPLR 3404 come into play. Lax conduct before the case has been placed on the trial calendar by the filing

---

[34]   Gray v. Crouse-Irving Memorial Hosp., Inc., 107 A.D.2d 1038, 486 N.Y.S.2d 540 (4th Dep't 1985); see generally Darko v. New York City Transit Authority, 13 Misc. 3d 203, 819 N.Y.S.2d 456 (Sup. Ct., Bronx County 2006) (discussing conflict among departments).

[35]   See § 370.

[36]   See, e.g., Siegel v. Commack School Dist., 107 A.D.3d 687, 966 N.Y.S.2d 215 (2d Dep't 2013); Jedraszak v. County of Westchester, 102 A.D.3d 924, 958 N.Y.S.2d 490 (2d Dep't 2013); Wasielewski v. Town of Cheektowaga, 281 A.D.2d 944, 722 N.Y.S.2d 674 (4th Dep't 2001).

[37]   CPLR 3404 is treated in § 376.

[38]   Hillegass v. Duffy, 148 A.D.2d 677, 539 N.Y.S.2d 426 (2d Dep't 1989).

[39]   Lopez v. Imperial Delivery Service, Inc., 282 A.D.2d 190, 725 N.Y.S.2d 57 (2d Dep't 2001). All departments have since adopted the *Lopez* view. See Johnson v. Sam Minskoff & Sons, Inc., 287 A.D.2d 233, 735 N.Y.S.2d 503 (1st Dep't 2001) (SPR 120:3); Chauvin v. Keniry, 4 A.D.3d 700, 773 N.Y.S.2d 142 (3d Dep't 2004); In re Giangualano (Birnbaum), 99 A.D.3d 1221, 951 N.Y.S.2d 439 (4th Dep't 2012), lv. denied 101 A.D.3d 1700, 957 N.Y.S.2d 261.

of the note of issue and certificate of readiness must, therefore, be remedied by resort to CPLR 3216.[40]

As will be seen, the caselaw on CPLR 3404 governing the restoration of a stricken case to the trial calendar is generous,[41] even as to cases marked off several years earlier. Under *Lopez*, that generosity will no longer be applied to pre-note of issue laxness where CPLR 3216 reigns with its strict 90-day demand requirement.

CPLR 3126—don't confuse it with CPLR 3216—may also play a role on this scene. Under CPLR 3126, a sanction up to and including a dismissal can be imposed for a plaintiff's willful failure to perform disclosure obligations. The issue usually comes up at the pre-note of issue stage and hence might seem to put CPLR 3126 in conflict with CPLR 3216. While a CPLR 3126 dismissal for failure to proceed with disclosure can indeed be envisaged as a category of neglect to prosecute,[42] it has been treated as independent of the requirements in CPLR 3216 and therefore a source of dismissal that does not have to pursue the CPLR 3216(b)(3) 90-day demand steps.[43]

The defendant's motion to dismiss the plaintiff's claim is the situation in most of the CPLR 3216 cases. But CPLR 3216 is generic in terminology and can work for a plaintiff moving against a counterclaim, a co-defendant moving against a cross-claim, etc.[44]

A CPLR 3216 dismissal of the plaintiff's claim does not bar the plaintiff from defending against any counterclaim that may remain standing.[45]

Plaintiffs who would relieve their cases of any threat from CPLR 3216 should serve their pleadings and bills of particulars timely, set up all of their disclosure proceedings promptly and in accordance with any timetables set forth in a preliminary conference order,[46] pressure the defendants to do the same—in letters of which copies are inserted in the file for potential future use in resisting CPLR 3216 motions—and otherwise fulfill whatever the certificate of readiness requirement mandates. That will clear the path for the filing of the note of issue even if a 90-day demand of CPLR 3216 should appear, and it will help to remove the spectre of CPLR 3216 from the case.

§ 376. Dismissal of Abandoned Cases; CPLR 3404

Distinct from the dismissal for neglect to prosecute under CPLR 3216, the subject of the previous section, is the dismissal under CPLR 3404. The CPLR 3216 dismissal is aimed at cases so delayed that they have never reached the trial calendar. CPLR 3404, entitled "Dismissal of abandoned cases," is directed to cases that have reached the trial calendar, but have afterwards been struck from it. The striking, or marking "off," usually

---

[40] See also 22 N.Y.C.R.R. § 202.27, applicable in the supreme and county courts and directed at certain defaults before and after the filing of the note of issue. The specific role played by the sometimes draconian application of this rule is explored in Johnson v. Brooklyn Hosp. Center, 295 A.D.2d 567, 744 N.Y.S.2d 215 (2d Dep't 2002), noted in SPR 133:3.

[41] See § 376.

[42] See Andrea v. Arnone, Hedin, Casker, Kennedy and Drake, Architects and Landscape Architects, P.C., 5 N.Y.3d 514, 806 N.Y.S.2d 453, 840 N.E.2d 565 (2005).

[43] See on that subject the lead note in SPR 126:1; see also 22 N.Y.C.R.R. § 202.27 (permitting dismissal of actions based on pre-note of issue defaults without 90-day demand).

[44] It is less likely that these claims, or a third-party claim, will meet want of prosecution objections because they usually depend on the initiative with which the plaintiff is driving the main claim. See Commentary C3216:9 on McKinney's CPLR 3216.

[45] Chin v. Chin, 44 A.D.2d 812, 355 N.Y.S.2d 422 (1st Dep't 1974).

[46] See § 77D.

results from a party's failure to appear at a duly scheduled "calendar call," whether conducted by a judge or by the clerk; or because a party appeared at the call without being ready to proceed and without a good reason for an adjournment, or for still other reasons. Some of these fall under the heading of "Engagement of Counsel," a catch-all phrase and the caption of an important rule that sets up criteria and priorities to guide adjournment of a case in one court based on the engagement of one of the attorneys in some other.[1]

Whatever the reason for the striking, unless the court makes some direction to the contrary, CPLR 3404 requires that the case be restored to the calendar within one year afterwards or it shall be "deemed abandoned and ... dismissed ... for neglect to prosecute." In other words, the plaintiff, whose default is usually the one that invokes CPLR 3404, had best move to restore the case within a year or a dismissal will attend the case. Furthermore, the dismissal purports to be automatic: CPLR 3404 directs that the clerk, without any need to involve the judge, make "an appropriate entry without the necessity of an order."

For a long time, the line between CPLR 3216, which applies before the note of issue has been filed and the case has been added to the trial calendar, and CPLR 3404, which applies after it has been added but has then been struck, was blurred. The mission of each statute was sometimes confused with the other. The Second Department in Lopez v. Imperial Delivery Service, Inc.[2] addressed this overlap and endeavored to draw a line between the two statutes, as discussed in more detail in the earlier treatment of CPLR 3216.[3] The other departments have followed the reasoning of the *Lopez* decision.[4]

Statute of Limitations Consequences of CPLR 3404 Dismissal

The dismissal under CPLR 3404 is explicitly labeled a "neglect to prosecute" and, therefore, if the original statute of limitations has expired when the dismissal occurs, the plaintiff may be foreclosed from receiving the benefit of a six-month extension to sue again under CPLR 205(a).[5] That will depend on whether the court dismissing the action has "set forth on the record the specific conduct constituting the neglect, which conduct shall demonstrate a general pattern of delay in proceeding with the litigation."[6] As noted above, CPLR 3404 permits the clerk to make an entry dismissing the action without the necessity of a court order and that will often result in the lack of recitation needed to prevent the plaintiff from being able to invoke CPLR 205(a)'s gift. The defendant may consider making a motion to dismiss under CPLR 3404 if the stricken case is not restored within a year and requesting that specific language be included in the order to ensure that CPLR 205(a) is placed out of plaintiff's reach. That procedure may wake sleeping

---

[1]　See Part 125 of the Uniform Rules. A violation of this rule can ultimately lead to a default. See Malachi v. Good Samaritan Hosp., 245 A.D.2d 492, 666 N.Y.S.2d 721 (2d Dep't 1997); § 369.

[2]　Lopez v. Imperial Delivery Service, Inc., 282 A.D.2d 190, 725 N.Y.S.2d 57 (2d Dep't 2001).

[3]　See § 375; SPR 110:1.

[4]　See Johnson v. Sam Minskoff & Sons, Inc., 287 A.D.2d 233, 735 N.Y.S.2d 503 (1st Dep't 2001) (SPR 120:3); Chauvin v. Keniry, 4 A.D.3d 700, 773 N.Y.S.2d 142 (3d Dep't 2004); In re Giangualano (Birnbaum), 99 A.D.3d 1221, 951 N.Y.S.2d 439 (4th Dep't 2012), lv. denied 101 A.D.3d 1700, 957 N.Y.S.2d 261.

[5]　See Schwartz v. Mandelbaum & Gluck, 266 A.D.2d 273, 275, 698 N.Y.S.2d 252, 254 (2d Dep't 1999); Pomerantz v. Cave, 10 A.D.2d 569, 195 N.Y.S.2d 437 (1st Dep't 1960).

[6]　CPLR 205(a); see § 52.

dogs,[7] but it will often be desirable to make the argument regarding neglect and delay before the court that has witnessed it first-hand.

The practitioner also has to distinguish, for CPLR 205(a) purposes, between a dismissal under CPLR 3404, which may render the case beyond CPLR 205(a)'s reach, and other kinds of analogous but not identical dismissals, which may or may not receive a new six month statute of limitations. If, for example, the plaintiff's case is dismissed for failure to select a jury and proceed to trial, it would seem at first blush to be a neglect to prosecute. But that depends on whether the trial judge, who made the dismissal, intended it as such and "set forth on the record the specific conduct constituting the neglect, which conduct shall demonstrate a general pattern of delay in proceeding with the litigation."[8] A record indicating that that was the intention will usually mean no new period from CPLR 205(a),[9] while one suggesting that the dismissing judge did not regard the activity as a neglect to prosecute does earn the CPLR 205(a) limitations' extension.[10] These can be close questions and a plaintiff is wise to assume the worst, taking precautions accordingly. The cautious plaintiff should not automatically accept the dismissal and just try to sue over, but should instead try to get the case restored before dismissal, or perhaps, if it has already been dismissed, try to vacate the dismissal and restore the case to the calendar.[11]

Restoring the Case to the Calendar

Whether the motion to restore is made before or after a dismissal, the plaintiff must recognize that this is a category of default and must be addressed with care. Judicial hesitancy to bar a stricken case from restoration to the calendar under CPLR 3404 is most manifest in Basetti v. Nour.[12] There, the Second Department reconsidered the burden of proof imposed on the plaintiff in different CPLR 3404 contexts and held that as long as the restoration motion is made within the year, there is no need to excuse the default at all—in other words, an excuse is needed only when the motion to restore is made after the year.[13] Even there, moreover, the tolerant caselaw on CPLR 3404 will apparently still apply.[14]

Until the Court of Appeals has weighed in on the matter, it may be advisable to include the usual default duet when moving to restore an action to the trial calendar: an excuse for the default and an affidavit of merits.[15] The courts may be less generous in certain areas, and plaintiffs who assume the worst are more likely to do their best. Sometimes the court may also require a showing that the defendant would not be

---

[7] See Okun v. Tanners, 11 N.Y.3d 762, 867 N.Y.S.2d 25, 896 N.E.2d 660 (2008) (defendant's motion to dismiss action as abandoned prompted plaintiff's cross-motion to restore the case).

[8] CPLR 205(a).

[9] See Wright v. L. C. Defelice & Son, Inc., 22 A.D.2d 962, 256 N.Y.S.2d 63 (2d Dep't 1964), aff'd, 17 N.Y.2d 586, 268 N.Y.S.2d 345, 215 N.E.2d 522 (1966); Marrero v. Crystal Nails, 114 A.D.3d 101, 106, 978 N.Y.S.2d 257, 260 (2d Dep't 2013) (examining dismissal under CPLR 3126).

[10] Schuman v. Hertz Corp., 17 N.Y.2d 604, 268 N.Y.S.2d 563, 215 N.E.2d 683 (1966), rev'g 23 A.D.2d 646, 257 N.Y.S.2d 400 (1st Dep't 1965).

[11] See the discussion under the heading below, "Restoring the Case to the Calendar." The dismissal can be treated as the equivalent of a default and the motion to vacate it can be based on CPLR 5015(a)(1).

[12] Basetti v. Nour, 287 A.D.2d 126, 731 N.Y.S.2d 35 (2d Dep't 2001); see Brannigan v. Board of Educ. of Levittown Union Free School Dist., 307 A.D.2d 945, 763 N.Y.S.2d 471 (2d Dep't 2003).

[13] This view has also been adopted by the First Department. See Johnson v. Rivera, 10 A.D.3d 288, 781 N.Y.S.2d 22 (1st Dep't 2004).

[14] See SPR 110:1; 114:1.

[15] Renne v. Roven, 29 A.D.2d 866, 288 N.Y.S.2d 415 (2d Dep't 1968).

prejudiced by restoration of the case,[16] which suggests that the mere fact of delay does not by itself give rise to a presumption of prejudice.

The "shall be deemed abandoned and shall be dismissed" language of CPLR 3404, when the year has passed without restoration after the case has been marked off the calendar, has the ring of the absolute to it. But the Court of Appeals has held it to create only a presumption of abandonment and a rebuttable one at that. The key decision establishing that point is Marco v. Sachs,[17] a case that had been hanging fire in the courts for a quarter of a century—a page out of Dickens. Nonetheless, the Court found that at the time of the calendar dismissal, other activity connected with the case, including the pendency of three appeals, indicated that there was no intention to abandon it.

If a year has passed after the case has been stricken from the trial calendar and the action is presumably dismissed, the plaintiff must stand ready to produce a reasonable excuse for the default and an affidavit of merits. In Okun v. Tanners,[18] the Court of Appeals demonstrated that at this juncture, the plaintiff's motion to restore will be carefully scrutinized. In *Okun*, there was a 20-month delay in pursuing the action after it had been stricken from the trial calendar, and that pursuit came via a cross-motion to restore the case in response to the defendant's motion to dismiss it as abandoned. The Court ruled that "plaintiff's conclusory and unsubstantiated claim of law office failure does not constitute a reasonable excuse for the 20-month delay in pursuing the action" and that "plaintiff's inactivity between the time the action was marked off the calendar and defendant's motion to dismiss fail[ed] to rebut the presumption of abandonment that arose pursuant to CPLR 3404."[19]

The courts have actually required a four part showing by plaintiff at this juncture: 1) a potentially meritorious cause of action, 2) a reasonable excuse for the delay in prosecuting the action, 3) a lack of intent to abandon the action, and 4) a lack of prejudice to the defendants.[20] When the court does restore the case to the calendar, it may condition the restoration on the payment of a sum of money to the defendant, presumably compensating the defendant for its inconvenience,[21] and will sometimes stress that the payment must be made by the plaintiff's attorney personally, i.e., without reimbursement from the client.[22] In counties and among judges with crowded calendars, a judge may even admonish a defendant for not being vigorous enough in opposing a restoration motion, as a judge did in one case that had been on the calendar 68 times![23]

It must also be remembered that the calendar is just as much the courts' concern as it is the parties'. Hence, even if the defendant is willing to stipulate to the restoration of a stricken case, restoration under CPLR 3404 is not guaranteed. The best it will do is

---

[16]   See Wells Fargo Bank, N.A. v. Buffenmyer, 134 A.D.3d 1578, 21 N.Y.S.3d 921 (4th Dep't 2015).

[17]   Marco v. Sachs, 10 N.Y.2d 542, 226 N.Y.S.2d 353, 181 N.E.2d 392 (1962).

[18]   *Okun,* 11 N.Y.3d at 763, 867 N.Y.S.2d at 26.

[19]   *Okun,* 11 N.Y.3d at 763, 867 N.Y.S.2d at 26.

[20]   *Wells Fargo Bank, N.A.,* 134 A.D.3d at 1578, 21 N.Y.S.3d at 921; Sierra R. v. Jamaica Hosp. Medical Center, 101 A.D.3d 701, 702, 955 N.Y.S.2d 198 (2d Dep't 2012).

[21]   See, e.g., Barrada v. Target Const. Corp., 31 A.D.2d 810, 299 N.Y.S.2d 708 (2d Dep't 1969); Hood v. City of New York, 4 Misc. 3d 627, 631–33, 781 N.Y.S.2d 431, 434–35 (Sup. Ct., Bronx County 2004).

[22]   See Schickler v. Seifert, 45 A.D.2d 816, 357 N.Y.S.2d 225 (4th Dep't 1974) (payment of $1,000 required).

[23]   Butter v. Brookdale Hospital, 67 Misc. 2d 727, 324 N.Y.S.2d 502 (Sup. Ct., Kings County 1971).

count as a factor in the exercise of discretion by the court, but the court has the final word on matters affecting its calendars.[24]

Uniform Rule 202.27 and Defaults

The rules play a role here, implementing and overlapping CPLR 3216 and CPLR 3404. Uniform Rule 202.27, applicable in the supreme and county courts, is a rule with draconian potential that applies not only when the call of a "calendar" is not answered, but also when a party does not appear at a duly scheduled "conference."[25] The rule suggests, but does not mandate, the imposition of consequences that are the equivalent of the death penalty in civil cases when one side or the other defaults—such as a default judgment and inquest for the plaintiff when the defendant defaults, or a dismissal of the action when the plaintiff defaults. Uniform Rule 202.27, which seems to be at odds with the regime established by the legislature under CPLR 3216 and CPLR 3404, can apply both before and after the filing of the note of issue.

CPLR 3404's Applicability

CPLR 3404 assumes that the case was properly on the calendar. If it was removed from the calendar, not for failure to appear at a calendar call, but because the note of issue was stricken upon a finding that the case was not yet ready for calendar placement, CPLR 3404 and its one-year restoration restriction doesn't apply. In that situation, the case returns to pre-note of issue status, where, if the defendant or the court then seeks the case's dismissal for want of prosecution, the steps prescribed in CPLR 3216 must be followed.[26]

CPLR 3404 is applicable by its own terms to only the supreme and county courts, but lawyers should check into the rules of other courts in which they may find themselves. In Chavez v. 407 Seventh Avenue Corp.,[27] for example, the court pointed out that Rule 208.14(c) of the civil court's rules had, like CPLR 3404, a one-year restoration provision, but it did not contain the automatic dismissal feature. The court therefore held that automatic dismissal would not occur in that court. Absent such a lower court rule on point, CPLR 3404 may still find application in the lower court through the general provision of the lower court act adopting the CPLR for matters not otherwise addressed in the act.[28]

E. MODE OF TRIAL

Table of Sections

§ 377.   Triability by Jury

§ 378.   Demand and Waiver of Trial by Jury

---

[24]   See Incorporated Village of Thomaston v. Biener, 84 A.D.2d 781, 443 N.Y.S.2d 887 (2d Dep't 1981). If the case does get removed from the trial calendar by stipulation of the parties, it is likely to fall outside the CPLR 3404 category and therefore not invoke the one-year-to-restore requirement. See Gorski v. St. John's Episcopal Hosp., 36 A.D.3d 757, 830 N.Y.S.2d 196 (2d Dep't 2007).

[25]   The rules have at least two kinds of conferences, one a "preliminary conference" (see § 77D) and one a "pretrial conference" (see § 374), but any sort of scheduling conference is likely subject to 22 N.Y.C.R.R. § 202.27's guillotine.

[26]   Travis v. Cuff, 28 A.D.3d 749, 814 N.Y.S.2d 681 (2d Dep't 2006). The CPLR 3216 steps are discussed in § 375. They weren't followed in *Travis*, making it error for the lower court to dismiss the case.

[27]   Chavez v. 407 Seventh Ave. Corp., 39 A.D.3d 454, 833 N.Y.S.2d 219 (2d Dep't 2007).

[28]   See § 3; see, e.g., Uniform Dist. Ct. Act § 2102.

§ 379.	Triability by Referee
§ 380.	Triability by the Court
§ 381.	Advisory Jury

§ 377. Triability by Jury

Because different calendars are often kept for jury and nonjury cases, the time when the case first goes on the calendar is usually the occasion to determine the mode of trial as well, i.e., whether the facts are to be tried by a jury, the court, or a referee. Even under the Individual Assignment System, that remains the assumption because the paper that puts the case on the calendar, the note of issue, is also the paper that includes a jury demand if a jury is desired.[1] That's the requirement of CPLR 4102(a), discussed in the next section. The mission of this one is to note which cases are triable by jury.

CPLR 4101 provides for the actions in which trial by jury is required. For the most part, they are the actions evolved through the common law courts, as opposed to those developed in equity (chancery), which continue to be triable by the court.

The most numerous of the law actions is the simple money action, listed in CPLR 4101(1). Causes of action for money only, whether sounding in tort—such as the prolific personal injury, property damage, and wrongful death actions, based on negligence, warranty, breach of a statutory duty, or strict products liability—or in contract—like the common actions for goods sold and delivered, services rendered, money loaned, damages for breach, etc.—are all triable by jury.

In all actions, issues of law are for the court to determine, whatever the mode of trial of the facts.

In gauging whether to allow a jury trial, the courts tend to look at the relief being sought, at least if it's responsive to the facts pleaded. In the event of a conflict, the pleaded facts control the demand for relief. Where, for example, P demands only money from D (law), but the complaint manifests that P is entitled to an accounting from D (equity) if he is entitled to anything, the pleaded facts control the demand[2] and a jury would not be allowed.

If the demand for relief is responsive to the facts pleaded and manifests a claim at law, the court is likely to allow a jury today even though the claim may have been interposed in a form generally regarded as equitable. Where, for example, a shareholder brought a derivative action in behalf of a corporation, joining the corporation as a defendant along with the alleged wrongdoers, but without seeking any relief from the corporation, the court allowed trial by jury. It noted that the action sought money only without any equitable demand; that it would have been triable by jury had it been brought, as the plaintiff claimed it should have been, by the corporation itself; and that the claim's appearance in derivative rather than direct context should therefore not deprive a party of the substantial right to be heard by a jury. The court stressed the language of CPLR 4101(1), which, without addressing contexts, allows a trial by jury in

---

[1]	See the note of issue form contained in § 371.

[2]	See, e.g., Geddes v. Rosen, 22 A.D.2d 394, 255 N.Y.S.2d 585 (1st Dep't 1965), aff'd, 16 N.Y.2d 816, 263 N.Y.S.2d 10, 210 N.E.2d 362.

any action "in which a party demands and sets forth facts which would permit a judgment for a sum of money only."[3]

Paragraph 2 of CPLR 4101 lists other actions triable by jury. These include ejectment, dower,[4] waste, abatement of and damages for a nuisance, replevin (an action to recover a chattel), and the action to compel the determination of a claim to real property.[5]

Paragraph 3 in CPLR 4101 is a reminder that a jury will also be allowed in any other actions in which it is either constitutionally guaranteed or afforded as a matter of legislative grace. The relatively infrequent cases that appear today on CPLR 4101 are more likely to involve this paragraph than the first two. The New York Constitution guarantees trial by jury "in all cases in which it has heretofore been guaranteed by constitutional provision,"[6] and the Court of Appeals held In re Garfield's Estate[7] that this right cannot be divested by authorizing "a court of equity," meaning a court in some other context than a plenary law action, to take jurisdiction of the claim.

In *Garfield*, a surrogate's court case, A was an attorney seeking to recover for services rendered to the testator. He made a claim for them by petitioning for an accounting in the surrogate's court.[8] The executrix resisted A's claim, thus making a trial necessary, and demanded a jury. A maintained that since the claim was asserted in an accounting proceeding in the surrogate's court, it took on an equitable air and lost its jury right. The Court of Appeals held that the claim's appearance in this context was not decisive. The claim itself was one for money only and not governed by any equitable principles and it was therefore triable of constitutional right by jury, on the executrix's demand, even in the surrogate's court.[9]

A tracing of the constitutional sources preserving trial by jury starts with New York's first constitution, that of 1777. It guaranteed trial by jury in all cases in which it had "heretofore been used."[10] This was intended to carry forward with constitutional protection trial by jury in all cases in which the common law afforded it. Later constitutions, through that of 1894, used similar terminology. The effect was to bestow a constitutional guarantee of trial by jury on all cases in which the legislature, between the 1777 and 1894 constitutions, had offered it only as a matter of legislative grace. Among the actions and proceedings in which that happened, for example, and in which today the right to trial by jury is therefore a constitutional one, is the so-called "discovery

---

[3]   Fedoryszyn v. Weiss, 62 Misc. 2d 889, 310 N.Y.S.2d 55 (Sup. Ct., Nassau County 1970).

[4]   Dower actions are growing scarcer with the passing years, and are likely nonexistent today. Dower was abolished in New York except as to marriages entered into before September 1, 1930. See Real Prop. Law § 190.

[5]   This action is authorized and governed by Article 15 of the Real Property Actions and Proceedings Law.

[6]   N.Y. Const. art. I, § 2.

[7]   In re Garfield's Estate, 14 N.Y.2d 251, 251 N.Y.S.2d 7, 200 N.E.2d 196 (1964).

[8]   Authorization for making the claim in this mode after it has been rejected by the personal representative is in SCPA 1808.

[9]   Had A, rather than the executrix, demanded the jury, a jury would not have been allowed for the reason that A's submission of the claim to the surrogate's court was voluntary. A had the option—which the executrix had not—of bringing the claim as an ordinary money action in some other court after its rejection, see SCPA 1810, in which other court either party could have demanded a jury.

[10]   N.Y. Const. 1777, Art. XLI.

proceeding" in the surrogate's court, by which the personal representative can seek data about assets belonging to the decedent and compel the possessor to hand them over.[11]

The 1894 constitution was the last one to use the "heretofore used" language. The 1938 constitution gives the jury guarantee only to cases in which jury trial had been previously "guaranteed by constitutional provision"—language still applicable.[12] The result is that all cases on which the legislature conferred the right of trial by jury after 1894 get it today only from statute, if at all, and not as a constitutional right.

If a demand is made for a jury in a case not specified for jury trial in any current statute, the judge must determine whether a jury was required at common law or offered by a statute enacted between 1777 and 1894.[13] It is not a frequent inquiry, but as the discourses in *Garfield* and in the later Court of Appeals treatment in Motor Vehicle Mfrs. Ass'n of U.S., Inc. v. State[14] indicate, it can be a complex one.

In the *Motor Vehicle* case, the constitutionality of the procedure set up by New York's so-called Lemon Law was at issue. The procedure calls for arbitration of a dispute between a car buyer and the car's manufacturer, but only at the option of the buyer. This, complained the manufacturer, divested it of the right to trial by jury. The Court analyzed the remedies offered to the owner by the Lemon Law—either replacement of the vehicle or a refund of the full purchase price—and found both of them equitable in nature. Hence, held the Court, there was no divestiture of the right to trial by jury and the Lemon Law procedure was upheld.

There are a number of statutes besides CPLR 4101 that authorize trial by jury. Jury is allowed in divorce cases[15] and in most annulment actions.[16] It is allowed also in the ubiquitous summary proceeding to recover the possession of real property, the common landlord-tenant forum,[17] but valid waiver provisions commonly found in leases make trial by jury in summary proceedings infrequent.[18] CPLR provisions other than 4101 may also offer jury trial.[19] Whether these and similar statutes have constitutional underpinnings is an inquiry needed only if the legislature should by mere statute attempt to rescind the right to trial by jury in the particular instance.[20]

The fact that among the actions in which trial by jury is preserved are those in which it was used prior to 1777 accounts for the main surviving distinction today between law and equity, despite the merger of the two systems. In pre-1777 New York, when it was an English colony, jury trial was allowed in law actions, but not in chancery (equity) suits.[21] The merger of law and equity in many respects obscured the differences

---

[11]   See In re Goldfarb's Estate, 18 Misc. 2d 773, 188 N.Y.S.2d 55 (Sur. Ct., New York County 1959). The discovery proceeding is today governed by SCPA 2103 and 2104, whose predecessors had been added by L.1870, ch. 359, 394.

[12]   See N.Y. Const. art. I, § 2.

[13]   See Matter of DES Market Share Litigation, 79 N.Y.2d 299, 304, 582 N.Y.S.2d 377, 591 N.E.2d 226 (1992); In re Luria's Estate, 63 Misc. 2d 675, 313 N.Y.S.2d 12 (Sur. Ct., Kings County 1970).

[14]   Motor Vehicle Mfrs. Ass'n of U.S., Inc. v. State, 75 N.Y.2d 175, 551 N.Y.S.2d 470, 550 N.E.2d 919 (1990).

[15]   Dom. Rel. Law § 173.

[16]   Dom. Rel. Law § 143.

[17]   RPAPL 745.

[18]   As to waiver of jury trial, see § 378.

[19]   See, e.g., CPLR 3034(3), treated in § 609.

[20]   See generally 2d Rep. Leg. Doc. No. 13, pp. 217 to 218 (1958).

[21]   See *Matter of Luria,* 63 Misc. 2d at 676–80, 313 N.Y.S.2d at 14–17.

between the two. With the additional factor of the liberalization of practice and procedure, claims previously associated with one context can now arise in different ones. It is the changed-context claim that is likely to account for the relatively few instances in which a traceback of the claim, to determine its pre-1777 antecedents and hence its triability by jury, is needed today. This was so in the *Garfield* case, for example, where a simple money claim (law) appeared in an "accounting" context (presumably equity) in the surrogate's court, the Court of Appeals downgrading the context and awarding the right to a jury based on the relief sought. Similar conclusions explain how a jury is awarded on a simple money claim interposed in a corporation's behalf in a derivative suit.[22]

Perhaps the most interesting case in which inquiry may be needed into the right to trial by jury is the declaratory judgment action, which did not come into being in New York until long after the merger of law and equity. Because the declaratory action is not taken up until later in this book, however, treatment of trial by jury in that category is postponed until then.[23]

Sometimes trial by jury, otherwise required, has been abolished by the constitution or by a statute with constitutional sanction. A notable illustration here is the worker's compensation claim.[24]

CPLR 4101 declares that "equitable defenses and equitable counterclaims" are to be tried by the court. This applies even though they are interposed in what is otherwise a law action. Where, for example, P sues for money on a contract and D counterclaims for reformation of that contract, the reformation claim is clearly equitable and if tried separately from the main claim, which it may be, does not get a jury. The same would be true even if all the defendant wants to accomplish with that "counterclaim" is to avoid liability on the plaintiff's claim, i.e., where the defendant is in effect using the equitable "counterclaim" as an equitable defense. Under prior law, much effort was spent determining whether a counterclaim was being used as a mere "defense" to the main claim, in which case it would go to a jury if the main claim did, or as a true "counterclaim," in which event the court would try it. CPLR 4101 spares that effort by directing the court to try it without a jury whatever category it falls under.[25]

The nature of this kind of "counterclaim/defense" will be looked at by the court, which will determine whether a jury is required, even where it's twice removed from the main claim. For example, assume P sued for money, D pleaded release as a defense, and P in a reply then sought to rescind the release. Whether regarded as a counterclaim or as a defense, the rescission demand contained in the reply was held equitable and not triable by jury. Furthermore, since everything else in the case depended first on the rescission demand, it was even granted a separate and prior trial.[26]

---

[22]   See Fedoryszyn v. Weiss, note 3, above, and accompanying text.

[23]   See § 439.

[24]   N.Y. Const. art. I, § 18.

[25]   See Menado Corp. v. Indemnity Ins. Co. of North America, 53 Misc. 2d 533, 279 N.Y.S.2d 84 (N.Y. City Civ. Ct. 1967).

[26]   See Rill v. Darling, 44 Misc. 2d 174, 253 N.Y.S.2d 184 (Sup. Ct., Madison County 1964). For the origin of this problem and the distinction between an equitable and a legal defense, see 2d Rep. Leg. Doc. No. 13, p. 576 (1958).

A counterclaim interposed in its own right rather than just as an offset—by "offset" is meant a mere endeavor to neutralize the plaintiff's claim—will be independently measured for triability by jury, a matter discussed in the next section.

When there are both legal and equitable claims present, the court may have to do some careful analyzing to determine the proper allotment of the fact-finding function, a matter illustrated in Mercantile & General Reinsurance Co., plc v. Colonial Assur. Co.,[27] in which S was in the business of guaranteeing that capital equipment would have a stated and specific residual value at a designated future date. To make its product more attractive to customers, S secured insurance with X to back up its guarantees. X then reinsured with insurer P. Alleging that misrepresentations had been made by S, P later brought suit against both S and X for a formal rescission of the reinsurance contract. The rescission claim was equitable and triable by the court without a jury. But S counterclaimed against P for money damages in both contract and tort based on S's loss of customers. That claim sounded at law and was jury triable.

A jury was impaneled to hear the case and the judge gave the jury interrogatories covering both the legal and equitable claims. The answers revealed that the jury's verdict was for S: that S had made no misrepresentations and that it was P who breached the contract. The verdict was of course binding—at least tentatively—in respect of the law claim, but only advisory on the rescission claim, which, sounding in equity, was for the court to decide. Exercising its prerogative to disregard the advisory segment of the verdict, the trial court set aside the jury's finding that S had made no misrepresentations and found that S did indeed make them. It awarded P judgment rescinding the contract even though this nullified the verdict that the jury had awarded S on its money counterclaim.

The Court of Appeals upheld the trial court's power to do this, explaining that the facts in respect of the rescission claim did not overlap any of the facts the jury found on the law claim. It observed that

> [t]o find material misrepresentation [which supports rescission], the court did not need to contradict any of the factual findings the jury made in deciding the factual issues pertinent to the legal claim for breach of contract because a finding of material misrepresentation is not inconsistent with a finding that the parties entered into a contract. To the contrary, the very essence of a rescission action is to set aside a contract that is otherwise valid and binding.[28]

§ 378. Demand and Waiver of Trial by Jury

CPLR 4102 contains the basics about how to demand trial by jury and the ways in which a jury may be waived. We assume, for purposes of this discussion, that the case is one triable by jury.

Trial by jury must as a rule be affirmatively demanded, and the place to demand it is in the note of issue. Thus, if the party filing the note of issue[1] wants a jury trial, she must demand it in the note of issue. This is usually done simply by putting a check mark

---

[27]   Mercantile & General Reinsurance Co., plc v. Colonial Assur. Co., 82 N.Y.2d 248, 604 N.Y.S.2d 492, 624 N.E.2d 629 (1993).

[28]   Mercantile & General Reinsurance Co., 82 N.Y.2d at 253, 604 N.Y.S.2d at 493, 624 N.E.2d at 630. This case is the subject of the lead note in NYSLD No. 409. Its impact is explored at length in Bernard E. Gegan, *Turning Back the Clock on the Trial of Equitable Defenses in New York*, 68 St. John's L. Rev. 823 (1994).

[1]   CPLR 3402(a). Any party may file the note of issue.

in the appropriate box on a printed note of issue form.[2] If a party served with a note of issue not containing the demand wants a jury trial, the procedure is to serve and file a "demand" for trial by jury within 15 days after being served with the note of issue. If no party demands trial by jury in one of these ways, trial by jury is deemed waived by all parties.[3] A note of issue silent as to the right to trial by jury is therefore a waiver of it by the one filing the note.

The CPLR does allow the chief administrator of the courts to provide by local rules for the reverse: that a silent note of issue is deemed to demand the jury.[4] However, the party filing the note of issue, if she wants jury trial, does herself no harm by affirmatively making the demand for it in the note of issue even if such a rule is in force. A party who would rely on such a rule, in any event, had best ascertain that it is currently in force. Trial by jury is a substantial right and rule changes are easy to overlook.

Once trial by jury has been duly demanded by a party, the demand cannot be withdrawn without the consent of the other parties.[5] This is designed to enable each party to rely on a jury demand made by any other, obviating an additional demand and sparing a plethora of demands. CPLR 4102(a) requires the consent of all parties to the withdrawal of the jury demand "regardless of whether another party previously filed a note of issue without a demand."[6]

The one who first demands a jury may specify only certain issues on which trial by jury is sought.[7] Absent such a specification, the demand will be deemed to cover all issues.[8] If the demand is for only some issues, any other party may, within 10 days after service of the limited demand, serve and file a demand for jury trial of some or all of the rest of the issues.[9] In order to save the time and trouble of trial by jury, the rules may express a preference that if only some issues are to be tried by jury, those that are not should be tried first,[10] just in case they prove dispositive and make a jury trial unnecessary.

CPLR 4102(c) provides that a party will also waive trial by jury by failing to appear at the trial, by filing a written waiver with the clerk, or by waiving it orally in open court, and that these things will waive the jury even if that party is the one who previously demanded it. But if such a demand was duly made, any other party may—as noted— continue to rely on it. Therefore, an attempted waiver now by the one who demanded the jury will not cancel the jury if any other party still wants it. Thus, once a demand has been made by one party, some kind of waiver conduct will generally have to be shown against all parties before trial by jury will be cancelled.

In this era of calendar congestion, many judges, recognizing that a trial with a jury is much more demanding and time consuming than one without, welcome jury waivers. Sometimes they may even suggest the waiver. This is permissible only if no undue

---

[2]   See § 371 for the note of issue form.

[3]   CPLR 4102(a).

[4]   CPLR 4102(d).

[5]   CPLR 4102(a).

[6]   It took an amendment of CPLR 4102(a) in 1990 to restore this assurance, overruling Gonzalez v. Concourse Plaza Syndicates, Inc., 41 N.Y.2d 414, 393 N.Y.S.2d 362, 361 N.E.2d 1011 (1977).

[7]   CPLR 4102(b); see the note of issue form in § 371.

[8]   CPLR 4102(b).

[9]   CPLR 4102(b).

[10] See, e.g., 22 N.Y.C.R.R. § 202.40.

pressure is brought to bear by the judge. Judicial pressure is often difficult for a lawyer to resist, and if an appellate court finds on the record that the judge overstepped discretion in exacting the waiver, such as where the judge threatened to declare a mistrial and start over unless the case was continued before him without the jury, it will undo the coerced stipulation of waiver and remand the case for a new trial.[11]

Jury waiver can result in other ways than those recited by CPLR 4102(c). It can be waived in a contract between the parties,[12] and as long as no deceit is shown affecting the waiver of jury clause, a mere unawareness of the clause's existence will not necessarily undo the waiver.[13] There is some dispute about that, however.[14] In actions where there is a fraudulent inducement cause of action that challenges the validity of the underlying agreement, including the jury waiver clause, the party is entitled to a jury trial on the claim.[15] The waiver should in any event be clear and unequivocal, for it will be strictly construed against the party who drafted the instrument containing it.[16]

Even if the waiver is in an "adhesion" contract, it is apparently valid. It has been held valid, in any event, in one category often qualifying as an adhesion contract: the residential apartment lease. The lease waiver suffices to cancel jury trial in the summary proceeding, the usual landlord/tenant device designed to collect the rent or dispossess the tenant for non-payment or for holding over past term.[17] In actions between landlord and tenant "for personal injury or property damage," however, the waiver has been made ineffective by statute,[18] thus preserving the right to trial by jury in those categories[19] even if it has been waived in respect of the rent collection and dispossession claims.

A waiver resulting from a failure to comply with CPLR 4102, such as by omitting to demand a jury by the methods specified, can be relieved by the court "if no undue prejudice to the rights of another party would result."[20] Intentional waivers are not likely to be undone on this authority,[21] but if the waiver was inadvertent, such as where the paper first filed omitted the jury demand but was corrected shortly afterwards by a refiling with a paper containing the demand, it has been forgiven and the late demand accepted.[22] Needless to say, the party relying on such an amnesty is tempting fate. Trial by jury is too precious to let pass as a matter of right and then seek as a matter of

---

[11] Kay v. Tankel, 16 A.D.2d 96, 225 N.Y.S.2d 642 (1st Dep't 1962).

[12] See Tiffany At Westbury Condominium v. Marelli Development Corp., 34 A.D.3d 791, 826 N.Y.S.2d 623 (2d Dep't 2006).

[13] James Talcott, Inc. v. Wilson Hosiery Co., 32 A.D.2d 524, 299 N.Y.S.2d 460 (1st Dep't 1969); Estate of Greenberg, 102 Misc. 2d 308, 425 N.Y.S.2d 909 (App. Term, 1st Dep't 1979).

[14] See Colgate Const. Corp. v. Hill, 70 Misc. 2d 646, 334 N.Y.S.2d 1002 (Mount Vernon City Ct. 1972).

[15] J.P. Morgan Securities Inc. v. Ader, 127 A.D.3d 506, 506, 9 N.Y.S.3d 181 (1st Dep't 2015).

[16] Barrow v. Bloomfield, 30 A.D.2d 947, 293 N.Y.S.2d 1007 (1st Dep't 1968); 2475 Hughes Ave. Realty Corp. v. Gonzalez, 28 Misc. 3d 266, 897 N.Y.S.2d 830 (N.Y. City Civ. Ct. 2010).

[17] See Teitler v. Tetenbaum, 123 Misc. 2d 702, 477 N.Y.S.2d 544 (App. Term, 1st Dep't 1984); Belmont Theatre Corp. v. Bunny Cinema Corp., 71 Misc. 2d 379, 336 N.Y.S.2d 298 (N.Y. City Civ. Ct. 1972).

[18] Real Prop. Law § 259–c.

[19] See Avenue Associates, Inc. v. Buxbaum, 83 Misc. 2d 719, 373 N.Y.S.2d 814 (App.Term., 1st Dep't 1975), rev'g 83 Misc. 2d 134, 371 N.Y.S.2d 736 (N.Y. City Civ. Ct. 1975).

[20] CPLR 4102(e); Debevoise & Plimpton LLP v. Candlewood Timber Group LLC, 102 A.D.3d 571, 959 N.Y.S.2d 43 (1st Dep't 2013).

[21] See Fischer v. RWSP Realty, LLC, 53 A.D.3d 595, 597, 862 N.Y.S.2d 539, 541 (2d Dep't 2008); Heller v. Hacken, 40 A.D.2d 1012, 338 N.Y.S.2d 943 (2d Dep't 1972).

[22] See In re Mirsky's Estate, 81 Misc. 2d 9, 365 N.Y.S.2d 122 (Sur. Ct., New York County 1975); see also Tanger v. Ferrer, 100 A.D.3d 528, 954 N.Y.S.2d 86 (1st Dep't 2012).

discretion, which the court possesses in abundance in determining whether to forgive the waiver.

A waiver of trial by jury is itself waivable. If a contract waives trial by jury, for example, but a jury is demanded and no one makes a timely objection to it, trial by jury will proceed.[23]

The joinder of claims, or of different demands for relief in respect of but a single claim, is a sensitive area when jury trial is at stake and should be carefully considered. The rules come from clunky language in CPLR 4102(c). If a plaintiff has two or more entirely separate claims emanating from separate transactions, the plaintiff can under the rules of joinder sue on them in one action.[24] If one claim asks legal relief (jury) and the other equitable relief (no jury), the plaintiff will not, by the joinder, forfeit the right to a jury trial on the legal claim. But a plaintiff who joins claims or demands based on the same transaction, asking legal relief on one and equitable relief on the other, or in the alternative, waives trial by jury entirely. Thus, the plaintiff who seeks both money damages (jury) and an injunction (no jury) based on the same transaction will be held to waive trial by jury even on the money claim. Furthermore, if a party has contractually waived a right to trial by jury on a claim, and joins it with a claim for which it has a right to a jury trial, the party waives its right to a jury trial on both claims if they arise from the same transaction.[25]

In Cioffi v. S.M. Foods, Inc.,[26] plaintiff commenced an action for personal injuries and also attempted to pierce a defendant's corporate veil to hold its principals individually liable. The court noted that piercing a corporate veil does not constitute an independent cause of action against the corporation. While the piercing of a corporate veil is equitable in nature, the court concluded that plaintiffs' personal injury action sought only legal relief in the form of money damages and reliance on the equitable theory of piercing the corporate veil did not amount to a waiver of the right to a jury trial.

The plaintiff's pleading of legal and equitable claims arising out of the same transaction does not affect the defendant, however, who can still demand a jury on the money claim.[27]

Similarly, CPLR 4102(c) prescribes that a defendant who interposes a counterclaim, cross-claim, or third-party claim, itself jury triable, in an action in which the main claim is not jury triable, does not waive the jury on the new claim. This is so even though all of the claims emanate from the same transaction. Thus, where P sues for specific performance (no jury) and D counterclaims for money damages (jury) on the same contract, D is entitled to jury trial of the counterclaim. But when the claims are reversed, and P brings a claim triable by jury and D meets it with a related counterclaim not triable by jury, there is presently a conflict. Some courts hold that D waives trial by jury

---

[23]   See Sapp v. Propeller Co. LLC, 12 A.D.3d 218, 784 N.Y.S.2d 532 (1st Dep't 2004); Import Alley of Mid-Island, Inc. v. Mid-Island Shopping Plaza, Inc., 103 A.D.2d 797, 477 N.Y.S.2d 675 (2d Dep't 1984).

[24]   CPLR 601; see § 126.

[25]   See *Tiffany at Westbury Condo.,* 34 A.D.3d at 792, 826 N.Y.S.2d at 624.

[26]   Cioffi v. S.M. Foods, Inc., 129 A.D.3d 888, 894, 10 N.Y.S.3d 620, 627 (2d Dep't 2015).

[27]   *Heller,* 40 A.D.2d at 1013, 338 N.Y.S.2d at 944; Vinlis Const. Co. v. Roreck, 23 A.D.2d 895, 260 N.Y.S.2d 245 (2d Dep't 1965).

even on P's law claim in that situation.[28] Others say no and preserve D's right to jury trial on the law claim on the theory that a contrary holding would only encourage D to bring his equitable claim separately because by so doing he would at least preserve the right to demand a jury trial in P's law action.[29]

Suppose that the interposer of the law claim wants a jury trial, is entitled to it, and demands it. What happens if the nonjury claim, interposed by the other party, involves common issues of fact, as is likely to be the case when all the claims arise out of the same transaction? Take the example of P suing for damages for breach of a real property contract (jury triable with a jury duly demanded by P), with D counterclaiming for specific performance (for which there is no jury). Since each contends that the other breached the contract, the facts can ordinarily be determined only one way. The jury will have to try the facts on the damages claim while the court must resolve the same facts on the specific performance claim. If judge and jury disagree, there is an apparent dilemma, which seems to have no theoretical solution.

It does have a practical solution, however. As will be seen in a later section, the court has the power to convene an "advisory" jury even for cases triable by the court.[30] Exercising that power, the court can treat the jury, impaneled as of right for the damages claim, as an advisory one on the specific performance claim, and merely adopt the jury's findings, if supportable, to dispose of all the claims.[31]

Yet another possibility in this situation might be to have one claim tried before the other, which is usually in the court's discretion to do as a matter of the sequence of trial.[32] The problem this time is that if the nonjury claim is tried first and its results are sought to be given res judicata or collateral estoppel effect on the jury claim, it can amount to a back-door divestiture of trial by jury.[33] When the equitable claim is one to rescind a contract, the Court of Appeals has held that it may be decided by the court even if its effect is to bar jury-triable damages claims based on the same contract, interposed by other parties.[34] The Court does not apprehend this as a negation of the right to trial by jury because the right doesn't arise unless there's a contract and the court in the exercise of its equity powers can, by ordering a rescission, determine that there is none.[35]

Another situation that periodically arises is that in which the parties prepare for only one mode of trial, based on the claim initially interposed, only to have it appear at the trial itself that another mode is appropriate. This happens, for example, when P brings an equitable claim and has it processed all the way up to trial on the nonjury calendar. It is now tried by the judge, who finds that P, while not having made out a

---

[28] See Nationscredit Financial Services Corp. v. Turcios, 55 A.D.3d 806, 865 N.Y.S.2d 556 (2d Dep't 2008).

[29] See, e.g., International Playtex, Inc. v. CIS Leasing Corp., 115 A.D.2d 271, 495 N.Y.S.2d 864 (4th Dep't 1985).

[30] CPLR 4212; see § 381.

[31] See Motor Vehicle Mfrs. Ass'n of U.S., Inc. v. State, 75 N.Y.2d 175, 551 N.Y.S.2d 470, 550 N.E.2d 919 (1990), discussed in § 377; see also John W. Cowper Co., Inc. v. Buffalo Hotel Development Venture, 99 A.D.2d 19, 471 N.Y.S.2d 913 (4th Dep't 1984).

[32] CPLR 4011, 603; see Vinlis Const. Co. v. Roreck, 23 A.D.2d 895, 260 N.Y.S.2d 245 (2d Dep't 1965); §§ 129, 394.

[33] See *Import Alley of Mid-Island, Inc.*, 103 A.D.2d at 798, 477 N.Y.S.2d at 676–77.

[34] This is what occurred in the *Motor Vehicle Manufacturers* case discussed above.

[35] On this point, note also the Court of Appeals *Mercantile* decision in § 377.

claim for equitable relief, has established enough to warrant damages, a law recovery.[36] If D objects, on the reasonable ground that he would have been entitled to a jury had the case been processed, as it should have been, as a law claim, D must now be afforded an opportunity to demand a jury trial before the legal relief can ensue.[37] This can entail a whole new trial, before a jury. The court may even require an amended complaint, specifying legal relief,[38] and, as a calendar matter, order the case re-noticed for trial on a jury calendar.[39]

The converse of the above—a case starting out at law and therefore being tried by jury only to have it appear at the trial that equitable relief is permissible and is now sought by the plaintiff—is a rarity. Should it arise, it's not a serious problem. The jury can merely be dismissed, and the judge, in attendance all the while, can make the findings of fact bearing on the equitable claim. The court must be sensitive in this instance, however, to permit the defendant to introduce any defenses he may have to the equitable claim that were not relevant to the legal claim, such as the defense of laches or unclean hands.

§ 379. Triability by Referee

The CPLR provides that if the case is triable by neither a jury nor a referee, it is tried by the judge.[1] Triability by jury is the subject of the prior sections, trial by the judge the subject of the next one. Trial by referee is the subject of this one. When may a referee be the trier?

A referee is a person (usually a lawyer)[2] appointed by the court to conduct a hearing or to perform some court-related function. Also permitted to serve as a "referee" is a "judicial hearing officer," a retired judge who has been duly certified as able to perform judicial duties, or a court attorney reference employed by the Unified Court System.[3]

The CPLR recognizes three kinds of references: (1) to determine an issue; (2) to perform an act; and (3) to hear and report on an issue.[4] The terms of a reference are set forth in a court order.[5] The reference to determine, category 1, means that the referee hears the case as the court would and the decision is binding.

There are several kinds of category 2 references for the performance of acts found in and out of the CPLR. One CPLR kind is the assignment of a referee to supervise all disclosure proceedings in a case.[6] Other frequently met category 2 references include the

---

[36] An example would be a claim for specific performance found at the trial to be barred by laches, while a damages claim, which is not subject to the laches doctrine, is alive and sustainable. See § 36 (discussing laches).

[37] CPLR 4103.

[38] Newman v. Resnick, 38 Misc. 2d 94, 238 N.Y.S.2d 119 (Sup. Ct., New York County 1963).

[39] *Vinlis Construction*, 23 A.D.2d at 896, 260 N.Y.S.2d at 247–48.

[1] CPLR 4211.

[2] CPLR 4312(1).

[3] See CPLR 105. A 1983 amendment of CPLR 4301 included the judicial hearing officer in the "referee" definition. Related amendments in CPLR 4312, 4313, 4315, and 4321 are discussed in the Commentaries on those provisions in McKinney's CPLR.

[4] CPLR 4001; see Hunter v. Hunter, 54 Misc. 3d 477, 43 N.Y.S.3d 881 (Sup. Ct., Essex County 2016). One might consider as a fourth kind a reference to receive and report evidence, see CPLR 4311, which presumably means that the referee will not even suggest tentative conclusions, but leave them entirely to the judge.

[5] See 22 N.Y.C.R.R. § 202.43.

[6] CPLR 3104.

referee appointed to mortgage, lease, or sell real property in various contexts or to oversee the foreclosure settlement process required by CPLR 3408.[7] The reference to hear and report, category 3, makes the referee a kind of assistant to the court. The referee conducts a hearing and reports her findings and conclusions back to the court, which can accept or reject them. The report of a referee to report, in other words, is only a recommendation, while the decision of a referee to determine is binding, like the decision of a judge.

The provisions about referees are not in the best order in the CPLR. By its title, "Trial by a Referee," Article 43 would seem to reposit all one needs to know about referees, but while it does supply the general powers and procedures to be followed by referees, it is CPLR 4001 which in broad language invests the court with the power to appoint them. The appointment power in CPLR 4001, however, lacks specifics. These may be found in Article 43 for the reference to determine[8] and in Article 42 for the reference to report.[9] Article 42 also concerns trial by the court, but since the reference to report is only a recommendation, with the court retaining the power and responsibility of the final decision, Article 42 was deemed the proper place for it.

The reference to determine is authorized by CPLR 4317, which provides in subdivision (a) for the reference by consent of the parties and in subdivision (b) for the reference by court direction regardless of the parties' consent.

CPLR 4317(a) states that when the parties stipulate, "any issue" shall be determined by a referee, and it permits the parties to designate the referee themselves. This is accomplished with a stipulation and order. But in three listed instances, a reference to determine, even if desired by all parties, requires leave of court and the court to designate the referee: (1) matrimonial actions; (2) certain actions to dissolve a corporation or to receive or distribute its property; and (3) actions in which a defendant is an infant.

The matrimonial exception is designed to prevent the parties from obtaining a simple consent divorce or other matrimonial relief merely by appointing a referee who will give them what they want without regard to the evidence. The corporate dissolution exception contemplates the proceedings of Article 11 of the Business Corporation Law.[10]

The reference to determine without the parties' consent, which comes from CPLR 4317(b), is commonly known as a "compulsory reference." This category of reference is authorized in "long account" cases or to try damages if they are separately triable and don't require trial by jury.

The "long account" case is an old example of the compulsory reference. If the account involved is a "long" one in this sense, it can even take the fact-findings away from a jury, and, over the objections of a party, give them to a referee to determine, presumably a person of expertise in the subject involved. This is constitutional because New York's first constitution, that of 1777, guaranteed trial by jury only in cases in which it was

---

[7]   See RPAPL 1611, CPLR 3408(i).

[8]   CPLR 4317.

[9]   CPLR 4212. Provisions concerning referees also appear in the Uniform Rules. See 22 N.Y.C.R.R. § 202.43.

[10]   See Dalminter, Inc. v. Siderexport S.p.A., 23 A.D.2d 749, 258 N.Y.S.2d 954 (1st Dep't 1965). If the action is brought by the attorney-general, leave of court for the reference is not needed. CPLR 4317(a). See also Matter of Cohen, 215 A.D.2d 341, 627 N.Y.S.2d 40 (1st Dep't 1995) (order of reference to hear and report in valuation proceeding pursuant to Bus. Corp. Law § 1118 was permissible).

theretofore used,[11] and the pre-1777 practice was to allow the compulsory reference in long account cases.[12]

That a long account is involved, sufficient to invoke this compulsory reference provision, must appear from the plaintiff's statement of the cause of action in the complaint. If only a counterclaim manifests a long account, the compulsory reference may not be used unless the counterclaiming defendant in effect concedes the plaintiff's claim—because that's the way things were before 1777.[13] The quantity of items the account involves is not the sole, or even the main, criterion for determining whether it is a "long" one justifying the reference. Rather, it must be shown that the issues are "so numerous and tedious that it would be impossible for a jury to resolve them within the reasonable time limits of a trial."[14]

It need not be a law action that presents the long account and invokes the compulsory reference. An equity action—of which the accounting action itself would be the most relevant example—can do it, too,[15] although the contract action at law is the context from which the compulsory reference emerged.[16]

The compulsory reference has been cited by analogy to sustain the special system of appointing "housing judges" to the housing part of the New York City Civil Court pursuant to section 110 of its court act.[17]

The other provision of CPLR 4317(b), authorizing a nonconsensual reference "to determine an issue of damages separately triable and not requiring a trial by jury," was added by the CPLR's drafters because, they stated, the same reason justifying the compulsory reference of long account cases—their intricacy and difficulty—applies as well to the trial of complex damages issues.[18] When a jury trial is required and demanded for the damages issues, this provision acknowledges as much and excludes a reference.

Damages are "separately triable" in several situations. One is where summary judgment has been granted on liability and only damages remain to be tried.[19] If the case would have gone to trial by jury if there had been no summary judgment, the damages trial must also be by jury if a party insists.[20] By acknowledging this, CPLR 4317(b) wards off the risk of being found unconstitutional. An instance in which damages are "separately triable," but where a compulsory reference might be allowed, is where a default has conceded liability.[21] CPLR 3215(b) expressly authorizes a compulsory

---

[11]   The history of jury trial is discussed in § 377.

[12]   The leading case on the point, replete with historical traceback, is Steck v. Colorado Fuel & Iron Co., 142 N.Y. 236, 37 N.E. 1 (1894).

[13]   See Schaffer v. City Bank Farmers Trust Co., 269 N.Y. 336, 199 N.E. 503 (1936).

[14]   Schanback v. Schanback, 130 A.D.2d 332, 519 N.Y.S.2d 819 (2d Dep't 1987); Longo v. Adirondack Drilling, Inc., 14 A.D.2d 476, 217 N.Y.S.2d 905 (3d Dep't 1961).

[15]   See Thayer v. McNaughton, 117 N.Y. 111, 22 N.E. 562 (1889).

[16]   Steck v. Colorado Fuel & Iron Co., note 12, above.

[17]   See Glass v. Thompson, 51 A.D.2d 69, 379 N.Y.S.2d 427 (2d Dep't 1976). At the outset the housing judges were called "hearing officers."

[18]   See 2d Rep. Leg. Doc. No. 13 at pp. 250–51 (1958).

[19]   CPLR 3212(c); see § 285.

[20]   Caplan v. Tofel, 33 A.D.3d 748, 822 N.Y.S.2d 760 (2d Dep't 2006); see Commentary C3212:27 on McKinney's CPLR 3212.

[21]   For the right to jury trial in that situation, see Commentary C3215:7 on McKinney's CPLR 3215.

reference and provides that judgment may be entered "in accordance with the [referee's] report without any further application."

All we have just discussed concerns the reference to determine. The referee to determine has the same powers the court would have in carrying out a like function,[22] except that a referee can't relieve himself of his duties or appoint a successor. He has the power to punish for contempt a witness before him but no other contempt powers.[23] Therefore, he can't enforce a decision through the contempt power, as a judge might do on certain judgments. It has also been held that a referee may not decide to bifurcate[24] a trial, i.e., try liability and damages in separate segments. This conclusion is based on the language in CPLR 4311, which specifically states that the order assigning a referee shall direct the referee to determine "the entire action or specific issues." Therefore, the decision about what the referee is to try "will already have been made" by the court.[25]

The reference to report, because it amounts to only a recommendation rather than a final decision, is not quite so delicate. A reference made just "for hearing," without specifying what kind it is, will ordinarily be assumed to be a reference to hear and report.[26] Although the parties in a jury-triable case can waive the jury and agree instead to a reference to report (or, for that matter, even a reference to determine), this category of reference is mainly associated with court-triable issues. The main source of the reference to report is CPLR 4212, which allows the court to submit "any issue of fact required to be decided by the court" to a referee to report, but only "upon a showing of some exceptional condition requiring it or in matters of account."[27]

The reference to report may be sought under CPLR 4212 on the motion of a party. A motion for trial by a referee should ordinarily be made within 20 days after the note of issue is filed.[28] This presumably applies to the reference to determine as well as to the reference to report, but in either instance the 20 days should be subject to extension by stipulation of the parties or by court order.[29] An application for a reference should not be made before the note of issue is filed.[30]

Just as the reference to determine may be directed by the court sua sponte, so may a reference to report be made by the court "on its own initiative."[31] This suggests that the consent of the parties to a reference to report is not needed. That is indeed the assumption of much caselaw,[32] even including cases that demonstrate hostility to the reference.[33] The absence of consent is in any event an element to be considered by the

---

[22]   Bauer v. Special Brands NY, Inc., 138 A.D.3d 1048, 31 N.Y.S.3d 132 (2d Dep't 2016).

[23]   CPLR 4301; Hoffman v. Helm Capital Group, Inc., 104 A.D.3d 608, 609, 961 N.Y.S.2d 456 (1st Dep't 2013).

[24]   On bifurcation, see § 130.

[25]   Dunleavy v. White, 236 A.D.2d 316, 653 N.Y.S.2d 597 (1st Dep't 1997), involving a judicial hearing officer, who is considered a referee by CPLR 4301.

[26]   See Sternberg v. Sternberg, 88 A.D.2d 950, 451 N.Y.S.2d 187 (2d Dep't 1982).

[27]   As noted earlier in this section, if the account qualifies as a "long account" within the meaning of CPLR 4317(b), it is of course subject to a reference to determine rather than just a reference to report, and a compulsory one at that.

[28]   CPLR 4015.

[29]   CPLR 2004; see § 6.

[30]   See 22 N.Y.C.R.R. § 202.43(a), applicable to references in the supreme and county courts.

[31]   CPLR 4212.

[32]   See Llorente v. City of New York, 60 A.D.3d 1003, 876 N.Y.S.2d 478 (2d Dep't 2009).

[33]   See Wilder v. Silbert, 5 A.D.2d 1, 168 N.Y.S.2d 1005 (1st Dep't 1957).

court in deciding whether to refer the matter. Some cases indicate that the reference to report is restricted to only that which the parties consent to.[34] A constitutional argument can be urged against a reference to report made over a party's objection. It can be urged that the party has a right to have the case tried before a duly constituted judge of the court[35] and that this requirement is not met merely by having the judge review the referee's findings.[36] The argument, whichever way it may ultimately be resolved, loses currency if all parties consent to the reference.

Even assuming the court's power to make a reference to report without consent of all parties, the "exceptional condition" requirement of CPLR 4212 must still be met, and it is not met if the issue can be decided by the court "without extraordinary impingement on [its] regular business."[37]

Attitudes about references may be influenced by the condition of judicial calendars and may vary among departments and even from time to time within a given department. In Angelo v. Laremet Corp.,[38] for example, the Third Department said that as long as judges are available they should try all controverted issues, with or without a jury—as the nature of the case dictates—notwithstanding a statutory permission to refer them. Circumstances changed in the Third Department after that, with judges becoming scarcer, and the department more receptive to the use of referees.[39]

These factors are important if the court proposes to refer a matter without the parties' consent. Their import drops considerably and in most cases even disappears if the consent is present. If the parties consent, who is there to complain?

Practically speaking, it's the consensual reference to report that one sees more often. A reference to report is a good way to have the case heard by an expert on the particular subject or to expedite matters when a number of documents have to be analyzed.[40] The referee to report may be analogized in many ways to the old master in chancery, who acted as a kind of assistant to the chancellor in the carrying out of various judicial functions.[41] Vestiges of the master's role appear in Rule 53 of the Federal Rules of Civil Procedure, on which the CPLR's drafters occasionally drew in formulating the CPLR's referee provisions.[42]

As long as the parties consent to the reference, they will ordinarily be allowed to be their own judge of what condition suffices as "exceptional" enough to warrant it. Some very unexceptional situations have been voluntarily submitted to referees. Often an issue of personal jurisdiction is referred, whether complicated (as where a series of alleged longarm acts under CPLR 302 have to be parsed) or simple (as where the

---

[34]   See Fernald v. Vinci, 302 A.D.2d 354, 355, 754 N.Y.S.2d 668, 669 (2d Dep't 2003).

[35]   See, e.g., De Hart v. Hatch, 3 Hun 375, 6 Thomp. & C. 186 (Gen.T. 1st Dep't, 1875), which speaks of the court's duty to "entertain" a case as well as determine it.

[36]   Cf. L. H. Feder Corp. v. Bozkurtian, 48 A.D.2d 701, 368 N.Y.S.2d 247 (2d Dep't 1975).

[37]   Luppino v. Mosey, 103 A.D.3d 1117, 1119, 958 N.Y.S.2d 823 (4th Dep't 2013).

[38]   Angelo v. Laremet Corp., 23 A.D.2d 191, 259 N.Y.S.2d 428 (3d Dep't 1965).

[39]   See Keown v. Wright, 89 A.D.2d 932, 454 N.Y.S.2d 49 (3d Dep't 1982).

[40]   See Burlington Industries, Inc. v. Eastern Exp., Inc., 23 A.D.2d 841, 259 N.Y.S.2d 678 (1st Dep't 1965).

[41]   See La Buy v. Howes Leather Company, 352 U.S. 249, 77 S. Ct. 309, 1 L. Ed. 2d 290 (1957); In re Peterson (State Report Title: Ex Parte Peterson), 253 U.S. 300, 40 S. Ct. 543, 64 L. Ed. 919 (1920).

[42]   See 2d Rep. Leg. Doc. No. 13, p. 244 et seq. (1958).

question is whether or not the process server properly served the summons on the defendant).

Trial in the usual way will not be deemed waived by implication, so the agreement to refer must be clear from the order of reference and the referee must restrict herself to the matters referred.[43] The order of reference should be specific about the referee's obligations, i.e., whether the referee is to perform an act, hear all or only designated issues, report them, or report only the evidence offered on them, or decide them (if it's a reference to determine), etc. It may limit the referee's powers and fix a time and place for the hearing.[44] Unless the order of reference otherwise prescribes, a referee to report has the power to issue subpoenas, administer oaths, and preside over disclosure proceedings as well as the trial,[45] which is conducted in the same manner as a judge trying a nonjury case.[46]

The referee to report has 30 days, after the matter is submitted, in which to file the report with the assigning judge,[47] and the plaintiff has 15 days after notice of the filing of the report in which to move to confirm or reject the report.[48] If the plaintiff does not make the motion, the defendant has 30 days after the notice of filing to make it.[49] The court can reject the report in whole or in part, take additional testimony, make new findings, or even order a new hearing, but if no issues remain to be tried, the court must decide the case and direct judgment accordingly.[50] The referee to determine also has 30 days from submission in which to file, but in this instance, the thing filed is a decision rather than a report, and the decision stands as the decision of the court.[51] Unless authorized by administrative order, a referee cannot sign an order or judgment.

If all parties consent, the referee can be a layperson. Otherwise, the referee must be a duly qualified New York lawyer.[52] Parties can consent, for example, to a layperson who has much expertise in the subject matter involved. In matrimonial actions, only a judicial hearing officer or "special referee" so designated by the chief administrator of the courts may be used and may be designated even if all parties object.[53] Today, matrimonial parts throughout the State are staffed by court referees authorized by administrative order to

---

[43]   L. H. Feder Corp. v. Bozkurtian, 48 A.D.2d 701, 368 N.Y.S.2d 247 (2d Dep't 1975).

[44]   CPLR 4311.

[45]   CPLR 4201.

[46]   CPLR 4318, 4320(a).

[47]   CPLR 4320(b). A transcript of testimony and the exhibits must accompany the report unless the parties stipulate otherwise.

[48]   22 N.Y.C.R.R. § 202.44 elaborates the procedure for confirming or rejecting the report, placing the burden of the application on the plaintiff.

[49]   22 N.Y.C.R.R. § 202.44(a).

[50]   CPLR 4403.

[51]   CPLR 4319. In an extensive review of the history of the statutes on references, John Hancock Mut. Life Ins. Co. v. 491–499 Seventh Ave. Associates, 169 Misc. 2d 493, 644 N.Y.S.2d 953 (Sup. Ct., New York County 1996), concludes that CPLR 4319, concerning the time for rendering a decision, was not intended to govern a mere reference to report, which is governed instead by CPLR 4320. See the discussion of the *John Hancock* case in the Commentary on McKinney's CPLR 4319 and in SPR 57:3–4.

[52]   CPLR 4312(1). Provision is made to have three referees instead of one, but this is rare. If there should be three, proceedings are governed by CPLR 4316. Paragraphs 3 and 4 of CPLR 4312 disqualify as referees certain judicial and non-judicial personnel, and those associated with the lawyers in the case.

[53]   CPLR 4312(2). This provision is an effort to discourage consent divorces through the device of securing the services of amenable referees. It assumes that the parties, although having no voice in the selection of a referee, have nonetheless consented to a reference.

conduct pendente life proceedings. All but the judicial hearing officer and the "special" referee[54] must take an oath before embarking on their duties unless the oath is waived.[55]

The order of reference should determine "the basis and method of computing the referee's fees and provide for their payment," and the court may make an order for the referee's reasonable expenses.[56] In default of such a provision, the statutory rate would seem to apply.[57] That rate is unrealistically low,[58] but absent an order or stipulation directing as to the referee's fees, some courts hold that it applies. Others hold that the fee can be set at a higher figure by the court to fairly compensate the referee.[59] That's best done before the referred matter is heard, but it has been done afterwards.[60] Unless ordered or agreed otherwise, fees or expenses advanced to the referee may be recovered back by a winning party from the loser as part of a bill of costs.[61]

Dispute on these matters will be resolved by the court.[62] The referee is not to apply to the parties for money that hasn't been agreed to for the obvious reason that it can compromise his impartiality or the appearance of it.[63]

The additional expense incurred by the parties when a referee is used has been cited as further reason for limiting the use of referees to where the parties consent to it.[64]

§ 380. Triability by the Court

If the issues are not triable by jury, whether because jury trial is not available in the particular action or because a jury has been waived, and they have not been referred to a referee to determine, they must be decided by the court (the judge).[1] This means that the judge must decide fact issues not only when the judge is hearing the case alone but also when it has been heard by a referee to report or by an advisory jury.[2] The report of the referee or verdict of an advisory jury in that instance is only a recommendation and the final word lies with the judge.

Although the sequence of trial, i.e., the order in which the various trial steps are taken, is essentially the same whether a jury is present or the court is hearing the case

---

[54]   The "special" referee is an amorphous thing. The primary allusion by the CPLR's drafters to a "special" referee—that which now appears in CPLR 4312(2)—was deemed to require a "clarification" to indicate that the appellate division was to appoint him, see 5th Rep. Leg. Doc. No. 15 at p. 537 (1961), although it is not clear today whether a referee becomes "special" only when appointed by the appellate division. Apparently, a special referee is a "standing" one, such as a retired judge so designated, as opposed to one appointed on an ad hoc basis. The appointer of special referees today, in any event, is not the appellate division, but the chief administrator of the courts, and the adoption of the provisions on judicial hearing officers, who are retired judges (see CPLR 105), would seem to make the office of special referee superfluous anyway.

[55]   CPLR 4315.

[56]   CPLR 4321(1). The fees provision doesn't apply when a judicial hearing officer is the referee. CPLR 4321(2).

[57]   Pittoni v. Boland, 278 A.D.2d 396, 717 N.Y.S.2d 646 (2d Dep't 2000); Neuman v. Syosset Hosp. Anesthesia Group, P.C., 112 A.D.2d 1029, 493 N.Y.S.2d 26 (2d Dep't 1985).

[58]   It is presently $50 per day under CPLR 8003(a).

[59]   Blake Terrace Associates v. Sommers, 176 A.D.2d 394, 574 N.Y.S.2d 101 (3d Dep't 1991).

[60]   See O'Dwyer v. Robson, 103 A.D.2d 1036, 478 N.Y.S.2d 407 (4th Dep't 1984).

[61]   CPLR 4321(a).

[62]   See Davis v. Commercial Metals Co., 54 Misc. 2d 729, 283 N.Y.S.2d 366 (N.Y. City Civ. Ct. 1967).

[63]   National Bank of North America v. New Paltz Growers, Inc., 89 A.D.2d 647, 453 N.Y.S.2d 124 (3d Dep't 1982).

[64]   See Wilder v. Silbert, 5 A.D.2d 1, 168 N.Y.S.2d 1005 (1st Dep't 1957).

[1]   CPLR 4211.

[2]   The advisory jury is the subject of the next section.

alone,[3] it is less formal when there is no jury. The informality touches especially the rules of evidence, which are applied with less rigidity. While one periodically finds admonitions that even in a judge-tried case "the practice of overly admitting otherwise inadmissible evidence is not to be condoned,"[4] such admittings will not often necessitate a new trial. This is on the theory that since the appellate division in a judge-tried case stands in the position of the trial judge, it can disregard incompetent evidence in determining whether to uphold the decision and can render whatever judgment is appropriate to the proof as purged.

Before the case is finally submitted, the judge must allow the parties an opportunity to submit requests for findings of fact. These should be so numbered and phrased that the court may conveniently pass on them.[5] This has been held to mean that the requests should succinctly state, without being argumentative or repetitious, the ultimate facts on which the case turns, not the evidentiary facts on which they're bottomed.[6]

As measured from the final submission of the case, the judge has 60 days in which to render a decision unless the parties extend the time.[7] This is the same time a judge has in which to decide an ordinary motion and, as mentioned in that context,[8] the period is not jurisdictional and a late decision is not void.[9] Even a delay of 18 months, though found shocking, did not void the decision, especially not on the complaint of a loser who made no objection to the delay until he found out he'd lost.[10] A rule requires the chief administrator of the courts to get periodic accountings from all judges of any matters they have held for more than the maximum 60 days.[11] This helps to expedite decisions to a degree.

"The decision of the court may be oral or in writing and shall state the facts it deems essential." So provides CPLR 4213(b), disposing tersely of the court's obligation in judge-tried cases generally, but it goes on to require the judge to itemize damages in detail in the principal tort actions and in certain actions against public employers in order to facilitate the application of several other laws whose implementation requires a parsing of the verdict, such as the so-called "collateral source" rule,[12] contribution among tortfeasors,[13] and issues of joint and several liability.[14] These CPLR 4213(b) requirements in a court-tried case are akin to those imposed by CPLR 4111 in a jury case.[15]

---

[3]   CPLR 4011. The formalities of the trial stage are reserved for Chapter 15.

[4]   Dann v. Sands, 38 A.D.2d 661, 327 N.Y.S.2d 222, 223 (3d Dep't 1971); see Matter of Leon RR, 48 N.Y.2d 117, 122, 421 N.Y.S.2d 863, 397 N.E.2d 374 (1979).

[5]   CPLR 4213(a).

[6]   See Charles F. Ryan & Son, Inc. v. Lancaster Homes, Inc., 22 A.D.2d 186, 254 N.Y.S.2d 473 (4th Dep't 1964), aff'd, 15 N.Y.2d 812, 257 N.Y.S.2d 934, 205 N.E.2d 859 (1965); Capasso v. Capasso, 119 A.D.2d 268, 274, 506 N.Y.S.2d 686, 691 (1st Dep't 1986).

[7]   CPLR 4213(c).

[8]   See § 250.

[9]   Kessler v. Hunter, 53 Misc. 2d 965, 280 N.Y.S.2d 474 (Sup. Ct., Westchester County 1967); see Murov v. Celentano, 3 Misc. 3d 1, 4, 776 N.Y.S.2d 430, 431 (App. Term, 2d Dep't 2003) (addressing Uniform City Ct. Act § 1304, providing for a 30-day period in which a judgment is to be rendered in city courts).

[10]   Mix v. Tarazskiewicz, 24 A.D.2d 808, 263 N.Y.S.2d 784 (3d Dep't 1965).

[11]   See 22 N.Y.C.R.R. § 4.1 of the Rules of the Chief Judge.

[12]   CPLR 4545; see § 399.

[13]   CPLR Article 14; see §§ 169 to 177.

[14]   CPLR Article 16; see §§ 168A to 168D.

[15]   See the Commentaries on McKinney's CPLR 4111 and 4213.

An "oral" decision should be used only when rendered in open court and taken down by the stenographer. A written decision, no matter how terse, is preferable for many reasons, including appellate review, which is one of the main purposes of requiring that the essential facts found be stated.[16] Without those findings, the appellate court can't properly review the decision and may have to reverse and remand it for proper findings.[17] If the record before the appellate court is complete, however, it may, if it chooses, make the requisite findings itself and render a decision accordingly. This merely recognizes that in a court-tried case, the first-tier appellate court stands in the shoes of the trial judge.[18] Or the appellate court can take the middle step of holding the case in abeyance while remanding it to the lower court for findings and re-transmittal. This was done in a case that acts as a reminder that the parties' waiver of findings of fact, and of their right to make requests to find, does not relieve the trial judge of the responsibility under CPLR 4213(b) to state the essential facts that support the judgment.[19]

§ 381. Advisory Jury

CPLR 4212 authorizes the court on motion of a party or on its own motion to submit to an "advisory" jury any issue of fact triable by the court. There is no criterion set forth, and the provision applies when the case is not jury triable because of its nature or because a jury was waived.[1] When a jury is so used, the verdict, like the report of a referee, is only a recommendation that the court can accept or reject as it sees fit—thus the "advisory" title, which comes from the counterpart federal rule.[2] CPLR 4212 is also the provision that authorizes submission of an issue to a referee to report, but while that requires a showing of some "exceptional condition," no such limitation appends to a submission to an advisory jury. A party who would move such a submission must ordinarily make the motion within 20 days after the filing of the note of issue.[3]

Despite the absence of any stated restriction on its use or, indeed, of any standard at all, the advisory jury is relatively rare. It amounts to a luxury in an era when the courts in many parts of the state are behind in their jury calendars generally.

One of the most appropriate uses of the advisory jury is in the situation, previously discussed, in which legal and equitable issues in respect of the same transaction arise in the same action.[4] Suppose, for example, that P sues for specific performance of a contract (no jury) and D counterclaims for damages for breach of the same contract (jury). A jury will determine the counterclaim, but the court must decide the facts insofar as they relate to the main claim. The court can treat the jury, present as of right on the counterclaim, as an advisory one to try the main claim, too. Technically, the verdict in respect of the main claim will not bind the court, but if it has support in the record, if it would withstand any effort to overturn it were it the verdict of an of-right jury, and if

---

[16]   CPLR 4213(b); see Conklin v. State, 22 A.D.2d 481, 256 N.Y.S.2d 477 (3d Dep't 1965).

[17]   Sager v. Sager, 21 A.D.2d 183, 249 N.Y.S.2d 467 (3d Dep't 1964); see Reed v. Hudson, 7 Misc. 3d 136(A), 801 N.Y.S.2d 241, 2005 WL 1253308, *1 (App. Term, 2d Dep't 2005).

[18]   See In re Jeraldine C., 14 A.D.3d 560, 561, 789 N.Y.S.2d 180, 181 (2d Dep't 2005).

[19]   Nutone Inc. v. William E. Bouley Co., 38 A.D.2d 670, 327 N.Y.S.2d 256 (4th Dep't 1971).

[1]   See 2d Rep. Leg. Doc. No. 13, p. 240 (1958).

[2]   Fed. R. Civ. P. 39(c).

[3]   CPLR 4015. If the court submits issues to an advisory jury on its own initiative under CPLR 4212, the time limit of CPLR 4015 does not apply. See Wargo v. Wargo, 48 Misc. 2d 349, 265 N.Y.S.2d 37 (Sup. Ct., Erie County 1965).

[4]   See § 378.

the court's refusal to confirm it would cause it to conflict with the verdict rendered on the counterclaim—on which the verdict is binding—the court would do well, as a matter of the practical if not the technical, to adopt it in full.[5]

A judge may find an advisory jury particularly helpful in a case expected to produce much conflicting testimony. It enables the judge to apply a kind of community experience to the difficult fact-finding task. One judge, for example, called on an advisory jury on his own motion when counsel cautioned, at the outset of a trial of a family dispute over insurance proceeds, that the testimony would be especially conflicting and bitter.[6]

The procedures used in connection with an advisory jury are essentially the same as those used with the usual of-right jury,[7] but the final decision lies with the judge, who can confirm or reject the verdict in whole or in part and make different findings. A party who would move to confirm or reject the verdict of an advisory jury should do so within 15 days after it is rendered.[8]

If the case has already been tried without a jury, the court must render a decision. It can't avoid the duty by trying to impanel an advisory jury now to try the case over. That has been held an abuse of discretion and an Article 78 proceeding can be used to compel the judge to decide the case.[9]

F. SUBPOENAS AND OATHS

Table of Sections

§ 382.   Subpoenas; Issuance
§ 383.   Service of Subpoena
§ 384.   Motion to Quash Subpoena
§ 385.   Disobedience of Subpoena
§ 386.   Form of Subpoena
§ 387.   Notice to Produce
§ 388.   Oaths and Affirmations

§ 382. Subpoenas; Issuance

A subpoena is judicial process, a paper whereby a witness is subjected to the jurisdiction of the court and required to give relevant information or produce relevant materials "under penalty" (which is what "subpoena" means) of contempt for disobedience. Article 23 of the CPLR governs subpoenas.

CPLR 2301 recognizes two basic kinds of subpoena. The first and most common secures testimony from the witness. Its formal name is "subpoena ad testificandum," but the CPLR adopts the common practice of just calling it a "subpoena." The second is a

---

[5] Cf. Dellefield v. Blockdel Realty Co., 1 F.R.D. 689 (S.D.N.Y. 1941). There have been analogous instances in which the verdict of a jury, present in a case as of right for one claim, has been held binding on another claim that would not be jury triable if brought by itself. See Fitzgerald v. U.S. Lines Co., 374 U.S. 16, 83 S. Ct. 1646, 10 L. Ed. 2d 720 (1963).

[6] *Wargo*, 48 Misc. 2d at 353–54, 265 N.Y.S.2d at 43–44.

[7] CPLR 4212.

[8] CPLR 4403.

[9] See In re Island Improvement, Inc., 231 A.D. 837, 246 N.Y.S. 424 (2d Dep't 1930).

subpoena "duces tecum," which seeks a paper or thing rather than testimony.[1] The subpoena duces tecum is served on the person having possession or control of the item and is satisfied if the item is produced at the appointed time and place, whether by the person served or by some other person familiar with it.[2] If the issuer wants the testimony of the person served with the subpoena duces tecum as well as the paper or thing itself, the subpoena should contain both testimonial and duces tecum clauses, or two subpoenas should be served. CPLR 2305(b) provides that "[a] subpoena duces tecum may be joined with a subpoena to testify at a trial, hearing or examination or may be issued separately."[3]

In Buholtz ex rel. Rochester Philharmonic Orchestra, Inc. v. Board of Directors of Rochester Philharmonic Orchestra, Inc.,[4] the subpoenas served by plaintiff on several nonparties did not request the "production of books, papers or other things."[5] Rather, plaintiff's subpoenas provided draft affidavits for the recipients to sign and return to the court under threat of contempt. In granting the motion to quash the subpoenas, the court ruled that "the practice of requesting nonparties to create, rather than simply produce, records amounted to a misuse of the subpoena." Similarly, a subpoena may not be used to compel production of documents and records not in existence at the time of its service.[6]

The subpoena used in litigation, which is the one we are concerned with here,[7] ordinarily needs the context of an action or proceeding, whose caption and index number it bears. It is not an independent process.[8]

With only a few exceptions, there is no stated minimum or maximum time for the return of the subpoena. The issuer decides when and where the witness shall appear and the subpoena instructs accordingly.[9] Recognizing, however, that the court will consider all relevant factors in determining whether to invoke contempt if the subpoena is disobeyed, the issuer should afford the witness what in context amounts to a reasonable time.[10] A "forthwith" subpoena is permissible when the exigencies suggest it, but it is best left as the exception.

With the subpoena duces tecum, there is a special timing requirement designed to protect the other parties. A copy of the subpoena duces tecum must be served on the

---

[1]   A third kind, used in connection with the enforcement of money judgments, is called an "information subpoena." It's merely a set of interrogatories served and answered by mail. See CPLR 5224(a)(3), discussed in § 509.

[2]   CPLR 2305(b).

[3]   The quoted language was added to the statute in a 2003 amendment. It was an incident of a concurrent amendment made in CPLR 3120 to enable a mere subpoena duces tecum to secure a discovery from a nonparty, which had previously required a motion. See § 362. Forms of subpoenas are in § 386.

[4]   Buholtz ex rel. Rochester Philharmonic Orchestra, Inc. v. Board of Directors of Rochester Philharmonic Orchestra, Inc., 39 Misc. 3d 491, 960 N.Y.S.2d 613 (Sup. Ct., Monroe County 2013).

[5]   CPLR 2301.

[6]   See Liberty Mut. Ins. Co. v. City of New York Commission on Human Rights, 39 A.D.2d 860, 860, 332 N.Y.S.2d 971, 972 (1st Dep't 1972), aff'd, 31 N.Y.2d 1044, 342 N.Y.S.2d 70, 294 N.E.2d 855 (1973).

[7]   Various tribunals, agencies, committees, and other like creatures besides courts have the subpoena power. Their subpoenas qualify as "non-judicial" and involve the courts—and our attention—only in regard to applications to quash, modify, or enforce the subpoenas, to which reference will be made in ensuing sections.

[8]   See In re State Police Administrative Disciplinary Hearing on April 27, 2004, 13 A.D.3d 884, 885, 787 N.Y.S.2d 173, 174 (3d Dep't 2004); In re Blake's Estate, 51 Misc. 2d 42, 272 N.Y.S.2d 597 (Sur. Ct., Nassau County 1966).

[9]   See Application of Mullen, 177 Misc. 734, 31 N.Y.S.2d 710 (Queens County Ct. 1941).

[10]   See Commentary C2305:1 on McKinney's CPLR 2305, which also cites several special subpoena provisions having time minimums.

other parties "promptly" after the subpoenaed person has been served and must be so timed that it is "received" by the other parties before the time scheduled for the production of the papers or other things sought.[11]

As a rule, the issuance of a subpoena does not require leave of court.[12] An array of people have the power to issue it. A subpoena may be issued by the clerk, the judge (especially when there is no clerk),[13] an arbitrator, a referee, or any member of a board or commission empowered to hear or determine a matter requiring the taking of proof. Most importantly, the subpoena may be issued by the attorney of record of any party to an action, special proceeding, administrative proceeding, or arbitration.[14]

It is in fact the attorneys who most often issue subpoenas in New York practice. They do so on their own initiative, based only on the reasonable needs of the proceeding involved. This has long been the practice in New York, but only recently became so in federal practice.[15] The clerk also has this power, but exercises it less often, usually at the behest of a party appearing pro se. Whether issued by the clerk, attorney, judge, or any other authorized person, the litigation subpoena stands as process of the court and the contempt remedy stands behind it as the enforcement tool.

The subpoena may provide that the person appear on the date stated "and any recessed or adjourned date" of the trial or hearing, and if given reasonable notice of the adjourned time, no new subpoena is necessary.[16] Often at the end of a day during a continuing trial, the issuing lawyer will also ask the court to instruct the witness, if the witness is still needed, to return on the following day, which the court usually does as a matter of course.

It is appropriate at this juncture to interpose a practical advice. It is always best that the party secure the testimony of a favorable witness amicably, without the coercion of a subpoena. To this end, the party should be prepared to pay voluntarily all of the witness's actual expenses[17] in attending the trial or hearing, including the costs of transportation and lodging as well as reimbursement for any earnings the witness loses in order to give testimony.[18]

The amount of such payment was the subject of the dispute in Caldwell v. Cablevision Systems Corp.,[19] where an orthopedic surgeon was subpoenaed to testify as

---

[11]   CPLR 2303(a); see Commentary C2303:1A on McKinney's CPLR 2303; "Timing the Subpoena Duces Tecum" in SPR 142:3.

[12]   Some do require court leave, such as where the testimony of a prisoner is needed. See CPLR 2302(b). CPLR 2302(b) was amended in 2011 to add a new last sentence, providing that "[i]n the absence of an authorization by a patient, a trial subpoena duces tecum for the patient's medical records may only be issued by a court." This amendment was a companion to an amendment of CPLR 3122, which is discussed in § 363.

[13]   This recognizes that some courts, notably the justice courts in the state's towns and villages, do not have a regular court "clerk" to whom a civil litigant appearing pro se can turn for a subpoena.

[14]   CPLR 2302(a).

[15]   Fed. R. Civ. P. 45(a)(3); see § 641 (Practitioner's Edition); Commentary C45–5 on Fed. R. Civ. P. 45 in 28 U.S.C.A.

[16]   CPLR 2305(a). An additional fee is required, however, for each additional day. Fees are treated in the next section.

[17]   The statutory witness fees are nominal, as are the mileage fees (the rate per mile for travel expenses), which the witness also gets in certain instances. See CPLR 8001.

[18]   This is so notwithstanding that the sums expended will not necessarily be recoverable as a disbursement, which may be restricted to the statutory fees. See § 415.

[19]   Caldwell v. Cablevision Systems Corp., 20 N.Y.3d 365, 960 N.Y.S.2d 711, 984 N.E.2d 909 (2013) (SPR 234:1) (NYSLD No. 639).

a fact witness at trial regarding the notes he recorded when he evaluated plaintiff in an emergency room after her alleged fall. The notes stated that plaintiff informed him that she tripped over a dog rather than defendant's trench. During cross-examination, the doctor admitted that he was compensated by defendant for appearing based on his lost time from work in the sum of $10,000!

The Court of Appeals noted that, like the Second Department, it was "troubled by what appears to be a substantial payment to a fact witness in exchange for minimal testimony" of approximately one hour.[20] Nonetheless, it affirmed the order of the appellate division, which held that the substantial payment made by the defendant to the doctor did not require exclusion of the witness's testimony. The large payment did, however, mandate that the jury be charged regarding the suspect credibility of factual testimony from a witness who was paid so handsomely.

While acknowledging that CPLR 8001(a) prescribes "only the minimum that must be paid to a subpoenaed fact witness," the Court cautioned that attorneys may not "pay a witness whatever fee is demanded, however exorbitant it might be."[21] Judicial decisions and Rule 3.4(b)(1) of the New York Rules of Professional Conduct mandate that any compensation made to a fact witness be "reasonable" in relation to "the loss of time in attending, testifying, preparing to testify or otherwise assisting counsel." Furthermore, a lawyer cannot "pay, offer to pay or acquiesce in the payment of compensation to a witness contingent upon the content of the witness's testimony or the outcome of the matter."[22] The Court agreed with the trial court's conclusion that "the fee payment was fertile ground for cross-examination and comment during summation." In addition, the Court held that because defendant did not even attempt to justify such a large payment for one hour of testimony, the jury should have also been charged to assess whether the compensation was disproportionately more than what was reasonable for the loss of the doctor's time from work and, if so, whether it had the effect of influencing his testimony.[23]

The use of a subpoena with no compensation for lost time, while permissible, should be reserved for hostile witnesses who will not respond with anything less. In these circumstances, the lawyer issuing the subpoena had best have taken the witness's deposition before trial[24] so as not to be surprised by the witness's testimony. The subpoena is also useful for friendly or indifferent witnesses who have to be served with the subpoena for some practical reason, as where they need it to show their employers so as to be let off work, frequently the case with governmental employees.

Do the concerns noted by the Court of Appeals in *Caldwell* arise when a payment is made for physical evidence? In New York State Bar Association Opinion 997,[25] the evidence at issue was a surveillance tape recorded by a nonparty storeowner, which apparently showed that the defendant's actions caused the accident at issue. Under the CPLR, the plaintiff's lawyer could, of course, serve a subpoena requesting production of

---

[20] *Caldwell*, 20 N.Y.3d at 370, 960 N.Y.S.2d at 714, 984 N.E.2d at 912.

[21] *Caldwell*, 20 N.Y.3d at 370, 960 N.Y.S.2d at 714, 984 N.E.2d at 912.

[22] New York Rules of Professional Conduct, Rule 3.4(b).

[23] See NY PJI 1:90.4 ("Compensation of Fact Witnesses"). The *Caldwell* decision is discussed in further detail in Commentary C2303:9 to McKinney's CPLR 2303.

[24] See Cavaretta v. George, 270 A.D.2d 862, 706 N.Y.S.2d 291 (4th Dep't 2000); Kenford Co., Inc. v. Erie County, 41 A.D.2d 586, 340 N.Y.S.2d 300 (4th Dep't 1973); Commentary C3101:22 on McKinney's CPLR 3101.

[25] 2014 WL 8774728 (2014).

the tape.[26] Yet, as was apparently the case in *Caldwell*, there are times when a lawyer would rather secure the willing cooperation of a nonparty in lieu of seeking to compel the production of materials with the force of a subpoena. The opinion observed that New York's Rules of Professional Conduct are silent as to whether a lawyer may make a payment for evidence on behalf of a client. However, the Committee opined that "[s]uch payment may, depending on the circumstances, be an appropriate means of advancing a client's interests." The opinion notes several potential ethical limitations on the practice, but concludes that when these are not present, "a lawyer may purchase surveillance video . . . for use as evidence in contemplated or pending litigation."

§ 383. Service of Subpoena

CPLR 2303 requires that a subpoena be served in the same manner as a summons, which means that all of the alternatives of CPLR 308 are available.[1] Service by personal delivery under CPLR 308(1) is usually preferable to the other methods, especially when the subpoena has a short return time, because it entails but a single step and gets the job done quickly. The other methods are available if needed.

For a while, there were impediments to the use of the deliver-and-mail and affix-and-mail methods of paragraphs 2 and 4 of CPLR 308 for subpoena service because of the filing of proof of service requirements imposed by those provisions and principally because of their postponed "completion" of service.[2] Using them sometimes undermined the effectiveness of the subpoena by prompting the courts to withhold the contempt remedy when service complications appeared,[3] and the threat of contempt is the thing that gives the subpoena its teeth. The legislature met the problem with an amendment of CPLR 2303 in 1982, dispensing with the filing of proof of service in the subpoena service context and deeming service complete immediately upon the carrying out of the second of the two service steps that paragraphs 2 and 4 of CPLR 308 requires.[4] Similar problems can be met in trying to use the personal service by mail method of CPLR 312–a,[5] suggesting that it may be politic to avoid that provision for subpoena service, especially when the subpoena is returnable in only a few days or weeks.

The subpoena may be served, as may a summons, by any person 18 and over and not a party.[6]

The subpoenaed person must be paid a witness fee and mileage, and these must be "paid or tendered in advance."[7] It is customary to tender these sums along with the subpoena, and to pay them in cash, but a check has been held permissible.[8] A subpoenaed witness "cannot be compelled to attend without such payment" of fees.[9] Furthermore, if

---

[26]   See CPLR 3101(i), CPLR 3120(1)(i); see §§ 348, 362.

[1]   See §§ 66 to 75.

[2]   See §§ 72, 74; Commentary C2303:2 on McKinney's CPLR 2303.

[3]   See, e.g., Garrison Fuel Oil of Long Island, Inc. v. Grippo, 127 Misc. 2d 275, 486 N.Y.S.2d 136 (Nassau County Court 1985), involving the enforcement-of-judgment subpoena of CPLR 5224.

[4]   See §§ 72, 74. The amendment is discussed in Commentary C2303:2 on McKinney's CPLR 2303.

[5]   See § 76A.

[6]   CPLR 2103(a).

[7]   CPLR 2303. The sums applicable are found in CPLR 8001.

[8]   Osborne v. Miller, 67 Misc. 2d 824, 325 N.Y.S.2d 150 (Sup. Ct., New York County 1971).

[9]   In re Depue, 185 N.Y. 60, 77 N.E. 798 (1906).

witness fees are not tendered with the subpoena or before it is returnable, the witness may not be punished for disobeying it.[10]

As for the territorial reach of the subpoena, it may generally be served wherever the particular court's summons may be served, but there are some special restrictions in the lower courts.[11] In the supreme, county, surrogate's, and family courts, and in the court of claims, subpoena service is statewide on direct constitutional authority.[12] But a New York subpoena may not be served outside the state regardless of the court involved.[13] Even in situations in which, by analogy to summons service, authority might be spelled out for the service of a subpoena outside New York, the language used in section 2–b of the Judiciary Law, which speaks of subpoenas directed to persons "found in the state," has been applied to preclude extrastate service of a subpoena.[14] This is a needlessly restrictive interpretation,[15] but as long as it stands, a New York subpoena may not reach beyond New York borders whatever the bases or justifications may be in the particular situation. A party in need of an outsider's testimony must therefore turn to the pretrial disclosure devices[16] or the Uniform Interstate Depositions and Discovery Act[17] and must preserve the resulting product for use at the trial[18] unless, of course, the witness is willing to come into the state voluntarily.

If there is such willingness, and the out-of-state resident voluntarily appears to testify in an action, does that give the court power to direct the witness to return for further testimony on future days under penalty of contempt? Cherfas v. Wolf holds that it does.[19] The witness in *Cherfas*, P's accountant, was from New Jersey and came to testify because P's attorney said he had to, which was not true. The court says, however, that once the witness does appear he can be ordered to continue to appear, like a nonresident defendant who makes a general appearance in an action that would otherwise have lacked jurisdiction of him.[20]

Judiciary Law section 2–b gets a well deserved comeuppance from the First Department in Coutts Bank (Switzerland) Ltd. v. Anatian,[21] but while the whole court upholds the outcome, which in effect gives a CPLR 5224 subpoena some extraterritorial

---

[10]   Jaggars v. Scholeno, 6 A.D.3d 1130, 776 N.Y.S.2d 684 (4th Dep't 2004); see Commentary C2303:8 on McKinney's CPLR 2303.

[11]   See §§ 1101 and 1201 in each of the New York City Civil, Uniform District, Uniform City, and Uniform Justice court acts (McKinney's Vol. 29A, Parts 2 and 3).

[12]   N.Y. Const. art. VI, § 1(c).

[13]   Where a state has adopted the Uniform Interstate Depositions and Discovery Act, the New York subpoena can be readily converted to a subpoena of that state. See § 360.

[14]   See, e.g., Siemens and Halske, GmbH. v. Gres, 37 A.D.2d 768, 324 N.Y.S.2d 639 (1st Dep't 1971), but see the court's later and more expansive approach taken in its *Coutts* decision, discussed below.

[15]   See Commentary C2303:6 on McKinney's CPLR 2303.

[16]   See, e.g., CPLR 3108.

[17]   See § 360; Commentary on C3108:5 and C3108:6 on McKinney's CPLR 3108.

[18]   See § 358; Commentary C2303:7 on McKinney's CPLR 2303.

[19]   Cherfas v. Wolf, 20 Misc. 3d 1118(A), 867 N.Y.S.2d 15 (Sup. Ct., Kings County 2008) (nonparty witness who voluntarily entered the state to testify in a case and was directed to return as a continuing witness waived right to move to quash or vacate subpoena); Practice Commentary CPLR 2305, C2305:2 ("Recessed or Adjourned Date"). See the note on the case in SPR 203:4.

[20]   See § 112.

[21]   Coutts Bank (Switzerland) Ltd. v. Anatian, 275 A.D.2d 609, 713 N.Y.S.2d 45 (1st Dep't 2000).

effect, it does so in only a brief opinion sustaining a subpoena served by a substituted method pursuant to court order.[22]

The Court of Appeals in Standard Fruit & S. S. Co. v. Waterfront Commission of New York Harbor has held that if a corporation is subject to in-state service of the subpoena, thus avoiding the problem of extrastate service, the corporation may be required to produce knowledgeable officers and employees even if they are stationed outside the state.[23] Consistent with this, if testimony is sought from the employee of a corporate party, a CPLR 3106(d) deposition notice can be served on the corporation to compel the appearance of the employee even without service of a subpoena on the employee proper, and in this situation an independent basis for jurisdiction of the witness is not needed.[24] A 2008 amendment adding CPLR 2303–a helps implement the holding of *Standard Fruit*, at least with regard to a party. The new statute allows a party to serve a trial subpoena on an adverse party's attorney of record requiring the attendance at trial of a party or a "person within the party's control."[25] In this context, the statute also allows the trial subpoena to be served like any other interlocutory paper, which permits service to be made by regular mail.[26]

The provision of CPLR 2303 providing that the "manner" of service be the same as that used for a summons imports CPLR 308 as well the list of proper persons to serve in behalf of an entity or unit being subpoenaed.[27] Hence, when the subpoena is served on an entity or governmental unit of some kind, the person to be served may ordinarily be any person upon whom a summons could be served in an action brought against the entity or unit.[28]

When records are sought, the subpoena duces tecum should of course be addressed to the person who has custody of them. If the records are with some big entity with a central office in one place and several branches all around, it has been held that service either at the branch that has the records or at the central office will do.[29]

It has been held that a person, or in any event a New Yorker, served in New York with a subpoena issued out of an action or proceeding pending in a sister state need not respond to it.[30] There may be instances, however, in which the contacts of the served

---

[22] See Commentary C2303:6 on McKinney's CPLR 2303; SPR 104:1. All the information about the case comes from the concurring opinion of Presiding Justice Sullivan, offering an incisive treatment of Jud. Law § 2–b(1). The CPLR 5224 subpoena is used in the enforcement of judgments. See § 509.

[23] Standard Fruit & S. S. Co. v. Waterfront Commission of New York Harbor, 43 N.Y.2d 11, 400 N.Y.S.2d 732, 371 N.E.2d 453 (1977).

[24] See Sammy v. First American Title Ins. Co. of New York, 2015 WL 4597115 (Sup. Ct., Queens County 2015); see 23/23 Communications Corp., d/b/a Communications Diversified v. General Motors Corporation, 172 Misc. 2d 821, 660 N.Y.S.2d 296 (Sup. Ct., New York County 1997) (SPR 70:4) (service of trial subpoena).

[25] See Commentary C2303–a:1 on McKinney's CPLR 2303–a; SPR 189:2; see also Gyani v. Great Neck Medical Group, 35 Misc. 3d 278, 936 N.Y.S.2d 534 (Sup. Ct., Nassau County 2012) (SPR 241:1).

[26] See CPLR 2103(b); § 202.

[27] See § 69.

[28] See CPLR 311(a)(1) (service upon domestic or foreign corporation); § 70; see also Gihon LLC v. 501 Second Street, L.L.C., 50 Misc. 3d 1208(A), 28 N.Y.S.3d 648 (Sup. Ct., Kings County 2016) (ruling that subpoenas were improperly served on corporation and limited liability company because they were not delivered to the appropriate person in accordance with CPLR 311 and 311–a, respectively).

[29] See Application of Bott, 125 Misc. 2d 1029, 481 N.Y.S.2d 266 (Monroe County Court 1984), noting the time element that the lawyer has to be conscious of and taking a pragmatic approach to matters of this kind.

[30] See Doe v. Roe, 190 A.D.2d 463, 599 N.Y.S.2d 350 (4th Dep't 1993).

individual with the jurisdiction whose subpoena is involved suffice to justify the extraterritorial service and require a response.[31]

§ 384. Motion to Quash Subpoena

If the person served with a subpoena has some objection to it or wishes to test its validity, the remedy is a motion to quash, condition, or modify the subpoena under CPLR 2304. The motion should be made to the court in which the subpoena is returnable.[1] It should be made promptly and in any event before the return day. If the time is short, the motion can be brought on by order to show cause, abbreviating the notice time. If the subpoena is not returnable in a court, such as one issued for a deposition scheduled in a lawyer's office[2] or in conjunction with an administrative proceeding, a request to withdraw or modify the subpoena should first be made to the person who issued it.[3] If that does not avail, a motion to quash may be made to the court.

Whether a subpoena is, in fact, returnable in court has been the subject of conflicting decisions. In Brooks v. City of New York,[4] the court concluded that the phrase "returnable in a court" in CPLR 2304 "is not the same thing as returnable in a courthouse." Rather, it means that the subpoena is issued within a court action or proceeding. In Rubino v. 350 Madison Co., LLC,[5] the court reached a seemingly contrary conclusion and denied a motion to quash a subpoena served by a party to an action because "the correct procedure for objecting to a subpoena duces tecum ha[d] not been complied with."[6]

If the subpoena has not issued out of a court, the motion to quash or modify is made to the supreme court.[7] The applicable statute does not supply a venue, but since "[a] motion to quash a non-judicial subpoena is similar to a CPLR article 78 proceeding,"[8] the purpose of which is to review administrative action,[9] the proper venue in which to quash a subpoena issued out of an administrative proceeding, for example, would be a county in which an Article 78 proceeding could be brought against the agency.[10] If the subpoena issued out of an arbitration, the appropriate venue would be that set by statute for other applications in connection with the arbitration.[11]

A motion to quash challenges the validity of the subpoena or the jurisdiction of the issuing authority.[12] These categories can embrace a myriad of defects, however, ranging

---

[31]   See the discussion above and in SPR 26:4.

[1]   CPLR 2304.

[2]   See CPLR 3106(b) and Commentary C3110:4 on McKinney's CPLR 3110.

[3]   Rubino v. 330 Madison Co., LLC, 39 Misc. 3d 450, 958 N.Y.S.2d 587 (Sup. Ct., New York County 2013).

[4]   Brooks v. City of New York, 178 Misc. 2d 104, 678 N.Y.S.2d 479 (Sup. Ct., New York County 1998).

[5]   Rubino v. 330 Madison Co., LLC, 39 Misc. 3d 450, 958 N.Y.S.2d 587 (Sup. Ct., New York County 2013).

[6]   See Commentary C2304:4 to McKinney's CPLR 2304.

[7]   CPLR 2304. See Commentary C2304:4 on McKinney's CPLR 2304.

[8]   New York Republican State Committee v. New York State Com'n on Government Integrity, 138 A.D.2d 884, 526 N.Y.S.2d 264 (3d Dep't 1988).

[9]   See §§ 557 et seq.

[10]   CPLR 506(b); see New York Republican State Committee v. New York State Com'n on Government Integrity, 138 A.D.2d 884, 884, 526 N.Y.S.2d 264, 265 (3d Dep't 1988).

[11]   CPLR 7502(a); see § 591 (Practitioner's Edition).

[12]   In re 381 Search Warrants Directed to Facebook, Inc., 29 N.Y.3d 231, 55 N.Y.S.3d 696, 78 N.E.3d 141 (2017); Santangello v. People, 38 N.Y.2d 536, 381 N.Y.S.2d 472, 344 N.E.2d 404 (1976).

from the most substantive, such as where the subpoena seeks matter irrelevant to the proceeding,[13] to the most procedural, such as where there was some formal defect in its service. Other grounds, perhaps not technically sufficient to affect "validity" or "jurisdiction," may also be raised. Perhaps, for example, the demands of the subpoena are such that the witness can't afford to meet them on the meager fees[14] tendered. In this regard, when the party serving the subpoena seeks disclosure, it must bear any reasonable costs incurred by a nonparty in satisfying the subpoena.[15] The court is also empowered, on a motion to quash or modify, to impose any condition the court finds just,[16] and one condition the court may resort to is that the issuing party advance to the subpoenaed person, in addition to the nominal statutory fees, the reasonable actual cost of honoring the subpoena, especially when it is a subpoena duces tecum requiring the witness to go to expense to produce the papers or things sought. Conditionings of this kind are not frequent, probably because a party in need of a witness's testimony or materials will ordinarily advance such expenses voluntarily, thereby propitiating the witness and obviating the motion to condition and possibly even the subpoena itself.[17]

In Kapon v. Koch,[18] the Court of Appeals resolved a long simmering conflict at the intermediate appellate level and held that so long as disclosure sought from a nonparty is relevant to the prosecution or defense of an action, it must be produced.[19] The Court used the occasion to provide a helpful discussion of the corresponding burdens of proof imposed on a motion to quash a subpoena. The *Kapon* Court concluded that CPLR 3101(a)(4) merely requires that a subpoenaing party sufficiently state the "circumstances or reasons" that support disclosure from the nonparty, "either on the face of the subpoena itself or in a notice accompanying it."[20] If the subpoenaing party satisfies these requirements, which the Court described as "minimal," the subpoena will be facially sufficient. If the subpoena is facially sufficient, the movant has the burden of establishing that " 'the futility of the process to uncover anything legitimate is inevitable or obvious' . . . or [that] the information sought is 'utterly irrelevant to any proper inquiry.' "[21] If the movant meets this burden, the burden shifts back to the subpoenaing party to establish that the discovery sought is "relevant to the prosecution or defense of [the] action."[22]

§ 385. Disobedience of Subpoena

The disobedience of a subpoena issued in conjunction with a court proceeding is punishable as a contempt.[1] The disobedience also subjects the disobeyer, whether a party

---

[13]   See, e.g., Brodsky v. New York Yankees, 26 Misc. 3d 874, 887–88, 891 N.Y.S.2d 590, 599–600 (Sup. Ct., Albany County 2009); Temporary State Commission on Living Costs and Economy v. Bergman, 80 Misc. 2d 448, 363 N.Y.S.2d 977 (Sup. Ct., New York County 1975).

[14]   See CPLR 8001; see § 382.

[15]   See CPLR 3122(d); § 362.

[16]   CPLR 2304; see 1st Rep. Leg. Doc. No. 6(b), p. 165 (1957).

[17]   See § 382.

[18]   Kapon v. Koch, 23 N.Y.3d 32, 988 N.Y.S.2d 559, 11 N.E.3d 709 (2014).

[19]   See § 345.

[20]   *Kapon*, 23 N.Y.3d at 34, 988 N.Y.S.2d at 562, 11 N.E.3d at 711.

[21]   *Kapon*, 23 N.Y.3d at 38, 988 N.Y.S.2d at 565, 11 N.E.3d at 715 (internal quotation omitted).

[22]   *Kapon*, 23 N.Y.3d at 34, 37, 988 N.Y.S.2d at 562, 564, 11 N.E.3d at 711, 714; see Commentary C2304:1 to McKinney's CPLR 2304.

[1]   The procedures and penalties for punishing contempt are discussed in the enforcement chapter. See §§ 481 et seq.

or a nonparty witness, to the actual damages the disobedience causes the issuer as well as a penalty of up to $150. If the disobeyer is a party, civil penalties may also be imposed, up to and including the striking of the party's pleading.[2]

The disobedience of a non-judicial subpoena, which refers to one issued in an out-of-court proceeding like an administrative hearing or arbitration,[3] is not directly punishable as a contempt.[4] The issuer or the person in whose behalf the subpoena was issued must first move in the supreme court to compel compliance. If the court then orders compliance, further disobedience is a violation of the order and may now be the subject of contempt proceedings.[5] Here, too, the court, through the issuance of warrants, can command the sheriff to produce the witness before the appropriate body and to commit the witness to jail if need be until obedience is secured.

§ 386. Form of Subpoena

The following are illustrative forms for the testimonial subpoena and the subpoena duces tecum.

---

[2]   See CPLR 2308(a), which in addition to invoking the general contempt punishment authorizes the court to issue a warrant directing the sheriff to bring the witness to court forcibly and to jail the witness if the contumely continues. The civil sanctions authorized by CPLR 3126 and available against a party are so meaningful that it should rarely be necessary to invoke the contempt penalty against a party to an action, as opposed to a nonparty witness. See Commentary C3126:4 on McKinney's CPLR 3126.

[3]   See § 384.

[4]   See Commentary C2308:6 on McKinney's CPLR 2308; see Lyon Financial Services, Inc. v. Pinto Trading Co., 24 Misc. 3d 1237(A), 901 N.Y.S.2d 900, 2009 WL 2516876, *3 (Sup. Ct., Kings County 2009).

[5]   CPLR 2308(b); see Dias v. Consolidated Edison Co. of New York, Inc., 116 A.D.2d 453, 496 N.Y.S.2d 686 (1st Dep't 1986).

(a)   Form of testimonial subpoena.

SUPREME COURT OF THE STATE OF NEW YORK
COUNTY OF NEW YORK

A.B., Plaintiff, against C.D., Defendant.	Subpoena Index No. _____ Name of Assigned Judge _____

To E.F.

Greetings:

   You are hereby commanded to appear at a trial before the Hon. Martin Evans, a Justice of this Court, at [Part or Room Number], to be held at the Courthouse at 60 Centre Street, in the Borough of Manhattan, City of New York, on April 26, 2018, at 9 o'clock in the morning, and at any recessed or adjourned date and time of that trial, to testify and give evidence as a witness on behalf of the defendant in the above-captioned action. For a failure to attend you will be deemed guilty of a contempt of court as well as liable for all damages sustained by the defendant because of your failure and to a penalty of $150 as well.

   Dated April 19, 2018.

                                       _____

                                       Attorney for Defendant

                                       Address:

                                       Telephone Number:

   (b)   Form of subpoena duces tecum. The caption, introductory amenities, and signature read the same as in the testimonial subpoena above. "Duces Tecum" is added to "Subpoena" to the right of the caption and the body of the subpoena duces tecum can read:

You are hereby commanded to appear at a trial before the Hon. Martin Evans, a Justice of this Court, at [Part or Room Number] to be held at the Courthouse at 60 Centre Street, in the Borough of Manhattan, City of New York, on April 26, 2018, at 9 o'clock in the morning, and at any recessed or adjourned date of the trial, and to bring with you and produce at that time and place the following documents and things [describe them here as precisely as possible], of which you have custody or control. For your failure to do so you will be deemed guilty of a contempt of court as well as liable for all damages sustained by the defendant because of your failure and to a penalty of $50 as well.

   Although often phrased to require the person served to "appear" or "attend," a statute makes clear that a subpoena with only this general kind of "duces tecum" language is adequately met when any person able to identify the item and attest to its custody shows up at the appointed time and place with the papers or things sought.[1] It is for this reason that the issuer who wants testimony as well as materials from the subpoenaed person should serve that person with two subpoenas or with a subpoena having separately delineated testimonial and duces tecum clauses.[2]

§ 387. Notice to Produce

Quite apart from a subpoena, and finding its authority in caselaw rather than statute, is a device known as a "notice to produce." By the use of this notice, which is only a paper served by one attorney on an opposing attorney a reasonable time in advance of the trial, the recipient can be made to produce designated books and documents. This notice is bound up with the best evidence rule: its violation precludes the served party from using the items in evidence while permitting the serving party to introduce secondary evidence of them.[1] Reference to the item in a pleading is deemed the equivalent of a notice to produce the item and an adequate basis for secondary evidence if it is not produced.[2]

The sanctions of contempt, damages, and money penalties, which stand behind the subpoena, are irrelevant to the notice to produce. Barring the resisting party from using the materials while enabling the seeking party to introduce secondary evidence of them is the sole penalty.

Seeking a paper by such a notice, or even by a discovery notice before trial,[3] does not require the seeking party to use it in evidence after getting it.[4] The seeking party's purpose may have been merely to peruse the item to determine whether it is needed.

If the item is present in the courtroom, even this advance notice is not necessary. The attorney who wants the item can merely ask the court to compel its surrender by the attorney who has it, and if the item is relevant and not immunized by any exclusionary rule of evidence, the court will order it turned over.[5]

The notice to produce is thus a device for use between parties. When an item is sought from a nonparty witness who will not surrender it before trial, the compulsion of a subpoena duces tecum is required. It would be advisable to serve a formal CPLR 3120(1) notice on a party, too, if secondary evidence of the thing sought is not available to warrant use of the relatively frail notice to produce.

§ 388. Oaths and Affirmations

Two basic groups of people are authorized by the CPLR to administer oaths: those authorized to conduct hearings and take evidence and those authorized to take

---

[1]   CPLR 2305(b).

[2]   See § 382.

[1]   Smith v. Rentz, 131 N.Y. 169, 30 N.E. 54 (1892).

[2]   Lawson v. Bachman, 81 N.Y. 616, 1880 WL 1578 (1880), aff'd, 109 U.S. 659, 3 S. Ct. 479, 27 L. Ed. 1067 (1884).

[3]   CPLR 3111, 3120(1).

[4]   *Smith*, 131 N.Y. at 175, 30 N.E. at 56; see also Garabendian v. New York State Liquor Authority, 33 A.D.2d 980, 307 N.Y.S.2d 270 (4th Dep't 1970).

[5]   See Echtermacht v. Cohen, 24 A.D.2d 968, 265 N.Y.S.2d 422 (1st Dep't 1965); Whelan v. Gorton, 15 Misc. 625, 37 N.Y.S. 344 (N.Y. City Ct. 1896).

acknowledgements of deeds.[1] The first group embraces judges, arbitrators, administrative hearing officers, and the like. The second is the group taken by adoption from the Real Property Law's lists of those who may acknowledge deeds.[2] The clerk, for example, one of the leading oathgivers in litigation, is on one of the lists.[3] The notary public is the leading entry on the real property lists[4] and the chief oathgiver outside the courtroom. The affidavit, which is the principal item of proof on an ordinary motion, is usually sworn to before a notary.

Any form of oath is satisfactory, as long as "calculated to awaken the conscience and impress the mind of the person taking it in accordance with his religious or ethical beliefs."[5] The ceremony should be "solemn . . . an unequivocal act of assent to tell the truth."[6] As long as it is, it will be backed, at least theoretically, by the perjury penalties in the Penal Law, which defines "oath" to include "an affirmation and every other mode authorized by law of attesting" to what is said.[7] This "affirmation," by the way, is a form of oath, duly taken before one qualified to administer an oath and should not be confused with the "affirmation" authorized by CPLR 2106. The latter, it will be recalled,[8] is authorized for certain professionals in subscribing their statements. It dispenses with the formal swearing ceremony usually required of affiants and subjects the affirmer to perjury under its own terms. When those persons, including lawyers and doctors, take the stand in open court, they must go through the same swearing ceremony required of all witnesses.

CPLR 2309(c) requires, among other things, that an oath or affirmation taken outside the United States or Canada must, in order to be used in New York proceedings, be accompanied by a certificate of a governmental official of the foreign place authenticating the oathgiver's authority. This certificate is sometimes familiarly called a "flag."[9]

The difficulties in securing a "flag" were somewhat alleviated when CPLR 2106 was amended in 2015 to add a new subsection (b) to permit the use of an affirmation by any person who subscribes and affirms the statement while located outside the geographic boundaries of the United States and its territories.[10] It is important to note that the requirements of CPLR 2309(c) are still imposed when the oath or affirmation is made outside New York State, but within the United States and its territories.

---

[1] CPLR 2309(a). A number of other provisions also grant the power to administer oaths. See 2d Rep. Leg. Doc. No. 13, pp. 205–208 (1958).

[2] See Real Prop. Law §§ 298, 299, 301.

[3] Real Prop. Law § 298(2)(a). The provision includes clerks of courts "of record." That includes all of the courts of the state except the town and village courts, Jud. Law § 2, but the clerks of those courts get oath-administering powers elsewhere. See § 109 of the Uniform Just. Ct. Act. Hence the clerks of all New York courts have the power to administer oaths.

[4] Real Prop. Law § 298(1)(d).

[5] CPLR 2309(b).

[6] 2d Rep. Leg. Doc. No. 13, p. 204 (1958).

[7] Penal Law § 210.00(1).

[8] See § 205.

[9] It comes about by the adoption, by CPLR 2309(c), of whatever is currently required by the Real Property Law for deed acknowledgements.

[10] See § 205.

In Midfirst Bank v. Agho,[11] the Second Department reported "a significant upswing in the number of appeals where the parties are contesting the admissibility of affidavits executed outside of the state, without CPLR 2309(c) certificates of conformity." The issue is an important one and has plagued lawyers in all sorts of contexts, including on motions for summary judgment, applications for default judgments "in residential mortgage foreclosure actions reliant upon affidavits of out-of-state bank employees, motions in medical malpractice actions reliant upon out-of-state physician experts, motions in slip-and-fall actions reliant upon out-of-state witnesses, motions in actions brought pursuant to Insurance Law § 3420(a) [to recover on an unsatisfied judgment against an insured], motions in motor vehicle negligence actions reliant upon out-of-state experts, and motions in contract actions reliant upon out-of-state expert contractors . . . ."[12]

The *Midfirst* court stressed that a "certificate of conformity" required under CPLR 2309(c) is distinct from the "certificate of authentication" or "flag."[13] The certificate of conformity addresses the manner in which a foreign oath is taken and must attest that the oath was taken in accordance with the law of either the foreign jurisdiction or New York.[14] By contrast, the certificate of authentication "attests to the oathgiver's authority under the foreign jurisdiction to administer oaths."[15]

As far as the certificate of authentication is concerned, an affidavit will be in conformance with CPLR 2309(c) if it is acknowledged by, among others, a notary public in a foreign state.[16] The certificate of authentication is only "necessary when an out-of-state acknowledgment is provided by a foreign officer other than one enumerated in Real Prop. Law § 299, or when the acknowledgment is taken in foreign countries other than Canada, or by foreign mayors or chief civil officers not under seal."[17]

Even when an oath or affirmation is taken outside the state by a notary, CPLR 2309(c) still requires that it be accompanied by a proper certificate of conformity. "In other words," held the *Midfirst Bank* court, "a certificate of conformity is required whenever an oath is acknowledged in writing outside of New York by a non-New York notary, and the document is proffered for use in New York litigation."[18]

The courts are not of one mind regarding the effect of a failure to comply with CPLR 2309(c). The Second Department's decision in *Midfirst Bank* contains dicta noting that even if the affidavit was not accompanied by a proper certificate of conformity, this CPLR 2309(c) defect could "be corrected nunc pro tunc . . . or pursuant to CPLR 2001, which permits trial courts to disregard mistakes, omissions, defects, or irregularities at any

---

[11]   Midfirst Bank v. Agho, 121 A.D.3d 343, 344, 991 N.Y.S.2d 623, 625 (2d Dep't 2014).

[12]   *Midfirst Bank,* 121 A.D.3d at 344–45, 991 N.Y.S.2d at 625.

[13]   *Midfirst Bank,* 121 A.D.3d at 349, 991 N.Y.S.2d at 628.

[14]   See Real Prop. Law § 299–a(1).

[15]   *Midfirst Bank,* 121 A.D.3d at 349, 991 N.Y.S.2d at 628.

[16]   See Real Prop. Law § 299(1) to (5) (listing officers who may, for the conveyance of real property situated in New York, acknowledge the conveyance outside of New York, including foreign judges, mayors, notaries, commissioners, and other persons designated by the foreign state to take acknowledgments or proof of deeds to be recorded).

[17]   *Midfirst Bank*, 121 A.D.3d at 350, 991 N.Y.S.2d at 628–29.

[18]   *Midfirst Bank*, 121 A.D.3d at 350, 991 N.Y.S.2d at 629. The court also referenced Real Prop. Law § 309–b, entitled "Uniform forms of certificates of acknowledgement or proof without this state," which provides sample language for a "certificate of an acknowledgement" and a "certificate for a proof of execution." See § 201.

time during an action where a substantial right of a party is not prejudiced."[19] This dicta should not be a source of comfort for those facing a problem under CPLR 2309(c). In Scott v. Westmore Fuel Co., Inc.,[20] the First Department concluded that supreme court properly rejected an expert's affidavit "as inadmissible, given that the affidavit, which was notarized in New Jersey, was lacking a [CPLR 2309(c)] certificate of conformity . . . ."

---

[19]   *Midfirst Bank*, 121 A.D.3d at 350, 991 N.Y.S.2d at 630; see § 6.

[20]   Scott v. Westmore Fuel Co., Inc., 96 A.D.3d 520, 947 N.Y.S.2d 15 (1st Dep't 2012). This troublesome issue is explored in further detail in Commentary C2309:3 on McKinney's CPLR 2309.

Chapter 15

THE TRIAL

Analysis

A. **Introductory**
B. **Selecting a Jury**
C. **The Trial Proper**
D. **The Verdict**
E. **Trial Motions**

A. INTRODUCTORY

Table of Sections

§ 389. The Trial, Introductory

§ 389. The Trial, Introductory

With this chapter we arrive at the trial itself, propelled there by the calendar practices discussed in the opening sections of the last chapter. Whatever calendars the case has visited—and this will depend almost entirely on the practice of the particular judge or in the particular part or court—it has now endured to the day of trial, statistically quite an accomplishment today. If both the judge and the case are at last ready together, the case goes to trial, with the actual time to be determined by the judge, usually in consultation with the parties. In multi-judge courts that don't use the Individual Assignment System (IAS), this may mean that it will be sent by an "assignment judge" or equivalent person to a "part," i.e., a courtroom to which another judge has been assigned who is ready for another case. At this initial moment, however, the lawyers probably have neither the parties nor the witnesses with them. This is because the case may have to detour on its way to the courtroom so that the lawyers can pick a jury, which they usually do themselves as we shall see. This may take them to a different section of the courthouse where the jurors are waiting. The parties and witnesses do not as a rule show up until the jury selection process is completed and that can take some time.

Concentration throughout this chapter will be on trial by jury rather than on trial by the court or by a referee. Stressing trial by jury will offer more thorough insights into the trial process because (1) a number of important procedures that it involves, such as the impaneling of the jury at the outset and the judge's charge at the end, are not found at all in the other modes of trial; and because (2) those procedures and rules applicable to all modes of trial are more strictly applied when a jury is present, especially in regard to the rules of evidence, rulings on evidentiary objections, the summation, and post-trial motions. One experienced in the process of trial by jury can turn easily to trial by the court or a referee because the additional points to be absorbed for that conversion are few.[1]

Article 40 of the CPLR is entitled "Trial Generally" and contains a few basics applicable to one degree or another in all modes of trial. Some of these, too, are best viewed in jury-trial context and will be treated at appropriate junctures later in this chapter. A few can be noted and disposed of here:

The trial will almost invariably take place at the courthouse, but there is authority, if the parties stipulate, that all or part of it may take place elsewhere.[2] This is rarely invoked and should be reserved for unique exigencies, such as where a key witness can give testimony only from a hospital bedside.

CPLR 4014 provides that the trial "shall continue until it is completed" even though the particular term of court at which it began has expired. This of course does not preclude reasonable adjournments of the trial for any of myriad causes. The rule about adjournments is that they are in the discretion of the trial judge and will not be interfered with by an appellate court except in cases of clear abuse.[3]

Recognizing the inevitable problems of scheduling when conflicting demands are made by several courts on the time of one or more of the trial lawyers, an extensive provision, Uniform Rule section 125.1, endeavors to regulate when adjournments based on "engagement of counsel" should be made. The courts' individual rules then require that all such adjournments follow that rule.[4]

Courts try to be understanding when a lawyer faces conflicting demands, adjourning matters as need be, but conduct in a given case can exceed a court's patience as it did, for example, in McCluskey v. Ferriter.[5] There, despite multiple adjournments and warnings and several months' notice of trial, P's counsel did not show up, pleading that he was on trial in another county and couldn't get out of it. The trial court dismissed the action, remitting P to a malpractice claim against the lawyer. The appellate division, however, loath to impose the dire penalty of dismissal even here, reversed and reinstated the action, but only on the condition that P's lawyer pay all costs, expenses, and attorney's fees caused to D by the adjournments, and costs and disbursements on appeal as well.

Some of the Uniform Rules require that when a lawyer other than the attorney of record is to try the case, that lawyer must be identified in a filed writing within designated time limits.[6] There may also be court rules governing the absence of the attorney during the trial.[7]

---

[1] Some have already been covered in discussing the mode of trial. The few remaining ones can be unobtrusively integrated in this chapter as they become relevant. See § 379 on triability by referee and § 380 on triability by the court.

[2] CPLR 4013.

[3] See Case's Will v. Donovan, 24 A.D.2d 797, 263 N.Y.S.2d 861 (3d Dep't 1965).

[4] See 22 N.Y.C.R.R. § 202.32 (applicable in the supreme and county courts), 22 N.Y.C.R.R. § 205.13 (family court), 22 N.Y.C.R.R. § 206.17 (court of claims), 22 N.Y.C.R.R. § 207.33 (surrogate's court), 22 N.Y.C.R.R. § 208.25 (New York City Civil Court), 22 N.Y.C.R.R. § 212.25 (district courts), and 22 N.Y.C.R.R. § 210.25 (city courts).

[5] McCluskey v. Ferriter, 292 A.D.2d 244, 738 N.Y.S.2d 844 (1st Dep't 2002), rev'g 186 Misc.2d 849, 721 N.Y.S.2d 479 (Sup. Ct., New York County 2001).

[6] See, e.g., 22 N.Y.C.R.R. § 202.31, applicable in the supreme and county courts.

[7] See, e.g., 22 N.Y.C.R.R. § 202.36, applicable in the supreme and county courts.

B.   SELECTING A JURY

Table of Sections

§ 390.   Impaneling a Jury
§ 391.   Alternate Jurors
§ 392.   Challenges to Jurors

§ 390.   Impaneling a Jury

Trial by jury in a civil action today is by 6 persons under a 1972 amendment of CPLR 4104, which had previously offered a choice of 6 or 12.[1] An elaborate machinery goes to work before those 6 are selected, however, beginning with the process of aggregating the "array"—the large body of citizens who have been summoned to jury duty for a particular term of court and from which lawyers will ultimately draw a jury for their individual cases. The provisions for the basic qualifications of jurors and for the methods of summoning an array are in Article 16 of the Judiciary Law and in Part 128 of the Uniform Rules for the Jury System. The Judiciary Law provisions had been overhauled in 1977 to bring them up to date and make impanelment procedures more uniform throughout the State. The Uniform Rules that went into effect a decade or so later aimed farther in the same direction. Parts of the impanelment process are explicitly delegated to the Chief Administrator of the Courts or to the appellate division to prescribe by rule or other direction.[2]

The jurors must of course be selected at random, but as long as they meet the basic statutory qualifications[3] they can be selected from any number of sources, including voter registration lists and such other lists of county residents as the Chief Administrator may specify, including lists of utility subscribers, vehicle owners or operators, taxpayers, and even consent-filing volunteers.[4] Outside New York City, the official charged with carrying out the selection process is the person appointed to serve as the County Commissioner of Jurors; in the five counties of New York City, the county clerk serves as commissioner.[5]

The Chief Administrator prescribes the mechanical method for drawing jurors.[6] The use of electronic devices can be permitted as an alternative to the old fashioned ballot box, for which the law specifically provided prior to 1977.[7] The ballot box may still be an option, and it can serve as an illustration of a typical way of impaneling the basic array as well as the smaller array from which lawyers pick the jurors who will actually try the case:

---

[1]   The reduction from 12 to 6 is authorized by the constitution. N.Y. Const. art. VI, § 18(a). The number is also 6 in the lower courts, see § 1305 in each of the New York City Civil, Uniform District, Uniform City, and Uniform Justice Court Acts (McKinney's Vol. 29A, Parts 2 and 3), in some of which the smaller jury predates the amendment of CPLR 4104.

[2]   See Jud. Law §§ 506, 508, 522.

[3]   Jud. Law § 510.

[4]   Jud. Law § 506; 22 N.Y.C.R.R. § 128.3.

[5]   Jud. Law § 502; 22 N.Y.C.R.R. § 128.0.

[6]   22 N.Y.C.R.R. § 128.5.

[7]   See, e.g., § 668 of the Judiciary Law prior to its repeal by L.1977, ch. 316.

The name of each qualified person goes on a separate ballot, which is placed in a general ballot box with an aperture large enough to admit only a hand.[8] From this box are periodically drawn an array in numbers sufficient to meet the contemplated needs of the particular jury term.[9] The jurors so drawn are notified of when and where to appear, usually by a summons mailed by the commissioner or served by the sheriff at the commissioner's direction.[10] By a similar procedure, the names of the jurors who have appeared and are on hand, not having been for one reason or another excused, are again placed in a ballot box. It is from this one that a sufficient number of names are then drawn to meet the requirements of the waiting case or cases.

All of the names in these boxes are on separate ballots thoroughly mixed so that each has an equal chance of being pulled. An inadvertent and unprejudicial oversight in this connection need not vitiate the selection, however. In one instance, for example, in which the names of jurors returning from one case had been kept clipped together when reinserted into the ballot box for further call, and thus failed to circulate in the box freely and independently, a jury picked from that box was nonetheless held proper, and its verdict upheld.[11]

A statute that had contained generic lists of employments, statuses, and circumstances that disqualified categories of persons as jurors,[12] and another that contained a substantial list of exemptions,[13] were repealed in 1995. "Postponement and Excusal from Jury Service" is now governed by section 128.6–a of the Uniform Rules, which determines the methods whereby a juror may be allowed to postpone service or avoid it entirely. Hence, when the clerk draws names from the ballot box for a waiting case, all named are ordinarily on hand and ready to be questioned by the lawyers to determine whether they are individually fit to try the particular case. This involves an inquiry into their personal attitudes towards the subject matter, their relationship to the parties and lawyers, their unique biases or prejudices, etc., all of which concerns the subject of challenges (which are taken up two sections hence). This inquiry, commonly known as a "voir dire," is usually the first contact the lawyers have with the jurors, who up to this time have passed through the hands of others: clerks; commissioners; sheriffs; and diverse other non-judicial personnel connected with the basic impanelment process.

A sufficient number of jurors to constitute at least a petit jury (the jury of six that will try the case) are called for the voir dire, a replacement coming in for each juror excused in the course of the questioning until a fully satisfactory jury of six is assembled.[14] This questioning in New York civil practice is usually conducted by the lawyers themselves, without a judge present,[15] but a judge must attend if a party so requests.[16] A judge's failing to attend when duly requested has been held reversible error

---

[8]   This was the procedure prescribed by the old § 668.

[9]   Jud. Law § 508.

[10]   Jud. Law § 516; 22 N.Y.C.R.R. § 128.6.

[11]   See Chaffee v. Marsh, 2 A.D.2d 934, 156 N.Y.S.2d 376 (3d Dep't 1956).

[12]   Jud. Law § 511.

[13]   Jud. Law § 512.

[14]   If one or two alternate jurors are to be used (see § 391), they are picked and qualified at the same time. CPLR 4106.

[15]   Compare the federal practice under Fed. R. Civ. P. 47(a), which permits the judge to decide whether to conduct the examination or let the lawyers do it.

[16]   CPLR 4107.

that can undo a judgment.[17] The lawyers will often agree on which jurors are to be excused; if they can't, and a dispute in need of judicial resolution arises, it can be taken to the judge in chambers or the courtroom.

Jurors must respond candidly and honestly to all questions asked. Concealment of facts suggesting possible bias can vitiate a verdict.[18] It is in fact one of the few grounds on which a juror may be heard to impeach the verdict of the jury, as where juror A by affidavit attests to a fact revealed to him by juror B, but improperly withheld by B on the voir dire.[19]

§ 391. Alternate Jurors

If it is contemplated that the trial will be prolonged, increasing the prospect that the disability of a juror will void all prior proceedings and put all parties to the expense of starting afresh, it will be helpful to have an extra juror available who has heard all of the proceedings and can take the place of the one who has become disabled. CPLR 4106 provides for this by authorizing the impaneling of "one or more" extra jurors, along with the basic six, the extra ones to act as "alternate" jurors. When this is done, a panel of more than six will hear the whole case, but no alternate will participate in deliberations unless and until one of the regular six jurors is disabled. The first six qualified still constitute the jury.[1] The alternates are just standbys.

In Piacente v. Bernstein,[2] plaintiff requested that supreme court, pursuant to CPLR 4105 and 4106, empanel the first six jurors that had been selected and designate the remaining two jurors as alternate jurors. The court concluded that a local rule enacted in the Third Judicial District regarding jury selection procedures required that the six deliberating jurors be chosen randomly by the court clerk and denied plaintiff's request. Plaintiff moved under CPLR 4404(a) to set aside the verdict in the interest of justice, claiming that the violation of his statutory right to designate the first six jurors selected during voir dire denied him a fair trial. Supreme court granted the motion and set aside the verdict, and the Third Department affirmed. The court found no evidence in the record indicating that plaintiff waived any objection to supreme court's reliance on the Third Judicial District's jury selection rule, which "contravened plaintiff's substantial right to empanel the first six jurors that had been selected by the parties, pursuant to the 'mandatory procedure' set forth in CPLR 4105."[3]

Before 1972, only a judge could order that alternate jurors be drawn. A 1972 amendment to CPLR 4106 allows either party to have alternates drawn, but empowers the court to order otherwise. The effect is to switch the initiative to the parties, while keeping a veto power in the court.

While it was traditionally the contemplated long trial that prompted the selection of alternates, CPLR 4106 states no criteria. For obviously brief issues, an alternate may be a needless public expense and the court can intercede to preclude it.

---

[17]   See Baginski v. New York Telephone Co., 130 A.D.2d 362, 515 N.Y.S.2d 23 (1st Dep't 1987).

[18]   See, e.g., Holland v. Blake, 38 A.D.2d 344, 329 N.Y.S.2d 169 (3d Dep't 1972), aff'd, 31 N.Y.2d 734, 338 N.Y.S.2d 108, 290 N.E.2d 147.

[19]   See McHugh v. Jones, 258 A.D. 111, 16 N.Y.S.2d 332 (2d Dep't 1939), aff'd, 283 N.Y. 534, 29 N.E.2d 76 (1940).

[1]   CPLR 4105.

[2]   Piacente v. Bernstein, 127 A.D.3d 1365, 6 N.Y.S.3d 793 (3d Dep't 2015).

[3]   Piacente, 127 A.D.3d at 1367, 6 N.Y.S.3d at 795.

The when and how of substituting alternate jurors got the attention of the appellate division in Gallegos v. Elite Model Management Corp.[4] The court held that without the consent of all the parties, no substitution of alternate jurors may be made after deliberations have begun. The trial court had ordered substitution during deliberations after two original jurors were tainted because of a conversation with a party in the bathroom.

With consent to the substitution lacking, a problem arose in cases like *Gallegos* because the Court of Appeals has held that absent consent to trial by less than six jurors, the parties to a civil case have a constitutional right to a trial by a full six-member jury.[5] Consent was rarely forthcoming from all parties to allow for these deviations, i.e., consent to allow the alternate jurors to participate in the ongoing deliberations or a verdict by less than six jurors. Therefore, if a juror took ill during the deliberations, a mistrial was often declared, resulting in a waste of time and money for the litigants, the attorneys, and the court system.

In an attempt to address these problems, CPLR 4106 was amended in 2014 to permit the court, upon the request of a party, to allow one or more alternate jurors (instead of the previous maximum of two) to be drawn and then retained after final submission of a case to ensure their availability if needed during jury deliberations. Under the amendment, once deliberations have begun, the court may allow an alternate juror to participate in such deliberations, but "only if a regular juror becomes unable to perform the duties of a juror."

The amendment does not prescribe the method for selecting an alternate juror to participate in deliberations. A 2004 supreme court decision held that alternate jurors must be chosen at random rather than being chosen sequentially.[6] Subsequently, the First Department ruled that "[t]he trial court's procedure of randomly drawing an alternate juror to substitute for a discharged juror, rather than substituting an alternate juror sequentially according to the designation of alternate jurors, was permissible."[7] This leaves open the question of whether selecting alternate jurors sequentially is appropriate without consent.

§ 392. Challenges to Jurors

A challenge is an objection to jurors or, more frequently, to an individual juror. There are several kinds of challenges. The first is a challenge to the array, which is an objection to the whole panel; it can be either substantive, objecting to the basic statutory qualifications or disqualifications of jurors on the ground that they do not make for an array representative of the community, or procedural, objecting to some defect of form or method in the impanelment process. A challenge to the array is uncommon in civil actions; it is more likely to appear in a criminal context,[1] but it is infrequent there, too. Attorneys ordinarily reserve their challenges for individual jurors.

---

⁴   Gallegos v. Elite Model Management Corp., 28 A.D.3d 50, 807 N.Y.S.2d 44 (1st Dep't 2005) (SPR 178:4).

⁵   Sharrow v. Dick Corp., 86 N.Y.2d 54, 59–60, 629 N.Y.S.2d 980, 981–82, 653 N.E.2d 1150, 1151–52 (1995).

⁶   Xi Yu v. New York University Medical Center, 4 Misc. 3d 602, 781 N.Y.S.2d 416 (Sup. Ct., Queens County 2004).

⁷   Rivera v. New York City Transit Authority, 92 A.D.3d 516, 938 N.Y.S.2d 535 (1st Dep't 2012).

¹   See, e.g., People v. Young, 46 Misc. 2d 364, 259 N.Y.S.2d 577 (Seneca County Court 1965).

A challenge to an individual juror is known as a challenge to the poll or polls. There are two kinds, the peremptory challenge and the challenge for cause, the latter further subdivided into a challenge for principal cause and a challenge to the favor. Each of these will be discussed in turn after preliminaries are disposed of.

It is upon the voir dire that the questioning of potential jurors proceeds so as to determine whether any juror is subject to challenge. This questioning, as already noted, is generally conducted by the attorneys without a judge being present. A challenge for cause, if it has any colorable basis, often results in the mutual agreement of counsel to excuse the juror, thereby relieving the court of having to rule on the objection. If agreement is lacking and a ruling is necessary, the challenge is today tried and determined by the court. This is so whatever the ground of the objection, i.e., whether to the array or to the polls and whether the issue it poses is one of law or of fact.[2]

Challenges for cause are the subject of CPLR 4110. Subdivision (b) disqualifies persons related within the sixth degree to a party either by blood or marriage. The related party waives the objection by not raising it before the trial starts; any other party (who would presumably be the prejudiced one) has until 6 months after the verdict to raise it, although it should of course be raised as promptly as possible. This category of objection is known as one "for principal cause," which means that the existence of the relationship disqualifies the juror as a matter of law.[3]

The most common kind of challenge for cause is known as a challenge "to the favor," the subject of CPLR 4110(a). This one differs from the challenge for principal cause in that it poses an issue of fact rather than an issue of law. The difference rarely has practical significance; what little it has is likely to be felt more in the scope of review on appeal than at trial level.[4] An experienced attorney is usually reluctant to resist an arguable challenge made by the other side, and the experienced judge equally reluctant to overrule an objection that has a possible basis for the reason that doing so would tend to confer a tactical advantage on the objector: if she wins on the merits with the objectionable juror present, the objection will expire; but if she loses, she may have a trump card to lay before the appellate court. It is rarely necessary, therefore, to draw sharp lines between challenges for principal cause ("law" objections) and challenges to the favor ("fact" objections).

While not ordinarily present at the voir dire, the judge must attend it if requested to by one of the attorneys.[5] Objections not resolvable by stipulation can in any event be brought to the judge for rulings either to chambers or the courtroom.

A challenge to the favor can be based on anything tending to show that the juror can't judge the case indifferently. The factors that can support that showing are infinite.[6] The potential jurors at the voir dire are told about the kind of case it is, and the parties and their lawyers are identified. The questioning of jurors can then touch on anything reflecting on their capacity to maintain objectivity in the case. Fair subjects here are, among other things, any kind of relationship the juror may have to the parties or to their lawyers or to any other persons, such as witnesses, involved in the case whether the

---

[2]   CPLR 4108.

[3]   Butler v. Glens Falls, S.H. & Ft. E. St. R. Co., 121 N.Y. 112, 24 N.E. 187 (1890).

[4]   *Butler*, 121 N.Y. at 118–19, 24 N.E. at 190.

[5]   CPLR 4107.

[6]   See *Butler*, 121 N.Y. at 118, 24 N.E. at 190.

relationship is by blood, marriage, business, friendship, or anything else. Utter candor is the juror's obligation. As has already been indicated, a falsehood on the voir dire is one of the few revelations one juror may make of another after the verdict is in, even if it tends to destroy the verdict.

Any datum tending to show bias by the juror, in whatever direction it may carry the juror's inclination in the case, is a permissible topic of voir dire examination. Jury questionnaires can be used to ascertain if any potential bias exists.[7] This is important to note even before turning to some more specific content of CPLR 4110(a) because the things the statute enumerates are by no means exclusive. The statute merely lists a few frequently arising grounds and subjects them to challenges to the favor. The juror's employment by a party is listed as a ground for challenge to the favor,[8] for example, while the juror's employment by one of the lawyers or by a close friend or relative of a party is not. Yet, it would be equal ground for challenge. Another example: if a party is a corporation, the juror's status of shareholder is a listed objection, but his status as a creditor or debtor of the corporation is not; yet, it would still be a factor on which to base a challenge if there is any doubt about its effect on the juror's disinterest.

Since personal injury and wrongful death cases today are a big part of judicial calendars and are almost invariably defended by liability insurers, CPLR 4110(a) permits the jurors to be asked whether any has any position with or interest in such an insurer and authorizes a challenge to the favor against one who has. This may of course tend to suggest the presence of insurance to the jury, but the question may be asked if done without undue stress or histrionics. While neither the fact nor the sum of applicable insurance may be announced to the jury, its existence—in the compulsory insurance state of New York—has been statutorily recognized at least to the extent of allowing the voir dire question just noted.[9] Although it is probably safest to put the question in the identical terms in which CPLR 4110(a) casts it,[10] it has been held that related matters may also be investigated if done "without undue emphasis"—such as asking whether the jurors have heard through public media about the effect of negligence verdicts on insurance rates,[11] a datum that can prejudice a juror against the plaintiff.

If a municipality (city, village, town, or county) is a party, the fact that a juror is a resident or taxpayer of that municipality is not a ground for challenge to the favor;[12] it would often be difficult, if that were not the rule, to get a jury in cases in which a municipality is a party.[13]

---

[7] See Blaine v. International Business Machines Corp., 91 A.D.3d 1175, 1177, 937 N.Y.S.2d 405, 407 (3d Dep't 2012) (noting that "biases may be addressed through a comprehensive juror questionnaire sent to prospective jurors before jury selection and through the jury selection process itself").

[8] See *Blaine*, 91 A.D.3d at 1177, 937 N.Y.S.2d at 407 (noting that former employees are not covered by the rule).

[9] As part of pretrial disclosure during the action, a copy of the defendant's liability policy must be given to the plaintiff upon demand, but the policy and its content may still not be made known to the jury. See CPLR 3101(f); § 344.

[10] Is anyone among you "a shareholder, stockholder, director, officer or employee, or in any manner interested, in any insurance company issuing policies for protection against liability for damages for injury to persons or property[?]" CPLR 4110(a).

[11] See Graham v. Waite, 23 A.D.2d 628, 257 N.Y.S.2d 629 (4th Dep't 1965).

[12] CPLR 4110(a). Nor is a judge disqualified from presiding in a case involving a municipality merely because he is a resident or taxpayer of it. Jud. Law § 15, CPLR 4110–a.

[13] See the venue requirements applicable to an action against a municipality. CPLR 504.

Lawyers usually prefer to address questions to the jurors collectively, pursuing an individual juror with follow-up questions only when that juror's response to the collective question suggests it as a logical follow-up.

A party learning that a juror has withheld a pertinent datum on the voir dire, to that party's prejudice, should apprise the court promptly; withholding the objection until after a loss on the merits will likely forfeit it.[14]

Up to now, we have been discussing challenges for cause. An entirely different kind of challenge needs no ground at all, at least on the face of things: the peremptory challenge. Originally, CPLR 4109 gave "each party" three peremptories plus one for each alternate juror, taking cognizance of the situation in which there were more parties on one side than another by empowering the court to give additional challenges to the side with the fewer. A 1996 amendment altered this by giving three peremptories to each side rather than to each party and by allowing one additional peremptory challenge for each two alternates instead of for each one.[15] When there are several parties on a side, the court can allocate the side's peremptories among them.

Also prior to the 1996 amendment, if the interests on one side were antagonistic, each would get their own batch of peremptory challenges,[16] such as where there were co-defendant drivers of different cars in a personal injury case, each being patently hostile to the other. Whether there is to be an adjustment for mutual hostility among the members of a given side today is another matter awaiting definitive judicial resolution.

As long as a side's peremptory challenges last, the rule until recently was that the side can exercise them as arbitrarily as it pleases, with no reason being offered at all. A lawyer could take a dislike to a potential juror for as infinite a variety of reasons as there are people in the world. It could be based on something in the juror's background, comportment, or appearance which suggested a lack of sympathy with the questioner's cause; it could be a look, a nod, or the lawyer's own paranoia. Whatever it was, it remained a secret as long as the lawyer wished to keep it so.

While that is still largely the rule, an exception has been carved out for the peremptory challenge suspected of violating the Equal Protection Clause. Following the lead of the federal courts, the First Department held in Ancrum v. Eisenberg[17] that the Equal Protection Clause bars the discriminatory use of peremptory challenges against jurors in civil actions. The plaintiffs in the case were black and the defendant used all of his peremptory challenges against black jurors. A verdict for the defendant was overturned and the case remanded for a new trial. The court said that in a case like that, the party exercising the peremptory challenge must offer "a race-neutral explanation" that is "not mere pretext," which the defendant in *Ancrum* was unable to do.

---

[14]   See Gamell v. Mt. Sinai Hospital, 40 A.D.2d 1010, 339 N.Y.S.2d 31 (2d Dep't 1972).

[15]   There is an unresolved issue under the 1996 amendment about whether a third-party defendant is entitled to a separate set of peremptory challenges or must share the allotment that the main defendants get. See the lead note in SPR 50:1.

[16]   See Heiston v. Taylor, 281 A.D. 800, 119 N.Y.S.2d 452 (4th Dep't 1953).

[17]   Ancrum v. Eisenberg, 206 A.D.2d 324, 615 N.Y.S.2d 14 (1st Dep't 1994) (SPR 21:2).

In People v. Smocum,[18] the Court of Appeals adopted a three-part test for determining whether race was used as the basis for a peremptory challenge. It was a criminal case, but the rule applies in civil cases, too, albeit not seen there as often.[19]

The attorney often does best to save her peremptory challenges for last. It is helpful, for example, to have at hand a peremptory challenge to excuse a juror against whom the lawyer has made an unsuccessful challenge for cause. The juror may have been offended by the effort.

Trial lawyers develop their own preferences for the kinds of jurors they want in a given case or on a given side. Cultivating one's own predilections is one of the privileges of membership in the trial bar.

There is no stated time limit on the voir dire questioning process; the matter is left largely to judicial discretion. But that discretion can be breached. A rare example of it appears in Zgrodek v. McInerney,[20] which held that allowing only 15 minutes per round of questioning in a personal injury case with complicated damages issues was too short as a matter of law. The court discussed the time element in some depth, citing a publication on voir dire on the courts' website which states that "a reasonable time period to report on the progress of voir dire is after about two or three hours of actual voir dire."

Liability in the case had been conceded by D, but P, although awarded substantial damages by the jury, sought to set aside the verdict because of the voir dire restriction, apparently figuring the verdict would have been bigger with a more leisurely selected jury. The court granted P's motion and ordered the damages issues tried anew.

C. THE TRIAL PROPER

Table of Sections

§ 393.   Sequence of Trial
§ 394.   Separate Trial of Issues; Bifurcation
§ 395.   Right to Open and Close
§ 396.   Objections and Rulings
§ 397.   Summation
§ 398.   The Charge

§ 393. Sequence of Trial

The sequence of proceedings at a jury trial has been standardized by tradition, but if there are any issues in the case that are not jury triable, whether because not so by their nature or because trial by jury as to them has been waived, the preference of the rules is that they be disposed of before any proceedings involving the jury get under way. Indeed, the stated preference is that a jury not even be impaneled until nonjury issues are decided, especially when the issues may be dispositive of the case.[1]

If the nonjury issues are not dispositive, or if there are none in the case, trial by jury gets under way. After such initial discussions between court and counsel as are needed

---

18   People v. Smocum, 99 N.Y.2d 418, 757 N.Y.S.2d 239, 786 N.E.2d 1275 (2003).

19   See the discussion of the *Smocum* case and its three-part test in NYSLD No. 521.

20   Zgrodek v. McInerney, 61 A.D.3d 1106, 876 N.Y.S.2d 227 (3d Dep't 2009); (SPR 209:3).

1   See 22 N.Y.C.R.R. § 202.40.

to familiarize the judge with the case, or perhaps just to refresh the judge's recollection of it, the formal steps in a trial by jury follow this general order: the plaintiff makes an opening statement to the jury; the defendant does the same; the plaintiff calls her witnesses and puts in her case; the defendant does the same (each party cross-examining the other's witnesses); the defendant makes a closing argument ("summation") to the jury; the plaintiff does the same; the court charges the jury; and the jury retires, deliberates, and renders its verdict.[2] Through all of this runs the ever-present progression of objections, rulings, and related colloquies while the stenographer keeps track of it all. More serious discussions of evidentiary matters, or of legal points that hold some potential for prejudice if the jury should hear the dialogue, are taken out of the jury's hearing either at the bench or in chambers, or by excusing the jury.

At the trial's outset, the party who filed the note of issue—ordinarily the plaintiff—must furnish the court a set of marked pleadings.[3] Under the Individual Assignment System (IAS), the trial is not likely to be the judge's first contact with the case unless the "dual-track" system is in effect in the area, under which the case leaves the IAS judge and goes to a different judge for trial after the note of issue is filed.[4] If dual track does apply, however, or if the IAS is not used in the particular court, the marked pleadings may be the trial judge's first contact with the case. Marked pleadings offer a bird's-eye view of the issues.

The parties should also hand up any other papers or documents the court ought to have at the outset, such as formal admissions made under CPLR 3123 (which obviate trial of the issues admitted). A copy of any statute a party intends to rely on at the trial must also be submitted.[5] The court can direct the submission of trial memoranda and their exchange among counsel at the trial or even before it.[6]

The trial example we are using is the trial by jury, which enables us to see the trial at its most formal. Trial before a judge or referee is less rigidly structured. At the very outset, for example, a formal "opening" statement might be dispensed with. CPLR 4016 expressly authorizes an opening statement regardless of the mode of trial, but in the absence of a jury, the trial judge may just peruse the pleadings, impatiently waive off an opening statement as superfluous, and direct the plaintiff to call her first witness. Since an opening statement is designed to acquaint the fact trier with the issues and with what to look for in the proof, lawyers, recognizing that an experienced trial judge can often discern this from a scanning of the pleadings, will not press their formal right to "open"[7] unless the case is triable by jury.

After the openings, the witnesses are called and the evidence starts accumulating, the plaintiff going first. At this point, the rules of evidence take over. Objections and their preservation become a prime topic.[8] If the court finds it helpful, it can allow the

---

[2] CPLR 4011, although captioned "sequence of trial," is not intended to vary this traditional progression of events at a common law trial. Its principal mission is to authorize the trial of one issue before another, in the court's discretion as elaborated in § 394.

[3] CPLR 4012. Marked pleadings are described in § 222. This requirement of CPLR 4012 is picked up and expanded on by the Uniform Rules to include other papers. See, e.g., 22 N.Y.C.R.R. § 202.35 (applicable in the supreme and county courts).

[4] See § 77A.

[5] See, e.g., 22 N.Y.C.R.R. § 202.35.

[6] 22 N.Y.C.R.R. § 202.35.

[7] The right to open and close is treated in § 395.

[8] Objections and rulings are the subject of § 396.

jury to visit and view a premises relevant to the action.[9] After the evidence is closed, both sides having rested, the parties sum up, in inverse order to their openings.[10] Summation, about which there are a number of points to be made, is a separately treated topic,[11] as is the court's charge to the jury,[12] which in the sequence of the trial follows the summations. The jury then goes to its deliberations and in due course renders its verdict.

Only five of the six jurors are needed for a verdict in a civil action;[13] if five can't agree "after being kept together for as long as is deemed reasonable by the court"—this is popularly known as a hung jury—"the court shall discharge the jury and direct a new trial before another jury."[14] What a "reasonable" time is depends entirely on the facts of the particular case, the length of the trial, and the complexity of the issues.

The verdict will usually be followed by motions by the loser, a motion for judgment notwithstanding the verdict or for a new trial being the foremost examples of post-verdict motions. In the case of a money verdict, the plaintiff may seek to raise the sum or the defendant to lower it, which introduces the procedures known as additur and remittitur. These are also separate later topics.[15]

§ 394. Separate Trial of Issues; Bifurcation

CPLR 4011 allows the court to determine "the sequence in which the issues shall be tried and otherwise regulate the conduct of the trial in order to achieve a speedy and unprejudiced disposition of the matters at issue in a setting of proper decorum." It is not the purpose of CPLR 4011, however, although captioned "Sequence of trial," to vary the traditional order in which steps are taken at a jury trial as generally discussed in the prior section. An occasional variation in that sequence may be appropriate, and CPLR 4011—which is only a confirmation, anyway, of the powers of a common law judge[1]— may perhaps be cited to support it, but the rule's primary aim is to allow the court to direct that one issue be tried before another in a case with several (and separable) issues. Its assumption is that if a case has several issues and the trial of one of them separately from and prior to another will expedite the case, that one ought to be tried first. When there is still outstanding at trial time, for example, a defense like lack of jurisdiction, release, statute of limitations, or the like, which if resolved against the plaintiff can end the case then and there, the court can single it out for trial before the complaint's main issues on the merits are addressed.

If there are both jury and nonjury issues in the case, as when a jury trial of fewer than all issues has been demanded, the rules express a clear preference to have the nonjury issues disposed of first.[2]

---

[9]   CPLR 4110–c. See the Practice Commentary on that section in McKinney's CPLR.

[10]   CPLR 4016.

[11]   See § 397.

[12]   See § 398.

[13]   CPLR 4113(a). As to whether the same five jurors have to agree on all the issues in the case, see § 400.

[14]   CPLR 4113(b).

[15]   See §§ 405–407.

[1]   Martin v. Marshall, 25 A.D.2d 594, 266 N.Y.S.2d 992 (3d Dep't 1966).

[2]   22 N.Y.C.R.R. § 202.40. See § 393.

When the main issues for trial are the liability and damages phases of a personal injury or wrongful death action, and the liability issue is tried first, which is a common practice today, the bench and bar call this "bifurcation." Today, the rules do, too. The rule in point in the supreme and county courts, Uniform Rule section 202.42,[3] provides that judges are "encouraged" to order bifurcation. It doesn't say when a bifurcated trial is necessary; it merely provides guidance for such a trial when bifurcation is directed "by law or in the court's discretion." Bifurcation is preferred, in tort cases in any event, with the issue of liability tried first, for the obvious reason that if liability is negated, a damages trial, with all the frills upon it, is unnecessary.

The topic of bifurcation was previously discussed in the study of CPLR 603. That was the more appropriate place for it because an order of bifurcation is often directed in a pretrial order, grounded on CPLR 603 ("severance and separate trials"). If a direction for bifurcation should be made at the trial itself, however, no formal pretrial order having directed it, CPLR 4011 can be cited as the authority for it, along with the rules. The justifications for bifurcating will generally be similar whether ordained by pretrial order or directed at the trial itself, which makes the several considerations treated earlier[4] relevant here.

An appellate division review of some of the factors the trial judge should consider in deciding whether to order bifurcation appears in Carpenter v. County of Essex,[5] in which the court upholds a trial court's denial of bifurcation.[6]

§ 395. Right to Open and Close

The right to open and close—governed by CPLR 4016—is jealously guarded in a trial by jury because the party who has it gets both the first and the last word to the jury. The two things are a set: the party who makes opening remarks to the jury first has the right to deliver summation last. (The right to open and close was once before touched on when the subject of consolidation of actions was treated.[1] The topic there was how to adjust the right when there are multiple parties.)

The right to open and close is tied to the burden of proof. It belongs to the plaintiff almost invariably, but not quite. If the plaintiff does not have the affirmative burden of proof on any issue, and the defendant does, the defendant will get the open-and-close right, but that rare situation must be manifest from the pleadings themselves. If the defendant by answer denies any allegation of the complaint so as to put the plaintiff to the burden of proving the allegation, the plaintiff retains the right to open and close with respect to the whole case. The defendant will not be allowed to appropriate the right to open and close by attempting to concede the plaintiff's case even at the trial itself. This is designed to prevent a defendant, for whom the trial is not going well, from usurping at least the psychological advantage of closing to the jury by the simple expedient of

---

[3]   Similar rules should be looked for in other courts. See, e.g., 22 N.Y.C.R.R. § 208.35, applicable in the New York City Civil Court.

[4]   See § 130.

[5]   Carpenter v. County of Essex, 67 A.D.3d 1106, 888 N.Y.S.2d 278 (3d Dep't 2009). See 1A NY PJI3d 1:2A (2017).

[6]   The case is the subject of the lead note in SPR 219:1.

[1]   See § 128.

conceding all of the plaintiff's case and then addressing only a defense or counterclaim (on which the defendant has the burden of proof).[2]

If, on the other hand, the defendant has conceded the plaintiff's case in the answer, the plaintiff is not likely to dispute the defendant's right to open and close on a defense or counterclaim at the trial: the plaintiff will likely be there with a summary judgment already in hand, for which the plaintiff should have promptly moved when the answer and its concessions first arrived. Indeed, if the answer that conceded the plaintiff's claim offered only a defense, but no counterclaim, the plaintiff would likely have had the defense disposed of, one way or the other, by a pretrial motion to dismiss the defense under CPLR 3211(b), leaving no issues in the case at all and avoiding a trial altogether.

Contrary to popular misconception, a party is not rigidly bound by her opening statement. The omission of an item requisite to a prima facie case, for example, will not necessarily be fatal; it can be cured during the trial.[3] Judges are realistic about this and ordinarily will not permit even a variance between the pleading and the bill of particulars on the one hand, and the opening statement on the other, to undermine a case if there is still in prospect an evidentiary possibility of making out a claim.[4] CPLR 4401 does authorize judgment for a party "on the basis of admissions," but, as will be seen,[5] the admissions intended are those that absolutely preclude all possibility of judgment for the admitter rather than those that merely vary—from what the papers in the case show—some facts or even theories without prejudicing the other side or foreclosing a foundation for a victory on the merits. An "admission" during the opening is prone to be of the latter kind, and is therefore hardly a basis for judgment.

Sometimes, a party can end up as both a plaintiff and a defendant in the same case. In a two-car accident, for example, driver A, with a privately retained lawyer, may be suing driver B in one action, while driver B is suing A in a separate action in which A is represented by a lawyer retained by his insurance company. Should the two actions be consolidated, a not infrequent occurrence, a clamor goes up among the parties to win the right to open and close. It has been held that someone in A's position is not necessarily entitled to have opening and closing statements made by both his lawyers; the court retains discretion to determine how the right shall be allotted.[6]

May the specific amount sought by the plaintiff in a money action be mentioned in the opening or closing statements to the jury? This was an unsettled point for a while. Under Tate v. Colabello, the Court of Appeals held that it is "counsel's privilege" to suggest the sum in summation.[7] The right to do so in summation is now approved by CPLR 4016. For a while, the statute allowed it in the opening statement, too,[8] but only

---

[2]   See Lake Ontario Nat. Bank v. Judson, 122 N.Y. 278, 25 N.E. 367 (1890).

[3]   See Justice Rosenblatt's discussion in De Vito v. Katsch, 157 A.D.2d 413, 556 N.Y.S.2d 649 (2d Dep't 1990), New York's most detailed treatment of the subject to date.

[4]   See § 404 discussing CPLR 3025(c).

[5]   See § 402.

[6]   See Tomassi v. Town of Union, 58 A.D.2d 670, 395 N.Y.S.2d 747 (3d Dep't 1977), modified, 46 N.Y.2d 91, 412 N.Y.S.2d 842, 385 N.E.2d 581 (1978).

[7]   See § 397.

[8]   See the amendment of CPLR 4016 as treated in SPR 143:1. See also 1B NY PJI3d 2:277A ("Damages—Comment by Counsel During Closing Remarks").

for about a year. The legislature then had a change of heart, preserving the right for summation, but barring it from the opening.[9]

§ 396. Objections and Rulings

After the parties have opened to the jury, the witnesses are called and the evidence begins.

One of the essentials of the trial process is of course the rule that testimony at the trial be live from the witness on the stand. We may note an occasional, and assuredly rare, infraction. In Campaign for Fiscal Equity v. State,[1] for example, in which the court, conducting a bench trial, was faced with a list of some 140 witnesses in a case of public interest, it allowed their direct testimony to be injected in affidavit form. Even there, however, this was allowed only for the witnesses' direct testimony, the court adding the precautions that each witness initially take the stand to swear to the affidavit and then remain there, or be available to take the stand again, for live cross-examination.[2] The procedure was also restricted to fact testimony, excluding, e.g., expert testimony from the process.

During the trial, the law of evidence takes over, but a few essential things can be noted about the making and preservation of objections without undue trespass on the law of evidence, to which the objections will usually relate.

There is no magic word or formula for the making of objections. "Objection" is the most obvious and hence the most popular word, and so it remains the most frequent opening word in the usual counsel-and-court colloquy about the admissibility of a question, datum, or item. When a ruling is requested, the lawyer's obligation is to make known the action she thinks the court should take or her objection to the action already taken or proposed to be taken by the court;[3] the combination of words that so apprises the court is secondary.[4] If an evidentiary objection is sustained and an answer or item is consequently excluded, the aggrieved party should make an offer of proof for the sake of the record, describing the nature and purpose of the excluded item so as to enable the appellate court to adjudge its admissibility—its relevancy, competency, materiality, etc. In some instances, depending on the potential prejudice the offer of proof may have if made in front of the jury, the court may insist that it be made at the bench or otherwise beyond the jury's hearing or vision or in the jury's absence.

The failure to advise the court of an objection will have impact on the appellate process where it will restrict the scope of review. A "ruling" itself is not appealable; nor are a series of rulings. But the final judgment is appealable, and if appealed will bring up for review a number of things, including evidentiary rulings and remarks of the court. But the review will ordinarily embrace only those rulings and remarks to which objection was made.[5]

---

[9]   See SPR 156:2.

[1]   Campaign for Fiscal Equity v. State, 182 Misc. 2d 676, 699 N.Y.S.2d 663 (Sup. Ct., New York County 1999) (SPR 92:3).

[2]   The court cited examples of similar procedures used by federal judges in bench trials. The procedure would probably be entirely unsatisfactory in a trial by jury. See 22 N.Y.C.R.R. § 202.70(g), Com. Div. Rule 32(a) ("Direct Testimony by Affidavit").

[3]   CPLR 4017.

[4]   More punctilio is necessary for the charge to the jury, treated separately in § 398.

[5]   CPLR 5501(a)(3), (4). See §§ 526, 530.

If, upon an objection by the other side, the offerer responds with arguments justifying admissibility and the court hears both sides before ruling, the record in regard to the ruling should be adequate to preserve review at the behest of whichever party loses on the point. But even a lawyer's mere putting of a question, or tender of a document, should bear implicitly the contention that it's admissible, requiring no further objection on the offerer's part if, upon the sustaining of an adversary's objection, the question or item is excluded. If the appellate court is convinced from the record that the court was aware of the appellant's position on the ruling, it will deem an objection to the court's action on the matter to have been both made and preserved. This of course assumes that the matter is one of substance and that the party with the objection did not afterwards acquiesce in the ruling.

There is no requirement today to follow an unfavorable ruling with the word "exception" or any other word or words to indicate displeasure. As long as the loser's position on the point has been made known to the court, the unfavorable ruling is preserved for appellate review without the follow-up utterance of the pouty "exception"[6] at one time in favor—and still used today, unnecessarily but harmlessly, by some lawyers. The word "exception," instead of "objection," is sometimes heard in initial opposition to a question. It is just as effective. The use of either word or neither word or other words will bear no consequence as long as the party's grievance is made known.[7] But words of some kind should be used; a surly look is hard to record on a transcript.

In making an objection, it may be politic to omit any specification of ground at the outset. This is called a "general" objection. If the court sustains it and there is any ground at all to support it, the ruling will be upheld on appeal. If the objection is sustained on a particular ground, however, the appellate court may refuse to entertain any but the cited ground to determine the ruling's validity. If the cited ground is found invalid, the ruling may be overturned notwithstanding the existence of another ground, uncited, that might have supported it.[8] An exception to this rule is where the evidence excluded is found by the appellate court to be wholly incompetent by all standards, in which event exclusion will be approved despite the trial court's reliance on a specific but incorrect ground.

Matching this is the rule that if a general objection is overruled, and the evidence is received, the appellate court will uphold its receipt unless it is by all criteria incompetent.[9] If a sanguine objector, bent on deriving some tactical benefit from these rules, makes an objection generally, the offerer of the evidence, sensing this, should be able to keep the objector honest simply by asking the court to have the objector specify the ground relied on. Unless the evidence is patently incompetent, and the validity of the objection consequently obvious, the court is likely to be receptive to that suggestion.

Objections should be timely from a tactical as well as a technical point of view. If the objection is addressed to a question, it should be made before the question is answered and the answer is heard by the jury; if addressed to an item, it should be put when the item is tendered—before it is admitted into evidence and before the jury is made aware of its purpose or contents. If made afterwards, the objection becomes what is known as a motion to strike, i.e., to strike the answer from the record or the item from the evidence. Although called a "motion," it is really only a form of objection—a request

---

6   CPLR 4017.

7   See 2d Rep. Leg. Doc. No. 13, p. 213 (1958).

8   See Bloodgood v. Lynch, 293 N.Y. 308, 56 N.E.2d 718 (1944).

9   See Tooley v. Bacon, 70 N.Y. 34, 1877 WL 12006 (1877).

for a ruling. It is obviously less effective than a timely objection that prevents the answer or item from emerging in the first place, but it has its niche in trial practice.

Sometimes a witness is faster with an answer than the opposing lawyer is with an objection. Sometimes an answer or item depends for its evidentiary validity on something to come later, and is admitted by the court "subject to connection" with the later item, and the later item does not materialize or emerges much less potently than the court was led to believe. The appropriate remedy in these instances is a motion to strike. It is often accompanied by a court instruction that the jury disregard the particular question and answer, or the item. Although this may be unrealistic in many cases—how does one get a jury to unsee, unhear, or unknow something?—it is important, once again, in order to preserve the objection for review on appeal. If the matter admitted is found on appeal to have been so prejudicial that the instruction to disregard it could not work, a new trial will be ordered. (One may recall here the cartoon of a judge blandly instructing the jury to disregard the last answer as all 12 jurors sit there with their faces in shock and their hair up on end.)

A motion to strike may also be available to a party who, excusably, did not earlier realize that there was a valid evidentiary objection, and it is of course permissible when a perfectly valid question elicits a wholly unresponsive and prejudicial answer. The motion may also be the expedient whereby a judge, now convinced that he was in error in admitting an objectionable answer or item earlier, attempts to remedy the mistake later. The judge must take care to see that the jury understands the purpose of the motion to strike.

The most important note here, which may lend some sense to the motion to strike procedure, is that as far as the appellate process is concerned, the key word is "prejudice." No error, or even quantum of errors, in the course of evidentiary rulings, whether in response to early objections or to later motions to strike, will overturn the verdict unless the appellate court is convinced that the error materially prejudiced the losing party.

§ 397. Summation

The lawyer's closing statement to the jury is called the "summation," or sometimes the "argument."

Summations are made in inverse order to openings: the party who opens first sums up last.[1] The right to the final word has a psychological impact that makes it a forensic prize. However effective a defendant's summation may be, its most telling points may be blunted by an equally able plaintiff's summation that follows. Plaintiffs are generally comforted throughout their summations by the knowledge that the defendant will not get another chance to address this jury.

It is the right of counsel in summation to comment on every fact relevant to the case and arguably supported by the evidence. Allowed the widest latitude, the attorney will be interrupted by the court only when necessary to prevent prolixity, waste of time, or totally unjustifiable comment,[2] which means making statements on matters not in evidence or indulging arguments having no basis whatever in the proof—including

---

[1]   CPLR 4016. See the discussion of the right to open and close in § 395.

[2]   Williams v. Brooklyn Elevated R. Co., 126 N.Y. 96, 26 N.E. 1048 (1891).

appeals to prejudice or passion.[3] Overstepping those bounds, even if the trial judge does not intervene, can bring reversal on appeal and necessitate a retrial.[4] Sometimes an appellate court will grant a new trial because of the cumulative effect of a series of unwarranted comments in summation,[5] even though perhaps none individually would justify it.

Irrelevancies and absurdities in quantity will turn the trick as where in a personal injury case, the plaintiff's lawyer leads off by buttering up the judge, pledges his love for the venue, and then offers discourse on his deprived youth and a large cast of unbilled characters ranging from Perry Mason to the immortal bard.[6] In such a case, it's not that the lawyer is pressing for unsupported conclusions. It's that the aggregate of the asininities will so divert the jurors from the issues that the rights of the parties will be lost in the morass.

When summation exceeds all reasonable frontiers of propriety, the opposing lawyer need not stand by in silence. He may object during the summation,[7] asking for a court direction that counsel desist and that improper remarks be disregarded.[8] One lawyer should not, however, interrupt another's summation for anything less than palpably improper and potentially prejudicial conduct or comment. It should be a courtesy among lawyers that each allow the other an unfettered opportunity for argument, which is what a summation is.

If attorneys are abiding by the expected amenities, there may be no need to have the stenographer record the summations. A hint of trouble, however, should prompt a request that the summations be taken down and it has been held reversible error for the court to refuse such a request.[9] The difficulty of reviewing objectionable comments without a verbatim record may itself require a new trial,[10] or amount to a waiver of the objections.[11]

A frequent topic on summation, and a legitimate one, is the other party's failure to call a given witness, especially if because of relationship the witness's testimony would presumably favor that party and the witness's absence has not been explained, such as where the plaintiff does not call his own physician in a personal injury case or a party does not call his own employee.[12]

What about mentioning specific sums in summation, an especially sensitive matter in an action for personal injury or wrongful death? Until the early 1980s, there was no uniform practice around the State about allowing the plaintiff in a tort case to state in summation the amount demanded in the complaint, although there was appellate

---

[3]   See Cherry Creek Nat. Bank v. Fidelity & Casualty Co. of New York, 207 A.D. 787, 202 N.Y.S. 611 (4th Dep't 1924).

[4]   See McCabe v. Queensboro Farm Products, Inc., 21 A.D.2d 675, 250 N.Y.S.2d 91 (2d Dep't 1964).

[5]   See Bishin v. New York Cent. R. Co., 20 A.D.2d 921, 249 N.Y.S.2d 778 (2d Dep't 1964).

[6]   See Laughing v. Utica Steam Engine and Boiler Works, 16 A.D.2d 294, 228 N.Y.S.2d 44 (4th Dep't 1962).

[7]   Samuel v. Porchia, 40 A.D.2d 697, 336 N.Y.S.2d 387 (2d Dep't 1972).

[8]   Layton Sales & Rentals, Inc. v. Somat Realty Corp., 39 A.D.2d 640, 331 N.Y.S.2d 164 (4th Dep't 1972).

[9]   Robinson v. Ferens, 33 A.D.2d 688, 306 N.Y.S.2d 530 (2d Dep't 1969).

[10]   See Devine v. Keller, 32 A.D.2d 34, 299 N.Y.S.2d 249 (3d Dep't 1969).

[11]   See Leven v. Marguerite, 52 A.D.2d 970, 383 N.Y.S.2d 120 (3d Dep't 1976).

[12]   See the extended treatment of this subject in Seligson, Morris & Neuburger v. Fairbanks Whitney Corp., 22 A.D.2d 625, 257 N.Y.S.2d 706 (1st Dep't 1965); 1A NY PJI3d 1:75 (Missing Witness Charge).

division caselaw allowing it based on the rule that the content of the pleadings may always be revealed to the jury.[13] The money demand (the "ad damnum") in a tort case was usually so unrealistic[14] (and often still is) that a strong argument can be made against its divulgence to the jury. The point was clarified when the Court of Appeals held in Tate v. Colabello[15] that it is "counsel's privilege" to suggest to the jury the sum counsel believes appropriate as damages in an unliquidated damages case like one involving personal injuries, and in conjunction with that to reveal also the amount demanded in the complaint. An important concomitant is that the jury be charged that the ultimate determination of damages is up to them, an instruction the trial court had properly made in *Tate*.

Resolving a conflict in the cases about whether the sum sought may be mentioned to the jury in a medical malpractice action,[16] the legislature amended CPLR 4016 in 2003 to hold that it may be in all money actions.[17]

The precursor of CPLR 4016 in the early studies of the CPLR's drafters included a provision expressly authorizing the court to limit the time for opening and closing statements,[18] a provision afterwards omitted, apparently with the intent to leave the time allotment to judicial discretion to be exercised on a case-by-case basis without any statutory hints.[19]

§ 398. The Charge

The charge, which follows the parties' summations, is the court's address to the jury in which it instructs them on the law applicable to the diverse issues in the case. It is made by the judge by direct address in person.[1] The jury are advised that they will determine all issues of fact. The law charged advises them of the legal impact of their fact-findings. The charge thus enables the jury, as necessary, to convert their conclusions of fact into conclusions of law and render a verdict accordingly. The court should therefore tell the jury not only what the law is, but also what the factual contentions of the parties are with respect to the legal principles charged.[2] It should discuss the evidence and relate it to the rules of law, including a careful delineation for the jury of which party has the burden of proof on each issue and how the discharge of that burden is to be gauged. General or abstract principles of law, no matter how correct, are frowned on because they are not helpful to a jury unless made relevant to the issues of fact that it is the jury's responsibility to resolve.[3]

---

[13]   See, e.g., Rice v. Ninacs, 34 A.D.2d 388, 312 N.Y.S.2d 246 (4th Dep't 1970).

[14]   Plaintiffs' lawyers had to keep their demands high because the verdict could not exceed the demand, a restriction afterwards abandoned. See § 217.

[15]   Tate by McMahon v. Colabello, 58 N.Y.2d 84, 459 N.Y.S.2d 422, 445 N.E.2d 1101 (1983).

[16]   See Bechard v. Eisinger, 105 A.D.2d 939, 481 N.Y.S.2d 906 (3d Dep't 1984), and Braun v. Ahmed, 127 A.D.2d 418, 515 N.Y.S.2d 473 (2d Dep't 1987).

[17]   The amendment allowed the sum sought to be mentioned in the opening to the jury as well, but the legislature changed its mind about that a year later and restricted that right to the summation. See § 395.

[18]   See 2d Rep. Leg. Doc. No. 13, p. 212 (1958).

[19]   See 5th Rep. Leg. Doc. No. 15, p. 517 (1961).

[1]   The use of tape, for example, has been held impermissible. See Fogel v. Lenox Hill Hosp., 127 A.D.2d 548, 512 N.Y.S.2d 109 (1st Dep't 1987).

[2]   Arroyo v. Judena Taxi, Inc., 20 A.D.2d 888, 248 N.Y.S.2d 952 (1st Dep't 1964).

[3]   Green v. Downs, 27 N.Y.2d 205, 316 N.Y.S.2d 221, 265 N.E.2d 68 (1970).

Elaborate itemization of the verdict is required today in the major tort actions as a result of amendments expanding or creating substantive rights affecting damages. The right of defendants to have "collateral source" payments credited against the verdict,[4] to have contribution rights determined among themselves,[5] to have their "joint" liability cancelled under certain circumstances,[6] to pay certain parts of the plaintiff's "future" damages in installments instead of in one lump sum (in what is known as a "structured judgment")[7]—all of these turn in some measure on what the jury finds each individual item of damages to be and the share of fault of each party with respect to it. The statutes enacted or amended to accomplish this itemization task, in CPLR 4111, are subdivisions (d) with respect to the medical malpractice categories of action[8] and (e) for the other tort actions.[9] It is the obligation of the court to assure that the charge to the jury clarifies the jury's obligation to furnish these detailed itemizations.[10]

The "collateral source" rule of CPLR 4545 noted above entitles the defendant (in effect, the liability insurer) to have credited against the verdict payments the plaintiff has received, or will receive "with reasonable certainty," from outside sources that duplicate items of damages awarded in the verdict.[11] CPLR 4545(a) instructs that any required collateral source reduction "shall be made by the trial court after . . . the jury's verdict" has been rendered, but it doesn't specify the procedures to be used or a time limit on when the defendant can request the collateral source hearing. In Firmes v. Chase Manhattan Automotive Finance Corp.,[12] the Second Department concluded that "an application for a collateral source hearing may be timely made any time before the judgment is entered." The plaintiff may not, by arranging to have a judgment entered without notice, deprive the defendant of a hearing on possible collateral source reductions.[13]

In New York, several volumes of "Pattern Jury Instructions" ("PJI") are available, which set forth representative charges in a number of different civil actions. These are drawn by a diverse group of trial and appellate justices and scholars, and are accompanied by detailed commentary that is updated annually. The treatise contains a remarkable compilation of New York law, and can serve as a valuable research tool in a wide array of substantive areas.[14] While the pattern charges are not binding on trial judges, and often need to be adopted to the facts of a particular case, they represent well-respected authority. The charges and comments have been found of great value by the

---

[4]   CPLR 4545. See §§ 180, 399.

[5]   CPLR Article 14. See §§ 172 et seq.

[6]   CPLR Article 16. See §§ 168A et seq.

[7]   See CPLR Articles 50–A and 50–B. See § 409.

[8]   Subdivision (d) was amended in 2003 in an attempt to produce still greater specificity in the medical categories for the purposes of applying the structured judgment statute, CPLR Article 50–A. See Practice Commentary on McKinney's CPLR 4111; 1B NY PJI3d 2:277 ("Damages—General").

[9]   Subdivision (e) had been (f) before (e) was repealed in 2009 and (f) relettered (e) in amendments—L.2009, ch. 494, Part F—designed to clarify the application of the collateral source rule. See § 180 and § 399, and the discussion of the amendments in SPR 216:1–2.

[10]   Subdivision (e) of CPLR 4111 has a similar but narrower mission, addressed only to actions against certain public employers. There, the benefits of the collateral source rule are the subject aimed at.

[11]   The disclosure of collateral source payments is discussed in § 348.

[12]   Firmes v. Chase Manhattan Automotive Finance Corp., 50 A.D.3d 18, 852 N.Y.S.2d 148 (2d Dep't 2008).

[13]   Turuseta v. Wyassup-Laurel Glen Corp., 91 A.D.3d 635, 937 N.Y.S.2d 76 (2d Dep't 2012) (SPR 242:3).

[14]   PJI is available on Westlaw.

judiciary and bar,[15] and have been favorably cited by the New York Court of Appeals and the appellate division on numerous occasions.[16]

Because the charge is a key part of the trial, lawyers must be alert to advise the court thoroughly on the law as each contends it to be. It is the responsibility of every trial advocate to see to it that the judge is made aware of every law relevant to the facts and favorable to the client, and this includes statutes, rules, regulations, ordinances, decisions, and any other sources that may qualify as "law" and govern the rights of the parties. The lawyer does this in what is called a "request to charge," governed today by CPLR 4110–b, which was added to the CPLR in 1973. The section permits any party at the close of the evidence to submit "written requests that the court instruct the jury on the law as set forth in the requests."[17] The court is required to rule on the requests before summation and out of the jury's hearing so as to enable counsel to adjust their summations accordingly.[18]

Before the addition of CPLR 4110–b, practices varied, but probably the most common one was to save requests to charge until after summation, submitting them before the judge's charge or even after it (when they would amount to requests for additional charges or substitutes for objectionable portions of the charge already delivered). That is still done. The submission of requests to charge before summation is something a party "may" do under CPLR 4110–b, which leaves the option to the party. And even if the option is picked up, it need not preclude further requests after summation or even after the court's main charge.

It will probably take some time before CPLR 4110–b succeeds, if it ever does, in making it a norm for the parties to submit their requests to charge before summation, although much benefit may come of it. It avoids, for example, the occasional fiasco in which a lawyer delivers a fine summation built around an anticipated rule of law that then doesn't materialize in the charge. Early submission of a request to charge can educate the lawyer about what the judge sees as the applicable rule of law on each issue, which necessarily teaches the lawyer something about how to construct the argument to the jury. In fact, CPLR 4110–b contemplates such requests to charge not just before summation but even "at such earlier time during the trial as the court reasonably directs." In potentially long trials, or in trials involving complex issues, for example, it is especially advantageous both to judge and counsel that each understand the other's position on the governing legal principles. It can assist the lawyer in presenting evidence and the court in ruling on its admissibility. Indeed, it is good practice in long or complex trials to submit at the outset, to both court and adversary, a legal memorandum setting out, to the extent tactically appropriate in advance of trial, one's specific postures on the legal issues involved.

---

[15]   See, e.g., Celle v. Filipino Reporter Enterprises Inc., 209 F.3d 163, 174 (2d Cir. 2000) ("These draft instructions—with extensive citations to cases, statutes and secondary authorities—are kept up-to-date by a distinguished group of New York Supreme Court Justices and law professors. They are relied upon in New York courts and in federal courts in diversity actions."); Acerra v. Trippardella, 34 A.D.2d 927, 311 N.Y.S.2d 522 (1st Dep't 1970).

[16]   See, e.g., Burlington Ins. Co. v. NYC Transit Authority, 29 N.Y.3d 313, 57 N.Y.S.3d 85, 79 N.E.3d 477 (2017); Mazella v. Beals, 27 N.Y.3d 694, 706, 37 N.Y.S.3d 46, 54, 57 N.E.3d 1083, 1091 (2016).

[17]   CPLR 4110–b uses the word "file" rather than "submit," which betrays its federal origin. (The provision is modeled on Fed. R. Civ. P. 51.) What the lawyer should do is submit at least one copy to the court and give one to each of the other parties in the action.

[18]   See the Practice Commentary on McKinney's CPLR 4110–b.

While CPLR 4017 governs the making and preservation of objections generally in the course of a trial, CPLR 4110–b has a more specific instruction about objections concerning the court's charge to the jury. It provides that "no party may assign as error the giving or the failure to give an instruction unless he objects thereto before the jury retires to consider its verdict." And the party must specify "the matter to which he objects and the grounds of his objection." The court is directed to afford the objectant an opportunity to make the objection out of the jury's hearing.

The technical deadline, then, for the making of an objection affecting the charge, whether the objection is to the court's refusal to charge as requested or to something contained in the court's charge as already made, is before the jury retires. But if on the facts counsel has acted with apparent diligence in at least trying to make objections timely, they will be preserved. Thus, where the judge indicated that he wished to have objections heard in chambers, and the chambers conference followed the jury's retirement to deliberate, the objections were deemed timely; the appellate court noted that a prompt recall of the jury at that early moment, for such further instruction as a sustaining of the objection might have called for, would have had scant impact on the jury's deliberative process.[19]

The trial court has broad power to recall a jury for further instructions. It usually does this when it is the jury that requests it, such as where the jury is confused on a point and wants it clarified. But the recall may also be made on the court's initiative,[20] which can be triggered by a party's request.

The main consequence of a failure to make a timely objection to a charge or to the rejection of a request to charge is that the objectant may be held to have waived the objection on appeal. An error in connection with the charge, as is true of trial errors in general, is preserved for appellate review only when duly objected to.[21] In other words, a failure to except to a given instruction may make it the "law of the case."[22] There is an important exception, however: if the appellate division finds the error in respect of the charge "fundamental," it can order a new trial in the interest of justice even though the error was not objected to.[23] This appellate power is not undone by CPLR 4110–b.[24]

Of course, even an error properly objected to in the charge will not be ground for reversal unless found to be prejudicial. Harmless error, even in the charge to the jury, is ignored.[25]

---

[19]   Meagher v. Long Island R. Co., 27 N.Y.2d 39, 313 N.Y.S.2d 378, 261 N.E.2d 384 (1970).

[20]   See Barreto v. Calderon, 31 A.D.2d 896, 297 N.Y.S.2d 799 (1st Dep't 1969).

[21]   CPLR 4017, 5501(a)(3).

[22]   See Olsen v. St. Margaret of Scotland Roman Catholic Church, 21 A.D.2d 827, 251 N.Y.S.2d 512 (2d Dep't 1964). The "law of the case" doctrine is a species of intra-action res judicata. See § 448.

[23]   See, e.g., Jemison v. Goodman, 49 A.D.2d 1011, 373 N.Y.S.2d 926 (4th Dep't 1975).

[24]   DiGrazia v. Castronova, 48 A.D.2d 249, 251–2, 368 N.Y.S.2d 898, 902 (4th Dep't 1975). The case illustrates what can qualify as an error so "fundamental" as to mandate a new trial.

[25]   See, e.g., Lieberman v. Washington Square Hotel Corp., 40 A.D.2d 647, 336 N.Y.S.2d 518 (1st Dep't 1972).

D. THE VERDICT

Table of Sections

§ 399.   Kinds of Verdict

§ 400.   Delivery of the Verdict

§ 401.   Defective Verdicts; Impeachment

§ 399.   Kinds of Verdict

The verdict is the determination of the jury on the issues submitted. It can be either general or special. A "general" verdict is one in which the jury merely finds in favor of a party; it is pronounced in just that conclusory way and the various component findings that account for it remain unspoken. "We find in favor of the defendant." Or: "We find for the plaintiff in the sum of $175,000." The "special" verdict is a statement by the jury of the facts it has found. What it essentially constitutes is the jury's answers to questions submitted to it, sometimes very detailed questions. The court then reviews the answers and determines which party is to have judgment.[1]

The general verdict is still in use today, but losing ground to the special verdict, especially in tort cases. With the expansion in the 1970s of contribution rights among tortfeasors,[2] closely followed by the adoption of a rule of comparative negligence applicable to a tort plaintiff to replace the traditional New York rule of contributory negligence,[3] and with the adoption in the 1980s of the collateral source rule,[4] and the rule adjusting joint liability among tortfeasors,[5] the need to have the jury reveal its specific findings of percentages of fault in personal injury and wrongful death cases gave the special verdict new vogue. Elaboration by the jury of allotments of fault and items of damages in tort cases was ultimately made mandatory.[6] It has even been held that if there are issues of comparative negligence in a case, it is reversible error for the judge to elicit only a general verdict unless the parties stipulate to it.[7]

The special verdict entails the submission to the jury of written questions susceptible of brief answer, or written forms of the various alternative findings the jury can choose from, or some other equivalent method to elicit written findings. Whichever device is used, the charge must of course clarify the jury's obligations on all of the issues involved. The parties must be alert to assure that all the questions of interest to their side are submitted. If an issue duly raised by the pleadings or evidence is not among the proposed submissions, the interested party must demand its inclusion before the jury retires. Otherwise, trial by jury of the omitted issue may be waived and a consent implied to the court's determining it; or, in default of an express judicial finding, the issue will be deemed resolved in accordance with the judgment.[8] This is designed, when a special

---

[1]   CPLR 4111(a).

[2]   CPLR 1401–1404. See § 172.

[3]   CPLR 1411. See § 168E.

[4]   CPLR 4545, noted in § 180.

[5]   CPLR Article 16. See §§ 168A et seq.

[6]   CPLR 4111; see § 398. A similar set of requirements applies to the judge in a judge-tried case under CPLR 4213. See the Commentaries on McKinney's CPLR 4111 and 4213.

[7]   See Russo v. Jess R. Rifkin, D.D.S., P.C., 113 A.D.2d 570, 497 N.Y.S.2d 41 (2d Dep't 1985).

[8]   CPLR 4111(b).

verdict is used, to prevent invalidation of the whole trial through the inadvertent omission of but one issue.[9]

The special verdict is especially appropriate when several different grounds are alleged in support of a claim. Suppose, for example, that a jury renders a general verdict for P on a claim allegedly supported by two grounds. An appellate court finds one of the grounds unsupported by the record, but cannot determine whether the jury relied on that one, which would require a reversal,[10] or the valid one, which could bring affirmance. The court has no choice in that situation but to reverse and remand for a new trial.[11] A special verdict, by clarifying whether the supportable ground was sustained by the jury, can avoid that. This has frequently prompted appellate courts, on remanding for a new trial in an instance of multiple theories, to require that a special verdict be used.[12]

The court has yet a third way of submitting the case to the jury. It is known as a general verdict accompanied by answers to interrogatories, a kind of mixture of general and special verdicts. It clarifies the jury's constituent findings, but also enables the jury to draw the conclusions they believe the findings justify. This device comes from CPLR 4111(c),[13] which also provides for the situation in which there is conflict between the conclusion (the general verdict) and one of the answers. As long as the answers are consistent with each other, they will ordinarily prevail over the general verdict. The underlying theory is that the components of the jury's findings are more revealing than its conclusions.[14] But the court retains discretion to send the jury back for further deliberations or to order a new trial. When one of the answers is in conflict with the general verdict and it also appears that the answers are not consistent among themselves, further deliberations or a new trial are the court's only options; judgment in accordance with the answers would be precluded.[15]

Suppose, for example, that in a tort case governed by New York's comparative negligence rule, P and each of the two defendants A and B are found guilty of 40% fault. That would total an impossible 120% and the answers, without even having to consider how they stack up against the general verdict, would necessitate further deliberations or a new trial.

The special verdict by itself is probably a neater tool to discern the jury's intentions, but whether to use it alone or in combination with the general verdict, giving rise to the general verdict accompanied by interrogatories, is left to the court's discretion. The Court of Appeals has observed that the technique of submitting interrogatories to the jury is "especially well suited to cases with multiple parties and legal theories,"[16] to which we

---

[9]   See 2d Rep. Leg. Doc. No. 13, pp. 234–35 (1958). This provision was adapted from Fed. R. Civ. P. 49(a).

[10]   See Blair v. New York University College of Dentistry, 15 A.D.2d 211, 222 N.Y.S.2d 1 (1st Dep't 1961).

[11]   See Hamilton v. Presbyterian Hospital of City of New York, 25 A.D.2d 431, 267 N.Y.S.2d 656 (1st Dep't 1965).

[12]   See, e.g., Corbett v. Brown, 32 A.D.2d 27, 32, 299 N.Y.S.2d 219, 224 (3d Dep't 1969).

[13]   CPLR 4111(c) is modeled on Fed. R. Civ. P. 49(b).

[14]   See and compare Chevalier v. Farrell, 58 Misc. 2d 991, 296 N.Y.S.2d 896 (Sup. Ct., Rensselaer County 1968).

[15]   CPLR 4111(c).

[16]   Marine Midland Bank v. John E. Russo Produce Co., Inc., 50 N.Y.2d 31, 427 N.Y.S.2d 961, 405 N.E.2d 205 (1980).

may add issues of comparative and contributory fault. No uniform criteria have yet been developed for whether to use the interrogatories with or without a general verdict. Even appellate courts, when remanding cases for new trials, sometimes seem to suggest one or the other indifferently.[17]

As a matter of tactics, plaintiffs' attorneys in tort cases, especially those involving serious injuries but questionable liability, prefer the general verdict alone and put the special verdict at the bottom of their list of options. Their fear is that a jury bent on finding facts without at all times being aware of their legal impact will be more prone to find for the defendant. The fear had more basis under the now-superseded contributory negligence rule where a finding of any negligence on the plaintiff's part destroyed the case. It lost much of its justification under the superseding rule of comparative negligence,[18] which allows a negligent plaintiff to recover for at least the defendant's proportionate share of the plaintiff's damages.

The collateral source rule was noted earlier in the discussion of the jury charge.[19] Amendments to CPLR 4545 in 2009 and some important caselaw warrant a further word about it here. Now governed in personal injury actions by subdivision (a) of CPLR 4545,[20] the collateral source rule allows a defendant tortfeasor to show that items of damages claimed by the plaintiff are essentially duplicated by payments the plaintiff has received, or will receive "with reasonable certainty," from outside ("collateral") sources. The burden of proof there is on the defendant, and the burden is of course heaviest when the plaintiff has been awarded future economic damages and the defendant must show to a "reasonable certainty" that collateral recoveries will be received by P in duplication of those damages.

The Second Department's decision in Kihl v. Pfeffer[21] treats the issue in depth. In *Kihl*, the court parses a number of items in a personal injury verdict, juxtaposes them with outside sources claimed likely to duplicate them, and attempts to make a reasonable application of the perhaps inherently unreasonable "reasonable certainty" standard of CPLR 4545(a). The defendant did not discharge its burden of proof in *Kihl* and was therefore not allowed any collateral source deductions.

Disputed collateral source issues are usually resolved at a post-verdict hearing. In a follow-up to *Kihl*, yet another major Second Department case addressed how much the defendant has to show in order to secure such a hearing. Firmes v. Chase Manhattan Automotive Finance Corp.[22] says that "the defendant must tender some competent evidence from available sources that the plaintiff's economic losses may in the past have been, or may in the future be, replaced, or the plaintiff indemnified, from collateral sources."

The *Firmes* court acknowledges that the defendant is entitled to discovery from the plaintiff to secure data for potential use in a collateral source hearing, and recites the several methods available for it, including the usual disclosure proceedings that occur

---

[17]　Compare Gandy v. Wuster, 25 A.D.2d 478, 266 N.Y.S.2d 544 (4th Dep't 1966) with *Corbett*, 32 A.D.2d at 32–33, 299 N.Y.S.2d at 224–25.

[18]　CPLR Article 14–A; see § 168E.

[19]　See § 398.

[20]　It was lettered (c) before the 2009 amendment.

[21]　Kihl v. Pfeffer, 47 A.D.3d 154, 848 N.Y.S.2d 200 (2d Dep't 2007) (SPR 192:1).

[22]　Firmes v. Chase Manhattan Automotive Finance Corp., 50 A.D.3d 18, 852 N.Y.S.2d 148 (2d Dep't 2008) (SPR 194:1).

during the pretrial period.[23] CPLR 4545(a), in directing that "[a]ny collateral source deduction . . . shall be made by the trial court after . . . the verdict," specifies that "[t]he plaintiff may prove his or her losses and expenses at the trial irrespective of whether such sums will later have to be deducted from the plaintiff's recovery."

That helps, of course, because until the verdict is in the plaintiff doesn't know what part of it (if any) may parallel a collateral source receipt. Some plaintiffs, however, forego pursuing certain categories of damages, such as medical expenses, because they have already been paid for these losses and the amounts will almost certainly be deducted from the verdict at the collateral source hearing. This has caused health insurers to attempt to intervene in the plaintiff's action in the hope of asserting these damages and recovering them through a right of subrogation. The matter is controversial and pits three major forces against each other in a battle royal: liability insurers; health insurers; and the personal injury bar.[24]

§ 400. Delivery of the Verdict

When the jury have reached a verdict, they advise the court, which arranges for them to return to the courtroom to make formal delivery of the verdict while all parties are present or represented. Only five of the six jurors need agree on the verdict;[1] unlike a jury's verdict in a criminal action, the civil verdict need not be unanimous. But unless the parties stipulate otherwise, all six must participate in the deliberations. If, without the parties' permission, one juror is absent, for whatever reason, a verdict of the others will be invalidated even though it is a verdict of five.[2] The theory is that the absent juror might have disagreed and persuaded at least one other juror to do likewise, thus precluding a verdict or perhaps even tilting the verdict the other way.

If there's a stipulation to accept a jury of fewer than six, it has been held that all parties must subscribe to it; that if only one party does, the verdict is invalid no matter who wins it. In one case, for example, in which one of the six jurors took ill and had to be excused, P consented to five but D would not go along. The court allowed the five to proceed anyway and the five then produced a unanimous verdict for D, who promptly reexamined his conscience, found a jury of five okay after all, and magnanimously offered to accept the verdict. The appellate division looked this gift horse in the mouth and kicked it and the verdict out; it held that a party will not be allowed to exploit such a no-lose situation.[3]

If the case is divisible into segments and the jury must decide each of them, it should not be necessary for the same five jurors to agree on everything. Where, for example, five of the six agree on the defendant's liability in a personal injury case but a different five then agree on what the plaintiff's damages are—different jurors dissenting on each phase—the verdict should stand. At least one case had held otherwise,[4] but its holding

---

[23]   See § 348.

[24]   See § 180; Patrick Connors, *New Laws After Fasso Leave Health Insurer Out in the Cold*, N.Y.L.J., Jan. 28, 2010, at 243 (no. 18).

[1]   CPLR 4113(a).

[2]   See Measeck v. Noble, 9 A.D.2d 19, 189 N.Y.S.2d 748 (3d Dep't 1959).

[3]   Waldman v. Cohen, 125 A.D.2d 116, 512 N.Y.S.2d 205 (2d Dep't 1987). If the trial is likely to be prolonged, the answer to the prospect of an incapacitated juror is an alternate or several alternate jurors. See § 391. In the *Waldman* case, the alternate jurors had been excused.

[4]   Murphy v. Roger Sherman Transfer Co., 62 Misc. 2d 960, 310 N.Y.S.2d 891 (App. Term, 1st Dep't 1970).

seems untenable in a system that recognizes the bifurcated trial,[5] which allows the two phases even to be tried separately, and by separate juries.

While it is not necessarily inconsistent for a juror voting against liability to participate afterwards in the assessment of P's damages, what of the liability phase itself? If liability is at issue between or among defendants, perhaps with the comparative fault of the plaintiff thrown in for good measure, and an apportionment of the shares of fault of all is necessary, is consistency required on the part of each juror? Can the juror who votes P free of fault on the 5–1 vote holding P guilty of comparative negligence, for example, then be one of the majority on another 5–1 vote finding P's precise percentage of fault? The Second Department said yes in Schabe v. Hampton Bays Union Free School Dist.[6] and adopted the "any five" rule. Extensively reviewing the issue, the court held that while consistency must be maintained from question to question on the special verdict as a whole, "individual juror voting patterns" need not be consistent.

Also part of the *Schabe* holding is that jurors are free to argue on each subsequent issue and can't be "bound" by how they voted on an earlier one. Otherwise, the casting of a dissenting vote on any question would reduce the dissenter's influence "to a state of practical impotence," said *Schabe*, and create "a mandate for continued unanimity among the other jurors on the remaining questions."

On yet another key point, *Schabe* held that it is permissible to tell a jury the effect that their answers will have on the outcome of the case, lest they just speculate and possibly end up guessing wrong.[7]

A party can determine whether a given juror supports the verdict by polling the jury after the verdict has been delivered. Conducting such a poll is a party's absolute right.[8] The poll is conducted by asking each juror whether the verdict is his or hers, thus revealing the juror's individual support for, or opposition to, the verdict. A polling question so propounded as to inquire only whether the verdict delivered is the verdict of the *jury* is improper because even a juror who individually disagreed with it may be misled to answer yes to the question.[9] In a bifurcated tort trial in which liability and damages are being tried separately, but to the same jury, a polling of the jury after a finding of liability can be deferred until after trial of the damages phase after which the jury can be polled on both parts.[10] It would seem appropriate, however, to poll in respect of the liability finding immediately, to determine whether the finding is truly the jury's, because if it isn't, the damages trial can prove a waste.

When a five-sixths verdict is rendered sustaining liability in the bifurcated trial situation, and there is some doubt about whether the holdout juror on liability even

---

5   See § 130.

6   Schabe v. Hampton Bays Union Free School Dist., 103 A.D.2d 418, 480 N.Y.S.2d 328 (2d Dep't 1984).

7   The issue arose in *Schabe* in the common context of a bifurcated trial. The jury, having imputed 41% fault to P during the liability trial, didn't know whether the figure they were producing now, on the damages trial, was the actual amount P would get or a figure that the 41% would then reduce. *Schabe* acknowledges conflict on the several points it decides, notably on the "any five" rule, both in New York and nationally. The case is the subject of the lead note in NYSLD No. 301.

8   Duffy v. Vogel, 12 N.Y.3d 169, 878 N.Y.S.2d 246, 905 N.E.2d 1175 (2009) (6–1 decision). *Duffy* holds the right sacrosanct and rejects a verdict in which the trial court refused a plaintiff's polling request as "unnecessary" after the verdict came in for the defendants. The case is the subject of the lead note in NYSLD No. 592.

9   See O'Brien v. Mix, 14 A.D.2d 832, 220 N.Y.S.2d 652 (4th Dep't 1961).

10   Pickering v. Freedman, 32 A.D.2d 649, 300 N.Y.S.2d 742 (2d Dep't 1969).

participated in the deliberations on damages, the juror in question may be asked about that during the polling process.[11] Whichever way the holdout juror may have been disposed to vote on the issue of damages, all parties are entitled to have all jurors take part in the deliberations and doubt about whether all of them did can vitiate the verdict.

The jury delivers its verdict in the courtroom, usually orally. But an alternative is the sealed verdict, in which the jury writes its verdict down and delivers the writing to a designated court official. It's in the court's discretion to order a sealed verdict, which is used, for example, when the judge or the lawyers can't stand by and be available to return to the courtroom when the verdict is reached. The sealing of the verdict enables the jury to be dispersed, to reassemble in the courtroom at a later time, designated by the judge when the verdict is unsealed and formally delivered. An opening of the sealed verdict is deferred until then primarily to enable polling to take place. A sealed verdict is otherwise treated the same as an oral one.[12]

If the verdict is improper in form but its substantive content is clearly discernible, the court can correct it to reflect its legal impact. Thus, where the jury in a personal injury case, finding defendants A and B negligent in respective proportions of 70% and 30%, also tried to restrict the liability of each to his own share, the court corrected the verdict to permit entry of judgment against each defendant for 100% of the plaintiff's damages.[13] Percentages of fault among joint tortfeasors dictated their contribution rights among themselves at the time, but the plaintiff was entitled to a joint and several judgment against each defendant.[14]

If the jury can't deliver a verdict because of irreconcilable disagreement among them "after being kept together for as long as is deemed reasonable by the court," they are a hung jury and are discharged. The discharge of a hung jury results in a new trial before a new jury.[15]

Assuming that a valid verdict has been rendered, the next step is its entry. The clerk is required to enter in the minutes the details of the verdict, along with a specification of the time and place of the trial, the names of the jurors and witnesses, and any directions of the court about subsequent proceedings.[16] The "clerk" who does this is usually the non-judicial employee assigned to the particular courtroom. If that person acts also as the "judgment" clerk, her own minutes will supply whatever data about the verdict is needed to verify the validity of a judgment later presented for entry. (A judgment based on a verdict must refer to the verdict and state the result of it.)[17] In urban areas, where the judgment clerk, with whom the judgment is formally "entered,"[18]

---

[11]   See Sharrow v. Dick Corp., 86 N.Y.2d 54, 629 N.Y.S.2d 980, 653 N.E.2d 1150 (1995) (NYSLD No. 427).

[12]   See the dissenting opinion of Dowling, J., in Wirt v. Reid, 138 A.D. 760 at 779, 123 N.Y.S. 706 at 720 (1st Dep't 1910).

[13]   Gleich v. Volpe, 32 N.Y.2d 517, 346 N.Y.S.2d 806, 300 N.E.2d 148 (1973).

[14]   Under the later adjustment of joint and several liability with the adoption of Article 16 of the CPLR, defendants who are found 50% or less at fault in some tort actions are freed of joint liability with respect to non-economic damages. See §§ 168A et seq.

[15]   CPLR 4113(b).

[16]   CPLR 4112.

[17]   CPLR 5011.

[18]   See § 418.

is a separate official, the common practice is to take to the judgment clerk an extract from the minutes of the clerk who attended in the courtroom, attesting to the verdict.

§ 401. Defective Verdicts; Impeachment

A general rule in New York is that jurors may not be heard to impeach their verdict. This means that they can't, with affidavits or testimony or in any other way, adduce anything that would tend to overturn the verdict once it's been delivered. The primary intent of this rule is to keep sacrosanct the processes and deliberations of the jury and to insulate the verdict from later revelations of what went on in the jury room.[1]

The rule is not applicable, however, to the prejudicial conduct of a juror outside the jury room even if the conduct is learned of by another juror inside. So, for example, where a juror made an unauthorized visit to the scene of the occurrence at issue in the case, the visit could be revealed by other jurors and the verdict overturned.[2]

The most common exception to this rule of nonimpeachment is where a juror has lied or deliberately concealed a material fact on the voir dire. For a long time, this has been a basis for entertaining a co-juror's affidavit attesting to the falsehood or concealment even though learned of in the jury room or courtroom or during some jury recess. A new trial was mandated, for example, where it was shown that a juror concealed an ethnic prejudice against the defendant.[3] It is also permissible for the court to put the offending juror on the stand in such an instance to ascertain the facts in a testimonial hearing.[4]

There is no established rule barring a juror from revealing the jury's deliberations after the trial is over and the jury has been dismissed, but the courts frown on outright post-trial investigations of jurors, probing their deliberations and relationships. It is felt to constitute an undue harassment of jurors and an undermining of the jury process.[5] The primary design of the anti-impeachment rule, in fact, is to divest such fishing expeditions of their most hoped-for reward—the overturning of the verdict—a candid acknowledgment that many a verdict could be assailed if jury deliberations could be revealed and made the basis for post-trial motions to invalidate the verdict.[6]

Efforts to clarify what the verdict in fact is are a wholly different matter. Here, affidavits of the jurors are acceptable. In one case, for example, involving a sealed verdict, several jurors had changed their minds—which they are entitled to do before the verdict is recorded—and tried to communicate as much to the judge before the verdict was opened. Their change of mind had changed the verdict, but they could not get through to the judge in time. Their affidavits to show this were entertained. Although it might at first seem an attempt to impeach the verdict, it was in essence quite the

---

[1]   Persons other than jurors are not subject to this anti-impeachment rule, but nor are they privy to the jury's deliberations. They thus have scant opportunity to reveal them. Invasion of the secrecy of the jury room is in any event a criminal contempt. See People ex rel. Choate v. Barrett, 9 N.Y.S. 321 (Gen. Term 1890), aff'd, 121 N.Y. 678, 24 N.E. 1095 (1890).

[2]   Bainton v. Board of Ed. of City of New York, 57 Misc. 2d 140, 292 N.Y.S.2d 229 (App. Term, 2d Dep't 1968).

[3]   People v. Leonti, 262 N.Y. 256, 186 N.E. 693 (1933).

[4]   Leonti, 262 N.Y. at 258, 186 N.E. at 696.

[5]   See Gamell v. Mt. Sinai Hospital, 40 A.D.2d 1010, 339 N.Y.S.2d 31 (2d Dep't 1972).

[6]   See the discussion in People v. De Lucia, 20 N.Y.2d 275, 282 N.Y.S.2d 526, 229 N.E.2d 211 (1967).

contrary: an endeavor to show that the verdict as recorded was not the verdict they reached.[7]

There are some well known categories of defective verdict. One of them is the "compromise" verdict, which can be discerned as such merely by looking at it in light of the evidence. It therefore requires no affidavits from jurors. A good illustration of a compromise verdict when New York followed the contributory negligence rule—under which any negligence at all on the part of the plaintiff destroyed the case entirely[8]— would sometimes appear in a tort action involving extensive injuries (and hence damages), but doubtful liability. A verdict for the plaintiff in a grossly inadequate sum would manifest that the jury was sympathetic to the plaintiff, but did not really find the defendant at fault, "compromising" by faulting the defendant while underassessing the damages. Such a verdict could not stand.[9] The comparative negligence rule,[10] under which the plaintiff with a share of fault is allowed to recover, but with damages reduced by that share, validates that kind of verdict today and removes it from the tainted "compromise" category.

There may be other evidences of irreconcilable compromise. In one case, for example, P sued D for negligence in permitting a certain hair spray to come in contact with P's forehead. D impleaded T, the manufacturer, alleging that the spray itself was defective. Clearly, D's application of the product would not have caused the injury if the product itself were not defective. A finding that D was liable, but that T was not, was therefore inconsistent and could not stand.[11]

Another kind of presumably defective verdict is the "quotient" verdict, appearing in tort and other unliquidated damages cases. Each of the jurors jots down the damages figure he or she deems appropriate and these are then added up and divided by the number of jurors. Many a verdict is reached that way. If all jurors stood firm on their own figures, there would never be a verdict. The courts recognize this.[12] The only thing that makes a "quotient" verdict invalid, therefore, is the jurors' advance agreement to be bound by the quotient no matter what it comes to. If they reach for a quotient with the understanding that they can then deliberate on it before concluding themselves, the verdict is good.[13]

Unlike the "compromise" verdict, whose invalidity appears on its face, proof that the verdict is an invalid "quotient" one must come from a juror. It entails, in other words, divulging the deliberations and therefore runs into the anti-impeachment rule. Rare, therefore, is the money verdict attackable as a "quotient" one.

---

[7] Spielter v. North German Lloyd S.S. Co., 232 A.D. 104, 249 N.Y.S. 358 (1st Dep't 1931).

[8] The contributory negligence rule was replaced by the comparative negligence rule, CPLR Article 14–A, as of September 1, 1975. See § 168E.

[9] See Lallo v. W. T. Grant Co., 31 A.D.2d 941, 298 N.Y.S.2d 802 (2d Dep't 1969).

[10] CPLR 1411, 1413.

[11] Toner v. Constable, 61 Misc. 2d 586, 306 N.Y.S.2d 323 (N.Y. City Civ. Ct. 1968), modified on other grounds, 61 Misc. 2d 591, 307 N.Y.S.2d 231 (App. Term, 1st Dep't 1969).

[12] See Hamilton v. Owego Waterworks, 22 A.D. 573, 48 N.Y.S. 106 (3d Dep't 1897), aff'd 163 N.Y. 562, 57 N.E. 1111 (1900).

[13] Honigsberg v. New York City Transit Authority, 43 Misc. 2d 1, 249 N.Y.S.2d 296 (N.Y. City Civ. Ct. 1964).

E. TRIAL MOTIONS

Table of Sections

§ 402.   Motion for Judgment During Trial

§ 403.   Motion for Mistrial

§ 404.   Motion to Conform the Pleadings to the Proof

§ 405.   Post-Trial Motion for Judgment

§ 406.   Motion for New Trial on the "Weight of the Evidence"

§ 407.   Additur and Remittitur

§ 408.   Motions for "Judgment," Compared

§ 402. Motion for Judgment During Trial

CPLR 4401 provides the motion for judgment during trial. It reads:

> Any party may move for judgment with respect to a cause of action or issue upon the ground that the moving party is entitled to judgment as a matter of law, after the close of the evidence presented by an opposing party with respect to such cause of action or issue, or at any time on the basis of admissions. Grounds for the motion shall be specified. The motion does not waive the right to trial by jury or to present further evidence even where it is made by all parties.

The main motion authorized by this provision is better known to the bar as the motion for a "directed verdict." That terminology is still used, but in official CPLR parlance today, it is simply a motion for "judgment as a matter of law" under CPLR 4401.

A party may make this motion only after the other side's case is in so that it is not seen at the outset of the trial unless it is based on "admissions." A motion based on admissions is authorized "at any time."

One might see at the beginning of a trial, however, a CPLR 3211 dismissal motion based on certain grounds, like lack of subject matter jurisdiction, failure to state a cause of action, or failure to join a party, the grounds set forth in paragraphs 2, 7, and 10 of CPLR 3211(a), because those grounds are not governed by the usual time restrictions of CPLR 3211(e) and may therefore be made at any time. While it is technically permissible, a party's withholding a CPLR 3211(a) dismissal motion until the trial is not likely to get a warm reception. Postponement until the trial of a motion that could have avoided a trial shows undue delay, whatever the technical permission of CPLR 3211 may be. It would also be a violation of the spirit, if not the letter, of the certificate of readiness rule.[1]

A traditional pretrial motion that the courts did sometimes see at the opening of a trial was the motion for summary judgment under CPLR 3212, which until 1997 had no outer time restriction. It was then given one, however, with the explicit design of barring the practice of saving a summary judgment motion for the trial, i.e., forcing any party with a summary judgment aspiration to make the motion either before the filing of the note of issue or within a set number of days after it.[2] Under the amendment, the practice

---

[1]   See § 370.

[2]   See CPLR 3212(a), discussed in § 279.

of saving a summary judgment motion for the trial has presumably been dissolved, but one may wonder how this will play out. If the case is truly one for summary judgment, but a motion for it at the outset of the trial is barred, the trial proof itself, pretty soon after it gets under way, should manifest the one-sidedness of the case and readily produce a CPLR 4401 motion for judgment at some point during the trial.

While a motion for judgment based on admissions is authorized "at any time," one must today be circumspect about what will satisfy as an admission for this purpose. The courts are justifiably reticent about putting an abrupt end to a case—after it has survived all the pretrial stages and at last arrived at trial—before the parties have put in their evidence. The motion for judgment based on admissions will therefore be granted only when counsel "deliberately and intentionally states or admits some fact that in any view of the case is fatal to the action,"[3] and counsel obviously does not make a habit of that. The admissions should be of a kind intended as the virtual equivalent of a pleading rather than some mere evidentiary statement that the party is not precluded from contradicting with other evidence.[4] A formal admission made under CPLR 3123, if sufficient to warrant judgment against the admitter as a matter of law, should suffice, but it is tactically unlikely that the opposing party—who would presumably have initiated and secured the admission during the pretrial stage—would have saved the admission to use on a dispositive motion at the trial when she could have used it to ground a summary judgment motion under CPLR 3212 long before.

Much of the caselaw on this phase of CPLR 4401 involves the plaintiff's opening to the jury and whether counsel made some fatal admission during it. The complaint will not be dismissed on the opening statement, however, unless it plainly appears that there is really no issue of fact holding the case up; that taking as true every fact the plaintiff alleges and resolving in the plaintiff's favor every fact the defendant disputes, the plaintiff still has no case.[5] An admission in the opening that amounts to nothing more than an immaterial variance from the complaint or bill of particulars, or even from a deposition, will not ground a dismissal. Where, for example, the complaint and bill of particulars in a tort case alleging a failure of supervision by school officials charged that unauthorized hardballs were used in a certain game, and on the opening to the jury counsel said instead that softballs were used, this was no judgment-grounding admission: a prima facie case was made out on the opening regardless of discrepancies in the size and texture of the ball.[6]

Practically speaking, if the trial looks to be a short one (not more than a day or two), if both sides are at hand with their witnesses, and if there is nothing in the plaintiff's case so summarily defective that it would have lent itself to a dismissal with some pretrial device like a motion to dismiss or for summary judgment, a dismissal on the plaintiff's opening is best avoided even by a judge with serious doubts. There is no harm in waiting until the plaintiff has called witnesses and put in her case.

In an authoritative decision on this matter in De Vito v. Katsch,[7] the court said that a dismissal based on the plaintiff's opening to the jury has to be reserved for a most

---

[3]   Hoffman House v. Foote, 172 N.Y. 348, 351, 65 N.E. 169 (1902).

[4]   See Martin Fireproofing Corp. v. Maryland Cas. Co., 45 Misc. 2d 354, 257 N.Y.S.2d 100 (Sup. Ct., Erie County 1965), aff'd, 26 A.D.2d 910, 275 N.Y.S.2d 375 (4th Dep't 1966).

[5]   Runkel v. City of New York, 282 A.D. 173, 123 N.Y.S.2d 485 (2d Dep't 1953).

[6]   Rivera v. Board of Ed. of City of New York, 11 A.D.2d 7, 201 N.Y.S.2d 372 (1st Dep't 1960).

[7]   De Vito v. Katsch, 157 A.D.2d 413, 556 N.Y.S.2d 649 (2d Dep't 1990).

unique case; that a strong general rule exists against so narrowly based a dismissal. The court must give the plaintiff the benefit of every doubt, examining the pleadings to determine whether there is anything in them that amounts to a conceding away by the plaintiff of an element indispensable to the plaintiff's case. In *De Vito*, the trial court had dismissed the action after the plaintiff said on her opening that she would not be calling any first-hand witnesses. The appellate division reversed, holding that the plaintiff had to be given a chance to establish her case by circumstantial evidence.

It is after the evidence is in, either on the plaintiff's side or on both sides, that the meaty motion of CPLR 4401—what bench and bar will probably always call the motion for a directed verdict[8]—makes its appearance. It is not based on anything as flighty as indecisive statements in jury openings; it is based on the evidence itself. To see that this evidentiary foundation is complete enough for a court-directed judgment, CPLR 4401 authorizes the motion for judgment only after the movant's adversary has completed her case.

The only stated criterion is that the movant is entitled to judgment "as a matter of law." The standard has been phrased in these general terms to recognize the limitless variety of fact situations that can invoke it. The judge may grant the motion, which of course takes the case out of the jury's hands, only when convinced that the jury could not find for the other party by any rational process;[9] when, in support of the party against whom it proposes to order judgment, the court can find "no evidence and no substantial inferences;"[10] when reasonable minds reacting to the evidence could not differ and would have to conclude just one way.[11] The court must accept as true all of the evidence offered by the party against whom the motion for judgment aims and must even resolve in that party's favor all questions relating to the credibility of witnesses.[12] There are many word combinations one may summon to describe a situation appropriate to a motion for judgment, but it is essentially a matter of an experienced reaction to a given fact pattern. Piling up a lot of generalizations doesn't help.[13]

Since the essence of the movant's posture when judgment is sought under CPLR 4401 is that there is no fact issue to be tried, the very making of the motion was at one time deemed a concession that no fact issue existed. This meant that even if the motion was denied, the movant by its mere making was held to waive all further right to trial by jury. That is no longer the case. CPLR 4401 in express language assures the movant that the making of an unsuccessful motion for judgment does not waive trial by jury or the right to present further evidence. The movant need not even "reserve" those rights

---

[8]   A "directed verdict" does not contemplate, and has not for a long time, that the jury will actually retire and then come back with the verdict the court has directed. In today's practice, the old terminology is just shorthand for the situation in which the judge during the trial takes the case away from the jury and directs judgment as a matter of law.

[9]   Prince v. City of New York, 21 A.D.2d 668, 250 N.Y.S.2d 107 (1st Dep't 1964).

[10]   African Metals Corporation v. Bullowa, 288 N.Y. 78, 81, 41 N.E.2d 466, 468 (1942).

[11]   Cesario v. Chiapparine, 21 A.D.2d 272, 250 N.Y.S.2d 584 (2d Dep't 1964). In one situation, a special statute mandates dismissal after the plaintiff's case is in: in an action for medical malpractice based "solely" on lack of informed consent, the plaintiff is required to produce expert medical testimony on the issue and a failure to do so requires dismissal notwithstanding that other proof may support the plaintiff's claim. See CPLR 4401–a.

[12]   Hurder v. Samuel Kosoff & Sons, Inc., 23 A.D.2d 804, 258 N.Y.S.2d 1 (4th Dep't 1965).

[13]   See § 408, comparing the CPLR 4401 motion for judgment during trial with the CPLR 3212 motion for summary judgment before trial and the CPLR 4404 motion for judgment after trial. Note also that the motion for judgment under CPLR 4401 is not the occasion for "weighing" the evidence, which is a post-trial phenomenon governed by CPLR 4404, treated later. See § 406.

when she makes the motion.[14] These assurances obtain even when all parties move for judgment under CPLR 4401.[15]

The requirement that each party await the conclusion of the other's case before moving for judgment is designed to afford all parties a day in court. The general assumption is that the party has offered everything he has and if his case is still legally inadequate, an end may as well be put to it now. But if it appears that some deficiency in one party's case can possibly be remedied when some other party, even an adverse party, puts in her evidence, the court will deny the motion and let the case go on. If P sues A and B in tort, for example, and it appears that some defect in P's case may be filled in by A or B, who are hostile to each other, the court should not grant judgment against P at the close of P's proof.[16]

There is a tie-in between CPLR 4401 and CPLR 5013. The latter provides that a dismissal against a plaintiff before the close of the plaintiff's evidence is not on the merits (which means that a dismissal made at that point will not bar a fresh suit), while a dismissal after the close of the plaintiff's evidence does qualify as a merits determination (which would subject a new action to the defense of res judicata).[17] The juncture at which CPLR 4401 authorizes its main motion for judgment is therefore a juncture at which, if the motion is granted, the movant will ordinarily draw the added advantage of the res judicata doctrine.

The court does have power to provide otherwise, however, i.e., to give res judicata effect to a dismissal made before the close of the plaintiff's evidence or to deprive of res judicata effect a dismissal made after.[18] Whether the court will exercise this discretionary power depends on the state of the evidence. If the dismissal is based, for example, on a failure of proof that the plaintiff may yet be able to come up with, the dismissal after the close of plaintiff's case should be without prejudice, i.e., not on the merits.[19] But if there is no indication that curative proof exists, the dismissal at that stage should not be qualified and should thus be left to stand as a judgment on the merits.[20]

The appending of a qualification may also occur through pretrial motion practice, serving a punitive purpose when the plaintiff has been guilty of neglecting the case. An order entered on the plaintiff's default in failing to serve a bill of particulars pursuant to a conditional preclusion order, for example, dismissing the complaint "upon the merits" or "with prejudice," has been held to bar a second action. The court said that while the power to qualify a dismissal made before the plaintiff's case has been put in is "sparingly exercised," it is appropriate to exercise it when "the only purpose of new litigation is to

---

[14]   Woodard v. Motor Vehicle Acc. Indemnification Corp., 23 A.D.2d 215, 259 N.Y.S.2d 918 (3d Dep't 1965).

[15]   Application of LaManna, 23 A.D.2d 957, 259 N.Y.S.2d 987 (4th Dep't 1965).

[16]   See, e.g., Simon v. Lowenthal, 169 Misc. 718, 8 N.Y.S.2d 484 (N.Y.C. Mun. Ct. 1938).

[17]   CPLR 5013 refers to the "proponent" of the evidence, thus imposing its res judicata consequences on counterclaims, cross-claims, and the like, as well as on the plaintiff's main claim. The latter is used in our examples. A CPLR 4401 judgment against a plaintiff counts as the "judgment dismissing a cause of action" referred to in CPLR 5013.

[18]   CPLR 5013.

[19]   See Harsco Corp. v. Rodolitz Realty Corp., 61 Misc. 2d 644, 307 N.Y.S.2d 531 (Sup. Ct., Queens County 1969). An alternative to a dismissal in this instance, of course, especially when the witness or document needed to remedy the failure of proof is close at hand, is a mere adjournment.

[20]   Hansen v. City of New York, 274 A.D. 196, 80 N.Y.S.2d 249 (1st Dep't 1948), aff'd, 299 N.Y. 136, 85 N.E.2d 905 (1949).

circumvent the preclusion decree."[21] The "continual disregard" of court orders in bill of particulars practice is seen as one of those "exceptional circumstances" that warrant the appending of a fatal qualification to the dismissal.[22]

If the dismissal has not been specified to be without prejudice, and there is nothing in the record to corroborate that it was intended to be, even the judge who ordered the dismissal may be precluded from later amending it to add the qualification; it may amount to the judge's sitting as an appellate court over himself.[23] But if the record does support that this was the court's initial intention and the omission of the qualification was inadvertent, a nunc pro tunc amendment should be permissible.[24]

As a general and salutary rule, the courts prefer to deny CPLR 4401 motions during the trial in deference to the CPLR 4404 motion after it. The reasons for this are discussed later.[25]

§ 403. Motion for Mistrial

The motion for a mistrial is a device to cancel or discontinue a trial in order to start it afresh before a new jury or continue it at a later time before the same one. It used to be known as a motion "to withdraw a juror,"[1] which resulted in an incomplete jury and a breakdown of the trial. It was the device alighted on as a good way to remedy certain prejudicial defects in the course of a trial by jury. It is commonly known today as a simple "mistrial" motion, but the CPLR doesn't even use that terminology. The governing provision is CPLR 4402, whose caption is "Motion for continuance or new trial during trial." Its substance is one sentence:

At any time during the trial, the court, on motion of any party, may order a continuance or a new trial in the interest of justice on such terms as may be just.

The statute offers the alternatives of a mere continuance (i.e., adjournment) or an outright new trial before a new jury if necessary. Which, if any, step to take depends on the defect to be remedied and perhaps even on whether it was inadvertent or contrived. Inadvertent and unobtrusive mentions of the existence of insurance in a personal injury case, for example, have been held curable by a mere instruction, while a deliberate attempt by the plaintiff to show that insurance exists[2] or by the defendant to show that it does not[3] will necessitate a new trial before a new jury.

Misconduct that may necessitate a new trial is not restricted to that of a party or lawyer. The intemperate comments or conduct of a judge, for example, suggesting the judge's prejudice against a party or cause, will require a new trial and may even occasion

---

[21]   Palmer v. Fox, 28 A.D.2d 968, 283 N.Y.S.2d 216 (4th Dep't 1967), aff'd, 22 N.Y.2d 667, 291 N.Y.S.2d 361, 238 N.E.2d 751 (1968).

[22]   See Mitchell v. Kiamesha Concord, Inc., 94 A.D.2d 914, 463 N.Y.S.2d 626 (3d Dep't 1983), and the discussion in § 241.

[23]   If the application is prompted by newly discovered evidence not known about during the earlier trial, the applicant's remedy is to make a motion to vacate the judgment and request a new trial under CPLR 5015(a)(2). See § 428.

[24]   CPLR 5019(a).

[25]   See § 405.

[1]   See Schultze v. Huttlinger, 150 A.D. 489, 135 N.Y.S. 70 (1st Dep't 1912).

[2]   See the discussion in Ismail v. City of New York, 18 Misc. 2d 818, 181 N.Y.S.2d 848 (Sup. Ct., Queens County 1959).

[3]   Rendo v. Schermerhorn, 24 A.D.2d 773, 263 N.Y.S.2d 743 (3d Dep't 1965).

an appellate reprimand.[4] The misconduct of a juror will do the same as where a juror walks the plaintiff home during the trial and assures her that everything will be okay.[5]

There are no arbitrary limits on the trial judge's power to declare a mistrial. Whatever the source of the prejudicial conduct, if it deprives an innocent party of a fair trial, the court can make it the basis of a mistrial.

If the defect is something that does not induce jury bias and is curable by a mere adjournment, a new trial is not necessary under CPLR 4402 and a mere continuance will be ordered. This is appropriate where, for example, a key witness has not appeared in time, or has taken temporarily ill and cannot show up for a few days, or where some surprise element has arisen at the trial and a party needs some time to secure evidence to meet it. A refusal to order an adjournment when it is reasonable to do so will meet appellate censure as in one case where the judge would not wait half an hour for the imminent arrival of medical experts.[6] Even an adjournment of several weeks may be appropriate in order secure the testimony of a key witness.[7]

A party who deems himself irrevocably prejudiced by some piece of conduct during the trial should move for a mistrial promptly upon learning of it. He cannot hold the datum as a trump card, speculating on a favorable verdict and moving the mistrial only if he doesn't get it.[8]

The use of the words "on motion of any party" in CPLR 4402 indicates that a mistrial may not be granted by the court sua sponte. Instances exist, however, in which the court has done that,[9] and as a practical matter there is no cure for it if it is done before the verdict is rendered: there is no verdict to reinstate and a new trial is necessary anyway. A judge bent on granting a mistrial because of something prejudicial occurring during the trial, whether through his own conduct or another person's, should advise the presumably prejudiced party of the court's willingness to entertain a mistrial motion. Under the rule discussed in the prior paragraph, a party failing to respond to that invitation may be held to have waived a mistrial.

If a mistrial is declared, the case should be rescheduled for trial. A specific rule may even require it.[10]

§ 404. Motion to Conform the Pleadings to the Proof

CPLR 3025(c) provides that "the court may permit pleadings to be amended before or after judgment to conform them to the evidence, upon such terms as may be just including the granting of costs and continuances." This is really an adjunct of the liberalization of pleadings. Its purpose is to have the final judgment dictated as much as is reasonable by what the evidence actually reveals at the trial rather than by what the pleadings and bill of particulars alleged it would be.

The courts are today quite free with the amendment as long as no party can claim prejudice because of it. Prejudice is the key, and a legitimate claim of surprise is the key

---

[4]   See, e.g., Habenicht v. R.K.O. Theatres, Inc., 23 A.D.2d 378, 260 N.Y.S.2d 890 (1st Dep't 1965).

[5]   See Campbell v. Towber, 46 Misc. 2d 891, 261 N.Y.S.2d 458 (Sup. Ct., Kings County 1965).

[6]   Murphy v. City of New York, 273 A.D. 492, 78 N.Y.S.2d 191 (1st Dep't 1948).

[7]   See Bruce v. Hospital for Special Surgery, 34 A.D.2d 963, 312 N.Y.S.2d 765 (2d Dep't 1970).

[8]   Schein v. Chest Service Co., 38 A.D.2d 929, 330 N.Y.S.2d 147 (1st Dep't 1972).

[9]   See, e.g., Jaworski v. New Cassel Fuel Corp., 21 A.D.2d 753, 251 N.Y.S.2d 929 (2d Dep't 1964).

[10] See, e.g., 22 N.Y.C.R.R. § 202.45, applicable in the Supreme and County courts.

to whether there's prejudice. As long as the papers in the case advised the other side sufficiently of the transaction, occurrence, or event out of which the claim or defense arises—to such an extent that a diligent lawyer could be deemed to have been on notice that the matter now sought to be changed or added by amendment could reasonably have been expected to arise at the trial—the purpose of the rule is fulfilled and the amendment permissible.[1]

The amendment is not available to add a new substantive claim, otherwise barred by the statute of limitations and clearly beyond what the other side could have expected,[2] but mere changes in theory are permissible. A classic instance of this in New York is the case of Diemer v. Diemer.[3] A husband's separation complaint had pleaded cruel and inhuman treatment as its ground. On appeal the court substituted, and sustained, the ground of abandonment, holding that the proved underlying wrong, which was the wife's refusal to have sexual relations with her husband, constituted abandonment as a matter of law.

As long as it is clear that the responsive proof would have been the same, whichever conclusory theory or ground had been pleaded, permitting such an amendment is sound modern practice. But if there is any reasonable possibility that the other party would have prepared different proof with which to respond to the altered ground—a party in this position should show the court that this is so—the amendment should be denied or, at worst, an adjournment had to permit the gathering of such proof.

The amendment is always good for mere technical defects, such as to amend an equity complaint to include an inadvertently omitted allegation that there is no adequate remedy at law.[4]

One of the main functions of the amendment is to divest of impact unprejudicial variances between pleadings and proof. Pleadings for this purpose include the bill of particulars. A CPLR 3025(c) amendment can give effect to trial evidence that varies from both the pleading and the bill as long as there is no prejudice. Where, for example, a deposition or other pretrial disclosure device puts the other party on notice of what later emerges at the trial, the claim of prejudice dissolves and the amendment lies.[5] Trial proof within the purview of the complaint may ground the amendment even if the bill of particulars does not embrace the matter, as where the bill alleges only that the defendant passed a stop sign and the trial proof shows there was no stop sign, but reveals other grounds of negligence embraced in the complaint.[6]

The trial itself is the usual scene of an amendment under CPLR 3025(c), which becomes relevant when the proof establishes something arguably omitted from, or at variance with, the papers in the case. The motion is usually oral and is made right in the courtroom to the trial judge. It need not await an adversary's objection—to the effect,

---

[1]   See Kimso Apartments, LLC v. Gandhi, 24 N.Y.3d 403, 998 N.Y.S.2d 740, 23 N.E.3d 1008 (2014) (permitting defendant to amend answer under CPLR 3025(c) to assert a counterclaim that did not prejudice plaintiff).

[2]   McGough v. State, 41 Misc. 2d 78, 244 N.Y.S.2d 1007 (Ct. Cl. 1963).

[3]   Diemer v. Diemer, 8 N.Y.2d 206, 203 N.Y.S.2d 829, 168 N.E.2d 654 (1960). An amendment had not even been formally moved for in the *Diemer* case.

[4]   See American-Russian Aid Ass'n v. City of Glen Cove, 41 Misc. 2d 622, 246 N.Y.S.2d 123 (Sup. Ct., Nassau County 1964), aff'd, 23 A.D.2d 966, 260 N.Y.S.2d 589 (2d Dep't 1965).

[5]   Di Benedetto v. Lasker-Goldman Corp., 46 A.D.2d 909, 363 N.Y.S.2d 5 (2d Dep't 1974).

[6]   Pogor v. Cue Taxi Service, Inc., 43 Misc. 2d 487, 251 N.Y.S.2d 635 (N.Y. City Civ. Ct. 1964), aff'd, 45 Misc. 2d 933, 258 N.Y.S.2d 60 (App. Term, 1st Dep't 1965).

e.g., that the new matter is incompetent or irrelevant because not embraced by the pleading or bill of particulars—but often does. It can be made as a formal written motion, but that's unnecessary. Whether oral or written, the motion should in any event be made only to the trial judge, as is true of trial and post-trial motions generally.[7]

An actual "amendment" of the pleadings under CPLR 3025(c) is not necessary. The court, if it grants the motion, can merely recite in the order that the pleadings are "deemed" amended to conform to the evidence and, indeed, even an "order" for this purpose is not required. Since the motion and its surrounding colloquy ordinarily takes place at the trial, the stenographer takes it all down and the transcript then evinces everything needed. Should a party aggrieved by the court's action on the motion wish to appeal it, she can do so as part of an appeal from the final judgment.[8] A party wishing to appeal it independently might try to secure the entry of a formal order on the court's ruling and appeal that.[9]

An appellate court as well as the trial court can conform the pleadings to the proof,[10] and may even do so sua sponte.[11] It has been done even in the Court of Appeals: the *Diemer* case discussed above is an example of it.

CPLR 3025(c) allows the amendment to be made conditional. The conditions include the granting of costs and continuances. These are not often needed, but they may be useful. Suppose, for example, that a party does wish at the trial to change an allegation or add an item and that an arguable claim of surprise is made against it. The objector convinces the court that he is unprepared, not unreasonably, to meet the new matter, but the court is equally convinced that a short adjournment is all that is needed to enable that party to secure the witness or proof required. The court can permit the amendment and give the objector that chance, continuing the case and even requiring the party who moved for the amendment to pay the objector the costs of securing the belated proof. This is of course cutting things close even with so generous a rule as CPLR 3025(c): an amendment at the trial stage that requires an adversary to get new proof to meet it is not always remediable by mere conditions and is therefore not granted for the asking.

Twice before we have seen a motion to amend a complaint to increase the "ad damnum"—the amount demanded in the wherefore clause of a money complaint. An attempt to secure this amendment after trial and verdict was one instance, evolving from what seemed an absolute "No" for a while to at least a conditional "Yes."[12] The other was an attempt to secure the amendment by motion under CPLR 3025(b), in advance of the trial. That one, as we saw, has a better chance, but is still not granted for the mere asking.[13]

What of an endeavor to secure an ad damnum amendment not before or after the trial, but during it? A motion for an increased ad damnum made at the trial under CPLR 3025(c) may involve elements applicable to either or both of the previously treated

---

[7] CPLR 4405. Note also the 15-day time limit in that provision. See § 405.

[8] CPLR 5501(a). See § 530.

[9] CPLR 5701(a)(2)(iv), (v). Unless reduced to an order, a disposition qualifying as a mere "ruling" will not be appealable separately. See § 526.

[10] Dampskibsselskabet Torm A/S v. P. L. Thomas Paper Co., 26 A.D.2d 347, 274 N.Y.S.2d 601 (1st Dep't 1966).

[11] Harbor Associates, Inc. v. Asheroff, 35 A.D.2d 667, 317 N.Y.S.2d 897 (2d Dep't 1970).

[12] See § 217.

[13] See § 237.

motions. If, for example, the standard for a pretrial amendment requires a showing that the need to increase the damages demand was only just discerned, and that the motion to amend is made on the heels of the new discovery, such a showing is likely to be required as well when the motion is made at the trial. Attitudes may vary from department to department on these essentially discretionary matters.[14] It will also be remembered that judicial rejection of the motion, when delayed until after the verdict, may be predicated on the insurance factor: that if the figure to which the increase is now sought exceeds the defendant's insurance coverage, it will now be too late for the defendant to secure counsel of his own choice and the verdict, to the extent of the difference, will have to be paid out of his personal assets as a fait accompli.[15] The same is true—if the ad damnum is to jump from within to beyond coverage—when the motion is made during the trial, albeit before the verdict: it is still too late for the defendant to get an attorney of her private choosing. Even if the ad damnum amendment is made during the trial, therefore, it does not always have clear sailing.

§ 405. Post-Trial Motion for Judgment

The post-trial motion comes from CPLR 4404, subdivision (a) governing in jury trials and subdivision (b) in nonjury trials. The motion comes after the verdict or decision; a motion for judgment before that time belongs technically under CPLR 4401 as a motion "during" the trial even though it may be made after both sides have rested.

CPLR 4404(a) provides that after a verdict is rendered the court can set it aside and either (1) grant judgment to whichever party is entitled to it as a matter of law or (2) order a new trial on the ground that the verdict is "contrary to the weight of the evidence." The first item is by this time a familiar one: the "matter of law" standard is the same as that used for judgment during the trial under CPLR 4401. There the bar knows it as a motion for a "directed verdict"; here, since it entails discarding a verdict already rendered, it becomes the equally well known "judgment notwithstanding the verdict" or judgment "n.o.v."[1] Both have criteria in common with the pretrial motion for summary judgment.[2]

The "weight of the evidence" phenomenon is quite different and will be returned to in a moment.

Because the standards for judgment as a "matter of law" are largely the same whether the motion is made before the verdict under CPLR 4401 or after it under CPLR 4404(a), the court can grant it at either time, but ordinarily prefers to await the verdict. This is especially so when the motion for judgment is made at the end of all the evidence. If made before that time, as where the defendant moves for judgment under CPLR 4401 at the end of the plaintiff's case, its grant at least spares further trial. But when a motion for judgment is made after both sides have rested, there is nothing left to try and there

---

[14]   See, for example, Natale v. Pepsi-Cola Co., 7 A.D.2d 282, 182 N.Y.S.2d 404 (1st Dep't 1959), a First Department case taking a rigid position that afterwards seemed to relax, while the more relaxed attitude of the Third Department seemed to grow stricter. See Commentary C3025:14 on McKinney's CPLR 3025. Movements of this kind have been known to reverse themselves, however, and the lawyer must keep track of current local attitudes.

[15]   See § 217.

[1]   This stands for non obstante veredicto, Latin for "notwithstanding the verdict."

[2]   All three are compared in § 408.

is thus little to gain and much to lose by granting the motion at that time rather than after submitting the case to the jury and awaiting its verdict.

The reason is obvious: the judge is authorized to grant judgment as a "matter of law" only when she believes that on this record, reasonable minds could not differ and there is therefore only one way a jury can go. The difficulty is that reasonable minds may differ about whether reasonable minds may differ, and among them may be the reasonable minds that inhabit the appellate court. If the trial judge grants judgment for a side under CPLR 4401 without letting a jury pass on the issues, an appellate court that disagrees with the judge's action has no verdict to reinstate and must therefore order a new trial, wasting the earlier one. But if the trial court waits until a verdict is in, saving its action for CPLR 4404 and granting judgment notwithstanding the verdict (should the jury have found the other way), a disagreeing appellate court has a verdict to reinstate. This is no small economy, and it accounts for the widespread practice among judges of letting a fully tried case go to the jury before ruling on a motion for judgment.[3]

There is also the possibility, of course, and perhaps even the probability, that the jury will react to the evidence just as the judge did, finding for the party whom the judge also finds entitled to judgment. That would make it unnecessary for the judge to act at all. Hence, "[u]nless it appears that the defendant's case will consume an inordinate amount of the trial court's time, the better practice is to submit the case to the jury."[4]

If the court finds the verdict to be against the "weight of the evidence," it orders a new trial rather than directing judgment for the opposing party. This is a long recognized alternative for the court when it sets aside a verdict on a post-trial motion under CPLR 4404(a). The elusive criteria for "weighing" the evidence are treated in the next section.

A party may make a CPLR 4404 motion after the trial even though he made no CPLR 4401 motion during it, or move for judgment n.o.v. after the verdict without having moved for judgment before it. One is not a condition precedent to the other. Still, a party who loses the verdict and wants judgment n.o.v. is in a more consistent position if she can show that she moved for judgment as a matter of law before the jury retired.

Each party does well to make a motion—even if it is only pro forma—for judgment under CPLR 4401 at the close of the evidence, on which the court may rule, or instead reserve decision until after the jury renders a verdict. At one time, the court could not act on its own motion to grant judgment after the verdict unless an earlier motion had been made for a directed verdict and the judge had reserved decision on it. That requirement, too, has been abandoned: CPLR 4404 authorizes the post-trial motion by either a party or by the court sua sponte.

If there are separable issues in the case, a post-trial motion under CPLR 4404 can address them individually, and this is so even if they are all part of but one cause of action. A common example of this is where the court sustains a jury finding of liability

---

[3] See, for example, Muszynski v. City of Buffalo, 49 Misc. 2d 957, 268 N.Y.S.2d 753 (Sup. Ct., Erie County 1966), which discusses the matter and where subsequent appellate steps illustrate it. The trial court did not grant a motion to dismiss the complaint after the close of the evidence, waiting for the verdict, which was for the plaintiff. The appellate division then reversed and reinstated the verdict, 33 A.D.2d 648, 305 N.Y.S.2d 163 (4th Dep't 1969), and was affirmed by the Court of Appeals in 29 N.Y.2d 810, 327 N.Y.S.2d 368, 277 N.E.2d 414 (1971).

[4] Rosario by Vasquez v. City of New York, 157 A.D.2d 467, 549 N.Y.S.2d 661 (1st Dep't 1990).

in a personal injury case, but directs a new trial on the issue of damages. This involves procedures known as "additur" and "remittitur," which are discussed later.[5]

The post-trial motion is usually made promptly upon the delivery of the verdict, and made orally in the courtroom. In addition to such an oral application, however, each party aggrieved by the verdict is entitled to make one formal, written motion under CPLR 4404. For the written motion, the several requirements of CPLR 4405 and 4406 must be met. The motion may be made only to the judge who presided at the trial and must be made within 15 days after the verdict.[6] If a judgment has been entered in the interim, the granting of the motion can incidentally vacate the judgment.[7]

The taking of an appeal from a final judgment in the case will not cut off the trial court's power to grant a post-trial motion under CPLR 4404,[8] but argument or submission of the appeal will. Given the short time limit for the making of a CPLR 4404 motion, the idea that an appeal will have advanced to that stage while the trial court's time to act on a CPLR 4404 motion is still open is a procedural fantasy. It must be noted, however, that an appeal from an order on a CPLR 4404 motion will not bring up for review all issues that affect the final judgment.[9]

Only one formal post-trial motion under CPLR 4404 is allowed, and if any party against whom the motion is made would himself make a CPLR 4404 application, that party must now do so by the expedient of a cross-motion.[10] The 15-day period in which to make a CPLR 4404 motion is not a statute of limitations, however, and so is subject to discretionary extension by the court under CPLR 2004.[11] But since the plain purpose of the time restriction is to put an expeditious end to the case, a delay will not be kindly received.

There is some interplay between CPLR 4404 and CPLR 5015(a), the statute that authorizes vacatur of judgments on certain grounds. The losing party who finds the CPLR 4404 door closed may find relief under CPLR 5015(a).[12]

In a nonjury, or "bench," trial, the post-trial motion is governed by CPLR 4404(b). The technical rules, such as the time for the making of the motion—measured now from "decision" instead of "verdict"—are the same as govern the trial by jury, but the court's powers are of course more extensive. In a court-tried case, the judge on the post-trial motion can make new findings and conclusions, take additional testimony if need be, and render a new and entirely different decision; while in a trial by jury, the judge's powers are necessarily more restricted.

---

  [5]   See § 407.

  [6]   CPLR 4405. The reference in CPLR 4405 to "this article" is meant to be a reference to only the post-trial motion of CPLR 4404.

  [7]   CPLR 4404(a).

  [8]   CPLR 4405.

  [9]   Rivera v. Montefiore Medical Center, 123 A.D.3d 424, 998 N.Y.S.2d 321 (1st Dep't 2014), aff'd, 28 N.Y.3d 999, 41 N.Y.S.3d 454, 64 N.E.3d 274 (2016).

  [10]   CPLR 4406.

  [11]   See Johnson v. Suffolk County Police Dept., 245 A.D.2d 340, 665 N.Y.S.2d 440 (2d Dep't 1997); Casey v. Slattery, 213 A.D.2d 890, 623 N.Y.S.2d 942 (3d Dep't 1995).

  [12]   See § 428.

On an appeal, the appellate court stands in the same position as the trial court. In a judge-tried case, it can therefore make whatever findings it determines the trial court should have made and render judgment itself.[13]

§ 406. Motion for New Trial on the "Weight of the Evidence"

When the court sets aside a verdict on a post-trial motion under CPLR 4404(a), it has the alternative of granting a new trial instead of awarding outright judgment to the other side. The new trial is the route the court takes when, while not confident that any party is entitled to judgment as a matter of law, it nonetheless finds the verdict contrary to the "weight of the evidence." Here, CPLR 4404(a) allows a new trial "in the interest of justice," but neither of the quoted phrases is very informative. Precision about what is meant is elusive if not impossible: the "weight" of the evidence involves the judge's viscera as much as her intellect. There are really three different situations to be distinguished, among which the new trial based on the weight of the evidence is the middle one:

The first situation requires the court to keep hands off, merely confirming the verdict and directing that judgment be entered on it: there are issues of fact that can be resolved either way and it is for the jury to resolve them. If the facts give rise to conflicting inferences, for example, it is for the jury to draw the inferences.[1] If the issue is one of credibility, it is for the jury to determine who is telling the truth.[2] If reasonable minds may differ, in short, it is for the jury to determine who prevails.[3] Most verdicts fall into this category.

The third category is the matter-of-law situation. This one involves more than the mere "weight" of the evidence;[4] this is the situation in which—in the judge's thinking—reasonable minds could not differ and the judgment can go only one way.

In between the two, and without sharp lines on either side, is the elusive but often visited "weight of the evidence" terrain. Here, the court is dissatisfied with the verdict, enough to reject it, but not quite enough to direct judgment notwithstanding it. The key is the judge's common sense reaction to the evidence[5] because there can of course be no precise standard by which to "weigh" it. The scale is in the court's exclusive keeping and not every judge will read it the same way. A lawyer inexperienced in trial practice may even be surprised to learn that the weighing of the evidence is left entirely to the court's discretion and that this discretion may be exercised to set aside the verdict even where the evidence may be technically sufficient to sustain it.[6]

Since the plaintiff has the burden of proof, it has been held that a verdict for the defendant can be set aside only when the evidence preponderates greatly in the plaintiff's favor,[7] i.e., that the scale must tip sharply in order for the judge to set aside a

---

[13]   See, e.g., Mellon v. Street, 23 A.D.2d 210, 259 N.Y.S.2d 900 (3d Dep't 1965).

[1]   Rosen v. Motor Vehicle Acc. Indemnification Corp., 22 A.D.2d 671, 253 N.Y.S.2d 297 (1st Dep't 1964).

[2]   Sherman v. Smith, 23 A.D.2d 642, 256 N.Y.S.2d 947 (1st Dep't 1965).

[3]   McDonald v. Metropolitan St. Ry. Co., 167 N.Y. 66, 60 N.E. 282 (1901).

[4]   Lakin v. Motor Vehicle Acc. Indemnification Corp., 23 A.D.2d 488, 255 N.Y.S.2d 678 (1st Dep't 1965).

[5]   Micallef v. Miehle Co., Division of Miehle-Goss Dexter, Inc., 39 N.Y.2d 376, 384 N.Y.S.2d 115, 348 N.E.2d 571 (1976).

[6]   See Cohen v. Hallmark Cards, Inc., 45 N.Y.2d 493, 410 N.Y.S.2d 282, 382 N.E.2d 1145 (1978), and the extended discussion in *McDonald*, 167 N.Y. at 69, 60 N.E. at 283.

[7]   Tannenbaum v. Mandell, 51 A.D.2d 593, 378 N.Y.S.2d 468 (2d Dep't 1976).

defendant's verdict, while it perhaps need tilt only moderately to set aside a plaintiff's verdict.

A setting aside of a verdict as against the weight of the evidence produces only a new trial; it does not authorize a judgment for a different party.

The court finds the verdict against the weight of evidence when there is something about the case that arouses its suspicions and makes it uncomfortable, although it cannot say clearly that the result can go in only one direction. It may be some testimony that strikes the court as incredible or a story it finds morally improbable.[8] It may be some misconduct on the part of counsel that the judge thinks may have influenced the verdict.[9] It may be any of a number of other factors manifest in a plethora of cases over the years because this power to set aside a verdict and grant a new trial is an inherent one. CPLR 4404(a) is merely a codification of it.[10]

The point at which a judge concludes that a new trial is required

is not fixed on the caprice of judicial individualism; it is rather arrived at by a synthesis of all the experience that the judge has had; in the beginning as a law student, in the later controversies of law practice, in the hearing of cases and the writing of decisions, in the sum of all that he has absorbed in the courtroom and in the library.[11]

It is another of those moments, in other words, that a judge can recognize but cannot always describe, which is why one may observe that it is as much visceral as intellectual. Since the new trial may be granted even where the evidence is sufficient to support the verdict,[12] it may be argued that the grant of a new trial deprives the winning party of the right to trial by jury. From one standpoint, that may be so, but it is so only to the extent that the case goes to a new jury, not to final judgment. It is a kind of compromise with which the law has long since made peace.

Since the motion for a new trial on the weight of the evidence is governed by CPLR 4404(a), it is subject to the several requirements of CPLR 4405 and 4406, discussed in the last section. It can be made as a written motion, for example, in addition to having been made the subject of an oral motion in the courtroom. If it is made in writing, it must be made within 15 days after the verdict is delivered. In either form, it must be directed to the judge who presided at the trial; it is only that judge who holds the scale on which the evidence in the case may be "weighed."

§ 407. Additur and Remittitur

If the verdict for damages in a money action is inadequate or excessive, the court can try to raise or lower the figure by the devices of additur and remittitur.[1] As a general

---

[8]   See, e.g., Bottalico v. City of New York, 281 A.D. 339, 119 N.Y.S.2d 704 (1st Dep't 1953).

[9]   See, e.g., Robinson v. Klein, 21 A.D.2d 778, 250 N.Y.S.2d 977 (1st Dep't 1964).

[10]   McCarthy v. Port of New York Authority, 21 A.D.2d 125, 248 N.Y.S.2d 713 (1st Dep't 1964). To illustrate the broad range of grounds on which the power to order a new trial may be based, the *McCarthy* case cites the indexes of annotations following CPLR 4404 and CPLR 5015 in McKinney's CPLR. A hung jury is also, of course, ground for a new trial. CPLR 4113(b), 4404(a).

[11]   Mann v. Hunt, 283 A.D. 140, 141, 126 N.Y.S.2d 823, 824 (3d Dep't 1953).

[12]   *McDonald*, 167 N.Y. at 69, 60 N.E. at 283. See Recommendations with Respect to Motions for Directed Verdicts and Similar Practice Motions, 15th Jud. Conf. Rep. 241, 276 (1949).

[1]   The word "remittitur" also defines the sending back of a case from an appellate to a lower court for the entry of judgment or further proceedings, see § 545, but that's not the definition that concerns us here.

rule, the court cannot raise or lower the sum directly, at least not in personal injury and like cases involving unliquidated damages, because the setting of damages is strictly a jury function.[2] But the court can grant a new trial "unless" the defendant stipulates to a higher sum ("additur") or the plaintiff stipulates to a lower one ("remittitur"). This is really a kind of "weight of the evidence" phenomenon.[3] It is a step not infrequently taken at either trial or appellate level. It will sometimes happen, in fact, that after the trial judge has exacted one reduction (or increase), the appellate court will exact yet another.[4]

The figure set by the court, and the one to which the party is required to stipulate or face a new trial, represents the minimum (in the case of additur) or the maximum (in the case of remittitur) found by the court to be permissible on the facts. Each of those terminals, in other words, is treated in effect as a matter-of-law terminal whether it is technically that or not. That would insulate the procedure from the accusation that it unconstitutionally denies a party trial by jury. The Court of Appeals considers it an exercise of the trial and intermediate appellate courts' inherent constitutional powers,[5] a matter "committed to the discretion of the trial court and the Appellate Division," and hence beyond the Court of Appeals' review powers.[6]

Of course, if each terminal is deemed the legal bottom or top of the case—and they are treated that way—the trial or intermediate appellate court should be able to set the outside figure directly and order judgment accordingly, in which event the requirement of a stipulation would be superfluous. However that may be, it is well established in unliquidated damage cases that the court may not affect the figure by such direct action; that it can at best order a new trial unless the party affected stipulates to the court-set figure.

The figure used by the judge in these situations is, once again, the product of her whole experience brought to bear on the facts that have been tried before her.[7] What is maximum or minimum to one judge is not necessarily so to another, of course, and, as already noted, appellate judges will disagree, too. This accounts for the many varied illustrations of additur and remittitur that roam through the cases. A remittitur can reduce the verdict to a fraction of what the jury has set,[8] and an additur can multiply it several fold.[9] A verdict of X dollars set by the jury can be remitted down to Z dollars by the trial court, and then readjusted up to Y dollars—yet a third figure—by an appellate court.[10]

The traditional standard for altering the verdict is that its sum is so great or so small that the court finds that it "shocks the conscience." That standard was relaxed in 1986 in tort actions, including the common personal injury and wrongful death actions

---

[2]   Kupitz v. Elliott, 42 A.D.2d 898, 347 N.Y.S.2d 705 (1st Dep't 1973); Ferro v. Maline, 31 A.D.2d 779, 296 N.Y.S.2d 967 (4th Dep't 1969).

[3]   CPLR 4404(a). See § 406.

[4]   See, e.g., Saltzberg v. Kiamesha Concord, Inc., 24 A.D.2d 876, 264 N.Y.S.2d 428 (2d Dep't 1965), aff'd, 17 N.Y.2d 847, 271 N.Y.S.2d 283, 218 N.E.2d 323 (1966).

[5]   See O'Connor v. Papertsian, 309 N.Y. 465, 131 N.E.2d 883 (1956).

[6]   Tate by McMahon v. Colabello, 58 N.Y.2d 84, 459 N.Y.S.2d 422, 445 N.E.2d 1101 (1983).

[7]   See Mann v. Hunt, 283 A.D. 140, 126 N.Y.S.2d 823 (3d Dep't 1953).

[8]   See, e.g., Rivera v. Monticello Central School Dist., 51 A.D.2d 616, 377 N.Y.S.2d 822 (3d Dep't 1976), sustaining a remittitur from $602,345 to $39,845.

[9]   See, e.g., Mollitor v. Smith, 24 A.D.2d 497, 261 N.Y.S.2d 204 (2d Dep't 1965).

[10]   See, e.g., Williams v. Sterling Estates, Inc., 26 A.D.2d 841, 274 N.Y.S.2d 407 (2d Dep't 1966).

in which additur and remittitur are most often seen,[11] when an amendment of CPLR 5501(c) permitted the alteration of the verdict on the lighter finding that the award "deviates materially from what would be reasonable compensation." The amendment authorized this only for the appellate division, however, and for a while it appeared that the trial court would still be limited to the "shocks the conscience" standard. The futility of having the trial court apply a standard different from that applicable on appellate review prompted the courts to hold that the "deviates materially" standard, while applicable in terms only to the appellate division under CPLR 5501(c), must be applied by the trial courts as well, superseding the "shocks the conscience" criterion.[12] The "deviates materially" standard is also applicable in an action in a federal court within New York when subject matter jurisdiction in the federal court is based on diversity of citizenship and state law is therefore applicable to substantive issues.[13]

The new trial that results if the stipulation exacted on an additur or remittitur is not forthcoming is usually limited to damages only, but it can be for liability as well if in the particular case liability is intertwined with damages, as where there are difficult questions of impact or causation in a personal injury case.[14]

Suppose that after a verdict of liability and damages, the court does order a new trial of the damages aspect unless the plaintiff stipulates to accept less (remittitur) or the defendant stipulates to pay more (additur). At one time, the party's so stipulating was held to bar that party's appeal even of the liability finding on the ground that signing the stipulation deprived the party of "aggrieved" status. The Court of Appeals changed course on that and now holds that aggrievement remains as to liability in that situation and that appeal of it is therefore permissible.[15] In an additur situation, the defendant is not required to expressly specify an amount that it considers reasonable to preserve the claim that the additur was excessive. In Oakes v. Patel,[16] defendants adequately preserved their argument in opposing plaintiffs' motion for a new trial by asserting that the first jury's award was reasonable and "that an additur in any amount would be inappropriate." A similar set of rules should apply to a plaintiff challenging a remittitur.

Preservation of a claim of excessive additur or insufficient remittitur is, however, only one aspect of the problem. "The party that wants to challenge the amount of an additur or remittitur on appeal must do so before a new trial takes place." This is due to the fact that "[t]he chief benefit of the devices known as additur and remittitur is that, when they are accepted, they spare the parties and the court the burden and expense of a second trial."[17] Allowing appellate review of an additur or remittitur after the second trial "removes the benefit" and affords "the party opposing the device on appeal the tactical advantage of already knowing what the second jury has awarded. Furthermore,

---

[11] The actions affected are those in which an itemized verdict is required under CPLR 4111.

[12] See Wendell v. Supermarkets General Corp., 189 A.D.2d 1063, 592 N.Y.S.2d 895 (3d Dep't 1993); Prunty v. YMCA of Lockport, Inc., 206 A.D.2d 911, 616 N.Y.S.2d 117 (4th Dep't 1994).

[13] See Gasperini v. Center for Humanities, Inc., 518 U.S. 415, 116 S. Ct. 2211, 135 L. Ed. 2d 659 (1996).

[14] See Oakes v. Patel, 20 N.Y.3d 633, 647, 965 N.Y.S.2d 752, 759, 988 N.E.2d 488, 495 (2013).

[15] See Adams v. Genie Industries, Inc., 14 N.Y.3d 535, 903 N.Y.S.2d 318, 929 N.E.2d 380 (2010) (NYSLD No. 607).

[16] *Oakes*, 20 N.Y.3d at 642, 965 N.Y.S.2d at 756, 988 N.E.2d at 492.

[17] *Oakes*, 20 N.Y.3d at 642, 965 N.Y.S.2d at 756, 988 N.E.2d at 492.

the *Oakes* Court observed that appellate review of an additur or remittitur on an appeal from the final judgment in the second trial would not be available.[18]

Therefore, if a party will not accept an additur or remittitur and desires to appeal, it may need to seek a stay from the trial or appellate court before the second trial is conducted.[19] If a stay is not granted and appellate review cannot be had before the second trial, the "party's only remaining option is to reject the additur or remittitur and retry the case." This was the remedy opted for by the defendants in *Oakes* and the Court held that "[t]hey are not entitled to another remedy because they are displeased with the result."[20]

In sum, the party confronted with an additur or remittitur order can (1) accept the new trial by refusing the stipulation, (2) accept the court-set figure by giving the stipulation, or (3) appeal the order.[21] It should also be noted that the other party may be dissatisfied with the court-set figure as well as with the verdict. Thus, even if the stipulation is accepted by the party and final judgment is entered on the changed figure, the other side can still appeal it.[22] And of course, as noted, these goings-on as to damages do not bar an appeal on the issue of liability.

Whether a party will accept the additur or remittitur and give the stipulation will of course depend on how that party appraises the chances of doing better on a new trial. If the substituted figure is not too far from the supposed mark, the party may be prone to accept the stipulation rather than risk the vagaries of a second trial. In one case, for example, a plaintiff with a $75,000 verdict refused to remit it to $30,000, preferring a new trial. The new trial brought the plaintiff a verdict of only $16,000, and the court upheld it.[23]

§ 408. Motions for "Judgment," Compared

We have seen at this stage no fewer than three motions for a merits "judgment," each of which takes the case out of the jury's hands and has the court determining which party wins. The first was the motion for summary judgment under CPLR 3212, which is made before the trial; the second, the motion under CPLR 4401 for judgment during the trial; and the third, the motion under CPLR 4404 for judgment after the trial. What relationship do they have, if any?

Every motion for judgment that takes the case away from the jury assumes that there is no material issue of fact to be tried and is necessarily sui generis. It turns on the experience of the judge and his ability to discern when there is something to try and when there is not. Hence, the criteria must be stated generally. The CPLR 4401 and 4404 motions are at least built on testimony and evidence at the trial. The CPLR 3212 motion, on the other hand, is not, and is perhaps the more difficult because the judge can depend only on affidavits and other writings, not having the courtroom advantage

---

[18] See, e.g., Barker v. Tennis 59th Inc., 65 N.Y.2d 740, 492 N.Y.S.2d 30, 481 N.E.2d 570 (1985) ("Appellate Division order granting a new trial which is here sought to be reviewed, did not 'necessarily affect' the final judgment."); see § 530.

[19] See CPLR 5519; § 535.

[20] *Oakes*, 20 N.Y.3d at 643, 965 N.Y.S.2d at 757, 988 N.E.2d at 492.

[21] Mormon v. Serkanic, 25 A.D.2d 526, 267 N.Y.S.2d 661 (2d Dep't 1966).

[22] Saltzberg v. Kiamesha Concord, Inc., 24 A.D.2d 876, 264 N.Y.S.2d 428 (2d Dep't 1965), aff'd, 17 N.Y.2d 847, 271 N.Y.S.2d 283, 218 N.E.2d 323 (1966). See CPLR 5501(a)(5).

[23] See Reinertsen v. George W. Rogers Const. Corp., 519 F.2d 531 (2d Cir. 1975).

of hearing the testimony and observing the demeanor and credibility of the witnesses. And yet the root criterion of all of these motions for judgment is the same: that the movant is entitled to judgment as a matter of law.

Judges can identify these situations far more readily than they can articulate them, and both the judiciary and legislature have even defined one in terms of the other, as if one of them could draw sharp definition by analogy to another no sharper. The justification for granting a motion for summary judgment before trial under CPLR 3212, for example, depends on whether the showing is such as would warrant the granting of a CPLR 4401 motion for judgment during the trial.[1] The grant of the CPLR 4401 motion depends in turn on whether, if the case were to go to the jury and the jury were to find the other way, the judge would have to grant judgment notwithstanding the verdict under CPLR 4404.[2]

The practical teaching of this interplay is that the verbalization of when judgment is due as a matter of law is an exercise in semantics, if not futility. Each of these motions may draw eclectically on the experience of the others, but "experience" is likely to be the only building material. When a court proposes to put a summary and permanent seal on a case, a few words in a book are no substitute for a few years in the courtroom.

---

[1]   CPLR 3212(b).

[2]   See Tirschwell v. Dolan, 21 A.D.2d 923, 251 N.Y.S.2d 91 (3d Dep't 1964).

Chapter 16

THE JUDGMENT

Analysis

A. Contents of Judgment
B. Interest
C. Fees, Costs and Disbursements
D. Recording the Judgment
E. Recording Satisfaction
F. Vacating Judgments and Orders
G. Renewal of Judgment
H. Declaratory Judgment

A. CONTENTS OF JUDGMENT

Table of Sections

§ 409.   Content of Judgment
§ 410.   Interlocutory Judgment

§ 409. Content of Judgment

A judgment is the resolution of the dispute and the note on which the action or proceeding ends. It is the embodiment of the verdict or decision, to which it must refer, and if it is the result of a default it must refer to that. All actions and proceedings in the usual courts of civil jurisdiction today end in a "judgment."[1] The "final order" that used to end a special proceeding before the CPLR arrived in 1963 is no longer used[2] and the "decree" that once terminated an equity action had given way to a simple "judgment" long before that when law and equity merged.[3]

There is no rigid form for a judgment. It varies according to the needs of the particular case. The money judgment, the most common in litigation, is also the most familiar and probably as close as we come to a "standard" judgment.[4] A money judgment is rendered in dollars and cents, unless based on a claim "denominated in a currency other than [that] of the United States," in which event the court is to render judgment in the foreign currency, with a conversion into U.S. currency at the rate of exchange applicable at the time of entry.[5]

---

[1] CPLR 5011.

[2] See CPLR 411, RPAPL 747.

[3] An exception is the surrogate's court, whose proceedings continue to end in what is denominated a "decree," see SCPA 602, which is still nothing more than a "judgment."

[4] A common form of money judgment is contained in § 417.

[5] Jud. Law § 27(b).

At one time, and in fact until quite recently, it could be said that the only item needing change on the bottom line of a money judgment from one case to another was the amount involved. That changed in the mid 1980s when the legislature prescribed use of a "periodic payment" judgment[6] in the unintentional tort actions, designed to spread out over a period of years—instead of awarding as an immediate lump sum—a portion of the projected future damages found to have been sustained by the plaintiff.[7]

At the other end of the spectrum is the judgment of injunction, which must carefully address the facts of the particular case and delineate the defendant's obligations with respect to them. Here an omission can seriously undermine enforcement of the judgment, which has to depend on contempt proceedings.

The verdict or decision, which the judgment merely reflects, establishes the rights of the parties regardless of the source from which the supporting evidence comes. It is no longer necessary that it be the plaintiff's proof that implicates the defendant, or the defendant's that defeats the plaintiff. Where P's case against defendant A has a gap, for example, it can be filled by proof put in by defendant B.[8] Likewise in a third-party context: proof adduced by X, the third-party defendant, can defeat P's claim against D, the main defendant, even though D stands mute.[9] The judgment will be determined by the whole of the evidence, without regard to the channel through which it came.

CPLR 5011 provides that the judgment "may be either interlocutory or final." A "final" judgment is the one we have been discussing, and the one to which almost all discussion about judgments relates. The interlocutory judgment is the subject of the next section. Except for appeal of the judgment and for the few narrow grounds on which a judgment can be set aside,[10] the final judgment terminates the controversy and sets the stage for enforcement.

A judgment can determine the whole case or only part of it. It can determine one cause of action and leave others for later. It can even decide part of but a single cause of action, or give judgment as to some, but not all, parties.[11] The needs of the particular case will dictate, and to the extent that part, but not all, of the case is sent to judgment, the court has several tools to help it make the division. The first and most obvious is the severance, available at any appropriate juncture of an action[12] or special proceeding.[13] Where, for example, on a motion to dismiss under CPLR 3211, or for summary judgment under CPLR 3212, only one cause of action is disposed of but others remain to be tried,

---

[6] It is sometimes popularly referred to as a "structured judgment," after the "structured settlement" terminology that had evolved earlier when the parties were able to agree on that form of judgment.

[7] See CPLR Article 50–A (CPLR 5031–5034, 5036–5039), enacted in 1985, governing medical, dental, and podiatric malpractice actions, and CPLR Article 50–B (CPLR 5041–5049), governing the rest of the personal injury, injury to property, and wrongful death actions. (The two Articles are virtually identical and could have been enacted as one.) Some of the complications in this category of judgment are explored in 1B NY PJI3d 2:277 ("Damages—General").

[8] See Simon v. Lowenthal, 169 Misc. 718, 8 N.Y.S.2d 484 (N.Y.C. Mun. Ct. 1938). There was a statute so providing expressly, § 212(2) of the old Civ. Prac. Act (repealed 1963), but a counterpart does not appear in the CPLR because the matter is apparently deemed implicit in sound modern practice without the need of a statutory statement.

[9] CPLR 1008; see § 163.

[10] CPLR 5015(a); see §§ 426–431.

[11] CPLR 5012.

[12] CPLR 603; see § 129.

[13] CPLR 407; see § 547.

the order of disposition may include a severance of the concluded claim and leave the undecided claims for trial.

A single judgment can dispose of the entire case no matter how many claims or parties are involved. It will merely go through its recitations in some logical sequence until the rights of all parties with respect to all claims are clarified. If in the court's discretion claims or parties are so profuse that the embodiment of all of their rights in a single paper is unduly confusing, the court can, with or without a severance, direct that separate papers reflect the rights involved, cross-referencing one paper to another if need arises. It is flexibility that the general language of CPLR 5011 aims for.

Also to be included in the judgment are costs and disbursements. If the judgment is for money, interest may also have to be added. These things are discussed in subsequent sections.[14]

§ 410. Interlocutory Judgment

CPLR 5011 provides that the judgment may be interlocutory or final. When used alone, "judgment" usually means a final judgment. An interlocutory judgment, which is not common today, is one lacking finality in some respect. It decides part, but not all, of the case,[1] or it decides all of it, but postpones conclusiveness for a designated time or until a designated event. A prime example until 1968 was the matrimonial action, where an annulment or divorce would first go to interlocutory judgment and not become "final" until three months later. The three months were a cooling-off period during which the parties would, so the legislature hoped, reunite, preserve the marriage, and make the entry of a final judgment unnecessary. The statutes so providing[2] were repealed in 1968 in conjunction with the legislature coming to grips with reality and the liberalization of New York's divorce laws. Today divorce and annulment judgments become final immediately, permitting remarriage, or at least a change of relationship status on Facebook, without a waiting period.

The interlocutory judgment remains available to the court whenever it has some appropriate aid to offer. It is sometimes used by the court in the bifurcated personal injury or wrongful death action to reflect that liability has been found and to signal that the liability finding may be separately appealed before damages are tried. Without such an interlocutory judgment, or a prior order granting partial summary judgment on liability,[3] an appeal would not yet lie. The trial judge determines whether to authorize such a judgment, which in effect gives the court the say as to whether to allow an immediate appeal of the liability determination.[4]

A major treatment of the subject appears in Bank of N.Y. v. Ansonia Assocs.,[5] in which a jury found gross negligence in a ceiling fall case, grounding punitive damages, which set the stage for discovery proceedings with respect to the defendants' net worth. The defendants were denied the interlocutory judgment that would have permitted an

---

[14] See §§ 411–415.

[1] See Moza v. Sun Mut. Ins. Co., 13 Abb. Pr. 304, 22 How. Pr. 60, 1861 WL 4956 (Sup. Ct. 1861).

[2] Former Dom. Rel. Law §§ 241–242.

[3] See § 285.

[4] See Jack Parker Const. Corp. v. Williams, 35 A.D.2d 839, 317 N.Y.S.2d 911 (2d Dep't 1970).

[5] Bank of New York v. Ansonia Associates, 172 Misc. 2d 70, 656 N.Y.S.2d 813 (Sup. Ct., New York County 1997) (SPR 69:3).

immediate appeal of the liability finding. Hence the trial had to continue through the damages phase.

The use of an interlocutory judgment in those contexts—money actions at law—is analogous to its more traditional use in the accounting action in equity. It was, and may still be, used there to reflect whether there is a *right* to an accounting. That will require the court to determine whether the conditions precedent to that equitable right have been met, such as the existence of a fiduciary relationship between the parties,[6] before the accounting itself is allowed. In neither instance, however, is the interlocutory judgment indispensable. The finding on the first phase (liability) need not, except in connection with the appellate process discussed, be reduced to an interlocutory judgment in order for the case to proceed into the second phase (damages). The requisite finding can just be held in abeyance, reduced neither to an order nor a judgment, while the rest of the case proceeds.

By the general language of CPLR 5011, it is today open to the court to direct the use of an interlocutory judgment whenever in the court's view it has a useful function to serve. In Rupert v. Sellers,[7] for example, P sued D for punitive damages and sought disclosure as to D's wealth. The court held that D's wealth was relevant on a punitive damages assessment, since the money to be awarded has to be enough to make a dent in D's assets, but that the subject was not ripe for investigation unless and until D was found guilty of malice, a prerequisite to the imposition of punitive damages.[8] The court held that disclosure on the wealth topic must therefore abide a special verdict establishing malice. Once such a verdict is rendered, the court can reflect it in an interlocutory judgment, thus setting the stage for both disclosure and trial on the subject of D's wealth. But here, again, it is a mere option for the court. If the court finds it unnecessary, as where no immediate appeal is sought from the finding of malice and no other right is asserted that can be shown to depend on the entry of an interlocutory judgment, it need not be used.

If the court does direct an interlocutory judgment, and the later moment arrives when the case becomes ripe for a final one, the party entitled to the final judgment can move for it.[9] If by the terms of the interlocutory judgment the right to a final one becomes automatic with the mere passage of time or the mere occurrence of some readily proved condition, even a motion should not be necessary. In such circumstances, the clerk, upon appropriate proof, should be able to enter the final judgment.

B.　INTEREST

Table of Sections

§ 411.　　Allowance of Interest

§ 412.　　Rate of Interest

---

[6]　See Kaminsky v. Kahn, 23 A.D.2d 231, 259 N.Y.S.2d 716 (1st Dep't 1965), rev'd (in effect) on other grounds, 20 N.Y.2d 573, 285 N.Y.S.2d 833, 232 N.E.2d 837 (1967).

[7]　Rupert v. Sellers, 48 A.D.2d 265, 368 N.Y.S.2d 904 (4th Dep't 1975).

[8]　See generally 1B NY PJI3d 2:278 ("Damages—Punitive").

[9]　CPLR 5016(e).

§ 411. Allowance of Interest

Interest is the cost of use of another's money.[1] The CPLR provides for it on litigated obligations that culminate in a judgment. There are three distinct periods to be considered, governed respectively by CPLR 5001, 5002, and 5003:

I.   Interest on the cause of action from its accrual until the verdict or the decision, if the case is tried by the court;

II. Interest on the verdict or decision until judgment is entered; and

III. Interest on the judgment from entry until payment.

Interest in categories II and III attaches uniformly to all money obligations once reduced to verdict or judgment, including money awards incidental to equitable relief. This is not so of category I, however, where there are a number of points to note.

Category I Interest

All actions for money seeking in essence to recover for property loss, whether sounding in contract or tort, get interest as a matter of right in category I. This is so if the action is one at law, in any event, which means that it is so in most categories of money actions, almost all of which sound at law. If the money demand is incidental to an equitable claim, however, whether to allow category I interest and the rate and date from which it will accrue is left to the court's discretion.[2] In categories II and III, the interest lies as a matter of right on money claims without regard to their legal or equitable origins.

The main exceptions to category I are the personal injury and punitive damages claims, neither of which carries interest from accrual to verdict, although both carry interest in categories II and III. Denial of interest on the personal injury claim, which includes not just the negligent torts but some of the intentional ones as well,[3] of course means that one of the most common claims in litigation does not draw interest until a verdict or decision is rendered in court. The Advisory Committee considered altering this, but decided against it because it involves "difficult policy considerations" and entails speculative assessments of potential future losses, especially in regard to the element of pain and suffering that is such a key part of these cases.[4] Even when the personal injury has a contract ground to rest on, as it frequently does today when a product has caused the injury and the theory of breach of warranty supports the claim, it will not draw interest from accrual, i.e., interest in category I.[5]

The wrongful death claim, governed by a special statute,[6] gets interest from the time of death until the verdict or decision, at which time CPLR categories II and III take

---

[1]   Love v. State, 78 N.Y.2d 540, 544, 577 N.Y.S.2d 359, 361, 583 N.E.2d 1296, 1298 (1991).

[2]   CPLR 5001(a).

[3]   Such as defamation. See Rupert v. Sellers, 50 N.Y.2d 881, 430 N.Y.S.2d 263, 408 N.E.2d 671 (1980).

[4]   See 3d Rep. Leg. Doc. No. 17, p. 88 (1959).

[5]   Gillespie v. Great Atlantic & Pacific Tea Co., 26 A.D.2d 953, 276 N.Y.S.2d 372 (2d Dep't 1966), modified, 21 N.Y.2d 823, 288 N.Y.S.2d 907, 235 N.E.2d 911 (1968).

[6]   EPTL 5–4.3; Toledo v. Iglesia Ni Christo, 18 N.Y.3d 363, 367–68, 939 N.Y.S.2d 282, 286, 962 N.E.2d 773, 773 (2012).

over. This is because the wrongful death claim is economic in nature and seeks recovery of pecuniary losses.[7]

When a property damage or wrongful death claim, each of which does get interest from accrual, is joined with a personal injury claim, which does not, the plaintiff had best ask the court to instruct the jury to bring back separate verdicts on each claim so that those entitled to category I interest can be given their allotment. A failure to request the separate verdicts will waive the interest altogether.[8] In this age of the special verdict,[9] which when properly used reveals the details of the jury's determination, an inadvertent merging of the personal injury and property damage elements is less likely than it once was.

Since interest is designed to compensate for the loss of use of money, money to be awarded as punitive damages, which requires a showing of the defendant's malice, is denied category I interest on the theory that these damages are not designed to compensate, but rather to punish.[10] Once reduced to verdict, which establishes the plaintiff's entitlement to the money, the category II interest does attach to punitive damages, as does the category III interest when judgment is entered.

In determining when the cause of action accrued for purposes of category I interest, it will often be satisfactory to adopt and apply the same accrual moment applicable under CPLR 203(a) in determining the start of the statute of limitations. But CPLR 5001(b) recognizes that this will not always be so and permits the court to handle the interest problem flexibly, directing that interest be computed "from the earliest ascertainable date the cause of action existed."

When items of damage, all incidents of a single claim, accrue at different times, a separate interest computation is made for each, measured from its own accrual. Where P is suing D on a note that calls for monthly interest payments, for example, and several installments are overdue when P sues on the note, P is entitled under CPLR 5001(b) to have separate interest computations made on each overdue installment, measured independently from the due date of each.[11]

If the individual accrual dates can't be ascertained, "a single reasonable intermediate date" can be set by the court, with interest on the aggregate of the damages measured from that time.[12] In a contract case, for example, the date of breach was clear, but money payable under the contract fell due at different times and the record was not clear about when. The court picked out a point midway between the breach and the contract's expiration date and measured interest from that moment.[13] In other instances, in which discerning the appropriate dates is difficult, as in an action for unfair

---

[7]　　See Johnson v. Manhattan & Bronx Surface Transit Operating Authority, 71 N.Y.2d 198, 203–04, 524 N.Y.S.2d 415, 418, 519 N.E.2d 326, 328 (1988).

[8]　　See Helman v. Markoff, 255 A.D. 991, 8 N.Y.S.2d 448 (2d Dep't 1938), aff'd, 280 N.Y. 641, 20 N.E.2d 1012 (1939); see Brandt Corp. v. Warren Automatic Controls Corp., 37 A.D.2d 563, 564, 322 N.Y.S.2d 291, 293 (2d Dep't 1971).

[9]　　See § 399.

[10]　　See 3d Rep. Leg. Doc. No. 17, p. 88 (1959); Stassou v. Casini & Huang Const., Inc., 14 A.D.3d 695, 789 N.Y.S.2d 225 (2d Dep't 2005).

[11]　　See Spodek v. Park Property Development Associates, 96 N.Y.2d 577, 733 N.Y.S.2d 674, 759 N.E.2d 760 (2001) (NYSLD No. 505) (holding that this computation does not amount to compounding of interest).

[12]　　CPLR 5001(b).

[13]　　City of New York v. Coastal Oil New York, Inc., 2000 WL 648365 (S.D.N.Y. May 18, 2000).

competition where pinpointing the moment of damage accrual involves conjecture, the category I interest may be held to start only upon commencement of the action.[14]

The accrual moment used to calculate category I interest is often just a question of fact. If the point is in doubt, the facts should be litigated and the matter left to the jury or other fact trier.[15] If the case is being tried to a jury and the jury is discharged without having fixed the interest-starting date, the plaintiff may be in trouble. The clerk may be able to fix the interest on an affidavit if the facts on which interest depends have been incidentally determined and are clear on the record, and there have even been special instances in which an appellate court has awarded interest for the first time.[16] If, however, interest depends on facts that the plaintiff neglected to litigate, the result can be a substantial forfeiture. In one case, for example, inattention to the facts on which interest depended resulted in a forfeiture of some $88,000.[17] With dates in hand, the clerk makes the actual computation of interest and adds it to the basic damages for inclusion in the verdict or decision.[18] The total then bears interest as part of category II.

In category I—with the exception of the personal injury and punitive damages cases already noted—interest on a money claim is so routinely awarded and infrequently disputed that the applicable statute, CPLR 5001(a), rarely gets a probing visit from the courts. It got one from the Court of Appeals in Manufacturer's & Traders Trust Co. v. Reliance Ins. Co.,[19] in the interesting context of an interpleader action. The Court held that the winning claimant is not entitled to interest from the loser because there is no "sum awarded" (as CPLR 5001(a) requires) against the loser in an interpleader case. The case just produces a judicial direction as to who, as between competing claimants, is entitled to the funds held by the stakeholder.

Category II Interest

Category II interest, which is governed by CPLR 5002, is as a general rule the least important category of interest and therefore often ignored by lawyers. It contemplates that the whole of the verdict or decision, including the category I interest awarded, will be added together, and that category II interest will then run on that sum until a judgment is formally entered, at which point category III interest takes over. But since the time between rendition of the verdict and the formal entry of judgment is usually brief (a diligent lawyer will seldom let more than a few days elapse before getting judgment entered),[20] interest here is likely to be negligible. Sometimes when entering judgment the clerk will just measure category I interest on the claim until the moment of entry of judgment, thus in effect disregarding category II.

---

[14] See De Long Corp. v. Morrison-Knudsen Co., 20 A.D.2d 104, 244 N.Y.S.2d 859 (1st Dep't 1963), the point discussed here being afterwards affirmed in 14 N.Y.2d 346, 251 N.Y.S.2d 657, 200 N.E.2d 557 (1964).

[15] See 1B NY PJI3d 2:313 ("Damages—Property—Interest").

[16] Compare Newburger, Loeb & Co., Inc. v. Gross, 611 F.2d 423, 432–34 (2d Cir. 1979) (affirming district court's grant of prejudgment interest, and awarding additional prejudgment interest given support in record), with Paddington Partners v. Bouchard, 34 F.3d 1132, 1139–44 (2d Cir. 1994) (reversing award of interest on Rule 60 motion to amend judgment because district court was required to make a finding of fact regarding the dates from which such interest would run).

[17] See Lee v. Joseph E. Seagram & Sons, Inc., 592 F.2d 39 (2d Cir. 1979), a federal diversity action in which interest was governed by New York law, so that CPLR 5001 applied.

[18] CPLR 5001(c); see § 417 containing a sample form of judgment.

[19] Manufacturer's & Traders Trust Co. v. Reliance Ins. Co., 8 N.Y.3d 583, 838 N.Y.S.2d 806, 870 N.E.2d 124 (2007) (NYSLD No. 572).

[20] The act of "entry" of the judgment is discussed in § 418.

The only difference is one of compounding, anyway: if the category I interest is included in the sum on which category II interest is computed, the plaintiff will earn interest on interest between verdict and judgment, whereas deferring the addition of all interest until judgment is entered skips that step.[21]

In some instances, however, the category II interest can take on importance. That will be so whenever there is a long period between verdict and judgment. This can happen, for example, in a bifurcated trial of a personal injury claim in which a verdict of liability on phase one is reduced to an interlocutory judgment and is separately appealed before damages are tried.[22] It has been held that if the appeal upholds liability, whatever damages are then assessed will receive category II interest from the original liability verdict.[23]

The matter becomes most significant in a personal injury action, where category I interest is not allowed. In those actions, interest gets its start only from the verdict, i.e., in category II. This should at least prompt second thoughts by a defendant before taking a separate appeal from the liability finding in a bifurcated trial. Delay in settlement, which category I in effect rewards by withholding interest on a personal injury claim, will not necessarily carry advantages once a liability verdict is in, even though damages have yet to be tried. The same can be said where the plaintiff has been awarded partial summary judgment on liability, as category II interest will begin to run from that moment.[24]

Similar questions arise in this situation:

Suppose that a personal injury judgment for the plaintiff, including damages, is appealed, and the appellate court orders a new trial. Will a new verdict for the plaintiff, and whatever its damage award may be, carry category II interest from the old (the reversed) verdict? It has been held that it will, at least where the defendant is found to have unreasonably prolonged the appellate process.[25] But absent a finding of unreasonable delay, the court may hold that the interest will run only from the new verdict. These are not academic points. In one case, for example, in which category II interest upon a new trial was held to run from the new rather than the old verdict, the difference in interest amounted to more than $6,500 in 1966 dollars.[26]

---

[21] Suppose, for example, that on October 18 the plaintiff is awarded a verdict of $20,000 on a property damage claim accruing exactly three years earlier. At 9% per year, interest on that sum would be $5,400, and the verdict should then be treated as one for $25,400. Assume judgment is entered three days later, on October 21. If category II interest is distinctly treated, the sum of $25,400 would bear three days interest, amounting to about $18.79, for a total of $25,418.79, to go in as the initial judgment figure. If category II is skipped, and interest on $20,000 is computed for three years and three days, the total comes to about $25,414.79. The difference is only about $4.00, which accounts for the frequent bypassing of the second category. As discussed in a moment, increased damages and greater time between verdict and entry of judgment will warrant the computation of category II interest.

[22] See § 410.

[23] Trimboli v. Scarpaci Funeral Home, Inc., 37 A.D.2d 386, 326 N.Y.S.2d 227 (2d Dep't 1971), aff'd, 30 N.Y.2d 687, 332 N.Y.S.2d 637, 283 N.E.2d 614 (1972). Even the State is subject to interest from the time of the verdict or decision when it unsuccessfully appeals a liability finding in a bifurcated trial. Gunnarson v. State, 70 N.Y.2d 923, 524 N.Y.S.2d 396, 519 N.E.2d 307 (1987).

[24] See §§ 280, 285. A stipulation as to liability does not trigger the accrual of category II interest under CPLR 5002. Mahoney v. Brockbank, 142 A.D.3d 200, 205, 35 N.Y.S.3d 459, 463 (2d Dep't 2016), leave to appeal granted, 29 N.Y.3d 904, 2017 WL 1224136 (2017).

[25] See Beyer v. Murray, 33 A.D.2d 246, 306 N.Y.S.2d 619 (4th Dep't 1970).

[26] See Lindwall v. Talent Cab Corp., 51 Misc. 2d 381, 273 N.Y.S.2d 261 (Sup. Ct., New York County 1966), aff'd 27 A.D.2d 647, 276 N.Y.S.2d 565 (1st Dep't).

In Love v. State,[27] a decision fixing claimant's damages was not rendered by the court until more than 10 months after the trial on damages had concluded, but neither party was responsible for the delay. The Court of Appeals held that category II interest related back to the earlier liability finding, rejecting the suggestion that the interest should be given a relation back only when the defendant is found to have caused delay in the trial of the damages issue.

Category III Interest

Category III interest runs on the judgment until it is satisfied. The judgment should technically include all interest awarded under categories I and II, but as noted above, the second category is sometimes disregarded. The moment from which category III interest runs is the "entry" of the judgment. For this purpose, an order directing the payment of money may be docketed as if it were a judgment[28] and will draw category III interest from the docketing.[29]

The plaintiff is entitled to category III interest as a matter of right. While prejudgment interest is not classified as a "penalty," post-judgment interest is generally deemed a penalty for the delayed payment of a judgment.[30] Therefore, when the delay in paying the judgment is caused solely by the plaintiff, the right to category III interest may be deemed waived or denied through an estoppel.[31]

Interest in Wrongful Death Actions

In wrongful death cases that involve both past (pre-verdict) and future (post-verdict) losses, the Court of Appeals has prescribed how to compute interest.[32] In Toledo v. Iglesia Ni Christo,[33] the Court held that in awarding category I interest in a wrongful death action, it was appropriate to discount future wrongful death damages back to the date of decedent's death and award interest on that sum from the date of death to the date of verdict.

It is not clear how interest is to be figured under the "periodic payment" provisions governing judgments in tort cases that involve an award of future damages.[34] The court can be called upon for instructions if the parties can't agree about interest. When a periodic payment judgment has been rendered, and the problem is the debtor's failure to make payment pursuant to it, the matter of interest is left to the court.[35]

---

[27] Love v. State, 78 N.Y.2d 540, 577 N.Y.S.2d 359, 583 N.E.2d 1296 (1991) (NYSLD No. 384).

[28] CPLR 2222; see Han Soo Lee v. Riverhead Bay Motors, 134 A.D.3d 656, 21 N.Y.S.3d 624 (1st Dep't 2015) (allowing category III interest, but denying category II interest); Commentary C2222:1 on McKinney's CPLR 2222; § 250 (discussing CPLR 2222).

[29] CPLR 5003. The statute refers to the "docketing" of the order as a judgment, but the word would be better read as "entered" if it is to govern the lower as well as the supreme and county courts. See § 421.

[30] ERHAL Holding Corp. v. Rusin, 252 A.D.2d 473, 675 N.Y.S.2d 138 (1st Dep't 1998).

[31] Juracka v. Ferrara, 120 A.D.2d 822, 501 N.Y.S.2d 936 (3d Dep't 1986).

[32] See Milbrandt v. A.P. Green Refractories Co., 79 N.Y.2d 26, 580 N.Y.S.2d 147, 588 N.E.2d 45 (1992) (NYSLD No. 386).

[33] Toledo v. Iglesia Ni Christo, 18 N.Y.3d 363, 939 N.Y.S.2d 282, 962 N.E.2d 773 (2012).

[34] Articles 50–A and 50–B of the CPLR (CPLR 5031–5034, 5036–5039, 5041–5049).

[35] CPLR 5034, 5044.

Interest on Arbitration Awards

The award of an arbitrator is deemed the equivalent of a court decision so as to carry category II interest under CPLR 5002.[36] The interest will be computed accordingly when the arbitration award is confirmed into a judgment through the procedures of CPLR 7510 and 7514, met later.[37] If the matter in arbitration involves a breach of contract, which would be entitled to category I interest as of right, the issue must be raised for the arbitrator to determine. A party cannot seek category I interest when confirming the award unless it was awarded by the arbitrator.[38]

What happens in the situation in which, for one reason or another, the damages issues are arbitrated after a verdict of liability in a court action? When the arbitrator decides on damages and the award is confirmed into a judgment, does the interest get measured only from the moment of the arbitration award, or does it get measured from the old liability finding? In Grobman v. Chernoff,[39] the Court of Appeals held that it runs from the old liability finding.

Interest on Settlements

Before 1992, there was no stated time limit within which the sum agreed to in a settlement of an action had to be paid. With the 1992 enactment of CPLR 5003–a, a time limit was imposed. When the action is settled, it is the plaintiff's obligation under the statute to draw up a release and "tender" a copy of it on the settling defendant by personal delivery or registered or certified mail, return receipt requested,[40] along with a copy of a stipulation discontinuing the action. If the settlement requires judicial approval, as it does when the claim is that of an infant, a copy of the order approving the settlement must also be included.[41] Within 21 days from the tender of those papers, the defendant must pay the amount of the settlement.[42]

If the settlement isn't paid in full on time, the plaintiff may seek the entry of a judgment without notice against the defendant for the entire amount of the settlement, plus costs, disbursements, and interest on that amount, measured from the date of the tender. The consequence of not paying the stated amount of the settlement on time, in other words, is that costs and disbursements will now be added to it, along with interest.[43] If only a partial payment of the settlement is made on time, the defendant must pay interest on sums already paid under the settlement, and not solely on the unpaid amount.[44]

---

[36]   Board of Ed. of Cent. School Dist. No. 1 of Towns of Niagara, Wheatfield, Lewiston and Cambria v. Niagara-Wheatfield Teachers Ass'n, 46 N.Y.2d 553, 558, 415 N.Y.S.2d 790, 793, 389 N.E.2d 104, 107 (1979); Svenson v. Swegan, 133 A.D.3d 1279, 1281, 20 N.Y.S.3d 278, 281 (4th Dep't 2015).

[37]   See §§ 601 and 605 (Practitioner's Edition).

[38]   Levin & Glasser, P.C. v. Kenmore Property, LLC, 70 A.D.3d 443, 896 N.Y.S.2d 311 (1st Dep't 2010) ("[b]ecause petitioner could have sought [pre-award] interest from the arbitrators, it is barred from seeking it from the court in its petition to confirm the award.").

[39]   Grobman v. Chernoff, 15 N.Y.3d 525, 914 N.Y.S.2d 731, 940 N.E.2d 557 (2010) (NYSLD No. 614).

[40]   CPLR 5003–a(g).

[41]   CPLR 5003–a(d).

[42]   See CPLR 5003–a(a). Governmental defendants are allowed 90 days. See CPLR 5003–a(b), (c).

[43]   It was held in O'Meara v. A & P, Inc., 169 Misc. 2d 697, 647 N.Y.S.2d 424 (Sup. Ct., Westchester County 1996), that while interest in this situation runs only from the time of the plaintiff's tender of the settlement papers, the costs and disbursements awarded will be for the whole of the action.

[44]   See Mann v. All Waste Systems, Inc., 293 A.D.2d 656, 741 N.Y.S.2d 272 (2d Dep't 2002).

May a "high-low" agreement count as a "settlement" under CPLR 5003–a? The question arose in Cunha v. Shapiro.[45] A "high-low" agreement, which aims at the damages portion of the trial, stipulates that the plaintiff will not get less than a stated figure (in *Cunha*, $75,000) and the defendant will not have to pay more than a stated figure (in *Cunha*, $325,000), no matter what the verdict produces. The verdict in *Cunha*, a personal injury case, was brought in for $400,000, invoking the $325,000 maximum, a break for D. Failing to fulfill its obligation under the statute to tender a release to D, P was held entitled to no CPLR 5003–a interest, at least in this situation, where one of the "high-low" settlement figures supplied D's ultimate obligation.

If neither settlement terminal agreed to by the parties has to be applied, because the verdict falls somewhere between them, does the statute become inapplicable, i.e., does the agreement cease to be a "settlement" under CPLR 5003–a? If so, then P would presumably be entitled to interest measured all the way back to the earlier finding of liability.[46]

It has been held that the procedures of CPLR 5003–a do not apply to a settlement made before commencement of the action.[47]

Interest in Equitable Actions

It has already been noted that money obligations emerging in an equitable context draw interest as a matter of right in categories II and III, but not category I. Whether to award category I interest at all—and the rate and date from which it is to run if awarded—is in the court's discretion on an equitable claim. Argument sometimes arises, therefore, as to whether a given claim is equitable or legal. In this connection, an action brought on a separation agreement has been held to draw category I interest as of right because it amounts to claim at law,[48] while a money claim arising out of a matrimonial action or out of an equitable action involving the monetary rights of the family may have to depend on judicial discretion for this class of interest.[49]

While lawyers who do not comply with the Letter of Engagement Rule[50] may be entitled to recover their fees on a quantum meruit basis,[51] they may not be entitled to a substantial amount of category I interest.[52] There is some authority, however, that the awarding of category I interest on a quantum meruit cause of action is required under New York.[53]

Computing and Compounding Interest

Whichever of the three categories is involved, all matters relating to interest should be resolved within the action, if need be by a motion to amend, to resettle, or to modify

---

[45] Cunha v. Shapiro, 42 A.D.3d 95, 837 N.Y.S.2d 160 (2d Dep't 2007).

[46] See SPR 185:2.

[47] State Farm Mut. Auto. Ins. Co. v. Mamadou, 17 Misc. 3d 600, 844 N.Y.S.2d 680 (Sup. Ct., Kings County 2007).

[48] Iaizzo v. Gerard, 210 A.D.2d 204, 620 N.Y.S.2d 266 (2d Dep't 1994).

[49] See Sinclair v. Wieder, 48 A.D.2d 866, 369 N.Y.S.2d 18 (2d Dep't 1975).

[50] 22 N.Y.C.R.R. Part 1215.

[51] See Seth Rubenstein, P.C. v. Ganea, 41 A.D.3d 54, 833 N.Y.S.2d 566 (2d Dep't 2007).

[52] See Patrick M. Connors, *Issues Remain for Lawyers Not Complying With Part 1215*, N.Y.L.J., Sept. 15, 2008 at 53.

[53] See Stillman v. InService America Inc., 738 F. Supp. 2d 480 (S.D.N.Y. 2010), aff'd, 455 Fed. Appx. 48 (2d Cir. 2012).

the judgment. Interest may not ordinarily be sought in a separate action or after judgment has been entered.[54] The Court of Appeals decision in CRP/Extell Parcel I, L.P. v. Cuomo[55] vividly makes the point. In *CRP/Extell*, the attorney general ordered the sponsor of a condominium offering to return down payments to purchasers. The sponsor commenced an Article 78 proceeding challenging the attorney general's determinations, but the supreme court denied the petition, directed the release and return of the down payments with accumulated escrow interest, and dismissed the proceeding. After the sponsor returned the down payments and accumulated escrow interest, the purchasers made a motion and obtained an award of statutory interest under CPLR 5001 totaling $4.9 million. Because the purchasers did not seek this substantial relief until after the final judgment dismissing the Article 78 proceeding was entered, the Court of Appeals affirmed the appellate division's vacatur of the award. The Court held that once the supreme court dismissed the petition and judgment was entered, it no longer possessed jurisdiction to entertain the post-judgment motion for statutory interest.

The *CRP/Extell* decision should be contrasted with the Court's prior decision in Kiker v. Nassau County.[56] In *Kiker*, the Court permitted a municipal entity an amendment of a judgment to reflect the special municipal interest rate several years after the clerk mistakenly entered interest at the higher regular rate allowed in CPLR 5004. The authority for the belated correction rests in CPLR 5019(a), which permits the court to correct clerical errors but does not countenance belated judicial steps, such as allowing a new demand for interest to be pursued after the matter has already been reduced to judgment.

Except when computing category II interest on a verdict that includes category I interest, or computing category III interest on a judgment that includes interest under either of the first two categories, there is no compounding of interest under the CPLR. In other words, there is no compounding of interest within a category. Therefore, if a judgment for $100,000 is outstanding for five years, for example, at 9% a year,[57] the interest to be computed at this moment would be $45,000, which is a straight $9,000 a year for five years.

Deviation of Statutory Right to Interest in a Contract

As we discuss in the next section, a contract can fix a different rate of interest than the 9% allowed by CPLR 5004. In J. D'Addario & Co., Inc. v. Embassy Industries, Inc.,[58] the Court of Appeals held that a contract can also trump the parties' statutory right to category I interest under CPLR 5001(a). In *J. D'Addario*, the parties to a real estate contract agreed that the "sole remedy" for the seller and the "sole obligation" of the purchaser in the event of the purchaser's default would be an award of the down payment and that the seller had "no further rights" against the defaulting purchaser. The Court held that this contractual language trumped the right to statutory interest in CPLR 5001(a). In sum, the seller was entitled to an award of the entire down payment ($650,000), but not category I interest ($227,406). It is likely that the holding in *J.*

---

[54] See Ferguson v. City of New York, 67 Misc. 2d 812, 324 N.Y.S.2d 894 (Sup. Ct., Orange County 1971), modified, 39 A.D.2d 569, 331 N.Y.S.2d 735 (2d Dep't 1972).

[55] CRP/Extell Parcel I, L.P. v. Cuomo, 27 N.Y.3d 1034, 33 N.Y.S.3d 148, 52 N.E.3d 1174 (2016).

[56] Kiker v. Nassau County, 85 N.Y.2d 879, 626 N.Y.S.2d 55, 649 N.E.2d 1199 (1995); see § 420.

[57] The rate of interest is the subject of a separate section, § 412.

[58] J. D'Addario & Co., Inc. v. Embassy Industries, Inc., 20 N.Y.3d 113, 957 N.Y.S.2d 275, 980 N.E.2d 940 (2012) (NYSLD No. 638).

D'Addario could be used as authority to permit parties to a contract to waive their statutory rights to category II and category III interest.

Examining the relatively large number of recent decisions addressing interest, it is apparent that the statutory interest rate of 9% in CPLR 5004 is well worth a fight in our current economic times. These cases also demonstrate that the transactional lawyers who draft agreements can provide a valuable service to their clients if they are knowledgeable concerning the workings of Article 50 of the CPLR.

§ 412. Rate of Interest

Sections 5001 through 5003 provide for when interest is to be allowed. The rate of interest to be applied, however, is left to CPLR 5004.[1]

Prior to 1972, CPLR 5004 adopted and applied the so-called "legal" rate, i.e., the prevalent rate applicable to ordinary commercial loans. That rate was supplied by section 5–501 of the General Obligations Law, commonly known as the usury statute. In later years, that statute did not set a straight rate for interest, leaving it instead to the State Banking Board[2] to set from time to time in response to current economic conditions.[3] For a time before 1972, therefore, the rate applicable to litigated obligations, as supplied through adoption by CPLR 5004, was the prevalent loan rate applicable during the period that the particular obligation was outstanding. If there were several different rates applicable during its life, because of periodic statutory or Banking Board changes, several computations would be made so as to use each applicable rate for each applicable period. The procedure posed no serious problems and had the merit of keeping the litigation rate the same as the current "legal" rate, thus offering neither benefit nor detriment to, for example, one defaulting on a loan. The defaulter would ordinarily pay the same rate after default and a judgment (governed by CPLR 5004) as it had contracted to pay before it.

In 1972, however, CPLR 5004 was amended to supply a straight 6% rate and to discontinue the practice of adopting the current legal rate. Subsequently, in 1981, the rate was raised to 9% where it still stands now. The amendment's assumption was apparently that there would be no serious commercial disadvantage in applying a different rate in litigation than had been stipulated in a contract between the parties. It is at least theoretically incongruous, however, to reward a defaulting debtor, who has borrowed money on a promise to pay 12% interest, by charging him 3% less for the money after he defaults. Furthermore, it is difficult to justify imposing a 9% interest on unpaid personal injury judgments in our current economic climate. That is how things work out, though, with perhaps one important exception:

In categories II and III, discussed in the prior section, the 9% rate of CPLR 5004 applies without variation and does so on all money claims once reduced to a verdict or decision,[4] or to a judgment.[5] In those categories, the 9% governs whether the money claim arose at law or in equity, in contract or in tort. In category I, however, some

---

[1]   An exception is the money claim arising in equity, in which category I interest, as governed by CPLR 5001(a), is fixed by the court in its discretion. Category II and III interest, however, is at the CPLR 5004 rate even in equity cases.

[2]   Superintendent of Financial Services today.

[3]   See Banking Law § 14–a.

[4]   CPLR 5002.

[5]   CPLR 5003.

variations must be noted. If the money claim arose in equity (few do),[6] interest from accrual until verdict, if allowed at all, will be at whatever rate the court's discretion dictates.[7] The nice question that arises in category I concerns the law action consisting of a money claim based on contract.

Can the contract itself fix a different rate than that allowed by CPLR 5004? An important appellate division decision in 1975, Astoria Federal Savings and Loan Association v. Rambalakos,[8] held that it can. In 2011, the Court of Appeals reached the same conclusion in NML Capital v. Republic of Argentina,[9] which unambiguously holds that a contract can recite that its stipulated interest rate will apply not merely to interest on the claim until verdict or decision (CPLR 5001, category I interest) and on the verdict or decision until the entry of judgment (CPLR 5002, category II interest), but on the judgment itself (CPLR 5003, category III interest) until the judgment is paid. It is merely a matter of the contract so providing clearly. Using language to the effect that the contract rate will govern "until the principal is paid" will do the job of assuring the contract rate in all three categories of interest. A lender's draftsman should consider using similar language in the contract if the point is open to negotiation and the contract rate is being set higher than the CPLR 5004 litigation rate, while the borrower possessed of any bargaining power should go along with such a provision only if the proposed contract rate is lower than the CPLR 5004 rate.

The lender must of course see to it that the contract stipulates a rate no greater than the current usury rate,[10] so as to insulate the transaction from a charge of usury and, under New York law, lose it all.[11] Adopting the contractual language in *NML Capital* will at least secure to the lender the higher interest rate set by the contract. Failing to do that can bring about a substantial forfeiture of interest, as it did in one case in which the interest lost came to $17,000.[12]

What interest rate applies to a foreign judgment after it has been converted into a New York judgment: the New York 9% or the rate the foreign law prescribes? In an 1887 decision, Wells, Fargo & Co. v. Davis,[13] the Court of Appeals held for the New York rate, but in Hospital Service Plan of New Jersey v. Warehouse Production & Sales Employees

---

[6] An example would be a judgment awarding specific performance of a contract to convey land, with incidental damages caused by the delay in conveying.

[7] CPLR 5001(a).

[8] Astoria Federal Sav. and Loan Ass'n v. Rambalakos, 49 A.D.2d 715, 372 N.Y.S.2d 689 (2d Dep't 1975) (involving bond and mortgage specifying that interest would be at the rate of 8.5% "until the principal is fully paid"); see also Citibank, N.A. v. Liebowitz, 110 A.D.2d 615, 487 N.Y.S.2d 368 (2d Dep't 1985).

[9] NML Capital v. Republic of Argentina, 17 N.Y.3d 250, 928 N.Y.S.2d 666, 952 N.E.2d 482 (2011) (NYSLD No. 620).

[10] See Banking Law § 14–a(1).

[11] Gen. Oblig. Law §§ 5–521, 5–511(2); see Lloyd Capital Corp. v. Pat Henchar, Inc., 80 N.Y.2d 124, 127, 589 N.Y.S.2d 396, 398, 603 N.E.2d 246, 248 (1992).

[12] See Chipetine v. McEvoy, 238 A.D.2d 536, 657 N.Y.S.2d 88 (2d Dep't 1997) (SPR 78:4).

[13] Wells, Fargo & Co. v. Davis, 105 N.Y. 670, 12 N.E. 42 (1887); see Abu Dhabi Commercial Bank PJSC v. Saad Trading, Contracting and Financial Services Co., 117 A.D.3d 609, 613, 986 N.Y.S.2d 454, 459 (1st Dep't 2014) (New York's statutory post-judgment interest rate should apply to the English judgment domesticated in New York).

Union,[14] many years later, the Second Department held for the foreign rate. Other cases then joined the fray and the issue is now in conflict.[15]

The "except" clause in CPLR 5004 is a reminder that if a different rate of interest is set in any particular kind of case or situation, CPLR 5004 defers to it. A low rate of interest is set on certain judgments against municipalities, for example.[16] A number of other statutes, whether providing for 9% as does CPLR 5004, or a lower rate, do not simply prescribe the rate but provide that the interest awarded "shall not exceed" the stated rate. For a long while, the courts appeared to be disregarding the qualification and just applying the stated rate outright. This practice was overturned by the Court of Appeals in 1997 in Rodriguez v. New York City Housing Authority,[17] a case involving the 9% rate specified in section 157(5) of the Public Housing Law, governing housing authorities. Holding that the 9% in that situation is just a maximum, the Court remanded the case for the trial court to determine what an appropriate rate would be within the maximum.

Because a number of similar statutes stipulating a rate for other entities do so in the same "shall not exceed" language that section 157(5) does—like section 3–a of the General Municipal Law for municipalities in general, and section 16 of the State Finance Law for the state itself, each stipulating 9% but with the "shall not exceed" qualification—the issue became a controversial one. Some of the "shall not exceed" statutes have maximums even less than 9%, with some as low as 3% or 4%. Under *Rodriguez*, an application of any of these statutes now requires a determination, apparently on a case-by-case basis, of an appropriate rate to choose—within the stated maximum—for the period involved. In determining that rate in a given case, must equity opportunities (i.e., not just fixed obligations, such as government bonds) be considered by the court? A divided Court of Appeals said yes in Denio v. State.[18]

When a federal judgment has been converted into a New York judgment through the transcripting procedure,[19] and enforcement now proceeds in the New York State courts, which rate of interest applies to the judgment: New York's 9%, or the federal rate, which is substantially lower? The Second Department in Hartman v. Morganstern, a legal malpractice action, observed that "there is no case law or statute requiring a New York State court to apply the Federal interest rate as opposed to the higher New York State interest rate" when a federal judgment is docketed in a New York State court, which suggests that a creditor with an unpaid federal judgment should resort to the New York transcripting procedure pronto.[20] What is there to lose?

---

[14]   Hospital Service Plan of New Jersey v. Warehouse Production & Sales Emp. Union, 76 A.D.2d 882, 429 N.Y.S.2d 31 (2d Dep't 1980) (where interest on New Jersey judgment was 8%, rather than 6% New York rate existing at that time, judgment debtor required to pay higher rate to satisfy judgment).

[15]   See the summary in SPR 21:3.

[16]   See Gen. Mun. Law § 3–a; 3d Rep. Leg. Doc. No. 17, p. 92 (1959).

[17]   Rodriguez v. New York City Housing Authority, 91 N.Y.2d 76, 666 N.Y.S.2d 1009, 689 N.E.2d 903 (1997).

[18]   Denio v. State, 7 N.Y.3d 159, 818 N.Y.S.2d 802, 851 N.E.2d 1153 (2006) (NYSLD No. 560).

[19]   See CPLR 5018(b); § 422.

[20]   Hartman v. Morganstern, 28 A.D.3d 423, 814 N.Y.S.2d 169 (2d Dep't 2006) (SPR 176:2). In FCS Advisors, Inc. v. Fair Finance Co., Inc., 605 F.3d 144 (2d Cir. 2010) (SPR 222:2), the court held that for post-judgment interest in a federal action, the federal rate governs unless the parties in "clear, unambiguous and unequivocal language" stipulate otherwise. See also Schipani v. McLeod, 541 F.3d 158, 164–65 (2d Cir. 2008) (noting that "[i]n a diversity case, state law governs the award of prejudgment interest" but "[i]n contrast, post-judgment interest is governed by federal statute").

If enforcement of the judgment proceeds in federal court, the Second Circuit has ruled that "federal district courts must apply the federal rate of post-judgment interest to judgments rendered in diversity actions, even when those judgments have been docketed in state court."[21] The court also expressly noted, however, that it was not addressing whether federal law preempted the application of New York's post-judgment interest rates in state court enforcement proceedings.[22]

Should the interest rate depend on the nature of the claim underlying the federal judgment? In Turner v. CSX Transportation, Inc.,[23] involving a claim under the Federal Employers Liability Act that was tried and went to judgment in state court, the court held interest a substantive issue and that the federal rate should therefore apply. The *Turner* court cited the U.S. Supreme Court's 1988 decision in Monessen Southwestern Ry. Co. v. Morgan,[24] which held so with respect to prejudgment interest. *Turner* says a similar rule should be applied to post-judgment interest.[25]

C. FEES, COSTS, AND DISBURSEMENTS

Table of Sections

§ 413.   Fees, Costs, and Disbursements, Generally

§ 414.   Costs

§ 414A.   "Frivolity" Sanctions

§ 415.   Disbursements

§ 416.   Taxation of Costs and Disbursements

§ 417.   Form of Judgment

§ 413. Fees, Costs, and Disbursements, Generally

Fees are sums fixed by statute for the taking of various steps in litigation. They are usually payable to the county clerk or a court-related officer for the taking of some official step, but the article that provides for them, Article 80 of the CPLR, sets up a fee schedule for a variety of other things as well. A perusal of the article, vast and varied though it is, will offer a quick perspective of it. When it is the business of the person to whom the fee is payable to collect it, such as the clerk of the court, the sheriff, a stenographer, etc., that official can be trusted to advise the party of precisely what the fee is. (While it may be better to give than to receive, the receiver usually has the better memory of what's due.) When the recipient is someone less knowledgeable, the party may have to be a little more punctilious about checking about fees. A subpoenaed witness must be paid a fee,[1] for example, and many a witness is not initially aware of this requirement. If the witness learns of it later, however, and before the subpoena's return day, his nonappearance is not likely to be punished for contempt if the fee was not duly tendered.

The fees of the clerk for the performance of various acts are among those covered by Article 80. The fee for the assignment of an index number to the case, for example, is in

---

[21]   Cappiello v. ICD Publications, Inc., 720 F.3d 109, 112 (2d Cir. 2013).

[22]   *Cappiello*, 720 F.3d at 113 n.4.

[23]   Turner v. CSX Transportation, Inc., 23 Misc. 3d 527, 878 N.Y.S.2d 543 (Sup. Ct., Erie County 2009) (SPR 206:2).

[24]   Monessen Southwestern Ry. Co. v. Morgan, 486 U.S. 330, 108 S. Ct. 1837, 100 L. Ed. 2d 349 (1988).

[25]   *Turner*, 23 Misc. 3d at 529–30, 878 N.Y.S.2d at 545.

[1]   CPLR 8001; see § 383.

CPLR 8018(a); for making a motion or placing a case on the calendar, in CPLR 8020(a); for demanding a trial by jury, in CPLR 8020(c); etc. Fees for doing identical acts may differ between and among counties, especially between urban and rural ones, under either some CPLR provision or under a local law. A constitutional attack on geographical discrepancies of this kind in New York, based on both due process and equal protection grounds, was rejected and the differences held permissible.[2] Courts that have their own court acts (all courts of original jurisdiction do except the supreme and county courts) may have their own fee schedules.[3] These prevail over the fee schedules of Article 80 of the CPLR to the extent of any inconsistency.[4]

Costs and disbursements differ from "fees." Briefly, costs are an arbitrary statutory sum that the winner gets from the loser. Disbursements are the winner's out-of-pocket expenses (as a general rule not including an attorney's fee) that are also recovered from the loser. Ensuing sections elaborate.

§ 414. Costs

"Costs" under the CPLR are an arbitrary figure generally allowed the winner against the loser. They are designed as solace to the winner for the trouble and expense of litigation, theoretically engendered by her adversary's failure to deal with her fairly. They are not, as is sometimes thought, a substitute for an attorney's fee or even a theoretical equivalent.[1] Attorney's fees, the major expense of a litigant, are not generally recoverable in American jurisprudence, and New York follows the mainstream. Attorney's fees may be awarded, along with other sanctions,[2] for frivolous conduct in litigation, but this should not be confused with an award of attorney's fees merely as a part of the winner's recovery.

In a few selected categories of action, the legislature has varied the general rule and allowed an attorney's fee, such as in class actions[3] and in certain actions against the state or its agencies under the "Equal Access to Justice Act."[4] A notable example of Congress's authorizing attorney's fees is in federal civil rights litigation,[5] jurisdiction of which is concurrent in both federal and state courts[6] and in both the fee provision is applicable.

The failure to make it a general rule to include an attorney's fee in the winner's recovery is often criticized. A study by the Judicial Conference in 1971, for example, dug into the issue and came up with ameliorative recommendations, which got nowhere. The

---

[2] See Manes v. Goldin, 400 F. Supp. 23 (E.D.N.Y. 1975) (Three-Judge District Court), aff'd, 423 U.S. 1068, 96 S. Ct. 851, 47 L. Ed. 2d 80 (1976).

[3] See, for example, § 1911 in each of the New York City Civil, Uniform District, Uniform City, and Uniform Justice Court Acts, McKinney's Vol. 29A, Parts 2 and 3.

[4] CPLR 101.

[1] See Harlan v. Weiner, 80 Misc. 2d 723, 364 N.Y.S.2d 270 (N.Y. City Civ. Ct. 1974).

[2] See § 414A.

[3] CPLR 909.

[4] CPLR Article 86. A fee will not be awarded if the state's position is found "substantially justified" or "special circumstances make an award unjust." CPLR 8601; see Fried, *Attorneys' Fees Against the State: The Equal Access to Justice Act,* N.Y.L.J., Apr. 2, 1990, at 1.

[5] See 42 U.S.C.A. § 1988.

[6] See 42 U.S.C.A. § 1983.

study justly criticized "costs" in this country, including New York, as "a monumental absurdity."[7] When we see a bit later the amount of those costs, we can accept the epithet.

We should first discuss when costs are allowed, which is the mission of Article 81 of the CPLR, and then discuss their amount, as separately supplied by Article 82.

The party who wins the judgment gets costs against the loser unless statute says otherwise or the court determines that on the facts of the particular case it would not be fair to allow costs.[8] That's the rule applicable at trial level when the case is disposed of, and a similar rule governs costs on an appeal.[9] Costs on a motion are discretionary with the court.[10]

The court can deny costs to the winner, either at trial or appellate level, and can do so on any ground that touches discretion, such as where a brief is found inadequate on the one hand[11] or too long on the other.[12] If the court finds warrant for it on the facts, it can not only deny costs to the winner, but make the winner pay costs to the loser.[13]

The common procedure is for the winner to draw up a bill of costs and submit it to the clerk, who peruses it for accuracy and includes the sum in the judgment if it passes muster.[14] This procedure is known as "taxing" costs.[15]

If P's claim against D fails without reaching the merits, as where it has been dismissed for want of jurisdiction, and costs are awarded to D against P in conjunction with that dismissal, a later action by P against D on the same claim will be stayed until the costs are paid.[16]

If D has interposed a counterclaim and lost on it while P has lost on the main claim, both parties being losers, D is ordinarily deemed the prevailing party so as to get costs, but the court can vary that, too, if need be.[17] If P sues A and B, and prevails against A, but not B, P ordinarily gets costs against A while B gets them against P.[18]

Article 81 also has the provision that denies costs to the winner in a money action if the damages awarded show that the claim was sued on in too high a court and could have been brought in a lower one. To get costs in a supreme court action, for example, P must recover at least $6,000 if the case was brought in any county in New York City,[19] the theory being that if P does not recover at least that much, the case should have been brought in the New York City Civil Court. Outside New York City, where there is

---

[7]   Crane, Adequacy of Costs Allowable in Litigation, 16th Jud. Conf. Rep. 246–47 (1971). The Judicial Conference is now the Office of Court Administration. See § 5.

[8]   CPLR 8101.

[9]   CPLR 8107.

[10]   CPLR 8106.

[11]   Tsomis v. Benenson, 23 A.D.2d 654, 257 N.Y.S.2d 894 (1st Dep't 1965).

[12]   Tri-State Pipe Lines Corp. v. Sinclair Refining Co., 24 A.D.2d 756, 264 N.Y.S.2d 138 (1st Dep't 1965).

[13]   See, e.g., Schiff v. Loomer, 23 A.D.2d 481, 255 N.Y.S.2d 482 (1st Dep't 1965).

[14]   See § 417 for a form of judgment including costs.

[15]   Taxation of costs and the procedure for having the court review the costs is discussed in § 416.

[16]   See, e.g., Prudential Oil Corp. v. Phillips Petroleum Co., 83 A.D.2d 453, 445 N.Y.S.2d 438 (1st Dep't 1981), where the earlier costs award to D was in a federal court.

[17]   See Michaels v. Cooper, 245 A.D.2d 1103, 666 N.Y.S.2d 92 (4th Dep't 1997).

[18]   Montague v. Hunt, 50 Misc. 2d 442, 270 N.Y.S.2d 771 (Sup. Ct., Greene County 1966).

[19]   CPLR 8102(1).

generally a wider variety of lower courts to pick from, the minimum recovery in order for the winner to get costs in a supreme court action is $500.[20]

It should be noted that an award of costs in an appellate court does not mean costs in all courts unless the appellate court so provides in the particular case.[21] A litigant in doubt in this regard should secure a clarification from the appellate court, such as with a motion to clarify or resettle the dispositive order. Furthermore, the supreme court cannot order a party to pay the cost of printing the appellate record. These costs must be awarded in the appellate context in the decision on appeal.[22]

The amount of costs is supplied by Article 82 of the CPLR. Perusing the sums allowed confirms that while they are not as nominal as they used to be,[23] they have no relationship at all to the actual cost of litigation. In an action in the supreme court, for example, costs are $200 if the case terminates before the note of issue is filed, an additional $200 if it terminates after that, but before the trial, and an additional $300, for a grand total of $700, if the case has gone to trial.[24] In the lower courts, there may be different costs schedules, just as there may be different fee schedules.[25]

Motion costs, if awarded, may not exceed $100.[26]

The costs provisions applicable to an action also apply to a special proceeding.[27]

Another phenomenon distinct from costs, but relevant to them, is known as "security for costs." This is a device ordinarily used against a nonresident plaintiff to make sure that if the plaintiff loses the case he will not return home and leave the defendant with a costs judgment that can be enforced only in the plaintiff's home state. Security for costs is provided for by Article 85 of the CPLR. The defendant ordinarily seeks it by ex parte motion,[28] which if granted requires the plaintiff to furnish a $500 bond in New York City ($250 elsewhere).[29] The initial penalty for not furnishing the bond is a stay of the plaintiff's action, but it can ripen into an outright dismissal.[30] There is no time limit on when a defendant can move for security for costs.[31]

§ 414A. "Frivolity" Sanctions

The sanction of an attorney's fee and other costs and expenses and even a punitive money penalty for a frivolous litigation practice became a vigorous and controversial

---

[20] CPLR 8102(2).

[21] See Barton Realty Corp. v. Mangan, 25 A.D.2d 730, 268 N.Y.S.2d 869 (1st Dep't 1966).

[22] Derr v. Fleming, 108 A.D.3d 854, 855–56, 970 N.Y.S.2d 100, 102 (3d Dep't 2013).

[23] They were increased in 1989.

[24] CPLR 8201.

[25] See, e.g., Article 19 in the New York City Civil Court Act and in the Uniform District, City, and Justice Court Acts, McKinney's Vol. 29A, Parts 2 and 3.

[26] CPLR 8202. Appellate costs are provided in CPLR 8203–8204.

[27] City of Buffalo v. J. W. Clement Co., 28 N.Y.2d 241, 263, 321 N.Y.S.2d 345, 364, 269 N.E.2d 895, 908 (1971); see Meehan v. Nassau Community College, 242 A.D.2d 155, 159, 675 N.Y.S.2d 354, 357 (2d Dep't 1998) (special proceeding to confirm an arbitration award).

[28] CPLR 8501(a).

[29] CPLR 8503.

[30] CPLR 8502.

[31] Cie Noga, S.A. v. Heather Financial Corp., 130 Misc. 2d 1086, 1088, 498 N.Y.S.2d 985, 987 (Sup. Ct., New York County 1986).

topic in the mid-1980s with the adoption of CPLR 8303–a and afterwards Part 130–1 of the Rules of the Chief Administrator.

Before that, the most common and most visible source of an award of attorney's fees seen in New York practice was the penalty imposed against a party as a condition for getting out from under a default.[1] The situation there is that a party has been guilty of so serious a default that the court, on motion of the other side, has clear power to make the default stick. Doing so, however, exacts a forfeiture of the party's claim or defense and is often viewed by the judges as too severe, a draconian requisition that penalizes the client for what is most often the fault of the lawyer. The judicial predilection in this category has therefore been to excuse the default, but only on the condition that the defaulter's lawyer pay the other side (or some worthy outside source like the Lawyers' Fund for Client Protection)[2] a sum of money commensurate with the defaulter's delay and his proffered excuse. The court may require the lawyer to pay this out of pocket, not to be reimbursed by the client, or may allot it between client and lawyer.

Pleading defaults have been the most common illustration of this,[3] but they are not the only ones. Defaults in connection with a bill of particulars under CPLR 3042,[4] disclosure under CPLR 3126,[5] a failure to prosecute under CPLR 3216,[6] and calendar calls under CPLR 3404,[7] are other examples. The money sanction in this category is a penalty imposed on the offender almost as a favor—a slap on the wrist offered in lieu of capital punishment. Considering that a malpractice action and disciplinary proceedings can confront the lawyer if the default sticks, this appraisal is no exaggeration. The offense has reached the stage, in other words, at which the court has clear statutory power to impose a full default, and implicit in that ultimate power is the power to do something less. The something less is the attorney's fee imposed as a condition for excusing the default. (The defaulter can always refuse the condition and accept the default!)

These sources of attorney's fees remain intact and active. Quite another source today is the attorney's fee imposed for a "frivolous" litigation practice. The defaults just enumerated can often themselves qualify as frivolous conduct, of course, but separate and apart from them, and standing on its own, is what the bar has come to know outright as the "frivolity" sanction of Part 130–1 and CPLR 8303–a.

After the Second Department Appellate Division handed down two cases in 1985, holding that the courts have "inherent" power to impose the sanction of an attorney's fee for a "frivolous" litigation practice,[8] the Court of Appeals rejected the conclusion as

---

[1] As noted in § 414, attorney's fees are not generally recoverable in New York practice except in a few special categories. In those categories, they are assessed by the court as part of the victory. The attorney's fees that are the subject of the present section are imposed after special findings of misconduct by the lawyer or client in connection with the litigation itself.

[2] See, e.g., McLoughlin v. Henke, 130 Misc. 2d 1091, 499 N.Y.S.2d 332 (Sup. Ct., Queens County 1986), one of the first cases to designate the fund the recipient of a "default" sanction.

[3] See § 231.

[4] See § 241.

[5] See § 367.

[6] See § 375.

[7] See § 376.

[8] Gabrelian v. Gabrelian, 108 A.D.2d 445, 489 N.Y.S.2d 914 (2d Dep't 1985), so held of courts of original jurisdiction for the bringing of frivolous actions. LTown Ltd. Partnership v. Sire Plan, Inc., 108 A.D.2d 435, 489 N.Y.S.2d 567 (2d Dep't 1985), aff'd as modified, 69 N.Y.2d 670, 511 N.Y.S.2d 840, 503 N.E.2d 1377 (1986), so held of appellate courts with respect to frivolous appeals.

premature. It held in A.G. Ship Maintenance Corp. v. Lezak[9] that it was not yet necessary to decide whether courts have "inherent" power to impose frivolity sanctions because it perceived the courts as having such authority through rule-making powers delegated by the legislature.[10] It also held that whatever the source of such a power, it should not be exercised on an "ad hoc" basis, but only by a "plenary rule" containing guideposts and standards.

Meanwhile, in 1985, the legislature enacted and in 1986 amended and expanded CPLR 8303–a, a statute that unequivocally authorizes attorney's fees in the "frivolity" category in designated tort actions—the usual unintentional torts: personal injury, property damage, and wrongful death cases, including those based on medical malpractice. CPLR 8303–a permits a court to award "costs and reasonable attorneys' fees" of up to $10,000 against any party found to have interposed a frivolous claim or defense in such an action. CPLR 8303–a did not (and still does not) apply to other categories of action, however, such as contract, corporate, commercial, property, or matrimonial actions, or to special proceedings. Part 130–1 of the Rules was designed to remedy that.

Part 130–1 was first circulated by the Office of Court Administration in July of 1987, calling for comment from bench and bar.[11] Among the responders were some legislators who asked OCA to hold up on the rule until the legislature had a chance to look into it. OCA obliged, and the originally proposed effective date of January 1, 1988, was put off. When the 1988 legislative session passed with no action, OCA returned to the rule, redrafted it after considering the comments that the initial circulation had elicited, and promulgated it with a January 1, 1989, effective date. It took effect on that day and has been doing its work ever since.

Much of the agitation over CPLR 8303–a, which was a controversial subject from the outset, gave way to greater agitation when Part 130–1 entered the scene, a tumult akin to that enveloping Rule 11 of the Federal Rules of Civil Procedure, on which, indeed, important parts of Part 130–1 are modeled.[12]

A number of points must be made about Part 130–1, in the course of which we will coordinate it with CPLR 8303–a.

1. The rule authorizes two distinct categories of money punishment for frivolous conduct. The first, generally referred to as "costs," awards costs and reasonable attorney's fees that reimburse actual expenses incurred by the other side because of the frivolous conduct. This is best described as a "compensatory" award. The second, which is the one that officially gets the name "sanction," is a separate money assessment imposed as a punishment for the frivolous conduct. This is best described as a "punitive" award. At the outset, a $10,000 cap applied to both categories together.[13] An amendment

---

[9] A.G. Ship Maintenance Corp. v. Lezak, 69 N.Y.2d 1, 511 N.Y.S.2d 216, 503 N.E.2d 681 (1986).

[10] The Court cited Article VI, § 30, of the State Constitution and § 211(1)(b) of the Jud. Law as the source.

[11] It was originally numbered Part 130, but renumbered Subpart 130–1 afterwards. In the text, it is referred to as Part 130–1.

[12] See Chase, *Sanctions in State Courts*, N.Y.L.J., Oct. 22, 1987, at 1, in which the view is expressed that "the disadvantages of judicial sanctions are likely to outweigh the advantages" and that "the federal experience [on which the New York rule is built] is not comforting."

[13] An early case imposing the full $10,000 is Winters v. Gould, 143 Misc. 2d 44, 539 N.Y.S.2d 686 (Sup. Ct., New York County 1989), applying it against a tricky character who used the delays of the court system to live rent free off several landlords.

that took effect March 1, 1998, retains the cap on the punitive award but removes it from the compensatory award.

2.   The "costs" (compensatory award) go to the person—party or lawyer—who sustained the expense caused by the frivolous conduct. The "sanction" (punitive award) has a different destination: if the money is assessed against the party, it goes to the clerk for deposit into the public treasury; if it's assessed against the lawyer, it goes to the Lawyers' Fund for Client Protection, the fund set up to recompense the victims of dishonest lawyers.

3.   The assessment may be made against either the party, the attorney, or both, wherever the court finds the fault to lie. When it is made against the attorney, the rule provides that

> it may be against the attorney personally or upon a partnership, firm, corporation, government agency, prosecutor's office, legal aid society or public defender's office with which the attorney is associated . . . .

Is an insurer subject to the Part 130–1 sanction? In Saastomoinen v. Pagano,[14] the supreme court held that in personal injury litigation, where the defendant's insurer supplies and controls the defense, the insurer is the real party in interest and may therefore be subjected to the sanctions provisions, CPLR 8303–a and Part 130–1. The court thereupon imposed a sanction directly on the insurer for refusing to concede liability on clear-cut facts and forcing the case to trial. The appellate division reversed, however, rejecting the lower court's "real party in interest" theory and holding that the insurer is not a party and hence not subject to the sanctions rule.[15]

The case posed a problem mainly because it stood as a barrier against something many judges deemed important in tort litigation: the power to require the defendant's insurer to attend a settlement conference. A rule afterwards promulgated by the Office of Court Administration conferred that power on the court in specific terms. Uniform Rule 202.26(e) provides that "the court may order parties, representatives of parties, representatives of insurance carriers or persons having an interest in any settlement, including those holding liens on any settlement or verdict, to also attend in person or telephonically at the settlement conference." The failure to attend can lead to a sanction against the insured, as illustrated in Perez-Wilson v. McPhee.[16] In Carnegie Associates Ltd. v. Miller,[17] the supreme court granted defendants' motion to dismiss the plaintiff's complaint and to strike the reply to their counterclaims due to plaintiff's failure to proceed with a court-ordered mediation. The First Department modified, concluding that "neither CPLR 3126 nor Uniform Rule 202.26(e) authorizes such a sanction in these circumstances."

Unfortunately, the penalty prescribed in Uniform Rule 202.26(e) for a failure to comply with its attendance requirements is inadequate, noting only that it may be deemed a default under CPLR 3404. That's the provision that would allow the striking of the case from the trial calendar, something that neither plaintiff nor defendant should suffer if an insurer fails to attend a pretrial conference.

---

[14]   Saastomoinen v. Pagano, 183 Misc. 2d 781, 704 N.Y.S.2d 796 (Sup. Ct., Nassau County 2000).

[15]   Saastomoinen v. Pagano, 278 A.D.2d 218, 717 N.Y.S.2d 274 (2d Dep't 2000). See SPR 92:2; SPR 102:2.

[16]   Perez-Wilson v. McPhee, 23 Misc. 3d 1053, 874 N.Y.S.2d 779 (Sup. Ct., New York County 2009).

[17]   Carnegie Associates Ltd. v. Miller, 94 A.D.3d 404, 946 N.Y.S.2d 107 (1st Dep't 2012) (SPR 241:3).

4. Note the inclusion of the "government agency" in the rule. That includes not only those agencies that have their own legal staffs, but also those that the Attorney-General's office represents in court.[18]

5. On the punitive segment of Part 130–1, there is yet a further consideration. If it is strictly punitive, as it appears to be, there may be difficulty about applying it not only against the State, but even against municipalities,[19] although its application to the individual lawyers who represent the state or municipality is apparently permissible.

6. The rule's target of any "frivolous conduct" at all in litigation means that it includes not just a frivolous claim or defense, but a frivolous motion, appeal, or any other piece of conduct that can earn the ignominious "frivolity" label. In this regard, which can prove to be an important one, it differs from CPLR 8303–a. Coordinating 8303–a with Part 130–1 poses some questions.

7. Under CPLR 8303–a, sanctions are imposable only for a frivolous claim or defense. In tort cases governed by CPLR 8303–a, there was some doubt at the outset whether Part 130–1 could also be applied in those cases, thereby authorizing sanctions for (e.g.) a frivolous motion or other conduct. Subdivision 5 of Part 130–1 says that the rule "shall not apply to requests for costs or attorney's fees subject to the provisions of CPLR 8303–a." At first glance that seems to say that Part 130–1 doesn't apply in the tort cases at all, so that nothing but a frivolous claim or defense would do the job in those cases. But the exception[20] says that what the rule doesn't apply to is a "request" subject to CPLR 8303–a, and the only "request" subject to that provision is one relating to a claim or defense. Since a request relating to something like a motion or appeal or other step is not subject to CPLR 8303–a, one may conclude that Part 130–1 is free to operate on these other things in tort cases. Since many cases in which Part 130–1 sanctions have been applied are tort cases that also fall under CPLR 8303–a, the expansive interpretation suggested is apparently the interpretation followed. This is no small matter.

8. Whatever definitive answer the courts may give the question in tort cases, the courts clearly have the power to address any kind of frivolous conduct in other actions (contract, commercial, property, matrimonial, etc.), where there is no CPLR 8303–a to confuse matters.

9. There are some other exceptions to take note of. The rule does not apply in the small claims parts[21] or to certain proceedings in the family court.[22]

---

[18] There is some doubt about whether the rule applies to the State itself, as when the State is sued for money in an ordinary court of claims action. In authorizing costs and sanctions, Part 130.1 says the rule applies "except where prohibited by law." Section 27 of the Court of Claims Act bars costs and attorney's fees in a court of claims suit. So clear was this barrier in legislative thinking, in fact, that it took an amendment of § 27 in 1987 to refer to CPLR 8303–a explicitly, a statutory sanctions provision. It was thought that without the amendment, § 27 would be a barrier to the application of CPLR 8303–a in the court of claims. It would seem to follow that if an unamended § 27 would have barred the sanctions contained in a statute, it would a fortiori bar those promulgated in a mere rule like Part 130–1. And the language of § 27 would seem to erect the barrier in both directions, i.e., preclude an assessment against any party to the court of claims suit, not just the State.

[19] See and compare the Court of Appeals decision in Sharapata v. Town of Islip, 56 N.Y.2d 332, 452 N.Y.S.2d 347, 437 N.E.2d 1104 (1982).

[20] Part 130–1.5.

[21] There are small claims parts in the New York City Civil Court and in each of the district and city courts. See §§ 581–583. In the town and village courts, which also have small claims parts, the rule does not apply at all—to the small claims or any other part. (Most of the judges of those courts are not lawyers.)

[22] Part 130–1.1.

10. The fact that a "proceeding" as well as an action is included means that special proceedings are included. That embraces Article 78 proceedings contesting administrative action, where a finding that a determination was "arbitrary and capricious" is among the grounds for overturning a determination.[23] It's interesting to speculate whether there is any appreciable difference between "arbitrary and capricious" on the one hand and "frivolous" on the other? If there isn't, the agency or its lawyer would be sanctionable whenever the determination is rejected as arbitrary and capricious. (Needless to say, that hasn't been the conclusion reached, but the idea does lend a light note to break up this dark discourse on sanctions).

11. The summary proceeding (the landlord-tenant device) is a category of special proceeding and is included in Part 130–1.[24] Summary proceedings are brought in the hundreds of thousands annually. Especially when based on non-payment of rent, they often meet defenses that can qualify as frivolous—the obvious product of desperation of a tenant, simply unable to pay, who will interpose anything the imagination can conjure up to keep a roof over the family for the time being, but:

12. All awards under Part 130–1 lie in the court's discretion. That discretion may have a special role to play in summary and other proceedings that often involve disadvantaged parties.

13. The first-tier appellate court retains the power of plenary review of any sanction imposed, as to the facts, the law, and the court's discretion. The sometimes vilified interlocutory appeal[25] may prove a hero on this scene, standing by to facilitate appellate review of an individual judge's action under Part 130–1 should it be perceived as excessive in a given case.

A serious problem with the appellate step under the sanctions rule is pointed out in Honeycrest Holdings, Ltd. v. Integrated Brands, Inc.,[26] in which P's law firm was sanctioned by the trial judge for falsifying a temporary restraining order. The sanction had been imposed by the court on its own motion, not the opposing party's (D), and when P appealed the sanction order, D did not oppose the appeal. This left no one to argue in the appellate division in support of the sanction, resulting in a reversal which cancelled the sanction with the statement that

[u]nder the circumstances of this case, the Supreme Court improvidently exercised its discretion in imposing sanctions upon the appellants [the sanctioned lawyers].

Honeycrest manifests how the rule's invitation to the judge to act sua sponte in the application of a sanction can be frustrated through the simple fact of an unopposed appeal.

14. Neither costs nor sanctions can be the product of a moment's judicial whim or bad temper. Part 130–1.2 permits the award

---

[23] CPLR 7803(3). See § 561.

[24] Indeed, Part 130–1.4 makes sure that the powers conferred by the rule belong also to the judges of the Housing Part of the New York City Civil Court.

[25] See § 526. An interlocutory appeal implies the appeal of an order that disposes of some intermediate step in the case, short of a final judgment.

[26] Honeycrest Holdings, Ltd. v. Integrated Brands, Inc., 283 A.D.2d 398, 723 N.Y.S.2d 892 (2d Dep't 2001).

only upon a written decision setting forth the conduct . . ., the reasons why the court found the conduct to be frivolous, and the reasons why the court found the amount awarded or imposed to be appropriate.

15. The rule requires that the sum granted be entered as a judgment, which would seem to allow—if, indeed, it does not require—that it be a judgment separate from the judgment on the merits.

16. There must be "a reasonable opportunity to be heard" on the issue of a Part 130–1 award. So provides Part 130–1.1(d), but it says that the form of the hearing "shall depend upon the nature of the conduct and the circumstances of the case." This is a hedge. It avoids dictating any specific place or point as more appropriate to a hearing than any other. Presumably the court can order an immediate hearing on a costs or sanctions application, suspending further attention to the merits of the case while the hearing goes forward, or postpone it to some later point, perhaps depending on what the allegedly frivolous conduct affected (the whole case? just a defense? some incidental step like a motion? etc.).

A discussion of what kind of hearing is required appears in Bruckner v. Jaitor Apartments Co.,[27] where the court said that if a motion is made for sanctions, the return day of the motion is the hearing. Reviewing earlier cases, the court also noted that when the offense occurs right in front of the judge, no further hearing is necessary.

17. The award can be sought either by motion, or by cross-motion, or by the court on its own motion. It has been held that a request for sanctions may not be asserted as a separate claim.[28]

18. A key question throughout, of course, is what constitutes "frivolous" conduct. Part 130–1.1(c) defines frivolity to include conduct that is "completely without merit in law and cannot be supported by a reasonable argument for an extension, modification or reversal of existing law," language the gist of which is borrowed from Rule 11 of the Federal Rules of Civil Procedure. It also includes conduct taken "to delay . . . harass or maliciously injure another," and the assertion of "material factual statements that are false."

19. Lest it occur to a party to try to use Part 130–1 to harass the other side, another part of Part 130–1.1(c) includes as frivolous conduct the making of an unjustified frivolity motion under Part 130–1.

The drafters did not want to encourage some of the so-called "satellite" litigation that was generated by the federal provision. Some judges wearied of a practice they found all too common under the sanctions rule: cross-moving for a sanction as almost a "knee-jerk" reaction to a motion on the ground that the motion was frivolous. Often the frivolous step was not the motion that the cross-motion aimed at, but the cross-motion itself, the court in one case condemning the practice and punishing it.[29]

This kind of automatic reaction was discouraged in federal practice with the amendment of Rule 11 of the Federal Rules of Civil Procedure that introduced the so-called "safe-harbor" provision, under which motion papers for a sanction may be served

---

[27] Bruckner v. Jaitor Apartments Co., 147 Misc. 2d 796, 555 N.Y.S.2d 563 (N.Y. City Civ. Ct. 1990).

[28] See, e.g., Osborn v. Wemer, N.Y.L.J., Oct. 14, 2003, at 20, col.3 (Sup. Ct., Westchester County; Dillon, J.) (SPR 145:4).

[29] See Shelley v. Shelley, 180 Misc. 2d 275, 688 N.Y.S.2d 439 (Sup. Ct., Westchester County 1999).

right off, but can't be filed with the court for three weeks, giving the parties a chance to resolve the matter between themselves and spare the court (and themselves) the burden of yet another sanction motion.[30]

20. Yet another part of Part 130–1.1(c) requires the court to see whether "the conduct was continued when its lack of legal or factual basis was apparent, or was brought to the attention of counsel or the party." Thus a lawyer who was in any measure hoodwinked by the client, believing the claim, defense, motion (or whatever) meritorious at first and only later learning otherwise, is given a chance to discontinue the frivolous pursuit at that time. Doing so avoids the rule; failing to invokes it.

Is Part 130–1 an end run around the holding of Drago v. Buonagurio,[31] in which the Court of Appeals held in 1978 that even when a defendant is sued without any ground whatever, the defendant can't recover damages against the plaintiff's lawyer? The Court held that no existing theory of law would support such a claim, rejecting negligence, abuse of process, malicious prosecution, and "prima facie tort" theories, and rejecting as well an invitation to fashion a new theory to support the claim. The Court said that this would have to be done through legislation. Part 130–1 has in effect adopted, through judicial regulation, the "wrongful suit" claim that *Drago* rejected, and this appears to be all the more accurate a conclusion under the 1998 amendment that removed the $10,000 cap from the compensatory assessment allowed by the rule.

* * *

There has been a steady accumulation of cases applying Part 130–1 sanctions.

The Court of Appeals' first review of the rule occurred in Minister, Elders and Deacons of Reformed Protestant Dutch Church of City of New York v. 198 Broadway, Inc.,[32] where the Court imposed a $2,500 sanction for a frivolous appeal and dilatory conduct. After that, in Intercontinental Credit Corp. Div. of Pan American Trade Development Corp. v. Roth,[33] the Court imposed a $5,000 sanction for a frivolous motion to reargue.

In the lower courts the imposition of sanctions has ranged wide. A "vendetta" against the defendant occasioned a sanction of $2,000 in Jones v. Camar Realty Corp.,[34] where the court acted sua sponte in exacting $2,000 from the plaintiff's lawyer, whom it found to be on a vendetta not only against the defendant landlord but also, "it would seem, the courts." The occasion was the denial of a motion seeking reargument of a previously denied motion for leave to appeal an appellate term order. The lawyer threatened to prosecute unmeritorious claims against the landlord and make him spend lots of money defending them. The case was an early warning to parties and lawyers who may once have felt insulated in uttering threats like that.

---

[30]   See § 631 (Practitioner's Edition).

[31]   Drago v. Buonagurio, 46 N.Y.2d 778, 413 N.Y.S.2d 910, 386 N.E.2d 821 (1978).

[32]   Minister, Elders and Deacons of Reformed Protestant Dutch Church of City of New York v. 198 Broadway, Inc., 76 N.Y.2d 411, 559 N.Y.S.2d 866, 559 N.E.2d 429 (1990) (NYSLD No. 367).

[33]   Intercontinental Credit Corp. Div. of Pan American Trade Development Corp. v. Roth, 78 N.Y.2d 306, 574 N.Y.S.2d 528, 579 N.E.2d 688 (1991).

[34]   Jones v. Camar Realty Corp., 167 A.D.2d 285, 561 N.Y.S.2d 916 (1st Dep't 1990).

If the motive for interposing a claim is found to be malicious, the claimant has been held subject to the sanction of Part 130–1 even if the claim is found to have some colorable basis.[35]

Sexist comments directed against a female attorney in the course of a deposition brought a $1,000 sanction against the offender in Principe v. Assay Partners,[36] half being a compensatory assessment to cover the cost of the sanctions motion and the other half a punitive measure.

It has been held frivolous, and made the subject of a sanction, to take evasive steps to try to avoid the judge who has been assigned to the case. Such an attempt was made in International 800 Telecom Corp. v. Kramer, Levin, Nessen, Kamin & Frankel,[37] where a company was sued in New York County and lost. In an effort to undo the result (which was presumably destined to failure under the res judicata doctrine anyway), the company then brought another action, and, to avoid assignment to the same judge, brought it in Rockland County. The opposing parties then moved before the original judge in New York County to declare the Rockland action a related one and have it transferred back to New York. The motion was granted and a sanction imposed.

Under the separate Part 130–2, costs or a punitive sanction may be imposed for failing to show up, or for showing up late, at a scheduled court appearance. Under Part 130–2, however, the maximum is $2,500, and it caps both categories: costs and a punitive sanction together can't exceed $2,500 under that rule.[38]

Cases on Part 130–1 sanctions proliferate. The few noted in this section are a mere sampling.

The requirement that the actual signature of an attorney appear on "[e]very pleading, written motion, and other paper, served on another party or filed or submitted to the court" is also part of Part 130–1, where it appears in subdivision (a) of Part 130–1.1–a.[39] Subdivision (b) then provides that the signature constitutes an automatic certification by the signer "that, to the best of that person's knowledge, information and belief, formed after an inquiry reasonable under the circumstances, the presentation of the paper or the contentions therein are not frivolous." No actual certification form or ritual is required. The signing itself constitutes the certification, and a false certification of course grounds a sanction. That's why the signing requirement is contained in the sanctions rule itself: to stress the individual responsibility of the lawyer to make a reasonable effort to ascertain the truth or accuracy of the content of the paper signed.

The signing aspect of the rule is separately treated in the chapter on papers, met earlier.[40]

---

[35]   See Gordon v. Marrone, 202 A.D.2d 104, 616 N.Y.S.2d 98 (2d Dep't 1994) (SPR 29:3).

[36]   Principe v. Assay Partners, 154 Misc. 2d 702, 586 N.Y.S.2d 182 (Sup. Ct., New York County 1992).

[37]   International 800 Telecom Corp. v. Kramer, Levin, Nessen, Kamin & Frankel, 155 Misc. 2d 975, 591 N.Y.S.2d 313 (Sup. Ct., New York County 1992) (SPR 2:3).

[38]   See SPR 35:1 and 67:1.

[39]   The numbering system used for Part 130–1 is sometimes misleading, but all of the provisions are at hand under "Part 130" of the rules, occupying just a little more than two pages in the annually recompiled "McKinney's New York Rules of Court."

[40]   See § 201.

§ 415. Disbursements

In contrast with "costs," which under the CPLR are arbitrary sums awarded to the winner, disbursements are the winner's out-of-pocket expenditures, which the winner also gets back from the loser. The rule is that the party to whom costs are awarded also recovers disbursements.[1] It's not rigid, however; the court can allow disbursements to a party not awarded costs, and if the winner has won judgment of at least $50, he must be allowed disbursements even if costs are denied him by the court for one reason or another.[2] The disbursements recoverable, however, are those listed in Article 83 of the CPLR, and as a perusal of the main list in CPLR 8301(a) quickly shows, not every expenditure that a party makes is recoverable. Indeed, one of the most significant expenses in litigation, the deposition, is limited to a disbursement of $250 even though the actual expenditure is likely to be well beyond that.[3]

After listing specific recoverable disbursements in its earlier paragraphs, CPLR 8301(a) then allows in paragraph 13 "such other reasonable and necessary expenses as are taxable according to the course and practice of the court, by express provision of law or by order of the court." This paragraph produces most of the caselaw on disbursements. The provision has been held applicable only to the expenses of a party, not those of a nonparty witness,[4] who is limited to the set (and modest) witness fees of CPLR 8001. The fees of an expert witness are not recoverable as a disbursement under any subdivision in CPLR 8301 unless extraordinary circumstances are established.[5] Therefore, the party who wants to use the expert must defray the expert's expenses and actual fee without expecting to recover these as disbursements.

There is some flexibility in the "reasonable and necessary" phrase of CPLR 8301(a)(13). A judicial push can send it one way or another on a given claim of disbursement. Some courts, advocating uniformity, suggest that rules of court should provide a more detailed treatment of what items may be considered taxable disbursements. Until such rules are adopted, the matter is left to the discretion of the individual judge.[6] Others take a restrictive view of the disbursement statute, holding that any expansion of the list should await legislative action.[7] A party unclear on local practice should inquire of the clerk and of local practitioners. Because a given expenditure, although disputed, may be insufficient to warrant a judicial contest, the establishment of a uniform list more thorough than that of CPLR 8301(a) is not likely to emerge through the cumbersome common law method. It will more likely require a legislative or regulatory effort, perhaps by the Office of Court Administration.

---

[1]   CPLR 8301(a).

[2]   CPLR 8301(c).

[3]   CPLR 8301(a)(9).

[4]   Davis Sportswear, Inc. v. Parker, Duryee, Benjamin, Zunino and Malone, 49 Misc. 2d 77, 266 N.Y.S.2d 573 (Sup. Ct., New York County 1966). The court suggests that the witness may recover those expenses in a plenary action if worth the witness's while.

[5]   Alvarado v. Dillon, 67 A.D.3d 1214, 1216, 888 N.Y.S.2d 673, 676 (3d Dep't 2009); Van Patten v. Sylvia, 76 Misc. 2d 899, 352 N.Y.S.2d 565 (Sup. Ct., Schenectady County 1974).

[6]   See Muffoletto v. Rivera, 54 Misc. 2d 114, 281 N.Y.S.2d 549 (Sup. Ct., Erie County 1967).

[7]   North Oyster Bay Baymen's Ass'n v. Town of Oyster Bay, 150 A.D.3d 865, 55 N.Y.S.3d 258 (2d Dep't 2017); Marcus v. New York City Housing Authority, 80 A.D.2d 844, 436 N.Y.S.2d 771 (3d Dep't 1981).

The printing of a record on appeal, because it does involve substantial expenditure, comes in for occasional dispute in the disbursement context.[8] It has been held, for example, that the cost of printing a record when a less expensive method than printing is available will not be allowed as a disbursement.[9] In one case, a third-party defendant went to a printing expense of $800 to appeal a $450 judgment. The expense was termed "profligate" and was disallowed; a figure applicable to an alternative and cheaper method was substituted.[10]

The fees statutorily exacted of a party under Article 80 of the CPLR are usually recoverable as disbursements but not all are. Poundage, for example, which is a percentage of property levied on by a sheriff, is a statutory expense under Article 80,[11] but not a taxable disbursement under Article 83. Instead, the sheriff collects the poundage out of the property levied on.[12] Thus, the poundage is the debtor's burden, which can be a very substantial sum indeed and can slip into the picture almost surreptitiously against a debtor able and willing to pay, but just a bit dilatory in doing so.[13] Poundage in the thousands of dollars can become due the sheriff for doing little more than serving a paper.[14]

In certain categories of action, notably those affecting real property, additional allowances may be made to the winner.[15] And in any kind of contested action in which the winner can convince the court that the case was "difficult or extraordinary" (the court is not easily convinced), it can award up to $3,000 as an "additional allowance."[16]

§ 416. Taxation of Costs and Disbursements

The practice is for the winning party to get up a bill of costs, including all disbursements she deems herself entitled to and to present it to the clerk along with the judgment when it's presented for entry. The bill of costs should be supported by affidavits. The clerk is required to review it without waiting for a party's objection. The procedure bears the imposing name of "taxation" of costs, but it has nothing to do with taxation as the term is generally understood. If satisfied that the expenses claimed are permissible, the clerk inserts their total in the judgment as costs and disbursements.[1]

The step is usually taken without notice to the other side. In that case, however, when the winner gets costs taxed as requested and included in the judgment, he must immediately serve a copy of the bill of costs on the adverse party. He can just include the bill of costs with a copy of the judgment when he serves it with notice of entry. The

---

[8]   See CPLR 8301(a)(6); Hartmann v. Fox, 87 A.D.2d 885, 449 N.Y.S.2d 536 (2d Dep't 1982) (defendant could not recover as a disbursement his printing expenses for the record and brief submitted on an appeal in which plaintiff was awarded costs and disbursements).

[9]   Lew Morris Demolition Co. Inc. v. Board of Ed. of City of New York, 80 Misc. 2d 944, 365 N.Y.S.2d 109 (N.Y. City Civ. Ct. 1974); see also CPLR 5529(a)(1).

[10]   Society of New York Hospital v. Mogensen, 81 Misc. 2d 1089, 370 N.Y.S.2d 354 (App. Term, 1st Dep't 1975). As might be expected, it was a government agency that got the "profligate" label: in this case, ironically, the New York City Commissioner of Social Services.

[11]   CPLR 8012(b).

[12]   DeLia v. DeLia, 32 A.D.2d 987, 302 N.Y.S.2d 5 (3d Dep't 1969).

[13]   See Cabrera v. Hirth, 87 A.D.3d 844, 928 N.Y.S.2d 706 (1st Dep't 2011); see § 495.

[14]   See, e.g., Considine v. Pichler, 72 A.D.2d 103, 422 N.Y.S.2d 429 (1st Dep't 1979).

[15]   See CPLR 8302, 8303.

[16]   CPLR 8303(a)(2).

[1]   CPLR 8401.

adverse party then has 5 days within which to move to "retax" the costs.[2] Alternatively, the party seeking costs can initially give notice of their taxation,[3] thus compelling the other side to put in, at the specified return time, any objections she may have.

Any party dissatisfied with an item taxed (or refused taxation) by the clerk may have the court, by motion or notice, review the item.[4]

The procedure for taxing costs and disbursements is extensively reviewed in East Thirteenth Street Community Ass'n v. New York State Urban Development Corp.[5]

§ 417. Form of Judgment

The following is a sample form of judgment as used in an ordinary money action tried by jury (in this example, damages for breach of contract).

SUPREME COURT OF THE STATE OF NEW YORK
COUNTY OF NEW YORK

A.B., Plaintiff,	
against	Judgment
	Index No. _____
C.D., Defendant.	

The issues in this action having duly been tried before Justice Martin B. Stecher and a jury at Trial Term, Part XIV of this court, held at the courthouse at 60 Centre Street on April 26, 2018, and the plaintiff and defendant having appeared by their respective attorneys, Roland Garrulous and Vera Voluble, and the jury on April 26, 2018, having rendered a verdict for plaintiff against defendant for damages of $40,000, with interest thereon from October 18, 2015, and the plaintiff's costs and disbursements having been duly taxed by the clerk in the sum of $_____,

Now, on motion of Roland Garrulous, plaintiff's attorney, it is

ORDERED, ADJUDGED AND DECREED, that plaintiff A.B., recover of defendant C.D., the sum of $40,000, with interest thereon from October 18, 2015, amounting to $_____, together with costs and disbursements as taxed in the sum of $_____, making in all the sum of $_____, and that the plaintiff have execution therefor.

Judgment signed May 3, 2018.

_____
                                            Clerk

A few comments on the form. The blanks are filled in by the clerk, who computes the interest based on the appropriate dates. The form used here, which is typical, shows

---

[2]   CPLR 8403.

[3]   CPLR 8402.

[4]   CPLR 8404.

[5]   East Thirteenth Street Community Ass'n v. New York State Urban Development Corp., 164 Misc. 2d 589, 625 N.Y.S.2d 418 (Sup. Ct., New York County 1995) (SPR 38:1).

how interest from verdict until judgment, as authorized by CPLR 5002, is often omitted as a separate step.[1]

D. RECORDING THE JUDGMENT

Table of Sections

§ 418.   Entry of Judgment

§ 419.   The Judgment-Roll

§ 420.   Correcting the Judgment; Nunc Pro Tunc Changes

§ 421.   Docketing the Judgment

§ 422.   Transcripting Judgments Between Courts and Counties

§ 423.   Changes Affecting Judgments and Dockets

§ 418.   Entry of Judgment

The judgment, which is usually drafted by the winner, is brought to the clerk for signing and entry. The CPLR provides that formal "entry" occurs when, after the judgment "has been signed by the clerk, it is filed by him."[1] The fact of entry is recorded by the clerk in what is officially denominated a "judgment-book," which court clerks are required to maintain.[2] Once the judgment is entered, the winner should serve on the loser a copy of the judgment with notice of entry; it is this service that starts the loser's appeal time.[3] If the judgment contemplates enforcement, as it usually does when the plaintiff is the winner, it is entry that marks the moment that enforcement may be sought.

"Entry" should not be confused with "docketing," although it often is. Technically, the "docketing" of the judgment is its recording in a set of alphabetized books; it is the step that makes the judgment a lien on the defendant's real property. Docketing a judgment is thus a step distinct from entry, although both steps are almost simultaneous in the supreme and county courts[4] because the county clerk, in whose office the real property docket books are maintained, is ex officio also the clerk of both courts.[5] In lower courts, however, there is no such "docketing"; when used in those courts, the term usually intends to connote nothing more than "entry." This topic (including the real property lien) is elaborated in the later treatment of docketing.[6]

When the judgment is based on the general verdict of a jury, the clerks often handle it without specific instruction from the court. The procedure in that situation, especially in the more populous counties (where the "clerk's" office has many personnel), is to secure from the clerk in attendance during the trial a statement describing the verdict—this is sometimes called an "extract" from the clerk's minutes—which the winner takes to the "judgment" clerk along with the draft of the judgment. The extract establishes the fact of the verdict and suffices to permit entry of judgment. If a special verdict was used—

---

[1]   See § 411.

[1]   CPLR 5016(a). The "judgment-roll," discussed in the next section, is presented to the clerk at the same time that the judgment is tendered for entry.

[2]   CPLR 9702(1).

[3]   CPLR 5513(a). See § 533.

[4]   CPLR 5018(a).

[5]   County Law §§ 525, 909.

[6]   See § 421.

i.e., a list of questions submitted to the jury, which has become a much more common practice today—the judge translates the jury's answers into the appropriate result and directs judgment accordingly.[7] If an extract is used, it reflects the judge's directions. When there is no jury, the decision of the judge determines the judgment to be entered.[8]

Until recently, there was no time limit on how long the winner had to get judgment entered. The deterrent to delay was the appellate point already made: that the loser's appeal time remains open until the winner serves a copy of the judgment on the loser with notice of entry. Occasionally laches was applied to exact a forfeiture against a dilatory submitter,[9] but that was rare.

With the adoption of the Uniform Rules in 1986, a 60-day period was imposed as a time limit for the entry of a judgment or order. The rule in point in the supreme and county courts is Uniform Rule section 202.48. It brings the 60-day limit into play when the decision calls for a settlement or submission of the judgment and starts the 60 days from the time of the filing of the decision. The Court of Appeals has held that the 60-day period won't start unless the decision calls explicitly for settlement or submission.[10]

Sometimes the decision will contain no such direction. It is still a good idea to see to it that all judgments are drawn and entered promptly, whether technically subject to the 60-day requirement or not.

"Abandonment" of the victory is the explicit consequence imposed by the rule for letting the 60 days—when it's applicable—pass.[11] Uniform Rule section 202.48 applies to orders as well as judgments.

A money judgment has a form well-recognized by lawyers. The judgment in non-money actions can be more complicated. If dispute on the form arises, the court will resolve it on motion.

There are a few points to be noted about the situation in which a party dies before judgment is entered. If the verdict or decision has already been rendered before a party dies, the entry of judgment is allowed, either for or against the deceased and may even be made in the names of the original parties. But no verdict or decision may be rendered against a party who has died.[12] In that instance, the decedent's personal representative must be substituted before the case can proceed. If substitution does not take place within a reasonable time, the action may be dismissed as against the side needing substitution.[13]

When entering judgment in a case involving multiple defendants, the plaintiff must keep a few points in mind. If the defendants' liability is joint and several, as is often the case with joint tortfeasors, the entry of judgment against one—if the plaintiff should be

---

[7]   CPLR 5016(b).

[8]   CPLR 5016(c).

[9]   See, e.g., Vickery v. Village of Saugerties, 106 A.D.2d 721, 483 N.Y.S.2d 765 (3d Dep't 1984) (4 year delay in submitting order), aff'd 64 N.Y.2d 1161, 490 N.Y.S.2d 735, 480 N.E.2d 349 (1985).

[10]   See § 250.

[11]   See § 250; Farkas v. Farkas, 11 N.Y.3d 300, 869 N.Y.S.2d 380, 898 N.E.2d 563 (2008) (reversing appellate division order concluding that violation of 60-day rule resulted in forfeiture of $750,000 judgment).

[12]   CPLR 5016(d).

[13]   CPLR 1021. See §§ 184 et seq. for discussion of the procedure for substitution and connected problems.

entitled to judgment against that one but not against the others[14]—should pose no problem. Each bears an individual liability in that instance, not irrevocably linked to the others. The plaintiff in that situation should see to it, however, that an order of severance is also entered, or that a severance direction is included in the judgment or order being entered, so as to separate and leave for independent adjudication the claims not now going to judgment. The severance direction is easy to secure and should be asked for when applying to enter judgment.[15] Sometimes the clerk will enter a severance order without direction.[16]

If the liability is joint only, however, such as the liability of partners on a contract claim against the partnership,[17] rather than joint and several (statistically the more frequent liability among joined defendants), and through one event or another the plaintiff deems herself entitled to a judgment against one defendant, but not all of them, the plaintiff must be cautious about entering a separate judgment against the one. It is safe to do so when the one has confessed judgment because in that situation a statute states expressly that such entry does not bar the continued pursuit of the others.[18] But if one, but not all, of the defendants should default, it has been held that the intentional entry of judgment against the defaulting one will merge (and thus destroy) the claim against the others.[19]

Such are the rigors of this "joint" liability. The theory is that any one of the nondefaulters, if successful on the merits, would succeed for all (thus making her cohort's earlier default academic). A plaintiff unaware of these consequences, who enters judgment against a defaulting joint-only debtor, should move to vacate it promptly upon discovery of the mistake.[20] The court should be receptive to such a vacatur motion, considering the substantive disaster—forfeiture of the plaintiff's claim against the others—to be visited upon so minor a procedural oversight. The Court of Appeals has held that this rule about joint debtors should not apply unless the plaintiff, in entering judgment against one, intentionally waives his rights against the others.[21] A plaintiff entering judgment against only one debtor cannot be said to have intentionally waived his rights against the others if the one does not pay.

Simple though it be—and there are few things any simpler—the step of "entry" is a key one and its careless disregard can bring a substantial forfeiture. In Firstar Equipment Finance v. Jonathan Travel & Tours, Inc.,[22] for example, C won judgment.

---

[14]   This can happen, for example, where some but not all of the defendants default or confess judgment.

[15]   See CPLR 5012.

[16]   The clerk does this, for example, when entering a default judgment against fewer than all defendants. See CPLR 3215(a).

[17]   Partnership Law § 26(2).

[18]   CPLR 3218(d).

[19]   See Salem v. Seigel, 126 N.Y.S.2d 214 (Sup. Ct., New York County 1953), in which the partner who suffered a default judgment proved to be insolvent. These procedural peculiarities are the trappings of the common law's distinction between "joint" and "joint and several" liabilities, an anachronism that has been justly criticized. See Werner, *Shared Liability: An Alternative to the Confusion of Joint, Several, and Joint and Several Obligations*, 42 Alb. L. Rev. 1 (1977). Inroads into "joint and several liability" were made with the enactment of Article 16 of the CPLR effective in 1986. See §§ 168A–168D.

[20]   The right to move to vacate a default judgment is available not only to the defendant against whom it was taken but also in appropriate circumstances to the plaintiff who took it. See § 427.

[21]   United States Printing & Lithograph Co. v. Powers, 233 N.Y. 143, 135 N.E. 225 (1922).

[22]   Firstar Equipment Finance v. Jonathan Travel & Tours, Inc., 2001 WL 36113094 (Sup. Ct., New York County 2001), aff'd, 292 A.D.2d 275, 738 N.Y.S.2d 853 (1st Dep't 2002).

Without first securing its entry, C issued an execution to the sheriff, who levied it. Creditor X then came along and prevailed in a priority race with C, all because of the want of the mere entry of C's judgment.[23]

In Lesnick and Mazarin v. Carvalho,[24] involving real property, it was the debtor who lost out. The judgment creditor (JC) had won and entered the judgment, and it stood of record as a lien against JD. But JD now succeeded in getting the judgment vacated, and it would have been dissolved as a lien had JD merely secured entry of the order granting the vacatur. But JD didn't. The judgment thus remained a lien, giving JC priority over the person to whom JD then tried to sell the land.[25]

§ 419. The Judgment-Roll

The party at whose instance judgment is entered prepares a "judgment-roll," which is submitted with the judgment and which the clerk files when entering the judgment.[1] The judgment-roll consists of the basic papers in the case. It contains the summons, pleadings, judgment, orders "involving the merits or necessarily affecting the final judgment," and any admissions that may have been made in the action (the presence of which would have dispensed with proof of the matters admitted).[2] These contents are specified in CPLR 5017(b), which then goes on to list additional contents of the judgment-roll in specific instances, e.g., in a contested action, or on a default, or upon judgment by confession, etc.[3] If there is doubt as to whether a given paper belongs in the judgment-roll, it is usually best just to include it.

Gathering together the judgment-roll is a light task. Quite often the papers required are already in the court's file of the case, which enables the clerk to put the judgment-roll together without further papers from the party.[4] The party need only determine which papers, required as part of the judgment-roll, are not already on file, putting these together with those already on file to compose the judgment-roll and handing the whole of it over to the clerk, who will usually put it back into the file, immediately or ultimately. The file is the permanent repository of the judgment-roll where it may then be inspected as a public record.

Usually the original of each paper or document is included in the judgment-roll, but this is more a matter of practice than mandate: unless otherwise expressly required, copies instead of originals are appropriate either for service (on a party) or filing (with the clerk).[5]

§ 420. Correcting the Judgment; Nunc Pro Tunc Changes

CPLR 5019(a) provides that "a judgment or order shall not be stayed, impaired or affected by any mistake, defect or irregularity in the papers or procedures in the action

---

[23]   See SPR 114:4.

[24]   Lesnick and Mazarin v. Carvalho, 299 A.D.2d 412, 749 N.Y.S.2d 563 (2d Dep't 2002).

[25]   See SPR 131:2.

[1]   CPLR 5017(a).

[2]   The main source of admissions is CPLR 3123. See § 364.

[3]   In the procedure known as the Simplified Procedure for Court Determination of Disputes, a kind of judicial arbitration, see § 609 (Practitioner's Edition), the content of the judgment-roll is specified in CPLR 3036(7).

[4]   See CPLR 5017(a).

[5]   CPLR 2101(e). See § 201.

not affecting a substantial right of a party." It provides express permission for either the trial or appellate court to cure the mistake. Even errors of substance are correctible under this provision, as where the defendant was found to have title but the plaintiff secured entry of a judgment that recited title to be in himself,[1] as long as the record offers clear support for what was intended. In another case with sufficient record support, the Court of Appeals allowed a municipal party (a county), several years after judgment, an amendment to reflect the special municipal interest rate that the clerk had mistakenly entered at the higher regular rate.[2]

The statute may not be used to reopen a trial, as was attempted, unsuccessfully, in *Fleming v. Sarva*,[3] where the defendant moved to alter the court's damages findings on the contention that there was error in the determination. The court denied the motion, stating that "[t]he court cannot increase or decrease the amount of damages where there has been no clerical error." Appeal should have been the route pursued; it was in *Fleming*, but it raised only issues of liability, not damages.

An absence of record support for the change sought will of course find the court reluctant to make it. No change will be allowed by an appellate court, for example, if the context suggests that the trial court was simply changing its mind on a matter already decided. The trial judge may not sit as an appellate court over herself. The Court of Appeals has said that

> [t]he rule has long been settled and inflexibly applied that the trial court has no revisory or appellate jurisdiction to correct by amendment error in substance affecting the judgment. It cannot, by amendment, change the judgment . . . to meet some supposed equity subsequently called to its attention . . . . It cannot correct judicial errors either of commission or omission . . . . Clerical errors or a mistake in the entry of the judgment or the omission of a right or relief to which a party is entitled as a matter of course may alone be corrected . . . through an amendment.[4]

The kinds of mistakes contemplated for correction here are mere ministerial ones, not those involving new exercises of discretion or a further turn of the fact-finding wheel. The rule permits the correction of clerical errors, such as where the judgment included interest the clerk was not permitted to insert,[5] but it does not countenance belated judicial steps of a substantive nature, such as allowing an expansion of a money demand after a party has already pursued the claim to judgment,[6] or allowing a new demand for interest to be pursued after the matter has already been reduced to judgment.[7]

A decision permissible when the contest is on, in other words, may not be sought in the guise of an amendment or a resettlement after the contest is over. A judgment dismissing an action "with prejudice," for example, may not be resettled to substitute

---

[1]   Stormville Mountain Homes, Inc. v. Zurhorst, 35 A.D.2d 562, 313 N.Y.S.2d 178 (2d Dep't 1970).

[2]   See Kiker v. Nassau County, 85 N.Y.2d 879, 626 N.Y.S.2d 55, 649 N.E.2d 1199 (1995). See § 411.

[3]   Fleming v. Sarva, 15 Misc. 3d 892, 833 N.Y.S.2d 887 (Sup. Ct., Nassau County 2007).

[4]   Herpe v. Herpe, 225 N.Y. 323, 327, 122 N.E. 204, 205 (1919).

[5]   See Aetna Cas. & Sur. Co. v. Whitestone General Hosp., 142 Misc. 2d 67, 70, 536 N.Y.S.2d 373, 375 (Sup. Ct., New York County 1988).

[6]   See First Nat. City Bank v. Elsky, 62 Misc. 2d 880, 312 N.Y.S.2d 325 (N.Y. City Civ. Ct. 1970) (reviewing permissible and impermissible amendments under CPLR 5019(a)).

[7]   See CRP/Extell Parcel I, L.P. v. Cuomo, 27 N.Y.3d 1034, 33 N.Y.S.2d 148, 52 N.E.3d 1174 (2016); § 411.

"without prejudice" if the record does not confirm that "without prejudice" was the court's unambiguous intention.[8] But if there is support in the record, as where the stenographer's minutes plainly record it, even so momentous a change can be considered part of the mere "ministerial" category and thereby permitted by simple amendment under CPLR 5019(a).

It is only an "amendment" that this rule bars from effecting substantial changes unsupported in the record. Substantial changes may indeed be permissible, but they must be sought either through the appellate process or by an outright motion to vacate the judgment,[9] such as on the basis of newly discovered evidence. The procedure to "vacate" the judgment, however, contemplating a fresh judgment embodying the change sought, is simply a motion,[10] so if it can be shown that the opposing party has had full notice of the nature of the change being sought and a fair opportunity to meet it, perhaps the court can just treat the motion to "amend" as one to "vacate."[11]

There must be notice. In one case, for example, where the trial court effected a substantial change in a judgment on its own motion, with neither side advised, the appellate court held the change improper.[12] A formal motion by one side on notice to the other would probably have supported the change.

A closely analogous problem here involves the so-called nunc pro tunc order. Here the party is seeking not only to amend or alter a judgment or order, or to secure its belated entry, but to have the alteration reflect that it is being given retroactive effect as of a stated earlier time. This is permissible only "when a ruling has in fact been made, but is improperly evidenced by a defective mandate."[13] An order or judgment may then be made to reflect what was done and to give it effect as of its earlier doing.[14] That is what is known as a "nunc pro tunc" (now for then) order. It is sought when, for one reason or another, the party must make the judgment effective as of an earlier date.

The most common instance of this need was the divorce action when the judgment had to first be interlocutory and remain so for three months (during which the marriage subsisted) before final judgment could be entered: death during that period, or merely failing to secure the final judgment when the period expired, posed substantial nunc pro tunc questions. Earlier treatment of them, when abatement of claims was discussed,[15] spares us further discourse here, except to note once again that the interlocutory judgment requirement has been abolished and a divorce judgment today becomes final immediately, like any other judgment.

This development on the divorce front reduced the nunc pro tunc order's arena considerably but not entirely. Even without the requirement of interlocutory judgment, the divorce action remains one of the few that abate on the death of a party. It is hence a fertile and continuing source of nunc pro tunc questions when death intervenes. A key factor is whether a decision granting a divorce was definitively made before the party

---

[8]   See, e.g., Johnson v. Societe Generale S.A., 94 A.D.3d 663, 664–65, 943 N.Y.S.2d 74, 76–77 (1st Dep't 2012).

[9]   See *Herpe*, 225 N.Y. at 327, 122 N.E. at 205.

[10]   See CPLR 5015(a)(2); §§ 426, 428.

[11]   See, e. g, Horan v. Town of Brookhaven, 29 A.D.2d 563, 286 N.Y.S.2d 450 (2d Dep't 1967).

[12]   Baum v. Baum, 40 A.D.2d 1000, 347 N.Y.S.2d 960 (2d Dep't 1972).

[13]   Merrick v. Merrick, 266 N.Y. 120, 122, 194 N.E. 55, 56 (1934).

[14]   Farber v. U.S. Trucking Corp., 26 N.Y.2d 44, 50, 308 N.Y.S.2d 358, 363, 256 N.E.2d 521, 524 (1970).

[15]   See § 185.

died, even if not yet reduced to a formal judgment. If it was, the nunc pro tunc order is permissible even though substantial rights turn on it. In one case, for example, the children of H's first marriage sought a nunc pro tunc judgment on a clearly made decision divorcing his second marriage (he died before judgment was entered), in the hope of denying widowhood to the second wife and thus increasing their own Social Security allotment. The lower court refused the order on the ground that the second wife's property rights would be divested; it relied technically on the fact that the divorce did not exist at the earlier time, despite the then existing right to enter the judgment securing it. The appellate court reversed and allowed the nunc pro tunc judgment, holding that "[n]o vested rights of either party will be impaired by the entry of the judgment *nunc pro tunc*."[16] One may even argue that refusing the nunc pro tunc order would itself have qualified as the divestiture of vested rights: the rights won when the divorce decision was rendered.

CPLR 5016(d) contains perhaps the law's strongest clue to what the legislature wishes to be the rule when death occurs after a decision has been made but before the decision has been reduced to judgment. The statute regards the decision as the key element and the judgment an adjunct of it, permitting and perhaps even mandating (judgment "shall" be entered) that judgment ensue. With such a spur, a nunc pro tunc order should be permissible for any judgment when the right sought to be retroactivated was a right at the earlier time, duly decided and unambiguously apparent, and when all that is now sought is a paper—a judgment or order—saying so. That a substantial right may be affected by giving the judgment nunc pro tunc effect is better cited to support than to oppose the step. Litigation is designed to affect substantial rights.

§ 421. Docketing the Judgment

Quite apart from the "entry" of the judgment is its "docketing," which makes the judgment a lien on the defendant's real property. The docketing of the judgment is significant only when it takes place in the office of the county clerk of the real property's county; it is there that the docketing makes the judgment a lien.[1] (Liens on personal property are a different matter.)[2] Since the county clerk is ex officio the clerk of both the supreme court and the county court in the county,[3] a docketing of a judgment of either court with its "clerk" refers to the county clerk. Accordingly, the "docketing" in that office accomplishes the lien. With other courts, however, such as the New York City Civil Court and the district, city, town, and village courts, a "docketing" of a judgment with the court's clerk brings about no lien at all; in fact, the use of the word "docketing" in those courts is a misnomer for "entry." To make a judgment of one of those other courts a lien on real property, a transcripting procedure, elaborated in the next section, is used.

Keeping in mind that we are now talking only about money judgments in the supreme and county courts, we can examine the docketing procedure:

For each year or for a period of years, the clerk maintains alphabetized docket books. When the clerk files the judgment-roll upon entering the judgment,[4] she must also

---

[16]   Jayson v. Jayson, 54 A.D.2d 687, 387 N.Y.S.2d 274 (2d Dep't 1976), reversing 83 Misc. 2d 417, 373 N.Y.S.2d 497 (Sup. Ct., Nassau County 1975).

[1]   CPLR 5203(a). For further discussion of the judgment as a lien on real property, see § 517.

[2]   See §§ 518–520.

[3]   County Law §§ 525, 909.

[4]   CPLR 5017(a).

docket the judgment.[5] She does this by recording in the docket books, under the surname of the judgment debtor, the various data about the judgment.[6] Any searcher can then find, under an individual's name, whether there is any judgment outstanding against him in the county, whether it is still a timely lien against his real property, and any other datum concerning the judgment that may afterwards have been recorded on the docket. This docketing procedure is required for all money judgments, but if requested by the judgment creditor it is also available for judgments in actions directly affecting real property.[7] If the clerk maintains what is known as a "block index"—a set of records listing all realty in the county by section and lot—a judgment involving real property can be "docketed" there instead of in the alphabetized dockets. The block-index alternative is not available for money judgments, however.[8]

If there are two or more judgment debtors on the judgment, the docketing is made separately in the surname of each, but the details of the judgment need be recorded only under the name of the first debtor listed in the judgment; under the others goes a cross-reference to the first one and the searcher is put in touch with the relevant facts that way.[9] If the action was brought against a number of named parties, but not all were served with a summons and thus subjected to personal jurisdiction, the words "not summoned" must be written next to the name of the unserved ones to clarify that the judgment is not effective against them.[10] Ordinarily no entry at all should be made in the name of an unserved defendant, since the judgment is void as to her; there should thus be no occasion for having to write "not summoned" next to her name.[11] Even in the case of a joint liability, such as that of a partnership on a contract, the service of the summons on Partner A but not Partner B makes the judgment so ineffective against B that when a subsequent action is brought against B—as it may be to seek from him whatever remains unpaid on a judgment against the partnership itself or Partner A— the earlier judgment is not even res judicata of the facts. Partner B may therefore interpose defenses that could have been raised in the earlier action.[12]

Changes affecting the judgment or its impact as a lien can be reflected on the docket as they arise, thus enabling all searchers to find, centralized in the county of rendition, the judgment's subsequent history.

---

[5]   CPLR 5018(a).

[6]   See CPLR 5018(c), listing the information the docket is to contain.

[7]   The provisional remedy of notice of pendency of Article 65 of the CPLR, also available in actions directly affecting real property, will carry out the function of giving notice to potential buyers and encumbrancers before and during real property actions. Because it is available as a notice-giver even in advance of judgment, it should be considered for use in such actions.

[8]   CPLR 5018(a).

[9]   CPLR 5018(c).

[10]   CPLR 5018(a).

[11]   Apparently CPLR 1501 is the culprit that accounts for an entry being made next to the name of an unserved debtor, thus necessitating this "not summoned" addendum for CPLR 5018(a). CPLR 1501, applicable to cases of joint liability, authorizes judgment to be taken even against an unserved defendant, apparently theorizing that only by so doing will a collective liability be spelled out (such as will enable partnership assets to be reached on a judgment good as against the partnership on the basis that at least one partner was summoned, see CPLR 310). Because the partnership and like creatures have no identity apart from their members, there is ordinarily no separate set of books to reflect their liabilities; these can be reflected only by making an entry next to the name of each member, even if a "not summoned" qualification is needed to insulate an unserved member from personal liability. This procedure may overlook that today a partnership can be named and sued in its partnership name, CPLR 1025, without naming any individual partner at all.

[12]   CPLR 1502.

§ 422. Transcripting Judgments Between Courts and Counties

When a judgment is entered in a court other than the supreme or county court, it is not a lien on real property anywhere. Nor is a judgment docketed in one county a lien in any other. How can it be made so? The procedure is known as "transcripting" the judgment. A transcript is a paper containing the essential data about the judgment,[1] certified by the clerk with whom the judgment is filed or docketed. Its filing with the county clerk of another county makes it a lien on real property in that county, too. To achieve uniformity in its content, there is a statutory form of transcript.[2]

A judgment creditor with a judgment from a lower court who would make it a lien on real property must apply to the clerk of the lower court for a transcript[3] and then file the transcript with the county clerk of the home county—the county in which the judgment was rendered—who must thereupon docket the judgment in the usual alphabetical docket books. That gives the judgment the same effect as one entered and docketed in an original supreme court action in that county,[4] which accomplishes two things: it makes the judgment a lien on the defendant's real property in that county and it enables the judgment to be enforced as if it were a supreme court judgment.[5] Similar steps can be taken, and with the same accomplishments, for a federal, sister-state, or foreign country judgment, as follows:

Federal judgment: For a federal judgment on file in any federal court in New York, a transcript of the judgment can be secured from the clerk of the federal court and may be filed with the county clerk of any county. The filing requires the docketing of the judgment by that clerk, makes the judgment a real property lien in the county of docketing, and enables the judgment to be enforced as if rendered by the New York Supreme Court.[6]

Note that this docketing is permissible only for federal judgments filed in New York federal courts. To accomplish the same thing for a federal judgment rendered outside New York, a simple additional step, authorized by federal law, must be taken. A certified copy of the federal judgment is secured from the rendering court and is then filed with the clerk of a New York federal court, which gives it the "same effect" as if the latter rendered it.[7] Having such effect, a transcript of it, given now by the New York federal court, may be filed with any county clerk in the State.[8]

---

[1]   An order directing the payment of money may be treated as a judgment, CPLR 2222, and therefore transcripted and docketed under these provisions.

[2]   See Jud. Law § 255–c.

[3]   See § 1502 in the New York City Civil, Uniform District, Uniform City, and Uniform Justice Court Acts, McKinney's Vol. 29A, Parts 2 and 3. For surrogate's court decrees and orders, see SCPA 603. For family court support orders, see Fam. Ct. Act § 475.

[4]   CPLR 5018(a).

[5]   Some of the various devices of CPLR Article 52 for the enforcement of a money judgment may then be captioned and made returnable in the supreme court instead of in the lower court where the judgment was rendered. This becomes important for enforcing judgments of certain lower courts, in which some of these devices may not be available. See § 493.

[6]   CPLR 5018(b).

[7]   28 U.S.C.A. § 1963. See the Commentary on the 1988 revision of that section in the U.S.C.A. Alternatively, a federal judgment rendered outside New York can skip the § 1963 procedure and seek direct registration in New York under CPLR Article 54. See § 435.

[8]   The federal judgment's docketing in a New York State court also makes available the enforcement devices in CPLR Article 52, and these will even bear the caption of a New York Supreme Court judgment and make use of the New York sheriff rather than the federal marshal. See Knapp v. McFarland, 462 F.2d 935 (2d

Sister-state judgment: The judgment of a court of another state[9] must first be converted into a New York judgment before being enforceable in New York. This can be accomplished by mere registration in most cases;[10] or, in any case, by a motion-action seeking quick summary judgment;[11] or through an ordinary plenary action based on the sister-state judgment. In whatever court this is done, the sister-state judgment becomes a judgment of that court; further transcripting steps are taken accordingly.[12]

Foreign-country judgment: The judgment, again, must first be converted into a New York judgment, either by a motion-action[13] or by a plenary action.[14] If successfully converted, it becomes a judgment of the New York court in which the action or motion-action was brought, the transcripting procedures now to follow accordingly.

Thus may the judgments of various courts be made into New York judgments and docketed with a county clerk. All such judgments, however, including an original New York one, will stand as a lien only on the defendant's real property in the county of docketing. In order to make the judgment a lien in other counties, a transcript is secured from the county clerk of the home county, which may then be filed with the county clerk of any other county, whereupon the judgment gets docketed and becomes a lien there.[15]

A judgment creditor can get as many transcripts from the home county clerk as she requests[16] for filing in as many counties as she pleases. The judgment becomes a lien in each. It is a common practice in some metropolitan areas for attorneys who do a lot of collection work (enforcement of money judgments) to secure a handful of transcripts for each judgment rendered, filing them in the home and surrounding counties on the premise that the judgment debtor may, presently unknown to the creditor, have some real property nearby.

The foregoing shows that for the purpose of docketing the judgment in other counties, the home county serves as a kind of clearing house, not only for supreme court and county court judgments originally docketed there, but also for lower court judgments and even foreign judgments docketed there by transcript.[17] For example, to make a New York City Civil Court judgment rendered in Kings County, a lien on the defendant's real property in Erie County, a transcript must be secured from the civil court clerk and filed with the county clerk in Kings County and yet another transcript obtained from the latter. It is this one that may be filed with the county clerk of Erie County.

Cir. 1972). Even protective measures, available for the judgment debtor under the New York procedure, become applicable to a transcripted federal judgment. See Wandschneider v. Bekeny, 75 Misc. 2d 32, 346 N.Y.S.2d 925 (Sup. Ct., Westchester County 1973).

[9]   This would embrace the courts of the District of Columbia and of the territories of the United States as well, which are the equivalent of state courts for full faith and credit purposes. See U.S. Const. art. IV; 28 U.S.C.A. § 1738.

[10]   CPLR Article 54; See § 435.

[11]   CPLR 3213. See §§ 288 et seq.

[12]   If the procedure used is the Article 54 registration, the judgment becomes the equivalent or a supreme court judgment. CPLR 5402(b).

[13]   CPLR 3213, which may also be used for foreign-country judgments.

[14]   The filing and registration procedures of CPLR Article 54 are not available for the judgments of foreign countries.

[15]   CPLR 5018(a).

[16]   A fee is paid for each. See CPLR 8016(a).

[17]   This clearing house function of the county clerk's office was the result of 1959 legislation, L.1959, ch. 238, 631. See Study, *Proposed Uniform Procedure Relating to Judgments and Their Enforcement,* 4th Jud. Conf. Rep. 130 (1959).

At one time there was no way of knowing in what other counties or courts a given judgment had been docketed by transcript. It is now required, however, that whenever a county clerk dockets a judgment by transcript, he must notify the issuing clerk by mail, who is then required to note on the main docket the other place or places of docketing.[18] If, for example, the county clerk of the home county has issued a dozen transcripts and these have been filed in a dozen different counties, the procedure described will show this on the home county clerk's records and offer the peruser all needed information about where the judgment has been docketed and become a real property lien. It is of course important to know this in order to record a satisfaction of the judgment, and other changes in its status, on all dockets that reflect it.

This whole transcripting procedure, whether from a lower court to the county clerk's office or from one county clerk's office to another, touches only the enforcement of the judgment and its effect as a lien. Only for those purposes does it have the effect of a supreme court judgment. For any other purpose it must continue to be treated only as a judgment of the court that originally rendered it. A motion to vacate the judgment, for example, must be made to the original court; the transcripting procedure does not authorize entertainment of such a motion by any other court or in any other county.[19]

§ 423. Changes Affecting Judgments and Dockets

Any number of things can occur to affect a judgment after it has been docketed with the home county clerk or, through a transcript, elsewhere. It may be desirable and perhaps even necessary to have these changes reflected on some or all of these dockets. A subsequent judgment or order may have reversed, vacated, or modified the judgment, for example, or the judgment may have been assigned by the judgment creditor to another. The judgment creditor may have died and his personal representative succeeded to his interest. Or, through one device or another, the judgment may have been wholly or partly satisfied.

When any change occurs in the judgment, such as by reversal, vacatur, or modification, the change should first be made on the records of the clerk of the court that rendered the judgment. If it is a lower court, such as a city court, whose judgment had previously been transcripted into the county clerk's office, a certificate[1] can then be secured from the lower court clerk attesting to the change. This certificate can be filed with the home county clerk, who then records the change on her docket. Alternatively, instead of the certificate, a certified copy of the judgment or order making the change may be filed with the home county clerk.[2]

Once the change has been recorded on the dockets of the home county clerk, whether directly (because the judgment or order making the change is one by the supreme or county court) or indirectly (through the certificate of a lower court clerk or a certified copy of a lower court judgment or order), it is the certificate of the home county clerk that will thereafter be procured in order to reflect the change on the dockets of any other county clerk with whom the judgment has previously been transcripted, once again

---

[18] CPLR 5018(a). The transcript has a stub to facilitate this and to help the issuing clerk to identify the judgment. See 22 N.Y.C.R.R. § 202.47.

[19] Wood v. Ford, 78 A.D.2d 585, 432 N.Y.S.2d 572 (4th Dep't 1980).

[1] The certificate is essentially the same in form as a transcript and has also been made uniform by statute. Jud. Law § 255–c.

[2] CPLR 5019(b).

making the home county clerk's office the central clearing house for all outside-county activities involving inside-county judgments.[3] When the certificate of the home county clerk is filed with any other county clerk whose docket contains the judgment, an entry must be made on the latter to reflect the change.

The same path is followed when, by judgment, order, or written instrument, the ownership of the judgment changes, such as through an order substituting a personal representative in place of a deceased judgment creditor or through an instrument assigning the judgment to another. If this is done by court order, the order should be certified; if it is done by an instrument, the instrument should be acknowledged. These requirements, which are contained in CPLR 5019(c), have been interpreted strictly by at least one court, which deemed a notarized assignment of a judgment ineffective because it was not acknowledged in the form required for the recording of a deed under the Real Property Law.[4] Most courts are not as rigid in enforcing a similar requirement contained in CPLR 2309(c), which states that an oath or affirmation taken outside New York must be "accompanied by such certificate or certificates as would be required to entitle a deed acknowledged without the state to be recorded within the state if such deed had been acknowledged before the officer who administered the oath or affirmation."[5] Upon the filing of the paper reflecting the change of the ownership of the judgment, the clerk notes the change on the docket,[6] and the path for indicating the change on the dockets of the other clerks is again the same, with the home county clerk's office again acting as the clearing house.[7]

Persons who come into an interest in a judgment should make sure the judgment debtor knows about it. The person to whom a judgment creditor has assigned a judgment, for example, should notify the judgment debtor promptly. The mere filing of the assignment, whatever notice it may give the world at large, does not put the judgment debtor herself on notice. If the unnotified debtor then pays the judgment as if the original creditor still owned it—as where she pays it to a sheriff levying execution on a judgment obtained by the judgment creditor's own judgment creditor—she is fully protected. The debtor need not search county records every time she makes a payment on a judgment.[8]

E. RECORDING SATISFACTION

Table of Sections

§ 424.   Satisfaction-Piece

§ 425.   Entry of Satisfaction

---

[3]   CPLR 5019(d).

[4]   See Chase Bank USA, N.A. v. Cardello, 27 Misc. 3d 791, 896 N.Y.S.2d 856 (N.Y. City Civ. Ct. 2010); but see Musah v. Houslanger & Associates, PLLC, 2012 WL 5835293 (S.D.N.Y. 2012) (declining to follow *Chase Bank* because of the Second Circuit's holding "that an assignment of judgment is effective even without a 5019(c) filing").

[5]   See § 388.

[6]   CPLR 5019(c).

[7]   CPLR 5019(d).

[8]   See Tri City Roofers, Inc. v. Northeastern Indus. Park, 61 N.Y.2d 779, 473 N.Y.S.2d 161, 461 N.E.2d 298 (1984).

§ 424. Satisfaction-Piece

A satisfaction-piece is an acknowledged instrument attesting to the complete or partial satisfaction of a judgment. It is the instrument used when the judgment debtor voluntarily pays the judgment. Today it is the judgment creditor's obligation not only to execute the satisfaction-piece when the judgment is paid, but also to see to its filing with the appropriate clerk so that the judgment may be reflected as paid on the court's records. The appropriate clerk is the one who originally entered the judgment or, in the case of a lower court judgment which has been docketed in the county clerk's office by transcript, the county clerk. The satisfaction-piece recites the book and page where the judgment is docketed and upon its filing the clerk must enter the satisfaction on his dockets.[1] Within 10 days after the filing, the judgment creditor must mail a copy of the satisfaction-piece to the judgment debtor.[2]

If the judgment has been docketed in yet other counties, the judgment creditor is also responsible for having the satisfaction reflected on their dockets. The creditor must obtain certificates from the home county clerk, now indicating the satisfaction, and file one in each of the other counties in which docketing has taken place.[3] This requirement applies, however, only when the satisfaction is complete; if it is only partial, the requirement for certificating the satisfaction into other counties does not apply,[4] although the requirement for filing it in the home county does.[5] A judgment creditor who fails to make the required filings within 20 days after getting full satisfaction is subject to a $100 penalty, which the judgment debtor can seek either in a plenary action or in a small claims proceeding.[6]

The judgment creditor's attorney of record may execute the satisfaction-piece, but only during the 10-year period following entry of the judgment.[7] After that the law assumes that the attorney's authority has expired, and the paying judgment debtor had best pay the judgment creditor directly or secure new evidence of the attorney's continuing authority. It is good practice for the judgment debtor to draw a check to the judgment creditor and her attorney jointly[8] or to have both sign a receipt for a cash payment, thus insulating the judgment debtor from any lawyer-lien disputes that may arise between the creditor and the creditor's lawyer.

The judgment debtor is not helpless if he is not given a satisfaction-piece after satisfying the judgment in whole or in part. He can obtain a court order directing that

---

[1]   CPLR 5021(a)(1).

[2]   CPLR 5020(a).

[3]   The home county clerk's dockets will list the other counties in which docketing has occurred. See § 422.

[4]   CPLR 5020(d).

[5]   CPLR 5020(a).

[6]   CPLR 5020(c). The courts in whose small claims part the penalty can be sought are the New York City Civil Court and the district and city courts. It should also be permissible in the small claims part of the town and village courts, which got a small claims part in 1975, see Article 18 of the Uniform Justice Court Act, McKinney's Vol. 29A, Part 2, but they are not listed in the earlier amended (1974) CPLR 5020(c). If New York City is the judgment creditor, the judgment debtor must serve on it a demand that the satisfaction-piece be executed and filed, and the penalty will apply only if 20 days then expire without compliance. Other creditors are not entitled to such demands.

[7]   CPLR 5020(b).

[8]   See Hafter v. Farkas, 498 F.2d 587 (2d Cir. 1974).

an entry of satisfaction be made on the dockets. The order is sought upon motion, which should be brought on by order to show cause.[9]

There is also a remedy for a judgment debtor ready and willing to pay the judgment, but unable to locate the judgment creditor so as to pay and obtain a satisfaction-piece. CPLR 5020–a sets up a procedure that culminates in the debtor's merely depositing with the clerk a certified check in the amount of the judgment.[10]

§ 425. Entry of Satisfaction

As the prior section discusses, a voluntary payment of the judgment usually results in the filing of a satisfaction-piece in the appropriate clerk's office, which then requires that an entry of the satisfaction be made on the docket of the judgment.[1] Whenever a judgment has been satisfied in whole or in part, the judgment debtor is entitled to have it mirrored on the record. If she cannot secure a satisfaction-piece, or if for any other reason the home dockets have not yet been made to reflect a satisfaction that was in fact made, whether in whole or in part and whether made voluntarily or not, the judgment debtor need only move the court, by order to show cause, for an order directing the entry of an appropriate satisfaction.[2]

If the judgment creditor should refuse a tender of complete or partial satisfaction, an infrequent but occasional phenomenon, the judgment debtor may seek an order permitting him to deposit the money into court. This motion, too, is brought on by order to show cause, which enables the court to determine who should be notified of it. A deposit so made entitles the debtor to an entry of satisfaction.

When the judgment debtor makes such a motion, he must satisfy the court that there are no outstanding executions on the judgment on which a sheriff's fee may be due.[3] This prevents the debtor from evading the additional charges that might be due the sheriff on the execution by seeking to deposit the money into court instead of paying it over to the sheriff. In this lies a special lesson to the dallying judgment debtor who plans to pay the judgment, but who does not pay it promptly, or bond it during an appeal, or make some other arrangement with the judgment creditor before the sheriff levies. The levy may cost the judgment debtor dear. In one case, for example, it cost a debtor fully able to pay the judgment an extra $30,000.[4]

The deposit into court under this provision will stop the running of interest, but the deposit procedure should not be used without good reason because it entails a possibly needless court application. Good reason would be an inability to locate the creditor. It has been held that if the creditor is available, a tender to him is a condition precedent to a deposit of the money into court.[5]

---

[9]   CPLR 5021(a)(2); see § 425.

[10] For the purpose and impact of this statute, see the Commentary on McKinney's CPLR 5020–a.

[1]   CPLR 5021(a)(1).

[2]   CPLR 5021(a)(2).

[3]   CPLR 5021(a)(3).

[4]   See Thornton v. Montefiore Hosp., 117 A.D.2d 552, 498 N.Y.S.2d 828 (1st Dep't 1986). See § 495.

[5]   Meilak v. Atlantic Cement Co., 30 A.D.2d 254, 291 N.Y.S.2d 639 (3d Dep't 1968); see MacKenzie v. MacKenzie, 17 Misc. 3d 346, 841 N.Y.S.2d 433 (Sup. Ct., Essex County 2007) (no tender found where defendant never delivered the judgment amount plus legal interest to plaintiff).

Another step, entailing a deposit into court but not calling for a motion, may help the judgment debtor who can't locate the creditor.[6] It does not bring about a recording of satisfaction,[7] but it saves the debtor continuing enforcement expenses.[8]

The execution referred to earlier is one of the devices for enforcing a money judgment under Article 52 of the CPLR. It is a paper issued to the sheriff requiring the sheriff to seek property of the judgment debtor to sell towards payment of the judgment. The details of its procedures come later,[9] but some discussion of the "return" of the execution is appropriate now.

The return is the sheriff's statement of his proceedings on the execution, including whether it brought about any satisfaction of the judgment. The sheriff makes this return to the clerk of the court out of which the execution issued.[10] If it shows satisfaction of the judgment to any extent, the clerk must reflect it on her records.[11] When a payment is made pursuant to the execution, the sheriff is also required upon request to give the judgment debtor a certified copy of the execution and the return showing the satisfaction.[12] The judgment debtor can file this with the clerk of the county in which the execution was levied, who must docket the satisfaction accordingly. This contemplates a situation in which, for example, a supreme court judgment of county X is enforced in county Y. The execution bears the caption of the home county, county X, and it is to the clerk of that county that a return will be sent. But the execution may be delivered for levy to the sheriff of any county.[13] If delivered to the sheriff of Y, who finds property of the debtor there and successfully levies, the Y sheriff must still make his return to the X clerk. That return will assure reflection of the satisfaction on the home dockets in X, but if the judgment has been transcripted into Y it may still remain of record there notwithstanding the successful levy in that very county. The requirement of the certified copy, delivered by sheriff to debtor, immediately offers the debtor a document that he can file locally in Y to evince the satisfaction.[14]

Executions must generally be returned, satisfied or not, within 60 days after issuance.[15] Perhaps overlooking that requirement, or perhaps because the requirement

---

[6]   See CPLR 5020–a.

[7]   To accomplish a recording of satisfaction, a motion under CPLR 5021 would be necessary.

[8]   See the Commentary on McKinney's CPLR 5020–a.

[9]   See §§ 494 et seq., discussing CPLR 5230, the source of the execution. We refer here to an ordinary execution against property as opposed to the "income execution" of CPLR 5231, which is a levy against the debtor's wages or other income, treated in § 502.

[10]   CPLR 5230(c).

[11]   CPLR 5021(b). The statute says "docket," having in mind the county clerk, whose dockets manifest the real property liens. But the provision applies by adoption to the lower courts as well, where "records" would be a more appropriate term than "dockets," although the terms are often carelessly interchanged. See § 701(c) in each of the New York City Civil, Uniform District, Uniform City, and Uniform Justice Court Acts, McKinney's Vol. 29A, Parts 2 and 3. The cited section in the court acts should be consulted whenever a CPLR enforcement device involving the sheriff is involved; it clarifies the device's use in the lower court and provides for necessary adjustments, including references to the enforcement officers of the lower court.

[12]   CPLR 5021(b).

[13]   CPLR 5230(b).

[14]   Alternatively, the debtor can wait until the return is recorded on the X county's dockets and then get a certificate of satisfaction from the X clerk for filing in Y. CPLR 5021(c).

[15]   CPLR 5230(c).

is sometimes disregarded when there has been no satisfaction at all, a more specific instruction to the sheriff has been enacted for small claims judgments.[16]

If the judgment has been docketed outside the home county, via transcripts, a home county satisfaction resulting from any of the methods discussed—voluntary satisfaction, court order, court deposit on order, or satisfied execution—can be certificated onto other-county dockets by the same route. The home county clerk, on whose dockets the satisfaction is recorded, issues the certificate, which other county clerks must file, recording the satisfaction on their dockets accordingly.[17] If the initial satisfaction is recorded on the records of a lower court, a certificate of the latter's clerk, so indicating, can be filed with the home county clerk to get the datum onto her dockets, after which the latter's certificates will be used to reach dockets in other counties.

F. VACATING JUDGMENTS AND ORDERS

Table of Sections

§ 426.   Motion to Vacate Judgment or Order, Generally
§ 427.   Excusable Default
§ 428.   Newly Discovered Evidence
§ 429.   Fraud or Misconduct
§ 430.   Lack of Jurisdiction
§ 431.   Reversal of Underlying Judgment
§ 432.   Conditioning the Vacatur
§ 433.   Restitution

§ 426. Motion to Vacate Judgment or Order, Generally

CPLR 5015(a) is a frequently invoked provision in New York practice. It lists the principal grounds on which a judgment or order may be vacated. It provides (verbatim) that "[t]he court which rendered a judgment or order may relieve a party from it upon such terms as may be just, on motion of any interested person with such notice as the court may direct, upon the ground of:

1.   excusable default, if such motion is made within one year after service of a copy of the judgment or order with written notice of its entry upon the moving party, or, if the moving party has entered the judgment or order, within one year after such entry; or

2.   newly-discovered evidence which, if introduced at the trial, would probably have produced a different result and which could not have been discovered in time to move for a new trial under section 4404; or

3.   fraud, misrepresentation, or other misconduct of an adverse party; or

---

[16]   CPLR 5021(b). Expressly stating that a return of execution is necessary even if unsatisfied, CPLR 5021(b) requires a return on small claims judgments within 90 days after the sheriff has received the "judgment," meaning the execution. ("Sheriff" here includes whoever the enforcement officer of the particular lower court may be, for which see § 701 in the lower court acts, note 11, above). This was done to expedite identification of deadbeat judgment debtors in small claims actions and to facilitate punitive damage suits against them when it is shown that they can pay, but just refuse to. See § 1812 in the New York City Civil, Uniform District, Uniform City, and Uniform Justice Court Acts, McKinney's Vol. 29A, Parts 2 and 3. For enforcement of a small claims judgment, see § 583.

[17]   CPLR 5021(c). For elaboration of the transcript route, see § 422.

4. lack of jurisdiction to render the judgment or order; or

5. reversal, modification or vacatur of a prior judgment or order upon which
    it is based."

The five enumerated categories cover just about all possible grounds on which a
vacatur might be sought. Should a ground arise not expressly listed, however, and not
susceptible, even with a little push, of being lodged under a listed ground—most are
susceptible—the lawyer can take note that thorough as the list may seem, it is not
exhaustive. The court has inherent discretionary power to vacate its judgments and
orders for good cause shown, not limited by the CPLR 5015(a) list.[1] The Advisory
Committee stressed this.[2]

The procedure for seeking the vacatur—vacatur is what CPLR 5015(a) has
primarily in mind when it speaks of allowing a court to "relieve" a party of a judgment
or order—is a motion made to the court that rendered it. That a transcript of a lower
court judgment may have been filed in the county clerk's office, or a transcript of any
court's judgment filed in another county, does not authorize any other than the court
that rendered the judgment, or courts along its appellate path, to vacate it. The supreme
court, for example, cannot vacate a New York City Civil Court judgment merely because
the latter has been docketed in the county clerk's office by transcript. The transcript
procedure is only an aid to enforcement, not a substitution of tribunals for redoing the
merits.[3] The same is true of a supreme court judgment rendered in county X, afterwards
transcripted into county Y: ordinarily only X can entertain a vacatur motion.[4]

The requirement in CPLR 5015(a) that the vacatur motion be made "with such
notice as the court may direct" means that it should be brought on by order to show
cause. This recognizes that applications of this kind can take place long after the
judgment was rendered and that uncertainties can arise concerning, for example, the
continued authority of the other side's lawyer. The court in the order to show cause can
take cognizance of the applicable facts, including lapse of time, and direct accordingly
about whom and how to serve.

While it is of course the losing party who usually moves to vacate a judgment, under
CPLR 5015 a party may even move to vacate her own judgment. A plaintiff may be
allowed to vacate a default judgment she obtained against the defendant, for example,
so as to add a fraud claim based on newly discovered evidence.[5]

It is not even indispensable that the person moving the vacatur have been a party
to the action. One who was not a party may be allowed to move to vacate the judgment
if he demonstrates a legitimate interest in doing so. In one case, for example, P, in taking
a default judgment against D Corporation, concealed certain facts, and this concealment

---

[1] G.F.A. Advanced Systems, Ltd. v. Local Ocean LLC, 137 A.D.3d 479, 26 N.Y.S.3d 285, 285–86 (1st
Dep't 2016).

[2] See 3d Rep. Leg. Doc. No. 17, p. 204 (1959). Fed. R. Civ. P. 60(b), on which CPLR 5015(a) is based,
has a paragraph 6 which, after earlier paragraphs enumerate specific grounds, authorizes vacatur of a
judgment or order for "any other reason that justifies relief." The New York provision omits that as superfluous
in view of the New York caselaw that reaches the same conclusion. See Woodson v. Mendon Leasing Corp., 100
N.Y.2d 62, 68, 760 N.Y.S.2d 727, 731, 790 N.E.2d 1156, 1160 (2003).

[3] See § 422.

[4] See Wood v. Ford, 78 A.D.3d 585, 432 N.Y.S.2d 572, 572–73 (4th Dep't 1980); see Lipp v. Port
Authority of New York and New Jersey, 17 Misc. 3d 667, 671, 847 N.Y.S.2d 405, 408–09 (Sup. Ct., Queens
County 2007), aff'd, 57 A.D.3d 953, 871 N.Y.S.2d 307 (2d Dep't 2008).

[5] Cooke v. Wozen Equities, Inc., 143 Misc. 3d 578, 540 N.Y.S.2d 629 (Sup. Ct., New York County 1988).

gave P more of a judgment than he was entitled to. When D proved insolvent and could not pay the judgment, P thereupon sued X on a charge that X looted D. The claim against X depended on the validity of the judgment P had against D. This was held to give X a sufficient interest to move to vacate the P v. D judgment, which X did on the ground of fraud or misconduct, the ground set forth in paragraph 3 of CPLR 5015(a).[6]

Ensuing sections will treat each listed category of CPLR 5015(a) separately.

§ 427. Excusable Default

The first category of vacatur ground listed in CPLR 5015(a) is excusable default, a ground that in some measure overlaps that supplied by CPLR 317. Both provisions were compared and contrasted earlier.[1] The reader may find it helpful to review that discussion before continuing here; it clarifies, among other things, that the 1-year period purporting to restrict this ground of vacatur is not a period of limitation and is therefore not rigidly applied, and that a motion to vacate a default in New York practice, whether based on CPLR 317 or 5015(a)(1), should be accompanied by (1) an excuse for the default and (2) an affidavit of merits.[2]

The courts are liberal in vacating default judgments. They want disputes resolved on the merits and are therefore inclined, practically speaking, to accept a generous range of excuses, sometimes even vacating deliberate defaults,[3] but there is a limit to their patience and from time to time a warning is issued to potential defaulters. One defendant, for example, who apparently suffered the default because he deemed himself execution-proof, moved for vacatur only when it appeared that the plaintiff had discovered a way to get at the defendant's property. His motion was denied.[4] If the default is beyond all excusing, it has been said that masses of neither "contriteness nor penitence" will help the defendant,[5] but that view is not universal. Other courts may open the default and allow the defaulter to repent under a hefty money sanction.

One ordinarily thinks of the defendant as the party making a motion to vacate a default judgment, which is of course the more common situation, but CPLR 5015(a)(1) contemplates that for good cause shown a plaintiff may move to vacate a default judgment entered in his own favor. Where it appeared, for example, that a default judgment based only on a loan would have been dischargeable in the defendant's bankruptcy, the plaintiff was allowed to open the judgment so as to add and litigate a fraud ground (substantiating it in his papers), which would survive bankruptcy.[6]

---

[6] Oppenheimer v. Westcott, 47 N.Y.2d 595, 419 N.Y.S.2d 908, 393 N.E.2d 982 (1979). Another point made in *Oppenheimer* is that the availability to X of a plenary action to vacate the judgment does not preclude the use of the simpler CPLR 5015(a) motion as an alternative.

[1] See § 108.

[2] The assumption in the present section is that the court obtained jurisdiction and the defendant is seeking to open the default only to be allowed to defend on the merits, a matter in the court's discretion. When the motion is based exclusively on lack of jurisdiction, the governing paragraph of CPLR 5015(a) is 4, not 1, and involves no discretion, and requires no affidavit of merits, as discussed more fully in § 430.

[3] See, e.g., Hensey Properties, Inc. v. Lamagna, 23 A.D.2d 742, 258 N.Y.S.2d 495 (1st Dep't 1965). If the court vacates a deliberate default, it should impose a substantial costs assessment against the defaulter, as it did in *Hensey*.

[4] Murphy v. Hall, 24 A.D.2d 892, 264 N.Y.S.2d 782 (2d Dep't 1965).

[5] Beetz v. City of New York, 73 A.D.2d 925, 423 N.Y.S.2d 503 (2d Dep't 1980).

[6] See Manufacturers Nat. Bank of Troy v. Soltys, 49 Misc. 2d 261, 267 N.Y.S.2d 237 (Montgomery County Court 1966); see also Cooke v. Wozen Equities, Inc., 143 Misc. 2d 578, 540 N.Y.S.2d 629 (Sup. Ct., New York County 1988). It would be difficult for a plaintiff to do this kind of thing today unless the plaintiff can

If the court vacates the default, it can do so in whole or in part. If it deems liability to be inadequately contested in the defendant's moving affidavit of merits, for example, but finds a genuine issue raised about damages, it can vacate the default judgment only to the extent of permitting a damages trial.[7]

The defaults contemplated by CPLR 317 and 5015(a)(1) are defaults on which a judgment has already been rendered or an order already made on the default. A party should of course be able to undo a default before it has been formally converted into the form of an order or judgment: that these provisions allow the default to be opened after entry affords authority a fortiori for the court's entertaining the application before entry.

An assumption under these provisions is that the defaulting party had no hearing in respect of the matter defaulted, which is usually the case when the default consists of a failure to appear in the action. But keep in mind that a "default" can be imposed for other behavior than failing to make an initial response to process, such as for repeated failures to make disclosure despite opportunities to do so. In the latter situation, the recalcitrant party has had his hearing and CPLR 5015(a)(1) does not support a motion to vacate the "default."[8] The procedure in that situation is for the defaulter to appeal the judgment, not move to vacate it.[9]

A motion to vacate a default judgment must of course be addressed to the court, whether based on CPLR 317 or 5015(a)(1). But if all parties stipulate to the vacatur, the clerk can do the vacating upon the filing of the stipulation.[10] It has been held, however, that not even a stipulation between the parties—whatever other rights it may affect between them—will undo a sheriff's execution sale already conducted in enforcement of the default judgment.[11]

The motion to vacate a default judgment is ordinarily made on the initiative of a party to the particular action. But a series of abuses in the consumer area, coming to the fore in the 1960s and 1970s, resulted in the enactment of a provision[12] authorizing the en masse vacatur of default judgments found to have been the product of consistent abuse at the hands of a given plaintiff or plaintiffs.[13] The change eased service requirements and reduced instances of "sewer service," but it still appears and came to the fore again in 2009 when it prompted the intervention of the attorney general.[14]

---

show that he had no notice of the fraud in time to include a claim based on it in the earlier action. See the discussion of the "transactional analysis" test in § 447, in the res judicata chapter.

[7]   See Borek, Stockel & Co. v. Slevira, 203 A.D.2d 314, 609 N.Y.S.2d 679 (2d Dep't 1994); Schutzer v. Berger, 40 A.D.2d 725, 337 N.Y.S.2d 71 (2d Dep't 1972).

[8]   See Champion v. Wilsey, 150 A.D.2d 833, 540 N.Y.S.2d 594 (3d Dep't 1989).

[9]   See Clarke v. United Parcel Service, Inc., 300 A.D.2d 614, 614–15, 752 N.Y.S.2d 395, 396 (2d Dep't 2002); Achampong v. Weigelt, 240 A.D.2d 247, 658 N.Y.S.2d 606 (1st Dep't 1997) (SPR 61:4); but see Lauer v. City Of Buffalo, 53 A.D.3d 213, 862 N.Y.S.2d 675 (4th Dep't 2008) (holding that a party who fails to comply with the terms of a conditional order can move under CPLR 5015(a)(1) to vacate the "default"). The *Lauer* decision is discussed in detail in Commentary C3126:13 on McKinney's CPLR 3126.

[10]   CPLR 5015(b).

[11]   Roosevelt Hardware v. Green, 72 A.D.2d 261, 424 N.Y.S.2d 276 (2d Dep't 1980).

[12]   Originally Jud. Law § 217–a, now subdivision (c) of CPLR 5015.

[13]   Fraud, misrepresentation, illegality, unconscionability, lack of adequate service, and other "violations of law" are listed as the abuses sufficient to trigger this procedure. CPLR 5015(c). The provision is sometimes called "Thompson's Law," after Justice Edward Thompson, whose default-vacatur activities as administrative chief of the New York City Civil Court paved the way for this codification.

[14]   See the discussion of sewer service in § 71.

This category of collective default vacatur is initiated by the administrative head of the particular court when evidence exists of extended abuse; it is a category apart and should not be confused with the ordinary motion to vacate a default judgment under CPLR 5015(a)(1).

§ 428. Newly Discovered Evidence

The key word in paragraph 2 of CPLR 5015(a) is "probably." Newly discovered evidence will not suffice to open the judgment and permit retrial of the merits unless the court is convinced that the new evidence would "probably" change the result. A mere showing of possibility is insufficient. So is a showing that the new evidence is merely cumulative or relevant only to a witness's credibility.

Perhaps the best known illustration of this motion, while by no means the only one, is the post-judgment appearance of a key witness to the event, unknown-of or unlocatable earlier in spite of diligent effort.[1]

There is no stated time limit for a motion to vacate based on newly discovered evidence. The law implies a reasonable time,[2] and what is reasonable is determined sui generis.

Newly discovered matter such as would reopen the judgment must, as a rule, be competent evidence, although occasionally even incompetent evidence may be allowed to do it if it tends "dramatically" to undermine the original judgment, as where H discovered, after W was granted a separation from him, that W at the time of the trial was pregnant by another man.[3] Entertaining presumably incompetent evidence for this purpose, however minds may disagree about its utility, has analogy in the summary judgment area, where incompetent evidence has sometimes been entertained to defeat a summary judgment motion.[4]

A further requirement for a motion under CPLR 5015(a)(2) is that the newly discovered evidence could not have been discovered in time to move for a new trial under CPLR 4404. Since a motion under CPLR 4404 must be made within 15 days after the decision or verdict,[5] the discovery of the new evidence before the expiration of that 15-day period would presumably fit that motion and therefore preclude this one. This is playing things a bit close, however, and the courts are justifiably reluctant to deny newly discovered evidence motions, otherwise meritorious, that are near these time lines, even if on the wrong side of them. If, for example, the evidence is discovered towards the end of the 15-day period, but nonetheless in time to move under CPLR 4404, a failure to make that motion would technically forfeit the objection altogether, the CPLR 4404 motion being too late and the CPLR 5015(a)(2) motion not being available because the CPLR 4404 motion was.

The courts have tried various ways around this potential injustice,[6] but the shortest answer is that the 15-day period purporting to restrict the CPLR 4404 motion, since it

---

[1]   See Cizler v. Cizler, 19 A.D.2d 819, 243 N.Y.S.2d 614 (1st Dep't 1963).

[2]   See 3d Rep. Leg. Doc. No. 17, p. 205 (1959).

[3]   See Delagi v. Delagi, 34 A.D.2d 1005, 313 N.Y.S.2d 265 (2d Dep't 1970). The source of the alleged incompetence of the evidence in the *Delagi* case was the doctor-patient privilege.

[4]   See § 281.

[5]   CPLR 4405.

[6]   See, e.g., Tollin v. Elleby, 77 Misc. 2d 708, 354 N.Y.S.2d 856 (N.Y. City Civ. Ct. 1974).

is not a statute of limitations, is presumably subject to discretionary extension by the court.[7] In that light, a motion based on CPLR 5015(a)(2) which could have been made just a little earlier under CPLR 4404 can be treated as a late—but excusably late—CPLR 4404 motion.

§ 429. Fraud or Misconduct

"Fraud, misrepresentation, or other misconduct of an adverse party" is ground for vacating the judgment under paragraph 3 of CPLR 5015(a).[1] Of course, the court must be convinced that the conduct complained of is something that could have affected the outcome.

The fraud involved can qualify as either "intrinsic" or "extrinsic." The main point of deciding which it is has to do with where the motion may be made. If the fraud is "intrinsic," it can as a rule be acted on only by direct attack, which means on direct appeal or by a motion to vacate the judgment made to the court that rendered it. If it is "extrinsic," it can also be the basis of a collateral attack, i.e., a separate action to enjoin its enforcement or a refusal by some other court to recognize the judgment when its validity arises in some context before that court.

An effort to draw a sharp line between the two categories of fraud is not rewarding. Extrinsic fraud is generally considered to be that conduct which deprives a party of a full trial or has the effect of preventing a party from fully presenting her case. Examples would be where there have been false representations that the action has been discontinued, or will be dropped, or that judgment will be taken only for X relief—prompting a default—with Y relief then being applied for and granted in violation of the understanding.[2] A judgment based on a fraudulent instrument, on the other hand, or perjured testimony, or any other item presented to and acted on by the court, whatever its fraudulent component, is just an intrinsic fraud and may hence be acted on only through direct attack.[3] Airtight distinctions are probably impossible, but perhaps a reasonably accurate general statement is that conduct which in effect denies a hearing is extrinsic while conduct that injects fraud into the hearing is intrinsic.

In line with the commanding position of the Full Faith and Credit Clause[4] governing state judgments, which requires State 2 to recognize any judgment of State 1 rendered with jurisdiction regardless of any error that the court may have made on the merits,[5] it would be helpful to characterize as "extrinsic" only that fraud which divests State 1 of jurisdiction. Only then would full faith and credit authorize a collateral attack on the judgment. But while that may seem like a good answer, it merely puts the question in different terms: what fraud will deprive State 1 of jurisdiction? If the party seeking to undo the judgment will seek the undoing by a motion to vacate made to the rendering court, which can entertain the fraud ground whatever its category, a collateral reward will be that there will be no need to determine which "trinsic" it is.

---

[7]   See CPLR 2004; § 6.

[1]   Paragraph 3 is modeled on Fed. R. Civ. P. 60(b)(3).

[2]   See the extended treatment in Tamimi v. Tamimi, 38 A.D.2d 197, 328 N.Y.S.2d 477 (2d Dep't 1972).

[3]   See Crouse v. McVickar, 207 N.Y. 213, 100 N.E. 697 (1912); Stewart v. Citimortgage, Inc., 122 A.D.3d 721, 722, 996 N.Y.S.2d 638, 639–40 (2d Dep't 2014).

[4]   U.S. Const. art. IV, § 1.

[5]   V.L. v. E.L., 136 S. Ct. 1017, 1020, 194 L. Ed. 2d 92 (2016); Fauntleroy v. Lum, 210 U.S. 230, 28 S. Ct. 641, 52 L. Ed. 1039 (1908).

A paragraph 3 objection often overlaps some other paragraph of CPLR 5015(a). The fraud ground, for example, even if only of the "intrinsic" variety, is likely to overlap paragraph 2 of CPLR 5015(a) since the fraudulent conduct now uncovered is likely to qualify as "newly-discovered evidence" as well. If an overlap there be, so much the better for the movant, who should join all grounds. Where, for example, post-judgment motion pictures taken of a personal injury plaintiff who presented a sad physical picture during the trial show a sudden recovery afterwards—better known to fraud than to science— the new data would constitute newly discovered evidence as well as showing fraud. The fraud in that case would probably be an "intrinsic" fraud, but, whatever its category, it would invoke paragraph 2 as well as paragraph 3 of CPLR 5015(a).[6]

Facts that establish an "extrinsic" fraud, on the other hand, which can be seen as affecting the court's jurisdiction, may also invoke the jurisdictional ground of paragraph 4, discussed in the next section. Again, the movant should join all grounds when more than one seem to apply.

If the fraud does get stamped "extrinsic," it technically dispenses with an affidavit of merits as part of the moving papers because it is deemed to go to jurisdiction.[7] But here the movant may be too easily misled. Since it is often difficult if not impossible to predict in advance which "trinsic" describes the case, the inclusion of a strong affidavit of merits can do no harm.

The Advisory Committee intended the "fraud" of paragraph 3 to have broad meaning, citing Ladd v. Stevenson,[8] a major New York case on the power of a court to vacate its judgments in the interest of justice.[9] Under the *Ladd* case, the power of the court to relieve a party from a judgment taken through mistake, inadvertence, surprise, or excusable neglect "does not depend on any statute, but is inherent."[10]

On the question of time, the rule is the same here as for the newly discovered evidence motion of paragraph 2. There being no stated time, a reasonable time will govern the motion to vacate on the ground of fraud or misconduct, with the court determining reasonableness on a sui generis basis.

§ 430. Lack of Jurisdiction

If the court lacked jurisdiction to render the judgment or order, the motion to vacate should be based on paragraph 4 of CPLR 5015(a). The motion can rest on a lack of subject matter jurisdiction, but more frequently it's based on a lack of personal jurisdiction. Whichever it is, CPLR 5015(a)(4) applies but the court will perhaps not cite it. The reason is that lack of jurisdiction is so deep a defect, and so obviously a basis for vacatur, that a statute authorizing the vacatur on this ground is like the proverbial fifth wheel. For the same reason, the jurisdictional defect permits the vacatur motion without a time limit: the judgment in this instance is theoretically void and the order sought under CPLR 5015(a)(4) is not what makes it so; the order merely declares it to be so, cancelling of

---

6   See, e.g., Cohen v. Crimenti, 24 A.D.2d 587, 262 N.Y.S.2d 364 (2d Dep't 1965).

7   Shaw v. Shaw, 97 A.D.2d 403, 467 N.Y.S.2d 231 (2d Dep't 1983); see Avenoso v. Avenoso, 266 A.D.2d 326, 698 N.Y.S.2d 301 (2d Dep't 1999); see § 430.

8   Ladd v. Stevenson, 112 N.Y. 325, 19 N.E. 842 (1889).

9   See 3d Rep. Leg. Doc. No. 17, p. 204 (1959).

10   *Ladd*, 112 N.Y. at 332, 19 N.E. at 844.

record a judgment that has had the presumption to stand on the books without a jurisdictional invitation.[1]

There is a substantial difference in purpose between this motion and those of the earlier paragraphs of CPLR 5015(a). The others, such as the default opener of paragraph 1 and the newly discovered evidence ground of paragraph 2, seek to vacate the judgment so as to clear the way for a trial, or for a new trial, while the motion under paragraph 4 seeks to vacate the judgment and dismiss the underlying action altogether. Often when the alleged want of jurisdiction has led the defendant to default, she will join paragraphs 4 and 1 in the alternative: move to vacate the judgment and dismiss the action under paragraph 4 or, if jurisdiction should be found present, open the default and defend on the merits under paragraph 1.[2]

If the motion is based on paragraph 4 alone—want of jurisdiction—no affidavit of merits is necessary because "[s]uch a judgment is a nullity, irrespective of the question of merit."[3] Indeed, it would not even be proper to make the vacatur of the judgment conditional, such as by requiring the defendant to appear and defend the case on the merits or to waive a defense, such as the statute of limitations. The court in such an instance is "without authority to take any action other than to dismiss."[4]

As already noted, it is generally a good idea for the defendant to hedge his bets, however, and make the motion in the alternative—to vacate the judgment and (1) dismiss for want of jurisdiction or, if the court finds jurisdiction present, (2) to open the default and permit the defendant to defend on the merits. Since the second alternative requires the affidavit of merits even if the first does not, the affidavit of merits should be included not as an adjunct of the first part of the motion, but of the second. The bottom line is that it should be included. To omit it because the first part—the jurisdictional ground—doesn't require it is to forfeit the second part—the discretionary vacatur—altogether: the defendant would have to prevail on the jurisdictional point or lose everything, including the very substantial right to a hearing on the merits. That would be putting too many eggs in one basket.

If the defect is one of subject matter jurisdiction, it is as a rule unwaivable. But if it goes to personal jurisdiction, it is of course subject to waiver. A waiver can occur, for example—if it hasn't already occurred within the action—where a defendant makes payments on the judgment for a considerable time after its rendition[5] or settles the matter.[6]

Some objections occasionally thought of as "jurisdictional" are not so in either the subject matter or personal sense. In matrimonial actions, for example, it is often

---

[1] See Fed. R. Civ. P. 60(b)(4), for the counterpart provision in the federal rules, whose ground is simply that "the judgment is void."

[2] The consequence of specifying only the jurisdictional ground in this situation is illustrated in City of Albany Indus. Development Agency v. Hampton Investors, 175 A.D.2d 466, 572 N.Y.S.2d 747 (3d Dep't 1991).

[3] Shaw v. Shaw, 97 A.D.2d 403, 404, 467 N.Y.S.2d 231, 234 (2d Dep't 1983). The U.S. Supreme Court has so held even as a matter of federal constitutional law. See Peralta v. Heights Medical Center, Inc., 485 U.S. 80, 108 S. Ct. 896, 99 L. Ed. 2d 75 (1988).

[4] Community State Bank v. Haakonson, 94 A.D.2d 838, 463 N.Y.S.2d 105 (3d Dep't 1983).

[5] See, e.g., Star Credit Corp. v. Ingram, 71 Misc. 2d 787, 337 N.Y.S.2d 245 (N.Y. City Civ. Ct. 1972).

[6] Lomando v. Duncan, 257 A.D.2d 649, 650, 684 N.Y.S.2d 569, 569–70 (2d Dep't 1999) ("defendant's partial satisfaction of the judgment against him in order to obtain a release of the lien on his real property amounted to a partial settlement of the action which impliedly acknowledged the validity of the judgment"). See § 111 (discussing waiver of defense of lack of personal jurisdiction).

necessary to show that at least one of the parties was a resident of the state for a minimum of 1 year prior to the commencement of the action;[7] it is a condition precedent to the maintenance of the matrimonial action, a substantive element of the cause of action itself. But it is not a requirement of "jurisdiction" within the meaning of CPLR 5015(a)(4). Hence an error in this respect by the trial court, entertaining the action despite the absence of residence, does not void the judgment and subject it to attack indefinitely.[8] If it did, the judgment would be undependable, a particularly critical prospect in the matrimonial realm.

§ 431. Reversal of Underlying Judgment

If the judgment or order is based on some other judgment or order, and the latter is in some way undermined, as by reversal, modification, or vacatur, the dependent judgment can similarly be cancelled or adjusted by motion under CPLR 5015(a)(5). The most likely context for this happening is where a sister-state or foreign country judgment has been converted into a New York one,[1] only to be afterwards undone in some way at home.

The provision also applies to original New York judgments. For example, P sued D, who impleaded X—an ordinary indemnity situation—but D won against P, which naturally gave X judgment against D on the third-party claim because there was nothing to indemnify. Only P appealed, but he succeeded, and the judgment for D was reversed. On motion by D under CPLR 5015(a)(5) after remand from the appellate court, X's judgment dismissing D's indemnity claim was also vacated. The court held that the revival of P's claim against D automatically reinstated D's indemnity claim against X.[2]

The Court of Appeals issued a major decision on CPLR 5015(a) in Nash v. Port Authority of New York and New Jersey,[3] where the plaintiff entered a $4.4 million judgment against the defendant Port Authority after successfully prosecuting her lawsuit for injuries sustained during the first World Trade Center bombing in 1993. The liability phase of her case was jointly tried with other plaintiffs and was then followed by her own separate trial on damages. The judgment in her action became final when the Port Authority did not appeal a final order of the appellate division to the Court of Appeals, a decision they would deeply regret.

Although the victory seemed complete, a second tragedy of sorts befell plaintiff in the form of a subsequent decision from the Court of Appeals in an action commenced by Antonio Ruiz, who was also injured in the bombing and whose action was jointly tried with plaintiff's during the liability phase. The Ruiz action remained in the appellate pipeline and, approximately two months after plaintiff's judgment had become final, the Court of Appeals ultimately dismissed it, concluding that the governmental immunity

---

[7] Dom. Rel. Law § 230. "Residence" here is usually construed to mean "domicile." See Black v. Black, 108 A.D.3d 842, 843–44, 968 N.Y.S.2d 722, 723–24 (3d Dep't 2013).

[8] See Lacks v. Lacks, 41 N.Y.2d 71, 390 N.Y.S.2d 875, 359 N.E.2d 384 (1976).

[1] This conversion can take place either through an ordinary plenary action, a motion-action under CPLR 3213, or, in the case of judgments entitled to full faith and credit, by the simple registration procedure of Article 54 of the CPLR.

[2] Frank L. Ciminelli Const. Co., Inc. v. City of Buffalo, 110 A.D.2d 1075, 1076, 488 N.Y.S.2d 932, 934 (4th Dep't 1985); see Springer v. Keith Clark Pub. Co., 191 A.D.2d 922, 923–24, 594 N.Y.S.2d 904, 905–06 (3d Dep't 1993) (on facts of case, CPLR 5015(a)(5) did not mandate, nor did the interest of justice require, reinstatement of this third-party complaint after plaintiff's action was reinstated in part).

[3] Nash v. Port Authority of New York and New Jersey, 22 N.Y.3d 220, 980 N.Y.S.2d 880, 3 N.E.3d 1128 (2013).

doctrine insulated the Port Authority from tortious liability for injuries sustained in the bombing.[4]

Four days after the Court of Appeals' decision in Mr. Ruiz's action, the Port Authority moved to vacate plaintiff's judgment pursuant to CPLR 5015(a)(5), arguing that the reversal of the liability determination in the *Ruiz* action required a vacatur of plaintiff's judgment, which depended on that liability determination. Plaintiff argued that the supreme court lacked jurisdiction to vacate her final judgment under this provision because the Port Authority failed to timely appeal the appellate division order in her action, which affirmed her judgment on both liability and damages.

A divided Court of Appeals concluded that plaintiff's substantial judgment was subject to vacatur under CPLR 5015(a)(5) based on the reversal of the liability determination against the Port Authority in the *Ruiz* action.[5] While the court agreed with plaintiff's contention that "her judgment had, in fact, become final when the Port Authority failed to appeal within the requisite time period," it nonetheless concluded that CPLR 5015(a)(5) could provide a pathway to its vacatur.[6] In language that may limit the applicability of its holding in future cases, the Court ruled that "[CPLR] 5015(a)(5) applies in a case like this one where a joint trial on liability results in a single order entered in two cases, and where, after a separate trial on damages in one of the cases, that order is reversed on appeal."[7] The majority still reversed, however, because it appeared that the courts below believed that they were required to vacate plaintiff's judgment after the Court's decision holding that the governmental immunity doctrine insulated the Port Authority from liability in Mr. Ruiz's action. The Court emphasized that the introductory language in CPLR 5015(a), which provides that a court "may relieve" a party from a judgment or order "upon such terms as may be just," highlights that a court's determination to vacate a judgment under CPLR 5015(a)(5) is discretionary, not mandatory. The Court of Appeals remitted the matter to supreme court to allow it to conduct an analysis of the pertinent facts and exercise its discretion on the motion to vacate.

On remand, the supreme court again vacated the $4.4 million judgment under CPLR 5015(a)(5) in the exercise of its discretion, but the appellate division reversed.[8] The court emphasized that when the Port Authority decided not to appeal either the liability or the damages determination in plaintiff's action, but to instead challenge the *Ruiz* judgment, it abandoned any claim that it was not liable to plaintiff. Furthermore, the court found that the Port Authority represented to the Court of Appeals that a reversal in the *Ruiz* action would not affect actions such as plaintiff's, which were final. While a court possesses limited authority under CPLR 5015(a)(5) to vacate a final judgment, the First Department ruled that it "must be sparingly exercised lest final judgments be subject to never-ending attack, undermining the sanctity and finality of judgments."[9]

---

[4]   In re World Trade Center Bombing Litigation, 17 N.Y.3d 428, 933 N.Y.S.2d 164, 957 N.E.2d 733 (2011).

[5]   *Nash*, 22 N.Y.3d at 225, 980 N.Y.S.2d at 884, 3 N.E.3d at 1132.

[6]   *Nash*, 22 N.Y.3d at 224, 980 N.Y.S.2d at 883, 3 N.E.3d at 1131.

[7]   *Nash*, 22 N.Y.3d at 225, 980 N.Y.S.2d at 884, 3 N.E.3d at 1132.

[8]   Nash v. Port Authority of New York and New Jersey, 131 A.D.3d 164, 167, 14 N.Y.S.3d 17, 19 (1st Dep't 2015).

[9]   *Nash*, 131 A.D.3d at 166, 14 N.Y.S.3d at 19.

CPLR 5015(a)(5)'s counterpart on the federal side, Rule 60(b)(5), in addition to contemplating the vacatur motion when the underlying judgment has been reversed or vacated, also allows it when the underlying judgment has been "satisfied, released, or discharged."[10] New York does not necessarily require a motion to vacate in that instance, contemplating instead the making of appropriate entries on the dockets to reflect the satisfaction. If the judgment debtor can secure from the creditor a satisfaction-piece in respect of the underlying judgment, even if foreign, duly acknowledged and otherwise in conformity with New York requirements,[11] it can be filed with the county clerk of the New York county with whom the foreign judgment was first docketed, resulting in an entry of satisfaction and thereby a cancellation of the judgment as a lien on the defendant's real property.[12] If the debtor has paid the underlying judgment and cannot secure the required satisfaction piece, she need only make a motion to the New York court, proving the satisfaction, and the court will order that it be entered of record and the docket adjusted accordingly.[13]

There is no stated time limit on a vacatur motion under CPLR 5015(a)(5). A reasonable time is therefore the standard, with the court to gauge reasonableness on the facts of the particular case.

§ 432. Conditioning the Vacatur

There is express authority in CPLR 5015(a) for the court to allow the vacatur "upon such terms as may be just." The conditions can include the granting of costs and disbursements for the trial or appellate levels or both, an attorney's fee, and such other sums as would defray actual expenses to which the other side has been put.[1] If the vacating of the judgment contemplates further proceedings, as where a default is opened and a trial on the merits is directed, or where a retrial results from newly discovered evidence, the judgment can be made to stand as security for the plaintiff pending the trial's outcome,[2] or the defendant can be required to post a bond in the amount of all or part of the judgment.[3]

There are no arbitrary limits on the court's discretion in fixing terms under CPLR 5015(a), as long as the ground relied on can be disposed of as a matter of discretion. The ground of paragraph 4, of course—want of jurisdiction—cannot. Hence, when the defendant moves to vacate the judgment solely on the ground of want of jurisdiction, the court cannot impose a condition, like exacting an appearance from the defendant or requiring the waiver of some defense.[4]

---

[10]   Fed. R. Civ. P. 60(b)(5).

[11]   See CPLR 5020.

[12]   CPLR 5021(a)(1).

[13]   CPLR 5021(a)(2). See § 424.

[1]   See, e.g., Workman v. Amato, 231 A.D.2d 627, 647 N.Y.S.2d 793 (2d Dep't 1996) (conditioning vacatur of default judgment upon the payment of the sum of $5,000 to compensate the plaintiff for the cost of its expert witness as well as for the inconvenience and additional legal work caused by defendant's delay in moving to vacate); Hensey Properties, Inc. v. Lamagna, 23 A.D.2d 742, 258 N.Y.S.2d 495 (1st Dep't 1965).

[2]   See, e.g., Treitel v. Arnold Chait, Ltd., 20 A.D.2d 711, 247 N.Y.S.2d 373 (2d Dep't 1964).

[3]   See, e.g., Sabre, Inc. v. Paras Exims, Inc., 60 A.D.3d 563, 563–64, 876 N.Y.S.2d 29, 29–30 (1st Dep't 2009).

[4]   Community State Bank v. Haakonson, 94 A.D.2d 838, 463 N.Y.S.2d 105 (3d Dep't 1983); see § 430.

§ 433. Restitution

If the judgment or order to be vacated or modified has already been paid in whole or in part, whether voluntarily or by execution or some other device for the enforcement of a money judgment, the judgment debtor may be entitled to have the money repaid. CPLR 5015(d) covers this by authorizing the court to direct the judgment creditor to make restitution. It adopts for this purpose the provision that authorizes restitution after an appeal has undone some part of a judgment.[1]

The restitution can be directed in the order granting the vacatur or modification, or by a later order. The important point is that the allowance of this relief by order clarifies that the judgment debtor will not be put to the burden of a separate plenary action to recover what has already been paid. The remedy is a mere motion. The lower courts, including the New York City Civil Court and the district, city, town, and village courts, also have this restitution power in respect of their judgments.[2]

An order directing restitution is the equivalent of an ordinary money judgment and may be docketed and enforced as such,[3] which makes the usual enforcement devices of Article 52 of the CPLR available. But despite its being an "order" to pay the money back, it is not ordinarily enforceable through the contempt punishment.[4]

The restitution requirement can have especially serious consequences in tort cases. When a tort defendant appeals a money judgment, the common practice is for the defendant (usually through its liability insurer) to secure a stay of enforcement by bonding the judgment.[5] It's unusual for the insurer to instead pay the judgment in the meantime, but that's what was done in Polipo v. Sanders,[6] the plaintiff collecting $500,000 while the case was on appeal. Reversal resulted, and now the insurer sought restitution. Rejecting the plaintiff's contentions that he had changed his life style after getting the money and that the insurer's payment amounted in any event to a waiver, the court ordered the restitution.[7]

The insurer's purpose was to save the interest that it would have had to pay had it lost on the appeal. Weighing that against the prospect that the plaintiff would squander the money and make it unavailable for restitution, however, suggests that this kind of gamble is not always a wise one for the insurer.

G. RENEWAL OF JUDGMENT

Table of Sections

§ 434.   Renewal of New York Judgment

§ 435.   Registration of Full Faith and Credit Judgment

---

[1]   See CPLR 5523.

[2]   See § 212 in the New York City Civil, Uniform District, Uniform City, and Uniform Justice Court Acts, McKinney's Vol. 29A, Parts 2 and 3, and CPLR 101.

[3]   CPLR 2222.

[4]   See Marlee, Inc. v. Bittar, 257 N.Y. 240, 177 N.E. 434 (1931). Cf. CPLR 5105.

[5]   See CPLR 5519(a)(2).

[6]   Polipo v. Sanders, 170 Misc. 2d 833, 650 N.Y.S.2d 941 (Sup. Ct., Bronx County 1996), aff'd, 245 A.D.2d 2, 666 N.Y.S.2d 406 (1st Dep't 1997).

[7]   The segment of the interim recovery that went to the lawyer as a contingent fee must also be returned. See Abrahami v. UPC Const. Co., Inc., 248 A.D.2d 272, 670 N.Y.S.2d 457 (1st Dep't 1998) (SPR 78:3).

§ 434. Renewal of New York Judgment

A plaintiff with a foreign judgment—a judgment rendered by a court in a sister state or foreign country—must, in order to enforce the judgment in New York, first take some step to convert it into a New York judgment. If the judgment is one of a foreign country, an action will have to be brought on the judgment, either in conventional form or by use of the summary judgment device of CPLR 3213;[1] if the judgment is one of a sister state or other American jurisdiction entitled to full faith and credit,[2] it has the even better option of the simple registration procedure of Article 54, treated in the next section.

A creditor with a New York judgment need not bother with any further proceedings on it: the judgment is ripe for enforcement and the creditor need only go about exploiting the enforcement devices. It would be idle to bring a new action on the judgment because a new one would ordinarily be no better than the old one. A New York action on a New York judgment is therefore precluded—except in a few instances. CPLR 5014 recognizes three such instances.

The first is where the real property lien of the original judgment has expired. Although a New York money judgment has a life of 20 years,[3] it is a lien against real property for only 10.[4] After the 10 years have expired without satisfaction of the judgment, the creditor is permitted to sue on it afresh so as to get a new judgment and hence a new 10-year lien.[5] The original 10-year period is measured from the filing of the judgment-roll in the original rendering court, which means that no new 10-year period will start at some later docketing, such as through the filing of a transcript of the judgment in some other county.[6]

The second exception involves certain default judgments. If a defendant who has failed to appear in a New York action was not served with the summons by personal delivery, and a default judgment was entered, the defendant may move to open the default under CPLR 317. The courts, liberal to begin with in vacating defaults, are especially so when a secondary method of service was used.[7] The plaintiff's default judgment in that situation is therefore insecure, which CPLR 5014(2) recognizes by allowing the plaintiff, if able to effect personal delivery of the summons in a second action, to sue on the earlier judgment[8] and secure a second and more secure one. It is an option left with the plaintiff. It is not exercised very often.

The last part of CPLR 5014, paragraph 3, is an omnibus provision enabling the court to authorize an action on a New York judgment in any situation that appeals to judicial

---

[1] See §§ 288 and 290. As the cited sections manifest, the CPLR 3213 motion device is ordinarily preferable to the ordinary plenary action.

[2] See § 471 in the chapter on res judicata, Chapter 17, for a discussion of which judgments get full faith and credit.

[3] CPLR 211(b).

[4] CPLR 5203(a).

[5] CPLR 5014(1).

[6] See CPLR 5203(a). The "first docketing" mentioned in CPLR 5014(1) should, for the sake of uniformity, be construed as also referring to the filing of the judgment-roll. It might otherwise give a lower court judgment, docketed by transcript with a county clerk several years after the judgment was rendered, a longer lien period than intended.

[7] See § 108.

[8] An endeavor to base such second action directly on the underlying claim in disregard of the first judgment would face the defense of res judicata. See § 450.

discretion. Under this paragraph, leave of court is necessary, which requires a motion;[9] under paragraphs 1 and 2, leave is not required.

Activity under CPLR 5014 in recent years has centered on its paragraph 1. Suppose that a judgment creditor, still unable to enforce the judgment and mindful that its 10-year lien on the defendant's real property is about to expire, brings an action under CPLR 5014(1) several months before the 10-year lien of the first judgment expires. Is that permissible? Some caselaw had held such an action premature.[10] But if a new action is not commenced until after the expiration of the original 10-year lien period, whatever time it takes to secure a new judgment would be a period in which there is no lien, which would enable another of the debtor's creditors to jump into the gap with priority.[11] Recognizing this, the legislature amended CPLR 5014 in 1986 to overrule the caselaw and permit the renewal action as early as 1 year prior to the expiration of the initial 10-year lien period. The new judgment is designated a "renewal judgment" and its 10-year lien begins when the first judgment's lien expires, thereby closing any gap in the continuity of the lien.

The renewal suit must be brought early enough within that last year so that, if renewal is granted, judgment can be *rendered* within the year. The judgment creditor's failure to do that in Gletzer v. Harris,[12] delaying suit until the very end of the year, forfeited the lien of the judgment and created a gap into which other waiting creditors were able to step. A jurisdictional issue confronted the creditor in *Gletzer*, because the judgment debtor had since moved from the state and it was apparently assumed by all that jurisdiction would have to be secured all over again against the now-no-longer-resident debtor. It's arguable, however, that the judgment should have been renewable, without new process, by mere registration under Article 54 of the CPLR, just as sister-state judgments are.[13]

If the second action is permissible, it should in any event be able to qualify as an action on a judgment and thus be entitled to at least the expedited procedures of CPLR 3213, which means that it can be brought on by service of a summons with summary judgment motion papers instead of a complaint.[14] As noted, if the renewal is sought under paragraph 1 of CPLR 5014, it shouldn't even have to go through that; it should qualify for the simple registration device of CPLR Article 54. Although Article 54 aims at a "foreign" judgment, it would be consistent with the article's purpose to apply it as well to a New York judgment ripe for renewal under CPLR 5014.

A plaintiff who has a claim against several persons, jointly or severally, and who sues and gets a judgment against only one of them, is not precluded by CPLR 5014 from bringing suit on the judgment against the others if the judgment has not been satisfied.[15] But while the second suit in that situation may be technically "based" on the original

---

[9]   The motion must be on notice to such persons as the court directs, which means that it should be brought on by an order to show cause in which the court can include those directions.

[10]   See, e.g., Brookhaven Memorial Hospital, Inc. v. Hoppe, 65 Misc. 2d 1000, 319 N.Y.S.2d 564 (Dist. Ct., Suffolk County 1971).

[11]   See the Commentary on McKinney's CPLR 5014.

[12]   Gletzer v. Harris, 12 N.Y.3d 468, 882 N.Y.S.2d 386, 909 N.E.2d 1224 (2009).

[13]   See the discussion in the lead note in NYSLD No. 594.

[14]   See §§ 288 and 290.

[15]   That is what CPLR 5014 intends to convey by its reference to Gen. Oblig. Law § 15–102. Nor, if the judgment is unsatisfied, is such an action against one debtor an election of remedies as against the others. See CPLR 3002(a).

judgment, it is really a new suit on the same underlying liability: the new defendant, because not a party to the earlier action, may not be visited with any res judicata or collateral estoppel consequences coming out of it.[16]

§ 435. Registration of Full Faith and Credit Judgment

Article 54 of the CPLR sets up a procedure for the simple New York registration of an out-of-state judgment, obviating an action on the judgment and even the motion-action of CPLR 3213. It applies, however, only to judgments "entitled to full faith and credit,"[1] which means the judgments of sister states, the federal courts, the United States territorial courts, and the courts of the District of Columbia.[2] The procedures in Article 54 do not apply to the judgment of a foreign country, which must therefore rely on the conventional action or the CPLR 3213 motion/action.[3]

Article 54 is the adoption, somewhat modified, of the Uniform Enforcement of Foreign Judgments Act.[4] It differs from Article 53, the Uniform Foreign Country Money-Judgments Recognition Act,[5] in two important respects. First, Article 53 is addressed only to foreign country judgments, while Article 54 is addressed to judgments of domestic courts. Second, Article 53 is not concerned with procedure, but rather with the substantive question of what foreign judgments are entitled to recognition. Article 54 leaves to federal statutory and decisional law the question of whether substantive recognition of a given American judgment is required by "full faith and credit."[6] It assumes entitlement and simply sets up an expeditious registration procedure.

A "judgment," as we use the word in this chapter, includes a mere order as well, as long as it has sufficient finality where rendered to make it enforceable there. The phrase used by CPLR 5401, in fact, is "judgment, decree, or order . . . ."

Generally speaking, all judgments rendered by American courts with jurisdiction must be accorded full faith and credit. Since Article 54 assumes that such a judgment is at hand, we make the same assumption here and leave to the later res judicata chapter the details of when full faith and credit is mandated.[7]

The only two categories of full faith and credit judgments that the statute explicitly bars from use of the registration procedure are (1) the judgment rendered in F-1 (the first forum) on the defendant's default in appearing,[8] and (2) the judgment by

---

[16] See CPLR 1502.

[1] CPLR 5401.

[2] See § 471 for further discussion of full faith and credit.

[3] Those routes remain as options for the full faith and credit judgment, too. See CPLR 5406. But in view of the great facility of the registration procedure, they would not ordinarily be used.

[4] CPLR 5408. See Kulzer, *The Uniform Enforcement of Foreign Judgments Act*, 13th Jud. Conf. Rep. 248 (1968), the background study of the uniform acts from which Article 54 of the CPLR emerged.

[5] CPLR 5309.

[6] See § 471.

[7] See § 471.

[8] CPLR 5401; see Schulz v. Barrows, 94 N.Y.2d 624, 628, 709 N.Y.S.2d 148, 150, 730 N.E.2d 946, 948 (2000). If the defendant did appear, but defaulted at some later stage of the proceedings, the resulting judgment does qualify for registration. See Shine, Julianelle, Karp, Bozelko & Karazin, P.C. v. Rubens, 192 A.D.2d 345, 345–46, 596 N.Y.S.2d 20, 21 (1st Dep't 1993); L & W Air Conditioning Co., Inc. v. Varsity Inn of Rochester, Inc., 82 Misc. 2d 937, 371 N.Y.S.2d 997 (Sup. Ct., Monroe County 1975), aff'd, 56 A.D.2d 735, 392 N.Y.S.2d 853 (4th Dep't 1977).

confession.[9] Those judgments, even if valid and entitled to full faith and credit, must seek conversion in a conventional action or with a CPLR 3213 motion.

The "confession of judgment" to which CPLR 5401 denies registration is narrowly construed in New York, but consent judgments in general do qualify for Article 54 registration. It has been held, for example, that an order entered in the foreign action "upon notice and consent of both parties" is entitled to registration.[10] Only the device commonly known as the formal "confession" of judgment, and especially, of course, the "cognovit" judgment, are barred from CPLR 5401 use.[11]

It has been held that a support award contained in a foreign judgment calling for periodic payments but not yet reduced to a final arrears judgment—a common situation in matrimonial and family court litigation—may not use the registration procedures of Article 54.[12] What the creditor really wants in that situation is to have the New York court "adopt" the foreign judgment as its own so as to make the New York judicial machinery available for an application for an arrears judgment. Whether New York will allow that is treated elsewhere.[13]

The procedure for registration is for the judgment creditor to get the judgment authenticated[14] and, within 90 days, file it with the county clerk of any county in the State.[15] An affidavit must also be filed attesting that the judgment was not rendered by default or confession and that its enforcement has not been stayed.[16] The affidavit must also state the sum still remaining unpaid on the judgment—this would of course apply only if the judgment is one for money, as most are[17]—and the name and last known address of the judgment debtor. The clerk's obligation upon that filing is to treat the judgment the same as if rendered by the New York Supreme Court, which makes it fully enforceable as such.[18] The applicant upon the filing must pay the appropriate fee,[19] whereupon the clerk assigns the judgment its own file and index number.[20] That index number should then appear on all enforcement papers, which should be captioned in the New York Supreme Court.

CPLR 5402(b) states that the filing converts the judgment into one of the New York Supreme Court even to the extent that "the same procedures, defenses and proceedings for opening, vacating or staying" a supreme court judgment apply to it. This is misleading and should be treated circumspectly by the courts. The only ground on which

---

[9]   CPLR 5401.

[10]   Mallan v. Samowich, 94 A.D.2d 249, 97 A.D.2d 364, 464 N.Y.S.2d 122 (1st Dep't 1983).

[11]   See §§ 299 et seq.

[12]   Glotzer v. Glotzer, 112 Misc. 2d 851, 447 N.Y.S.2d 603 (Sup. Ct., New York County 1982).

[13]   See § 290.

[14]   CPLR 5402(a). For authentication, see CPLR 4540.

[15]   Although any county is permissible, the judgment creditor would do well, for general convenience, to choose a county where the judgment debtor has property because the judgment will act as a lien on that property. See CPLR 5203(a). For further discussion of the judgment as a lien on real property, see § 517.

[16]   For example, the enforcement of a Massachusetts judgment is stayed by Mass. R. Civ. P. 62(d), which provides that "the taking of an appeal from a judgment shall stay execution upon the judgment during the pendency of the appeal."

[17]   CPLR 5402(a). A separate statute authorizes the New York filing of another state's child custody decree and gives the decree so filed the effect of a New York custody decree for enforcement purposes. See Dom. Rel. Law §§ 77–d and 77–e.

[18]   CPLR 5402(b).

[19]   See CPLR 8018(a).

[20]   CPLR 5405.

New York can refuse recognition to a full faith and credit judgment is lack of jurisdiction in the first court. No quantum of error on the merits or anything else not going to the jurisdiction of the first court is an excuse for refusing recognition,[21] unless it is shown that the original rendering court itself would permit attack on its judgment on the particular ground. A showing, for example, that an item of newly discovered evidence—such as finding a new witness not earlier known about—would not be allowed to upset the judgment under the law of the rendering court would also preclude New York from refusing recognition on that ground, notwithstanding the contrary assumption of CPLR 5402(b) and even though New York may allow vacatur of its own judgments on that ground.[22] CPLR 5402(b) should be taken in this respect to mean only that New York must make its procedures available to present the grounds, not as suggesting that New York law dictates what grounds will suffice.

In respect of enforcement, there are indications that New York law will govern even in particulars that give the registered judgment wider impact than it would have had at home. It has been held, for example, that a Pennsylvania judgment duly registered under Article 54 is entitled to enforcement against 10% of the defendant's wages, as authorized by New York law,[23] even though Pennsylvania allows no levy against wages at all.[24] Interest on the judgment, on the other hand, has been held to run at the rate prescribed by the law of the place of the judgment's rendition, not by New York law.[25]

Within 30 days after the filing, the judgment creditor must mail notice of the filing to the judgment debtor at its last known address.[26] The proceeds of any execution on the judgment cannot be distributed to the judgment creditor until 30 days after the creditor's filing of proof of service of the notice, providing an incentive to file proof of service as soon as possible.[27] The notice and waiting period are designed to give the judgment debtor a chance to move to vacate the judgment or otherwise attack the registration, as where the judgment debtor can show that the judgment was rendered by default or confession in the first forum and may therefore not exploit the registration procedure of Article 54.

Although any defect in the first forum's jurisdiction can of course be made the basis for vacating the registered judgment, the presence of first-forum jurisdiction is apparently all that is needed to justify registration. The background of Article 54 suggests that there is no need to demonstrate that New York has jurisdiction over the defendant. The assumption appears to be that the defendant got full due process in the first court and that there now remains only the need to enforce the judgment, which can proceed wherever the judgment debtor's property may be found and with no demonstration of personal jurisdiction over the judgment debtor in that place. Indeed, the state-to-state registration procedure of Article 54 has been viewed as equivalent to the county-to-county transcripting of a supreme court judgment within New York State

---

[21]   See V.L. v. E.L., 136 S. Ct. 1017, 1020, 194 L. Ed. 2d 92 (2016); Fauntleroy v. Lum, 210 U.S. 230, 28 S. Ct. 641, 52 L. Ed. 1039 (1908).

[22]   See CPLR 5015(a)(2); see § 428.

[23]   See CPLR 5231.

[24]   See People's Nat. Bank v. Hitchcock, 104 Misc. 2d 647, 428 N.Y.S.2d 850 (Sup. Ct., Broome County 1980).

[25]   Hospital Service Plan of New Jersey v. Warehouse Production & Sales Emp. Union, 76 A.D.2d 882, 429 N.Y.S.2d 31 (2d Dep't 1980). There appears to be a conflict on this point. See the discussion in § 412.

[26]   CPLR 5403.

[27]   CPLR 5403.

under CPLR 5018(a).[28] The notice requirement of CPLR 5403 is not necessarily for the purpose of inviting the judgment debtor to test New York's jurisdiction, but to enable the debtor to get the judgment vacated, as where (for another example) the debtor can show that the judgment has been paid.[29]

If the underlying judgment has been stayed in the first forum because of an appeal or a motion to vacate or the like, the judgment debtor can move to stay the overlaid New York judgment as well, but only upon a showing that if the first forum required security as a condition for a stay of enforcement, the security there has been given.[30] Additionally, if the judgment debtor can demonstrate a ground that would, under New York law, entitle a domestic judgment to be stayed, the debtor can move to stay the registered judgment on a like ground.[31] This would invoke CPLR 5240, for example, the provision authorizing a court to make protective orders in conjunction with the enforcement of a money judgment.[32] As discussed earlier, however, it would not allow an attack on a validly rendered judgment if the ground of the attack, although recognized by New York law, is not recognized by the law of the place where the judgment was rendered. If there is some doubt about whether a given vacatur ground would be entertained by the first forum, the New York court can stay local enforcement for just long enough to enable the judgment debtor to make the motion to vacate in the other jurisdiction and have the court there, rather than the New York court, determine the issue.

The registration procedure has a respected forebear in federal court practice, where statute[33] has for a long time authorized the registration of federal judgments between and among districts anywhere in the federal system. The availability of this federal registration procedure was even cited by the Second Circuit in a dictum suggesting that the Article 54 procedure does not apply to federal judgments,[34] but after further consideration the court held that it does,[35] pointing out significant differences between the two procedures.[36]

The federal alternative remains, however. The federal route converts any federal judgment into the equivalent of one rendered by a federal court in New York, and New York treats the latter the same as a New York judgment by allowing it to be transcripted into and throughout the State system. It was in the context of transcripting, in fact, that the federal registration statute was met and treated earlier.[37]

H. DECLARATORY JUDGMENT

Table of Sections

§ 436.   Declaratory Judgment, Generally

§ 437.   Uses of Declaratory Judgment

---

[28] See the Judicial Conference CPLR Report to the 1969 Legislature, Feb. 1, 1969, p. 46.

[29] See the Judicial Conference CPLR Report to the 1970 Legislature, Jan. 2, 1970, p. 27.

[30] CPLR 5404(a); see Evoy v. Amandio, 34 Misc. 3d 410, 932 N.Y.S.2d 874 (Sup. Ct., New York County 2011) (SPR 251:4) (merely appealing the underling judgment will not invoke a stay under CPLR 5404(a)).

[31] CPLR 5404(b).

[32] See § 522.

[33] 28 U.S.C.A. § 1963.

[34] See Knapp v. McFarland, 462 F.2d 935 (2d Cir. 1972).

[35] See Keeton v. Hustler Magazine, Inc., 815 F.2d 857 (2d Cir. 1987) (NYSLD No. 334).

[36] See Commentary C5402:3 on McKinney's CPLR 5402.

[37] See § 422.

§ 438.   Procedure in Declaratory Action; Limitations of Time

§ 439.   Trial by Jury in Declaratory Action

§ 440.   Judgment in Declaratory Action

§ 441.   Need for Follow-Up Relief

§ 436. Declaratory Judgment, Generally

The declaratory judgment action is primarily a creature of the 20th century and is therefore without direct ancestors either at law or in equity. It is not an unduly complicated procedural device, but its few elements can touch any of several junctures of a litigation and make it a bit difficult to niche chronologically in a text treatment. We have put it here, at the end of the treatment of judgments, because the foundation it requires needs a few building blocks from matters already treated. If its sudden appearance in present context seems abrupt, perhaps that explanation will soften the transition.

A declaratory action is like any other except that it contemplates a judgment that will merely declare the rights of the parties in respect to the matter in controversy and let things go at that. It differs from all of the traditional forms of action, inherited from the courts of common law and chancery, whose judgments go to enforcement either by execution or contempt. The main distinguishing factor of the declaratory action, therefore, is the absence of coercive enforcement. As a rule, the declaratory action can be brought by any person involved in a genuine civil controversy who feels that a mere judicial declaration of rights vis-a-vis the other side will do the job.

"The general purpose of the declaratory judgment is to serve some practical end in quieting or stabilizing an uncertain or disputed jural relation either as to present or prospective obligations."[1]

The declaratory judgment formally entered New York practice with the Civil Practice Act in 1921,[2] although the likes of it had been around for a time.[3] It is a useful and now well ensconced device with a variety of functions, as the next section will demonstrate. It is so much an accepted part of practice today that one must wonder why it had to be so cautiously approached during its early years.

There are only two basic provisions about the declaratory judgment in the CPLR, both of them brief and general. The first is CPLR 3001, which supplies the remedy:

The supreme court may render a declaratory judgment having the effect of a final judgment as to the rights and other legal relations of the parties to a justiciable controversy whether or not further relief is or could be claimed. If the court declines to render such a judgment it shall state its grounds.

The second provision is CPLR 3017(b), which concerns the relief clause:

In an action for a declaratory judgment, the demand for relief in the complaint shall specify the rights and other legal relations on which a declaration is requested and state whether further or consequential relief is or could be claimed and the nature and extent of any such relief which is claimed.

---

[1]   Walsh v. Andorn, 33 N.Y.2d 503, 507, 355 N.Y.S.2d 329, 332, 311 N.E.2d 476, 478 (1974).

[2]   Civ. Prac. Act § 473 (repealed 1963).

[3]   See Commentary C3001:2 on McKinney's CPLR 3001.

Just about everything the CPLR wants to say about the declaratory judgment is said in those two statutes. The rest is caselaw.

A genuine dispute—or "actual controversy" as it is called in the later adopted federal declaratory judgment provision[4]—is necessary for a declaratory judgment action. In common with an action in the federal courts, no New York action may be used to secure a mere advisory opinion, and this is as true of the declaratory action as of any other.[5] CPLR 3001 also says that the controversy must be "justiciable," but in this context, the word is apparently used only to confirm that there must be an actual controversy.[6]

It is sometimes thought that a declaratory action may be brought only when the facts are conceded and only the law is disputed. This unfortunate mistake probably comes from confusing the declaratory action with the action on submitted facts of CPLR 3222.[7] Although a case that poses only questions of law may make it ideal for a declaratory judgment,[8] there may indeed be fact issues in the action—and there usually are.[9] Indeed, if the parties do agree on the facts they can draw up a CPLR 3222 submission and with it seek a mere declaratory judgment, which simply shows that the declaratory action can use the same broad range of procedural tools as any other action.

As a newcomer on the scene—a scene occupied by judges and lawyers trained in the common law and its respect for precedent—the declaratory action was at first approached with suspicion. The idea took root that declaratory relief is "usually unnecessary where a full and adequate remedy is already provided by another well-known form of action."[10] One may occasionally hear echoes of that overly cautious approach, but it has in large measure been abandoned. Underlying it may have been the fear that the right of trial by jury could be infringed, or a statute of limitations circumvented, by allowing a declaratory action where one with the right to trial by jury or with a short limitations' period might otherwise have to be resorted to. Those are legitimate apprehensions, but they are met head on today, resolving questions of mode

---

4 28 U.S.C.A. § 2201.

5 See In re Workmen's Compensation Fund, 224 N.Y. 13, 119 N.E. 1027 (1918); Premier Restorations of New York Corp. v. New York State Dept. of Motor Vehicles, 127 A.D.3d 1049, 5 N.Y.S.3d 888 (2d Dep't 2015) (plaintiff pleaded "a hypothetical injury which would be contingent upon the occurrence of events which may or may not come to pass at some point in the future"). An exception to this rule today is the New York Court of Appeals' certification procedure, under which the court answers questions of New York law for federal and sister-state courts. See § 528A.

6 See, e.g., Jacob Goodman & Co. v. New York Tel. Co., 309 N.Y. 258, 128 N.E.2d 406 (1955), cited on the "justiciable controversy" point in 3d Rep. Leg. Doc. No. 17, p. 48 (1959). In what is probably its most common context, the separation of powers among the three branches of government, "justiciability" is used to describe issues appropriate to judicial resolution as opposed to those that belong to the legislative or executive branches. See New York State Inspection, Sec. and Law Enforcement Employees, Dist. Council 82, AFSCME, AFL-CIO v. Cuomo, 64 N.Y.2d 233, 485 N.Y.S.2d 719, 475 N.E.2d 90 (1984) (NYSLD No. 305). "Justiciability" problems met in the federal courts are more involved with the separation of powers problem than they are with the absence of a genuine controversy. See, e.g., Flast v. Cohen, 392 U.S. 83, 88 S. Ct. 1942, 20 L. Ed. 2d 947 (1968).

7 The action on submitted facts is discussed in § 304.

8 See, e.g., Morgenthau v. Erlbaum, 59 N.Y.2d 143, 150–51, 464 N.Y.S.2d 392, 396, 451 N.E.2d 150, 154 (1983); Dun & Bradstreet v. City of New York, 276 N.Y. 198, 206, 11 N.E.2d 728, 732 (1937).

9 See, e.g., Rockland Power & Light Co. v. City of New York, 289 N.Y. 45, 43 N.E.2d 803 (1942).

10 See James v. Alderton Dock Yards, 256 N.Y. 298, 305, 176 N.E. 401, 404 (1931). The Court in *James* was apprehensive that the declaratory judgment was being sought as a means of securing a premature lien, for which the plaintiff might otherwise have had to wait. It is submitted that if, but for that, declaratory relief would help, the declaration can be granted but the lien denied or postponed.

of trial[11] and statute of limitations[12] by direct address without necessarily denying the declaratory form of relief.

It is in fact a paradox to insist that P pursue D by coercive means when all P wants is a judicial statement resolving their dispute. It's like ordering a person to threaten a neighbor with a stick when all he wants to do is have the neighbor sit down to table and reason together.

CPLR 3017(b) makes clear that declaratory relief need not be sought by itself, but can be joined with a demand for more traditional relief. It usually is. A demand for a declaratory judgment is often joined with a demand for an injunction or for money damages. There is no bar to either, or to the joinder of any other category of legal or equitable relief to which the plaintiff fancies himself entitled along with the declaration.

A plaintiff who makes a mistake of form, moreover, and brings a declaratory action when the relief desired must be sought in other guise, should still not face a dismissal as long as the complaint states any recognizable claim under the law and jurisdiction over the parties has been secured. The worst that should happen is that the declaratory action gets converted to the more appropriate form.[13] It can even be converted into a special proceeding, such as one under Article 78 of the CPLR, if the relief sought is the stuff of that article.[14] The converse is also true, and many an Article 78 proceeding has been treated as a declaratory action.[15]

§ 437. Uses of Declaratory Judgment

One hesitates to set forth examples of declaratory actions, lest the examples used be taken as in any way exhaustive. There is no arbitrary restriction on the kind or character of claim that may be brought in declaratory form. A few prominent categories have found the declaratory action unusually helpful, however, and have used it prodigiously. These should be highlighted, but with the warning that they should not be taken as suggesting in any way the exclusion of the device from other contexts.

The matrimonial area is one of the leading beneficiaries of the declaratory action. Doubts about the validity of a divorce, for example, especially a foreign one purporting to rest on a rem foundation (the so-called "ex parte" divorce), can be resolved in a declaratory action. This can be brought either by the proponent of the divorce, to declare it valid, or by the other side, to declare it void. Alternatively, the action can declare on the validity of the marriage itself, whether or not tied in with a divorce or with any other category of matrimonial action.[1] There must of course be a genuine dispute about the marital status. W was denied a judgment declaring that she was married to H, for example, when despite a showing that H and his girlfriend were living together openly

---

[11]   On trial by jury in declaratory actions, see § 439.

[12]   On statute of limitations in declaratory actions, see § 438.

[13]   See CPLR 103(c).

[14]   See, e.g., Town of Fishkill v. Royal Dutchess Properties, Inc., 231 A.D.2d 511, 648 N.Y.S.2d 107 (2d Dep't 1996); Verbanic v. Nyquist, 41 A.D.2d 466, 344 N.Y.S.2d 406 (3d Dep't 1973). The Article 78 proceeding is treated in §§ 557 et seq.

[15]   See e.g., Lakeland Water Dist. v. Onondaga County Water Authority, 24 N.Y.2d 400, 301 N.Y.S.2d 1, 248 N.E.2d 855 (1969); see also Press v. Monroe County, 50 N.Y.2d 695, 702, 431 N.Y.S.2d 394, 397, 409 N.E.2d 870, 873 (1980) (discussing instances where courts converted Article 78 proceedings into declaratory judgment actions pursuant to CPLR 103(c)).

[1]   See Long v. Long, 281 A.D. 254, 119 N.Y.S.2d 341 (1st Dep't 1953); see Krieger v. Krieger, 25 N.Y.2d 364, 368, 306 N.Y.S.2d 441, 444, 254 N.E.2d 750, 751–52 (1969).

and having children, there was no colorable record of a marriage between them and hence no basis on which W would need a declaration.[2]

Insurance disputes have also lent themselves well to declaratory treatment. In ordinary casualty, disability, burglary, and fire insurance cases, for example, the action can determine such things as whether a loss was sustained and whether the policy was in effect at the time of the allegedly insured event.

In the liability insurance area, in view of the dominance of tort claims on court calendars today, the declaratory action has been a unique aid. Whenever there is a dispute about whether a liability policy covers a particular case, a declaratory action (often referred to as a "DJ action" in this context) can make the determination and can usually do it promptly. The principal appearance of this example is where the insurer has disclaimed coverage in a tort case, or wishes to, whether by reason of the policy's alleged lapse, the inapplicability of its terms, a failure of notice, the insured's want of cooperation, or any other reason. The first manifestation of the dispute is usually when the insurer receives a summons and complaint served on its insured, the defendant in a pending tort action, and refuses to defend. Both sides confront a dilemma. If the refusal continues, the insured must retain counsel, while the insurer, should the disclaimer ultimately be found invalid, may find itself liable on a claim already gone to judgment and with the right to defend it on the merits with counsel of its choice forfeited.

Resolution of whether the insurer must undertake the defense of the tort action, i.e., whether the policy is in force and applicable to the claim, may be resolved in a separate declaratory action brought while the tort action pends. It may be brought by either insurer against insured or vice-versa. Recognizing that the injured person, the plaintiff in the personal injury action, also has an interest in the resolution of this issue, some courts allowed the declaratory action to be brought by the injured person. After the Court of Appeals held in Lang v. Hanover Ins. Co.,[3] that this type of declaratory judgment action violated section 3420 of the Insurance Law, the so-called "direct action" statute, the legislature amended both CPLR 3001 and section 3420 in 2008 to allow the injured person the requisite standing. CPLR 3001 now provides that "[a] party who has brought a claim for personal injury or wrongful death against another party may maintain a declaratory judgment action directly against the insurer of such other party," but only if the disclaimer dispute centers on the insured's alleged failure to provide timely notice of the incident within the time required by the policy.[4]

If the fact on which coverage depends is one that would have to be resolved within the tort action itself, such as whether a driver had permission to use a vehicle (on which finding the owner's liability as well as the applicability of the insurance policy would depend), the insurer will be required to defend and a declaratory action will be rejected[5] or a declaration made that a defense is required.

The declaratory action is often used to test the validity, on constitutional or other grounds, or the scope, of a contested statute, ordinance, rule, regulation, or other law.

---

[2] See Somberg v. Somberg, 263 N.Y. 1, 188 N.E. 137 (1933). For criticism of this decision, see Commentary C3001:9 on McKinney's CPLR 3001.

[3] Lang v. Hanover Ins. Co., 3 N.Y.3d 350, 787 N.Y.S.2d 211, 820 N.E.2d 855 (2004) (NYSLD No. 540).

[4] See Ins. Law § 3420(a)(6); see also the Commentary C3001:10 on McKinney's CPLR 3001; SPR 201:1.

[5] See Allstate Ins. Co. v. Santiago, 98 A.D.2d 608, 469 N.Y.S.2d 343, 344 (1st Dep't 1983). A separate declaratory action will be allowed, however, if for some unique reason the decisive issue is removed from the tort action. See Aetna Cas. & Sur. Co. v. Lauria, 54 A.D.2d 183, 388 N.Y.S.2d 432 (4th Dep't 1976).

As long as the action is not an attempt to avoid a criminal prosecution and have the facts that would otherwise be tried in the criminal case tried instead in the declaratory action, a person with a genuine interest in the particular provision or its scope may seek the declaration.[6] Although nothing stops a declaratory action from presenting issues of fact, if this type of challenge poses only questions of law, it may be that much more conducive to a declaration.[7]

Use of a declaratory action to test the validity of a statute is also available in the administrative area. If, however, the plaintiff's attack is not on the validity of the applicable law but only on the propriety of the proceedings taken under it, the plaintiff must ordinarily pursue administrative channels before going to court. This is the well known doctrine of the exhaustion of administrative remedies, a precondition to judicial action, and when the dispute finally goes to court it is usually in a proceeding under Article 78 of the CPLR rather than a declaratory action.[8] The line between what is properly the function of an Article 78 proceeding and what is properly the function of a declaratory action is in fact one of the more obscure borders in litigation, often resulting in a rejection of the one brought because the other is found to be proper. But if the defect is one in form only, under the CPLR the worst that happens in that situation is a conversion from improper to proper form, with jurisdiction retained.[9]

The which-shall-it-be contest with Article 78 also illustrates how the plaintiff can end up with some incidental procedural advantage should an action in declaratory form be sustained. The venue of an Article 78 proceeding is restricted to the choices offered by CPLR 506(b), for example, while venue in a declaratory action is governed by CPLR 503, 504, and 505, which can offer a preferable venue allotment in a given case.[10]

A declaratory action will not be allowed to evade a criminal prosecution. It will therefore not be entertained when it appears to be an endeavor, by a plaintiff whose activities may be running afoul of the penal law, to force out of a civil action findings that would otherwise have to be made in an outright criminal prosecution. For that basic proposition, Reed v. Littleton[11] is a major case in point.

P in *Reed* sued in the supreme court for a declaration that stated activities were "not in violation" of certain penal law provisions. The court refused to entertain the case, noting that even if it found a violation to exist—i.e., made a finding against the potential criminal defendant—its holding would not be binding in a later criminal action because of the different burdens of proof: "a fair preponderance of the evidence" in the declaratory action (the usual civil burden) as against "beyond a reasonable doubt" (the criminal standard).

More recently, the Court of Appeals has noted that "[t]he general rule is that, once a criminal action has been initiated, a criminal defendant may not bring a declaratory

---

[6]   See the Commentary C3001:13 on McKinney's CPLR 3001.

[7]   See, e.g., Cayuga Indian Nation of New York v. Gould, 14 N.Y.3d 614, 904 N.Y.S.2d 312, 930 N.E.2d 233 (2010).

[8]   See, e.g., Slater v. Gallman, 38 N.Y.2d 1, 377 N.Y.S.2d 448, 339 N.E.2d 863 (1975). For treatment of Article 78, see §§ 557 et seq.

[9]   CPLR 103(c); see § 563.

[10]   See, e.g., W. T. Wang, Inc. v. New York State Dept. of Taxation and Finance, 108 Misc. 2d 641, 438 N.Y.S.2d 453 (Sup. Ct., New York County 1981), rev'd on other grounds, 88 A.D.2d 825, 451 N.Y.S.2d 130 (1st Dep't 1982), aff'd, 58 N.Y.2d 1021, 448 N.E.2d 1348, 462 N.Y.S.2d 437 (1983). A statute of limitations difference is not so easily avoided, however. See § 438.

[11]   Reed v. Littleton, 275 N.Y. 150, 9 N.E.2d 814 (1937).

judgment action to raise a statutory interpretation or other issue that can be adjudicated in the criminal prosecution."[12] The mere fact that a party is a criminal defendant, however, does not preclude her "from raising issues in a declaratory judgment action that cannot be resolved in the criminal action and that, even if sustained, will not supply a basis to prevent the prosecution or collaterally attack the conviction."[13]

While the courts have been especially sensitive to prevent the declaratory action from affecting a criminal action already pending, they appear to be less hesitant when the effect is on a future prosecution only. In Morgenthau v. Erlbaum,[14] for example, a criminal court judge, finding unconstitutional a statute dispensing with jury trial in certain cases, was about to use a jury. A district attorney brought a declaratory action in the supreme court to determine that the statute was valid and a jury unnecessary. The Court of Appeals allowed the action, but made the declaration applicable only to future cases (not to the specific criminal case that triggered the declaratory action).

Perhaps this distinction can be explained by the courts' greater willingness to adjudicate in declaratory form an issue about the procedure to be followed at the criminal trial than an issue about the guilt or innocence of the accused, which involves issues of fact. Indeed, if the facts are not in dispute, it has been held that the declaratory action may be used to determine whether conceded conduct comes within a penal law.[15]

Another advantage of the declaratory action is the initiative it will sometimes offer a person who is involved in a dispute but unable to find among the traditional kinds of action one that will enable her to bring it to court. In one case, for example, P was a composer who wanted a document construed as giving no rights in his compositions to D. It appeared, however, that P had no action at law—he maintained that the document was not a contract and hence that a contract did not exist—and none in equity either, such as for rescission or injunction. P might have waited, and brought the dispute to court with an injunction or damages claim after D actually pirated the property on the strength of the document, but it was held that P did not have to wait. He was allowed to get his claim resolved in a declaratory action.[16]

Similarly, where P does have other remedies but the others would be defensive only—P could do no better in existing modes than wait to be sued and then put his case in by way of defense—declaratory action lies and offers P a way to take the initiative.[17] The need to commence a declaratory judgment action in a defensive posture has arisen under the Fee Dispute Resolution Program implemented through Part 137 of the Rules of the Chief Administrator. Under the program, a client may pursue arbitration of a fee dispute with an attorney.[18] When a client is aggrieved by an arbitration award and claims that she owes the attorney nothing for the representation, or something less than the amount awarded by the arbitrator, she "may commence an action on the merits of

---

[12] *Cayuga Indian Nation*, 14 N.Y.3d at 633, 904 N.Y.S.2d at 321, 930 N.E.2d at 242.

[13] *Cayuga Indian Nation*, 14 N.Y.3d at 633 n.8, 904 N.Y.S.2d at 321 n.8, 930 N.E.2d at 242 n.8.

[14] Morgenthau v. Erlbaum, 59 N.Y.2d 143, 464 N.Y.S.2d 392, 451 N.E.2d 150 (1983).

[15] See New York Foreign Trade Zone Operators v. State Liquor Authority, 285 N.Y. 272, 34 N.E.2d 316 (1941) (distinguishing *Reed* decision); see also *Morgenthau*, 59 N.Y.2d at 150–51, 464 N.Y.S.2d at 396, 451 N.E.2d at 154.

[16] Kalman v. Shubert, 270 N.Y. 375, 1 N.E.2d 470 (1936).

[17] See *New York Foreign Trade Zone Operators*, 285 N.Y. at 278, 34 N.E.2d at 320.

[18] 22 N.Y.C.R.R. § 137.6(c) and (d).

the fee dispute in a court of competent jurisdiction within 30 days after the arbitration award has been mailed."[19] This will allow for de novo review of the fee dispute.[20]

The client aggrieved by the arbitration in this scenario cannot ordinarily commence an action for a money judgment because that is not the relief she is seeking. In effect, the client is usually seeking a declaration that she does not owe the lawyer for the claimed services and the only appropriate vehicle for obtaining such relief is a declaratory judgment action. Clients attempting to pursue this relief met jurisdictional obstacles because of the limitations on the subject matter jurisdiction of the lower courts to grant declaratory relief.[21] Effective January 1, 2011, the lower court acts were amended to provide jurisdiction to the lower courts to entertain declaratory judgment actions commenced by a party aggrieved by a Part 137 arbitration award.[22]

§ 438. Procedure in Declaratory Action; Limitations of Time

There is very little that is special about the procedure in a declaratory action. The remedy is generally restricted to the supreme court,[1] but its procedures follow those of any other action: summons, pleadings, bill of particulars, parties, disclosure, venue, trial, etc.[2] The same rules of both personal and rem jurisdiction apply. If there are issues of fact, a trial is necessary. If not, summary judgment is permissible. Whether a trial must be by jury is discussed later.[3]

It has been held that a declaratory judgment may be rendered in a special proceeding.[4] This does not mean, however, that a plaintiff may bring a special proceeding whenever declaratory relief is sought. It merely means that if the special proceeding has been authorized by statute in the particular kind of case,[5] relief in it can be demanded in declaratory form.

Earlier discussion touched on the problem of the statute of limitations in declaratory actions.[6] The "problem" is an attempt by a tardy plaintiff to circumvent an expired statute with the declaratory device. Since the declaratory action has no ancestor at law, it comes under none of the periods devised by Article 2 of the CPLR for law actions and

---

[19]   22 N.Y.C.R.R. § 137.8(a).

[20]   22 N.Y.C.R.R. § 137.8(a); see Tray v. Thaler & Gertler, LLP, 17 Misc. 3d 617, 842 N.Y.S.2d 713 (Dist. Ct., Nassau County 2007).

[21]   See, e.g., *Tray*, 17 Misc.3d at 620–21, 842 N.Y.S.2d at 715–17 (discussing cases).

[22]   See Commentary C3001:20 on McKinney's CPLR 3001; 2011 Commentary on § 212–a(b) of the New York City Civil Court Act.

[1]   CPLR 3001. The surrogate's court has often entertained proceedings that are in the nature of a declaratory judgment action. See the Commentary C3001:20 on McKinney's CPLR 3001. Under § 212–a of the New York City Civil Court Act, that court has jurisdiction of a declaratory action to test the validity of an insurance disclaimer.

[2]   We may note parenthetically that CPLR 3001 is concerned with declaratory judgments only by the courts. An administrative agency can issue a "declaratory ruling" on statutes and rules that are within its enforcement obligations. The statute that authorizes it, § 204 of the State Administrative Procedure Act, was broadly construed in Power Authority of State of N.Y. v. New York State Dept. of Environmental Conservation, 58 N.Y.2d 427, 461 N.Y.S.2d 769, 448 N.E.2d 436 (1983). See the Commentary C3001:20 on McKinney's CPLR 3001.

[3]   See § 439.

[4]   State Division of Human Rights v. State, 77 Misc. 2d 597, 354 N.Y.S.2d 287 (Sup. Ct., Rensselaer County 1973); see Shipman v. City of New York Support Collection Unit, 183 Misc. 2d 478, 483, 703 N.Y.S.2d 389, 392 (Sup. Ct., Bronx County 2000).

[5]   See CPLR 103(b).

[6]   See § 36.

therefore falls under the 6-year "residual" period of CPLR 213(1), which governs equity actions and all other actions for which no limitation is otherwise prescribed.

The 6 years is a relatively generous period, however, and the plaintiff does not get it automatically just by seeking declaratory relief. That would make it too easy for a plaintiff to evade the shorter period prescribed for an alternative remedy that might be just as effective in the particular case. To guard against this, the Court of Appeals adopted in Solnick v. Whalen[7] what may be described as a kind of next-nearest-context standard: the period applicable to the declaratory action is the shorter one that governs the action or proceeding that would have been the one brought if the declaratory action had not been invented. The Court said in *Solnick* that

> [a] salutary result of the application of the limitation period appropriate to the other form of judicial proceeding will be to preclude resort by a dilatory litigant to the declaratory remedy for the purpose of escaping a bar of time which has outlawed the other procedure . . . .[8]

Solnick concerned the health commissioner's disallowance of a Medicaid reimbursement. An Article 78 proceeding, governed by the 4-month limitation period of CPLR 217(1), would have been the usual procedure to contest the commissioner's action. The plaintiff, too late under that measure, got no longer of a period by suing for a declaration.[9]

By contrast, in Saratoga County Chamber of Commerce, Inc. v. Pataki,[10] plaintiffs commenced a declaratory judgment action seeking both a determination that a gaming compact between the State and Native American tribes was unconstitutional and an injunction against the use of State funds to implement it. Applying the next-nearest-context rule, the Court noted that the desired relief could not be sought against executive officials under CPLR Article 78 and, therefore, the 4-month statute of limitations under CPLR 217(1) did not apply. Quoting from its decision in *Solnick*, the Court ruled that because no other form of proceeding existed for the resolution of the claims tendered in the declaratory judgment action, the 6-year catch-all statute of limitations in CPLR 213(1) applied.

It is especially important to note this next-nearest-context rule in a proceeding to contest a real estate tax assessment. The proceeding is usually governed by a short period, one measured in terms of days or months. Yet it would not be difficult to contest the assessment in terms of a declaratory judgment, such as with an attack on the constitutionality of the rate schedule on which the assessment is based, which involves no issue unique to the particular case. But if the taxpayer expects to get more time by resorting to the declaratory action, the plan won't work. Emphasizing that municipal funding depends on the prompt disposition of all assessment disputes, the Court of Appeals has held that the shorter period applicable to the usual review proceeding will apply in assessment contests even if the specific issue raised is appropriate to a declaratory action.[11] If the attack on the assessment is that it violates 42 U.S.C. § 1983,

---

[7]   Solnick v. Whalen, 49 N.Y.2d 224, 425 N.Y.S.2d 68, 401 N.E.2d 190 (1980) (NYSLD No. 246).

[8]   *Solnick*, 49 N.Y.2d at 230, 425 N.Y.S.2d at 71–72, 401 N.E.2d at 194.

[9]   See also Gress v. Brown, 20 N.Y.3d 957, 958 N.Y.S.2d 675, 982 N.E.2d 595 (2012); § 566.

[10]   Saratoga County Chamber of Commerce, Inc. v. Pataki, 100 N.Y.2d 801, 766 N.Y.S.2d 654, 798 N.E.2d 1047 (2003).

[11]   Press v. Monroe County, 50 N.Y.2d 695, 431 N.Y.S.2d 394, 409 N.E.2d 870 (1980) (NYSLD No. 252).

however, the federal civil rights statute, which carries a 3-year statute of limitations, the Second Circuit has held that the 3 years would have to be allowed for the federal ground.[12]

Although difficult, because of its relative youth, to characterize as either wholly legal or wholly equitable, the declaratory action "is governed by equitable principles." Thus spoke the Court of Appeals in Krieger v. Krieger,[13] proceeding to apply the laches doctrine, an equitable defense, to the declaration sought there. H had waited until 12 years after W divorced him, and until after W had remarried, before bringing an action to declare the divorce void. The Court held the action barred by laches.[14] Thus, if the declaration is sought in what amounts to an equitable context, as in the *Krieger* case, it may get the benefit of the 6-year period of CPLR 213(1)[15] only to be undone by the laches doctrine, which can be applied even to bar a claim timely under the applicable statute of limitations.[16]

§ 439. Trial by Jury in Declaratory Action

The declaratory judgment action did not arrive on the New York scene until almost a century after the 1840's merger of law and equity and a century and a half after New York's 1777 Constitution, which marks the State's original moment of inheritance of the distinctions between common law and chancery. Therefore, it is impossible to award the declaratory action to either the law or equity category.

Inability to niche it poses problems in several areas, some already touched on. Some kind of determination of the "equitable" or "legal" nature of the relief sought may be necessary, for example, to discern the applicable statute of limitations in a declaratory action.[1]

It has also been seen that if the particular dispute involved in the case is found to be essentially "equitable" in nature, defenses traditionally associated with equity, such as laches, will be allowed despite prosecution of the claim in declaratory form.[2] In such instances, notwithstanding that the passkey to whether the claim is legal or equitable is usually the relief sought, the court is looking beyond the relief—which, as "declaratory" in nature, will offer no key at all—to the underlying nature of the claim asserted. It is applying a kind of next-nearest-context rule, asking, in effect, what kind of action would most likely have been used to present this claim had the declaratory judgment action not been created?

This kind of next-nearest-context rule should also be applied to determine whether the action is in essence equitable, and therefore triable by the court, or legal, and therefore triable by jury. That rule was applied by the Second Department in

---

[12] See Cloverleaf Realty of New York, Inc. v. Town of Wawayanda, 572 F.3d 93 (2d Cir. 2009). The decision undermines the *Press* case, which *Cloverleaf* apparently overlooked, but the undermining would only occur when the complaining taxpayer has the federal argument available but has omitted it from the original contest, not likely to happen often. *Cloverleaf* is the subject of lead notes in Issues 597 and 598 of the NYSLD.

[13] Krieger v. Krieger, 25 N.Y.2d 364, 306 N.Y.S.2d 441, 254 N.E.2d 750 (1969).

[14] The laches defense is discussed in § 36.

[15] Most of the equity actions also lack specific niches in Article 2 and hence fall into the 6-year catchall provision, as the declaratory judgment does when standing on its own.

[16] In *Krieger*, the statute of limitations was itself no bar because a void judgment, which the divorce was alleged to be, is not subject to the bar of the statute.

[1] See § 438.

[2] See Krieger v. Krieger, 25 N.Y.2d 364, 371, 306 N.Y.S.2d 441, 446, 254 N.E.2d 750, 753 (1969).

Independent Church v. Board of Assessors of Nassau County,[3] involving a challenge to a tax assessment. The most likely judicial context to raise such an issue before the declaratory judgment arrived on the scene was found to be an action to vacate the assessment as a lien, an equitable action. Hence, no jury.[4]

The federal courts had faced a similar issue earlier. In its major pronouncement, Simler v. Conner,[5] the U.S. Supreme Court took the same approach. A client's suit against his lawyer for a declaration of how much of a fee was due was held to be in essence a law action and therefore triable by jury. If no declaratory action had been available, the next-nearest-context to put the question would have been an action by the lawyer against the client to collect the fee, a simple money action triable by jury. It apparently makes no difference, in applying the next-nearest-context approach, that the more conventional plaintiff-defendant roles are reversed, and it should not. The right to trial by jury, as long as it remains available for use in civil actions, is too important a right to hold forfeit through the artifice of a simple declaration.

§ 440. Judgment in Declaratory Action

If a plaintiff in an ordinary action fails to establish entitlement to relief, the result is a dismissal of the complaint. In a declaratory action, "the court should make a declaration, even though the plaintiff is not entitled to the declaration he seeks."[1] A mere dismissal is not appropriate.[2] The court must determine the rights of the parties to the dispute involved and, if the defendant prevails, the declaration should simply go the defendant's way.[3]

If the defendant should move to "dismiss" the complaint in a declaratory judgment action for failure to state a cause of action under CPLR 3211(a)(7), it will only present for consideration the issue of whether a cause of action for declaratory relief is set forth and not the question of whether the plaintiff is entitled to a favorable declaration.[4] Therefore, a motion to dismiss a cause of action for declaratory judgment should be denied if the pleading "is sufficient to invoke the court's power to render a declaratory judgment . . . as to the rights and other legal relations of the parties to a justiciable controversy."[5] If, however, there are no questions of fact, the motion should be treated as one seeking a declaration in defendant's favor and treated accordingly.

---

[3]   Independent Church of Realization of Word of God, Inc. v. Board of Assessors of Nassau County, 72 A.D.2d 554, 420 N.Y.S.2d 765 (2d Dep't 1979).

[4]   See also Anesthesia Associates of Mount Kisco, LLP v. Northern Westchester Hosp. Center, 59 A.D.3d 481, 482, 873 N.Y.S.2d 202, 203–04 (2d Dep't 2009) (plaintiff not entitled to jury trial where cause of action for declaratory relief most closely resembled rescission, which is equitable in nature).

[5]   Simler v. Conner, 372 U.S. 221, 83 S. Ct. 609, 9 L. Ed. 2d 691 (1963).

[1]   Hirsch v. Lindor Realty Corp., 63 N.Y.2d 878, 881, 483 N.Y.S.2d 196, 197, 472 N.E.2d 1024, 1025 (1984).

[2]   Savik, Murray & Aurora Const. Management Co., LLC v. ITT Hartford Ins. Group, 86 A.D.3d 490, 494, 927 N.Y.S.2d 634, 638 (4th Dep't 2011); Hubert v. Lumbermens Mut. Cas. Co., 117 A.D.2d 964, 965, 498 N.Y.S.2d 931, 932 (3d Dep't 1986).

[3]   See Justice Court Mut. Housing Co-op., Inc. v. Sandow, 50 Misc. 2d 541, 270 N.Y.S.2d 829 (Sup. Ct., Queens County 1966).

[4]   North Oyster Bay Baymen's Ass'n v. Town of Oyster Bay, 130 A.D.3d 885, 16 N.Y.S.3d 555 (2d Dep't 2015).

[5]   *North Oyster Bay Baymen's Ass'n*, 130 A.D.3d at 890, 16 N.Y.S.3d at 560.

As is true of any judgment in any action, the court can shape its judgment in a declaratory action to suit the needs of the occasion.[6] If the court declines to render a declaration altogether, it must state its grounds.[7]

It will be recalled that the declaration need not be sought alone but can be joined with any other relief the plaintiff is entitled to, legal or equitable.[8] If the proof sustains a right to such other relief, the judgment should include it along with the declaration.

A duly rendered declaratory judgment is entitled to the full benefits of the res judicata and collateral estoppel doctrines,[9] which means that it is also entitled to full faith and credit from other American jurisdictions.[10]

§ 441. Need for Follow-Up Relief

Since CPLR 3017(b) expressly permits the complaint in a declaratory action to include any other relief the plaintiff has a right to, there is no reason for the plaintiff's withholding any relief due at the time. Indeed, the courts prefer that everything connected with the dispute be resolved at once so that a second action will not be necessary.[1] But if a declaratory judgment is forthcoming, and the party's rights as declared are afterwards violated, the party may bring a second action for the needed subsequent relief. If, for example, the first judgment's violation causes the plaintiff money damages, the plaintiff can seek the damages in a new action.[2]

While it is clear that such follow-up relief, if the need for it is the consequence of the declaration's flouting, may be pursued in a second plenary action, a plaintiff would ordinarily prefer to seek the relief by mere motion, instead, such as a motion to reopen or modify the original judgment to insert the additional relief. The motion would bear the caption of the original declaratory action and require no new ritual of summons service or pleadings. Fact issues, should they arise on the motion, could be expeditiously tried,[3] and fairness would be better served by sparing the plaintiff a second plenary action after the apparently frustrated victory in the first. We have on several occasions advocated the allowance of a simple motion for follow-up relief,[4] and there may be tacit authority for such a procedure from the Court of Appeals. In Berlitz Publications, Inc. v. Berlitz,[5] the plaintiff sought to enforce the provisions of an earlier declaratory judgment by an application "at the foot of the judgment," in essence a motion for follow-up relief. The Court denied the relief on the merits, but presumably it would not have reached the

---

[6]   First Nat. Stores, Inc. v. Yellowstone Shopping Center, Inc., 21 N.Y.2d 630, 290 N.Y.S.2d 721, 237 N.E.2d 868 (1968); see Town of Hardenburgh, Ulster County v. State, 52 N.Y.2d 536, 540, 439 N.Y.S.2d 303, 304, 421 N.E.2d 795, 796 (1981).

[7]   CPLR 3001.

[8]   CPLR 3017(b).

[9]   See Rockland Power & Light Co. v. City of New York, 289 N.Y. 45, 43 N.E.2d 803 (1942); Sabatino v. Capco Trading, Inc., 27 A.D.3d 1019, 813 N.Y.S.2d 237 (3d Dep't 2006).

[10]   Spadaro v. Newark Ins. Co., 21 A.D.2d 226, 249 N.Y.S.2d 753 (4th Dep't 1964), aff'd, 15 N.Y.2d 1000, 260 N.Y.S.2d 16, 207 N.E.2d 611 (1965).

[1]   See Silverstein v. Continental Cas. Co., 23 A.D.2d 801, 258 N.Y.S.2d 485 (4th Dep't 1965), aff'd, 17 N.Y.2d 845, 271 N.Y.S.2d 282, 218 N.E.2d 323 (1966).

[2]   Dale Renting Corp. v. Bard, 39 Misc. 2d 266, 240 N.Y.S.2d 488 (Sup. Ct., Kings County 1963), aff'd, 19 A.D.2d 799, 243 N.Y.S.2d 420 (2d Dep't). See the Commentary C3001:5 on McKinney's CPLR 3001.

[3]   See CPLR 2218; § 251.

[4]   See the Commentaries C3001:6 on McKinney's CPLR 3001 where an analogy is made to practice in connection with the enforcement devices.

[5]   Berlitz Publications, Inc. v. Berlitz, 37 N.Y.2d 878, 378 N.Y.S.2d 363, 340 N.E.2d 730 (1975).

merits if the motion method had been found inadequate to introduce them. Several courts have so read the *Berlitz* case and allowed a simple motion for follow-up relief in this context.[6]

---

[6]   See, e.g., Korn v. Gulotta, 186 A.D.2d 195, 197–98, 587 N.Y.S.2d 960, 962 (2d Dep't 1992); Auer v. Dyson, 125 Misc. 2d 274, 479 N.Y.S.2d 102 (Sup. Ct., Oneida County 1984), aff'd, 112 A.D.2d 803, 491 N.Y.S.2d 1022 (4th Dep't 1985).

Chapter 17

RES JUDICATA

Analysis

A.   Introductory
B.   General Requisites
C.   Comparison with Other Doctrines
D.   Res Judicata in Particular Situations
E.   Collateral Estoppel
F.   Identity of Parties
G.   Identifying the Issue
H.   Multiparty Situations
I.   Different Courts
J.   Procedural Incidents

A. INTRODUCTORY

Table of Sections

§ 442.   Res Judicata, Introductory
§ 443.   Members of the Res Judicata Family

§ 442. Res Judicata, Introductory

The doctrine of res judicata is designed to put an end to a matter once duly decided. It forbids relitigation of the matter as an unjustifiable duplication, an unwarranted burden on the courts as well as on opposing parties. Its main predicate is that the party against whom it is being invoked has already had a day in court and, if it was not satisfactory, the proper course was to appeal the unsatisfactory result rather than ignore it and attempt its relitigation in a separate action.

The phrase "res judicata" has taken on several meanings. In its technical sense, res judicata—thing adjudicated—is applicable only when a party is attempting to relitigate her whole cause of action. It intervenes in that instance to foreclose not only matters litigated, but also those that might have been litigated.[1] This has come to be called "claim preclusion," to be distinguished from the doctrine of collateral estoppel, which the Restatement denominates "issue preclusion,"[2] terminology that the New York courts have been using increasingly, but not exclusively.[3] The differences between them will be

---

[1]   Schuylkill Fuel Corp. v. B. & C. Nieberg Realty Corp., 250 N.Y. 304, 165 N.E. 456 (1929).

[2]   Restatement (Second) of Judgments § 27.

[3]   See, e.g., Koch v. Consolidated Edison Co. of New York, Inc., 62 N.Y.2d 548, 479 N.Y.S.2d 163, 468 N.E.2d 1 (1984), cert. den. 469 U.S. 1210, 105 S.Ct. 1177, 84 L.Ed.2d 326 (1985). The courts began to use the new terms as early as the tentative drafts of the Second Restatement. See, e.g., Pace v. Perk, 81 A.D.2d 444, 440 N.Y.S.2d 710 (2d Dep't 1981).

seen more clearly in subsequent sections as these and related doctrines, such as the election of remedies and the law of the case, are compared and contrasted.

The other use of "res judicata," and the one more commonly met in practice, is really a shorthand term that takes in all of these doctrines. There is a tendency, harmless enough when taken generally rather than strictly, to denominate as "res judicata" any situation in which a party is foreclosed from something in a later action because of something that happened or failed to happen in an earlier one. In this more popular sense, "res judicata" is not so much a doctrine as it is a policy—the policy of avoiding duplication when there is no good reason for duplicating. The thread that ties all the related doctrines together is their common aim of implementing some phase of that policy. If one keeps that broad purpose always in mind, the great pliability of "res judicata" itself, as well as of all its family members, will not take the lawyer by surprise. As long as the attorney is properly forewarned, the myriad of conditions and exceptions and qualifications with which the topic—and therefore this chapter—is replete will all fall into place as appropriate servants of an important and flexible policy rather than as unruly offspring of a rigid doctrine.

There is nothing rigid about res judicata. And there is nothing rigid about any of its family either. Each case must be decided on its own facts. There are a host of cases on res judicata, but only a small fraction of them contain the guideposts by which to judge future cases. In common with caselaw on such things as the bill of particulars and summary judgment, the majority of res judicata decisions are mere illustrations of a result appropriate to the facts of the case at hand.

Guideposts for res judicata are almost exclusively the products of caselaw. In the realm of New York practice, that makes the subject unique as statutes play no major role here. There are, to be sure, occasional statutes or rules that touch the doctrine, in effect if not explicitly, but these are few and they address specific situations.

CPLR 3216(a), for example, provides that a dismissal for neglect to prosecute is "not on the merits,"[4] and CPLR 3217(c) has instructions about when a voluntary discontinuance is "without prejudice" or "on the merits."[5]

Perhaps the most significant CPLR dictate about when a result is "on the merits"— a shorthand description often used to invoke res judicata—is that of CPLR 5013. It governs a dismissal of a claim during the trial and provides that the dismissal is "on the merits" if made after the plaintiff's whole case is in, but not if made before.[6] In the overall context of res judicata, however, these and a few other statutes and rules, dispositive as they may be in a given case, play a small role. Recognizing how dependent each case is on its own peculiar facts, the legislature has maintained a hands-off policy: res judicata is, and continues to be, a common law doctrine. This makes it one of the few areas of New York practice that can turn for help to the American Law Institute's Restatement. The one most relevant here is the Restatement (Second) of Judgments.[7]

---

[4]   See § 375.

[5]   See § 298.

[6]   See § 402.

[7]   The treatise is available on Westlaw.

§ 443. Members of the Res Judicata Family

Vocabulary always plays a significant role in New York practice, but particularly so in this chapter. It will be helpful at this early juncture to list and briefly define a number of doctrines often thought of as members or close friends of the res judicata family. Later sections will elaborate with finer distinctions and with citations, but as popularly used in New York practice the coterie's respective functions run this way:

(1) Res Judicata. This one is the parent and in popular usage it often lends its name to the others, a handy title to describe the whole clan. As indicated in the prior section, the res judicata doctrine in its narrower and more technical sense is concerned with an endeavor to relitigate a whole claim, rather than only parts of it. In this sense it has given way to the term "claim preclusion."

(2) Collateral Estoppel. This is the most influential member of the family. More often than not a judge or lawyer saying "res judicata" really means collateral estoppel. Each doctrine is usable only against a party who had a day in court on the relevant issue in the first action or proceeding and lost on it, but while res judicata is looking for an attempt to duplicate the whole case, collateral estoppel is looking for less. Collateral estoppel scans the first action and takes note of each issue decided in it. Then if the second action, although based on a different cause of action, attempts to reintroduce the same issue, collateral estoppel intervenes to preclude its relitigation and to bind the party against whom the doctrine is being invoked to the way the issue was decided in the first action. "Issue preclusion" is the newer terminology, but collateral estoppel still hangs on. The two phrases are usually used to mean the same thing, and we use the terms in this book interchangeably.

Judge Cardozo's famous *Schuylkill* case[1] can illustrate the collateral estoppel, or "issue preclusion," doctrine. P contracted to supply coal to five defendants. They did not pay for a delivery and P sued them for it. They claimed their liability was several only, while P claimed it was joint, making each defendant liable for coal delivered to any one of the others. P won on the point and the defendants' liability under the contract was found joint. P then made another delivery under the same contract and again had to sue for it. The defendants again pleaded that their liability was several. Since it was based on a later delivery, the second action presented a separate cause of action and could not be foreclosed by the res judicata, or "claim preclusion," doctrine itself. But since the issue of the nature of the defendants' liability under this very contract had been litigated in the first action, collateral estoppel bound the defendants to the earlier holding on that issue and established for all purposes in the second action that the defendants' liability was joint.

We should note that although the collateral estoppel doctrine operates on a smaller item, i.e., an "issue" decided in the first action rather than on the whole claim, it operates on a broader plain and hence with more influence. It will rear its head whenever the same issue appears, while res judicata will not show up unless it is convinced that there is an attempt to relitigate a cause of action. As caselaw manifests, the reappearance of an "issue" is much more frequent than the reappearance of the whole "claim," which

---

[1]   Schuylkill Fuel Corp. v. B. & C. Nieberg Realty Corp., 250 N.Y. 304, 165 N.E. 456 (1929).

makes collateral estoppel the star performer on this stage—and incidentally shows why "issue preclusion" and "claim preclusion" are handier terms.[2]

(3) Election of Remedies. Res judicata and collateral estoppel generally require a final judgment on the merits. The election of remedies doctrine does not, intervening (or trying to) whenever a plaintiff with a choice of two or more remedies sues on fewer than all of them. The plaintiff is deemed to have "elected" the one sued on, which results in a waiver of the rest. The election doctrine has been restricted by both caselaw and statute. Since it often becomes relevant at the pleading stage of an action, it was treated at that point—including contrasts with res judicata[3]—which spares duplication here.

(4) Splitting. This is another member of the res judicata family, and a sibling, if not a twin, of the election of remedies doctrine. The splitting doctrine in New York is largely confined to instances in which a plaintiff with a single money claim omits part of what is due when she sues. The part omitted is waived. This was also the subject of earlier treatment.[4]

(5) Law of the Case. This doctrine recognizes that res judicata, strictly speaking, operates only when there has been a final judgment on the merits. The doctrine of law of the case endeavors to accomplish similar results within an action before judgment is reached. It thus provides that once a point has been decided in a case, it cannot be relitigated within it, although it may be raised on appeal. The doctrine was met previously during discussion of the effect of orders disposing of motions under CPLR 3211, the motion to dismiss, and CPLR 3212, the summary judgment motion,[5] and will be returned to in greater depth later in this chapter.[6]

(6) Direct Estoppel. This is not a terribly useful term and seldom appears in New York cases, but it may be helpful to note its technical meaning and function. Its area of operation is where a prior action has been dismissed on a ground that does not reach the merits, and thus does not preclude a second action, but nonetheless disposes of an issue that may arise in a later action on the same claim. The Second Restatement gives this example:

Relying on longarm jurisdiction, P sues D, a nonresident, for injuries suffered when P was hit by a car driven in the state by X on D's behalf. D pleads that X lacked permission and is upheld, the action being dismissed for lack of jurisdiction, which depends on permission. But suppose that the substantive liability of D also depends on permission. When P sues D and obtains jurisdiction in a second action, D may plead the want of permission, found only in regard to jurisdiction in the first action, as dispositive of the merits in the second because the issue is the same, or so the Restatement concludes by way of illustrating what is sometimes called "direct estoppel."[7] It is not certain in New York practice, however, that an issue disposed of on a jurisdictional dismissal in the first action will be given merits impact in the second.[8]

---

[2]   The study of collateral estoppel as distinct from res judicata begins in § 457.

[3]   See § 218.

[4]   See § 220.

[5]   See §§ 276 and 287.

[6]   See § 448.

[7]   See Restatement (Second) of Judgments § 27, Illus. 3.

[8]   See § 92.

(7) Full Faith and Credit. This doctrine is one of federal, constitutional, and statutory law.[9] It requires that the judgments of American courts rendered with jurisdiction be given recognition by all other American courts. It is a kind of mandatory, interstate, res judicata. It's the subject of distinct treatment near the end of this chapter.[10]

(8) Comity. The judgments of foreign countries, unlike those of American courts, are not within the Full Faith and Credit Clause and the states are therefore free to formulate their own rules of recognition. If the State does recognize the judgment, it is giving that judgment "comity," or respect. In the realm of the conflict of laws, "comity" has come to describe, casually but helpfully, the whole topic of the recognition of the judgments of foreign nations.[11]

From among this stately procession of related doctrines, at least one of them can usually be found to preclude relitigation of an issue when it is truly inexcusable. Still other doctrines may be summoned or fitted out for the maverick case which, while unjustifiably attempting relitigation, slyly evades all of the res judicata family members described. Suppose, for example, that D has made a motion to dismiss an action for want of jurisdiction. Before the motion is heard, P brings a second action, which D promptly moves to dismiss based on the pendency of the first action. D is talking out of both sides of his mouth here, and yet he nicely sidesteps all of the existing doctrines. The court in such a case can invoke a simple *equitable estoppel* against D, or find that with his jurisdictional motion in action #1 he has *waived* the right to claim its pendency in action #2, or has *consented* to the second suit.[12] Although perhaps not within any of the blood line of res judicata, a situation like this poses the same kind of inconsistency of position that the res judicata family was born to battle.

The equitable estoppel doctrine serves as a kind of general backup whenever the facts elude one of the more standard doctrines. In one case, for example, P contracted to sell certain plants to D, which D contracted to furnish to X for use on a building project. When X postponed the order, D sued X and won, pleading that the plants were ready and in accord with specifications. Then, in a later suit by P against D, D tried to show that the plants did not satisfy those specifications. Issue preclusion might have been invoked against D, but issue preclusion is generally designed for use against a party who lost in the first action, while here, D won in that action. No matter, held the court: the doctrine of "estoppel against inconsistent positions" is available to do the job.[13]

The caselaw consistently serves the theme of the res judicata tribe, manifesting that a resourceful judge will not suffer a blatant disregard of the family's policy merely because a case dropped by when no one doctrine was at home.

Sometimes the visitor may find the premises occupied by a friend while the family is away, and with the friend quite ready to do the family's bidding. The doctrine of stare decisis is such an ally and it can take hold of a case just as it is about to slip away from

---

[9]   U.S. Const. art. IV, § 1; 28 U.S.C.A. § 1738.

[10]   See § 471.

[11]   See § 472.

[12]   See Commentary C3211:17 on McKinney's CPLR 3211 and Moreo v. Regan, 140 A.D.2d 313, 314, 527 N.Y.S.2d 547 (2d Dep't 1988); see also § 262.

[13]   Environmental Concern, Inc. v. Larchwood Const. Corp., 101 A.D.2d 591, 476 N.Y.S.2d 175 (2d Dep't 1984).

the premises. This is illustrated in a later section where stare decisis and the role it plays alongside res judicata are treated.[14]

The concepts of "merger" and "bar" are merely different ways of describing res judicata in different contexts. They also occupy a separate section.[15]

B. GENERAL REQUISITES

Table of Sections

§ 444. Necessity of Final Judgment

§ 445. Res Judicata for Order

§ 446. Necessity for Disposition on "Merits"

§ 447. Preclusion for "Might Have Been Litigated" Items

§ 444. Necessity of Final Judgment

As a general rule, the res judicata doctrine—collateral estoppel included for this purpose—requires a final judgment on the merits.[1] It has been said, therefore, that a verdict or decision not reduced to judgment will not do.[2] The purpose of this rule is to assure finality, however, and if finality is clear, the source of it should be secondary. Indeed, the CPLR provides that if the ministerial act of entering judgment is all that is necessary after the merits have been duly determined in a verdict or decision, judgment may follow even if the losing party dies in the interim.[3] This can be taken as establishing the CPLR's view that a showing of finality is more important than the name of the paper that embodies it. The key is whether the adjudication is "sufficiently firm," as the Restatement puts it,[4] and a firm one should qualify as a "final judgment," whatever its name.

A settlement made without an action having been brought does not get res judicata or collateral estoppel effect, but it will often get the equivalent if the claim is sued on in violation of the settlement. The issue now becomes a matter of contract. The defense of release,[5] for example, can be interposed against the claim and will usually do the job, at least where the action attempts to interpose the whole of the settled claim. A settlement within an action can provide for the entry of a judgment embodying its terms.[6] When it does, the result is a consent judgment, and a consent judgment does get res judicata treatment.[7]

If a judgment for which preclusive effect is sought is itself based on an earlier judgment, domestic or foreign, and the earlier one has been vacated or reversed or

---

[14] See § 449.

[15] See § 450.

[1] Today a special proceeding culminates in a "judgment," just as an action does. CPLR 411. See § 556. It used to end in a "final order," but as the equivalent of a judgment that, too, got full res judicata effect. See Bannon v. Bannon, 270 N.Y. 484, 1 N.E.2d 975 (1936).

[2] Rudd v. Cornell, 171 N.Y. 114, 63 N.E. 823 (1902); Towne v. Asadourian, 277 A.D.2d 800, 722 N.Y.S.2d 187 (3d Dep't 2000).

[3] CPLR 5016(d).

[4] Restatement (Second) of Judgments § 13.

[5] CPLR 3018(b), 3211(a)(5), see § 263.

[6] See CPLR 2104.

[7] See § 451.

otherwise undone, it is of course divested of its finality and the remedy to cancel the second judgment is a motion to vacate it on the ground of the undoing of the first.[8] Until that is done, however, the second one will stand. Indeed, there is authority that a second judgment will even prevail over an earlier one involving the same claim if there should be an inconsistency between them.[9]

If it becomes necessary to pinpoint the moment of a judgment's "finality," the general rule is that it becomes final as of the date it is "rendered," as the Restatement has it,[10] or, in New York practice, at least as of its formal moment of "entry."[11] The fact that the time in which to appeal the judgment is still open, or even that an appeal has in fact been taken and is pending, does not divest the judgment of its finality in New York.[12] The judgment is still entitled to its res judicata effect. But the fact of the appeal's pendency may be made the basis of a stay application in the second action—the action in which it is sought to apply the res judicata doctrine—to await the outcome of the appeal in the first.[13]

If, after a final judgment is rendered, all of the parties settle in a stipulation that prescribes that no judgment shall be entered, or that a judgment previously entered shall be vacated, must the courts enforce the agreement, thereby cancelling the judgment and depriving it of collateral estoppel effect? The U.S. Supreme Court held in U.S. Bancorp Mortgage Co. v. Bonner Mall Partnership[14] that courts need not honor such a stipulation. Equitable principles govern in this scenario and by settling, the loser forfeits the equitable right of vacatur. The matter has yet to be resolved by the New York Court of Appeals, but *Bancorp* is favorably cited by the appellate division in Paramount Communications v. Gibraltar Cas. Co.[15] where the court adopts a similar rule for New York, holding that the parties can't get a judgment vacated merely by settling the action and including vacatur as a condition of the settlement. To the argument that settlement would be encouraged by permitting such an automatic vacatur, the court answers that the practice could, in some ways, discourage settlements.

Perhaps those who seek most often to erase judgments with settlements are manufacturers who face numerous lawsuits because of a defective product. Their obvious aim is to deny others, and perhaps numerous others, a free ride on the issue of liability once liability has been found against them in one of the actions. The impact of such a judgment as a precedent is mentioned briefly but strongly in the *Bancorp* case.[16]

---

[8]   See CPLR 5015(a)(5); § 431.

[9]   See § 471.

[10]   See Restatement (Second) of Judgments § 13.

[11]   CPLR 5016; see § 418.

[12]   See Parkhurst v. Berdell, 110 N.Y. 386, 18 N.E. 123 (1888); 77 Water St., Inc. v. JTC Painting & Decorating Corp., 148 A.D.3d 1092, 50 N.Y.S.3d 471 (2d Dep't 2017).

[13]   CPLR 2201. Compare Commentary C2201:11 on McKinney's CPLR 2201.

[14]   U.S. Bancorp Mortg. Co. v. Bonner Mall Partnership, 513 U.S. 18, 115 S. Ct. 386, 130 L. Ed. 2d 233 (1994).

[15]   Paramount Communications v. Gibraltar Cas. Co., 212 A.D.2d 490, 623 N.Y.S.2d 850 (1st Dep't 1995) (noted in SPR 35:3); see Foster Wheeler L.L.C. v. Affiliated FM Ins. Co., 33 Misc. 3d 1204(A), 938 N.Y.S.2d 227 (Sup. Ct., New York County 2011) (denying motion to vacate decision and order on motion).

[16]   Where parties to an arbitration agreement stipulate that no award made in the arbitration will have estoppel impact, some courts have upheld the agreement and denied the estoppel. See, e.g., Kerins v. Prudential Property & Cas., 185 A.D.2d 403, 585 N.Y.S.2d 637 (3d Dep't 1992) (SPR 21:3).

§ 445. Res Judicata for Order

Since the res judicata doctrine is so frequently mentioned as requiring a "final judgment," it will be helpful if we break in briefly at this point to discuss the extent to which the doctrine can apply to an adjudication embodied in a mere "order."

In New York, an order entered on a motion is ordinarily entitled to the same res judicata and collateral estoppel treatment that a judgment gets as long as the other requisites of those doctrines—finality, opportunity to contest, identity of issue, etc.—are met.[1] This is especially significant when the order made on the motion is dispositive rather than interlocutory or intermediate. An order granting a motion for summary judgment, for example, would ordinarily get res judicata treatment in an attempted second action.[2]

Questions like this are usually avoided by getting a formal "judgment" entered on the order, but a failure to do that should not be controlling. If it is unclear whether a particular issue was passed on in the course of deciding a motion—this is more relevant to collateral estoppel (issue preclusion) than to res judicata (claim preclusion)—the doctrine will not apply.[3]

In applying the preclusion doctrines to an order, one must of course be mindful of the ground on which the order rests. An order granting a motion for summary judgment based on the overall merits of the case will get full claim preclusion treatment, for example, while one based on a narrower ground, such as want of jurisdiction or incapacity of a party, will be dispositive only of the particular objection and will not preclude a new action that meets and overcomes the objection.[4]

Motions within actions that result in orders denying them are usually interlocutory rather than final, in the sense that the action continues. While they do not get res judicata treatment as such, they get the relative equivalent—for whatever issue is disposed of in the order denying the motion—under the doctrine known as "the law of the case," separately discussed below.[5]

§ 446. Necessity for Disposition on "Merits"

The general rule is that the earlier judgment must be on the "merits" to invoke the preclusion doctrines.[1] But "merits" in this sense is taken today as meaning only that the earlier disposition can have no greater effect in the second action than it was intended to be given when made in the first. On a straight application of res judicata, or claim preclusion, such as an attempt at relitigation by a plaintiff who lost on the merits after a full trial in the first action, no doubt should arise. The earlier judgment disposed of the merits once and for all and unless it is directly overturned, as on appeal, it will preclude a new action.

---

[1]   Vavolizza v. Krieger, 33 N.Y.2d 351, 352 N.Y.S.2d 919, 308 N.E.2d 439 (1974).

[2]   See § 287.

[3]   See Royal Business Funds Corp. v. Ehrlich, 78 Misc. 2d 305, 356 N.Y.S.2d 407 (Sup. Ct., New York County 1974), aff'd, 45 A.D.2d 823, 356 N.Y.S.2d 1015 (1st Dep't); see Commentary C3212:21 on McKinney's CPLR 3212.

[4]   See §§ 276, 287.

[5]   See § 448.

[1]   See, e.g., Rudd v. Cornell, 171 N.Y. 114, 63 N.E. 823 (1902).

But in other situations, the earlier disposition must be subjected to closer scrutiny, especially when the earlier result was a dismissal of the claim on a motion of some kind. The key question is, what kind? A general summary judgment motion, as noted in the prior section, or a CPLR 3211 motion treated as one for summary judgment,[2] is intended to dispose of the whole case and will invoke full claim preclusion if a new action is brought on the same cause of action. But the dismissal of an earlier action on some lesser ground, touching on some curable defect clearly not intended to foreclose the merits, keeps the merits open for a second round.

Examples of this would be a dismissal for lack of prosecution,[3] or a voluntary discontinuance,[4] which do not ordinarily constitute adjudications on the merits,[5] although a second action may well face the bar of the statute of limitations.[6] A number of the objections listed as dismissal grounds in CPLR 3211(a) also come in for only limited res judicata application. They are deemed an adjudication of only the narrow ground predicating the dismissal even though the dismissal is embodied in a formal judgment.[7] Illustrations here would be dismissals based on lack of jurisdiction (subject matter, personal, or rem),[8] the plaintiff's lack of capacity to sue at the time of the earlier action (e.g., the plaintiff was an infant and tried to bring suit in her own behalf),[9] and the failure to join a necessary party (omitted in the earlier action but joined in the present one).[10] Res judicata applies, but it operates only on the ground on which the earlier adjudication rests and in these situations the ground was not one disposing of the merits of the claim. The doctrinal element in this context is a kind of hybrid between claim preclusion and issue preclusion: the thing dismissed in round one was the "claim"; but the dismissal was predicated on what might be considered a single and nondispositive "issue."

Of course, if a given ground is the common sense equivalent of a general merits disposition, it will be given res judicata effect if relitigation is attempted. Examples here would be where the earlier action was dismissed on such grounds as release or payment or, indeed, where the earlier action was itself dismissed based on res judicata or collateral estoppel emanating from a still earlier action.[11]

It will be noted that in this last batch of examples, the earlier disposition resulted from a motion rather than after trial. Nonetheless, the disposition was—or in any event should have been—embodied in a "judgment" closing out the first action.

Suppose the dismissal motion in the earlier action was denied, with the denial being embodied in an order and the action continuing because of the denial. Can the matter determined then be raised again *within* the action? Or is res judicata unavailable

---

[2]   CPLR 3211(c) authorizes this treatment. See § 270.

[3]   See § 375.

[4]   See § 298.

[5]   See CPLR 3216(a), 3217(c).

[6]   See CPLR 205(a); § 52.

[7]   See § 276; see also Landau v. LaRossa, Mitchell & Ross, 11 N.Y.3d 8, 862 N.Y.S.2d 316, 892 N.E.2d 380 (2008) (prior judgment dismissing the first complaint "without prejudice" on the basis of the plaintiff corporation's lack of capacity was not entitled to res judicata effect in the second action brought by the corporation's successor).

[8]   CPLR 3211(a)(2), (8), (9).

[9]   CPLR 3211(a)(3).

[10]   CPLR 3211(a)(10).

[11]   See CPLR 3211(a)(5).

because the disposition is not on the "merits," or "final"? The "law of the case" doctrine, treated two sections hence, will be found to preclude relitigation in that situation so that if "res judicata" itself proves unwilling, it will also find itself unneeded.

§ 447. Preclusion for "Might Have Been Litigated" Items

Res judicata in its strict sense operates to bar not only matters that were actually put in issue in the prior action but also those that might have been. The classic statement of the rule is this language of Judge Cardozo in the *Schuylkill* case:[1]

A judgment in one action is conclusive in a later one, not only as to any matters actually litigated therein, but also as to any that might have been so litigated, when the two causes of action have such a measure of identity that a different judgment in the second would destroy or impair rights or interests established by the first.[2]

The purpose of this rule is to prevent a party from seeking in a later action to inject matters (theories, grounds, counts, defenses, etc.) that could and should have been used in the first action but weren't. This is the claim preclusion doctrine in operation, or res judicata in its technical sense (as opposed to collateral estoppel or issue preclusion). Therefore, it requires a determination of whether the second action involves the same "cause of action" as the first.

The best general standard for determining this is the Restatement Second's, which deems the causes the same if they arise out of the same transaction or series of connected transactions.[3] If, for example, P sues D in ejectment because of an encroachment and wins judgment, but cannot enforce the judgment because of a recalcitrant sheriff, P cannot thereafter sue for equitable relief, hoping for a judgment that would make the defendant remove the encroachment himself.[4] P had but one cause of action and could not break it down into segments and bring separate suit on each. In the example, the plaintiff won the first suit on the merits. The same rule would apply when the plaintiff loses the first action on the merits as where P with a personal injury claim sues D only in negligence and the jury finds for D. P cannot thereafter sue D for the same injury on counts of breach of warranty or strict products liability, or any other ground that P could have included, but omitted, in the first action.

Until 1981, this rule was shackled with unusual exceptions when the plaintiff lost based on some threshold objection, like the statute of frauds or the statute of limitations. A judgment of dismissal based on one of those grounds was held to bar a second action based on the same theory, but not to foreclose a second action on a different theory even though the cause of action was the same.[5] A second action was allowed on a quantum meruit claim, for example, when the earlier suit in contract was dismissed under the statute of frauds for want of a writing.[6] And a second suit based on fraud, for another example, timely under its unique limitations' measure, was allowed even though the first

---

[1]   Schuylkill Fuel Corp. v. B. & C. Nieberg Realty Corp., 250 N.Y. 304, 165 N.E. 456 (1929).

[2]   *Schuylkill*, 250 N.Y. at 306–307, 165 N.E. at 457.

[3]   Restatement (Second) of Judgments § 24(1). Section 24(2) suggests that a "transaction" or related "series" of them must be determined "pragmatically," weighing such considerations as time, place, origin, and motivation, and treating also the parties' understanding and expectations.

[4]   See Hahl v. Sugo, 169 N.Y. 109, 62 N.E. 135 (1901). This overlaps with the election of remedies doctrine, a subject returned to below. *Hahl* was also met in § 218, and will be met again in § 478.

[5]   See § 212 (comparing "cause of action" with "theories" or "grounds" for recovery).

[6]   Smith v. Kirkpatrick, 305 N.Y. 66, 111 N.E.2d 209 (1953).

action, in contract, was dismissed as time barred.[7] The reason for this was the courts' endeavor to abate the harsh consequences of the election of remedies doctrine as it was applied at common law,[8] but in so doing the courts seriously undermined the res judicata (claim preclusion) doctrine, most particularly the "might have been litigated" standard that is part of it. These matters were explored in more detail in the treatment of the election of remedies doctrine earlier[9] and need no repetition here, except to cite again the two Court of Appeals cases that overruled the older cases in 1981 and restored the claim preclusion doctrine to its predominant present role.

Those cases are O'Brien v. City of Syracuse,[10] and Smith v. Russell Sage College.[11] Under them, a plaintiff omitting a count or ground from the earlier action will pay the price of a res judicata forfeiture. No longer can the affixation of an "election of remedies" label circumvent it. The res judicata rule is designed to encourage a plaintiff to put in everything relative to the claim. The *O'Brien* and *Smith* cases implement that rule.[12] In *O'Brien*, the plaintiff was barred from bringing a second action against a city on a trespass count after the first action, based on a wrongful taking, failed. The trespass count could have been joined in the first action and arose out of the same transaction as the wrongful taking. In *Smith*, the plaintiff brought a second action on a ground still timely under the statute of limitations after the earlier action on a different count and with a different time measure was dismissed as too late. As in *O'Brien*, the second ground could have been joined in the first action and arose out of the same transaction that was the basis for the first action. The plaintiff had notice of the second ground in time to join it in the first action, at least through the process of amendment. Only if the plaintiff legitimately and excusably lacked knowledge of the second ground in time to join it in the first action would the tightened claim preclusion doctrine permit a second action.

The Court of Appeals calls this the "transactional analysis" approach. It bars all claims arising out of a given transaction, occurrence, or event once any of the claims so arising is litigated to a final judgment or its equivalent.[13]

The "might have been litigated" rule does not apply when the consequences of an earlier criminal action are sought to be used in a later civil one.[14] Only the points actually decided in the criminal action may be exploited for civil use.[15] The criminal defendant can therefore conduct his defense without having to pay any attention to the civil impact that omitted matters would otherwise have.

Nor will the "might have been litigated" rule apply to multiple taxpayer suits. There, claim preclusion in the second action will attend only matters actually litigated in the first. So held the Court of Appeals in Murphy v. Erie County,[16] and in context to suggest that this should also be the rule in class actions generally. The class members

7   Fitzgerald v. Title Guarantee & Trust Co., 290 N.Y. 376, 49 N.E.2d 489 (1943).

8   See Strong v. Reeves, 280 A.D. 301, 114 N.Y.S.2d 97 (3d Dep't 1952), aff'd, 306 N.Y. 666, 116 N.E.2d 497 (1953).

9   See § 218.

10   O'Brien v. City of Syracuse, 54 N.Y.2d 353, 445 N.Y.S.2d 687, 429 N.E.2d 1158 (1981).

11   Smith v. Russell Sage College, 54 N.Y.2d 185, 445 N.Y.S.2d 68, 429 N.E.2d 746 (1981).

12   The cases are the subject of the lead note in NYSLD No. 267.

13   In re Hunter, 4 N.Y.3d 260, 269, 794 N.Y.S.2d 286, 291, 827 N.E.2d 269, 274 (2005).

14   For a general discussion of civil use of criminal findings, see § 453.

15   See Vavolizza v. Krieger, 33 N.Y.2d 351, 352 N.Y.S.2d 919, 308 N.E.2d 439 (1974).

16   Murphy v. Erie County, 28 N.Y.2d 80, 320 N.Y.S.2d 29, 268 N.E.2d 771 (1971). As to what a "taxpayer" suit is, see § 136.

should not be barred with anything but issues actually litigated and decided in the class suit.[17]

Some recent cases have been applying a stronger dose of the "might have been litigated" rule in matrimonial litigation, affecting financial claims between the parties in divorce and like actions. The court clearly has power, for example, to determine an issue between the spouses concerning title to real property, but injection of the issue was once thought to be permissive rather than mandatory. It is now deemed mandatory so that a failure to inject the title issue into a matrimonial action is held to waive it.[18]

The same rule was applied for a time to a personal injury claim between the spouses,[19] but the Court of Appeals in Xiao Yang Chen v. Fischer[20] reached a different conclusion, holding that while the personal injury claim may be litigated in the matrimonial action, it doesn't necessarily have to be. Hence, its omission from the divorce action does not necessarily bar a separate suit on the claim afterwards as long as fault allegations are not actually litigated in the divorce action. The Court observed, however, that "the better practice would be to include a reservation of rights in the judgment of divorce."[21]

C. COMPARISON WITH OTHER DOCTRINES

Table of Sections

§ 448.   Law of the Case
§ 449.   Relation to Stare Decisis
§ 450.   "Merger" and "Bar"

§ 448. Law of the Case

Since the doctrine of res judicata technically requires a final judgment on the merits in one action and an attempted relitigation in a second, it has no application within an action. The doctrine of the "law of the case" was devised to close that gap. It applies to various stages of the same action or proceeding[1] and its purpose is to avoid the re-injection of issues already determined within it.[2]

For practical purposes, the doctrine of the law of the case can be considered a kind of intra-action issue preclusion. It has already been met in this book, with examples, in discussing the res judicata effect of an order disposing of a motion to dismiss under CPLR 3211.[3]

The doctrine is almost entirely the product of caselaw. It has been described by the Court of Appeals as "amorphous," and while met principally in civil actions, it has been applied in criminal cases too. We note the point here because—perhaps ironically—it

---

[17]   Res judicata as applied to class actions and other representative actions is treated in § 454.

[18]   Boronow v. Boronow, 71 N.Y.2d 284, 286, 525 N.Y.S.2d 179, 519 N.E.2d 1375 (1988).

[19]   See SPR 155:2.

[20]   Xiao Yang Chen v. Fischer, 6 N.Y.3d 94, 810 N.Y.S.2d 96, 843 N.E.2d 723 (2005).

[21]   *Xiao Yang Chen*, 6 N.Y.3d at 100, 810 N.Y.S.2d at 102, 843 N.E.2d at 727.

[1]   People v. Evans, 94 N.Y.2d 499, 706 N.Y.S.2d 678, 727 N.E.2d 1232 (2000); McGrath v. Gold, 36 N.Y.2d 406, 369 N.Y.S.2d 62, 330 N.E.2d 35 (1975).

[2]   Brown v. State, 250 A.D.2d 314, 681 N.Y.S.2d 170 (3d Dep't 1998).

[3]   See § 276.

was in a criminal action that the court offered perhaps its most incisive discourse on the law of the case rule.[4]

Once a point is decided within a case, the doctrine of the law of the case makes it binding not only on the parties, but on the court as well. No other judge of coordinate jurisdiction may undo the decision.[5] The order embodying the finding is open to appellate review, but it may not be negated by any other judge of the same court.[6] Indeed, if a later application is seen to affect a prior order, the preference of the CPLR is that the later application be made to the same judge who disposed of the prior one.[7]

The res judicata doctrine, including claim preclusion and issue preclusion, and the doctrine of the law of the case collectively assure finality for judicial dispositions whether made in a final judgment ending an action or in an interlocutory order within the action. This can be seen just by contrasting the grant and denial of a dismissal motion under CPLR 3211, which offers the best illustration.

Suppose, for example, that D moves to dismiss a money claim on the ground of payment under CPLR 3211(a)(5). The court grants the motion. This establishes that the claim has been paid and contemplates a final judgment dismissing the action. An endeavor to dispute the point again in a future case will be foreclosed either by res judicata (claim preclusion) itself as where the identical claim is sued on again, or collateral estoppel (issue preclusion), as where the claim is a different one but whether this particular debt was paid becomes a relevant issue in the subsequent action. If the court denies the motion, however, this establishes that payment has not been made, but it contemplates only an order denying the motion. The case goes on, but the doctrine of the law of the case will prevent the defendant from again trying to show that the claim was paid unless the motion was denied without prejudice.

A disposition claiming to be the law of the case will usually be found to be embodied in a court order, but that's not indispensable.[8] If the court's decision on a point is clear, for example, it concludes other coordinate judges whether embodied in a formal order or not.[9]

In some situations in which special circumstances suggest the need for speedy resolution of temporary matters, findings made for the temporary purpose will not bind the judge who has to decide the merits of the case later. So, for example, the findings of a judge on a motion for a preliminary injunction will not conclude the trial judge who later has to decide whether to grant a permanent injunction.[10] The preliminary injunction is only a status quo retainer and it would be unseemly to let the findings made in its grant or denial—and made expeditiously just to keep things intact while the merits

---

[4]   See People v. Evans, 94 N.Y.2d 499, 706 N.Y.S.2d 678, 727 N.E.2d 1232 (2000), discussed in the lead note in NYSLD No. 483.

[5]   State of N.Y. Higher Educ. Services Corp. v. Starr, 158 A.D.2d 771, 551 N.Y.S.2d 363 (3d Dep't 1990).

[6]   See George W. Collins, Inc. v. Olsker-McLain Industries, Inc., 22 A.D.2d 485, 257 N.Y.S.2d 201 (4th Dep't 1965), holding that the doctrine applies even to prevent Judge 2 from granting a consolidation motion denied by Judge 1.

[7]   CPLR 2221; see § 253. This issue has become academic in courts that use the Individual Assignment System inaugurated in 1986, under which a case goes to but a single judge at the outset and remains with that judge throughout. See § 77A for a discussion of the IAS and its exceptions.

[8]   In re Estate of Levinson, 11 A.D.3d 826, 828, 784 N.Y.S.2d 165 (3d Dep't 2004), lv. denied 4 N.Y.3d 704, 792 N.Y.S.2d 1, 825 N.E.2d 133 (2005).

[9]   See George W. Collins, Inc., 22 A.D.2d at 489, 257 N.Y.S.2d at 205.

[10]   See § 329.

are investigated—dictate those merits. The same is true of applications for temporary support in matrimonial and other family law contexts. Public policy requires that such applications be disposed of expeditiously, lest the needs of a family go wanting. Nonetheless, certain findings may be required even before such temporary orders can be made, such as the extent of the family's needs or a spouse's or parent's resources or even with respect to the validity of the marriage or of a divorce purporting to dissolve it.

Findings on any of those or similar issues made for the purpose of awarding temporary relief do not bind the court when it later makes a final judgment. Indeed, to encourage the trial bench at judgment time to reach findings on these matters independently of the presumably hastier findings made earlier, the appellate courts virtually insist that judicial thinking not be impeded by the earlier doings.[11] This is so even if the temporary findings were the product of a testimonial hearing rather than just motion papers and affidavits, which are the more usual basis.[12]

The justifying rationale in these special situations is sometimes said to be that since the earlier findings were made on only a motion, they cannot under res judicata conclude the action.[13] Since the law of the case doctrine designs to give conclusive effect even to motions within actions, it is sounder to consider these temporary relief situations as merely an exception to the doctrine, and a reasonable one.

§ 449. Relation to Stare Decisis

The doctrine of stare decisis makes the common law what it is by giving judicial precedents the effect of law, i.e., binding if from direct appellate level and at least persuasive if from some other source. The doctrine differs from res judicata in that it applies only to issues of law while the res judicata family touches both issues of law and issues of fact.

Stare decisis is also more flexible. This is not to say that res judicata and its progeny are rigid—ensuing sections will demonstrate the contrary—but they are not quite as pliable as stare decisis. If a claim or an issue between the same parties is found to be identical with one previously adjudicated between them, even though there is much judgment to be exercised in making such a finding of identity, the res judicata doctrine must be applied and relitigation foreclosed. The doctrine is operating on only one claim, or one issue, and between the same parties.

The mission of stare decisis is broader: to set precedents for cases generally. To determine whether to apply a precedent from an earlier case to a legal issue in a later one involving a similar or identical claim, much else comes into play. From what court does the precedent come? When was it decided? Have there been intervening changes in the law itself, from statute or later caselaw, or from changing times and diverging attitudes? Stare decisis and its elasticity enable the judge to consider factors like these before invoking the doctrine while they play a smaller role, if they play one at all, in the realm of res judicata. As Justice Frankfurter observed, "stare decisis is a principle of policy and not a mechanical formula of adherence to the latest decision, however recent and questionable."[1]

---

[11]   See, e.g., Haber v. Haber, 20 A.D.2d 858, 248 N.Y.S.2d 83 (1st Dep't 1964).

[12]   Bannon v. Bannon, 270 N.Y. 484, 1 N.E.2d 975 (1936).

[13]   *Bannon*, 270 N.Y. at 489, 1 N.E.2d at 977.

[1]   Helvering v. Hallock, 1940–1 C.B. 223, 309 U.S. 106, 119, 60 S. Ct. 444, 451, 84 L. Ed. 604 (1940).

Stare decisis often acts as a good back-up when the need for flexibility makes res judicata itself inappropriate despite the presence of its several ingredients. This is notably the case with the periodic assessments of real property. If from the time of an earlier assessment there has been no change in either the facts concerning the land and its surroundings or in the rules of law applicable to the assessment, the case would seem to be tailor made for res judicata. But the doctrine doesn't apply. Public policy dictates that in the interest of the whole community, a finding for an earlier period not bind for a later one, lest, for example, error at an earlier time with respect to a given taxpayer do continuing damage to a later one, or, on the contrary, to the whole body of taxpayers by requiring others to pick up the first one's share of the tax load. A leading case so holding points out that if all things are the same as they were before, stare decisis can be turned to for aid,[2] nicely compromising the need for flexibility on the one hand with the need for consistency on the other.

A point that often arises in connection with stare decisis in New York is the extent to which—when the Court of Appeals has not yet spoken—an appellate division precedent in one department binds in another. The trial courts in one department should follow an appellate division precedent set in another until the local appellate division addresses the matter,[3] but among the departments themselves the holding of one is persuasive, but not binding, on the others.[4] If two departments have issued conflicting rulings on a point of law, a trial judge in neither can follow the holding that it deems to comport most closely with the law.[5] The doctrine of stare decisis does not require a supreme court judge to follow a decision of a supreme court in another judicial district.[6]

§ 450. "Merger" and "Bar"

These are two theoretical subdivisions of the res judicata doctrine. If the plaintiff is the winner, the cause of action "merges" in the judgment, which technically means that the judgment supersedes the underlying cause of action to such an extent that it disappears.[1] If the defendant wins, the judgment "bars" any later action by the plaintiff on the underlying claim.[2] This dichotomy has doubtful practical significance today; if used at all, it should be used carefully, especially the "merger" doctrine, which can do more harm than good when applied thoughtlessly.

The merger doctrine merely seeks to prevent suit from being duplicated on the claim, preferring to regard the judgment as its superseder. This is usually just fine with the plaintiff who, other things being equal, would prefer a judgment any time. But make one of those other things unequal, and merger rigidly applied does needless damage. If there is anything about the underlying claim that offers the plaintiff some advantage, for example, it should retain its identity and peer right through the judgment to make itself felt. If the original claim gave the plaintiff some kind of lien, for example, surely a

[2]   People ex rel. Watchtower Bible & Tract Soc., Inc. v. Haring, 286 A.D. 676, 146 N.Y.S.2d 151 (3d Dep't 1955).

[3]   See People v. Turner, 5 N.Y.3d 476, 481–482, 806 N.Y.S.2d 154, 840 N.E.2d 123 (2005).

[4]   Phelps v. Phelps, 128 A.D.3d 1545, 9 N.Y.S.3d 519 (4th Dep't 2015); Mountain View Coach Lines, Inc. v. Storms, 102 A.D.2d 663, 476 N.Y.S.2d 918 (2d Dep't 1984).

[5]   See Darko v. New York City Transit Authority, 13 Misc. 3d 203, 206, 819 N.Y.S.2d 456, 458 (Sup. Ct., Bronx County 2006).

[6]   D'Alessandro v. Carro, 123 A.D.3d 1, 6, 992 N.Y.S.2d 520, 523 (1st Dep't 2014).

[1]   See Restatement (Second) of Judgments § 18.

[2]   Restatement (Second) of Judgments § 19.

judgment on it should not destroy the lien.[3] New York subscribes to the healthy view that the merger doctrine will not be allowed to undermine benefits inhering in the claim merely because it has gone to judgment. If, for example, the question is whether a judgment survives the later bankruptcy of the judgment debtor, and the answer depends on the judgment's underlying cause of action, the court will readily pierce the "merger" technicality and look right through to the cause.[4] The essential nature of the primary claim is not necessarily lost when judgment ensues.[5] Indeed, when a claim has been fully litigated, courts should be sensitive to see to it that the judgment is a reward rather than a deprivation.

Exceptions to merger will be spelled out whenever necessary, even to assure just a procedural right associated with the original claim. P had judgment against D in a Massachusetts court, for example, and then sued on it in New York. D, a corporation, had by that time surrendered its authority to do business in New York and pleaded lack of jurisdiction. P countered that under New York law D had agreed to continuing New York jurisdiction if the liability sued on was, as it was here, incurred in New York. D answered that the Massachusetts judgment merged that liability and agreement and that the New York court could not consider it. The court did consider it, however, sustaining jurisdiction and holding that merger will be carried no further than the ends of justice require.[6] A judgment against a defendant is not to be turned into a sword for the defendant to use against the plaintiff, in other words, as a strict use of "merger" would sometimes seem to have it.

When a court is asked for a provisional remedy in an action based on a judgment already rendered, it should be permissible if the availability of the remedy depends on the nature of the underlying claim, for the court to pierce the judgment and look at the claim. A provisional remedy often involved with this question in New York was the order of attachment because at one time several of the grounds for allowing it turned on the nature of the claim asserted.[7] Some caselaw had earlier held that the piercing could not take place for this purpose; that the merger would obscure the claim and leave visible only a cause of action on a "judgment."[8] A later amendment of the attachment statute, however,[9] makes suit on a judgment an independent ground for attachment and thus makes the prior caselaw academic, at least in respect of an attachment. Should a different remedy, provisional or otherwise, be sought in an action on a judgment, however, the question of merger would subsist and should be resolved along the lines indicated above.

The "bar" doctrine, applicable when the defendant in the first action is the winner, has not posed equivalent issues in New York. Whether an earlier judgment will in fact preclude ("bar") the plaintiff from a second suit on the same claim will of course depend on the ground of the first action's dismissal. A jurisdictional or like disposition, which

---

3   See Restatement (Second) of Judgments § 18, cmt. g.

4   See In re Williams, 208 N.Y. 32, 101 N.E. 853 (1913) (involving alimony).

5   See State of Wisconsin v. Pelican Ins. Co., 127 U.S. 265, 8 S. Ct. 1370, 32 L. Ed. 239 (1888).

6   Jay's Stores, Inc. v. Ann Lewis Shops, Inc., 15 N.Y.2d 141, 256 N.Y.S.2d 600, 204 N.E.2d 638 (1965).

7   Those grounds were contained in subdivisions 5, 6, and 8 of CPLR 6201, which were repealed in 1977.

8   See, e.g., McCormick v. American Press Publications, Inc., 52 Misc. 2d 297, 275 N.Y.S.2d 429 (Sup. Ct., New York County 1966).

9   Now numbered subdivision 5 of CPLR 6201.

contemplates and allows a new action if the earlier objection can be cured, of course does not act as a "bar."[10]

D. RES JUDICATA IN PARTICULAR SITUATIONS

Table of Sections

§ 451.   Application to Default and Consent Judgments

§ 452.   Application to Counterclaims

§ 453.   Civil Use of Criminal Findings

§ 454.   Res Judicata in Representative and Class Situations

§ 455.   Res Judicata for Jurisdictional Issues

§ 456.   Res Judicata for Administrative and Arbitral Decisions

§ 451. Application to Default and Consent Judgments

A judgment by default or on consent must be given claim preclusion effect,[1] barring new suit on the same claim. The judgment would not be much good otherwise. The more difficult question is whether a judgment of this kind should be given the more influential effects of collateral estoppel (issue preclusion) as well. As a general rule, New York does give default and consent judgments that effect.

A collateral estoppel lies for any issue duly pleaded in and legitimately a part of the action in which a default was suffered. Reich v. Cochran[2] so held even of the summary proceeding to recover the possession of real property, finding that a default judgment established the validity of the lease and precluded a collateral attempt in a later proceeding to cancel it. A consent judgment was given similar effect in Canfield v. Elmer E. Harris & Co.[3] where the judgment consented to had been entered in an earlier action involving D's status as a holdover tenant. When P consented to judgment for D,[4] everything underlying the judgment was deemed resolved in D's favor, including the fact that D was not a holdover tenant, and P was bound by that finding in a subsequent proceeding involving the same issue.

Hence, an actual contest is not necessary for collateral estoppel; the only required showing is that the issues were necessary to the determination, contested or not. This is true in New York of both the default judgment[5] and the consent judgment,[6] but not without argument. While few dispute that claim preclusion—res judicata itself, in its technical sense—must attend default and consent judgments, there is criticism of New

---

[10]   See § 276.

[1]   Martins v. Wood, 251 A.D.2d 465, 675 N.Y.S.2d 544 (2d Dep't 1998); Walston & Co. v. Klein, 44 Misc. 2d 607, 254 N.Y.S.2d 734 (Sup. Ct., New York County 1964), aff'd, 24 A.D.2d 559, 260 N.Y.S.2d 831 (1st Dep't 1965).

[2]   Reich v. Cochran, 151 N.Y. 122, 45 N.E. 367 (1896).

[3]   Canfield v. Elmer E. Harris & Co., 252 N.Y. 502, 170 N.E. 121 (1930).

[4]   The consent in this instance was not an outright judgment by confession, such as that authorized by CPLR 3218, see § 299, but rather a stipulation for judgment absolute used in appellate practice, see § 527, which amounts to a consent judgment and was so treated by the Court of Appeals in the *Canfield* case.

[5]   119 Rosset Corp. v. Blimpy of N.Y. Corp., 65 A.D.2d 683, 409 N.Y.S.2d 735 (1st Dep't 1978); Trecot v. Taxter, 69 Misc. 2d 248, 329 N.Y.S.2d 139 (Sup. Ct., Nassau County 1972).

[6]   In re DeChiaro's Estate, 35 Misc. 2d 485, 230 N.Y.S.2d 604 (Sup. Ct., Nassau County 1962).

York's giving them issue preclusion effect as well.[7] The main objections are that this gives small judgments too much influence, requires clairvoyance of defendants, penalizing them for not foreseeing how a light (or absent) defense in one case can come back to haunt them collaterally in another.

And it deters settlements. Even an offer to compromise under CPLR 3221, which is just a category of consent judgment, has been given estoppel effect, binding a defendant who made such a compromise in P's property damage action and holding D concluded as well in P's later—and possibly unexpected but much more substantial—personal injury action.[8] Although consistent with the overall New York view, a result like that does tend to discourage compromise offers and was of course not the intention of CPLR 3221.

Perhaps the criticisms, including this writer's,[9] can today be met with more recent suggestions from the Court of Appeals. In a series of important later decisions, notably the *DeWitt* and *Schwartz* cases,[10] a number of sui generis factors have been set up as a kind of check list for a judge to go over before according an earlier judgment issue preclusion impact in a later suit. Those factors, listed and discussed in a later section,[11] are at least as relevant to default and consent judgments as they are to contested ones and ought to be considered in all of them. By applying them, almost on a sui generis basis, a flexibility is introduced sufficient to deny issue preclusion effect to earlier default and consent judgments whenever one of the listed components suggests it—such as the smallness of the earlier claim and, as a result, the laxity of the defense made against it. The result of such a fresh approach will be the overturning of some earlier precedents that gave default and consent judgments collateral estoppel effect arbitrarily, without attention to such individual factors as the Court of Appeals requires treatment of today.

That's the way things are going. Two cases separated by three decades can illustrate. In the first,[12] a default judgment of $79.16 in an action by P against D for property damage was held under collateral estoppel to require dismissal of D's later suit against P for personal injury. In the second, a default judgment on a $750 fee claim by a physician against a patient was denied estoppel effect in the patient's later action against the physician for medical malpractice.[13]

Independent evaluation of each case is the only practical solution to an attempt to give issue preclusion effect to a default or consent judgment. It seems a fair response to the problem, and a complete one to the critics.

§ 452. Application to Counterclaims

Res judicata ordinarily applies in full measure to claims interposed by way of counterclaim, cross-claim, third-party claim, and the like as long as there was sufficient

---

[7] See, e.g., Maurice Rosenberg, *Collateral Estoppel in New York*, 44 St. John's L. Rev. 165, 173–181 (1969).

[8] Card v. Budini, 29 A.D.2d 35, 285 N.Y.S.2d 734 (3d Dep't 1967).

[9] See Commentary C3221:2 on McKinney's CPLR 3221.

[10] B. R. DeWitt, Inc. v. Hall, 19 N.Y.2d 141, 278 N.Y.S.2d 596, 225 N.E.2d 195 (1967), and Schwartz v. Public Adm'r of Bronx County, 24 N.Y.2d 65, 298 N.Y.S.2d 955, 246 N.E.2d 725 (1969), discussed in §§ 466 and 467.

[11] See § 467.

[12] Roberts v. Strauss, 108 N.Y.S.2d 733 (Sup. Ct., New York County 1951).

[13] Kossover v. Trattler, 82 A.D.2d 610, 442 N.Y.S.2d 554 (2d Dep't 1981). See the discussion in the concurring opinion of Justice Gibbons.

jurisdiction in the first action to dispose of the claim.[1] In this connection it's important to recall that New York does not have, as the federal system has,[2] a compulsory counterclaim rule: a rule that makes a counterclaim "compulsory" and forces its interposition (under the threat of waiver) if it arises out of the same transaction or event that grounds the plaintiff's main claim. All counterclaims are supposed to be permissive in New York, but we have already seen how misleading that notion can be; how the doctrine of collateral estoppel (issue preclusion) can invade a second action, brought now on the previously withheld counterclaim, and, with findings from the earlier action, dictate its result. That prior discussion during treatment of counterclaims in the pleadings chapter[3] also showed how a defendant's interposition of certain matter as a mere defense in the first action can have the same effect as if it had been used as a counterclaim, barring it from use as a separate claim later. This is a kind of waiver doctrine, and it is an erratic and perilous thing in a practice that presumes to label all counterclaims permissive. Its illustration is best seen in the case of Musco v. Lupi,[4] also met and discussed during that earlier treatment, which the reader would do well to review here.[5]

Now assume that the plaintiff commences an action in federal court, where counterclaims are "compulsory,"[6] and the defendant withholds a counterclaim that arises out of the same transaction or occurrence as plaintiff's claim? Can the defendant in the federal court action then turn to a New York State court and commence an action to assert that claim under our permissive counterclaim rule? In Paramount Pictures Corp. v. Allianz Risk Transfer AG,[7] the First Department ruled that "the later assertion in a state court action of a contention that constituted a compulsory counterclaim (FRCP rule 13[a]) in a prior federal action between the same parties is barred under the doctrine of res judicata." This principle of law required dismissal of the complaint in the state court action.

Although not mentioned in the *Paramount Pictures* decision, we wonder if the result reached is compelled by the doctrine of full faith and credit.[8] The doctrine requires that the judgments of American courts rendered with jurisdiction be given recognition by all other American courts. If there is some difference between the law of the first forum (F-1) and the second forum (F-2) on the effect to be given the F-1 judgment, F-2 will ordinarily apply the F-1 rules on the theory that to do otherwise would be according less than full credit or comity to the F-1 judgment.[9] In that the claim would be barred if it was asserted in a federal court based on the compulsory counterclaim rule and res judicata, it should be similarly barred in a New York action.[10]

---

[1]   In respect of counterclaims, see Restatement (Second) of Judgments §§ 21–23.

[2]   Fed. R. Civ. P. 13(a).

[3]   § 224.

[4]   Musco v. Lupi, 6 Misc. 2d 930, 164 N.Y.S.2d 84 (Sup. Ct., Orange County 1957).

[5]   See § 224.

[6]   See §§ 224, 632.

[7]   Paramount Pictures Corp. v. Allianz Risk Transfer AG, 141 A.D.3d 464, 468, 36 N.Y.S.3d 11, 15 (1st Dep't 2016), lv. granted, 28 N.Y.3d 909, 47 N.Y.S.3d 224, 69 N.E.3d 1020.

[8]   See §§ 443, 471.

[9]   See Restatement (Second) of Judgments § 87 ("[f]ederal law determines the effects under the rules of res judicata of a judgment of a federal court").

[10]   See Commentary C3019:2 on McKinney's CPLR 3019.

§ 453. Civil Use of Criminal Findings

It often happens that a single occurrence will give rise to both civil and criminal proceedings. A simple example is an assault. It is clear that a civil judgment against a party cannot be used against that party in a later criminal prosecution for the reason that the burden of proof differs: the civil assault finding rests on a "fair preponderance of the evidence" while the prosecutor in the criminal action has the heavier burden of satisfying the jury "beyond a reasonable doubt." To import the civil finding into, and make it dictate the result of, the criminal action would violate the criminal law standard.

But in the reverse situation that is not a problem. It should be theoretically as well as practically palatable to permit a plaintiff suing a defendant for the civil consequences of his act to make use of a prior criminal conviction of the defendant for the same act. The wrongful act having been proved in the earlier criminal action "beyond a reasonable doubt," that would more than amply cover the "fair preponderance," which is the plaintiff's burden in a civil suit. Notwithstanding this, the courts for a long time did not permit the criminal result to bind the defendant in a civil action, allowing the criminal conviction to qualify at most as only prima facie evidence for the fact trier to consider in the civil case.[1] This was based on the "mutuality" doctrine,[2] which was interred in B. R. Dewitt, Inc. v. Hall,[3] setting the stage for its abandonment in the criminal-to-civil situation as well.

The abandonment took place in S.T. Grand, Inc. v. City of New York,[4] which required the civil action to import and be bound by the criminal conviction. In *Grand*, bribery in connection with a contract was involved and X was duly convicted of the crime. When X later brought civil suit to recover on the same contract, the defendant was allowed to use the conviction as conclusive proof that the contract was illegal, barring X's civil recovery. The usual requirements that the issue be the same and that X be shown to have had a full opportunity to litigate the earlier (in this case the criminal) proceeding were held to be the sole governing criteria and the Court of Appeals confirmed this again in Vavolizza v. Krieger.[5]

Both *Grand* and *Vavolizza* involved only the "shield" use of res judicata and collateral estoppel, i.e., the plaintiff in the later civil action was the previously convicted person, and the defendant in the civil action was the one seeking to use the estoppel as a defense. But what of the situation in which the civil plaintiff is the victim, and the civil defendant the convict? May the victim make "sword" use of the conviction, and march off with an affirmative victory in the civil case based on the conviction of the same defendant in the earlier criminal action? It has been held that he may; that whether the use to which the estoppel is put in the civil action is affirmative or defensive should make no difference as long as the estopped issue is the same and the civil tribunal is satisfied that there was a full opportunity for the defendant in the criminal action to litigate it.[6]

---

[1]   See Schindler v. Royal Ins. Co., 258 N.Y. 310, 179 N.E. 711 (1932).

[2]   For discussion of this doctrine, see § 460.

[3]   B. R. DeWitt, Inc. v. Hall, 19 N.Y.2d 141, 278 N.Y.S.2d 596, 225 N.E.2d 195 (1967), discussed in §§ 466 and 467.

[4]   S. T. Grand, Inc. v. City of New York, 32 N.Y.2d 300, 344 N.Y.S.2d 938, 298 N.E.2d 105 (1973).

[5]   Vavolizza v. Krieger, 33 N.Y.2d 351, 352 N.Y.S.2d 919, 308 N.E.2d 439 (1974).

[6]   Read v. Sacco, 49 A.D.2d 471, 375 N.Y.S.2d 371 (2d Dep't 1975).

The "full opportunity" is the key. In one leading case, for example, Gilberg v. Barbieri,[7] a city court conviction for harassment—a petty offense not qualifying even as a misdemeanor—was denied estoppel effect in a civil suit by the victim against the same defendant for assault. The Court of Appeals described the criminal action as a "relatively minor" one that the defendant could not be expected to defend "with the same vigor" he would a regular criminal action. "The brisk, often informal, way in which these matters must be tried," said the court, "as well as the relative insignificance of the outcome, afford the party neither opportunity nor incentive to litigate thoroughly."

Gilberg is an example of the full and fair opportunity test in action. The test plays a dominant role in the res judicata domain today. It requires case by case analysis of a number of factors, elaborated below.[8]

§ 454. Res Judicata in Representative and Class Situations

In the usual representative situations that one encounters in the courts, res judicata has full operation. Once the representative has litigated the matter, the represented person is fully bound. So it is with the fiduciary (executor, administrator, guardian, etc.) of a person or estate, or the trustee of a trust: the beneficiaries, or represented persons whatever their designation, are bound by the judgment that binds the representative.[1]

This rule also applies to the well-known "class action."[2] The fact that all of the class members are—and constitutionally may be—bound by the judgment[3] is among the reasons why the courts keep such close control of the class action. When res judicata is invoked for a prior class judgment, the court must look carefully into a number of factors, including the adequacy of the representation and of course whether there was truly an identity of interest between the representatives who were the named plaintiffs, and who conducted the class action, and the members of the class now sought to be bound.[4]

The rule that res judicata precludes litigation of matters that "might have been litigated," as discussed in an earlier section,[5] does not apply rigidly to class actions. The Court of Appeals has so held of taxpayer actions, for example,[6] a variety of class action. As a rule, therefore, the class action judgment will bind only as to matters actually litigated and not necessarily those that merely might have been.

§ 455. Res Judicata for Jurisdictional Issues

Jurisdictional determinations get res judicata treatment, ordinarily limited, of course, to the jurisdictional point itself.[1] Principles of personal jurisdiction support this conclusion readily. Where, for example, D appears in the first action and moves to dismiss it on the grounds (e.g.) that notice was inadequate or that the court lacked a jurisdictional basis, a determination against D on that motion binds him. If D should

---

[7]   Gilberg v. Barbieri, 53 N.Y.2d 285, 441 N.Y.S.2d 49, 423 N.E.2d 807 (1981).

[8]   See § 467.

[1]   In re Sullivan's Will, 123 N.Y.S.2d 159 (Sur. Ct., Kings County 1953).

[2]   The class action is treated in §§ 139–147.

[3]   See Hansberry v. Lee, 311 U.S. 32, 61 S. Ct. 115, 85 L. Ed. 22 (1940). Even members of the plaintiff class who are not residents of the forum state can be bound by the judgment. See § 144.

[4]   See Restatement (Second) of Judgments § 41, cmt. e.

[5]   See § 447.

[6]   See Murphy v. Erie County, 28 N.Y.2d 80, 320 N.Y.S.2d 29, 268 N.E.2d 771 (1971).

[1]   Johnson v. Muelberger, 340 U.S. 581, 71 S. Ct. 474, 95 L. Ed. 552 (1951).

afterwards default, or even contest and lose on the merits, the later forum will be bound to recognize that the first court had jurisdiction as well as accept its result on the merits.[2] The same is true when D, after losing in the first forum on the jurisdictional point, does not defend the action and a default judgment on the merits is entered against D. The adverse decision on the jurisdictional issue confirms the jurisdiction and res judicata seals it for recognition in all future cases.[3]

Appearing in the first action, in other words, marks the voluntary submission of the jurisdictional question to the first court. A second court before whom the issue of the first court's jurisdiction arises must discontinue its inquiry into the first court's jurisdiction as soon as it is demonstrated that D appeared in the first action and raised and lost on the jurisdictional point, or appeared and simply failed to raise it.[4] The second court cannot, in the guise of re-adjudicating jurisdictional facts, subvert the recognition due the first judgment on the merits.[5]

The answer is different if D did not appear in the first action. In that case, the second court may litigate the first one's jurisdiction. Each defendant is entitled to a day in court on the question of jurisdiction just as on any other issue. The law is that D can seek that day in the second court as long as he did not appear in the first. In that instance, when the second court is looking into the first one's jurisdiction, it must cease its inquiry and award recognition to the judgment upon being shown that the first court did have jurisdiction. Conversely, if it is shown, on proper proof, that the first court did not have jurisdiction, the judgment may be denied recognition.[6] If this discourse sounds more like one on the Federal Full Faith and Credit Clause than it does on New York internal law, it is because the issues are similar in both, but the caselaw more profuse on the full faith and credit subject.[7]

Rem jurisdictional determinations get res judicata treatment, too, but only to the extent that the judgment affects the res on which jurisdiction was based. The second court may look into the question of whether the first had any rem jurisdiction at all, at least where D did not appear in the first action, but upon being satisfied that rem jurisdiction was present it must treat that issue as res judicata. The judgment will have no impact beyond the subject res, however; it cannot touch D's personal liability.[8] So, for example, if the only jurisdiction the first forum had as against D was quasi in rem based on the attachment of D's property, its judgment is effective only to the extent of the property attached and cannot preclude D if and when D is later sued in personam for a part of the claim still due—as where the attached assets did not suffice to cover the whole demand. The earlier judgment is not entitled to collateral estoppel effect in that

---

[2]   Baldwin v. Iowa State Traveling Men's Ass'n, 283 U.S. 522, 51 S. Ct. 517, 75 L. Ed. 1244 (1931).

[3]   Vander v. Casperson, 12 N.Y.2d 56, 236 N.Y.S.2d 33, 187 N.E.2d 109 (1962). See § 111.

[4]   Davis v. Davis, 305 U.S. 32, 59 S. Ct. 3, 83 L. Ed. 26 (1938).

[5]   Coe v. Coe, 334 U.S. 378, 68 S. Ct. 1094, 92 L. Ed. 1451 (1948).

[6]   Williams v. State of N.C., 325 U.S. 226, 65 S. Ct. 1092, 89 L. Ed. 1577 (1945). This is the second of the *Williams'* cases, the first being 317 U.S. 287, 63 S.Ct. 207 (1942); the second makes the point that occupies us here. (If the first court lacked jurisdiction, moreover, the second court not only may, but probably must deny the first judgment res judicata effect for due process reasons).

[7]   Full faith and credit as such is separately treated in § 471 where several of these matters are returned to.

[8]   Restatement (Second) of Judgments § 30(2).

situation,[9] even if it involved the identical issues. Not even the "splitting" doctrine will be applied here[10] because of the first forum's obvious jurisdictional limitations.

It is this rule that accounts for the so-called "divisible divorce" doctrine in the matrimonial area. An example of divisible divorce is where a husband, H, has gotten a valid ex parte divorce—ex parte in this context means that personam jurisdiction over the defendant spouse was lacking in the divorce court—from his wife, W, in the first forum. The basis of the first court's divorce jurisdiction was that the "matrimonial res" was present there through H's domicile.[11] In a second action, this one in personam, W sues H for alimony and support. H there contends (1) that he is not W's husband because of the earlier divorce judgment and (2) that the earlier judgment also extinguished W's monetary rights. The first contention is correct because the first court had rem jurisdiction of the marital status and that sufficed for the divorce. But the second is wrong because in order to affect W's monetary rights, the first court needed personam jurisdiction of W, which it lacked. The "divisible" item is the relief sought: the status and money phases are segregated and the earlier judgment allowed res judicata effect only on the jurisdictionally secure item: the status. Since there was no personam jurisdiction in the first forum to support a monetary adjudication, however, a second action may be brought for that.[12]

The res judicata treatment of jurisdictional issues is not hard to conceptualize when personam or rem jurisdiction is the topic. Since those categories of jurisdictional objection are in any event waivable, even a holding of jurisdiction by a court that does not have it, as long as D appeared, can be accepted on any of several theories, e.g., that D with the appearance consented to have the first court decide the question, or waived the objection by failing to raise it or not appealing an adverse determination of it, or is estopped from now contending that jurisdiction was absent after having submitted the issue to the first court. But suppose that the issue is one of subject matter rather than of personal or rem jurisdiction. Unlike the latter two, subject matter jurisdiction cannot be conferred by consent, waiver, estoppel, laches, or anything else.[13] Suppose that the first court's subject matter jurisdiction is called in issue and the court holds, upon D's due appearance and submission of the question, that it has jurisdiction. Does the holding get res judicata treatment? Difficult though the concept may be—how can a court that lacks basic power over a case literally "talk itself" into it?—it usually does. Even issues of subject matter jurisdiction must be laid to rest sooner or later. Based on this need, the U.S. Supreme Court has several times applied res judicata to issues of subject matter jurisdiction, or in any event to issues contended or assumed to involve subject matter jurisdiction. It has done so, for example, in real property[14] and matrimonial[15] cases.

---

[9]   Benadon v. Antonio, 10 A.D.2d 40, 197 N.Y.S.2d 1 (1st Dep't 1960), modified, 10 A.D.2d 929, 205 N.Y.S.2d 800 (1st Dep't).

[10]   The splitting doctrine is treated in § 220.

[11]   See § 102.

[12]   Vanderbilt v. Vanderbilt, 354 U.S. 416, 77 S. Ct. 1360, 1 L. Ed. 2d 1456 (1957); Estin v. Estin, 334 U.S. 541, 68 S. Ct. 1213, 92 L. Ed. 1561 (1948).

[13]   See § 8.

[14]   See Durfee v. Duke, 375 U.S. 106, 84 S. Ct. 242, 11 L. Ed. 2d 186 (1963).

[15]   See Sherrer v. Sherrer, 334 U.S. 343, 68 S. Ct. 1087, 92 L. Ed. 1429 (1948). For further treatment of *Sherrer*, which requires res judicata treatment for adjudications of subject matter and personal jurisdiction alike, see § 471.

When more than one state is involved, the Full Faith and Credit Clause is implicated[16] and the requirements imposed by the U.S. Supreme Court's interpretation of it must be met. But when no supervening federal requirement is present, New York's view is that a court's determination that it has subject matter jurisdiction will be binding—assuming of course that the bound party appeared—only when it turns on an issue of fact rather than an issue of law. If the first court's holding that it has subject matter jurisdiction amounts only to a legal conclusion, the facts not being in dispute, collateral attack is open, i.e., a second court may determine the first's subject matter jurisdiction afresh, no matter what the first may have said about it. So held the New York Court of Appeals in Friedman v. State,[17] an unusual situation involving a removed judge and his right to collect his salary.

A better example is a federal example:

Suppose that P sues D in a federal district court based on diversity of citizenship.[18] P is a citizen of New York and contends that D is a citizen of Vermont, D insisting, however, that he, too, is a New Yorker. D's citizenship, which is roughly the equivalent of "domicile" in this context,[19] is a question of fact, but its resolution will dictate whether or not there is diversity—which is clearly a question of subject matter jurisdiction in federal practice. If D moves to dismiss the federal action for want of diversity and loses, the court finding him a citizen of Vermont, that issue of fact gets res judicata effect even though subject matter jurisdiction turns on it.

The Second Restatement takes the position that adjudications of subject matter jurisdiction are entitled to res judicata treatment unless the doctrine's underlying policy (finality) is outweighed by the need to prevent the first court in a given case from expanding its own sphere of competence. Several factors are listed for consideration, including whether the case was "plainly" beyond the first court's subject matter jurisdiction.[20] This is healthy hedging in a tough area.

Retaining such flexible standards would at least prevent a city court judge from giving away title to the General Electric Company, or a justice of the peace from rendering a divorce. The Court of Appeals' holding in the *Friedman* case, that the second court's inquiry into the first's subject matter jurisdiction is always open when it turns only on a legal conclusion rather than on a determination of fact, would cover situations like the two noted and thus give the second court leeway, at least in clear-cut instances, to determine for itself whether the first court had subject matter jurisdiction, unbound by what the first court may have had to say on the point.

§ 456. Res Judicata for Administrative and Arbitral Decisions

It is becoming increasingly clear that parties to an administrative proceeding must bear in mind that the results of what they are participating in may have consequences beyond the proceeding. The Court of Appeals has been giving administrative determinations what appears to be increasing collateral estoppel (issue preclusion) effect. Developments on this front have been intense in recent years, traceable mainly to

---

[16] U.S. Const. art. IV, § 1.

[17] Friedman v. State, 24 N.Y.2d 528, 301 N.Y.S.2d 484, 249 N.E.2d 369 (1969).

[18] 28 U.S.C.A. § 1332.

[19] See § 611 (Practitioner's Edition).

[20] Restatement (Second) of Judgments § 12(1).

Ryan v. New York Telephone Co.,[1] decided in 1984. Arbitration awards, too, have come in for some collateral estoppel treatment as manifest in Matter of Ranni's Claim,[2] among other cases. The ensuing discussion may overlap topics not treated in detail until later, such as collateral estoppel[3] and identity of parties.[4] This is a by-product of accelerating developments in res judicata in the area of administrative and arbitral determinations in recent years. It should not be necessary, but some readers may be more comfortable scanning the footnoted sections before undertaking the present one.

It stands to reason that even determinations of tribunals other than courts must be given claim preclusion treatment, or they would have diminished value. Hence, the general rule is that the determination of any tribunal vested with the power to conduct a hearing and decide an issue, whether a board, commission, agency, or the like, is entitled to the same claim preclusion treatment as a duly rendered judicial judgment.[5]

The administrative agency, which proliferates in this bureaucratic age, is the primary beneficiary of this rule. Res judicata appends to its quasi-judicial decisions[6] as long as the agency is acting within its jurisdiction. Indeed, if it is, and the determination is given res judicata effect by the State it serves, it must also be given binding effect in other American jurisdictions to whatever extent the home jurisdiction dictates.[7]

In Auqui v. Seven Thirty One Ltd. Partnership, the Court declared that:

> Quasi-judicial determinations of administrative agencies are entitled to collateral estoppel effect where the issue a party seeks to preclude in a subsequent civil action is identical to a material issue that was necessarily decided by the administrative tribunal and where there was a full and fair opportunity to litigate before the tribunal.[8]

That test was not satisfied in *Auqui* because the defendant failed to establish that the determination of the Workers' Compensation Board that plaintiff had no further causally related disability and no further need for treatment was sufficiently identical to the issues in plaintiff's personal injury action. In reaching its conclusion that collateral estoppel should not be applied, the Court stressed that in a proceeding under the Workers' Compensation Law, the focus "is on a claimant's ability to perform the duties of his or her employment."[9] By contrast, a negligence action seeking recovery for personal injuries is concerned with "the larger question of the impact of the injury over the course

---

[1]   Ryan v. New York Telephone Co., 62 N.Y.2d 494, 478 N.Y.S.2d 823, 467 N.E.2d 487 (1984).

[2]   Matter of Ranni's Claim, 58 N.Y.2d 715, 458 N.Y.S.2d 910, 444 N.E.2d 1328 (1982).

[3]   See § 457.

[4]   See §§ 458 to 461.

[5]   Goodkind v. WFS Inv'rs Corp., 192 A.D.2d 694, 597 N.Y.S.2d 130 (2d Dep't 1993); Jones v. Young, 257 A.D. 563, 14 N.Y.S.2d 84 (3d Dep't 1939).

[6]   See Auqui v. Seven Thirty One Ltd. Partnership, 22 N.Y.3d 246, 980 N.Y.S.2d 345, 3 N.E.3d 682 (2013). By quasi-judicial is meant a decision in a particular instance following an administrative hearing as opposed to such administrative functions as rule-making, investigation, etc.

[7]   See Magnolia Petroleum Co. v. Hunt, 320 U.S. 430, 64 S. Ct. 208, 88 L. Ed. 149 (1943). Thomas v. Washington Gas Light Co., 448 U.S. 261, 100 S. Ct. 2647, 65 L. Ed. 2d 757 (1980), comes close to overruling the *Magnolia* case, but doesn't quite muster the votes for it. It does show, however, that *Magnolia* stands in some disrepute for requiring blind deference by a court in State Two to an administrative determination in State One, in apparent disregard of State Two's own substantial interest in the resolution of the matters at issue.

[8]   *Auqui*, 22 N.Y.3d at 255, 980 N.Y.S.2d at 348, 3 N.E.3d at 685.

[9]   *Auqui*, 22 N.Y.3d at 256, 980 N.Y.S.2d at 349, 3 N.E.3d at 686.

of plaintiff's lifetime."[10] While acknowledging that there is typically some overlap of the issues determined in the two proceedings, the Court held that they are not sufficiently identical to visit collateral estoppel on the plaintiff in his personal injury action.

As demonstrated from the above, it is not the res judicata (claim preclusion) aspect of the determination of a non-judicial tribunal that has made waves in recent years, but the collateral estoppel (issue preclusion) aspect. Staying with the administrative determination for the moment (returning to the arbitration award later), we can take note of a major development, the *Ryan* case.

Ryan involved a misconduct finding made against a claimant in an administrative proceeding, which finding resulted in a denial of the unemployment benefits the claimant was seeking. The claimant then brought an action in court, trying to establish false arrest and like claims against his employer. The claims failed when the administrative finding of misconduct (theft from the employer) was allowed preclusion use against the claimant. The Court of Appeals applied the full and fair opportunity test that had evolved only a few years earlier[11] and found it satisfied in the hearing conducted before the agency, which in *Ryan* was the department of labor.

The case was controversial for several reasons. One was that the employee had only a union official to represent him before the agency, not a lawyer. The Court of Appeals responded that this was the employee's choice; that he could have used a lawyer if he wanted to. The rejoinder from lawyers practicing before administrative agencies is that employees of modest means do not have so potentially expensive an option.

More important still is the argument that an administrative proceeding cannot be said to satisfy the "full and fair opportunity" requirement for a variety of reasons. The pretrial disclosure devices of Article 31 of the CPLR, for example, vaunted as the treasured source of truth-seeking and trial preparation in the courts, are unavailable before agencies. And the rules of evidence do not apply strictly in administrative proceedings. To some lawyers, *Ryan* means that procedural rights like these, jealously guarded in direct litigation, are being desanctified through the indirect format of the collateral estoppel doctrine applied to agency proceedings.[12]

The Court of Appeals appears nevertheless to be adhering to the basic view that the procedural weaknesses of the administrative process do not by themselves mean that a full and fair opportunity was lacking. Citing *Ryan* and applying the full opportunity test several years later in Allied Chemical v. Niagara Mohawk Power Corp.,[13] the Court granted estoppel to an administrative determination, but it handed down on the same day two other cases in which estoppel was denied in similar contexts.[14] The indication was that while the basic rule of issue preclusion will apply to an administrative

---

[10]   *Auqui*, 22 N.Y.3d at 256, 980 N.Y.S.2d at 349, 3 N.E.3d at 686.

[11]   See § 467.

[12]   A lead note in NYSLD No. 310 discusses the expanding uses of collateral estoppel in administrative contexts, including *Ryan*.

[13]   Allied Chemical, an Operating Unit of Allied Corp. v. Niagara Mohawk Power Corp., 72 N.Y.2d 271, 532 N.Y.S.2d 230, 528 N.E.2d 153 (1988).

[14]   Staatsburg Water Co. v. Staatsburg Fire Dist., 72 N.Y.2d 147, 531 N.Y.S.2d 876, 527 N.E.2d 754 (1988), and Halyalkar v. Board of Regents of State of N.Y., 72 N.Y.2d 261, 532 N.Y.S.2d 85, 527 N.E.2d 1222 (1988), both decided on July 7, 1988, the same day as the *Allied* case.

determination, it will apply only if the determination survives the scrutiny of the full opportunity test.[15]

An interesting historical note is that criticism of the *Ryan* case proved powerful enough to produce an amendment of Labor Law section 623 overruling the case in its unemployment insurance setting. Perhaps ironically, the amendment overrules the *Ryan* result only in the specific *Ryan* context: the unemployment insurance proceeding. The fact is, however, that the *Ryan* decision has impact far beyond that. The Court of Appeals used the *Ryan* decision as just a base, taking off from there into the general proposition that credits an administrative hearing as the virtual equal of a court hearing for estoppel purposes. In view of the legislative closing of the base, one might have expected the courts to ground some of the other craft that took off from it, but that does not appear to have happened. Or, to use another metaphor, the seed may have been tainted, but there was no general recall of the plants that grew out of it.

Turning to the arbitration award, we may note that the claim preclusion doctrine clearly applies to it. The award gets collateral estoppel treatment,[16] including even the award of a panel in a foreign nation if the parties have duly bound themselves to arbitrate there and the procedures that were followed comport with domestic notions of due process.[17] Any other conclusion would undermine the important and expanding arbitration process,[18] which has done much to prevent the total collapse of the overworked judicial process by drawing a good part of the dispute resolution business to itself.

Suppose there was an earlier arbitral award and the issue of whether to give it estoppel effect arises in a later arbitration. The Court of Appeals held in In re Falzone that the matter must be left to the second-round arbitrator to determine.[19] If the second round happens to be a court action, on the other hand, and the court is called on to determine the estoppel effect of the earlier award, the court determines whether to give it estoppel effect. Any error by the court can be reviewed and corrected on appeal. By contrast, if an arbitrator erred in not applying collateral estoppel, the limited scope of judicial review of arbitral awards would normally leave the award undisturbed.[20]

The claim preclusion effect of arbitral awards made under the hit-and-run coverage of an insurance policy needs special consideration by lawyers if they plan any kind of conventional common law action based on a vehicle accident. Should a vehicle other than the hit-and-run vehicle also be involved in the accident, for example, and an arguable claim of fault can be made against it so as to permit a conventional action, the award in the arbitration may be accepted, prima facie, as being the total damages due for non-economic loss in the action. If the arbitration award is paid in full, it can bar the claim

---

[15] See the lead note in NYSLD No. 344, comparing the three cases.

[16] Clemens v. Apple, 65 N.Y.2d 746, 492 N.Y.S.2d 20, 481 N.E.2d 560 (1985).

[17] See Gilbert v. Burnstine, 255 N.Y. 348, 174 N.E. 706 (1931). While earning res judicata treatment, an arbitral award does not count as a precedent under the stare decisis doctrine because arbitrators are not bound by the rules of substantive law. See SCM Corp. v. Fisher Park Lane Co., 40 N.Y.2d 788, 390 N.Y.S.2d 398, 358 N.E.2d 1024 (1976).

[18] Arbitration is the subject of Article 75 of the CPLR and is treated at length in chapter 22 beginning in § 586.

[19] In re Falzone (New York Cent. Mut. Fire Ins. Co.), 15 N.Y.3d 530, 914 N.Y.S.2d 67, 939 N.E.2d 1197 (2010).

[20] See § 602.

against the defendant in the court action. So held a divided Court of Appeals in Velazquez v. Water Taxi, Inc.[21]

Applying the issue preclusion rule (the collateral estoppel doctrine) to an arbitration award is a more difficult matter than applying claim preclusion—more difficult even than with the administrative decision because the arbitration process has even fewer safeguards than the administrative process has. The substantive law, applicable in administrative proceedings, ordinarily does not apply in arbitration, and neither does the bulk of the state's procedural law, including the rules of evidence.[22] Nevertheless, the Court of Appeals has indicated that even an arbitration award may come in for issue preclusion treatment.

That appears to be the thrust of the *Ranni* case mentioned at the outset, in which an arbitration award, approving an employee's discharge, had found him insubordinate. The award was held to bind in a later administrative proceeding in which the employee sought unemployment benefits.[23] Benefits would fail if the employee was guilty of misconduct, and the insubordination finding imported from the arbitration was allowed to establish just that, and deny benefits.

Awards emanating from no-fault insurance arbitrations have also been making some of the law on this front. In one case, for example, a plaintiff involved in a vehicle accident sought no-fault benefits from her insurer for certain injuries, but the arbitrator found that she did not sustain them. That finding was held to bind her when she then sought to recover in court, for the same injuries, from the other vehicle involved in the accident.[24]

That the Court of Appeals intends to retain issue preclusion effect for arbitral determinations is manifest in Clemens v. Apple,[25] in which, in a brief memorandum, the Court cited and analogized to the *Ryan* case as if there were nothing to differentiate arbitral from administrative proceedings. It stressed in *Clemens*, however, that the one against whom the estoppel worked was the party who chose arbitration as a forum, the implication being that an award would not bind a party, in the issue preclusion sense, if that party had no say in whether the claim would go to arbitration as happens in the compulsory and quasi-compulsory arbitrations (of which no fault-arbitration is a variety) appearing in increasing numbers today.[26]

On the commercial side of arbitration, collateral estoppel was applied in Guard-Life Corp. v. S. Parker Hardware Mfg. Corp.[27] to allow one party in a court action, who was not a party to the arbitration, to make estoppel use of an arbitration finding against a person who was a party to both. P got an arbitration award against X for $75,000 for breach of contract, but was apparently unable to collect it. P then brought a court suit

---

[21] Velazquez v. Water Taxi, Inc., 49 N.Y.2d 762, 426 N.Y.S.2d 467, 403 N.E.2d 172 (1980) (noting "this might well be a different case" if plaintiff established that the arbitrator adjudicated only the dollar value of the hit-and-run vehicle's apportioned share of the liability).

[22] See § 586.

[23] It would appear to make no difference that the award was being applied in an administrative proceeding instead of in a court. If the award has collateral estoppel effect in a court, it presumably has it before an agency as well.

[24] Kilduff v. Donna Oil Corp., 74 A.D.2d 562, 424 N.Y.S.2d 282 (2d Dep't 1980).

[25] *Clemens*, 65 N.Y.2d at 749, 492 N.Y.S.2d at 21, 481 N.E.2d at 56.

[26] See § 603.

[27] Guard-Life Corp. v. S. Parker Hardware Mfg. Corp., 50 N.Y.2d 183, 428 N.Y.S.2d 628, 406 N.E.2d 445 (1980).

against D for inducing X's breach. D was allowed an estoppel in the action to the extent of limiting the amount of P's damages to $75,000. Thus was D, who was not a party to the arbitration, allowed to make use of its damages findings against P, who was. And the best of it from D's viewpoint is that because D was not part of the arbitration, he himself is not bound by the $75,000 damages figure and is hence free in the action to prove that P's damages are less.

This situation, which gives someone like D the best of both worlds, is not a rare phenomenon on the res judicata scene today.[28] Its counterpart for the other side—the one who was a party to both proceedings—is the worst of both worlds: being subject to estoppel use of negative aspects of the first proceeding while afterwards being barred from using its positive elements vis-a-vis one not a party to that earlier proceeding. In Baldwin v. Brooks, for example,[29] another no-fault case in the tort area, P was hit by O's car (driven by D) and brought a no-fault arbitration against O's insurer and won on a causation issue. Then P brought a regular tort action against O and D and wanted an estoppel against them on that issue. The court held that P may not have it because O and D were not parties to the first action; their insurer was the party. Unlike ordinary liability coverage, where insurer and insured are in privity, in no-fault the insurer's obligation runs directly to the injured person and there is no link between insured and insurer sufficient to bind one to an adverse finding made in a proceeding involving the other. But the court observes (citing other decisions) that because P is a party to both proceedings, arbitral findings adverse to P may be used by a party to a later action who was not a party to the no-fault proceeding.

A point of special interest to attorneys involves the arbitration of fee disputes with clients. When lawyer and client agree to arbitrate their dispute about the lawyer's fee before an arbitral forum, such as a committee of a bar association, and the lawyer prevails in the arbitration, collateral estoppel can insulate the lawyer from an action for legal malpractice.[30] Attorneys can still agree to arbitrate fee disputes and legal malpractice claims with clients today,[31] but even if they do not, Part 137 of the Rules of the Chief Administrator requires the lawyer to provide the client with an opportunity to arbitrate certain fee disputes.[32] If the client elects arbitration, the lawyer must participate in the process,[33] but any award is subject to de novo review at the option of either the client or the lawyer.[34] If, however, de novo review is not timely sought, or the lawyer and client mutually agree to arbitration of fee disputes that is final and binding,[35] the award will not be subject to de novo review. Any arbitral award that has not been

---

[28]   See § 460.

[29]   Baldwin v. Brooks, 83 A.D.2d 85, 443 N.Y.S.2d 906 (4th Dep't 1981).

[30]   See Altamore v. Friedman, 193 A.D.2d 240, 602 N.Y.S.2d 894 (2d Dep't 1993) (SPR 24:3).

[31]   See New York Rules of Professional Conduct, Rule 1.8, cmt. 14 ("This paragraph [Rule 1.8(h)] does not, however, prohibit a lawyer from entering into an agreement with the client to arbitrate legal malpractice claims, provided such agreements are enforceable and the client is fully informed of the scope and effect of the agreement.").

[32]   22 N.Y.C.R.R. § 137.2(a).

[33]   22 N.Y.C.R.R. § 137.11.

[34]   22 N.Y.C.R.R. § 137.8.

[35]   See 22 N.Y.C.R.R. § 137.2(c), (d).

challenged through de novo review or under CPLR 7511, can be entitled to res judicata and collateral estoppel.[36]

E. COLLATERAL ESTOPPEL

Table of Sections

§ 457.   Collateral Estoppel, Introductory

§ 457. Collateral Estoppel, Introductory

The doctrine of collateral estoppel was at one time used principally in cases involving an indemnity relationship of some kind, often in conjunction with a vouching-in notice,[1] to assure that the indemnitor would be bound by the same findings that bound the indemnitee and to avoid what has been termed the "absurd result of having the indemnitor exonerated, while the indemnitee was held liable."[2] Currently, it has far broader range, no longer limited to indemnity or any other category; its expanded mission today is to implement in substantially all situations "the sound principle that, where it can be fairly said that a party has had a full opportunity to litigate a particular issue, he cannot reasonably demand a second one."[3] Unlike res judicata itself, which applies only when the same cause of action is repeated—for which reason it often goes under the name of "claim preclusion" today—collateral estoppel applies when the second cause of action is distinct or different, applying to issues rather than to whole claims or defenses.[4] The Second Restatement calls it "issue preclusion" and notes that it applies alike to issues of fact and issues of law.[5]

On several previous occasions,[6] mention was made of Schuylkill Fuel Corp. v. B. & C. Nieberg Realty Corp.,[7] an opinion by Judge Cardozo that is probably the most quoted on the distinction between res judicata and collateral estoppel. The part that succinctly states the difference is this:

> A judgment in one action is conclusive in a later one, not only as to any matters actually litigated therein, but also as to any that might have been so litigated, when the two causes of action have such a measure of identity that a different judgment in the second would destroy or impair rights or interests established by the first . . . . It is not conclusive, however, to the same extent when the two causes of action are different, not in form only . . ., but in the rights and interests affected. The estoppel is limited in such circumstances to the point actually determined . . . .[8]

---

[36]   See § 603 for a further discussion of arbitration under Part 137. There is a three-part treatment of the rule in SPR 117:1–119:1.

[1]   See § 168 for discussion of the vouching-in procedure.

[2]   Schwartz v. Public Adm'r of Bronx County, 24 N.Y.2d 65, 69, 298 N.Y.S.2d 955, 958, 246 N.E.2d 725, 728 (1969).

[3]   *Schwartz*, 24 N.Y.2d at 69, 298 N.Y.S.2d at 958, 246 N.E.2d at 728.

[4]   Bonde v. General Sec. Ins. Co. of Canada, 55 Misc. 2d 588, 285 N.Y.S.2d 675 (Sup. Ct., Albany County 1967).

[5]   Restatement (Second) of Judgments § 27.

[6]   E.g., § 447.

[7]   Schuylkill Fuel Corp. v. B. & C. Nieberg Realty Corp., 250 N.Y. 304, 165 N.E. 456 (1929).

[8]   *Schuylkill*, 250 N.Y. at 306–307, 165 N.E. at 457.

The first quoted sentence is the doctrine of res judicata, or claim preclusion; the next two are the doctrine of collateral estoppel or issue preclusion. The estoppel inquiry is whether an issue involved here was disposed of there and whether the party sought to be bound with it here was a party there, had a fair chance to have the issue determined in her favor there, and lost.[9]

F. IDENTITY OF PARTIES

Table of Sections

§ 458.   Identity of Estopped Party

§ 459.   Different Capacities

§ 460.   Identity of Estopping Party; "Mutuality" of Estoppel

§ 461.   "Privity"

§ 458. Identity of Estopped Party

Collateral estoppel, or "issue preclusion," can often be used today by one who was not a party to the first action. An earlier rule known as "mutuality of estoppel" had held otherwise, but has since been abandoned.[1] But the law is adamant that the doctrine may not be used against one who was not a party to the first action because that would deny that person a hearing[2] and raise issues of due process. So, for example, when a car and bus collide and the car driver, suing the bus company in tort, is found innocent of comparative fault and wins, the driver still cannot defend with that victory a later action brought against him by a bus passenger. The passenger was not a party to the earlier suit.[3] This means that the jury in the second action may, disagreeing with the jury in the first, find that the car driver was at fault.

It may, indeed. Inconsistencies like that are always a possibility when not all claims arising from a single occurrence are tried together. Consolidation and joint trial can reduce the likelihood of such separate actions, but even those devices can work only when all claims are pending in the same court system. When several different courts are involved—the supreme court and the court of claims, federal and state courts, courts in different states, etc.—the prospects for inconsistency increase.

If the party to be estopped in action two was not a party to action one, she must at least be shown to be in "strict privity" with the party who lost in the first action.[4] Privity as used in this sense means a relationship of a kind that enables the court to be perfectly comfortable in visiting the consequences of the first action on the party to the second one.[5] Some of these situations are obvious, such as decedent/representative, trustee/beneficiary, guardian/ward, committee/incompetent, and the like; clearly, a

---

[9]   Zabriskie v. Zoloto, 22 A.D.2d 620, 257 N.Y.S.2d 965 (1st Dep't 1965); see 303 Realty Corp. v. Albert, 154 A.D.2d 590, 546 N.Y.S.2d 417 (2d Dep't 1989).

[1]   On mutuality of estoppel, see § 460.

[2]   Cases in which a party may not have been joined individually but who had a representative as a stand-in are exceptions, the class action being one example of this. See § 454.

[3]   See Neenan v. Woodside Astoria Transp. Co., 261 N.Y. 159, 184 N.E. 744 (1933).

[4]   People v. Lo Cicero, 14 N.Y.2d 374, 251 N.Y.S.2d 953, 200 N.E.2d 622 (1964).

[5]   See People ex rel. Spitzer v. Applied Card Systems, Inc., 11 N.Y.3d 105, 123, 863 N.Y.S.2d 615, 626, 894 N.E.2d 1, 12–13 (2008).

judgment rendered in an action involving such a representative is binding in a later action on the person represented.[6]

Even less obvious situations may be found to involve at base a relationship sufficient to invoke this "privity" concept, or whatever else one would call it. Control of the earlier litigation is the key feature. The Second Restatement holds bound one who, although not a party to the earlier action, "controls or substantially participates in the control" of the case.[7] Whether the participation or control is ample enough to generate the estoppel is at root a sui generis question and will be decided as such. Where an executor in the second action, for example, was found to have in fact controlled the first action, although not technically a party to it, he was held bound by the judgment.[8] Control therefore satisfies as "privity" in the collateral estoppel sense.

So does a merger of interests. A corporation in the second action, for example, may be held bound by the results of the earlier action if a party to the earlier action was the sole or main shareholder of the corporation and the court is convinced on the facts that the one can be said to have been doing the bidding of the other.[9]

If two parties share interests in some respect but are not in privity in all respects necessary to satisfy the court of the fairness of applying the estoppel doctrine, it will not be applied. This is so even if the same person is nominally the party in both actions, a not infrequent occurrence in the insurance area when subrogation is involved. Suppose, for example, that in a vehicle accident situation P collects from her own insurer for property damage and that the insurer, now subrogated to P, brings a proceeding in P's name to collect from the other car. The latter's win in that proceeding will not conclude P in P's separately brought personal injury action arising out of the same accident. P lacked control of the property damage claim, which was in the complete dominion of the insurer, and this divests the case of the needed "privity" or "control" or "participation" or whatever other word one wants to use when the court, on an analysis of the fairness factors, finds it unfair to work an estoppel.[10]

Being merely a witness in the first action, and even coming in with a lawyer and having the lawyer examine other witnesses during the trial, will not necessarily establish the needed control to invoke this privity concept. So, where the driver of a car was not a party to the first action, although the owner and the other car's people were, the driver could not be bound by a judgment against the owner even though the driver was a witness in the earlier action and, more significantly still, even though the owner's liability was derivative of the driver's.[11]

If it is shown that a party's representation in the first action was inadequate and the circumstances suggest that the party was not responsible for this, she will not be bound. This does not mean that the party gets out from under merely because he had a

---

[6]   See Restatement (Second) of Judgments § 41; as to assignors and assignees, § 55.

[7]   Restatement (Second) of Judgments § 39.

[8]   Watts v. Swiss Bank Corp., 27 N.Y.2d 270, 317 N.Y.S.2d 315, 265 N.E.2d 739 (1970).

[9]   See ACE Holding, LLC v. N.Y. State Office of the State Comptroller, 2009 WL 3713140 (Sup. Ct., New York County 2009); Warren v. Monroe County, 51 Misc. 2d 292, 273 N.Y.S.2d 107 (Sup. Ct., Monroe County 1966).

[10]   See Terman v. Gonta, 26 A.D.3d 160, 807 N.Y.S.2d 566 (1st Dep't 2006); Anderson v. Snyder Tank Corp., 44 A.D.2d 761, 354 N.Y.S.2d 241 (4th Dep't 1974).

[11]   See, e.g., Willsey v. Strawway, 44 Misc. 2d 601, 255 N.Y.S.2d 224 (Sup. Ct., Chemung County 1963), aff'd, 22 A.D.2d 973, 254 N.Y.S.2d 830 (3d Dep't 1964).

poor lawyer; it takes a more unique circumstance than that. An example would be a tort situation in which the same driver is a defendant in one action and a plaintiff in another. As a defendant, he will likely be represented by an attorney assigned by his insurance carrier; as a plaintiff, he will have his own lawyer. If the insurance policy substantially limits the insurer's liability and the defense for this reason falls short on effort, such as by "throwing in" the policy and foregoing appeal after an unfavorable verdict (so as to avoid further expense), the court may refuse to hold the result binding in the second action where the former defendant is now the plaintiff pursuing his own claim with his own lawyer. It may even happen that such separate actions will be consolidated, further obscuring things. The court can still cut through the morass, determine whether the representation was adequate, and withhold the estoppel if it was not.[12]

Analogously, a patient's lawsuit against a dentist for malpractice is not concluded by the dentist's being exonerated of the alleged wrongdoing in a disciplinary proceeding. While the patient had filed the grievance that initiated the proceeding and testified at the hearing, where she appeared with her attorney, her participation was as a witness only: she was allowed no participation at all as the case went through administrative appeal steps. Under such circumstances, the patient cannot be said to have had the kind of full and fair opportunity against the dentist that could estop her from pressing her case against him in the law action.[13]

Apparently in conflict with that is a later case from a lower court in which a nonparty to the first action who volunteered an affidavit there was made to pay an estoppel price for it in her own action later. D-1, the driver of car one, sued D-2. P, a passenger in D-1's car, was not a party, but when D-1 and D-2 each moved for summary judgment against the other, P put in an affidavit vigorously contending that D-1 was negligent and not entitled to summary judgment. D-1 got summary judgment anyway. Then, in P's separate action against D-1, D-1 was awarded a collateral estoppel against P on the issue of D-1's fault. The court found that P, even though not a party to the first action—and obviously not in privity with its loser (D-2)—had a full and fair opportunity to litigate the issue of D-1's fault in the earlier action, and lost on it.[14]

An interesting question is whether nonparty P could have appealed the D-1 judgment in the earlier action. A full day in court in New York practice includes the appellate process if the loser wants to use it.[15] A situation in which an appeal is for one reason or another foreclosed would fall short of the "full" day required to invoke an estoppel under this rule.

When one person's claim is wholly derivative of another's, it has been held that a determination that the latter has no claim binds the would-be deriver whether or not she is a party to the determination. So, where a husband sued X for personal injuries and a jury found for X, his wife, although not a party, was bound by that determination

---

[12] See, e.g., Huston v. DeLeonardis, 44 A.D.2d 110, 353 N.Y.S.2d 771 (1st Dep't 1974).

[13] David v. Biondo, 92 N.Y.2d 318, 680 N.Y.S.2d 450, 703 N.E.2d 261 (1998). The case is the subject of the lead note in NYSLD No. 468.

[14] Augustine v. Sugrue, N.Y.L.J., May 19, 2003, at 33, col.1 (Sup. Ct., Queens County; Taylor, J.). Would P's inability to appeal the adverse finding in the first action—because P was not a party to it—lead to a different conclusion? See the last paragraph in § 465.

[15] See § 465.

and could not maintain a subsequent action against X for such derivative claims as the loss of her husband's services and consortium.[16]

§ 459.　Different Capacities

If a person has several capacities, a judgment against that person in an action involving one capacity will not necessarily bind her in a second one involving the other. So, for example, if a person appears as a personal representative—executrix or administratrix—in action one, the judgment will not be binding when she pursues her rights as an individual in action two, and vice versa.[1] The assumption underlying this rule is that a proper job of representation necessarily entails a setting aside of one's individual interest so that neither the fruits nor the consequences of a judgment rendered in the one capacity should bind in the other.[2] If the person appears in both capacities, however, interposing both individual and represented claims, such as a father suing for his child's personal injuries (a representative claim) as well as for the father's own medical expenditures or for the loss of services of the child (individual claims), he will be bound in both capacities.

§ 460.　Identity of Estopping Party; "Mutuality" of Estoppel

At one time, even though X had had a full day in court on a particular issue in the first action and lost on it, Y could not have a collateral estoppel on that issue against X in a second action if Y was not himself a party to the first one.

This was known as the doctrine of "mutuality of estoppel." Its predicate was that since X, had he won in the first action, could not have made any later estoppel use of his victory as against Y for the simple reason that Y had not yet been heard and thus could not be bound by the judgment, then Y should not be able to make any estoppel use of the judgment against X if X should be the loser. The mutuality doctrine was upheld by the Court of Appeals,[1] and was adhered to even when some rethinking appeared to be in order,[2] but it steadily lost credit until the Court of Appeals itself finally abandoned it entirely, declaring it a "dead letter" in B.R. DeWitt, Inc. v. Hall[3] in 1967. It remains a dead letter today.

In *DeWitt*, a truck and jeep collided. The truck driver sued the jeep owner for personal injuries and won. The truck owner then sued the jeep owner for property damage and sought to make estoppel use of the truck driver's earlier victory. He was allowed it notwithstanding that had the jeep owner won in the earlier action he could not have used that victory against the truck owner simply because the truck owner was not also a party to the first action.

---

[16]　Fischbach v. Auto Boys, Inc., 106 N.Y.S.2d 416 (Sup. Ct., Kings County 1951), rev'd on other grounds, 279 A.D. 1035, 112 N.Y.S.2d 283 (2d Dep't 1952).

[1]　Juan C. v. Cortines, 89 N.Y.2d 659, 657 N.Y.S.2d 581, 679 N.E.2d 1061 (1997); Hellstern v. Hellstern, 279 N.Y. 327, 18 N.E.2d 296 (1938).

[2]　See Restatement (Second) of Judgments § 36, and its accompanying illustrations.

[1]　See Haverhill v. International R. Co., 244 N.Y. 582, 155 N.E. 905 (1927) aff'g 217 A.D. 521, 217 N.Y.S. 522 (4th Dep't 1926).

[2]　See Elder v. New York & Pennsylvania Motor Exp., 284 N.Y. 350, 31 N.E.2d 188 (1940). The *Elder* facts will be treated in the course of some tort examples later. See § 466.

[3]　B. R. DeWitt, Inc. v. Hall, 19 N.Y.2d 141, 278 N.Y.S.2d 596, 225 N.E.2d 195 (1967).

The Court of Appeals said the test applied should be the identity of issue test[4] despite the absence of a total identity of parties, citing Israel v. Wood Dolson Co.,[5] a 1956 pronouncement of the Court and a major development along this line. *Israel* held that there is no need to show that the party seeking to use the estoppel was a party to the first action; that it is necessary to show only that the party against whom it is used in the second was a party to the first and thus had a full day in court on the issue.

In the first action in *Israel*, P had sued D for breach of contract and lost, no breach being proved. In the second action, P sued X for inducing D's breach of the same contract. Although X was not a party to the first action, he was allowed an estoppel to establish that this contract had not been breached. A showing of a breach being an indispensable element to P's success in the second action, P lost the action because of the estoppel. *Israel* holds that it is not necessary for a party to have had a day in court against a particular litigant; it is sufficient that he had it on the identical issue.

Unbound by any adverse finding in the first action because not a party to it, while able to make use of a favorable finding emanating from it because for that purpose she does not have to be a party to it, a second-round party can today get the best of two worlds. Where, for example, there are several parties involved in the first action, the nonparty can use collateral estoppel against a first action loser while being immune to any use of it by a first action winner.

Given the enthusiastic judicial use of devices like consolidation and joint trial if separate actions arising out of the same occurrence should be brought today, this best-of-both-worlds phenomenon is not very frequent, but can and does occur. Suppose, for example, that passenger A in car one is injured in a two-car collision and sues both drivers, winning only against the first driver. Then passenger B, not a party to that action, separately sues the same drivers. B can have an estoppel against the first driver, who lost in the first action, but the second driver, who won in the first action, cannot have an estoppel against B.[6] B is therefore entitled to litigate afresh the second driver's liability, which of course opens the door to a conflicting determination.

One of the more frequent sources of separate actions, and potential conflicts, is the accident involving the liability of both the State, which can be sued only in the court of claims, and a private person, who must be sued in some other court.[7]

Mutuality's abandonment can create the above anomalies, but they are easier to live with than a rule that arbitrarily mandates relitigation whenever parties are not totally parallel. The law today looks at the first action's loser and asks whether that person had a full hearing on the dispositive issue; if she had, it's of secondary importance that a nonparty may want to use it.

§ 461. "Privity"

Also necessary to put into perspective in a collateral estoppel (issue preclusion) discussion is the loose-limbed doctrine called "privity," which has wiggled in and out of

---

[4]   The identity of issue test is discussed in § 462.

[5]   Israel v. Wood Dolson Co., 1 N.Y.2d 116, 151 N.Y.S.2d 1, 134 N.E.2d 97 (1956).

[6]   See Jacobs v. Del Guercio, 67 Misc. 2d 606, 324 N.Y.S.2d 773 (Sup. Ct., New York County 1971).

[7]   See § 470.

the cases. Unlike "mutuality," which seemed easy enough to understand (if not agree with), "privity" in collateral estoppel context was always muddy.

When applied to the second action party against whom the estoppel is sought, "privity," as we have seen,[1] has a clear enough meaning: it takes on its traditional connotation, requiring a legal relationship of a kind that would allow the loss of the first action (or of an issue in it) by X to be justly visited upon Y in the second action. X as decedent and Y as X's personal representative would be an example. These are clear instances of "privity."

The murky area is where X in the second action is the one who wants to use the collateral estoppel. May X do so only if she has some connection, some "privity," with a winner in the first action? The First Restatement said that before a person in the second action can be either the victim or the beneficiary of the first action's result, she must be shown to have been either a party to the first action or else "in privity" with a party.[2] The Second Restatement abandons that idea; it contains no counterpart for the "privity" rule,[3] at least insofar as it concerns the user of collateral estoppel.

New York joined early in the abandonment of the privity requirement when the estoppel was used only defensively in the second action, but the doctrine still hovered about when offensive use was sought. In Cummings v. Dresher,[4] for example, the driver of car one and his passenger sued the driver[5] of the second car for personal injuries. The passenger won but the first-car driver, found guilty of contributory negligence—at a time when any contributory negligence on the part of a plaintiff would bar the claim entirely— did not. In a subsequent action by the driver of the second car (the first action's defendant) against the driver and owner of the first car, the first-car owner, although not a party to the first action, was allowed a defensive estoppel against the second-car driver: the affirmative negligence found against the second-car driver in the first action was held to constitute contributory negligence against him in his posture as plaintiff in the second action, foreclosing his recovery. While a legal link of a kind that might be called "privity" could be found to exist between the owner and driver of the first car, that would not avail the owner in Cummings because the driver lost the first action. It was the passenger who won, and whose victory the owner wanted to use, and was allowed to. That had to mean either that there is "privity" between a car's owner and one who is a mere passenger in it or, as seems more likely, that "privity" is just not required, at least for an estoppel used defensively.[6]

Despite that indication, the Court of Appeals in the later case of B.R. DeWitt, Inc. v. Hall,[7] in which estoppel was used offensively, still listed a kind of "privity" as a significant factor. A truck owner, suing a jeep owner for property damage in a collision, was allowed estoppel use of the truck driver's previous victory against the same defendant for personal injuries. When recapitulating the factors deemed significant in allowing the estoppel, the Court in DeWitt mentioned that the truck owner "derived" his

---

[1]   See § 458.

[2]   Restatement (First) of Judgments § 83.

[3]   See also the Reporter's Memorandum at p. xii of Tentative Draft No. 2 of the Second Restatement.

[4]   Cummings v. Dresher, 18 N.Y.2d 105, 271 N.Y.S.2d 976, 218 N.E.2d 688 (1966).

[5]   Both actions also involved the second car's owner, but the driver suffices for the example.

[6]   See the dissenting opinion in the Cummings case, 18 N.Y.2d at 110, 271 N.Y.S.2d at 979, 218 N.E.2d at 691.

[7]   B. R. DeWitt, Inc. v. Hall, 19 N.Y.2d 141, 278 N.Y.S.2d 596, 225 N.E.2d 195 (1967).

right from the driver, thus giving that link some significance even though adding that the owner and driver "do not technically stand in . . . privity."[8]

The New York bar awaited further word. Was that kind of liaison, or something like it, whether labeled "privity" or something else, to remain a requirement for estoppel, or was it to expire at last? Its death knell, or at least a major tug at the bell, came in the Court of Appeals statement in Schwartz v. Public Administrator.[9] The Court, citing both *Cummings* and *DeWitt*, observed that it had "already discarded, as irrelevant . . . the fact that there may or may not have been any significant jural relationship between the party seeking to invoke the doctrine and the prior victor."[10] The final round, and the apparent interment of the privity doctrine, awaited the mid-1980s, when the Court of Appeals permitted the use of collateral estoppel by different victims of a multiparty accident. Until then, the privity concept had been one of the stalwarts in avoiding the problem of whether to allow (e.g.) a victory by passenger one to be used by the hundred other passengers involved in the same train or plane accident.[11]

It was not a vehicle accident case that finally met the issue head on, however; it was a blackout in New York City. After one citizen who suffered damages in the blackout recovered a judgment against the grossly negligent electric utility, other citizens damaged by the same event were allowed a free estoppel ride on the liability issue. And shortly after that, a cancer-causing drug case added yet another nail to the privity coffin. When a woman damaged by her mother's earlier ingestion of a dangerous drug recovered a judgment from the drug's manufacturer, other women so damaged by the same drug were allowed to invoke the first one's victory on liability issues through the estoppel route. The blackout case is Koch v. Consolidated Edison Co. of New York.[12] The drug case is Kaufman v. Eli Lilly and Co.[13] Together they appeared to have written finis to the privity requirement.[14]

The "privity" concept in this context had no more relevance or utility than the "mutuality" doctrine had. If the New York courts have indeed abandoned it, they have done well. Insofar as it purports to require a link between a first action winner and a second action estoppel user, the privity notion under present lights is unnecessary. The identity of issue test, to which we next turn, seems able to offer the needed protection without help from "privity."

There remain cases, however, in which a link between the second action user and the first action winner, whether referred to as privity or anything else, continues to play an important role. In one interesting case, for example, an assaulted person was found to be in privity with the assaulter:

P was a shopkeeper shot by D. In a prosecution in which P testified for the State, D was convicted of the crime, including a finding that D was guilty of an intent to injure P.

---

[8]   *DeWitt*, 19 N.Y.2d at 148, 278 N.Y.S.2d at 602, 225 N.E.2d at 189.

[9]   Schwartz v. Public Adm'r of Bronx County, 24 N.Y.2d 65, 298 N.Y.S.2d 955, 246 N.E.2d 725 (1969). The *Schwartz* case is discussed more fully in § 467.

[10]   *Schwartz*, 24 N.Y.2d at 70, 298 N.Y.S.2d at 958–59, 246 N.E.2d at 728.

[11]   See Example K in § 468.

[12]   Koch v. Consolidated Edison Co. of New York, Inc., 62 N.Y.2d 548, 479 N.Y.S.2d 163, 468 N.E.2d 1 (1984).

[13]   Kaufman v. Eli Lilly and Co., 65 N.Y.2d 449, 492 N.Y.S.2d 584, 482 N.E.2d 63 (1985).

[14]   The cases are treated in more detail later, in the discussion of the full and fair opportunity test. See § 467.

Then P brought a civil suit against D for damages for the assault and got a big default judgment against D. D resided with his parents, who had a homeowner's policy that covered D as an insured, and now P sued the insurer to have it make good on the judgment. The insurer disclaimed on the ground that the policy explicitly excluded coverage of an injury "intended by the Insured." The Court sustained the disclaimer, holding that the criminal judgment established the insured's intent to injure and that the finding bound P. The Court also indicated that even if P had not testified at the criminal trial, P would have been estopped because P was in "privity" with D in respect of the insurance issue.[15]

What about a patient's lawsuit against a dentist for malpractice after the dentist has been exonerated of wrongdoing by a disciplinary board? Not binding, held the Court of Appeals in David v. Biondo;[16] the patient is free to prove malpractice. While the patient had filed the grievance that initiated the disciplinary proceeding and testified at the hearing before the five-member panel, she was not allowed any other participation. The court said that the patient could not be said to have had the kind of full and fair opportunity against the dentist that could estop her from pressing her case against him in the law action.

Can the cases be distinguished in that in the latter, the victim's contention at the administrative hearing (that the dentist was a malpractitioner) was consistent with her position in the court action, while in the first case the victim's testimony at the criminal trial indicated the wrongdoer's intent to harm, not at all consistent with the victim's later endeavor, in trying to get at the policy proceeds, to show that the wrongdoer had no such intent?[17]

A major later pronouncement by the Court of Appeals on collateral estoppel in general, and on "privity" in particular, is contained in the decision in Buechel v. Bain.[18] In *Buechel*, the court waded through a complicated fact pattern to pin on two lawyers, B and C, an unfavorable result rendered against their partner, A, in an earlier action involving the partnership's agreement with the client. A sued the client and made B and C, with whom there had been a falling out, additional defendants. The client counterclaimed against A to set aside the transaction that had been profiting all three partners, but did not cross-claim against B and C for the same relief. Some shred of relationship at that time apparently continued with B and C and the client was loath to disrupt it. When the rupture was complete and the client now got around to suing B and C in a second action, they claimed they were not active participants in the first action and thus couldn't be bound by the findings made in it.

The court held B and C bound. They were linked—in privity—with A on the issue of protecting the agreement, had a full and fair opportunity to defend the agreement whether they thought it politic or not to do so in that unusual context, and were bound

---

[15] D'Arata v. New York Cent. Mut. Fire Ins. Co., 76 N.Y.2d 659, 563 N.Y.S.2d 24, 564 N.E.2d 634 (1990). The "privity" concept was reviewed in two later cases involving its attempted use between insurers: State Farm etc. v. Sceviour, N.Y.L.J., Sept. 8, 2006, at 26, col.1 (Sup. Ct., Nassau County; Winslow, J.), concerning liability insurance; and Town of Wilton v. Tarrant Mfg. Co., Sup. Ct., Saratoga County, June 13, 2006 (Index No. 2005–2585; Nolan, J.), concerning fire insurance. Both are reviewed and contrasted in the lead note in SPR 179:1.

[16] David v. Biondo, 92 N.Y.2d 318, 680 N.Y.S.2d 450, 703 N.E.2d 261 (1998), treated in the lead note in NYSLD No. 468.

[17] See the discussion of these cases in the lead note in NYSLD No. 468.

[18] Buechel v. Bain, 97 N.Y.2d 295, 740 N.Y.S.2d 252, 766 N.E.2d 914 (2001).

by the result, which was that the agreement amounted to an overreaching by the partnership and was invalid.[19]

G. IDENTIFYING THE ISSUE

Table of Sections

§ 462.   Identity of Issue Test

§ 463.   Law and Fact, Ultimate and Evidentiary

§ 464.   Underlying Facts Bind, Litigated or Not

§ 465.   Gratuitous Findings

§ 462. Identity of Issue Test

If the first inquiry in any attempt to use collateral estoppel is whether it's being used only against one who has already had a day in court, then the second would have to be whether the issue on which the estoppel is sought was passed upon during that earlier court day. This is the identity of issue test, and two of its chief proponents are Israel v. Wood Dolson Co.[1] and Schwartz v. Public Administrator.[2]

In *Israel*, a commercial setting, an earlier holding that a plaintiff/defendant contract was not breached collaterally estopped the plaintiff from contending in a second action that a breach was induced by one X. In *Schwartz*, a tort case, a passenger's recovery from both his own and the other car's drivers, establishing the negligence of both, estopped one driver from afterwards suing the other by importing as contributory negligence in the second action—at a time when the rule was that any contributory negligence on the part of the plaintiff barred the claim altogether—the affirmative negligence established in the first. In each instance, the Court carefully examined the issue on which estoppel was sought and satisfied itself that it was the same as the one passed on earlier.

Examples today are numerous. P had a claim against the State because of an alleged trespass by a state contractor. P first sued the contractor in the supreme court where the contractor won. P then sued the State in the court of claims. The State's liability was found to be derivative of the contractor's and since the contractor had none, then under collateral estoppel neither had the State.[3]

Sometimes it will happen that a dismissal on a seemingly jurisdictional ground will be found upon closer scrutiny to dispose of a piece of the merits as well—perhaps even enough to work an estoppel when the merits are met in another court later. Suppose, for example, that P sues D in a federal court alleging a federal constitutional violation. The basis of federal subject matter jurisdiction is that a federal question is involved. Assume that the federal court, looking into the matter, dismisses the action for want of a substantial federal question as sometimes happens. It is presumably only a jurisdictional dismissal, but if the federal issue was found inadequate even for mere jurisdiction, how can a later court, which has secured jurisdiction, uphold the issue on its merits? The earlier judgment in that situation, whether purporting to be a mere

---

[19]   The *Buechel* case is treated at length in NYSLD No. 507.

[1]   Israel v. Wood Dolson Co., 1 N.Y.2d 116, 151 N.Y.S.2d 1, 134 N.E.2d 97 (1956).

[2]   Schwartz v. Public Adm'r of Bronx County, 24 N.Y.2d 65, 298 N.Y.S.2d 955, 246 N.E.2d 725 (1969).

[3]   Bronxville Palmer, Limited v. State, 18 N.Y.2d 560, 277 N.Y.S.2d 402, 223 N.E.2d 887 (1966).

jurisdictional dismissal or not, may well be given conclusive effect on the merits when the merits are reached in the second action.[4]

The inquiry into the nature of the issue must be a careful one. Sometimes a single statute or part of it can be the source of several kinds of dismissal, only some of which carry final estoppel consequences. A good example is the motion to dismiss for failure to state a cause of action under CPLR 3211(a)(7). The motion can be based either on the pleading's failure to verbalize a good claim (i.e., the pleading is defective on its face), or it can be based on the claim's lack of substantive merit, summarily established by affidavits and other proof even though the pleading on its face is fine. The first kind of dismissal will work an estoppel if the complaint in the second action is "virtually identical" to the complaint in the first,[5] but there will be no estoppel if the earlier pleading defect is remedied.[6] If the dismissal was of the second variety, establishing not just that the pleading was poor but that the plaintiff had no claim, it of course does get estoppel effect.[7] Today, under the Court of Appeals decisions in Miglino v. Bally Total Fitness of Greater New York, Inc. and Rovello v. Orofino Realty Co.,[8] this latter category of disposition is likely only if the court elected to treat the CPLR 3211(a)(7) motion as one for summary judgment.[9]

The burden of showing that the issue on which collateral estoppel is sought is the same as one disposed of in the earlier action is on the party who wants the estoppel. But if the resisting party—the one against whom the estoppel is sought—has anything to show to avoid the estoppel, such as that she did not have a full opportunity to contest the issue in the earlier action, the resister has the burden on that score and must go forward with it. So holds the *Schwartz* case,[10] a leading one in New York. *Schwartz* lists a number of factors for the court to consider in determining whether to award an estoppel.[11] When one of these factors is cited by the party resisting the estoppel to get out from under it, that party carries the burden. Caselaw suggests with good reason that in the final analysis collateral estoppel is sui generis, that its "crowning consideration" is fairness, that rigidity has no place in its application, and that "all the circumstances" of the prior action must be examined to determine whether the estoppel is to be allowed.[12]

If the earlier judgment could have proceeded on any of several distinct facts or theories and it is unclear which of them actually accounts for it, there can be no estoppel and the matter is open for litigation anew. If, for example, an earlier decision concerning a lease can be accounted for either by a finding that no such lease was made or that it was made but its ostensible maker had no authority to make it, and the earlier record

---

[4] See Becker v. Levitt, 81 Misc. 2d 664, 366 N.Y.S.2d 940 (Sup. Ct., Nassau County 1975).

[5] See McKinney v. City of New York, 78 A.D.2d 884, 433 N.Y.S.2d 193 (2d Dep't 1980).

[6] See Deacon's Bench, Inc. v. Hoffman, 101 A.D.2d 971, 477 N.Y.S.2d 447 (3d Dep't 1984); Allston v. Incorporated Village of Rockville Centre, 25 A.D.2d 545, 267 N.Y.S.2d 564 (2d Dep't 1966). *Allston* was an action. The same rule applies to a dismissed special proceeding. Searles v. Main Tavern Inc., 28 A.D.2d 1136, 284 N.Y.S.2d 652 (2d Dep't 1967).

[7] See § 276 and Commentaries C3211:67 and C3211:68 on McKinney's CPLR 3211.

[8] Miglino v. Bally Total Fitness of Greater New York, Inc., 20 N.Y.3d 342, 961 N.Y.S.2d 364, 985 N.E.2d 128 (2013); Rovello v. Orofino Realty Co., Inc., 40 N.Y.2d 633, 389 N.Y.S.2d 314, 357 N.E.2d 970 (1976). See § 265.

[9] See § 270.

[10] *Schwartz*, 24 N.Y.2d at 73, 298 N.Y.S.2d at 962, 246 N.E.2d at 730.

[11] These factors will be explored in detail when the multiparty tort cases are treated later. See § 467.

[12] Read v. Sacco, 49 A.D.2d 471, 375 N.Y.S.2d 371 (2d Dep't 1975).

does not clarify which ground was used, neither can support an estoppel in the second action.[13]

An even more common source of this kind of problem has been the multi-party tort case in which use of estoppel in the second action is frustrated by the fact that a general verdict in the first action obscured the grounds that produced it. Suppose, for example, that P sues a car owner for personal injuries sustained in an accident, and two issues are litigated: whether the driver was negligent and whether the driver had permission to drive (which would be necessary in order to hold in the owner). The jury brings back a general verdict for the owner. The resulting judgment cannot be the source of a later estoppel on either of the two issues because it did not clarify precisely what the jury found on each: a finding in the owner's favor on either of the issues could adequately account for the judgment, depriving it of its clarity and hence its estoppel use.[14]

A special verdict embodying all of the jury's findings in the form of answers to questions would clarify the findings and expedite their use for estoppel purposes in later actions.[15] In this connection, the advent of New York's comparative negligence rule (replacing the contributory negligence rule), applicable to claims arising on or after September 1, 1975,[16] along with a number of other developments,[17] has diminished this kind of estoppel problem by increasing the use of special verdicts. The special verdict always supports issue preclusion better than a general verdict.

§ 463. Law and Fact, Ultimate and Evidentiary

hen the whole of an issue arising in a second action was disposed of in the first one, and the lines of the issue in both contexts are identical, the estoppel doctrine applies with no difficulty. This is so whether the issue can be characterized as one of law or one of fact because collateral estoppel (issue preclusion) as a general rule applies to both kinds. Indeed, it would be untenable to permit the doctrine and its polices to be evaded merely by stamping the issue "law" or "fact" or, for that matter, "mixed"; the line between the two is often blurred.[1]

When the lines of the issue are not entirely parallel, and when there are some strands connected to it in the first action that do not adhere to it in the second, a closer scrutiny may be necessary to determine whether to invoke the doctrine. A good illustration of this problem and of its pragmatic resolution is Hinchey v. Sellers.[2] Simplifying the facts for purposes of illustration: X was a passenger in a car driven by D and owned by O. It went off the road in New York and X was killed. P was X's administrator and because D was a New Hampshire resident, P brought a wrongful death suit against D in a New Hampshire court. O was not a party there but it was claimed that O's insurance covered the accident. The insurer disclaimed, however, on the ground that D was driving without O's permission within the meaning of the policy. The issue was tested in a declaratory action in New Hampshire, involving P, D, and the

---

[13] Lewis v. Ocean Navigation & Pier Co., 125 N.Y. 341, 26 N.E. 301 (1891).

[14] See Manard v. Hardware Mut. Cas. Co., 12 A.D.2d 29, 207 N.Y.S.2d 807 (4th Dep't 1960).

[15] See Kret by Kret v. Brookdale Hosp. Medical Center, 93 A.D.2d 449, 462 N.Y.S.2d 896 (2d Dep't 1983), aff'd, 61 N.Y.2d 861, 473 N.Y.S.2d 970, 462 N.E.2d 147 (1984).

[16] CPLR 1411–1413. See § 188E.

[17] See § 399.

[1] See Restatement (Second) of Judgments § 28, cmt. b.

[2] Hinchey v. Sellers, 7 N.Y.2d 287, 197 N.Y.S.2d 129, 165 N.E.2d 156 (1959).

insurer, and resolved in favor of the insurer: it was found that D did not have permission to drive the car and hence that the insurance did not cover.

In a later action in New York, P sued O on the same cause of action, O's liability being predicated on New York's statute imputing the driver's conduct to the owner when the car is driven with permission.[3] O invoked collateral estoppel on that point, however, claiming that the lack of permission established in the New Hampshire action was conclusive upon P in this action as well. P countered that the issue was not the same; that while perhaps called "permission" in both instances, its scope and content was different in each: in the New Hampshire action, the issue was permission under the insurance policy while in the instant action it was permission under the New York statute; and the "ultimate legal issue" was not necessarily the same.

The Court of Appeals agreed that the "ultimate legal issue" was not the same in both cases, but, digging into the detailed evidentiary findings on which the issue was resolved in the first action, the court found enough in its foundation to support an estoppel in the second action. Comparing the findings on which "permission" was found to be lacking under the insurance policy, in other words, with the findings necessary to establish want of "permission" under the New York statute, the court found the necessary parallels and upheld the estoppel. The "ultimate" issue was concededly not the same because what would satisfy as "permission" under the insurance contract would not necessarily satisfy as "permission" under the statute. But this merely meant that the estoppel would not be automatic, that it would instead entail an examination of all the fact findings—the "evidentiary" details—on which the New Hampshire conclusion of non-permission was based, to see whether any one or a combination of them should happen to parallel the New York statute's constituents as well.

The particular finding that did the job in *Hinchey* was New Hampshire's determination, one of many, that when O lent the car, the permission was conditioned on the borrower's not letting D into the car at all and that D was allowed into the car in disregard of that stipulation. That destroyed "permission" under the insurance policy; upon independent later examination by the New York courts, it was found that such a violation would also undo "permission" under the New York statute. In that lay the parallel, and down came the estoppel.

The lesson is that an issue need not qualify as "ultimate" to invoke the estoppel. The doctrine will not be undone by a label. If an examination of the record, going into as much detail as need be, reveals that enough was determined—and fairly determined— in the first action to conclude an issue in the second, it is of secondary importance that the fact found to do the job is an "ultimate" fact or something less. Indeed, if we may draw an analogy to pleadings, the pre-CPLR distinction made between "ultimate" and "evidentiary" facts was found to be a useless pursuit and was, with much profit, abandoned.[4] A court can well point to that in the estoppel realm as well.[5] The disposition must be governed by the reality rather than the caption.

---

[3] See Veh. & Traf. Law § 388.

[4] See § 207.

[5] The Second Restatement rejects the attempt to draw a line between ultimate and evidentiary facts, suggesting that the more appropriate question to ask is whether, whatever the label, the parties and fact trier recognized the issue as important and necessary and tried and determined it accordingly. See Restatement (Second) of Judgments § 27, cmt. j.

§ 464. Underlying Facts Bind, Litigated or Not

The concept usually met, and generally valid, in collateral estoppel ("issue preclusion") is that it will attach only to matters actually litigated as opposed to claim preclusion (res judicata itself in its stricter sense), which also forecloses matters that could have been litigated.[1] But now a qualification: the estoppel or issue preclusion doctrine will apply not only to matters actually litigated, but also to all that are necessarily established by the earlier judgment, litigated or not. Where a judgment of a particular kind can be accounted for only by the existence of a certain combination of findings, each of those findings will be deemed established by the judgment. A judgment of separation, for example, necessarily establishes that there was a valid marriage because without a valid marriage there is nothing to separate. So, where H sued W for separation and won, and in a later action W sued H for annulment (which seeks to establish that the marriage was not valid to begin with), the first judgment was deemed to establish the marriage's validity and W was estopped from claiming otherwise. The annulment action failed.[2]

Similarly, P's judgment against D for negligent personal injury under the old rule of contributory negligence (which barred P from all recovery if found guilty of any negligence at all) necessarily established (1) that D was negligent and (2) that P was not. The estoppel could thereafter be exploited accordingly. The estoppel would attach to such a judgment even if it had been based only on a general verdict that did not expressly report its underlying findings, for the reason that no other combination of findings could legally account for the judgment. Note, however, that a contrary general verdict under the old contributory negligence rule—one in favor of D against P—would not lend itself to collateral estoppel use because any of several sets of findings could explain it and the set actually used would not be known: P was negligent and D was not; both were negligent; neither was. Any of these combinations could account for a defendant's general verdict under a contributory negligence rule.[3]

A key lesson emerging from the foregoing is that when a given finding necessarily underlies a judgment, and the judgment's very existence can be explained only by assuming the fact to be thus and so, the fact may become the basis of an estoppel even if it was not litigated in the earlier action. Estoppel does not invariably demand that the point be shown to have been disputed in the first action. "Whatever is necessarily implied in the former decision, is for the purpose of the estoppel deemed to have been actually decided" as are also "conclusions of law or fact, which necessarily flow from a judgment, although not expressly found."[4]

This phase of the estoppel rule can be summed up as the basic proposition that any finding essential to the judgment constitutes a component of that judgment and lends itself to an estoppel.[5]

---

[1]   Schuylkill Fuel Corp. v. B. & C. Nieberg Realty Corp., 250 N.Y. 304, 165 N.E. 456 (1929).

[2]   Statter v. Statter, 2 N.Y.2d 668, 163 N.Y.S.2d 13, 143 N.E.2d 10 (1957). In *Statter*, it was alleged that newly discovered evidence undermined a fact found in the earlier action. That is not ordinarily an excuse to deny an estoppel. The remedy in that situation is a motion, made and captioned in the first action itself, to vacate the first judgment and reopen the case for a new trial. See CPLR 5015(a)(2) and § 428.

[3]   The use of a special verdict avoids this problem by announcing all findings explicitly. See the discussion towards the end of § 462.

[4]   Pray v. Hegeman, 98 N.Y. 351, 358, 1885 WL 10563 (1885).

[5]   Hinchey v. Sellers, 7 N.Y.2d 287, 197 N.Y.S.2d 129, 165 N.E.2d 156 (1959).

The estoppel can of course be met and offset today with a showing by the other side that the earlier action did not offer a "full and fair opportunity" to litigate the issue, such as for want of a stake big enough to make a vigorous defense worthwhile.[6] In Kossover v. Trattler,[7] for example, a judgment for a physician on a $750 claim against a patient for a fee was denied estoppel effect in the patient's later action against the physician for medical malpractice, even though recovery of the fee necessarily presumed the legitimacy of the medical service rendered. The first judgment in *Kossover* had been rendered by default.[8] In Chisholm-Ryder Co. v. Sommer & Sommer,[9] in contrast, the earlier adjudication occurred in a contested action by attorneys seeking a fee for their services. They were granted summary judgment for the fee and the judgment was given estoppel effect in a later action by the client, who was now attempting to show malpractice in the rendition of the legal services. The court said that "the prior action between these parties necessarily determined that services were performed by the attorneys for the client and that compensation was due them."[10]

§ 465. Gratuitous Findings

In the prior section, we met the rule that a fact or conclusion that is a necessary part of a judgment will be entitled to an estoppel even if it was not actually litigated. We now meet the converse: even an issue actually litigated may be denied the estoppel if it was not necessary to the judgment.

To earn an estoppel, a fact must be shown to be material and relevant to the resolution of the legal issue involved in the first action.[1] Gratuitous findings will not support an estoppel. Where, for example, W sued H for abandonment but did not make out a ground, judgment for H became appropriate dismissing the abandonment charge without further ado. When the court went further, therefore, and found affirmatively that it was W who abandoned H, the finding was deemed gratuitous and barred from estoppel use.[2] One basis for this rule is that once enough has been found to justify a judgment, further findings lose their decisiveness and hence do not invite the responsibility, care, and attention that all judicial findings deserve. Estoppel, in other words, does not apply to unessential facts, and this is so even though they may be put in issue by the pleadings and directly decided.[3]

While that would appear to be the general rule, an exception may have to be carved out today if on the facts of a given case a finding may have been technically "gratuitous," but is found to have been the product of much "care and attention" by the trial judge. The apprehensions underlying the "gratuitous finding" rule—the fear that deliberation

---

[6]   See § 467 and more particularly items 2 and 4 on the list of factors enumerated there.

[7]   Kossover v. Trattler, 82 A.D.2d 610, 442 N.Y.S.2d 554 (2d Dep't 1981).

[8]   See the discussion of this point in the concurring opinion of Justice Gibbons in *Kossover*, 82 A.D.2d at 610, 442 N.Y.S.2d at 554.

[9]   Chisholm-Ryder Co., Inc. v. Sommer & Sommer, 78 A.D.2d 143, 434 N.Y.S.2d 70 (4th Dep't 1980).

[10]   When lawyer and client agree to arbitrate their dispute about the lawyer's fee, and the lawyer prevails in the arbitration, it has been held that the arbitration victory insulates the lawyer from an action for legal malpractice. See Altamore v. Friedman, 193 A.D.2d 240, 602 N.Y.S.2d 894 (2d Dep't 1993), noted in SPR 24:3; § 456.

[1]   Zabriskie v. Zoloto, 22 A.D.2d 620, 257 N.Y.S.2d 965 (1st Dep't 1965).

[2]   Silberstein v. Silberstein, 218 N.Y. 525, 113 N.E. 495 (1916).

[3]   *Silberstein*, 218 N.Y. at 528–29, 113 N.E. at 496, and cases there cited.

will be lax because the result lacks impact—are apparently not at hand in that situation. So directs Malloy v. Trombley,[4] unless the case is to be put down as strictly sui generis.

A and B in *Malloy*, tort claimants from different cars involved in the same accident, sued the State in the court of claims but made out no case. When the judge dismissed as against the State, he then found, gratuitously, that both A and B were contributorily negligent. The record indicated such careful deliberation in his doing so, however, that the finding was allowed estoppel use in a supreme court action between A and B where, under the rule of contributory negligence applicable at the time, it resulted in a dismissal.[5]

Shortly after *Malloy* came down, the Court of Appeals distinguished it in O'Connor v. G & R Packing Co.[6] on the basis that in *O'Connor* a finding of fault on the part of P was just a general statement made by the court on dismissing at the end of P's case. Thus a different defendant, now sued by P in respect of the same accident, could not invoke the earlier judgment against P.

Sometimes the rule against awarding an estoppel to what the court deems an "unnecessary" finding will be invoked even when the finding seems relevant and material to the first action. This is especially so when the issue was resolved against the party who, nevertheless, won the first action. The case of Karameros v. Luther[7] will illustrate. W sued H for separation, but lost when the court found that a separation ground was not made out. The court also found that there was a valid marriage between the parties. Then H sued W for annulment on the ground that W lacked capacity to marry (because she already had an undivorced husband). W defended on the ground that the earlier action had found that her marriage with H was valid and that this estopped H from now pleading that it was not. The Court held that H was not estopped; it found that although the validity of the marriage may be an indispensable part of a judgment that grants a separation,[8] the earlier judgment in this case denied the separation, and in that context a finding on the validity of the marriage amounted to an unnecessary finding.

How can one justify this? A finding on the validity of a marriage is hardly an irrelevant item in a separation action, whichever way the case may go. Is there some magic order in which issues must be tried? There is not, but the result in *Karameros* can be defended on a different ground. In *Karameros*, it was W, the loser in the first action, who in the second action wanted an estoppel on the marriage issue to use against H, the earlier winner. Suppose, however, that while H was the winner of the first action, H seriously disputed the finding of the marriage's validity, contending throughout the first action that the marriage was invalid. What could H do after the court had found against him on the issue and held the marriage valid, but nevertheless gave him judgment on the merits dismissing the separation claim based on W's failure to spell out a ground for separation? As the winner, H presumably could not appeal: he would lack aggrieved

---

4   Malloy v. Trombley, 50 N.Y.2d 46, 427 N.Y.S.2d 969, 405 N.E.2d 213 (1980).

5   Today, under the comparative negligence rule, see § 168E, a dismissal would not be the result unless perhaps the finding was of 100% fault of the party who is later the plaintiff in the supreme court. But if the court of claims should allot precise percentages of fault between A and B, or among A, B, and the State, the allotment between A and B would likely be available for estoppel use in the supreme court action between A and B.

6   O'Connor v. G & R Packing Co., 53 N.Y.2d 278, 440 N.Y.S.2d 920, 423 N.E.2d 397 (1981).

7   Karameros v. Luther, 279 N.Y. 87, 17 N.E.2d 779 (1938).

8   See Statter v. Statter, 2 N.Y.2d 668, 163 N.Y.S.2d 13, 143 N.E.2d 10 (1957); § 464.

status sufficient to support an appeal.[9] The result would be that the adverse finding on the marriage issue would stand against him without his having been able to secure appellate review.

A full day in court in New York practice includes the appellate process if the loser wants it, and a situation in which an appeal is foreclosed can thus be regarded as an inadequate day in court. The Restatement takes that position, too, holding that the estoppel will not apply against a person who could not have obtained appellate review of the earlier judgment.[10]

H. MULTIPARTY SITUATIONS

Table of Sections

§ 466.   Multiparty Situations; a Perspective
§ 467.   The Full and Fair Opportunity Test; Factors to Consider
§ 468.   Multiparty Vehicle Tort Examples

§ 466. Multiparty Situations; a Perspective

The extent to which one not a party to the first action may make estoppel use of something coming out of it has already been discussed. The topic of "mutuality" covered it.[1] And the topic of "privity" treated whether such an aspiring user would have to show at least some kind of relationship to the person who prevailed in the first action.[2] Framing those subjects, as it does just about everything in the realm of collateral estoppel, or "issue preclusion," is the rule that the issue sought to be foreclosed must be shown to be the same in both actions. That also had its own section.[3] The ensuing treatment of multiparty situations will involve those topics and will review them, but the reader turning to the present section may find it helpful to review those earlier sections to strengthen perspective for this one. Although by no means unique to tort— multiparty problems of course arise in commercial and property and other settings as well—the tort area, with its calendar-dominating vehicle cases in New York, has been the most active and even volatile area of collateral estoppel in New York practice. And so it ends up with the lion's share of attention.

For a while the courts drew a distinction between what they regarded as "defensive" versus "offensive" use of collateral estoppel, allowing the estoppel in the first category but not in the second. Good Health Dairy Products Corporation v. Emery,[4] a 1937 Court of Appeals decision, allowed an estoppel to a vehicle owner, the defendant in action two, based on a victory his driver had against the other vehicle in the first action. The owner, who was not a party to the first action, was using estoppel "defensively," i.e., to escape liability as a defendant. Shortly afterwards, the Court of Appeals in Elder v. New York & Pennsylvania Motor Express,[5] refused to allow "offensive" use of an estoppel in a

---

[9]   See § 525.

[10]   Restatement (Second) of Judgments § 28(1). For this reason the decision in Augustine v. Sugrue, N.Y.L.J., May 19, 2003, at 33, col.1 (Sup. Ct., Queens County; Taylor, J.), note 13 in § 458, is questionable.

[1]   See § 460.

[2]   See § 461.

[3]   See § 462.

[4]   Good Health Dairy Products Corporation v. Emery, 275 N.Y. 14, 9 N.E.2d 758 (1937).

[5]   Elder v. New York & Pennsylvania Motor Exp., 284 N.Y. 350, 31 N.E.2d 188 (1940).

similar context. It was another collision case. The owner of vehicle one sued the owner of vehicle two for property damage and won. The driver of vehicle one, not a party to the first action, then sued ("offensive" use) the same defendant for personal injuries and sought an estoppel based on the owner's victory in the first action. The Court denied the estoppel, distinguishing the *Good Health* case because there the estoppel was used as a shield while in *Elder* the driver was trying to use it as a sword. While the Court of Appeals had been willing to carve out an exception to the then-applicable mutuality rule so as to allow defensive use of estoppel by a first action nonparty, it was not willing to make a similar exception for offensive use, so mutuality ruled the roost in *Elder* and estoppel was refused.

Not until 1967, when B.R. DeWitt, Inc. v. Hall[6] finally interred the mutuality doctrine, did the Court of Appeals firmly align itself behind even offensive use of estoppel by those not parties to the first action. The driver of car one sued the driver of car two for personal injuries and won. The owner of car one then sought to use that victory to establish the same defendant's liability in a later action for property damage. Removing the barrier of mutuality, the court allowed the estoppel.

The immediate question that came to the fore was whether *Elder* was overruled.[7] It was not, and for yet other reasons it is not at all clear that *Elder* is passe. In *Elder*, the first action was by the vehicle owner for property damage and the second action by the driver for personal injuries; in *DeWitt*, it was the other way around. The dissent in *DeWitt*[8] stressed this distinction, warning that while it might be permissible to bind a defendant to the result of a substantial personal injury action—when it is the first one brought as it was in *DeWitt*—it does not at all follow that the defendant should be similarly bound by the result of a property damage action if that is the initial suit as it was in *Elder*. The stakes are different, for one thing. It may be more provident to interpose against a modest property damage claim an equally modest defense, and to let the office novice try the case for the experience rather than bring out the senior trial lawyers, whose fees would be disproportionate to the damages claimed. To bestow an estoppel on the result, however, when the much higher stakes of a personal injury claim are later involved, would be unfair, although it may be quite fair in reverse circumstances—where the first action was on a substantial personal injury claim and was vigorously defended—to allow an estoppel from that one to bind the later and presumably more nominal property damage claim.

In a given case even those ideas can reverse themselves, suggesting an estoppel for a property damage claim involving a solid gold sports car and a fortune in damages so as to make it bind a later personal injury claim amounting to less money. There are a myriad of individual factors to consider on a case by case basis, in other words, before a court can make a sound judgment on whether to work an estoppel, and this is the warning of the three-judge dissent in *DeWitt*. The majority of four take this warning to heart, for at the end of the majority opinion in *DeWitt* are a number of individual factors that the court carefully lists and finds satisfied.

Those factors amount to what is in essence a checklist for the judges to consult and apply in every estoppel case. The list will be parsed and its items treated individually in

---

6   B. R. DeWitt, Inc. v. Hall, 19 N.Y.2d 141, 278 N.Y.S.2d 596, 225 N.E.2d 195 (1967).

7   A case clearly overruled by *DeWitt* is Haverhill v. International R. Co., 244 N.Y. 582, 155 N.E. 905 (1927), whose result was dictated entirely by want of mutuality.

8   *DeWitt*, 19 N.Y.2d at 148, 278 N.Y.S.2d at 602, 225 N.E.2d at 199.

the next section, entitled "the full and fair opportunity test." Stretched with additional items from Schwartz v. Public Administrator[9] and further expanded with items from yet other cases and from the Restatement, the list is today the essence of collateral estoppel, or "issue preclusion," in multiparty situations. It is a sui generis consulting table designed to avoid arbitrary conclusions and enable an intelligent judgment to be made only after weighing factors present in the particular case. It will necessarily require a more thoughtful effort by advocates and a more sensitive analysis by judges than was required earlier, but that is a small price to pay to be rid of such arbitrary and often irrelevant dogmas as "mutuality" and "privity," "offensive use" and "defensive use," and other like notions that were once allowed to block a thoughtful application of the collateral estoppel doctrine.

§ 467. The Full and Fair Opportunity Test; Factors to Consider

When seeking to apply collateral estoppel (issue preclusion) in multiparty cases, lawyers and judges must keep at hand today a list of factors to consider on a case by case basis. The components, while not restricted to multiparty cases, are especially relevant to them, so all are listed here even though they may have bearing as well in other instances not involving multiple parties. The components are principally drawn from: (1) B. R. DeWitt, Inc. v. Hall,[1] (2) Schwartz v. Public Administrator,[2] (3) the factors listed in the Second Restatement,[3] and (4) other cases suggesting elements warranting individual treatment. For convenience and for later reference, it will be helpful to number the items treated. And to the end that as many factors as possible may be listed, we will risk some overlapping by making the list profuse.

1. *Sameness of issue.* It will always be necessary to determine that the issue is the same in both actions. The majority in *DeWitt* stressed this, finding that the issues as framed by the pleadings in that case were the same as those in the earlier action.

The *Schwartz* case offers a good illustration here. In *Schwartz*, a passenger in one vehicle sued the drivers of both vehicles and won against both. The contributory negligence rule, barring all recovery by a plaintiff guilty of any negligence at all, was applicable at the time, and so, in the second action, when driver one sued driver two, the latter sought to import and establish as contributory negligence against driver one in the second action the affirmative negligence found against both drivers in the first action. The courts had said no to this for years,[4] suspicious that the issues were not necessarily the same; that the negligence of the drivers vis-à-vis a passenger was not necessarily negligence as to one another. Satisfying themselves that the negligence issue was the same in both actions, i.e., that the negligence of both drivers as against the passenger was also negligence as against each other, the court in *Schwartz* overruled earlier caselaw and allowed the estoppel.[5]

---

[9]   Schwartz v. Public Adm'r of Bronx County, 24 N.Y.2d 65, 298 N.Y.S.2d 955, 246 N.E.2d 725 (1969).

[1]   B. R. DeWitt, Inc. v. Hall, 19 N.Y.2d 141, 278 N.Y.S.2d 596, 225 N.E.2d 195 (1967).

[2]   Schwartz v. Public Adm'r of Bronx County, 24 N.Y.2d 65, 298 N.Y.S.2d 955, 246 N.E.2d 725 (1969).

[3]   Restatement (Second) of Judgments §§ 28 and 29.

[4]   See, e.g., Glaser v. Huette, 232 A.D. 119, 249 N.Y.S. 374 (1st Dep't 1931), aff'd, 256 N.Y. 686, 177 N.E. 193.

[5]   A thoughtful dissent by Judge Bergan in the *Schwartz* case, 24 N.Y.2d at 76, 298 N.Y.S.2d at 964, 246 N.E.2d at 732, suggests that still other factors must be considered, especially in regard to jury sympathy based on the differing contexts of the two actions. See the discussion under item 10 later in this section.

The door is always open to a showing that the issues differ, however, no matter how alike they may seem on the surface. Suppose, for example, that G is a teenage girl driving a car with P, her friend, as a passenger. The car is chased by F, G's father, on a disciplinary mission but at so high a rate of speed that an accident occurs, killing P. P's estate sues both G and F and recovers judgment against both. Then G sues F, her father, who pleads that the negligence established in P's favor against both F and G in the earlier action constitutes contributory negligence—the contributory negligence rule was still at work in this case—against G in the context of the second action, barring it.

Does it bar the second action? The court can well find on facts like these that the negligence issues are not the same; that the duty owed by G to P may have been found breached in respects not applicable to the duties existing between G and F; that it may have been reasonable for G to run for her life from F, but negligent to take P with her, a ground that might explain P's victory against G in the first action, but which might count in G's favor when interposed between G and F in the second. In short, the issues of duty and breach can be deemed different and, if they are, there is no estoppel.[6] Issue sameness is one of the primary colors in the estoppel spectrum.

2. Vigor of defense in first action. This is on the *DeWitt* list. The court there notes that the earlier action was in fact defended with full vigor. (In *DeWitt* there was every reason to put in a strong defense because the earlier action was the personal injury claim, the one with the higher stakes.) The door must be kept open to a showing that the defense in the earlier action was not vigorous, however, presumably with a citation of some reason (e.g., small stakes) to justify the laxity. A harassment conviction in a city court, for example, was denied estoppel effect in a later civil action for damages against the same defendant for the reason that the earlier action was a "relatively minor" nonjury case and the defendant could not be faulted for not defending it vigorously.[7]

Another example may be where X as a defendant in an earlier action was represented by a lawyer assigned by X's insurer, as happens in tort litigation, while in the present action X is a plaintiff appearing through a lawyer of her own choosing. The mere fact of different lawyers may not ipso facto avoid an estoppel, but if any laxity or patent indifference or incompetence on the part of X's lawyer in the first action can be demonstrated, the court would lend an ear to that when considering whether to allow an estoppel in the second action.

3. Link between #2 user and #1 winner. This is the old "privity" business in its most disorderly sense. The *DeWitt* majority gave it at least passing mention,[8] but it has apparently left the scene almost entirely since then. For a long time it appeared to be the main barrier to the use of collateral estoppel in mass accident cases. Where, for example, 50 bus passengers are injured in an accident and passenger one sues and wins on the issue of the carrier's fault, the want of a legal link to the winner would have precluded use of estoppel by the 49 other passengers. Then, following *DeWitt*, the Court of Appeals said in the *Schwartz* case itself that it has "discarded, as irrelevant to a proper consideration of the issues in this area, the fact that there may or may not have been any significant jural relationship between the party seeking to invoke the doctrine and

---

6   See Terwilliger v. Terwilliger, 52 Misc. 2d 404, 276 N.Y.S.2d 8 (Sup. Ct., Tompkins County 1966).

7   Gilberg v. Barbieri, 53 N.Y.2d 285, 441 N.Y.S.2d 49, 423 N.E.2d 807 (1981). See § 453.

8   See § 461.

the prior victor."[9] Then in the 1980s came the *Koch*[10] and *Kaufman*[11] cases, mentioned earlier,[12] stressing the identity of issue and full opportunity tests and dispensing with any "privity" or other link between the first action winner and the second action user. Both cases involved mass torts.

Koch involved the vast New York City blackout of 1977. A grocer afterwards sued for food spoilage and, winning, established the gross negligence of the defendant, the electric utility. The Court of Appeals held in *Koch* that all others damaged by the blackout may, in their own suits, make estoppel use of the liability issue against the utility. The court reviewed the elements of the full and fair opportunity test and found them met, notably in the fact that the utility knew of the collateral estoppel potential and had every incentive to defend the grocer's suit "fully and vigorously."

In the *Kaufman* case, another major statement by the Court of Appeals on the "offensive" use of collateral estoppel by nonparties to the first action, the Court of Appeals indicated that the plaintiff, who claimed to have developed a cancerous condition because of her mother's ingestion years earlier of the drug DES, could be permitted estoppel use of a prior plaintiff's victory against the same defendant (a drug company) on a similar claim.[13]

4. *Size of claim.* This was mentioned in the second item listed above, but we give it an independent statement here because it is expressly listed as a factor in the *Schwartz* case. It connotes, simply, that if the earlier claim was a small one, the court is free to determine whether it was too small to earn estoppel treatment for its result.

5. *Forum of prior litigation. Schwartz* lists this. The fact that the earlier adjudication comes from a different court, however, or even from a different court system—federal, sister-state, or foreign country—will not always be a factor against estoppel, but it must be kept open to investigation. If, for example, an adjudication for a substantial sum comes from a court in which procedure is lax and informality the norm (even the town and village courts, which are staffed mainly by nonlawyers, have up to $3,000 civil jurisdiction today), a court in the second action should be allowed to weigh that fact in before giving the judgment scope beyond its own contemplation.[14] Similarly, if a judgment comes from a court system of a foreign country about whose procedures we know little[15] or whose jurisprudence is at all suspect, a more trenchant investigation is in order. This factor expressly authorizes that investigation. Several later sections treat more specific problems met when different courts are involved.[16]

6. *Use of initiative.* This is on the *Schwartz* list. It overlaps size of claim (the fourth item above)—since size of claim will often affect initiative—and vigor of defense (the second item above). Whatever factor the party against whom the estoppel is sought can show to justify a want of initiative in the earlier action, the door is open to the

---

[9]   *Schwartz*, 24 N.Y.2d at 70, 298 N.Y.S.2d at 958–9, 246 N.E.2d at 728.

[10]   Koch v. Consolidated Edison Co. of New York, Inc., 62 N.Y.2d 548, 479 N.Y.S.2d 163, 468 N.E.2d 1 (1984).

[11]   Kaufman v. Eli Lilly and Co., 65 N.Y.2d 449, 492 N.Y.S.2d 584, 482 N.E.2d 63 (1985).

[12]   See § 461.

[13]   *Kaufman* posed an additional and different problem, which precluded a simple estoppel. See the discussion under caption 16, below.

[14]   See Restatement (Second) of Judgments § 29(2).

[15]   See Restatement (Second) of Judgments § 28(3).

[16]   See §§ 469, 470, and 471.

showing. This has perhaps extra importance in New York, where a default judgment has also been held entitled to collateral estoppel use.[17] While the general rule may be to that effect, a showing that the earlier judgment was rendered by default can be a weighty factor in convincing the second court to deny it estoppel effect.[18]

7. *Extent of the litigation.* This is another item from the *Schwartz* list, and again it overlaps previously listed items. This one can be deemed to take in a hitherto unmentioned element: the context from which the issue, sought to be precluded, emerges in the first action. If the issue had its own clear niche there, meriting and getting appropriate attention, it may earn an estoppel. If on the other hand it was obscured by a mass of other issues in a complicated or prolonged litigation, the court would be free to find it too inadequately considered to deserve estoppel treatment.

8. *Competence and experience of counsel.* The *Schwartz* list recognizes this factor, which has special bearing in the situation mentioned in item two, above: where the party is appearing with a lawyer of her own choice in the second action while having been represented only by a lawyer assigned by her insurance company in the first. An example would be where a passenger sues driver one and wins when driver one is found to be at fault. Then driver one sues driver two, also involved in the accident, who pleads estoppel. Driver one shows that the lawyer assigned to defend her by the insurer in the earlier action commenced by the passenger was inexperienced and ineffective. On such a showing, the estoppel may be denied.

9. *Availability of new evidence.* This item from the *Schwartz* list confirms that it may sometimes be permissible to deny an estoppel to a previously decided issue on the ground that new evidence has since come to the fore in the interim, which could have changed the result. In an earlier case by X against D, for example, D may have been found liable for damages caused by a certain drug. By the time Y brings suit against D for damages caused by the same drug, a new test may have been devised establishing the drug as harmless. Collateral estoppel will not preclude the new evidence.[19] This basis for refusing an estoppel will usually be restricted to multiparty situations. Contrast the situation in which the parties involved are the same in both actions, in which event the courts prefer that the new evidence be made the basis for a motion to vacate the first judgment (and have the earlier action retried) rather than used to ground a refusal, in a second action, to accord the earlier judgment an estoppel.[20]

10. *Indication of compromise verdict.* If it appears that there was some ingredient in the earlier verdict to suggest that it was a compromise—based, for example, on sympathy or prejudice rather than strictly responsive to the law as applied to the evidence—the *Schwartz* case says that this can be considered by the court in determining whether to award an estoppel.[21] Relevant here is a point made by the dissent in the *Schwartz* case, where a passenger in car one first sued the drivers of both vehicles and won against both. Then, when one of the drivers sued the other, the majority allowed an

---

[17]   See § 451.

[18]   See the concurring opinion in Kossover v. Trattler, 82 A.D.2d 610, 442 N.Y.S.2d 554 (2d Dep't 1981).

[19]   See Vincent v. Thompson, 50 A.D.2d 211, 377 N.Y.S.2d 118 (2d Dep't 1975).

[20]   CPLR 5015(a)(2); § 428. See Statter v. Statter, 2 N.Y.2d 668, 163 N.Y.S.2d 13, 143 N.E.2d 10 (1957); § 464.

[21]   An argument that the verdict in the earlier action was a compromise verdict was attempted in *Kaufman*, 65 N.Y.2d at 453–58, 492 N.Y.S.2d at 65–69, 482 N.E.2d at 586–90, but did not work. See the discussion of *Kaufman* in the lead note in NYSLD No. 309.

estoppel to establish the plaintiff driver as contributorily negligent and to bar his recovery. His injuries were serious, the dissent noted pragmatically, and if he had been able to sue the other driver without having been first sued by a passenger, he would likely have won before the jury. He was thus being penalized by the coincidence that there happened to be a passenger, in whose action against both drivers the jury's sympathy would tend to favor the passenger.[22] This does not suggest a compromise verdict, but rather a verdict influenced by sympathy. Indeed, in the view of the *Schwartz* dissent, the problem was perhaps just the opposite: sympathy such as might have favorably disposed the jury towards the driver was allowed too small rather than too large a role in the earlier action, in which the driver's injuries were not in issue. Whatever it was, it is obvious that it did not persuade the majority of the Court of Appeals in *Schwartz*.

The major appearances of the compromise and sympathy factors in tort litigation were found during the reign of the old rule of contributory negligence. They have less significance under New York's current rule of comparative negligence, which is built on compromise: each side sustaining its share of fault and damages being adjusted accordingly.

11. Differences in applicable law. Suppose that injured persons come from several states, and actions have been brought in two of them. Assume further that each state has a different rule, one a rule of comparative and the other a rule of contributory negligence, and that each, under choice of law principles applicable in the conflict of laws, is free to apply its own rule, and chooses to. Suppose that the earlier action from which the estoppel is sought was tried under a contributory negligence rule, which allowed the jury to find for the plaintiff only by finding the plaintiff altogether free from fault. That may have encouraged the jury to impose fault on the defendant for the whole of the occurrence, while a jury allowed to apply a comparative negligence rule might have made at least a pro rata reduction in the share of fault allotted to the defendant. It might then be unfair to allow other plaintiffs suing the same defendant to claim an estoppel imposing total fault on the defendant if a comparative negligence rule is applicable in the later case. This would illustrate what *Schwartz* calls "differences in the applicable law."

An intervening change in the law, such as to suggest a different result under the rule now applicable than that reached under the prior rule, is also a ground on which to deny an estoppel.[23]

12. Foreseeability of future litigation. This last item on the *Schwartz* list is also on the Restatement's, which terms the situation possible but considers lack of foreseeability "rare."[24] Lack of foreseeability should therefore be a significant factor only when the context is such that the court can readily accept a party's claim of surprise, e.g., when a reasonably attentive lawyer diligently going about her business could not be expected to contemplate that what is being done here now can have repercussions there later. When many have been damaged by a tort, the tortfeasor usually knows it. In the *Koch* case, for

---

[22] The Restatement might include these phenomena in what it describes as "imperfections in the adjudicative process," and would allow their consideration so as not to extend them unduly by allowing them to dictate in the second action as well as the first. See Restatement (Second) of Judgments § 29, cmt. g.

[23] See Restatement (Second) of Judgments § 28(2).

[24] Restatement (Second) of Judgments § 28(5), cmt. i.

example,[25] in which a utility was held bound by a finding of liability for blackout damages suffered by a grocer, the Court stressed the fact that the utility knew of the collateral estoppel potential of the earlier action and had every incentive to defend the grocer's suit "fully and vigorously."

13. Different burdens of proof. Passenger P sues drivers A and B and wins against A but not B. It may be that the jury did not find by a fair preponderance of the evidence that B was free of negligence, but merely that the evidence was evenly divided,[26] and that because P had the burden of proof on the issue of B's negligence, P simply failed to sustain it. Now B sues A and seeks an offensive estoppel. It would be permissible to allow it to B to the extent of establishing A's affirmative negligence, a commodity reasonably importable from the first action, but should B have the estoppel on the issue of B's own negligence as well (exonerating B from any charge of fault and precluding A from showing otherwise)? No fair preponderance of the evidence having yet established whether and in what degree B was negligent, it would remain an open issue in the second action, requiring litigation.[27]

14. Avoidance of prejudice by joinder. The Restatement lists for consideration the availability of joinder-of-party devices in the first action.[28] It mentions intervention,[29] for example, but there is little indication from New York caselaw that one not a party to the first action should be denied estoppel use of its result merely because he might have intervened in the first action.[30] This item has so far been given little weight in New York estoppel law.

15. Inconsistency of prior determinations. The Restatement suggests that consideration be given to whether the determination sought to be made binding here was itself inconsistent with a still earlier determination.[31] This can become relevant in mass accident cases, for example, like one involving a number of train passengers. One sues and loses; a second sues and wins. Now the others sue and of course want to play up the second one's victory. The fact that there were two prior actions with inconsistent results diminishes the force that might otherwise propel estoppel.

An example in point is the 2008 decision of the Court of Appeals in Gaston v. American Transit Ins. Co.,[32] which was P-4's tort action against the driver and owner of a car. When the car's liability insurer disclaimed coverage, P-4 introduced two judgments from actions by prior plaintiffs, P-1 and P-2, against the same car, in which the disclaimer was disallowed and the insurance held applicable. That would ordinarily have given P-4 an estoppel on the coverage issue. But the insurer was able to introduce a

---

[25]   See caption 3, "Link between #2 user and #1 winner," above.

[26]   See Restatement (Second) of Judgments § 28(4).

[27]   See Nesbitt v. Nimmich, 34 A.D.2d 958, 312 N.Y.S.2d 766 (2d Dep't 1970), aff'd, 30 N.Y.2d 622, 331 N.Y.S.2d 438, 282 N.E.2d 328 (1972).

[28]   Restatement (Second) of Judgments § 29(3).

[29]   Restatement (Second) of Judgments § 29(3), cmt. e.

[30]   Indeed, CPLR 1013 makes intervention so available in these common accident situations that a failure to move to intervene, or perhaps to move for consolidation under CPLR 602 where separate actions have been brought, could all too often be used to defeat the estoppel doctrine. There is no significant indication in New York law that these omissions will be allowed to undermine the estoppel doctrine.

[31]   Restatement (Second) of Judgments § 29(4).

[32]   Gaston v. American Transit Ins. Co., 11 N.Y.3d 866, 873 N.Y.S.2d 250, 901 N.E.2d 743 (2008) (NYSLD No. 590).

judgment from an action against the same car by yet another person (P-3) in which it was the insurer who won on the disclaimer issue. The court denied the estoppel.

16. Tactical oversight in prior action. When the result of an action is sought to affect a myriad of others, the Court of Appeals has indicated that the action had best show a strong, foible-free record. If a tactical oversight taints the record, the Court is disinclined to give the judgment the broad impact that collateral estoppel has, however binding (and damaging) the oversight may have been on the loser in the earlier action itself.

The court sends this message by pointing to the earlier litigation from which the plaintiff in the *Kaufman* case[33] sought to derive an estoppel. A "concerted action theory" had been submitted to the jury in the earlier action as a basis on which to establish liability against the several drug companies producing the drug DES. Legal acceptance of the theory was in dispute at the time,[34] and it might not have been submitted to the jury if the defendant had properly challenged it. But the defendant failed to make that challenge, and the verdict went for the plaintiff in the first action. Because of that, the court would not allow the plaintiff in the second action an estoppel based on "concerted action." This concededly waters down collateral estoppel somewhat, the Court acknowledged, but "policy reasons . . . outweigh" simple use of the estoppel doctrine in cases of "mass tort liability."

* * *

The list can be expanded further—it is not exhaustive—but enough has been listed above to alert the reader to the sui generis nature of the inquiry and the numerous factors that go into it. For good measure, the Second Restatement leaves the door open to any "other compelling circumstances" that might be shown to suggest that an estoppel should be withheld.[35]

§ 468. Multiparty Vehicle Tort Examples

Building on the factors listed in the prior sections and some of the cases cited there, we can review the rules applicable in multiparty vehicle negligence situations through a series of examples using abbreviations to facilitate reference. Assume throughout that there are several vehicles involved in an accident, and a progression of owners, drivers, and passengers. D-1 will indicate the driver of the first vehicle, O-2 the owner of the second vehicle, P-3 a passenger in the third vehicle, and so forth. The assumption will be that each action is for personal injuries; if it is instead for property damage, the letters PD will be used. In each example, the line-up of the parties in the first action will be given, putting the winner in parenthesis, followed by the line-up of the parties in the second action with an underlining of the party seeking the estoppel. That will afford a perspective of the whole situation at just a glance. We will make the examples as profuse as possible, starting with just a two-party situation and then expanding. So that this excursion can serve as a review of the whole multiparty area, all but a few of the examples will be used to make only one major point. In deference to that purpose,

---

[33] *Kaufman*, 65 N.Y.2d at 449, 492 N.Y.S.2d at 584, 482 N.E.2d at 63.

[34] The dispute was afterwards addressed by the Court of Appeals in Hymowitz v. Eli Lilly and Co., 73 N.Y.2d 487, 541 N.Y.S.2d 941, 539 N.E.2d 1069 (1989).

[35] Restatement (Second) of Judgments § 29(8).

incidental matters that could be extracted from each example will not necessarily be treated.

A.   #1   (D-1)   v.   D-2

#2   D-2   v.   <u>D-1</u>

Assuming the applicable rule to be one of contributory negligence,[1] in which any fault on the part of a party precludes that party's recovery, D-1 in the above example is entitled to a full estoppel against D-2 in the second action. The first judgment established D-2's negligence as well as D-1's freedom from negligence, either of which, imported into the second action, supports an estoppel.

B.   #1   D-1   v.   (D-2)

#2   <u>D-2</u>   v.   <u>D-1</u>

Unless in the above example there was a special verdict in the first action clarifying the precise basis on which D-2 won, there can be no estoppel in the second action for either side. A general verdict would not reveal enough to support an estoppel.[2]

C.   #1   (D-1)   v.   D-2

#2   P-2   v.   <u>D-1</u>
                        <u>O-2</u>

Neither defendant in the second action can estop P-1. D-1 can't even though he won the first action because P-1 was not a party to the first action and cannot be visited with any negative consequence emerging from it.[3] D-2 will be denied the estoppel for that reason, and, as the loser in the first action, would just as soon forget about it anyway.

D.   #1   (D-1)   v.   D-2

#2   D-2   v.   <u>D-1</u>
                        <u>O-1</u>

Both defendants in the second action are entitled to an estoppel against D-2. D-1, the first action winner, is of course entitled to it. The additional point made here is that O-1, although not a party to the first action, may also make use of the estoppel—in this case defensively. Want of mutuality would at one time have barred it, but is no longer a barrier.[4]

---

[1]   That will be the assumption in these examples unless otherwise indicated. Much of the law in this area was made during the reign of the contributory negligence rule and the cases involving it continue to offer strong guidance on collateral estoppel in general. A comparative negligence illustration appears later, as Example L, with its different elements noted. The comparative negligence rule is concerned with relative responsibility for the damages rather than for just the occurrence, which can of course have a bearing on estoppel questions. See § 168E.

[2]   See the discussion in § 462.

[3]   See § 458.

[4]   See §§ 460 and 466.

E.   #1   (O-1)   v.   O-2   PD
                           D-2

     #2   O-2   v.   D-1   PD
                      ‾‾‾‾
                       O-1

No estoppel for any side in the second action. The issues are different. This introduces the influential decision in Mills v. Gabriel,[5] which holds that a driver's affirmative negligence is imputed to the owner under New York law[6] only when the owner is sued as a defendant—the statutory purpose being to increase the likelihood of a solvent source of recovery for an injured person—but not when that owner is suing as a plaintiff for his own property damage.[7] In the above example, therefore, the issue in the first action was D-2's affirmative negligence, which was imputed to O-2 under the New York statute. When O-2 became plaintiff in the second action, however, D-2's negligence in operation became irrelevant because now it would not be imputed to O-2. But what of O-1's responsibility? Could the first action not be deemed to establish that O-1 was free of fault and thus entitled to an estoppel on that issue in the second action? The answer is again no, and for the same reason. When O-1 sued as plaintiff in the first action, D-1's negligence was not in issue because it could not be imputed to O-1. But with O-1 as defendant in the second action, an imputation is in order, and hence D-1's negligence in operation of the vehicle must be tried. In the second action, in other words, D-2's negligence, although adjudicated in the first action, is not in issue, but D-1's negligence, not adjudicated in the first action, is.

F.   #1   (P-1)   v.   D-2
                       O-2

     #2   O-2   v.   D-1   PD
                      ‾‾‾‾

No estoppel will be allowed to D-1 in the second action for the same reasons assigned in the prior example. While D-2's negligence was at issue in the first action and was imputed there to O-2, that's not in issue in the second action. Therefore, nothing coming out of the first action can estop O-2 in the second. D-1's negligence was not in issue in the first action, but it is in the second and must be tried. If it could be shown that in the first action O-2 was held to account not just for his driver's negligent operation of the car but for something for which O-2 was individually at fault, an estoppel could result. If the first action establishes, for example, that O-2 was found liable for knowingly allowing the car to be driven with defective brakes, which contributed to the accident, this would constitute an independent basis of fault on O-2's part, importable from the first action

---

[5]   Mills v. Gabriel, 259 A.D. 60, 18 N.Y.S.2d 78 (2d Dep't 1940), aff'd, 284 N.Y. 755, 31 N.E.2d 512.

[6]   See Veh. & Traf. Law § 388.

[7]   It is assumed that the car is not being operated on the owner's business, which can alter the *Mills v. Gabriel* conclusion. Some courts cast doubt on the continued vitality of the *Mills* case in light of the Court of Appeals' more recent decision in *Schwartz v. Public Administrator* (§ 467). See, e.g., Donato v. Cataffo, 69 Misc. 2d 705, 330 N.Y.S.2d 536 (Sup. Ct., Kings County 1972). But it is submitted that unless the courts wish to reconsider *Mills'* underlying policy reasons—that of imputing negligence when the owner is a defendant so as to improve the injured plaintiff's chance to satisfy a judgment while freeing the owner from the imputation when he is himself a property damage plaintiff—the *Mills* holding is not incompatible with present estoppel law. See Schuyler v. Perry, 69 A.D.3d 33, 886 N.Y.S.2d 228 (2d Dep't 2009) (following *Mills*).

so as to establish O-2 as contributorily negligent in the second and to bar his recovery under the contributory negligence rule that we are assuming governs these examples.

> G.   #1   (D-1)   v.   D-2
>
>   #2   <u>O-1</u>   v.   D-2   PD

O-1 is entitled to an estoppel establishing D-2's affirmative negligence in the second action. This is in essence the *DeWitt* case.[8] The dimension it adds is the allowance of offensive use of estoppel to one not a party to the first action. Presumably, there is no issue of O-1's comparative negligence, but if there were, such as where O-1 is charged with some independent act of negligence not raised or litigated in the first action, it would have to be litigated in the second.

> H.   #1   (O-1)   v.   D-2   PI
>
>   #2   <u>D-1</u>   v.   D-2   PD

At first blush this would seem to lend itself to the same conclusions as the prior example, in which estoppel was allowed. The distinction is that the positions of D-1 with a personal injury claim and O-1 with a property damage claim are reversed in order of time, and this is a distinction with a difference. This fact pattern is in essence the *Elder* case,[9] which refused the estoppel. Even after *DeWitt*, which allowed the estoppel when the personal injury claim was the first tried, the question whether there should be an estoppel when the sequence is reversed is still open. As already discussed,[10] it is not certain that an estoppel will obtain. A sui generis inquiry will be necessary to determine whether to allow the fruits of a property damage case, presumably involving a modest sum, to govern a later personal injury claim for a lot more. All of the factors listed in the prior section would have to be carefully negotiated.

> I.   #1   (P-1)   v.   D-1
>   D-2
>
>   #2   D-1   v.   <u>D-2</u>

Unless something is affirmatively demonstrated to suggest that the negligence issues are not the same—i.e., that the context is such that negligence by both of the drivers against the passenger would not necessarily constitute negligence between themselves—estoppel applies and D-2 is entitled to a dismissal of the second action. (Remember that these examples assume the applicability of the contributory rather than comparative negligence rule.) This is the *Schwartz* situation, previously discussed.[11] Usually, the negligence issues are the same in these situations and an estoppel will apply. An example of where it would not apply, however, was also previously cited: a case in which D-1's conduct might be found reasonable as against D-2 while being found tortious as against P-1.[12]

---

[8]   B. R. DeWitt, Inc. v. Hall, 19 N.Y.2d 141, 278 N.Y.S.2d 596, 225 N.E.2d 195 (1967). See § 466.

[9]   Elder v. New York & Pennsylvania Motor Exp., 284 N.Y. 350, 31 N.E.2d 188 (1940).

[10]   See § 466.

[11]   See Caption 1, "Sameness of issue," in § 467.

[12]   See the last paragraph in Caption #1, "Sameness of issue," in § 467.

J.　#1　P-1　v.　O-1 ⎤ P-1 wins against O-1
　　　　　　　　　D-1 ⎬ and D-1, but the
　　　　　　　　　D-2 ⎦ verdict exonerates D-2

　　#2　O-2　v.　D-1　　PD
　　　　 ‾‾‾　　　O-1

This fact pattern, invoking a number of principles, is a challenging review. O-2 can probably have an estoppel. The fact that O-2 was not a party to the first action is no barrier because that involves the mutuality doctrine, which the *DeWitt* case abandoned.[13] The same case confirms that such a first action nonparty can make offensive, not just defensive, use of the estoppel in the second action. The fact that the findings against D-1 and O-1, which are sought for use in the second action, accrued in favor of someone in the first action (P-1) with whom O-2 lacked "privity" also has no bearing today.[14] The next and last matter is whether the negligence issues are the same: would the fact that D-1 and O-1 were found culpable in this accident vis-a-vis P-1 also establish their culpability with respect to O-2's car? If the answer is yes, O-2 should have an estoppel; if not, he should not. This is in essence the *Schwartz* case, the subject of example I, above: unless something is shown to satisfy the court that the negligence issues in the two contexts differ, the estoppel applies. Nothing in this example having been shown to suggest a difference in the issues, there ought to be an estoppel.

K.　#1　(P-1)　v.　O-1

　　#2　P-2　v.　O-1
　　　　 ‾‾‾

This ostensibly simple situation was for a long time the major open question in the estoppel realm. It involves the mass accident, such as 100 people killed or injured in (e.g.) a bus or plane crash. A passenger sues the owner, driver, or manufacturer of any vehicle involved and wins. Are all the other 99 passengers to get a free estoppel ride on the coattails of the first successful passenger? The courts' long insistence on a showing of "privity" or a like link between the #2 user and the #1 winner[15] was the barrier to the estoppel ride. That barrier was later lifted, and with its lifting, the estoppel train took off. Other things being equal, P-2 in the above example is entitled to estoppel against O-1 on the issue of O-1's liability.[16] Damages issues are of course unique to each injured person and would have to be litigated or otherwise resolved individually.

L.　#1　(P-1)　v.　D-1
　　　　　　　　　D-2

　　#2　P-2　v.　D-1
　　　　 ‾‾‾　　　D-2

We use this two-car example to see what happens when the comparative negligence rule applies.[17] It applies in New York to all accidents occurring on or after September 1,

---

[13] See § 466.

[14] See § 461.

[15] See, e.g., Cobbs v. Thomas, 55 Misc. 2d 800, 286 N.Y.S.2d 943 (Sup. Ct., Dutchess County 1968), aff'd, 31 A.D.2d 719, 296 N.Y.S.2d 557 (2d Dep't).

[16] See § 461 and caption 3 on the list in § 467.

[17] CPLR Article 14–A. See § 188E.

1975. The rule introduced new elements into the estoppel picture. Assume in the above example (in addition to assuming, of course, that there is no barrier to one passenger using another's victory, the stuff of the last example), that P-1, duly seat-belted, is found in the first action to have no fault at all. D-1 and D-2 are found equally responsible (50%–50%) for the accident. As long as nothing is shown in the second action to indicate that any fault on P-2's part contributed to his own injury, P-2 should have a straight estoppel establishing the defendants' fault, leaving only the measure of P-2's damages to be tried. Even the drivers' 50% shares as found in the first action would be a basis for estoppel in the second.

The above would be an instance in which responsibility for the occurrence and for the injuries is the same. But note that under the comparative negligence rule, the culpable conduct involved is not that which caused the accident but rather the "damages."[18] If it can be shown, therefore, that the damages-causing conduct in P-1's action is not the same as in P-2's, the issue would not be deemed disposed of by the first action and would require litigation in the second.

Suppose, for instance, that P-1 was not wearing a seat belt, although it was readily at hand, and that in the first action this failure accounted for 90% of P-1's injuries[19] even though each defendant driver was found 50% responsible for the occurrence. Estoppel must be imported accordingly. To the extent that in the second action the issue arises out of the drivers' responsibility for the occurrence, an estoppel could establish that each was 50% at fault. But when the ratio of accountability for P-2's injuries arises in the second action, as it necessarily will, the matter will be open to litigation, enjoying no estoppel from the first action.

If, for example, P-2 is found by the second jury to have worn a seat belt, the drivers' respective shares of fault in causing the accident may be found applicable to P-2's damages as well. But if P-2 was not wearing a seat belt, or was guilty of any other act or omission contributing to his own injuries, such as engaging in horseplay in the car or sitting perched on the sun roof while the car was at high speed, the ratios of responsibility for P-2's damages could not be dictated by the findings in respect of P-1 in the first action and would need trial.

Under the comparative negligence rule, in other words, whenever the first-round plaintiff is found to have contributed in any measure to his own injuries, an estoppel in respect of responsibility for P-2's injuries in the second action will not result. This is so notwithstanding that any proportions of fault in causing the occurrence—the accident itself—may be an estoppel basis if they become relevant in the second action. If it should be found in the second action, for example, that P-2 suffered total damages of $100,000 and that P-2 was 60% responsible for his own damages, and the drivers between them accountable for 40% of P-2's injuries, the first action finding that each driver had 50% responsibility for the occurrence could then be applied to their collective 40% responsibility in the second action, resulting there in respective contributive shares of 20%. That would produce a joint and several judgment for P-2 against the drivers for $40,000, with their contributive shares $20,000 each.

---

[18]   CPLR 1411.

[19]   See Spier v. Barker, 35 N.Y.2d 444, 363 N.Y.S.2d 916, 323 N.E.2d 164, 80 A.L.R.3d 1025 (1974). See Veh. & Traf. Law § 1229–c(8); § 223.

Here's another interesting and important point to keep in mind. If D-1 and D-2 both have adequate insurance, or are both solvent and able to pay any judgment that P-2 might get, P-2 will be content to import and apply their respective 50% shares. But suppose D-2 lacks adequate coverage or resources to pay a judgment. Here, P-2 may want a chance to show that D-1's share was greater than 50% for the obvious reason that the more imputable to D-1 the greater the chance of collecting. Since P-2 was not a party to the first action and therefore can't be bound by the 50%–50% shares imputed to the two defendants there, P-2 should be free in the second action to try to prove that D-1's share exceeded 50%.

I. DIFFERENT COURTS

Table of Sections

§ 469.   Effect When Different Courts Involved

§ 470.   Nonjury Determinations; Court of Claims Problems

§ 471.   Recognition of Domestic Judgments; Full Faith and Credit

§ 472.   Recognition of Foreign-Country Judgments; "Comity"

§ 469. Effect When Different Courts Involved

If a court decides an issue clearly within its range of subject matter jurisdiction, there may be no reason for refusing its judgment estoppel treatment merely because the court is one of limited or inferior jurisdiction. Any other rule would make the dispositions of such courts insecure, and a court system like New York's, with a profusion of lower and special courts, could ill afford that. But the distribution of judicial business among the various courts does occasionally account for a few estoppel dilemmas. These usually occur when a court, in the course of adjudicating a case properly before it, is required, perhaps only as an incident, to pass on something that is really the plenary business of some other court. Often the incidental item arises as part of a defense.

The general rule in New York today is that limitations on subject matter jurisdiction apply only to affirmative claims, not to defenses; that a court may entertain—and, indeed, a defendant may not be precluded from interposing—any defense she has to a claim whether the defense is legal or equitable and regardless of the court in which the claim appears. Statutes in some of the lower court acts confirms this expressly,[1] rejecting all prior efforts to deprive a defendant of a legitimate defense under the guise of subject matter jurisdiction. All of the lower courts, with the exception of Town and Village courts, also have unlimited monetary jurisdiction on counterclaims.[2]

One proceeding with a potential for this kind of jurisdictional dilemma is the summary proceeding to recover possession of real property (the so-called "landlord-tenant" device brought for non-payment of rent or holding over after the expiration of the lease). The proceeding is within the jurisdiction of all of the state's lower courts,[3] but its function is to determine only the immediate right to possession of the premises; it is not designed to try title.[4] In the great majority of cases, no title question arises; the

---

[1]   See § 905 in the New York City Civil Court Act and in the Uniform District, Uniform City, and Uniform Justice Court Acts (McKinney's Vol. 29A, Parts 2 and 3).

[2]   See §§ 14, 19, 20, and 21.

[3]   See §§ 19, 20, 21, and 22.

[4]   The summary proceeding is treated in §§ 571 to 580.

respondent tenant does not dispute the landlord's title. But every now and again the respondent does, injecting into the middle of a summary proceeding the defense that the respondent has title or that the petitioner-landlord has not. The court is obliged to reach a determination of the right to possession, and a defense of want of title may well hold the effective answer to that claim of right.

So it is that a lower court entertaining a summary proceeding will occasionally have to pass, expressly or tacitly, on a title question. If a court without jurisdiction to adjudicate title questions, such as a town, village, city, or district court, does so in that context, is the adjudication binding in a higher court in a later plenary test of title? The answer is usually no. Recognizing that the summary proceeding is almost invariably the product of a court of limited jurisdiction, a statute provides that the judgment in it shall not preclude an action "for affirmative equitable relief" barred from the summary proceeding because of the court's limited jurisdiction if the equity action is commenced within 60 days after the judgment's entry.[5] Indeed, the statute provides that the judgment shall not even bar "an action to recover the possession of real property," which can be taken to suggest that not even the possessory right adjudicated in the summary proceeding is binding in a plenary action presenting the same issues later. It should not be so taken, however; issues legitimately a part of a summary proceeding are entitled to issue preclusion effect.[6] But title is not such an issue, so as far as title is concerned, the judgment in the summary proceeding is ordinarily no bar to a later plenary test of title, a view supported by caselaw old[7] and young.[8]

It is permissible, however, for a stipulation to resolve a title question, even if given within a summary proceeding, on the theory that it is the parties' agreement that resolves the issue in that case and that the level of court from which the agreement-embodying judgment comes is secondary.[9]

Practical advice to a summary-proceeding respondent who has a genuine defense of title and wants to keep it out of the lower court is to immediately institute a separate action, such as one for a declaratory judgment or other title-testing procedure in the supreme court, and move in that action to remove and consolidate the summary proceeding.

The limited subject matter jurisdiction of a lower court entertaining a summary proceeding can also pose difficulties in other situations. For example, in 172 Van Duzer Realty Corporation v. Globe Alumni Student Assistance Association,[10] the Court rejected the defendants' argument that the doctrine of res judicata barred plaintiff in a supreme court action from pursuing damages based on an acceleration clause where those

---

[5]   RPAPL 747(2).

[6]   See Reich v. Cochran, 151 N.Y. 122, 45 N.E. 367 (1896), discussed in its other aspects in § 451.

[7]   Willis v. McKinnon, 37 Misc. 386, 75 N.Y.S. 770 (Sup. Ct., Delaware County 1902), aff'd, 79 A.D. 249, 79 N.Y.S. 936 (3d Dep't 1903), aff'd, 178 N.Y. 451, 70 N.E. 962 (1904).

[8]   See O'Frias v. Melton, 32 A.D.2d 1046, 303 N.Y.S.2d 785 (2d Dep't 1969), aff'd, 27 N.Y.2d 638, 313 N.Y.S.2d 765, 261 N.E.2d 670 (1970). If the summary proceeding involved is not of the run-of-the-mill type, however, such as to recover possession of an apartment, but a more sophisticated one in which it appears that the parties deliberately let the title issue go forward in the lower court, estoppel may attach to it. See the discussion of the *Nissequogue* case in § 576.

[9]   The Court of Appeals affirmance in the *O'Frias* case, 32 A.D.2d at 1046, 303 N.Y.S.2d at 785, stressed the presence of a stipulation there.

[10]   172 Van Duzer Realty Corp. v. Globe Alumni Student Assistance Ass'n, Inc., 24 N.Y.3d 528, 2 N.Y.S.3d 39, 25 N.E.3d 952 (2014).

damages had not been recovered in a prior New York City Civil Court action awarding plaintiff possession of the premises. The *Van Duzer* Court ruled that the civil court did not possess subject matter jurisdiction to address a claim for the balance of rent due under the acceleration clause in the holdover proceeding.[11] Therefore, such damages could be sought in the subsequent supreme court action and were not barred by the doctrine of res judicata.[12] It is important to remember that in this scenario the doctrine of collateral estoppel could, however, apply to factual determinations made in the prior action.[13]

An analogous problem arises when a family court, legitimately passing on a proper piece of its business such as a support proceeding, incidentally passes on the validity of a marriage or the validity of a divorce purporting to dissolve the marriage, issues that the respondent may have raised as defenses. They are relevant defenses and the family court respondent is entitled to have them heard, but the Court of Appeals has held that determinations on those issues do not bind in later plenary tests of the marriage in the supreme court, which has exclusive jurisdiction of marital actions. Thus, a family court holding that a marriage does not exist because a disputed divorce is found good,[14] or, conversely, that a marriage does exist because the divorce is found bad,[15] does not get estoppel treatment in the supreme court even though it may be dispositive of the main issues involved in the family court proceeding.[16]

We may also note parenthetically that a court with subject matter jurisdiction of a claim is not divested of it by anything contained in a defense,[17] whatever the estoppel impact may be of an adjudication made in respect of the defense. A different rule would be tantamount to giving a defendant a veto power over the plaintiff's choice of forum: the mere interposition of the defense would divest the court of its jurisdiction.

The lower the court making an adjudication, the more likely is an estoppel problem of this nature to arise. At the lowest rung of the judicial ladder, the small claim, there is a statutory restriction on the res judicata doctrine. The statute is treated in the small claims chapter,[18] but we may note here that it is the collateral estoppel doctrine (issue preclusion) and not res judicata in its technical sense (claim preclusion) that the statute withholds from a small claims judgment.[19]

In other areas which lack statutory guidance, but in which policy suggests strictures on incidental findings made in lower court or special court proceedings, the New York courts seem ready enough to implement the policy, but they lack a clear set of guideposts. Relevant decisions seem murky and evasive. A cure would be to recognize that the

---

[11] See § 19.

[12] See Parker v. Blauvelt Volunteer Fire Co., Inc., 93 N.Y.2d 343, 349, 690 N.Y.S.2d 478, 482, 712 N.E.2d 647, 650 (1999) ("res judicata is inapplicable where the plaintiff 'was unable to . . . seek a certain remedy or form of relief in the first action because of the limitations on the subject matter jurisdiction of the courts or restrictions on their authority to entertain . . . multiple remedies or forms of relief in a single action, and the plaintiff desires in the second action . . . to seek that remedy or form of relief '") (quoting Restatement (Second) of Judgments § 26(1)(c)).

[13] *Parker*, 93 N.Y.2d at 349–50, 690 N.Y.S.2d at 482–83, 712 N.E.2d at 651.

[14] See Loomis v. Loomis, 288 N.Y. 222, 42 N.E.2d 495 (1942).

[15] See Tcholakian v. Tcholakian, 29 A.D.2d 848, 287 N.Y.S.2d 920 (1st Dep't 1968).

[16] See Restatement (Second) of Judgments § 31(3).

[17] See Mohar Realty Co. v. Smith, 46 Misc. 2d 849, 260 N.Y.S.2d 685 (App. Term, 2d Dep't 1965).

[18] Chapter 21 (Practitioner's Edition), §§ 581 et seq.

[19] See § 585 (Practitioner's Edition).

limited or special nature of the court from which the issue seeking the estoppel comes, or the issue's relatively incidental status in its lower court context, are themselves items that must be weighed into the balance before a determination is made of whether the issue has earned an estoppel. Treat this factor, in other words, as one of the sui generis items to be considered in applying the full and fair opportunity test.[20]

An approach of that kind would also hold the key to a still more embarrassing situation: that in which a state court finding on an exclusively federal issue seeks recognition in a federal court. In the prior examples we've been using, the courts were at least arms of the same sovereign. Here we have courts of two different sovereigns. Suppose, for example, that in a contract action in a state court a defendant interposes as a defense the invalidity of a patent involved in the contract. Were that issue the subject of a direct action (such as one for patent infringement), it would be a matter of exclusively federal jurisdiction.[21] Will the state court's adjudication of the patent issue in defense context be binding in a later federal action involving the same issue? It depends on a number of factors, but it is by no means to be deemed automatically binding.[22]

The federal doctrine of "pendent jurisdiction," now codified as "supplemental jurisdiction," occasionally presents some sticky res judicata problems in state courts. The doctrine permits a federal court to entertain a state claim of which it would otherwise lack subject matter jurisdiction when it is joined with a related federal claim, the two arising out of the same event or connected series of events. The federal claim acts as the equivalent of a jurisdictional crutch. The res judicata problem arises when the federal claim is dismissed on its merits early in the federal litigation. If the disposition clearly addresses the merits of the pendent state claim as well, it will of course be entitled to res judicata effect in a state court later. But when the disposition of the state claim is unclear, and the plaintiff, believing that the state claim was not a merits dismissal, commences a new state-court action on it, how shall the state court determine the issue? The point was the subject of address in two phases of McLearn v. Cowen & Co., one from the New York Court of Appeals[23] and the other from the federal Second Circuit.[24]

The case began as a federal district court action. It was based on federal securities violations and a connected state claim was included. The federal claims were dismissed in what amounted to a merits disposition. The plaintiff then brought a state action on the state claim. A divided New York Court of Appeals, perusing the federal record, found the dismissal to be a merits disposition of the state claim as well. Three judges dissented; finding the federal dismissal equivocal at best, they would have entertained the state action. The plaintiff then went back to the federal court with a motion to clarify that the federal dismissal did not reach the merits of the state claim. This led to the Second Circuit decision, which, disagreeing with the New York Court of Appeals, held that the federal *McLearn* dismissal was not a merits termination of the state claim, opening it up

---

[20]   The test and its list of factors is in § 467. Note caption 5 on the list. The Restatement also lists differences in courts as one of the factors warranting individual consideration in an estoppel test. See Restatement (Second) of Judgments § 28(3).

[21]   See 28 U.S.C.A. § 1338.

[22]   See the Reporter's Note on § 28 in Restatement (Second) of Judgments.

[23]   McLearn v. Cowen & Co., 48 N.Y.2d 696, 422 N.Y.S.2d 60, 397 N.E.2d 750 (1979).

[24]   McLearn v. Cowen & Co., 660 F.2d 845 (2d Cir. 1981).

to litigation in the state court. The Second Circuit was also divided on the point, and even the two majority judges had different rationales.[25]

Meriting separate treatment is the case in which an estoppel is asked for a prior New York Court of Claims judgment. That poses the difficulty of according estoppel in a jury case to an adjudication made in a nonjury case. It's the subject of the next section.

§ 470. Nonjury Determinations; Court of Claims Problems

An additional question that collateral estoppel sometimes poses is whether the doctrine may foreclose in a jury case an issue decided in a nonjury case. It has been held that an issue found in a jury-tried case can be the basis of an estoppel in a case in which no jury trial is permitted[1]—which confirms the use of a jury-tried law judgment to foreclose issues in a court-tried equity action. But what of the converse situation, most often involving the court of claims, in which there is no trial by jury?[2]

A claimant who loses in a court of claims action is usually subject to the estoppel consequences of the loss even though it entails application of the estoppel in a later jury case in some other court. The claimant has been held to subject herself to this merely by bringing suit in the court of claims, or at least by suing there first.[3] So, for example, where P had a negligence claim against both the State and D, and sued the State in the court of claims (he could not and still cannot sue D, a private person, there) and lost on being found guilty of contributory negligence—at a time when contributory negligence barred a plaintiff's claim entirely—D was allowed to use that loss against P in a later P v. D suit in the supreme court.[4] The theory sometimes cited is that the claimant could have had a jury pass on the issues by bringing the supreme court action first.[5] In this age of the crowded calendar and the delayed trial, however, such an approach can be faulted for overlooking the statute of limitations. Especially when the second action would have to be brought in the court of claims, which has for the State a shorter statute than applies against other defendants,[6] the plaintiff who sues first in some other court and then waits patiently for a determination may find his patience rewarded with a statute of limitations dismissal of the court of claims suit attempted later.

Other problems arise from the separateness of the court of claims. Had P sued the State first and the State wished to implead D, the private person, as an indemnifying or contributing tortfeasor, it would have been precluded from doing so because impleader does not lie in the court of claims.[7] A victory for P in the court of claims is thus barred

---

[25] The cases are treated in more detail in editions 240 (lead note) and 265 of the New York State Law Digest. The doctrine of supplemental jurisdiction is the subject of § 614 in this book (Practitioner's Edition).

[1] Albero v. State, 31 A.D.2d 694, 295 N.Y.S.2d 965 (3d Dep't 1968), aff'd, 26 N.Y.2d 630, 307 N.Y.S.2d 469, 255 N.E.2d 724 (1970).

[2] It has been held that if the first action could have been tried by jury but the jury was waived, the estoppel can visit the second action without impediment. See, e.g., Vincent v. Thompson, 79 Misc. 2d 1029, 361 N.Y.S.2d 282 (Sup. Ct., Nassau County 1974), rev'd on other grounds, 50 A.D.2d 211, 377 N.Y.S.2d 118 (2d Dep't 1975).

[3] See Planty v. Potter-DeWitt Corp., 27 A.D.2d 401, 279 N.Y.S.2d 938 (3d Dep't 1967).

[4] Hires v. New York Cent. R.R., 24 A.D.2d 1075, 265 N.Y.S.2d 895 (4th Dep't 1965); Chaffee v. Lawrence, 282 A.D. 875, 124 N.Y.S.2d 425 (2d Dep't 1953). On the federal side, the U.S. Supreme Court has held a nonjury result binding in a later jury-triable action. See Parklane Hosiery Co., Inc. v. Shore, 439 U.S. 322, 99 S. Ct. 645, 58 L. Ed. 2d 552 (1979), offering a review of the subject.

[5] See Jones v. Young, 257 A.D. 563, 14 N.Y.S.2d 84 (3d Dep't 1939).

[6] See Ct. of Claims Act § 10.

[7] People v. Delaware & Hudson R. R. Corp., 42 A.D.2d 618, 344 N.Y.S.2d 488 (3d Dep't 1973).

from estoppel use against D for the obvious reason that D was not a party to the court of claims action. Hence, these court of claims barriers to impleader and other joinder devices usually make it impossible for the dispute to touch others involved in the occurrence, and with this unhappy denouement for the claimant: if he loses in the court of claims, the loss can be used against him by others; but if he wins in the court of claims, he cannot make use of his victory against anyone else who was not a party to the court of claims action. The worst of both worlds, in other words.

This has posed special problems in the apportioning of damages among tortfeasors[8] as we can illustrate with a case that involved the application of the comparative negligence rule and in which the supreme court suit came first.

P, a passenger injured while in D's car when it slid on some ice, a condition for which the State was responsible, sued D in the supreme court, established some fault on the part of D, and won a $40,000 verdict against D. Now D sued the State for contribution in the court of claims, which found the State responsible for 40% of P's damages, but it applied the 40% to the $40,000 figure, and this it could not do, at least not yet. It might hold, by way of estoppel, that P's damages could not now be found to *exceed* $40,000 because D was a party to the earlier action and can be estopped from seeking contribution from the State based on anything higher than the $40,000 figure the supreme court action produced, but since the State was not a party to that action, it was now free to try to establish that P's damages were less than that.[9]

§ 471. Recognition of Domestic Judgments; Full Faith and Credit

The Full Faith and Credit Clause of the Federal Constitution,[1] combined with Congress's implementation and expansion of it in the full faith and credit statute,[2] requires that all American courts recognize each others' judgments. While the constitutional provision itself refers only to the states, the statute goes further and by language and construction includes, in addition to the state courts, all of the federal courts and the courts of the territories and possessions of the United States and of the District of Columbia. Each of these courts must recognize the validly rendered judgments of the others and give them essentially the same preclusive effect the rendering jurisdiction expects for its judgments.[3]

The term "American" courts can for convenience be used to describe the above courts collectively. The courts of foreign nations are not under the full faith and credit umbrella; their judgments can at best ask for "comity," a doctrine to be looked at in the next section.

As applied to an American judgment, the full faith and credit doctrine is in essence only res judicata applied interstate and made mandatory. Full faith and credit applies to the American judgment as long as the rendering court, F-1, had jurisdiction. Jurisdiction is in almost all cases the sole inquiry. As soon as the second forum (F-2) ascertains that F-1 had jurisdiction, the F-2 inquiry must end and the F-1 judgment

---

[8] See Artibee v. Home Place Corp., 28 N.Y.3d 739, 49 N.Y.S.3d 638, 71 N.E.3d 1205 (2017); § 168C; SPR 13:4.

[9] See La Buda v. State, 86 A.D.2d 692, 446 N.Y.S.2d 534 (3d Dep't 1982).

[1] U.S. Const. art. IV, § 1.

[2] 28 U.S.C.A. § 1738.

[3] See, e.g., Taylor v. Sturgell, 553 U.S. 880, 891 n.4, 128 S. Ct. 2161, 2171 n.4, 171 L. Ed. 2d 155 (2008); Gargiul v. Tompkins, 790 F.2d 265 (2d Cir. 1986).

must be recognized on its merits and be given the same preclusive effect of the rendering jurisdiction.[4] That is so no matter what error there may have been on F-1's part in reaching the merits: as long as F-1 had jurisdiction, any error that F-1 made on the merits must be reviewed by direct attack in F-1[5] and not by collateral attack in F-2.[6]

F-2 may examine the question of whether F-1 had jurisdiction. If the defendant did not appear in the F-1 proceeding, F-2 may decide the question of F-1's jurisdiction for itself—looking into the usual jurisdictional prerequisites of basis, notice, and opportunity to be heard. Although F-2 must give "proper weight" to what F-1 may have held as to its own jurisdiction, F-2 is not bound by the F-1 holding in this instance and may, upon appropriate proof, determine that F-1 did not have jurisdiction even in the teeth of F-1's own determination that it did.[7] The theory is that the F-1 defendant is entitled to a day in court on the question of F-1's jurisdiction and that she must be allowed that day in F-2 as long as she did not appear in F-1.

It is in fact this phenomenon of federal constitutional law that lends jeopardy to the so-called "ex parte" divorce, the divorce rendered in F-1 with no personal jurisdiction of the defendant spouse.[8] It is always open to the defendant, if the F-1 divorce should be questioned in F-2, to show that F-1 had no jurisdiction at all, not even the "rem" jurisdiction that might have obtained if the plaintiff spouse was found an F-1 domiciliary—the very fact question on which F-1's jurisdiction in this instance depends and which F-2 can decide for itself by virtue of the defendant's nonappearance in F-1. The question of F-1's jurisdiction remains open, in other words, and any person remarrying on the strength of such an ex parte divorce runs the risk of having F-2 reject the divorce upon determining that F-1 lacked jurisdiction. All this, when the defendant does not appear in the F-1 proceeding.

If the defendant does appear in F-1, the full faith and credit doctrine takes on some added magic: it forecloses reinvestigation of, and binds F-2 to recognize, not just the result on the merits, but also the fact of F-1's jurisdiction. Here the theory is that by appearing in F-1 the defendant had a direct opportunity to raise and litigate the jurisdictional question. If he did litigate it and lost on it, the holding of F-1's jurisdiction of course binds him.[9] But even if he appeared in the F-1 action without raising a jurisdictional issue, he is foreclosed on it just the same because the opportunity to litigate it was there whether used or not.[10] This rule applies whether the jurisdictional issue goes to personal or to subject matter jurisdiction.[11] A sister-state divorce rendered on the defendant spouse's appearance, whether in person or through an attorney, invokes this

---

[4] See V.L. v. E.L., 136 S. Ct. 1017, 194 L. Ed. 2d 92 (2016).

[5] By direct attack is meant either an appeal in F-1 or a motion to the F-1 court itself to vacate the judgment.

[6] Fauntleroy v. Lum, 210 U.S. 230, 28 S. Ct. 641, 52 L. Ed. 1039 (1908); see *V.L.*, 136 S. Ct. at 1020–21 (Georgia decree allowing plaintiff to adopt her lesbian partner's two biological children was entitled to full faith and credit in Alabama).

[7] Williams v. State of N.C., 325 U.S. 226, 65 S. Ct. 1092, 89 L. Ed. 1577 (1945).

[8] This is the category of divorce that depends on "rem" jurisdiction of the marital status. F-1 gets this rem jurisdiction if the plaintiff is a domiciliary of F-1. See § 102.

[9] Baldwin v. Iowa State Traveling Men's Ass'n, 283 U.S. 522, 51 S. Ct. 517, 75 L. Ed. 1244 (1931).

[10] See Johnson v. Muelberger, 340 U.S. 581, 71 S. Ct. 474, 95 L. Ed. 552 (1951) and Cook v. Cook, 342 U.S. 126, 72 S. Ct. 157, 96 L. Ed. 146 (1951).

[11] Sherrer v. Sherrer, 334 U.S. 343, 68 S. Ct. 1087, 92 L. Ed. 1429 (1948).

rule of jurisdictional foreclosure. In common parlance, this type of divorce is called "bilateral."

Just as the ex parte sister-state divorce is insecure, at least until F-2 confirms F-1's jurisdiction, so the bilateral one is airtight for the very reason that the Full Faith and Credit Clause of the Federal Constitution bars F-2 from even questioning F-1's jurisdiction.

As noted above, the foregoing applies only to American judgments. Those of foreign countries, not coming in for full faith and credit and therefore compelled to rely on "comity" at best, are separately treated in the next section.

Once it is determined to recognize the F-1 judgment, whether via full faith and credit because it comes from an American court or through comity that has been granted to a foreign country judgment, the rest is usually just a matter of applying the rules of res judicata and collateral estoppel of F-1. If there is some difference between the law of F-1 and F-2 on the scope to be given the F-1 judgment, F-2 will ordinarily apply the F-1 rules on the theory that to do otherwise would be according less than full credit or comity to the F-1 judgment.[12]

Suppose that F-2 is obliged to recognize an F-1 judgment but fails to, rendering judgment for X although Y, the F-1 winner, should have prevailed. If the validity of both judgments now arises before F-3, which earlier judgment prevails? It has been held that the F-2 judgment, the later in time, prevails; that if F-2 failed to recognize the F-1 judgment, the failure was error which should have been reviewed by appeal in F-2.[13] But if two actions are riding to judgment at the same time, the one arriving at judgment first is the one ordinarily entitled to res judicata treatment even if the other action was commenced first. For res judicata purposes, the moment of judgment, and not the moment of commencement, is ordinarily the key time.

Special problems have always attended the recognition of child custody decrees. As a matter of federal constitutional law, the U.S. Supreme Court never applied the Full Faith and Credit Clause to custody decrees,[14] and New York took the position that the clause was not operative in the custody sphere at all.[15] Implementing a uniform act, New York ultimately adopted a special statute[16] to govern the recognition of child custody adjudications made by other American courts, resting recognition on whether the jurisdictional basis on which the other court purported to ground custody is analogous to one that New York authorizes.[17] This was in effect a voluntary undertaking by the state legislature, but Congress itself intervened and made recognition mandatory in many instances with a statute, § 1738A of Title 28 of the U.S. Code, set right next to the main full faith and credit statute, § 1738. In stated situations, the statute applies the Full Faith and Credit Clause to custody determinations. It encourages intercourt

---

[12]   See Magnolia Petroleum Co. v. Hunt, 320 U.S. 430, 64 S. Ct. 208, 88 L. Ed. 149 (1943). Although not directly overruled, the *Magnolia* case is undermined by the *Thomas* case, cited in § 456. See also Johnson v. Muelberger, 340 U.S. 581, 71 S. Ct. 474, 95 L. Ed. 552 (1951).

[13]   Treinies v. Sunshine Mining Co., 308 U.S. 66, 60 S. Ct. 44, 84 L. Ed. 85 (1939).

[14]   See the concurrence of Justice Frankfurter in May v. Anderson, 345 U.S. 528, 73 S. Ct. 840, 97 L. Ed. 1221 (1953).

[15]   See, e.g., Bachman v. Mejias, 1 N.Y.2d 575, 154 N.Y.S.2d 903, 136 N.E.2d 866 (1956).

[16]   See § 77–b of the Dom. Rel. Law.

[17]   See §§ 76 et seq. of the Dom. Rel. Law.

communication on custody problems, a practice on which New York had embarked under its own statutes even before the federal mandate took effect.[18]

§ 472. Recognition of Foreign-Country Judgments; "Comity"

In the prior section, only American judgments were discussed because only they get full faith and credit. The judgments of foreign countries are not within the full faith and credit requirement, and as long as there is nothing else to require recognition, such as a treaty between the United States and the particular nation,[1] the best that the foreign country judgment can hope for is what is termed "comity." Loosely, this means courtesy, respect, or mutual accommodation;[2] practically, it means that each sovereign, including the State of New York, can decide for itself which foreign country judgments it will recognize and which it won't.

New York's position is stated mainly, but not exclusively, in Article 53 of the CPLR, which adopts in essence the Uniform Foreign Country Money-Judgments Recognition Act.[3] The Act dictates in some detail which foreign money judgments must be recognized[4] and which need not be.[5] For example, CPLR 5304(a)(2) generally provides that a foreign judgment will not be enforced in New York "if the foreign court did not have personal jurisdiction over the defendant." An exception to this broad rule is recognized in CPLR 5305(a)(3), which states that a "foreign country judgment shall not be refused recognition for lack of personal jurisdiction if . . . the defendant prior to the commencement of the proceedings had agreed to submit to the jurisdiction of the foreign court with respect to the subject matter involved."

In Landauer Ltd. v. Joe Monani Fish Co., Inc.,[6] the Court applied its prior precedent in concluding that recognition of a foreign judgment "is not repugnant to our notion of fairness if defendant was a party to a contract in which the parties agreed that disputes would be resolved in the courts of a foreign jurisdiction and defendant was aware of the ongoing litigation in that jurisdiction but neglected to appear and defend." The *Landauer* Court reiterated that in these circumstances, as "long as the exercise of jurisdiction by the foreign court does not offend due process, the judgment should be enforced in New York "without 'microscopic analysis' of the underlying proceedings."[7]

These recognition standards were easily met in *Landauer* where the contracts between the parties contained a provision giving the English courts exclusive jurisdiction over any disputes arising from the transactions. Furthermore, the record established that, through its counsel, defendant had ample notice of the lawsuit before the default judgment was entered in England. Therefore, the Court of Appeals granted plaintiff's

---

[18]   See, e.g., Vernon v. Vernon, 100 N.Y.2d 960, 967, 768 N.Y.S.2d 719, 722–23, 800 N.E.2d 1085, 1088–89 (2003); Vanneck v. Vanneck, 49 N.Y.2d 602, 427 N.Y.S.2d 735, 404 N.E.2d 1278 (1980).

[1]   Treaties play an insignificant role in the area of foreign judgments at the moment, but an important international convention, to which the United States is a signatory, does govern international arbitration awards and thus dictates to the States on their recognition. Chapter 2 of Title 9 of the U.S.C.A. contains Congress' implementing provisions for this treaty.

[2]   See Franzen v. Zimmer, 35 N.Y.S. 612 (Sup. Ct., Monroe County 1895).

[3]   See CPLR 5309.

[4]   CPLR 5303. The act does not address "non-money judgments." CPLR 5301(b).

[5]   CPLR 5304.

[6]   Landauer Ltd. v. Joe Monani Fish Co., Inc., 22 N.Y.3d 1129, 1131, 985 N.Y.S.2d 463, 465, 8 N.E.3d 839, 840 (2014).

[7]   *Landauer*, 22 N.Y.3d at 131, 985 N.Y.S.2d at 465, 8 N.E.3d at 841.

CPLR 3213 motion for summary judgment in lieu of complaint[8] to afford recognition to the English judgment in New York despite defendant's contention that it had not been properly served in England.

It is important to note that while recognition of a foreign country judgment is not compelled by full faith and credit, the standard established by the Court of Appeals in *Landauer* for recognition of such judgments may limit the defenses that would otherwise be available when a party seeks to enforce the judgment of a sister-state. In the latter situation, a defendant who has not appeared in the sister-state can always raise the defense of lack of proper service in that state to defeat enforcement of the judgment in New York.[9] Not so if recognition of a foreign country judgment is sought in New York. In this situation, lack of proper service in the foreign jurisdiction will not necessarily require that the judgment be denied recognition in New York if: 1) the parties agreed to submit the dispute at hand to the foreign tribunal; and 2) defendant was aware of the litigation in the foreign jurisdiction but failed to appear.

Article 53, which became law in 1970, was not added because of any special need New York had for guidance in this respect. The State has always been generous in recognizing foreign country judgments even without statutory or constitutional pressures, insisting essentially on nothing more than that the judgment be shown to have been based on principles of jurisdiction and due process analogous to our own, thus comporting with our own sense of fairness.[10] This attitude continues. Comity under New York caselaw should therefore assure recognition to any money judgment that would have gotten it before Article 53 was adopted. It has even been said that the article is merely a codification of caselaw.[11] And comity would of course continue to be given to non-money judgments that would have earned it before, because to them, Article 53 is not applicable at all.[12]

The motive behind the New York adoption of Article 53 was not to prescribe what New York has to do for foreign judgments, but with what the mere existence of Article 53 on the New York statute books would accomplish for New York judgments seeking recognition elsewhere. It was felt that foreign tribunals, especially those that insist on reciprocity, would be more likely to recognize a New York judgment if shown a New York statutory scheme manifesting a ready willingness to reciprocate, especially one based on a uniform act that has achieved some currency domestically and some familiarity overseas.[13] To judges in civil law nations, as opposed to common law nations, it is apparently insufficient, for ready recognition of a New York judgment, to show reciprocal generosity through New York caselaw. A statute is what they want to see, and Article 53 is the New York showpiece. Probably for the reason that New York caselaw has been

---

[8]   See § 290 for a discussion of CPLR 3213.

[9]   See Vertex Standard USA, Inc. v. Reichert, 16 A.D.3d 1163, 791 N.Y.S.2d 892 (4th Dep't 2005) (affirming dismissal of action seeking to enforce California judgment entered upon defendants' default because plaintiff failed to satisfy California's requirements for service of process); see also § 471.

[10]   See Cowans v. Ticonderoga Pulp & Paper Co., 246 N.Y. 603, 159 N.E. 669 (1927), aff'g on opinion in Cowans v. Ticonderoga Pulp & Paper Co., 219 A.D. 120, 219 N.Y.S. 284 (3d Dep't 1927).

[11]   CIBC Mellon Trust Co. v. Mora Hotel Corp. N.V., 100 N.Y.2d 215, 221, 762 N.Y.S.2d 5, 9, 792 N.E.2d 155, 159 (2003); see Island Territory of Curacao v. Solitron Devices, Inc., 489 F.2d 1313 (2d Cir. 1973).

[12]   See CPLR 5307.

[13]   See *CIBC*, 100 N.Y.2d at 221, 762 N.Y.S.2d at 9, 792 N.E.2d at 159; Kulzer, The Uniform Foreign Money Judgments Recognition Act, 13th Ann. Jud. Conf. Rep., p. 194, at 195 (1968). Professor Kulzer's study offers extensive background on what later became in essence Article 53 of the CPLR.

at least as liberal as Article 53 in acknowledging foreign judgments,[14] the article and its progenitors and counterparts have received "scant judicial attention."[15]

The article must be perused, however, in conjunction with any issue involving recognition of a foreign country money judgment, especially when an outright adoption of that judgment is sought, whether by plenary action or by the motion-action of CPLR 3213, the latter being of course the more expeditious and hence the preferable tool.[16]

The same "last-in-time" rule that governs the recognition of inconsistent sister-state judgments under the Full Faith and Credit Clause[17] has also been applied by New York under its comity doctrine. Hence, if two foreign judgments are inconsistent, the later of the two will be the one that New York recognizes.[18]

What about the situation in which the defendant appeared in, and contested the jurisdiction of, the foreign court, which ruled against it on the jurisdictional issue before rendering its judgment on the merits? CIBC Mellon Trust Co. v. Mora Hotel Corp. N.V.,[19] involving an English judgment, is on the point. The Court observed that if the defendant had stuck only to the jurisdictional issue in the foreign court, it might have preserved the issue for the New York court to consider de novo.[20] On the *CIBC* record, however, whatever chance the defendants had on that score was forfeit on a record showing that the defendant did not so limit itself, but argued the merits of the case as well.[21]

Excepted from the recognition requirement of Article 53 are foreign judgments for "taxes, a fine or other penalty, or a judgment for support."[22] The statutory basis for denying enforcement of such foreign judgments "is predicated on the classification and purpose of the judgment, not the court that issued it, making no differentiation between foreign civil and foreign criminal judgments."[23] The exception for "a judgment for support" does not bar a foreign support judgment's recognition as a simple matter of comity, however,[24] a holding that should keep the door similarly ajar for the other judgments as well when no strong public policy appears to be jeopardized.[25] This is not an expresio unius situation, in other words: Article 53's mandate of recognition for some judgments is not an absolute mandate against it for others.

---

[14]   See, e.g., von Engelbrechten v. Galvanoni & Nevy Bros., Inc., 59 Misc. 2d 721, 300 N.Y.S.2d 239 (N.Y. City Civ. Ct. 1969), aff'd, 61 Misc. 2d 959, 307 N.Y.S.2d 381 (App. Term, 1st Dep't 1970), extending recognition farther than a treaty in the case appeared to require but did not preclude.

[15]   See Overmyer v. Eliot Realty, 83 Misc.2d 694 at 701, 371 N.Y.S.2d 246 at 255 (Sup. Ct., Westchester County 1975).

[16]   See §§ 288 and 290.

[17]   See the discussion in § 471.

[18]   See Ackerman v. Ackerman, 517 F. Supp. 614 (S.D.N.Y. 1981), aff'd, 676 F.2d 898 (2d Cir. 1982).

[19]   CIBC Mellon Trust Co. v. Mora Hotel Corp. N.V., 100 N.Y.2d 215, 762 N.Y.S.2d 5, 792 N.E.2d 155 (2003).

[20]   See CPLR 5305(a)(2).

[21]   The *CIBC* decision is the subject of the lead note in NYSLD No. 523. The case also discusses what has come to be known as a *Mareva* order, an injunction designed to operate on a defendant's property outside the forum state.

[22]   CPLR 5301(b).

[23]   Harvardsky Prumyslovy Holding, A.S.-V Likvidaci v. Kozeny, 117 A.D.3d 77, 80, 983 N.Y.S.2d 240, 242 (1st Dep't 2014) (Article 53 permits recognition of a foreign country judgment issued by a criminal court awarding a sum of money as compensation for damages sustained by a victim of a fraudulent scheme).

[24]   Downs v. Yuen, 298 A.D.2d 177, 748 N.Y.S.2d 131 (1st Dep't 2002).

[25]   See Commentary C5301:2 on McKinney's CPLR 5301.

It has been held that a hefty award of attorney's fees in a foreign judgment in a country that allows them is not necessarily a "penalty" for this purpose. In Blacklink Transport v. Von Summer,[26] the country was Australia. Attorney's fees of some $89,000 were awarded to D after P refused D's settlement offer of $7,000 and then won less than that at the trial. Australia is a common law country, and a democratic one, indicating that we harbor no suspicions about the fairness of its courts. Hence, *Blacklink* holds that the allowance of attorney's fees, while a step that New York does not follow internally, is not such a deep violation of New York public policy as to constitute a "penalty" under our statute and require rejection of the Australian judgment.

In an action on a foreign judgment, the service of the papers in the underlying action may have been governed by the Hague Convention, a treaty to which the United States is a party.[27] In John Galliano, S.A. v. Stallion, Inc.,[28] where recognition of a French judgment was sought, the Court of Appeals held that as long as the procedure used to obtain personal jurisdiction in the foreign court is not "fundamentally unfair, the propriety of the service under the Hague Convention was an issue for the court in France." Finding that the procedure used in France was "not repugnant to our notion of fairness," the *John Galliano* Court concluded that the recognition requirements of CPLR Article 53 were met and affirmed the appellate division's recognition of the foreign judgment in New York.

In Chevron Corp. v. Naranjo,[29] the plaintiff sought to invoke the act to secure an injunction in New York and abroad barring enforcement of a huge Ecuadorean judgment that had been rendered against it. The court dismissed the action without reaching the merits, determining only that Article 53, which was applicable in this federal action, could not be invoked by the plaintiff because it operates only when the judgment creditor brings a New York action on the foreign judgment. In that instance, it allows the judgment debtor to interpose certain defenses to the suit, such as where the judgment is shown to come from a corrupt court system or to have been obtained by fraud.[30] *Chevron* alleged both of those things, and more, but the court found no occasion to consider any of them because they are defenses that don't become ripe for judicial decision until an action is brought in New York to enforce the foreign judgment.

J. PROCEDURAL INCIDENTS

Table of Sections

§ 473   Evidentiary Sources to Establish Matters Estopped

§ 474.   Estoppel Only for Given Issue

§ 475.   Raising the Issue; Burden of Proof

---

[26] Blacklink Transport Consultants PTY Ltd. v. Von Summer, 18 Misc. 3d 1113(A), 856 N.Y.S.2d 496 (Sup. Ct., New York County 2008).

[27] See § 100.

[28] John Galliano, S.A. v. Stallion, Inc., 15 N.Y.3d 75, 81–82, 904 N.Y.S.2d 683, 686, 930 N.E.2d 756, 759 (2010) (NYSLD No. 606).

[29] Chevron Corp. v. Naranjo, 667 F.3d 232 (2d Cir. 2012) (SPR 242:3).

[30] See CPLR 5304(a)(1) and (b)(3).

§ 473. Evidentiary Sources to Establish Matters Estopped

In resolving any issue of res judicata or collateral estoppel, any competent source can be considered to determine what matters were disposed of in the earlier action. Hopefully, the judgment itself will reveal what's needed. Perhaps the judgment will require a juxtaposition with the pleadings to determine the issues raised and decided. The pleadings may of course be looked to. A transcript of the earlier proceedings may also be examined, including the charge to the jury, which is a likely source to resolve what the issues were, and any special verdict. Indeed, the trial itself may not have followed the pleadings; issues outside the pleadings may have been raised and disposed of, and as a general rule, these are also entitled to estoppel treatment.[1]

If the aggregate of the papers in the earlier action, including a trial transcript, do not reveal with clarity the issues disposed of, extrinsic evidence may be received. It may even be received to show that the record in the prior action does *not* accurately reflect what issues were determined.[2]

§ 474. Estoppel Only for Given Issue

Collateral estoppel works on individual issues, not necessarily on the whole case. This has already been noted at several points, but is worth repeating. If the issue precluded is at the crux of the case, it will of course be wholly dispositive. So, for example, where P sues D for inducing X to breach a P-X contract, and an earlier action involving P established that there was no contract, the estoppel attaching to that issue destroys P's whole case against D, entitling D to summary judgment.[1]

If the estoppel visits only a given issue without disposing of the whole case, the unprecluded issues must stand for trial. So, to cite a frequent example, where P-1, injured in an accident, recovers a judgment for personal injuries against D after D is found to have caused the accident and P-1 is found free of comparative fault, a second person, P-2, suing D for personal injuries incurred in the same accident, may have an estoppel establishing D's fault, but will have to litigate any issue raised about P-2's own comparative negligence. And of course the issue of P-2's damages, not relevant to the first action, will have to be resolved in the second one. In that situation, P-2, although not entitled to summary judgment on her whole case, will be entitled to have it summarily determined that D was at fault in causing the accident.[2]

There must of course be a genuine issue as to the unprecluded matter; mere unfounded allegations of such an issue will not suffice as may sometimes be seen in a tort case involving a passenger against whom not even a colorable accusation of comparative fault can be made.[3]

In all tort situations involving a second action plaintiff different from the one who succeeded in the first action, damages will have to be tried even though there may be a full estoppel on issues going to liability. In that situation, summary judgment may be granted as to liability and an immediate trial ordered of damages.[4] Conversely, however,

---

[1]   See Bronxville Palmer, Limited v. State, 18 N.Y.2d 560, 277 N.Y.S.2d 402, 223 N.E.2d 887 (1966).

[2]   See Restatement (Second) of Judgments § 27, cmt. f.

[1]   See Israel v. Wood Dolson Co., 1 N.Y.2d 116, 151 N.Y.S.2d 1, 134 N.E.2d 97 (1956); § 460.

[2]   See Quick v. O'Connell, 53 Misc. 2d 1091, 281 N.Y.S.2d 120 (Sup. Ct., Jefferson County 1967).

[3]   See, e.g., Jacobs v. Del Guercio, 67 Misc. 2d 606, 324 N.Y.S.2d 773 (Sup. Ct., New York County 1971).

[4]   CPLR 3212(c).

if it is the same plaintiff who is suing for the same injuries in both actions—a different defendant being sued in each, as commonly happens in New York when the State itself is one of the defendants and can be sued only in the court of claims—collateral estoppel may even alight upon the amount found as damages in the first action and entitle the second action defendant to a holding that whatever may be found as to that defendant's liability in the second action, the plaintiff's damages may not be allowed to exceed the sum they were set at in the earlier action.[5] Indeed, whatever the first defendant may have paid in satisfaction of that first judgment will have to be credited against whatever judgment the plaintiff may recover for the same wrong against the second defendant.[6] Any other conclusion would authorize a double recovery, and nothing about res judicata or collateral estoppel supports that.

§ 475. Raising the Issue; Burden of Proof

The doctrines of res judicata and collateral estoppel are affirmative defenses for the defendant to plead and prove.[1] They can be taken as affirmative defenses in the answer or, at the defendant's option, may be raised by a motion to dismiss instead.[2] If taken by answer, they can then be made the basis of a motion for summary judgment.[3] If the defense becomes available only after the action has been pending for a while, and the responding time has already expired—as where the action from which the estoppel emerges has only just gone to judgment—the remedy is a motion to amend the responsive pleading in the pending action to insert the defense,[4] joined, if appropriate, with a demand for summary judgment based on the new defense.

Note that while the official descriptions of these doctrines, in both the pleading[5] and motion[6] provisions, are "res judicata" and "collateral estoppel," they cover the whole family of res judicata doctrines, by whatever name any one of them may go by—claim preclusion, issue preclusion, merger, bar, election of remedies, splitting, etc.[7] As a general rule, the pleading-or-motion option is available for all of them.

The burden is on the party relying on the estoppel to show identity of issue and to establish that the issue was necessarily decided in the earlier action. If the party against whom the doctrine is invoked then has anything to show to indicate that he did not have a full and fair opportunity to meet the issue in the earlier action,[8] the burden of that showing is on him.[9]

---

[5]   See La Buda v. State, 86 A.D.2d 692, 446 N.Y.S.2d 534 (3d Dep't 1982); § 470.

[6]   As to all of these matters, see Goines v. Pennsylvania R. Co., 6 A.D.2d 531, 179 N.Y.S.2d 960 (1st Dep't 1958).

[1]   CPLR 3018(b). See § 223.

[2]   CPLR 3211(a)(5), (e). See § 274.

[3]   CPLR 3212. See § 283.

[4]   CPLR 3025(b). See § 237.

[5]   CPLR 3018(b).

[6]   CPLR 3211(a)(5).

[7]   See §§ 443 and 450.

[8]   The ingredients that go into the full and fair opportunity test are set forth in § 467.

[9]   Schwartz v. Public Adm'r of Bronx County, 24 N.Y.2d 65, 73, 298 N.Y.S.2d 955, 962, 246 N.E.2d 725, 730 (1969). The distribution of burden of proof was noted earlier during treatment of the identity of issue test. See § 462.

Chapter 18

ENFORCEMENT OF JUDGMENTS

Analysis

Introductory
> PART I.   ENFORCEMENT OF NON-MONEY JUDGMENTS
A.   **Judgments Involving a Chattel or Realty**
B.   **Enforcement by Contempt**
> PART II.   ENFORCEMENT OF MONEY JUDGMENTS
A.   **In General**
B.   **Property Subject to Enforcement**
C.   **Devices in Perspective**
D.   **Property Executions**
E.   **Income Execution**
F.   **The "Supplementary Proceedings"**
G.   **Incidental Matters**
H.   **Priorities and Liens**
I.   **Protection Against Abuse**
J.   **Contempt as Back-Up Device**

INTRODUCTORY

Table of Sections

§ 476.   Enforcement of Judgments, Generally

§ 476.   Enforcement of Judgments, Generally

In many respects, this topic gives law its ultimate test. We learn that law is divided into substantive and procedural segments. The whole of the substantive law determines whether the plaintiff has a right and the whole of the procedural law, at considerable expense to the plaintiff, hears everyone out, determines whether the plaintiff has a claim, and gives the plaintiff a judgment if she has. If that judgment can't be enforced, law is bound to fall several notches in the esteem of the plaintiff, which makes the enforcement of judgments a key moment in a test of the system.

The traditional division of judgments for enforcement purposes was into law and equity, law judgments enforceable by execution and equity judgments by contempt. Much of the tradition survives, but in applying the experience of the years, which has shown the money judgment to pose more enforcement problems than all the other categories combined, the legislature has reordered its division into (1) non-money judgments and (2) money judgments. To that we may add yet a third category, the declaratory judgment, which as a creature of the 20th Century has no direct ancestors either at law or in equity.

The first two categories involve what is sometimes called "coercive" relief, some kind of pressure on the defendant or a taking of the defendant's property, while the declaratory judgment involves no coercive step at all. In a manner of speaking, the declaratory judgment has no enforcement stage. It merely declares the rights of the parties between or among themselves; the context is such that the declaration alone, embodied in a judgment, is assumed to resolve the dispute. We speak here of the declaratory judgment in its pure form. The plaintiff who seeks it can of course join demands for other relief,[1] and if other relief is awarded, the judgment on the other relief will pursue the usual coercive enforcement channels. The few words to be said about the enforcement stage of the declaration itself were said when the device was studied earlier[2] and need no repetition.

The first category we turn to now, the non-money judgment, includes equity decrees for such as injunction and specific performance. These are backed by the contempt punishment, as they always were. But also in the non-money grouping are ejectment and replevin, two categories of law judgment that are not as a rule enforced by contempt, but rather by execution. Article 51 of the CPLR governs the enforcement of non-money judgments, supplying the few devices needed to enforce them.

One of these, the receivership "to carry the judgment into effect," applies alike to equity and law judgments having specific property as their "subject."[3] It is merely the post-judgment or enforcement counterpart of the provisional receivership supplied by Article 64 of the CPLR[4] and is in fact governed by the several provisions of that article, which was treated earlier.[5] Receivership therefore needs no further discussion, but it should be counted among the small stockpile of devices—the rest to be treated in Part I of this chapter—for the enforcement of a non-money judgment.

Part II will treat the money judgment, whose enforcement arsenal is a much bigger one. Article 52 governs the enforcement of money judgments[6] which, as the most common kind rendered by the courts, is our major study. For sheer quantity of governing statute as well as caselaw, the money judgment is the bull of the enforcement market.

---

[1]   See § 436.

[2]   See §§ 436 and 440.

[3]   CPLR 5106.

[4]   See CPLR 6401.

[5]   See §§ 332 and 333.

[6]   See CPLR 5101.

PART I. ENFORCEMENT OF NON-MONEY JUDGMENTS
A. JUDGMENTS INVOLVING A CHATTEL OR REALTY

Table of Sections

§ 477.   Judgment Awarding Possession of Chattel

§ 478.   Judgment Awarding Possession of Realty

§ 479.   Judgment Directing Sale of Realty

§ 480.   Judgment Directing Conveyance of Realty

§ 477. Judgment Awarding Possession of Chattel

This is the last stage of a replevin action, whose final judgment is governed by CPLR 7108, part of the article on the provisional-like remedy of seizure of a chattel studied earlier.[1] It will be recalled that if the plaintiff has won in a replevin action, the judgment awards the plaintiff possession of the chattel. If the plaintiff does not already have the chattel (she might have gotten it through the prejudgment order of seizure),[2] the judgment must also fix the value of the chattel.[3] This enables the sheriff to enforce the judgment like an ordinary money judgment if the sheriff should be unable to locate the chattel and restore its possession to the plaintiff. The value of the chattel is fixed as of the time of the trial.[4]

The method of enforcement of the judgment is an execution, a paper drawn by the plaintiff's attorney and delivered to the sheriff of the county where the chattel is. It basically follows the requirements applicable to an execution on a money judgment,[5] except that it first directs the sheriff to restore the chattel's possession to the plaintiff, instructing the sheriff to levy as if on a money judgment only if the chattel can't be located in the county.[6]

This is an effective remedy, even if the plaintiff ends up with the monetary value of the chattel instead of the chattel itself, but only if there is nothing unique about the chattel. Money will of course not make amends for the loss of a unique chattel, for which reason, when uniqueness has been demonstrated, the replevin article expressly authorizes a judgment directing the defendant to hand the chattel over under the penalty of contempt.

The uniqueness of the chattel authorizes a judgment in alternative form, enforceable either by the usual remedy of execution or by the equitable device of contempt, as the plaintiff chooses.[7]

---

[1]   See §§ 337 et seq.

[2]   See § 340.

[3]   CPLR 7108(a). See § 342.

[4]   It has been held that fixing it as of some earlier time, such as the commencement of the action, is reversible error that may require a new trial. Colonial Funding Corp. v. Bon Jour Intern. Ltd., 148 A.D.2d 654, 539 N.Y.S.2d 405 (2d Dep't 1989).

[5]   CPLR 5230. See §§ 494 et seq.

[6]   CPLR 5102.

[7]   CPLR 7109(b). See § 342.

§ 478. Judgment Awarding Possession of Realty

The main situation in which a possessory dispute over real property arises today involves the landlord-tenant relationship where the procedure for recovering possession is the summary proceeding of Article 7 of the Real Property Actions and Proceedings Law.[1] Summary proceedings, which number in the hundreds of thousands each year in New York, are usually based on non-payment of rent or holding over after the expiration of a lease. If the landlord wins in the proceeding and is awarded possession, the enforcement procedures are to be found not in the CPLR, but in the Real Property Actions and Proceedings Law in the same article that governs the rest of the summary proceeding.[2] The advent of the summary proceeding reduced other forms of action to recover possession of land to what amounts by comparison to an infinitesimal number, including the ancient ejectment action.

If the relationship between disputants does not fall within the reach of the summary proceeding,[3] resort may still be had, of course, to the plenary ejectment or a like action.[4] These may be used, for example, against squatters, interlopers, trespassers, encroachers, etc., and even against outright tenants if based on something besides non-payment of rent, holding over, or one of the other enumerated summary proceeding grounds.[5] When it is used, ejectment still qualifies traditionally as a law action, which has two major consequences: it is constitutionally triable by jury,[6] and the process of enforcement for a resulting judgment is still an execution.[7]

The execution is drawn by the plaintiff's lawyer and delivered to the sheriff of the real property county. It directs the sheriff to do what must be done to restore the plaintiff to possession. In other respects it follows CPLR 5230, which supplies the detail and procedure on the ordinary execution on a money judgment.[8] Execution is a satisfactory remedy if enforcement is a straightforward and trouble-free prospect, as where some portable object has to be removed from the land or a few trespassers put off. Theoretically, however, the sheriff is required to restore possession in any case at all if the execution so directs, whether this entails the removal of a pebble or a skyscraper, an undersized squatter or an army. But theory and practice diverge here. Hahl v. Sugo[9] stands as a mighty illustration of the frustration of the execution remedy when the sheriff deems the job too big.

The *Hahl* execution entailed the removal of a wall and the sheriff returned the execution as "impracticable" to levy. Perhaps an Article 78 proceeding in the nature of mandamus would lie to compel the sheriff to perform the duty, with the sheriff hiring such people or equipment as may be required. (The plaintiff may be required to pay, in

---

[1] See RPAPL 701, 711.

[2] See RPAPL 749.

[3] The summary proceeding is treated in Part III of Chapter 20 (Practitioner's Edition), commencing with § 571.

[4] Since the forms of action have been abolished, CPLR 103(a), it is not necessary to give the action any name at all.

[5] See RPAPL 711.

[6] See N.Y. Const. art. I, § 2; CPLR 4101(2). The right to jury trial is also given in a summary proceeding, RPAPL 745, but the lease between the parties usually waives it. See §§ 377 and 378.

[7] CPLR 5102. "Judgment" includes "order" for this purpose, should it happen to be an order that returns possession. See, e.g., Dom. Rel. Law § 234.

[8] See §§ 494 et seq.

[9] Hahl v. Sugo, 169 N.Y. 109, 62 N.E. 135 (1901).

advance, all connected expenses, which may later be recouped from the defendant). With the proper people and equipment, the sheriff can do just about any job, but pragmatic lawyers try to avoid this fatiguing course. In a situation at all likely to involve difficulties of enforcement, they bring, instead of ejectment, an equitable claim against the defendant, one that tries the identical facts but results in a judgment directing the defendant to remove the encroachment himself, under threat of contempt. The law usually allows this. The very existence of *Hahl* and like cases manifests the inadequacy of the legal remedy and thus supplies a traditional element needed to invoke the court's equity jurisdiction.

This lesson must be applied not at the end of an action, however, when seeking enforcement, but at the beginning, when determining what remedy to choose. The best idea when enforcement looms as a problem is to sue in equity, or at minimum to add an equitable count to the complaint. If the claim succeeds on its merits, responsibility for removing the encroachment or otherwise troubling to return possession to the plaintiff will fall on the defendant itself.[10]

We are concerned here only with the enforcement stage of a real property action. Nothing said above should be taken as suggesting a fine line between an action that tries the right to possession of real property and one that tries title to it. As long as a plenary action is used—a summary proceeding tries only the right to possession—and the court in which it is brought has jurisdiction of real property actions, the abolition of the forms of action permits adjudication of both ownership and possessory rights, whatever procedural differences may attend the enforcement steps afterwards.

§ 479. Judgment Directing Sale of Realty

Most of the actions likely to end in a sale of real property, such as partition and mortgage foreclosure, are addressed and governed by the Real Property Actions and Proceedings Law, including the incidents of the sale.[1] The CPLR thus has little to say about the sale. Its main concern is to see that the sale takes place in the county of the real property. This and its few other directions appear in CPLR 5103.

The venue provisions of Article 5 of the CPLR will usually assure that an action involving real property is tried only in the county in which it is situated.[2] But it will sometimes happen that it is tried elsewhere as where the parties waived venue[3] or where the real property claim was joined with another claim as to which a different county was permissible venue, in which event a county proper for any of the claims becomes a proper one for all of them.[4] If it should happen that a judgment (or order) directing the sale of the real property is rendered in other than its situs county, a certified copy of the judgment or order must be filed with the county clerk of the situs, who must then enter it. This is to assure that the county clerk's office in the county of the real property will always remain a dependable repository of records concerning local real property. Indeed,

---

[10]   This is an election of remedies problem. For that aspect of the *Hahl* case, see § 218.

[1]   For partition, see RPAPL Article 9; for foreclosure, RPAPL Article 13.

[2]   See CPLR 507. See § 121.

[3]   See CPLR 509. See § 123.

[4]   CPLR 502.

the buyer at the sale is not required to pay the purchase money or accept a deed until appropriate entry has been made on home county records.[5]

The sale itself must take place in the real property county, conducted either by the sheriff of that county or by a referee, as the court designates. If the property is situated in more than one county, the court can order it sold in any of them, or, if feasible, the property can be divided into parcels with each parcel sold in its own county.[6]

§ 480. Judgment Directing Conveyance of Realty

If the judgment directs the defendant to convey title to the plaintiff, or any party to convey title to another, such as in the common action for specific performance of a contract to sell real property, there are several modes of enforcement. If the property is not in the state, which assumes that the action has been able to get by a forum non conveniens objection, the court cannot act directly against the property and so can do no more than direct the defendant—presumably there's personal jurisdiction of the defendant—under penalty of contempt, to make a deed to the plaintiff in form satisfactory to the real property jurisdiction. A refusal would then require contempt proceedings, the subject of later sections.

Contempt is theoretically available in that kind of case even if the real property is in New York, as long as personal jurisdiction has been secured over the defendant, but when the property is in the state, the court has the alternative of simply directing the sheriff to make the conveyance in the recalcitrant party's behalf.[1] The court will usually prefer this alternative, which lets the judgment act in rem.[2] The deed should be made by the sheriff of the real property county. When properly executed, the deed enters county records as if fully executed by the party and accomplishes a total conveyance. This is also approximately what occurs when a money judgment is enforced by the levy of execution against real property: it is also the sheriff who deeds the property to the buyer at the sale.[3]

B. ENFORCEMENT BY CONTEMPT

Table of Sections

§ 481.   Enforcement by Contempt; Grounds
§ 482.   Criminal and Civil Contempt Distinguished; Punishment
§ 483.   Constitutionality of Contempt Procedure
§ 484.   Procedure to Punish for Contempt

§ 481. Enforcement by Contempt; Grounds

CPLR 5104 provides that if any judgment or order, interlocutory or final, is not enforceable under Article 52 or pursuant to CPLR 5102, it is enforceable by contempt.

---

[5]   CPLR 5103(a).

[6]   CPLR 5103(b). Cf. Bridgehampton Nat. Bank v. White, 63 Misc. 2d 853, 313 N.Y.S.2d 258 (Suffolk County Court 1970). Distinguish this situation, in which specific real property is the subject of the action and the judgment itself is directing its sale, from the sale of real property on an execution pursuant to an ordinary money judgment. The latter also takes place in the situs, but is governed in detail by CPLR 5236. See § 500.

[1]   See CPLR 5107.

[2]   See Garfein v. McInnis, 248 N.Y. 261, 162 N.E. 73 (1928).

[3]   CPLR 5236(f). See § 500.

The categories thereby excluded from the contempt remedy are the money judgment, for which Article 52 lays out the array of enforcement tools, and the judgment awarding possession of either real or personal property, for which CPLR 5102 supplies execution as the enforcement device.[1] For other judgments the remedy is a contempt proceeding.

The usual equity judgments come under this category, notably the injunction, but special statutes have also made even some money judgments directly enforceable by contempt.[2] Directions for the payment of alimony or support contained in a matrimonial decree, for example, are so enforceable,[3] as is a judgment directing the payment of money into court.[4]

If a trustee or other fiduciary is directed to pay money because of a wilful breach of trust, the direction is enforceable by contempt.[5] The fiduciaries who fit into that category include a trustee, a personal representative of a decedent, a committee or conservator, and a guardian. In a given set of circumstances, the category can embrace still others, such as an escrowee[6] and even corporate officials.[7] A plaintiff who would invoke the contempt penalty in these instances had best be sure that the judgment itself recites the facts manifesting that the dereliction arises out of the required fiduciary connection.[8]

Even a replevin judgment, ordinarily enforceable only by an execution directing the sheriff to seize the chattel and return it to the plaintiff, can be converted into one enforceable by contempt if the chattel is unique and the judgment specifically instructs the defendant to return it.[9]

Insofar as a "judgment" of a given kind or category is enforceable by contempt, so is a court "order" of the same kind or category if it is otherwise properly made. There is no distinction between a judgment and an order in this regard.[10]

The disobedience of a subpoena is also a contempt of court[11] and sometimes even the disobedience of a mere notice may be.[12]

---

[1]   See §§ 477 and 478 for treatment of the judgments awarding possession of property, and Part II of this chapter, §§ 485 et seq., for the enforcement of money judgments.

[2]   Although it is not directly available to enforce an ordinary money judgment, the contempt remedy stands behind several of the incidental devices that are, and thus becomes at least an indirect enforcement tool for money judgments. See § 523.

[3]   Dom. Rel. Law § 245.

[4]   CPLR 5105(1).

[5]   CPLR 5105(2).

[6]   Avalon East, Inc. v. Monaghan, 43 Misc. 2d 401, 251 N.Y.S.2d 290 (Sup. Ct., New York County 1964).

[7]   Gould v. Jacobs, 44 Misc. 2d 990, 256 N.Y.S.2d 20 (Sup. Ct., New York County 1964), aff'd, 24 A.D.2d 934, 263 N.Y.S.2d 1004 (1st Dep't 1965).

[8]   Gould v. Jacobs, 44 Misc. 2d 990, 256 N.Y.S.2d 20 (Sup. Ct., New York County 1964), aff'd, 24 A.D.2d 934, 263 N.Y.S.2d 1004 (1st Dep't 1965). For general discussion of what it takes to satisfy CPLR 5105(2) as a "fiduciary" relationship, see the dissenting opinion in National Sur. Corp. v. Silver, 23 A.D.2d 398, 402, 261 N.Y.S.2d 511, 515 (1st Dep't 1965), adopted by the Court of Appeals in 17 N.Y.2d 477, 266 N.Y.S.2d 983, 214 N.E.2d 162 (1965).

[9]   CPLR 7109(b). See § 342.

[10]   CPLR 5104. The Advisory Committee intended this identity of treatment. See 3d Rep. Leg. Doc. No. 17, pp. 223, 230 (1959).

[11]   Jud. Law § 753(A)(5). See § 385.

[12]   The restraining notice of CPLR 5222, one of the devices for the enforcement of a money judgment, is an example. It requires no judicial authorization. See § 508. For the broad lists of behavior punishable as a contempt of court, see Jud. Law §§ 750, 753.

The process of contempt is sometimes used in other phases of the litigation process, not necessarily limited to final judgments and orders. The provisional remedy of preliminary injunction, for example, and its short-lived master of ceremonies, the temporary restraining order,[13] are devices wholly dependent on the contempt remedy for enforcement. And without the threat of contempt to hold over a subpoenaed person, the subpoena would lose much of its effect, especially when addressed to nonparty witnesses against whom the threat of civil sanctions within the action, such as preclusion orders and defaults, are meaningless. Even the device of an internal stay of proceedings, authorized by the CPLR in general terms and in some situations more specifically,[14] and having numerous functions, may have to depend on the ogre of contempt to deter violations.[15]

The present study, therefore, consisting of this and the next three sections, which constitute something like a mini-chapter on the contempt remedy, is relevant not exclusively to the enforcement of judgments—although the remedy does serve as the enforcement device for certain judgments—but germane as well to all of the judicial processes that have to turn to contempt for implementation. While the contempt punishment may therefore be relevant at many stages of litigation, we have placed its study here, in the enforcement chapter, as the most logical repository. Appropriate references made at its other points of relevancy lead back to this one.

In whatever instance the contempt remedy is invoked, the fact of the contempt must be established to the satisfaction of the court, and this requires a motion or proceeding of some kind. (We are not concerned here with that other variety of contempt, the one committed in the "immediate view and presence" of the court, such as insolent conduct, which is summarily punishable.)[16] The motion or proceeding that brings on the contempt application itself is taken up three sections hence. One of its key inquiries will be whether the alleged contemnor had adequate notice of the direction he was required to obey, which depends heavily on whether he was properly served with the papers containing the direction, a matter we look into now.

Whenever the disobedience of a given direction is punishable as a contempt, the party who wishes to keep the remedy available should follow closely any instructions about service of the paper that contains the direction. A subpoena, for example, must be served in the same manner as a summons.[17] A restraining notice in connection with the enforcement of a money judgment must be served in the same manner as a summons or by registered or certified mail.[18] An order to show cause containing a temporary restraining order must be served as the order itself prescribes. In each of these instances, where there is a specific direction about service, it should be followed to the letter. Some categories of judgments and orders enforceable by contempt have special service

---

[13] See §§ 327 and 330.

[14] See CPLR 2201 (treated in § 255); CPLR 3211(a)(4) (§ 262); and § 5519 (§ 535).

[15] See, e.g., Hunter v. National Transp. Co., 273 A.D. 487, 78 N.Y.S.2d 225 (1st Dep't 1948).

[16] This is known as summary contempt and usually falls under the criminal contempt category. See Jud. Law § 750(A)(1) and Katz v. Murtagh, 28 N.Y.2d 234, 321 N.Y.S.2d 104, 269 N.E.2d 816 (1971). Civil and criminal contempts are distinguished in § 482.

[17] CPLR 2303. See § 383.

[18] CPLR 5222(a).

instructions. A matrimonial judgment or order directing alimony or support, for instance, must be personally served in order to lay a contempt foundation.[19]

In El-Dehdan v. El-Dehdan,[20] the Court of Appeals outlined the elements necessary to establish civil contempt under Judiciary Law section 753 ("Power of courts to punish for civil contempts"):

First, "it must be determined that a lawful order of the court, clearly expressing an unequivocal mandate, was in effect." Second, "[i]t must appear, with reasonable certainty, that the order has been disobeyed." Third, "the party to be held in contempt must have had knowledge of the court's order, although it is not necessary that the order actually have been served upon the party." Fourth, "prejudice to the right of a party to the litigation must be demonstrated."

The plaintiff in *El-Dehdan*, a matrimonial action, sought civil contempt penalties against her spouse who failed to comply with an order requiring him to deposit in escrow the proceeds of the sale of properties which were the subject of a prior equitable distribution determination. The Court held that plaintiff met her burden by establishing the above four elements by clear and convincing evidence.

The *El-Dehdan* Court also stressed that neither Judiciary Law section 753 nor its prior caselaw impose a "willfulness" requirement for civil contempt. Judiciary Law section 750, which governs criminal contempt, does contain such a requirement as it only permits a court to impose punishment for criminal contempt for "[w]illful disobedience to its lawful mandate."[21]

If there is no special provision in point, CPLR 5104 governs the enforcement of a judgment or order by contempt. It requires that the judgment or order to be obeyed be certified[22] and that the certified copy be served on the person from whom compliance is sought.

Will defects in service of the paper to be obeyed preclude contempt punishment if the party to be served knew of the direction, from whatever source, and disobeyed it anyway? The New York cases are not in the tidiest state in this area, but the Court of Appeals has said that even the absence of service—let alone technical defects in it—is no excuse for disobedience if there was knowledge of the direction,[23] and has indicated that the knowledge can come about even by telephone.[24] Even those not parties to the action out of which an injunction arises are therefore punishable for contempt if, although aware of the injunction, they act with or under the enjoined party and disobey it.[25] Nor can an enjoined person evade contempt by procuring another to do the

---

[19]   Dom. Rel. Law § 245.

[20]   El-Dehdan v. El-Dehdan, 26 N.Y.3d 19, 29, 19 N.Y.S.3d 475, 481, 41 N.E.3d 340, 346 (2015).

[21]   Jud. Law § 750(A)(3).

[22]   Certification is not a problem today. It no longer has to be made by the clerk. The attorney can make it. CPLR 2105.

[23]   See, e.g., Daly v. Amberg, 126 N.Y. 490, 27 N.E. 1038 (1891); see also *El-Dehdan*, 26 N.Y.3d at 29, 19 N.Y.S.3d at 481, 41 N.E.3d at 346.

[24]   See McCormick v. Axelrod, 59 N.Y.2d 574, 466 N.Y.S.2d 279, 453 N.E.2d 508 (1983).

[25]   People ex rel. Stearns v. Marr, 181 N.Y. 463, 74 N.E. 431 (1905). *Stearns* says that there is no distinction between criminal and civil contempt insofar as service of the paper to be obeyed is concerned, and that for civil contempt, not even actual knowledge of the direction is needed—although it is for criminal contempt, where the element of intent is a key factor. The differences between these contempts are discussed in § 482.

proscribed thing, or by resorting to subterfuge, such as by forming a corporation to do it. Upon proof that such person is behind the scenes calling the shots, the contempt will reach him.[26]

The reader should be aware that there is also authority to the contrary: cases that take a more rigid line about service of the paper to be obeyed and that withhold the contempt punishment if service is not carried out to the letter, notwithstanding that the contemnor had knowledge.[27] As the prior footnote indicates, some courts sway back and forth on the point, but any holding disregarding knowledge and letting the contemnor off because he was not perfectly served not only conflicts with clear pronouncements of the Court of Appeals, but also encourages evasion of judicial process. The function of the contempt remedy is to uphold judicial process and the reasonable expectations of those who turn to it. Distinctions that disregard actual knowledge and turn on overly nice procedural points are not in harmony with that purpose.

As the ensuing sections show, the contempt remedy is a hard study. It demands distinctions between criminal and civil contempt; it is riddled with confused procedures under decrepit governing statutes in need of revision, but never given it. Furthermore, the statutes are made the more difficult to apply because of inconsistent judicial interpretations. Judicial trepidation to apply the remedy even in situations where it would appear to be appropriate is therefore no surprise.

This trepidation appears to have lost some of its significance in light of a more recent and less complicated tool that has been placed in the hands of the judges: the frivolity sanction, treated in depth earlier.[28] In many situations in which contempt would earlier have been the only cure, a frivolity sanction is now available, and with the judges evidently more receptive to it than they have been to the contempt device.[29]

§ 482. Criminal and Civil Contempt Distinguished; Punishment

For several purposes, it is necessary to draw a line between criminal and civil contempt.

Criminal contempt is an offense against public justice. It is designed to vindicate and uphold the authority of the judiciary. Hence the penalty for it is punitive. If the penalty is a fine, the money goes into the public treasury.

---

[26] See Mead Johnson & Co. v. Rosen, 16 A.D.2d 337, 228 N.Y.S.2d 204 (1st Dep't 1962).

[27] See, e.g., R. C. Gluck & Co. v. Tankel, 12 A.D.2d 339, 211 N.Y.S.2d 602 (1st Dep't 1961), which said that service on the attorney instead of the party is inadequate. For that proposition it cited Shakun v. Shakun, 17 Misc. 2d 935, 936, 187 N.Y.S.2d 439, 440 (Sup. Ct., Kings County 1959), which squarely held that the requirement for serving a certified copy of the judgment must be strictly obeyed and that if the service is not carried out just so, "knowledge of the judgment is immaterial." A later phase of that same case (*Shakun*) went to the appellate division, however, which said just the opposite: that actual knowledge is adequate for contempt even if service was not made. 11 A.D.2d 724, 204 N.Y.S.2d 694 (2d Dep't 1960). In 1964, after the CPLR took effect, the same court, now treating § 245 of the Dom. Rel. Law (regarding money in matrimonial actions), said that under § 245 personal service on the husband "would appear to be a prerequisite to holding him in contempt." Kohn v. Kohn, 21 A.D.2d 881, 251 N.Y.S.2d 781, 783 (2d Dep't 1964). A decade later, the court backtracked and said that service is not needed for contempt; knowledge suffices. Yorktown Central School Dist. No. 2 v. Yorktown Congress of Teachers ("YCT"), 42 A.D.2d 422, 348 N.Y.S.2d 367 (2d Dep't 1973). A distinction could perhaps be made on the ground that different subject matter and different statutes were involved from case to case, but the more candid conclusion is that the cases are just in conflict.

[28] See § 414A.

[29] See SPR 68:2.

Civil contempt is for the violation of a private right. The penalty imposed for it is designed to compensate or otherwise further the right of the party in whose favor the judicial direction was made.[1] Hence if the penalty imposed for a civil contempt is a monetary assessment, it goes to the aggrieved party. The penalty for civil contempt is designed to redress a party's right, while the penalty for criminal contempt is designed to punish the contemnor so that he will stop treading, and not tread again, on the dignity of the judicial arm of the sovereign.[2]

The same act can be both a criminal and civil contempt,[3] and often is. It's sometimes hard to tell which it is;[4] more accurately, it is often hard to tell at what point a contempt becomes a criminal one. Any disobedience of a judicial mandate that is punishable by contempt and injures the party on whose behalf the mandate issued is forthwith a civil contempt, but it does not become a criminal one until it reaches such a stage that it threatens the dignity of the court itself.[5] That is where the murky line appears.

Whether behavior has attained that level is an inquiry individual to the particular case. The reason for the distinction is historical and, today, statutory. The Judiciary Law perpetuates the distinction and appends different punishments to each class of contempt. One may criticize the distinction as overlooking the obvious—that any disobedience of a judicial mandate is an affront to the court and a threat to the system—but arguments of that kind must at this late stage be saved for the legislature. Justified or not, the differences are real.

Another difference, fostered by the U.S. Supreme Court in regard to federal mandates and influential with the New York courts on state mandates, is that punishment for criminal contempt is imposable even though it is ultimately determined that the mandate (judgment, order, etc.) should not have issued because it was improper or even beyond jurisdiction.[6] Punishment for civil contempt, on the other hand, is cancelled upon such a determination,[7] but a party advised that an order is beyond jurisdiction disobeys it at risk because he can still be visited with a criminal contempt. In New York, unfortunately, and very ironically, that prospect often lacks in terrorem impact because of the weakness of the penalties imposable for criminal contempt, as we shall shortly see.

The main catalog of conduct that qualifies as a criminal contempt in New York is contained in section 750 of the Judiciary Law. The civil contempt roster is in section 753

---

[1]   King v. Barnes, 113 N.Y. 476, 21 N.E. 182 (1889).

[2]   People v. Court of Oyer and Terminer, 101 N.Y. 245, 4 N.E. 259 (1886).

[3]   See, e.g., Beth-El Hospital, Inc. v. Davis, 231 N.Y.S.2d 635 (Sup. Ct., Kings County 1962), aff'd, 18 A.D.2d 1138, 239 N.Y.S.2d 535 (2d Dep't 1963); see § 481.

[4]   See, e.g., State v. New York Movers Tariff Bureau, Inc., 48 Misc. 2d 225, 264 N.Y.S.2d 931 (Sup. Ct., New York County 1965).

[5]   People ex rel. Stearns v. Marr, 181 N.Y. 463, 74 N.E. 431 (1905).

[6]   The major federal case is U.S. v. United Mine Workers of America, 330 U.S. 258, 67 S. Ct. 677, 91 L. Ed. 884 (1947), admitting as the singular exception (where even criminal contempt would be cancelled) only the case in which the power to make the mandate is not even arguably within the lower court's power. For the New York law, see Mount Sinai Hospital, Inc. v. Davis, 8 A.D.2d 361, 188 N.Y.S.2d 298 (1st Dep't 1959). It is obviously only an appellate court that can determine that lower court jurisdiction was lacking; the party therefore must, at the risk of criminal contempt, obey the mandate at least until an appellate court so determines.

[7]   Bachman v. Harrington, 184 N.Y. 458, 77 N.E. 657 (1906).

of that law,[8] in CPLR 5104, and in diverse other places.[9] Some of the distinctions between criminal and civil contempt were emphasized by the Court of Appeals in El-Dehdan v. El-Dehdan,[10] discussed in the prior section.

Presumably the criminal contempt—the variety of contempt that at least sounds more serious—would carry the more severe punishment. Not so in New York. Criminal contempt against an individual is in almost all instances punishable by a fine of not more than $1,000 or by jail for not more than 30 days, or both[11]—an astounding situation. It confronts a criminal contemnor with a price he can usually afford and at worst the prospect of a month's confinement. The civil contempt penalty, incongruously, has sharper teeth and supplies the higher incentive to obey New York judicial process.

Civil contempt carries as a fine any sum that will indemnify the injured party for the actual loss caused by the contempt.[12] The fine must be measured by the injury caused to the contempt's victims and not by the nature of the contempt. It must be formulated "not to punish an offender, but solely to compensate or indemnify private complainants."[13] Damages must be proved by the injured party and can include an attorney's fee.[14] Absent proof of damages, the party gets only costs plus an arbitrary $250.[15] The nature and extent of the punishment necessarily depends on the facts of the individual case and rests largely in the court's discretion.[16] The punishment in the case of a civil contempt can also include jail, and the term of it is not limited if the mandate calls for the doing of an act which the contemnor still has the power to do. He can be jailed until he does it.[17] Where, for example, a woman wilfully refused to obey a court order directing that she stop concealing a child and produce him in court, she was kept in jail a year and even more while her refusal persisted.[18] Confinement in that situation is coercive rather than punitive. When the jailing is for a contempt for the doing of a forbidden act which now can't be undone, or for some other past recalcitrance, it is punitive and is limited to six months.[19] Here, too, the jailing is not necessarily alternative, but can be additional to a compensatory assessment.

---

[8]   See § 481.

[9]   CPLR 5251, for example, imposes contempt as the remedy for the disobedience of several of the devices of Article 52 used in the enforcement of money judgments.

[10]   El-Dehdan v. El-Dehdan, 26 N.Y.3d 19, 29, 19 N.Y.S.3d 475, 481, 41 N.E.3d 340, 346 (2015).

[11]   Jud. Law § 751(1). Fines in the case of contumacious unions or hospitals (as opposed to individuals) are not arbitrarily limited and can be substantial. Jud. Law § 751(2), (3). Criminal contempt of the kind under discussion here is also a crime and may be prosecuted as such, Penal Law §§ 215.50, 215.51, leading to more prolonged imprisonment and greater fines, see, e.g., Penal Law §§ 70.00, 70.15, 80.05, 80.10, but prosecutions of this kind are obviously more cumbersome than the proceedings authorized by the Judiciary Law, are not frequent, and are hence not a robust deterrent to criminal contempt of court. Penal Law § 215.54 provides that an adjudication of criminal contempt under Jud. Law § 750(A) does not bar a Penal Law prosecution for it, but that the previous punishment shall be considered by the court before sentence. There is also the possibility, of course, that the second proceeding will be barred on grounds of double jeopardy.

[12]   Jud. Law § 773.

[13]   State v. Unique Ideas, Inc., 44 N.Y.2d 345, 405 N.Y.S.2d 656, 376 N.E.2d 1301 (1978).

[14]   Quantum Heating Services Inc. v. Austern, 121 A.D.2d 437, 503 N.Y.S.2d 137 (2d Dep't 1986).

[15]   Jud.L. § 773. See Levine v. 97 Realty Corp., 21 A.D.2d 655, 249 N.Y.S.2d 715 (1st Dep't 1964).

[16]   In re Hildreth, 28 A.D.2d 290, 284 N.Y.S.2d 755 (1st Dep't 1967).

[17]   Jud. Law § 774(1).

[18]   People ex rel. Feldman v. Warden, New York City Correctional Institute for Women, 46 A.D.2d 256, 362 N.Y.S.2d 171 (1st Dep't 1974), aff'd, 36 N.Y.2d 846, 370 N.Y.S.2d 913, 331 N.E.2d 691 (1975).

[19]   Jud. Law § 774(1).

The imposition of a jail sentence as a punitive rather than coercive measure for a civil contempt poses constitutional issues. Must the proof on the contempt application be established beyond a reasonable doubt, for example, the criminal standard? The courts have been troubled by this.[20] The application often seeks punishment for both categories of contempt, however, and insofar as a punitive jailing may be called for, the criminal aspect of the application, properly processed, supports it and enables the court to sidestep the issue in its civil aspect.[21]

All jailings for contempt must be reviewed at intervals of not more than 90 days.[22]

§ 483. Constitutionality of Contempt Procedure

The next section will discuss the procedure for invoking the contempt punishment, but in order to avoid encumbering it with constitutional issues, we address the constitutional points in this section and leave the next one to do its job uncluttered.

Because contempt proceedings can lead to fines and jailings, they must meet minimal constitutional standards analogous to those met and discussed in the provisional remedies.[1] As they stood before 1977, the New York contempt procedures, which are contained in Article 19 of the Judiciary Law, did not on their face meet those standards, or so a three-judge federal district court[2] held in Vail v. Quinlan.[3] Under the name of Juidice v. Vail, however, that decision was reversed by the U.S. Supreme Court[4] with instructions that the district court on remand not entertain the case, i.e., that it "abstain" under the doctrine of Younger v. Harris.[5]

The *Younger* doctrine requires, in the interests of federalism and comity, that the federal courts not interfere unduly with the states' administration of their laws when the area is one of sensitive state interest and when there is an adequate opportunity for a prompt and thorough airing of all the issues in the state court itself. Review of federal issues by the U.S. Supreme Court is preserved in that instance by letting the case go through the state system to the highest state court, from which review can then be sought from the U.S. Supreme Court.[6]

---

[20] See the majority and dissenting opinions in N.A. Development Co. Ltd. v. Jones, 99 A.D.2d 238, 472 N.Y.S.2d 363 (1st Dep't 1984). A discussion of the constitutionality of the contempt procedure when a warrant has issued for the seizure of the contemnor appears in § 483.

[21] This happened in *Jones*, 99 A.D.2d at 238, 472 N.Y.S.2d at 363, in which the dissenting justices complain with good reason that the Judiciary Law's contempt provisions "are long overdue for legislative review and revision."

[22] See Jud. Law § 774(2), CPLR 2308(c). Provision is made for notice to other parties to the action out of which the contempt arose. For the moment when each 90-day period starts to run, see People ex rel. Oppenheimer v. Rosoff, 82 Misc. 2d 199, 368 N.Y.S.2d 969 (Sup. Ct., New York County 1975).

[1] See §§ 307, 315, and 338.

[2] A "three-judge district court" was a special ad hoc panel set up to hear (among other things) an action to enjoin the enforcement of a state statute on grounds of repugnancy to the Federal Constitution. Congress in 1976 abolished the three-judge court system in all but a few instances, leaving these matters to the usual one-judge district court. See Pub. L. 94–381, Aug. 12, 1976, 90 Stat. 1119, repealing 28 U.S.C.A. §§ 2281 and 2282 and amending 2284.

[3] Vail v. Quinlan, 406 F. Supp. 951 (S.D.N.Y. 1976).

[4] Juidice v. Vail, 430 U.S. 327, 97 S. Ct. 1211, 51 L. Ed. 2d 376 (1977).

[5] Younger v. Harris, 401 U.S. 37, 91 S. Ct. 746, 27 L. Ed. 2d 669 (1971). The federal abstention doctrines in general are treated in § 613 (Practitioner's Edition).

[6] See 28 U.S.C.A. § 1257.

The major objection voiced by the district court was that one of the possibilities under the New York contempt procedures was that at some point or another an alleged contemnor could be arrested by the sheriff and incarcerated without a hearing.[7] The district court indicated that if the seizure of the contemnor were solely for the purpose of bringing him to court for a hearing, before incarceration, the procedures might pass muster. Tacit in the U.S. Supreme Court's reversal of the district court was that, even assuming a preincarceration hearing is constitutionally mandated, such a requirement might be interpolated by the state courts if given a chance to review the matter themselves. Indeed, the New York courts proved ready to do just that,[8] and interpolation in this fashion had many times in the past been recognized as a way of avoiding due process objections.[9]

The problem was in any event abated in 1977 legislation which provided that when an arrest is made pursuant to a warrant issued in a contempt proceeding, the warrant must command the sheriff to bring the defendant "forthwith" before the court.[10]

In many cases, the contemnor had already been given opportunities for a hearing and adequate notice in connection with each of them, but disregarded them all. The district court attitude in *Vail* was: no matter, due process requires an actual hearing before imprisonment, not just an opportunity. The U.S. Supreme Court, in reversing, was at pains to refute that. It stressed the many opportunities the contemnor in *Vail* had already had for a hearing but had ignored: he was given notice of the underlying action itself, a minor money claim against him, and defaulted; after a default judgment was entered and a subpoena served on him to elicit data about his assets[11] he ignored the subpoena, which was his second default; when contempt proceedings were thereupon instituted for disobedience of the subpoena, by an order to show cause offering him yet another hearing opportunity, he ignored that as well, and that was default number three. Only afterwards did the next step, the warrant of arrest, issue. By observing that the contemnor "had ignored for a period of nine months every stage of the state court proceedings"[12] and forfeited one opportunity after another for a hearing, the U.S. Supreme Court, although concluding only to direct the district court to abstain and let the state courts have a go at the issues, was hinting as closely as it could, without actually deciding, that the New York statutes even as then constituted were not offensive to due process.

Therein lies the important constitutional lesson of the *Vail* case: a general admonition that an opportunity for a hearing, rather than an actual one, is all that due process requires. There may still be occasions for testing that proposition under New York law, but it is not likely be in the contempt area. The 1977 contempt legislation appears to contemplate that even when arrest results—previous hearing opportunities

---

[7] Section 757 of the Judiciary Law, as then constituted, authorized the court, upon issuance of a warrant, to direct the sheriff to arrest the defendant and bring him before the court "either" forthwith or at a later time.

[8] See, e.g., Walker v. Walker, 51 A.D.2d 1029, 381 N.Y.S.2d 310 (2d Dep't 1976).

[9] See National Equipment Rental, Limited v. Szukhent, 375 U.S. 311, 84 S. Ct. 411, 11 L. Ed. 2d 354, 7 Fed. R. Serv. 2d 23 (1964), distinguishing but seeming more to overrule Wuchter v. Pizzutti, 276 U.S. 13, 48 S. Ct. 259, 72 L. Ed. 446, 57 A.L.R. 1230 (1928). See also Agur v. Wilson, 498 F.2d 961 (2d Cir. 1974), cert. den. 419 U.S. 1072, 95 S.Ct. 661, 42 L.Ed.2d 669 (1974).

[10] L.1977, ch. 437, amending Jud. Law §§ 772, 773.

[11] The subpoena was issued pursuant to CPLR 5224. See § 509.

[12] *Vail*, 430 U.S. at 330, 97 S.Ct. at 1214.

having been ignored or not—the next stop must generally be the courthouse if there has not already been a hearing. Jail is to follow only if the judge, after hearing the contemnor, orders it, and that satisfies the demands of due process.

§ 484. Procedure to Punish for Contempt

If the alleged contemnor was not a party to the action out of which the contempt arises, it has been held that the application to punish for contempt must take the form of a special proceeding.[1] If the alleged contemnor was a party, the more usual situation, the procedure to punish for contempt is a motion,[2] which may be brought on by the usual notice of motion or by the alternative of an order to show cause.[3] As a mere motion, it should bear the caption of the action or proceeding out of which the contempt arises and should ordinarily be sought from the court in the county in which the action or proceeding was brought.[4]

Specifically designated a motion, the application should not, as long as the contemnor was a party, be deemed a separate special proceeding, unless perhaps it seeks to punish a contempt emanating from a non-judicial proceeding, such as one before an administrative agency. In that instance, there would be no pending court action or proceeding to supply the context for a motion. If denominated a motion in such an instance, and it is found that a special proceeding would have been the proper form (and of course assuming that jurisdiction over the alleged contemnor has been secured), the motion should simply be converted into a special proceeding, or, indeed, merely be deemed one.[5]

If an ordinary notice of motion is used, the motion must be made on no fewer than 10 and no more than 30 days notice. The notice must also contain on its face, in at least eight-point boldface type in capital letters, this admonition: WARNING: YOUR FAILURE TO APPEAR IN COURT MAY RESULT IN YOUR IMMEDIATE ARREST AND IMPRISONMENT FOR CONTEMPT OF COURT.[6] The papers must be served on the contemnor himself unless the court directs service on his attorney (which ordinarily means that an order to show cause is being used).[7] Actually the applicant probably does best to serve copies of the motion papers on attorney and client both.

How shall the papers be served? All the applicable statute[8] says is that the papers bringing on a contempt motion "shall be served" on the party. This has been held to mean that ordinary mail service will do; that personal delivery is not required.[9] At least that

---

1   Long Island Trust Co. v. Rosenberg, 82 A.D.2d 591, 442 N.Y.S.2d 563 (2d Dep't 1981). The procedure in special proceedings is governed by Article 4 of the CPLR, treated in §§ 547 et seq.

2   Jud. Law § 756.

3   Before 1977, the show cause procedure had to be used exclusively. Jud. Law § 757 and Dom. Rel. Law § 245 so required. Amendments of those statutes in L.1977, ch. 437, made the show cause procedure a mere alternative, as it is for motions generally.

4   See Shapiro v. Shapiro, 60 Misc. 2d 622, 303 N.Y.S.2d 565 (Sup. Ct., Queens County 1969).

5   See CPLR 103(c); § 4.

6   Jud. Law § 756.

7   Jud. Law § 761.

8   Jud. Law § 761.

9   New York Higher Ed. Assistance Corp. v. Cooper, 65 A.D.2d 906, 410 N.Y.S.2d 687 (3d Dep't 1978).

is so of civil contempt.[10] With criminal contempt, some courts require personal service.[11] The lawyer who wants to tie up all loose ends in any doubtful situation should use the personal service alternative. It is worth remembering that the judges are not anxious to impose the contempt punishment and that procedural defects that may be deemed harmless in other contexts can prove destructive in this one: a convenient hook for a hesitant judge to hang his hat on.

Upon the motion's return, recognizing that a fine or imprisonment may be imposed, statute requires the judge to advise the contemnor that she has the right to counsel. If the contemnor cannot afford counsel, the court may in its discretion assign counsel.[12]

The court must determine whether the alleged contemnor is guilty of the contempt charged and, if he is, what kind of contempt it is and what the punishment will be. If there is a factual dispute as to D's conduct unresolvable from the papers on the motion, a hearing will be necessary and will investigate all relevant factors. The statute requires a hearing,[13] and the right to a hearing would in any event be implied.[14]

An issue of fact requiring a trial does not necessarily require a trial by jury. The general rule, in fact, has been held to be that neither category of contempt, civil or criminal, requires trial by jury for historical reasons,[15] and the Court of Appeals has confirmed that even for criminal contempt a trial by jury is not mandatory because the potential imprisonment upon conviction (30 days) falls into the "petty" category under applicable U.S. Supreme Court standards.[16]

If the contempt arises in connection with a procedure under the CPLR for the enforcement of a judgment,[17] a showing that the contemnor—the judgment debtor in this instance—has not the means to comply requires a denial of the application to punish. The denial is of course without prejudice to renewal upon proof that the debtor's financial condition has changed.[18]

---

[10] See the discussion in Department of Housing Preservation and Development v. Arick, 131 Misc. 2d 950, 503 N.Y.S.2d 489 (N.Y. City Civ. Ct. 1986), cited approvingly in Department of Housing Preservation and Development of City of New York v. 24 West 132 Equities, Inc., 137 Misc. 2d 459, 524 N.Y.S.2d 324 (App. Term, 1st Dep't 1987), aff'd, 150 A.D.2d 181, 540 N.Y.S.2d 711 (1st Dep't 1989), before being reversed on just a timeliness point in 137 Misc.2d 1079, 526 N.Y.S.2d 51 (App. Term, 1st Dep't 1988).

[11] See, e.g., Lu v. Betancourt, 116 A.D.2d 492, 496 N.Y.S.2d 754 (1st Dep't 1986). A detailed treatment of the subject, noting departmental differences, appears in the *Arick* case, 131 Misc.2d at 950, 503 N.Y.S.2d at 489.

[12] Jud. Law § 770.

[13] Jud. Law § 772. See CPLR 2218, made applicable to the contempt application by Jud. Law § 772's adoption of general motion practice. It authorizes the immediate trial of any issues of fact arising on the motion.

[14] See Agur v. Wilson, 498 F.2d 961 (2d Cir. 1974), cert. den. 419 U.S. 1072, 95 S.Ct. 661, 42 L.Ed.2d 669 (1974).

[15] See Department of Housing Preservation and Development of City of New York v. Chance Equities, Inc., 135 Misc. 2d 375, 515 N.Y.S.2d 709 (N.Y. City Civ. Ct. 1987).

[16] See Rankin on Behalf of Bd. of Ed. of City of New York v. Shanker, 23 N.Y.2d 111, 295 N.Y.S.2d 625, 242 N.E.2d 802 (1968), and Morgenthau v. Erlbaum, 59 N.Y.2d 143, 464 N.Y.S.2d 392, 451 N.E.2d 150 (1983), discussing the applicable constitutional requirements and how New York procedures fare under them.

[17] These procedures arise under Article 52 of the CPLR, governing the enforcement of money judgments. Some of the devices supplied by Article 52 are enforced by the contempt penalty under CPLR 5251. See § 523.

[18] Jud. Law § 770. Reference to the offender's financial condition implies applicability only to money judgments. Other judgments are also backed by the contempt penalty, however. See CPLR 5104; § 481.

An order adjudging a person in contempt may be made conditional, i.e., "unless" the contemnor does a particular thing or makes a specified payment within a stated time.[19] This affords the contemnor a chance to purge the contempt.

When the contempt arises out of a procedure for the enforcement of a judgment, including a direction for the payment of money under a matrimonial judgment or order, a special purging procedure is offered even if the contemnor does not respond to the contempt motion. The court in that case is required to make a conditional commitment order, the condition being that the contemnor purge the contempt within 10 days after being personally served with the order. If the 10-day period lapses without performance, as proved by an affidavit furnished to the court, a warrant may now be issued by the court directing the arrest of the contemnor. Upon that arrest, in fulfillment of constitutional requirements, the contemnor will be brought forthwith to court to be heard.[20] If the punishment includes a fine, a similar 10-day conditional purging order is permissible, and the court may in its discretion include a provision requiring the contemnor to supply an undertaking conditioned upon his paying the fine and performing any act required by the judgment or order.[21]

If the contemnor appears on the return day of the original contempt motion, and the facts are thereupon determined and establish the contempt to the satisfaction of the court, the punishment imposed need not be conditional.

All of the foregoing should be taken to apply whether the contempt involved is of the civil or criminal variety. The statutes supplying the procedural instruction, despite their 1977 amendment and improvement, assume their applicability only to civil contempt,[22] but they would appear to apply to criminal contempt as well. Since the distinctions between civil and criminal contempt are based on the conduct that constitutes the contempt and the nature of the punishment to be imposed for it, there should be little difference in the procedural steps by which the contemptuous conduct is proved and the punishment imposed.[23] Perhaps we may be allowed to pause here to observe that the need constantly to deduce and infer and extrapolate in order to make sense of the Judiciary Law's contempt provisions gives credence to the observation made in N.A. Development Co. Ltd. v. Jones:[24] that the Judiciary Law's contempt provisions "are long overdue for legislative review and revision."

Although the mechanics for invoking the punishment should be the same whether the offense involved is civil or criminal or both,[25] the contempt proceeding itself has been held to be of a civil nature. To make this point clear, the Court of Appeals has used words to the effect that criminal contempt arising out of a civil action "constitutes a civil special

---

[19]   See, e.g., Denberg v. Denberg, 21 A.D.2d 863, 251 N.Y.S.2d 90 (1st Dep't 1964).

[20]   Jud. Law § 772.

[21]   Jud. Law § 773.

[22]   See, e.g., Jud. Law §§ 756, 761.

[23]   See Jud. Law § 751(1), which clearly applies only to criminal contempt. Section 754 provides that any contempt other than one committed in the immediate view and presence of the court (which is what is commonly known as "summary" contempt) may be punished only after the party charged is notified and given a reasonable opportunity to defend. The procedures supplied in this and subsequent sections of the Judiciary Law, which have grounded discussion up to this point, are the most obvious as well as the most convenient source of procedural guidance for the criminal contempt application notwithstanding their reference to civil contempt.

[24]   N.A. Development Co. Ltd. v. Jones, 99 A.D.2d 238, 245, 472 N.Y.S.2d 363, 368 (1st Dep't 1984) (Sandler, J., dissenting).

[25]   See People ex rel. Stearns v. Marr, 181 N.Y. 463, 74 N.E. 431 (1905).

proceeding."[26] The intent was to require that rules of civil rather than criminal procedure govern the criminal contempt application; it was not intended to require that the application be treated as an independent special proceeding—as opposed to a mere motion—but some courts have been led to that anyway.[27] If the clerk treats it as a separate proceeding, he may insist on a separate index number and filing fee. Even so, it has been held that the failure to secure the number in advance is curable nunc pro tunc without loss of jurisdiction.[28] Ordinarily the application should not be treated as a distinct proceeding. At least as against one who was a party to the underlying action or proceeding, it should be considered a mere motion arising out of that action or proceeding. This is what section 756 of the Judiciary Law obviously intends by authorizing the motion procedure. Having the context of the original action or proceeding, the motion should need no new file number (or filing fee).

We noted at the end of section 481 that the judges' trepidation about imposing the contempt penalty appears to have lost some of its significance in light of the more recent adoption of the sanctions rule, Part 130, treated in depth in section 414A earlier; that in many situations in which contempt would earlier have been the only cure, a frivolity sanction is now available, and with the judges apparently more comfortable with it. There may even be an interplay between the two categories, as in Astrada v. Archer.[29]

A lawyer in *Astrada* had been found guilty of frivolous conduct and fined the maximum penal sum allowed under the rule, $10,000. Of special note is that the court imposed the punishment and fine on its own motion, reciting at the very outset of the decision that there are "no appearances" on this application; that this was a "sua sponte Order by the Court." The fine was directed to be paid into the Lawyer's Fund for Client Protection, to which the court sent a copy of the decision. Several months later, after the Fund advised that the money had not been received, the court held the lawyer in contempt.

---

[26]   See Douglas v. Adel, 269 N.Y. 144, 146, 199 N.E. 35, 36 (1935).

[27]   See, e.g., Board of Ed. of City School Dist. of City of New Rochelle v. Zeluck, 60 Misc. 2d 1090, 304 N.Y.S.2d 697 (Sup. Ct., Westchester County 1969).

[28]   See In re Lakeland Federation of Teachers, Local 1760, 65 Misc. 2d 397, 317 N.Y.S.2d 902 (Sup. Ct., Westchester County 1971) (decided prior to adoption of commencement by filing system).

[29]   Astrada v. Archer, N.Y.L.J., Dec. 4, 2008, at 27, col. 3 (Sup. Ct., Kings County; Schack, J.) (SPR 205:4).

PART II. ENFORCEMENT OF MONEY JUDGMENTS

A. IN GENERAL

Table of Sections

§ 485.   Enforcement of Money Judgments, Introductory

§ 485. Enforcement of Money Judgments, Introductory

The money judgment dominates the area of "enforcement of judgments." This is so for two reasons. The first, as we saw in Part I of this chapter, is that the enforcement of the non-money judgment is a less complicated affair, usually involving but a single device, while the money judgment can involve many. Even when contempt is sought, which can entail the issuance of a warrant and the arresting and jailing of the defendant, the enforcement road of a non-money judgment is seldom a long one. The second reason is that there are many more money judgments seeking enforcement than there are other kinds. Article 52 governs the enforcement of the money judgment.

Ironically, in what is probably the most numerous category of money action today, the personal injury tort, enforcement is less frequently an issue. Since the defendant's liability is most often backed by insurance, the plaintiff's quest is to get the judgment; the insurer sooner or later makes it good, of course limited by the amount of the insurance policy, and this often obviates enforcement. But in commercial, property, and matrimonial cases and, indeed, uninsured tort cases or those in which damages exceed the defendant's insurance coverage, enforcement is a frequent problem.

The structure of Article 52 resembles that of Article 31, the CPLR's disclosure article. The opening section, CPLR 5201, tells us what property of the defendant may be applied to the judgment, just as CPLR 3101 lists the basic disclosure criteria. CPLR 5201 also carves out some exceptions, which 3101 does, too. Most of the rest of Article 52 is devoted to supplying a series of devices to aid enforcement (as Article 31 supplies a series of devices to aid disclosure) and such other items as the ordering of liens and priorities. The two articles even have in common a "protective order." CPLR 5240 does for Article 52 and the enforcement devices what CPLR 3103 does for Article 31 and the disclosure devices: it sets forth in one place an omnibus judicial power to intervene in the use of any device so as to prevent, on a case by case basis, any unjustified harassment or oppression. This frees Article 52 to supply each device without having to incorporate protective or punitive provisions at every turn.

Lawyers bent on familiarizing themselves with the enforcement of judgments should make a general study of each of the devices and its particular function. Only by knowing the function of all of them can they make an intelligent choice of which one to use in a given situation, and the situations are endlessly variable.

If the judgment debtor has no assets whatever, and no job or other income source, Article 52 offers no comfort. The law can draw no blood from a stone. But if the debtor does have leviable property or income, however ingeniously he has tried to conceal it, imagination and effort brought to bear by the lawyer should be able with Article 52's aid to identify and get through to the property. The legislature has tried in Article 52 to produce a series of devices designed, alone or in combination, to cover the field. There are ways to reach possessory interests when title is lacking, and ownership when the right to possession is lacking; to get at tangibles hands can touch, and intangibles as incorporeal as a cause of action; to obtain property in plain view so that a sheriff can levy, and property concealed so that it must first be sought out and then the debtor made to produce it. There is a tool to reach income to a limited percentage, and a tool to reach more of the income when it is clear that the debtor can afford more. The fact that there is income may be plain, or deducible from a state of facts. There are devices for property that needs to be retained and managed in order to be valuable, and property whose value can be realized only through sale; for property with worth that a public auction can exploit, and property that requires a private sale; for property that can be seized immediately, and property that can be reached only later; for property the debtor has herself, and property that is hers but is held by another; and on and on. Further, the creditor may know nothing at all about the debtor's assets and finances to begin with, and may need assistance to find out about them or about a third person who controls the asset.

For all of these situations Article 52, through one or a mixture of its devices, has aid to give. By having a general picture of all of the devices—briefly listed in a later section[1] and then treated individually—the lawyer can quickly identify the situations appropriate to each of them.

The moment as of which the judgment becomes enforceable is the moment of its entry. As a general rule, the judgment creditor may then dive into Article 52 and extract whichever devices suit her particular purpose. There is no priority in the use of the devices. No device is a condition precedent to the use of any other; the sequence of their use is for the judgment creditor to decide. Nor is there any general limit on the number of times a single device may be used. If abuse arises, the cure is an ad hoc protective order under CPLR 5240.

To the general rule that a judgment creditor is entitled to seek enforcement of a money judgment immediately upon entry and, for its full sum, is an important exception enacted in the mid-1980s for the periodic rather than lump sum payment of portions of certain tort judgments. Popularly known as the "structured judgment," it is embodied in two articles of the CPLR, Article 50–A for medical, dental, and podiatric malpractice actions, and Article 50–B for all other personal injury, injury to property, and wrongful death actions.[2]

The main limitation on the use of the enforcement devices to aid the collection of a money judgment is, as one might suspect, money. Some of the devices involve substantial lawyering, which means they will be costly to the judgment creditor. Depositions to aid disclosure, motions seeking orders of one kind or another, dealings with the enforcement officer, and other steps in pursuit of an elusive judgment debtor can be expensive. If their cost is disproportionate to the amount of the judgment being enforced, the creditor may have to abandon enforcement for reasons of simple economics. This is a misfortune to the judgment creditor and an unflattering comment on the system, but it is really only

---

[1] See § 492.

[2] Article 50–A appeared in 1985. Article 50–B, which followed in 1986, was almost identical to Article 50–A and could easily have been integrated with Article 50–A instead of being made a separate article. The two as originally enacted are compared and the few paltry differences between them at the time are noted in the Commentaries on McKinney's CPLR Articles 50–A and 50–B. Article 50–A was amended in 2003 in some important particulars. These are discussed in the extensive 2003 Supplementary Practice Commentaries of Thomas F. Gleason on McKinney's CPLR Article 50–A.

the enforcement phase of a more serious problem needing legislative attention: ready and reasonably priced access to court and counsel by all.

If the judgment creditor emerges from a strenuous enforcement effort without having satisfied the judgment, and the judgment debtor does have assets that might have been applied to the judgment, the fault will not lie with Article 52 for having failed to supply appropriate aids; it will likely be attributable to the economic unfeasibility of pursuing those aids any further. If the stakes are high enough, though, and the hope of realizing on the judgment is real, Article 52 will not be found wanting.

Just as economics may dictate whether a significant effort may be made to pursue the debtor at all, so will it also dictate how far a creditor wants the pursuit to go. From one point of view, the enforcement of judgments is the place to which most other law topics ultimately lead. The assumption is that if the plaintiff has a right and the right is pursued to judgment, it only remains to get the judgment enforced. But there are several subjects, which follow rather than precede the enforcement of judgments, that the judgment creditor should have in mind during or even before the enforcement journey.

A judgment creditor may find that she is not alone in pursuit of the debtor, who may be in such financial extremis that his creditors are legion. At this point the topic becomes what law school curricula often denominated "creditors' rights," a battleground that determines priorities in the assets of a declining debtor. If the progression continues, the law and the law schools also have a name for the next topic: "bankruptcy." The "enforcement" topic can lead to these other two, which are studies in themselves and beyond the scope of Article 52, but that they lurk just around the corner warns the judgment creditor to be sensitive about the debtor's economic status; pressing the judgment debtor too far, especially when others are also pressing, can result in the creditor's collecting a good deal less than a little patience earlier on might have earned, or nothing at all. Sometimes accepting less than the law technically authorizes, or letting the judgment debtor stretch payments over a longer period than the law requires, is the more provident course. The enforcement of judgments is ruled by pragmatists. Theoreticians have no fun at this party.

The main groupings in the ensuing study will be property subject to enforcement, the devices available to get at the property, liens and priorities in the property, and protective orders. With other incidents integrated at appropriate junctures, that will be the progression.

B. PROPERTY SUBJECT TO ENFORCEMENT

Table of Sections

§ 486.   Property Applicable to the Judgment, Introductory
§ 487.   Examples of Leviable Property Rights
§ 488.   Creditor Stands in Debtor's Shoes
§ 489.   Contingent Intangibles
§ 490.   Exemptions
§ 491.   Proper Garnishee

§ 486. Property Applicable to the Judgment, Introductory

The general rule under the CPLR is that any property interest of a judgment debtor, which by law the debtor may assign or transfer, may be sought for application to the judgment. The rule is embodied in subdivision (b) of CPLR 5201. It recognizes the futility of trying to list specifically all of a person's possible property interests in an age when "property" takes on so many varied and often sophisticated forms.

This standard is a decided improvement over the old Civil Practice Act, which, in trying to supply such a list, found itself on a quest without end.[3] Property rights and interests are as variable as the human engagements that create them, and just as extensive. The CPLR wisely abandons any effort to identify them all and says instead that any property interest the judgment debtor has, other than that rare sort that the law has made unassignable, may be appropriated and applied to the judgment, no matter how difficult the steps needed to accomplish the application. Problems in getting through to the property and realizing on it are the reason for the CPLR's broad variety of enforcement devices. These, with some imagination and initiative, will usually be found to supply what is needed. Property real and property personal; property tangible and property intangible; debts owed and debts claimed; present interests and future interests—for all of these there are ways and means available. For the moment, we ask only what property is worth pursuing. The mechanics of the pursuit come later.

Most property interests are assignable. The most significant interest that is not is a cause of action the judgment debtor has against a third person for personal injuries,[4] as where the judgment debtor has been involved in an accident and has not yet recovered on a claim for damages arising out of it. But the courts have made a distinction between the transfer of the personal injury claim itself, which is not permitted, and the transfer of the potential proceeds of the claim, which are.[5] The judgment creditor may therefore pursue the proceeds,[6] which become leviable when the judgment debtor wins judgment or obtains a settlement in the personal injury suit.

A second inquiry the judgment creditor must make is whether the particular property is exempt from seizure. Some property, mainly the basics of domestic life, is statutorily insulated from the owner's creditors. We will come back to this later with a treatment of the CPLR's exemption lists.[7]

A third inquiry must be made in the event the property interest to be pursued is a "debt" allegedly owed to the judgment debtor, or a cause of action the debtor has against a third person. Interests of that nature, which are of course intangible, are supposedly leviable only if "past due or . . . yet to become due, certainly or upon demand."[8] This is designed to avoid judicial involvement with intangibles that may never ripen into a

---

[3]   See, e.g., §§ 687, 687–a, and 688 of the Civ. Prac. Act (repealed 1963).

[4]   Gen. Oblig. Law § 13–101.

[5]   See Grossman v. Schlosser, 19 A.D.2d 893, 244 N.Y.S.2d 749 (2d Dep't 1963). For a more extended discussion of the general differences between assignment of a claim and assignment of its proceeds, see Stathos v. Murphy, 26 A.D.2d 500, 276 N.Y.S.2d 727 (1st Dep't 1966), aff'd, 19 N.Y.2d 883, 281 N.Y.S.2d 81, 227 N.E.2d 880 (1967).

[6]   Iguanti v. Kronish, 52 Misc. 2d 306, 276 N.Y.S.2d 130 (Sup. Ct., Bronx County 1966).

[7]   See § 490.

[8]   CPLR 5201(a).

significant property right, as where they depend on a contingency that may never occur. This category of excluded property has been a problem for the New York courts.[9]

Examples of property rights, both obvious and subtle, that are pursuable (as a matter of law) and worth pursuing (as a matter of economics) will appear in the course of the next few sections.

There is an interplay here between attachment and execution. Any property interest applicable to the satisfaction of a judgment is also applicable to a prejudgment order of attachment.[10] But rather than list separately the property on which the provisional remedy of attachment may be levied, the CPLR concentrates all attention—and avoids needless duplication—on post-judgment enforcement, afterwards making the fruits of the whole project available for attachment as well in a simply worded statute, CPLR 6202, which provides that "[a]ny debt or property against which a money judgment may be enforced as provided in section 5201 is subject to attachment." The main difference between the two is that the purpose of the attachment is to keep the property out of the debtor's hands for the time being, not to convert it to money for payment over to the plaintiff, while conversion and payment are very much the purpose of the post-judgment enforcement devices.

Recognizing that under the CPLR the same property interests lend themselves to prejudgment attachment and post-judgment enforcement indifferently, cases involving either are cited interchangeably throughout the chapter.

In this connection, the category of quasi in rem jurisdiction should be remembered. In that category a plaintiff finding New York property of a nondomiciliary defendant tries to use it as a jurisdictional basis to try a claim against the defendant in a New York court and secure a judgment good to the extent of the property even without personal jurisdiction of the defendant. That category of jurisdiction was vastly reduced by the U.S. Supreme Court in Shaffer v. Heitner[11] in 1977. Many of the cases clarifying property interests of one kind or another[12] involved this jurisdictional use of the attachment. These cases are still good law on the subject of leviable property, but ironically, their future utility for jurisdictional attachments—the very realm that produced them—is much curtailed.

§ 487.   Examples of Leviable Property Rights

Tangible real or personal property owned outright by the defendant and not within any of the exemption provisions can of course be applied to the judgment, but so can a myriad of other interests. Title to the property is reachable even if the right of possession has been partly divested; the encumbered right of title can be sold for whatever a buyer is willing to pay for it. Conversely, a present right of possession may be levied on even if a right of repossession or outright title lies elsewhere[1] as long as the right, however

---

    [9]   See § 489.

    [10]   The provisional remedy of attachment was treated in an earlier chapter. See §§ 313 et seq.

    [11]   Shaffer v. Heitner, 433 U.S. 186, 97 S. Ct. 2569, 53 L. Ed. 2d 683 (1977). The *Shaffer* case, including the few instances in which it still allows quasi in rem use of an attachment, is treated in § 104.

    [12]   See, e.g., ABKCO Industries, Inc. v. Apple Films, Inc., 39 N.Y.2d 670, 385 N.Y.S.2d 511, 350 N.E.2d 899 (1976). The *ABKCO* case is discussed at length in § 489, which is concerned with contingent intangible interests of a judgment debtor and their availability to creditors.

    [1]   See General Motors Acceptance Corp. v. Maloney, 46 Misc. 2d 251, 259 N.Y.S.2d 211 (Sup. Ct., Queens County 1965).

limited, has anything of economic value that might entice a buyer. If it lacks at least that value, it will be useless to the judgment creditor not as a matter of law, but as a matter of economics. Indeed, appraisal of the particular interest is an important preliminary for the judgment creditor, lest she go to needless expense in pursuit of what turns out to be an unwelcome duet: leviable but worthless.

Intangible interests, including money belonging to or owed to the judgment debtor, are subject to levy and are infinite in their variety. Some of these incorporeal interests have economic value so real and so direct that a judgment creditor would prefer them to any kind of tangible property. Others are more remote and take greater effort to reduce to money. Others are so contingent that they may never amount to a thing and hence are not even worth an effort.

An example of a popular intangible that probably qualifies as the judgment creditor's favorite treasure, if the creditor is lucky enough to find it, is a bank account the debtor has in New York. Even though the bank may have numerous branches, it is best as a rule to pursue enforcement of the account, such as with a levy of execution or the service of a restraining notice—devices to be met in due course—only at the branch where the account is actually maintained. This recommendation is based on the "separate entity" rule, which has been applied for almost a century by several New York state and federal courts interpreting New York law.[2] Under the rule, a restraining notice or turnover order served on a bank branch in New York is only effective as to assets held in accounts maintained at that specific branch, but will not have any effect on assets held in other branches.

With the advent of modern communication technology, some courts concluded that the separate entity rule was no longer necessary and that the service of a restraining notice or turnover order on the bank's main office in New York was legally effective against assets held in another branch of the bank. Although the separate entity rule had been breaking creditors' hearts in enforcement proceedings dating back to 1916, it was never expressly addressed by the New York Court of Appeals until it answered a question certified by the Second Circuit in 2014 in Motorola Credit Corp. v. Standard Chartered Bank.[3]

The stakes were high in *Motorola*, as the plaintiff sought to enforce a judgment in excess of $3 billion by serving a CPLR 5222 restraining order on the New York branch of defendant Standard Chartered Bank, a foreign bank incorporated and headquartered in the United Kingdom. The bank did not possess any of defendant's property at its New York branch, but did locate approximately $30 million of defendant's assets in its branches in the United Arab Emirates (U.A.E.) and placed a freeze on them in accordance with the restraining order. Regulatory authorities in the U.A.E. and Jordan acted quickly and unilaterally debited about $30 million from the bank's account in the U.A.E. Central Bank. In May 2013, the bank sought relief by claiming, among other things, that the restraining order subjected it to double liability and violated New York's

---

[2]   See, e.g., Therm-X-Chemical & Oil Corp. v. Extebank, 84 A.D.2d 787, 444 N.Y.S.2d 26 (2d Dep't 1981) ("in order to reach a particular bank account the judgment creditor must serve the office of the bank where the account is maintained"); Det Bergenske Dampskibsselskab v. Sabre Shipping Corp., 341 F.2d 50, 53–54 (2d Cir. 1965) (concluding that the separate entity rule prohibited a restraint on funds located in a separate branch in New York that had not been served).

[3]   Motorola Credit Corp. v. Standard Chartered Bank, 24 N.Y.3d 149, 996 N.Y.S.2d 594, 21 N.E.3d 223 (2014).

separate entity rule because it essentially froze assets located in an overseas branch of the bank.

The *Motorola* Court concluded that the "separate entity" rule is indeed alive and well and "prevents a judgment creditor from ordering a garnishee bank operating branches in New York to restrain a judgment debtor's assets held in foreign branches of the bank."[4] The majority recounted the history of the rule and its rationale, including international comity and the possibility of double liability, which was a real danger for the bank in the *Motorola* litigation. The Court also rejected the argument that its blockbuster decision in Koehler v. Bank of Bermuda Ltd.,[5] necessarily abrogated the separate entity rule.

The account at issue in *Motorola* was overseas, and the Court expressly noted that it was not addressing a separate, but very important, issue of "whether the separate entity rule has any application to domestic bank branches in New York or elsewhere in the United States."[6] Until the Court specifically addresses this issue, the safest course is to levy an execution or serve a restraining notice at the bank branch where the account at issue is maintained. This will not be difficult when the branch is in New York, but will prove troublesome when the account is located in a branch in another state, or outside the United States.

Is it possible that a bank could be subject to personal jurisdiction in New York based on its operation of a branch in the state? If so, can this provide a basis for service of a restraining notice or turnover order on the foreign branch where the debtor's assets are sitting? The answers to these critical questions raise issues concerning the scope of the United States Supreme Court's holding in Daimler AG v. Bauman,[7] which addressed a forum state's ability to subject a corporation to personal jurisdiction.[8] In this regard, it should be noted that the majority in *Motorola* distinguished *Koehler* on the ground that "[i]t would appear that the judgment creditor [therein] also served the bank itself in Bermuda, not only its New York subsidiary, providing yet another reason for the inapplicability of the separate entity rule in that case."[9]

As long as the deposited money is the debtor's, the creditor can reach the account with ease. It has been held that even a deposit made by the debtor in his own name, but in trust for another—the so-called "Totten Trust"[10]—is money belonging to the depositor until his death and may be reached by his creditors.[11]

If the judgment debtor, D, has a joint bank account with another, A, the judgment creditor can pursue it: there is a presumption that each joint tenant is entitled to all of

---

[4]   *Motorola*, 24 N.Y.3d at 156, 996 N.Y.S.2d at 595, 21 N.E.3d at 224.

[5]   Koehler v. Bank of Bermuda Ltd., 12 N.Y.3d 533, 883 N.Y.S.2d 763, 911 N.E.2d 825 (2009); see § 491. The majority distinguished *Koehler*, noting that the separate entity rule was not raised by the foreign bank in that case, nor discussed by the Court. *Motorola*, 24 N.Y.3d at 161, 996 N.Y.S.2d at 599, 21 N.E.3d at 228.

[6]   *Motorola*, 24 N.Y.3d at 159 n.2., 996 N.Y.S.2d at 597 n.2, 21 N.E.3d at 226 n.2

[7]   Daimler AG v. Bauman, 571 U.S. 117, 134 S. Ct. 746, 187 L. Ed. 2d 624 (2014).

[8]   See §§ 82, 86, 95; *Motorola*, 24 N.Y.3d at 160, n.4, 996 N.Y.S.2d at 598 n.4, 21 N.E.3d at 227 n.4 (noting issues of personal jurisdiction arising under *Daimler*).

[9]   *Motorola*, 24 N.Y.3d at 161 n.5, 996 N.Y.S.2d at 599 n.5, 21 N.E.3d at 228 n.5. Legislation repealing the separate entity rule has been proposed by New York's Advisory Committee on Civil Practice. See Report of the Advisory Committee on Civil Practice, January 2015, p. 49.

[10]   See In re Totten, 179 N.Y. 112, 71 N.E. 748 (1904).

[11]   Abraham & Straus, Division of Federated Dept. Stores, Inc. v. Feynman, 71 Misc. 2d 928, 337 N.Y.S.2d 654 (Dist. Ct., Suffolk County 1972).

the account. The presumption is rebuttable, however, with the burden on the joint owners to rebut it. If they do rebut it, as by showing that the money was all put in by A, with D added as a party only for A's convenience, the pursuit may bear less fruit, or none at all because the levy is good only to the extent of D's "actual interest," which is subject to disproof.[12]

Until the presumption of D's interest is rebutted, the quest is usually worthwhile. A bank will sometimes refuse to release funds in a joint account, however, until satisfied of the part belonging to the judgment debtor, putting the creditor to the burden of a court application to resolve the matter.[13]

The interest of a judgment debtor as a beneficiary under a decedent's estate may be reached by her creditor.[14] If it appears that such a beneficiary would not get the use of the money or property, however, as where she is in a country that would not let her have it, the money may be directed into a kind of impoundage deposit.[15] If it is, the deposit can be reached by the beneficiary's creditors, as can almost any funds in custodia legis in which the debtor has a present interest,[16] at least to the extent that the debtor herself could reach the funds were she not subject to any foreign fetters.

In the commercial area, assets worth pursuing against a judgment debtor include all variety of debts evidenced by commercial paper or accounts receivable.[17] Even if an account has been encumbered, the debtor may still retain an equity in it. Any equity the debtor may have in it, or in any other property he may have pledged or otherwise given to another for some security purpose, may be levied.[18]

The several varieties of tenancy ownership in real property may be reached by the creditor to the extent of the tenant's interest. In this sphere, the most troublesome has always been the tenancy by the entirety, in which spouses have coequal rights in the property. It has been held that the creditor of only one spouse can reach that spouse's interest, but judges have had trouble in determining just what it is that gets reached. If the property produces income, the creditor can be allowed the debtor-spouse's share of it, but the courts are loath to allow the creditor to share possession of the asset with the non-debtor spouse. In a few cases the courts have made this category of property interest unavailable as a practical matter when the asset involved was the family residence, declaring either that the right of possession is not reachable as a matter of law,[19] or that, whether theoretically reachable or not, it should be insulated with an ad hoc protective order under CPLR 5240.[20] This may mean that all the creditor takes here is a kind of lien against the property, to become fully leviable only if and when the non-debtor spouse

---

[12] See Viggiano v. Viggiano, 136 A.D.2d 630, 523 N.Y.S.2d 874 (2d Dep't 1988).

[13] See, e.g., Household Finance Corp. v. Rochester Community Sav. Bank, 143 Misc. 2d 436, 541 N.Y.S.2d 160 (N.Y. City Ct. 1989). It has been held that when a judgment creditor brings a proceeding to get at the debtor's funds in a joint account, the other joint holder is an indispensable party. See SPR 122:3.

[14] In re Pallonetti's Estate, 48 Misc. 2d 814, 265 N.Y.S.2d 976 (Sur. Ct., Kings County 1965).

[15] See SCPA 2218.

[16] See In re Leikind's Estate, 22 N.Y.2d 346, 292 N.Y.S.2d 681, 239 N.E.2d 550 (1968).

[17] See International Ribbon Mills, Ltd. v. Arjan Ribbons, Inc., 36 N.Y.2d 121, 365 N.Y.S.2d 808, 325 N.E.2d 137 (1975).

[18] Fitchburg Yarn Co. v. Wall & Co., Inc., 46 A.D.2d 763, 361 N.Y.S.2d 170, 16 U.C.C. Rep. Serv. 229 (1st Dep't 1974).

[19] See Berlin v. Herbert, 48 Misc. 2d 393, 265 N.Y.S.2d 25 (Dist. Ct., Nassau County 1965).

[20] See Gilchrist v. Commercial Credit Corp., 66 Misc. 2d 791, 322 N.Y.S.2d 200 (Sup. Ct., Nassau County 1971).

predeceases the debtor spouse (who would thereupon succeed to the whole of the property), or to lapse into nothingness if the non-debtor spouse is the survivor. Or, if divorce should undo the marriage and convert the tenancy by the entirety into a tenancy in common, the debtor-spouse's creditor will now be able to levy because the debtor's interest will be transferable to a buyer.[21]

Real property in all of its diverse modern forms of ownership may be sought for application to a judgment, including cooperatives, condominiums, and mobile homes, subject, of course, to the applicable exemption if the property is the debtor's principal residence. Here it is important to note that a judgment debtor's interest in a cooperative apartment, at one time thought to be real property for all purposes and therefore lienable by the mere docketing of the judgment in the county of the apartment's location,[22] was held by the Court of Appeals in State Tax Commission v. Shor to be personal property for enforcement purposes.[23] Liens on personal property do not arise on the mere docketing of a judgment, with the result in *Shor* that the creditor lost all priority, and some $100,000, for relying on the property's assumed status as real property. This means that a judgment creditor in pursuit of the judgment debtor's interest in a cooperative apartment must make the greater effort needed to lien personal property,[24] even though for other purposes, such as the residential exemption, the cooperative apartment remains classified as real property.[25] The condominium differs from the cooperative in that the law requires the condominium to be treated as real property for all purposes.[26]

A legitimate arrangement between a judgment debtor and those with whom he deals will be honored even though it may have the effect of curtailing the value that the property right involved might otherwise have to a judgment creditor. If the debtor's title is subject to a third person's right of possession, for example, or if the debtor's right of possession is subject to a third person's title, what the judgment debtor is left with is necessarily less valuable than if she had the whole interest outright. Still, the creditor can reach nothing more than the debtor has,[27] or, looked at more optimistically, can reach at least what the debtor has.

The law will not tolerate an arbitrary attempt, in an arrangement between the debtor and some third person, to put an otherwise leviable asset beyond the reach of the debtor's creditors. If, for example, G owes D money evidenced by paper, the paper cannot without some special and commercially legitimate reason place the debt it represents beyond the reach of D's creditors.[28] A legitimate reason ought to earn judicial recognition, however, as where G leases to D a delicate and expensive instrument which D is equipped to handle, but which the world at large is not: if the arrangement provides for reversion of the asset if taken from D, or if a taking is merely threatened, and the provision is in its nature reasonable, it should be upheld. Here it would be a legitimate

[21] See Hohenrath v. Wallach, 37 A.D.2d 248, 323 N.Y.S.2d 560 (2d Dep't 1971). Entirety problems are further discussed in § 522, dealing with protective orders.

[22] See § 421.

[23] State Tax Commission v. Shor, 43 N.Y.2d 151, 400 N.Y.S.2d 805, 371 N.E.2d 523 (1977).

[24] See §§ 518–20. The problem of obtaining a lien on personal property is the subject of a lead note in NYSLD No. 216.

[25] CPLR 5206(a)(2). See § 490.

[26] Section 339–g of the Real Prop. Law.

[27] See § 488 following.

[28] See Oppenheimer v. Dresdner Bank A. G., 50 A.D.2d 434, 377 N.Y.S.2d 625 (2d Dep't 1975), aff'd, 41 N.Y.2d 949, 394 N.Y.S.2d 634, 363 N.E.2d 358 (1977). Note also in this connection N.Y. UCC § 9–401.

protection to the third person, not a calculated evasion designed to "judgment-proof" the debtor.

When dealing with an intangible property interest, it is often important to fix its situs since it can be dealt with by a New York court only if found to have in some sense a New York situs. If D, the judgment debtor, in turn has a debtor (G), for example, what is the situs to be affixed to the debt that G owes D so that a New York judgment creditor of D can seize it? In Harris v. Balk,[29] it was held that the situs of the debt is wherever G is, and that if G happens into the state of someone who has a claim or judgment against D, that creditor can seize the debt by serving G with appropriate process,[30] thereby requiring G to pay the debt not to D, but to the creditor.

Although the intangible's situs in the situation just discussed has been fixed, the same intangible may not have the same situs in other contexts. The situs of an intangible, said Judge Cardozo, is a legal fiction and varies from one context to another, being fixed by "a common sense appraisal of the requirements of justice and convenience in particular conditions."[31] A leasehold interest, for example, has been held to be where the real property is, rather than where the tenant is,[32] a contrast to the mobility ascribed to the debt in *Harris*.[33]

If a debt—the intangible we have been alluding to—is to be seized, the seizure must be effected through the "garnishee," the person whom the CPLR defines as one who, among other things, owes a debt to the judgment debtor.[34] Determining the proper garnishee is therefore often just another way of fixing the "situs" of the debt itself.[35]

Further illustrations of property interests subject to levy and the extent to which the levy may proceed when the debtor's interest is less than whole are in the next section, which demonstrates how the creditor's standing to reach an asset depends on the debtor's own standing in it.

§ 488. Creditor Stands in Debtor's Shoes

When the asset or interest that the judgment creditor wants to apply to the judgment belongs to the judgment debtor only in part, it is only that part that is subject to enforcement. Any right or interest lodged legitimately in a third person remains there, and a levy can proceed only on the debtor's right as is. So, for example, in the common situation in which the judgment debtor is a mortgagor and has deposited with the mortgagee escrow moneys to cover taxes and assessments on the realty, those moneys are for the mortgagee's security and can't be reached by the mortgagor's creditors without the mortgagee's leave.[1] The judgment creditor stands in the shoes of the

---

[29]   Harris v. Balk, 198 U.S. 215, 25 S. Ct. 625, 49 L. Ed. 1023 (1905). *Harris* is cited here only for its reflections on the situs of an intangible. The aspect of the *Harris* case that affects quasi in rem jurisdictional use of a debt has been largely overruled. See § 104.

[30]   In New York, the process is an order of attachment if the seizure is before judgment, CPLR 6214(a), or an execution if after. CPLR 5232(a).

[31]   Severnoe Securities Corporation v. London & Lancashire Ins. Co., 255 N.Y. 120, 124, 174 N.E. 299, 300 (1931).

[32]   See Glassman v. Hyder, 23 N.Y.2d 354, 296 N.Y.S.2d 783, 244 N.E.2d 259 (1968).

[33]   Further discussion of these matters is in § 489.

[34]   CPLR 105.

[35]   Determining the proper garnishee is the subject of § 491.

[1]   Valerio v. College Point Sav. Bank, 48 Misc. 2d 91, 264 N.Y.S.2d 343 (Sup. Ct., Suffolk County 1965). The addition of subdivision (g) to CPLR 5205 in 1978 specifically exempts from the reach of creditors such

judgment debtor, and if a given property, asset, interest, or deposit is unavailable to the debtor, it is unavailable to the creditor. If in the hands of the debtor the asset is available but encumbered, it can be levied, but only as encumbered. We can call this the stand-in-the-shoes rule, and it can answer many questions.

Applied to an escrow fund, this rule of vicarious standing will intervene to allow the judgment creditor to reach the fund upon a showing that the judgment debtor could do so himself. In the foregoing example of the mortgage escrow, the debtor could not, and so neither could his creditor. But when escrow money in different context was sufficiently in the debtor's control to be reached by him, his judgment creditor was allowed to reach it.[2]

The rule can serve in many instances, whether involving a tangible or intangible interest or property. Where the judgment debtor has pledged stock as collateral for a loan, for example, the judgment creditor will be allowed to levy on the collateral only to the extent of its value over and above the interest of the pledgee. If, allowing for as much of the stock as is necessary to secure the balance still due on the loan, there is something left, that's what the creditor can levy on.[3] If, on the other hand, the collateral is less than the obligation it secures, it leaves nothing for the debtor to touch, which means there is nothing for the creditor to touch either.[4]

Similarly, if the judgment debtor has possession of chattels under a valid conditional sales contract allowing repossession by the conditional seller if default should occur in the contract's terms, a judicial sale of the debtor's possessory right will convey subject to the conditional seller's repossessory right, which the latter can pursue no matter where the chattels may end up.[5] If the right of possession in such a situation has value, it is worth pursuing; otherwise it is not.

The foregoing are situations in which the judgment debtor owns or is using property of some kind on which another has a lien or equivalent encumbrance. But now look at the lien or encumbrance itself. It, too, is property, and may be reached by the judgment creditor of the one who holds the lien. A mortgagee on an ordinary real property mortgage makes a good judgment debtor, for example: her judgment creditor can levy on the mortgage and the buyer at the judicial sale will then become entitled to the mortgage payments as they become due and to all other rights conferred on the mortgagee by the terms of the mortgage.

The mortgage is one of the most common of liens, but less familiar ones are also reachable, whatever mechanical adjustments may be needed to facilitate the reaching.

If the judgment debtor has no right to the money or property, then neither has the judgment creditor, even though the money may be due in conjunction with a transaction

---

money as the debtor may have deposited as security for a lease of real property or in connection with utility services.

[2] See Koroleski v. Badler, 32 A.D.2d 810, 303 N.Y.S.2d 221 (2d Dep't 1969), in which the debtor's "control" of the fund was found ample enough to support a levy.

[3] See U. R. C. Inc. v. Applied Images Inc., 106 Misc. 2d 1034, 431 N.Y.S.2d 859 (Sup. Ct., Nassau County 1980); see also Cohen v. First Nat. City Bank, 49 Misc. 2d 141, 267 N.Y.S.2d 146 (N.Y. City Civ. Ct. 1966), which suggests several routes whereby to effect the seizure mechanically.

[4] See Key Lease Corp. v. Manufacturers Hanover Trust Co., 117 A.D.2d 560, 499 N.Y.S.2d 66 (1st Dep't 1986).

[5] See Intermediate Credit Corp. v. Overseas Nat. Airways, Inc., 41 Misc. 2d 522, 245 N.Y.S.2d 749 (Sup. Ct., Queens County 1963).

in which the judgment debtor was much involved, and perhaps even the key figure. Where, for example, hospital services are furnished to the judgment debtor or his family and payments are due from X to the hospital under an insurance arrangement, the stand-in-the-shoes rule will clarify that the debtor's judgment creditor may make no levy: since the money is due to the hospital rather than the judgment debtor, the debtor has no right to it and so neither has his judgment creditor derivatively.[6]

Even a special and seemingly personal right, like the cause of action an insured person has against his liability insurer for unreasonably failing to settle a tort claim made against the insured—a so-called "bad faith" claim by insured against insurer— may be pursued under the step-into-the-shoes principle. Hence, when injured persons recovered a judgment against the insured which was not fully paid, they were allowed the appointment of a receiver to bring suit in the insured's behalf against the insurer on the bad faith claim.[7]

To all of the foregoing conclusions we must append the assumption that the judgment debtor's transactions have been lawful and fraud-free. Indeed, an attempt by a debtor to insulate his property from his creditors by conveying it or encumbering it without fair consideration will be presumed fraudulent, without regard to actual intent, if the debtor is at the time insolvent or will be made so by the transfer.[8] The creditors may pursue the property into the hands of the gratuitous transferee.[9] Moreover, if the gratuitous transfer occurs while the transferor is a defendant in a money action which the plaintiff later wins, the transfer is presumed fraudulent against that plaintiff (now judgment creditor) merely upon a showing that the defendant (now judgment debtor) has not paid the judgment and without regard to the defendant's solvency.[10]

Assuming fair consideration for the judgment debtor's various undertakings, and their basic bona fides, all existing encumbrances, restrictions, and qualifications on the debtor's property rights will as a rule modify accordingly the rights of the judgment creditor. The creditor who steps into the debtor's shoes may walk only on terrain open to the debtor himself.

§ 489. Contingent Intangibles

CPLR 5201(b), which sets a broad measure for "property" applicable to a judgment, includes intangible property rights and interests as well as the tangible. We have even seen that some categories of intangible, such as a bank account, are even favored by creditors for the ease with which they can be levied on. But now attention must be directed to the troublesome subdivision (a) of CPLR 5201, which singles out one category of intangible interest—a "debt" allegedly owed to the judgment debtor—and provides

---

[6]   See Security Nat. Bank v. Associated Hospital Service, 63 Misc. 2d 731, 313 N.Y.S.2d 561 (Sup. Ct., New York County 1970).

[7]   Oppel v. DeGangi, 84 A.D.2d 549, 443 N.Y.S.2d 177 (2d Dep't 1981).

[8]   Debt. & Cred. Law § 273.

[9]   Debt. & Cred. Law § 278. The statute offers several remedies. One is to disregard the transfer and try to levy on the transferred property. Blue Giant Equipment Corp. v. Tec-Ser, Inc., 92 A.D.2d 630, 459 N.Y.S.2d 948 (3d Dep't 1983). This may prove an impractical course, however, because the sheriff will usually refuse to levy against property not standing plainly in the judgment debtor's name and right. Another, more burdensome to the judgment creditor but more productive, is a separate action or proceeding against the gratuitous transferee to set aside the transfer. See Crete Concrete Corp. v. Josephs, 66 Misc. 2d 837, 322 N.Y.S.2d 935 (Sup. Ct., Rockland County 1971), modified on other grounds, 39 A.D.2d 543, 332 N.Y.S.2d 601 (2d Dep't 1972).

[10]   Debt. & Cred. Law § 273–a.

that the debt may be subjected to levy only if it is "past due or . . . yet to become due, certainly or upon demand of the judgment debtor . . . ." "Its purpose is to preclude enforcement against a debt—or a cause of action, which it also includes[1]—if the debt depends on a contingency that may never occur. It was adopted almost verbatim from the old Civil Practice Act,[2] but it could have used a little rethinking.

There are some interests that depend on contingencies too remote for the law to bother with. An obligation to pay the debtor only if A survives B and C moves to Budapest should not waste the court's or even the debtor's time. But there are other debts and claims that are less remote, or, despite remoteness, have economic value sufficient to entice a buyer at a judicial sale. A debt or claim with a value of that kind ought to be leviable whether contingent or not, but subdivision (a) as constituted would seemingly bar enforcement against all debts contingent on anything more than the mere passage of time or the mere demand of the judgment debtor.

The courts have manifested impatience with this. In the famous case of Seider v. Roth,[3] the Court of Appeals disregarded CPLR 5201(a) and held leviable the obligations of a liability insurer to "defend" and to "indemnify" its insured under a liability insurance policy—obligations which, at a judicial sale, would net nothing.[4] Were *Seider* to be allowed precedential scope, subdivision (a) of CPLR 5201 would disappear altogether: the obligations in nearly every other case even arguably within subdivision (a) were, whatever the nature of their contingencies, less contingent than those in *Seider*. The case of Glassman v. Hyder,[5] for example, involved rents due under a lease of real property in another state. The one who leased the property had a New York presence, just as the insurance company (which "owed" the obligations to defend and indemnify) had in *Seider*, and certainly the obligation to pay rent under the lease is no more contingent than the *Seider* obligation to defend or to indemnify under the insurance policy. Nonetheless, the Court of Appeals in the *Glassman* case held the rents to be unleviable contingencies within the meaning of subdivision (a). The theory was apparently that something might occur, before a rent payment came due, to cancel the lease and with it the obligation to pay.[6] *Seider* and its progeny were distinguished for failing to make any effort "to classify contractual duties as between debt and property."[7]

It was not clear what would be accomplished by stressing a distinction between "debt" and "property." Was this some kind of hint that an interest of a given kind might be treated as either—leviable if treated as "property" under subdivision (b) of CPLR 5201 although barred from levy as too contingent if treated as a "debt" under subdivision (a)? That is apparently what the Court of Appeals did indeed mean, as it later clarified in

---

[1]   The line between a "debt" and "cause of action" is often imperceptible, a matter returned to at the end of this section.

[2]   Civ. Prac. Act § 687(a)(1) (repealed 1963). See 3d Rep. Leg. Doc. No. 17, p. 101 (1959).

[3]   Seider v. Roth, 17 N.Y.2d 111, 269 N.Y.S.2d 99, 216 N.E.2d 312 (1966). The history of the *Seider* case, which was overruled by the U.S. Supreme Court on federal constitutional grounds in Rush v. Savchuk after 14 controversial years of life, is treated in detail in § 105.

[4]   So incapable were these obligations of conversion into any kind of pecuniary consequence, that the court later discarded them and held instead that the thing attached in these *Seider*-based cases is the face amount of the policy itself. See § 105.

[5]   Glassman v. Hyder, 23 N.Y.2d 354, 296 N.Y.S.2d 783, 244 N.E.2d 259 (1968).

[6]   There is indication that rents already due may be levied. See Mobil Oil Corp. v. Lovotro, 65 Misc. 2d 729, 318 N.Y.S.2d 989 (Monroe County Court 1971).

[7]   *Glassman*, 23 N.Y.2d at 359, 296 N.Y.S.2d at 786, 244 N.E.2d at 261.

ABKCO Industries, Inc. v. Apple Films, Inc.,[8] the most illuminating and helpful decision yet made in this difficult arena.

In *ABKCO*, a nondomiciliary (D) made a contract with a New York corporation (G), licensing G to show a certain film and obligating G to pay D a certain percentage of the profits. Nothing was yet due to D under the contract when the action was brought; indeed, under the D-G arrangement a balance was owing by D to G at the time rather than the vice-versa needed for a levy. The court said that the right that D had against G could be treated *either* as a "debt" under CPLR 5201(a) *or* as "property" under 5201(b), and held that the levy would be allowed if it passed muster under either. Since the "property" criterion of 5201(b) is satisfied upon a simple showing that the right asserted is assignable, without regard to its contingent nature, the contractual obligation, clearly an assignable one in *ABKCO*, was held leviable despite the fact that it was a contingency that would have been barred from levy if held up to measure under 5201(a).

This is a sound rule. When left to subdivision (b) as "property," economic reality rather than legal technicality becomes the standard, as it ought to. If a right allegedly held by D against G is levied in behalf of P—a judgment creditor of D—its economic significance and hence its utility as an enforcement asset is measured by what a buyer would be willing to pay for this "right" at a public auction—the auction being the method used for converting property into money under an execution.[9] In the *ABKCO*, case a buyer would likely have offered a tidy sum: the right was to a percentage of profits under the D-G contract and the contract involved a film starring the Beatles, a young English quartet who were an international synonym for money during their heyday beginning in the 1960s. An asset of that value, or of any significant value, is surely one that ought to be leviable by its owner's creditors. When the defendant protested that the obligation depended on a contingency that might never occur—the film might fail—the creditor asked for an opportunity to take that chance. The Court of Appeals obliged by characterizing the contractual obligation as "property" under subdivision (b), thereby freeing it of the strictures imposed on a "debt" by subdivision (a), and making it leviable.

To be eligible for "property" treatment under subdivision (b), all that need be shown is that the property is assignable and that it has a New York situs. It was on the situs element, in fact, that the *ABKCO* case distinguished *Glassman*. The rents in *Glassman*, both before and after *ABKCO*, would be barred as a "debt" under subdivision (a) because of their contingency, but why would they not qualify as "property" so as to be leviable under subdivision (b)? The Court in *ABKCO* answered this by noting that the "property" in *Glassman* was a leasehold interest; that a leasehold has its situs where the real property is; and that the situs was not New York in the *Glassman* case. So the *Glassman* rents were leviable neither under subdivision (a), because contingent, nor (b), because

---

8   ABKCO Industries, Inc. v. Apple Films, Inc., 39 N.Y.2d 670, 385 N.Y.S.2d 511, 350 N.E.2d 899 (1976). Although it concerned the quasi in rem jurisdictional use of an attachment, a category of jurisdiction much reduced if not abolished by Shaffer v. Heitner, 433 U.S. 186, 97 S. Ct. 2569, 53 L. Ed. 2d 683 (1977), see § 104, the *ABKCO* case is not at all undone by the *Shaffer* case. *ABKCO* is concerned only with defining what a leviable contingent interest is. The use that may be made of that kind of interest is a different question, with which *ABKCO* is not concerned. The interest *ABKCO* involves, for example, will be fully available for attachment, but perhaps only when the attachment is being used for mere security rather than for jurisdiction. (It's only the jurisdictional use that *Shaffer* bars.) And it is in any event pursuable by judgment creditors during the post-judgment enforcement stage of a case. Lawyers should keep these factors in mind as they peruse the *ABKCO* decision, lest they fail to appreciate its utility.

9   CPLR 5232–5233. Details about levying against personal property, including intangibles, are met later. See §§ 496, 497, and 498.

not geographically reachable in New York. Had the rents been due on New York property, they would have been leviable under this standard.[10]

An important difference between *Seider* and *ABKCO* is that the contractual obligations in *Seider* lacked economic value of any kind that might invite a significant bid at an auction. In the words of Judge (later Chief Judge) Breitel, "before any intangible right has practical significance as an asset to be levied upon or attached, it must give promise of being translatable into an economically valuable tangible."[11] In *ABKCO*, it had that promise. In stark contrast to *Seider*, which offered for sale an insurer's obligation to defend and indemnify a tort case, in *ABKCO* a queue of bidders for the potential profits of a Beatles film would probably have circled the globe. It surely helps enforcement that the courts take practical realities like this into consideration. The Court of Appeals in *ABKCO*, incidentally, which is now the ruling precedent in this realm, did not even accord *Seider* the courtesy of mention.

Translatability into something of economic value can also distinguish (and justify) levies against other kinds of insurance rights than the obligations arising under the liability policy involved in *Seider*. Where D has sustained a burglary loss, for example, and has a claim against his insurer (G), a seizure of that claim by one of D's creditors is permissible,[12] and economically worth a try. A bidder may be willing to pay something substantial for the right to pursue the claim.

The distillation of the foregoing is that as long as a New York situs can be spelled out for the intangible at issue, it can be given "property" treatment under CPLR 5201(b) and subjected to levy. The Court of Appeals' attitude is that the levy can be tried, in any event. If there is anything contingent about the item levied, it may be reflected in what its judicial sale attracts, and in that sense a CPLR 5201(b) treatment may be chancy. The new theme, however, is that it ought to be the judgment creditor who is allowed to determine whether the chance is worth taking.

Even before *ABKCO*, courts sometimes allowed a contingent debt or obligation to be treated as leviable property under subdivision (b) if it was perceived as having some economic substance that could make the levy worthwhile.[13] Cases forbidding levy by literal application of the "contingency" rule, on the other hand, notwithstanding that the obligation involved did have real economic potential, imposed a needless restriction on the judgment creditor.[14] Those cases are implicitly overruled by the *ABKCO* decision, at least if a New York situs can be found for the obligation or right involved.

Wages or salary to be earned by a judgment debtor, or trust income to become due, could easily be placed under the contingent-debt category and barred from levy by CPLR 5201(a) if not made exceptions to it. But exceptions they are, and hence leviable: wages and trust income may be levied to the extent of 10% under the income execution provision

---

[10] In that event, of course, the real property itself would have been leviable, relegating the rents question to the academic.

[11] Simpson v. Loehmann, 21 N.Y.2d 305, 315, 287 N.Y.S.2d 633, 641, 234 N.E.2d 669, 674–5, 1968 A.M.C. 1214 (1967) (concurring opinion).

[12] See Baumgold Bros. v. Schwarzschild Bros., 276 A.D. 158, 93 N.Y.S.2d 658 (1st Dep't 1949), aff'd, 302 N.Y. 628, 97 N.E.2d 357 (1951).

[13] See, e.g., M. F. Hickey Co. v. Port of New York Authority, 23 A.D.2d 739, 258 N.Y.S.2d 129 (1st Dep't 1965).

[14] See, e.g., Fredrick v. Chicago Bearing Metal Co., 221 A.D. 588, 224 N.Y.S. 629 (1st Dep't 1927).

of CPLR 5231,[15] and the judgment debtor can be directed to pay an even higher percentage under another enforcement device known as an installment payment order.[16]

An interesting review of the *ABKCO* case emerges from the complicated fact pattern in the Second Circuit decision in Alliance Bond Fund, Inc. v. Grupo Mexicano De Desarrollo[17] The plaintiffs in *Alliance* were U.S. holders of notes issued by a Mexican company in conjunction with the building of toll roads in Mexico. On default, the Mexican government itself became embroiled, undertaking to make good on instruments to be exchanged for certain receivables, but it wasn't clear whether Mexico would step in only with respect to receivables held by Mexicans, or those held by others as well.

Through the adoption of state law that Rule 69(a) of the Federal Rules of Civil Procedure prescribed for enforcement steps, the New York rule about assignability became relevant. As the Second Circuit viewed the case, all enforcement in New York would be stymied if it were found that Mexico would not recognize assignability of the obligations sought. The case was therefore remanded for findings on the issue of whether Mexico would.

In the course of the opinion, the court treated at length CPLR 5225 and 5227, which provide for the "turnover" procedures that facilitate getting at property when a proper garnishee is amenable to New York jurisdiction.[18] It was argued that anything qualifying as "property" under CPLR 5201 is necessarily property as well for the "turnover" purpose of CPLR 5225 and 5227, but the court rejected the argument. It held that for a turnover order to work, the judgment creditor must proceed "against the person having the ability to produce the asset," and whether the persons pursued in *Alliance* had that ability turned on Mexico's intentions. Hence the remand to explore the issue.

Addressing a similar issue in Commonwealth of Northern Mariana Islands v. Canadian Imperial Bank of Commerce,[19] on a certified question from the Second Circuit, the Court of Appeals held that a New York bank could not be compelled in a CPLR 5225(b) turnover proceeding to deliver property held by its foreign subsidiary, even though it may have had the ability to require its subsidiary to produce the asset.[20]

The lesson is that while CPLR 5201, abetted by *ABKCO*, licenses the pursuit of any assignable asset, it does not guarantee a New York situs for the asset pursued. Findings were needed before a New York situs could be fixed for the assets in *Alliance*, and CPLR 5225 or 5227 could not help until such findings were made.

The *ABKCO* decision was scrutinized once again in Verizon New England, Inc. v. Transcom Enhanced Services, Inc.,[21] where petitioner commenced a turnover proceeding contending that respondent's oral, at-will, prepayment service agreement with the judgment debtor constituted a debt or property interest subject to a CPLR 5222(b) restraining notice. Pursuant to the agreement, respondent promised to pay the judgment

---

[15]   See §§ 502 et seq. The counterpart of the 10% levy is in CPLR 5205(d), which exempts 90% of this income.

[16]   CPLR 5226. See § 511.

[17]   Alliance Bond Fund, Inc. v. Grupo Mexicano De Desarrollo, S.A., 190 F.3d 16 (2d Cir. 1999).

[18]   See § 510.

[19]   Commonwealth of Northern Mariana Islands v. Canadian Imperial Bank of Commerce, 21 N.Y.3d 55, 967 N.Y.S.2d 876, 990 N.E.2d 114 (2013).

[20]   The *Commonwealth of Northern Mariana Islands* decision is discussed in further detail in § 491.

[21]   Verizon New England, Inc. v. Transcom Enhanced Services, Inc., 21 N.Y.3d 66, 967 N.Y.S.2d 883, 990 N.E.2d 121 (2013) (NYSLD No. 641).

debtor in advance for various services it opted to receive in the future. The Court ruled that because the affirmed findings of fact of the courts below established that respondent prepaid for the services it received from the debtor, "there was no debt past due or yet to become due under the definition of CPLR 5201(a)."[22]

Next, the court considered whether, under CPLR 5201(b), the oral agreement was an attachable property interest subject to restraint under CPLR 5222(b). The *Verizon* Court noted that while *ABKCO* held that a contractual agreement could constitute contingent property interests subject to enforcement under CPLR 5201(b) and attachment under CPLR Article 62, the licensing agreement in that case "set forth an obligation to pay the debtor, which constituted the 'principal feature of economic significance' of the agreement."[23] By contrast, the at-will, oral agreement in *Verizon* that was in place at the moment the restraining notice was served contained no obligation on the part of respondent to continue using the judgment debtor's services. Quoting from *ABKCO*, the Court held that "there was no debt, and no obligation 'certain to become due.' "[24]

One final matter. CPLR 5201(a) defines a "debt" as including a "cause of action" that the judgment debtor may have against a third person (a "garnishee"). The line between an outright "debt" on the one hand and a mere "cause of action" on the other is at best a shaky one. If G concedes the obligation, it would be a "debt" that G owes to D. If G denies it, or merely denies part of it, it would be a "cause of action" that D has against G. For purposes of determining leviability under CPLR 5201, there should be no need to stress the distinction, which touches the mechanics of perfecting the levy more than it does the initial levy itself.[25] Whichever category the given right is deemed to fall under, its leviability should be adjudged by the *ABKCO* standards, and an assignable "cause of action" with an economic potential should be just as leviable under CPLR 5201(b) as an outright "debt" is. To whatever extent a "debt," unleviable under subdivision (a) of CPLR 5201, can be levied as "property" under subdivision (b), so, therefore, should a "cause of action" be.

§ 490. Exemptions

A number of items of personal property as well as certain real property are exempt from application to a judgment. The main exemption sections are CPLR 5205 for personal property and 5206 for real property. These are old sections, inherited with only a few adjustments from prior law because the revisors felt that any extensive changes were beyond their function. A perusal of both sections will manifest their age. Old or not, the items they list may not be sought for enforcement. In general, they are what the legislature deems to be the necessities of life, which not even a person's judgment creditors should be allowed to reach.

---

[22] *Verizon*, 21 N.Y.3d at 71, 967 N.Y.S.2d at 885–86, 990 N.E.2d at 123–24.

[23] *Verizon*, 21 N.Y.3d at 71, 967 N.Y.S.2d at 886, 990 N.E.2d at 124.

[24] *Verizon*, 21 N.Y.3d at 71, 967 N.Y.S.2d at 886, 990 N.E.2d at 124.

[25] "Perfecting" the levy is a popular term used to describe the follow-up steps that must be taken to convert levied property into money to pay the judgment. These subsequent steps will prove more demanding when one is pursuing a "cause of action" that G resists, entailing the equivalent of a plenary suit by the judgment creditor, standing in D's shoes, against G, and a regular trial. Perfection is of course easier when G concedes the "debt" and just pays it over to the sheriff to the credit of the judgment that the sheriff is levying on. The distinction between the levy and its perfection is discussed in detail later. See § 496.

The CPLR lists are not exhaustive, moreover. A number of other provisions in the consolidated laws also contain exemptions.[1]

CPLR 5205(a) exempts the basic household goods: appliances, certain books, domestic animals, wearing apparel, household furniture, and tools essential for the judgment debtor's work. In 1976 a television set was added,[2] a legislative indication that it has become one of the necessities of the modern age. Perhaps the smartphone should now be added.

The listing of an item of personal property as exempt under CPLR 5205 does not prevent the owner from using the property as security for a loan. Specifically liening it in that fashion is not barred by CPLR 5205.[3]

While CPLR 5205(c) exempts the principal of a trust created for the judgment debtor, the exemption does not apply to any remainder interest the debtor may have in the trust.[4] Income from the trust, moreover, is only 90% exempt. The trust income exemption is contained in the first paragraph of CPLR 5205(d), whose second paragraph makes the well known 90% exemption for wages. The net result is that as a rule only 10% of either trust income or wages is applicable to the judgment. (The device used to secure the 10% is the income execution of CPLR 5231.)[5]

Note the opening language of CPLR 5205(d), which permits more than 10% to be levied if a court finds, after examining into the needs of the judgment debtor's family, that the debtor can afford more. Those findings are made on a motion for what is known as an installment payment order,[6] met and discussed later.[7] Caselaw has also held that since the 90% exemption is designed to preserve that segment for the needs of the judgment debtor's family, the exemption ceases to apply when it is the family that is seeking the money, such as for support,[8] thus enabling a court to direct payment of whatever is needed without a percentage limitation.

Any income paid or payable to someone on public welfare is altogether exempt from levy[9] as is the welfare payment itself.[10] Alimony payments to a wife and support payments to a child under a matrimonial judgment, when the recipient is the judgment debtor, are also immune in full (rather than just to the extent of 90%), but only

---

    [1]   Many of these are enumerated in the Advisory Committee's Third Report. See Leg. Doc. No. 17, p. 93 (1959).

    [2]   CPLR 5205(a)(5).

    [3]   State v. Avco Financial Service of New York Inc., 50 N.Y.2d 383, 429 N.Y.S.2d 181, 406 N.E.2d 1075 (1980).

    [4]   See Sherman v. Kirshman, 261 F. Supp. 858 (S.D.N.Y. 1966).

    [5]   See §§ 502 et seq.

    [6]   CPLR 5226.

    [7]   See § 511.

    [8]   See Fordyce v. Fordyce, 80 Misc. 2d 909, 365 N.Y.S.2d 323 (Sup. Ct., Nassau County 1974).

    [9]   Soc. Serv. Law § 137–a. See, however, Prior v. Cunningham, 33 A.D.2d 853, 306 N.Y.S.2d 22 (3d Dep't 1969), aff'd, 27 N.Y.2d 502, 312 N.Y.S.2d 677, 260 N.E.2d 871 (1970), which holds that while the exemption applies to the expressly listed "wages, salary, commissions, or other compensation" paid to a public welfare recipient, it does not go beyond that. The case is unclear about what other kinds of leviable income the debtor may have, and about why, if he has other income from which payments on the judgment could be directed, he is receiving public assistance.

    [10]   Soc. Serv. Law § 137.

presumptively; if the court finds that some part can be spared for the judgment creditor, it can order payment of that part.[11]

There is frequent controversy about the extent to which federal law insulates from levy a debtor's pension or welfare plan that falls under ERISA (the Employee Retirement Income Security Act),[12] a federal law designed to preserve retirement plans for workers who have been promised a pension. Several key questions under it are the subject of conflicting decisions around the country. The New York Court of Appeals has held that federal law is not totally preemptive in ERISA cases; that there are some situations in which the creditor can reach a pension plan, including one in which it is shown that the plan's "very creation" was fraudulent.[13]

Special Problems with Exempt Income

There is a constitutional requirement to advise the judgment debtor about the possibly exempt status of his property when enforcement steps are taken. The requirement occasioned amendments of several statutes in 1982,[14] but these did not suffice to avoid some serious abuses and finally, in 2008, the legislature acted again.

The background is that there is a perennial difficulty with exempt income, of whatever category, which often finds its way into the bank account of a judgment debtor of little means, or who is disabled. The money's exempt status is often unknown to the bank or other depository. When a judgment creditor would issue something like an execution or restraining notice to the bank, the bank would therefore honor the levy or restraint by removing money from the account, or freezing what's there, almost literally taking the bread out of the debtor's mouth. A further effort to meet this problem was made in Chapter 575 of the Laws of 2008, known as the 2008 Exempt Income Protection Act (EIPA), which added a new CPLR 5222–a[15] and amended CPLR 5205, 5222, 5230, 5231, and 5232.

The debtor addressed is the "natural person" depositor only, not a corporate or like debtor. If the debtor's account consists of exempt income, the amendment seeks to stop the enforcement devices at the bank's very threshold. With a number of restrictions, it prevents the device from getting into the bank at all, or in any event into the debtor's account. The reason, of course, is that moneys in the account may be the only funds available for the debtor's support.[16]

An income execution under CPLR 5231 would be the device most likely to be involved when exempt funds in an account are threatened, but other devices might also appear in this situation. North Shore University Hosp. at Plainview v. Citibank Legal

---

[11]   CPLR 5205(d)(3).

[12]   29 U.S.C.A. §§ 1001 et seq.

[13]   See Planned Consumer Marketing, Inc. v. Coats and Clark, Inc., 71 N.Y.2d 442, 527 N.Y.S.2d 185, 522 N.E.2d 30 (1988), treated in the lead note in NYSLD No. 345.

[14]   CPLR 5222, 5232, and 5234. See § 508 and Commentary C5222:11 on McKinney's CPLR 5222.

[15]   See Distressed Holdings, LLC v. Ehrler, 113 A.D.3d 111, 119, 976 N.Y.S.2d 517, 523 (2d Dep't 2013) (noting "purpose of CPLR 5222–a is to protect judgment debtors from having funds that are exempt from judgment enforcement restrained and seized by judgment creditors").

[16]   An example of the kind of problem aimed at is Contact Resource Services, LLC v. Gregory, 10 Misc. 3d 968, 806 N.Y.S.2d 407 (Rochester City Ct. 2005) (SPR 174:3). Treatment of Chapter 575 itself appears in an extended note in SPR 202:3.

Service Intake Unit,[17] discussing the 2008 amendments, holds that a judgment creditor can't make use of any enforcement device—in that case, a turnover order under CPLR 5225(b)[18] was the one tried—to get at the bank account if the funds in the account answer to the statutory descriptions and the effect would be to circumvent the exemption. If the judgment creditor doesn't know whether exempt funds are in the account, the court suggests starting out with the device of the information subpoena to get the needed information—the subpoena can be served on the bank or the debtor or yet others[19]— resorting to the restraining notice,[20] turnover order, or any other coercive device only after ascertaining that the funds sought are not exempt.[21]

An extended treatment of CPLR 5222–a and its intended workings appeared in Midland Funding LLC v. Singleton,[22] in which the court reviewed the many papers that went back and forth between and among the parties and the bank at which the account was being levied. Apparently, all of the demanding steps of the statutory procedure followed by the judgment creditor (JC) and the bank were faithful to the elaborate requirements of the statute, but the judgment debtor (JD) nevertheless defaulted on all of them. The court enumerated four such defaults: failure to appear in the underlying action (which produced the default); failure to move to vacate the default and the attempted enforcement steps; failure to oppose the JC's motion objecting to her claim of exemption; and finally, failure to appear at the two evidentiary hearings, "even though the JD was advised by the court and the JC's attorney of the date, time, and place" of each. From these repeated defaults, the court drew "adverse inferences" against the JD and held that the portion of the funds in the account that were the subject of the exemption dispute were not exempt and hence were subject to levy.

By contrast, in LR Credit 22, LLC v. Eggleston,[23] a "JD" competently pursued his obligations, going to considerable trouble and expense in doing so, including retaining the services of a lawyer. The court found that the "JC", on the other hand, was remiss in its obligations. It noted that JC had received information demonstrating that all of the funds in JD's account were exempt, and yet failed to instruct the bank, as required, to release the funds to JD. The court observed that JC had "callously disregarded" its obligations under the statute and granted JD an award against JC of $1,000 as a penalty, costs of $50 (the maximum allowed by Uniform City Court Act section 1906(a)), and attorney's fees incurred by JD.

The Court of Appeals had its first major address to CPLR 5222–a in Cruz v. TD Bank, N.A.,[24] in which it entertained certified questions in two federal actions in which JDs brought putative class actions seeking injunctive relief and money damages against their banks. Plaintiffs alleged violations of the EIPA arising out of restraints placed on their accounts held at bank branches in New York.

---

[17]   North Shore University Hosp. at Plainview v. Citibank Legal Service Intake Unit, 25 Misc. 3d 655, 883 N.Y.S.2d 898 (Dist. Ct., Nassau County 2009).

[18]   See § 510.

[19]   See § 509.

[20]   See § 508.

[21]   See the discussion in SPR 214:3.

[22]   Midland Funding LLC v. Singleton, 35 Misc. 3d 410, 943 N.Y.S.2d 373 (Dist. Ct., Nassau County 2012).

[23]   LR Credit 22, LLC v. Eggleston, 37 Misc. 3d 653, 951 N.Y.S.2d 658 (Jamestown City Ct. 2012) (SPR 249:3).

[24]   Cruz v. TD Bank, N.A., 22 N.Y.3d 61, 979 N.Y.S.2d 257, 2 N.E.3d 221 (2013) (NYSLD No. 649).

In a decision that contains an expansive discussion of not only the procedures required under CPLR 5222–a, but of several of the enforcement devices in CPLR Article 52, the Court of Appeals addressed whether JDs possess a private right of action for money damages and injunctive relief against banks that violate the EIPA's procedural requirements. CPLR 5222–a(b)(3) requires a bank to serve a copy of any restraining notice it receives on the JD, along with the accompanying exemption notice and exemption claim forms. The statute specifically provides, however, that the "inadvertent failure by a depository institution to provide the notice . . . shall not give rise to liability on the part of the depository institution."

The Court rejected plaintiffs' argument that, by explicitly providing that banks cannot be liable for inadvertently failing to serve the forms required by CPLR 5222–a(b)(3), the legislature intended that financial institutions could be liable for all other failures to comply with the statute, whether inadvertent or otherwise. If the legislature intended to impose a new form of liability on banks in this context, the Court concluded that it would have expressly provided for it in the statute. The *Cruz* Court noted that Article 52 has long contained various remedies and enforcement mechanisms, which predated the EIPA, and that they can be turned to by a JD seeking relief from a garnishee or JC.

Furthermore, the Court pointed to provisions in CPLR 5222–a that expressly permit a JD to recover money damages arising from noncompliance with the EIPA against JCs who initiate the exemption notice process.[25] These penalties were, in fact, imposed by the court under the statute in the *LR Credit 22* decision, discussed above.

The Real Property Exemption

One major point to note about CPLR 5206, which contains the real property exemption, is the amount of the exemption. For many years under CPLR 5206(a), it was $10,000. A 2005 amendment quintupled it to $50,000.[26]

A second is that the exemption applies only to the judgment debtor's "homestead," i.e., principal residence.

The exemption applies whether the residence consists of land and building, shares in a cooperative apartment, units in a condominium, or a mobile home. The place must be a "principal residence" in order to qualify for the exemption, however; a mere vacation retreat, for example, will not do.[27] If the debtor's equity exceeds $50,000, the balance may be reached by the judgment creditor, but it takes a special proceeding under CPLR 5206(e) to compel the sale of the property. When the residence is a cooperative apartment, which is real property for purposes of the exemption, but may be treated as personal property in other respects,[28] the source of the special proceeding to accomplish this may be ambiguous.[29] The availability of a special proceeding under several statutes

---

[25]   See CPLR 5222–a(g) (where "the court finds that the judgment creditor disputed the claim of exemption in bad faith . . . the judgment debtor shall be awarded costs, reasonable attorney fees, actual damages and an amount not to exceed one thousand dollars").

[26]   L.2005, ch. 623, effective August 30, 2005. See SPR 166:2.

[27]   See In re Galcia's Estate, 59 Misc. 2d 511, 299 N.Y.S.2d 723 (Sur. Ct., New York County 1969).

[28]   See § 487.

[29]   See Swatzburg v. Swatzburg, 137 Misc. 2d 1042, 523 N.Y.S.2d 399 (Sup. Ct., New York County 1987).

makes the matter academic, however.[30] When the real property is sold, the first $50,000 goes to the judgment debtor, in whose hands it is exempt for a year thereafter.[31]

The Fourth Department Case of Wyoming County Bank & Trust Co. v. Kiley[32] presented the issue of whether the landowner is entitled to assert the $10,000 (now $50,000) exemption against a foreclosing mortgagee. Under the terms of CPLR 5206(a), the exemption clearly does not apply against a purchase money mortgagee. The *Wyoming* case holds that it doesn't apply against any other kind of mortgagee either; that the exemption is usable only against a creditor trying to enforce an ordinary money judgment and that a mortgage foreclosure judgment is not such.[33] Nor is the foreclosure of a mechanic's lien.[34]

It was held in First Federal Sav. and Loan Ass'n of Rochester v. Brown,[35] that should there be a mortgage foreclosure—which entails a sale of the property—and a surplus left after the mortgage is satisfied, the surplus will not enjoy the $10,000 (now $50,000) exemption even if an ordinary judgment creditor is the one pursuing it; that the exemption lasts only while the premises are occupied by the family. The court explained that the surplus is personal property while the exemption applies only to real property.

The exemption applies only to the satisfaction of a civil money judgment, moreover. It has no application to a fine imposed by a criminal court.[36]

The real property exemption has an important role on the bankruptcy scene. As authorized by federal law, New York has enacted statutes[37] that opt out of the federal bankruptcy exemptions scheme and make New York exemptions exclusive. Under them, each spouse, when both file in bankruptcy, may claim a real property exemption under CPLR 5206. When both file, therefore, the exemption doubles, to what would now be $100,000.[38]

§ 491. Proper Garnishee

Since a "garnishee" is defined as anyone who has possession of property belonging to the judgment debtor or in which the debtor has an interest, or who owes a debt to the debtor,[1] identifying the proper person to treat as a garnishee is an important step. It is

---

[30]   See, e.g., CPLR 5225, 5227, and the summary of the *Swatzburg* case, CPLR 5225, 5227, in NYSLD No. 344.

[31]   CPLR 5206(e). See also Sailors' Snug Harbor in City of New York v. Tax Commission of City of New York, 26 N.Y.2d 444, 311 N.Y.S.2d 486, 259 N.E.2d 910 (1970).

[32]   Wyoming County Bank & Trust Co. v. Kiley, 75 A.D.2d 477, 430 N.Y.S.2d 900 (4th Dep't 1980).

[33]   Other departments subscribe to the *Wyoming* view. See First Nat. Bank of Glens Falls v. G.F. Clear, Inc., 103 A.D.2d 951, 479 N.Y.S.2d 802 (3d Dep't 1984); Citibank, N.A. v. Cambel, 119 A.D.2d 720, 501 N.Y.S.2d 133 (2d Dep't 1986).

[34]   See Robert S. Moore, Inc. v. Whittaker, 142 Misc. 2d 708, 538 N.Y.S.2d 415 (Schoharie County Court 1989).

[35]   First Federal Sav. and Loan Ass'n of Rochester v. Brown, 78 A.D.2d 119, 434 N.Y.S.2d 306 (4th Dep't 1980).

[36]   See People v. McArdle, 55 N.Y.2d 639, 446 N.Y.S.2d 256, 430 N.E.2d 1309 (1981), involving a conviction for welfare fraud.

[37]   See §§ 282 to 284 of the Debt. & Cred. Law, added in 1982.

[38]   See John T. Mather Memorial Hosp. of Port Jefferson, Inc. v. Pearl, 723 F.2d 193, 195 (2d Cir. 1983) ("The purpose of the New York legislation was clearly to provide joint debtors the opportunity to make a 'fresh start' " with a doubling of the homestead exemption).

[1]   CPLR 105.

often through a garnishee that enforcement is carried out. In most instances there is no difficulty. If the property is a bank account, for example, the garnishee is the bank. If it is a chattel, the garnishee is the one who has custody of it; if a debt, the one who owes it; if a cause of action, the one against whom it lies. These are common situations. Subdivision (c) of CPLR 5201, in listing the proper garnishee in a few instances, has merely selected some special situations in which it was felt that some statutory instruction about proper garnishee would be helpful.

When the judgment debtor has an interest in an estate or trust, the proper garnishee is the fiduciary—the executor or administrator of the estate, the trustee or equivalent of the trust, etc.[2] When the debtor has an interest in a partnership, any other partner is the proper garnishee.[3] This works even when the judgment is between the partners. Where, for example, in a three-person partnership, partner A has a judgment against partners B and C, B and C each qualify as a garnishee with respect to the judgment rendered against the other.[4]

Special note should be made of the situation in which the pursued asset is a debt represented by some piece of commercial paper. If the paper is negotiable, the paper itself is the asset, deemed property "capable of delivery"; the proper garnishee is not necessarily the person owing the debt, but the person who has custody of the paper.[5] This is so not only of a negotiable instrument for the payment of money, but also of a negotiable document of title under Article 7 of the Uniform Commercial Code.[6]

If the paper representing the interest is nonnegotiable, the paper is not deemed the asset; the proper garnishee is the one who owes the debt or the one who has possession of the property.

A similar distinction is made when the asset sought to be reached is the judgment debtor's shares in a corporation or other share-issuing association. If the shares are represented by duly issued and outstanding certificates, these are deemed the property and the person who has them is the garnishee.[7] If no certificates are outstanding, the garnishee is the corporation or association itself.[8]

It is only the judgment debtor's property that the judgment creditor may pursue in the hands of the garnishee, not the garnishee's own property. If, for example, the garnishee owes a debt to the debtor, the creditor may, through appropriate devices, require payment of the debt to him instead of to the debtor. The creditor may not,

---

[2]   CPLR 5201(c)(2).

[3]   CPLR 5201(c)(3). The judgment creditor holding a judgment against an individual partner may not levy against any particular asset of the partnership because each such asset is collectively the partnership's and does not belong to any given partner. The creditor's remedy here is to levy execution, or to get what is called a "charging order" under § 54 of the Partnership Law, against the debtor partner's interest in the partnership. (For purposes of achieving priority, such as in a race with another creditor, the levy is preferable to the charging order. See § 520.) Only if the judgment is rendered against the partnership itself may the partnership's assets be pursued. See CPLR 5201(b) (second sentence).

[4]   See Jones v. Palermo, 105 Misc. 2d 405, 432 N.Y.S.2d 288 (Sup. Ct., New York County 1980).

[5]   CPLR 5201(c)(4). For discussion of what property is "capable of delivery," see § 497.

[6]   This is in conformity with what the Code itself provides on the subject. See N.Y. UCC § 7–602. It is designed to protect the bailee of goods by authorizing him to reject a levy on the goods in his possession unless the negotiable document is surrendered.

[7]   CPLR 5201(c)(4).

[8]   CPLR 5201(c)(1).

however, go after any other property belonging to the garnishee,[9] at least not until appropriate follow-up proceedings have been taken and these have produced a judgment in favor of the judgment creditor directly against the garnishee.[10]

A fringe benefit emerges from taking note of who the proper garnishee is in these several situations. As noted in the section on "contingent intangibles,"[11] almost any kind of assignable interest is leviable today if a New York situs can be found for it. Finding the garnishee is just another way of finding the asset's "situs": if the garnishee has a New York presence, the debtor's asset in the garnishee's hands will usually be found to have a New York situs, too. Where, for example, the garnishee owes the judgment debtor a debt, not represented by a negotiable instrument, the garnishee's physical presence in New York fixes New York as the situs of the debt.[12] Where the asset being pursued is a claim that the judgment debtor has against the garnishee, the garnishee's New York presence enables suit on the claim to be brought in New York and thus, again, gives the claim a New York situs. Even in the case of a debt represented by a negotiable instrument, which is deemed property with the proper garnishee being its custodian, one can treat the interest as having a New York situs as long as the garnishee is in New York. This is so even if the instrument or document is in the garnishee's custody at an out-of-state location.

A leading case so holding is the Court of Appeals decision in Koehler v. Bank of Bermuda Ltd.,[13] which held that a Bermuda bank with a New York branch could be treated as a garnishee with a New York presence, enabling a New York court to direct the garnishee to deliver certain stock certificates on deposit with it in Bermuda to a petitioner who brought a special proceeding in New York. The petitioner was a judgment creditor with a Maryland judgment—duly converted into a New York judgment—against the judgment debtor who owned the stock. The creditor sought to seize the stock with a New York enforcement device: a delivery or "turnover" order under CPLR 5225(b). It worked, although barely: the court was divided 4–3 and the dissent raised some difficult issues.[14]

The decision in *Koehler* must now be viewed in light of the Court's 2014 decision in Motorola Credit Corp. v. Standard Chartered Bank,[15] which held that the " 'separate entity' rule prevents a judgment creditor from ordering a garnishee bank operating branches in New York to restrain a judgment debtor's assets held in foreign branches of the bank." A two-judge dissent in *Motorola*, joined by the author of *Koehler*, concluded, among other things, that the Court's opinion could not be reconciled with *Koehler*, which the majority attempted to do on several occasions.[16] The decisions in *Koehler* and *Motorola* demonstrate that judgment enforcement in our global economy can lead to

---

[9]   See Smith v. Amherst Acres, Inc., 43 A.D.2d 792, 350 N.Y.S.2d 236 (4th Dep't 1973).

[10]   This can happen, for example, if a garnishee resists the levy. The judgment creditor can bring a special proceeding against the garnishee, in which a money judgment can be rendered for the creditor directly against the garnishee. This judgment may then be enforced against property of the garnishee, who in this situation has become a judgment debtor. See §§ 496 and 510.

[11]   See § 489.

[12]   See Harris v. Balk, 198 U.S. 215, 25 S. Ct. 625, 49 L. Ed. 1023 (1905), and the discussion in § 487.

[13]   Koehler v. Bank of Bermuda Ltd., 12 N.Y.3d 533, 883 N.Y.S.2d 763, 911 N.E.2d 825 (2009).

[14]   The case is treated more extensively in the lead note in NYSLD No. 595 and in a follow-up Outside Counsel column in the New York Law Journal of July 28, 2009 (page 4).

[15]   Motorola Credit Corp. v. Standard Chartered Bank, 24 N.Y.3d 149, 996 N.Y.S.2d 594, 21 N.E.3d 223 (2014).

[16]   The *Motorola* decision is discussed in further detail in § 487.

some very close and difficult calls. This is due, in part, to the fact that most of the devices relied upon in this area were drafted over a half-century ago.

What if the debtor's property is not held by a bank with a New York branch, as in *Koehler*, but by a New York bank's foreign subsidiary? In Commonwealth of Northern Mariana Islands v. Canadian Imperial Bank of Commerce,[17] the Court of Appeals held "that for a court to issue a post-judgment turnover order pursuant to CPLR 5225(b) against a banking entity, that entity itself must have actual, not merely constructive, possession or custody of the assets sought." In short, the mere fact that a New York bank's subsidiary might have possession or custody of a judgment debtor's assets is not sufficient to compel the bank to produce those assets in New York. CPLR 5225(b) permits a judgment creditor to commence a special proceeding "against a person in *possession or custody* of money or other personal property in which the judgment debtor has an interest," commonly known as a turnover proceeding. The petitioner in *Northern Mariana Islands* contended that the phrase "possession or custody" in CPLR 5225(b) includes the concept of control and that the subdivision is, therefore, "applicable to garnishees with constructive possession of a judgment debtor's assets." Petitioner argued that because the New York bank could, in effect, order its subsidiary to turn over the assets of the judgment debtor to it in New York, it could be compelled to do so under CPLR 5225(b).

The Court rejected the argument, emphasizing that "[t]he plain language of section 5225(b) refers only to 'possession or custody,' excluding any reference to 'control.'"[18] Tracing the legislative history of the subdivision, the Court concluded that exclusion of the word "control," which had been present in the predecessor Civil Practice Act provisions, "signaled a purposeful legislative modification of the applicable scope, of turnover statutes."[19] The Court referenced several CPLR provisions that include the word "control," reasoning that its absence in CPLR 5225(b) was purposeful and was intended to require actual possession or custody by the garnishee.

Considering that this was an effort to enforce a New York judgment, a construction that aids enforcement should, as between competing possibilities, be the one selected. A leasehold interest in real property, however, as mentioned during the earlier discussion of the *Glassman* and *ABKCO* cases,[20] has been held to be where the real property is, putting rents beyond levy when the property is outside New York, notwithstanding that the lessee, i.e., the rent payer, also has a New York presence (such as where it is a corporation doing business in many places, including New York).

Although the state is not subject to the enforcement procedures of Article 52 when it is the judgment debtor, it may be and often is a garnishee and is in general subject to the provisions of Article 52 affecting garnishees.[21] Without statutory authorization, however, the federal government and its agencies may not be compelled to serve as garnishees on New York process, even when a federal employee is the judgment debtor

---

[17]   Commonwealth of Northern Mariana Islands v. Canadian Imperial Bank of Commerce, 21 N.Y.3d 55, 57, 967 N.Y.S.2d 876, 878, 990 N.E.2d 114, 115 (2013) (NYSLD No. 641).

[18]   *Northern Mariana Islands*, 21 N.Y.3d at 60, 967 N.Y.S.2d at 879, 990 N.E.2d at 117.

[19]   *Northern Mariana Islands*, 21 N.Y.3d at 61–62, 967 N.Y.S.2d at 880, 990 N.E.2d at 118.

[20]   See § 489.

[21]   CPLR 5207. An example of the garnishment contemplated would be the salary of a state employee who is the judgment debtor. By statute, however, tax refunds or credits due the judgment debtor as the taxpayer are not garnishable. Tax Law § 7.

and only her salary is sought to be garnished.[22] The procedure in that situation is to pursue the money only after it has reached the judgment debtor's hands. That could be done with an installment payment order under CPLR 5226.[23]

C. DEVICES IN PERSPECTIVE

Table of Sections

§ 492. The Enforcement Devices, Introductory
§ 493. Courts in Which Enforcement Devices Available

§ 492. The Enforcement Devices, Introductory

There are eight enforcement devices in Article 52; nine, if we include contempt, which aids enforcement only indirectly. The following is the list, with the CPLR provisions that supply and implement the particular device.

1.	Property execution	CPLR 5230.
	Levy and sale of	
	— personal property	CPLR 5232–3.
	— real property	CPLR 5235–5236.
2.	Income executions	CPLR 5231, 5241–2.
*3.	Restraining notice	CPLR 5222.
*4.	Disclosure in aid of enforcement	CPLR 5223–4.
*5.	Delivery order or judgment	CPLR 5225, 5227.
*6.	Installment payment order	CPLR 5226.
7.	Receivership	CPLR 5228.
8.	Arrest	CPLR 5250.
9.	Contempt	CPLR 5251.

* The asterisked devices are the ones that rely for implementation on the contempt punishment.

The list follows the order in which the devices appear in Article 52, except for the two categories of execution. These have been taken out of their CPLR sequence and listed first mainly because all courts have jurisdiction of them, whereas not all courts have jurisdiction of the others, a matter to be elaborated in the next section. The others, numbers 3 through 9, are collectively known to the bar as the "supplementary proceedings," a terminology borrowed from prior law. Technically the term is not accurate today because the devices in the main are not "proceedings" in the sense of separate special proceedings.[1] They are for the most part just enforcement devices

---

[22] A statutory example of where the United States can be a garnishee in a state court proceeding is where it concerns a support or alimony obligation of a federal employee. See, e.g., Diaz v. Diaz, 568 F.2d 1061 (4th Cir. 1977).

[23] See § 511.

[1] The details of the procedures in special proceedings are met in a later chapter. See §§ 547 et seq.

captioned in the very action that produced the judgment, usually entailing nothing more than a motion, and some don't even require that. There are, however, a few special proceedings expressly authorized, such as to require garnishees and other third persons to honor enforcement devices they have not honored voluntarily. These will be met in the course of the individual treatment given each device in subsequent portions of the chapter.

Later sections will also go into some detail about which of the devices give their user a priority or lien on the defendant's personal property,[2] but for the present bird's eye view we can note that the devices that do this are the property execution, number 1 on the above list, and the delivery and receivership orders, numbers 5 and 7.[3] The restraining notice, number 3 on the list, does not give priority under the CPLR, a fact that some lawyers have overlooked to their detriment.[4]

As to the sequence in which the devices must be used, there is none. The judgment creditor can use whichever ones suit the particular purpose at hand, beginning with any one of them and finishing with any other, with no particular progression except that which the judgment creditor has decided suits the case best. The CPLR has no direction about it, preferring for this, as it prefers for enforcement generally, to leave the correction and avoidance of all abuses to individual protective orders under CPLR 5240.[5]

None of the enforcement devices is available against the State when it is a judgment debtor, but the State and its agencies do remain subject to all of the Article 52 devices when the state is a garnishee.[6] If a genuine dispute arises as to whether the State as garnishee is in fact indebted to the judgment debtor, the guise of an enforcement proceeding will not be able to resolve it, as it might with a private garnishee, because it would usurp the jurisdiction of the court of claims, which has exclusive power to hear claims against the State.

Under Rule 69(a) of the Federal Rules of Civil Procedure, state practices and procedures are in large measure adopted for enforcement of the judgments of local federal courts, thus making these New York devices, which in the language of the federal rule are "proceedings supplementary to and in aid of judgment," available to the federal courts situated in New York.[7]

§ 493. Courts in Which Enforcement Devices Available

Courts that have civil jurisdiction usually have jurisdiction of the two execution devices: the property execution and the income execution, the first two devices on the prior section's list. All of the state's lower courts have, including the New York City Civil

---

[2]   A lien on real property is accomplished by mere docketing. See § 517.

[3]   See §§ 519 and 520. An income execution, number 2 on the list, also earns priority, but only with respect to income and only as against other income execution users. See § 504.

[4]   See §§ 508 and 520.

[5]   The protective order is treated in § 522.

[6]   CPLR 5207. See Bankers Trust Co. v. State Dept. of Audit and Control, 28 A.D.2d 272, 284 N.Y.S.2d 594 (3d Dep't 1967).

[7]   See § 641 (Practitioner's Edition).

Court, the district and city courts,[1] and even the town and village courts.[2] But devices 3 through 9 on the list, collectively known informally as the supplementary proceedings, are beyond the jurisdiction of some of the lower courts and must be sought—when a judgment of one of those courts is involved—in the supreme court or in a county court. Which courts have and which courts lack this jurisdiction is determined by CPLR 5221.

In subdivision (a), CPLR 5221 lists the courts that have the necessary jurisdiction. In terms, the subdivision simply lists the courts in which a "special proceeding" authorized by Article 52 may be brought. The enforcement devices of Article 52 are for the most part not special proceedings, however; they are mere adjuncts of the original action that gave rise to the judgment. But subdivision (b) of CPLR 5221, by listing the implements whereby the other enforcement devices are exploited, restricts them to only the courts listed in subdivision (a). Thus the two subdivisions between them account for restricting jurisdiction of the so-called "supplementary proceedings" to the courts listed in subdivision (a).

The supreme court and the county courts entertain all of the enforcement devices involving their judgments.[3] So do the New York City Civil Court[4] and the district courts.[5] The city courts, too, but with respect to city court judgments the county court is made an alternative forum for enforcement.[6]

The town and village courts lack jurisdiction of the "supplementary proceeding" devices; when one of those devices is used to enforce a judgment of a town or village court, it is captioned in and seeks the aid of either the supreme court or a county court.[7]

Neither do the surrogates' courts entertain these devices to enforce their judgments.[8]

CPLR 5221 also supplies venue for most of the Article 52 devices.[9]

To the extent that any judicial aid is needed, the aim of CPLR 5221 is to require the judgment creditor to seek it only in a place convenient to the person against whom the device is used. A lower court, for example, even if it can entertain all of the enforcement

---

[1]   See Article 15 of the New York City Civ. Ct. Act, and of the Uniform Dist. Ct. Act, and Uniform City Ct. Act, McKinney's Vol. 29A, Part 3. Execution against real property, however, does not issue out of those courts; a transcripting procedure is invoked and the supreme court is used. See § 1505 in each of the cited acts.

[2]   See Article 15 of the Uniform Just. Ct. Act, McKinney's Vol. 29A, Part 2. Again, as mentioned in the prior note, the court's execution may not be levied against real property; the supreme court is used for that after the judgment has been transcribed. See Uniform Just. Ct. Act § 1505. The surrogate's court does not ordinarily entertain the money judgment enforcement devices, not even the executions; the supreme court acts as the enforcement arm. See SCPA 605. But the surrogate's court does handle the contempt punishment for equity and certain other of its own judgments. See SCPA 606, 607.

[3]   CPLR 5221(a)(4).

[4]   CPLR 5221(a)(3).

[5]   CPLR 5221(a)(2).

[6]   CPLR 5221(a)(1).

[7]   CPLR 5221(a)(4). An outright conversion of a lower court judgment into one of the supreme court for enforcement purposes can occur if the lower court judgment has been docketed by transcript with the county clerk of the home county. See CPLR 5018(a). When that is done, the judgment creditor has the option, for CPLR 5221 purposes, of treating the judgment as one of either the lower court that rendered it or the supreme court.

[8]   SCPA 605. See note 2.

[9]   It is sometimes necessary to bring a special proceeding to aid in the perfection of an execution, see, e.g., CPLR 5232(a), 5225, 5227. When it is, the court and venue restrictions of CPLR 5221(a) apply even though the particular lower court can otherwise entertain its own executions.

devices, will be allowed to do so only if the person involved resides or works in the county in which the lower court is located, or, in the case of the New York City Civil Court, in New York City. If the person lives and works elsewhere, but within the state, court applications should be addressed to the supreme court or county court of the county of that person's residence or work. If she neither lives nor works in the state, the applications go to the supreme court or county court of the county in which the person is served with the necessary papers or the county in which judgment was rendered.[10] If the needed court is not in session in the right county, the proceeding may be brought in an adjoining county or any other county in the same judicial district.[11] These rules apply whether the person against whom the device or proceeding is aimed is the judgment debtor proper, or a garnishee, or some other third person.[12] They sound more complicated than they actually are. This phase of the rules is just a "where to do" reference chart, which can be consulted as needed when the lawyer is about to use a given device or initiate a special proceeding.

Defects in the use of CPLR 5221 will usually be mere venue errors, correctible with a change of venue or, in an appropriate case, deemed waived. They can sometimes be jurisdictional, however.

An example of a mere venue mistake is where, on a supreme court judgment, an enforcement proceeding has been brought in the wrong county. The respondent's failure to object to it will constitute a waiver of the wrong venue,[13] and even a timely objection should result in nothing worse than a change of venue to the right county.[14] But if enforcement is sought from a court without any jurisdiction at all under the varied terms of CPLR 5221(a), as where it is sought from a county court to enforce a district court judgment, the defect has been held jurisdictional.[15]

It should not be serious even in that instance, however: a judgment has a 20-year life,[16] and if the enforcement was sought any time within that period—but not, of course, near its very end—there would be nothing to stop the judgment creditor from pivoting right about and bringing the device or proceeding afresh in the right court. A dismissal (and thus a new start) may not even be necessary; transfer to the right court may be an alternative, by analogy to the transfer powers that courts have in connection with actions initially brought in the wrong courts.[17]

With respect to the town and village courts, it's worth noting that one of the reasons for allowing judgments of other courts to seek full enforcement in their courts of rendition while requiring those of the town and village courts to invoke aid from higher courts is that the town and village courts usually lack the facilities and staff needed to process the supplementary devices, which often require much judicial attention. There are, moreover, a number of incidental equitable powers connected with these devices,

---

[10]   CPLR 5221(a)(4).

[11]   CPLR 5221(a)(5).

[12]   An exception is the deposition taken of the judgment debtor (as opposed to some third person). In that instance, the county in which the action is pending is made a proper deposition venue even if the debtor neither lives nor works there. See CPLR 5224(c), adopting the venue provision of CPLR 3110(1). See § 509.

[13]   See Silbert v. Silbert, 25 A.D.2d 570, 267 N.Y.S.2d 744 (2d Dep't 1966).

[14]   CPLR 511, 103(b).

[15]   See Garrison Fuel Oil of Long Island, Inc. v. Grippo, 127 Misc. 2d 275, 486 N.Y.S.2d 136 (Nassau County Court 1985).

[16]   CPLR 211(b).

[17]   See § 24 in the chapter on subject matter jurisdiction.

including injunctions and orders enforceable by contempt, which the legislature has seen fit to withhold from the town and village courts, whose judges need not even be lawyers, and usually aren't.

It should be remembered, also, that CPLR 5221 and its offering of various courts designs only to aid enforcement. Only for the enforcement purpose, therefore, may a lower court judgment sometimes be treated like a judgment of a higher or different court. Note that this does not give the latter any power to trifle with the merits of the other court's judgment. A motion to vacate the judgment, for example,[18] would have to be made to the rendering court, as would any other kind of motion to modify, correct, resettle, or otherwise touch its merits.

It was noted earlier that a judgment of a lower court or of a federal court can be made the equivalent of a supreme court judgment through the simple procedure of docketing the judgment, with a transcript, in a county clerk's office.[19] Either the supreme court or a county court may then be used for enforcement of the judgment so docketed,[20] but it should be remembered that the person against whom enforcement is sought, including the judgment debtor himself, may not yet have been brought within the jurisdiction of the court being turned to for enforcement. If the device involved requires an actual application to the court, it may therefore be necessary to use a method of service that secures personal jurisdiction of the person involved. Where a federal judgment has been so docketed, for example, and an application to punish for contempt has to be made after (e.g.) an enforcement subpoena has been disobeyed, a mere motion served by ordinary mail may not suffice to secure the needed jurisdiction of the contemnor. A special proceeding, brought on by service of the initiatory papers in the same manner as a summons,[21] may be required.[22]

When a transcript of a lower court judgment is filed with the county clerk—for the purpose of converting the lower court judgment into a supreme court judgment for enforcement purposes—need a new filing fee be paid, as it would have to be for a new action brought in the higher court? An opinion issued by the Comptroller's office says no.[23]

A counseling point about terminology: various devices to be met in this chapter may sometimes be described as issuing "out of" a given court. This merely means that its caption bears the name of that court and that its issuance is upon the authority of that court; it does not necessarily mean that a judge issued it. Several devices, for example, do not need a judge's input, at least not at the outset, such as the restraining notice of CPLR 5222 and the subpoenas of CPLR 5224. They bear the signature of the judgment creditor's lawyer and are valid process just that way. They are nonetheless deemed to issue "out of" the higher court being used for enforcement and whose name their captions carry.

---

[18] See CPLR 5015.

[19] See § 422.

[20] See CPLR 5221(a)(4).

[21] CPLR 403(c). See § 553.

[22] See Federal Deposit Ins. Corp. v. Richman, 98 A.D.2d 790, 470 N.Y.S.2d 19 (2d Dep't 1983).

[23] The opinion is dated November 16, 2000. See SPR 98:1, 105:4.

D. PROPERTY EXECUTIONS

Table of Sections

§ 494.   The Executions, Generally
§ 495.   Property Execution, Issuance, and Contents
§ 496.   Levy on Personal Property
§ 497.   Property "Capable of Delivery"
§ 498.   Selling the Personal Property
§ 499.   Levy on Real Property
§ 500.   Selling the Real Property
§ 501.   Sheriff's Return

§ 494. The Executions, Generally

There are two categories of execution. The first is the property execution authorized by CPLR 5230. It can be levied against personal property under CPLR 5232 and 5233 or against real property under CPLR 5235 and 5236. The second is the income execution, supplied for money judgments in general by CPLR 5231, which operates against 10% of the judgment debtor's income, and for family support money in particular by CPLR 5241, which allows a greater percentage.

There is no priority of use among the executions. One can be used before or instead of the other. There is no requirement that a property execution be tried first.[1] Nor, in the case of the property execution, is there any priority between real and personal property: either class of property can be levied in whatever sequence the judgment creditor and sheriff work out, subject of course to variation by the court through a protective order under CPLR 5240. A preliminary court order is not required for either execution; it is just issued by the judgment creditor's lawyer and sent to the sheriff of the proper county. All of this will appear in more detail as the executions are taken up separately in ensuing sections.

An execution can be issued at any time during the 20-year period of the judgment's life[2] until the judgment is satisfied.

A sheriff or other court officer charged with carrying out an execution and failing to is subject to the compulsion of an Article 78 proceeding in the nature of mandamus.[3] The sheriff derelict in his duties also faces personal liability to the judgment creditor.[4]

§ 495. Property Execution, Issuance, and Contents

The main provision on the property execution is CPLR 5230, which, by its address to the "sheriff" as the enforcement officer, manifests its preoccupation with the supreme court and the county courts, for both of which the sheriff acts as the enforcement official.

---

[1]   Compare § 684 of the old Civ. Prac. Act (repealed 1963).

[2]   CPLR 211(b). Under CPLR 5014 the judgment can be renewed; if it is, it will get a new 20-year period. See § 434.

[3]   Liggett v. Pichler, 142 A.D.2d 206, 534 N.Y.S.2d 973 (1st Dep't 1988). Article 78 proceedings are studied beginning with § 557.

[4]   In Wang v. Bartel, 163 Misc. 2d 600, 624 N.Y.S.2d 735 (App. Term, 2d Dep't 1994), for example, noted in SPR 45:4, the court sustained a damages action by a judgment creditor suing a deputy sheriff for disregard of his duties.

With a little help from the lower court acts, CPLR 5230 also serves in the lower courts, which dictate that when the enforcement provisions are applied there, the word "sheriff" shall be deemed a reference to the court's own enforcement officer, should it be someone other than the sheriff.[1] In the New York City Civil Court, for example, the city marshals and the New York City sheriff both serve as enforcement officers and either may be turned to by the judgment creditor.[2] With these adjustments, CPLR 5230 is the uniform guidepost for property executions in all the state's courts.

As a result of legislation in 1997 and 1998, executions on supreme court judgments that are to be levied in New York City may be directed to a city marshal as an alternative to the sheriff.[3]

The execution may be issued by the clerk of the court or—the more common practice—by the judgment creditor's lawyer. No leave is needed. It may be directed to the sheriff of any county, and should of course be delivered to the sheriff of a county in which the judgment debtor has property.[4] For this purpose, no filing of a transcript is needed in the county in which enforcement is sought. Transcripting is not ordinarily a condition precedent to enforcement,[5] at least not when a supreme court or county court judgment rendered in one county is being levied in another: enforcement can proceed in the latter even though the judgment has not been docketed there.[6] But if a lower court judgment is being enforced in other than the lower court itself, it must have been docketed, by transcript, with the home county clerk, and in that situation, the execution must specify the date of the transcript's filing.

This last is a requirement of CPLR 5230(a), which also specifies the basics of what an execution must contain. Every execution must specify the court in which the judgment was entered, the date of its entry, the original amount of the judgment, the sum still due, and of course the names of the judgment creditor and judgment debtor.

As a practical matter, the lawyer should also accompany the execution with a note of some kind describing and locating the judgment debtor's property so that the sheriff can levy on it. The assumption that the sheriff will search for property himself is a bit too optimistic. That can be a demanding task, and even with the best intentioned sheriff, other duties ordinarily impede such searches. The statement identifying property is not mandated by the statute, however.[7] Indeed, the judgment creditor may be using the execution just to secure priority in the distribution of the judgment debtor's assets since

---

[1] See § 701(b) in the New York City Civ. Ct. Act, Uniform Dist. Ct. Act, Uniform City Ct. Act, and Uniform Just. Ct. Act, McKinney's Vol. 29A, Parts 2 and 3. As used in this chapter, "sheriff" includes the particular lower court's enforcement officers. To the extent that any further adjustments are needed to make the CPLR's execution provisions workable in a given lower court, they can be found in Article 15 of the cited court acts.

[2] New York City Civ. Ct. Act § 701(a).

[3] See SPR 61:3 and 75:2, and the Commentaries on § 1609 of the New York City Civ. Ct. Act. Reference to a sheriff will henceforth be deemed to include the city marshals when the execution is delivered in New York City.

[4] CPLR 5230(b).

[5] The transcripting procedure is described in § 422.

[6] Of course, if it has not been docketed there it will not be a lien on real property in that county, see § 517, which suggests that when it is real property that the judgment creditor is after, a transcripting would be wise just as a precaution to prevent another creditor from inadvertently securing priority.

[7] Some caselaw suggests that such a statement should accompany the execution. See, e.g., Princeton Bank & Trust Co. v. Berley, 57 A.D.2d 348, 394 N.Y.S.2d 714 (2d Dep't 1977).

the mere delivery of the execution makes it a lien on the debtor's personal property.[8] Because of this automatic lien effect, the failure of a sheriff to accept and receipt an execution only because it is not accompanied by a statement about the defendant's property can result in a liability for the sheriff.[9]

The creditor must be circumspect about identifying property as the debtor's. If the execution does specify property, a garnishee is entitled to rely on it. If the sheriff levies on the specified property, therefore, and it turns out that the property does not belong to the judgment debtor, "it is the creditor and not the garnishee who is liable for damages to the actual owner."[10] The creditor in need of information about the debtor's property can turn to CPLR 5223 and 5224, the provisions on disclosure in aid of enforcement.

If jurisdiction in the action that produced the judgment was based solely on the attachment of the judgment debtor's local assets, there being no personal jurisdiction of the debtor, the judgment may be enforced only against the previously attached assets. In that case the execution must state this limitation and direct that only the attached assets be levied.[11]

There is also a special limitation when the judgment is for a debt for which a mortgage was given as security. The policy of the law is to have the mortgagee bring a regular foreclosure action if there is a default, a procedure that preserves the mortgagor's right of redemption.[12] So, while the mortgagee can, if it chooses, ignore the mortgage and just bring an ordinary money action on the underlying debt (the note or bond), the mortgagee will find at the enforcement stage that the one property against which the execution may not be levied is the mortgaged property itself, lest the important right of redemption be circumvented. Accordingly, the execution in that instance must identify the mortgage by the book and page of its recording, describe (locate) the mortgaged property, and direct that no levy be made against it.[13]

A judgment debtor must be advised about the possibly exempt status of her property.[14] If a notice has previously been served on the judgment debtor advising to that effect,[15] the execution should say so.[16] If the execution does not contain the statement, the sheriff can include an appropriate notice about exempt property when he levies. It is the obligation of the judgment creditor to assure that this notice is given.[17]

In the case of a third-party (impleader) judgment, the rule is that there can be no enforcement of the judgment by way of execution or any other device unless and until

---

[8]   For liens and priorities, see §§ 518 et seq.

[9]   See the discussion in SPR 31:2.

[10]   Chin Sung Yu v. Riggs Nat. Bank of Washington, D.C., 248 A.D.2d 235, 670 N.Y.S.2d 187 (1st Dep't 1998).

[11]   CPLR 5230(a). This occurs in the quasi in rem category of jurisdiction, which was much reduced by the U.S. Supreme Court in Shaffer v. Heitner, 433 U.S. 186, 97 S. Ct. 2569, 53 L. Ed. 2d 683 (1977), discussed in § 104, but still has some residual use.

[12]   See RPAPL 1352.

[13]   CPLR 5230(a).

[14]   Exemptions are discussed in § 490.

[15]   Such an advice must be furnished, for example, when a restraining notice is used under CPLR 5222.

[16]   This is a requirement spelled out indirectly from subdivision (c) of CPLR 5232, added in 1982 to meet constitutional objections directed at several of the CPLR's enforcement devices. See § 508.

[17]   See the 1982 Commentaries C5222:11 and C5232:5 on McKinney's CPLR 5222 and 5232. The requirement is statutory, and the statutes implement constitutional demands, so there are in fact two bases for upsetting enforcement steps that fail to fulfill the notice requirement.

the defendant has made some payment to the plaintiff on the main judgment. The rule recognizes that a third-party judgment is almost always designed to indemnify the defendant for whatever she may have had to pay the plaintiff on the main judgment.

A violation of this rule with an effort to collect the third-party judgment before collection has been made on the main judgment can be remedied by an application for a protective order under CPLR 5240, quashing or limiting the execution. In rare instances, notably those involving a personal injury defendant who has been subjected to extra liability because her liability insurer has unreasonably failed to defend or indemnify her in the action, or to negotiate a settlement in good faith, execution has been allowed before actual payment of the main claim. Indeed, even a separate indemnity suit by insured against insurer for such an "excess"—the amount by which the liability imposed on the insured exceeds the insurance coverage—has been sustained before the insured has paid it out.[18] This recognizes the injustice of requiring an unfairly treated insured person to liquidate her assets only to discharge a liability for which the insurer may have to indemnify her anyway.[19]

Before we turn to the levy of the execution, covered in the following sections, a note of warning to the judgment debtor is appropriate. If the debtor does plan to pay the judgment, or in any event to appeal it and seek a stay of enforcement during the appeal, the debtor should take the appropriate step promptly. Delaying it, so that a levy goes forward, even if it can now be stopped in its tracks, may incur substantial poundage fees to the sheriff that could have easily been avoided. One defendant who delayed bonding a judgment in connection with an appeal, for example, had to pay $30,000 in otherwise avoidable poundage.[20] Not even the reversal of the judgment—on which the execution and its poundage were based—with a resulting dismissal of the complaint, will save the defendant the poundage.[21]

§ 496. Levy on Personal Property

The execution can be levied on personal property in either of two ways.

If the property is capable of delivery, and is not in the possession of one who has a superior right to its possession under (for example) a pledge or lease, the sheriff levies on it by taking it into his custody. When he does, the sheriff serves a copy of the execution on the person from whom the property is taken. This is levy by seizure under subdivision

---

[18] See Henegan v. Merchants Mut. Ins. Co., 31 A.D.2d 12, 294 N.Y.S.2d 547 (1st Dep't 1968), and compare Colpan Realty Corp. v. Great Am. Ins. Co., 83 Misc. 2d 730, 373 N.Y.S.2d 802 (Sup. Ct., Westchester County 1975).

[19] On rare occasions the courts have allowed a recovery over of this kind, before payment of the main judgment, even in noninsurance cases. See, e.g., Bonwit-Teller, Division of 721 Corp. v. Rosenstiel, 75 Misc. 2d 108, 347 N.Y.S.2d 753 (N.Y. City Civ. Ct. 1968). Except in the insured-versus-insurer situations, however, a prepayment recovery from a third-party defendant is not permitted. See § 175.

[20] Thornton v. Montefiore Hosp., 117 A.D.2d 552, 498 N.Y.S.2d 828 (1st Dep't 1986). After convincing the judgment creditor, P, to hold off execution to give D time to bond the judgment while D appealed, D delayed until P finally had the execution levied. D was a hospital and the levy held up D's payroll. D then got P to withdraw the levy, but the sheriff would not waive poundage. Of course, if the judgment should then be reversed on appeal, D would be able to recover the amount of the poundage from the plaintiff as a disbursement. See Herbert H. Levess & Co. v. Celebrity Knitwear, Inc., 130 Misc. 2d 1055, 498 N.Y.S.2d 974 (Sup. Ct., New York County 1986).

[21] See SPR 148:4.

(b) of CPLR 5232.[1] The sheriff's next duty is to sell the property.[2] Execution in this instance is subject to the requirement that it be returned by the sheriff within 60 days after issuance unless the judgment creditor gives the sheriff an additional 60 days. This requirement comes from subdivision (c) of CPLR 5230. It recognizes that since the execution gives its issuer priority in the debtor's personal property,[3] it should be levied and perfected expeditiously so as not to unfairly delay other waiting judgment creditors. If there are no other creditors, however, the judgment creditor can continue to give the sheriff 60-day extensions.[4]

If the property is not capable of delivery, the method of levy is for the sheriff to serve a copy of the execution on the garnishee,[5] which must be made in the same manner as a summons. This is known as levy by service and is governed by subdivision (a) of CPLR 5232.[6] When levy is by service instead of by seizure in the first instance, the 60-day limitation on the return time does not apply.[7]

Whatever the method of levy, the sheriff must be certain not to interfere with the rights of third persons. Trespassing on those rights can bring personal liability to the sheriff and his sureties. "Innocent mistake will not exculpate him, nor erroneous direction by the judgment creditor . . . . If in doubt, [the sheriff] would have the right to secure indemnification from the party seeking to have him act before proceeding to make levy."[8]

The sheriff's liability to third persons if he interferes with their rights in the course of the levy is addressed by the Court of Appeals in Cla-Mil East Holding Corp. v. Medallion Funding Corp.,[9] which holds that as long as the judgment creditor relies for the levy entirely on the enforcement officer—in *Cla-Mil* a marshal, but the holding applies as well to a sheriff—damage done to the property of a third person in the course of the levy is the responsibility of the enforcement officer, not the judgment creditor. The case, an unsuccessful action by the third person, a landlord, to make the judgment creditor pay for the damages caused by the levy, offered an opportunity to treat more extensively the procedures and liabilities—and protective options—of enforcement officers.[10]

---

[1]   The question periodically arises about whether the sheriff can break down the outer door of a residence—there is usually no problem about other places—to get at the property. On this subject, see the annotation in 57 ALR 210.

[2]   CPLR 5233, treated in § 498.

[3]   See §§ 519 and 520.

[4]   CPLR 5230(c).

[5]   Contrast these levy alternatives with levy of an attachment. Attachment, designed as it is to serve as security rather than enforcement, is ordinarily levied by delivery of a copy of the order of attachment to the garnishee regardless of the nature of the property, CPLR 6214(a). There, levy by seizure is required only if the plaintiff indemnifies the sheriff. CPLR 6215. With an execution, the initial levy is required to be by seizure if the property is capable of delivery; it may initially be made by mere service only if the property is not deliverable.

[6]   A CPLR 318 agent of the garnishee may be served with the execution in the garnishee's behalf, but no other agent (such as the secretary of state in the case of a corporation) may be. If the State is the garnishee, service instructions are contained in CPLR 5231(h), which CPLR 5232(a) adopts.

[7]   Kennis v. Sherwood, 82 A.D.2d 847, 439 N.Y.S.2d 962 (2d Dep't 1981).

[8]   See Meritum Corp. v. Pichler, N.Y.L.J., Sept. 10, 1980, at 7, col. 2 (Sup. Ct., New York County; Gammerman, J.); § 520.

[9]   Cla-Mil East Holding Corp. v. Medallion Funding Corp., 6 N.Y.3d 375, 813 N.Y.S.2d 1, 846 N.E.2d 431 (2006).

[10]   The treatment is in the lead note of NYSLD No. 555.

Notice of the levy must be given to the judgment debtor. CPLR 5232 was one of the statutes declared unconstitutional in the early 1980s for not requiring that notice be given to the judgment debtor about the possibly exempt status of the property being pursued for enforcement. It was amended in 1982 by adding a subdivision (c) to repair the omission.[11] The requirement is that if a proper notice[12] has not already been served on the judgment debtor, the sheriff must serve it on the debtor along with a copy of the execution. This service, which may be made by the sheriff by either personal delivery or by ordinary first class mail, must be made within four days after the sheriff has served the execution on the garnishee.[13]

The choice of the initial method of levy depends on whether the property involved is "capable of delivery." If it is, levy is by seizure under subdivision (b) of CPLR 5232; otherwise it's by service under subdivision (a), where it then requires careful follow-up steps needed to preserve it. These follow-up steps are commonly known as "perfecting" the levy.

For the sake of illustrating the perfection steps, it will be assumed that the property is not "capable of delivery."[14] The assumption will be that the levy is being made against (e.g.) a debt owed by the garnishee to the judgment debtor, not represented by an instrument and thus not amenable to a summary "seizure" by the sheriff in the first instance. That will do as an example.

In order for this levy-by-service to be effective, the garnishee must, at the time he is served with the execution, either owe a debt to the judgment debtor or have possession of some property in which the judgment debtor has an interest. As long as either is the fact at levy time, the levy applies not just to that debt or property, but also to any other property of the defendant that may afterwards come into the garnishee's possession. This includes any debts the garnishee owes to the debtor that may later fall due.[15] If the property is the judgment debtor's, but stands in the name of another, or if for any other reason there is some possibility that the garnishee may not know that some property of which he has possession belongs to the judgment debtor, the judgment creditor can describe and identify that property in a notice accompanying the execution, whereupon the levy applies to it. But the creditor had best be sure about this; the creditor is liable in damages if, using such a notice, he turns out to be mistaken and the mistake has injured the true owner.[16]

The obligation of the garnishee is to transfer the levied property to the sheriff and to pay to the sheriff rather than to the judgment debtor all matured debts owed to the debtor, executing such documents as may be needed to effect the transfer—a kind of attornment. As soon as the garnishee has made such a transfer, turning over to the

---

[11] The amendment and its requirements are discussed in Commentary C5232:5 on McKinney's CPLR 5232.

[12] The notice is fleshed out by subdivisions (d) and (e) of CPLR 5222, where it is part of the enforcement device known as the restraining notice. See § 508.

[13] CPLR 5232(c).

[14] What "capable of delivery" means is taken up in the next section.

[15] The requirement that the garnishee possess something of the debtor's at levy time in order to preserve validity has a counterpart in the restraining notice provision of CPLR 5222(b). See § 508.

[16] CPLR 5232(a).

sheriff everything he has belonging to the judgment debtor, the levy loses effect and applies to no other property coming into the garnishee's possession thereafter.[17]

This transfer should be made within 90 days after the levy, the levy being the moment that the garnishee is served with a copy of the execution. An outright transfer to the sheriff perfects and concludes the levy, now requiring only a sale by the sheriff of the personal property that has come into his possession. The levy must be perfected one way or another during that 90-day period,[18] however, and if the garnishee has not made a voluntary transfer to the sheriff within that time, the judgment creditor is going to have to take some other "perfection" step before the 90 days expire.[19]

Two other steps are available, either of which will perfect the levy, at least to the extent of satisfying the 90-day requirement. One is for the judgment creditor to commence a special proceeding against the uncooperative garnishee,[20] and its mere commencement within the 90 days satisfies the requirement; the proceeding need not be heard or determined within that time. The second alternative, and often the simplest one, is for the creditor merely to secure an extension of the 90-day period. This the creditor can do by motion, and the extension will be whatever time the court allows, not necessarily limited to 90-day spurts.[21] An extension is not granted just for the asking, however. Aware that other judgments creditors may be waiting in the wings, the court must be satisfied that the judgment creditor is proceeding with diligence.

During the 90 days, or whatever extended period the court allows, the garnishee is required to preserve the levied property, allowing no one but the sheriff at it unless the court directs otherwise. A garnishee who violates this prohibition, although not subject to the contempt punishment,[22] bears personal liability to the judgment creditor for any resulting damages, which the creditor can recover in the special proceeding noted earlier.

If none of the steps discussed above is taken within the 90 days, the levy becomes void and its injunctive effect dissolves.[23] It is unwise, therefore, for the judgment creditor to let the 90 days pass without seeing to it that some appropriate protective step is taken. In one case, for example, in which a garnishee bank had sent a check in fulfillment of the levy, but the check was lost, the bank asked the creditor's lawyer to make out a lost check form. The lawyer passed the buck by saying it was the sheriff who should make out the lost check form. While the buck passed, so did the 90 days, and the levy failed.[24] A simple motion to extend the 90 days, made before the period expired, would probably have sufficed to preserve the levy.

The 90-day period is not relevant when the initial levy is by seizure under subdivision (b); it's designed to recognize the need for extra time when the property is not amenable to simple seizure, the scenario contemplated by subdivision (a). The subdivision (b) seizure is governed by the 60-day period of CPLR 5230(c), which requires that the execution be completed and returned within that time. The 60 days run from

---

[17]   CPLR 5232(a).

[18]   Here is another analogy to the attachment device. See § 321.

[19]   CPLR 5232(a).

[20]   The proceeding contemplated is governed by CPLR 5225 or 5227. See § 510. The garnishee in that proceeding can assert her defenses or otherwise explain why the property was not handed over.

[21]   CPLR 5232(a).

[22]   See CPLR 5251.

[23]   CPLR 5232(a).

[24]   Wordie v. Chase Manhattan Bank, N.A., 140 A.D.2d 435, 529 N.Y.S.2d 1 (2d Dep't 1988).

the issuance of the execution, while the 90 days applicable under 5232(a) run from the levy. In each instance the time allowed is felt to be adequate for expeditious enforcement in the particular circumstances; other judgment creditors waiting in line should not be put off any longer than necessary.[25]

§ 497. Property "Capable of Delivery"

This is an apt juncture at which to address the phrase "capable of delivery" as used in CPLR 5232 and elsewhere in the CPLR.[1] Parts of this discourse will touch on a few items, like priorities and liens, not treated until later, but the phrase is too fundamental a part of the levying of executions to be put off. Anticipatory references will be just brief enough to understand the role that priorities and liens play in making the "capable of delivery" phrase loom larger today than it did under prior law.

Since whether or not a given property is "capable of delivery" will determine whether it is to be levied by initial seizure under CPLR 5232(b) or by initial service under CPLR 5232(a) (in the latter case, with subsequent steps to perfect the levy), we must analyze it carefully in this context. Nowhere in the CPLR is there a comprehensive description of what makes property "capable of delivery," although a few property interests otherwise unlikely to fit without a little push have been brought within the standard. A property interest consisting of a debt represented by a negotiable instrument, for example, has been strictly categorized as "capable of delivery": the instrument itself is deemed the property and the one holding the instrument rather than the one owing the debt is deemed the garnishee through whom enforcement is pursued.[2]

We may reasonably deduce that any intangible obligation, whether debt or cause of action or otherwise, not represented by a negotiable instrument is property "not capable of delivery" and is to be treated as such for enforcement.[3] The question is, is that the only thing that falls beyond the standard? Is everything else, including all interests in a tangible chattel, to be deemed "capable of delivery" without regard to anything else?

Common sense suggests that a pragmatic definition is needed for "capable of delivery" as used in Article 52. Any situation in which the sheriff cannot readily lay hands on the property interest involved, and by some means take immediate actual or at least constructive custody of it, should be deemed to involve property "not capable of delivery" and therefore to permit levy by service under subdivision (a) of CPLR 5232 instead of being restricted to levy be seizure under subdivision (b). To say otherwise would often frustrate the levy of an execution when there is no need to.[4] Several prominent illustrations come to mind.

Assume a debt represented by a negotiable instrument. The CPLR clearly deems the instrument "capable of delivery." Now suppose the garnishee who has custody of the instrument will not surrender it, or even tell the sheriff where it is. Is execution to fail completely? Is levy by service under subdivision (a), which would work nicely in that

---

[25]   See Vance Boiler Works, Inc. v. Co-Operative Feed Dealers, Inc., 46 Misc. 2d 654, 260 N.Y.S.2d 303 (Sup. Ct., Wayne County 1965).

[1]   E.g., CPLR 6215.

[2]   CPLR 5201(c)(4). See § 491.

[3]   See 3d Rep. Leg. Doc. No. 17, p. 296 (1959).

[4]   The situation would be all the more lamentable because in some situations it is only the levy itself, rather than the mere delivery of the execution to the sheriff, that affords the judgment creditor a priority in the property interest involved. See §§ 519 and 520.

situation, to be precluded because the property is technically "capable of delivery" and thus subject to levy only by seizure under subdivision (b), even though initial seizure has been frustrated? That showing should trigger CPLR 5232(a), enabling levy to be made just by serving the garnishee and leaving to the subsequent perfection process such steps as are needed to persuade the garnishee to deliver the instrument. If the garnishee refuses, the judgment creditor may bring a special proceeding against the garnishee as a perfection step under CPLR 5232(a), and this will likely persuade the garnishee to hand over the instrument under pain of facing a direct judgment for its sum. CPLR 5232(a) would thus serve well, while CPLR 5232(b), by insisting on an initial seizure when none is possible, would not work at all.

Another example would be where the property is a chattel of some kind that the garnishee has in her residence or some other place inaccessible to the sheriff.[5] The sheriff can't readily seize it and, were subdivision (b) to preempt, no levy would be possible. This practical impediment should by itself translate the property from capable to incapable of seizure and thereby authorize levy by service under subdivision (a).

Yet another illustration would be where the garnishee has the property, and the sheriff can easily lay hands on it, but when it is under pledge or lease to the garnishee, who therefore has a right to its continued possession. CPLR 5232(b) itself precludes seizure in that case, and by implication authorizes levy by service under subdivision (a), which is meaningful: the service of the execution on the garnishee will warn her that when her possessory right terminates she must give the chattel to the sheriff rather than back to the judgment debtor, thus protecting the judgment creditor's interest. Here is a piece of pragmatism built right into CPLR 5232 itself, and it can be cited as inviting a pragmatic approach to the other levy situations.

If reasonable means exist for the sheriff to effect an immediate seizure, even if it entails only constructive custody—as by chaining and locking the working parts of a big piece of machinery so as to make it inoperable, or designating some person on the premises as the sheriff's custodian—the case can be deemed one for subdivision (b) and levy by seizure can be required. But if no such reasonable means exist, whether because the property is concealed, or inaccessible, or is for any other reason unseizable even constructively, a levy by service should be permissible under subdivision (a).

The argument may be heard that if the property is not capable of immediate seizure, the judgment creditor need not bother about the execution device at all; that the creditor can just turn to one of the other devices, such as a delivery application under CPLR 5225(b) or 5227. The trouble with that, as we shall see, is that these other devices do not give the judgment creditor a lien on the affected property until the order or judgment sought is actually granted, entered, and filed, which can be a long way off, while an execution will afford the judgment creditor a lien directly upon levy by the sheriff, and sometimes even upon mere delivery of the execution to the sheriff.[6] The prior law counterparts of today's restraining notice[7] and disclosure subpoena[8] did create liens for

---

5   See § 496.
6   See the discussion of liens in §§ 519 and 520.
7   CPLR 5222.
8   CPLR 5224.

their user,[9] but today neither does.[10] If they did, either would serve as a lien-giver just as effectively as an execution, because either is promptly servable without court leave, just as an execution is. This change from prior to present law makes fast access to the execution all the more important today for the lien it instantly secures.[11] Echoing CPLR 5232(b), old caselaw holds that if property is "capable of delivery" it must be levied by seizure and that if there is no seizure, there is no levy.[12] This is not inconsistent with what is urged here, which suggests only that the phrase be interpreted pragmatically.[13]

It's always preferable, especially from the judgment creditor's point of view, to have the levy made by immediate seizure, and the sheriff remains under obligation to seize whenever it is feasible. If a seizure can be readily effected, a sheriff turning instead to a levy by service under CPLR 5232(a) would be effecting no levy at all, which can well damage the judgment creditor should some competitor achieve priority as a result. For that, the sheriff would be liable to the creditor,[14] which suggests that the sheriff himself would prefer to turn to levy by service under subdivision (a) only when not reasonably able to effect levy by seizure under subdivision (b).

A practical definition of what "capable of delivery" means thus need not be apprehended as inviting laxity on the part of enforcement officers. In fact, increasing the use of levy by service gives the judgment creditor closer control of enforcement proceedings: the execution and/or levy gives the creditor priority, at least for a time, which protects the creditor while he now turns to other devices for enforcement aid without undue concern about whether or not they are also lien-givers.

§ 498. Selling the Personal Property

Any levied personal property that comes into the sheriff's possession and which is not itself money (legal tender) must be sold by the sheriff at public auction pursuant to CPLR 5233. In fact, the sheriff is required to sell not only property that comes to him through an execution, but also that which he gets through any other Article 52 device, such as a delivery order.[1] The sheriff must give notice of the sale[2] and is authorized to sell the property, tangible or intangible, as a unit, in lots, or in such other form as in his judgment will best attract bidders.[3] If the situation poses any urgency, the court can order immediate sale or other disposition, dispensing with the formal auction requirements.[4] It will exercise that power, for example, in the case of perishables, or

---

[9]   See Civ. Prac. Act § 781 (repealed 1963); Wickwire Spencer Steel Co. v. Kemkit Scientific Corporation, 292 N.Y. 139, 54 N.E.2d 336, 153 A.L.R. 208 (1944).

[10]   See City of New York v. Panzirer, 23 A.D.2d 158, 259 N.Y.S.2d 284 (1st Dep't 1965).

[11]   Graze v. Bankers Trust Co., 45 Misc. 2d 610, 257 N.Y.S.2d 483 (Sup. Ct., New York County 1965), illustrates how one who diligently makes a CPLR 5225 application as well as serves both a 5222 restraining notice and a 5224 subpoena still loses out to another judgment creditor in whose behalf a simple execution levy is made.

[12]   See, e.g., Pach v. Gilbert, 124 N.Y. 612, 27 N.E. 391 (1891).

[13]   The interpretation suggested would also appear to be the only one permissible under the liberal construction edict of CPLR 104.

[14]   See § 520.

[1]   CPLR 5225. See § 510.

[2]   CPLR 5233(b) provides for the notice methods.

[3]   CPLR 5233(a).

[4]   CPLR 5233(c).

where the property involved has only momentary value, such as a news article or film clip on a topic of current interest.

If an issue arises about whether particular property is saleable, such as contraband, the sheriff can apply to the court for instructions.[5]

From whatever is realized at the sale, the sheriff deducts his fees and expenses and any taxes that may be due, paying the balance to the judgment creditor towards satisfaction of the judgment; if anything remains, it of course goes to the judgment debtor.[6]

§ 499. Levy on Real Property

A levy on real property is easier in its first stage than one on personal property, mainly because it initially involves neither a "seizure" nor even the service of the execution on the garnishee—the methods of a personal property levy.[1] With the sale of the real property, it is the second stage, treated in the next section, that becomes more involved, mainly because of CPLR 5236 and its demanding set of statutory requirements for the sale.

The first thing the judgment creditor should see to when she has an eye to the debtor's real property is that the judgment has been docketed in the county clerk's office of the real property county. It is the docketing that makes the judgment a lien on the real property in that county and prevents others from slipping in with a priority while its sale is being carried out.[2]

The initial lien of the judgment is only 10 years, however,[3] while the life of the judgment is 20.[4] This means that if the judgment is more than 10 years old when the levy is sought (the levy being permissible any time during the life of the judgment), the enforcement will be going forward at a time when the judgment has lost its lien value. For that situation, CPLR 5235 has a special procedure whereby the judgment can once again be made a lien, at least for a long enough time to enable the sheriff to sell the property.

To accomplish this, the judgment creditor delivers an execution to the sheriff of the real property county and has the sheriff file with its county clerk a "notice of levy," which describes the judgment, the execution, and the property. This is then indexed in the same manner as a notice of pendency.[5] The judgment thereupon becomes a lien once again and remains a lien until the execution is returned by the sheriff,[6] which will not occur until the sale has been completed. The sheriff now goes ahead with the sale.

During the first 10 years of the judgment, when—as long as the judgment has been duly docketed in the real property county—it retains its original lien value, this filing of a notice of levy is unnecessary. If the sheriff has received an execution from the judgment creditor, he simply proceeds with the sale. If the judgment creditor wants to avoid a

---

5   Subdivision (d), added to CPLR 5233 in a 1979 amendment, so authorizes.

6   CPLR 5234(a).

1   CPLR 5232 contains the methods for levying against personal property.

2   For treatment of the docketing of judgments between and among courts, see §§ 421 and 422.

3   CPLR 5203(a). See § 517.

4   CPLR 211(b).

5   For the methods of indexing a notice of pendency, see § 335.

6   CPLR 5203(a).

priority gap, as when the levy occurs near the tail end of the 10-year lien period, she can, during the last year of that period, commence an action to renew the judgment and secure a fresh 10-year lien.[7]

The CPLR has no requirement, incidentally, that a levy on personal property be attempted before the defendant's real property is levied. The judgment creditor can go after real property directly, subject to an ad hoc protective order varying the progression if the court sees fit.[8]

§ 500. Selling the Real Property

The requirements for the sale of real property under an execution are more profuse and detailed than those for personal property. The statute in point, CPLR 5236, has come in for a number of amendments, several resulting from a study conducted during the early years of the CPLR.[1] Although its ultimate impact is on the creditor and debtor, the statute is of more immediate moment to the sheriff, who must conduct the sale, and to the title companies, which will end up paying the bill if some oversight causes a title to fail. The title companies, in fact, have been the principal overseers of CPLR 5236 and the advocates of most of its amendments.

The sale of the real property is, as with personal property, by public auction, but with a more elaborate set of notice requirements. The sheriff must post notice of the sale in at least three public places in the town or city in which the real property is located and publish the notice in a newspaper in the real property's county. These exactions and their time instructions are in CPLR 5236(c),[2] which also requires the sheriff to notify the judgment debtor and all others who are shown of record to have any lien on or interest in the real property as of a certain day, fixed with reference to the projected date of sale. The judgment creditor must furnish the sheriff a list of these other lienholders. The requirement that they be notified is to enable them to take such steps as they feel necessary to protect their own interests. The auction at which the sale is conducted takes place, unless duly postponed, between the 8th and 9th week following the first publication of the notice of sale.[3]

Among those included on the creditors' list will be other judgment creditors of the same debtor, if their judgments have been made liens against the property. Upon getting notice from the sheriff, they must deliver their own executions to him, which entitles them to take their proper place in line for the sale's proceeds.[4] Even a creditor whose judgment lien is senior to that of the judgment being levied on must, upon being notified, deliver an execution. A failure to do so forfeits his lien.[5] If the senior creditor does deliver it, however, he will have first crack at the proceeds of the sale, even though it's at another judgment creditor's initiative that the sale is taking place. Proceeds must be distributed

---

[7]   CPLR 5014. See § 434.

[8]   CPLR 5240. See § 522.

[1]   See Sale of Real Property Pursuant to an Execution under the CPLR, 10th Jud. Conf. Rep. 120 (1965).

[2]   The typical posting locations are on bulletin boards found in post offices, municipal buildings (state or local courthouse lobby, county DMV, county clerk, county treasurer, town hall, village hall, etc.), convenience stores, libraries, and banks. See also RPAPL 231(2)(b) (prescribing similar notice requirements in certain foreclosure sales).

[3]   CPLR 5236(a), (d).

[4]   CPLR 5236(g).

[5]   CPLR 5236(e); Meadow Brook Nat. Bank v. Goodkin, 53 Misc. 2d 1099, 280 N.Y.S.2d 978 (Sup. Ct., Nassau County 1966), aff'd, 28 A.D.2d 648, 282 N.Y.S.2d 441 (2d Dep't 1967).

by the sheriff in the order of lien priority of the judgments on which he has received executions.[6] A junior judgment creditor can only hope (as can, indeed, the levying judgment creditor himself if he has confronted senior judgment liens) that there will be enough proceeds for all.

Other categories of senior lienholders, such as a mortgagee, retain their liens, to which the buyer at the sale takes subject, but junior lienors are wiped out by the sale. For that reason, a mortgagee or other lienor junior to the judgment being levied on is also allowed to share in any surplus that an execution sale on that judgment may produce.[7]

Whatever is left over from the sale's proceeds after payment of all fees, expenses, and taxes (in that order) and execution issuers and junior lienors (in the order of seniority among them), goes to the judgment debtor.[8] Other provisions govern the sheriff's conveyance to the buyer at the sale,[9] and issues arising if the buyer's title should for some reason fail.[10] Any party with an objection to the sheriff's proceedings may raise it by a motion to the court either under CPLR 5238, a special provision concerned with property levies, or CPLR 5240, the omnibus protective order provision applicable to all of Article 52.

If the judgment is for a mortgage debt on the subject real property and was entered in a money action on the debt instead of in an action to foreclose the mortgage that secures the debt, the real property cannot be levied on pursuant to the judgment because it would circumvent the right of redemption as it exists in mortgage foreclosure context.[11]

Since the real property will be sold to the highest bidder under CPLR 5236, without reference to whether or not the bid equals the judgment debtor's actual equity in the property, unhappy situations arise when the discrepancy is substantial. This is especially the case when the real property is a residence. There have been instances of the family home being sold for substantially less than the family's equity. The sale has nevertheless been upheld when the proceedings were regular and especially when the bidder was a stranger to them.[12]

The problem is the worse because there is no right of redemption here as there is in mortgage foreclosure—the right within a stated time to get up the money to pay off the debt, cancel the proceedings, and get property back. That is, there is no right of redemption explicitly set forth. With a protective order under CPLR 5240, however, the court can give the judgment debtor more time to seek the money to pay the judgment, postponing the sale for that purpose, and this amounts to a de facto right of redemption.

---

[6] CPLR 5236(g)(1). For priorities and liens with respect to real property, see § 517.

[7] Bank Leumi Trust Co. of New York v. Liggett, 115 A.D.2d 378, 496 N.Y.S.2d 14 (1st Dep't 1985).

[8] CPLR 5236(g)(2). If the property was the judgment debtor's principal residence, $50,000 is of course an exemption, CPLR 5206(a), and goes to the judgment debtor; the creditors ordinarily share only what is left after the $50,000 is subtracted. See § 490.

[9] CPLR 5236(f).

[10] CPLR 5237. Innocent purchasers are usually protected when their dispute is with one whose lien is junior to that of the levying judgment creditor (through whom their interests have come). See, e.g., First Federal Sav. & Loan Ass'n of Port Washington v. McKee, 61 Misc. 2d 693, 305 N.Y.S.2d 589 (Sup. Ct., Nassau County 1969).

[11] CPLR 5236(b). See § 495.

[12] See, e.g., In re Bachner, 82 Misc. 2d 107, 368 N.Y.S.2d 749 (Sup. Ct., Nassau County 1975), where the bid was claimed to be only 41% of the equity's market value.

The Court of Appeals, in Rondack Const. Services, Inc. v. Kaatsbaan Intern. Dance Center, Inc.,[13] also points out that a right to redeem actually does exist in execution cases under CPLR 5236(a), but only before a judicial sale. The statute provides for at least eight weeks to elapse between the posting of notice of the auction and the auction itself, a period which is in effect a redemption period because the debtor's tender of all due within that time undoes the enforcement step and preserves the property for the debtor, which is what occurred in *Rondack*.

If it appears that a private sale of the property, through the usual channels of advertisement or brokerage, will likely get a better price than what might be expected of the public auction under CPLR 5236, the court on motion can appoint a receiver to make such a sale.[14] The courts are sympathetic to judgment debtors faced with the loss of their residential equity for less than its worth. In one memorable case, in which an equity of $13,000 was about to go for $197.25, and to someone in apparent privity with the judgment creditor—who may of course join the bidders, but whose presence makes the court all the more suspicious—the court set aside the sale despite the fact that it fulfilled all applicable requirements.[15]

What is the sum to be credited against the judgment after the sale: the bid price or the actual market value of the property (should it be higher)? In the mortgage foreclosure realm, a statute requires that the higher market value price be credited.[16] There is no such direction with respect to the levy of execution on a judgment, however, and the bid price is therefore the one ordinarily used to determine the sum by which the judgment shall be reduced after the sale. There is authority, however, at least when the judgment creditor is the winning bidder, for borrowing from the mortgage foreclosure realm the rule crediting the debtor with the market value. That was the position taken by the supreme court in Wandschneider v. Bekeny,[17] in 1973, and it was later adopted and followed by the appellate division in Yellow Creek Hunting Club, Inc. v. Todd Supply, Inc.[18] While this will not restore the property, it will at least credit the owner with its true value in reduction of the debt. Without that crediting, the debt will be reduced based only on the bid, and an inadequate bid will mean that the debtor has lost her property without even being able to reduce her obligation by the property's worth.

Judicial intervention of this kind shows that the law has at least some remedies for avoiding injustices, as long as they (and the situations needing remedy) are called to the court's attention.[19] What is mainly needed to avoid abuse is ready access to competent counsel by all, regardless of economic station, a matter of urgency that has not earned a fair share of legislators' attention, probably for reasons they would assign to economic factors.

---

[13] Rondack Const. Services, Inc. v. Kaatsbaan Intern. Dance Center, Inc., 13 N.Y.3d 580, 896 N.Y.S.2d 278, 923 N.E.2d 561 (2009).

[14] CPLR 5228. See § 512.

[15] Community Capital Corp. v. Lee, 58 Misc. 2d 34, 294 N.Y.S.2d 336 (Sup. Ct., Nassau County 1968).

[16] RPAPL 1371(2).

[17] Wandschneider v. Bekeny, 75 Misc. 2d 32, 346 N.Y.S.2d 925 (Sup. Ct., Westchester County 1973).

[18] Yellow Creek Hunting Club, Inc. v. Todd Supply, Inc., 145 A.D.2d 679, 535 N.Y.S.2d 222 (3d Dep't 1988). The *Yellow Creek* case is discussed in the lead note in NYSLD No. 351.

[19] Further examples of judicial intervention to prevent injustice appear in § 522, where the protective order is treated.

§ 501. Sheriff's Return

A return is a statement of the sheriff's doings in connection with the execution and of any success the sheriff has had on the levy. The sheriff makes the return to the clerk of the court out of which the execution issued. If the judgment has in any measure been satisfied, the clerk must record as much on his dockets.[1] The general rule is that the property execution must be returned within 60 days after issuance.[2] As a rule, this is feasible only on a personal property levy, and even there, only when the levy is made by seizure under subdivision (b) of CPLR 5232 rather than by service under subdivision (a), which has its own time provisions.[3] The 60-day period may be extended by the judgment creditor's attorney, but only once as a matter of right; recognizing that other judgment creditors may be waiting, the statute permits further extensions only if none of these others has an execution outstanding in the hands of the same sheriff.[4]

As will be seen, a judgment creditor's delivery of an execution to a sheriff secures for that creditor a lien on the judgment debtor's personal property.[5] That lien is lost when the execution is returned unsatisfied.[6]

The 60-day limitation on return of the execution must also be deemed inapplicable when real property is being levied. The time required for a real property sale under CPLR 5236 goes well beyond 60 days. The docketing of the judgment, moreover, is the step that gives a judgment its real property lien, which therefore does not, as a personal property lien does, depend on the moment that an execution is delivered to the sheriff. Since the moment of delivery does not have that significance in a real property situation, there is less need for rigidity about when a return is needed; the parties should instead concentrate on the sale procedures of CPLR 5236 and see that they are fulfilled with reasonable diligence. Any problems arising in connection with the sheriff's proceedings can be resolved by the court on motion.[7]

The sheriff is required to keep a complete set of execution records, which must include the date of the execution's issuance, the date and time of its delivery to the sheriff (these to be endorsed on the execution itself and all the more important because they determine priorities), the date of the execution's return, the amount due at delivery time, and anything still due at return time.[8]

E. INCOME EXECUTION

Table of Sections

§ 502.   Income Execution, Contents and Service

§ 503.   Income Execution; Computing the 10%

§ 504.   Priorities Among Income Executions

---

[1]   CPLR 5021(b).

[2]   CPLR 5230(c).

[3]   See §§ 496 and 497.

[4]   CPLR 5230(c).

[5]   See §§ 519 and 520.

[6]   International Ribbon Mills, Ltd. v. Arjan Ribbons, Inc., 36 N.Y.2d 121, 365 N.Y.S.2d 808, 325 N.E.2d 137 (1975). This does not preclude issuance of a second execution, but the time between the return of the old and the issuance of the new may enable another judgment creditor to slip in with priority.

[7]   See CPLR 5238.

[8]   CPLR 5230(d).

§ 505.   Employer's Obligations on Income Execution
§ 506.   Sheriff's Obligation on Income Execution
§ 507.   Modifying the Income Execution
§ 507A. Special Income Execution for Support

§ 502. Income Execution, Contents and Service

CPLR 5231, which is the primary subject of this section, contains one of the CPLR's most popular, but complicated, judgment enforcement devices: the 10% income execution. An income execution operates on the judgment debtor's income from wages and any other source, such as a trust.[1] It operates on 10% of the income, requiring payment of that percentage to the sheriff on each due date. It acts as a continuing levy, unlike an ordinary property execution, which loses validity when the garnishee hands over whatever he presently has belonging to the judgment debtor.[2] It also constitutes an exception to CPLR 5201(a), which precludes levy against contingent intangibles: the income execution operates on income as it comes due even though its effectiveness is premised on continuing services.

The income execution for money judgments in general is supplied and governed by CPLR 5231, the subject that we take up here and in the several sections following. (There is a special income execution for support in family matters, CPLR 5241, which is treated as a distinct subject afterwards.)[3] By allowing levy on 10%, CPLR 5231 is the counterpart of CPLR 5205(d), the provision that exempts 90% of income. By force of habit, the income execution under CPLR 5231 is also what bench and bar usually have in mind when they use the word "garnishment." The income execution is of course only one kind of garnishment, however; any levy on a debtor's assets in the hands of a third person, including a levy under an ordinary property execution, is also a category of "garnishment."[4]

CPLR 5231 sets up a procedure that most often leads to a two-step service of the income execution, as is explained in more detail below. The "first service" is made by the sheriff upon the judgment debtor, and it requires the debtor to make installment payments.[5] This service affords the debtor the opportunity to honor the execution and avoid the embarrassment of any "second service" of the execution on the person who owes the judgment defendant money, such as an employer. If the judgment debtor fails to pay

---

[1]   See CPLR 5231(a) (requiring income execution to specify, among other things, "the name and address of the person or entity from whom the judgment debtor is receiving or will receive money"); CPLR 5231(b) (noting that income execution can be issued "[w]here a judgment debtor is receiving or will receive money from any source . . . ."); CPLR 5231(g) (form statement required to be contained in any income execution delivered to a sheriff defines "Gross Income" as including "income from trusts"). The implication that only earnings are aimed at by CPLR 5231 was removed by 2015 and 1990 amendments, clarifying that trust and like income is included as well. Because earnings are by far the most common income source that CPLR 5231 is used on, the treatment of the income execution in this and the ensuing sections will assume that the levied item is earnings and that the payer is an employer, but the terms are intended to include as an "employer" any trustee or other garnishee required to make the payments, and to include as "wages" or "earnings" all forms of compensation for personal services as well as trust income.

Most of the subdivisions of CPLR 5231 were relettered as part of an extensive 1987 amendment of the statute. Because many pre-1987 cases refer to the old lettering, a chart coordinating the subdivisions before and after the amendment appears in a footnote at the end of § 503.

[2]   CPLR 5232(a).
[3]   See § 507A.
[4]   See the definition of "garnishee" in CPLR 105.
[5]   See CPLR 5231(d).

installments for a period of twenty days, or if the sheriff is unable to serve an income execution upon the judgment debtor within twenty days after the execution is delivered to the sheriff, the second step service is required.[6] This second step service is not on the judgment debtor, but rather on the person "from whom the judgment debtor is receiving or will receive money."[7]

The income execution is drawn by the lawyer and delivered directly to the sheriff. Its form is largely prescribed by statute.[8] It requires no court order or other preliminary permission, as it once did; nor is an attempt at any other device a condition precedent to use of an income execution, as was the case under old law.[9] It can be the first enforcement device used; in fact, if the creditor knows that income is the debtor's only asset, it is likely to be the first, last, and only device used. It is probably the most commonly relied on enforcement device and in a sense it is the last refuge of the judgment creditor who has a modest judgment against an unpropertied judgment debtor. Hence there is much caselaw on the income execution.

In addition to the contents generally prescribed for executions by CPLR 5230, the income execution contains the name and address of the employer—or other person (such as a trustee), but the employer will do for our examples—from whom the debtor is receiving money, the frequency of the payments and their amount, and the amount to be deducted. It is delivered to the sheriff, who first serves it on the judgment debtor himself—before any turn is made to the employer for payment. This procedure is known as "first service."[10] The debtor must be allowed at least 20 days to start paying over the 10%, a CPLR innovation designed to spare the debtor the embarrassment, or worse, of having the income execution served on his employer, and to spare the latter the bother, if possible. The income execution must therefore contain a notice to the judgment debtor advising him of his obligation and warning that default will result in service on the employer, which is commonly referred to as "second service."[11]

Because the "first service" of the income execution is made on the judgment debtor, it is to the sheriff of the debtor's county (if that is not the same as his employer's) that the attorney must initially deliver it. Only if the judgment debtor is a nonresident of the state may it be delivered straight to the sheriff of the employer's county.[12] The sheriff serves the income execution on the judgment debtor in the same manner as a summons[13] or by certified mail with return receipt requested. If the certified mail method is used, additional copies must then be sent to the debtor by regular mail both to his residence and to his last known place of employment. The sheriff must serve the debtor within 20 days after receiving the execution, a requirement designed to require expeditious treatment of this popular device.[14]

Twenty days also measures the judgment debtor's chance to make the payments himself. If the debtor fails within that time to pay an installment—the 20 days run from

---

[6]   CPLR 5231(e).

[7]   CPLR 5231(e).

[8]   CPLR 5231(g).

[9]   See § 684 of the old Civ. Prac. Act (repealed 1963).

[10]   CPLR 5231(d).

[11]   CPLR 5231(a); CPLR 5231(e).

[12]   CPLR 5231(b).

[13]   See CPLR 308; §§ 66 to 76A.

[14]   CPLR 5231(d).

the service of the execution on the debtor—the sheriff is then empowered to make "second service" on the employer.[15] There must be flexibility, however. The debtor's salary may be paid monthly, for example, with the first payment due more than 20 days after he has been served. The sheriff will usually supply such additional time as is reasonable in these situations. A judgment debtor proceeding in good faith usually need only contact the sheriff's office to secure the additional time, a process that is usually also to the creditor's advantage.

If the debtor defaults on this opportunity to start making payments on the income execution, as many do, or if the sheriff is unable to serve the debtor within 20 days after delivery of the execution, the sheriff may make "second service" on the employer.[16]

If the employer is in the same county, it can be the same sheriff who now serves the employer. The sheriff need only serve another copy of the income execution, for which reason it may be helpful to deliver several copies to the sheriff, but this is not required.

A 2015 amendment to CPLR 5231(e) clarifies that the "second service" of the income execution can be made in "any county in which the person or entity from whom the judgment debtor is receiving or will receive money has an office or place of business . . . ." This revision recognizes the reality that "second service" is not made on the judgment debtor, but rather on "the person or entity from whom the judgment debtor is receiving or will receive money," which is most typically the judgment debtor's employer. As noted in the Memorandum in Support of the Bill, many employers actually require that income executions be forwarded to a central office, regardless of the state or county in which the judgment debtor is employed. Thus, the amendment clarifies that "second service" is not restricted to the county in which the judgment debtor resides or works. Rather, such "second service" can be made in any county in which, for example, the judgment debtor's employer has an office or place of business.

If "the person or entity from whom the judgment debtor is receiving or will receive money," such as an employer, is in a different county than the one in which the judgment debtor resides, the likelihood is that the first sheriff will just return the execution, unsatisfied, to the attorney for the judgment creditor. The attorney will now have to deliver another copy of the income execution to the sheriff of "any county in which the person or entity from whom the judgment debtor is receiving or will receive money has an office or place of business."[17] This should also be done within 20 days after the first sheriff's return because the execution will otherwise lose the priority that the first delivery secured.[18] The sheriff's method of serving the employer is, again, by personal delivery[19] or by certified mail with return receipt requested.[20]

Sheriffs in certain counties have interpreted the recent amendments to CPLR 5231(e) as permitting them to make second service of an income execution in "any"

---

[15]   CPLR 5231(e).

[16]   CPLR 5231(e).

[17]   CPLR 5231(e).

[18]   CPLR 5231(j). Priorities are discussed in § 504.

[19]   CPLR 308; §§ 66 to 76A.

[20]   CPLR 5231(e). A CPLR 318 agent can be served if the employer has one, but no other designated agent, such as the secretary of state in the case of a corporate employer, is servable in this instance. Special requirements concerning service and its incidents applicable to certain governmental units as employers, including municipalities and the state itself (which is a permissible garnishee under CPLR 5207), are contained in CPLR 5231(h).

county in New York State. Under this reading of the statute, for example, a sheriff in Saratoga County could make second service under CPLR 5231(e) by personally serving the income execution on the judgment debtor's employer in Niagara County. That interpretation is rather dubious and is not supported by the amended language of the statute or by its legislative history.

The amendments to CPLR 5231(e) are designed to allow second service of an income execution under CPLR 5231(e) to be made in "any county *in which the person or entity from whom the judgment debtor is receiving or will receive money has an office or place of business.*"[21] The language does not, however, broaden an enforcement officer's powers to make service in "any county" in the State. The validity of any income execution served in such fashion will be in serious doubt, leading to battles between creditors to void the income execution.[22]

There is a question, today, about whether an income execution is available if the judgment debtor neither resides nor works in New York, as may be the case where the New York judgment against him was based on longarm jurisdiction. Under the old Civil Practice Act, the mere fact that the employer was present in New York, even though the defendant lived elsewhere and worked for the employer elsewhere, was sufficient not only for post-judgment income execution, but (by adoption) even for prejudgment attachment. So held Morris Plan Industrial Bank v. Gunning,[23] but the viability of the case today is doubtful regarding prejudgment attachment. Whatever the merits of an income levy attempted with a prejudgment attachment, a good case can be made out for a post-judgment income execution against a nonresident judgment debtor whose employer has a New York presence. As long as the New York judgment itself was rendered with jurisdiction, even though the debtor neither lives nor works in the state, his obligation to pay a New York judgment is good ground for arguing that the coincidental New York presence of his employer may be reasonably exploited to satisfy the judgment. But is it permissible under CPLR 5231, which as a whole seems to contemplate that the judgment debtor either lives or works in New York?

The courts are in disagreement. Some hold that income execution is not permitted in that instance;[24] others, that it is, and at least one of these has said that the part requiring preliminary service on the debtor before the employer may be served can be met by delivering the execution to an enforcement officer in the foreign state and having him serve the judgment debtor,[25] a procedure that can meet stiff resistance from the foreign official. The matter awaits definitive resolution.

§ 503. Income Execution; Computing the 10%

The standards for computing exactly how much has to be deducted on the income execution are in subdivision (b) of CPLR 5231, and even more informative is the actual

---

[21] CPLR 5231(e) (emphasis added).

[22] See V. Loewer's Gambrinus Brewing Co. v. Lithauer, 36 Misc. 539, 540, 73 N.Y.S. 947, 947–48 (App. Term 1901) (Manhattan marshal "had [no] power to perform any official function in Kings county, so that all the defendant did there in the way of taking and retaining possession of the property was tortiously done and conferred no rights whatever either upon him or the judgment creditor he assumed to represent").

[23] Morris Plan Industrial Bank of New York v. Gunning, 295 N.Y. 324, 67 N.E.2d 510 (1946).

[24] E.g., Brown v. Arabian Am. Oil Co., 53 Misc. 2d 182, 278 N.Y.S.2d 256 (Sup. Ct., Suffolk County 1967); Kaplan v. Supak & Sons Mfg. Co., 46 Misc. 2d 574, 260 N.Y.S.2d 374 (N.Y. City Civ. Ct. 1965).

[25] Oystermen's Bank & Trust Co. v. Manning, 59 Misc. 2d 144, 298 N.Y.S.2d 355 (Sup. Ct., New York County 1969).

form, supplied by subdivision (g), which has to be included in the income execution itself. The percentage of the deduction is 10%, which is the maximum that New York law allows under CPLR 5231, but federal law[1] exempts part of the debtor's earnings altogether and restricts the computation base, on which the 10% is to be computed, to only what is left over.[2]

A key figure under the federal standard is the current hourly minimum wage multiplied by 30, and a key phrase is "disposable earnings." "Disposable earnings" means the debtor's net income after deductions for sums that the law requires to be withheld: taxes, Social Security, unemployment insurance, and the like, but not including deductions for voluntary withholdings like union dues or insurance plan payments. The debtor's weekly "disposable earnings" must be at least 30 times the current minimum hourly wage before the income execution becomes operative; that basic sum is deemed essential for the debtor's family needs.

If the earnings do not exceed that figure, there can presumably be no income deduction at all. If they do exceed it, the 10% presumably works only on the excess. The basic sum, in other words, is exempt.[3] That, in any event, is our thinking on the subject, but we have injected a "presumably" or two as a hedge in a realm that is still in need of definitive resolution.[4]

Restrictions apply when deductions are already being made from the debtor's income for support and related family purposes. If those deductions are 25% or more of the debtor's disposable earnings, there can be no income levy at all on a CPLR 5231 execution.[5] If they do not exceed 25%, a levy is allowed, but the 10% authorized by CPLR

---

[1]   15 U.S.C.A. §§ 1671–1677.

[2]   These federal standards were explicitly incorporated into CPLR 5231 in an amendment in 1987 after the prior CPLR 5231 scheme had been invalidated in Follette v. Vitanza, 658 F. Supp. 492 (N.D.N.Y. 1987), in part for failing to take the federal statutory requirements into consideration. Other reasons cited for the invalidation were that the New York provisions failed to advise the judgment debtor about the possibly exempt status of her income or about remedies she might pursue to protect her rights. The amendment answers those objections as well, but before it could be drafted and put through the cumbersome legislative process, a subsequent order had to be issued by the court to preserve existing income executions, which numbered in the thousands. The order directed remedial steps in the interim. Follette v. Cooper, 658 F. Supp. 514 (N.D.N.Y. 1987). These matters, and the flurry of activity that surrounded the two *Follette* decisions, are described in the lead note in NYSLD No. 328.

[3]   This is in contrast with the way New York computed the 10% before 1987, when a basic weekly $85 was the key figure, and it was a gross rather than net measure—no withholding at all could be considered. Nor was it just a threshold, and once the $85 was reached, the whole $85 became subject to levy: a debtor earning $84 a week, for example, was immune from income levy while one earning $86 had $8.60 deducted. Caselaw confirmed those methods of computation—see, e.g., County Trust Co. v. Berg, 65 Misc. 2d 533, 318 N.Y.S.2d 154 (Sup. Ct., Kings County 1971); Slocum-Dickson Medical Group v. General Elec. Co., 66 Misc. 2d 363, 320 N.Y.S.2d 883 (Oneida County Court 1971)—although an occasional voice in the wilderness, guided by logic because of having inadvertently overlooked the statute's stubborn history, held that take-home pay (after legally required deductions) should be the computation base. See, e.g., County Trust Co. v. Duerr, 52 Misc. 2d 411, 275 N.Y.S.2d 910 (Sup. Ct., Westchester County 1966). The general background of the income execution under its pre-1987 standards is treated in a series of articles by this writer appearing in the New York Law Journal editions of May 18–20, 1971.

[4]   After doing some canvassing during 2009 in the offices of several county sheriffs and with some New York City marshals, we've encountered some who disagree not only with some of our figurings, but also among themselves. How come no definitive caselaw on this? Whatever the importance of the issue in a statewide perspective, or to the individual judgment debtor, the economic stakes in any given case are apparently too low to press for a final decision through the courts. We did a lead note on this subject, with several different formulae discussed, in SPR 215:1.

[5]   A special income execution, CPLR 5241, itself designed to aid in the collection of support money, does not have this restriction. A clause in the form supplied by CPLR 5231(g) explicitly advises that nothing in CPLR 5231 limits income deductions for support purposes.

5231 plus the sum being deducted for support cannot together exceed 25% of disposable earnings. To the extent of the excess, it is the CPLR 5231 execution that has to be reduced. It was argued in one case—in which a support order was already garnishing more than 25% and this exhausted the earnings segment that would otherwise have been available for an ordinary judgment creditor—that the 25% is really just the coordinate of a 75% reserve for family needs and that the support order should be deemed to come out of the 75%, leaving the 25% available to income execution leviers. The Second Circuit rejected the argument, finding no Congressional intent "to protect the rights of creditors," only a purpose "to limit the ills" that come from unrestricted garnishment.[6]

Mandatory support deductions already being made against a support debtor under CPLR 5241 and 5242, the special support income execution statutes, are applied to reduce a CPLR 5231 levy,[7] but incongruously, it has been held that payments conscientiously being made by the support debtor pursuant to the terms of a divorce judgment do not reduce the levy.[8]

A supervening factor is that all the earnings of one who is receiving public assistance are exempt from income levy under New York law,[9] as are the public assistance payments themselves.[10] These exemptions apply whether the money is still in the hands of the disbursing agency or has already reached the hands of the judgment debtor or his bank account, if the money on deposit is shown to be welfare receipts.[11] Indeed, if the content of the debtor's account is from any exempt source at all—and there are others—a 2008 package of amendments tries to prevent the levy from reaching the debtor's account in the first place.[12]

All income based on personal services qualifies for income execution, "whether denominated as wages, salary, commission, bonus, or otherwise, and includes periodic payments pursuant to a pension or retirement program."[13] The label is secondary. Even "irregular" payments are to be reached.[14] If the payments are other than weekly, such as monthly or quarterly or even less regular than that, they are to be averaged out to what they amount to by the week and to face income execution if by that measure they meet the current standards.[15] The judgment debtor should think twice before starting any arguments about whether the payments, however irregular, are for personal services and therefore subject to the income execution. It is to his advantage to have it assumed that they are. A contrary holding, which frees the earnings from the 10% levy, will

---

[6] Long Island Trust Co. v. U.S. Postal Service, 647 F.2d 336 (2d Cir. 1981), decided when the federal standards were applicable, but before they had been included in CPLR 5231 explicitly.

[7] CPLR 5231(b)(iii).

[8] See Tilden Financial Corp. v. Corwin, 149 Misc. 2d 544, 566 N.Y.S.2d 457 (Sup. Ct., New York County 1990). *Tilden* acknowledges that it is only the "scoundrel" who benefits from this, but says that the legislature must correct the problem. Criticizing *Tilden*, but not to the extent of just honoring outright these other support payments being made by the judgment debtor, American Exp. Centurion v. Melia, 155 Misc. 2d 587, 589 N.Y.S.2d 290 (N.Y. City Civ. Ct. 1992) says that what the court should do is hold a hearing, modifying the CPLR 5231 payments with a protective order if necessary.

[9] Soc. Serv. Law § 137–a.

[10] Soc. Serv. Law § 137.

[11] Consumer Credit Corp. v. Lewis, 63 Misc. 2d 928, 313 N.Y.S.2d 879 (Dist. Ct., Nassau County 1970).

[12] The 2008 law adds a new § 5222–a to the CPLR and makes incidental amendments in CPLR 5205, 5222, 5230, 5231, and 5232. See § 490, the section on exemptions.

[13] CPLR 5231(c)(i).

[14] See 6th Rep. Leg. Doc. No. 8, p. 496 (1962).

[15] In re Ostergren's Will, 49 Misc. 2d 894, 268 N.Y.S.2d 906 (Sur. Ct., Kings County 1966).

subject them instead to a 100% levy. In his haste to be rid of the 10% levy, in other words, a debtor may overlook that it is the counterpart of a 90% exemption.

As applied to sums earned before the income execution is delivered to the sheriff, the limitations attach only to earnings for services rendered within the preceding 60 days.[16] Earnings more than 60 days old are subject to total levy, not just 10%.[17] A threatened hardship in a particular case, were a full levy to proceed as authorized, can be met through an individual protective order applied for under either CPLR 5231(i), allowing modification of income executions in particular, or CPLR 5240, the general protective order provision.[18] Conversely, future earnings, all of them presumably 90% exempt, can theoretically be allowed to accumulate beyond the needs of the debtor's family. Here the judgment creditor's remedy would be an installment payment order under CPLR 5226, where the court addresses the facts of the individual case and is empowered to direct payment of more than 10% if the debtor can afford it.[19]

Complications can also arise when the employer has made advances of salary payments to the employee—advances that the employer would ordinarily be entitled to deduct from further earnings. It has been held that the employer can apply post-execution earnings against legitimate pre-execution advances, thus taking that segment of them out of the category of the debtor's "earnings" and putting it beyond reach of the income execution. The theory is that it is the employer's money, not the debtor's, until all is paid back.

So it is for pre-execution advances. Post-execution advances will not be allowed to impede the levying creditor, however,[20] lest collusion be encouraged between a debtor and an unduly cooperative employer. Employers have to be careful about such things. A perusal of the footnoted case suggests that the law is not as clear as it might be. The situation might even be analogized to where the employer itself is a judgment creditor of its employee—one of several judgment creditors—and the employer tries to take advantage of its dual creditor/garnishee role to give itself an advantage. One such person who tried to do that, not adhering strictly to the income execution procedures, ended up not only losing priority, which it had initially achieved by proper procedure, but with personal liability to another creditor who played strictly according to the rules.[21]

CPLR 5231 is an important part of New York practice, and as the discussion indicates, the 1987 amendment of CPLR 5231 was a fundamental one. Part of the amendment was a relettering of most of the subdivisions of CPLR 5231, throwing out of kilter references made to them in numerous pre-1987 cases. A chart coordinating the subdivisions before and after the amendment, which may be helpful for reference, is therefore set forth in the footnote.[22]

---

[16]   CPLR 5205(d)(2).

[17]   A good treatment of these matters appears in Girard Trust Bank v. Gotham Football Club, Inc., 31 A.D.2d 142, 295 N.Y.S.2d 741 (1st Dep't 1968).

[18]   See § 522.

[19]   See § 511.

[20]   See Larry Goldwater, Inc. v. C. B. Snyder Nat. Realty Co., 48 Misc. 2d 669, 265 N.Y.S.2d 542 (N.Y. City Civ. Ct. 1965).

[21]   See Franklin Nat. Bank v. Rayno Distributors, Inc., 43 Misc. 2d 651, 252 N.Y.S.2d 123 (App. Term, 2d Dep't 1964). By reimbursing itself directly rather than through an income execution, the employer was apparently trying to avoid poundage, a percentage the sheriff gets for collecting money on an execution. See CPLR 8012(b).

[22]   The following charts the 1987 reordering of CPLR 5231:

§ 504. Priorities Among Income Executions

The scheme of priorities governing personal property in general[1] does not apply to the income execution, which has its own system under CPLR 5231(j). Priority among different creditors, when several have judgments against the same debtor, is in the order in which they deliver income executions to the sheriff or other enforcement officer in the county or smaller unit—city or town, relevant when lower court judgments are being enforced by local marshals or constables—in which the judgment debtor resides or is employed. The 10% levy operates on only one judgment at a time, at least until a court directs otherwise, such as on a motion for an installment payment order,[2] and continues until the judgment with priority is fully paid. Number two on the priority line does not come in for anything at all until that time. Number three then awaits satisfaction of number two, etc. This shows how important priority is. By beating out others even by just a day, a judgment creditor may monopolize the 10% income levy against a debtor for years.

If the judgment debtor balks or cannot be found by the sheriff, necessitating "second service" on the employer,[3] the priority earned by initial delivery will remain in effect while the sheriff now serves the employer. If the latter is in a different county, requiring issuance of another execution to that county's sheriff, the initial delivery to the first sheriff will still determine priority provided that the delivery to the second sheriff is made within 20 days after the execution's return by the first one. The lesson to the judgment creditor's lawyer is to act fast in these situations. When the first delivery is to an enforcement officer other than a sheriff, such as a New York City marshal, and the second one goes to a sheriff, there is some question about whether the initial delivery to the lower-court enforcement officer can qualify as a priority-giver that adheres through

Pre-1987 Subdivision	Result of 1987 Amendment
(a)	Remained (a)
(b)	Remained (b) but amended to defer to federal maximums
New subd. (c) added, defining earnings	
(c)	Relettered (d)
(d)	Relettered (e)
(e)	Relettered (f) and amended with minor conforming change
New subd. (g) added, prescribing form of notice to be given debtor	
(f)	Relettered (h)
(g)	Relettered (i)
(h)	Relettered (j)
(i)	Relettered (k)

[1]   It's in CPLR 5234, treated in §§ 518 et seq.

[2]   See § 511.

[3]   CPLR 5231(e); see § 502.

the sheriff's proceedings. Caselaw is divided,[4] but it is more compatible with the lower court acts, which equate all enforcement officers with the sheriff,[5] to uphold the continuity of priority in that situation.

If the priority battle is between an ordinary judgment creditor using CPLR 5231 and a support creditor (wife, child, etc.) using CPLR 5241,[6] the support creditor prevails, and without regard to which came first.[7] Other interests, such as a governmental unit with a tax lien, may also compete for the debtor's wages, and may be allowed a kind of simultaneous enforcement.[8] Again, hardship in these instances can be alleviated on a case by case basis through a protective order issued by the court.

A judgment creditor may be persuaded to voluntarily accept less than 10% by agreement with the employer. This has been held acceptable as long as there is no competing judgment creditor waiting in the wings. The service on the employer of #2's income execution mandates cancellation of the agreement made with #1 and the full resumption of the 10% levy on #1 as of that moment, to the end that #1's income execution be satisfied as soon as possible to make way for #2.[9]

§ 505. Employer's Obligations on Income Execution

When served with the execution, the employer or other garnishee must withhold 10% each payday and turn it over to the sheriff. If the employment is terminated, so is the employer's obligation on the execution, unless the employment resumes within 90 days, in which event whatever falls due after resumption also faces the 10% levy.[1]

If the employer fails to make each appropriate deduction and pay it to the sheriff, the judgment creditor may bring a special proceeding against the employer to compel it, and to collect accrued installments. If the income execution issued out of a lower court not listed in CPLR 5221(a),[2] it has been held that the proceeding must be brought in the

---

[4] Republic Associates, Inc. v. McRae, 46 Misc. 2d 1098, 261 N.Y.S.2d 777 (Sup. Ct., Westchester County 1965), for example, holds that the priority remains, while Schleimer v. Gross, 46 Misc. 2d 931, 261 N.Y.S.2d 670 (Sup. Ct., Nassau County 1965), holds that it is lost.

[5] See § 701 in the New York City Civ. Ct. Act, Uniform Dist. Ct. Act, Uniform City Ct. Act, and Uniform Just. Ct. Act, McKinney's Vol. 29A, Parts 2 and 3.

[6] See § 507A.

[7] CPLR 5241(h), 5242(c). Before the so-called "payroll deduction order" of § 49–b of the Pers. Prop. Law was replaced by CPLR 5242, there was a conflict as to the effect to be given a payroll deduction order competing with an income execution. Some courts held that the deduction order got priority, even holding that its mere issuance works an automatic suspension of any outstanding income execution, at least until a court reinstated the execution. See, e.g., Beahm v. Beahm, 47 Misc. 2d 900, 263 N.Y.S.2d 533 (Fam. Ct., Richmond County 1965). Others held that both work simultaneously until a court intervenes. E.g., Costa v. Chevrolet-Tonawanda, Division of General Motors Corp., 53 Misc. 2d 252, 278 N.Y.S.2d 275 (Buffalo City Ct. 1963), ultimately approved by the Appellate Division in 24 A.D.2d 732, 263 N.Y.S.2d 319 (4th Dep't 1965). The conflict was noted in Lincoln Nat. Bank & Trust Co. of Central New York v. Colgan, 71 Misc. 2d 908, 337 N.Y.S.2d 412 (Syracuse City Ct. 1972). But there was in any event agreement that whatever the initial rule locally followed, the court on motion could always vary it with an individually tailored protective order.

[8] See, e.g., Royal Business Funds Corp. v. Rooster Plastics, Inc., 53 Misc. 2d 181, 278 N.Y.S.2d 350 (Sup. Ct., New York County 1967).

[9] See Spatz Furniture Corp. v. Lee Letter Service, Inc., 52 Misc. 2d 291, 276 N.Y.S.2d 219 (N.Y. City Civ. Ct. 1966), aff'd, 54 Misc. 2d 359, 282 N.Y.S.2d 624 (App. Term, 1st Dep't 1967).

[1] CPLR 5231(f).

[2] See § 493.

supreme court or a county court.[3] If it is found in the proceeding that the income execution is valid, and that the employer failed without justification to make the required 10% deduction, the employer (or other garnishee) will be held personally liable to the judgment creditor for all that should have been withheld, up to the amount due on the judgment.[4]

An employer is forbidden to discharge an employee on the sole ground that her wages are being subjected to an income execution or series of them, or, indeed, to refuse to hire a person in the first place because of a history of income levies elsewhere. Both damages and reinstatement can be directed against an employer who violates this rule.[5]

§ 506. Sheriff's Obligation on Income Execution

The sheriff must serve the income execution within the stated time limits.[1] Since personal delivery is no longer indispensable, certified mail having been made an alternative, there is no reason for delay if the sheriff has been given the appropriate names and addresses.

The sheriff should compute the interest due on the judgment from the time of its entry to the time it is satisfied and see to it that the interest is regularly added to the principal sum of the judgment and that the employer/garnishee is kept abreast of the running total. The sheriff must continue to levy until the whole judgment, with interest included, is collected. If the garnishee is not advised of interest due, and pays out until the principal sum is satisfied, the judgment creditor has no further claim against the garnishee.[2]

With an ordinary property execution, the sheriff is sometimes required to make a return within 60 days after issuance. That period does not apply to an income execution[3] where the sheriff's principal obligation is to accumulate the regularly received payments and to account and pay them over to the judgment creditor periodically—at least once every 90 days.[4]

The sheriff's "return" in this instance can apparently await the moment when the judgment has been fully paid, or such earlier moment when the execution loses effect, such as where the employment or trust terminates. Should any earlier need arise to reflect on the clerk's dockets the satisfaction made of the judgment to date, the sheriff can be asked to make a partial return earlier. Alternatively, the judgment creditor can

---

[3]   CPLR 5221(a)(4). See First Westchester Nat. Bank of New Rochelle v. Lewis, 42 Misc. 2d 1007, 249 N.Y.S.2d 537 (Westchester County Court 1964), so holding for an enforcement motion, which would a fortiori apply to a special proceeding. See CPLR 5221(b).

[4]   Franklin Nat. Bank v. Brita Homes Corp., 35 A.D.2d 550, 313 N.Y.S.2d 248 (2d Dep't 1970). In the *Franklin* case, the judgment creditor brought a plenary action against the employer to collect this money, but under CPLR 5231(e), a special proceeding suffices and is of course the cheaper and faster course. See § 547.

[5]   See CPLR 5252, another part of which, discussed in Commentary C5252:1 on McKinney's CPLR 5252, adds contempt as a remedy.

[1]   CPLR 5231(d), (e).

[2]   National Sur. Corp. v. R.H. Macy & Co., Inc., 116 Misc. 2d 780, 455 N.Y.S.2d 1007 (Sup. Ct., New York County 1982). The implication is that the judgment creditor must seek his remedy against the sheriff. Perhaps nothing prevents the creditor from issuing a new income execution to collect the interest still unpaid, but if some other creditor has since come into priority, there may a long delay in collection.

[3]   See CPLR 5230(c).

[4]   CPLR 5231(k).

be asked for a partial satisfaction piece,[5] which the judgment debtor can file. Or the court on motion can order entry of whatever satisfaction has been made.[6]

§ 507. Modifying the Income Execution

Either judgment creditor or judgment debtor can move at any time to modify an income execution pursuant to CPLR 5231(i). As with a special proceeding, it has been held that the motion may not be made in a court not listed in CPLR 5221(a),[1] which means that in the case of income executions issued out of a town or village court, the motion to modify must be made in the supreme or a county court.[2]

This motion to "modify" is at root only a specialized kind of protective order, and the general protective order provision itself, CPLR 5240, would probably supply all needed modification authority without any special help from CPLR 5231(i). Whichever provision is used, the motion for the modification is generally brought on by order to show cause. Examples of protective modifications, including adjustments needed when an income execution and an installment payment order compete against the same judgment debtor, are met in later sections.[3]

§ 507A. Special Income Execution for Support

CPLR 5241, supplying a more generous, expansive, and self-executing income execution than 5231 offers, was added to the CPLR in 1985 to aid in the enforcement of a support obligation. The support obligation can come from a judgment, decree, or order of a court, temporary or final, or even from a mere "agreement or stipulation incorporated by reference" in the court paper.[1] It is available for support obligations only. Among the advantages of the 5241 execution are that it reaches higher percentages than the 10% to which CPLR 5231 is restricted; that the sheriff's or other enforcement officer's office does not have to be used (as it must be for the CPLR 5231 execution); and that a judgment for accumulated "arrears" is not a necessary preliminary to the enforcement of a CPLR 5241 execution.

In addition to the persons who can issue any execution—the sheriff or other enforcement official, the clerk, or the creditor's lawyer—a "support collection unit" or other agency responsible for support collection can issue a CPLR 5241 execution.[2] A copy of the execution must be served on the debtor,[3] who then has 15 days in which to apply to the court with his defense, which, as will be shown, is limited to a "mistake of fact." When the execution has been issued by a support collection unit, the debtor's defense takes the form of a "submission" to the unit instead of to the court. If the unit rejects the submission, it notifies the debtor and advises that the income execution will now be served on his employer.[4]

---

[5]   CPLR 5020.

[6]   CPLR 5021(a)(2).

[1]   See § 505.

[2]   CPLR 5221(a)(4), 5221(b).

[3]   See §§ 511 and 522.

[1]   CPLR 5241(a)(1).

[2]   See CPLR 5241(a)(9), (b).

[3]   CPLR 5241(d).

[4]   CPLR 5241(e).

The sheriff's office is not used. The creditor can effect the levy just by serving the execution on the employer, and while the service may be made in the same manner as a summons, it is also allowed by the simple alternative of "regular mail."[5]

The amount of the deduction that has to be made from income under CPLR 5241 varies between 50% and 65%, depending on whether the debtor is also supporting a spouse or child other than the creditor and on how long the debtor has been in arrears.[6] The computations are based on the debtor's "disposable earnings," the standard also used on an ordinary income execution under CPLR 5231.[7]

The contents of the CPLR 5241 execution, more detailed than for other executions, are explicitly laid out in the statute.[8] It takes priority "over any other assignment, levy or process,"[9] which of course includes an ordinary income execution issued in behalf of some other judgment creditor under CPLR 5231, even if the latter preceded the CPLR 5241 execution.[10]

Simultaneously enacted with CPLR 5241 was CPLR 5242, supplying an "income deduction order for support enforcement" in replacement of the payroll deduction order that had previously been used for this purpose.[11] Resort to the court for an order under CPLR 5242 is discouraged in the hope that the CPLR 5241 execution will be used instead,[12] but the question of how tightly locked the courthouse door will be is a question that may take some litigating. It has been held that no 5242 application may be made until a 5241 execution has at least been attempted.[13]

The purpose of CPLR 5241 is to expedite the collection of support money and to deter dilatory conduct by the support debtor by restricting the debtor's defenses. The recognized defense is a "mistake of fact."[14] The courts have had trouble with the phrase, which is defined to include a computation error, a mistake in identifying the debtor, or a showing that the support order does not exist or was vacated.[15] It is the debtor's burden to show that he is not in default in making the required payments,[16] and the courts, while noting this,[17] have occasionally upheld defenses on bases other than a mistake of fact. In one case, for example, husband H showed that wife W had twice before altered bills and checks upwards, that H had held up several checks in the past only because W had moved without advising him of her change of address, and that some 18 previous checks sent to W had not been cashed. Noting that there had been no problem for almost a decade, during which H apparently fulfilled his obligations under a separation decree,

---

5   CPLR 5241(f).

6   See CPLR 5241(g).

7   See § 503.

8   CPLR 5241(c).

9   CPLR 5241(h).

10   CPLR 5241(h).

11   Pers. Prop. Law § 49–b, repealed when CPLR 5242 took over.

12   CPLR 5241 and 5242 are discussed in the McKinney's Commentaries on CPLR 5241 and 5242.

13   Scarey v. Scarey, 131 Misc. 2d 252, 499 N.Y.S.2d 866 (Sup. Ct., Schoharie County 1986).

14   CPLR 5241(e).

15   CPLR 5241(a)(8).

16   "Default" is defined as a failure to make three payments, or allowing arrears to accumulate beyond a month's worth. CPLR 5241(a)(7).

17   Blackman v. Blackman, 131 A.D.2d 801, 517 N.Y.S.2d 167 (2d Dep't 1987).

and citing due process requirements, the court granted H's motion to vacate a CPLR 5241 income execution.[18]

F. THE "SUPPLEMENTARY PROCEEDINGS"

Table of Sections

§ 508.   Restraining Notice
§ 509.   Disclosure in Aid of Enforcement
§ 510.   Delivery Order or Judgment
§ 511.   Installment Payment Order
§ 512.   Receivership
§ 513.   Arrest

§ 508. Restraining Notice

With the restraining notice of CPLR 5222, we begin the series of devices that bench and bar know collectively, albeit informally, as the "supplementary proceedings."[1] The notice is issued by the judgment creditor's attorney (the court clerk is also authorized to issue it), may be served on the judgment debtor or a garnishee, and enjoins the person served from giving over the defendant's property except to the sheriff or pursuant to court order. It is in every sense an injunction, and acts as such under the signature of the lawyer without a court order or any other preliminary leave. It is not a special proceeding, but a mere post-judgment adjunct of the action itself and bearing its caption. Disobedience of a restraining notice is punishable as a contempt of court.[2]

If the judgment creditor has any indication about who may have possession of some of the debtor's property, the restraining notice is a good thing to serve promptly, after the entry of judgment, on any such persons. It acts as a kind of freeze on such of the debtor's assets as the served person may have, during which the judgment creditor can use other devices, such as an execution, to try to have the property turned over. It buys time, in other words. It may be served on any garnishee, with the exception of the judgment debtor's employer,[3] but special restrictions apply when the notice attempts to reach the exempt contents of the judgment debtor's bank account.[4]

The restraining notice must name all of the parties to the action, specify those for and against whom the judgment was rendered, the court and date of rendition, the amount of the judgment, and the amount of it still unsatisfied. It is then required to set forth subdivision (b) of CPLR 5222, which contains the injunctive language, and to advise that disobedience will constitute a contempt of court. The notice is served either in the same manner as a summons or by registered or certified mail with return receipt requested.[5] Any nonparty 18 or over may effect the service; it need not be the sheriff.

---

[18]   Shutt v. Shutt, 133 Misc. 2d 81, 506 N.Y.S.2d 611 (Sup. Ct., Oneida County 1986).

[1]   See § 492.

[2]   CPLR 5251.

[3]   CPLR 5222(a). The employer is excepted only in respect of wages where the income execution of CPLR 5231 is deemed adequate.

[4]   See § 490, the section on exemptions.

[5]   CPLR 5222(a), which also contains some special instructions for serving restraints on state agencies. Subdivision (g) of CPLR 5222, added in 1994, permits the restraining notice to be served in the form of a magnetic tape instead of a signed paper, but with several provisos. See SPR 20:2.

When a state unit is the garnishee, service of the restraining notice must be made on the head of the unit and also on the state department of audit and control.[6] This double-service requirement is not just a pro forma thing; it has been held that the failure to serve the department makes the notice invalid.[7]

CPLR 5222(a) requires that the copy of the restraining notice being served "contain an original signature or copy of the original signature" of the issuer. The statement of such a requirement in CPLR 5222, the product of a 1991 amendment, is now probably superfluous in light of the later amendment of the sanctions rule, Rule 130–1, to require the actual signing of all papers served in litigation.[8]

CPLR 5222 was one of several enforcement devices declared unconstitutional in 1982 for failure to require notice to the judgment debtor about the possibly exempt status of her property and to advise the debtor about procedures to protect any exemptions.[9] The legislature promptly amended three of the provisions—CPLR 5222, 5232, and 5234—to meet the objection, with CPLR 5222 selected to do the bulk of the job. The core amendment was the addition of subdivisions (d) and (e) to CPLR 5222, requiring such a notice and setting forth the specific form to be used for it.[10] Doubts were expressed at first about whether the amendments adequately met the constitutional objections, but it was later held that they do.[11]

A failure to give the notice that CPLR 5222 requires has been held to void the restraining notice and any follow-up enforcement steps that depend on it.[12] The failure can also give rise to a damages claim. That was held to be so even under the pre-amendment status of the enforcement devices,[13] but on that point there is some dispute.[14]

While the restraining notice is most effective when served on a garnishee, it may be used against the judgment debtor himself. When served on the judgment debtor, it lasts the life of the judgment or until the judgment is satisfied. It purports to preclude the debtor from in any way divesting himself of unexempt property except by instruction of the sheriff or the court. Of course, the restraining notice has a better potential when served on a third-person—a garnishee—who, because of obvious personal risks, will not go quite as far out on a limb to protect the judgment debtor as the debtor is wont to do for himself (such as by secreting assets in violation of the notice).

A restraining notice served on a garnishee is effective only if, when served, the garnishee owes a debt to or has property belonging to the judgment debtor. If the garnishee has such debt or property at that moment, the restraint will apply to that property as well as to all other property "thereafter coming into" the garnishee's

---

[6]   CPLR 5222(a).

[7]   Remo Drug Corp. v. State, 145 Misc. 2d 300, 546 N.Y.S.2d 529 (Ct. Cl. 1989).

[8]   See § 414A. Before the adoption of this requirement, conformed rather than actually signed papers could be served in most instances.

[9]   See Deary v. Guardian Loan Co., Inc., 534 F. Supp. 1178 (S.D.N.Y. 1982), and the lead note in NYSLD No. 270).

[10]   The amendments are discussed in Commentary C5222:11 on McKinney's CPLR 5222.

[11]   McCahey v. L.P. Investors, 774 F.2d 543 (2d Cir. 1985).

[12]   Weinstein v. Gitters, 119 Misc. 2d 122, 462 N.Y.S.2d 553 (Sup. Ct., Suffolk County 1983).

[13]   See Warren v. Delaney, 98 A.D.2d 799, 469 N.Y.S.2d 975 (2d Dep't 1983).

[14]   See Cais v. Pichler, 123 Misc. 2d 275, 473 N.Y.S.2d 719 (N.Y. City Civ. Ct. 1984).

possession.[15] If the garnishee lacks any such property or obligation at the moment of service, the restraint never takes effect at all.

The restraint precludes the garnishee from selling, assigning, transferring, or otherwise disposing of the obligation or property to anyone but the sheriff, unless the sheriff or court directs otherwise.[16] Even a transfer to the judgment debtor's assignee for the benefit of creditors has been held to violate the restraint.[17] In the case of a garnishee, the restraint retains its injunctive effect for only a year after its service (in contrast with the life-of-the-judgment run it gets when served on the judgment debtor), unless extended by protective order under CPLR 5240.

The garnishee may be unaware that property in its possession belongs to the judgment debtor, or it may think that a debt it owes is due not to the judgment debtor, but to someone else. The garnishee is subject to the restraint only if it "knows or has reason to believe" that the judgment debtor has an interest in the property; any ambiguity in this respect jeopardizes the restraint. The judgment creditor is therefore authorized to identify, in the restraining notice itself, the debt or property aimed at. If the creditor does that, the property identified falls under the restraint regardless of who the garnishee thinks the owner may be. But a judgment creditor must be reasonably sure about this; a wrong guess makes the creditor liable to the rightful owner for any damages caused by the wrongful restraint.[18] The garnishee who honors the process is not liable if the property designation is incorrect.[19]

The restraint is usually operative against all the debtor's property in the possession of the garnishee, regardless of the amount of the judgment. The restraining notice is not the occasion for measuring the value of the property (if other than outright money) held by the garnishee. But if the garnishee does owe just a monetary debt to the judgment debtor it can, by withholding twice the amount of the judgment, free all other money and property from the restraint.[20]

Once having served the restraint on the garnishee, the judgment creditor is expected to take prompt proceedings through other devices to get hold of the property, and to resolve such disputes as may arise about whom the property belongs to. That's the reason for giving the restraint only a year of life. Nor can the judgment creditor, for these same reasons, let the year pass and just serve a second restraint. A second one needs court leave.[21]

---

[15]   CPLR 5222(b). See Laborers Union Local 1298 of Nassau and Suffolk Counties Vacation Fund v. Frank L. Lyon & Sons, Inc., 66 Misc. 2d 1042, 323 N.Y.S.2d 229 (Sup. Ct., Nassau County 1971).

[16]   It has been held that although the sheriff is the one to whom the property is delivered, its direct delivery to the judgment creditor will not be penalized if no damage is shown. In re Wooton's Estate, 79 Misc. 2d 673, 361 N.Y.S.2d 137 (Sur. Ct., Schenectady County 1974).

[17]   International Ribbon Mills, Ltd. v. Arjan Ribbons, Inc., 36 N.Y.2d 121, 365 N.Y.S.2d 808 (1975). Involved there was a transfer by the judgment debtor; the rule would presumably be the same if the transfer were by a garnishee.

[18]   CPLR 5222(b).

[19]   See, by analogy, Chin Sung Yu v. Riggs Nat. Bank of Washington, D.C., 248 A.D.2d 235, 670 N.Y.S.2d 187 (1st Dep't 1998) (noted in SPR 76:2), so holding in respect of an execution. The garnishee is entitled to rely on the property identifications made in the execution. See CPLR 5209, 5232(a).

[20]   See, by analogy, *Chin Sung Yu*, 248 A.D.2d at 235, 670 N.Y.S.2d at 187, so holding in respect of an execution. The garnishee is entitled to rely on the property identifications made in the execution. See CPLR 5209, 5232(a).

[21]   CPLR 5222(c).

As is true of all of the enforcement devices other than the executions, the restraining notice may issue only out of the courts listed in CPLR 5221(a), which excludes it from the town and village courts. A restraint in respect of the judgments of those courts is permissible, but it must issue out of the supreme court or a county court.[22]

The restraining notice does not secure a lien for its user. This is important to note. While the notice requires no court application or sheriff assistance and can for that reason be quickly served by the judgment creditor so as to effect an immediate restraint, it had best be followed with expeditious steps using one of the lien-giving devices. In this connection we return to an advantage earlier attributed to the restraining notice. We said that it buys time. We now qualify that to note that it does so only when no other judgment creditor is pursuing the same judgment debtor. If there is another, and that creditor secures a lien through one of the devices that gives one, she will prevail against the creditor who served the restraining notice notwithstanding a showing that the latter was more diligent overall.[23] A general stay of enforcement of the judgment, not accompanied by any bond or other security protecting the judgment creditor, does not cancel the restraint, although it does suspend any follow-up steps, such as payment over of the property to the sheriff.[24]

The contempt punishment, which backs the restraining notice, may be invoked even against one not served with the notice but who knows of its service on someone else and wilfully participates in its violation.[25] And while contempt is the statutorily stated remedy,[26] it is not the exclusive one. The violator is also liable in damages to the judgment creditor, who may seek the damages in an action or even in a mere special proceeding, such as one brought to compel a garnishee to honor an execution.[27]

Suppose, for example, that P effects a restraint on D's bank account by duly serving it on the branch where D keeps his account. Negligently overlooking the restraint, the bank (garnishee) lets D withdraw the money through one of its other offices or branches. That happened in one case, for example, and when P brought an action against the bank for its omission,[28] one of the defenses was that the bank's conduct was not wilful but, at worst, only negligent. Holding that negligence is all it takes for liability, the court held the bank liable to P for the amount D was allowed to withdraw.

It was held in Zemo Leasing Corp. v. Bank of New York[29] that a bank should have until the close of business of the day following its receipt of a restraining notice in which to effectuate the notice against a depositor's account. In *Zemo*, where the judgment debtor withdrew funds after the bank had received a mailed restraint earlier in the day, the court held that the bank was not liable for the withdrawal; that it needed time to process the restraint and wasn't given enough time in this case. Practitioners advising

---

[22] CPLR 5221(b), (a)(4). See § 493.

[23] The lawyer should take careful note of these lien factors, which are treated in §§ 518 et seq.

[24] See Nardone v. Long Island Trust Co., 40 A.D.2d 697, 336 N.Y.S.2d 325 (2d Dep't 1972).

[25] Ivor B. Clark Co. v. Hogan, 296 F. Supp. 407 (S.D.N.Y. 1969).

[26] CPLR 5251. The procedure to punish for contempt is treated in §§ 481 et seq.

[27] See CPLR 5232(a).

[28] Mazzuka v. Bank of North America, 53 Misc. 2d 1053, 280 N.Y.S.2d 495 (N.Y. City Civ. Ct. 1967). A plenary action for this relief would not be necessary today. A special proceeding under CPLR 5227, which is faster and cheaper, can do the job. See the *Nardone* case, note 24 and § 510.

[29] Zemo Leasing Corp. v. Bank of New York, 158 Misc. 2d 991, 602 N.Y.S.2d 503 (Sup. Ct., Rockland County 1993), noted in SPR 10:3.

banks may want to be more cautious. Effectuating the restraint forthwith is the best advice.

We've been using examples involving bank accounts. We must now take note that quite often the money in the account is from an exempt source and has been reached by the creditor only because neither the creditor nor the bank knew of the exemption. This has often resulted in the unlawful seizure of a disadvantaged debtor's bread money, which in 2008 generated a new CPLR 5222–a and amendments to CPLR 5205, 5222, 5230, 5231, and 5232, all seeking to protect the exempt funds of judgment debtors that enforcement devices had been reaching improperly, often when the debtors lacked the wherewithal to protect themselves. The restraining notice was also playing a role in that injustice; hence, CPLR 5222 is among the 2008 amendments. The earlier section on exemptions discusses the 2008 legislation.[30]

While a showing of wilfulness is not necessary in order to hold the garnishee—bank or otherwise—to the consequences of a violation of CPLR 5222, it must be shown that the garnishee had knowledge of the restraining notice, which of course depends on proper service. In one case, for example,[31] the garnishee did not know of the notice and paid the money to the judgment debtor. The notice had been served by mail and was received and signed for by a laborer who had worked for the garnishee for only one day and who did not turn the notice over to an appropriate official. The judgment creditor did not succeed against the garnishee. The case seems to make the creditor responsible for those who receive the garnishee's mail. Perhaps a more constructive lesson to the judgment creditor is not to sit back after a restraining notice has been served—by whatever means—but to contact the garnishee shortly afterwards to inquire whether it was received and whether it's being honored.

Although contempt or a damages action may be available against a garnishee who violates the restraint, a transferee who pays fair consideration for the property will prevail over the judgment creditor even though the transferee takes through the violator. A gratuitous transferee, based merely on the equities, may be subordinated to the interests of the judgment creditor whose restraint was disobeyed,[32] but since even a lien-getting judgment creditor may have to defer to a transferee who pays fair consideration,[33] a fortiori a judgment creditor who relies on the restraint of CPLR 5222, which does not even give a lien, is also made to defer to such a transferee.

§ 509. Disclosure in Aid of Enforcement

In the discussion of the enforcement devices up to now, the tacit assumption has been that the judgment creditor knows what and where the judgment debtor's assets are. As likely as not, however, the creditor will know little or nothing about them. CPLR 5223 and 5224 offer aid on that front. They authorize disclosure and supply subpoenas to implement it.

CPLR 5223 provides that any time before the judgment is satisfied or vacated, the judgment creditor may compel disclosure of "all matter relevant to the satisfaction of the

---

[30]   See § 490.

[31]   Security Trust Co. of Rochester v. Magar Homes, a Div. of R. John Magar and Son Development Corp., 92 A.D.2d 714, 461 N.Y.S.2d 103 (4th Dep't 1983).

[32]   See *International Ribbon Mills*, 36 N.Y.2d at 124, 365 N.Y.S.2d at 810, 325 N.E.2d at 138, and the discussion of priorities in §§ 518 et seq.

[33]   See CPLR 5202, discussed in § 519.

judgment," a broad criterion authorizing investigation through any person shown to have any light to shed on the subject of the judgment debtor's assets or their whereabouts. The creditor can effect service of a subpoena on that person, who may be the judgment debtor himself, a friend or relative who may have information on the subject, a garnishee or one reasonably thought to be a garnishee, including the debtor's bank, accountant, broker, employer, etc. Even the judgment debtor's attorney may have to reveal data about the debtor's finances.[1]

Service of a CPLR 5224 subpoena does not commence a special proceeding. Like the pretrial disclosure subpoena and the trial subpoena, it is merely captioned in the action itself—even though the action in this case has already gone to judgment—and is deemed an adjunct of it. It can be used before, with, or after any other enforcement device. It is common, for example, and often wise, to serve the subpoena with a CPLR 5222 restraining notice. Since neither the subpoena nor the notice requires court leave, and because each constitutes judicial process under the signature of the creditor's attorney who acts as an officer of the court, both can be drawn and served promptly.

Like the restraining notice, the subpoena of CPLR 5224 is one of the so-called "supplementary proceedings" and may issue only out of courts listed in CPLR 5221(a), which means that when sought in respect of the judgment of a town or village court, the subpoena must bear the caption of the supreme court or a county court and seek in that court whatever implementation or enforcement is needed.[2]

In addition to describing the usual obligation of its recipient—requiring attendance at a designated time and place, production of an item, response to questions, etc.—the subpoena must name all of the parties to the action, state the court in which the judgment was rendered, the date and amount of the judgment, and the amount still outstanding. And it must of course advise that a failure to comply will be a contempt of court.

CPLR 5224 does not adopt for enforcement disclosure the whole gamut of pretrial disclosure devices that CPLR Article 31 offers during the pretrial phase of an action. It deems adequate an offering of subpoenas and makes three kinds available:

(1) The usual testimonial subpoena. This produces a deposition. It requires attendance for examination at a designated time and place. The examination may be on oral or written questions,[3] and is analogous to the pretrial depositions supplied by Article 31.[4] This subpoena must be served in the same manner as a summons.[5] When the deposition is of a third party, it has been held that the judgment debtor has no absolute right to attend it.[6]

(2) The subpoena duces tecum. This requires the production of books and records and other papers at a designated time and place,[7] just as it does at the pretrial and trial

---

[1]   See Lang, *Aids to Collecting After Judgment*, N.Y. St. B.J. 58 (1987).

[2]   See § 493.

[3]   CPLR 5224(a)(1).

[4]   See §§ 354 and 359.

[5]   CPLR 2303, CPLR 308. See the Commentaries on McKinney's CPLR 2303.

[6]   See ITT Commercial Finance Corp. v. Bailey, 166 Misc. 2d 24, 631 N.Y.S.2d 225 (Sup. Ct., Chautauqua County 1995) (SPR 36:2). But nor is there any standing rule to bar the debtor's attendance. In excluding the debtor in the *ITT* case, the court invoked CPLR 5240, the protective order provision, citing as a reason the debtor's prior efforts to favor other creditors.

[7]   CPLR 5224(a)(2).

stages. It is the approximate equivalent of the pretrial discovery device of CPLR 3120. This subpoena is also served in the same manner as a summons, and, limited only by the "relevant" standard of CPLR 5223, it can pursue any item reflecting on the debtor's assets. It can, for example, require production of a joint tax return filed by debtor and spouse, and their accountant can be subpoenaed for her copy if they do not have one.[8] It has been held that these subpoenas may not be served outside the state even though they are but the enforcement phase of a New York judgment rendered with all needed jurisdiction and even though there would be ample basis for extraterritorial service against the judgment debtor or other person sought to be served.[9]

Resolving what had been a murky issue in the caselaw, a 2006 amendment adding a subdivision (a–1) to CPLR 5224 explicitly allows the securing of materials by in-state service of a subpoena duces tecum on the person controlling the materials even if the materials themselves are outside the state. The amenability of that person to in personam New York jurisdiction is deemed to be an adequate basis for that.[10]

(3) The information subpoena. This is a third kind of subpoena, not used as such in pretrial or trial practice, but explicitly offered for enforcement aid by CPLR 5224(a)(3). All it really is, though, is a set of interrogatories sent and answered by mail, and for that reason, it does have a counterpart among the pretrial disclosure devices.[11] Service of the information subpoena, unlike the first two subpoenas, need not be in the same manner as a summons. It may alternatively be served by registered or certified mail with return receipt requested.[12] Accompanying the subpoena are the original and a copy of the questions with a prepaid and self-addressed return envelope.

The recipient must serve a sworn response to all questions within seven days after being served. If the recipient does not respond within the required time, and the judgment creditor can show that the knowledge that the recipient could have imparted would have enabled the creditor to lay hands on the debtor's property through one of the other Article 52 devices, is the recipient liable to the creditor for the loss? Several cases say no,[13] but if the proof is strong that the judgment creditor's loss can be traced to the recipient's delay in the furnishing of the required data, it is suggested that other courts may not let the recipient off so lightly.[14] In Corpuel v. Galasso,[15] where a fine of $1 1/2 million dollars was imposed on the debtor's wife for not cooperating in the enforcement of the judgment against her husband, the root of the contempt was the ignoring of a

---

[8]   See Siemens & Halske, GmbH. v. Gres, 77 Misc. 2d 745, 354 N.Y.S.2d 762 (Sup. Ct., New York County 1973), aff'd, 43 A.D.2d 1021, 353 N.Y.S.2d 395 (1st Dep't 1974).

[9]   See, e.g., Israel Discount Bank Limited v. P. S. Products Corp., 65 Misc. 2d 1002, 319 N.Y.S.2d 554 (Sup. Ct., New York County 1971), applying Jud. Law § 2–b with, it is submitted, needless rigidity. See Commentary C2303:6 on McKinney's CPLR 2303; § 99. There are proposals afoot to allow extrastate subpoena service, at least on the judgment debtor proper. See § 383.

[10]   The placement of this new "(a–1)"—captioned just that—is peculiar. It appears after paragraphs 3 and 4 of CPLR 5224(a), which deal with the information subpoena (to be discussed shortly), while its own subject matter is relevant only to the subpoena duces tecum of subdivision (a)(2). See the note on the amendment in SPR 177:4. Relevant also in this connection are the conflicting *Gryphon* and *Hotel 71* cases treated in § 510.

[11]   CPLR 3130 et seq.; see § 361.

[12]   CPLR 5224(a)(3).

[13]   See, e.g., Syndicate Bldg. Corp. v. City University of New York, 159 Misc. 2d 898, 607 N.Y.S.2d 551 (Ct. Cl. 1993); Miller v. Saretsky, 171 Misc. 2d 404, 654 N.Y.S.2d 970 (Sup. Ct., Suffolk County 1996).

[14]   The disobedience, unless excused, is in any event a contempt of court. How the contempt punishment interplays with issues of the recipient's personal liability to the judgment creditor is discussed in SPR 56:3.

[15]   Corpuel v. Galasso, 240 A.D.2d 531, 659 N.Y.S.2d 65 (2d Dep't 1997) (SPR 71:2).

subpoena. Even with third persons having no relationship to the judgment debtor, attorneys must ask themselves how they would advise a client showing up with an information subpoena and asking how to respond. The advice should be to respond in full and on time. By no means should the attorney offer any assurance that the client won't face liability for disregarding, or even just unreasonably delaying, a response to the notice.

Shown in recent years that information subpoenas have been served indiscriminately on third persons who turn out to have no knowledge whatever about the debtor's assets, and that "[t]hese subpoenas have become overly burdensome and voluminous in nature and labor intensive to businesses," the legislature in 2006 altered CPLR 5224(a)(3) with a corrective amendment that prescribes a certification procedure in these situations.[16]

Returning now to the other devices—brought on with a regular subpoena or a subpoena duces tecum under paragraph 1 and/or 2 of CPLR 5224(a)—the deposition is set up on at least 10 days notice unless the court directs less (which would require a preliminary court application). The provision in point, CPLR 5224(c), contemplates a formal session not only for the deposition, but also for the discovery brought on by the subpoena duces tecum. The discovery need not necessitate a session, however; if the parties can agree on some other procedure, such as the creditor's attorney just visiting the subpoenaed person's office to inspect or copy the papers or records sought, that would of course be acceptable.

The venue of the deposition session is taken from CPLR 3110. The proper county for it is therefore the deponent's residence or business county, or, if the debtor is the deponent, the county in which the judgment was rendered.[17] The caselaw on CPLR 3110 should also be deemed to govern the question of where, within the county, the deposition may be held.[18] The mechanics and incidents of conducting the examination are in CPLR 5224(d); those for preparing and signing the deposition, in CPLR 5224(e). Both have close parallels in Article 31, which by adoption in CPLR 5224(c) says which officers may conduct the examination.[19]

A judgment debtor served with a subpoena gets no fees, but any other person served does. In the case of the testimonial subpoena and the subpoena duces tecum, the sums are one day's witness fee plus mileage.[20] The fees here are no more realistic than they are in the case of pretrial or trial subpoenas, and here, there is even a ludicrous follow-up: a second examination of the judgment debtor (who gets no fee) within a year after a prior examination needs court leave; a second examination of some other person does not.[21] The reason: the requirement to pay witnesses' fees is deemed a sufficient safeguard against abuse! A second examination can in any event be cancelled by individual protective order under CPLR 5240 if it is found useless or abusive.

---

[16] See SPR 178:2.

[17] CPLR 3110(1), (2). The alternative of the county in which the judgment was rendered would not necessarily be available if venue were governed by CPLR 5221(a), which governs most other enforcement steps.

[18] See § 355; Commentary C3110:4 on McKinney's CPLR 3110.

[19] See CPLR 3113, 3114, and 3116; §§ 356–57.

[20] See CPLR 8001; § 383. For the information subpoena the fee used to be fifty cents, but it was dispensed with in a 1994 amendment of CPLR 5224(b). The amendment had no appreciable effect on world trade.

[21] CPLR 5224(f).

The one-year restriction on follow-up examinations of the judgment debtor does not apply if the second deposition is occasioned by the debtor's unjustified refusal to answer questions at the first examination. Even if it did apply, the court in such an instance would be expected to grant leave for a second examination anyway.[22]

Disclosure is not precluded merely because the assets that the judgment creditor is trying to get at are assets held by the judgment debtor outside the state. The judgment debtor is himself within the court's jurisdiction, and this enables the court to direct that the debtor make disclosure here about assets there.[23]

This principle and New York State's broad post-judgment disclosure tools were put to the test in Republic of Argentina v. NML Capital,[24] where plaintiff possessed a multibillion-dollar federal court judgment against Argentina and sought disclosure from two nonparty banks regarding the debtor's assets located outside the United States. On a motion to quash the subpoenas, Argentina asserted that the banks' compliance with the subpoenas would infringe on its sovereign immunity and violate the Foreign Sovereign Immunities Act ("FSIA"). The federal district court rejected the argument and compelled the banks to comply with the subpoenas duces tecum at issue. The Second Circuit affirmed the district court, concluding that "because the Discovery Order involves discovery, not attachment of sovereign property, and because it is directed at third-party banks, not at Argentina itself, Argentina's sovereign immunity is not infringed."[25]

The United States Supreme Court affirmed, emphasizing that Federal Rule of Civil Procedure 69(a)(2) permits a judgment creditor to obtain discovery permitted under either the broad standard set forth in the Federal Rule of Civil Procedure 26(b)(1) or the rules of practice of the state where the district court sits. The High Court noted that CPLR 5223 permits disclosure of "all matter relevant to the satisfaction of [a] judgment" and quoted from this section of the text, observing that New York law permits "investigation [of] any person shown to have any light to shed on the subject of the judgment debtor's assets or their whereabouts."[26] The narrow question before the United States Supreme Court was whether a subpoena issued under these broad discovery standards violated the Foreign Sovereign Immunities Act. The Court held that it did not.

What if the assets targeted by the discovery request are beyond the jurisdictional reach of the court to which the request is made? Could the court still permit discovery to proceed if the judgment creditor establishes that the assets are recoverable under the laws of the jurisdiction in which the assets are located? The Court did not answer these issues, but they are likely to arise in the near future because of New York's "separate entity" rule, which "prevents a judgment creditor from ordering a garnishee bank operating branches in New York to restrain a judgment debtor's assets held in foreign branches of the bank."[27]

---

[22] See City of New York v. Marchese, 74 Misc. 2d 367, 343 N.Y.S.2d 547 (Sup. Ct., Queens County 1973).

[23] See Raji v. Bank Sepah-Iran, 139 Misc. 2d 1026, 529 N.Y.S.2d 420 (Sup. Ct., New York County 1988). This is consistent with the amendment concerning the subpoena duces tecum—the 2006 addition of subdivision (a–1) noted earlier—which requires even nonparties in control of property outside the state to submit to in-state disclosure about it.

[24] Republic of Argentina v. NML Capital, Ltd., 134 S. Ct. 2250, 189 L. Ed. 2d 234 (2014).

[25] EM Ltd. v. Republic of Argentina, 695 F.3d 201, 205 (2d Cir. 2012).

[26] *Republic of Arg.*, 134 S. Ct. at 2254.

[27] Motorola Credit Corp. v. Standard Chartered Bank, 24 N.Y.3d 149, 156, 996 N.Y.S.2d 594, 595, 21 N.E.3d 223, 224 (2014); see § 510.

§ 510. Delivery Order or Judgment

CPLR 5225 and 5227 supply the device commonly known as a delivery or payment order. It is also called a "turnover" order, but in fact it takes the form of an order only when it runs against the judgment debtor himself. When it runs against a garnishee or other third person, as indeed it may, it is not an order at all, but an outright judgment. This results because the procedure for seeking the delivery from the judgment debtor is a mere motion bearing the caption of the main action,[1] while the procedure for seeking it from a third person is a special proceeding.[2]

CPLR 5225 applies if it is property or money that is being sought; CPLR 5227, when it is a debt owed to the judgment debtor. Because the line between "money" and a "debt" is often difficult or impossible to draw, lawyers base their applications on both provisions together, an acceptable step because procedurally they are just about the same. The only significant difference between 5225 and 5227, in fact, is that the latter contemplates only a special proceeding because it always aims at a third person (the garnishee who owes the judgment debtor a debt), while CPLR 5225, concerned with personal property, contemplates either a special proceeding or a motion, depending on who has the property. If a third person (garnishee) has it, a special proceeding is used; if the judgment debtor has it, motion practice is used. CPLR 5225—which we use in this section as including CPLR 5227—thus has a double mission, involved when either debtor or garnishee has possession of the property, and it supplies a motion or special proceeding accordingly. Procedural steps properly taken, but under the label of the wrong provision, can be treated as rightly denominated and the error can be disregarded with the aid, if need be, of the conversion statute, CPLR 103(c).

One situation appropriate for a CPLR 5225 delivery order is where the property or money is located in the judgment debtor's residence, which as a rule effectively places it beyond a sheriff's reach under an execution.[3] Upon proof that the judgment debtor has property applicable to enforcement, whether in his residence or elsewhere, the court on motion can make an order directly instructing the judgment debtor to deliver it or pay it over. It can do this for a painting in the debtor's living room, shares of stock in a desk drawer, a negotiable instrument in a safe, money in a mattress, ad infinitum.

As long as the debtor is subject to the court's personal jurisdiction, a delivery order can be effective even when the property sought is outside the state.[4] Creditors seeking such property, tangible as well as intangible, will find especially gratifying the First Department's decision in Gryphon Domestic VI, LLC v. APP Intern. Finance Co., B.V.,[5] a field day for those involved in the enforcement of judgments against evasive foreign judgment debtors who, however foreign, are subject to New York personal jurisdiction. In Hotel 71 Mezz Lender LLC v. Falor,[6] the Court of Appeals, in a similar vein, held that a defendant's interest in a foreign limited liability company is subject to New York

---

[1] CPLR 5225(a).

[2] CPLR 5225(b), 5227. A special proceeding ends in a judgment, CPLR 411, not an order. See § 556.

[3] See § 496.

[4] See Starbare II Partners, L.P. v. Sloan, 216 A.D.2d 238, 629 N.Y.S.2d 23 (1st Dep't 1995) (noted in SPR 40:3), involving artwork in New Jersey.

[5] Gryphon Domestic VI, LLC v. APP Intern. Finance Co., B.V., 41 A.D.3d 25, 836 N.Y.S.2d 4 (1st Dep't 2007) (SPR 197:1).

[6] Hotel 71 Mezz Lender LLC v. Falor, 14 N.Y.3d 303, 900 N.Y.S.2d 698, 926 N.E.2d 1202 (2010) (NYSLD No. 603).

attachment; that personal jurisdiction of the defendant, even if not a domiciliary of the state, enables the court to attach the defendant's interests in foreign companies.

In virtually all of these situations, the tool that makes the enforcement effort worthwhile—the logistical implement that effectuates the seizure of the property—is the CPLR 5225/5227 turnover order.

In the cases discussed above, there was personal jurisdiction of the judgment debtor. Similar enforcement opportunities arise when personal jurisdiction of the debtor may be lacking, but there's personal jurisdiction of a garnishee—an entity or person controlling the sought-after property of the debtor. An example is Koehler v. Bank of Bermuda Ltd.,[7] in which the pursued property consisted of stock owned by the debtor, but the certificates for which were on deposit with a bank in Bermuda. The bank was treated as the garnishee in the case and held subject to jurisdiction because of a branch the bank maintained in New York.[8] By contrast, in Commonwealth of Northern Mariana Islands v. Canadian Imperial Bank of Commerce,[9] the Court held that a New York bank subject to a CPLR 5225(b) turnover proceeding could not be compelled to deliver property held by its foreign subsidiary because it was not "in possession or custody" of the property as required by the statute.[10]

The *Koehler* and *Northern Mariana Islands* decisions must also be viewed in light of the Court's 2014 decision in Motorola Credit Corp. v. Standard Chartered Bank,[11] which held that the " 'separate entity' rule prevents a judgment creditor from ordering a garnishee bank operating branches in New York to restrain a judgment debtor's assets held in foreign branches of the bank." A two-judge dissent in *Motorola*, joined by the author of *Koehler*, concluded, among other things, that the Court's opinion could not be reconciled with *Koehler*, which the majority attempted to do on several occasions. The enforcement device at issue in *Motorola* was a CPLR 5222 restraining notice, yet the Court's opinion is a must read for those relying on *Koehler* in an attempt to enforce a judgment through a CPLR 5225/CPLR 5227 payment or delivery order.

Securing the proof that will convince the court that the judgment debtor has such money or property can of course be a problem in CPLR 5225/5227 situations, but no order will be made without it. Here the exploitation of the disclosure tools of CPLR 5223/4 will of course help.

The cases illustrating this turnover device are most often those with big judgments and big prospects of enforcement. The need of investigatory proof and the close attention of a lawyer makes them so expensive as to be practicable only for big judgments, or those held by wealthy creditors. Otherwise the cost of the procedure will be disproportionate to the judgment being enforced. Assuming that the judgment belongs to a modest creditor like a small contractor or storekeeper or salesman—public attention often forgets the humble status of many creditors as it concentrates on the needs of the

---

[7]   Koehler v. Bank of Bermuda Ltd., 12 N.Y.3d 533, 883 N.Y.S.2d 763, 911 N.E.2d 825 (2009).

[8]   A number of issues arise under *Koehler*, a 4–3 decision of the court. These are discussed in the lead note in NYSLD No. 595 and in a follow-up article on the case done as an Outside Counsel column in the New York Law Journal of July 28, 2009 (page 4).

[9]   Commonwealth of Northern Mariana Islands v. Canadian Imperial Bank of Commerce, 21 N.Y.3d 55, 967 N.Y.S.2d 876, 990 N.E.2d 114 (2013).

[10]   The *Koehler* and *Northern Mariana Islands* decisions are discussed in further detail in § 491.

[11]   Motorola Credit Corp. v. Standard Chartered Bank, 24 N.Y.3d 149, 996 N.Y.S.2d 594, 21 N.E.3d 223 (2014); see § 487.

debtors—these factors are but another example of how economics can limit access to the courts.

Assuming that the appropriate jurisdiction is present and the requisite proof at hand to make a CPLR 5225/CPLR 5227 application—motion or special proceeding— worthwhile, we can turn to its mechanics and its other features.

The application is made on notice, but the moving papers must be served either in the same manner as a summons or by registered or certified mail with return receipt requested. If the applicant's proof is firm and the court is convinced, it will order the debtor to make the appropriate delivery. If money is involved, the debtor will be directed to pay it to the creditor towards satisfaction of the judgment; if property is involved, the direction will be to deliver it to the sheriff, who will then sell it at public auction,[12] just as the sheriff would sell property levied on an execution.[13] Disobedience of the order by the judgment debtor is a contempt of court and punishable as such.[14]

A special proceeding rather than a mere motion is required when the property is held or a debt is owed by a third person, i.e., a garnishee. The reasons for this are that the garnishee was not a party to the main action, is not part of its caption, and has yet to be subjected to the court's jurisdiction. While a motion is only an application in the context of an action, a special proceeding is an independent application and hence more appropriate when addressed to a person being brought within jurisdiction for the first time.

The judgment creditor brings the proceeding as petitioner, whether under CPLR 5225 or 5227—as already noted, we regard them as interchangeable in this section— against the garnishee as respondent. The procedures that govern the proceeding come from Article 4 of the CPLR. Service of the initiatory papers[15] are made in the same manner as a summons unless an order to show cause is used and directs otherwise.[16] Failure to join the garnishee in the proceeding will of course mean that the garnishee cannot be bound by what the proceeding decides.[17]

An additional requirement imposed is that the judgment debtor, who is not necessarily a named party in the proceeding, be advised of the proceeding in a notice served either in the same manner as a summons or by registered or certified mail with return receipt requested. The debtor can be allowed to intervene in the proceeding.

For various reasons it is often a good idea for the creditor/petitioner to name the judgment debtor as an actual party to the proceeding. In some instances, it may even be indispensable, as when the property entails a special processing of some kind and the judgment debtor appears to be an essential part of it. In Sochor v. IBM Corp.,[18] for example, the property that the judgment creditor was seeking enforcement against was a pension plan established by the debtor's employer, and the plan's activation required the debtor to make an election from among various options available under it. The court

---

[12] CPLR 5233.

[13] CPLR 5225(a).

[14] CPLR 5251; see § 523.

[15] These are a petition and notice of petition. CPLR 402, 403(a), (b); see § 553.

[16] CPLR 403(c), (d). The special proceeding and its procedures are met later. See §§ 547 et seq.

[17] Kennis v. Sherwood, 82 A.D.2d 847, 439 N.Y.S.2d 962 (2d Dep't 1981).

[18] Sochor v. International Business Machines Corp., 60 N.Y.2d 254, 469 N.Y.S.2d 591, 457 N.E.2d 696 (1983).

held that the debtor had to be within the jurisdiction of the court in the proceeding in order for the court either to compel the debtor to make the election or to enable the court to make it for him. If there should be some kind of jurisdictional problem in locating the debtor for service, as was apparently the problem in *Sochor*, the answer is not to omit the debtor as a party, but to exploit some special method of service of process, like service by a court-invented means under CPLR 308(5).[19]

If there are any other claimants to the property or money involved, they can be allowed to intervene, if, indeed, the judgment creditor has not already joined them in the first place, or the garnishee interpleaded them. Interpleader may be especially appropriate here if conflicting claims are being made to the property or debt, but its use in this context will ordinarily require court leave.[20]

The special proceeding, in short, can be converted into a full-fledged test of precisely whom the disputed property or debt belongs to, which is all CPLR 5225(b) and 5227 mean by their cross-references to CPLR 5239.[21]

When interests in it are disputed, the property cannot be applied to the satisfaction of the judgment unless and until the special proceeding resolves that it belongs to the judgment debtor. If the proceeding finds that it belongs to someone else, this enforcement step, as far as this judgment creditor is concerned, fails. But the special proceeding is plenary and can try any fact issues arising between and among all those properly before the court; an ordinary plenary action, in other words, is rendered unnecessary.[22] If the particular dispute would in more conventional context be jury triable, the right to trial by jury remains. If demanded, a jury will be impaneled in the special proceeding itself.[23]

In Colonial Surety Co. v. Lakeview Advisors, LLC,[24] the Fourth Department concluded that a special proceeding "under CPLR 5225 and 5227 against a party other than the judgment debtor is an outgrowth of the 'ancient creditor's bill in equity,' which was used after all remedies at law had been exhausted." The judgment creditor in this situation is seeking legal relief to the extent she desires an adjudication of whether the third-party owes a money debt to the judgment debtor and also equitable relief in that she wants any such debt to be paid to her and not the judgment debtor. In that the judgment creditor's use of CPLR 5225 and 5227 in *Colonial Surety* was "in furtherance of both legal and equitable relief," the court ruled that it was not entitled to a jury trial.[25] The *Colonial Surety* court noted in dicta that prior caselaw had concluded that the respondent in a proceeding under CPLR 5225(b) and 5227 did possess a right to a jury trial and could demand it.[26]

---

[19] See Commentary C5225:5 on McKinney's CPLR 5225; § 99.

[20] CPLR 401.

[21] For discussion of the versatility of CPLR 5239, see § 521.

[22] See Ruvolo v. Long Island R. Co., 45 Misc. 2d 136, 256 N.Y.S.2d 279 (Sup. Ct., Queens County 1965); First Small Business Inv. Corp. v. Zaretsky, 46 Misc. 2d 328, 259 N.Y.S.2d 700 (Sup. Ct., Queens County 1965).

[23] See 1965 Commentary on McKinney's CPLR 5225; Leedpak, Inc. v. Julian, 78 Misc. 2d 519, 356 N.Y.S.2d 1011 (Sup. Ct., New York County 1974).

[24] Colonial Sur. Co. v. Lakeview Advisors, LLC, 125 A.D.3d 1292, 1295, 3 N.Y.S.3d 800, 804 (4th Dep't 2015).

[25] See CPLR 4102(c); § 209.

[26] *Colonial Surety*, 125 A.D.3d at 1294, 3 N.Y.S.3d at 803; see Leedpak, Inc. v. Julian, 78 Misc. 2d 519, 356 N.Y.S.2d 1011 (Sup. Ct., New York County 1974).

The proceeding may also be used by the judgment creditor to collect damages caused by a garnishee who did not properly carry out the requirements of a restraining notice or an execution. There, too, a plenary action, although permissible,[27] is no longer necessary.[28]

The special proceeding of CPLR 5225 is available not only against a garnishee legitimately holding property or money of the judgment debtor, such as a bank or warehouse, but also against a "transferee" of the judgment debtor. This would mean any transferee against whom the judgment creditor has (or may possibly have) a higher right, such as a gratuitous transferee.[29] This touches on the realm of the fraudulent transfer made by a debtor to frustrate creditors. A person who has a judgment against that debtor is entitled to set aside such a transfer,[30] but at one time had to bring a regular plenary action to accomplish this. Today, once again, the special proceeding under CPLR 5225 or 5227 can be used.[31]

If the property or money is found to be the debtor's, or if the rights of the judgment creditor are found superior to those of the transferee, the court will direct the respondent (garnishee or transferee) to pay to the judgment creditor enough money to satisfy the judgment; and if the money paid does not suffice, to deliver to the sheriff enough of the debtor's other personal property (the sheriff will sell it) to pay the rest.[32]

These directions are embodied in a final judgment in the proceeding. If money is involved, the judgment will usually take the form of a money judgment running against the respondent, who would then be subject to the Article 52 enforcement devices directly, just like any judgment debtor. It has been held, moreover, that the judgment may take the form of a specific direction to the respondent to hand over the money or to deliver designated property to the sheriff, disobedience of which can even subject the respondent to the contempt punishment.[33]

The special proceedings of CPLR 5225 or 5227 are also the ones contemplated as a "perfection" step when a garnishee fails to respond to a levy of execution.[34]

If a document of any kind is needed to effect a payment or delivery of the subject money or property, and it is within the power of the person against whom a CPLR 5225 or 5227 motion or special proceeding has been brought to make or deliver the document, that person can be required to.[35] This would embrace the making, indorsement, or negotiation of any kind of commercial paper, including a bill or note or withdrawal slip for money, a bond or share of stock or other evidence of ownership, a document of title or the like—whatever piece of paper, in short, will facilitate realization of the property

---

[27] See Mazzuka v. Bank of North America, 53 Misc. 2d 1053, 280 N.Y.S.2d 495 (N.Y. City Civ. Ct. 1967).

[28] See Nardone v. Long Island Trust Co., 40 A.D.2d 697, 336 N.Y.S.2d 325 (2d Dep't 1972).

[29] See § 519.

[30] See American Sur. Co. of N.Y. v. Conner, 251 N.Y. 1, 166 N.E. 783, 65 A.L.R. 244 (1929).

[31] See Siemens and Halske, GmbH. v. Gres, 32 A.D.2d 624, 299 N.Y.S.2d 908 (1st Dep't 1969).

[32] If a receiver has been duly appointed under CPLR 5228, see § 512, the court will direct delivery of the property to the receiver instead of to the sheriff for sale.

[33] See Carl B. Nusbaum, Inc. v. Calale, 45 Misc. 2d 903, 258 N.Y.S.2d 8 (Orange County Court 1965). The court apparently deems a judgment under CPLR 5225 or 5227 the equivalent of the "order" for which contempt is authorized by CPLR 5251. Contempt can be justified on the alternative theory that the judgment is simply an equitable one, acting in personam on the respondent and just as susceptible of contempt enforcement as any judgment emanating from an equity action. See CPLR 103(b).

[34] CPLR 5232(a). See § 496.

[35] CPLR 5225(c), 5227.

interest involved.[36] When the interest aimed at is a debt not yet due, a situation contemplated by CPLR 5227, the paper the respondent may be directed to make would be an attornment or some similar kind of commitment to pay the debt to the judgment creditor when it does fall due, instead of to the judgment debtor. The court can even render a judgment against the respondent for the debt, but if the debt is not yet due, this would require a stay of either entry or execution until the due date.

A garnishee or other third person who has paid or given to the judgment creditor or sheriff money or property of the judgment debtor, pursuant to regular Article 52 procedures in enforcement of the judgment, is relieved of the obligation to the judgment debtor and may use such payment or delivery as a complete defense if afterwards sued by the judgment debtor.[37]

An order under CPLR 5225(a), which should be deemed to include a judgment under CPLR 5225(b) or 5227, gives the judgment creditor who gets it a lien on the subject personal property as of the moment of entry of the judgment or order.[38]

Only the courts listed in CPLR 5221(a) may entertain motions or special proceedings under CPLR 5225 or 5227. The effect of this is to exclude the town and village courts from entertaining them. When sought in respect of a judgment of one of those courts, the application is made to the supreme court or to a county court.[39]

§ 511. Installment Payment Order

A useful device against a judgment debtor trying to conceal income, and in a variety of other situations, is the installment payment order of CPLR 5226. It's brought on by mere motion, captioned in the original action. The motion papers are served on the judgment debtor in the same manner as a summons or by registered or certified mail with return receipt requested. The court on the motion can direct the debtor to make regular payments to the judgment creditor in any sum it finds the debtor able to afford, not limited by the 10% that restricts the income execution of CPLR 5231. The 10% is the corollary of CPLR 5205(d), which exempts 90% of income, but it will be recalled that the exemption is not absolute; the court can invade any part of the 90% that it finds "unnecessary for the reasonable requirements of the judgment debtor and his dependents," and it is the installment payment motion of CPLR 5226 that supplies the occasion for the court to make those findings. It is always a sui generis inquiry, for which reason it requires strong proof, often through diligent use of enforcement disclosure under CPLR 5223 and 5224.

The application can therefore generate much expense in time, effort, and money, which makes the device—akin in this regard to the delivery order of CPLR 5225 and 5227—practicable only when the judgment is a big one or the judgment creditor well off.

The court on the motion must consider all of the usual family obligations of the debtor. The needs of the debtor's dependents will be reviewed, as well as his obligations to other creditors, especially judgment creditors, including any who have issued income executions or secured wage assignments. Items not falling within family requirements

---

[36] See Jack London Productions, Inc. v. Samuel Bronston Productions, Inc., 22 A.D.2d 870, 254 N.Y.S.2d 397 (1st Dep't 1964).

[37] CPLR 5209. See § 515.

[38] CPLR 5234(c), 5016(a). See §§ 518 et seq.

[39] See § 493.

are not likely to earn consideration, as one bachelor debtor found out when he unsuccessfully attempted to have the court factor in his expenses for dating, a credit card, the New York Athletic Club, a golf club, and a wine and food society—everything, in other words, short of maid service on a yacht.[1]

No single factor is decisive; all relevant ingredients figure. The court will simply direct the judgment debtor to pay, at designated intervals, whatever in overall context the court thinks the debtor can afford. That these findings are made on notice, and only after a careful analysis of the debtor's needs, insulates the installment payment device from any blunderbuss due process attack.

The rendering of services without adequate compensation is one of the evasions explicitly addressed by CPLR 5226. Thus, where the debtor worked for a corporation whose assets were owned mainly by his wife, and claimed he did so gratis, the court fixed the reasonable value of his services and from that sum directed that the debtor pay a designated sum to the judgment creditor every month.[2]

Where the judgment debtor was receiving regular income from her son, who said he would stop payments if any part of them were allowed to her creditor, the court nonetheless directed her to pay a stipulated sum per month based on what she had been receiving, saying that the payments would have to continue only as long as income from her son continued, in effect daring the son to cut her off.[3]

The invisible means of support is another evasion that a well-prepared CPLR 5226 motion can pierce. A judgment debtor was shown, for example, to be managing to get on quite well with $700 in monthly living expenses—this in 1963—but, he swore, no salary. Where was he getting the money? Loans, he said. He was apparently employed by someone, and a hearing was ordered to determine what his talents were and what his services were worth.[4] With temerity enough to tell a court that he was living off monthly loans, his services were probably worth a good deal.

A simple situation for an installment order is where the judgment debtor is guilty of no concealment, but is shown to be earning enough to pay his judgment creditor more than the 10% to which an income execution is restricted. The debtor's income may be found ample enough, in fact, to pay one judgment creditor on the 10% execution and another an additional sum ordered under CPLR 5226.[5] When a series of income executions were outstanding against the same debtor, for example, each waiting its proper turn since only one goes forward at a time,[6] another enterprising judgment creditor was able to convince the court, on a CPLR 5226 motion, that the debtor could afford more than 10%. He ended up getting the affordable balance while the queued-up income executioners gawked.[7]

It is feasible enough for the court to make a CPLR 5226 order even after a CPLR 5231 income execution has taken hold because the order factors in the income execution

---

[1] Yamamoto v. Costello, 73 Misc. 2d 592, 342 N.Y.S.2d 33 (Sup. Ct., Nassau County 1973).

[2] Frooks v. Clurman, 76 N.Y.S.2d 187 (Sup. Ct., Kings County 1942), aff'd, 266 A.D. 859, 43 N.Y.S.2d 861 (2d Dep't 1943).

[3] Lewshap Realty Co. v. Shubert, 182 Misc. 343, 44 N.Y.S.2d 65 (N.Y. City Ct. 1943).

[4] See Kosow v. Greenberg, N.Y.L.J., Sept. 20, 1963, at 12, col. 6 (Sup. Ct., Nassau County; Albert, J.).

[5] See, e.g., Widder Bros. Inc. v. Kaffee, 19 A.D.2d 817, 243 N.Y.S.2d 601 (1st Dep't 1963).

[6] CPLR 5231(h).

[7] Schwartz v. Goldberg, 58 Misc. 2d 308, 295 N.Y.S.2d 245 (Sup. Ct., Bronx County 1968).

and directs payment of only what the debtor can afford after considering it. Difficulty is in store for the debtor, however, when things are the other way around—when, while the installment order of one creditor is being paid, another comes along with an income execution, peremptorily demanding 10%. If the debtor can't afford both, the remedy is a motion under CPLR 5231(i) to modify or abate the income execution in deference to the installment order, or a motion under CPLR 5240 for a protective order abating either.

The installment payment order is also the tool of the creditor whose debtor's income derives from sources not reachable with an income execution. Where, for example, the debtor works for a federal agency (which is not ordinarily amenable to income execution),[8] and he does not voluntarily make 10% deductions himself, he can be subjected to an installment payment order. Once the wages come into his hands they lose whatever federal exemption they had before disbursement.[9] The CPLR 5226 order would do like service when the employer is an out-of-state or foreign one beyond New York jurisdiction, but where the judgment debtor remains within jurisdiction. One may even urge that the order be entertained even if the judgment debtor, too, is now outside New York, under a kind of "continuing jurisdiction" theory. If the judgment itself is good, personam jurisdiction having fully obtained in the underlying action, it ought to be deemed to continue for enforcement purposes even if the judgment debtor moves from the state after judgment or was never a domiciliary to begin with—as where longarm jurisdiction was used to secure jurisdiction in the action. Continuing jurisdiction theories have constitutional support in a sufficient number of analogous situations[10] to suggest that an extension of it to the enforcement of ordinary money judgments would find equal footing.[11]

An extensive treatment of the CPLR 5226 device and its application appears in Balanoff v. Niosi,[12] an especially helpful decision because it considers not just the judgment debtor's regular income from her employment but also maintenance income she's receiving from her former spouse.[13]

The installment payment order is backed by the contempt punishment.[14] It's another of the devices that can't be entertained by town or village courts. To be used with a judgment of one of those courts, the installment payment order must be sought from the supreme court or a county court.[15]

§ 512. Receivership

We have already met two kinds of CPLR receivership: first the provisional remedy of Article 64, under which a receiver is appointed to take charge of specific property that's

---

[8] See Reeves v. Crownshield, 274 N.Y. 74, 8 N.E.2d 283 (1937).

[9] Erenerol v. McCarthy, 20 A.D.2d 798, 248 N.Y.S.2d 464 (2d Dep't 1964).

[10] See, e.g., Michigan Trust Co. v. Ferry, 228 U.S. 346, 33 S. Ct. 550, 57 L. Ed. 867 (1913) (removal of estate fiduciary); Ohlquist v. Nordstrom, 143 Misc. 502, 257 N.Y.S. 711 (Sup. Ct., Chautauqua County 1932), aff'd, 238 A.D. 766, 261 N.Y.S. 1039 (4th Dep't 1933), aff'd, 262 N.Y. 696, 188 N.E. 125 (application for contribution judgment from joint tortfeasor); Schneidman v. Schneidman, 188 Misc. 765, 65 N.Y.S.2d 876 (Sup. Ct., Kings County 1946) (alimony modification in divorce judgment); see § 99.

[11] See Kaplan v. Supak & Sons Mfg. Co., 46 Misc. 2d 574, 260 N.Y.S.2d 374 (N.Y. City Civ. Ct. 1965), and the discussion in Commentary C5226:5 on McKinney's CPLR 5226.

[12] Balanoff v. Niosi, 16 A.D.3d 53, 791 N.Y.S.2d 553 (2d Dep't 2005).

[13] The *Balanoff* case is the subject of the lead note in SPR 162:1.

[14] CPLR 5251.

[15] CPLR 5221. See § 493.

the subject of an action and who functions to preserve the property during the action's pendency;[1] and the post-judgment receivership designed to carry out a judgment rendered in an action of that kind.[2] The receivership of CPLR 5228, which we take up now, is also a post-judgment variety, but it's designed to aid enforcement of an ordinary money judgment and may therefore operate on any property belonging to the judgment debtor that's applicable to enforcement.

Under CPLR 5228, in common with just about all receiverships, the receiver can be authorized to manage and preserve designated property, but unlike some of the others, notably the provisional receivership of Article 64, the CPLR 5228 receiver can be authorized to sell the property—that may indeed be the main purpose of this category of receivership—so as to convert it to money to pay the judgment. The order of appointment specifies the receiver's powers as well as the property to be received.

The receivership is sought by motion brought on by order to show cause, in which the court determines the notice steps. As far as practicable, says CPLR 5228(a), the court should direct that notice be given to the judgment debtor and to other judgment creditors; any of the others can then ask that the receiver be designated to act both for them as well as for the original movant. If a receiver has already been appointed in behalf of one judgment creditor, another may simply move to extend the receivership to her judgment as well.[3]

The provisions of CPLR 6402 through 6405, which are the parts of the provisional remedy article that govern a receiver's oath, bond, accounts, and removal, are made applicable by adoption to the CPLR 5228 receivership, too.

The receivership is one of the less used of the enforcement devices. One of its prime uses is where it's shown that a private sale of some item of the debtor's property, real or personal, will likely bring a substantially higher price than would the public auction that a sheriff is required to conduct when levying an execution. This is especially the case when the debtor's residence is involved: a receiver can use the usual channels of newspaper advertisements, brokers, etc.

A receivership to sell is not limited to real property, however. It can be used for personal property, too, such as shares in a corporation.[4] A receivership has been held especially appropriate when the property interest involved is intangible, lacks a ready market, and presents nothing that a sheriff can work with at an auction, such as the interest of a psychiatrist/judgment debtor in a professional corporation of which he is a member.[5]

Another good use of this device is where the interest sought is a cause of action the judgment debtor has against a third person (garnishee). Knowing that anything he recovers may be quickly gobbled up by his waiting creditor, a judgment debtor may lack incentive to pursue the claim. A receiver can be appointed to bring the suit in the debtor's behalf. A receivership for this purpose is even allowable to a creditor with a personal injuries judgment when it can be shown that the judgment debtor's insurer unreasonably failed to negotiate and the verdict exceeds the debtor/insured's coverage. The debtor has

---

[1]   See § 332.

[2]   CPLR 5106. See § 476.

[3]   CPLR 5228(b).

[4]   See Myer, Matter of, 273 A.D. 387, 77 N.Y.S.2d 660 (1st Dep't 1948).

[5]   Udel v. Udel, 82 Misc. 2d 882, 370 N.Y.S.2d 426 (N.Y. City Civ. Ct. 1975).

in that instance what the bar calls an "excess" or "bad faith" claim against the insurer. The judgment creditor does not own the claim; it belongs technically to the debtor-insured. But it's deemed a property right of the debtor susceptible of receivership, and a receiver can be appointed at the creditor's behest to sue the insurer on the claim,[6] with the proceeds of course to go towards the judgment. (Often the judgment debtor in that situation will facilitate things by merely assigning his "excess" claim to the judgment creditor.)[7]

It is also permissible to have a receiver appointed to manage a property—instead of sell it—collecting profits and making payments on the judgment out of them. This is not a favored use, however. It prolongs enforcement and involves the court, which acts as the receiver's overseer, in extended management. Sale of the whole property and quick conversion to money is preferred, so that a receivership-to-manage would likely be allowed only when the situation is one in which continued management is clearly the only way to realize on the property's value.

A bank can be appointed receiver.[8] So, for that matter, can the judgment creditor himself. But a judgment creditor so appointed is not entitled to compensation, while a receiver other than the judgment creditor is, getting both expenses and such commissions (on the moneys received and disbursed by him) as the appointing court allows, not to exceed 5%.[9]

After deducting for expenses, compensation, and any taxes involved in the proceedings, the receiver must pay over the balance of the receipts to the judgment creditor towards satisfaction of the judgment. Should there be anything left over after that, it of course goes back to the judgment debtor.[10] If a delivery order for personal property is made under CPLR 5225 while a receivership is outstanding, the property is delivered for sale to the receiver instead of the sheriff.[11]

The CPLR 5228 receivership is another of the enforcement devices excluded from use in the town and village courts. Should one be sought in respect of a judgment of one of those courts, it must be applied for to the supreme court or to a county court.[12]

The receivership does have lien value: the judgment creditor who secures the receivership gets a lien on the property ordered received as of the entry of the order.[13]

§ 513. Arrest

If it is shown that the judgment debtor is hiding in or is about to leave the state with unexempt property, CPLR 5250 provides that the court on ex parte motion can issue a warrant directing the sheriff to seize the debtor and bring him before the court. The court may then order the debtor to furnish an undertaking that he will appear for an examination about his assets and that he will obey any restraining notice directed against him.

---

[6] See Oppel v. DeGangi, 84 A.D.2d 549, 443 N.Y.S.2d 177 (2d Dep't 1981).

[7] See the note on "Bad Faith Claims" in SPR 104:3.

[8] Franklin Nat. Bank v. Hall, 51 Misc. 2d 736, 273 N.Y.S.2d 810 (N.Y. City Civ. Ct. 1966).

[9] CPLR 5228(a).

[10] CPLR 5234(a).

[11] CPLR 5228(a).

[12] CPLR 5221(a). See § 493.

[13] CPLR 5234(c). See §§ 518 et seq.

This is a rarely used provision. Body execution as a tool for the enforcement of a money judgment was abolished by the CPLR, and the provisional remedy of civil arrest that was carried into the CPLR as Article 61 was repealed in 1979. The instant arrest is a narrowly tailored cousin of those devices designed mainly to enable the judgment creditor to arrange for an examination of a debtor whose evasiveness has frustrated subpoena service. The theory is that if the debtor can be served with a subpoena, the contempt proceedings that back it—which can themselves end in arrest and jailing—would do the job and make arrest under CPLR 5250 unnecessary.[1]

If the judgment debtor is not shown to be hiding in or about to leave New York, no quantity of property in his possession will justify an arrest under CPLR 5250. Nor would it be necessary: the judgment debtor and his property would be available for the whole run of Article 52's other enforcement devices.

Arguments about constitutionality can be made about this device, but it is too rarely used (if it is used at all) to generate much caselaw or to warrant further attention.

G. INCIDENTAL MATTERS

Table of Sections

§ 514.   Death of Judgment Debtor
§ 515.   Protecting the Garnishee
§ 516.   Prejudgment Enforcement

§ 514. Death of Judgment Debtor

Generally speaking, the death of the judgment debtor prevents further efforts at enforcement from proceeding through the court that rendered the judgment and requires that payment be sought in the surrogate's court that will be administering the debtor's estate. CPLR 5208, the main provision in point, bars all further enforcement steps except upon leave of the surrogate. The main reason for this is that the judgment must now line up with all of the other obligations of the decedent, seeking its priority pursuant to section 1811 of the Surrogate's Court Procedure Act, which gives preference to certain other items, mainly taxes.[1]

Even an execution already issued and in the sheriff's hands when the debtor dies, fails, at least insofar as the debtor's personal property is concerned, remitting its issuer to the surrogate's court. But if a levy has already been made, it can apparently proceed to perfection and sale. In the case of real property on which the judgment has been made a lien through docketing in the county clerk's office—a lien against real property does not depend on delivery of executions or their levy[2]—it has been held that the debtor's death does not preclude levy and sale afterwards; that the sheriff can proceed with the sale as long as the execution was issued before the debtor's death.[3] Based on that authority, it was then held that a restraining notice issued and served before death retains its effect,[4] but there is some doubt about what that should be. The court's

---

[1]   See 3d Rep. Leg. Doc. No. 17, p. 315 (1959).

[1]   SCPA 1811(2). See the Commentaries on McKinney's SCPA 1811.

[2]   See § 517.

[3]   Oysterman's Bank & Trust Co. v. Weeks, 35 A.D.2d 580, 313 N.Y.S.2d 535 (2d Dep't 1970).

[4]   Plaza Hotel Associates v. Wellington Associates, Inc., 84 Misc. 2d 777, 378 N.Y.S.2d 859 (Sup. Ct., New York County 1975).

rationale was that while the debtor's death precludes new enforcement steps from being initiated without leave of the surrogate, it does not nullify such steps as have already been taken.

In some regards it does, however. Priorities, for example, secured by judgment creditors before death can, upon death, be superseded by those of SCPA 1811.[5] And if the surrogate's court under the SCPA can reorder priorities, it should logically also have jurisdiction to take hold of the property against which the priorities are being asserted. It would therefore seem that a restraining notice (which does not even earn a priority for its user under the CPLR)[6] cannot bar the surrogate from control of the affected property, or SCPA 1811 from its say as to who shall have it.

The reason why issues like this do not often arise is that they are ultimately a problem only when the estate is insolvent. As long as the estate can pay all of its debts, the worst its creditors confront is some delay. As long as the creditor gets paid, it is ordinarily of small moment whether the payment comes from liquidation of a given estate asset on which the creditor may earlier have had a lien, or from some other asset in which she had no special right at all.

Recognizing the time element, and that an indefinite delay in the surrogate's proceedings can unfairly impede the judgment creditor, the CPLR provides that if no executor or administrator is appointed for the decedent within 18 months after his death, enforcement can proceed through the original court without leave of the surrogate. The procedure for the judgment creditor to use in that situation is to move the original court for leave to continue enforcement, doing so by order to show cause (in which the court can determine how and upon whom notice shall be served).[7]

If the judgment debtor died a domiciliary of a state other than New York, so that it is the probate or like court of that state that is taking on the main administration of the decedent's estate, CPLR 5208 can still be given scope and effect. (Ancillary letters[8] may ultimately be necessary. If they are, they're sought from the New York Surrogate's Court insofar as any local assets of the decedent are affected.) Proceedings in this nondomiciliary situation are not entirely clear, especially when the local creditors' claims have been reduced to judgment. The singular theme of the SCPA in this situation, however, is that local assets should not be let out of the state unless and until local creditors have been paid their just claims, the property to act in effect as security. That theme is sounded for the protection of all local creditors,[9] and it should a fortiori guide proceedings for those who have achieved the even higher status of judgment creditor.

CPLR 5208 is concerned only with a judgment rendered against the decedent before he died. This must be distinguished from a judgment rendered against the representative of the estate in some action or proceeding after death. Although

---

[5] See the extensive treatment in 3d Rep. Leg. Doc. No. 17, p. 126 (1959). Although as a group judgment creditors may be subordinated to other creditors of the decedent, they at least retain their competitive lien positions among themselves. SCPA 1811(2)(c).

[6] See § 520.

[7] CPLR 5208.

[8] Ancillary letters are those that appoint someone as fiduciary to administer the local assets of one who died domiciled, and whose main estate is being administered, elsewhere. See SCPA 1604, 1607, 1608.

[9] See SCPA 1610(2).

enforcement in that situation, too, requires leave of the surrogate,[10] it is not governed by CPLR 5208.

§ 515. Protecting the Garnishee

In several situations under Article 52, a garnishee who has property of the judgment debtor or who owes a debt to the judgment debtor may be required to deliver or pay it to the judgment creditor instead, or to the sheriff. The garnishee may be obliged to do so on an execution or on some category of Article 52 order or judgment, such as a delivery or "turnover" order under CPLR 5225. Whenever, pursuant to an execution or order, the garnishee makes the required payment or delivery, the garnishee is discharged from any further obligation to the judgment debtor to the extent of it.[1] Thus, if the judgment debtor should afterwards bring suit against the garnishee on the same obligation, the garnishee's prior payment or delivery pursuant to an enforcement device duly issued at the behest of the judgment debtor's judgment creditor will be a good defense. It will also be entitled to full faith and credit if the suit is brought in another American jurisdiction.[2]

One thing the garnishee should make sure of in the New York enforcement proceedings is that the property or debt belongs to or is owed to the judgment debtor, and not to some third person, especially if the execution has identified the judgment debtor but no specific property. If there is any doubt, the garnishee should withhold the property or debt until a court, with jurisdiction of the third person (who would then be bound by all findings), determines the property to be the judgment debtor's. At that point, the garnishee may safely pay it over. Doing so without that determination—and jurisdiction of the third person—subjects the garnishee to double liability: the third person, in a later suit against the garnishee, would not be bound by any earlier proceedings purporting to adjudicate that the property belonged to the judgment debtor.

If an execution has specifically designated property, however, the garnishee who complies is protected; in that situation "it is the creditor and not the garnishee who is liable for damages to the actual owner."[3]

If, because of any risk perceived, the garnishee does refuse to turn over money or property in violation of an execution, the garnishee can expect a special proceeding from the judgment creditor to force the turn-over.[4] But that's just what the doctor orders here. The garnishee can use that proceeding to secure the protective determination needed. If the judgment creditor has voluntarily joined the other claimants in that proceeding, as he is likely to do if the garnishee has pointed to them as the reason for withholding payment, judgment in that proceeding will bind them. If they have not been initially joined, the garnishee as respondent in that proceeding can move to interplead them,[5] thus converting the proceeding into the equivalent of defensive interpleader.[6] The

---

[10]   See EPTL 11–4.6.

[1]   CPLR 5209. An order as used in this provision should be deemed to embrace a judgment as well since a delivery direction against a garnishee under CPLR 5225(b) or 5227 will often emanate from a special proceeding, which ends in a judgment rather than an order. CPLR 411; see § 556.

[2]   Harris v. Balk, 198 U.S. 215, 25 S. Ct. 625, 49 L. Ed. 1023 (1905).

[3]   Chin Sung Yu v. Riggs Nat. Bank of Washington, D.C., 248 A.D.2d 235, 670 N.Y.S.2d 187 (1st Dep't 1998) (noted in SPR 76:2).

[4]   See CPLR 5232(a), 5225(b), 5227.

[5]   CPLR 401.

[6]   See CPLR 1006(b); see § 148.

garnishee can initiate the proceeding,[7] but it's usually more comfortable to leave the initiative on that to the judgment creditor who, because collection of the judgment is meanwhile suspended, can be expected to seize it.

§ 516. Prejudgment Enforcement

The moment that permits enforcement to go forward is the entry of the judgment so that practically speaking all enforcement is a post-judgment procedure. But CPLR 5229 allows two of the enforcement devices to be used during the brief interval after rendition of the verdict or decision, but before the formal entry of judgment. These are the examination (disclosure) in regard to assets (otherwise governed by CPLR 5223 and 5224 in post-judgment use) and the restraint against divestiture of those assets (governed after judgment by CPLR 5222). When sought at this prejudgment moment, however, a court order is required. It is sought by motion to the trial judge. For that reason it can be an oral motion, made right after the decision or verdict comes in, but whether oral or written it is rarely used, probably because the full panoply of enforcement devices will become available as soon as a judgment is formally entered and that can usually be effected within a day or so.

One situation in which CPLR 5229 has special utility is where an interlocutory judgment establishes liability, but where a final judgment must still abide a trial of damages. A restraint in the interim can prevent the defendant from selling off his property and frustrating collection of the ultimate judgment. It is not ordinarily germane in a bifurcated trial in a personal injury case because in that instance, an insurer will usually be paying the ultimate judgment anyway. But it would be helpful in an accounting action, for example, in which liability has gone to interlocutory judgment and where there is some apprehension about the defendant's divestiture of assets before the damages phase can be tried.[1]

Under CPLR 5229, the defendant can apparently be directed by the court to submit to immediate questioning about his assets by the plaintiff's lawyer, but that also presupposes that the lawyer has prepared the questioning, which is usually not the case.

It is not necessary, for this prejudgment relief, to show that the defendant is actually disposing of assets. Nor is the pendency of a motion to vacate the verdict or decision a bar.[2]

All in all CPLR 5229 is benevolent, but not popular. It may come in handy from time to time though, and the practitioner should keep it in the arsenal. It is not restricted— as are the more popular supplementary proceedings—to the courts listed in CPLR 5221(a);[3] it makes its examination and restraint available in any court with jurisdiction to render a civil judgment.

Indeed, CPLR 5229 applies in federal practice, too, and it is in fact a federal case that gives the statute its most extensive treatment.[4]

---

[7]　See CPLR 5239, treated in § 521.

[1]　See Kaminsky v. Kahn, 46 Misc. 2d 131, 258 N.Y.S.2d 1000 (Sup. Ct., New York County 1965), modified on other grounds 23 A.D.2d 231, 259 N.Y.S.2d 716 (1st Dep't).

[2]　See Gallegos v. Elite Model Mgmt. Corp., N.Y.L.J., Sept. 4, 2003, at 18, col. 1 (Sup. Ct., New York County; York, J.), noted in SPR 151:4.

[3]　See § 493.

[4]　See Sequa Capital Corp. v. Nave, 921 F. Supp. 1072 (S.D.N.Y. 1996), noted in SPR 45:4.

H. PRIORITIES AND LIENS

Table of Sections

§ 517.   Priorities and Liens on Real Property

§ 518.   Rights in Personal Property, Introductory

§ 519.   Rights in Personal Property; Judgment Creditor Versus Transferee

§ 520.   Rights in Personal Property; Judgment Creditors Among Themselves

§ 521.   Proceeding to Determine Adverse Claims

§ 517. Priorities and Liens on Real Property

Obtaining a lien on the judgment debtor's real property is an easy affair mechanically, at least when contrasted with personal property. It's simply a matter of getting the judgment docketed with the county clerk of the county where the real property is located. That docketing, which is an entry under the debtor's name in a set of alphabetized books or an entry on a block index if one is maintained,[1] makes the judgment a lien with nothing more required.[2] But it is only a lien on real property in that county. To make it a lien elsewhere, a transcript of the judgment is secured from the home county clerk and filed with the county clerk of the other county in which a lien is sought, whereupon the judgment is docketed in that county and becomes a lien there, too.

The docketing of a judgment is practically automatic when rendered in the supreme court or a county court, because the county clerk is ex officio the clerk of those courts and anything she does as court clerk she does as county clerk as well. So, when a judgment in an action in one of those courts is entered and docketed, and the judgment-roll is filed—events that occur at just about the same time[3]—the judgment immediately becomes a lien on the judgment debtor's local real property. If the judgment was rendered in a lower court, however, a transcript of the judgment must be secured from that court's clerk and filed with the county clerk before a real property lien is effected. The procedures for transcripting judgments between and among courts was the subject of earlier treatment, which the reader may find it convenient to review at this point.[4]

The lien lasts 10 years—measured not from the time of docketing, but from the filing of the judgment roll,[5] which is essentially the moment the judgment was entered.[6] As indicated, that moment and the moment of docketing are the same in a supreme court or county court action, but not with a lower court judgment, such as one of a city court. There, the lien will not take effect until docketing by transcript with the county clerk; nevertheless, the 10-year lien period will have started when the judgment was entered in the lower court. Where, for example, judgment in an Albany City Court action is entered in 1988, but not docketed with the Albany county clerk until 1990, the lien will have only eight years left at docketing time. The first two years will have been lost as lien time.

---

[1]   CPLR 5018(a).

[2]   CPLR 5203(a).

[3]   CPLR 5018(a); see § 418.

[4]   See §§ 421 and 422.

[5]   CPLR 5203(a).

[6]   CPLR 5017(a).

CPLR 5203(a) determines the effect of the lien. It provides that no transfer by the judgment debtor of any interest in the liened real property is effective against the judgment creditor after the lien takes effect. It then carves out a set of six exceptions, as follows:

1.   The lien of course defers to senior judgment liens, so that a buyer at a sale on an execution being levied on a judgment with a senior lien takes free of the junior judgment, and the proceeds of the sale go first to satisfy the senior judgment creditor.[7]

2.   If the judgment debtor gave back a purchase money mortgage when he bought the property, that mortgagee prevails over the judgment creditor even if the judgment stood of record when the debtor bought.[8] This situation can arise when a judgment debtor buys the land after judgment against him has been docketed, which suggests that the judgment creditor may have been lax in pursuit of the judgment debtor and thereby failed to uncover the money that the debtor later used towards purchase of the property.

3.   Any purchaser at a judicial sale takes free of judgment liens, including those senior to the judgment being levied.[9] The reason for this is that when real property is sold on execution, the sheriff notifies all the other judgment creditors, senior and junior alike,[10] who must then issue their own executions. The proceeds of the sale are then distributed in the order in which each judgment became a lien on the real property.[11] Seniority is thus recognized by that route and all judgment creditors lose their liens on the real property although they of course retain their other rights against the judgment debtor to the extent that the proceeds of the sale do not satisfy their judgments.[12]

4.   If the judgment was entered after the death of the judgment debtor, it does not get a lien,[13] at least not in the technical way it otherwise would. The judgment creditor must in that case turn to the surrogate's court for satisfaction of the judgment.[14]

5.   A judgment against the State or its agencies or against a municipal corporation does not become a lien against real property.[15] This avoids the specter of a sheriff trying to auction off City Hall or the Capitol.

6.   If the judgment was rendered against an executor or administrator in his or her representative capacity,[16] the judgment does not become a lien against real property. This enables the fiduciary to pass title to a buyer without the encumbrance of a judgment standing against the land.[17] The judgment creditor's security in this instance is the overall assets of the estate—if there are any—or the bond of the fiduciary, if one was given.

---

[7]   CPLR 5203(a)(1).

[8]   CPLR 5203(a)(2).

[9]   CPLR 5203(a)(3).

[10]   CPLR 5236(c).

[11]   CPLR 5236(g)(1).

[12]   CPLR 5236(e). See § 500.

[13]   CPLR 5203(a)(4).

[14]   CPLR 5208. See § 514.

[15]   CPLR 5203(a)(5).

[16]   This is to be distinguished from where the judgment was rendered against the decedent, as contemplated by #4 on the list. In the present situation, the judgment runs directly against the fiduciary, albeit for something done in his or her representative capacity.

[17]   CPLR 5203(a)(6).

It was noted in number 4 on the list that if the judgment was entered after the death of the judgment debtor, it gets no lien. If it was entered and became a lien before the judgment debtor's death, however, it does retain its competitive position as against other judgment creditors, but satisfaction must now be sought through the surrogate's court.[18] In fact, if there was less than two years left on the judgment lien when the judgment debtor died, the lien is extended to two years from death,[19] a provision designed to give the judgment creditor, frustrated in enforcement by the death of the debtor, some time to put the claim before the estate representative or surrogate without losing the lien.

The docketing is the key moment if the creditor has competitors, and most especially so if the debtor/owner of the real property resorts to a quick bankruptcy filing. Under federal law, the mere bankruptcy filing gives the bankruptcy trustee an immediate lien,[20] and if the winner in the New York action has not yet secured and docketed a judgment, the trustee takes priority over the New York winner. A major injustice results in this scenario if the winner has already prevailed in the New York action, but has not yet reduced the victory to a judgment and docketed it. The entry and docketing can be done fast, but fast as it might be done there is still a brief interim in which a crafty debtor can frustrate the winner with a bankruptcy filing, as happened, for example, in the Second Circuit's decision Musso v. Ostashko.[21]

A 2010 amendment adding a subdivision (c) to CPLR 5203[22] sought to meet the problem when the successful party just needs a few days to arrange for docketing. CPLR 5203(c) provides that as long as the docketing is made within 30 days after the court has made "an oral or written determination on the record" awarding ownership of an interest in real property to the party, the docketing shall be "deemed" made on the day just prior to that determination, but "solely" for purposes of giving the judgment priority over the lien created by "the simultaneous or later" bankruptcy filing.

The seniority of liens applies essentially to where the judgment debtor was the owner of the real property when the liens arose. A pro-rata sharing rule applies for after-acquired real property, i.e., real property that the judgment debtor comes into after the docketing of the judgment. If the judgment debtor gets the real property by inheritance, for example, after several judgments have been docketed and would have stood as real property liens against him if he had any, one does not take priority over another; all share pro rata.[23]

The lien of a judgment can be lifted by court order if, in conjunction with an appeal, the judgment debtor has given an undertaking sufficient to secure the judgment creditor.[24]

---

[18] CPLR 5208. See also SCPA 1811, which clarifies that although the lien progression continues to dictate priorities among judgment creditors, SCPA 1811(2)(c), they may as a group become subordinated to other interests, notably those of the sovereign for taxes and other obligations. SCPA 1811(2)(a), (b). These matters are further discussed in § 514.

[19] CPLR 5208 (last sentence).

[20] 11 U.S.C.A. § 544.

[21] Musso v. Ostashko, 468 F.3d 99 (2d Cir. 2006). See also Bank of New York v. Nies, 96 A.D.2d 166, 468 N.Y.S.2d 278 (4th Dep't 1983) (discharge in bankruptcy does not impair judgment liens that attached to real property of debtor prior to bankruptcy).

[22] L.2010, ch. 427; SPR 231:1.

[23] Hulbert v. Hulbert, 216 N.Y. 430, 111 N.E. 70 (1916).

[24] CPLR 5204.

We have previously discussed the interplay between the life of a judgment, which is 20 years, and its life as a lien against real property, which is only 10. Since execution can be made at any time during the life of the judgment, it is possible that when it is sought during the second decade of the judgment's life, it will be made while the judgment is not a lien, raising the possibility that some other creditor's lien may intervene. One remedy for that situation is CPLR 5235, which permits a "notice of levy" to be used, offering a brief renewal of the lien for the time it takes to complete an execution sale of the real property.[25] Another is for the judgment creditor to move to extend the original 10-year period to cover the time necessary to conduct the execution sale, but this is less helpful than CPLR 5235 because it's permissible only if the creditor duly delivered an execution to the sheriff before the 10 years expired. The court is also empowered by order to stretch the 10 years by whatever time enforcement of the judgment was stayed, such as in conjunction with an appeal or a motion to vacate the judgment.[26]

The best remedy, however, available only since CPLR 5014 was amended in 1986 to allow it, is for the judgment creditor, during the year preceding the expiration of the 10-year lien, to bring an action to renew the judgment. That produces a new 10-year lien and avoids the gap that would otherwise occur between the expiration of the original 10-year lien and the time of actual sale of the real property during the period following.[27]

§ 518. Rights in Personal Property, Introductory

With real property, a filing with the county clerk puts the world on notice of the interest claimed in the filed paper. It accomplishes this so thoroughly that the simple expedient of a filing has been made almost the exclusive method for determining lien rights in real property. The mobility of personal property—which includes everything from multi-ton tangibles to mere choses in action with no corporeal substance at all—prevents a mere filing from doing so perfect a job.

Only for orders secured under Article 52 of the CPLR has the legislature decided on the moment of filing as the determining point for priorities in personal property; it was felt that with orders, the time of filing is as good as any other. And here the moment of filing that counts is that of the filing of the enforcement order, not of the original judgment. For executions, in contrast, priority arrives in some instances with mere delivery to the sheriff, in others only with actual levy. Determining priorities in personal property is the mission of CPLR 5202 when the judgment creditor is vying with a transferee of the judgment debtor, and of CPLR 5234 when judgment creditors are competing among themselves. Each gets separate treatment in the sections following.[1]

---

[25]   See the discussion in § 499.

[26]   CPLR 5203(b).

[27]   See § 434.

[1]   The Advisory Committee had initially decided on a scheme of priorities in personal property based on filing with the county clerk or, in the case of a nonresident debtor, with the secretary of state, see 2d Rep. Leg. Doc. No. 17, p. 101 (1959), but this was afterwards rejected by the legislature. The present schemes of priority contained in CPLR 5202 and 5234 are not the Advisory Committee's work. To the extent that they carry forward prior law, which in significant degree they do, they are criticized by the committee as "extremely uncertain, unnecessarily complex and virtually devoid of rational justification . . . ." 2d Rep. Leg. Doc. No. 17, at p. 103 (1959). The legislature, apparently postulating that provisions invoking so enthusiastic a rebuke can't be all bad, kept them on.

The only liens created by the CPLR are judgment liens, and it is therefore only in respect of judgment creditors that the CPLR resolves priorities. The CPLR does not in any way purport to resolve all of the limitless disputes that can arise among an equally limitless variety of other interests, and situations involving other interests are by no means rare. A judgment creditor pursuing a debtor will often find that he is not alone. He may recognize a few judgment creditors among his rivals, but be taken aback by the myriad of others with liens emanating from mortgages or pledges, the rendering of services, the sale of goods, the undertaking of a venture, the imposition of taxes, and more. In a race like that, the CPLR does not dictate the winner; it declares only the lien moment of the judgment creditor, not of other creditors. Nor does any other single source, statutory or otherwise, array all of the others. Some may get their liens from statutes, some from common law. When all come together, therefore, nothing plain dictates the line of march. They are an undisciplined mob, and the judge may have a big job sorting them all out.

But if the CPLR does not order the race, it at least supplies the track. With CPLR 5239, whose later treatment will cite a few examples of these lien battles,[2] the CPLR offers a special proceeding whereby any one of the competitors can bring all of the others into court for a test of priorities. When competition gets to that stage, however, it goes beyond the subject of the "enforcement of judgments" and expands into what a law school curriculum sometimes describes as "creditors' rights." And if things cannot be worked out in proceedings involving the various creditors' rights, the next step will lead to yet another subject: bankruptcy. Those are topics beyond the CPLR, but in the ensuing sections, we will at least go as far as the CPLR does.

§ 519. Rights in Personal Property; Judgment Creditor Versus Transferee

A distinction is made between the judgment creditor who uses an execution and one who uses an Article 52 device that gives rise to an order. The execution will be treated first.

CPLR 5202(a) provides that a creditor using an execution gets priority in the judgment debtor's personal property as of the moment he delivers the execution to the sheriff. The priority affects debts and other intangible interests as well as tangible property.

The statute does not in terms require that the sheriff to whom the delivery is made be the sheriff of the county where the property has its situs, but that would be a very sound idea. There is even room for a finding that this is the only sheriff to whom a delivery of the execution will secure a priority for the judgment creditor. The legislature indicated that it was essentially adopting prior law in this instance,[1] and prior law specified that the proper sheriff was the one with jurisdiction to levy,[2] which could only be the sheriff of a county in which the property itself can be found or a proper garnishee subjected to jurisdiction.

---

[2] See § 521.

[1] See 6th Rep. Leg. Doc. No. 8, p. 456 (1962).

[2] Civ. Prac. Act § 679(1) (repealed 1963).

Assuming that the execution has been delivered to the right sheriff, it gives the judgment creditor a higher right than a later transferee of the judgment debtor, with two stated exceptions:

1.   A transfer after the execution is delivered, but before it is levied, gives the transferee a right superior to the creditor's as long as the transferee is shown to have paid fair consideration for the property.[3]

2.   A transfer after the levy (but obviously before payment or delivery of the proceeds to the levying creditor) for fair consideration also gives the transferee a right superior to the judgment creditor's, but in this instance only if it is shown that the transferee had no knowledge of the levy,[4] which is necessarily a question of fact in each case.

A further distinction between the two exceptions is that the second one applies only when the debt or property is not "capable of delivery," a term investigated in an earlier section in conjunction with a levy of execution.[5] In general, the definition suggested in that section would probably do here as well. If the property is "capable of delivery," the sheriff is required to levy an execution by seizing the property itself;[6] and if the sheriff does that, the property would be in the sheriff's hands and could not afterwards be transferred by the judgment debtor or garnishee. If, on the other hand, the property is not capable of delivery, it would have to be levied on by the mere service of the execution.[7] In that situation, whatever the property is would remain in the hands of the debtor or garnishee until later steps bring it into the sheriff's custody, even though the levy itself was technically effected by the sheriff's mere service of the execution. A transferee can be unaware of a levy by service and—relying on the fact that no sheriff has taken the property—part with fair consideration for it. Thus, although the transfer takes place after the levy has theoretically been accomplished, the transferee can still be allowed to prevail, but only if he shows that he took in ignorance of the levy. If he knew of the levy, he will lose out to the judgment creditor.

The approach is not perfect. There are a number of situations one can conjure up in which a proposed transferee should be put to the burden of making inquiries that would lead to knowledge of the levy, but this is one of those areas in which the legislature apparently felt that the factual variations are too extensive to admit of qualifications, and that a set rule, even if not ideal, would be better. The lesson to the judgment creditor is to get the levy perfected both by pressure on the sheriff as well as through his own steps, such as an application for a delivery order under CPLR 5225 or 5227. Only when the property interest pursued is effectively taken into the sheriff's hands, such as a debt finally paid over to the sheriff or an attornment or other commitment made by the

---

[3]   CPLR 5202(a)(1). "Fair consideration" for all purposes of CPLR 5202 is as defined by § 272 of the Debt. & Cred. Law. It includes an antecedent debt, see International Ribbon Mills, Ltd. v. Arjan Ribbons, Inc., 36 N.Y.2d 121, 365 N.Y.S.2d 808, 325 N.E.2d 137 (1975), including an antecedent mortgage, Ruppert v. Community Nat. Bank, 22 A.D.2d 165, 254 N.Y.S.2d 341 (1st Dep't 1964), aff'd, 16 N.Y.2d 589, 261 N.Y.S.2d 52, 209 N.E.2d 100 (1965), or similar obligation, thus protecting a transferee to whom the transfer has been made in fulfillment of the earlier obligation.

[4]   CPLR 5202(a)(2).

[5]   See § 497.

[6]   CPLR 5232(b).

[7]   CPLR 5232(a).

garnishee to pay the debt to the judgment creditor or sheriff at some later time, is the door to a lien-robbing transfer closed.

Besides an execution, the other Article 52 lien-givers are orders that the article authorizes, such as the delivery order of CPLR 5225 and the receivership order of CPLR 5228. Each specifies the property involved, and it is that property to which the lien attaches. A judgment creditor who has "secured" such an order[8]—this should be taken to mean the moment the order is filed[9]—prevails over a later transferee of the judgment debtor except one who pays fair consideration for the property and had no notice of the order. For this purpose an "order" should be deemed to include a "judgment" as well, a judgment being what a judgment creditor gets who brings a special proceeding against a garnishee under CPLR 5225(b) or 5227, two of the lien-giving devices of Article 52.

The same risks of transfer faced by an execution-using creditor under subdivision (a) of CPLR 5202, as described above, can also be met by an order-securing creditor under subdivision (b). The judgment creditor should close the door to transfers as soon as possible by keeping up the pressure to get possession of the subject property.

The transfer adequate to defeat the judgment creditor must in any event be for fair consideration. If it is not, it qualifies as fraudulent and can be set aside by the judgment creditor in either a separate plenary action or, better, in a special proceeding under CPLR 5225(b), 5227, or 5239.[10]

A judgment creditor who takes no step to secure a lien with some lien-giving device of Article 52, i.e., who issues no execution and secures no Article 52 order, leaves the door wide open to transfers that can readily frustrate collection of the judgment.[11]

§ 520. Rights in Personal Property; Judgment Creditors Among Themselves

When it comes to the rights of judgment creditors among themselves, CPLR 5234 governs priorities and liens in the judgment debtor's personal property: subdivision (b) governing when all the competing creditors are using executions and subdivision (c) governing when some are using Article 52 devices implemented by court orders.

When two or more executions[1] are issued in behalf of different judgment creditors against the same judgment debtor and are delivered to the same enforcement officer,[2] priority in the proceeds of the execution sale is determined by the order of delivery of the

---

[8]   CPLR 5202(b).

[9]   One can deduce this by analogy to CPLR 5234(c), which expressly says "filing." And in both instances this should be deemed to mean "entry" as defined in CPLR 5016(a).

[10]   Debt. & Cred. Law § 273–a. See § 510.

[11]   See, e.g., County Nat. Bank v. Inter-County Farmers Co-op. Ass'n, 65 Misc. 2d 446, 317 N.Y.S.2d 790 (Sup. Ct., Sullivan County 1970).

[1]   Since a prejudgment order of attachment can seize property to the credit of the attaching plaintiff, a timely attachment will prevail over later levies of post-judgment execution, even on judgments rendered in actions commenced long before the action in which the attachment issued. For this reason, orders of attachment are treated the same as executions in CPLR 5234(b) and (c). The word "execution" is therefore used in this section of the text as including an attachment, and the words "judgment creditor" as including an attaching plaintiff.

[2]   The words "enforcement officer" include whoever services the particular court: the sheriff for the supreme court and the county courts, the sheriff and city marshals together for the New York City Civ. Ct. (see § 701 of its court act, McKinney's Vol. 29A, Part 3), marshals or constables for the justice courts (see Uniform Just. Ct. Act § 110, McKinney's Vol. 29A, Part 2), etc. The marshals have also been given certain powers under CPLR Article 52 in supreme court actions in New York City. See CPLR 105(s–1).

executions.[3] What was said about the proper sheriff in the prior section applies here, too: although this part of the statute does not expressly require that the sheriff used be the sheriff of the county in which the personal property has its situs, the situs sheriff was probably intended, and is the logical choice in any event. The second sentence of CPLR 5234(b), moreover, does specify the situs sheriff, and in context to suggest that the sheriff of the situs county—or of one of the situs counties if the property has a multiple situs—is the one intended in all CPLR 5234 situations.

The mission of the second sentence is to dictate priorities when executions have been delivered to different enforcement officers and all have jurisdiction to levy. This can happen, for example, when judgment creditor A delivers a supreme court execution to the New York City sheriff and judgment creditor B delivers a New York City Civil Court execution to a city marshal, both concerning an asset with a New York City situs. Here the moment of delivery is not the key time, but rather the moment of levy. When there are but two executions involved, the one levied first gets first crack at the proceeds and the other gets the balance provided that the non-levying officer makes a demand for such balance on the levying officer. When three or more executions are involved, the levying officer collects the proceeds and his judgment creditor gets first priority in them; the other officers must make a demand on that sheriff to share in the proceeds; they get priority for their judgment creditors in the order in which they make their demands. One whose execution is returned before the levy is made does not share in the proceeds,[4] which is also true, of course, of those whose delivery of an execution does not take place until after the proceeds have been distributed.

The officer who unreasonably fails to levy and returns execution unsatisfied while another officer levies successfully, thus denying the judgment creditor what would otherwise have been his proper share of the proceeds, may be sued for the damages caused by the dereliction. It is not a popular remedy in the courts—sheriffs and other enforcement officers are not big fans either—but it is ancient law that dereliction in respect of judicial process renders the enforcement officer fully liable for whatever damages he causes.[5] (Hence the requirement that enforcement officers be bonded.) Damage suits against sheriffs, while not frequent, do appear from time to time.[6] Their infrequency should not prompt enforcement officers, bonded or not, to lose sight of their liabilities.

The present assumption is that the sheriff has not gone far enough. Another example of a sheriff's liability is when the sheriff goes too far and becomes subject to liability to a third party.[7] Where, for example, the sheriff levies in behalf of creditor C against property of debtor D, which the sheriff knows to be subject to a security

---

[3]   This part of CPLR 5234 is analogous to the priorities scheme set up for income executions by CPLR 5231(j). Having its own priority statute, the income execution is not governed by CPLR 5234.

[4]   See International Ribbon Mills, Ltd. v. Arjan Ribbons, Inc., 36 N.Y.2d 121, 365 N.Y.S.2d 808, 325 N.E.2d 137 (1975).

[5]   See Root v. Wagner, 30 N.Y. 9, 1864 WL 4115 (1864).

[6]   Wang v. Bartel, 163 Misc. 2d 600, 624 N.Y.S.2d 735 (App. Term, 2d Dep't 1994), for example, noted in SPR 45:4, sustained a damages action by a judgment creditor suing a deputy sheriff for alleged disregard of his obligations.

[7]   See § 496.

agreement that D had previously made in favor of S, the sheriff and his sureties are liable to S.[8]

When the competing judgment creditors have all used orders under Article 52 instead of executions, such as delivery orders under CPLR 5225 or 5227 or receivership orders under CPLR 5228, the time of the filing of those orders[9] determines priority among them.[10] If some creditors are using executions and others rely on orders, the execution creditors have their priorities set in the order of levy, the others as of the time their orders are filed. Here an additional limitation is imposed on the judgment creditor who has secured and filed an order: he must see to it that the transfer it requires, whether to himself, to the sheriff, or to a receiver, is completed within 60 days after the filing unless the order specifies otherwise or an extension order is secured and filed within those 60 days. Else that creditor loses priority.[11] If he contemplates trouble in securing actual transfer, the judgment creditor should ask, when originally applying for a delivery order under CPLR 5225 or 5227 or for a receivership order under CPLR 5228, that an appropriate extended time period be included in the order.

A garnishee may come under pressure from a number of creditors claiming priorities. A garnishee who is not clear on its obligations should await court action and see to it, whatever form the court procedure takes, that all of the claimants are made parties. In one case, for example, a debt owed by G to D had been duly assigned by D to A. Afterwards J, a judgment creditor of D, issued an execution, which was levied by service on G. G paid the debt to J and because of that was held liable to A for the amount paid.[12]

If the use of some enforcement device has secured a lien and an appeal has been or is now taken from the judgment, the lien can be released by the judgment debtor (appellant) by furnishing an undertaking on the appeal adequate to secure the judgment creditor.[13]

It is important for the judgment creditor to remember that under the CPLR, the only devices that give liens are the executions and the orders. There is no priority secured by the service of either a restraining notice under CPLR 5222 or a subpoena under CPLR 5224, whatever those devices can otherwise accomplish, and notwithstanding that they did give liens under prior law. Some practitioners, weaned on the old law or absorbing it from epic sagas of the old folks around the campfire, have overlooked this and consequently lost priority for their clients.[14] Nor is it a question of diligence. A diligent judgment creditor who goes to the trouble of serving both a restraining notice and a subpoena and even making an application under CPLR 5225 for a delivery order will still lose out to another creditor who merely has a sheriff levy execution in the interim.[15]

---

[8]   See Meritum Corp. v. Pichler, N.Y.L.J., Sept. 10, 1980, at 7, col. 2 (Sup. Ct., New York County; Gammerman, J.).

[9]   Filing and entry are virtually synonymous. See CPLR 5016(a).

[10]   An "order" in this sense must be deemed to include a "judgment" rendered against a garnishee in a special proceeding brought under CPLR 5225(b) or 5227.

[11]   CPLR 5234(c).

[12]   See Lincoln Rochester Trust Co. v. S. C. Marasco Steel, Inc., 66 Misc. 2d 295, 320 N.Y.S.2d 864 (Monroe County Court 1971).

[13]   CPLR 5204.

[14]   See City of New York v. Panzirer, 23 A.D.2d 158, 259 N.Y.S.2d 284 (1st Dep't 1965).

[15]   See Graze v. Bankers Trust Co., 45 Misc. 2d 610, 257 N.Y.S.2d 483 (Sup. Ct., New York County 1965).

The levy is a lien-giver; the restraining notice and the subpoena are not. Nor is the mere application for an order; it is only the filing of the order—which obviously implies its granting—that gives the lien.

When the judgment debtor happens to be a member of a partnership, a common device for pursuing his interest in the partnership is a charging order under section 54 of the Partnership Law. An application under that provision may also result in an order appointing a receiver of the debtor partner's interest. But neither order will afford a lien until it is filed so that even in that situation, the judgment creditor does better by issuing an execution to the sheriff and having the sheriff levy on the debtor/partner's interest.[16] (The charging order contemplated by section 54 is not an exclusive remedy. An ordinary levy of execution is permissible, and, when priorities are involved, preferable because of the lien it promptly secures.)[17]

When none of the competing creditors has taken a lien-giving step under CPLR 5234, the latter can be deemed inapplicable, leaving the individual equities of the case to determine who should be awarded priority. In one case, for example, a judgment creditor issued a CPLR 5222 restraining notice to the judgment debtor, after which the debtor, violating the notice, made an assignment for the benefit of creditors. While conceding that the CPLR 5222 notice gave no lien, the court held that a creditor who has been diligent enough to convert his claim into a judgment should on equitable principles prevail over other creditors who have not.[18]

§ 521. Proceeding to Determine Adverse Claims

As mentioned earlier, the only liens created by the CPLR are judgment liens, and they are therefore the only ones among which the CPLR purports to set priorities. The situation will often arise, however, in which creditors of various stripes and with diverse claims of lien will be competing with judgment creditors to get at the assets of the judgment debtor. Neither the CPLR nor any other single statute purports to enumerate all of these interests or to set down a comprehensive list of how priorities are to be determined among them.[1] The CPLR's only offering, in these multi-creditor pursuits, is a special proceeding designed to enable the claims of all of them to be expeditiously brought to court; however, their substantive priorities may be adjudicated after they get there. CPLR 5239 supplies this special proceeding, which may be brought by "any interested person" against "the judgment creditor or other person" with whom a priority dispute exists. Between this proceeding and the special proceedings authorized by CPLR 5225(b) and 5227, the judgment creditor has a selection of priority-determining proceedings to choose from.

If the competitors are both judgment creditors, and one has a CPLR lien superior to the other's, the superior one will of course win. If neither has secured a lien, however, the governing principles will be drawn from outside the CPLR, from statute, caselaw, or equity. In one such case, for example, in which the competition was between the State

---

[16] CPLR 5201(c)(3).

[17] See *Princeton Bank & Trust Co. v. Berley*, 57 A.D.2d 348, 394 N.Y.S.2d 714 (2d Dep't 1977). Unless the judgment is against the partnership itself, no partnership asset can be reached directly. See § 491.

[18] In re *Nassau Expressway, Borough of Queens, City of New York*, 56 Misc. 2d 602, 289 N.Y.S.2d 680 (Sup. Ct., Queens County 1968), cited with approval in *Arjan*, 36 N.Y.2d at 125, 365 N.Y.S.2d at 811, 325 N.E.2d at 139.

[1] See § 518.

Tax Commission and a bank, the commission prevailed under the rule that other things being equal, the sovereign and its agencies come first.[2]

When creditors with other than judgment liens are among the competitors, CPLR 5239 is equally available; there have been a number of cases that illustrate how it paves the way to the courthouse even though the CPLR will not have the sole say as to who wins after they enter. Many other statutes purporting to confer liens may have to be considered, along with the judgment liens of the CPLR and cases announcing other equities. Properly perfected liens under the Uniform Commercial Code, for example, such as those of a factor in inventory and accounts receivable, are often found in competition with judgment creditors in CPLR 5239 proceedings.[3] So are liens under the Workers' Compensation Law, Social Services Law, and Tax Law, etc., in addition to the myriad that come out of the Lien Law itself.[4]

The basic difference between the CPLR 5239 proceeding and those under CPLR 5225(b) or 5227 is that the latter two are brought by the judgment creditor, while the CPLR 5239 proceeding may be brought by any interested person (judgment creditor included). Any interested persons, including adverse claimants, may be joined as respondents in any of these proceedings. If the language of CPLR 5225(b) and 5227 seems narrower than that, the proceeding can instead be based on CPLR 5239[5] or, better still, on all of them together, gaining maximum scope that way. The only stated time limitation for the CPLR 5239 proceeding is that it be brought before the property involved has actually been applied (i.e., the proceeds distributed) towards satisfaction of a judgment. It is that requirement, in fact, from which we infer that CPLR 5239 can be exploited only when at least one of the competitors, even if only one of a dozen, is a judgment creditor.

Intervention is also expressly authorized by CPLR 5239, so that any claimant not already joined can move to be let in.

The proceeding is initiated by serving on the respondents (claimant, sheriff, receiver, etc.)[6] a notice of petition, "in the same manner as a notice of motion." That kind of service, which may be by mere mail to the respondent's lawyer,[7] would be satisfactory only if the particular respondent had been a party to the main action. If he was not, it is safer to make service in the same manner as a summons, recognizing that this

---

[2] See In re Robbins' Estate, 74 Misc. 2d 793, 346 N.Y.S.2d 86 (Sur. Ct., Suffolk County 1973).

[3] See, e.g., William Iselin & Co. v. Burgess & Leigh Limited, 52 Misc. 2d 821, 276 N.Y.S.2d 659, 3 U.C.C. Rep. Serv. 1168 (Sup. Ct., New York County 1967).

[4] See, e.g., Lacaille v. Feldman, 44 Misc. 2d 370, 253 N.Y.S.2d 937 (Sup. Ct., New York County 1964), and Neilson Realty Corp. v. Motor Vehicle Acc. Indemnification Corp., 47 Misc. 2d 260, 262 N.Y.S.2d 652 (Sup. Ct., Queens County 1965). The *Neilson* case also illustrates the overlapping between and among CPLR 5225(b), 5227 and 5239. The proceeding was captioned under CPLR 5227, but was essentially a lien battle of the kind primarily contemplated by CPLR 5239. Any proceeding brought under one of those provisions should be treatable as the equivalent of any of the others as long as all interested parties are before the court and have had an opportunity for a full hearing.

[5] CPLR 5239 was amended to expand its utility as a tool for or against competing claimants. See 10th Jud. Conf. Rep. 120, 144–145, 151–152 (1965).

[6] Although not expressly required, it is often a good idea to serve notice of the proceeding on the judgment debtor, D, as well. Certainly that is so if D's rights may be affected beyond the impact of the judgment itself. If, for example, the judgment creditor claims that G owes a debt to D, and tries to levy it, X may claim that the money is owed to him and not to D. If G then brings a proceeding against the judgment creditor and X, but without joining D, and the court determines that the money is owed to X, that determination would probably not bind D, and G may therefore confront a double liability later.

[7] CPLR 2103(b).

respondent has yet to be subjected to the court's jurisdiction.[8] The proceeding will be governed generally in its procedures by Article 4 of the CPLR.[9] When served on the respondent—each respondent—the petition should be accompanied by a notice of petition.[10] If an execution levy is among the things involved, the proceeding may be brought in the county of levy. It can in any event be brought in a county authorized by CPLR 5221(a), which, as applied here, would mean in any county in which any of the respondents either lives or works.[11] If on balance the county chosen turns out to be inconvenient, a change of venue would be permissible on motion.[12]

The proceeding can try any issue of fact arising in respect of any of the claims. It is no longer necessary that a plenary action be brought if an issue of fact appears.[13] If a jury would otherwise be required to try the fact, it can be demanded and would have to be allowed.[14] When ordering a trial, the court can determine who shall hold the disputed property in the meantime and whether such person will have to furnish a protective bond.

The court can render judgment in the proceeding for whatever is warranted after the issues have been resolved. The court's ultimate goal is to determine who shall finally have the disputed property. In conjunction with that, it can declare the priority of all claimed liens and incidentally vacate any order, execution, or levy. It can award damages to any party establishing a legal right to them. The proceeding can even be used as a vehicle to set aside a fraudulent conveyance if the fraudulent transferee is a party— something that used to require a separate plenary action.

If the court in the proceeding finds that any claim interposed is fraudulent, it can require the claimant to pay to any other party the damages caused, including attorney's fees incurred in the proceeding.[15]

I. PROTECTION AGAINST ABUSE

Table of Sections

§ 522.   Protective Order

§ 522. Protective Order

CPLR 5240, the statute on protective orders in the enforcement of judgments, provides that

> the court may at any time, on its own initiative or the motion of any interested
> person, and upon such notice as it may require, make an order denying,

---

[8]   See the Commentary on McKinney's CPLR 5239. Cf. Joseph Durst Corp. v. Leader, 51 Misc. 2d 72, 272 N.Y.S.2d 448 (Sup. Ct., New York County 1966).

[9]   Article 4 and its handful of provisions, which govern in special proceedings, are treated in §§ 550 et seq.

[10]   See CPLR 403(b). The petition is the pleading in a special proceeding; the notice of petition is the initiatory process.

[11]   See § 493.

[12]   CPLR 5240, 511, 103(b).

[13]   See, e.g., First Small Business Inv. Corp. v. Zaretsky, 46 Misc. 2d 328, 259 N.Y.S.2d 700 (Sup. Ct., Queens County 1965).

[14]   See the discussion of this matter in § 510.

[15]   CPLR 5239.

limiting, conditioning, regulating, extending or modifying the use of any enforcement procedure. Section 3104 is applicable to procedures under this article.

By centering in one place this pervasive judicial power to right, on a case by case basis, any wrong in connection with any of the numerous Article 52 procedures, the statute frees all of them to go about their missions without each of them having to contemplate and cure abuses. CPLR 5240 is to Article 52, in fact, what the protective order of CPLR 3103 is to the disclosure article, Article 31.[1] Even the provision of the disclosure article that authorizes the designation of a judge or the appointment of a referee to supervise a given procedure, CPLR 3104, is adopted for Article 52 use by CPLR 5240.

The protective order can be granted by the court sua sponte, but it is more often sought on motion of the judgment debtor or other interested person. An order to show cause is the procedure, which is what CPLR 5240 contemplates by directing the court to determine upon whom and how to make service, but an ordinary notice of motion duly served on all needed parties should also be acceptable.

Examples of the uses of a protective order abound. It has been used to vary the sale time of real property otherwise dictated by CPLR 5236,[2] for example, and to vacate an income execution issued after an installment payment order was entered against the judgment debtor.[3] When addressed to an income execution, CPLR 5240 shares power with CPLR 5231(i), which explicitly authorizes the court to modify an income execution. Any protective step affecting an income execution, such as one reducing it from 10% to 5% upon a showing that the debtor can afford no more,[4] can find authority in either provision. Further ideas for what a protective order can accomplish—it can go as far as to preclude use of a given device altogether if the court finds it to be vain or unnecessarily abusive or remit a seeker from one device to another—can be found by checking the examples contained in the legislative notes on the analogous CPLR 3103,[5] and in cases on that provision as well as on CPLR 5240.

While it has been said that CPLR 5240 does not countenance radical departures from the framework of Article 52,[6] the statute has indeed come in for some liberal, if not radical, applications. In the case of Wandschneider v. Bekeny,[7] for example, the court used CPLR 5240 to borrow from the mortgage foreclosure realm and apply to execution sales the rule that the underlying debt will be credited with the market value of the real property sold on the execution, thus reducing the judgment debtor's debt by his actual market equity in the levied premises even though the sale's winning bid is for substantially less.[8]

In cases involving a judgment debtor's tenancy by the entirety of the family residence, applications of CPLR 5240 have been generous, and frequent. In one case, for

---

[1] See § 353.

[2] See Olsen v. Robaey, 45 Misc. 2d 33, 256 N.Y.S.2d 103 (Sup. Ct., Suffolk County 1965).

[3] See Rush v. Rush, N.Y.L.J., Nov. 26, 1963, at 15, col. 5 (Westchester County Court 1963).

[4] See First Westchester Nat. Bank of New Rochelle v. Lewis, 42 Misc. 2d 1007, 249 N.Y.S.2d 537 (Westchester County Court 1964).

[5] The notes follow McKinney's CPLR 3103.

[6] See Kaplan v. Supak & Sons Mfg. Co., 46 Misc. 2d 574, 260 N.Y.S.2d 374 (N.Y. City Civ. Ct. 1965).

[7] Wandschneider v. Bekeny, 75 Misc. 2d 32, 346 N.Y.S.2d 925 (Sup. Ct., Westchester County 1973).

[8] The Third Department has also adopted this position. See § 500.

example, the court held that the judgment creditor could presently do nothing against such premises; that the judgment would be deemed a mere lien against the premises, to be denied any effectuation unless and until the judgment debtor is shown to have outlived his or her spouse, at which point the debtor would take full title and be subject to levy; or the spouses voluntarily sell the property, at which point the judgment could be applied against the debtor spouse's share of the proceeds.[9] In another such case citing CPLR 5240 and the family's needs, the court simply precluded levy against the residence, at least for a time, but on the condition that the judgment debtor pay a specified (and modest) sum monthly towards the judgment.[10] In yet another case, the court precluded levy for a year, directing the judgment creditor to try other enforcement devices in the interim, with leave to seek court permission to relevy if the others did not work.[11] All of these are judicial acknowledgments that any levy against the family home at the behest of the creditor of only one of the spouses would be an intolerable interference with family life. Cases that take this position (not all do) are in effect creating a de facto exemption for the residence in these situations.

While the courts are sympathetic to cases in which a residence is being levied on, their powers under CPLR 5240 are not unlimited. In one case with much appeal to conscience, for example, in which the judgment debtor was an elderly man with his abandoned 7-year-old granddaughter in his charge, the court noted the age of the judgment (some 9 years) and that no part of it had been paid. It did not cancel the levy against the residence, but stayed it for six months to enable the judgment debtor to find new quarters, with the proviso that $750 per month be paid towards the judgment in the interim.[12]

Other examples of protective orders connected with the execution sale of real property appeared earlier.[13]

After the judgment debtor's property has been duly sold to a bona fide purchaser at an execution sale, the protective order provision of CPLR 5240 may not be used to undo the sale.[14]

The protective order shield has been found to have two sides, occasionally flipping over and protecting the judgment creditor from the judgment debtor's spouse playing fast and loose in a tenancy by the entirety case. In one such case, the judgment was for $900 against husband H, which wife W could have altogether removed from even lien effect against the property just by paying the judgment. But she did not. She instead bid $1,000 at the sale, but was outbid by X who, when H and W later divorced, became a tenant in common with W, enabling X to bring a partition action against W, which he

---

[9]   See Hammond v. Econo-Car of North Shore, Inc., 71 Misc. 2d 546, 336 N.Y.S.2d 493 (Sup. Ct., Nassau County 1972).

[10]   Holmes v. W. T. Grant, Inc., 71 Misc. 2d 486, 336 N.Y.S.2d 601 (Sup. Ct., Nassau County 1972).

[11]   Gilchrist v. Commercial Credit Corp., 66 Misc. 2d 791, 322 N.Y.S.2d 200 (Sup. Ct., Nassau County 1971). Nassau County has had a disproportionate share of problems with residential properties sold pursuant to small judgments, accounting for the number of Nassau cases with protective order steps designed to guard against abuse.

[12]   Federal Deposit Ins. Co. v. Lapadula, 137 Misc. 2d 559, 521 N.Y.S.2d 391 (Sup. Ct., Nassau County 1987).

[13]   See § 500.

[14]   Guardian Loan Co., Inc. v. Early, 47 N.Y.2d 515, 419 N.Y.S.2d 56, 392 N.E.2d 1240 (1979). The court stressed the absence of any special equities in the case and added that "mere inadequacy of price" is not by itself ground to set aside the sale.

did. Now W moved under CPLR 5240 to vacate the old execution sale, pleading unsophistication in legal matters. A suspect plea; she did, after all, bid $1,000 at the sale when for $100 less she could have paid off the judgment and avoided the sale altogether. But what she was looking to do was win at the sale, in which case she would have (1) won 100% of the residence and (2) wiped out the liens of all other judgment creditors of H as well.[15] The tacit reaction of the court was that if she was as unsophisticated as she claimed, then the naive shall inherit the earth. The court held that even if CPLR 5240 could go this far, which it doubted, W did not present the equities to deserve it; it denied her motion to undo the sale.[16]

There is also caselaw manifesting that a protective order will not protect a judgment debtor from her own deliberate folly. A spectacular lesson on that front is House v. Lalor.[17] P had a $350 small claims judgment against D, which D—a wealthy woman who despised P—flatly refused to pay. The judgment finally went to enforcement through an execution against a cooperative apartment that D owned, and D ended up losing an equity of $185,000 in the apartment! The big winners were the bidder at the auction and future defendants who could take the *House* case as a lesson about what the court described as the "obstinacy" of the defendant in resisting enforcement.

J. CONTEMPT AS BACK-UP DEVICE

Table of Sections

§ 523.   Contempt Enforcement of Certain Devices

§ 523. Contempt Enforcement of Certain Devices

Contempt is not available as a direct tool for enforcing the ordinary money judgment. But it does serve as the remedy that gives force to a number of the Article 52 enforcement devices and by so doing becomes by indirection an enforcement remedy for money judgments. CPLR 5251 provides that the following behavior constitutes contempt of court:

1. Wilful disobedience of one of the CPLR 5224 disclosure subpoenas or false swearing at any examination or in response to any questions;

2. Wilful disobedience of a CPLR 5222 restraining notice;

3. Wilfully defacing or removing notices of upcoming sales of property, such as in conjunction with levies and sales of personal property[1] or real property;[2]

4. Wilful disobedience of any order issued under Article 52, among which would be:

    a. a delivery order under CPLR 5225 or 5227;

    b. an installment payment order under CPLR 5226;

---

[15]   CPLR 5236(c), (e), (g). See § 500.

[16]   Murphy v. Grid Realty Corp., 73 Misc. 2d 1071, 343 N.Y.S.2d 670 (Sup. Ct., Nassau County 1973).

[17]   House v. Lalor, 119 Misc. 2d 193, 462 N.Y.S.2d 772 (Sup. Ct., New York County 1983), summarized in NYSLD No. 286.

[1]   CPLR 5233(b).

[2]   CPLR 5236(c).

    c.   an order directing that property be surrendered to a receiver appointed under CPLR 5228;

    d.   prejudgment orders directing an examination or restraint under CPLR 5229; and

    e.   a protective order under CPLR 5240.

When an application under CPLR 5225(a) is brought against a judgment debtor, it contemplates an order brought on by motion and the disregard of the order would clearly invoke the contempt penalty under CPLR 5251. A nicer question is whether contempt is available against a garnishee in connection with a delivery proceeding brought under CPLR 5225(b) or 5227. Against a garnishee or other third person, the delivery device is not a motion culminating in an order, but a special proceeding that culminates in a "judgment."[3] Shall the "order" listed in CPLR 5251 be deemed to embrace the "judgment," so as to subject a recalcitrant garnishee to contempt for a failure to obey a delivery judgment rendered in the special proceeding? Or, indeed, shall these provisions be construed to allow an "order" to be entered against the garnishee, instead of a judgment, and invoke CPLR 5251 by that route?

The matter is not free from doubt. If the court in the special proceeding renders an ordinary money judgment in favor of the judgment creditor against the garnishee, the judgment will then qualify for all of the Article 52 devices, including those that ultimately invoke the contempt remedy. But the court in that proceeding is not restricted to a money judgment alone; sitting as a court of equity, it can apparently make a judgment directing the garnishee to turn over specific property. Disobedience in that case will be a contempt, if not under CPLR 5251, then under the basic contempt provisions of the Judiciary Law.[4] Authority does exist for holding a garnishee in contempt in conjunction with directions issued under CPLR 5225 and 5227.[5]

Even when clearly available, contempt is not necessarily the exclusive remedy. A judgment creditor suffering damages caused by the disregard of an Article 52 device may in some instances bring a money claim against the one who caused the damages, such as a garnishee bank that permits the judgment debtor to draw from an account in disregard of a restraining notice.[6]

CPLR 5251 merely lists the conduct that will be deemed contemptuous. The procedures for determining and punishing the contempt are to be found, as with any contempt, in the Judiciary Law.[7] Their essentials are set forth in Part I of this chapter,[8] in conjunction with the enforcement of non-money judgments. Contempt is the principal enforcement tool for equitable judgments, for example, and whenever it is properly invoked, whether directly on an equity judgment, or indirectly, as for the devices enumerated in CPLR 5251 in aid of a money judgment, the same Judiciary Law

---

    [3]   CPLR 411; see § 570.

    [4]   See Jud. Law § 753(A)(3); see §§ 481 et seq.

    [5]   See Carl B. Nusbaum, Inc. v. Calale, 45 Misc. 2d 903, 258 N.Y.S.2d 8 (Orange County Court 1965). See § 510.

    [6]   See Mazzuka v. Bank of North America, 53 Misc. 2d 1053, 280 N.Y.S.2d 495 (N.Y. City Civ. Ct. 1967), and § 508.

    [7]   Jud. Law Article 19, §§ 750–781.

    [8]   See § 484.

instructions must be followed. Everything contained in the subchapter on contempt in Part I, therefore, has parallel application here.[9]

Only the courts listed in CPLR 5221(a) have the power to punish for contempt since those are the courts that can entertain the Article 52 devices listed in CPLR 5221.[10] This excludes the town and village courts. Contempt proceedings in respect of Article 52 devices connected with judgments rendered in those courts should be brought in the supreme court or a county court.[11]

---

[9]   See §§ 481 et seq.

[10]   See CPLR 5221(b).

[11]   See § 493. With respect to prejudgment enforcement under CPLR 5229, however, which is authorized for use in all courts (see § 516), even these lower courts can be deemed to have the contempt power.

Chapter 19

APPEALS

Analysis

A.   **Introductory**
B.   **Appealability**
C.   **Reviewability**
D.   **Taking the Appeal**
E.   **Perfecting the Appeal**
F.   **Incidental Appellate Practice**
G.   **Concluding the Appeal**

A.   INTRODUCTORY

Table of Sections

§ 524.   Appeals, Introductory
§ 525.   "Aggrieved" Party

§ 524. Appeals, Introductory

Three articles of the CPLR govern appeals. Article 57 governs appealability to the appellate division and Article 56 appealability to the Court of Appeals, while Article 55, entitled "Appeals Generally," supplies the procedure and incidentals of the appellate process and determines the scope of review.

Despite these three articles, in appellate practice one can never rely exclusively on the CPLR. The rules of the particular appellate court where the appeal lies become indispensable and must be consulted. The rules of the appellate court will likely have more to say, at least in regard to the mechanics of the appeal, than the CPLR. Indeed, at several key junctures, after making a rather detailed instruction about procedure, the CPLR casually announces that the appellate division can change all of this for their own departments if they wish. We will take note of when they do, and references to court rules in this chapter will be more frequent than encountered elsewhere in our study.

The rules can differ from department to department and from court to court, not only in detail, but also in topic selected for coverage, thus warning even the practitioner who has troubled to learn well the rules of one appellate court that she cannot safely apply them in another.

There are no so-called "Uniform Rules" for the appellate courts, as there are, at least nominally, for the trial courts. Lawyers taking an appeal to a court they are not yet familiar with are best advised not just to check out specific matters as they arise, but to read the court's rules through. It will flag a number of things they may not otherwise have grasped. Once tackled, the rules prove much less forbidding than they seem when first approached.

A newcomer on the scene, CPLR 2112, entitled "Filing of papers in the appellate division by electronic means," became effective in 2015 and shows some promise to reduce the differences in the rules among the departments in the appellate division. The new law authorizes the use of mandatory e-filing in the appellate division at the discretion of each department. Each department is permitted to adopt e-filing rules for: 1) appeals, 2) motions for permission to appeal, 3) commencement of any proceeding over which the court has original jurisdiction, and 4) the filing and service of papers in pending actions and proceedings. CPLR 2112 recommends that "[t]o the extent practicable, rules promulgated by the appellate division in each judicial department pursuant to this section shall be uniform."[1] It is our hope that all four departments in the appellate division will find it practicable in every instance, but the rules have not yet been issued.

The rules of the various appellate courts may be found in the state's Official Compilation of Codes, Rules and Regulations, where they comprise part of Title 22 and on court websites. They will be cited here either with that identification, abbreviated to N.Y.C.R.R., or simply as Rule so-and-so. They are found more conveniently in McKinney's "New York Rules of Court" pamphlet, a single soft-cover volume recompiled annually.

When we cite rules, the citations will be to the rules of the Court of Appeals and the four departments of the appellate division. There are other appellate courts of which one must take account, however, when dealing with the lower trial courts. In the First and Second Departments, there are appellate terms, to which appeals go from the New York City Civil and Criminal Courts and the district, city, town, and village courts.[2] In the Second Department, even appeals from the county courts in civil matters go to appellate term.[3] In the Third and Fourth Departments, the county courts sit as appellate courts over city, town, and village courts. When the appeal is from any of these lower courts, the practitioner's first look should be at Article 17 of the Uniform Court Acts.[4] It will be a brief consultation, but it will advise of what is appealable and where the appeal goes: Article 17 in the lower court acts supplies only a few variants from the ordinary appellate practice contained in Article 55 of the CPLR, which it then adopts in full,[5] so that lawyers will find themselves directed right back to the CPLR and to the rules of court for most of what they need even for the lower reaches of the appellate process. In this connection, the lawyer should note that the appellate term has its own rules,[6] which must be consulted by anyone taking an appeal to that court.

In the study of appeals, among the first questions to ask is what court the appeal goes to, which is just another way of asking about the subject matter jurisdiction of the appellate courts. We met that in Chapter 2, where as each trial court's jurisdiction was studied, reference was included to the appellate path of its judgments and orders. The

---

[1]   CPLR 2112.

[2]   22 N.Y.C.R.R. §§ 640.1, 730.1; see § 13.

[3]   22 N.Y.C.R.R. § 730.1.

[4]   These are the New York City Civ. Ct. Act, Uniform Dist. Ct. Act, Uniform City Ct. Act, and Uniform Just. Ct. Act (town and village) found in McKinney's Volume 29A.

[5]   See § 1703 in each of the four Uniform Acts.

[6]   22 N.Y.C.R.R. Parts 640 (First Department), 731 (Second and Eleventh Districts in Second Department), and 732 (Ninth and Tenth Districts in Second Department).

chart of the court system found there should quickly refresh recollection about which appellate court one appeals to from a given court.[7]

The next question to ask is one of venue, which overlaps jurisdiction, but can be easily ascertained. If appeal is to the county court, it is to that of the lower court's county. If appeal is to an appellate term, the appellate term rules determine which one to go to.[8] Supreme court appeals go to the appellate division of the department in which the judgment or order was entered.[9] It is permissible, however, for that appellate division to send the appeal to another department in furtherance of justice, as when their own rules or administrative orders are being contested in the case and the court wishes to avoid even the appearance of prejudice.[10] This amounts to the court's disqualifying itself, not a frequent occurrence.[11]

If an appeal is taken to the wrong court altogether, as where it has been taken to the Court of Appeals when it should have gone to an appellate division, it is simply transferred to the right court.[12] The court to which the appeal is erroneously taken can even effect the transfer sua sponte.[13]

The next question is, what may be appealed? This comes under the heading of "appealability" and is the first major topic to be studied.[14] Asking what may or may not be appealed is just another way of inquiring into the subject matter jurisdiction of the appellate court. When an appellate tribunal dismisses an appeal because the particular judgment or order is not "appealable," it is announcing in effect that it lacks jurisdiction of the subject matter of the appeal.

We start with study of the first level of appeal, principally appeal from the supreme court to the appellate division, in the course of which we readily integrate appeals from lower courts to their appropriate appellate courts. By adoption of many CPLR procedures in the lower court acts, appealability has been made parallel with that of supreme court judgments and orders.

The lawyer new to the scene will note how much broader appealability is in the New York system than in the federal courts where appeals usually must await a final judgment.[15]

We then take up the appeal to the New York Court of Appeals,[16] which is narrower than the appellate division appeal not only as to what may be appealed, "appealability," but also as to what the court may review, "reviewability." "Reviewability," or "scope of

---

[7]　See § 9.

[8]　See 22 N.Y.C.R.R. §§ 640.1 (First Department) and 730.1 (Second Department).

[9]　An exception is the order changing venue in a supreme court action, where appeal is to the department in which the motion was heard and determined, despite the entry of the order in the transferor county. CPLR 511(d); see § 123.

[10]　CPLR 5711.

[11]　To relieve congestion in the appellate division of the overworked Second Department, where the time between perfection of the appeal and oral argument can be over 18 months as of this writing, some of the appeals to it may be sent to other departments. See *Outside Counsel,* N.Y.L.J., Apr. 23, 1990, at 1, noting the choice of law issues that can arise in transferred cases. Whether such a detour applies in a given case at a given time is a matter for which inquiry can be made of the clerk.

[12]　N.Y. Const. art. VI, § 5(b).

[13]　See, e.g., Biggs v. Town of Huntington, 35 N.Y.2d 904, 364 N.Y.S.2d 895, 324 N.E.2d 363 (1974).

[14]　See §§ 526 to 528A.

[15]　See § 642 (Practitioner's Edition).

[16]　See §§ 527 to 528A.

review," is the next topic in line,[17] followed by the mechanics of taking,[18] perfecting,[19] concluding,[20] and implementing the appeal and its determination.

In New York, the general rule is that the only thing that may be appealed is a "judgment" or an "order."[21] There may be no appeal from a decision, verdict, report, opinion, ruling, or anything else but a "judgment" or an "order." This rule admonishes the lawyer to have whatever it is that aggrieves her reduced to either the one or the other, as may be appropriate.[22] Nor will it avail to label as a judgment or order something not formally that, such as a judge's memorandum.[23] If a statute or court rule makes a given disposition the equivalent of an order, however, it may be appealed, as has been held, for example, with the transcript of a preliminary conference.[24]

Appeal from a court of original instance is of course from the judgment or order entered with its clerk. Appeal from an appellate court is from the appellate court's order, entered in the office of its clerk, and not from any judgment or order that the lower court may ministerially enter based on the appellate order upon remand. This requirement clarifies the obligation of the appellant and avoids confusion about which paper gets appealed. Mistakes in this regard are supposedly remediable, anyway.[25]

As a general rule, an appeal cannot be taken before the appealable paper has been formally entered.[26] An appeal taken before entry, although otherwise ripe, is at worst premature, and the defect is one that the appellate court can ignore.[27] It can treat the notice of appeal from a decision "as a premature notice of appeal from an order," but the court must be convinced that the interests of justice warrant this generosity.[28] It is ordinarily so simple to get an order entered on a decision already made that some special reason indeed should be cited to the court to invoke this power. If any difficulty should arise, a motion can be made to either the original or the appellate court to compel both the entry of the order and the filing of the papers on which the order was based.[29] This

---

[17]　See §§ 529 to 530.

[18]　See §§ 531 to 535.

[19]　See §§ 536 to 540.

[20]　See §§ 543 to 545.

[21]　CPLR 5512(a).

[22]　In a few narrow instances, statutes purport to allow an appeal to be taken from the "determination" of an administrative agency or the "award" of an arbitration panel, but this should not be confused with the more common path of judicial review of agency action, which starts with an Article 78 proceeding in the supreme court, see §§ 557 et seq., culminating in a fully appealable "judgment," CPLR 7806, or with the more limited review of an arbitration award. The statutes that purport to make such a "determination" or "award" appealable to the Court of Appeals—CPLR 5601(d), 5602(a)(1)(ii), and 5602(b)(2)(ii)—are also of questionable constitutional validity since there appears to be nothing in the relevant part of N.Y. Const. art. VI, § 3 to support such an appeal.

[23]　See In re Lynn's Estate, 22 A.D.2d 810, 254 N.Y.S.2d 771 (2d Dep't 1964).

[24]　See, e.g., Herbert v. City of New York, 126 A.D.2d 404, 510 N.Y.S.2d 112 (1st Dep't 1987), and the lead note in SPR 5:1.

[25]　See CPLR 5512(a). Timeliness, however, is measured from the service of the appellate order, not the lower court order, and CPLR 5512(a) in this regard may be something of a trap. See § 553.

[26]　The time in which to appeal, which generally runs not from entry but from the later moment when the appellant is served with the judgment or order with notice of entry, CPLR 5513, is treated in detail later. See § 533.

[27]　CPLR 5520(c); see Matter of Ryan v. Nolan, 134 A.D.3d 1259, 1261 n.1, 21 N.Y.S.3d 469, 471 n.1 (3d Dep't 2015).

[28]　See, e.g., Scott v. Vassar Bros. Hosp., 133 A.D.2d 76, 518 N.Y.S.2d 422 (2d Dep't 1987).

[29]　CPLR 5512(b).

may become necessary for an ex parte order, for example, i.e., one made out of court and whose papers have not yet been channeled back to the courthouse.

An ex parte order cannot be appealed directly; the procedure for the adverse party is to move on notice to vacate the order and then, if the motion is denied, appeal the order of denial. But even for that purpose it may be necessary to get the ex parte order onto the clerk's records and its underlying papers into the court's files. These appellate steps should not be confused with the procedure whereby an ex parte order may be vacated under CPLR 5704 by a motion made directly to the appellate division or appellate term, and sometimes to but one of its judges. That direct procedure, usually more expeditious and less expensive than an appeal, is discussed in the earlier chapter on motion practice.[30] A court's sua sponte order is the equivalent of an ex parte order for this purpose. It can't be appealed directly, but an appeal does lie from an order, made on notice, denying a motion to vacate the sua sponte order.[31]

§ 525. "Aggrieved" Party

Only an "aggrieved" party, or one duly substituted in place of an aggrieved party,[1] may appeal the judgment or order.[2] We all know the meaning of the word from our experiences on the battlefield of love, but its use has posed problems in the civil procedure realm. The drafters of the CPLR retained it for inability to find a better one, leaving its resolution to caselaw.[3] Its basic purpose, of course, is to assure that no one with a mere academic interest in the outcome, or with no interest at all, will be allowed status to appeal.

One must be aggrieved in some real sense in order to be an appellant. Where, for example, an original answer has been superseded by an amended one, an order directed to the original one becomes irrelevant and an appeal from it will not be allowed[4] because no one can be aggrieved by an irrelevancy. The issue can become a good deal more complex, however, and an attorney with any doubt about the client's aggrievement in this appellate sense would do well to check the caselaw under CPLR 5511, the statute that requires the aggrieved status.

Lack of aggrievement is what precludes appeal from a judgment or order entered on a default. The party does not become aggrieved until he has moved to vacate the default and the motion has been denied. It is therefore the order on the motion to vacate that becomes the appealable paper. If there has been a contest on the question of damages at an inquest, however, even though liability has been established through a default, appeal does lie from the determination of damages.[5] This is consistent with the prevalent rule that it takes a contest to generate aggrievement.

---

[30]   See § 244.

[31]   Sholes v. Meagher, 100 N.Y.2d 333, 763 N.Y.S.2d 522, 794 N.E.2d 664 (2003) (NYSLD No. 524).

[1]   See §§ 184 et seq.

[2]   CPLR 5511.

[3]   See 2d Rep. Leg. Doc. No. 13, p. 321 (1958).

[4]   See, e.g., Oceancrest Homes, Inc. v. Golfbay Country Club, Inc., 2 A.D.2d 756, 153 N.Y.S.2d 331 (2d Dep't 1956).

[5]   See James v. Powell, 19 N.Y.2d 249, 279 N.Y.S.2d 10, 225 N.E.2d 741 (1967).

One agreeing to a judgment can't be aggrieved by it, for which reason a consent judgment is also unappealable.[6] But again, a plaintiff's accepting a judgment that includes a favorable determination on an issue of liability will not preclude the plaintiff from securing review of the sum awarded if he contends that it should be more. Nor will appeal be precluded even by his accepting payment of the lower sum, as long as objections to it have been duly preserved.[7] This is merely an example of where a party, although winning the case, has not prevailed on every part of it. If the part on which he came up short can in a practical sense be regarded as affecting a substantial right, the party can be accorded "aggrieved" status notwithstanding that the overall victory in the case was his.

Suppose that after a verdict of liability and damages, the court orders a new trial of the damages phase unless the plaintiff stipulates to accept less ("remittitur") or the defendant stipulates to pay more ("additur").[8] At one time the party who so stipulated could not then appeal the liability finding on the ground that signing the stipulation denied the party "aggrieved" status. The Court of Appeals changed course on that and now holds that aggrievement remains as to liability in that situation and that appeal of the liability finding is therefore permissible notwithstanding the stipulation on damages.[9]

This kind of aggrievement problem arises from time to time on the liability determination in a matrimonial action where important rights may depend on the particular ground on which a divorce or separation is granted.[10]

A prevailing party should be alert to these situations. Having won below, the winner's not unreasonable assumption is that if anyone appeals, it should be the loser. But if the loser does appeal, the winner's further assumption may be that he can accomplish whatever he needs just by opposing the loser's appeal. That is often the case, but not always. If the respondent—the overall winner who is opposing the appeal[11]— asked for any kind of affirmative relief below and was denied it, that party should himself consider taking an appeal or a cross-appeal in respect of the denial. Stated otherwise, the rule is that the nonappealing party cannot be granted affirmative relief.

Suppose, for example, that P and D each allege that the other breached the same contract and each seeks damages, D by way of counterclaim. If the judgment denies both of them damages, D's opposition to P's appeal, although it will entitle him to show everything relevant to support a denial of damages to P, will not necessarily earn D appellate review of the denial of the damages D sought on the counterclaim. That would be affirmative relief, and the party who seeks it should, notwithstanding that it was his adversary's initiative that has produced the appeal, independently appeal or cross-appeal from the judgment or order, or the aspect of it that denied the affirmative relief sought.[12] This does not mean two appeals or two records, or double expense. It usually

---

[6] See City Bank Farmers Trust Co. v. Macfadden, 13 A.D.2d 395, 216 N.Y.S.2d 215 (1st Dep't 1961), aff'd, 12 N.Y.2d 1035, 239 N.Y.S.2d 680, 190 N.E.2d 24 (1963).

[7] See Cornell v. T. V. Development Corp., 17 N.Y.2d 69, 268 N.Y.S.2d 29, 215 N.E.2d 349 (1966).

[8] Additur and remittitur are the subject of § 407.

[9] See Adams v. Genie Industries, Inc., 14 N.Y.3d 535, 903 N.Y.S.2d 318, 929 N.E.2d 380 (2010), the subject of the lead note in NYSLD No. 607.

[10] See, e.g., Becker v. Becker, 36 N.Y.2d 787, 369 N.Y.S.2d 697, 330 N.E.2d 646 (1975).

[11] CPLR 5511.

[12] See, e.g., City of Rye v. Public Service Mut. Ins. Co., 34 N.Y.2d 470, 358 N.Y.S.2d 391, 315 N.E.2d 458 (1974).

only requires serving a notice of cross-appeal after receiving the other side's notice of appeal, ensuring the record contains copies of both, and that the briefs address both issues.[13]

A controversy may become academic or moot—"mootness" is usually the name applied to this phenomenon—if something occurs during the appellate process to suggest that the appellant no longer has incentive to press the appeal forward. An example would be where the time for the implementation of the particular appellant's right has now passed or the status from which her interest springs has changed or for any of a number of other reasons. New York takes a realistic view of whether to allow the appeal to proceed in such a situation, allowing it when "the controversy is of a character which is likely to recur not only with respect to the parties before the court but with respect to others as well."[14]

The precedential impact of a decision, in other words, may be a reason for letting the appeal go through. If the appellant or some other party has lost interest and refrains from strong advocacy or from any at all, this is something to be considered. But in cases of public interest, it often happens that others have applied for and been granted leave to file briefs amicus curiae.[15] If the court feels that these adequately assure adversary representation on the appeal, it can continue the appeal regardless of the original party's lost enthusiasm.

While perhaps seen more often at appellate level, the mootness doctrine has also been applied to bar a would-be litigant from bringing an action in the first place.[16]

B. APPEALABILITY

Table of Sections

§ 526. Appeals to Appellate Division
§ 527. Appeals to Court of Appeals as of Right
§ 528. Appeals to Court of Appeals by Permission
§ 528A. Certification to Court of Appeals by Other Courts

§ 526. Appeals to Appellate Division

CPLR 5701 is the key section here, determining which judgments and orders of the supreme court or county courts may be appealed,[1] which are appealable as of right, and which need permission. Few need permission. By adoption, CPLR 5701 also determines

---

[13] CPLR 5513(c); see § 533.

[14] East Meadow Community Concerts Ass'n v. Board of Ed. of Union Free School Dist. No. 3, Nassau County, 18 N.Y.2d 129, 135, 272 N.Y.S.2d 341, 346, 219 N.E.2d 172, 175 (1966).

[15] Amicus curiae means friend of the court. It denotes the situation in which a nonparty with an interest in the case wishes to submit a brief and support a particular side. The nonparty moves the appellate court for leave to file a brief amicus curiae. See, e.g., 22 N.Y.C.R.R. § 500.23 (Court of Appeals rule for nonparty seeking to file an amicus brief). Whether to grant the motion is in the court's discretion and usually depends on how much additional education the court believes it can draw from the amici. If the court feels that all sides are already represented in full, it will deny leave.

[16] See, e.g., Dreikausen v. Zoning Bd. of Appeals of City of Long Beach, 98 N.Y.2d 165, 746 N.Y.S.2d 429, 774 N.E.2d 193 (2002), and the note on it in NYSLD No. 513.

[1] Appeals from the county courts in civil matters in the Second Department go to an appellate term instead of the appellate division. N.Y. Const. art. VI, § 8(d); 22 NYCRR § 730.1. Elsewhere they go to the appellate division.

what may be appealed from a surrogate's court to an appellate division[2] and from the New York City Civil Court and the district, city, town, and village courts to their respective appellate courts.[3] Court of claims appeals go to the local appellate division.[4] Appeals from the family court are governed by the Family Court Act.[5]

CPLR 5701 has a number of parts, which should be taken up seriatim.

Appealability of Judgments

First, the appealability of judgments. CPLR 5701(a)(1) makes all judgments appealable, whether final or interlocutory, unless the judgment is only a ministerial one being entered on an appellate order that has already disposed of all issues in the action.[6] Which judgments are "final" for appeal purposes is a question more often met on appeal to the Court of Appeals and is discussed below.[7]

An example of an interlocutory judgment would be one entered upon a finding of liability in a "bifurcated" personal injury trial, damages issues having been held in abeyance for separate trial later, if warranted.[8] By appellate invitation, in fact, trial judges have been using the interlocutory judgment as a kind of appeal-control tool. The liability phase is separately appealable only if the trial judge authorizes the entry of an interlocutory judgment on it. If the judge finds no reason for delay and wants the damages phase to go forward immediately, the judge merely refuses to permit entry of an interlocutory judgment and thereby forecloses a separate appeal.[9]

Appealability of Orders

The appealability of orders, as opposed to judgments, is governed by CPLR 5701(a)(2). It is here that New York is unique in its generosity, making a broad range of nonfinal—also called "intermediate" or "interlocutory"—orders immediately appealable without waiting for final judgment. Many need not be appealed immediately, but can be saved and later reviewed as part of an appeal from the final judgment, provided they "necessarily affect" the judgment.[10] But if the appellate calendars are any gauge, this waiting alternative is little exploited and does not in significant measure discourage immediate and separate appeals from intermediate orders. These are a significant part

---

[2]   See SCPA 2701, also providing that the "decree" of a surrogate is to be deemed a "judgment" for appellate purposes.

[3]   Section 1702 in the New York City Civ. Ct. Act, Uniform Dist. Ct. Act, Uniform City Ct. Act, and the Uniform Just. Ct. Act, which is just a tailored version of CPLR 5701, mildly altered to fit the lower courts.

[4]   See Ct. of Claims Act § 24. Before 1978, the Third Department adjudicated court of claims appeals arising in the First and Second Departments.

[5]   See Fam. Ct. Act, Article 11.

[6]   Further appeal, if sought in that instance, is taken from the appellate order, rather than from a judgment entered on it in the lower court on remand. See CPLR 5611.

[7]   See § 527. The question of finality is relatively unimportant at the first level of appeal (to the appellate division, an appellate term, or a county court) because even if the determination is not final, as will be seen shortly, the order embodying it is likely to be appealable anyway. Finality is normally required at Court of Appeals level.

[8]   See CPLR 5011; § 410. The bifurcated trial is the subject of § 130.

[9]   See Jack Parker Const. Corp. v. Williams, 35 A.D.2d 839, 317 N.Y.S.2d 911 (2d Dep't 1970). A major treatment of when and whether to allow such an interlocutory judgment appears in Bank of New York v. Ansonia Associates, 172 Misc. 2d 70, 656 N.Y.S.2d 813 (Sup. Ct., New York County 1997), noted in § 410 and SPR 69:3.

[10]   CPLR 5501(a)(1); see § 530 on scope of review.

of appellate division calendars and place New York at the opposite end of the spectrum from federal practice.

Although federal practice, like New York's, allows appeal from final dispositions,[11] an appeal from an interlocutory order in federal practice is rarely allowed. This practice sits in stark contrast with the unusually generous New York attitude. In the federal courts, precious few nonfinal orders can be appealed as a matter of right,[12] most notable among them applications connected with injunctions.[13] In the New York courts, precious few can't be.

Setting the New York CPLR provision down verbatim will manifest the provisions that account for this broad appealability. CPLR 5701(a)(2) provides that an order in New York is appealable if it:

(i)   grants, refuses, continues, or modifies a provisional remedy; or

(ii) settles, grants, or refuses an application to resettle a transcript or statement on appeal; or

(iii) grants or refuses a new trial; except where specific questions of fact arising upon the issues in an action triable by the court have been tried by a jury, pursuant to an order for that purpose, and the order grants or refuses a new trial upon the merits; or

(iv) involves some part of the merits; or

(v)   affects a substantial right; or

(vi) in effect determines the action and prevents a judgment from which an appeal might be taken; or

(vii) determines a statutory provision of the state to be unconstitutional, and the determination appears from the reasons given for the decision or is necessarily implied in the decision; or

(viii) grants a motion for leave to reargue made pursuant to subdivision (d) of rule 2221 or determines a motion for leave to renew made pursuant to subdivision (e) of rule 2221 . . . .

The culprits that account for the generous appealability of nonfinal dispositions are obviously subparagraphs (iv) and (v) on this list, which authorize appeal if the order involves any part of the "merits," or, even if it does not involve the merits, just affects some "substantial right." These two provisions act like enormous magnets, overlapping the other listed grounds, making some if not all of them superfluous, and drawing in so much that it is futile even to start a list of orders included. It is easier to set forth a few orders that have been found to escape these bountiful standards, and in the relatively uncommon instance when such an escapee is identified, we have the anomaly of a party troubling to appeal an order only to be told by the appellate court that his "right," which has prompted the appeal, is not "substantial."

---

[11]   See 28 U.S.C.A. § 1291.

[12]   See § 642 (Practitioner's Edition).

[13]   See 28 U.S.C.A. § 1292(a). Subdivision (b) of that section sets up a procedure whereby the district judge can set the stage for the interlocutory appeal of other orders in certain instances. Fed. R. Civ. P. 54(b) has a like mission in cases involving multiple claims or parties. See § 642 (Practitioner's Edition).

The courts have held that these standards, open-hearted though they are, do not include an order continuing an examination before trial,[14] or rulings in connection with questions at the examination itself, even if reduced to an order.[15] The same is true, of course, of mere "rulings" during the trial.[16] It was said in Brown v. Micheletti[17] that "[g]enerally, decisions made by the court during the course of a trial of an action are deemed trial rulings, not orders, whether or not they are reduced to a writing in the form specified for orders . . . ."[18]

In Lieblich v. Saint Peter's Hospital of City of Albany,[19] the court noted that an exception to the above rule regarding examinations before trial exists where the order concerning the examination "involves some part of the merits" under CPLR 5701(a)(2)(iv), or "affects a substantial right" of a party under CPLR 5701(a)(2)(v). The Third Department ruled that the three orders at issue, one of which denied plaintiff's motion to compel defendant doctor to answer certain questions, fell within these two most generous provisions and were therefore appealable.

It is difficult to discern the standard that invokes these two expansive provisions when one seeks to appeal from an order concerning questions at a deposition. The complaint in *Lieblich* alleged that the decedent was overmedicated during the course of a medical procedure and, following his respiratory arrest, was improperly resuscitated. The supreme court denied plaintiff's motion to compel the defendant doctor to answer disputed questions regarding his care and treatment of decedent, finding that the questions were improper. Did this order "involve[ ] some part of the merits" or "affect[ ] a substantial right" of the plaintiff? Certainly, but the appellate division does not normally entertain appeals from such orders and the cases cited by the *Lieblich* court in reaching this conclusion do not involve orders in connection with questions posed at a deposition.

The appealability of orders on motions to reargue or renew, the subject of subparagraph (viii), was discussed earlier.[20]

Other orders that have been held unappealable include an order directing the immediate trial of an issue of fact arising on a motion[21] or referring the issue of fact to a referee to hear and report.[22] But the rule is not invariable: when the issues were found "serious" and in need of a "lengthy hearing," appeal from the reference order was allowed.[23] Are any of these rights insubstantial?

---

[14]   See Alterman v. Maimonides Hospital of Brooklyn, 25 A.D.2d 864, 270 N.Y.S.2d 134 (2d Dep't 1966).

[15]   See Taylor v. New York City Housing Authority, 83 A.D.3d 929, 920 N.Y.S.2d 706 (2d Dep't 2011); Kaplan v. State, 36 A.D.2d 655, 318 N.Y.S.2d 127 (3d Dep't 1971).

[16]   See Matter of Leo T., 87 A.D.2d 297, 451 N.Y.S.2d 147 (1st Dep't 1982).

[17]   Brown v. Micheletti, 97 A.D.2d 529, 468 N.Y.S.2d 160 (2d Dep't 1983).

[18]   This has been held to apply to pretrial evidentiary rulings as well. "It is well settled," said Maguire v. Rebaglia, 232 A.D.2d 380, 648 N.Y.S.2d 142 (2d Dep't 1996), in dismissing an appeal, "that no appeal lies from an order adjudicating [even] in advance of trial the admissibility of evidence."

[19]   Lieblich v. Saint Peter's Hosp. of City of Albany, 112 A.D.3d 1202, 977 N.Y.S.2d 780 (3d Dep't 2013).

[20]   See § 254 and the lead note in SPR 86:1. An order denying a motion to resettle a prior order has been held unappealable. Balboa Ins. Co. v. Herbin, 50 A.D.2d 526, 375 N.Y.S.2d 7 (1st Dep't 1975).

[21]   Bagdy v. Progresso Foods Corp., 86 A.D.2d 589, 446 N.Y.S.2d 137 (2d Dep't 1982).

[22]   Stern v. Stern, 24 A.D.2d 489, 260 N.Y.S.2d 810 (2d Dep't 1965).

[23]   See Stowell v. Berstyn, 26 A.D.2d 828, 274 N.Y.S.2d 120 (2d Dep't 1966).

It has been held that an order granting or denying a motion to dismiss a complaint made at or after trial, or for judgment at that time, is not appealable,[24] perhaps because the motion was oral or perhaps because it embodies a mere "ruling." Sometimes the holding of nonappealability is even accompanied by the statement that no "substantial right" is involved.[25] If the situation is one in which the court's "ruling" would set the stage for a final judgment, as where it denies a motion to overturn a verdict or dismiss a complaint after the plaintiff has just won, the judgment can be promptly entered and appealed and there is no reason why time need be wasted on entering a mere "order" to embody the ruling.[26] But if that's not the case, it is difficult to understand why an order granting or denying a motion to dismiss a complaint, or a motion for judgment, does not involve a "substantial right," especially in light of how many less significant orders have been held to meet this standard.

The holdings that deny appealability are at best erratic, perhaps describable as just an occasional effort by the appellate courts to protect their calendars from the pair of vultures that occupy subparagraphs (iv) and (v) of CPLR 5701(a)(2).

Appeals from temporary alimony orders in matrimonial actions, while allowable, are not encouraged; the courts prefer that the case be tried promptly.[27] At least part of the rationale for this is that appellate review of merely temporary findings is idle since the temporary findings, with or without an appellate imprimatur, do not bind the trial judge who must make the requisite permanent findings later.[28]

All of the appealable orders generously embraced in paragraph 2 of CPLR 5701(a) are the result of motions made on notice. When the order results from a motion made without notice—i.e., an ex parte motion—it is not appealable under paragraph 2. In that instance, CPLR 5701(a)(3) governs. It contemplates that the party aggrieved by the ex parte order will move, on notice, to vacate or modify it, and it allows an appeal from the order disposing of that motion.[29]

This procedure is also applicable to an order that a court makes on its own motion, which has been held to be a species of ex parte order.[30]

There is little problem about requiring a motion on notice before an ex parte order can be made appealable, as long as there is an adverse party—someone on whom to serve the notice to vacate or modify. But what happens when there is no adverse party—when the proceeding at trial level is one of those rare ones that involve no adverse party and envision only an ex parte application for the particular relief?

---

[24]   Tribolati v. Lippman, 24 A.D.2d 769, 264 N.Y.S.2d 6 (2d Dep't 1965).

[25]   See, e.g., Covell v. H.R.H. Const. Corp., 24 A.D.2d 566, 262 N.Y.S.2d 370 (2d Dep't 1965), aff'd, 17 N.Y.2d 709, 269 N.Y.S.2d 718, 216 N.E.2d 710 (1966).

[26]   In addition, the entry of final judgment precludes the continuance of an appeal from a nonfinal order. See § 530.

[27]   See, e.g., Goldstein v. Goldstein, 35 A.D.2d 777, 317 N.Y.S.2d 77 (4th Dep't 1970).

[28]   See § 448 in the Res Judicata chapter.

[29]   See § 524. These appellate steps should not be confused with the procedure whereby an ex parte order may be vacated under CPLR 5704 by a motion made directly to the appellate division or appellate term, and sometimes to but one of its judges. That direct procedure, usually more expeditious and less expensive than an appeal, is discussed in the earlier chapter on motion practice. See § 244.

[30]   Sholes v. Meagher, 100 N.Y.2d 333, 763 N.Y.S.2d 522, 794 N.E.2d 664 (2003), treated in the lead note in NYSLD No. 524.

A change of name proceeding is an example.[31] It seldom has an adverse party. The appealability problem obviously becomes academic as long as the court grants the relief sought. But if the court refuses and review is sought by an appellate court, the petitioner bumps into the two-sided problem that: (1) no appeal lies from an ex parte determination and (2) there is no one on whom to serve a notice of motion to vacate the ex parte disposition so as to produce an appealable order. There may still be some routes up, but the courts are presently in conflict about what they are.[32]

Subdivision (c) of CPLR 5701 provides that any order not appealable as of right may be appealed by permission of the judge who made the order or, if the judge refuses, by a justice of the appellate court. An application may be made to the latter directly, without first applying to the judge who made the order.[33]

Orders explicitly falling into the permission-needed category are those made in the course of an Article 78 proceeding[34] and those granting or denying corrective motions made against pleadings under CPLR 3024, like the motion for a more definite statement and the motion to strike scandalous or prejudicial matter.[35] Were these few not specified, one would be hard pressed to find gainful employment for subdivision (c).

As discussed above, CPLR 5701(c) allows a motion for leave to appeal from any order that is not appealable of right under subdivision (a). But before the stage is set for this motion, the order must be shown to be one that neither involves the merits nor affects a substantial right, else it would be appealable as a matter of right under CPLR 5701(a)(2)(iv) and (v). One wonders what chance an order like has to get the court to exercise its discretion and turn on the appellate machinery voluntarily? It's like asking a judge to allow an appeal because of the established unimportance of the issue.

Subdivision (c) was originally devised to accompany a scheme that was planned to be more restrictive of appeals as of right, which would have left a handsome residuum of orders for which it would be worthwhile to seek leave.[36] But that proposal was rejected and appealability as of right was restored in full measure, leaving subdivision (c), which was not recast, with little role.

Appeal by permission, in fact, is an altogether rare procedure at the first appellate level, i.e., on appeal from a court of original jurisdiction. It becomes a frequent and important device only at the second level. Appeal to the Court of Appeals, for example, requires leave in not just a few instances, but in most instances. We turn to this subject in the next section. An appeal to the appellate division from another appellate court sometimes requires leave, as when the appeal is sought from an order of an appellate term. The leave in that instance is sought from the appellate term or, if refused there, from the appellate division.[37]

---

[31] See Civ. Rights Law §§ 60 et seq.

[32] See Matter of Joint Diseases North General Hosp., 148 A.D.2d 873, 539 N.Y.S.2d 511 (3d Dep't 1989). The problem is the subject of a two-part treatment in the lead notes in NYSLD No. 356 and 357.

[33] Section 1702(c) of the New York City Civ. Ct. Act, Uniform Dist. Ct. Act, Uniform City Ct. Act, and Uniform Just. Ct. Act, McKinney's Vol. 29A, Parts 2 and 3, is to the same effect.

[34] CPLR 5701(b)(1). Article 78 is studied later. See §§ 557 et seq.

[35] CPLR 5701(b)(2), (3). These motions are treated in § 230.

[36] See 2d Rep. Leg. Doc. No. 13, pp. 117 to 119 (1958).

[37] So provides subdivision (a) of CPLR 5703. This provision also requires a stipulation for judgment absolute in certain cases, a procedure more often met in conjunction with an appeal to the Court of Appeals and which is therefore reserved for treatment there. See § 527.

When the appeal is from an order of a county court sitting as an appellate tribunal, such as on an appeal from a city, town, or village court disposition,[38] subdivision (b) of CPLR 5703 governs and the appeal to the appellate division may be taken of right.[39]

This provision has given rise to some bizarre caselaw, generated by too literal a construction of the statutory language. The statute is addressed to an appeal of a county court order rendered after reviewing a lower court "judgment." The Third and Fourth departments—the only ones that exploit this appellate aspect of county court jurisdiction (the other two use the appellate term)—agree that "judgment" does not include "order." This means that when the county court has reviewed a mere order of the lower court, further appeal of right to the appellate division is barred. The Third Department has allowed a motion for leave to appeal in that situation, however,[40] while the Fourth Department bars even that.[41] This led to an anomaly, and a patent injustice, in Ellingsworth v. City of Watertown,[42] causing CPLR 5703(b) to do what it was never intended to: make the county court a court of last resort.

P in Ellingsworth sued D in a city court, which denied D's dismissal motion in an order that was of course not final. Even as an interlocutory order, however, it was appealable to the county court, and D took the appeal. The county court reversed and dismissed the action, producing an order that now amounted to a final disposition. That county court order should have been appealable to the appellate division because it was in every sense final, putting an end to the case. But it was held not to be appealable because what it disposed of was a city court *order*, not a city court *judgment*.[43]

When permission is required, the criteria for determining whether to grant it are left to the discretion of the tribunal applied to. Influential ingredients that help tilt that discretion include the precedential impact of the point involved, the public nature of the case, the newness of the issue, and the fact that the decision below may be in conflict with decisions of other lower courts.[44]

The grant of leave may be conditional. It can require, for example, that a moving defendant post security to pay the judgment in the event of an affirmance.[45]

§ 527. Appeals to Court of Appeals as of Right

Appealability to the Court of Appeals is narrower and more complex than to the appellate division. Finality plays a larger role, and so does the appeal by permission. There are conditions and qualifications, especially on appeals by permission, which sometimes require several references back and forth between CPLR sections; lawyers may feel themselves running out of fingers as they try to mark places while flipping pages. Some of the restrictions are built into the constitution itself.[1]

---

[38]   See Uniform Just. Ct. Act § 1701.

[39]   The same is provided when a Special Term sits as an appellate court, which it rarely does today.

[40]   See Cammarota v. Bella Vista Development Corp., 88 A.D.2d 703, 451 N.Y.S.2d 309 (3d Dep't 1982).

[41]   Gastel v. Bridges, 110 A.D.2d 146, 493 N.Y.S.2d 674 (4th Dep't 1985).

[42]   Ellingsworth v. City of Watertown, 113 A.D.2d 1013, 494 N.Y.S.2d 587 (4th Dep't 1985).

[43]   These results are further discussed in the Commentaries on McKinney's CPLR 5703.

[44]   See Handy v. Butler, 183 A.D. 359, 169 N.Y.S. 770 (2d Dep't 1918).

[45]   Rosenberg v. Rosenberg, 24 A.D.2d 26, 263 N.Y.S.2d 586 (1st Dep't 1965).

[1]   Court of Appeals jurisdiction is covered by N.Y. Const. art. VI, § 3.

It will be best to study the applicable provisions in the order of their CPLR appearance, promptly making whatever cross-references are needed and explaining what they accomplish. For this reason the reader in search of a quick perspective on Court of Appeals jurisdiction, which is governed by Article 56 of the CPLR, may find it helpful to have a copy of the CPLR handy during the ensuing treatment.

CPLR 5601 governs appeals as of right—appeals that involve no preliminary leave of any court. Subdivision (a) is the provision in point when an order of the appellate division finally determines an action originating in the supreme court, a county court, surrogate's court, family court, court of claims, or administrative agency.

Under subdivision (a), the order is appealable as of right to the Court of Appeals only "where there is a dissent by at least two justices on a question of law" in favor of the appellant. This is all that's left after a 1985 amendment of subdivision (a). Before the amendment, appeal of right was allowed when only one justice dissented, and, even when the decision was unanimous, it was allowed whenever the decision itself was one of reversal or modification. Generally speaking, a unanimous affirmance by the appellate division was the only disposition not appealable of right under subdivision (a). Now, generally no unanimous decision of any kind is appealable of right; it requires permission, as we shall see in the next section. An exception is where a construction of the New York or Federal Constitution is directly involved, in which case even a unanimous decision is appealable of right.[2]

Even in the two-justice dissent situation, allowing appeal of right, a 3–2 disagreement among the appellate division on an undecisive issue, or even the presence of an opinion concurred in by two justices and formally denominated a "dissent," does not assure an appeal of right under subdivision (a). The posture of the two-justice dissent must be such as would turn the case the appellant's way.

Suppose, for example, that an action has been dismissed on two grounds. On appeal, the appellate division affirms with two dissenters who disagree about ground one, but who support the dismissal on ground two. Since they would also dismiss, their dissent would not be "in favor of" the appellant and hence would not support an appeal of right.[3] In this situation, although they may style their position a "dissent," they are in essence concurring in result.

In Reis v. Volvo Cars of North America,[4] the defendant appealed from an order as of right on a two-judge dissent in the appellate division. The plaintiff, who was also aggrieved by the order because the majority dismissed his failure to warn claims, similarly sought to appeal as of right. The Court dismissed the plaintiff's appeal because the two-justice dissent in the appellate division was not in plaintiff's favor. Unfortunately, plaintiff did not move for permission to appeal from that portion of the order under CPLR 5602(a), which is always advisable in these circumstances.[5] Therefore, the Court determined that "the portion of the order unfavorable to plaintiff was beyond its review."

---

[2] See CPLR 5601(b)(1).

[3] See Christovao v. Unisul-Uniao de Coop. Transf. de Tomate Do Sul Do Tejo, S.C.R.L., 41 N.Y.2d 338, 392 N.Y.S.2d 609, 360 N.E.2d 1309 (1977).

[4] Reis v. Volvo Cars of North America, 24 N.Y.3d 35, 993 N.Y.S.2d 672, 18 N.E.3d 383 (2014).

[5] See § 528.

Turning to the matters that could be reviewed on the appeal,[6] the *Reis* Court observed that "an appeal properly taken under CPLR 5601(a) brings up for review all issues that the Appellate Division decided adversely to the appellant, even those on which no Appellate Division justice dissented."[7] This was a critical point of appellate practice in this matter because while the Court did not agree with the two-judge dissent's conclusion that the trial court improperly charged the jury on customary business practices, it did rule that the appellate division majority erred in concluding that it was proper to charge the jury on special knowledge. Therefore, the Court reversed the judgment and remitted the case for a new trial.

The *Reis* decision highlights several important aspects of appellate practice in the New York Court of Appeals. There is also a lesson to be drawn from the outcome of the case. When a party finds herself in the Court of Appeals as a respondent, she must carefully examine if she desires any affirmative relief previously denied below. If so, she is "aggrieved" and must either cross-appeal as of right or, more commonly, seek permission to appeal to the Court.[8] The plaintiff's failure to do so in *Reis* meant he could not receive the affirmative relief ultimately sought in the Court of Appeals, i.e., reinstatement of that portion of the jury's verdict based on the failure to warn claim.

Cases originating in courts other than those listed in CPLR 5601(a), as enumerated above, do not reach the Court of Appeals as of right. Their first-tier appeals go to appellate courts below the appellate division, presently to either an appellate term or to a county court, and only a further appeal goes to the appellate division.[9] If the case is then to go to the Court of Appeals, which would mean a third appellate step, it needs leave from the appellate division.[10] If it doesn't get leave, that's usually the end of the line. It means in effect that for most of the state's lower courts, the appellate division serves as the court of last resort.

Superseding the above is the appeal from a trial-level final judgment if the appeal presents only the question of the validity of a New York or federal statute under the New York or Federal Constitution. Here the appeal not only lies of right; it by-passes all intermediate appellate courts and goes directly to the Court of Appeals from the court of original instance.[11] An example is the case that determined the constitutionality of New York's no-fault statute in the tort realm, which went directly from the supreme court to the Court of Appeals.[12]

To take advantage of this direct appeal route, the constitutional question must be "substantial,"[13] the Court of Appeals of course being the ultimate judge of that. And it must be the only question presented on the appeal; the Court of Appeals can't consider anything else.[14] If the issue is insubstantial, or if the appeal adds any other question, it

---

[6]   See CPLR 5501; § 530.

[7]   *Reis*, 24 N.Y.3d at 41, 993 N.Y.S.2d at 676, 18 N.E.3d at 387.

[8]   See §§ 525, 528.

[9]   CPLR 5703. Subdivision (a) of CPLR 5703 governs appeals from an appellate term, which require leave. Subdivision (b) governs appeals from other appellate courts, mainly a county court sitting as such, but there an appeal to the appellate division may be taken as of right.

[10]   CPLR 5602(b)(2).

[11]   CPLR 5601(b)(2). The statute applies only to a court "of record," an arbitrary distinction today that excludes only the town and village courts. See Jud. Law § 2.

[12]   Montgomery v. Daniels, 38 N.Y.2d 41, 378 N.Y.S.2d 1, 340 N.E.2d 444 (1975).

[13]   See, e.g., Gerzof v. Gulotta, 40 N.Y.2d 825, 387 N.Y.S.2d 568, 355 N.E.2d 797 (1976).

[14]   N.Y. Const. art. VI, § 3(b)(2).

does not lie to the Court of Appeals at all and if taken there it will be transferred to where it belongs.[15]

A word is in order about what "final" means. It has usually been given a pragmatic interpretation, meaning a judgment or order that puts an end to the case, or to a logically separable part of it, and leaves nothing else in respect of it to be decided. We will cite a few examples, but a practitioner with any doubt should check the annotations.

An appellate division order granting summary judgment on only one of several claims is final as to that one, allowing appeal as to it, but not as to the other claims still left standing.[16] Similarly, the dismissal of a counterclaim is final even if the main claim remains to be tried, and in instances like these, the dismissed claim, if not actually severed, may be deemed so in order to set the stage for its appeal. This is sometimes known as the doctrine of implied severance, but it should be relied on only when the counterclaim is completely independent of the main claim.[17] Earlier indications of a less stringent attitude[18] are inappropriate to rely on today, especially after the Court of Appeals decision in Burke v. Crosson,[19] which reviews and adjusts the "implied severance" rule to make it depend entirely on the relatedness of the claims involved. When some but not all claims are resolved, holds *Burke*, an implied severance will be deemed to occur

> only if the causes of action [that are resolved] do not arise out of the same transaction or continuum of facts or out of the same legal relationship as the unresolved causes of action.

If they do arise out of the same transaction, an implied severance will presumably not occur, barring an appeal until the unresolved matters also go to final judgment.[20]

An order denying a stay of arbitration, in effect compelling arbitration and thus taking the dispute out of the court system, is, as far as the courts are concerned, final, and may be treated as such for appellate purposes.[21] Indeed, even a disposition denying arbitration and thus retaining the case in court may be final enough for this appellate purpose if the disposition about arbitrability is made in a special proceeding, as most such dispositions are, instead of in the context of an action.[22] The special proceeding is an independent one, and its disposition, whether for or against arbitration, is usually embodied in a judgment terminating the proceeding and therefore "final" in that context.[23]

When finality is required for the appeal, as it is in the instances discussed so far, the paper that disposes of the issues is the one to be appealed. Thus, when an order of

---

[15] See Merced v. Fisher, 38 N.Y.2d 557, 381 N.Y.S.2d 817, 345 N.E.2d 288 (1976).

[16] See Northern Operating Corp. v. Town of Ramapo, 26 N.Y.2d 404, 311 N.Y.S.2d 286, 259 N.E.2d 723 (1970).

[17] See Lizza Industries, Inc. v. Long Island Lighting Company, 36 N.Y.2d 754, 368 N.Y.S.2d 830, 329 N.E.2d 664 (1975).

[18] See Sirlin Plumbing Co. v. Maple Hill Homes, Inc., 20 N.Y.2d 401, 283 N.Y.S.2d 489, 230 N.E.2d 394 (1967).

[19] Burke v. Crosson, 85 N.Y.2d 10, 623 N.Y.S.2d 524, 647 N.E.2d 736 (1995).

[20] The *Burke* case is treated in the lead note in NYSLD No. 424.

[21] Wilaka Const. Co. v. New York City Housing Authority, 17 N.Y.2d 195, 269 N.Y.S.2d 697, 216 N.E.2d 696 (1966).

[22] See § 591 (Practioner's Edition).

[23] CPLR 411. Special proceedings are treated in detail in Chapter 20.

the appellate division is the final one and leaves nothing further to be decided below, the appeal should be taken from the appellate division order and not from any judgment or order afterwards entered on it in the original court. So provides CPLR 5611, which also recognizes that although the order may be final, it may include a condition whereby finality can be defeated, such as an order dismissing a complaint with leave to replead within a specified time. In such an instance, the order is not to be deemed "final" until the time for doing the conditional act passes without the act's being done. Doing the act, of course, such as by repleading in the example, divests the order of its finality.

In additur and remittitur situations—situations in which the court below has raised or lowered a verdict in response to a party's contention that the amount awarded was either too little (additur) or too much (remittitur)[24]—a variety of steps may follow, involving the parties, the trial court, and the appellate division. These variations can seriously complicate the issue of what follow-up event is the "final" one that can set the stage for Court of Appeals review. Recognizing these difficulties in Whitfield v. City of New York,[25] the Court outlines several scenarios and endeavors to pinpoint in each of them the step that constitutes the "final" one needed for an appeal (or a motion for leave when leave is required) to the Court of Appeals. Despite the court's best efforts at clarification in *Whitfield*, however, there may still be confusion about which disposition is the properly appealable one in a given situation. Perhaps the only safe course for a party bent on securing appellate review in these and yet other multipaper situations in appellate practice generally, and Court of Appeals practice especially, is to appeal everything in sight and as often as need be.[26]

A few nonfinal dispositions are appealable as of right to the Court of Appeals. The most infamous and deadly of these is the often misunderstood "stipulation for judgment absolute" supplied by CPLR 5601(c). It is relevant when the appellate division grants a new trial, or affirms an order granting a new trial, in a case originating in any of the five courts listed earlier in this section (supreme, county, surrogate's and family courts, and the court of claims) or in an administrative agency. The party who won the judgment at trial wants to keep it and would therefore like to overturn the appellate division order that grants the new trial. But such an order is not final and thus not appealable as of right. It has been made so, however, by CPLR 5601(c), but with the proviso that the appellant stipulate that in the event of affirmance, "judgment absolute shall be entered against him." This means that if the Court of Appeals finds the appellate division to be within its powers in granting a new trial, and hence affirms the order granting it, it will not mean a new trial at all; it will mean that the appellant has lost everything: the trial court judgment that the appellant wanted to reinstate as well as the second chance (the new trial) that the appellate division had offered.

This is a dangerous procedure which an appellant should not use unless the appeal presents only questions of law and not a breath of appellate division discretion, and few appellants of such a mind can be sure the Court of Appeals will see the case the same way. Since appellate division discretion in ordering a new trial is vast, an appellant should not test it with CPLR 5601(c), which is a CPLR version of Russian Roulette. All the Court of Appeals has to do is find that the appellate division has acted anywhere

---

[24] Additur and remittitur are the subject of § 407, and some appellate issues are discussed there.

[25] Whitfield v. City of New York, 90 N.Y.2d 777, 666 N.Y.S.2d 545, 689 N.E.2d 515 (1997).

[26] That's the conclusion reached in the extensive lead note on *Whitfield* in NYSLD No. 458.

within the nearly unlimited confines of its discretion in granting a new trial, and the lightning will strike.

Appellate lawyers who have made the mistake of using this device, or who (more likely) have been frantically retained of counsel by others who did, should consider asking opposing counsel to stipulate to withdraw the appeal altogether. Absent cooperation from the other side, the appellant can move the Court of Appeals to let it withdraw the stipulation (in effect asking that its own appeal be dismissed, and with good riddance). The motion will likely be granted, but the Court may impose costs as a condition.[27] It is also advisable to make the motion before oral argument takes place. The Court of Appeals has indicated that it will not entertain the motion once the appeal has been argued,[28] and it is not wise to hope for an exception.

If the stipulation is given, it must be one that will, in the event of affirmance, dispose of everything because the purpose of this small opening in the wall of finality is to create at least the possibility of a final determination. Stipulating to judgment absolute solely on the issue of liability therefore doesn't suffice, and an appeal based on such a conditional stipulation won't be entertained for the reason that an affirmance would not put an end to the case: there would still have to be a trial of the damages issues.[29]

A similar judgment absolute procedure is set up for an appellate term order granting a new trial if it is to be appealed to the appellate division.[30] It has no less peril than the one we have been discussing.

An important point about the judgment absolute procedure is made in City of New York v. Scott,[31] addressing the lower courts "judgment absolute" provision, but presumably applicable as well to the other major sources of the device. The court says that if the party who appeals the order directing a new trial takes the case up by filing the stipulation, and the appellate court, even though affirming, does not order judgment absolute at the end of the case, but instead includes in its remittitur the right to a hearing on an issue, the case remains alive and continues. If the remittitur is in error in this respect—it would have been expected to direct judgment absolute against the appellant—the court says that the aggrieved person should apply to the appellate court to have the error corrected.

Another instance in which an appeal of right lies to the Court of Appeals is under CPLR 5601(d). In that situation, there has been an earlier appeal to the appellate division and its order on that occasion could not be appealed because it was not final; the case was remanded to the lower court for further proceedings. Now those proceedings have been concluded in a final judgment and the case is ready to go up again. If the appellant seeks review of only those points previously decided by the appellate division— it would be idle to take them back to the same court again—she can appeal the judgment directly to the Court of Appeals, skipping the appellate division. It's optional. She can instead go back to the appellate division, but should do that only if she seeks review of

---

[27] See Rattray v. Raynor, 10 N.Y.2d 494, 225 N.Y.S.2d 39, 180 N.E.2d 429 (1962).

[28] See Shtekla v. Topping, 18 N.Y.2d 961, 277 N.Y.S.2d 694, 224 N.E.2d 116 (1967).

[29] See Lusenskas v. Axelrod, 81 N.Y.2d 300, 598 N.Y.S.2d 166, 614 N.E.2d 729 (1993).

[30] See CPLR 5703(a), where the appeal, even with the stipulation, lies only by permission. There is yet another stipulation instance, in CPLR 5602(b)(2)(iii), which also requires leave.

[31] City of New York v. Scott, 178 Misc. 2d 836, 680 N.Y.S.2d 819 (N.Y. City Civ. Ct. 1998).

new matters not covered on the earlier appeal, thereupon setting the stage for a total review by the Court of Appeals afterwards, of both the old and new issues.

Suppose, for example, that the trial court on D's motion dismisses P's claim for failure to serve a notice of claim. P appeals and the appellate division reverses, finding the notice properly served and remanding for a trial of the merits. P wins on that trial and D wants to appeal the judgment. If the only point D wants reviewed is the one concerning the notice of claim, D can take a direct appeal to the Court of Appeals, but D will be limited to that issue alone and may not raise any others that the appellate division has not yet had a go at.

Two additional showings are required for this kind of appeal. One is that the prior appellate order "necessarily affects" the later judgment.[32] The order in the notice of claim example of course does that, since a judgment for P would be canceled if the notice of claim were no good. The other is that the absence of finality was the only thing that prevented the prior order from reaching the Court of Appeals. The prior order, in other words, must be shown to satisfy the other ingredients, besides finality, needed for an appeal of right to the Court of Appeals under CPLR 5601(a).[33] Today, as noted at the outset, the only surviving ingredient in subdivision (a) that will assure appeal as of right is a showing that two justices dissented. The prior order in the notice of claim example satisfied one of the requirements of the pre-1985 version of subdivision (a), viz., that the appellate division disposition was one of reversal, but today that by itself would not do. A showing that two justices dissented would be required. When CPLR 5601(d) is satisfied in all respects but this last one, appeal as of right still being barred for want of a two-justice dissent, direct appeal will still lie, but only by permission.[34] Appeal by permission is the subject of the next section.

When direct appeal to the Court of Appeals is available under this provision because, for example, there was a two-judge dissent on a question of law on the initial appeal to the appellate division,[35] the appellant must elect whether to invoke it, or instead to appeal to the intermediate appellate court, where the new matters can also be reviewed. Choosing the direct appeal waives review of the new matters.[36] If an appeal is first taken to the intermediate appellate court, and then the appeal to the Court of Appeals is pursued, the appellant should seek leave to appeal from those new matters not addressed by the prior two-judge dissent. Those matters will not be before the Court of Appeals on the appeal as of right.

Finally, on CPLR 5601(d), an administrative determination or an arbitration award may be directly appealed to the Court of Appeals, but only where (1) it was to an agency or an arbitrator rather than to a court that the appellate division remitted the proceedings after the earlier appeal; (2) where the agency or arbitrator has now followed through and produced a "final" determination or award; and (3) where the other

---

[32]   See § 530.

[33]   See Buffalo Elec. Co. v. State, 14 N.Y.2d 453, 253 N.Y.S.2d 537, 201 N.E.2d 869 (1964).

[34]   Such a case will fall under CPLR 5602(a)(1)(ii) if it involves one of the higher trial courts (any of the five listed earlier in this treatment), or under CPLR 5602(b)(2)(ii) if it involves one of the lower courts.

[35]   CPLR 5601(a).

[36]   See Parker v. Rogerson, 35 N.Y.2d 751, 361 N.Y.S.2d 916, 320 N.E.2d 650 (1974).

requirements of CPLR 5601(d), as discussed above, have been met. This aspect of CPLR 5601(d) poses constitutional issues.[37]

§ 528. Appeals to Court of Appeals by Permission

The governing provision on appeals to the Court of Appeals by permission is CPLR 5602, divided into two categories. Subdivision (a) provides for cases in which the permission may be sought from either the appellate division or the Court of Appeals. Subdivision (b) provides for cases in which only the appellate division can grant the permission. Subdivision (a) is further divided. CPLR 5602(a)(1) is directed to an action originating in any of the five higher courts (supreme, county, surrogate's and family courts, or the court of claims) or in an administrative agency. An appellate division order finally determining such an action and not appealable of right under CPLR 5601 may be appealed by permission under subparagraph (i) of CPLR 5602(a)(1).

Subparagraph (ii) of CPLR 5602(a)(1), authorizing a direct appeal to the Court of Appeals, is the counterpart of CPLR 5601(d), treated earlier.[1]

When permission to appeal is sought under subdivision (a), the one seeking it may first move the appellate division and, if unsuccessful, then move the Court of Appeals. Alternatively, the aggrieved party may simply move directly before the Court of Appeals. The procedure is by the basic steps of a motion, but with special additional requirements, usually coming from the rules of the appellate court, to be met later.[2]

When the application is made to the appellate division, the court decides for itself what vote it will require for a grant of leave. But when the application is made to the Court of Appeals, a statute requires that it be granted if any two judges vote for it.[3] As in the U.S. Supreme Court with a denial of certiorari, so with the New York Court of Appeals: "denial of a motion for leave to appeal is not equivalent to an affirmance and has no precedential value."[4]

Following the logical progression, i.e., seeking appellate division leave first, and only if that fails seeking leave from the Court of Appeals, gives the appellant two bites of the apple. It also affords the movant some extra time to put together the best possible set of papers before the Court of Appeals, assuming the motion there is necessary. Moving the Court of Appeals in first instance waives the two-step procedure and forfeits one of the bites.

What happens when the would-be appellant seeks leave from both courts at the same time? The two-bite option would remain if the Court of Appeals were to dismiss as premature the motion made to itself, thus allowing the appellate division to rule first. The Court in fact did that in its 1958 decision in Wild v. Bartol.[5] But it overruled *Wild* in Lumsby v. Donovan,[6] holding that in this dual-motions situation the Court "has the

---

[37] There appears to be no constitutional support for an appeal from a "determination" or "award." See § 524.

[1] See § 527. For the background of CPLR 5602(a)(2), concerning proceedings involving public officers, boards, and agencies in certain instances, see 2d Rep. Leg. Doc. No. 13, p. 110 (1958), and F. J. Zeronda, Inc. v. Town Bd., of Town of Halfmoon, 37 N.Y.2d 198, 371 N.Y.S.2d 872, 333 N.E.2d 154 (1975).

[2] See § 541.

[3] CPLR 5602(a).

[4] Brooklyn Hospital v. Lennon, 45 N.Y.2d 820, 409 N.Y.S.2d 210, 381 N.E.2d 608 (1978).

[5] Wild v. Bartol, 5 N.Y.2d 792, 180 N.Y.S.2d 322, 154 N.E.2d 574 (1958).

[6] Lumsby v. Donovan, 10 N.Y.3d 951, 862 N.Y.S.2d 463, 892 N.E.2d 857 (2008).

power to entertain the motion without waiting for the Appellate Division to issue its determination." It then did entertain the motion in *Lumsby*, and denied it on the merits. Since a second bite of the apple is available only when the appellate division is allowed to go first, the result was the elimination of bite two.

CPLR 5602(b), which authorizes only the appellate division to grant leave to appeal to the Court of Appeals, has two paragraphs. Paragraph 1 authorizes the grant of leave from an appellate division order that does not finally determine an action.[7] If the motion is granted, the appellate division certifies to the Court of Appeals the questions of law it finds presented, and the Court of Appeals can review only the question(s) certified.[8] Paragraph 2 is concerned with actions originating in the lower courts, which would include the New York City Civil Court and the district, city, town, and village courts, and is broken down into three subparagraphs, which should be treated independently.

If the case gets to the appellate division, and that court's order finally determines it, the order would be appealable to the Court of Appeals as of right if it involved a construction of the state or Federal Constitution,[9] but when the constitutional construction is absent, the mission of subparagraph (i) of CPLR 5602(b)(2) is to require appellate division permission before the case can go any higher.

Subparagraph (ii) of CPLR 5602(b)(2), like CPLR 5602(a)(1)(ii) mentioned at the outset, is also a counterpart of CPLR 5601(d), authorizing direct appeal to the Court of Appeals by leave when CPLR 5601(d) does not offer it as a matter of right. CPLR 5601(d) was discussed towards the end of the last section and has better context for understanding there.

Finally, subparagraph (iii) of CPLR 5602(b)(2) is another stipulation for judgment absolute situation. It differs from the main one, found in CPLR 5601(c), in two ways. First, it applies to actions originating in the state's lower trial courts while the main one applies to those originating in the higher trial courts. Second, it requires appellate division leave to go to the Court of Appeals, while under the main one the appeal lies as a matter of right. With that differentiation, the two are parallel.

The stipulation for judgment absolute provisions apply when the appellate division has ordered a new trial. Before being allowed to appeal that order, the would-be appellant must stipulate that if the order is affirmed by the Court of Appeals, judgment absolute will be entered against him. It's a perilous course and must be traveled with caution.[10]

A uniform requirement when the appellate division grants leave to appeal to the Court of Appeals, whether under subdivision (a) of CPLR 5602, where it shares with the Court of Appeals itself the power to grant such leave, or under subdivision (b), where it holds the power alone, is that the appellate division state in the order granting leave that in its opinion questions of law have arisen which ought to be reviewed.[11] When the

---

[7]   An exception here is the order granting a new trial or hearing, which is left to the procedure of the stipulation for judgment absolute. See § 527. CPLR 5602(b)(1) accomplishes this by cross-referencing CPLR 5601(c) and 5602(b)(2)(iii)—the provisions containing the stipulation requirement. Another exception involves the situation of CPLR 5602(a)(2), mentioned in note 1 above.

[8]   See generally, Patrician Plastic Corp. v. Bernadel Realty Corp., 25 N.Y.2d 599, 307 N.Y.S.2d 868, 256 N.E.2d 180 (1970).

[9]   See CPLR 5601(b)(1), treated in § 527.

[10]   We expatiate on this in § 527.

[11]   CPLR 5713.

order being appealed is not final, such as one that merely upholds jurisdiction, the order granting leave must also indicate whether lower court fact findings have been affirmed, reversed, modified, or not considered, specifying those that are reversed or modified and setting forth any new findings of fact.[12] All of this has bearing on the scope of review to which the order can be subjected in the Court of Appeals, whose power to review the facts is severely circumscribed.[13]

As noted above,—when the appellate division grants leave to appeal from a nonfinal order under CPLR 5602(b), the appellate division certifies the question of law deemed decisive of its determination.[14] If the question certified turns out to be one that the Court of Appeals can't review—and the Court of Appeals is of course the final judge of that— the appeal will be dismissed.[15] Similarly, even if the certified question states that the "determination was made as a matter of law and not in the exercise of discretion," the Court of Appeals is not bound by the appellate division's characterization in its certification order.[16] Instead, the Court will make an independent determination of whether the appellate division's decision nonetheless reflects a discretionary balancing of interests. If an appellate division's determination is deemed to be discretionary in nature, the Court of Appeals' review is limited to whether the intermediate appellate court abused its discretion as a matter of law.[17]

§ 528A. Certification to Court of Appeals by Other Courts

The New York courts must decide issues only in the context of an actual controversy. Advisory opinions, in which an answer to a law question is supplied, but resolution of the dispute is left to some other court system to resolve, are not permissible. A narrow exception to this rule has been carved out, but only for the New York Court of Appeals.

At the request of the U.S. Supreme Court, a federal court of appeals, or the highest court of a sister state, the New York Court of Appeals can now supply the answer to a question of New York law, i.e., render the previously unauthorized advisory opinion. The authorization—the product of a constitutional referendum in the mid-1980s[1]—was designed to recognize the frequency with which, in our mobile federal society, questions of New York law arise in other forums from which no direct route is available to the New York Court of Appeals, the only court that can supply definitive answers to questions of New York law.

Implementation of the procedure, which is commonly known as the "certification" procedure because it requires the requesting court to "certify" the issue of law it wants answered, required a rule of court, which the Court of Appeals promptly adopted.[2] The rule supplies the guideposts and procedures for invoking the certification process and makes clear that even when the certification request is made by a proper court, whether

---

[12] CPLR 5713.

[13] See § 529.

[14] N.Y. Const. art. VI, § 3(b)(4); CPLR 5713.

[15] See Rosemont Enterprises, Inc. v. Irving, 41 N.Y.2d 829, 393 N.Y.S.2d 392, 361 N.E.2d 1040 (1977); Arthur Young & Company v. Leong, 40 N.Y.2d 984, 390 N.Y.S.2d 927, 359 N.E.2d 435 (1976).

[16] Pegasus Aviation I, Inc. v. Varig Logistica S.A., 26 N.Y.3d 543, 26 N.Y.S.3d 218, 46 N.E.3d 601 (2015).

[17] Andon ex rel. Andon v. 302–304 Mott Street Associates, 94 N.Y.2d 740, 745, 709 N.Y.S.2d 873, 876, 731 N.E.2d 589 (2000); see § 529.

[1] It added a paragraph 9 to N.Y. Const. art. VI, § 3(b).

[2] 22 N.Y.C.R.R. § 500.27.

to accept and act on the request is still left to the discretion of the Court of Appeals. Entertaining the request on its merits is not mandatory, no matter which court puts the question.

The first invocation of the new procedure, and a successful one, was at the behest of the U.S. Court of Appeals for the Second Circuit in Kidney v. Kolmar Laboratories, Inc.,[3] in which the New York Court of Appeals answered the certified question in a per curiam opinion. The Second Circuit then acted on it by applying the response and closing out the case,[4] also taking the occasion to express its pleasure at having available this new and direct route by which to resolve issues of New York law. These appear frequently before the Second Circuit, principally when the basis for federal subject matter jurisdiction is the diversity of citizenship of the parties.

In order "to enhance understanding . . . and to provide an illustration of a form of Certificate that evidently complies with the certification procedure of the New York Court of Appeals," the Second Circuit set forth in full in its *Kidney* opinion a copy of the certificate that it used.

Whether the Court of Appeals accepts and acts on a given certificate is a sui generis determination. The Court retains control of all issues, from the basic one of whether to accept the certificate in the first place right down to the details of how the case should be presented, briefed, and argued.

While the *Kidney* case got the certification procedure off to a cordial start,[5] it did not become quite the herald that the Second Circuit had hoped it would. Several Second Circuit requests for certification were turned down for one reason or another afterwards. An early illustration of a rejected request is Rufino v. United States,[6] in which the New York Court of Appeals noted that the same questions were pending in a case presently before the appellate division and that it would be "unquestionably preferable . . . to secure the benefit afforded by our normal process—the considered deliberation and writing of our intermediate appellate court." Another is Retail Software Services, Inc. v. Lashlee,[7] in which the Second Circuit, having before it a question of whether a state statute provided extraterritorial jurisdiction over the defendant, asked the Court of Appeals for an answer. Although the Court initially accepted the question for review, it ultimately rejected the request, concluding that the issue "did not comport with the constitutional requirement that the question certified may be determinative of the cause . . . pending in the certifying court."[8] The rule in point[9] requires a showing that the issue "may be determinative," but it does not say determinative of what. It appears, however, that the Court of Appeals will answer a certified question of New York State law even if

---

[3]   Kidney by Kidney v. Kolmar Laboratories, Inc., 68 N.Y.2d 343, 509 N.Y.S.2d 491, 502 N.E.2d 168 (1986).

[4]   Kidney by Kidney v. Kolmar Laboratories, Inc., 808 F.2d 955 (2d Cir. 1987).

[5]   See the lead note in NYSLD No. 329.

[6]   Rufino v. U.S., 69 N.Y.2d 310, 514 N.Y.S.2d 200, 506 N.E.2d 910 (1987).

[7]   Retail Software Services, Inc. v. Lashlee, 71 N.Y.2d 788, 530 N.Y.S.2d 91, 525 N.E.2d 737 (1988).

[8]   N.Y. Const. art. VI, § 3(b)(9).

[9]   22 N.Y.C.R.R. § 500.27.

a Federal Constitutional issue remains to be decided by the court that has invoked the certification procedure.[10]

The denial of a certification request can lead to conflict and embarrassment, but this may be unavoidable in our nation's judicial system. In the *Rufino* case, for example, the Second Circuit asked the Court of Appeals to answer a key issue of damages in a tort case—whether New York recognizes the "loss of enjoyment of life" as a damages element distinct from the standard element of pain and suffering. When the Court of Appeals rejected the certification, the Second Circuit, forced to prognosticate, predicted that the New York Court would hold the "enjoyment of life" element to be distinct from pain and suffering. But when the issue finally arrived before the Court of Appeals, which it did in McDougald v. Garber,[11] the court went the other way, holding the element to be just another one to be factored in under "suffering."

These dispositions apparently cooled the enthusiasm with which the Second Circuit originally greeted the certification procedure. Hence, certifications slowed down for a while after the *McDougald* case, but increased again soon enough.

Certification requests now arrive at the New York Court of Appeals regularly, sometimes involving an issue that is arguably of too little precedential importance to be worth the Court's time. In Carney v. Philippone,[12] for example, the Court accepted a certification involving a narrow issue of a particular municipality's tax law. The issue was likely to arise infrequently and was of interest to only those in that municipality, and to few even there. It was hardly the kind of thing the New York Court of Appeals would have accepted for review from an order of the appellate division, whose decision on the issue would have by itself clarified the matter for the future guidance of the few who might need it. A federal Second Circuit decision in point would likely earn the same respect.

It has been suggested that the same standards that the New York Court of Appeals uses for granting leave to appeal from an appellate division order should be applied as well to the acceptance of a certified question from an outside court.[13] Using that standard would likely keep a case like *Carney* out.

C. REVIEWABILITY

Table of Sections

§ 529.　　　Reviewability in Particular Courts

§ 530.　　　Scope of Review from Final Judgment

---

[10]　See Schoenefeld v. State, 25 N.Y.3d 22, 6 N.Y.S.3d 221, 29 N.E.3d 230 (2015), reversing and remanding, conforming to answer to certified question, 821 F.3d 273 (2d Cir. 2016). The problem is discussed in the lead note in NYSLD No. 346.

[11]　McDougald v. Garber, 73 N.Y.2d 246, 538 N.Y.S.2d 937, 536 N.E.2d 372 (1989).

[12]　Carney v. Philippone, 1 N.Y.3d 333, 774 N.Y.S.2d 106, 806 N.E.2d 131 (2004).

[13]　See 22 N.Y.C.R.R. § 500.22(b)(4) (Court of Appeals Rule requiring that motions for leave to appeal in civil cases state "why the questions presented merit review . . ., such as that the issues are novel or of public importance, present a conflict with prior decisions of this Court, or involve a conflict among the departments of the Appellate Division."). The issue is discussed in the lead note in NYSLD No. 532.

§ 529. Reviewability in Particular Courts

The fact that the losing party can appeal the judgment or order does not guarantee an appellate review of the point that has caused aggrievment. Reviewability and appealability are not the same.

Scope of review is governed by CPLR 5501 and should be considered as posing two questions. The first, which we treat in this section, is, what powers of review does the particular appellate court have? The second, which we turn to in the next section, is, how much of the case is open to review when an order or final judgment is appealed?

The appellate division, being a division of the supreme court, reviews both questions of law and questions of fact,[1] the latter including exercises of discretion. An appellate term has similar review powers,[2] as does a county court when sitting in an appellate capacity.[3]

This pervasive review power allows the appellate court at the first tier of appeal to stand in the place of the nisi prius judge and do whatever that judge should have done.[4] The appellate court must of course respect a jury verdict and is bound by it to the same extent the trial judge is. But to the extent that the supreme court, for example, can set aside a verdict and grant judgment notwithstanding it, or order a new trial on the ground that the verdict is contrary to the weight of the evidence, or order an "additur" or "remittitur" raising or lowering the damages found by the jury, or otherwise affect the verdict, so can the appellate division.[5] In matters like that, however, which depend on a judicial reaction to what amounts to the whole record, the appellate court is not quick to substitute itself for the trial judge, recognizing the latter's advantage in having observed the demeanor of the witnesses and otherwise having enjoyed the vivid perceptions offered at the trial itself. But it has the power to.[6]

On appeals in court-tried cases (bench trials), the trial judge's powers being broader, so are the appellate court's. If the record is adequate, the court on reversing need not send the case back for retrial, or for the trial judge to act, but can render whatever judgment the trial judge should have rendered.[7] Hence, one does not often hear arguments in conjunction with review in the appellate division over whether a given question is one of law or one of fact. In that court it makes little difference.

It makes a great deal of difference, however, in the Court of Appeals because that Court is authorized to review only questions of law. The exception, in which the court can review the facts, is where the appellate division has reversed or modified a judgment and in doing so has found new facts and ordered a final judgment based on them.[8] The

---

[1]   CPLR 5501(c).

[2]   CPLR 5501(d).

[3]   See §§ 1701 and 1702(d) in the Uniform City Ct. Act and Uniform Just. Ct. Act, McKinney's Vol. 29A, Parts 2 and 3. Section 1702(d) is designed to assure that an exercise of discretion will also be reviewable, lest the power to review the facts not be deemed to embrace it, which it does.

[4]   For reviewability purposes, reference hereafter will be to the appellate division, but with the understanding that scope of review in the other first-tier appeal courts—the appellate term and county courts—is essentially the same.

[5]   Thompson v. City of New York, 60 N.Y.2d 948, 471 N.Y.S.2d 50, 459 N.E.2d 159 (1983).

[6]   Northern Westchester Professional Park Associates v. Town of Bedford, 60 N.Y.2d 492, 470 N.Y.S.2d 350, 458 N.E.2d 809 (1983).

[7]   See, e.g., Society of New York Hospital v. Burstein, 22 A.D.2d 768, 253 N.Y.S.2d 753 (1st Dep't 1964).

[8]   CPLR 5501(b).

exception recognizes that it is New York policy to offer one appellate review of the facts, and the Court of Appeals is the only court positioned to conduct that review when the appellate division is the first fact-finder.[9]

In Rocky Point Drive-In, L.P. v. Town of Brookhaven,[10] the Court ruled that "[w]hen the Appellate Division decides that a factual finding is against the weight of the evidence, that is itself a new finding of fact." That circumstance opens the door to permit the Court of Appeals to review the factual record to determine which factual findings "more nearly comport with the weight of the evidence."[11] Rather than simply ascertaining if there was factual support in the record for the appellate division's decision, the *Rocky* Court reviewed the entire factual record and ultimately concluded that "the Appellate Division's findings more nearly comported with the weight of the evidence." The bottom line in *Rocky Point* was that the appellate division order was affirmed based primarily on the Court of Appeals' factual determination rather than its review of a question of law.

For the most part, it is not difficult to distinguish between a question of law and a question of fact. We can at least say that each realm has a host of recognizable occupants. But given the number of issues and questions that arise in the course of litigation, there are always more than enough entries in the gray area in between to manufacture problems and caselaw. The interpretation and construction of documents, for example, such as contracts and trust instruments and the like, while often involving subjective intent (which strikes the senses as touching the facts rather than the law), are treated as law matters and are therefore reviewable by the Court of Appeals.[12]

Whether a given court has power to do a particular thing, or entertain a particular item or request for relief, is clearly a law question and thus within the ken of the Court of Appeals.[13] This, indeed, is how the Court occasionally gets involved with exercises of discretion.

An exercise of discretion on a given matter, which can run the gamut from whether to allow the amendment of a pleading or an extension of time to serve a bill of particulars or take any other of a hundred steps in litigation, to such heavier issues as whether to allow the late service of a complaint or to dismiss an action for want of prosecution, and including an army of other things that proliferate in litigation and which no few pages can hope to list, qualifies as an issue of fact that the Court of Appeals cannot, and will not, review.

"Discretion" may be of several different categories. One, for example, "is the familiar scope of choice in the resolution of questions of fact"; another, the discretion "to grant or

---

[9] See Da Silva v. Musso, 53 N.Y.2d 543, 444 N.Y.S.2d 50, 428 N.E.2d 382 (1981). An exception in the criminal area, in which the Court of Appeals reviews the facts, is where the judgment is of death—N.Y. Const. art. VI, § 3—a penalty that has not yet been extended to civil actions.

[10] Rocky Point Drive-In, L.P. v. Town of Brookhaven, 21 N.Y.3d 729, 737, 977 N.Y.S.2d 719, 723, 999 N.E.2d 1164, 1168 (2013) (NYSLD No. 648).

[11] *Rocky Point*, 21 N.Y.3d at 738, 977 N.Y.S.2d at 723, 999 N.E.2d at 1168; see also Pegasus Aviation I, Inc. v. Varig Logistica S.A., 26 N.Y.3d 543, 552, 26 N.Y.S.3d 218, 223, 46 N.E.3d 601 (2015) ("Where the Appellate Division reaches a factual conclusion different from that reached by the trial court, 'the scope of our review is limited to determining whether the evidence of record . . . more nearly comports with the trial court's findings or with those of the Appellate Division' ").

[12] See, e.g., Gitelson v. Du Pont, 17 N.Y.2d 46, 268 N.Y.S.2d 11, 215 N.E.2d 336 (1966).

[13] Dittmar Explosives, Inc. v. A. E. Ottaviano, Inc., 20 N.Y.2d 498, 285 N.Y.S.2d 55, 231 N.E.2d 756 (1967).

to withhold a remedy prayed for."[14] Whatever the category, the basic rule is the same. As long as what the lower court has done can find solid ground anywhere within the generous outer limits of the extensive range "discretion" occupies, the Court of Appeals will not substitute its discretion for the lower court's even if, had it been the lower court, it would have alighted on a different part of the range.

But when those outer limits are passed—and only the Court of Appeals can be the ultimate judge of where those limits lie—the lower court's doing exceeds its powers and constitutes an "abuse of discretion," which magically transforms an unreviewable question of fact into a reviewable question of law.[15] And if it is alleged that the lower court, in exercising discretion, has failed to take account of any factor entitled to consideration, that also poses a reviewable law question.[16]

The adequacy, inadequacy, or even over-adequacy, of the record in respect of a given finding can convert what seems to be an issue of fact into one of law. It is clear that an appellate division affirmance of a trial court's finding of fact poses no law question and cannot be reviewed by the Court of Appeals,[17] but that of course assumes there is evidence in the record adequate to support the finding. An issue of whether the record contains such supportive evidence—and here again the Court of Appeals will be the ultimate judge—is one of law and can be reviewed by the Court of Appeals.[18] Conversely, a record may point so compellingly to a given fact that a failure to find it can be regarded as an error of law and set the stage for review by the Court of Appeals.[19] It's at the fringes of normalcy, in other words, that the record tips beyond the realm of fact and falls into the category of law: on the one side too deficient to admit the finding and on the other too ample to exclude it.

If there is no specific issue of law in the case, as where the Court of Appeals sees the record as presenting only issues of fact and in its judgment the facts found below are supported by the record, the Court has nothing to do but affirm. The Court has noted that this type of determination, "although appealable, is beyond the scope of our review."[20]

With the diminution in the appeal of right, however, and the concomitant expansion of the appeal by permission, discrepancies between appealability and reviewability inevitably diminish. The court will presumably withhold permission if it sees in a case no significant point of law that warrants review. The narrowing of the channel for the appeal of right[21]—presumably a more likely source of cases that have a way to get up, but little to posit for review once they get there[22]—has already cut off much of the traffic.

---

[14]   Patron v. Patron, 40 N.Y.2d 582, 583–4, 388 N.Y.S.2d 890, 891, 357 N.E.2d 361, 362 (1976).

[15]   *Patron*, 40 N.Y.2d at 583–84, 388 N.Y.S.2d at 891, 357 N.E.2d at 362.

[16]   See Irrigation & Indus. Development Corp. v. Indag S. A., 37 N.Y.2d 522, 375 N.Y.S.2d 296, 337 N.E.2d 749 (1975).

[17]   See, e.g., Farr v. Newman, 14 N.Y.2d 183, 250 N.Y.S.2d 272, 199 N.E.2d 369, 4 A.L.R.3d 215 (1964).

[18]   See Joseph E. Seagram & Sons, Inc. v. Tax Commission of City of New York, 14 N.Y.2d 314, 251 N.Y.S.2d 460, 200 N.E.2d 447 (1964).

[19]   See, e.g., Lazarus v. Bowery Sav. Bank, 16 N.Y.2d 793, 262 N.Y.S.2d 717, 209 N.E.2d 889 (1965).

[20]   See, e.g., Vadala v. Carroll, 59 N.Y.2d 751, 463 N.Y.S.2d 432, 450 N.E.2d 238 (1983).

[21]   See § 527.

[22]   The *Vadala* case in note 20, for example, got to the Court of Appeals merely on the basis that the appellate division had reversed the trial court. Under CPLR 5601(a), that was, but is no longer, a basis for an appeal of right. See § 527.

As discussed in section 527, CPLR 5601(a) allows an appeal as of right to the Court of Appeals from an appellate division order containing "a dissent by at least two justices on a question of law in favor of the party taking such appeal." In Reis v. Volvo Cars of North America,[23] the Court observed that "an appeal properly taken under CPLR 5601(a) brings up for review all issues that the appellate division decided adversely to the appellant, even those on which no appellate division justice dissented." This was a critical point of appellate practice in *Reis* because while the Court did not agree with the two-judge dissent's conclusion that the trial court improperly charged the jury on customary business practices, it did rule that the majority at the appellate division erred in concluding that it was proper to charge the jury on special knowledge. Therefore, the Court reversed the judgment and remitted the case for a new trial.

Also shown in earlier sections treating appealability to the Court of Appeals was that an appeal may sometimes be taken there directly from a court of original jurisdiction. One example is where there has been an earlier appeal to the appellate division, whose disposition on that occasion was not final—thus precluding further appeal at that time—because it contemplated further proceedings in the trial court. The judgment resulting upon the later completion of those trial-court proceedings is the one that can be appealed directly to the Court of Appeals.[24] The point we make now is that if this direct appeal route is used, the only matters that the Court of Appeals can review are those encompassed by the prior nonfinal determination of the appellate division, not any new matters raised by the trial court's later judgment.[25] So limited, this simply amounts to a postponed appeal of matters the appellate division has already passed on.

If the appellant would have the new matter reviewed as well, the second appeal must also be taken to the appellate division, with further appeal from everything to abide that court's disposition of the new matter.[26]

§ 530. Scope of Review from Final Judgment

The issue to be reviewed on an appeal from an intermediate order is ordinarily narrow; the order has usually disposed of just one issue and that's the only one to be looked into by the appellate court. But an appeal from the final judgment in the case opens the door wider, and the loser, and for some purposes even the winner, will try to squeeze through it with all manner of grievances and objections touching many parts of the case. Subdivision (a) of CPLR 5501 determines just how much is opened for review upon an appeal from a final judgment, and for this purpose, an order that amounts to the equivalent of a judgment in that it disposes of the whole case will also qualify as a judgment and earn the same scope of review.[1] That it may have been labeled an "order" is not decisive,[2] and this includes as well an order of the appellate division that finally

---

[23] Reis v. Volvo Cars of North America, 24 N.Y.3d 35, 41, 993 N.Y.S.2d 672, 676, 18 N.E.3d 383, 387 (2014); see § 527.

[24] CPLR 5601(d), 5602(a)(1)(ii), (b)(2)(ii).

[25] CPLR 5501(b).

[26] See the discussion of CPLR 5601(d) in § 527.

[1] See Hurd v. Lis, 126 A.D.2d 163, 513 N.Y.S.2d 278 (3d Dep't 1987).

[2] See State v. Wolowitz, 96 A.D.2d 47, 468 N.Y.S.2d 131 (2d Dep't 1983).

determines the action and contemplates nothing more than the ministerial entry of a judgment on it.[3]

Subdivision (a) of CPLR 5501 provides that an appeal from a final judgment brings up for review:

1. any nonfinal judgment or order which necessarily affects the final judgment, including any which was adverse to the respondent on the appeal from the final judgment and which, if reversed, would entitle the respondent to prevail in whole or in part on that appeal, provided that such nonfinal judgment or order has not previously been reviewed by the court to which the appeal is taken;

2. any order denying a new trial or hearing which has not previously been reviewed by the court to which the appeal is taken;

3. any ruling to which the appellant objected or had no opportunity to object or which was a refusal or failure to act as requested by the appellant, and any charge to the jury, or failure or refusal to charge as requested by the appellant, to which he objected;

4. any remark made by the judge to which the appellant objected; and

5. a verdict after a trial by jury as of right, when the final judgment was entered in a different amount pursuant to the respondent's stipulation on a motion to set aside the verdict as excessive or inadequate; the appellate court may increase such judgment to a sum not exceeding the verdict or reduce it to a sum not less than the verdict.

Number 1 on the list raises a number of points. It introduces the sometimes difficult and pesky inquiry of whether an intermediate order or interlocutory judgment "necessarily affects" the final judgment. One test, not perfect but seemingly helpful, is to ask this question: assuming that the nonfinal order or judgment is erroneous, would its reversal overturn the judgment? If it would, it's a reviewable item; if it would not, and the judgment can stand despite it, it is not reviewable.

The above test was rejected as too narrow by the Court of Appeals in Siegmund Strauss, Inc. v. East 149th Realty Corp.,[4] where it applied a far more generous standard. In *Siegmund Strauss*, plaintiff commenced an action seeking a declaration that it was entitled to sole possession of property it leased to operate its wholesale business. The defendants counterclaimed against plaintiff and commenced a third-party action against plaintiff's principals asserting various tort claims. Plaintiff and its principals moved to dismiss the counterclaims and third-party action for failure to state a cause of action and the supreme court granted the motion. Defendants did not appeal this interlocutory order.

After the filing of the note of issue, defendants moved for leave to amend their answer, counterclaims, and cross-claims, and to file a third-party complaint to assert various claims, this time grounded in breach of contract. The supreme court denied the

---

[3]   See De Long Corp. v. Morrison-Knudsen Co., 14 N.Y.2d 346, 251 N.Y.S.2d 657, 200 N.E.2d 557 (1964).

[4]   Siegmund Strauss, Inc. v. East 149th Realty Corp., 20 N.Y.3d 37, 956 N.Y.S.2d 435, 980 N.E.2d 483 (2012).

motion as untimely. The defendants appealed this second interlocutory order to the appellate division, but did not perfect the appeal.

After a bench trial, the court declared plaintiff to be the lawful tenant of the premises and a final judgment was entered. The defendants appealed from the final judgment and also sought review of the two prior interlocutory orders. The First Department affirmed the judgment and held that the appeal from the judgment did not bring up for review the prior interlocutory orders under CPLR 5501(a)(1). Applying the test recited above, the court concluded that these orders did not "necessarily affect" the final judgment because, if they were reversed, the judgment declaring plaintiff to be entitled to possession of the leased premises would not be disturbed. In sum, while reversal of the interlocutory orders would have permitted the claims against plaintiff and its principals to go forward, it would not have affected the judgment awarding plaintiff possession of the real property.

The Court of Appeals reversed. It concluded that to meet CPLR 5501(a)(1)'s "necessarily affects" standard, defendants were not required to show that reinstatement of their counterclaims and third-party action would completely overturn the judgment declaring plaintiff to be entitled to possession of the premises. Rather, it was sufficient to demonstrate that supreme court's dismissal of the counterclaims and third-party action "necessarily removed that legal issue from the case (i.e., there was no further opportunity during the litigation to raise the question decided by the prior non-final order) . . . ."[5]

Under this broad standard, the Court concluded that the appellate division erred in holding that defendants' appeal from the final judgment did not bring up for review the interlocutory order granting dismissal of the counterclaims and third-party action under CPLR 3211(a)(7). That order necessarily removed the legal issue of whether defendants had properly stated a cause of action from the case, and there was no further opportunity during the litigation to raise the issue. The Court remitted the action to the First Department for review of supreme court's first interlocutory order in conjunction with the appeal of the final judgment.

Defendants' persistent efforts reaped rewards. On remand, the First Department reinstated the counterclaims and third-party action.[6]

The Court returned to the subject once again, less than six months later, in Oakes v. Patel,[7] where one of several defendants in a medical malpractice action moved to amend its answer to assert a defense of release. The motion, which was made between the first and second trials in the matter, was denied. Defendants sought to review that order on the appeal from the final judgment in the second trial pursuant to CPLR 5501(a)(1), contending that it "necessarily affect[ed] the final judgment."

The Court confessed that its decisions interpreting CPLR 5501(a)(1) "may not all be consistent" and acknowledged that "application of the 'necessarily affects' rule to orders granting or denying motions to amend pleadings has been particularly vexing."[8] After

---

[5]   *Siegmund Strauss*, 20 N.Y.3d at 43, 956 N.Y.S.2d at 439, 980 N.E.2d at 487.

[6]   Siegmund Strauss, Inc. v. East 149th Realty Corp., 104 A.D.3d 401, 960 N.Y.S.2d 404 (1st Dep't 2013) (NYSLD No. 637, p. 4).

[7]   Oakes v. Patel, 20 N.Y.3d 633, 965 N.Y.S.2d 752, 988 N.E.2d 488 (2013) (NYSLD No. 640). Appellate issues presented by additur and remittitur are also discussed in the *Oakes* decision. See § 407.

[8]   *Oakes*, 20 N.Y.3d at 644, 965 N.Y.S.2d at 757, 988 N.E.2d at 493.

reviewing some of its conflicting decisions in this area, the Court ultimately concluded that it could no longer "adhere to the rule that the grant or denial of a motion to amend is always unreviewable on appeal from a final judgment."[9] Therefore, it overruled some of its prior decisions holding to the contrary.

The Court held that "[t]here will be times, of which this is one" when an order granting or denying a motion to amend " 'necessarily affects' the final judgment under any common sense understanding of those words."[10] In *Oakes*, defendant's motion to amend its answer to add the defense of release, "if granted, would have added a new defense to the case—one that defendants argue, with at least colorable justification, would have significantly changed the case's result." As in *Siegmund Strauss*, the Court once again set forth a generous interpretation of CPLR 5501(a)(1), holding that "when an order granting or denying a motion to amend relates to a proposed new pleading that contains a new cause of action or defense—the order necessarily affects the final judgment."[11] The Court then reviewed the order, but concluded that the denial of the motion to amend was within the sound discretion of the trial court.[12]

Some examples from prior caselaw demonstrate CPLR 5501(a)(1)'s limitations and probably remain good law even under the broad standards for review in *Siegmund Strauss* and *Oakes*. An order directing temporary alimony may not be reviewed as part of a later final judgment in a matrimonial action because its reversal would not undermine the judgment's foundation: the ingredients of the order, however similar they may be on some matters to the ingredients of the final judgment, are wholly independent of it.[13] Equally independent, whatever its individual importance, is an order granting or denying a preliminary injunction, so that an appeal from a later final judgment will not bring it up for review: whether the final judgment—including such permanent injunctive relief as it may contain—is supported by the record does not turn one way or the other on whether a case was made out for a temporary injunction earlier.[14]

While the liberal standards for review of interlocutory orders outlined in *Siegmund Strauss* and *Oakes* are helpful, there is, in fact, no airtight way to determine whether an order "necessarily affects" the final judgment so as to assure review. Some cases have held, for example, that an order denying a pretrial deposition[15] or a bill of particulars[16] does not necessarily affect the final judgment and, strictly speaking, this is so. There is no assurance that, if the deposition or bill had been allowed, the judgment would "necessarily" have gone the other way or even been affected.

Yet it is clear that CPLR 5501(a)(1) does not invariably require such a showing. In Matter of Aho,[17] for example, the Court of Appeals held that an order denying a change of venue does affect the final judgment and may be reviewed as part of its appeal, and yet there is no guarantee there, either, that had the venue been changed the judgment

---

⁹   *Oakes*, 20 N.Y.3d at 644, 965 N.Y.S.2d at 757–58, 988 N.E.2d at 493.

¹⁰   *Oakes*, 20 N.Y.3d at 644, 965 N.Y.S.2d at 758, 988 N.E.2d at 493.

¹¹   *Oakes*, 20 N.Y.3d at 644–45, 965 N.Y.S.2d at 758, 988 N.E.2d at 493.

¹²   See § 237.

¹³   See, e.g., Caplin v. Caplin, 33 A.D.2d 908, 307 N.Y.S.2d 486 (2d Dep't 1970).

¹⁴   Cinerama, Inc. v. Equitable Life Assur. Soc. of U.S., 38 A.D.2d 698, 328 N.Y.S.2d 160 (1st Dep't 1972).

¹⁵   See Dulber v. Dulber, 37 A.D.2d 566, 322 N.Y.S.2d 862 (2d Dep't 1971), aff'd, 29 N.Y.2d 408, 328 N.Y.S.2d 641, 278 N.E.2d 886 (1972).

¹⁶   See Collins v. McWilliams, 185 A.D. 712, 173 N.Y.S. 850 (1st Dep't 1919).

¹⁷   In Matter of Aho, 39 N.Y.2d 241, 383 N.Y.S.2d 285, 347 N.E.2d 647 (1976).

would "necessarily" have differed. The intangibles that distinguish one county from another, however, whether measurable or not, are formidable, and a trial lawyer would corroborate that if the venue order does not "necessarily" affect the judgment, it comes close enough to justify review within the intendment of CPLR 5501. But then, trial lawyers may be heard to plead the same thing for the order denying them a deposition or doing anything else that affects preparation for the courtroom.

The more generous approach manifest in the *Aho* case can be justified, not because it expands review upon appeal from a final judgment, but because it may have the salutary effect—by assuring later review of borderline "necessarily affects" interlocutory orders—of sparing separate and immediate appeals from them. With the broad appealability New York allows of interlocutory orders, that may be a worthwhile saving. Under a less generous reviewability standard, a lawyer bent on getting the order reviewed would be obliged to appeal it independently.

Some orders by their very nature "necessarily" affect the judgment and are assured review as part of an appeal from a final judgment. Included here are those which, had they gone the other way, would have dismissed the case at the threshold and thereby blocked the judgment altogether. A prime example is the order denying a motion to dismiss the complaint for failure to state a cause of action[18] since a judgment for the plaintiff would not have come on had the action earlier been dismissed.

Failure to state a cause of action is today only one of many grounds for dismissal offered by CPLR 3211(a), and if a denial of a dismissal on the one ground "necessarily" affects" the judgment, so should a denial on any of the other 3211(a) grounds. Thus, an order denying a motion to dismiss based on lack of personal jurisdiction[19]—the ubiquitous vehicle for testing, among other things, whether there is longarm jurisdiction under CPLR 302 or proper service under CPLR 308—necessarily affects the judgment and is preserved for review. Indeed, dismissals denied under provisions other than CPLR 3211 should also qualify for review, such as an order denying a dismissal for failure to serve a complaint under CPLR 3012, for failure to make disclosure under CPLR 3126, or for want of prosecution under CPLR 3216.

The probable reason why one does not run into this point more often is the free availability of the interlocutory appeal—the separate and immediate appeal from a nonfinal order—under CPLR 5701(a)(2).[20] That route is apparently preferred by New York practitioners, for objectionable nonfinal orders in general and for those affecting jurisdiction in particular. Why should a defendant burden itself, the assumption goes, with defending on the merits by postponing review of an order sustaining jurisdiction if the order can, as it can in New York, be appealed immediately?

A suggestion emerging from all that has been said, if we press for one, is that if there is any doubt at all about whether an appeal from a final judgment would preserve a given kind of order for review, and the order is one the loser definitely wants reviewed, she should opt for the immediate appeal route and spare herself the guesswork.

If the loser does that, however, and the appeal of the interlocutory order is still pending undetermined when later final judgment is entered, the earlier appeal will be

---

[18] Schamber Chemical Co. v. Ross & Kominsky Plumbing & Heating Co., 259 A.D. 784, 18 N.Y.S.2d 368 (4th Dep't 1940).

[19] CPLR 3211(a)(8).

[20] See § 526.

dismissed: under *Matter of Aho*, the entry of final judgment precludes the continuance of an appeal from a nonfinal order.[21] But if the order does qualify as one that "necessarily affects" the final judgment, it will get its review as part of the now appealed final judgment notwithstanding the dismissal of the earlier interlocutory appeal.[22]

This aspect of *Matter of Aho* can result in calamitous consequences. For example, in Smith v. Town of Colonie,[23] plaintiff did not file a notice of appeal from the final judgment, but appealed only from a nonfinal order partially granting defendant's motion for summary judgment and limiting plaintiff's failure to warn claim. The court dismissed the appeal, noting that plaintiff's right to appeal from the nonfinal order terminated upon the entry of the final judgment after trial. While the interlocutory order necessarily affected the final judgment and would have been reviewable on appeal from the final judgment under *Siegmund Strauss* "inasmuch as it removed legal issues from the case," the failure to appeal from the final judgment prevented the court from reviewing it.

A party who has won the final judgment will not ordinarily appeal it,[24] but if the loser does, the winner may want review of other things that occurred during the action. The winner would be the respondent on the appeal, but some of these other things may have gone against him and one of them, if reversed in his favor, might itself support the judgment even if the court were otherwise disposed to uphold the appellant's position and overturn it. Any nonfinal order with this judgment-supporting potential may, at the respondent's behest, be reviewed on the appeal, which is what CPLR 5501(a)(1) means to allow by sweeping under scope of review such orders as were "adverse to the respondent."

Take this example. D makes a pretrial motion under CPLR 3211(a)(5) to dismiss P's money claim on the ground of release. The court finds the release invalid and denies the motion. No immediate appeal is taken. The case goes to trial and the jury brings in a verdict for D, on which judgment is rendered. P appeals the judgment, alleging various errors in evidentiary rulings. D, the respondent, is entitled to have the appellate court review the pretrial order that held the release invalid. If the release is good, it would uphold the final judgment—"entitle the respondent [D] to prevail"—even though P, having established that there was prejudicial error in rulings at the trial, might otherwise be entitled to a reversal. It just establishes that the appellant's day in the appellate court may be made the respondent's, too.

It must be stressed that only a prior "nonfinal" order can get reviewed as part of the appeal from the final judgment. If the prior order qualifies as "final" in its own right, it does not fall under CPLR 5501(a)(1) and is not preserved for later review,[25] which is a warning to the aggrieved person who wants such an order reviewed to take an appeal from it forthwith.

---

[21]   See *Matter of Aho*, 39 N.Y.2d at 248, 383 N.Y.S.2d at 289, 347 N.E.2d at 651.

[22]   Austrian Lance & Stewart, P. C. v. Jackson, 50 A.D.2d 735, 375 N.Y.S.2d 868 (1st Dep't 1975).

[23]   Smith v. Town of Colonie, 100 A.D.3d 1132, 952 N.Y.S.2d 923 (3d Dep't 2012).

[24]   A winner may occasionally be accorded "aggrieved" status sufficient to appeal a judgment in his own favor, as where one of the important grounds on which he relied, and which may carry future consequences, was decided against him (other grounds having been present to support the judgment). See § 525.

[25]   Crystal v. Manes, 130 A.D.2d 979, 516 N.Y.S.2d 823 (4th Dep't 1987). P's complaint in *Crystal* had five claims. An order dismissed four of them in 1986, which P did not appeal. The fifth and last claim was dismissed in 1987. P did appeal that dismissal and as part of it wanted the 1986 order reviewed. The review was held unavailable; the prior order was final as to the four claims it dismissed. See § 527.

Finally, on paragraph 1 of CPLR 5501(a)—all said so far is the discharge of that one provision—is the assurance the CPLR offers that orders reviewable under it need not be specified in the notice of appeal, as was once required.[26] These "necessarily affects" orders are automatically reviewable as long as the final judgment has been properly appealed.

There is no coordinate provision expanding the scope of review of a mere order—unless it qualifies on the facts of a particular case as the equivalent of a final judgment,[27] not a common occurrence. The ordinary intermediate (nonfinal) order is narrower than a judgment, usually disposing of just one issue, and an appeal from that order will review just that one issue. But should there be several matters disposed of in the order, with review sought of all of them, it is best to follow the practice followed with judgments and appeal "from each and every part" of the order. It has been held that "[a]n appeal from only part of an order constitutes a waiver of the right to appeal from the other parts of that order."[28]

If a given order disposes of several things, therefore, the appellant should be careful not to phrase the notice of appeal too narrowly. If all the issues disposed of aggrieve the appellant, the appellant should see to it that the notice of appeal covers them all. Picking and choosing can be perilous, as it proved to be in City of Mount Vernon v. Mount Vernon Housing Authority.[29]

The order in that case had granted D's cross-motion to dismiss P's complaint, while also denying P's motion for leave to amend the complaint. P appealed from "that part of the order" that denied the motion to amend the complaint, but not from the part that granted the dismissal. When P later asked the appellate division for leave to amend the notice of appeal to assert that it was also an appeal from the dismissal part, the court denied the motion, holding that the failure to appeal the dismissal part was a defect that deprived the appellate division of jurisdiction to review it.

Paragraphs 3 and 4 of CPLR 5501(a) are the passageways through which come up for review any alleged errors made by the trial court in any of its myriad rulings, made on points of evidence or otherwise, and any prejudicial remarks the judge may have made. A proviso here is that the record manifest that the appellant duly made known his objection to the ruling or remark if there was opportunity to do so, whether by using the word "objection" or "exception" or any other language. The key is that the grievance was made known to the judge; the words used to convey it are secondary.

There is a broad and general rule of preservation that the court will not review on appeal any points not raised in the court below, a wholesome requirement designed to avoid waste.[30] Its principal rationale is that if the matter had been duly raised below, it might have prevailed there and the grievance been avoided. The rule is not absolute, however, and the appellate division, exercising its broad discretion to grant a new trial in the interests of justice, may be influenced by something not technically presented and preserved below. There is even indication that the Court of Appeals may sometimes

---

[26]   See Civ. Prac. Act § 580 (repealed 1963).

[27]   See the *Hurd* and *Wolowitz* cases in notes 1 and 2, and the text at those points.

[28]   Royal v. Brooklyn Union Gas Co., 122 A.D.2d 132, 504 N.Y.S.2d 519 (2d Dep't 1986).

[29]   City of Mount Vernon v. Mount Vernon Housing Authority, 235 A.D.2d 516, 652 N.Y.S.2d 771 (2d Dep't 1997).

[30]   See Kolmer-Marcus, Inc. v. Winer, 32 A.D.2d 763, 300 N.Y.S.2d 952 (1st Dep't 1969), aff'd, 26 N.Y.2d 795, 309 N.Y.S.2d 220, 257 N.E.2d 664 (1970).

consider something of that nature if special circumstances exist. The Court has also confirmed that it may entertain matter raised in the trial court, but skipped at appellate division level, although it is rare for it to do so and there is usually good reason when it does.[31]

An exception to the rule that the appellate court will not consider matters outside the record exists when the particular matter involves something undeniable, or which in any event would not generate factual issues needing trial-level resolution. An issue of the existence and content of the rules of a certain entity are an example of this.[32] This is analogous to the doctrine of judicial notice if it is not the doctrine itself. But no lawyer should assume that unpreserved matters have a decent chance of creeping up for appellate review. It is better to leave this subject with the warning that dependence on appellate willingness to entertain something outside the record, which it was both appropriate and feasible to put into the record, is unwise.

Paragraph 5 of CPLR 5501(a) assures review of the amount of the verdict in instances in which, through the use of the additur or remittitur devices,[33] the judgment ends up in a different sum. So, for example, if the verdict is for $100,000, and the court on D's motion orders a new trial unless P stipulates to take $40,000 instead (remittitur), which P accepts, D's appeal from the judgment enables P, without bothering to cross-appeal, to bring up for review the propriety of the reduction and permits the appellate court to restore any part of the sum remitted.

D. TAKING THE APPEAL

Table of Sections

§ 531.   Taking an Appeal; How
§ 532.   Subsequent Orders
§ 533.   Time to Appeal or Move for Leave
§ 534.   Omissions, Defects, and Time Extensions
§ 535.   Injunctions and Stays

§ 531. Taking an Appeal; How

A distinction must be made between "taking" an appeal and what the bar loosely refers to as "perfecting" it. The perfection steps are the involved and expensive ones, consisting of securing the transcript, drawing the record, writing the briefs, getting the whole business printed or otherwise reproduced, serving and filing everything in the required number of copies, getting onto the appellate court's calendar, and, finally, arguing or submitting the appeal. The "taking" of the appeal, in contrast, although it confronts a rigid time limitation, is probably the easiest step in civil practice. It's just the service and filing of a paper, or at worst several papers.

CPLR 5515(1) provides that an appeal is taken "by serving on the adverse party a notice of appeal and filing it in the office where the judgment or order of the court of original instance is entered . . . ." Although the statute says "the adverse party," it is best

---

[31]   See Telaro v. Telaro, 25 N.Y.2d 433, 306 N.Y.S.2d 920, 255 N.E.2d 158 (1969).

[32]   See, e.g., Crawford v. Merrill Lynch, Pierce, Fenner & Smith, Inc., 35 N.Y.2d 291, 361 N.Y.S.2d 140, 319 N.E.2d 408 (1974).

[33]   For discussion of these devices, see § 407.

to serve a copy on each of the other parties to the action, whether adverse or not and whether they are deemed affected by the appeal or not. (Let them judge that for themselves, as agrievement is in the eye of the beholder.) Note that the copy to be filed is filed with the clerk of the court of original instance, not with the clerk of the appellate court. This is so even when the appeal is being taken from an intermediate appellate court to a higher one. The court to which the appeal is taken gets notice of it through other means, which we will return to later.

If the action is governed by e-filing, legislation passed in 2015 provides that the filing and service of a notice of appeal under CPLR 5515(1) is subject to the e-filing rules.[1] That means that any notice of appeal in an e-filed action must be electronically filed and served.[2] The new legislation will also have an impact on the time to serve and file the notice of appeal under CPLR 5513(a).[3]

The notice of appeal contains the caption of the action and specifies the party who is appealing, the judgment or order or part of it being appealed, and the court to which the appeal is being taken.[4] Its contents are standard and straightforward. The whole body of an ordinary notice of appeal from a final judgment can read:

> Please take notice that the defendant Jones hereby appeals to the Appellate Division of the Third Department from a judgment of this court [the court having been specified in the caption] in favor of plaintiff Smith for $35,000, entered with the clerk on June 1, 2010, and from every part thereof.

The appeal, since it is in this case from a final judgment, will bring up for review all of the nonfinal dispositions specified in CPLR 5501(a), discussed earlier,[5] and will do so automatically, i.e., without their being specified in the notice of appeal.[6]

The notice of appeal need not be served by personal delivery or by any other service-of-summons prescription. Like any other intra-action paper, it is served pursuant to CPLR 2103. This means that it is served on the other party's attorney and that it may be served by ordinary mail provided the action is not governed by e-filing.[7] Some attorneys prefer registered or certified mail, which is not required. Dispute over whether service was made is rare, but the precaution of registration or certification can ordinarily do no harm. The filing with the clerk can also be effected by a mere mailing.

The appeal is "taken" when the duly addressed and stamped envelopes containing the notices of appeal are dropped into the mailbox.[8]

The foregoing is the procedure when the appeal is being taken as of right. When leave is required, no formal notice of appeal is used. The would-be appellant merely makes the motion for leave to appeal, doing so within the time a notice of appeal would

---

[1] CPLR 2111(c).

[2] See § 202.

[3] See § 533.

[4] CPLR 5515(1).

[5] See § 530.

[6] The record must contain the relevant supporting papers, of course, and the briefs must direct attention to any nonfinal disposition of which review is sought. See Austrian Lance & Stewart, P. C. v. Jackson, 50 A.D.2d 735, 375 N.Y.S.2d 868 (1st Dep't 1975).

[7] See CPLR 2111(c). The time requirements for doing these things in appellate practice are treated in § 533.

[8] CPLR 2103(b)(2).

have to be served in an of-right case. If the motion is granted, the entry of the order granting the motion is deemed the taking of the appeal.[9]

When the appeal is being taken to the Court of Appeals, a statute requires that the clerk of the original court, with whom the notice of appeal is filed, forthwith send a copy of it to the clerk of the Court of Appeals.[10] When appeal to that Court is being allowed by leave of the appellate division, the latter's clerk sends to the clerk of the Court of Appeals a copy of the order granting permission.[11] By those means the Court of Appeals is promptly apprised of the appeal and can track its business more closely. These requirements are not imposed by statute when the appeal is to the appellate division, but the latter's rules may have similar exactions.[12]

An additional requirement the practitioner should note when the appeal is to the Court of Appeals is that within 10 days after the service of the notice of appeal (or entry of an order granting leave), the appellant must file a "Preliminary Appeal Statement" with the clerk, accompanied by several other papers.[13] This facilitates the court's review of its jurisdiction in the case. Court of Appeals jurisdiction is narrow, and the court often reviews its jurisdiction without waiting for a request by a party.[14]

§ 532. Subsequent Orders

When an order is being appealed, what effect shall be given to a later motion to reargue or renew the motion that gave rise to the order, or to a motion to resettle it? This has been a matter troublesome enough to earn some special statutory attention. It also takes us back to the discussion of some of the follow-up motions in the chapter on Motion Practice.[1]

The prime lesson to the would-be appellant aggrieved by the original order is to appeal it—the *original* order. If the subsequent motion, whether made by the appellant or by any other party, is made so promptly that the time to appeal the original order is still open, it must still be remembered that the judge is likely to take some time before deciding the new motion. The appellant should not await the outcome of the new motion before taking an appeal from the original order. If the appellant intended to appeal the original, but waited to see what would happen with the later application, he may find that he has forfeited the appeal altogether.

CPLR 5517(a) lists several subsequent activities that it specifically says shall not affect the appeal from the original order, thus assuring that the appeal will not be mooted or otherwise cancelled by these later doings. For purposes of discussion, it is useful to treat items not on the list as well as the listed ones, to assume that a timely appeal has been taken from the original order, and to ask what, if any, effect the later activity will have on the original order.

---

[9]   CPLR 5515(1).

[10]   CPLR 5515(2).

[11]   CPLR 5515(3).

[12]   See, e.g., 22 N.Y.C.R.R. §§ 600.17 and 670.2(e), the respective rules of the First and Second departments. Absent such a rule, the first notice the appellate court gets of the case may be later on, when the record is filed, or perhaps when a motion is made. Compare the more uniform method statutorily provided in criminal cases. See Crim. Proc. Law 460.10(1)(e).

[13]   See 22 N.Y.C.R.R. § 500.9, part of the Court of Appeals rules.

[14]   See 22 N.Y.C.R.R. § 500.10.

[1]   See § 254.

First, a motion to reargue. If the motion is denied, it has no effect at all on the appeal. And the order denying a motion to reargue is not itself appealable, so the appellant had better have taken an appeal from the original order. If the motion to reargue has been duly and timely made by the appellant, and has been granted, and the appellant has obtained in that grant just what he would have wanted from the appeal, he naturally has no further cause to prosecute the appeal. He can discontinue it or withdraw it.[2] If the motion to reargue has been granted but has essentially adhered to the original determination, it has no effect on a pending appeal from the original,[3] which goes right on through.

Next, a motion to resettle the original order. A denial of that motion has no effect on the appeal. Since as a rule an order denying a motion to resettle may not be appealed,[4] it is again important to have appealed the original order. The granting of a motion to resettle has no effect on the original appeal,[5] but here we must again look at what the resettlement order does. If it makes so substantial a change in the order—this is not likely, but it is possible—that it has dissolved the appellant's grievance, it is once again a situation in which the appellant may wish to withdraw the appeal.[6]

It is especially perilous for an appellant to refrain from taking an appeal from the original order on the assumption that the original is defective in some way and that the defect bars its appeal. The appellant may think that the order must first be resettled before being appealable. There would be no harm, however, in taking an appeal from the original order as a precaution: a resettlement motion can be made while the appeal from the original order is pending, and it would be chancy indeed to wait and appeal only from the order on the resettlement motion. This is true even if the order is resettled in exactly the way the appellant wishes.

One of the requirements applicable to an order, for example, is that it "recite the papers used on the motion."[7] It has been held, however, that the failure of the order to recite the papers does not bar an appeal from it and that an appellant who does not appeal the order on time, waiting instead for the outcome of a motion to resettle the order (so as to include a recitation of the papers) and appealing only the resettled order instead, forfeits the appeal altogether.[8] If the matter on which resettlement is granted, in other words, would not have affected the appealability of the original order and the respect in which it aggrieved the appellant, the prospect of appeal is gone. The resettled matter in the new order would pose nothing the appellant needs reviewed—it is not, after all, the order's failure to recite the papers that the appellant was seeking to get reviewed—and the appellant who guesses that the time in which to appeal the original order is automatically extended by the granting of a resettled one is guessing wrong.

---

[2]   The other side, of course, now aggrieved by the change made by the order granting the motion to reargue, can take an appeal from it. An order granting reargument, in contrast with one denying it, is appealable. See § 254.

[3]   CPLR 5517(a)(1).

[4]   See In re Reed, 230 A.D. 764, 244 N.Y.S. 217 (2d Dep't 1930).

[5]   CPLR 5517(a)(2).

[6]   In this situation again, as with the substantial change made by the grant of a motion to reargue illustrated at note 2, above, the very fact that the change divests the appellant of her grievance should aggrieve the adverse party and permit that party, if so disposed, to appeal the order granting resettlement.

[7]   CPLR 2219(a).

[8]   Singer v. Board of Educ. of City of New York, 97 A.D.2d 507, 468 N.Y.S.2d 25 (2d Dep't 1983).

Then there is the motion to renew. In contrast with the motion to reargue, the motion to renew is based on new or additional proof. A denial of the motion to renew does not have an effect on the appeal,[9] but by implication an order granting the motion does. This contemplates that the grant will affect the original order in some substantial way, perhaps even abating the original appeal. It would be a happy abatement for the appellant if the order granting the renewal motion actually gives the appellant what he wants. An order either granting or denying a motion to renew is appealable, however, so that whatever the disposition of the motion is, if it does not give the appellant everything and he still retains a grievance worth appealing, he should take an appeal from the order disposing of the renewal motion.

Prior to the 1999 amendment of CPLR 2221, the rule had been that the jurisdiction of a trial-level judge to entertain a motion to reargue is not cut off by the fact that an appeal from the original order has been taken; that it would only be the submission of the appeal that would cut off the lower court's jurisdiction.[10] Some courts have held that the new law does not allow the motion to reargue at any time during an appeal's pendency; that it must be made within 30 days after the service of notice of entry of the original order.[11]

The better view is that the pendency of the appeal is a period during which—as under prior law—a motion to reargue may be made to the lower court notwithstanding that the 30-day period has expired.[12]

Several of the orders discussed above are themselves appealable, whether they affect the original appeal or not. In addition to orders granting or denying renewal motions, an order granting (as opposed to denying) reargument is appealable; even an order granting resettlement is if it makes a substantial change,[13] unlike the example above in which the only change made was the insertion into the order of a list of the papers on which it was based. To secure review of any of these, the appellant who has duly appealed the original order need not take a separate appeal. CPLR 5517(b) provides that the appellate court, on the main appeal, may also review any of the subsequent orders we have been discussing.[14] The appellant need only include in the record a copy of the subsequent order and the papers it is based on and speak to it in his brief.

The independent appealability of some of these subsequent orders would seem to be relevant, then, only for one who has not appealed the original order.

While CPLR 5517 is helpful, it is still not a source of total security for the careful lawyer. The latter's course, when she is bent on appeal and wants to keep all loose ends tucked in, is to appeal everything in sight: the original order as well as any subsequent one having bearing on the original and not clearly unappealable by itself (such as an

---

[9] CPLR 5517(a)(3).

[10] William H. Van Vleck, Inc. v. Klein, 50 Misc. 2d 622, 271 N.Y.S.2d 64 (Sup. Ct., Kings County 1966). See § 254.

[11] See, e.g., Kern v. City of Rochester, 3 Misc. 3d 948, 775 N.Y.S.2d 505 (Sup. Ct., Monroe County 2004). The amendment did not intend this result; its aim was merely to codify prior caselaw. See the discussion in SPR 151:2–3.

[12] See, e.g., Itzkowitz v. King Kullen Grocery Co., Inc., 22 A.D.3d 636, 804 N.Y.S.2d 350 (2d Dep't 2005), noted in SPR 167:2. The 30-day period that generally limits the time to reargue comes from CPLR 2221(d)(3), but the caselaw rule holding that the pendency of an appeal from the same order continues to be an alternative period for the motion to reargue should still be applicable.

[13] Kaehler v. Phoenix Ins. Co., 38 A.D.2d 683, 327 N.Y.S.2d 254 (4th Dep't 1971).

[14] See, e.g., Rever v. Nelson, 23 A.D.2d 505, 256 N.Y.S.2d 368 (2d Dep't 1965).

order denying reargument). This does not mean multiple records and great additional expense; it merely means the service and filing of an additional notice of appeal from each of the later orders, the inclusion in the record—a single record serves for all—of copies of the later orders, their underlying papers, and the notices of appeal from them, and, of course, whatever attention the party wants to give the later doings in his brief. If any one of the appealed orders proves unappealable, the appellate court will dismiss the appeal from that one. But that's no problem. As long as any of the items appealed is the properly appealable order, the whole appeal will proceed through its good offices. One sees from time to time an appellate decision reviewing everything through the one order that it has found appealable, while dismissing appeals taken from the others as "superfluous."[15] The appellate court, after all, has the final say on what the appealable paper is.

Although CPLR 5517 directs itself only to an appeal from an order, its lessons can by analogy be applied to an appeal from a judgment, especially the lesson of the last paragraph. A judgment, too, is subject to subsequent motions. If not a motion to reargue or renew, then in any event to a motion to resettle or modify or the like. If one who would appeal the judgment is aggrieved as well by a later resettlement order and has any doubt as to whether an appeal from the one preserves review of the other, he does well to appeal both.

Of course, a party who is aggrieved only by the subsequent order, and not by the original—such as the winner on the original motion who has been deprived of his victory by an order granting reargument or renewal and overturning the original (as several times already noted) should appeal only the subsequent order.

An analogous situation in which a would-be appellant can become confused about which paper to appeal from involves the granting of a motion to dismiss or for summary judgment. The winner may first get an order entered to reflect the disposition, and it of course behooves the loser to appeal from that. But while that appeal is pending, the winner may then get a judgment entered on the order. Cautious appellants used to appeal from the judgment as well, especially after the Court of Appeals decision in *Matter of Aho*,[16] which said that in this situation the mere entry of the judgment terminates the appeal from the order. An amendment of CPLR 5501(c)[17] obviated the second appeal by providing that the notice of appeal from an order dismissing or granting summary judgment

shall be deemed to specify a judgment upon said order entered after service of the notice of appeal and before entry of the order of the appellate court . . . .

Some attorneys may choose to take an appeal from the judgment anyway.[18] In these multipaper situations, the cautious appellate lawyer is prone to appeal everything in sight, and as often as need be.[19]

---

[15]   See, e.g., In re Bingham's Will, 7 N.Y.2d 1, 25, 194 N.Y.S.2d 465, 483, 163 N.E.2d 301, 314 (1959) (clarification in dissenting opinion).

[16]   Matter of Aho, 39 N.Y.2d 241, 383 N.Y.S.2d 285, 347 N.E.2d 647 (1976).

[17]   L.1997, ch. 474.

[18]   See the discussion in SPR 60:3.

[19]   See the discussion of the *Whitfield* case in § 527.

§ 533. Time to Appeal or Move for Leave

An appeal as of right must be taken within 30 days after the appellant has been served with a copy of the objectionable judgment or order, with notice of its entry.[1] Not until that service will the 30 days start to run, and it makes no difference that the appellant knows of the entry from other sources. The point is illustrated in Dobess Realty Corp. v. City of New York,[2] where the city was one of several defendants and had earned a dismissal. The other defendants remained in and went to trial, judgment ultimately going against them. Proper service of the judgment with notice of entry was made on those defendants, starting their appeal time running, but the city never made such service and hence the time for the plaintiffs to appeal the old dismissal order made in favor of the city was still alive, and the plaintiffs took advantage of it.

The court mentioned that the earlier judgment referred to the city's victory in its recital but not decretal paragraph, perhaps suggesting that mention in both paragraphs might have made a difference. It is not a point worth challenging. One in the position of the city in the *Dobess* case should draw, obtain entry of, and serve a copy of its judgment of dismissal with notice of entry, and do it all promptly. Whatever is done should be done thoughtfully and not be allowed to loiter for want of attention. And the rule that imposes a time limit on submitting orders and judgments for entry should be kept firmly in mind.[3]

As a rule, the winning party should serve the judgment or order (with notice of entry) on the loser. Cases appeared, however, in which the service was made by the court or clerk, and that service was held to start the appellant's appeal time running. This created some confusion and an amendment of CPLR 5513 in 1996 overruled those cases and provides that the loser's appeal time won't start until a party does the serving.[4]

A subsisting exception to the rule that the winner's service on the loser starts the appeal time is where the loser himself serves the judgment or order and notice of entry. Either side can get the paper entered and effect service of it on the other side, but it is usually the potential respondent who does so—having won below, the respondent is the one with the incentive to get the appeal time running and (hopefully) out of the way. But the would-be appellant can effect the entry if so disposed, and serve the paper with notice of entry on the respondent. If he does, however, his 30 days to appeal run from that time.[5]

The court can't vary these rules; it cannot, for example, curtail the appellant's appeal time by striking from the order or judgment a requirement that notice of entry be given.[6] Conversely, the court cannot, nor can even the parties by stipulation, extend the time to appeal beyond the statutory allotment.[7] What few extension possibilities exist are discussed in the next section.

---

[1]   CPLR 5513(a).

[2]   Dobess Realty Corp. v. City of New York, 79 A.D.2d 348, 436 N.Y.S.2d 296 (1st Dep't 1981).

[3]   See §§ 250, 418.

[4]   When leave is required, the same rule applies to the time in which to move for leave to appeal. See the discussion in SPR 47:2.

[5]   CPLR 5513(a).

[6]   See In re Martz' Will, 16 N.Y.2d 939, 264 N.Y.S.2d 925, 212 N.E.2d 441 (1965).

[7]   See Ocean Accident & Guarantee Corp., Ltd v. Otis Elevator Co., 291 N.Y. 254, 52 N.E.2d 421 (1943).

If the order or judgment to be appealed is served by mail, five days are added to the 30-day appeal time, making it 35 days.[8] Clearly that's the case when the winner serves the judgment or order. But when the loser does, and makes the service by mail, does the loser also stretch his own appeal time from 30 to 35 days? There was a conflict on the matter, but it was resolved—in the loser's favor—by a 1999 amendment that added a subdivision (d) to CPLR 5513. The amendment explicitly allows even the loser the extra five days. Since only a lawyer of limited gifts would rely on an extension of time devised not for him, the server, but for his adversary, the servee, the amendment is sometimes called the Dumb Lawyer's Rule.

In the world of electronic filing,[9] most documents are never mailed through the postal service. When a paper is filed through the New York State Courts Electronic Filing system ("NYSCEF") in a case in which other attorneys or parties have recorded their consent or their representation, the filing of the document with NYSCEF automatically causes service to occur on the other participating attorneys or parties.[10] The NYSCEF system immediately transmits an e-mail message to all of the attorneys participating in e-filing containing a link to the document, and a party responding to the paper will not be the beneficiary of CPLR 2103(b)(2)'s five day add-on.

Therefore, if a party in an e-filed action files an order or judgment, with notice of entry, it will immediately be served on all other parties to the action.[11] As noted above in section 531, in actions subject to e-filing, the filing and service of a notice of appeal under CPLR 5515(1) is subject to the e-filing rules.[12] That means that any notice of appeal in those actions must be electronically filed and served. In that the order or judgment, with notice of entry, from which appeal is being sought in those actions will almost always be served electronically, the thirty day appeal time in CPLR 5513(a) will not be the recipient of CPLR 2103(b)(2)'s five day add-on.

Before being allowed to start the other side's appeal time, the paper served must include notice of "entry." The Court of Appeals has given this a strict construction, holding in Reynolds v. Dustman[13] that the omission of the word "entry" from the paper served will not start the appeal time. The omission in *Reynolds* resulted in the sustaining of an appeal taken almost half a year after the service of the paper that the server thought would start the 30-day appeal time.[14]

In situations in which an order sometimes precedes a judgment, with the judgment later being entered "on" the order, a failure to timely appeal the order will not necessarily bar an appeal from the judgment. "It has been repeatedly held," for example, "that a party may appeal from a judgment entered based upon an order granting a motion for summary judgment, despite the fact that the time in which to appeal from the underlying

---

[8]   Albany Engineering Corp. v. Hudson River, 110 A.D.3d 1220, 1222 n.1, 973 N.Y.S.2d 391, 393 n.1 (3d Dep't 2013). The source of the additional time is CPLR 2103(b)(2), which provides that whenever a period of time to perform an act is measured from the service of a paper, and the paper is served by mail, the responding party gets five additional days to perform the act. If an order or judgment, with notice of entry, is served via mail outside New York State, an amendment to CPLR 2103(b)(2) will now permit service and filing of the notice of appeal within 36 days. See § 202.

[9]   See § 63A.

[10]   See 22 N.Y.C.R.R. § 202.5–b(f)(2)(ii) ("Service of interlocutory documents in an e-filed action.").

[11]   See 22 N.Y.C.R.R. § 202.5–b(h)(3).

[12]   CPLR 2111(c).

[13]   Reynolds v. Dustman, 1 N.Y.3d 559, 772 N.Y.S.2d 247, 804 N.E.2d 411 (2003).

[14]   See the discussion of *Reynolds* in NYSLD No. 532.

order has elapsed."[15] If the order itself has been appealed, on the other hand, it will also be deemed an appeal from a later judgment entered "on" the order, obviating a separate appeal from the judgment.[16] The cautious practitioner should not refrain from appealing the order on the assumption that he can just appeal the overlaying judgment when it comes in later, at least not when they dispose of the same thing.

For the winner of a dispositive motion like this, a better and more economical practice is to get the order and judgment entered simultaneously—both embodied in one paper if the clerk will accept it—and serve both, or the consolidated one, on the loser with notice of entry.

When an appeal is taken from an appellate court, the appealable paper is the order of the appellate court rather than any judgment or order that the trial court may enter on it on remand. CPLR 5512(a) so provides, but then, in a seemingly generous gesture, it adds that if a "timely" appeal is taken from the wrong paper in such an instance, it can simply be deemed taken from the right paper and the defect ignored. This may be more of a trap than a reassurance, however, because, whichever paper the appeal is formally taken from, the timeliness of the appeal will apparently be measured from the service of notice of entry of the *appellate* order.[17] If that is so, the only mistake that CPLR 5512(a) forgives is an erroneous reference, in the notice of appeal, to the overlaying lower court judgment or order rather than to the appellate order itself—a piddling gift.

The same rules of timeliness apply when the appeal is not as of right but needs permission. The difference is that within the applicable period the aspiring appellant, instead of serving a notice of appeal, must make the motion for leave to appeal, i.e., serve the motion papers that bring on the motion.[18] The mailing of the motion papers within the applicable time satisfies this requirement even though the motion may not be heard or disposed of until after the period expires. When the situation is one in which leave can be sought from two courts (as from the appellate division or, if it refuses leave, from the Court of Appeals),[19] the 30 days in which to move for the second court's permission is computed from the service of the first court's order denying leave with notice of entry, again with the caveat that if the would-be appellant is the one who has done the serving, it is his own service that starts the time running.[20]

The party moving for permission to appeal must make the motion returnable at least 8 days, but not more than 15 days after service of the notice of the motion.[21] He must ascertain what the motion days are in the court to which the motion is being made[22] and should then pick the first motion day available following the 8th day after the notice of motion is served. Failing to serve the supporting papers and brief at least 8 days prior to the return day can result in a dismissal of the motion.[23]

---

[15] Flynn v. City of Long Beach, 108 A.D.2d 840, 485 N.Y.S.2d 565 (2d Dep't 1985).

[16] A 1997 amendment of CPLR 5501(c) so provides. See the discussion at the end of § 532.

[17] See Rodolitz v. Neptune Paper Products, Inc., 22 N.Y.2d 383, 292 N.Y.S.2d 878, 239 N.E.2d 628 (1968).

[18] CPLR 5513(b).

[19] See CPLR 5602(a), 5703(a); see § 528.

[20] CPLR 5513(b).

[21] CPLR 5516.

[22] See § 541.

[23] See Dellaratta v. International House of Pancakes, 46 N.Y.2d 936, 415 N.Y.S.2d 211, 388 N.E.2d 348 (1979).

The judgment or order served on the appellant should be an exact copy of the original in the clerk's file. It has been held that the service of an incorrect copy of the judgment or order to be appealed, "containing . . . a substantial alteration of the original," won't start the appellant's appeal time running.[24] It is probably best as a rule of thumb to serve only a photostatic copy of the original, which will automatically pick up hand-written changes, cross-outs, initials, and everything else.

If any issue of timeliness arises, it is ordinarily raised by a motion to dismiss the appeal and is based on affidavits stating the facts relevant to service.[25] The motion is made to the court to which the appeal is being taken, not to the lower court, since it really has to do with the appellate court's jurisdiction.[26]

It may happen that more than one party will want to appeal or move for leave to appeal. If party X serves a notice of appeal (or motion papers for leave where leave is required) before party Y does, Y need only serve his own notice of appeal (or motion papers for leave) in response. Y may even get a time extension in that situation. Y may use whatever is left of the original 30-day period and will in any event get 10 days from the service of X's notice of appeal or motion papers regardless of where the original 30-day period may now stand. This is known as a cross-appeal.[27] It does not entail two records or sets of briefs; one serves for both and the record contains whatever is needful to either.

To be on the safe side, each party prevailing on an order or judgment should serve its own notice of entry on the loser rather than depending on a coparty's service, unless several parties are united in interest enough to jointly sign the notice of entry. The risk, otherwise, is that the loser's time to appeal may be open indefinitely against a winner who failed to serve a notice of entry even after the period has long since run against another winner who did make such service.[28]

Extensions of time are the subject of the next section.

§ 534. Omissions, Defects, and Time Extensions

Various omissions and defects can appear in conjunction with an appeal, but those appearing at the "taking" as opposed to the "perfection" stage are the ones that make the most trouble. They hold the potential for forfeiture of the appeal and are the ones best to avoid. An attempt is sometimes made to divide defects into those that concern the time element and those that do not, but it's a superficial effort. On deeper analysis, almost all of the serious defects can be shown to involve time because if time were not a barrier, the whole step could be taken over and done right.

CPLR 2004 recognizes that there are numerous time periods in the CPLR for the doing of many things. It allows the court to extend any of them for good cause shown "except where otherwise expressly prescribed by law." The time in which to take an appeal is one of the exceptions, and it's rigid. CPLR 5514(c) precludes any extension of

---

[24]   Masters, Inc. v. White House Discounts, Inc., 119 A.D.2d 639, 500 N.Y.S.2d 790 (2d Dep't 1986).

[25]   See Nancy C. v. John J. O'C., 50 A.D.2d 800, 375 N.Y.S.2d 630 (2d Dep't 1975).

[26]   Runkel v. Homelsky, 137 N.Y.S.2d 870 (Sup. Ct., Kings County 1955).

[27]   See CPLR 5513(c).

[28]   A note on this point, built around Blank v. Schafrann, 206 A.D.2d 771, 615 N.Y.S.2d 107 (3d Dep't 1994), appears in SPR 27:3.

time in which to take an appeal, or move for leave to appeal, with only a few narrow exceptions:

If the appellant makes a mistake as to method, taking an appeal of right in a case in which leave is required, or seeking leave when an appeal lies of right, the time in which to take the right step may be recomputed. The time will run anew from the dismissal of the appeal, as where the appellant appeals of right in a case that requires leave, or—vice versa—from the denial of an application for leave when leave is unnecessary because the appeal lies of right. Caselaw has given the mistaken appellant another leg-up in this situation. Although the statute says the new time runs from the dismissal or denial itself,[1] it has been construed by the Court of Appeals to start from the usual service of the order (in this case the one dismissing the appeal or denying the motion for leave) with notice of entry, so as to conform to what attorneys generally understand of appellate practice—and, for that matter, of civil practice in general—and to avoid a needless additional trap.[2] It is also provided that if an appeal has been taken by permission, i.e., permission was granted, only to have it discovered later that permission was not necessary, the appeal shall not be dismissed as long as the motion for permission was made within the time limited for the taking of an appeal as of right.[3] This postulates that permission was needlessly granted, but concludes that since the appeal is here it should be prosecuted just as if properly taken as of right.

The taking of an appeal, or the making of a motion for leave to appeal, requires the dual procedure of serving the notice on the adverse party and filing it with the clerk. If the party takes one of those steps on time, but omits the other, she can be allowed an extension of time to do the other. Any of the courts involved can grant this extension: the original court, the appellate court, or even the intermediate appellate court when the case is stepping from one appellate tribunal to another.[4]

An extension of time may be secured if the attorney for the would-be appellant becomes in some way disabled,[5] but not if the attorney has merely been voluntarily discharged by the client.[6] Time may also be extended to allow for substitution of a party when something happens to require it.[7] It must be shown that the attorney's disability or the substitution-requiring event occurred before the appeal time expired.

Having dutifully set forth the several exceptions, we can now stress the great rigidity of the time for taking an appeal or for moving for leave to take an appeal. The two major obduracies of civil practice attend this time period: it is (1) a statute of limitations that cannot be extended, except upon the narrow grounds stated, and (2) the passing of the period is even deemed to divest the appellate court of jurisdiction.[8] This jurisdiction is of the most austere kind, moreover—subject matter jurisdiction—so that not even mutual consent of the parties can reopen the door once the passing of the time

---

[1]   CPLR 5514(a).

[2]   See Park East Corp. v. Whalen, 38 N.Y.2d 559, 381 N.Y.S.2d 819, 345 N.E.2d 289 (1976).

[3]   CPLR 5520(b).

[4]   CPLR 5520(a); see Gamble v. Gamble, 23 A.D.2d 887, 259 N.Y.S.2d 910 (2d Dep't 1965). In some circumstances, when one party has been timely served with a notice of appeal, the statute may be applied to extend the time to appeal with respect to another party. See Leonard v. Regan, 167 A.D.2d 790, 563 N.Y.S.2d 348, 64 Ed. Law Rep. 1163 (3d Dep't 1990).

[5]   See CPLR 5514(b).

[6]   Siegel v. Obes, 112 A.D.2d 930, 492 N.Y.S.2d 447 (2d Dep't 1985).

[7]   See CPLR 1022.

[8]   See, e.g., Curran v. City of Rochester, 50 A.D.2d 1059, 376 N.Y.S.2d 284 (4th Dep't 1975).

period has closed it.[9] The appellate court and its personnel, without waiting for the adverse party's initiative, often sift through notices of appeal and motions for leave to appeal and any other papers before them for any evidence of untimeliness and, for that matter, any other jurisdictional defects, dismissing appeals and motions when they find one. Sometimes the court will merely raise the issue rather than raise and dispose of it sua sponte, eliciting the parties' address to the matter in correspondence through the clerk.

A defect in mere form, as where the caption is imperfect or where the judgment or order being appealed is not accurately described in the notice of appeal, may be ignored by the appellate court "when the interests of justice so demand,"[10] which presumably means when no one would be prejudiced by the error, as where the other side knew what was intended.

Prematurity of the appeal is also an ignorable defect if by the time the defect is called to the court's attention the appeal would lie.[11] This can occur when, for example, an over-zealous appellant has taken an appeal before waiting to be served with the appealable paper and notice of its entry, or, indeed, when he has not even waited for the paper to be entered. An appellant in that league doubtless subscribes to Emerson's view that nothing great can be accomplished without enthusiasm.

§ 535. Injunctions and Stays

It is recognized that the need to retain status quo in the situations provided for by Article 63 of the CPLR, which supplies the provisional remedies of preliminary injunction and temporary restraining order, may also be felt at the appellate stage of the case. CPLR 5518 therefore allows the appellate division in such situations[1] to entertain applications for the injunctive remedies after an appeal has been taken in the action, or a motion made for leave to appeal, including applications seeking an injunction initially as well as applications to modify or vacate an injunction already granted.

Quite apart from, and in no event to be confused with, the injunctions authorized by Article 63 is the well known stay of enforcement of the judgment pending appeal. Here CPLR 5519 supplies the governing provisions and in some detail. This category of stay seeks to prevent the respondent—assume the plaintiff is the respondent and the defendant the appellant—from realizing on the judgment or order[2] while an appeal is taking place, the appellant's hope being that the appeal will succeed and get the disposition reversed. If that does happen, but without a stay having been granted, and the judgment has meanwhile been enforced, e.g., a money judgment has been paid through property of the appellant levied on by the sheriff, the appellant will afterwards be put to the trouble of seeking restitution.[3] In the meantime, the appellant may have been divested of valuable property without any guarantee that such restitution as might later be ordered against the respondent will be collectible; the respondent may have

---

[9] See Haverstraw Park, Inc. v. Runcible Properties Corporation, 33 N.Y.2d 637, 347 N.Y.S.2d 585, 301 N.E.2d 553 (1973).

[10] CPLR 5520(c).

[11] CPLR 5520(c).

[1] The situations in which the injunctive remedies are available are set forth in CPLR 6301. See § 327.

[2] CPLR 5519 speaks throughout of a "judgment or order." We use the word "judgment" henceforth in this section to embrace both.

[3] See CPLR 5523, 5015(d); § 433.

squandered the money and become insolvent in the interim. A stay of enforcement avoids that.

Under subdivision (a) of CPLR 5519, which provides for a stay without a court order, the stay results automatically in several situations. When the appellant is the State or one of its political subdivisions or an officer or agency of either, for example, its mere service of a notice of appeal, or of a paper known as an "affidavit of intention to move for permission to appeal," automatically stays enforcement of any judgment rendered against it.[4] This may not be too important when the State itself is the appellant, at least on a money judgment, because none of the procedures available for its enforcement are available against the State anyway.[5] But it may be of moment when something other than a money judgment is involved, or when others in this governmental category are appealing. An inquiry should be made into what government creatures qualify here. Some officials with a colorable claim to governmental status have been held to be beyond it, and therefore not entitled to an automatic stay, including, for example, the senior officials of the New York City Transit Authority.[6]

The state's municipalities—the cities, counties, towns, and villages—are among the major beneficiaries of this automatic stay.

When the stay takes effect, it operates to stay proceedings to "enforce" the judgment or order. To use a simple example, a plaintiff's money judgment against a city can't be enforced after the city takes an appeal from the judgment. But how does the stay operate when an order does no more, for example, than deny a motion to dismiss? There was for a time no uniform view among the several departments. Three of the four held that only the enforcement of the particular judgment or order is stayed, while the First Department held that the stay operates to suspend all further proceedings in the action.[7] Then in 2008, in All American Crane Service, Inc. v. Omran,[8] the First Department withdrew from that view and went along with the other three departments.

In *Crane*, a city code provision prohibited a certain procedure by crane operators. They sued to bar its enforcement and won in the supreme court, which issued an injunction order against the city to stop it from seeking enforcement. The city appealed the order and argued that its appeal invoked the automatic stay provision of subdivision (a)(1) of CPLR 5519. Rejecting the argument, the court held that when the appealed decision directs the city not to do something—as in *Crane*—the automatic stay is not operative to allow the city to do the prohibited thing during the pendency of the appeal.

---

[4]   CPLR 5519(a)(1).

[5]   See CPLR 5207.

[6]   Ronan v. Levitt, 73 Misc. 2d 35, 341 N.Y.S.2d 176 (Sup. Ct., Albany County 1973), aff'd, 42 A.D.2d 10, 344 N.Y.S.2d 624 (3d Dep't).

[7]   See the lead notes in SPR 20:1 and 34:1. The question of what the automatic stay operates on when a municipality or other governmental unit appeals has been a thorny issue. In a concerted effort to meet and resolve the issue, in respect of both stays and injunctions, the Second Department handed down a quartet of cases in 1996, each addressing a different aspect of the question: Pokoik v. Department of Health Services of County of Suffolk, 220 A.D.2d 13, 641 N.Y.S.2d 881 (2d Dep't 1996); Pickerell v. Town of Huntington, 219 A.D.2d 24, 641 N.Y.S.2d 887 (2d Dep't 1996); Schwartz v. New York City Housing Authority, 219 A.D.2d 47, 641 N.Y.S.2d 885 (2d Dep't 1996); and State v. Town of Haverstraw, 219 A.D.2d 64, 641 N.Y.S.2d 879 (2d Dep't 1996). The four cases are treated in the lead note in SPR 44:1.

[8]   All American Crane Service, Inc. v. Omran, 2008 WL 3304212 (1st Dep't 2008).

The court said that "the automatic stay provision of CPLR 5519(a)(1) [is] inapplicable herein as the injunction challenged is prohibitory in nature."[9]

A municipality has sometimes been known to take a totally groundless appeal just to secure the automatic stay of CPLR 5519(a)(1), but that has been held a frivolous practice under Rule 130–1 and can subject the municipality to monetary sanctions.[10]

Administrative agencies are also beneficiaries of the automatic stay, which generated controversy in licensing situations and produced an amendment to CPLR 5519(a)(1) in 1988 providing that when the license of a small corporation or partnership has been administratively revoked, and the revocation cancelled by the supreme court in an Article 78 proceeding[11] so that the license now revives, the automatic stay of the supreme court judgment that results when the agency takes an appeal exists for only 15 days, i.e., suspends the license only for that 15 days. At the end of the 15 days, the license revives again. If the agency wants the stay extended, so that the license will not be valid while the appeal pends, it must move for a discretionary stay under subdivision (c) of CPLR 5519, which we take up later.

Nongovernmental litigants get an automatic stay only if they file a bond or take some other step to secure the respondent. A defendant appealing an ordinary money judgment, for example, gets a stay of enforcement without a court order when he serves a notice of appeal or the "affidavit of intention" described above, but only if he gives an undertaking to pay the judgment in the event it is affirmed or the appeal dismissed.[12] Stays without a court order when other than money judgments are involved, including judgments with specific property as their subject, are also provided for upon meeting certain conditions, such as by placing personal property in neutral custody during the appeal;[13] or, if the judgment calls for the execution of an instrument, by making the instrument and depositing it with the clerk.[14] In some of those situations, and in still others, a bond is once again exacted as a condition to an automatic stay.[15]

The bond usually covers only the pendency of the particular appeal, and its obligation dissolves if the appellant prevails. Even a reopening of only the liability question may be considered an appellate success adequate to cancel the bond, notwithstanding retention of the damages figure while liability goes back for a retrial.[16]

If the situation is one in which the defendant (D) has to bond the judgment in order to stay its execution during an appeal, D had best bond it promptly. If D does not, and P has the sheriff levy the judgment, D becomes liable for poundage to the sheriff[17] even if D then does bond the judgment and spares the sheriff all further steps. In one recent

---

[9] The *Crane* case is the subject of the lead note in SPR 200:1.

[10] See Matter of Troy Police Benev. and Protective Ass'n, Inc. (City of Troy), 223 A.D.2d 995, 636 N.Y.S.2d 499, 153 L.R.R.M. (BNA) 2505 (3d Dep't 1996), noted in SPR 41:3.

[11] Article 78 is treated beginning with § 557.

[12] CPLR 5519(a)(2). If the judgment directs the payment of money in installments, paragraph 3 of 5519(a) governs the bond. For all of the undertakings mentioned in CPLR 5519, as for undertakings generally under the CPLR, Article 25 provides the details. See § 206.

[13] CPLR 5519(a)(4).

[14] CPLR 5519(a)(5).

[15] See paragraphs 3, 4, and 6 of CPLR 5519(a).

[16] See La Rocco v. Federal Insurance Co., 35 N.Y.2d 806, 362 N.Y.S.2d 461, 321 N.E.2d 551 (1974), rev'g 42 A.D.2d 475, 349 N.Y.S.2d 135 (3d Dep't 1973).

[17] See CPLR 8012.

case, this delay by D, a hospital, cost it $30,000 that it could have saved by being just a few days prompter.[18]

On appeal from a judgment against an insured in an ordinary personal injury action defended by an insurer—whose solvency is assumed—an automatic stay results (to the extent of the insurance policy's coverage but not beyond) when the insurer takes certain prescribed steps.[19] If the judgment exceeds the coverage, however, the insured would have to give a bond to stay enforcement with respect to the balance unless the insurer opts to furnish a full bond, which it may do.

A special provision applies in medical, dental, and podiatric malpractice actions when the plaintiff has had judgment for more than $1 million. It provides that if an appeal is taken by the defendant and an undertaking is given either for $1 million or for the amount of the defendant's malpractice insurance policy, whichever is greater, the appellate court must stay enforcement proceedings during the appeal if it finds "a reasonable probability that the judgment may be reversed or determined excessive."[20] The attainment of this stay is that it can enable a bonding of $1 million to stay enforcement of a judgment that may be for much more than that.[21]

In those situations in which an undertaking is exacted as a condition of a stay, the direction is that the undertaking be "given." What constitutes a "giving"? If the appellant tenders it to the respondent, who accepts it and thereupon refrains from attempting to enforce the judgment, that should do the job. If it is tendered and rejected, the appellant can apparently satisfy the requirement, and earn the stay, by filing the undertaking with the clerk.[22] If any enforcement procedure should be taken in violation of a stay that the appellant assumes has taken effect, the appellant should promptly move to vacate whatever step has been taken, preferably with an order to show cause in which an interim and unambiguous stay can be included. The motion is best made to the court of original jurisdiction since it is there that the enforcement will be attempted.[23]

In any situation in which no provision is made for an automatic stay, the appellant can apply for a court-ordered stay under subdivision (c) of CPLR 5519, which allows the application to be made to the appellate court, to the original court, or even to an intermediate appellate court when the latter's order is being appealed. This stay, which lies entirely in the court's discretion, is of course the one turned to when the automatic stay provisions aren't applicable, or aren't used, but the court's powers are not restricted to those cases. The court under subdivision (c) has power even over the automatic stays and can vacate, limit, or modify them.[24]

When granted, a discretionary stay can be conditional. One of the more popular conditions is that the appeal be prosecuted promptly.[25] Any relevant factor may be

---

[18] Thornton v. Montefiore Hosp., 117 A.D.2d 552, 498 N.Y.S.2d 828 (1st Dep't 1986).

[19] CPLR 5519(b).

[20] CPLR 5519(g).

[21] See the Commentary on McKinney's CPLR 5519(g).

[22] See Rhoades v. Adelman, 145 N.Y.S.2d 766 (Sup. Ct., New York County 1955).

[23] See, e.g., CPLR 5240, the provision authorizing a protective order in any situation involving the enforcement of a money judgment.

[24] If the state or other governmental unit is the party favored by the stay, the stay can be altered only by the court to which the appeal is being taken. CPLR 5519(c), (a)(1).

[25] See, e.g., Kiamesha Development Corp. v. Guild Properties, Inc., 3 N.Y.2d 981, 169 N.Y.S.2d 741, 147 N.E.2d 247 (1957).

considered by the court in exercising its discretion. The stay will be denied, for example, if the court suspects that the appeal has a dilatory aim. The presumptive merit of the appeal will also be an element.[26]

The stay provision also contemplates the circumstance in which the appellant loses at the first appellate level. It keeps the stay in effect through the next level of appeal provided that the second appeal is taken, or leave for it is moved for, within five days after the appellant is served with notice of the entry of the first appellate court's order determining the appeal there.[27] There is some caselaw suggesting that this automatic second-step stay will not result if the initial stay was granted by court order under CPLR 5519(c) without an undertaking,[28] but this is a questionable conclusion. The provision in point on the second-step stay, CPLR 5519(e), does not purport to distinguish between sources of the original stay. The Court of Appeals appears to be of this view.[29]

When the further appeal is one that requires a motion for leave, and leave is granted, any stay applicable during the pendency of the motion continues until five days after the appeal is determined; when leave is denied, it continues until five days after the movant is served with the order of denial with notice of entry.[30]

A municipal appellant that does not pursue the next appellate step during the allowed five-day period nevertheless gets a new automatic stay when the step is finally taken, even if taken after the five days.[31]

E. PERFECTING THE APPEAL

Table of Sections

§ 536. "Perfecting" the Appeal, Introductory
§ 537. The Transcript
§ 538. The Record
§ 539. The Briefs and Appendices
§ 540. Calendar Practice and the Argument

§ 536. "Perfecting" the Appeal, Introductory

After the appeal has been formally taken, whether of right or after the entry of an order granting permission, a record of the case has to be put together. If the appeal is from an order, or from a judgment rendered without testimony in open court, such as one resulting from a dismissal under CPLR 3211 or summary judgment under CPLR 3212, there will ordinarily have been no open-court testimony and therefore no stenographic transcript to secure. This will eliminate one of the main expenses of the

---

[26] See Application of Mott, 123 N.Y.S.2d 603, 608 (Sup. Ct., Oswego County 1953).

[27] CPLR 5519(e). Similar protections are set forth when leave to appeal is needed.

[28] See DFI Communications, Inc. v. Greenberg, 55 A.D.2d 887, 391 N.Y.S.2d 8 (1st Dep't 1977).

[29] After the *DFI* holding by the appellate division, 55 A.D.2d at 887, 391 N.Y.S.2d at 8, that the CPLR 5519(c) stay would not continue through the second stage, the appellant moved the Court of Appeals for a stay. The Court denied it as "unnecessary," which could only mean that in its view the earlier stay did continue, contrary to the appellate division's view. See DFI Communications, Inc. v. Greenberg, 41 N.Y.2d 1017, 395 N.Y.S.2d 639, 363 N.E.2d 1384 (1977).

[30] CPLR 5519(e)(i) and (ii).

[31] Summerville v. City of New York, 97 N.Y.2d 427, 740 N.Y.S.2d 683, 767 N.E.2d 140 (2002). The case is the subject of a note in NYSLD No. 510.

appellate process. But if there has been a trial or hearing, a transcript will be needed, and the ordering of it is one of the first steps in what is loosely called "perfecting" the appeal.

"Perfecting" are the steps that process the appeal: ordering and securing a transcript, drawing up a record, writing, serving and filing the briefs, getting the case onto the appellate court's calendar for argument, and, finally, arguing and submitting the case.

It is primarily on the initiative of the appellant that the appeal gets perfected. The burden is on the one initiating the appellate process to secure the transcript and put together a record. The respondent's main job is to see that the record also contains everything he may wish to rely on; other than that, the respondent's attention will be directed to drawing his brief, principally a defensive activity designed to answer the appellant's points and sustain the lower court's doings.

Article 55 turns its attention to the "perfection" phase of the appellate process starting with CPLR 5525, which concerns the transcript. It then attends to the record (CPLR 5526) or a statement in lieu of a record (CPLR 5527), to the briefs (CPLR 5528, 5529, and 5530), and to a few other incidentals.

One who consults Article 55 for the first time may be surprised to find nothing about the argument of the case, about how one brings the argument on, or about the time allowed for it. Nor will anything be found about such basic matters as motion days in the court, should the need to make a motion arise; or about preargument conferences, if there should be such a practice in a given appellate court. These things come almost exclusively from the rules of the particular appellate court, and they aren't uniform. Even those parts of the perfection process that the CPLR does speak to, such as the record and the briefs, are themselves so heavily addressed in the individual rules of court that in some instances a CPLR provision may be virtually eclipsed. This is not to suggest that the CPLR has lost sovereignty, but only to acknowledge an unusually potent regent. Any appellate practitioner can vouch that in perfecting an appeal the rules of court are surely that.

In the few sections following, therefore, as the perfection process builds around the CPLR, references to rules of court will be more frequent. This will have the effect, not of extending the discourse, but of curtailing it. The matters involved are mechanical; little is to be gained by repeating step-by-step procedures first outlined by the CPLR and then expanded by an individual court's rules. Calling attention to these provisions rather than repeating them will be the mission. Citations of rules will be mainly to those of the appellate division departments, with occasional reference to the rules of the Court of Appeals. The practitioner must also keep in mind that each of these courts is the sole proprietor of its own rules and can change them at will and on short notice. Our rule citations are therefore only samples, and calling attention to them or to illustrative ones among them is intended only to narrow the lawyer's research, never to substitute for it.[1]

Both the CPLR and the rules have many time restrictions on perfecting the appeal, but these are not applied as strictly as the time for taking the appeal in the first place.

---

[1]　Finding the courts' rules is not the burden it once was. Law libraries have the official compilation, which is Title 22 of the New York Code of Rules and Regulations, and McKinney's Consolidated Laws publishes all of them together in a soft cover pamphlet, "McKinney's New York Rules of Court," recompiled and distributed annually.

This is something of a paradox. The taking of the appeal is among the easiest and quickest steps in practice, yet the failure to take it within the prescribed time is fatal: the court lacks power to grant discretionary extensions. The perfection process, on the other hand, is time consuming and expensive, but the time periods applicable to it are not rigid and can be extended. Notwithstanding this, the frequent willingness of lawyers to delay whenever they are given to understand that delay may be forgiven has prompted an occasional tightening up on these requirements and an occasional warning.[2]

The lawyer planning anything less than strict adherence to the time limits placed on the perfection steps by local rules of court had better make inquiry about what the consequences of a time lapse will be: attitudes differ from time to time and from court to court. A little check into the local status of strictness will be worthwhile. The grapevine should advise if rules or recent cases do not. Adherence to the letter will of course obviate the inquiry, but some lawyers feel that there is tradition to be honored. They may not wish to jeopardize their credentials with unseemly diligence! Yet diligence does have its rewards, as may be detected by looking at the other side of the coin. If the local attitude is strict, or the lapse serious, the result can be a dismissal of the appeal for want of prosecution—a result just as devastating on appeal as it is at trial level. It's in effect a forfeiture on the merits. It's significant enough, in any event, to warrant a separate section later on.[3]

There are several different ways recognized or at least allowed by the CPLR for getting together the record of the case or the parts of it needed for appellate review. The four departments of the appellate division, in fact, have culled from Article 55 three alternative methods. Each court has, to one extent or another, promulgated rules designed to implement them. These are elaborated later,[4] but can be briefly listed now:

One is the procedure of coming up on a full record—the most expensive means, but optional only.[5] A second is known as the "Appendix System," whereby an appendix to the brief (or to each brief) contains what is needed from the record without reproduction of the whole record.[6] The third is an agreed statement instead of a record, the least expensive method, but also apparently the least used because it requires the kind of agreement between lawyers that the adversary system does not foster.[7] Treatment of these topics and the other constituents of the perfection process are the function of the next few sections.

The Court of Appeals requires a "Preliminary Appeal Statement" and provides a form for it in its Rule 500.9. Because its jurisdiction is much narrower than that of the appellate division, the Court has given notice in its Rule 500.10 that it may examine its

---

[2]   See, for example, the statement of the clerk of the Court of Appeals, advising that thenceforth extensions in conjunction with appeals to the Court of Appeals would be granted only upon a showing of "extraordinary circumstances." N.Y.L.J., Dec. 3, 1973, at 1, cols. 3 to 4.

[3]   See § 542.

[4]   See §§ 538 and 539.

[5]   See 22 N.Y.C.R.R. §§ 600.5(c) (First Department), 670.9(a) (Second Department), 800.4(a) (Third Department), 1000.4(a) (Fourth Department). CPLR 5528(a)(5) authorizes this full-record method at appellate division option.

[6]   CPLR 5528(a)(5); 22 N.Y.C.R.R. §§ 600.5(a) (First Department), 670.9(b) (Second Department), 800.4(b) (Third Department), 1000.3(d) (Fourth Department). The appendix method may be made mandatory in designated instances by court rule. See, e.g., 22 N.Y.C.R.R. § 500.14, a Court of Appeals rule.

[7]   CPLR 5527; 22 N.Y.C.R.R. §§ 600.5(b) (First Department), 670.9(c) (Second Department), 800.4(d) (Third Department), 1000.4(c) (Fourth Department).

jurisdiction of the appeal on its own motion. And under another rule, Rule 500.11, it can select some appeals to set on a more summary path to possible resolution. The selection of a case for this special treatment is often triggered by something about it that suggests to the Court at the outset that the case can be disposed of expeditiously: something among the papers filed with it so far, or on the decision, record and briefs in the lower appellate court, or on the jurisdictional statement itself.

The parties are advised by the clerk if their case is selected for this treatment. A case so selected may be detoured from the usual "perfection" route and will be if the Court does decide that the merits can be disposed of without putting the case through the usual perfection process. It will not be, however, if the Court terminates the sua sponte consideration, in which event the clerk advises the parties and a new perfection schedule is set.[8]

Electronic Filing of Records and Briefs

In addition to the prescribed number of hard copies of the record and brief that must be filed and served, the New York Court of Appeals now requires that all records and briefs be electronically filed.[9] These documents, known as digital companion briefs and records, are electronically filed with the clerk's office by uploading them to the Court of Appeals Public Access and Search System (Court-PASS).[10] The digital companion briefs and records must comply with the technical specifications and instructions for submission, available from the clerk's office, or risk rejection.[11]

The Court of Appeals has many rules on redaction that can make finalizing the record somewhat onerous in particular cases.[12] Digital submissions must include the Court's "confidential and sensitive materials attestation form" to ensure compliance with the Court's sealing and redaction requirements.[13]

The First Department also requires electronic filing and service of records and briefs.[14] A memorandum issued by the First Department in July 2013 outlines the court's electronic filing requirements under sections 600.10 and 600.11 of the court's rules. In general, each party perfecting or answering an appeal must electronically file one PDF copy of each of the papers in addition to filing and serving the required paper copies. Papers in civil, criminal, and Family Court matters must all be e-mailed to separately provided e-mail addresses. The memorandum can be found on the First Department's website.[15]

As of this writing, there are no rules for the electronic filing of records and briefs in the Second, Third, or Fourth Departments, but they are likely on the way. Chapter 237 of the Laws of 2015 authorizes the use of mandatory e-filing in the Appellate Division at the discretion of each department. Each department is permitted to adopt e-filing rules

---

[8]   See 22 N.Y.C.R.R. § 500.11(i).

[9]   See 22 N.Y.C.R.R. § 500.2(a).

[10]   See Frequently Asked Questions—Court-Pass—Digital Filing available at: https://www.nycourts. gov/ctapps/digfilingfaq.htm.

[11]   22 N.Y.C.R.R. § 500.2(b), (f); Technical Specifications and Instructions for Submission of Briefs and Record Material in Digital Format available at https://www.nycourts.gov/ctapps/techspecs.htm.

[12]   See 22 N.Y.C.R.R. § 500.5.

[13]   See the Technical Specifications and Instructions for Submission referenced above.

[14]   See 22 N.Y.C.R.R. § 600.11 ("Perfecting and hearing of appeals; calendar; adjournments").

[15]   See http://www.courts.state.ny.us/courts/AD1/PDFs/EmailFilingRule6.pdf.

for: 1) appeals, 2) motions for permission to appeal, 3) commencement of any proceeding over which the court has original jurisdiction, and 4) the filing and service of papers in pending actions and proceedings.[16] The law excludes from mandatory e-filing those same actions that are excluded from it in the trial courts.[17] Thankfully, the legislation recommends that "[t]o the extent practicable, rules promulgated by the appellate division in each judicial department pursuant to this section shall be uniform."[18] It is our hope that all four departments in the appellate division will find it practicable in every instance.

The future looks bright in this respect. On June 1, 2017, the Office of Court Administration circulated a "Request for Public Comment on Proposed Rules for Electronic Filing in the Appellate Division of Supreme Court." Lawyers prosecuting appeals should check the status of these proposed rules. The hope here is that all departments could ultimately adopt one unified system for perfecting an appeal electronically in the appellate division.

§ 537. The Transcript

A transcript is the typed-out manuscript of testimony and other colloquy of a trial or hearing, taken down verbatim by the court stenographer (also called court reporter) in his minutes. Appeal from a final judgment after a trial usually needs a transcript; so does an appeal from an order in the infrequent instances in which it was not decided on papers alone, but required an open-court hearing. The average order involves no live testimony and hence needs no transcript. The procedure for getting the transcript, needed as part of an appellate record or for a brief's appendix, is set forth in CPLR 5525. The appellant, within the time to appeal, serves the court stenographer with a request for the transcript and deposits the necessary fee.[1]

The parties can stipulate that only a portion of the minutes be transcribed,[2] which can result in quite a saving. Absent mutual agreement, a transcription of the whole is required. It has been held that the court is without power to require a resisting party to accept less.[3] If less is feasible, both sides should be receptive to a stipulation. The transcript is expensive,[4] and the loser may end up paying for all of it as a disbursement.[5]

If the parties can unite on a single factual statement of the whole case, they can forego a transcript altogether and prosecute the appeal on a "statement in lieu of record on appeal," but this, as already noted,[6] is apparently asking too much of the adversary system. Hence a statement of this kind is not often the appeal method used.

---

[16]   See CPLR 2112 ("Filing of papers in the appellate division by electronic means").

[17]   See § 63.

[18]   CPLR 2112.

[1]   CPLR 5525(a).

[2]   CPLR 5525(b).

[3]   See Perry v. Tauro, 21 A.D.2d 804, 250 N.Y.S.2d 898 (2d Dep't 1964).

[4]   See CPLR 8002.

[5]   CPLR 8301(a)(13); see Sterling Optical Co. v. University of State of N.Y., 56 Misc. 2d 54, 287 N.Y.S.2d 961 (Sup. Ct., Albany County 1968) (citing to former CPLR 8301(a)(12), prior to renumbering of subdivisions).

[6]   See § 536. The statement is authorized by CPLR 5527 and is one of the three distinct methods of prosecuting an appeal.

After the transcript has been drawn up, the court stenographer serves two copies of it on the appellant who ordered it, or as many copies as have otherwise been ordered,[7] whereupon the appellant can review it and propose changes in it to conform with his recollection. The appellant then serves a copy of the transcript and proposed changes on the respondent, who reviews it and proposes her own changes. Hopefully they can resolve disputes and come up with a settled transcript without court aid. If they can't, they must follow a prescribed procedure for having the court settle the transcript,[8] which it is the court's duty to do.[9] A procedure is also set forth whereby the transcript will be deemed settled if a respondent who has been served with it does not respond within a certain time.[10] Certification of the transcript in that instance is by the stenographer,[11] otherwise it is certified by the parties together or by the court.[12] In any instance, a stipulation by the parties will be gladly received in place of certification.[13]

When the transcript is settled by one means or another and there is no agreement between the parties working things out otherwise, the appellant usually ends up with both copies of the transcript. The appellant's next prescribed obligation with respect to it is when he serves his brief on the respondent: the appellant must at that time either serve a copy of the transcript on the respondent or else file it with the clerk of the trial court.[14] The serving is preferable because it saves the respondent the trouble of having to consult the transcript at the courthouse (which can be a distance away), so it amounts to a courtesy as well, but there is nothing in the CPLR to preclude the clerk from letting the respondent borrow and remove the filed copy if the appellant has opted for the filing rather than the service.

Court rules can vary the time requirements stated in CPLR 5525 or require that only a single transcript be prepared, and in that case the single copy will have to serve for all parties and the court.[15]

If there has been testimony, but no transcript, a procedure is set up whereby the appellant can get together a statement of the proceedings from "the best available sources, including his recollection," and serve it on the respondent. Both sides can then either work out its terms or present it to the court for settlement.[16]

If the appellant relies in any measure on proceedings at the trial itself, which will almost invariably be the case on an appeal from a judgment or order made after a testimonial hearing, the transcript will be a key item. If it's deficient, or if an unsettled transcript is so replete with errors and omissions as to be uncorrectable, or if no stenographer was used and no transcript is available and the parties' statement is undependable, the court may simply throw up its hands and remand the case for a whole

---

[7]   CPLR 5525(a).

[8]   CPLR 5525(c)(1).

[9]   See Wahrhaftig v. Space Design Group, Inc., 28 A.D.2d 940, 281 N.Y.S.2d 500 (3d Dep't 1967).

[10]   CPLR 5525(c)(2), (3).

[11]   CPLR 5525(c)(2).

[12]   CPLR 5525(c)(1).

[13]   CPLR 5532.

[14]   CPLR 5525(c)(1).

[15]   CPLR 5525(a), (e). See, e.g., 22 N.Y.C.R.R. §§ 600.5(f) (First Department) and 800.6(a) (Third Department).

[16]   CPLR 5525(d). This is derived from what is presently Rule 10(c) of the Federal Rules of Appellate Procedure.

new trial.[17] While the appellate court has the power to permit defects in the transcript to be remedied and can grant a continuance for the purpose, it may not be disposed to review the case at all if no transcript or statement is submitted. In that instance, it is possible that the court will see "no alternative but to accept the findings of the trial court" and affirm.[18]

We will assume that the transcript, or statement, is now ready for use on the appeal. How it is used is the subject of the next two sections.

§ 538. The Record

The content and form of the record on appeal are prescribed by CPLR 5526, but the rules of the particular appellate court will usually be found to address the subject as well, sometimes adding a few items.[1]

On appeal from a final judgment, the record contains the notice of appeal, the judgment-roll,[2] a settled transcript if there was testimony,[3] any relevant exhibits used below, copies of all reviewable orders,[4] and any opinions written in the case. On an appeal from an order or from an interlocutory judgment, the record consists of the notice of appeal, the order or judgment being appealed, a transcript if there is one, the papers and exhibits on which the order or judgment is based, and any opinions in the case. All papers printed or reproduced must be on paper 11 × 8 1/2 inches.[5]

The appellant, who puts together the record on appeal, must include in it all of the "papers and other exhibits upon which the judgment or order was founded."[6] The appellant may not put the record together selectively; he may not include only materials favorable to his own side while omitting matter favorable to the other.[7]

The record must be adequate for appellate review of whatever it is that is being questioned. Even a stipulation by all parties approving the record will not earn appellate review of an issue if the record is found inadequate. The appeal in such a case is likely to be stricken from the appellate calendar, if already on it, with, at best, leave to remedy the defects and move to restore the case.[8] The failure to assemble a proper record as prescribed by CPLR 5526 will not always warrant dismissal of the appeal. In Martinez v. Premium Laundry Corp.,[9] for example, defendant failed to identify any material information omitted from the record on appeal that was relevant to a determination of

---

[17] See Ernest LL v. Rosemary LL, 50 A.D.2d 706, 375 N.Y.S.2d 495 (3d Dep't 1975).

[18] See, e.g., Hayden v. Sclafani, 45 A.D.2d 942, 359 N.Y.S.2d 324 (2d Dep't 1974). Alternatively, a "dismissal" of the appeal may be the outcome in such a situation. For most purposes the difference would be academic.

[1] See 22 N.Y.C.R.R. §§ 600.10 (First Department); 670.10–a, 670.10–b, 670.10–c (Second Department); 800.5(a) (Third Department); 1000.4 (Fourth Department).

[2] CPLR 5017(b). See § 419.

[3] If no stenographic transcript was made, a statement of the proceedings may be used. CPLR 5525(d).

[4] CPLR 5501(a) determines which prior orders are reviewable. See § 530.

[5] CPLR 5526.

[6] CPLR 5526.

[7] See 2001 Real Estate v. Campeau Corp. (U.S.), Inc., 148 A.D.2d 315, 538 N.Y.S.2d 531 (1st Dep't 1989).

[8] See Guarnacci v. Ferguson, 29 A.D.2d 839, 287 N.Y.S.2d 471 (4th Dep't 1968).

[9] Martinez v. Premium Laundry Corp., 137 A.D.3d 419, 25 N.Y.S.3d 867 (1st Dep't 2016).

the issues raised and the appellate division concluded that the record was sufficiently complete to address the merits.

A cross-appellant, i.e., a party also appealing but serving a notice of appeal after another party has already served one should not assume that the whole burden of putting the record together is on the first appellant. The particular court's rules should be checked on this. In one case, for example, when a cross-appellant, without the main appellant's consent and in violation of a court rule, merely included a copy of the notice of cross-appeal in his brief and tried to use only the record furnished by the main appellant, the cross-appeal was dismissed.[10]

Although a deficient record will impede or altogether prevent appellate review, especially when the deficiencies are in the transcript discussed in the prior section, on the other side is the rule that records and materials not offered or received in evidence at the trial are improper to include on the appeal, either in the record, in the briefs, or anywhere else.[11] Even the inclusion of an affidavit not properly part of the record below has been "severely condemned," with a warning that "counsel do not help their cases by attaching to briefs matters dehors the record."[12] Such matters will ordinarily be disregarded by the appellate court, permitted neither to buttress nor to weaken the case as the record shows it.

It is provided by CPLR 5530(a) that the appellant shall file the record on appeal with the appellate court when he files his briefs,[13] and all of this is done, according to that provision, within 20 days after the transcript is settled.[14] The respondent then has 15 days in which to file and serve her briefs, manifesting the ungenerosity of these time allotments. On the face of things, the respondent, whose defensive posture on the appeal mandates that she review the appellant's brief carefully before drawing her own, has only 15 days to do that, and to write her own brief, and to get everything reproduced and filed. Furthermore, it may be that she does not even have a copy of the transcript, which may have been filed with the clerk instead of being served on her, that option belonging to the appellant under CPLR 5525(c) if the parties don't otherwise agree.

CPLR 5525(e) recognizes this problem, however, by authorizing the appellate division to vary these time requirements in their own departments, and the rules adopted pursuant to this authority do indeed supply different time limitations.[15] The lesson, once again, is not to rely solely on the CPLR for these matters, but to consult the rules or the appellate clerk if the rules are not clear. Some departments, while not rigidly applying the CPLR time limits, may set an outside time of their own for concluding the appeal, which the Court of Appeals has also done.[16] All courts of course reserve to themselves the power to enlarge time on a case by case basis, but one court may be

---

[10] Kapchan v. Kapchan, 104 A.D.2d 358, 478 N.Y.S.2d 689 (2d Dep't 1984).

[11] See Ro-Stan Equities, Inc. v. Schechter, 44 A.D.2d 577, 353 N.Y.S.2d 224 (2d Dep't 1974).

[12] Terner v. Terner, 44 A.D.2d 702, 354 N.Y.S.2d 161, 162 (2d Dep't 1974).

[13] On appeals from lower courts, the clerk forwards the record to the appellate court. See § 1704 in the New York City Civ. Ct. Act, Uniform Dist. Ct. Act, Uniform City Ct. Act, and in the Uniform Just. Ct. Act (McKinney's Vol. 29A, Parts 2 and 3).

[14] When cross-appeals are taken, i.e., when both sides are dissatisfied and are appealing, the plaintiff gets the appellant status in the appellate court; or, where an appeal is from one appellate court to another, the appellant in the lower one keeps that status in the higher one. CPLR 5530(b).

[15] See, e.g., 22 N.Y.C.R.R. § 800.9, the Third Department rule. The Court of Appeals has also addressed these matters in its rules. See 22 N.Y.C.R.R. § 500.12.

[16] 22 N.Y.C.R.R. §§ 500.15 and 500.16.

stricter than another and a party not adhering to the letter of the time requirements should ascertain local indulgence in advance.

The printing of the record is not required. It may be reproduced by offset printing, mimeographing, or any other method of reproduction offering clear black on white copy on paper 11 × 8 1/2 inches.[17] Indeed, the use of printing, when found unreasonable and unnecessary by the court, may result in denying the printing expense as a disbursement, even if the offender is a successful appellant. In one case, for example, the appellant went to a printing expense of $800 to appeal a $450 judgment—a cost found in context to be "profligate" and denied by the court as a disbursement.[18]

How many copies of the record will be needed? This is determined almost entirely by individual court rule and will depend also on the method of appeal being used. The appellant opting to come up on a full record[19] may be burdened with reproducing many copies.[20] If instead the appellant elects the appendix system,[21] only a single copy of the record, usually the original itself, is filed with the appellate court. This, again, is to be found in the rules of court. When it is the original record which, unreproduced, is to leave the trial court and go to the appellate court, the responsibility for transmitting it may be placed by rule on the clerk instead of the parties.[22] When the record is filed with the appellate court, it is accompanied by a statement describing the case and containing the several items of data listed in CPLR 5531, including a statement of the method of appeal being used.[23]

Lost in the course of the foregoing discussion is the third appellate method: the "statement in lieu of record on appeal" offered by CPLR 5527. This can be used only when the questions raised on the appeal "can be determined without an examination" of the record and when all parties are able to unite on a single statement, which may include portions of the transcript or other items in the record. But if the controversy between the parties is one on which they can now, after trial, draw an agreed statement, it is likely to be one on which they could have used the peaceful procedures of CPLR 3222—the "action on submitted facts"[24]—to bring their controversy to court in the first place, dispensing with adversary procedures altogether. Hence it is not likely that a dispute not amenable to such a mutual statement at the outset will suddenly become so after the bruising ordeal of a trial. But CPLR 5527 is optimistic. It briefly sets forth the statement's requirements, and if the parties can find enough common ground, not to resolve their controversy, but just to articulate it together, they will find savings in exploiting it.

---

[17]   The basic permission for these alternatives is in CPLR 5529(a)(1), directed to briefs and appendices, but under court rules it may apply as well to the record when the record is to be reproduced. See, e.g., 22 N.Y.C.R.R. § 600.10, the First Department rule.

[18]   *Society of New York Hospital v. Mogensen*, 81 Misc. 2d 1089, 1090, 370 N.Y.S.2d 354, 355 (App. Term, 1st Dep't 1975). Involved there was § 1705 of the New York City Civil Court Act, but the disbursement denial was built mainly around former CPLR 8301(a)(12) (currently numbered CPLR 8301(a)(13)), allowing only "reasonable and necessary expenses" as a disbursement, which makes the *Society* case relevant in other courts as well.

[19]   The full record is one of the three alternative appellate routes. See § 536.

[20]   See, e.g., 22 N.Y.C.R.R. § 670.9, the Second Department rule.

[21]   Since the "appendix" is appended to the brief, it is treated in the next section.

[22]   See, e.g., 22 N.Y.C.R.R. § 600.5(a), the First Department rule.

[23]   CPLR 5531(7).

[24]   See § 304.

If the CPLR 5527 statement is used, it is submitted to the trial court for correction and approval. As approved, the statement is by itself the record on appeal and is printed as a joint appendix.[25]

The statement must be adequate for appellate review. The parties' agreement can no more force the court to work with an inadequate statement than it can to compel a review on an inadequate record.[26]

§ 539. The Briefs and Appendices

Three provisions are concerned with the briefs and appendices. CPLR 5528 governs their content, CPLR 5529 their form, and CPLR 5530 their filing and service. Once again, court rules play a major role, the CPLR in several instances expressly inviting the rules to vary things as they choose.[1] Subdivisions (a) and (b) of CPLR 5528 provide for the contents of the briefs and appendices of the appellant and respondent, respectively; the rules then confirm, add to, or otherwise elaborate the list.[2] The major item meriting attention here is the appendix.

The appendix method is one of the three set forth by the CPLR and recognized by the appellate division rules.[3] A second is the appeal on a full record. This one requires multiple reproductions of the record and is too costly in some cases, measured by the stakes involved. The third is CPLR 5527's statement in lieu of a record, the most desirable method, but also the least used because of its requirement, difficult to implement, that the parties agree on almost everything to be presented to the appellate court.

When an appendix is used, the rules of court usually require that only a single copy of the full record, or only the original, be filed with the appellate court. The one copy is kept available for the appellate judges for reference if the appendices should prove inadequate or if for any reason a judge should want to consult the record proper.

The appendix, contained in the brief or bound separately, selectively reproduces only "such parts of the record . . . as are necessary to consider the questions involved."[4] If it does its job properly, it will give the appellate court everything needed for review, thus obviating reference to the record itself. That, in fact, is a major function of an appendix. An appendix properly compiled by the appellant and included in her brief will make it unnecessary for the respondent to include any at all in his. This is because the appellant is required to include in her appendix not only the part of the record relevant to her side, but also "those parts the appellant reasonably assumes will be relied upon by the respondent."[5] Whatever appeal method is used, it is "highly unprofessional" for the appellant to include only materials favorable to his own side and omit matter favorable to the other. An appellant who did that in one case was scolded by the appellate division, the practice "deplored," and the summary judgment that had been granted

---

[25] See CPLR 5528(d), discussed in the next section. CPLR 5527 specifically says that the statement "shall be printed," but its Article 55 context would appear to allow the alternatives of offset printing or mimeographing or xeroxing, etc., as is allowed for an appendix itself. See CPLR 5529(a)(1).

[26] See Guarnacci v. Ferguson, 29 A.D.2d 839, 287 N.Y.S.2d 471 (4th Dep't 1968).

[1] See, e.g., CPLR 5528(a)(5), 5530(c).

[2] See, e.g., 22 N.Y.C.R.R. § 600.10(c), (d), the First Department rules.

[3] See § 536.

[4] CPLR 5528(a)(5).

[5] CPLR 5528(a)(5).

against the appellant in the trial court unanimously affirmed.[6] If the respondent finds the appendix contained in the appellant's brief inadequate, he adds an appendix to his own brief, to contain only such additional parts as are necessary for his side.[7] The parties can in the alternative agree on a single appendix, called a "joint appendix," which when used is filed with the appellant's brief.[8]

The contents of appendices, as well as of the briefs themselves, should also be checked against local rule requirements.[9]

In order to encourage use of the appendix method without inviting unreasonably lengthy appendices—compiled in an excess of caution—the Court of Appeals has held that an outright affirmance should not be visited on a case solely because its appendix is inadequate. In that instance, the proper course is to require a further appendix or to dismiss the appeal unless an adequate appendix is filed within a set time. It held so in E.P. Reynolds, Inc. v. Nager Electric Company,[10] acknowledging that the appendix in the case was inadequate. It was about 13 pages in length, extracted from a trial transcript of over 950 pages, and it sought reversal on the ground of the insufficiency of the evidence, a ground that may require consultation of the whole record.

If testimony is included in the appendix, it should be set forth in the order of its transcript appearance, not in some different sequence, such as in the alphabetical order of the witnesses' names. The appendix may contain an alphabetical index, of course, but the testimony itself should be in the chronological order of its presentation. Anything else is likely to be found unacceptable.[11] The courts sometimes have occasion to note "an increasing tendency . . . to disregard the requirements prescribed for the use of the appendix method and to submit appendices which are inadequate and incomplete" and have held this to be an abuse of the system and an intolerable imposition on appellate courts.[12] Noncompliance can also bear costs sanctions.[13]

The foregoing is not to suggest that the appellate court insist on perfect appendices. The court does have a copy of the whole record and any judge wishing to can visit the clerk's office, or have the record sent up by the clerk, to check out such things as the appendix may have inadvertently omitted. The Advisory Committee took note of this possibility,[14] but it is a recourse to be indulged only as an appellate favor when the appendix has been compiled with reasonable competence and care, not as a substitute for one thrown together haphazardly.

---

[6]   2001 Real Estate v. Campeau Corp. (U.S.), Inc., 148 A.D.2d 315, 538 N.Y.S.2d 531 (1st Dep't 1989). The appellant was "only interested in having this court examine fully its own arguments," the court remarked, and the respondent "was compelled to submit its own extensive supplemental record," which was about three times the size of the one the appellant submitted.

[7]   CPLR 5528(b).

[8]   CPLR 5528(d). When the full record rather than the appendix method is used, each judge gets a copy of the complete record; and each party's brief, instead of reproducing any part of the record, cites as need be to the relevant portions of it.

[9]   See, e.g., 22 N.Y.C.R.R. §§ 670.10.2 and 670.10.3, applicable in the Second Department. A Court of Appeals rule allows use of the appendix used in the appellate division if it is otherwise in conformity with Court of Appeals requirements. See 22 N.Y.C.R.R. § 500.14.

[10]   E. P. Reynolds, Inc. v. Nager Elec. Co., 17 N.Y.2d 51, 268 N.Y.S.2d 15, 215 N.E.2d 339 (1966).

[11]   See, e.g., Kimberly-Clark Corp. v. Power Authority, 35 A.D.2d 330, 316 N.Y.S.2d 68 (4th Dep't 1970).

[12]   Lo Gerfo v. Lo Gerfo, 30 A.D.2d 156, 158, 290 N.Y.S.2d 1005, 1007 (2d Dep't 1968).

[13]   CPLR 5528(e). See O'Rourke v. Long, 41 N.Y.2d 219, 391 N.Y.S.2d 553, 359 N.E.2d 1347 (1976).

[14]   See 2d Rep. Leg. Doc. No. 13, p. 350 (1958).

The form of briefs and appendices is in CPLR 5529. Briefs and appendices do not require printing. Offset printing, mimeographing, xeroxing, or any other competent black on white method of reproduction on 11 × 8 1/2-inch paper suffices.[15] What was mentioned in the prior section, in discussing the record, holds true also for the briefs and appendices: a voluntary printing when the economic significance of the case puts the expense out of proportion may be disallowed as a disbursement even to a successful appellant and may be publicly castigated as "profligate."[16]

An amendment of CPLR 5529(a) that took effect January 1, 2003, lets each appellate court prescribe for itself "the size of margins and type of briefs and appendices and the line spacing and the length of briefs."[17]

The time for the service and filing of the briefs and appendices, and the number of copies required, is the subject of CPLR 5530, whose subdivision (c) invites the individual rules of the appellate courts to modify the CPLR 5530 requirements at will.[18]

When leave to appeal is required, as it is with the Court of Appeals most often and with lower appellate courts occasionally,[19] the motion for leave will involve the record and may entail, along with motion papers, a set of briefs.[20] Since the would-be appellant must convince the appellate court of the merits of the grievances, and the opposing party (the potential respondent) is obliged to refute them, the briefs pro and con take on the content and form of an outright appeal. They should; the applicant on that motion cannot safely save a thing for the appeal proper because there will be none if the brief does not convince the court to grant leave. When leave is forthcoming—the majority of motions for leave to appeal are denied—the parties are then confronted with the appeal itself, and in that situation they often ask what, if anything, their appeal briefs should contain which their permission briefs did not. If they did their jobs right, the answer is: not much. The appeal briefs can iron out rough spots in the earlier ones, but the lawyer should not be concerned that their substance is virtually the same. Indeed, if anything of true substance appears only in the appeal brief, having been overlooked in the earlier motion brief, the movant may be considered lucky that the motion was granted without it. Conversely, a respondent in that position may well wonder whether, had the point been included in his papers resisting the motion, the motion for leave to appeal might have been denied.

There is no central and uniform limit on the size of briefs, but, as noted above, individual appellate courts are free to devise limits if they wish.[21] Oversized briefs are not often a problem, but they do appear from time to time and can face the embarrassment of appellate censure. The Court of Appeals, in a rare address to the problem, condemned a 284–page brief for its useless redundancies, irrelevancies, and

---

[15]   CPLR 5529(a).

[16]   See Society of New York Hospital v. Mogensen, 81 Misc. 2d 1089, 370 N.Y.S.2d 354 (App. Term, 1st Dep't 1975).

[17]   The amendment is discussed in SPR 129:3.

[18]   See, e.g., 22 N.Y.C.R.R. § 800.9(a), the Third Department rule.

[19]   See CPLR 5602, 5701(c), 5703(a).

[20]   See, e.g., 22 N.Y.C.R.R. §§ 500.21 and 500.22.

[21]   CPLR 5529(a)(3); see, e.g., 22 N.Y.C.R.R. §§ 500.13(c) (Court of Appeals Rule on word and page limits), 600.10(d)(1) (First Department rule on word and page limits), 670.10.3(a)(3) (Second Department rule on word and page limits); 800.8(a) (Third Department rule on page limits); 1000.4(f)(3) (Fourth Department rule on page limits).

aimlessness.[22] Pithiness is not merely admired by the appellate courts; it is likely to be far more effective than prolixity.

The First Department's Rules of Practice require, among other things, that the appellant's brief contain "an index or table of contents including the titles of the points urged in the brief" and "the argument for the appellant, which shall be divided into points by appropriate headings distinctively printed."[23] Relying on these provisions in DaSilva v. Everest Scaffolding, Inc.,[24] the First Department ruled that defendant's "argument that it is also entitled to contractual indemnification by third-party defendant is not properly before us since it is not included in the table of contents or as a point heading in the argument in [appellants'] main brief, as required by this Court's rules." The *DaSilva* court's interpretation of Rule 600.10 is a stringent one, but should be followed by all lawyers seeking appellate relief in the First Department.

§ 540. Calendar Practice and the Argument

On the question of appealability, the constitution and the statutes have the say. The same is true of scope of review. The early procedural steps of taking the appeal are also largely dictated by statute, but as the perfection stage is reached—securing the transcript and putting together the record and briefs—statutes begin to share power with individual rules of court. Now, arriving at calendar practice in the appellate courts, statutes leave the stage and the court rules become virtually the whole cast. At trial level, calendar practice is largely under the governance of the rules; at appellate level, it is almost entirely so. Our mission here will be to call attention to the several steps still left in perfecting the appeal and to cite at least a sample rule at each juncture.

The first question is how to get on the court's calendar. The practice will differ from court to court, perhaps entailing the filing of a "note of issue."[1] The rules will also determine how the parties are notified of when the case comes on for argument and how much time will be allowed for it,[2] and relevant instruction if there is—or if there is required to be—a submission without argument. In the Court of Appeals, for example, although appeals are argued orally, motions for leave to appeal ordinarily are not.[3]

In some departments, there are what are denominated the "Enumerated" and "Non-Enumerated" calendars. These are just lists of judgments and orders coming under one category or the other; the ones the appellate division deems the more important are listed as "enumerated" and the more pedestrian the "nonenumerated."[4] The consequence of the difference is that appeals in the "enumerated" category, or most of them, are orally argued, while the "unenumerated" appeals ordinarily are not.[5] In other departments there may be rules that perform an equivalent role in different terminology.[6]

In some departments there is a requirement of a "preargument conference" to take place in designated cases—a procedure designed to make another attempt at restricting

---

[22] See Slater v. Gallman, 38 N.Y.2d 1, 377 N.Y.S.2d 448, 339 N.E.2d 863 (1975).

[23] 22 N.Y.C.R.R. § 600.10(d)(2)(i), (iv).

[24] DaSilva v. Everest Scaffolding, Inc., 136 A.D.3d 423, 25 N.Y.S.3d 141 (1st Dep't 2016).

[1] See, e.g., 22 N.Y.C.R.R. § 600.11 (First Department).

[2] See, e.g., 22 N.Y.C.R.R. § 670.20 (Second Department).

[3] See 22 N.Y.C.R.R. § 500.21(a).

[4] See, e.g., 22 N.Y.C.R.R. § 600.4 (First Department).

[5] See 22 N.Y.C.R.R. § 600.11(f) (First Department).

[6] See, e.g., 22 N.Y.C.R.R. § 1000.11, the Fourth Department rule.

the issues and possibly securing settlement, akin to the purpose of the pretrial conference at trial level.[7] The various departments that have adopted such procedures take them quite seriously and will not suffer a disregard of their requirements. When a conference was duly set up under the Second Department rule, for example, and the respondents' attorney did not attend it, the court, under a provision authorizing sanctions,[8] refused to consider the respondents' brief.[9]

One of the few phases of appellate calendar practice that the CPLR does address is the preference, but the address is terse. CPLR 5521 states that "preferences in the hearing of an appeal may be granted in the discretion of the court to which the appeal is taken." It sets no standard, however, leaving it entirely to the individual courts. Some of the courts have rules that speak to the matter,[10] but even the absence of a governing rule does not seem to make much difference. The court can grant a preference whenever, on a sui generis basis, the facts warrant it. We can analogize here to the discretionary grounds on which special preferences are granted at trial level,[11] but the appellate preference is not the coveted prize that the one at trial level is. An appellate court abreast of its calendar may sometimes have more trouble keeping the parties moving than vice-versa.

For all calendar matters, the attorneys should consult the rules, and for what the rules don't cover, they should consult the clerk. The clerk's staff will usually be found courteous and willing to help and, of course, knowledgeable. And if the clerk wants things done a certain way, the lawyer should not be quick to see the contrary in the applicable statutes or rules. The matter can be discussed, but when it comes to calendar practice, the odds in a contest between the law and the clerk are with the clerk.

F. INCIDENTAL APPELLATE PRACTICE

Table of Sections

§ 541.   Motions in Appellate Courts
§ 542.   Dismissal of Appeal for Want of Prosecution

§ 541. Motions in Appellate Courts

One does not usually associate a "motion" with the appellate process, except perhaps the motion for leave to appeal, but there are a number of occasions when relief sought from an appellate court, sometimes incidental and sometimes final, is sought by motion. If a stipulation between the parties can't resolve an incidental dispute, for example, or a stipulation is not sufficient, it will usually take a motion to resolve it—as where an enlargement of time after a certain point in the appellate process has by rule been made to require court approval.[1] The rule of thumb about motions in an appellate court can be derived from the motion practice at trial level: any incidental order that the court has the power to make can be moved for by any interested party.

---

[7]   See, e.g., 22 N.Y.C.R.R. § 670.4, the Second Department rule. See § 374 for the analogy to the pretrial conference at trial level.

[8]   22 N.Y.C.R.R. § 670.4(b).

[9]   Romanelli v. Associated Marble Industry, Inc., 365 N.Y.S.2d 264 (2d Dep't 1975).

[10]   See, e.g., 22 N.Y.C.R.R. § 600.12 (First Department).

[11]   CPLR 3403(a)(3). See § 373.

[1]   See, e.g., 22 N.Y.C.R.R. § 670.8(d) (Second Department).

Several of the things already met require a motion. The provisional remedy of injunction does, and we now note that the motion for it can be made during the appellate stage of the litigation.[2] The appellate court is an alternative motion forum (the trial court the other) for a stay of enforcement during an appeal when the stay requires a motion, which it does when an automatic stay is not available.[3]

Most of the motions that appear in the appellate courts are during the appellate process itself, that is, after the appeal has been taken, but before it has been decided. The main one before that time is of course the motion for permission to appeal, made by the aspiring appellant. One seen after that time is the motion to reargue made by the appellate loser. These are such key motions in appellate practice, in fact, that special rules will often be found directed to them. The Court of Appeals rule on motions devotes much of its attention, in fact, to the motion for leave to appeal[4] and to one extent or another all of the departments of the appellate division regulate that motion. The same is true of the motion to reargue, treated in a later section.[5]

On the mechanics and procedural incidentals of motion practice, the appellate rules again must be the first resort. There will usually be something in point,[6] and if the applicable rule has all the answers, inquiry need go no further. If it does not, one may then consult the CPLR's general article on motion practice, Article 22. If on a given occasion an Article 22 provision does not seem to fit—it is devised, after all, with courts or original jurisdiction in mind—there is no remaining option but to call the clerk.

§ 542. Dismissal of Appeal for Want of Prosecution

The ultimate penalty for failing to bring the appeal to fruition is a dismissal for want of prosecution, the appellate equivalent of a trial-level dismissal on the same ground, and every bit as serious. When the time for the taking of a required step passes without the taking, the appeal starts to become ripe for such a dismissal. Most appellate courts, recognizing the bar's need for clear guidance on the matter, have rules directed to dismissals and calendar strikings of this kind.[1] A motion to dismiss is supplied, and the rules may also contain an automatic dismissal for a given omission. An appellate court can, moreover, direct a dismissal sua sponte—a prospect all the more likely when the court has already granted an extension of time and it has been abused.[2]

If the court does not keep surveillance on its cases, and the respondent is not particularly vigilant, the appeal may hang around for years without getting perfected, but the absence of sua sponte action by the court or early motion initiative by the respondent is no guarantee that a long delayed case is going to sneak through to a disposition on the merits. The court may entertain a dismissal request on the argument of the appeal itself, in fact, and grant the dismissal instead of reaching the merits.[3]

---

[2]   CPLR 5518.

[3]   CPLR 5519(c).

[4]   22 N.Y.C.R.R. § 500.22.

[5]   See § 544.

[6]   On motion practice generally, see 22 N.Y.C.R.R. §§ 500.21–500.25 (Court of Appeals), 600.2(a) (First Department), 670.5 (Second Department), 800.2(a) (Third Department), 1000.13 (Fourth Department).

[1]   See, e.g., 22 N.Y.C.R.R. § 500.16 (Court of Appeals rule).

[2]   See, e.g., Eller v. Eller, 44 A.D.2d 582, 353 N.Y.S.2d 244 (2d Dep't 1974).

[3]   See, e.g., Weingrad & Weingrad v. Kevelson, 44 A.D.2d 523, 353 N.Y.S.2d 216 (1st Dep't 1974).

The court can, and often does, grant a dismissal motion conditionally, the condition being that the appellant will serve and file the required papers or otherwise perfect the appeal within a stated time, but the appellant's lawyer cannot safely assume that this will always be the result. As has been noted several times already, attitudes on these matters may differ from court to court, or from time to time in the same court, and the indulgence of one moment may become the impatience of another. The lawyer uninitiated in these fluctuations would do well to read Tonkonogy v. Jaffin,[4] which acknowledges prior laxity and warns that the reins are again being tightened. It also stresses the appellant's obligations when faced with a motion to dismiss for want of prosecution. As a category of default, opposition to the motion requires (1) reasons satisfactorily explaining the delay and (2) affidavits averring the merits of the appeal.[5] The lawyer ready to subscribe to the letter of the court's requirements is relieved of having to look into whether the local temper is in a cycle of generosity or sternness. The dilatory lawyer, by contrast, may find himself spending more time on that line of inquiry than on the appeal.

The motion to dismiss an appeal for want of prosecution is addressed to the sound discretion of the court,[6] and the appellant who would stay in court should address that discretion with something substantial.

This category of dismissal may carry even greater consequences than a want of prosecution dismissal does in the trial court. In the trial court, it is not deemed a dismissal on the merits, so that if the original statute of limitations on the claim is still alive—it rarely is—it can be sued on again without meeting the defense of res judicata.[7] But it has been held that dismissal of an appeal for want of prosecution does act as a disposition on the merits—the merits just as they were found below. So held a divided Court of Appeals in Bray v. Cox,[8] in which an earlier appellate division order had been appealed and the appeal dismissed for nonprosecution. The case then went back to trial and another appeal was taken, this one from the final judgment. The appellant then sought to raise in the Court of Appeals the same point presented on the prior—the dismissed—appeal. The Court held that the dismissal acted as a bar to all questions that were presented, but never reached on the earlier appeal.

A close look at the *Bray* case shows quite a forfeiture. As was noted earlier, New York is unusually generous in its allowance of the interlocutory appeal.[9] The party aggrieved by a nonfinal determination has the option of taking it up for review with an immediate appeal, or in some cases of waiting for final judgment and, if the judgment is unfavorable, appealing the judgment and getting the old order reviewed as part of it.[10] The party who elects the immediate appeal and then lets it lapse forfeits both avenues of review and is stuck forever with the determination that aggrieved him. Here is how one appellate division sums up the impact of the *Bray* case:

> Where a party appeals from an intermediate order, [and] thereafter abandons
> the appeal for failure to perfect, and the appeal is then dismissed by an

---

4   Tonkonogy v. Jaffin, 21 A.D.2d 264, 249 N.Y.S.2d 934 (1st Dep't 1964).

5   See §§ 108, 427.

6   Tonkonogy v. Jaffin, 21 A.D.2d 264, 249 N.Y.S.2d 934 (1st Dep't 1964).

7   See § 375.

8   Bray v. Cox, 38 N.Y.2d 350, 379 N.Y.S.2d 803, 342 N.E.2d 575 (1976).

9   See § 526.

10   See § 530.

appellate court, the party is estopped for reasons of judicial economy from seeking review of issues which could have been raised on the appeal from the intermediate order . . . .[11]

Hence, an appellant who appeals an interlocutory order must be especially sensitive not to let the appeal lapse merely because he has appealed from a later judgment—or, indeed, from a later order rendered on reargument or renewal and posing the same issues as the original order, as occurred in Rubeo v. National Grange Mut. Ins. Co.[12]

The appellant who for whatever reason decides not to prosecute the earlier appeal should take formal steps to withdraw it, or, in an appropriate situation, move for an extension of time to perfect it. What bothered the court in *Rubeo* was the appellant's "complete indifference toward the court system" by ignoring the procedural steps prescribed for the prosecution of an appeal.

G. CONCLUDING THE APPEAL

Table of Sections

§ 543. Disposition of Appeal
§ 544. Reargument
§ 545. Remittitur

§ 543. Disposition of Appeal

The appellate court will direct whatever result is warranted by its review of the appeal's merits. Subdivision (a) of CPLR 5522 provides that the appellate court may "reverse, affirm, or modify, wholly or in part, any judgment, or order before it, as to any party," and that it shall "render a final determination or, where necessary or proper, remit to another court for further proceedings." The appellate court, in other words, may, within its powers of review, do whatever it thinks has to be done.

If the reviewing court is the appellate division, whose powers are coextensive with the trial court's, it can order a new trial in a money action unless the plaintiff stipulates to take less in damages or the defendant stipulates to pay more—the devices commonly known as "remittitur" and "additur," treated elsewhere.[1]

If restitution in conjunction with the result is called for, as where a levy has gone forward against the property of the defendant and the case is afterwards reversed and the judgment overturned on the appeal, the court can direct the restitution.[2] So can the trial court itself when a judgment's vacatur is called to its attention.[3] When the record before the appellate court is complete and nothing is to be gained by a new trial, the

---

[11] See Montalvo v. Nel Taxi Corp., 114 A.D.2d 494, 494 N.Y.S.2d 406 (2d Dep't 1985), where D had previously appealed an order denying a motion to vacate his default in answering. He then let the appeal lapse and the appeal was dismissed. When judgment was later entered against him after inquest, D appealed the judgment and tried to get the old default order reviewed as part of it. He did not succeed.

[12] Rubeo v. National Grange Mut. Ins. Co., 93 N.Y.2d 750, 697 N.Y.S.2d 866, 720 N.E.2d 86 (1999). The *Rubeo* case is treated in the lead note of NYSLD No. 478.

[1] See § 407. Subdivision (b) of CPLR 5522 requires the appellate division, upon rendering an additur or remittitur, to list the factors it considered. This category of "remittitur" should not be confused with the one (treated in § 545) that merely connotes the sending back of a case from an appellate court to a lower court.

[2] CPLR 5523.

[3] See CPLR 5015(d); see § 433.

court's disposition will be an order directing final judgment; or, in the case of the Court of Appeals, perhaps an order, after determining the law, remitting the case to the appellate division for further findings of fact, if found necessary. If the record is insufficient for final judgment, even if it affects only damages, for example, further proceedings will be needed, and these will take whatever form the appellate order of disposition directs.[4]

On an appeal in a case involving an indemnity claim asserted by way of a cross-claim between co-defendants or a third-party claim against an impleaded defendant, it has generally been understood that if the main judgment that P has against D is overturned, the overturning must carry down as well a third-party judgment that D has against co-defendant X or third-party defendant X for indemnification or contribution to D in respect of P's claim, and that is so even if X has not appealed.[5] That should still be the rule when the thing to be indemnified—P's main claim—is the claim that falls. How can an indemnification claim running only in favor of D against X to indemnify D for what D has to pay P be retained under any circumstances when D has paid P nothing, and will not have to?

But now consider this situation. P fell on a sidewalk and sued C, a city, and G, a garage, winning against both. Only C appealed, and won on the appeal when it was held that there was no defect in the sidewalk. That holding would have let G off too had G appealed. But G did not appeal. Does G get the advantage of co-defendant C's victory? The Court of Appeals in Hecht v. City of New York[6] said no: the nonappealing G may not have the fruits of the victory of appellant C. G thus ended up facing a liability alone—C is apparently out even as an indemnitor or contributor—for something for which the simple precaution of an appeal, and perhaps just the copying of C's briefs, would have released G altogether.

The lesson to every party in a case in which some adverse party has appealed is to project all possible results of the appeal and, if any of them can affect the client's interest adversely, take an appeal as a precaution.[7] If the 30-day period for an original appeal has expired, there will still be the 10-day period for a cross-appeal measured from the other party's service of its notice of appeal.[8]

How should *Hecht* play out in a clear-cut indemnification situation? There, as noted above, a third-party defendant (the indemnitor) will be given the benefit of an appellate victory by the main defendant (the indemnitee). But what of the converse, in which the third-party defendant is the successful appellant and the defendant the party that failed to appeal. *Hecht* would suggest that the defendant could not be given the advantage of the third-party defendant's victory, but the matter isn't clear.

The Court of Appeals has not reconciled its cases,[9] and especially in view of criticism of the *Hecht* decision as too strict,[10] some attorneys may be disposed to disregard *Hecht* and refrain from appealing in analogous situations. Caution suggests, however, that a

---

[4] See, e.g., Frenchman & Sweet, Inc. v. Philco Discount Corp., 21 A.D.2d 180, 249 N.Y.S.2d 611 (4th Dep't 1964).

[5] See, e.g., Salerno v. New York Cent. R. Co., 21 A.D.2d 850, 251 N.Y.S.2d 394 (4th Dep't 1964).

[6] Hecht v. City of New York, 60 N.Y.2d 57, 467 N.Y.S.2d 187, 454 N.E.2d 527 (1983).

[7] See the discussion of the *Hecht* case in the lead note in NYSLD No. 285.

[8] CPLR 5513(c); see § 533.

[9] See and compare Sharrow v. Dick Corp., 86 N.Y.2d 54, 629 N.Y.S.2d 980, 653 N.E.2d 1150 (1995).

[10] See Newman, *Appellate Practice,* N.Y.L.J., Oct. 20, 1983.

losing party, otherwise content not to appeal, should reconsider if some other losing party does appeal.[11]

Hecht does need further elaboration from the Court of Appeals. Some lower courts have distinguished the case as stating only a "general rule," such as Koscinski v. St. Joseph's Medical Center.[12] *Koscinski* involved two defendants who each cross-moved for dismissal in opposition to P's motion to restore a case to a calendar. The cross-motions were denied, but only D-1 appealed, winning a reversal and dismissal. D-2 was afterwards allowed, on a motion to "renew," to exploit the appellate victory of D-1.

The Second Circuit decision in Hegger v. Green[13] is a stark example of the consequences of failing to appeal in a multi-defendant case. P brought a wrongful death claim against hospital H and doctor D and got a half-million dollar verdict. There was some reduction for comparative fault on the decedent's part, and there was an apportionment of fault between H and D. D's total liability under the original judgment, after considering all things including potential contribution from H, was some $96,000. D did not appeal, but P and H did. P convinced the appellate court that there had been no comparative fault and hence that no deduction was permissible for it. H convinced the appellate court that H was not at fault at all. D did not convince the appellate court of anything because D did not appeal and was not there to state his case. The result was that D's exposure, $96,000 before the appeal, was more than $500,000 after it.[14]

A lawyer with a client so situated who fails to preserve the client's standing before the appellate court with a proper appeal had best have a carefully considered reason for standing pat, or an ample malpractice policy.

The different powers of review of the Court of Appeals and the appellate division, the Court of Appeals being restricted to law questions while the appellate division is able to review the facts as well, have created certain problems on Court of Appeals review. In formulating its dispositive order, the Court of Appeals is helped by knowing whether the appellate division has based its determination on the law, on the facts, or on both. To that end, the appellate division is required in several common instances to state in its order precisely what it has relied on in that respect.[15] After it has disposed of any questions of law, the Court of Appeals is then better situated to determine what to do with the case, e.g., direct final judgment because no facts remain to be reviewed, remand to the appellate division to review facts not previously reviewed, remand to the trial court for a retrial because that is what the appellate division says it would have done on the facts if it should be found to be in error on the law, etc.

Absent such specific indications from the appellate division as to how it has disposed of the facts, the Court of Appeals is required to presume that the appellate division has not considered the facts,[16] which becomes relevant if the Court of Appeals disposition is one of reversal or modification. If in that situation it appears that the appellate division has not considered the facts, whether because it has said as much or because its silence on the matter has invoked the presumption, the Court of Appeals must remit the case to

---

[11]   See the discussions in NYSLD No. 427 and SPR 27:3.

[12]   Koscinski v. St. Joseph's Medical Center, 47 A.D.3d 685, 850 N.Y.S.2d 162 (2d Dep't 2008) (SPR 195:3).

[13]   Hegger v. Green, 646 F.2d 22 (2d Cir. 1981).

[14]   The *Hegger* case is treated in the lead note in NYSLD No. 259.

[15]   See CPLR 5712(b), (c).

[16]   CPLR 5612(a).

the appellate division for consideration of the facts raised[17] in an instance in which it might otherwise have been able to direct a final judgment and bring the case to an end.

Whenever the Court of Appeals has before it an appeal on certified questions submitted by the appellate division,[18] the Court does not simply answer the questions and send back the answers; it is also required to direct entry of the appropriate judgment or order,[19] i.e., to dispose of the case just as it would on any appeal.

Another point of interplay between the two courts concerns the fact that a final determination in the appellate division is appealable to the Court of Appeals of right if there are two dissenting justices in the appellate division,[20] for which reason the latter's order determining an appeal must state whether there are any dissents.[21]

An opinion is not required from the appellate court and it is therefore in the court's discretion, and in the discretion of each judge or justice, whether to write one. But if the case is one of reversal or modification and no opinion is written, the appellate court must at least "briefly state the grounds of its decision."[22]

§ 544. Reargument

The party who lost the appeal can move to reargue it, which implies an ability to convince the court that it overlooked something or misapprehended the law or the facts, which in turn explains why the great majority of reargument motions are denied. Good chance or not, it is the loser's last one, and the magnetism of a last hurrah is, for many a loser, irresistible. The number of reargument motions is therefore substantial and for that reason almost all courts have a rule directed to them. The attorney considering such a motion should check carefully into any time limitations the local rule may impose on a motion to reargue.[1]

Also important to take note of here is the general rule, previously met at trial level, but relevant on appeal as well, that a motion to renew may not be permitted to take advantage of changes in the law occurring after the court has handed down its decision unless the time in which to appeal the decision, or to take a further appeal from it, is still open.[2] This is a necessary adjunct of the rule that "there must be an end to lawsuits and the time to take an appeal cannot forever be extended."[3]

The motion to reargue, which involves no new proof or points—and sometimes a court rule will explicitly preclude reargument motions from raising new points[4]—must be distinguished from the situation in which new proof has been discovered and is felt to be sufficient to change the result of the case. The expedient for the presentation of the new matter is not a motion to reargue in the appellate court, but a motion in the trial

---

[17] CPLR 5613.

[18] See CPLR 5713.

[19] CPLR 5614.

[20] CPLR 5601(a); see § 527.

[21] CPLR 5712(a).

[22] CPLR 5522(a). For a brief time, between 1975 and 1977, this was also required when the decision was an affirmance. See Commentary C5522:3 on McKinney's CPLR 5522.

[1] See, e.g., 22 N.Y.C.R.R. § 500.24 (Court of Appeals rule).

[2] See § 254.

[3] In re Huie, 20 N.Y.2d 568, 572, 285 N.Y.S.2d 610, 612, 232 N.E.2d 642, 644 (1967).

[4] The Court of Appeals rule, 22 N.Y.C.R.R. § 500.24(d), can again serve as the example.

court under CPLR 5015(a)(2) to vacate the judgment or order and rehear the issue, or try the case anew.

Because the vast majority of reargument motions are denied, one may even say that it is almost futile to move to reargue, especially in the Court of Appeals. When the case is not even one for an appeal as of right, moreover, but requires leave, and leave has been moved for and denied, the chance of obtaining permission to reargue the motion for leave stands on an even lower level of likelihood. That's nevertheless what a defendant sought in Intercontinental Credit Corp. v. Roth.[5] What he found, instead, in addition to the predictable denial of the motion for leave to reargue the motion for leave, was $5,000 worth of frivolity sanctions under Part 130–1 of the Rules: one $2,500 allotment debited to him, and one to his lawyer.

§ 545. Remittitur

The determination of the appellate court is embodied in an order, which is entered in the office of the appellate court's clerk.[1] If further proceedings are contemplated, a copy of the order together with the appellate record is remitted to the clerk of the court required to conduct such further proceedings.[2] That would usually be the court of original jurisdiction, as where a new trial has been ordered. But it can instead be an appellate court, as where the Court of Appeals, determining issues of law, remits the case to the appellate division for a review of the facts if there has not yet been one.[3] If no further proceedings are called for, as where the appellate determination is final, the case gets remitted to the original court, whose clerk enters the appellate order and any judgment it may call for.[4]

If further proceedings are required, they should be conducted in conformity with the intentions of the appellate court as embodied in the order. If there has been an opinion in the case that sheds any light on intentions, it must of course be consulted. In the average case, further proceedings will require nothing very unusual: a retrial on all or some issues, a reassessment of damages, new findings by a judge or referee, etc. If perfect implementation of the appellate order has been rendered impossible by changed conditions—an occurrence more likely to appear when equitable relief is involved, but not frequent even in that situation—the trial court should adapt its proceedings to implement the appellate order as nearly as may be. The Court of Appeals has said that "adapting relief to the exigencies of new conditions ... is not nullification, but enforcement."[5]

If there should be any need to correct a remittitur, i.e., the appellate order accompanying the record on its trip back to the lower court, as where the order does not accurately reflect the appellate disposition intended, a motion to amend the remittitur

[5] Intercontinental Credit Corp. Div. of Pan American Trade Development Corp. v. Roth, 78 N.Y.2d 306, 574 N.Y.S.2d 528, 579 N.E.2d 688 (1991).

[1] CPLR 5524(a).

[2] CPLR 5524(b). This "remittitur" merely means the return of a case to the court it came from, either for further proceedings or for final judgment. It is to be distinguished from the word as used in its "additur-remittitur" context where it implies a reduction of damages for excessiveness. See § 407.

[3] See CPLR 5613; see § 543.

[4] CPLR 5524(b).

[5] Rudiger v. Coleman, 228 N.Y. 225, 233, 126 N.E. 723, 726 (1920).

should be made to the appellate court from which it comes. No other court is authorized to effect such an amendment.

It may also happen that the losing party wants to try to take the case to the U.S. Supreme Court, which may be permissible if a federal right is involved.[6] If the order and the opinion do not make clear the involvement of a federal issue, an amendment of the order of remittitur can be sought from the appellate court to clarify whether a federal issue was passed on.

On rare occasions, an appellate remittitur will go lost, as it did in Fry v. Village of Tarrytown.[7] Saying that "for this court to proceed, a copy of the remittitur must be entered in the . . . Clerk's Office," the court held itself to be without jurisdiction to take further proceedings, denying a request for them "without prejudice to renewal after the filing of the remittitur." If the remittitur can't be located, an application can ordinarily be made to the appellate court for a new one.

---

[6]   28 U.S.C.A. § 1257. The route to the U.S. Supreme Court from a state court today is by petition for a writ of certiorari exclusively. A 1988 amendment eliminated the appeal of right. See the Commentary on the 1988 Revision in 28 U.S.C.A. § 1257.

[7]   Fry v. Village of Tarrytown, 176 Misc. 2d 275, 671 N.Y.S.2d 633 (Sup. Ct., Westchester County 1998).

Chapter 20

SPECIAL PROCEEDINGS

Analysis

PART I.   THE SPECIAL PROCEEDING, IN GENERAL

PART II. THE ARTICLE 78 PROCEEDING

A.   **Introductory**

B.   **Scope of the Proceeding**

C.   **Procedural Basics**

D.   **Mechanics**

§ 546. Special Proceedings, Introductory

The purpose of this chapter is to cover the "special proceeding," an expeditious device available in certain instances.

The first segment will discuss special proceedings generally, including a detailed treatment of Article 4 of the CPLR, whose purpose is to supply a central repository of governing rules for special proceedings. The next will treat the Article 78 proceeding, whose principal function is to supply judicial review of administrative determinations. It's among the most important and frequently used procedures in practice today. The same may be said of the summary proceeding—the device whereby the landlord-tenant dispute, for either rent or repossession—goes to court. The summary proceeding is the final item in this chapter.

PART I.　THE SPECIAL PROCEEDING, IN GENERAL

Table of Sections

§ 547.　　The "Special Proceeding," Described

§ 548.　　Statute of Limitations in Special Proceedings

§ 549.　　Venue in Special Proceedings

§ 550.　　Procedure in Special Proceedings

§ 551.　　Parties to Special Proceedings

§ 552.　　Pleadings in Special Proceedings

§ 553.　　Bringing the Proceeding

§ 554.　　Motions in Special Proceedings

§ 555.　　Disclosure in Special Proceedings

§ 556.　　Hearing and Disposition of Special Proceeding

§ 547.　The "Special Proceeding," Described

A special proceeding is a quick and inexpensive way to implement a right. It's as plenary as an action, culminating in a judgment, but is brought on with the ease, speed, and economy of a mere motion. Combining the best of both worlds, the special proceeding is of course preferable to the ordinary action, but it may be used only when explicitly authorized by law in a particular case. The rule is that it takes an ordinary action to prosecute a right "except where prosecution in the form of a special proceeding is authorized."[1]

When a given procedure is authorized for both an action and a special proceeding, the CPLR mentions only the "action" because the action is defined to include a special proceeding.[2]

Statutes authorizing special proceedings abound, both in and out of the CPLR. Some of the special proceedings authorized by the CPLR itself and already met in this book are the proceeding to settle an infant's claim,[3] the proceeding by an attaching plaintiff against a garnishee to compel the garnishee to deliver property to the levying sheriff,[4] and the several supplied for the enforcement of a money judgment.[5] Some to be studied shortly are the Article 78 proceeding[6] and those supplied for testing the arbitrability of a dispute or the validity of an arbitral award.[7] A special proceeding is also used in the supreme court to determine matters relating to a trust.[8]

Outside the CPLR are many other statutes authorizing special proceedings. These may be found in various parts, likely and unlikely, of the consolidated laws. One of the likely ones is the well-known summary proceeding to recover the possession of real

---

[1]　CPLR 103(b).

[2]　CPLR 105(b). Procedure in special proceedings is treated in § 550.

[3]　CPLR 1207. See § 200.

[4]　CPLR 6214(d). See § 321.

[5]　CPLR 5225(b), 5227, 5239. See §§ 510 and 521.

[6]　See §§ 557 et seq.

[7]　See § 591 (Practitioner's Edition).

[8]　CPLR 7701.

property,[9] taken up later.[10] Although the principal device for determining and punishing a contempt of court today is a mere motion, there may still be occasions to use a special proceeding for it.[11]

The legislature has authorized a special proceeding for the litigation of many other categories of dispute. Its speed has made it appropriate to test election squabbles, for example, especially preelection challenges carried on under the pressure of an approaching election.[12] A special need for a procedure quicker than a ponderous action presumably underlies most if not all of the legislative enactments that allow the proceeding. It's a kind of indirect way of offering a given category of dispute a special preference. It is permitted, for example, as the means to get a dangerous dog destroyed or securely confined[13] or to have a person declared an incapacitated person and have a guardian appointed for him[14] where the need to act fast is plain.

Whether the legislative motive in allowing a special proceeding in a given instance is plain or not, its availability is always good news to the petitioner,[15] the person with the claim. It will spare the petitioner the burdensome trappings of an ordinary action and permit the application to be brought on promptly.

There is no formula for determining when a special proceeding is permissible. Whatever the theoretical purpose may be for authorizing a special proceeding, the legislature has sometimes supplied it arbitrarily. The would-be petitioner must therefore ascertain that there is statutory authority for bringing a special proceeding instead of an action. Absent such authorization, the rule is that the case must be prosecuted in the form of an ordinary action.

There are a few exceptions. Sometimes when an application has to be made and there's no procedural guidance for it, the courts have directed that the device of the special proceeding be used. They've done this with the application for leave to file a late notice of claim, for example,[16] and with the application for preaction disclosure.[17]

What happens when a petitioner mistakenly brings a special proceeding and it is not authorized; when a regular action should have been brought instead? There used to be a dismissal for this defect, but no longer. If the defect is the only one—jurisdiction having been duly acquired over the parties—the remedy is for the court to convert the case into an action. New York no longer tolerates a dismissal for this relatively innocent error.[18]

The conversion is effected by the court's ordering the process and pleadings in the proceeding to be deemed the process and pleadings in an action, the case to be henceforth treated as having been properly brought. The court may prescribe any other conversion

---

[9]   RPAPL Article 7.

[10]   See §§ 571 et seq. (Practitioner's Edition).

[11]   See § 484.

[12]   See Elec. Law Article 16 generally and §§ 16–116 in particular.

[13]   Agric. & Mkts. Law § 121.

[14]   Mental Hyg. Law §§ 81.05 et seq.

[15]   Parties to the special proceeding are petitioner and respondent instead of plaintiff and defendant. See § 551.

[16]   See Billone v. Town of Huntington, 188 A.D.2d 526, 591 N.Y.S.2d 437 (2d Dep't 1992). See § 32.

[17]   See Robinson v. Government of Malaysia, 174 Misc. 2d 560, 664 N.Y.S.2d 907 (Sup. Ct., New York County 1997). See § 352.

[18]   See CPLR 103(c).

steps it deems appropriate. If there are several claims or counterclaims or cross-claims present in a given case, for example, some of which should be actions and others special proceedings, the court may sever any that should be prosecuted in different form and direct that they proceed accordingly.[19]

Conversely, an action for relief that should have been sought in a special proceeding may be converted into one.

Sometimes the mistake made by the petitioner is not in bringing an action when a proceeding is proper, but in attempting to "appeal" an objectionable determination. In that situation, a simple conversion can't help. The reason is that jurisdiction of the other side must be obtained, and while the procedures of an action include the jurisdiction-getting device of service of process,[20] an appeal does not. Hence, a dismissal may be the result,[21] without prejudice to the commencement of a proceeding. Time, however, can run out in the interim, which makes the statute of limitations—a sensitive issue in all cases—an especially sensitive one in special proceedings. It's the next topic.

§ 548. Statute of Limitations in Special Proceedings

In most categories of special proceeding, problems of timeliness seldom arise. This is probably because the special proceeding has been primarily designed by the legislature for situations calling for speed and dispatch, and it would be especially perverse for the petitioner—the one who presumably needs the relief quickly—to let it ride for any time at all, much less for a time adequate to raise a limitations' problem.

When the problem does arise, it is primarily in a case in which the allotted time period is unusually short. It is only four months, for example, in the Article 78 proceeding,[1] and only 20 days in the proceeding to test the arbitrability of a dispute after arbitration has been demanded.[2] As one may expect, therefore, those are two special proceedings that raise limitations' issues often. In other categories with time limitations as short or even shorter, however, time problems may appear less frequently simply because of the principals' continuous alertness to the need for judicial relief. This is notably the case in nomination and election disputes where, despite very short limitations,[3] issues of timeliness are relatively infrequent because the parties will usually have their attorneys perched on the courthouse steps.[4]

In yet other categories of special proceeding, the barrier of time may seem altogether absent, for a combination of reasons. The summary proceeding, the prolific device for the landlord-tenant dispute, for example, involves claims that usually spring from contract

---

[19]   See CPLR 407.

[20]   See § 553.

[21]   See Common Council of City of Gloversville v. Town Bd. of Town of Johnstown, 144 A.D.2d 90, 536 N.Y.S.2d 881 (3d Dep't 1989).

[1]   CPLR 217(1). The Article 78 proceeding is the subject of more detailed study later. See § 566.

[2]   CPLR 7503(c). See § 593, in the arbitration chapter (Practitioner's Edition). One must remember that the 5 and 6-day add-on periods in CPLR 2103(b)(2) apply only to papers served via regular mail within an already commenced and pending litigation. They do not apply to papers served in an administrative proceeding or other out-of-court proceedings, such as an arbitration. See § 202.

[3]   See Elec. Law Article 16.

[4]   A good treatment of these issues in election cases appears in Van Wie and Houdek, *Outside Counsel*, N.Y.L.J., July 11, 2005, at 4. Any lawyer, and especially one not expert in the subject, with the temerity to represent either primary or election candidates will find the article helpful.

and which therefore earn a six-year period of limitations.[5] On top of that is the relief: the landlord seeks in the proceeding either rent or the premises; and the landlord who waits six years for that has not been a notable drain on judicial attention.

The first question to ask is: where does one find the statute of limitations applicable to a given special proceeding? The most likely place is the statute that expressly authorizes the proceeding; it's in any event the first place to look.[6] If there's nothing about time there or in any other provision specifically devised for the particular proceeding,[7] it would be governed, at the outer limit, by the six-year residual provision applicable to ordinary actions not having a specific period.[8] If the relief demanded sounds in equity, such as where it consists of an injunction or like direction, the petitioner must also guard against the sui generis defense of laches.[9] One seeking to have a dangerous dog destroyed, for example, should not bring the proceeding several years after the animal's bite if in the interim it has won prizes for gentleness.

The filing of the petition constitutes the moment of commencement of the proceeding for statute of limitations purposes.[10] Before 1992, when the filing system was adopted for use in the supreme and county courts, it was the service of the initiatory papers that marked commencement, not their filing.[11] The interplay of the filing and service requirements, which can of course affect the statute of limitations, is treated below.[12]

§ 549. Venue in Special Proceedings

The proper venue of a special proceeding must be found in the provision that authorizes the particular special proceeding either expressly or inferentially. CPLR 506(a), which is addressed to the venue of special proceedings "generally" and which may therefore be assumed to set the proper venue, does no such thing. All it does is take whatever county the special statute offers as proper venue in the given instance and authorizes the proceeding to be brought in that county or any other "within the judicial district," just as occurs with the venue of ordinary motions.[1] It was in fact an analogy to motion practice and to the similarity the procedure in a special proceeding bears to it that prompted the Advisory Committee to offer these alternatives.[2]

The point is that one must find the initially proper county of venue in or through the statute supplying the particular proceeding.[3] That statute will usually be found to resolve the venue question. The special proceeding to settle an infant's claim, for

[5] CPLR 213(2). See §§ 35, 566.

[6] CPLR 7503(c) and some of the sections in Article 16 of the Election Law are examples of statutes that authorize special proceedings and also stipulate time limits for them.

[7] The statute of limitations for an Article 78 proceeding, for example, although not contained in Article 78 itself, is contained in another statute, CPLR 217(1), explicitly addressed to it. See § 35.

[8] CPLR 213(1), 101, 103(b). See § 35.

[9] The laches doctrine is discussed in § 36.

[10] CPLR 304(a); see § 45.

[11] See Matter of Fernandez, 130 A.D.2d 657, 515 N.Y.S.2d 588 (2d Dep't 1987).

[12] See §§ 550, 553.

[1] See CPLR 2212(a); § 245.

[2] See Fin. Rep. Advy. Comm., Adv. Draft (Ed. Thompson Co. Jan. 4, 1961), p. A–162, afterwards embodied in 5th Rep. Leg. Doc. No. 15, p. 74 (1961).

[3] CPLR 506(b) supplies the venue for the Article 78 proceeding and is separately studied later. See § 565.

example, is brought in the county in which an action could have been brought had there been no settlement.[4] A special proceeding in aid of the enforcement of a money judgment is brought where the respondent lives or works;[5] one to compel arbitration is brought where the agreement requiring arbitration specifies or in other counties listed in the applicable statute when the agreement is silent.[6] Those are CPLR provisions authorizing special proceedings. Statutes outside the CPLR that authorize special proceedings may also be found to dictate venue.[7]

Once the county of proper venue is found from the special statute, CPLR 506(a) can operate on it, authorizing venue in any other county in the same judicial district. CPLR 506(a) and its alternatives will not be applicable, however, if the law authorizing the given proceeding has "otherwise prescribed." Precisely what qualifies as an "otherwise prescribed" prescription is not clear. If the authorizing law sets down a proper venue county, but without language indicating that it is to be the only proper one, presumably CPLR 506(a) can be allowed to supply its alternatives. Any specific limiting language, however, indicating that the venue set is the only one authorized, should trigger the "otherwise" clause of CPLR 506(a) and withhold the alternatives.

The matter may not be terribly important because even a wrong guess will lead to a mere change of venue to the county the court deems the proper one.[8] The same provision that declares that the selection of a wrong venue is not a jurisdictional defect in an action should apply to a special proceeding as well.[9]

This is especially comforting when one encounters a statute authorizing a special proceeding without any indications at all about venue. Where should the proceeding be brought in such a case? Following through on the CPLR's direction to apply the CPLR in general to any proceeding not having a specific provision addressed to the given procedural matter at hand,[10] the petitioner can presumably borrow for the proceeding the venue instructions that CPLR 503 offers in detail for actions. The county of residence of either party would then be proper venue.[11]

Note that CPLR 506(a), in authorizing venue "in any county within the judicial district where the proceeding is triable," appears to address itself only to the supreme court. It is that court with which Article 5 of the CPLR is preoccupied; the quoted provision is in fact borrowed from the venue provision applicable to motion practice in the supreme court,[12] not in other courts. But this borrowing overlooks that although the supreme court is the proper forum for many, and perhaps even most, special proceedings, it is not the exclusive forum for all of them. The proceeding to destroy a dangerous animal, for example, is authorized for and is usually brought in the lower courts, including the town and village courts.[13] The ubiquitous summary proceeding to recover

---

[4] CPLR 1207.

[5] CPLR 5221(a).

[6] CPLR 7502(a).

[7] See, e.g., Mental Hyg. Law § 81.05.

[8] CPLR 511. Those parts of CPLR 511 supplying the special "demand" procedure for changing the venue of an action, however (see § 123), are not feasible to apply in a special proceeding and should not be used there.

[9] CPLR 509, 101, 103(b). See § 116.

[10] CPLR 103(b).

[11] See CPLR 503(a).

[12] CPLR 2212(a).

[13] See Agric. & Mkts. Law § 121, specifying a "municipal judge or justice."

the possession of real property, a species of special proceeding, is almost invariably allotted to the lowest court of civil jurisdiction servicing the area in which the real property is located.[14] Even some of the CPLR's own provisions authorizing special proceedings confer jurisdiction on courts other than the supreme court.[15] Whenever that is so, and the proceeding is being brought in other than the supreme court, the alternatives of CPLR 506(a) would likely be irrelevant and should therefore be deemed inapplicable.

§ 550. Procedure in Special Proceedings

Article 4 of the CPLR governs the special proceeding and is the main source of procedural guidance for it. But it's not the sole source. The first place to look for any procedural instruction for a given special proceeding is of course in the provision that authorizes the proceeding. Some authorizing provisions are so replete with instruction that little or no recourse to Article 4 of the CPLR is needed. An example of this is the summary proceeding to recover possession of real property under RPAPL Article 7, for which recourse to the CPLR is rarely necessary. Another example is the Article 78 proceeding. Recognizing the numerous cases the article generates, the legislature has supplied within Article 78 itself the basic procedures for it, for the most part independent of Article 4, to which an Article 78 proceeding therefore turns only rarely.

Both of these articles, for the very reason of their frequency and importance in practice, are studied individually later.[1] Most statutes authorizing special proceedings do only that, however, leaving procedure to the guidance of CPLR Article 4, sometimes entirely and sometimes with only one or two variations dictated by the authorizing statute, perhaps addressed to such issues as how or upon whom to serve the initiatory papers.[2]

To whatever extent it purports to speak to a given procedure, the special authorizing statute governs to the exclusion of Article 4. The progression of governance in special proceedings, therefore, is (1) the authorizing statute, (2) Article 4 of the CPLR, and (3) the CPLR in general. Since Article 4 usually has all that's needed, reference to the CPLR at large is not frequent.

The mission of the next few sections is to examine the procedures prescribed by Article 4, the very existence of which now frees the legislature to authorize a special proceeding for any given purpose without having to devise procedure afresh when it does. The special problems met in special proceedings because of the adoption of the "filing" system for commencing cases in the supreme and county courts are treated in the section on "Bringing the Proceeding."[3]

§ 551. Parties to Special Proceedings

The one who brings the special proceeding is called the "petitioner" and the one it is brought against is called the "respondent"; they're the equivalent of what the plaintiff

---

[14] See § 572 (Practitioner's Edition).

[15] See, e.g., CPLR 1207, 5221(a).

[1] See §§ 557 et seq. (Article 78 proceedings) and §§ 571 et seq. (summary proceedings) (Practitioner's Edition).

[2] See, e.g., CPLR 1207, 7503(c).

[3] § 553.

and defendant are in an ordinary action.[1] Since most special proceedings involve adversaries, the great majority have respondents. On occasion there may be no adverse party, however, such as may happen with a special proceeding to dispose of an infant's or incompetent's real property. There the question of whether there shall be notice to anyone at all is left to the court's discretion.[2]

If the authorizing statute requires notice of the proceeding to be given "as directed by the court,"[3] or to be served upon "such persons"[4] or "such other persons"[5] as the court may direct, or involve similar judicial discretion, this signifies that the court will be consulted at the very outset for a determination of who the adversaries are or, in any event, who shall be given notice of the proceeding. In these instances, the thing to do is bring the proceeding on with an order to show cause—one of the options for commencing a special proceeding[6]—which will enable the court to supervise the matter. If the court finds the application of interest to no one but the petitioner, as in a proceeding for a change of name sought by a competent adult,[7] it can dispense with notice altogether. When it does, it can proceed with the petition forthwith—there is no one to notify—and even determine it on the merits summarily if the papers are adequate.[8]

The party-joining devices available without leave of court in an ordinary action after its commencement, such as impleader under CPLR 1007 and the joinder of additional parties on a counterclaim or cross-claim under CPLR 3019(d), are available in a special proceeding, but only by leave of court.[9] The idea is to prevent an adverse party from using those devices to delay a special proceeding, leaving it to the court to determine whether the joinder is appropriate. As long as court leave is secured, any of the panoply of joinder devices can be used in a special proceeding, including intervention and interpleader in addition to those just mentioned.

§ 552. Pleadings in Special Proceedings

The initial pleading in a special proceeding is the "petition," the equivalent of the complaint in an action. It must in general comply with the requirements applicable to a complaint.[1] CPLR 3013, the core provision applicable to the complaint, applies as well to the petition in a special proceeding.[2] Any pleading direction contained in the statute authorizing the particular special proceeding would of course have to be followed. By listing specific requirements, the authorizing statute is able to control more directly the information deemed relevant to the dispute involved in the given proceeding.[3] Absent a pleading instruction in the authorizing statute, the petition need only comply with the usual (and liberal) CPLR demands. Unlike the complaint in an action, the petition in a

---

[1]   CPLR 401.

[2]   See, e.g., RPAPL 1721.

[3]   E.g., CPLR 1207.

[4]   E.g., Elec. Law §§ 16–116.

[5]   E.g., CPLR 5239.

[6]   See § 553.

[7]   See Civ. Rights Law § 62.

[8]   When the proceeding is ex parte, a question of appealability arises when the relief sought by the petitioner is denied. See § 526.

[9]   CPLR 401.

[1]   CPLR 402.

[2]   See Boll v. Shanly, 34 A.D.2d 875, 310 N.Y.S.2d 847 (3d Dep't 1970).

[3]   See, e.g., Mental Hyg. Law § 81.08.

special proceeding is usually accompanied by affidavits, and because these supply more detail than a pleading does, the presence of affidavits often reduces dependence on the pleadings. The sufficiency of a pleading in a special proceeding, in fact, should be measured by the supporting affidavits as well as by the pleading itself; the affidavits can be taken as filling any gaps otherwise discernible in the pleading.

The responsive pleading is an "answer," just as it is in an action, but CPLR 402 requires an answer only "where there is an adverse party," recognizing, as discussed in the prior section, that some special proceedings have more. In the few that don't, the proceeding is being brought in fact or in effect ex parte, in which event the petition must state whether any prior application was made for similar relief and, if so, what happened on it, why is this petition being brought anew, etc. This recognizes that when there is no adverse party, there is no one to balance the petitioner's one-sided presentation; it's analogous to the requirement imposed on a party making an ex parte motion in an ordinary action.[4]

The answer may contain a counterclaim, and presumably it may contain a cross-claim if there should be multiple respondents. The interposition of a counterclaim or cross-claim against a party and nonparty together, which would entail the joinder now of the nonparty, requires court leave.[5] Some caselaw suggests that leave is required even for a cross-claim being used against one already a party,[6] but that should not be a problem. If the court finds that for one reason or another the cross-claim should not be heard in the present proceeding, it can simply sever it.[7]

A counterclaim must be replied to, just as it must be in an action, but a cross-claim needs an answer only if the pleading containing it demands one.[8] Note, however, that in an action, an answer without a counterclaim may not be voluntarily replied to (court leave is required), while in a special proceeding, the petitioner may serve a reply to new matter contained in an answer even if no counterclaim is asserted.[9]

Any further pleadings require court leave, just as in an action.[10]

§ 553. Bringing the Proceeding

CPLR 403 supplies the procedure for the commencement of the proceeding. Since the procedure is analogous to the making of a motion within an action, the reader looking for a broad perspective may find it profitable, for comparison purposes, to review motion mechanics at this point.[1]

The petitioner commences the special proceeding by filing a petition with the clerk.[2] The notice of petition or order to show cause, which will specify the time and place of the hearing and enumerate the supporting affidavits that accompany the petition,[3] need not

---

[4]   See CPLR 2217(b); § 244.

[5]   See § 551.

[6]   See Balaban v. Phillips, 138 Misc. 2d 990, 526 N.Y.S.2d 347 (N.Y. City Civ. Ct. 1988).

[7]   CPLR 603. See § 129.

[8]   See CPLR 3011.

[9]   CPLR 402.

[10]   CPLR 402, 3011.

[1]   See § 247.

[2]   CPLR 304(a); see § 45.

[3]   CPLR 403(a), (d).

be filed along with the petition.[4] Before 2001, it had to be, but this was found to create special statute of limitations problems.[5] Hence, while the notice of petition must still accompany the petition when it's served, it need not—though it may—accompany the petition when it's filed. It must be kept in mind, of course, that it's the filing of the petition that measures whether the applicable statute of limitations has been satisfied.

The notice of petition or order to show cause is process, the counterparts of the summons in an action. The petition is the pleading, the counterpart of the action's complaint. We will begin our discussion with the notice of petition and petition method of commencing a special proceeding, and return later to the order to show cause alternative.

The notice of petition, as will be seen, must among other things set a return day for the proceeding. This will entail consultation with the rules of the judge who will hear the case and when the petition is filed there will usually have as yet been no judge assigned. Hence, the Uniform Rules require that the petition be filed with a Request for Judicial Intervention (RJI).[6] The filing of an RJI identifies the case at the very outset and gets it assigned to a judge,[7] who can then be consulted for approval of a return day. A return day has to be included in the notice of petition, and the notice of petition must accompany the petition when service is made,[8] so it would be convenient for the petitioner to have in hand a proper return day to insert into the notice of petition before effecting service. (More on the issue of what return date to insert in the notice of petition appears below.)

Just as in an action where the summons and complaint must be served on the defendant within a set period after their filing, so in a special proceeding must the notice of petition and petition be served on the respondent within a set period after the filing of the petition. In an action, the period for service is 120 days, running from the filing itself.[9] In a special proceeding, the period for service is not calculated from the filing of the petition. Rather, the period for service is whatever is left on the statute of limitations, plus 15 days.[10] This may be convoluted, but it is a matter that has to be attended to warily. The time element must be negotiated with care because it quickly becomes intermeshed with the statute of limitations—and the statute of limitations in a special proceeding is usually a short one.[11] While it is the filing of the petition that marks commencement, a failure to effect service of the petition and notice of petition within the

---

[4]　CPLR 304(a).

[5]　See the discussion of the 2001 amendment in the lead note in SPR 116:1 and in a follow-up note in SPR 120:3–4.

[6]　See, e.g., 22 N.Y.C.R.R. §§ 202.6, 202.9 (applicable in the supreme and county courts); § 77C. The official form prescribed for the RJI is reprinted in § 77C.

[7]　See § 77B. 22 N.Y.C.R.R. § 202.8(b), which governs the making of a motion in a case not yet assigned to a judge, has a detailed procedural prescription for a motion, which 22 N.Y.C.R.R. § 202.9 borrows to apply to a special proceeding.

[8]　The mere notice that CPLR 305(b) permits to be used instead of a complaint at the outset of an action, see § 60, is not an available alternative in a special proceeding. See Lebow v. Village of Lansing Planning Bd., 151 A.D.2d 865, 542 N.Y.S.2d 840 (3d Dep't 1989); and Cruz v. N.Y.C. Department of Education, N.Y.L.J., Jan. 19, 2010 (decision dated Jan. 5), at 18, col.3 (Sup. Ct., New York County; Scarpulla, J.) (SPR 222:4).

[9]　See § 63.

[10]　See CPLR 306–b. The actual language of the statute is that if the applicable statute of limitations is four months or less, the 15-day provision applies. Because most proceedings are in that range—the Article 78 proceeding, for example, has a four-month statute of limitations under CPLR 217—we just assume in this discussion that the 15-day provision is the applicable one.

[11]　See § 548.

required time can also, at least where not excused, produce a dismissal with statute of limitations consequences.

The court can extend the 15-day period "upon good cause shown or in the interest of justice."[12]

The hearing or "return" day may not be set for earlier than the 8th day after the papers are served. The answer and its supporting affidavits must then be served at least two days before the return day,[13] which raises the same problem met with motions: answering papers served at that time, since they are usually served by mail, may not reach the petitioner before the return day. The problem is avoided in the special proceeding much as it is in motion practice within an action: by CPLR 403(b) making available an alternative set of time requirements.

In the special proceeding, instead of using a minimum 8-day notice period, the petitioner can opt to give at least 12 days notice, i.e., set a return day at least 12 days away from the time the initiatory papers are served. The petitioner who does that can then demand, in the notice of petition, that the respondent's answering papers be served at least 7 days before the return day.[14] This helps assure receipt of the papers in advance of the hearing. The petitioner's reply in that instance, if there is to be a reply, must be served at least one day before the return day.[15]

These time provisions apply to almost all special proceedings. Occasionally, a given category of proceeding will have its own time requirements, such as the Article 78 proceeding and the summary proceeding to recover possession of real property.[16] Special time provisions applicable to an individual proceeding supersede the general provisions contained in Article 4 of the CPLR.

Recognizing that it has the same jurisdiction-getting function that a summons has in an action, the statute requires that the petition and notice of petition and all accompanying papers be served in the same manner as a summons.[17] This means that the simple mail method widely used for intra-action motions[18] is not available to commence a special proceeding.[19]

Service is governed by CPLR 308 and the other statutes on service of process.[20] Any of the prescribed methods contained in CPLR 308 may be used, but it is usually preferable to use the personal delivery method of 308(1). The deliver-and-mail method of 308(2) and the affix-and-mail method of 308(4), since both postpone "completion" of

---

[12]   See § 63 discussing these provisions in the context of an action where they have similar application.

[13]   CPLR 403(b).

[14]   CPLR 403(b). The analogous provision for motions is CPLR 2214(b), but note that the time periods are not the same. The 2007 amendments to CPLR 2214(b) changing the outer notice period from 12 to 16 days, see § 247, were not similarly incorporated into CPLR 403(b).

[15]   CPLR 403(b).

[16]   See §§ 567, 573, et seq. (Practitioner's Edition).

[17]   CPLR 403(c).

[18]   CPLR 2103(b)(2); see § 202.

[19]   It's also awkward to try to use the mail method of CPLR 312–a in a special proceeding, although CPLR 312–a is technically available for it. See § 76A.

[20]   See §§ 66 to 76A.

service until 10 days after proof of service is filed, can become sticky to apply in a special proceeding.[21]

As alluded to above, there is an important alternative to the notice of petition in a special proceeding that is not available in an action. The special proceeding, like a motion, may be brought on by an order to show cause instead of by an ordinary notice of petition.[22]

The order to show cause alternative holds the answer to many a service dilemma. Whenever difficulty arises in making personal delivery of the papers, or any other problem appears of the kind that in motion practice would prompt a show cause application instead of an ordinary notice of motion, the petitioner need merely exploit the show cause method to start the proceeding. In the order to show cause, the judge can direct as to method of service, time of return (abbreviating the otherwise applicable notice minimums), etc.[23]

The use of an unauthorized method of service without an order to show cause, at least when the papers are shown to have been actually received, has sometimes been sustained on the theory that since an order to show cause could have authorized the method at the outset, it can be sustained by a kind of nunc pro tunc order afterwards.[24] This is not a universal view, however,[25] and since we are dealing here with jurisdiction-getting papers, careless petitioners are courting trouble when they devise methods on their own in the hope of securing judicial approval later.

Before 2001, there were some occasions when an order to show cause, ordinarily a help, would instead prove a hindrance if sought near the end of the statute of limitations. The order to show cause requires finding a judge to sign the order and that may consume some time. An ordinary notice of petition, on the other hand, may be filed without preliminary judicial input, formally commencing the action then and there and satisfying the statute of limitations.

Difficulties in this regard were largely avoided by the 2001 amendment that made the filing of the petition alone constitute commencement.[26] The amendment removed a number of other potential problems as well, by introducing a measure of flexibility into the service requirement—flexibility of a kind that did not exist when process (a notice of petition or an order to show cause) had to accompany the petition at filing time. This flexibility is shown in Jordan v. City of New York,[27] a personal injury case against a

---

[21]   See §§ 72, 74; Long Island Jewish Med. Ctr. v. Sovereign Bank, 15 Misc. 3d 1041, 838 N.Y.S.2d 413 (Sup. Ct., Queens County 2007). The proceeding in *Sovereign* was brought under CPLR 5225 to aid in the enforcement of a money judgment. Service was attempted under CPLR 308(2), the deliver-and-mail provision, but that requires the filing of the affidavit of service and the affidavit was not filed. The court therefore held service "not yet complete" and dismissed the petition.

[22]   CPLR 403(d).

[23]   The advantages of the show cause application are many. See § 248.

[24]   See, e.g., Fagenson v. First-York 86th St. Corp., 73 Misc. 2d 1069, 343 N.Y.S.2d 774 (Sup. Ct., New York County 1973).

[25]   See Graffagnino v. Motor Vehicle Acc. Indemnification Corp., 48 Misc. 2d 441, 264 N.Y.S.2d 483 (Sup. Ct., New York County 1965).

[26]   A classic illustration of how the order to show cause could hurt rather than help prior to the 2001 amendment may be seen in Krenzer v. Town of Caledonia, 167 Misc. 2d 708, 634 N.Y.S.2d 927 (Sup. Ct., Monroe County 1995), aff'd, 233 A.D.2d 882, 649 N.Y.S.2d 863 (4th Dep't 1996), in which an inability to find a judge at the last minute resulted in the expiration of the statute of limitations before an order to show cause could be signed.

[27]   Jordan v. City of New York, 38 A.D.3d 336, 833 N.Y.S.2d 8 (1st Dep't 2007).

municipality in which petitioner P failed to serve a notice of claim within the 90 days allowed by General Municipal Law section 50–e. When P now brought a special proceeding for leave to file a late notice, using the show cause procedure to bring the proceeding on, P missed—by just a bit—a deadline for service set by the court in the order to show cause. The lower court held that this made service a "nullity" and dismissed the proceeding, but the appellate division, reversing, pointed out that since all of this affected only service, not filing, the court had discretion to extend the time and, on the facts, should have.[28]

While problems with service of process do not encumber filing under the amendment, they can still encumber service itself, and the time for it. Petitioners should therefore keep in mind that while the proceeding may have been safely insulated from the statute of limitations for the moment with the timely filing of the petition, there is still the matter of securing service within the 15-day period allowed by CPLR 306–b. Furthermore, the service must comply with the notice periods in CPLR 403(b) or the time frames set by the judge in the order to show cause. Attorneys should take sharp note of this. The 2001 amendment was a boon to petitioners by relieving pressure up front, at filing time, but petitioners should not let it become the occasion for just postponing the pressure for a few days by being lax about effecting service.

The general rule in an action or a special proceeding is that the papers served must be the same as the papers filed.[29] Hence, it may be a good idea to file the notice of petition or order to show cause, along with all accompanying papers, before or at the same time as their service. This amounts to a second filing, with the filing of the petition to interpose the claim under CPLR 304(b) being the first. While it doesn't meet the statute of limitations pressure that the filing of the petition meets, it's still a good general practice in special proceedings to see that the court's file contains the same papers that were served on the respondent, even if they're inserted into the file long after it is opened.

Of course, while the rule now is that the notice of petition need not be filed when the initial petition is, there's nothing stopping it from being filed at the same time, and many practitioners prefer that course, at least when there are no other barriers, such as problems about a proper return date. Petitioners must in any event keep in mind the 15-day time limit for effecting service, and the fact that it runs from the expiration of the statute of limitations.

An interesting issue arises when the order to show cause procedure is used, in which the court prescribes the details of service. Suppose that on appeal the lower court itself is found to have been in error in its instructions on service. This happened in Standifer v. Goord, for example,[30] where service was required on the attorney general and on the corrections commissioner. The order to show cause that the petitioner presented to the court so provided, but the court then issued its own order calling for service on only the attorney general. Since the fault was the court's, the appellate division remanded to have the petitioner's version executed, extending the time for service under CPLR 306–b for that purpose.

We stress once again that in the common practice of preparing a notice of petition, the lawyer may encounter difficulty in setting a return day because it is likely at this

---

[28]   See SPR 195:4.

[29]   See § 63.

[30]   Standifer v. Goord, 285 A.D.2d 912, 727 N.Y.S.2d 823 (3d Dep't 2001).

early stage that no judge has yet been assigned to the case. That, indeed, is the reason why the petitioner must file an RJI with the petition itself. Without having an assigned judge, it's often impossible to set a "firm" return day in the notice of petition since the actual day of the hearing will largely depend on the judge's own calendar.

The Court of Appeals has held in this regard that all the petitioner need do—as long as the initial filing is timely—is fix a return date in the notice of petition that satisfies applicable notice requirements.[31] Later changes in the return date, such as those made by the judge, will then not invalidate the proceeding.[32]

Even with that high-court assurance, the petitioner may feel more comfortable checking with the clerk of the particular county to ask how things are done locally.

§ 554. Motions in Special Proceedings

The profusion of motion practice seen in actions has no counterpart in special proceedings for the reason that the proceeding itself is analogous to a motion and is designed to go to hearing and determination promptly. It is permissible, however, to make a motion in a special proceeding, but if the motion is made before the return day of the proceeding itself, it must be made returnable at the same time.[1] A respondent who has a formal legal objection to the proceeding, for example, like want of jurisdiction, can move to dismiss based on it.[2] But alternatively, all the respondent need do is incorporate the objection as a defense in the answer and supply proof of it in his supporting affidavits. The court will consider it just as thoroughly as had it been raised by motion. Since a motion, in other words, is just a device to speed a point to the court's attention, the proceeding itself, replete with an oncoming return day, offers all the context needed to get the objection ruled on quickly.

Then when would a motion be appropriate? It may prove helpful when the purpose is to raise and secure the adjudication of a threshold defense whose favorable determination will altogether obviate an answer on the merits and when by the nature of the case an answer on the merits would be a time-consuming procedure. Defenses like want of jurisdiction, statute of limitations, and res judicata, for example, and others equally separable from the merits, may put a summary end to the proceeding.

If the dismissal motion is unsuccessful, the court may permit the respondent to answer. CPLR 404(a) so provides and supplies also the time for the service of an answer and a procedure for the petitioner to re-notice the hearing on the merits.

While it is usual for the court to allow the respondent to answer on the merits if a legal objection, such as a threshold defense, fails, it isn't automatic. If the court determines that an answer can add nothing, for reasons unique to the case, it can in its discretion deny leave to answer,[3] which means in effect that the petitioner wins on the merits.

---

[31] For these, see CPLR 403(b) for special proceedings in general and 7804(c) for the Article 78 proceeding.

[32] National Gypsum Co. Inc. v. Assessor of Town of Tonawanda, 4 N.Y.3d 680, 797 N.Y.S.2d 809, 830 N.E.2d 1137 (2005) (NYSLD No. 546).

[1] CPLR 406.

[2] CPLR 404(a).

[3] See, e.g., Matter of Dodge, 25 N.Y.2d 273, 303 N.Y.S.2d 847, 250 N.E.2d 849 (1969).

Since any motion made by the respondent in advance of the proceeding's return day (as most motions in special proceedings are) must be made returnable on that day, there will often be too little time to enable the petitioner to respond to the motion. Problems on this score have no clear solution and must be left to the court to resolve on a case by case basis. If it seems reasonable in the particular case, keeping always in mind that expedition is a prime aim of a special proceeding, the court can of course grant an adjournment to enable the petitioner to meet the motion. One court, pondering the matter, concluded that an "ad hoc adjournment procedure appears to be the only option available to the court."[4]

When the answer to a petition contains new matter, the petitioner can respond to it in a reply or, again, with a motion, this one denominated a motion to strike the new matter.[5]

There is some authority under pre-CPLR law to the effect that a party can raise a legal objection by oral motion on the return day,[6] but that is not a sound practice. The same authority confirms that the movant's contention must in any event be supported in the papers already submitted to the court, and it takes little effort to draw and serve a page or two in addition, including one formally denominated a "notice of motion," announcing that a formal motion application is being made.

CPLR 405 supplies a few corrective motions in special proceeding practice. Either party can move to correct a defect in the record and either can make against a pleading the same corrective motions available in an action.[7] These corrective motions, for which special procedural instruction is set forth,[8] are not frequent. Pleading defects in the special proceeding context are even less significant than in an action—and today they have a diminished role even in an action—because each party's pleading rests also on supporting papers—for the most part detailed affidavits—and these can be looked at to cure pleading defects.

The requirement that a fee be paid for the making of any motion in a supreme or county court action, adopted as an incidental part of the state budget in 2003, applies to special proceedings, but it does not apply to the commencement of the special proceeding itself, alike though it is in procedure to a motion made in an ordinary action.[9]

§ 555. Disclosure in Special Proceedings

Recognizing that among the main purposes of a special proceeding are speed and economy, the disclosure devices, so pervasively relied on in an action—and for the most part available there by mere notices served between the parties—are available in a special proceeding only by leave of court. And it takes good cause to invoke judicial discretion to allow the disclosure. The only disclosure device excepted from the leave

---

[4]   Goldman v. McCord, 120 Misc. 2d 754, 466 N.Y.S.2d 584 (N.Y. City Civ. Ct. 1983).

[5]   CPLR 404(b).

[6]   See Rockwell v. Morris, 12 A.D.2d 272, 211 N.Y.S.2d 25 (1st Dep't 1961), aff'd, 10 N.Y.2d 721, 219 N.Y.S.2d 268, 176 N.E.2d 836.

[7]   CPLR 405(a). See CPLR 3024(a), (b); § 230.

[8]   CPLR 405(b), (c).

[9]   This was clarified in a memorandum sent to the county clerks by the Office of Court Administration dated October 16, 2003. The problems of fee collection are almost all logistical. See §§ 243 et seq. The fee for an index number must, however, be paid at the time of the filing of the petition. See § 78.

requirement, and therefore available by mere notice even in a special proceeding, is the notice to admit contained in CPLR 3123.[1]

A bill of particulars, which is not a disclosure device but an amplification of a pleading, has for that reason been held available on mere demand in a special proceeding.[2] Considering again, however, that in a special proceeding detail comes from affidavits supporting the pleadings, a bill of particulars should rarely be needed, or allowed. While not a disclosure device as such, the bill of particulars entails steps akin to one and a demand for a bill of particulars should not be allowed to become a standard practice. Like the disclosure devices, it would detour the mission the legislature has in mind for the special proceeding.

The requirement of leave of court for the disclosure devices does not apply in the surrogate's court, even though its regular business is carried on in a series of special proceedings, or in the special proceeding relating to an express trust under Article 77 of the CPLR, which is brought in the supreme court.[3] In those cases, Article 31 of the CPLR applies on its own terms, which makes most of the disclosure devices available without preliminary leave of court.

§ 556. Hearing and Disposition of Special Proceeding

Each party furnishes to the court all papers it has served in the proceeding. Any papers needed for the determination but not already in the court's possession are to be furnished by the petitioner. If the respondent has a needed paper, the petitioner can require its production at the hearing by including with the petition a demand to that effect. The papers furnished to the court ordinarily go into the court's permanent file.[4]

If no triable issues are raised and the papers before the court are adequate for a determination, the court is required to make the determination summarily. This is analogous to what the court does on an ordinary summary judgment motion within an action. The court's powers on such a motion have for that reason been made applicable to the determination of the proceeding.[5]

If any triable issue of fact arises precluding a summary disposition, the statute directs that it be tried "forthwith," and by jury if a jury would otherwise be required.[6] "Forthwith" is a relative word, however, connoting only that the matter should be tried as soon as practicable under all the circumstances, with the judge considering the urgency of the cause in the context of other exigencies before the court that may have even higher priority. In any event, a special preference for the trial is the least the court should grant the case under the "forthwith" direction.

Whether a jury trial is demandable depends of course on what kind of a proceeding is involved. The relief for which trial by jury is centrally authorized by the CPLR[7] does not very often appear in the special proceeding context, but if it should, or if there is

---

[1]   CPLR 408. Recognizing the imminence of the proceeding's return day, and that the admissions are usually sought for use on that day, CPLR 408 sets forth shorter time requirements for the notice to admit than are applicable in an action under CPLR 3123, the CPLR's principal notice to admit statute.

[2]   See, e.g., Western Printing & Lithographing Co. v. McCandlish, 55 Misc. 2d 607, 286 N.Y.S.2d 59 (Sup. Ct., Dutchess County 1967).

[3]   CPLR 408. See § 352.

[4]   CPLR 409(a).

[5]   CPLR 409(b).

[6]   CPLR 410.

[7]   See CPLR 4101(1), (2).

some specific statutory conferral of the right of trial by jury in a given proceeding,[8] the court must give the parties a chance to demand a jury.[9]

The special proceeding culminates in a "judgment," just as an action does,[10] determining the rights of the parties.[11] The judgment is usually a final one, but it can be made interlocutory if the court contemplates a need for some subsequent step. In one case, for instance, where the court rendered a judgment requiring a party to appoint an arbitrator, the court noted that the party's failure to appoint one would justify the court's doing so in that party's behalf, that a further application could be made to the court for such relief if it should become necessary, and that the judgment now being rendered should be deemed merely an interlocutory one in order to facilitate such follow-up relief.[12]

---

[8] See, e.g., Mental Hyg. Law § 81.11(f) (incompetency proceeding); RPAPL 745 (summary proceeding to recover real property).

[9] CPLR 410.

[10] Prior to the CPLR a special proceeding ended in what was called a "final order." See, e.g., Civ. Prac. Act § 1300 (repealed 1963).

[11] CPLR 411.

[12] Miller v. Ives, 79 Misc. 2d 184, 359 N.Y.S.2d 640 (Sup. Ct., New York County 1974).

PART II. THE ARTICLE 78 PROCEEDING

A. INTRODUCTORY

Table of Sections

§ 557.   Article 78 Proceeding, Introductory

§ 557. Article 78 Proceeding, Introductory

The Article 78 proceeding supersedes the common law writs of mandamus, prohibition, and certiorari to review, supplying in replacement of all three of them a uniform device for challenging the activities of an administrative agency in court. The administrative agency is the major apparatus today for the conduct of government, the unit through which regulation reaches down to the people on an individual basis. The difficulty of sharply delineating the writs is what produced the Article 78 proceeding.

While the Article 78 proceeding has occasional uses against other than administrative agencies—it's available even against judges in certain instances—the administrative agency is its primary target. In our bureaucratic age, this means that the Article 78 proceeding is among the most popular and important devices in practice. A volume of the state reports would feel presumptuous on its library shelf if it didn't offer a handsome number of Article 78 cases on its pages. So broad and general is the proceeding's grasp that it does not even purport to name the agencies it takes in. It refers to its target as every "body or officer," which it defines as "every court, tribunal, board, corporation, officer, or other person, or aggregation of persons, whose action may be affected" by anything that would have been within the purview of the three superseded common law writs.[1] Today, all of these entities and individuals are subject to Article 78.

The proceeding first went onto the books in 1937 as Article 78 of the Civil Practice Act, the CPLR's predecessor. The proper lines of each of the three old writs had become blurred over the years as the courts sought to apply the writs to ever expanding varieties of administrative action. Also expanding, therefore, were instances in which applicants inadvertently pursued the wrong writ altogether. One proceeding designed to do the job of all three of the writs would, it was felt, spare the bar this recurring mistake.[2]

For the most part it did, but only procedurally. For the purpose of getting into court, it was sufficient just to bring an "Article 78" proceeding without identifying which of the three predecessor writs would earlier have done the job. But when the courts got around to deciding the merits of the proceeding, they found that the substantive reach of the earlier writs was still germane. The new device had paved the way to the courthouse, but had not altered the function of the court after arrival. Each old writ was designed to remedy a different grievance, and despite Article 78's smoother access to the court, "the nature of the alleged grievance [still] determines . . . the form of the hearing before the

---

[1]   CPLR 7802(a). In a few instances, notably those involving determinations of the Unemployment Insurance Appeal Board and the Workers' Compensation Board, Article 78 is not used; the route is direct appeal, and the appeal goes to the Appellate Division, Third Department. See Lab. Law § 624; Work. Comp. Law § 23.

[2]   See 3d Jud. Council Rep. 129, 172 (1937).

court to which the aggrieved party is entitled, the questions to be determined at such hearing, and the relief which the court has power to grant."[3]

While only the mechanics were facilitated, that was gift enough. Dependence on the proceeding became so heavy and the "Article 78" caption in the Civil Practice Act so firmly ensconced in the bar's affections, that the Advisory Committee thought it best not to part the proceeding from its title when it devised the CPLR; the committee saw to it that the successor provisions were situated in the same-numbered article slot they had in the old Civil Practice Act: Article 78.

Since the collective scope and extent of the three writs still dictate the scope and extent of permissible judicial review under Article 78, as will be manifest in ensuing sections which discuss the questions that the court may ask and answer in an Article 78 proceeding, judicial opinions often open with a statement that this is an Article 78 proceeding "in the nature of" certiorari, mandamus, or prohibition—whichever it is—thus narrowing for the reader the expected terrain of the inquiry.

Briefly stated, the basic function of each of the three writs (and the aggregate function of Article 78) is not hard to set down on paper. Certiorari reviews an administrative determination taken after a judicial-type hearing or, as it is often described, a "quasi judicial" hearing. Mandamus compels action admitting of no discretion and so clearly required as to be merely ministerial. Prohibition prevents a body for exceeding its jurisdiction. If every Article 78 proceeding fell squarely within one of those three categories, the article would be less of a study than it is. But Article 78 does not have such clear sailing. Nor did its predecessor writs in their latter years. Many cases straddle the line between categories, or hover near their outer fringes. Those are the ones that cause lingering problems for Article 78. But with the new device in hand, the courts met and managed them all.

CPLR 7803, which prescribes the scope of Article 78 review, does so in the form of a list of questions. It provides that the only questions that may be raised in an Article 78 proceeding are:

1. whether the body or officer failed to perform a duty enjoined upon it by law;

2. whether the body or officer proceeded, is proceeding or is about to proceed without or in excess of jurisdiction;

3. whether a determination was made in violation of lawful procedure, was affected by an error of law or was arbitrary and capricious or an abuse of discretion, including abuse of discretion as to the measure or mode of penalty or discipline imposed; or

4. whether a determination made as a result of a hearing held, and at which evidence was taken [this is the "quasi judicial" hearing], pursuant to direction by law is, on the entire record, supported by substantial evidence.

The first, second, and fourth of the listed questions pertain distinctly to but one of the old writs: number 1 is the old mandamus question; number 2 the prohibition question; and number 4 the certiorari question. That leaves number 3, which is actually

---

[3]   Newbrand v. City of Yonkers, 285 N.Y. 164, 174–5, 33 N.E.2d 75, 80 (1941).

several questions, and these are the ones often found in the cloudy areas between the writs instead of at the sunny center of any one of them.

The best way to compartmentalize a study is to do each old writ in a separate section, integrating in each the CPLR 7803 question that pertains to it. The next three sections are thus captioned after the three writs and cover, respectively, questions 1, 2, and 4 of CPLR 7803, along with the part of question 3 in any possible way relevant to the inquiry. Then a fourth section, entitled the "mandamus-certiorari borderline"—the major problem area—will cover what remains to be said of question 3.

The very process of reviewing administrative action necessarily entails an occasional look into an agency's internal workings, but that's just an incident of Article 78, not its main aim. The article builds a path from the agency to the courthouse; its preoccupation is with judicial supervision rather than with the agency's internal workings, which are governed by the State Administrative Procedure Act (SAPA).

The SAPA, which became effective in September 1976, supplies for the first time in New York a uniform set of instructions for administrative procedure in and before the state's numerous agencies. Its articles address rule making[4] and adjudicatory proceedings,[5] with a special one on licenses and their revocation.[6] While the SAPA is the supplier of the internals of the administrative process, Article 78 is its judicial supervisor, the vent and window through which light and air expose and refresh the dank milieu of that ubiquitous and indispensable phenomenon of our civilization: the administrative agency.

The administrative agency can be a regulator, investigator, prosecutor, and defender, or any one, or any combination of them. It can act as a jury, a judge, or a warden, by turns or together. It's also an important source of employment for political figures who might otherwise turn to crime. Its blessings, in other words, are many, but mixed.

It's Article 78 that makes the administrative agency tolerable.

By laying a red carpet to the courthouse door to review agency action and by dictating the scope of that review inside, Article 78 is itself a kind of administrative law lesson. Hence, while our aim is only to determine the function of the courts in watch-dogging the administrative process, what ensues in the next handful of sections may occasionally go into the process itself. The overlapping is unavoidable, but we'll try to keep it to a minimum. After those few sections will come the mechanics of the Article 78 proceeding, which are a quicker study.

B. SCOPE OF THE PROCEEDING

Table of Sections

§ 558.   Mandamus

§ 559.   Prohibition

§ 560.   Certiorari

§ 561.   Mandamus-Certiorari Borderline

---

[4]   SAPA Article 2.

[5]   SAPA Article 3.

[6]   SAPA Article 4.

§ 562.   Judicial Review of Penalty or Discipline

§ 563.   Overstepping Outer Borders of Article 78

§ 558. Mandamus

The first of the questions that may be raised in an Article 78 proceeding is "whether the body or officer failed to perform a duty enjoined upon it by law."[1] This is from the old writ of mandamus. An Article 78 proceeding in the nature of mandamus is used to compel the performance of a duty that is merely ministerial in nature and involves no exercise of judgment or discretion. It's allowable, for example, to compel election officials to issue absentee ballots to voters entitled to them, there being nothing but the ministerial act of sending them the ballots,[2] but not to compel the comptroller to bring an action to test the legality of the state budget because whether to do so involves his judgment and discretion.[3] This judgment-and-discretion exclusion is what keeps Article 78 from being used to compel most categories of executive action: the demonstration that the activity entails any substantial discretion removes any mandamus possibility, whatever other remedy may be appropriate.[4] Mandamus is designed to require the performance of a positive duty, not a discretionary one. The right to that duty's performance must therefore be free of reasonable doubt or controversy.[5]

Even money payable by a public official can be ordered paid through an Article 78 proceeding in the nature of mandamus if the duty to pay is indisputable. Hence, the proceeding serves as the enforcement device to collect unpaid judgments rendered against governmental units, including municipalities. Nor is a judgment needed in order to manifest that the obligation to pay is clear enough to justify mandamus; an undisputed agreement can offer the needed certainty.[6]

The exclusion of mandamus from the realm of executive (as opposed to merely administrative) activity is clearest when the issues involved are public rather than private. Thus, Article 78 will not be allowed to compel a mayor to fill a judicial vacancy even though that is clearly a mayoral function.[7] But it does serve as the remedy to implement a discretion-free right asserted against an administrator or agency. In the civil service area, for example, if the petitioner in taking an examination shows that an answer he furnished is as good as the one the respondents selected, and demonstrates this clearly enough to leave no room for a contrary view, he is entitled to a mandamus

---

[1]   CPLR 7803(1).

[2]   See Hudson v. Nehill, 25 Misc. 2d 1025, 206 N.Y.S.2d 918 (Sup. Ct., Rensselaer County 1960).

[3]   Posner v. Levitt, 37 A.D.2d 331, 325 N.Y.S.2d 519 (3d Dep't 1971).

[4]   An improper attempt to invoke Article 78 to affect executive action brought about a Court of Appeals discourse on the line between "political" and "justiciable" issues in New York State Inspection, Sec. and Law Enforcement Employees, Dist. Council 82, AFSCME, AFL-CIO v. Cuomo, 64 N.Y.2d 233, 485 N.Y.S.2d 719, 475 N.E.2d 90 (1984), the "political" category being beyond judicial review altogether. See § 136.

[5]   Petz v. Property Clerk of 68th Squad, Brooklyn, N.Y., 149 N.Y.S.2d 179 (Sup. Ct., Kings County 1956).

[6]   See, e.g., Fehlhaber Corp. v. O'Hara, 53 A.D.2d 746, 384 N.Y.S.2d 270 (3d Dep't 1976). As to whether Article 78 in the nature of mandamus can exact money from the State without a formal action in the court of claims, see State Div. of Human Rights on Complaint of Geraci v. New York State Dept. of Correctional Services, 90 A.D.2d 51, 456 N.Y.S.2d 63 (2d Dep't 1982).

[7]   Blaikie v. Wagner, 46 Misc. 2d 441, 259 N.Y.S.2d 890 (Sup. Ct., New York County 1965).

direction that his answer is good.[8] In Article 78 context, this merely means a judgment directing that the answer be accepted and that the examination be regraded accordingly.

Examples of Article 78 in the nature of mandamus and its vast range of uses can fill a book as indeed they almost do: the small-print annotations on CPLR 7801 and 7803 in McKinney's Consolidated Laws of New York run for many pages, with a myriad of illustrations. They are an ideal start for a lawyer stepping into the realm, a reservoir of suggestions and analogies.

Article 78 in the nature of mandamus is also available against corporations, private as well as public, because corporations derive their charter and existence from state law and therefore take on a quasi-governmental status, at least for the purpose of a mandamus-type remedy. But as with all mandamus cases, the remedy lies only when the right to it is clear and involves no arguable discretion. A common and acceptable example is a proceeding against corporate officials to compel them, at the behest of an appropriate petitioner, to permit an inspection of corporate books and records.[9]

The categories of corporation that are subject to Article 78 proceedings run the whole gamut as long as the right to what is sought is so clear as to fall into the realm of the merely ministerial. The corporation need not on the one hand be wholly commercial nor on the other strictly governmental. Both kinds are included along with in-betweens as well. Incorporated universities and like non-commercial entities, for example, are subject to Article 78. But the article does not apply to a partnership[10] or to an unincorporated association[11] or to like creatures not owing their status to the State.[12] Unincorporated labor unions are in that category, and therefore escape Article 78 proceedings.[13]

The erroneous use of Article 78 against one not subject to it is not as serious today as it once was: as long as a substantive right is asserted, the worst that will happen is a conversion of the proceeding into an ordinary action.[14]

While most often used against agencies and bodies corporate, Article 78 in the nature of mandamus has some uses against a court or, more specifically, a judge. It can be used, for example, to compel the judge to render a decision as where the judge has failed to do so within a statutorily allotted time, but it can't dictate what that decision will be, which is a matter of judicial judgment and discretion.[15] The merits of a judicial decision are utterly beyond a mandamus-type review although, as will be seen, Article 78 in the nature of prohibition may sometimes be used to overturn a decision in extraordinary situations.[16] An exception to this, in which Article 78 has been explicitly

---

[8] See Dolan v. Krone, 16 N.Y.2d 917, 264 N.Y.S.2d 703, 212 N.E.2d 155 (1965).

[9] See, e.g., Morris v. Pepsi-Cola Co., 21 A.D.2d 651, 249 N.Y.S.2d 565 (1st Dep't 1964).

[10] Two Eleven Co. v. Harrison, 66 Misc. 2d 245, 319 N.Y.S.2d 897 (Sup. Ct., New York County 1971).

[11] See Weidenfeld v. Keppler, 84 A.D. 235, 82 N.Y.S. 634 (1st Dep't 1903), aff'd, 176 N.Y. 562, 68 N.E. 1125.

[12] There is some indication, however, that even an unincorporated creature will be subject to a mandamus-type remedy if, while it does not have the entity status of a corporation, it is nonetheless formed pursuant to statutory direction. See Importers' & Exporters' Ins. Co. v. Rhoades, 239 N.Y. 420, 146 N.E. 648 (1925).

[13] See, e.g., Phalen v. Theatrical Protective Union No. 1, Intern. Alliance of Theatrical and Stage Emp., AFL-CIO, 22 N.Y.2d 34, 290 N.Y.S.2d 881, 238 N.E.2d 295 (1968).

[14] CPLR 103(c). See § 563.

[15] See, e.g., Briggs v. Lauman, 21 A.D.2d 734, 250 N.Y.S.2d 126 (3d Dep't 1964).

[16] See § 559.

authorized to challenge and review a judicial determination, is a determination summarily punishing a contempt committed in the court's presence.[17]

Action strictly legislative rather than administrative is also beyond the reach of Article 78. A legislative body can't be mandamused in regard to anything within its prerogative.

The dispute over whether the legislature can be judicially compelled to raise judges' salaries, which went to the Court of Appeals in a trio of 2010 cases[18] and which was of course in the thick of this kind of controversy, was brought to court as a "hybrid CPLR article 78 proceeding/declaratory judgment action," evincing that as long as the relief is judicially cognizable—the major point of difficulty in those cases—some kind of procedural routing can be found for it.

The rule against Article 78 interfering in the legislative process applies not only to the State legislature itself, but to municipal legislatures as well. Thus a resolution by the New York City Board of Estimate adopting a map change cannot be reviewed under Article 78.[19] Even the order of an administrative agency, if wholly legislative in character, may for that reason fall beyond Article 78, such as when the agency is performing a legislatively delegated rate-fixing function.[20]

The uses of Article 78 were expanded by the State Administrative Procedure Act (SAPA), which took effect in 1976. The article was made available to secure judicial review of rules promulgated by an agency.[21] Another part of the SAPA enables a person to secure a declaratory ruling from an agency on whether a given statute or rule, within the agency's jurisdiction to enforce, applies to that person or to a designated property or state of facts, and authorizes the use of Article 78 to review the ruling.[22]

The general utility of Article 78 is implicitly acknowledged whenever the proceeding is extended to some new purpose. Under the Freedom of Information Law, for example, which seeks to increase public access to governmental records,[23] a denial of access is made reviewable under Article 78.[24]

Is any one of these last few items a "mandamus" use of Article 78? It would be, if there were no discretion involved. Is it Article 78 in the nature of "certiorari"? It would

---

[17]   CPLR 7801(2). See Kahn v. Backer, 21 A.D.2d 171, 249 N.Y.S.2d 572 (1st Dep't 1964). Out-of-court contumacious conduct (such as disobedience of an injunction), proved in a contempt proceeding and punished by the court after a hearing, is not within this provision and not subject to Article 78 review.

[18]   Maron v. Silver, 14 N.Y.3d 230, 899 N.Y.S.2d 97, 925 N.E.2d 899 (2010).

[19]   See Porter Flushing Realty Co. v. New York City Planning Commission, 21 A.D.2d 864, 251 N.Y.S.2d 125 (1st Dep't 1964). In zoning matters especially, the line is hard to draw between administrative and quasi-administrative decisions on the one hand, justifying Article 78 review, and genuine legislative activity on the other, precluding Article 78 review. See Bar Harbour Shopping Ctr., Inc. v. Andrews, 23 Misc. 2d 894, 196 N.Y.S.2d 856 (Sup. Ct., Nassau County 1959). If the act is legislative, a test of its validity must technically be sought in a declaratory judgment action. Today, however, the mistaking of the remedy is cured by a mere procedural conversion into proper form. Todd Mart, Inc. v. Town Bd. of Town of Webster, 49 A.D.2d 12, 370 N.Y.S.2d 683 (4th Dep't 1975). See § 563.

[20]   See, e.g., Lakeland Water Dist. v. Onondaga County Water Authority, 24 N.Y.2d 400, 301 N.Y.S.2d 1, 248 N.E.2d 855 (1969). The case indicates that if a hearing had been statutorily required, Article 78 might be appropriate for review. (In that case, of course, the Article 78 proceeding would be in the nature of certiorari, not mandamus. See § 560.).

[21]   SAPA § 205.

[22]   SAPA § 204.

[23]   Pub. Off. Law §§ 84–90.

[24]   Pub. Off. Law § 89(4)(b).

be if a full-fledged hearing were required before the application could be denied. (As will be seen, certiorari is a review based on a full record after a quasi-judicial hearing.) What happens when there is some element of discretion allotted to the agency, but that no hearing is required, thus putting the case beyond the clear grasp of either category? There we have one of the situations that still straddles the line between the two old writs. Article 78's grand favor is that it admits the thing to court astride the dividing line although there may be some trouble later when the court has to decide just how much it can review.[25]

That mandamus is designed to require the performance of a positive duty rather than a discretionary one does not exclude mandamus from every scene that involves some exercise of discretion. When there is a clear duty to perform a given act, the fact that some exercise of discretion must be made in the course of performing it does not prevent a court from entertaining mandamus to see that the act is performed. The Court of Appeals clarified this in Natural Resources Defense Council, Inc. v. New York City Department of Sanitation,[26] in which a city sanitation department was required by law to set up a recycling program and mandamus was brought by a public interest group to make it do that. The use of the word "may" at many points in the enabling act permitted diverse exercises of discretion to be made by the department in carrying out this mandate, but, held the Court, the fact that exercises of discretion lie along the way does not prevent the courts from making sure the department takes the trip.

It must be noted that although "mandamus" as such is usually thought of as a device designed exclusively to compel something, it has evolved another and equally important function: that of merely reviewing administrative action without necessarily compelling a particular act. In this respect—another one responsible for muddying the waters between the two writs—it resembles certiorari. But certiorari is technically applicable only when there is a hearing required by law, when the record produced at the hearing is the sole basis on which the determination can rest, and when the so called "substantial evidence" rule is the review standard.[27] When the hearing need not be of the plenary quasi-judicial kind, but merely allows an opportunity for the petitioner to supply the agency what evidence she wishes, when the agency can in the particular situation consider evidence not produced at the "hearing" but coming to the agency's knowledge through other channels, and when judicial review is not limited to the substantial evidence test, it can't technically be certiorari.[28] It is technically "mandamus" on those facts, but more a kind of mandamus to "review" than the more common mandamus to "compel."

In one case, for example, a petitioner was denied a liquor license on two grounds: (1) he failed to supply assurances that he would operate a restaurant on the premises and (2) the area already had sufficient licensees. The court in an Article 78 proceeding found that his assurances were sufficient and that the first ground was therefore an inadequate basis for refusing a license. The second ground was found supportable, however, and so the court could not "compel" the issuance of the license. But nor could it approve a refusal: the refusal was based on two grounds and the agency might not wish

---

[25]   See § 561.

[26]   Natural Resources Defense Council, Inc. v. New York City Dept. of Sanitation, 83 N.Y.2d 215, 608 N.Y.S.2d 957, 630 N.E.2d 653 (1994), noted in NYSLD No. 414.

[27]   See CPLR 7803(4).

[28]   See 125 Bar Corp. v. State Liquor Authority, 24 N.Y.2d 174, 299 N.Y.S.2d 194, 247 N.E.2d 157 (1969).

to refuse if limited—as it would now be limited as a result of the court's decision—to but one of the grounds. That was for the agency to decide, and so the matter was remitted to the agency.[29]

This was a good example of mandamus to "review," and the presence in the case of an element of discretion was yet another factor that kept the case out of the "compel" category. Actually, the case is an example of Article 78's eschewal of labels. Were it merely a question of going into court, we could forget distinctions altogether. Article 78 gets all of these things into the courtroom without a caption. Once there, however, the old distinctions may hang on: they determine which of the four categories of questions enumerated in CPLR 7803 will control the judicial inquiry. With mandamus to "compel," question 1 of CPLR 7803 is the inquiry. With mandamus to "review," question 3 the inquiry.[30] When all the requisites of "certiorari" are present, number 4 supplies the controlling question.[31]

The doctrine of the exhaustion of administrative remedies, embodied in the requirement of CPLR 7801(1) that the determination be "final" before being subject to an Article 78 proceeding, applies to mandamus to review. It means that if there are further (and reasonable) administrative steps available to secure a change in the result, the party must pursue them before going to court. The finality requirement applies as well to certiorari, but in either instance caselaw clarifies that if it is plain that pursuit of further administrative relief would be futile, it will be dispensed with and an Article 78 proceeding will be deemed ripe.[32]

The courts are also sensitive, of course, to guard against the invocation of judicial jurisdiction for controversies not yet ripe at all. This is not a problem when the Article 78 proceeding is in the nature of certiorari or mandamus to review, i.e., where a determination has already been made and it is merely a question of having to take further steps before pursuing a judicial remedy. But it can appear in something like a mandamus to compel, such as where the petitioner, insisting that he is entitled to something from the respondent, was never refused it because he never asked for it. Thus, where petitioner sought a certain phone service but did not ask the phone company for it, the court found an Article 78 proceeding, predicated on an anticipatory refusal by the company, premature, and dismissed it.[33] This is consistent with the exhaustion doctrine.

§ 559. Prohibition

Question 2 listed in CPLR 7803 as a permissible one for an Article 78 proceeding is "whether the body or officer proceeded, is proceeding or is about to proceed without or in excess of jurisdiction." This is from the old writ of prohibition. A judge before whom the Article 78 proceeding comes will often identify it, at the outset of an opinion, as one "in the nature of prohibition."

---

[29]   Rochester Colony, Inc. v. Hostetter, 19 A.D.2d 250, 241 N.Y.S.2d 210 (4th Dep't 1963).

[30]   See § 561.

[31]   See § 560.

[32]   See, e.g., Kurk v. Medical Soc. of Queens County, Inc., 46 Misc. 2d 790, 260 N.Y.S.2d 520 (Sup. Ct., Queens County 1965), rev'd on other grounds, 24 A.D.2d 897, 264 N.Y.S.2d 859 (2d Dep't), aff'd, 18 N.Y.2d 928, 276 N.Y.S.2d 1007, 223 N.E.2d 499 (1966).

[33]   See Rubano v. New York Tel. Co., 43 Misc. 2d 149, 250 N.Y.S.2d 373 (Sup. Ct., Westchester County 1964).

Article 78 in the nature of prohibition appears against judges more often than the other categories do. This is because prohibition does not lie against strictly administrative action, but only against judicial and quasi-judicial action.[1] When brought against an administrative official, the latter must therefore be shown to be exceeding jurisdiction in some quasi-judicial capacity. If the official's activity is strictly administrative, it is technically "mandamus" that the petitioner is seeking whether to compel favorable action at the outset or to review unfavorable action already taken.

It is often said that prohibition is available only to forestall rather than review action,[2] but that statement, like almost every other purportedly facile statement about the old writs, can be misleading. Quasi-judicial activity taken without jurisdiction does not become valid merely because it has already gone to a determination. If the taker lacked jurisdiction at the outset and would at that time have been subject to prohibition, he is just as subject to it, and his determination just as subject to annulment, in a prohibition proceeding brought afterwards. If these distinctions seem hard to digest, we can remind ourselves once again that at least for the purpose of getting into court one need not identify the "nature" of what is sought at all. One need only label it an Article 78 proceeding.

Prohibition is an extraordinary remedy, available at best only as a matter of judicial discretion and not as a matter of right. Given an extraordinary showing, however, such as that there is a risk of violation of the double jeopardy rule,[3] or that the respondent lacks jurisdiction on the very face of the complaint brought before him, prohibition will issue to enjoin even a criminal action.[4] In Soares v. Carter,[5] the Court of Appeals affirmed the granting of a writ of prohibition enjoining a city court judge from enforcing his orders compelling the prosecution of criminal matters after the district attorney decided to discontinue them. Under the doctrine of separation of powers, the courts lack the power to compel the prosecution of criminal actions and any attempt by a judge to compel prosecution through the use of contempt powers constitutes an excess of jurisdiction.

While courts are naturally loath to restrain exercises of jurisdiction by another court, they will do so when the latter, by the very exercise, threatens fundamental constitutional rights. Prohibition has issued, for example, to prevent the seizure of an allegedly obscene film when the proceedings were found to have inadequate procedural safeguards under the First Amendment.[6]

The use of prohibition must always be related to a want of jurisdiction, or at least to an exercise of power so excessive as to be its equivalent. Whether the threatened excess is sufficiently extraordinary to trigger the device is sometimes hard to tell. In one case, for example, applications had been made to vacate two convictions, one on the ground that the defendant was under age and the other on the ground that he did not have counsel. The latter was held to be a defect so basic that the trial court itself retained

---

[1]   See, e.g., Dobler v. Kaplan, 27 Misc. 2d 15, 211 N.Y.S.2d 96 (Sup. Ct., Suffolk County 1961), aff'd, 18 A.D.2d 1093, 220 N.Y.S.2d 701 (2d Dep't 1963).

[2]   See, e.g., Bradford v. Helman, 24 A.D.2d 937, 264 N.Y.S.2d 930 (1st Dep't 1965).

[3]   See Di Lorenzo v. Murtagh, 36 N.Y.2d 306, 367 N.Y.S.2d 761, 327 N.E.2d 805 (1975).

[4]   See, e.g., Powell v. Criminal Court of City of New York, New York County, 44 Misc. 2d 838, 255 N.Y.S.2d 1 (Sup. Ct., New York County 1964).

[5]   Soares v. Carter, 25 N.Y.3d 1011, 10 N.Y.S.3d 175, 32 N.E.3d 390 (2015).

[6]   See Milonas v. Schwalb, 65 Misc. 2d 1042, 319 N.Y.S.2d 327 (Sup. Ct., New York County 1971).

jurisdiction to vacate the conviction on motion, and, jurisdiction being present, prohibition would not lie to stop it. The other, that based on age, was found not to be of such a fundamental kind; the trial court thus lacked power to vacate the conviction on that ground and prohibition lay to prevent its attempting to.[7]

Niceties of this kind are hard to apply, and are perhaps even undetectable until a court has passed on the particular ground. Indeed, the Court of Appeals has candidly held that the "magnitude" of the issue may be the key factor. So it said in Lee v. County Court of Erie County,[8] reaffirming what it had occasion to point out before: that Article 78 in the nature of prohibition is available not only to restrain an unwarranted assumption of jurisdiction, but also to stop a court from exceeding its "powers" in a case in which it concededly has jurisdiction. Theoretical standards like that are elusive to the attorney who has to apply them in practice. Translating them into the practical means that the advocate's burden is to establish the situation as truly extraordinary.

What is truly "extraordinary"? If we may analogize, it may be akin to the "special circumstances" rule applied in New York in the forum non conveniens area. When a case has no New York contacts with either the parties or the subject matter, the courts insist on some good reason for entertaining the action.[9] So with prohibition, where the petitioner must show some special reason why a court should prevent a case from even starting, some unique factor explaining why the case should not go forward at all and why an attack should not be postponed until after judgment, when a review of the proceedings can be undertaken.

The violation of fundamental constitutional rights by the very fact that the petitioner must endure a trial is one such special circumstance, already mentioned. Another is the unavailability—or in any event the manifest inadequacy in the particular case—of the ordinary process of appeal.

Prohibition has therefore become a kind of review route when the usual appellate door is closed, but only in very special circumstances. A mere showing that a determination is unappealable will by no means suffice.[10] Nor can prohibition be turned to by one who had the appeal route available, but let the time for taking it lapse.[11] It is not available merely to correct substantive or procedural errors of the trial court, no matter how grievous. Only when the court threatens to act in excess of its "powers" may prohibition be turned to, and among the factors the court will consider in determining whether a court's powers have been exceeded are the gravity of the harm to the petitioner, the capacity of a later appeal to undo the harm, and the efficacy of other channels of redress.[12] Where, for example, the petitioner has a strong claim of want of jurisdiction or "excess" of powers against a court, and would, if compelled to pursue other remedies, remain incarcerated in the interim, the extraordinary case for prohibition is

---

    [7]   See Hogan v. Court of General Sessions of New York County, 296 N.Y. 1, 68 N.E.2d 849 (1946). The case was precipitated by earlier restrictions on criminal vacatur motions, apparently since removed. See Crim. Proc. Law § 440.10.

    [8]   Lee v. County Court of Erie County, 27 N.Y.2d 432, 318 N.Y.S.2d 705, 267 N.E.2d 452 (1971).

    [9]   See § 28.

    [10]   See Nigrone v. Murtagh, 36 N.Y.2d 421, 369 N.Y.S.2d 75, 330 N.E.2d 45 (1975).

    [11]   Roberts v. County Court of Wyoming County, 39 A.D.2d 246, 333 N.Y.S.2d 882 (4th Dep't 1972), aff'd, 34 N.Y.2d 246, 356 N.Y.S.2d 853, 313 N.E.2d 335 (1974).

    [12]   See La Rocca v. Lane, 37 N.Y.2d 575, 376 N.Y.S.2d 93, 338 N.E.2d 606 (1975).

at hand.[13] The petitioner's burden is to convince the prohibition court that the other court is guilty of an arrogation of power, if not of an outright want of jurisdiction.

If its extraordinary elements are otherwise present, the remedy of prohibition is not limited to criminal cases. It can be used, for example, when the petitioner, a corporation, can show that being compelled to go through a civil trial would constitute an undue burden on its interstate commerce. Suppose, for example, that the petitioner is a defendant in such an action and has moved to dismiss based on the commerce objection, and the motion is denied. It can appeal the order of denial to the appellate division. If it does and the order is affirmed, however, the order will be nonfinal, which may preclude further appeal to the New York Court of Appeals.[14] It has been held that a petitioner in that situation may bring a separate prohibition proceeding, that being put through a trial may unduly disrupt its commerce, and that this suffices to make the case extraordinary enough to invoke prohibition.[15] It boils down to a matter of judicial discretion and to how much the petitioner can show to invoke it. The petitioner must show either that there is no other remedy at all or that all the others are inadequate.[16] Instead of merely demonstrating error in respect of but a part of the case, the petitioner should show that the abuse consists in entertaining the case at all.[17]

The requirement of finality, important as a condition precedent to certiorari and sometimes to mandamus as well,[18] is not applicable to prohibition. This recognizes that with prohibition the defect under attack is a want of subject matter jurisdiction or an exercise of power so excessive as to be its equivalent, which presumably authorizes an attack at any juncture.[19]

An Article 78 proceeding in the nature of prohibition is brought in the supreme court, except when aimed at a justice of that court or a judge of the county court, in which case it's commenced in the appellate division.[20]

§ 560. Certiorari

Question 4 on the list of questions that CPLR 7803 allows in an Article 78 proceeding is "whether a determination made as a result of a hearing held, and at which evidence was taken, pursuant to direction by law is, on the entire record, supported by substantial evidence."

This is from the old writ of certiorari to review.[1] The fact that the determination results from a required evidentiary hearing is what invokes the certiorari remedy and

---

[13] See *La Rocca*, 37 N.Y.2d at 580, 376 N.Y.S.2d at 98, 338 N.E.2d at 610.

[14] See CPLR 5601(a); §§ 527–28.

[15] See Baltimore Mail S. S. Co. v. Fawcett, 269 N.Y. 379, 199 N.E. 628, 1936 A.M.C. 141 (1936), cert. den. 298 U.S. 675, 56 S.Ct. 939.

[16] Schuyler v. State University of New York at Albany, 31 A.D.2d 273, 297 N.Y.S.2d 368 (3d Dep't 1969).

[17] See State v. King, 36 N.Y.2d 59, 364 N.Y.S.2d 879, 324 N.E.2d 351 (1975).

[18] CPLR 7801(1).

[19] See Civil Service Emp. Ass'n v. Helsby, 31 A.D.2d 325, 297 N.Y.S.2d 813 (3d Dep't 1969), aff'd, 24 N.Y.2d 993, 302 N.Y.S.2d 822, 250 N.E.2d 230.

[20] CPLR 506(a). See § 565.

[1]   Another certiorari, this one to inquire into detention, is set forth in Article 70 of the CPLR. See CPLR 7001. It is seldom heard from today, having been replaced verbally, if not actually, by the writ of habeas corpus. It was technically the writ used when an inquiry into detention was sought without having the detained person immediately produced, a kind of habeas corpus without the corpus. This is still permissible, see CPLR 7003(a),

with it the substantial evidence criterion. If there is no requirement for a hearing, or the hearing permitted in the particular situation is not of the plenary evidentiary ("quasi judicial") kind, the review standards will be those of mandamus. The practical difference is discussed in the next section.

Although the hearing must be one required by law, it is not necessary that the requirement be express; an implied one is enough, and one will be implied whenever the agency's exercise of a statutory power can adversely affect a substantial right of the petitioner. Thus, where the prospect was the revocation of the petitioner's hack license, a hearing requirement was implied from a silent statute.[2] If neither a right nor a statutory hearing requirement is present, however, any "hearing" voluntarily tendered to the petitioner is a matter of grace rather than a requirement of law and hence not reviewable under the certiorari standard.[3] It will still be Article 78 that brings the case to court, but the review standard will be taken from subdivision 3 of CPLR 7803, generally associated with mandamus to review, and not subdivision 4, the certiorari standard.

The hearing required must be of the judicial or quasi-judicial kind,[4] the kind that the State Administrative Procedure Act (SAPA) defines as one "in which a determination of the legal rights, duties or privileges of named parties thereto is required by law to be made only on a record and after an opportunity for a hearing."[5] The SAPA calls it an "adjudicatory proceeding," and supplies for it a central repository of requirements applicable to all agencies.[6] The hearing that the SAPA calls "adjudicatory" is what the older caselaw means by "judicial or quasi-judicial." The determination resulting from it is therefore reviewable by certiorari. In present Article 78 parlance, this means that its review is under the substantial evidence standard of CPLR 7803(4), which works out well: it's the same standard the SAPA itself adopts for its adjudicatory proceedings.[7]

When an adjudicatory hearing is required, even a quasi-legislative determination like a rate-making order involving a public utility has been held to qualify for certiorari review under Article 78.[8]

Another characteristic of the certiorari case, and a natural concomitant of the substantial evidence rule, is that the determination cannot be based on anything outside the record and will be overturned if it is.[9] When less than a quasi-judicial hearing is permitted, on the other hand, and the review is therefore through mandamus instead of certiorari, matter outside the record, such as data gathered by the agency's own investigators, may form part of the basis for the decision.[10]

---

but in either instance the procedure is a special proceeding under Article 70 of the CPLR, and in neither should the proceeding be confused with the certiorari-to-review purpose of an Article 78 proceeding.

    [2]   See Hecht v. Monaghan, 307 N.Y. 461, 121 N.E.2d 421 (1954).

    [3]   See London Sporting Club, Inc. v. Helfand, 3 Misc. 2d 431, 152 N.Y.S.2d 819 (Sup. Ct., New York County 1956), aff'd, 6 A.D.2d 775, 175 N.Y.S.2d 152 (1st Dep't 1958).

    [4]   Testa v. Wickham, 51 Misc. 2d 968, 274 N.Y.S.2d 421 (Sup. Ct., Albany County 1966), aff'd, 28 A.D.2d 780, 280 N.Y.S.2d 829 (3d Dep't 1967).

    [5]   SAPA § 102(3).

    [6]   SAPA Article 3, §§ 301 to 307.

    [7]   See SAPA § 306(1).

    [8]   See Lakeland Water Dist. v. Onondaga County Water Authority, 24 N.Y.2d 400, 301 N.Y.S.2d 1, 248 N.E.2d 855 (1969).

    [9]   Simpson v. Wolansky, 38 N.Y.2d 391, 380 N.Y.S.2d 630, 343 N.E.2d 274 (1975).

    [10]   See 125 Bar Corp. v. State Liquor Authority, 24 N.Y.2d 174, 299 N.Y.S.2d 194, 247 N.E.2d 157 (1969).

The "substantial evidence" test replaces the old "legal residuum" standard, a largely unworkable one, and is roughly analogous to the standard used by the courts in setting aside a jury verdict because the evidence does not support it.[11] The real measure, whatever the wording, is whether the determination strikes the court as rational on the record.[12]

Except for the rules of privileged communications, which must be observed in quasi-judicial hearings before administrative agencies, the rules of evidence are not binding in such hearings.[13] The main entry through this open door is hearsay, but it has been held that "substantial" reliance on hearsay will not be acceptable and that a determination unduly dependent on it will not be upheld if it has the effect of undermining a party's right of cross-examination.[14] Since the SAPA also recognizes this right in administrative "adjudicatory" (i.e., quasi-judicial) proceedings,[15] the rule against undue dependence on hearsay subsists.

The requirement of finality ordinarily applies to a determination sought to be reviewed by certiorari. In familiar administrative parlance, this is known as the doctrine of the exhaustion of administrative remedies: the loser must pursue an appellate route within the agency, if one is available, before turning to the courts with an Article 78 proceeding.[16] The doctrine has some application in mandamus, too, but in either situation it's applied pragmatically: where, despite the availability of an internal administrative appeal, it is plain on the facts of the particular case that pursuing the appeal would be futile, an Article 78 proceeding will be deemed ripe enough.[17]

The Court of Appeals has held . . . that the exhaustion rule is not inflexible and need not be followed when the action is challenged as either unconstitutional or outside of a grant of power, when resort to an administrative remedy would be futile or when its pursuit would cause irreparable injury . . . .[18]

When the applicable remedy is mandamus to review, the agency has already acted and the act is the thing to be reviewed. An analogous situation, usually involving mandamus to compel—as opposed to either certiorari or mandamus to review—is where the agency has not acted because the petitioner has not asked it to. There an Article 78 proceeding may be dismissed for prematurity,[19] a result at home with the exhaustion doctrine if not a precise example of it.

§ 561. Mandamus-Certiorari Borderline

Since questions 1, 2, and 4 on CPLR 7803's list each has a clear antecedent among the old writs, they were treated first and number 3 saved for last. Number 3 lists several

---

[11] See *Testa*, 51 Misc. 2d at 970–71, 274 N.Y.S.2d at 424, aff'd, 28 A.D.2d 780, 280 N.Y.S.2d 829.

[12] Pell v. Board of Ed. of Union Free School Dist. No. 1 of Towns of Scarsdale and Mamaroneck, 34 N.Y.2d 222, 356 N.Y.S.2d 833, 313 N.E.2d 321 (1974). See § 561.

[13] SAPA § 306(1).

[14] See Erdman v. Ingraham, 28 A.D.2d 5, 280 N.Y.S.2d 865 (1st Dep't 1967).

[15] SAPA § 306(3).

[16] See CPLR 7801(1).

[17] See the discussion in § 558.

[18] Caso v. New York State Public High School Athletic Ass'n, Inc., 78 A.D.2d 41, 45–46, 434 N.Y.S.2d 60, 63–64 (4th Dep't 1980).

[19] See, e.g., Rubano v. New York Tel. Co., 43 Misc. 2d 149, 250 N.Y.S.2d 373 (Sup. Ct., Westchester County 1964).

questions that may be presented in an Article 78 proceeding. These are the nomads that have not found a stable domicile within any one of the writs, the migrants that seem to criss-cross the common frontier of mandamus and certiorari and make things hard for the census taker. Compelled to allot each of them to but a single writ, we would most often have to give them to mandamus; but clearly, as we shall see, they sometimes belong to certiorari. For a few lingering reasons, some already discussed and some to come, and in spite of the alleged fusion of all the writs into the singular Article 78 proceeding, it does become necessary on occasion to pinpoint the category. From the nature of the questions set forth in CPLR 7803(3), the only one of the three writs not in the contest under it is prohibition.

The questions that subdivision 3 lists as permissible in an Article 78 proceeding are these:

> whether a determination was made in violation of lawful procedure, was affected by an error of law or was arbitrary and capricious or an abuse of discretion, including abuse of discretion as to the measure or mode of penalty or discipline imposed . . . .

The last item, judicial review of a penalty or discipline imposed by an agency, is reserved for the next section. The rest of subdivision 3 we take up here.

Any substantial violation of applicable procedure is a basis for overturning an administrative determination, without regard to whether the category is mandamus or certiorari. A "procedural" violation will most often be concerned with some aspect of the hearing. The ultimate example of it would be the failure to grant any hearing at all when one is required. This is so whether the hearing required is the full quasi-judicial one seen in the certiorari category, or something less, which would allocate it to mandamus.[1] With the quasi-judicial proceeding, the one the State Administrative Procedure Act (SAPA) calls an "adjudicatory proceeding" and for which its Article 3 prescribes procedure in some detail, a substantial violation of one of the prescribed procedures would constitute a "violation of lawful procedure" as contemplated by CPLR 7803(3). Denying a party the right to cross-examine a witness,[2] or basing a finding of fact on something outside the record,[3] would be prime examples.

Subdivision 3's listing of an "error of law" as a permissible question is in one sense superfluous. If it means an error in procedure, it's covered by the first item, just noted. If it means an error of substance, it's covered by almost everything else listed in CPLR 7803. Whether a determination is arbitrary and capricious or an abuse of discretion, for example, which are other questions set forth in subdivision 3, or is supported by "substantial evidence," the test contained in subdivision 4, are all questions of law or in any event so intertwined with the legal issues in the case that they would cover and preserve review for whatever legal conclusions the decision depends on.

The same is true of the broadly phrased mandamus and prohibition questions appearing in subdivisions 1 and 2 of CPLR 7803. If for any reason these broad review standards should not be found adequate in a given case to secure review of the legal issue involved, and the amenability of the issue to judicial review must stand or fall on its own, the "error of law" under subdivision 3 can be relied on. A disputed construction of

---

[1]   See George v. Fiore, 62 Misc. 2d 429, 308 N.Y.S.2d 744 (Sup. Ct., Erie County 1970).

[2]   SAPA § 306(3).

[3]   SAPA § 302(3).

some provision in the agency's enabling act, for example, or of some other statute or rule applicable to the case, would always find a way to review under the "error of law" banner if not under some other.

Whether the determination is "arbitrary and capricious"—one of the best known phrases in administrative law—has been the subject of much discourse. It's the "arbitrary and capricious" test, rather than the "substantial evidence" test of subdivision 4, that applies when the determination is not required to be based on a full evidentiary hearing, i.e., the quasi-judicial hearing or what the SAPA calls the "adjudicatory" hearing. This is another way of saying that the "arbitrary and capricious" test is a phenomenon of mandamus, not certiorari, to which the "substantial evidence" test belongs.[4]

What is arbitrary and capricious? It is action taken "without sound basis in reason and . . . without regard to the facts."[5] Whether the facts on which the determination is based were adduced at a hearing or otherwise, the determination is "arbitrary and capricious" if the court finds that the conclusion drawn from them, or the administrative action taken based on them, is untenable as a matter of law.

The arbitrary and capricious test is usually associated with mandamus to review rather than mandamus to compel, in case the reader sees a difference. The fact that mandamus to compel covers the question listed in subdivision 1 of CPLR 7803—"whether the body or officer failed to perform a duty enjoined upon it by law"—suggests inferentially that any mandamus-type case reached by subdivision 3 is necessarily some other kind of mandamus. But this is an illusion, too. Intermixing is frequent and conceptually feasible. If there was a duty "enjoined . . . by law" under subdivision 1, for example, the failure to perform it would also be "arbitrary and capricious" under subdivision 3. This kind of overlap offers no difficulty. The writ referenced in either case is mandamus.

A more interesting question is the extent to which the "arbitrary and capricious" test of subdivision 3, which is mandamus, differs from the "substantial evidence" test of subdivision 4, which is certiorari. Article 78 does not cancel the need to categorize, remember; it merely postpones it until after the case is safely in court. By virtue of the very fact that subdivisions 3 and 4 supply different tests, the need presumably arises once again to determine whether the case is a mandamus case for application of the "arbitrary and capricious" standard of subdivision 3 or a certiorari case for application of the "substantial evidence" test of subdivision 4.

But we submit that the tests are virtually indistinguishable. A decision found to be "arbitrary and capricious" cannot be said to be supported by "substantial evidence." And a decision found to be unsupported by "substantial evidence" is necessarily "arbitrary and capricious." The Court of Appeals appears to have acknowledged that there is no difference. It has held that "rationality is what is reviewed under both the substantial

---

[4]   See Colton v. Berman, 21 N.Y.2d 322, 287 N.Y.S.2d 647, 234 N.E.2d 679 (1967). The arbitrary and capricious test was also the one adopted by the Court of Appeals to apply to the judicial review of an award in compulsory arbitration. See Caso v. Coffey, 41 N.Y.2d 153, 391 N.Y.S.2d 88, 359 N.E.2d 683 (1976), treated in § 603 (Practitioner's Edition). The scope of review of an award in the more common voluntary arbitration is more restrictive. See § 602 (Practitioner's Edition).

[5]   Pell v. Board of Ed. of Union Free School Dist. No. 1 of Towns of Scarsdale and Mamaroneck, 34 N.Y.2d 222, 231, 356 N.Y.S.2d 833, 839, 313 N.E.2d 321, 325 (1974).

evidence rule and the arbitrary and capricious standard."[6] A decision failing either test as irrational, in other words, must necessarily fail the other test as well.

It helps to have this Court of Appeals acknowledgment on the books. It relieves a judge from having to hunt out the invisible niceties once thought to differentiate the tests. For the purpose of determining how the tests differ, it tells the judge that they really do not differ at all; that in this respect there is nothing to pick between subdivisions 3 and 4.

For yet other purposes, alas, there is still a need to pick. A certiorari case under subdivision 4 gets transferred to the appellate division for initial determination,[7] while a mandamus case under subdivision 3 gets heard in first instance in the supreme court. Thus, just as we are about to assure ourselves that there is no longer a need to identify precisely whether the case is mandamus or certiorari, we find an arbitrary statute which, by directing different levels of initial review, perpetuates the ungratifying need to continue to categorize with punctilio.[8]

The "abuse of discretion" is yet another review basis, and presumably a distinct one, for overturning the determination. Discretion is the power to reach any of several decisions within certain confines. Only a decision beyond those confines constitutes an "abuse" of discretion such as a court will overturn, but the courts are of course the ultimate judge of the confines. If the administrative decision is within the outer limits of discretion, a court will not substitute its judgment for the agency's: as long as the agency's determination is within the borders of discretion—as perceived by the court— it qualifies as a question of fact.[9] But when it passes those borders—as perceived by the court—it becomes an "abuse," and an abuse of discretion is a question of law. "Abuse of discretion" is yet another separately verbalized review standard under subdivision 3 of CPLR 7803.

An "abuse of discretion," legally and lexicographically, is just another way of defining something that is "arbitrary and capricious."[10] But since "arbitrary and capricious" can also describe a decision wanting in "substantial evidence," the "substantial evidence" test must be the same as the "abuse of discretion" test, and each would have to be the same as the other. If singled out and instructed to describe how the CPLR distinguishes it, each of these tests could take a page out of a Marx Brothers routine and say simply, "It thinks I look alike!"

In its context in CPLR 7803(3), the "abuse of discretion" test appears to offer a basis for determining the adequacy of fact findings distinct from the "arbitrary and capricious" and "substantial evidence" tests. It is not limited, in other words, to measuring whether an administratively imposed penalty or discipline is sustainable. The caselaw, however, suggests that the penalty and discipline category is indeed the principal sphere of influence of the "abuse of discretion" standard. Its operation in that realm, of great

---

6   See *Pell*, 34 N.Y.2d at 231, 356 N.Y.S.2d at 839, 313 N.E.2d at 325.

7   CPLR 7804(g). See § 568.

8   For a few other lingering purposes, too, there remains a need to categorize. See §§ 566 and 569.

9   See Angelo J. Martone & Son, Inc. v. Nassau County, 42 Misc. 2d 804, 249 N.Y.S.2d 353 (Sup. Ct., Nassau County 1964).

10   See Douglas v. Miller, 55 Misc. 2d 303, 285 N.Y.S.2d 174 (Sup. Ct., Westchester County 1967), aff'd, 31 A.D.2d 889, 298 N.Y.S.2d 911 (2d Dep't 1969).

practical significance because of the judicial reins it puts on agency-imposed punishments, is the subject of the next section.

§ 562. Judicial Review of Penalty or Discipline

After authorizing review of whether there has been an "abuse of discretion," CPLR 7803(3) adds the phrase "including abuse of discretion as to the measure or mode of penalty or discipline imposed." This explicitly overrules the earlier notion that the courts lack power to review punishments administratively imposed.[1] Today, in fact, the courts have come to scrutinize quite closely alleged administrative excesses in the imposition of penalties, and cases claiming such excesses are perhaps the most frequent setting for the appearance of the "abuse of discretion" standard.

The question often if not always appears in a certiorari context because an administratively imposed punishment or forfeiture is usually imposed only after there has been a full quasi-judicial hearing. This in turn means that the official review standard is the "substantial evidence" test of subdivision 4, and yet it is subdivision 3 that contains the authority for the court to review alleged excesses in any punishment imposed, further establishing subdivision 3 as a kind of catchall. The courts have no trouble with this. They test the adequacy of the agency's fact findings by the substantial evidence test of subdivision 4 and the fairness of the measure of the punishment by the abuse of discretion test of subdivision 3.[2] Sometimes the courts will even be found using the word "arbitrary" or some other mandamus-type language to describe the punishment imposed by the agency,[3] but on closer analysis, it will more likely be a certiorari situation. The distinction retains significance as already mentioned and to be returned to yet again[4] because it determines whether the supreme court can pass on the issues initially or must transfer the case straightaway to the appellate division.[5]

As if distinguishing between "arbitrary and capricious," "abuse of discretion," and "supported by substantial evidence," is not chore enough, there's yet another criterion added when the measure of punishment is the issue: the "shocks the conscience" standard. The Court of Appeals confirmed this in Featherstone v. Franco,[6] holding that the courts are not to interfere unless the penalty imposed by the agency "shocks the conscience" of the court, which it didn't do in *Featherstone*.

In that case, a tenant violated the rules of a public housing authority by refusing to agree to exclude her violent son from her apartment after he proved a threat to her and the community. The Court upheld the authority's power to terminate the tenancy on that ground. The sanction of eviction on those facts does not "shock the conscience," and that's the criterion the courts are to apply in determining whether to overturn or abate an administrative sanction.

The governing provision, CPLR 7803(3), says that "abuse of discretion" is the review standard. The Court in *Featherstone* amplifies this by saying that when reviewing

---

[1] See, e.g., Sagos v. O'Connell, 301 N.Y. 212, 93 N.E.2d 644 (1950).

[2] See, e.g., Pomilio v. Lee, 21 A.D.2d 299, 250 N.Y.S.2d 339 (4th Dep't 1964).

[3] See, e.g., Shander v. Allen, 28 A.D.2d 1150, 284 N.Y.S.2d 142 (3d Dep't 1967), aff'd, 24 N.Y.2d 974, 302 N.Y.S.2d 599, 250 N.E.2d 81 (1969).

[4] See § 568.

[5] See CPLR 7804(g), treated in § 568.

[6] Featherstone v. Franco, 95 N.Y.2d 550, 720 N.Y.S.2d 93, 742 N.E.2d 607 (2000). The case is the subject of the lead note in NYSLD No. 494.

administrative sanctions, an "abuse" is to be deemed to occur only if the conscience is shocked.

When the judicial conscience is sufficiently jolted, judicial alteration of the punishment becomes more likely, as some earlier cases can illustrate, albeit not necessarily under a "shocks the conscience" banner. Alteration sometimes occurs after the court has rejected some of the agency's underlying findings. In one case, for example, after some administrative findings had been rejected by the court, a civil service pharmacist's dismissal was cancelled and a mere 15-day suspension substituted as the maximum warranted by the findings left over.[7] In other instances, the court may adopt the agency's findings in full but differ on the punishment they support as in one case in which the court rejected an agency decision revoking a realtor's license and imposed a short suspension instead despite full affirmance of the agency's findings of his "untrustworthiness."[8] In these instances, the court is substituting, in place of the agency's higher penalty, a lower one that the court feels to be the highest one permissible as a matter of law. The court is treating the matter as in effect a question of law, which every "exercise" of discretion becomes when it goes so far afield—as the court defines the field—that it spills over into an "abuse."

Under the *Featherstone* standard, these reductions in administrative penalties are presumably made because the court's conscience is shocked. There would of course be less occasion for judicial review, and a great saving in judicial energy, if a conscience could be installed and maintained at administrative level, but that appears to be beyond present technology.

If a suspension or like punishment has already been suffered, but its term has ended, an Article 78 proceeding may still lie to review it. The proceeding may be allowed in order to cleanse the record and remove the odium that can otherwise adhere to the petitioner.[9]

§ 563. Overstepping Outer Borders of Article 78

While the Article 78 proceeding may be used today for any category of relief formerly available under any of the three old writs of mandamus, prohibition, or certiorari, it will sometimes happen that the relief the petitioner seeks does not identify with any of the three writs and is beyond the purview of Article 78 altogether. The result in that case used to be a dismissal. Today, as long as a legally cognizable claim is stated and the proper parties are before the court, the result will be a simple conversion from proceeding to action—the action that should have been brought in the first place.[1] This is a boon to the petitioner who has mistaken her remedy. It spares the need to sue anew and it measures the timeliness of the action, for limitations' purposes, from the moment of commencement of the proceeding.

This shows that the lines separating the old writs now contained within Article 78 are not the only muddy ones; the line that purports to define the outer limits of Article 78 will also blur from time to time. While Article 78 may be proper, for example, to determine whether a statute has been applied in a constitutional manner, it may not be

---

[7]   Pomilio v. Lee, 21 A.D.2d 299, 250 N.Y.S.2d 339 (4th Dep't 1964).

[8]   Ancis v. Lomenzo, 31 A.D.2d 615, 295 N.Y.S.2d 784 (1st Dep't 1968).

[9]   See, e.g., Leo Newman's Theatre Ticket Office, Inc. v. DiCarlo, 46 Misc. 2d 549, 260 N.Y.S.2d 221 (Sup. Ct., New York County 1965).

[1]   CPLR 103(c). See § 4.

used to test whether the statute is constitutional on its face, for which the declaratory judgment action has been held the proper remedy.[2] The line is sometimes hard to draw, and for one who wishes to raise both objections it may be impossible. It is comforting to know that as long as the parties are right and personal jurisdiction has been obtained over them, the worst that will visit a wrong guess as to form will be a procedural conversion.

While in most special proceedings the notice time for the hearing can be as short as eight days,[3] in the Article 78 proceeding, it is ordinarily at least 20 days,[4] which makes it more analogous to the time a defendant has to respond to a summons in an action.[5] Hence, when the court proposes to convert an Article 78 proceeding into an action, the respondent cannot even complain about short notice. And even if there were a time differential, the defect could be met by the court's extending the responding time rather than refusing to convert.

The availability of simple conversion into proper form can be credited with encouraging the courts, at least in cases close to Article 78's outer limits, to abandon altogether a search for the line and just get on with the merits,[6] a healthy accomplishment. But the petitioner must demonstrate some kind of right. A failure to do at least that will still result in a dismissal. In this respect, a careful examination of Article 78 and all of its old writ categories will often aid the lawyer in determining whether the client even has an enforceable right or is really looking for some special privilege or concession not available at all.[7] It may also happen that a remedy has been lodged exclusively in administrative channels without provision for judicial review. That, too, although an infrequent phenomenon today, will result in a dismissal.[8]

Of course the petitioner must remain sensitive to the statute of limitations. While a conversion from one form to another may be easy enough when the statute of limitations on each of them is still open, it will not help if the court finds the proceeding brought to be the proper one, but too late, and the action to which conversion is sought, while still timely under its own statute of limitations, seeks a remedy not available on the facts. The best example of this, and the most common, is the petitioner's attempt to convert her untimely Article 78 proceeding into a declaratory judgment action.[9]

C. PROCEDURAL BASICS

Table of Sections

§ 564. Parties in Article 78 Proceeding

§ 565. Venue of Article 78 Proceeding

§ 566. Statute of Limitations in Article 78 Proceeding

---

[2] See Kovarsky v. Housing and Dev. Admin. of City of New York, 31 N.Y.2d 184, 335 N.Y.S.2d 383, 286 N.E.2d 882 (1972).

[3] CPLR 403(b). See § 553.

[4] See § 567.

[5] See CPLR 320(a), 3012(a). See § 110.

[6] See, e.g., Albany Medical Center Hospital v. Breslin, 47 Misc. 2d 208, 262 N.Y.S.2d 285 (Sup. Ct., Albany County 1965).

[7] See, e.g., Irving v. Finger Lakes State Parks Commission, 12 Misc. 2d 1087, 174 N.Y.S.2d 291 (Sup. Ct., Schuyler County 1958).

[8] See, e.g., Werfel v. Agresta, 36 N.Y.2d 624, 370 N.Y.S.2d 881, 331 N.E.2d 668 (1975).

[9] See the discussion of this matter in § 438 and § 566.

§ 564. Parties in Article 78 Proceeding

CPLR 7802 addresses the subject of parties to an Article 78 proceeding. It supplements CPLR 401, which defines the parties in special proceedings generally.[1] The person aggrieved by the administrative result, who brings the proceeding, is called, as in special proceedings in general, the petitioner.

The opposing party may occasionally contest the petitioner's "standing to sue," a loose caption designed to preclude litigation at the behest of a person who has no personal stake in the outcome different from that of any other citizen.[2] The "standing" barrier has not been a high one in New York. Not high, in any event, when contrasted with federal practice.[3] It climbed up a bit, however, after the decision in New York State Ass'n of Nurse Anesthetists v. Novello,[4] handed down in 2004, in which a divided Court of Appeals held that nurse anesthetists lacked "standing" to contest a health department "guideline" even though it impacted directly on their jobs.[5]

Perhaps the *Anesthetists* case was just an aberration. More will doubtless be heard on the point. The Court of Appeals had previously indicated that the right to challenge administrative action should be enlarged rather than diminished.[6]

CPLR 7802(a) provides that the "body or officer" against which (or whom) an Article 78 proceeding may be maintained—denominated the "respondent"—"includes every court, tribunal, board, corporation, officer, or other person, or aggregation of persons, whose action may be affected by a proceeding under this article." The main entry under this sweeping caption is of course the administrative agency, but executive and judicial personnel are also included as long as a clear case for Article 78 relief can be made out. The applicability of Article 78 to private corporations, commercial and otherwise, occurs primarily when the relief sought is in the nature of mandamus. These matters were treated earlier.[7]

The respondent is usually designated by name, but there is authority to use the official title of the respondent's office instead, subject always to the court's power to require names to be added.[8] If the petitioner's right subsists, it is also permissible to maintain the proceeding against a person whose term of office has expired.[9] When the respondent is an individual sued in his official capacity and dies or otherwise ceases to hold office, the proceeding can be continued against his successor. If the official title was used, without designation of names, it is not even necessary to effect a substitution.[10] This suggests that if the petitioner did use the name of the individual respondent, a

---

[1] See § 551.

[2] See, e.g., Blaikie v. Wagner, 46 Misc. 2d 441, 259 N.Y.S.2d 890 (Sup. Ct., New York County 1965), holding that a citizen-taxpayer-resident of New York City has no standing to compel the mayor to fill judicial vacancies. See also § 136 (discussing standing to sue).

[3] See § 612 (Practitioner's Edition).

[4] New York State Ass'n of Nurse Anesthetists v. Novello, 2 N.Y.3d 207, 778 N.Y.S.2d 123, 810 N.E.2d 405 (2004).

[5] See the discussion of the *Anesthetists* case in the lead note in NYSLD No. 533.

[6] See, e.g., Dairylea Cooperative, Inc. v. Walkley, 38 N.Y.2d 6, 377 N.Y.S.2d 451, 339 N.E.2d 865 (1975), discussed in § 136.

[7] See § 558.

[8] CPLR 1023.

[9] CPLR 7802(b). The successor in office may also be joined.

[10] CPLR 1019.

substitution order is required in order to insert the name of the successor. Quite often this is not done, however, and since the official title is also included in the caption, the proceeding is merely deemed to be against the office and the case goes through to judgment on the merits, which is as things ought to be.

The initial papers determine who the parties are. After the proceeding is commenced, the joinder, impleader, or interpleader of any other party requires a court order as is true of special proceedings in general.[11] If the court determines that any other person has an interest in the proceeding, whether on the petitioner's or the respondent's side, it can require that such person be notified, and it can allow intervention by interested persons at any time.[12] It has been held, in fact, that while intervention still requires a court order,[13] the court's power to permit intervention is even broader in an Article 78 proceeding than in an action.[14]

A justice, judge, referee, or judicial hearing officer is sometimes the respondent in an Article 78 proceeding as has been seen.[15] If the grievance against such judicial entity arises out of an action or proceeding pending before it, the petitioner is required to designate as additional respondents all of the parties to that pending action or proceeding and to serve on them copies of all the Article 78 papers. These are the special requirements of subdivision (i) of CPLR 7804.

The judicial respondent, J, does not have to appear in the Article 78 proceeding unless the court conducting the proceeding otherwise directs. If J elects not to appear, the other parties are notified of this and the results of the Article 78 proceeding bind J. If J does elect to appear, J is entitled to be represented by the attorney general. One of the statute's hopes is that the other parties to the underlying case, now joined as respondents, will conduct the defense in the Article 78 proceeding, thereby obviating an appearance by the judge and his representation by the attorney general.

§ 565. Venue of Article 78 Proceeding

The venue of an Article 78 proceeding is prescribed by CPLR 506(b), which permits the proceeding to be brought

in any county within the judicial district where the respondent made the determination complained of or refused to perform the duty specifically enjoined upon him by law, or where the proceedings were brought or taken in the course of which the matter sought to be restrained originated, or where the material events otherwise took place, or where the principal office of the respondent is located . . . .

The range is broad, and all the broader because one of the additional venue options afforded motions within an action[1] is afforded the Article 78 proceeding as well: the proceeding may be brought not only in a county answering to one of the above descriptions but, as the opening language evinces, in any other county in the same judicial district. Although this permits some forum shopping, its primary justification is that it offers the petitioner convenient alternatives when a supreme court session is not

---

[11] CPLR 401.

[12] CPLR 7802(d); Elinor Homes Co. v. St. Lawrence, 113 A.D.2d 25, 494 N.Y.S.2d 889 (2d Dep't 1985).

[13] CPLR 401, 1012, 1013.

[14] See, e.g., Helms v. Diamond, 76 Misc. 2d 253, 349 N.Y.S.2d 917 (Sup. Ct., Schenectady County 1973).

[15] See § 558.

[1] See CPLR 2212(a); § 245.

being held in one of the described counties. Except for certain instances in which it must be initiated in the appellate division, which we will see in a moment, an Article 78 proceeding belongs jurisdictionally to the supreme court alone.[2] CPLR 506(b) merely tells us what counties within the supreme court the proceeding is to be brought in.

The remedy for a wrong venue in an Article 78 proceeding is the same as in an action: a mere change of venue to the right county.[3] Like an action, a special proceeding may not be dismissed for improper venue,[4] a failure to object to improper venue is a waiver of the objection,[5] and an ensuing judgment on the merits is valid.[6]

A change of venue is permissible not only when the venue has been laid in a wrong county, but also when based on one of the so-called "discretionary" grounds: to secure an impartial trial when a proper county would not be able to offer one or to serve the convenience of material witnesses.[7]

When an Article 78 proceeding is brought against a justice of the supreme court or a judge of a county court, it's initiated in the appellate division,[8] one of the few instances in which the appellate division exercises its original jurisdiction. This recognizes the incongruity of allowing one supreme court justice to review another's activity. For this purpose, judges of the county court,[9] especially because they exercise plenary jurisdiction of felonies, are deemed to be on an equal plane with the supreme court and can also be subjected to Article 78 only in the appellate division. In rural counties, a judge can sit on multiple benches and may concurrently serve as both a county court and surrogate's court judge. If a proceeding is brought against such a judge in her capacity as a surrogate, it must originate in supreme court because a surrogate's court judge is not listed in CPLR 506(b)(1).[10]

If some other person, such as a district attorney, must also be included as a respondent, it has been held permissible to include that person in the proceeding brought in the appellate division, but the converse is not permissible: the presence of some other person as a respondent does not enable the whole proceeding to be brought in the supreme court.[11]

---

[2]   CPLR 7804(b).

[3]   CPLR 510(1). See Progressive Northern Ins. Co. v. Secondino, Sup. Ct., Westchester County, Dec. 4, 2000 (Index No. 13133/00; Lefkowitz, J.). CPLR 511, which governs the procedure for a change of venue, should also govern in an Article 78 proceeding to the extent feasible, but the special "demand" procedure that subdivision (b) of CPLR 511 sets up for a change of venue in an action (see § 123) is mechanically awkward in a special proceeding and should not be used there.

[4]   See Travelers Indem. Co. of Illinois v. Nnamani, 286 A.D.2d 769, 730 N.Y.S.2d 522 (2d Dep't 2001), and the lead notes in SPR 99:1 and SPR 101:1, which discuss the remedies for a special proceeding in which the selected venue violates the rule.

[5]   See HVAC & Sprinkler Contractors Ass'n, Inc. v. State Univ. Const. Fund, 80 Misc. 2d 1047, 364 N.Y.S.2d 422 (Sup. Ct., Nassau County 1975).

[6]   CPLR 509.

[7]   CPLR 510(2), (3). See § 124.

[8]   CPLR 506(b)(1).

[9]   CPLR 506(b)(1) also refers to the court of "general sessions," which entertained the felonies in New York County prior to September 1, 1962, but was abolished on that date and superseded by the supreme court. N.Y. Const. art. VI, § 35(a). This reference is now superfluous.

[10]   Tonawanda Seneca Nation v. Noonan, 27 N.Y.3d 713, 37 N.Y.S.3d 36, 57 N.E.3d 1073 (2016) ("[T]he determination of venue for an article 78 proceeding against a multi-bench judge turns on the capacity in which the judge was serving when taking the challenged action.").

[11]   Pollak v. Mogavero, 114 A.D.2d 640, 494 N.Y.S.2d 476 (3d Dep't 1985).

If the proceeding is against certain governmental respondents, including the commissioner of education, the tax commissioner, the comptroller, and some half dozen others enumerated, a special provision authorizes venue only in the supreme court in Albany County, the seat of government.[12] This list supersedes the more generous list of venue alternatives contained in the opening language of subdivision (a), quoted above and applicable to other respondents. Even the provision that authorizes venue in any other county in the same judicial district appears to be inapplicable to the respondents enumerated in subdivision (b), leaving Albany County as the sole proper venue.[13]

There is no need to raise this to the level of a jurisdictional issue, however. Should the proceeding be brought and entertained in the supreme court in a county other than Albany without objection to venue, the court should be able to dispose of it on the merits.

§ 566. Statute of Limitations in Article 78 Proceeding

The statute of limitations in an Article 78 proceeding is short. It's four months, supplied and governed by CPLR 217(1), whose treatment we have reserved until now. CPLR 217(1) provides that the four months start to run when

the determination to be reviewed becomes final and binding upon the petitioner . . . or after the respondent's refusal, upon the demand of the petitioner . . . to perform its duty . . . .

The first one enumerated, which measures the four months from the time the determination "becomes final," is generally the starting point for an Article 78 proceeding in the nature of certiorari while the second one, measured from the respondent's refusal to perform his duty after demand has been duly made, is the usual one for an Article 78 proceeding in the nature of mandamus. The lines to neither one can be described as straight and unswerving; however, so here again, the lawyer may note yet another instance in which distinctions between the old writs subsist despite Article 78's embrace of them all.[1]

When the consequence attending a wrong guess is a limitations' dismissal, the practitioner should not be guessing at all. The petitioner with any doubt should bring the proceeding fast and leave to the scholars the pinpointing of which writ is involved and which technical starting time goes with it. The judges themselves will disagree on whether a given Article 78 proceeding smacks of one writ or the other, with the result that each may start the four months from a different moment.[2]

The "determination" of which CPLR 217(1) speaks, and whose moment of finality starts the four months, applies not only to what is strictly speaking "certiorari," where the determination follows a quasi-judicial hearing mandated by law, but also to "mandamus to review," where an administrative determination involves discretion but does not require a plenary hearing. The involvement of discretion, therefore, is one

---

[12]   CPLR 506(b)(2).

[13]   CPLR 506(a). See Posner v. Rockefeller, 33 A.D.2d 683, 305 N.Y.S.2d 852 (1st Dep't 1969), aff'd, 25 N.Y.2d 720, 307 N.Y.S.2d 224, 255 N.E.2d 563.

[1]   See 2d Rep. Leg. Doc. No. 13, p. 394 (1958).

[2]   See, e.g., Colodney v. New York Coffee & Sugar Exch., Inc., 2 N.Y.2d 149, 157 N.Y.S.2d 573, 138 N.E.2d 810 (1956) (majority and dissenting opinions).

strong indicator that the "final determination" moment starts the four months,[3] but it's not always a certain one.[4]

Another test, equally well known, is to ask whether what the petitioner seeks is something to which she has a clear legal right—that is, something of a mere ministerial nature—for (1) if the thing demanded is not of that kind, the case will stay in the "review" category and the "final determination" will remain the trigger; while (2) if it is of that kind, it will be the refusal after demand that starts the four months. This is so whether or not the determination followed a hearing of the judicial or quasi-judicial kind, or an informal hearing, or no hearing at all. Where, for example, petitioners, liquor licensees, sought to annul a license issued by the state liquor authority to one who would be competing with the petitioners, the four months ran from the date of the issuance of the license; it was held to be "final and binding" at that time.[5] Since the issuance of a liquor license rested in the discretion of the respondent, the proceeding, whether analogized to certiorari or to mandamus, was one for "review" within the meaning of CPLR 217(1) and the four months thus ran from the time the determination became final and binding.

Once the determination has reached that stage, the four months start to run and the "petitioner cannot, by renewing the application, extend the limitation" because that would enable the petitioner to "toll the statute ad infinitum, and make an absurdity" of it.[6]

The lawyer who is not very happy with some of these distinctions can find company among hosts of other lawyers who are listed as petitioners' counsel in Article 78 cases dismissed over the years as untimely. Close divisions, even on appellate benches in these matters,[7] attest to the difficulty of drawing the right line, and they seem to be a steady progression. In Waterside Associates v. New York State Dept. of Environmental Conservation,[8] for example, the petitioner wanted the respondent, the environmental conservation department, to stop designating areas of a certain parcel as wetlands. The petitioner made a permit application that it hoped would start a process to accomplish that. The respondent would not process the application and sent a form letter saying so. Was this the "refusal" that would trigger the four months of an Article 78 proceeding? Four judges said yes and three judges said no. Whatever the stakes, all was lost by a single vote, and in the highest tribunal of the State. And it was lost not on some great matter of public policy—some profound issue that tries men's souls—but on a dispute over the moment that starts the four-month period for bringing an Article 78 proceeding against an administrative agency.[9]

---

[3]   See Alliano v. Adams, 2 A.D.2d 532, 157 N.Y.S.2d 119 (1st Dep't 1956), aff'd, 3 N.Y.2d 801, 166 N.Y.S.2d 4, 144 N.E.2d 645 (1957).

[4]   See and compare Foy v. Brennan, 285 A.D. 669, 140 N.Y.S.2d 132 (1st Dep't 1955) with *Alliano*.

[5]   Cohen v. State Liquor Authority, 25 A.D.2d 773, 269 N.Y.S.2d 525 (2d Dep't 1966).

[6]   Mallen v. Morton, 199 Misc. 805, 811, 99 N.Y.S.2d 521, 528–29 (Sup. Ct., New York County 1950).

[7]   See, e.g., Owners Committee on Elec. Rates, Inc. v. Public Service Com'n of State of N.Y., 150 A.D.2d 45, 545 N.Y.S.2d 416 (3d Dep't 1989), rev'd, 76 N.Y.2d 779, 559 N.Y.S.2d 957, 559 N.E.2d 651 (1990).

[8]   Waterside Associates v. New York State Dept. of Environmental Conservation, 72 N.Y.2d 1009, 534 N.Y.S.2d 915, 531 N.E.2d 636 (1988).

[9]   The *Waterside* case and the dilemma of determining the starting time of the Article 78 statute of limitations is the subject of the lead note in NYSLD No. 354. In another case that never reached the merits and in which the hapless petitioner had to deal with not one agency but three, the four-month period for Article 78 review was apparently held to run from the time the petitioner failed to furnish papers to one agency that it had already furnished to another. See Essex County v. Zagata, 91 N.Y.2d 447, 672 N.Y.S.2d 281, 695 N.E.2d 232 (1998), treated in the lead note in NYSLD No. 463.

If the would-be petitioner arrives at the lawyer's office with enough time left under all measures, the lawyer should consider himself twice blessed—once for the client and once for the client's punctuality—and fly to court. The only time the attorney can be excused for a late suit is when the client arrives too late in the first place.

A subsequent Court of Appeals case on this apparently unsolvable dilemma is In re City of New York,[10] in which a hapless eminent domain victim was educated on the difficulty. Then came Comptroller of City of New York v. Mayor of City of New York[11] and after that Walton v. New York State Dept. of Correctional Services.[12] *Walton* produced a majority opinion, a concurrence, and a dissent, but no safe guidepost. Nor has any corrective legislation appeared.

The fly-to-court doctrine remains, to our thinking, the safest course to follow in this muddled area, but the path can be paved with frustration for the lawyer and client concerned about spending valuable time and money in the endeavor under review. In Ranco Sand and Stone Corp. v. Vecchio,[13] for example, the town board, acting as the lead agency under SEQRA, issued a positive declaration on petitioner's proposed rezoning that required a draft environmental impact statement (DEIS). The petitioners, obviously concerned with the substantial costs required to prepare a DEIS, commenced an article 78 proceeding seeking to annul the positive declaration. The Court of Appeals held that a positive declaration of this sort is ripe for judicial review when two requirements are satisfied: 1) the administrative action must "impose an obligation, deny a right or fix some legal relationship as a consummation of the administrative process"; and 2) "there must be a finding that the apparent harm inflicted by the action may not be prevented or significantly ameliorated by further administrative action or by steps available to the complaining party."[14]

The petitioner in *Ranco* established the first requirement for ripeness, but not the second. Petitioner's contention that it could not recoup the substantial costs in preparing a DEIS (allegedly between $75,000 and $150,000) even if it was ultimately successful in obtaining the rezoning, was not sufficient to establish the harm requirement. In reaching its conclusion, the Court emphasized the importance of avoiding piecemeal review of each determination made in the SEQRA process, which would add further delay to an already lengthy ordeal. Rather than constituting final agency action ripe for review, a positive declaration imposing a DEIS requirement is usually only an initial step in the SEQRA process.

When the case is clearly a mandamus-to-compel one, and the four-month measure is from demand and then refusal to act, another thing the courts look out for is a delayed demand. Postponing the demand would obviously be an easy way for a petitioner to avoid

---

10   In re City of New York, 6 N.Y.3d 540, 814 N.Y.S.2d 592, 847 N.E.2d 1166 (2006); see also Kahn v. New York City Dept. of Educ., 18 N.Y.3d 457, 940 N.Y.S.2d 540, 963 N.E.2d 1241 (2012) (NYSLD No. 628) (administrative decisions were "final and binding" within the meaning of CPLR 217(1) as of the dates when petitioners' probationary service ended, not on the dates that internal review concluded).

11   Comptroller of City of New York v. Mayor of City of New York, 7 N.Y.3d 256, 819 N.Y.S.2d 672, 852 N.E.2d 1144 (2006) (NYSLD No. 561).

12   Walton v. New York State Dept. of Correctional Services, 8 N.Y.3d 186, 831 N.Y.S.2d 749, 863 N.E.2d 1001 (2007) (NYSLD No. 568).

13   Ranco Sand and Stone Corp. v. Vecchio, 27 N.Y.3d 92, 29 N.Y.S.3d 873, 49 N.E.3d 1165 (2016).

14   *Ranco*, 27 N.Y.3d at 98–99, 29 N.Y.S.3d at 877, 49 N.E.3d at 1169.

the limitation; hence, the laches doctrine can get invoked here.[15] Where the petitioner was removed from office, for example, and without excuse delayed a demand for reinstatement, his proceeding was dismissed for laches.[16] Of course, if a reasonably diligent petitioner is not aware of the facts that would prompt him to make the demand, his delay in making it is excusable and laches does not apply.[17]

Up to now, we have been talking about certiorari and mandamus. A word should be said about prohibition. With prohibition, the very applicability of the four-month statute of limitations of CPLR 217(1) is questionable. It has from time to time been applied to an Article 78 proceeding in the nature of prohibition,[18] but since the proceeding in such an instance is one that implies a lack of jurisdiction on the part of the respondent that would presumably be a continuing one—it can be argued that the four months may be measured from any point during the jurisdiction's continued exercise.

That would be so, in any event, when the objection is addressed strictly to the respondent's lack of subject matter jurisdiction, the traditional arena of prohibition. But the writ's function (and Article 78's function as its successor) has been extended to that ill-defined realm, previously discussed, in which jurisdiction exists but "power" is exceeded.[19] The petitioner objecting to this exercise of "power" would do well, at least until we have a further clarification of the matter, to commence the proceeding within four months of its first perceived exercise.

CPLR 217(1) also addresses the disabilities of infancy and insanity, should the petitioner be under either disability when the four months are set to begin. It permits the court in such an instance to extend the four months for a period of up to two years.

The moment of the claim's interposition for limitations' purposes is when the petition is filed in court. The petition is then served with the notice of petition or order to show cause, as the statute permits use of this procedural tool.[20] The service of these initiatory papers must be effected within whatever is left of the applicable statute of limitations plus 15 days, the exotic formula for special proceedings supplied by CPLR 306–b. The interplay of the filing and service requirements under this system, which affect the statute of limitations and can be demanding, is treated in depth in the section on special proceedings generally.[21]

CPLR 7804(c), which governs the service of the initial papers in an Article 78 proceeding, adds the requirement that when the respondent is a state body or officer (as opposed to one at municipal level, for example), service must also be made on the attorney general through a prescribed procedure. If service is timely made on the respondent but late on the attorney general, however, it has been held that all is

---

[15]   See Sheerin v. New York Fire Dept. Articles 1 and 1B Pension Funds, 46 N.Y.2d 488, 495–96, 414 N.Y.S.2d 506, 387 N.E.2d 217 (1979) (noting that in "an article 78 proceeding in the nature of mandamus, proof of unexcused delay without more may be enough" to invoke laches); Austin v. Board of Higher Ed. of City of New York, 5 N.Y.2d 430, 186 N.Y.S.2d 1, 158 N.E.2d 681 (1959).

[16]   Peruzzin v. Test, 282 A.D. 550, 125 N.Y.S.2d 353 (4th Dep't 1953).

[17]   O'Connell v. Kern, 287 N.Y. 297, 39 N.E.2d 246 (1942); see Chevron U.S.A., Inc. v. Commissioner of Environmental Conservation, 86 A.D.3d 838, 927 N.Y.S.2d 452, 455 (3d Dep't 2011) (SPR 238:3) (reversing a finding of laches where "there was no prior case law addressing the proper procedure for seeking a return of an overpayment of [the] fees" at issue).

[18]   See, e.g., Feldman v. Matthews, 32 Misc. 2d 996, 223 N.Y.S.2d 604 (Sup. Ct., Monroe County 1962).

[19]   See § 559.

[20]   CPLR 7804(c). See § 567.

[21]   See § 553.

preserved. The reason is that the purpose of this provision is to assure a defense by the attorney general if the named respondent does not have separate counsel,[22] not to make the attorney general the party.[23] Conversely, though, and for the same reason, timely service on the attorney general is not a substitute for timely service on the named respondent, and where the respondent was served late, the proceeding was dismissed under the statute of limitations.[24]

Another note of warning. CPLR 217(1) defers to any statute that requires that a given Article 78 proceeding be brought in less than four months. Review of a village board of appeals in a zoning matter, for example, gets only 30 days from the decision's filing with the village clerk,[25] and there are other similar examples.[26] The lawyer dealing with any municipal, governmental, or quasi-governmental body should, upon losing a decision, make the applicable statute of limitations the first point of research. If there is nothing specific addressed to the particular proceeding, the four months of CPLR 217(1) will apply. Exceptional sensitivity to time issues must be exercised in election cases where, for obvious reasons, the time in which to bring remedial proceedings is short.[27] Furthermore, if the time for its bringing has expired, the petitioner cannot, by labeling the proceeding one under Article 78 instead of under the Election Law, secure the former's more favorable four-month period.[28]

Discussed elsewhere, and at length,[29] is the situation in which a petitioner who is too late for the Article 78 relief appropriate to his case tries to disguise his claim as one for a declaratory judgment, in the hope of securing the longer statute of limitations applicable to that. The petitioner, arguing that what was done to him is a violation of the constitution—it's not hard to plead that—may phrase his claim as one to declare invalid the statute or other law on which the respondent based its action. This has often been tried, but seldom achieved the longer time period.[30]

It's always risky for a claimant with a gripe against a governmental unit of any kind to forgo the Article 78 device in the expectation of getting a longer time for suit by bringing a plenary action of some kind instead. The mistake will often have fatal statute of limitations consequences as it did in New York City Health and Hospitals Corp. v. McBarnette,[31] which contains an extensive discussion of the point.[32]

---

[22] See Commentary C2214:30 on the analogous provision of McKinney's CPLR 2214.

[23] Chem-Trol Pollution Services, Inc. v. Ingraham, 42 A.D.2d 192, 345 N.Y.S.2d 714 (4th Dep't 1973).

[24] Cohen v. State Tax Commission, 51 A.D.2d 79, 378 N.Y.S.2d 507 (3d Dep't 1976).

[25] Village Law § 7–712–c.

[26] A list of others appears in 2d Rep. Leg. Doc. No. 13, p. 550 (1958). The list needs updating, but even a current one is no substitute for specific inquiry in the individual case when the statute of limitations is hovering about.

[27] See the several proceedings supplied by Article 16 of the Election Law.

[28] See Mansfield v. Epstein, 5 N.Y.2d 70, 180 N.Y.S.2d 33, 154 N.E.2d 368 (1958), and Murray v. Lord, 46 A.D.2d 721, 361 N.Y.S.2d 96 (4th Dep't 1974), aff'd, 35 N.Y.2d 737, 361 N.Y.S.2d 909, 320 N.E.2d 644.

[29] See § 438.

[30] See, e.g., Gress v. Brown, 20 N.Y.3d 957, 958 N.Y.S.2d 675, 982 N.E.2d 595 (2012); see also Commentary C3001:18 on McKinney's CPLR 3001.

[31] New York City Health and Hospitals Corp. v. McBarnette, 84 N.Y.2d 194, 616 N.Y.S.2d 1, 639 N.E.2d 740 (1994).

[32] See also the lead note in NYSLD No. 416.

D. MECHANICS

Table of Sections

§ 567. Bringing the Proceeding

§ 568. Hearing and Determination; Transfer to Appellate Division

§ 569. Trial of Issue of Fact in Article 78 Proceeding

§ 570. Judgment and Enforcement in Article 78 Proceeding

§ 567. Bringing the Proceeding

The procedure for commencing the Article 78 proceeding is similar to that applicable to special proceedings in general, which makes the discussion in section 553 relevant here, and profitable to review. But Article 78 prefers its own statement for certain particulars, setting them forth in CPLR 7804(c).

The technical moment of the commencement of the proceeding for statute of limitations purposes is the filing of the petition. Also, as elaborated in section 553, the notice of petition or order to show cause, which act as process and which must of course accompany the petition when service is made, need no longer be filed with the petition at the outset.[1]

In common with special proceedings in general, the requirement for service is that it be made by the 15th day after the statute of limitations is scheduled to expire. The petitioner has the balance of the statute of limitations, in other words, as measured from the petition's filing, plus 15 days. The court can extend the 15-day period "upon good cause shown or in the interest of justice."[2]

In common with special proceedings in general, the notice of petition must set a return day for the proceeding, but the period of notice is longer. The return day can't be set for earlier than the 20th day after service, in contrast to the 8-day minimum applicable to other special proceedings.[3] The respondent's answer must be served at least 5 days before the return day, and the petitioner who would then serve a reply must do so at least 1 day before. Setting the return day for earlier than the 20th day has sometimes been held a jurisdictional defect,[4] but more recently it has been said that "short notice should be excused unless the error is substantial or it causes prejudice."[5] Under that view, it would be incumbent on the respondent to show "that the defect prevented it from adequately responding" to the claim,[6] which a mistake of only a day or a few days is not likely to do.

---

[1]   This is the result of a 2001 amendment. Before it, the notice of petition had to be filed with the petition in order to satisfy the statute of limitations. See the lead note in SPR 116:1.

[2]   CPLR 306–b. See § 63 discussing these provisions in the context of an action where they have similar application.

[3]   CPLR 403(b). See § 553.

[4]   See, e.g., Dickerson v. Jensen, 33 A.D.2d 890, 307 N.Y.S.2d 559 (4th Dep't 1969).

[5]   Marmo v. Department of Environmental Conservation, 134 A.D.2d 260, 520 N.Y.S.2d 442 (2d Dep't 1987). See also Bloeth v. Marks, 20 A.D.2d 372, 247 N.Y.S.2d 410 (1st Dep't 1964), involving a pro se petitioner, and Griswald v. Village of Penn Yan, 244 A.D.2d 950, 665 N.Y.S.2d 177 (4th Dep't 1997).

[6]   Szklowin v. Planning Bd. of Town of Blooming Grove, 115 Misc. 2d 1045, 455 N.Y.S.2d 70 (Sup. Ct., Orange County 1982).

The petitioner who is really pressed for time can simply bring the proceeding on by order to show cause, in which the court can set an earlier return than the otherwise required 20 days.

The alternative of the order to show cause procedure is available for the Article 78 proceeding just as it is for special proceedings generally[7] and for motions in actions.[8] The very fact that an order to show cause is an available alternative in a special proceeding suggests that the remedy when an ordinary notice of petition is used with fewer than 20 days notice is for the court simply to award more time, putting the return day off as needed. However that may be, the rushed petitioner should use the order to show cause procedure specifically; it's inadvisable to use an ordinary notice of petition and then set a return day earlier than the statute prescribes.

Whether an order to show cause or a regular notice of petition is used, the petitioner must remember that when the respondent is a body or officer of the State rather than one of a municipal or other level, service must also be made on the attorney general.[9]

Labeling the papers a notice of motion instead of a notice of petition has been held harmless error,[10] but it can lead to confusion in the clerk's office. A motion has the context of a pending action with an index number already assigned, while an Article 78 proceeding is an independent application and requires its own index number and the payment of a fee for it. As with special proceedings in general, the papers initiating an Article 78 proceeding must be accompanied by a Request for Judicial Intervention (RJI),[11] which gets the case assigned to a judge.[12] For the reasons suggested earlier, it may be helpful to file the notice of petition or order to show cause with the petition even if it is no longer required.[13]

Pending its decision on the merits, the court can stay the enforcement of the determination (of which review is sought) and any further proceedings by the respondent, imposing conditions as it sees fit.[14] It can do this on either the motion of a party or on its own motion. The value of a stay, which gives the aggrieved person some breathing space while a court looks into the administrative activity, can be attested to by many lawyers. One way of seeking the stay is by opting to bring the proceeding on by order to show cause and by requesting that the court include a stay in the order.[15]

Pleadings in an Article 78 proceeding are much the same as in any proceeding, with a few variations. They must be verified, for example,[16] but the consequence of a failure to verify should be no greater in the proceeding than it is in an action.[17] There is even

---

[7]   CPLR 403(d).

[8]   CPLR 2214(d). See § 248.

[9]   CPLR 7804(c).

[10]   *Marmo*, 134 A.D.2d at 261, 520 N.Y.S.2d at 443.

[11]   See § 553.

[12]   This requirement comes from the Uniform Rules. The relevant rules here are 22 N.Y.C.R.R. §§ 202.6, 202.8(b), and 202.9, applicable in the supreme and county courts. The official RJI form is reprinted in § 77C.

[13]   See § 553.

[14]   CPLR 7805.

[15]   In this connection, however, the practitioner must bear in mind the restriction imposed by CPLR 6313(a). It precludes the issuance of a temporary restraining order against "a public officer, board or municipal corporation" if the effect of it is "to restrain the performance of statutory duties." See § 330.

[16]   CPLR 7804(d).

[17]   See § 235.

authority, especially when prompt objection is not made, for disregarding the defect altogether.[18] Since the pleadings are usually accompanied by sworn affidavits, which set forth the facts more abundantly, an absence of a formal verification of the pleadings is not likely to be prejudicial.

Another pleading variation in an Article 78 proceeding is that a reply is mandatory not only when the respondent's answer contains a counterclaim, but also when there is "new matter in the answer or where the accuracy of proceedings annexed to the answer is disputed."[19] A reply is technically required, in other words, if the petitioner wants to dispute the correctness of the administrative record.

If there is a record, as there often is—and it is often voluminous—and the court does not already have it, it is the respondent's obligation to furnish it to the court, which the respondent does by filing with the answer "a certified transcript of the record of the proceedings."[20] This is no mean attainment: without the statute imposing this burden on the respondent, many a petitioner would be in no position to press forward with the proceeding.

The court can also direct the respondent to supply any omissions it detects in the record. If no record is filed at all, the court may take such remedial steps as it deems fit, including a dismissal of the respondent's answer with leave to serve a new one with a record annexed to it.[21]

If the respondent has "an objection in point of law" to the petition, CPLR 7804(f) gives the respondent the option of including it as a defense in the answer or making a motion to dismiss based on it. This was intended to draw a limited analogy to an action; the "objections" intended for this alternative treatment are of the kind listed in CPLR 3211(a),[22] and more particularly those on the CPLR 3211(a) list that do not go to the merits and thus make possible a disposition that may spare the court the effort of having to reach the merits at all.[23] Objections based on a want of jurisdiction or on the statute of limitations are perhaps the most common examples.

When the objection is taken by motion, the motion must be noticed "within the time allowed for answer."[24] Since the answering time is 20 days, this gives the respondent enough time to notice a motion, but just barely. The motion must be made returnable at the same time and place set by the Article 78 proceeding in the notice of petition.[25]

---

[18] See CPLR 3022; Ferro v. Lavine, 46 A.D.2d 313, 362 N.Y.S.2d 591 (3d Dep't 1974).

[19] CPLR 7804(d). In other special proceedings, a reply is optional even in those situations. See CPLR 402.

[20] CPLR 7804(e). It has been held that this applies only to the Article 78 proceeding itself, however. It does not require the furnishing of a transcript during the various administrative stages of the dispute that preceded the commencement of the proceeding. Rivera v. Smith, 137 A.D.2d 281, 528 N.Y.S.2d 930 (3d Dep't 1988).

[21] See Occhino v. Hostetter, 21 A.D.2d 744, 250 N.Y.S.2d 120 (4th Dep't 1964).

[22] See § 257 and 4th Rep. Leg. Doc. No. 20, p. 181 (1960).

[23] See Hop-Wah v. Coughlin, 118 A.D.2d 275, 504 N.Y.S.2d 806 (3d Dep't 1986), rev'd on other grounds, 69 N.Y.2d 791, 513 N.Y.S.2d 115, 505 N.E.2d 625 (1987).

[24] Note the requirement, added in 2003, that a fee of $45 be paid for the making of any motion, which applies to special proceedings as well as to actions. The subjects of motion fees in general and special proceedings in particular are discussed in § 243 and § 554.

[25] CPLR 406.

The statute says that if the motion is denied, the court "shall" permit the respondent to answer.[26] Despite the mandatory tone of this subdivision, the Court of Appeals has observed that a court need not permit a respondent to serve an answer after denying a motion to dismiss "if the facts are so fully presented in the papers of the respective parties that it is clear that no dispute as to the facts exists and no prejudice will result from the failure to require an answer."[27] If, after the denial of a motion to dismiss, there are still triable issues of fact, or the motion addresses only one of several issues, the respondent should be permitted to serve an answer to the petition.[28]

The courts frown on the making of a motion by a respondent on the presumably narrow ground of a single defense while at the same time including on the motion all the evidence the respondent has on the merits and asking that it be allowed to serve an answer if the motion is denied. It amounts to the respondent's attempt to get two bites at the apple. "The statute does not contemplate successive hearings on issues of fact, at least unless the court finds some good reason for so ordering."[29]

But what remedy? The statute does say, after all, that the court "shall" permit an answer if the motion is denied, not merely that it "may" do so. While there is some indication that the difference from the language governing a special proceeding in CPLR 404(a) was intended,[30] if it is plain from all the papers that the respondent has nothing with which to answer and that further proceedings would be wasteful, the court should not prolong the petitioner's agony. It should be able to close the case out with a judgment. Some courts lean in that direction, especially when the issues are of law rather than of fact and require no trial.[31] Others suggest that the court may invoke CPLR 3211(c) and treat the motion as one for summary judgment, notifying the parties to submit any additional proof they may have and thereby obviating yet another court hearing. The First Department has said that

> it is difficult to see what appropriate purpose is served by permitting the denial of the motion to be followed by an answer that raises no new factual or legal issue . . . .[32]

If the motion is denied and the court does allow an answer, CPLR 7804(f) provides for the time within which the respondent must serve it and for the petitioner's time for re-noticing the hearing.

---

[26]   CPLR 7804(f). This is in contrast to CPLR 404(a), applicable to special proceedings in general, which provides only that the court "may" permit an answer in that situation.

[27]   Kickertz v. New York University, 25 N.Y.3d 942, 944, 6 N.Y.S.3d 546, 547, 29 N.E.3d 893, 894 (2015).

[28]   *Kickertz*, 25 N.Y.3d at 944, 6 N.Y.S.3d at 547–48, 29 N.E.3d at 894–95; Nassau BOCES Cent. Council of Teachers v. Board of Co-op. Educ. Services of Nassau County, 63 N.Y.2d 100, 102, 480 N.Y.S.2d 190, 469 N.E.2d 511 (1984).

[29]   R. Bernstein Co. v. Popolizio, 97 A.D.2d 735, 468 N.Y.S.2d 888 (1st Dep't 1983).

[30]   See 5th Rep. Leg. Doc., p. 755 (1961).

[31]   See, e.g., DeVito v. Nyquist, 56 A.D.2d 159, 391 N.Y.S.2d 747 (3d Dep't 1977), aff'd, 43 N.Y.2d 681, 401 N.Y.S.2d 25, 371 N.E.2d 788.

[32]   230 Tenants Corp. v. Board of Standards and Appeals of City of New York, 101 A.D.2d 53, 474 N.Y.S.2d 498 (1st Dep't 1984).

§ 568. Hearing and Determination; Transfer to Appellate Division

The Article 78 proceeding is brought in the supreme court.[1] The supreme court will ordinarily dispose of the whole case, but with a big proviso. CPLR 7804(g) provides that if the "substantial evidence" question[2] is raised

the court shall first dispose of such other objections as could terminate the proceeding, including but not limited to lack of jurisdiction, statute of limitations, and res judicata, without reaching the substantial evidence issue. If the determination of the other objections does not terminate the proceeding, the court shall make an order directing that it be transferred for disposition to . . . the appellate division . . . .

The mere presence of the substantial evidence question, in other words, which means that the proceeding is one in the nature of "certiorari," will trigger this transfer requirement if some other objection does not terminate the proceeding. And the procedure is just that—a transfer, not an appeal.

The reason for the transfer is partly historical and partly a recognition that a "substantial evidence" review of an administrative record is analogous to an appellate review of a court-made record and for that reason merits quick deposit before the appellate tribunal.[3]

The reason for not allowing the petitioner to initiate the proceeding in the appellate division, requiring instead that it be commenced in the supreme court and allowing the supreme court to determine whether to transfer it, is to enable the supreme court to rule on potentially dispositive issues that may obviate consideration of the substantial evidence question. The several such issues listed are illustrative only. The objections intended are perhaps best taken to be the same as those intended by the phrase "objections in point of law" as used in CPLR 7804(f), discussed in the prior section: threshold objections that are capable of disposing of the case without reaching the merits, like a number of the objections that CPLR 3211(a) lists for use in actions.[4]

There is some suggestion, however, that any legal issue separate from the substantial evidence question—which is itself a question of law—can qualify as an objection that the trial-level judge can pass on even though not necessarily of the CPLR 3211(a) variety, such as in one case where the question of law was who among certain categories of persons was responsible for a certain tax.[5]

---

[1]   CPLR 7804(b). If the proceeding is against a supreme court justice or a county court judge, it's brought initially in the appellate division. CPLR 506(b)(1). See § 565. There are some other rare exceptions in which an Article 78 proceeding is initiated in the appellate division instead of the supreme court, such as one to review of a decision of the tax appeals tribunal, which goes directly to the Third Department Appellate Division. See Tax Law § 2016.

[2]   CPLR 7803(4).

[3]   See 2d Rep. Leg. Doc. No. 13, p. 402 (1958). In some instances, special statutes supersede this transfer requirement and mandate that special term dispose of all the issues initially, including the substantial evidence question. This is notably so of zoning and land use cases. See, e.g., Town Law § 267–c(1) and Village Law § 7–712–c(1).

[4]   See Hop-Wah v. Coughlin, 118 A.D.2d 275, 504 N.Y.S.2d 806 (3d Dep't 1986), rev'd on other grounds, 69 N.Y.2d 791, 513 N.Y.S.2d 115, 505 N.E.2d 625 (1987).

[5]   See Komp v. State Tax Commission, 56 Misc. 2d 824, 290 N.Y.S.2d 297 (Sup. Ct., Albany County 1968).

If the substantial evidence question is in the case, and the connected issue is tied in with the merits and would logically be decided in the course of applying the substantial evidence criterion, the issue should not be passed on by the supreme court but left to the appellate division.[6] One can argue interminably on this matter,[7] but evasive as a sharp definition of "objections" may seem, the price of guessing wrong is not high. Consider the following background:

Before a 1990 amendment that produced the language quoted above, the statement of CPLR 7804(g) was that the supreme court "may" pass on the objections before sending the case up, suggesting that it did not have to; that it could just leave the whole case to the appellate division. Some justices, for example, disposed of only such clear-cut merits-avoiding objections as lack of jurisdiction and the statute of limitations, as the 1990 amendment now specifically directs. It was not of great moment, however, because CPLR 7804(g) went on to provide, as it still does, that "when the proceeding comes before it, whether by appeal or transfer, the appellate division shall dispose of all issues in the proceeding."

If the supreme court has already disposed of some issues, therefore, the appellate division, when the case gets transferred up, can simply conduct an appellate-type review of those issues while making the initial review of the substantial evidence question. Note, however, that the presence of the substantial evidence question requires a transfer of the whole case to the appellate division and that a transfer is more expeditious than an appeal.

The requirement of transfer when a substantial evidence issue is presented, i.e., in a "certiorari" case, is a principal source of the continuing necessity to pinpoint which old writ the Article 78 proceeding involves. If, for example, the case is really a mandamus situation and involves the "arbitrary and capricious" standard, it should be kept at special term and the whole of it initially decided there. What happens, then, when the lower court incorrectly deems it a certiorari situation involving the "substantial evidence" test and sends the case up? This has happened, and can happen frequently, but the courts have made their peace with the problem. The appellate division can just keep the case and decide all of it on the merits, even if it should not have been transferred.[8] The Court of Appeals has upheld the appellate division's power to do this.[9]

The converse can also occur: the proceeding may be an authentic certiorari case and invoke the "substantial evidence" test requiring a transfer up, but be erroneously deemed a mandamus case by the trial judge and kept and decided by the supreme court applying the "arbitrary and capricious" standard. On subsequent appeal, the appellate division can just disregard the supreme court disposition, and, treating the case as having been properly transferred up in the first place, dispose of all of the issues, including the substantial evidence issue, de novo.[10]

The transfer purpose has perpetuated arguments about what makes a case a "certiorari" one (transferable) or a "mandamus" one (nontransferable). One court may

---

[6]   See, e.g., Dan's Living Room, Limited v. State of N.Y. Liquor Authority, 31 A.D.2d 799, 298 N.Y.S.2d 291 (1st Dep't 1969), aff'd, 25 N.Y.2d 759, 303 N.Y.S.2d 513, 250 N.E.2d 574.

[7]   This transfer provision of CPLR 7804(g) is the subject of the lead note in NYSLD No. 235.

[8]   See Pauling v. Smith, 46 A.D.2d 759, 361 N.Y.S.2d 16 (1st Dep't 1974).

[9]   125 Bar Corp. v. State Liquor Authority, 24 N.Y.2d 174, 299 N.Y.S.2d 194, 247 N.E.2d 157 (1969).

[10]   See Daigle v. State Liquor Authority, 35 A.D.2d 901, 315 N.Y.S.2d 706 (3d Dep't 1970).

say, for example, that it turns on whether a hearing is required by law regardless of the kind of hearing it is,[11] while another may hold that it turns on the kind of hearing it is regardless of whether required or not.[12] One case will sometimes try to distinguish the other without much success. The only saving factor is the flexibility that the appellate courts have built into the realm. As frequent as errors may be—nisi prius judges keeping cases that should be transferred, or transferring cases that should be kept—the appellate court, however it gets the case, seems willing to dispose of it on the merits. Nor need there be any apprehension that so generous a reaction will prompt a party to seek an undue advantage. An error in this connection, after all, is an error by the supreme court justice, not by the petitioner's attorney, who must in any event commence the proceeding in the supreme court.

§ 569. Trial of Issue of Fact in Article 78 Proceeding

Most Article 78 proceedings are resolved on papers alone. Rarely does an Article 78 proceeding present an issue of fact requiring a trial, but CPLR 7804(h) recognizes that this does happen from time to time and provides that "if a triable issue of fact is raised . . . it shall be tried forthwith."

When the Article 78 proceeding is essentially a mandamus one, for example, and there was no hearing conducted before the agency and hence no transcript to review, it may not be possible to determine from the papers alone whether the administrative activity was arbitrary and capricious. In such an instance, a determination of the facts on which the activity—such as the denial of a license—depends will sometimes require a trial.[1] In a certiorari situation, on the other hand, which implies that there was a full hearing that developed all the facts, the court's function is to determine whether the findings and conclusions are supported by substantial evidence in the record. Here, therefore, the appearance of factual disputes requiring a trial by the court should be still less frequent.[2]

Whatever the frequency of its arising, if an issue of fact does arise, is it triable by jury? CPLR 7804(h) does not say, and CPLR 410, which governs special proceedings in general and to which we should be able to turn for aid, offers none. It merely says that the court must give the parties an opportunity to demand a jury "if" the issues are so triable. It just begs the question.

If the Article 78 proceeding is in the nature of mandamus, there is apparently a right to trial by jury of issues of fact,[3] and a constitutional one at that.[4] There is some suggestion that a jury trial may also be required to try issues of fact arising in the

---

[11]   See, e.g., Metropolitan Theater Ticket Agents Guild, Inc. v. DiCarlo, 48 Misc. 2d 208, 264 N.Y.S.2d 650 (Sup. Ct., New York County 1965).

[12]   See, e.g., Consolidated Edison Co. of New York, Inc. v. Kretchmer, 68 Misc. 2d 545, 327 N.Y.S.2d 375 (Sup. Ct., Kings County 1971).

[1]   See, e.g., Yetta's Rest., Inc. v. State Liquor Authority, 47 Misc. 2d 436, 262 N.Y.S.2d 743 (Sup. Ct., New York County 1965). The court must of course be circumspect here. It should not, in the review context of Article 78, try any fact issue that's the agency's function to dispose of. The court's function is merely to determine whether the agency's finding is supportable, suggesting a remand to the agency for a hearing or for a further hearing if it appears that a key fact is at issue and has not yet been tried. As the *Yetta's* case manifests, this is another elusive line on the Article 78 field.

[2]   See Rochester Colony, Inc. v. Hostetter, 19 A.D.2d 250, 241 N.Y.S.2d 210 (4th Dep't 1963).

[3]   See People ex rel. Desiderio v. Connolly, 212 A.D. 102, 207 N.Y.S. 525 (4th Dep't 1925); Arnold v. Dumpson, 78 Misc. 2d 703, 356 N.Y.S.2d 784 (Sup. Ct., New York County 1974).

[4]   See 3d Ann. Jud. Council Rep. 169 (1937).

certiorari situation, but the problem seems to have arisen so infrequently that the conclusion is tenuous at best.[5] A court faced with the problem and doubtful as to whether a jury is required would do well to impanel one anyway as it has the power to do.[6]

It is generally agreed that an issue of fact arising in an Article 78 proceeding in the nature of prohibition, which will occasionally happen, is not triable by jury,[7] for the reason that prohibition tests jurisdiction and jurisdictional issues are traditionally resolved by the court.

CPLR 7804(h)'s direction that a triable issue of fact arising in an Article 78 proceeding be tried "forthwith" does not mean that everything in sight must be deferred to it. It means in essence that the case is entitled to a special trial preference.[8] How special the preference is must of course depend on the exigencies of the particular case and the other preferred cases standing by in competition for the court's attention.

CPLR 7804(h) also recognizes that the proceeding may have been initiated in the appellate division as it is when brought against a supreme court justice or a county court judge.[9] It provides that if the triable issue of fact arises before the appellate division, it can be ordered tried either by a referee or by a trial term of the supreme court, the matter being remitted for that purpose. But the remission is only temporary: the verdict, report, or decision—rendered after the trial—is returned to the appellate division, and the latter renders the judgment in the case.[10]

§ 570. Judgment and Enforcement in Article 78 Proceeding

The Article 78 proceeding culminates in a "judgment" as all special proceedings do today.[1] CPLR 7806 provides in part that

> the judgment may grant the petitioner the relief to which he is entitled or may dismiss the proceeding either on the merits or with leave to renew. If the proceeding was brought to review a determination, the judgment may annul or confirm the determination in whole or in part, or modify it, and may direct or prohibit specified action by the respondent.

In that statement, a good deal more detailed for the Article 78 proceeding than the counterpart provision is for judgments in an action,[2] the legislature is merely assuring that the court has the requisite power to render any judgment appropriate to the case. If the record is complete enough to enable the court to render a final judgment on the merits, the court will do that; if the case entails a correction of errors and requires further proceedings by the respondent, the correction will be made and back will go the case.

---

[5]   3d Ann. Jud. Council Rep. 188 (1937), which states its conclusion hedgingly but is cited and relied on in turn in 2d Rep. Leg. Doc. No. 13, p. 404 (1958).

[6]   CPLR 4212. It can qualify as only an "advisory" jury, but the difference between that and a jury of right vanishes if the judge happens to agree with the verdict. See § 381.

[7]   See 3d Ann. Jud. Council Rep. p. 167 (1937).

[8]   See Mulligan v. Lackey, 33 A.D.2d 991, 307 N.Y.S.2d 371 (4th Dep't 1970).

[9]   See CPLR 506(b)(1). See § 565.

[10]   CPLR 7804(h) refers to an "order" to be made in the case but should also be construed, if the need arises, to include the "judgment" that formally terminates an Article 78 proceeding. CPLR 7806.

[1]   CPLR 411. See § 556. When reading older cases, which refer to a "final order," one should keep in mind that under prior law, Civ. Prac. Act § 1300 (repealed 1963), the "final order" was the culmination of a special proceeding and served as the equivalent of the "judgment" used today.

[2]   CPLR 5011.

Although not expressly listed, a remand to the agency for further proceedings is very much a part of the court's power.

The power to modify a determination, included in CPLR 7806, includes the power to reduce a punishment meted out as part of the administrative process. This was at one time precluded; the court's power was limited to canceling the punishment or penalty, if deemed necessary, with a remand of the case to the agency to fix a different one. Today the court can do it all. The power to review abuses of discretion "as to the measure or mode of penalty or discipline," expressly conferred by CPLR 7803(3),[3] is deemed to carry, as a logical concomitant, the power to reduce a punishment down to what the court finds to be the maximum permissible, should the agency have gone too far.[4]

The power to "direct or prohibit" specified action is explicit in the statute. A judgment in an Article 78 proceeding that embodies those directions, or, indeed, any other directions needed to secure to the petitioner the Article 78 relief ordered, is enforceable by contempt proceedings.[5] Since many of these directions amount in effect to injunctions, it is reasonably clear today that even outright injunctive relief, if appropriate, is available in an Article 78 proceeding.[6] Although one occasionally hears repeated the older view that it is not,[7] the better view would have to be that it is, at least in cases near the borders of Article 78 itself, i.e., in cases seeking relief arguably if not clearly within the scope of any of the three old writs of mandamus, prohibition, or certiorari. The line between the writs on one side and the injunction on the other is yet another obscure one.[8] The CPLR attitude, that even if the line is identified in a given case it should result in nothing worse than a conversion from wrong form (proceeding) to right form (action),[9] buttresses the view that if it is not clearly perceptible, the form brought should be kept and the relief shaped to the case without further regard to form.

Finally, there is the matter of whether money damages may be awarded in an Article 78 proceeding. CPLR 7806 assumes that they may be, but provides that

> any restitution or damages granted to the petitioner must be incidental to the primary relief sought by the petitioner and must be such as he might otherwise recover on the same set of facts in a separate action or proceeding suable in the supreme court against the same body or officer in its or his official capacity.

This provision, not added to CPLR 7806 until the last of the legislative reports preceding adoption of the CPLR,[10] allows damages, but only on a combination of narrow grounds.

---

[3]   This provision comes from § 1296(5–a) of the Civil Practice Act, which took effect in 1955 and was repealed in 1963.

[4]   See Mitthauer v. Patterson, 8 N.Y.2d 37, 201 N.Y.S.2d 321, 167 N.E.2d 731 (1960). The use of Article 78 to review and alter administrative punishment and discipline was the subject of separate treatment earlier. See § 562.

[5]   CPLR 5104, Jud. Law §§ 750, 753.

[6]   See Policemen's Benev. Ass'n of Westchester County, Inc. v. Board of Trustees of Village of Croton-on-Hudson, 21 A.D.2d 693, 250 N.Y.S.2d 523 (2d Dep't 1964).

[7]   E.g., Teuch v. Murphy, 45 Misc. 2d 81, 256 N.Y.S.2d 25 (Sup. Ct., New York County 1965).

[8]   See 3d Jud. Council Rep. at 157–59 (1937).

[9]   CPLR 103(c). See § 4.

[10]   See 6th Rep. Leg. Doc. No. 8, p. 677 (1962).

The first requirement is that the relief be "incidental" to the primary relief sought in the Article 78 proceeding. The Court of Appeals held in Gross v. Perales[11] that money is incidental if a grant of the relief that is the primary aim of the Article 78 proceeding would make it a "statutory duty" of the respondent to pay the petitioner the sum sought.

The facts of the *Gross* case can illustrate. The petitioner, P, was a city agency providing public assistance benefits to individuals, and the respondent, R, the state department that oversaw the program and had to reimburse P for a segment of the payments. Regulations required P to terminate or reduce benefits under certain circumstances. R audited P to determine compliance. P fulfilled the requirements of all statutes and rules, but R also applied "internal audit guidelines" that imposed more stringent requirements of which P had no notice, docking P $20 million in reimbursements for not fulfilling them. The court held R's action arbitrary and capricious, set the action aside, and directed R to pay the $20 million as "incidental" relief.

Setting aside an administrative determination as arbitrary and capricious is the primary stuff of Article 78, the Court said, and since the setting aside in this case made it obligatory for R to reimburse P the sum withheld, the money was just an incident and the statute was satisfied: there was nothing else for a court to determine.

The second requirement of CPLR 7806 is a showing that damages would lie if sought in a separate supreme court action against the same respondent, which appears to be just a way of ascertaining whether the respondent would be subject to a money suit in the supreme court. The Court of Appeals in *Gross* found in CPLR 7806 an intention to let the supreme court entertain the whole proceeding.[12] This would pose no problem if the respondent were a municipal agency, but a problem of immunity looms if the respondent, as a state agency, qualifies as the alter ego of the State, for the reason that while the State has of course waived sovereign immunity in behalf of itself and those entities that qualify as its alter egos, it has done so only to allow suit in the court of claims.[13] Under the *Gross* decision, it would seem that the waiver now extends jurisdiction to the supreme court as well when the damages sought are incidental to a legitimate Article 78 proceeding.

If the money damages, as "incidental" to the proceeding, may be included there, the logical next question is, *must* they be? Is there a waiver if they are not so that a separate suit for the damages later can be defeated with the res judicata or "splitting" doctrine?[14] The New York Court of Appeals will have to answer that question. Until it does, Article 78 petitioners are perhaps best advised to include in the proceeding a demand for whatever damages can possibly be deemed "incidental" to it. Prior to the *Gross* case, the Second Circuit had to answer the waiver question in a case seeking damages for a civil rights violation.[15] The plaintiff had previously brought an Article 78 proceeding in the

---

[11]   Gross v. Perales, 72 N.Y.2d 231, 532 N.Y.S.2d 68, 527 N.E.2d 1205 (1988).

[12]   Citing the bill jacket of the 1962 law that enacted CPLR 7806, the Court said that all the legislature intended to do with the "incidental" damages language was immunize the State "from paying consequential damages in cases where a state agency improperly denied, revoked or suspended a petitioner's license."

[13]   Cf. Burgos v. State, 40 Misc. 2d 971, 244 N.Y.S.2d 479 (Ct. Cl. 1963), decided before CPLR 7806 became effective.

[14]   See § 220.

[15]   42 U.S.C.A. § 1983.

state court involving the same dispute but did not include there the claim for money damages. The court said there was no waiver and sustained the claim.[16]

If a damages award is made as part of an Article 78 judgment, that part would presumably be enforceable, as would any money judgment, by the procedures of Article 52 of the CPLR.[17] Contempt would then be the enforcement device only for the non-money parts of the judgment.[18]

---

[16]   See Davidson v. Capuano, 792 F.2d 275 (2d Cir. 1986), discussed in the lead note in NYSLD No. 319.

[17]   See CPLR 5101.

[18]   See CPLR 5104.

Table of Cases

12 Baker Hill Road, Inc. v. Miranti, 506

23/23 Communications Corp., d/b/a Communications Diversified v. General Motors Corporation, 809, 955

34 Funding Associates, Inc. v. Pollak, 495

77 Water St., Inc. v. JTC Painting & Decorating Corp., 1095

119 Rosset Corp. v. Blimpy of N.Y. Corp., 1105

125 Bar Corp. v. State Liquor Authority, 1374, 1379, 1400

125 Church Street Development Co. v. Grassfield, 34

172 Van Duzer Realty Corp. v. Globe Alumni Student Assistance Ass'n, Inc., 34, 1149

230 Tenants Corp. v. Board of Standards and Appeals of City of New York, 1398

303 Realty Corp. v. Albert, 1119

381 Search Warrants Directed to Facebook, Inc., In re, 956

423 South Salina Street, Inc. v. City of Syracuse, 59, 70

509 Sixth Ave. Corp. v. New York City Transit Authority, 86

805 Third Ave. Co. v. M.W. Realty Associates, 512

885 W.E. Residents Corp. v. Coronet Properties Co., 172

1405 Realty Corp. v. Napier, 186

1417 Bedford Realty Co. v. Sun Oil Co., 872

1501 Corp. v. Leilenok Realty Corp., 606, 654

2001 Real Estate v. Campeau Corp. (U.S.), Inc., 1334, 1338

2475 Hughes Ave. Realty Corp. v. Gonzalez, 937

3505 Realty Corp. v. Weinberger, 24

5303 Realty Corp. v. O & Y Equity Corp., 780

2138747 Ontario, Inc. v. Samsung C & T Corp., 49

A & M Exports, Ltd. v. Meridien Intern. Bank, Ltd., 770

A. C. Israel Commodity Co. v. Banco Do Brasil, S.A., 761

A. Millner Co. v. Noudar, Lda., 231

A.G. Ship Maintenance Corp. v. Lezak, 1033

A.J. Pegno Const. Corp. v. City of New York, 576

AABCO Sheet Metal Co., Inc. v. Lincoln Center for Performing Arts, Inc., 271

Abbott v. Page Airways, Inc., 512, 584

Abitol v. Schiff, 656

ABKCO Industries, Inc. v. Apple Films, Inc., 744, 755, 1185, 1194

ABKCO Industries, Inc. v. Lennon, 52, 220

Aboujdid v. Singapore Airlines, Ltd., 167

Abraham & Straus, Division of Federated Dept. Stores, Inc. v. Feynman, 1187

Abrahami v. UPC Const. Co., Inc., 1069

Abrahao v. Perrault, 532

Abramowitz v. Berger, 589

Abrams v. Pecile, 804

Abschagen v. Goldfarb, 338

Abu Dhabi Commercial Bank PJSC v. Saad Trading, Contracting and Financial Services Co., 1026

ACE Holding, LLC v. N.Y. State Office of the State Comptroller, 1120

ACE Securities Corp. v. DB Structured Products, Inc., 88

Acerra v. Trippardella, 985

Achampong v. Weigelt, 1061

Ackerman v. Ackerman, 1158

Ackerman v. City of New York, 587

Ackerman v. Price Waterhouse, 86, 96

ACLI Intern. Inc. v. E. D. & F. Man (Coffee) Ltd., 284

Adamo v. Kirsch Beverages, Inc., 894

Adams v. Genie Industries, Inc., 1009, 1284

Addesso v. Shemtob, 666

Adolph E. by Susan E. v. Lori M., 432

Advance Music Corp. v. American Tobacco Co., 504

Aetna Cas. & Sur. Co. v. F & F Maintenance, Inc., 626

Aetna Cas. & Sur. Co. v. Lauria, 1079

Aetna Cas. & Sur. Co. v. Whitestone General Hosp., 1047

African Metals Corporation v. Bullowa, 997

Agawam Trading Corp. v. Mayer Malbin Co., 786

Aguilera v. Pistilli Const. & Development Corp., 163

Agur v. Wilson, 1176, 1178

Aho, Matter of, 1309, 1318

AIG Financial Products Corp. v. Penncara Energy, LLC, 49

Akalski v. Counsell, 884

Akely v. Kinnicutt, 342, 358

Alava v. Peninsula General Hospital, 853

Albanese v. Albanese, 8

Albano v. Schwab Bros. Trucking, Inc., 815

Albany Engineering Corp. v. Hudson River, 1320

Albany Indus. Development Agency, City of v. Hampton Investors, 1065

Albany Medical Center Hospital v. Breslin, 1386

Albemarle Theatre, Inc. v. Bayberry Realty
Corp., 554
Albero v. State, 1152
Albert Levine Associates, Inc. v. Hudson,
270
Alfred E. Mann Living Trust v. ETIRC
Aviation S.a.r.l., 190
Alkalaj v. Alkalaj, 307
All American Crane Service, Inc. v. Omran,
1325
All Funds on Deposit in any Accounts
Maintained in Names of Meza or De
Castro, United States v., 276
Allegretti-Freeman v. Baltis, 822
Allen v. Auto Specialties Mfg. Co., 248
Allen v. Canadian General Elec. Co. Ltd.,
248
Allen v. Crowell-Collier Pub. Co., 800
Allende v. New York City Health and
Hospitals Corp., 90
Alliance Bond Fund, Inc. v. Grupo Mexicano
De Desarrollo, S.A., 1196
Alliano v. Adams, 1391
Allied Chemical, an Operating Unit of
Allied Corp. v. Niagara Mohawk Power
Corp., 1114
Allied Intern. Fund, Inc. v. Gladtke, 719
Allis-Chalmers Mfg. Co. v. Malan Const.
Corp., 515
All-State Credit Corp. v. Riess, 514
Allstate Ins. Co. v. Santiago, 1079
Allston v. Incorporated Village of Rockville
Centre, 1128
Alrose Oceanside, LLC v. Mueller, 577
Alston v. State, 74
Alston v. Transport Workers Union of
Greater New York, 81
Altamore v. Friedman, 1117, 1132
Alterman v. Maimonides Hospital of
Brooklyn, 1288
Altman v. City of New York, 869
Altman v. Kelly, 888
Altona Citizens Committee, Inc. v. Town of
Altona, 7
Alvarado v. Dillon, 1040
Ambac Assur. Corp. v. Countrywide Home
Loans, Inc., 811
Ambrose v. Wurlitzer Co., 850
American Exp. Centurion v. Melia, 1231
American List Corp. v. U.S. News and
World Report, Inc., 583
American Lumbermens Mut. Cas. Co. of
Illinois v. Cochrane, 124
American Motorists Ins. Co. v. Oakley, 382
American Recreation Group, Inc. v.
Woznicki, 233, 243
American Sur. Co. of N.Y. v. Conner, 1251
American-Russian Aid Ass'n v. City of Glen
Cove, 1001
Amherst Synagogue v. Schuele Paint Co.,
Inc., 894

Amins v. Life Support Medical Equipment
Corp., 231
Amsterdam Hospitality Group, LLC v.
Marshall-Alan Associates, Inc., 644
Ancis v. Lomenzo, 1385
Ancrum v. Eisenberg, 973
Anderson v. Anderson, 472
Anderson v. Armentano, 644
Anderson v. Carlson, 544
Anderson v. Carney, 104
Anderson v. Snyder Tank Corp., 1120
Andesco, Inc. v. Page, 784
Andon ex rel. Andon v. 302–304 Mott Street
Associates, 803, 1300
Andre v. Pomeroy, 680, 682
Andrea v. Arnone, Hedin, Casker, Kennedy
and Drake, Architects and Landscape
Architects, P.C., 113, 900, 926
Andrew Carothers, M.D., P.C. v.
Progressive Ins. Co., 38
Andrew v. Hurh, 824
Anesthesia Associates of Mount Kisco, LLP
v. Northern Westchester Hosp. Center,
1085
Angelo J. Martone & Son, Inc. v. Nassau
County, 1383
Angelo v. Laremet Corp., 944
Annunziato v. City of New York, 97
Anonymous v. Anonymous, 244
Anonymous, In re, 30
Anthony DeMarco & Sons Nursery, LLC v.
Maxim Const. Service Corp., 557
Antone v. General Motors Corp., Buick
Motor Div., 123
Apicella v. Valley Forge Military Academy
and Jr. College, 663
Aranzullo v. Collins Packing Company, 267
Arce v. Sybron Corp., 174
Ardelean v. Affuso, 523
Arena Bagels, Inc. v. Brooklyn Bagels, Inc.,
698
Arett Sales Corp. v. Island Garden Center
Queens, Inc., 583
Argento v. Wal-Mart Stores, Inc., 364
Arkwright v. Steinbugler, 324
Armonk Snack Mart, Inc. v. Robert Porpora
Realty Corp., 493
Armored Motor Service of America, Inc. v.
Gribbon, 793
Armour v. Broadman, 473
Armstrong v. Peat, Marwick, Mitchell &
Co., 578, 674, 687
Arnold v. Dumpson, 1401
Aronov v. Regency Gardens Apartments
Corp., 642
Arons v. Jutkowitz, 880, 883, 884, 907
Arp Films, Inc. v. Marvel Entertainment
Group, Div. of Cadence Industries Corp.,
53
Arpels v. Arpels, 765
Arroyo v. Board of Educ. of City of New
York, 923

Arroyo v. Fourteen Estusia Corp., 581

Arroyo v. Judena Taxi, Inc., 983

Arthur Young & Company v. Leong, 1300

Artibee v. Home Place Corp., 32, 409, 1153

Arts4All, Ltd. v. Hancock, 897

Arvelo ex rel. Arvelo v. City of New York, 62

Asabor v. Archdiocese of New York, 683

Asahi Metal Industry Co., Ltd. v. Superior Court of California, Solano County, 224, 250, 284, 390

Ashcroft v. Iqbal, 507, 655

Ashland Equities Co. v. Clerk of New York County, 782

Ashline v. Kestner Engineers, P.C., 895

Askey v. Occidental Chemical Corp., 365

Assenzio v. A.O. Smith Water Products, 637

Association of Bar of City of New York, In re, 22

Association of Data Processing Service Organizations, Inc. v. Camp, 348

Astoria Federal Sav. and Loan Ass'n v. Rambalakos, 1026

Astrada v. Archer, 1180

AT&T Mobility LLC v. Concepcion, 366

Athanasiou v. Esposito, 924

Atkinson v. Superior Court In and For Los Angeles County, 384

Atlas Arm Co. v. Smith, 690

Atlas Credit Corp. v. Ezrine, 719, 720

ATM One, LLC. v. Escobar, 716

Audiovox Corp. v. Benyamini, 907

Auer v. Dyson, 1087

Augsbury Corp. v. Petrokey Corp., 263

Auqui v. Seven Thirty One Ltd. Partnership, 1113

Aurora Loan Services, LLC v. Taylor, 347

Austin v. Board of Higher Ed. of City of New York, 1393

Austin v. McPherson, 635

Austrian Lance & Stewart, P. C. v. Jackson, 1311, 1314

Avalon East, Inc. v. Monaghan, 1169

Avco Financial Service of New York Inc., State v., 1198

Avena v. Ford Motor Co., 377

Avenoso v. Avenoso, 1064

Avenue Associates, Inc. v. Buxbaum, 937

Aversa v. Taubes, 824

Aversano v. Town of Brookhaven, 132

Avgush v. Berrahu, 186

AXA Equitable Life Ins. Co. v. Kalina, 835

Axelrod & Co. v. Telsey, 550, 552

Ayala v. Boss, 702

Aybar v. Aybar, 215, 216, 263, 264

Ayliffe and Companies, Application of, 838

Azzopardi v. St. Vincent's Medical Center of Richmond, 39

B & F Bldg. Corp. v. Liebig, 517

B & M Kingstone, LLC v. Mega Intern. Commercial Bank Co., Ltd., 264

B. R. DeWitt, Inc. v. Hall, 1106, 1108, 1122, 1124, 1135, 1136, 1145

B. W. Acceptance Corp. v. Richmond, 545

B.B.Y. Diamonds Corp. v. Five Star Designs, Inc., 635

B.F. v. Reproductive Medicine Associates of New York, LLP, 89

B.M.C. Mfg. Corp. v. Tarshis, 391

Babcock v. Jackson, 124

Baby Boy O., In re, 5

Baby Show Exhibition Co. v. Crowell Pub. Co., 516

Bachman v. Harrington, 768, 1173

Bachman v. Mejias, 1155

Bachner, In re, 1223

Baehre v. Rochester Dental Prosthetics, Inc., 719

Baer v. Law Offices of Moran & Gottlieb, 93, 120

Baez v. New York City Health and Hospitals Corp., 118

Bagdon v. Philadelphia & Reading Coal & Iron Co., 264

Bagdy v. Progresso Foods Corp., 1288

Baginski v. New York Telephone Co., 969

Baidoo v. Blood-Dzraku, 190, 192

BAII Banking Corp. v. Northville Industries Corp., 808

Bainton v. Board of Ed. of City of New York, 993

Baker v. Commercial Travelers Mut. Acc. Ass'n, 113

Baker v. General Mills Fun Group, Inc., 846

Baker v. Gundermann, 695

Baker v. Julius Pollak & Sons, 324

Bal v. Court Employment Project, Inc., 132

Balaban v. Phillips, 1359

Balancio v. American Optical Corp., 922

Balanoff v. Niosi, 1254

Balanta v. Stanlaine Taxi Corp., 704

Balboa Ins. Co. v. Herbin, 1288

Balbuena v. IDR Realty LLC, 389

Baldwin v. Brooks, 1117

Baldwin v. Iowa State Traveling Men's Ass'n, 1110, 1154

Ballestero v. HAF Edgecombe Associates, L.P., 171

Baltimore & O.R. Co. v. Joy, 457

Baltimore Mail S. S. Co. v. Fawcett, 54, 1378

Banasik v. Reed Prentice Division of Package Machinery Co., 682

Banco Ambrosiano, S.P.A. v. Artoc Bank & Trust Ltd., 283

Banco Do Brasil v. Madison S. S. Corp., 266

Bank Leumi Trust Co. of New York v. Liggett, 1223

Bank of New York Mellon v. Jinks, 557

Bank of New York Mellon v. Piercey, 489

Bank of New York v. Ansonia Associates, 336, 1015, 1286

Bank of New York v. Nies, 1263

Bankers Trust Co. v. State Dept. of Audit and Control, 1207

Bannon v. Bannon, 1094, 1102
Banque De France v. Supreme Court of State of New York, 55
Baptiste v. Harding-Marin, 651
Bar Harbour Shopping Ctr., Inc. v. Andrews, 1373
Barasch v. Micucci, 11, 298, 558
Baratta v. Kozlowski, 80, 529
Barch v. Avco Corp., 332
Barker v. Conley, 650, 661
Barker v. O'Grady, 551
Barker v. Tennis 59th Inc., 1010
Barlow v. Sun Chemical Co., 85
Barnes v. County of Onondaga, 120
Barnes v. Quigley, 503
Barnes v. Shul Private Car Service, Inc., 888
Baron v. Bobroy, Inc., 39
Barouh Eaton Allen Corp. v. International Business Machines Corp., 867, 868
Barrada v. Target Const. Corp., 929
Barrera v. City of New York, 587
Barreto v. Calderon, 986
Barrett v. Jacobs, 671
Barrett v. Watkins, 686
Barrett v. Wojtowicz, 81
Barrick v. Barrick, 501
Barrier Systems, Inc. v. A.F.C. Enterprises, Inc., 691
Barringer v. Zgoda, 647
Barrow v. Bloomfield, 937
Barry v. American Home Assur. Co., 50
Barton Realty Corp. v. Mangan, 1031
Basetti v. Nour, 928
Bata v. Bata, 46, 53
Batavia Kill Watershed Dist. in County of Greene v. Charles O. Desch, Inc., 541
Bauer v. Special Brands NY, Inc., 943
Baum v. Baum, 1048
Bauman v. Fisher, 268
Baumgartner v. Baumgartner, 168
Baumgold Bros. v. Schwarzschild Bros., 288, 1195
Baumis v. General Motors Corp., 492
Bausch & Lomb Inc. v. Hydron Pacific, Ltd., 770
Baxt v. Cohen, 924
Bay Crest Ass'n v. Paar, 39
Bay Ridge Air Rights, Inc. v. State, 397
Bayonne Block Co., Inc. v. Porco, 517
Bazakos v. Lewis, 73
Bazile v. City of New York, 120
BDO USA, LLP v. Phoenix Four, Inc., 714
Beahm v. Beahm, 1234
Beatty v. Donley, 852
Becan, In re, 469, 471
Bechard v. Eisinger, 524, 983
Beck v. Renahan, 387
Becker v. Becker, 1284
Becker v. Levitt, 1128
Beckerman v. Walter J. Munro, Inc., 394
Bedingfield v. Dairymaid Farms, Inc., 906

Beece v. Guardian Life Ins. Co. of America, 537
Beekman v. City of New York, 362
Beetz v. City of New York, 1060
Beiny, Matter of, 875
Beja v. Jahangiri, 221, 290
Bell Atlantic Corp. v. Twombly, 507, 655
Bell v. Bell, Kalnick, Klee & Green, 172
Bell v. New York Higher Educ. Assistance Corp., 626
Bellefeuille v. City and County Sav. Bank, 399, 400
Bellen v. Baghei-Rad, 824
Bellepointe, Inc. v. Kohl's Dept. Stores, Inc., 263
Bellini v. Gersalle Realty Corp., 580
Bello v. Transit Authority of New York City, 536
Belmont Theatre Corp. v. Bunny Cinema Corp., 937
Belpasso v. Port Authority of New York and New Jersey, 62
Belscher v. New York State Teachers' Retirement System, 33
Beltran v. Borstein, 915
Benadon v. Antonio, 286, 297, 519, 530, 708, 1111
Bender v. New York City Health & Hospitals Corp., 60
Bennett v. St. John's Home, 678
Bennett v. Troy Record Co., 818
Bensaull v. Fanwood Estates, 319
Benson v. Eastern Bldg. & Loan Ass'n, 314
Bensusan Restaurant Corp. v. King, 253
Bentivegna v. Meenan Oil Co., Inc., 654
Benware v. Schoenborn, 160
Berg v. Flower Fifth Ave. Hospital, 886
Bergassi, LLC v. Ikon Solutions, Inc., 715
Berlin v. Herbert, 1188
Berlitz Publications, Inc. v. Berlitz, 1086
Berman v. Town of Liberty, 688
Berman, Matter of, 467
Bermejo v. New York City Health and Hospitals Corp., 333
Bermudez v. City of New York, 11
Bernard by Bernard v. City School Dist. of Albany, 559
Berry Petroleum Co. v. Adams and Peck, 354
Berry v. St. Peter's Hosp. of City of Albany, 449
Best Van Lines, Inc. v. Walker, 228
Beth-El Hospital, Inc. v. Davis, 1173
Beyer v. Murray, 1020
Beyer, In re, 470
Bhonlay v. Raquette Lake Camps, Inc., 316
Bianchi v. Federal Ins. Co., 861
Bianchi v. Galster Management Corp., 807
Bianco v. Ligreci, 610
Bichler v. Eli Lilly & Co., 854
Bierzynsky v. New York Cent. R. Co., 914
Bigelow v. Acands, Inc., 859

Biggs v. Town of Huntington, 1281
Billone v. Town of Huntington, 1353
Binderman v. Kazdan, 34
Bingham's Will, In re, 1318
Birmingham v. Squires, 321
Biscone v. JetBlue Airways Corp., 605, 634
Bishin v. New York Cent. R. Co., 982
Bissell v. New York State Dept. of Transp., 675
Bittner v. Motor Vehicle Acc. Indemnification Corp., 473
Black River Associates v. Newman, 255
Black v. Black, 277, 1066
Black v. Oberle Rentals, Inc., 252
Blackburn v. Blackburn, 696
Blacklink Transport Consultants PTY Ltd. v. Von Summer, 1159
Blackman v. Blackman, 1237
Blaikie v. Wagner, 1371, 1387
Blaine v. International Business Machines Corp., 325, 972
Blair v. New York University College of Dentistry, 988
Blake Terrace Associates v. Sommers, 946
Blake's Estate, In re, 950
Blanco v. American Tel. & Tel. Co., 84
Blank v. Schafrann, 1322
Blatz v. Benschine, 183, 660
Bleiler v. Bodnar, 73
BLF Realty Holding Corp. v. Kasher, 45
Blinds To Go (U.S.), Inc. v. Times Plaza Development, L.P., 538
Bliss v. Jaffin, 636
Block v. Fairbairn, 581, 833
Bloeth v. Marks, 1395
Bloodgood v. Lynch, 980
Bloom v. Cunard Line, Ltd., 364
Blue Giant Equipment Corp. v. Tec-Ser, Inc., 1192
Blueberry Investors Co. v. Ilana Realty Inc., 578
Blumenstyk v. Singer, 604
Blumenthal v. Allen, 352
Blye v. Globe-Wernicke Realty Co., 732
Board of Ed. of Cent. School Dist. No. 1 of Towns of Niagara, Wheatfield, Lewiston and Cambria v. Niagara-Wheatfield Teachers Ass'n, 1022
Board of Ed. of City School Dist. of City of New Rochelle v. Zeluck, 1180
Board of Ed. of Half Hollow Hills Central School Dist. of Huntington and Babylon v. Half Hollow Hills Teachers Ass'n, Inc., 270
Board of Ed. of Hudson City School Dist. v. Sargent, Webster, Crenshaw & Folley, 79, 423
Board of Ed. of Scotia-Glenville Central School Dist. v. Shapiro, 636
Board of Managers of the Mews at North Hills Condominium v. Farajzadeh, 39
Bobowski v. Toomey, 914

Boddie v. Connecticut, 191, 293, 465
Boden v. Arnstein, 379
Boehm v. Dillon, 723
Boley v. Kaymark, 139
Boll v. Shanly, 1358
Bolsinger v. Bolsinger, 471
Bombard v. Albany County, 830
Bonde v. General Sec. Ins. Co. of Canada, 1118
Bonesteel's Will, In re, 162
Bonilla v. Tutor Perini Corp., 110
Bonk v. Hodgkins, 28
Bonnette v. Long Island College Hosp., 494
Bonwit-Teller, Division of 721 Corp. v. Rosenstiel, 1214
Borden v. 400 East 55th Street Associates, L.P., 360
Borek, Stockel & Co. v. Slevira, 1061
Borgia v. City of New York, 89
Boris v. Flaherty, 379, 452
Born to Build LLC v. Saleh, 854
Boronow v. Boronow, 1100
Boryszewski v. Brydges, 347
Boss v. American Express Financial Advisors, Inc., 48
Bossak v. National Surety Co. of New York, 343
Bossey ex rel. Bossey v. Camelback Ski Corp., 229
Bossuk v. Steinberg, 164, 180
Bosurgi v. Chemical Bank New York Trust Co., 863
Bott, Application of, 955
Bottalico v. City of New York, 1007
Bouleris v. Cherry-Burrell Corp., 403, 404
Bowen v. Fiore, 882
Bowery Sav. Bank v. Ward, 570
Boyle v. Starwood Hotels & Resorts Worldwide, Inc., 50
Brackett v. Griswold, 457
Bradford v. Eden, 737
Bradford v. Helman, 1376
Bradley v. Plaisted, 318
Brady by Brady v. Wyeth Laboratories, Inc., 874
Braff v. Par-Du Leasing, Inc., 332
Brandes v. Harris, 837
Brandon v. Chefetz, 363
Brandt Corp. v. Warren Automatic Controls Corp., 1018
Brandt v. Hashinsky, 120
Brannigan v. Board of Educ. of Levittown Union Free School Dist., 928
Brastex Corp. v. Allen Intern., Inc., 738
Braun v. Ahmed, 524, 983
Braun v. C. E. P. C. Distributors, Inc., 723
Braun v. St. Vincent's Hospital & Medical Center, 179
Braun v. State, 32
Braunston v. Anchorage Woods, Inc., 780
Brause 59 Co. v. Bridgemarket Associates, 167

Bray v. Cox, 1343
Bray v. Gluck, 634
Bredin v. Buchman, 899
Brenner v. Title Guarantee & Trust Co., 358, 360
Briarpatch Ltd., L.P. v. Briarpatch Film Corp., 596
Brick v. Cohn-Hall-Marx Co., 79
Brickner v. Linden City Realty, Inc., 502
Bridgehampton Nat. Bank v. White, 1168
Briger, Estate of, 616
Briggs v. Lauman, 1372
Briggs v. Spencerport Road Plaza, Inc., 816
Brill v. Brill, 644
Brill v. City of New York, 674
Brink's Exp. Co. v. Burns, 332
Brock v. Bua, 104
Brockman v. Turin, 716
Broder v. Broudarge, 778
Brodsky v. New York Yankees, 957
Brodvin v. Hertz Corp., 536
Broida v. Bancroft, 53
Bronxville Knolls, Inc. v. Webster Town Center Partnership, 644
Bronxville Palmer, Limited v. State, 1127, 1160
Brooke Group Ltd. v. JCH Syndicate 488, 50
Brookhaven Memorial Hospital, Inc. v. Hoppe, 1071
Brooklyn Bank v. Barnaby, 108
Brooklyn Floor Maintenance Co. v. Providence Washington Ins. Co., 828
Brooklyn Hospital v. Lennon, 1298
Brooklyn Navy Yard Asbestos Litigation, In re, 411
Brooks Bros. v. Tiffany, 573
Brooks v. City of New York, 956
Brooks v. Dalsheim, 315
Brothers v. Florence, 81
Brown & Guenther v. North Queensview Homes, Inc., 82
Brown v. Arabian Am. Oil Co., 1229
Brown v. City of New York, 58, 61
Brown v. Erie-Lackawanna R. Co., 251
Brown v. Lockheed Martin Corp., 263
Brown v. Lockwood, 531
Brown v. Micheletti, 627, 1288
Brown v. Sagamore Hotel, 173
Brown v. State, 31, 1100
Brown v. Waryas, 453
Brown, Application of, 469
Bruce v. Hospital for Special Surgery, 1000
Bruckner v. Jaitor Apartments Co., 1037
Brunswick Corp. v. Aetna Cas. & Sur. Co., 814
Bryant v. Finnish Nat. Airline, 214
Buckley v. National Freight, Inc., 493
Buckley v. Redi-Bolt, Inc., 259
Buckner v. D & E Motors, Inc., 174
Buechel v. Bain, 1126
Buffalo Elec. Co. v. State, 1297

Buffalo, City of v. J. W. Clement Co., 1031
Buffalo, City of v. State Bd. of Equalization and Assessment, 453
Buffone v. Aronson, 845
Buholtz ex rel. Rochester Philharmonic Orchestra, Inc. v. Board of Directors of Rochester Philharmonic Orchestra, Inc., 950
Bulkley v. Bulkley, 162
Bullard v. Bullard Orchards, Inc., 698
Bulman v. Bulman, 786
Bulova Watch Co., Inc. v. Celotex Corp., 87
Bumpus v. New York City Transit Authority, 460, 839
Bundy v. City of New York, 428
Bunker v. Bunker, 397
Buran v. Coupal, 105
Burger King Corp. v. Rudzewicz, 223, 239
Burgos v. State, 1404
Burke v. Aspland, 37
Burke v. Crosson, 1294
Burke v. Yudelson, 821
Burlington Industries, Inc. v. Eastern Exp., Inc., 944
Burlington Ins. Co. v. NYC Transit Authority, 985
Burnham v. Superior Court of California, County of Marin, 130
Burns v. Pace University, 115
Burstin v. Public Service Mut. Ins. Co., 611
Buscher v. Ehrich, 163
Bush Terminal Bldgs. Co. v. Luckenbach S.S. Co., 425
Busler v. Corbett, 139
Butler v. Catinella, 654, 658
Butler v. Glens Falls, S.H. & Ft. E. St. R. Co., 971
Butter v. Brookdale Hospital, 929
Buxton v. Ruden, 865
C.K.S., Inc. v. Helen Borgenicht Sportswear, Inc., 398
C.S.A. Contracting Corp. v. New York City School Const. Authority, 63
Caban v. Caban, 294
Cabrera v. Hirth, 1041
Cadichon v. Facelle, 922
Caffaro v. Trayna, 97, 104, 579
Cahill v. Lat, 93
Caiazzo v. Volkswagenwerk A.G., 421, 436
Cais v. Pichler, 1239
Calamari v. Panos, 72, 104, 122
Calcano v. Rodriguez, 681
Calder v. Jones, 227
Caldwell v. Cablevision Systems Corp., 951, 952
Calhoun v. Pickett, 882
Calise v. Heartland Medical Services, P.C., 438
Callanan Industries, Inc. v. Sovereign Const. Co., Ltd., 315
Callegari v. Davis & Partners, LLC, 675
Camarda v. Vanderbilt, 652, 653

Cammarota v. Bella Vista Development Corp., 1291
Campaign for Fiscal Equity v. State, 979
Campbell v. Holt, 81
Campbell v. Regency Towers, Inc., 904
Campbell v. Smith, 781
Campbell v. Towber, 1000
Campos v. Payne, 874, 881
Canfield v. Elmer E. Harris & Co., 1105
Capasso v. Capasso, 947
Capital Newspapers Division-Hearst Corp. v. Vanderbilt, 572
Capitol Records, LLC v. Harrison Greenwich, LLC, 70
Caplan v. Tofel, 942
Caplash v. Rochester Oral & Maxillofacial Surgery Associates, LLC, 612
Caplin v. Caplin, 1309
Cappelluti v. Sckolnick, 93
Cappiello v. ICD Publications, Inc., 1028
Capri Beachwear, Inc. v. AAA Stretch, Inc., 908
Capruso v. Village of Kings Point, 77, 86
Capuano v. Tishman Const. Corp., 681
Carbon Capital Management, LLC v. American Exp. Co., 136
Carbone v. Alverio, 696
Card v. Budini, 511, 1106
Card v. Polito, 713
Cardy v. Frey, 587
Carey v. Sugar, 739, 758
Carl A. Morse, Inc. (Diesel Const., Division) v. Rentar Indus. Development Corp., 733
Carl B. Nusbaum, Inc. v. Calale, 1251, 1276
Carlin v. Patel, 440
Carlton Group, Ltd. v. Property Markets Group, Inc., 318
Carnegie Associates Ltd. v. Miller, 1034
Carney v. Philippone, 1302
Caronia v. Peluso, 488
Caronia v. Philip Morris USA, Inc., 83
Carpenter v. County of Essex, 335, 977
Carpenter v. Weatherwax, 297
Carpinelli v. Manhattan Bottling Corp., 881
Carr v. Carr, 278
Carrasquillo v. Holliswood Hosp., 118
Carrera v. Carrera, 166
Carriage Hill, Inc. v. Lane, 453
Carrick v. Central General Hospital, 104, 111
Carroll v. Gammerman, 8
Carroll v. Kenin, 769
Carroll v. President and Com'rs of Princess Anne, 774
Carruthers v. Jack Waite Mining Co., 340
Carter v. Phillips, 764
Carver Federal Savings Bank v. Shaker Gardens, Inc., 162
Carver v. Nassau County Interim Finance Authority, 113
Case v. Indian Motocycle Co., 358
Case's Will v. Donovan, 966

Caselli v. City of New York, 58
Casey v. Slattery, 1005
Casey v. State, 441
Caso v. Coffey, 1382
Caso v. New York State Public High School Athletic Ass'n, Inc., 1380
Cassevah v. Mack, 685
Cassissi v. Yee, 552
Castellano v. Norwegian Christian Home and Health Center, Inc., 583
Casten v. Tannenbaum, 690
Castro v. United Container Machinery Group, Inc., 388
Castrovinci v. Edwards, 455
Caton v. Caton, 295
Cattat v. Alfa Romeo, Inc., 850, 873
Cavaretta v. George, 952
Cayo v. Saggar, 268
Cayuga Indian Nation of New York v. Gould, 1080, 1081
CDR Creances S.A.S. v. Cohen, 899
Cedar Rapids Engineering Co. v. Haenelt, 788
Celle v. Filipino Reporter Enterprises Inc., 985
Cellura v. Cellura, 124
Celotex Corp. v. Catrett, 683
Central New York Regional Market Authority v. John B. Pike, Inc., 489
Central Valley Concrete Corp. v. Montgomery Ward & Co., 492
Cerami v. City of Rochester School Dist., 119
Ceravit Corp. AG v. Black Diamond S. S. Corp., 55
Cerrato v. Thurcon Const. Corp., 662
Cesar v. United Technology of New York, 50
Cesario v. Chiapparine, 997
Chabert v. Robert & Co., 787
Chaffee v. Lawrence, 1152
Chaffee v. Marsh, 968
Chambers v. Mirkinson, 75, 93
Chambland v. Brewer, 551
Champion v. Wilsey, 1061
Champlain Creameries v. Hovey, Stanter & Co., 324
Chance v. Guaranty Trust Co. of New York, 108
Chapel v. Mitchell, 394
Charles F. Ryan & Son, Inc. v. Lancaster Homes, Inc., 947
Charles F. Winson Gems, Inc. v. D. Gumbiner, Inc., 704
Charles v. Long Island College Hosp., 399
Chartener v. Kice, 119
Chase Bank USA, N.A. v. Cardello, 1054
Chase Manhattan Bank, N.A. v. Marcovitz, 695
Chase Nat. Bank of City of New York v. Turner, 167
Chase Scientific Research, Inc. v. NIA Group, Inc., 72

Chauvin v. Dayon, 168
Chauvin v. Keniry, 925, 927
Chavez v. 407 Seventh Ave. Corp., 930
Chemprene, Inc. v. X-Tyal Intern. Corp.,
    310
Chem-Trol Pollution Services, Inc. v.
    Ingraham, 1394
Cherfas v. Wolf, 954
Cherry Creek Nat. Bank v. Fidelity &
    Casualty Co. of New York, 982
Chester, N.Y., Town of v. Laroe Estates,
    Inc., 449
Chevalier v. Farrell, 988
Chevron Corp. v. Naranjo, 1159
Chevron Oil Co. v. Atlas Oil Co. of Utica,
    101
Chevron U.S.A., Inc. v. Commissioner of
    Environmental Conservation, 1393
Chianese v. Meier, 414
Chicago Dressed Beef Co. v. Gold Medal
    Packing Corp., 692
Childs v. Levitt, 492
Chimenti v. American Express Co., 369
Chin Sung Yu v. Riggs Nat. Bank of
    Washington, D.C., 1213, 1240, 1259
Chin v. Chin, 926
Chipetine v. McEvoy, 1026
Chiques v. Sanso, 912
Chisholm v. Mahoney, 857
Chisholm-Ryder Co., Inc. v. Sommer &
    Sommer, 1132
Chittenden v. Chittenden, 278
Choate, People ex rel. v. Barrett, 993
Christian v. Hashmet Management Corp.,
    702
Christovao v. Unisul-Uniao de Coop.
    Transf. de Tomate Do Sul Do Tejo,
    S.C.R.L., 1292
Chung v. Kim, 45
CIBC Mellon Trust Co. v. Mora Hotel Corp.
    N.V., 1157, 1158
Ciccone v. Glenwood Holding Corp., 576
Ciceron v. Jamaica Hosp., 89
Cie Noga, S.A. v. Heather Financial Corp.,
    1031
Cinerama, Inc. v. Equitable Life Assur. Soc.
    of U.S., 1309
Cioffi v. S.M. Foods, Inc., 504, 505, 938
Cirale v. 80 Pine St. Corp., 811, 812
Citibank Eastern, N. A. v. Minbiole, 701
Citibank N. A., In Interest of Dale Olds Inc.
    v. Hamilton, 488
Citibank, N.A. v. Cambel, 1202
Citibank, N.A. v. Liebowitz, 1026
Citibank, N.A. v. McGarvey, 210
Citigroup Inc. v. City Holding Co., 234
Citimortgage, Inc. v. Espinal, 704
Citizens for St. Patrick's v. City of
    Watervliet Zoning Board of Appeals, 771
Citizens Utilities Co. v. American
    Locomotive Co., 87

City Bank Farmers Trust Co. v. Macfadden,
    1284
City Commission on Human Rights v. Regal
    Gardens, Inc., 763
Ciunci v. Wella Corp., 576, 723
Civil Service Emp. Ass'n v. Helsby, 1378
Cizler v. Cizler, 1062
Cla-Mil East Holding Corp. v. Medallion
    Funding Corp., 1215
Clarcq v. Chamberlain Mobile Home
    Transport, Inc., 531
Clark v. Bilt-Rite Land Corp., 649
Clark v. Mosher, 381
Clark v. New York State Dept. of Motor
    Vehicles, 872
Clarke v. Fidelity & Cas. Co. of New York,
    403
Clarke v. Laidlaw Transit, Inc., 644
Clarke v. United Parcel Service, Inc., 1061
Clearwater Realty Co. v. Hernandez, 631
Clemens v. Apple, 1115, 1116
Cleveland v. Farber, 393
Cloverleaf Realty of New York, Inc. v. Town
    of Wawayanda, 74, 1084
CMRC Corp., Ltd. v. State, 815
Coast to Coast Energy, Inc. v. Gasarch, 258
Cobbs v. Thomas, 1146
Cocchi v. State, 31, 329
Codling v. Paglia, 87
Coe v. Coe, 1110
Coffey v. Orbachs, Inc., 893
Coffin Bros. & Co. v. Bennett, 731
Cogen Properties, Ltd. v. Griffin, 649
Cogen v. Robin Klinger Children's
    Entertainment, 689
Cohen v. Crimenti, 1064
Cohen v. Douglas L. Elliman & Co., 352
Cohen v. First Nat. City Bank, 1191
Cohen v. Hallmark Cards, Inc., 1006
Cohen v. Heine & Co., 891
Cohen v. M. Keizer, Inc., 786
Cohen v. Manufacturers Safe Deposit Co.,
    724
Cohen v. Pearl River Union Free School
    Dist., 59
Cohen v. Shure, 484
Cohen v. State Liquor Authority, 1391
Cohen v. State Tax Commission, 1394
Cohen, Matter of, 941
Cohn v. Lionel Corp., 512
Cohoes Housing Authority v. Ippolito-Lutz,
    Inc., 115
Colbert v. Home Indem. Co., 818
Colbert v. International Sec. Bureau Inc.,
    303
Cole v. Long Island Lighting Co., 404
Cole-Hatchard v. Nicholson, 719
Coleman by Coleman v. Richards, 824
Coleman v. Kirkey, 830
Colgate Const. Corp. v. Hill, 937
Colichio v. Bailey, 102
Collins v. AA Trucking Renting Corp., 495

Collins v. Jamestown Mut. Ins. Co., 818
Collins v. McWilliams, 1309
Colodney v. New York Coffee & Sugar
  Exch., Inc., 1390
Colonial Funding Corp. v. Bon Jour Intern.
  Ltd., 795, 1165
Colonial Sur. Co. v. Lakeview Advisors,
  LLC, 1250
Colpan Realty Corp. v. Great Am. Ins. Co.,
  1214
Colt Industries Shareholder Litigation v.
  Colt Industries Inc., 373
Colton v. Berman, 1382
Columbia Broadcasting System, Inc. v.
  Roskin Distributors, Inc., 491
Commissioners of State Ins. Fund v. Trio
  Asbestos Removal Corp., 32
Committee for G. I. Rights v. Callaway, 355
Common Council of City of Gloversville v.
  Town Bd. of Town of Johnstown, 1354
Community Bd. 7 of Borough of Manhattan
  v. Schaffer, 645
Community Capital Corp. v. Lee, 1224
Community State Bank v. Haakonson,
  1065, 1068
Competello v. Giordano, 666
Complexions, Inc. v. Industry Outfitters,
  Inc., 54
Comptroller of City of New York v. Mayor of
  City of New York, 1392
Computer Strategies, Inc. v. Commodore
  Business Machines, Inc., 738
Conant v. Schnall, 544
Concrete Pipe & Products Corp. v. Modern
  Bldg. Materials, Inc., 230
Confidential Lending, LLC v. Nurse, 713
Conklin v. Draper, 94
Conklin v. State, 948
Connecticut v. Doehr, 746
Connell v. City of New York, 907
Connell v. Hayden, 100
Connolly v. 129 East 69th Street Corp., 677
Considine v. Pichler, 1041
Consolidated Airborne Systems, Inc. v.
  Silverman, 554
Consolidated Edison Co. of New York, Inc.
  v. Alston, 789
Consolidated Edison Co. of New York, Inc.
  v. Church of St. Cecilia, 791
Consolidated Edison Co. of New York, Inc.
  v. Kretchmer, 1401
Constantine v. Diello, 880
Construction by Singletree, Inc. v. Lowe,
  685, 826
Consumer Credit Corp. v. Lewis, 1231
Contact Resource Services, LLC v. Gregory,
  1199
Conway v. Elite Towing & Flatbedding
  Corp., 825
Conway, People v., 599
Cook v. Cook, 1154

Cooke v. Wozen Equities, Inc., 598, 1059,
  1060
Coonradt v. Walco, 583, 610
Cooperatieve Centrale Raiffeisen-
  Boerenleenbank, B.A. v. Navarro, 694,
  695
Copeland v. Salomon, 64, 779
Corbett v. Brown, 988, 989
Corbo v. Stephens, 187
Corchado v. City of New York, 679
Corcoran v. National Union Fire Ins. Co. of
  Pittsburgh, Pa., 543
Cordero v. Grant, 602
Cordner v. Metropolitan Life Ins. Co., 384
Cornell University v. Livingston, 189
Cornell v. Cornell, 457
Cornell v. T. V. Development Corp., 1284
Corona Courts, Inc. v. Frank G. Shattuck
  Co., 816
Corpuel v. Galasso, 1244
Corradetti v. Dales Used Cars, 485
Correa, People v., 24
Corsello v. Verizon New York, Inc., 122
Costa v. Chevrolet-Tonawanda, Division of
  General Motors Corp., 1234
Costanza v. City of New York, 536
Costello v. Hapco Realty, Inc., 686
Costello v. North Shore University Hosp.
  Center for Extended Care and
  Rehabilitation, 118
Costigan & Co., P.C. v. Costigan, 596, 608
Cotteral v. City of New Rochelle, 899
Coty v. County of Clinton, 678
Countryman v. Watertown Housing
  Authority, 310
County Nat. Bank v. Inter-County Farmers
  Co-op. Ass'n, 1267
County Nat. Bank v. Vogt, 718, 719, 721
County Trust Co. v. Berg, 1230
County Trust Co. v. Duerr, 1230
Court of Oyer and Terminer, People v., 1173
Courtney v. Olsen, 880
Coutain v. Coutain, 209
Coutts Bank (Switzerland) Ltd. v. Anatian,
  271, 954
Covell v. H.R.H. Const. Corp., 1289
Cowans v. Ticonderoga Pulp & Paper Co.,
  1157
Cowles' Will, In re, 352
CPC Intern. Inc. v. McKesson Corp., 245
Cracco v. Cox, 68
Cramer v. Henderson, 350, 468
Crandall's Estate, In re, 456
Cranesville Block Co., Inc. v. Spring
  Apartments, LLC, 99, 148
Crawford v. Liz Claiborne, Inc., 677
Crawford v. Merrill Lynch, Pierce, Fenner
  & Smith, Inc., 1313
Created Gemstones, Inc. v. Union Carbide
  Corp., 691
Creative Woodworking Co. v. Bohn, 508

Credit Agricole Indosuez v. Rossiyskiy
  Kredit Bank, 763
Crete Concrete Corp. v. Josephs, 1192
Crimmins v. Polhemus, 570
Crook v. E.I. du Pont de Nemours Co., 159
Croop v. Odette, 122
Cross Properties, Inc. v. Brook Realty Co.,
  Inc., 770
Crouse v. McVickar, 1063
Crow v. Gleason, 108
CRP/Extell Parcel I, L.P. v. Cuomo, 1024,
  1047
Crume v. Clarence Central School Dist. No.
  1, 59
Cruz v. TD Bank, N.A., 1200
Crystal v. Manes, 1311
Cummings v. Dresher, 542, 1124
Cunha v. Shapiro, 1023
Curran v. City of Rochester, 1323
Curriere v. Roeill, 329
Curry v. Davis, 686
Curry v. Moser, 420
Curtiss-Wright Corp. v. Intercontinent
  Corp., 108
Cushing-Murray v. Adams, 341
Cushman & Wakefield, Inc. v. John David,
  Inc., 667
Custodi v. Town of Amherst, 422
Cuzdey v. American Motorists Ins. Co., 55
Cwick v. City of Rochester, 602
Cypress v. Newport News General and
  Nonsectarian Hospital Ass'n, 355
D. H. Overmyer Co. Inc., of Ohio v. Frick
  Co., 719, 720
D.P.C. Corp. v. Jobson, 545
D'Alessandro v. Carro, 1103
D'Ambrosio v. City of New York, 444
D'Amico v. Correctional Medical Care, Inc.,
  665
D'Arata v. New York Cent. Mut. Fire Ins.
  Co., 1126
Da Silva v. Musso, 1304
Daar v. Yellow Cab Co., 355
Dahlstrom v. Gemunder, 532
Daigle v. State Liquor Authority, 1400
Daimler AG v. Bauman, 52, 214, 221, 223,
  228, 263, 563, 656, 1187
Dain & Dill, Inc. v. Betterton, 334
Dairylea Cooperative, Inc. v. Walkley, 345,
  1387
Dairymen's League Co-op. Ass'n v. Brundo,
  326
Dale Renting Corp. v. Bard, 1086
Daliendo v. Johnson, 671
Dalminter, Inc. v. Dalmine, S. p. A., 690
Dalminter, Inc. v. Siderexport S.p.A., 941
Daly v. Amberg, 1171
Dampskibsselskabet Torm A/S v. P. L.
  Thomas Paper Co., 682, 1002
Dan's Living Room, Limited v. State of N.Y.
  Liquor Authority, 1400

Daniel J. v. New York City Health and
  Hospitals Corp., 89, 119
Danko v. F. W. Woolworth Co., 518
Dann v. Bernstein, 695
Dann v. Sands, 947
Darko v. New York City Transit Authority,
  925, 1103
DaSilva v. Everest Scaffolding, Inc., 1340
Data Tree, LLC v. Romaine, 821
David v. Bauman, 379, 452
David v. Biondo, 1121, 1126
David v. Mallilo & Grossman, 42
Davidson v. Capuano, 1405
Davies, State v., 225
Davis Sportswear, Inc. v. Parker, Duryee,
  Benjamin, Zunino and Malone, 1040
Davis v. City of New York, 61, 89
Davis v. Commercial Metals Co., 946
Davis v. Davis, 1110
Davis v. William Rosenzweig Realty
  Operating Co., 528
Davis, Matter of, 836
Davis, People v., 24
Dawley v. McCumber, 577
Day v. Davis, 524
De Candido v. Young Stars, Inc., 766
De Hart v. Hatch, 944
De La Bouillerie v. De Vienne, 46
De Long Corp. v. Morrison-Knudsen Co.,
  1019, 1307
De Lucia, People v., 993
De Mato v. Suffolk County, 551
De Milt v. Tax Appeals Tribunal of State of
  N.Y., 485
De Rentiis v. Lewis, 290
De Rijdt v. Robert Straile Co., 455, 458
De Sapio v. Kohlmeyer, 835
De Vito v. Katsch, 978, 996, 997
De Witt v. Abraham Bros. Horse & Mule
  Co., 160
Deacon v. Witham, 638
Deacon's Bench, Inc. v. Hoffman, 1128
Deary v. Guardian Loan Co., Inc., 1239
Deason v. Deason, 191, 465
Debevoise & Plimpton LLP v. Candlewood
  Timber Group LLC, 937
DeCarvalhosa v. Adler, 189
DeChiaro's Estate, In re, 1105
Decisionware, Inc. v. Systems Equipment
  Lessors, Inc., 272
Decker v. Gardner, 776
Deer Park Associates v. Town of Babylon,
  865
Defendini, In re, 633
Defina v. Daniel, 635
Dehaney v. New York City Transit
  Authority, 841
DeJac v. DeJac, 50
Delagi v. Delagi, 1062
Delagi v. Volkswagenwerk A.G. of
  Wolfsburg, Germany, 219

Delair v. T. Southworth Tractor & Mach. Co., 325

Delaware & Hudson R. R. Corp., People v., 1152

Delgado v. City of New York, 693

Delgado v. Fogle, 882

DeLia v. DeLia, 1041

Dellaratta v. International House of Pancakes, 1321

Dellefield v. Blockdel Realty Co., 949

Deloitte, Haskins, and Sells, Matter of, 838

Delta Diagnostic Radiology, P.C. v. Travelers Property Cas. Co. of America, 808

Denberg v. Denberg, 1179

Denio v. State, 1027

Denner v. Katz, 44

Denning v. Lettenty, 210

Dennis v. City of New York, 685

Dennis v. Stout, 636

Denny v. Ford Motor Co., 78

Dentists' Supply Co. of N.Y. v. Cornelius, 527

Denton v. Noyes, 309

Depalois v. Pellegrino, 64, 170

Department of Housing Preservation and Development of City of New York v. 24 West 132 Equities, Inc., 1178

Department of Housing Preservation and Development of City of New York v. Chance Equities, Inc., 1178

Department of Housing Preservation and Development of City of New York v. Koenigsberg, 168

Department of Housing Preservation and Development v. Arick, 1178

Depue, In re, 953

Dero Enterprises, Inc. v. Georgia Girl Fashions, Inc., 232

DeRonda v. Greater Amsterdam School Dist., 668

Derr v. Fleming, 1031

DES Market Share Litigation, Matter of, 933

Desiderio, People ex rel. v. Connolly, 1401

DeSilva by DeSilva v. Rosenberg, 886

Det Bergenske Dampskibsselskab v. Sabre Shipping Corp., 1186

Detraglia v. Grant, 872

Deutsche Bank AG v. Vik, 265

Deutsche Bank Nat. Trust Co. v. Kuldip, 557

Deutsche Bank Nat. Trust Co. v. Young, 612

Deutsche Bank Securities, Inc. v. Montana Bd. of Investments, 232, 234, 242

Devadas v. Niksarli, 93

Devine v. Keller, 982

DeVita v. Macy's East, Inc., 490

DeVito v. Nyquist, 1398

Dexter v. 16th Street Holdings, L.L.C., 484, 673

DFI Communications, Inc. v. Greenberg, 1328

Di Bartolo v. American & Foreign Ins. Co., 898

Di Benedetto v. Lasker-Goldman Corp., 1001

Di Gilio v. William J. Burns Intern. Detective Agency, 911

Di Lorenzo v. Murtagh, 1376

Di Menna v. Cooper & Evans Co., 505

Di Prospero v. Ford Motor Co., 619

Di Sabato v. Soffes, 679, 680

Dias v. Consolidated Edison Co. of New York, Inc., 958

Diaz v. Diaz, 1206

Diaz v. Paterson, 734, 781

Dickerson v. Jensen, 1395

Dickinson v. Houston, 658

Dickinson, United States v., 509

Didner v. Keene Corp., 441

Diemer v. Diemer, 503, 1001

Dietrich's Will, In re, 846

DiGiovanni v. Pepsico, Inc., 845

Digital Centre, S.L. v. Apple Industries, Inc., 53

DiGrazia v. Castronova, 986

Dillenbeck v. Hess, 880

Dime Savings Bank of New York, FSB v. Higner, 711

DiMichel v. South Buffalo Ry. Co., 816

Dimmerling v. Andrews, 286

Dinallo v. DAL Elec., 634

Dinnerstein v. Max's Gas Station, 760

Dioguardi v. Durning, 507

DiPiano v. Truchly, 825

Dissolution of Rencor Controls Inc., In re, 682

Dissolution of Stony Creek Preserve, Inc., In re, 174

Distressed Holdings, LLC v. Ehrler, 1199

Dittmar Explosives, Inc. v. A. E. Ottaviano, Inc., 1304

Dixie Dinettes, Inc. v. Schaller's Furniture, Inc., 53

Dixon v. Globe Realty Of New York, Inc., 438

Dixon v. Roy, 774

Dobbins v. Clifford, 94

Dobess Realty Corp. v. City of New York, 1319

Dobkin v. Chapman, 184, 188, 213

Dobler v. Kaplan, 1376

Dodge, Matter of, 1364

Dodumoff v. Lyons, 916

Doe v. Roe, 955

Doe v. State, 97

Doe, In re, 472

Dolan v. Krone, 1372

Dolce v. Powalski, 93

Dole v. Dow Chemical Co., 336, 394, 397, 423, 424, 425

Dolgin Eldert Corp., In re, 490, 493

Dolgow v. Anderson, 187, 363, 368
Domestic Finance Corp. v. Milner, 507
Dominion of Canada General Ins. Co. v.
    Pierson, 302
Donas v. European American Bank and
    Trust Co., 379
Donato v. Cataffo, 1144
Donawitz v. Danek, 290
Donenfeld v. Brilliant Technologies Corp.,
    647
Donnelly v. Donnelly, 137
Doran & Associates, Inc. v. Envirogas, Inc.,
    770
Dorfman, Application of, 304
Dormer v. Suffolk County Police Benev.
    Ass'n, Inc., 77
Dossous v. Corporate Owners Bayridge
    Nissan, Inc., 616
Doughney v. Fauset, 173
Douglas v. Adel, 1180
Douglas v. Miller, 1383
Doundoulakis v. Town of Hempstead, 429
Dowling v. Mosey, 495
Downs v. Yuen, 1158
Doyle v. American Home Products Corp.,
    114
Doyle v. Buturlinsky, 533
Drago v. Buonagurio, 1038
Dreger v. New York State Thruway
    Authority, 110
Dreikausen v. Zoning Bd. of Appeals of City
    of Long Beach, 1285
Dresdner v. Goldman Sachs Trading Corp.,
    648
Drexel Burnham Lambert, Inc. v. D'Angelo,
    284
Drice v. Queens County Dist. Attorney, 575
Drooker v. South Nassau Communities
    Hosp., 419
Drumgold v. AVA Service Corp., 676
Drummy v. Oxman, 125
Duban v. Platt, 520
Dudley v. Kerwick, 375
Duffy v. Horton Memorial Hosp., 106
Duffy v. Vogel, 991
Dugas v. Bernstein, 616, 617
Dulber v. Dulber, 1309
Dulberg v. Mock, 501
Dun & Bradstreet v. City of New York, 1077
Dunham v. Hilco Const. Co., Inc., 686
Dunleavy v. White, 943
Dunn v. Dunn, 649
Dunn v. Medina Memorial Hosp., 824
DuPont v. Bronston, 271
Durfee v. Duke, 1111
Durgom v. Durgom, 181, 273
Dyer v. Cahan, 113
Dynamic Medical Imaging P.C. v. State
    Farm Fire and Cas. Co., 644
E. P. Reynolds, Inc. v. Nager Elec. Co., 1338
E.B. Metal & Rubber Industries, Inc. v.
    Washington County, 692

E.H.A. Successor Corp. v. Vogel, 777
E.K. v. New York Hospital-Cornell Medical
    Center, 461
Early v. Nassau County, 875
Easley v. New York State Thruway
    Authority, 33
East Asiatic Co. v. Corash, 578
East End Laboratories, Inc. v. Altaire
    Pharmaceuticals, Inc., 846
East Meadow Community Concerts Ass'n v.
    Board of Ed. of Union Free School Dist.
    No. 3, Nassau County, 1285
East Thirteenth Street Community Ass'n v.
    New York State Urban Development
    Corp., 1042
Eaton v. Chahal, 846
Eaton v. Equitable Life Assur. Soc. of U.S.,
    Inc., 298, 558
Echevarria v. Sadker, 317
Echtermacht v. Cohen, 960
Edelman v. Edelman, 541
Edelman v. Holmes Private Ambulances,
    Inc., 885
Edenwald Contracting Co., Inc. v. City of
    New York, 576
EDP Hosp. Computer Systems, Inc. v.
    Bronx-Lebanon Hosp. Center, 924
Edward Shapiro, P.C., In re, 477
Edwards v. Erie Coach Lines Co., 520
Edwards v. Rockaway Storage, Inc., 497
Edwin F. Guth Co. v. Gurland, 520
Egon J. Salmon, Inc. v. Tamarin, 914
Ehrenfeld v. Bin Mahfouz, 238
Eidelberg v. Zellermayer, 693
Eidlitz v. Rothschild, 551
EIFS, Inc. v. Morie Co., Inc., 868
Eighth Judicial Dist. Asbestos Litigation, In
    re, 493, 822
Einstoss' Estate, In re, 308, 454
Eisen v. Carlisle and Jacquelin, 357, 368
Eisenbach v. Metropolitan Transp.
    Authority, 119
Eisenberg v. Citation-Langley Corp., 274,
    741
Eisenberg v. Rockland County, 682
El-Dehdan v. El-Dehdan, 1171, 1174
Elder v. New York & Pennsylvania Motor
    Exp., 1122, 1134, 1145
Eldre Components, Inc. v. Kliman, 766
Elias, In re, 331
Elinor Homes Co. v. St. Lawrence, 1388
Ellenberg v. Sydharv Realty Corp., 393, 397
Eller v. Eller, 1342
Ellingsworth v. City of Watertown, 1291
Elliot v. Green Bus Lines, Inc., 107
Elman v. Ziegfeld, 581
Elton Leather Corp. v. First General
    Resources Co., 738
EM Ltd. v. Republic of Argentina, 1246
Emberger's Estate, In re, 552
Emery v. Pease, 504

Emigrant Mortgage Co. Inc. v. Corcione, 207
Emigrant Sav. Bank v. Elan Management Corp., 778
Emil v. James Felt & Co., Inc., 69
Empire Mut. Ins. Co. v. Palladino, 8
Employers' Fire Ins. Co. v. Cotten, 786
Engel by Engel v. Lichterman, 483, 564
Environmental Concern, Inc. v. Larchwood Const. Corp., 1093
Epstein v. Consolidated Edison Co. of New York, 844, 887
Erbesh v. Schwartz, 590
Erdman v. Ingraham, 1380
Erenerol v. McCarthy, 1254
ERHAL Holding Corp. v. Rusin, 1021
Erickson v. Macy, 112
Erie R. Co. v. Tompkins, 125
Ernest LL v. Rosemary LL, 1334
Esposito v. Metropolitan Transp. Authority, 684
Essex County v. Zagata, 1391
Essex v. Newman, 597, 598
Estabrook & Co. v. Masiello, 881
Estates Roofing Co., Inc. v. Savo, 843
Estin v. Estin, 1111
Etra v. Matta, 243
Etter v. Littwitz, 765
Etzion v. Etzion, 869
Eugene Di Lorenzo, Inc. v. A.C. Dutton Lumber Co., Inc., 298, 557
Eugenia J. Fiala v. Metropolitan Life Insurance, 369
Eugenia J. Fiala v. Metropolitan Life Insurance., 370
Eujoy Realty Corp. v. Van Wagner Communications, LLC, 604
European American Bank & Trust Co. v. Schirripa, 695
Eurycleia Partners, LP v. Seward & Kissel, LLP, 518
Evans v. Hawker-Siddeley Aviation, Ltd., 68
Evans v. Planned Parenthood of Broome County, Inc., 258
Evans, People v., 1100, 1101
Everitt v. Everitt, 307, 573, 703
Evoy v. Amandio, 1075
Executive Plaza, LLC v. Peerless Ins. Co., 82
Export Ins. Co. v. Mitsui S. S. Co., 48
Exxon Mobil Corp. v. Allapattah Services, Inc., 357
F. I. duPont, Glore Forgan & Co. v. Chen, 179
F. J. Zeronda, Inc. v. Town Bd., of Town of Halfmoon, 1298
Fagenson v. First-York 86th St. Corp., 1362
Fairchild Camera & Instrument Corp. v. Barletta, 845
Faison v. Lewis, 67
Fajardo v. St. Joseph's Medical Center, 854

Falco v. Pollitts, 535
Falk v. Goodman, 671, 684
Falk v. Kalt, 907
Falzerano v. DeLuca, 647
Falzone (New York Cent. Mut. Fire Ins. Co.), In re, 1115
Fantasy Records, Inc. v. Travelers Indem. Co., 751
Fantis Foods, Inc. v. Standard Importing Co., Inc., 253
Farage v. Ehrenberg, 92, 651
Faragiano ex rel. Faragiano v. Town of Concord, 413
Farber v. Breslin, 650
Farber v. U.S. Trucking Corp., 1048
Farca v. Semah, 866
Farkas v. Cedarhurst Natural Food Shoppe Inc., 680
Farkas v. Farkas, 625, 1044
Farr v. Newman, 1305
Fasano v. City of New York, 473
Fashion Page, Ltd. v. Zurich Ins. Co., 163
Fassig's Estate, In re, 471
Fasso v. Doerr, 449
Fauntleroy v. Lum, 1063, 1074, 1154
FCNB Spiegel Inc. v. Dimmick, 220
FCS Advisors, Inc. v. Fair Finance Co., Inc., 1027
Featherstone v. Franco, 1384
Federal Deposit Ins. Co. v. Lapadula, 1274
Federal Deposit Ins. Corp. v. Richman, 1210
Fedoryszyn v. Weiss, 932
Fehlhaber Corp. v. O'Hara, 1371
Feinberg's Estate, In re, 68
Feingold v. Walworth Bros., 895
Feinstein v. Bergner, 180, 561
Feld v. Ginsburg, 156
Felder v. Casey, 59, 70
Feldman v. Matthews, 1393
Feldman v. New York City Health & Hospitals Corporation, 435
Feldman v. New York City Transit Authority, 625
Feldman, People ex rel. v. Warden, New York City Correctional Institute for Women, 1174
Feldsberg v. Nitschke, 858
Felix v. County of Nassau, 922
Feng Wang v. A & W Travel, Inc., 849
Ferdico v. Zweig, 309
Ferguson v. City of New York, 1024
Fermas v. Ampco System Parking, 575
Fernald v. Vinci, 944
Fernandez v. Vukosa, 536
Fernandez, Matter of, 1355
Ferrante Equipment Co. v. Lasker-Goldman Corp., 403
Ferro v. Lavine, 1397
Ferro v. Maline, 1008
Fidelity Nat. Title Ins. Co. v. Smith, 294

Fiedelman v. New York State Dept. of Health, 486

Fields ex rel. Peterson v. Wendy's Old Fashioned Hamburgers of New York, Inc., 868

Figgs v. County of Suffolk, 57

Figueroa v. Figueroa, 457

Filannino v. Triborough Bridge and Tunnel Authority, 676

Fine v. Di Stanti, 699, 700

Finegold v. Lewis, 818

Finn Hannevig & Co. v. Frankel, 568

Fiore v. Oakwood Plaza Shopping Center, Inc., 720

Fireman's Fund Ins. Co. v. D'Ambra, 753

Firmes v. Chase Manhattan Automotive Finance Corp., 822, 984, 989

First Federal Sav. & Loan Ass'n of Port Washington v. McKee, 1223

First Federal Sav. and Loan Ass'n of Rochester v. Brown, 1202

First Nat. Bank of Glens Falls v. G.F. Clear, Inc., 1202

First Nat. Bank of Rochester v. Volpe, 590

First Nat. City Bank v. City of New York Finance Administration, 7

First Nat. City Bank v. Elsky, 488, 1047

First Nat. Stores, Inc. v. Yellowstone Shopping Center, Inc., 1086

First Small Business Inv. Corp. v. Zaretsky, 1250, 1272

First Westchester Nat. Bank of New Rochelle v. Lewis, 1235, 1273

Firstar Equipment Finance v. Jonathan Travel & Tours, Inc., 1045

Firth v. State of New York, 85, 86

Fischbach v. Auto Boys, Inc., 1122

Fischbarg v. Doucet, 231

Fischer v. RWSP Realty, LLC, 937

Fish & Richardson, P.C. v. Schindler, 894

Fish v. Conley, 102

Fisher v. Fossett, 880

Fishkill, Town of v. Royal Dutchess Properties, Inc., 1078

Fishman v. Fishman, 192

Fishman v. Pocono Ski Rental Inc., 515

Fishman v. Sanders, 213, 295

Fitchburg Yarn Co. v. Wall & Co., Inc., 1188

Fitzgerald v. Lyons, 75

Fitzgerald v. Title Guarantee & Trust Co., 525, 1099

Fitzgerald v. U.S. Lines Co., 505, 949

Fizette v. Riverview Plaza, Inc., 584

Flagg Bros., Inc. v. Brooks, 734

Flame S.A. v. Worldlink Intern. (Holding) Ltd., 263

Flamenbaum, In re, 76, 538

Flanagan v. Mount Eden General Hospital, 65, 94

Flanigen v. Mullen & Gunn, Inc., 811

Flast v. Cohen, 348, 1077

Fleet Finance Inc. v. Nielsen, 711

Fleming v. Graham, 388

Fleming v. Sarva, 1047

Flemming v. Barnwell Nursing Home and Health Facilities, Inc., 377

Flemming v. Williams, 290

Fletcher v. Hatch, 473

Flick v. Stewart-Warner Corp., 262

Flintkote Co. v. American Mut. Liability Ins. Co., 649

Flood v. Re Lou Location Engr., 444

Flores v. Lower East Side Service Center, Inc., 388

Florsz v. Ogruk, 421

Flowers for Robinson v. Lyell Metal Co., Inc., 820, 869

Flowers v. City of New York, 803

Flynn v. City of Long Beach, 1321

Flynn v. Sinclair Oil Corp., 668

Fogel v. Lenox Hill Hosp., 983

Foitl v. G.A.F. Corp., 559

Foley v. D'Agostino, 501, 513, 518, 652

Foley v. Roche, 620

Follette v. Cooper, 1230

Follette v. Vitanza, 1230

Fontana v. Town of Hempstead, 56

Fontanetta v. Doe, 644

Food Fair, Inc. v. Board of Assessment Review of Town of Niskayuna, 874

Forbes v. Boynton, 290

Forcelli v. Gelco Corp., 490

Ford v. Unity Hospital, 261

Fordyce v. Fordyce, 1198

Foreign Cars of New Paltz, Inc. v. Hennessy, 671

Forman v. Henkin, 804, 805

Forte v. Perry, 844

Fosmire v. Nicoleau, 598

Fossella v. Dinkins, 535

Foster Wheeler L.L.C. v. Affiliated FM Ins. Co., 1095

Four Seasons Hotels Ltd. v. Vinnik, 660, 667

Fowler v. Bowery Sav. Bank, 527

Fox Chase Knitting Mills v. Handal, 544

Fox v. City of Utica, 130, 144

Fox v. Gower, 169

Fox v. Tioga Const. Co., Inc., 330

Foy v. 1120 Ave. of Americas Associates, 172

Foy v. Brennan, 1391

Fraley v. Desilu Productions, Inc., 656, 664

Franchise Acquisitions Group Corp. v. Jefferson Valley Mall Ltd. Partnership, 114

Francilion v. Epstein, 41

Frank L. Ciminelli Const. Co., Inc. v. City of Buffalo, 1066

Frank Pompea, Inc. v. Essayan, 647

Frank v. Meadowlakes Development Corp., 408, 411

Frankart Furniture Staten Island, Inc. v. Forest Mall Associates, 580

Frankel Associates, Inc. v. Dun & Bradstreet, Inc., 43
Frankel v. Berman, 399
Frankel v. Vernon & Ginsburg, LLP, 826
Franklin Nat. Bank v. Brita Homes Corp., 1235
Franklin Nat. Bank v. Hall, 1256
Franklin Nat. Bank v. Rayno Distributors, Inc., 1232
Franzen v. Zimmer, 1156
Freccia v. Carullo, 707
Fredrick v. Chicago Bearing Metal Co., 1195
Free In Christ Pentecostal Church v. Julian, 616
Free Park Associates v. Cepeda, 816
Freedman v. Black, 912
Fregoe v. Fregoe, 535
Freidman v. Fayenson, 801, 855, 891
Fremay, Inc. v. Modern Plastic Machinery Corp., 52, 221
French v. Banco Nacional de Cuba, 166
Frenchman & Sweet, Inc. v. Philco Discount Corp., 1345
Friar v. Vanguard Holding Corp., 363, 374, 378
Fried v. Carlucci & Legum, Cascione, Chechanover & Purcigliotti, P.C., 621
Friedlander v. Roxy Theatre, Inc., 458
Friedler v. Palyompis, 865
Friedman v. Great Atlantic & Pac. Tea Co., 24
Friedman v. Law, 319
Friedman v. State, 1112
Friends of Animals, Inc. v. Associated Fur Mfrs., Inc., 684
Fromkin v. Loehmann's Hewlett, Inc., 318
Fromm v. Glueck, 543
Frooks v. Clurman, 1253
Frummer v. Hilton Hotels Intern., Inc., 217
Frutiger's Estate, In re, 492
Frutos v. Shapiro, 683
Fry v. Village of Tarrytown, 142, 301, 1349
Frydman v. Arcure, 43
Fuentes v. Shevin, 730
Fulford v. Baker Perkins, Inc., 576
Funk v. Barry, 623, 624
Furey v. Milgrom, 182
FYM Clinical Laboratory, Inc. v. Perales, 661
G. A. C. Commercial Corp. v. La Pardo Bros. Excavating Contractors, Inc., 791
G.F.A. Advanced Systems, Ltd. v. Local Ocean LLC, 1059
Gabrelian v. Gabrelian, 1032
Gaetano v. Erwin, 765
Gaffey v. Shah, 571
Gaglia v. Wells, 880
Gaillard v. Lavine, 362
Gaines v. City of New York, 113
Galcia's Estate, In re, 1201
Galdon v. Ring, 885

Galgay v. Bulletin Co., Inc., 226, 229, 242
Galich, Application of, 528, 529
Gallegos v. Elite Model Management Corp., 970
Gallewski v. H. Hentz & Co., 81
Gallo Painting, Inc. v. Aetna Ins. Co., 684
Gamble v. Gamble, 1323
Gamell v. Mt. Sinai Hospital, 973, 993
Gamiel v. Curtis & Riess-Curtis, P.C., 654
Gamiel v. Sullivan & Liapakis, P.C., 141
Gammarata v. Bill's Garage, Inc., 853
Gandy v. Wuster, 989
Garabendian v. New York State Liquor Authority, 960
Garabettian v. Garabettian, 165
Garbellotto v. Montelindo Compagnie Navegacion, S. A., 253
Garcia v. Hilton Hotels Intern., 77, 507
Garcia v. Jesuits of Fordham, Inc., 633
Garcia v. Riverbay Corp., 904
Garcia v. Stickel, 856
Gardner & North Roofing & Siding Corp. v. Demko, 316
Gardner v. Alexander Rent-A-Car, Inc., 518
Garfein v. McInnis, 279, 1168
Garfield's Estate, In re, 932
Gargiul v. Tompkins, 1153
Garrison Fuel Oil of Long Island, Inc. v. Grippo, 953, 1209
Garthon Business Inc. v. Stein, 48
Gasperini v. Center for Humanities, Inc., 1009
Gass v. Hahn, 57
Gastel v. Bridges, 1291
Gaston v. American Transit Ins. Co., 1141
Gavigan v. Otis Elevator Co., 819
Gaynor v. Rockefeller, 370
Gazerwitz v. Adrian, 308
Gear Up, Inc. v. City of New York, 557
Geary v. Geary, 277, 292
Geddes v. Rosen, 381, 931
Geffner v. Mercy Medical Center, 814, 819
Gehring v. Goodman, 478
Geico General Ins. Co. v. Weislee, 836
Geidel v. Niagara Mohawk Power Corp., 320
Gelbman v. Gelbman, 433
Gelfand v. Tanner Motor Tours, Limited, 218
Geller v. Port Jefferson Obstetrics and Gynecology, P.C., 586
General Aniline & Film Corp. v. Photo-Marker Corp., 330
General Foods Corp. v. State, 32
General Motors Acceptance Corp. v. Ayanru, 788
General Motors Acceptance Corp. v. Maloney, 1185
General Stencils, Inc. v. Chiappa, 121
George Cohen Agency, Inc. v. Donald S. Perlman Agency, Inc., 392, 395, 400

George Doulaveris & Son, Inc. v. P.J. 37 Food Corp., 196

George Reiner & Co., Inc. v. Schwartz, 230

George v. Fiore, 1381

George v. Mt. Sinai Hospital, 110

George v. Sparwood Realty Corp., 512

George W. Collins, Inc. v. Olsker-McLain Industries, Inc., 1101

Georgi v. Texas Co., 527

Gerard v. Inglese, 680

Gerenstein v. Williams, 780

Germain, Matter of Estate of, 626

Gershel v. Porr, 142

Gershman v. Ahmad, 713

Gerzof v. Gulotta, 1293

Getz v. Harry Silverstein, Inc., 715

Giangualano (Birnbaum), In re, 925, 927

Gibbons v. Groat, 331

Gibbs v. Kings Auto Show Inc., 654

Gibbs v. St. Barnabas Hosp., 589, 900

Giblin v. Nassau County Medical Center, 109

Gibraltar Management Co., Inc. v. Grand Entrance Gates, Ltd., 70

Gibson v. Meehan, 121

Giglio v. NTIMP, Inc., 705

Gihon LLC v. 501 Second Street, L.L.C., 955

Gilberg v. Barbieri, 1109, 1137

Gilbert v. Burnstine, 1115

Gilchrist v. Commercial Credit Corp., 1188, 1274

Gillespie & Co. of New York v. Coleport Fabrics, Inc., 266

Gillespie v. Great Atlantic & Pacific Tea Co., 1017

Gillmore v. J. S. Inskip, Inc., 248

Ginsburg v. Hearst Publishing Co., 50

Giordano v. College of Staten Island, 123

Giordano v. Market America, Inc., 84

Girard Trust Bank v. Gotham Football Club, Inc., 1232

Giryluk v. Giryluk, 719

Gitelson v. Du Pont, 1304

GK v. JK, 715

Gladden v. Logan, 921

Glamm v. Allen, 56

Glaser v. Huette, 1136

Glass v. Thompson, 942

Glasser v. Keller, 181

Glassman v. Hyder, 232, 730, 757, 1190, 1193

Gleich v. Volpe, 992

Glendon v. Glendon, 167

Glens Falls Ins. Co. v. Wood, 403

Gletzer v. Harris, 1071

Glicksman v. Board of Education/Central School Bd. of Comsewogue Union Free School Dist., 634

Global Custom Integrations, Inc. v. JDP Wholesale Enterprises, Inc., 486

Global Financial Corp. v. Triarc Corp., 124

Glogowski v. Rapson, 471, 473

Glotzer v. Glotzer, 1073

Gluckselig v. H. Michaelyan, Inc., 555

Gochee v. Wagner, 434

Godell v. Greyhound Rent A Car, Inc., 577

Goffredo v. City of New York, 627

Goines v. Pennsylvania R. Co., 1161

Gokey v. Massey, 780

Goldberg v. Camp Mikan-Recro, 104, 110

Goldberg v. Freedman, 848

Goldberg v. Sitomer, Sitomer & Porges, 103

Goldenberg v. Westchester County Health Care Corp., 10, 144, 208, 301

Goldfarb's Estate, In re, 933

Goldheart Int'l Ltd. v. Vulcan Constr. Corp., 200, 596

Goldin v. New York and Presbyterian Hosp., 675

Goldman Sachs Mortg. Co. v. Mares, 69

Goldman v. McCord, 1365

Goldner v. Lendor Structures, Inc., 893

Goldstein v. Gold, 780

Goldstein v. Goldstein, 1289

Gomez v. New York City Transit Authority, 908

Gomez v. State, 808

Gonyea v. Avis Rent A Car System, Inc., 490

Gonzales v. Armac Industries, Ltd., 439

Gonzales v. Harris Calorific Co., 248

Gonzalez v. Concourse Plaza Syndicates, Inc., 936

Gonzalez v. Ford Motor Co., 459

Gonzalez v. Industrial Bank (of Cuba), 454

Good Health Dairy Products Corporation v. Emery, 1134

Goodemote v. McClain, 117

Goodkind v. WFS Inv'rs Corp., 1113

Goodman v. Solow, 303

Goodwin, People v., 622

Goodyear Dunlop Tires Operations, S.A. v. Brown, 214, 247

Goot v. Board of Ed. of Waterford Halfmoon High School, Saratoga County, 902

Gordon v. Marrone, 1039

Gordon v. Sea Crest Health Care Center, LLC, 198

Gorie v. Gorie, 863

Gorski v. St. John's Episcopal Hosp., 930

Goshen v. Mutual Life Ins. Co. of New York, 644

Gotay v. Breitbart, 91, 92

Gould v. Jacobs, 1169

Grace v. Law, 91, 309

Graffagnino v. Motor Vehicle Acc. Indemnification Corp., 1362

Graham v. Board of Sup'rs, Erie County, 354, 768

Graham v. Waite, 972

Grand Bahama Petroleum Co., Ltd. v. Asiatic Petroleum Corp., 54

Grand Jury Investigation in New York County, In re, 830

Grandison v. College Truck Renting Corp., 268

Grant v. City of New York, 924

Grant v. Miles Shoes, 160

Grassel v. Albany Medical Center Hosp., 825

Grasso v. Nassau County, 61, 62

Gray v. American Radiator & Standard Sanitary Corp., 244

Gray v. Crouse-Irving Memorial Hosp., Inc., 925

Graze v. Bankers Trust Co., 1220, 1269

Graziano v. Indemnity Ins. Co. of North America, 316

Great American Ins. Co. of New York v. Castleton Commodities Intern. LLC, 813

Great Northern Associates, Inc. v. Continental Cas. Co., 654

Great Northern Tel. Co. v. Yokohama Specie Bank, 344

Greco v. Wellington Leasing Ltd. Partnership, 907

Green Bus Lines, Inc. v. Consolidated Mut. Ins. Co., 538

Green by Cage v. Staten Island University Hosp., 841

Green v. Disbrow, 108

Green v. Downs, 983

Green v. Fairway Operating Corp., 496

Green v. Gross and Levin, LLP, 171, 173

Green v. Morningside Heights Housing Corp., 174

Green v. Vogel, 915

Greenberg v. City of Yonkers, 334, 336

Greenberg, Estate of, 937

Greenhaus v. Milano, 614

Greenpoint Properties, Inc. v. Carter, 674

Greenwood v. White, 268

Greer v. Smith, 371

Gress v. Brown, 1083, 1394

Gribbins v. Rushford Lake Recreation Dist., 557

Griffin Bros., Inc. v. Yatto, 507

Griffin v. Griffin, 280

Grimaldi v. Guinn, 234

Grisi v. Shainswit, 597

Griswald v. Village of Penn Yan, 1395

Grobman v. Chernoff, 1022

Groesbeck v. Morgan, 76

Gross v. Cross, 173

Gross v. Perales, 1404

Gross v. Shields, 769

Gross v. State Cooperage Export Crating & Shipping Co., 763

Grossman v. Schlosser, 1184

Group IX, Inc. v. Next Printing & Design Inc., 484, 672

Grskovic v. Holmes, 155

Grupo Mexicano de Desarrollo S.A. v. Alliance Bond Fund, Inc., 763

Gryphon Domestic VI, LLC v. APP Intern. Finance Co., B.V., 1247

Guaman v. Tran, 631

Guardian Loan Co., Inc. v. Early, 1274

Guard-Life Corp. v. S. Parker Hardware Mfg. Corp., 1116

Guarino v. Sharzer, 89

Guarnacci v. Ferguson, 1334, 1337

Gucci America, Inc. v. Weixing Li, 264

Guffanti v. National Surety Co., 358

Guggenheim v. Guggenheim, 616

Guggenheimer v. Ginzburg, 501, 653

Gugliano v. Levi, 820

Guilderland, Town of v. Texaco Refining and Marketing, Inc., 106

Guiliana v. Chiropractic Institute of N. Y., 553

Gumperz v. Hofmann, 165

Gunn v. Sound Shore Medical Center of Westchester, 830

Gunnarson v. State, 1020

Gushlaw v. Roll, 826

Guzy v. New York City, 113

Gyani v. Great Neck Medical Group, 955

H.J. Heinz Co. v. Currie, 767

Ha v. T.W. Smith Corp., 704

Haar v. Armendoris Corporation, 231

Haas v. Scholl, 43

Habenicht v. R.K.O. Theatres, Inc., 1000

Haber v. Haber, 1102

Habiby v. Habiby, 551

Hacker v. City of New York, 335

Hafter v. Farkas, 1055

Hahl v. Sugo, 527, 1098, 1166

Hahn Automotive Warehouse, Inc. v. American Zurich Ins. Co., 85

Hahn v. Wylie, 778

Haines v. Cook Elec. Co., 583

Haire v. Long Is. R.R. Co., 815

Hairston v. Metro-North Commuter R.R., 817

Hall v. Coburn Corp. of America, 355

Halligan v. Glazebrook, 889

Hallock v. Bogart, 895

Hallock v. State, 493

Hallock, Helvering v., 1102

Halloran v. Don's 47 West 44th Street Restaurant Corp., 449

Halucha v. Jockey Club, 100

Halyalkar v. Board of Regents of State of N.Y., 1114

Hamer v. City of New York, 824

Hamilton v. Miller, 882

Hamilton v. Owego Waterworks, 994

Hamilton v. Presbyterian Hospital of City of New York, 988

Hamm v. Richards, 334

Hammer v. Rosen, 119

Hammerman v. Louis Watch Co., 317

Hammond v. Econo-Car of North Shore, Inc., 1274

Han Soo Lee v. Riverhead Bay Motors, 621, 1021
Handy v. Butler, 1291
Haney, In re Estate of, 456
Hanna v. Stedman, 384
Hanover Fire Ins. Co. v. Morse Dry Dock & Repair Co., 75
Hanover Ins. Co. v. Finnerty, 662
Hanover Ins. Co. v. Lama, 867
Hansberry v. Lee, 354, 1109
Hansen v. City of New York, 998
Hanson v. Denckla, 223, 226, 230
Hanson v. Hanson, 515
Harari-Raful v. Trans World Airlines, Inc., 336
Harbor Associates, Inc. v. Asheroff, 1002
Hardenburgh, Ulster County, Town of v. State, 1086
Harding v. Noble Taxi Corp., 459
Hargrave v. Oki Nursery, Inc., 246
Harkness v. Doe, 461
Harlan v. Weiner, 1029
Harlem River Consumers Co-op., Inc. v. Manufacturers Hanover Trust Co., 400
Harrington v. Cramer, 319
Harrington v. Palmer Mobile Homes, Inc., 677
Harris v. Balk, 282, 761, 1190, 1204, 1259
Harris v. Krauss, 496
Harris v. Miller, 700
Harris v. Niagara Falls Bd. of Educ., 142
Harris v. Processed Wood, Inc. (P.W.I., Inc.), 819
Harris v. Shearson Hayden Stone, Inc., 366
Harry Winston, Inc. v. Waldfogel, 229
Harsco Corp. v. Rodolitz Realty Corp., 998
Hart Island Committee v. Koch, 766
Hart's Estate, In re, 482
Hartford Accident & Indemnity Co. v. First Nat. Bank & Trust Co. of Hudson, 403
Hartley v. Ring, 830
Hartman v. Morganstern, 1027
Hartmann v. Fox, 1041
Harvardsky Prumyslovy Holding, A.S.-V Likvidaci v. Kozeny, 1158
Harvey v. Chemie Grunenthal, G.m.b.H., 244
Harvey v. Colonial Home Imp. Co., 315
Harvin v. Chiusano, 915
Hatch v. Tran, 539
Hauzinger v. Hauzinger, 810
Haverhill v. International R. Co., 1122, 1135
Haverstraw Park, Inc. v. Runcible Properties Corporation, 1324
Haverstraw, Town of, State v., 1325
Hawkins v. Genesee Hospital, 805
Hayden v. Sclafani, 1334
Hayward v. Willard Mountain, Inc., 820
HCG Mezzanine Development Fund, L.P. v. Jreck Holdings, LLC, 695
Headley v. Noto, 716

Heaney v. Purdy, 644
Hearn 45 St. Corporation v. Jano, 76
Hearst Corp. v. Goldberger, 254
Hecht v. City of New York, 399, 1345
Hecht v. Monaghan, 1379
He-Duan Zheng v. American Friends of Mar Thoma Syrian Church of Malabar, Inc., 159
Heffron v. Jennings, 28, 40
Hegger v. Green, 1346
Heiston v. Taylor, 973
Helfant v. Sobkowski, 624
Heller Financial, Inc. v. Wall Street Imports, Ltd., 757
Heller v. Hacken, 937, 938
Heller v. Louis Provenzano, Inc., 578
Heller v. U.S. Suzuki Motor Corp., 78, 86, 88
Hellstern v. Hellstern, 1122
Helman v. Dixon, 543
Helman v. Markoff, 1018
Helme v. Buckelew, 274
Helms v. Diamond, 1388
Hemingway v. Pelham Country Club, 609
Henbest & Morrisey Inc. v. W.H. Ins. Agency Inc., 652
Henderson v. Henderson, 304
Hendler & Murray, P.C. v. Lambert, 835
Henegan v. Merchants Mut. Ins. Co., 1214
Henry M. Riebesehl, Estate of, 879
Henry Sash & Door Co. v. Medi-Complex Limited, 514
Henry v. City of New York, 118
Hensey Properties, Inc. v. Lamagna, 297, 1060, 1068
Herbert H. Levess & Co. v. Celebrity Knitwear, Inc., 1214
Herbert v. City of New York, 1282
Herle's Estate, In re, 582
Hernandez v. City of New York, 575
Hernandez v. Ezrow, 587
Hernandez v. New York City Health and Hospitals Corp., 118
Herpe v. Herpe, 1047, 1048
Herrick v. Watters, 76
Hertz Corp. v. Luken, 664, 665
Hertz, Newmark and Warner v. Fischman, 232
Herzog v. Brown, 662
Heslin v. County of Greene, 118
Heslin v. Schechter, 459
Hess v. Pawloski, 222
Hickman v. Taylor, 812, 813
Hidalgo v. 4–34–68, Inc., 708
Higby Enterprises, Inc. v. City of Utica, 664
Higgins v. Blauvelt, 169
Higgins, In re, 921
Hildreth, In re, 1174
Hillegass v. Duffy, 925
Hinchey v. Sellers, 1129, 1131
Hipsley v. Hipsley, 790
Hires v. New York Cent. R.R., 1152

Hirsch v. Lindor Realty Corp., 1085
Hirsch v. New York City Dept. of Educ., 557
Hochberg v. Davis, 596
Hochberg v. Hochberg, 802
Hochheiser v. Alin, 874
Hodes v. City of New York, 887
Hodges v. Beattie, 7
Hoeft v. MVL Group, Inc., 810
Hoenig v. Westphal, 885
Hoesten v. Best, 85
Hoff v. Dugan, 456
Hoffman House v. Foote, 996
Hoffman v. Boston & Maine R.R., 326
Hoffman v. Helm Capital Group, Inc., 943
Hoffstaedter v. Lichtenstein, 516, 533
Hogan v. Court of General Sessions of New
  York County, 1377
Hohenrath v. Wallach, 1189
Hohmann v. Packard Instrument Co., 360
Holihan v. Regina Corp., 905
Holland v. Blake, 969
Hollendonner v. Kiem, 649
Hollow v. Hollow, 141, 189
Holloway v. Brooklyn Union Gas Co., 392
Holloway v. New York City Transit
  Authority, 508
Holmes v. City of New York, 456
Holmes v. Greenlife Landscaping, Inc., 320
Holmes v. W. T. Grant, Inc., 1274
Holodook v. Spencer, 432
Holzman v. Manhattan and Bronx Surface
  Tr. Operating Authority, 836
Hom-De-Lite Realty Corp. v. Trimboli, 752
Home Ins. Co. v. Dick, 757
Home Sav. Bank v. Chiola, 489
Honeycrest Holdings, Ltd. v. Integrated
  Brands, Inc., 1036
Honeywell, Inc. v. Technical Bldg. Services,
  Inc., 770, 772
Honigsberg v. New York City Transit
  Authority, 994
Hood v. City of New York, 904, 929
Hope v. Fortunato, 331, 675, 908
Hopkins v. Lincoln Trust Co., 81
Hopper v. Commissioner of Taxation and
  Finance, 41
Hop-Wah v. Coughlin, 1397, 1399
Horan v. Syosset Hospital, 584
Horan v. Town of Brookhaven, 1048
Horn v. 197 5th Ave. Corp., 856
Horn v. Ketchum, 393
Hornok v. Hornok, 615
Hornung v. Mucci, 41
Horoch v. State, 32
Horowitz v. Incorporated Village of Roslyn,
  176, 562
Horsemen's Benev. & Protective Ass'n (New
  York Division), State v., 581
Horton's Estate, Matter of, 492
Hospital Service Plan of New Jersey v.
  Warehouse Production & Sales Emp.
  Union, 1027, 1074

Hotel 71 Mezz Lender LLC v. Falor, 1247
Hotel New Yorker Pharmacy, Inc. v. New
  Yorker Hotel Corp., 331
House v. Lalor, 1275
House v. Schwartz, 462
Household Finance Corp. v. Rochester
  Community Sav. Bank, 1188
Houston v. Trans Union Credit Information
  Co., 649, 687
Howard S. v. Lillian S., 802
Howard v. Allen, 290
HSBC Bank USA, N.A. v. Carchi, 888
HSBC Bank USA, N.A. v. Clayton, 704
Hubbard, Westervelt & Mottelay, Inc. v.
  Harsh Bldg. Co., 233
Hubert v. Lumbermens Mut. Cas. Co., 1085
Hudson v. Eck, 610
Hudson v. Nehill, 1371
Huebner v. Caldwell & Cook, Inc., 360
Huerta-Saucedo v. City Bronx Leasing Inc.,
  681, 692
Hui v. New Clients, Inc., 765
Huie, In re, 1347
Hulbert v. Clark, 67
Hulbert v. Hulbert, 1263
Humbach v. Goldstein, 449
Hunter v. Hunter, 940
Hunter v. National Transp. Co., 1170
Hunter, In re, 1099
Huntington Utilities Fuel Corp. v.
  McLoughlin, 183
Hurd v. Lis, 1306
Hurder v. Samuel Kosoff & Sons, Inc., 997
Huston v. DeLeonardis, 1121
Huston v. Rao, 41, 45
HVAC & Sprinkler Contractors Ass'n, Inc.
  v. State Univ. Const. Fund, 1389
HVT, Inc. v. Safeco Ins. Co. of America, 323
Hydromatics, Inc. v. County Nat. Bank, 581
Hyman v. Booth Memorial Hosp., 458
Hyman v. Hillelson, 659
Hymowitz v. Eli Lilly and Co., 1142
I. H. P. Corp. v. 210 Central Park South
  Corp., 504
Iacovangelo v. Shepherd, 540, 574, 666
Iaizzo v. Gerard, 1023
Iannone v. Iannone, 271
Iguanti v. Kronish, 1184
ILMS Realty Ass'n v. Madden, 719
Ilyayeve v. The City of New York, 430, 431,
  546
Immediate v. St. John's Queens Hospital,
  539
Imor v. Imor, 310
Import Alley of Mid-Island, Inc. v. Mid-
  Island Shopping Plaza, Inc., 938, 939
Importers' & Exporters' Ins. Co. v. Rhoades,
  1372
Incorporated Village of Island Park v.
  Island Park-Long Beach, Inc., 447
Incorporated Village of Laurel Hollow v.
  Laverne, Inc., 650, 662

Incorporated Village of Thomaston v. Biener, 930

Independent Church of Realization of Word of God, Inc. v. Board of Assessors of Nassau County, 1085

Independent Health Ass'n, Inc. v. Grabenstatter, 449

Independent Health Ass'n, Inc. v. Murray, 766

Indestructible Metal Products Co. v. Summergrade, 637

Industrial Consultants, Inc. v. H. S. Equities, Inc., 125

Industrial Development Foundation of Auburn, N. Y., Inc. v. U.S. Hoffman Machinery Corp., 530

IndyMac Bank, F.S.B. v. Yano-Horoski, 207

Infanto v. Infanto, 30

Ingraham v. Carroll, 253

Inset Systems, Inc. v. Instruction Set, Inc., 254

Insurance Co. of North America v. ABB Power Generation, Inc., 125

Intercontinental Credit Corp. Div. of Pan American Trade Development Corp. v. Roth, 1038, 1348

Interman Indus. Products, Ltd. v. R.S.M. Electron Power, Inc., 694, 695

Intermeat, Inc. v. American Poultry Inc., 283

Intermediate Credit Corp. v. Overseas Nat. Airways, Inc., 1191

International 800 Telecom Corp. v. Kramer, Levin, Nessen, Kamin & Frankel, 1039

International Harvester Co. of America v. Commonwealth of Kentucky, 214

International Mill. Co. v. Columbia Transp. Co., 55

International Playtex, Inc. v. CIS Leasing Corp., 939

International Ribbon Mills, Ltd. v. Arjan Ribbons, Inc., 1188, 1225, 1240, 1242, 1266, 1268, 1270

International Shoe Co. v. State of Wash., Office of Unemployment Compensation and Placement, 129, 222, 281, 384

International Text-Book Co. v. Tone, 54, 221

Interstate Equipment Corp. v. Bell, 691

IRB-Brasil Resseguros, S.A. v. Inepar Investments, S.A., 49

Irons v. Roberts, 717

Irrigation & Indus. Development Corp. v. Indag S. A., 1305

Irving v. Finger Lakes State Parks Commission, 1386

Isaf v. Pennsylvania R. Co., 174

Islamic Republic of Iran v. Pahlavi, 47

Island Improvement, Inc., In re, 949

Island Territory of Curacao v. Solitron Devices, Inc., 1157

Island Wholesale Wood Supplies, Inc. v. Blanchard Industries, Inc., 241

Ismail v. City of New York, 999

Israel Discount Bank Limited v. P. S. Products Corp., 1244

Israel v. Wood Dolson Co., 1123, 1127, 1160

Israelson v. Bradley, 783

Italian Colony Restaurant v. Wershals, 303

ITT Commercial Finance Corp. v. Bailey, 1243

Itzkowitz v. King Kullen Grocery Co., Inc., 633, 1317

Ives v. Darling, 163

Ivor B. Clark Co. v. Hogan, 1241

Izquierdo v. Cities Service Oil Co. (Pa.), 646

J. D'Addario & Co., Inc. v. Embassy Industries, Inc., 1024

J. McIntyre Machinery, Ltd. v. Nicastro, 247

J.A. Preston Corp. v. Fabrication Enterprises, Inc., 770

J.P. Morgan Securities Inc. v. Ader, 937

J.P. Morgan Securities Inc. v. Vigilant Ins. Co., 644

Jack London Productions, Inc. v. Samuel Bronston Productions, Inc., 1252

Jack Parker Const. Corp. v. Williams, 336, 1015, 1286

Jackson v. Jackson, 279

Jackson v. Strong, 504

Jacob Goodman & Co. v. New York Tel. Co., 1077

Jacobellis v. State of Ohio, 672

Jacobs v. Del Guercio, 1123, 1160

Jacobs v. Johnston, 907

Jacobs v. Peress, 906

Jacox v. Jacox, 465

Jaggars v. Scholeno, 954

Jaliman v. JMJ Films, Inc., 720

Jamaica Savings Bank v. Spiro, 489

James Talcott, Inc. v. Wilson Hosiery Co., 937

James Talcott, Inc. v. Winco Sales Corp., 545

James v. Alderton Dock Yards, 1077

James v. Powell, 702, 897, 1283

James-Smith v. Rottenberg, 577

Janis, In re Estate of, 490

Janssen v. Incorporated Village of Rockville Centre, 667, 668

Javorek v. Superior Court, 290

Jaworower v. Rovere, 489

Jaworski v. New Cassel Fuel Corp., 1000

Jay's Stores, Inc. v. Ann Lewis Shops, Inc., 1104

Jayell Films v. A.F.E. Corp., 652, 663

Jayson v. Jayson, 1049

JBGR, LLC v. Chicago Title Ins. Co., 644

JCD Farms, Inc. v. Juul-Nielsen, 580

Jedraszak v. County of Westchester, 925

Jefferds v. Ellis, 788

Jeffrey M. Rosenblum, P.C. v. Casano, 35

Jemison v. Goodman, 986

Jenks v. Murphy, 463

Jeraldine C., In re, 948

Jered Contracting Corp. v. New York City Transit Authority, 518

Jericho Group, Ltd. v. Mid-Town Development Ltd. Partnership, 714

Jervis, Estate of v. Teachers Ins. and Annuity Ass'n, 139

Jessamy v. Doran Group, 309

Jewish Center of Baldwin v. Winer, 137

Jiannaras v. Alfant, 373

Jing Xue Jiang v. Dollar Rent a Car, Inc., 824

JMJ Contract Management, Inc. v. Ingersoll-Rand Co., 798, 808

Jobse v. Connolly, 859

Johantgen v. Hobart Mfg. Co., 886

John Galliano, S.A. v. Stallion, Inc., 1159

John Hancock Mut. Life Ins. Co. v. 491–499 Seventh Ave. Associates, 945

John J. Campagna, Jr., Inc. v. Dune Alpin Farm Associates, 647, 648

John J. Kassner & Co., Inc. v. City of New York, 82

John T. Brady & Co. v. City of New York, 908

John T. Mather Memorial Hosp. of Port Jefferson, Inc. v. Pearl, 1202

John W. Cowper Co., Inc. v. Buffalo Hotel Development Venture, 939

John Wiley & Sons, Inc. v. Grossman, 557

Johns v. Van Brunt Motors, Inc., 141

Johnson v. Brooklyn Hosp. Center, 926

Johnson v. Manhattan & Bronx Surface Transit Operating Authority, 1018

Johnson v. Muelberger, 278, 1109, 1154, 1155

Johnson v. New York City Health & Hospitals Corp., 800, 853

Johnson v. Proskauer Rose LLP, 91

Johnson v. Rivera, 928

Johnson v. Sam Minskoff & Sons, Inc., 925, 927

Johnson v. Societe Generale S.A., 1048

Johnson v. Suffolk County Police Dept., 1005

Johnson v. Ward, 225, 237

Joiner v. City of New York, 109

Joint Diseases North General Hosp., Matter of, 1290

Jones ex rel. Cline v. 636 Holding Corp., 674

Jones v. Camar Realty Corp., 1038

Jones v. Greyhound Bus Lines, 123

Jones v. Kalache, 419, 420, 430, 538

Jones v. Maphey, 920

Jones v. Palermo, 1203

Jones v. Putnam Hosp. Center, 828

Jones v. Vetter, 459

Jones v. Young, 1113, 1152

Joosten v. Gale, 707

Jordan v. City of New York, 1362

Joseph Durst Corp. v. Leader, 1272

Joseph E. Seagram & Sons, Inc. v. Tax Commission of City of New York, 1305

Joseph Francese, Inc. v. Enlarged City School Dist. of Troy, 109

Joseph P. Suchy, Inc. v. Stuerzel, 70

JPMorgan Chase Bank, N.A. v. Maurer, 117

Juan C. v. Cortines, 1122

Judith S. v. Howard S., 12

Juidice v. Vail, 1175

Juracka v. Ferrara, 1021

Jurkowski ex rel. Cosgrove v. Sheehan Memorial Hosp., 587

Jusino v. New York City Housing Authority, 902

Juskowitz v. Hahn, 844

Justice Court Mut. Housing Co-op., Inc. v. Sandow, 1085

Justino v. Fassi, 723

K.M. ex rel. Mobley v. Mobley, 169

Kaehler v. Phoenix Ins. Co., 1317

Kagen v. Kagen, 24, 469

Kahn v. Backer, 1373

Kahn v. New York City Dept. of Educ., 1392

Kahn v. Samson Management Corp., 557

Kalechman v. Drew Auto Rental, Inc., 434

Kalir v. Ottinger, 496, 635

Kalman v. Neuman, 751

Kalman v. Shubert, 1081

Kamchi v. Weissman, 520

Kaminsky v. Kahn, 1016, 1260

Kamp v. In Sportswear Inc., 309

Kandel v. Tocher, 818, 819

Kapchan v. Kapchan, 1335

Kaplan v. Kaplan, 838, 873

Kaplan v. Meskin, 30

Kaplan v. Reuss, 311

Kaplan v. State, 1288

Kaplan v. Supak & Sons Mfg. Co., 1229, 1254, 1273

Kapon v. Koch, 800, 806, 807, 835, 848, 873, 957

Karameros v. Luther, 1133

Karasek v. LaJoie, 73

Karlin v. Avis, 180

Karlsberg v. Hunter Mountain Ski Bowl, Inc., 316

Karrat v. Merhib, 255

Katz v. Goodyear Tire and Rubber Co., 325, 326

Katz v. Murtagh, 1170

Katz v. Posner, 833

Kaufman v. Clearview Gardens Federal Credit Union, 905

Kaufman v. Eli Lilly and Co., 1125, 1138

Kavanagh v. Ogden Allied Maintenance Corp., 883

Kay v. Tankel, 937

Kearns v. Johnson, 323

Keenan v. Munday, 856

Keene v. Chambers, 339

Keeton v. Hustler Magazine, Inc., 227, 1075
Kel Management Corp. v. Rogers & Wells, 559
Kelliher v. New York Cent. & H.R.R. Co., 96
Kellogg v. Freeland, 533
Kellogg v. Match Supply Co., 566
Kellogg v. Office of Chief Medical Examiner of City of New York, 61
Kelly v. Long Island Lighting Co., 426
Kelly v. Stanmar, Inc., 306, 657
Kelly v. Tarnowski, 885
Kelly v. Yannotti, 334, 396
Kelson v. Nedicks Stores, Inc., 323
Kemelhor v. Furness, Withy & Co., 82
Kemp, People v., 622
Kenford Co., Inc. v. Erie County, 324, 814, 952
Kennedy v. Bethlehem Steel Co., 425
Kennedy v. City of Yonkers, 410
Kenneths Fine Repairs, LLC v. State, 686
Kenney v. Zimmerman, 591
Kennis v. Sherwood, 1215, 1249
Kenron Awning & Window Corp. of Eastern New York v. Abbott, 316
Kent Development Co., Inc. v. Liccione, 332, 648
Kenworthy v. Town of Oyster Bay, 683
Keown v. Wright, 944
Kerins v. Prudential Property & Cas., 1095
Kerlin v. Green, 587
Kern v. City of Rochester, 1317
Kerrigan, Matter of, 626
Kessler v. Hunter, 947
Kevorkian v. Harrington, 647
Key Lease Corp. v. Manufacturers Hanover Trust Co., 1191
Keyes v. McLaughlin, 555
Keys v. Leopold, 76
Kharmah v. Metropolitan Chiropractic Center, 411
Khela v. City of New York, 57
Kheyfets v. El Amari, Inc., 353
Khlevner v. Khlevner, 145
KI 12, LLC v. Joseph, 557
Kiamesha Concord, Inc. v. Pullman, 460
Kiamesha Development Corp. v. Guild Properties, Inc., 1327
Kickertz v. New York University, 1398
Kidd v. Delta Funding Corp., 367
Kidney by Kidney v. Kolmar Laboratories, Inc., 348, 1301
Kieley v. Central Complete Combustion Mfg. Co., 748
Kihl v. Pfeffer, 897, 989
Kiker v. Nassau County, 1024, 1047
Kilduff v. Donna Oil Corp., 1116
Kimberly-Clark Corp. v. Power Authority, 1338
Kimso Apartments, LLC v. Gandhi, 575, 590, 1001
Kinder Morgan Energy Partners, LP v. Ace American Ins. Co., 488

King v. Barnes, 1173
King, State v., 1378
Kirama v. New York Hosp., 854
Kirkman/3HREE, Inc. v. Priority AMC/Jeep, Inc., 712
Kirsch v. Lubin, 124
Kirschbaum v. Eschmann, 532
Kitson & Kitson v. City of Yonkers, 752
Kittinger v. Churchill Evangelistic Ass'n, 646
Klaxon Co. v. Stentor Electric Mfg. Co., 125
Kleeman v. Rheingold, 149
Kleeschulte v. Blair, 884
Klein v. Mount Sinai Hosp., 556
Klevens Const. Co., Inc. v. State, 848
Kliment v. McKinsey & Co., Inc., 72, 80
Klinger v. Dudley, 435
Knapp v. McFarland, 1051, 1075
Knauer v. Long Island Airports Limousine Service Corp., 508
Kneisel v. QPH, Inc., 830
Knight v. Maybee, 567
Koch v. Consolidated Edison Co. of New York, Inc., 367, 1089, 1125, 1138
Kochenthal v. Kochenthal, 233
Koehler v. Bank of Bermuda Ltd., 282, 1187, 1204, 1248
Kohn v. Kohn, 1172
Kohn v. Tri-State Hardwoods, Ltd., 705
Kolchins v. Evolution Markets, Inc., 644
Kolmer-Marcus, Inc. v. Winer, 1312
Kolnacki v. State, 524
Kolodzinski v. Ferreiras, 181
Komp v. State Tax Commission, 1399
Komyathy v. Board of Ed. of Wappinger Central School Dist. No. 1, 774
Konig v. WordPress.com, 836
Konrad v. 136 East 64th Street Corp., 874
Koolery v. Lindemann, 396
Kooper v. Kooper, 806
Koos v. Ludwig, 552
Kopeloff v. Arctic Cat, Inc., 826
Korn v. Gulotta, 1087
Korn v. Korn, 627
Kornfeld v. Wagner, 41
Koroleski v. Badler, 1191
Koschak v. Gates Const. Corp., 317
Koscinski v. St. Joseph's Medical Center, 636, 1346
Kosiba v. City of Syracuse, 352
Kossover v. Trattler, 1106, 1132, 1139
Koump v. Smith, 880, 881
Kovacs v. Castle Restoration and Const., Inc., 588
Kovarsky v. Brooklyn Union Gas Co., 359, 361
Kovarsky v. Housing and Dev. Admin. of City of New York, 1386
Kowalczyk v. Village of Monticello, 514, 537
Kowalski v. Knox, 887
Kozlowski v. Alcan Aluminum Corp., 829
Kozlowski, People v., 814

Kramer v. Vogl, 226

Kraus v. Kraus, 69

Krause v. American Guarantee & Liability Ins. Co., 396

Kregg v. Maldonado, 804

Krenitsky v. Ludlow Motor Co., 454

Krenzer v. Town of Caledonia, 1362

Kret by Kret v. Brookdale Hosp. Medical Center, 1129

Kreutter v. McFadden Oil Corp., 233

Krieger v. Krieger, 1078, 1084

Kroese v. General Steel Castings Corp., 340

Krupp v. Aetna Life & Cas. Co., 684

Kuehne & Nagel, Inc. v. Baiden, 682

Kulers v. State, 899

Kulko v. Superior Court of California In and For City and County of San Francisco, 293

Kulpa v. Jackson, 259

Kupitz v. Elliott, 1008

Kurk v. Medical Soc. of Queens County, Inc., 1375

Kurzweil v. Story & Clark Piano Co., 793

Kutner v. Hodnett, 167

Kwiatek v. Buffalo Truck Sales & Service, 589

Kyriacou v. Village of Airmont, 717

L & W Air Conditioning Co., Inc. v. Varsity Inn of Rochester, Inc., 1072

L.B. Foster Co. v. Terry Contracting, Inc., 577

L.F. Dommerich & Co. v. Diener & Dorskind, Inc., 581

L.F. O'Connell Associates, Inc. v. State, 74

L.F. Rothschild, Unterberg, Towbin v. McTamney, 242

L.H. Feder Corp. v. Bozkurtian, 944, 945

L-3 Communications Corp. v. SafeNet, Inc., 341, 657

La Buda v. State, 1153, 1161

La Buy v. Howes Leather Company, 944

La Marque v. North Shore University Hosp., 490

La Rocca v. Lane, 1377

La Rocco v. Federal Insurance Co., 1326

LaBarbera v. New York Eye and Ear Infirmary, 94

LaBate v. Meyerbank Elec. Co., 576

LaBello v. Albany Medical Center Hosp., 89

Laborers Union Local 1298 of Nassau and Suffolk Counties Vacation Fund v. Frank L. Lyon & Sons, Inc., 1240

Lacaille v. Feldman, 1271

LaCarrubba v. Naclerio, 729

Lacharite v. Ducatte, 751

Lachoff v. Lachoff, 802

Lacks v. Lacks, 1066

Ladd v. Stevenson, 296, 1064

Laddcap Value Partners, LP v. Lowenstein Sandler P.C., 855

LaFreniere v. Capital Dist. Transp. Authority, 674

LaJoy v. State, 865

Lake Louise Marie Community Ass'n v. Lake Louise Marie Corp., 783

Lake Minnewaska Mountain Houses, Inc. v. Smiley, 859

Lake Ontario Nat. Bank v. Judson, 978

Lakeland Federation of Teachers, Local 1760, In re, 1180

Lakeland Water Dist. v. Onondaga County Water Authority, 1078, 1373, 1379

Lakeside Concrete Corp. v. Pine Hollow Bldg. Corp., 177

Lakin v. Motor Vehicle Acc. Indemnification Corp., 1006

Lallo v. W. T. Grant Co., 994

LaManna, Application of, 998

LaMarca v. Pak-Mor Mfg. Co., 252

Lamendola v. Slocum, 882

Lancer v. Lancer, 463

Landau v. LaRossa, Mitchell & Ross, 110, 349, 646, 1097

Landauer Ltd. v. Joe Monani Fish Co., Inc., 1156

Landolphi v. Wilhelmsen, 267

Lane v. Mercury Record Corp., 503

Lang v. Hanover Ins. Co., 1079

Lang, In re, 30

Langemyr v. Campbell, 651

Lansingburgh Realties, Inc. v. Commissioner of Assessments and Taxation of City of Troy, 632

Lanzi v. Brooks, 518

Lape v. Lape, 703

Lapensky v. Gordon, 806

Laprease v. Raymours Furniture Co., 731, 787, 790

LaRosa v. Edward J. Furhmann & Co., 394

Larry Goldwater, Inc. v. C. B. Snyder Nat. Realty Co., 1232

Lasker-Goldman Corp. v. Delma Engineering Corp., 395

Lassiter v. Department of Social Services of Durham County, N. C., 464

Lastowski v. Norge Coin-O-Matic, Inc., 433

Laudico v. Sears, Roebuck and Co., 104

Lauer v. City Of Buffalo, 899, 1061

Laughing v. Utica Steam Engine and Boiler Works, 982

LaVigna v. Capital Cities/ABC, Inc., 492

Law Offices Binder & Binder, P.C. v. O'Shea, 833

Lawrence, In re, 92

Lawson v. Bachman, 960

Layton Sales & Rentals, Inc. v. Somat Realty Corp., 982

Lazar v. Merchants' Nat. Properties, Inc., 455

Lazarus v. Bowery Sav. Bank, 1305

Leader v. Maroney, Ponzini & Spencer, 139

Leber-Krebs, Inc. v. Capitol Records, 750

Lebow v. Village of Lansing Planning Bd., 1360

LeConte v. City of New York, 132
Lederman v. McLean Trucking Co., 501
Lee v. County Court of Erie County, 1377
Lee v. Gucker, 473
Lee v. Joseph E. Seagram & Sons, Inc.,
    1019
Leedpak, Inc. v. Julian, 1250
Leeds v. Leeds, 687
LeFevre v. Cole, 661
Leff v. Our Lady of Mercy Academy, 836
Lefkowitz v. Nassau County Medical
    Center, 881
Lefrak v. Robinson, 571
Legget's Trust, In re, 470
Lehigh Valley Industries, Inc. v.
    Birenbaum, 246
Lehman Bros., Inc. v. Hughes Hubbard &
    Reed, L.L.P., 115
Lehmann v. Kingston Plaza, Inc., 521
Leighton v. Roper, 224
Leikind's Estate, In re, 1188
Leist v. Goldstein, 633
Lemke v. Lemke, 802
Lentlie v. Egan, 571
Leo Newman's Theatre Ticket Office, Inc. v.
    DiCarlo, 1385
Leo T., Matter of, 1288
Leon RR, Matter of, 947
Leonard v. Regan, 1323
Leone v. Lohmaier, 350
Leonti, People v., 993
Lepkowski v. State, 572
Lerman v. Church, 189
Lermit Plastics Co., Inc. v. C. W. Lauman &
    Co., Inc., 576
Lerwick v. Kelsey, 535
Lesnick and Mazarin v. Carvalho, 1046
Lester v. Lester, 465
Lester v. New York State Office of Parks,
    Recreation & Historic Preservation, 486
Lettiere v. Martin Elevator Co., Inc., 439
Leutloff v. Leutloff, 575
Leven v. Marguerite, 982
Levin & Glasser, P.C. v. Kenmore Property,
    LLC, 1022
Levin v. Levin, 482
Levine v. 97 Realty Corp., 1174
Levine v. Bornstein, 898
Levine v. National Transp. Co., 162
Levine v. Shell Oil Co., 394
Levine, Application of, 837
Levinson, In re Estate of, 1101
Levitt v. Kinori, 277
Levkovich v. Vivian Hotel Corp., 322
Levy v. Levy, 256
Lew Morris Demolition Co. Inc. v. Board of
    Ed. of City of New York, 1041
Lewin v. County of Suffolk, 62
Lewis v. Borg-Warner Corp., 398
Lewis v. Lewis, 458
Lewis v. MTA Bus Co., 584

Lewis v. New York City Transit Authority,
    120
Lewis v. Ocean Navigation & Pier Co., 1129
Lewshap Realty Co. v. Shubert, 1253
Liang v. Hart, 619
Liberty Affordable Housing, Inc. v. Maple
    Court Apartments, 644
Liberty Mut. Ins. Co. v. City of New York
    Commission on Human Rights, 950
Liberty Taxi Management, Inc. v.
    Gincherman, 684
Libow v. Brill, 914
Licci ex rel. Licci v. Lebanese Canadian
    Bank, SAL, 237
Licci v. Lebanese Canadian Bank, 235, 237
Lichtman v. Mount Judah Cemetery, 483
Lichtyger v. Franchard Corp., 358
Lieb v. Lieb, 256
Lieberman v. Washington Square Hotel
    Corp., 986
Lieblich v. Saint Peter's Hosp. of City of
    Albany, 852, 856, 1288
Liebling v. Yankwitt, 303, 666
Liemer v. Kings Highway Hosp. Center,
    Inc., 866
Liggett v. Pichler, 1211
Ligoure v. City of New York, 815
Lincoln Nat. Bank & Trust Co. of Central
    New York v. Colgan, 1234
Lincoln Rochester Trust Co. v. S. C.
    Marasco Steel, Inc., 1269
Lindenman v. Kreitzer, 72
Lindwall v. Talent Cab Corp., 1020
Ling Ling Yung v. County of Nassau, 176
Linton v. Unexcelled Fire-Works Co., 539
Lipco Elec. Corp. v. ASG Consulting Corp.,
    870
Lipin v. Bender, 844, 898
Lipp v. Port Authority of New York and
    New Jersey, 1059
Lisa C.-R. v. William R., 845
Livingston v. Blumenthal, 689
Lizza Industries, Inc. v. Long Island
    Lighting Company, 1294
Llana v. Town of Pittstown, 338
Llorente v. City of New York, 943
Lloyd Capital Corp. v. Pat Henchar, Inc.,
    1026
Lo Cicero, People v., 1119
Lo Gerfo v. Lo Gerfo, 1338
Lobel v. Hilltop Village Cooperative, No. 4,
    557
Loew v. McInerney, 550
Logan v. Esterly, 428
Lomando v. Duncan, 1065
Lombardo v. Pecora, 805
London Sporting Club, Inc. v. Helfand, 1379
Long Island City Sav. and Loan Ass'n v.
    Suggs, 13
Long Island Diagnostic Imaging, P.C. v.
    Stony Brook Diagnostic Associates, 654

Long Island Jewish Med. Ctr. v. Sovereign Bank, 1362
Long Island Lighting Co. v. New England Petroleum Corp., 325
Long Island Trust Co. v. Porta Aluminum Corp., 791
Long Island Trust Co. v. Rosenberg, 1177
Long Island Trust Co. v. U.S. Postal Service, 1231
Long v. Long, 1078
Longines-Wittnauer Watch Co. v. Barnes & Reinecke, Inc., 226, 227, 243, 251
Longo v. Adirondack Drilling, Inc., 942
Loomis v. Civetta Corinno Const. Corp., 522, 579
Loomis v. Loomis, 1150
Lopez ex rel. Farias v. State, 114
Lopez v. Imperial Delivery Service, Inc., 925, 927
Lopez v. Quickset Printers, Inc., 209
Lorenzo v. Bussin, 108
Louis R. Shapiro, Inc. v. Milspemes Corp., 647, 715
Louis Sherry Ice Cream Co. v. Kroggel, 694
Love v. State, 1017, 1021
LR Credit 22, LLC v. Eggleston, 1200
LTD Trading Enterprises v. Vignatelli, 191
LTown Ltd. Partnership v. Sire Plan, Inc., 1032
L-Tron Corp. v. Davco Systems, Inc., 836
Lu v. Betancourt, 1178
Luboch v. Sidey's Inc., 717
Luce v. Pierce Muffler Shops, 160
Lucido v. Mancuso, 578
Luckern v. Lyonsdale Energy Ltd. Partnership, 461
Lumbermens Mut. Cas. Co. v. Morse Shoe Co., 604
Lumsby v. Donovan, 1298
Luppino v. Mosey, 944
Luria's Estate, In re, 933
Lusenskas v. Axelrod, 1296
Lustig v. Congregation B'Nai Israel of Midwood, 660
Lutza v. Bollacker, 587
Lyebyedyev v. Hoffman, 676
Lynch v. Carlozzi, 119
Lynn's Estate, In re, 1282
Lyon Financial Services, Inc. v. Pinto Trading Co., 958
Lyons v. Butler, 924
Lyons, United States v., 68
M & S Mercury Air Conditioning Corp. v. Rodolitz, 689
M. F. Hickey Co. v. Port of New York Authority, 1195
M. Farbman & Sons, Inc. v. New York City Health and Hospitals Corp., 820
M. Katz & Son Billiard Products, Inc. v. G. Correale & Sons, Inc., 229
M. Kramer & Sons, Inc. v. Facilities Development Corp., 576

Macchia v. Russo, 164
MacDonald v.Howard, 582
Machnick Builders, Ltd. v. Grand Union Co., 296
Mack v. Mendels, 117
Mack v. Stanley, 777
MacKenzie v. MacKenzie, 1056
MacLeod v. County of Nassau, 143
Madden v. Atkins, 462
Madden v. Town of Greene, 604
Maddux v. Schur, 145, 634
Madeline D'Anthony Enterprises, Inc. v. Sokolowsky, 682
Maggio v. 24 West 57 APF, LLC, 674, 676
Maglich v. Saxe, Bacon & Bolan, P.C., 695
Magnolia Petroleum Co. v. Hunt, 1113, 1155
Maguire v. Rebaglia, 1288
Mahon, Mahon, Kerins & O'Brien, LLC v. Moskoff, 380
Mahoney v. Brockbank, 1020
Mahoney v. Turner Const. Co., 494, 823
Maidman v. Stagg, 421
Majique Fashions, Ltd. v. Warwick & Co., Ltd., 284
Makeun v. State, 440
Malachi v. Good Samaritan Hosp., 927
Malatestinic v. Board of Educ. of City of New York, 8
Malay v. City of Syracuse, 115
Maldonado v. Maryland Rail Commuter Service Admin., 563
Malkan v. State, 74
Mallan v. Samowich, 1073
Mallen v. Morton, 1391
Malloy v. Trombley, 1133
Maloney v. McMillan Book Co., 530
Maloney v. Union Free School Dist. No. 7, 587
Mammarella v. Consolidated Edison Co. of New York, Inc., 591
Mamoon v. Dot Net Inc., 571
Manard v. Hardware Mut. Cas. Co., 1129
Manchester v. Braender, 108
Mandel v. Kent, 39
Mandell v. Moses, 462
Manes v. Goldin, 1029
Manganaro v. Estwing Mfg. Co., 390, 548
Manganello v. Park Slope Advanced Medical PLLC, 686
Mango v. Long Island Jewish-Hillside Medical Center, 617
Manhattan Telecommunications Corp. v. H & A Locksmith, Inc., 707, 711
Maniscalco v. New York City Transit Authority, 681
Mann ex rel. Akst v. Cooper Tire Co., 845, 894
Mann v. All Waste Systems, Inc., 1022
Mann v. Compania Petrolera Trans-Cuba S.A., 451
Mann v. Hunt, 1007, 1008

Mansfield v. Epstein, 1394
Manufacturer's & Traders Trust Co. v. Reliance Ins. Co., 1019
Manufacturers Nat. Bank of Troy v. Soltys, 1060
Marano v. Mercy Hosp., 829
Marco v. Sachs, 929
Marcucilli v. Alicon Corp., 518
Marcus v. Antell, 648
Marcus v. New York City Housing Authority, 1040
Mareno v. Kibbe, 660
Margerum v. City of Buffalo, 56
Margolies v. Encounter, Inc., 770
Marguess v. City of New York, 886, 887
Maria E. v. 599 West Associates, 418
Marin, Matter of, 488
Marine Midland Bank v. John E. Russo Produce Co., Inc., 988
Marine Trust Co. of Western New York v. Collins, 856
Marinelli v. Shifrin, 689
Marino v. Proch, 68
Markoff v. South Nassau Community Hosp., 112, 187
Marks v. Solomon, 826
Marlee, Inc. v. Bittar, 1069
Marmo v. Department of Environmental Conservation, 1395
Maron v. Silver, 1373
Marraccini v. Ryan, 517
Marracino v. Alexander, 651
Marrero v. Crystal Nails, 114, 928
Marrone v. John A. Johnson & Sons, Inc., 399
Marsala v. Weinraub, 418
Marshall v. Zimmerly's Exp., 586
Marte v. Graber, 158
Martin Fireproofing Corp. v. Maryland Cas. Co., 996
Martin v. Curran, 462
Martin v. Edwards Laboratories, Div. of American Hosp. Supply Corp., 83
Martin v. Julius Dierck Equipment Co., 78
Martin v. Marshall, 976
Martin v. Portexit Corp., 496
Martin v. State, 572
Martin v. State Liquor Auth., 660
Martin v. Suarez, 912
Martinez v. Premium Laundry Corp., 594, 673, 1334
Martinez v. State, 865
Martinkovic v. Chrysler Leasing Corp., 916
Martins v. Wood, 1105
Martz' Will, In re, 1319
Maryland Cas. Co. v. Byrne, 107
Marzello v. Kiamesha Concord, Inc., 326
Mashreqbank PSC v. Ahmed Hamad Al Gosaibi & Bros. Co., 47, 51
Massachusetts, Commonwealth of v. Mellon, 348

Mastan v. Desormeau Dairy-Vend Service, Inc., 174
Masters, Inc. v. White House Discounts, Inc., 1322
Masterson v. Valley Nat. Bank of Long Island, 669
Masterwear Corp. v. Bernard, 823
Mastropierro v. Bennett, 181
Matheson v. Joy-Kar Taxi, Inc., 915
Matthew H. v. County of Nassau, 335
Matthews v. Matthews, 292, 293
Matthews v. Schusheim, 461
Maxson v. Delaware, L. & W.R. Co., 75
May v. Anderson, 1155
Maydanik v. Cieri, 166
Mayer v. Albany Medical Center Hospital, 875
Mayes v. Leipziger, 232
Mazarakis v. Bronxville Glen I Ass'n, 899
Mazella v. Beals, 985
Mazie v. Mazie, 488
Mazzocki v. State Farm Fire & Cas. Co., 367
Mazzuka v. Bank of North America, 1241, 1251, 1276
MBIA Ins. Corp. v. Credit Suisse Securities (USA) LLC, 864
McArdle, People v., 1202
McCabe v. Queensboro Farm Products, Inc., 387, 393, 395, 401, 982
McCabe v. The Inc. Village of Flower Hill, 616
McCahey v. L.P. Investors, 1239
McCann v. Harleysville Ins. Co. of New York, 804
McCarthy v. Port of New York Authority, 1007
McCarthy v. Volkswagen of America, Inc., 119
McCarty v. Community Hosp. of Glen Cove, 829
McCaskey, Davies and Associates, Inc. v. New York City Health & Hospitals Corp., 574
McCasland v. McCasland, 280, 293
McCaslin v. Peterson, 268
McCluskey v. Ferriter, 966
McCord v. Ghazal, 155
McCormack v. Gomez, 130
McCormick v. American Press Publications, Inc., 1104
McCormick v. Axelrod, 1171
McDermott v. City of New York, 398, 443
McDermott v. McDermott, 322
McDermott v. Torre, 91
McDonald v. Ames Supply Co., 162, 174
McDonald v. Metropolitan St. Ry. Co., 1006, 1007
McDougald v. Garber, 1302
McDowell & Walker, Inc. v. Micha, 676
McFall v. Compagnie Maritime Belge S.A., 423

McGee v. International Life Ins. Co., 223
McGinnis v. Bankers Life Co., Des Moines, Iowa, 503
McGoldrick v. Whitney M. Young, Jr. Health Center, Inc., 828
McGough v. State, 1001
McGowan v. Bellanger, 304
McGrath v. Gold, 1100
McHugh ex rel. Kurtz v. Fitzgerald, 816, 844
McHugh v. Jones, 969
MCK Building Assocs. v. St. Lawrence Univ., 781
McKee Elec. Co. v. Rauland-Borg Corp., 226
McKenna v. Forsyth & Forsyth, 72
McKenzie Banking Co. v. Billinson, 53
McKenzie v. St. Elizabeth Hospital, 584, 822
McKinney v. City of New York, 1128
McKnight v. Bank of New York & Trust Co., 350
McLearn v. Cowen & Co., 664, 1151
McLoughlin v. Henke, 1032
McMahon v. McMahon, 714
McMahon, State v., 571
McMann v. Ballantyne Marine, Inc., 700
McMaster v. Gould, 274
McMurray v. New York State Div. of Housing and Community Renewal, 67
McNamara Realty, Inc. v. Hutchinson, 320
McNeil v. Tomlin, 180, 185
McNellis v. American Box Bd. Co., 230
McNerney v. New York Polyclinic Hospital, 859
McNulty v. McNulty, 811
Mead Johnson & Co. v. Rosen, 1172
Mead v. Bloom, 445
Meadow Brook Nat. Bank v. Goodkin, 1222
Meagher v. Long Island R. Co., 986
Meany v. Supermarkets Gen. Corp., 625
Measeck v. Noble, 990
Mechanics Exchange Sav. Bank v. Chesterfield, 781
Mechta v. Scaretta, 339
Meckert v. Sears Roebuck & Co., 863
Media Corp. of America v. Motif Mfg. Co., Inc., 224, 390
Medina ex rel. Valentin v. Gold Crest Care Center, Inc., 324
Meed v. Nassau County Police Dept., 56
Meehan v. Nassau Community College, 1031
Meilak v. Atlantic Cement Co., 1056
Meis v. ELO Organization, LLC., 388
Meiselman v. McDonalds Restaurants, 144
Melcher v. Greenberg Traurig, LLP, 71
Melendez v. City of New York, 810
Meleo v. Rochester Gas and Elec. Corp., 441
Melino v. Tougher Heating & Plumbing Co., 582
Melissa "G" v. North Babylon Union Free School Dist., 804

Mellon v. Street, 1006
Memphis Cotton Oil Co., United States v., 509
Menado Corp. v. Indemnity Ins. Co. of North America, 934
Mendel v. Pittsburgh Plate Glass Co., 87
Mendelowitz v. Xerox Corp., 874
Mendon Ponds Neighborhood Ass'n. v. Dehm, 10, 145
Mendoza v. Highpoint Associates, IX, LLC, 670, 896
Mendoza v. Mendoza, 307, 573
Meng v. Allen, 656, 664
Menin v. Menin, 465
Mercado v. City of New York, 335
Mercantile & General Reinsurance Co., plc v. Colonial Assur. Co., 935
Merced v. Fisher, 1294
Merchandise Nat. Bank of Chicago v. Lister, 186
Merigone v. Seaboard Capital Corp., 168
Mermelstein v. Kalker, 893
Merrick v. Merrick, 650, 1048
Merrill Lynch, Pierce, Fenner & Smith, Inc. v. Global Strat Inc., 897
Merrill Realty Co., Inc. v. Harris, 321
Merritt Hill Vineyards Inc. v. Windy Heights Vineyard, Inc., 22
MetLife Auto & Home v. Joe Basil Chevrolet, Inc., 898
Metropolitan Theater Ticket Agents Guild, Inc. v. DiCarlo, 1401
Metz v. People, 766
Meurer v. Meurer, 777
Meyers v. American Locomotive Co., 28
Micallef v. Miehle Co., Division of Miehle-Goss Dexter, Inc., 422, 1006
Michaels v. Cooper, 1030
Micheli Contracting Corp. v. Fairwood Associates, 171, 782
Michelsen v. Brush, 757
Michigan Trust Co. v. Ferry, 271, 1254
Micro-Spy, Inc. v. Small, 133
Midfirst Bank v. Agho, 479, 962, 963
Midland Funding LLC v. Singleton, 1200
Midonick v. Peppertree Hill Development Corp., 324
Miglino v. Bally Total Fitness of Greater New York, Inc., 653, 661, 664, 687, 1128
Mihlovan v. Grozavu, 660
Milbrandt v. A.P. Green Refractories Co., 1021
Miller v. Board of Assessors, 571
Miller v. General Elec. Co., 486
Miller v. Ives, 1367
Miller v. Kingston Diagnostic Center, 884
Miller v. Miller, 637
Miller v. Rivard, 93
Miller v. Saha, 854
Miller v. Saretsky, 1244
Miller v. Surf Properties, Inc., 218
Miller v. Waters, 132, 144, 146

Millerton Agway Co-op., Inc. v. Briarcliff Farms, Inc., 671
Milliken v. Meyer, 212, 222
Mills v. Gabriel, 1144
Mills v. Monroe County, 56
Milne v. Chandler and Hatlee, 425
Milonas v. Schwalb, 1376
Mingone v. State, 63
Minichiello v. Rosenberg, 290
Minister, Elders and Deacons of Reformed Protestant Dutch Church of City of New York v. 198 Broadway, Inc., 1038
Mirabella v. Banco Indus. de la Republica Argentina, 578
Mirisoloff v. Monroe, 638
Mirsky's Estate, In re, 937
Mitchell v. Kiamesha Concord, Inc., 589, 999
Mitchell v. New York Hosp., 445
Mitchell v. Olar, 102
Mitchell v. W. T. Grant Co., 734
Mittelman v. Mittelman, 186
Mittenthal v. Mittenthal, 696
Mitthauer v. Patterson, 1403
Mix v. Tarazskiewicz, 947
Mobil Oil Corp. v. Lovotro, 1193
Mohar Realty Co. v. Smith, 1150
Moise v. Brown, 329
Moldavsky v. Nevins, 720
Molino v. Sagamore, 316
Mollitor v. Smith, 1008
Monahan v. Hartka, 12
Mondello v. New York Blood Center-Greater New York Blood Program, 100, 105
Monessen Southwestern Ry. Co. v. Morgan, 1028
Monex Financial Services Ltd. v. Dynamic Currency Conversion, Inc., 682
Montague v. Hunt, 1030
Montalvo v. Air Dock Systems, 646
Montalvo v. Nel Taxi Corp., 1344
Montana v. Incorporated Village of Lynbrook, 58
Montcalm Pub. Corp. v. Pustorino, 666
Monte Pub. Co. v. Cohen, 789
Montgomery v. Daniels, 1293
Montreal Trust Co., United States v., 260
Moore v. Maddock, 96
Moore v. Metropolitan Life Ins. Co., 355
Moore v. Washington, 454
Mora v. Saint Vincent's Catholic Medical Center of New York, 854
Morales v. County of Nassau, 419
Moray v. Koven & Krause, Esqs., 310
Morell v. Balasubramanian, 32
Moreo v. Regan, 1093
Morey v. Sealright Co., 513
Morgan v. State, 422
Morgenstern v. Freudenberg, 279
Morgenthau v. Avion Resources Ltd., 272
Morgenthau v. Erlbaum, 1077, 1081, 1178

Moriarity v. Butler Bin Co., 466
Mormon v. Serkanic, 1010
Morning Glory Media, Inc. v. Enright, 790, 793
Moroff, In re, 477
Morris Investors, Inc. v. Commissioner of Finance of City of New York, 111
Morris Plan Industrial Bank of New York v. Gunning, 730, 756, 1229
Morris v. Pepsi-Cola Co., 1372
Morrison v. Budget Rent A Car Systems, Inc., 166
Morse v. Penzimer, 795
Morton v. Morton, 704
Mosca v. Pensky, 801
Moser v. Boatman, 230
Moses H. Cone Memorial Hosp. v. Mercury Constr. Corp., 649
Mosey v. County of Erie, 821
Mosheyeva v. Distefano, 607
Moss v. Frost Hempstead Corp., 224
Mossip v. F. H. Clement & Co., 118
Motor Vehicle Mfrs. Ass'n of U.S., Inc. v. State, 933, 939
Motorola Credit Corp. v. Standard Chartered Bank, 1186, 1204, 1246, 1248
Mott, Application of, 1328
Mount Sinai Hospital, Inc. v. Davis, 1173
Mount Vernon, City of v. Best Development Co., 460
Mount Vernon, City of v. Mount Vernon Housing Authority, 1312
Mountain View Coach Lines, Inc. v. Storms, 1103
Moussa v. State, 821
Moustakas v. Bouloukos, 310
Moza v. Sun Mut. Ins. Co., 1015
Mravlja v. Hoke, 858
Mrwik v. Mrwik, 209
Muffoletto v. Rivera, 1040
Mulder v. A.S. Goldman & Co., Inc., 746
Mullane v. Central Hanover Bank & Trust Co., 127, 294
Mullen, Application of, 950
Muller v. Sturman, 91
Mulligan v. Lackey, 1402
Multari v. Glalin Arms Corp., 402, 706
Municipal Mortgage Co. v. 461 Eighth Ave. Co., 174
Murov v. Celentano, 947
Murphy v. City of New York, 1000
Murphy v. Erie County, 1099, 1109
Murphy v. Grid Realty Corp., 1275
Murphy v. Hall, 1060
Murphy v. Roger Sherman Transfer Co., 990
Murray v. City of New York, 59, 576
Murray v. Lord, 1394
Musah v. Houslanger & Associates, PLLC, 1054
Musco v. Conte, 387, 397
Musco v. Lupi, 542, 1107

Muscoreil By Vigneri v. Pool Mart, Inc., 807
Musso v. Ostashko, 1263
Muszynski v. City of Buffalo, 1004
Mutual Home Dealers Corp. v. Alves, 302
Myer, Matter of, 1255
Myers v. Overton, 137
Myers v. Slutsky, 705
N.A. Development Co. Ltd. v. Jones, 1175, 1179
Nadeau v. Tuley, 780
Nader v. General Motors Corp., 582
Nama Air Cargo Co., Ltd. v. Unitrans Consol. Inc., 849
Nancy C. v. John J. O'C., 1322
Napierski v. Finn, 829
Naples v. City of New York, 253
Nappi v. St. John's Cemetery, 924
Nardone v. Long Island Trust Co., 1241
Nardone v. Morris A. Fierberg Co., 448
Nasaba Corporation v. Harfred Realty Corporation, 76
Nash v. Port Authority of New York and New Jersey, 1066, 1067
Nasir v. Tait, 846
Nassau BOCES Cent. Council of Teachers v. Board of Co-op. Educ. Services of Nassau County, 1398
Nassau Expressway, Borough of Queens, City of New York, In re, 1270
Nassau Roofing & Sheet Metal Co., Inc. v. Celotex Corp., 664
Natale v. Pepsi-Cola Co., 1003
National Audubon Soc., Inc. v. Sonopia Corp., 738
National Bank of North America v. New Paltz Growers, Inc., 946
National Equipment Rental, Limited v. Dec-Wood Corp., 269
National Equipment Rental, Limited v. Graphic Art Designers Inc., 269
National Equipment Rental, Limited v. Szukhent, 188, 269, 1176
National Gypsum Co. Inc. v. Assessor of Town of Tonawanda, 1364
National Microtech, Inc. v. Satellite Video Services, Inc., 610
National Sur. Corp. v. R.H. Macy & Co., Inc., 1235
National Sur. Corp. v. Silver, 1169
National Union Fire Ins. Co. of Pittsburgh, Pa. v. Worley, 48
National Westminster Bank, USA v. State, 783
Nationscredit Financial Services Corp. v. Turcios, 939
Natixis Real Estate Capital Trust 2007-HE2 v. Natixis Real Estate Holdings, LLC, 653
Natter v. Isaac H. Blanchard Co., 339
Natural Resources Defense Council, Inc. v. New York City Dept. of Sanitation, 1374

Naujokas v. H. Frank Carey High School, 522
Navillus Tile, Inc. v. LC Main, LLC, 12
Necchi S.p.A. v. Nelco Sewing Mach. Co., 808
Neenan v. Woodside Astoria Transp. Co., 1119
Nehmadi v. Davis, 643
Neil v. New York City Housing Authority, 673
Neill v. Ridner, 244
Neilson Realty Corp. v. Motor Vehicle Acc. Indemnification Corp., 1271
Nelson v. Cross & Brown Co., 381
Nelson v. Fraboni, 169
Nemetsky v. Banque De Developpement De La Republique Du Niger, 286
Neroni v. Follender, 481
Nesbitt v. Nimmich, 1141
Netherlands Shipmortgage Corp., Ltd. v. Madias, 54
Neuman v. Dunham, 291
Neuman v. Frank, 872
Neuman v. Syosset Hosp. Anesthesia Group, P.C., 946
Neumark v. New York City Police Property Clerk, 57
Neumeier v. Kuehner, 124
Nevelson v. Piesner, 324
New England Industries v. Margiotti, 167
New England Merchants Nat. Bank v. Iran Power Generation and Transmission Co., 189
New England Mut. Life Ins. Co. v. Brandenburg, 340
New York Cent. Mut. Fire Ins. Co. v. Czumaj, 487
New York City Asbestos Litigation, In re, 63, 411, 442
New York City Asbestos Litigation, Matter of, 866
New York City Asbestos Litigation: Brooklyn Naval Shipyard Cases, 442
New York City Health and Hospitals Corp. v. McBarnette, 1394
New York Civil Liberties Union v. City of Saratoga Springs, 821
New York County Data Entry Worker Product Liability Litigation, In re, 822
New York County DES Litigation, Matter of, 84
New York Foreign Trade Zone Operators v. State Liquor Authority, 1081
New York Higher Educ. Assistance Corp. v. Cooper, 1177
New York Higher Educ. Services Corp., State of v. Starr, 669, 1101
New York Hosp. Medical Center of Queens v. Microtech Contracting Corp., 389
New York Life Ins. Co. v. Dunlevy, 282, 384
New York Mortg. Agency, State of v. Linkenberg, 704

New York Movers Tariff Bureau, Inc., State v., 552, 1173

New York Republican State Committee v. New York State Com'n on Government Integrity, 956

New York Skyline, Inc., In re, 492

New York State Ass'n of Nurse Anesthetists v. Novello, 347, 1387

New York State Defenders Ass'n v. New York State Police, 821

New York State Higher Educ. Services Corp. v. Bandler, 117

New York State Higher Educ. Services Corp. v. Fabrizio, 69

New York State Inspection, Sec. and Law Enforcement Employees, Dist. Council 82, AFSCME, AFL-CIO v. Cuomo, 348, 1077, 1371

New York, City of v. Britestarr Homes, Inc., 498

New York, City of v. Coastal Oil New York, Inc., 1018

New York, City of v. Long Island Airports Limousine Service Corp., 337

New York, City of v. Marchese, 1246

New York, City of v. Panzirer, 1220, 1269

New York, City of v. Scott, 1296

New York, City of v. West Winds Convertibles Int'l, Inc., 614

New York, In re City of, 1392

New York, State of v. County of Sullivan, 439

Newbrand v. City of Yonkers, 1369

Newburger, Loeb & Co., Inc. v. Gross, 1019

Newburgh, City of v. Hauser, 810

Newcomb v. Middle Country Cent. School Dist., 60

Newcomb's Estate, In re, 317

Newell v. Huston, 602

Newell v. Woodward, 500

Newman v. Resnick, 940

Newman v. State, 487

Ng v. Chalasani, 492

Niagara Mohawk Power Corp. v. Town of Moreau Assessor, 816

Nickerson v. City of New York, 390

Nicodene v. Byblos Restaurant, Inc., 140

Nigrone v. Murtagh, 1377

Nilsa B. B. v. Clyde Blackwell H., 256

Nix v. Grand Lodge of Intern. Ass'n of Machinists and Aerospace Workers, 361

NML Capital v. Republic of Argentina, 1026

Noble v. Cole, 826

Nolechek v. Gesuale, 433

Nomako v. Ashton, 801, 802, 898

Norex Petroleum Ltd. v. Blavatnik, 116, 126

Norkin v. Hoey, 843

Norman Co. v. Nassau County, 392, 397

Normoyle v. New York City Transit Authority, 680

North British & Mercantile Ins. Co. v. Central Vermont R. Co., 82

North County Communications Corp. v. Verizon New York, Inc., 491

North Georgia Finishing, Inc. v. Di-Chem, Inc., 735

North Oyster Bay Baymen's Ass'n v. Town of Oyster Bay, 1040, 1085

North Shore University Hosp. at Plainview v. Citibank Legal Service Intake Unit, 1200

Northern Blvd. & 80th St. Corp. v. Siegel, 729

Northern Mariana Islands, Commonwealth of v. Canadian Imperial Bank of Commerce, 1196, 1205, 1248

Northern Operating Corp. v. Town of Ramapo, 1294

Northern Westchester Professional Park Associates v. Town of Bedford, 1303

Northway Engineering, Inc. v. Felix Industries, Inc., 536, 581

Northwestern Telegraph Co. v. Western Union Telegraph Co., 375

Norton v. Nguyen, 824

Notarius v. Hess Oil & Chemical Corp., 331

Notaro v. Bison Const. Corp., 685

Nowacki v. Becker, 663

Nussenblatt v. Nussenblatt, 511

Nutone Inc. v. William E. Bouley Co., 948

Nykorchuck v. Henriques, 89, 90

O'Brien v. City of Syracuse, 526, 1099

O'Brien v. Contreras, 144

O'Brien v. Mix, 991

O'Connell v. Kern, 1393

O'Connor v. G & R Packing Co., 1133

O'Connor v. O'Connor, 184

O'Connor v. Papertsian, 1008

O'Dwyer v. Robson, 946

O'Frias v. Melton, 1149

O'Hara v. Tidewater Oil Co., 577

O'Meara v. A & P, Inc., 1022

O'Neill v. Ho, 853, 854

O'Rourke v. Long, 1338

Oakes v. Patel, 1009, 1010, 1308

Oakley v. County of Nassau, 664

Oberly v. Bangs Ambulance Inc., 584

Occhino v. Hostetter, 1397

Ocean Accident & Guarantee Corp., Ltd v. Otis Elevator Co., 1319

Oceancrest Homes, Inc. v. Golfbay Country Club, Inc., 1283

Offner v. Rothschild, 44

Ohio ex rel. Popovici, State of v. Agler, 166

Ohlquist v. Nordstrom, 271, 1254

Okun v. Tanners, 928, 929

Ole Olsen, Limited, State v., 654

Olean Urban Renewal Agency v. Herman, 682

Olsen & Chapman Const. Co. v. Village of Cazenovia, 551

Olsen v. Bankers' Trust Co., 345

Olsen v. Robaey, 1273
Olsen v. St. Margaret of Scotland Roman
  Catholic Church, 986
Olson v. Jordan, 555
Oluwatayo v. Dulinayan, 681, 692
One West Bank v. Chapilliquen, 659
Oneida Nat. Bank & Trust Co. of Central
  New York v. Unczur, 467, 472
Onofrio v. Playboy Club of New York, Inc.,
  372, 374
Onorati v. National Automatic Laundry &
  Cleaning Council, Inc., 508
Oppel v. DeGangi, 1192, 1256
Oppenheimer v. Dresdner Bank A. G., 1189
Oppenheimer v. Westcott, 1060
Oppenheimer, People ex rel. v. Rosoff, 1175
Organek v. Harris, 673
Orient Mid-East Lines, Inc. v. Albert E.
  Bowen, Inc., 232, 238
Orix Credit Alliance, Inc. v. Grace
  Industries, Inc., 691
Orlik v. National Carbon Co., 574
Ortega v. City of New York, 892, 898
Osborne v. Miller, 953
Oshrin v. Celanese Corp. of America, 612
Osowski v. AMEC Const. Management,
  Inc., 441
Osserman v. Osserman, 811
Ostergren's Will, In re, 1231
Osterhoudt v. Wal-Mart Stores Inc., 895
Ostrov v. Rozbruch, 605
Otto v. Royal Palm Bar, 210
Otto v. Wegner, 400
Oustecky v. Farmingdale Lanes, Inc., 174
Outdoor Supply Co. v. Westhome Sec.
  Corp., 137
Overmyer v. Eliot Realty, 1158
Overseas Reliance Tours & Travel Service,
  Inc. v. Sarne Co., 683
Owens v. Patent Scaffolding Co., Division of
  Harsco Corp., 70
Owens v. Sokol, 860
Ownbey v. Morgan, 731
Owners Committee on Elec. Rates, Inc. v.
  Public Service Com'n of State of N.Y.,
  1391
Oxford Paper Co. v. S. M. Liquidation Co.,
  53
Oyague v. Schwartz, 145
Oyster Bay, Town of v. Lizza Industries,
  Inc., 86
Oysterman's Bank & Trust Co. v. Weeks,
  1257
Oystermen's Bank & Trust Co. v. Manning,
  1229
P. Ballantine and Sons v. Boston Celtics
  Basketball Club, 699
P.H. Carlyon, Inc. v. Roberts, 108
PacAmOr Bearings, Inc. v. Foley, 186
Pacamor Bearings, Inc. v. Molon Motors &
  Coil, Inc., 229
Pace v. Perk, 541, 577, 1089

Pach v. Gilbert, 1220
Paddington Partners v. Bouchard, 1019
Padilla v. Greyhound Lines, Inc., 328
Pallonetti's Estate, In re, 1188
Palmer v. Fox, 589, 999
Palumbo v. Innovative Communications
  Concepts, Inc., 857
Pampris v. Egnasher, 680
Papa v. Burrows, 668
Paparella v. Paparella, 256
Pappalardo v. Westchester Rockland
  Newspapers, 518
Paragon Homes, Inc. v. Carter, 270
Paramount Communications v. Gibraltar
  Cas. Co., 1095
Paramount Pictures Corp. v. Allianz Risk
  Transfer AG, 542, 1107
Pardee v. Mutual Ben. Life Ins. Co., 807
Park East Corp. v. Whalen, 1323
Parke-Bernet Galleries, Inc. v. Franklyn,
  231
Parker v. Blauvelt Volunteer Fire Co., Inc.,
  1150
Parker v. Mack, 131, 144, 508
Parker v. New York Tel. Co., 872
Parker v. Port Authority of New York and
  New Jersey, 100
Parker v. Rogerson, 1297
Parkhurst v. Berdell, 1095
Parklane Hosiery Co., Inc. v. Shore, 1152
Parks v. Leahey & Johnson, P.C., 497
Parmenter v. State, 81
Parr Meadows Racing Ass'n, Inc. v. White,
  729, 785
Parsons v. Hytech Tool & Die, Inc., 882
Paskus, Gordon and Hyman v. Peck, 555
Pataki v. Kiseda, 819
Paterno v. Laser Spine Institute, 234, 252,
  563
Patrician Plastic Corp. v. Bernadel Realty
  Corp., 11, 161, 1299
Patron v. Patron, 1305
Patterson v. Turner Const. Co., 804
Patti v. State, 402
Paul Conte Cadillac, Inc. v. C.A.R.S.
  Purchasing Service, Inc., 298
Pauling v. Smith, 1400
Paulus v. Christopher Vacirca, Inc., 711
Payne v. Civil Service Emp. Ass'n, 322
Payne v. New York, S. & W.R. Co., 510
Pearl v. City of Long Beach, 123
Pearson v. Pearson, 696
Pease & Elliman, Inc. v. 926 Park Ave.
  Corp., 690
Peerless Ins. Co. v. Michael Beshara, Inc.,
  544
Pegasus Aviation I, Inc. v. Varig Logistica
  S.A., 876, 896, 1300, 1304
Pell v. Board of Ed. of Union Free School
  Dist. No. 1 of Towns of Scarsdale and
  Mamaroneck, 1380, 1382
Pelley, Application of, 836

Pendleton v. City of New York, 103
Penguin Group (USA) Inc. v. American
  Buddha, 254
Pennington v. Fourth Nat. Bank of
  Cincinnati, Ohio, 282
Penn-Ohio Steel Corp. v. Allis-Chalmers
  Mfg. Co., 583
Pennoyer v. Neff, 129, 222, 266, 282, 285,
  293, 748
Penoyar v. Kelsey, 729, 745
People's Nat. Bank v. Hitchcock, 1074
Peoples Trust Co. of Malone v. O'Neil, 108
Peralta v. Heights Medical Center, Inc.,
  1065
Perez v. Fitzgerald, 73
Perez v. Paramount Communications, Inc.,
  106, 353
Perez v. Time Moving & Storage, 845, 851
Perez-Wilson v. McPhee, 1034
Pernet v. Peabody Engineering Corp., 518,
  582
Perrone v. Jim Doyle Ford, Inc., 99
Perry v. Tauro, 1332
Peruzzin v. Test, 1393
Peter-MacIntyre v. Lynch Intern., Inc., 483
Petersen v. Talisman Sugar Corp., 355
Peterson v. Spartan Industries, Inc., 259,
  642
Peterson, In re, 944
Petker v. Rudolph, 471
Petnel v. American Tel. & Tel. Co., 75
Petrogradsky Mejdunarodny
  Kommerchesky Bank v. National City
  Bank of New York, 352, 383
Petrova v. Roberts, 167
Petz v. Property Clerk of 68th Squad,
  Brooklyn, N.Y., 1371
Phalen v. Theatrical Protective Union No.
  1, Intern. Alliance of Theatrical and
  Stage Emp., AFL-CIO, 7, 1372
Phelps v. Phelps, 1103
Philadelphia Indem. Ins. Co. v. Goggins-
  Starr, 44, 45
Philip Shlansky & Bro. v. Grossman, 331
Phillips Petroleum Co. v. Shutts, 373
Phillips v. Chevrolet Tonawanda Division of
  General Motors Corp., 400
Phillips v. Joseph Kantor & Co., 684
Phillips v. Tietjen, 315
Pi Ju Tang v. St. Francis Hosp., 115
Piacente v. Bernstein, 969
Piccinich v. Forest City Tech Place
  Associates, 461
Pickerell v. Town of Huntington, 1325
Pickering v. Freedman, 991
Pierce v. International Harvester Co., 333,
  390
Pierson v. City of New York, 60
Pina v. Flik Intern. Corp., 857
Pine Street Homeowners Ass'n v. 20 Pine
  Street LLC, 660
Pinna v. Davis, 240

Piquette v. City of New York, 610
Pittoni v. Boland, 946
Plachte v. Bancroft Inc., 912
Plank v. Watson Bowman Acme Corp., 670
Planned Consumer Marketing, Inc. v. Coats
  & Clark, Inc., 654, 1199
Planned Indus. Centers, Inc. v. Eric
  Builders, Inc., 811
Planty v. Potter-DeWitt Corp., 1152
Plateis v. Flax, 616
Plath v. New York State Olympic Regional
  Development Authority, 33
Platman v. Pham Thu Duc, 850
Plaza ex rel. Rodriguez v. New York Health
  and Hospitals Corp. (Jacobi Medical
  Center), 61
Plaza Hotel Associates v. Wellington
  Associates, Inc., 1257
Plemmenou v. Arvanitakis, 497
Ploski v. Riverwood Owners Corp., 846
Plummer ex rel. Heron v. New York City
  Health and Hospitals Corp., 90
Plummer v. New York City Health and
  Hospitals Corp., 90
Podolsky v. Devinney, 289
Pogor v. Cue Taxi Service, Inc., 590, 1001
Pokoik v. Department of Health Services of
  County of Suffolk, 1325
Polansky v. Paugh, 184
Policemen's Benev. Ass'n of Westchester
  County, Inc. v. Board of Trustees of
  Village of Croton-on-Hudson, 1403
Polipo v. Sanders, 1069
Pollak v. Mogavero, 1389
Pollicina v. Misericordia Hosp. Medical
  Center, 24
Poly Const. Corp. v. Oxford Hall
  Contracting Corp., 332
Pomerantz v. Cave, 927
Pomilio v. Lee, 1384, 1385
Porter Flushing Realty Co. v. New York
  City Planning Commission, 1373
Porter v. Kingsbrook OB/GYN Associates,
  P.C., 460
Posada v. Pelaez, 140
Posner v. Levitt, 1371
Posner v. Rockefeller, 1390
Post v. 120 East End Ave. Corp., 24
Poulard v. Papamihlopoulos, 100
Powell v. Criminal Court of City of New
  York, New York County, 1376
Power Authority of State of N.Y. v. New
  York State Dept. of Environmental
  Conservation, 1082
Powers v. Foley, 12
Pray v. Hegeman, 1131
Premier Restorations of New York Corp. v.
  New York State Dept. of Motor Vehicles,
  1077
Premo v. Cornell, 524
Presidential Realty Corp. v. Michael Square
  West, Ltd., 230

Press v. Monroe County, 74, 1078, 1083, 1084
Price Paper and Twine Co. v. Miller, 766
Price v. Booth, 454
Price v. Brody, 907
Priel v. Linarello, 45
Prince v. City of New York, 997
Princeton Bank & Trust Co. v. Berley, 719, 1212, 1270
Principe v. Assay Partners, 1039
Prior v. Cunningham, 1198
Proskauer Rose Goetz & Mendelsohn LLP v. Munao, 101
Prospero v. Prospero, 313
Provident Tradesmens Bank & Trust Co. v. Patterson, 342
Prudential Ins. Co. of America v. Stone, 99
Prudential Lines, Inc. v. Firemen's Ins. Co. of Newark, N. J., 631
Prudential Oil Corp. v. Phillips Petroleum Co., 1030
Prudential Property and Cas. Ins. Co. v. Holtzman, 210
Prunty v. YMCA of Lockport, Inc., 1009
Psaroudis v. Psaroudis, 888
Psathas v. Catskill Regional Off-Track Betting Corp., 176
Public Service Mut. Ins. Co. v. Zucker, 484
Pugach, Application of, 470
Puleo v. Shore View Center for Rehabilitation and Health Care, 315, 324
Punwaney v. Punwaney, 864
Puro v. Puro, 693
Pustilnik v. Pustilnik, 519
Pyne v. 20 E. 35 Owners Corp., 116
Q.P.I. Restaurants Ltd. v. Slevin, 710
QFI, Inc. v. Shirley, 693
Qian v. Dugan, 825
Quadrozzi Concrete Corp. v. Mastroianni, 95
Quality Ford of Mt. Vernon, Inc. v. Metro Auto Leasing, Inc., 790
Quantum Heating Services Inc. v. Austern, 1174
Quick v. O'Connell, 1160
Quinn v. Spitale, 430
Quinones v. NYRAC, 120
Quintanilla v. Harchack, 893
R. Bernstein Co. v. Popolizio, 1398
R. C. Gluck & Co. v. Tankel, 1172
Rab v. Colon, 911, 913
Rabinowitz v. Bernstein, 899
Rae v. Hotel Governor Clinton, Inc., 332
Rae v. Kestenberg, 717, 720
Raes Pharmacy, Inc. v. Perales, 621
Raharney Capital, LLC v. Capital Stack LLC, 53
Rahi v. Fang, 100
Rait v. Jacobs Bros., 172
Raji v. Bank Sepah-Iran, 1246
Rakowski v. Irmisch, 850

Ranco Sand and Stone Corp. v. Vecchio, 1392
Rand v. Hearst Corp., 659
Rand v. Lockwood, 468
Randall v. Randall, 169
Rangolan v. County of Nassau, 412
Rankin on Behalf of Bd. of Ed. of City of New York v. Shanker, 1178
Ranni's Claim, Matter of, 1113
Raoul v. Olde Village Hall, Inc., 665
Raschel v. Rish, 175
Raspante v. Trans. Supply & Management, Inc., 267
Rattray v. Raynor, 1296
Rawstorne v. Maguire, 212
Ray v. Marine Midland Grace Trust Co., 356
Raybin v. Raybin, 684
Raymond v. Honeywell, 446
Raymond v. Marchand, 518
RDLF Financial Services, LLC v. Bernstein, 310
Read v. Sacco, 1108, 1128
Rebell v. Trask, 492
Rechler Equity B–1, LLC v. AKR Corp., 478
Reckson Associates Realty Corp. v. Blasland, Bouck & Lee, Inc., 648
Recovery Racing, LLC v. Sunrise Motors, LLC, 654
Rector, Church Wardens and Vestrymen of St. Bartholomew's Church in City of New York v. Committee to Preserve St. Bartholomew's Church, Inc., 808
Red Hook/Gowanus Chamber of Commerce v. New York City Bd. of Standards and Appeals, 341
Redfield v. Critchley, 296
Reed v. Hudson, 948
Reed v. Littleton, 1080
Reed v. Shoratlantic Development Co., Inc., 660
Reed, In re, 1316
Reeves v. Crownshield, 1254
Regency Club at Wallkill, LLC v. Appel Design Group, P.A., 91
Regency Club at Wallkill, LLC v. Bienish, 719, 721
Regnell v. Page, 740
Reich v. Cochran, 1105, 1149
Reich v. Manhattan Boiler & Equipment Corp., 436
Reichenbach v. Corn Exchange Bank Trust Co., 323
Reilly v. Sicilian Asphalt Paving Co., 510
Reinertsen v. George W. Rogers Const. Corp., 1010
Reis v. Volvo Cars of North America, 1292, 1306
Reliance Ins. Co. v. PolyVision Corp., 111
Remo Drug Corp. v. State, 1239
Rendo v. Schermerhorn, 999
Renne v. Roven, 928

Renwick v. Town of Allegany, 575
Republic Associates, Inc. v. McRae, 1234
Republic Aviation Corp. v. Republic Lodge
   No. 1987, Intern. Ass'n of Machinists, 767
Republic of Argentina v. NML Capital, Ltd.,
   1246
Resch v. Briggs, 148
Resource Funding Co. v. McNamara, 622
Retail Software Services, Inc. v. Lashlee,
   239, 1301
Reurs v. Carlson, 448
Rever v. Nelson, 1317
Reybold v. Reybold, 168
Reyes-Peralta v. Ngernak, 148
Reynolds Securities, Inc. v. Underwriters
   Bank & Trust Co., 701
Reynolds v. Dustman, 1320
Reynolds v. Morka Enterprises, Inc., 439
Rhoades v. Adelman, 1327
Rhulen Agency, Inc. v. Gramercy
   Brokerage, Inc., 490
Ribolow, In re, 921
Rice v. Ninacs, 983
Rich Products Corp. v. Diamond, 180
Rich v. Lefkovits, 491, 663
Rich v. Rich, 301, 752
Richardson Greenshields Sec., Inc. v. Lau,
   596
Richardson v. Orentreich, 89
Richardson v. Vajiradhammapadip Temple,
   76
Richardson, United States v., 348
Richbell Information Services, Inc. v.
   Jupiter Partners L.P., 809, 864
Ricker v. Lajoie, 290
Rickert v. Travelers Ins. Co., 671
Rife v. Union College, 576
Rifenburg v. Liffiton Homes, Inc., 298
Riland v. Frederick S. Todman & Co., 654
Rill v. Darling, 934
Rima v. Rossie Iron-Works, 471
Rinaldi v. Viking Penguin, Inc., 86
Rintala v. Shoemaker, 290
Rios v. Donovan, 797, 829, 831, 833, 869,
   874
Risko v. Alliance Builders Corp., 442
River Ridge Living Center, LLC v. ADL
   Data Systems, Inc., 683
Rivera v. Albany Medical Center Hosp., 829
Rivera v. Board of Ed. of City of New York,
   996
Rivera v. Glen Oaks Village Owners, Inc.,
   830
Rivera v. Laporte, 713
Rivera v. Montefiore Medical Center, 825,
   1005
Rivera v. Monticello Central School Dist.,
   1008
Rivera v. New York City Transit Authority,
   860, 970
Rivera v. Smith, 1397
Rivers v. Birnbaum, 826

Rivieccio, United States v., 781
Riviello v. Waldron, 443
Rizk v. Cohen, 89
Rizzuti v. Laucella, 895
Robbins v. Goldstein, 784
Robbins' Estate, In re, 1271
Robert S. Moore, Inc. v. Whittaker, 1202
Robert Stigwood Organisation, Inc. v.
   Devon Co., 690
Roberts v. County Court of Wyoming
   County, 1377
Roberts v. Northington, 557
Roberts v. Strauss, 1106
Robins v. Finestone, 510
Robinson v. City of New York, 109, 121
Robinson v. Ferens, 982
Robinson v. Government of Malaysia, 1353
Robinson v. June, 408
Robinson v. Klein, 1007
Robinson v. Oceanic Steam Nav. Co., 16, 52
Robinson v. Robins Dry Dock & Repair Co.,
   81
Robinson, Application of, 168
Rocanova v. Equitable Life Assur. Soc. of
   U.S., 643
Roche v. Udell, 854
Rochester Colony, Inc. v. Hostetter, 1375,
   1401
Rochester Radio Supply Co., Inc. v. State,
   585
Rochester, City of v. Chiarella, 672
Rochester, City of v. Diksu Corp., 533
Rock v. Reed-Prentice Division of Package
   Machinery Co., 438
Rockaway Boulevard Wrecking & Lumber
   Co. v. Raylite Elec. Corp., 332
Rockefeller v. Moront, 94
Rockland Power & Light Co. v. City of New
   York, 1077, 1086
Rockwell v. Morris, 1365
Rocky Point Drive-In, L.P. v. Town of
   Brookhaven, 1304
Rodgers v. Rodgers, 189, 769
Rodi v. Landau, 419
Rodolitz v. Greater New York Mut. Ins. Co.,
   818
Rodolitz v. Neptune Paper Products, Inc.,
   1321
Rodrigues v. N & S Building Contractors,
   Inc., 388
Rodriguez v. City of New York, 681
Rodriguez v. Manhattan Medical Group,
   P.C., 94
Rodriguez v. New York City Housing
   Authority, 1027
Roeck v. Columbia-Greene Medical Center,
   807
Roecklein v. American Sugar Refining Co.,
   344
Roff v. Green Hills of Glenham
   Condominium Ass'n, Inc., 669
Rogoff v. San Juan Racing Ass'n, Inc., 540

Rokina Optical Co., Inc. v. Camera King, Inc., 701, 702

Rolm Corp. v. F. Garofalo Elec. Co., Inc., 485

Romanelli v. Associated Marble Industry, Inc., 1341

Romano v. Romano, 67

Romano v. Steelcase Inc., 803

Rome Cable Corp. v. Tanney, 399

Rome Sentinel Co. v. Boustedt, 457

Ronan v. Levitt, 1325

Rondack Const. Services, Inc. v. Kaatsbaan Intern. Dance Center, Inc., 1224

Ronder & Ronder, P.C. v. Nationwide Abstract Corp., 670

Ronga v. Alpern, 784

Rook v. 60 Key Centre, Inc., 824

Roosevelt Hardware v. Green, 1061

Root v. Wagner, 1268

Rosado v. Mercedes-Benz of North America, Inc., 878

Rosado v. Valvo, 805

Rosario by Vasquez v. City of New York, 1004

Rosario v. General Motors Corp., 828

Rosemont Enterprises, Inc. v. Irving, 1300

Rosen v. Motor Vehicle Acc. Indemnification Corp., 1006

Rosen v. Rosen, 192

Rosenberg v. Rosenberg, 1291

Rosenblatt v. Birnbaum, 351, 467

Rosenfeld v. A. H. Robins Co., Inc., 362

Rosenfeld v. Hotel Corp. of America, 224, 274, 458

Rosenman Colin Freund Lewis & Cohen v. Edelman, 605

Rosenshein v. Rosenshein, 631

Rosenstrauss v. Women's Imaging Center of Orange County, 538

Rosenthal v. Agate, 614

Rosner v. Globe Valve Corp., 552

Ross Realty v. V & A Fabricators, Inc., 34

Ross v. Jamaica Hosp. Medical Center, 115, 651

Ross v. Pawtucket Mut. Ins. Co., 396

Ross v. Ross, 522

Rossi v. Blue Cross and Blue Shield of Greater New York, 811, 812

Ro-Stan Equities, Inc. v. Schechter, 1335

Rotella v. Wegmans Food Mkts., Inc., 626

Roth v. State University of New York, 132

Rothkopf v. Rothkopf, 613

Rothschild v. Carolina Coach Co., 915

Rothschild v. Finkelstein, 712

Rothschild v. Thompson, 232

Rothstein v. Tennessee Gas Pipeline Co., 84

Rouse v. Champion Home Builders Co., 533

Rovello v. Orofino Realty Co., Inc., 652, 653, 660, 1128

Rowell v. Gould, Inc., 132

Rowlee v. Dietrich, 620

Roy v. Hartogs, 44

Royal Business Funds Corp. v. Ehrlich, 1096

Royal Business Funds Corp. v. Rooster Plastics, Inc., 1234

Royal v. Brooklyn Union Gas Co., 1312

Rozz v. Law Offices of Saul Kobrick, P.C., 571

Rubano v. New York Tel. Co., 1375, 1380

Rubeo v. National Grange Mut. Ins. Co., 1344

Rubiano v. Kelly, 659

Rubin v. Deckelbaum, 490

Rubin v. Lesser, 743

Rubinfeld v. City of New York, 412

Rubino v. 330 Madison Co., LLC, 956

Rubino v. G. D. Searle & Co., 853

Rudd v. Cornell, 1094, 1096

Rudiger v. Coleman, 1348

Ruffin v. Lion Corp., 10, 141, 145, 195, 273

Rufino v. United States, 1301

Runcie v. Bankers Trust Co., 377

Runkel v. City of New York, 996

Runkel v. Homelsky, 1322

Rupert v. Sellers, 869, 1016, 1017

Ruppert v. Community Nat. Bank, 1266

Rush v. Savchuk, 287

Russ-Kap, Inc. v. Connolly, 157

Russo v. City of New York, 625

Russo v. Jess R. Rifkin, D.D.S., P.C., 987

Ruvolo v. Long Island R. Co., 1250

Ruzicka v. Rager, 544

Ryan v. Beavers, 418

Ryan v. Great Atlantic & Pac. Tea Co., 324

Ryan v. Michelsen, 828, 885

Ryan v. New York Telephone Co., 1113

Ryan v. State, 33

Ryan v. Town of Cortlandt, 608

Ryan, Matter of v. Nolan, 621, 1282

Ryder v. Travelers Ins. Co., 453

Rye, City of v. Public Service Mut. Ins. Co., 1284

S. & C. Clothing Co. v. United States Trucking Corporation, 344

S. T. Grand, Inc. v. City of New York, 1108

S.L. Benfica Transp., Inc. v. Rainbow Media, Inc., 693

Saastomoinen v. Pagano, 1034

Sabatino v. Capco Trading, Inc., 1086

Sabre, Inc. v. Paras Exims, Inc., 1068

Saccente v. Toterhi, 816

Sack v. Low, 125

Sacks v. Sacks, 278

Sacks v. Town of Thompson, 583

Safadjou v. Mohammadi, 190

Safier v. Cohl, 647

Sage Realty Corp. v. Proskauer Rose LLP, 665

Sager v. Sager, 948

Sagos v. O'Connell, 1384

Sailors' Snug Harbor in City of New York v. Tax Commission of City of New York, 1202

Sakow, In re, 781
Salander v. Central General Hosp., 840
Salem v. Seigel, 1045
Salemeh v. Toussaint ex rel. Local 100 Transp. Workers Union, 462
Salerno v. New York Cent. R. Co., 1345
Salmon, In re, 598
Saltzberg v. Kiamesha Concord, Inc., 1008, 1010
Sammy v. First American Title Ins. Co. of New York, 809, 835, 955
Sampson v. Lancaster, 456
Samuel v. Porchia, 982
San Jose, City of v. Superior Court, 355
Sanchez v. National R.R. Passenger Corp., 495, 567, 604
Sanfilipo v. Baptist Temple, Inc., 829
Santana v. City of New York, 673
Santangello v. People, 956
Santoli v. 475 Ninth Ave. Associates, LLC, 612
Santulli v. Englert, Reilly & McHugh, P.C., 71, 80
Sapichino v. City of New York, 907, 908
Sapp v. Propeller Co. LLC, 938
Saratoga County Chamber of Commerce, Inc. v. Pataki, 77, 1083
Sarno v. Florida East Coast Ry. Co., 243
Sartwell v. Field, 729, 745, 767
Save the Pine Bush, Inc. v. Common Council of City of Albany, 346
Savik, Murray & Aurora Const. Management Co., LLC v. ITT Hartford Ins. Group, 1085
Savino v. Demiglia, 59, 67
Sawh v. Bridges, 897
Sayeedi v. Walser, 236
Sbarra Real Estate, Inc. v. Lavelle-Tomko, 644
Scantlebury v. New York City Health and Hospitals Corp., 58, 61
Scarey v. Scarey, 1237
Scaringe v. Kinley, 571
Scaringi v. Elizabeth Broome Realty Corp., 133
Scattergood v. Jamaica Water Securities Corp., 660
Schabe v. Hampton Bays Union Free School Dist., 991
Schachter v. Massachusetts Protective Ass'n, 553
Schaeffer v. Schaeffer, 802
Schaffer v. City Bank Farmers Trust Co., 942
Schamber Chemical Co. v. Ross & Kominsky Plumbing & Heating Co., 1310
Schanback v. Schanback, 942
Schauer v. Joyce, 429
Scheckter v. Ryan, 721
Schein v. Chest Service Co., 1000
Schenck v. State Line Telephone Co., 525
Scheuering v. Scheuering, 619

Schickler v. Seifert, 929
Schiff v. Loomer, 1030
Schimansky v. Nelson, 715
Schindler v. Royal Ins. Co., 1108
Schipani v. McLeod, 1027
Schleimer v. Gross, 1234
Schmidt v. Board of Co-op. Educational Services of Nassau County, 64
Schmidt v. Merchants Despatch Transp. Co., 79, 83
Schneidman v. Schneidman, 271, 1254
Schoenefeld v. Schneiderman, 488
Schoenefeld v. State, 487, 1302
Scholastic Inc. v. Pace Plumbing Corp., 12, 67, 502, 509, 510, 513, 537, 553, 658
Schrank v. Lederman, 75
Schroeder v. City of New York, 294
Schultze v. Huttlinger, 999
Schulz v. Barrows, 699, 1072
Schuman v. Hertz Corp., 928
Schunk v. Schunk, 919
Schutzer v. Berger, 1061
Schuyler v. Perry, 1144
Schuyler v. State University of New York at Albany, 1378
Schuylkill Fuel Corp. v. B. & C. Nieberg Realty Corp., 525, 1089, 1091, 1098, 1118, 1131
Schwartz v. Binder, 335
Schwartz v. Goldberg, 1253
Schwartz v. Lois Associates, 75
Schwartz v. Mandelbaum & Gluck, 927
Schwartz v. New York City Housing Authority, 1325
Schwartz v. Public Adm'r of Bronx County, 121, 805, 1106, 1118, 1125, 1127, 1128, 1136, 1161
Schwartz v. Schwartz, 5
Schweber v. Berger, 492
Schwinger v. Hickok, 280
Sciara v. Surgical Associates of Western New York, P.C., 853
SCM Corp. v. Fisher Park Lane Co., 102, 1115
Scollo v. Good Samaritan Hosp., 845
Scott Shoe-Machinery Co. v. Dancel, 137
Scott v. Columbia Memorial Hosp., 924
Scott v. Vassar Bros. Hosp., 1282
Scott v. Westmore Fuel Co., Inc., 685, 963
Sea Trade Maritime Corp. v. Coutsodontis, 696
Seaman-Andwall Corp. v. Wright Mach. Corp., 694
Sears Roebuck & Co. v. Austin, 794
Sears, Roebuck & Co. v. Enco Associates, Inc., 79
Seattle Pacific Industries, Inc. v. Golden Valley Realty Associates, 874
Secor v. Sturgis, 530
Secreto v. International Business Machines Corp., 487

Security Nat. Bank v. Associated Hospital
    Service, 1192
Security Nat. Bank v. Village Mall at
    Hillcrest, Inc., 778, 779
Security Pacific Nat. Bank v. Evans, 349
Security Trust Co. of Rochester v. Magar
    Homes, a Div. of R. John Magar and Son
    Development Corp., 1242
Segway of New York, Inc. v. Udit Group,
    Inc., 697
Seidenberg v. Rosen, 886
Seider v. Roth, 287, 288, 1193
Seligson, Morris & Neuburger v. Fairbanks
    Whitney Corp., 982
Semenetz v. Sherling & Walden, Inc., 258
Seplow v. Century Operating Co., 769
Sequa Capital Corp. v. Nave, 1260
Serani v. Rowe, 568
Serio v. Rhulen, 582
Seth Rubenstein, P.C. v. Ganea, 1023
Severnoe Securities Corporation v. London
    & Lancashire Ins. Co., 1190
Shady Grove Orthopedic Associates, P.A. v.
    Allstate Ins. Co., 363
Shaffer v. Heitner, 214, 276, 277, 281, 292,
    305, 384, 736, 738, 761, 1185, 1213
Shaid v. Consolidated Edison Co. of New
    York, Inc., 637
Shakun v. Shakun, 1172
Shander v. Allen, 1384
Shanker v. 119 East 30th, Ltd., 175
Shanty Hollow Corp. v. Poladian, 594
Shapiro v. Shapiro, 1177
Shapiro, In re, 477
Shapolsky v. Shapolsky, 502, 553
Sharapata v. Town of Islip, 1035
Sharkey v. Locust Valley Marine, Inc., 590
Sharp Export Limited v. Mulco Products,
    Inc., 225
Sharrock v. Dell Buick-Cadillac, Inc., 732
Sharrow v. Dick Corp., 399, 970, 992, 1345
Sharrow v. Inland Lines, 67
Shaw v. Lewis, 344, 512
Shaw v. Shaw, 1064, 1065
Shea v. Johnson, 671
Sheerin v. New York Fire Dept. Articles 1
    and 1B Pension Funds, 1393
Sheftman v. Balfour Housing Corp., 402
Shelley v. Shelley, 1037
Shepard v. St. Agnes Hospital, 705
Sheridan Const. Corp., Application of, 777
Sherk v. Sherk, 524
Sherman v. Kirshman, 1198
Sherman v. M. Lowenstein & Sons, Inc.,
    820
Sherman v. Smith, 1006
Sherrer v. Sherrer, 304, 1111, 1154
Shine, Julianelle, Karp, Bozelko & Karazin,
    P.C. v. Rubens, 1072
Shipman v. City of New York Support
    Collection Unit, 1082
Shirley D. v. Carl D., 256

Sholes v. Meagher, 1283, 1289
Sholom & Zuckerbrot Realty Corp. v.
    Coldwell Banker Commercial Group, Inc.,
    665
Shtekla v. Topping, 1296
Shu Yiu Louie v. David & Chiu Place
    Restaurant, Inc., 742
Shulga v. Ashcroft, 680
Shumsky v. Eisenstein, 86, 91, 96
Shutt v. Shutt, 1238
Sibley v. Lake Anne Realty Corp., 132
Siegel v. Commack School Dist., 925
Siegel v. Northern Boulevard & 80th St.
    Corp., 761
Siegel v. Obes, 1323
Siegmund Strauss, Inc. v. East 149th
    Realty Corp., 1307, 1308
Siemens and Halske, GmbH. v. Gres, 954,
    1244, 1251
Sierra Club v. Village of Painted Post, 346
Sierra R. v. Jamaica Hosp. Medical Center,
    929
Silberberg v. Hotpoint Division of General
    Elec. Co., 815
Silberstein v. Silberstein, 1132
Silbert v. Silbert, 1209
Silver v. Great Am. Ins. Co., 46, 383
Silverstein v. Continental Cas. Co., 1086
Silvestris v. Silvestris, 521
Sim v. Farley Equipment Co. LLC, 665
Simcuski v. Saeli, 122
Simler v. Conner, 1085
Simmons v. Mercer, 710
Simon v. Lowenthal, 998, 1014
Simon v. Mehryari, 620
Simon v. Usher, 323
Simoneit v. Mark Cerrone, Inc., 681
Simonson v. International Bank, 221
Simpson v. Loehmann, 288, 289, 305, 1195
Simpson v. Wolansky, 1379
Sinclair v. Wieder, 1023
Singer v. Board of Educ. of City of New
    York, 1316
Singer v. Federated Dept. Stores, Inc., 78
Singh v. Mohamed, 635
Singh v. Singh, 869
Sinley v. Estco, Inc., 170, 468
Sinnott v. Feiock, 786
Sirlin Plumbing Co. v. Maple Hill Homes,
    Inc., 1294
Skagen v. New York City Emp. Retirement
    System, 435
Skaneateles Sav. Bank v. Modi Associates,
    108
Skoler v. Rimberg, 783
Skyline Agency, Inc. v. Ambrose Coppotelli,
    Inc., 309
Slate v. Schiavone Const. Co., 140, 565
Slater v. Gallman, 1080, 1340
Slavuter v. Slavuter, 619
Sloan v. Beard, 631

Slocum-Dickson Medical Group v. General Elec. Co., 1230
Slovik v. Wang, 706
Small v. Lorillard Tobacco Co., Inc., 366
Smiley, In re, 464
Smith v. Amherst Acres, Inc., 1204
Smith v. City of Troy, 924
Smith v. Coe, 533
Smith v. Giuffre Hyundai, Ltd., 157
Smith v. IG Second Generation Partners, L.P., 699
Smith v. Kirkpatrick, 525, 668, 1098
Smith v. Pach, 663
Smith v. Rentz, 960
Smith v. Robilotto, 808
Smith v. Russell Sage College, 526, 1099
Smith v. Sapienza, 433
Smith v. Schnabel, 915
Smith v. Scott, 58
Smith v. Town of Colonie, 1311
Smith v. Wilson, 184
Smith v. Witteman Co., 315
Smocum, People v., 974
Snegur v. Grupo Iberostar, 236
Sniadach v. Family Finance Corp. of Bay View, 730
Snyder v. Harris, 357
Soares v. Carter, 1376
Sochor v. International Business Machines Corp., 1249
Society Milion Athena v. National Bank of Greece, 361, 371
Society of New York Hospital v. Burstein, 1303
Society of New York Hospital v. Mogensen, 1041, 1336, 1339
Society of Plastics Industry, Inc. v. County of Suffolk, 346
Sol Lenzner Corp. v. Aetna Cas. & Sur. Co., 394
Solarino v. Noble, 574, 576
Solicitor for Affairs of His Majesty's Treasury v. Bankers Trust Co., 382
Solkav Solartechnik, G.m.b.H. (Besicorp Group, Inc.), Matter of, 8
Solnick v. Whalen, 1083
Solomon R. Guggenheim Foundation v. Lubell, 71, 85
Somberg v. Somberg, 1079
Somer & Wand, P.C. v. Rotondi, 171
Somerset R. R. Corp. v. Graham, 769
Sommer v. Federal Signal Corp., 394
Sommerfield v. Office of the Comptroller, 62
Sorge v. Parade Publications, Inc., 85
Sortino v. Fisher, 565, 919
Sosnowski v. Kolovas, 662
Soto v. Freda, 144, 562
Soto v. Soto, 470
Southampton, Town of v. Salten, 610
Sovereign Bank v. Calderone, 488
Spadaro v. Newark Ins. Co., 1086

Spatz Furniture Corp. v. Lee Letter Service, Inc., 1234
SPCA of Upstate New York, Inc. v. American Working Collie Ass'n, 228
Spector v. Berman, 164
Spectrum Systems Intern. Corp. v. Chemical Bank, 811, 812, 814, 819
Spielter v. North German Lloyd S.S. Co., 994
Spier v. Barker, 1147
Spindell v. Brooklyn Jewish Hospital, 668
Spinnell v. Doris L. Sassower, P.C., 45
Spitzer, People ex rel. v. Applied Card Systems, Inc., 1119
Spodek v. New York State Com'r of Taxation and Finance, 138
Spodek v. Park Property Development Associates, 1018
Sporn v. Hudson Transit Lines, 327
Sporn v. MCA Records, Inc., 71
Spring Valley, Village of v. Village of Spring Valley Housing Authority, 448
Springer v. Keith Clark Pub. Co., 1066
St. Clair v. Yonkers Raceway, Inc., 347
St. Hilaire v. White, 827
St. Paul Fire & Marine Ins. Co. v. Town of Hempstead, 576
Staatsburg Water Co. v. Staatsburg Fire Dist., 1114
Stafford Sec. Co. v. Kremer, 545
Stafford v. International Harvester Co., 125
Standard Fruit & S. S. Co. v. Waterfront Commission of New York Harbor, 955
Standard Wine & Liquor Co. v. Bombay Spirits Co., 230
Standifer v. Goord, 1363
Stanley Elec. Service, Inc. v. City of New York, 647
Stantec Consulting Group (Fonda-Fultonville Cent. School Dist.), In re, 82
Star Credit Corp. v. Ingram, 1065
Starbare II Partners, L.P. v. Sloan, 1247
Starr v. Johnsen, 661
Stassou v. Casini & Huang Const., Inc., 1018
State Bank of Albany v. Murray, 472
State Bd. of Equalization and Assessment v. Kerwick, 660
State Div. of Human Rights on Complaint of Geraci v. New York State Dept. of Correctional Services, 1371
State Div. of Human Rights v. State, 1082
State Farm Fire & Cas. Co. v. Tashire, 385
State Farm Ins. Co. v. Brother Transp., Inc., 319
State Farm Mut. Auto. Ins. Co. v. Mamadou, 1023
State Farm Mut. Auto. Ins. Co. v. Westlake, 434
State Police Administrative Disciplinary Hearing on April 27, In re, 950
State Tax Commission v. Shor, 1189

Stathos v. Murphy, 1184
Statter v. Statter, 1131, 1133, 1139
Stearns, People ex rel. v. Marr, 1171, 1173, 1179
Steck v. Colorado Fuel & Iron Co., 942
Stefaniw v. Cerrone, 490
Stein v. Wainwright's Travel Service, Inc., 924
Steinbach v. Relief Fire Ins. Co., 527
Steinberg v. Goodman, 671
Steinway, In re, 23
Stephan B. Gleich & Associates v. Gritsipis, 701
Sterling Fifth Associates v. Carpentille Corp., Inc., 491
Sterling Optical Co. v. University of State of N.Y., 1332
Stern v. Chemical Bank, 694, 695
Stern v. Four Points, 235
Stern v. Stern, 1288
Stern v. Worth, 167
Sternberg v. Sternberg, 943
Stewart v. Citimortgage, Inc., 1063
Stewart v. Keyes, 81
Stewart v. Volkswagen of America, Inc., 262
Stillman v. InService America Inc., 1023
Stilloe v. Contini, 89
Stines v. Hertz Corp., 752
Stoner v. Culligan, Inc., 531
Stora v. City of New York, 114
Stormville Mountain Homes, Inc. v. Zurhorst, 1047
Storrs v. Holcomb, 338, 657
Stowell v. Berstyn, 627, 688, 1288
Straub v. Yalamanchili, 884
Strawbridge v. Curtiss, 356, 385
Strong v. Reeves, 525, 1099
Strosberg v. Kiamesha Concord, Inc., 326
Students Challenging Regulatory Agency Procedures (SCRAP), United States v., 348
Studio A Showroom, LLC v. Yoon, 606
Sturcke v. Link, 752, 753
Stuyvesant v. Weil, 157
STX Panocean (UK) Co., Ltd. v. Glory Wealth Shipping Pte Ltd., 263
Suddin v. Lynbrook Gardens Co., 321
Suffolk Chiropractic Center v. Geico Ins. Co., 51
Sugar v. Curtis Circulation Co., 739
Suleiman v. Miamor Transp. Corp., 702, 709
Sullivan & Donovan, L.L.P. v. Bond, 601, 602
Sullivan v. Murphy, 355
Sullivan's Will, In re, 1109
Summerlin, United States v., 68
Summerville v. City of New York, 1328
Summit Const. Services Group, Inc. v. Act Abatement, LLC, 243
Sun Life Ins. and Annuity Co. of New York v. Braslow, 380

Sunrise Toyota, Ltd. v. Toyota Motor Co., 219
Supreme Automotive Mfg. Corp. v. Continental Cas. Co., 684
Supreme Tribe of Ben Hur v. Cauble, 354, 356
Svendsen v. Smith's Moving & Trucking Co., 734
Svenson v. Swegan, 1022
Swatzburg v. Swatzburg, 1201
Sweets' Estate v. Behrens, 769
Swezey v. Merrill Lynch, Pierce, Fenner & Smith, Inc., 341
Sybron Corp. v. Wetzel, 253
Syndicate Bldg. Corp. v. City University of New York, 1244
Syracuse Plaster Co. v. Agostini Bros. Bldg. Corp., 315
Syracuse, City of v. Hogan, 504
Szklowin v. Planning Bd. of Town of Blooming Grove, 1395
Szolosi v. Long Island R. Co., 554
T./P. Children, Matter of, 879, 890
T.E.A. Marine Automotive Corp. v. Scaduto, 181
T.R. America Chemicals, Inc. v. Seaboard Sur. Co., 107
Taca Intern. Airlines, S. A. v. Rolls-Royce of England, Limited, 217
Taconic Inn Corp. v. Holsapple, 314
Taft v. Shaffer Trucking, Inc., 428
Taieb v. Hilton Hotels Corp., 297
Tamburello v. Mooney, 120
Tamburo v. P & C Food Markets, Inc., 156
Tamimi v. Tamimi, 1063
Tanbro Fabrics Corp. v. Beaunit Mills, Inc., 330, 344
Tanger v. Ferrer, 937
Tannenbaum v. Mandell, 1006
Tashenberg v. Breslin, 318
Tatar v. Port Authority of New York and New Jersey, 663
Tate by McMahon v. Colabello, 522, 586, 983, 1008
Tate-Mitros v. MTA New York City Transit, 825
Tauza v. Susquehanna Coal Co., 214
Taylor v. Blair, 886
Taylor v. Interstate Motor Freight System, 46
Taylor v. John Doe, 874
Taylor v. New York City Housing Authority, 1288
Taylor v. Sturgell, 1153
Taylor, Application of, 836
Tcholakian v. Tcholakian, 1150
Tebedo v. Nye, 254
Teichman by Teichman v. Community Hosp. of Western Suffolk, 450
Teichman v. Ker, 569
Teitelbaum Holdings, Ltd. v. Gold, 492, 715
Teitler v. Tetenbaum, 937

Tejeda v. Dyal, 907

Telaro v. Telaro, 1313

Teleprompter Manhattan CATV Corp. v. State Bd. of Equalization and Assessment, 448

Temporary State Commission on Living Costs and Economy v. Bergman, 957

Tender Loving Care Agency, Inc. v. Hladun, 652

Tenenbaum v. Setton, 137

Tener v. Cremer, 869, 870, 871, 872, 877

Terio v. Spodek, 617

Terman v. Gonta, 1120

Terner v. Terner, 1335

Terry v. Munger, 527

Terwilliger v. Terwilliger, 1137

Testa v. Wickham, 1379, 1380

Teuch v. Murphy, 1403

Tewari v. Tsoutsouras, 11, 198

Textile Technology Exchange, Inc. v. Davis, 303, 667

Thayer v. McNaughton, 942

The Bank Bldg. v. Mehling, 690

Thelma Sanders & Associates, Inc. v. Hague Development Corp., 781

Thermoid Co. v. Fabel, 167

Therm-X-Chemical & Oil Corp. v. Extebank, 1186

Thoma v. Ronai, 681

Thomas v. Alleyne, 828

Thomas v. Washington Gas Light Co., 1113

Thome v. Benchmark Main Transit Associates, LLC, 535

Thompson v. City of New York, 1303

Thompson v. Cuadrado, 659

Thompson v. Iannucci, 655

Thompson v. Mather, 852

Thompson v. Raymond Kramer, Inc., 454

Thompson v. Swiantek, 829

Thompson-Starrett Co. v. Otis Elevator Co., 394

Thornton v. Montefiore Hosp., 1056, 1214, 1327

Thorp v. Adams, 167

Thrasher v. U.S. Liability Ins. Co., 189

Thropp v. Erb, 760

Tienken v. Benedictine Hosp., 825

Tiernan v. Missouri New York World's Fair Commission, 166

Tierney v. State, 32

Tiffany At Westbury Condominium v. Marelli Development Corp., 937, 938

Tilden Financial Corp. v. Corwin, 1231

Tillman v. Guaranty Trust Co. of New York, 85

Tintner v. Marangi, 916

Tirado v. Miller, 643, 907

Tirschwell v. Dolan, 1011

Title Guarantee & Trust Co. v. Hicks, 101

Titus v. Poole, 110

Tjepkema v. Kenney, 306, 647

Toal v. Staten Island University Hosp., 836

Tobia v. Town of Rockland, 156

Todd Mart, Inc. v. Town Bd. of Town of Webster, 1373

Todd-Buick v. Smith, 729

Toledo v. Iglesia Ni Christo, 1017, 1021

Tollin v. Elleby, 1062

Tomasino v. William Morrow & Co., Inc., 85

Tomassi v. Town of Union, 978

Tomeo v. Beccia, 496

Tonawanda Seneca Nation v. Noonan, 1389

Toner v. Constable, 994

Tonkonogy v. Jaffin, 1343

Tooley v. Bacon, 980

Torres v. Board of Educ. of City of New York, 856

Torres v. Jones, 705

Totero v. World Telegram Corp., 187

Totten, In re, 1187

Tower v. Chemical Bank, 881

Town Bd. of Town of Fallsburgh v. National Sur. Corp., 575

Towne v. Asadourian, 1094

Tran v. New Rochelle Hosp. Medical Center, 805, 817

Traub v. Dinzler, 387

Travelers Indem. Co. of Illinois v. Nnamani, 315, 1389

Travelers Indem. Co. v. United Diagnostic Imaging, P.C., 836

Travelers' Ins. Co. v. Mulligan, 567

Travis v. Cuff, 930

Tray v. Thaler & Gertler, LLP, 1082

Trecot v. Taxter, 1105

Treen Motors Corporation v. Van Pelt, 569, 571

Treinies v. Sunshine Mining Co., 1155

Treitel v. Arnold Chait, Ltd., 1068

Tri City Roofers, Inc. v. Northeastern Indus. Park, 1054

Tribolati v. Lippman, 1289

Trimboli v. Scarpaci Funeral Home, Inc., 335, 1020

Tri-State Pipe Lines Corp. v. Sinclair Refining Co., 1030

Troy Police Benev. and Protective Ass'n, Inc. (City of Troy), Matter of, 1326

Troy Sand & Gravel Co., Inc. v. Town of Nassau, 806

Tsomis v. Benenson, 1030

Tuper v. Tuper, 74, 519

Turner v. CSX Transportation, Inc., 1028

Turner, People v., 1103

Turuseta v. Wyassup-Laurel Glen Corp., 984

Twiddy v. Standard Marine Transport Services, Inc., 581

Twitchell v. MacKay, 523

Two Eleven Co. v. Harrison, 1372

U. R. C. Inc. v. Applied Images Inc., 1191

U.S. Bancorp Mortg. Co. v. Bonner Mall Partnership, 1095

U.S. Bank Nat. Ass'n v. GreenPoint Mortgage Funding, Inc., 845, 879, 880

U.S. Fidelity & Guaranty Co. v. E. W. Smith Co., 123

Udel v. Udel, 1255

Ugarriza v. Schmieder, 680

Ultrashmere House, Ltd. v. 38 Town Associates, 328

Underpinning & Foundation Constructors, Inc. v. Chase Manhattan Bank, N.A., 653

Ungewitter v. Toch, 522

Unicon Management Corp. v. Koppers Co., 260

Unique Ideas, Inc., State v., 1174

Unitarian Universalist Church of Central Nassau v. Shorten, 448, 453

United Bank Ltd. v. Cambridge Sporting Goods Corp., 859, 866

United Enterprises, Ltd. v. Hill, 647

United Equity Services, Inc. v. First Am. Title Ins. Co. of New York, 669

United Jewish Appeal-Federation of Jewish Philanthropies of New York, Inc. v. Young Men's and Young Women's Hebrew Ass'n, Inc., 602

United Mine Workers of America, United States v., 259

United Services Auto. Ass'n v. Graham, 453

United Services Auto. Ass'n v. Kungel, 145

United States Printing & Lithograph Co. v. Powers, 1045

Unterberg v. Scarsdale Imp. Corp., 43

Urbach v. City of New York, 404

US Bank Nat. Ass'n v. Konstantinovic, 704

Usher v. Usher, 317, 661

V. Loewer's Gambrinus Brewing Co. v. Lithauer, 1229

V.L. v. E.L., 695, 1063, 1074, 1154

Vaage v. Lewis, 50, 290

Vadala v. Carroll, 1305

Vail v. Quinlan, 1175

Valdimer v. Mount Vernon Hebrew Camps, Inc., 473

Valentino v. State, 32

Valerio v. College Point Sav. Bank, 1190

Valstrey Service Corp. v. Board of Elections, Nassau County, 391

Valz v. Sheepshead Bay Bungalow Corporation, 157

Van Patten v. Sylvia, 1040

Van Vooren v. Cook, 468

Vance Boiler Works, Inc. v. Co-Operative Feed Dealers, Inc., 1218

Vandenburgh v. Columbia Memorial Hosp., 819

Vander v. Casperson, 304, 1110

Vanderbilt v. Vanderbilt, 1111

Vandermark v. Jotomo Corp., 661

Vandermast v. New York City Transit Authority, 61

Vanderveer v. Magedson, 711

VanDyke v. Jefferson Anesthesiology, P.C., 863

Vanneck v. Vanneck, 1156

Vargas v. City of New York, 882

Varkonyi v. S. A. Empresa De Viacao Airea Rio Grandense (Varig), 47

Varner v. Winfield, 830

Varsity Transit, Inc. v. Board of Educ. of City of New York, 58

Vasquez v. Soto, 678

Vasquez v. Superior Court, 355

Vastola v. Maer, 103

Vaughns v. Kirkland, 644

Vavolizza v. Krieger, 1096, 1099, 1108

Vazquez v. Beharry, 557

Vega v. Mount Sinai-NYU Medical Center and Health System, 829

Vega v. Restani Const. Corp., 670, 671, 683

Velasquez v. Pine Grove Resort Ranch, Inc., 332

Velazquez v. Water Taxi, Inc., 1116

Velez v. Craine & Clark Lumber Corp., 77, 87

Velez v. Hunts Point Multi-Service Center, Inc., 873, 876

Velez v. Port Authority of New York and New Jersey, 320

Venizelos v. Venizelos, 491

Vera v. Republic of Cuba, 264

Verbanic v. Nyquist, 1078

Vergari v. Pierre Productions, Inc., 765

Verizon New England, Inc. v. Transcom Enhanced Services, Inc., 1196

Vernon v. Vernon, 1156

Vertex Standard USA, Inc. v. Reichert, 1157

Vickers v. Home Federal Sav. and Loan Ass'n of East Rochester, 361, 363, 368, 369

Vickery v. Village of Saugerties, 623, 1044

Victor Auto Parts, Inc. v. Cuva, 157

Victorson v. Bock Laundry Mach. Co., 77, 87

Vidal v. Sheffield Farms Co., 328

Video Corp. of America v. Frederick Flatto Associates, Inc., 80

Viggiano v. Viggiano, 1188

Vigilant Ins. Co. of America v. Housing Authority of City of El Paso, Tex., 69

Vigo S. S. Corp. v. Marship Corp. of Monrovia, 330

Vilas v. Plattsburgh & M.R. Co., 309

Villa v. Vetuskey, 861

Villafane v. Banner, 466

Vinal v. New York Cent. R. Co., 905

Vincent v. Seaman, 783, 868

Vincent v. Thompson, 1139, 1152

Vinlis Const. Co. v. Roreck, 938, 939, 940

Viscosi v. Merritt, 132

Vista Surgical Supplies, Inc. v. Travelers Ins. Co., 497

Viviane Etienne Medical Care, P.C. v. Country-Wide Ins. Co., 682, 684, 857, 874

Volkswagenwerk Aktiengesellschaft v. Schlunk, 273

Von Arx, A. G. v. Breitenstein, 54

von Engelbrechten v. Galvanoni & Nevy Bros., Inc., 1158

VOOM HD Holdings LLC v. EchoStar Satellite L.L.C., 876, 896, 898

Voss v. Netherlands Ins. Co., 683

Vrooman v. Vrooman, 318

VSL Corp. v. Dunes Hotels and Casinos, Inc., 50

W. T. Grant Co. v. Srogi, 112

W. T. Grant Co. v. Uneeda Doll Co., 395, 513

W. T. Wang, Inc. v. New York State Dept. of Taxation and Finance, 1080

W. U. Tel. Co. v. Com. of Pa., by Gottlieb, 383

Wachtel v. Diamond State Engineering Corporation, 28

Wagner v. Cornblum, 694

Wahler v. Thompson, 267

Wahrhaftig v. Space Design Group, Inc., 908, 1333

Walborsky v. Wolf, 862

Walden v. Fiore, 216, 246, 563

Waldman v. Allen, 586

Waldman v. Cohen, 990

Waldo v. Schmidt, 22

Waljohn Waterstop, Inc. v. Webster, 165

Walker Memorial Baptist Church v. Saunders, 768

Walker v. Foreman, 711

Walker v. Walker, 1176

Wallace v. Ford, 612

Wallace v. McDonald, 355

Wallace v. Merrill Lynch Capital Services, Inc., 664

Wallace, Estate of Matter of, 837, 839

Wally G. ex rel. Yoselin T. v. New York City Health and Hospitals Corp., 56, 60

Walsh v. Andorn, 1076

Walsh v. New York State Liquor Authority, 767

Walston & Co. v. Klein, 1105

Walton v. New York State Dept. of Correctional Services, 1392

Walton v. Strong Memorial Hosp., 94

Wandschneider v. Bekeny, 1052, 1224, 1273

Wang v. Bartel, 1211, 1268

Ward v. City of Schenectady, 537

Ward v. Mehar, 840

Ware v. Grossman, 492

Ware v. Manhattan and Bronx Surface Transit Operating Authority, 176

Wargo v. Wargo, 948, 949

Warner v. Buffalo Drydock Co., 383

Warner v. Bumgarner, 899

Warner v. Orange County Regional Medical Center, 904

Warren v. Delaney, 1239

Warren v. Monroe County, 1120

Warsowe Acquisition Corp. v. DeNoble, 656

Washington v. Borough of Manhattan Community College, 61

Wasielewski v. Town of Cheektowaga, 925

Wasserman v. Wasserman, 271

Watchtower Bible & Tract Soc., Inc., People ex rel. v. Haring, 1103

Waterside Associates v. New York State Dept. of Environmental Conservation, 1391

Watkins v. Board of Educ. of Port Jefferson Union Free School Dist., 8

Watso v. City of New York, 103

Watts v. Phillips-Jones Corporation, 351

Watts v. Swiss Bank Corp., 1120

Waverly Central School Dist., State v., 57, 68

Way v. George Grantling Chemung Contracting Corp., 389

Webb & Knapp v. United Cigar-Whelan Stores Corp., 633

Webb v. Greater New York Auto. Dealers Ass'n, Inc., 488

Webb v. Tire and Brake Distributor, Inc., 888

Weber v. Kowalski, 39, 911

Weicker v. Weicker, 553, 554

Weidenfeld v. Keppler, 1372

Weigel v. Cook, 528

Weill v. Erickson, 182, 613

Weinbaum's Estate, In re, 637

Weinberg v. Hertz Corp., 365

Weingrad & Weingrad v. Kevelson, 1342

Weinheimer v. Hoffman, 430

Weinstein v. Gindi, 849

Weinstein v. Gitters, 1239

Weinstein v. Haft, 619

Weisgold v. Kiamesha Concord, Inc., 818

Weiss v. Deloitte & Touche, LLP, 636

Weiss v. Glatt Pack Kosher, Inc., 174

Weissman v. Sinorm Deli, Inc., 694, 699

Wells Fargo Bank Minnesota, Nat. Ass'n v. Mastropaolo, 646

Wells Fargo Bank, N.A. v. Buffenmyer, 929

Wells Fargo Bank, N.A. v. Daskal, 704

Wells Fargo Bank, N.A. v. Eitani, 111, 705

Wells Fargo Bank, N.A. v. Frierson, 621

Wells Fargo Bank, N.A. v. Gerasimou, 580

Wells, Fargo & Co. v. Davis, 1026

Wendell v. Supermarkets General Corp., 1009

Werfel v. Agresta, 1386

Werner Spitz Const. Co. v. Vanderlinde Elec. Corp., 102

Wesco Ins. Co. v. Vinson, 144

West v. Aetna Cas. & Sur. Co., 800

West v. City of New York, 157

Westchester Joint Water Works v. Assessor of City of Rye, 112

Western Elevating Ass'n v. Chapman, 875

Western Printing & Lithographing Co. v. McCandlish, 1366
Westwood Associates v. Deluxe General, Inc., 47
Whalen v. Kawasaki Motors Corp., 442
Wharton v. 241 Corp., 297
Wharton v. Wharton, 646, 647
Whelan v. Gorton, 960
Whitaker v. Whitaker, 233
White House Manor, Ltd. v. Benjamin, 494
White v. Adler, 531
Whiteman Osterman & Hanna, LLP v. Albany-Troy Neurosurgical Associates, P.C., 578
Whitfield v. City of New York, 1295
Whitfield v. State, 589
Whitlow v. Martin, 871
Wickham v. Liberty Mut. Ins. Co., 309
Wickham v. Socony Mobil Oil Co., 813
Wickwire Spencer Steel Co. v. Kemkit Scientific Corporation, 1220
Widder Bros. Inc. v. Kaffee, 1253
Wilaka Const. Co. v. New York City Housing Authority, 1294
Wilcox v. Winter, 635
Wild v. Bartol, 1298
Wildeb Rest., Inc. v. Jolin Restaurant, Inc., 700
Wilder v. Silbert, 943, 946
Wilkinson v. British Airways, 868
Wilkinson v. Skinner, 682, 686
Willette v. Willette, 604
William A. White & Sons v. Scott, 756
William H. Van Vleck, Inc. v. Klein, 1317
William Iselin & Co. v. Burgess & Leigh Limited, 1271
William Iser, Inc. v. Garnett, 210, 782
William L. Bonnell Co. v. Katz, 221
Williams by Williams v. Niske by Niske, 442
Williams ex rel. Fowler v. Nassau County Medical Center, 59
Williams v. Brooklyn Elevated R. Co., 981
Williams v. City of New York, 335
Williams v. D. A. H. Const. Corp., 428
Williams v. Long Island R. R., 522
Williams v. New York City Health and Hospitals Corp., 444
Williams v. State of North Carolina, 277, 1110, 1154
Williams v. Sterling Estates, Inc., 1008
Williams, In re, 1104
Williamson ex rel. Lipper Convertibles, L.P. v. PricewaterhouseCoopers LLP, 91
Willis v. McKinnon, 1149
Willmark Service System, Inc., In re, 22, 599
Willsey v. Strawway, 1120
Wilson v. Galicia Contracting & Restoration Corp., 899
Wilson v. Garcia, 70
Wilson v. Iseminger, 81

Wilson v. Lufthansa German Airlines, 809
Wilton v. Seven Falls Co., 649
Windhurst v. Town of Thompson, 323
Windy Ridge Farm v. Assessor of Town of Shandaken, 341, 657
Wings & Wheels Exp. Inc. v. Sisak, 389
Winters v. Gould, 1033
Wirt v. Reid, 992
Wisconsin v. Pelican Ins. Co., State of, 1104
Wiseman v. American Motors Sales Corp., 832, 863
Wishni v. Taylor, 191
Wolf Popper Ross Wolf & Jones, Application of, 837
Wolff v. Laverne Inc., 919
Wolfson v. Nassau County Medical Center, 890, 893
Wolin v. St. Vincent's Hosp. and Medical Center of New York, 844, 887
Wolodkowicz v. Seewell Corp., 829, 831
Wolowitz, State v., 1306
Women in City Government United v. City of New York, 853
Wood v. Ford, 1053, 1059
Woodard v. Motor Vehicle Acc. Indemnification Corp., 998
Woodburn Court Associates I v. Wingate Management Co., Inc., 460
Woods v. Interstate Realty Co., 54
Woods v. M.B.D. Community Housing Corp., 139
Woods v. New York City Dept. of Sanitation, 61
Woodson v. Mendon Leasing Corp., 707, 708, 1059
Woodward v. Eighmie Moving & Storage, Inc., 707
Wooton's Estate, In re, 1240
Wordie v. Chase Manhattan Bank, N.A., 1217
Workman v. Amato, 1068
Workmen's Compensation Fund, In re, 1077
World Trade Center Bombing Litigation, In re, 811, 812, 1067
Worldwide Carriers Limited v. Aris S. S. Co., 752, 753
World-Wide Volkswagen Corp. v. Woodson, 223, 249, 284
Wright v. Farlin, 557
Wright v. L. C. Defelice & Son, Inc., 928
Wuchter v. Pizzutti, 188, 1176
Wyandanch Volunteer Fire Co., Inc. v. Randon Const. Corp., 87
Wyatt v. City of New York, 159
Wydallis v. U.S. Fidelity & Guar. Co., 112
Wygocki v. Milford Plaza Hotel, 849
Wyman v. Morone, 522
Wyoming County Bank & Trust Co. v. Kiley, 1202
Xi Yu v. New York University Medical Center, 970
Xiao Yang Chen v. Fischer, 1100

Yamamoto v. Costello, 1253
Yardarm Club Hotel, Inc. v. Morgan, 581
Yarusso v. Arbotowicz, 117
Yearwood v. Yearwood, 465
Yellow Creek Hunting Club, Inc. v. Todd
    Supply, Inc., 1224
Yesuvida v. Pennsylvania R. Co., 52
Yetta's Rest., Inc. v. State Liquor Authority,
    1401
Yonkers Contracting Co., Inc. v. Port
    Authority Trans-Hudson Corp., 107
Yonkers Fur Dressing Co. v. Royal Ins. Co.,
    492, 715
Yorktown Central School Dist. No. 2 v.
    Yorktown Congress of Teachers ("YCT"),
    1172
Young v. Franklyn, 508
Young v. New York City Health & Hospitals
    Corp., 90
Young v. Young, 638
Young, People v., 970
Younger v. Harris, 1175
Yu Hui Chen v. Chen Li Zhi, 849
Yun Tung Chow v. Reckitt & Colman, Inc.,
    683
Zabriskie v. Zoloto, 1119, 1132
Zahn v. International Paper Co., 357
Zaidi v. New York Bldg. Contractors, Ltd.,
    611
Zakarias v. Radio Patents Corp., 836
Zamir v. Hilton Hotels Corp., 856
Zarnoch v. Luckina, 663
Zausner v. Fotochrome, Inc., 515
Zegarelli v. Hughes, 817, 869
Zellman v. Metropolitan Transp. Authority,
    829
Zelman, Estate of v. Scibelli, 721
Zemo Leasing Corp. v. Bank of New York,
    1241
Zenatello v. Pons, 738
Zenith Bathing Pavilion v. Fair Oaks S.S.
    Corporation, 743
Zerilli-Edelglass v. New York City Transit
    Authority, 123
Zgrodek v. McInerney, 974
Zilken v. Leader, 862
Zillman v. Meadowbrook Hospital Co., Inc.,
    430
Zimmerman v. Mingo, 212
Ziperman v. Frontier Hotel of Las Vegas,
    229
Zletz v. Wetanson, 897
Zona v. Oatka Restaurant and Lounge, Inc.,
    430
Zottola v. AGI Group, Inc., 238
Zubulake v. UBS Warburg LLC, 870, 871,
    880, 896
Zuckerman v. 234–6 W. 22 Street Corp.,
    109
Zuckerman v. City of New York, 429, 682
Zurich Ins. Co. v. White, 393
Zwaal, United States v., 179

Table of Statutes and CPLR Citations

**NEW YORK, MCKINNEY'S
CONSTITUTION**

Art. I, § 2 .... 932, 933, 1166
Art. I, § 18 934
Art. VI 24
Art. VI, § 1(a) 23
Art. VI, § 1(c) 18, 23, 29, 30, 31, 36,
   38, 954
Art. VI, § 2(a) 20
Art. VI, § 3 ....1282, 1291, 1304
Art. VI, § 3(a) 20
Art. VI, § 3(b) 20, 1300
Art. VI, § 3(b)(2) 21, 1293
Art. VI, § 3(b)(4) 1300
Art. VI, § 3(b)(9) 21, 1301
Art. VI, § 4(b) 21
Art. VI, § 5(b) 1281
Art. VI, § 6(c) 23
Art. VI, § 6(e) 146
Art. VI, § 7(b) 24, 469
Art. VI, § 8 27
Art. VI, § 8(c) 27
Art. VI, § 8(d) 1285
Art. VI, § 9 31
Art. VI, § 10 27
Art. VI, § 11(a) 27
Art. VI, § 11(b) 29
Art. VI, § 12(a) 29
Art. VI, § 12(c) 29
Art. VI, § 13(a) 30
Art. VI, § 13(c) 30
Art. VI, § 14 29
Art. VI, § 15(a) 33, 34
Art. VI, § 15(b) 33, 34
Art. VI, § 16(b) 36
Art. VI, § 16(c) 36
Art. VI, § 16(d) 35, 36
Art. VI, § 16(h) 35
Art. VI, § 17(a) 36
Art. VI, § 18(a) 967
Art. VI, § 19(b) 28, 40
Art. VI, § 19(d) 40
Art. VI, § 19(e) 40
Art. VI, § 19(f) 40
Art. VI, § 19(i) 40
Art. VI, § 19(k) 912
Art. VI, § 20(a) 18, 38
Art. VI, § 20(c) 38
Art. VI, § 26(a) 603
Art. VI, § 28(a) 8
Art. VI, § 28(b) 8
Art. VI, § 28(c) 8
Art. VI, § 30 1033
Art. VI, § 35(a) 1389
Art. XLI 932

**NEW YORK, MCKINNEY'S
AGRICULTURE AND MARKETS LAW**

§ 121 .... 1353, 1356

**NEW YORK, MCKINNEY'S
BANKING LAW**

§ 14–a 1025
§ 14–a(1) 1026
§ 200(a) 264

**NEW YORK, MCKINNEY'S BUSINESS
CORPORATION LAW**

Art. 12 777
§ 304 .... 175, 220, 261, 263, 264
§§ 304–307 5
§ 306 .... 175, 195, 262, 274, 297
§ 306(b) 220
§ 307 .... 175, 195, 213, 262, 264, 274
§ 307(b) 262
§ 626 375
§ 1118 941
§ 1301 221
§ 1301(b) 221
§ 1304(b) 52
§ 1312 .... 53, 221, 516
§ 1312(a) 54
§ 1314 .... 51, 52, 53, 221
§ 1314(a) 51
§ 1314(b) 51, 52
§ 1314(b)(5) 52

NEW YORK CIVIL PRACTICE ACT

§ 19 183
§ 34 69
§ 48(2) 71
§ 181 919
§ 193 337
§ 195 355
§ 210 349
§ 212(1) 344
§ 212(2) 1014
§ 227 183
§ 237–a 299, 301
§ 241 500
§ 262 .... 541, 652
§§ 285 et seq. 379
§ 288 799
§ 473 1076
§ 580 1312
§ 679(1) 1265
§ 684 .... 1211, 1227
§ 687 1184
§ 687(a)(1) 1193
§ 687–a 1184
§ 688 1184
§ 781 1220
§ 1093 786
§ 1300 .... 1367, 1402

NEW YORK, MCKINNEY'S CIVIL
PRACTICE LAW AND RULES
(CPLR)

Art. 4 1177
Art. 5 .... 315, 1356
Art. 9 358
Art. 12 170
Art. 14 .... 421, 425, 947
Art. 14–A... 421
Art. 16 .... 406, 411, 947
Art. 31 791
Art. 50–A... 1014
Art. 50–B... 1014
Art. 52 .... 1051, 1267
Art. 55 1329
Art. 64 777
Art. 70 153
Art. 75 .... 25, 154
Art. 78 .... 73, 150, 153, 1372
101.....................3, 4, 29, 30, 31, 34, 36, 763,
    1029, 1069, 1355, 1356
103(a) 6, 1166
103(b) 7, 107, 447, 1082, 1209,
    1251, 1272, 1352, 1355, 1356
103(c)..............7, 8, 62, 699, 839, 1078, 1080,
    1177, 1247, 1353, 1372, 1385, 1403
104...........9, 10, 11, 729, 731, 745, 747, 1220
105...................4, 10, 255, 278, 286, 314, 321,
    343, 466, 568, 737, 756, 940, 946, 1190,
    1202, 1226
105(b) 7, 107, 146, 1352
105(e) 146
105(f) 151, 153, 154
105(j) 117, 168
105(p) 150
105(s–1)...................................... 762, 1267
105(u) 495, 567, 604, 744, 769
107...................................... 12, 505
201....................................12, 66, 68, 82, 107
202....................116, 123, 124, 125, 126, 291
203.. 103
203(a) 83, 98, 1018
203(b) 100, 568
203(b)(5).. 101
203(c)............................98, 99, 103, 104, 105
203(d) 101, 102, 103, 104, 107
203(f) 103, 104, 105, 107, 110, 111,
    122, 564, 579
203(g) 84, 95, 96, 525
204(a) 108, 109
204(b) 109
205(a) 104, 109, 110, 111, 112, 113,
    114, 115, 116, 125, 126, 131, 137, 260,
    557, 561, 565, 651, 658, 693, 705, 716,
    900, 920, 922, 923, 927, 928, 1097
206(a)(2) 85
206(b) 96
206(d) 108
207.. 117
207(1) 183
207(3) 117, 183

208 .... 90, 93, 117, 118, 119, 120
209 120
209(c) 81
210 120
210(a) 97, 120
210(b) 121, 158
211 68
211(b) 68, 69, 72, 1070, 1209, 1211, 1221
212 69
212(a) 69
213 .... 69, 576
213(1).............. 69, 70, 71, 75, 76, 77, 1083,
    1084, 1355
213(2)............ 69, 71, 72, 79, 80, 85, 96, 101,
    397, 527, 1355
213(8) 79, 95, 525
214 .... 70, 73, 75
214(2) 71, 79
214(3) 71
214(4) 70, 71, 79, 86, 527
214(5) 70, 73, 77
214(6) 71, 72, 73, 79, 80, 81, 88, 91, 96
214(c)(4).. 84
214–a 73, 75, 84, 88, 89, 94, 95, 101,
    119, 651
214–c.................... 79, 81, 83, 84, 95, 97, 405
214–c(1) 83
214–c(2) 83, 84
214–c(3) 84
214–c(4) 84
214–c(5) 84, 95
214–d 71
215 73
215(3) 73, 85
215(5) 73
216 .... 382, 383
216(a)(1).. 382
216(a)(2).. 382
216(a)(3).. 382
216(b).. 383
217 .... 77, 195, 1360
217(1) 73, 1083, 1354, 1355, 1390, 1391,
    1392, 1393, 1394
217–a 68, 75
241(6).. 72, 86
301 .... 52, 54, 117, 128, 211, 212, 213,
    219, 229, 235, 247, 263, 269, 272, 274,
    283, 563
302 ..... 52, 117, 128, 167, 183, 193, 212, 215,
    216, 219, 220, 223, 224, 225, 229, 237,
    238, 240, 244, 247, 251, 257, 258, 260,
    261, 262, 264, 266, 267, 270, 274, 277,
    278, 279, 283, 308, 383, 384, 385, 573,
    655, 664, 944, 1310
302(a) 224, 225, 227, 231, 232, 234, 235,
    238, 239, 244, 245, 251, 260, 262, 269
302(a)(1).......... 187, 216, 225, 226, 227, 228,
    229, 230, 231, 233, 234, 235, 236, 237,
    238, 239, 240, 241, 242, 243, 244, 252,
    253, 279, 280, 284, 642
302(a)(2).... 188, 243, 244, 245, 257, 267, 268

302(a)(3) 235, 244, 245, 246, 247, 249, 250, 251, 252, 253, 254
302(a)(3)(i)................................ 246, 248, 251
302(a)(3)(ii) 246, 251, 252, 253, 254, 284, 563
302(a)(4) 255, 279, 280, 339
302(b) 30, 233, 255, 256, 257, 277, 293
302(c)....................................... 257, 308, 573
302(d) 238, 239
303...................................... 167, 265, 266
304.....................66, 101, 130, 192, 751, 902
304(a) 98, 99, 116, 130, 138, 201, 597, 772, 1355, 1359, 1360
304(b) 138, 1363
305(a) 105, 106, 135, 145, 158, 160, 321, 351, 353, 516, 889
305(b) 26, 99, 130, 131, 132, 133, 134, 135, 136, 138, 144, 159, 161, 192, 300, 301, 307, 508, 509, 524, 555, 556, 560, 561, 573, 655, 700, 706, 836, 1360
305(c)..................................156, 157, 158, 159
306.. 208, 706
306(a) 209
306(b) 209
306(c)...................................... 183, 184, 209
306(d) 208
306(e) 208
306–a(b) 208
306–b..................98, 116, 130, 138, 139, 140, 141, 149, 150, 179, 182, 189, 209, 286, 294, 461, 464, 565, 698, 748, 753, 782, 794, 873, 1360, 1363, 1393, 1395
307.. 128, 176
308....117, 128, 149, 160, 161, 163, 164, 165, 172, 177, 178, 179, 180, 182, 183, 184, 186, 191, 192, 195, 209, 210, 268, 269, 272, 274, 280, 294, 480, 487, 561, 613, 614, 697, 709, 712, 748, 791, 953, 955, 1227, 1228, 1243, 1310, 1361
308 et seq. 128
308(1) 161, 163, 164, 177, 178, 179, 181, 187, 191, 295, 697, 953
308(2) 116, 140, 161, 163, 164, 172, 173, 175, 178, 179, 180, 181, 182, 183, 186, 187, 191, 196, 486, 662, 697, 782, 1362
308(3) 161, 178, 179, 182, 183, 186, 191, 261, 272, 295
308(4) 116, 140, 161, 178, 180, 182, 183, 184, 185, 186, 187, 191, 486, 662
308(5) 117, 140, 141, 161, 171, 177, 185, 187, 188, 189, 190, 191, 192, 268, 294, 295, 409, 461, 562, 597, 1250
308(6) 182, 186
309.............................163, 177, 193, 468, 470
309(a) 168, 169, 173, 181, 350, 468
309(b) 169, 468
309(c).. 169, 468
310..........................160, 163, 170, 172, 1050
310(a) 170
310–a... 170, 171
310–a(a) 170, 171

310–a(b) 171
310–a(c) 171
311 .... 163, 176, 177, 191, 748, 955
311(1) 163
311(4) 562
311(a).........................58, 175, 176, 177, 272
311(a)(1)... 160, 163, 172, 174, 176, 177, 213, 220, 697, 955
311(a)(4)... 176
311(b).............................. 141, 191, 409, 597
311–a...171, 955
312.. 176
312–a 161, 164, 169, 170, 178, 181, 193, 195, 208, 480, 561, 562, 706, 953, 1361
312–a(a) 193
312–a(b)..194, 208
312–a(c) 193
312–a(d) 193
312–a(e) 194
312–a(f) 194
313 ..... 29, 117, 128, 161, 165, 169, 181, 188, 195, 212, 213, 225, 256, 269, 272, 273, 274, 280, 390
314 ... 117, 193, 277, 278, 280, 286, 294, 383, 656, 791
314(1)........................... 192, 256, 257, 277
314(2)..279, 384
314(3) 280, 285, 286, 293, 742, 746, 747, 748, 749, 754, 788
315 .... 192, 294, 656, 747
316 .... 294, 295, 747
316(a)...295, 706
316(b)..295
317 .... 189, 295, 296, 297, 298, 1060, 1061, 1070
318 .... 179, 182, 183, 261, 295, 1215, 1228
320(a) 133, 181, 299, 300, 304, 351, 489, 491, 554, 555, 658, 662, 697, 1386
320(b)..301
320(c) 289, 291, 292, 305
320(c)(1) 305, 308, 748, 759
320(c)(2) 301, 306, 307
320(d)...300
3201 717
321(a)...308
321(b)................................... 92, 309, 479
321(b)(2)..309
321(c)...310
325 .... 40, 41, 42, 918
325(a).. 40, 41
325(b)..41, 42, 45
325(c) 42, 43, 912, 918
325(d)............... 42, 43, 44, 45, 912, 913, 918
325(g)..40
326 40
327 .... 48, 51, 383, 642
327(a)............................. 47, 50, 51, 52, 645
327(b)...................................... 48, 49, 52
328(a)...837
328(b)...837
401 .... 402, 447, 1250, 1259, 1358, 1387, 1388

402............................1249, 1358, 1359, 1397
403................................. 7, 751, 1359
403(a) 1249, 1359
403(b) 1249, 1272, 1361, 1363, 1364, 1386, 1395
403(c)............62, 470, 480, 1210, 1249, 1361
403(d) 470, 482, 698, 1249, 1359, 1362, 1396
404(a) 1364, 1398
404(b) 1365
405.. 1365
405(a) 1365
405(b) 1365
405(c).................................... 1365
406 .... 1364, 1397
407 .... 1014, 1354
408 .... 799, 839, 1366
409(a) 1366
409(b) 1366
410.....7, 1013, 1094, 1247, 1259, 1276, 1294, 1367, 1402
501 .... 315, 316, 323
503......................313, 314, 889, 1080, 1356
503(a) 314, 317, 321, 1356
503(b) 318
503(c) 318
503(d) 319
503(e) 318
503(f) 321
504........................ 320, 972, 1080
504(1) 319
504(2) 319
504(3) 319
505 1080
505(a) 320
505(b) 319
506(a) 1355, 1356, 1357, 1378, 1390
506(b) 320, 956, 1080, 1355, 1388, 1389
506(b)(1) 22, 1389, 1399, 1402
506(b)(2) 1390
507 .... 314, 320, 1167
508.................................. 314, 321
509.............314, 315, 1167, 1356, 1389
509–511 602
510 324
510(1) 324, 1389
510(2) 324, 325, 1389
510(3) 324, 1389
511...........................1209, 1272, 1356, 1389
511(a) 316, 322, 323, 324
511(b) 316, 322, 323, 324, 484, 1389
511(c).................................... 326
511(d) 322, 326, 1281
513 314
513(a) 321
513(b) 321
513(c).................................... 322
601....................330, 333, 343, 400, 530, 938
601(a) 327, 328
601(b) 343

602 ... 315, 328, 329, 332, 380, 381, 392, 393, 397, 450, 453, 1141
602(a) 329, 333, 363
602(b) 329, 542
603 .... 329, 333, 334, 343, 382, 392, 398, 401, 546, 663, 939, 977, 1014, 1359
901(a) 359, 360, 361, 363
901(a)(1) 360
901(a)(2) 361
901(a)(5) 362, 363
901(b) 363
901–909 ....355, 364, 365, 371, 374
902 ....360, 364, 365, 367, 368
902(1) 370
903 ....365, 369, 373
904 368
904(a) 361, 367, 370
904(b) 367, 370
904(c) 368
904(c)(III)..368
904(d) 369
905 377
906(1) 361
906(2) 361
907 ....375, 376, 377
908 ....376, 377, 715
909 ....377, 378, 1029
1001 ....337, 342
1001(a) 337, 338
1001(b) 338, 339, 341, 342, 352, 383, 657
1001(b)(1) 339, 657
1001(b)(4) 341, 657
1001(b)(5) 340
1002 ....330, 343, 512
1002(a) 38, 328, 342, 343, 345, 358
1002(b) 344, 400, 527
1002(c)..343
1003 .... 104, 106, 157, 158, 159, 338, 351, 353, 574, 579
1004 .... 173, 349, 350, 351, 448, 468
1005 ....355, 356, 361
1005(a) 358
1005(b) 375
1005(b)(1)..376
1006(a) 352, 378, 380
1006(b) 352, 378, 379, 1259
1006(c)..381
1006(d) 379, 380
1006(f) 379, 380
1006(g)..384
1007 .... 380, 386, 389, 390, 426, 546, 547, 1358
1008 .... 107, 390, 398, 399, 400, 805, 1014
1009 ....106, 400, 435, 574
1010 ....390, 393, 396, 404
1011 ....402, 551
1012 .... 446, 447, 448, 449, 453, 1388
1012(a) 447, 451
1012(a)(1)..447
1012(a)(2).........................376, 448, 451
1012(a)(3)..452
1012(b)(3)..447

1012(c) 447
1013 ....376, 446, 447, 448, 449, 452, 453, 1141, 1388
1014 453
1015–1022 454
1015 224
1015(a) 454
1015(b) 455
1016 455
1017 455
1018 455
1019 .... 459, 1387
1021 ....224, 457, 458, 1044
1022 .... 459, 1323
1023 .... 459, 1387
1024 .... 460, 461
1025 ....170, 173, 462, 1050
1026 460
1101(a) 462, 463
1101(b) 463
1101(c) 463
1101(d) 464
1101(e) 464
1101(f) 464
1102 464
1102(a) 464
1102(b) 465
1102(c) 465
1102(d) 465
1201 ....119, 120, 170, 309, 466, 467, 468, 469, 470, 646
1202 .... 170, 469
1202(a)(1) 470
1202(a)(2) 469
1202(a)(3) 470, 472
1202(b) 470
1202(c) 470
1203 472
1204 471
1206 .... 433, 473
1207 ....472, 1352, 1356, 1357, 1358
1208 .... 472, 473
1208(d) 473
1209 472
1210 .... 433, 469
1211 473
1401 ....423, 424, 425, 427, 428, 431, 546
1401–1404 987
1402 .... 427, 429, 432
1403 ....427, 430, 431, 546
1404(b) 428
1411 ....39, 336, 420, 422, 426, 427, 987, 994, 1147
1411–1413 1129
1412 ....419, 420, 506, 538, 681
1413 .... 420, 506, 994
1501 1050
1502 ....172, 566, 1050, 1072
1600 .... 405, 406, 412
1601 .... 406, 407, 408, 409
1601(1) 406, 409, 410, 411, 413, 417
1601(2) 411, 445

1602 .... 406, 408, 413, 414, 415
1602(1) 411
1602(1)(a) 414
1602(2)(ii) 428
1602(2)(iii) 407
1602(2)(iv) 407, 412, 413, 415
1602(4) 414
1602(5) 408
1602(6) 416, 417, 432
1602(8) 412
1603 .... 418, 419, 536
2001 ..... 10, 11, 141, 142, 143, 144, 145, 146, 148, 155, 156, 195, 196, 208, 274, 393, 479, 562, 685, 697, 962
2004 .... 10, 11, 12, 66, 198, 322, 485, 548, 556, 588, 663, 697, 856, 924, 943, 1005, 1063, 1322
2005 .... 11, 298, 558, 559, 921
2101 475
2101(a) 475, 477
2101(c) 147, 476
2101(d) 476
2101(e) 478, 1046
2101(f) 479
2101(g) 478
2102 .... 147, 486, 746
2102(c) 144, 147
2103 .... 481, 1314
2103(a) 137, 209, 273, 953
2103(b) 160, 481, 482, 487, 708, 864, 955, 1271
2103(b)(1) 482
2103(b)(2) 323, 482, 484, 486, 547, 548, 593, 608, 609, 617, 633, 672, 746, 792, 847, 848, 867, 873, 1314, 1320, 1354, 1361
2103(b)(4) 889
2103(b)(5) 482
2103(b)(6) 482, 485, 608, 617
2103(c) 481, 889
2103(d) 481
2103(e) 158, 400, 488, 489, 548, 611, 616, 834
2103(f) 152
2108(f)(1) 482
2103–a 476, 889
2103–a(a) 889
2104 .... 489, 490, 493, 556, 612, 714, 834, 1094
2105 .... 479, 1171
2106 .... 193, 495, 496, 497, 568, 961
2106(b) 496
2110 152
2111 .... 23, 152
2111(a) 31, 150, 152
2111(b)(2)(A) 150, 151
2111(b)(2)(B) 30, 150
2111(b)(2)(C) 35, 150
2111(b)(2–a) 151
2111(b)(3) 151
2111(b)(3)(A) 151
2111(b)(3)(B) 151

2111(c) 152, 1314, 1320
2112...........................22, 23, 152, 1280, 1332
2201..............637, 638, 648, 765, 1095, 1170
2211...........593, 605, 611, 612, 614, 619, 677
2212...........600, 601, 602, 603, 615, 772, 775
2212(a) 322, 332, 600, 601, 620,
    1355, 1356, 1388
2212(b) 599, 602, 603, 615
2212(c) 602
2212(d) 322, 600, 601, 602, 615
2213... 600
2213(c) 600
2214......7, 594, 604, 605, 606, 607, 608, 609,
    610, 611, 614, 618, 619, 643, 917, 1394
2214(a) 603, 604, 605, 612
2214(b) 607, 608, 609, 610, 611, 612, 613,
    617, 618, 697, 771, 1361
2214(c)..............197, 605, 606, 607, 634, 641,
    654, 655
2214(d) 482, 609, 613, 614, 698, 757, 1396
2215........................616, 617, 618, 619, 676
2215(a) 617
2215(b) 617
2217.. 630, 631
2217(a) 631
2217(b) 598, 615, 729, 743, 771, 1359
2217(c) 632
2217(d) 600
2218..................627, 661, 662, 688, 689, 698,
    1086, 1178
2219(a) 597, 619, 620, 624, 629, 1316
2220...........620, 622, 623, 624, 625, 626, 627
2220(a) 620
2220(b) 621, 669
2221.................606, 630, 631, 632, 633, 634,
    635, 1101, 1317
2221(a) 632, 636
2221(a)(2) 599
2221(b) 600
2221(d) 632
2221(d)(2) 635
2221(d)(3) 633, 634, 1317
2221(e).. 634
2221(e)(2) 633
2221(e)(3) 633, 634, 635
2221(f) 636
2222....................621, 691, 1021, 1051, 1069
2223... 627
2301 .... 949, 950
2302(a) 951
2302(b) 881, 951
2303...............480, 697, 848, 869, 951, 952,
    953, 954, 955, 1170, 1243, 1244
2303(a) 873, 876, 951
2303–a.. 955
2304...............................807, 835, 956, 957
2305 .... 950, 954
2305(a) 951
2305(b) 950, 960
2308...............................870, 878, 892, 958
2308(a) 835, 870, 958
2308(b) 958

2308(c) 1175
2309 .... 479, 963
2309(a) 961
2309(b) 961
2309(c) 496, 961, 962, 963, 1054
2501(1) 498
2501(2) 498
2502 742
2502(d) 479
2506 498
2507 498
2508 498
2512 776
3001 .... 29, 1076, 1077, 1079, 1080,
    1082, 1086, 1394
3002 527
3002(a) 527, 1071
3002(b) 527
3002(c) 527
3002(d) 527
3002(e) 528
3002(f) 528
3004 516
3011 .... 419, 543, 547, 550, 551, 552,
    555, 1359
3012 ... 99, 133, 134, 298, 390, 548, 555, 557,
    558, 559, 1310
3012(a)..... 131, 133, 181, 481, 488, 543, 547,
    554, 1386
3012(b)............ 99, 113, 131, 133, 298, 300,
    555, 556, 557, 642
3012(c) 131, 181, 351, 547, 554, 662
3012(d)............................ 556, 557, 558, 559
3012–a 113, 198, 556
3012–b 197, 198, 517, 556, 704
3012–b(d) 517
3013 .... 67, 500, 501, 502, 503, 505,
    506, 507, 508, 509, 511, 514, 517, 518,
    524, 537, 539, 1358
3014 .... 344, 395, 503, 509, 510, 511,
    512, 513, 514, 521, 529, 534, 537, 539,
    553
3015 .... 502, 514, 515, 516, 517, 520
3015(a) 56, 515, 516, 534
3015(b) 516
3015(c) 516
3015(d) 516, 517, 534
3015(e) 517
3016 .... 502, 517, 518, 519, 520
3016(b) 518, 519
3016(c) 519
3016(d) 519
3016(e) 519, 520, 583
3016(f)................................... 520, 533, 566, 584
3016(g) 506, 520, 584
3016(h) 520
3017 .... 521, 522
3017(a) 501, 503, 521, 522
3017(b) 1076, 1078, 1086
3017(c) 131, 522, 523, 524, 579, 703, 836
3018 .... 159, 503, 514, 532, 534, 535,
    536, 537, 539

3018(a) 531, 534, 551, 702
3018(b) 67, 419, 515, 535, 536, 540, 649, 650, 1094, 1161
3019............................... 265, 543, 1107
3019(a) 265, 303, 541, 544
3019(b) 303, 391, 546, 547
3019(c)................................... 543
3019(d) 541, 545, 547, 1358
3020.............................. 566, 567, 568
3020(a)................................. 566, 567
3020(b)(1).. 566
3020(b)(2).. 566
3020(c)... 567
3020(d) 568, 570
3020(d)(1).. 568
3020(d)(2).. 568
3020(d)(3)................................... 568, 569
3021.. 569, 570
3022............................... 571, 572, 1397
3024...............300, 503, 509, 552, 553, 554, 573, 891, 1290
3024(a) 501, 552, 594, 1365
3024(b) 552, 1365
3024(c)..............131, 300, 554, 573, 594, 669
3025........104, 573, 575, 576, 579, 667, 1003
3025(a) 133, 158, 307, 353, 419, 540, 551, 572, 575, 576, 586, 665, 666
3025(b) 41, 102, 103, 307, 431, 540, 551, 574, 575, 577, 578, 579, 587, 666, 1002, 1161
3025(c)..................503, 522, 579, 590, 978, 1000, 1001, 1002
3025(d) 573, 574, 580
3026.....................502, 503, 510, 572
3034(3) 933
3036(7) 1046
3041...................................581, 582, 584, 833
3042............................... 585, 590, 1032
3042(a) 585
3042(b) 586
3042(c)................................585, 586, 587, 588
3042(d) 435, 585, 586, 588, 589, 895
3042(e)... 586, 844
3043... 586, 587
3043(a) 582, 583, 584
3043(b) 586
3043(c) 583
3044.. 567, 584, 585
3101................493, 519, 801, 802, 805, 806, 807, 809, 810, 811, 812, 814, 816, 817, 818, 819, 821, 822, 825, 826, 835, 840, 842, 844, 869, 878, 952, 1181
3101(a) 581, 791, 797, 798, 799, 800, 801, 805, 806, 807, 809, 814, 817, 819, 820, 851, 864, 865, 869, 873, 883, 885
3101(a)(1) 805, 808, 869
3101(a)(2) 805, 806, 808
3101(a)(3) 805, 806, 807, 835
3101(a)(4) 805, 806, 807, 808, 835, 957
3101(b) 810, 811, 812, 813, 814, 822, 823
3101(c)..............812, 813, 814, 822, 823, 878
3101(d) 686, 814, 815, 819, 825

3101(d)(1) 823, 827, 829, 840
3101(d)(1)(i) 26, 685, 823, 824, 825, 826, 827, 828, 885
3101(d)(1)(ii)..................................807, 823
3101(d)(1)(iii)...........................26, 823, 828
3101(d)(2) 802, 812, 813, 814, 815, 816, 818, 819, 820, 821, 822, 823, 830, 831, 878, 885
3101(e)..816
3101(f)..801, 972
3101(g)...819, 869
3101(h)............824, 839, 840, 841, 842, 868, 878, 895
3101(i)....................805, 816, 817, 869, 953
3102 .... 143, 836, 837, 838, 839, 879, 907
3102(a)..831, 832
3102(b)...833
3102(c) 143, 208, 791, 835, 839, 847, 851
3102(d)..837, 847
3102(e) 837, 838, 863
3102(f)..838
3103 ....798, 799, 801, 806, 833, 844, 845, 868, 879, 887, 898, 907, 1181, 1273
3103(a).....823, 824, 843, 844, 848, 849, 852, 854, 868, 879
3103(b)...843
3103(c) 844, 898
3104 ....846, 940, 1273
3104(a)..845, 851
3104(b) 845, 846, 851
3104(c) 846
3105 834
3106 808
3106(a) 834, 847, 848
3106(b) 806, 808, 835, 843, 848, 849, 875, 892, 956
3106(c) 838
3106(d).....................................808, 809, 955
3107 ....757, 847
3108 ....809, 832, 861, 863, 864, 954
3109 863
3109(a)..862
3109(b)..862
3110 ....843, 848, 849, 850, 873, 891, 956, 1245
3110(1).........................849, 862, 1209, 1245
3110(2)..849, 1245
3110(3)...850
3111 ....848, 875, 876, 879, 960
3112 848
3113 ....845, 851, 853, 854, 1245
3113(a)..850, 851
3113(a)(2)..851
3113(a)(3)..851
3113(b).....................851, 852, 854, 862, 891
3113(c) 851, 852, 853
3113(d)..854
3114 ....854, 878, 1245
3115 855
3115(a) 854
3115(b)..853, 854
3115(c) 851, 855

3115(d) 853, 855
3115(e) 862
3116 .... 675, 1245
3116(a) 841, 856
3116(b) 856
3116(c) 857
3116(d) 848, 856, 857
3117 ....847, 858, 860, 866, 867
3117(a) 857, 860, 861
3117(a)(1) 857, 858, 861
3117(a)(2) 858, 860, 867
3117(a)(3) 834, 859, 860, 866
3117(a)(4) 860
3117(b) 860
3117(c) 861
3117(d) 861
3118 889
3119 .... 838, 863
3120 ....206, 642, 757, 817, 831, 834,
      838, 839, 841, 850, 857, 867, 868, 869,
      870, 871, 872, 873, 874, 875, 876, 877,
      878, 879, 880, 890, 892, 893, 950, 1244
3120(1) 869, 870, 873, 960
3120(1)(i) 347, 817, 841, 877, 953
3120(1)(ii) 581, 872, 874
3120(2) 872, 873, 874, 877
3120(3) 873, 876
3120(b) 838, 869
3121 ....815, 850, 877, 878, 881, 882, 883,
      884, 885, 890, 893
3121(a) 73, 479, 834, 880, 881, 882, 883,
      884, 885
3121(b) 815, 820, 885
3122 ....876, 877, 878, 881, 883, 951
3122(a) 877, 878, 890
3122(a)(1) 883, 893
3122(a)(2) 881
3122(b) 812, 877, 878
3122(c) 877
3122(d) 871, 877, 879, 957
3122–a 685, 873, 874
3122–a(a) 873
3122–a(a)(1–4) 873
3122–a(d) 873
3123 ....834, 839, 844, 865, 885, 886, 887,
      888, 889, 890, 975, 996, 1046, 1366
3123(a) 885, 886, 887
3123(b) 888
3123(c) 888, 889, 894
3124 ....803, 831, 835, 852, 853, 868, 879,
      883, 890, 891, 892, 893, 894, 900
3125 892
3126 ....113, 114, 115, 588, 589, 590, 642,
      701, 835, 840, 852, 876, 879, 888, 890,
      892, 893, 894, 895, 896, 897, 898, 899,
      900, 924, 926, 928, 958, 1032, 1034, 1061,
      1310
3126(1) 895, 897, 898
3126(2) 895, 896, 897
3126(3) 113, 701, 849, 897, 898, 899, 900
3130 .... 865, 866, 1244
3130(1) 585, 865, 866

3131 .... 865, 866, 867, 875
3132 .... 834, 867, 868
3133 867
3133(a) 867, 868
3133(b) 841, 868
3133(c) 868
3140 .... 802, 815, 820
3211 .... 300, 301, 302, 303, 332, 571,
      573, 606, 610, 627, 639, 640, 641, 642,
      643, 644, 645, 650, 652, 654, 655, 656,
      659, 660, 661, 662, 664, 665, 666, 667,
      668, 669, 672, 686, 688, 760, 995, 1014,
      1092, 1093, 1097, 1100, 1101, 1128, 1310,
      1328
3211(8) 656
3211(a) 133, 137, 301, 302, 306, 540, 573,
      574, 576, 640, 642, 643, 644, 645, 646,
      649, 650, 651, 653, 656, 662, 663, 665,
      666, 669, 687, 688, 693, 714, 760, 995,
      1097, 1310, 1397, 1399
3211(a)(1) 641, 644, 645
3211(a)(10) 338, 383, 657, 664, 1097
3211(a)(11) 520
3211(a)(2) 50, 301, 514, 645, 664,
      688, 1097
3211(a)(3) 53, 349, 646, 688, 1097
3211(a)(4) 49, 315, 381, 637, 646,
      647, 648, 649, 1170
3211(a)(5) 67, 112, 515, 649, 650,
      651, 666, 669, 673, 688, 1094, 1097, 1101,
      1161, 1311
3211(a)(6) 544, 651, 663
3211(a)(7) 77, 501, 606, 610, 644,
      650, 652, 653, 654, 655, 658, 660, 664,
      665, 667, 673, 687, 1085, 1128, 1308
3211(a)(8) 141, 164, 301, 514, 540,
      642, 655, 658, 661, 662, 666, 688, 1097,
      1310
3211(a)(9) 306, 656, 688, 1097
3211(a)(e) 515
3211(b) 137, 302, 563, 564, 641, 650, 654,
      657, 658, 659, 660, 661, 663, 667, 688,
      689, 692, 978
3211(c) 627, 641, 652, 653, 657, 659, 660,
      661, 662, 663, 668, 672, 688, 1097, 1398
3211(d) 259, 641, 642, 664, 669, 685
3211(e) 67, 131, 137, 141, 142, 145,
      164, 168, 301, 302, 349, 491, 514, 515,
      540, 555, 574, 576, 642, 645, 654, 656,
      658, 659, 662, 663, 664, 665, 666, 667,
      668, 673, 687, 995, 1161
3211(f) 300, 573, 669
3212 .... 381, 532, 606, 610, 627, 639,
      641, 645, 652, 653, 659, 660, 661, 662,
      664, 665, 666, 667, 670, 672, 674, 683,
      686, 687, 688, 692, 695, 942, 995, 996,
      997, 1010, 1011, 1014, 1092, 1096, 1161,
      1328
3212(a) 302, 331, 484, 594, 656, 659, 663,
      672, 673, 674, 675, 676, 677, 678, 679,
      685, 687, 906, 995

3212(b) 607, 635, 641, 645, 655, 670, 671, 682, 685, 686, 826, 1011
3212(c) 688, 942, 1160
3212(d) 644
3212(e).............................333, 687, 689, 691
3212(e)(2) 690
3212(f) 673, 683, 685
3212(g) 681, 691, 692
3213.................567, 597, 610, 639, 693, 694, 695, 696, 697, 698, 699, 700, 1052, 1066, 1070, 1071, 1072, 1073, 1157, 1158
3214(b) 610, 669, 670, 672
3215.................402, 555, 639, 700, 701, 702, 703, 707, 708, 710, 712, 942
3215(a) 333, 701, 706, 709, 710, 1045
3215(b) 521, 701, 702, 709, 942
3215(c).......................305, 401, 704, 705, 710
3215(d) 705, 706
3215(e).. 706
3215(f) 133, 147, 210, 706, 707, 708, 709, 712
3215(g) 708, 709, 710, 711, 713
3215(g)(1) 308, 710, 711
3215(g)(2) 489, 710
3215(g)(3) 711, 712
3215(g)(3)(i).............................. 711, 713
3215(g)(3)(ii) 712
3215(g)(3)(iii) 712
3215(g)(4) 712, 713
3215(g)(4)(i)............................. 712
3215(g)(4)(ii) 712
3215(g)(4)(iii) 712
3215(i) 703
3216.................113, 114, 398, 487, 639, 642, 833, 919, 920, 921, 922, 923, 924, 925, 926, 927, 930, 1032, 1310
3216(a) 920, 922, 1090, 1097
3216(b) 923
3216(b)(2) 922
3216(b)(3) 484, 920, 922, 923, 924, 925, 926
3216(c) 923, 925
3216(d) 923
3216(e)................................. 923, 924, 925
3217.................112, 115, 352, 639, 714, 715, 717, 760
3217(a)(1) 713, 714
3217(a)(2) 714
3217(b) 715, 716
3217(c)................................716, 1090, 1097
3218.........................639, 717, 719, 721, 1105
3218(a) 717, 718
3218(a)(1) 718
3218(a)(2) 718
3218(a)(3) 718
3218(b) 478, 720
3218(c).. 721
3218(d) 718, 1045
3219.. 722
3220.. 722
3221.. 722, 1106
3222......................639, 723, 724, 1077, 1336

3222(a) 723
3222(b)(1) 724
3222(b)(2) 724
3222(b)(3) 22, 724
3222(b)(4) 724
3222(b)(5) 724
3401 .... 901, 903, 906
3402 .... 534, 839, 903
3402(a) 197, 486, 903, 904, 906, 935
3402(b) 905
3403 911
3403(a) 913, 917
3403(a)(1)... 914
3403(a)(3)... 915, 916, 1341
3403(a)(4)... 914
3403(a)(5)... 914
3403(a)(6)... 914, 915
3403(b)... 905, 916
3404 .... 113, 538, 918, 925, 926, 927, 928, 929, 930, 1032, 1034
3405 .... 6, 34, 35, 37, 38
3406 .... 113, 198, 201, 903
3406(a) 198
3408 .... 198, 207, 704, 941
3408(a) 198, 207
3408(i) 941
3409 198
3420 1079
4001 .... 940, 941
4011 .... 334, 382, 939, 947, 975, 976, 977
4012 .... 534, 975
4013 966
4014 966
4015 .... 943, 948
4016 .... 331, 975, 976, 977, 978, 981, 983
4016(b) 524
4017 .... 979, 980, 986
4101 .... 931, 932, 933, 934
4101(1) 931, 1366
4101(2)... 1166, 1366
4102 .... 935, 937
4102(a) 505, 904, 931, 936
4102(b) 936
4102(c) 331, 504, 505, 936, 937, 938, 1250
4102(d) 936
4102(e) 937
4103 .... 504, 940
4104 967
4105 969
4106 .... 968, 969, 970
4107 .... 968, 971
4108 971
4109 973
4110 .... 851, 971
4110(a) 325, 971, 972
4110(b) 325
4110–a 972
4110–b 985, 986
4110–c 976
4111 .... 947, 984, 987, 1009
4111(a) 987
4111(b) 987

4111(c) 988
4111(e) 984
4112 992
4113(a) 976, 990
4113(b) 976, 992, 1007
4201 945
4211 .... 940, 946
4212 .... 505, 939, 941, 943, 944, 948,
   949, 1402
4213 .... 947, 987
4213(a) 947
4213(b) 947, 948
4213(c) 947
4301 .... 940, 943
4311 .... 940, 943, 945
4312 .... 940, 945
4312(1) 940, 945
4312(2) 945, 946
4313 940
4315 .... 940, 946
4316 945
4317 941
4317(a) 941
4317(b) 941, 942, 943
4318 945
4319 945
4320 945
4320(a) 945
4320(b) 945
4321 940
4321(1) 946
4321(2) 946
4321(a) 946
4401 .... 671, 978, 995, 996, 997, 998,
   999, 1003, 1004, 1010, 1011
4401–a 997
4402 .... 999, 1000
4403 .... 945, 949
4404 .... 997, 999, 1004, 1005, 1007,
   1010, 1011, 1062, 1063
4404(a) ... 969, 1003, 1004, 1005, 1006, 1007,
   1008
4404(b) 1005
4405 .... 1002, 1005, 1007, 1062
4406 .... 1005, 1007
4501 810
4502 810
4503 810
4504 810
4505 810
4511(a) 519
4511(b) 519, 520
4518 .... 684, 857
4518(a) 685, 873
4519 684
4533–b 437
4540 1073
4545 .... 449, 450, 451, 947, 984, 987, 989
4545(a) 984, 989, 990
4547 823
5001 .... 1017, 1019, 1024, 1026
5001(a) 1017, 1019, 1024, 1025, 1026

5001(b) 1018
5001(c) 1019
5002 .... 621, 682, 1017, 1019, 1020,
   1022, 1025, 1026, 1043
5003 .... 621, 1017, 1021, 1025, 1026
5003–a 1022, 1023
5003–a(a) 1022
5003–a(b) 1022
5003–a(c) 1022
5003–a(d) 1022
5003–a(g) 1022
5004 .... 621, 1024, 1025, 1026, 1027
5011 .... 992, 1013, 1014, 1015, 1016,
   1286, 1402
5012 .... 333, 691, 1014, 1045
5013 .... 998, 1090
5014 .... 1070, 1071, 1211, 1222, 1264
5014(1) 1070, 1071
5014(2) 1070
5014(3) 1070
5015 .... 295, 296, 298, 492, 613, 703, 1007,
   1059, 1210
5015(a) 296, 615, 707, 1005, 1014, 1058,
   1059, 1060, 1062, 1063, 1064, 1065, 1066,
   1067, 1068
5015(a)(1) 189, 295, 296, 297, 298,
   302, 557, 707, 928, 1060, 1061, 1062
5015(a)(2) 634, 999, 1048, 1062,
   1063, 1074, 1131, 1139, 1348
5015(a)(3) 721
5015(a)(4) 274, 296, 302, 711, 1064, 1066
5015(a)(5) 1066, 1067, 1068, 1095
5015(b) 1061
5015(c) 178, 703, 1061
5015(d) 1069, 1324, 1344
5016 1095
5016(a) 1043, 1252, 1267, 1269
5016(b) 1044
5016(c) 691, 1044
5016(d) 454, 457, 1044, 1049, 1094
5016(e) 1016
5017(a) 1046, 1049, 1261
5017(b) 1046, 1334
5018(a) ... 171, 1043, 1050, 1051, 1052, 1053,
   1075, 1208, 1261
5018(b) 1027, 1051
5018(c) 1050
5019(a) 999, 1024, 1046, 1048
5019(b) 1053
5019(c) 1054
5019(d) 1054
502 .... 314, 1167
5020 .... 1068, 1236
5020(a) 1055
5020(b) 1055
5020(c) 1055
5020(d) 1055
5020–a 1056, 1057
5021 1057
5021(a)(1) 1055, 1056, 1068
5021(a)(2) 1056, 1068, 1236
5021(a)(3) 1056

5021(b) 1057, 1058, 1225
5021(c)... 1057, 1058
5031–5034 .... 1014, 1021
5034.. 1021
5036–5039.................................. 1014, 1021
5041–5049................................. 1014, 1021
5044 1021
5101...................................... 1164, 1405
5102...528, 529, 795, 1165, 1166, 1168, 1169
5103.. 1167
5103(a) 1168
5103(b) 1168
5104........892, 1168, 1169, 1171, 1174, 1178,
    1403, 1405
5105... 1069
5105(1) 1169
5105(2) 1169
5106..............................777, 779, 1164, 1255
5107 .... 279, 1168
5201 ....754, 1181, 1196, 1197
5201(a) 288, 291, 292, 755, 1184, 1192,
    1193, 1194, 1195, 1197, 1226
5201(b) 754, 755, 1184, 1192, 1193, 1194,
    1195, 1197, 1203
5201(c)... 756, 1203
5201(c)(1) 1203
5201(c)(2) 287, 1203
5201(c)(3) 1203, 1270
5201(c)(4) 287, 1203, 1218
5202.................................1242, 1264, 1266
5202(a) 1265, 1267
5202(a)(1) 1266
5202(a)(2) 1266
5202(b) 1267
5203 .... 721, 1263
5203(a) 1049, 1070, 1073, 1221,
    1261, 1262
5203(a)(1) 1262
5203(a)(2) 1262
5203(a)(3) 1262
5203(a)(4) 1262
5203(a)(5) 1262
5203(a)(6) 1262
5203(b) 1264
5203(c) 1263
5204.. 1263, 1269
5205.................754, 1190, 1197, 1198, 1199,
    1231, 1242
5205(a) 1198
5205(a)(5) 1198
5205(c) 1198
5205(d) 1196, 1198, 1226, 1252
5205(d)(2) 1232
5205(d)(3) 1199
5206......................................754, 1201, 1202
5206(a) 1201, 1202, 1223
5206(a)(2) 1189
5206(e).. 1201, 1202
5207...........................1205, 1207, 1228, 1325
5208................1257, 1258, 1259, 1262, 1263
5209...............................1240, 1252, 1259
5221.................1208, 1209, 1210, 1254, 1277

5221(a) 1208, 1209, 1234, 1236,
    1241, 1243, 1245, 1252, 1256, 1260, 1272,
    1277, 1356, 1357
5221(a)(1)..1208
5221(a)(2)..1208
5221(a)(3)..1208
5221(a)(4)................. 1208, 1209, 1210, 1235,
    1236, 1241
5221(a)(5)...1209
5221(b) 1208, 1235, 1236, 1241, 1277
5222 ..... 1169, 1186, 1199, 1206, 1210, 1213,
    1216, 1219, 1231, 1238, 1239, 1242, 1243,
    1248, 1260, 1269, 1270, 1275
5222(a) 1170, 1238, 1239
5222(b) 1196, 1197, 1216, 1238, 1240
5222(c) 1240
5222(g) 1238
5222–a 1199, 1200, 1201, 1231, 1242
5222–a(b)(3)...1201
5222–a(g)..1201
5223 .... 837, 1213, 1242, 1244, 1246, 1252,
    1260
5223–5224 1206
5224 .... 271, 837, 890, 953, 954, 955, 1176,
    1210, 1213, 1219, 1242, 1243, 1244, 1252,
    1260, 1269, 1275
5224(a) 1245
5224(a)(1)..1243
5224(a)(2)..1243
5224(a)(3).........................950, 1244, 1245
5224(b) 1245
5224(c) 1209, 1245
5224(d) 1245
5224(e) 1245
5224(f)..1245
5225 ..... 1196, 1202, 1206, 1208, 1217, 1220,
    1247, 1249, 1250, 1251, 1252, 1256, 1259,
    1266, 1267, 1269, 1275, 1362
5225(a) 1247, 1249, 1252, 1276
5225(b) 1196, 1200, 1204, 1205,
    1219, 1247, 1248, 1250, 1252, 1259, 1267,
    1269, 1270, 1271, 1276, 1352
5225(c)..1251
5226 .... 271, 1196, 1198, 1206, 1232, 1252,
    1253, 1254, 1275
5227 ..... 1196, 1202, 1206, 1208, 1217, 1219,
    1241, 1247, 1248, 1249, 1250, 1251, 1252,
    1259, 1266, 1267, 1269, 1270, 1271, 1275,
    1276, 1352
5228 .... 777, 1206, 1224, 1251, 1255, 1256,
    1267, 1269, 1276
5228(a) 1255, 1256
5228(b) 1255
5229 .... 837, 847, 1260, 1276, 1277
5230 .... 435, 721, 1057, 1165, 1166,
    1199, 1206, 1211, 1212, 1227, 1231
5230(a) 288, 305, 1212, 1213
5230(b) 1057, 1212
5230(c) 1057, 1215, 1217, 1225, 1235
5230(d) 1225
5231 .... 730, 756, 757, 1057, 1074,
    1196, 1198, 1199, 1206, 1211, 1226, 1229,

1230, 1231, 1232, 1234, 1236, 1237, 1238, 1252, 1253
5231(a) 1226, 1227
5231(b) 1226, 1227, 1229
5231(b)(iii)... 1231
5231(c)(i) 1231
5231(d) 480, 1226, 1227, 1235
5231(e).....480, 1227, 1228, 1229, 1233, 1235
5231(f) 1234
5231(g) 1226, 1227, 1230
5231(h) 1215, 1228, 1253
5231(i) 1232, 1236, 1254, 1273
5231(j) 1228, 1233, 1268
5231(k) 1235
5232.....................288, 750, 762, 1199, 1211, 1213, 1216, 1218, 1219, 1221, 1231, 1239, 1242
5232–5233................................. 1194, 1206
5232(a) 1190, 1208, 1215, 1216, 1217, 1218, 1219, 1220, 1226, 1240, 1241, 1251, 1259, 1266
5232(b) 1215, 1216, 1218, 1219, 1220, 1225, 1266
5232(c).. 1213, 1216
5233.....................288, 750, 762, 1211, 1215, 1220, 1249
5233(a) 1220
5233(b) 1220, 1275
5233(c) 1220
5234........762, 1199, 1233, 1239, 1264, 1267, 1268, 1270
5234(a) 1221, 1256
5234(b) 292, 1267, 1268
5234(c).......................1252, 1256, 1267, 1269
5235.................................1211, 1221, 1264
5235–5236.. 1206
5236........750, 1168, 1211, 1221, 1222, 1223, 1224, 1225, 1273
5236(a) 1222, 1224
5236(b) 1223
5236(c)..............................1222, 1262, 1275
5236(d) 1222
5236(e)..............................1222, 1262, 1275
5236(f) 1168, 1223
5236(g) 1222, 1275
5236(g)(1) 1223, 1262
5236(g)(2) 1223
5237... 1223
5238.. 1223, 1225
5239......1250, 1260, 1265, 1267, 1270, 1271, 1272, 1352, 1358
5240....................401, 721, 1075, 1181, 1182, 1188, 1207, 1211, 1214, 1222, 1223, 1232, 1236, 1240, 1243, 1245, 1254, 1272, 1273, 1274, 1275, 1276, 1327
5241......1211, 1226, 1230, 1231, 1234, 1236, 1237, 1238
5241(a)(1) 1236
5241(a)(7) 1237
5241(a)(8) 1237
5241(a)(9) 1236
5241(b) 1236

5241(c) 1237
5241(d) 1236
5241(e) 1236, 1237
5241(f).. 1237
5241(g) 1237
5241(h) 1234, 1237
5241–5242 1206
5242 .... 1231, 1234, 1237
5242(c) 1234
5250 .... 1206, 1256, 1257
5251 ..... 1174, 1178, 1206, 1217, 1238, 1241, 1249, 1251, 1254, 1275, 1276
5252 1235
5301 1158
5301(b) 696, 1156, 1158
5303 1156
5304 1156
5304(a)(1) 1159
5304(a)(2) 1156
5304(b) 239
5304(b)(3) 1159
5304(b)(4) 239
5305(a)(2) 1158
5305(a)(3) 1156
5307 1157
5309 .... 1072, 1156
5401 .... 696, 1072, 1073
5402 1075
5402(a) 1073
5402(b) 1052, 1073, 1074
5403 .... 1074, 1075
5404(a) 1075
5404(b) 1075
5405 1073
5406 1072
5408 1072
5501 .... 304, 1293, 1303, 1310
5501(a)... 669, 1002, 1306, 1307, 1312, 1313, 1314, 1334
5501(a)(1) 304, 1286, 1308, 1309, 1311
5501(a)(3)..979, 986
5501(a)(4)..979
5501(a)(5) 1010
5501(b) 915, 1303, 1306
5501(c) 22, 1009, 1303, 1318, 1321
5501(d) 1303
5511 .... 1283, 1284
5512(a) 1282, 1321
5512(b) 1282
5513 .... 623, 634, 1282, 1319, 1320
5513(a) 115, 634, 1043, 1314, 1319, 1320
5513(b) 1321
5513(c) 1285, 1322, 1345
5514(a) 1323
5514(b) 1323
5514(c) 12, 459, 1322
5515(1) 152, 1313, 1314, 1315, 1320
5515(2) 1315
5515(3) 1315
5516 1321
5517 .... 1317, 1318
5517(a) 1315

5517(a)(1) 1316
5517(a)(2) 1316
5517(a)(3) 1317
5517(b) 1317
5518.. 1324, 1342
5519........637, 1010, 1170, 1324, 1325, 1326
5519(a) 1325
5519(a)(1) 1325, 1326, 1327
5519(a)(2) 498, 1069, 1326
5519(a)(3) 1326
5519(a)(4) 1326
5519(a)(5) 1326
5519(a)(6) 1326
5519(b) 1327
5519(c)................1326, 1327, 1328, 1342
5519(e) 1328
5519(e)(i) 1328
5519(e)(ii) 1328
5519(g) 1327
5520(a) 1323
5520(b) 1323
5520(c) 1282, 1324
5521.. 1341
5522.. 1347
5522(a) 1344, 1347
5522(b) 1344
5523......................................1069, 1324, 1344
5524(a) 1348
5524(b) 1348
5525.....................................1329, 1332, 1333
5525(a) 1332, 1333
5525(b) 1332
5525(c) 1335
5525(c)(1) 1333
5525(c)(2) 1333
5525(c)(3) 1333
5525(d) 1333, 1334
5525(e) 1333, 1335
5526................................620, 1329, 1334
5527...............1329, 1330, 1332, 1336, 1337
5528...................................... 1329, 1337
5528(a) 1337
5528(a)(5) 1330, 1337
5528(b) 1337, 1338
5528(d) 1337, 1338
5528(e)... 1338
5529................................1329, 1337, 1339
5529(a) 1339
5529(a)(1) 1041, 1336, 1337
5529(a)(3) 1339
5530................................1329, 1337, 1339
5530(a) 1335
5530(b) 1335
5530(c) 1337
5531.. 1336
5531(7) 1336
5532.. 1333
5601... 1292, 1298
5601(a) 1293, 1297, 1305, 1306,
    1347, 1378
5601(b)(1) 1292, 1299
5601(b)(2) 18, 21, 1293

5601(c) 1295, 1299
5601(d) 1282, 1296, 1297, 1298,
    1299, 1306
5602 ....1298, 1339
5602(a) 1292, 1298, 1299, 1321
5602(a)(1)...1298
5602(a)(1)(ii) 1282, 1297, 1299, 1306
5602(a)(2) 1298, 1299
5602(b) 1299, 1300
5602(b)(1) 1299
5602(b)(2) 1293, 1299
5602(b)(2)(ii) 1282, 1297, 1306
5602(b)(2)(iii) 1296, 1299
5611 ....1286, 1295
5612(a) 1346
5613 ....1347, 1348
5614 1347
5701 ....22, 24, 28, 29, 1285, 1286
5701(a)...1289
5701(a)(1) 669, 1286
5701(a)(2)... 200, 599, 669, 1286, 1287, 1289,
    1310
5701(a)(2)(i) 759
5701(a)(2)(iv) 1002, 1288, 1290
5701(a)(2)(v) 303, 554, 1002, 1288, 1290
5701(a)(3)...1289
5701(b)(1)...1290
5701(b)(2) 554, 1290
5701(b)(3) 554, 1290
5701(c) 1290, 1339
5703 ....1291, 1293
5703(a) 22, 27, 1290, 1293, 1296,
    1321, 1339
5703(b) 1291
5704 ....599, 614, 776, 1283, 1289
5704(a) 599, 776
5704(b) 599, 776
5711 1281
5712(a) 1347
5712(b) 1346
5712(c) 1346
5713 ....1299, 1300, 1347
6001 ....619, 727, 728, 729
6201 .... 286, 292, 737, 738, 739, 741,
    743, 745, 747, 750, 758, 780, 1104
6201(1) 753, 760
6201(3) 285, 764
6201(5)...285
6202 ....287, 730, 737, 754, 1185
6203 762
6203(1) 762
6203(2) 762
6204 761
6205 742
6210 ....740, 742, 743, 770
6211 ....286, 740, 742
6211(a) 598, 742, 744
6211(b) 740, 741, 743, 744, 745, 746, 747,
    750, 758, 759
6212 286
6212(a) 740, 743, 744
6212(b) 497, 742, 760, 785

6212(c) 744, 746
6212(d) 746
6212(e) 761
6213 .... 286, 293, 747, 748, 749, 753, 754
6214 .... 749, 751, 755
6214–6216 737
6214(a) 286, 745, 747, 749, 1190, 1215
6214(b) 291, 292, 747, 749, 750, 751
6214(c) 751
6214(d) 752, 761, 1352
6214(e) 747, 751, 752, 754, 755
6215 .... 745, 749, 751, 1215, 1218
6216 .... 286, 749, 751, 761
6218 750
6218(a) 750
6218(b) 750
6219 .... 741, 750
6220 757
6221 761
6222 759
6223 .... 740, 741, 759
6223(a) 740, 758, 759
6223(b) 740, 743, 758, 759
6224 759
6225 .... 760, 761
6226 762
6301 .... 614, 763, 764, 765, 767, 769,
    771, 773, 1324
6311 .... 771, 775
6311(1) 768, 772, 775
6311(2) 775
6312 766
6312(a) 769
6312(b) 497, 742, 765, 769, 772, 785
6313 .... 614, 772, 773
6313(a) 598, 771, 772, 773, 774, 917, 1396
6313(b) 772
6313(c) 497, 742, 772
6314 .... 775, 776
6315 .... 769, 770
6330 .... 765, 774
6401 .... 779, 1164
6401(a) 777, 778, 779
6401(b) 777, 778, 779
6401(c) 779
6402 778
6402–6405 1255
6403 .... 497, 778
6404 778
6405 778
6501 .... 749, 780, 781, 783
6511(a) 782
6511(b) 782
6511(c) 782
6512 .... 782, 783
6513 781
6514 .... 783, 784
6514(a) 782, 783
6514(b) 782, 784
6514(c) 784
6514(d) 783
6514(e) 783

6515 .... 497, 784
6515(1) 784
6515(2) 784
6516 781
7001 1378
7003(a) 1378
7005 136
7101 785
7102 .... 730, 731, 787, 788
7102(a) 789, 791, 793, 794
7102(b) 791, 793, 794
7102(c) 788
7102(c)(5) 731, 790
7102(c)(6) 789
7102(d)(1) 731, 787, 790
7102(d)(2) 789
7102(d)(3) 788
7102(d)(4) 790, 792
7102(e) 789
7102(f) 792, 794
7103 .... 731, 793
7103(a) 792
7103(b) 793
7103(c) 793
7103(d) 793, 794
7104 .... 731, 787
7105 793
7106(a) 793
7107 793
7108 .... 787, 1165
7108(a) 529, 793, 795, 1165
7108(b) 795
7109(a) 764
7109(b) 787, 795, 1165, 1169
7110 .... 730, 731, 790
7112 .... 787, 791
7501 270
7502 .... 109, 270
7502(a) 315, 956, 1356
7502(a)(iii) 8
7503 .... 109, 270
7503(a) 637, 651
7503(c) 12, 487, 1354, 1355, 1357
7510 .... 73, 270, 1022
7511 .... 270, 1118
7514 .... 270, 1022
7514(a) 73
7701 1352
7801 1372
7801(1) 1375, 1378, 1380
7801(2) 1373
7802 1387
7802(a) 619, 1368, 1387
7802(b) 1387
7802(d) 447, 1388
7803 ..... 1369, 1370, 1372, 1375, 1378, 1379,
    1380, 1381, 1382, 1383
7803(1) 597, 619, 1371
7803(3) 1036, 1381, 1383, 1384, 1403
7803(4) 1374, 1379, 1399
7804(b) 1389, 1399
7804(c) 1393, 1395, 1396

7804(d) 566, 1396, 1397
7804(e)... 1397
7804(f) 1397, 1398, 1399
7804(g) 1383, 1384, 1399, 1400
7804(h) 1401, 1402
7804(i) 1388
7805.. 1396
7806......................1282, 1402, 1403, 1404
8001............951, 953, 957, 1028, 1040, 1245
8001(a) 952
8002.. 1332
8003(a) 946
8004(a) 778
8004(b) 778
8012.. 1326
8012(b) 1041, 1232
8016(a) 1052
8018(a) 208, 1029, 1073
8020.. 904
8020(a) 597, 603, 611, 1029
8020(c) 1029
8020(d) 493
8101.. 1030
8102... 24, 241
8102(1) 24, 1030
8102(2) 24, 1031
8106.. 1030
8107.. 1030
8201.. 1031
8202.. 1031
8203–8204.. 1031
8301.. 1040
8301(a) 904, 1040
8301(a)(12) 1332, 1336
8301(a)(13) 1040, 1332, 1336
8301(a)(6) 1041
8301(a)(9) 1040
8301(c) 1040
8302.. 1041
8303.. 1041
8303(a)(2) 1041
8303–a.....................1032, 1033, 1034, 1035
8401.. 1041
8402.. 1042
8403.. 1042
8404.. 1042
8501(a) 53, 1031
8502.. 1031
8503.. 1031
8601.. 1029
9401.. 22
9702(1) 1043
9802.. 56

NEW YORK, MCKINNEY'S
CIVIL RIGHTS LAW

§§ 60 et seq... 1290
§ 62 1358

NEW YORK, MCKINNEY'S
COUNTY LAW

§ 52(1)... 56
§ 525 .... 1043, 1049

§ 525(1) 146
§ 909 .... 146, 1043, 1049

NEW YORK, MCKINNEY'S DEBTOR
AND CREDITOR LAW

§ 272 1266
§ 273 1192
§ 273–a................................... 1192, 1267
§ 278 1192
§§ 282 to 284....................................... 1202

NEW YORK, MCKINNEY'S
DOMESTIC RELATIONS LAW

Art. 7..30
§§ 75–a through 75–l 278
§ 75–d 257
§ 76 278
§§ 76 et seq. 256, 278, 1155
§ 76–f 50
§ 77–b..1155
§ 77–d 1073
§ 77–e 1073
§ 81 469
§ 140(e) 456
§ 143 933
§ 170(7) 74, 519
§ 172(1) 447
§ 173 933
§ 210 74
§ 211 .... 192, 566, 707
§ 230 .... 277, 292, 1066
§ 232 ....191, 192
§ 232(b) 209
§ 233 .... 292, 727, 737
§ 234 1166
§ 236 .... 201, 255, 270, 469, 802
§ 240 .... 255, 469
§§ 241–242..1015
§ 243 .... 292, 727, 728, 737
§ 245 .... 615, 1169, 1171, 1172, 1177

NEW YORK, MCKINNEY'S
EDUCATION LAW

§ 2(13) 175
§ 3813...430

NEW YORK, MCKINNEY'S
ELECTION LAW

Art. 16..................................... 1353, 1354
§ 16–116................................ 914, 1353, 1358

NEW YORK, MCKINNEY'S ESTATES,
POWERS AND TRUSTS LAW

5–4.1 .... 67, 74, 96, 97
5–4.3 1017
5–4.4 579
11–3.2 456
11–4.6 1259

NEW YORK, MCKINNEY'S
EXECUTIVE LAW

§ 142–a..497

NEW YORK, MCKINNEY'S GENERAL ASSOCIATIONS LAW

§ 13 .... 173, 462
§ 15 462
§ 16 462
§ 17 462
§ 18 319

NEW YORK, MCKINNEY'S GENERAL BUSINESS LAW

§ 11 .... 136, 137
§ 13 137
§ 250 261
§ 340 369
§ 342–b 369
§ 399–dd 480

NEW YORK, MCKINNEY'S GENERAL CONSTRUCTION LAW

§ 20 .... 65, 68, 481
§ 24 .... 65, 68, 481
§ 25 .... 65, 481
§ 25–a 65, 68, 481
§ 25–b 71
§ 37–a 456
§ 66 .... 55, 850

NEW YORK, MCKINNEY'S GENERAL MUNICIPAL LAW

§ 3–a 1027
§ 50–(i) 97
§ 50–b 74
§ 50–e 55, 56, 57, 59, 70, 74, 75, 142, 516, 614, 1363
§ 50–e(1) 61
§ 50–e(1)(a) 55
§ 50–e(2) 57
§ 50–e(3)(a) 57
§ 50–e(3)(c) 58
§ 50–e(3)(d) 58
§ 50–e(3)(f) 57, 58
§ 50–e(5) 59, 60, 61, 62, 109, 143, 144, 614
§ 50–e(6) 57, 58
§ 50–e(7) 61
§ 50–e(f) 176
§ 50–h 58
§ 50–i 59, 70, 74, 75, 109
§ 50–i(1) 56
§ 50–i(1)(b) 62, 109
§ 50–i(1)(c) 74, 75, 97
§ 51 347
§ 53 57

NEW YORK, MCKINNEY'S GENERAL OBLIGATIONS LAW

§ 5–335 450
§ 5–511(2) 1026
§ 5–521 1026
§ 5–1401 .... 48, 49
§ 5–1402 48
§ 5–1402(1) 49, 52
§ 5–1501B(1) 479
§ 11–101 429
§ 13–101 1184

§ 13–105.. 545
§ 15–102.. 1071
§ 15–108.. 409, 411
§ 15–108(b) 438
§ 15–108(c) 438, 440
§ 15–108(d) 438, 440
§ 17–101... 107
§ 17–103(1) 82
§ 17–103(4)(b) 82, 121

NEW YORK, MCKINNEY'S INSURANCE LAW

§ 107(a)(41) 175, 261
§ 167(7) 291, 292
§ 1212... 261
§ 1212(b) 175
§ 1213... 261
§ 3420..................................... 291, 1079
§ 3420(a) 962
§ 3420(a)(6) 1079
§ 3420(g) 434
§ 5102(a) 520, 583
§ 5102(d) 520, 583
§ 5104(a) 583
§ 5501(b) 914

NEW YORK, MCKINNEY'S JUDICIARY LAW

Art. 7–A 460
Art. 16... 967
Art. 19.. 1175
Art. 19, §§ 750–781 1276
§ 2 .... 961, 1293
§ 2–b 954, 1244
§ 2–b(1) 955
§ 5 136
§ 15 972
§ 27(b) 1013
§ 53 21
§ 56 21
§ 90 22
§ 179 29
§ 190(1) 28
§ 190(3) 27, 28
§ 190(4) 28, 469
§ 190–a 28
§ 210(2) 8
§ 210(3) 8
§ 211 9
§ 211(1)(b) 1033
§ 211(2) 8
§ 212 9
§ 213 9
§ 214 9
§ 217–a 178, 1061
§ 229(3) 3
§ 255–c 1051, 1053
§ 461 21
§ 462 21
§ 470 .... 487, 488
§ 475 311
§ 487 71
§ 502 967

§ 506 967
§ 508 .... 967, 968
§ 510 967
§ 511 968
§ 512 968
§ 522 967
§ 668 .... 967, 968
§ 750 ....1169, 1171, 1403
§ 750(A) 1174
§ 750(A)(1) 1170
§ 750(A)(3) 1171
§ 751(1) 1174, 1179
§ 751(2) 1174
§ 751(3) 1174
§ 753 ....1169, 1171, 1403
§ 753(A)(3) 1276
§ 753(A)(5) 1169
§ 756 ....615, 1177, 1179
§ 757 .... 615, 1177
§ 761 .... 1177, 1179
§ 770 1178
§ 772 ....1176, 1178, 1179
§ 773 ....1174, 1176, 1179
§ 774(1) 1174
§ 774(2) 1175

NEW YORK, MCKINNEY'S FAMILY COURT ACT

Art. 5–B 257
Art. 11 1286
§ 131 30
§ 154 256
§ 154(b) 30
§ 165 30
§ 165(a) 5
§ 442 270
§ 443 270
§ 475 1051
§ 580–101 257
§ 641 30
§ 661 469
§ 812 30
§ 1111 .... 22, 30

NEW YORK, MCKINNEY'S COURT OF CLAIMS ACT

§ 8 23
§ 9 .... 23, 31
§ 9(3) 32
§ 9(9) 31
§ 10 .... 75, 1152
§ 10(6) 74
§ 10(7) 84
§ 10(8)(a) 74
§ 11 176
§ 11(b) 568, 572
§ 11(c) 74
§ 24 .... 22, 31, 1286
§ 27 1035

NEW YORK, MCKINNEY'S UNIFORM INTERSTATE AND INTERNATIONAL PROCEDURE ACT

§ 1.03(a)(2) 243

NEW YORK, MCKINNEY'S UNIFORM JUSTICE COURT ACT

Art. 11 799
Art. 15 1208
Art. 18 .... 37, 1055
§ 109 961
§ 110 1267
§ 204 37
§ 208 .... 37, 543
§ 209 101
§ 213 .... 38, 313
§ 400 .... 98, 136, 208
§ 501 309
§ 701 1234
§ 701(b) 1212
§ 902(a)(1) 158
§ 1505 1208
§ 1701 .... 28, 38, 1303
§ 1702 1286
§ 1702(c) 1290
§ 1702(d) 1303
§ 1703 1280
§ 1704 1335
§ 1809(2) 309
§ 1813 157
§ 1814 157
§ 2101 37
§ 2300(b)(1) 37
§ 2300(b)(2) 37

NEW YORK CITY CIVIL COURT ACT

Art. 3 313
Art. 4 34
Art. 11 799
Art. 15 1208
Art. 18 34
Art. 18–A 309
§ 110 34
§ 202 33
§ 203 33
§ 204 33
§ 205 .... 34, 379
§ 208 543
§ 208(b) 34
§ 208(c) 34
§ 208(c)(2) 543
§ 212–a 1082
§ 212–a(b) 1082
§ 213 34
§ 400 130
§ 400(3) 138, 142
§ 404 .... 45, 224
§ 404(a)(1) 236
§ 408 402
§ 411 140
§ 701 .... 34, 1234, 1267
§ 701(a) 1212
§ 701(b) 1212
§ 902 556
§ 902(a) 508
§ 902(a)(1) 131, 158

§ 903 508
§ 1301 903
§ 1609 1212
§ 1701 34
§ 1702.. 1286
§ 1702(c) 1290
§ 1704 1335
§ 1705 1336
§ 1813.. 157
§ 1814 157
§ 2102 34

NEW YORK, MCKINNEY'S UNIFORM CITY COURT ACT

Art. 4 36
Art. 11 799
Art. 15 1208
Art. 18.. 37
Art. 18–A.. 309
§ 102 36
§ 203 36
§ 204 36
§ 205 .... 36, 379
§ 208 543
§ 208(b).. 36
§ 213 .... 36, 313
§ 400 130
§ 400(3).. 138, 142
§ 404 224
§ 408 402
§ 411 140
§ 701 1234
§ 902 131
§ 1304 947
§ 1701 .... 28, 36, 1303
§ 1702 1286
§ 1702(c) 1290
§ 1702(d).. 1303
§ 1704 1335
§ 1906(a) 1200
§ 2102 36

NEW YORK, MCKINNEY'S UNIFORM DISTRICT COURT ACT

Art. 3 313
Art. 4 35
Art. 11 799
Art. 15 1208
Art. 18.. 35
Art. 18–A.. 309
§ 202 35
§ 203 35
§ 204 35
§ 205 .... 35, 379
§ 208 543
§ 208(b).. 35
§ 400 130
§ 400(3).. 138, 142
§ 404 224
§ 408 402
§ 411 140
§ 701 1234
§ 701(b).. 1212

§ 902 131
§ 902(a)(1)... 158
§ 1701 35
§ 1702.. 1286
§ 1702(c) 1290
§ 1704.. 1335
§ 1813.. 157
§ 1814.. 157
§ 2102.. 36, 930

NEW YORK, MCKINNEY'S LABOR LAW

Art. 10.. 412
§ 200 676
§ 240 412
§ 240(1) 676
§ 241 412
§ 241(6) 676
§ 623 1115
§ 624 1368
§ 807 .... 763, 772
§ 808 763

NEW YORK, MCKINNEY'S LIEN LAW

§ 17 12
§ 43 781
§ 181 732
§ 200 732
§ 201 732
§ 201–a 732
§ 202 732
§ 204 732

NEW YORK, MCKINNEY'S MENTAL HYGIENE LAW

Art. 81... 169, 467
§ 81.05.. 1356
§§ 81.05 et seq. 1353
§ 81.08.. 1358
§ 81.11(f) 1367

NEW YORK, MCKINNEY'S MILITARY LAW

§ 304 638
§ 308 120

NEW YORK, MCKINNEY'S NAVIGATION LAW

§ 74 261

NEW YORK, MCKINNEY'S NOT-FOR-PROFIT CORPORATION LAW

§ 720–a.. 520

NEW YORK, MCKINNEY'S PARTNERSHIP LAW

§ 26(2) 1045
§ 51(2)(c) 756
§ 52 756
§ 54 .... 756, 1203, 1270
§ 115 171
§ 121–109.. 171

NEW YORK, MCKINNEY'S PENAL LAW

Ch. 210 495
§ 70.00 1174
§ 70.15 1174
§ 80.05 1174
§ 80.10 1174
§ 210.00(1) 961
§ 210.10 566
§ 210.15 566
§ 215.50 1174
§ 215.51 1174
§ 215.54 1174
§ 255.17 566

NEW YORK, MCKINNEY'S PERSONAL PROPERTY LAW

§ 49–b 1234, 1237
§ 302(9) 545
§ 403(4) 545

NEW YORK, MCKINNEY'S PUBLIC AUTHORITIES LAW

§ 1744(2) 63
§ 2980 63
§§ 2980–2982 63

NEW YORK, MCKINNEY'S PUBLIC HOUSING LAW

§ 157(5) 1027

NEW YORK, MCKINNEY'S PUBLIC OFFICERS LAW

§§ 84–90 .... 811, 820, 1373
§ 87(2)(a) 821
§ 89 821
§ 89(4)(b) 1373
§ 96–a 480

NEW YORK, MCKINNEY'S REAL PROPERTY LAW

Art. 12 275
§ 190 932
§ 254(10) 779
§ 259–c 937
§ 298 961
§ 298(1)(d) 961
§ 298(2)(a) 961
§ 299 .... 961, 962
§ 299(1) to (5) 962
§ 299–a(1) 962
§ 301 961
§ 309–a 479
§ 309–b 479, 962
§ 339–g 321, 1189
§ 339–n(7) 261
§ 391 275

NEW YORK, MCKINNEY'S REAL PROPERTY ACTIONS AND PROCEEDINGS LAW

Art. 7 .... 7, 402, 1166, 1353
Art. 9 1167
Art. 13 1167

§ 231(2)(b) 1222
§ 701 1166
§ 701(1) 28
§ 711 1166
§ 735 186
§ 735(1) 196
§ 741 .... 566, 571
§ 745 .... 933, 1166, 1367
§ 747 1013
§ 747(2) 1149
§ 749 1166
§ 1304 153
§ 1304(5) 151
§ 1321(1) 704
§ 1331 781
§ 1352 1213
§ 1371(2) 1224
§ 1721 1358

NEW YORK, MCKINNEY'S SOCIAL SERVICES LAW

§ 137 .... 1198, 1231
§ 137–a 1198, 1231

NEW YORK, MCKINNEY'S STATE FINANCE LAW

Art. 7–A 347
§ 6 1027
§§ 123 to 123(j) 347

NEW YORK, MCKINNEY'S STATE ADMINISTRATIVE PROCEDURE ACT

Art. 2... 1370
Art. 3.. 1370, 1381
Art. 3, §§ 301 to 307 1379
Art. 4... 1370
§ 102(3) 1379
§ 204 .... 1082, 1373
§ 205 1373
§ 302(3) 1381
§ 306(1) 1379, 1380
§ 306(3) 1380, 1381

NEW YORK, MCKINNEY'S SURROGATE'S COURT PROCEDURE ACT

§ 102 .... 5, 29, 839
§ 201 29
§ 201(2) 29
§ 201(3) 29
§ 209(6) 29
§ 210 .... 29, 223
§ 211 29
§ 301 .... 98, 138
§ 404 471
§ 602 1013
§ 603 1051
§ 605 1208
§ 606 1208
§ 607 1208
§ 708 261
§ 708(1) 271
§ 1002 455
§ 1002(1) 121, 459

§ 1604 1258
§ 1607 1258
§ 1608 1258
§ 1610(2) 1258
§ 1701 469
§ 1750 et seq. 469
§ 1808 932
§ 1811 .... 1257, 1263
§ 1811(2) 1257
§ 1811(2)(a) 1263
§ 1811(2)(b) 1263
§ 1811(2)(c) 1258, 1263
§ 2103 933
§ 2104 933
§ 2218 1188
§ 2701 .... 22, 29, 1286

NEW YORK, MCKINNEY'S TAX LAW
§ 7 1205
§ 2016 .... 22, 1399

NEW YORK, MCKINNEY'S TOWN LAW
§ 65(3) 56
§ 267–c(1) 1399

NEW YORK, MCKINNEY'S UNIFORM COMMERCIAL CODE
Art. 7 1203
§ 2–102 69
§ 2–105 69
§ 2–302 720
§ 2–319 226
§ 2–725 .... 69, 74, 398
§ 2–725(1) 79, 82
§ 2–725(2) 86, 87
§ 3–122(1)(b) 85
§ 3–122(3) 85
§ 3–306 545
§ 3–307(1) 516
§ 3–803 403
§ 7–602 1203
§ 8–114(1) 516
§ 9–318(1)(b) 545
§ 9–401 1189

NEW YORK, MCKINNEY'S VEHICLE AND TRAFFIC LAW
§ 253 ..... 5, 169, 188, 195, 222, 224, 244, 260, 261, 268, 269, 274
§ 254 268
§ 311 432
§ 312 432
§ 388 .... 266, 434, 703, 1130, 1144
§ 1225–d(2)(a) 872
§ 1229–c(8) 536, 1147

NEW YORK, MCKINNEY'S VILLAGE LAW
§ 7–712–c 1394
§ 7–712–c(1) 1399

NEW YORK, MCKINNEY'S WORKERS' COMPENSATION LAW
§ 11 .... 388, 389, 413, 414, 426, 427
§ 23 1368

NEW YORK CITY ADMINISTRATIVE CODE
§§ 20–403—20–410 481

NEW YORK LAWS
1870, ch. 359 933
1870, ch. 394 933
1959, ch. 238 1052
1959, ch. 631 1052
1968, ch. 645 456
1971, ch. 1051, § 1 787
1973, ch. 1034 802
1975, ch. 109, § 8 914
1977, ch. 316 967
1977, ch. 437 .... 1176, 1177
1977, ch. 860 739
1980, ch. 715 732
1981, ch. 115 472
1984, ch. 827 687
1986, ch. 220 643
1987, ch. 312 463
1992, ch. 216 98
1992, ch. 698 .... 119, 467
1992, ch. 698, § 4 169
1993, ch. 98 798
1996, ch. 635 427
1997, ch. 474 1318
2003, ch. 296 447
2003, ch. 62, Part J 597
2003, ch. 62, Part J, § 28 493
2005, ch. 623 1201
2009, ch. 494, § 8 450
2009, ch. 494, Part F 984
2010, ch. 427 1263

UNITED STATES

UNITED STATES CONSTITUTION
Art. IV 1052
Art. IV, § 1 .... 695, 1063, 1093, 1112, 1153
Art. VI 23
Amend. V 810
Amend. XIV 810

UNITED STATES CODE ANNOTATED

9 U.S.C.A.—Arbitration
Ch. 2 1156

11 U.S.C.A.—Bankruptcy
§ 108(c) 109
§ 544 1263

15 U.S.C.A.—Commerce and Trade
§§ 1671–1677 1230

17 U.S.C.A.—Copyrights
§ 507(b) 70

28 U.S.C.A.—Judiciary and Judicial Procedure
§ 1257 .... 1175, 1349
§ 1291 1287
§ 1292(a) 1287
§ 1292(b) 1287
§ 1331 356

§ 1332 ....125, 356, 385, 1112
§ 1332(c) 516
§ 1333 275
§ 1333(1) 275
§ 1334 23
§ 1335 385
§ 1335(a) 385
§ 1335(a)(1) 385
§ 1338 1151
§ 1338(a) 23
§ 1351 166
§ 1367 357
§ 1391(a) 385
§ 1397 385
§ 1404(a) 50, 314
§ 1406(a) 314
§ 1407 333
§ 1441 330
§ 1446 330
§§ 1604–1607 166
§§ 1605–1607 174
§ 1608(a) 173
§ 1608(b) 173
§ 1608(c) 174
§ 1608(d) 174
§ 1608(e) 174
§ 1738 ....695, 1052, 1093,
   1153, 1155
§ 1738A 1155
§ 1781 809
§ 1963 .... 1051, 1075
§ 2201 1077
§ 2281 1175
§ 2282 1175
§ 2284 1175
§ 2361 385
§ 2415 68

29 U.S.C.A.—Labor
§§ 1001 et seq. 1199

42 U.S.C.A.—The Public Health and Welfare
§ 1983 ....59, 70, 74, 1029, 1083, 1404
42 U.S.C.A. § 1988 1029

50 U.S.C.A.App.—War and National Defense
§ 3931 210
§ 3931(d) 638

STATUTES AT LARGE
94–381 (1976) 1175

STATE STATUTES

WEST'S ANNOTATED CALIFORNIA CODE OF CIVIL PROCEDURE
§ 410.10 223

ILLINOIS COMPILED STATUTES
735, § 5/2–209 .... 223, 262

MASSACHUSETTS GENERAL LAWS ANNOTATED
Ch. 223A, § 3(b) 243

Table of Court Rules

NEW YORK CODE OF RULES AND REGULATIONS

Tit. 22

§ 100.3(B)(6)(d) 919
§ 118.1 9
§ 125.1 904
§ 128.0 967
§ 128.3 967
§ 128.5 967
§ 128.6 968
§ 130–1 596
§ 130–1.1 .... 477, 842
§ 137.11 1117
§ 137.2(a) 1117
§ 137.6(c) 1081
§ 137.6(d) 1081
§ 137.8 1117
§ 137.8(a) 1082
§ 202.1(a) 27
§ 202.3 902
§ 202.3(c)(2) 199, 200
§ 202.5 .... 475, 476, 478, 480
§ 202.5(d) 147, 148, 208
§ 202.5(d)(1) 709
§ 202.5(e)(3) 480
§ 202.5–b(d)(1) 152
§ 202.5–b(d)(1) 147, 148
§ 202.5–b(d)(1) 154
§ 202.5–b(e)(1) 478, 485, 486
§ 202.5–b(f)(2)(ii) 594, 597, 609, 621, 622, 624, 626, 1320
§ 202.5–bb(a)(1) 478, 486, 594, 609, 621
§ 202.5–bb(e)(3) 152
§ 202.5–bb(e)(3) 151
§ 202.5–bb(e)(3) 152
§ 202.6 .... 1360, 1396
§ 202.6(a) 615, 772
§ 202.7 ....846, 848, 879, 892, 894, 900
§ 202.7(a) 588
§ 202.7(c) 588
§ 202.7(e) 600, 603, 605, 615, 775
§ 202.8(a) 891
§ 202.8(b) 595, 599, 600, 607, 608, 609, 611, 612, 613, 615, 619, 631, 1360, 1396
§ 202.8(e)(1) 665
§ 202.9 .... 1360, 1396
§ 202.8(a) 600
§ 202.8(e) 611
§ 202.12 .... 911, 922
§ 202.12(c) 205, 206, 207
§ 202.12(c)(2) 824, 871, 877
§ 202.12(c)(6) 42
§ 202.13 913
§ 202.13(a) 43
§ 202.13(b) 44
§ 202.13(c) 44

§ 202.13(d) 44
§ 202.13(e) 44
§ 202.13(f) 44
§ 202.13(h) 44
§ 202.13(i) 44
§ 202.15 .... 851, 854, 857
§ 202.16 .... 201, 802, 865
§ 202.17 .... 815, 850, 882, 885
§ 202.21 ....839, 902, 903, 906, 907
§ 202.22(a) 901, 902, 903, 904
§ 202.22(a)(2) 902
§ 202.24 913
§ 202.24(b) 916
§ 202.24(d) 916
§ 202.25 913
§ 202.25(a) 917
§ 202.26 .... 201, 205
§ 202.26(e) 918
§ 202.26(g)(2) 44
§ 202.27 .... 926, 930
§ 202.27(b) 114
§ 202.27–a 709
§ 202.27–a(i) 148, 709
§ 202.27–a(j) 709
§ 202.27–b 709
§ 202.28 714
§ 202.31 966
§ 202.32 966
§ 202.35 975
§ 202.36 966
§ 202.40 .... 936, 974, 976
§ 202.42 .... 335, 336
§ 202.43 .... 940, 941, 943
§ 202.44 945
§ 202.45 1000
§ 202.46(a) 702, 709
§ 202.47 1053
§ 202.48(a) 623, 624, 625
§ 202.48(b) 625
§ 202.48(c)(2) 623, 624, 625, 626, 627
§ 202.56 .... 198, 201, 903, 906
§ 202.59 802
§§ 202.59–202.61 815
§ 202.60 802
§ 202.61 802
§ 202.64 914
§ 202.67 472
§ 202.69 333
§ 202.70 .... 596, 669, 672
§ 202.70(a) 153
§ 202.70(b) 153
§ 202.70(c) 25, 26, 153
§ 202.70(g) 807, 828, 868, 979
§ 205.7 475
§ 205.13 966
§ 206.5 475
§ 206.8 595
§ 206.9 595

§ 206.10	205	§ 221.1(a)	853, 854, 855, 891
§ 206.11	851	§ 221.2(c)	851, 855
§ 206.12	903, 906	§ 500.2(a)	1331
§§ 206.13 et seq.	901	§ 500.2(f)	1331
§ 206.17	966	§ 500.5	1331
§ 206.19	335	§ 500.9	1315
§ 206.21	802	§ 500.10	1315
§ 207.4	475	§ 500.11(i)	1331
§ 207.33	966	§ 500.12	1335
§ 207.37	623	§ 500.13(c)	1339
§ 208.3	199	§ 500.14	1330, 1338
§ 208.4	475	§ 500.15	1335
§ 208.7	508	§ 500.16	1335, 1342
§ 208.10	595	§ 500.21	1339, 1340
§ 208.11	595	§§ 500.21–500.22	1342
§ 208.12	851	§ 500.22	1339
§ 208.13	882	§ 500.22(b)(4)	1302, 1342
§ 208.14	901	§ 500.23	1285
§ 208.16	715	§ 500.24	1347
§ 208.17	903, 906	§ 500.27	348, 1300, 1301
§§ 208.17 et seq.	901	§ 600.4	1340
§ 208.20	913	§ 600.5(a)	1336
§ 208.21	913	§ 600.5(c)	1330
§ 208.22	917	§ 600.5(f)	1333
§ 208.25	966	§ 600.10	1334, 1336
§ 208.32	709	§ 600.10(c)	1337
§ 208.33	623	§ 600.10(d)	1337
§ 208.35	335, 977	§ 600.10(d)(1)	1339
§ 208.36	472	§ 600.10(d)(2)(i)	1340
§ 210.4	475	§ 600.10(d)(2)(iv)	1340
§ 210.8	595	§ 600.11	1331, 1340
§ 210.9	595	§ 600.12	1341
§ 210.10	205	§ 600.17	1315
§ 210.12	851	§ 640.1	27, 33, 34, 1280, 1281
§ 210.13	882	§ 670.10.3(a)(3)	1339
§ 210.14	901	§ 670.10–a	1334
§ 210.16	714	§ 670.10–b	1334
§ 210.17	903, 906	§ 670.10–c	1334
§§ 210.17 et seq.	901	§ 670.2(e)	1315
§ 210.20	913	§ 670.20	1340
§ 210.21	913	§ 670.4	1341
§ 210.22	917	§ 670.8(d)	1341
§ 210.25	966	§ 670.9	1336
§ 210.33	623	§ 670.9(a)	1330
§ 210.36	472	§ 670.9(b)	1330
§ 212.3	199	§ 670.9(c)	1330
§ 212.4	475	§ 730.1	1280, 1281, 1285
§ 212.7	508	§ 730.1(b)	27
§ 212.10	595	§ 730.1(b)(1)	34
§ 212.11	595	§ 730.1(b)(2)	33
§ 212.12	851	§ 730.1(d)	27, 28, 35, 36, 38
§ 212.13	882	§ 800.4(a)	1330
§ 212.14	901	§ 800.4(b)	1330
§ 212.16	715	§ 800.4(d)	1330
§ 212.17	903, 906	§ 800.5(a)	1334
§§ 212.17 et seq.	901	§ 800.6(a)	1333
§ 212.20	913	§ 800.8(a)	1339
§ 212.21	913	§ 800.9	1335, 1339
§ 212.22	917	§ 1000.3(d)	1330
§ 212.25	966	§ 1000.4	1334
§ 212.33	623	§ 1000.4(a)	1330
§ 212.36	472	§ 1000.4(c)	1330

§ 1000.4(f)(3) 1339
§ 1000.11 1340

RULES OF THE CHIEF JUDGE

Rules of the Chief Judge 4.1 947

FEDERAL RULES OF APPELLATE PROCEDURE

Fed. R. App. P. 10(c) 1333

FEDERAL RULES OF CIVIL PROCEDURE

1 10
3 .... 98, 130, 197
4 ....70, 137, 179, 193
4(b) 130
4(c)(1) 130
4(c)(2) 137
4(c)(2)(C)(ii) 193
4(d) 193
4(e)(2)(B) 179
4(k) 385
4(k)(1)(A) 224
4(m) 130, 138, 139, 141
4(n)(2) 288
5(d)(1) 197
8 .... 507, 508
8(a) 514, 516
9(b) 519
11 .... 1033, 1037
12(b) 540, 655
12(b)(6) 77, 655
13 1107
13(a) 542, 1107
13(b) 542
13(g) 546
15(c) 103, 105, 564
16 918
19 342
19(a) 337, 338
22 385
23 ....355, 356, 357, 366, 368, 369
23(a) 359
23(b) 364
23(b)(3) 359, 365
23(c)(1) 364
23(c)(2) 368
23(c)(3) 369, 377
23(d) 376
24(a) 448, 449
24(b) 452
26–37 ....798, 807, 814, 840
26(a)(1)(A)(i) 829
26(a)(1)(A)(iv) 801
26(a)(2)(B) 827
26(b)(1) 799, 1246
26(b)(4)(A) 827
26(c) 843
26(e) 839, 840
26(e)(1) 840
26(e)(2) 840
28(b) 864
30(b)(4) 854

33 865
37(e) 897
37(e)(2) 798
37(e)(2)(B) 897
39(c) 948
41(a) 717
42(a) 330
45 951
45(a)(3) 951
45(d)(1)(D) 871
47(a) 968
49(a) 988
49(b) 988
51 985
53 944
54(b) 1287
60(b) 1059
60(b)(3) 1063
60(b)(4) 1065
60(b)(5) 1068
64 753
65 763
69(a) 1196, 1207
69(a)(2) 1246
82 356
84 12

FEDERAL RULES OF EVIDENCE

408 823

Index

References are to Sections

ABANDONMENT
Arbitration agreements, § 589
Calendar practice, dismissal of abandoned cases, § 376
Collateral estoppel
    mutuality of estoppel doctrine, § 460
    privity doctrine, § 461
Common law forms of action, § 4
Dismissal of abandoned cases, § 376
Motions, § 250
Mutuality of estoppel doctrine, § 460
Privity doctrine, collateral estoppel, § 461
Statute of limitations, dismissal of abandoned cases, § 376

ABATEMENT OF CLAIMS
Substitution of parties, § 185

ABRIDGEMENT STATUTES
Limitations of actions, altering the period, § 38

ABSTENTION DOCTRINE
Federal practice, § 613

ABUSE
Disclosure, protection against abuse, § 353
Money judgments, enforcement, protective order, § 522
Sanctions for abusive conduct in litigation, § 414A

ACCELERATED JUDGMENTS
    Generally, § 256, § 297
Abandoned cases, dismissal motion, § 376
Abortive motion, salvaging something from, summary judgment, § 286
Actions subject to, summary judgment, § 280
Affidavits, proof, summary judgment, § 281
Affirmative defenses usable, dismissal motion, § 263
Appearance, default after; 5 days notice of time, § 296
Application, § 295
Capacity to sue, lack of, dismissal motion, § 261
Complaint, motion in lieu of conversion,
    summary judgment, § 292
    denial, effect of, summary judgment, § 292
    generally, summary judgment, § 288
    judgment as basis for, summary judgment, § 290
    money instrument as basis for motion, summary judgment, § 289
    procedure, summary judgment, § 291
Consumer credit transactions, § 295
Contract action, breach of; twenty-day notice requirements, § 296
Corporations served pursuant to BCL Section 306; twenty-day notice requirements, § 296

Counterclaim non-interposable, dismissal motion, § 264
    summary judgment, § 285
Cross-motion, time to make, summary judgment, § 279
Deadlines, court rules imposing, summary judgment, § 279
Default Judgments (this index)
Defenses
    affirmative defenses usable, dismissal motion, § 263
    documentary evidence, defense based on, dismissal motion, § 259
    motion to dismiss defense, dismissal motion, § 269
Defined, summary judgment, § 278
Discontinuance (this index)
Dismissal Motion (this index)
Documentary evidence, defense based on, dismissal motion, § 259
Effect of discontinuance, § 298
Extending responding time, dismissal motion, § 277
Failure to appear, defined, § 293
Failure to prosecute, dismissal motion, § 375
Federal practice
    dismissal motion, § 635
    summary judgment, § 635
    vacating in, § 629
Five-day notice requirements, § 296
Forum non conveniens, dismissal motion, § 28
Good cause to entertain late motion, summary judgment, § 279
Grounds for, dismissal motion, § 258
Immediate trial of fact issue
    dismissal motion, § 271
    summary judgment, § 284
Indispensable party, for, dismissal motion, § 268
Jurisdiction
    personal jurisdiction, lack of, dismissal motion, § 266
    rem jurisdiction, lack of, dismissal motion, § 267
    subject matter jurisdiction as basis, dismissal motion, § 260
Late motion, good cause to entertain, summary judgment, § 279
Leave to replead, dismissal motion, § 275
Methods of discontinuance, § 297
Military service, affidavit that defendant is not in, § 79
Money instrument as basis for motion in lieu of complaint, summary judgment, § 289
Notice of application, § 296
    discontinuance by, § 297
One year after default, taking proceedings to enter, § 296

Option to plead instead of move, dismissal
     motion, § 274
Order, discontinuance by, § 297
Other action pending, dismissal motion, § 262
Papers on application, § 295
Partial, summary judgment, § 285
Personal jurisdiction, lack of, dismissal motion,
     § 266
Pretrial, summary judgment, § 402
Procedure, dismissal motion, § 257
Proof on, summary judgment, § 281
Rem jurisdiction, lack of, dismissal motion, § 267
Requirements, § 256
Res judicata, § 276, § 287, § 402, § 451
Salvaging something from abortive motion,
     summary judgment, § 286
Searching record, summary judgment, § 282
Single motion rule, dismissal motion, § 273
Standing to sue, lack of, dismissal motion, § 261
Stipulations
     discontinuance by, § 297
     extending time to move for, summary
          judgment, § 279
Subject matter jurisdiction as basis, dismissal
     motion, § 260
Summary Judgment (this index)
Taking, § 293
Time or date
     for application, § 294
     for motion, dismissal motion, § 272
     to move for, summary judgment, § 279
Twenty-day notice requirements, § 296
Vacating default judgments
          generally, § 108
          affidavit of merits, § 108
Waiver, dismissal motion, § 274
Want of prosecution, dismissal motion, § 375

ACCIDENTS
Class actions, mass accident cases, § 142
Personal injury cases, accrual of claim, § 40
Reports by employees, disclosure, § 348
Stipulations, ground for setting aside, § 204

ACCOUNTS AND ACCOUNTING
Bank accounts, money judgments, enforcement,
     § 522
Bill of particulars, § 238
Compulsory reference, long account cases, § 379
Disclosure, accounting action, § 344
Long account cases, compulsory reference, § 379
Mutual account, limitations of actions, § 50
Statute of limitations
     malpractice, accountants, accrual,
          continuous treatment theory, § 42
     multiple recovery theories against
          accountants, § 37
Temporary receivers, § 332

ACCRUAL
     Generally, § 40
Authority, breach of warranty of; discovery
     accrual, § 43
Borrowing statute, § 57
Continuous representation exception, malpractice
     claim, § 42

Continuous treatment exception, medical
     malpractice, § 42
Continuous wrongs, § 40
Defamation, § 40
Delayed-accrual rules, § 40
Discovery rule, § 40, § 43
Exposure cases, discovery accrual, § 43
Foreign claims, § 57
Fraud, discovery accrual, § 43
Joining claims and, § 40
Medical malpractice, § 42
Nonresidents, § 57
Out-of-state, § 57
Statute of Limitations (this index)
Warranties, § 41

ACKNOWLEDGMENTS
Requirements, § 201

ACTIONS AND PROCEEDINGS
Accompanying papers, service of process,
     summons, and papers, service of process,
     summons, and papers, § 60
Accrual of claim, malpractice, § 42
Actual controversy, declaratory judgments, § 436
Add-ons for recipient of paper, service of process,
     summons, and papers, § 202
Adequately protecting interests of class,
     representative parties, § 141
Administrative Proceedings (this index)
Affidavits of service, service of process, summons,
     and papers, § 202
Affix-and-mail, service of process, summons, and
     papers, § 71, § 73, § 74
Agent for service, designation of, service of
     process, summons, and papers, § 73
Age of persons authorized to serve, service of
     process, summons, and papers, § 63
All parties, service on, service of process,
     summons, and papers, § 203
Altering initiatory papers after filing but before
     service, service of process, summons, and
     papers, § 63
Amendment allowing for correction of many filing
     mistakes, service of process, summons, and
     papers, § 63
Appeal
     Court of appeals, § 527
     electronic filing and perfecting appeal,
          § 536
     stay of proceedings, § 535
Appearance by defendant; response to CPLR
     305(b) notice, service of process, summons,
     and papers, § 60
Appellate division, electronic filing, § 11
Arbitration, stay of proceedings, § 592
Article 78 proceeding
     arbitrary and capricious test, § 561
     primary mission to review decisions, § 4
     review of penalty or discipline, § 561
Associations, service of process, summons, and
     papers, § 68
Attachment; summons service within 60 days,
     service of process, summons, and papers,
     § 319

Attorneys
    initiatory papers, service of process, summons, and papers, **§ 202**
    process server's acts, attorney for plaintiff accountable for, service of process, summons, and papers, **§ 63**
Bare summons, service of process, summons, and papers, **§ 60, § 231**
Board, court or commission, service of process, summons, and papers, **§ 70**
Children, service of process, summons, and papers, **§ 68, § 195**
Civil judicial proceeding, defined, **§ 6**
Class Actions (this index)
Clerk of court, filing
    commencement of action, **§ 63**
    electronic filing, service of process, **§ 202**
    refusal to accept papers, commencement of action, **§ 63**
    service of process, summons, and papers, **§ 63**
Commencement of Action (this index)
Commission, court or board, service of process, summons, and papers, **§ 70**
Complaint accompanying summons
    form of summons served with complaint, service of process, summons, and papers, **§ 61**
    requirements, service of process, summons, and papers, **§ 60**
Completion of service, service of process, summons, and papers, **§ 202**
Conciliation proceedings, jurisdiction, **§ 16**
Conditions precedent to suit, **§ 32**
Consensual electronic filing, **§ 63A**
Conservatees, service of process, summons, and papers, **§ 68**
Consolidation of Actions (this index)
Continuous treatment
    exception to accrual of claim, malpractice, **§ 42**
    toll for derivative claim, malpractice, **§ 42**
Corporations, service of process, summons, and papers, **§ 68, § 70, § 296**
Correction of many filing mistakes, amendment allowing, service of process, summons, and papers, **§ 63**
Counties and actions with mandatory electronic filing, **§ 63A**
Court, board or commission, service of process, summons, and papers, **§ 70**
Court of claims, electronic filing, **§ 17**
Court-ordered service, service of process, summons, and papers, **§ 75**
CPLR 305(b) notice. Default notice; CPLR 305(b), infra
CPLR 305(b) notice, service of process, summons, and papers, **§ 60, § 60**
Credibility of procrastinator affected, service of process, summons, and papers, **§ 231A**
Curing technical defects in service, service of process, summons, and papers, **§ 76B**
Declaratory Judgments (this index)
Default judgment, vacating, service of process, summons, and papers, **§ 108**

Default notice; CPLR 305(b)
    appearance by defendant; response to notice, service of process, summons, and papers, **§ 60**
    defined, service of process, summons, and papers, **§ 60**
    form, service of process, summons, and papers, **§ 62**
    requirements, service of process, summons, and papers, **§ 60**
    response to notice, service of process, summons, and papers, **§ 60**
Defendant's side as class, **§ 146**
Defined, **§ 4, § 139**
    special proceedings, **§ 547**
Deliver-and-mail, service of process, summons, and papers, **§ 71, § 72**
Derivative claim, continuous treatment toll, malpractice, **§ 42**
Disclosure, special proceedings, **§ 555**
Discovery rule and malpractice, **§ 43**
Discretion of court, class actions, **§ 147**
Disposition, of special proceedings, **§ 556**
Dram shop actions, contribution, **§ 172**
E-filing, service of process, summons, and papers, **§ 202**
Electronic Filing (this index)
Enticement into jurisdiction, service of process, summons, and papers, **§ 67**
Estates and trusts, service of process, summons, and papers, **§ 68**
Exceptions to mandatory electronic filing, **§ 63A**
Expert disclosure in malpractice actions, malpractice, **§ 348A**
Extending time for service, service of process, summons, and papers, **§ 63**
Facsimile, by, service of process, summons, and papers, **§ 202**
Federal practice
    commencement of action, **§ 621**
Federal practice, service of process, summons, and papers, **§ 624, § 625**
Filing, commencement, **§ 63**
Fluid recovery, class actions, **§ 145**
Follow-up relief, need for declaratory judgments, **§ 441**
Foreign actions
    disclosure to aid, **§ 352**
    jurisdiction, **§ 28**
Foreign nations and agencies, service of process, summons, and papers, **§ 68**
Foreign object exception to accrual of claim, malpractice, **§ 42**
Forms
    default notice 305(b), summons served with, service of process, summons, and papers, **§ 62**
    summons served with complaint, service of process, summons, and papers, **§ 61**
Forum non conveniens, stay of proceedings, **§ 28**
Guardians, service of process, summons, and papers, **§ 68**
Hearings, special proceedings, **§ 556**

Immunity from service
    diplomatic immunity, service of process,
        summons, and papers, § 68
    sovereign immunity, service of process,
        summons, and papers, § 68
    voluntarily in state, service of process,
        summons, and papers, § 68
Incapacitated persons, service of process,
    summons, and papers, § 68, § 195
Incompetents and conservatees, service of
    process, summons, and papers, § 68
Incorrect initiatory papers failing to name
    defendant, court invoking CPLR 2001 to
        forgive, electronic filing, § 63A
Index number, commencement of action, § 77
Individual Assignment System, consolidation of
    actions, § 128
Infants, service of process, summons, and papers,
    § 68
Initiatory papers versus interlocutory papers,
    service of process, summons, and papers,
    § 202
Insurance disputes, declaratory judgments, § 437
Interlocutory papers versus initiatory papers,
    service of process, summons, and papers,
    § 202
Interrogatories, service of process, summons, and
    papers, § 361
Issuance of summons, service of process,
    summons, and papers, § 60
Joint tort liability adjustment; third-party
    practice, malpractice, § 168C
Joint trial and consolidation of actions, § 127,
    § 128
Judgment
    class actions, § 147
    judgment declaratory action, § 440
Judicial administration, suits involving, proper
    parties, § 187
Jury trial, declaratory judgments, § 439
Late e-filing after county clerk rejected hard-copy
    filing, supreme court refusing to forgive,
    § 63A
Late notice, leave to serve, service of process,
    summons, and papers, § 32
Law office failure for late service of pleadings,
    service of process, summons, and papers,
    § 231
Laws, rules and administrative orders governing
    electronic filing, § 63A
Limitations of time, declaratory judgments, § 438
Limited liability partnerships, service of process,
    summons, and papers, § 68
Limited partnerships, service of process,
    summons, and papers, § 68
Local actions, venue, § 116, § 121
Longarm jurisdiction, malpractice, § 88
Mail
    affix-and-mail, service of process, summons,
        and papers, § 71, § 73, § 74
    deliver-and-mail, service of process,
        summons, and papers, § 71, § 72
    first-class mail, service of process,
        summons, and papers, § 202

ordinary mail, service of process, summons,
    and papers, § 202
personal delivery, service of process,
    summons, and papers, § 66, § 76A
Malpractice (this index)
Mandatory electronic filing
    generally, § 63A
    counties and actions with, § 63A
    exclusions, § 63A
    opting out, § 63A
Matrimonial actions
    declaratory judgments, § 437
    service of process, summons, and papers,
    § 76
Medical malpractice
    accrual of claim, § 42
    continuous treatment exception to accrual
        of claim, § 42
    continuous treatment toll for derivative
        claim, § 42
    derivative claim, continuous treatment toll
        for, § 42
    discovery rule and, § 43
    expert disclosure in malpractice actions,
        § 348A
    foreign object exception to accrual of claim,
        § 42
    joint tort liability adjustment; third-party
        practice, § 168C
    longarm jurisdiction, § 88
    Statute of Limitations (this index)
    2-years and six months period, § 35, § 42
Methods, generally, service of process, summons,
    and papers, § 66, § 202
Motions
    service of process, summons, and papers,
        § 246, § 247, § 249, § 250
    special proceedings, § 554
    stay of proceedings, § 255
Municipal entities, service of process, summons,
    and papers, § 70
Neglect proceedings, jurisdiction, § 16
New classes of actions, supreme court
    jurisdiction, § 12
New parties, need to add, service of process,
    summons, and papers, § 231A
New York City Civil Court, electronic filing, § 19
Notice, class actions, § 143
Notice of claim, service of process, summons, and
    papers, § 32, § 32, § 231A
Numerosity requirement, class actions, § 141
120 days after filing to effect service, service of
    process, summons, and papers, § 63
Opting out
    class actions, § 144
    mandatory filing, electronic filing, § 63A
Order allowing class actions, § 142
Outside state, service, service of process,
    summons, and papers, § 100
Overnight delivery, service of process, summons,
    and papers, § 202
Parties, to special proceedings, § 551
Partnerships, service of process, summons, and
    papers, § 68
Paternity proceedings, jurisdiction, § 16

Personal delivery
  apartment house, service of process, summons, and papers, § 66
  concealing summons invalidating service, service of process, summons, and papers, § 66
  corporations, service of process, summons, and papers, § 70
  deliver-and-mail, service of process, summons, and papers, § 71, § 72
  due diligence, service of process, summons, and papers, § 66
  family members, to, service of process, summons, and papers, § 66
  generally, service of process, summons, and papers, § 59, § 66
  mail, service of process, summons, and papers, § 66, § 76A
  person, to, service of process, summons, and papers, § 66
  redelivery, service of process, summons, and papers, § 66
  substituted service, service of process, summons, and papers, § 71
Physical office requirement, service of process, summons, and papers, § 202
Pleadings
  complaint accompanying summons
    form of summons served with complaint, service of process, summons, and papers, § 61
    requirements, service of process, summons, and papers, § 60
  credibility of procrastinator affected, service of process, summons, and papers, § 231A
  default, service of process, summons, and papers, § 231A
  defect in summons service, service of process, summons, and papers, § 231A
  federal courts; late service, service of process, summons, and papers, § 231A
  generally, service of process, summons, and papers, § 231
  jurisdictional defects, service of process, summons, and papers, § 231A
  law office failure for late service, service of process, summons, and papers, § 231
  leave time for trouble, service of process, summons, and papers, § 231A
  new parties, need to add, service of process, summons, and papers, § 231A
  notice, inadequate, service of process, summons, and papers, § 231A
  relation back doctrine, dispensing reliance on, service of process, summons, and papers, § 231A
  responding time, service of process, summons, and papers, § 231
  special proceedings, § 552
  statute of limitations, service of process, summons, and papers, § 231A

timely filing but late service, service of process, summons, and papers, § 231A
  wrong person, serving, service of process, summons, and papers, § 231A
Prior law, class actions, § 140
Procedure, declaratory judgments, § 438
Procedure, special proceedings, § 550
Proof of, service of process, summons, and papers, § 79
Publication, service by; rem jurisdiction, service of process, summons, and papers, § 107
Public authorities, service of process, summons, and papers, § 70
Questions of law or fact common to class, § 141
Recovery of statutory penalty, class actions barred, § 141
Relation back doctrine, dispensing reliance on, service of process, summons, and papers, § 231A
Rem jurisdiction and service by publication, service of process, summons, and papers, § 107
Replevin, commencement of action, § 341
Requirements, service of process, summons, and papers, § 59
Requirements of class actions, § 141
Res judicata, § 139, § 454, § 456
Response
  CPLR 305(b) notice, response by defendant to, service of process, summons, and papers, § 60
  summons, to, service of process, summons, and papers, § 231
Rules, laws and administrative orders governing electronic filing, § 63A
Sabbath, service on, service of process, summons, and papers, § 63
Saturdays, service on, service of process, summons, and papers, § 63, § 202
Service of Process and Papers (this index)
Settlement of class actions, § 147
Sewer service, service of process, summons, and papers, § 71
Signature on papers, electronic filing, § 201
Sovereign immunity, service of process, summons, and papers, § 68
Special Proceedings (this index)
Starting actions by electronic filing, § 63A
State, on, service of process, summons, and papers, § 70
Statute of limitations
  new action following termination of prior action, service of process, summons, and papers, § 52
  special proceedings, § 548
  3-year period, professionals, nonmedical malpractice cases, § 35
  tolling, stay of proceedings, § 51
  2-years and six months period, medical malpractice of professionals, § 35
Statutory instructions on service, specific, service of process, summons, and papers, § 202
Stay of Proceedings (this index)

Submitted on facts
        generally, § 304
        disposition of submission, § 305
Subpoenas, service of process, summons, and
        papers, § 383
Substituted service, service of process, summons,
        and papers, § 71
Summary Proceedings (this index)
Sunday, service on, service of process, summons,
        and papers, § 63
Surrogate's court, electronic filing, § 15
Technical defects in service, curing, service of
        process, summons, and papers, **§ 76B**
Time computation, service of process, summons,
        and papers, § 202
Transient service, service of process, summons,
        and papers, § 59
Transitory actions, venue, § 116, § 118
2-years and six months period, malpractice, **§ 35,**
        § 42
Typicality of claims of class representatives,
        § 141
Unincorporated associations, service of process,
        summons, and papers, § 68
Uses, declaratory judgments, § 437
Venue (this index)
Warrant and stay, summary proceedings, § 580
When and by whom summons served,
        commencement of action, service of process,
        summons, and papers, § 63
Wrong person, serving, service of process,
        summons, and papers, § 231A

AD DAMNUM CLAUSE
Amendment of damages, § 237
Closing statement; mentioning amount
        demanded in complaint, § 396
Damages
        amendment of, § 237
        closing statement; mentioning amount
            demanded in complaint, § 396
Defined, § 217
Leave to amend, § 25
Money actions, pleading, § 217

ADDITUR
        Generally, § 407
Court of appeals, finality, § 527

ADDRESSES
Arbitration, party serving notice of intention to
        arbitrate, § 593
Attachment order, address of plaintiff's lawyer,
        § 316
Disclosure, § 350, § 365
Papers, form of, § 201

ADJOURNMENT
Arbitration hearing, § 597
Motions, § 247
Summary proceedings, § 578
Trial, § 389

ADMINISTRATION OF COURTS
Chief administrator's role, § 5
Procedure, § 5

ADMINISTRATIVE PROCEEDINGS
Appeal to court of appeals, § 527
Article 78 proceeding
        arbitrary and capricious test, § 561
        primary mission to review decisions, § 4
        review of penalty or discipline, § 561
Res judicata, § 456

ADMISSIONS
Answer, § 221
Arbitration, failure to appear, § 600
Disclosure; request for admission, § 350, § 364
Notice to admit, § 364
Pretrial conferences, § 374
Summary judgment motion, proof, § 281
Time, notice to admit, § 364
Trial motions, § 402

ADMISSION TO PRACTICE OF LAW
Appellate division, § 11
Court of Appeals, rules of, § 10

ADOPTION
Concurrent jurisdiction, § 16
Family court jurisdiction, § 16

ADVERSE POSSESSION
Affirmative defense, § 223
Statute of limitations, 10-year period, § 35

ADVISORY JURY
        Generally, § 381
Pleading equitable and legal claims, § 209

ADVISORY OPINIONS
Court of appeals, § 10, § 528A
Federal courts, § 612
Standing to sue, § 136

AFFIDAVITS
        Generally, § 205
Affix and mail service, § 74
Attachment, § 316
Confession of judgment, § 300
Default judgments
        affidavit that defendant is not in military
            service, § 79
        vacation, affidavit of merits, § 108
Defined, § 205
Electronic signatures, § 205
Ex parte motions, § 244
Jurors, verdict clarification, § 401
Motions
        cross motions, § 249
        reply affidavits, § 246
Preliminary injunctions, § 329
Proof of service, § 79
Reply affidavits, motions, § 246
Seizure of chattel, § 339
Service, affidavits of, § 202
Summary judgment motion, proof, § 281
Temporary receivership, motion papers, § 333
Vacating defaults, affidavit of merits, § 108

AFFIRMATIONS
        Generally, § 205
Electronic signatures, § 205
Oaths and Affirmations (this index)

AFFIRMATIVE DEFENSES
Generally, § 214, § 215, § 223
Adverse possession, § 223
Arbitration and award
generally, § 223
dismissal motion, defenses usable, § 263
Bankruptcy, discharge in
generally, § 223
dismissal motion, defenses usable, § 263
Collateral estoppel
generally, § 223
for detailed treatment see **Collateral Estoppel** (this index)
dismissal motion, defenses usable, § 263
Comparative negligence rule, culpable conduct of plaintiff, § 223
Defamation, truth as, § 223
Disability
generally, § 223
dismissal motion, defenses usable, § 263
Discharge in bankruptcy
generally, § 223
dismissal motion, defenses usable, § 263
Dismissal motion, defenses usable on, § 263
Fraud, § 223
Illegality, § 223
Infancy or other disability
generally, § 223
dismissal motion, defenses usable, § 263
Joint liability tort defendants with culpability of 50% or less, § 223
Laches, § 223
Limitations of actions
generally, § 223
dismissal motion, defenses usable, § 263
Motion to dismiss, defenses usable in, § 263
Payment
generally, § 223
dismissal motion, defenses usable, § 263
Plaintiff, culpable conduct, of comparative negligence rule, § 223
Pleading, § 215, § 223, § 223
Privilege, qualified, § 223
Qualified privilege, § 223
Release
generally, § 223
dismissal motion, defenses usable, § 263
Res judicata
generally, § 223
for detailed treatment see **Res Judicata** (this index)
dismissal motion, defenses usable, § 263
Standing to sue, § 223
Statute of Frauds
generally, § 223
dismissal motion, defenses usable, § 263
Statute of limitations, § 34, § 223
pleading, § 223
suspension of remedy, theory, § 34
Statute of Limitations
generally, § 223
dismissal motion, defenses usable, § 263
Truth in defamation action, § 223
Types of, § 223

AGE
Service of papers; age of persons authorized to serve, § 63

AGENTS
Attorney as agent, § 96
Election of remedies, § 218
Foreign agencies, § 61
Jurisdiction
generally, § 96
longarm jurisdiction; agency theory, § 95
Longarm jurisdiction; agency theory, § 95
Mandamus against, § 558
Physical and mental examinations, § 363
Pleading, verification, § 233
Public agency, substitution of parties, § 186
Service of process, designation of agent to receive, § 73
State agencies
automatic stays, § 535
Court of claims, jurisdiction, § 17
Summons, service on, § 73
Verification of pleading, § 233

ALIMONY
Longarm jurisdiction, § 90

AMENDED PLEADINGS
Ad damnum, § 237
Bill of particulars, § 240
Conditional order granting amendment, § 237
As of course, § 236
Interposition of claim; statute of limitations, § 49
Leave, by, § 237
Merits, consideration of, § 237
Service of pleadings and responsive pleadings, § 237
Statute of limitations
interposition of claim, § 49
leave, amendment by, § 237
Summons
generally, § 64
parties, changing, § 65
Supplement pleading, motion to, § 237

ANSWER
Generally, § 221
Admissions, § 221
Affirmative defenses, § 223
Cross-claims, § 227, § 228
Cross-motions, § 249
Denials, § 221
Dismissal motion extending responding time, § 277
Form of answer; cross-claims, § 228
Marked pleadings, § 222
Summary proceedings, § 576

APPEALS
Generally, § 9, § 10, § 524
Admission to practice, § 10, § 11
Advisory opinion, § 10
Aggrieved party, § 525
Appeals to appellate division, § 526
Appellate Division (this index)
Appellate process, § 541
Appellate terms, § 9

Appendices, § 539
Article 78 proceedings, transfer of, § 568
Briefs
  electronic filing of records and, § 536
  perfecting appeal, § 539
Calendar practice and argument, § 540
Certification to Court of Appeals by other courts,
  § 528A
City courts, § 21
County courts, § 14
Court of Appeals (this index)
Court of claims, § 17
Criminal judgment appeal, § 10
Decision of Appellate division in Court of
  Appeals, § 10
Defects, § 534
Digital format, submission of documents in, § 10
Direct appeal, § 9
Discretion of court, § 11
Disposition, § 543
District courts, § 20
E-filings, mandatory, § 11
Electronic filing of records and briefs, § 536
Ex parte application, order on, § 244
Extension of time, § 6, § 534
Facts, review of, § 10
Federal practice, § 642
Final judgment, scope of review from, § 530
First Department, § 11
Fourth Department, § 11
Injunctions, § 535
Judgments, appealability of, § 526
Judicial departments, § 11
Law and facts, review of both, § 11
Move for leave, § 533
Omissions, § 534
Orders, of, § 526
Organization, § 11
Perfecting appeal
  generally, § 536
  appendices, § 539
  briefs, § 539
  calendar practice and argument, § 540
  electronic filing of records and briefs, § 536
  record, § 538
  transcripts, § 537
Permission, by, § 528
Reargue or renew motions, § 254
Reargument, § 544
Record, § 538
Remittitur, § 545
Reviewability
  final judgment, scope of review from, § 530
  particular courts, in, § 529
As of right, § 527
Second Department, § 11
Small claims, § 584
Stays, § 535
Subsequent orders, § 532
Supreme court, from, § 12
Surrogate's court, § 15
Taking appeal
  defects, § 534
  injunctions, § 535
  move for leave, § 533

omissions, § 534
procedure, § 531
stays, § 535
subsequent orders, § 532
time extensions, § 534
time to appeal, § 533
Third Department, § 11
Time extensions, § 534
Time to appeal, § 533
Transcripts, § 537
Want of prosecution, dismissal of appeal for,
  § 542

APPEARANCE
  Generally, § 109
Adding claims, § 114
CPLR 305(b) notice, response by defendant to,
  § 60
Default judgment after; 5 days notice of time,
  § 296
Defined, § 109
How and when to appear, § 110
Informal, § 112
Jurisdiction
  longarm jurisdiction, § 91
  objection to, making and preserving, § 111
  rem actions, § 113
Limited, § 109, § 113
Longarm jurisdiction, § 91
Objection to jurisdiction, making and preserving,
  § 111
Procedure, § 110
Qualified, § 109
Rem actions, § 113
Representation by attorney, § 115
Restricted, § 109
Special, § 109

APPELLATE DIVISION
  Generally, § 11
Admission to practice, § 11
Appeals to, § 526
Article 78 proceedings, transfer of, § 568
Discretion of court, § 11
E-filings, mandatory, § 11
First Department, § 11
Fourth Department, § 11
Judicial departments, § 11
Law and facts, review of both, § 11
Organization, § 11
Second Department, § 11
Third Department, § 11

APPELLATE TERMS
  Generally, § 9, § 13
First Department, § 13
Second Department, § 13

APPRAISALS
Arbitration, § 608

ARBITRATION
  Generally, § 586
Abandonment, arbitration agreements, § 589
Adjournment of hearing, § 597
Agreement to, § 588
Appraisal proceeding, § 608

Arbitrability, § 589
Arbitrator's role, § 596
Attachment, § 599
Attorney-client fee dispute resolution program,
  § 603
Awards
       generally, § 600
    attorney-client fee dispute resolution
      program, § 603
    compulsory arbitration, scope of review in,
      § 603
    confirmation, § 601
    courts involvement other than supreme
      court, § 606
    judgment on, § 605
    modification, application for, § 604
    scope of review, § 602, § 603
    supreme court, courts involvement other
      than, § 606
    vacating, § 602
Compel or stay, applying to, § 592
Compulsory arbitration, scope of review in, § 603
Consolidation, § 598
Court applications, generally, § 591
Courts involvement other than supreme court,
  § 606
Custody proceedings, § 587
Defined, § 586
Disclosure from arbitrators, § 345
Evidence, § 586, § 597
Federal Arbitration Act compared, § 607
Form, § 591
Hearing, § 597
Impleader, § 598
Injunctions, preliminary, § 599
Interest on awards, § 411
Judgment on awards, § 411, § 605
Modification of award, application for, § 604
Notice of intention to arbitrate, § 593
Preliminary injunctions, § 599
Provisional remedies, § 599
Public policy issues, § 587
Remedies, § 599
Res judicata, § 456
Separability, § 589
Simplified Procedure, § 609
Small claims; court-annexed arbitration of claims
     under stated sums, § 585B
Specific performance, award, § 587
Statute of limitations, § 35, § 590
Stay or compel, applying to, § 592
Supreme court, courts involvement other than,
  § 606
Termination, arbitration agreements, § 589
Threshold questions, § 589, § 590
Trial of threshold question, § 594
Valuation or appraisal proceeding, § 608
Venue, § 591
Visitation, § 587
Waiver of, § 595

ARREST
Enforcement of money judgments and, § 513

ARTICLE 78 PROCEEDINGS
  Generally, § 557

Affidavits, accompanying pleadings, § 567
Albany County, venue of proceeding against
    certain respondents, § 565
Answer, § 567
Appellate division, transfer to, § 568
Arbitrary and capricious test, § 561
Body against which proceeding maintained, § 564
Certiorari, § 560, § 561
Commencement of proceedings, § 567
Comptroller, Albany County as venue of
    proceeding against, § 565
Determination, § 568
Discipline or penalty, judicial review of, § 562
Education, Commissioner of, Albany County as
    venue of proceeding against, § 565
Enforcement of judgments, § 570
Fact, trial of issue of, § 569
Forum shopping, § 565
Freedom of Information Law, denial of request
    reviewable, § 558
Hearings and determination, § 568
Impleader, § 564
Incorporated universities, § 558
Interpleader, § 564
Intervention, § 564
Issue of fact, issue of, § 569
Joinder of parties, § 564
Judge as respondent, § 564
Judgments, § 570
Judicial hearing officer as respondent, § 564
Judicial review of penalty or discipline, § 562
Justice as respondent, § 564
Labor unions, unincorporated, § 558
Laches, § 566
Limitations, § 563
Mandamus, § 558, § 561
Name of respondent, § 564
Non-commercial entities, § 558
Officer against whom proceeding maintained,
  § 564
Official title of respondent, § 564
Parties, § 564
Penalty or discipline, judicial review of, § 562
Petitioner, § 564
Pleadings, § 567
Primary mission to review decisions, § 4
Prohibition, § 559
Reply, § 567
Request for Judicial Intervention (RJI), § 567
Respondent, § 564
    name or official title of respondent, § 564
Restrictions, § 563
Review of penalty or discipline, § 561
Standing to sue, challenging, § 564
State Administrative Procedure Act (SAPA, § 557
Statute of limitations, § 35, § 566
Tax commisioner, Albany County as venue of
    proceeding against, § 565
Trial of issue of fact, § 569
Unincorporated labor unions, § 558
Universities, incorporated, § 558
Venue, § 565

ASSIGNMENTS
Counterclaim against assignee-plaintiff, § 226

ASSOCIATIONS
Service of process, summons and papers, § 68

ASSUMPTION OF RISK
Comparative negligence, § 168E

ATTACHMENT
          Generally, § 313
Annulling, § 325
Applying for, § 316
Arbitration, § 599
Constitutionality, § 315
Defined, § 313
Discharge, § 325
Disclosure to aid, § 324
Discretionary, as, § 317
Disposition of property, § 326
Disputes, § 326
Examples of interplay of requirements, § 322
Federal practice, § 640
Garnishee defined, § 313
Grounds for, § 314
Levy
                    generally, § 320
          perfecting, § 321
          personal property, § 320
          real property, § 320
          seizure, by, § 320
          service, by, § 320
90-day period, § 318
One-day period, § 318
Order, generally, § 313
Perfecting levy, § 321
Priorities, § 326
Property attachable, § 323
Remedies, defendant's, § 325
Service of summons
          levy, service by, § 320
          60 days, within, § 319
60-day period, § 318
10-day period, § 318
Time periods, § 318
Types of property attachable, § 323
Undertakings, action on plaintiff's, § 325
Vacatur, § 325

ATTORNEYS
Address on papers, § 201
Admission to Practice of Law (this index)
Agent, as; jurisdiction, § 96
Appearance; representation by attorney, § 115
Appellate division, admission to practice of law,
          § 11
Arbitration, attorney-client fee dispute resolution
          program, § 603
Court of Appeals, rules and admission to practice
          of law, § 10
Disclosure duties under Rules of Professional
          Conduct, § 352A
Name, address and telephone number on papers,
          § 201
Poor persons, appointment of attorney for, § 192
Process server's acts, attorney for plaintiff
          accountable for, § 63
Rules for admission to practice of law, § 10

Service process
          initiatory papers, § 202
          process server's acts, attorney for plaintiff
                    accountable for, § 63
Telephone numbers on, § 201
Work product rule, § 347, § 348

AUDIO TAPES
Disclosure; privileged communications, § 348

AUTOMOBILES
Motor Vehicles (this index)

BANKRUPTCY
Contribution, § 176
Joint tort liability adjustment; third-party
          practice, § 168C
Riviello problem, § 176

BIFURCATED TRIAL
          Generally, § 130, § 394
Defined, § 130
Jurisdiction, § 23
Trifurcation and, § 130
Wrongful death, § 394

BILL OF PARTICULARS
          Generally, § 238
Amending, § 240
Burden of proof, to be supplied by party with,
          § 238
Defined, § 238
Demands in, § 238
Disclosure device, as, § 238
Limitations on use, § 238
Penalties against demanding party, § 241
Pleading, curing omission of detail, § 216
Procedure, § 239
Purpose, § 238
Remedies, § 241
Supplementing, § 238, § 240
Variances, § 242
Verification, § 238

BONDS AND UNDERTAKINGS
          Generally, § 206
Attachment and action on plaintiff's undertaking,
          § 325
Surety defined, § 206

BORROWING STATUTE
Statute of limitations, § 57

BREACH OF TRUST
Pleading, particularity requirement, § 216

BURDEN OF PROOF
Bill of particulars to be supplied by party with,
          § 238
Collateral estoppel, § 475
Comparative negligence, § 168E
Disclosure, § 344
Joint tort liability adjustment; third-party
          practice, § 168D
Longarm jurisdiction, § 93
Res judicata, § 475

CALENDAR PRACTICE
          Generally, § 368

Abandoned cases, dismissal of, § 376
Appeals, § 540
Calendar defined, § 368
Certificate of readiness, note of issue and, § 369
Consolidation of actions and Individual Assignment System (IAS), § 128
Defined, § 368
Disclosure after case on, § 352
Dual track system of assignment, Individual Assignment System (IAS), § 77A
Ex parte order, judicial intervention (RJI), § 77B
Forms
    certificate of readiness, § 371
    note of issue, § 371
    request for judicial intervention (RJI), § 77C
Individual Assignment System (IAS) (this index)
Motions
    Individual Assignment System (IAS), § 243
    request for judicial intervention (RJI), § 243
Note of Issue (this index)
Obtaining, Individual Assignment System (IAS), § 78
Preferences
    general, § 372
    special, § 373
Preliminary conference and request for judicial intervention (RJI), § 77B
Pretrial conferences, note of issue, § 374
Request for Judicial Intervention (RJI) (this index)
Statement of readiness, § 370
Trial assignment part (TAP), Individual Assignment System (IAS), § 77A

CAPACITY
Standing to Sue (this index)

CAPTIONS
Requirements, § 201

CERTIFICATE OF READINESS
Form, § 371
Note of issue and, § 369

CHANGE OF VENUE
    Generally, § 116
Convenience of material witness, ground, § 124
Demand procedure, § 123
Discretionary grounds, § 124
Effecting, § 125
Grounds, § 124
Impartial trial as issue, § 124
Improper to proper county, from, § 123
Material witnesses, for convenience of, § 124
Third party defendants, § 124

CHATTEL
Rem jurisdiction, § 103
Replevin (this index)

CHILDREN
Appointment, procedure to appoint guardian ad litem, § 197

Authority of guardian ad litem, § 198
Contribution; non-supervision of child, § 175
Definition of guardian ad litem, § 196
Distinguishing guardian ad litem from other guardianships, § 196
Guardians
    generally. **Guardians** (this index)
    Guardian Ad Litem (this index)
Litigation concerning, guardian ad litem, § 193
Qualifications for guardian ad litem, § 198
Representation of **Guardian Ad Litem** (this index)
    Guardians (this index)
Rights regarding guardians ad litem, § 198
Risks if no representative present, guardian ad litem, § 199
Service of process, summons and papers, § 68, § 195
Service of process on guardians, § 68, § 195
Settlement of infant's claim, § 200
Statute of limitations; infancy as disability resulting in toll, § 54
Support
    income execution, § 507A
    longarm jurisdiction, § 90

CHOICE OF FORUM
Factors, § 616
Forum non conveniens doctrine, § 618
Removal, § 619
Statute of limitations, § 615
Venue, § 617

CITIES
Venue, actions against, § 120

CITY COURTS
    Generally, § 21
Appeals, § 21
Jurisdiction, § 21
Monetary jurisdiction, § 21
Summary proceedings, § 21

CIVIL CONTEMPT
Contempt (this index)

CIVIL JUDICIAL PROCEEDINGS
Defined, § 6

CIVIL PRACTICE LAW AND RULES (CPLR)
    Generally
Action defined, § 4
Adoption of rules, § 2
Articles, organization of, § 2
Citation of, § 2
Effective date, § 2
Historical background, § 2
Law and equity distinction abolished, § 4
Purpose of publication, § 1
Rules, organization of, § 2
Uniform acts and, § 3

CLASS ACTIONS
    Generally, § 139
Adequately protecting interests of class, representative parties, § 141
Defendant's side as class, § 146
Defined, § 139

Discretion of court, § 147
Fluid recovery, § 145
Judgment, § 147
Notice of, § 143
Numerosity requirement, § 141
Opting out, § 144
Order allowing, § 142
Prior law, § 140
Questions of law or fact common to class, § 141
Requirements, § 141
Res judicata, § 139, § 454
Settlement, § 147
Typicality of claims of class representatives,
    § 141

CLERKS OF COURT
Filing with, § 63
Late e-filing after county clerk rejected hard-copy
    filing, supreme court refusing to forgive, §
    63A
Refusal to accept papers, § 63, § 63A

CLOSING STATEMENTS
    Generally, § 396
Amount demanded in complaint, § 396
Right to close, § 395
COLLATERAL ESTOPPEL
Abandonment
    mutuality of estoppel doctrine, § 460
    privity doctrine, § 461
Burden of proof, § 475
Defined, § 443
Evidence
    burden of proof, § 475
    sources to establish matters estopped,
        § 473
Gratuitous findings, § 465
Identity of issue test
        generally, § 462
        gratuitous findings, § 465
        law and fact, § 463
        underlying facts binding, § 464
Identity of parties
        different capacities, § 459
        estopped parties, § 458
        mutuality of estoppel, § 460
        privity, § 461
Individual issues, applicable to, § 474
Multiparties
        generally, § 466
        full and fair opportunity test, § 467
        vehicle tort examples, § 468
Mutuality of estoppel, § 460
Privity, § 461
Res judicata and, § 443
Vehicle tort examples, multiparty, § 468

COLLATERAL SOURCE RULE
    Generally, § 398
Health insurance, § 180
Intervention and, § 180
Verdict, § 399

COMITY DOCTRINE
Res judicata, § 443, § 472

COMMENCEMENT OF ACTION
Accompanying papers, service of process, § 60
Add-ons for recipient of paper, service of process,
    § 202
Affidavits of service, service of process, § 202
Affix-and-mail, service of process, § 71, § 73, § 74
Agent for service, designation of, service of
    process, § 73
Age of persons authorized to serve, service of
    process, § 63
All parties, service on, service of process, § 203
Altering initiatory papers after filing but before
    service, service of process, § 63
Amendment allowing for correction of many filing
    mistakes, service of process, § 63
Appeals, perfecting, electronic filing, § 536
Appearance by defendant; response to CPLR
    305(b) notice, service of process, § 60
Appellate division, electronic filing, § 11
Associations, service of process, § 68
Attachment; summons service within 60 days,
    service of process, § 319
Attorneys
    initiatory papers, service of process, § 202
    process server's acts, attorney for plaintiff
        accountable for, service of process,
        § 63
Bare summons, service of process, § 60, § 231
Board, court or commission, service of process,
    § 70
Children, service of process, § 68, § 195
Clerk of court, filing with
        generally, § 63
        refusal to accept papers, § 63
Commission, court or board, service of process,
    § 70
Complaint accompanying summons
        form of summons served with complaint,
            service of process, § 61
        requirements, service of process, § 60
Completion of service, service of process, § 202
Consensual, electronic filing, § 63A
Conservatees, service of process, § 68
Corporations, service of process, § 68, § 70, § 296
Correction of many filing mistakes, amendment
    allowing, service of process, § 63
Counties and actions with mandatory, electronic
    filing, § 63A
Court, board or commission, service of process,
    § 70
Court of claims, electronic filing, § 17
Court-ordered service, service of process, § 75
CPLR 305(b) notice. Default notice; CPLR 305(b),
    infra
CPLR 305(b) notice, service of process, § 60, § 60
Credibility of procrastinator affected, service of
    process, § 231A
Curing technical defects in service, service of
    process, § 76B
120 days after filing to effect service, service of
    process, § 63
Default judgment, vacating, service of process,
    § 108

Default notice; CPLR 305(b)
    appearance by defendant; response to
        notice, service of process, § 60
    defined, service of process, § 60
    form, service of process, § 62
    requirements, service of process, § 60
    response to notice, service of process, § 60
Deliver-and-mail, service of process, § 71, § 72
E-filing, service of process, § 202
Electronic Filing (this index)
Enticement into jurisdiction, service of process,
    § 67
Estates and trusts, service of process, § 68
Exceptions to mandatory filing, electronic filing, §
    63A
Extending time for service, service of process,
    § 63
Facsimile, by, service of process, § 202
Federal practice, generally, § 621
Federal practice, service of process, § 624, § 625
Foreign nations and agencies, service of process,
    § 68
Forms
    default notice 305(b), summons served
        with, service of process, § 62
    summons served with complaint, service of
        process, § 61
Guardians, service of process, § 68
Immunity from service
    diplomatic immunity, service of process,
        § 68
    sovereign immunity, service of process, § 68
    voluntarily in state, service of process, § 68
Incapacitated persons, service of process, § 68,
    § 195
Incompetents and conservatees, service of
    process, § 68
Incorrect initiatory papers failing to name
    defendant, court invoking CPLR 2001 to
    forgive, electronic filing, § 63A
Index number, § 77
Infants, service of process, § 68
Initiatory papers versus interlocutory papers,
    service of process, § 202
Interlocutory papers versus initiatory papers,
    service of process, § 202
Interrogatories, service of process, § 361
Issuance of summons, service of process, § 60
Late e-filing after county clerk rejected hard-copy
    filing, supreme court refusing to forgive,
    electronic filing, § 63A
Late notice, leave to serve, service of process, § 32
Law office failure for late service of pleadings,
    service of process, § 231
Laws, rules and administrative orders governing,
    electronic filing, § 63A
Limited liability partnerships, service of process,
    § 68
Limited partnerships, service of process, § 68
Mail
    affix-and-mail, service of process, § 71, § 73,
        § 74
    deliver-and-mail, service of process, § 71,
        § 72
    first-class mail, service of process, § 202

ordinary mail, service of process, § 202
    personal delivery, service of process, § 66,
        § 76A
Mandatory e-filing
    counties and actions with, electronic filing,
        § 63A
    exclusions, electronic filing, § 63A
    generally, electronic filing, § 63A
    opting out, electronic filing, § 63A
Matrimonial actions, service of process, § 76
Methods, generally, service of process, § 66, § 202
Motions, service of process, § 246, § 247, § 249,
    § 250
Municipal entities, service of process, § 70
New parties, need to add, service of process,
    § 231A
New York City Civil Court, electronic filing, § 19
Notice of claim, service of process, § 32, § 32,
    § 231A
Opting out of mandatory filing, electronic filing, §
    63A
Outside state, service, service of process, § 100
Overnight delivery, service of process, § 202
Partnerships, service of process, § 68
Personal delivery
    apartment house, service of process, § 66
    concealing summons invalidating service,
        service of process, § 66
    corporations, service of process, § 70
    deliver-and-mail, service of process, § 71,
        § 72
    due diligence, service of process, § 66
    family members, to, service of process, § 66
    generally, service of process, § 59, § 66
    mail, service of process, § 66, § 76A
    person, to, service of process, § 66
    redelivery, service of process, § 66
    substituted service, service of process, § 71
Physical office requirement, service of process,
    § 202
Pleadings
    complaint accompanying summons
        form of summons served with
            complaint, service of process,
            § 61
        requirements, service of process, § 60
    credibility of procrastinator affected,
        service of process, § 231A
    default, service of process, § 231A
    defect in summons service, service of
        process, § 231A
    federal courts; late service, service of
        process, § 231A
    generally, service of process, § 231
    jurisdictional defects, service of process,
        § 231A
    law office failure for late service, service of
        process, § 231
    leave time for trouble, service of process,
        § 231A
    new parties, need to add, service of process,
        § 231A
    notice, inadequate, service of process,
        § 231A

relation back doctrine, dispensing reliance on, service of process, § 231A

responding time, service of process, § 231

statute of limitations, service of process, § 231A

timely filing but late service, service of process, § 231A

wrong person, serving, service of process, § 231A

Proof of, service of process, § 79

Publication, service by; rem jurisdiction, service of process, § 107

Public authorities, service of process, § 70

Relation back doctrine, dispensing reliance on, service of process, § 231A

Rem jurisdiction and service by publication, service of process, § 107

Replevin, § 341

Requirements, service of process, § 59

Response
    CPLR 305(b) notice, response by defendant to, service of process, § 60
    summons, to, service of process, § 231

Rules, laws and administrative orders governing, electronic filing, § 63A

Sabbath, service on, service of process, § 63

Saturdays, service on, service of process, § 63, § 202

Service of papers and, electronic filing, § 202

Service of Process and Papers (this index)

Sewer service, service of process, § 71

Signature on papers, electronic filing, § 201

Sovereign immunity, service of process, § 68

State, on, service of process, § 70

Statute of limitations; new action following termination of prior action, service of process, § 52

Statutory instructions on service, specific, service of process, § 202

Subpoenas, service of process, § 383

Substituted service, service of process, § 71

Summary proceedings, service of process, § 575

Sunday, service on, service of process, § 63

Surrogate's court, electronic filing, § 15

Technical defects in service, curing, service of process, § 76B

Time computation, service of process, § 202

Transient service, service of process, § 59

Unincorporated associations, service of process, § 68

When and by whom summons served, commencement of action, service of process, § 63

Wrong person, serving, service of process, § 231A

COMMERCIAL PAPER

Leviable property right, § 487

Pleading, signatures, § 215

Promissory notes, jurisdiction under CPLR 302(a)(1), § 86

Proper garnishee, enforcement of judgments, § 491

Signatures, pleading, § 215

Summary judgment, negotiable instrument as basis for CPLR 3213 motion, § 289

COMMON CARRIERS

Venue, § 119

COMMON LAW

Abandonment, common law forms of action, § 4

COMPARATIVE NEGLIGENCE

Generally, § 168E

Assumption of risk, § 168E

Burden of proof, § 168E

Contributory negligence and, § 168E

Culpable conduct, § 223

COMPLAINTS

Impleader complaint negating main claim, § 158

Summary judgment in lieu of. **Summary Judgment** (this index)

Summons with
    form of summons served with complaint, § 61
    requirements, § 60

COMPROMISE OR SETTLEMENT

Amount, determination of, contribution, § 172

Apportionment rule, contribution, § 171

Article 14 requirements, contribution, § 172

Bankruptcy, contribution, § 176

Child, non-supervision of, contribution, § 175

Class actions, § 147

Cross-claims, contribution, § 227

Defined, contribution, § 169

Delay in signing settlement agreements, § 204

Difficulties in dividing fault, contribution, § 175

Disclosure; privileged communications, § 348

Discretionary tools in handling, contribution, § 177

Dole v. Dow Chemical Co., contribution, § 170, § 171

Dram Shop cases, contribution, § 172

Equitable share payment, contribution, § 172

Excess, judgment limited to; prior contribution rules compared, contribution, § 174

Fewer than all tortfeasors, settlement with, contribution, § 176

Generally, contribution, § 169

High/low and settlement agreements, disclosure of, § 204

Historical background, contribution, § 170

Impleader
    proportionate share determination, contribution, § 175
    spouse, applicability of insurance to impleaded, contribution, § 175

Indemnifiction distinguished, contribution, § 169, § 176

Interest on, § 411

Joint tort liability adjustment; settlement under General Obligations Law Section 15–108, § 168C

Methods of seeking, contribution, § 173

Motor vehicle, imputation of control to owner present in, contribution, § 175

Multiparty problem, contribution, § 175

Offer to compromise, § 303

Passive-active dichotomy, contribution, § 170

Pre-Dole, contribution, § 174

Prior contribution rules compared, contribution, § 174

Relative culpability and determination of, contribution, § 172

Res judicata effect of, § 204

Sequence of trial, contribution, § 177

Signing agreements, delay in, § 204

Spouse, applicability of insurance to impleaded, contribution, § 175

Statute of limitations for contribution claim, 6-year period, contribution, § 35

Stipulations of, § 204

CONDITIONS PRECEDENT TO SUIT
Generally, § 32

CONFERENCES
Preliminary Conference (this index)
Pretrial conference, § 77D
Pretrial conferences, § 374

CONFESSION OF JUDGMENT
Generally, § 299
Affidavit for, § 300
Effect of confessed judgment, § 301
Enforcement, § 301
Filing, § 301
Vacating, § 302

CONFIDENTIAL INFORMATION
Redaction of personal information in papers, § 201

CONFIDENTIALITY
Privileged Communications (this index)

CONSENT
Judgments; res judicata, § 451
Transfer between courts
    with consent, § 26
    without consent, § 27

CONSERVATEES
Incompetents and Conservatees (this index)

CONSOLIDATION
Arbitration, § 598
Interpleader, § 151

CONSOLIDATION OF ACTIONS
Generally, § 127
Individual Assignment System, § 128
Joint trial and, § 127, § 128

CONSTRUCTION AND INTERPRETATION
Civil judicial proceeding, § 6
Extension of time, § 6
Liberal construction, § 6
Mistakes, omissions, defects and irregularities, § 6

CONSUMER CREDIT TRANSACTIONS
Default judgments, § 295
Venue, § 122

CONTEMPT
Generally, § 481
Attorney fees, civil contempt, § 482
Attorneys, contemnor's right to, § 484

Conditional orders, § 484

Constitutionality of procedure, § 483

Corporate officials, direction to pay money, willful breach of trust, § 481

Costs, civil contempt, § 482

Criminal and civil contempt, distinguished, § 482

Damages, civil contempt, § 482

Defects in service of the paper to be obeyed, § 481

Disobedience of subpoena, § 385

Distinction between criminal and civil contempt, § 482

Enforcement of money judgments, § 523

Enforcement of Non-Money Judgments (this index)

Fiduciaries, direction to pay money, willful breach of trust, § 481

Fines, § 482

Hearings, § 484

Imprisonment, § 483

Procedure to punish for, § 484

Purging contempt, § 484

Replevin judgment, enforcement, unique chattel, § 481

Right to counsel, § 484

Stay of proceedings, willful violation, § 255

Subpoenas, disobedience, § 385

Trustees, direction to pay money, willful breach of trust, § 481

CONTRACTS
Arbitrate, agreement to, § 588
Default against natural person in breach of contract action; twenty-day notice requirements, § 296
Election of remedies
    conversion and contract, § 218
    reformation, § 218
    rescission, damages plus, § 218
Interest in, deviation of statutory right to, § 411
Jurisdiction
    longarm jurisdiction; contracts anywhere clause, § 86A
    written agreement, by, § 98
Longarm jurisdiction; contracts anywhere clause, § 86A
Sales contracts, statute of limitations; 4-year period, § 35
Statute of limitations, 6-year period, § 35
Venue, agreement to fix, § 117

CONTRIBUTION
Generally, § 169
Amount, determination of, § 172
Apportionment rule, § 171
Article 14 requirements, § 172
Bankruptcy, § 176
Child, non-supervision of, § 175
Cross-claims, § 227
Defined, § 169
Difficulties in dividing fault, § 175
Discretionary tools in handling, § 177
Dole v. Dow Chemical Co., § 170, § 171
Dram Shop cases, § 172
Equitable share payment, § 172
Excess, judgment limited to; prior contribution rules compared, § 174

Fewer than all tortfeasors, settlement with, § 176
Historical background, § 170
Impleader
        proportionate share determination, § 175
        spouse, applicability of insurance to
                impleaded, § 175
Indemnifiction distinguished, § 169, § 176
Methods of seeking, § 173
Motor vehicle, imputation of control to owner
        present in, § 175
Multiparty problem, § 175
Passive-active dichotomy, § 170
Pre-Dole, § 174
Prior contribution rules compared, § 174
Relative culpability and determination of, § 172
Sequence of trial, § 177
Spouse, applicability of insurance to impleaded,
        § 175
Statute of limitations for contribution claim, 6-
        year period, § 35

CONTRIBUTORY NEGLIGENCE
Comparative negligence theory replacing, § 168E

CONVERSION
Election of remedies; conversion and contract,
        § 218

COPYRIGHTS
Statute of limitations, copyright infringement, 6-
        year period, § 35

CORPORATIONS
Default against corporations served pursuant to
        BCL Section 306; twenty-day notice
        requirements, § 296
Disclosure from, § 345
Doing business test, § 82, § 83
Foreign Corporations (this index)
Forum non conveniens, § 29
Jurisdiction
        doing business test, § 82, § 83
        general jurisdiction, § 82
        presence doctrine, § 82
        specific jurisdiction, § 82
        unlicensed plaintiff corporation and, § 30
Service of process, summons and papers, § 68,
        § 70, § 296
Unlicensed plaintiff corporation and jurisdiction,
        § 30
Venue, § 119

CORRECTIVE MOTIONS
Defined, § 230

COSTS
        Generally, § 414
Appellate award, § 414
Civil contempt, § 482
Defined, § 414
Depositions, § 354
Disclosure, § 353, § 362
Ex parte motions, security for costs, § 414
Frivolous conduct in litigation, sanction, § 414A
Judgments, § 413, § 414
Lis pendens, § 336
Motion costs, § 414

Notice to admit, § 364
Poor Persons (this index)
Retaxing the costs, § 416
Security for costs, § 414
Special proceedings, § 414
Taxation of costs, § 416

COUNSEL
Attorneys (this index)

COUNTERCLAIMS
        Generally, § 224
Assignee-plaintiff, against, § 226
Defined, § 224
Dismissal motion; non-interposable counterclaim,
        § 264
Equitable recoupment doctrine, § 226
Federal practice, § 632
Interposition of claim; statute of limitations, § 48,
        § 49
Parties with several capacities, § 225
Reply, § 224, § 229
Res judicata, § 452
Several capacities, parties with, § 225
Summary judgment, § 285

COUNTIES
Venue, actions against, § 120

COUNTY COURTS
        Generally, § 14
Appeals, § 14
Jurisdiction, § 14
Monetary limitations, § 14
Organization, § 14
Real property actions, § 14

COURT OF APPEALS
        Generally, § 9, § 10
Admission to practice, rules for, § 10
Advisory opinion, § 10
Appellate division decision, § 10
Certification to Court of Appeals by other courts,
        § 528A
Criminal judgment appeal, § 10
Digital format, submission of documents in, § 10
Direct appeal, § 9
Facts, review of, § 10
Federal practice, § 642
Permission, by, § 528
As of right, § 527

COURT OF CLAIMS
        Generally, § 16
Appeals, § 17
E-filing, § 17
Joint tort liability adjustment; third-party
        practice, § 168C
Judges, § 17
Jurisdiction, § 17, § 17
Res judicata issues, § 470
State, action against, § 17
State employees, suit against, § 17

COURT OF CLAIMS ACT
        Generally, § 3, § 17
Service on state and, § 70

COURT SYSTEM
Chart, § 9
Judicial departments, § 9
Organization, § 9

CRIMINAL CONTEMPT
Contempt (this index)

CRIMINAL PROCEDURE
Court of Appeals, appeal of criminal judgment to, § 10

CROSS-CLAIMS
Generally, § 227
Answer, § 227, § 228
Apportionment claims, § 227
Contribution, § 227
Defined, § 227
Federal practice, § 632
Indemnification, § 227

CROSS-MOTIONS
Generally, § 249
Add-ons, § 249
Answering papers, § 249
Defined, § 249
Motions (this index)
Notice, § 249
Relief on, § 249
Service with answering papers, § 249
Summary judgment motion, time to make, § 279

CUSTODY PROCEEDINGS
Appointment of guardian, § 196
Arbitration, § 587
Family court jurisdiction, § 16

DAMAGES
Ad damnum clause
    amendment of, § 237
        closing statement; mentioning amount
            demanded in complaint, § 396
Additur, § 407
Amount of contribution, determination of, § 172
Apportionment rule, contribution, § 171
Article 14 contribution requirements, § 172
Assumption of risk, § 168E
Bankruptcy, § 176
Burden of proof, § 168E
Child, non-supervision of, contribution, § 175
Closing statement; mentioning amount
    demanded in complaint, § 396
Comparative Negligence (this index)
Contribution (this index)
Contributory negligence and, § 168E
Cross-claims, contribution, § 227
Culpable conduct, § 223
Defined, § 169
Difficulties in dividing fault, contribution, § 175
Discretionary tools in handling contribution, § 177
Dole v. Dow Chemical Co., § 170, § 171
Dram Shop cases, § 172
Election of remedies, § 218
Enforcement of Money Judgments (this index)
Equitable share payment, § 172

Excess, judgment limited to; prior contribution
    rules compared, § 174
Fewer than all tortfeasors, settlement with, § 176
Historical background of contribution, § 170
Impleader
        proportionate share determination, § 175
        spouse, applicability of insurance to
            impleaded, § 175
Indemnifiction distinguished from contribution, § 169, § 176
Methods of seeking contribution, § 173
Motor vehicle, imputation of control to owner
    present in, § 175
Multiparty problem, § 175
Passive-active dichotomy, § 170
Pre-Dole, § 174
Prior contribution rules compared, § 174
Relative culpability and determination of
    contribution, § 172
Remittitur, § 407
Sequence of trial, § 177
Settlement or Compromise (this index)
Spouse, applicability of insurance to impleaded, § 175
Statute of limitations for contribution claim, 6-
    year period, § 35

DEATH
Enforcement of money judgments; death of
    judgment debtor, § 514
Statute of limitations
        tolling of limitations period, death of
            plaintiff or potential defendant, § 55
        wrongful death, § 35, § 44, § 55
Substitution of parties, § 184

DEBT
Defined, enforcement of judgments, § 489

DECEIT
Fraud (this index)

DECLARATORY JUDGMENTS
Generally, § 436
Actual controversy, § 436
Follow-up relief, need for, § 441
Insurance disputes, § 437
Judgment declaratory action, § 440
Jury trial, § 439
Limitations of time, § 438
Matrimonial actions, § 437
Procedure, § 438
Uses, § 437

DECREES
Judgments and Decrees (this index)

DEFAMATION
Foreign defamation judgment, recognition of, § 86
Particularity of statement required in pleading
    action for, § 216
Single publication rule, § 40
Statute of limitations, § 40

DEFAULT
Excusable; vacating judgments, § 427
Judgments. **Default Judgments** (this index)

Service of Process, Summons and Papers (this index)

DEFAULT JUDGMENTS
Appearance, default after; 5 days notice of time, § 296
Application, § 295
Consumer credit transactions, § 295
Contract action, breach of; twenty-day notice requirements, § 296
Corporations served pursuant to BCL Section 306; twenty-day notice requirements, § 296
Failure to appear, defined, § 293
Federal courts, vacating in, § 629
Five-day notice requirements, § 296
Inquest on damages, § 293
Military service, affidavit that defendant is not in, § 79
Notice of application, § 296
One year after default, taking proceedings to enter, § 296
Papers on application, § 295
Res judicata, § 451
Taking, § 293
Time for application, § 294
Twenty-day notice requirements, § 296
Vacating
        generally, § 108
        affidavit of merits, § 108

DEFECTS
Mistakes, Omissions, Defects and Irregularities (this index)

DEFENSES
Affirmative Defenses (this index)
Collateral Estoppel (this index)
Dismissal Motion (this index)
Res Judicata (this index)
Summary proceedings, § 576

DEFINITIONS
Abridgement statute, limitations of actions, § 38
Action, § 4
Ad damnum, pleadings, § 217
Additur, trial motions, § 407
Affidavit, § 205
Ancillary jurisdiction, § 614
Appearance, § 109
Arbitrary and capricious, administrative actions, § 561
Arbitration, § 586
Attachment, § 313
Bar, res judicata, § 450
Bifurcated trial, § 130
Bill of particulars, § 238
Calendar, § 368
Calendar practice, § 368
Certiorari, § 560
Civil contempt, § 482
Civil judicial proceeding, § 6
Class action, § 139
Collateral attack, judgments, § 8
Collateral estoppel, § 443
Comity, § 443
Compulsory counterclaim, federal practice, § 224

Consolidation, joinder of claims and actions, § 127
Contribution, § 169
Corrective motion, § 230
Costs, § 414
Counterclaim, § 224
Criminal contempt, § 482
Cross-claim, § 227
Cross-motions, § 249
Debt, enforcement of judgments, § 489
Default notice, summons served without complaint, § 60
Defensive interpleader, § 148
Diplomatic immunity, summons service, § 68
Direct estoppel, res judicata, § 443
Disbursements, judgments, § 415
Discharge of attachment, § 325
Docketing, judgments, § 418
Domicile, venue, § 118
Election of remedies, res judicata, § 443
Equitable share, contribution under CPLR Article 14, § 172
Execution, judgments, satisfaction, § 425
Ex parte motion, § 243
Extract, recording judgments, § 418
Extrinsic fraud, vacating judgments and orders, § 429
Failure to appear, taking default judgment, § 293
Fees, judgments, § 413
Final judgment, § 410
Fluid recovery, class actions, § 145
Full faith and credit, res judicata, § 443
Garnishee, enforcement of judgments, § 313
General jurisdiction, § 8
General verdict, § 399
Guardian ad litem, § 196
Informal appearance, § 112
Inquest, default judgment, § 293
Interest, judgments, § 411
Interlocutory judgment, § 410
Interpleader, § 148
Interposition, limitations of actions, § 45
Interrogatories, § 361
Intervention, § 178
Joint and several liability, tortfeasors, § 168A
Joint trial, § 127
Judgment, § 409
Justiciability, federal courts, § 612
Levy, attachment, personal property, § 320
Limited appearance, § 113
Local action, venue, § 121
Longarm jurisdiction, § 85
Merger, res judicata, § 450
Merits, res judicata, § 446
Mootness, federal practice, § 612
Motion, § 4
Mutual account, limitations of actions, § 50
Mutuality of estoppel doctrine, § 460
Neglect to prosecute, statute of limitations, § 52
Note of issue, § 369
Notice of pendency, § 334
Nunc pro tunc order, correcting judgments, § 420
Occurrence, permissive joinder of parties, § 134
Order to show cause, § 248
Ouster agreement, forum non conveniens, § 28

Perfection, attachment, levy, § 321
Personal jurisdiction, § 8
Petition, special proceedings, § 552
Petitioner, special proceedings, § 551
Preference, calendar, § 372
Prohibition, § 559
Protective order, § 353
Provisional remedies, § 306
Quasi in rem jurisdiction, § 101
Quotient verdict, § 401
Redelivery, service of summons, § 66
Referee, trial, § 379
Related counterclaim, pleadings, § 226
Relief clause, § 217
Remittitur, trial motions, § 407
Rem jurisdiction, § 8
Replevin, § 337
Reply, pleadings, § 229
Residence
        jurisdictional basis, § 81
        venue, § 118
Res judicata, § 442, § 443
Respondent, special proceedings, § 551
Restricted appearance, longarm jurisdiction, § 91
Ripeness, federal courts, § 612
Separate trial, joinder of claims and actions,
        § 127
Settle order, motion practice, § 250
Severance, joinder of claims and actions, § 127
Small claims, § 581
Special proceedings, § 547
Special verdict, § 399
Specific jurisdiction, § 84
Splitting, res judicata, § 443
Standing to sue, § 136
Stay, motion practice, § 255
Stipulation, § 351
Strictly in rem jurisdiction, § 101
Subject matter jurisdiction, § 8
Subpoena duces tecum, § 382
Subpoenas, § 382
Summary judgment, § 278
Summation, trial, § 397
Supplement, pleadings, § 237
Surety, bonds and undertakings, § 206
Taxing costs, § 414
Tender, accelerated judgment, § 303
Transitory action, venue, § 118
Uniform acts, § 3
Venue, § 116
Verdict, § 399
Verification, pleadings, § 232
Void judgment, jurisdiction, § 8

DEMAND FOR RELIEF
Generally, § 217

DENTISTS
Statute of Limitations (this index)

DEPOSITIONS
        Generally, § 350, § 354
Any person, use of deposition of, § 358
Commission or letters rogatory, § 350, § 360
Corrections, § 357
Costs, § 354

Demand, § 362
Effect of using, § 358
Executing, § 357
Former party to action, use of deposition of, § 358
Impeachment of deponent, use for, § 358
Letters rogatory, § 350, § 360
Notice, § 354
Objections, § 356
Part of, use of, § 358
Place of, § 355
Scheduling, § 354
Stenographers, § 357
Taking, § 356
Transcript, § 357
Translations, § 356
Uniform Rules for conduct of, § 355
Use of, § 358
Written questions, on, § 359

DERIVATIVE CLAIMS
Statute of limitations
        generally, § 35
        continuous treatment toll, § 42

DIPLOMATIC IMMUNITY
Summons service, § 68

DISABILITIES
Statute of limitations, § 54

DISBURSEMENTS
Defined, § 415
Judgments (this index)

DISCLOSURE
        Generally, § 343
Accident reports, privileged communications,
        § 348
Before action commmenced, order compelling
        disclosure, § 352
Address, demand for, § 350, § 365
Admission, request for, § 350, § 364
Admit, notice to, § 364
Arbitrators, § 345
Attachment, to aid, § 324
Attorney's duties under Rules of Professional
        Conduct, § 352A
Audio tapes of party, privileged communications,
        § 348
Bill of Particulars (this index)
Burden of proof, § 344
Calendar, after case on, § 352
Case on calendar, disclosure after, § 352
Compelling disclosure, motion for
        generally, § 362
        order, § 352, § 366
        sanctions for nondisclosure, § 367
        statute of limitations issues, § 367
Conditional immunity, overcoming, privileged
        communications, § 348
Contents and timing of notice or subpoena, § 362
Corporation, § 345
Costs, § 362
Criteria, § 344
Depositions (this index)
Devices, § 350
        bill of particulars, § 238

Discovery and inspection, § 350, § 362
During or after trial, § 352
Electronically stored information, § 77D, § 362
Enforcement of money judgments, § 509
Expert reports, privileged communications, § 348
Experts (this index)
Federal Practice (this index)
Films, privileged communications, § 348
Foreign action, to aid, § 352
Freedom of Information Law, § 348
Freedom of Information Law, privileged
    communications, § 348
Hi/lo and settlement agreements, disclosure of,
    § 204
Identification of experts, § 348A
Insurer's file, materials, in privileged
    communications, § 348
International, § 345
Interrogatories (this index)
Land, entry upon and inspection of, § 362
Litigation hold and preservation letters,
    implementing, § 362
Material and necessary criteria, § 344
Mediators, § 345
Medical malpractice actions, experts, § 348A
Method of bringing disclosure, § 351
Nonparties
    from, § 345
    discovery against, § 352
Notices
        generally, § 351
        admit, notice to, § 364
        depositions, § 354
        physical and mental examinations, § 363
Order compelling disclosure, § 352
Orders of court
    before action commenced, order compelling
        disclosure, § 352
    case on calendar, disclosure after, § 352
    compelling disclosure, § 366
    during or after trial, § 352
    instances where order initially required,
        § 352
    nonparties, disovery against, § 352
    prisoners, § 352
    protective orders, § 353
    special proceedings, § 352
    state, by, § 352
Parties, from, § 345
Parties, statcments, of privileged
    communications, § 348
Photographs, privileged communications, § 348
Physical and mental examinations, § 350, § 363
Preservation of information, § 352, § 362
Priority of use, § 350
Prior responses, supplementing, § 352A
Prisoners, § 352
Privileged Communications (this index)
Privileged matters, expert reports, § 348
Protective orders, § 353
Relevancy standard, § 344
Requirements, § 344
    supplement prior responses, § 352A
Sanctions for nondisclosure, § 367
Settlements, privileged communications, § 348

Social media sites, on, § 344
Special circumstances, further disclosure
    permitted on showing of, § 348A
Special proceedings, § 352, § 555
State, by, § 352
Statement of expected testimony, experts, § 348A
Statute of limitations issues and compelling,
    § 367
Stipulation, § 351
Subpoenas (this index)
Supplement prior responses, requirement to,
    § 352A
Surveillance tapes, privileged communications,
    § 348
Timing of notice or subpoena, § 362
Trade secrets, protection against disclosure,
    § 353
Video, privileged communications, § 348
Witnesses and parties, statements, of privileged
    communications, § 348
Witnesses (this index)
Work product, attorney's, privileged
    communications, § 347, § 348

DISCONTINUANCE
    Generally, § 297
Effect of, § 298
Methods, § 297
Notice, by, § 297
Order, by, § 297
Stipulation, by, § 297

DISCOVERY
Disclosure (this index)
Federal practice
        generally, § 636
        criteria, § 637
        devices, § 638
        exclusions, § 637
        protective orders, § 639
        sanctions, § 639

DISCOVERY RULE
Statute of limitations, accrual of claim, § 40, § 43

DISMISSAL MOTION
    Generally, § 257
Abandoned cases, § 376
Affirmative defenses usable, § 263
Capacity to sue, lack of, § 261
Counterclaim, non-interposable, § 264
Defenses
        affirmative defenses usable, § 263
        documentary evidence, defense based on,
            § 259
        motion to dismiss defense, § 269
Documentary evidence, defense based on, § 259
Extending responding time, § 277
Failure to prosecute, § 375
Federal practice, § 635
Forum non conveniens, § 28
Grounds for, § 258
Immediate trial of fact issue, § 271
Indispensable party, for, § 268
Jurisdiction
        personal jurisdiction, lack of, § 266
        rem jurisdiction, lack of, § 267

subject matter jurisdiction as basis, § 260
Leave to replead, § 275
Option to plead instead of move, § 274
Other action pending, § 262
Personal jurisdiction, lack of, § 266
Procedure, § 257
Rem jurisdiction, lack of, § 267
Res judicata effect of disposition, § 276, § 402
Single motion rule, § 273
Standing to sue, lack of, § 261
Subject matter jurisdiction as basis, § 260
Summary judgment, treating motion as, § 270,
§ 283
Time for motion, § 272
Waiver, § 274
Want of prosecution, § 375

DISTRICT COURTS
Generally, § 20
Appeals, § 20
Judges, § 20
Jurisdiction, § 20

DIVORCE ACTIONS
Pleading particularity requirement, § 216

DOCKETING OF JUDGMENTS
Changes affecting, § 423
Requirements, § 421

DOCTRINES
Abstention doctrine, § 613
Comity doctrine, res judicata, § 443, § 472
Equitable recoupment doctrine, § 226
Fiduciary shield doctrine, longarm jurisdiction,
§ 87
Forum non conveniens doctrine, § 618
Law of the case doctrine, res judicata and, § 443,
§ 448
Mutuality of estoppel doctrine, § 460, § 460
Pendent jurisdiction, federal doctrine of, § 469
Presence doctrine, jurisdiction over corporation,
§ 82
Privity doctrine, collateral estoppel, § 461
Relation back doctrine, dispensing reliance on,
§ 231A
Seider v. Roth doctrine, in rem, § 105
Splitting doctrine, election of remedies, § 220
Stare decisis doctrine, § 449

DOCUMENTARY EVIDENCE
Defense based on; dismissal motion, § 259

DOING BUSINESS IN NEW YORK
Corporation, jurisdiction over, § 82, § 83

DOMICILE OR RESIDENCE
Defined
personal jurisdiction, basis for, § 81
venue, § 118
Forum non conveniens, § 28
Jury selection, municipality as party, juror as
resident, § 392
Personal jurisdiction, as basis for, § 81
Venue in transitory actions, § 118

DOWER
Jury trial, § 377

DRAM SHOP CASES
Contribution, § 172

DUE PROCESS
Personal jurisdiction, § 58, § 80

E-FILING
Electronic filing (this index)

ELECTION OF REMEDIES
Agent and undisclosed principal, § 218
Within an action, § 219
Contracts (this index)
Conversion and contract, § 218
Damages, § 218
Rescission, damages plus, § 218
Separate actions, § 218
Several persons, action against, § 218
Splitting doctrine, § 220

**ELECTRONICALLY STORED
INFORMATION (ESI)**
Discovery, § 77D, § 362

ELECTRONIC COMMUNICATIONS
Appeals, perfecting, § 536
Appellate division, § 11
Commencement of actions by, generally, § 63A
Consensual, § 63A
Counties and actions with mandatory, § 63A
Court of claims, § 17
Electronic Filing (this index)
Exceptions to mandatory filing, § 63A
Incorrect initiatory papers failing to name
defendant, court invoking CPLR 2001 to
forgive, § 63A
Late e-filing after county clerk rejected hard-copy
filing, supreme court refusing to forgive, §
63A
Laws, rules and administrative orders governing,
§ 63A
Longarm jurisdiction; transacting business
through electronic communication, § 86
Mandatory
generally, § 63A
counties and actions with, § 63A
exclusions, § 63A
opting out, § 63A
New York City Civil Court, § 19
Opting out of mandatory filing, § 63A
Passive website; longarm jurisdiction, § 86
Rules, laws and administrative orders governing,
§ 63A
Service of papers and, § 202
Signature on papers, § 201
Social media sites, disclosure of information on,
§ 344
Surrogate's court, § 15

ELECTRONIC FILING
Appeals, perfecting, § 536
Appellate division, § 11
Commencement of actions by, generally, § 63A
Consensual, § 63A
Counties and actions with mandatory, § 63A
Court of claims, § 17
Exceptions to mandatory filing, § 63A

Incorrect initiatory papers failing to name defendant, court invoking CPLR 2001 to forgive, § 63A

Late e-filing after county clerk rejected hard-copy filing, supreme court refusing to forgive, § 63A

Laws, rules and administrative orders governing, § 63A

Mandatory
    generally, § 63A
    counties and actions with, § 63A
    exclusions, § 63A
    opting out, § 63A

New York City Civil Court, § 19

Opting out of mandatory filing, § 63A

Rules, laws and administrative orders governing, § 63A

Service of papers and, § 202

Signature on papers, § 201

Surrogate's court, § 15

EMPLOYERS AND EMPLOYEES

Accident reports by employees, disclosure, § 348

Court of Claims, suit against state employees, § 17

Disclosure of accident reports by employees, § 348

Income execution, employer's obligations on, § 505

Joint tort liability adjustment, plaintiff's employer at fault, § 168C

Notice of claim, employees of municipal entities, § 32

Plaintiff's employer, action against, § 155, § 168C

State employees, suit against Court of Claims, § 17

Third-party action against plaintiff's employer, § 155, § 168C

ENFORCEMENT OF MONEY JUDGMENTS
    Generally, § 476, § 485

Arrest, § 513

Contempt, § 523

Contingent intangibles, § 489

Courts in which enforcement devices available, § 493

Creditor standing in debtor's shoes, § 488

Death of judgment debtor, § 514

Delivery order on, § 510

Devices for, § 492, § 493

Disclosure in aid of enforcement, § 509

Execution on judgments
    generally, § 494
    contents, § 495
    delivery, property capable of, § 497
    Income Execution (this index)
    issuance, § 495
    levy on personal property, § 496
    real property, levy on, § 499
    return of, sheriff's, § 501
    selling personal property, § 498
    selling real property, § 500
    sheriff's role, generally, § 495

Exemptions, § 490

Garnishee
    proper, § 491
    protecting, § 515

Income Execution (this index)

Installment payment order, § 511

Leviable property rights, examples of, § 487

Liens. Priorities and liens, infra

Pre-judgment enforcement, § 516

Priorities and liens
    adverse claims, proceeding to determine, § 521
    judgment creditor versus transferee, § 519
    personal property, rights in, § 518, § 519, § 520
    real property, § 517

Property subject to, § 486

Protective orders, § 522

Receivership, § 512

Restraining notice, § 508

Subpoenas, § 509

ENFORCEMENT OF NON-MONEY JUDGMENTS
    Generally, § 476

Chattel, awarding possession of, § 477

Contempt, by
    constitutionality of procedure, § 483
    criminal and civil contempt distinguished, § 482
    grounds, § 481
    punish, procedure to, § 484

Real property
    generally, § 478
    conveyance of property, § 480
    sale of, judgment directing, § 479

EQUITABLE ACTIONS

Interest on, § 411

EQUITABLE ESTOPPEL

Statute of limitations, estopping defendant from pleading, § 56

EQUITABLE RECOUPMENT DOCTRINE

Counterclaims, § 226

EQUITY ACTIONS

Statute of limitations, § 36

ESI

Electronically Stored Information (ESI) (this index)

ESTATES

Service of process, summons and papers, § 68

ESTOPPEL

Collateral Estoppel (this index)

Direct, § 443

Statute of limitations, estopping defendant from pleading, § 56

EVIDENCE

Arbitration
    presentation, § 586
    rules of evidence, inapplicable, § 597

Attachment application, § 316

Bill of particulars not usable to obtain, § 238

Burden of Proof (this index)

Collateral estoppel
> burden of proof, § 475
> evidentiary sources to establish matters
> > estopped, § 473

Conforming pleadings to proof, motion for, § 404

Default application, § 295

Defense based on documentary evidence, motion
> to dismiss, § 259

Disclosure (this index)

Documentary evidence, defense based on;
> dismissal motion, § 259

Leave to replead, § 275

Motion for new trial on weight of evidence, § 406

Motion to dismiss, defense based on documentary
> evidence, § 259

Newly discovered evidence; vacating judgments,
> § 428

New trial on weight of evidence, motion for
> judgment, § 406

Pleading, inclusion in, § 207

Preliminary injunctions, § 329

Presumptions (this index)

Service, proof, § 79

Sources to establish matters estopped, § 473

Spoliation of evidence, § 367

Summary judgment, § 281

Witnesses (this index)

EXAMINATION BEFORE TRIAL
Depositions (this index)

EXECUTION ON JUDGMENTS
> Generally, § 494

Contents, § 495, § 502

Delivery, property capable of, § 497

Employer's obligations on income execution,
> § 505

Enforcement of Money Judgments (this
> index)

Income execution
> > generally, § 502
> > contents, § 502
> > employer's obligations, § 505
> > modification, § 507
> > priorities among, § 504
> > service, § 502
> > sheriff's obligations on, § 506
> > support, special execution for, § 507a
> > 10%, computing, § 503

Issuance, § 495

Levy on personal property, § 496

Modification, income execution, § 507

Priorities among income execution, § 504

Real property, levy on, § 499

Return of, sheriff's, § 501

Selling personal property, § 498

Selling real property, § 500

Service, income execution, § 502

Sheriff
> obligations, on income execution, § 506
> role, generally, § 495

Support, special execution for income execution,
> § 507A

10%, computing, income execution, § 503

EX PARTE MOTIONS
> Generally, § 244

Affidavits, § 244

Appeal of order on, § 244

Attachment application, § 316

Costs, security for, § 414

Defined, § 243

Request for judicial intervention, § 244

Vacating order on, § 244

Venue, ex parte supreme court motions, § 245

EXPERTS
Disclosure
> further disclosure permitted on showing of
> > special circumstances, § 348A
> identification of, § 348A
> medical malpractice actions, § 348A
> statement of expected testimony, § 348A

Privileged matters, expert reports, § 348

EXTENSION OF TIME
Appeals, § 6, § 534

Construction and interpretation, § 6

Dismissal motion extending responding time,
> § 277

Factors considered, § 6

Service of papers, § 63

Statute of Limitations (this index)

Summary judgment motion, § 279

FACSIMILE
Service of papers, § 202

FACTS, ACTION ON SUBMITTED
Action on Submitted Fact (this index)

FAILURE TO PROSECUTE
Want of Prosecution (this index)

FAMILY COURT
> Generally, § 16

Adoption, jurisdiction over, § 16

Adoption proceedings
> concurrent jurisdiction, § 16
> family court jurisdiction, § 16

Appeals, § 526

Conciliation proceedings, jurisdiction, § 16

Concurrent jurisdiction, adoption proceedings,
> § 16

Custody, jurisdiction over, § 16

Custody proceedings, jurisdiction, § 16

Family Court Act, § 16

Guardianship, jurisdiction over, § 16

Guardianship proceedings, jurisdiction, § 16

Impleader, limited use, § 167

Infants, jurisdiction, § 196

Judges, § 16

Jurisdiction, § 16

Juvenile delinquency, jurisdiction over, § 16

Juvenile delinquency proceedings, jurisdiction,
> § 16

Longarm jurisdiction, § 90

Neglect, jurisdiction over, § 16

Neglect proceedings, jurisdiction, § 16

Paternity proceedings, jurisdiction over, § 16

Persons in need of supervision, jurisdiction over,
> § 16

Subpoena service, statewide, § 383
Supervision, persons in need of, jurisdiction over, § 16

FEDERAL PRACTICE
Abstention doctrine, § 613
Appeals to Court of Appeals, § 642
Choice of forum
       factors, § 616
       forum non conveniens doctrine, § 618
       removal, § 619
       statute of limitations, § 615
       venue, § 617
Commencement of action, generally, § 621
Comparison of New York and, § 610
Counterclaims, § 632
Cross-claims, § 632
Defaults, vacating, § 629
Disclosure. Discovery, infra
Discovery
       generally, § 636
       criteria, § 637
       devices, § 638
       exclusions, § 637
       protective orders, § 639
       sanctions, § 639
Dismissal motions, § 635
Enforcement of judgments, § 641
Entry of judgments, § 641
Extraterritorial jurisdiction, § 626
Forms, § 620
Forum non conveniens doctrine, § 618
Judgments, § 641
Jurisdiction
       personal jurisdiction, infra
       subject matter jurisdiction, infra
Justiciability, § 612
Laches, § 615
Mandatory filing system, § 633
Mootness, § 612
Motions
       generally, § 634
       dismissal, § 635
       summary judgment, § 635
Orders, § 641
Papers, § 633
Parties, § 630
Personal jurisdiction
       generally, § 622
       defaults, vacating, § 629
       extraterritorial jurisdiction, § 626
       longarm statute, § 626
       objections, raising and preserving, § 628
       rem jurisdiction, § 627
Pleadings, § 631
Protective orders, § 639
Provisional remedies, § 640
Rem jurisdiction, § 627
Ripeness, § 612
Sanctions; discovery, § 639
Service methods, § 624
Standing, § 612
Statute of limitations, § 615, § 625
Subject matter jurisdiction
       generally, § 611
       abstention doctrine, § 613

       case or controversy requirement, § 612
       justiciability, § 612
       mootness, § 612
       ripeness, § 612
       standing, § 612
       supplemental jurisdiction, § 614
Summary judgment, § 635
Summons
       issuance, § 623
       service, § 624, § 625
       time limits on, § 625
Supplemental jurisdiction, § 614
Vacatur, § 641
Venue, § 617

FEES
Defined, § 413
Judgments, § 413
Motions, § 243

FIDUCIARY SHIELD DOCTRINE
Longarm jurisdiction, § 87

FILING
Clerk of court, filing with, § 63
Confession of judgment, § 301
Federal practice, § 633
Foreclosure action, filing certificate of merit in, § 77
General filing requirements, § 77
Index number, § 77
Motions, § 243, § 247, § 250
Notice of pendency, § 335
Service of Process and Papers (this index)

FILMS
Disclosure; privileged communications, § 348

FOIL
Freedom of Information Law (FOIL) (this index)

FORECLOSURES
Certificate of merit, filing, § 77
Statute of limitations for mortgage foreclosure action, 6-year period, § 35

FOREIGN CLAIMS
Statute of limitations, § 57

FOREIGN CORPORATIONS
Unlicensed plaintiff corporation and jurisdiction, § 30
Venue, § 119

FOREIGN COUNTRIES
Particularity of statement required in pleading; foreign country's laws, § 216
Service of process, summons and papers, § 68

FOREIGN JUDGMENTS
       Generally, § 422
Defamation judgment, recognition of, § 86
Res judicata and recognition of, § 472

FOREIGN LAW
Pleading, § 216

FORMS

Generally, § 7
Cross-claims; form of answer, § 228
Federal practice, § 620
Judgment, § 417
Motions (this index)
Official forms, § 7
RJI, § 77C
Subpoenas, § 386
Summons
complaint, served with, § 61
default notice 305(b), summons served with, § 62
Verification of pleadings, § 234

FORUM, CHOICE OF

Factors, § 616
Forum non conveniens doctrine, § 618
Removal, § 619
Statute of limitations, § 615
Venue, § 617

FORUM NON CONVENIENS

Clauses, § 28
Corporations, § 29
Discretionary factors, § 28
Dismissal motion, § 28
Doctrine, generally, § 618
Federal practice, § 618
Historical background, § 28
Objections, § 28
Ouster agreement, § 28
Service of suit clause, § 28
Stay of proceedings, § 28

FRAUD

Particularity of statement required in pleading action for, § 216
Statute of limitations, discovery accrual, § 43
Vacating judgment, § 429

FREEDOM OF INFORMATION LAW

Denial of access reviewable under Article 78 proceeding, § 558
Disclosure; privileged communications, § 348
Impact on pretrial disclosure, § 348

FRIVOLOUS CONDUCT

Sanctions, § 414A

FULL FAITH AND CREDIT JUDGMENT

Registration of, § 435
Res judicata and, § 443, § 471

GARNISHMENT

Generally, § 313, § 476, § 485
Annulling, § 325
Applying for, § 316
Arbitration, § 599
Arrest, § 513
Attachment (this index)
Constitutionality, § 315
Contempt, § 523
Contingent intangibles, § 489
Courts in which enforcement devices available, § 493
Creditor standing in debtor's shoes, § 488
Death of judgment debtor, § 514

Defined, § 313
Delivery order on, § 510
Devices for, § 492, § 493
Discharge, § 325
Disclosure in aid of enforcement, § 509
Disclosure to aid, § 324
Discretionary, as, § 317
Disposition of property, § 326
Disputes, § 326
Enforcement of Money Judgments (this index)
Examples of interplay of requirements, § 322
Execution on judgments
generally, § 494
contents, § 495
delivery, property capable of, § 497
Income Execution (this index)
issuance, § 495
levy on personal property, § 496
real property, levy on, § 499
return of, sheriff's, § 501
selling personal property, § 498
selling real property, § 500
sheriff's role, generally, § 495
Exemptions, § 490
Federal practice, § 640
Garnishee
defined, § 313
proper, § 491
protecting, § 515
Grounds for, § 314
Income Execution (this index)
Installment payment order, § 511
Leviable property rights, examples of, § 487
Levy
generally, § 320
attachment levy, turning over property to sheriff, § 326
perfecting, § 321
personal property, § 320
real property, § 320
seizure, by, § 320
service, by, § 320
Liens. Priorities and liens, infra
90-day period, § 318
One-day period, § 318
Order, generally, § 313
Perfecting levy, § 321
Pre-judgment enforcement, § 516
Priorities and liens
adverse claims, proceeding to determine, § 521
attachment levy, turning over property to sheriff, § 326
judgment creditor versus transferee, § 519
personal property, rights in, § 518, § 519, § 520
real property, § 517
Property attachable, § 323
Property subject to, § 486
Protective orders, § 522
Receivership, § 512
Remedies, defendant's, § 325
Restraining notice, § 508

Service of summons
    levy, service by, § 320
    60 days, within, § 319
60-day period, § 318
Subpoenas, § 509
10-day period, § 318
Time periods, § 318
Turning over property to sheriff, complete
    protection, § 326
Types of property attachable, § 323
Undertakings, action on plaintiff's, § 325
Vacatur, § 325

GOVERNMENTAL ENTITIES
Municipalities (this index)
Service of process, summons and papers, § 70
Statute of limitations for actions against, 1 year
    and 90 days, § 35
Substitution of parties, public bodies or officers,
    § 187
Venue, § 120

GUARDIAN AD LITEM
Generally, § 193
Appointment, procedure for, § 197
Authority of, § 198
Defined, § 196
Distinguished from other guardianships, § 196
Qualifications, § 198
Rights, § 198
Risks if no representative present, § 199

GUARDIANS
Generally, § 193
Guardian Ad Litem (this index)
Service of process, § 68, § 195

HOSPITAL RECORDS
Authorizations for, § 363

HUSBAND AND WIFE
Communications between, privileged matter,
    § 346
Contribution; applicability of insurance to
    impleaded spouses, § 175
Infant married to adult spouse, spouse may
    appear for infant, § 193
Matrimonial Actions (this index)
Rem jurisdiction of marital status, § 102

IAS
Individual Assignment System (IAS) (this
    index)

IMMUNITY
Service of process, summons and papers
    sovereign immunity, § 68
    voluntarily in state, § 68

IMPANELING A JURY
Generally, § 390

IMPLEADER
Third-Party Practice (this index)

INCAPACITATED PERSONS
Incompetents and Conservatees (this index)

INCOME EXECUTION
Generally, § 502
Contents, § 502
Employer's obligations, § 505
Modification, § 507
Priorities among, § 504
Service, § 502
Sheriff's obligations on, § 506
Support, special execution for, § 507A
10%, computing, § 503

INCOMPETENTS AND CONSERVATEES
Appointment of conservators, § 194
Committee for, § 194
Legal representation
    generally, § 194
    service distinguished, § 195
Service of process, summons and papers, § 68,
    § 195
Settlement of incapacitated person's claim, § 200
Substitution of parties, § 184

INCONVENIENT FORUM
Forum Non Conveniens (this index)

INDEMNIFICATION
Contribution distinguished, § 169, § 176
Cross-claims, § 227
Joint tort liability adjustment; third-party
    practice, § 168C
Third-party practice, § 157

INDIGENTS
Poor Persons (this index)

INDIVIDUAL ASSIGNMENT SYSTEM (IAS)
Generally, § 77A, § 78
Consolidation of actions and, § 128
Dual track system of assignment, § 77A
Motions, § 243
Obtaining, § 78
Trial assignment part (TAP, § 77A

INFANTS
Children (this index)

INJUNCTIONS
Appeals, § 535
Applying for, § 329
Arbitration, § 599
Discretion, § 328
Federal practice, § 640
Modifying, § 331
Preliminary injunctions, § 327
Required showing, § 328
Temporary restraining orders, § 330
Vacating, § 331
Yellowstone injunction, enforcement in summary
    proceeding, § 580

INQUEST
Defined, taking default judgment, § 293

IN REM JURISDICTION
Rem Jurisdiction (this index)

INSANITY
Statute of limitations; insanity as disability
    resulting in toll, § 54

INSTALLMENT PAYMENTS
Enforcement of money judgments, § 511

INSURANCE
Contribution; applicability of insurance to
    impleaded spouses, § 175
Declaratory judgments, § 437
Disclosure of materials in liability insurer's file;
    privileged communications, § 348
Health insurance and collateral source rule,
    § 180
No-fault requirement; pleadings, § 216
Subrogation; health insurers, § 180
Third-party practice, § 160

INTENTIONAL TORTS
Statute of limitations, 1-year period, § 35

INTEREST
Judgments (this index)

INTERLOCUTORY JUDGMENTS
    Generally, § 410
Bifurcated trial, § 410
Defined, § 410

INTERNET
Electronic Communications (this index)

INTERPLEADER
    Generally, § 148
Consolidation, § 151
Defensive interpleader, § 148
Defined, § 148
Discharge of stakeholder, § 149
Discretionary tools, § 151
Federal courts, § 154
Joint trial, § 151
Jurisdictional issues
        generally, § 152
        rem jurisdiction as interpleader basis,
          § 153
Liberal use, § 149
Mode of trial, § 150
Procedure, § 148
Rem jurisdiction as interpleader basis, § 153

INTERPOSITION OF CLAIM
Statute of Limitations (this index)

INTERPRETATION
Construction and Interpretation (this index)

INTERROGATORIES
    Generally, § 350, § 361
Answers, service of, § 361
Defined, § 361
General verdict accompanied by answers to,
    § 399
Objections, service of, § 361
Restrictions on use, § 361
Service of, § 361
Use of, § 361

INTERSTATE COMMERCE
Interference with, § 31

INTERVENTION
    Generally, § 178

Collateral source rule and, § 180
Defined, § 178
Health insurers, § 180
Inadequate representation and intervention of
    right, § 180
Permissive, § 182
Procedure for, § 181
Property cases, as of right in, § 181
Request for Judicial Intervention (RJI) (this
    index)
Right, as of
        generally, § 179
        inadequate representation, § 180
        property cases, § 181
        special statutes, § 179
Special proceedings, § 178
Timeliness, § 181

IRREGULARITIES
**Mistakes, Omissions, Defects and
    Irregularities** (this index)

ISSUE PRECLUSION
Collateral Estoppel (this index)

JOINDER OF CLAIMS
    Generally, § 126
Consolidation, § 127
Procedure, § 126

JOINDER OF PARTIES
Add or drop parties, motion to, § 138
Adequately protecting interests of class,
    representative parties, class actions, § 141
Class Actions (this index)
Defendant's side as class, class actions, § 146
Defined, class actions, § 139
Discretion of court, class actions, § 147
Drop or add, motion to, § 138
Fluid recovery, class actions, § 145
Generally, class actions, § 139
Judgment, class actions, § 147
Misjoinder, § 138
Necessary parties
        generally, § 131
        CPLR requirements, § 132
        dismissal
            motion for indispensable party, § 268
            nonjoinder, avoiding dismissal for,
              § 133
Notice of, class actions, § 143
Numerosity requirement, class actions, § 141
Opting out, class actions, § 144
Order allowing, class actions, § 142
Permissive joinder
        generally, § 134
        alternative, joinder in the, § 135
        occurrence, defined, § 134
Prior law, class actions, § 140
Questions of law or fact common to class, class
    actions, § 141
Real party in interest, § 137
Requirements, class actions, § 141
Res judicata, class actions, § 139, § 454
Settlement, class actions, § 147
Standing to sue, § 136

Typicality of claims of class representatives, class actions, § 141

JOINT AND SEVERAL LIABILITY
Defined, tortfeasors, § 168A

JOINT TORT LIABILITY ADJUSTMENT
Third-Party Practice (this index)

JOINT TRIAL
Generally, § 127
Consolidation and, § 127
Defined, § 127
Interpleader, § 151
Severance, § 127

JUDGMENTS
Defined, § 409
Interest
defined, § 411

JUDGMENTS AND DECREES
Abandonment
mutuality of estoppel doctrine, collateral estoppel, § 460
privity doctrine, collateral estoppel, § 461
Accelerated Judgments (this index)
Actual controversy, declaratory judgments, § 436
Affidavit for confession of judgment, § 300
Appealability, § 526
Appearance, default after; 5 days notice of time, § 296
Application for default judgment, § 295
Arbitration awards, § 411, § 605
Arrest, enforcement of money judgments, § 512
Article 78 proceedings, judgment and enforcement in, § 570
Burden of proof, collateral estoppel, § 475
Chattel, awarding possession, enforcement of nonmoney judgments, § 477
Class actions, § 147
Collateral Estoppel (this index)
Comparison of motions for judgment, § 408
Conditioning vacatur, § 432
Confession of Judgment (this index)
Consumer credit transactions, default judgment, § 295
Contempt
constitutionality of procedure, enforcement of non-money judgments, § 483
criminal and civil contempt distinguished, enforcement of non-money judgments, § 482
grounds, enforcement of non-money judgments, § 481
money judgments, enforcement of, § 523
punish, procedure to , enforcement of nonmoney judgments, § 484
Contents, § 409
enforcement of money judgments, § 495
Contingent intangibles, enforcement of money judgments, § 489
Contract
breach of; twenty-day notice requirements, default judgment, § 296
Contract, deviation of statutory right to interest in, § 411

Corporations served pursuant to BCL Section 306; twenty-day notice requirements, default judgment, § 296
Correcting, § 420
Costs, § 413, § 414
Courts in which enforcement devices available, enforcement of money judgments, § 493
Creditor standing in debtor's shoes, enforcement of money judgments, § 488
Death of judgment debtor, enforcement of money judgments, § 514
Declaratory Judgments (this index Default judgment, vacating, § 108
Default Judgments (this index)
Defined
collateral estoppel, § 443
Delivery
order on, enforcement of money judgments, § 510
property capable of, enforcement of money judgments, § 497
Devices for, enforcement of money judgments, § 492, § 493
Disbursements
generally, § 413), § 415
taxation of costs and, § 416
Disclosure in aid of enforcement, enforcement of money judgments, § 509
Discontinuance (this index)
Docketing, § 421, § 423
Effect of
confessed judgment, § 301
discontinuance, § 298
Enforcement of confessed judgment, § 301
Enforcement of Money Judgments (this index)
Enforcement of Non-Money Judgments (this index)
Entry of, § 418
Equitable actions, interest on, § 411
Evidence
burden of proof, collateral estoppel, § 475
sources to establish matters estopped, collateral estoppel, § 473
Excusable default, § 427
Execution on judgments
contents, enforcement of money judgments, § 495
delivery, property capable of, enforcement of money judgments, § 497
generally, enforcement of money judgments, § 494
issuance, enforcement of money judgments, § 495
levy on personal property, enforcement of money judgments, § 496
real property, levy on, enforcement of money judgments, § 499
return of, sheriff's, enforcement of money judgments, § 501
selling personal property, enforcement of money judgments, § 498
selling real property, enforcement of money judgments, § 500

sheriff's role, generally, enforcement of money judgments, **§ 495**

Exemptions, enforcement of money judgments, **§ 490**

Failure to appear, defined, default judgment, **§ 293**

Federal, **§ 422**

Federal practice, **§ 641**
    vacating default judgment in, **§ 629**

Fees, **§ 413**

Filing confessed judgment, **§ 301**

Five-day notice requirements, default judgment, **§ 296**

Follow-up relief, need for declaratory judgments, **§ 441**

Foreign country judgments, **§ 422**

Form, **§ 417**

Fraud, **§ 429**

Frivolity sanctions, **§ 414A**

Full faith and credit, registration of, **§ 435**

Garnishee
    proper, enforcement of money judgments, **§ 491**
    protecting, enforcement of money judgments, **§ 515**

Gratuitous findings, collateral estoppel, **§ 465**

Identity of issue test
    generally, collateral estoppel, **§ 462**
    gratuitous findings, collateral estoppel, **§ 465**
    law and fact, collateral estoppel, **§ 463**
    underlying facts binding, collateral estoppel, **§ 464**

Identity of parties
    different capacities, collateral estoppel, **§ 459**
    estopped parties, collateral estoppel, **§ 458**
    mutuality of estoppel, collateral estoppel, **§ 460**
    privity, collateral estoppel, **§ 461**

Individual issues, applicable to, collateral estoppel, **§ 474**

Installment payment order, enforcement of money judgments, **§ 511**

Insurance disputes, declaratory judgments, **§ 437**

Interest
    allowance of, **§ 411**
    arbitration award, **§ 411**
    category of, **§ 411**
    computing and compounding, **§ 411**
    contract, deviation of statutory right to interest in, **§ 411**
    equitable actions, **§ 411**
    rate, **§ 412**
    settlements, **§ 411**
    wrongful death actions, **§ 411**

Interlocutory, **§ 410**

Issuance, enforcement of money judgments, **§ 495**

Judgment-roll, **§ 419**

Jurisdiction, lack of, **§ 430**

Jury trial, declaratory judgments, **§ 439**

Leviable property rights, examples of, enforcement of money judgments, **§ 487**

Levy on personal property, enforcement of money judgments, **§ 496**

Liens. Priorities and liens, infra

Limitations of time, declaratory judgments, **§ 438**

Matrimonial actions, declaratory judgments, **§ 437**

Matter of law, as, **§ 402**

As a matter of law, **§ 402**

Methods of discontinuance, **§ 297**

Military service, affidavit that defendant is not in, default judgment, **§ 79**

Misconduct, **§ 429**

Money judgments, enforcement of, **§ 476, § 485**

Motion, generally, **§ 426**

Multiparties
    full and fair opportunity test, collateral estoppel, **§ 467**
    generally, collateral estoppel, **§ 466**
    vehicle tort examples, collateral estoppel, **§ 468**

Mutuality of estoppel, collateral estoppel, **§ 460**

Newly discovered evidence, **§ 428**

Non-money judgments, enforcement of, **§ 476**

Notice by discontinuance, **§ 297**

Notice of application, default judgment, **§ 296**

Nunc pro tunc charges, **§ 420**

One year after default, taking proceedings to enter, **§ 296**

Order of discontinuance, **§ 297**

Papers on application, default judgment, **§ 295**

Particularity of statement required in pleading, **§ 216**

Post-trial motion for, **§ 405**

Pre-judgment enforcement, enforcement of money judgments, **§ 516**

Priorities and liens
    adverse claims, proceeding to determine, enforcement of money judgments, **§ 521**
    judgment creditor versus transferee, enforcement of money judgments, **§ 519**
    personal property, rights in, enforcement of money judgments, **§ 518, § 519, § 520**
    real property, enforcement of money judgments, **§ 517**

Privity, collateral estoppel, **§ 461**

Procedure, declaratory judgments, **§ 438**

Property subject to, enforcement of money judgments, **§ 486**

Protective orders, enforcement of money judgments, **§ 522**

Real property
    conveyance of property, enforcement of nonmoney judgments, **§ 480**
    levy on, enforcement of money judgments, **§ 499**
    money judgments, enforcement of, **§ 499**
    non-money judgments, enforcement of, **§ 478**
    sale of, judgment directing, enforcement of nonmoney judgments, **§ 479**

Receivership, enforcement of money judgments, **§ 512**

Recording
    changes affecting judgments and dockets, **§ 423**

correcting judgment, § 420
docketing judgment, § 421, § 423
entry, § 418
judgment-roll, § 419
nunc pro tunc charges, § 420
satisfaction
    entry of, § 425
    satisfaction-piece, § 424
transcripting judgments between courts
    and counties, § 422
Renewal, § 434, § 435
Replevin, § 342
Res Judicata (this index)
Restitution, § 433
Restraining notice, enforcement of money
    judgments, § 508
Return of, sheriff's, enforcement of money
    judgments, § 501
Reversal of underlying judgment, § 431
Satisfaction of
    entry of, § 425
    satisfaction-piece, § 424
Selling personal property, enforcement of money
    judgments, § 498
Selling real property, enforcement of money
    judgments, § 500
Settlements, interest on, § 411
Sheriff's role, generally, enforcement of money
    judgments, § 495
Sister-state, § 422
Small claims, judgment and enforcement, § 583
Stipulation of discontinuance, § 297
Subpoenas, enforcement of money judgments,
    § 509
Summary Judgment (this index)
Summary proceedings, § 579
Taking, default judgment, § 293
Third-party judgment, enforcement of, § 165
Time for application, default judgment, § 294
Transcripting judgments between courts and
    counties, § 422
Trial motions, judgment during, § 402
Twenty-day notice requirement, default
    judgment, § 296
Uses of declaratory judgments, § 437
Vacating Judgments and Orders (this index)
Vehicle tort examples, multiparty, collateral
    estoppel, § 468
Wrongful death actions, interest in, § 411

**JUDICIAL INTERVENTION, REQUEST
FOR**
Request for Judicial Intervention (RJI) (this
index)

JURISDICTION
Generally, § 5, § 58
Agents
    generally, § 96
    longarm jurisdiction; agency theory, § 95
Aggregating or reducing claims, § 23
Agreement, by written, § 98
Alimony, longarm, § 90
Appearance (this index)
Bifurcated trial, § 23
Burden of proof, longarm, § 93

Categories of, in rem, § 101
Chattel, in rem, § 103
Child support, longarm, § 90
City courts, § 21
Conditions precedent to suit, § 32
Consent to personal jurisdiction based on
    designation of agent in New York, longarm,
    § 95
Continuing jurisdiction, § 99
Contracts anywhere clause, longarm, § 86A
Corporations (this index)
County courts, § 14
Court of claims, § 17
Defamation actions, longarm, § 86
Default judgment
    vacating in federal practice, § 629
Defined
    longarm, § 85
    in rem, § 8
Dismissal Motion (this index)
District courts, § 20
Electronic communication, transacting business
    through, longarm, § 86
Enforcement of Judgments (this index)
Extraterritorial jurisdiction in federal practice,
    § 626
Family actions, longarm, § 90
Family court, § 16
Federal Practice (this index)
Fiduciary shield doctrine, longarm, § 87
Forum Non Conveniens (this index)
General, § 8
Historical background, longarm, § 84
Interpleader
    generally, § 152
    rem jurisdiction as interpleader basis,
    § 152, § 153
Interstate commerce, interference with, § 31
Lack as basis for dismissal motion, § 266, § 267
Limited, § 8
Longarm Jurisdiction (this index)
Marital status, in rem, § 102
Matrimonial actions
    continuing jurisdiction, § 99
    longarm, § 90
    longarm jurisdiction, § 90
    sequestration in, in rem, § 106
Medical malpractice, longarm, § 88
Merits versus, longarm, § 92
Motorist; nonresident motorist statute, longarm,
    § 84, § 97
New York City civil court, § 19
Nonresident motorist statute, longarm, § 84, § 97
Notice of claim, § 32
Objections, raising and preserving in federal
    practice, § 628
Overlap of longarm bases, longarm, § 94
Personal Jurisdiction (this index)
Pleading, § 215
Pleadings, § 215
Publication, service by, in rem, § 107
Quasi in rem
    generally, § 101, § 104
    all property in New York, § 104
    minimal contacts, § 104

no other forum, § 104
procedure, § 104
Real property, longarm, § 89
Reducing or aggregating claims, § 23
Rem Jurisdiction (this index)
Replevin, in rem, § 103
Res judicata, § 455, § 469
Res judicata, in rem, § 455
Restricted appearance, longarm, § 91
Seider v. Roth doctrine, in rem, § 105
Service of Process, Summons and Papers
(this index)
Specific jurisdiction, defined, § 84
Stream of commerce test, longarm, § 87
Strictly in rem, § 101
Subject Matter Jurisdiction (this index)
Substantial revenue from goods used or
consumed in New York, longarm, § 87
Summary proceedings, § 572
Support, action for, longarm, § 90
Supreme court, § 12
Surrogate's court, § 15
Tortious acts
fiduciary shield doctrine, longarm, § 87
generally, longarm, § 87
medical malpractice, longarm, § 88
merits versus jurisdiction, longarm, § 92
outside state, act, longarm, § 87
without state, act, longarm, § 87
Town courts, § 22
Transaction of any business under CPLR
302(a)(1), longarm, § 86
Transfers Between Courts (this index)
Types of, § 8
Unlicensed plaintiff corporation, § 30
Vacating judgment for lack of, § 430
Village courts, § 22

JURY
Generally, § 377
Alternate jurors, § 391
Cause, challenges for, § 392
Challenges to jurors, § 392
Charge, § 398
Declaratory judgments, jury trial and, § 439
Demand and waiver of trial by, § 378
Dower actions, § 377
Impaneling, § 390
Instructions to, § 398
Lying jurors, impeachment of verdict, § 401
Selection
alternate jurors, § 391
cause, challenges for, § 392
challenges to jurors, § 392
impaneling jury, § 390
Sequence of trial, § 393
Waiver
generally, § 378
invalidation of waiver
transfer of case down on consent, § 26
transfer of case up for more relief,
§ 25
Simplified Procedure for court
determination of dispute, § 609

JUSTICIABILITY
Subject matter jurisdiction, federal practice,
§ 612

LACHES
Generally, § 36
Affirmative defense, § 223
Article 78 proceeding, § 566
Consolidation motions, § 128
Federal practice, § 615
Impleader, § 156
Specific performance of contract, application, § 36
Statute of limitations, § 36

LANDLORD AND TENANT
Summary Proceedings (this index)

LAW OFFICE FAILURE
Service of pleading, § 231
Want of prosecution, dismissal for, § 375

LAW OF THE CASE DOCTRINE
Res judicata and, § 443, § 448

LAWYERS
Attorneys (this index)

LEASES
Summary Proceedings (this index)

LETTERS ROGATORY
Depositions, § 350, § 360

LEVY
Attachment (this index)

LIBEL AND SLANDER
Defamation (this index)

LICENSES
Unlicensed plaintiff corporation and jurisdiction,
§ 30

LIENS
Enforcement of Money Judgments (this
index)

LIMITATIONS OF ACTIONS
Statute of Limitations (this index)

LIMITED LIABILITY PARTNERSHIPS
Service of process, summons and papers, § 68

LIMITED PARTNERSHIPS
Service of process, summons and papers, § 68

LIS PENDENS
Notice of Pendency (this index)

LONG ACCOUNT CASES
Compulsory reference, § 379

LONGARM JURISDICTION
Generally, § 58, § 85
Agency theory, § 95
Alimony, § 90
Appearance, restricted, § 91
Burden of proof, § 93
Child support, § 90
Consent to personal jurisdiction based on
designation of agent in New York, § 95

Contracts anywhere clause, § 86A
Defamation actions, § 86
Defined, § 85
Electronic communication, transacting business
    through, § 86
Family actions, § 90
Federal practice, § 626
Fiduciary shield doctrine, § 87
Historical background, § 84
Matrimonial actions, § 90
Medical malpractice, § 88
Merits versus, § 92
Motorist; nonresident motorist statute, § 84, § 97
Nonresident motorist statute, § 84, § 97
Overlap of longarm bases, § 94
Real property, § 89
Restricted appearance, § 91
Stream of commerce test, § 87
Substantial revenue from goods used or
    consumed in New York, § 87
Support, action for, § 90
Tortious acts
            generally, § 87
            fiduciary shield doctrine, § 87
            medical malpractice, § 88
            merits versus jurisdiction, § 92
            outside state, act, § 87
            without state, act, § 87
Transaction of any business under CPLR
    302(a)(1), § 86

MAIL
Affix-and-mail, § 71, § 73, § 74
Deliver-and-mail, § 71, § 72
First-class mail, § 202
Ordinary mail, § 202
Personal delivery, § 66, § 76A
Service of Process, Summons and Papers
    (this index)

MALPRACTICE
Statute of limitations
        3-year period, professionals, nonmedical
            cases, § 35
        2-years and six months period, medical
            professionals, § 35

MARKED PLEADINGS
Answer, § 222

MATRIMONIAL ACTIONS
Declaratory judgments, § 437
Jurisdiction
        continuing jurisdiction, § 99
        longarm jurisdiction, § 90
Longarm jurisdiction, § 90
Particularity of statement required in pleading
    action for, § 216
Rem jurisdiction, § 102, § 106
Service of process, § 76
Statute of limitations for distributive award, 6-
    year period, § 35
Supreme court, § 16

MEDIATION
Disclosure from mediators, § 345

MEDICAL MALPRACTICE
Accrual of claim, § 42
Continuous treatment exception to accrual of
    claim, § 42
Continuous treatment toll for derivative claim,
    § 42
Derivative claim, continuous treatment toll for,
    § 42
Disclosure of experts, § 348A
Discovery rule and, § 43
Expert disclosure in malpractice actions, § 348A
Foreign object exception to accrual of claim, § 42
Joint tort liability adjustment; third-party
    practice, § 168C
Longarm jurisdiction, § 88
Statute of Limitations (this index)
2-years and six months period, § 35, § 42

MEDICAL PROFESSIONALS
Accrual of statute of limitations, § 42
Continuous treatment exception to accrual of
    statute of limitations, medical malpractice,
    § 42
Malpractice
        expert disclosure in malpractice actions,
            § 348A
        joint tort liability adjustment; third-party
            practice, § 168C
        longarm jurisdiction, § 88
        Statute of Limitations (this index)
Statute of Limitations (this index)

MENTAL AND PHYSICIAL EXAMINATIONS
Disclosure, § 350, § 363
Hospital records, authorizations for, § 363
Notices, § 363
Who is subject to, § 363

**MENTAL EXAMINATIONS, PHYSICAL AND
Physical and Mental Examinations** (this
    index)

MINORS
Children (this index)

MISCONDUCT
Vacating judgment, § 429

MISREPRESENTATION
Pleading, particularity requirement, § 216

MISTAKE
Pleading, particularity requirement, § 216

**MISTAKES, OMISSIONS, DEFECTS AND
    IRREGULARITIES**
        Generally, § 6
Amendment allowing for correcting of many filing
        mistakes, § 63
Appeals, taking, § 534
Construction and interpretation, § 6
Correction, § 6
Depositions, § 357
Electronic filing of incorrect initiatory papers
        failing to name defendant, court invoking
        CPLR 2001 to forgive, § 63A
Judgment, correcting, § 420
Pleadings, corrective motions for, § 230

Service of pleadings, defect in, § 231A
Transfers between courts; mistake in choice of
   court, § 24
Verification of pleadings, remedy for, § 235

MISTRIAL
Motion for, § 403

MONEY JUDGMENTS
   Generally, § 313, § 476, § 485
Annulling, § 325
Applying for, § 316
Arbitration, § 599
Arrest, enforcement, § 513
Attachment (this index)
Constitutionality, § 315
Contempt, enforcement, § 523
Contents, income execution, § 502
Contingent intangibles, enforcement, § 489
Courts in which enforcement devices available,
   § 493
Creditor standing in debtor's shoes, enforcement,
   § 488
Death of judgment debtor, enforcement, § 514
Defined, § 313
Delivery order on, enforcement, § 510
Devices for enforcement, § 492, § 493
Discharge, § 325
Disclosure in aid of enforcement, § 509
Disclosure to aid, § 324
Discretionary, as, § 317
Disposition of property, § 326
Disputes, § 326
Employer's obligations, income execution, § 505
Enforcement of Money Judgments (this
   index)
Examples of interplay of requirements, § 322
Execution on judgments
      generally, § 494
      contents, § 495
      delivery, property capable of, § 497
      Income Execution (this index)
      issuance, § 495
      levy on personal property, § 496
      real property, levy on, § 499
      return of, sheriff's, § 501
      selling personal property, § 498
      selling real property, § 500
      sheriff's role, generally, § 495
Exemptions, enforcement, § 490
Federal practice, § 640
Garnishee
      proper, § 491
      protecting, § 515
Garnishee defined, § 313
Grounds for, § 314
Income Execution (this index)
Installment payment order, enforcement, § 511
Leviable property rights, examples of,
   enforcement, § 487
Levy
      generally, § 320
      perfecting, § 321
      personal property, § 320
      real property, § 320
      seizure, by, § 320

service, by, § 320
Liens. Priorities and liens, infra
Modification, income execution, § 507
90-day period, § 318
One-day period, § 318
Order, generally, § 313
Perfecting levy, § 321
Pre-judgment enforcement, § 516
Priorities, § 326
Priorities among income execution, § 504
Priorities and liens
      adverse claims, proceeding to determine,
         enforcement, § 521
      judgment creditor versus transferee,
         enforcement, § 519
      personal property, rights in enforcement,
         § 518, § 519, § 520
      real property, enforcement, § 517
Property attachable, § 323
Property subject to enforcement, § 486
Protective orders, enforcement, § 522
Receivership, enforcement, § 512
Remedies, defendant's, § 325
Restraining notice, enforcement, § 508
Service, income execution, § 502
Service of summons
      levy, service by, § 320
      60 days, within, § 319
Sheriff's obligations on income execution, § 506
60-day period, § 318
Statute of limitations, 20-year period, § 35
Subpoenas, enforcement, § 509
Support, special execution for income execution,
   § 507A
10%, computing income execution, § 503
10-day period, § 318
Time periods, § 318
Types of property attachable, § 323
Undertakings, action on plaintiff's, § 325
Vacatur, § 325

MOOTNESS
Subject matter jurisdiction, federal practice,
   § 612

MORTGAGES
Statute of limitations for mortgage foreclosure
   action, 6-year period, § 35

MOTIONS
   Generally, § 243
Abandoned cases, dismissal motion, § 376
Abandonment, § 250
Accelerated Judgments (this index)
Adjournment, § 247
Affidavits, ex parte motions, § 244
Affirmative defenses usable, dismissal motion,
   § 263
Appealability of orders on motions to reargue or
   renew, § 254
Appeal of order on ex parte motions, § 244
Attachment application, ex parte motions, § 316
Capacity to sue, lack, of dismissal motion, § 261
Contents, § 246
Corrective motions, pleadings, § 230
Costs, security for ex parte motions, § 414

Counterclaim, non-interposable, dismissal motion, § 264

Court, providing to, § 246

Cross-motions
generally, § 249
add-ons, § 249
answering papers, § 249
defined, § 249
notice, § 249
relief on, § 249
service with answering papers, § 249
summary judgment motion, time to make, § 279

Deciding, § 250

Defenses, dismissal motion
affirmative defenses usable, § 263
documentary evidence, defense based on, § 259
motion to dismiss defense, § 269

Defined, § 4, § 243

Disclosure, compelling. **Disclosure** (this index)

Discovery, compelling, § 362

Dismissal Motion (this index)

Documentary evidence, defense based, on dismissal motion, § 259

Entering order, § 250

Ex Parte Motions (this index)

Extending responding time, dismissal motion, § 277

Failure to prosecute, dismissal motion, § 375

Federal practice
generally, § 634
dismissal, § 635
summary judgment, § 635

Federal practice, dismissal motion, § 635

Fees, § 243

Filing, § 243, § 247, § 250

Forms
court order, § 251
notice of motion, § 251
show cause order, § 251

Forum non conveniens, dismissal motion, § 28

Forum non conveniens; dismissal motions, § 28

Grounds, for dismissal motion, § 258

IAS, § 243

Immediate trial of fact issue, dismissal motion, § 271

Inadequate notice, § 247

Indispensable party, for dismissal motion, § 268

Individual court rules, § 243

Joinder of parties, motion to add or drop parties, § 138

Jurisdiction, dismissal motion
personal jurisdiction, lack of, § 266
rem jurisdiction, lack of, § 267
subject matter jurisdiction as basis, § 260

Leave to replead, dismissal motion, § 275

Memorandum of law, § 246

Negotiating rules, § 247

Notices
cross-motions, § 249
form, § 252
requirements, § 247

Option to plead instead of move, dismissal motion, § 274

Oral argument, § 247

Oral versus written, § 243

Order filed, § 250

Other action pending, dismissal motion, § 262

Papers, § 246

Permission of court to make, § 243

Personal jurisdiction, lack, of dismissal motion, § 266

Pleadings, corrective motions for, § 230

Procedure, dismissal motion, § 257

Reargue, § 254

Reducing decision to written order, § 250

Rem jurisdiction, lack, of dismissal motion, § 267

Renew, § 254

Request for judicial intervention, ex parte motions, § 244

Res judicata effect of disposition, dismissal motion, § 276, § 402

Return date, picking, § 247

RJI, § 243

Service, § 246, § 247, § 249, § 250

Settle order, § 250

Show cause orders, § 248, § 252

Single motion rule, dismissal motion, § 273

Special proceedings, § 554

Standing to sue, lack, of dismissal motion, § 261

Stay of proceedings, § 255

Subject matter jurisdiction as basis, dismissal motion, § 260

Submit order, § 250

Subpoenas, quashing, § 384

Summary Judgment (this index)

Supplement pleading, motion to, § 237

Time for making, § 243

Time for motion, dismissal motion, § 272

Time to decide, § 250

Trial Motions (this index)

Uniform Rules, § 243

Vacating Judgments and Orders (this index)

Vacating order on ex parte motions, § 244

Venue, § 245

Venue, ex parte supreme court motions, § 245

Waiver, dismissal motion, § 274

Want of prosecution, dismissal motion, § 375

Where made, § 245

Withdrawal, § 247

Written versus oral, § 243

MOTOR VEHICLES

Collateral estoppel; multiparty vehicle tort examples, § 468

Contribution; imputation of control to owner present in vehicle, § 175

Joint tort liability adjustment and exception; third-party practice, § 168C

Longarm jurisdiction; nonresident motorist statute, § 84, § 97

MUNICIPALITIES

Service of process, summons and papers, § 70

Statute of limitations for actions against, 1 year and 90 days, § 35

Venue, § 120

MUTUAL ACCOUNT

Defined, limitations of actions, § 50

MUTUALITY OF ESTOPPEL
Abandonment, § 460
Collateral estoppel, identity of estopping party, § 460
Defined, § 460

NECESSARY PARTIES, JOINDER OF
Joinder of Parties (this index)

NEGLECT PROCEEDINGS
Family court jurisdiction, § 16

NEW TRIAL
Motion for new trial on weight of evidence, § 406

NEW YORK CITY
Venue, actions against, § 120

NEW YORK CITY CIVIL COURT
Generally, § 19
E-filing, mandatory, § 19
Judges, § 19
Jurisdiction, § 19
Pleadings, § 211
Procedure, § 19
Small claims court, § 19

NEW YORK CITY CIVIL COURT ACT
Generally, § 3

NEW YORK CITY CRIMINAL COURT
Generally, § 18
Lesser offenses, § 18
Misdemeanors, § 18

NONJURY TRIAL
Generally, § 380

NONRESIDENTS
Longarm Jurisdiction (this index)

NOTARY PUBLIC
Generally, § 205

NOTE OF ISSUE
Calendar practice, § 369, § 371
Certificate of readiness and, § 369
Form, § 371
Pretrial conferences, § 374

NOT-FOR-PROFIT ENTITIES
Pleadings, § 216

NOTICE OF CLAIM
Contents, § 32
Employees of municipal entities, § 32
Late notice, application for leave to serve, § 32
Public authorities, § 32
Service, § 32, § 231A
Statute of limitations, § 32, § 35

NOTICE OF PENDENCY
Generally, § 334
Cancellation of notice, § 336
Defined, § 334
Federal practice, § 640
Filing, procedure for, § 335
Specific performance, use, § 334

NOTICES
Arbitrate, notice of intention to, § 593
Class actions, § 143
Default judgment application, § 296
Depositions, § 354
Disclosure (this index)
Discontinuance, § 297
Enforcement of money judgments; restraining notice, § 508
Late notice, leave to serve, § 32
Lis pendens. **Notice of Pendency** (this index)
Motions (this index)
Notice of Claim (this index)
Notice of Pendency (this index)
Physical and mental examinations, § 363
Produce, notice to, § 387
Service of Process, Summons and Papers (this index)
Summary proceedings, notice of petition, § 573

NUNC PRO TUNC JUDGMENTS
Generally, § 420

OATHS AND AFFIRMATIONS
Requirements, § 388

OBJECTIONS
Appearance; making and preserving jurisdictional objection, § 111
Depositions, § 356
Federal practice; raising and preserving jurisdictional objections, § 628
Forum non conveniens, § 28
Jurors, challenges to, § 392
Trial process, § 396

OFFICE OF COURT ADMINISTRATION (OCA)
Role of, § 5

OMISSIONS
Mistakes, Omissions, Defects and Irregularities (this index)

OPENING STATEMENTS
Judge, trial before, § 393
Right to open, § 395

ORDERS, VACATING
Vacating Judgments and Orders (this index)

ORDER TO SHOW CAUSE
Show Cause Orders (this index)

PAPERS
Acknowledgments, § 201
Address, § 201
Affidavits, § 205
Affirmations, § 205
Captions, § 201
Confidential information, redaction of personal, § 201
Copies versus originals, § 201
Defects in form, § 201
Exhibits, size of, § 201
Form of, § 201
Motions (this index)
Names on, § 201

Originals versus copies, § 201
Service of Process, Summons and Papers
    (this index)
Signature rule, § 201
Size of papers and print size, § 201
Stipulations, § 204
Subscription by attorney on all papers, § 201
Telephone numbers, § 201

PARTIES
Abatement of claims, substitution of parties,
    § 185
Additional claims among parties, third parties,
    § 164
Add or drop parties, motion for joinder of parties,
    § 138
Adequately protecting interests of class,
    representative parties, class actions, § 141
Advantages, third parties, § 155
Amendment of summons to change parties, § 65
Appeals and aggrieved party, § 525
Arbitration, third parties, § 598
Article 78 proceedings, § 564
Attorney, appointment for poor persons, § 192
Bankruptcy, third parties joint tort liability,
    § 168C
Burden of proof, third parties joint tort liability,
    § 168D
Capacities, difference and identity of parties,
    § 459
Class actions
    generally, § 139
    adequately protecting interests of class,
        representative parties, § 141
    defendant's side as class, § 146
    defined, § 139
    discretion of court, § 147
    fluid recovery, § 145
    judgment, § 147
    notice of, § 143
    numerosity requirement, § 141
    opting out, § 144
    order allowing, § 142
    prior law, § 140
    questions of law or fact common to class,
        § 141
    requirements, § 141
    res judicata, § 139, § 454
    settlement, § 147
    typicality of claims of class representatives,
        § 141
Collateral Estoppel (this index)
Collateral source rule and, intervention, § 180
Comparative negligence, third parties, § 168E
Complaint negating main claim, third parties,
    § 158
Conservatorship, substitution of parties, § 184
Consolidation
    interpleader, § 151
    joinder of claims, § 127
Contribution
    proportionate share determination, third
        parties, § 175
    spouse, applicability of insurance to
        impleaded, third parties, § 175
    third parties joint tort liability, § 168C

Court of claims, Article 16 and, third parties joint
    tort liability, § 168C
CPLR requirements, necessary parties, § 132
Death of party, substitution of parties, § 184
Defendant
    as class, class actions, § 146
    third party rights, § 163
Defensive interpleader, interpleader, § 148
Defined, class actions, § 139
Discharge of stakeholder, interpleader, § 149
Disclosure from, § 345
Discretionary tools, interpleader, § 151
Discretion of court, class actions, § 147
Dismissal, discretionary powers of, third parties,
    § 161
Drop or add, motion for joinder of parties, § 138
Employer
    action against plaintiff's, third parties,
        § 155, § 168C
    fault, plaintiff's, third parties joint tort
        liability, § 168C
Enforcement of judgment, third parties, § 165
Estopped parties, § 458
Exceptions, third parties joint tort liability,
    § 168C
Federal practice, § 630
    interpleader, § 154
50%-or-less tortfeasor, third parties joint tort
    liability, § 168B
Fluid recovery, class actions, § 145
Full and fair opportunity test, multiparties, § 467
General Obligations Law Section 15–108, third
    parties joint tort liability, § 168C
Health insurers, intervention, § 180
Identity of parties
    different capacities, § 459
    estopped parties, § 458
    mutuality of estoppel, § 460
    privity, § 461
Impleader. **Third-Party Practice** (this index)
Inadequate representation and intervention of
    right, intervention, § 180
Incompetency, substitution of parties, § 184
Indemnification
    impleader basis, third parties, § 157
    third parties joint tort liability, § 168C
Indigent persons, § 190
Indispensable party, necessary party, motion for,
    § 268
Insurance cases, third parties, § 160
Intentional conduct and reckless disregard cases
    excepted, third parties joint tort liability,
    § 168C
Interpleader (this index)
Intervention (this index)
Joinder of Claims (this index)
Joinder of Parties (this index)
Joint tort liability adjustment
    bankruptcy, third parties, § 168C
    burden of proof, third parties, § 168D
    contribution and indemnification, third
        parties, § 168C
    court of claims, Article 16 and, third
        parties, § 168C

employer at fault, plaintiff's, third parties, § 168C

exceptions, third parties, § 168C

generally, third parties, § 168A

indemnification, third parties, § 168C

intentional conduct and reckless disregard cases excepted, third parties, § 168C

medical malpractice and successive tortfeasor cases, third parties, § 168C

motor vehicle exception, third parties, § 168C

non-delegable duty exception, third parties, § 168C

nonparty tortfeasor share not considered, third parties, § 168C

50%-or-less tortfeasor, third parties, § 168B

reckless disregard cases excepted, third parties, § 168C

requirements, third parties, § 168C

settlement under General Obligations Law Section 15–108, third parties, § 168C

successive tortfeasor cases, third parties, § 168C

Joint trial, interpleader, § 151

Judgment

class actions, § 147

enforcement of, third parties, § 165

Jurisdictional issues

generally, interpleader, § 152

rem jurisdiction as interpleader basis, interpleader, § 153

Liberal use, interpleader, § 149

Medical malpractice and successive tortfeasor cases, third parties joint tort liability, § 168C

Misjoinder, joinder of parties, § 138

Mode of trial, interpleader, § 150

Motor vehicle exception, third parties joint tort liability, § 168C

Multiparties

generally, § 466

full and fair opportunity test, § 467

vehicle tort examples, § 468

Mutuality of estoppel, § 460

Necessary parties, joinder of. **Joinder of Parties** (this index)

Non-delegable duty exception, third parties joint tort liability, § 168C

Nonjoinder, avoiding dismissal for, necessary parties, § 133

Nonparty tortfeasor share not considered, third parties joint tort liability, § 168C

Notice of, class actions, § 143

Numerosity requirement, class actions, § 141

Opting out, class actions, § 144

Order allowing, class actions, § 142

Permissive, intervention, § 182

Permissive joinder

generally, § 134

alternative, joinder in the, § 135

occurrence, defined, § 134

Poor Persons (this index)

Premature suit, as, third parties, § 159

Prior law, class actions, § 140

Privileges conferred on persons qualifying as poor, § 192

Privity, identity of parties, § 461

Procedure

interpleader, § 148

intervention, § 181

joinder of claims, § 126

secure status as poor person, § 191

substitution of parties, § 186

third parties, § 156

Proper parties

real party in interest, § 137

standing to sue, § 136

Property cases, as of right in, intervention, § 181

Public body or officer as party, substitution, § 187

Questions of law or fact common to class, class actions, § 141

Real party in interest, § 137

Reckless disregard cases excepted, third parties joint tort liability, § 168C

Rem jurisdiction as interpleader basis, interpleader, § 153

Requirements

class actions, § 141

third parties joint tort liability, § 168C

Res judicata, class actions, § 139, § 454

Right, as of

generally, intervention, § 179

inadequate representation, intervention, § 180

property cases, intervention, § 181

special statutes, intervention, § 179

Separate trial, third parties, § 161

Service of Process, Summons and Papers (this index)

Settlement

class actions, § 147

General Obligations Law Section 15–108, third parties joint tort liability, § 168C

Several capacities, parties with; counterclaims, § 225

Severance, third parties, § 161

Special proceedings, § 551

intervention, § 178

Standing to sue, § 136

Statute of limitations

impleader claims, third parties, § 162

Statute of limitations, plaintiff adding direct claim against third parties; interposition of claim, § 49

Substitution of Parties (this index)

Successive impleaders, third parties, § 166

Successive tortfeasor cases, third parties joint tort liability, § 168C

Third-Party Practice (this index)

Timeliness, intervention, § 181

Transcript costs, poor persons, § 192

Transfer of interests, substitution of parties, § 184

Typicality of claims of class representatives, class actions, § 141

Unknown parties, substitution of parties, § 188

Vehicle tort examples, multiparties, § 468

Vouching-in, third parties, § 168

PARTNERSHIPS
Service of process, summons and papers, § 68
Venue, § 119

PENALTIES
Bill of particulars; penalties against demanding
    party, § 241
Statute of limitations for forfeiture or penalties,
    3-year period, § 35

PENDENT JURISDICTION
Federal doctrine of, § 469

PERFECTING APPEAL
    Generally, § 536
Appendices, § 539
Briefs, § 539
Calendar practice and argument, § 540
Electronic filing of records and briefs, § 536
Record, § 538
Transcripts, § 537

PERSONAL DELIVERY
Apartment house, service of process, § 66
Concealing summons invalidating service, service
    of process, § 66
Deliver-and-mail, service of process, § 71, § 72
Dorporations, service of process, § 70
Due diligence, service of process, § 66
Family members, to, service of process, § 66
Mail, service of process, § 66, § 76A
Person, to, service of process, § 66
Redelivery, service of process, § 66
Service of process, § 59, § 66
Substituted service, service of process, § 71

PERSONAL INJURY ACTIONS
Bifurcated trial, § 394
Interrogatories, § 361
Statute of limitations, 3-year period, § 35
Verdicts, § 399

PERSONAL JURISDICTION
    Generally, § 58
Agency theory, longarm, § 95
Agreement, by written, § 98
Alimony, longarm, § 90
Appearance
    longarm, restricted, § 91
    in rem actions, § 113
Basis for, § 80
Burden of proof, longarm, § 93
Categories of, in rem, § 101
Chattel, in rem, § 103
Child support, longarm, § 90
Consent to personal jurisdiction based on
    designation of agent in New York, longarm,
    § 95
Continuing jurisdiction, § 99
Contracts anywhere clause, longarm, **§ 86A**
Corporate presence doctrine, § 82
Defamation actions, longarm, § 86
Default judgment
    vacating in federal practice, **§ 629**
Default judgment, vacating, § 108
Defined, § 8
    longarm, § 85

in rem, § 8
Dismissal motion based on lack of, **§ 266, § 267**
Domicile as basis, § 81
Due process, **§ 58, § 80**
Electronic communication, transacting business
    through, longarm, § 86
Extraterritorial jurisdiction in federal practice,
    § 626
Family actions, longarm, § 90
Federal practice, **§ 622**
        generally, **§ 622**
    defaults, vacating, **§ 629**
    extraterritorial jurisdiction, **§ 626**
    longarm statute, **§ 626**
    objections, raising and preserving, **§ 628**
    rem jurisdiction, **§ 627**
Fiduciary shield doctrine, longarm, § 87
Historical background, longarm, § 84
Interpleader, in rem, § 152
Longarm Jurisdiction (this index)
Marital status, in rem, § 102
Matrimonial actions
    longarm, § 90
    sequestration in, in rem, § 106
Medical malpractice, longarm, § 88
Merits versus, longarm, § 92
Motorist; nonresident motorist statute, longarm,
    § 84, § 97
Nexus requirement, § 58
Nonresident motorist statute, longarm, **§ 84, § 97**
Objections, raising and preserving in federal
    practice, **§ 628**
Overlap of longarm bases, longarm, § 94
Pleading, § 215
Prior action dismissed for failure to obtain;
    statute of limitations, § 52
Publication, service by, in rem, § 107
Quasi in rem
        generally, **§ 101, § 104**
    all property in New York, **§ 104**
    minimal contacts, **§ 104**
    no other forum, **§ 104**
    procedure, **§ 104**
Real property, longarm, § 89
Rem Jurisdiction (this index)
Replevin, in rem, § 103
Res judicata, in rem, § 455
Restricted appearance, longarm, § 91
Seider v. Roth doctrine, in rem, § 105
Service of Process, Summons and Papers
    (this index)
Stream of commerce test, longarm, § 87
Strictly in rem, § 101
Substantial revenue from goods used or
    consumed in New York, longarm, § 87
Support, action for, longarm, § 90
Tortious acts
    fiduciary shield doctrine, longarm, § 87
    generally, longarm, § 87
    medical malpractice, longarm, § 88
    merits versus jurisdiction, longarm, § 92
    outside state, act, longarm, § 87
    without state, act, longarm, § 87
Transaction of any business under CPLR
    302(a)(1), longarm, § 86

Transfers between courts, § 27

PERSONAL PROPERTY
Attachment (this index)
Enforcement of Money Judgments (this
index)

PHOTOGRAPHS
Disclosure; privileged communications, § 348

PHYSICAL AND MENTAL EXAMINATIONS
Disclosure, § 350, § 363
Hospital records, authorizations for, § 363
Notices, § 363
Who is subject to, § 363

PHYSICIANS
Medical Professionals (this index)
Statute of Limitations (this index)

PLEADINGS
Generally, § 207
Abolition, theory of pleadings rule, § 209
Ad damnum, amendments, § 237
Ad damnum, money actions, § 217
Admissions, answer, § 221
Affirmative, § 208
Affirmative Defenses (this index)
Agent and undisclosed principal, election of
remedies, § 218
Alternative, § 214
Amended Pleadings (this index)
Answer (this index)
Apportionment claims, cross-claims, § 227
Article 78 proceedings, § 567
Assignee-plaintiff, counterclaims against, § 226
Background, § 207
Basic requirements, § 208
Bill of Particulars (this index)
Breach of trust, particularity requirement, § 216
Complaint (this index)
Conditional order granting amendment, § 237
Conforming pleadings to proof, motion for, § 404
Contribution, cross-claims, § 227
Conversion and contract, election of remedies,
§ 218
Corrective motions, § 230
Counterclaims (this index)
Course, amendments as of, § 236
Cross-Claims (this index)
Cross-motions, answer, § 249
Damages, election of remedies, § 218
Defamation, particularity requirement, § 216
Defective, remedy, for verification of pleadings,
§ 235
Defensive, § 208
Defined, verification of pleadings, § 232
Demand for relief, § 217
Denials, answer, § 221
Dismissal motion, non-interposable counterclaim,
§ 264
Dismissal motion extending responding time,
answer, § 277
Divorce actions, particularity requirement, § 216
Election of Remedies (this index)
Eligibility to verify, verification of pleadings,
§ 233

Equitable recoupment doctrine, § 226
Factual, statements as, § 208
Federal and lower courts compared, § 211
Federal practice, § 631, § 632
Cross-claims, § 632
Foreign law, § 216
Form, of verification of pleadings, § 234
Form of answer; cross-claims, answer, § 228
Forms, § 210
Fraud, particularity requirement, § 216
Good or services, schedule of, § 216
Goods or services, schedule of; particularity
requirement, § 216
Hypothetical, § 214
Inconsistency, § 214
Indemnification, cross-claims, § 227
Indorsement pleading, money actions, § 211
Interposition of claim; statute of limitations, § 48,
§ 49
Interposition of claim; statute of limitations,
amendments, § 49
Judgment, suit on; particularity requirement,
§ 216
Judgments, § 216
Jurisdiction, § 215
Leave to amend, § 237
Limitations of actions
affirmative defense, § 34
specific matters, pleading of, § 215
Lower and federal courts compared, § 211
Marked pleadings, answer, § 222
Merits, consideration of amendments, § 237
Misrepresentation, particularity requirement,
§ 216
Mistake, particularity requirement, § 216
Money actions, indorsement pleading, § 211
New York City Civil Court, § 211
Not-for-profit entities, § 216
Notice of claim, § 32
Numbering, § 212
Official forms, generally, § 210
Omission of detail, curing, § 216
Omissions, remedy, answer, § 216
Particularity requirement
generally, § 215, § 216
defamation, § 216
divorce actions, § 216
foreign country's laws, § 216
fraud, § 216
goods or services, schedule of, § 216
judgment, suit on, § 216
no-fault requirement, § 216
separation, § 216
Personal jurisdiction, § 215
Purpose, of verification of pleadings, § 232
Relief, demand for, § 217
Repetition of prior statements, § 213
Reply, § 224, § 229
Requirements, § 208
Rescission, damages plus, election of remedies,
§ 218
Res judicata, § 452
Schedule of good or services, § 216
Separate actions, election of remedies, § 218
Separate statement and numbering, § 212

Separation, particularity requirement, § 216
Service of pleadings and responsive pleadings, amendments, § 237
Service of Process, Summons and Papers (this index)
Services or goods, schedule of, § 216
Several capacities, parties with, § 225
Several persons, action, against election of remedies, § 218
Special proceedings, § 552
Splitting doctrine, election of remedies, § 220
Statements
    deemed repeated, § 213
    factual, statements as, § 208
    separate statement and numbering, § 212
Statute of frauds, § 215
Statute of limitations
    affirmative defense, § 34
    Amendments
        interposition of claim, § 49
        leave, amendment by, § 237
    specific matters, pleading of, § 215
Summary judgment, § 285
Summary proceedings, answer, § 576
Summons
    Amendments
        generally, § 64
        parties, changing, § 65
Supplement pleading, motion to amend, § 237
Techniques of pleading, § 214
Theory of the pleadings rule abolished, § 209
Undue influence, particularity requirement, § 216
Verification of Pleadings (this index)
Who may verify, verification of pleadings, § 233
Wilful default, particularity requirement, § 216
Within an action, election of remedies, § 219
Writings, § 213

PODIATRISTS
Statute of Limitations (this index)

POOR PERSONS
    Generally, § 190
Attorney, appointment of, § 192
Privileges conferred on persons qualifying as, § 192
Procedure to secure status s, § 191
Transcript costs, § 192

POVERTY
Poor Persons (this index)

PREEMPTION
Federal Arbitration Act, § 607

PREFERENCES
Calendar practice
    general, § 372
    special, § 373

PREFERENCES AND PRIORITIES
Adverse claims, proceeding to determine, § 521
Judgment creditor versus transferee, § 519
Personal property, rights in, § 518, § 519, § 520
Real property, § 517

PRELIMINARY CONFERENCE
Generally, § 77B, § 77D

PRELIMINARY INJUNCTIONS
Affidavits, § 329
Appeals, effect on bond, § 329
Arbitration, use, § 599
Attorney fees, bonds and undertakings, § 329
Authorization, designated situations, § 327
Bonds and undertakings, § 329
Burden of proof, § 328
Complaint, § 329
Contempt, enforcement by, § 481
Costs, bonds and undertakings, § 329
Damages, bonds and undertakings, § 329
Enforcement by contempt, § 481
Federal practice, § 640
Grounds, § 327
Irreparable damage, required showing, § 328
Modifying, § 331
Proof, § 329
Requirements, § 327
Service, notice of motion, § 329
Stay of proceedings, distinguished, § 327
Temporary restraining order, distinguished, § 330
Undertakings, § 329
Vacating, § 331

PRESENCE DOCTRINE
Jurisdiction over corporation, § 82

PRESUMPTIONS
Abandoned cases, dismissal, § 376
Jurisdiction, court of general jurisdiction, § 8
Statute of limitations, action on previouslyrendered judgment, § 35

PRETRIAL CONFERENCE
    Generally, § 77D, § 374
Electronic discovery issues, § 77D
Procedure, § 77D

PRIMA FACIE
Summary judgment, showing of entitlement to, § 281

PRIORITIES
Enforcement of Money Judgments (this index)

PRISONERS
Disclosure, § 352

PRIVILEGED COMMUNICATIONS
    Generally, § 346
Accident reports, § 348
Audio tapes of party, § 348
Conditional immunity, overcoming, § 348
Expert reports, § 348
Films, § 348
Freedom of Information Law, § 348
Insurer's file, materials in, § 348
Parties, statements of, § 348
Photographs, § 348
Settlements, § 348
Surveillance tapes, § 348
Video, § 348

Witnesses and parties, statements of, § 348
Work product, attorney's, § 347, § 348

PRIVITY
Collateral estoppel, § 461

PRIVITY DOCTRINE
Collateral estoppel, § 461

PROCEEDINGS
Actions and Proceedings (this index)

PROCESS, SERVICE OF
Service of Process, Summons and Papers
(this index)

PROCESS SERVERS
Attorney for plaintiff accountable for process
server's acts, § 63
Personal delivery, § 66

PRODUCTION OF DOCUMENTS
Notice to produce, § 387

PROMISSORY NOTES
Commercial Paper (this index)

PROOF OF SERVICE
Requirements, § 79

PROPERTY
Attachment (this index)
Enforcement of Money Judgments (this
index)
Injury to
interrogatories, § 361
Intervention, § 181
Real Property (this index)
Receivership (this index)
Rem jurisdiction, § 103

PROTECTIVE ORDERS
Enforcement of money judgments, § 522
Federal practice, § 639
Good faith affirmation requirement on disclosure
motions, § 353
Requirements, § 353

PROVISIONAL REMEDIES
Generally, § 306
Attachment (this index)
Constitutional requirements, § 307
Federal developments, § 307
Federal practice, § 640
Injunctions (this index)
Interposition of claim; statute of limitations, § 46
New York developments, § 307
Receivership (this index)
Types of, § 306

PUBLICATION
Rem jurisdiction and service by, § 107

PUBLIC AUTHORITIES
Notice of claim, leave to serve late, § 32
Service of process, summons and papers, § 70
Venue, § 120

PUBLIC OFFICERS
Substitution of parties, § 187

PURGING CONTEMPT
Generally, § 484

QUALIFIED PRIVILEGE
Affirmative defenses, § 223

QUASI IN REM
Generally, § 101, § 104
All property in New York, § 104
Minimal contacts, § 104
No other forum, § 104
Procedure, § 104

QUASI IN REM JURISDICTION
Rem Jurisdiction (this index)

REAL PARTY IN INTEREST
Generally, § 137

REAL PROPERTY
Adverse possession, 10-year statute of limitations
period, § 35
Attachment (this index)
Conveyance of property, enforcement of non-
money judgments, § 480
County courts, actions in, § 14
Enforcement of Money Judgments (this
index)
Enforcement of Non-Money Judgments (this
index)
Entry upon and inspection of, § 362
Execution on judgments
real property, levy on, § 499
selling real property, § 500
Jurisiction, longarm, § 89
Levy, attachment, § 320
Longarm jurisdiction, § 89
Non-money judgments, enforcement of, § 478
Personal jurisdiction, § 89
Priorities and liens, real property, § 517
Sale of, judgment directing, enforcement of
nonmoneyjudgments, § 479
Specific performance, enforcement of judgment
directing conveyance, § 480
Summary Proceedings (this index)
Venue, § 121

REAL PROPERTY ACTIONS AND
PROCEEDINGS LAW (RPAPL)
Generally, § 3
Summary Proceedings (this index)

RECEIVERSHIP
Accounts and accounting, temporary, § 332
Affidavits and motion papers, temporary
receivers, § 333
Applying for, § 333
Enforcement of money judgments, § 512
Federal practice, § 640
Garnishment, § 512
Money judgments, enforcement of, § 512
Requirements, § 333
Temporary, § 332

RECORDS
Hospital records, authorizations for, § 363
Summary judgment, searching record for, § 282

REFEREES
Compensation and fees, § 379
Defined, § 379
Depositions, conducting, § 356
Time, reports, § 379
Triability by, § 379

RELATION BACK DOCTRINE
Service of pleadings; dispensing reliance on
    doctrine, § 231A
Statute of limitations, § 65, § 231A

RELATIVES
Disqualification from taking depositions, § 356
Jurors related to parties, challenge for cause,
    § 392

REMITTITUR
Generally, § 407
Appeals, § 545

REM JURISDICTION
Generally, § 101, § 103
Appearance in rem actions, § 113
Attachment (this index)
Categories of, § 101
Chattel, § 103
Defined, § 8
Dismissal motion based on lack of, § 267
Federal practice, § 627
Interpleader, § 152
Marital status, § 102
Matrimonial actions, sequestration in, § 106
Publication, service by, § 107
Quasi in rem
           generally, § 101, § 104
        all property in New York, § 104
        minimal contacts, § 104
        no other forum, § 104
        procedure, § 104
Replevin, § 103
Res judicata, § 455
Seider v. Roth doctrine, § 105
Strictly in rem, § 101

REMOVAL
Federal courts, § 619

REPLEVIN
Generally, § 337
Action, commencement, § 341
Applying for, § 339
Commencing action, § 341
Constitutionality of preliminary seizure, § 338
Defined, § 337
Enforcement of non-money judgments, § 476
Judgments, § 342
Jurisdiction, in rem, § 103
Personal jurisdiction, in rem, § 103
Rem jurisdiction, § 103
Subsequent proceedings, § 340
Unique chattel, enforcement, § 481

REPLY
Generally, § 229
Counterclaims, § 224, § 229
Further pleadings, § 229
Requirements, § 229

REQUEST FOR JUDICIAL INTERVENTION
    (RJI)
Generally, § 77B
Ex parte order, § 77B
Form, § 77C
Motions, § 243
Preliminary conference and, § 77B

RESIDENCE
Domicile or Residence (this index)

RES JUDICATA
Generally, § 442
Administrative decisions, § 456
Arbitral decisions, § 456
Burden of proof, § 475
Civil use of criminal findings, § 453
Class actions, § 139, § 454
Collateral estoppel, § 443
Comity, § 443, § 472
Consent judgments, § 451
Counterclaims, § 452
Courts, effect of involvement of different, § 469
Default judgments, § 451
Defined, § 442, § 443
Direct estoppel, § 443
Dismissal motion, res judicata effect of
    disposition of, § 276, § 402
Domestic judgments, recognition of, § 471
Election of remedies, § 443
Final judgment, necessity of, § 444
Foreign country judgments, recognition of, § 472
Full faith and credit, § 443, § 471
Jurisdictional issues, § 455, § 469
Law of the case doctrine, § 443, § 448
Merger and bar, § 450
Merits, necessity for disposition on, § 446
Might have been litigated items, preclusion for,
    § 447
Motions, effect of disposition, dismissal motion,
    § 276, § 402
Nonjury determinations; court of claims issues,
    § 470
Order, for, § 445
Pendent jurisdiction, federal doctrine of, § 469
Rem jurisdiction, § 455
Representative and class situations, § 454
Settlement, res judicata effect of, § 204
Small claims, § 585
Splitting, § 443
Stare decisis doctrine, § 449
Summary judgment, § 287
Supplemental jurisdiction, § 469
Types of relief, § 443

RESTITUTION
Vacating judgment, effect of, § 433

RESTRAINING NOTICES
Enforcement of money judgments, § 508

RIPENESS
Subject matter jurisdiction, § 612

RJI
Request for Judicial Intervention (RJI) (this
    index)

SANCTIONS
Federal practice; discovery, § 639
Frivolity sanctions, § 414A
Nondisclosure, for, § 367

SATURDAYS, SUNDAYS AND HOLIDAYS
Service of summons
    add-ons for recipient of paper, § 63
    Sabbath, on, § 63
    Saturdays, on, § 63, § 202
    Sunday, on, § 63
Statute of limitations, last day of period, § 34

SCHOOLS AND SCHOOL DISTRICTS
Venue, actions against, § 120

SEIDER V. ROTH DOCTRINE
In rem jurisdiction, § 105

SEIZURE
Attachment (this index)
Chattel, of. **Replevin** (this index)

SELECTION OF JURY
Jury (this index)

SEPARATE TRIAL
    Generally, § 127, § 394
Bifurcated trial, § 130, § 394
Severance and, § 127, § 129
Third-party practice, § 161

SEPARATION ACTIONS
Particularity of statement required in pleadings,
    § 216
Pleading particularity requirement, § 216

SERVICE OF PROCESS, SUMMONS AND
    PAPERS
Accompanying papers, § 60
Add-ons for recipient of paper, § 202
Affidavits of service, § 202
Affix-and-mail, § 71, § 73, § 74
Agent for service, designation of, § 73
Age of persons authorized to serve, § 63
All parties, service on, § 203
Altering initiatory papers after filing but before
    service, § 63
Amendment allowing for correction of many filing
    mistakes, § 63
Appearance by defendant; response to CPLR
    305(b)notice, § 60
Associations, § 68
Attachment; summons service within 60 days,
    § 319
Attorneys
    initiatory papers, § 202
    process server's acts, attorney for plaintiff
        accountable for, § 63
Bare summons, § 60, § 231
Board, court or commission, § 70
Children, § 68, § 195
Clerk of court, filing with, § 63
Commencement of action, generally, § 63
Commission, court or board, § 70
Complaint accompanying summons
    form of summons served with complaint,
        § 61

requirements, § 60
Completion of service, § 202
Conservatees, § 68
Corporations, § 68, § 70, § 296
Correction of many filing mistakes, amendment
    allowing, § 63
Court, board or commission, § 70
Court-ordered service, § 75
CPLR 305(b) notice, § 60, § 60
CPLR 305(b) notice. Default notice; CPLR 305(b),
    infra
Credibility of procrastinator affected, § 231A
Curing technical defects in service, § 76B
Default, pleadings, § 231A
Default judgment, vacating, § 108
Default notice; CPLR 305(b)
    appearance by defendant; response to
        notice, § 60
    defined, § 60
    form, § 62
    requirements, § 60
    response to notice, § 60
Defect in summons service, pleadings, § 231A
Deliver-and-mail, § 71, § 72
E-filing, § 202
Enticement into jurisdiction, § 67
Estates and trusts, § 68
Extending time for service, § 63
Facsimile, by, § 202
Federal practice, § 624, § 625
    late service, pleadings, § 231A
Foreign nations and agencies, § 68
Forms
    default notice 305(b), summons served
        with, § 62
    summons served with complaint, § 61
Guardians, § 68
Immunity from service
    diplomatic immunity, § 68
    sovereign immunity, § 68
    voluntarily in state, § 68
Incapacitated persons, § 68, § 195
Incompetents and conservatees, § 68
Infants, § 68
Initiatory papers versus interlocutory papers,
    § 202
Interlocutory papers versus initiatory papers,
    § 202
Interrogatories, § 361
Issuance of summons, § 60
Jurisdictional defects, pleadings, § 231A
Late notice, leave to serve, § 32
Law office failure for late service of pleadings,
    § 231
Leave time for trouble, pleadings, § 231A
Limited liability partnerships, § 68
Limited partnerships, § 68
Mail
    affix-and-mail, § 71, § 73, § 74
    deliver-and-mail, § 71, § 72
    first-class mail, § 202
    ordinary mail, § 202
    personal delivery, § 66, § 76A
Matrimonial actions, § 76

Methods
generally, § 66, § 202
Motions, § 246, § 247, § 249, § 250
Municipal entities, § 70
New parties, need to add, § 231A
Notice of claim, § 32, § 32, § 231A
120 days after filing to effect service, § 63
Outside state, service, § 100
Overnight delivery, § 202
Partnerships, § 68
Personal delivery
generally, § 59, § 66
apartment house, § 66
concealing summons invalidating service,
§ 66
corporations, § 70
deliver-and-mail, § 71, § 72
due diligence, § 66
family members, to, § 66
mail, § 66, § 76A
person, to, § 66
redelivery, § 66
substituted service, § 71
Physical office requirement, § 202
Pleadings
generally, § 231
complaint accompanying summons
form of summons served with
complaint, § 61
requirements, § 60
credibility of procrastinator affected,
§ 231A
default, § 231A
defect in summons service, § 231A
federal courts; late service, § 231A
jurisdictional defects, § 231A
law office failure for late service, § 231
leave time for trouble, § 231A
new parties, need to add, § 231A
notice, inadequate, § 231A
relation back doctrine, dispensing reliance
on, § 231A
responding time, § 231
statute of limitations, § 231A
timely filing but late service, § 231A
wrong person, serving, § 231A
Proof of, § 79
Publication, service by; rem jurisdiction, § 107
Public authorities, § 70
Relation back doctrine, dispensing reliance on,
§ 231A
Rem jurisdiction and service by publication,
§ 107
Requirements, § 59
Response
CPLR 305(b) notice, response by defendant
to, § 60
summons, to, § 231
Sabbath, service on, § 63
Saturdays, service on, § 63, § 202
Sewer service, § 71
Sovereign immunity, § 68
State, on, § 70
Statute of limitations pleadings, § 231A

Statute of limitations; new action following
termination of prior action, § 52
Statutory instructions on service, specific, § 202
Subpoenas, § 383
Substituted service, § 71
Summary proceedings, § 575
Sunday, service on, § 63
Technical defects in service, curing, § 76B
Time computation, § 202
Timely filing but late service, pleadings, § 231A
Transient service, § 59
Unincorporated associations, § 68
When and by whom summons served,
commencement of action, § 63
Wrong person, serving, § 231A

SETTLEMENT OR COMPROMISE
Amount, determination of, contribution, § 172
Apportionment rule, contribution, § 171
Article 14 requirements, contribution, § 172
Bankruptcy, contribution, § 176
Child, non-supervision of, contribution, § 175
Class actions, § 147
Contribution (this index)
Cross-claims, contribution, § 227
Defined, contribution, § 169
Delay in signing settlement agreements, § 204
Difficulties in dividing fault, contribution, § 175
Disclosure; privileged communications, § 348
Discretionary tools in handling, contribution,
§ 177
Dole v. Dow Chemical Co., contribution, § 170,
§ 171
Dram Shop cases, contribution, § 172
Equitable share payment, contribution, § 172
Excess, judgment limited to; prior contribution
rules compared, contribution, § 174
Fewer than all tortfeasors, settlement with,
contribution, § 176
Generally, contribution, § 169
High/low and settlement agreements, disclosure
of, § 204
Historical background, contribution, § 170
Impleader
proportionate share determination,
contribution, § 175
spouse, applicability of insurance to
impleaded, contribution, § 175
Indemnifiction distinguished, contribution, § 169,
§ 176
Interest on, § 411
Joint tort liability adjustment; settlement under
General Obligations Law Section 15–108,
§ 168C
Methods of seeking, contribution, § 173
Motor vehicle, imputation of control to owner
present in, contribution, § 175
Multiparty problem, contribution, § 175
Offer to compromise, § 303
Passive-active dichotomy, contribution, § 170
Pre-Dole, contribution, § 174
Prior contribution rules compared, contribution,
§ 174
Relative culpability and determination of,
contribution, § 172
Res judicata effect of, § 204

Sequence of trial, contribution, § 177
Signing agreements, delay in, § 204
Spouse, applicability of insurance to impleaded, contribution, § 175
Statute of limitations for contribution claim, 6-year period, contribution, § 35
Stipulations of, § 204

SETTLEMENTS
Incapacitated person's claim, § 200
Infant's claim, § 200

SEVERANCE
Generally, § 127
Separate trial and, § 127, § 129
Third-party practice, § 161

SHERIFFS
Execution on judgments. **Enforcement of Money Judgments** (this index)
Income execution, obligations, § 506
Obligations, on income execution on judgments, § 506
Role in execution on judgments, generally, § 495
Statute of limitations; delivery of summons to sheriff, § 47

SHOW CAUSE ORDERS
Motions, § 248, § 251

SIGNATURES
Affirmations, electronic signatures, § 205
E-filed actions, § 201
Papers, form of, § 201
Settlement agreements, delay in signing, § 204
Stipulation signed by nonparty, § 204

SLANDER
Defamation (this index)

SMALL CLAIMS
Generally, § 581
Appeals, § 584
Arbitration; court-annexed arbitration of claims under stated sums, § 585B
Commercial part, § 585A
Court-annexed arbitration of claims under stated sums, § 585B
Defined, § 581
Hearings, commencement of, § 582
Incidental procedure, § 582
Judgment and enforcement, § 583
Res judicata, § 585
Specific performance not permissible, § 583

SMALL CLAIMS COURT
New York City civil court, § 19

SOCIAL MEDIA SITES
Disclosure of information on, § 344

SOVEREIGN IMMUNITY
Service of process, summons and papers, § 68

SPECIAL PROCEEDINGS
Generally, § 4, § 546, § 547
Article 78 Proceedings (this index)
Commencement of, § 553
Defined, § 547

Disclosure, § 555
Disposition of, § 556
Hearings, § 556
Motions, § 554
Parties to, § 551
Pleadings, § 552
Procedure, § 550
Statute of limitations, § 548
Summary Proceedings (this index)
Venue, § 549

SPECIFIC PERFORMANCE
Arbitration award, § 587
Laches doctrine, application, § 36
Lis pendens, use, § 334
Realty, enforcement of judgment directing conveyance, § 480
Small claims, not permissible, § 583

SPLITTING DOCTRINE
Election of remedies, § 220

SPOUSES
Communications between, privileged matter, § 346
Contribution; applicability of insurance to impleaded spouses, § 175
Infant married to adult spouse, spouse may appear for infant, § 193
Matrimonial Actions (this index)
Rem jurisdiction of marital status, § 102

STAKEHOLDERS
Interpleader (this index)

STANDING TO SUE
Generally, § 136
Affirmative defenses, § 223
Dismissal motion based on lack of capacity to sue, § 261
Federal practice, § 612
Subject matter jurisdiction, § 612

STARE DECISIS DOCTRINE
Res judicata and, § 449

STATE, ACTIONS AGAINST
Service of process, summons and papers, § 70

STATUTE OF FRAUDS
Pleading, § 215

STATUTE OF LIMITATIONS
Generally, § 33
Abandoned cases, dismissal of, § 376
Abridgement statute, § 38
Absence from state, tolling for defendant's, § 53
Accrual of claim
generally, § 40
authority, breach of warranty of; discovery accrual, § 43
borrowing statute, § 57
continuous representation exception, malpractice claim, § 42
continuous treatment exception, medical malpractice, § 42
continuous wrongs, § 40
defamation, § 40

delayed-accrual rules, § 40
discovery rule, § 40, § 43
exposure cases, discovery accrual, § 43
foreign claims, § 57
fraud, discovery accrual, § 43
joining claims and, § 40
medical malpractice, § 42
nonresidents, § 57
out-of-state, § 57
warranties, § 41
Adverse possession, 10-year period, § 35
Affirmative defense, § 34, § 223
Alterations, § 38
Amended pleadings
interposition of claim, § 49
leave, amendment by, § 237
Applicable periods, generally, § 35
Application of, § 34
Arbitration, § 35, § 590
Article 78 proceedings, § 35, § 566
Authority, breach of warranty of; discovery accrual, § 43
Borrowing statute, § 57
Calculating, § 33
Catch-all period, residual; 4-year period, § 35
Clerk of court, delivery to, § 47
Continuous representation exception to accrual of claim, malpractice claim, § 42
Continuous treatment exception to accrual of claim, medical malpractice claim, § 42
Continuous wrongs, § 40
Contracts, 6-year period, § 35
Contribution claim, 6-year period, § 35
Copyright infringement, 6-year period, § 35
Counterclaims; interposition of claim, § 48, § 49
CPLR, periods outside, § 35
Death
tolling of limitations period; death of plaintiff or potential defendant, § 55
wrongful death, § 35, § 44, § 55
Defamation, § 40
Delayed-accrual rules, § 40
Dental malpractice. Medical malpractice, infra
Derivative claims
generally, § 35
continuous treatment toll for, § 42
Disabilities as tolls, § 54
Disclosure, compelling, § 367
Discovery rule, accrual of claim, § 40, § 43
Equitable estoppel, § 56
Equity actions, § 36
Estopping defendant from pleading limitation, § 56
Exposure cases, discovery accrual, § 43
Extension of time
generally, § 6, § 50
estopping defendant from pleading limitation, § 56
termination of prior action, new action where, § 52
Federal practice, § 615, § 625
Foreign claims, § 57
Foreign object exception to accrual of claim, § 42
Forfeiture or penalties, 3-year period, § 35
4-month period, § 35

4-year period, Uniform Commercial Code, § 35
Fraud, discovery accrual, § 43
Holidays, last day of period, time for commencing action, § 34
Impleader claims, § 162
Infancy as disability resulting in toll, § 54
Insanity as disability resulting in toll, § 54
Intentional torts, 1-year period, § 35
Interposition of claim
generally, § 45
amended pleadings, § 49
clerk of court, delivery to, § 47
counterclaims, § 48, § 49
defined, § 45
existing party, amended pleading to add claim against, § 49
joint tortfeasors, § 45
new party, amended pleading to add, § 49
provisional remedy as, § 46
sheriff or clerk, delivery to, § 47
third-party defendant, plaintiff adding direct claim against, § 49
united in interest, § 45
Laches, § 36
Lengthen or shorten period, agreements to, § 39
Malpractice claim
continuous representation exception to accrual of claim, § 42
continuous treatment exception to accrual of statute of limitations, medical malpractice, § 42
medical malpractice, infra
3-year period, professionals, nonmedical cases, § 35
Matrimonial action, distributive award, 6-year period, § 35
Medical malpractice
accrual of claim, § 42
continuous treatment exception to accrual of claim, § 42
continuous treatment toll for derivative claim, § 42
derivative claim, continuous treatment toll for, § 42
discovery rule and, § 43
foreign object exception to accrual of claim, § 42
2-years and six months period, § 35, § 42
Money judgment, 20-year period, § 35
Mortgage foreclosure action, 6-year period, § 35
Multiple theories, § 37
Municipalities, actions against, § 35
New action following termination of prior action
generally, § 52
calculating six month period, § 52
neglect to prosecute, dismissal for, § 52
personal jurisdiction, prior action dismissed for failure to obtain, § 52
service requirements, § 52
subject matter jurisdiction, prior action dismissed for failure to obtain, § 52
Nonresidents; borrowing statute, § 57
Notice of claim, § 32, § 35
1-year period, § 35
Out-of-state accrual of claim, § 57

Penalties or forfeiture, 3-year period, § 35
Personal injury actions, 3-year period, § 35
Personal jurisdiction, prior action dismissed for
    failure to obtain, § 52
Podiatric malpractice. Medical malpractice, supra
Property, injury to; 3-year period, § 35
Provisional remedy as interposition of claim, § 46
Relation back doctrine, § 65, § 231A
Sales contracts, 4-year period, § 35
Saturday, last day of period, time for commencing
    action, § 34
Service of papers
    new action following termination of prior
        action, § 52
    timeliness of, § 231A
Sheriff or clerk, delivery to, § 47
Shorten or lengthen period, agreements to, § 39
Six month extension for new action. New action
    following termination of prior action, supra
6-year period, § 35
Special proceedings, § 548
Strict tort or products liability, 3-year period,
    § 35, § 37
Subject matter jurisdiction, prior action
    dismissed for failure to obtain, § 52
Sunday, last day of period, time for commencing
    action, § 34
Suspension of remedy reckoning, § 34
10-year period, § 35
Termination of prior action, new action where.
    New action following termination of prior
    action, supra
Third-party defendant, plaintiff adding direct
    claim against; interposition of claim, § 49
3-year period, § 35
Tolling of generally, § 50
    absence from state, tolling for defendant's,
        § 53
    agreements, § 39
    continuous treatment toll for derivative
        claim, § 42
    death of plaintiff or potential defendant,
        § 55
    disabilities as tolls, § 54
    infancy, § 54
    insanity, § 54
    stayed, where action, § 51
    wrongful death, § 55
20-year period, § 35
2-years and six months period, medical
    professionals, § 35
Uniform Commercial Code, 4-year period, § 35,
    § 41
Want of prosecution, dismissal for, § 375
Warranties, § 35, § 37, § 41
Wrongful death, § 35, § 44, § 55

STAY OF PROCEEDINGS
Appeals, § 535
Arbitration, § 592
Forum non conveniens, § 28
Motion practice, § 255
Statute of limitations, tolling of, § 51
Summary proceedings, warrant and stay, § 580

STENOGRAPHERS
Depositions, § 357

STIPULATIONS
Accident, ground for setting aside, § 204
Collusion, ground for setting aside, § 204
Disclosure, § 351
Discontinuance, § 297
Fraud, ground for setting aside, § 204
Grounds for setting aside, § 204
Mistake, ground for setting aside, § 204
Nonparty, stipulation signed by, § 204
Oral, § 204
Requirements, § 204
Settlement, of, § 204
Summary judgment motion, extending time to
    make, § 279

STRICT LIABILITY
Statute of limitations for strict tort or products
    liability, 3-year period, § 35, § 37

SUBJECT MATTER JURISDICTION
    Generally, § 611
Abstention doctrine, § 613
Case or controversy requirement, § 612
Defined, § 8
Dismissal motion and, § 260
Federal Practice (this index)
Justiciability, § 612
Lack of, effect of, § 8
Mootness, § 612
Prior action dismissed for failure to obtain;
    statute of limitations, § 52
Ripeness, § 612
Standing, § 612
Supplemental jurisdiction, § 614

SUBPOENAS
    Generally, § 382
Ad testificandum, § 382
Content and timing of, § 362
Defined, § 382
Disobedience of, § 385
Duces tecum, § 382, § 386
Enforcement of money judgments, § 509
Form, § 386
Issuance, § 382
Quash, motion to, § 384
Service, § 383
Testimonial, form of, § 386

SUBSTITUTION OF PARTIES
    Generally, § 184
Abatement of claims, § 185
Conservatorship, § 184
Death of party, § 184
Incompetency, § 184
Procedure, § 186
Public body or officer as party, § 187
Transfer of interests, § 184
Unknown parties, § 188

SUMMARY JUDGMENT
    Generally, § 278
Abatement, grant of summary judgment based
    on, § 283

Abortive motion, salvaging something from, § 286
Actions subject to, § 280
Admissions, written, proof, § 281
Affidavits, proof, § 281
Attorney's affidavit, probative force, § 281
Complaint, motion in lieu of
    generally, § 288
    conversion, § 292
    denial, effect of, § 292
    judgment as basis for, § 290
    money instrument as basis for motion,
      § 289
    procedure, § 291
Conversion, motion in lieu of complaint, § 292
Counterclaim, § 285
Cross-motion, time to make, § 279
Damages, immediate trial of fact issue, § 284
Deadlines, court rules imposing, § 279
Defined, § 278
Denial
    effect of motion in lieu of complaint, § 292
    key fact in exclusive knowledge of moving
      party, § 281
Depositions, proof, § 281
Dismissal motion; treating as summary
    judgment, § 270, § 283
District of Columbia judgments, basis for CPLR
    3213 motion, § 290
Effect of counterclaim, § 285
Effect of res judicata, § 287
Evidence, viewed in light most favorable to party
    moved against, § 281
Fact issue, immediate trial of, § 284
Federal practice, § 635
Foreign country judgment, basis for CPLR 3213
    motion, § 290
Good cause to entertain late motion, § 279
Grounds, § 283
Immediate trial of fact issue, § 284
Judgment as basis for motion in lieu of
    complaint, § 290
Key fact in exclusive knowledge of movant party,
    § 283
Late motion, good cause to entertain, § 279
In lieu of complaint, motion
    generally, § 288
    conversion, § 292
    denial, effect of, § 292
    judgment as basis for, § 290
    money instrument as basis for motion,
      § 289
    procedure, § 291
Money instrument as basis for motion in lieu of
    complaint, § 289
Motions
    abortive motion, salvaging something from,
      § 286
    federal practice, § 635
    in lieu of complaint, generally, § 288
    res judicata effect, § 287
    salvaging something from abortive motion,
      § 286
    time to move for, § 279
Opposition party, evidence viewed in light
    favorable to, § 281

Partial, § 285
Party
    evidence viewed in light favorable to
      opposition, § 281
    not granting judgment due to plaintiff's
      weaknesses in motions, § 281
Pretrial, § 402
Prima facie showing of entitlement to judgment,
    § 281
Procedure, motion in lieu of complaint, § 291
Proof, generally, § 281
Proof on, § 281
Record, searching, § 282
Res judicata effect, § 287
Salvaging something from abortive motion, § 286
Searching record, § 282
Sister-state judgments, basis for CPLR 3213
    motion, § 290
Stipulations extending time to move for, § 279
Time to move for, § 279
Trial of fact issue, immediate, § 284
Written admissions, proof, § 281

SUMMARY PROCEEDINGS
    Generally, § 572
Answer and defenses, § 576
City courts, § 21
Defenses, § 576
Enforcement of judgments in, § 580
Incidental procedure, § 577
Judgments, § 579, § 580
Jurisdiction, § 572
Notice of petition, § 573
Petition, § 574
RPAPL application, § 571
Service in, § 575
Stay, warrant and, § 580
Trial, § 578
Warrant and stay, § 580
Yellowstone injunction, § 580

SUMMATION
Closing Statements (this index)

SUMMONS
Accompanying papers, service of process, § 60
Add-ons for recipient of paper, service of process,
    § 202
Affidavits of service, service of process, § 202
Affix-and-mail, service of process, § 71, § 73, § 74
Agent for service, designation of, service of
    process, § 73
Age of persons authorized to serve, service of
    process, § 63
All parties, service on, service of process, § 203
Altering initiatory papers after filing but before
    service, service of process, § 63
Amendment
    generally, § 64
    correction of many filing mistakes, service
      of process, § 63
    parties, changing, § 65
Appeals, perfecting, electronic filing, § 536
Appearance by defendant; response to CPLR
    305(b) notice, service of process, § 60
Appellate division, electronic filing, § 11

Associations, service of process, § 68

Attachment; summons service within 60 days, service of process, § 319

Attorneys
    initiatory papers, service of process, § 202
    process server's acts, attorney for plaintiff accountable for, service of process, § 63

Bare summons, service of process, § 60, § 231

Board, court or commission, service of process, § 70

Children, service of process, § 68, § 195

Clerk of court, filing with, § 63

Commencement of action
    electronic filing, § 63A
    service of process, § 63

Commission, court or board, service of process, § 70

Complaint accompanying summons
    form of summons served with complaint, service of process, § 61
    requirements, service of process, § 60

Completion of service, service of process, § 202

Consensual, electronic filing, § 63A

Conservatees, service of process, § 68

Corporations, service of process, § 68, § 70, § 296

Correction of many filing mistakes, amendment allowing, service of process, § 63

Counties and actions with mandatory electronic filing, § 63A

Court, board or commission, service of process, § 70

Court of claims, electronic filing, § 17

Court-ordered service, service of process, § 75

CPLR 305(b) notice. Default notice; CPLR 305(b), infra

CPLR 305(b) notice, service of process, § 60

Credibility of procrastinator affected, service of process, § 231A

Curing technical defects in service, service of process, § 76B

120 days after filing to effect service, service of process, § 63

Default judgment, vacating, service of process, § 108

Default notice; CPLR 305(b)
    appearance by defendant; response to notice, service of process, § 60
    defined, service of process, § 60
    form, service of process, § 62
    requirements, service of process, § 60
    response to notice, service of process, § 60

Deliver-and-mail, service of process, § 71, § 72

Diplomatic immunity, service of process, § 68

E-filing, service of process, § 202

Electronic filing, § 63A

Electronic Filing (this index)

Enticement into jurisdiction, service of process, § 67

Estates and trusts, service of process, § 68

Exceptions to mandatory filing, electronic filing, § 63A

Exclusions to mandatory electronic filing, § 63A

Extending time for service, service of process, § 63

Facsimile, by, service of process, § 202

Federal Practice (this index)

Foreign nations and agencies, service of process, § 68

Forms
    default notice 305(b), summons served with, service of process, § 62
    summons served with complaint, service of process, § 61

Guardians, service of process, § 68

Immunity from service
    diplomatic immunity, service of process, § 68
    sovereign immunity, service of process, § 68
    voluntarily in state, service of process, § 68

Incapacitated persons, service of process, § 68, § 195

Incompetents and conservatees, service of process, § 68

Incorrect initiatory papers failing to name defendant, court invoking CPLR 2001 to forgive, electronic filing, § 63A

Infants, service of process, § 68

Initiatory papers versus interlocutory papers, service of process, § 202

Interlocutory papers versus initiatory papers, service of process, § 202

Interrogatories, service of process, § 361

Issuance, § 623
    federal practice, § 623
    service of process, § 60

Late or delayed
    e-filing after county clerk rejected hard-copy filing, supreme court refusing to forgive, electronic filing, § 63A
    notice, leave to serve, service of process, § 32

Law office failure for late service of pleadings, service of process, § 231

Laws, rules and administrative orders governing, electronic filing, § 63A

Limited liability partnerships, service of process, § 68

Limited partnerships, service of process, § 68

Mail
    affix-and-mail, service of process, § 71, § 73, § 74
    deliver-and-mail, service of process, § 71, § 72
    first-class mail, service of process, § 202
    ordinary mail, service of process, § 202
    personal delivery, service of process, § 66, § 76A

Mandatory, electronic filing
    generally, § 63A
    counties and actions with, § 63A
    exclusions, § 63A
    opting out, § 63A

Matrimonial actions, service of process, § 76

Methods, generally, service of process, § 66, § 202

Motions, service of process, § 246, § 247, § 249, § 250

Municipal entities, service of process, § 70

New parties, need to add, service of process, § 231A

New York City Civil Court, electronic filing, § 19
Notice of claim, service of process, § 32, § 231A
Opting out of mandatory electronic filing, § 63A
Outside state, service, service of process, § 100
Overnight delivery, service of process, § 202
Partnerships, service of process, § 68
Personal delivery
    apartment house, service of process, § 66
    concealing summons invalidating service,
        service of process, § 66
    corporations, service of process, § 70
    deliver-and-mail, service of process, § 71,
        § 72
    due diligence, service of process, § 66
    family members, to, service of process, § 66
    generally, service of process, § 59, § 66
    mail, service of process, § 66, § 76A
    person, to, service of process, § 66
    redelivery, service of process, § 66
    substituted service, service of process, § 71
Physical office requirement, service of process,
    § 202
Pleadings
    complaint accompanying summons
        form of summons served with
            complaint, service of process,
            § 61
        requirements, service of process, § 60
    credibility of procrastinator affected,
        service of process, § 231A
    default, service of process, § 231A
    defect in summons service, service of
        process, § 231A
    federal courts; late service, service of
        process, § 231A
    generally, service of process, § 231
    jurisdictional defects, service of process,
        § 231A
    law office failure for late service, service of
        process, § 231
    leave time for trouble, service of process,
        § 231A
    new parties, need to add, service of process,
        § 231A
    notice, inadequate, service of process,
        § 231A
    relation back doctrine, dispensing reliance
        on, service of process, § 231A
    responding time, service of process, § 231
    statute of limitations, service of process,
        § 231A
    timely filing but late service, service of
        process, § 231A
    wrong person, serving, service of process,
        § 231A
Proof of, service of process, § 79
Publication, service by; rem jurisdiction, service
    of process, § 107
Public authorities, service of process, § 70
Relation back doctrine, dispensing reliance on,
    service of process, § 231A
Rem jurisdiction and service by publication,
    service of process, § 107
Requirements, service of process, § 59

Response
    CPLR 305(b) notice, response by defendant
        to, service of process, § 60
    summons, to, service of process, § 231
Rules, laws and administrative orders governing,
    electronic filing, § 63A
Sabbath, service on, service of process, § 63
Saturdays, service on, service of process, § 63,
    § 202
Service, federal practice, § 624, § 625
Service of papers, and electronic filing, § 202
Service of Process, Summons and Papers
    (this index)
Sewer service, service of process, § 71
Signature on papers, electronic filing, § 201
Sovereign immunity, service of process, § 68
State, on, service of process, § 70
Statute of limitations; new action following
    termination of prior action, service of
    process, § 52
Statutory instructions on service, specific, service
    of process, § 202
Subpoenas, service of process, § 383
Substituted service, service of process, § 71
Summary proceedings, service of process, § 575
Sunday, service on, service of process, § 63
Supplemental, § 65
Surrogate's court, electronic filing, § 15
Technical defects in service, curing, service of
    process, § 76B
Time computation, service of process, § 202
Time limits, § 625
    federal practice, § 625
Transient service, service of process, § 59
Unincorporated associations, service of process,
    § 68
Voluntarily in state, service of process, § 68
When and by whom summons served,
    commencement of action, service of process,
    § 63
Wrong person, serving, service of process, § 231A

SUNDAYS
Saturdays, Sundays and Holidays (this index)

SUPPLEMENTAL JURISDICTION
Subject matter jurisdiction and federal practice,
    § 614

SUPPORT ENFORCEMENT
Income execution, § 507A
Longarm jurisdiction, § 90

SUPREME COURT
    Generally, § 12
Appeals from, § 12
Applicability of CPLR to, § 3
Arbitration awards; courts involvement other
    than supreme court, § 606
Categories of action and assignment to
    Commercial Division, § 12A
Commercial Division, § 12A
CPLR, applicability of, § 12
Jurisdiction, § 12
Matrimonial actions, § 16
Monetary thresholds, Commercial Division,
    § 12A

Rules of Practice, Commercial Division, **§ 12A**

SURROGATE'S COURT
Generally, **§ 15**
Appeals, **§ 15**
Court act, governing, **§ 3**
Decedent's estates, jurisdiction, **§ 15**
E-filing, mandatory, **§ 15**
Governing act, **§ 3**
Inter vivos trusts, jurisdiction, **§ 15**
Judges, **§ 15**
Jurisdiction, **§ 15**
Lifetime inter vivos trusts, jurisdiction, **§ 15**
Number of judges, **§ 15**
Procedure, generally, **§ 15**
Process, service of, **§ 15**
Service of process, **§ 15**
Subject matter jurisdiction, **§ 15**
Surrogate's Court Procedure Act (SCPA), **§ 3,
§ 15**
Term of judges, **§ 15**
Uniform rules, **§ 3**

**SURROGATE'S COURT PROCEDURE ACT
(SCPA)**
Generally, **§ 3, § 15**

SURVEILLANCE
Disclosure of surveillance tapes; privileged
communications, **§ 348**

SUSPENSION OF REMEDY THEORY
Affirmative defense, **§ 34**

TAXES
Costs and disbursements, **§ 416**

TAXING COSTS
Defined, **§ 414**

TELEPHONE NUMBERS
Papers, form of, **§ 201**

TEMPORARY RECEIVERSHIP
Generally, **§§ 332 et seq.**
Accounts and accounting, **§ 332**
Application, **§ 333**
Compensation and salaries, **§ 332**
Extension beyond judgment, **§ 333**
Motion for appointment, **§ 333**
Notice, motion for appointment, **§ 333**
Powers, **§ 332**

TEMPORARY RESTRAINING ORDERS
Generally, **§ 330**
Contempt, enforcement by, **§ 481**
Federal practice, **§ 640**
Preliminary injunction, distinguished, **§ 330**
Requirements, **§ 330**
Vacating, **§ 331**

TENDER
Generally, **§ 303**

TERMINATION
Arbitration agreements, **§ 589**

THIRD-PARTY PRACTICE
Generally, **§ 155, § 167**

Additional claims among parties, **§ 164**
Advantages, **§ 155**
Arbitration, **§ 598**
Comparative negligence, **§ 168E**
Complaint negating main claim, **§ 158**
Contribution
proportionate share determination, **§ 175**
spouse, applicability of insurance to
impleaded, **§ 175**
Defendant's rights, **§ 163**
Dismissal, discretionary powers of, **§ 161**
Employer, action against plaintiff's, **§ 155,
§ 168C**
Enforcement of judgment, **§ 165**
Indemnification as impleader basis, **§ 157**
Insurance cases, **§ 160**
Joint tort liability adjustment
generally, **§ 168A**
bankruptcy, **§ 168C**
burden of proof, **§ 168D**
contribution and indemnification, **§ 168C**
court of claims, Article 16 and, **§ 168C**
employer at fault, plaintiff's, **§ 168C**
exceptions, **§ 168C**
50%-or-less tortfeasor, **§ 168B**
indemnification, **§ 168C**
intentional conduct and reckless disregard
cases excepted, **§ 168C**
medical malpractice and successive
tortfeasor cases, **§ 168C**
motor vehicle exception, **§ 168C**
non-delegable duty exception, **§ 168C**
nonparty tortfeasor share not considered,
§ 168C
reckless disregard cases excepted, **§ 168C**
requirements, **§ 168C**
settlement under General Obligations Law
Section 15–108, **§ 168C**
successive tortfeasor cases, **§ 168C**
Judgment, enforcement of, **§ 165**
Laches, **§ 156**
Premature suit, as, **§ 159**
Procedure, **§ 156**
Separate trial, **§ 161**
Severance, **§ 161**
Statute of limitations on impleader claims, **§ 162**
Successive impleaders, **§ 166**
Time for impleader, **§ 156**
Vouching-in, **§ 168**

TIME LIMITATIONS
Statute of Limitations (this index)

TORTS
Collateral estoppel; multiparty vehicle tort
examples, **§ 468**
Comparative Negligence (this index)
Contribution (this index)
Longarm Jurisdiction (this index)
Statute of Limitations (this index)
Third-party practice; joint tort liability
adjustment.
Third-Party Practice (this index)

TOWN COURTS
Generally, **§ 22**

Geographical restriction, § 22
Jurisdiction, § 22
Justice of peace, § 22
Small claims part, § 22

TOWNS
Venue, actions against, § 120

TRADE SECRETS
Protection against disclosure, § 353

TRANSCRIPTS
Appeals, § 537
Poor persons, § 192

TRANSFERS BETWEEN COURTS
Generally, § 24
Ad damnum clause, leave to amend, § 25
Consent to transfer down
　　with consent, § 26
　　without consent, § 27
Mistake in choice of court, § 24
Personal jurisdiction issues, § 27
Transfer down on consent, § 26
Transfer down without consent, § 27
Transfer up for more relief, § 25

TRANSITORY ACTIONS
Venue, § 118

TRANSLATIONS
Depositions, § 356
Foreign-language documents, discovery and
　　inspection, § 362

TRIAL
Generally, § 389
Additur, § 407
Adjournments, § 389
Admissions, based on, § 402
Arbitration and trial of threshold question, § 594
Bifurcated Trial (this index)
Calendar Practice (this index)
Closing statements, § 395, § 396
Comparison of motions for judgment, § 408
Consolidation of Actions (this index)
Defined, § 130
Directed verdict, motion for, § 402
Disclosure (this index)
Discretion of court, adjournments, § 389
Dismissal motion; immediate trial of fact issue,
　　§ 271
Engagement of counsel rule, § 389
Introduction, § 389
Joint Trial (this index)
Judgment during trial, motion for, § 402
Jurisdiction, § 23
Jury (this index)
Mistrial, § 403
Motions. **Trial Motions** (this index)
New trial on weight of evidence, motion for
　　judgment, § 406
Nonjury trial, § 380
Objections and rulings, § 396
Opening statements, § 395
Place, § 389
Post-trial motion for judgment, § 405
Referee, by, § 379

Remittitur, § 407
Res Judicata (this index)
Separate Trial (this index)
Sequence of, § 393
Severance (this index)
Summary judgment; immediate trial of fact issue,
　　§ 284
Summary proceedings, § 578
Trifurcation and, § 130
Verdict (this index)
Witnesses (this index)
Wrongful death, § 394

TRIAL MOTIONS
Additur, § 407
Admissions, based on, § 402
Comparison of motions for judgment, § 408
Judgment during trial, motion for, § 402
Mistrial, § 403
New trial on weight of evidence, motion for
　　judgment, § 406
Post-trial motion for judgment, § 405
Remittitur, § 407

TRUSTS
Service of process, summons and papers, § 68

TRUSTS AND TRUSTEES
Inter vivos trusts, surrogate court jurisdiction,
　　§ 15
Lifetime inter vivos trusts, surrogate court
　　jurisdiction, § 15
Surrogate court jurisdiction, § 15

UNDERTAKINGS
Bonds and Undertakings (this index)

UNDUE INFLUENCE
Pleading, particularity requirement, § 216

UNIFORM ACTS
Defined, § 3

UNIFORM CITY COURT ACT
Generally, § 3, § 21

UNIFORM COMMERCIAL CODE
Statute of limitations; 4-year period, § 35, § 41

UNIFORM DISTRICT COURT ACT
Generally, § 3, § 20

UNIFORM JUSTICE COURT ACT
Generally, § 3

UNIFORM RULES
Generally, § 3
Depositions, § 355
Motions, § 243

UNINCORPORATED ASSOCIATIONS
Service of process, summons and papers, § 68
Venue, § 119

VACATING JUDGMENTS AND ORDERS
Conditioning vacatur, § 432
Excusable default, § 427
Federal practice, § 641
Fraud, § 429
Jurisdiction, lack of, § 430

Misconduct, § 429
Motion, generally, § 426
Newly discovered evidence, § 428
Restitution, § 433
Reversal of underlying judgment, § 431

VEHICLES
Motor Vehicles (this index)

VENUE
Generally, § 116
Agreement to fix venue, § 117
Arbitration, § 591
Article 78 proceedings, § 565
governmental agency, § 120
Assignee of claim, transitory actions, § 118
Associations, unincorporated, § 119
Change of venue
generally, § 116
convenience of material witness, ground,
§ 124
demand procedure, § 123
discretionary grounds, § 124
effecting, § 125
grounds, § 124
impartial trial as issue, § 124
improper to proper county, from, § 123
material witnesses, for convenience of,
§ 124
third party defendants, § 124
Change of Venue (this index)
Cities, actions against, § 120
Common carriers, § 119
Consumer credit cases, special venue
requirements in, § 122
Contracts, fixing, § 117, § 123
Convenience of material witness, ground, change
of venue, § 124
Cooperative apratments, cases involving, § 121
Corporations, § 119
Counties, actions against, § 120
Defined, § 116
Discretionary grounds, change of venue, § 124
Discretionary grounds for change of venue, § 124
Domicile or residence, transitory actions, § 118
Federal practice, § 617
Foreign corporations, § 119
Governmental entities, § 120
Impartial trial as issue; change of venue, § 124
Improper to proper county, change of venue from,
§ 123
Individually-owned business, § 119
Local actions, § 121
Material witnesses, change of venue for
convenience of, § 124
Motions
requirement to change venue, § 116
Motions, where made, § 245
New York City, actions against, § 120
Partnerships, § 119
Principal office, § 119
generally, § 119
corporations, § 119
partnerships, § 119
Public authorities, § 120
Real property, § 121

Residence, § 118
School districts, actions against, § 120
Seizure of chattel, § 121
Special proceedings, § 549
Special venue requirements, in consumer credit
cases, § 122
Third party defendants, change of venue, § 124
Towns, actions against, § 120
Transitory actions, § 118
Unincorporated associations, § 119
Villages, actions against, § 120

VERDICT
Generally, § 399
Affidavits of jurors, clarification, § 401
Clarification, affidavits of jurors, § 401
Collateral source rule, § 399
Compromise verdict, § 401
Defective, § 401
Defined, § 399
Delivery of, § 400
Directed verdict, motion for, § 402
General, § 399
Impeachment, § 401
Interrogatories, general verdict accompanied by
answers to, § 399
Kinds, § 399
Lying jurors, impeachment of verdict, § 401
Oral verdicts, § 400
Personal injury, § 399
Polling the jury, § 400
Quotient verdict, § 401
Special, § 399
Types of, § 399
Wrongful death, § 399

VERIFICATION OF PLEADINGS
Generally, § 232
Bill of particulars, § 238
Defective, remedy for, § 235
Defined, § 232
Eligibility to verify, § 233
Form of, § 234
Purpose of, § 232
Who may verify, § 233

VIDEOTAPES
Disclosure; privileged communications, § 348

VILLAGE COURTS
Generally, § 22
Geographical restriction, § 22
Jurisdiction, § 22
Small claims part, § 22
Village police justice, § 22

VILLAGES
Venue, actions against, § 120

VISITATION
Arbitration, § 587

VOLUNTARY DISCONTINUANCE
Discontinuance (this index)

WAIVERS
Arbitration, § 595
Demand and waiver of trial by jury, § 378

Dismissal motion, § 274

WANT OF PROSECUTION
Appeal dismissed for, § 542
Dismissal for, § 375, § 542

WARRANTIES
Accrual in warranty cases, statute of limitations,
    § 41
Statute of limitations, § 35, § 37, § 41

WARRANTS
Summary proceedings, warrant and stay, § 580

WHEREFORE CLAUSE
Pleadings, demand for relief, § 217

WIFE
Husband and Wife (this index)

WILFUL DEFAULT
Pleading, particularity requirement, § 216

WITNESSES
Change of venue for convenience of material
    witnesses, § 124
Disclosure
    names of witnesses, § 349
    nonparty witness, § 352
    statements of witnesses, § 348

WORDS AND PHRASES
Definitions (this index)

WORKERS' COMPENSATION
Grave injury under, § 155

WORK PRODUCT
Materials prepared for litigation, § 348
Privileged matters, § 347, § 348

WRONGFUL DEATH
Bifurcation, trial, § 394
Interlocutory judgment, bifucated action, § 410
Interrogatories, § 361
Judgments, interest on, § 411
Statute of limitations, § 35, § 44, § 55
Verdicts, § 399

YELLOWSTONE INJUNCTION
Enforcement in summary proceeding, § 580